The Bare Facts Video Guide

1998 Edition

Craig Hosoda

Additional copies of this book (volume purchases also available) can be purchased from:

The Bare Facts
P.O. Box 3255
Santa Clara, CA 95055-3255
U.S.A.

Voice and facsimile: (408) 249-2021
e-mail: chosoda@barefacts.com
World Wide Web: http://www.barefacts.com

Cover Design: Robert Steven Pawlak Design
San Francisco, California.

ISBN 0-9625474-8-4

HOW TO USE THIS BOOK

The book is divided into two sections: Actresses and Titles. In the Actress section, everyone is listed alphabetically by last name. A • in front of a name denotes they are new to this edition. An asterisk (*) after someone's name denotes they have a magazine listing in *The Bare Facts Magazine Guide* and *The Bare Facts Video Guide CD-ROM.* (See "Other Products" on page v.)

Under each name are films, TV shows and cable TV shows that a person has appeared in. The non-nudity titles are listed to help you remember who a particular person is. If they have appeared nude in something, the title is in bold face. Following the title is the year the film was released, then the character name. "n.a." for the character name is an abbreviation for "not available." Under the title is a • to ••• rating and the time when the nudity occurs. Lastly, is a brief description of how the person appears in the scene.

In the Title section, Films, Made for Cable TV Movies and video tapes that have nude scenes (of someone in the Actress section) are listed. A • in front of a title denotes that it is new to this edition. Under each entry, are the cast and character names. The nude scenes for the cast members are listed under their names. If a person is listed in the Title section, they have a listing in the Actress section. Note that a film can have more nude scenes than are listed—I only list nude scenes of people who are in the Actress section.

Time definitions:	Very, very brief:	Need to use PAUSE to see one frame
	Very brief:	Use SLOW MOTION to see under 1 second
	Brief:	About 1 second
	No comment:	2 to 15 seconds
	Long scene:	Longer than 15 seconds

Rating definitions:	•	Yawn. Usually too brief or hard to see for some reason.
	••	Okay. Check it out if you are interested in the person.
	•••	Wow! Don't miss it. The scene usually lasts for a while.

The ratings are approximate guides to how much nudity an actress has in a scene. More weight is given on how famous she is, how well lit and clear the scene is, if it's a close shot and the length of time they stay still so you can see clearly. So if an actress has an erotic love scene but they don't show any skin or they are topless but their backs are toward the camera, it won't get rated.

To help you find the nude scenes quickly and accurately, the location on video tape is specified in hours:minutes format rather than counter numbers since different VCR's have different counters. Most VCR's sold now have real-time counters. The time starts at 0:00 after the last film company logo disappears (Universal, Paramount, etc.).

In the descriptions, "breasts" means you see both breasts, "full frontal nudity" means you see both breasts and the pubic area, "lower frontal nudity" means you see the pubic area and "nude" means you see both breasts, the pubic area and the buns.

Actresses who have appeared nude in only one film and are never seen anywhere else are not included because this book helps you locate someone unclothed that you've seen somewhere else before. (They will be listed in *The Bare Facts Video Guide One Timer Supplement.*) Exceptions are actresses who are listed in *The Bare Facts Magazine Guide* and some adult film actresses.

INTRODUCTION

It used to be that people did nude scenes in films at the beginning of their careers trying to get their "big break." Once they established themselves, they announced they would not be doing any more nudity and hoped everyone would forget their earlier performances. Phoebe Cates for example. But more and more actors and actresses are surprising us by doing nude scenes later in their careers (Sigourney Weaver and Julie Andrews). Fortunately, there are a few who do nudity in just about every film they are in. Sylvia Kristel and Marilyn Chambers for example. This book compiles all of these unbashful actresses into one reference to help you locate their nude scenes on video tape to save you time and money. I have listed a few close calls like Janine Turner in *Monkey Shines* and Christina Applegate in *Streets*.

Actresses that *look* like they have done nudity in films, but have used body doubles instead, are also noted. A body double is another person who is used for nude scenes when an actress is too modest. You can usually spot a body double in a movie when there is a nude body without seeing a face.

I have spent my time concentrating on getting the greatest *number* of people into this book as possible. Therefore, you'll find the entries for some people like Laura Gemser or Claudia Jennings, incomplete since it's relatively easy to locate films they have nude scenes in. Obviously, I haven't been able to view all the movies ever made (yet), so there will be films with nude scenes that I have missed. (I still haven't even started looking at Russ Meyers' films!)

I realize that I don't always use the best English in my descriptions, "Right breast making love." Please try not to laugh out loud too much! I'd rather be succinct and to the point, because I know this book isn't going to win a Pulitzer Prize.

If you find any mistakes or have additions, please write to me and they will be corrected in the next edition. I have a long list of nude scenes compiled from reader's letters which I need to verify because occasionally, scenes have been incorrectly remembered or have been cut from the film on the video release.

I only review video tapes, not the theatrical release in movie theaters, so you won't see times for *Titanic* or *Wild Things* in this edition because they weren't on video tape when this book was being prepared. But you can be assured that they will be in the next edition!

Enjoy!

THANKS, THANKS AND MORE THANKS!

First of all, I need to thank my wife, Marie, for her help and patience putting up with all my video tape viewing. I also need to thank my children, Christopher and Melanie, for going to school and going to sleep at night so I can watch video tapes. Thanks also to my parents and the rest of my family for all their help and support.

Thank you to Dave Dell'Aquila of Dell'Aquila Data Systems, in San Jose, who is my 4th Dimension Consultant. Without his help, I couldn't have set up the database, imported the data, generated the Title section or completed the CD-ROM. Also thank you to Ron Dell'Aquila of Protron D.C., in Santa Clara, who programmed the export from 4th Dimension into FrameMaker. Thank you to both Dave and Ron for their continued support.

Thanks to all my friends who have helped:
Marty Brenneis, Robert L. Brown, Mike Covey, Shauna Edridge, Sam Kattuah, Heather King, Holly King, James Marlowe, Huu-Quyen Ngo, Emily Nguyen, Mike Santomauro, Mark Shapiro and Valerie Smith.

Thanks to the personalities who have provided information or answered questions:
India Allen, Tia Bella, Linda Blair, Tia Carrere, Tamara Clatterbuck, Elise Daniels, Jennifer Delora, Denise Duff, Nikki Fritz, Monique Gabrielle, Schae Harrison, David Heavener, Lori Jo Hendrix, Cory Lane, Summer Leigh, Jacklyn Lick, Jacqueline Lovell, Yvette McClendon, Tim Matheson, Shelley Michelle, Midori, Jeannie Millar, Nikki Nova, Linda O'Neil, Kira Reed, Debbie Rochon, Scott Schwartz, Taylor St. Claire, Lisa Stahl, Peggy Trentini, Kendra Tucker and Taryn White.

Thanks to all the business relations who have helped:
David Barraclough/Titan Books, Ltd., Rick Bitzeberger/General Media Entertainment, John Blanford/MVP Home Entertainment, Tony Borg/Playboy Entertainment Group, Inc., Kirk Bowman/Pictor Home Entertainment, Robert Corn-Revere/Hogan & Hartson, John Cross/Hot Body International, David DeCoteau/Cinema Home Video, Lian DesMarias/Unapix Entertainment Inc., Frank Djeng/Tai Seng Video Marketing Inc., Dean Edward/Full Moon Pictures, Richard Gabai/Check Entertainment IFC, Dan Golden, Dean Goldfarb/DG Distributors Inc., Andy Green/New Vision Video, Penn Jillette, Kevin King/Image 2000, Bruce Kluger/Playboy Enterprises, Inc., Steven Kramer/The Picture Palace, Chad Kunimoto/Macdaddy Entertainment Inc., Dick Lane/Amazing Fantasy Entertainment, Becky LeBeau/Soft Bodies, Robert Lombard/Creative Image Management, Steve Lustgarten/Leo Home Video, Laura Malek/Playboy Enterprises, David McCarter/NicheWare, Scott Messing/Catalogic, Mark Ouimet/Publishers Group West, Jim Pehling/Consolidated Printers, Fred Olen Ray/American Independent Productions, Neil Reshen/Media Management, Patrick Riley, Angus Robertson/Magenta Systems Ltd, Cristiane Roget/Sales, Inc., Tony Rosen/Troma Team Video, Pedro Santos, Norman Scherer/Video Oyster, Bill Seip/American Video Center, Seema & Pankaj Shah/American Video Center, Pat Siciliano/Amazing Fantasy Entertainment, Michael J. Shoel/Phoenix Distributors, Rick Sloane/Rick Sloane Productions, Debbie Sleezer/Playboy Entertainment Group, Inc., Irv Slifkin/Movies Unlimited, Sherry Sortes/Hot Body International, Kristy Spaven, Barry L. Stern, David Stevens/Publishers Group West, Gabor Szabo/United Video Corporation, Christy Taylor/Hot Body International and Anna Vallois/Titan Books Ltd. and Jim Wynorski.

THANKS TO THE MEDIA

Thanks to all the media people who have enabled me to spread word about *The Bare Facts* through newspapers, books, magazines, radio and television:

Andy Barber/KHTT-FM, Jason Barr/CFNY, Ken Boxer/KCTV Television, Ken Butler/Butler & Associates, Ken Carriere/TV Guide Canada, Gary Dell'Abate/Infinity Broadcasting, Doug Dingler/WWGZ, Scott Einsinger/E! Entertainment Network, Wendy Gatlin/WGLX, Mark Harris/WMMS, Mitchell Horsley/WLGC, Tom Jorgensen/WKEW, Edward Margulies/ Movieline magazine, Mercedes Martinez/KMXB, Mike Mayo/Roanoke Times & World-News, Debbie McFadden/WOC, Mike McKelly/WRKR, Jack O'Neal/WFPS-WFRL, Darian O'Toole/ KBGG, Ben Olins/The Guardian, Jim Richards/CFRB, Howard Stern/Infinity Broadcasting, Stuart Takehara/Arrow 108, Nicole von Ruden/Entertainment Tonight, Scott Voorhees/KGDE and Jerry Wright/KLYV.

THANKS TO MY CONTRIBUTORS

Thanks to all the people who have sent me additions and corrections:

A very special thank you to Erich Mees who has provided a lot of hard to find information for the book.

These individuals have gone beyond the call of duty:

Craig Anthony, Randel J. August, Tim Barnes, Matt Bear, José X. Bonastre, Edward Dolan, Daniel J. Dudych, Anders Engstrom, Brett Fairbairn, John Flukas, Stephen Grace, Mark Havelin, Michael S. Jones, Dave Lachance, The Million Dollar Kid, Michael L. Pierce, R.L. Roberts, Angus Robertson, R.W. Schaefer, David Stephens, Bret Suval and A. Warner.

A big thank you also to:

Tony Alter, Ray Angelo, Emil Babel, Keith Bailey, Eric Battershell, Harry Beams, Steven Bell, Larry Booty, Dick Bowen, George Brintakis, James Cartwright, Dusty Chalk, Alan Coito, N.B. Deal, Jack Delahanty, Patrick Dunphy, Nate Elsner, Elliot Fabric, Tim Fielding, Ben Fischer, Eric Fleming, Matt Forgit, Travis Garrett, John Giannes, Lawrence M. Green, James R. Green Jr., David Guntner, Jesse Hahm, C.P. Hall, Rodney Hall, Glenn Hart, Tilman Hausherr, Dieter Heller, Dan Hindes, Hans Hornstein, Gary Imhoff, Rob Jacob, Gene Kelly, Tom Kelly, Kopyguard Kevin, Joshua Keypour, Ed Kodi, Santo A. LaNasa III, Tom MacQueen, James W. Marcel, Thomas Maronick, Kostas Maudides, Rick Miles, Mike Moniz, Sean Neal, Tom Neet Jr., Andrew Nystrom, John Pauly, Jason Pendergast, John Pini, Keith Pusavat, Lisa-Marie Reed, Joseph A. Ricely, Curtis Roberts, Steven W. Roberts, Marc Rosaaen, Rick Rosenholm, Robert Sardo, Steve Schmied, Norman Shackelford, Kip Simonsen, David Slattery, Wallace Sliwinski, David Spivack, Allen Stenhouse, Dwight Stone, Tim Strafford, Walter Teague, Carlton A. VanLear, Kevin Walker, Tony Ward, Dave Webb, Jim Welke, Tony Weltzin and Gabriel Zee.

Note: If you send additions and/or corrections and don't want your name printed in the next edition, please use a pseudonym like "The Million Dollar Kid" above.

OTHER PRODUCTS

The following Bare Facts products are available only via mail-order direct from The Bare Facts, they are not available in stores.

CD-ROM
The 1998 CD-ROM version of *The Bare Facts Video Guide* is available. Both the Macintosh and Windows versions are on one CD-ROM. It includes actress data up to December 1997, magazine, "one timer" and actor information. The price is $39.95.

Magazine Supplement
The *Playboy* and *Penthouse* magazine references were moved to a separate supplement to keep the main book a manageable size. It includes data up to March 1997. *The Bare Facts Magazine Guide 1997* costs $19.95.

One Timer Supplement
Actresses who do nudity in one film and are never seen again in anything else, are listed in *The Bare Facts Video Guide One Timer Supplement 1997*. You never know if last year's "one timer" will be today's overnight sensation! It includes data up to March 1997. It costs $19.95.

Newsletter
We publish a newsletter 3 times a year between Editions. Get up-to-date information on important new celebrity nude scenes. I receive preview video tapes from the studios, so there will be reviews for video tapes that are about to arrive at your local video store. There will also be sections for reader letters, questions and answers, tidbits on celebrity nudity and ads you can place for video swap requests with other readers. The subscription for 3 issues is $24 per year. If you order before the 3 issues are ready, we will mail each one to you as they become available. If you order after an issue is done, we will mail the back issue immediately, then the remaining issues when they are available.

Video Tapes for Sale
We offer some video tapes for sale, such as *Different Strokes* with Dana Plato, *All Nude Glamour* with Sara St. James (a.k.a. Jacqueline Lovell), *Scream Queen Hot Tub Party* with Kelli Maroney, *Risk* with Karen Sillas, *The Turning* with Gillian Anderson, *Naked Instinct* with Michelle Bauer and many more. Write, call, fax or e-mail for more information.

Contacting The Bare Facts
We can process credit card orders in addition to check or money orders. Shipping is $3.00 per order, except when ordering only the Newsletters. To receive more information on any of the products, please contact us:

U.S. Postal Service:	The Bare Facts P.O. Box 3255 Santa Clara, CA 95055-3255 U.S.A.
Voice Mail and Fax:	Call (408) 249-2021 to leave a voice-mail message or send a fax order.
Fax-Back Service:	Call (408) 249-2021 with your fax machine and listen to the instructions.
e-mail:	chosoda@barefacts.com
World Wide Web:	http://www.barefacts.com

Actresses

Aames, Angela

Films:

Fairytales (1979). . . . . Little Bo Peep
- ••• 0:14—Nude with The Prince in the woods.

H.O.T.S. (1979) . . . . Boom-Boom Bangs
a.k.a. T & A Academy
- • 0:21—Breasts parachuting into pool.
- • 0:39—Breasts in bathtub playing with a seal.
- • 1:33—Breasts while playing football.

...All the Marbles (1981) . . . . Louise
a.k.a. The California Dolls
- •• 0:21—Breasts, when caught in Peter Falk's motel room by Iris, then sitting on the bed, while talking with Falk.

The Best of Sex and Violence (1981). . . . . . . Little Bo Peep
- • 0:18—Brief breasts in scene from *Fairytales.*
- • 0:20—Brief right breast in scene from *Fairytales.*

Famous T & A (1982) . . . . Little Bo Peep
(No longer available for purchase, check your video store for rental.)
- •• 0:50—Breasts scene from *Fairytales.*

The Lost Empire (1983) . . . . .Heather McClure
- ••• 0:31—Breasts and buns taking a shower while Angel and White Star talk to her.

Scarface (1983). . . . . Woman at the Babylon Club
Bachelor Party (1984) . . . . Mrs. Klupner
Basic Training (1984). . . . . .Cheryl
- • 0:19—Brief breasts in bathtub.

Chopping Mall (1986). . . . . Miss Vanders
a.k.a. Killbots

• Abel, Dominique

Films:

Celestial Clockwork (1993; French/Portugese). . . . . .Gaby
a.k.a. Mecánicas celestes

Made for Cable TV:

Red Shoe Diaries: Four on the Floor (1995; Showtime) . . . . .Julia
- • 0:15—Breasts, while getting out of her wet clothes.
- • 0:18—Breasts, while making love with Nick Corri.
- • 0:21—Left breast, while making love with Corri.

Abigail

Films:

Alvin Purple (1973; Australian) . . . . .Girl in See-Through
Alvin Rides Again (1974; Australian) . . . . Mae
- ••• 0:12—Breasts in store with Alvin.

The Adventures of Eliza Fraser (1976; Australian) . . . . Buxom Girl
- • 0:01—Breasts when Martin pulls the sheets off her.

Breaking Loose (1988; Australian) . . . . Helen

Able, Sheri

Films:

The Evil Below (1991) . . . . .Tracy
- • 0:10—Buns, in two piece swimsuit on boat.
- • 0:21—Right breast, with Max behind curtain. Hard to see.

Ultimate Desires (1991). . . . . .Carlos' Girlfriend
a.k.a. Silhouette

Abril, Victoria *

Films:

Comin' At Ya! (1982). . . . . Abilene
The Moon in the Gutter (1983; French/Italian). . . . . . . Bella
a.k.a. La Lune dans Le Caniveau
- • 0:28—Left breast, while riding on swing and getting felt by Gérard Depardieu.
- •• 1:26—Breasts, while lying in bed. Dark.
- ••• 1:27—Nude, getting out of bed and arguing with Depardieu. Long scene. Subtitles get in the way sometimes.
- • 1:50—Upper half of right breast, popping out of the top of her dress when Depardieu leans her back on the counter.

On the Line (1984; Spanish) . . . . Engracia
- ••• 0:16—Breasts getting undressed to make love with Mitch.
- • 0:29—Very brief breasts, making love in bed with Mitch.

L'Addition (1985; French) . . . . .Patty
Padre Nuestro (1985). . . . . Cardenala
Baton Rouge (1988; Spanish) . . . . Dr. Ana Alonso
- • 0:41—Brief buns, when sitting on her office desk, before making love with Antonio Banderas.
- • 0:48—Right breast, while sitting in bed after stabbing Leon.

Tie Me Up! Tie Me Down! (1990; Spanish) . . .Marina Osorio
- ••• 0:24—Full frontal nudity playing with a frogman toy in the bathtub.
- • 0:34—Buns and brief side of right breast, getting dressed.
- •• 0:44—Breasts while changing clothes, then on TV while Maximo watches.
- •• 1:09—Breasts while changing clothes.
- ••• 1:16—Right breast, then breasts while making love in bed with Ricky.

High Heels (1991; Spanish) . . . . Rebecca Giner
- • 0:31—Breasts, when her dress falls down slightly while hanging on a pole and making love with Lethal.

Lovers (1992; Spanish). . . . . .Luisa
a.k.a. Amantes
- • 0:28—Buns, while lowering herself onto Paco.

Intruso (1993; Spanish) . . . . .Luisa
- • 0:53—Partial breasts behind glass shower door. Partial right breast and buns while making love with Angel in the shower.
- • 1:03—Brief breasts, taking off her nightgown and getting into bed with Angel.
- • 1:04—Partial buns, while making love in bed with Angel. Dark.
- • 1:06—Brief right breast, while making love with her husband in bed. Brief buns, when getting out of bed.

Jimmy Hollywood (1993). . . . . Lorraine
Kika (1994; Spanish) . . . . Andrea Caracortada (Scarface)
French Twist (1996; French). . . . . Loli
- •• 0:19—Full frontal nudity, while in bed with her husband.
- • 0:23—Very brief left breast, when getting back into bed.
- • 0:45—Left breast, while sitting in bathtub with Marijo.
- •• 0:58—Brief buns and very, very brief side of right breast, when leaving the room.
- • 1:00—Very brief buns, when standing up to make love with her husband.
- •• 1:01—Nude, getting out of bed and walking around the house.
- • 1:04—Buns visible through opening in apron.
- • 1:06—Brief buns, when turning over on couch with her husband. Long shot. Very, very brief partial breasts, when sitting up.

Ackerman, Leslie

Films:

Cracking Up (1977). . . . . .n.a.
The First Nudie Musical (1979) . . . . .Susie
Hardcore (1979) . . . . Felice
- • 0:44—Breasts in porno house with George C. Scott.

Blame It on the Night (1984). . . . . Shelley

TV:

Skag (1980) . . . . Barbara Skagska

• Adams, April

Films:

Teenage Catgirls in Heat (1993) . . . . Storm Catgirl

Eve's Beach Fantasy (1997) . . . . Eve

• 0:01—Breasts and buns during fantasy.

• 0:23—Very brief left breast, popping out of her bra, when turning over in bed.

•• 0:30—Breasts, while in back seat of limousine during fantasy with a guy.

• 0:36—Brief left breast, when standing up in restaurant in dream.

• 0:38—Very brief left breast, popping out of her bra, when turning over in bed.

••• 0:47—Nude, while trying on different swimsuits and clothes in bathroom.

••• 0:55—Nude, when taking off robe and taking a shower.

• 1:02—Brief breasts and buns in flashback of 0:47 scenes.

• 1:05—Buns in swimsuit during photo shoot.

• 1:09—Buns in lingerie, while posing during photo session.

••• 1:15—Nude, while making love with the photographer.

Adams, Brooke

Films:

Shock Waves (1977) . . . . Rose

Days of Heaven (1978) . . . . Abby

Invasion of the Body Snatchers (1978) . . . Elizabeth Driscoll

•• 1:43—Brief breasts behind plants when Sutherland sees her change into a pod person. Hard to see because plants are in the way.

• 1:48—Breasts walking through the pod factory pointing out Sutherland to everybody. Long shot, hard to see.

Cuba (1979) . . . . Alexandra Pulido

Tell Me a Riddle (1980) . . . . Jeannie

The Dead Zone (1983) . . . . Sarah Bracknell

Utilities (1983) . . . . Marion

Almost You (1984) . . . . Erica Boyer

Key Exchange (1985) . . . . Lisa

• 0:45—Very brief right breast getting into the shower with her boyfriend, then hard to see behind the shower curtain.

The Unborn (1991) . . . . Virginia Marshall

• 1:12—Right breast, while breast feeding her baby creature.

Gas, Food, Lodging (1992) . . . . Nora

Made for Cable Movies:

The Last Hit (1993; USA) . . . . Anna

Made for Cable TV:

Picture Windows: Song of Songs (1995; Showtime) . . . . Angie Varnas

Miniseries:

Lace (1984) . . . . Pagan

Lace II (1985) . . . . Pagan

Made for TV Movies:

Bridesmaids (1989) . . . . Pat

Stephen King's "Sometimes They Come Back" (1991) . . . Sally

TV:

O.K. Crackerby (1965-66) . . . . Cynthia Crackerby

Adams, Joey Lauren *

Films:

Coneheads (1993) . . . . Christina

Dazed and Confused (1993) . . . . Simone

The Program (1993) . . . . Louanne

S.F.W. (1994) . . . . Monica Dice

• 0:31—Brief upper half of right breast, then left breast, while making love in bed with Stephen Dorff.

Sleep With Me (1994) . . . . Lauren

Bio-Dome (1995) . . . . Monique

Mallrats (1995) . . . . Gwen

• 0:29—Brief breasts, while in dressing room before guy's head comes crashing through the wall.

Michael (1996) . . . . Anna

Chasing Amy (1997) . . . . Amy

TV:

Second Noah (1996) . . . . Joey

Adams, Kim

Films:

Ted & Venus (1991) . . . . Linda

• 0:16—In sheer leotard in dance studio.

••• 0:30—Breasts, reciting poetry while in bed at night.

Leaving Las Vegas (1995) . . . . Sheila

Hoodlum (1997) . . . . Show Girl

Adams, Lynne

Films:

Street Smart (1987) . . . . Reporter

Wild Thing (1987; U.S./Canadian) . . . . Edwina

The Carpenter (1988; Canadian) . . . . Alice

Blood Relations (1989; Canadian) . . . . Sharon Hamilton

Forbidden Love: The Unashamed Stories of Lesbian Lives (1992; Canadian) . . . . Mitch

• 1:17—Breasts, while with another woman.

Johnny Mnemonic (1995) . . . . Rocket Launcher Yakuza

Silent Hunter (1995) . . . . Anna

• 1:03—Very brief left breast, while pulling up her blouse to taunt Miles O'Keeffe.

Grace of My Heart (1996) . . . . Kindly Nurse

Habitat (1996; Canadian) . . . . Tara Fisher

• 1:30—Brief breasts in torn outfit after explosion.

Made for Cable Movies:

Hiroshima (1995; Canadian/Japanese; Showtime) . . . . Reporter

Adams, Maud *

Films:

The Christian Licorice Store (1971) . . . . Cynthia Vicstrom

The Girl in Blue (1973; Canadian) . . . . Paula/Tracy

a.k.a. U-turn

• 1:16—Side view of right breast, while sitting on bed with Scott.

The Man with the Golden Gun (1974; British) . . Andrea Anders

Killer Force (1975; Swiss/Irish) . . . . Claire Chambers

Rollerball (1975) . . . . Ella

Laura (1979) . . . . Sarah

a.k.a. Shattered Innocence

Tattoo (1981) . . . . Maddy

• 0:22—Very brief breasts taking off clothes and putting a bathrobe on.

•• 0:23—Breasts opening bathrobe so Bruce Dern can start painting.

•• 0:25—Brief breasts getting into the shower to take off body paint.

•• 0:58—Brief breasts and buns getting out of bed.

•• 1:04—Breasts, knocked out on table before Dern starts tattooing her.

••• 1:07—Breasts looking at herself in the mirror with a few tattoos on.

•• 1:24—Breasts lying on table masturbating while Dern watches through peep hole in the door.

••• 1:36—Full frontal nudity taking off robe then making love with Dern (her body is covered with tattoos).
Target Eagle (1982) . . . . . Carmen
Octopussy (1983; British) . . . . . Octopussy
Hell Hunters (1985) . . . . . Amanda Hoffman
Nairobi Affair (1986) . . . . . Anne Malone
Jane and the Lost City (1987; British) . . . . . Lola Pagola
The Women's Club (1987) . . . . . Angie Blake
Angel III: The Final Chapter (1988) . . . . . Nadine
Intimate Power (1989; Canadian) . . . . . Sineperver
A Man of Passion (1989) . . . . . Susana
The Kill Reflex (1990) . . . . . Crystal Tarver
Silent Night, Deadly Night 4: Initiation (1990) . . . . . Fima
Ringer (1996) . . . . . Leslie Polokoff

Made for TV Movies:
Playing for Time (1980) . . . . . Mala

TV:
Chicago Story (1982) . . . . . Dr. Judith Bergstrom
Emerald Point N.A.S. (1983-84) . . . . . Maggie Farrell

Adams, Rhonda *

Video Tapes:
Playboy Video Calendar 1996 (1995) . . . . . July
••• 0:27—Nude in house after surprise birthday party.
••• 0:28—Nude in warehouse.
Playboy's Girls of the Internet (1996) . . . . . Herself
••• 0:10—Nude, while at the beach with two other women.

Adams, Stephanie *

Video Tapes:
Playboy Video Calendar 1994 (1993) . . . . . April
••• 0:15—Nude with brightly colored props in studio.
••• 0:17—Nude (down to stockings and garter belt) in hot office fantasy.
Playboy's Playmate Review 1993 (1993) . . Miss November
••• 0:12—Nude in house and in bed.
Playboy's Sexy, Steamy, Sultry (1993) . . . . . Playmate
Playboy's Women of Color (1994) . . . . . Playmate
••• 0:30—Nude, while in motion and in still photos.
••• 0:33—Nude, while posing in studio.
••• 0:35—Nude in warehouse fantasy.

Adams, Stephanie (2) *

Adult Films:
Centerfold Strippers (1994) . . . . . Herself

Adams, Tracey

See: Blaisdell, Deborah.

• *Addison, Joie*

Films:
What Do You Say to a Naked Lady? (1970) . . . . Girl in Elevator
The Love-Thrill Murders (1971) . . . . . Carol
•• 0:53—Breasts and buns with Chris during party, while everyone else watches.
•• 1:13—Nude, getting placed on and tied to dining cart.
••• 1:17—Breasts, while talking and tied to dining cart, then getting killed.
• 1:20—Side of right breast and lower frontal nudity, while lying dead on dining cart.

Adell, Traci *

Films:
Dumb & Dumber (1994) . . . . . Sexy Woman
Deadly Currency (1995) . . . . . Julia
Playback (1995) . . . . . Galaxy Club Waitress
TNT (1997) . . . . . Barbara

Made for Cable TV:
Dream On: Hey Diddle Diddle (1996; HBO) . . . . Woman #3
•• 0:05—Breasts, when joining Martin in the shower.

Video Tapes:
Playboy Video Centerfold: Anna-Marie Goddard (1994) . . . . . Runner-Up Playmate
••• 0:43—Nude in lingerie in sequence with a small pool and chair.
Playboy Video Calendar 1996 (1995) . . . . . June
••• 0:22—Nude posing in studio in various outfits.
••• 0:24—Nude in art studio.

Adjani, Isabelle

Films:
Story of Adele H. (1975; French) . . . . . Adele Hugo
The Tenant (1976; French) . . . . . Stella
The Driver (1978) . . . . . The Player
The Bronte Sisters (1979; French) . . . . . Emily
Nosferatu, The Vampire (1979; French/German) . . Lucy Harker
Possession (1981; French/German) . . . . . Anna/Helen
• 0:04—Breasts in bed.
• 0:16—Breasts lying in bed when Sam Neill pulls the covers over her.
••• 0:47—Right breast, then breasts lying in bed with Neill.
• 1:08—Right breast, while lying on the floor with Neill, then sitting up.
Quartet (1981; British/French) . . . . . Marya Zelli
•• 1:06—Breasts in bed with Alan Bates.
Next Year if All Goes Well (1983; French) . . . . . Isabelle
• 0:27—Brief right breast, lying in bed with Maxime.
One Deadly Summer (1984; French) . . . . . Eliane
•• 0:21—Brief breasts changing in the window for Florimond.
••• 0:32—Nude, walking in and out of the barn.
• 0:36—Brief left breast lying in bed when Florimond gets up.
• 0:40—Buns and breasts taking a bath.
• 1:41—Part of right breast, getting felt up by an old guy, then right breast then brief breasts.
•• 1:47—Breasts in bedroom with Florimond.
Subway (1985; French) . . . . . Helena
Ishtar (1987) . . . . . Shirra Assel
• 0:27—Very brief left breast flashing herself to Dustin Hoffman at the airport while wearing sunglasses.
Camille Claudel (1989; French) . . . . . Camille Claudel
Queen Margot (1994; French) . . . . . Marguerite of Valois (Margot)
a.k.a. La Reine Margot
•• 1:41—Full frontal nudity, while making love with Le Mole.
Diabolique (1996) . . . . . Mia Baran
• 0:03—Nude in bathroom.
• 0:05—Very, very brief right breast, while lying on the floor.

Agbayani, Tetchie

Films:
The Dolls (1984; German) . . . . . Lee
a.k.a. The Story of the Dolls
• 0:12—Brief right breast, several times, while fighting with Pedro on the beach.
••• 0:24—Breasts and buns, while undressing and taking a bubble bath with the other models.
•• 0:39—Buns and right breast, then full frontal nudity while posing on beach for Tom.
••• 0:41—Full frontal nudity, while making love on the beach with Tom.
•• 0:57—Buns, while making love with Tom.
• 0:58—Breasts in magazine photos.

• 1:01—Brief breasts in magazine photos.
• 1:03—Nude in magazine photos.
•• 1:04—Nude, while running on beach in flashback.
• 1:10—Very brief right breast, during tribal ceremony.
••• 1:12—Breasts, getting paint taken off her in bed, then sitting up.
• 1:24—Brief buns, while on the ground with Tom.

The Emerald Forest (1985) . . . . Caya
• 1:48—Breasts in the river when Kachiri is match making all the couples together.

Gymkata (1985) . . . . .Princess Rubali

The Money Pit (1986) . . . . .Florinda

Rikky & Pete (1988; Australian) . . . . Flossie
• 0:58—Brief upper half of left breast in bed with Pete when Rikky accidentally sees them in bed.
••• 1:30—Breasts in black panties dancing outside the jail while Pete watches from inside.

Mission Manila (1989) . . . . Maria

Indio 2: The Revolt (1990) . . . . Mrs. Morrell

Deathfight (1993) . . . . .n.a.

Agcaoili, Adriana

Films:

Dark Tide (1993) . . . . .Lia
• 1:14—Very, very brief right breast, while getting her blouse ripped open on table by Richard Tyson.

Fortunes of War (1993) . . . . Young Thai Nun

Behind Enemy Lines (1996) . . . . Chique

Ager, Suzanne

a.k.a. Amy Page.

Films:

Crocodile Dundee II (1988) . . . . Hooker

The Alien Within (1990) . . . . .Erin West
(Contains footage from *The Evil Spawn* woven together with new material.)

Mob Boss (1990) . . . . Pool Girl

Shock 'Em Dead (1990) . . . . Groupie 3

Smooth Talker (1990) . . . . .Candy (The 976-GIRL)
• 0:23—Left breast and partial buns, while lying on the floor dead.
• 0:24—More left breast, while lying dead on the floor. Lit with red light.
• 0:35—Left breast, while lying dead on the floor. Very brief buns in G-string.

Angel Eyes (1991) . . . . Nurse Stewart

Camp Fear (1991) . . . . .n.a.
a.k.a. Millenium Countdown

Evil Toons (1991) . . . . Terry
••• 0:31—Breasts and buns in G-string, taking off clothes to put on her pajamas.
•• 1:09—Right breast, while on the floor getting her pajamas ripped open by Roxanne.
•• 1:10—Brief breasts when Roxanne rips the pajamas all the way down.

Inner Sanctum (1991) . . . . Maureen

The Bikini Carwash Company (1992) . . . . Foxy
(Unrated version reviewed.)
• 0:59—Buns in G-string, doing strip routine.

Buford's Beach Bunnies (1992) . . . . Boopsie Underall
•• 0:19—Breasts in the shower.
• 0:20—Brief breasts when her towel falls off in front of telegram guy.
• 0:36—Buns, in red two piece swimsuit at the beach.
• 0:37—Buns, while walking up the stairs.

Fatal Justice (1992) . . . . Diana
••• 0:12—In black body suit, then breasts and buns in G-string while making love with her boyfriend.
• 0:36—Breasts while changing clothes behind room divider. Hard to see.

Inner Sanctum 2 (1994) . . . . .Maureen
(Unrated version reviewed.)

Aguilar, Orietta

Films:

La Ruletera (1987; Mexican) . . . . .n.a.

Barbarian Queen II: The Empress Strikes Back (1989) . . . . Erigina
•• 0:14—Breasts during fight in mud with Lana Clarkson.

Agutter, Jenny

Films:

East of Sudan (1964; British) . . . . Asua

Gates to Paradise (1968; British/German) . . . . Maud

I Started Counting (1970; British) . . . . Wynne

The Railway Children (1971; British) . . . . Bobbie

Walkabout (1971; Australian/U.S.) . . . . Girl
•• 0:57—Nude, while swimming in the water.
•• 1:00—Breasts, while getting dressed.
•• 1:19—Breasts, when surprised in the house by David Gulpilil.
•• 1:37—Nude, when swimming outdoors with her little brother and Gulpilil.

Logan's Run (1976) . . . . .Jessica
• 1:05—Very brief breasts and buns changing into fur coat in ice cave with Michael York.

The Eagle Has Landed (1977; British) . . . . Molly Prior

Equus (1977; British) . . . . Jill Mason
••• 2:00—Nude in loft above the horses in orange light, then making love with Alan.

China 9, Liberty 37 (1978; Italian) . . . . Catherine
a.k.a. Gunfire
(Hard to find this video tape. *Gunfire* has the nude scenes cut out.)
•• 0:06—Full frontal nudity (long shot), while undressing to bathe in a stream. Close up shot of breasts partially under the water when she is sitting in the stream.
•• 0:35—Breasts, after taking off her dress outdoors with Clayton.
•• 0:47—Brief buns and side of right breast, when standing up in bathtub. Brief breasts, while getting dried off.
•• 1:09—Breasts and partial buns, while making love in bed with Clayton.

Dominique is Dead (1978; British) . . . . .Miss Ballard
a.k.a. Dominique

Survivor (1980; Australian) . . . . .Hobbs

Sweet William (1980; British) . . . . .Ann
• 0:27—Buns, while standing on balcony with Sam Waterston.
•• 0:28—Breasts sitting on edge of the bed while talking with Waterston.
• 0:44—Brief left breast when Waterston takes her blouse off in the living room.

An American Werewolf in London (1981) . . . . . Alex Price
• 0:41—Brief right breast in bed with David Naughton. Dark, hard to see.

Riddle of the Sands (1984; British) . . . . .Clara Dollman

Secret Places (1984; British) . . . . .Miss Lowrie

Dark Tower (1987) . . . . Carolyn Page

Child's Play 2 (1990) . . . . Joanne Simpson

Darkman (1990) . . . . Uncredited Doctor

Made for Cable TV:
Dream On: No Deposit, No Return (1992; HBO) . . . . Ellen
Miniseries:
The Buccaneers (1995; U.S./British). . . . . Idina Hatton
Made for TV Movies:
The Man in the Iron Mask (1977) . . . . Louise de la Valliere
Beulah Land (1980). . . . . Lizzie Corlay
Silas Marner (1985; British) . . . . Nancy Lammeter

Aimee, Anouk

Films:
La Dolce Vita (1960; Italian/French). . . . . Maddalena
Lola (1961; French/Italian) . . . . .Lola
Sodom and Gomorrah (1962; U.S./French) . . . . Queen Bera
A Man and a Woman (1966; French). . . . . .Anne Gauthier
Justine (1969; Italian/Spanish). . . . . .Justine
•• 0:36—Nude, while frolicking in the ocean.
The Model Shop (1969) . . . . .Lola
The Tragedy of a Ridiculous Man (1981; Italian)
. . . . Barbara Spaggiari
Success is the Best Revenge (1984; British)
. . . . Monique de Fontaine
A Man and a Woman: 20 Years Later (1986; French)
. . . . .Anne Gauthier
Dr. Bethune (1993; Canadian/French)
. . . . Marie-Frances Coudaire
Ready to Wear (1994) . . . . Simone Lowenthal
a.k.a. Prêt-à-porter

Aiton, Lisa Bradford

See: Bradford-Aiton, Lisa.

Akers, Andra

Films:
Moment by Moment (1978). . . . . Naomi
Desert Hearts (1986) . . . . .Silver
• 1:16—Left breast, while sitting in windowsill with Patricia Charboneau.
Video Tapes:
E. Nick: A Legend in His Own Mind (1984) . . . . Aunt Mona

Akesson, Monica

Films:
Novel Desires (1991) . . . . .Model
••• 0:17—Buns, then breasts while making love outside during story.
••• 0:18—Breasts making love on picnic table with Eric.
The Swindle (1991) . . . . Tom's Last Hurrah
••• 1:17—Breasts, then full frontal nudity, posing on couch for Tom.
Last Dance (1992). . . . . .Body Double

Akkemay

Films:
Army Brats (1984; Dutch) . . . . Madeline Gisberts
•• 0:22—Breasts in the shower with her boyfriend.
• 0:26—Brief breasts, taking off towel and putting on robe while arguing with her mother.
• 0:32—Brief breasts while changing tops.
• 0:47—Brief breasts while sunbathing outside (seen through binoculars).
• 1:24—Breasts in bed with her boyfriend.
The Assault (1986; Dutch). . . . . Sandra

Alaouie, Afifi

Films:
Steel Frontier (1994) . . . . Shay

Austin Powers: International Man of Mystery (1997)
. . . . '60s Model
Made for Cable Movies:
Dead Weekend (1995; Showtime) . . . . Amelia B
•• 0:15—Breasts, while making love with Stephen Baldwin in barn.

Alard, Nelly

Films:
Eating (1990). . . . . .Martine
••• 0:06—Breasts, several times while sunbathing, then getting up and walking by pool, sitting down and tying a blouse around her waist.
Venice/Venice (1992). . . . . Jeanne

*Alberico, Natasha **

Video Tapes:
Playboy's College Girls (1994) . . . . Herself
••• 0:01—Nude, while drying off in bedroom after a shower, then dressing.
••• 0:03—Nude, with a muscular guy in B&W segment.

*Albert, Laura **

Films:
Angel III: The Final Chapter (1988) . . . . Nude Dancer
• 0:00—Brief breasts dancing in a casino. Wearing red G-string.
• 0:01—Brief breasts dancing in background.
• 0:06—Side view of left breast and buns, while yelling at Molly for taking her picture.
Bloodstone (1988) . . . . Kim Chi
• 0:05—Very brief side view of left breast turning around in pool to look at a guy.
Death By Dialogue (1988). . . . . Linda
••• 0:29—Breasts in white panties, while making love on top of her boyfriend.
•• 0:57—Breasts after pulling her dress top down in nightmare, then yanking her boyfriend's head off.
Glitch (1988) . . . . Topless
• 0:33—Brief breasts auditioning for Todd and Bo by taking off her top.
The Jigsaw Murders (1988). . . . . .Blonde Stripper
••• 0:19—Breasts and buns in black G-string, stripping during bachelor party in front of a group of policemen.
Party Plane (1988) . . . . Uncredited Auditioning Woman
•• 0:30—Breasts, taking off blue dress during audition. She's wearing a white ribbon in her ponytail.
The Unnameable (1988) . . . . .Wendy Barnes
•• 0:46—Left breast while lying on floor kissing John, then brief buns when he pulls her panties down.
Blood Games (1989) . . . . .Babe
Dr. Alien (1989). . . . . Rocker Chick #3
a.k.a. I Was a Teenage Sex Mutant
••• 0:21—Breasts in black outfit during dream sequence with two other rocker chicks.
Dr. Caligari (1989) .Mrs. Van Houten
••• 0:05—Breasts taking off yellow towel, then sitting in bathtub.
•• 0:07—Lying down, making love with guy wearing a mask.
••• 0:10—Breasts taking orange bra off, then lying back and playing with herself.
•• 0:11—More breasts, lying on the floor.
•• 0:12—More breasts, lying on the floor again.
• 0:30—Brief left breast with big tongue.
Roadhouse (1989). . . . . .Strip Joint Girl
•• 0:45—Breasts and buns dancing on stage, wearing a hat.

Stone Cold (1991) . . . . Joe's Girlfriend
- • 0:11—Buns, in bed when waking up. Very brief right breast.

Live By the Fist (1992). . . . . Helen Ferris
The Unnameable II (1992) . . . . Guest Corpse
Naked Gun 33 1/3: The Final Insult (1993) . . . . Stunts
Automatic (1994) . . . . Stunt Player
Double Dragon (1994) . . . . Stunts
Fist of the North Star (1995) . . . . Stunts
Hellraiser: Bloodline (1996) . . . . Stunt Double Rimmer
Starship Troopers (1996) . . . . Stunts

Made for Cable Movies:

Rebel Highway: Roadracers (1994; Showtime) . . . . Stunts

Made for Cable TV:

Tales From the Crypt: The Man Who was Death (1989; HBO) . . . . Go-Go Dancer
- • 0:20—Brief breasts a couple of times dancing in a cage in a nightclub.

Dream On: The First Episode (1990; HBO) . . . . Whipped Cream Girl
Dream On: Pants on Fire (1991; HBO). . . . . Tanya
- •• 0:16—Breasts sitting up on the couch, talking to Martin.

Dream On: Take Two Tablets, And Get Me to Mt. Sinai (1995; HBO) . . . . Martin's Lover

Alda, Rutanya

Films:

The Long Goodbye (1973) . . . . Marloe's Neighbor
Pat Garrett and Billy the Kid (1973). . . . . Ruthie Lee
(Uncut Director's version reviewed.)
- •• 1:35—Breasts, while sitting on bed with James Coburn. (She's the only girl wearing a necklace.)

Scarecrow (1973) . . . . Woman in Camper
Swashbuckler (1976). . . . . Bath Attendant
The Deer Hunter (1978) . . . . Angela
The Fury (1978) . . . . Kristen
When a Stranger Calls (1979) . . . . Mrs. Mandrakis
Mommie Dearest (1981). . . . . Carol Ann
Amityville II: The Possession (1982). . . . . Deloris Montelli
Girls Nite Out (1982) . . . . Barney
a.k.a. Scared to Death
Vigilante (1983) . . . . Vickie
Racing with the Moon (1984). . . . . Mrs. Nash
Rappin' (1985) . . . . Cecilia
The Stuff (1985) . . . . Psychologist
Hot Shot (1986) . . . . Georgia Kristidis
Apprentice to Murder (1987) . . . . Elma Kelly
Black Widow (1987) . . . . Irene
Gross Anatomy (1989) . . . . Mama Slovak
Prancer (1990) . . . . Aunt Sarah
Article 99 (1992). . . . . Ann Travis
Leaving Normal (1992). . . . . Palmer House Nurse
The Dark Half (1993). . . . . Miriam Cowley
The Ref (1993) . . . . Linda
a.k.a. Hostile Hostages
Steel (1997) . . . . Mrs. Hunt

Made for Cable Movies:

Laguna Heat (1987; HBO). . . . . n.a.
They (1993; Showtime). . . . . Sue Madehurst

Made for Cable TV:

Tales From the Crypt: Deadline (1991; HBO). . . . . Mildred

Made for TV Movies:

Double Jeopardy (1996) . . . . Gabriel Neuland

Alda, Ruth

Films:

Greetings (1968). . . . . Linda (Shoplifter)
- • 0:59—Undressing on bed in sheer bra while Robert De Niro films her.

Hi, Mom! (1971). . . . . "Be Black Baby" Audience Member
The Panic in Needle Park (1971) . . . . Admitting Nurse

*Alden, Stacey **

Films:

Grotesque (1987) . . . . n.a.
A Nightmare on Elm Street 3: The Dream Warriors (1987). . . . . Marcie
- ••• 0:49—Breasts and buns in white G-string, taking off nurse's uniform and seducing Joey in hospital room. Then giving him the tongue before turning into Freddy Kruger.

Alessandrini, Toni

Films:

The Sex and Violence Family Hour (1983; Canadian) . . . . Body Flash Dancer
- •• 1:05—Buns in one piece leotard, while dancing in a studio. Nude after taking it off to put on a robe.

Bachelor Party (1984) . . Desiree, Woman Dancing with Donkey
- • 1:24—Buns, in G-string, while dancing with donkey during party.

Hell Squad (1986) . . . . Night Club Waitress
Marked for Murder (1990) . . . . Toni
- • 0:38—Breasts while serving drinks to Winfield in bar.
- •• 0:40—Breasts while talking with Wings Hauser in bar.
- •• 0:42—Buns in G-string and breasts, when bringing drinks to Hauser.

Vice Academy, Part 2 (1990) . . . . Aphrodisia
- • 0:33—Breasts in dressing room.
- ••• 0:34—Breasts and buns in G-string, dancing in club.

Vice Academy, Part 3 (1991) . . . . Stripper
- •• 0:26—Breasts taking off dress on stage.
- •• 0:27—More breasts on stage (about five times).
- • 0:28—More breasts giving her money to the robbers.
- • 0:34—Buns in G-string, while dancing on stage.

Mind, Body & Soul (1992). . . . . Priestess Tura
- •• 1:05—Breasts under fishnet body stocking during occult dance in a house.

Pleasure in Paradise (1992) . . . . Lingerie Girl/First
- •• 0:51—In black lingerie, then breasts and buns in G-string, while dancing in bar.

Alexander, Adriana

Films:

Barb Wire (1995). . . . . Redhead

Video Tapes:

Playboy's Sisters (1995). . . . . Herself/Friend & Confidant
- ••• 0:42—Nude while posing with her sister in country farmhouse fantasy.

Alexander, Annastasia

a.k.a. Raven Alexander.

Films:

Anthony's Desire (1993) . . . . Dancer
- ••• 0:04—Nude, on stage stripping out of black dress. Wearing gloves.
- •• 0:22—Full frontal nudity, while stretching in the background on the left.
- •• 0:54—Breasts while lying on her back in the middle of the group of women.
- • 1:02—Breasts, while sitting in the background on the left.

Midnight Confessions (1993) .... Britt
(Unrated version reviewed.)
••• 0:37—Nude, while performing oral sex on a customer.
Sex and the Single Alien (1993)................. Roxana
••• 0:09—Breasts and buns in string lingerie, while dancing on stage.
•• 0:25—Breasts, while dancing on stage.
Witchcraft V: Dance with the Devil (1993) ..... Sacrifice
••• 1:15—Nude, undressing and getting sacrificed on table. Long scene.
Video Tapes:
Love Scenes: Volume 2 (1992) .... Lisa Carey
•• 1:36—Nude, while swimming under water with David, Tom and Suzanne.
••• 1:38—Breasts, while on boat with David and Tom, then during food fight with ice cream and chocolate.
••• 1:45—Nude, during orgy on boat with David, Tom and Suzanne.

Alexander, Barbara Lee

See: Niven, Barbara.

Alexander, Jane

Chairperson of the National Endowment for the Arts (1993-1997).
Films:
The Great White Hope (1970).................... Eleanor
A Gunfight (1971)........................ Nora Tenneray
The New Centurions (1972) .... Dorothy
The Betsy (1978)...................... Alicia Hardeman
Kramer vs. Kramer (1979) .... Margaret Phelps
Brubaker (1980) .... Lillian
Night Crossing (1981).....................Doris Strelzyks
Testament (1983) .... Carol Wetherly
City Heat (1984)...............................Addy
Sweet Country (1985) ....Anna
• 1:39—Brief side view of left breast after getting out of bed.
Square Dance (1987) ....Juanelle
a.k.a. Home is Where the Heart Is
Made for TV Movies:
Playing for Time (1980).......................Alma Rose
Stay the Night (1992).................Blanche Kettmann

Alexander, Khandi

Films:
A Chorus Line (1985) .... Dancer
Streetwalkin' (1985) ....Star
Army of One (1993) ....Maralena
CB4 (1993)... Sissy
• 0:51—In bra and brief partial buns in panties on bed on top of Chris Rock. Side view of right breast, twice, while letting Allen Payne and Chris Rock poke it (Don't see her face, probably a body double).
Greedy (1993).....................................Laura
Menace II Society (1993).................. Karen Lawson
Poetic Justice (1993) ....Simone
Sugar Hill (1993)........................... Ella Scuggs
What's Love Got to Do With It (1993) ....Darlene
House Party 3 (1994) ....Janelle
Made for TV Movies:
To My Daughter with Love (1994)................. Harriet
Robin Cook's "Terminal" (1996) .... Dr. Levy
TV:
ER (1995) .... Jackie Benton
NewsRadio (1995-97) ....Catherine Duke

Alexander, Nina

See: Parton, Julia.

Alexander, Raven

See: Alexander, Annastasia.

• Alexandra, Charlotte

Films:
Immoral Tales (1975; French)...... Therese the Philosopher
•• 0:32—Breasts, undressing by herself in room.
•• 0:34—Breasts and buns, in bed while playing with a cucumber.
••• 0:36—Breasts and buns.
•• 0:38—Buns and breasts while lying in bed.
Goodbye Emmanuelle (1977) .... Chloe
••• 0:17—Breasts and brief lower frontal nudity with another girl.
••• 0:20—Nude, walking around the house while everybody is eating breakfast.

Alexandra, Tiana

Real name: Thi Thanh Nga.
Wife of the late producer/writer Stirling Silliphant.
Films:
The Killer Elite (1975) .... Tommie
Catch the Heat (1987) ....Checkers Goldberg
• 0:20—Left breast, several times, while in the shower.
From Hollywood to Hanoi (1993) .... Herself

Alfred, Rebekah

Films:
Bikini Summer (1991) .... D.A. Rachel Green
•• 1:20—In bra, then breasts and buns in dressing room, trying on swimsuit after everyone has left.
Video Tapes:
Score with Chicks (1992).................. Cast Member

Alhanti, Iris

Films:
Kramer vs. Kramer (1979) ....n.a.
Partners (1982)................................ Jogger
•• 0:21—Breasts in the shower when Ryan O'Neal opens the shower curtain.

Aliff, Lisa

Films:
Dragnet (1987)...................................April
Remote Control (1987) .... Heroine
Trained to Kill (1988)...................... Jessie Revels
Playroom (1989)............................... Jenny
a.k.a. Schizo
•• 0:23—Breasts making love on top of Christopher.
Damned River (1990)..........................Anne
• 0:32—Very, very brief top of right breast in open blouse, then half of right breast in wet blouse washing her hair.
• 0:50—Very brief breasts struggling with Ray when he rips her top open. Don't see her face.
Made for TV Movies:
Love and Betrayal (1989).........................Patty

Alise, Esther

a.k.a. Esther Elise.
Films:
Deathrow Game Show (1988)................ Groupie
•• 0:08—Breasts in bed with Chuck.

Hollywood Chainsaw Hookers (1988). . . . . Lisa
••• 0:25—Breasts playing with a baseball bat while a John photographs her.
Midnight Cabaret (1988) . . . . Dancer
Vampire at Midnight (1988) . . . . Lucia Giannini
••• 1:01—In black lingerie, then breasts and buns while taking off clothes to wish Roger a happy birthday.

*Allain, Valerie **
Films:
Club de Rencontres (1986; French). . . . . Cricri
Aria (1987; U.S./British). . . . . Young Girl in Blue
• 0:22—Brief breasts with another girl in a weight lifting room walking around with muscular guys.
• 0:25—Brief breasts again.
•• 0:27—Nude in front of a weight lifter.
• 0:29—More nude, posing while the guys walk by.
Alouette, Je te Plumerai (1988) . . . . n.a.
TV:
French in Action (1987) . . . . Mireille Belleau
(Never wore a bra in this French language instructional series.)

• *Allan, Jennifer **
Video Tapes:
Playboy Video Calendar 1998 (1997) . . . . April
••• 0:14—Nude, while posing during apartment fantasy.
••• 0:16—Nude, while posing indoors.
Playboy's Fast Women (1997) . . . . Playmate

*Allen, Ashley **
Video Tapes:
Playboy Video Calendar 1994 (1993) . . . . March
••• 0:10—Nude on bed and in various lingerie outfits.
••• 0:12—Nude, lit with different lights.
Playboy's Playmate Review 1993 (1993) . . . . .Miss August
••• 0:32—Nude in a field and on horseback.
••• 0:33—Nude outside posing by freeway.
Playboy's Sexy, Steamy, Sultry (1993). . . . . Playmate
Playboy's The Girls of Hawaiian Tropic (1994)
. . . . Hawaiian Earth
••• 0:40—Nude, while posing at a black sand beach.

*Allen, Ginger Lynn **
Former adult film actress.
Films:
Vice Academy (1988) . . . . Holly
• 1:20—Buns, in white lingerie outfit when graduation robe gets torn off.
Wild Man (1988) . . . . Dawn Hall
•• 0:24—Breasts taking off her dress in front of Eric, then making love with him.
Cleo/Leo (1989) . . . . Karen
••• 0:39—Full frontal nudity getting out of the shower, getting dried with a towel by Jane Hamilton, then in nightgown.
••• 0:57—Full frontal nudity getting out of the shower and dried off again.
Dr. Alien (1989) . . . . Rocker Chick #1
a.k.a. I Was a Teenage Sex Mutant
••• 0:21—Breasts in red panties during dream sequence with two other rocker chicks.
Edgar Allan Poe's "Buried Alive" (1989) . . . . Debbie
• 0:12—Very, very brief left breast, while struggling with the other girls in the kitchen.
Hollywood Boulevard II (1989) . . . . Candy Chandler
•• 0:33—Breasts in screening room with Woody, the writer.
Vice Academy, Part 2 (1990) . . . . Holly
• 0:44—Buns in black bra, panties, garter belt and stockings.
•• 1:04—Buns in G-string, then breasts dancing with Linnea Quigley on stage at club.
Young Guns II (1990) . . . . Dove
Leather Jackets (1991). . . . . Bree
•• 0:39—Breasts on stage for Mickey's bachelor party. Buns, in G-string. Made up to look like Geisha Girls.
Vice Academy, Part 3 (1991) . . . . Holly
Whore (1991) . . . . Wounded Girl
a.k.a. If you're afraid to say it... Just see it
Mind, Body & Soul (1992). . . . . Brenda
•• 0:13—Breasts in open blouse while getting raped in jail by a guard.
••• 0:17—Breasts while talking with her boyfriend in open blouse and dripping candle wax on him.
••• 1:10—Breasts while lying in bed with her boyfriend, Sean.
Trouble Bound (1992) . . . . Uncredited Adult Film Actress
•• 0:22—Breasts on TV in motel room that Kit and Harry are watching.
Bound and Gagged: A Love Story (1993) . . . . .Leslie
••• 0:13—Breasts, while making love on kitchen counter with Chris Mulkey, then on the floor.
0:43—Very, very brief inner half of right breast, when her blouse is opened by Elizabeth.
• 0:48—Breasts, in back seat of car when a guy tries to "help" her.
The Stranger (1994) . . . . Sally Womack
Ultimate Taboo (1994) . . . . n.a.
TV:
SuperForce (1991-92) . . . . Crystal
NYPD Blue: Tempest In a C-Cup (Nov 16, 1993) . . Monique
• 0:22—Brief buns in G-string, while dancing in front Sipowicz at his table.
• 0:23—Brief buns in G-string, while closing door in backstage room with Sipowicz.
Video Tapes:
B-Movie Queens Revealed: The Making of "Vice Academy" (1993) . . . . Holly
• 0:35—Buns in T-back, dancing on stage with Linnea Quigley from *Vice Academy 2.*
•• 0:38—Breasts, dancing on stage with Quigley from *Vice Academy 2.*
Ginger Lynn Allen's Lingerie Gallery (1994) . . . . . Herself
Ginger Lynn Allen's Lingerie Gallery, Part 2 (1995) . . n.a.
CD-ROM:
Wing Commander III (1994) . . . . Chief Tech Rachel

*Allen, India **
Ex-wife of TV sportscaster Bill Macatee.
Films:
Round Numbers (1990). . . . . Swimsuit Model
Wild Cactus (1992). . . . . Alex
(Unrated version reviewed.)
••• 0:21—Buns and breasts, making love in bed on top of Naughton.
••• 0:34—Breasts, while pouring maple syrup on herself and making love with Naughton in the kitchen. Yummy!
••• 1:10—Nude, getting into and out of the shower.
••• 1:13—Nude, getting lotion rubbed on her by Maggie.
•• 1:18—Breasts, while making love in bed with Randall.
•• 1:20—Lower frontal nudity when Randall gets out of bed.
Almost Hollywood (1994) . . . . Herself
•• 0:55—Left breast, then breasts, while in bed with Dirk.
• 1:02—Brief buns, while wearing lingerie on the set.
The Force (1994). . . . . Cop #1

Seduce Me: Pamela Principle 2 (1994) . . . . Elaine
- •• 0:19—Breasts when Charles opens her pajamas in bed to try to make love with her.
- ••• 0:27—Breasts and buns, while taking a shower.
- •• 1:13—Nude, walking outside and getting into spa, then in spa. Medium long shots.
- ••• 1:25—Nude, when making love with her lover in shower while Charles watches from outside.

Silk Degrees (1994) . . . . Sheila
- •• 0:02—Breasts, while making love in bed with Degrillo.

Video Tapes:

Playboy Video Calendar 1989 (1988) . . . . January
- ••• 0:01—Nude.

Playboy Video Centerfold: India Allen (1988) . . . . Playmate of the Year 1988
- ••• 0:05—Nude in still photos.
- ••• 0:06—Nude in a field and by the side of a motel.
- ••• 0:09—Nude in and outside of house during the day and at night.
- ••• 0:12—Breasts and buns while exercising. Nice and sweaty.
- •• 0:13—Nude posing on chair in house. Quick cuts.
- ••• 0:15—Nude and in lingerie, while dancing. Color and B&W.
- •• 0:18—Nude while dancing in a sheer dress.
- ••• 0:19—Nude in bed. Lit with a swinging lamp, then continuous light.

Playboy's Playmates of the Year: The '80s (1989) . . . . Playmate of the Year 1988
- ••• 0:03—Nude, posing in chair.
- ••• 0:04—Nude, exercising and dancing around the house.
- ••• 0:06—Nude in bed.
- •• 0:52—Breasts in chair. Full frontal nudity in bed.

Playmates at Play (1990) . . . . Hoops, Hardbodies

The Best of Video Playmate Calendars (1992) . . Playmate
- •• 0:39—Breasts and buns in B&W music video.
- •• 0:40—Nude in bed.
- ••• 0:41—Nude in more B&W and color music video segments.
- ••• 0:42—Nude in bed.

Playboy's Playmates Revisited (1998) . . . . Playmate
- ••• 0:20—Nude in old footage and still photos.
- ••• 0:27—Full frontal nudity in new footage.

Allen, Karen

Films:

Animal House (1978) . . . . Katherine "Katy" Fuller
- • 1:21—Brief buns putting on shirt when Boone visits her at her house.

Manhattan (1979) . . . . TV Actor
The Wanderers (1979) . . . . Nina
Cruising (1980) . . . . Nancy
A Small Circle of Friends (1980) . . . . Jessica
- • 0:47—Brief breasts in bathroom with Brad Davis. Don't see her face.
- • 0:48—Very brief breasts, pushing Davis off her. Then very, very brief half of left breast turning around to walk to the mirror.

Raiders of the Lost Ark (1981) . . . . Marion Ravenwood
Shoot the Moon (1982) . . . . Sandy
Split Image (1982) . . . . Rebecca
Starman (1984) . . . . Jenny Hayden
Until September (1984) . . . . Mo Alexander
- •• 0:41—Breasts in bed making love with Thierry Lhermitte.
- •• 1:13—Breasts and buns walking from bed to Lhermitte.
- • 1:25—Brief breasts jumping out of bathtub.

Backfire (1987) . . . . Mara
- • 0:48—Lots of buns, then brief breasts with Keith Carradine in the bedroom.
- • 1:00—Brief breasts in the shower.

The Glass Menagerie (1987) . . . . Laura
Scrooged (1988) . . . . Claire Phillips
Sweet Talker (1991; Australian) . . . . Julie
Malcolm X (1992) . . . . Miss Dunne
Ghost in the Machine (1993) . . . . Terry Monroe
King of the Hill (1993) . . . . Miss Mathey
The Sandlot (1993) . . . . Mom

Made for Cable Movies:

Secret Weapon (1990) . . . . Ruth

Made for Cable TV:

Voyage (1993; USA) . . . . Kit

Made for TV Movies:

Challenger (1990) . . . . Christa McAuliffe

TV:

East of Eden (1981) . . . . Abra
The Road Home (1994-95) . . . . Alison Matson

• *Allen, Krista*

Films:

Raven (1996) . . . . Cali Goodwin
- •• 0:39—Partial right breast, then breasts, while making love with Martin.
- • 1:23—Breasts, while making love in bed with Martin.
- • 1:25—Brief breasts, when sitting up in bed.

Liar, Liar (1997) . . . . Busty Woman in Elevator

Made for Cable TV:

Full Frontal Comedy (1995; Showtime) . . . . Woman of Full Frontal Comedy

TV:

Days of Our Lives (1996-) . . . . Billie Reed

Allen, Nancy

Ex-wife of stand-up comedian Craig Shoemaker.
Ex-wife of director Brian De Palma.

Films:

The Last Detail (1973) . . . . Nancy
Forced Entry (1975) . . . . Hitchhiker
Carrie (1976) . . . . Chris Hargenson
- •• 0:01—Nude, in slow motion in girls' locker room behind Amy Irving.

I Wanna Hold Your Hand (1978) . . . . Pam
1941 (1979) . . . . Donna
Dressed to Kill (1980) . . . . Liz Blake
- • 1:36—Breasts (from above), buns and brief right breast in shower.

Home Movies (1980) . . . . Kristina
- • 1:14—Very brief left breast when bending over while sitting on bed and again when reaching up to touch Keith Gordon's face.

Blow Out (1981) . . . . Sally
- • 0:58—Brief upper half of right breast with the sheet pulled up in B&W photograph that John Travolta examines.

Strange Invaders (1983) . . . . Betty Walker
The Buddy System (1984) . . . . Carrie
Not for Publication (1984) . . . . Lois Thorndyke
The Philadelphia Experiment (1984) . . . . Allison
Terror in the Aisles (1984) . . . . Hostess
Robocop (1987) . . . . Anne Lewis
Sweet Revenge (1987) . . . . Jillian Grey
Poltergeist III (1988) . . . . Patricia Gardner
Limit Up (1989) . . . . Casey Falls
Robocop 2 (1990) . . . . Anne Lewis

The Turning (1992). . . . . Glory Lawson
Robocop 3 (1993). . . . . Anne Lewis
Made for Cable Movies:
Memories of Murder (1990; Lifetime) . . . . n.a.
Acting on Impulse (1993; Showtime) . . . . Cathy Tomas
Made for Cable TV:
The Outer Limits: Valerie 23 (1995; Showtime) . . . . Rachel Rose
The Outer Limits: Mary 25 (1998; Showtime) . . . . . Rachel Rose
Made for TV Movies:
The Man Who Wouldn't Die (1995) . . . . n.a.

Allen, Rosalind

a.k.a. Rosalind Ingledew.
Films:
Perfect (1985). . . . . Sterling
8 Million Ways to Die (1986). . . . . Tote Lady
Three Men and a Little Lady (1990) . . . . Pretty Girl
To Die For 2 (1991) . . . . Nina
a.k.a. Son of Darkness: To Die For II
- • 0:37—Breasts a few times in bed, while making love with Max.

Children of the Corn II: The Final Sacrifice (1992) . . . . . .Angela
Naked Gun 33 1/3: The Final Insult (1993) . . . . Bobbi
Ticks (1993) . . . . Holly Lambert
Love Affair (1994) . . . . Quantas Flight Attendant
Pinocchio's Revenge (1996) . . . . Jennifer Garrick
- • 0:38—Breasts, while making love with David in bed.

Made for Cable TV:
Dream On: The First Episode (1990; HBO) . . . . .Lauren
Dream On: Trojan War (1990; HBO) . . . . .Lauren
Made for TV Movies:
Ray Alexander: A Taste for Justice (1994). . . . . . Patricia Radcliff
Dallas: J.R. Returns (1996). . . . . Julie Cunningham
TV:
All My Children . . . . Noelle Keaton
Santa Barbara . . . . .Gretchen Richards
Seaquest DSV (1994-95). Wendy Smith

Allen, Sabrina

See: Moran, Stacy.

*Alley, Kirstie **

Ex-wife of actor Parker Stevenson.
Films:
Star Trek II: The Wrath of Kahn (1982) . . . . .Lt. Saavik
Blind Date (1984). . . . . Claire Simpson
a.k.a. Deadly Seduction
(Not to be confused with *Blind Date* (1987) with Bruce Willis.)
Deadly Seduction has Kirstie Alley's nude scene cut out.
- • 0:12—Brief breasts making love in bed with Joseph Bottoms. Dark, hard to see anything.

Runaway (1984) . . . . Jackie
Summer School (1987). . . . . .Robin Bishop
Shoot to Kill (1988). . . . . .Sarah
Look Who's Talking (1989) . . . . Mollie
Loverboy (1989) . . . . Joyce Palmer
Look Who's Talking Too (1990) . . . . Mollie
Madhouse (1990) . . . . .Jessie
Sibling Rivalry (1990) . . . . Marjorie Turner
Look Who's Talking Now! (1993) . . . . .Mollie Ubriacco
It Takes Two (1995). . . . . .Diane Barrows
Village of the Damned (1995). . . . . Dr. Susan Verner
Deconstructing Harry (1997) . . . . Joan
For Richer or Poorer (1997). . . . . .Caroline Sexton
Made for Cable TV:
The Hitchhiker: Out of the Night (1985; HBO) . . . . . . Angelica
Miniseries:
North and South (1985) .Virgilia Hazard
North and South, Book II (1986) . . . . .Virgilia Hazard
Made for TV Movies:
Sins of the Past (1984). . . . . Patrice
A Bunny's Tale (1985) . . . . Gloria Steinem
The Prince of Bel Air (1986). . . . . .Jamie Harrison
Stark: Mirror Images (1986). . . . . .Maggie
David's Mother (1994) . . . . .Sally Goodson
Radiant City (1996). . . . . Gloria
The Last Don (1997) . . . . Rose Marie
TV:
Masquerade (1983-84) . . . . .Casey Collins
Cheers (1987-93) . . . . Rebecca Howe
Veronica's Closet (1997-) . . . . Veronica "Ronnie" Chase

Allman, Cie

Films:
Blame It on the Vodka (1992) . . . . Annette Robertson
- • 0:30—Brief right breast, while making love in bed with Christopher.
- •• 0:55—Breasts, while making love in bed with Herman and Karen.
- ••• 1:08—Breasts, while making love in a car with Greg. Long scene.

Renegade: Fighting Cage (1993) . . . . Cheetah
(Nudity added for video release.)
- •• 0:46—Breasts in bed, while making love with a guy.

Trapped (1993) . . . . Buxom Blonde
a.k.a. The Killing Jar

Almgren, Susan

Films:
Separate Vacations (1985; Canadian) . . . . . . .Helene Gilbert
- •• 1:05—Breasts and buns in G-string before getting into bed and then in bed with David Naughton.
- • 1:07—Breasts and buns in bed, then in bathroom with Naughton.

Shades of Love: Lilac Dream (1987). . . . . .n.a.
Stalked (1994; Canadian/Australian) . . . . .Jeweled Lady
Made for Cable Movies:
Deadly Surveillance (1991; Showtime) . . . . .Rachel
- • 0:00—Very, very brief right breast, while getting dressed. Don't see her face. B&W.
- • 0:12—Breasts in the shower. Long shot.
- •• 0:34—Breasts in the shower with Nickels.
- ••• 0:54—Buns, in black panties and bra, then breasts in room with Michael Ironside.

Twin Sisters (1992). . . . . Sophie
- •• 0:06—Breasts and buns, while making love in bed with a guy.

Alonso, Maria Conchita

Films:
Fear City (1984) . . . . Silver Chavez
Moscow on the Hudson (1984) . . . . Lucia Lombardo
- •• 1:17—Breasts in bathtub with Robin Williams.

Touch and Go (1984) . . . . Denise
A Fine Mess (1986) . . . . Claudia Pazzo
Extreme Prejudice (1987) . . . . Sarita Cisneros
- •• 0:27—Brief breasts in the shower while Nick Nolte is in the bathroom talking to her.

The Running Man (1987) . . . . .Amber Mendez
Colors (1988). . . . . .Louisa Gomez
- ••• 0:48—Breasts making love in bed with Sean Penn.

Con el Corazón en la Mano (1988; Mexican). . . . . n.a.
• 0:38—Very, very brief right breast, while turning over in bed with her husband.
• 0:39—Breasts several times, taking a bath.
•• 1:15—Breasts while ripping off her dress. Long shot, side view, standing while kissing a guy.
Vampire's Kiss (1989) . . . . Alva
Predator 2 (1990) . . . . Leona
McBain (1991) . . . . Christine
Teamster Boss (1992) . . . . .Carmen
The House of Spirits (1993) . . . . .Transito
•• 0:18—Breasts and buns, undressing and starting to make love with Jeremy Irons.
Roosters (1993). . . . . Chata
Caught (1996). . . . . .Betty
• 0:31—Brief breasts in mirror tiles when seen by Nick and before closing the door.
•• 0:44—Breasts, while making love with Nick.
• 1:00—Buns, when in the shower with Nick, when almost caught by Edward James Olmos.
Acts of Betrayal (1997) . . . . .Eva Ramirez

Made for Cable Movies:
Blood Ties (1986; Italian; Showtime). . . . . Caterina
•• 0:35—Brief breasts when Vincent Spano rips her dress off.

Made for Cable TV:
Women: Stories of Passion-La Limpia (1996; Showtime) . . . . Sophia
•• 0:10—In bra, then breasts, while remembering her first husband.
••• 0:19—In bra, then breasts, while making love with Doug.
The Outer Limits: The Vaccine (1998; Showtime) . . . . n.a.

Made for TV Movies:
MacShayne: The Final Roll of the Dice (1994) . . . . Cindy Evans
Sudden Terror: The Hijacking of School Bus #17 (1996) . . . . . . Marta Caldwell
My Husband's Secret Life (1998). Toni

Video Tapes:
Dance It Up: Hot Fitness (1991) . . . . Herself

*Alphen, Corinne **

a.k.a. Corinne Wahl.
Ex-wife of actor Ken Wahl.

Films:
Hot T-Shirts (1980). . . . . Judy
• 1:10—In yellow outfit dancing in wet T-shirt contest. Brief breasts while flashing the crowd.
New York Nights (1981) . . . . The Debutante
•• 0:10—Breasts, making love in the back seat of a limousine with the rock star.
••• 1:38—Breasts dancing in the bedroom while the Financier watches from the bed.
Brainwaves (1983) . . . . .Lelia Adams
• 0:03—Brief side of right breast, reaching out to turn off the water faucets in the bathtub.
• 0:05—Full frontal nudity, getting electrocuted in the bubble bath.
• 0:50—Brief right breast, during Kaylie's vision.
C.O.D. (1983). . . . . Cheryl Westwood
• 0:21—Brief breasts changing clothes in dressing room while talking to Zacks.
• 1:25—Brief breasts taking off her blouse in dressing room scene.
Spring Break (1983; Canadian) . . . . Joan
Equalizer 2000 (1986). . . . . Karen
Amazon Women on the Moon (1987). . . . . Shari
••• 1:13—In black bra, then breasts on TV while Ray watches.

Screwball Hotel (1988) . . . . .Cherry Amour
• 0:46—Buns, in black outfit on bed with Norman.

Alt, Carol

Supermodel.

Films:
Portfolio (1983) . . . . Herself
• 0:28—Brief right breast, while adjusting black, see-through blouse.
Bye Bye Baby (1989; Italian) . . . . Sandra
• 0:09—Part of right breast, while in the shower.
My Wonderful Life (1989; Italian) . . . . Marina
A Family Matter (1990) . . . . .Nancy
•• 1:08—Buns, in panties. Brief side view of left breast with Eric Roberts.
Millions (1990) . . . . Beta
Beyond Justice (1992) . . . . Christine Sanders
Deadly Past (1994) . . . . Saundra
Ring of Steel (1994). . . . . Tanya
Body Armor (1996) . . . . Agent Monica McBride
Private Parts (1997) . . . . Gloria

TV:
Thunder in Paradise (1993-94) . . . . Kelly La Rew

Video Tapes:
Sports Illustrated's 25th Anniversary Swimsuit Video (1989) . . . . .Model
(The version shown on HBO left out two music video segments at the end. If you like buns, definitely watch the video tape!)

Always, Julie

Films:
Hardbodies (1984) . . . . .Photo Session Hardbody
•• 0:40—Breasts with other girls posing breasts getting pictures taken by Rounder. She's wearing blue dress with a white belt.
The Rosebud Beach Hotel (1985). . . . . .Bellhop
•• 0:22—Breasts, in open blouse, undressing with two other bellhops. She's the blonde on the left.
•• 0:44—Breasts, playing spin the grenade, with two guys and the two other bellhops. She's on the left.

Ambuehl, Cindy

Films:
The Naked Truth (1992) . . . . Miss Italy
Phantasm III: Lord of the Dead (1994). . . . . Edna
Body Count (1995) . . . . Janet Hood
• 0:34—Brief close-up of buns, when bending over in sauna and Robert Davi sees her tattoo. Don't see her face.
Dark Breed (1996). . . . . .Burgess
Meet Wally Sparks (1996) . . . . Lola Larue
• 1:10—Very, very brief breasts on fax that David Ogden Stiers slams on his desk. B&W.
• 1:20—Very, very brief left breast in color photo. Difficult to see.

Made for Cable TV:
Dazzling Women of Sports (1989; ESPN). . . . . Herself
Fallen Angels: Since I Don't Have You (1993; Showtime) . . . . Auditioning Blonde #2
(Available on the video tape *Fallen Angels One.*)

TV:
Blue Skies (1994). . . . . .n.a.
Head Over Heels (1997-) . . . . Valentina

*Ames, Denise **

Films:
Danger Zone III: Steel Horse War (1991) . . . . .n.a.

The Last Boy Scout (1991) .... Jacuzzi Party Girl
- 0:11—Brief left breast and buns in swimsuit bottom, while getting out of the spa.

Harley Hot Rod High (1995) .... Ex-wife
Dinosaur Valley Girls (1996).................. Hea-Thor
(Director's Cut reviewed.)
- 0:25—Brief breasts, when the dinosaur takes her top off and Tony carries her away.
- •• 0:46—Breasts and partial buns, while making love with Tony in cave.
- •• 1:27—Breasts, while sitting on lounge chair by the pool.

Fire In My Heart (1996)............................ n.a.
(Not available in the U.S. yet.)
Lovers, Liars and Thieves (1996) .... Flattop
Non-Fat (1996)........................... Femme Fatale

• Ames, Lynsey

See: Blair, Lindsay.

Amick, Mädchen

Model.

Films:

The Borrower (1989)........................... Megan
Don't Tell Her It's Me (1990)...................... Mandy
I'm Dangerous Tonight (1990) .... Amy O'Neil
Stephen King's "Sleepwalkers" (1992)....... Tanya Robertson
Twin Peaks: Fire Walk With Me (1992)......... Shelly Johnson
Dream Lover (1994)...................... Lena Reardon
(Unrated version reviewed.)
- •• 0:24—Breasts and buns, while making love with James Spader.
- 0:26—Brief buns and left breast while making love in dining room with Spader.
- ••• 0:29—Right breast, while lying in bed. Nude getting out of bed and walking to bathroom.

Trapped in Paradise (1994) .... Sarah Collins
The Courtyard (1995)........................... Lauren
Wounded (1996) .... Julie Clayton

Made for Cable Movies:

Love, Cheat & Steal (1993; Showtime) . . . Lauren Harrington
- 0:26—Buns, when Roberts rips her pants off. Don't see her face.
- 0:47—Brief back side of right breast, twice, getting out of bed and putting on robe.

Made for Cable TV:

Fallen Angels: Love and Blood (1995; Showtime) .... Trina
0:09—Falling back onto bed and pulling up her dress, showing her panties to Kiefer Sutherland.

Made for TV Movies:

The Great American Sex Scandal (1989) .... Stephanie

TV:

Twin Peaks (1990-91) .... Shelly Johnson
Central Park West (1995) .... Carrie Fairchild
CPW (1996) .... Carrie Fairchild

Amidou, Souad

Films:

A Man and a Woman (1966; French) ..... Francoise Gauthier
Life Love Death (1969; French/Italian)........ Francois Toledo
Petit Con (1986; French)........................... Salima
- •• 0:42—Breasts, after taking off her top and getting into bed, while Michel watches her.
- 0:50—Breasts, while lying in bed, then making love with Michel. Dark.
- 0:53—Breasts, getting out of bed and getting back in.

Amis, Suzy *

Films:

Fandango (1985) .... The Girl
The Big Town (1987) .... Aggie Donaldson
- 0:56—Very brief lower half of right breast, when falling back onto bed with Matt Dillon.

Plain Clothes (1988) .... Robin Torrence
Rocket Gibraltar (1988)............................ Aggie
Twister (1989)............................... Maureen
Where the Heart Is (1990) .... Chloe McBain
- 0:08—Breasts during her art film. Artfully covered with paint, with a bird. Breasts again in the third segment.
- 0:09—Breasts during the film again. Hard to see because of the paint. Last segment while she narrates.

Rich in Love (1992)......................... Rae Odom
The Ballad of Little Jo (1993)............. Jo Monaghan
- 0:12—Buns and left breast in reflection in mirror. Hard to see her face clearly.
- ••• 1:16—Breasts, while on bed with Tinman.

Two Small Bodies (1993)................ Eileen Maloney
- 0:57—Very, very brief back side view of right breast after taking off bra.

Watch It (1993)................................. Anne
Blown Away (1994).............................. Kate
Nadja (1995)............................... Cassandra
One Good Turn (1995) .... Laura Forrest
The Usual Suspects (1995).................. Edie Finneran
The Beneficiary (1996) .... Connie Roos
The Ex (1996) .... Molly Kenyon
- 0:22—Very brief upper part of left breast, when Nick Mancuso is on top of her in bed.

Cadillac Ranch (1997) .... C.J. Crowley
Firestorm (1997) .... Jennifer

Made for TV Movies:

Dead by Midnight (1997) .... Dr. Sarah Flint
Last Stand at Saber River (1997) .... Martha

Ammann, Renee

a.k.a. Renee Griffin and Jerri Reneé Griffin.

Films:

Showdown in Little Tokyo (1991) .... Angel
- •• 0:15—In black bra. Breasts in lingerie and stockings (mostly right breast) just before getting killed.
- 0:34—Right breast, on TV during playback of her execution.

Encino Man (1992) .... Fresh Nug
Cyborg 2: Glass Shadow (1993) .... Davena
- 0:04—Brief breasts, several times, while making love with a guy before she blows up.

Death Match (1994)................ Danielle Richardson
- •• 1:07—Breasts, when getting into shower with John. Breasts and partial buns, while making love in bed.

Number One Fan (1994) .... Blair Madsen
- ••• 0:18—In black bra, in bedroom with Chad McQueen, then breasts and buns while making love with him on the bed.
- 0:21—Brief right breast, while lying in bed in the morning
- •• 0:26—Breasts, while making love with McQueen in the kitchen.
- 0:28—Very brief, upper half of right breast, while standing outside with McQueen.
- 0:39—Brief breasts in open trench coat with Chad McQueen. Brief breasts while straddling over him during struggle.

The Stoned Age (1994) . . . . Lanie
•• 0:46—Brief breasts in bedroom with Hubbs, then brief right breast in bed with him.
• 0:47—Brief breasts, while sitting up in bed when Joe interrupts her session with Hubbs.
• 0:58—Brief breasts, while making love with Hubbs in bed.
• 1:06—Left breast, twice, while sleeping in bed when Joe comes in the room.
• 1:08—Left breast, twice again, after Joe's hallucination.
The Great White Hype (1996) . . . . Angel
Made for Cable Movies:
Ladykiller (1996; Showtime). Jennifer
••• 0:44—Breasts while wearing panties, when Richard undoes her overalls, then making love with him on the floor.
•• 0:50—Buns and breasts, while taking a shower behind clear plastic shower curtain.

Amore, Gianna *

Films:
Screwball Hotel (1988) . . . . Mary Beth
Nothing But Trouble (1991) . . . . Party Girl
Video Tapes:
Wet & Wild (1989). . . . . Model
Playmates at Play (1990) . . . . . Free Wheeling, Gotta Dance
Playboy Video Calendar 1992 (1991) . . . . January
••• 0:01—Nude in Italian restaurant fantasy.
••• 0:02—Nude in classical music fantasy in warehouse.
Playboy's 21 Playmates (1996). . . . . Playmate
••• 0:32—Full frontal nudity in still photos.
••• 0:33—Nude in pizza restaurant.

Amy-Rochelle

See: Rochelle, Amy.

Anders, Avalon *

Films:
Bikini Summer 2 (1992) . . . . Clarice
••• 0:11—Breasts in sexy outfit, acting as a dominatrix with Harry in his office.
•• 0:13—More breasts, while spanking Harry in his office.
• 0:33—Buns and brief left breast, while teasing Harry.
•• 0:37—In black body stocking, then breasts with Harry in his office.
••• 0:41—More breasts in white corset with Harry.
Buford's Beach Bunnies (1992) . . . . Santa's Helper
Sorority House Party (1992). . . . . Miranda
• 1:05—Breasts and buns under sheer purple body suit.
Die Watching (1993) . . . . Marie
••• 0:40—In pink outfit doing strip tease while getting videotaped by Christopher Atkins, then breasts. Long scene.
• 0:52—Brief breasts, seen on TV monitor.
The Great Bikini Off-Road Adventure (1994)
. . . . Paulina Smalls
•• 0:01—Breasts, while sunbathing and lying on ground and spraying herself with water.
•• 0:16—Breasts, while sunbathing outside on the rocks with Tisha.
••• 0:21—Breasts, while undoing her swimsuit top in front of two guys out in the desert.
• 0:31—Brief buns, while in swimsuit.
••• 0:44—Breasts, while posing on a jeep for a customer with a camera.
••• 0:50—Breasts and buns, while posing outside for a customer.
••• 1:02—Breasts and buns during water fight.

Wish Me Luck (1995) . . . . Geanie
(Unrated version reviewed.)
••• 0:00—Breasts during opening credits.
••• 0:16—Breasts, while in shower in the locker room.
• 0:19—Breasts in front of lockers, then in bra.
•• 1:01—Breasts, while making love in bed with a guy.
••• 1:25—Breasts, while dancing during the end credits.
Raven (1996). . . . . Uncredited Marcia
Rebecca's Secret (1997). . . . . Ally
••• 0:14—Buns in G-string and breasts, while dancing and making love with Jonathan.
• 0:19—Buns in lingerie, while modeling outdoors.
••• 1:04—Breasts, while making love with Jonathan in bed.
Made for Cable TV:
Red Shoe Diaries: Burning Up (1994; Showtime). . . . . Ruby
•• 0:15—Breasts and buns in G-string, while dancing on stage in club.
•• 0:18—Breasts and buns in G-string, while making love with the fireman in restroom stall.
Hot Springs Hotel: To Your Health (1998; Showtime). . . . . Cory
Video Tapes:
California Girl Fox Hunt Bikini Competition #6 . . Avalon
••• 0:02—Buns in sexy one piece swimsuit.
• 0:47—Buns during review.
Hot Body Video Magazine #1: Premiere Edition (1992)
. . . . Model
••• 0:41—Buns and breasts modeling, sunbathing and dancing. Great, long scenes.
Hot Body Video Magazine #9: The Best Of Hot Body Video Magazine (1994) . . . . Herself
Raw Adventures (1994). . . . . Herself
Hot Body Hall of Fame: Traci Dali (1995) . . . . Herself
•• 0:51—Nude in various clips.
Playboy's Hot Wheels & High Heels Biker Babes (1997)
. . . . Biker Bash/Avalon
••• 0:33—Nude, while Tylyn video tapes her posing on motorcycle.

Anders, Lola *

Video Tapes:
Penthouse Paradise Revisited (1992) . . . . Pet

Andersen, Bibi

Real life transsexual.
Films:
The Law of Desire (1987; Spanish). Ada
High Heels (1991; Spanish) . . . . Chon
Acción Mutante (1993; Spanish) . . . . Lujo's Guest
Kika (1994; Spanish) . . . . Susana
••• 0:40—Nude, while standing on balcony and singing, then inside apartment with Peter Coyote.
• 1:15—Brief buns, with Coyote on TV monitor.
• 1:23—Nude, on balcony and inside apartment on TV monitor.
• 1:24—Nude, while lying on floor dead, getting wrapped in a blanket by Coyote.
• 1:30—Brief breasts, while lying dead in bathtub when discovered by Ramon.

Anderson, Erika *

Films:
Nightmare on Elm Street 5: The Dream Child (1989) . . . Greta
Zandalee (1991) . . . . Zandalee Martin
(Unrated version reviewed.)
••• 0:02—Nude, taking off robe and dancing around the room.

••• 0:21—Nude, undressing, then in bed with Judge Reinhold. Long scene.
•• 0:30—Right breast, then breasts making love in bed with Nicolas Cage.
•• 0:32—Breasts as Cage paints on her with his finger.
••• 0:45—Left breast, then breasts and lower frontal nudity on floor with Cage.
•• 0:47—Nude, getting massaged by Cage with an oil and cocaine mixture.
• 0:48—Brief breasts getting into bed with Reinhold. Slightly out of focus.
•• 1:09—Breasts opening her dress for Reinhold while lying on a river bank, then making love with him at night in bed.

Quake (1992) .... Jenny Sutton
• 0:05—Breasts, getting out of the shower and drying herself off. More breasts, putting on bra.
• 0:40—Breasts in photos from 0:05 in darkroom.
•• 0:50—Breasts on table when Steve Railsback rips her bra off.
•• 0:51—Breasts, in drugged sleep while Railsback takes pictures of her.
• 0:52—More breasts asleep, then awake.

Object of Obsession (1994)................... Margaret
• 0:11—Brief breasts, several times, while making love when imagining herself in a movie that she's watching on TV. Don't see her face.
•• 0:29—Beasts, while making love in bed with Scott Valentine.
• 0:46—Brief buns, while making love in bed with Valentine.
• 1:00—Very, very brief right breast, while shaving her legs in the bathtub.
• 1:07—Brief partial right breast, while under Harvey in bed.

Made for Cable TV:
Dream On: B.S. Elliot (1992; HBO) .... Marina
Red Shoe Diaries: Liar's Tale (1994; Showtime)
.... Joanna Dunston
••• 0:19—In bra, then breasts and partial lower frontal nudity while making love with Jack at his house. Intercut with Audie England's nude scenes.

TV:
Twin Peaks (1990-91) ....Emerald/Jade

• Anderson, Gillian

Films:
The Turning (1992) .... April Cavanaugh
• 0:47—In bra, then very brief side of left breast when the bra is pulled down.
•• 0:48—Very brief right breast, seen from over her left shoulder as Clifford eases her backward.

The X-Files (1998)......................... Dana Scully

TV:
The X-Files (1993-)........................ Dana Scully

• Anderson, Kathryn

Made for Cable TV:
The Outer Limits: Bodies of Evidence (1997; Showtime)
.... Woman
• 0:07—Left breast, while killing her lover, Dr. Somerset, with acid.
• 0:34—Brief left breast in flashback.

Dead Man's Gun: The Highwayman (1998; Showtime)
.... Jeanette Barrett

Anderson, Kim *

Films:
Fatal Skies (1989) .... Cindy
• 0:48—Buns in lingerie, while posing for Lance in his office.

Hot Times at Montclair High (1989) ....Bridgette
Small Time (1991).................... Woman on Street

Made for Cable TV:
Dream On: Am I Blue (1995; HBO) .... Porno Actress
•• 0:08—Breasts and very brief partial lower frontal nudity in two porno video tapes that Martin watches.
• 0:18—Brief left breast, while sitting on bed next to the porno actor.

Video Tapes:
Swimwear Illustrated: On Location (1986).... Swimsuit Model (Blonde hair.)
Rock Video Girls (1991)...................... Herself (Brunette hair.)
• 0:02—Dancing in wet T-shirt. Buns and brief breasts on the beach (some in B&W).

Anderson, Leigh *

Video Tapes:
Penthouse: The Ultimate Pet Games (1996) .... Pet
••• 0:13—Nude during badminton segment.
••• 0:17—Nude, while posing in front of a cabin.
••• 0:21—Nude during oil wrestling segment.
••• 0:36—Breasts during pool volleyball game.

Anderson, Melody

Films:
Flash Gordon (1980)........................ Dale Arden
Dead and Buried (1981) ....Janet
The Boy in Blue (1986; Canadian) ....Dulcie
• 0:07—Brief cleavage while making love with Nicolas Cage, then very brief top half of right breast when a policeman scares her.

Firewalker (1986) .... Patricia Goodwyn
Final Notice (1989) ....Kate Davis
Speed Zone (1989) .... Lee
Landslide (1992) .... Claire Trinavant

Made for Cable Movies:
Hitler's Daughter (1990) ....n.a.
Marilyn & Bobby: Her Final Affair (1993; USA)
.... Marilyn Monroe

Made for TV Movies:
Policewoman Centerfold (1983) .... Jan Oaks
• 0:51—Very brief partial side of right breast, while kneeling on bed during photo shoot.

Ladies of the Night (1986) .... Claudia

TV:
Manimal (1983) .... Brooke McKenzie

Anderson, Pamela

See: Lee, Pamela.

Anderson, Pat *

Films:
Dirty O'Neil (1974).................................Lisa
Newman's Law (1974) .... Sharon
Cover Girl Models (1975) ....Barbara
• 0:12—Very brief breasts, taking off dress during fitting session.
• 0:22—Right breast, while making love in bed with a guy.
•• 0:24—Breasts, when getting out of bed.
• 1:02—Brief breasts, after undoing her halter top to get the attention of policeman.

Summer School Teachers (1975) . . . . Sally
- •• 0:52—Breasts and buns, posing for photos, then in bed with Bob.
- • 1:05—Side view of right breast in photo in magazine.

TNT Jackson (1975) . . . . Elaine
- •• 0:58—Buns and breasts, getting out of the shower and putting robe on.

Bloodfist III: Forced to Fight (1991) . . . . Elaine
- • 0:55—Buns and breasts in clip from movie *TNT Jackson* that the inmates watch while Diddler gets stabbed to death.

Body Waves (1991). . . . . Elaine
- • 0:41—Breasts, getting out of the shower in drive-in movie from *TNT Jackson.*

Anderson, Stephanie

Films:

Buford's Beach Bunnies (1992) . . . . Marilyn
Death Becomes Her (1992) . . . . Marilyn Monroe
Calendar Girl (1993) . . . . Marilyn Monroe
- • 0:46—Buns and very brief back side of rght breast, while standing at the beach, taking off her wig behind the two bad guys.

*Andersson, Bibi **

Films:

The Seventh Seal (1956; Swedish). Mia
Brink of Life (1957; Swedish). . . . . Hjordis
Wild Strawberries (1957; Swedish) . . . . Sara
The Magician (1959). . . . . Sara
Duel at Diablo (1966) . . . . Ellen Grange
Persona (1966; Swedish). . . . . Nurse Alma
The Passion of Anna (1969; Swedish) . . . . Eva Vergerus
The Touch (1971; U.S./Swedish) . . . . Karen Vergerus
- • 0:31—Breasts, while in bed with Elliott Gould.
- ••• 0:56—Breasts, while kissing Gould.
- • 1:13—Very, very brief right breast, when washing Gould's hair in the sink.

Scenes from a Marriage (1973; Swedish). . . . . Katarina
I Never Promised You a Rose Garden (1977) . . . . Dr. Fried
Quintet (1979) . . . . Ambrosia
Twice a Woman (1979) . . . . Laura
- • 0:05—Breasts taking off her bra and putting a blouse on.
- • 0:06—Brief side view of left breast, getting into bed, brief left breast lying back in bed.

Exposed (1983). . . . . Margaret
Babette's Feast (1987; Danish). . Swedish Court Lady-in-Waiting
a.k.a. Babettes Gaestebud

Made for TV Movies:

Wallenberg: A Hero's Story (1985). Maj

Andersson, Harriet

Films:

Monika (1952; Swedish) . . . . Monika
a.k.a. Sommaren Med Monika
- • 0:42—Brief back side of left breast, while sitting down next to water. Buns while getting up to run to water.
- • 1:33—Buns and long shot of right breast in Harry's flashback. This scene lasts longer than the 0:42 one.

Sawdust and Tinsel (1955; Swedish) . . . . Anne
a.k.a. The Naked Night
Smiles of a Summer Night (1957; Swedish). . . . Petra the Maid
Dreams (1960; Swedish) . . . . Doris
A Lesson in Love (1960; Swedish) . . . . Nix
Through a Glass Darkly (1962; Swedish) . . . . Karin
Cries and Whispers (1972; Swedish) . . . . Agnes
Fanny and Alexander (1983; Swedish/French/German). . Justina

• *Andrea, Alex **

Video Tapes:

Babes, Bikes & Beyond (1994) . . . . Herself
- ••• 0:09—Breasts and buns in T-back.

Andreeff, Starr

Films:

Skullduggery (1983; Canadian). . . . . Irene
Dance of the Damned (1988) . . . . Jodi
- •• 0:03—Breasts dancing in black bikini bottoms on stage in a club.
- •• 1:08—Breasts in the bar with the vampire.

Ghoulies II (1988) . . . . Alice
Out of the Dark (1988) . . . . Camille
The Terror Within (1988). . . . . Sue
Streets (1989) . . . . Policewoman on Horse
Syngenor (1990) . . . . Susan
Driving Me Crazy (1991). . . . . Legs
Scanner Cop (1993) . . . . Glenda
Amityville Dollhouse (1996). . . . . Claire
Vampire Journals (1996) . . . . Iris

Made for Cable Movies:

Breast Men (1997; HBO) . . . . Scrub Nurse

Made for TV Movies:

The Deliberate Stranger (1986) . . . . Jane Maxwell

TV:

General Hospital . . . . Jessica Holmes

*Andress, Ursula **

Ex-wife of the late photographer/director/actor John Derek.

Films:

Dr. No (1962; British) . . . . Honey
Four for Texas (1963). . . . . Maxine Richter
Fun in Acapulco (1963) . . . . Margarita Douphine
Nightmare in the Sun (1964). . . . . Marsha Wilson
Once Before I Die (1965). . . . . Alex
What's New, Pussycat? (1965; U.S./French) . . . . Rita
The Blue Max (1966) . . . . Countess Kasti
- • 1:26—Very, very brief half of left breast, lying on her back in bed.
- • 1:47—(0:04 into tape 2) Very brief half of right breast, while kneeling down in front of Peppard in hotel room. Very, very brief breasts under towel around her neck when she stands up.
- • 1:48—(0:05 into tape 2) Very, very brief silhouette of right breast, while lying back down in bed with George Peppard in bedroom.

Casino Royale (1967; British) . . . . Vesper Lynd
Anyone Can Play (1968; Italian). Norma
The Southern Star (1969; French/British). . . . . . Erica Kramer
- • 1:07—Buns, walking into lake to wash herself. Long shot.
- • 1:08—Breasts seen through water while she talks to George Segal.

Perfect Friday (1970; British) . . . . Lady Britt Dorsett
Red Sun (1972; French/Italian/Spanish). . . . . Cristina
- • 1:12—Almost side view of right breast, then left breast while changing tops in room while Charles Bronson watches.

Loaded Guns (1975) . . . . Laura
- • 0:32—Buns, lying in bed with a guy.
- ••• 0:33—Breasts and buns getting out of bed. Full frontal nudity in elevator.
- •• 0:40—Nude getting out of bed and putting dress on.
- ••• 0:48—Nude getting into bathtub, breasts in tub, nude getting out and drying herself off.

• 1:00—Buns while getting undressed and hopping in to bed.
• 1:02—Brief side view of right breast while getting dressed.

The Sensuous Nurse (1975; Italian) . . . . Anna
•• 0:16—Breasts and buns in bed after making love with Benito.
•• 0:22—Nude swimming in pool while Adonais watches.
••• 0:50—Nude slowly stripping and getting in bed with Adonais.
••• 1:10—Nude getting into bed.

Stateline Motel (1975; Italian). . . . . Michelle Nolton
a.k.a. Last Chance for a Born Loser
••• 0:34—Left breast, then breasts on bed with Oleg.

The Loves and Times of Scaramouche (1976; Italian) Josephine
The Fifth Musketeer (1977) . . . . Mlle De La Valliere

Slave of the Cannibal God (1979; Italian) . . . . n.a.
•• 0:33—Breasts taking off shirt and putting on a T-shirt.
••• 1:07—Nude getting tied to a pole by the Cannibal People and covered with red paint.
• 1:20—Brief peek at buns under her skirt when running away from the Cannibal People.

Tigers in Lipstick (1979) . . . . . . The Stroller and The Widow
• 0:50—Very brief breasts when top of slip accidentally falls down.
• 0:51—More breasts with the photographer.

Clash of the Titans (1981) . . . . Aphrodite

Famous T & A (1982) . . . . Herself
(No longer available for purchase, check your video store for rental.)
••• 0:15—Full frontal nudity scenes from *Slave of the Cannibal God.*

The Chinatown Murders: Man Against the Mob (1989) . . . . Betty Starr

Video Tapes:

Playboy Video Magazine, Volume 1 (1982) . . . . Herself
•• 0:58—Breasts in still photos from *Playboy* pictorial.

• Andrews, Brittany

Adult film actress.

Films:

Eve's Beach Fantasy (1997). . . . . Jamie
••• 0:22—Breasts and buns, while making love with Roland.

Video Tapes:

Nude Models Summerhouse (1996) . . . . n.a.
Penthouse: The Art of Massage (1996) . . . . Model

Andrews, Julie

Wife of director Blake Edwards.

Films:

Americanization of Emily (1964) . . . . Emily
Mary Poppins (1964) . . . . Mary Poppins
(Academy Award for Best Actress.)
The Sound of Music (1965). . . . . Maria
Hawaii (1966) . . . . Jerusha Bromley
Thoroughly Modern Millie (1967). . . . . Millie Dillmoun t
Darling Lili (1970) . . . . Lili Smith
• 1:12—Very, very brief left breast, when doing strip tease and tossing aside yellow outfit to duck behind curtain.

The Tamarind Seed (1974; British) . . . . Judith Farrow
10 (1979) . . . . Sam
Little Miss Marker (1980) . . . . Amanda
S.O.B. (1981) . . . . Sally Miles
•• 1:19—Breasts pulling the top off her red dress during the filming of a movie.

Victor/Victoria (1982) . . . . Victor/Victoria
The Man Who Loved Women (1983) . . . . Marianna
That's Life! (1986) . . . . Gillian Fairchild
Duet for One (1987). . . . . Stephanie Anderson
• 0:28—Very brief left breast in gaping blouse in bathroom splashing water on her face because she feels sick, then wet T-shirt.
••• 1:06—Breasts stretching, lying in bed.
• 1:07—Very brief buns and very brief right breast, when she rolls off the bed onto the floor.

A Fine Romance (1992; Italian) . . . . Pamela Picquet

Made for TV Movies:

Our Sons (1991) . . . . Audrey Grant

TV:

The Julie Andrews Hour (1972-73). . . . . Hostess
Julie (1992) . . . . Julie Carlisle

• Angel

Made for Cable TV:

Erotic Confessions: An Erotic Christmas Carol (1997; Cinemax) . . . . Cynthia
•• 0:04—In white lingerie outfit, then breasts, while fooling around with Gary in his office.
• 0:10—Brief breasts in flashbacks.

Erotic Confessions: Off the Menu (1997; Cinemax) . . . . Coralyn
••• 0:09—Brief breasts, while looking at herself in the mirror, then full frontal nudity while caressing herself on the bed.
••• 0:20—Breasts, while making love with a guy in the women's restroom.

Angel, Vanessa

Films:

Spies Like Us (1985) . . . . Russian Rocket Crewmember
Another Chance (1989) . . . . Jacky Johanssen
• 0:26—Sort of breasts under water in spa. Hard to see because of the bubbles.

King of New York (1990). . . . . British Female
Homicidal Impulse (1992). . . . . Deborah
a.k.a. Killer Instinct
(Unrated version reviewed.)
•• 0:13—In bra, then breasts making love with Scott Valentine in his office on top of the photocopier (Don't see her face).
•• 0:24—Breasts and buns, while making love in bed (you can see her face a little bit).
••• 0:30—In black bra, then breasts while making love (don't see her face).
• 0:39—Very brief breasts in flashes during Valentine's drug induced visions.

Stop! Or My Mom Will Shoot (1992). . . . . Stewardess
Sleep With Me (1994) . . . . Marianne
Kingpin (1996) . . . . Claudia
Kissing a Fool (1998). . . . . Natasha

TV:

Baywatch (1992-93) . . . . Megan
Reasonable Doubts (1992-93). . . . . Officer Peggy Eliot
Weird Science (1994-97) . . . . Lisa

Angeli, Pier

Ex-wife of singer Vic Damone.
Identical twin sister of actress Marisa Pavan.

Films:

Silver Chalice (1954) . . . . Deborra
Somebody Up There Likes Me (1956) . . . . Norma
Sodom and Gomorrah (1962; U.S./French). . . . . Ildith
Battle of the Bulge (1965) . . . . Louise

The Folds of the Flesh (1970; Italian) .... Falesse/Ester
- 0:16—Upper half of left breast, sticking out of nightgown, twice, while leaning over Michael after stabbing him.
- 0:45—Right breast, when Pascal pulls down her nightgown. Don't see her face.

Octaman (1971) .... n.a.

Ann, Tiffany

Video Tapes:

Hot Body International: #2 Miss Puerto Vallarta (1990) .... Contestant
- •• 0:29—Breasts wearing pasties and buns, in G-string.
- •• 0:58—Buns, posing in wet, green two piece swimsuit.

Hot Body International: #4 Spring Break (1992) .... Contestant
- 0:36—Barely there wet T-shirt. Brief right breast, when bending over.

Hot Body Competition: The Best of Hot Body (1994) .... Herself
- ••• 0:58—Buns in swimsuits. Breasts under pasties.

Ann-Margret *

Wife of actor Roger Smith.

Films:

Pocketful of Miracles (1961) .... Louise
State Fair (1962) .... Emily Porter
Bye Bye Birdie (1963) .... Kim McAfee
The Pleasure Seekers (1964) .... Fran Hobson
Viva Las Vegas (1964) .... Rusty Martin
Bus Riley's Back in Town (1965) .... Laurel
The Cincinnati Kid (1965) .... Melba
Murderer's Row (1966) .... Suzie Solaris
The Swinger (1966) .... Kelly Olsson
Tiger and the Pussycat (1967; U.S./Italian) .... Carolina
C.C. & Company (1970) .... Ann
- 1:01—Buns and breasts, while making love with Joe Namath.

R.P.M. (1970) .... Rhoda
- •• 0:07—Brief left breast and buns getting out of bed talking with Anthony Quinn.

Carnal Knowledge (1971) .... Bobbie
- 0:48—Breasts and buns, while making love in bed with Jack Nicholson. Dark.
- •• 0:49—Buns and brief breasts, lying in bed, then getting out and into shower with Nicholson.
- 1:07—Brief side view of left breast putting a bra on in the bedroom.
- 1:08—In black bra and panties, while sitting in bed talking with Nicholson.

The Outside Man (1973; U.S./French) .... Nancy
The Train Robbers (1973) .... Mrs. Lowe
Tommy (1975; British) .... Nora Walker
The Twist (1976) .... Charlie Minerva
Joseph Andrews (1977; British/French) .... Lady Boaby
The Last Remake of Beau Geste (1977) ..... Lady Flavia Geste
The Cheap Detective (1978) .... Jezebel Desire
Magic (1978) .... Peggy Ann Snow
- ••• 0:44—Right breast, lying on her side in bed talking to Anthony Hopkins.

The Villain (1979) .... Charming Jones
Middle Age Crazy (1980; Canadian) .... Sue Ann
I Ought to Be in Pictures (1982) .... Stephanie
Lookin' to Get Out (1982) .... Patti Warner
Return of the Soldier (1983; British) .... Jenny
Twice in a Lifetime (1985) .... Audrey
52 Pick-Up (1986) .... Barbara Mitchell
A New Life (1988) .... Jackie
A Tiger's Tale (1988) .... Rose
- 0:45—Side view of left breast in bra, then breasts jumping up after fire ants start biting her. Brief buns running along a hill. Long shot, probably a body double.

Newsies (1992) .... Medda Larkson
Grumpy Old Men (1993) .... Ariel
Grumpier Old Men (1995) .... Ariel Gustafson

Made for Cable Movies:

Nobody's Children (1994; USA) .... Carol Stevens

Miniseries:

Queen (1993) .... Sally Jackson
Scarlett (1994) .... n.a.

Made for TV Movies:

Our Sons (1991) .... Luanne Barnes
Blue Rodeo (1996) .... Maggie Yearwood

TV:

Homestead (1998-) .... n.a.

Annabi, Amina

Films:

The Sheltering Sky (1990) .... Mahrnia
- •• 0:20—Left breast, then breasts in tent with John Malkovich.
- •• 0:22—Right breast while lying down with Malkovich, breasts when he gets up.

The Advocate (1993; British/French) .... Samira

a.k.a. The Hour of the Pig
- 0:42—Brief breasts, while talking with Colin Firth.
- •• 1:07—Left breast, while making love with Firth.

Annarino, Karen

Films:

Party Plane (1988) .... Judy
- 0:06—Very brief side view of left breast when Lee peeks through window. Don't see her face.
- 0:10—Very, very brief side of right breast when another guy goes to peek. Don't see her face.
- 0:22—Breasts behind shower door, while putting on towel.

Virtuosity (1995) .... TV Reporter

• Anne, Deborah *

Video Tapes:

Playboy's The Girls of Hawaiian Tropic (1994) .... Paradise
- ••• 0:01—In white bra and panties, then nude while posing outdoors during the day.

Anne, Tiffany

See: Lain, Chasey.

Annen, Glory

Films:

Justine (1977; British) .... Prostitute

a.k.a. Cruel Passion

Felicity (1978; Australian) .... Felicity
- •• 0:02—Breasts taking off leotard in girl's shower room, then nude taking a shower.
- 0:05—Buns, then left breast, then right breast undressing to go skinny dipping.
- •• 0:10—Breasts and buns at night at the girl's dormitory with Jenny.
- •• 0:15—Breasts undressing in room in front of Christine.
- 0:16—Left breast, while touching herself in bed.
- ••• 0:20—Lots of lower frontal nudity trying on clothes, bras and panties in dressing room. Brief breasts and buns.

••• 0:25—Buns and breasts taking a bath. Full frontal nudity when Steve peeks in at her.
• 0:31—Brief full frontal nudity losing her virginity on car with Andrew.
••• 0:38—Full frontal nudity in bath with Mei Ling and two other girls, then getting massaged. Long scene.
••• 0:58—Full frontal nudity in bed with Miles.
••• 1:13—Full frontal nudity with Mei Ling making love on bed. Long scene.
• 1:20—Left breast, while making love standing up.
•• 1:21—Breasts and buns making love with Miles.
•• 1:27—Nude making love again with Miles.
• 1:29—Buns, while in the water with Miles.

Spaced Out (1980; British) . . . . Cosia
a.k.a. Outer Touch
••• 0:23—Breasts talking to the other two space women. Long scene.
• 0:31—Very brief breasts changing clothes while dancing.
•• 0:43—Breasts in bed with Willy.
••• 1:08—Breasts lying down.

The Lonely Lady (1983). . . . . Marion
• 0:07—Brief left breast in back seat of car with Ray Liotta. Dark, hard to see.

Alien Prey (1984; British) . . . . Jessica
• 0:22—Breasts unbuttoning blouse to sunbathe.
•• 0:34—Breasts taking off top, getting into bed with Josephine, then making love with her.
• 0:36—Buns, while rolling on top of Josephine.
••• 0:38—More breasts when Josephine is playing with her.
• 0:39—More buns in bed. Long shot.
• 0:46—Left breast and buns standing up in bathtub.
•• 1:05—Breasts getting out of bed and putting a dress on.
•• 1:19—Breasts in bed with Anders. Brief buns when he rips her panties off.

Supergirl (1984; British) . . . . Midvale Protestor

Annesley, Imogen

Films:

Playing Beatie Bow (1986; Australian). . . . . Abigail

Howling III: The Marsupials (1987). . . . . Jerboa
• 0:42—Very brief breasts taking off dress in barn to give birth. Breasts are covered with make-up.

Kiss the Night (1988; Australian). . . . . Sacha

Strapless (1990; British). . . . . Imogen

Annis, Francesca *

Films:

Saturday Night Out (1963; British) . . . . Jean

Macbeth (1972; British). . . . . Lady Macbeth
• 1:41—Buns, while walking around after the bad guys have attacked and looted the castle. Side view of left breast, hard to see because it's covered by her hair.

Dune (1984) . . . . Lady Jessica

Under the Cherry Moon (1986) . . . . Mrs. Wellington

Made for Cable Movies:

Doomsday Gun (1994; HBO) . . . . Sophie

Made for Cable TV:

Tales From the Crypt: A Slight Case of Murder (1996; HBO) . . . . Sharon Bannister

Miniseries:

Masterpiece Theatre: Lilli (1979) . . . . Lilli Langtree

Made for TV Movies:

The Richest Man in the World: The Story of Aristotle Onassis (1988). . . . . Jacqueline Kennedy Onassis

Parnell & The Englishwoman (1991). . . . . . . Katharine O'Shea

Anspach, Susan

Films:

Five Easy Pieces (1970) . . . . Catherine Van Oost

The Landlord (1970) . . . . Susan Enders

Play It Again, Sam (1972) . . . . Nancy

Blume in Love (1973) . . . . Nina Blume

The Big Fix (1978). . . . . Lila

Running (1979). . . . . Janet Andropolis

Gas (1981; Canadian) . . . . Jane Beardsley

Montenegro (1981; British/Swedish) . . . . Marilyn Jordan
•• 1:08—Full frontal nudity, while taking a shower.
• 1:28—Right breast, while making love with Montenegro.

Blood Red (1988) . . . . Widow

Into the Fire (1988) . . . . Rosalind Winfield
a.k.a. Legend of Lone Wolf
•• 0:22—Left breast, under trench coat when she first comes into the house, briefly again in the kitchen.
•• 0:31—Breasts in bedroom standing up with Wade.

Back to Back (1990) . . . . Madeline Hix

The Rutanga Tapes (1991). . . . . Kate Simpson

Made for Cable Movies:

Gone Are the Dayes (1984; Disney). . . . . n.a.

Made for Cable TV:

The Hitchhiker: Dead Man's Curve (HBO) . . . . Claudia
(Available on *The Hitchhiker, Volume 2.*)
• 0:14—Buns (probably a body double) in a hotel room with a guy.

Made for TV Movies:

Cagney & Lacey: The Return (1994) . . . . Deborah Nelson

TV:

The Doctors. . . . . Angela Carter

The Yellow Rose (1983). . . . . Grace McKenzie

Anthony, Lysette *

Films:

Krull (1983). . . . . Lyssa

Looking for Eileen (1988; Dutch) . . . . Marjan/Eileen/Karnen
(Not available on video tape.)
Breasts.

Without a Clue (1988). . . . . Fake Leslie

The Pleasure Principal (1991; British). . . . . Charlotte

Switch (1991) . . . . Liz
• 0:05—Brief breasts in spa with JoBeth Williams and Felicia, trying to kill Steve.

Husbands and Wives (1992) . . . . Sam

The Advocate (1993; British/French) . . . . . . Filette d'Auferre
a.k.a. The Hour of the Pig
• 1:03—Brief full frontal nudity, after dropping her dress for Colin Firth.

Face the Music (1993). . . . . Julie Sanson

Look Who's Talking Now! (1993). . . . . Samantha

Save Me (1993) . . . . Ellie
(Unrated version reviewed.)
0:31—Upper half of right breast in bra, while making love in convertible Mustang with Hamlin.
••• 0:39—Nude, while sleeping then making love in bed with Hamlin.
•• 0:49—Breasts in spa with Hamlin. Long shot of buns, when getting out. Breasts again while putting on swimsuit.
••• 0:52—In bra, then breasts while making love with Hamlin in front of fireplace.
• 1:05—Breasts, when Hamlin forces himself on her in stairway of parking garage.

A Brilliant Disguise (1994) . . . . Michele Ramsey
•• 0:44—Breasts and buns, while making love with Andy.

The Hard Truth (1994). .Lisa Kantrell
0:04—In black bra and panties.
0:22—In black bra in office with Jonah.
••• 0:39—In black bra, then breasts, while making love with Jonah.
Dead Cold (1995) . . . . .Alicia
Dr. Jekyll and Ms. Hyde (1995) . . . . Sarah Carver
Dracula: Dead and Loving It (1995). . . . . Lucy
The Fiancé (1997) . . . . Faith Moore
Misbegotten (1997) . . . . Caitlin Bourke
Made for Cable Movies:
A Ghost in Monte Carlo (1990) . . . . Mistral
Target of Suspicion (1995) . . . . .Jennifer
Trilogy of Terror II (1996; USA) . . . .
Laura/Bobby's Mom/Dr. Simpson
Made for Cable TV:
Tales From the Crypt: Forever Ambergris (1993; HBO)
. . . . Bobbi
••• 0:08—Right breast in mirror, then breasts while making love with Ike when Roger Daltrey peeks in.
••• 0:24—Breasts, while making love with Daltrey in bed.
Miniseries:
Princess Daisy (1983) . . . . Lady Sarah
Made for TV Movies:
Ivanhoe (1982) . . . . Lady Rowena
Jack the Ripper (1988). Mary Jane Kelly
The Lady and the Highwayman (1989) . . . . Lady Panthea Vyne
TV:
Dark Shadows (1991) . . . . Angelique

Anthony, Olga

Films:
Macbeth (1972; British). . . . . Dancer
The Mutations (1973; British) . . . . Bridget
a.k.a. Freakmaker
•• 0:20—Breasts, while lying unconscious on table in Donald Pleasance's laboratory, being undressed by Tom Baker.

*Antonelli, Laura **

Films:
Dr. Goldfoot and the Girl Bombs (1966; Italian) . . . . . Rosanna
Man Called Sledge (1971; Italian) . . . . Ria
High Heels (1972; French) . . . . .Martine
a.k.a. Docteur Popaul
• 0:35—Breasts, while undressing and Jean-Paul Belmondo watches. Long, long shot.
• 0:36—Briefly nude when Belmondo watches through opera glasses.
••• 0:53—Breasts and buns, getting out of bed and walking around.
• 0:55—Buns, getting a shot while lying on examination table.
•• 0:56—Breasts, twice, sitting naked on examination table.
• 1:30—Brief side of right breast during flashback of 0:56 scene.
• 1:31—Brief full frontal nudity, while running around her house and Mia Farrow watches. Long shot.
Without Apparent Motive (1972; French) . . . . Juliette Vaudreuil
How Funny Can Sex Be? (1973)
. . . . Miscellaneous Personalities
• 0:01—Brief breasts taking off swimsuit.
• 0:04—Brief breasts in bathtub covered with bubbles.
• 0:26—Breasts getting into bed.
• 0:36—Breasts making love in elevator behind frosted glass. Shot at fast speed.
• 1:08—In sheer white nun's outfit during fantasy sequence. Brief breasts and buns. Nice slow motion.
• 1:24—In black bra and panties, then breasts while changing clothes.
Malicious (1974; Italian) . . . . Angela
• 1:14—Breasts after undressing while two boys watch from above.
•• 1:27—Breasts, undressing under flashlight. Hard to see because the light is moving around a lot.
• 1:29—Breasts and buns running around the house.
Till Marriage Do Us Part (1974; Italian) . . . . Eugenia
•• 0:58—Nude in the barn, while lying on hay after guy takes off her clothes.
•• 1:02—Full frontal nudity standing up in bathtub while maid washes her.
•• 1:07—Right breast with chauffeur in barn.
•• 1:36—Breasts surrounded by feathers on the bed while priest is talking.
The Innocent (1976; Italian) . . . . Julianna
••• 0:41—Breasts in bed with her husband.
••• 0:53—Full frontal nudity in bed when her husband lifts her dress up.
The Divine Nymph (1977; Italian) . . . . . . Manoela Roderighi
•• 0:10—Full frontal nudity reclining in chair.
• 0:18—Right breast in open blouse sitting in bed. Lower frontal nudity while getting up.
Wifemistress (1977; Italian) . . . . Antonia De Angelis
• 1:22—Brief upper half of left breast in bed with Clara and her husband.
Tigers in Lipstick (1979). . . . . The Pick Up
Secret Fantasy (1981). . . . . Costanza Vivaldi
(Breasts a lot. Only the best are listed.)
••• 0:16—In black bra in Doctor's office, then left breast, then breasts getting examined.
•• 0:18—In black bra and panties in another Doctor's office. Breasts and buns.
•• 0:19—Breasts getting X-rayed. Brief breasts lying down.
•• 0:32—Breasts and buns when Nicolo drugs her and takes Polaroid photos of her.
•• 0:49—Breasts and buns posing around the house for Nicolo while he takes Polaroid photos.
•• 0:53—Breasts and buns during Nicolo's dream.
••• 1:12—Breasts in Doctor's office.
•• 1:14—Breasts and buns in room with another guy.
•• 1:16—Breasts on train while workers "accidentally" see her.
•• 1:20—Breasts on bed after being carried from bathtub.
•• 1:25—Breasts dropping dress during opera.
•• 1:27—More breasts scenes from 0:49.
Passion of Love (1982). . . . . .Clara
a.k.a. Passion D'Amor
• 0:05—Brief side of right breast, while undressing by the fire. Long shot.
Chaste and Pure (1984; Italian) . . . . Rosa
• 0:35—Breasts and brief partial lower frontal nudity, while lying in bed and undressing, posing for Fernanado's Polaroid photos.
• 0:58—Brief breasts, twice, falling out of her dress, while running through the woods at night.
La Venexiana (1986) . . . . Angela
Collector's Item (1988) . . . . Marie Colbert
a.k.a. The Trap
• 0:20—Lower frontal nudity, then right breast while making love with Musante. Dark.

Antonia

See: Dorian, Antonia.

Anulka

See: Dziubinska, Anulka.

Anuszek, Martine

Films:

The Other Woman (1992). . . . . Sheila
(Unrated version reviewed.)
- •• 0:31—Buns and side of left breast, posing with Traci for Elysse at the beach.
- ••• 0:32—Full frontal nudity, posing with Traci at the beach.
- • 0:33—Breasts and buns, running in the surf. Long shot.
- •• 0:40—Breasts at the beach during Jessica's flashbacks.

Video Tapes:

Penthouse: Fast Cars/Fantasy Women (1992)
. . . . Ferrari California Spyder
- ••• 0:34—In lingerie, then nude, while posing with car.

Anwar, Gabrielle

Films:

Manifesto (1988) . . . . .Tina
a.k.a. A Night of Love
If Looks Could Kill (1991) . . . . Mariska
a.k.a. Teen Agent
Wild Hearts Can't Be Broken (1991) . . . . .Sonora Webster
Scent of a Woman (1992). . . . . .Donna
For Love or Money (1993) . . . . Andy Hart
a.k.a. The Concierge
The Three Musketeers (1993) . . . . Queen Anne
Body Snatchers (1994) . . . . Marti Malone
- • 0:49—Very, very brief breast while in bathtub when pod creature falls on top of her.
- ••• 1:13—Several brief breast shots, while sitting up, looking at Tim and writhing around on bed in infirmary.

The Grave (1995) . . . . .Jordan
Innocent Lies (1995) . . . . Celia Graves
- • 1:21—Partial buns in hiked up dress in office with Stephen Dorff.

Things to Do in Denver When You're Dead (1996) . . . . Dagney

Made for Cable Movies:

In Pursuit of Honor (1995; HBO) . . . . .Jessica Stuart
Sub Down (1997; USA). . . . . n.a.

Made for Cable TV:

Fallen Angels: Dead-End for Delia (1993; Showtime). . . . . Delia
(Available on the video tape *Fallen Angels Two.*)

Apollonia *

Real name is Patty Kotero.
Singer.

Films:

Amor Ciego (1980; Mexican) . . . . Patty
- • 0:32—Breasts, while getting out of hammock.
- ••• 0:52—Right breast, when standing up, then breasts while kissing Daniel. More breasts while in bed.
- ••• 0:59—Buns, while making love in bed, then breasts afterwards.
- •• 1:11—Breasts, after taking off her towel and putting Daniel's hand on her left breast.
- •• 1:15—Breasts, while turning over, then lying in bed.

Heartbreaker (1983) . . . . Rose
Purple Rain (1984). . . . . .Apollonia
- •• 0:20—Brief breasts, after taking off jacket before jumping into lake.

Ministry of Vengeance (1989) . . . . Zarah
Back to Back (1990) . . . . .Jesse Duro
Black Magic Woman (1990) . . . . Cassandra Perry
- • 0:18—Brief side of left breast with Mark Hamill. Don't see her face.
- • 0:25—Very brief upper half of left breast, while in shower with Hamill.

TV:

Falcon Crest (1985-86) . . . . Apollonia

Applegate, Christina

Films:

Streets (1989) . . . . Dawn
1:09—Very, very brief almost side view of left breast, while kissing her boyfriend, Sy. His hand is over her breast. Not really a nude scene, but I'm including it because people might send this in as an addition.

Don't Tell Mom the Babysitter's Dead (1991) . . . . .Swell
Across the Moon (1994) . . . . Kathy
Vibrations (1994). . . . . .Anamika
Wild Bill (1995) . . . . Lurline
Mars Attacks! (1996) . . . . .Sharona

Made for TV Movies:

Dance 'Til Dawn (1988) . . . . Patrice Johnson

TV:

Heart of the City (1986-87). . . . . Robin Kennedy
Married ...with Children (1987-97) . . . . .Kelly Bundy

Applegate, Colleen

a.k.a. Adult film actress Shauna Grant.

Video Tapes:

Nudes in Limbo (1983) . . . . .Model
Penthouse Love Stories (1986). . . . . Service Station Woman
- ••• 0:10—Nude, making love in a bedroom. Long scene.

Penthouse: On the Wild Side (1988) . . . . Colleen
- ••• 0:39—Breasts in lingerie on bed. Nude on the floor.

Appleseth, Mary Ann

Films:

Slumber Party '57 (1976) . . . . .Jo Ann
- •• 1:18—Left breast with movie star getting interviewed. Don't see her face. Breasts a couple of more times, but still don't see her face.

Planet of Dinosaurs (1978) . . . . .n.a.

Araya, Zeudi

Films:

The Body (1980) . . . . .Princess
- • 0:26—Silhouette of right breast, then breasts and buns, while running in the dark at the beach.
- •• 0:27—Full frontal nudity, while lying down at the beach with Alan.
- •• 0:38—Breasts, while opening her dress top to tease Alan, then on bed making love.
- • 1:00—Right breast in open dress, while playing in the surf with Alan.
- • 1:13—Brief breasts while on the beach, making love with Alan.

Hearts and Armour (1983). . . . . Marfisa

Archer, Anne

Daughter of actor John Archer and actress Marjorie Lord.

Films:

Cancel My Reservation (1972). Crazy
The Honkers (1972). . . . . .Deborah Moon
The All-American Boy (1973). . . . . Drenna Valentine

Lifeguard (1975). . . . . Cathy
- 1:04—Very brief nipple while kissing Sam Elliott. Need to crank the brightness on your TV to the maximum. It appears in the lower right corner of the screen as the camera pans from right to left.

Trackdown (1976). . . . . Barbara
Paradise Alley (1978). . . . . Annie
Good Guys Wear Black (1979). . . . . Margaret
Hero at Large (1980). . . . . J. Marsh
Raise the Titanic (1980; British) . . . . Dana Archibald
Green Ice (1981; British) . . . . Holbrook
The Naked Face (1984). . . . . Ann Blake
Too Scared to Scream (1985) . . . . Kate
The Check is in the Mail (1986). . . . . Peggy Jackson
Fatal Attraction (1987) . . . . Ellen Gallagher
Love at Large (1990) . . . . Miss Dolan
Narrow Margin (1990) . . . . Hunnicut
Eminent Domain (1991; Canadian/French) . . . . Mita
Body of Evidence (1992). . . . . Joanne Braslow
(Unrated version reviewed.)
1:12—Nude scene on video playback is body double Shawn Lusader.

Patriot Games (1992) . . . . Dr. Cathy Ryan
Family Prayers (1993) . . . . n.a.
Short Cuts (1993). . . . . Claire Kane
- 1:49—(0:6 into Part 2) Very brief side view of buns, while hiking up nightgown and sitting on edge of tub.

Clear and Present Danger (1994) . . . . Candy Ryan

Made for Cable Movies:
The Last of His Tribe (1992; HBO) . . . . Henriette Kroeber
Nails (1992; Showtime). . . . . Mary Niles
0:16—Breasts and buns belong to body double Shelley Michelle.

Directed By: Leslie's Folly (1994; Showtime) . . . . Leslie
The Man in the Attic (1995; Showtime). . . . . . Krista Heldmann
(Nudity is done by a body double.)
Indiscretion of an American Wife (1998; Lifetime) . . Julia Burton

Made for Cable TV:
Directed By: Present Tense, Past Perfect (1995; Showtime) . . . . Kate

Miniseries:
Seventh Avenue (1977). . . . . Myrna Gold

Made for TV Movies:
Because Mommy Works (1994). . . . . n.a.
Jane's House (1994). . . . . Mary Parker
My Husband's Secret Life (1998) . . . . . . Theresa "Sissy" Sullivan

TV:
Bob & Carol & Ted & Alice (1973) . . . . Carol Sanders
The Family Tree (1983) . . . . Annie Benjamin Nichols
Falcon Crest (1985). Cassandra Wilder

• Ardant, Fanny *

Films:
The Family (1987; Italian/French) . . . . Adriana
Afraid of the Dark (1992; British/French) . . . . Miriam
Colonel Chabert (1994; French) . . . . Countess Ferraud
Sabrina (1995) . . . . Irene
Ridicule (1996; French) . . . . Countess of Blayac
- 0:06—Brief buns and side of left breast while getting powdered. Long shot.

Argento, Asia

Daughter of Italian director Dario Argento and actress Daria Nicolodi.

Films:
The Church (1991; Italian). . . . . Lotte
a.k.a. La Chiesa
Trauma (1992). . . . . Aura Petrescu
- •• 0:27—Breasts, after taking off bra in bathroom.

Queen Margot (1994; French) . . . . Charlotte
a.k.a. La Reine Margot
- 1:13—Brief lower frontal nudity while in bed with Henri.

Argo, Allison

Films:
Between the Lines (1977) . . . . Dancer
- 0:28—Breasts dancing on stage.

Cry From the Mountain (1986) . . . . Laurie Matthews

TV:
Ladies' Man (1980-81) . . . . Susan

Ariane

Model.

Full name is Ariane Koizumi.

Films:
The Year of the Dragon (1985). . . . . Tracy Tzu
- 0:59—Very brief breasts when Mickey Rourke rips her blouse off in her apartment.
- •• 1:14—Nude, taking a shower in her apartment.
- •• 1:18—Breasts straddling Rourke, while making love on the bed.

King of New York (1990) . . . . Dinner Guest
Skin Art (1993) . . . . Lin
- 1:00—Left breast when Will pulls her lingerie top down and kisses her.

Made for Cable Movies:
Women & Men 2: Three Short Stories (1991; HBO). . . . . . Alice

Ariel, Brigitte *

Films:
Rosebud (1975). . . . . Sabine
- 0:11—Very, Very brief part of right breast, while lying in bed when her boyfriend, Patrice, sits up. Brief left breast, when scooting up behind him.
- 0:19—Buns while sleeping on bed, then lower frontal nudity after terrorist wakes her up. Buns, while standing on deck of boat (she's first in line).

Piaf—The Early Years (1982) . . . . Edith Piaf

Aries, Anna

Films:
The Omega Man (1971) . . . . Woman in Cemetary Crypt
Rage (1972). . . . . n.a.
Invasion of the Bee Girls (1973). . . . . Cora Kline
- •• 0:55—Buns and breasts getting transformed into a Bee Girl.
- ••• 1:00—Breasts getting out of the bee transformer.

Armitage, Alison

See: York, Brittany.

Armstrong, Bess

Films:
Four Seasons (1981) . . . . Ginny Newley
- 0:38—Brief buns, twice, while skinny dipping in the water with Nick.

Jekyll & Hyde... Together Again (1982) . . . . Mary

High Road to China (1983) . . . . Eve
Jaws 3 (1983) . . . . Kathryn Morgan
The House of God (1984) . . . . Cissy Anderson
(Not available on video tape.)
Breasts.
Nothing in Common (1986) . . . . Donna Mildred Martin
Second Sight (1989) . . . . Sister Elizabeth
Serial Mom (1993) . . . . Uncredited
The Skateboard Kid (1993) . . . . Maggie
Dream Lover (1994) . . . . Elaine
(Unrated version reviewed.)
The Perfect Daughter (1996) . . . . Jill Michaelson

Made for Cable TV:
Tales From the Crypt: What's Cookin' (1992; HBO) . . . . . . Erma

Miniseries:
Lace (1984) . . . . Judy Hale

Made for TV Movies:
The Lakeside Killer (1979) . . . . n.a.
Take Me Home Again (1994) . . . . Connie
Danielle Steel's "Mixed Blessings" (1995) . . . . Pilar
She Stood Alone: The Tailhook Scandal (1995) . . . Barbara Pope
Stolen Innocence (1995) . . . . Becky Sapp
She Cried No (1996) . . . . Denise Connell

TV:
On Our Own (1977-78) . . . . Julia Peters
All Is Forgiven (1986) . . . . Paula Russell
Married People (1990-91) . . . . Elizabeth Meyers
My So-Called Life (1994-95) . . . . Patty

Armstrong, Katherine

Films:
The Arrival (1990) . . . . n.a.
Crash and Burn (1990) . . . . Christine
••• 1:00—Breasts taking a shower before being killed.
Ambition (1991) . . . . Roseanne
••• 1:13—Buns in G-string, then breasts in Clancy Brown's apartment.
Street Soldiers (1991) . . . . Julie
Silk Degrees (1994) . . . . Nicole
• 1:05—Very, very brief breast, when in water, while killing Mark Hamill.

Armstrong, Kerry

Films:
Key Exchange (1985) . . . . The Beauty
Hunting (1990; Australian) . . . . Michelle Harris
• 0:29—Side view of left breast in steamy shower.
•• 0:35—Breasts, making love with John Savage in bed. Seen on video monitors.
• 1:00—Breasts and upper half of buns, making love with Savage.
• 1:02—Brief buns, turning over in bed.
• 1:26—Very, very brief breasts, getting her dress top yanked down. Breasts, long shot, getting raped on dining table. Left breast, lying on the floor afterwards.

Made for Cable TV:
Ocean Girl (1994-95; Disney; Australian/U.S./British) . . . . Dr. Dianne Bates

Armstrong, Melinda *

a.k.a. Melinda Greene.

Films:
Casual Sex? (1988) . . . . Uncredited Exercise Instructor
In the Cold of the Night (1989) . . . . Laser Model 2
Bikini Summer (1991) . . . . Cheryl
• 0:07—Very brief breasts and partial buns, in bathroom when Chet interrupts her.
• 0:25—Close-up of buns in swimsuit, while bending over.
••• 0:35—Nude in swimming pool and talking to Burt. Nice, long scene.
•• 0:49—Breasts and buns, trying on swimsuits, then having a water fight with Shelley Michelle.
• 0:51—Buns in swimsuit, while at the beach.
••• 1:17—Full frontal nudity in swimming pool flashback.
The Naked Gun 2 1/2: The Smell of Fear (1991) . . . . Uncredited Model
Alien Intruder (1992) . . . . Tammy
•• 0:29—In two piece swimsuit, then nude in shower during Maxwell Caulfield's virtual reality experience.
• 0:30—Very, very brief right breast, while putting on robe while walking on balcony.
• 0:54—Breasts, while lying dead on beach.
Bikini Summer 2 (1992) . . . . Venessa
••• 0:05—Breasts and buns, while taking a shower.
••• 0:52—Breasts, taking off swimsuit top in bedroom. Breasts and buns, taking a shower.
•• 0:54—Breasts and buns in T-back panties, taking off robe and getting into bed, then sitting up to eat breakfast.
Encino Man (1992) . . . . Mountain Nug
Assault of the Party Nerds II: The Heavy Petting Detective (1993) . . . . Babe #1
Deep Down (1993) . . . . Holly
(Unrated version reviewed.)
•• 0:08—Left breast in open blouse, while making love with a boy.
•• 0:21—Full frontal nudity, while making love with a boy in Andy's dream.
•• 0:26—Breasts, while on bed with a boy in Andy's daydream.
Jailbait (1993) . . . . Dawn
a.k.a. Streetwise
• 0:43—Brief buns in G-string, then breasts, while talking to C. Thomas Howell in room in sex club.

Video Tapes:
Hot Body Video Magazine #2: Double Trouble (1992) . . . . Model
•• 0:00—Breasts during opening credits.
••• 0:03—In white bra, then breasts, buns in panties, posing outside.
••• 0:25—Breasts and buns (on the left), changing swimsuits.
Nude Daydreams (1993) . . . . Daydream 1
••• 0:01—Nude in and out of lingerie. Long scene.
Hot Body Competition: The Best of Hot Body (1994) . . . . Herself
••• 0:11—Buns in swimsuits. Breasts while trying on lingerie.
Raw Adventures (1994) . . . . Pacific Ocean
••• 0:15—Nude, while taking off her swimsuit and posing at the beach.
• 0:20—Breasts, while posing outdoors.

Armstrong, Rebekka *

Films:
Mortuary Academy (1988) . . . . Nurse
Hider in the House (1989) . . . . Attractive Woman
• 0:47—Brief breasts in bed with Mimi Roger's husband when she surprises them.
Immortalizer (1990) . . . . June
• 0:16—Breasts getting blouse taken off by nurse.
••• 0:29—Breasts when a worker fondles her while she's asleep.

Instant Karma (1990) . . . . Jamie
Angel 4: Undercover (1993) . . . . Catfight Groupie
• 0:41—Brief breasts, while with a band member and another woman in dressing room.

Music Videos:
Give Me the Keys/Huey Lewis & the News . . . . n.a.

Video Tapes:
Playboy Video Centerfold: Rebekka Armstrong . . . . Playmate
Playboy Video Calendar 1987 (1986) . . . . Playmate
Playboy Video Magazine, Volume 10 (1986) . . . . Playmate
••• 0:40—Nude in song and dance number in car repair shop.
Sexy Lingerie (1988) . . . . Model
Wet & Wild (1989) . . . . Model
Playboy Video Centerfold: Kerri Kendall (1990) . . . . Playmate
••• 0:33—Nude.
Playmates at Play (1990) . . . . Gotta Dance
Wet & Wild II (1990) . . . . Model
Sexy Lingerie III (1991) . . . . Model
Ultimate Sensual Massage (1991) . . . . Seduction
••• 0:39—Nude, during massage session in surreal outdoor setting.
Wet & Wild III (1991) . . . . Model
The Best of Wet and Wild (1992) . . . . Model
Intimate Workout For Lovers (1992) . . . . Sensual Exercise
••• 0:11—Nude, exercising in living room and exercise room.

Arneric, Neda

Films:
The Sensual Man . . . . Caterina
Shaft in Africa (1973) . . . . Jazar
•• 1:19—Buns and breasts, after taking off dress in cabin on boat with Richard Roundtree.
•• 1:20—Very brief lower frontal nudity, then buns and breasts when Roundtree brings her into the bathroom.
•• 1:21—Breasts and buns, in bed with Roundtree.
• 1:23—Brief partial right breast, lying in bed. Buns and partial breasts, sitting up.

*Arnett, Sherry **

Video Tapes:
Playboy Video Centerfold: Sherry Arnett . . . . . . Playmate
Playboy Video Calendar 1987 (1986) . . . . Playmate
Playboy Video Calendar 1988 (1987) . . . . Playmate

Arnold, Caroline

Films:
Vindicator (1986; Canadian) . . . . Lisa
a.k.a. Frankenstein '88
•• 0:40—Breasts in bed with a jerk, then putting her blouse on.
Meatballs III (1987) . . . . Ida (Girl in VW Bug)

Aronson, Judie

Films:
Friday the 13th, Part IV—The Final Chapter (1984) . . . . Samantha
• 0:26—Brief breasts and very brief buns taking clothes off to go skinny dipping.
• 0:29—Brief breasts under water pretending to be dead.
•• 0:39—Breasts and brief buns taking off her T-shirt to go skinny dipping at night.
American Ninja (1985) . . . . Patricia
Weird Science (1985) . . . . Hilly
After Midnight (1989) . . . . Jennifer

Cool Blue (1990) . . . . Cathy
•• 1:03—Breasts in bed on top of Woody Harrelson.
The Sleeping Car (1990) . . . . Kim
•• 0:42—Brief breasts on top of David Naughton making love. Brief breasts three times after he hallucinates.
Desert Kickboxer (1991) . . . . Claudia

TV:
Pursuit of Happiness (1987-88) . . . . Sara Duncan

Arquette, Patricia

Sister of actress Rosanna and actors Alexis and David Arquette.
Granddaughter of actor Cliff Arquette a.k.a. Charlie Weaver.
Daughter of actor/director Lewis Arquette.
Wife of actor Nicolas Cage.

Films:
Pretty Smart (1986) . . . . Zero
A Nightmare on Elm Street 3: The Dream Warriors (1987) . . . . Kristen Parker
Far North (1988) . . . . Jilly
Prayer of the Rollerboys (1990) . . . . Casey
The Indian Runner (1991) . . . . Dorothy
Trouble Bound (1992) . . . . Kit
Ethan Frome (1993) . . . . Mattie Silver
Inside Monkey Zetterland (1993) . . . . Grace Zetterland
True Romance (1993) . . . . Alabama Whitman
(Unrated version reviewed.)
• 0:11—Brief breasts, while lying in bed with Christian Slater. [On the wide screen laser disc version only: Right breast two more times and partial left breast (••).]
Ed Wood (1994) . . . . Kathy O'Hara
Holy Matrimony (1994) . . . . Havana
Beyond Rangoon (1995) . . . . Laura Bowman
Flirting With Disaster (1996) . . . . Nancy Coplin
Infinity (1996) . . . . Arline
The Secret Agent (1996) . . . . Winnie
Lost Highway (1997) . . . . Renee Madison/Alice Wakefield
•• 0:12—Brief side view of right breast and buns, after taking off robe.
•• 0:15—Breasts (in slow motion), while making love under Bill Pullman.
••• 1:32—In bra and panties, then breasts when being forced to strip at gunpoint in front of Robert Loggia.
• 1:54—Breasts and partial buns, while making love outdoors at night, lit by car's headlights. Overexposed shot looks almost like B&W.
• 1:56—Breasts and buns, leaving Getty and walking up the stairs.

Made for Cable Movies:
Wildflower (1991; Lifetime) . . . . Alice Guthrie

Made for Cable TV:
Tales From the Crypt: Four Sided Triangle (1990; HBO) . . . . Mary Jo

Made for TV Movies:
Dillinger (1991) . . . . Polly
Betrayed by Love (1994) . . . . Deanne

*Arquette, Rosanna **

Sister of actress Patricia and actors Alexis and David Arquette.
Granddaughter of actor Cliff Arquette a.k.a. Charlie Weaver.
Daughter of actor/director Lewis Arquette.

Films:
Gorp (1980) . . . . Judy
S.O.B. (1981) . . . . Babs
• 0:21—Brief breasts taking off white T-shirt on the deck of the house. Long shot, hard to see.

The Executioner's Song (1982). . . . . Nicole Baker
(European Version reviewed.)
••• 0:30—Brief breasts in bed, then getting out of bed. Buns, walking to kitchen.
••• 0:41—Breasts in bed with Tommy Lee Jones.
••• 0:48—Breasts on top of Jones making love.
•• 1:36—Right breast and buns, standing up getting strip searched before visiting Jones in prison.
Off the Wall (1982) . . . . Pam
Baby, It's You (1983) . . . . Jill
•• 1:17—Left breast, making love in bed with Vincent Spano.
The Aviator (1984) . . . . .Tilly Hansen
After Hours (1985) . . . . Marcy
Desperately Seeking Susan (1985) . . . . Roberta Glass
• 0:24—Upper half of breasts in bubble bath.
• 0:46—Breasts while getting dressed when Aidan Quinn sees her through the fish tank. Long shot, hard to see.
• 1:22—Very, very brief left breast, when getting up after lying down with Quinn.
Silverado (1985) . . . . .Hannah
8 Million Ways to Die (1986). . . . . .Sarah
Nobody's Fool (1986) . . . . Cassie
Amazon Women on the Moon (1987). . . . . Karen
The Big Blue (1988) . . . . .Johana
Black Rainbow (1989; British) . . . . Martha Travis
••• 0:50—Breasts in bed with Hulce, then walking to bathroom.
New York Stories (1989) . . . . .Paulette
...Almost (1990; Australian) . . . . Wendy
Flight of the Intruder (1991) . . . . .Callie
The Linguini Incident (1991). . . . . Lucy
Fathers and Sons (1992) . . . . Miss Athena
Don't Hang Up (1993) . . . . Sarah Weiss
Nowhere to Run (1993). . . . . Clydie
••• 0:11—In white bra and panties, undressing in bathroom, then nude, getting into the shower while Jean-Claude Van Damme peeks in through the window.
••• 1:01—In bra, then breasts while making love in bed with Van Damme.
Pulp Fiction (1994) . . . . Jody
Search and Destroy (1995) . . . . Lauren Mikheim
Crash (1996; Canadian). . . . . Gabrielle
(NC-17 version reviewed.)
•• 1:14—Left breast, while having sex in Mercedes with James Spader.
Deceiver (1997) . . . . Mrs. Kennesaw
Gone Fishin' (1997) . . . . Rita
Trading Favors (1997) . . . . .Alex
Made for Cable Movies:
Sweet Revenge (1990) . . . . Kate
The Wrong Man (1993; Showtime) . . . . .Missy
•• 0:34—Buns in black panties, then breasts, taking off her dress at the beach and going into the water. Medium long shot.
••• 1:15—Breasts after taking off bra and dancing on table in room, then putting on dress afterwards. Very nice, long scene.
• 1:23—Very, very brief part of right breast in open robe and very brief side view of buns while in bed on top of Anderson.
Miniseries:
Son of Morning Star (1991) . . . . Libby Custer
Made for TV Movies:
In the Deep Woods (1992) . . . . .Joanna
Nowhere to Hide (1994). . . . . Sarah Blake
TV:
Shirley (1979-80) . . . . Debra Miller

• *Arroyave, Karina*
Films:
Falling Down (1993) . . . . Angie
The Cowboy Way (1994). . . . . Rosa
Trial By Jury (1994) . . . . Mercedes
Dangerous Minds (1995). . . . . .Josy
187 (1997). . . . . Rita
• 0:19—Very, very brief left breast, while putting her bra back on in shed after getting discovered by John Heard.
• 0:52—Brief right breast, while lying nude on Samuel L. Jackson's couch.
Made for TV Movies:
Friends at Last (1995) . . . . Ramona
TV:
As the World Turns (1989-94) . . . . .Bianca

• *Artecona, Christine* *
Twin sister of Jacqueline Artecona.
Video Tapes:
Playboy's Twins & Sisters Too (1997) . . .Workout Together
••• 0:26—Nude, while working out on exercise equipment with her twin sister.

• *Artecona, Jacqueline* *
Video Tapes:
Playboy's Twins & Sisters Too (1997) . . .Workout Together
••• 0:26—Nude, while working out on exercise equipment with her twin sister.

Arth, Emily *
Video Tapes:
Playboy Video Calendar 1990 (1989) . . . . May
••• 0:23—Nude.
Playboy Video Playmate Six-Pack 1992 (1992) . .Playmate

Arthur, Sean'a
a.k.a. Shana Arthur.
Films:
Body Waves (1991). . . . . Dream Girl
•• 0:02—Brief buns in swimsuit, walking into office.
••• 0:03—Breasts, taking off her bathing suit top during Rick's dream.
•• 0:07—Breasts and side view of buns in swimsuit bottom, during Dooner's fantasy.
Dance with Death (1991) . . . . .Sherilyn
• 0:42—Buns, while dancing on stage with Lola.
Uncaged (1991) . . . . Dancer
a.k.a. Angel in Red
•• 0:44—Buns in lingerie. Breasts dancing on stage.
Black Belt (1992). . . . . Reporter

Arthur, Stacy *
Mrs. Ohio 1990.
Video Tapes:
Playboy Video Calendar 1992 (1991) . . . . October
••• 0:39—Buns in lingerie. Full frontal nudity fantasizing in bed.
••• 0:41—Nude in various locations around the house.
Playboy's Playmate Review 1992 (1992) . . . . Miss January
••• 0:18—Nude, dancing on back of truck, then using a pottery wheel.
Sexy Lingerie IV (1992) . . . . .Model

Asha

See: Siewkumar, Asha.

Ashbrook, Daphne

Films:

Gimme an "F" (1981) ....Phoebe Willis
a.k.a. T & A Academy 2

Sunset Heat (1991)..............................Julie
a.k.a. Midnight Heat
(Unrated version reviewed.)
• 1:06—Brief breasts in silhouette, while making love with Michael Paré. Dark.
•• 1:07—More breasts, while on top of Paré, then lying down.

Automatic (1994) .... Nora Rochester

Made for TV Movies:

That Secret Sunday (1986) .... Collie
Daughters of Privilege (1990) .... Mary Hope
Intruders (1992) .... Lesley Hahn
Poisoned by Love: The Kern County Murders (1993).....Dyna
Jake Lassiter: Justice on the Bayou (1995) ..... Susan Corrigan

TV:

Our Family Honor (1985-86)............. Officer Liz McKay
Fortune Dane (1986).............Kathy "Speed" Davenport

Ashe, Danni *

Adult film actress.

Video Tapes:

Soft Bodies: Double Exposure (1994) .... Herself
••• 0:02—In blue bra and panties, then nude, on sofa.
••• 0:10—In sheer white lingerie, then nude outside.
••• 0:14—In blue two piece swimsuit, then nude in spa.

All Nude Glamour (1995) .... Danni
••• 0:05—Nude, while posing indoors. Some behind-the-scenes shots included. Long scene.
•• 0:09—Full frontal nudity, while talking dirty.

Soft Bodies: Pillow Talk (1996) .... Herself
••• 0:02—In lingerie, then nude, while posing on chair indoors.
••• 0:08—In dress, then nude, while posing on chair outdoors.
••• 0:12—In bra and panties, then nude in bathroom, then in bubble bath.
•• 0:37—Breasts, after taking off her top and doing cheerleader moves outdoors with Becky LeBeau.

CD-ROM:

Crystal Fantasy (1995).......................... Danni

Ashland, Brittany

a.k.a. Adult film actress Tanya Rivers and Hillary Winters.

Films:

Psycho Cop 2 (1992) .... Go Go Dancer #1
• 0:21—Breasts on film that the guys are watching at bachelor party. (She's the blonde.)
• 1:17—Breasts and buns in white panties in film during end credits.

Video Tapes:

Starlet Screen Test III (1992) .... Brigitte Williams
••• 0:34—Breasts in silhouette during audition, then nude with the lights on and playing with ice.

Ashley, Elizabeth

Films:

The Carpetbaggers (1964) .... Monica Winthrop

The Marriage of a Young Stockbroker (1971)...... Nan
• 0:49—Very, very brief partial right breast, while adjusting her bikini top.
• 1:26—Buns through shower door in women's locker room.

Paperback Hero (1973; Canadian)............... Loretta
••• 0:37—Nude in shower with Keir Dullea. Long scene.
••• 0:39—Breasts, straddling Dullea in the shower.

92 in the Shade (1975) ....Jeannie Carter
Rancho Deluxe (1975)...................... Cora Brown
The Great Scout and Cathouse Thursday (1976) ... Nancy Sue
Coma (1978).............................. Mrs. Emerson
Paternity (1981) .... Sophia Thatcher
Split Image (1982)............................... Diana
Dragnet (1987) .... Police Commissioner Jane Kilpatrick
A Man of Passion (1989) .... Gloria
Vampire's Kiss (1989)......................... Dr. Glaser

Made for Cable Movies:

Harnessing Peacocks (1995; British; A&E) ...... Grandmother

Made for Cable TV:

The Hitchhiker: Out of the Night (1985; HBO)........Woman

Miniseries:

The Buccaneers (1995; U.S./British)............Mrs. Closson

Made for TV Movies:

Svengali (1983) .... Eve Swiss
In the Best Interest of the Children (1992)........ Carla Scott

TV:

Another World........................... Emma Ordway
Evening Shade (1990-94) .... Frieda Evans

Ashley, Erin Weidner

Films:

Out for Justice (1991) .... Hooker

Midnight Tease 2 (1995) .... Shane
• 0:05—Breast breasts and buns in T-back, garter belt and stockings while dancing on stage.
• 0:53—Brief breasts, while dancing on stage.
••• 0:55—Breasts and buns, while dancing on stage.
•• 1:00—Breasts while dancing on stage.

Ashley, Jennifer *

Films:

Your Three Minutes Are Up (1973) .... Teenage Driver

The Centerfold Girls (1974) ....Charly
• 0:34—Breasts taking off blouse while changing clothes.
•• 0:49—Breasts and buns posing for photographer outside with Glory.

The Pom Pom Girls (1976) .... Laurie
• 1:02—Brief breasts (on the left), taking off her white blouse in locker room. Brief buns, taking off panties and pulling down her cheerleader body suit.

Tintorera (1977)............................... Kelly
• 0:27—Buns and brief side of left breast, taking off her dress and swimming to the boat. She's the first one to undress.
•• 0:28—Breasts and buns, while on boat deck and getting into hammock with Steven.
•• 0:29—Breasts, when sleeping in hammock and getting out. Brief nude in water, while swimming from the boat.
• 1:11—Breasts, while taking off her yellow top. Dark.
• 1:12—Brief breasts, while doing backstroke in water near Cynthia.
• 1:14—Brief breasts, while getting pulled out of the water by Steven, then lying on her back on beach.

Horror Planet (1980; British) ....Holly
a.k.a. Inseminoid

Partners (1982) .... Secretary
Chained Heat (1983; U.S./German)................Grinder
The Man Who Loved Women (1983).........David's Mother

Ashley, Kaitlyn

Adult film actress.
a.k.a. Kelly J. Hoffman.

Adult Films:

Breeders (1996) . . . . n.a.
Beautiful (1998) . . . . n.a.

Films:

Indecent Behavior 3 (1995) . . . . Candy
•• 0:02—Nude, while in bedroom with Mr. Cowens.

Stripshow (1995) . . . . Dancer
• 0:10—Buns in T-back, then breasts while dancing on stage.
• 0:40—Breasts and buns in T-back, while on stage.
•• 1:12—Breasts while on stage.
•• 1:15—Breasts and buns in T-back, while dancing on stage, intercut with Tané McClure.

Babe Watch: The Forbidden Parody (1996). . . . . . . Bambi
•• 0:07—Breasts, while trying on swimsuit in dressing room.
• 0:20—Buns in swimsuit, while skating in parking lot. Brief breasts, when her swimsuit top comes off after falling on Derek.
• 1:01—Brief buns, after being rescued at the beach.
• 1:15—Buns in pink swimsuit, then brief breasts, while dancing on stage.

Ashley, Kirsten

Films:

The Rain Killer (1990) . . . . Dancer #2
• 0:32—Nude, dancing on stage in club. Backlit too much.
• 0:49—Buns, then brief nude on stage in club. Slightly out of focus.

Sex Crimes (1991) . . . . Dancer

Made for Cable TV:

Erotic Confessions: Inspiration (1995; Cinemax) . . . . . . Andrea
(Available on video tape in *Erotic Zone: Inspiration.*)

Ashley, Susan

Made for Cable TV:

Dream On: What I Did for Lust (1991; HBO) . . . . . Marsha
•• 0:01—Breasts in Eddie's dressing room with a sweater over her head.

Video Tapes:

Rock Video Girls (1991). . . . . .Herself

• Ashton, Juli *

Adult film actress.

Video Tapes:

Playboy's Night Calls (1998). . . . . .Herself
••• 0:00—Nude throughout.

Ashton, Vali

Films:

Blue Desert (1990) . . . . Young Woman
Die Watching (1993) . . . . Nola Carlisle
• 1:00—Buns in white panties and right breast while making love with Atkins.

Mortal Danger (1993). . . . . Counselor

Aspen, Jennifer

Films:

Sometimes They Come Back ...Again (1995)
. . . . Maria Moore
•• 1:13—Left breast, after taking off her blouse, while with Vinnie.

A Very Brady Sequel (1996). . . . . .Kathy Lawrence

Made for TV Movies:

The Secret She Carried (1996) . . . . .Toni

TV:

NYPD Blue: Taillights's Last Gleaming (Feb 18, 1997) . . . . .n.a.

Assan, Ratna *

Films:

Papillon (1973) . . . . Zoraima
• 1:54—Breasts, first seeing Steve McQueen.
•• 1:55—Breasts, helping clean up McQueen on the beach and in the ocean.
•• 1:56—Breasts, walking on the beach with McQueen.
•• 1:57—Breasts, getting off boat and watching a guy open oysters.
•• 2:00—Breasts, on beach, walking with McQueen while holding a torch.

Asti, Adrianna

Films:

Before the Revolution (1964; Italian) . . . . Gina
Ludwig (1973; Italian) . . . . Lila Von Buliowski
Down the Ancient Staircase (1975; Italian) . . . . Gianna
The Inheritance (1978; Italian). . . . . .Teta Ferramonti
Caligula (1980) . . . . Ennia
(X-rated, 147 minute version.)
• 0:27—Breasts at side of bed with Malcolm McDowell when he feels her breasts.
•• 0:54—Breasts lying down surrounded by slaves. Mostly her right breast.

Chimere (1989; French) . . . . .Alice's Mother

Astley, Pat

Films:

Playbirds (1978; British) . . . . Doreen Hamilton
•• 0:00—Breasts posing for photo session.

Don't Open Till Christmas (1984; British). . . . . Sharon
••• 0:19—Breasts in sexy gold outfit while posing for photo session. Nice, long scene.
•• 0:22—Breasts flashing while wearing a Santa outfit for Cliff.
•• 0:24—Breasts in Santa outfit when the killer checks her out while holding a razor.
•• 0:26—Breasts, sitting on bed opening her robe for policemen.

Atwood, Kathryn

Films:

To Die For 2 (1991). . . . . Nurse
a.k.a. Son of Darkness: To Die For II

A Woman, Her Men and Her Futon (1992) . . . . . . Waitress #2
Deep Down (1993) . . . . Waitress #2
(Unrated version reviewed.)
• 0:07—Brief right breast in gaping dress top while cleaning table when Andy sees her.

Jason Goes to Hell—The Final Friday (1993)
. . . . .Alexis, the blonde camper
(Unrated Director's Original Cut reviewed.)
•• 0:26—Breasts, after taking off wet blouse after skinny dipping with her friends.

S.F.W. (1994). . . . . Pebbles Goren
Cyber Tracker 2 (1995) . . . . Blair

Auger, Claudine

Films:

Thunderball (1965; British) . . . . .Domino Dervall
The Head of the Family (1967; Italian/French) . . . . .Adriana
• 1:18—Very brief side of right breast, while putting Marco's shirt on.

Black Belly of the Tarantula (1972; Italian) . . . . Laura

Summertime Killer (1973) . . . . Michele Dobvien
Lovers and Liars (1979; Italian) . . . . Elisa
The Associate (1982; French/German) . . . . Agnes
a.k.a. L'Associe
Secret Places (1984; British) . . . . Sophy Meister

Austin, Julie

Films:
Elves (1989) . . . . Kirsten
Night of the Wilding (1990) . . . . Betty
•• 0:14—Side of left breast, taking off bra in bathroom. Breasts in shower.
• 0:16—More breasts in the shower.
• 0:17—Breasts visible behind shower door.
Smooth Talker (1990) . . . . Ms. Weston
Twisted Justice (1990) . . . . Andrea Leyton
Made for Cable Movies:
Extreme Justice (1993; HBO) . . . . Cindy

*Austin, Lynne **

Video Tapes:
Playboy Video Centerfold: Lynne Austin . . . . Playmate
Playboy Video Calendar 1989 (1988) . . . . May
••• 0:17—Nude.
Sexy Lingerie (1988) . . . . Model
Wet & Wild (1989) . . . . Model
Playboy's Fantasies II (1990) . . . . n.a.
Playboy's Sexy, Steamy, Sultry (1993) . . . . Playmate

Austin, Teri

Films:
Terminal Choice (1985; Canadian) . . . . Lylah Crane
• 0:14—Full frontal nudity, covered with blood on operating table. Long shot.
• 0:21—Right breast, on table being examined by Ellen Barkin. Dead, covered with dried blood.
• 0:26—Very brief left breast under plastic on table, hard to see.
Vindicator (1986; Canadian) . . . . Lauren Lehman
a.k.a. Frankenstein '88
• 0:30—Very brief left breast and buns in mirror getting out of the bubble bath covered with bubbles. Long shot, hard to see anything.
Dangerous Love (1988) . . . . Dominique
Raising Cain (1992) . . . . Karen
Made for Cable TV:
Bedtime (1996; Showtime) . . . . Jane
Bedtime: Episode 3 (1996; Showtime) . . . . Jane
•• 0:06—In bra, then left breast, while in hotel room with Craig.
• 0:13—Brief right breast, when sitting on food cart, making love with Craig, then very brief right breast, while lying on bed under Craig.
Bedtime: Episode 4 (1996; Showtime) . . . . Jane
• 0:12—Brief breasts, when remembering her affair with Craig.
Bedtime: Episode 5 (1996; Showtime) . . . . Jane
Made for TV Movies:
Laura Lansing Slept Here (1988) . . . . Melody Gomphers
False Witness (1989) . . . . Sandralee
TV:
Knots Landing (1985-89) . . . . Jill Bennett

Austine, Nicola

Films:
Not Tonight Darling (1971; British)
. . . . At the West Side Health Club
Suburban Wives (1973; British) . . . . Jean
The Adventures of a Private Eye (1974; British)
. . . . Wife in Bed
•• 0:00—Breasts and buns, getting out of bed to take a shower.
Old Dracula (1975; British) . . . . Playboy Bunny

Avery, Belle

Films:
Repossessed (1990) . . . . Gym Receptionist
Made for Cable Movies:
Sketch Artist (1992; Showtime) . . . . Krista
• 1:11—Right breast, while making love with Paul by swimming pool. Long shot, don't see her face very well.

Avery, Margaret

Films:
Cool Breeze (1972) . . . . Lark/Mercer's Mistress
Terror House (1972) . . . . Edwina
Hell Up in Harlem (1973) . . . . Sister Jennifer
••• 0:42—Breasts in bed, while making love with Fred Williamson.
Magnum Force (1973) . . . . Prostitute
Which Way Is Up? (1977) . . . . Annie Mae
The Fish That Saved Pittsburgh (1979) . . . . Toby Millman
The Color Purple (1985) . . . . Shug Avery
The Return of the Superfly (1990) . . . . Francine
Riverbend (1990) . . . . Bell Coleman
Mardi Gras for the Devil (1993) . . . . Miss Sadie
Cyborg 3: The Recycler (1995) . . . . Doc Edford
White Man's Burden (1995) . . . . Megan Thomas
Made for Cable Movies:
The Set-Up (1995; Showtime) . . . . Olivia Dubois
Miniseries:
The Jacksons: An American Dream (1992) . . . . Martha

Aviles, Angel

Films:
Chain of Desire (1992) . . . . Isa
• 0:14—In bra in bed with Jesus, then breasts. Dark.
Equinox (1992) . . . . Anna Gutierrez
Jailbait (1993) . . . . Pizza Girl
a.k.a. Streetwise
Mi Vida Loca (My Crazy Life) (1994) . . . . Sad Girl
Desperado (1995) . . . . Zamira
The Low Life (1995) . . . . Latina Girlfriend
Scorpion Spring (1995) . . . . Nadia

Axelrod, Lisa

Films:
Click: Calendar Girl Killer (1989) . . . . Jennifer
•• 0:58—Breasts, while on bed in photography studio with Andy.
• 0:59—Breasts, while making love in bed with Andy. Hard to see because of the strobe lights.
• 1:00—Brief breasts and buns in G-string getting killed. Still lit with strobe lights.
• 1:01—Brief breasts, dead, covered with blood, after crashing through glass in door.
Night Angel (1989) . . . . Double
Roadhouse (1989) . . . . Party Girl

Coldfire (1990) . . . . Dancer
- •• 0:11—Breasts, twice, dancing on stage.
- • 0:13—Brief breasts, getting pushed off the stage.

Axelrod, Nina

Films:

Roller Boogie (1979) . . . . .Bobby's Friend

Motel Hell (1980) . . . . Terry
- •• 1:01—Breasts sitting up in bed to kiss Vincent.
- • 1:04—Very brief breasts in tub when Bruce breaks the door down, then getting out of tub.

Brainstorm (1983) . . . . Simulator Technician

Cross Country (1983; Canadian) . . . . Lois Hayes
- • 0:28—Brief buns and sort of breasts, getting fondled by Richard.
- • 1:05—Very, very brief breasts, while fighting outside the motel in the rain with Johnny.

Cobra (1986) . . . . .Waitress

Critters 3 (1991) . . . . Mrs. Briggs

Ayer, Lois

a.k.a. Adult film actress Lois Ayers or Sondra Stilman.

Films:

Tougher Than Leather (1988) .Charlotte

Video Tapes:

In Search of the Perfect 10 (1986) . . . . Perfect Girl #2
- ••• 0:08—In swimsuit, then breasts exercising by the pool.

Wet Water T's (1987) . . . . .Herself
- ••• 0:55—Breasts during boxing match. Long scene.

Ayres-Hamilton, Leah

Films:

All That Jazz (1979) . . . . Nurse Capobianco

The Burning (1981) . . . . Michelle

Eddie Macon's Run (1983) . . . . Chris

Bloodsport (1987) . . . . Janice

Hot Child in the City (1987) .Rachel
- • 1:12—Very brief breasts in the shower with a guy. Long shot, hard to see anything.

The Player (1992) . . . . Sandy

TV:

The Edge of Night . . . . Valerie Bryson

9 to 5 (1983) . . . . Linda Bowman

Azhari, Ayu

Films:

Diamond Run (1988; Indonesian) . . . . Aileen

a.k.a. Java Burn

Without Mercy (1996) . . . . Tanya
- • 0:30—Very brief breasts with John by sofa.
- • 0:31—Brief breasts, several times, while making love in bathtub with John.
- • 0:54—Buns, while in bed with John.

*Bach, Barbara **

Wife of singer/former *Beatles* drummer Ringo Starr.

Films:

Black Belly of the Tarantula (1972; Italian) . . . . .Jenny

Stateline Motel (1975; Italian) . . . . .Emily

a.k.a. Last Chance for a Born Loser

The Spy Who Loved Me (1977; British) . . Major Anya Amosova

Force Ten from Navarone (1978) . . . . Maritza
- • 0:32—Brief breasts, while taking a bath in the German officer's room.

Screamers (1978; Italian) . . . . Amanda

a.k.a. The Island of the Fishmen

a.k.a. Something Waits in the Dark

The Humanoid (1979; Italian) . . . . Lady Agatha

Jaguar Lives (1979) . . . . .Anna

Great Alligator (1980; Italian) . . . . Alice Brandt

Caveman (1981) . . . . Lana

The Unseen (1981) . . . . .Jennifer

Up the Academy (1981) . . . . Bliss

Give My Regards to Broad Street (1984; British) . . . . .Journalist

Miniseries:

Princess Daisy (1983) . . . . Vanessa Valerian

*Bach, Catherine **

Films:

Nicole (1972) . . . . Sue

a.k.a. The Widow's Revenge
- •• 1:01—Brief breasts, twice, undressing to put on nightgown on boat. Nice shots, but too brief.
- •• 1:10—Very brief side view of breasts, three times, getting felt by Leslie Caron. Don't see either Bach's or Caron's face.

The Midnight Man (1974) . . . . Natalie

Thunderbolt and Lightfoot (1974) . . . . .Melody

Hustle (1975) . . . . Peggy Summers

Cannonball Run II (1984) . . . . Marcie

Street Justice (1988) . . . . Tamarra

Driving Force (1990) . . . . Harry

Masters of Menace (1990) . . . . Kitty Wheeler

The Nutt House (1992) . . . . Benefit Reporter

Rage and Honor (1992) . . . . Captain Murdoch

Made for TV Movies:

Dukes of Hazzard: Reunion! (1997) . . . . .Daisy

TV:

The Dukes of Hazzard (1979-85) . . . . Daisy Duke

African Skies (1992-93) . . . . .Margo

Bach, Pamela

Wife of actor/singer David Hasselhoff.

Films:

Appointment with Fear (1988) . . . . Samantha
- • 0:56—Breasts getting into the spa. Long shot, hard to see.

Nudity Required (1989) . . . . Dee Dee

TV:

Baywatch (1991-92) . . . . Kay Morgan

• *Bachar, Carmit*

Films:

North (1994) . . . . Texas Dancer

Made for Cable TV:

Red Shoe Diaries: Forbidden Zone (1996; Showtime) . . . . .Trouble Girl
- • 0:05—Brief full frontal nudity in open jacket. B&W.
- • 0:07—Very brief breasts. B&W. Superimposed over Beverly Johnson's face.
- • 0:09—Very brief breasts superimposed over flames. B&W.
- • 0:10—Nude, while making love with a guy in grainy B&W shots. Brief full frontal nudity in open jacket again.

Red Shoe Diaries: Banished (1998; Showtime) . . . . . . .Dancer 1

*Bachman, Cheryl **

Films:

Renegade: Fighting Cage (1993) . . . . Ring Card Girl
(Nudity added for video release.)

Blue Chips (1994) . . . . .Uncredited Girl at Party

Video Tapes:

Playboy Video Calendar 1993 (1992) . . . . April
••• 0:14—Nude in studio setting.
••• 0:16—Nude outside on rocks and in bathtub.

Playboy's Playmate Review 1992 (1992) . . . Miss October
••• 0:30—Nude on rooftop and then outside in a field.

Playboy's Sexy, Steamy, Sultry (1993). . . . . .Playmate

Backlinie, Susan *

Films:

Jaws (1975) . . . . Chrissie Watkins
• 0:02—Brief back side of right breast, while taking off her clothes and running on the beach. Seen mostly in silhouette.
• 0:03—Brief left breast (seen from the shark's point-of-view from underneath), while swimming in the water. Dark.

Day of the Animals (1976). . . . . Mandy Young

1941 (1979). . . . . .Polar Bear Girl
• 0:02—Brief breasts and buns, while taking off robe and running into the ocean. Dark, hard to see. This is a parody of her part in *Jaws*.
• 0:05—Buns, while hanging on submarine periscope.
• 0:06—Very, very brief left breast when getting back into the water.

Terror in the Aisles (1984) . . . . Swimmer
• 0:51—Breasts, under water from *Jaws*.

Badler, Jane

Films:

The First Time (1981) . . . . Karen
a.k.a. Doin' It

Black Snow (1989) . . . . Shelby Collins

Easy Kill (1989) . . . . Jade
• 0:35—Brief breasts, while sitting in spa with slit wrists. Brief crotch shot when Frank Stallone carries her out of the spa.
• 0:43—Brief right breast, while making love in bed with Stallone.
• 1:07—Left breast, while making love in bed with Stallone. Don't see her face.

Miniseries:

V (1983) . . . . Diana

TV:

One Life to Live (1977-81). . . . . Melinda Kramer
The Doctors (1981-82) . . . . Natalie Bell
Falcon Crest (1986-87) . . . . Meredith Braxton
Highwayman (1987-88) . . . . Tania Winthrop
Mission: Impossible (1989-90). . . . . .Shannon Reed

Baer, Meridith

Films:

The Sister-In-Law (1974) . . . . Deborah Holt
• 0:58—Breasts, while lying down on the ground in the woods to make love with John Savage.
• 1:00—Left breast, while kissing John Savage.

Coach (1978) . . . . .Janet
Private Lessons (1981). . . . . .Miss Phipps

Bagdasarian, Carol

Films:

The Strawberry Statement (1970) . . . . Telephone Girl
Charge of the Model T's (1979). . . . . .n.a.

The Octagon (1980) . . . . Aura
• 1:18—Brief side view of right breast, while taking off her blouse, sitting on bed next to Chuck Norris.

The Aurora Encounter (1985) . . . . Alain

Made for TV Movies:

The Amazing Howard Hughes (1977) . . . . Jean Peters

Baird, Bobbi

Video Tapes:

Hot Body Video Magazine #3: Blonde Fever (1993) . . . . .Coming Attractions
•• 0:55—Breasts.

Hot Body Video Magazine #4: Extra Sexy (1993) . . . . .Covergirl
•• 0:02—Breasts during introduction.
••• 0:43—Breasts and side of buns, while posing on pool table.
•• 0:49—Breasts under sheer purple bodysuit, then breasts after taking it off.
••• 0:51—In sexy swimsuit in spa, then breasts and buns.

Hot Body Video Magazine #9: The Best Of Hot Body Video Magazine (1994) . . . . Herself

Baird, Jeanne

Films:

The D.I. (1957) . . . . .Mother

The Gay Deceivers (1969) . . . . Mrs. Conway
• 0:51—Very brief buns, coming out of the bathroom and going back in when Danny shows up.

Nightforce (1986) . . . . .Mrs. Hanson

Baird, Roxanne

Films:

Open House (1987). . . . . .Allison
•• 1:12—Buns and brief side view of left breast walking to swimming pool, then breasts getting out of the pool before the killer gets her.

Black Belt II: Fatal Force (1988) . . . . .Karen Pendleton

Baker, Alretha

Films:

Dance with Death (1991) . . . . Sunny
••• 0:23—Breasts and buns in G-string, dancing on stage and falling off because she's on drugs.

The Baby Doll Murders (1992). . . . . Rhodes Receptionist

Baker, Carroll *

Films:

You've Got to Have Heart. . . . . .Lucia
a.k.a. At Last, At Last
•• 1:23—Left breast, while in cabin, consoling Giovanni.
•• 1:24—More left breast, while with Giovanni.
•• 1:25—Right breast while making love.

Baby Doll (1956) . . . . Baby Doll
Giant (1956) . . . . Luz Benedict II
How the West was Won (1963) . . . . Eve Prescott
The Carpetbaggers (1964). . . . . Rina
Harlow (1965) . . . . Jean Harlow
Sylvia (1965) . . . . Sylvia West
Orgasmo (1968) . . . . Kathryn West

The Sweet Body of Deborah (1968). . . . . Deborah
(Not available on video tape.)
Breasts.

Paranoia (1969; Italian/French) . . . . Kathryn West
• 0:13—Buns and partial glimpses of breasts, in shower with Peter.
• 0:16—Very, very brief upper half of right breast when Peter rips her dress.
•• 0:17—Buns, while lying in bed with Peter.
• 0:25—Brief buns, under mesh black robe.

Bloodbath (1976). . . . . Treasure
a.k.a. The Sky is Falling
• 0:16—Outline of left breast in see-through blouse when kneeling in the ocean to urinate.
• 0:50—Very brief buns, while mooning her mute lover.
My Father's Wife (1976; Italian) . . . . .Lara
a.k.a. Confessions of a Frustrated Housewife
• 0:03—Right breast making love in bed with her husband, Antonio.
•• 0:06—Breasts standing in front of bed talking to Antonio.
••• 0:18—Breasts kneeling in bed, then getting out and putting a robe on while wearing beige panties.
Andy Warhol's Bad (1977; Italian) . . . . .Mrs. Aiken
The World is Full of Married Men (1979; British)
. . . . Linda Cooper
• 0:19—Brief left breast, while sitting up in bathtub covered with bubbles.
The Body (1980). . . . . .Madeliene
• 1:19—Brief left breast, twice, while making love with Alan. Close-up shot.
• 1:20—Buns, when getting letter out of drawer. Brief left breast when sitting on bed.
The Watcher in the Woods (1981; British). . . . . . . Helen Curtis
Star 80 (1983). . . . . Dorothy's Mother
The Secret Diary of Sigmund Freud (1984) . . . . . . Mama Freud
Ironweed (1987). . . . . .Annie Phelan
Kindergarten Cop (1990) . . . . .Eleanor Crisp
Skeletons (1996). . . . . .Nancy Norton
Whiskey Down (1996). . . . . Momie
The Game (1997) . . . . Ilsa
Made for Cable Movies:
North Shore Fish (1997; Showtime) . . . . Arlyne
Made for Cable TV:
Tales From the Crypt: The Trap (1991; HBO). . . Mother Paloma
Made for TV Movies:
Judgment Day: The John List Story (1993) . . . . .Alma List
A Kiss to Die For (1993). .Mrs. Graham
Men Don't Tell (1993). . . . . Ruth
Dalva (1996). . . . . .Mom
Heart Full of Rain (1997). . . . . Edith Pearl Dockett

Baker, Cheryl

Films:
The Sex and Violence Family Hour (1983; Canadian)
. . . . .Body Flash Dancer
•• 1:16—Nude after taking off one piece swimsuit during interview.
Lethal Weapon (1987). . . . . Girl in Shower #1
Die Hard (1988) . . . . .Woman with Man
• 0:22—Brief breasts in office with a guy when the terrorists first break into the building.
Roadhouse (1989). .Well-Endowed Wife
L.A. Story (1991) . . . . .Changing Room Woman
• 0:18—Brief breasts in dressing room, when Steve Martin sees her.

Baker, Cynthia

Films:
Risky Business (1983) . . . . Test Teacher
Blood Diner (1987). . . . . Cindy
••• 0:44—Nude outside by fire with her boyfriend, then fighting a guy with an axe.
Beach Fever (1988). . . . . .Hooker #2
The Fugitive (1993). . . . . .Woman In Car
U.S. Marshals (1998). . . . . .Mama Conroy

Baker, Georgette

Films:
Private Road (1987) . . . . Maria
••• 0:29—Breasts taking off her dress and getting into bed, then making love with Greg Evigan.
I Will Dance on Your Grave: Lethal Victims (1992) . . . . Lupe

Baker, Kai

Films:
Armed Response (1986) . . . . Pam
Stormquest (1988). . . . . Arr
• 0:37—Very, very brief left breast, while struggling with Zar in the water.
American Eagle (1990) . . . . .Angela Argente

Baker, Kirsten

Films:
California Dreaming (1978). . . . . Karen
Gas Pump Girls (1978). . . . . June
• 0:05—Breasts, when her graduation gown gets torn off during ceremony, after April's.
Teen Lust (1978). . . . . .Carol Hill
a.k.a. Girls Next Door
• 0:45—Brief side view of left breast, while changing clothes in her bedroom.
Midnight Madness (1980). . . . . .Sunshine
Friday the 13th, Part II (1981) . . . . Terry
•• 0:45—Breasts and buns taking off clothes to go skinny dipping.
• 0:47—Very brief breasts jumping up in the water.
• 0:48—Full frontal nudity and buns getting out of the water. Long shot.
Sector 13 (1982). . . . . Sue
Terror in the Aisles (1984) . . . . .Terry
•• 1:03—Breasts and buns, undressing to go skinny dipping from *Friday the 13th, Part II.*
Weeds (1987) . . . . Kirsten
Island Fury (1989). . . . . .Candy
Made for TV Movies:
The Seduction of Miss Leona (1980) . . . . Sue
TV:
James at 15 (1978) . . . . Christina Kollberg

Baker, LeeAnne

Films:
Breeders (1986) . . . . Kathleen
••• 0:28—Nude, undressing from her nurse outfit in the kitchen, then taking a shower.
• 0:59—Brief breasts in alien nest. (She's the blonde in front.)
•• 1:08—Breasts in alien nest.
•• 1:09—Breasts in alien nest again. (Behind Alec.)
• 1:11—Breasts behind Alec again. Then long shot when nest is electrocuted. (On the left.)
Mutant Hunt (1987) . . . . .Pleasure Droid
Necropolis (1987). . . . . Eva
• 0:04—Right breast, while dancing in skimpy black outfit during vampire ceremony.
• 0:38—Brief breasts in front of three evil things. (Before she has special make-up to make it look like she has six breasts).
Psychos in Love (1987) . . . . Heavy Metal Girl
••• 0:25—Breasts, undressing in room in front of Joe.
Galactic Gigolo (1988). . . . . Lucy
a.k.a. Club Earth
• 0:08—Breasts in hot tub behind Eoj.

Baker, Marina *

Films:

Casanova (1987). . . . . .Lucretia

Video Tapes:

Playboy Video Calendar 1988 (1987) . . . . .Playmate

Wet & Wild (1989). . . . . .Model

Playboy Video Playmate Six-Pack 1992 (1992). . Playmate

Baker, Penny *

Films:

Real Genius (1985) . . . . Ick's Girl at Party

The Men's Club (1986). . . . . Lake

•• 1:13—Breasts while lying in bed with Treat Williams.

Million Dollar Mystery (1987) . . . . Charity

Video Tapes:

Playboy Video Magazine, Volume 4 (1983) . . . . .Playmate

Playboy Video Magazine, Volume 5 (1983) . . . . .Playmate

••• 1:03—Full frontal nudity, in outdoor bathtub.

•• 1:04—Full frontal nudity on a chair in a field.

•• 1:09—Miscellaneous breasts shots.

••• 1:11—Full frontal nudity in an Asian-theme bedroom set.

Wet & Wild (1989). . . . . .Model

Playboy Video Centerfold: Anna-Marie Goddard (1994) . . . . .Playmate

• 0:28—Brief breasts, in still photo during retrospective.

Playboy's 21 Playmates: Volume II (1996) . . . . . .Playmate

••• 0:32—Nude in still photos.

••• 0:33—Full frontal nudity in oriental theme bedroom.

Baker, Sylvia

Films:

Roadhouse (1989). . . . . .Table Dancer

Video Tapes:

Centerfold Screen Test, Take 3 (1988) . . . . Herself

••• 0:38—Nude after taking off dress during audition.

Starlet Screen Test II (1991) . . . . Herself

••• 0:01—Nude on couch (same segment from *Centerfold Screen Test, Take 3.*)

Bakke, Brenda *

Films:

Last Resort (1985) . . . . .Veroneeka

•• 0:36—Breasts in the woods with Charles Grodin.

Hardbodies 2 (1986) . . . . .Morgan

•• 0:34—Buns, getting into bathtub, then breasts, taking a bath.

Death Spa (1987) . . . . .Laura

••• 0:05—Very brief lower frontal nudity, while taking off pants in locker room. Don't see her face. Then nude, in steam room.

Fast Gun (1987) . . . . Julie Comstock

Dangerous Love (1988). . . . . .Chris

Scavengers (1988). . . . . Kimberly Blake

Fist Fighter (1989). . . . . Ellen

Nowhere to Run (1989) . . . . Joanie

Solar Crisis (1992). . . . . Claire Beeson

Twogether (1992). . . . . .Allison McKenzie

(Unrated version reviewed.)

•• 0:08—Breasts and buns, while making love in bed with Nick Cassavetes.

•• 0:10—Brief breasts, several times, while making love with Cassavetes.

•• 0:24—Lower frontal nudity, while posing in a bra for drawing by Cassavetes.

• 1:50—Brief buns and partial breasts with Cassavetes in bed in flashback.

Gunmen (1993). . . . . Maria

Hot Shots! Part Deux (1993) . . . .Michelle Rodham Huddleston

Lone Justice II (1993). . . . . .n.a.

Demon Knight (1994) . . . . Cordelia

• 0:21—Brief partial breasts, while sitting on Thomas Haden Church's lap in bed.

Gunhed (1994; Japanese) . . . . .Texas Air Ranger Sergeant Nim

Starquest (1995) . . . . Zinovitz

Under Siege 2: Dark Territory (1995). . . . . Gilder

L.A. Confidential (1997) . . . . Lana Turner

Shelter (1997) . . . . Helena

• 0:25—Brief upper half of right breast in bloody, open blouse in car.

• 1:02—Brief breasts, several times, while making love with Martin.

Made for Cable Movies:

The Fixer (1997) . . . . .CJ

• 0:12—Very, very brief left breast, while making love with Jon Voight in bed.

Made for TV Movies:

Danielle Steel's "Secrets" (1992) . . . . Sandy Warwick

TV:

Brisco County Jr. (1993-94) . . . . .Frances

Ned Blessing (1993) . . . . Wren

American Gothic (1995-96). . . . . .Selena Coombs

Bako, Brigitte

Films:

One Good Cop (1991) . . . . Mrs. Garrett

Dark Tide (1993). . . . . Andi

• 0:26—Very brief tip of left breasts in bathtub. Brief breasts, while covering up when Richard Tyson looks at her.

• 0:27—Right breast, under water after Tyson leaves.

••• 0:43—Breasts, while making love with Tyson in underground pool. Great!

••• 1:05—Breasts, while sitting in bathtub, with a snake crawling up her chest.

A Man in Uniform (1994; Canadian/Australian) . . . . Charlie Warner

Replikator (1994). . . . . .Kathy Mosko

Strange Days (1995). . . . . Iris

• 0:54—Breasts and very brief lower frontal nudity when the killer rips her blouse open, rapes and kills her in replay of a clip.

Double Take (1997). . . . . Nikki Capelli

Made for Cable Movies:

Red Shoe Diaries (1992; Showtime). . . . . Alex

(Unrated video tape version reviewed.)

(Most of the scenes where you don't see her face are a body double.)

• 0:26—Buns and breasts, getting out of bathtub with Jake.

• 0:35—Very brief buns when Tom rips off her panties.

•• 0:36—Several brief breasts shots while making love with Tom in bed.

• 0:40—Brief breasts, leaning back on bed with Tom.

Made for Cable TV:

Strangers: Stone Heart (1996; HBO) . . . . .Jayce

Balaski, Belinda

Films:

Bobbie Jo and the Outlaw (1976). . . . . .Essie Beaumont

••• 0:29—Breasts in pond with Marjoe Gortner and Lynda Carter.

• 0:43—Very brief breasts, when Gortner pushes her into a pond.

Cannonball (1976; U.S./Hong Kong) . . . . .Maryanne

Food of the Gods (1976). . . . . Rita
Piranha (1978) . . . . Betsy
Till Death (1978). . . . . n.a.
The Howling (1981) . . . . Terry Fisher
Amazon Women on the Moon (1987). . . . . Bernice Pitnik
Gremlins 2: The New Batch (1990) . . . . . . Movie Theatre Mom
Matinee (1993). . . . . Stan's Mom

Made for Cable Movies:

Rebel Highway: Runaway Daughters (1994; Showtime) . . . . Mrs. Nicholson
The Second Civil War (1997; HBO) . . . . Graphic Designer

Made for TV Movies:

Deadly Care (1987). . . . . Terry

• *Balasko, Josiane*

Also writer and director.

Films:

This Sweet Sickness (1977; French). . . . . Nadine
a.k.a. dites-lui que je l'aime
Too Beautiful for You (1990; French). . . . . . . Colette Chevassus
Dead Tired (1995; French) . . . . Herself
a.k.a. Grosse Fatigue
French Twist (1996; French). . . . . Marijo
- 0:46—Partial right breast, while sitting in bathtub with Victoria Abril.

Balding, Rebecca

Films:

Silent Scream (1980) . . . . Scotty Parker
- 0:50—Brief right breast while making love in bed with Jack.

The Boogens (1981). . . . . Trish Michaels
(Not available on videotape.)
- 0:31—Buns, twice, while getting caught in the hallway with a towel wrapped halfway around herself.
- •• 0:55—Breasts, while making love with Mark on the floor of the cabin.

Made for TV Movies:

Deadly Game (1977). . . . . Amy Franklin
The Gathering (1977) . . . . Julie Pelham
The French-Atlantic Affair (1979). . . . . Harriet Kleinfeld
The Gathering, Part II (1979) . . . . Julie Pelham

TV:

Lou Grant (1977) . . . . Carla Mardigian
Soap (1978-81). . . . . Carol David
Makin' It (1979) . . . . Corky Crandall

Baldwin, Elizabeth

Films:

Knight Moves (1992) . . . . Christine Eastman
Mirror Mirror III (1996). . . . . Carolyn
- •• 0:46—Breasts, while making love in bed with Billy Drago.
- 0:49—Very, very brief tip of right breast, when putting bra on.
- •• 1:11—Breasts, while making love with a guy in bed.
- 1:13—Brief buns, while walking into bathroom.

Made for Cable TV:

Sherman Oaks: Season 2, Episode 7 (1996; Showtime) . . . . Chris Weaver
Sherman Oaks: Season 2, Episode 10 (1996; Showtime) . . . . Chris Weaver
- 0:10—Buns in sexy outfit while in bed with Billy.

Baldwin, Janit

Films:

Prime Cut (1972) . . . . Violet
- 0:25—Very brief nude, being swung around when Gene Hackman lifts her up to show to Lee Marvin.
- 0:41—Brief breasts putting on a red dress.

Gator Bait (1973) . . . . Julie
- •• 0:27—Breasts and buns walking into a pond, then getting out and getting dressed.
- 0:35—Very brief right breast, twice, popping out of her dress when the bad guys hold her.
- 0:40—Brief left breast struggling against two guys on the bed.

Ruby (1977) . . . . Leslie Claire
Where the Buffalo Roam (1980) . . . . n.a.
Humongous (1982; Canadian) . . . . Carla Simmons

Made for TV Movies:

Born Innocent (1974) . . . . n.a.

Baldwin, Judith

Films:

The Seven Minutes (1971). . . . . Fremont's Girlfriend
Evel Knievel (1972) . . . . Sorority Girl
The Stepford Wives (1975) . . . . Mrs. Cornell
Talking Walls (1982) . . . . n.a.
No Small Affair (1984). . . . . Stephanie
- ••• 0:36—In white bra, panties and garter belt, then breasts in Jon Cryer's bedroom trying to seduce him.

Made in U.S.A. (1988). . . . . Dorie
Pretty Woman (1990) . . . . Susan
Exit to Eden (1994) . . . . Priscilla/Los Angeles

TV:

The Bold and the Beautiful (1987). . . . . Beth Logan

• *Balk, Fairuza*

Films:

Return to Oz (1985) . . . . Dorothy
Valmont (1989). . . . . Cécile
- 1:16—Buns, when Valmont kisses her and plays with her before deflowering her. Don't see her face with the rest of her body.

Gas, Food, Lodging (1992) . . . . Shade
Imaginary Crimes (1994). . . . . Sonya
Tollbooth (1994). . . . . Doris
- 0:20—Very, very brief blurry breasts, while making love in bed on top of Will Patton (right after the doll is stuck in the garbage disposal).
- 0:21—Very, very brief blurry breasts, while making love on top of Patton some more (right after the garbage disposal starts). Very, very brief breasts seen through the blinds.

The Craft (1996) . . . . Nancy
The Island of Dr. Moreau (1996) . . . . Aissa
Things to Do in Denver When You're Dead (1996) . . . . Lucinda
The Marker (1997) . . . . Bella Soto

Made for Cable Movies:

Shame (1992; Lifetime) . . . . Lizzie Curtis

Made for TV Movies:

The Worst Witch . . . . Midred Hubble
Poor Little Rich Girl: The Barbara Hutton Story (1987) . . . . Barbara (Age 12)
Deadly Intentions...Again? (1991). . . . . Stacey
The Danger of Love (1992) . . . . Lisa
Murder in the Heartland (1993) . . . . Caril Ann Fugate
Shadow of a Doubt (1995) . . . . Angel Harwell

• Ball, Angeline

Films:

The Commitments (1991; U.S./British) . . . . Imelda Quirke
My Girl 2 (1994) . . . . .Maggie Muldovan
Brothers in Trouble (1997). . . . . .Mary

Made for Cable TV:

Picture Windows: Two Nudes Bathing (1995; Showtime) . . . . Simone

•• 0:18—Breasts, while lying in bed with Charley Boorman.
• 0:19—Brief right breast, when Boorman gets back into bed.

Ballard, Joy

Films:

976-EVIL II: The Astral Factor (1991) . . . . .Stripper

Video Tapes:

BabeWatch, Episode 1: Lingerie Fantasies (1994) . . . . Herself

••• 0:05—Nude, while trying on lingerie in a bathroom. Long scene.
••• 0:51—Nude, while posing on chair outside. Long scene.
••• 0:55—Nude, after end credits.

Baltay, Julie

Films:

Caroline at Midnight (1993). . . . . Dream Lover

• 0:31—Right breast, while in bed during Jack's dream. Don't see her face.

Dinosaur Island (1993) . . . . .Cave Girl

Baltron, Donna

Films:

Hide and Go Shriek (1988) . . . . Judy Ramerize

•• 0:56—In white bra and panties, then breasts after undressing seductively in front of her boyfriend.

Shallow Grave (1988) . . . . Rose
Death Becomes Her (1992) . . . . Madeline Body Double
Intent to Kill (1992). . . . . Girl in Bar
The Naked Truth (1992) . . . . .Miss Cuba
Bikini Squad (1993) . . . . Muffy

•• 0:38—Breasts, while on sofa with David after taking off her bra.

It's Pat (1994) . . . . Second Stripper

Made for Cable Movies:

Virtual Seduction (1995; Showtime) . . . . .2nd Woman at Restaurant

Made for Cable TV:

Dream On: Reach Out and Touch Yourself (1993; HBO) . . .Lola

TV:

Down the Shore (1993). . . . . Cheyenne
NYPD Blue: Tempest In a C-Cup (Nov 16, 1993) . . . . Ingrid

• 0:21—Brief buns, several times, while dancing on stage.
• 0:22—Brief buns in G-string, while walking up to table in front of Metavoy.
• 0:23—Almost left breast, after taking off her top in front of Metavoy.

Video Tapes:

Morgan Fairchild Stress Management (1991) . . . . Herself

• Bandera, Vaitiare

Films:

U.S. Marshals (1998) . . . . .Stacia Vela

Made for Cable TV:

Stargate SG-1: Children of the Gods (1997; Showtime) . . . . Sha're

•• 1:01—Full frontal nudity, when her body is examined and taken over by the alien.

Bang, Joy

Films:

Cisco Pike (1971) . . . . Lynn

• 0:45—Very, very brief right breast, seen under Kris Kristofferson's arm at the beginning of the scene in bed with Merna.

Pretty Maids All in a Row (1971). . . . . Rita

• 0:57—Brief breasts in car with Rock Hudson.
• 1:01—Right breast, in car with Hudson. Dark. More right breast, while getting dressed.

Red Sky at Morning (1971) . . . . Corky
Play It Again, Sam (1972) . . . . Julie
Dead People (1974). . . . . Toni
Night of the Cobra Woman (1974; U.S./Philippines) . . . Joanna

Banks, Laura

Films:

Star Trek II: The Wrath of Kahn (1982) . . . . Uncredited Khan's Navigator
Wheels of Fire (1984). . . . . Stinger

a.k.a. Desert Warrior

• 0:49—Brief breasts when Trace rips her top open outside.

Demon of Paradise (1987). . . . . Cahill
Hexed (1993) . . . . 1st Reporter

a.k.a. All Shook Up

Barba, Vana

Films:

Vios Ke Politia (1988; German) . . . . .n.a.
Mediterraneo (1991; Italian). . . . . Vassilissa

•• 1:03—Side of left breast, while in bed with Antonio.

Barbeau, Adrienne

Ex-wife of director John Carpenter.

Films:

The Fog (1980) . . . . Stevie Wayne
The Cannonball Run (1981). . . . . Marcie
Escape from New York (1981) .Maggie
Swamp Thing (1981) . . . . Alice Cable

• 1:03—Side view of left breast washing herself off in the swamp. Long shot.

Creepshow (1982). . . . . Wilma Northrup
The Next One (1983) . . . . Andrea Johnson
Back to School (1986) . . . . .Vanessa
Open House (1987). . . . . Lisa Grant

• 0:27—In black lace lingerie, then very brief half of left breast making love with Joseph Bottoms on the floor.
•• 1:15—Brief side view of right breast getting out of bed at night to look at something in her briefcase.
••• 1:16—Brief breasts taking off bathrobe and getting back into bed. Kind of dark.

Cannibal Women in the Avocado Jungle of Death (1988) . . . . Dr. Kurtz
Two Evil Eyes (1991) . . . . .Jessica
Father Hood (1993). . . . . Celeste
Silk Degrees (1994) . . . . Violet

Made for Cable Movies:

Doublecrossed (1991; HBO) . . . . Debbie Seal
Rebel Highway: Jailbreakers (1994; Showtime) . . . Mrs. Norton

Bram Stoker's Burial of the Rats (1995; Showtime) .... The Queen

Made for Cable TV:

Dream On: Bad Girls (1992; HBO) .... Gloria Gantz

Miniseries:

The Burden of Proof (1992)................. Silvia Hartnell

TV:

Maude (1972-78) ....Carol

Barber, Frances

Films:

The Missionary (1982; British).................Mission Girl

Acceptable Levels (1983; British)...................... Jill

A Zed and Two Noughts (1985; British) ..... Venus de Milo

- ••• 0:22—Breasts, sitting in bed, talking to Oliver, then nude while getting thrown out of his place.

Castaway (1986).................... Sister Saint Winifred

Prick Up Your Ears (1987; British) ....Leonie Orton

Sammy and Rosie Get Laid (1987; British).... Rosie Hobbs

- • 1:09—Very brief breasts, while bending over to kiss Danny. More brief breasts while making love (short cuts). 1:21—Partial right breast while sitting in bubble bath with Sammy.

We Think the World of You (1988; British)........... Megan

Young Soul Rebels (1991; British) ....Ann

Soft Top, Hard Shoulder (1992; British)......... Miss Trimble

Made for TV Movies:

Mystery! The Death of the Self (1995)............... Nicole

Barber, Glynnis

Films:

Terror (1979; British).............................Carol

Yesterday's Hero (1979; British).................... Susan

The Hound of the Baskervilles (1983; British)... Beryl Stapleton

The Wicked Lady (1983; British) .... Caroline

- ••• 0:58—Breasts and buns making love with Kit in the living room. Possible body double.

Edge of Sanity (1988) ....Elisabeth Jekyll

Déjà Vu (1998) .... Claire

TV:

Blake's 7 (1981; British).......................... Soolin

Dempsey and Makepeace (1984-86) .... Detective Sergeant Harriet Makepeace

Barbieri, Paula *

Films:

The Dangerous (1994) ....Paula

Night Eyes 4 ...Fatal Passion (1995) ..... Dr. Angela Cross

- •• 0:01—Buns and breasts, while taking a shower.
- •• 0:53—Breasts, while making love with Steve on the floor.
- •• 0:59—Breasts and buns, while making love with Steve in a stairwell.
- •• 1:06—Breasts, while making love with Steve in bed.
- • 1:12—Breasts, while making love with Steve in the kitchen.

Made for Cable TV:

Red Shoe Diaries: Double or Nothing (1993; Showtime) ....The Girl

(Available on the video tape *Red Shoe Diaries 5: Weekend Pass.*)

- • 0:02—Brief breasts, while making love in bed.
- • 0:03—Brief breasts, in open blouse, while fighting with Carl.
- • 0:15—Brief breasts and buns, while making love with Tommy.
- •• 0:16—Breasts and very brief partial lower frontal nudity several times while making love with Tommy in bed and outside in the rain.
- •• 0:18—Left breast, while making love with Tommy.
- • 0:19—Buns, while getting out of bed and putting on panties.
- • 0:29—Left breast while starting to make love with Tommy on pool table. More breasts in long shot.

Bardot, Brigitte *

Ex-wife of director Roger Vadim.

Films:

Doctor at Sea (1955; British) .... Helene Colbert

...and God created woman (1957; French) .... Juliette

- • 0:40—Very brief side view of right breast getting out of bed.

A Very Private Affair (1962; French/Italian)............... Jill

Contempt (1963; French/Italian)............. Camille Javal

- • 0:04—Buns.
- • 0:54—Buns, while lying on rug.
- • 1:30—Buns, while lying on beach. Long shot.

Dear Brigitte (1965) .... Herself

Head Over Heels (1967) .... Cecile

a.k.a. A Coeur Joie!

Shalako (1968; British) ....Countess Irini Lazaar

- • 1:38—Brief partial back side of right breast, when Sean Connery catches her washing herself.

Ms. Don Juan (1973)................................ Joan

- • 0:19—Left breast in bathtub.
- •• 1:19—Breasts through fish tank. Buns and left breast, then brief breasts in mirror with Paul.

Famous T & A (1982) .... Joan

(No longer available for purchase, check your video store for rental.)

- • 0:25—Buns, then brief breasts in scene from *Ms. Don Juan.*

Barkin, Ellen

Ex-wife of actor Gabriel Byrne.

Films:

Diner (1982) .... Beth

Daniel (1983) .... Phyllis Isaacson

Eddie and the Cruisers (1983) ....Maggie

Tender Mercies (1983)......................... Sue Anne

The Adventures of Buckaroo Banzai, Across the 8th Dimension (1984)...................................Penny Priddy

Harry and Son (1984) .... Katie

Terminal Choice (1985; Canadian) .... Mary O'Connor

Desert Bloom (1986)............................... Starr

Down by Law (1986).......................... Laurette

The Big Easy (1987) ....Anne Osborne

- • 0:32—Brief buns, when jumping up in kitchen after pinching a guy who she thinks is Quaid.

Made in Heaven (1987)............................ Lucille

Siesta (1987) .... Diane

- ••• 0:03—Brief full frontal nudity long shot taking off red dress, breasts, brief buns standing up, then full frontal nudity lying down.
- • 1:22—Right nipple sticking out of dress while imagining she's with Gabriel Byrne instead of the reality of getting raped by taxi driver.
- • 1:23—Brief lower frontal nudity, very brief silhouette of a breast, then brief buns some more while with Byrne. Dark, hard to see.
- • 1:24—Lower frontal nudity, with torn dress while lying in bed after the taxi driver gets up.
- • 1:26—Very brief lower frontal nudity, while running down road and her dress flies up as police cars pass by.

- 1:28—Very brief side view of right breast putting on dress in bed just before Isabella Rossellini comes into the bedroom to attack her. Long distance shot.

Johnny Handsome (1989) .... Sunny Boyd
Sea of Love (1989) .... Helen Cruger
- 1:13—Brief upper half of buns, while lying in bed with Pacino.

Switch (1991) .... Amanda Brooks/Steve
Mac (1992) .... Oona
Man Trouble (1992) .... Joan Spruance
Into the West (1993) .... Kathleen
This Boy's Life (1993) .... Caroline Wolff
Bad Company (1994) .... Margaret Wells
Wild Bill (1995) .... Calamity Jane
The Fan (1996) .... Jewel Stern
Mad Dog Time (1996) .... Kira Everly
Fear and Loathing in Las Vegas (1998) .... The North Star Waitress

Made for Cable Movies:
Act of Vengeance (1986) .... Annette
Blood Money: The Story of Clinton and Nadine (1988; HBO) .... Nadine Powers
Original title: *Clinton and Nadine.*

Barkin, Marcie

Films:
Chesty Anderson, U.S. Navy (1975) .... Pucker
The Van (1977) .... Sue
- 0:52—Brief breasts and very brief partial buns, while making love with Jack in back of van.
- 0:54—Very brief right breast, twice, while lying in back of van with Jack.

Barnes, Priscilla *

Films:
Delta Fox (1977) .... Karen
- 0:36—Left breast undressing in room for David. Very dark, hard to see.
- 0:38—Very brief breasts struggling with a bad guy and getting slammed against the wall.
- 0:39—Very brief blurry left breast, while running in front of the fireplace.
- 0:40—Breasts sneaking out of house. Brief breasts getting into Porsche.
- 0:49—Brief right breast reclining onto bed with David. Side view of left breast several times while making love.
- 1:29—Very brief side view of left breast in David's flashback.

Texas Detour (1977) .... Claudia Hunter
- ••• 1:03—Breasts, changing clothes and walking around in bedroom. Wearing white panties. This is her best breasts scene.
- 1:11—Breasts sitting up in bed with Patrick Wayne.

Tintorera (1977) .... Girl from Bar
- 1:12—Brief breasts, while pouring beer over her head. Breasts seen from under water, while she turns around while wearing white panties. Breasts, while dropping her beer in the water.
- 1:14—Breasts, while on the beach after the shark attack (on the left).

Seniors (1978) .... Sylvia
- •• 0:18—Breasts at the top of the stairs while Arnold climbs up the stairs while the rest of the guys watch.

The Last Married Couple in America (1980) .... Helena Dryden
Sunday Lovers (1980; Italian/French) .... Donna
Traxx (1988) .... Mayor Alexandria Cray
License to Kill (1989) .... Della Churchill
Lords of the Deep (1989) .... Claire
Stepfather III: Father's Day (1992) .... Christine Davis
- 1:27—Very brief buns, sitting down in bubble bath.

Talons of the Eagle (1992; Canadian) ..... Cassandra Hubbard
Erotique (1993) .... Taboo Parlor/Claire
- •• 0:30—Breasts and brief partial buns, while in bed with Camilla Søeberg.

Ava's Magical Adventure (1994) .... Sarah
The Crossing Guard (1995) .... Verna
- ••• 0:37—Breasts while walking backstage into dressing room and talking with Jack Nicholson.

Mallrats (1995) .... Ivannah
- •• 0:58—Breasts, after opening her blouse and feeling her breasts to "read" the fortunes for the two boys. Ordinarily this would have rated a three, but the second, special-effect nipple on her right breast is rather distracting.

Made for Cable Movies:
Attack of the 5' 2" Women (1994; Showtime) .... Crystal
Made for TV Movies:
Perry Mason: The Case of the Reckless Romeo (1992) .... Brenda Kingsley
TV:
The American Girls (1978) .... Rebecca Tomkins
Three's Company (1981-84) .... Terri Alden

Baron, Carla

Films:
Hack-O-Lantern (1987) .... Vera
a.k.a. Halloween Night
- 0:16—Breasts, while in bubble bath. Breasts and buns, getting out of bathtub after getting scared by a rubber spider.
- 0:44—Brief breasts, while in bed with Brian when caught by Joey.

The Jigsaw Murders (1988) .... Script Girl
Necromancer (1988) .... Gail
- 0:42—Brief breasts getting out of bed with Paul. Dark.

Sorority Babes in the Slimeball Bowl-O-Rama (1988) ... Frankie

Barondes, Elizabeth

Films:
Oscar (1991) .... Theresa
The Cool Surface (1992) .... Actress
Don't Do It (1994) .... Waitress/Phone Sex
Night of the Scarecrow (1995) .... Claire
The Girl Gets Moe (1997) .... Monica
- 0:41—Very brief left breast, while making love with Tony Danza. Don't see her face.

Made for Cable Movies:
Full Body Massage (1995; Showtime) .... Alice
- 0:22—Brief breasts, while sitting in pond with Bryan Brown. Medium long shot.
- 0:36—Nude, taking off towel, and lying on ground for Hopi Medicine Man. Medium long shot.
- •• 0:51—Breasts, while making love with Bryan Brown in bed.
- •• 0:58—Breasts, while in pond with Brown.

Not of This Earth (1995; Showtime) .... Amanda Sayles
- •• 0:35—Breasts, while sunbathing on lounge chair outside.

TV:
Lois & Clark: The New Adventures of Superman (1993-97) .... Lucy

• Barranco, Maria

Films:
Women on the Verge of a Nervous Breakdown (1988; Spanish) .... Candela

Tie Me Up! Tie Me Down! (1990; Spanish) .... Médica
Don Juan, My Love (1991; Spanish) .... Doña Ines
Zafarinas (1994; Spanish).........................Elisa
a.k.a. Morirás en Chafarinas
- 0:51—Very, very brief side view of right breast in open military shirt when she shifts position in bed with Jorge Sanz.
- 0:52—Very, very brief upper half of right breast, just before opening the shower curtain to leave the shower. The US version cuts off the bottom of the screen with a black bar for the subtitles, so more may be seen in the original, non-subtitled version.

Mouth to Mouth (1996; Spanish) .... n.a.
a.k.a. Boca a Boca

Barrault, Marie-Christine *

Films:

My Night at Maud's (1970; French) ....Francoise
Cousin, Cousine (1975; French)................. Marthe
- •• 1:05—Breasts in bed with her lover, cutting his nails.
- • 1:07—Brief side view of right breast, while giving him a bath.
- ••• 1:16—Breasts with penciled tattoos all over her body.
- • 1:33—Braless in see-through white blouse saying "goodbye" to everybody.

The Daydreamer (1975; French) .... Lisa
The Medusa Touch (1978; British).................. Patricia
Stardust Memories (1980)......................... Isabel
Table for Five (1983)............................ Marie
A Love in Germany (1984; French/German) ....Maria Wyler
- • 0:23—Right breast, in bed with her lover when Pauline peeks from across the way.
- •• 0:28—Right breast in bedroom with Karl. Very brief lower frontal nudity getting back into bed. Long scene.
- ••• 0:43—Breasts in bedroom with Karl. Subtitles get in the way! Long scene.

Swann in Love (1984; French/German)..... Madame Verdunn
a.k.a. Un Amour de Swann

Barrese, Katherine

Films:

Homer & Eddie (1989) ....Waitress
Jezebel's Kiss (1990)........................... Jezebel
- •• 0:36—Full frontal nudity washing herself off in kitchen after having sex with the sheriff.
- • 0:42—Brief buns, going for a swim in the ocean. Dark.
- ••• 0:48—Breasts taking off her robe in front of Hunt, then making love with him.
- • 0:58—Brief right breast and buns while Malcolm McDowell watches through slit in curtain. Long shot.
- • 1:09—Right breast and buns getting undressed. Long shot. Closer shot of buns, putting robe on.
- ••• 1:12—Breasts making love with McDowell. More breasts after.

Payback (1994)........................Woman in Prison
(Special director's cut reviewed.)

Barrett, Alice

Films:

Incoming Freshman (1979).............Boxing Student
- •• 0:43—Breasts answering a question during Professor Bilbo's fantasy.
- • 0:55—Breasts in another of Bilbo's fantasies.
- • 1:18—Breasts during end credits.

Mission Hill (1982) ....Laura Doyle

TV:

Another World (1989-96) .... Frankie Frame

Barrett, Jamie

Films:

Club Life (1987) .... Sissy
House of the Rising Sun (1987) ....Janet
- • 1:04—Very brief breasts making love with Louis.

Barrett, Nitchie

Films:

Preppies (1984)............................ Roxanne
- • 0:11—Brief breasts changing into waitress costumes with her two friends.

She-Devil (1989) .... Bob's Secretary
A Time to Die (1991) .... Sheila
- • 0:12—Buns, getting out of bed.
- •• 0:16—Breasts making love in bed with Sam.

Barrett, Victoria

Films:

Hot Resort (1984) .... Jane
Hot Chili (1985) ....Victoria Stevenson
- • 0:55—Very brief close up shot of right breast when it pops out of her dress. Don't see her face.

Three Kinds of Heat (1987) ....Terry O'Shea

Barrick, Melissa

Films:

The Pamela Principle (1992). . . Uncredited Steve's Girlfriend
(Unrated version reviewed.)
- ••• 0:45—Breasts and buns in red G-string, then lower frontal nudity, while playing strip-card game with Steve.

The Bikini Carwash Company II (1993)........... Cyndi
(Unrated version reviewed.)
- ••• 0:38—In black lingerie, then breasts during kitchen commercial.
- ••• 0:42—Breasts and buns under black body stocking in "Rock Me" music video number.
- ••• 0:46—In lingerie, then breasts during repairman commercial.
- • 0:52—Brief breasts, while making out on kitchen table.
- • 1:28—Breasts during music video number at the carwash.

• Barrientos, Marie

Films:

Street Smart (1987)................. Hispanic Prostitute
- • 0:06—Brief breasts and buns, when getting beat up by a customer when Morgan Freeman opens the door.

Hangin' with the Homeboys (1991) .... Party Woman
Blackout (1995)................................ Cindy

Made for Cable TV:

Subway Stories (1997; HBO) .... Ragged Woman

Barringer, Pat

Films:

Orgy of the Dead (1965).................... Shirley/Gold
Agony of Love (1966) .... Barbara Thomas
- •• 0:10—Breasts, after taking off bra, then on bed with the customer. Upper half of buns in pulled down panties.
- ••• 0:16—Breasts and buns, standing in front of bathroom mirror, then taking a bath and drying herself off.
- •• 0:19—Breasts, while making love with the Beatnik and his girlfriend.
- • 0:29—Brief breasts several times during nightmare with money.
- • 0:38—Brief breasts while wearing panties, in bed with a Conventioneer.

- ••• 0:42—Breasts, while lying on bed and getting out of bed after making love with the Conventioneer.
- • 0:43—Breasts, while sitting up after making love with the other Conventioneer.
- • 0:54—In white bra and panties on bed, then breasts several times with a customer.
- •• 1:02—In white bra, taking off her clothes in front of a customer. Then breasts while wearing panties while she poses and he messily eats a lot of food.
- • 1:16—Brief breasts, while turning over in bed before seeing her husband.

Psychopathia Sexualis (1966). . . . . Dancer
a.k.a. On Her Bed of Roses
- ••• 0:34—Breasts, while belly dancing during party (she's the second dancer). Long scene.

Barrington, Rebecca

Films:

Dance or Die (1988) . . . . n.a.
The Newlydeads (1988). . . . . Blanche
- • 0:08—Right breast, while making out with her fiancee, Bull, in the car.
- • 1:01—Right breast, peeking out of the top of her body suit.
- • 1:02—Brief buns, while on the floor with Bull.

Living to Die (1990) . . . . Married Woman
- • 0:23—In red bra, blindfolded and tied to a lounge chair, then breasts while getting photographed.
- • 0:27—Breasts in chair when Wings Hauser talks to her.

• *Barry, Michelle*

Films:

Femalien (1995) . . . . Girl Cop, Theatre Woman
Virtual Encounters (1995). . . . . . . Policewoman/S&M Girl 2
(Unrated version reviewed.)
- ••• 0:29—Stripping on stage while dressed as a policewoman. In black bra and T-back, then nude after dancing and taking off all her clothes, then making love with a guy on stage. Long scene.
- ••• 1:07—Full frontal nudity in black outfit, while making love and dribbling hot candle wax on the other girl.

Barry, Wendy

Films:

Savage Dawn (1984) . . . . Lipservice
- • 1:01—Breasts, after taking off top in room in front of Richard Lynch.
- •• 1:03—Breasts and buns after getting up with Lynch, then getting dressed.

3:15—The Moment of Truth (1986) . . . . Lora
Knights of the City (1986). . . . . Jasmine
Young Lady Chatterley II (1986)
. . . . Sybil, Maid in Hot House
- • 0:12—Breasts in hot house with the Gardener.

Barrymore, Drew *

Former model for *Guess?* jeans.

Films:

Altered States (1980). . . . . Margaret Jessup
E.T. The Extraterrestrial (1982). Gertie
Firestarter (1984). . . . . Charlie McGee
Irreconcilable Differences (1984) . . . . Casey Brodsky
Cat's Eye (1985) . . . . Girl
Far From Home (1989) . . . . Joleen Cox
See You in the Morning (1989) . . . . Cathy
Motorama (1991) . . . . Fantasy Girl
No Place to Hide (1991) . . . . Tinsel Hanley
Waxwork II: Lost in Time (1991) . . . . Vampire Victim
Doppelganger: The Evil Within (1992) . . . . Holly Gooding
- •• 0:23—Breasts in shower when water turns blood red. Great shot, but ruined by the red water.
- • 0:26—Brief side of left breast in kitchen with Patrick.

Poison Ivy (1992). . . . . Ivy
(Unrated version reviewed.)
(Body double used for nude scenes in European version.)
Wayne's World 2 (1993) . . . . Bjergen Kjergen
Bad Girls (1994) . . . . Lilly Laronette
(Extended version reviewed.)
- • 0:15—Brief right breast while frolicking in the water with the other women.
- • 1:15—Left breast in mirror while putting on dress in front of bad buy.

Boys on the Side (1994). . . . . Holly
- • 0:22—Very brief breasts, twice, when pulling up her blouse to tease Billy Wirth while he's tied up in a chair.
- • 1:10—Brief breasts, while fooling around in bed with Matthew McConaughey.

Batman Forever (1995) . . . . Sugar
Mad Love (1995). . . . . Casey
Everyone Says I Love You (1996) . . . . Skylar
Scream (1996). . . . . Casey
The Wedding Singer (1997). . . . . Julia

Made for Cable Movies:

Guncrazy (1992; Showtime) . . . . Anita
- • 1:24—Brief buns, while in bed on top of her boyfriend. Don't see her face.

Sketch Artist (1992; Showtime) . . . . Daisy

Made for TV Movies:

The Amy Fisher Story (1993) . . . . Amy Fisher
(Body double nude scene added for video tape version.)
0:28—Brief right breast and partial lower frontal nudity in bed with Joey is a body double.

TV:

2000 Malibu Road (1992) . . . . Lindsay

Bartel, Cheryl *

Films:

Centerfold (1995). . . . . Billie
- •• 0:28—Breasts, while talking with Gail outside by pool.
- ••• 0:33—Breasts and buns, while making love with a guy in the massage room.
- •• 0:56—Nude, while undressing on diving board and diving into the pool during a party.
- • 0:59—Breasts, while starting to make love with the senator in the stable.
- •• 1:11—Breasts and buns, while tied by her wrists, having sex with the senator in the stable.

Austin Powers: International Man of Mystery (1997) . . . Fembot

Made for Cable Movies:

Sawbones (1995; Showtime). . . . . Beautiful Woman
- •• 0:40—Breasts, while lying on operating table, unable to move.
- • 0:55—Breasts, several times, while lying dead on coroner's examination table.

Made for Cable TV:

Full Frontal Comedy (1995; Showtime)
. . . . Woman of Full Frontal Comedy
Women: Stories of Passion-Blind Love (1996; Showtime)
. . . . Tina Russel
- • 0:02—Breasts while wearing pasties and buns in G-string, when in dressing room.
- • 0:14—Brief buns in G-string, while in dressing room.

Barton, Diana

Films:

Skin Deep (1989) . . . . .Helena
Wizards of the Lost Kingdom, Part 2 (1991) . . . . Freyja
Body of Influence (1992). . . . . Jennifer
(Unrated version reviewed.)
No Escape, No Return (1993) . . . . Woman #2
Sexual Malice (1993) . . . . Christine
(Unrated version reviewed.)

- • 0:13—Brief buns in panties, taking off robe and getting into bed.
- ••• 0:32—Breasts in shower, then nude getting out and putting on a robe.
- •• 0:33—Left breast in open robe, looking at herself in the mirror.
- ••• 0:36—Breasts and buns in hotel room when takes her robe off and makes love with her in bed.
- •• 0:42—Breasts while making love in surf under pier at the beach.
- ••• 0:48—In white bra, panties and stockings, then buns and breasts while making love.
- •• 0:55—Breasts and buns while making love in dressing room of clothing store.
- ••• 1:04—Breasts, while in bed with a black girl while Quinn takes photos.
- • 1:13—Breasts, while in spa with Edward Albert.

TV:

The Young and the Restless (1994-95) . . . . .Mari Jo Mason

Video Tapes:

Eden (1992). . . . . Andrea

- ••• 0:05—Breasts, undressing, making love, then getting dressed in locker room with Ian. Long scene.
- ••• 0:37—Breasts, taking off her swimsuit top to tease Ian. More breasts and buns while making love with him on the sofa.

Basil, Toni

Singer and Choreographer.

Films:

Pajama Party (1964) . . . . Pajama Girl
Easy Rider (1969) . . . . .Mary

- • 1:24—Brief right breast (her hair gets in the way) and very, very brief buns, taking off clothes in graveyard during hallucination sequence.
- • 1:26—Very brief buns, when climbing on something (seen through fish-eye lens).
- • 1:27—Buns, while lying down (seen through fish-eye lens).

Sweet Charity (1969) . . . . Dancer in "Rhythm of Life" Number
Five Easy Pieces (1970) . . . . Terry Grouse
The Last Movie (1971) . . . . Rose
Mother, Jugs & Speed (1976) . . . . .Addict
Angel III: The Final Chapter (1988) . . . . Hillary
Slaughterhouse Rock (1988) . . . . Sammy Mitchell
Eating (1990) . . . . Jackie
Rockula (1990) . . . . Phoebe

Basinger, Kim *

Wife of actor Alec Baldwin.

Films:

Hard Country (1981) . . . . Jodie Lynn Palmer
Motherlode (1982) . . . . Andrea Spalding
The Man Who Loved Women (1983) . . . . .Louise "Lulu"
Never Say Never Again (1983) . . . . Domino Vitale

- • 1:48—Very brief buns in wet lingerie, when getting pulled onto rescue boat.

The Natural (1984) . . . . .Memo Paris
Fool For Love (1985) . . . . May
9 1/2 Weeks (1986) . . . . Elizabeth

- • 0:27—Blindfolded while Mickey Rourke plays with an ice cube on her. Brief right breast.
- • 0:54—Very brief left breast, while rolling over in bed.
- ••• 1:11—In wet lingerie, then breasts making love in a wet stairwell with Rourke.
- • 1:19—Doing a sexy dance for Rourke in a white slip.
- • 1:22—Buns, showing off to Rourke on building.
- • 1:44—Brief buns, putting on pants and getting out of bed.

No Mercy (1986). . . . . .Michel Duval
Blind Date (1987) . . . . Nadia Gates
Nadine (1987). . . . . Nadine Hightower
My Stepmother Is An Alien (1988). . . . . Celeste Martin
Batman (1989) . . . . .Vicki Vale
The Marrying Man (1991). . . . . Vicki Anderson
a.k.a. Too Hot to Handle
Cool World (1992) . . . . .Holli Would
Final Analysis (1992) .Heather Evans

- •• 0:21—Brief breasts, while making love in bed under Richard Gere. Dark.

The Getaway (1993). . . . . .Carol McCoy
(Unrated version reviewed.)

- •• 0:18—In bra and panties in bedroom with Alec Baldwin, then nude (kind of silhouette).
- • 0:25—Very brief left breast and lower frontal nudity while pulling down towel behind steamy shower door. Hard to see.
- • 1:29—Side view of buns in the shower.
- ••• 1:30—Breasts and buns, while making love with Baldwin. Nice. Very, very brief lower frontal nudity.

The Real McCoy (1993). Karen McCoy
Wayne's World 2 (1993) . . . . .Honey Hornée
Ready to Wear (1994) . . . . Kitty Porter
a.k.a. Prêt-à-porter
L.A. Confidential (1997) . . . . Lynn Bracken

Miniseries:

From Here to Eternity (1979). . . . . .Lorene Rogers

Made for TV Movies:

Katie: Portrait of a Centerfold (1978). . . . . .Katie McEvera

TV:

Dog and Cat (1977) . . . . Officer J.Z. Kane
From Here to Eternity (1980). . . . . .Lorene Rogers

Music Videos:

Mary Jane's Last Dance/Tom Petty (1993) . . . . .n.a.

Video Tapes:

Playboy Video Magazine, Volume 10 (1986)
. . . . 9 1/2 Weeks

- • 0:32—Brief right breast in ice cube scene.
- • 0:34—Brief right breast during slide show scene.
- • 0:37—Brief breasts in wet stairwell scene.

Basler, Marianne

Films:

A Soldier's Tale (1988; New Zealand). . . . . Belle

- • 0:19—Brief breasts, while undressing in bedroom for Gabriel Byrne.
- •• 0:21—Breasts in bed with Byrne.
- •• 1:02—Buns and brief breasts while washing herself when Byrne sees her.

Softly From Paris III (1990) . . . . .n.a.
Overseas (1991; French) . . . . Gritte
Farinelli (1995; Swiss/French/Belgian) . . . . Countess Mauer
a.k.a. Farinelli: il castrato

Bass, Victoria

Films:

Too Scared to Scream (1985) . . . . Cynthia Oberman

••• 0:08—Breasts and buns, undressing and hanging up her dress in closet, then walking to shower.

•• 0:10—Brief breasts, getting out of the shower.

The Bodyguard (1992) . . . . Woman in Green

Traces of Red (1992) . . . . Susan Dobson

The Specialist (1994). . . . . Socialite

The Maddening (1995) . . . . Lisa

Plato's Run (1996). . . . . Matty

TV:

Who's the Boss? . . . . Wanda

Bassett, Angela

Films:

F/X (1986) . . . . TV Reporter

Boyz N the Hood (1991). . . . . Reva Styles

City of Hope (1991) . . . . Reesha

•• 1:20—Breasts in bed with Joe Morton.

Critters 4: They're Invading Your Space (1992). . . . . Fran

•• 0:25—Buns in nice, tilt-up shot with partial back side view of right breast, but you don't see her face.

Innocent Blood (1992) . . . . U.S. Attorney Sinclair

Malcolm X (1992). . . . . Betty Shabazz

Passion Fish (1993) . . . . Dawn/Rhonda

What's Love Got to Do With It (1993) . . . . Tina Turner

Strange Days (1995) . . . . Lornette "Mace" Mason

Vampire in Brooklyn (1995). . . . . Rita

Waiting to Exhale (1995). . . . . Bernadine

Contact (1997) . . . . Rachel Constantine

Miniseries:

The Jacksons: An American Dream (1992). . . Katherine Jackson

Bastedo, Alexandra

Films:

This, That and the Other (1970; British) . . . . Angie

Wedding Night (1970; Irish) . . . . Gloria

The Ghoul (1975; British) . . . . Angela

Made for Cable Movies:

Draw! (1984; HBO) . . . . Bess

• 0:52—Silhouette of right breast, leaning over Kirk Douglas while making love in bed.

Bastell, Victoria

Films:

Bad Lieutenant (1992). . . . . Bowtay

•• 0:10—Breasts and brief side view of buns in bed with another woman. Brief side view of right breast, while dancing with Harvey Keitel.

Romeo Is Bleeding (1994). . . . . Girl #1

• 0:03—Breasts, (she's the blonde) while frolicking in bed with a brunette woman and a guy. Very brief buns in panties in mirror.

• 0:31—Breasts, in room with a brunette woman and a guy.

• Bates, Ashley

Films:

Virtual Encounters (1995) . . . . Erica

(Unrated version reviewed.)

Sexual Roulette (1996) . . . . Nikki

(Unrated version reviewed.)

•• 0:09—Breasts and buns in T-back, while dancing on stage, then coming to talk at the bar.

Bates, Jo Anne

Films:

Perfect Timing (1984) . . . . Karen

••• 0:21—Nude, while getting ready to have her picture taken.

Heavenly Bodies (1985). . . . . Girl in Locker Room

Immediate Family (1989). Home Buyer

Deadly Sins (1994; Canadian) . . . . Rita

Fear (1996) . . . . Julie Masse

Misbegotten (1997). Dr. Rory Sorenson

Made for Cable TV:

The Outer Limits: Under the Bed (1995; Showtime)

. . . . French Mother

Bates, Kathy

Films:

Straight Time (1978). . . . . Selma Darin

Come Back to the Five and Dime, Jimmy Dean, Jimmy (1982)

. . . . Stella May

Two of a Kind (1983). . . . . Furniture Man's Wife

The Morning After (1986) . . . . Woman on Mateo Street

Summer Heat (1987). . . . . Ruth Stanton

Arthur 2 On the Rocks (1988) . . . . Mrs. Canby

High Stakes (1989) . . . . Jill

Men Don't Leave (1989) . . . . Lisa Coleman

Dick Tracy (1990) . . . . Mrs. Green

Misery (1990) . . . . Annie Wilkes

(Academy Award for Best Actress.)

White Palace (1990) . . . . Rosemary Powers

At Play in the Fields of the Lord (1991) . . . Hazel Quarrier

• 2:22—(0:52 into tape 2) Nude, covered with mud and leaves, going crazy outside after her son dies.

Fried Green Tomatoes (1991) . . . . Evelyn Couch

a.k.a. Fried Green Tomatoes at the Whistle Stop Café

Shadows and Fog (1991). . . . . Prostitute

Prelude to a Kiss (1992). . . . . Leah Blier

Used People (1992). . . . . Bibby

A Home of Our Own (1993) . . . . Frances Lacey

Curse of the Starving Class (1994). . . . . Ella Tate

North (1994). . . . . Alaskan Mom

Angus (1995) . . . . Meg Bethune

Dolores Claiborne (1995) . . . . Dolores Claiborne

Diabolique (1996). . . . . Shirley Vogel

The War at Home (1996). . . . . Maurine Collier

Primary Colors (1998) . . . . Libby Holden

Made for Cable Movies:

Hostages (1993; HBO). . . . . Peggy Say

The Late Shift (1996; HBO) . . . . Helen Kushnick

Miniseries:

Stephen King's "The Stand" (1994). . . . . Rae Flowers

• Batten, Cyia

Made for Cable Movies:

Marshal Law (1995; Showtime). . . . . Petal

Sins of the Mind (1997; USA) . . . . Allegra

Made for Cable TV:

Red Shoe Diaries: Tears (1995; Showtime) . . . . The Narrator

• 0:01—Brief right breast in red fabric.

• 0:15—Breasts, while in red fabric.

•• 0:24—Breasts under sheer black dress, then breasts and buns while dancing with Sasha.

Red Shoe Diaries: Banished (1998; Showtime). . . . Dancer 3

• 0:20—Breasts, after untying her dress in front of the angel.

• 0:22—Breasts, while lying on the ground and being carried by the angel.

Made for TV Movies:

W.E.I.R.D. World (1995) . . . . n.a.

Bauer, Belinda

Films:

The American Success Company (1979) . . . . .Sarah

Winter Kills (1979). . . . . Yvette Malone

•• 0:46—Breasts making love in bed with Jeff Bridges, then getting out of bed.

• 1:25—Breasts, dead as a corpse when sheet uncovers her body.

Flashdance (1983). . . . . .Katie Hurley

Timerider (1983). . . . . Clair Cygne

The Rosary Murders (1987). . . . . Pat Lennon

UHF (1989). . . . . Mud Wrestler

Act of Piracy (1990; South African/U.S.) . . . . . . Sandy Andrews

Robocop 2 (1990). . . . . .Juliette Faxx

Servants of Twilight (1991) . . . . Christine Scavello

Necronomicon: Book of the Dead (1993) . . . . Nancy Gallmore

Poison Ivy 2: Lily (1995) . . . . Angela Falk

Made for Cable Movies:

A Case for Murder (1993; USA). . . . . Joanna Gaines

Made for Cable TV:

The Hitchhiker: Love Sounds (HBO) . . . . Veronica Hoffman

• 0:15—Brief breasts, making love in the house with Kerry.

•• 0:22—Breasts, making love in the boat.

Made for TV Movies:

Starcrossed (1985) . . . . Mary

Bauer, Jaime Lyn *

(Yes, her name is spelled Jaime.)

Films:

The Centerfold Girls (1974) . . . . Jackie

•• 0:04—Breasts getting out of bed and walking around the house.

••• 0:14—Breasts getting undressed in the bathroom.

•• 0:15—Brief breasts and buns putting on robe and getting out of bed, three times.

Young Doctors in Love (1982). . . . . Cameo

TV:

The Young and the Restless (1973-82)

. . . . Lauralee (Laurie) Brooks Prentiss

Bare Essence (1983) . . . . Barbara Fisher

The Young and the Restless (1984)

. . . . Lauralee (Laurie) Brooks Prentiss

Days of Our Lives (1993-). . . . . .Laura Horton

• *Bauer, Kristin*

Films:

Galaxis (1995). . . . . Commander

Glory Daze (1995) . . . . Dina

•• 0:20—Breasts, in sexy black rubber outfit, then breasts while in Ben Affleck's bedroom.

Romy and Michele's High School Reunion (1997)

. . . . Kelly Possenger

TV:

The Crew (1995-96) . . . . Maggie

Total Security (1997). .Geneva Renault

Bauer, Michelle *

a.k.a. Michelle McClellan briefly when her ex-husband threatened to sue for using "Bauer."

a.k.a. Former adult film actress Pia Snow.

The two easiest adult video tapes to find are *Cafe Flesh* and *Bad Girls.*

Films:

Homework (1982) . . . . .Uncredited Dream Groupie

••• 1:01—Breasts with two other groupies, groping Tommy while he sings. (She has a flower in her hair and is the only brunette.)

Monaco Forever (1984) . . . . Nazi Woman

••• 0:20—In black bra and panties, then breasts, undressing out of Nazi outfit.

Cave Girl (1985) . . . . Locker Room Student

•• 0:05—Breasts with four other girls in the girls' locker room undressing, then running after Rex. She's the first to take her top off, wearing white panties, running and carrying a tennis racket.

Tomboy (1985) . . . . .Uncredited Girl in Corvette

• 1:16—Brief breasts, while opening her dress in Corvette.

Armed Response (1986) . . . . .Stripper

• 0:41—Breasts, dancing on stage.

Cyclone (1986) . . . . .Uncredited Shower Girl

• 0:06—Very brief buns and side of left breast walking around in locker room. (Passes several times in front of camera.)

Reform School Girls (1986). . . . . . . .Uncredited Shower Girl

•• 0:25—Breasts, then nude in the shower.

Roller Blade (1986). . . . . Bod Sister

• 0:11—Breasts, being held by Satacoy's Devils.

••• 0:13—More breasts and buns in G-string during fight. Long scene.

• 0:16—Brief breasts twice, getting rescued by the Sisters.

•• 0:33—Breasts during ceremony with the other two Bod Sisters. Buns also.

••• 0:35—Full frontal nudity after dip in hot tub. (Second to leave the tub.)

•• 0:40—Nude, on skates with the other two Bod Sisters. (She's on the left.)

Screen Test (1986) . . . . Dancer/Ninja Girl

•• 0:04—Breasts dancing on stage.

••• 0:42—Nude, with Monique Gabrielle, making love in a boy's dream.

Lust for Freedom (1987) . . . . Jackie

•• 0:37—In bra, then breasts after undressing in prison cell with Lynn.

• 0:40—Lower frontal nudity and left breast when removing her panties.

Nightmare Sisters (1987) . . . . Mickey

••• 0:39—Breasts standing in panties with Melody and Marci after transforming from nerds to sexy women.

••• 0:40—Breasts in the kitchen with Melody and Marci.

••• 0:44—Full frontal nudity in the bathtub with Melody and Marci. Excellent, long scene.

••• 0:47—Breasts in the bathtub. Nice close up.

••• 0:48—Still more breasts in the bathtub.

•• 0:53—Breasts in bed with J.J.

Phantom Empire (1987) . . . . Cave Bunny

•• 1:13—Breasts after losing her top during a fight, more breasts until Andrew puts his jacket on her.

The Tomb (1987) . . . . .Nefartis

Demonwarp (1988) . . . . .Betsy

•• 0:41—Breasts, after taking off her T-shirt to get a tan in the woods.

•• 0:43—Left breast, while lying down, then brief breasts getting up when the creature attacks.
•• 0:47—Breasts, while putting blood-stained T-shirt back on.
•• 1:19—Breasts, while strapped to table, getting ready to be sacrificed.
• 1:22—Breasts, while lying on stretcher, dead.

Hollywood Chainsaw Hookers (1988) . . . . Mercedes
••• 0:09—Nude in motel room with a John just before chainsawing him to pieces.

The Jigsaw Murders (1988). . . . . Cindy Jakulski
• 0:20—Brief buns on cover of puzzle box during bachelor party.
• 0:21—Brief breasts in puzzle on underside of glass table after the policemen put the puzzle together.
• 0:29—Very brief breasts when the police officers show the photographer the puzzle picture.
• 0:43—Very brief breasts long shots in some pictures that the photographer is watching on a screen.

Sorority Babes in the Slimeball Bowl-O-Rama (1988) Lisa
••• 0:12—Breasts, while brushing herself in the front of mirror when Brinke Stevens takes a shower.
• 0:14—Brief full frontal nudity when the three nerds fall into the bathroom.
••• 0:40—Breasts, while taking off her bra.
••• 0:43—More breasts, while undoing garter belt.
•• 0:46—More breasts, while in locker room.
•• 0:47—More breasts, while taking off stockings.
• 1:04—Full frontal nudity, while sitting on the floor by herself.
•• 1:05—Full frontal nudity, while getting up after the lights go out. Kind of dark.

Warlords (1988) . . . . Harem Girl
••• 0:14—Breasts, getting her top ripped off, then shot by a bad guy.

Wild Man (1988). . . . . .Trisha Collins
• 1:02—In sheer white lingerie with Eric. Buns also.
••• 1:06—Breasts on couch making love with Eric. Brief lower frontal nudity.

Assault of the Party Nerds (1989) . . . . .Muffin
• 0:16—Side view of left breast kissing Bud.
••• 0:20—Breasts lying in bed seen from Bud's point of view, then sitting up by herself.
• 1:15—Brief right breast, then breasts in bed with Scott.

Beverly Hills Vamp (1989). Kristina
• 0:12—Buns and brief side view of right breast in bed biting a guy.
•• 0:38—Breasts trying to get into Kyle's pants.

Deadly Embrace (1989) . . . . .Female Spirit of Sex
•• 0:22—Breasts caressing herself during fantasy sequence.
••• 0:28—Breasts taking off tube top and caressing herself.
••• 0:40—Breasts and buns kissing blonde guy. Nice close up of him kissing her breasts.
• 0:42—Side of left breast lying down with the guy.
• 1:03—Buns and side of right breast with the guy.

Dr. Alien (1989) . . . . Coed #1
a.k.a. I Was a Teenage Sex Mutant
••• 0:53—Breasts taking off her top (she's on the left) in the women's locker room after another coed takes hers off in front of Wesley.

Murder Weapon (1989). . . . . .Girl in Shower on TV
• 1:00—Brief left breast on TV that the guys are watching. Scene from *Nightmare Sisters*.

Naked Obsession (1990) . . . . Uncredited Dancer
(Unrated version reviewed.)
• 0:11—Very brief breast, when pulling down her blue blouse after pushing a customer back. Brief breasts, when kneeling on all fours.

Puppet Master III: Toulon's Revenge (1990). Lili
• 0:15—Brief breasts bringing the phone to the General while he takes a bath.
•• 0:43—Breasts, twice, making love on top of the General.

Virgin High (1990). . . . . Miss Bush

Camp Fear (1991) . . . . Body Double for Betsy Russell
a.k.a. Millenium Countdown

The Dwelling (1991). . . . . .n.a.

Evil Toons (1991). . . . . Mrs. Burt
•• 0:48—Breasts opening her lingerie for Burt. Buns, while walking away in G-string.

Inner Sanctum (1991)
. . . . Body Double for Margaux Hemingway
• 0:09—Left breast, body double in office for Margaux Hemingway.
•• 0:23—Breasts body double for Hemingway, while in bed with Joseph Bottoms.

Lady Avenger (1991) . . . . Annalee
••• 0:30—Breasts, making love in bed on top of J.C.
••• 0:52—Breasts, making love in bed on top of Ray.

Spirits (1991). . . . . Sister Mary
••• 0:21—Breasts, taking off nun's habit, trying to seduce Erik Estrada. Brief lower frontal nudity and buns also. Long scene.

Chickboxer (1992) . . . . .Greta "Chickboxer" Holtz
••• 0:57—Full frontal nudity, making love with a guy in bed.

Hellroller (1992) . . . . .Michelle Novak
••• 0:30—Breasts taking a bath.

Assault of the Party Nerds II: The Heavy Petting Detective (1993) . . . . Muffin
•• 0:47—Breasts, while making love with Bud in bed.

Dinosaur Island (1993). . . . . June
••• 0:20—Breasts (she has white necklaces on), while bathing in a stream with April and May, then bathing the guys.
••• 0:22—More breasts, while bathing the guys.
• 0:38—Brief upper half of left breast, popping out of bikini top after winning fight with the Queen.
••• 1:07—Breasts, while making love outside at night with Turbo.

Naked Instinct (1993) . . . . Michelle
••• 0:10—Full frontal nudity with Virgin Rich Kid after taking off her maid outfit and making love with him on bed. Long scene.
••• 0:13—More full frontal nudity with him on top of her.
••• 0:43—Full frontal nudity with Frat Bully and making love with him. Long scene.
••• 1:07—Breasts and buns in red panties, making love with the Therapist. Long scene.
••• 1:10—Full frontal nudity making love on the floor, with her on top.
••• 1:11—More full frontal nudity with him on top.
••• 1:13—More full frontal nudity making love on her hands and knees.

One Million Heels B.C. (1993). . . . . Cavegirl
••• 0:10—Half of right breast, while in skimpy top, under Rose in bed. Nude in the shower with Rose.
•• 0:12—Breasts, while sitting on bed.
••• 0:13—Full frontal nudity while trying on lingerie.
••• 0:21—Nude, while soaping Savannah and Rose in the spa.

- • 0:25—Brief full frontal nudity taking off her towel in bedroom.
- ••• 0:26—Breasts and buns, while getting dressed on bed.

Blonde Heaven (1994) . . . . Amanda Blackwell
- ••• 1:08—Nude, while making love with Pluto.

Attack of the 60 Foot Centerfold (1995) . . . . . . Dr. Joyce Mann

Bikini Drive-In (1995) . . . . Dyanne Lynn
(Unrated version reviewed.)
- ••• 0:40—Breasts and buns in swimsuit relaxing by the pool and swimming. Some under water shots.
- ••• 0:43—Breasts, after getting out of the pool after talking on the phone, then getting oil rubbed on her breasts by her servant.

Vampire Vixens From Venus (1995) . . . . Shampay
- •• 0:58—Breasts, while on the floor with her boyfriend.

Maximum Revenge (1997) . . . . Shana

Video Tapes:

Nudes in Limbo (1983) . . . . Model

Best Chest in the West (1984) . . . . Michelle
- ••• 0:24—In two piece swimsuit, then breasts and buns.

Love Skills: A Guide to the Pleasures of Sex (1984) . . . . Model
- ••• 0:34—Full frontal nudity, caressing herself in front of a mirror.

Candid Candid Camera, Volume 4 (1985) . . . . Model
- ••• 0:08—Full frontal nudity, undressing while complaining about a bad tan from a tanning salon.
- ••• 0:50—Nude, posing in front of a guy, asking his opinion on her poses. Long scene.

Terror on Tape (1985) . . . . . . Unsatisfied Video Store Customer

Candid Candid Camera, Volume 5 (1986) . . Debbie White
- ••• 0:34—Buns, pulling down her pants while a guy rubs purple paint on her rear.

Centerfold Screen Test, Take 2 (1986) . . . . Marsha
- ••• 0:12—Breasts taking off her dress for Mr. Johnson. Then full frontal nudity. Nice, long scene.

In Search of the Perfect 10 (1986) . . . . Perfect Girl #10
- ••• 0:53—In yellow outfit stripping in office. Breasts and buns in G-string bottom.

Penthouse Love Stories (1986). . . . . Therapist's Patient
- ••• 0:45—Nude, making love in Therapist's office with his assistant.

Night of the Living Babes (1987) . . . . Sue
- •• 0:44—Breasts chained up with Chuck and Buck.
- ••• 0:46—More breasts chained up.
- • 0:50—Breasts getting rescued with Lulu.

Playboy Video Magazine, Volume 12 (1987) . . . . Candid Candid Camera
- •• 0:35—Lower nudity when her skirt falls down whenever she sneezes.

Penthouse: On the Wild Side (1988) . . . . Punk or Bust Hairdresser
- • 0:32—Breasts in black leather outfit.
- ••• 0:34—Nude while wearing black leather outfit, making love with Julie Parton.

Scream Queen Hot Tub Party (1991) . . . . Herself
- •• 0:00—Full frontal nudity during opening credits.
- •• 0:07—Breasts taking off pink outfit and putting on red teddy.
- • 0:12—Buns, while walking up the stairs.
- ••• 0:33—Nude, stripping out of blue dress in scene from *Hollywood Chainsaw Hookers.* Long scene.
- ••• 0:38—In black lingerie, then stripping to breasts to demonstrate the proper Scream Queen use of a chainsaw.
- ••• 0:44—Breasts taking off her swimsuit top and soaping up with the other girls.
- •• 0:46—Breasts in still shot during the end credits.

Jewel Naked Around the World (1995). . . . . Herself
- • 0:39—Brief breasts and buns in several clips from *In the Flesh.*

If I'm So Famous, How Come Nobody's Ever Heard of Me? (1996) . . . . Herself
- • 0:16—Brief breasts in still photo on table during convention.

*Baxter, Amy Lynn **

Films:

Summer's Games (1987) . . . . Boxer/Girl from Penthouse
- •• 0:04—Breasts opening her swimsuit top after contest. (1st place winner.)
- •• 0:18—Breasts during boxing match.

Spring Fever USA (1988) . . . . Amy (Car Wash Girl)
a.k.a. Lauderdale

Summer Job (1989) . . . . Susan
- •• 0:10—Breasts changing in room with the other three girls. More breasts sitting on bed.
- • 0:34—Brief breasts when her swimsuit top pops off after saving a guy in swimming pool.
- • 0:45—In white lingerie, brief breasts on stairs, flashing her breasts (wearing curlers).
- • 1:23—Breasts pulling her top down talking to Mr. Burns.

Affairs of the Heart (1992). . . . . Josie Hart
- •• 0:00—Breasts during opening credits.
- •• 0:02—Breasts and buns in G-string, while posing for photos.
- ••• 1:09—Breasts posing in Santa cap during photo session.
- •• 1:13—Breasts with Richard during smoky dream scene.

Bikini Bistro (1995) . . . . Judy
(Unrated version reviewed.)
- ••• 0:12—Nude, while changing into a swimsuit in room with the two other girls.
- • 0:53—Nude, while changing into swimsuit.
- ••• 0:56—Breasts and buns, while making love in back room with Russel.

Broadcast Bombshells (1995). . . . . Kendall Saranski
- •• 0:05—Breasts, while wearing black panties, changing clothes in dressing room.
- ••• 0:43—Full frontal nudity, while changing clothes in room with the other two girls.
- ••• 0:55—In white bra, then nude, while making love with Neil. Long scene.
- ••• 1:14—Full frontal nudity, while making love with Neil backstage.

In the Flesh (1995) . . . . Dancer

Blood Bullets Buffoons (1996) . . . . n.a.

Video Tapes:

Wet Water T's (1987). . . . . Herself
- ••• 0:33—Breasts in black lingerie bottoms, then buns in G-string, dancing on stage in a contest.
- •• 0:38—Breasts during judging.
- •• 0:39—Breasts during semi-finals.
- ••• 0:40—Breasts dancing with the other women during semi-final judging.
- ••• 0:43—Breasts during finals.
- •• 0:47—Breasts during final judging.
- ••• 0:48—Breasts dancing after winning first place.

Penthouse Centerfold—Amy Lynn (1991) . . . . Pet

Penthouse Passport to Paradise/Hawaii (1991) . . . Model
- ••• 0:49—Undressing on boat in white swimsuit top and white panties, then full frontal nudity.

Penthouse Pet of the Year Playoff 1991 (1992) . . . . . Pet
••• 0:02—Full frontal nudity during Hollywood starlet/photographer segment.
••• 0:04—Full frontal nudity on bed during interview.
•• 0:06—Full frontal nudity in still photos.
••• 0:08—Nude, while posing on boat.
••• 0:14—Nude, while posing with large sculptures.
••• 0:19—Nude, while wearing black wig and posing in house and playing with food (including a banana!).
Penthouse Pet of the Year Winners 1992: Brandy & Amy (1992). . . . . Pet
Penthouse Forum Letters: Volume 1 (1993)
. . . . .Maid to Order/The Maid
••• 0:21—Breasts, taking off bra and playing with herself while watching the owners of the house make love. Buns in panties.
Penthouse The Great Pet Hunt—Part II (1993) . . . . . . Pet
••• 0:34—Breasts and buns in T-back after stripping out of bride outfit on stage. More fun while playing with oil.
Playboy's Girls of Radio: Talk, Rock and Shock (1995)
. . . . Herself
••• 0:06—Nude, when shaving her legs and pubic region (!) while in bathroom. More nude while taking a bath with Tempest.

Baxter, Arlene *

Video Tapes:
Playboy Video Calendar 1995 (1994) . . . . February
••• 0:05—Nude in cabin. Nude in apartment.

Baxter, Lynsey

Films:
The French Lieutenant's Woman (1981) . . . . .Ernestina
Real Life (1984; British) . . . . Jackie
The Girl in a Swing (1989; U.S./British) . . . . Barbara
The Pleasure Principal (1991; British). . . . . Sammy
The Cold Light of Day (1995; German). . . . . . Milena Tatour
• 1:17—Side view of left breast, while making love in bed with Richard E. Grant. Kind of dark.
Made for TV Movies:
I Spy Returns (1994) . . . . Santina

Baxter, Meredith

a.k.a. Meredith Baxter-Birney.
Ex-wife of actor David Birney.
Wife of actor Michael Blodgett.
Films:
Ben (1972) . . . . Eve Garrison
Stand Up and Be Counted (1972) . . . . .Tracy
All the President's Men (1976). . . . . Debbie Sloan
Jezebel's Kiss (1990) . . . . Virginia De Leo
One More Mountain (1994) . . . . Margaret Reed
Made for TV Movies:
Beulah Land (1980). . . . . Lauretta Pennington
Burning Bridges (1990). . . . . .n.a.
A Mother's Justice (1991) . . . . Lilah Comminger
A Woman Scorned: The Betty Broderick Story (1992)
. . . . Betty Broderick
Darkness Before Dawn (1993) . . . . .Mary Ann Grand
Her Final Fury: Betty Broderick, the Last Chapter (1993)
. . . . Betty Broderick
For the Love of Aaron (1994). . . . . .Margaret Gibson
My Breast (1994) . . . . Joyce Wadler
•• 0:19—Left breast, while the doctor feels her during breast examination.
Betrayed: A Story of Three Women (1995) . . . Amanda Nelson
After Jimmy (1996) . . . . .n.a.
The Inheritance (1997) . . . . Beatrice Hamilton
TV:
Bridget Loves Bernie (1972). . . . . . Bridget Fitzgerald Steinberg
Family (1976-80). . . . . Nancy Lawrence Maitland
Family Ties (1982-89) . . . . Elyse Keaton
The Faculty (1996) . . . . Flynn

Bay, Sara

See: Neri, Rosalba.
Films:
Deadly Sanctuary (1968; British/Spanish) . . . . Florette

Baye, Nathalie

Films:
Day for Night (1973; French). Assistant
Mado (1976; French). . . . . Catherine
The Man Who Loved Women (1977; French)
. . . . Martine Desdoit
Beau Pere (1981; French). . . . . Charlotte
I Married a Shadow (1982; French) . . . . Helene
The Return of Martin Guerre (1983; French)
. . . . Bertrande de Rols
• 0:59—Brief side view of left breast, making love in bed on top of Martin. Don't see her face.
Detective (1985; French/Swiss) . . . . Francoise Chenal
Honeymoon (1985; French/Canadian) . . . . Cécile
• 1:00—Brief breasts, while sitting on bed with John Shea.
C'est La Vie (1990; French) . . . . Lena
The Man Inside (1990) . . . . Christine
Every Other Weekend (1995). . . . . Camille Valmont
Made for Cable Movies:
And the Band Played On (1992; HBO). . . . . Dr. Francoise Barre

Baynes, Henrietta

Films:
Nijinsky (1980; British). . . . . Magda
Tales of Erotica (1995). . . . . Mrs. Kirsch
• 0:30—Brief upper half of breasts, while wearing lingerie and playing with a vibrator by herself.

Beacham, Stephanie *

Films:
The Games (1970). . . . . .Angela Simmonds
The Nightcomers (1971; British) . . . . . . Miss Margaret Jessel
• 0:13—Brief left breast lying in bed having her breasts fondled.
••• 0:30—Breasts in bed with Marlon Brando while a little boy watches through the window.
•• 0:55—Breasts in bed pulling the sheets down.
The Devil's Widow (1972; British) .Janet
Dracula A.D. 1972 (1972; British) . . . . Jessica Van Helsing
a.k.a. Dracula Today
And Now the Screaming Starts (1973; British)
. . . . Catherine Fengrifen
The Confessional (1977; British) . . . . .Vanessa
a.k.a. House of Mortal Sin
Schizo (1977; British). . . . . Beth
a.k.a. Amok
a.k.a. Blood of the Undead
Horror Planet (1980; British) . . . . Kate
a.k.a. Inseminoid
Troop Beverly Hills (1989) .Vicki Sprantz
Made for Cable Movies:
Foreign Affairs (1993; TNT) . . . . .Rosemary Radley

Miniseries:
Napolean and Josephine (1987) . . . . Therese
Made for TV Movies:
Danielle Steel's "Secrets" (1992) . . . . Sabina Quarles
To Be The Best (1992) . . . . Arabella
TV:
The Colbys (1985-87) . . . . Sable Scott Colby
Dynasty (1988-89) . . . . Sable Colby
Sister Kate (1989-90) . . . . Sister Katherine Lambert
Seaquest DSV (1993-94) . . . . Dr. Kristin Westphalen

Beal, Cindy

Films:
My Chauffeur (1986) . . . . Beebop
Slavegirls from Beyond Infinity (1987) . . . . Tisa
(Wearing skimpy outfits during most of the movie.)
••• 0:36—Breasts on beach wearing white panties.
• 1:05—Left breast leaning back on table while getting attacked by Zed.

Beall, Sandra

Films:
Easy Money (1983) . . . . Maid of Honor
A Night in Heaven (1983) . . . . Slick
• 1:09—Brief close up of left breast in shower with Christopher Atkins.
The Cotton Club (1984) . . . . Myrtle Fay
Birdy (1985) . . . . Shirley
Key Exchange (1985) . . . . Marcy
••• 1:14—Breasts on bed taking off her clothes and talking to Daniel Stern.
Loverboy (1989) . . . . Robin
State of Grace (1990) . . . . Steve's Date

Beals, Jennifer

Films:
Flashdance (1983) . . . . Alex
The Bride (1985) . . . . Eva
• 0:53—Standing in wet white nightgown in the rain, while talking to Sting.
Split Decisions (1988) . . . . Barbara Uribe
Vampire's Kiss (1989) . . . . Rachel
Club Extinction (1990) . . . . Sonja Vogler
a.k.a. Doctor M
• 1:16—Brief side of left breast rolling over in bed with Hartmann. Don't see her face, but probably her.
•• 1:17—Brief breasts in bed with Hartmann when he kisses her right breast, then brief right breast.
Blood & Concrete: A Love Story (1991) . . . . Mona
• 0:10—Buns, in pulled up slip on bed with Billy Zane. Brief, out-of-focus shot of her left breast. Don't see her face.
In the Soup (1992) . . . . Angelica
Indecency (1992) . . . . Ellie
Day of Atonement (1993; French) . . . . Joyce Ferratti
Caro Diario (1994) . . . . Herself
Dead on Sight (1994) . . . . Rebecca Darcy
Mrs. Parker and the Vicious Circle (1994) . . Gertrude Benchley
Devil in a Blue Dress (1995) . . . . Daphne Monet
Four Rooms (1995) . . . . Angela
The Prophecy II (1997) . . . . Valerie Rosales
•• 0:16—Very brief upper half of buns, brief breasts, very brief left breast, while making love in bed with Russell Wong.
Made for Cable Movies:
Twilight of the Golds (1997; HBO) . . . . Suzanne
The Spree (1998; TMC) . . . . Xinia Kelly
Made for Cable TV:
The Outer Limits: Bodies of Evidence (1997; Showtime)
. . . . Robin Dysart
TV:
2000 Malibu Road (1992) . . . . Perry Quinn

Beaman, Lee Anne

Films:
Mirror Images (1991) . . . . Rebecca
••• 1:11—Buns in G-string, then breasts in conference room, undressing in front of Jeff Conaway and Carter.
The Other Woman (1992) . . . . Jessica Mathews
(Unrated version reviewed.)
••• 0:17—Nude, undressing and getting into the shower.
•• 0:40—Breasts in the bathtub.
•• 0:51—Buns, while lying in bed in the fetal position.
••• 1:09—Nude, on the floor making love with Traci. Interesting camera angles.
••• 1:13—Nude, getting up and out of bed, taking a shower, then making love with Carl. Long scene.
•• 1:23—Breasts on floor with Traci during video playback on TV.
••• 1:34—Buns, in long shot, taking off robe to greet Zmed. Breasts and buns in bed with him.
Sins of the Night (1993) . . . . Sue Ellen
(Unrated version reviewed.)
•• 0:46—In black bra and G-string panties under sheer robe while drunk in her house, then breasts.
Tropical Heat (1993) . . . . Carolyn
••• 0:10—Nude, taking her clothes off outside by swimming pool, then getting in and making love with Rick Rossovich. Long scene.
•• 0:14—Breasts, while sitting at bar in swimming pool with Rossovich.
Improper Conduct (1994) . . . . Kay
(Unrated version reviewed.)
•• 0:12—Full frontal nudity while in the shower.
•• 1:02—Breasts while in photocopy room with John Loughlin.
••• 1:07—In red bra and panties, then buns and breasts while making love with John Loughlin in motel room.
•• 1:16—In black bra and panties, then breasts while in office with Steven Bauer.
Irresistible Impulse (1995) . . . . Jeannine Miller
•• 0:47—Breasts, while lying in hammock, then in sheer black robe when talking with Richard.
• 1:03—Buns in panties, while walking away and on the beach.
••• 1:05—Buns and breasts, while making love with Richard on the beach, then on a hammock, then inside the house.
•• 1:07—Breasts and buns in spa, then getting out.
•• 1:31—Breasts, while making love with Simon in bed, then sitting up in bed afterwards.
Tainted Love (1995) . . . . Sara Baldwin
• 0:24—Brief breasts, while in bathtub.
•• 0:29—Breasts and partial buns, while talking with Chantal in steam room.
• 0:41—Brief buns, while walking into spa and talking with Chantal.
•• 0:53—Breasts, while making love with Michael on boat.
• 0:54—Buns in T-back, while kissing Michael on boat.
•• 1:03—Breasts, while making love with Michael in back seat of limousine.
• 1:19—In black bra, then buns in panties, while in her apartment with Michael.

Twisted Passion (1995) . . . . Truck Stop Waitress
a.k.a. Shades of Gray

Béart, Emmanuelle *

Model for *Borghese* cosmetics.

Films:

Date with an Angel (1987) . . . . Angel
- 1:14—Breasts, when bathing in pond in forest while Michael E. Knight watches from the bushes. Long shot, don't really see anything. In a closer shot, her hair covers breasts.

Manon of the Spring (1987; French). . . . . Manon
- 0:11—Brief nude dancing around a spring playing a harmonica.

La Belle Noiseuse (1992; French) . . . . Marianne
- •• 1:11—Full frontal nudity, after taking off robe and posing in studio.
- •• 1:24—Left breast and lower frontal nudity while posing.
- •• 1:27—Full frontal nudity after finishing posing and putting on robe.
- •• 1:34—Nude, after taking off robe and getting ready to pose.
- ••• 1:38—Nude, after taking off robe and getting ready to pose while leaning on stool.
- ••• 1:43—Nude, after taking off robe and posing while sitting on chair.
- •• 1:49—Nude, lying on chair after taking off robe.
- •• 1:51—Nude, after taking off robe and posing on floor.
- ••• 1:53—Nude, while kneeling on bench while posing.
- ••• 1:57—Full frontal nudity while posing on stool, then sitting on chairs and sitting on floor. Long scene.
- • 2:03—(0:00 into tape 2) Full frontal nudity while posing on bench.
- •• 2:06—(0:03 into tape 2) Nude, while getting off bench and putting on robe.
- •• 2:10—(0:07 into tape 2) Breasts and buns, after taking off robe and sitting on bench.
- ••• 2:16—(0:13 into tape 2) Breasts, while posing on stool, then full frontal nudity, getting up off stool and putting on robe.
- ••• 2:33—(0:30 into tape 2) Nude, after taking off robe, and posing on mattress on the floor.
- ••• 2:42—(0:39 into tape 2) Nude, while walking around the studio, looking at the paintings, then sitting on mattress on the floor. Long scene.
- •• 2:57—(0:54 into tape 2) Buns and breasts, when sitting on mattress on the floor. Full frontal nudity while lying down, then getting up, putting on robe and walking away.
- •• 3:17—(1:14 into tape 2) Breasts and buns, while standing and posing.
- •• 3:20—(1:17 into tape 2) Right beast, while standing and posing. Long shot at first, then closer shot.

Divertimento (1992; French) . . . . Marianne
(A shorter, slightly re-edited version of *La Belle Noiseuse.*)

Un Coeur en Hiver (1993; French). . . . . Camille
L'Enfer (1994; French). . . . . .Nelly
Mission: Impossible (1996) . . . . Claire

Beatty, Debra

Films:

Sorority House Party (1992) . . . . Mennonite Fury Woman

Animal Instincts 2 (1993) . . . . Cindy
- •• 0:24—Full frontal nudity, while posing for Eric in his studio and putting a robe on.

Anthony's Desire (1993) . . . . Dancer
- ••• 0:04—Full frontal nudity, while stripping out of green dress on stage with other women.
- •• 0:22—Breasts, while sitting on stage on the right.
- • 1:02—Left breast, while sitting behind Annastasia Alexander on the left side of the stage.

Hollywood Dreams (1993). . . . . Sara
a.k.a. L.A. Dreams
(Unrated version reviewed.)
- ••• 0:11—Breasts after taking off her top in office for audition in front of Lou.
- ••• 0:19—Nude, diving into pool and getting out, then making love at Lou's.
- •• 0:24—Left breast and partial lower frontal nudity while lying on bed on a set.
- •• 0:39—Breasts while making love with Robby on bed in bedroom set.
- • 1:06—Side of right breast while getting made up.

The Perfect Gift (1993) . . . . Beatrice
Strike a Pose (1993) . . . . .Model
Witchcraft 6: The Devil's Mistress (1993). . . . . .Keli
(Unrated version reviewed.)
- ••• 0:50—Breasts, while sitting in bubble bath, then nude, while making love with Will in the tub.
- ••• 1:06—Full frontal nudity getting into the bathtub, then washing herself.
- • 1:11—Brief right breast, while washing herself.

Surf, Sand and Sex (1994). . . . . Second Woman
- ••• 0:12—Breasts and buns, while fantasizing about doing a strip dance routine in front of one customer in gentleman's club, then making love with him on stage. Long scene.
- • 1:08—Breasts again during end credits.

Caged Heat 3000 (1995) . . . . Billie
- •• 0:14—Breasts, while in showers, throwing sponge at Kira.
- •• 0:28—Brief breasts, while standing in the showers, then whipping a guy.

Cyborg 3: The Recycler (1995) . . . . Pleasure Unit #2

Forbidden Passions (1995) . . . . .Mara
- ••• 0:07—Breasts, while making love with her husband, Stephen.
- • 0:12—Brief breasts when standing up and talking with Stephen, then sitting back in bed.
- •• 0:14—Nude, while by herself in a beach like setting.
- ••• 0:26—Full frontal nudity while posing for the painter, then letting him paint on her, then making love with him.
- ••• 1:02—Breasts, while making love with Amy.
- •• 1:14—Breasts, while making love with Bob.

Midnight Tease 2 (1995) . . . . Sandra
- •• 1:05—Breasts and buns in T-back while dancing on stage with Griffin Drew.

Dead Tides (1997). . . . . Body Double for Tawny Kitaen
- • 0:43—Brief buns, while making out with Roddy Piper. Don't see her face.
- • 0:55—Brief buns, while making love with Piper. Don't see her face.

Made for Cable TV:

Love Street: Cross Current (1994; Showtime) . . . . . . Laura
- •• 0:08—Breasts and buns, while making love with her husband.
- •• 0:18—Breasts while starting to make love with Greg.
- ••• 0:21—Buns and breasts, while making love with Greg.

Erotic Confessions: Friends and Lovers (1996; Cinemax)
. . . . Jean
(Available on video tape in *Erotic Confessions, Volume 2: Intrigue.*)
- • 0:03—In braless wet blouse, while horsing around with Mike.

••• 0:07—Breasts, while sunbathing on lounge chair and talking with Mike, then breasts and buns in the shower.
••• 0:12—Nude, undressing, then making love with Mike.

Erotic Confessions: Fringe Benefits (1997; Cinemax). . Lilli
• 0:00—Breasts, while posing with two blonde models.
•• 0:03—Breasts and buns, while posing with two blonde models.
••• 0:05—Breasts, while posing on bed during photo session.
••• 0:08—Nude, while making love with Miguel on bed.

Beatty, Linda

See: Carpenter, Linda.

Beauchamp, Michelle

Made for Cable TV:

Red Shoe Diaries: You Make Me Want to Wear Dresses (1994; Showtime). . . . . Maria

Red Shoe Diaries: Forbidden Zone (1996; Showtime) . . . . Bella
• 0:07—Very, very brief breasts while dancing right after Beverly Johnson says "Bella."
• 0:16—Very brief breasts, while spinning around during dance when Angelica runs away.

Beaudoin, Michelle

Films:

Bad Company (1994). . . . . Wanda
• 0:11—Brief right breast in bed with John.

Made for Cable TV:

The Outer Limits: White Light Fever (1995; Showtime) . . . . Jessie Wells

Poltergeist: The Legacy/Ghost in the Road (1996; Showtime) . . . . .Wendy Barton

TV:

Sabrina, The Teenage Witch (1996-) . . . . Jenny Kelly

Beccarie, Claudine

Films:

The Mark (1976; Italian) . . . . .Huana
•• 0:25—Nude, while leaning out of doorway, walking to bed, lying on it and answering the phone.
•• 0:36—Breasts, in open blouse, while making love with Francis.
••• 0:41—Full frontal nudity, while running in ocean in slow motion. Orange colored tint.
•• 1:15—Breasts on the beach with Francis. Orange colored tint.

Inhibition (1984; Italian). . . . . .Carol
• 0:11—Brief lower frontal nudity in open nightgown walking into bedroom.
• 0:23—Brief buns and left breast in dressing room.
• 0:51—Brief lower frontal nudity, while sitting on a swing.
••• 0:57—Nude masturbating in bed.
••• 1:00—Nude sitting, then being mean to Anna in a bathtub.
• 1:10—Full frontal nudity under sheer black nightgown greeting Robert.
••• 1:11—Nude, making love in bed with Robert.
•• 1:29—Breasts, making love in bed with Peter.
• 1:32—Brief breasts waking up in bed in the morning.

Beck, Dixie

Films:

Body Strokes (1995) . . . . Karen
•• 0:14—Breasts, while making love with Leo.
•• 0:50—Full frontal nudity, while making love with Leo.
•• 1:13—Breasts, with Rachel and Leo.
• 1:19—Brief right breast, while posing with Rachel.
• 1:20—Brief right breast, while posing with Rachel.
••• 1:25—Breasts and buns, while making love with Leo.
•• 1:29—Breasts, while posing for Leo.
• 1:32—Breasts, while posing with Beth and Claire.

Scoring (1995) . . . . Abbey

Tainted Love (1995) . . . . Marie

Video Tapes:

Playboy's Real Couples: Sex in Dangerous Places (1995) . . . . Up on the Roof/Woman
• 0:45—Brief buns, while mooning the camera at the beach.
••• 0:52—Nude while making love with James and Shayna.

Beck, Kimberly

a.k.a. Kimberly Clark.

Films:

Yours, Mine and Ours (1968). . . . . Janette North

Massacre at Central High (1976) . . . . .Theresa
• 0:32—Nude romping in the ocean with David. Long shot, dark, hard to see anything.
•• 0:42—Breasts on the beach making love with Andrew Stevens after a hang glider crash.

Roller Boogie (1979) . . . . Lana

Friday the 13th, Part IV—The Final Chapter (1984) . . . . . . Trish

Maid to Order (1987) . . . . .Kim

Nightmare At Noon (1987). . . . . Sherry Griffith
a.k.a. Deathstreet USA

The Big Blue (1988). . . . . Sally

Friday the 13th, Part VII: The New Blood (1988) . . . . Tricia/Prologue

Messenger of Death (1988). . . . . Piety Beecham

Operation: Paratrooper (1988) . . . . .Kim
a.k.a. Private War

Playroom (1989) . . . . .Secretary
a.k.a. Schizo

Adventures in Dinosaur City (1992). . . . . Chanteuse

Frozen Assets (1992) . . . . Voice-Over Actress

Killing Zoe (1994) . . . . .Woman Customer

Independence Day (1996). .Housewife

Made for Cable TV:

Sex, Shock and Censorship in the 90's (1993; Showtime) . . . . Marsha Miller

Made for TV Movies:

In the Deep Woods (1992) . . . . Margot

TV:

Peyton Place (1965) . . . . .Kim Schuster

Lucas Tanner (1974-75). . . . . .Terry Klitsner

General Hospital (1975) . . . . Samantha Chandler

Rich Man, Poor Man—Book II (1976-77). . . . . Diane Porter

Capitol (1982-83) . . . . Julie Clegg

Becker, Brooke

Films:

Cat Chaser (1988). . . . . .Philly

Deadly Rivals (1992) . . . . Shallie Kittle
• 0:14—Breasts visible under sheer white blouse while talking to Andrew Stevens in auditorium.

Becker, Desiree

Films:

Good Morning, Babylon (1987; Italian/French). . . . . . Mabel
• 1:06—Brief breasts in the woods making love.

Made for Cable TV:

The Hitchhiker: Out of the Night (1985; HBO). . . . . Kathy
•• 0:12—Brief breasts lying in the steam room talking to Peter, then close up of breasts.

Bedelia, Bonnie

Aunt of actor Macaulay Culkin.

Films:

The Gypsy Moths (1969) . . . . Annie Burke
- 0:28—Very, very brief right breast, while opening and folding her robe together while walking up the stairs. Partially hidden by shadow.

Lovers and Other Strangers (1970) . . . . Susan Henderson
The Big Fix (1978). . . . . Suzanne
Heart Like a Wheel (1983) . . . . Shirley Muldowney
The Boy Who Could Fly (1986) . . . . Charlene
The Stranger (1986). . . . . Alice Kildee
- 0:15—Brief right breast sticking up from behind her lover's arm making love in bed during flashback sequence (B&W).
- 0:19—Brief left breast turning over in hospital bed when a guy walks in. Long shot, hard to see.
- •• 0:38—Right breast again making love (B&W).

Violets Are Blue (1986) . . . . Ruth Squires
Die Hard (1988) . . . . Holly McClane
The Prince of Pennsylvania (1988). . . . . Pam Marshetta
Fat Man and Little Boy (1989). . . . . Kitty Oppenheimer
Die Hard 2 (1990). . . . . Holly McClane
Presumed Innocent (1990) . . . . Barbara Sabich
Needful Things (1993) . . . . Polly Chalmers
Judicial Consent (1994) . . . . Gwen
- 0:24—Brief left breast while making love with Billy Wirth at his place. Don't see her face.

Speechless (1994) . . . . Annette

Made for Cable Movies:

Somebody Has to Shoot the Picture (1990; HBO) . . . . Hannah McGrath
- 1:15—Upper half of left breast, while lying in bed with Roy Scheider.

Directed By: The Gift (1994; Showtime) . . . . n.a.
Homecoming (1996; Showtime) . . . . Eunice

Made for Cable TV:

Fallen Angels: The Quiet Room (1993; Showtime) . . . . Sally Creighton
(Available on the video tape *Fallen Angels Two.*)
Outer Limits: Worlds Apart (1996; Showtime) . . . . Nancy

Made for TV Movies:

Memorial Day (1983) . . . . n.a.
Switched at Birth (1991) . . . . Regina Twigg
A Mother's Right: The Elizabeth Morgan Story (1992) . . . . Dr. Elizabeth Morgan
The Fire Next Time (1993) . . . . Suzanne Morgan
Legacy of Sin: The William Colt Story (1995). . . . . Jill Colt
Shadow of a Doubt (1995) . . . . Robin Harwell
Her Costly Affair (1996). . . . . Dr. Diane Weston

TV:

Love of Life . . . . Sandy Porter
The New Land (1974). . . . . Anna Larsen

Bega, Leslie

Films:

For Keeps (1988). . . . . Carlita
Mobsters (1991) . . . . Anna Lansky
a.k.a. Mobsters—The Evil Empire
Uncaged (1991) . . . . Micki
a.k.a. Angel in Red
- •• 0:02—Breasts on top of a customer, in bed.
- •• 0:16—Breasts in bed with Evan.
- 0:42—Brief breasts with Evan on the floor.

The American President (1995) . . . . White House Staffer Laura
Power 98 (1996) . . . . Denise
Lost Highway (1997) . . . . Raquel

TV:

Head of the Class (1986-89) . . . . Maria Borges

Behr, Jena *

a.k.a. Jennifer Behr.

Films:

Sex & Money (1994). . . . . X-The Slave

Made for Cable TV:

Erotic Confessions: Gifts (1996; Cinemax) . . . . Naydeen
(Available on video tape in *Erotic Confessions, Volume 2: Intrigue.*)
- ••• 0:03—In white bra and panties, then nude, while making love with Tom in lab.

Hot Line: Hannah's Surprise (1996; Cinemax) . . . . Lisa
- ••• 0:03—Buns in white lingerie, then breasts, while in motel room with her husband.
- ••• 0:08—Breasts, while making love with her husband in bed.
- ••• 0:18—Breasts, while making love on bed with Angelique.

Video Tapes:

Playboy Night Dreams (1993). . . . . . Arresting Development
- ••• 0:47—Nude, after stripping out of police officer uniform then making love.

Supermodels Go Wild (1993) . . . . Model
- ••• 0:00—Nude throughout.

Playboy's Erotic Fantasies: Forbidden Liaisons (1995) . . . . Cast Member

Behr, Melissa

Films:

The Marrying Man (1991) . . . . Dee
a.k.a. Too Hot to Handle
Bad Channels (1992) . . . . Nurse Ginger
Blue Flame (1993) . . . . Jack
- 0:49—Brief side view of left breast, then brief partial glimpses of breasts as she circles Brian Wimmer. Partial upper half of right breast, when held by Wimmer.

Dollman vs. the Demonic Toys (1993) . . . . Nurse Ginger

Made for Cable TV:

Red Shoe Diaries: The Boxer (1997; Showtime) . . . . . . Kate
- 0:25—Breasts and side view of buns, while making love with Max. Mostly in silhouette.

Beimpold, Ulrike

Films:

Private Passions (1983) . . . . Laura
- •• 0:28—Left breast, then breasts in bed with Toni.

The Cop and the Girl (1985; Austrian/West German) . . . . Prostitute

Beldam, Lia *

Films:

The Shining (1980) . . . . Young Woman in Bath
- ••• 1:12—Full frontal nudity getting out of bathtub while Jack Nicholson watches.

• Belén, Ana

Pop singer/actress in Spain.

Films:

The Perfect Husband (1995; Spanish) . . . . Theresa Brock
- 0:43—Breasts and buns under sheer white robe while in bathroom.
- 0:45—Brief beasts, while making love with Tim Roth in bed.
- 0:58—Partial breasts, while sitting in mud bath when Roth caresses her.

•• 1:27—Breasts, while in the shower with Roth when discovered by her husband.

Bell, Catherine

Films:

Death Becomes Her (1992). . . . . Lisle Body Double
•• 1:19—Buns, while getting out of swimming pool and drying herself off. (2 long shots and 1 close-up.)
Men of War (1994) . . . . Grace
Crash Dive (1996). . . . . Lisa

Made for Cable TV:

Dream On: Those Who Can't, Edit (1994; HBO). . . . . . Kay
••• 0:01—Breast, while starting to make love with Martin in his apartment.
Hot Line: The Brunch Club (1995; Cinemax) . . . . Cat
(Available on video tape in *Hot Line 3*.)
•• 0:13—Breasts and buns, while making love with Derrick in her office at night.

TV:

JAG (1997-) . . . . Sarah MacKenzie

Bell, Jeannie *

Films:

Black Gunn (1972) . . . . Lisa
Mean Streets (1973) . . . . Diane
• 0:07—Breasts dancing on stage with pasties on.
• 1:00—Breasts backstage wearing pasties.
The Klansman (1974) . . . . Mary Anne
Policewomen (1974) . . . . Pam Harris
•• 0:02—Buns and breasts changing clothes during prison break.
••• 1:28—Brief breasts changing into military clothes outside next to truck.
Three the Hard Way (1974). . . . . Polly
TNT Jackson (1975) . . . . Diana "TNT" Jackson
••• 0:43—Breasts, getting her blouse ripped off by the bad guys. More breasts during fight (notice her panties change from black to white to black).
• 0:45—Brief breasts, almost hitting Joe.
••• 0:50—Breasts, while making love with Charlie.
The Choirboys (1977). . . . . Fanny Forbes
Sex on the Run (1979; German/French/Italian) . . . . Slave Girl
a.k.a. *Some Like It Cool*
a.k.a. *Casanova and Co.*
••• 0:01—Breasts, reading book in large bath with Marisa Berenson.
••• 0:24—Breasts, giving Berenson a back massage.
Bloodfist III: Forced to Fight (1991) . . Diana "TNT" Jackson
•• 0:55—Breasts several times in movie *TNT Jackson* that the inmates watch while Diddler gets stabbed to death.
Body Waves (1991) . . . . Diana "TNT" Jackson
•• 0:43—Breasts in open top in drive-in movie from *TNT Jackson.*

Bell, Josie

Films:

Bright Lights, Big City (1988) . . . . Runway Model
SnakeEater (1988) . . . . The Kid
• 0:39—Very brief side view of right breast and buns, when walking past open doorway while Lorenzo Lamas watches. Medium long shot.
A Family Matter (1990). . . . . Cissy

Beller, Kathleen

Films:

The Godfather, Part II (1974) . . . . Girl in "Senza Mama"
The Betsy (1978). . . . . Betsy Hardeman
••• 0:12—Nude getting into swimming pool.
•• 1:14—Breasts lying under Tommy Lee Jones.
Movie Movie (1978) . . . . Angie Popchik
Promises in the Dark (1979) . . . . Buffy Koenig
Surfacing (1980). . . . . Kate
• 0:22—Very brief buns, pulling down pants to change. Dark, hard to see.
• 0:23—Very brief right breast undressing. Dark, hard to see.
• 0:24—Very, very brief breasts turning over in bed.
• 0:25—Buns, while standing next to bed.
••• 1:23—Breasts washing herself in the water. One long shot, one side view of right breast.
Fort Apache, The Bronx (1981) . . . . Theresa
The Sword and the Sorcerer (1982) . . . . Alana
• 0:54—Side view of buns, lying face down getting oil rubbed all over her.
Touched (1982). . . . . Jennifer
Cloud Waltzing (1986) . . . . Meredith Tolliver
Time Trackers (1989). . . . . R.J. Craig

Miniseries:

Blue and the Gray (1982) . . . . Kathy Reynolds
Dynasty: The Reunion (1991) . . . . Kirby

Made for TV Movies:

Mary White (1977) . . . . Mary White
Are You in the House Alone? (1978) . . . . Gail

TV:

Search for Tomorrow (1971-74) . . . . Liza Walton
Dynasty (1982-84) . . . . Kirby Anders
Bronx Zoo (1987-88) . . . . Callahan

Belli, Agostina

Films:

Bluebeard (1972) . . . . Caroline
• 1:31—Brief left breast lying on grass getting a tan.
•• 1:32—Breasts taking off clothes and lying on the couch.
Blood in the Streets (1974; French/Italian). . . . . Maria
The Seduction of Mimi (1974; Italian) . . . . Rosalia
The Purple Taxi (1977; French/Italian/Irish) . . . Anne Taubelman
Holocaust 2000 (1978) . . . . Sara Golen
•• 0:50—Breasts in bed making love with Kirk Douglas.

Belliveau, Cynthia

a.k.a. Cyd Belliveau.

Films:

Loose Screws (1986; Canadian). . . . . Mona Lott
Goofballs (1987) . . . . n.a.
Night Friend (1987; Canadian) . . . . Maggie
The Dark (1993) . . . . Tracy
•• 0:29—In slip, then bra, then breasts, while making love on bed in motel with Hunter.

Made for Cable Movies:

The Spider and the Fly (1994; USA). . . . . Blair

Made for Cable TV:

E.N.G. (1989-90; Lifetime; Canadian) . . . . Terri Morgan

Made for TV Movies:

Breach of Faith: A Family of Cops II (1997) . . . . Melanie

Bellomo, Sara

a.k.a. Adult film actress Roxanne Blaze.

Films:

Beach Babes From Beyond (1993) . . . . Xena
••• 0:01—Breasts and very brief lower frontal nudity while in shower and getting dressed with Luna and Sola during opening credits.
•• 0:32—Buns, in swimsuit at the beach.

• 0:58—Buns, while dancing in swimsuits and boots on stage at beach during bikini contest.

Cave Girl Island (1994) . . . . Xena

a.k.a. Beach Babes 2: Cave Girl Island

•• 0:02—Breasts, when meeting Moon and kissing him.

••• 0:05—Nude, while making love with Moon. Long scene.

•• 0:17—Breasts, while sexily playing with a banana.

••• 0:22—Breasts, while making love with Moon some more.

•• 1:05—Nude, during party on spaceship.

Seduce Me: Pamela Principle 2 (1994) . . . . Inger

•• 0:33—Breasts, twice, while walking past Charles in house.

• 0:50—Breasts, while sitting in spa. (She's on the left.)

•• 1:01—Breasts, while making love (loudly) on bed when Charles passes by open door. Dark.

Bikini Drive-In (1995) . . . . Carrie

(Unrated version reviewed.)

••• 0:05—Breasts, after taking off her purple swimsuit top at the beach and rubbing suntan lotion on herself.

••• 0:15—Buns and breasts, while making love in bathtub with her boyfriend.

• 0:24—Breasts under red top, when wiping her face off after water fight while cleaning the drive-in.

Virtual Encounters (1995). . . . . First Encounter Woman

(Unrated version reviewed.)

••• 0:12—Nude, while making love with a guy in outdoor setting during first VR experience. (This is part of a clip from *Cave Girl Island*.)

Belmonte, Anastacia

Films:

Treacherous (1993) . . . . Maria

Made for Cable TV:

Love Street: Ex-Girlfriend (1994; Showtime) . . . . . . Maggie

• 0:02—Very brief buns, then brief buns in panties after fight with Parker.

• *Belvedere, Vittoria* *

Films:

Gentle Into the Night (1996) . . . . Serena

• 1:03—Very brief right breast, while photographed in bed with a guy.

• 1:15—Very brief right breast in B&W photo.

Bender, Te-See

Films:

Demon Knight (1994) . . . . Party Babe 6

• 1:02—Very brief left breast with other Party Babes in Dick Miller's fantasy. She licks the tip of a long neck beer bottle.

Dillinger and Capone (1994). . . . . Brunette Hooker

• *Bendix, Simone*

Films:

The Informant (1996; Irish/U.S.) . . . . Samantha

• 1:19—Breasts, while lying in bed after making love with her boyfriend.

••• 1:20—Breasts and buns, getting out of the bed, answering the phone, then sitting in bed, then nude when dressing with Cary Elwes.

Made for Cable Movies:

Lie Down with Lions (1994; Lifetime) . . . . Lleve

TV:

Space Precinct (1994) . . . . Jane Castle

Bening, Annette *

Wife of actor Warren Beatty.

Films:

The Great Outdoors (1988) . . . . Kate Craig

Valmont (1989) . . . . Marquise de Merteuil

• 0:10—Very brief, hard to see right breast, while reaching up to kiss Jeffrey Jones.

The Grifters (1990). . . . . Myra Langtry

•• 0:36—In bra and panties in her apartment, then breasts lying in bed "paying" her rent. Kind of dark.

••• 1:06—Nude, walking down the hall to the bedroom and into bed.

• 1:30—Very brief right breast, dead in morgue. Long shot.

Postcards from the Edge (1990). . . . . Evelyn Ames

Bugsy (1991). . . . . Virginia Hill

Guilty by Suspicion (1991). . . . . Ruth Merrill

Regarding Henry (1991) . . . . Sarah Turner

Love Affair (1994) . . . . Terry McKay

The American President (1995) . . . . Sydney Ellen Wade

Richard III (1995; British) . . . . Queen Elizabeth

Mars Attacks! (1996) . . . . Barbara Land

Made for TV Movies:

Manhunt for Claude Dallas (1986). . . . . Ann Tillman

Hostage (1988) . . . . Jill

Bennett, Angela

Films:

Fatal Games (1984). Sue Allen Baines

•• 0:21—Full frontal nudity in the sauna with Teal Roberts.

• 0:23—Nude, running around the school, trying to get away from the killer. Dark.

Punchline (1988) . . . . Nurse

• *Benson, Kelly*

Films:

Drop Dead Fred (1991) . . . . Natalie

The Final Cut (1995) . . . . Dead Body

White Tiger (1995). . . . . The Brunette

• 0:27—Breasts, while sitting up in bed with Cary Hiroyuki Tagawa.

Wounded (1996). . . . . Cohen's Secretary

Benson, Vickie

Films:

Private Resort (1985). . . . . Bikini Girl

• 0:21—In blue two piece swimsuit, showing her buns, then brief breasts with Reeves.

• 1:11—Buns and very brief left breast, in locker room, trying to slap Reeves.

Hollywood Erotic Film Festival (1986) . . . . . . Thin Walls/Yvette

Las Vegas Weekend (1986) . . . . Amanda

• 1:12—Breasts and buns, while making love in bed with Percy.

My Chauffeur (1986). . . . . Party Girl

The Wraith (1986) . . . . Waitress

• 0:59—Breasts in bed with Packard when Loomis interrupts them.

Cheerleader Camp (1987) . . . . Miss Tipton

a.k.a. Bloody Pom Poms

• 0:27—Brief breasts undressing in her bedroom.

Blue Movies (1988) . . . . Andrea

Mortuary Academy (1988) . . . . Salesgirl

Bentley Konkel, Dana

Films:

Bad Girls from Mars (1990) . . . . Martine
•• 0:28—Breasts taking off her blouse in office.
•• 0:59—Breasts several times wrestling with Edy Williams.

Death Merchant (1990). . . . . Jason's Girlfriend
• 0:35—Brief breasts undressing for shower during dream.

The Invisible Maniac (1990) . . . . Newscaster
• 1:22—Brief breasts on monitor doing the news.

Repo Jake (1990). . . . . .Jenny

Sorority House Massacre 2 (1990) . . . . .Janey
••• 0:23—Breasts in bedroom talking to Suzanne and looking in the mirror. Buns, while getting dressed in black bodysuit.
• 0:48—Left breast, sticking out of bodysuit, covered with blood, when the girls discover her dead.

Benton, Barbi *

Films:

Hospital Massacre (1982) . . . . .Susan Jeremy
a.k.a. X-Ray
••• 0:31—Breasts getting examined by the Doctor. First sitting up, then lying down.
••• 0:34—Great close up shot of breasts while the Doctor uses stethoscope on her.

Deathstalker (1983). . . . . Codille
•• 0:39—Breasts struggling while chained up and everybody is fighting.
• 0:47—Right breast, struggling on the bed with Deathstalker.

TV:

Hee Haw (1971-76) . . . . Regular
Sugar Time! (1977-78) . . . . .Maxx

Video Tapes:

Playboy Video Magazine, Volume 9. . . . . .Herself

Benton, Suzanne

Films:

That Cold Day in the Park (1969) . . . . Nina
• 0:38—Side view of left breast putting top on. Long shot.
• 1:05—Breasts taking off her clothes and getting into the bathtub. Another long shot.

Catch-22 (1970). . . . . Dreedle's WAC
Best Friends (1975). . . . . Kathy

A Boy and His Dog (1976). . . . . Quilla June
•• 0:29—Nude, getting dressed while Don Johnson watches.
• 0:45—Right breast lying down with Johnson after making love with him.

Bentzen, Jane

Films:

Nightmare at Shadow Woods (1983) . . . . .Julie
a.k.a. Blood Rage

Made for Cable Movies:

A Breed Apart (1984; HBO). . . . . Reporter
••• 0:55—Left breast in bed with Powers Booth, then full frontal nudity getting out of bed and putting her clothes on.

Benussi, Femi

Films:

The Hawks and the Sparrows (1967; Italian) . . . . Luna
The Biggest Bundle of Them All (1968). . . . Uncle Carlo's Bride
Hatchet for the Honeymoon (1969; Spanish/Italian) . . . . . . n.a.
a.k.a. Blood Brides
The Italian Connection (1973; U.S./Italian) . . . . .Nana

My Father's Wife (1976; Italian). . . . . Patricia
a.k.a. Confessions of a Frustrated Housewife
• 0:33—Close up view of left breast.
•• 0:51—Right breast, while making love in bed with Claudio. Breasts after.

Benz, Donna Kei *

Films:

Looker (1981) . . . . Ellen

The Challenge (1982). . . . . Akiko
• 1:23—Breasts making love with Scott Glenn in motel room. Could be a body double. Dark, hard to see anything.

Pray for Death (1986) . . . . Aiko Saito
Moon in Scorpio (1987) . . . . Nurse Mitchell

• Berben, Iris

Films:

Love 600 (1969; German) . . . . Eva
a.k.a. Stehaufmädchen
• 1:11—Very brief left breast when Erik gets out of bed.

Companeros (1971) . . . . .Lola
The Killer Condom (1997; German) . . . . Dr. Doris Riffleson

Berdot, Trisha

Films:

Under Lock and Key (1994). . . . . Zelda
•• 0:03—Breasts and buns while in the shower.

Caged Hearts (1995) . . . . Lisa
Dragon Fury (1995). . . . . Dixie Dancer

Berenson, Marisa *

Films:

Death in Venice (1971; Italian/French). . . Frau Von Aschenbach
Cabaret (1972) . . . . .Natalia Landauer
Barry Lyndon (1975; British) . . . . .Lady Lyndon
Killer Fish (1979; Italian/Brazilian) .Ann
Sex on the Run (1979; German/French/Italian) . . . . The Caliph's Wife
a.k.a. Some Like It Cool
a.k.a. Casanova and Co.

S.O.B. (1981) . . . . Mavis
•• 1:20—Breasts in bed with Robert Vaughn.

The Secret Diary of Sigmund Freud (1984) . . Emma Herrmann
Trade Secrets (1989; French). . . . . Jeanne
Night of the Cyclone (1990) . . . . Francoise
White Hunter Black Heart (1990). . . . . Kay Gibson

Made for Cable Movies:

Notorious (1992; Lifetime) . . . . Katarina

Miniseries:

Sins (1986) . . . . Luba Tcherina

Made for TV Movies:

Playing for Time (1980). . . . . Elzvieta

Berg, Carmen *

Video Tapes:

Playboy Video Calendar 1989 (1988) . . . . July
••• 0:25—Nude.

Sexy Lingerie (1988) . . . . .Model
Wet & Wild (1989) . . . . .Model
Playboy's 21 Playmates: Volume II (1996) . . . . . .Playmate
••• 0:25—Full frontal nudity in still photos.
••• 0:26—Nude, while posing and dancing on rooftop and other locations.

Bergan, Judith-Marie

Films:

Abduction (1975) . . . . Patricia
- 0:08—Very brief buns and very brief lower frontal nudity on sofa when terrorists break into her apartment and kidnap her.
- 0:19—Lower frontal nudity several times, when blindfolded and raped on bed by one of the terrorists.
- •• 0:41—Breasts, after taking off T-shirt while sitting on chair in front of Carol.
- 0:49—Breasts on B&W video monitors in playback of scene at 0:41.
- •• 1:10—Full frontal nudity, after taking off her clothes in bedroom in front of Dory and Frank.
- 1:24—Brief breasts, while making love in bed with Dory.

Rage (1995) . . . . .Gladys

Made for Cable Movies:

Two Voices (1997; Lifetime). . . . . .n.a.

TV:

Maggie (1981-82). . . . . Buffy Croft
Domestic Life (1984). . . . . .Candy Crane
All Is Forgiven (1986) . . . . .Cecile Porter-Lindsey
NYPD Blue: Black Men Can Jump (Mar 1, 1994)
. . . . .Carolyn Case

Bergen, Candice

Former model.
Wife of the late French director Louis Malle.
Daughter of ventriloquist Edgar Bergen.

Films:

The Group (1966). . . . . .Lakey Eastlake
The Adventurers (1970). . . . . Sue Ann
Getting Straight (1970). . . . . Jan
Soldier Blue (1970). . . . . .Cresta Marybelle Lee
- 0:57—Close-up of buns, in open skirt while in back of wagon when Peter Strauss tries to cover her up. Don't see her face.

Carnal Knowledge (1971) . . . . Susan
The Hunting Party (1971; British) . . . . Melissa Ruger
T. R. Baskin (1971). . . . . .T.R. Baskin
Bite the Bullet (1975) . . . . .Miss Jones
The Wind and the Lion (1975) . . . . Eden Pedecaris
A Night Full of Rain (1978; Italian) . . . . Lizzy
- •• 1:04—Right breast, while in car with Giancarlo Giannini.

Oliver's Story (1978) . . . . .Marcie Bonwit
Starting Over (1979) . . . . .Jessica Potter
- 1:29—Very, very brief left breast in bed with Reynolds when he undoes her top. You see her breast just before the scene dissolves into the next one. Long shot, hard to see.

Rich and Famous (1981) . . . . Merry Noel Blake
Gandhi (1982) . . . . .Margaret Bourke-White
Stick (1985). . . . . Kyle

Made for TV Movies:

Mayflower Madam (1987). . . . . Sydney Biddle Barrows
Mary & Tim (1996) . . . . .Mary Horton

TV:

Murphy Brown (1988-98) . . . . Murphy Brown

Berger, Debra

Films:

Rosebud (1975). . . . . Gertrude Fryer
- 0:19—Brief upper half of buns, while on deck of boat with the other girls and the terrorists (she's last in line).

Emanuelle in Bangkok (1976; Italian). . . . . Debra
- •• 1:15—Full frontal nudity, while taking a bath with Laura Gemser.
- 1:21—Breasts, while making love in bed with Gemser.

Nana (1982) . . . . .Satin
Naked Massacre (1983). . . . . .n.a.
Dangerously Close (1986) .Ms. Hoffman
Lightning, The White Stallion (1986) . . . . Lili Castle

Berger, Katia

Films:

Nana (1982) . . . . Nana
The Moon in the Gutter (1983; French/Italian). . . Catherine
a.k.a. La Lune dans Le Caniveau
- 0:04—Right breast a couple of times, while lying dead on sidewalk.
- 1:24—Left breast, dead, while lying on table that Gérard Depardieu looks at during dream-like scene.
- 1:25—Brief right breast in close-up.

Tales of Ordinary Madness (1983; Italian) . . . Girl on Beach
- ••• 1:30—Full frontal nudity, taking off her clothes in front of Ben Gazzara at the beach.

Berger, Senta

Films:

Ambushers (1967). . . . . Francesca
If It's Tuesday, This Must Be Belgium (1969) . . . . Herself
When Women Had Tails (1970; Italian) . . . . .Felli
- 0:22—Buns, while lying in pit.
- 1:08—Buns, while getting carried around.
- 1:30—Buns, after her boyfriend gets caught in tree.

When Women Lost Their Tails (1971; Italian) . . . . .Felli
- 0:13—Very long shot of buns, while walking into pond.

Cross of Iron (1977) . . . . Eva
- 0:55—Brief buns, while taking off her nightgown in bedroom.

Killing Cars (1986). . . . . Marie

Berger, Sophie

Films:

Emmanuelle IV (1984) . . . . Maria
- •• 0:46—Full frontal nudity putting on robe.
- 0:49—Buns, taking off robe in front of Mia Nygren.

Love Circles Around the World (1984) . . . . Dagmar
a.k.a. Love Circles
- ••• 0:38—Breasts in women's restroom in casino making love with a guy in a tuxedo.
- ••• 0:43—Breasts in steam room wearing a towel around her waist, then making love.

Bergman, Sandahl *

Films:

All That Jazz (1979) . . . . Sandra
- •• 0:51—Breasts and buns in T-back while dancing on scaffolding during a dance routine.

Xanadu (1980) . . . . .A Muse
Airplane II: The Sequel (1982) . . . . Officer #1
Conan the Barbarian (1982) .Valeria
- •• 0:49—Brief left breast making love with Arnold Schwarzenegger.

She (1983) . . . . .She
- •• 0:22—Breasts getting into a pool of water to clean her wounds after sword fight.

Red Sonja (1985). . . . . Queen Gedren
Hell Comes to Frogtown (1987) . . . . Spangle
Kandyland (1987) . . . . .Harlow Divine

Programmed to Kill (1987) . . . . Samira
a.k.a. The Retaliator
• 0:11—Brief side view of right breast taking off T-shirt and leaning over to kiss a guy. Don't see her face.
Stewardess School (1987) . . . . Wanda Polanski
Raw Nerve (1991) . . . . Gloria Freedman
Body of Influence (1992) . . . . Clarissa
(Unrated version reviewed.)
Loving Lulu (1992) . . . . Lulu
••• 0:35—Breasts, making love with Sam.
• 0:42—Brief buns and brief breasts in shower with Sam.
• 0:57—Brief right breast in bathroom, twice, with Sam.
Lipstick Camera (1993) . . . . Lilly Miller
• 0:19—Buns, while in T-back panties, while making love with Flynn in bed.
• 1:18—Buns on monitor during video playback.
Possessed by the Night (1993) . . . . Peggy Hansen
••• 0:06—Breasts and buns, while making love with Ted Prior in bed.
• 0:08—More right breast and buns, while lying in bed after making love.
0:26—In white bra and panties in bedroom with Prior.
0:58—Briefly in bra in bathroom.
• 0:59—Breasts, while in bathtub.
1:02—In white bra and panties, after undressing while Shannon Tweed hold Prior at gunpoint.
••• 1:03—Breasts, while lying in bed after Prior rips her bra and panties off.
•• 1:14—Breasts, while changing tops in bedroom.
Ice Cream Man (1994) . . . . Marion Cassera
Inner Sanctum 2 (1994) . . . . Sharon Reed
(Unrated version reviewed.)
Night of the Archer (1994) . . . . Marla Miles
The Assault (1996) . . . . Helen
Made for TV Movies:
Getting Physical (1984) . . . . Nadine Cawley
In the Arms of a Killer (1992) . . . . Nurse Henninger
Revenge on the Highway (1992) . . . . Python
Video Tapes:
The Firm Aerobic Workout With Weights, Vol. 3 . . . . Instructor

Bergstrom, Helena *

Films:
House of Angels (1993; Swedish) . . . . Fanny Zander
• 1:13—Nude, standing with her friends near the water. Medium long shot.

Berkley, Elizabeth *

Films:
Molly & Gina (1993) . . . . Kimberly Sweeney
Showgirls (1995) . . . . Nomi Malone
(NC-17 version reviewed.)
••• 0:23—Breasts and buns in T-back, while doing strip routine on stage at Cheetah's.
••• 0:25—Breasts and buns in T-back backstage.
••• 0:28—Breasts and buns in T-back, then nude when doing lap dance for Kyle MacLachlan while Gina Gershon watches.
•• 0:35—Nude, while dancing on stage with Penny.
• 0:36—Breasts, while walking and talking to Phil.
••• 0:40—Breasts after taking off her bra during audition and afterward while talking with Gershon.
••• 0:47—Breasts, while dancing with James in his house.
••• 1:00—Breasts and buns in T-back, during dance number on stage.
•• 1:01—Breasts and buns in G-string, while walking down the stairs backstage.
•• 1:10—Breasts when Gershon pulls her top off and kisses her.
••• 1:11—Breasts and buns in G-string, while backstage behind Nicky, sitting at make-up table.
••• 1:24—Nude, after taking off dress and going for a swim in MacLachlan's pool, then making love with him. Nice!!
• 1:26—Brief buns, while getting dressed.
• 1:29—Buns in G-string during audition.
••• 1:38—Breasts in leather outfit and buns in G-string while dancing on stage.
•• 1:40—Breasts, while running down the stairs.
••• 1:43—Breasts and buns in G-string, while dancing on stage.
•• 1:56—Breasts after taking off her top with Carver, then beating him up.
White Wolves II: Legend of the Wild (1995) . . . . Crystal
The First Wives Club (1996) . . . . Phoebe LaVelle
The Real Blonde (1998) . . . . Tina
Made for Cable TV:
Perversions of Science: Planely Possible (1997; HBO) . . . . . Ruth
Made for TV Movies:
Saved by the Bell Hawaiian Style (1992) . . . . Jesse
Saved by the Bell: Wedding in Las Vegas (1994) . . . . Jesse
TV:
Saved by the Bell (1989-94) . . . . Jesse

Berland, Terri

Films:
The Strangeness (1980) . . . . Cindy Flanders
Pink Motel (1982) . . . . Marlene
••• 1:18—Breasts, dropping her sheet in room in front of Max and Skip.
The Sting II (1983) . . . . One of O'Malley's Girls

Bernard, Sue *

Film writer and producer.
Films:
Faster Pussycat, Kill! Kill! (1966) . . . . Linda
The Killing Kind (1973) . . . . Tina
• 0:00—Breasts during gang rape.
• 0:19—Breasts again during flashback.
• 1:12—Brief breasts again several times during flashbacks.
The Witching (1983) . . . . Nancy
a.k.a. Necromancy
(Originally filmed in 1971 as *Necromancy*, additional scenes were added and re-released in 1983.)
• 1:03—Brief breasts in bed with Michael Ontkean.

Bernhard, Sandra *

Comedienne.
Films:
Cheech & Chong's Nice Dreams (1981) . . . . Girl Nut
King of Comedy (1983) . . . . Masha
The House of God (1984) . . . . Angel Dutton
(Not available on video tape.)
Track 29 (1988; British) . . . . Nurse Stein
Heavy Petting (1989) . . . . Herself/Comedienne
Without You I'm Nothing (1990) . . . . . . Various Characters
••• 1:20—Dancing in very small pasties on stage. Buns in very small G-string. Long scene.
Hudson Hawk (1991) . . . . Minerva Mayflower
Truth or Dare (1991) . . . . Herself
Inside Monkey Zetterland (1993) . . . . Imogene
Unzipped (1995) . . . . Herself

Made for Cable Movies:
The Late Shift (1996; HBO) . . . . Herself
Made for Cable TV:
The Hitchhiker: O. D. Feeling (HBO) . . . . n.a.
Tales From the Crypt: Top Billing (1991; HBO) . . Sheila Winters
Sandra After Dark (1992; HBO) . . . . Hostess
••• 0:47—Breasts and buns, taking off bra and panties and getting into bed.
Directed By: Museum of Love (1996; Showtime). . . . . Kitty
Made for TV Movies:
Freaky Friday (1995) . . . . Frieda Debny
TV:
Roseanne (1992-97) . . . . Nancy Thomas

Bernstein, Caron

Films:
Who's the Man? (1993). . . . . Kelly
Made for Cable TV:
Red Shoe Diaries: The Game (1994; Showtime). . . . . . . Lily
• 0:04—Left breast in open blouse with John.
••• 0:07—Breasts, while doing various things around the house, including caressing herself.
•• 0:08—Breasts, while making love with John while blindfolded.
•• 0:10—Breasts and buns in panties, taking off raincoat outside in the rain.
•• 0:14—Breasts, while playing game with neighbor couple, then making love with John while watching the couple also make love.
•• 0:18—Breasts and brief buns, while making love in restroom with a sailor in a fantasy.
Red Shoe Diaries: The Art of Loneliness (1996; Showtime) . . . . Frances
••• 0:21—Breasts and buns, while making love with Bobby. Sometimes she's blindfolded and sometimes her hands are tied.

Berridge, Elizabeth

Films:
Natural Enemies (1979). . . . . Sheila Steward
The Funhouse (1981) . . . . Amy Harper
•• 0:03—Brief breasts taking off robe to get into the shower, then very brief breasts getting out to chase Joey.
Amadeus (1984) . . . . .Constanze
Smooth Talk (1985). . . . . June
Five Corners (1988). . . . . .Melanie
When the Party's Over (1991) . . . . Frankie
Made for TV Movies:
Silence of the Heart (1984) . . . . .Penny Jacobs
Home Fires Burning (1989) . . . . .Francine Tibbetts
Montana (1990) . . . . Lavetta
TV:
Texas (1981-82) . . . . Allison Linden
The Powers That Be (1992) . . . . Charlotte
The John Larroquette Show (1993-96) . . . . . Officer Eve Eggers

Bertinelli, Valerie

Wife of guitarist Eddie Van Halen.
Films:
Number One with a Bullet (1987) . . . . Teresa Barzak
Made for TV Movies:
Young Love, First Love (1979) . . . . Robin Gibson
The Seduction of Gina (1984) . . . . .Gina Breslin

Ordinary Heroes (1986) . . . . Maria Pezzo
• 0:28—Brief silhouette of breast in darkened room backlit by window, when she takes off her blouse while on top of Richard Dean Anderson in bed.
Pancho Barnes (1988) . . . . Pancho Barnes
Taken Away (1989) . . . . Stephanie Monroe
In a Child's Name (1991). . . . . Angela Cimarelli
Murder of Innocence (1993) . . . . Laurie Wade
The Haunting of Helen Walker (1995) . . . . Helen Walker
Two Mothers for Zachary (1996) . . . . .Jody Ann Shaffell
Night Sins (1997) . . . . .Megan O'Malley
TV:
One Day at a Time (1975-84) . . . . .Barbara Cooper Royer
Sydney (1990). . . . . Sydney
Café Americain (1993-95) . . . . .Holly

Besch, Bibi

Mother of actress Samantha Mathis.
Films:
The Long Dark Night (1977) . . . . .Marge
a.k.a. The Pack
Hardcore (1979) . . . . .Mary
The Beast Within (1982) . . . . Caroline MacCleary
•• 0:06—Breasts, getting her blouse torn off by the beast while she is unconscious. Dark, hard to see her face.
Star Trek II: The Wrath of Kahn (1982). . . . . . .Dr. Carol Marcus
The Lonely Lady (1983). . . . . Veronica
Date with an Angel (1987) . . . . .Grace Sanders
Who's That Girl? (1987). . . . . .Mrs. Worthington
Kill Me Again (1989) . . . . Jack's Secretary
Steel Magnolias (1989) . . . . Belle Marmillion
Tremors (1989) . . . . Megan, The Doctor's Wife
Betsy's Wedding (1990). .Nancy Lovell
Lonely Hearts (1991) . . . . .Maria Wilson
My Family (1995) . . . . Mrs. Gillespie
Made for Cable Movies:
Dead Solid Perfect (1988; HBO). . . . . .Rita
Made for Cable TV:
Tales From the Crypt: Revenge Is the Nuts (1994; HBO) . . .n.a.
Made for TV Movies:
Death of a Centerfold: The Dorothy Stratten Story (1981) . . . . .Hilda
Doing Time on Maple Drive (1992). . . . . Lisa
Abandoned and Deceived (1995) . . . . Iris
TV:
Secrets of Midland Heights (1980-81) . . . . . . Dorothy Wheeler
The Hamptons (1983) . . . . Adrienne Duncan Mortimer
Freshman Dorm (1992). . . . . Mrs. Flynn

Best, Alyson

Films:
Pacific Banana (1980; Australian). . . . . Mandy
Brothers (1984; Australian) . . . . Janine Williams
Man of Flowers (1984; Australian) . . . . Lisa
•• 0:04—Undressing out of clothes, in bra, panties and stockings in front of Charles, then full frontal nudity, then getting dressed.
•• 0:13—Full frontal nudity after taking off robe and sitting on chair for art class.
• 0:36—Brief breasts while in bed with a guy.

Beswicke, Martine

Films:
From Russia with Love (1963; British) . . . . Zora
Saturday Night Out (1963; British) .n.a.
Thunderball (1965; British) . . . . .Paula Caplan

One Million Years B.C. (1966; U.S./British) . . . . Nupondi
Slave Girls (1968) . . . . Kari
a.k.a. Prehistoric Women
Dr. Jekyll and Sister Hyde (1971) . . . . Sister Hyde
• 0:25—Breasts, opening her blouse and examining her breasts after transforming from a man.
• 0:27—Left breast, feeling herself.
• 0:44—Brief buns, taking off coat to put on a dress.
Seizure (1973). . . . . The Queen
The Happy Hooker Goes Hollywood (1980)
. . . . Xaviera Hollander
•• 0:05—Brief breasts in bedroom with Dick Miller.
••• 0:22—Brief buns, jumping into the swimming pool, then breasts next to the pool with Adam West.
• 0:27—Breasts in bed with West, then breasts waking up.
Melvin and Howard (1980) . . . . Real Estate Woman
Cyclone (1986) . . . . Waters
The Offspring (1986) . . . . Katherine White
Evil Spirits (1990) . . . . Vanya
Miami Blues (1990) . . . . Noira
Trancers II (1991) . . . . Nurse Trotter
Life on the Edge (1992) . . . . Linda James
Wide Sargasso Sea (1993) . . . . Aunt Cora
Night of the Scarecrow (1995) . . . . Barbara
TV:
Aspen (1977) . . . . Joan Carolinian

Betchley, Leigh

Films:
Novel Desires (1991) . . . . Susan
••• 0:13—Breasts in warehouse making love with Sandman. Long scene.
••• 0:15—More breasts while talking to Sandman.
Knockouts (1992) . . . . Brooke
• 0:04—Brief breasts while putting on white bra in dressing room.
• 0:26—Very brief left breast after winning strip poker game.
••• 0:41—Breasts while taking off lingerie, while wearing blue panties.
••• 0:44—Breasts while posing in space costume for photographs.
• 0:46—Brief right breast while posing in front of blinds.
Uninhibited (1993) . . . . Rocket's Wife
••• 0:54—Breasts, while making love on top of Escobar.
Hollywood Passions (1994) . . . . Connie
• 0:33—Brief breasts, while dressing.
California Heat (1995) . . . . Boudoir Bikini Girl
• 0:01—Very brief buns in black body suit, while posing for Jack.

Betzler, Geri

See: Trilling, Zoe.

*Beyer, Tanya **

Video Tapes:
The Best of Wet and Wild (1992) . . . . Model
Playboy Playmates in Paradise (1992) . . . . Playmate
Playboy Video Calendar 1993 (1992) . . . . March
•• 0:09—Breasts under sheer dress. Full frontal nudity by pool.
••• 0:11—Nude indoors and outdoors.
Wet & Wild IV (1992) . . . . Model
Playboy's Playmate Review 1993 (1993) . . . Miss February
••• 0:06—Nude, dancing in front of a big screen TV.
••• 0:08—Nude on fountain in front of a house.
Playboy's Sexy, Steamy, Sultry (1993) . . . . Playmate
Sexy Lingerie: Dreams & Desire (1994) . . . . Playmate

*Bianca, Raquel **

Films:
Golden Balls (1993; Spanish) . . . . Ana, the Maneater
Abducted II: The Reunion (1994) . . . . Maria Marcolini
•• 0:57—Breasts, after taking off her wet blouse in Vern's cave.
••• 1:04—Breasts, while making love with a good looking guy.
• 1:17—Breasts, while on cliff with Vern.

• Bick, Susie

Films:
Princess Caraboo (1994) . . . . n.a.
Ready to Wear (1994) . . . . Model
a.k.a. Prêt-à-porter
Flirt (1995) . . . . Model
•• 0:28—Full frontal nudity, while standing, then putting on dress.

*Biffignani, Monique **

Video Tapes:
Rock Video Girls 2 (1992) . . . . Herself
• 0:49—Right breast under gauze and buns in G-string after being unwrapped as a mummy.
Sexy Lingerie IV (1992) . . . . Model

Billings, Dawn Ann

Films:
Trancers III (1993) . . . . Jana
Warlock: The Armageddon (1993) . . . . Amanda Sloan
• 0:10—Very brief side of left breast, walking through hallway while taking off robe. Brief breasts, while walking past doorway.
A Brilliant Disguise (1994) . . . . . . Brunette in French Restaurant
Virtual Combat (1995) . . . . Greta
Human Desires (1996) . . . . Zoe
•• 0:11—Breasts, while making love in bed with Julia in bed.
••• 0:49—In bra and panties, then breasts and buns, while making love with Dean on sofa.

*Billingsley, Jennifer **

Films:
Blood Hunt . . . . Laura
Lady in a Cage (1964) . . . . Elaine
The Young Lovers (1964) . . . . Karen
The Spy With My Face (1966) . . . . Taffy
C.C. & Company (1970) . . . . Pom Pom
•• 0:14—Breasts, when her biker friends cheer her on while she's bathing in a pond.
• 0:54—Breasts in pulled up blouse, while struggling on the ground with Joe Namath.
Welcome Home, Soldier Boys (1972) . . . . Broad
White Lightning (1973) . . . . Lou

*Bingham, Traci **

Films:
Demon Knight (1994) . . . . Party Babe 2
• 1:02—Brief breasts, several times with other Party Babes in Dick Miller's fantasy. She's in yellow bikini bottoms and says "You've had a long, hard day Uncle Willy."
Made for Cable TV:
Dream On: Am I Blue (1995; HBO) . . . . Porno Actor 3
TV:
The Young and the Restless . . . . n.a.
Baywatch (1996-98) . . . . Jordan

Video Tapes:

The Darker Image Swimsuit Calendar: Behind the Scenes (1996) . . . . Herself

• 0:16—Brief buns in two piece swimsuit in B&W.

Binoche, Juliette *

Films:

Hail, Mary (1985; French) . . . . Juliette
a.k.a. Je Vous Salve, Marie

Rendez-Vous (1986; French). . . . . Anne "Nina" Larrieu

• 0:07—Brief breasts in dressing room when Paulot surprises her and Fred.

••• 0:25—Side of left breast, then breasts and buns in empty apartment with Paulot.

•• 0:32—Full frontal nudity in bed with Quentin.

•• 0:35—Buns, then brief breasts in bed with Paulot and Quentin. Full frontal nudity getting out.

•• 1:08—Breasts taking off her top in front of Paulot in the dark, then breasts lying on the floor.

• 1:11—Right breast, making love on the stairs. Dark.

Bad Blood (1987; French) . . . . Anna

The Unbearable Lightness of Being (1988) . . . . Tereza

• 1:33—Brief breasts while jumping onto couch.

• 1:35—Buns, while lying on couch when Lena Olin pulls her panties down.

• 1:36—Buns, while sitting in front of fire being photographed, then running around, when trying to hide.

• 1:53—Very brief left breast, then very, very brief right breast, while in bed with Lewis.

• 2:18—Left breast and lower frontal nudity in The Engineer's apartment.

Damage (1992; French/British) . . . . Anna
(Unrated Director's cut reviewed.)

• 0:52—Brief breasts while sitting on floor and making love with Jeremy Irons.

•• 1:31—Breasts on bed after getting caught by Iron's son.

Blue (1993; French/Polish) . . . . Julie

White (1993; French/Polish) . . . . Cameo

Red (1994; French) . . . . Julie Vignon

The Horseman on the Roof (1995; French) . . . . Pauline

• 1:48—Breasts, while Angelo rubs her down with alcohol to help her over her bout with cholera. Don't see her face with her body.

A Couch in New York (1996; French/U.S.). . . . . Beatrice
a.k.a. Un Divan a New York

The English Patient (1996) . . . . Hana
(Won an Academy Award for Best Supporting Actress in 1996.)

•• 1:54—(0:48 into Tape 2) Left breast, while lying in bed.

Made for Cable Movies:

Women & Men 2: Three Short Stories (1991; HBO) . . . . . Mara

Wuthering Heights (1994; TNT) . . . . Cathy

Bird, Minah

Films:

Oh, Alfie! (1975; British) . . . . Gloria
a.k.a. Alfie Darling

The Stud (1978; British). . . . . Molly

•• 0:26—Breasts in bed when Tony is talking on the telephone.

Birkin, Jane *

Mother of actress Charlotte Gainsbourg.

Films:

Blow-Up (1966; British/Italian). . . . . Teenager

• 1:06—Breasts, while changing clothes in David Hemming's studio.

• 1:08—Brief breasts while frolicking with Hemmings and the other teenage girl in the studio. Very, very brief lower frontal nudity under Hemmings.

Ms. Don Juan (1973). . . . . Clara

• 0:58—Lower frontal nudity lying in bed with Brigitte Bardot.

• 1:00—Brief breasts in bed with Bardot. Long shot.

•• 1:01—Full frontal nudity getting dressed. Brief breasts in open blouse.

Dark Places (1974; British) . . . . Alta

Catherine & Co. (1975; French) . . . . Catherine

• 0:07—Breasts, standing up in the bathtub to open the door for another woman.

•• 0:09—Side view of left breast, while taking off her blouse in bed.

••• 0:10—Breasts, sitting up and turning the light on, smoking a cigarette.

•• 0:17—Right breast, while making love in bed.

•• 0:24—Breasts taking off her dress, then buns jumping into bed.

•• 0:36—Buns and left breast posing for a painter.

• 0:45—Breasts taking off dress, walking around the house. Left breast, inviting the neighbor in.

Stuntwoman (1981) . . . . Herself

Dust (1985; French/Belgian). Magda

• 1:17—Brief breasts and buns, taking off robe and pounding the wall. Very dark.

Le Petit Amour (1988; French). . . . . Mary-Jane
a.k.a. Kung Fu Master

Daddy Nostalgie (1991; French) . . . . Caroline

La Belle Noiseuse (1992; French) . . . . Liz

Divertimento (1992; French) . . . . Liz
(A shorter, slightly re-edited version of *La Belle Noiseuse.*)

Bisignano, Jeannine *

Films:

Body Rock (1984) . . . . Girl

My Chauffeur (1986) . . . . Party Girl

• 1:23—Breasts, several times, after taking off her white blouse in the back of the limousine. (She's the only brunette.)

Ruthless People (1986) . . . . Hooker in Car

• 0:40—Breasts in the same scene three times on TV while Danny De Vito watches.

• 0:49—Left breast hanging out of the car when the Chief of Police watches on TV. Closest shot.

Stripped to Kill II (1988) . . . . Sonny

• 0:06—Buns, while wearing a black bra in dressing room.

••• 0:38—Breasts and buns during strip dance routine in white lingerie.

License to Kill (1989). . . . . Stripper

Made for Cable Movies:

Lies of the Twins (1991; USA) . . . . Biker Girl

Bisset, Jacqueline *

Films:

Cul-de-sac (1966) . . . . Jacqueline

Casino Royale (1967; British). . . . . Miss Goodthighs

Two for the Road (1967; British) . . . . Jackie

Bullitt (1968) . . . . Cathy

The Detective (1968). . . . . Norma McIver

The Sweet Ride (1968) . . . . Vicki Cartwright
(Not available on video tape.)
Breasts.

The Secret World (1969; French) . . . . Wendy

Airport (1970) . . . . Gwen Meighen

The Grasshopper (1970) . . . . Christine Adams
a.k.a. The Passing of Evil
a.k.a. Passions
Believe in Me (1971) . . . . Pamela
The Mephisto Waltz (1971) . . . . .Paula Clarkson
• 0:48—Very brief right and side view of left breast in bed with Alan Alda.
•• 1:45—Very brief breasts twice under bloody water in blood covered bathtub, dead. Discovered by Kathleen Widdoes.
Secrets (1971) . . . . .Jenny
• 0:49—Very brief lower frontal nudity, putting panties on while wearing a black dress.
••• 1:02—Brief buns and a lot of breasts on bed making love with Raoul.
The Life and Times of Judge Roy Bean (1972) . . . . . . Rose Bean
Stand Up and Be Counted (1972). . . . . .Sheila Hammond
The Thief Who Came to Dinner (1973) . . . . .Laura
The Magnificent One (1974; French/Italian) . . Tatiana/Christine
Murder on the Orient Express (1974; British)
. . . . Countess Andrenyi
The Spiral Staircase (1975; British). . . . . Helen
End of the Game (1976; Italian/German) . . . . . . Anna Crawley
St. Ives (1976). . . . . Janet Whistler
The Deep (1977) . . . . Gail Berke
••• 0:01—Scuba diving underwater in a wet T-shirt.
• 0:08—More wet T-shirt, getting out of water, onto boat.
The Greek Tycoon (1978) . . . . .Liz Cassidy
Who is Killing the Great Chefs of Europe? (1978) . . . . .Natasha
When Time Ran Out! (1980) .Kay Kirby
Inchon (1981). . . . . Barbara Hallsworth
Rich and Famous (1981) . . . . Liz Hamilton
Famous T & A (1982) . . . . .Jenny
(No longer available for purchase, check your video store for rental.)
••• 0:31—Breasts scene from *Secrets*.
Class (1983) . . . . Ellen
Under the Volcano (1984). . . . . .Yvonne Firmin
High Season (1988; British) . . . . Katherine Shaw
• 0:56—Brief breasts doing the backstroke in the water with Kenneth Branagh, then left breast while lying down. Hard to see, everything is lit with blue light.
Scenes from the Class Struggle in Beverly Hills (1989) . . . . Clare
The Maid (1990). . . . . Nicole Chantrelle
Wild Orchid (1990) . . . . Claudia
Crime Broker (1994) . . . . Holly Soames
Dangerous Beauty (1998) . . . . Paola Franco
Made for Cable Movies:
Forbidden (1985) . . . . Nina von Halder
End of Summer (1995; Showtime) . . . . Christine
Miniseries:
Anna Karenina (1985) . . . . .Anna Karenina
Napolean and Josephine (1987) . . . . Josephine de Beauharnais
Lots of cleavage.
Made for TV Movies:
Leave of Absence (1994) . . . . .Nell
Once You Meet a Stranger (1996). . . . . .Sheila Gaines

Bissett, Josie

Wife of actor Rob Estes.
Spokesmodel for Soft & Dri deodorant.
Films:
Desire (1989; Italian) . . . . Jessica Harrison
••• 0:28—Breasts and buns, while making love in bed with her boyfriend. Long scene.
•• 0:32—Brief breasts, getting out of bed and getting dressed.
••• 0:45—Breasts, while making love with the taxi boy.
••• 0:51—Breasts, playing the piano while getting caressed and kissed.
••• 0:55—Breasts, while lying in bed.
•• 1:16—Breasts in bed with an older man.
• 1:17—Brief breasts in bed while wearing a brunette wig (she's supposed to be her mother).
• 1:20—Side view of left breast on top of a guy in bed in slow motion. (Wearing a wig).
• 1:21—More left breast (still wearing wig).
• 1:27—Left breast, while in bed in flashbacks.
All-American Murder (1991). . . . . .Tally Fuller
• 1:01—Brief breasts in Polaroid photographs that Charlie Schlatter looks at. Hard to see.
• 1:07—Very brief breasts several times during B&W flashbacks.
• 1:12—Breasts on top of the Dean during Joanna Cassidy's B&W flashbacks. Quick cuts.
The Book of Love (1991) . . . . Lily
The Doors (1991) . . . . Robby Krieger's Girlfriend
I Posed for Playboy (1991). . . . . .Claire Baywood
a.k.a. Posing: Inspired by Three Real Stories
(Shown on network TV without the nudity.)
Mikey (1992). . . . . .Jessie
Made for TV Movies:
Danielle Steel's "Secrets" (1992) . . . . .Gaby Smith
Deadly Vows (1994) . . . . Bobbi Gilbert
Dare to Love (1995) . . . . Jessica Wells
Baby Monitor: Sound of Fear (1997) . . . . .Ann
TV:
Doogie Howser, M.D. (1990) . . . . Christa Benson
Hogan Family (1990-91) . . . . Cara
Melrose Place (1992-98) . . . . .Jane Andrews Mancini

Bittle, Dottie

Video Tapes:
Hot Body Video Magazine #3: Blonde Fever (1993)
. . . . Covergirl/Fashion
•• 0:00—Breasts during introduction.
••• 0:30—Full frontal nudity, while changing clothes with Nova and Samantha.
••• 0:40—Buns in two piece swimsuit, then nude by and in swimming pool.
••• 0:45—Nude, while stripping out of one of her sexy outfits.
••• 0:51—Nude, while posing on bed.
Hot Body International: Dreamgirl II (1995). . . . . Herself
Hot Body International: Steamed Heat (1995) . . . Herself
• 0:11—Buns in swimsuit, while posing outdoors with two other models.

Bittner, Carrie

a.k.a. Adult film actress Alicyn Sterling.
Films:
Malibu Summer (1991) . . . . Lisa
Bikini Summer 2 (1992). . . . . Sandra
• 0:15—Buns in two piece swimsuit, while walking with Sandy.
•• 0:38—Breasts (she's the blonde), taking off her T-shirt and jumping into the pool with Sandy.
• 0:40—Very brief breasts, while running past some guys.
•• 0:42—More breasts, while running around the backyard.
•• 0:44—More breasts and buns in swimsuit, while running around some more.

Night Rhythms (1992) . . . . Elaine
(Unrated version reviewed.)
••• 0:06—Right breast, then breasts and lower frontal nudity while talking on the phone and playing with herself. Long scene.
Video Tapes:
Penthouse Satin & Lace: An Erotic History of Lingerie (1992) . . . . Model

Black, Karen *

Films:
Easy Rider (1969) . . . . Karen
Five Easy Pieces (1970) . . . . Rayette Dipesto
Cisco Pike (1971) . . . . Sue
•• 0:47—Breasts, getting dressed in bedroom.
Drive, He Said (1972) . . . . Olive
• 1:15—Brief breasts screaming in the bathtub when she gets scared when a bird flies in.
• 1:19—Brief lower frontal nudity running out of the house in her bathrobe.
Little Laura and Big John (1972) . . . . Laura
Portnoy's Complaint (1972) . . . . The Monkey
Airport 1975 (1974) . . . . Nancy
The Great Gatsby (1974) . . . . Myrtle Wilson
The Day of the Locust (1975) . . . . Faye
Nashville (1975) . . . . Connie White
Burnt Offerings (1976) . . . . Marion
Capricorn One (1978) . . . . Judy Drinkwater
In Praise of Older Women (1978; Canadian) . . . . Maya
•• 0:35—Breasts in bed with Tom Berenger.
Separate Ways (1979) . . . . Valentine Colby
• 0:04—Breasts and in panties changing while her husband talks on the phone, then in bra. Long shot.
•• 0:18—Breasts in bed, while making love with Tony Lo Bianco.
•• 0:36—Breasts taking a shower, then getting out.
Chanel Solitaire (1981) . . . . Emilienne D'Alencon
Killing Heat (1981) . . . . Mary Turner
•• 0:41—Full frontal nudity giving herself a shower in the bedroom.
Come Back to the Five and Dime, Jimmy Dean, Jimmy (1982) . . . . Joanne
Can She Bake a Cherry Pie? (1983) . . . . Zee
• 1:02—Very brief upper half of left breast in bed when she reaches up to touch her hair.
Savage Dawn (1984) . . . . Rachel
Cut and Run (1985; Italian) . . . . Karin
Eternal Evil (1985; Canadian) . . . . Janus
Invaders from Mars (1986) . . . . Linda
Dixie Lanes (1987) . . . . Zelma
Miss Right (1987; Italian) . . . . Amy
• 0:47—Brief breasts jumping out of bed and running to get a bucket of water to put out a fire.
The Invisible Kid (1988) . . . . Mom
It's Alive III: Island of the Alive (1988) . . . . Ellen Jarvis
Out of the Dark (1988) . . . . Ruth
Bad Manners (1989) . . . . Mrs. Fitzpatrick
Homer & Eddie (1989) . . . . Belle
Night Angel (1989) . . . . Rita
Zapped Again! (1989) . . . . Homeroom Teacher
The Children (1990; British/German) . . . . Sybil Lollmer
Club Fed (1990) . . . . Sally Rich
Evil Spirits (1990) . . . . Ella Purdy
Haunting Fear (1990) . . . . Dr. Julia Harcourt
Mirror Mirror (1990) . . . . Mrs. Gordon
Overexposed (1990) . . . . Mrs. Trowbridge
Twisted Justice (1990) . . . . Mrs. Granger
Auntie Lee's Meat Pies (1991) . . . . Auntie Lee
Blood Money (1991) . . . . Barrett
a.k.a. The Killer's Edge
Children of the Night (1991) . . . . Karen Thompson
Caged Fear (1992) . . . . Blanche
The Double O Kid (1992) . . . . Mrs. Elliot
Final Judgment (1992) . . . . Mrs. Sorrel
Hitz (1992) . . . . Tiffany Powers
a.k.a. Judgment
The Player (1992) . . . . Cameo
Rubin & Ed (1992) . . . . Rula
Bound and Gagged: A Love Story (1993) . . . . Carla
Crimetime (1996; U.S./British) . . . . Millicent Hargreave
Dinosaur Valley Girls (1996) . . . . Ro-Kell
(Director's Cut reviewed.)
Made for Cable TV:
The Hitchhiker: Hired Help (1985; HBO) . . . . . Mrs. Kay Mason
(Available on *The Hitchhiker, Volume 1*.)
The Hunger: Ménage À Trois (1997; Showtime) . . . . Miss Gati
Made for TV Movies:
Trilogy of Terror (1974)
. Millicent Larimore/Therese Larimorex/Julie Eldridgex/Amelia
Tales of the City (1994) . . . . Herself
TV:
The Second Hundred Years (1967-68) . . . . . . Marcia Garroway

Black, Nicole

a.k.a. Adult film actress Nicole Noir.
Films:
Simply Irresistible (1983) . . . . Mata Hari
(R-rated version. *Irresistible* is the X-rated version.)
•• 1:14—Full frontal nudity, while tied to a chair.
Video Tapes:
Nudes in Limbo (1983) . . . . Model

Blackburn, Greta

Films:
48 Hrs. (1982) . . . . Lisa
•• 0:13—Breasts and buns in bathroom in hotel room with James Remar.
The Concrete Jungle (1982) . . . . Lady in Bar
Chained Heat (1983; U.S./German) . . . . Lulu
Yellowbeard (1983) . . . . Mr. Prostitute
Party Line (1988) . . . . Angelina
• 0:01—Partial side of left breast in open dress, while standing and kissing Curtis.
•• 0:02—Breasts in bed with Curtis. Brief breasts after rolling off him when Leif Garrett comes in.
Death Feud (1989) . . . . Jenny
Under the Boardwalk (1989) . . . . Mrs. Vorpin
My Blue Heaven (1990) . . . . Stewardess
Life on the Edge (1992) . . . . Joanie Hardy
Miniseries:
V: The Final Battle (1984) . . . . Lorraine

Blackman, Joan

Films:
Career (1959) . . . . Barbara
Blue Hawaii (1961) . . . . Maile Duval
Kid Galahad (1962) . . . . Rose Grogan
Vengeance of Virgo (1972) . . . . n.a.
Macon County Line (1974) . . . . Carol Morgan
Pets (1974) . . . . Geraldine Mills
• 0:46—Brief side view of left breast, while getting out of bed after making love with Bonnie.

Moonrunners (1975). . . . . Reba
They Came From Within (1975; Canadian) . . . Elevator Mother
a.k.a. Shivers
One Man (1979; Canadian) . . . . n.a.
Return to Waterloo (1986) . . . . Mother, Horsley Station

Blair, Kimberly

Films:

The Affair (1995). . . . . Bobbie Pins
Over the Wire (1995). . . . . Sascha
••• 0:00—In bra and panties, when dancing and stripping in front of a guy, then breasts and buns, while making love.
Witchcraft 7: Judgement Hour (1995) . . . . Gina
(Unrated version reviewed.)
••• 0:09—Full frontal nudity, getting out of shower and drying herself off, then putting on panties and bra. Long scene.
••• 0:11—Breasts and very brief lower frontal nudity, after taking off bra and making love with her boyfriend in bed. Long scene.
• 0:15—Buns in panties, after police raid the apartment.
Stripteaser 2 (1997) . . . . Lisa

Made for Cable TV:

Beverly Hills Bordello: Reunion (1997; Showtime)
. . . . Beautiful Woman
•• 0:20—Nude, while having sex with Jack in bedroom.

Blair, Linda *

Films:

Way We Live Now (1970) . . . . Sara Aldridge
The Exorcist (1973). . . . . Regan
Airport 1975 (1974) . . . . Janice Abbott
Exorcist II: The Heretic (1977). . . . . Regan
Roller Boogie (1979). . . . . Terry Barkley
Hell Night (1981) . . . . Marti
Chained Heat (1983; U.S./German) . . . . Carol
••• 0:30—Breasts in the shower.
•• 0:56—In bra, then breasts in the Warden's office when he rapes her.
Savage Streets (1984) . . . . Brenda
••• 1:05—Breasts, while sitting in the bathtub thinking.
Night Patrol (1985) . . . . Sue
• 1:19—Brief left breast, in bed with The Unknown Comic.
Savage Island (1985). . . . . Daly
Nightforce (1986). . . . . Carla
Grotesque (1987) . . . . Lisa
Red Heat (1987; U.S./German) . . . . Chris Carlson
••• 0:56—Breasts in shower room scene.
••• 1:01—Brief breasts getting raped by Sylvia Kristel while the male guard watches.
Silent Assassins (1988). . . . . Sara
Up Your Alley (1988). . . . . Vickie Adderly
W. B., Blue and the Bean (1988) . . . . Nettie
a.k.a. Bail Out
Witchery (1988) . . . . Jane Brooks
Bedroom Eyes II (1989) . . . . Sophie Stevens
• 0:31—Buns, in bed with Wings Hauser.
• 0:33—Brief left breast under bubbles in the bathtub. Don't see her face.
A Woman Obsessed (1989). . . . . Evie Barnes
Zapped Again! (1989). . . . . Miss Mitchell
Dead Sleep (1990; Australian). . . . . Maggie Healey
Repossessed (1990). . . . . Nancy Aglet
Fatal Bond (1991; Australian) . . . . Leonie
•• 0:25—Brief right breast out of her slip, while making love on top of Joe in bed.
Double Blast (1993) . . . . Claudia
Sorceress (1994) . . . . Amelia
Prey of the Jaguar (1996). . . . . Cody Johnson
Scream (1996). . . . . Obnoxious Reporter

Made for TV Movies:

Born Innocent (1974) . . . . Chris Parker
Sarah T.: Portrait of a Teenage Alcoholic (1975). . . . . Sarah
Sweet Hostage (1975). . . . . Doris Mae Withers
Calendar Girl, Cop, Killer? The Bambi Bembenek Story (1992)
. . . . Jane Mader
Perry Mason: The Case of the Heartbroken Bride (1992)
. . . . Hannah Hawkes

• *Blair, Lindsay*

a.k.a. Lynsey Ames.

Films:

Illicit Confessions (1997). . . . . Jo
••• 0:51—Breasts and buns, while making love with Mark on the floor in front of the fireplace.

Made for Cable TV:

Intimate Sessions: Karen (1998; Showtime). . . . . Karen
••• 0:06—Breasts, while making love with Andrew in bed.
••• 0:13—Buns and breasts, while making love with Andrew in supply closet.
•• 0:20—In black bra, then breasts and buns, while making love with Andrew in restaurant supply closet.

Blaisdell, Deborah

a.k.a. Adult film actress Tracey Adams.

Films:

The Lost Empire (1983) . . . . Girl Recruit
• 0:42—Brief buns and breasts, turning over on exam table.
Screen Test (1986) . . . . Dancer
• 1:20—Brief breasts, twice, dancing on stage. Long shot.
Student Affairs (1987). . . . . Kelly
••• 0:26—Breasts sitting up in bed talking to a guy.
Wildest Dreams (1987) . . . . Joan Peabody
• 1:10—Brief breasts during fight on floor with two other women.
Wimps (1987) . . . . Roxanne Chandless
• 1:22—Brief breasts and buns taking off clothes and getting into bed with Francis in bedroom.
Enrapture (1989) . . . . Martha
••• 0:10—Breasts undressing in her apartment with Keith.
•• 0:17—Left breast, in bed with Keith, then brief breasts.

Blake, Megan

Films:

Invasion U.S.A. (1985). . . . . Girl Friend
It Takes Two (1988). . . . . Megan
Mortuary Academy (1988) . . . . Tammy
Pass the Ammo (1988) . . . . Cherry
Infinity (1989). . . . . Karen
• 0:40—Very brief breasts, while bathing in pond.
• 1:20—Brief buns and side of right breast, while being carried by the guy. (It looks like there is tape over her nipples.)
Digital Man (1995) . . . . Lt. Thompson
Dream Man (1995) . . . . Ballet Mistress

Blake, Stephanie

a.k.a. Stella Blalack, Cimmaron and Rosalind Moreland.

Films:

The Big Bet (1985) . . . . Mrs. Roberts
••• 0:04—Breasts sitting on bed, then making love with Chris.
•• 0:37—Nude on bed with Chris. Shot at fast speed, he runs between bedrooms.
•• 0:59—Full frontal nudity in bed again. Shot at fast speed.

The Sure Thing (1985) . . . . Barmaid
Ferris Bueller's Day Off (1986) . . . . Singing Nurse
Over the Top (1987) . . . . Ticket Agent
Danger Zone II: Reaper's Revenge (1988)
. . . . Tattooed Topless Dancer
••• 0:47—Breasts, dancing on stage in bikini bottoms.
The Invisible Maniac (1990) . . . . Mrs. Cello
•• 0:42—Breasts opening her blouse for Chet.
•• 0:52—Breasts in her office trying to seduce Dr. Smith. Nice close up of right breast.
Whore (1991) . . . . Stripper in Big T's
a.k.a. If you're afraid to say it... Just see it
• 0:35—Buns, in G-string on stage.
••• 0:36—Breasts, dancing on stage in a club.
The Mambo Kings (1992) . . . . Stripper

Blakely, Susan *

Films:
Savages (1972) . . . . Cecily
The Way We Were (1973) . . . . Judianne
The Lords of Flatbush (1974) . . . . Jane Bradshaw
The Towering Inferno (1974) . . . . Patty Simmons
Capone (1975) . . . . Iris Crawford
•• 1:13—Breasts, taking off her clothes outside in front of Ben Gazzara.
• 1:22—Left breast, while lying in bed with Gazzara.
••• 1:23—Nude, getting out of bed and getting dressed, then more breasts while fooling around with Gazzara.
Report to the Commissioner (1975) . . . . Patty Butler
• 1:07—Brief buns, running around in apartment with Slick.
• 1:08—Brief breasts, taking off robe and getting into shower while Michael Moriarty tries to hide.
Airport '79: The Concorde (1979) . . . . Maggie
Over the Top (1987) . . . . Christine Hawk
Blackmail (1991) . . . . Lucinda Sullivan
Made for Cable Movies:
Wildflower (1991; Lifetime) . . . . Ada Guthrie
Color Me Perfect (1996; Lifetime) . . . . Linda
Made for Cable TV:
The Hitchhiker: Remembering Melody (1984; HBO)
. . . . Melody
••• 0:17—Right breast in shower with Ted and brief breasts in the bathtub.
Miniseries:
Rich Man, Poor Man (1976) . . . . Julie Prescott Abbott Jordache
Made for TV Movies:
Broken Angel (1988) . . . . Catherine Coburn
Ladykillers (1988) . . . . Lilah Corbett
The Incident (1989) . . . . Billie
Murder Times Seven (1990) . . . . Gert Kiley
And the Sea Will Tell (1991) . . . . Gail Bugliosi
Against Her Will: An Incident in Baltimore (1992) . . . . Billie
Intruders (1992) . . . . Leigh Holland
No Child of Mine (1993) . . . . Peggy Young
Honor Thy Father & Mother (1994) . . . . Abramson
Co-Ed Call Girl (1996) . . . . Teri Halbert

Blakiston, Caroline

Films:
The Magic Christian (1970; British) . . . . Esther
Sunday, Bloody Sunday (1971) . . . . Rowing Wife
• 1:09—Brief right breast in open dress during fight at party.
The Return of the Jedi (1983) . . . . Mon Mothma

Blanchard, Vanessa

Films:
Witchfire (1986) . . . . Liz
•• 0:52—Brief breasts in bed and then the shower.
Uphill All the Way (1987) . . . . Velma

Blaze, Roxanne

See: Bellomo, Sara.

Blee, Debra

Films:
The Beach Girls (1982) . . . . Sarah
••• 1:22—Brief breasts opening her swimsuit top on the beach.
Savage Streets (1984) . . . . Rachel
Sloane (1984) . . . . Cynthia Thursby
• 0:15—Very brief breasts during attempted rape.
The Malibu Bikini Shop (1985) . . . . Jane
Hamburger—The Motion Picture (1986) . . . . Mia Vunk

Blondi

Adult film actress.
a.k.a. Marjorie Miller and Blondi Bee.
Films:
Party Favors (1987) . . . . Bobbi
•• 0:04—Breasts in dressing room, taking off red top and putting on black one.
• 0:23—Brief breasts when blouse pops off while delivering pizza.
••• 0:27—Breasts and buns in G-string doing a strip routine outside.
• 0:31—Brief breasts flapping her blouse to cool off.
••• 1:04—Breasts doing a strip routine in a little girl outfit. Buns, in G-string. More breasts after.
• 1:16—Nude taking off swimsuit next to pool during final credits.
Video Tapes:
The Girls of Malibu (1986) . . . . Marjorie
••• 0:06—In two piece swimsuit. Breasts riding a motorcycle. Full frontal nudity posing on it. Nude outside.
In Search of the Perfect 10 (1986) . . . . Perfect Girl #3
••• 0:14—Breasts in back of car.
Best Buns on the Beach (1987) . . . . Blondi
••• 0:06—Breasts, stripping on stage during dance routine. Buns, in G-string.
•• 0:52—Breasts and buns with all the contestants during review.
••• 0:53—Breasts and buns in final pose-off.
•• 0:57—Breasts and buns winning the contest.
••• 0:58—More slow motion breasts and bun shots during the final credits.
Night of the Living Babes (1987)
. . . . Mondo Zombie Girl Darlene
••• 0:12—Breasts wearing dark purple wig and long gloves, with the other Mondo Zombie Girls.
••• 0:16—More breasts and buns in bed with Buck.
• 0:50—Breasts on the couch with the other Zombie Girls.
• 0:52—Breasts on the couch again.
The Perfect Body Contest (1987) . . . . Jennifer
••• 0:46—Buns, in two piece swimsuit, then breasts.
• 0:50—Breasts on stage with the other contestants.
High Society Centerspread Video #3: Blondi (1990)
. . . . Herself

Bloom, Claire

Films:
The Illustrated Man (1969) . . . . Felicia

Three into Two Won't Go (1969; British)..... Frances Howard
A Severed Head (1971; British) ....Honor Klein
- • 1:10—Breasts, while leaning up, then right breast while sitting up in bed with Richard Attenborough.

A Doll's House (1973; British) ....Nora Helmer
Islands in the Stream (1977) .... Audrey
Clash of the Titans (1981)........................ Hera
Deja Vu (1984) .... Eleanor Harvey
Queenie (1987)...........................Vicky Kelley
Sammy and Rosie Get Laid (1987; British)............. Alice
Shameless (1994; British) ....Liz
Mighty Aphrodite (1995) .... Amanda's Mother
Daylight (1996)......................... Eleanor Trilling

Miniseries:
Brideshead Revisited (1981; British)......... Lady Marchmain

Made for TV Movies:
Promises to Keep (1985)........................... Sally
It's Nothing Personal (1993) .... Evelyn Whitloff

TV:
As the World Turns ....n.a.

Bloom, Lindsay

Films:
Cover Girl Models (1975) .... Claire
- • 0:11—Brief right breast, after taking off swimsuit top during photo session.
- • 0:32—Brief left breast, while putting on robe in bathroom.
- •• 0:57—Brief breasts, while struggling with bad guy.

Six Pack Annie (1975) .... Annie
Texas Detour (1977) .... Sugar McCarthy
French Quarter (1978) .. "Big Butt" Annie/Policewoman in Bar
H.O.T.S. (1979) ....Melody Ragmore
a.k.a. T & A Academy
- • 0:28—Very brief right breast on balcony.
- • 1:34—Brief breasts, while throwing football. (She's the quarterback.)

The Main Event (1979) ....Girl in Bed
The Happy Hooker Goes Hollywood (1980) .... Chris

TV:
Dallas (1982) .... Bonnie Robertson
Mike Hammer (1984-87) ....Velda

Blount, Lisa

Films:
9/30/55 (1977).............................Billie Jean
Dead and Buried (1981) .... Girl on the Beach
- • 0:06—Brief breasts on the beach getting her picture taken by a photographer.

An Officer and a Gentleman (1982) ....Lynette Pomeroy
Radioactive Dreams (1984).................. Miles Archer
Cease Fire (1985) .... Paula Murphy
Cut and Run (1985; Italian)................... Fran Hudson
What Waits Below (1986) ....Leslie Peterson
Nightflyers (1987)........................... Audrey
Prince of Darkness (1987) .... Catherine
South of Reno (1987) .... Anette Clark
Great Balls of Fire (1989)..................... Lois Brown
Out Cold (1989) .... Phyllis
Blind Fury (1990) .... Annie Winchester
Femme Fatale (1990) ....Jenny
Judicial Consent (1994)..................... Theresa Lewis
Stalked (1994; Canadian/Australian) .... Janie

Made for Cable TV:
The Hitchhiker: One Last Prayer (HBO) .... Miranda

Made for TV Movies:
Unholy Matrimony (1988) ....Karen Stockwell
In Sickness and in Health (1992) ....Carmen
Murder Between Friends (1994) ....Janet Myers

TV:
Sons & Daughters (1991) ....Mary Ruth
Profit (1996) .... Bobbi

• *Blue, Skye*

Adult film actress.

Films:
Sex and the Single Alien (1993).................. Ruth
- •• 0:45—Breasts and buns, while dancing on stage with Merry.
- •• 1:08—Breasts in white lingerie while dancing on stage again with Merry.

Dark Secrets (1995)......................... Dominatrix
Boogie Nights (1997)...... Uncredited Actress in Hot Tub 2
- • 1:42—Buns and breasts while in hot tub with another actress during filming of a movie. (She's the blonde.)

Blueberry

Films:
One Man Force (1989) .... Santiago's Girlfriend

Video Tapes:
Rock Video Girls 2 (1992) .... Herself
- • 0:28—Buns in G-string under sheer body stocking.

Blye, Margaret

Films:
Waterhole 3 (1967)....................Billie Copperod
The Sporting Club (1971) ....Janey
- • 0:31—Breasts, sunbathing on rock when seen by James. Medium long shot.

Ash Wednesday (1973) .... Kate
The Entity (1983) ....Cindy Nash

TV:
Kodiak (1974) .... Mandy

Bockrath, Tina *

Films:
Totally Exposed (1991) ....Lillian Tucker
- •• 0:00—Buns and breasts, turning over on tanning table during opening credits.
- • 0:01—Brief full frontal nudity, lying on tanning table.
- •• 0:03—Briefly nude, while getting out of bed and putting on towel, talking to Bill.
- ••• 1:01—Full frontal nudity, turning over on tanning table. Full frontal nudity, dropping her towel in reception area.
- ••• 1:02—Buns, walking back to the room. Nude, taking off towel and lying on massage table.
- ••• 1:04—Nude, sitting up on table and standing up with Bill.

Made for Cable TV:
Tales From the Crypt: Abra Cadaver (1991; HBO) ....Paula/Cadaver
- • 0:04—Breasts (in B&W) pretending to be a corpse during practical joke.

Video Tapes:
Playboy Video Calendar 1991 (1990) .... January
- ••• 0:01—Nude.

Sexy Lingerie II (1990).........................Model
Playboy's Girls of Spring Break (1991) .... Herself
- ••• 0:30—Breasts and buns in panties, while dancing in Western theme segment with Brittney Powell.

Bodnar, Jenna

Films:

Spirit of the Night (1994) . . . . .Tara Wexford

- • 0:01—Brief buns in panties and brief partial right breast, while making out with a guy in a daydream.
- • 0:18—In bra, then brief breasts, while making out with Michelle and Alek on sofa.
- • 0:27—Brief breasts, when the spirit takes off her clothes and enters her body.
- • 0:28—Buns while in the shower. Brief breast, while examining herself in the bathroom, very brief full frontal nudity after knocking a glass off the shelf.
- ••• 0:42—Full frontal nudity, while caressing herself outdoors at night. Long scene.
- • 0:47—Very brief full frontal nudity in bedroom during flashback.
- ••• 0:49—In wet body suit, then nude, while posing for photographs, then making love with Jacob. Great, long scene.
- • 1:11—Breasts in B&W photos.

The Affair (1995) . . . . Alexis

- •• 0:06—Full frontal nudity, after dropping towel in her bedroom.
- ••• 1:03—Full frontal nudity, while making love with Linda in bedroom.

Cellblock Sisters: Banished Behind Bars (1995) . . Manny

- •• 0:30—Buns and breasts, while sitting on bench with other inmates when first entering prison.
- •• 0:44—Full frontal nudity, while in the showers with her girl gang, giving Gail Harris a hard time.

Friend of the Family 2 (1996). . . . . Maddy

a.k.a. Innocence Betrayed

- • 0:21—Left breast when starting to make love with Alex in bed.
- ••• 0:30—In lingerie, then breasts and buns, while making love with Alex in bed.

Midnight Temptations 2 (1997). . . . . Southern Woman

- ••• 0:50—Breasts, while making love with the Confederate soldier.

Made for Cable Movies:

Breast Men (1997; HBO) . . . . .Capsulotomy Patient

Made for Cable TV:

Love Street: Truth of the Heart (1995; Showtime)
. . . . .Vanessa

- •• 0:02—Brief buns, after dropping towel, then breasts while in bathtub talking with Alex.
- ••• 0:04—Breasts, while making love with Alex in bathtub and on bed.
- •• 0:05—Buns and right breast, after getting out of bed.
- ••• 0:23—Breasts, while making love with the terrorist.

Erotic Confessions: The Address (1996; Cinemax)
. . . . Celeste

- •• 0:09—Breasts, while making love with John in the bathtub.
- ••• 0:10—Buns and breasts, getting up off the floor and sitting on bed. Nude, getting into bed with John.
- •• 0:13—Full frontal nudity, while making love with John in bed and standing with him on the floor.
- • 0:15—Very brief breasts in bed. Seen in reflection in the mirror.

Erotic Confessions: Off the Menu (1997; Cinemax)
. . . . Annabelle

- •• 0:20—Full frontal nudity, while making love with Giddeon in the kitchen. Sometimes playing with food.

Intimate Sessions: Joy (1998; Cinemax) . . . . Joy

- •• 0:06—Breasts, while caressing herself and talking on the phone with Sean.
- ••• 0:11—In white bra and panties, then breasts, while talking on the phone, then making love in bed with Sean. Long scene.
- •• 0:19—In bra and panties, then breasts and buns, while making love in bed with Sean.

Intimate Sessions: Renee (1998; Cinemax). . . . . Susan

Bogenshutz, April *

Spokesmodel contestant on *Star Search.*

Films:

Raw Justice (1994) . . . . Donna

a.k.a. Good Cop, Bad Cop

- • 0:08—In bra and panties, taking off her clothes. Buns and right breast while getting into the shower.
- ••• 0:09—Full frontal nudity while taking a shower and getting out, then struggling with the killer.

Bohrer, Corinne

Films:

The Beach Girls (1982) . . . . .Champagne Girl
I, the Jury (1982) . . . . .Soap Opera Actress
My Favorite Year (1982). . . . . Bonnie
Zapped! (1982) . . . . Cindy
Joysticks (1983) . . . . Patsy Rutter
Surf II (1984) . . . . .Cindy Lou
Cross My Heart (1987) . . . . Susan
Police Academy 4: Citizens on Patrol (1987) . . . . Laura
Stewardess School (1987) . . . . Cindy Adams
Vice Versa (1988). . . . . Sam
Aurora: Operation Intercept (1994) . . . . Sharon Pruett

a.k.a. Operation Intercept

The Coriolis Effect (1994) . . . . Suzy

- • 0:01—Partial breasts, while making love with Dana Ashbrook on kitchen table.

Heidi Fleiss: Hollywood Madam (1995; British/Canadian)
. . . . Actor

Made for Cable Movies:

Dead Solid Perfect (1988; HBO) . . . . Janie Rimmer

- ••• 0:31—Nude, getting out of bed to get some ice for Randy Quaid. Nice scene!

Made for Cable TV:

Dream On: What I Did for Lust (1991; HBO) . . . . Chloe

Made for TV Movies:

Revenge of the Nerds IV: Nerds in Love (1994)
. . . . Jeanie Humphrey

TV:

E/R (1984-85) . . . . .Nurse Cory Smith
Free Spirit (1989-90) .Winnie Goodwin
Man of the People (1991) . . . . Constance
Double Rush (1995). . . . . .Zoe

Bohringer, Romane

Daughter of French actor Richard Bohringer.

Films:

Savage Nights (1992; French). . . . . Laura

a.k.a. Les Nuits Fauves

- • 0:29—Half of left breast, while making love in bed with Jean.
- • 0:30—Left breast.
- • 0:34—Full frontal nudity while going to closet to get a T-shirt. Dark, medium long shot.
- ••• 0:41—Left breasts, then breasts, while in bed with Jean.

The Accompanist (1993; French). . . . . Sophie Vasseur

a.k.a. L'accompagnatrice

Colonel Chabert (1994; French) . . . . Sophie

Total Eclipse (1995; French/British) . . . . Mathilde
• 0:37—Very brief partial left breast, when covering herself up after breast feeding.
••• 0:51—Buns, while lying face down on bed, then breasts, with David Thewlis in bed and out.

*Boisson, Christine **

Films:

Emmanuelle (1974; French) . . . . Marie-Ange
(R-rated version reviewed.)
•• 0:16—Full frontal nudity diving into swimming pool. Also buns, under water.
••• 0:19—Breasts outside in hanging chair with Sylvia Kristel.
Identification of a Woman (1983; Italian) . . . . Ida
Le Passage (1986; French). . . . . Catherine Diez
Dreamers (1987). . . . . Sima
Sandra (1989; French) . . . . Sandra

Bolin, Kim

Films:

Bad Love (1992) . . . . Porn Actress #1
Witchcraft V: Dance with the Devil (1993) . . . . . Secretary
••• 1:09—Breasts, while making love with the Reverend on the sofa.

*Bolling, Tiffany **

Films:

Tony Rome (1967) . . . . Photo Girl
The Marriage of a Young Stockbroker (1971)
. . . . Girl in the Rain
Bonnie's Kids (1973) . . . . Ellie
•• 0:21—Breasts, modeling in office.
• 1:16—Brief right breast making love in bed.
Wicked, Wicked (1973) . . . . Lisa James
The Centerfold Girls (1974) . . . . Vera
• 1:02—Brief breasts in photograph.
••• 1:12—Breasts in the shower.
• 1:21—Brief breasts in motel bed getting raped by two guys after they drug her beer.
The Wild Party (1975) . . . . Kate
Kingdom of the Spiders (1977) . . . . Diane Ashley
The Vals (1982). . . . . Valley Attorney and Parent
Love Scenes (1984). . . . . Val
a.k.a. Ecstacy
•• 0:01—Side view of left breast in bed with Peter.
••• 0:06—Breasts getting photographed by Britt Ekland in the house.
• 0:09—Brief breasts opening her bathrobe to show Peter.
• 0:12—Breasts in bathtub with Peter.
••• 0:19—Breasts lying in bed talking with Peter, then making love.
•• 0:43—Breasts acting in a movie when Rick opens her blouse.
•• 0:57—Nude behind shower door, then breasts getting out and talking to Peter.
•• 0:59—Breasts making love tied up on bed with Rick during filming of movie.
•• 1:07—Breasts, then full frontal nudity acting with Elizabeth during filming of movie.
•• 1:17—Full frontal nudity getting out of pool.
•• 1:26—Breasts with Peter on the bed.
Open House (1987) . . . . Judy Roberts

Made for TV Movies:

Key West (1973) . . . . Ruth

TV:

The New People (1969-70). . . . . Susan Bradley

Bonet, Lisa

Ex-wife of singer Lenny Kravitz.

Films:

Angel Heart (1987) . . . . Epiphany Proudfoot
(Original Unedited Version reviewed.)
• 1:01—Brief left breast, twice, in open dress during voodoo ceremony.
••• 1:27—Breasts in bed with Rourke. It gets kind of bloody.
• 1:32—Breasts in bathtub.
• 1:48—Breasts in bed, dead. Covered with a bloody sheet.
Bank Robber (1993). . . . . Priscilla
•• 0:36—Buns, while lying on bed, waiting for Patrick Dempsey.
•• 0:37—Breasts, while making love in bed with Dempsey.
•• 1:05—Brief breasts while making love in bed with Dempsey.
Dead Connection (1993) . . . . Catherine Briggs
• 0:58—Breasts, while making love in bed with Michael Madsen.
New Eden (1994) . . . . Lily
• 1:02—Brief back side of left breast while in bed with Stephen Baldwin.

TV:

The Cosby Show (1984-87). . . . . Denise Huxtable
A Different World (1987-89) . . . . Denise Huxtable
The Cosby Show (1989-92). . . . . Denise Huxtable-Kendall

Bonet, Nai

Films:

Soul Hustler (1975) . . . . Helena
• 0:54—Very, very brief buns, when putting on night shirt in bedroom with Fabian Forte.
The Greatest (1977; U.S./British) . . . . Suzie Gomez
Fairytales (1979). . . . . Sheherazade
• 0:29—Buns and very brief left breast doing a belly dance and rubbing oil on herself.
Nocturna (1979). . . . . Nocturna

Bonham Carter, Helena

Films:

A Room with a View (1986; British) . . . . Lucy Honeychurch
Lady Jane (1987; British) . . . . Lady Jane Grey
• 1:19—Breasts kneeling on the bed with Guilford.
• 2:09—Side view of right breast and very, very brief breasts sitting by fire with Guilford.
Maurice (1987; British) . . . . Young Lady at Cricket Match
Getting It Right (1989) . . . . Minerva Munday
•• 0:18—Breasts a couple of times in bed talking to Gavin. It's hard to recognize her because she has lots of make-up on her face.
Hamlet (1990; British/French) . . . . Ophelia
Howards End (1992) . . . . Helen Schlegel
Where Angels Fear to Tread (1992) . . . . Caroline Abbott
Francesco (1994; Italian/German) . . . . Chiara
Mary Shelley's Frankenstein (1994) . . . . Elizabeth
Mighty Aphrodite (1995) . . . . Amanda
Twelfth Night (1996; British). . . . . Olivia
The Wings of the Dove (1997; British) . . . . Kate Croy
••• 1:30—Nude, while sitting on bed in bedroom, then making love with Merton.

Made for TV Movies:

A Hazard of Hearts (1987). . . . . Serena Staverly
Fatal Deception: Mrs. Lee Harvey Oswald (1993)
. . . . Marina Oswald
Mystery! A Dark-Adapted Eye (1995). . . . . Faith Severn
Merlin (1998) . . . . Morgan le Fey

Bonnaire, Sandrine

Films:

A Nos Amours (1984; French) . . . . Suzanne
- • 0:17—Brief breasts, pulling dress top down to put on nightgown.
- •• 0:34—Breasts sitting up in bed talking to Bernard. Brief side view of buns.
- • 0:42—Very brief side view of left breast while waking up in bed.
- • 0:57—Very brief lower frontal nudity, while getting out of bed with Martine and her boyfriend. Long shot of buns, while hugging Bernard in the background (out of focus).

Police (1985; French). . . . . .Lydie
- ••• 0:49—Full frontal nudity, undressing in front of Gérard Depardieu, then getting out of the shower.

Vagabond (1985; French) . . . . Mona
Monsieur Hire (1990; French) . . . . Alice
Prague (1991; French/British) . . . . .Elena
The Plague (1992; French/British). . . . . .Martine Rambert
- ••• 0:53—Breasts, while in bathroom, examining herself for the plague.

La Cérémonie (1996) . . . . Sophie

Bonner, Gillian *

Video Tapes:

Playboy Video Calendar 1997 (1996) . . . . .November
- ••• 0:45—In lingerie and nude, while posing indoors.
- ••• 0:46—In lingerie and nude, while posing in a warehouse.

Bonner, Sharona

See: LeBeau, Becky.

Bonvoisin, Berangere

Films:

Good Morning, Babylon (1987; Italian/French) . . . . .Mrs. Moglie Griffith
La Lectrice (1989; French) . . . . . Joel's Mother/Hotel Waitress
a.k.a. The Reader
- • 1:15—Brief breasts while sitting in bed with Jocelyne and a guy.

Dr. Petiot (1994; French). . . . . Georgette Petiot

Boorman, Katrine

Films:

Excalibur (1981; British) . . . . Igrayne
- • 0:14—Right breast, then breasts in front of the fire when Uther tricks her into thinking that he is her husband and makes love to her.

Dream One (1984; British/French). . . . Duchka/Nemo's Mother
Marche A L'Hombre (1984; French). . . . . Katrina
Hope and Glory (1987; British) . . . . Charity
Camille Claudel (1989; French) . . . . .Jessie
French Twist (1996; French) . . . . Emily Crumble

Booth, Connie

Films:

Monty Python and the Holy Grail (1974; British) . . . . The Witch
Romance with a Double Bass (1974; British) . . . . Princess Costanza
- •• 0:10—Very brief buns, going into the water to retrieve her fishing float, then full frontal nudity while yelling at a guy who steals her clothes.
- •• 0:11—Full frontal nudity, while walking around, looking for her clothes.
- ••• 0:18—Breasts, while holding her hand over her eyes.
- •• 0:20—Brief left breast, while reaching up to close the bass case.

84 Charring Cross Road (1987) . . . . Lady from Delaware
Hawks (1988; British). . . . . .Nurse Jarvis
High Spirits (1988; U.S./British) .Marge
Leon the Pig Farmer (1993; British) . . . . Yvonne Chadwick

Miniseries:

The Buccaneers (1995; U.S./British). . . . . Miss March

Made for TV Movies:

How to Irritate People (1968; British). . . . . Various

TV:

Fawlty Towers (British). . . . . Polly

Borel, Annik

Films:

Weekend with the Babysitter (1970) . . . . .Doris
Truck Turner (1974) . . . . Stalingrad
- • 0:38—Brief breasts, twice, in slow motion while running to stab Isaac Hayes' partner.

Boris, Angel *

Films:

Exit (1995) . . . . .Dancer 2
- ••• 0:15—Breasts and buns in green T-back, while dancing on stage with another dancer.

South Beach Academy (1997) . . . . .Extra

TV:

Beverly Hills, 90210 (1997-98). . . . . Emma Bennett

Video Tapes:

Playboy's The Girls of Hawaiian Tropic (1994) . . . . Moonlit Beach
- ••• 0:06—Nude, while dancing at the beach at night.

Playboy's Girls of South Beach (1996). . . . . Herself
- ••• 0:29—Nude while doing various things.

Wet & Wild VIII: Bottoms Up (1996) . . . . .Playmate
Playboy Video Calendar 1998 (1997) . . . . November
- ••• 0:44—Nude, while posing outdoors.
- ••• 0:47—Nude, while posing in an auto showroom.

Botsford, Sara

Films:

By Design (1982; Canadian) . . . . Angie
- • 0:23—Full frontal nudity in the ocean. Long shot, hard to see anything.
- • 1:08—Brief side view of left breast making love in bed while talking on the phone.

Deadly Eyes (1982; Canadian). . . . . Kelly Leonard
- • 0:42—Breasts several times, making love with Paul.

Still of the Night (1982). . . . . .Gail Phillips
Murder By Phone (1983; Canadian). . . . . Ridley Taylor
a.k.a. Bells
Jumpin' Jack Flash (1986) . . . . Lady Sarah Billings
Legal Eagles (1986) . . . . .Barbara
The Gunrunner (1989; Canadian) . . . . Maude

Made for Cable Movies:

The Fixer (1997) . . . . Bonnie

Made for Cable TV:

E.N.G. (1989-90; Lifetime; Canadian) . . . . Ann Hildebrand

Made for TV Movies:

Fatal Memories (1992). . . . . Janice
My Breast (1994). . . . . Eve

TV:

As the World Turns . . . . Lilith McKechnie
Wright Verdicts (1995). . . . . Mercedes De Pedroso

Bouche, Sugar

Films:

Heavenly Bodies (1985)........................Stripper
- 0:16—Breasts doing stripper-gram for Steve.

Graveyard Shift (1987)................Fabulous Frannie
- ••• 0:12—Breasts doing a stripper routine on stage.
- • 0:24—Brief breasts in the shower.

Bouchet, Barbara *

Films:

A Global Affair (1964)............................Girl
Good Neighbor Sam (1964)..................Receptionist
Sex and the Single Girl (1964)...................Frannie
What a Way to Go (1964)...................Girl on Plane
In Harm's Way (1965)...................Liz Eddington
- • 0:05—Very, very brief right breast, while waving to Hugh O'Brian from the water (B&W).

Agent for H.A.R.M. (1966).....................Ava Vestak
Casino Royale (1967; British)................Moneypenny
Danger Route (1968; British)........................Mari
Sweet Charity (1969)..............................Ursula
Black Belly of the Tarantula (1972; Italian).........Maria Zani
Maniac Mansion (1972; Italian).......................n.a.
Cry of a Prostitute: Love Kills (1975; Italian)......Margie
- • 0:30—Brief left breast, lying in bed with Rico.
- • 0:31—Brief breasts in bed, with Rico when he starts making love with her.
- •• 0:50—Breasts in panties and robe, walking angrily around her room.

Down the Ancient Staircase (1975; Italian)............Carla
Blood Feast (1976; Italian)...........................n.a.
Duck in Orange Sauce (1976; Italian)................Patty
Sex with a Smile (1976; Italian)
........................"One for the Money" segment
- ••• 0:50—Breasts sitting up in bed with a guy in bed, then lying down, wearing glasses.

Death Rage (1978; Italian)..........................n.a.

Made for TV Movies:

The Scarlet and the Black (1983).............Minna Kappler

• Bouchez, Elodie

Films:

Tango (1993; French)...................Girl in Aeroplane
Wild Reeds (1994; French).......................Maite
- • 1:39—Brief right breast, while out in the woods with Henri, then brief partial right breast, while sitting on the ground. Very brief left breast after lying on her back just before Henri starts to feel her. Brief lower frontal nudity, while lying on her back.

The Proprietor (1996).........................Young Girl

Boulting, Ingrid

Daughter of British director Roy Boulting.

Films:

The Last Tycoon (1976)................Kathleen Moore
- • 0:56—Buns and side of right breast taking off her dress in unfinished beach house in front of Robert De Niro.
- •• 0:58—More buns, lying down afterwards.
- • 1:00—Buns, getting up and putting dress on. Very brief side of left breast.
- • 1:02—Brief right breast when De Niro takes her dress off.

Deadly Passion (1985)..............Martha Greenwood
- • 0:46—Brief buns taking off clothes and jumping into pool. Long shot.
- •• 0:47—Breasts getting out of pool and kissing Brent Huff. Right breast in bed.
- • 0:54—Breasts in whirlpool bath with Huff.
- ••• 1:02—Breasts, wearing white panties and massaging herself in front of a mirror.
- •• 1:31—Breasts taking off clothes and jumping into bed with Huff.

Bouquet, Carole

Model for *Chanel* cosmetics.

Films:

That Obscure Object of Desire (1977; French/Spanish)
....Conchita
- ••• 0:53—Breasts in bedroom.
- ••• 1:01—Breasts in bed with Fernando Rey.

For Your Eyes Only (1981)................Melina Havelock
Bingo Bongo (1983)...............................Laura
Dream One (1984; British/French)..............Rals-Akrai
Too Beautiful for You (1990; French).....Florence Barthelemy
A Business Affair (1993; British/French)......Kate Swallow
- • 0:37—Buns and right breast, while lying in bed next to Christopher Walken.
- • 1:11—Buns, while lying on tanning bed.

Tango (1993; French).....................Female Guest
Dead Tired (1995; French)........................Herself
a.k.a. Grosse Fatigue

Boushel, Joy

Films:

Pick-Up Summer (1979; Canadian)................Sally
- ••• 0:56—Breasts playing pinball, then running around.

Terror Train (1980; Canadian).......................Pet
- •• 0:49—Breasts, while wearing panties in sleeper room on train with Mo.

Quest For Fire (1981)......................Tribe Member
Humongous (1982; Canadian).............Donna Blake
- •• 0:09—Breasts looking out the window. More breasts in the room in the mirror.
- • 0:48—Breasts undoing her top to warm up Bert.

Thrillkill (1984)................................Maggie
The Fly (1986)................................Tawny
- • 0:54—Very brief breasts viewed from below when Jeff Goldblum pulls her by the arm to get her out of bed.

Keeping Track (1988).............................Judy
Look Who's Talking (1989)......................Melissa

Bow, Clara

Films:

Down to the Sea in Ships (1923)..............Dot Morgan
Dancing Mothers (1926).................Kitten Westcourt
Mantrap (1926)...................................Alverna
It (1927)......................................Betty Lou
Wings (1927)..........................Mary Preston
- • 1:22—It looks like very, very brief left breast (blurry) when military guys walk in on her and she stands up straight while in front of a mirror.

The Wild Party (1929).......................Stella Ames

Bowker, Judi

Films:

Brother Sun, Sister Moon (1973; British/Italian).........Clare
East of Elephant Rock (1976; British)..........Eve Proudfoot
Clash of the Titans (1981)..................Andromeda
- • 1:41—Buns and partial side view of right breast getting out of bath. Don't see her face.

The Shooting Party (1985; British)............Olivia Lilburn

Miniseries:

Ellis Island (1984)..................Georgiana O'Donnell

Anna Karenina (1985) . . . . Kitty
Sins (1986) . . . . Natalie Junot
Made for TV Movies:
In This House of Brede (1975) . . . . Joanne
Count Dracula (1977; British) . . . . Mina

*Bowser, Sue **

Films:
Stripes (1981) . . . . Mud Wrestler
Doctor Detroit (1983) . . . . Dream Girl
Into the Night (1985) . . . . Girl on Boat
•• 0:24—Breasts taking off blouse with Jake on his boat after Michelle Pfeiffer leaves.

Boyd, Tanya

Films:
Black Shampoo (1976) . . . . Brenda
Ilsa, Harem Keeper of the Oil Sheiks (1976) . . . . Satin
The Happy Hooker Goes Hollywood (1980) . . . . Sylvie
• 0:39—Brief breasts in jungle room when an older customer accidentally comes in.
Wholly Moses (1980) . . . . Princess
Jo Jo Dancer, Your Life Is Calling (1986) . . . . Alicia
Loving Lulu (1992) . . . . Background
Made for Cable Movies:
The Disappearance of Christina (1993) . . . . Banker
TV:
Days of Our Lives (1994-) . . . . Celeste

Boyle, Lara Flynn

Films:
Poltergeist III (1988) . . . . Donna Gardner
How I Got Into College (1989) . . . . Jessica Kailo
May Wine (1990; French) . . . . Cammie
The Rookie (1990) . . . . Sarah
The Dark Backward (1991) . . . . Rosarita
Eye of the Storm (1991) . . . . Sandra
Mobsters (1991) . . . . Mara Motes
a.k.a. Mobsters—The Evil Empire
Equinox (1992) . . . . Berverly Franks
Red Rock West (1992) . . . . Suzanne
Wayne's World (1992) . . . . Stacy
Where The Day Takes You (1992) . . . . Heather
The Temp (1993) . . . . Kris Bolin
Baby's Day Out (1994) . . . . Laraine
Farmer & Chase (1994) . . . . Hillary
• 0:52—Very brief side right breast, when rolling over underneath Todd Field in bed.
The Road to Wellville (1994) . . . . Ida Muntz
•• 0:16—Breasts, while sitting on bed in Matthew Broderick's fantasy.
••• 0:55—Breasts, while sitting in bed, talking with Broderick. Nice long scene, although she's made up to look sick.
Threesome (1994) . . . . Alex
• 0:52—Buns, while walking and diving into lake to go skinny dipping.
• 0:54—Partial buns, while lying on lake shore with Baldwin and Charles.
• 1:21—Partial buns, while lying in bed between Baldwin and Charles.
The Big Squeeze (1996) . . . . Tanya
Afterglow (1997) . . . . Marianne
Made for Cable Movies:
Past Tense (1994; Showtime) . . . . . . Tory Bass/Sabrina James
• 0:10—In black bra with Scott Glenn. Brief breasts two times. You don't see her face very well and one is a medium long shot.
• 0:13—Supposedly her breasts, while making love with another guy during video playback on TV.
• 0:15—Very brief buns in flashback while on top of Glenn on the floor. Medium long shot.
• 0:28—Breasts, several times, during video playback on TV. Don't see her face very well.
Cafe Society (1995; Showtime) . . . . Pat Ward
• 0:18—Brief side view of right breast, while making love with Frank Whaley. Don't see her face.
Miniseries:
Amerika (1987) . . . . Jessie Bradford
TV:
Twin Peaks (1990-91) . . . . Donna Hayward
The Practice (1997-) . . . . Helen Gamble

*Boyle, Lisa **

a.k.a. Cassandra Leigh.
Films:
Midnight Witness (1992) . . . . Heidi
•• 1:11—Breasts, while getting out of bed. Buns and breasts some more, seen in mirror.
Concealed Weapon (1994) . . . . Polish Emigree
•• 0:07—Breasts in ripped open dress top, while getting molested by the American guy.
•• 0:10—Breasts in open dress top when the American guy caresses her breasts with gun before killing her.
I Like to Play Games (1994) . . . . Suzanne
•• 0:13—Breasts, while making out with Michael in alley.
••• 0:15—In black bra and panties in bed, then breasts and partial lower frontal nudity.
• 0:24—In white lingerie, then wet white lingerie while in bathtub with Michael.
••• 0:25—Full frontal nudity while in bed with Michael.
•• 0:32—Breasts and partial lower frontal nudity in black leather strap outfit in Michael's office.
••• 0:35—Breasts and buns in leather strap outfit in motel room with Michael (including dropping hot wax on him).
••• 0:40—Breasts and lower frontal nudity, while making love.
• 0:44—Left breast, while playing with an ice cube in limousine.
••• 0:52—Breasts and buns, while watching Michael make love with Tiffany.
••• 0:54—Breasts and buns, while joining in and making love with Michael and Tiffany.
• 1:02—Left breast, while making love with Michael in punk club.
••• 1:06—Nude, while making love outside with Michael next to the pool.
• 1:16—Brief right breast in ripped blouse, during fight with Michael.
• 1:21—Breasts, while in bed, when Michael wakes her up.
• 1:25—Left breast, in pulled down blouse in pool during struggle with Michael.
Midnight Tease (1994) . . . . Samantha
•• 0:02—Breasts in lingerie outfit, walking up to her stepfather and slicing his throat.
• 0:11—Buns in T-back and in bra, while undressing, then lying on bed.
•• 0:12—Breasts in lingerie outfit, while killing her stepfather in dream.

•• 0:24—Breasts, after opening her leather jacket on table in front of Dr. Saul.
••• 0:37—Breasts, while making love with Dr. Saul in his office.
••• 0:44—Breasts and buns in T-back while dancing on stage with Mantra.
•• 0:47—Breasts while talking with Mantra in dressing room.
•• 0:50—Breasts in lingerie outfit in dream, while slitting Mantra's throat.
••• 0:53—Full frontal nudity while taking a shower behind clear plastic curtain.
•• 0:58—In white bra and panties, then breasts and buns after stripping out of schoolgirl outfit. Intercut with flashbacks of her stepfather's suicide.

Alien Terminator (1995) . . . . Rachel
•• 0:18—Breasts, while making out with Pete in maintenance tunnel.
••• 0:19—More breasts, while making out some more.
•• 0:31—Breasts, while taking a shower, then putting on T-shirt.

Bad Boys (1995) . . . . Girl Decoy

Caged Heat 3000 (1995) . . . . Kira
•• 0:14—Breasts and buns in shower scene.
••• 0:34—Breasts, while being fondled by a guy when she's asleep.

Criminal Hearts (1995) . . . . Claire

Dream Master: The Erotic Invader (1995) . . . . September
•• 1:17—Breasts, while tied to a bed by Devora.
••• 1:20—Buns and breasts, while making love on top of Grant in bed.

Friend of the Family (1995) . . . . Montana
a.k.a. Elke's Erotic Nights
(Unrated version reviewed.)
•• 0:02—Breasts, while making out with a guy in the pool at night, then during argument with Linda.
••• 0:23—Breasts and buns, while making love outside on the grass at night with another guy.
••• 0:35—Breasts, while making love in the back seat of a convertible car with a guy.

Showgirls (1995). . . . . Sonny
(NC-17 version reviewed.)

Starquest (1995) . . . . Veiled Woman
••• 0:45—Breasts while posing in desert during virtual reality session.

The Nutty Professor (1996). . . . . Sexy Girl

Face/Off (1997) . . . . Cindee

Lost Highway (1997) . . . . Marian
• 2:04—Brief breasts, while acting in a movie. (She's on the right while another woman is on the left.) B&W.

Made for Cable Movies:

When the Bullet Hits the Bone (1996; Showtime) . . . . Uncredited Desert Girl
•• 0:25—Brief breasts, while in desert in Michelle Johnson's vision.

Made for Cable TV:

Red Shoe Diaries: Double or Nothing (1993; Showtime) . . . . Uncredited Dancer
(Available on the video tape *Red Shoe Diaries 5: Weekend Pass.*)
• 0:11—Brief breasts and buns in T-back, dancing in bar and putting a blindfold on Tommy.

Red Shoe Diaries: Emily's Dance (1993; Showtime) . . . . European Version Dancer
••• 0:25—Breasts and buns in T-back, while dancing in music video.

Sex, Shock and Censorship in the 90's (1993; Showtime) . . . . Psychiatrist's Receptionist
•• 0:42—Breasts in Robert Hays' daydream when the pixelation effect to censor her breasts has a hard time keeping up with her movements.

Dream On: The Courtship of Martin's Father (1994; HBO) . . . . Lisa
••• 0:03—Breasts, after taking off her lingerie in Martin's bedroom. Very brief buns, going into bathroom.

Love Street: The Mechanics of Desire (1994; Showtime) . . . . Lizabeth
• 0:02—Brief frontal nudity, putting on robe.
••• 0:12—In black bra, then breasts, making love with Guy, while her husband watches.
•• 0:19—Full frontal nudity, making love with Roxie in bathroom, while watched by Boyle's husband. Tied by wrists to faucet in bathtub.
•• 0:24—Breasts, while kissing her husband in gas station restroom.
• 0:26—Brief breasts, then brief right breast in open blouse when her husband brings gas station attendant in to restroom.

Music Videos:

I Shot the Sheriff/Warren G.. . . . . n.a.

Love Is Hard On Your Knees/Aerosmith . . . . n.a.

Video Tapes:

Playboy's Rising Stars and Sexy Starlets (1996) . . Herself
•• 0:02—Breasts, in strap outfit from *I Like to Play Games.*
••• 0:05—Nude, while dancing in front of a guy on soundstage.

Bracci, Teda

Films:

C.C. & Company (1970) . . . . Pig

R.P.M. (1970) . . . . Student

The Big Bird Cage (1972) . . . . Bull Jones
•• 0:15—Breasts in front of the guard, Rocco.
• 0:51—Very brief right breast, then left breast during fight with Pam Grier. Brief left breast standing up in rice paddy.

The Centerfold Girls (1974) . . . . Rita
• 0:18—Breasts taking off her clothes in the living room in front of everybody.

The Trial of Billy Jack (1974). . . . . Teda

The World's Greatest Lover (1977). . . . . Whore #3

Bracco, Lorraine

Wife of actor/director Edward James Olmos.
Ex-wife of actor Harvey Keitel.

Films:

The Pick-Up Artist (1987) . . . . Carla

Someone to Watch Over Me (1987) . . . . Ellie Keagan

The Dream Team (1989) . . . . Riley

GoodFellas (1990). . . . . Karen Hill

Switch (1991) . . . . Sheila Faxton

Talent for the Game (1991) . . . . Bobbie Henderson

Medicine Man (1992) . . . . Dr. Rae Crane

Radio Flyer (1992). . . . . Mary

Traces of Red (1992) . . . . Ellen Schofield

Being Human (1994). . . . . Anna

Even Cowgirls Get the Blues (1994) . . . . Delores Del Ruby
• 0:49—Brief lower frontal nudity, after pulling down her pants with the other cowgirls.

The Basketball Diaries (1995). . . . . Jim's Mother

Hackers (1995) . . . . Margo

Made for Cable Movies:

Scam (1993; Showtime) . . . . Maggie Rohrer

Made for TV Movies:
Getting Gotti (1994) .... Diane Giacalone

Brackett, Sarah

Films:
The Third Secret (1964; British) .... Nurse
Battle Beneath the Earth (1968; British) .... Meg Webson
Emily (1976; British) .... Margaret
• 0:09—Buns, while looking out the window at Koo Stark.
Priest of Love (1980) .... Athsah Brester
The Lords of Discipline (1983) .... Mrs. Durrell

*Bradford-Aiton, Lisa **

Films:
Screwball Hotel (1988) .... Punk Singer
Video Tapes:
Penthouse The Great Pet Hunt—Part II (1993) ...... Pet
••• 0:01—Breasts and buns in T-back while dancing on stage. (She's a great dancer.)

Bradigan, Bond

Films:
Steele Justice (1987) .... Reporter
Out of the Dark (1988) .... Hooker/Lee
•• 1:04—Buns, wearing corset, black stockings and garter belt. Long shot breasts, then breasts in bathroom.

Brady, Janelle

Films:
Class of Nuke 'Em High (1986) .... Chrissy
•• 0:26—Breasts sitting on bed in the attic with Warren.
• 0:31—Brief breasts scene from 0:26 superimposed over Warren's nightmare.
Teen Wolf Too (1987) .... History Student

*Braga, Sonia **

Films:
Dona Flor and Her Two Husbands (1978; Brazilian) . . . Flor
• 0:13—Buns and brief breasts with her husband, Vadinho.
•• 0:15—Breasts, while lying on the bed.
• 0:17—Brief buns, twice, when getting out of bed.
•• 0:54—Breasts, while making love on the bed with Vadinho.
•• 0:57—Breasts, while lying on the bed.
••• 1:41—Breasts, while kissing Vadinho.
Lady on the Bus (1978; Brazilian) .... n.a.
• 0:11—Brief left breast.
••• 0:12—Breasts, then buns, then full frontal nudity in bed getting her slip torn off by her newlywed husband. Long struggle scene.
•• 0:39—Right breast standing with half open dress, then breasts lying in bed, then getting into the pool.
••• 0:48—Breasts and buns on the beach after picking up a guy on the bus.
• 0:54—Brief breasts in bed dreaming.
• 1:02—Brief breasts in waterfall with bus driver.
•• 1:05—Breasts in cemetery after picking up another guy on the bus.
• 1:13—Breasts on the ground with another guy from a bus.
• 1:16—Left breast sitting on sofa while her husband talks.
I Love You (1982; Brazilian) .... Maria
a.k.a. Eu Te Amo
••• 0:34—Full frontal nudity making love with Paulo.
•• 0:36—Breasts sitting on the edge of the bed.
• 0:49—Breasts running around the house teasing Paulo.
•• 0:50—Briefly nude in blinking light. Don't see her face.
• 0:53—Breasts eating fruit with Paulo.
••• 0:54—Breasts wearing white panties in front of windows with Paulo. Long scene.
• 1:03—Left breast standing talking to Paulo.
• 1:10—Left breast talking to Paulo.
• 1:15—Very brief full frontal nudity, several times, in Paulo's flashback in blinking light scene.
••• 1:23—Breasts with Paulo during an argument. Dark, but long scene.
•• 1:28—Breasts walking around Paulo's place with a gun. Dark.
•• 1:33—Various breasts scenes.
Gabriela (1984; Brazilian) .... Gabriela
•• 0:26—Breasts leaning back out the window making love on a table with Marcello Mastroianni.
••• 0:27—Nude, taking a shower outside and cleaning herself up.
• 0:32—Right breast in bed.
•• 0:38—Nude, making love with Mastroianni on the kitchen table.
•• 0:45—Nude, getting in bed with Mastroianni.
• 1:13—Full frontal nudity, on bed with another man, then getting beaten up by Mastroianni.
••• 1:17—Nude, changing clothes in the bedroom.
•• 1:32—Breasts and buns making love outside with Mastroianni. Lots of passion!
Kiss of the Spider Woman (1985; U.S./Brazilian)
.... Leni/Marta/Spider Woman
The Milagro Beanfield War (1988) .... Ruby Archuleta
Moon Over Parador (1988) .... Madonna Mendez
The Rookie (1990) .... Liesl
Roosters (1993) .... Juana
•• 0:26—Right breast and lower frontal nudity, while lying in bed with Edward James Olmos.
Two Deaths (1994; British) .... Ana Puscasu
•• 0:44—Breasts, when Michael Gambon takes her top off during dinner party in front of several men.
•• 1:23—Breasts, while Gambon gropes her.
Made for Cable Movies:
The Last Prostitute (1991; Lifetime) .... Loah
The Burning Season (1994; HBO) .... Regina de Carvalho
Made for Cable TV:
Tales From the Crypt: This'll Kill Ya (1992; HBO) . . Sophie
• 0:12—Very brief left breast, twice, while sitting on Dylan McDermott's lap in bathroom.
• 0:13—Very brief right breast, when kissing McDermott in bathroom. Breasts, while lying back on bed.
Made for TV Movies:
Streets of Laredo (1995) .... Maria
TV:
Homestead (1998-) .... Carlota Alvarez

Brahms, Penny

Films:
The Wrong Box (1966; British)..... Twitering Female on Moor
2001: A Space Odyssey (1968; British/U.S.) .... Stewardess Girl
Hammerhead (1968) .... Frieda
Games That Lovers Play (1970) .... Constance
•• 0:08—Breasts outside with a customer.
•• 0:10—Breasts again putting dress back on.
Dracula A.D. 1972 (1972; British) .... Hippy Girl
a.k.a. Dracula Today

• *Brammall, Bridget*

Films:

Paper Mask (1991; British) . . . . Girl in Bed
•• 0:17—Breasts in bed with Matthew, while he is checking out her anatomy.

Loaded (1996) . . . . Shop Assistant

Brando, Rikki

Films:

Zipperface (1991) . . . . Sherry

The Bikini Carwash Company (1992) . . . . Amy
(Unrated version reviewed.)
• 0:15—Brief breasts when Stanley steals her bikini top.
• 0:30—Brief breasts during water fight.
• 0:31—Brief breasts at car wash.
• 0:43—Brief right breast, while making love with Donovan.
•• 0:44—Buns and breasts, making love with Donovan.
•• 0:59—Breasts, making out in car with Donovan.
••• 1:00—More breasts in car with Donovan.
• 1:02—Brief breasts in car wash.
•• 1:12—Breasts posing for photos.

Buford's Beach Bunnies (1992) . . . . Lauren Beatty
•• 0:54—Breasts in bed with Jeeter.

The Bikini Carwash Company II (1993) . . . . Amy
(Unrated version reviewed.)
••• 0:09—Breasts with the other three girls, celebrating in office during music video number.
•• 1:09—Buns in lingerie, then breasts in dressing room with Marshall.

*Brandt, Brandi **

Ex-wife of Mötley Crüe bassist Nikki Sixx.

Films:

Wedding Band (1989) . . . . Serena (Gypsy Wedding)

Video Tapes:

Playboy Video Calendar 1989 (1988) . . . . November
••• 0:41—Nude.

Glamour Through Your Lens—Outdoor Techniques (1989) . . . . Herself

Playmates at Play (1990) . . . . Easy Rider

Playboy's 21 Playmates (1996) . . . . Playmate
••• 0:39—Nude in still photos.
••• 0:40—Nude in biker fantasy.

Brandy

See: Ledford, Brandy.

Brannon, Sandi

Films:

A Killing Affair (1985) . . . . Sara
•• 0:08—Breasts, sitting up in bed, then kissing Pink.

Dead Aim (1987) . . . . Misty
• 0:05—Buns in G-string, while dancing on stage during opening credits.
• 0:09—Breasts, while dancing on stage with the other girls (wearing a white bottom).
••• 1:02—Breasts and buns in G-string doing dance routine.
• 1:14—Very brief right breast, several times, while covered with blood, lying dead on bed.

*Braxton, Brandi Lee **

Video Tapes:

Penthouse: The Ultimate Pet Games (1996) . . . . Pet
••• 0:02—Nude during obstacle course segment.
••• 0:29—Nude in tug-of-war segment.
••• 0:42—Nude during squirt gun segment.

Breeze, Crystal

Adult film actress.

a.k.a. Lisa Marie Stagno.

Adult Films:

Fresh Meat #2 (1995) . . . . n.a.

Films:

Lust for Freedom (1987) . . . . Lynn
•• 0:38—Breasts, after taking off her top in prison cell with Michelle Bauer.
• 0:40—Breasts and brief buns, while kissing Bauer.
• 0:41—Left breast, while kissing Bauer on bed.
•• 0:42—Close up of breasts, while Bauer makes love with her.
•• 1:22—Breasts, after taking off her top in prison cell to ask a favor from the guard.

Wild Child (1991) . . . . Jan
• 0:30—Breasts, while sitting on the edge of the pool, then running around in black swimsuit bottoms.
••• 0:59—Breasts, while making love with Jack in the kitchen. Long scene.

Liquid Dreams (1992) . . . . Neuroid Reactor
(Unrated version reviewed.)

Army of One (1993) . . . . Body Double for Kristian Alfonso
•• 0:34—Breasts and buns, while undressing and getting into shower. Body double for Kristian Alfonso.

Bremmer, Leslee

Films:

Hardbodies (1984) . . . . Photo Session Hardbody
• 0:02—Breasts in the surf when her friends take off her swimsuit top during the opening credits.
•• 0:40—Breasts with other topless girls posing for photographs taken by Rounder. She takes off her dress and is wearing a black G-string.

Paradise Motel (1985) . . . . . . Uncredited Girl Leaving Room
• 0:38—Breasts buttoning her pink sweater, leaving motel room.

School Spirit (1985) . . . . Sandy
• 1:18—Breasts on a guy's shoulder in pool. (She's on the right, wearing red swimsuit bottoms.)

My Chauffeur (1986) . . . . Party Girl
• 1:24—Buns and brief breasts in back of the limousine, taking off her yellow outfit.
• 1:25—Breasts, while sleeping when Penn and Teller leave the limousine.

Reform School Girls (1986) . . . . Uncredited Shower Girl
•• 0:25—Brief breasts in the shower three times. Walking from left to right in the background, full frontal nudity by herself with wet hair, breasts walking from left to right.

Another Chance (1989) . . . . Girl in Womanizer's Meeting

Video Tapes:

Best Chest in the West (1984) . . . . Leslee
••• 0:29—In black, two piece swimsuit, then breasts and buns.
• 0:32—More breasts during judging and winning the 2nd round.

E. Nick: A Legend in His Own Mind (1984) . . . . Nymphet/Announcer
• 0:03—Breasts, while getting dressed in bunny costume with other nymphets.
• 0:09—Partial buns, in lingerie on video tape.
• 0:38—Breasts under wet, white T-shirt, while playing volleyball in pool with other Nymphets.

Centerfold Screen Test (1985) . . . . Herself
• 0:22—Breasts under fishnet top. (Practically see-through top.)
•• 0:24—Dancing, wearing the fishnet top and black G-string.

••• 0:28—Closer shot, dancing, while wearing the top.
Best Chest in the West II (1986). . . . . Herself
• 0:49—Dancing in pink top. Buns, in G-string.
The Girls of Malibu (1986) . . . . Leslee
••• 0:01—In two piece swimsuit, then nude, posing outside.
Starlet Screen Test (1986). . . . . Leslee
••• 0:11—Nude, taking off towel in hot tub.
Best Chest in the U.S. (1987) . . . . Bernadette
• 0:25—Buns in G-string.
Hot Body International: #1 Miss Cancun (1990)
. . . . Contestant
•• 0:25—Buns in two piece swimsuit.
Starlet Screen Test II (1991) . . . . Lauren
••• 0:41—Breasts and buns, in swimsuit bottom, dancing on stage.
Starlets Exposed! Volume II (1991) . . . . Leslee
(Same as *The Girls of Malibu.*)
••• 0:40—Breasts, then nude, taking off two piece swimsuit in garden.

Breneman, April

Films:
Wish Me Luck (1995) . . . . .Joyce
(Unrated version reviewed.)
Witchcraft 7: Judgement Hour (1995) . . . . Keli
(Unrated version reviewed.)
•• 0:40—Nude, while making love with Will in bed.
•• 0:57—Nude, while making love with Will in the living room.
•• 1:08—Breast, while in bed with Martin.
Street Corner Justice (1996) . . . . .Newswoman
L.A. Confidential (1997) . . . . Look-Alike Dancer

Brennan, Eileen

Films:
The Last Picture Show (1971) . . . . .Genevieve
Scarecrow (1973) . . . . .Darlene
• 0:27—Brief breasts in bed when Gene Hackman takes off her bra and grabs her breasts.
The Sting (1973). . . . . Billie
Daisy Miller (1974) . . . . .Mrs. Walker
Hustle (1975) . . . . Paula Hollinger
The Great Smokey Roadblock (1976) . . . . .Penelope
Murder by Death (1976). . . . . Tess Skeffington
The Cheap Detective (1978) . . . . Betty DeBoop
FM (1978). . . . . Mother
Private Benjamin (1980) . . . . Captain Doreen Lewis
Clue (1985). . . . . .Mrs. Peacock
The New Adventures of Pippi Longstocking (1988)
. . . . .Miss Bannister
Rented Lips (1988) . . . . Hotel Desk Clerk
Texasville (1990) . . . . Genevieve Morgan
White Palace (1990) . . . . Judy
I Don't Buy Kisses Anymore (1992) . . . . Frieda
Made for Cable Movies:
If These Walls Could Talk (1996; HBO). . . . . Tessie
Made for Cable TV:
Tales From the Crypt: Till Death Do We Part (1994; HBO)
. . . . Ruth
Made for TV Movies:
My Old Man (1979) . . . . Marie
Deadly Intentions...Again? (1991). . . . . Charlotte
Taking Back My Life: The Nancy Ziegenmeyer Story (1992)
. . . . Vicky Martin
Poisoned by Love: The Kern County Murders (1993)
. . . . Martha Catlin
Precious Victims (1993) . . . . Minnie Gray
My Name is Kate (1994) . . . . Barbara Mannix
Take Me Home Again (1994) . . . . Sada
Freaky Friday (1995) . . . . Principal
Trail of Tears (1995) . . . . .Clara
TV:
13 Queens Boulevard (1979) . . . . .Felicia Winters
Private Benjamin (1981-83) . . . . .Captain Doreen Lewis

• *Brennan, Kaitlin*

See: Reed, Kira.

Brenneman, Amy

Films:
Casper (1995) . . . . Amelia Harvey
Heat (1995). . . . . Eady
Daylight (1996). Madelyne Thompson
Fear (1996) . . . . .Laura Walker
TV:
NYPD Blue (1993-94) . . . . Janice Licalsi
NYPD Blue: Pilot (Sep 21, 1993) . . . . Janice Licalsi
• 0:41—In white bra and panties in room with Kelly. Buns and brief right breast while in bed.
NYPD Blue: 4B or not 4B (Sep 28, 1993) . . . . . Janice Licalsi
• 0:25—Brief breasts, while on top of Kelly in bed.
NYPD Blue: Ice Follies (Nov 30, 1993). . . . . Janice Licalsi
• 0:38—Most of left breast, while making love in bed with John.
• 0:39—Brief buns, while getting out of bed.

Brentano, Amy

Films:
Blood Sisters (1986) . . . . Linda
••• 0:12—Breasts, getting out of bed.
•• 0:14—Breasts, walking around. Right breast, in bed with Russ. Brief upper half of buns.
Breeders (1986). . . . . .Gail
• 0:59—Long shot of buns, getting into the nest.
• 1:07—Breasts in nest, throwing her head back.
•• 1:08—Brief breasts, writhing around in the nest, then breasts, arching her back.
• 1:11—Breasts, long shot, just before the nest is destroyed.
Robot Holocaust (1986). . . . . Irradiated Female
Prime Evil (1987) . . . . Brett
••• 1:13—Breasts removing her gown (she's in the middle) with Cathy and Judy.

Bresee, Bobbie *

Films:
Mausoleum (1983) . . . . Susan Farrell
••• 0:25—Breasts and buns wrapping a towel around herself in her bedroom.
•• 0:26—Breasts on the balcony showing herself to the gardener.
• 0:29—Breasts in the garage with the gardener. Brief, dark, hard to see.
• 0:32—Brief left breast, while kissing Marjoe Gortner.
• 1:10—Breasts in the bathtub talking to Gortner. Long shot.
Armed Response (1986) . . . . .Anna
Star Slammer—The Escape (1986). . . . . Marai
Surf Nazis Must Die (1986) . . . . Smeg's Mom
Evil Spawn (1987). . . . . Lynn Roman
• 0:14—Very brief half of right breast in bed with a guy.
••• 0:36—Breasts and side view of buns in bathroom looking at herself in the mirror, then taking a shower.

The Alien Within (1990) . . . . Lynn Roman
(Contains footage from *The Evil Spawn* woven together with new material.)
- 0:12—Very brief half of right breast in bed with a guy.
- ••• 0:37—Breasts and side view of buns in bathroom looking at herself in the mirror, then taking a shower.

*Breton, Patty **
Video Tapes:

Playboy's Cheerleaders (1996). . . . . .Cheerleader
- ••• 0:32—Nude (she's the first to take her bra off) outside during car wash with two other cheerleaders.

Playboy's Women Behaving Badly (1997) . . . . All Wet
- ••• 0:02—Nude, while undressing in locker room with her two girlfriends in locker room, then taking a shower. (She's wearing earrings.)

*Bridges, Elisa **
Video Tapes:

Playboy Video Calendar 1996 (1995) . . . . September
- ••• 0:35—Nude outdoors in Western theme segment.
- •• 0:37—Nude in dusty attic type fantasy.

Playboy Video Centerfold: Julie Lynn Cialini (1995)
. . . . Playmate of the Year Runner-Up
- 0:42—Briefly nude during introduction.
- ••• 0:43—Nude in colorful house.
- ••• 0:47—Nude, doing things around a farm.
- ••• 0:49—Nude in outdoor bedroom fantasy.
- ••• 0:52—Nude in still photos.
- ••• 0:53—Nude in living doll segment.

Playboy's Girls Next Door: Naughty and Nice (1998)
. . . . Playmate

Bridges, Krista
Films:

Soft Deceit (1994) . . . . Ed's Girlfriend
- 0:07—Left breast, while sleeping in bed, brief breasts, when Ed gets up out of bed.
- 0:08—Brief side view of left breast, when Ed gets back in bed to kiss her.

Made for Cable Movies:

BloodKnot (1995; Showtime) . . . . .Julie

*Brighton, Connie **
Video Tapes:

Playboy's Playmate Review 3 (1985). . . . . Playmate

Playboy Video Centerfold: Kerri Kendall (1990)
. . . . Playmate
- ••• 0:31—Nude.

*Brigitte, Simone **
Video Tapes:

Penthouse Pet Rocks (1995). . . . . Pet

*Brimhall, Cynthia **
Films:

Hard Ticket to Hawaii (1987). . . . . Edy
- •• 0:47—Breasts changing out of a dress into a blouse and pants.
- •• 1:33—Breasts during the end credits.

Picasso Trigger (1989). . . . . Edy
- •• 0:59—Breasts in weight room with a guy.

Guns (1990). . . . . .Edy Stark
- 0:26—Buns in G-string, while singing and dancing at club.
- •• 0:27—Breasts in dressing room.
- 0:53—Buns, in black one piece outfit and stockings, while singing in club. Nice legs!

Do or Die (1991) . . . . .Edy Stark
- 0:31—Most of buns, wearing white lingerie outfit, singing and dancing at night.
- ••• 0:36—Breasts and buns, making love with Lucas on floor in front of fire.

Every Breath (1992). . . . . Kris

Fit To Kill (1993) . . . . .Edy Stark
- •• 1:00—Breasts under sheer white body suit while posing for her boyfriend while he photographs her.

Hard Hunted (1993). . . . . .Edy Stark
- ••• 0:50—Breasts in bedroom while making love with Lucas.
- •• 1:18—Left breast, then breasts in bed with Lucas.

Video Tapes:

Playboy Video Calendar 1987 (1986) . . . . .Playmate

Playboy Video Magazine, Volume 10 (1986) . . . .Playmate
- ••• 0:53—Nude in still photos, then in the woods after riding motorcycle and then in the desert.

Sexy Lingerie (1988) . . . . Model

Playmates at Play (1990) . . . . Easy Rider

Playboy's Playmates Revisited (1998). . . . . .Playmate
- ••• 0:48—Nude in old footage and still photos.
- ••• 0:53—Nude in new footage.

Brin, Michele
a.k.a. Michelle Lamothe.

Films:

Secret Games (1991) . . . . .Julianne
(Unrated version reviewed.)
(Nude a lot, only the best are listed.)
- •• 0:03—Left breast, while lying in bed with Billy Drago.
- ••• 0:08—Breasts and buns, while taking a shower.
- •• 0:09—Breasts under sheer white robe, trying to entice Drago.
- 0:12—Brief left breast, while getting out of bed. Breasts, while picking clothes out of closet.
- ••• 0:34—Breasts, sunbathing with the other girls. (She's wearing brown framed sunglasses.)
- ••• 0:38—Breasts in bed, making love with Martin Hewitt.
- ••• 0:43—Buns and breasts making love in bed with Drago.
- ••• 0:48—Breasts, while tied to the bed.
- ••• 0:54—In white bra and panties, then nude taking them off and putting new ones on.
- ••• 1:10—Breasts, while lying in bed with Hewitt.
- ••• 1:13—Breasts and buns, making love with Hewitt in bathtub.
- •• 1:15—Breasts under sheer robe.
- •• 1:32—Buns in G-string, then breasts, getting into bed and making love with Drago.

Sins of the Night (1993) . . . . Laura Winters
(Unrated version reviewed.)
- 0:05—In black bra and panties in her house with her lover. Brief buns in G-string while Jack takes photos.
- ••• 0:06—Breasts, while making love with her lover. Long scene.
- •• 0:14—Breasts and buns, getting out of bed.

Strike a Pose (1993). .Miranda Cross
- ••• 0:06—Breasts, while making love with Nick at night outside by a fire. Long scene.
- ••• 0:32—In black bra and panties, then breasts while making love with Nick. Long scene.
- 0:40—Buns in panties that are squished against a glass door.
- ••• 1:06—Brief left breast in bed, then breasts and buns while making love with Nick.

Sexual Intent (1994) .... Barbara Hayden
• 0:28—Breasts, on balcony after John talks to her on cellular phone. Long shot.
• 0:47—Breasts during fantasy with John while she's watching video tape of an interview.
••• 0:49—In bra and panties, then breasts and buns while making love with John in her office.
•• 0:54—Breasts, while sitting in bathtub.
Scoring (1995) .... Della
Made for Cable TV:
Dream On: Up All Night (1992; HBO)............. Ariel
••• 0:14—Breasts, taking off her dress and walking down hallway during Martin's dream.
Video Tapes:
Eden 6 (1994)............................ Ginny Lynch

Brisebois, Danielle

Films:
The Premonition (1976) .... Janie
King of the Gypsies (1978) .... Young Tita
Big Bad Mama II (1987).............Billy Jean McClatchie
••• 0:12—Breasts with Julie McCullough playing in a pond underneath a waterfall.
Kill Crazy (1989).............................. Libby
•• 0:39—Breasts taking off top to go skinny dipping with Rachel.
• 0:46—Very brief right breast, while lying on ground with a bad guy while getting raped. Buns, getting turned over before being shot.
As Good As It Gets (1997)........................ Singer
TV:
All In the Family (1978-83) .... Stephanie Mills
Knots Landing (1983-84) .... Mary-Frances Sumner

Brittany, Tally

See: Chanel, Tally.

*Broady, Eloise **

Films:
Dangerous Love (1988)......................... Bree
••• 0:06—Breasts changing into lingerie in the mirror.
To Die For (1988) ....Girl at Party
Troop Beverly Hills (1989)................. Starlet at Party
Weekend at Bernie's (1989).......................Tawny
a.k.a. Hot and Cold
• 0:35—Buns in two piece swimsuit, coming into Bernie's house to get the ski boat keys.
Video Tapes:
Playboy Video Calendar 1989 (1988) ....December
••• 0:45—Nude.
Wet & Wild III (1991)..........................Model
The Best of Wet and Wild (1992) ....Model
Playboy Video Playmate Six-Pack 1992 (1992). . Playmate

Brochet, Anne

Films:
Cyrano De Bergerac (1990; French) .... Roxanne
All the Mornings of the World (1992; French) . . Madeleine
a.k.a. Tout Les Matins Du Monde
• 0:46—Nude by river bank while running to hide behind tree when seen by Marin. Long shot.
•• 0:56—Left breast, while opening her dress and letting Marin feel and kiss her breast.
• 1:06—Brief breasts, after opening her blouse for Marin in the hallway.
• 1:08—Brief upper half of right breast while holding Marin's hand.
•• 1:20—Lower frontal nudity under nightgown, while getting out of bed.
Barjo (1993; French) .... Fanfan

Brockman, Ungela

Films:
From Dusk Till Dawn (1995) .... Bar Dancer
Showgirls (1995)............................. Annie
(NC-17 version reviewed.)
• 0:09—Brief breasts in dressing room, when Gay passes by.
• 1:17—Buns, while getting dressed backstage.
Starship Troopers (1996) .... Corporal Birdie

• *Broderick, Beth*

Films:
If Looks Could Kill (1987)................... Newswoman
Slammer Girls (1987)........................... Abigail
Student Affairs (1987) .... Alexis
Young Nurses in Love (1987).....................Putnam
Stealing Home (1988) .... Sexy Neighbor
The Bonfire of the Vanities (1990) .... Caroline Heftshank
Thousand Pieces of Gold (1990) ....Berthe
ShadowHunter (1992)......................Bobby Cain
Made for Cable Movies:
Breast Men (1997; HBO) .... Terri (Voice Only)
Made for Cable TV:
Women: Stories of Passion-The Bitter and the Sweet (1997; Showtime) ....Ellie
•• 0:09—Breasts, while rubbing lotion on herself during Timothy's flashback.
• 0:12—Breasts, while making love on bed with Timothy.
•• 0:14—Breasts, while lying in bed next to Timothy.
•• 0:15—Breasts, while in bathtub, talking with Timothy.
•• 0:17—Breasts, while making love in bed with Timothy.
• 0:19—Brief left breast, when sitting up in bed.
Made for TV Movies:
In the Deep Woods (1992) ....Myra
TV:
Glory Days (1990)........................Sheila Jackson
Hearts Afire (1992-93).....................Dee Dee Starr
The Five Mrs. Buchanans (1994) .... Delilah Buchanan
Sabrina, The Teenage Witch (1996-).........Zelda Spellman

Broderson, Nicole

Films:
Anthony's Desire (1993) .... Dancer
• 0:54—Buns, while sitting on her stomach in the middle of the group of women. Tattoo on her right butt cheek.
Video Tapes:
Penthouse Forum Letters: Volume 2 (1994) ....The Loving Nurse/Nurse
••• 0:01—Nude, while making love in hospital bed with a patient.

• *Bronwyn Moore, Lisa*

Films:
Hollow Point (1995) ....Vicky
Made for Cable Movies:
More Tales of the City (1998; Canadian/U.S.; Showtime) .... Bus Ticket Seller
Made for Cable TV:
The Hunger: The Other Woman (1998; Showtime). . . Beth
• 0:21—Brief breasts, while making love with Nicholas Campbell.

- 0:23—Brief right breast, when caught with Campbell by Joanna Cassidy.

Brooke, Sandy

Films:

Bits and Pieces (1985) . . . . Mrs. Talbot

- ••• 1:03—Breasts in bathtub washing herself before the killer drowns her. Very brief right breast when struggling.
- • 1:09—Brief breasts under water in bathtub, dead.

Star Slammer—The Escape (1986). . . . . .Taura

- ••• 0:21—Breasts in jail putting a new top on. In braless white T-shirt for most of the rest of the film.
- •• 1:09—Breasts changing into a clean top.

The Terror on Alcatraz (1986) . . . . Mona

- • 0:05—Right breast on bed getting burned with a cigarette by Frank.

Nightmare Sisters (1987) . . . . .Amanda Detweiler
Deep Space (1988) . . . . .Woman in House

Brooks, Angela *

Video Tapes:

Playboy's Girls of Spring Break (1991) . . . . .Herself

- •• 0:25—Buns in still photos. Dancing in white lingerie. Breasts and buns in swimming pool.

Brooks, Elisabeth *

Films:

The Howling (1981) . . . . Marsha

- •• 0:46—Full frontal nudity taking off her robe in front of a campfire.
- • 0:48—Breasts sitting on Bill by the fire.

Deep Space (1988) . . . . Mrs. Ridley
The Forgotten One (1989) . . . . .Carla
Jaded (1989) . . . . Rita

TV:

Doctors' Hospital (1975-76) . . . . Nurse Connie Kimbrough

Brooks, Iris

Films:

I Drink Your Blood (1970) . . . . Sylvia
Up the Sandbox (1972) . . . . Vicki
Is There Sex After Death? (1975)
. . . . .Breast Development Student

- ••• 1:18—Breasts in open blouse with Buck Henry.

Brooks, Randi *

a.k.a. Randi Brazen.

Films:

Looker (1981) . . . . .Girl in Bikini
Deal of the Century (1983) . . . . .Ms. Della Rosa
The Man with Two Brains (1983) . . . . Fran

- •• 1:11—Brief breasts showing Steve Martin her breasts in front of the hotel. Buns, changing in the hotel room, then wearing black see-through negligee.

Tightrope (1984) . . . . Jamie Cory

- ••• 0:20—Nude, taking off her robe and getting into the spa.
- • 0:24—Buns and side of left breast, dead in the spa while Clint Eastwood looks at her.

Hamburger—The Motion Picture (1986) . . . . . . Mrs. Vunk

- •• 0:52—Brief breasts in helicopter with a guy.

Terrorvision (1986) . . . . .Cherry
Cop (1988) . . . . Jeanie Pratt

TV:

Wizards and Warriors (1983) . . . . Witch Bethel
The Last Precinct (1986) . . . . Officer Mel Brubaker
Mancuso, FBI (1989-90) . . . . Jean St. John

Brown, Blair

Films:

The Choirboys (1977) . . . . .Kimberly Lyles
Altered States (1980). . . . . Emily Jessup

- • 0:10—Brief left breast making love with William Hurt in red light from an electric heater.
- •• 0:34—Breasts lying on her stomach during Hurt's mushroom induced hallucination.
- • 1:39—Buns, sitting in hallway with Hurt after the transformations go away.

One Trick Pony (1980). . . . . Marion
Continental Divide (1981) . . . . .Nell
A Flash of Green (1984). . . . . Catherine "Kat" Hubble

- • 1:30—Very brief right breast moving around in bed with Ed Harris.

Strapless (1990; British). . . . . Dr. Lillian Hempel
Passed Away (1992) . . . . .Amy Scanlan
The Day My Parents Ran Away (1994). . . . . Judy Miller

Made for Cable TV:

Days and Nights of Molly Dodd (1989-91; Lifetime)Molly Dodd

Miniseries:

Wheels (1978). . . . . Barbara Lipton
Space (1987). . . . . Penny Hardesty Pope

Made for TV Movies:

And I Alone Survived (1978) . . . . Lauren Elder
Hands of a Stranger (1987) . . . . Diane Benton
Extreme Close-Up (1990) . . . . .Margaret
Those Secrets (1992). . . . . .n.a.
Rio Shannon (1993) . . . . .n.a.
The Gift of Love (1994) . . . . Helen
Moment of Truth: To Walk Again (1994) . . . . .n.a.

TV:

Captains and the Kings (1976) . . . Elizabeth Healey Hennessey
Days and Nights of Molly Dodd (1987-88) . . . . . . Molly Dodd
Feds (1997). . . . . .Erica Stanton

Brown, Bobbi *

Films:

Betrayal of the Dove (1992) . . . . Dancer

- •• 1:03—Buns in outfit, then breasts while dancing on stage.

Video Tapes:

BabeWatch, Episode 3: Sex Kittens (1994). . . Bobbi Brown

- ••• 0:07—Breasts, wearing a skirt, while dancing in house with her girlfriend.
- ••• 0:28—Nude, while taking a shower, then joined by her girlfriend.

Penthouse Forum Letters: Volume 2 (1994)
. . . . The Window Washer/Lover

- ••• 0:46—Nude, making love with another woman on sofa, on kitchen counter and on bed.

Brown, Cindy *

Video Tapes:

Playboy Video Calendar 1996 (1995) . . . . February

- •• 0:05—In lingerie and nude in a warehouse. Sometimes playing with basketball.
- ••• 0:07—Nude, on rotating turntable wearing jewelry.

Wet & Wild: Hot Holidays (1995). . . . . .Playmate

Brown, Juanita

Films:

Willie Dynamite (1973) . . . . Sola
Caged Heat (1974) . . . . .Maggie
a.k.a. Renegade Girls

- • 0:25—Breasts in shower scene.

Foxy Brown (1974) . . . . .Claudia

Brown, Judy

Films:

The Big Doll House (1971) . . . . Marnie Collier
- • 0:03—Very brief breasts while getting blouse taken off and searched before going to jail.
- •• 0:04—Right breast getting examined by the doctor. Brief left breast. Long scene.
- •• 0:32—Breasts after Pam Grief leaves shower room.
- ••• 1:06—Breasts a lot while tied down on table by the guard. Mostly left breast. Long scene.
- • 1:42—Breasts while changing blouse while riding in back of truck.

Willie Dynamite (1973) . . . . .Georgia
Slaughter's Big Rip-Off (1975) . . . . Norja
The American Success Company (1979) . . . . n.a.
Independence Day (1983) . . . . Janis

Brown, Julie

Comedienne.
Singer–"The Homecoming Queen's Got a Gun."
Not to be confused with former MTV Video Jockey "Downtown" Julie Brown.

Films:

Any Which Way You Can (1980) . . . . .Candy
Bloody Birthday (1980) . . . . Beverly
- ••• 0:13—Dancing in red bra, then breasts while two boys peek through hole in the wall, then buns. Nice, long scene.

Police Academy II: Their First Assignment (1985) . . . . Chloe
Earth Girls are Easy (1989) . . . . .Candy
Timebomb (1990) . . . . .Uncredited Waitress at Al's Diner
Nervous Ticks (1991) . . . . Nancy Rudman
The Spirit of '76 (1991) . . . . Ms. Liberty
The Opposite Sex ...and How to Live with Them (1992) . . . Zoe
Shakes the Clown (1992) . . . . Judy
Clueless (1995) . . . . Ms. Stoeger
Spy Hard (1996) . . . . Cigarette Girl

Made for Cable Movies:

Medusa: Dare to be Truthful (1991; Showtime) . . . . . . .Medusa
Attack of the 5' 2" Women (1994; Showtime) . . . . .Tonya Hardly/Lenora Babbitt
Out There (1995; Showtime) . . . . Joleen

Made for Cable TV:

Just Say Julie (1990; MTV) . . . . Hostess

TV:

The Edge (1992-94) . . . . Cast Member

Brown, Linda *

Films:

Pleasure in Paradise (1992) .Heather
- • 0:02—Full frontal nudity, while getting out of the shower and wrapping a towel around herself.
- ••• 0:41—Breasts while in bed, making love with Rob. Long scene.

• Brown, Lisa Ann *

Films:

Stripteaser 2 (1997) . . . . Sindy
- ••• 0:05—Breasts and buns in red T-back, while dancing on stage. Long scene.
- ••• 0:25—Breasts and buns in T-back, while dancing on stage with Sylvia.
- •• 0:41—Breasts and buns, while dancing on stage with Sylvia.
- • 0:46—Breasts, while showing Angie around the upstairs room.
- • 0:48—Breasts, while showing Angie around the upstairs room.
- •• 0:57—Breasts, while chained by her wrists in upstairs room.
- ••• 1:01—Breasts and buns in panties on stage with Junior in dream.
- •• 1:08—Breasts and buns, while dancing for customers in upstairs room (wearing mask).

Brown, Robin *

Video Tapes:

Penthouse Satin & Lace II: Hollywood Undercover (1992) . . . . Pet
Penthouse The Great Pet Hunt—Part I (1992) . . . . Pet
Making of the "Carousel Girls' Calendar" (1993) . . . . Miss January
- ••• 0:09—Nude during photo shoot.
- ••• 0:13—Nude during interview segment.

The Penthouse All-Pet Workout (1993) . . . . Pet
- • 0:00—Right breast during introduction.
- •• 0:03—Brief nude shots while getting undressed and suited up.
- ••• 0:21—Nude on sofa inside.
- ••• 0:43—Nude with the other girls, exercising, working with equipment, in the pool and spa.

Penthouse DreamGirls (1994) . . . . Robin
- ••• 0:14—Nude, in a house in lingerie, by a window, in a bubble bath.

Brown, Robin Joi

Films:

Test Tube Teens From the Year 2000 (1993) . . . . .Victoria
a.k.a. Virgin Hunters
- ••• 0:31—Breasts, in the showers (she's on the left) with Annie while Vin and Naldo watch.

Hard Drive (1994) . . . . Assistant Examiner
(Unrated version reviewed.)
Final Equinox (1995) . . . . .Piper
- •• 0:45—Nude, while making love in bed with a guy.

Brown, Sara Suzanne

Films:

The Last Boy Scout (1991) . . . . Dancer
- • 0:19—Brief breasts and buns in T-back, twice, while dancing in club.

The Bikini Carwash Company (1992) . . . . .Sunny
(Unrated version reviewed.)
- • 0:15—Brief breasts when Stanley steals her bikini top.
- •• 0:25—Breasts, washing windshield and side window.
- ••• 0:26—More breasts while window washing.
- •• 0:30—Breasts during water fight.
- •• 0:31—Breasts at car wash.
- •• 0:35—Breasts running after a guy who stole her bikini top.
- ••• 0:46—Breasts and buns in G-string, hand washing a customer with Rita.
- ••• 0:47—Breasts and buns, dancing inside car wash.
- •• 0:53—Breasts outside at car wash.
- ••• 1:02—Nude, soaped up in car wash with Melissa and Rita.
- ••• 1:12—Breasts, posing for photos.
- •• 1:15—Breasts when Stanley takes her top off.

The Bikini Carwash Company II (1993) . . . . .Sunny
(Unrated version reviewed.)
- ••• 0:09—Breasts with the other three girls, celebrating in office during music video number.
- •• 0:16—Breasts at carwash during music video number. (Wearing yellow bikini bottoms.)

- 0:24—Buns in lingerie in offices of The Miracle Network with Rita.
- 0:27—Brief breasts, twice, while flashing her breasts in office.

••• 1:16—In black lingerie, then breasts in office fantasy.
•• 1:29—Breasts and buns in bikini bottoms during music video number at the carwash.

Mirror Images II (1993) . . . . Prostitute
••• 0:13—In red bra and panties, then breasts and buns while making love with Clete in motel room. Long scene.

Secret Games 2—The Escort (1993). . . . . Irene
(Unrated version reviewed.)
••• 0:32—Undressing in bedroom, then nude while making love with Martin Hewitt in bed.
• 0:53—Breasts, while making love next to dining room table with Hewitt.
•• 1:00—Breasts, while lying in bed with Hewitt.
••• 1:20—Nude, while making love with Hewitt in bed.

Test Tube Teens From the Year 2000 (1993) . . . . . . Reena
a.k.a. Virgin Hunters
•• 0:03—In black bra and panties, then buns in panties and breasts stripping out of her jumpsuit during Vin's day dream.

Killer Looks (1994). . . . . Diane
(Unrated version reviewed.)
• 0:01—Buns, while in two piece swimsuit in pool.
• 0:02—Buns and breasts after getting out of pool and taking off swimsuit top.
••• 0:04—Full frontal nudity while making love with the plumber.
••• 0:26—Breasts, while making love in spa with her husband.
• 0:30—Breasts, while putting bra on in bedroom.
••• 0:41—Nude while making love with Mickey in bed.
• 0:47—Briefly nude, while getting into bed.
• 0:50—Full frontal nudity in flashbacks while on bed with Mickey.
• 0:59—Breasts in open dress top, while trying to get back away from Cynthia's advances.
•• 1:23—In bra and panties, then breasts, while blindfolded and making out with Janine Lindemulder and Lené Hefner on stairway.
••• 1:25—Nude, while in the shower.

Lover's Leap (1995) . . . . Rita
••• 0:18—Nude, while making love in bed with Charlie.
••• 0:21—Nude, when walking and standing out on the balcony in the morning.
•• 0:49—Breasts, while sunbathing out in pool with Billie.

Made for Cable TV:
Dream On: Tie Me Sister Lu Down, Sport (1995; HBO) . . . . Penny
• 0:01—Breasts with Martin in his apartment, before getting interrupted by the property manager.

Brown, Tricia

Films:
Vamp (1986) . . . . Candi
• 0:32—Brief breasts doing strip tease.
Phantom Empire (1987) . . . . Cavegirl
Hollywood Chainsaw Hookers (1988) . . . . Ilsa
•• 0:37—Breasts while Jack is tied up in bed.

*Browne, Leslie **

Films:
The Turning Point (1977) . . . . Emilia Rogers
• 0:51—Brief side view of right breast, while lying in bed with Mikhail Baryshnikov at the end of the love scene. Don't see her face.
Nijinsky (1980; British) . . . . Romula
• 1:34—Very brief breasts, twice, on the floor when Nijinksy rips her dress off. Dark.
Dancers (1987) . . . . Nadine

*Bruce, Andi **

Films:
Summer's Games (1987) . . . . News Anchor
• 0:12—Brief right breast, while turning around to look at monitor.
• 0:42—Breasts turning around to look at the monitor.
Screwball Hotel (1988) . . . . Bobbi Jo

*Bruinooge, Lucienne **

Films:
The Secrets of Love—Three Rakish Tales (1986) . . . . Marietta
• 0:02—Buns, while getting spanking.
•• 0:27—Breasts, while lying in bed.

Brunaux, Olivia

Films:
The Secrets of Love—Three Rakish Tales (1986) . . . . Célestine
• 1:03—Brief breasts and buns fantasizing.
••• 1:14—Breasts and buns in the greenhouse making love.
••• 1:18—Breasts while kneeling in the greenhouse and making love.
Grand Guignol (1987; French) . . . . Coco
Cayenne Palace (1989; French) . . . . Alice
Bitter Moon (1994) . . . . Cindy

*Bryant, D'Andrea **

Films:
Nothing But Trouble (1991) . . . . Party Girl
Video Tapes:
Sexy Lingerie II (1990). . . . . Model

*Bryant, Pamela **

Films:
Don't Answer the Phone (1979) . . . . Sue Ellen
•• 0:28—Breasts in the killer's photo studio when he rips her jacket off and kills her.
H.O.T.S. (1979) . . . . Teri Lynn
a.k.a. T & A Academy
• 1:33—Breasts during football game.
Separate Ways (1979) . . . . Cocktail Waitress
Looker (1981) . . . . Reston Girl
Lovely But Deadly (1981) . . . . Gloria
Lunch Wagon (1981) . . . . Marcy
a.k.a. Lunch Wagon Girls
a.k.a. Come 'N' Get It
•• 0:04—Breasts while changing tops in room in gas station with Rosanne Katon while a guy watches through key hole.
• 0:55—Left breast, several times, in van with Bif.
Private Lessons (1981). . . . . Joyce
• 0:03—Very brief right breast, changing in the house while Billy and his friend peep from outside.
Scorpion (1986) . . . . Flight Attendant

Trapped (1993) . . . . Laura Armstrong
a.k.a. The Killing Jar
• 0:04—Brief breasts on TV monitor.
• 0:05—Brief buns and right breast in mirror while changing clothes in the bathroom.
•• 0:11—Breasts, while starting to make love in backyard with Curtis.
• 0:15—Brief breasts in bathroom with her husband while he fantasizes about Monica.
• 0:24—Breasts, while on TV.
•• 0:27—Breasts, while in shower, getting out and getting dressed.
• 0:29—Brief right breast when it slips out of nightgown while she lies in bed.
• 0:32—Brief left breast when masked guy cuts her nightgown strap open.
• 0:48—Brief side of left breast on TV.
••• 0:50—Nude, getting into bathtub, in bathtub, then getting dragged around house by guy.

TV:
B.J. and the Bear . . . . n.a.

Buchanan, Yvette

Films:
Night Eyes (1990) . . . . Baby Doll
(Unrated version reviewed.)
• 0:07—Brief left breast, then breasts making love in bathroom with Ronee.

The Malibu Beach Vampires (1991) . . . . . . The Rocket Scientist
Roots of Evil (1991) . . . . Hooker
(Unrated version reviewed.)

*Buchfellner, Ursula **

a.k.a. Ursula Fellner.
Films:
Popcorn and Ice Cream (1978; West German) . . . . . Yvonne
a.k.a. Sex and Ice Cream
••• 0:30—Nude with the hotel manager, Vivi and Bea.
• 0:40—Breasts in open dress at the disco.

Bloodline (1979) . . . . Murder Victim
The Manhunters (1980; French/Spanish/German)
. . . . Laura Crawford
• 0:06—Buns and side view breasts, walking around the house. Long shot.
• 0:08—Breasts taking a bath.
•• 0:10—Breasts in the bathtub.
• 0:15—Full frontal nudity getting pulled out of the tub unconscious.
• 0:19—Brief right breast when a kidnapper opens her blouse while she's tied up.
• 0:43—Very brief breasts, while running through the jungle.
• 0:58—Brief lower frontal nudity, then breasts captured by the natives.
•• 1:04—Breasts, unconscious, while tribe women undress her.
•• 1:05—Full frontal nudity tied to a pole.
•• 1:06—Nude, getting dragged into a hut.
•• 1:10—Full frontal nudity taking a shower under waterfall with three tribe women.
•• 1:12—Full frontal nudity, lying down while three tribe women put flowers on her.
•• 1:23—Breasts and buns, getting carried away by the cannibal creature.
• 1:26—Buns, being carried by the creature.
•• 1:27—Breasts on the ground.
•• 1:29—Buns and right breast, getting carried down the mountain side.
••• 1:30—Breasts on the boat with Peter.

Buckman, Tara

Films:
Rollercoaster (1977). . . . . Coaster Attendant
Hooper (1978). . . . . Debbie
The Cannonball Run (1981). . . . . Jill
Silent Night, Deadly Night (1984) . . . . Mother (Ellie)
• 0:12—Brief right breast twice when the killer dressed as Santa Claus, rips her blouse open. Breasts lying dead with slit throat.
• 0:18—Very, very brief breasts during Billy's flashback.
• 0:43—Brief breasts a couple of times again in another of Billy's flashbacks.

Never Too Young to Die (1986) . . . . Sacrificed Punkette
Silent Night, Deadly Night, Part 2 (1986). . . . . Mother
• 0:09—Very brief right breast, with Santa Claus during flashback.
• 0:14—Very brief breasts on ground during flashback.
• 0:22—Very, very brief blurry breasts during flashback.
• 0:47—Very, very brief breasts during flashback.

Terminal Exposure (1988) . . . . Mrs. Karrothers
The Loves of a Wall Street Woman (1989). . Brenda Baxter
• 0:00—Breasts taking a shower, opening the door and getting a towel.
•• 0:06—Breasts changing clothes in locker room in black panties. Nice legs!
••• 0:18—Breasts in bed making love with Alex.
•• 0:31—Breasts in bed with Alex making love.
•• 0:40—Breasts in black panties dressing in locker room.
• 0:46—Brief breasts lying in bed, talking to her lover, side view of buns. Long shot.
••• 1:16—Breasts making love in bed with Alex.

The Marilyn Diaries (1990) . . . . Jane
•• 0:53—Breasts and buns, taking off robe and getting into bathtub. Left breast, in tub reading diary.
•• 0:54—Breasts in and getting out of tub. Very brief lower frontal nudity.
•• 1:27—Breasts in bathtub talking with John.

Object of Desire (1991) . . . . Angie
• 0:12—Breasts, leaning up on massage table.
••• 0:14—Breasts, getting dressed so Derrick can see.
•• 0:23—Breasts, making love with Derrick in her dressing room.
••• 0:28—Breasts in bathtub with Derrick.
• 0:43—Right breast, while making love in bed with Derrick.
• 0:50—Side view of buns, while lying in bed.
•• 0:51—Right breast, while sitting up in bed, then full frontal nudity.
••• 0:55—Breasts, opening her blouse in Steve's office in front of him.
••• 1:09—Full frontal nudity, posing for photographer in studio. Also side view of his buns.
• 1:12—Brief breasts in magazine photos.
••• 1:18—Breasts changing clothes in dressing room.

Xtro 2, The Second Encounter (1991) . . . . Dr. Julie Casserly
Round Trip to Heaven (1992). . . . . Phyllis
Blindfold: Acts of Obsession (1993) . . . . Barmaid

TV:
Lobo (1980-81) . . . . Brandy

Buckner, Bari

Films:
Uninvited (1993) . . . . Emma

Made for Cable TV:
Hot Line: Where Were We? (1996; Cinemax)
.... Stefanie Brenner
• 0:02—Right breast, while making love with Allen in bed.
••• 0:07—Breasts and buns, after taking off her lingerie top while in bed with Allen, making love then stopping. Long scene.
•• 0:13—Breasts and buns, while dancing in the backyard to get Allen excited.
• 0:14—Buns, getting up after hearing the gardener in the backyard.
••• 0:23—Breasts and buns, while making love with Allen on the living room floor.

Buick, Denise
Films:
Full Contact (1992) .... Tori
••• 0:31—Buns in T-back, then in bra, then breasts, while doing strip routine on stage.
•• 0:39—Buns in T-back and breasts while dancing on stage.
•• 1:02—Breasts and buns, while making love with Luke.
Made for Cable TV:
Compromising Situations: Let Your Fingers Do the Walking (1995; Showtime)............................ Barbara
Video Tapes:
Inside Out 4 (1992) .... Claudia/What Anna Wants... (Unrated version reviewed.)
••• 1:08—Nude in bed with William while Anna takes photos.

Bujold, Genevieve
Films:
King of Hearts (1966; French/Italian)............ Colombine (Letterboxed French version with English subtitles.)
The Thief of Paris (1967; French/Italian) .... Charlotte
Anne of the Thousand Days (1969; British) ...... Anne Boleyn
The Trojan Women (1972; British)............... Cassandra
Kamouraska (1973; Canadian/French)........... Elisabeth
Nude in long shot.
Earthquake (1974) .... Denise
Obsession (1976) .... Elizabeth Courtland/Sandra Portinari
Swashbuckler (1976)..................... Jane Barnet
• 1:00—Very brief side view nude, diving from the ship into the water. Long shot, don't really see anything.
• 1:01—Buns and brief side of left breast seen from under water.
Coma (1978) .... Dr. Susan Wheeler
Murder by Decree (1979)................... Annie Crook
Last Flight of Noah's Ark (1980) .... Bernadette Lafleur
Final Assignment (1981) .... Nicole Thomson
Monsignor (1982) .... Clara
••• 1:05—Breasts getting undressed and climbing into bed while talking to Christopher Reeve.
Choose Me (1984) .... Dr. Love
Tightrope (1984) .... Beryl Thibodeaux
Trouble in Mind (1986).......................... Wanda
Dead Ringers (1988) .... Claire Niveau
•• 0:49—Very brief right breast in bed with Jeremy Irons, then brief breasts reaching for pills and water. Dark, hard to see.
The Moderns (1988)..................... Libby Valentin
False Identity (1990)........................... Rachel
Paper Wedding (1991; Canadian).................. Claire
Oh, What a Night (1992) .... Eva
The Adventures of Pinocchio (1996) .... Leone
Made for TV Movies:
Red Earth, White Earth (1989).................. Madeline

Buono, Cara
Films:
Gladiator (1992) .... Dawn
Waterland (1992; British/U.S.) .... Jody Dobson
• 0:38—Brief breasts, while sitting in chair in classroom during Jeremy Irons' daydream.
The Cowboy Way (1994)......................... Teresa
Kicking and Screaming (1995)..................... Kate
Killer: A Journal of Murder (1995) .... Esther Lesser

Burana, Lily Braindrop *
Made for Cable TV:
Wild Cards (1996; HBO)....................... Herself
•• 0:06—Buns in lingerie, while dancing in club.
•• 0:35—Buns and brief breasts, in lingerie, while dancing in club.

Burch, Tracey
Films:
Marked for Death (1990) .... Sexy Girl #1
• 0:39—Brief breasts on bed with Jimmy when Steven Seagal bursts into the room. (She's the blonde.)
Dance with Death (1991) .... Whitney
••• 0:03—Breasts and buns in G-string, dancing on stage.
••• 0:05—More breasts and buns while dancing.

Burger, Annette *
a.k.a. Elizabeth Burger.
Films:
Virtual Desire (1995) .... Cora
••• 0:50—In tight, white braless dress, then nude while making love with Brad. Long scene.

Burger, Michele
Films:
Emmanuelle 5 (1986)....................... Girl No. 3
••• 0:42—Breasts, while talking with the two other girls. Wearing a blue head band.
•• 0:44—Breasts, while drinking champagne with the other harem girls.
The Newlydeads (1988) .... Bikini Girl
Party Plane (1988)........................... Carol
• 0:31—Breasts, squirting whipped cream on herself for her audition.
•• 0:38—Breasts doing a strip tease routine on the plane.
••• 1:02—Breasts mud wrestling with Renee on the plane.
• 1:09—Breasts in the cockpit, covered with mud.
•• 1:17—Breasts in serving cart.
Payback (1988).............................. Laura
• 0:08—Brief breasts sitting up in bed just before getting shot, then brief breasts twice, dead in bed.
Roadhouse (1989)...................... Strip Joint Girl
Ninja Academy (1990) .... Nudist

Burgoyne, Victoria
Films:
Death Ship (1980; Canadian) .... Lori
Stealing Heaven (1988; British/Yugoslavian) ..... Prostitute
• 0:28—Left breast, taking off her top. Side view of right breast and buns.
•• 0:29—Breasts lying in bed.

Burke, Michelle
Films:
Coneheads (1993)............................ Connie
Dazed and Confused (1993) .... Jodi

The Last Word (1994) . . . . Sara
•• 0:09—Brief breasts and buns in T-back, when spinning around while dancing on stage.
Major League II (1994) . . . . Nikki Reese

Burkett, Laura

Films:
Blood Beach (1981). . . . . .Girl in Sand
Avenging Angel (1985). . . . . Blonde Hooker
Daddy's Boys (1988). . . . . Christie
••• 0:17—Breasts in room with Jimmy.
•• 0:20—Left breast, while making love with Jimmy in bed again.
• 0:21—Brief breasts during Jimmy's nightmare.
• 0:43—Brief breasts in bed again, then getting dressed.
• 0:53—Brief breasts in bed consoling Jimmy.
• 1:11—Left breast, while in bed with Jimmy.
Rush Week (1989) . . . . Rebecca Winters
•• 0:43—Breasts in the shower, talking to Jonelle.
• 0:55—Brief breasts getting dressed after modeling session.

*Burlingame, Tiffany **

Video Tapes:
Penthouse Women In & Out of Uniform (1995) . . . . . Pet
••• 0:02—Nude as an astronaut in a solo fantasy.
••• 0:08—Nude as a dentist assistant, with Tammy Parks in dental office.
••• 0:22—Nude as a paramedic, with Parks, while the guy watches from gurney inside ambulance.
••• 0:38—Nude as a policewoman with Janine Lindemulder and Julia Ann in squad room.
••• 0:41—Nude as a judge, in courthouse with Lindemulder and Julia Ann.
Penthouse: The Ultimate Pet Games (1996) . . . . Pet
••• 0:02—Nude during obstacle course segment.
••• 0:13—Nude during badminton segment.
••• 0:21—Nude during oil wrestling segment.
••• 0:29—Nude in tug-of-war segment.
••• 0:33—Nude, while making love with Leslie Glass in cabin (includes the use of honey and chocolate syrup).
••• 0:36—Breasts during pool volleyball game.
••• 0:42—Nude during squirt gun segment.
CD-ROM:
Penthouse Interactive Virtual Photo Shoot, Disc 4 (1995). . . . . Pet

Burnette, Kim

a.k.a. Veronica Cash.
Films:
Da Vinci's War (1992) . . . . .Monique
••• 0:49—Breasts, kneeling by herself, while putting on a show for the bad guy.
The Pamela Principle (1992) . . . . Pamela
(Unrated version reviewed.)
•• 0:18—Brief breasts, when Miss Fontana accidentally opens the dressing room door.
••• 0:27—Full frontal nudity, while getting dressed in her bedroom while talking on the phone. In panties, then in bra.
0:34—Breasts under sheer black lingerie.
••• 0:36—Breasts and buns in G-string while stripping out of skirt and stockings in front of Carl, then making love on sofa and the floor.
••• 0:39—Breasts in white panties and stockings while doing splits and stretching out.
• 1:12—Left breast, with Carl in the doorway.
• 1:23—Side of right breast, while taking off dress and putting on bra. Brief buns in G-string while taking off stockings.
••• 1:29—Breasts and brief lower frontal nudity, while making love in bed with Felicia.
•• 1:30—Breasts, while in front of Carl.
Made for Cable TV:
Red Shoe Diaries: Talk To Me Baby (1992; Showtime) . . Regina
(Available on the video tape *Red Shoe Diaries 3: Another Woman's Lipstick.*)

Burns, Bobbi

Films:
New York Nights (1981). . . . . .The Authoress
•• 0:16—Breasts on the couch outside with the rock star, then breasts in bed.
I, the Jury (1982). . . . . Sheila Kyle
• 0:01—Brief side view of right breast, while in bed with Armand Assante.
Q (1982) . . . . .Sunbather
•• 0:06—Breasts taking off swimsuit top and rubbing lotion on herself.

Burns, Catherine

Films:
Last Summer (1969). . . . . .Rhoda
• 1:31—Very brief breasts struggling with Stacy, Peter and Dan. Long shot.
Me, Natalie (1969) . . . . .Hester
Red Sky at Morning (1971) . . . . .Marcia Davidson

Burns, Janell

Video Tapes:
Hot Body International: #3 Lingerie Special (1992) . . . . Contestant
•• 0:31—Buns in one piece body suit.
Hot Body International: #5 Miss Acapulco (1992) . . . . Contestant
••• 0:14—Breasts and buns in swimsuit in pool. Breasts applying flowers to her breasts, then taking them off.
•• 0:16—Breasts taking off bikini top outside next to pool.
Hot Body Competition: The Best of Hot Body (1994) . . . . Herself
••• 0:08—Breasts and buns in swimsuit.

Burns, Kelly

a.k.a. Kehli O'Byrne.
Films:
K2 (1991) . . . . Pam
Knight Moves (1992) . . . . .Debi Rutledge
•• 0:08—Breasts and partial lower frontal nudity, while making love in bed with Christopher Lambert.
Dark Angel: The Ascent (1994) . . . . Angel
Tainted Love (1995) .Chantal Benteen
• 0:27—Brief breasts, while changing clothes in locker room.
•• 0:29—Full frontal nudity, while talking with Sara in steam room.
•• 0:58—In black bra, then breasts and buns, while making love with Franz on factory floor.
• 1:00—Breasts, while lying dead on bed with her wrists tied to the bed.
Twisted Passion (1995) . . . . .Gray Goodman
a.k.a. Shades of Gray
•• 0:09—Breasts, when Jack opens her dress, then makes love with her.

••• 0:41—Breasts and buns, when making love with Frank at night. Playing with fluorescent paint on each other, then in the shower.

Watch Me (1995) . . . . .Elise

• 0:00—Buns in panties and left breast during opening credits.

••• 0:18—Full frontal nudity, after pouring breakfast drink on herself and rubbing it all over while watching Alex and Samantha make love in other apartment.

• 0:30—Brief breasts, when caressing herself while watching Alex and Samantha make love in other apartment.

••• 0:32—Full frontal nudity, while caressing herself more after seeing Paul photographing her from another apartment.

• 0:36—Brief partial breasts in B&W photos.

• 0:40—Brief breasts in video playback.

•• 0:42—Breasts, while changing blouses in laundry room with Samantha.

• 0:44—Brief breast in video playback.

• 0:52—Breasts, caressing herself while watching Paul and Samantha make love in other apartment.

• 0:55—Brief buns in panties under short skirt, while dancing by herself in front of mirror.

•• 0:59—Breasts, while in studio, being photographed by Paul.

••• 1:18—Nude, while making love with Paul.

Made for Cable Movies:

Piranha (1995; Showtime) . . . . Gina Green

•• 0:52—Breasts on row boat after taking off her swimsuit top when Wechsler video tapes her. More breasts when in and under the water, getting attacked by the piranha.

Terminal Virus (1995; Showtime) . . . . .Shara

•• 0:55—Breasts, while making love in the lab with Joe.

Made for Cable TV:

Hot Line: Double Exposure (1996; Cinemax)
. . . . Melissa Jennings

(Available on video tape in *Hot Line 2*.)

•• 0:07—In black bra, then breasts, while indoors with a guy when Nick takes photos from outside.

•• 0:09—Breasts, while making love with a guy on the floor.

••• 0:18—In black lingerie, then breasts, while making love with Nick.

••• 0:23—Buns in T-back, then breasts while making love with Nick in his office.

Women: Stories of Passion-Reading for Pleasure (1997; Showtime). . . . . Wife

• 0:01—Breasts, during fantasy while reading a book.

•• 0:04—Breasts, while making love in bed with her husband.

•• 0:12—Breasts, while reading a book in spa outdoors.

•• 0:13—Breasts, while talking with her husband outdoors by the pool.

••• 0:17—Breasts and buns, after taking off her swimsuit and making love with her husband in bed. Some quick shots while swimming in pool.

•• 0:20—Brief buns and breasts, while lying outdoors with her husband, then walking away.

• 0:23—In bra, then brief left breast, while making love with her husband on desk.

• 0:24—Brief breasts, while making love some more.

Made for TV Movies:

Elvis and the Colonel: The Untold Story (1993). . . . . . . Priscilla

Video Tapes:

Playboy's Rising Stars and Sexy Starlets (1996) . . .Herself

•• 0:43—Full frontal nudity, in a clip from *Watch Me*.

••• 0:47—Nude, while making love with a guy in country house segment.

Burrell, Gretchen *

Films:

Pretty Maids All in a Row (1971). . . . . Marjorie

• 0:05—Partial side of right breast, in office with Rock Hudson.

• 0:07—Breasts on the couch in Hudson's office.

Burstyn, Ellen

Films:

Goodbye Charlie (1964) . . . . Franny

Alex in Wonderland (1970) . . . . Beth

• 1:19—Breasts, while sitting in bed, then putting her nightgown on.

Tropic of Cancer (1970). . . . . Mona

••• 0:02—Full frontal nudity, while lying on bed.

•• 0:03—Right breast while lying on her back in bed.

•• 0:04—Nude, getting out of bed to get bugs off her.

The Last Picture Show (1971) . . . . Lois Farrow

King of Marvin Gardens (1972) . . . . Sally

• 0:50—Brief breasts, while kneeling on the floor and turning around to shoot squirt guns.

The Exorcist (1973) . . . . .Chris

Harry and Tonto (1974). . . . . .Shirley

Alice Doesn't Live Here Anymore (1975) . . . . Alice Hyatt
(Academy Award for Best Actress.)

Providence (1977; French/Swiss). . . . . .Sonia Langham

A Dream of Passion (1978) . . . . Brenda

Same Time Next Year (1978). . . . . .Doris

Resurrection (1980). . . . . .Edna McCauley

The Ambassador (1984) . . . . .Alex Hacker

••• 0:06—Breasts opening her robe to greet her lover.

••• 0:07—Brief breasts making love in bed.

••• 0:29—Breasts in a movie while her husband, Robert Mitchum, watches.

Twice in a Lifetime (1985) . . . . Kate

Hanna's War (1988). . . . . .Katalin Senesh

Dying Young (1991) . . . . Mrs. O'Neil

Grand Isle (1991) .Mademoiselle Reisa

The Cemetery Club (1993) . . . . Esther Moskowitz

When a Man Loves a Woman (1993). . . . . .Emily

Roommates (1994) . . . . Judith

How to Make an American Quilt (1995) . . . . .Hy

The Spitfire Grill (1996). . . . . Hannah Fergeson

Deceiver (1997). . . . . Mook

Made for Cable Movies:

Act of Vengeance (1986). . . . . Margaret Yablonski

Primal Secrets (1994) . . . . .Frances Griffin

Made for TV Movies:

Pack of Lies (1987) . . . . .Barbara Jackson

When You Remember Me (1990) . . . . Nurse Cooder

Taking Back My Life: The Nancy Ziegenmeyer Story (1992)
. . . . .Wilma

Shattered Trust: The Shari Karney Story (1993) Joan Delvecchio

Getting Gotti (1994) . . . . Jo Giacalone

Getting Out (1994) . . . . Arlie's Mother

Follow the River (1995) . . . . Gretel

My Brother's Keeper (1995). . . . . Helen

A Deadly Vision (1997) . . . . .Yvette Watson

TV:

The Doctors. . . . . Dr. Kate Bartok

The Iron Horse (1967-68) . . . . Julie Parsons

The Ellen Burstyn Show (1986-88). . . . . Ellen Brewer

Burton, Jennifer Leigh

a.k.a. Jennifer Jarrett.

Films:

Desire (1994). . . . . Cynthia Hoffman
- • 0:18—Brief partial breasts, while blindfolded and rubbing perfume on herself before getting killed.

I Like to Play Games (1994) .Tiffany
- •• 0:53—Nude, when rubbing oil on Michael while Lisa Boyle watches.
- •• 0:57—Breasts and buns, while making love with Michael and Boyle in bed.

Play Time (1994). . . . . Lindsey

(Unrated version reviewed.)
- •• 0:01—Nude, while making love in bed with Joe.
- • 0:05—Buns in purple swimsuit by the pool and in the kitchen with Geena.
- ••• 0:07—Breasts while on lounge chair, rubbing lotion on herself next to Geena.
- •• 0:10—Nude in fantasy.
- •• 0:11—Breasts and buns, while running into the house with Geena to hide from the pool man.
- ••• 0:13—Breasts and buns, while dancing and masturbating in front of Geena (who is masturbating on the sofa). Steamy!
- ••• 0:16—Breasts, while on patio and talking with Geena in the pool.
- ••• 0:18—Buns in panties and breasts, while undressing for Joe in bedroom.
- •• 0:26—Breasts, when undressing in office and caressing Geena while masturbating.
- •• 0:32—Right breast, then breasts, while making love with Joe.
- ••• 0:36—Breasts and partial buns, masturbating and caressing Geena on bed, while Joe watches from closet.
- •• 0:41—Full frontal nudity, while sitting in spa and talking with Geena and Joe.
- ••• 0:44—Breasts and buns in panties in bedroom, caressing Connie while Joe watches.
- ••• 0:48—Breasts and buns, while making love with Geena and Joe in spa.
- ••• 0:53—Full frontal nudity while caressing herself in sauna so Brad can see her.
- ••• 1:03—In sheer blouse and black bra in Brad's office. Breasts and buns in panties after taking off her clothes and making love.
- • 1:11—Buns in panties while in bed with Brad.
- ••• 1:12—Nude, while making love in bed with Brad.
- •• 1:14—Breasts, when talking with Brad while lying in bed.
- • 1:18—Right breast, then breasts and buns, while in bed with Brad.
- ••• 1:35—Full frontal nudity, after taking off her swimsuit and rubbing lotion on Geena while the guys watch.

Caged Hearts (1995). . . . . Ranch Inmate

Killing For Love (1995) . . . . .Zoe
- ••• 0:33—Full frontal nudity, while making love with Paul in bed.
- •• 1:01—Full frontal nudity, while making love with Paul in the kitchen, then getting dressed.
- •• 1:08—Breasts, while trying to seduce Jay Richardson on sofa.

Nighttime Lover (1995). . . . . .Cynthia

a.k.a. Call Girl
- •• 0:01—Nude, while posing for photographs with another model.

Watch Me (1995) . . . . Samantha
- • 0:04—Brief breasts while on sofa.
- ••• 0:08—Nude, while making love with Alex. He has her tied by her wrists and blindfolded.
- ••• 0:16—Full frontal nudity, while lying on table when Alex blindfolds her, rubs raw egg on her body, then makes love with her.
- ••• 0:30—Full frontal nudity, when blindfolded, making love with Alex while Elise watches from other apartment.
- • 0:44—In black lingerie, then buns and breasts, while undressing when Paul video tapes her.
- ••• 0:49—Nude while being video taped some more, then making love with Paul.
- ••• 1:00—Nude, while making love with Alex during Elise's flashback.
- •• 1:14—Buns, while in kitchen with Alex. Full frontal nudity, while blindfolded in chair with Alex.

Made for Cable TV:

Red Shoe Diaries: How I Met My Husband (1993; Showtime) . . . . Dominatrix #1

Red Shoe Diaries: Burning Up (1994; Showtime) . . . Fire Victim

Red Shoe Diaries: Runway (1994; Showtime). . . . . . . Coco
- 0:01—In black bra.
- 0:19—Lower half of buns, while sitting next to Miguel.
- • 0:21—Brief breasts (she's on the right) while watching Alia and Miguel making love.

Erotic Confessions: Watching Vanessa (1995; Cinemax) . . . . .Vanessa
- ••• 0:04—Nude, when making love in house with Brad while being watched by someone outside. Long scene.
- ••• 0:14—Nude, undressing in the house, sitting on sofa, eating ice cream, then rubbing it all over herself.
- •• 0:16—Nude, while taking a shower.
- ••• 0:31—Full frontal nudity, while making love in bed with the newsman.

Erotic Confessions: Southern Hospitality (1997; Cinemax) . . . . Amy
- • 0:03—Brief breasts, while making love with Anthony in bed.
- ••• 0:12—Nude, while making love with Anthony in bed.

Erotic Confessions: The Hat Check Boy (1997; Cinemax) . . . . .Tracy
- •• 0:17—Breasts, while making love with Skip in hat check room.
- ••• 0:21—Breasts and buns while making love in apartment with Skip and Katherine.

Red Shoe Diaries: Dime A Dance (1997; Showtime) . . . . Darcy
- • 0:01—Brief right breast, twice, in flashbacks.
- •• 0:17—In bra, then breasts while making love with Michael in back seat of car. Almost B&W.

Beverly Hills Bordello: Inspiration (1998; Showtime) . . . . Helen
- •• 0:09—Nude, while in bedroom with Henry.
- ••• 0:14—Nude, while making love with Henry.

Video Tapes:

Playboy's Sensual Fantasy for Lovers (1993) . . Pretending
- 0:16—In wet, braless white blouse.
- ••• 0:17—Nude, in stable after undressing and making love.
- • 0:47—Full frontal nudity during review.

Playboy's Rising Stars and Sexy Starlets (1996) . . . Talent
- • 0:43—Brief full frontal nudity, while lying down in clip from *Watch Me.*

Burton, Kate

Films:

Big Trouble in Little China (1986) . . . . .Margo
Life With Mikey (1993) . . . . .Mrs. Burns
The First Wives Club (1996) . . . . Woman in Bed
Looking for Richard (1996) . . . . n.a.

Made for Cable Movies:

Love Matters (1993; Showtime). . . . . Deborah
(Unrated version reviewed.)

- 0:05—Brief breasts, getting turned over on bed during video playback.
- 0:09—Very brief side view of right breast, while making love in bed with Tony Goldwyn during video playback.

Mistrial (1996; HBO) . . . . Katherine Donahue

Miniseries:

Ellis Island (1984) . . . . Vanessa Ogden

TV:

Home Fires (1992) . . . . Anne Kramer
Monty (1994-95) . . . . .Fran Richardson

Bush, Jovita

Films:

Cool Breeze (1972) .Beauty Contestant
The Cheerleaders (1973). . . . . Bonnie

- 0:02—Brief breasts, while taking off blouse in the locker room.
- •• 0:28—Brief breasts with the other cheerleaders in locker room.
- •• 0:54—Side view of right breast, while at slumber party.
- ••• 0:58—Nude, while running around at slumber party/orgy.
- 1:00—Brief buns and left breast, when football player lifts her up.
- 1:13—Breasts, with the other cheerleaders in back seat at carwash.

Fox Style (1974) . . . . Bonnie

- 1:02—Brief right breast while in dressing room, changing clothes.

• Bussières, Pascale

Films:

When Night is Falling (1995; Canadian). . . . . Camille

- 0:00—Full frontal nudity, while swimming under water, sometimes with another woman. Sometimes it's hard to see because of the distorted view.
- 0:50—Brief side view of left breast, while making love in bed with Martin.
- •• 0:56—Breasts, while making love in bed with Petra.
- 1:08—Right breast, while making love in bed with Petra.
- 1:11—Brief breasts, when sitting up in bed with Petra.
- 1:13—Very brief partial left breast, after throwing pillow aside to get out of bed.

  1:22—Partial breasts, while swimming under water.
- 1:25—Brief buns, while lying on top of Petra.

Thunder Point (1996) . . . . n.a.

Butler, Bridget

Films:

Sunset Heat (1991) . . . . Lady in New York
a.k.a. Midnight Heat
(Unrated version reviewed.)

- 0:00—Buns, lying in bed.
- 0:01—Buns, when Michael Paré takes off her shirt. Buns and partial left breast lying on him in bed.

Sunset Strip (1992) . . . . .Candice
Amore! (1993) . . . . Barbie

Butler, Cher *

Video Tapes:

Wet & Wild (1989) . . . . .Model
Playmates at Play (1990) . . . . .Bareback

• Butler, Yancy

Films:

Hard Target (1993) . . . . Natasha Binder
Drop Zone (1994). . . . . .Jessie Crossman
Fast Money (1995) . . . . Francesca
The Ex (1996) . . . . Deidre Kenyon

- 0:11—Brief back side of right breast, while getting into bathtub with Frank, then drowning him.
- 1:02—Brief buns and partial back side of right breast, when taking off her dress in her apartment with Nick Mancuso, so that Suzy Amis can see. Medium long shot.

Made for Cable Movies:

The Hit List (1993; Showtime). . . . . .Jordan Henning

Made for Cable TV:

Perversions of Science: Given the Heir (1997; HBO)
. . . . Lisa Giroux

TV:

Mann & Machine (1992). . . . . .Eve Edison
South Beach (1993). . . . . .Kate Patrick
Brooklyn South (1997-) . . . . Ann-Marie Kersey
NYPD Blue: I Love Lucy (Apr 22, 1997) . . . . . .Lucinda Hastings

Buxbaum, Ingrid

Films:

Stars and Bars (1988) . . . . Photographer

Made for Cable Movies:

Traveling Man (1989; HBO) . . . . Uncredited Salesgirl

- ••• 0:05—Breasts and buns while wearing G-string, dancing during sales meeting.

Buxton, Judy

Films:

The Bawdy Adventures of Tom Jones (1976; British)
. . . . Lizzy

- 0:39—Brief breasts in bed several times, helping to keep Tom Jones and Prudence hidden.

The Devil Within Her (1976; British) . . . . Sheila
Aces High (1977; British). . . . . French Girl

Byrbo, Hana

See: Novak, Lenka.

Byrd-Nethery, Miriam

Films:

The Big Bus (1976) . . . . Farm Family Member
Lies (1984; British). . . . . Night Nurse
The Offspring (1986) . . . . Eileen Burnside

- 0:26—Breasts in bathtub filled with ice while her husband tries to kill her with an ice pick.
- 0:29—Very brief right breast, dead in bathtub while her husband is downstairs.

Summer Heat (1987). . . . . .Aunt Patty
Walk Like a Man (1987). Toy Store Clerk
Stepfather 2 (1989). . . . . Sally Jenkins
Leatherface: The Texas Chainsaw Massacre III (1990) . . . Mama
The Raven Red Kiss-Off (1990). . . . . .Motel Manager

TV:

Mr. T and Tina (1976) . . . . .Miss Llewellyn

Byrne, Patti T.
Films:
Fuzz (1972) . . . . Abigail
Night Call Nurses (1972) . . . . Barbara
a.k.a. Young LA Nurses 2
•• 0:59—Breasts several times in bed with the Doctor.

Byrnes, Maureen
Films:
Cry Uncle (1971) . . . . Lena Right
• 0:16—Breasts and buns in bed with two other girls while spanking Dominic. Hard to see because the negative image is projected.
••• 0:46—Brief breasts with Connie when Jake peeks in the window. Full frontal nudity, talking with Jake at the doorway.
• 0:48—Breasts, making love with Jake in bed.
•• 0:49—Nude, getting out of bed after knocking out Jake.
••• 0:50—Full frontal nudity, while interrogating Jake.
•• 0:53—Breasts, in room with gun while covering Jake.
•• 0:54—Full frontal nudity, while shooting gun and leaving.
Hurry Up, Or I'll Be 30 (1973) . . . . Flo
Sugar Cookies (1973) . . . . Dola
•• 0:37—Right breast while Gus is on top of her, then breasts and buns.
Goin' South (1978) . . . . Mrs. Warren

Byun, Susan
Films:
Crime Lords (1990) . . . . Monahan
•• 1:06—Left breast, then right breast, while making out with Wayne Crawford on the couch.
Dead Connection (1993) . . . . Sarah
• 0:50—Very, very brief left breast while catching shirt that Michael Madsen throws to her.
Deadly Target (1994) . . . . Diana
Extramarital (1998) . . . . Masseuse
Video Tapes:
Inside Out 4 (1992) . . . . Lee Anne/Three on a Match
(Unrated version reviewed.)
••• 0:58—Breasts, changing blouse in the bathroom.

Caballero, Katia
Films:
Beyond Innocence (1988) . . . . Marthe Foscari
•• 0:29—Breasts, after taking off nightgown in bed with Paul, then making love.
•• 0:31—Buns, brief lower frontal nudity and side view of right breast, while looking out the window.
• 0:32—Very brief right breast, while putting on robe.
• 0:37—Breasts, while in bed with Paul after he moves the covers down.
•• 1:08—Left breast, while lying in bed with Paul.
Interview With the Vampire: The Vampire Chronicles (1994) . . . . Woman in Audience

Cabasa, Lisa Ann
Films:
Wild at Heart (1990) . . . . Reindeer Dancer
•• 0:30—Breasts standing while Mr. Reindeer talks on the phone. More breasts dancing in front of him.
One Night Stand (1997) . . . . Armani Model
Made for Cable Movies:
Lies of the Twins (1991; USA) . . . . Caryn

Cable, Tawnni *
Made for Cable Movies:
Marilyn & Bobby: Her Final Affair (1993; USA) . . . . Jayne
Video Tapes:
Playboy Video Calendar 1990 (1989) . . . . March
••• 0:13—Nude.
Playboy Video Centerfold: Tawnni Cable (1990) . . . . Playmate
••• 0:00—Nude throughout.
Playmates at Play (1990) . . . . Gotta Dance
Wet & Wild II (1990) . . . . Model
Eden (1992) . . . . Uncredited Girl in Exercise Room
Playboy Playmates in Paradise (1992) . . . . Playmate
Playboy's Sexy, Steamy, Sultry (1993) . . . . Playmate
Sexy Lingerie: Dreams & Desire (1994) . . . . Picture Perfect/Blue
•• 0:10—Nude while posing with two other models.
Wet & Wild: The Locker Room (1994) . . . . Playmate
Centerfold Fantasies (1997) . . . . Herself
• 0:31—Brief buns in swimsuit.

Cadell, Ava *
Films:
Confessions of a Window Cleaner (1974; British) . . . . School Girl
Nude in shower scene with other school girls.
Happy Housewives (1975; British) . . . . Schoolgirl
• 0:39—Buns, when caught by the Squire and getting spanked.
The Hound of the Baskervilles (1977; British) . . . . Maid
The Golden Lady (1979; British) . . . . Anita
Spaced Out (1980; British) . . . . Partha
a.k.a. Outer Touch
•• 0:41—Left breast making love on bed with Cliff.
•• 0:42—Nude wrestling on bed with Cliff.
• 0:43—Brief left breast lying in bed alone.
•• 1:08—Breasts sitting on bed.
Smokey and the Bandit III (1983) . . . . Blond
Commando (1985) . . . . Girl in Bed
• 0:46—Very brief breasts three times in bed when Arnold Schwarzenegger knocks a guy through the motel door into her room.
Jungle Warriors (1985) . . . . Didi Belair
a.k.a. Captive Women 9
• 0:50—Brief breasts getting yellow top ripped open by Sybil Danning.
Not of This Earth (1988) . . . . Second Hooker
•• 0:41—Breasts in cellar with Paul just before getting killed with two other hookers. Wearing a gold dress.
Do or Die (1991) . . . . Ava
•• 0:20—Buns and brief breasts, getting dressed in motor home. Lots of buns shots, wearing swimsuit.
Lunch Box (1991) . . . . Maggie Dancer
• 1:01—Brief buns in swimsuit while kneeling next to Waldo by pool.
• 1:03—Brief buns in lingerie while in bed with Waldo.
Amore! (1993) . . . . Mrs. Scarborough
Fit To Kill (1993) . . . . Ava
•• 1:13—Half of right breast, sticking out of bra. Buns in G-string.
•• 1:14—Left breast, while making love with Petrov in radio station while still talking on the air.
••• 1:17—Breasts in spa with Petrov.
Hard Hunted (1993) . . . . Ava
••• 0:38—Breasts in spa with Becky while doing radio show.

Made for Cable TV:
Pillow Previews (Playboy) . . . . Hostess

Cady, Shawn

Films:
Nine Months (1995) . . . . Roller Blade Girl
Made for TV Movies:
Dalva (1996) . . . . Young Dalva
• 0:01—Very, very brief partial buns when her dress flies up while riding a horse. Note that she's wearing panties from the wrong time period (they look very '90s, not something you would see 20 years ago.)
• 0:03—Very brief buns again, while riding on horseback.

Caffaro, Cheri *

Films:
Ginger (1970) . . . . Ginger
••• 1:06—Breasts, taking off her top in front of Rodney and lying on top of him in bed.
•• 1:10—Full frontal nudity, getting up off the bed.
• 1:22—Sort of breasts during recollection of her rape. Hard to see.
• 1:23—Breasts, taking off her towel in front of Jimmy.
••• 1:32—Nude, on bed handcuffed behind her back by Rex, then getting molested by him. Long scene.
The Abductors (1971) . . . . Ginger
• 0:23—Breasts under sheer green blouse while talking with Ken Stanton.
••• 0:52—Nude, while making love with Stanton on the floor.
•• 1:01—Breasts, when getting molested by a bad guy while she's tied to a pole.
• 1:05—Breasts in open blouse outside after escaping.
•• 1:20—Breasts, after taking off blouse and washing Stanton in the shower while he's tied up.
A Place Called Today (1972). . . . . Cindy Cartwright
•• 0:14—Full frontal nudity covered with oil or something writhing around on the bed.
• 1:21—Brief side view of right breast undressing in the bathroom.
• 1:23—Brief full frontal nudity getting kidnapped by two guys.
•• 1:30—Nude when they take off the blanket.
• 1:35—Brief breasts just before getting killed.
Girls Are For Loving (1973) . . . . Ginger
• 0:02—Breasts under sheer pink nightie.
• 0:04—Buns, while lying on bed with her boyfriend.
• 0:18—Full frontal nudity, after taking off towel and getting into pool with Ronnie St. Clair.
•• 0:19—Breasts in front of mirror, putting on make-up while talking to Clay.
•• 0:26—Buns and breasts in pasties after song and dance number on stage.
••• 0:29—In sheer black nightie, then breasts while making love with Jim Whitney.
•• 0:32—Breasts in black nightie during martial arts fight.
••• 0:44—Buns and breasts at beach with bad guy, then fighting with him.
•• 1:07—Nude on table, while held down by bad guys.
••• 1:08—Full frontal nudity, when tied by wrists and ankles to the bed, talking to Ronnie, then making love with William while Ronnie watches.
•• 1:16—Buns and breasts, while getting untied by Clay during rescue.
Savage Sisters (1974) . . . . Jo Turner
Too Hot To Handle (1975) . . . . Samantha Fox
•• 0:06—Breasts wearing a black push-up bra and buns in black G-string.
• 0:13—Full frontal nudity lying on boat.
••• 0:39—Breasts making love in bed with Dominco.
••• 0:55—Full frontal nudity taking off clothes and lying in bed.
• 1:06—Brief left breast in bed with Dominco.

Cagan, Andrea

Films:
Captain Milkshake (1970) . . . . Melissa
The Hot Box (1972) . . . . Bunny
•• 0:16—Breasts cleaning herself off in stream behind Ellie and getting out.
• 0:21—Breasts sleeping in hammock. (She's the third girl from the front, stretching.)
••• 0:45—Breasts in stream while bathing with the other three girls.
Teenager (1975) . . . . n.a.

Cain, Sharon

a.k.a. Adult film actress Sharon Kane.
Films:
Preppies (1984). . . . . Exotic Dancer
Slammer Girls (1987) . . . . Rita
• 0:23—Brief breasts changing clothes under table in the prison cafeteria.
•• 1:01—Breasts walking around an electric chair trying to distract a prison guard.
Violated (1987) . . . . Party Guest
California Hot Wax (1992) . . . . Loretta
•• 0:55—Breasts, changing in car wash maintenance room in front of Scott.
•• 0:59—Breasts in and out of swimming pool with Scott.
The Perfect Gift (1993) . . . . Pajama Party Guest
Video Tapes:
Inside Out 4 (1992) . . . . Video Mate
(Unrated version reviewed.)
•• 1:14—Breasts on TV.
••• 1:16—Breasts in Dave's living room.
• 1:17—Nude, making love with Dave in fast speed.
••• 1:18—Breasts and buns, on sofa with Dave.
• 1:19—More breasts in fast speed.
••• 1:20—Nude in Dave's living room.
• 1:22—Nude on TV again.
Playboy Night Dreams (1993) . . . . Do Not Disturb
••• 0:36—Breasts and buns, when in panties, after getting locked out of her hotel room. Nude, while making love with a guy in his hotel room.

Calabrese, Gina

Films:
Goin' All the Way (1981). . . . . n.a.
•• 0:12—Left breast, in the girls' locker room shower. Standing on the left.
The Vals (1982) . . . . Annie
• 0:04—Breasts changing clothes in bedroom with three of her friends. Long shot, hard to see.
• 0:15—Right breast, while making love with a guy at a party.

Camden, Danone

See: Simpson, Danone.

• Cameron

Films:

Sunset Strip (1992) .... Crystal
•• 0:17—Breasts and buns in G-string, while dancing on stage.
•• 0:38—In red dress, then breasts while doing strip routine.
•• 1:03—In dress, then breasts while stripping. Buns in body stocking.
• 1:16—Breasts in music video.
Star Trek Generations (1994)............... Ensign Kellogg
Tales From the Hood (1995) ....n.a.

TV:

Star Trek: The Next Generation .... Ensign Kellogg

Cameron, Cissie

See: Colpitts-Cameron, Cissie.

Cameron, Joanna *

Films:

B.S. I Love You (1971)................... Marilyn/Michele
(Not available on video tape.)
Pretty Maids All in a Row (1971) .... Yvonne

TV:

Secrets of Isis (1975-78) .... Isis

Camille, Sharen

Films:

Death Benefit (1996)..................... Melissa Wilkens

Made for Cable Movies:

Psycho IV: The Beginning (1990; Showtime) ....Holly
•• 0:13—In bra, then breasts while in bedroom with Henry Thomas.

Camp, Colleen *

Films:

The Battle For the Planet of the Apes (1973)
.... Uncredited Julie
Smile (1974) .... Connie Thompson
• 0:47—Side profile of right breast and buns in dressing room while Little Bob is outside taking pictures.
The Swinging Cheerleaders (1974) .... Mary Ann
Fox Fire (1976) ....n.a.
a.k.a. Fox Force
a.k.a. She Devils in Chains
Death Game, The Seducers (1977).............. Donna
a.k.a. Mrs. Manning's Weekend
• 0:16—Buns, in spa with Sondra Locke trying to get George in with them.
• 0:47—Brief breasts jumping up and down on the bed while George is tied up.
•• 1:16—Breasts behind stained glass door taunting George. Hard to see.
Cat in the Cage (1978) .... Gilda Riener
• 0:36—Very brief left breast twice, while making love in bed with Bruce.
Apocalypse Now (1979) ....Playmate
The Game of Death (1979) .... Anne Morris
Cloud Dancer (1980) .... Cindy
The Deadly Games (1980)......................... Randy
a.k.a. The Eliminator
They All Laughed (1981)................... Christy Miller
The Seduction (1982) .... Robin
Smokey and the Bandit III (1983) .... Dusty Trails
Valley Girl (1983)...................... Sarah Richman
Doin' Time (1984).............................Catlett
The Joy of Sex (1984) .... Liz Sampson
Clue (1985)...................................Yvette
D.A.R.Y.L. (1985) .... Elaine
Police Academy II: Their First Assignment (1985)..... Kirkland
The Rosebud Beach Hotel (1985)..................Tracy
Police Academy 4: Citizens on Patrol (1987)
.... Mrs. Kirkland-Tackleberry
Walk Like a Man (1987).........................Rhonda
Illegally Yours (1988)...................... Molly Gilbert
Track 29 (1988; British) ....Arlanda
Wicked Stepmother (1989) .... Jenny
My Blue Heaven (1990).................Margaret Snow
The Magic Bubble (1992) ....Deborah
The Vagrant (1992) .... Judy Dansig
Wayne's World (1992)................. Mrs. Vanderhoff
Greedy (1993)................................... Patti
Last Action Hero (1993)........................ Ratcliff
Naked in New York (1993) .... Auditioner
Sliver (1993) .... Judy Marks
Die Hard with a Vengeance (1995) .... Connie Kowalski
Three Wishes (1995) .... Neighbor's Wife
The Associate (1996)................. Detective Jones
House Arrest (1996)................................n.a.
Speed 2: Cruise Control (1997).................. Debbie

Made for Cable Movies:

The Right to Remain Silent (1995; Showtime)
.... Mrs. Buford Lowry

Made for Cable TV:

Tales From the Crypt: Korman's Kalamity (1992; HBO)
....Mildred

Made for TV Movies:

Addicted to his Love (1988)................... Ellie Snyder
Backfield in Motion (1991) .... Laurie
For Their Own Good (1993) ....Chris

TV:

Tom (1994-95) .... Kara

• Campbell, Jennifer

Films:

The Raven Red Kiss-Off (1990)....... Ballantyne's Mistress
• 1:10—Brief breasts, while in bed with Bernie, then in background out of focus.
Animal Instincts 2 (1993)........................Mary
Blood Warriors (1993) .... Karen Stone

TV:

Robin's Hoods (1994-95).................. Annie Beckett
Baywatch (1998-)....................... Neely Kapshaw

• Campbell, Katherine

See: Fabian, Ava.

Campbell, Nell

Films:

Barry McKenzie Holds His Own... (1974; Australian)
.... Narida Breeley
• 0:15—Brief buns, while sitting on a chair on stage, talking with Barry in the audience. Brief buns and breasts, when Barry gets up on stage.
Lisztomania (1975; British)........................Olga
••• 1:04—Breasts in bed several times with Roger Daltrey when Ringo Starr comes in.
•• 1:06—Breasts in bed, sitting up and drinking.
••• 1:07—More breasts in bed with a gun after Starr leaves.
The Rocky Horror Picture Show (1975; British).. Columbia
• 1:17—Top of breasts popping out of her blouse during song and dance on stage.
Journey Among Women (1977; Australian) .... Meg

Jubilee (1977) . . . . Crabs
• 0:37—Brief breasts in bed with a new lover, Happy Days.
••• 1:31—Breasts, after taking off her T-shirt in laundromat while talking with the policeman. Buns, when making love with him in bed.

Pink Floyd The Wall (1982) . . . . Groupie

• *Campbell, Neve **

Films:

The Dark (1993) . . . . Jesse

Northern Passage (1994; Canadian) . . . . Nepeese
• 0:16—Brief buns, while walking into the river, long shot.

The Craft (1996) . . . . Bonnie

Scream (1996) . . . . Sidney

Scream 2 (1997) . . . . Sidney Prescott

Wild Things (1998) . . . . Suzie Troller

Made for TV Movies:

I Know My Son Is Alive (1994) . . . . Beth

The Canterville Ghost (1996) . . . . Ginny Otis

TV:

Catwalk (1992-93) . . . . Daisy McKenzie

Party of Five (1994-) . . . . Julia Salinger

Cannon, Dyan

Films:

Such Good Friends (1971) . . . . Julie Messinger
(Not available on video tape.)
0:03—Breasts under loose knit shawl, but you can't really see anything.
1:10—Breasts under shawl again.
1:13—Full frontal nudity in a Polaroid photograph that director Otto Preminger had made of a body double composited with Dyan Cannon's head.
1:16—Left breast under shawl while brushing her hair.

• *Canovas, Anne*

Films:

High Frequency (1988; Italian) . . . . Sylvie

Vincent and Theo (1990; British/French/U.S.) . . . . Marie
• 0:32—Three very, very brief breast shots in gaping nightgown, when getting up off the floor and yelling at Paul Rhys.

Ready to Wear (1994) . . . . Violetta Romney
a.k.a. Prêt-à-porter

*Cantrell, Cady **

Video Tapes:

Playboy Video Calendar 1993 (1992) . . . . May
••• 0:19—Nude outside on bridge and in boat.
••• 0:21—Nude in studio setting.

Playboy Video Centerfold: Cady Cantrell (1992) . . . . Playmate

Playboy Video Playmate Six-Pack 1992 (1992) . . Playmate

Wet & Wild IV (1992) . . . . Model

Playboy's Playmate Review 1993 (1993) . . . . . . Miss April
••• 0:15—Nude while modeling in studio photo session.
••• 0:17—Nude, outside in southern belle style segment.

Playboy's Sexy, Steamy, Sultry (1993) . . . . Playmate

Capetillo, Christina

Films:

Single White Female (1992) . . . . Exotic Applicant

Made for Cable TV:

Red Shoe Diaries: Alphabet Girl (1995; Showtime) . . . . Vanessa
••• 0:04—Breasts and buns, while undressing and making love with Matias.
• 0:06—Brief breasts and buns, when in bed and Matias starts taking photos.
• 0:17—Breasts after taking off blouse in Matias's office to show him she wants the job.
••• 0:23—Breasts, while making love with Carroll for the last time.

Capra, Jordana

Films:

Pass the Ammo (1988) . . . . Mary Trenton

After Midnight (1989) . . . . Vanessa

Hired to Kill (1990) . . . . Joanna

Watch It (1993) . . . . Call Girl
• 1:26—Brief partial buns, while making love with Michael in coat room during concert.

Access Denied (1996) . . . . Martha Riley

Street Corner Justice (1996) . . . . TV Newswoman

Made for Cable TV:

Erotic Confessions: Madelyn's Laundry (1996; Cinemax) . . . . Ms. Locke
(Available on video tape in *Erotic Confessions, Volume 4: Pleasure.*)

TV:

Sonny Spoon (1988) . . . . Monique

Capri, Ahna

Films:

Company of Killers (1970) . . . . Mary Jane Smythe

Darker than Amber (1970) . . . . Del

Payday (1972) . . . . Mayleen
• 0:20—Left breast in bed sleeping, then right breast with Rip Torn.
••• 0:21—Breasts sitting up in bed smoking a cigarette and talking to Torn. Long scene.

Enter the Dragon (1973) . . . . Tania
• 0:47—Very brief left breast three times in open blouse in bed with John Saxon.

The Specialist (1975) . . . . Londa Wyeth
••• 0:10—Breasts, while in bed, talking on the phone.
••• 0:28—Breasts on couch, posing for Bert.
•• 1:09—Breasts, sitting up in bed and putting robe on.

Capshaw, Kate

Wife of director Steven Spielberg.

Films:

A Little Sex (1982) . . . . Katherine
• 0:10—Brief buns under T-shirt, when running away from table after stuffing a pancake down Tim Matheson's underwear.
• 0:29—Breasts, while sitting on bed next to Matheson. Seen through out-of-focus candles.

Best Defense (1984) . . . . Laura

Dreamscape (1984) . . . . Jane DeVries

Indiana Jones and the Temple of Doom (1984) . . . . Willie Scott

Windy City (1984) . . . . Emily

Power (1986) . . . . Syndey Betterman

SpaceCamp (1986) . . . . Andie

Black Rain (1989) . . . . Joyce

Love at Large (1990) . . . . Ellen McGraw

My Heroes Have Always Been Cowboys (1991) . . . . Jolie Meadows

Just Cause (1994) . . . . Laurie Armstrong
Love Affair (1994) . . . . Lynn Weaver
How to Make an American Quilt (1995) . . . . Sally
The Locusts (1997) . . . . Mrs. Potts

Made for Cable Movies:

The Quick and the Dead (1987; HBO). . . . . n.a.
Next Door (1994; Showtime) . . . . Karen Coler

Made for TV Movies:

Code Name: Dancer (1987) . . . . Anne Goodwin

TV:

The Edge of Night (1981) . . . . Jinx Avery Mallory
Black Tie Affair (1993) . . . . Margo

Cara, Irene

Films:

Aaron Loves Angela (1975) . . . . Angela
Sparkle (1976). . . . . Sparkle
Fame (1980) . . . . Coco

- • 1:57—Brief breasts during "audition" on a B&W TV monitor.

Killing 'Em Softly (1981) . . . . Jane Flores
D.C. Cab (1983) . . . . Herself
City Heat (1984) . . . . Ginny Lee
Certain Fury (1985) . . . . Tracy

- • 0:32—Getting undressed to take a shower. Very brief side views of left breast.
- • 0:35—Very brief breasts in shower after Tatum O'Neal turns on the kitchen faucet. Hard to see because of the shower door.
- •• 0:36—Frontal nudity and side view of buns, behind shower door while Sniffer comes into the bathroom.
- •• 0:39—Breasts several times when Sniffer tries to rape her and she fights back.
- • 0:41—Buns, kneeling on floor. Overhead view.

Caged in Paradiso (1989) . . . . Eva

Miniseries:

Roots: The Next Generation (1979). . . . . . Bertha Palmer Haley

Cardan, Christina

Films:

Chained Heat (1983; U.S./German). . . . . Miss King
Glitch (1988). . . . . Non SAG

- • 0:47—Brief breasts in spa taking off her swimsuit top.

Carder, Elizabeth

Films:

Night Shift (1982). . . . . Dolores
Talking Walls (1982) . . . . Bored Girl

- •• 0:20—Breasts, making love in the Sheep Room.
- • 1:09—Very brief left breast, in bed.

Cardone, Nathalie

Films:

Drole D'Endroit Pour Une Recontre (1988; French) . . . . . Sylvie
The Little Thief (1989; French) . . . . Mauricette
a.k.a. La Petite Voleuse

- •• 1:19—Breasts in convent arguing with a nun, then getting a shot.

L'Enfer (1994; French). . . . . Marylin

Carides, Gia

Sister of actress Zoë Carides.

Films:

Bliss (1985; Australian). . . . . Lucy Joy

- • 1:25—Brief breasts during nightmare. Cockroaches crawl out of cut between her breasts. Pretty gross. (The cockroaches—not her.)

The Coca-Cola Kid (1985; Australian) . . . . Chambermaid
Backlash (1986; Australian) . . . . Nikki Iceton
Strictly Ballroom (1993; Australian) . . . . Liz Holt
Bad Company (1994) . . . . Julie Amis
Brilliant Lies (1996; Australian). . . . . Susy

Made for Cable TV:

The Adventures of Captain Zoom in Outer Space (1995)
. . . . Vesper

TV:

Ultraman: Towards the Future (1990; Australian/Japanese)
. . . . Jean Echo

Carides, Zoë

Sister of actress Gia Carides.

Films:

Death in Brunswick (1990; Australian) . . . Sophie Papafagos

- • 0:28—Side of left breast, while on top of Neill.
- • 0:29—Right breast, while lying in bed with Neill.

Police Rescue (1994; Australian). . . . . .Constable Lorrie Gordon
Brilliant Lies (1996; Australian). . . . . Katy

Carl, Kitty

Films:

Your Three Minutes Are Up (1973) . . . . Susan
The Centerfold Girls (1974) . . . . Sandi

- •• 0:45—Breasts taking off her top while sitting on the bed with Perry.
- • 0:51—Breasts while on the beach, dead. Long shot, hard to see.

Kitty Can't Help It (1975). . . . . n.a.
Carhops (1980) . . . . n.a.

Carlisi, Olimpia

Films:

Catch-22 (1970) . . . . Luciana

- • 1:04—Breasts lying in bed talking with Alan Arkin.

Casanova (1976; Italian) . . . . Isabella
The Tragedy of a Ridiculous Man (1981; Italian) . . . . Chiromat
Rendez-Vous (1986; French) . . . . n.a.

Carlisle, Anne *

Films:

Liquid Sky (1984) . . . . Margaret/Jimmy
Perfect Strangers (1984). . . . . Sally

- • 0:34—Left breast, while making love in bed with Johnny.

Desperately Seeking Susan (1985) . . . . Victoria
Suicide Club (1988). . . . . Catherine

Carlson, Karen

Films:

Shame, Shame, Everybody Knows Her Name (1969)
. . . . Susan Barton
The Student Nurses (1970) . . . . Phred
a.k.a. Young LA Nurses

- • 0:08—Breasts in bed with the wrong guy.
- ••• 0:50—In bed with Jim, breasts and buns getting out, then breasts sitting in chair. Long scene.
- • 1:02—Brief breasts in bed.

The Candidate (1972) . . . . Nancy McKay

Black Oak Conspiracy (1977) . . . . Lucy
Matilda (1978) . . . . Kathleen Smith
The Octagon (1980) . . . . Justine
Fleshburn (1984). . . . . Shirley Pinter

Made for TV Movies:

A Horse for Danny (1995) . . . . Mrs. Slauson

TV:

American Dream (1981) . . . . Donna Novak
Two Marriages (1983-84) . . . . Ann Daley
Dallas (1987) . . . . Mrs. Scottfield

Carlson, Linda

Films:

Honey, I Blew Up the Kid (1992) . . . . Nosey Neighbor
The Pickle (1992) . . . . Bernadette
- •• 0:12—In white bra and panties under stockings, after taking off her clothes in hotel room in front of Danny Aiello, then breasts.

The Beverly Hillbillies (1993) . . . . Aunt Pearl

Made for TV Movies:

A Place for Annie (1994) . . . . Gerry

TV:

Westside Medical (1977). . . . . Dr. Janet Cottrell
Kaz (1978-79). . . . . Katie McKenna
Newhart (1984-88). . . . . Bev Dutton

Carlsson, Ing-Marie

Films:

My Life as a Dog (1985; Swedish) . . . . Berit
- • 0:51—Very briefly nude when Ingemar falls through the skylight while trying to peek at her posing as a sculptor's model.

House of Angels (1993; Swedish) . . . . Eva Agren
The Slingshot (1994; Swedish) . . . . Karin Adamsson

Carlton, Hope Marie *

Films:

Hard Ticket to Hawaii (1987). Taryn
- •• 0:07—Breasts taking a shower outside while talking to Dona Speir.
- ••• 0:23—Breasts in the spa with Speir looking at diamonds they found.
- ••• 0:40—Breasts and buns on the beach making love with her boyfriend, Jimmy John.
- •• 1:33—Breasts during the end credits.

A Nightmare on Elm Street 4: The Dream Master (1988) . . . . Pin-Up Girl
- • 0:21—Brief breasts swimming in a waterbed.

Slaughterhouse Rock (1988) . . . . Krista Halpern
- • 0:09—Brief right breast, taking off her top in bedroom with her boyfriend.
- •• 0:49—Breasts, getting raped by Richard as he turns into a monster.

Terminal Exposure (1988). . . . . Christie
- ••• 1:11—Breasts in bathtub licking ice cream off a guy.

How I Got Into College (1989) . . . . Game Show Hostess
Picasso Trigger (1989). . . . . Taryn
- ••• 0:56—Breasts and buns in spa with a guy.

Savage Beach (1989) . . . . Taryn
- • 0:32—Breasts changing clothes in airplane with Dona Speir.
- •• 0:48—Nude, going for a swim on the beach with Speir.

Round Numbers (1990) . . . . Mitzi
- • 0:39—Left breast, twice, while turning around in steam room in Kate Mulgrew's imagination.

Side Out (1990) . . . . Vanna
Slumber Party Massacre 3 (1990) . . . . Janine
(Unrated version reviewed.)
Bloodmatch (1991) . . . . Connie Angel
Ghoulies III, Ghoulies Go To College (1991) . . . . . Veronica
- • 0:25—Brief right breast, while lying in bed with her boyfriend.
- • 0:53—Buns in black panties, bra and stockings while dancing around in her bedroom. Almost breasts, after taking off her bra.
- • 0:55—Brief breasts, while dancing in her bedroom.
- • 0:57—Brief buns and breasts, while taking a shower.

Miniseries:

Stephen King's "The Stand" (1994). . . . . Sally Campion

Video Tapes:

Playboy Video Magazine, Volume 9 . . . . Playmate
Playmate Playoffs. . . . . Playmate
Playboy Video Centerfold: Teri Weigel (1986) . . Playmate
Sexy Lingerie (1988) . . . . Model
Playmates at Play (1990) . . . . Flights of Fancy

CD-ROM:

Noctropolis (1994) . . . . Stiletto

• Carlton, Melissa

Films:

Hide and Seek (1994) . . . . Courtney
Lebensborn (1996) . . . . Kari Berman
- • 0:09—Brief upper half of right breast while taking a shower.
- • 0:20—Breasts, while lying on exam table and getting dressed.
- • 0:40—Brief left breast in open blouse, trying to help her brother get aroused so he can donate sperm.
- • 0:46—Left breast and buns, while starting to make love with Eric in bedroom.
- • 0:49—Brief back side of left breast, when getting out of bed.
- • 1:21—Brief breasts, while dreaming about manually stimulating her brother.
- •• 1:22—Breasts, while dreaming about making love with Eric and then her brother.
- •• 1:33—Breasts, taking off her T-shirt and getting into bed with her brother.

• Carlton-Luff, Rebekah

Films:

Leprechaun 4 In Space (1996) . . . . Princess Zarina
- •• 1:05—Breasts, when opening her top in front of the soldiers.

TV:

Baywatch (1995). . . . . Tracy

Carmack, Cody *

Films:

Affairs of the Heart (1992). . . . . Itchy
- ••• 0:45—Breasts taking off her bikini top with her husband.

Marilyn Chambers: Bedtime Fantasies (1996) . . . . n.a.

Carmack, Kona *

Video Tapes:

Playboy's Hard Bodies (1995). . . . . Herself
- ••• 0:46—Nude, while posing at the beach by herself and two other women.

Playboy Video Calendar 1997 (1996) . . . . July
- ••• 0:28—Breasts, while posing at the beach.
- ••• 0:29—Nude, while undressing by herself in a deserted train station.

Carney, Bridget

Films:

Hard to Die (1990) . . . . Shayne Hobbie
a.k.a. Tower of Terror
••• 0:24—Breasts and buns while taking a shower. Long scene.

Sorority House Massacre 2 (1990) . . . . Candy
••• 0:40—Breasts and buns in G-string, dancing in club.

Night of the Warrior (1991). . . . . Sarah

Martial Law II: Undercover (1992) . . . . Flash Dancer

Video Tapes:

Scream Queen Hot Tub Party (1991). . . . . Shayne
••• 0:17—Breasts and buns in shower from *Hard to Die*.

Carnon, Angela

Films:

Guess What Happened to Count Dracula (1970). . . . . . . Nurse

Pleasure Unlimited/Sensous Wife (1972) . . . . n.a.
a.k.a. Drop Out Wife

Innocent Sally (1973) . . . . n.a.
a.k.a. The Dirty Mind of Young Sally

Video Vixens (1973). . . . . Mrs. Gordon
•• 1:13—Full frontal nudity making love with Mr. Gordon in bed in various positions. Shot at fast speed.

Alice Goodbody (1975) . . . . Harmonica Girl
••• 1:07—Buns and lower frontal nudity playing a harmonica without her mouth. (Never see her face.)
• 1:20—Buns, during end credits.

Young and Wild (1975) . . . . n.a.

Carol, Jean

a.k.a. Jeannie Daly.

Films:

Payback (1988). . . . . Donna Nathan
••• 0:24—Breasts opening her pink robe for Jason while reclining on couch.

TV:

The Guiding Light . . . . Nadine Cooper

Carol, Linda

Films:

School Spirit (1985) . . . . Hogette

Reform School Girls (1986). . . . . Jennifer Williams
•• 0:05—Nude in the shower.
• 0:56—Breasts in the back of a truck with Norton.
•• 1:13—Breasts getting hosed down by Edna.

Back to the Beach (1987) . . . . Bridgette

Future Hunters (1987). . . . . Michelle
• 0:35—Very brief right breast and lower frontal nudity, stepping through doorway and wrapping robe around herself.
•• 0:36—Breasts in open robe in hotel room with the bad guys.

No Man's Land (1988) . . . . Party Girl

Carnal Crimes (1991). . . . . Elise
• 0:01—Very brief left breast, while rolling over in bed.
• 0:05—In wet lingerie and very brief side view of right breast in shower fantasy.
• 0:07—Breasts in B&W photo collage.
• 0:09—Full frontal nudity under sheer nightie, trying to get Stanley into bed.
• 0:11—Breasts in B&W photo again.
• 0:24—Brief right breast outside window opening her top while watching Renny & Mia make out.
• 0:26—Brief upper half of right breast when bum molests her.
••• 0:28—Breasts posing for Renny with Mia.
••• 0:29—Full frontal nudity making love with Renny and Mia.
• 0:30—Brief buns, sleeping in bed.
••• 0:38—Breasts making love with the baker. Long scene.
• 0:49—Breasts in B&W photo again.
• 1:02—Brief side view of right breast in gaping blouse.
• 1:33—Side view of buns in dominatrix outfit.

Fear of Scandal (1992; Italian) . . . . Anna
• 0:21—Brief left breast, while making love with a guy in bed.
•• 0:42—Left breast, while making love in bed.
•• 0:43—Breasts, while covering herself with the bed covers.

Made for Cable Movies:

Prey of the Chameleon (1992; Showtime) . . . . Nurse
• 0:00—Breasts several times, making love with a guy in restroom. Dark.

Video Tapes:

Inside Out 2 (1992). . . . . The Hitchhiker/The Hitchhiker
(Unrated version reviewed.)
••• 1:17—Breasts undressing in room, while a guy watches from across the way. Long scene. B&W.

Caron, Leslie

Films:

Daddy Long Legs (1955) . . . . Julie

The Glass Slipper (1955) . . . . Ella

Gigi (1958) . . . . Gigi

Fanny (1961). . . . . Fanny

Father Goose (1964) . . . . Catherine Freneau

Is Paris Burning? (1966; U.S./French). . . . . Francoise

Promise Her Anything (1966; British). . . . . Michele O'Brien

The Head of the Family (1967; Italian/French) . . . . . . Paola
• 0:22—Very brief upper half of left breast while sitting at drafting table and breast feeding her baby.

Madron (1970; U.S./Israeli) . . . . Sister Mary

Nicole (1972) . . . . Nicole
a.k.a. The Widow's Revenge

The Man Who Loved Women (1977; French) . . . . Vera

Valentino (1977; British) . . . . Nazimova

Goldengirl (1979) . . . . Dr. Lee

Dangerous Moves (1985; Swiss) . . . . Henia Liebskind

Courage Mountain (1990). . . . . Jane Hillary

Damage (1992; French/British) . . . . Elizabeth Prideaux
(Unrated Director's cut reviewed.)

Miniseries:

Master of the Game (1984) . . . . Solange

Made for TV Movies:

QB VII (1974) . . . . Angela Kelno

Carothers, Veronica *

Films:

Mankillers (1987). . . . . Shannon Smith

Phoenix the Warrior (1988) . . . . Suga

Fatal Skies (1989) . . . . Toni
•• 0:31—Buns, while putting on swimsuit bottom.
•• 0:32—Breasts, while putting on swimsuit top.

Kinjite (1989) . . . . Blonde Hostess

Vice Academy, Part 3 (1991) . . . . Loretta

Mind, Body & Soul (1992) . . . . Sacrifice Girl
••• 0:02—Breasts when her dress is ripped open during occult ceremony while tied by her wrists.
•• 0:26—Left breast several times and very, very brief right breast in black outfit (her face is covered with a hood) during occult ceremony.

Good Girls Don't (1993) . . . . Bimbo Jeannie

Vice Academy, Part 4 (1994). . . . . Amber
• 0:11—Brief partial buns, while getting a tattoo from Scabia.

Carpenter, Linda *

a.k.a. Playboy Playmate Linda Beatty.

Films:

Apocalypse Now (1979). . . . . Playmate
- 1:01—Breasts in centerfold photo, hung up for display. Long shot.

A Different Story (1979) . . . . Chastity
(R-rated version reviewed.)
- 1:33—Very brief breasts in shower, shutting the door when Meg Foster discovers her with Perry King.

Carr, Judy

a.k.a. Adult film actress Juliet Anderson.

Films:

It's Called Murder Baby (1982) . . . . Adrian Ross
(R-rated version of the adult film *Dixie Ray, Hollywood Star.*)
- 1:21—Brief breasts, sitting up on bed in background.

Carr, Laurie Ann *

Films:

Mortuary Academy (1988) . . . . Nurse

Video Tapes:

Wet & Wild (1989). . . . . Model

Playboy's 21 Playmates: Volume II (1996) . . . . . . Playmate
- ••• 0:06—Nude in still photos.
- ••• 0:07—In lingerie and nude in house.

Carr, Tanya

Video Tapes:

Hot Body International: #2 Miss Puerto Vallarta (1990)
. . . . Contestant
- • 0:15—Very, very brief breasts, while flashing.
- •• 0:24—Buns, in two piece swimsuit, then breasts wearing pasties.
- •• 0:56—Wearing pasties.

Hot Body International: #4 Spring Break (1992)
. . . . Contestant
- ••• 0:42—Breasts popping out of wet T-shirt, quite a few times. Buns in G-string.
- • 0:58—Brief breasts several times winning 3rd place in wet T-shirt contest.

Hot Body Competition: The Best of Hot Body (1994)
. . . . Herself
- ••• 0:42—Buns in swimsuits. Breasts while wearing pasties.

Carrera, Barbara *

Films:

Embryo (1976) . . . . Victoria
- •• 1:10—Brief buns and breasts in the mirror after making love with Hudson.
- • 1:11—Left breast sticking out of bathrobe.

The Island of Dr. Moreau (1977) . . . . Maria

When Time Ran Out! (1980) . . . . Iolani

Condorman (1981). . . . . Natalia

I, the Jury (1982) . . . . Dr. Charolette Bennett
- ••• 1:02—Nude on bed making love with Armand Assante. Very sexy.
- • 1:45—Brief breasts, while in hallway kissing Assante.
- • 1:46—Brief left breast, while falling to the floor. Breasts while lying on the floor wounded.

Lone Wolf McQuade (1983) . . . . Lola

Never Say Never Again (1983) . . . . Fatima Blush

Wild Geese II (1985; British) . . . . Kathy

The Underachievers (1987). Katherine

Love at Stake (1988). . . . . Faith Stewart

Loverboy (1989) . . . . Alex Barnett

Wicked Stepmother (1989). Priscilla
- • 1:14—Very, very brief upper half of right breast peeking out of the top of her dress when she flips her head back while seducing Steve.

Point of Impact (1993) . . . . Eva
- • 0:39—In wet white swimsuit, after getting out of swimming pool.
- • 0:40—Very brief breasts, while swimming under water past underwater window.
- •• 0:51—Close up of left breast, while making love with Paré.
- • 0:53—Brief left breast, after getting out of bed.
- ••• 0:59—Breasts and buns in T-back, while swimming under water in pool.
- •• 1:00—Breasts, while making love outside with Paré.
- •• 1:02—Breasts in shower with Paré and on bed in wet sheet.

Night of the Archer (1994) . . . . Victoria de Fleury

Tryst (1994). . . . . Julia
- • 1:03—Partial right breast, then left breast while making love in bed with Todd.

Made for Cable Movies:

Sawbones (1995; Showtime)
. . . . Rita Baldwin
- • 1:06—Buns, several times, while lying on operating table. Don't see her face very well.

Miniseries:

Masada (1981) . . . . Sheva
- •• 0:56—Breasts, after taking off her dress top in bedroom with Peter O'Toole. (Nude scene added for video tape release.)

TV:

Centennial (1978-79) . . . . Clay Basket

Dallas (1985-89) . . . . Angelica Nero

Video Tapes:

Playboy Video Magazine, Volume 1 (1982) . . . . . . Herself
- •• 0:01—Nude in still photos. Nude in scenes from *I, the Jury.*
- •• 0:30—Breasts in still photos.
- ••• 0:32—Nude in scenes from *I, the Jury.*

• Carrera, Christy *

Video Tapes:

Hot Body International: Dreamgirl II (1995). . . . . Herself

Hot Body International: Steamed Heat (1995)
. . . . Herself
- • 0:32—Brief breasts, after taking off her black top.

Playboy's Voluptuous Vixens (1997). . . . . Featured

Carrera, Tamara

Films:

Back to the Future, Part II (1989). . . . . Jacuzzi Girl

Blonde Heaven (1994) . . . . Dee
- •• 0:05—Breasts, after taking off dress top while being video taped.
- • 0:06—Breasts, while taking a shower.
- •• 0:09—Breasts, while making love in the shower with a guy.

Under Lock and Key (1994). . . . . Inmate

Video Tapes:

Hot Body International: #2 Miss Puerto Vallarta (1990)
. . . . Contestant

Hot Body International: #4 Spring Break (1992) . . . Contestant

Beverly Hills Workout (1993) . . . . Herself
- •• 0:08—Breasts and buns in T-back, while working out in backyard.
- ••• 0:27—Nude, while dancing and posing in backyard.
- ••• 0:45—Nude, while posing outdoors.

Carrere, Tia

Films:

Aloha Summer (1988) . . . . Lani Kepoo

Fatal Mission (1990) . . . . Mai Chang

- 0:22—Side view of right breast while changing tops. Dark, hard to see, but it is her.

Harley Davidson and The Marlboro Man (1991) . . . . . . Kimiko

Little Sister (1991) . . . . Adrienne

Showdown in Little Tokyo (1991) . . . . Minako

(Nudity is done by a body double.)

Wayne's World (1992) . . . . Cassandra

Quick (1993) . . . . Janet Sakamoto

Rising Sun (1993) . . . . Jingo Asakuma

Treacherous (1993) . . . . Dr. Jessica Jamison

Wayne's World 2 (1993) . . . . Cassandra

Hostile Intentions (1994) . . . . Nora

True Lies (1994) . . . . Juno Skinner

Hollow Point (1995) . . . . Diane Norwood

The Immortals (1995) . . . . Gina

Jury Duty (1995) . . . . Monica

High School High (1996) . . . . Victoria Chapell

Natural Enemy (1996) . . . . Christina

Kull the Conqueror (1997) . . . . Akivasha

Top of the World (1997) . . . . Rebecca Mercer

Made for Cable Movies:

Intimate Strangers (1991; Showtime) . . . . Mino

- 0:34—In black lingerie in Nick's apartment. Very brief side of right breast in bed with him.

Made for Cable TV:

Tales From the Crypt: On a Dead Man's Chest (1992; HBO) . . . . Scarlett

Made for TV Movies:

Nothing But the Truth (1995) . . . . Simone Gideon

TV:

General Hospital (1986-87) . . . . Jade Soong

Music Videos:

Ballroom Blitz/Wayne's World (1992) . . . . Herself

CD-ROM:

The Daedalus Encounter (1995) . . . . Ari

Carrico, Monica

Films:

Lucky 13 (1984) . . . . Charlene Andrews

a.k.a. Running Hot

a.k.a. Highway to Hell

- 0:02—Brief buns and partial left breast under water, while masturbating in bathtub.
- 0:48—Brief buns, after taking off her panties to go skinny dipping.
- •• 0:50—Breasts sitting on a rock after skinny dipping with Eric Stoltz.
- •• 0:51—Breasts and buns after getting out of water and picking up clothes.
- •• 1:03—Breasts in bed making love with Stoltz.
- ••• 1:15—Breasts while lying in bed with Stoltz.

Guilty by Suspicion (1991) . . . . Nelly Lesser

Carrillo, Elpidia

Films:

The Border (1982) . . . . Maria

- 1:19—Half of right breast and half of left breast, after opening her blouse in shack with Jack Nicholson.

Beyond the Limit (1983) . . . . Clara

- •• 0:31—Breasts making love with Richard Gere. Long scene.
- •• 1:08—Breasts talking to Gere. Another long scene.

Under Fire (1983) . . . . Sandanista (Leon)

Let's Get Harry (1986) . . . . Veronica

Salvador (1986) . . . . Maria

- 0:21—Very brief right breast, lying in a hammock with James Woods. Very brief buns and side of left breast when getting out of the hammock.

Predator (1987) . . . . Anna

The Assassin (1989) . . . . Elena

Dangerous Passion (1990) . . . . Angela

Predator 2 (1990) . . . . Anna

My Family (1995) . . . . Isabel Magaña

- 1:26—Brief left breast in bed with Jimmy Smits.
- 1:30—Breasts, after talking and crying with Smits.
  1:34—Brief right breast, dead, while under plastic cover in morgue.

Made for Cable Movies:

The Lightning Incident (1991; USA) . . . . Dolores

• Carroll, Diahann

Films:

Carmen Jones (1954) . . . . Myrt

Porgy and Bess (1959) . . . . Clara

The Split (1968) . . . . Ellie

Claudine (1974) . . . . Claudine

- 0:17—Very brief tip of left breast, while sitting up in bubble bath.
- •• 0:18—Brief partial left breast, while sitting in bubble bath after she puts hand towel down when she's talking with James Earl Jones.

The Five Heartbeats (1991) . . . . Eleanor Potter

Miniseries:

Roots: The Next Generation (1979) . . . . Zeona/Mrs. Simon Haley

Made for TV Movies:

I Know Why the Caged Bird Sings (1979) . . . . Vivan

TV:

Julia (1968-71) . . . . Julia Baker

Dynasty (1984-87) . . . . Dominique Deveraux

Lonesome Dove: The Series (1994-95) . . . . Ida Grayson

Carroll, Jill

Films:

The Vals (1982) . . . . Sam

Heart Like a Wheel (1983) . . . . John's Girlfriend

The Man Who Loved Women (1983) . . . . . . Sue the Baby Sitter

Psycho II (1983) . . . . Kim

Something Wicked this Way Comes (1983) . . . . . . Teenage Girl

Funland (1987) . . . . Denise Wilson

Snowballing (1987) . . . . Cheryl

The Unholy (1988) . . . . Millie

- 1:10—Very brief upper half of left breast, while talking in the courtyard with Ben Cross.

Made for TV Movies:

American Harvest (1987) . . . . Calla Bergstrom

Carroll, Regina

Films:

Brain of Blood (1971; Philippines) . . . . Tracey Wilson

Blazing Stewardesses (1975) . . . . Lori

Jessi's Girls (1976) . . . . Claire

- •• 0:58—Breasts and buns in hay with Indian guy. Don't see her face.

Carson, Rachelle

Films:

Kill Crazy (1989)............................Rachel
- •• 0:39—Breasts taking off top to go skinny dipping with Libby.

Eating (1990)................................Cathy

Carter, Elan *

Video Tapes:

Playboy Video Calendar 1995 (1994)........ September
- ••• 0:35—Nude posing outside a house. Nude in a large apartment.

Carter, Finn

Ex-wife of actor Steven Weber.

Films:

How I Got Into College (1989)............... Nina Saatchi
Tremors (1989)........................Rhonda Le Beck
Sweet Justice (1991).....................Sunny Justice

Made for Cable TV:

The Outer Limits: Beyond the Veil (1996; Showtime) ....Courtney
- • 0:31—Very brief side view of left breast, twice, while making love in bed with Michael O'Keefe.

Made for TV Movies:

Love in Another Town (1997)...................... Amy

TV:

As the World Turns (1985-88)...........Sierra Montgomery
NYPD Blue: Girl Talk (Mar 19, 1996)........... Ellen Lippert
Secret Service Guy (1997)...........................n.a.

Carter, Lynda

Miss World U.S.A. 1973.

Films:

Bobbie Jo and the Outlaw (1976) ....Bobbie Jo Baker
- • 0:10—Partial side of left breast, while changing blouses in her bedroom.
- ••• 0:17—Left breast, several times, while making love with Marjoe Gortner.
- •• 0:27—Brief left breast, making love with Gortner again at night.
- • 0:31—Very brief left breast, then very brief breasts in pond with Gortner experimenting with mushrooms.

I Posed for Playboy (1991) ....Meredith Lanahan
a.k.a. Posing: Inspired by Three Real Stories
(Shown on network TV without the nudity.)

Made for Cable Movies:

A Prayer in the Dark (1997; USA) ....Emily Hayworth

Made for TV Movies:

Rita Hayworth: The Love Goddess (1983)...... Rita Hayworth
Mickey Spillane's Mike Hammer: Murder Takes All (1989) .... Helen Durant
Danielle Steel's "Daddy" (1991) .... Charlotte Sampson

TV:

Wonder Woman (1976-79) .... Yeoman Diana Prince/Wonder Woman
Partners in Crime (1984)................. Carole Stanwyck
Hawkeye (1994-95)..................... Elizabeth Shields

Cartlidge, Katrin *

Films:

Sacred Hearts (1984; British)......................Doris
Naked (1993; British)..........................Sophie
- •• 0:16—Breasts, while making love around the house with David Thewlis.
- •• 1:17—In black bra and panties in bed with Greg Cruttwell. Breasts, while putting on her dress while sitting on bed.
- • 1:23—Brief right breast in gaping dress, when getting up off the floor.

Before the Rain (1995; U.S./French) ....Anne
- • 0:35—Breasts, seen behind shower door, while taking a shower.

Breaking the Waves (1996; Danish)................. Dodo

Made for Cable Movies:

Nobody's Children (1994; USA).................. Viorica

Cartwright, Nancy

Films:

Flesh + Blood (1985) ....Kathleen
- • 0:28—Brief breasts showing Jennifer Jason Leigh how to make love. Long shot.

Going Undercover (1988; British) .... Stephanie

Cartwright, Veronica

Sister of actress Angela Cartwright.

Films:

The Birds (1963)........................Cathy Brenner
Inserts (1976) ....Harlene
- •• 0:16—Breasts sitting on bed with Richard Dreyfuss.
- ••• 0:31—Nude on bed with Stephen Davies making a porno movie for Dreyfuss. Long scene.

Goin' South (1978)..........................Hermine
Invasion of the Body Snatchers (1978)........Nancy Bellicec
Alien (1979) ....Lambert
Nightmares (1983) .... Claire
The Right Stuff (1983)................... Betty Grissom
Flight of the Navigator (1986)............. Helen Freeman
My Man Adam (1986) .... Elaine Swit
- • 1:09—Side view of right breast lying on tanning table when Adam steals her car keys. Long shot, hard to see.

Wisdom (1986).................... Samantha Wisdom
The Witches of Eastwick (1987).............. Felicia Alden
Valentino Returns (1988) .... Pat Gibbs
- ••• 0:33—Breasts, while sitting in bed with Frederic Forrest. Fairly long scene.

False Identity (1990)............................ Vera
Man Trouble (1992) ....Helen Dextra
Mirror Mirror 2: Raven Dance (1993) ....Sister Aja
Candyman: Farewell to the Flesh (1995)........... Octavia

Made for Cable Movies:

Hitler's Daughter (1990)............................n.a.
Dead In the Water (1991)................ Victoria Haines
Directed By: On Hope (1994; Showtime) .. Woman in Grocery

Made for TV Movies:

It's Nothing Personal (1993)..................... Barbara
My Brother's Keeper (1995)......................... Pat
The Lottery (1996) ....Mrs. Dunbar

TV:

Daniel Boone (1964-66) .... Jenima Boone

Case, Catherine

Films:

The Jigsaw Murders (1988)................. Stripper #2
- • 0:27—Brief breasts in black peek-a-boo bra posing for photographer.

Dr. Caligari (1989).............Patient with Extra Hormones
Scanner Cop (1993) .... Nurse in Harrigan's Room

TV:

NYPD Blue: Jumpin' Jack Fleishman (Jan 18, 1994) ....Dawn, The Hygienist

Caselli, Chiara

Films:

My Own Private Idaho (1991) . . . . Carmella
• 1:17—Breasts and buns in very brief, quick cuts with Keanu Reeves.
Especially on Sunday (1993) . . . . Bride
Fiorile (1994; Italian) . . . . Chiara

Casey, Elana

Films:

Candy Stripe Nurses (1974) . . . . Zouzou
The Boob Tube (1975) . . . . Greta Van Allen
• 0:27—Buns, while lying in bed with Dr. Carstens.
••• 0:48—Breasts, taking off her blouse in bed, then making love with Natalie.
• 1:01—Buns and side of left breast on sofa.
••• 1:11—Nude, opening the door.
••• 1:12—Breasts during orgy on the couch.
• 1:16—Brief breasts in hallway.

Cash, Rosalind

Films:

Klute (1971) . . . . Pat
The Omega Man (1971) . . . . Lisa
•• 1:09—Side view of left breast and upper half of buns getting out of bed. Buns and breasts sitting in bed.
• 1:21—Side view breasts in beige underwear while trying on clothes.
Hickey and Boggs (1972) . . . . Nyona
The New Centurions (1972) . . . . Lorrie
The All-American Boy (1973) . . . . Poppy
Uptown Saturday Night (1974) . . . . Sarah Jackson
The Monkey Hustle (1976) . . . . Mama
Wrong is Right (1982) . . . . Mrs. Ford
The Adventures of Buckaroo Banzai, Across the 8th Dimension (1984) . . . . John Emdall
Go Tell It On the Mountain (1984) . . . . Aunt Florence
Death Spa (1987) . . . . Sgt. Stone
Tales From the Hood (1995) . . . . Dr. Cushing

Made for TV Movies:

A Dangerous Affair (1995) . . . . Dr. Robertson

Cash, Veronica

See: Burnette, Kim.

Casini, Stefania *

Films:

1900 (1976; Italian) . . . . Epileptic Girl
(NC-17 version reviewed.)
•• 2:02—Breasts taking off her top, more breasts in bed with Robert De Niro and Gerard Depardieu.
••• 2:04—Breasts sitting up in bed, then nude while having a seizure.
Andy Warhol's Bad (1977; Italian) . . . . PG
Suspiria (1977; Italian) . . . . Sara
The Belly of an Architect (1987; British/Italian) . . . . Flavia Speckler
••• 1:15—Lower frontal nudity, in open robe with Brian Dennehy. Then buns and breasts on couch. Kind of a long shot.

• Cass, Crystal

Made for Cable TV:

Outer Limits: Paradise (1996; Showtime) . . . . Alien
The Outer Limits: Bits of Love (1997; Showtime) . . . . Claire
• 0:09—Breasts, while taking off her dress in front of Jon Tenney.
•• 0:10—Breasts, while making love in bed with Tenney.
Dead Man's Gun: The Healer (1997; Showtime) . . . . Young Anna
• 0:20—Breasts, while fooling around with Dalton in the hay.
Outer Limits: Rite of Passage (1998; Showtime) . . . . K'ren
• 0:07—Nude, while walking to Brav, trying to get him interested.

Cassidy, Joanna

Films:

Bank Shot (1974) . . . . El
The Laughing Policeman (1974) . . . . Monica
Stay Hungry (1976) . . . . Joe Mason
The Late Show (1977) . . . . Laura Birdwell
Stunts (1977) . . . . Patti Johnson
Our Winning Season (1978) . . . . Sheila
The Glove (1980) . . . . Sheila Michaels
Night Games (1980) . . . . Julie Miller
• 0:44—Buns, while skinny dipping in the pool with Cindy Pickett.
•• 0:45—Brief full frontal nudity sitting up.
Blade Runner (1982) . . . . Zhora
•• 0:54—Breasts getting dressed after taking a shower while talking with Harrison Ford.
Under Fire (1983) . . . . Claire
Club Paradise (1986) . . . . Terry Hamlin
The Fourth Protocol (1987; British) . . . . Vassilieva
• 1:39—Brief left breast. She's lying dead in Pierce Brosnan's bathtub.
• 1:49—Same thing, different angle.
1969 (1988) . . . . Ev
Who Framed Roger Rabbit (1988) . . . . Dolores
May Wine (1990; French) . . . . Lorraine
Where the Heart Is (1990) . . . . Jean McBain
All-American Murder (1991) . . . . Erica Darby
Don't Tell Mom the Babysitter's Dead (1991) . . . . Rose
Lonely Hearts (1991) . . . . Erin Randall
Landslide (1992) . . . . Lucy Matterson

Made for Cable Movies:

Wheels of Terror (1990) . . . . Laura
Perfect Family (1992; USA) . . . . Janice
Barbarians at the Gate (1993; HBO) . . . . Linda Robinson
The Second Civil War (1997; HBO) . . . . Helena Newman

Made for Cable TV:

The Hunger: The Other Woman (1998; Showtime) . . . . Grace Wallace

Miniseries:

Hollywood Wives (1988) . . . . Maralee Gray
Grass Roots (1992) . . . . Ann Heath

Made for TV Movies:

Pleasures (1986) . . . . Lillian Benton
LIVE! From Death Row (1992) . . . . Alana Powers
Taking Back My Life: The Nancy Ziegenmeyer Story (1992) . . . . Geneva Overholser
The Tommyknockers (1993) . . . . Sheriff Ruth
The Rockford Files: I Still Love L.A. (1994) . . . . Kit
Eye of the Stalker: A Moment of Truth Movie (1995) . . . . Martha Knowlton
Sleep, Baby, Sleep (1995) . . . . Hannah Pierson

TV:

Shields and Yarnell (1977) . . . . Regular
The Roller Girls (1978) . . . . Selma "Books" Cassidy

240 Robert (1979-80) . . . . Deputy Morgan Wainwright
Buffalo Bill (1983-84) . . . . JoJo White
Falcon Crest (1983). Katherine Demery
The Family Tree (1983) . . . . Elizabeth Nichols
Codename: Foxfire (1985) . . . . Elizabeth "Foxfire" Towne
Dudley (1993). . . . . Laraine Bristol
Hotel Malibu (1994) . . . . Ellie Mayfield

Castel, Martina

Films:

Hollywood Hot Tubs 2—Educating Crystal (1989). . . . . . Hardie
Death Merchant (1990) . . . . Martina
Three for One (1991) . . . . n.a.
Total Exposure (1991) . . . . Cissy
- 1:06—Breasts in spa being questioned by a guy with a gun.

Catalano, Laura

Films:

The Santa Clause (1994). . . . . Veronica

Made for Cable Movies:

Escape Clause (1996; Showtime) . . . . Dark Haired Hooker
- 1:00—Breasts, with wrists tied behind her back in bedroom with Abe, when Andrew McCarthy comes in to save her.

Elvis Meets Nixon (1997; Showtime). . . . . . . TWA Ticket Agent

Cates, Georgina

Films:

An Awfully Big Adventure (1995; British) . . Stella Bradshaw
- •• 1:12—Breasts, when sitting up in bed and putting her bra on after making love with Alan Rickman.
- 1:22—Very brief right breast, while making love in bed with Rickman.
- 1:25—Partial left breast, while sitting in bed with Rickman.

Frankie Starlight (1995; Irish/British) . . . . Young Emma
- 0:42—Side view of right breast, while bathing herself.

Cates, Phoebe

Wife of actor Kevin Kline.

Films:

Paradise (1981) . . . . Sarah
- •• 0:23—Buns and breasts taking a shower in a cave while Willie Aames watches.
- 0:40—Very brief left breast caressing herself while looking at her reflection in the water.
- 0:43—Buns, getting out of bed to check out Aames' body while he sleeps.
- 0:46—Buns, washing herself in a pond at night.
- •• 0:55—Side view of her silhouette at the beach at night. Nude swimming in the water, viewed from below.
- 1:10—Breasts, while making love with Aames are a body double. Don't see her face.
- ••• 1:12—Nude swimming under water with Aames.
- 1:16—Breasts, while making love with Aames is a body double again.

Fast Times at Ridgemont High (1982) . . . . . . Linda Barrett
- ••• 0:50—Breasts getting out of swimming pool during Judge Reinhold's fantasy.

Private School (1983) . . . . Christine
- 1:21—Brief buns, while lying in sand with Mathew Modine.
- 1:24—Upper half of buns flashing with the rest of the girls during graduation ceremony.

Gremlins (1984) . . . . Kate
Date with an Angel (1987) . . . . Patty Winston
Bright Lights, Big City (1988) . . . . Amanda
Heart of Dixie (1989) . . . . Aiken
Shag (1989) . . . . Carson McBride
Gremlins 2: The New Batch (1990) . . . . Kate Beringer
I Love You to Death (1990) . . . . Uncredited Girl in Bar
Drop Dead Fred (1991) . . . . Elizabeth
Bodies, Rest & Motion (1993) . . . . Carol
My Life's In Turnaround (1993) . . . . Herself
Princess Caraboo (1994) . . . . Princess Caraboo/Mary

Miniseries:

Lace (1984) Lili
Lace II (1985) Lili

Made for TV Movies:

Baby Sister (1983) . . . . Annie

Catillon, Brigitte

Films:

La Lectrice (1989; French) . . . . Eric's Mother/Jocelyne

a.k.a. The Reader
- 0:27—Brief right breast and buns while lying in bed with a guy. Subtitles get in the way.
- 1:15—Very brief buns, while lying in bed with the hotel waitress and a guy.

Voyager (1991; German/French) . . . . Marianne
Un Coeur en Hiver (1993; French) . . . . Régine
The Proprietor (1996) . . . . Aristocratic Lady

Catkin, Carol

Films:

Not Tonight Darling (1971; British) . . . . Jill
- •• 1:02—Buns and left breast, while in the shower and out. Brief full frontal nudity when getting out of bed.

The Au Pair Girls (1972; British) . . . . Dawn

Cattrall, Kim *

Films:

Rosebud (1975). . . . . Joyce Donovan
- 0:19—Buns, while on deck of boat with the other girls and the terrorists (she's fourth in line).

Tribute (1980; Canadian) . . . . Sally Haines
Porky's (1981; Canadian) . . . . Honeywell
- 0:58—Brief buns, then very brief lower frontal nudity after removing skirt to make love in the boy's locker room.

Ticket to Heaven (1981; Canadian) . . . . Ruthie
City Limits (1984). . . . . Wickings
- •• 1:02—Right breast, while sitting up in bed with a piece of paper stuck to her.

Police Academy (1984) . . . . Karen Thompson
Turk 182 (1985) . . . . Danny Boudreau
Big Trouble in Little China (1986) . . . . Gracie Law
Mannequin (1987) . . . . Emmy
Masquerade (1988) . . . . Mrs. Brooke Morrison
- ••• 0:04—Breasts in bed with Rob Lowe.

Midnight Crossing (1988) . . . . Alexa Schubb
Smoke Screen (1988) . . . . Odessa Muldoon
- 0:31—Brief half of right breast, while sitting in bed with sheet pulled up on her.
- •• 1:16—Breasts in bed on top of Gerald.
- ••• 1:17—Breasts lying in bed under Gerald while he kisses her breasts.

The Return of the Musketeers (1989). . . . . Justine
The Bonfire of the Vanities (1990) . . . . Judy McCoy
Honeymoon Academy (1990) . . . . Chris
Star Trek VI: The Undiscovered Country (1991)
. . . . Lieutenant Valeris
Double Vision (1992; French/Canadian) . . . . Lisa/Caroline
Split Second (1992) . . . . Michelle
- •• 0:43—Breasts in the shower.

•• 0:45—Breasts in the shower, when Rutger Hauer opens the curtains.

Above Suspicion (1994) . . . . Gail
- •• 0:02—Breasts, while making love in bed with Nick and after getting interrupted by his beeper.
- • 0:19—Brief breasts, while getting out of the shower after making love with Nick.
- • 0:20—Brief buns and very brief side view of right breast, while taking off robe and getting into nightgown.
- • 0:22—Brief left breast in gaping nightgown in bed with Christopher Reeve.

Breaking Point (1994; Canadian) . . . . Allison Meadows
- • 0:41—Buns in T-back, then breasts, while making love with Busey. Don't see her face well.

Unforgettable (1995) . . . . Kelly
Where Truth Lies (1995) . . . . Racquel Chambers
Live Nude Girls (1996) . . . . Jamie
- •• 0:26—Buns in lingerie, while talking with Bob.
- • 0:30—Buns in lingerie, while talking with the Greenpeace boy and sitting on the table after making love with him.

Exception to the Rule (1997) . . . . Carla Rainer

Made for Cable Movies:
Miracle in the Wilderness (1991; TNT) . . . . Dora

Made for Cable TV:
Dream On: The Homecoming Queen (1994; HBO) . . . . Jeannie
The Outer Limits: Re-Generation (1997; Showtime) . . . . Rebecca Highfield
Sex and the City (1998- ; HBO) . . . . Samantha Jones
Sex and the City: Bay of the Married Pigs (1998; HBO) . . . . Samantha Jones
Sex and the City: Valley of the Twenty-Something Guys (1998; HBO) . . . . Samantha Jones
- • 0:07—Brief breasts, while making love with Jon in flashbacks.
- • 0:17—Breasts, rolling over after making love with Jon.

Miniseries:
The Bastard (1978) . . . . Anne Ware
- • 2:17—(0:31 into Tape 2) Very brief right breast when the Colonel rips her dress top down. I believe this blooper is even shown on regular broadcast TV!

Scruples (1980) . . . . Melanie
Wild Palms (1993) . . . . Paige Katz

Made for TV Movies:
The Rebels (1979) . . . . Anne Kent
Sins of the Past (1984) . . . . Paula
Running Delilah (1992) . . . . Delilah
The Heidi Chronicles (1995) . . . . Susan
Op Center (1995) . . . . Joanna Hood
Every Woman's Dream (1996) . . . . Liz
Robin Cook's "Invasion" (1997) . . . . Dr. Moran

TV:
Scruples (1980) . . . . Melanie Adams
Angel Falls (1993) . . . . Genna

• *Cavalier, Christine*
Films:
Santa Claws (1996) . . . . Laura Britton
- •• 0:06—Buns in G-string and breasts, while dancing and posing for videographer.

Scream Queens Naked Christmas (1996) . . . . n.a.

Cavalli, Marina Giulia
Made for Cable TV:
Red Shoe Diaries: Accidents Happen (1993; Showtime) . . . . Daria
(Available on the video tape *Red Shoe Diaries 4: Auto Erotica.*)
- ••• 0:15—Breasts, making love in bed with Zack.
- • 0:20—Brief breasts in bed with Zack on TV during playback.

Red Shoe Diaries: Some Things Never Change (1994; Showtime) . . . . Emma
- • 0:05—In black bra, while making love with Michael. Brief flashes of breasts.
- ••• 0:08—Breasts, while starting to make love on bed with Michael.
- •• 0:15—Breasts, while making love on stairway with Michael.

Cavalli, Valeria
Films:
A Blade in the Dark (1986; Italian) . . . . n.a.
Everybody's Fine (1991; Italian) . . . . Tosca
a.k.a. Stanno Tutti Bene
- • 0:54—Brief glimpses of left breast, after taking off her dress backstage at fashion show. Left breast, while breast feeding her baby.

Double Team (1997) . . . . Dr. Maria Trifioli

Cavazos, Lumi
Films:
Like Water for Chocolate (1993; Mexican) . . . . Tita
a.k.a. Como Agua Para Chocolate
- • 0:36—Left breast in gaping top when Pedro watches her grind corn.
- • 0:47—Brief breasts and lower frontal nudity in small room. Dark.
- •• 1:38—Nude, while making love and getting out of bed and covering Pedro with a blanket.

Bottle Rocket (1995) . . . . Inez

Cayer, Kim
Films:
Screwballs (1983) . . . . Brunette Cheerleader
Oddballs (1984) . . . . Miss Renoir
Loose Screws (1986; Canadian) . . . . Pig Pen Girl
Graveyard Shift (1987) . . . . Suzy
- •• 0:06—In black bra, then brief left breast when vampire rips the bra off.
- • 0:53—Brief breasts in junk yard with garter belt, black panties and stockings.

Psycho Girls (1987) . . . . n.a.
Model By Day (1994) . . . . Young Woman
(Shown on network TV without the nudity.)

Cayton, Elizabeth
See: Kaitan, Elizabeth.

Celedonio, Maria
Films:
One Man Force (1989) . . . . Maria
- • 0:30—Brief breasts, twice, while hiding John Matuzak in her apartment. Long shot.

Backstreet Dreams (1990) . . . . Maria M.
The Presence (1992) . . . . n.a.
How to Make an American Quilt (1995) . . . . Young Anna
Foxfire (1996) . . . . Zoe
The Substitute (1996) . . . . Lisa
Touch (1996) . . . . Alisha

Made for Cable Movies:
Rebel Highway: Dragstrip Girl (1994; Showtime) . . . . Pearl
Made for Cable TV:
Red Shoe Diaries: Hotline (1994; Showtime) . . . . Phone Sex Operator
Made for TV Movies:
Robin Cook's "Invasion" (1997) . . . . n.a.
TV:
NYPD Blue: Girl Talk (Mar 19, 1996) . . . . Lydia Garcia

Celeste
Video Tapes:
Penthouse Forum Letters: Volume 2 (1994) . . . . The Perfect Model/Model
••• 0:18—Nude, while posing, then making love with photographer in studio.
Penthouse Behind the Scenes (1995) . . . . Model
••• 0:10—Nude in interviews and behind the scenes footage.

Cellier, Caroline
Films:
Life Love Death (1969; French/Italian). . . . . Girl
This Man Must Die (1970) . . . . Helene Lawson
Femmes de Persone (1986; French) . . . . Isabelle
Petit Con (1986; French). . . . . .Annie Choupon
L'Année des Meduses (1987; French) . . . . .Claude, Chris' Mother
•• 0:02—Breasts taking off top at the beach.
•• 0:56—Breasts on boat at night with Romain.
•• 1:06—Breasts on the beach with Valerie Kaprisky.
• 1:14—Left breast, lying on beach with Romain at night.
Farinelli (1995; Swiss/French/Belgian) . . . . Margaret Hunter
a.k.a. Farinelli: il castrato

Chadwick, June
Films:
The Golden Lady (1979; British) . . . . Lucy
Forbidden World (1982) . . . . Dr. Barbara Glaser
•• 0:29—Breasts in bed making love with Jesse Vint.
•• 0:54—Breasts taking a shower with Dawn Dunlap.
The Last Horror Film (1984) . . . . Reporter
This is Spinal Tap (1984) . . . . Jeanine Pettibone
Headhunters (1988) . . . . Denise Giuliani
Rising Storm (1989) . . . . .Mila Hart
Backstab (1990) . . . . Mrs. Caroline Chambers
The Evil Below (1991) . . . . Sarah Livingston
• 0:08—Very, very brief left breast, while on the floor with Max after he takes off her bra.
• 0:45—Very brief left breast, while on the floor with Max. Different angle from 0:08.
Made for TV Movies:
Judith Krantz's "Dazzle" (1995). . . . . .Georgina
TV:
V: The Series (1984-85). . . . . .Lydia
Riptide (1986). . . . . .Lt. Joanna Parisi
Going to Extremes (1992-93) . . . . Dr. Alice Davis

Chambers, Carol
Films:
Dead Aim (1987) . . . . Nicole
• 0:15—Buns in G-string.
Sleepaway Camp II: Unhappy Campers (1988) . . . . Brooke

Chambers, Carrie
Films:
The Divine Enforcer (1991) . . . . .Kim
• 1:21—Upper half of right breast in bra, while strapped into a chair by Dan Stroud.
Wild Cactus (1992) . . . . Waitress
(Unrated version reviewed.)
The Bikini Carwash Company II (1993). . . . . .Chairwoman
(Unrated version reviewed.)
• 0:26—Brief back side of left breast in her office with Derek.
Desire (1994). . . . . .Nicole Meyers
•• 0:01—Breasts, while blindfolded and putting on perfume before getting killed.
Love is a Gun (1994) . . . . Ms. Preston's Body Double
• 0:25—Brief back side of right breast in the shower when Eric Roberts sees her.
• 0:43—Left breast, while making love in bed with Roberts.

Chambers, Marie
Films:
Street Asylum (1989). . . . . Dr. Cane
Eye For an Eye (1995) . . . . Parents of Murdered Children Group Member
Video Tapes:
Inside Out (1992) . . . . .Terry's Female Half/My Better Half
(Unrated version reviewed.)
•• 1:20—Breasts, while lying on couch with open robe.
• 1:21—Brief left breast in open robe, while standing up.
• 1:22—Brief right breast.
••• 1:24—Breasts, while kissing Terry and rolling around on the couch and on the floor.

Chambers, Marilyn *
Former adult film actress.
Films:
Rabid (1977; Canadian). . . . . Rose
•• 0:14—Breasts in bed.
•• 1:04—Breasts in closet selecting clothes.
•• 1:16—Breasts in white panties getting out of bed.
Angel of H.E.A.T. (1981) . . . . .Angel Harmony
a.k.a. The Protectors, Book I
•• 0:15—Full frontal nudity making love with an intruder on the bed.
• 0:17—Breasts in a bathtub.
•• 0:40—Breasts in a hotel room with a short guy.
• 0:52—Breasts getting out of a wet suit.
•• 1:01—Breasts sitting on floor with some robots.
• 1:29—Breasts in bed with Mark.
Deadly Force (1983) . . . . Actress in Video Tape
• 0:25—Breasts in adult video tape on projection TV.
My Therapist (1983). . . . . Kelly Carson
•• 0:01—Breasts in sex therapy class.
•• 0:07—Breasts, then full frontal nudity undressing for Rip. Long scene.
••• 0:10—Breasts undressing at home, then full frontal nudity making love on couch. Long scene. Nice. Then brief side view of right breast in shower.
• 0:18—Breasts on sofa with Mike.
•• 0:21—Breasts taking off and putting red blouse on at home.
••• 0:26—Nude in bedroom by herself masturbating on bed.
••• 0:32—Breasts exercising on the floor, buns in bed with Mike, breasts in bed getting covered with whipped cream.
•• 0:41—Left breast and lower frontal nudity fighting with Don while he rips off her clothes.
•• 1:08—Breasts and brief buns in bed.

Up 'n' Coming (1987) .... Cassie
(R-rated version reviewed, X-rated version available.)
••• 0:01—Nude, getting out of bed and taking a shower.
•• 0:08—Breasts making love in bed with the record producer.
• 0:30—Brief breasts in bed with two guys.
•• 0:47—Full frontal nudity getting suntan lotion rubbed on her by another woman.
•• 0:55—Breasts taking off her top at radio station.
Party Incorporated (1989) .... Marilyn Sanders
a.k.a. Party Girls
••• 0:56—In lingerie, then breasts in bedroom with Weston. Nice!
• 1:11—Brief breasts on the beach when Peter takes her swimsuit top off.
Breakfast in Bed (1990)............... Marilyn Valentine
•• 0:04—Full frontal nudity, getting out of bubble bath and drying herself off while talking to her manager.
••• 0:21—Breasts, taking off swimsuit top and sunbathing. Nude, swimming underwater.
•• 0:53—In bra, then breasts making love.
•• 1:16—Full frontal nudity, getting out of bed, putting on robe, then getting back in with Jonathan.
The Marilyn Diaries (1990) .... Marilyn
•• 0:02—Breasts in bathroom with a guy during party.
•• 0:26—In bra and panties in Istvan's studio, then breasts.
••• 0:27—Breasts in panties when Istvan opens her blouse.
•• 0:45—Breasts in trench coat, opening it up to give the Iranian secret documents.
• 0:47—Breasts when the Rebel Leader opens her trench coat.
• 0:48—Breasts with Colonel South.
•• 0:57—Breasts opening her top for Hollywood producer.
• 1:10—In swimsuit, then breasts with Roger.
••• 1:13—In black lingerie, then breasts making love with Chet.
• 1:19—Left breast, in flashback with Roger.
•• 1:25—In slip, then right breast, then breasts with Chet.
Marilyn Chambers' Bedtime Stories (1993)
.... Marilyn Chambers
•• 0:02—Breasts, after taking off towel, then opening and adjusting robe.
• 0:04—Brief breasts in bedroom, taking off robe.
• 1:02—Brief right breast on TV.
•• 1:14—Breasts while making love with Bob on bed.
•• 1:15—Breasts while making love with Bob on bed.
New York Nights (1994) .... Barbara Lowery
• 0:21—Breasts, while putting on lingerie for show.
• 0:28—Breasts, with Fred.
• 0:43—Brief breasts, while putting on lingerie.
••• 1:09—Breasts and buns, while making love with Stuart in bed.
• 1:27—Right breast, while making love in bed with a guy.
Bikini Bistro (1995) .... Marilyn
(Unrated version reviewed.)
••• 1:17—Nude, after opening her bra for Colin, then making love.
Marilyn Chambers: Bedtime Fantasies (1996) .... n.a.
Video Tapes:
Playboy Video Magazine, Volume 4 (1983) ...... Herself
•• 0:48—Breasts in scenes from miscellaneous films.
Marilyn Chambers: Wet & Wild Fantasies (1994)
.... Hostess
• 0:18—Partial breasts during segue.
• 0:20—Breasts again during another segue.
• 0:22—Breasts, while standing in the surf with binoculars. Breasts in a clip from a film.
• 0:26—Brief breasts, while standing in the surf.
• 0:28—Brief breasts, while in the surf.
•• 0:36—Nude while swimming under water.

Chambers, Patti

Films:
Psychos in Love (1987)..................... Girl in Bed
•• 0:02—Breasts, sitting in bed and stretching, just before getting killed.
My New Gun (1992)........................ Janice Phee

• Chambers, Rebecca

Films:
Prison Heat (1992).......................... Colleen
•• 0:15—Breasts, while drying off in the shower room and talking with Audrey.
••• 0:43—Breasts, while in the shower with Hellena.
Father of the Bride, Part II (1995)...... Young Woman at Gym

Champa, Jo

Films:
Salomé (1986; Italian) .... Salomé
•• 1:12—Nude under blue dress while dancing around.
• 1:20—Full frontal nudity under sheer blue dress while in jail cell.
• 1:27—Full frontal nudity in sheer dress while walking around.
The Family (1987; Italian/French) .... Young Adriana
Out for Justice (1991) .... Vicky Felino
Beretta's Island (1993).......................... Celeste
Direct Hit (1993)........................... Savannah
Little Buddha (1993) .... Maria
Monkey Trouble (1993)........................... Annie
Don Juan DeMarco (1994)................ Sultana Gulbeta
Honey Sweet Love (1995; Italian) .... Maria Addolorata

Champlin, Stephanie

Films:
The Perfect Gift (1993) .... Bathtub Girl One
Witchcraft 6: The Devil's Mistress (1993)...... 1st Victim
(Unrated version reviewed.)
• 0:02—Breasts, while lying dead in trunk of car.
Ice Cream Man (1994) .... Janet
Manhunt (1994) .... Woman in Bed
• 1:12—Breasts, buns and very brief lower frontal nudity in bed with Charlie before getting killed with him.
Silk n' Sabotage (1994) .... Lynn
•• 0:00—Breasts, while taking a shower.
• 0:01—Brief breasts after taking off towel in bedroom.
••• 0:03—Nude, while making love on sofa with Toby.
••• 0:05—In bra, then breasts, while trying on lingerie in bedroom.
• 0:06—Buns in black lingerie outfit.
•• 0:12—Breasts, while making love with Toby.
•• 0:16—Breasts, while looking at herself in bathroom mirror.
• 0:23—Buns in blue T-back swimsuit while at the beach with the other two girls.
••• 0:29—Brief buns in white T-back, when undressing in bedroom and rubbing lotion on her legs. Breasts and buns, while getting dressed and posing in front of mirror.
Wish Me Luck (1995)...................... Stephanie
(Unrated version reviewed.)
•• 0:16—Breasts, while in the shower in the locker room.

- 0:42—Brief buns in T-back under sheer black robe when she bends over.
- •• 0:47—Buns in panties and bra, then breasts in front of Eddie.
- 0:48—Breasts and buns in panties in bed, while talking with Eddie.

TV:

NYPD Blue: For Whom the Skell Rolls (Oct 18, 1994) .... Suzie
- 0:45—Very brief side view of buns, while getting spanked in video playback when Sipowicz tries to coerce Norman to say something nice about Kelly. (She's on the right.)

Video Tapes:

Nude Daydreams (1993) .... Daydream 10
- ••• 0:27—Breasts and partial buns (she's on the right) while playing violin in a musical trio.

Playboy's Erotic Fantasies: Forbidden Liaisons (1995) .... Nice Catch
- ••• 0:37—In bra, while undressing and making love in the park outside.

Chanda

Films:

Angel of Destruction (1994) .... Reena Jacobs
- ••• 0:09—Buns in lingerie, then breasts, while dancing on stage with Delilah.
- ••• 0:36—Breasts and buns in lingerie, while performing for music video with Delilah.

Dark Secrets (1995) .... Nancy Boyer

Lap Dancing (1995) .... Irene
- ••• 0:25—In bra and panties, then nude, while doing strip routine on stage in club. Long scene.
- 0:45—Brief breasts in flashbacks.
- 0:52—Breasts, while having sex in dark alley with a customer.

Chanel, Tally *

a.k.a. Tally Brittany.

Films:

Alien Warrior (1985) .... Barbara

a.k.a. King of the Streets
- •• 0:46—In white lingerie, then breasts and buns while undressing in room with the Police Captain.
- 1:03—Brief breasts and buns in flashback of 0:46 scene.

Bits and Pieces (1985) .... Jennifer

Free Ride (1986) .... Candy
- 0:53—Brief buns, wearing G-string, taking off her clothes on porch. Long shot.
- 0:57—Brief breasts in bedroom with Dan.

Sex Appeal (1986) .... Corinne
- 1:22—Brief breasts at the door of Tony's apartment when he opens the door while fantasizing about her.

The Nightstalker (1987) .... Brenda
- 0:54—Brief frontal nudity lying dead in bed covered with paint. Long shot, hard to see anything.

Run If You Can (1987) .... n.a.

Slammer Girls (1987) .... Candy Treat
- 0:56—Buns, in G-string, doing a dance routine wearing feathery pasties for the Governor in the hospital.

Warrior Queen (1987) .... Vespa
- ••• 0:09—Breasts hanging on a rope, being auctioned.
- ••• 0:20—Breasts and buns with Chloe.
- •• 0:37—Nude, before attempted rape by Goliath.
- •• 0:58—Breasts during rape by Goliath.

Hollywood Hot Tubs 2—Educating Crystal (1989) .... Mindy Wright

Knockouts (1992) .... Samantha Peters
- •• 0:15—Breasts taking off swimsuit top and getting ready for a bath.
- ••• 0:16—Breasts and buns, while undressing and getting into bathtub while Garth peeks in.
- ••• 0:25—Breasts during strip poker game.
- •• 0:26—Breasts and buns in G-string while walking to her bedroom.
- 0:29—Breasts while sitting on the bed.
- ••• 0:39—In white lingerie, then breasts while posing for photographs.
- •• 0:42—Breasts while Wesley helps put her top on.
- •• 0:43—Breasts while taking a shower (seen on TV monitor).
- ••• 0:47—Breasts while making love with Wesley.
- 0:59—Brief breasts while punching a bag (seen in mostly silhouette).
- 1:16—Breasts in shower in video playback.

L.A. Goddess (1992) .... Beverly
- •• 0:08—Breasts, while getting dressed in bathroom with Kathy.
- •• 0:17—Breasts and buns, while getting out of the shower.
- ••• 1:07—Buns (nice crotch shot) and breasts in bed while making love with Jeff Conaway and talking on the phone.

Dillinger and Capone (1994) .... Blonde Hooker

Chaney, Robin

Films:

Dinosaur Island (1993) .... Tara

Bikini Drive-In (1995) .... Snack Bar A-Go-Go Girl

(Unrated version reviewed.)
- 0:58—Brief buns in black lingerie outfit while dancing in the snack bar.
- 1:01—Brief buns in black lingerie in closer shot.
- 1:02—More brief buns.

• Chang, Corey Anne

Films:

The Beneficiary (1996) .... Lauren Powers
- 0:01—In braless blouse and panties, then very brief buns after ripping off her panties in B&W underwear commercial.
- •• 0:04—Breasts, opening her blouse in office in front of Ron Silver.

Phat Beach (1996) .... Corey

Chang, Lia

Films:

Frankenhooker (1990) .... Crystal
- 0:38—Buns, when Jeffrey draws a check mark on her.
- 0:40—Brief buns, fighting with the other girls over the drugs.

A Kiss Before Dying (1991) .... Shoe Saleslady

Wolf (1994) .... Desk Clerk

• Chant, Holley

Films:

Above Suspicion (1994) .... Nancy

The Last Word (1994) .... Angie

The Crow: City of Angels (1996) .... Holly Daze

The Killing Jar (1996) .... Katie

Event Horizon (1997) .... Claire
- 0:10—Very brief right breast, when Sam Neill starts to turn her around in chair.
- 1:08—Breasts, while sitting in bathtub and committing suicide in Neill's hallucination and later, when standing next to him.

Made for Cable TV:

Women: Stories of Passion-Mind's Eye (1997; Showtime) .... Anna

- ••• 0:08—Breasts, after taking off her blouse and looking at herself in the mirror.
- • 0:09—Breasts, during fantasy with Clay.
- •• 0:10—Breasts, while sitting in bathroom by herself.
- • 0:14—Brief full frontal nudity, while walking outside in the woods with Clay during her fantasy.
- •• 0:16—Full frontal nudity while making love with a guy and also sitting in bathtub.
- •• 0:22—Buns and breasts, while making love with Clay in bed.
- • 0:24—Brief buns, while walking outdoors.

Made for TV Movies:

A Child Lost Forever (1992) .... Linda

• Chanz, Nadine *

Video Tapes:

Playboy Video Calendar 1998 (1997) .... June

- ••• 0:22—In lingerie and nude, while posing in front of neon signs.
- ••• 0:24—In lingerie and nude in dark bedroom.

Chaplin, Geraldine

Daughter of actor Charlie Chaplin.
Granddaughter of Eugene O'Neill.

Films:

Doctor Zhivago (1965) .... Tonya
Cop-Out (1967; British) .... Angela Sawyer
The Three Musketeers (1973; British) .... Anne of Austria
Nashville (1975) .... Opal
Buffalo Bill and the Indians (1976) .... Annie Oakley
Roseland (1977) .... Marilyn
Welcome to L.A. (1977) .... Karen Hood

- •• 1:28—Full frontal nudity standing in Keith Carradine's living room.

Remember My Name (1978) .... Emily

- • 1:23—Very brief left breast, lying in bed, then right breast, with Anthony Perkins.

A Wedding (1978) .... Rita Billingsley
Bolero (1982; French) .... Suzan/Sara Glenn
The Moderns (1988) .... Nathalie de Ville
White Mischief (1988) .... Nina
The Return of the Musketeers (1989) .... Queen Anne
Barbara Cartland's "Duel of Hearts" (1990; British) .... Mrs. Miller
The Children (1990; British/German) .... Joyce Wheater
Chaplin (1992; British/U.S.) .... Hannah Chaplin
The Age of Innocence (1993) .... Mrs. Welland
Home for the Holidays (1995) .... Aunt Glady
Crimetime (1996; U.S./British) .... Thelma
Jane Eyre (1996) .... n.a.
Cousin Bette (1998) .... Adeline Hulot

Made for Cable Movies:

Mother Teresa: In the Name of God's Poor (1997; Family) .... Mother Teresa

Made for TV Movies:

A Foreign Field (1993) .... Beverley
Gulliver's Travels (1996) .... Empress Munodi
The Odyssey (1997) .... Eurycleia

Chappell, Crystal

Films:

Bigfoot: The Unforgettable Encounter (1994) .... Samantha
Lady in Waiting (1994) .... Elizabeth
(Unrated version reviewed.)

- • 0:39—Buns in T-back, while tied up on bed face-down. Don't see her face.
- • 0:42—Brief side view of buns in T-back and in bra in Michael Nouri's dream.

Made for Cable TV:

Poltergeist: The Legacy/Dream Lover (1998; Showtime) .... Jessica Lancy

- • 0:13—Very, very brief buns in Derek's vision.
- • 0:28—Back side of left breast, while making love with Derek in bed. Don't see her face.

TV:

Days of Our Lives .... Carly Manning

Charbonneau, Patricia

Films:

Desert Hearts (1986) .... Cay Rivvers

- • 1:05—Breasts, while sitting on the bed, waiting for Helen Shaver.
- • 1:06—Right breast, while talking to Shaver.
- • 1:08—Breasts, while kissing Shaver.
- ••• 1:10—Breasts, while making love in bed with Shaver.

Manhunter (1986) .... Mrs. Sherman
Call Me (1988) .... Anna

- •• 1:18—Brief left breast making love in bed with a guy, then breasts putting blouse on and getting out of bed.

Shakedown (1988) .... Susan Cantrell
Brain Dead (1989) .... Dana Martin

- • 0:43—Buns, on table with Bill Paxton. Briefly almost see side of left breast.

Robocop 2 (1990) .... Uncredited Engineer
K2 (1991) .... Jacki Metcalfe
Portraits of a Killer (1996; Canadian) .... Carolyn Price

Made for Cable TV:

Tales From the Crypt: Strung Along (1992; HBO) .... Ellen

Made for TV Movies:

C.A.T. Squad: Stalking Danger (1986) .... Nikki Pappas

TV:

Crime Story (1986-87) .... Inga Thorson
Wiseguy (1988-89) .... Carole Sternberg
Extreme (1995) .... Sheriff Lynn Roberts
Seaquest 2032 (1995-96) .... Morse

Charlie

See: Spradling, Charlie.

• Chase, Kimberly

Films:

Killing Obsession (1994) .... Annie Smith

- •• 0:31—Right breast, then breasts, while making love with Randy in photo studio.
- • 0:51—Breasts after Randy pulls her robe off.
- •• 1:09—Breasts and buns in panties, while undressing and changing into lingerie in bedroom.

Raven (1996) .... Sharon

Chase, Lynn

See: De Light, Venus.

Checa, Maria *

Video Tapes:

Sexy Lingerie: Dreams & Desire (1994) .... Playmate

- ••• 0:31—Nude in mansion with two other women.
- ••• 0:37—Nude.

Playboy Video Calendar 1996 (1995) . . . . March
••• 0:09—Nude while posing indoors.
••• 0:11—In lingerie, while in bedroom.
Playboy's Hot Latin Ladies (1995) . . . . Playmate/Host
••• 0:01—Nude, during introduction and during desert segment.
•• 0:49—Nude during segment.
Wet & Wild VIII: Bottoms Up (1996). . . . . Playmate

Chen, Joan *
Films:
Tai-Pan (1986). . . . . May May
• 0:56—Brief left breast washing herself, hard to see.
The Last Emperor (1987). . . . . Wan Jung
The Nightstalker (1987) . . . . Mai Wong
The Blood of Heroes (1989) . . . . Kidda
a.k.a. Salute of the Jugger
Turtle Beach (1992; Australian) . . . . Minou
a.k.a. The Killing Beach
••• 0:07—Brief buns, dropping robe and leaving room while talking to Greta Scacchi.
Heaven and Earth (1993) . . . . Mama
On Deadly Ground (1993) . . . . Masu
Temptation of a Monk (1993; Hong Kong)
. . . . Princess Scarlet/Violet
•• 1:39—Breast and upper half of buns, after opening her robe. (She has a shaved, bald head.)
Golden Gate (1994) . . . . Marilyn Song
The Hunted (1994). . . . . Kirina
• 0:10—Very brief half of right breast, then back half of right breast, while in hot tub in front of Christopher Lambert.
Judge Dredd (1995) . . . . Ilsa
Wild Side (1995). . . . . Virginia Chow
(Unrated version reviewed.)
• 0:39—Brief inside half of right breast, in open jacket with Anne Heche.
••• 0:40—Breasts, while making love in bed with Heche. You don't see as much of Chen as you do of Heche, but the scene is very erotic!
Precious Find (1996) . . . . Camilla Jones
Made for Cable Movies:
Dead Lock (1991; HBO) . . . . Noelle
Made for Cable TV:
Strangers: Small Sounds and Tilting Shadows (1992)
. . . . The Girl
(Available on video tape as *Strangers*.)
• 0:04—Brief left breast, while making love with Lambert Wilson. Dark.
• 0:05—Inner half of right breast, afterwards.
• 0:08—Very, very brief partial left breast a couple of times while washing herself.
Tales From the Crypt: Food For Thought (1993; HBO)
. . . . Connie
Made for TV Movies:
Shadow of a Stranger (1992) . . . . Vanessa
Steel Justice (1992) . . . . Nicole
TV:
Twin Peaks (1990-91) . . . . Jocelyn Packard

Chesser, Bethany
Films:
Showgirls (1995) . . . . Finalist Dancer
(NC-17 version reviewed.)
••• 0:40—Breasts while dancing during final audition with Elizabeth Berkley and another dancer.
That Thing You Do! (1996) . . . . Wisconsin Dancer

Chester, Holly
Films:
Ultimate Desires (1991). . . . . Streetgirl
a.k.a. Silhouette
Knight Moves (1992). . . . . Officer No. 2
SnakeEater III ...His Law (1992) . . . . Fran
••• 0:30—Breasts and buns in G-string while dancing on stage in club.

Cheung, Daphne
Films:
Rich Girl (1991). . . . . Oriental Temptress
• 1:14—Breasts, taking off her jacket in back room trying to get Rick to do drugs.
Roots of Evil (1991) . . . . Tina
(Unrated version reviewed.)
••• 0:09—Breasts in alley with a customer.
A Time to Die (1991). . . . . Sunshine
Mortal Danger (1993) . . . . Jan
Made for Cable Movies:
On Dangerous Ground (1995; Showtime). . . . . Su Yin

Chevalier, Catherine
Films:
Barbarella (1968; French/Italian) . . . . n.a.
Hellraiser II—Hellbound (1988) . . . . Tiffany's Mother
Riders of the Storm (1988) . . . . Rosita
Stormy Monday (1988). . . . . Cosmo's Secretary
Night Breed (1990). . . . . Rachel
• 1:12—Breasts in police jail, going through a door and killing a cop.
Jefferson in Paris (1995). . . . . Lady of the Court

Chiesa, Chana Jael
Video Tapes:
Inside Out (1992) . . . . My Secret Moments
(Unrated version reviewed.)
••• 0:42—Breasts, rubbing lotion on them, then with large cast of people during her fantasy as camera pulls back.
•• 0:44—Full frontal nudity, still in bed. Long shot.
Inside Out 4 (1992) . . . . Actress/Motivation
(Unrated version reviewed.)
• 0:13—Lower frontal nudity, dropping her shorts to show Dick her haircut.
••• 0:14—Nude, out in the desert with Dick, shooting a scene.
• 0:16—Breasts, while opening her blouse to show Dick her breasts, brief full frontal nudity, running to get into truck.
•• 0:17—Brief full frontal nudity, out in the desert with Dick again.

Chiles, Lois
Films:
The Way We Were (1973) . . . . Carol Ann
Coma (1978). . . . . Nancy Greenly
Moonraker (1979). . . . . Dr. Holly Goodhead
Raw Courage (1983) . . . . Ruth
Sweet Liberty (1986). . . . . Leslie
Broadcast News (1987) . . . . Jennifer Mack
Creepshow 2 (1987). . . . . Annie Lansing
•• 0:59—Brief breasts getting out of boyfriend's bed, then getting dressed.
Until the End of the World (1991) . . . . Elsa Farber
Diary of a Hitman (1992). . . . . Sheila
In the Eye of the Snake (1994; Swiss). . . . . Marc's Mother

The Babysitter (1995) . . . . Bernice Holsten
Bliss (1996) . . . . Eva
Curdled (1996) . . . . Katrina Brandt
Speed 2: Cruise Control (1997) . . . . Celeste

Made for Cable Movies:

Lush Life (1993; Showtime) . . . . Lucy

Made for TV Movies:

Burning Bridges (1990) . . . . Claire Morgan
Obsessed (1992) . . . . Louise

TV:

Dallas (1982-84) . . . . Holly Harwood

Chin, Lonnie *

Films:

Star 80 (1983) . . . . Playboy Mansion Guest

Video Tapes:

Playboy Video Magazine, Volume 1 (1982) . . . . . Playmate
•• 0:00—Full frontal nudity during introduction.
••• 0:15—Nude outside by pool.
••• 0:19—Nude posing in various clothes in clothes store.
••• 0:21—In bra and panties, then nude in garter belt and stockings in a house.

Playboy's Playmate Review 3 (1985) . . . . Playmate
Playboy's 21 Playmates (1996) . . . . Playmate
••• 1:10—Nude in still photos.
••• 1:11—Nude in mansion.

Chong, Rae Dawn *

Daughter of comedian/actor Tommy Chong.
Sister of actress Robbi Chong.
Ex-wife of actor C. Thomas Howell.

Films:

Quest For Fire (1981) . . . . Ika
• 0:37—Breasts and buns, running away from the bad tribe.
• 0:40—Breasts and buns, following the three guys.
• 0:41—Brief breasts behind rocks.
• 0:43—Brief side view of left breast, healing Noah's wound.
• 0:50—Right breast, while sleeping by the fire.
• 0:53—Long shot, side view of left breast after making love.
• 0:54—Breasts shouting to the three guys.
• 1:07—Breasts standing with her tribe.
• 1:10—Breasts and buns, walking through camp at night.
• 1:18—Breasts in a field.
• 1:20—Left breast, turning over to demonstrate the missionary position. Long shot.
• 1:25—Buns and brief left breast running out of bear cave.

Beat Street (1984) . . . . Tracy
Cheech & Chong's The Corsican Brothers (1984) . . . The Gypsy
City Limits (1984) . . . . Yogi
Fear City (1984) . . . . Leila
••• 0:26—Breasts and buns, dancing on stage.
• 0:50—Brief breasts in the hospital getting defibrillated to get her heart started.

American Flyers (1985) . . . . Sarah
The Color Purple (1985) . . . . Squeak
Commando (1985) . . . . Cindy
Running Out of Luck (1986) . . . . Slave Girl
•• 0:42—Left breast, while hugging Mick Jagger, then again while lying in bed with him.
•• 1:12—Left breast painting some kind of drug laced solution on herself.
•• 1:14—Right breast, while in prison office offering her breast to the warden.
• 1:21—Buns and left breast, in bed with Jagger during a flashback.

Soul Man (1986) . . . . Sarah
The Principal (1987) . . . . Hilary Orozco
The Squeeze (1987) . . . . Rachel Dobs
The Borrower (1989) . . . . Diana Pierce
Curiosity Kills (1990) . . . . Jane
Far Out Man (1990) . . . . Rae Dawn Chong
Tales From the Darkside, The Movie (1990) . . . . Carola
• 1:09—Left breast in blue light, twice, with James Remar. Don't see her face.

Amazon (1991) . . . . Paola
Common Bonds (1991) . . . . Ilene Curtis
Denial (1991) . . . . Julie
When the Party's Over (1991) . . . . MJ
• 0:03—Brief buns, while getting out of bed.

Time Runner (1992) . . . . Karen McDonald
Boca (1994) . . . . JJ
•• 0:25—Brief breasts, when Boca plays with Moema.
••• 0:29—Breasts, then nude while making love with Martin Kemp. Long scene.
••• 0:55—Brief breasts, after dancer pulls her up, then dancing after doing drugs.
• 1:09—Very brief right breast in gaping jacket when getting up off bed.
• 1:18—Brief right breast, then left breast in flashback.

Boulevard (1994) . . . . Ola
• 0:05—Breasts, while making love with a customer on bed.
• 0:30—Left breast then breasts, while sitting in bathtub, talking and smoking a joint with Kari Wüher.
• 0:45—Right breast, while taking a shower.
• 1:08—Breasts, while getting a massage from Wüher.
• 1:13—Partial buns, while dancing in club.

The Break ...Is All You Need (1994) . . . . Jennifer Hudson
Hideaway (1994) . . . . Rose Ornetto
Mask of Death (1994; Canadian) . . . . Cassandra Turner

Made for Cable Movies:

Prison Stories, Women on the Inside (1990; HBO) . . . . Rhonda
• 0:26—Very brief right breast several times in prison shower with Annabella Sciorra.

Power of Attorney (1995) . . . . Joan Armstrong
••• 0:50—Breasts, while making love in chair in office with Elias Koteas.

Made for Cable TV:

The Outer Limits: The Second Soul (1995; Showtime) . . . Karen
Poltergeist: The Legacy/The Spirit Thief (1997; Showtime) . . . . Tanya Moreau

Made for TV Movies:

Father & Son: Dangerous Relations (1993) . . . . Yvonne
Alibi (1997) . . . . Linda Garcia

Chong, Robbi

Daughter of comedian/actor Tommy Chong.
Sister of actress Rae Dawn Chong.

Films:

Cheech & Chong's The Corsican Brothers (1984) . . . Princess III
Far Out Man (1990) . . . . Dancer
Jimmy Hollywood (1993) . . . . Casting Secretary
Fatally Yours (1995) . . . . Bobbi

Made for Cable TV:

Red Shoe Diaries: Written Word (1995; Showtime) . . . . Professor Mennen
••• 0:11—Breasts, while in bed during fantasy with Davis.
• 0:16—Brief breasts, while lying in bed with Davis.
• 0:17—Brief breast and full frontal nudity, while lying in bed with Davis.

Poltergeist: The Legacy (1996- ; Showtime) . . . . Alex
Poltergeist: The Legacy/The Twelfth Cave (1996; HBO) . . . Alex

Chong, Shelby

Films:

Cheech & Chong's Next Movie (1980) . . . . Beautiful
Cheech & Chong's Nice Dreams (1981) . . . . Body Builder
Far Out Man (1990) . . . . .Tree
• 0:11—Very brief side view of left breast, in gaping blouse when she leans over to light a joint.
Relentless 2: Dead On (1991) .Waitress
The Spirit of '76 (1991). . . . . .Waitress

Chorak, Karen

See: Naples, Toni.

Choudhury, Sarita

Films:

Mississippi Masala (1992). . . . . Mina
• 1:11—Right breast when Denzel Washington sucks on it.
Wild West (1992; British). . . . . Rifat
The House of Spirits (1993) . . . . Pancha
• 0:17—Brief breasts when Jeremy Irons rips open her blouse and rapes her.
Fresh Kill (1994) . . . . Shareen Lightfoot
The Perez Family (1995) . . . . .Josette
Kama Sutra: A Tale of Love (1996) . . . . .Tara
(Unrated version reviewed.)
•• 0:25—Breasts, while starting to make love with Singh.
• 1:19—Left breast, while being examined by a doctor under a sheet.
••• 1:33—Full frontal nudity, when starting to make love with Maya.

Made for Cable Movies:

Down Came a Blackbird (1995; Showtime). . . . . Myrna

Made for Cable TV:

Subway Stories (1997; HBO). .Humera

Christensen, Alisa *

Films:

Whore (1991) . . . . .Lady in Toilet
a.k.a. If you're afraid to say it... Just see it
Bad Love (1992) . . . . Felicia
a.k.a. Wild Angel
Bounty Tracker (1992). . . . . Isabella
Deep Cover (1992) . . . . Ivy's Driver
The Immortals (1995) . . . . Stripper Shooter
• 0:17—Very brief breasts, twice, while shooting a shot gun in strip club office during robbery.
Wild Bill (1995). . . . . Mann's No. 10 Saloon Bargirl
Witchcraft 7: Judgement Hour (1995) . . . . .Lutz
(Unrated version reviewed.)
Mulholland Falls (1996) . . . . Spaghetti Girl
The Replacement Killers (1997). . . . . Stunts
Land of the Free (1998). . . . . Helene
•• 0:20—Brief breasts, while making love with Fitzpatrick in bed, then more breasts when walking to the bathroom, taking a shower and getting killed.

Made for Cable TV:

Tales From the Crypt: Cutting Cards (1990; HBO)
. . . . Blonde Woman
(Available on *Tales From the Crypt, Volume 3.*)

Christensen, Tonja *

Video Tapes:

Playboy Video Calendar 1993 (1992) . . . . December
••• 0:49—Nude in barn.
••• 0:50—Nude in house.
Playboy's Playmate Review 1992 (1992) . .Miss November
••• 0:02—Nude in hat and chair scenes in a house.
Playboy's Sexy, Steamy, Sultry (1993). . . . . .Playmate

Christian, Claudia

Films:

The Hidden (1987) . . . . Brenda Lee
Arena (1988). . . . . .Quinn
Clean and Sober (1988) . . . . Iris
Never on Tuesday (1988). . . . . Tuesday
(There are a lot of braless T-shirt shots of her throughout the film.)
• 0:43—Brief side view of right breast in the shower with Eddie during his fantasy.
Mom (1989) . . . . Virginia
Mad About You (1990) . . . . Casey
Maniac Cop 2 (1990) . . . . Susan Riley
Think Big (1990) . . . . Dr. Marsh
The Dark Backward (1991) . . . . Kitty
A Gnome Named Gnorm (1993). . . . . Samantha
a.k.a. Upworld
Hexed (1993). . . . . Hexina
a.k.a. All Shook Up
• 0:30—Tip of right breast, several times, while lying on her back in bed. (You can tell when the body double is used because of the bad wig.)
•• 0:31—Brief right breast, several times, while making love in bed.
• 0:34—Very brief inside of right breast in gaping coat, while raising knife. Brief buns, while getting pushed off bed.
The Chase (1994) . . . . Yvonne Voss

Made for Cable Movies:

Lies of the Twins (1991; USA) . . . . Felice
Strays (1991; USA) . . . . Claire Lederer
A Wing and a Prayer (1998; USA) .n.a.

Made for TV Movies:

Danielle Steel's "Kaleidoscope" (1990) . . . . Meagan
Columbo: It's All in the Game (1993) . . . . Lisa
Relentless: Mind of a Killer (1993) . . . . Leeann Hardy

TV:

Berrengers (1985) . . . . Melody Hughes
Babylon 5 (1994-97) . . . Lieutenant Commander Susan Ivanova

Christie, Julianne

Films:

Encino Man (1992) . . . . .Fresh Nug
It's Pat (1994) . . . . .Strip Club Hostess
The Nutty Professor (1996) . . . . Sporting Goods Clerk

Made for Cable TV:

Dead Man's Gun: Wages of Sin (1998; Showtime)
. . . . .Alexa Drake
• 0:32—Very, very brief bubble soap covered left breast, while in bathtub with Tim Matheson.

TV:

NYPD Blue: NYPD Lou (Oct 2, 1993). . . . . .Patty
• 0:39—Buns, a couple of times, getting out of bed with Kevin after getting caught by Andy's dad. Very brief breasts while getting dressed.
Public Morals (1996) . . . . .Corinne

Christie, Julie *

Films:

Billy Liar (1963) . . . . .Liz
Darling (1965). . . . . .Diana Scott
Doctor Zhivago (1965) . . . . Lara
Fahrenheit 451 (1967). . . . . Linda/Clarisse

Petulia (1968; U.S./British) .... Petulia Danner
McCabe and Mrs. Miller (1971) .... Mrs. Miller
Don't Look Now (1973).................... Laura Baxter
• 0:27—Brief breasts and lower frontal nudity, while sitting in bathtub and in front of mirror, talking with Donald Sutherland.
••• 0:30—Breasts, brief buns and brief partial lower frontal nudity, while making love with Sutherland in bed.
Shampoo (1975)................................ Jackie
Demon Seed (1977) .... Susan Harris
• 0:25—Side view of left breast, getting out of bed.
•• 0:30—Breasts and buns getting out of the shower while the computer watches with its camera.
Heaven Can Wait (1978).................... Betty Logan
Heat and Dust (1982)............................Anne
Return of the Soldier (1983; British).................. Kitty
Power (1986) .... Ellen Freeman
Miss Mary (1987) ....Miss Mary Mulligan
Fools of Fortune (1990)..................... Mrs. Quinton
Dragonheart (1996) ....Aislinn
Hamlet (1996)............................Gertrude
Afterglow (1997)......................... Phyllis Mann
Made for Cable Movies:
The Railway Station Man (1992; TNT)........Helen Cuffe
• 0:35—Buns, undressing to go skinny dipping. Brief side of left breast, running into the ocean. Long shot.
• 0:37—Buns, while walking out of the surf. Long shot.
Made for TV Movies:
Dadah is Death (1988) .... Barbara

Christine, Wendy *

Video Tapes:
Playboy's Girls of Spring Break (1991).......... Herself
••• 0:14—Full frontal nudity in still photos.
••• 0:16—Full frontal nudity, in spa at ski resort with her friend, Michelle Mullica.

Cialini, Julie *

Films:
Cover Me (1995)............................ Waitress
South Beach Academy (1997).................Phyllis Glass
TV:
High Tide (1994)............................. Annie
The New Price is Right (1994-95) ....Showcase Model
Video Tapes:
Playboy Video Calendar 1995 (1994) ....November
••• 0:44—Nude at a beach. Nude in a house.
Playboy Video Centerfold: Anna-Marie Goddard (1994) .... Runner-Up Playmate
••• 0:39—Nude in beach front (shot in a studio) sequence.
Playboy Video Centerfold: Jenny McCarthy (1994) ....Playmate
• 0:35—Buns while dancing in T-back.
••• 0:36—Nude in country setting segment.
•• 0:40—Breasts and buns in T-back while dancing around in city settings.
••• 0:42—Nude in still photos.
••• 0:43—Nude in fashion show fantasy.
••• 0:45—Nude, when posing in house while thinking about her lover.
Sexy Lingerie: Dreams & Desire (1994)............Playmate
Wet & Wild: The Locker Room (1994) ....Playmate
Playboy Video Calendar 1996 (1995) ....December
••• 0:48—Nude in studio posing in chair.
••• 0:50—In lingerie then nude in bedroom fantasy.
Playboy Video Centerfold: Julie Lynn Cialini (1995) ....Playmate of the Year
• 0:01—Nude during introduction.
• 0:02—Breasts and buns in swimsuit while fooling around outside.
••• 0:04—Nude, while in a bedroom.
••• 0:12—Nude in her apartment during air conditioner repairman fantasy.
••• 0:19—Nude in still photos.
••• 0:21—Nude, while dancing in studio.
••• 0:25—Nude outside, during biker guy fantasy.
••• 0:32—Nude during music video/dance segment.
••• 0:35—Nude in Victorian house fantasy.
Playboy's Girls of Radio: Talk, Rock and Shock (1995) .... Herself
••• 0:00—In blue bra and panties, then nude with three other women.
Wet & Wild: Hot Holidays (1995).................Playmate
Playboy The Best of Jenny McCarthy (1996) ..... Herself
••• 0:24—Nude, while dancing with 3 other Playmates with fire and ice from *Wet & Wild: The Locker Room.*
Playboy's Cheerleaders (1996) .... Cheerleader
••• 0:19—Nude, while making love with her football boyfriend in kitchen and playing with food.

Cicciolina

See: Staller, Ilona.

Ciesar, Jennifer

Films:
Lovers' Lovers (1993).......................... Blaire
(Body double used whenever you don't see her face. Body double has red fingernail polish.)
•• 0:29—Breasts and buns while in the shower.
• 1:07—In white bra and brief breasts while making love with Michael on bed.
1:13—In white bra and panties in bedroom.
Inner Sanctum 2 (1994) .... Jane
(Unrated version reviewed.)
Made for Cable TV:
Red Shoe Diaries: Kidnap (1994; Showtime) .... Sara McCleod
••• 0:17—Breasts, while making love outside with Tom at night.
•• 0:24—Nude, while making love in board room and in flashbacks with Tom.
Red Shoe Diaries: Hard Labor (1995; Showtime).....Aleta
•• 0:03—Breasts and buns, while making love in bed with David.
••• 0:27—Breasts and buns, while making love in bed with David.

Clair, Laureen E.

Films:
Zipperface (1991)...........................Elizabeth
• 0:23—Brief breasts, while putting on lingerie in front of mirror.
Wild Malibu Weekend! (1994) . . . "It's Only Plastic" Chorus Girl

Clark, Anna *

Video Tapes:
Playboy Video Calendar 1988 (1987) ....Playmate
Wet & Wild (1989) ....Model

Clark, Candy *

Films:

Fat City (1972) . . . . Faye
American Graffiti (1973) . . . . Debbie
I Will, I Will... For Now (1976) . . . . Sally Bingham
The Man Who Fell to Earth (1976; British). . . . . . Mary-Lou
(Uncensored version reviewed.)
•• 0:42—Breasts in the bathtub, washing her hair and talking to David Bowie.
•• 0:55—Breasts sitting on bed and blowing out a candle.
••• 0:56—Breasts in bed with Bowie.
••• 1:26—Full frontal nudity climbing into bed with Bowie after he reveals his true alien self.
• 1:56—Nude with Bowie, while making love and shooting a gun.
Citizen's Band (1977) . . . . Electra/Pam
The Big Sleep (1978; British) . . . . Camilla Sternwood
••• 0:18—Breasts, sitting in a chair when Robert Mitchum comes in after a guy is murdered.
• 0:30—Brief breasts in a photograph that Mitchum is looking at.
• 0:38—Breasts in the photos again. Out of focus.
•• 0:39—Breasts sitting in chair during recollection of the murder.
•• 1:03—Very brief full frontal nudity in bed, throwing open the sheets for Mitchum.
• 1:05—Very, very brief buns, while getting up out of bed.
When Ya Comin' Back Red Ryder (1979) . . . . Cheryl
(Not available on video tape.)
National Lampoon Goes to the Movies (1982) . . Susan Cooper
a.k.a. Movie Madness
Q (1982). . . . . Joan
Blue Thunder (1983). . . . . Kate
Hambone and Hillie (1984). . . . . Nancy
Cat's Eye (1985) . . . . Sally Ann
At Close Range (1986) . . . . Mary Sue
The Blob (1988) . . . . Fran Hewitt
Cool As Ice (1991) . . . . Grace
Buffy The Vampire Slayer (1992) . . . . Buffy's Mom
Original Intent (1992). . . . . Jessica Cameron
Radioland Murders (1994) . . . . Billy's Mom

Clark, Corrie

Films:

Deadly Sins (1994; Canadian). . . . . Beth
•• 0:25—In white bra, then breasts, while making love with Eric.
•• 0:54—In black bra and panties, then breasts, while making love with Eric on bed.
The Limbic Region (1996). . . . . Lake Girl
Made for Cable TV:
The Outer Limits: A Stitch in Time (1996; Showtime)
. . . . Young Theresa Givens
Outer Limits: Paradise (1996; Showtime) . . . . Young Sylvia
Made for TV Movies:
The Other Mother (1995) . . . . Young Carol

Clark, Dawn

Films:

The Happy Hooker Goes to Washington (1977) . . . Candy
• 1:18—Breasts, covered with spaghetti in a restaurant.
The Hollywood Knights (1980) . . . . Pom Pom Girl
•• 0:01—Breasts sunbathing outside with Fran Drescher and another Pom Pom Girl.
• 0:11—In bra, then brief breasts, changing clothes at night.
• 0:20—Breasts in B&W Polaroid photograph. Long shot.
Stripes (1981) . . . . Mud Wrestler

Clark, Kerrie

Not to be confused with actress Kerrie Klark.

Films:

Miami Blues (1990) . . . . Hooker
Sunset Heat (1991) . . . . Brandon's Model
a.k.a. Midnight Heat
(Unrated version reviewed.)
Wayne's World (1992) . . . . Girl in Car
Angel 4: Undercover (1993) . . . . Paula
••• 0:26—Breasts, while making love with Piston in bedroom.
•• 0:28—Very briefly nude, getting up out of bed. Breasts, while taking a shower.
The Beverly Hillbillies (1993)
. . . . Auditioning Woman in White Dress
Dark Breed (1996). . . . . Waitress
Made for TV Movies:
L.A. Johns (1997). . . . . Roger's Secretary

Clark, Kimberly

See: Beck, Kimberly.

Clark, Liddy

Films:

Blue Fin (1978) . . . . Ruth Pascoe
Kitty and the Bagman (1983; Australian) . . . Kitty O'Rourke
• 0:28—Very brief side view of right breast in pulled-down dress during fight with Big Lil. Very brief upper half of breasts when Big Lil drags her across the floor. Very, very brief upper half of right breast, just before grabbing Big Lil's hair.

Clark, Marlene

Films:

The Landlord (1970) . . . . Marlene
Slaughter (1972). . . . . Kim Walker
• 0:11—Very brief buns and right breast, getting thrown out of room by Jim Brown.
Night of the Cobra Woman (1974; U.S./Philippines) . . . . . Lena
Switchblade Sisters (1975). . . . . Muff

Clark, Sharon *

a.k.a. Sharon Weber or Sharon Clark Weber.

Films:

Lifeguard (1975). . . . . Tina
• 0:07—Brief side view of right breast undressing and getting into the shower.
• 0:08—Buns and brief breasts wrestling with Sam Elliott on the bed.
Lisa (1989) . . . . Porsche Passenger

Clark, Susan *

Wife of actor Alex Karras.

Films:

Coogan's Bluff (1968) . . . . Julie
Colossus: 'The Forbin' Project (1969) . . . . Cleo
Tell Them Willie Boy is Here (1969) . . . . Liz
• 0:21—Very brief buns when Robert Redford turns her over in bed.
Skin Game (1971) . . . . Ginger
Valdez is Coming (1971) . . . . Gay Erin
The Apple Dumpling Gang (1975)
. . . . Magnolia Dusty Clydesdale
Night Moves (1975) . . . . Ellen
• 1:09—Brief breasts in bed with Gene Hackman.
French Quarter (1978). . . . . Bag Stealer/Sue

Deadly Companion (1979; Canadian) . . . . Paula West
- 0:19—Brief left breast, while consoling Michael Sarrazin in bed, then brief side view of left breast.
- 0:20—Brief breasts sitting up in bed.

The North Avenue Irregulars (1979) . . . . Anne
Promises in the Dark (1979) . . . . Fran Koenig
Nobody's Perfekt (1981) . . . . Carol
Porky's (1981; Canadian). . . . . Cherry Forever

Made for TV Movies:

Babe (1975) . . . . Babe Didrickson Zaharias
(Emmy Award for Best Actress in a Special.)
Snowbound: The Jim and Jennifer Stolpa Story (1994)
. . . . Muriel Mulligan
Tonya & Nancy: The Inside Story (1994) . . . . . LaVona Harding

TV:

Webster (1983-89) . . . . . . Katherine Calder Young Papadapolis

Clarke, Caitlin

Films:

Dragonslayer (1981) . . . . Valerian
- 0:27—Body double's very brief side of left breast from under water.

Penn & Teller Get Killed (1989) . . . . Carlotta
Blown Away (1994). . . . . Rita

Made for TV Movies:

Mayflower Madam (1987). . . . . Virginia
Love, Lies and Murder (1991) . . . . Sandra Eden
Kiss and Tell (1996). . . . . Karen Wallace

TV:

Once a Hero (1979) . . . . Emma Greely

Clarke, Julie *

Films:

Can It Be Love (1992) . . . . Crystal
a.k.a. Spring Break Sorority Babes

Video Tapes:

Playboy Video Centerfold: Julie Clarke . . . . Playmate
Playboy Video Calendar 1992 (1991) . . . . February
- ••• 0:05—Breasts on stairs. Nude in warehouse, painting on the floor and on herself.
- ••• 0:07—Nude, putting oil on herself.

Playboy Playmates in Paradise (1992) . . . . Playmate
Playboy's Playmate Review 1992 (1992) . . . . . Miss March
- ••• 0:10—Nude in indoor pool, then in art studio and then on horseback.

Wet & Wild IV (1992) . . . . Model

Clarke, Melinda

Films:

Hot Under the Collar (1991) . . . . Monica
Out for Blood (1992). . . . . Laura
Return of the Living Dead 3 (1993). . . . . Julie Walker
- •• 0:16—Breasts, while in bed talking with her boyfriend, Curt.
- • 0:17—More breasts, while getting out of bed when Curt's dad comes home.
- • 1:07—Breasts under skimpy outfit after doing some severe body piercing.
- •• 1:25—Brief breasts when getting rescued by Curt.

Return to Two Moon Junction (1993)
. . . . Savannah Delongpre
- •• 0:37—Lying in bed in wet white lingerie, then left breast (close-up shot) while fantasizing about Jake.
- • 0:44—Upper half of buns, while in bed with Jake.
- •• 0:45—Buns and back half of right breast, while standing up and putting on dress.
- ••• 0:59—Breasts and very brief lower frontal nudity while making love with Jake.
- •• 1:01—Buns, while getting out of bed and putting a shirt on.
- • 1:09—Breasts, with Jake in bed.

Mulholland Falls (1996). . . . . Cigarette Girl
Spawn (1997) . . . . Jessica Priest

TV:

Days of Our Lives. . . . . Faith Taylor
Heaven Help Us (1994-95). . . . . Lexy Monroe

Clarkson, Lana *

Films:

Fast Times at Ridgemont High (1982) . . . . Mrs. Vargas
Deathstalker (1983) . . . . Kaira
- •• 0:26—Breasts when her cape opens, while talking to Deathstalker and Oghris.
- ••• 0:29—Breasts lying down by the fire when Deathstalker comes to make love with her.
- • 0:49—Brief breasts with gaping cape, sword fighting with a guard.

Scarface (1983) . . . . Woman at the Babylon Club
Blind Date (1984) . . . . Rachel
a.k.a. Deadly Seduction
(Not to be confused with *Blind Date* (1987) with Bruce Willis.)
- • 0:52—Brief breasts rolling over in bed when Joseph Bottoms sneaks in. Dark, hard to see.

Barbarian Queen (1985) . . . . Amethea
- •• 0:38—Brief breasts during attempted rape.
- ••• 0:48—Breasts being tortured with metal hand then raped by torturer.

Amazon Women on the Moon (1987). . . . . Alpha Beta
Barbarian Queen II: The Empress Strikes Back (1989)
. . . . Athelia
- ••• 0:14—Breasts during fight with Erigina in mud. More breasts afterwards.
- ••• 0:31—Left breast, while making love with Aurion outside.
- ••• 0:43—Breasts, tied up to torture rack.
- ••• 0:49—More breasts, tied up to torture rack.
- •• 0:51—Brief right breast then breasts several times, while lying down, tied to the rack.
- • 0:54—Very brief breasts when Aurion covers her up.

The Haunting of Morella (1989) . . . . Coel Deveroux
- ••• 0:17—Breasts, taking a bath, then getting out and wrapping a towel around herself.
- ••• 1:00—Breasts in white panties, standing under a waterfall.

Wizards of the Lost Kingdom, Part 2 (1991). . . . . Amathea
Vice Girls (1995) . . . . Jan Cooper
- •• 0:11—Breasts, while making out in restroom with John.

Another 9 1/2 Weeks (1996) . . . . Woman at Fashion Show

Clatterbuck, Tamara

Films:

The Borrower (1989) . . . . Michele Chodiss
Marked for Murder (1990). . . . . Barmaid
Set It Off (1996) . . . . Luther's Girlfriend
- • 1:20—Brief breasts, while making love with Luther in bed.

City of Industry (1997) . . . . Sunny
Phoenix (1998) . . . . Waitress

Made for Cable Movies:

The Perfect Bride (1991) . . . . Deidre
Blind Side (1993; HBO) . . . . Barbara Hall
- •• 1:13—In bra and panties, outside with Rutger Hauer by the spa. Then breasts several times.

Rebel Highway: Girls in Prison (1994; Showtime)
. . . . Actress on Newsreel

Made for TV Movies:
L.A. Johns (1997) . . . . Patty
Payback (1997) . . . . Janet
TV:
NYPD Blue: Closing Time (May 14, 1996) . . . . . Deena Farnham
The Young and the Restless (1998-) . . . . n.a.

Clayburgh, Jill

Films:
The Wedding Party (1969) . . . . Josephine Fish
Portnoy's Complaint (1972) . . . . Naomi
The Thief Who Came to Dinner (1973) . . . . Jackie
The Terminal Man (1974) . . . . Angela Black
Silver Streak (1976) . . . . Hilly Burns
Semi-Tough (1977) . . . . Barbara Jane Bookman
An Unmarried Woman (1978) . . . . Erica
•• 0:12—Brief breasts getting dressed for bed, kind of dark and hard to see.
•• 1:10—In bra and panties in guy's apartment, then brief breasts lying on bed.
Luna (1979) . . . . Caterina Silveri
Starting Over (1979) . . . . Marilyn Holmberg
• 0:45—Very brief upper half of breasts taking a shower while Burt Reynolds waits outside.
It's My Turn (1980) . . . . Kate Gunzinger
• 1:10—Brief upper half of left breast in bed with Michael Douglas after making love.
First Monday in October (1981) . . . . Ruth Loomis
I'm Dancing as Fast as I Can (1981) . . . . Barbara Gordon
Hanna K. (1984) . . . . Hanna Kaufman
Where Are the Children? (1986) . . . . Nancy Eldgridge
Shy People (1988) . . . . Diana
Rich in Love (1992) . . . . Helen Odom
Whispers in the Dark (1992) . . . . Sarah Green
Day of Atonement (1993; French) . . . . Sally White
Naked in New York (1993) . . . . Shirley
Fools Rush In (1997) . . . . Nan
Made for Cable Movies:
Sins of the Mind (1997; USA) . . . . Eve
When Innocence Is Lost (1997; Lifetime) . . . . Susan
Made for TV Movies:
Hustling (1975) . . . . Wanda
Female Instinct (1985) . . . . Mary
Reason for Living: The Jill Ireland Story (1991) . . . . . . Jill Ireland
Trial: The Price of Passion (1992) . . . . Judge Louise Parker
Firestorm: 72 Hours in Oakland (1993) . . . . . Anneliese Osborn
For the Love of Nancy (1994) . . . . Sally
Honor Thy Father & Mother (1994) . . . . Kitty Menendez
The Face on the Milk Carton (1995) . . . . Miranda Jessmon
TV:
Search for Tomorrow . . . . Grace Bolton

*Clément, Aurore **

Films:
Lovers and Liars (1979; Italian) . . . . Cora
Paris, Texas (1984; French/German) . . . . Anne
Mosca Addio (1987; Italian) . . . . Elena, Ida's Sister
El Sur (1988; Spanish) . . . . Irene Rios/Laura
Gemini: The Twin Stars (1988; U.S./Swiss) . . . . Mrs. Buffington

*Clery, Corrine **

Films:
Kleinhoff Hotel (1973) . . . . Pascale Rota
The Story of "O" (1975; French) . . . . O
(Nude a lot, only the best are listed.)
•• 0:04—Breasts in the back of car when her boyfriend pulls her blouse down and rips her bra off.
••• 0:08—Breasts, getting made up by two women.
•• 0:10—Left breast, while getting checked out.
•• 0:13—Frontal nudity, chained to chandelier and whipped.
•• 0:14—Breasts on couch.
•• 0:16—Breasts getting out of tub and sitting on bed.
••• 0:18—Breasts and brief buns, getting out of bed and whipped. Frontal nudity, getting up.
••• 0:20—Frontal nudity with two guys.
••• 0:22—Breasts, sitting in front of a mirror.
•• 0:24—Breasts, watching another woman have sex in library.
••• 0:27—Breasts sitting at table and eating.
••• 0:29—Breasts getting a bath.
•• 0:30—Breasts being led around blindfolded.
•• 0:33—Brief breasts, getting whipped and eating.
•• 0:42—Buns, while bent over sofa.
••• 0:43—Breasts with older man on sofa.
••• 0:44—Nude, taking off her skirt.
••• 0:59—Frontal nudity, reclining on bed, then sitting up.
•• 1:02—Breasts in room with older man when he opens her blouse.
••• 1:05—Breasts and buns in bedroom.
••• 1:06—Nude with other women, getting dressed in a corset.
••• 1:08—Breasts, getting chained to posts and whipped.
•• 1:13—Breasts in bed with another woman.
•• 1:14—Breasts before getting branded.
••• 1:17—Frontal nudity, getting out of tub and putting on robe.
•• 1:19—Breasts getting her blouse opened and breast sucked.
••• 1:21—Nude, making love in bed. Slightly overexposed.
••• 1:26—Tied up to posts by wrists.
•• 1:32—Breasts in open cape, while wearing a mask. Frontal nudity getting cape removed.
Covert Action (1978) . . . . Anne Florio
a.k.a. Sono Stato Un Agente Cia
The Switch (1978) . . . . Charlotte
a.k.a. The Con Artists
The Humanoid (1979; Italian) . . . . Barbar Gibson
Moonraker (1979) . . . . Corinne Dufour
I Hate Blondes (1981; Italian) . . . . Angelica
• 1:17—Left breast and upper half of buns, in bedroom with a guy when he tries to seduce her.
Yor: The Hunter from the Future (1983) . . . . Ka-Laa
Dangerous Obsession (1990; Italian) . . . . Carol Simpson
• 0:14—Right breast sticking out of lingerie while lying in bed.
•• 0:36—Full frontal nudity lying in bed waiting for her husband, then with him, then getting out of bed.
Forever (1992) . . . . n.a.

*Cleveland, Amanda **

a.k.a. Missy Cleveland.
Films:
Cheech & Chong's Next Movie (1980) . . . . Massage Girl
Blow Out (1981) . . . . Coed Lover/Shower Victim
• 0:01—Left breast in room while someone watches from the outside.
• 0:02—Breasts in shower and on TV monitor while killer stalks outside.
True Confessions (1981) . . . . Lois

Video Tapes:
Playboy Video Magazine, Volume 2 (1983)
. . . . .Herself/Playboy Playoffs

Cleveland, Missy *

See: Cleveland, Amanda.

Clifford, Veronica

Films:
Sebastian (1968; British) . . . . Ginny
Think Dirty (1970; British) . . . . Hot Dog Girl
a.k.a. Every Home Should Have One
Up Pompeii (1971; British) . . . . Boobia
Secret Places (1984; British). . . . . Miss Mallard
The Raggedy Rawney (1988; British). . . . . The Farmer's Wife
• 0:39—Left breast in open nightgown, while sleeping in bed when a boy peeks in the window.
Twenty-One (1991; British) . . . . .Bobby's Aunt

Clive, Teagan

a.k.a. Teagan.
Former body guard for David Lee Roth.
Films:
Armed and Dangerous (1986). . . . . Staff Member
Jumpin' Jack Flash (1986) . . . . Russian Exercise Woman
Obsession: A Taste For Fear (1987) . . . . . .Teagan Morrison
• 0:15—Brief upper half of right breast, when she lies back down in bed.
• 0:29—Buns, while lying dead, covered with plastic wrap.
• 0:37—Very brief buns in flashback to 0:29 scene.
Alienator (1989) . . . . Alienator
Interzone (1989) . . . . Mantis
Mob Boss (1990). . . . . .Noelle
Sinbad and the Seven Seas (1990). . . . . Soukra
Vice Academy, Part 2 (1990) . . . . Bimbo Cop
Music Videos:
California Girls/David Lee Roth . . . . Muscular Woman

Close, Glenn

Films:
World According to Garp (1982). . . . . .Jenny Fields
The Big Chill (1983) . . . . Sara
• 0:27—Breasts sitting down in the shower crying.
The Natural (1984) . . . . .Iris Gaines
The Stone Boy (1984) . . . . Ruth Hillerman
Jagged Edge (1985) . . . . Teddy Barnes
• 0:46—Side view of left breast, making love in bed with Jeff Bridges.
• 1:38—Very brief side view of right breast running down the hall taking off her blouse. Back is toward camera. Blurry shot.
Maxie (1985) . . . . .Jan/Maxie Malone
• 0:37—Very brief back half of left breast, while sitting up in bed.
Fatal Attraction (1987) .Alex Forrest
•• 0:17—Left breast when she opens her top to let Michael Douglas kiss her. Then very brief buns, falling into bed with him.
• 0:20—Brief right breast in freight elevator with Douglas.
••• 0:32—Breasts in bed talking to Douglas. Long scene, sheet keeps changing positions between cuts.
Dangerous Liaisons (1988) . . . . Marquise de Merteuil
Immediate Family (1989) . . . . Linda Spector
Hamlet (1990; British/French) . . . . Queen Gertrude
Meeting Venus (1990; British) . . . . Karin Anderson
Reversal of Fortune (1990). . . . . Sunny von Bülow
Hook (1991) . . . . Gutless
The House of Spirits (1993) . . . . Ferula
The Paper (1993). . . . . Alicia Clark
Mary Reilly (1995) . . . . Mrs. Farraday
101 Dalmatians (1996) . . . . .Cruella DeVil
Mars Attacks! (1996) . . . . First Lady Marsha Dale
Air Force One (1997). . . . . .Vice President Kathry Bennett
Paradise Road (1997). . . . . Adrienne Pargiter
Made for Cable Movies:
In the Gloaming (1997; HBO) . . . . .Janet
Made for TV Movies:
Something About Amelia (1984) . . . . Gail Bennett
Sarah Plain and Tall (1991) . . . . .Sarah Wheaton
Skylark (1993) . . . . Sarah Witting
Serving in Silence: The Margarethe Cammermeyer Story (1995) . . . . Colonel Margarethe Cammermeyer

Clunie, Michelle

Films:
Sunset Strip (1992). . . . . .Jonesy
••• 0:23—In black skirt and bra, then breasts and buns in G-string, while doing routine on stage.
• 1:16—Breasts in music video.
Erotique (1993) . . . . Let's Talk About Sex
Jason Goes to Hell—The Final Friday (1993)
. . . . .Deborah, the dark-haired camper
(Unrated Director's Original Cut reviewed.)
• 0:29—Brief right breast, while on top of Luke in tent.
••• 0:31—Breasts, while making love with Luke in tent before getting killed.
The Usual Suspects (1995). . . . . Sketch Artist
Made for Cable TV:
Hot Line: The Homecoming (1994; Cinemax)
. . . . .Jesse Summerfield
• 0:01—Breasts and brief buns, while making love during the opening credits.
• 0:08—Partial breasts while sitting in bubble bath.
•• 0:25—Breasts and buns, while making love with Daryl in attic.
Made for TV Movies:
Another Midnight Run (1994) . . . . Flight Attendant

• Cobo, Eva

Films:
Matador (1986; Spanish). . . . . .Eva Soler
•• 0:09—Breasts drying herself off after shower when Angel watches her through binoculars.
• 0:29—Full frontal nudity in bed with Diego.
Operation Condor (1990; Hong Kong) . . . . .Elsa

Cochran, Mimi

Films:
Talk Radio (1988). . . . . Girl #1
I Come in Peace (1990) . . . . Female Mechanic
Love Crimes (1991) . . . . Stunt Double for Sean Young
(Unrated version reviewed.)
Made for Cable TV:
Hot Line: The Brunch Club (1995; Cinemax)
. . . . .Kelly Andrews
(Available on video tape in *Hot Line 3*.)
• 0:02—Brief breasts and buns in fantasy with delivery boy. B&W.
•• 0:03—Breasts and buns in fantasy with delivery boy. B&W.
•• 0:05—Breasts, while wearing black panties, when undressing for bath.

•• 0:06—Breasts, while in bathroom and in bathtub with Alan.
•• 0:23—Breasts, while rubbing lotion on herself.
••• 0:24—In black lingerie, then breasts, while making love with Alan in bed.

Cochran, Shannon

Films:

The Babe (1992) . . . . Flapper

TV:

NYPD Blue (1993) . . . . Lois Snyder

NYPD Blue: Pilot (Sep 21, 1993) . . . . Lois Snyder
• 0:25—Very brief buns in panties and blurry breasts, while getting dressed after helping to set up Sipowicz.

Cochrane, Talie

Films:

The Love-Thrill Murders (1971) . . . . Ruth
•• 0:24—Breasts and buns, while undressing and talking with Faith.
••• 1:03—Nude, while dancing during party.

The Centerfold Girls (1974) . . . . .Donna

I Spit on Your Corpse (1974) . . . . Hitchhiker
a.k.a. Girls for Rent
• 0:47—Brief right breast, then breasts getting shot. More breasts, dead, covered with blood.

Fugitive Girls (1975) . . . . n.a.

Can I Do It 'Til I Need Glasses? (1976) . . . . n.a.

If You Don't Stop It You'll Go Blind (1979) . . . . n.a.

Cochrell, Elizabeth

a.k.a. Liza Cochrell.

Films:

The Big Bet (1985) . . . . Sister in Stag Film
••• 1:05—Breasts and buns, undressing and getting into bathtub in a video tape that Chris is watching.
•• 1:08—Breasts again on video tape, when Chris watches it on TV at home.

Free Ride (1986) . . . . Nude Girl #1
• 0:25—Brief buns taking a shower with another girl.

Sunset Strip (1986) . . . . Stripper

Cody, Marissa

Films:

Cover Story (1993) . . . . Allison
•• 0:02—Breasts, while making love with Matt in bed.
• 0:10—Brief breasts, while making love in B&W flashback.
• 0:12—Left breast, while reading a letter and making love with Matt, then dead in B&W flashbacks.
• 0:34—Very, very brief breasts in B&W flashback.
• 0:53—Very brief breasts, in B&W flashback.

Guyver 2: Dark Hero (1994) . . . . Mary

Coffey, Colleen

Films:

The Lawnmower Man (1992) . . . . Caroline Angelo
(Unrated Director's cut reviewed.)

The Mosaic Project (1994) . . . . Ash

Relentless 4: Ashes to Ashes (1994) . . . . .Jessice Parreti

Indecent Behavior 3 (1995) . . . . Ellie Maddox
••• 0:24—Breasts and buns, while making love in office with Billy.

The Beneficiary (1996) . . . . Commercial Voice

TV:

NYPD Blue: These Old Bones (Feb 6, 1996) . . . . n.a.

Coffey, Elizabeth

Transsexual. (Born a man.)

Films:

Pink Flamingos (1972) . . . . Woman in Park
•• 1:02—Right "breast," then penis, when flashing Raymond the flasher in the park. (Elizabeth was half way through his sex-change operation at the time.)

Female Trouble (1974) . . . . Ernestine
• 1:24—Right breast, while lying on cot in jail cell with Divine.
• 1:25—More right breast.
• 1:26—Brief lower frontal nudity when kissing Divine.

Colazzo, Dianne

a.k.a. Former under age adult film actress Alexandria Quinn.

Films:

Head of the Family (1996) . . . . Ernestina
•• 0:48—Breasts, while in bedroom, then making love with Lance.

Colbert, Claudette

Films:

Sign of the Cross (1932) . . . . Poppaea
• 0:19—Very, very brief upper half of breasts, several times, while in milk bath.
• 0:21—Very, very brief upper half of areola on left breast when telling Dacia to get in milk bath.

I Cover the Waterfront (1933) . . . . Julie Kirk

Cleopatra (1934) . . . . Cleopatra

It Happened One Night (1934) . . . . .Ellie Andrews

Tovarich (1937) . . . . .Grand Duchess Tatiana Petrovna

Drums Along the Mohawk (1939) . . .Lana "Magdelana" Martin

The Palm Beach Story (1942) . . . . Gerry Jeffers

Since You Went Away (1944) . . . . Anne Hilton

Guest Wife (1945) . . . . .Mary

Tomorrow Is Forever (1946) . . .Elizabeth MacDonald Hamilton

Without Reservations (1946) . . . . . . Christopher "Kit" Madden

The Egg and I (1947) . . . . Betty MacDonald

Three Came Home (1950) .Agnes Keith

Let's Make It Legal (1951) . . . . Miriam

Texas Lady (1955) . . . . Prudence Webb

Parrish (1961) . . . . Ellen McLean

• Colburn, Katie

Films:

Beach Babes From Beyond (1993) . . . . .Sally's Model
••• 0:20—Breasts, while posing in spa outside (she's in the middle) during catalog photo session with two other models.
• 1:02—Brief breasts, when swimsuit top flies off while dancing on stage during bikini contest (she's the first one).

Bikini Hotel (1996) . . . . .Eunice
• 0:32—Brief breasts, while taking off bikini top in front of registration desk.
• 0:38—Buns in T-back while making bed and vacuuming.
• 0:40—Buns in T-back while vacuuming.
• 0:47—Breasts, after taking off her bikini top during card game.
• 0:48—Buns in swimsuit, while gathering clothes.
• 0:51—Brief buns in T-back.
• 0:56—Breasts during card game.

Cole, Debra

Films:

Crossing Delancey (1988) . . . . Waitress

The Hot Spot (1990) ....Irene Davey
- • 1:26—Breasts sunbathing next to Jennifer Connelly at side of lake. Long shot.
- •• 1:27—Breasts talking with Connelly some more.

Coleman, Renee

Films:

After School (1987) .... September Lane
- •• 0:35—Breasts and buns getting into bathtub. Almost lower frontal nudity.

Rocket Gibraltar (1988)......................... Waitress
Who's Harry Crumb? (1989) .... Jennifer Downing
A League of Their Own (1992) ....Alice Gaspers
Pentathalon (1994)...............................Julia

Coleridge, Tania

Films:

Days of Thunder (1990) ....Russ Wheeler's Girlfriend
The Rain Killer (1990) .... Adele
- •• 0:28—Breasts on back of couch with Ray Sharkey. Left breast, after rolling onto the floor with Sharkey.
- • 0:32—Brief side view of right breast, in bed with Vince.
- • 0:53—Very brief tip of left breast, twice, in bubble bath.

Collings, Jeannie

Films:

Confessions of a Window Cleaner (1974; British).... Baby Doll
Happy Housewives (1975; British) .... Mrs. Wain
- • 0:16—Very, very brief right breast with the Newsagent's Daughter and Bob in the bathtub.

Carry On England (1976; British)............Private Edwards
Emily (1976; British).......................... Rosalind
- • 1:05—Brief breasts on the couch with Gerald while Richard watches.

Justine (1977; British) .... Prostitute
a.k.a. Cruel Passion

Collings, Lisa

Films:

Love is a Splendid Illusion (1970; British).... Amanda Dubarry
The Mutations (1973; British) .... Prostitute
a.k.a. Freakmaker
- • 1:04—Breasts, while opening her dress for Tom Baker.

Collins, Alana

See: Stewart, Alana.

Collins, Jo *

Films:

Fireball 500 (1966) .... Leander Fan
Video Tapes:

Playboy Video Centerfold: Donna Edmondson (1987) ....Playmate Update
- ••• 0:21—Breasts and buns in still photos.

Collins, Joan *

Films:

Decameron Nights (1953)......................... Maria
Stopover Tokyo (1957) .... Tina
Esther and the King (1960; U.S./Italian)............. Esther
Subterfuge (1969)......................... Anne Langley
The Executioner (1970; British) .... Sarah Booth
Quest for Love (1971; British) .... Ottilie
Fear in the Night (1972; British) .... Molly Charmichael
a.k.a. Dynasty of Fear
Tales From the Crypt (1972) .... Joanne Clayton
Dark Places (1974; British)......................... Sarah
Oh, Alfie! (1975; British) .... Fay
a.k.a. Alfie Darling
- ••• 1:00—Breasts lying in bed after Alfie rolls off her.

The Bawdy Adventures of Tom Jones (1976; British) ....Black Bess
The Devil Within Her (1976; British)............ Lucy Carlesi
Empire of the Ants (1977) ....Marilyn Fryser
The Big Sleep (1978; British) .... Agnes Lozelle
Fearless (1978) .... Bridgitte
- • 0:01—In bra and panties, then brief right breast during opening credits.
- •• 0:41—Breasts after doing a strip tease routine on stage.
- • 1:17—Undressing in front of Wally in white bra and panties, then right breast.
- • 1:20—Brief right breast lying dead on couch.

The Stud (1978; British)....................... Fontaine
- • 0:10—Brief left breast making love with Tony in the elevator.
- • 1:03—Brief breasts taking off dress to get in pool.
- • 1:04—Nude in the pool with Tony.

The Bitch (1979; British) .... Fontaine Khaled
- • 0:03—Brief breasts in the shower with a guy.
- •• 0:24—Brief breasts taking black corset off for the chauffeur in the bedroom, then buns getting out of bed and walking to the bathroom.
- • 1:01—Left breast after making love in bed.

Sunburn (1979)...................................Nera
Homework (1982)............................... Diane
Body double used for Joan's nude scene.
Miniseries:
Sins (1986) ....Helene Junot
Dynasty: The Reunion (1991) .... Alexis Morell Carrington Colby Dexter Rowan
Made for TV Movies:
Her Life as a Man (1984) .... Pam Dugan
The Cartier Affair (1985) .... Cartier Rand
Monte Carlo (1986).....................Katrina Petrovna
Annie: A Royal Adventure (1995).... Lady Edwina Hogbottom
TV:
Dynasty (1981-89)................ Alexis Carrington Colby
Pacific Palisades (1997) .... Christina Hobson
Video Tapes:
Joan Collins Personal Workout: Secrets of Fitness Beauty (1994) .... Herself

Collins, Pamela

Films:

Sweet Sugar (1972) ....Dolores
a.k.a. Hellfire on Ice
- • 0:26—Brief breasts when doctor tears her bra off.
- ••• 0:50—Breasts in the shower with Phyllis Davis.

So Long, Blue Boy (1973) .... Cathy
Famous T & A (1982) ....Dolores
(No longer available for purchase, check your video store for rental.)
- ••• 1:05—Breasts in scenes and outtakes from *Sweet Sugar.*

Collins, Pauline

Films:

Secrets of a Windmill Girl (1966; British) .... Pat Lord
Shirley Valentine (1989; British).......... Shirley Valentine
(If you like older women, check this out.)
- • 0:13—Brief left breast, while giving Joe a shampoo in the bathtub.
- •• 1:17—Brief breasts, while jumping from the boat into the water. Very brief breasts in the water.

•• 1:19—Buns, while hugging Tom Conti (possible body double—don't see her face). Left breast several times, while lying on deck, kissing Conti.

City of Joy (1992) . . . . Joan Bethel
Paradise Road (1997) . . . . Margaret Drummond

TV:

Upstairs, Downstairs . . . . Sarah

Collins, Roberta

Films:

The Big Doll House (1971) . . . . Alcott
••• 0:33—Breasts in shower. Seen through blurry window by prison worker, Fred. Blurry, but nice.
• 0:34—Brief left breast, while opening her blouse for Fred.

Unholy Rollers (1972) . . . . Jennifer
a.k.a. Leader of the Pack

The Arousers (1973) . . . . Call Girl
The Roommates (1973). . . . . Beth
Wonder Women (1973; Philippines) . . . . Laura

Caged Heat (1974). . . . . Belle
a.k.a. Renegade Girls
• 0:11—Very brief breasts getting blouse ripped open by Juanita.
••• 1:01—Breasts while the prison doctor has her drugged so he can take pictures of her.

Death Race 2000 (1975) . . . . Matilda the Hun
•• 0:27—Breasts being interviewed and arguing with Calamity Jane.

Train Ride to Hollywood (1975). . . . . Jean Harlow
The Witch Who Came From the Sea (1976) . . . . Clarissa
Death Wish II (1982). . . . . Woman at Party
Hardbodies (1984) . . . . Lana
School Spirit (1985) . . . . Helen Grimshaw
Hardbodies 2 (1986). . . . . Lana Logan
Vendetta (1986) . . . . Miss Dice

Collins, Ruth Corrine

Films:

Blood Sisters (1986) . . . . Prostitute

Sexpot (1986) . . . . Ivy Barrington
•• 0:09—Breasts on table, taking her dress off for Phillip.
• 0:41—Buns, in Damon's arms.
•• 0:51—Left breast, while in shower talking to Boopsie.

Doom Asylum (1987). . . . . Tina
•• 0:19—Breasts pulling up her top while yelling at kids below.

Firehouse (1987). . . . . Bubbles

Lurkers (1987) . . . . Jane (Model)
•• 0:13—Breasts, changing clothes with the other model.

Prime Evil (1987) . . . . Cathy
••• 0:15—Breasts making love with her boyfriend in bed.
• 0:16—More breasts sitting up and getting out of bed.
••• 0:27—Breasts, sitting up while the priest talks to her.
•• 1:13—Left breast, while removing her gown (she's on the left) with Brett and Judy.

Psychos in Love (1987) . . . . Susan
••• 0:42—Breasts, dancing and undressing in living room in front of Joe when caught by Kate.

Wildest Dreams (1987) . . . . Stella
••• 0:22—Breasts wearing panties in bedroom on bed with Bobby.
• 1:10—Brief breasts fighting on floor with two other women.

Alexa (1988) . . . . Marshall
• 0:01—Breasts a couple of times taking blue dress off and putting it on again. Long shot.

Galactic Gigolo (1988). . . . . Dr. Ruth Pepper
a.k.a. Club Earth
•• 0:47—Breasts, while stripping in front of Eoj.
• 0:49—Breasts, while getting tied up by Sammy.
• 0:53—Breasts in open cape while in the Goldberg's family room.
•• 0:55—Breasts, while getting rescued.

New York's Finest (1988). . . . . Joy Sugarman
• 0:04—Brief breasts with a bunch of hookers.
• 0:36—Breasts with her two friends doing push-ups on the floor.
•• 1:02—Breasts making love on top of a guy talking about diamonds.

Any Time, Any Play (1989) . . . . Kelly
•• 0:16—In black bra, then breasts after taking it off and walking into bathroom. Breasts under sheer white nightgown.
••• 0:32—Nude, while pouring drinks in bedroom, then making love with Vince in bed.
••• 0:41—Breasts, while wearing black panties, garter belt and stockings in dressing room with a friendly female saleswoman.
••• 0:52—Breasts, while making love in bed with Michael.

Cleo/Leo (1989) . . . . Sally
••• 0:08—Breasts getting dress pulled off by Leo.

Deadly Embrace (1989). . . . . Dede Magnolia
Exquisite Corpses (1989). . . . . Sue
Heaven Becomes Hell (1989). . . . . Rita

Party Incorporated (1989) . . . . Betty
a.k.a. Party Girls
• 0:07—Breasts on desk with Dickie. Long shot.
•• 1:08—Breasts in bed with Weston when Marilyn Chambers comes in.

Death Collector (1990) . . . . Annie Northbride
a.k.a. Tin Star Void

Eleven Days, Eleven Nights 2 (1990) . . . . . Dana Durrington
••• 0:14—Breasts while wearing stockings and making out with George on bed.

Dead Boyz Can't Fly (1992). . . . . Myra Kandinsky
• 0:14—Brief breasts while getting raped by Buzz in elevator.

Hellroller (1992) . . . . Eugene's Mother

*Collins, Tai **

Miss Virginia-U.S.A. 1983.

Films:

Enemy Gold (1993). . . . . Ava Noble
••• 0:20—Breasts and very brief lower frontal nudity in sauna. Breasts and buns, getting out of the sauna and into the shower.
••• 1:26—Breasts, while making love with Mark.

TV:

Baywatch (1992-93) . . . . n.a.

Video Tapes:

Playboy's Sensual Fantasy for Lovers (1993) . . . . . Games
••• 0:05—In white bra and panties, then full frontal nudity while in house, in bathtub, then making love in bed.
• 0:46—Nude during review.
• 0:49—Brief right breast during review.

*Collinson, Madeleine **

Identical twin sister of Mary Collinson.

Films:

Come Back Peter (1971; British) . . . . n.a.

The Love Machine (1971) . . . . Sandy
•• 1:22—Breasts in shower with Robin and her sister when Dyan Cannon discovers them all together. Can't tell who is who.

Twins of Evil (1971; British) . . . . Freida Gelhorn
- •• 1:07—Right breast, then brief breasts undoing dress, then full frontal nudity after turning into a vampire in bedroom.

Up in Smoke (1978) . . . . Pinup
- • 0:44—Brief breasts in centerfold photo on inside of restroom stall door.

Collinson, Mary *

Identical twin sister of Madeleine Collinson.

Films:

Come Back Peter (1971; British) . . . . n.a.

The Love Machine (1971) . . . . Debbie
- •• 1:22—Breasts in shower with Robin and her sister when Dyan Cannon discovers them all together. Can't tell who is who.

Twins of Evil (1971; British) . . . . Maria Gelhorn

Up in Smoke (1978) . . . . Pinup
- • 0:44—Brief breasts in centerfold photo on inside of restroom stall door.

Coloroso, Dotty

Films:

The Women's Club (1987) . . . . Cali
- • 0:11—Brief breasts getting angrily out of bed with Michael Paré.

Made for TV Movies:

Perry Mason: The Case of the Avenging Ace (1988) . . . . Amy Beth Sawyer

Colpitts-Cameron, Cissie

a.k.a. Cisse Cameron.

Films:

Beyond the Valley of the Dolls (1970) . . . . n.a.

Billy Jack (1971) . . . . Miss Eyelashes

The Happy Hooker Goes to Washington (1977) . . . . Miss Goodbody
- • 0:29—Very brief breasts when her top pops open during the senate hearing.

The Baltimore Bullet (1980) . . . . Sugar
- • 0:09—Breasts behind shower door after James Coburn gets out.

Porky's II: The Next Day (1983; Canadian) . . . . Graveyard Gloria/Sandy Le Toi
- • 0:26—Buns in G-string at carnival.
- •• 0:39—Breasts and buns in G-string, stripping for Pee Wee at cemetery.
- •• 0:40—More breasts, pretending to die.
- • 0:42—Breasts, being carried by Meat.

TV:

The Ted Knight Show (1978) . . . . Graziella

Colston, Karen

Films:

Sweetie (1989; Australian) . . . . Kay
- •• 0:24—Very brief side of right breast while sitting up in bed, then breasts in bed with Lou.
- • 0:25—Right breast while sitting up in bed and putting bra on.

The Piano (1993) . . . . Bluebeard's Wife

Colton, Diane *

Films:

Pleasure in Paradise (1992) . . . . Tiffany
- ••• 0:27—In black bra, then breasts while making love with Hansen. Long scene.

Combs, Holly Marie

Wife of actor Bryan Smith.

Films:

Sweet Hearts Dance (1988) . . . . Debs Boon

Born on the Fourth of July (1989) . . . . Jenny

Chain of Desire (1992) . . . . Diana

Dr. Giggles (1992) . . . . Jennifer Campbell

Simple Men (1992; U.S./British) . . . . Kim

A Reason to Believe (1995) . . . . Sharon
- ••• 1:06—Breasts, after taking off her blouse when making love with Wesley while Jay Underwood watches.

Made for TV Movies:

Danielle Steel's "A Perfect Stranger" (1994) . . . . Amanda

Love's Deadly Triangle: The Texas Cadet Murder (1997) . . . . Diane Zamora

Our Mother's Murder (1997) . . . . Alex Morell

TV:

Picket Fences (1992-96) . . . . Kimberly

Comshaw, Lisa

a.k.a. Lisa Sutton and Sandi Laine.

Films:

Almost Pregnant (1992) . . . . Body Double for Tanya Roberts
(Unrated version reviewed.)
- • 1:11—Close up shots of brief buns with a feather duster and getting bitten.
- • 1:12—Brief breasts and buns, with sentences projected on them.
- • 1:13— Close up of breasts, getting cupped by Gordon.

Housewife From Hell (1993) . . . . Melissa
- •• 0:03—Nude, after taking off robe in front of bathroom mirror (while wearing glasses), then getting into shower.
- •• 0:04—Breasts, while sitting in bathtub and talking to John.
- ••• 0:36—Breasts, while sitting in bubble bath and talking to John.
- • 0:48—In bra, buns in T-back while dancing in garage in between two other dancers.
- • 1:00—Breasts under white bodysuit.

Midnight Confessions (1993) . . . . Allyn
(Unrated version reviewed.)
- ••• 0:31—Breasts and buns, while making love with Monique Parent.

Scanner Cop (1993) . . . . Nurse in Operating Room

...And God Spoke (1994) . . . . Nude Ninja
- • 0:02—Brief breasts, while putting her sword away. (She's on the right, the first one to talk.)

Don Juan DeMarco (1994) . . . . Body Double for Woman in Restaurant
- • 0:05—Very, very brief partial right breast, while making love in bed.

Running Wild (1994) . . . . Pamela

Scanners: The Showdown (1994) . . . . Denise

Tough and Deadly (1994) . . . . Prostitute

Deadly Currency (1995) . . . . Jacuzzi Lady 2

Portrait in Red (1995) . . . . Rebecca Barlow
- • 0:07—Breasts, while having sex in bed with Sam.
- •• 0:15—Breasts and partial buns, while taking a shower.
- ••• 0:20—Nude, while having sex with a doctor on canvas on the floor, then killing him and smearing his blood around.
- •• 1:00—Left breast, while having sex on the floor with Adam.

Raven Hawk (1995) . . . . . . Uncredited Woman with Senator
- • 0:00—Brief breasts (three times), wearing panties and stockings in background while John De Lancie talks on the phone.

The Nurse (1996) . . . . Linda Henley

Illicit Confessions (1997). . . . . Andrea
••• 0:33—In black bra and panties, then full frontal nudity, while blindfolded and tied to fireplace, when having sex with Erica as her husband watches.

Made for Cable TV:
Erotic Confessions: At the Tone (1997; Cinemax) . . . Maryanne
Erotic Confessions: Behind the Lens (1997; Cinemax) . . . . Uncredited Marianne
• 0:05—Brief breasts in B&W photo.
••• 0:06—Nude, while posing for photographs with Robert while making love.
•• 0:09—Breasts and buns, while talking, then while making love with Monique Parent and Robert during photo shoot.

Made for TV Movies:
Come Die With Me: A Mickey Spillane's Mike Hammer Mystery (1994). . . . . Dominatrix

Video Tapes:
Buck Naked Line Dancing (1993). . . . . Dancer
••• 0:00—Breasts throughout. She's usually in the front in the left, wearing a choker.
Love Scenes: Volume 3 (1993) . . . . Barbara
1:00—In bra and panties, while watching Andreas dance, seen on monitor.
••• 1:07—Breasts, while making love with Andreas in living room. Dark.
Nude Daydreams (1993) . . . . Daydream 7
••• 0:22—Nude, while taking a shower.
Penthouse Forum Letters: Volume 1 (1993) . . . . Mystery Caller/Vicky
••• 0:40—In black bra, then breasts in her cubicle, squishing her breasts against the window.
••• 0:41—Nude, dancing in front of a different window.
••• 0:42—Breasts, while making love with Brad by the window.
•• 0:45—Breasts, taking off her clothes in the office with Tanya and Cindy in front of Brad.
Playboy Night Dreams (1993) . . . . Night Watch
••• 0:21—In bra, panties, garter belt and stockings in parking structure. Nude, while making love on car.
Playboy's Secret Confessions (1993) . . . . Here Comes the Judge/Gina
••• 0:50—Full frontal nudity, after taking off the judge's robe and making love with Spike on the judge's bench.
Babes, Bikes & Beyond (1994) . . . . Elaine
••• 0:04—Nude.
Playboy's Erotic Fantasies III (1994) . . . . Midnight Madness/Vampiress
••• 0:00—Nude, while making love with a guy and the other vampiress. (She's wearing snake arm bands.)
Single Alien Seeks Horny Earth Girl (1994) . . . . Tracy
Playboy's Erotic Fantasies: Forbidden Liaisons (1995) . . . . Double Exposure
••• 0:46—Full frontal nudity under and out of sheer white dress, making love in bed with a man and another woman.
Single Alien Seeks Horny Earth Girl (1995) . . . . Traci
•• 0:00—Nude in small window.
••• 0:03—Nude, while undressing and taking a shower.
• 0:10—Brief full frontal nudity in open robe.
••• 0:26—Breasts, while starting to make love with Zing, then putting her bra back on.
••• 0:34—Nude, after taking off lingerie and making love with Zing in bedroom.
••• 0:38—Breasts, while lying in bed with her wrists tied to the bed, making love with Zing.
Centerfold Fantasies (1997) . . . . Herself
••• 0:13—Nude, while posing in dining room.
••• 0:35—Nude, while posing outdoors on stairs.
••• 0:39—Nude, while cavorting around pool with the other girls.
••• 0:49—Nude, while walking around outdoors by the pool.

*Conaway, Cristi **

Films:
Doc Hollywood (1991) . . . . Receptionist
Batman Returns (1992) . . . . Ice Princess
Husbands and Wives (1992) . . . . Shawn Grainger
Nina Takes a Lover (1995) . . . . Friend
Intimate Betrayal (1996) . . . . Shelley
Underworld (1996) . . . . Julianne

Made for Cable Movies:
Attack of the 50 ft. Woman (1993; HBO) . . . . Honey
• 0:16—Very brief buns and back side of left breast, after getting out of bed and walking to the bathroom.
Any Place But Home (1997; USA) . . . . Carrie

Made for Cable TV:
Tales From the Crypt: 99 and 44/100% Pure Horror (1996; HBO) . . . . Willa

Miniseries:
Grass Roots (1992) . . . . Charlene Joiner

TV:
Timecop (1997-) . . . . Claire Hemmings

Condon, Iris

Films:
Party Plane (1988) . . . . Renee
• 0:29—Buns, in white lingerie during audition.
••• 0:48—Breasts, while on plane doing a strip tease routine.
••• 1:02—Breasts, while mud wrestling with Carol.
• 1:12—Left breast, covered with mud, holding the Mad Bomber.
• 1:17—Left breast, then breasts in trunk with the Doctor.
Pucker Up and Bark Like a Dog (1989). . . . Stretch Woman

Video Tapes:
In Search of the Perfect 10 (1986) . . . Perfect Girl #6/Jackie
••• 0:37—Breasts (she's the blonde) playing Twister with Rebecca Lynn. Buns in G-string.
Starlets Exposed! (1990) . . . . Iris
• 0:04—Brief breasts doing strippergram in office.
••• 0:05—Nude, taking a bubble bath and drying herself off.

Congie, Terry

Films:
Malibu Hot Summer (1981) . . . . Janice Johnson
a.k.a. Sizzle Beach
(*Sizzle Beach* is the re-released version with Kevin Costner featured on the cover. It is missing all the nude scenes during the opening credits before 0:06.)
• 0:09—Buns in the shower. Hard to see through the door.
••• 0:29—Breasts taking off her top and getting into bed with Steve, then making love.
• 1:09—Side view of left breast kissing Gary during the party.
•• 1:11—Breasts making love with Gary the next morning after the party.
Shadows Run Black (1981) . . . . Lee Faulkner
•• 0:22—Breasts, going for a swim in pool at night.
• 0:23—Breasts under water.

Connelly, Jennifer

Films:
Once Upon a Time in America (1984) . . . . Young Deborah
(Long version reviewed.)
Creepers (1985; Italian) . . . . Jennifer Corvino

Seven Minutes in Heaven (1985) . . . . Natalie
Labyrinth (1986) . . . . Sarah
Some Girls (1988) . . . . Gabriella
a.k.a. Sisters
The Hot Spot (1990) . . . . Gloria Harper
• 1:26—Buns, while lying next to Irene next to lake. Long shot.
••• 1:27—Breasts, while talking to Irene next to lake. Wow!
Career Opportunities (1991) . . . . Josie McClellan
The Rocketeer (1991) . . . . Jenny Blake
Higher Learning (1994) . . . . Taryn
Of Love and Shadows (1995) . . . . Irene
Far Harbor (1996) . . . . Ellie
• 0:34—Partial right breast under water, while sitting in bathtub.
Mulholland Falls (1996) . . . . Alison Pondi
• 0:02—In black bra, panties, garter belt and stockings during opening credits. Breasts when the guy takes her bra off. B&W.
• 0:17—Brief breasts, while kneeling on the bed during playback of B&W film.
• 0:26—Very, very brief side view of left breast, in flashback with Nick Nolte. Color.
• 1:09—Breasts, with Nolte when Melanie Griffith watches B&W film.
Inventing the Abbotts (1997) . . . . Eleanor Abbott
•• 0:17—Brief left breast several times, while making love with Billy Crudup in garage when seen by Joaquin Phoenix.
• 0:28—Very brief right breast, while making love with Crudup on the ground.
Dark City (1998) . . . . Emma Murdoch
Made for Cable Movies:
The Heart of Justice (1993; TNT) . . . . Emma Burgess

*Conner, Vanessa **

Video Tapes:
Playboy's Girls of Radio: Talk, Rock and Shock (1995) . . . . Herself
••• 0:16—In black bra and panties, then nude with four other women.

Conners, Julie

Films:
The Curious Female (1969) . . . . Andre Lewis/Girl #3
•• 1:12—Breasts while giving Pearl a back rub.
Count Yorga, Vampire (1970) . . . . Cleo

*Conrad, Kimberley **

Ex-wife of *Playboy* magazine publisher Hugh Hefner.
Video Tapes:
Playboy Video Calendar 1989 (1988) . . . . October
••• 0:38—Nude.
Playboy Video Calendar 1990 (1989) . . . . December
••• 1:03—Nude.
Playboy Video Centerfold: Kimberley Conrad (1989) . . . . Playmate of the Year 1989
••• 0:00—Nude throughout.
Playboy's Playmates of the Year: The '80s (1989) . . . . Playmate of the Year 1989
••• 0:44—Nude in still photos.
••• 0:49—Full frontal nudity in bathtub and in various scenes around the house.
• 0:53—In lingerie.
The Best of Video Playmate Calendars (1992) . . Playmate
••• 0:43—Breasts and buns in over exposed music video segment. Breasts while dancing in silk pajamas.
•• 0:44—In lingerie.
••• 0:45—Nude in outdoor fountain in slow motion.
•• 0:46—Nude in house, lit with a sliver of light.

*Conrad, Stevi **

a.k.a. Brittany Stone.
Films:
The Perfect Gift (1993) . . . . Pajama Party Guest
Femalien (1995) . . . . Angel
••• 0:34—In lingerie, while modeling for Kara in lingerie store. Nude, while making love with Gena.
Video Tapes:
Love Scenes: Volume 3 (1993) . . . . Robin
•• 0:41—Breasts, while tying Bill up to some trees outside.
••• 0:44—Nude, while making love in barn with Bill.
Body Language (1996) . . . . Fire Place/Sun Bath
••• 0:17—Nude, while caressing two other women in front of fire place.
••• 0:28—Nude, while sunbathing outdoors with Sara St. James and Lorissa McComas.
Erotic Heat (1996) . . . . Dining Room/Jacuzzi
••• 0:29—Nude, after stripping in kitchen and rubbing whipped cream all over herself.
••• 0:40—Nude, with the other girls in the spa.
Hot Body Competition: Bikinis & Bikes Contest (1996) . . . . Stevi Conrad
•• 0:35—Breasts and buns, while dancing on stage.
••• 0:36—Nude, while posing outdoors by pool.

Contouri, Chantal

Films:
Alvin Rides Again (1974; Australian) . . . . . . Boobs La Touche
• 1:15—Very brief lower frontal nudity, putting panties on in the car. Brief breasts, putting red dress on.
Barry McKenzie Holds His Own... (1974; Australian) . . . . . . Zizi
The Day After Halloween (1978; Australian) . . . . Madeline
a.k.a. Snapshot
Made for Cable Movies:
All the Rivers Run (1984; HBO) . . . . Julie

Cook, Kelly

See: Jaye, Kelly.

Cook, Tracy

Films:
SnakeEater III ...His Law (1992) . . . . Hildy Gardener
••• 0:27—Breasts, while making love with Lorenzo Lamas in bedroom.
Made for TV Movies:
Bermuda Grace (1994) . . . . Lady Harding

Cooke, Jennifer

Films:
Gimme an "F" (1981) . . . . Pam Bethlehem
a.k.a. T & A Academy 2
• 1:10—Wearing United States flag pasties frolicking with Dr. Spirit. Nice bouncing action.
Friday the 13th, Part VI: Jason Lives (1986) . . . . Megan
Made for Cable TV:
The Hitchhiker: Man's Best Friend (1985; HBO) . . . . Elanor
(Available on *The Hitchhiker, Volume 4.*)
• 0:19—Brief side view breasts getting undressed to take a shower.
Miniseries:
A Year in the Life (1986) . . . . Debbie Nesbit

TV:

The Guiding Light (1981-83) . . . . Morgan Nelson
V: The Series (1984-85) . . . . Elizabeth

Cooke, Victoria *

Video Tapes:

Playboy's Playmate Workout . . . . Playmate
Playboy Video Magazine, Volume 2 (1983)
. . . . Herself/Playboy Playoffs
Playboy's 21 Playmates: Volume II (1996) . . . . . . Playmate
••• 0:29—Nude in still photos.
••• 0:30—Full frontal nudity during centerfold photo session.

Coolidge, Rita *

Singer.
Ex-wife of singer/actor Kris Kristofferson.

Films:

Pat Garrett and Billy the Kid (1973). . . . . Maria
(Uncut Director's version reviewed.)
•• 1:48—Brief right breast, while sitting on bed and getting undressed with Kris Kristofferson.

Cooper, Jeanne

Mother of actors Corbin and Collin Bernsen.

Films:

The Redhead from Wyoming (1952) . . . . Myra
The Man from the Alamo (1953). . . . . Kate Lamar
Let No Man Write My Epitaph (1960) . . . . Fran
The Boston Strangler (1968) . . . . Cloe
There Was a Crooked Man (1970). . . . . Prostitute
• 0:18—Brief left breast trying to seduce the sheriff, Henry Fonda, in a room.
Kansas City Bomber (1972). . . . . Vivien
The All-American Boy (1973). . . . . Nola Bealer
Frozen Assets (1992). . . . . Zach's Mother

Made for TV Movies:

Beyond Suspicion (1993) . . . . Renata

TV:

Bracken's World (1970). . . . . Grace Douglas
The Young and the Restless (1973-) . . . . Katherine Chancellor-Sterling

Copley, Teri *

Films:

New Year's Evil (1981) . . . . Teenage Girl
• 0:49—Brief right breast in the back of the car with her boyfriend at a drive-in movie. Breast is half sticking out of her white bra. Dark, hard to see anything.
Down the Drain (1989) . . . . Kathy Miller
• 0:04—Full frontal nudity making love on couch with Andrew Stevens. Looks like a body double.
Masters of Menace (1990) . . . . Sunny
Transylvania Twist (1990) . . . . Marisa
Brain Donors (1992) . . . . Tina
Frozen Assets (1992). . . . . Peaches

Made for TV Movies:

I Married a Centerfold (1984) . . . . Debra
0:01—Briefly in wet swimsuit when getting out of pool. Hard to see, the credits get in the way.
In the Line of Duty: The F.B.I. Murders (1988). . . . . Vickie

TV:

We Got It Made (1983-84) . . . . Mickey McKenzie
I Had Three Wives (1985) . . . . Samantha

Cornell, Angela *

a.k.a. Sunare.

Films:

Beach Babes From Beyond (1993) . . . . Sally's Model
••• 0:20—Breasts, while posing in spa outside (she's on the left) during catalog photo session with two other models.
• 1:02—Brief breasts, when swimsuit top flies off while dancing on stage during bikini contest (she's the second one).

Made for Cable TV:

Red Shoe Diaries: Jake's Story (1993; Showtime)
. . . . Woman in Trailer
(Available on the video tape *Red Shoe Diaries 4: Auto Erotica.*)
••• 0:10—Breasts and buns while posing with a tattooed guy while Sheryl takes photos.
• 0:12—Brief breasts and buns in B&W flashback photos.
Red Shoe Diaries: The Game (1994; Showtime)
. . . . Uncredited Woman with John
• 0:21—Brief partial right breast while making love with John.
• 0:23—Brief breasts, twice, while making love with John.
Beverly Hills Bordello: Silence is Golden
(1997; Showtime) . . . . Casey
•• 0:04—Breasts, while sitting in bordello and talking with Shauna O'Brien.
••• 0:05—Breasts, while sitting in steam room and being caressed by O'Brien.
• 0:15—Brief breasts and buns in panties in bordello.
•• 0:16—Full frontal nudity, while talking to O'Brien in steam room.
••• 0:18—Full frontal nudity, while being caressed by O'Brien while Doug watches when he's tied up. Long scene.
• 0:24—Brief full frontal nudity, while sitting in steam room with O'Brien.

Video Tapes:

Beverly Hills Workout (1993) . . . . Herself
•• 0:04—Breasts, while working out on balcony with weights.
••• 0:24—Nude, while dancing and posing in backyard.
•• 0:42—Nude, while posing outdoors.
Playboy's College Girls (1994) . . . . Herself
••• 0:16—Nude, after taking off fencing outfit and popping balloons with fencing sword.
••• 0:18—Nude, while undressing out of sweaters and posing in studio.
Playboy's Erotic Fantasies: Forbidden Liaisons (1995)
. . . . Satisfaction Guaranteed
••• 0:13—Nude, in fountain with the plumber.

Corri, Adrienne

Ex-wife of actor Daniel Massey.

Films:

Corridors of Blood (1957; British) . . . . Rachel
Three Men in a Boat (1958). Clara Willis
Doctor Zhivago (1965) . . . . Amelia
A Clockwork Orange (1971) . . . . Mrs. Alexander
•• 0:11—Breasts through cut-outs in her top, then full frontal nudity getting raped by Malcolm McDowell and his friends.
Vampire Circus (1972; British) . . . . Gypsy Woman
Rosebud (1975). . . . . Lady Carter
Revenge of the Pink Panther (1978) . . . . Therese Douvier
A Study in Terror (1978; British) . . . . Angela
The Human Factor (1979). . . . . Sylvia

Corwin, Morena *

Video Tapes:

Playboy Video Calendar 1994 (1993) . . . . .November

••• 0:42—Breasts and buns, while walking around a house at night. Nude while painting in a field.

••• 0:45—Nude in B&W on sofa during dream, then in color when getting up out of bed.

Playboy's Playmate Review 1993 (1993) . . . . Miss September

••• 0:27—Nude in bed and dancing out in a field with a guy.

••• 0:30—Nude in pool and under water.

Playboy's Sexy, Steamy, Sultry (1993). . . . . .Playmate

Costa, Caroline

(Girl with the book in the beginning of each episode of *Compromising Situations.*)

Made for Cable TV:

Compromising Situations: The Surprise (1994; Showtime). . . . . Jill

••• 0:05—Buns and breasts sticking out of the top of lingerie outfit, then breasts, while giving Chris his birthday present in his office.

••• 0:20—Breasts and buns, while making love with Chris in hospital room.

• 0:23—Brief partial left breast, while lying in bed with Chris in the morning.

Costa, Cida *

Video Tapes:

Playboy International Playmates (1993) . . . . Cida

•• 0:04—Buns in still photos.

••• 0:05—Nude on the beach with colored fabric.

••• 0:46—Nude with Christina, trying on clothing at the beach.

••• 0:48—Breasts after taking off clothes and dancing.

Costa, Sara *

Films:

Weekend Pass (1984). . . . . Tuesday Del Mundo

••• 0:07—Buns in G-string, then breasts during strip dance routine on stage.

Stripper (1985). . . . . Herself

••• 0:16—Breasts doing strip dance routine.

••• 0:46—Breasts and buns dancing on stage in a G-string.

••• 1:12—Breasts doing another strip routine.

Video Tapes:

Hot Bodies (1988). . . . . Herself

••• 0:00—Nude, dancing on stage. Long scene. Dancing with a big boa snake.

••• 0:04—Breasts and buns in G-string.

Hot Body Video Magazine #1: Premiere Edition (1992) . . . . Lingerie Model/Sara

••• 0:26—Breasts and buns in room with three other models, trying on lingerie.

• Costello, Elizabeth

Made for Cable Movies:

House of the Damned (1996; Showtime) . . . Woman in Bed

a.k.a. Spectre

•• 0:30—Full frontal nudity while sleeping in bed in B&W vision, with a hand crawling up her body.

The Unspeakable (1996) . . . . .Mary Dumaski

a.k.a. Shadow of a Scream

Coté, Tina

Films:

Dark Side of Genius (1994). . . . . Anna/Kristi

•• 0:01—Breasts, while posing for painting, then getting killed during opening credits.

• 0:17—Brief breasts, while lying dead on sofa in a flashback.

• 0:22—Breasts and buns in G-string in Julian's studio (wearing a wig), then brief breasts (with blonde hair) in flashback.

• 0:32—Brief buns in G-string while posing on pedestal.

• 0:58—Breasts (blonde hair), while posing for paintings. Brief breasts (in wig) after Julian pushes her off the pedestal.

••• 1:02—Brief lower half of buns in long sweater, then breasts and upper half of buns, while making love with Julian in bed.

Heatseeker (1994) . . . . Jo

• 0:48—Breasts, while rolling on the floor in pain. Seen on TV monitor.

• 0:50—Breasts, while making love with Tung in Chance's bad dream.

Barb Wire (1995). . . . . .Woman in Bar

(Unrated version reviewed.)

Nemesis 2: Nebula (1995). . . . . Emily

Omega Doom (1995) . . . . .Blackheart

Mean Guns (1996) . . . . .Barbie

Courau, Clotilde

Films:

Map of the Human Heart (1992; Australian/Canadian) . . . . Rainee

The Pickle (1992) . . . . Francoise

• 0:58—Brief half of right breast in gaping bra when she helps Aiello back onto bed.

Court, Roma

Films:

Where Evil Lies (1994) . . . . Sadako

•• 0:42—Breasts and buns in panties, after undressing and making love with Kurt in front of the imprisoned girls.

Made for Cable Movies:

State of Emergency (1993; HBO). . . . . .Nurse #1

Last Exit to Earth (1996; Showtime). . . . . Syb 3

Courtney, Dori

Films:

Hollywood Hot Tubs 2—Educating Crystal (1989) . . . . Hot Tub Girl

•• 1:00—Breasts stuck in the spa and getting her hair freed.

Tango & Cash (1989) . . . . .Dressing Room Girl

• 1:06—Breasts, sitting in chair looking in the mirror in the background. Long shot.

Evil Spirits (1990). . . . . Bank Teller

Mob Boss (1990) . . . . Kathryn

••• 0:31—In black bra, talking with Eddie Deezen, then breasts. Nice close-up. Long scene.

Sorority Girls and the Creature from Hell (1990) . . . . Belinda

•• 0:06—Breasts, while drying herself off after shower. (Wearing panties.)

••• 0:08—More breasts, still drying herself off.

• 0:12—Brief right breast, while in car with J.J.

••• 0:35—Breasts while in spa with J.J.

• 0:37—Buns, then left breast, while in spa during Gerald's fantasy.

••• 0:41—Breasts after taking off her top by stream while J.J. gets killed.
•• 0:43—Breasts, while running around at night getting chased by the creature.

Camp Fear (1991) . . . . n.a.
a.k.a. Millenium Countdown

Whore (1991) . . . . Topless woman on TV
a.k.a. If you're afraid to say it... Just see it
• 0:14—Brief breasts on TV in old folks home in a scene from *Mob Boss.*

Courtney, Lorna

Films:

Ghoul School (1990) . . . . Mary

Affairs of the Heart (1992) . . . . Jane
••• 1:04—Breasts, making love in front of a fire in sleeping bag with Dick.

Comrades in Arms (1992) . . . . Anka

Cox, Christina

Films:

The Donor (1994) . . . . Angel
•• 0:07—Buns, after taking off white dress in bedroom with Jeff Wincott.

Street Law (1994) . . . . Kelly
a.k.a. Jungle Law
• 0:43—Brief close-up of buns, when Luis is feeling her up in raised skirt. Don't see her face.
• 0:44—Brief close-up of buns again.
• 1:08—Breasts, while making love in bed with Jeff Wincott. Don't see her face. In one shot you can see tape over her breasts.

Made for Cable Movies:

Mistrial (1996; HBO) . . . . Officer Ida Cruz

Made for TV Movies:

A Brother's Promise: The Dan Jansen Story (1996) . . . . . Natalie

No One Could Protect Her (1996) . . . . Det. Elizabeth Jordan

TV:

F/X: The Series (1996-98) . . . . Angie Ramirez

Cox, Courteney

Films:

Down Twisted (1987) . . . . Farah

Masters of the Universe (1987) . . . . Julie Winston

Cocoon, The Return (1988) . . . . Sara

Blue Desert (1990) . . . . Lisa Roberts
• 0:52—Silhouette of right breast, while standing up with Steve. Probably a body double. Very, very brief right nipple between Steve's arms lying in bed. Dark, hard to see.
•• 0:53—Left breast, lying in bed under Steve. A little hard to see her face, but it sure looks like her to me!

Curiosity Kills (1990) . . . . Gwen

Mr. Destiny (1990) . . . . Jewel Jagger

Shaking the Tree (1991) . . . . Kathleen

The Opposite Sex ...and How to Live with Them (1992) . . . . Carrie

Ace Ventura: Pet Detective (1993) . . . . Melissa

Scream (1996) . . . . Gale Weathers

The Commandments (1997) . . . . Rachel Luce
• 0:52—Very brief upper half of left breast, while making love in bed with Aidan Quinn.

Scream 2 (1997) . . . . Gale Weathers

Made for Cable Movies:

Sketch Artist II: Hands That See (1994; Showtime) . . . . . Emmy

Made for Cable TV:

Dream On: Come and Knock On Our Door... (1992; HBO) . . . . Alisha Littleton

Miniseries:

Till We Meet Again (1989) . . . . Freddy

Made for TV Movies:

Roxanne: The Prize Pulitzer (1989) . . . . Jacquie Kimberly

Battling for Baby (1992) . . . . Katherine

TV:

Misfits of Science (1985-86) . . . . Gloria Dinallo

Family Ties (1987-89) . . . . Lauren Miller

Trouble with Larry (1993) . . . . Gabriella

Friends (1994-) . . . . Monica Geller

Music Videos:

Dancing in the Dark/Bruce Springsteen . . . . Girl Who Goes Up on Stage

• *Coxx, Sindee*

Adult film actress.

Adult Films:

Breeders (1996) . . . . n.a.

Films:

Virtual Encounters (1995) . . . . S&M Girl 1
(Unrated version reviewed.)
••• 1:07—Full frontal nudity, in red outfit, while tied to the table, making love with another woman, getting hot candle wax dribbled on her.

Coyne, Ria *

Films:

Dolls (1987) . . . . n.a.

American Born (1989) . . . . Lupe

Corporate Affairs (1990) . . . . Mistress
•• 0:10—Left breast several times in back of car with Arthur.

Naked Obsession (1990) . . . . Cynthia
(Unrated version reviewed.)
•• 0:12—Breasts and buns, while dancing on stage in black lingerie.
• 0:13—Buns in G-string while dancing.
•• 0:14—More breasts and buns while dancing.

Batman Forever (1995) . . . . Socialite

Made for Cable TV:

Tales From the Crypt: Whirlpool (1994; HBO) . . . . . Velma
• 0:03—Breasts, while in bathroom when her husband, Jerry, is getting strangled in the bathtub.

Crampton, Barbara *

Films:

Body Double (1984) . . . . Carol Sculley
•• 0:04—Breasts, while making love in bed with another man when her husband walks in.

Fraternity Vacation (1985) . . . . Chrissie
••• 0:16—Breasts and buns in bedroom with two guys taking off her swimsuit.

Re-Animator (1985) . . . . Megan Halsey
(Unrated version reviewed.)
•• 0:10—Brief buns putting panties on, then breasts, putting bra on after making love with Dan.
•• 1:09—Full frontal nudity, lying unconscious on table getting strapped down.
• 1:10—Breasts getting her breasts fondled by a headless body.
• 1:19—Breasts on the table.

Chopping Mall (1986) . . . . Suzie
a.k.a. Killbots
•• 0:22—Brief breasts taking off top in furniture store in front of her boyfriend on the couch.
From Beyond (1986) . . . . Dr. Katherine McMichaels
•• 0:44—Brief breasts after getting blouse torn off by the creature in the laboratory.
• 0:51—Buns, while getting on top of Jeffrey Combs in black leather outfit.
Kidnapped (1986). . . . . Bonnie
••• 0:37—Breasts getting tormented by a bad guy in bed.
•• 1:12—Breasts after opening her pajamas for David Naughton.
•• 1:14—Breasts in white panties getting dressed.
Puppet Master (1989) . . . . Woman at Carnival
Trancers II (1991) . . . . Sadie Brady
Robot Wars (1992) . . . . Leda
Castle Freak (1995) . . . . Susan
TV:
The Guiding Light . . . . Melinda Sue Lewis
The Young and the Restless . . . . . . Leanna Randolph Newman
Days of Our Lives (1983) . . . . Trista Evans
The Bold and the Beautiful (1995-). . . . . Maggie

Crane, Chilton

Films:
Look Who's Talking Now! (1993). . . . . Girl's Mommy
Made for Cable TV:
Poltergeist: The Legacy/Man in the Mist
(1996; Showtime) . . . . Caroline
• 0:29—Brief right breast, while sitting up in bed to hug Samuel.
The Outer Limits: Dark Rain (1997; Showtime)
. . . . Pregnant Woman
The Outer Limits: Feasibility Study (1997; Showtime) . . . . . n.a.
Poltergeist: The Legacy/Rough Beast (1997; Showtime)
. . . . Tracy
Dead Man's Gun: The Resurrection of Joe Wheeler
(1998; Showtime) . . . . Emma Spence

Craven, Mimi

Films:
Swamp Thing (1981) . . . . Secretary
A Nightmare on Elm Street (1985) . . . . Nurse
Servants of Twilight (1991) . . . . Ms. Lindstrom
Mikey (1992). . . . . Rachel Trenton
•• 0:52—Breasts, sitting in bathtub when Mikey comes into the bathroom to talk.
Midnight Heat (1994) . . . . Alison Miller
• 0:08—Brief cleavage in open robe while standing at the window, then very brief breasts, hard to see because of fog on the window.
• 0:10—Breasts (don't see her face), while in bed with Kathrin Nicholson.
••• 0:17—In bra, garter belt and stockings, then breasts, while making love with Tim Matheson.
•• 0:34—Breasts in open robe, while making out with Matheson.
•• 0:36—Left breast, while making love with Matheson.
• 0:37—Breasts, while swimming in the pool, seen through water.
• 0:38—Breasts, while making love with Matheson in pool.
• 0:39—Breasts, while making love with Matheson in bed.
•• 1:02—Left breast, while lying in bed with Matheson.
Open Fire (1994). . . . . Lynne Tolbert
The Secretary (1994). Marcia Hastings

Last Gasp (1995) . . . . Goldie
••• 1:01—Breasts, while making love with Robert Patrick in kitchen.
Daddy's Girl (1996) . . . . Rachel Landers
Dogwatch (1996) . . . . Janet
•• 0:07—Breasts and buns in T-back, while dancing on stage.
Last Dance (1996) . . . . Stripper in Bar
Made for Cable Movies:
Disaster in Time (1992; Showtime) . . . . Carolyn
a.k.a. Timescape
Made for Cable TV:
Dream On: The Thirty-Seven Year Itch (1991; HBO)
. . . . Monica
••• 0:22—Breasts several times with Martin in his office.
Video Tapes:
Inside Out 4 (1992). . . . . Dolores/Put Asunder
(Unrated version reviewed.)
• 0:18—Left breast in bed with her husband.
••• 0:22—Breasts, lying in bed after making love with her husband.
Eden 5 (1993) . . . . Marla Burke
•• 0:06—Breasts and brief buns in bubble bath with Douglas.

Crawford, Cindy *

Supermodel and pin-up calendar girl.
Ex-wife of actor Richard Gere.
Model for *Revlon* cosmetics.
Model for *Diet Pepsi.*
Films:
Fair Game (1995) . . . . Kate McQuean
• 0:57—Back side of left breast, while changing clothes next to truck.
•• 1:09—Brief breasts, while making love with William Baldwin in the train. Brief breasts, when shooting the bad guy.
Unzipped (1995) . . . . Herself
TV:
House of Style (1992-95). . . . . Hostess
Video Tapes:
Cindy Crawford: Shape Your Body Workout (1992) . . . . Herself
Cindy Crawford: The Next Challenge (1993). . . . . Herself

• Crawford, Rachael

Films:
When Night is Falling (1995; Canadian) . . . . Petra
• 0:57—Brief breasts, while making love in bed on top of Camille.
Made for Cable Movies:
In His Father's Shoes (1997; Showtime) . . . . Celeste
Made for Cable TV:
The Outer Limits: Dark Rain (1997; Showtime)
. . . . Sherry McAllister
Made for TV Movies:
Treacherous Beauties (1994) . . . . Lois Parsons
TV:
On Thin Ice: The Tai Babilonia Story . . . . Tai Babilonia

Crawford, Sophia

On the *Mighty Morphin Power Rangers* TV show and movie, she does the martial arts/stunt work in the Pink Ranger costume. She started in the second year of the TV series.
Films:
Escape From Brothel (1991; Hong Kong) . . . . Blackmail Girl
• 0:12—Left breast, while making love in bed with a guy. Brief full frontal nudity, while sitting up in bed.
•• 0:13—Nude, while martial arts fighting the guy. Sometimes in slow motion. It looks like some frames were cut.

- ••• 0:14—Nude, while fighting some more, sometimes in slow motion (again, some frames are missing, especially when she does high kicks), before the guy gets even with her.

Gigolo and Whore (1991; Hong Kong) . . . . n.a.
Beauty Investigators (1992; Hong Kong) . . . . Brother Bee's Assistant
- •• 0:39—Breasts and buns, while taking a shower.
- • 0:40—Breasts under sheer white nightie.

Sword of Honor (1994) . . . . Vicky
- • 0:43—In bra and panties with Johnny, then (muscular) buns and brief right breast, twice.

Mighty Morphin Power Rangers: The Movie (1995) . . . . Stunts
Night Hunter (1995) . . . . Carmella
TV:
WMAC Masters (1998-) . . . . n.a.

Crespo, Teresa

Films:
Out of the Dark (1988) . . . . Debbie
Made for Cable Movies:
Nails (1992; Showtime) . . . . Elena Hernandez
- •• 0:44—Breasts, taking off her top in room with Dennis Hopper.

Cristal, Raquel

See: Drew, Griffin.

Crockett, Karlene

Films:
Charlie Chan & the Curse of the Dragon Queen (1981) . . . . Brenda Lupowitz
Eyes of Fire (1983) . . . . Leah
- • 0:44—Brief breasts sitting up in the water and scaring Mr. Dalton.
- • 1:16—Breasts talking to Dalton who is trapped in a tree. Brief breasts again when he pulls the creature out of the tree.

Massive Retaliation (1984) . . . . Marianne Briscoe
Return (1985) . . . . Diana
- • 0:46—Breasts sitting up and getting out of bed. Long shot.

Made for TV Movies:
Diary of a Hitchhiker (1979) . . . . Dana
The Promise of Love (1980) . . . . Tracy
Death of a Centerfold: The Dorothy Stratten Story (1981) . . . . Anna
Return to Mayberry (1986) . . . . Eunice Taylor

Crosby, Cathy Lee

Films:
The Laughing Policeman (1974) . . . . Kay Butler
Coach (1978) . . . . Randy
- • 0:31—Very brief side view of left breast when Michael Biehn opens the door while she's putting on her top.
- • 1:11—Very, very brief breasts in shower room with Biehn. Blurry, hard to see anything.

The Dark (1979) . . . . Zoe
The Player (1992) . . . . Cameo
Made for Cable Movies:
Untamed Love (1994; Lifetime) . . . . Maggie Bernard
TV:
That's Incredible (1980-84) . . . . Host

*Crosby, Denise **

Granddaughter of actor/singer Bing Crosby.
Films:
48 Hrs. (1982) . . . . Sally
- • 0:47—Very, very brief side view of half of left breast, while swinging baseball bat at Eddie Murphy.
- • 1:24—Very brief side view of right breast when James Remar pushes her onto bed.
- • 1:25—Very brief breasts, then very brief side view of right breast while attacking Nick Nolte.

The Trail of the Pink Panther (1982) . . . . Bruno's Moll
Curse of the Pink Panther (1983) . . . . Bruno's Moll
The Man Who Loved Women (1983) . . . . Enid
Desert Hearts (1986) . . . . Pat
Eliminators (1986) . . . . Nora Hunter
Arizona Heat (1988) . . . . Jill Andrews
- • 1:13—Brief upper half of left breast in shower with Larry.

Blackwater (1989) . . . . Sally
Miracle Mile (1989) . . . . Landa
Pet Sematary (1989) . . . . Rachel Creed
Skin Deep (1989) . . . . Angie Smith
Desperate Crimes (1991; Italian) . . . . Bella Blu
High Strung (1991) . . . . Melanie
Dolly Dearest (1992) . . . . Marilyn Reed
Relative Fear (1994) . . . . Connie
Dream Man (1995) . . . . Barbara
- •• 0:01—Breasts while blindfolded during opening credits. Slightly distorted.
- • 1:25—Brief breasts on video monitor.

Mutant Species (1995) . . . . Carol-Anne
Jackie Brown (1997) . . . . Public Defender
Made for Cable TV:
Red Shoe Diaries: You Have the Right to Remain Silent (1992; Showtime) . . . . Officer Lynn/Mona McCabe
(Available on the video tape *Red Shoe Diaries 2: Double Dare.*)
- ••• 0:22—Breasts, taking off her bra and making love with Nick on barber's chair.
- • 0:26—Brief buns, while sitting on Nick's lap in the chair.
- ••• 0:28—In black bra and panties, then breasts and buns. (Additional footage added for video tape.)

Red Shoe Diaries: The Psychiatrist (1995; Showtime) . . . . The Psychiatrist
Made for TV Movies:
My Wicked Ways... The Legend of Errol Flynn (1985) . . . . Diana Dyrenforth
TV:
Star Trek: The Next Generation (1987-88) . . . . Lt. Tasha Yar
Star Trek: The Next Generation (1991) . . . . Seela
Key West (1993) . . . . Chaucy

Crosby, Katja

Films:
It's Alive III: Island of the Alive (1988) . . . . Girl in Court
A Return to Salem's Lot (1988) . . . . Cathy
- •• 0:36—Breasts making love in bed with Joey.
- • 0:48—Side view of right breast kissing Joey outside next to a stream.

Crosby, Lucinda

Films:
Blue Thunder (1983) . . . . Bel-Air Woman
The Naked Cage (1985) . . . . Rhonda
Stitches (1985) . . . . Nurse #5
Blue Movies (1988) . . . . Randy Moon
- • 0:10—Breasts, while in a spa in a movie.

•• 0:11—Breasts, while kneeling on a table, shooting a porno movie.
••• 0:32—Breasts, while auditioning for Buzz.
• 1:02—Breasts, while on desk in a movie.
Pretty Woman (1990) . . . . Olsen Sister
Frankie & Johnny (1991) . . . . The Abused Neighbor
Exit to Eden (1994) . . . . Claudia/Trainer

Crosby, Mary

Daughter of actor/singer Bing Crosby.
Films:
Ice Pirates (1984) . . . . Princess Karina
Deadly Innocents (1988) . . . . Beth/Cathy
• 0:00—Very, very brief right breast in gaping nightgown when her husband grabs her wrist.
• 0:38—Brief upper back half of left breast in bathroom mirror after taking off her nightgown.
Tapeheads (1988) . . . . Samantha
Body Chemistry (1990) . . . . Marlee
Corporate Affairs (1990) . . . . Jessica Pierce
Eating (1990) . . . . Kate
The Berlin Conspiracy (1991) . . . . Ursula Schneider
Desperate Motive (1992) . . . . Marcie
Cupid (1996) . . . . Dana
Made for Cable TV:
Dream On: Flight of the Pedalbee (1995; HBO) . . . . Beverly
Miniseries:
North and South, Book II (1986) . . . . Isabel Hazard
TV:
Brothers & Sisters (1979) . . . . Suzi Cooper
Dallas (1979-81) . . . . Kristin Shepard

• Cross, Kendall

Made for Cable TV:
The Outer Limits: A Stitch in Time (1996; Showtime) . . . Allison
Dead Man's Gun: Mail Order Bride (1997; Showtime) . . . . Sarah Holbrook
• 0:13—Brief back sides of breasts, then brief buns, while changing clothes in bedroom.

• Cross, Marcia

Films:
Bad Influence (1990) . . . . Ruth Fielding
Female Perversions (1997) . . . . Eve's Mother
• 0:48—Very, very brief breast, while falling to the floor.
• 1:04—Very, very brief tip of right breast, just before being pushed back.
•• 1:11—Breasts, while tracing her right breast with a pen while straddling her husband.
••• 1:36—Brief right breast, then breasts, while opening her dress and tracing circles around her breasts with a pen, then being pushed onto the floor.
Made for TV Movies:
M.A.N.T.I.S. (1994) . . . . Carla
TV:
The Edge of Night (1984) . . . . Liz Correll
One Life to Live (1986-87) . . . . Kate Sanders Roberts
Knots Landing (1991-92) . . . . Victoria Broyard
Melrose Place (1992-97) . . . . Dr. Kimberly Shaw Mancini

Crouse, Lindsay

Films:
Between the Lines (1977) . . . . Abbie
• 0:52—Brief side view of right breast, lying in bed with John Heard.
Slap Shot (1977) . . . . Lily Braden
Prince of the City (1981) . . . . Carla Ciello
The Verdict (1982) . . . . Kaitlin Costello Price
Daniel (1983) . . . . Rochelle
Iceman (1984) . . . . Dr. Diane Brady
Places in the Heart (1984) . . . . Margaret Lomax
House of Games (1987) . . . . Margaret Ford
Communion (1989) . . . . Anne Strieber
Desperate Hours (1990) . . . . Chandler
Being Human (1994) . . . . Janet
The Indian in the Cupboard (1995) . . . . Jane
The Juror (1995) . . . . Tallow
The Arrival (1996) . . . . Ilana Green
Made for Cable Movies:
Chantilly Lace (1993; Showtime) . . . . Rheza
Parallel Lives (1994; Showtime) . . . . Una Pace
• 0:12—Very brief right breast in gaping dress, while bending over to make her bed on the sofa.
If These Walls Could Talk (1996; HBO) . . . . Frances White
Norma Jean & Marilyn (1996; HBO) . . . . Natasha Lyress
Made for TV Movies:
Final Appeal (1993) . . . . Dana Cartier
Out of Darkness (1994) . . . . Kim Donaldson

Crow, Emilia

a.k.a. Emilia Lesniak.
Films:
Scarface (1983) . . . . Echevera
Fear City (1984) . . . . Bibi
•• 0:16—Breasts, dancing at the Metropole club.
•• 1:00—Breasts, dancing on the stage.
9 Deaths of the Ninja (1985) . . . . Jennifer Barnes
Hollywood Vice Squad (1986) . . . . Linda
Hitz (1992) . . . . Chelsea Walker
a.k.a. Judgment
••• 0:27—Breasts and very brief upper half of lower frontal nudity, making love in bed with Jimmy. Lit with red light.
Made for Cable Movies:
Disaster in Time (1992; Showtime) . . . . Reeve
a.k.a. Timescape
• 0:18—Side view of left breast, sitting in front of vanity while Jeff Daniels watches. Long shot.

Crowley, Jeananne

Films:
Educating Rita (1983; British) . . . . Julia
Reilly: Ace of Spies (1984) . . . . Margaret
•• 0:52—Brief breasts, opening her blouse for her invalid husband.

• Croze, Marie-Josée

Made for Cable TV:
Hunger: A Matter of Style (1997; Showtime) . . . . . . Dominique
The Hunger: I'm Dangerous Tonight (1997; Showtime) . . . . Mimi Claudel
• 0:06—Breasts, while making love with Esai Morales in bed.
• 0:07—Brief breasts and buns, when waking up in bed.
•• 0:08—Brief breasts, when putting on her blouse.
• 0:21—Brief buns in bedroom with Morales.

Cruikshank, Laura

Films:
Ruthless People (1986) . . . . n.a.
Buying Time (1987) . . . . Jessica
•• 0:52—Breasts several times making love with Ron on pool table.

Cruz, Penelope *

Films:

Softly From Paris: Her & Him. . . . . Daphné/Javatte/Juliette

Jamón, Jamón (1992; Spanish). Silvia

••• 0:11—Right breast, then breasts, while making out with José Luis.

• 0:46—Breasts, while kneeling on ground in dream sequence.

• 1:02—Left breast sticking out of dress while José Luis has a temper tantrum.

1:03—In braless, wet white dress.

1:05—Partial buns, while kissing Raul.

••• 1:09—Breasts, while making love with Raul.

Belle Epoque (1993; Spanish) . . . . Luz

a.k.a. The Age of Beauty

Cruzat, Liza

Films:

Sweet Perfection (1988). . . . . Linda Johnson

a.k.a. The Perfect Model

• 0:31—Left breast, in bed with Mario. Don't see her face. Probably a body double.

Excessive Force (1993) . . . . Hooker

a.k.a. Men of War

Kissing a Fool (1998). . . . . Dara's Friend

Cser, Nancy

Films:

Joy (1983; French/Canadian) . . . . Unidentified

Perfect Timing (1984). . . . . Lacy

••• 0:56—Breasts getting photographed by Harry.

• 0:58—Breasts, making love with Harry.

• 1:01—Breasts.

Separate Vacations (1985; Canadian) . . . . Stewardess

Head Office (1986) . . . . Dantley's Secretary

Deceived (1991) . . . . Harvey's Girlfriend

A Man in Uniform (1994; Canadian/Australian). . . . Sheila Riggs

Made for Cable Movies:

BloodKnot (1995; Showtime) . . . . Connie

Cuevas, Diana

Films:

Invasion of Privacy (1992) . . . . Alex's Mother

(Unrated version reviewed.)

•• 0:01—Left breast, while in bedroom with her lover, while young Alex watches from closet.

Midnight Confessions (1993). . . . . Candice

(Unrated version reviewed.)

••• 0:51—Breasts and brief buns, while making love with her husband.

Sex and the Single Alien (1993). . . . . Merry

•• 0:45—Breasts and buns, while dancing on stage with Ruth.

•• 1:08—Breasts in black lingerie while dancing on stage again with Ruth.

Strike a Pose (1993) . . . . Model

Hollywood Passions (1994). . . . . Denise

•• 0:07—In bra, then breasts, after undressing and making out with Lou.

Money to Burn (1994) . . . . Beach Girl

Made for Cable TV:

Erotic Confessions: Inspiration (1995; Cinemax)

. . . . Judy Gold

(Available on video tape in *Erotic Zone: Inspiration.*)

••• 0:18—In bra, then breasts, when sitting on sofa while Nick rubs paints on her.

•• 0:19—Full frontal nudity, when posing for photos while covered with body paints.

Hot Springs Hotel: To Your Health (1998; Showtime)

. . . . Cecily Carrothers

••• 0:11—Breasts, while making love with Randy.

• 0:16—Left breast, while lying next to Randy afterwards.

••• 0:18—In bra and panties, then breasts, while making love with Ernest in bed.

Video Tapes:

Fantasies 2 (1992) . . . . Model

Nude Daydreams (1993) . . . . Daydream 3

• 0:07—Left breast, while playing piano, when another woman dances around ballet style.

Cufari, Lizz *

Video Tapes:

Playboy's Girls of Radio: Talk, Rock and Shock (1995)

. . . . Herself

••• 0:20—Nude in her office and in swimming pool.

Culliver Pierce, Katheryn *

Films:

Traces of Red (1992) . . . . Kimberly Davis

•• 0:11—Breasts in bed, dead with blood on her during James Belushi's recollection.

Biohazard The Alien Force (1994) . . . . Shana Alexander

••• 0:50—Breasts and buns, while making love on top of her boyfriend on the floor. Long scene.

•• 0:59—Breasts, while sitting up in bed during nightmare when her boyfriend morphs into creature.

• Cummings, Summer

Adult film actress.

Films:

Dark Secrets (1995) . . . . Uncredited Woman with Dominatrix

••• 0:03—Breasts and buns in strap outfit, while getting whipped, candle wax dripped on her, wrapped up in cellophane and hit with thorny roses. Long scene.

Boogie Nights (1997). . . . . . Uncredited Actress in Hot Tub 1

• 1:42—Buns and breasts while in hot tub with another actress during filming of a movie. (She's the brunette.)

Cummins, Juliette *

Former U.S. National Gymnast.

Films:

Lucky 13 (1984) . . . . Jenny

a.k.a. Running Hot

a.k.a. Highway to Hell

Friday the 13th, Part V—A New Beginning (1985)

. . . . Robin

••• 1:01—Breasts, wearing panties getting undressed and climbing into bed just before getting killed.

• 1:05—Very brief breasts, covered with blood when Reggie discovers her dead.

Psycho III (1986). . . . . Red

••• 0:39—Breasts making love with Duke in his motel room, then getting thrown out.

Slumber Party Massacre II (1987) . . . . Sheila

•• 0:24—In black bra, then breasts in living room during a party with her girlfriends.

Deadly Dreams (1988). Maggie Kallir

• 0:25—Breasts on bed, taking off her blouse and kissing Alex.

••• 0:55—Breasts and brief buns, making love with Jack in bed.

Click: Calendar Girl Killer (1989) . . . . Uncredited Model
••• 0:44—Buns in G-string, while undressing, then breasts and buns, dancing around in bathroom.
• 0:46—Partial breasts, while in bubble bath.
0:47—Slashed breasts, while in bathtub, after struggle with killer.

Cupisti, Barbara

Films:

The Key (1985; Italian) . . . . Lisa Rolfe
a.k.a. La Chiave
Terror at the Opera (1989; Italian) . . . . Albertini
The Church (1991; Italian) . . . . Lisa
a.k.a. La Chiesa
• 0:28—Very brief back side of right breast, while sitting up in bed. Side of right breast, while scooting over on bed while talking to Evald.
• 0:48—Very brief left breast in gaping nightgown, while scrambling for the phone. Very brief right breast in gaping nightgown when getting up off ground after jumping through window.
• 1:25—Breasts, while lying on slab and getting painted.
• 1:31—Breasts, while getting raped by beast.
Cemetery Man (1993; Italian) . . . . n.a.
a.k.a. Dellamorte Dellamore
Only You (1994) . . . . Anna

Curran, Lynette

Films:

Alvin Purple (1973; Australian) . . . . First Sugar Girl
•• 0:02—Brief full frontal nudity when Alvin opens the door.
Heatwave (1983; Australian) . . . . Evonne
Bliss (1985; Australian) . . . . Bettina Joy
The Year My Voice Broke (1987; Australian) . . . . Anne Olson
Women From Down Under (1995; Australian/New Zealand)
. . . . Just Desserts/Mrs. Fullilove

Currie, Cherie

Singer in The Runaways.
Identical twin sister of singer/actress Marie Currie Lukather.

Films:

Foxes (1980) . . . . Annie
Parasite (1982) . . . . Dana
Wavelength (1982) . . . . Iris Longacre
• 0:09—Brief side view of right breast and buns getting out of bed. Dark, don't really see anything.
The Rosebud Beach Hotel (1985) . . . . Cherie
Rich Girl (1991) . . . . Michelle

Currie, Sandee

See: Warren, Sandra.

*Currie, Sondra **

Daughter of actress Marie Harmon.
Sister of identical twin singers/actresses Cherie Currie and Marie Currie Lukather.

Films:

Teenage Seductress . . . . Terry
••• 0:14—Buns, while taking off robe in bedroom. Breasts, while looking at herself in bathroom mirror.
••• 0:16—Breasts, while in front of mirror again. More breasts while taking a shower.
• 0:24—Breasts, while in bed, trying to get Preston to join her.
• 1:14—Brief partial right breast, while lying on bed with Preston.

Mama's Dirty Girls (1974) . . . . n.a.
Policewomen (1974) . . . . Lacy Bond
••• 0:50—Breasts and buns taking off sheer robe and getting into bed, then making love with Frank.
Jessi's Girls (1976) . . . . Jessica
• 0:02—Nude in water cleaning up, then brief left breast getting dressed.
• 0:07—Breasts getting raped by four guys. Fairly long scene.
• 0:37—Breasts kissing Clay under a tree. Hard to see because of the shadows.
The Last Married Couple in America (1980) . . . . Lainy
•• 1:32—Breasts taking off her clothes in bedroom in front of Natalie Wood, George Segal and her husband.
The Concrete Jungle (1982) . . . . Katherine
Street Justice (1988) . . . . Mandy
Illicit Behavior (1991) . . . . Yolanda
(Unrated version reviewed.)
The Secretary (1994) . . . . Mary Quinn

Curtin, Jane

Films:

How to Beat the High Cost of Living (1980) . . . . . . Elaine
• 1:29—Close up breasts, taking off her bra. Probably a body double.
O.C. and Stiggs (1987) . . . . Elinore Schwab
Coneheads (1993) . . . . Prymaat

Made for Cable Movies:

Tad (1995; Family) . . . . Mary Todd Lincoln

Made for TV Movies:

Common Ground (1990) . . . . Alice McGoff

TV:

Saturday Night Live (1975-80)
. . . . Not Ready For Primetime Player
Kate and Allie (1984-90) . . . . Allie Lowell
Working It Out (1990) . . . . Sarah Marshall
3rd Rock From the Sun (1996-) . . . . Dr. Albright

*Curtis, Jamie Lee **

Daughter of actor Tony Curtis and actress Janet Leigh.
Wife of actor/writer/director Christopher Guest.

Films:

Halloween (1978) . . . . Laurie
The Fog (1980) . . . . Elizabeth Solley
Prom Night (1980) . . . . Kim
Terror Train (1980; Canadian) . . . . Alena
Halloween II (1981) . . . . Laurie
Road Games (1981; Australian) . . . . Hitch/Pamela
Trading Places (1983) . . . . Ophelia
••• 1:00—Breasts in black panties after taking red dress off in bathroom while Dan Aykroyd watches.
••• 1:09—Breasts and black panties taking off halter top and pants getting into bed with a sick Aykroyd.
The Adventures of Buckaroo Banzai, Across the 8th Dimension (1984) . . . . Dr. Sandra Banzai
Grandview, U.S.A. (1984) . . . . Michelle "Mike" Cody
••• 1:00—Left breast, lying in bed with C. Thomas Howell.
Love Letters (1984) . . . . Anna Winter
a.k.a. Passion Play
••• 0:31—Breasts in bathtub reading a letter, then breasts in bed making love with James Keach.
• 0:36—Brief breasts in lifeguard station with Keach.
••• 0:44—Brief breasts admiring a picture taken of her by Keach.
••• 0:46—Breasts and buns in bedroom undressing with Keach.

- 0:49—Breasts in black and white Polaroid photographs that Keach is taking.
- 1:07—Right breast, sticking out of slip, then right breast, while sleeping in bed with Keach.

Perfect (1985)............................ Jessie Wilson
Tall Tales and Legends: Annie Oakley (1985).....Annie Oakley
Amazing Grace and Chuck (1987) .... n.a.
A Man in Love (1987)........................ Susan Elliot
Dominick and Eugene (1988).............. Jennifer Reston
A Fish Called Wanda (1988) .... Wanda
Blue Steel (1989)......................... Megan Turner

- 1:27—Very, very brief buns twice when rolling out of bed, trying to get her gun. Dark.

My Girl (1991) .... Shelly DeVoto
Queens Logic (1991)............................ Grace
Forever Young (1992).......................... Claire
Mother's Boys (1994)........................... Jude

- 0:44—Very brief left nipple in open robe while sitting in chair when Gallagher enters her apartment. Very brief side view of breast in mirror as she turns around. Brief half of left breast in open robe while talking with Gallagher.
- 0:52—Brief side of left breast and buns, when walking past doorway while her son peeks. Don't see her face well.
- 0:55—Buns, standing up in bathtub to show C-section scar to her son. Don't see her face.

My Girl 2 (1994)....................... Shelly Sultenfuss
True Lies (1994) .... Helen Tasker

- 1:20—In black bra, buns in sexy panties, while doing strip routine in front of Arnold Schwarzenegger.

Fierce Creatures (1996)..................... Willa Weston
House Arrest (1996) .... Janet Beindorf

Made for TV Movies:

Death of a Centerfold: The Dorothy Stratten Story (1981) .... Dorothy Stratten
(Breasts in European version.)
She's in the Army Now (1981) .... Rita Jennings
The Heidi Chronicles (1995) .... Heidi Holland

TV:

Operation Petticoat (1977-78) .... Lt. Barbara Duran
Anything but Love (1989-92) .... Hannah Miller

Cutter, Lise

Films:

Buy and Cell (1988) .... Dr. Ellen Scott
Havana (1990) .... Patty

- 0:44—Most of side of left breast with Robert Redford. Very, very brief part of right breast while he turns her around. Very brief left breast when Redford puts a cold glass on her chest. Dark, hard to see.

Nickel & Dime (1992).................. Cathleen Markson
Shadowforce (1992)............................. Mary
Fleshtone (1994)..................... Jennifer Womak

- ••• 0:56—In black bra, then breasts while making love with Matthew in bathroom and on bed.
- ••• 0:58—Right breast, while lying on bed talking to Matthew. Brief partial left breast. Long scene.
- ••• 1:03—Buns and left breast while lying on bed, posing for Matthew.

Sioux City (1994) .... Allison

Made for TV Movies:

Desperado: The Outlaw Wars (1989)................ Nora

TV:

Equal Justice (1991) .... Andrea Kanin
Dangerous Curves (1992-93) .... Gina

Cyr, Myriam

Films:

Gothic (1986; British).......................... Claire

- •• 0:53—Left breast, then breasts while lying in bed with Gabriel Byrne.
- 0:55—Brief left breast lying in bed. Long shot.
- 1:02—Breasts, while sitting on pool table opening her top for Julian Sands. Special-effect with eyes in her nipples.
- 1:12—Buns and brief breasts covered with mud.

Frankenstein Unbound (1990)........... Information Officer
I Shot Andy Warhol (1996) .... Ultra Violet

*D'Abo, Maryam **

Cousin of actress Olivia d'Abo.

Films:

Xtro (1982) .... Analise

- ••• 0:25—Breasts making love with her boyfriend on the floor in her bedroom.
- •• 0:56—Brief breasts with her boyfriend again.

Until September (1984)........................ Nathalie
White Nights (1985) .... French Girl Friend
The Living Daylights (1987)..................Kara Milovy
Double Obsession (1992)................. Claire Burke

- 0:34—Breasts, while taking a shower. Seen behind plastic shower curtain.

Immortal Sins (1992; Spanish)..................... Susan
Shootfighter: Fight to the Death (1992) ....Cheryl
Leon the Pig Farmer (1993; British)...............Madeline
Tomcat: Dangerous Desires (1993) .... Jacki

- ••• 0:07—Breasts in bathroom mirror with Richard Grieco.

Tropical Heat (1993) .... Beverly

- •• 0:36—Breasts, several times, while in waterfall with Rick Rossovich.
- ••• 0:47—Breasts in bathtub, giving Rossovich a shave.
- 0:49—Partial left breast, while lying in bed and making love with Rossovich.
- 0:50—Brief breasts in bed, while under Rossovich.
- ••• 0:51—Breasts while in bed with Rossovich.

The Browning Version (1994) .... Diana Rafferty
Stalked (1994; Canadian/Australian) .... Brooke Daniels
Solitaire for 2 (1995; British) .... Caroline

Made for Cable TV:

Red Shoe Diaries: Another Woman's Lipstick (1993; Showtime)................................Zoe
(Available on the video tape *Red Shoe Diaries 3: Another Woman's Lipstick.*)

- •• 0:19—Nude, during fantasy. Don't see her face.
- 0:28—Brief left nipple in room with the Other Woman.
- ••• 0:29—Breasts in room with the Other Woman.

Tales From the Crypt: Well Cooked Hams (1993; HBO) .. Greta

Miniseries:

Master of the Game (1984).................. Dominique

Made for TV Movies:

Something Is Out There (1988)..................... Ta'ra

D'Abo, Olivia

Cousin of actress Maryam d'Abo.

Films:

Bolero (1984) .... Paloma

- 0:38—Nude covered with bubbles taking a bath.
- 1:05—Brief breasts in the steam room with Bo.
- 1:32—Breasts in the steam room talking with Bo. Hard to see because it's so steamy.

Conan the Destroyer (1984) .... Princess Jehnna

Bullies (1985) . . . . Becky Cullen
•• 0:39—In wet white T-shirt swimming in river while Matt watches.
Dream to Believe (1985; Canadian). . . . . Robin Crew
Into the Fire (1988) . . . . Liette
a.k.a. Legend of Lone Wolf
• 0:07—Very, very brief silhouette of left breast in bed with Wade.
•• 0:32—Breasts on bed with Wade. A little bit dark and hard to see.
•• 1:10—Breasts in the bathtub. (Note her panties when she gets up.)
The Spirit of '76 (1991). Chanel-6
Bank Robber (1993). . . . . Selina
• 0:03—Very, very brief right breast, when pulling the sheets over herself in bed. Brief breasts, while getting out of bed.
• 0:04—Brief, upper half of left breast at doorway, then brief partial left breast in mirror.
• 0:21—Brief side of right breast, while making love in bed with Chris.
• 1:10—Brief breasts, while turning over in bed after making love with Andy.
Greedy (1993). . . . . Molly
Point of No Return (1993). . . . . Angela
Wayne's World 2 (1993) . . . . Betty Jo
Clean Slate (1994). . . . . Judy
The Last Good Time (1994). . . . . Charlotte Zwicki
••• 1:01—Brief breasts, dropping her towel so Armin Mueller-Stahl can see her.
• 1:05—Brief partial right breast, letting Mueller-Stahl feel her breast.
• 1:06—Left breast, while straddling Mueller-Stahl in bed.
The Big Green (1995) . . . . Anna Montgomery
Kicking and Screaming (1995) . . . . Jane
Live Nude Girls (1996) . . . . Chris
•• 0:45—Breasts, while starting to make love in bed with Lora Zane.
••• 0:46—Breasts, while in bed with Zane. B&W.
Made for Cable Movies:
Midnight's Child (1992; Lifetime) . . . . Anna/Kirsten
Made for TV Movies:
Crash Course (1988). . . . . Maria Abeja
For Love and Glory (1993) . . . . Emily Doyle
TV:
The Wonder Years (1987-93). . . . . Karen Arnold
The Single Guy (1996-97). . . . . Marie Blake

D'Aloia, Tracy

See: Dali, Tracy.

D'Angelo, Beverly *

Films:
Annie Hall (1977) . . . . Actress in Rob's TV Show
First Love (1977). . . . . Shelley
• 0:05—Very, very brief half of left breast when her jacket opens up while talking to William Katt.
• 1:10—Brief breasts taking off her top in bedroom with Katt.
The Sentinel (1977) . . . . Sandra
• 0:33—Brief breasts playing cymbals during Raines' nightmare (in B&W).
• 1:24—Brief breasts long shot with zombie make-up, munching on a dead Chris Sarandon.
Hair (1979) . . . . Sheila
• 0:59—In white bra and panties, then breasts on rock near pond. Medium long shot.
••• 1:01—Breasts in panties getting out of the pond.
• 1:38—Side view of right breast changing clothes in car with George.
Coal Miner's Daughter (1980) . . . . Patsy Cline
Honky Tonk Freeway (1981) . . . . Carmen
Paternity (1981) . . . . Maggie
Finders Keepers (1983) . . . . Standish Logan
National Lampoon's Vacation (1983) . . . . . . Ellen Griswold
•• 0:18—Brief breasts while taking a shower in the motel. (Note she's wearing panties in the shower.)
• 1:19—Brief breasts taking off shirt and jumping into the swimming pool.
Highpoint (1984; Canadian) . . . . Lise Hatcher
National Lampoon's European Vacation (1985) . . Ellen Griswold
Big Trouble (1986). . . . . Blanche Ricky
Slow Burn (1986) . . . . Laine Fleischer
• 1:01—Breasts making love with Eric Roberts. Don't see her face. Part of lower frontal nudity showing tattoo.
Aria (1987; U.S./British). . . . . Gilda
In the Mood (1987). . . . . Francine Glatt
Maid to Order (1987) . . . . Stella
High Spirits (1988; U.S./British) . . . . Sharon
Cold Front (1989; Canadian). . . . . Amanda O'Rourke
National Lampoon's Christmas Vacation (1989)
. . . . Ellen Griswold
Daddy's Dyin'... Who's Got the Will? (1990) . . . . Evalita
Pacific Heights (1990) . . . . Ann
• 0:01—Sort of breasts in reflection on TV screen, then right breast, in bed with Michael Keaton.
• 0:03—Very brief buns, turning over on bed when two guys burst in to the house.
Lonely Hearts (1991) . . . . Alma
• 0:57—Brief side view of right breast, while getting into shower with Roberts.
• 0:58—Very brief left breast in shower after Roberts gets pushed by Louise.
• 0:59—Very brief buns, when Roberts punches Louise through the shower door.
The Miracle (1991; British). . . . . Renee
The Pope Must Die (1991). . . . . Veronica Dante
a.k.a. The Pope Must Diet
Man Trouble (1992) . . . . Andy Ellerman
Lightning Jack (1993; Australian). . . . . Lana
Eye For an Eye (1995) . . . . Dolly Green
Widow's Kiss (1995). Vivian Fairchild
• 0:15—Partial right breast, while lying in bed under Bruce Davison.
• 1:14—Right breast, while making love in bed with Paul.
Edie & Pen (1996). . . . . Barlady
A Rat's Tale (1997). . . . . Mrs. Dollart
Vegas Vacation (1997). . . . . Ellen Griswold
Made for Cable TV:
Tales From the Crypt: Werewolf Concerto (1992; HBO)
. . . . Janice Baird
Made for TV Movies:
A Child Lost Forever (1992). . . . . Jerry Sherwood
Trial: The Price of Passion (1992) . . . . . . Johnnie Faye Boudreau
Judgment Day: The John List Story (1993). . . . . Helen List
The Switch (1993). . . . . Dee Fine
Jonathan Stone: Threat of Innocence (1994) . . . . . Annie Hayes
Menendez: A Killing in Beverly Hills (1994) . . . . Kitty
TV:
Captains and the Kings (1976) . . . . Miss Emmy
Video Tapes:
The Kathy Kaehler Fitness System (1992). . . . . Exercise Student

D'Angelo, Mirella *

Films:

Caligula (1980) . . . . Livia

(X-rated, 147 minute version.)

•• 1:08—Buns and breasts in kitchen with Malcolm McDowell. Full frontal nudity on table when he rapes her in front of her husband-to-be.

Unsane (1982) . . . . Tilda

a.k.a. Tenebrae

Hercules (1983). . . . . Circe

D'Arbanville, Patti *

Ex-significant other of actor Don Johnson.

Films:

Rancho Deluxe (1975) . . . . Betty Fargo

• 0:14—Very brief back side of right breast, while making love with Jeff Bridges outside.

• 0:15—Side of right breast, while making love some more.

• 0:16—Very, very brief breasts, when jumping up after Bridges puts mask on. Breasts, while running after Bridges in field. Long shot with trees in the way, hard to see anything.

• 1:01—Very brief right breast, while adjusting sheets in bed after Bridges shoots gun.

Bilitis (1977; French) . . . . Bilitis

••• 0:25—Breasts, while copying Melissa undressing.

•• 0:27—Breasts, while on tree.

••• 0:31—Full frontal nudity, after taking off swimsuit with Melissa.

• 0:36—Buns, while cleaning herself in the bathroom.

•• 0:59—Breasts and buns, while making love with Melissa.

Big Wednesday (1978) . . . . Sally

The Fifth Floor (1978) . . . . Cathy Burke

The Main Event (1979) . . . . Donna

Time After Time (1979; British) . . . . Shirley

Hog Wild (1980; Canadian). . . . . Angie

Modern Problems (1981) . . . . Darcy

• 0:48—Very brief right breast in bed after Chevy Chase has telekinetic sex with her.

The Boys Next Door (1985) . . . . Angie

Real Genius (1985) . . . . Sherry Nugil

Call Me (1988) . . . . Cori

Fresh Horses (1988) . . . . Jean

Frame Up II (1991) . . . . Babs Griffith

a.k.a. Deadly Conspiracy

The Fan (1996) . . . . Ellen Renard

Father's Day (1997). . . . . Shirley Trainor

Made for Cable Movies:

Snow Kill (1990; USA) . . . . Lauren Crane

Made for TV Movies:

Crossing the Mob (1988) . . . . Lucy Conte

TV:

Wiseguy (1989-90) . . . . Amber Twine

Another World (1992-93) . . . . Christy Carson

South Beach (1993) . . . . Roxanne

New York Undercover (1994-97). . . . . Lt. Cooper

D'Errico, Donna *

Wife of Mötley Crüe bassist Nikki Sixx.

Films:

Baywatch: White Thunder at Glacier Bay (1997)

. . . . Donna Marco

TV:

Baywatch (1996-98) . . . . Donna Marco

Baywatch Nights (1996-97) . . . . Donna Marco

Video Tapes:

Playboy Video Centerfold: Stacy Sanches (1996)

. . . . Playmate

••• 0:36—Nude by old gas station outdoors.

••• 0:39—In lingerie and nude while posing out in the desert.

••• 0:42—Nude, while playing with paint in a studio.

••• 0:45—Nude in still photos.

•• 0:48—In lingerie, then nude in back of limousine with a guy in chauffeur fantasy.

•• 0:50—Breasts and buns by gas station in end segment.

D'Ortez, Cristobel

Films:

Outlaw of Gor (1987) . . . . Alicia

Edgar Allan Poe's "The Masque of the Red Death" (1989)

. . . . Dr. Karen

Wild Zone (1989) . . . . Mary

•• 1:19—Breasts in the brush, getting molested by a bad guy.

D'Pella, Pamella

Films:

Internal Affairs (1990) . . . . Cheryl

Illicit Behavior (1991) . . . . Marilyn

(Unrated version reviewed.)

Ted & Venus (1991) . . . . Gloria

••• 0:17—Breasts while undressing in locker room while talking to Linda.

Uncaged (1991) . . . . Ros

a.k.a. Angel in Red

Caged Heat 2: Stripped of Freedom (1993) . . . . Paula

••• 0:13—Breasts, while making love with the warden on sofa in his office.

••• 0:42—Brief buns in T-back and breasts, while dancing for the warden in his office.

Josh and S.A.M. (1993) . . . . Daughter on Bus

Made for Cable TV:

Tales From the Crypt: Only Sin Deep (1989; HBO) . . . . . Raven

TV:

The Young and the Restless . . . . Julia

• *Daans, Lara*

Films:

Fireballs (1988; Canadian) . . . . Bikini Contestant

Electra (1995) . . . . Karen

• 0:03—Buns in T-back, while dancing on stage.

•• 0:58—Breasts and buns in outfit, after taking off her top to entice Billy.

Made for Cable Movies:

Triplecross (1994; Showtime) . . . . Tiny's Pal

Dahl, Arlene

Ex-wife of actor Lex Barker.

Ex-wife of actor Fernando Lamas.

Mother of actor Lorenzo Lamas.

Films:

A Southern Yankee (1948) . . . . Sallyann Weatharby

Three Little Words (1950) . . . . Eileen Percy

Watch the Birdie (1950) . . . . Lucia Corlane

Here Come the Girls (1953) . . . . Irene Bailey

Slightly Scarlet (1956) . . . . Dorothy Lyons

Journey to the Center of the Earth (1959) . . . . Carla

Kisses for My President (1964) . . . . Doris Reid

Land Raiders (1970) . . . . Martha Carden

• 0:59—Very brief upper half of right breast, sticking out of her top in bed after struggle with George Maharis.

Night of the Warrior (1991) . . . . Edie Keane

Dahl, Elayne

Films:

Body Chemistry 3: Point of Seduction (1993) . . . . Brunette in Room

• 0:00—Breasts, while in room with a Krissy and Robert Forster.

Video Tapes:

Soft Bodies: Squeeze Play (1993). . . . . Herself

••• 0:21—In lingerie, then nude on bed.

••• 0:27—In lingerie, then breasts and buns on bed with Becky LeBeau.

••• 0:29—In dress, then in bra and panties, then nude on sofa.

•• 0:35—In outfit, then breasts, while outside on chair.

Dahms, Gail

Films:

The Silent Partner (1978) . . . . .Louise

• 0:31—Right breast in bathroom with another guy when Elliott Gould surprises them.

The Tomorrow Man (1979). . . . . .n.a.

Daily, Elizabeth *

a.k.a. E.G. Daily.

Singer.

Films:

The Escape Artist (1982) . . . . Sandra

Funny Money (1982). . . . . Cass

Ladies and Gentlemen, The Fabulous Stains (1982) . . . . .Motel Maid

(Not available on video tape.)

Street Music (1982) . . . . .Sadie

• 0:00—Nude behind shower door (can't see anything), then brief right breast while reaching for towel.

•• 0:24—Partial lower frontal nudity and left breast with Eddie.

• 1:07—Brief breasts while on top of Eddie on the floor.

•• 1:08—Brief breasts while getting dressed.

One Dark Night (1983). . . . . .Leslie

Valley Girl (1983) . . . . Loryn

•• 0:16—In bra through open jumpsuit, then brief breasts on bed with Tommy.

Wacko (1983) . . . . .Bambi

No Small Affair (1984). . . . . Susan

Streets of Fire (1984). . . . . Baby Doll

Fandango (1985) . . . . Judy

Pee Wee's Big Adventure (1985) . . . . Dottie

Bad Dreams (1988). . . . . Lana

Loverboy (1989) . . . . .Linda

Dogfight (1991) . . . . Marcie

Dutch (1991) . . . . Halley

a.k.a. Driving Me Crazy

Music Videos:

Young Turks/Rod Stewart . . . . Patty

Dakota, Deenie

Films:

Over Her Dead Body (1992) .Mary Lee

a.k.a. Enid Is Sleeping

Made for Cable Movies:

Grand Avenue (1996; HBO) . . . . .Justine

• 0:00—Very brief breasts, several times, while making love with her boyfriend in car.

Made for Cable TV:

Dream On: Bad Girls (1992; HBO). . . . . Claire Gantz

Dakour, Kim

Films:

Three Days to a Kill (1991) . . . . Yolanda

•• 0:31—Buns in white T-back, then breasts wearing tasseled pasties while dancing on stage.

• 1:11—Brief breasts, while fighting with Pepe on couch when he rapes her.

• 1:12—Brief buns, while lying on her stomach on the couch.

Caged Fear (1992). . . . . Mercedes

Dale, Cynthia

Sister of actress Jennifer Dale.

Films:

My Bloody Valentine (1981; Canadian) . . . . .Patty

Heavenly Bodies (1985) . . . . Samantha Blair

• 0:30—Brief breasts fantasizing about making love with Steve while doing aerobic exercises.

The Boy in Blue (1986; Canadian) . . . . Margaret

••• 1:15—Breasts standing in a loft kissing Nicolas Cage.

Moonstruck (1987) . . . . Sheila

Made for Cable Movies:

The Liberators (1987; Disney) . . . . Elizabeth Giddings

Thanks of a Grateful Nation (1998; Showtime) . . . . . Lisa Tuite

Made for TV Movies:

Sadie and Son (1987) . . . . .Paula Melvin

In the Eyes of a Stranger (1992). . . . . .Nancy

Dale, Jennifer *

Sister of actress Cynthia Dale.

Films:

Stone Cold Dead (1979; Canadian) . . . . Claudia Grissom

••• 0:05—Breasts, dancing on stage.

Suzanne (1980; Canadian). . . . . Suzanne

•• 0:29—Breasts when boyfriend lifts her sweatshirt up when she's sitting on couch doing homework.

•• 0:53—Breasts with Nicky on the floor.

Your Ticket is No Longer Valid (1982). . . . . Laura

•• 0:27—In black panties, then breasts when her husband fantasizes, then makes love with her.

• 1:23—Left breast in bed with Montoya, then sitting, waiting for Richard Harris.

Of Unknown Origin (1983; Canadian). . . . . .Lorrie Wells

Separate Vacations (1985; Canadian) . . . . .Sarah Moore

• 0:17—Brief right breast in bed with her husband after son accidentally comes into their bedroom.

•• 1:14—Breasts on bed with Jeff after having a fight with her husband.

• 1:19—Brief right breast, in bed with her husband.

The Adjuster (1991; Canadian). . . . . .Arianne

••• 0:46—Breasts, while making love on top of Elias Koteas and discussing her insurance adjustments. Dark but nice.

Cadillac Girls (1993; Canadian) . . . . Sally

••• 0:41—In bra, then breasts while making love in bedroom with Gregory Harrison.

Made for TV Movies:

John Woo's "Once a Thief" (1996). . . . . The Director

Dali, Tracy *

a.k.a. Tracy D'Aldia.

Films:

Back to the Future, Part II (1989). . . . . Jacuzzi Girl

Click: Calendar Girl Killer (1989) . . . . June

Pretty Woman (1990) . . . . .n.a.

Virgin High (1990) . . . . Christy

•• 0:04—Brief breasts several times when her blouse and bra pop open while talking to her parents.

Sunset Heat (1991) . . . . Carl's Pool Girl
a.k.a. Midnight Heat
(Unrated version reviewed.)
•• 1:08—Breasts in pool with Dennis Hopper. Breasts and buns, getting out of pool while wearing a G-string.
Bikini Summer 2 (1992) . . . . Anita
• 0:42—Brief buns, while bending over in maid outfit by the pool.
• 0:49—Buns, in black lingerie after taking off her maid outfit in front of Harry.
•• 0:51—Breasts in back seat of limousine, while making love with Harry.
• 0:55—Brief buns, while bending over in maid outfit.
• 1:00—Brief buns, while bending over in maid outfit.
Encino Man (1992) . . . . n.a.
Fast Getaway II (1994) . . . . n.a.
Kissing a Dream (1996) . . . . Laura
••• 0:51—Breasts and partial buns, while making love with Peter in office.
••• 1:04—Buns and breasts, while making love with Marc on lounge chair.
Made for Cable Movies:
Fatal Charm (1991; Showtime). . . . . Dream Girl
•• 0:11—Breasts in van with Christopher Atkins. Lots of diffusion.
• 0:20—Brief breasts in van during Amanda Peterson's fantasy.
Made for Cable TV:
Beverly Hills Bordello: Reunion (1997; Showtime)
. . . . Missy Allen
•• 0:04—Breasts, while in bedroom with Jack.
••• 0:08—Full frontal nudity, while making love with Jack in bedroom.
•• 0:11—Right breast, while talking with Jack afterward.
••• 0:13—Breasts and buns, while making love with Jack.
••• 0:23—Breasts and buns, while making love with Jack.
Video Tapes:
Fantasies 2 (1992) . . . . Model
Penthouse: Fast Cars/Fantasy Women (1992)
. . . . Porsche Speedster 1
••• 0:05—Nude (she's wearing the dark dress), while posing with car in grainy B&W video.
Score with Chicks (1992) . . . . Cast Member
Hot Body Competition: The Best of Hot Body (1994)
. . . . Herself
••• 0:33—Buns in lingerie and swimsuits. Breasts while trying on lingerie.
Hot Body Video Magazine #9: The Best Of Hot Body Video Magazine (1994) . . . . Herself
Hot Body Hall of Fame: Traci Dali (1995) . . . . Herself
••• 0:01—Stripping out of black outfit on balcony, then nude.
••• 0:06—Nude on the snow and in a spa.
••• 0:09—Nude, while stripping out of swimsuit in front of window.
•• 0:10—Nude, while posing next to swimming pool.
••• 0:11—Nude, while dancing in front of a black Testarossa.
••• 0:17—Nude, while posing and changing clothes during lingerie shoot.
••• 0:23—In lingerie, then nude, while posing on the floor in front of fireplace.
•• 0:27—In swimsuit, then nude, while posing out by pool.
Hot Body International: Dreamgirl II (1995) . . . . Herself
Hot Body International: Steamed Heat (1995) . . . . Herself
• 0:10—Buns in swimsuit, while posing outdoors with another model.
• 0:18—Buns in swimsuit, while posing outdoors with another model.
Playboy's Fast Women (1997) . . . . Cast

*Dalle, Béatrice **

Films:
Betty Blue (1986; French) . . . . Betty
••• 0:01—Breasts making love in bed with Zorg. Long sequence.
••• 0:30—Nude on bed having sex with boyfriend.
••• 1:03—Nude trying to sleep in living room.
••• 1:21—Breasts in white tap pants in hallway.
••• 1:29—Breasts lying down with Zorg.
••• 1:39—Breasts sitting on bathtub crying & talking.
On a Volé Charlie Spencer! (1987). . . . . Movie Star
Night on Earth (1992) . . . . The Blind Passenger
a.k.a. Une Nuit Sur Terre

Dalton, Kristen

Films:
Digital Man (1995) . . . . Gena
Hourglass (1995) . . . . Laughing Girl
The Sweeper (1995) . . . . Rachel
•• 1:04—Buns and breasts behind shower curtain, then behind glass, while making love with C. Thomas Howell.

Daly, Jeannie

See: Carol, Jean.

Daly, Tyne

Daughter of actor James Daly and actress Hope Newell.
Sister of actor Tim Daly.
Ex-wife of actor/director Georg Stanford Brown.
Films:
John and Mary (1969) . . . . Hilary
The Adultress (1973) . . . . Inez
• 0:21—Brief side view of right breast, while in room with Carl. Brief out of focus breasts in bed.
•• 0:51—Breasts, while outside with Hank.
••• 0:53—Breasts, while on a horse with Hank.
The Enforcer (1976) . . . . Kate Moore
Telefon (1977). . . . . Dorothy Putterman
Zoot Suit (1981) . . . . Alice
The Aviator (1984) . . . . Evelyn Stiller
Movers and Shakers (1985) . . . . Nancy Derman
Made for Cable Movies:
Tricks (1997) . . . . Sarah
Made for TV Movies:
Intimate Strangers (1977) . . . . Karen Renshaw
Face of a Stranger (1991) . . . . Dollie Madison
The Last to Go (1991) . . . . Mary Ellen
Scattered Dreams: The Kathryn Messenger Story (1993)
. . . . Kitty Messenger
Cagney & Lacey: The Return (1994) . . . . Mary Beth Lacey
Bye Bye Birdie (1995) . . . . Mae Peterson
Cagney & Lacey: The View Through the Glass Ceiling (1995)
. . . . Mary Beth Lacey
Cagney & Lacey: Together Again (1995) . . . . . Mary Beth Lacey
TV:
Cagney & Lacey (1982-88) . . . . Mary Beth Lacey
(Won four Emmy Awards.)
Christy (1994) . . . . Alice Henderson

Damiani, Donatella *

Films:

City of Women (1980; Italian/French) . . . . . Feminist on Roller Skates

Honey (1980; Italian) . . . . . The Landlady

• 0:24—Very, very brief right breast dodging Clio Goldsmith's hand while playfully drying her off with a towel.

• _Danes, Claire_

Films:

Little Women (1994) . . . . . Beth March

Home for the Holidays (1995) . . . . . Kitt

How to Make an American Quilt (1995) . . . . Young Geady Joe

To Gillian on her 37th Birthday (1996). . . . . Rachel Lewis

• 0:40—Brief buns in swimsuit, while walking on the beach next to Cindy.

• 0:41—Buns, while standing in swimsuit at the beach.

William Shakespeare's Romeo & Juliet (1996) . . . . . Juliet

The Rainmaker (1997). . . . . Kelly Riker

U Turn (1997) . . . . . Jenny

Les Miserables (1998) . . . . . Cosette

TV:

My So-Called Life (1994-95) . . . . . Angela Chase

Danielson, Lynn

Films:

Mortuary Academy (1988) . . . . . Valerie Levitt

Out of the Dark (1988) . . . . . Kristi

• 0:09—Brief breasts getting out of bed. More breasts outside getting photographed.

•• 1:01—Breasts in motel room making love with Kevin.

• 1:06—Left breast, while getting out of bed.

Nickel & Dime (1992). . . . . Destiny Charm

Ghoulies IV (1993) . . . . . Female Victim

Danner, Blythe

Films:

To Kill a Clown (1971). . . . . Lily Frischer

• 1:10—Side view of left breast sitting on bed talking to Alan Alda. Hair covers breast, hard to see. Buns, getting up and running out of the house.

1776 (1972) . . . . . Martha Jefferson

Hearts of the West (1975) . . . . . Miss Trout

Futureworld (1976). . . . . Tracy Ballard

The Great Santini (1980). . . . . Lillian Meechum

Man, Woman and Child (1983). . . . . Sheila Beckwith

Brighton Beach Memoirs (1986) . . . . . Kate

Another Woman (1988) . . . . . Lydia

Alice (1990). . . . . Dorothy

Mr. & Mrs. Bridge (1990) . . . . . Grace

The Prince of Tides (1991). . . . . Sallie Wingo

Husbands and Wives (1992) . . . . . Rain's Mother

Homage (1994). . . . . Katherine Samuel

To Wong Foo, Thanks for Everything! Julie Newmar (1995) . . . . . Beatrice

Mad City (1997) . . . . . Mrs. Banks

No Looking Back (1998) . . . . . Claudia's Mom

The X-Files (1998). . . . . Jana Cassidy

Made for Cable Movies:

Judgment (1990; HBO) . . . . . Emmeline Guitry

Made for Cable TV:

Tales From the Crypt: Maniac at Large (1992; HBO) . . . . . Margaret

Made for TV Movies:

Are You in the House Alone? (1978) . . . . . Ann

Money, Power, Murder (1989) . . . . . Jeannie

Cruel Doubt (1992). . . . . Bonnie Von Stein

Leave of Absence (1994) . . . . . Eliza

Oldest Living Confederate Widow Tells All (1994) . . . . . Bianca

TV:

Adam's Rib (1973). . . . . Amanda Bonner

Tattingers (1988-89) . . . . . Hillary Tattinger

Danning, Sybil *

a.k.a. Sybille Danninger.

Films:

Bluebeard (1972) . . . . . The Prostitute

• 1:08—Brief breasts kissing Nathalie Delon showing her how to make love to her husband.

• 1:09—Brief left breast, lying on the floor with Delon just before Richard Burton kills both of them.

Maiden Quest (1972) . . . . . Kriemhild

a.k.a. The Long Swift Sword of Siegfried

• 0:02—Breasts in bath, surrounded by topless blonde servants.

• 0:04—Breasts in the bath again.

••• 0:10—Nude in tub surrounded by breasts servant girls.

••• 0:12—Breasts on bed, getting rubbed with ointment by the servant girls.

•• 0:35—Breasts while in bed with Siegfried.

• 1:00—Breasts in bed with Siegfried.

••• 1:19—Breasts in bed with Siegfried.

Naughty Nymphs (1972; German). . . . . Elizabeth

a.k.a. Passion Pill Swingers

a.k.a. Don't Tell Daddy

••• 0:21—Nude taking a bath while yelling at her two sisters.

• 0:30—Breasts and buns throwing Nicholas out of her bedroom.

•• 0:38—Full frontal nudity running away from Burt.

The Three Musketeers (1973; British). . . . . Eugenie

The Four Musketeers (1975) . . . . . Eugenie

Albino (1976) . . . . . Sally

a.k.a. Night of the Askari

• 0:19—Breasts, then full frontal nudity getting raped by the Albino and his buddies.

The Loves of a French Pussycat (1976) . . . . . Andrea

••• 0:18—Breasts dancing with her boss, then in bed.

•• 0:24—Breasts and buns in swimming pool.

• 0:46—Breasts in bathtub with a guy.

• 1:03—Left breast sticking out of bra, then breasts.

The Twist (1976). . . . . Jacques' Secretary

•• 1:24—Brief breasts sitting next to Bruce Dern during his daydream.

God's Gun (1977) . . . . . Jenny

a.k.a. A Bullet from God

• 1:09—Right breast popping out of dress with a guy in the barn during flashback.

Cat in the Cage (1978). . . . . Susan Khan

• 0:24—Brief breasts getting slapped around by Ralph.

• 0:25—Brief left breast several times smoking and talking to Ralph, brief left breast getting up.

•• 0:30—Full frontal nudity getting out of the pool.

• 0:52—Black bra and panties undressing and getting into bed with Ralph. Brief left breast and buns.

• 1:18—Very brief right breast several times, struggling with an attacker on the floor.

Crossed Swords (1978; Panamanian). . . . . Mother Canty

Kill Castro (1978). . . . . Veronica

a.k.a. Cuba Crossing

Separate Ways (1979) . . . . . Mary

Battle Beyond the Stars (1980) . . . . . St. Exmin

The Day of the Cobra (1980) . . . . Brenda
• 0:41—Buns and side view of right breast getting out of bed and putting robe on with Lou. Long shot.
How to Beat the High Cost of Living (1980) . . . . .Charlotte
The Man with Bogart's Face (1980). . . . . .Cynthia
Nightkill (1981) . . . . .Monika Childs
The Salamander (1981). . . . . Lili Anders
Daughter of Death (1982) . . . . Susan
a.k.a. Julie Darling
•• 0:36—Breasts in bed with Anthony Franciosa.
• 0:38—Brief right breast under Franciosa.
Famous T & A (1982) . . . . Hostess
(No longer available for purchase, check your video store for rental.)
• 0:00—Brief side view of buns and partial left breast, getting dressed.
S.A.S. San Salvador (1982) . . . . .Countess Alexandra
• 0:07—Brief left breast, while lying on the couch and kissing Malko.
Talking Walls (1982) . . . . Bathing Beauty
Chained Heat (1983; U.S./German) . . . . Erika
••• 0:30—Breasts in the shower with Linda Blair.
Hercules (1983). . . . . .Arianna
Private Passions (1983) . . . . Katherine
Howling II: Your Sister is a Werewolf (1984). . . . . . Stirba
• 0:35—Left breast, then breasts with Mariana in bedroom about to have sex with a guy.
• 1:20—Very brief breasts during short clips during the end credits. Same shot repeated about 10 times.
Malibu Express (1984). . . . . Countess Luciana
• 0:13—Brief breasts making love in bed with Cody.
They're Playing with Fire (1984) . . . . Diane Stevens
••• 0:08—Breasts and buns making love on top of Jay in bed on boat. Nice!
•• 0:10—Breasts and buns getting out of shower, then brief side view of right breast.
•• 0:47—In black bra and slip, at home with Michael, then panties, then breasts and buns getting into shower.
••• 1:12—In white bra and panties in room with Jay then breasts.
Jungle Warriors (1985) . . . . Angel
a.k.a. Captive Women 9
• 0:53—Buns, while getting a massage.
Panther Squad (1986; French/Belgian) . . . . Ilona
Reform School Girls (1986) . . . . .Warden Sutter
Young Lady Chatterley II (1986) . . . . Judith Grimmer
••• 1:02—Breasts in the hut on the table with the Gardener.
Amazon Women on the Moon (1987). . . . . Queen Lara
Phantom Empire (1987) . . . . The Alien Queen
The Tomb (1987) . . . . .Jade
Warrior Queen (1987). . . . . Berenice
L.A. Bounty (1989) . . . . Ruger
Made for Cable TV:
The Hitchhiker: Face to Face (1984; HBO) . . . Gloria Loring
(Available on *The Hitchhiker, Volume 4*.)
•• 0:10—In red bra and panties, then right breast making love with Robert Vaughn.

Danon, Leslie

Films:
Beach Balls (1988) . . . . Kathleen
• 1:06—In bra, then brief breasts in car with Doug.
Marked for Death (1990) . . . . .Girl #1
The Double O Kid (1992) . . . . French Girl
Illusions (1992) . . . . Young Laura
Hail Caesar (1993) . . . . Annie
A Million to Juan (1993) . . . . Patricia
The Whispering (1994) . . . . .Lisa Smyths
Sometimes They Come Back ...Again (1995) . . . Lisa Porter
• 0:12—Brief breasts, when her dress is pulled off by her girl friend.
TV:
Tattooed Teenage Alien Fighters from Beverly Hills (1994)
. . . . Laurie Foster/Scorpio

Dante, Crisstyn

Films:
Midnight Crossing (1988) . . . . Body Double for Kim Cattrall
• 0:29—Brief left breast making love on small boat, body double for Kim Cattrall.
Phantom of the Mall: Eric's Revenge (1988)
. . . . Body Double for Ms. Whitman
•• 0:25—Breasts in bed about five times with Peter.
State Park (1988; Canadian). . . . . Blond in Net
• 0:45—Very, very brief left breast putting swimsuit top back on after being rescued from net by the guy in the bear costume.
Nightmare on Elm Street 5: The Dream Child (1989)
. . . . Body Double for Lisa Wilcox
Last Call (1990) . . . . Hooker

Danziger, Maia

Films:
Honky (1971) . . . . Sharon
The Magician of Lublin (1979) . . . . Magda
Dr. Heckyl and Mr. Hype (1980) . . . . Miss Finebum
High Stakes (1989) . . . . Veronica
Last Exit to Brooklyn (1990). . . . . Mary Black
• 0:10—Out of focus buns and right breast taking off her slip.
• 0:12—Very brief breasts making love with Harry. Breasts after.

Dare, Barbara

Adult film actress.
a.k.a. Stacey Nix.
Films:
Valet Girls (1987) . . . . .Uncredited Party Girl
• 1:10—Brief breasts, getting photographed while sitting on railing.
• 1:14—Brief breasts, popping out of birthday cake and putting a pie in Dirk's face.
Evil Toons (1991) . . . . Jan
••• 0:30—Breasts, taking off robe and putting on red nightgown.
•• 1:06—Breasts when her top is pulled down by Roxanne.
Video Tapes:
High Society Centerspread Video #10: Barbara Dare (1990). . . . . Herself
•• 0:01—Breasts undressing.
••• 0:03—Nude on bed with a guy video taping, then making love with her. Nice, long scene.
••• 0:08—Full frontal nudity during photo shoot and interview.
••• 0:13—Nude, on lounge chair, masturbating.
•• 0:18—Breasts, sitting in chair during interview.

Dare, Debra

See: Dutch, Deborah.

Darel, Florence

Films:
Tales of Four Seasons (1989; French). . . . . Natacha
a.k.a. Contes des Quatre Saisons

Uranus (1991; French). . . . . Marie-Anne
The Stolen Children (1993; Italian/French) . . . . Martine
à la mode (1994; French) . . . . Tonie
a.k.a. In Fashion
a.k.a. Fausto
•• 1:05—Full frontal nudity, while lying in bed with Fausto.

Darnell, Vicki

Films:
Senior Week (1987) . . . . Everett's Dream Teacher
•• 0:03—Breasts during classroom fantasy.
Alien Space Avenger (1988) . . . . Bordello Lady
Brain Damage (1988) . . . . Blonde in Hell Club
Frankenhooker (1990). . . . . Sugar
• 0:36—Brief middle part of each breast through slit bra during introduction to Jeffrey.
•• 0:37—Breasts, sticking out of black lingerie while getting legs measured.
• 0:38—Right breast, while sitting in chair.
• 0:39—Breasts through slit lingerie three times while folding clothes.
• 0:40—Buns, when fighting over drugs.
••• 0:41—Very brief right breast, sitting on bed (on the right) enjoying drugs. Breasts dancing with the other girls.
Sorority Girls and the Creature from Hell (1990)
. . . . Dancer
• 0:17—Breasts in bar in open blouse, while dancing on stage. Lit with red light.
• 0:24—More breasts dancing on stage.

Darrian, Racquel *

Adult film actress.
Used the name Kelly Jackson for her *Penthouse* pictorial.
Video Tapes:
High Society Centerspread Video #14: Racquel Darrian (1990). . . . . Herself
Penthouse Passport to Paradise/Hawaii (1991) . . . Model
••• 0:17—Undressing outside by a spa. In lingerie, then nude on a lounge chair and in the spa.
The Art of Desire (1992) . . . . n.a.

Das, Alisha

Films:
The Slugger's Wife (1985) . . . . Lola
Danger Zone II: Reaper's Revenge (1988) . . . . Francine
Nightwish (1988) . . . . Kim
(Unedited version reviewed.)
•• 1:09—Brief breasts, then left breast in open dress caressing herself while lying on the ground.
Firepower (1993) . . . . Lisa
Object of Obsession (1994). Charlotte

Dash, Stacey

Films:
Enemy Territory (1987) . . . . Toni Briggs
Moving (1988) . . . . Casey Pear
Blackwater (1989) . . . . Minnie
• 0:37—Upper half of buns and back side of right breast, while walking to and sitting on edge of bed.
• 0:44—Very brief side view of left breast, while propping herself up while lying on couch.
• 0:59—Brief right breast, while in bed on top of Julian Sands.
Mo' Money (1992) . . . . Amber Evans
Illegal in Blue (1994) . . . . Kari Truitt
••• 0:46—Breasts, while making love with Chris.
••• 1:08—Breasts, while making love with Chris in bed.
Renaissance Man (1994) . . . . Private Miranda Myers
Clueless (1995) . . . . Dionne
TV:
TV 101 (1988-89) . . . . Monique
Clueless (1996-97). . . . . Dionne
Clueless (1997-) . . . . Dionne

Datcher, Alex

Films:
Netherworld (1991) . . . . Mary Magdalene
Passenger 57 (1992) . . . . Marti Slayton
Rage and Honor (1992). . . . . Hannah the Hun
The Expert (1995) . . . . Dr. Alice Barnes
Jury Duty (1995) . . . . Sarah
Made for Cable Movies:
Last Exit to Earth (1996; Showtime). . . . . Heir Apparent
Made for Cable TV:
John Carpenter's Body Bags (1993; Showtime)
. . . . The Gas Station/Anne
Made for TV Movies:
Perry Mason: The Case of the Telltale Talk Show Host (1993)
. . . . Cathy Paxton
TV:
Goode Behavior (1996-97) . . . . Barbara Goode
Video Tapes:
Inside Out 3 (1992). . . . . Annie/The Wet Dream
••• 1:24—Breasts, taking off her blouse in front of the fish tank.
•• 1:25—Breasts, getting up when Dennis leaves.
• 1:26—Breasts, getting into bathtub. Long shot.
• 1:28—Breasts in bathtub.
• 1:29—Breasts in bathtub with Greg Louganis.

Davidovich, Lolita

a.k.a. Lolita David.
Films:
Class (1983) . . . . 1st Girl (motel)
The Pink Chiquitas (1986; Canadian). . . . . Pink Chiquita
Recruits (1986; Canadian). . . . . Susan
• 0:19—Very brief breasts when Steve bumps into her in the shower room.
•• 0:54—Right breast, then breasts while making out with Steve in car.
•• 0:56—Breasts, twice, while driving around in car with Steve, the Governor and his wife.
•• 0:58—Breasts, while getting out of the car.
The Big Town (1987). . . . . Black Lace Stripper
Blindside (1988; Canadian) . . . . Adele
•• 0:32—Breasts dancing on stage.
A New Life (1988) . . . . n.a.
Blaze (1989). . . . . Blaze Starr
• 0:09—In bra doing her first strip routine. Very brief side views of left breast under hat.
• 0:15—Strip tease routine in front of Paul Newman. At the end, she takes off bra to reveal pasties.
•• 0:48—Breasts on top of Newman, then side view of left breast.
The Inner Circle (1991; Italian) . . . . Anastasia
The Object of Beauty (1991) . . . . Joan
Boiling Point (1992; U.S./French). Vikki
Leap of Faith (1992) . . . . Marva
Raising Cain (1992) . . . . Jenny
Intersection (1993). Olivia Marshak
• 0:01—Breasts during Richard Gere's flashback. Don't see her face.
• 0:04—Very brief right breast while rolling over in bed.

•• 1:15—Brief breasts while pulling up her pajama tops during game of charades.

Cobb (1994) . . . . .Ramona
• 1:04—Brief breasts, while kneeling on bed with Tommy Lee Jones.

Younger & Younger (1994). . . . . Penny
Now and Then (1995) .Mrs. Albertson
Touch (1996) . . . . Antoinette Baker
Jungle 2 Jungle (1997) . . . . .Charlotte

Made for Cable Movies:

Prison Stories, Women on the Inside (1990; HBO). . . . . Lorretta
Keep the Change (1992; TNT) . . . . Ellen
Indictment: The McMartin Trial (1995; HBO) . . .Kee McFarlane
Dead Silence (1996; HBO) . . . . Sharon Foster

Made for Cable TV:

Perversions of Science: Dream of Doom (1997; HBO) . . . . Various Personalities
• 0:12—Breasts, while sitting and talking. B&W.

Made for TV Movies:

Harvest of Fire (1996) . . . . Sally Russell

Davidson, Eileen

Films:

Goin' All the Way (1981) . . . . BJ
••• 0:12—Breasts in the girls' locker room shower. Standing next to Monica.
••• 0:22—Exercising in her bedroom in braless pink T-shirt, then breasts talking on the phone to Monica.

House on Sorority Row (1983). . . . . Vicki
•• 0:16—Breasts and buns in room making love with her boyfriend.

Easy Wheels (1989). . . . . She Wolf

Eternity (1989) . . . . Dahlia/Valerie
• 0:33—In black bra and panties in dressing room. Brief buns standing in bathtub during Jon Voight's flashback.
• 0:52—Brief left breast, then breasts, in bed with Voight. Don't see face.

TV:

Santa Barbara . . . . .Kelly Capwell
The Young and the Restless . . . . Ashley Abbott
Broken Badges (1990-91) . . . . Bullet
Days of Our Lives (1993-). . . . . Kristen Blake

Davidtz, Embeth

Films:

Mutator (1989). . . . . .Jennifer

Sweet Murder (1990). . . . . .Laurie Shannon
• 0:40—Brief breasts behind wet shower door. Can't really see anything.

Till Death Do Us Part (1991) . . . . Cat
Army of Darkness (1992). . . . . Sheila
Schindler's List (1993). . . . . Helen Hirsch
Murder in the First (1994). . . . . .Mary McCasslin
Feast of July (1995) . . . . Bella Ford
Matilda (1996) . . . . Miss Honey
Fallen (1997). . . . . Gretta Miland
The Gingerbread Man (1998) . . . . .Mallory Doss

Made for Cable TV:

The Garden of Redemption (1997; Showtime) . . . . Adriana

Made for TV Movies:

Deadly Matrimony (1992). . . . . Dianne Masters

Davila, Azalea *

Films:

Blackout (1995) . . . . Mystery Woman
• 0:10—Brief breasts, while making love on top of Brian Bosworth. Don't see her face.

Unforgettable (1995) .Eddie's Girlfriend
Mulholland Falls (1996). . . . . Perino's Girl

Primal Fear (1996) . . . . Linda
• 1:11—Brief breasts, in Archbishop Rushman's office with Edward Norton and another boy seen on sex video playback.

Female Perversions (1997) . . . . Queen
• 0:56—Brief breasts, in open blouse while wearing a mask.

Made for Cable TV:

Dream On: Am I Blue (1995; HBO) . . . . Porno Actor 1
• 0:17—Brief breasts, while walking in a studio. (She's the brunette on the left.)
• 0:24—Breasts and very, very brief partial lower frontal nudity, while making love with a guy on TV.

Dream On: All About Louie (1996; HBO) . . . . Whitestone Babe #1
• 0:11—Brief breasts (she's the first one to walk into the office), while exchanging halter tops with another woman in Martin's office.

Davis, Carole *

Singer.

Used the name Tamara Kapitas for her *Penthouse* pictorial.

Films:

Piranha II: The Spawning (1981; Italian/U.S.). . . . . Jai

C.O.D. (1983). . . . . Contessa Bazzini
• 1:25—Brief breasts in dressing room scene in black panties, garter belt and stockings when she takes off her robe.

The Princess Academy (1986; U.S./Yugoslavian/French) . . . . Sonia
Mannequin (1987) . . . . Roxie
The Shrimp on the Barbie (1990) . . . . Domonique
• 0:58—Buns, in pool that is visible from inside restaurant. Don't see her face.
• 0:58—In black bra and panties, then breasts doing strip tease in front of Bruce. Very dark.

If Looks Could Kill (1991) . . . . Areola Canasta
a.k.a. Teen Agent

The Rapture (1991) . . . . Angie
• 0:20—Buns, on top of Vic in bed. Most of side of her right breast.
• 0:21—Very brief right breast, then very brief breasts while turning around to talk.

Made for Cable TV:

Hot Line: The Sitter (1996; Cinemax) . . . . . . Barbara Pollifumo
(Available on video tape in *Hot Line 3*.)
Sex and the City: The Power of Female Sex (1998; HBO) . . . . Amalita

Davis, Geena

Ex-wife of director Renny Harlin.

Ex-wife of actor Jeff Goldblum.

Films:

Tootsie (1982). . . . . April
Transylvania 6-5000 (1985). . . . . Odette
The Fly (1986). . . . . .Veronica Quaife
The Accidental Tourist (1988) . . . . Muriel
(Academy Award for Best Supporting Actress.)
Beetlejuice (1988) . . . . Barbara
Earth Girls are Easy (1989). . . . . .Valerie
Quick Change (1990) . . . . Phyllis

Thelma and Louise (1991). . . . . Thelma
Hero (1992) . . . . .Gale Gayley
A League of Their Own (1992) . . . . Dottie Hinson
Angie (1993). . . . . Angie Scacciapensieri
0:43—Brief left breast of body double after getting out of bathtub, before wrapping a towel around herself. Note that the mirror is not a mirror, but a hole in the wall.
Speechless (1994) . . . . Julia Mann
Cutthroat Island (1995). . . . . Morgan Adams
The Long Kiss Goodnight (1996) . . Samantha Caine/Charly
• 0:59—Brief side view of buns, while taking a shower. Hard to see because of all the steam.

TV:
Sara. . . . . .Sara McKenna
Buffalo Bill (1983-84) . . . . Wendy Killian

Davis, Judy

Wife of actor Colin Friels.

Films:
High Rolling (1977; Australian) . . . . Lynn
My Brilliant Career (1979; Australian) . . . . Syblla Melvyn
Winter of Our Dreams (1981) . . . . Lou
• 0:19—Brief left breast sticking out of yellow robe in bed with Pete.
• 0:26—Very brief side view of left breast taking off top to change. Long shot.
•• 0:48—Breasts taking off top and getting into bed with Bryan Brown, then brief right breast lying down with him.
The Final Option (1982; British) . . . . Frankie
a.k.a. Who Dares Win
Heatwave (1983; Australian) . . . . Kate
A Passage to India (1984; British) . . . . Adela Quested
Kangaroo (1986; Australian) . . . . Harriet Somers
High Tide (1987; Australian) Lilli
Alice (1990). . . . . Vicki
Barton Fink (1991) . . . . Audrey Taylor
Impromptu (1991) . . . . .George Sand
Naked Lunch (1991) . . . . Joan Frost/Joan Lee
Husbands and Wives (1992). . . . . Sally
• 1:07—Brief breasts, then brief left breast, while making love in bed with Liam Neeson.
Where Angels Fear to Tread (1992) . . . . .Harriet Herriton
The Ref (1993) . . . . Caroline Chasseur
a.k.a. Hostile Hostages
The New Age (1994). Katherine Witner
Absolute Power (1997) . . . . .Gloria Russell
Blood & Wine (1997) . . . . Suzanne Gates
Children of the Revolution (1997). . . . . Joan Fraser
Deconstructing Harry (1997). . . . . Lucy

Made for TV Movies:
A Woman Called Golda (1982) . . . . .Young Golda
One Against the Wind (1991) . . . . Mary Lindell
Serving in Silence: The Margarethe Cammermeyer Story (1995). . . . . .Diane Divelbess
The Echo of Thunder (1998) . . . . Gladwyn Ritchie

Davis, Neriah *

a.k.a. Neriah Napaul.

Films:
The Bikini Carwash Company (1992) . . . . Rita
(Unrated version reviewed.)
••• 0:15—Breasts taking off her bikini top so Stanley can "catch some fish" with it.
••• 0:18—Breasts and buns, making love with Big Bruce.
•• 0:43—Breasts and buns, making love with Big Bruce. (same as 0:18)
••• 0:45—Brief left breast, getting dressed. Then buns, after forgetting to put on her bikini bottoms.
••• 0:46—Breasts and buns in G-string, hand washing a customer with Sunny.
••• 0:47—Buns, bending over while wearing a cowboy outfit.
••• 0:48—Breasts and buns, dancing inside car wash with Sunny and Melissa.
••• 1:02—Nude, soaped up in car wash with Sunny and Melissa.
•• 1:11—Buns, posing while wearing cowboy outfit.
••• 1:13—Breasts and buns.
Meatballs 4 (1992) . . . . Neriah
• 0:05—Very brief buns, while getting her red towel pulled up by another girl while walking to the showers.
The Bikini Carwash Company II (1993). . . . . .Rita
(Unrated version reviewed.)
••• 0:09—Breasts with the other three girls, celebrating in office during music video number.
••• 0:16—Breasts at carwash during music video number. (Wearing pink bikini bottoms.)
• 0:24—Buns in lingerie in offices of The Miracle Network with Sunny.
• 0:27—Brief breasts while flashing her breasts in office.
••• 0:35—Breasts and buns in studio when she's caught without her clothes on.
• 1:15—Brief breasts and buns during clean up at the studio.
•• 1:29—Breasts and buns in swimsuit during music video number at the carwash.

Video Tapes:
Playboy Celebrity Centerfold: La Toya Jackson (1994) . . . . .Playmate
••• 0:36—Nude, during music video number out in the country.
••• 0:39—Nude in starry music video number. Sometimes in lingerie.
••• 0:42—Nude in still photos.
••• 0:43—In red bra and panties, then nude in music segment with artwork.
••• 0:47—Nude in farm music video segment.
Playboy Video Calendar 1995 (1994) . . . . July
••• 0:27—Nude outside on and near a train. Nude in starlight fantasy.

Davis, Patti *

Daughter of former President Ronald Reagan and former First Lady Nancy Reagan.

Films:
The Last Party (1993). . . . . Herself

Video Tapes:
Playboy Celebrity Centerfold: Patti Davis (1994) . . . . Herself
•• 0:02—Full frontal nudity while posing in water and on rocks.
••• 0:06—In lingerie, then nude on stage in futuristic fantasy.
••• 0:09—Nude in artistic fantasy with two muscular guys.
••• 0:16—Nude in still photos.
••• 0:19—Nude with a guy in beach fantasy.
••• 0:24—In white bra and panties, then nude while posing on couch.
••• 0:28—Nude in gym and shower in workout segment.
••• 0:37—In lingerie, then in bed with a man and another woman in futuristic dial-a-date fantasy. A few scenes where she's tied to the headboard by her wrists.

Davis, Phyllis

Films:

The Last of the Secret Agents? (1966) .... Beautiful Girl
The Swinger (1966) .... n.a.
Live a Little, Love a Little (1968) .... 2nd Secretary
Beyond the Valley of the Dolls (1970) .... Susan Lake
Sweet Sugar (1972) .... Sugar
a.k.a. Hellfire on Ice
(With brown hair.)
••• 0:34—Breasts in bed with a guard.
••• 0:50—Breasts in the shower with Dolores.
•• 0:57—Brief breasts in the bathroom.
The Day of the Dolphin (1973) .... Secretary
Terminal Island (1973) .... Joy Lange
••• 0:39—Breasts and buns in a pond, full frontal nudity getting out, then more breasts putting blouse on while a guy watches.
Train Ride to Hollywood (1975) .... Scarlett O'Hara
The Choirboys (1977) .... Foxy/Gina
•• 0:29—Breasts wearing pasties, under sheer pink robe.
The Best of Sex and Violence (1981) .... Sugar/Joy
•• 0:56—Breasts after bath and in bed in scenes from *Sweet Sugar.*
••• 0:59—Breasts and buns walking out of lake in scene from *Terminal Island.*
Famous T & A (1982) .... Sugar/Joy
(No longer available for purchase, check your video store for rental.)
••• 0:02—Nude in lots of great out-takes from *Terminal Island.* Check this out if you are a Phyllis Davis fan!
••• 0:51—Breasts in scenes from *Sweet Sugar.* Includes more out-takes.
••• 1:04—More out-takes from *Sweet Sugar.*
Guns (1990) .... Kathryn Hamilton

TV:

Love, American Style (1970-74) .... Repertory Player
Vega$ (1978-81) .... Beatrice Travis

Davis, Viveka

Films:

Shoot the Moon (1982) .... Jill
Morgan Stewart's Coming Home (1987) .... Emily
The End of Innocence (1989) .... Honey
Forbidden Sun (1989) .... Jane
Curly Sue (1991) .... Trina
Ricochet (1991) .... Babysitter
Man Trouble (1992) .... June Huff
Body Shot (1993) .... Rita
A Dangerous Woman (1993) .... Mercy
PCU (1994) .... Womynist #1

Made for Cable TV:

Women: Stories of Passion-As Always, Madelaine (1996; Showtime) .... Young Faith
••• 0:11—In slip, then breasts and buns, while making love in bedroom with Madelaine.
• 0:23—Brief breasts, while making love in bed with Madelaine.

Miniseries:

V (1983) .... Polly Maxwell
V: The Final Battle (1984) .... Polly Maxwell

Made for TV Movies:

I Can Make You Love Me: The Stalking of Laura Black (1993) .... Mary Ann
Naomi & Wynonna: Love Can Build a Bridge (1995) .... Wynonna Judd

TV:

V: The Series (1984-85) .... Polly Bernstein
Sweet Surrender (1987) .... Cak

Davis-Voss, Sammi

No relation to the late entertainer Sammy Davis, Jr.

Films:

Hope and Glory (1987; British) .... Dawn Rohan
A Prayer for the Dying (1987) .... Anna
Consuming Passions (1988; U.S./British) .... Felicity
The Lair of the White Worm (1988; British) .... Mary Trent
The Rainbow (1989) .... Ursula Brangwen
••• 0:21—Breasts and buns with Amanda Donohoe undressing, running outside in the rain, jumping into the water, then talking by the fireplace.
•• 0:30—Breasts and buns posing for a painter.
• 1:33—Brief right breast and buns getting out of bed.
••• 1:44—Nude running outside with Donohoe.
Horseplayer (1991) .... Randi
Shadow of China (1991; U.S./Japanese) .... Katherine
Indecency (1992) .... Nia
Four Rooms (1995) .... Jezebel
••• 0:10—Breasts, after taking off her top during witch ceremony.
••• 0:12—Breasts, while pouring sweat into cauldron and watching Ione Skye do her part.

Made for Cable Movies:

Chernobyl: The Final Warning (1991) .... Elena Mashenko
The Perfect Bride (1991) .... Stephanie

Made for Cable TV:

Red Shoe Diaries: You Make Me Want to Wear Dresses (1994; Showtime) .... Randi

Made for TV Movies:

Pack of Lies (1987) .... Julie

TV:

Homefront (1991-93) .... Caroline Hailey

Dawn, Angela

Video Tapes:

Hot Body International: #3 Lingerie Special (1992) .... Contestant
•• 0:13—Buns in body suit.
Hot Body International: #5 Miss Acapulco (1992) .... Contestant
•• 0:46—Buns, while dancing in orange two piece swimsuit.
Hot Body Video Magazine #1: Premiere Edition (1992) .... Street Scene/Model
••• 0:34—Buns in G-string and breasts during photo session on a Harley.
Hot Body Video Magazine #2: Double Trouble (1992) .... Feature Girl/Model
•• 0:01—Breasts during opening credits.
••• 0:28—Nude, taking off a red swimsuit and putting on a hot pink one.
••• 0:30—Outside on hay, in white bra and panties, then breasts and buns.
Hot Body Video Magazine #4: Extra Sexy (1993) .... Street Scene
•• 0:01—Breasts and buns during introduction.
••• 0:38—In two piece swimsuit, then breasts and buns while posing on a Harley-Davidson motorcycle.
Hot Body Competition: The Best of Hot Body (1994) .... Herself
•• 0:50—Buns in swimsuits.
Hot Body International: Dreamgirl II (1995) .... Herself

Dawn, Kimberly

See: Dawson, Kim.

Dawson, Kim

a.k.a. Kimberly Dawn.

Films:

Not of This Earth (1988) .... Girl in House
The Arrival (1990) .... Leslie
Bad Blood (1993) .... Chang's Girl
• 0:16—Breasts and brief partial lower frontal nudity while in bed with Chang.
The Perfect Gift (1993) .... Suzanne
Sexual Outlaws (1993)......................... Jeannie
••• 0:05—Breasts and buns in panties, then nude while changing lingerie, then posing on bed.
••• 0:07—Breasts and buns, while posing on bed.
••• 0:09—Breasts, while in bed with Rita.
Surf, Sand and Sex (1994)................. First Woman
••• 0:03—Full frontal nudity, in bathtub, then making love on bed with her first husband. Nice, long scene.
Ultimate Taboo (1994) .... n.a.
The Voyeur (1994) .... Brenda
•• 0:09—In pink bra, then breasts, while making out in bathroom with James during party.
• 0:21—Upper half of breasts and buns, while posing in lingerie in front of mirror.
• 0:25—Buns and upper half of breasts in lingerie, while making love with James in daydream.
• 0:31—Partial right breast in open blouse in James' daydream.
•• 0:33—Breasts in open blouse, while making love with James in his daydream.
••• 0:38—Upper half of breasts and buns in lingerie, while making love in room with James. Long scene.
••• 0:44—Nude, after taking off bra and panties, when making love in bed with James while his wrists are tied to the bed.
••• 0:55—Breasts on lounge chair, while James rubs lotion on her in front of some onlookers in his fantasy.
•• 0:56—Breasts, while wearing red panties, then putting on red dress, in bedroom with James.
••• 1:12—Nude, while making love with James in bed. Nice long scene.
Lap Dancing (1995) .... Sandy
••• 0:38—Nude, when making love with Jimmy in bed, while a blindfolded Lorissa McComas is sitting nearby.
••• 0:49—Nude, while doing strip routine on stage. Long scene.
Lurid Tales: The Castle Queen (1995) .... Older Sister
•• 0:01—Breasts, while making love with Charles.
•• 0:23—In black lingerie, then breasts, while making love with Tom.
• 1:12—Very, very brief breasts during flashbacks.
Maui Heat: Swimsuit Edition (1996) .... Laura Turner
••• 1:25—Nude, while making love with Jake on the beach at night.
Exposé (1997)........................... Mrs. Holmes
Stripteaser 2 (1997).................. Daphne Gulliani
••• 0:37—In bra, then breasts and partial buns, while making love with Nick in office.

Made for Cable TV:

Love Street: Hope's Creek (1993; Showtime)....... Jessica
0:18—Running through woods in slip, then in bra and panties.
••• 0:19—Breasts, while making love outside with Tucker.
• 0:22—Very brief buns, while putting on panties.
Erotic Confessions: At the Tone (1997; Cinemax).. Sandra
• 0:03—Breasts, while Scott caresses her.

Video Tapes:

Buck Naked Line Dancing (1993)............... Dancer
••• 0:00—Breasts throughout. She's in the back in the left.
Playboy's Erotic Fantasies: Forbidden Liaisons (1995) .... Piano Man
••• 0:21—In black lingerie after stripping in restaurant, then nude, while making love on the piano with the piano man.

Dax, Danielle

British alternative pop singer. Originally with the group the *Lemon Kittens.*

Films:

The Company of Wolves (1985) .... Wolfgirl
• 1:26—Brief buns and breasts running around outside. Her hair is in the way a lot.

Day, Alexandra

Films:

Erotic Images (1983) .... Logan's Girlfriend
•• 0:37—Breasts getting out of bed while Logan talks on the phone to Britt Ekland.
Boarding House (1984) .... Girl in Bathroom
Body Double (1984) .... Girl in Bathroom #1
Young Lady Chatterley II (1986)....... Jenny, Maid in Hut
••• 0:06—Breasts and buns in hut on the bed with the Gardener.
••• 0:28—Breasts taking bath with Harlee McBride.

Video Tapes:

The Girls of Penthouse (1984) .... Tattoo Woman & Use Me Woman
••• 0:34—Nude, getting tattooed by another woman, then making love with her.
••• 0:40—Nude, dancing and stripping off her clothes down to stockings and garter belt, then on bed. Quick cuts and strobe light make it hard to see.
Penthouse: On the Wild Side (1988) .... Honey Pot
••• 0:43—Breasts, getting honey dribbled on her, then getting it licked off by her lover.

Day, Catlyn

Films:

Kandyland (1987)............................... Diva
••• 0:50—Breasts wearing pasties doing strip routine.
• 1:06—Brief breasts talking on the telephone in dressing room.
• 1:12—Brief breasts during dance routine with the other girls.
Rented Lips (1988) .... Dancer
Wilding, The Children of Violence (1990) ... Officer Breedlove
Indecent Proposal (1993) .... Wine Goddess

• Dayne, Taylor *

Singer.

Films:

Love Affair (1994) .... Marissa

Made for Cable Movies:

Stag (1997; HBO)............................. Serena
• 0:16—Brief buns, when in bathroom with John Stockwell.
• 0:24—Brief partial buns, when being carried up the stairs.

de Aragon, Maria

Films:

Blood Mania (1970) . . . . Victoria
••• 0:11—Breasts while wearing panties and taking off her dress and getting into pool with the pool boy, then getting out.
• 0:26—Right breast, while doing amyl nitrate in bed with Dr. Cooper. Brief upper half of buns.
• 0:27—Breasts during the drug-induced visions.
•• 0:37—Breasts in front of mirror, after taking off nightgown. Seen from below.
••• 0:46—Breasts and buns, taking off her dress in front of Dr. Cooper.

Wonder Women (1973; Philippines) . . . . Linda

• de Cadenet, Amanda *

Films:

The Rachel Papers (1989; British) . . . . Yvonne
Blue Flame (1993). . . . . Hooker #2
Four Rooms (1995) . . . . Diana
Grace of My Heart (1996) . . . . Receptionist #2
Fall (1997) . . . . Sarah Easton
• 0:50—Partial left breast, while lying under Michael.

Made for Cable TV:

The Hunger: No Radio (1997; Showtime) . . . . Woman
• 0:05—Brief breasts, after Jamie rolls off her after having sex in bed.

de Capitani, Grace

Films:

Dog Day (1984; French) . . . . Lily
My New Partner (1984; French) . . . . Natasha
a.k.a. Les Ripoux
• 0:38—Brief side of left breast and buns, getting out of bathtub.
• 0:39—Brief buns and side view of left breast, when getting into bathtub. Breasts while talking to Thierry Lhermitte. Medium long shot.

• de Graaf, Marina

Films:

Mysteries (1978; Dutch) . . . . Sara
• 1:22—Buns and sides of breasts, while asleep on top of Rutger Hauer.

Antonia's Line (1996; Dutch). . . . . Deedee

de Haviland, Consuela

Films:

Betty Blue (1986; French) . . . . Lisa
The Unbearable Lightness of Being (1988) . . Tall Brunette
•• 2:10—In black bra, then lower nudity and side view of right breast while trying to seduce Daniel Day Lewis.

Barjo (1993; French) . . . . Claudie Hermelin

De La Croix, Raven *

Films:

Jokes My Folks Never Told Me (1976) . . . . n.a.
Up! (1976) . . . . Margo Winchester
Breasts.

The Chicken Chronicles (1977) . . . . Mrs. Worth
The Happy Hooker Goes to Washington (1977)
. . . . Uncredited Ice Cream Girl
• 0:31—Brief breasts, while lying on table, getting her rear end covered with ice cream.

The Blues Brothers (1980) . . . . n.a.
The Lost Empire (1983) . . . . White Star
••• 1:05—Breasts with a snake after being drugged by the bad guy.
•• 1:07—Breasts lying on a table.
•• 1:08—Breasts, getting up off table and punching a guy.

Screwballs (1983) . . . . Miss Anna Tomical
••• 1:08—Breasts during strip routine in nightclub.

Video Tapes:

Best Chest in the West (1984) . . . . Herself
••• 0:34—Breasts doing strip tease routine on stage.

De Leeuw, Lisa

Adult film actress.
a.k.a. Lisa Trego.

Films:

It's Called Murder Baby (1982) . . . . Dixie Ray
(R-rated version of the adult film *Dixie Ray, Hollywood Star.*)
• 0:26—Lower frontal nudity, raising her dress at the beach to prove to Nick that she never wears panties.
••• 0:42—Nude on table, getting massaged by Adrian.
•• 0:49—Full frontal nudity when Nick leaves the room.
•• 1:21—Breasts, getting up to get dressed.
• 1:22—Brief lower frontal nudity in open robe, while walking around the house.
••• 1:24—Breasts, opening her nightgown in front of Nick.

Up 'n' Coming (1987). . . . . Altheah Anderson
(R-rated version reviewed, X-rated version available.)
• 0:33—Very brief breasts by the pool when her robe opens.
• 0:48—Brief breasts, while walking around the house when her robe opens.
•• 0:49—Left breast talking with a guy, then breasts while walking into the bedroom.

De Light, Venus

a.k.a. Lynn Chase.

Films:

Stripper (1985) . . . . Herself
• 0:59—Brief breasts, on stage, blowing fire.
••• 1:07—Breasts and buns in black G-string, doing routine on stage, using fire.

Angel of Passion (1991) . . . . Carol
•• 0:15—Breasts taking a shower.
••• 0:19—Breasts and buns in G-string dancing outside next to pool at a birthday party.
••• 0:23—Breasts and buns in red lingerie in camper, then breasts while making love on top of Will.

Made for Cable TV:

Real Sex 5 (1993; HBO). . . . . Introducing Venus de Light
• 0:00—Brief breasts during opening credits.
• 0:01—Brief breasts during opening credits.
••• 0:02—Breasts and buns in T-back, dancing on stage with a dummy, a snake and feather fans.
••• 0:06—Breasts and buns, dancing on stage with a monkey, a bird and fire.

Video Tapes:

In Search of the Perfect 10 (1986) . . . . Perfect Girl #4
••• 0:18—Breasts talking on the phone and buns in G-string seen through the Nude-Cam.
••• 0:21—In two piece swimsuit, then breasts taking it off in the doorway.

The Stripper of the Year (1986) . . . . Venus De Light
••• 0:37—Nude, doing strip routine that includes fire tricks.
•• 0:53—Breasts on stage with the other contestants.
••• 0:55—Breasts as a finalist, then in dance-off.
•• 0:56—Breasts as the winner.

Hot Bodies (1988). . . . . Herself
•• 0:22—Breasts, dancing and taking off dress.
••• 0:24—Nude in large champagne glass prop.
••• 0:27—Nude dancing on stage.
••• 0:47—Breasts and buns in G-string stripping in nurse uniform.
••• 0:49—Breasts and buns, while on hospital gurney.
••• 0:52—Breasts and buns dancing with a life-size dummy prop.
Starlets Exposed! Volume II (1991) . . . . Venus
••• 0:43—Buns in G-string, then breasts dancing on stage with a life-size dummy and in a giant champagne glass.
Venus' Playhouse (1994) . . . . Herself
CD-ROM:
Venus' Playhouse (1994) . . . . Herself

De Liso, Debra

Films:
The Slumber Party Massacre (1982) . . . . Kim
• 0:08—Very brief breasts getting soap from Trish in the shower.
•• 0:29—In beige bra and panties, then breasts putting on a U.S.A. shirt while changing with the other girls.
Outrageous Fortune (1987). . . . . Ballet Double for Lauren
Iced (1988) . . . . Trina
• 0:11—In a bra, then briefly nude while making love with Cory in hotel room.
Dr. Caligari (1989). . . . . Grace Butter

de Medeiros, Maria *

Films:
1871 (1989; British) . . . . Maria
La Lectrice (1989; French). . . . . Silent Nurse
a.k.a. The Reader
Henry & June (1990). . . . . Anais Nin
• 0:50—Brief right breast, popping out of dress top.
•• 0:52—Breasts lying in bed with Richard E. Grant.
•• 1:13—Breasts in bed with Fred Ward, buns getting out. Right breast standing by the window.
••• 1:31—Breasts in bed with Brigitte Lahaie.
• 1:37—Nude under sheer black patterned dress.
•• 1:43—Close up of right breast as Ward plays with her.
•• 2:01—Left breast, then breasts after taking off her top in bed with Uma Thurman.
Meeting Venus (1990; British) . . . . Yvonne
Golden Balls (1993; Spanish). . . . . Marta (45 kilos)
Pulp Fiction (1994) . . . . Fabienne

De Mornay, Rebecca

Films:
Risky Business (1983). . . . . Lana
• 0:28—Briefly nude, while standing by the window with Tom Cruise.
Testament (1983) . . . . Cathy Pitkin
Runaway Train (1985) . . . . Sara
The Slugger's Wife (1985) . . . . Debby Palmer
The Trip to Bountiful (1986) . . . . Thelma
And God Created Woman (1988) . . . . Robin
(Unrated version.)
•• 0:06—Brief Left breast and buns in gymnasium with Vincent Spano. Brief right breast making love.
• 0:53—Brief buns and breasts in the shower when Spano sees her.
•• 1:02—Brief left breast with Langella on the floor.
••• 1:12—Breasts making love with Spano in a museum.
Feds (1988). . . . . Elizabeth De Witt
Dealers (1989). . . . . Anna Schuman
Backdraft (1991) . . . . Helen McCaffrey
The Hand That Rocks the Cradle (1992). . . . . Peyton
• 0:29—Upper half of right breast, breast feeding Claire's baby.
Guilty as Sin (1993). . . . . Jennifer Haines
The Three Musketeers (1993) . . . . Milady
Never Talk to Strangers (1995) . . . . Dr. Sarah Taylor
•• 0:34—In black bra, then breasts, while making love with Antonio Banderas.
••• 0:53—Breasts, while making love with Banderas in bed.
Made for Cable Movies:
By Dawn's Early Light (1990; HBO) . . . . Cindy Moreau
Blind Side (1993; HBO) . . . . Lynn Kaines
Made for Cable TV:
The Outer Limits: The Conversion (1995; Showtime)
. . . . Mystery Lady
Made for TV Movies:
An Inconvenient Woman (1991) . . . . Flo March
Getting Out (1994) . . . . Arlie Holsclaw
The Shining (1997) . . . . Wendy Torrance

De Moss, Darcy *

Films:
Gimme an "F" (1981) . . . . One of the "Ducks"
a.k.a. T & A Academy 2
Hardbodies (1984) . . . . Dede
••• 0:54—Breasts, while in the back seat of the limousine with Rounder.
Friday the 13th, Part VI: Jason Lives (1986) . . . . Nikki
Reform School Girls (1986) . . . . Knox
Can't Buy Me Love (1987). . . . . Patty
Return to Horror High (1987). . . . . Sheri Haines
• 0:21—Very brief left breast when her sweater gets lifted up while she's on some guy's back.
For Keeps (1988) . . . . Elaine
Friday the 13th, Part VII: The New Blood (1988)
. . . . Nikki/Prologue
Night Life (1989). . . . . Roberta Woods
Coldfire (1990) . . . . Maria
••• 0:27—Partial right breast and buns, lying in bed with Nick. Left breast, then breasts making love with him.
•• 0:30—Breasts in bathtub with Nick.
Living to Die (1990) . . . . Maggie Sams
• 0:32—Buns, getting out of spa while Wings Hauser watches without her knowing.
• 0:33—Buns, in long shot when Hauser fantasizes about dancing with her.
••• 0:56—In black bra, then breasts and buns making love with Hauser.
• 1:20—Breasts in mirror taking off black top for the bad guy.
Pale Blood (1990) . . . . Cherry
• 0:33—Very, very brief left breast, while opening her robe while posing on couch.
Vice Academy, Part 3 (1991) . . . . Uncredited Samantha
Forbidden Zone: Alien Abduction (1996). . . . . Sheri
a.k.a. Alien Abduction: Intimate Secrets
• 0:07—Brief breasts, taking off her red towel by pool.
• 0:19—Brief breasts, while talking about her experience with another woman.
• 0:20—Very brief breasts, while getting splashed with water in flashback.
•• 0:33—In bra, with the vet, then breasts when he soaps her up.
• 0:43—Breasts, when getting splashed with water again.
• 0:47—Brief partial right breast, while lying in bed.

• 0:58—Breasts during flashback with the vet.

Made for Cable Movies:

A Bucket of Blood (1995; Showtime) . . . . Alice

••• 0:55—Breasts, buns and very, very brief lower frontal nudity, after taking off her red dress to pose for Anthony Michael Hall, before he kills her. Long scene.

Made for Cable TV:

Erotic Confessions: Messy (1996; Cinemax). . . . . Alycia

(Available on video tape in *Erotic Confessions, Volume 2: Intrigue.*)

•• 0:10—Breasts and buns, with Cassandra in the kitchen.

••• 0:12—Breasts and buns, while making love with Jeff in the kitchen. Putting food on each other.

Erotic Confessions: Party for Two (1997; Cinemax) . . . . Carmella

• 0:02—In sheer white slip in front of the mirror, then in wet sheer white slip in the bathtub.

••• 0:08—Full frontal nudity, while making love with Ian.

••• 0:12—Breasts, while making love with Ian.

TV:

NYPD Blue: For Whom the Skell Rolls (Oct 18, 1994) . . . . .Denise

• 0:45—Very brief side view of buns, while getting spanked in video playback when Sipowicz tries to coerce Norman to say something nice about Kelly. (She's on the left.)

Video Tapes:

Aerobicise: The Ultimate Workout (1982) . . . . .Herself

Eden (1992). . . . . Randi

•• 1:21—Breasts, getting out of the water and putting on T-shirt.

••• 1:22—Breasts on beach, while making love with Abe.

•• 1:30—Brief breasts in bathroom.

Eden 2 (1992) . . . . Randi

••• 0:06—Breasts in sauna, while talking with Celine.

••• 0:25—Breasts, after waking up in bed with Celine.

••• 0:28—Breasts, taking off robe and putting on dress.

• 1:00—Brief breast, while making love with Celine.

••• 1:11—Breasts, in black panties, taking off her dress and diving into pool.

• 1:16—Breasts while frolicking in the ocean with Celine.

Eden 3 (1993) . . . . Randi

••• 1:36—In white bra and panties, then breasts while making love in bed with Josh.

Eden 4 (1993) . . . . Randi

• 0:27—Right breast, while in bed talking to Josh.

Eden 5 (1993) . . . . Randi

• 0:02—Brief left breast, while in bed with Josh.

• 0:20—Very brief tip of breast, while lying in bed with Josh.

• 0:44—Very brief left breast when Gabe tries to put the moves on her.

•• 1:03—In white bra, then breasts in bedroom with Gabe.

••• 1:15—Breasts, while making love on bed with Josh.

Eden 6 (1994) . . . . Randi

•• 0:06—Breasts and buns while making love in bed with Josh.

••• 1:09—Breasts, while taking off her top in front of mirror, then making love with Josh in bed. Nice close-up of Josh putting lotion on her breast.

••• 1:40—Breasts, with Josh. Seen in mirror.

• 2:00—Very, very brief side of right breast when Josh takes her dress off.

••• 2:01—Breasts and buns with Josh.

••• 2:14—Breast, while in bed with George.

*De Oliveira, Luma **

Films:

Boca (1994) . . . . Celeste

• 0:35—Breasts, after taking off her top at junk yard in a contest to win drugs from Boca. (She's wearing a pink dress.)

•• 0:38—Breasts while making love on table with Boca.

de Palma, Rossy

Films:

Women on the Verge of a Nervous Breakdown (1988; Spanish) . . . . .Marisa

Tie Me Up! Tie Me Down! (1990; Spanish) . . . . Drug Dealer on Scooter

Don Juan, My Love (1991; Spanish) . . . . . The Widow Prodoni

Acción Mutante (1993; Spanish) . . . . Lujo's Guest

Kika (1994; Spanish) . . . . Juana

Ready to Wear (1994) . . . . Pilar

a.k.a. Prêt-à-porter

• 2:05—Brief partial lower frontal nudity while standing with the other models after the "Lo" curtain goes up. (She's standing to the right of the model wearing a wedding veil.)

The Flower of My Secret (1995; Spanish). . . . . Rosa

a.k.a. La Flor de Mi Secreto

De Prume, Cathryn

Films:

Deadtime Stories (1985) . . . . .Goldi-lox

•• 1:08—Breasts taking a shower, quick cuts.

Five Corners (1988). . . . . Brita

Bloodhounds of Broadway (1989) . . . . Showgirl

Navy SEALS (1990) . . . . Bartender

Criss Cross (1992) . . . . Oakley

Terminal Velocity (1994) . . . . Karen

0:03—In white, braless blouse.

0:05—In wet, white braless blouse while getting interrogated.

Mrs. Winterbourne (1996). . . . . Renee

Made for TV Movies:

Love, Lies and Murder (1991) . . . . Linda Bailey Brown

TV:

Down the Shore (1992-93) . . . . Donna Shipko

De Ricci, Rona

a.k.a. Rona Freed.

Films:

The Penitent (1988). . . . . Celia Guerola

• 0:03—Breasts, while changing clothes in bedroom while Raul Julia watches. Mostly in silhouette.

• 0:27—In wet, white blouse, in the water with Armand Assante while he teaches her how to swim.

The Pit and the Pendulum (1991) . . . . Maria

••• 0:21—Full frontal nudity in front of Lance Henrickson and some other men while being examined.

• 0:28—Brief full frontal nudity during Henrickson's fantasy.

•• 0:59—Full frontal nudity when Henrickson slowly rolls her dress up to admire her before raping her.

De Rossi, Barbara

Films:

Stay As You Are (1978; Italian). . . . . n.a.

English language version.

La Cicala (The Cricket) (1983) . . . . Saveria

•• 0:39—Nude swimming under waterfall with Clio Goldsmith.

•• 0:43—Breasts undressing in room with Goldsmith.

- • 0:57—Brief right breast changing into dress in room.
- • 1:05—In wet white lingerie in waterfall with a guy, then in a wet dress.
- • 1:26—Very brief buns in bed with Anthony Franciosa.
- •• 1:28—Breasts in bathroom with Franciosa.
- • 1:36—Brief right breast making love with trucker.

Hearts and Armour (1983) . . . . Bradamante
- •• 1:05—Breasts while sleeping with Ruggero.

Made for Cable Movies:

Mussolini and I (1985; HBO) . . . . n.a.

Blood Ties (1986; Italian; Showtime). . . . . Luisa
- • 0:58—Brief breasts on couch when bad guy rips her clothes off.

de Rossi, Portia *

Films:

Sirens (1994; Australian) . . . . Giddy
- •• 1:15—Full frontal nudity while posing for painting.
- •• 1:24—Breasts while in pond with Elle Macpherson and Pru in Estelle's fantasy.
- • 1:30—Brief full frontal nudity on rock formation. Medium long shot. She's the first from the left.

Scream 2 (1997) . . . . Sorority Sister Murphy

TV:

Too Something (1995-96) . . . . Maria Hunter

de Sade, Ana

Films:

Return of a Man Called Horse (1976) . . . . Moonstar

Caveman (1981) . . . . .Grot's Mate

High Risk (1981) . . . . Nude

Cabo Blanco (1982) . . . . Rosa
- • 0:34—Brief breasts, lying in bed and talking to a guy.
- • 0:36—Brief right breast, twice, when he gets out of bed to look out the window.

Sorceress (1982) . . . . .Delisia
a.k.a. The Devil's Advocate

Triumphs of a Man Called Horse (1983; U.S./Mexican) . . . . Redwing

De Vasquez, Devin *

Star Search Winner 1986—Spokesmodel.

Films:

Can't Buy Me Love (1987). . . . . .Iris

House II: The Second Story (1987) . . . . The Virgin

Society (1989) . . . . .Clarisa
- ••• 0:37—Breasts, making love in bed with Billy.
- • 0:40—Left breast, while on sofa with Billy when her mother comes home.

Guns (1990). . . . . Cash
- • 1:12—Brief side of right breast and buns undressing for bath.

A Brilliant Disguise (1994) . . . . Gianna

A Low Down Dirty Shame (1994) . . . . Mendoza's Girl

Hard Time (1995) . . . . .Linda
- ••• 0:42—In body suit, then breasts and buns, while making love with Michael in bed.
- • 1:16—Breasts, while sitting in bubble bath.
- • 1:21—Brief partial right breast, while sitting in bubble bath.
- •• 1:26—Buns and breasts, while making love in bed with Michael and Angel.

Busted (1996) . . . . Casey
- • 0:05—Breasts and buns, while showering with Ava Fabian in the police showers. Sometimes with Corey Feldman.
- • 1:08—Breasts and buns while fooling around in bed with Ava and Martin.

Video Tapes:

Playboy Video Magazine, Volume 8 . . . . .Playmate

Playmate Playoffs. . . . . .Playmate

Playboy Video Calendar 1988 (1987) . . . . .Playmate

The Best of Video Playmate Calendars (1992). . .Playmate
- ••• 0:02—Nude during fantasy photo session.

Playboy's 21 Playmates: Volume II (1996) . . . . . .Playmate
- ••• 0:40—Nude in still photos.
- ••• 0:41—Nude, while posing for photographs.

Dean, Felicity

Films:

Crossed Swords (1978; Panamanian). . . . . Lady Jane

Success is the Best Revenge (1984; British) . . . . .n.a.

Steaming (1985; British) . . . . Dawn
- •• 1:12—Breasts, while painting on herself.

The Whistle Blower (1987; British). . . . . Cynthia Goodburn

Deane, Lezlie *

Films:

976-EVIL (1988). . . . . .Suzie
- • 0:34—Brief right breast in open leather jacket, making love on top of Spike. Brief breasts several times getting off him.
- •• 0:37—Brief breasts opening jacket after putting on underwear.

Girlfriend from Hell (1989) . . . . Diane

Midnight Ride (1990) . . . . Joan

Freddy's Dead: The Final Nightmare (1991). . . . . .Tracy

Almost Pregnant (1992) . . . . Party Girl
(Unrated version reviewed.)

To Protect and Serve (1992) . . . . Harriet
- • 0:47—Brief breasts in front of fireplace with C. Thomas Howell. Hard to see because candles get in the way.
- • 0:51—Brief breasts, getting up off the floor.
- • 1:18—Brief side view of left breast in mirror in bathroom. Long shot.

• *Deatcu, Elvira*

Films:

Bloodlust: Subspecies III (1993) . . . . Woman Victim
- •• 0:18—Breasts, after her blouse is lowered so vampires can feast on her. More breasts, while on the floor.

Vampire Journals (1996) . . . . Dreamy Girl

Deats, Danyi

Films:

The Allnighter (1987) . . . . Junkie

River's Edge (1987). . . . . Jamie
- • 0:03—Breasts, dead lying next to river with her killer. (All the shots of her breasts in this film aren't exciting unless you like looking at dead bodies).
- • 0:15—Close up breasts, then full frontal nudity when Crispin Glover pokes her with a stick.
- • 0:16—Full frontal nudity when the three boys leave.
- • 0:22—Full frontal nudity when all the kids come to see her body. (She's starting to look very discolored).
- • 0:24—Right breast when everybody leaves.
- • 0:30—Right breast when her body is dumped in the river.

DeBell, Kristine *

Films:

Alice in Wonderland (1977) . . . . Alice
(R-rated version reviewed.)
- • 0:10—Brief left breast, several times after shrinking.

- • 0:12—In braless wet sheet, after getting out of the water.
- • 0:14—Brief lower frontal nudity in open sheet during song and dance number.
- •• 0:16—Lower frontal nudity and breasts while getting licked by her new friends.
- •• 0:18—Full frontal nudity while putting new dress on.
- • 0:19—Left breast in gaping dress when sitting down on rock.
- ••• 0:22—Breasts, after taking off dress and playing with herself.
- • 0:40—Brief right breast, while lying on the ground with Tweedledum and Tweedledee.
- • 0:42—Brief breasts under dress while singing and dancing.
- •• 0:51—Full frontal nudity on bed with the king.
- ••• 0:59—Full frontal nudity getting bathed and primped by two women, then making love with them, then with the Queen. Brief buns, when getting up.
- • 1:05—Right breast in dress, while running from the Queen.
- •• 1:07—Nude while making love with her boyfriend after returning from Wonderland.
- ••• 1:10—Breasts, while running around in field in white dress, then riding a horse. Full frontal nudity in waterfall.
- •• 1:15—Nude during end credits.

Bloodbrothers (1978) . . . . Cheri
I Wanna Hold Your Hand (1978) . . . . Cindy the Hooker
Meatballs (1979; Canadian) . . . . A.L.
The Big Brawl (1980) . . . . Nancy
Willie and Phil (1980) . . . . Rena

- • 1:36—Breasts on the beach (mostly silhouette). Brief side of left breast.

T.A.G.: The Assassination Game (1982) . . . . Nancy
Cheerleaders Wild Weekend (1985). . . . . Debbie/Pierce
Club Life (1987) . . . . Fern

TV:

The Young and the Restless . . . . Pam Warren

Del Mar, Maria

Films:

Cold Sweat (1993) . . . . Joanne

- • 0:35—Brief breasts, opening her robe to get Ben Cross' attention. Brief breasts when he gets off of her.

Eclipse (1994; Canadian). . . . . Sarah

Made for Cable Movies:

Moonshine Highway (1995; Showtime) . . . . Ethyl Miller
Tails You Live, Heads You're Dead (1995; USA) . . . . Melanie

Made for Cable TV:

TekWar (1995; USA) . . . . Sam Houston

Del Sol, Laura

Films:

Carmen (1983; Spanish) . . . . Carmen

- • 1:14—Left breast, while lying in bed with Antonio.
- • 1:27—Brief partial left breast, standing up when Antonio catches her in wardrobe room with another dancer.

The Hit (1984) . . . . Maggie
The Stilts (Los Zancos) (1984; Spanish) . . . . Teresa
The Crew (1994). . . . . Camilla

*Delahunty, Justine **

a.k.a. Brittany Mays.

Video Tapes:

Penthouse Swimsuit Video 2 (1994) . . . . Pet
Penthouse Pet Rocks (1995). . . . . Pet

• *Delamere, Louise*

Films:

Shameless (1994; British) . . . . Sandy

- •• 0:25—Breasts, after Tony pulls her dress down while standing in front of open window.
- • 1:32—Very brief right breast, in B&W movie.

Judge Dredd (1995) . . . . Locker Judge

Delaney, Cassandra

Ex-wife of Country music singer John Denver.

Films:

Fair Game (1985; Australian). . . . . Jessica

- • 0:15—Buns and brief side of left breast, taking off her outfit and lying on bed.
- • 0:16—Breasts rolling over in bed.
- • 0:32—Brief left breast, taking off outfit to take a shower.
- •• 0:48—Brief breasts when the bad guys cut her blouse open. Breasts several times, while tied to front of truck.
- • 0:49—Brief left breast while getting up off the ground.
- • 0:50—Half of right breast, while sitting in the shower. Dark.

Rebel (1985; Australian) . . . . All-Girl Band Member
Hurricane Smith (1990). . . . . Julie

- •• 0:45—Breasts, while making love with Carl Weathers in bed.

Delaney, Gloria

Films:

The Human Tornado (1976) . . . . Hurricane Annie

- ••• 0:35—Full frontal nudity, taking off dress, exercising on bed, then making love with Rudy Ray Moore.

Blue Collar (1978). . . . . Party Girl 1

- • 0:33—Brief breasts, while standing in doorway, then hugging Yaphet Kotto.

Penitentiary (1979) . . . . Inmate
Crossroads (1986). Jukehouse Woman
Red Heat (1988) . . . . Intern
Number One Fan (1994). . . . . Nurse

Delaney, Kim

Films:

That Was Then... This Is Now (1985). . . . . Cathy Carlson
Campus Man (1987) . . . . Dayna Thomas
Hunter's Blood (1987). . . . . Melanie
The Drifter (1988) . . . . Julia Robbins

- • 0:11—Brief breasts making love with Miles O'Keeffe on motel floor.
- •• 0:21—Breasts in bed talking with Timothy Bottoms.

Hangfire (1990). . . . . Maria Slayton
Body Parts (1991) . . . . Karen Crushank
Darkman II: The Return of Durant (1994) . . . . Jill Randall
The Force (1994). . . . . Sarah
Temptress (1994) . . . . Karin Swann

- •• 0:14—Breasts, while making love with Chris Sarandon.
- • 0:44—Buns, making love on bed with Sarandon.

Serial Killer (1995). . . . . Selby Younger

Made for Cable Movies:

The Disappearance of Christina (1993) . . . . Lily Kroft
Tall, Dark and Deadly (1994; USA). . . . . Maggie

Made for Cable TV:

Tales From the Crypt: The Sacrifice (1992; HBO) . . . . Gloria Fielding

Made for TV Movies:

Cracked Up (1987) . . . . Jackie
Something Is Out There (1988). Mandy
The Broken Cord (1992) . . . . Suzanne
Jackie Collins' Lady Boss (1992). . . . . Lucky Santangelo

All Lies End in Murder (1997) . . . . n.a.
TV:
All My Children (1981-84). . . . . Jenny Gardner
Tour of Duty (1988-89) . . . . Alex Devilin
Fifth Corner (1992-93) . . . . Erica Fontaine
NYPD Blue (1995-) . . . . Detective Diane Russell
NYPD Blue: Boxer Rebellion (May 2, 1995)
. . . . Detective Diane Russell
• 0:57—Partial breasts, while in bed with Jimmy Smits.
NYPD Blue: Torah! Torah! Torah! (Oct 31, 1995)
. . . . Detective Diane Russell
0:55—Very brief partial breasts, while lying in bed with Jimmy Smits.
NYPD Blue: One Big Happy Family (Nov 7, 1995)
. . . . Detective Diane Russell
• 0:25—Buns and brief side of right breast, while in bed with Jimmy Smits.
NYPD Blue: A Tushful of Dollars (Feb 13, 1996)
. . . . Detective Diane Russell
•• 0:55—Very, very brief side view of right breast, then buns, while putting on shirt in bathroom.
NYPD Blue: Unembracable You (Dec 10, 1996)
. . . . Detective Diane Russell
• 1:02—Brief buns, while lying on top of Jimmy Smits in bed.
NYPD Blue: Bad Rap (Apr 29, 1997) . Detective Diane Russell
• 0:56—Very brief side of left breast, while sitting on Jimmy Smit's lap.
NYPD Blue: As Flies to Careless Boys Are We to the Gods or This Bud's For You (Sep 30, 1997)
. . . . Detective Diane Russell
0:56—Brief back half of right breast, twice, while in bathtub with Jimmy Smits.

Delany, Dana

Films:
The Fan (1981) . . . . Sales Woman
Almost You (1984) . . . . Susan McCall
Where the River Runs Black (1986) . . . . Sister Ana
Masquerade (1988). . . . . Anne Briscoe
Moon Over Parador (1988) . . . . Jenny
Patty Hearst (1989) . . . . Celina
Housesitter (1992). . . . . Becky
Light Sleeper (1992) . . . . Marianne
••• 0:46—Right breast, while lying on the floor with Willem Dafoe. Brief left breast when getting up. Lit with green light. (If this was anyone else, it would only get one •.)
Tombstone (1993). . . . . Josephine Marcus
The Enemy Within (1994) . . . . Betsy Corcoran
Exit to Eden (1994) . . . . Lisa
••• 0:37—Full frontal nudity, when getting out of the pool. Brief buns, while using Paul Mercurio as a chair.
•• 0:54—Brief right breast, when in bubble bath while talking with Mercurio. Buns, when standing up.
• 1:01—Buns in G-string, under sheer nightgown.
• 1:20—Left breast, when Mercurio rubs butter and sprinkles cinnamon on it.
•• 1:32—Partial buns, then breasts while making love with Mercurio in bed behind sheer curtain.
Fly Away Home (1996) . . . . Susan Barnes
Live Nude Girls (1996) . . . . Jill
•• 0:52—Buns in sheer panties, then bare buns after the mobster Don pulls the panties down and starts spanking her while she's bent over a desk.
Wide Awake (1998) . . . . Mrs. Beal
Made for Cable Movies:
Directed By: Texan (1994; Showtime) . . . . Anne
Choices of the Heart: The Margaret Sanger Story (1995; Lifetime). . . . . Margaret Sanger
Made for Cable TV:
Fallen Angels: Good Housekeeping (1995; Showtime)
. . . . Helen Fiske
0:16—Very brief back sides of breasts, after getting out of bubble bath and drying herself off.
Miniseries:
Wild Palms (1993) . . . . Grace Wyckoff
Made for TV Movies:
Donato and Daughter (1993) . . . . Lt. Dina Donato
a.k.a. Dead to Rights
For Hope (1996) . . . . Hope
True Women (1997) . . . . Sarah McClure
TV:
Love of Life (1979-80) . . . . Amy Russell
As the World Turns (1981). . . . . Haley Wilson
China Beach (1988-91) . . . . Nurse Colleen McMurphy
(Emmy Award in 1989.)

Delon, Nathalie

Films:
When Eight Bells Toll (1971; British). . . . . Charlotte
Bluebeard (1972) . . . . Erika
• 1:03—Breasts in bed, showing Richard Burton her breasts.
• 1:09—Brief right breast lying on the floor with Sybil Danning just before Richard Burton kills both of them.
The Godson (1972; Italian/French) . . . . Jan Lagrange
The Romantic Englishwoman (1975; British/French) . . Miranda
Game of Seduction (1976) . . . . . Countess Flora De Saint Gilles

Delora, Jennifer

Films:
Robot Holocaust (1986). . . . . Nyla
Sexpot (1986) . . . . Barbara
••• 0:28—In bra, then breasts with her two sisters when their bras pop off. (She's in the middle.)
•• 0:36—Breasts on bed with Gorilla.
• 1:32—Breasts during outtakes of 0:28 scene.
Deranged (1987). . . . . Maryann
• 1:09—Breasts in bed with Frank. Long shot.
Young Nurses in Love (1987). . . . . Bunny
Alexa (1988) . . . . Woman 2
• 0:42—Breasts undressing behind shelves.
New York's Finest (1988) . . . . Loretta Michaels
• 0:02—Brief breasts pretending to be a black hooker.
• 0:04—Brief breasts with a bunch of hookers.
• 0:36—Breasts with her two friends doing push-ups on the floor.
Sensations (1988) . . . . Della Randall
• 0:11—Brief breasts talking to Jenny to wake her up.
• 0:13—Brief breasts a couple of times in open robe.
•• 0:38—Breasts making love with a guy on bed.
Bedroom Eyes II (1989) . . . . Gwendolyn
•• 0:04—Undressing in hotel room with Vinnie. Breasts, then making love.
Cleo/Leo (1989) . . . . Bernice
Savage Lust (1989) . . . . Amanda
a.k.a. Deadly Manor
Club Fed (1990) . . . . Uncredited Girl at Pool
Frankenhooker (1990) . . . . Angel
• 0:36—Brief breasts during introduction to Jeffrey.
••• 0:41—Breasts dancing in room with the other hookers. (Nice tattoos!)
Fright House (1990) . . . . Dr. Victoria Sedgewick
Bad Girls Dormitory (1991) . . . . Lisa

Phantasy (1991) . . . . Fantasy
Suburban Commando (1991) . . . . Hooker
Dead Boyz Can't Fly (1992). . . . . Helen
Made for TV Movies:
Breaking Through (1996) . . . . Sister Anne

Delos Santos, Becky *

Video Tapes:
Playboy Video Calendar 1995 (1994) . . . . January
••• 0:01—Nude in room full on neon lights. Nude in a house.

Delpy, Julie

Films:
Detective (1985; French/Swiss) . . . . . . Wise Young Girl Groupie
Bad Blood (1987; French) . . . . Lise
The Passion of Beatrice (1988; French) . . . . Béatrice
• 0:58—Left breast, then breasts getting out of bed.
••• 1:11—Side view of right breast, holding dress after getting raped by her father. Nude, running to the door and barricading it with furniture.
•• 1:12—More nude, arranging furniture.
••• 1:13—Full frontal nudity, wiping her crotch and burning her clothes.
• 1:36—More of right breast, when her father puts soot on her face.
•• 1:37—Brief left breast, then breasts and brief buns standing with soot on her face. Long shot.
••• 1:44—Breasts taking a bath. Subtitles get in the way a bit.
La Noche Oscura (1989; Spanish) . . .Anna de Jesus/Virgin Mary
Europa Europa (1991; German). . . . . .Leni
Voyager (1991; German/French). . . . . Sabeth
The Three Musketeers (1993) . . . . .Constance
White (1993; French/Polish) . . . . Dominique Vidal
Before Sunrise (1994) . . . . Celine
Killing Zoe (1994) . . . . Zoe
•• 0:09—In black bra, then breasts, while in motel room with Eric Stoltz.
•• 0:10—Breasts, while making love on top of Stoltz in slow motion. Intercut with old B&W films.
• 0:12—Brief breasts, while lying in bed next to Stoltz.
• 0:18—Brief breasts in the shower, while struggling with Jean-Hughes Anglade, then outside hotel room.
Red (1994; French) . . . . Dominique Vidal
Younger & Younger (1994) . . . . .Melodie
An American Werewolf in Paris (1997) . . . . .Serafine

Delvaux, Claudine

Films:
Petit Con (1986; French). . . . . Maryse
•• 0:28—Right breast, while getting felt up by her husband in front of Michel.
Camille Claudel (1989; French). . . . . Concierge

Demitro, Papusha

Films:
Perfect Timing (1984) . . . . Bonnie O. Bendix
•• 0:26—Nude, taking off dress in photo studio and kissing Joe.
• 0:29—Breasts walking with Joe through the living room, then brief nude on the roof.
•• 0:32—Nude, walking into the kitchen and getting chocolate out of the refrigerator.
•• 0:34—Nude in bed with Joe.
••• 0:45—Nude in bedroom with Joe.
•• 1:03—Nude on bed with Joe.
Breaking All the Rules (1985; Canadian) . . . . Patty

Dempsey, Sandra

Films:
Video Vixens (1973). . . . . Actress
•• 0:05—Full frontal nudity, lying down getting make-up put on.
The Swinging Cheerleaders (1974) . . . . 1st Girl at Tryout
If You Don't Stop It You'll Go Blind (1979). . . . . .n.a.

• Dench, Judi

Films:
A Midsummer Night's Dream (1968; British) . . . . . . .Titania
• 0:21—Very brief breasts, while running through the woods before meeting Oberon.
• 0:22—Brief breasts, while giving a monologue. She's wearing plant-like pasties.
• 0:32—Brief breasts, several times, while in the woods with the fairies. She has green colored skin and plant-looking pasties.
• 0:51—Brief breasts, while talking to Bottom (he's got a donkey head). Her hair gets in the way.
• 0:53—Breasts, while standing behind Bottom when he's talking with the other fairies. Plant-like pasties get in the way.
• 1:57—Brief breasts, covered with the plant-like pasties again, while walking around in the house.
A Study in Terror (1978; British) . . . . Sally
GoldenEye (1995; British/U.S.) . . . . M
Hamlet (1996). . . . . .Hecuba
Jack & Sarah (1996; British/French) . . . . .Margaret
Mrs. Brown (1997) . . . . Queen Victoria

Deneuve, Catherine *

Films:
The Umbrellas of Cherbourg (1964) . . . . Genevieve Emery
Repulsion (1965). . . . . .Carol
Belle de Jour (1968; French). Séverine
• 0:52—Very brief partial left breast, then buns under sheer black fabric, while walking around in house.
1:05—Brief partial right breast, while sitting on bed. Subtitles get in the way.
The April Fool's (1969) . . . . Catherine Gunther
Mississippi Mermaid (1969; French)
. . . . Julie Roussel/Marion Vergano
•• 1:04—Breasts, changing from a blouse to a sweater while standing up in parked car.
•• 1:26—Brief breasts, taking off her blouse in bedroom.
La Grande Bourgeoise (1974; Italian). . . . . Linda Murri
Hustle (1975) . . . . Nicole Britton
Lovers Like Us (1975). . . . . .Nelly
a.k.a. The Savage
• 1:06—Brief left upper half of left breast in bed with Yves Montand. Dark.
••• 1:09—Breasts sitting up in bed.
Zig-Zag (1975; French) . . . . Marie
The Last Metro (1980). . . . . Marion
Je Vous Aime (1981) . . . . Alice
a.k.a. I Love You All
A Choice of Arms (1983; French). . . . . .Nicole
The Hunger (1983). . . . . Miriam
• 0:08—Brief breasts taking a shower with David Bowie. Probably a body double, you don't see her face.
Love Song (1985) . . . . .Margaux
Scene of the Crime (1987; French) .Lili
Indochine (1992; French) . . . . Eliane
The Convent (1995; Portugese/French). . . . . Hélène

My Favorite Season (1995; French) . . . . Emilie
a.k.a. Ma Saison Préférée
Thieves (1996; French) . . . . Marie Leblanc
a.k.a. Les Voleurs

• *Denicourt, Marianne*

Films:
La Lectrice (1989; French). . . . . Bella
a.k.a. The Reader
La Belle Noiseuse (1992; French). . . . . .Julienne
Divertimento (1992; French). . . . . .Julienne
(A shorter, slightly re-edited version of *La Belle Noiseuse.*)
Innocent Lies (1995) . . . . Maud Graves
My Sex Life... Or How I Got Into an Argument (1996; French) . . . . Sylvia
- 0:30—Brief buns, breasts and lower frontal nudity when Paul opens the dressing room door.
- 1:08—Breasts, while lying in bed, getting up and talking with Paul.
- 2:49—(1:27 into tape 2) Brief full frontal nudity, while playing pick-up sticks.

Made for Cable Movies:
Doomsday Gun (1994; HBO) . . . . .Monique

Denier, Lydie

Films:
The Nightstalker (1987) . . . . First Victim
- ••• 0:03—Breasts making love with big guy.

Bulletproof (1988) . . . . .Tracy
- •• 0:14—Breasts in Gary Busey's bathtub.
- • 0:20—Brief buns, putting on shirt after getting out of bed. Very, very brief side view of left breast.

Midnight Cabaret (1988) . . . . .Woman in White
Paramedics (1988) . . . . Liette
Red Blooded American Girl (1988) . . . . . . .Rebecca Murrin
- ••• 0:00—Breasts in bed wearing panties, garter belt and stockings. Buns, rolling over. Long scene.

Blood Relations (1989; Canadian) . . . . Marie
- •• 0:07—Left breast making love with Thomas on stairway.
- • 0:44—Brief left breast in bed with Thomas' father. Very brief cuts of her breasts in B&W.
- ••• 0:54—Full frontal nudity undressing for the Grandfather.

Satan's Princess (1989) . . . . Nicole St. James
- • 0:27—Full frontal nudity, getting out of pool.
- ••• 0:28—Full frontal nudity, next to bed and in bed with Karen.
- ••• 0:45—Breasts and buns, making love in bed with Robert Forster.

No Place to Hide (1991). . . . . Pamela Hanley
- • 0:03—Breasts, after opening her ballet costume in the wings backstage before getting sliced up with a knife.

Invasion of Privacy (1992) . . . . .Vicky
(Unrated version reviewed.)
- • 0:54—Brief breasts in her apartment dancing in front of Robby Benson while he video tapes her.
- ••• 1:19—Breasts on top of Benson in bed.

Wild Orchid II: Two Shades of Blue (1992). . . . Dominique
- ••• 0:28—Breasts, undressing from lingerie while Blue and Elle watch.

Mardi Gras for the Devil (1993). . . . . .Valerie
- ••• 0:50—Breasts, while making love in bed with Robert Davi.

Guardian Angel (1994) . . . . Nina
1:00—Brief buns, behind shower door.

Perfect Alibi (1994) . . . . .Janine
- • 0:37—Very brief side of left breast and buns, while making love in bed on top of Keith when discovered by Kathleen Quinlan. Dark.
- • 0:45—Brief partial left breast, while making love in bed with Keith.

To the Limit (1995) . . . . Frannie
The Assault (1996). . . . . Sammy Jo
Made for Cable TV:
Red Shoe Diaries: Talk To Me Baby (1992; Showtime) . . . . Elaine
(Available on the video tape *Red Shoe Diaries 3: Another Woman's Lipstick.*)
- • 0:13—Brief left breast several times, making love in bed with Richard Tyson.
- •• 0:14—Breasts and buns, taking off robe to shower with Rita.

TV:
General Hospital . . . . Yasmine Bernoudi
Tarzan (1991-93). . . . . Jane

Denise, Denise

Films:
Lady Sings the Blues (1972). . . . . .n.a.
Fox Style (1974) . . . . Cindy
- • 0:42—Brief breasts rolling over on her stomach on river bank with A. J.
- • 1:21—Most of right breast, while in bed with A.J.

Doctor Death: Seeker of Souls (1975) . . . . . . Girl with Flat Tire

• *Deno, Mari*

Made for Cable Movies:
Breast Men (1997; HBO). . . . . Pleased First-Op Girl
- • 0:40—Slightly bruised breasts, when examining them for the first time after her implant operation.

Made for Cable TV:
Love Street: Uninhibited Island (1994; Showtime) . . . . . Winnie

Derek, Bo *

Real name is Cathleen Collins.
Wife of the late director/photographer/actor John Derek.
Films:
Fantasies (1974) . . . . Anastasia
a.k.a. Once Upon a Love
- • 0:03—Left breast, in bathtub.
- •• 0:15—Breasts taking off top, then right breast, in bathtub.
- • 0:43—Breasts getting her dress top pulled down.
- • 0:59—Brief breasts in the water. Very brief full frontal nudity walking back into the house.
- • 1:00—Buns and left breast several times outside the window.
- • 1:17—Upper left breast, in bathtub again.

Orca, The Killer Whale (1977) . . . . Annie
10 (1979) . . . . Jennifer Hanley
- • 1:29—Brief buns and breasts taking off towel and putting on robe when Moore visits her. Long shot, hard to see.
- • 1:36—Brief breasts taking off dress trying to seduce Moore. Dark, hard to see.
- • 1:37—Breasts, lying in bed. Dark, hard to see.
- •• 1:41—Breasts, going to fix the skipping record. Long shot, hard to see. Buns, while jumping back into bed.
- • 1:43—Breasts and buns, while sitting up in bed.
- • 1:44—Breasts and buns in bed when Moore gets out.

A Change of Seasons (1980) . . . . Lindsey Routledge
- •• 0:00—Breasts in hot tub during the opening credits.

- 0:25—Side view of left breast in the shower talking to Anthony Hopkins.

Tarzan, The Ape Man (1981) .... Jane
- ••• 0:43—Nude taking a bath in the ocean, then in a wet white dress.
- • 1:35—Brief breasts painted all white.
- • 1:45—Breasts washing all the white paint off in the river with Tarzan.
- •• 1:47—Breasts during the ending credits playing with Tarzan and the orangutan. (When I saw this film in a movie theater, the entire audience actually stayed to watch the credits!)

Bolero (1984) .... Ayre McGillvary
- • 0:04—Brief breasts, stripping to panties, outside after graduating from school.
- ••• 0:19—Breasts making love with Arabian guy covered with honey, messy.
- ••• 0:58—Breasts making love in bed with Angel.
- ••• 1:38—Breasts during fantasy love making session with Angel in fog.

Ghosts Can't Do It (1989) .... Kate
- ••• 0:26—In one piece swimsuit on beach, then full frontal nudity taking it off. Brief buns covered with sand on her back. Long scene.
- ••• 0:32—Breasts, sitting and washing herself. Very brief buns, jumping into tub.
- •• 0:48—Full frontal nudity taking a shower.
- • 0:49—Very, very brief breasts and buns jumping into pool. Long shot. Full frontal nudity under water.
- • 0:52—Very, very brief partial breasts pulling a guy into the pool
- •• 1:12—Breasts behind mosquito net with her boyfriend.

Hot Chocolate (1992) .... B.J. Cassidy
- • 0:30—Brief side view of right breast, while pulling sheets up on herself in bed.

Shattered Image (1993) .... Helen
- • 1:12—Breasts, under water in spa, while talking with Jack Scalia.

Woman of Desire (1993) .... Christina Ford
(Unrated version reviewed.)
- • 0:07—Very brief right breast, while turning over in bed with Steven Bauer.
- • 0:14—Breasts, in photo that a detective finds on boat.
- ••• 0:19—Breasts, while sunbathing on boat, then nude after taking off bikini bottoms and diving into the water.
- 0:33—Breasts, while getting out of bed. Seen in "flashback-vision."
- •• 0:40—Breasts, while taking off blouse and putting on leather jacket in front of Jeff Fahey.
- ••• 0:41—Breasts and buns while making love with Fahey on a motorcycle inside. Great!
- •• 0:51—Breasts, in shower with Fahey.
- • 0:57—Breasts on floor, while making love with Fahey.
- 1:07—Sort of breasts on boat while sunbathing. Seen in "flashback-vision."

Tommy Boy (1995) .... Beverly

Video Tapes:

Playboy Video Magazine, Volume 1 (1982) .... Herself
- • 0:02—Breasts in still photos.
- •• 0:56—Breasts in still photos.
- •• 0:57—Breasts in scenes from *Fantasies.*
- •• 0:58—Breasts in still photos.

Dern, Laura

Daughter of actor Bruce Dern and actress Diane Ladd.

Films:

Alice Doesn't Live Here Anymore (1975)
.... Uncredited Girl with Ice Cream

Foxes (1980) .... Debbie

Ladies and Gentlemen, The Fabulous Stains (1982)
.... Jessica McNeil
(Not available on video tape.)

Teachers (1984) .... Diane

Mask (1985) .... Diana

Smooth Talk (1985) .... Connie

Blue Velvet (1986) .... Sandy Williams

Fat Man and Little Boy (1989) .... Kathleen Robinson

Wild at Heart (1990) .... Lula
- ••• 0:07—Breasts putting on black halter top.
- •• 0:26—Left breast, then breasts sitting on Nicolas Cage's lap in bed.
- •• 0:35—Breasts wriggling around in bed with Cage.
- • 0:41—Brief breasts several times making love with Cage. Hard to see because it keeps going overexposed. Great moaning, though.

Rambling Rose (1991) .... Rose
- •• 0:23—Right breast several times, while lying on bench with Robert Duvall while Lucas Haas peeks in.
- •• 1:16—Brief right breast, twice, when sheet drops while talking with Duvall in bedroom.

Jurassic Park (1993) .... Ellie Sattler

A Perfect World (1993) .... Sally Gerber

Citizen Ruth (1996) .... Ruth Stoops

Made for Cable Movies:

Afterburn (1992; HBO) .... Janet Harduvel

Down Came a Blackbird (1995; Showtime)
.... Helen McNulty
- • 0:40—Very, very brief partial left breast, while under water in a pool in flashback. B&W.
- • 1:21—Very brief breasts, while being pushed into a swimming pool, blindfolded and tied by wrists.
- • 1:23—Very, very brief breasts, while diving under the water to get Jan.

Made for Cable TV:

Fallen Angels: Murder, Obliquely (1993; Showtime)
.... Annie Ainsley
(Available on the video tape *Fallen Angels One.*)

Made for TV Movies:

Happy Endings (1983) .... Audrey Constantine

The Three Wishes of Billy Grier (1984) .... n.a.

Derval, Lamya

Films:

The Lonely Guy (1983) ...... One of "The Seven Deadly Sins"

Hellhole (1985) .... Jacuzzi Girl
- ••• 1:08—Breasts (she's on the right) sniffing glue in closet with another woman.
- ••• 1:12—Full frontal nudity in Jacuzzi room with Mary Woronov.

Howling IV: The Original Nightmare (1988) ...... Elanor
- •• 0:32—Brief left breast, then breasts making love with Richard. Nice silhouette on the wall.

Descombes, Colette

Films:

Unsatisfied (1964; Spanish) .... Suzanne

Paranoia (1969; Italian/French) .... Eva
- ••• 0:45—Breasts in bed with Peter, twice, when discovered by Carroll Baker.

- • 0:49—Brief left breast and upper half of right breast.
- ••• 0:50—Left breast, then breasts while sleeping in bed when Baker wakes up. Lit with red light.
- ••• 0:52—Right breast, while in bed with Baker.
- •• 1:02—Brief breasts while sleeping in bed with Peter.
- ••• 1:19—Breasts in bed with Peter, buns while getting out of bed.
- •• 1:22—Breasts in bed while sleeping.

Deshayes, Marie-Christine *

Films:

The French Woman (1979) .... Florence

a.k.a. Madame Claude

- •• 0:45—Breasts on bed dressed as a guy with a man dressed as a woman.

Desmond, Donna

Films:

Tender Loving Care (1974) .... Karen Jordan

- ••• 0:26—Breasts on waterbed with Reno, brief lower frontal nudity, making love. Long scene.
- • 0:39—Breasts and very brief buns getting out of bed.
- •• 0:55—Brief buns and breasts on bed with Dr. Traynor.

The Black Gestapo (1975) .... White Whore

Fugitive Girls (1975) .... n.a.

The Naughty Stewardesses (1978) .... Margie

a.k.a. Fresh Air

- •• 0:12—Breasts, while leaning out of the shower.

Detmers, Maruschka *

Films:

First Name: Carmen (1983; French) .... Carmen

- ••• 0:36—Breasts while standing by window with a guy.
- •• 0:40—Breasts several times while in bedroom with Joseph.
- • 0:42—Lower frontal nudity (out of focus) while talking to Joseph. Long scene.
- • 0:44—Brief lower frontal nudity with Joseph.
- • 0:46—More lower frontal nudity.
- •• 0:58—Nude, after Joseph takes off her robe.
- •• 1:07—Breasts while undressing in bedroom.
- ••• 1:08—Breasts in red panties, getting out of bed and walking through the house, sitting on couch and lying on bed. Long scene.
- •• 1:13—Brief full frontal nudity in bathroom and in shower.

Devil in the Flesh (1986; French/Italian) ...... Giulia Dozza

- • 0:20—Very brief side view of left breast and buns going past open door way to get a robe.
- ••• 0:27—Nude, talking to Andrea's dad in his office.
- • 0:55—Breasts putting a robe on. Dark.
- • 0:57—Breasts and buns in bedroom with Andrea.
- •• 1:09—Breasts in hallway with Andrea.
- ••• 1:22—Full frontal nudity holding keys for Andrea to see, brief buns.
- • 1:42—Lower frontal nudity, while dancing in living room in red robe.

Hanna's War (1988)........................ Hanna Senesh

The Mambo Kings (1992) .... Dolores Fuentes

- •• 0:47—Breasts several times, making love in bed with Antonio Banderas.

Hidden Assassin (1994) .... Simone Rosset

- •• 0:48—In black bra and panties, then breasts, getting into bathtub in front of Dolph Lundgren.

Devine, Loretta

Films:

Little Nikita (1988).................... Verna McLaughlin

- • 1:03—Very brief left breast in bed after Sidney Poitier jumps out of bed when River Phoenix bursts into their bedroom.

Sticky Fingers (1988) .... Diane

Stanley and Iris (1990)........................... Bertha

Livin' Large (1991)......................... Nadine Biggs

Caged Fear (1992)................................. Judy

Class Act (1992) .... Blade's Mom

Amos & Andrew (1993)............................. Ula

The Hard Truth (1994).................. Nichols' Secretary

Waiting to Exhale (1995) .... Gloria

Hoodlum (1997) .... Pigfoot Mary

Made for Cable Movies:

Clover (1997; USA) .... Everleen

Don King: Only in America (1997; HBO) ...... Connie Harper

TV:

A Different World (1987-88) .... Stevie Rallen

Sugar and Spice (1990).................. Loretta Fontaine

• Devos, Emmanuelle

Films:

My Sex Life... Or How I Got Into an Argument (1996; French)................................ Esther

- • 0:25—Very, very brief partial right breast, when reaching up to kiss Paul.
- •• 0:46—Brief breasts, when pulling her blouse and bra up in photo booth for Paul.
- • 0:47—Brief breasts in developed photograph.
- • 2:41—(1:19 into tape 2) Brief full frontal nudity while in the shower.

Artemisia (1997; French) .... Costanza

Dey, Neela

Films:

My First Wife (1985; Australian)............ Migrant Teacher

Naked Country (1985; Australian) .... Menyan

- • 0:27—Breasts when meeting Mary and Lance.
- •• 0:28—Breasts during wedding ceremony.
- • 1:03—Brief left breast, while on top of cliff.
- • 1:11—Very, very brief breasts during struggle in cave.

Dey, Susan *

Films:

Skyjacked (1972).......................... Elly Brewster

First Love (1977)..................... Caroline Hedges

- ••• 0:31—Breasts making love in bed with William Katt. Long scene.
- • 0:51—Breasts taking off her top in her bedroom with Katt.

Looker (1981) .... Cindy

- • 0:36—Buns, then brief breasts in computer imaging device. Breasts in computer monitor.

Echo Park (1986).................... Meg "May" Greer

- • 1:17—Brief glimpse of right breast, while doing a strip tease at a party.

The Trouble with Dick (1986) .... Diane

Bed of Lies (1992) .... Vickie Daniel

Made for Cable Movies:

Deadly Love (1995; Lifetime)............... Rebecca Barnes

Made for TV Movies:

Cage Without a Key (1975) .... n.a.

The Gift of Life (1982) .... Jolee Sutton

Sunset Limousine (1983) .... Julie

Lies and Lullabies (1993) .... Christina Kinsey

Whose Child Is This? The War for Baby Jessica (1993) . . . . Roberta DeBoer
Beyond Betrayal (1994). . . . . Joanna/Emma Doyle
Blue River (1995) . . . . Mrs. Sellers
Bridge of Time (1997). . . . . Madeleine Armstrong

TV:

The Partridge Family (1970-74). . . . . Laurie Partridge
Loves Me, Loves Me Not (1977) . . . . Jane
Emerald Point N.A.S. (1983-84) . . . . Celia Mallory Warren
L.A. Law (1986-92) . . . . Dep. D.A. Grace Van Owen
Love & War (1992-93) . . . . Wallis "Wally" Porter

di Lorenzo, Anneka *

Real name is Marjorie Thoreson.

Films:

Act of Vengeance (1974). . . . . Chris
a.k.a. The Rape Squad
(Not to be confused with the film with the same name starring Charles Bronson.)
••• 1:07—Buns and breasts, getting dressed in house. Seen from outside through simulated camera viewfinder.

The Centerfold Girls (1974). . . . . Pam

Caligula (1980). . . . . Messalina
(X-rated, 147 minute version.)
••• 1:16—Nude, making love with Lori Wagner. Long scene.

Video Tapes:

Penthouse: On the Wild Side (1988). . . . . Messalina
• 0:54—Nude with Lori Wagner during scenes from *The Making of Caligula.*

Di'Lazzaro, Dalila *

Films:

Andy Warhol's Frankenstein (1974; Italian/German/French) . . . . The Girl
•• 0:09—Breasts lying on platform in the lab.
• 0:37—Close up of left breast while the Count cuts her stitches. (Pretty bloody.)
• 0:43—Breasts, while strapped to table, covered with blood.
• 0:49—Breasts, while on table, all wired up.
• 1:03—Right breast lying on table. Long shot.
• 1:05—More right breast, long shot.
•• 1:06—More breasts on table, then standing in the lab.
•• 1:20—Brief right breast when Otto pulls her top down.
•• 1:23—Breasts on table again, then walking around. (Scar on chest.) Lower frontal nudity when Otto pulls her bandage down, then gross breasts when he removes her guts.

The Last Romantic Lover (1978) . . . . n.a.
Creepers (1985; Italian). . . . . Headmistress
Miss Right (1987; Italian) . . . . Art Student

Dial, Nikki *

Adult film actress.
a.k.a. Nicole Greiner.

Adult Films:

Endlessly (1993) . . . . n.a.

Video Tapes:

Big Bust Casting Call (1992). . . . . Roxanne
••• 0:09—In bra and panties, then nude during her audition.

The Lover's Guide to Sexual Ecstasy: A Sensual Guide to Lovemaking (1992) . . . . Advanced Foreplay
••• 0:25—In white bra, then nude, while making love with her lover.
••• 0:32—Breasts, while making love.
••• 0:36—Nude, while making love in bed in various positions.
••• 0:48—In white bra, then breasts and buns, in female superior positions.

Penthouse Pet of the Year Playoff 1992 (1992) . . . . Model
(Although listed in the credits, her part was cut in the final video tape.)

Intimate Secrets—How Women Love to be Loved (1993) . . . . Nicole
••• 0:13—In white bra and red panties, then full frontal nudity on couch.

Penthouse Pet of the Year Winners 1993: Mahalia & Julie (1994) . . . . Uncredited Cast Member
••• 0:18—Nude, while acting submissive to Mahalia. Wearing sunglasses.

Diamond, Michelle *

Video Tapes:

Playboy's College Girls (1994) . . . . Herself
••• 0:11—Nude, while posing on a grand piano.

Diaz, Maria

Films:

Fists of Iron (1994) . . . . Michelle
From Dusk Till Dawn (1995) . . . . Bar Dancer

Showgirls (1995) . . . . Yoga Dancer
(NC-17 version reviewed.)
••• 0:40—Breasts while dancing during final audition with Elizabeth Berkley and another dancer.

Extramarital (1998) . . . . Ann
•• 0:13—Brief back side of left breast after taking off bra. Breasts and partial buns, while making love with Bob (wearing a mask) in bed.
• 0:15—Brief full frontal nudity, when talking to Bob in bed afterwards.
• 0:28—Buns in lingerie.

Made for Cable Movies:

The Fear Inside (1992; Showtime) . . . . Reporter

Dick, Gina

Films:

Happy Birthday to Me (1980; Canadian) . . . . Waitress
Middle Age Crazy (1980; Canadian) . . . . Linda McAllister
Suzanne (1980; Canadian) . . . . Marilyn
My Bloody Valentine (1981; Canadian) . . . . Gretchen
Ticket to Heaven (1981; Canadian) . . . . Sandy

The Killer Instinct (1982; Canadian) . . . . Diana
a.k.a. Trapped
•• 1:15—Breasts, after Henry Silva rips her blouse open to taunt Nicholas Campbell.

TV:

High Hopes (1978; Canadian) . . . . Amy Sperry

• *Dickens, Kim*

Films:

Palookaville (1996) . . . . Laurie
Great Expectations (1997). . . . . Maggie

Truth or Consequences, N.M. (1997). . . . . . . Addy Monroe
• 1:24—Breasts, while making love in bed under Ray.

Zero Effect (1997). . . . . Gloria Sullivan

Dickerson, Pamela

Films:

I Like to Play Games (1994) . . . . Melody
• 0:00—Partial left breast, when getting fondled by Michael while playing chess.
0:01—Breasts, while on bed after taking off her dress for Michael.

Hourglass (1995). . . . . Model
Overkill (1995) . . . . Catherine Howard

Dickinson, Angie *

Ex-wife of songwriter Burt Bacharach.

Films:

Rio Bravo (1959) . . . . Feathers
Ocean's Eleven (1960). . . . . Beatrice Ocean
Cast a Giant Shadow (1966) . . . . Emma Marcus
The Chase (1966) . . . . Ruby Calder
Point Blank (1967). . . . . Chris
- • 0:51—Breasts in background putting dress on. Kind of a long shot.

Pretty Maids All in a Row (1971). . . . . Miss Smith
- • 1:04—Buns, in long shot, while lying on bed with Ponce.

Big Bad Mama (1974) . . . . Wilma McClatchie
- • 0:38—Buns, getting into bed with Tom Skerritt. Brief right breast, while on top of him.
- ••• 0:48—Breasts in bed with William Shatner.
- • 1:00—Very brief breasts, pulling the sheets up while lying in bed with Shatner.
- ••• 1:18—Breasts and brief full frontal nudity putting a shawl and then a dress on.

Dressed to Kill (1980) . . . . Kate Miller
- • 0:01—Brief side view behind shower door. Long shot, hard to see.
- 0:02—Frontal nude scene in shower is a body double, Victoria Lynn Johnson.
- • 0:24—Brief buns getting out of bed after coming home from museum with a stranger.

Klondike Fever (1980) . . . . Belinda McNair
Charlie Chan & the Curse of the Dragon Queen (1981) . . . . Dragon Queen
Death Hunt (1981) . . . . Vanessa
Big Bad Mama II (1987). . . . . Wilma McClatchie
- • 0:48—Very brief full frontal nudity putting on her shawl scene from *Big Bad Mama* superimposed over a car chase scene.
- •• 0:52—Breasts and brief buns (probably a body double) in bed with Robert Culp. You don't see her face with the body.

Even Cowgirls Get the Blues (1994). . . . . Miss Adrian
The Maddening (1995). . . . . Georgina Scudder
Sabrina (1995) . . . . Ingrid Tyson

Made for Cable Movies:

Treacherous Crossing (1992; USA). . . . . Beverly

Miniseries:

Pearl (1978) . . . . Midge
Hollywood Wives (1988) . . . . Sadie La Salle
Wild Palms (1993). . . . . Josie Ito

Made for TV Movies:

A Touch of Scandal (1984) . . . . Katherine Gilvey
Once Upon a Texas Train (1988) . . . . Maggie
Danielle Steel's "Rememberance" (1996) . . Margaret Fullerton

TV:

Police Woman (1974-78). . . . Sgt. Suzanne "Pepper" Anderson
Cassie and Company (1982) . . . . Cassie Holland

Dietrich, Cindi

Films:

The Man Who Loved Women (1983) . . . . Darla
Out of Control (1984) . . . . Robin
- • 0:29—Breasts taking off her red top. Long shot.

St. Elmo's Fire (1985) . . . . Flirt
Death Spa (1987) . . . . Linda
Made in U.S.A. (1988). . . . . Girl in Trans-Am

Made for TV Movies:

Mistress (1987) . . . . Rachel

Digard, Uschi *

Films:

Cherry, Harry & Raquel (1969) . . . . Soul
The Scavengers (1969) . . . . Lucile
The Beauties and the Beast (1973) . . . . Mary
Supervixens (1973) . . . . SuperSoul
Truck Stop Women (1974) . . . . Truck Stop Woman
- •• 0:18—Breasts getting arrested in the parking lot by the police officer, then buns and breasts getting frisked in a room.

Chesty Anderson, U.S. Navy (1975). . . . . . Baron's Girlfriend #1
The Killer Elite (1975) . . . . Uncredited Party Girl
- • 0:00—Brief right breast, while sitting in front of Robert Duvall at a party. Long shot. Continuity error: Note the next time you see her, the blouse is closed!

Fantasm (1976; Australian) . . . . Super Girl
The Kentucky Fried Movie (1977) . . . . . Woman in Shower
- •• 0:09—Breasts while getting them massaged in the shower, then squished breasts against the shower door.

Superchick (1978). . . . . Mayday
- ••• 0:42—Buns and breasts getting whipped acting during the making of a film, then talking to three people.

Beneath the Valley of the Ultravixens (1979) . . . . SuperSoul
If You Don't Stop It You'll Go Blind (1979) . . . . Various Characters
- •• 0:02—Breasts in bed and closets during opening credits.
- • 0:03—Breasts, pulling up her T-shirt during beginning credits.
- • 0:23—Brief breasts raising her hand in classroom.
- ••• 0:26—Breasts, while showing them to a guy and letting him feel them.
- • 0:36—Brief upper half of left breast, when it sticks out of her dress.
- ••• 0:52—Full frontal nudity (Contestant #1) on bed, waiting for Omar.
- •• 1:17—Breasts in class during end credits.

The Best of Sex and Violence (1981) . . . Truck Stop Woman
- • 0:47—Breasts getting chased by policeman in parking lot in scene from *Truck Stop Women.*

Famous T & A (1982) . . . . Truck Stop Woman
(No longer available for purchase, check your video store for rental.)
- •• 0:44—Breasts scenes from *Cherry, Harry & Raquel* and *Truck Stop Women.*

Dijkhuizen, Angelique *

Video Tapes:

Playboy International Playmates (1993) . . . . . . Angelique
- ••• 0:11—Full frontal nudity in still photos.
- ••• 0:12—Breasts undressing in bedroom and trying on lingerie and other clothing during cat burglar segment.
- ••• 0:50—Full frontal nudity in old castle.

Dillard, Victoria *

Films:

Coming to America (1988) . . . . Bather
- •• 0:04—Breasts, standing up in royal bathtub to announce "The royal penis is clean, Your Highness."

Internal Affairs (1990) . . . . Kee
Ricochet (1991). . . . . Alice
Deep Cover (1992) . . . . Betty
- • 0:52—Brief breasts, taking off her blouse to make love with Larry Fishburne.

The Glass Shield (1994). . . . . Barbara Simms
Killing Obsession (1994) . . . . Jean Wilson

Out of Sync (1995) . . . . Monica Collins
•• 1:24—Breasts and buns, taking off her swimsuit and showering.
Made for Cable Movies:
The Ditchdigger's Daughters (1997; Family) . . . . Tass
Made for Cable TV:
Statistically Speaking... (1995; Showtime). . . . . .Waitress
TV:
Spin City (1996-) . . . . Janelle

Dillaway, Denise

Films:
The Cheerleaders (1973). . . . . Claudia
• 0:08—Brief right breast, while in the car wash with Jon.
••• 0:23—Breasts and buns, while fooling around with Coach Gannon.
•• 0:28—Brief breasts with the other cheerleaders in locker room.
•• 0:49—Nude, while struggling on the ground with Sal outside.
• 0:56—Partial buns and partial breasts under sheer nightie.
• 1:13—Breasts, with the other cheerleaders in back seat at carwash.
Made for TV Movies:
Nightmare in Badham County (1976). . . . . Inmate
(Nudity added for video tape.)

Dillon, Melinda

Films:
Bound For Glory (1976) .Mary Guthrie
Close Encounters of the Third Kind (1977) . . . . . . .Jillian Guiler
Slap Shot (1977). . . . . Suzanne
••• 0:30—Right breast, lying in bed with Paul Newman, then breasts sitting up and talking. Nice, long scene.
F.I.S.T. (1978) . . . . Anna Zerinkas
Absence of Malice (1981) . . . . Teresa
A Christmas Story (1983) . . . . Mrs. Parker
Songwriter (1984). . . . . Honey Carder
Harry and the Hendersons (1987) . . . . Nancy Henderson
Spontaneous Combustion (1989) . . . . Nina
Staying Together (1989) . . . . Eileen McDermott
Captain America (1990) . . . . .Mrs. Rogers
The Prince of Tides (1991) . . . . Savannah Wingo
Sioux City (1994) . . . . .Leah Goldman
How to Make an American Quilt (1995) . . . . Mrs. Darling
To Wong Foo, Thanks for Everything! Julie Newmar (1995)
. . . . Merna
Entertaining Angels: The Dorothy Day Story (1996)
. . . . Sister Aloysius
Made for Cable Movies:
Nightbreaker (1989) . . . . Paula Brown
State of Emergency (1993; HBO) . . . . .Mrs. Anderson
Miniseries:
Space (1987) . . . . Rachel Mott
Made for TV Movies:
Shattered Spirits (1986) . . . . .Joyce Mollencamp
Judgment Day: The John List Story (1993) . . . . Eleanor
Confessions: Two Faces of Evil (1994) . . . . n.a.
Naomi & Wynonna: Love Can Build a Bridge (1995)
. . . . Polly Judd

Dion, Jami *

a.k.a. Dahlia Grey.
Adult Films:
Hidden Obsessions (1993). . . . . Bodyscapes
Wet (1998) . . . . n.a.
Films:
Sex & Money (1994). . . . . Bettina
••• 0:14—Nude, while posing.
••• 0:16—In tub with Taylor.
••• 0:31—Posing by herself.
Video Tapes:
Penthouse Satin & Lace II: Hollywood Undercover (1992). . . . . Pet
The Penthouse All-Pet Workout (1993) . . . . Pet
•• 0:00—Nude during introduction.
•• 0:03—Briefly nude, while getting undressed and suited up.
••• 0:28—Nude outside on sculpture and next to fence.
••• 0:43—Nude with the other girls, exercising, working with equipment, in the pool and spa.
Penthouse Pet of the Year Playoff 1993 (1993) . . . . . Pet
••• 0:01—Nude in house, on the beach, on bed, with an old T-bird.
Penthouse Pet of the Year Winners 1993: Mahalia & Julie (1994) . . . . Sneak Preview of Pet of the Year Playoff
••• 0:30—Nude while posing around a house.
The Girls of Penthouse, Volume 3 (1995). . . . . Pet
••• 0:01—Nude in still photos.
••• 0:02—Nude in motel.
••• 0:05—Nude outside and in a studio.
CD-ROM:
Penthouse Interactive Virtual Photo Shoot, Disc 3 (1993). . . . . Pet

Dionisio, Silvia

Films:
Andy Warhol's Dracula (1974; French/Italian) . . . . Perla
Fear (1980; French/Italian) . . . . Deborah
• 0:18—Brief breasts, while making out with Michael on the sofa.
• 0:32—Left breast in open sheer robe, while running from a hooded figure.
• 0:35—Breasts in open robe outside in the woods.
•• 0:38—Breasts, after her gown is ripped off while she's tied by her wrists.

Ditmar, Marita

Films:
Auditions (1978). . . . . Frieda Volker
•• 1:05—Breasts and partial buns with another woman and a guy.
Fairytales (1979). . . . . .S & M Dancer
• 0:38—Breasts wearing masks with two other S&M Dancers.

Divina, Guadalupe *

Video Tapes:
Playboy's Girls of Radio: Talk, Rock and Shock (1995)
. . . . Herself
••• 0:16—In pink slip, then nude with four other women.

Dix, Sophie

Films:
The Advocate (1993; British/French) . . . . Maria
a.k.a. The Hour of the Pig
••• 0:32—In nightgown, then nude, after taking it off and making love on top of Colin Firth in bed.
Second Best (1994) . . . . .Mary
Miniseries:
The Buccaneers (1995; U.S./British). . . . . Lady Honoria

Dobkin, Kaela

Films:

Kicking and Screaming (1995). . . . . Audra
- 1:04—Breasts, while sitting on bed, listening to a guy in dorm room. Medium long shot.
- 1:05—Brief breasts, while walking around in the dorm room.

Made for Cable TV:

Women: Stories of Passion-Blind Love (1996; Showtime) . . . . May
- 0:02—Partial left breast, then brief breasts, when opening her blouse while on stage during marionette routine.
- •• 0:08—Breasts, while lying on bed, during phone sex with Nick Corri.
- ••• 0:18—Breasts, while making love with Corri in hotel room when she's blindfolded.
- •• 0:22—Breasts, getting out of bed after taking off her blindfold.

TV:

Models Inc. (1994-95). . . . . Kristy

Dobrowolska, Gosia

Films:

Silver City (1985; Australian). . . . . Nina

A Woman's Tale (1991; Australian). . . . . .Anna
- 0:29—Brief breasts, while putting on blouse when standing at the door.

Careful (1992; Canadian) . . . . .Zenaida

The Custodian (1993) . . . . Josie

Resistance (1994; Australian). . . . . .Mrs. Wilson

Dockery, Erika

Films:

Basic Training (1984). . . . . Salesgirl 2
- 0:00—Brief breasts, whlie standing behind the desk.

Hardbodies (1984) . . . . Hardbody in Car

Doda, Carol

Films:

Head (1968) . . . . Sally Silicone

Honky Tonk Nights (1978) . . . . Belle Barnette
- ••• 0:17—Breasts changing blouses in bedroom with Doris Ann.
- 0:28—Left breast several times while making out with a guy.
- ••• 1:11—Breasts in bedroom with Doris Ann during flashback. (Different camera angle than 0:17.)

Video Tapes:

Playboy Video Magazine, Volume 3 (1983) . . . . Carol Doda A San Francisco Monument
- 0:22—Breasts in B&W before-silicone-injection photo (35 1/2-inch bust).
- •• 0:23—Breasts in B&W after-silicone-injection photo. (44-inch bust). Breasts while dancing on stage.
- 0:24—Brief breasts and buns, on stage in The Condor Club during her act.
- ••• 0:25—Breasts and buns in G-string. Lit with red light.
- ••• 0:26—Nude, taking off her clothes and running outside in a park. More breasts, on piano in The Condor Club.

Doherty, Shannen *

Ex-wife of actor/singer Ashley Hamilton (Son of actor George Hamilton and former wife Alana).

Films:

Night Shift (1982). . . . . Bluebird

Girls Just Want to Have Fun (1985) . . . . .Maggie Malene

Heathers (1989). . . . . Heather Duke

Almost Dead (1993) . . . . Katherine

Blindfold: Acts of Obsession (1993). . . . . Madeleine Dalton (The close-up shots of breasts where you don't see her face are body double shots.)
- ••• 0:07—Breasts, while making love.
- •• 0:08—Breasts while making love in the shower with Mike.
- ••• 0:21—Breasts, in bed, while making love with Mike.
- •• 0:39—Breasts, during photo session with pillows while posing for Mike. More breast flashes while in bed.
- 1:06—In black bra on desk in Judd Nelson's office. Brief, partial right breast, when he caresses it.

Mallrats (1995) . . . . Rene

Made for Cable Movies:

Rebel Highway: Jailbreakers (1994; Showtime) . . . . Angel

Made for TV Movies:

Obsessed (1992) . . . . Lorie Brindel

A Burning Passion: The Margaret Mitchell Story (1994) . . . . .Margaret Mitchell

Gone in the Night (1996) . . . . Cyndi Dowaliby

Friends 'til the End (1997) . . . . Heather Romley

Sleeping with the Devil (1997) . . . . .Rebecca Dubrovich

TV:

Little House: A New Begining (1982-83) . . . . Jenny Wilder

Our House (1986-88) . . . . Kris Witherspoon

Beverly Hills, 90210 (1990-94). . . . . Brenda Walsh

Dollarhide, April Dawn

Films:

Party Favors (1987) . . . . .n.a.

Caged Fury (1989) . . . . Rhonda Wallace
- 0:54—Briefly nude, after dropping towel and joining Kat in the showers.

Warlords 3000 (1992) . . . . Terrified Girl
- 0:11—Breasts, while struggling in room with bad guys who are trying to rape her.

Dombasle, Arielle *

Films:

Tess (1979; French/British). . . . . .Mercy Chant

The Story of "O" Continues (1981; French) . . . . . . Nathalie

a.k.a. Les Fruits de la Passion
- 0:17—Brief left breast, lying on her stomach in bed with Klaus Kinski.
- ••• 0:40—Full frontal nudity on bed, making love in front of O.
- 1:00—Very, very brief left breast, while grabbing her blouse out of Kinski's hands.

Le Beau Mariage (1982; French) . . . . Clarisse

Pauline at the Beach (1983; French) . . . . Marion
- 0:24—Brief breasts lying in bed with a guy when her cousin looks in the window.
- •• 0:43—Brief breasts in house kissing Henri, while he takes her white dress off.
- •• 0:59—Breasts walking down the stairs in a white bikini bottom while putting a white blouse on.

The Boss' Wife (1986) . . . . Mrs. Louise Roalvang
- 1:01—Brief breasts getting a massage by the swimming pool.
- ••• 1:07—Breasts trying to seduce Daniel Stern at her place.
- •• 1:14—Brief breasts in Stern's shower.

Trade Secrets (1989; French) . . . . Marguerite

Twisted Obsession (1990) . . . . Marion Derain

Celestial Clockwork (1993; French/Portugese) . . . . Celeste

a.k.a. Mecánicas celestes

Three Lives and Only One Death (1997) . . . . Helene

a.k.a. Trois Vies et Une Selue Mort

Made for Cable TV:
Red Shoe Diaries: Like Father, Like Son (1994; Showtime) . . . . Celeste
•• 0:04—In black bra, then breasts, while making love on bed with Jean-Claude. Then nude, getting out of bed and putting on robe.
• 0:06—Brief right breast, in gaping robe while cleaning up spilled bath water.
• 0:07—Very brief breasts, while wrapping robe around herself.
• 0:08—Very brief breasts, in Jamie's flashback while lying on the bed with Jenna.
• 0:10—Very brief right breast, then brief breasts, in more flashbacks.
0:14—In sheer nightgown in bedroom with Jamie.
••• 0:15—Breasts, while making love with Jamie on the bedroom floor.
Miniseries:
Lace II (1985) . . . . Maxine

Dommartin, Solveig

Films:
Wings of Desire (1987) . . . . Marion
a.k.a. Der Himmel Uber Berlin
• 0:34—Brief side of left breast, while putting robe on. (The film changes from B&W to color.)
Until the End of the World (1991) . . . . Claire Tourneur
••• 0:34—Left breast, then breasts, then full frontal nudity in bedroom with William Hurt and Winter.
Faraway, So Close (1993; German) . . . . Marion
a.k.a. In weiter Ferne, so nah!

Doná, Linda

Films:
Worth Winning (1989) . . . . Lady at the Paddock
Summer Dreams: The Story of the Beach Boys (1990) . . . . Karen Lamm
(Originally a made for TV movie.)
• 1:06—Silhouette of breasts while making love with Dennis Wilson.
Final Embrace (1991) . . . . Jeri
Future Kick (1991) . . . . Tye
Ricochet (1991) . . . . Wanda
•• 1:03—Breasts, undoing her dress, then buns, getting on bed to make love with Denzel Washington while he's drugged.
• 1:16—Buns, on top of Washington during video playback.
Switch (1991) . . . . Gay Club Patron
Delta Heat (1992) . . . . Tine Tulane
Showdown (1993) . . . . Kate
In the Heat of Passion II: Unfaithful (1994) . . . . . . Bartender #2
a.k.a. Behind Closed Doors
Made for Cable Movies:
Dead Solid Perfect (1988; HBO) . . . . Blonde
Made for Cable TV:
Dream On: One Ball, Two Strikes (1993; HBO). . . .Alannah
• 0:05—Very brief breasts in utility closet while making love with Martin.
•• 0:18—Breasts with Martin in his apartment.
••• 0:23—Breasts, while lying in bed with Martin.
Dream On: Take Two Tablets, And Get Me to Mt. Sinai (1995; HBO) . . . . Martin's Lover
Made for TV Movies:
In the Arms of a Killer (1992) . . . . Chrissy
TV:
General Hospital . . . . .Nancy Eckert

Donahoe, Terry

TV:
Sonny Spoon (1988) . . . . .Asst. D.A. Carolyn Gilder
Video Tapes:
Eden 2 (1992) . . . . Juliet
••• 0:57—Breasts in bed making love with Paul and after getting interrupted.

*Donatacci, Camille **

Wife of actor Kelsey Grammer.
Films:
Marilyn Chambers' Bedtime Stories (1993) . . . . Angelique
••• 0:34—Breasts and buns while changing lingerie in bedroom.
••• 0:42—Breasts, while making love with Chris on sofa.
••• 0:55—In pink bra and panties then right breast and buns in Chris' bedroom.
Private Parts (1997) . . . . .Bikini Girl in Westchester
Made for Cable TV:
Club MTV (1987-91; MTV) . . . . Dancer

*Donley, Kimberly **

Video Tapes:
Playboy Video Calendar 1994 (1993) . . . . .December
••• 0:47—Nude, while dancing in a studio with a black and white color theme.
••• 0:49—Nude, while on bed.
Playboy's Sexy, Steamy, Sultry (1993). . . . . .Playmate
Playboy's 21 Playmates (1996). . . . . .Playmate
••• 0:18—Nude in still photos.
••• 0:19—Nude in house.

Donnelly, Patrice

Films:
Personal Best (1982) . . . . Tory Skinner
•• 0:17—Nude after making love with Mariel Hemingway.
••• 0:31—Full frontal nudity in steam room with the other women.
• 1:03—Very brief right breast in open blouse and partial lower frontal nudity while getting into bed with Hemingway.
•• 1:10—Nude, while in the steam room with the other women again.
American Anthem (1987) . . . . Danielle
Made for Cable Movies:
The Celluloid Closet (1996; HBO) . . . . Tory Skinner
• 1:20—Brief buns, then breasts in clips from *Personal Best*.

*Donohoe, Amanda **

Wife of director Nicholas Broomfield.
Films:
Castaway (1986). . . . . Lucy Irvine
(Nude a lot, only the best are listed.)
••• 0:22—Breasts talking to Reed.
•• 0:32—Nude on beach after helicopter leaves.
•• 0:48—Full frontal nudity lying on her back on the rocks at the beach.
••• 0:51—Breasts on rock when Reed takes a blue sheet off her, then catching a shark.
••• 0:54—Nude yelling at Reed at the campsite, then walking around looking for him.
••• 1:01—Breasts getting seafood out of a tide pool.
•• 1:03—Breasts lying down at night talking with Reed in the moonlight.
••• 1:18—Breasts taking off bathing suit top after the visitors leave, then arguing with Reed.

Foreign Body (1986; British) .... Susan
- 0:37—Undressing in her bedroom down to lingerie. Very brief side view of right breast, then brief left breast putting blouse on.
- •• 0:40—Breasts opening her blouse for Ram.

The Lair of the White Worm (1988; British) .... Lady Sylvia Marsh
(Wears short black hair in this film.)
- 0:52—Nude, opening a tanning table and turning over.
- 0:57—Brief left breast licking the blood off a phallic-looking thing.
- 1:19—Brief breasts jumping out to attack Angus, then walking around her underground lair (her body is painted for the rest of the film).
- 1:22—Breasts walking up steps with a large phallic thing strapped to her body.

Dark Obsession (1989; British) .... Ginny
a.k.a. Diamond Skulls
- •• 0:01—Breasts getting felt by a pair of hands.
- ••• 0:41—Left breast, breasts, brief lower frontal nudity while making love with Gabriel Byrne.
- 0:47—In black bra and panties, then full frontal nudity getting into tub. Right breast while sitting in the tub.

Double Cross (1989) .... n.a.

The Rainbow (1989) .... Winifred Inger
- ••• 0:21—Nude with Sammi Davis undressing, running outside in the rain, jumping into the water, then talking by the fireplace.
- ••• 0:43—Full frontal nudity taking off nightgown and getting into bed with Davis, then right breast.
- ••• 1:44—Nude running outside with Davis.

Paper Mask (1991; British) .... Christine Taylor
- 0:53—Breasts in bed under Matthew, then on top of him.

The Madness of King George (1994) .... Lady Pembroke
Liar, Liar (1997) .... Miranda
One Night Stand (1997) .... Margaux

Made for Cable Movies:
Shame (1992; Lifetime) .... Diana Cadell
The Substitute (1993; USA) .... Laura Willingsley
Shame II: The Secret (1995; Lifetime) .... Diana Cadell

Made for TV Movies:
It's Nothing Personal (1993) .... Katherine Witloff
The Thorn Birds: The Missing Years (1996) .... Meggie

TV:
L.A. Law (1991-92) .... C.J. Lamb

Doody, Alison

Films:
A View to a Kill (1985) .... Jenny Flex
A Prayer for the Dying (1987) .... Siobhan
Taffin (1988; U.S./British) .... Charlotte
- 0:14—Very, very brief side view of right breast when Pierce Brosnan rips her blouse open. Long shot, hard to see.

Indiana Jones and the Last Crusade (1989) . . Dr. Elsa Schneider
Barbara Cartland's "Duel of Hearts" (1990; British) .... Lady Caroline Faye
Ring of the Musketeers (1992) .... Ann-Marie Athos
Major League II (1994) .... Flannery
Temptation (1994) .... Lee Reddick

Dorado, Lorraine

Video Tapes:
Becky Bubbles (1987) .... Herself
- ••• 0:09—Brief right breast and buns in black and white swimsuit, then breasts in pool.
- ••• 0:12—Breasts while playing on pool float with Becky and Brandi.
- ••• 0:14—Breasts getting in and out of pool, then rubbing lotion on herself.
- ••• 0:18—Breasts while playing on the grass in open swimsuit top.

Wild Bikinis (1987) .... Herself
- ••• 0:10—Breasts in pool and buns in swimsuit from *Becky Bubbles.*
- •• 0:35—Breasts playing with a ball on the grass with Jasaé.

Thunder and Mud (1989) .... Quisha/Sex Toy
- 1:02—Buns, while mud wrestling in white top and pink bikini bottom.
- ••• 1:06—Breasts, covered with mud after Leslie rips her top off.

L.A. Strippers (1992) .... Quisha Cori
- ••• 0:00—Breasts dancing on stage during introduction.
- ••• 0:05—In bra, then nude dancing on stage. Long scene.
- ••• 0:12—Breasts, then nude dancing.

• Doria *

Video Tapes:
Playboy's Night Calls (1998) .... Herself
- ••• 0:00—Nude throughout.

• Dorian, Angela

See: Vetri, Victoria.

Dorian, Antonia

Films:
Body Chemistry 3: Point of Seduction (1993) ..... Krissy
- 0:00—Breasts, while in room with a brunette woman and Robert Forster.

Dinosaur Island (1993) .... April
- ••• 0:20—Breasts (she has white head band on), while bathing in a stream with May and June, then bathing the guys.
- ••• 0:22—More breasts, while bathing the guys.
- ••• 0:53—Breasts, while making love outside with Skeemer.

Ghoulies IV (1993) .... Lady in Red
Tender Loving Care (1993) .... Nursing Grad
Munchie Strikes Back (1994) .... Cleopatra
Sorceress (1994) .... Trisha
Hard Bounty (1995) .... Junie Ray
Midnight Tease 2 (1995) .... Stephanie

Made for Cable Movies:
Wasp Woman (1995; Sci-Fi) .... Roommate
Vampirella (1996; Showtime) .... Vampire Girl #2

Video Tapes:
Soft Bodies: Party Favors (1992) .... Herself
- ••• 0:03—In black bra and panties in bed, then breasts and buns during photo session.
- ••• 0:08—Breasts, while on hammock outside.
- ••• 0:11—In white lace dress in living room by piano. Breasts and buns in G-string.
- ••• 0:18—Breasts and buns outside by pool with Becky LeBeau.

Dorman, Samantha *

Video Tapes:
The Best of Sexy Lingerie (1992) .... Model
Playboy Playmates in Paradise (1992) .... Playmate
Playboy Video Calendar 1993 (1992) .... August
- ••• 0:33—Full frontal nudity outside in a field and on swing.
- ••• 0:35—Nude in house in front of fire and on bed.

Playboy's Erotic Fantasies (1992) .... Cast Member

Playboy's Playmate Review 1992 (1992) . .Miss September
••• 0:06—Nude on boat, then in laboratory and then in surreal artistic setting.
Sexy Lingerie IV (1992) . . . . Model
Wet & Wild IV (1992) . . . . Model
Playboy's Erotic Fantasies II (1993) . . . . Model
Playboy's Sexy, Steamy, Sultry (1993) . . . . Playmate
Sexy Lingerie V (1993) . . . . Model

Dorsey, Fern

Films:

Love Crimes (1991) . . . . Colleen Dells
(Unrated version reviewed.)
••• 0:03—Breasts, getting photographed by Patrick Bergin.
McBain (1991) . . . . Dr. Elliott

*Doss, Terri Lynn **

Films:

Lethal Weapon (1987) . . . . Girl in Shower #2
Die Hard (1988) . . . . Girl at Airport
Roadhouse (1989) . . . . Cody's Girlfriend

Video Tapes:

Swimwear Illustrated: On Location (1986) . . . Swimsuit Model
Playboy Video Calendar 1989 (1988) . . . . March
••• 0:09—Nude.
Sexy Lingerie (1988) . . . . Model
Glamour Through Your Lens—Outdoor Techniques (1989) . . . . Herself
• 0:07—Buns in blue swimsuit bottom in wet yellow top in the pool.
Sexy Lingerie II (1990) . . . . Model

*Douglass, Robyn **

Films:

Breaking Away (1979) . . . . Katherine
Partners (1982) . . . . Jill
•• 1:00—Brief breasts taking off her top and getting into bed with Ryan O'Neal.
The Lonely Guy (1983) . . . . Danielle
• 0:05—Upper half of right breast in sheer nightgown in bed with Raoul while talking to Steve Martin. Great nightgown!
• 1:03—Very, very brief peek at left nipple when she flashes it for Martin so he'll let her into his party.
Romantic Comedy (1983) . . . . Kate

Made for TV Movies:

Her Life as a Man (1984) . . . . Carly Perkins

TV:

Battlestar Galactica (1980) . . . . Jamie Hamilton
Houston Knights (1987-88) . . . . .Lt. Joanne Beaumont

*Down, Lesley-Anne **

Films:

Countess Dracula (1972; British) . . . . Ilona
From Beyond the Grave (1973) . . . . .Rosemary Seaton
Brannigan (1975; British) . . . . Luana
The Pink Panther Strikes Again (1976) . . . . Olga
The Betsy (1978) . . . . Lady Bobby Ayres
• 0:38—Brief left breast and upper half of buns, while with Tommy Lee Jones.
• 0:57—Very brief left breast in bed with Jones.
A Little Night Music (1978) . . . . Anne Egerman
The One and Only Phyllis Dixey (1978) . . . . . . Phyllis Dixey
• 0:14—Side view of right breast, long shot, then right breast and buns in closer shot, while kneeling in front of altar in play.
• 0:29—Left nipple, visible between arm and hands during autobiographical strip tease on stage.
• 0:30—Very brief side view of buns, during fan dance on stage.
• 0:31—Brief breasts, after lifting fans at the end of fan dance. Medium long shot.
• 0:43—Brief breasts, after opening sheer wedding dress during dance on stage.
• 0:44—Very, very brief right breast when flipping coat from one side to the other.
• 1:05—Side of right breast and buns, while kneeling at altar. Medium long shot.
• 1:10—Brief left breast, under fur boa. Seen from side stage. Brief breasts after finishing.
The Great Train Robbery (1979; British) . . . . Miriam
Hanover Street (1979) . . . . Margaret Sallinger
• 0:22—In bra and slip, then brief breasts in bedroom with Harrison Ford.
Rough Cut (1980; British) . . . . Gillian Bramley
Sphinx (1981) . . . . Erica Baron
Nomads (1986) . . . . Flax
Scenes from the Goldmine (1987) . . . . Herself
Over the Line (1992) . . . . Elaine
0:46—Buns in the shower. Don't see her face.
0:47—Buns, while lying in bed. Don't see her face.
Death Wish V: The Face of Death (1993) . . . . Olivia Regent
Mardi Gras for the Devil (1993) . . . . Christine
In the Heat of Passion II: Unfaithful (1994) . . . . Jean
a.k.a. Behind Closed Doors
(Unrated version reviewed.)
Munchie Strikes Back (1994) . . . . Linda McClelland
BeastMaster III: The Eye of Braxus (1995) . . . . .Morgana
Meet Wally Sparks (1996) . . . . Hooker Nurse

Miniseries:

North and South (1985) . . . . Madeline Fabray
North and South, Book II (1986) . . . . Madeline Fabray
North and South, Book III: Heaven and Hell (1994) . . . . Madeline Main

Made for TV Movies:

A Family of Cops (1995) . . . . .Anna Novachek

TV:

Upstairs, Downstairs (1974-77) . . . . Georgina Worsley
Dallas (1990) . . . . Stephanie Rogers
Sunset Beach (1997-) . . . . Olivia Richards

Downes, Cathy

Films:

Winter of Our Dreams (1981) . . . . Gretel
• 0:41—Brief right breast putting top on while talking to Judy Davis.
•• 1:04—Breasts sitting up in bed at night.
• 1:11—Breasts sitting up in bed while Bryan Brown and Davis talk.
Monkey Grip (1983; Australian) . . . . Eve

*Downs, Brandi **

Video Tapes:

Becky Bubbles (1987) . . . . Herself
•• 0:11—Breasts in pool after Lorraine pushes her off the pool float.
••• 0:12—Breasts while playing on pool float with Lorraine and Becky.

••• 0:14—Breasts sunbathing on chair and putting her swimsuit back on.

Best Chest in the U.S. (1987) . . . . Charlene
••• 0:48—Breasts and buns, dancing in two piece swimsuit.
••• 0:54—Breasts on stage with the other finalists.
••• 0:57—Breasts winning.

The Perfect Body Contest (1987). . . . . Charlene
•• 0:18—Buns, in pink, two piece swimsuit, then breasts.
• 0:50—Breasts on stage with the other contestants.

Wild Bikinis (1987). . . . . Herself
• 0:09—Brief side of right breast, lying next to pool from *Becky Bubbles.*

Starlets Exposed! Volume II (1991) . . . . Charlene
(Same as *The Perfect Body Contest.*)
••• 0:21—Buns in pink two piece swimsuit, then breasts on stage doing strip routine.

• Doyle, Kathleen

Films:

Cannery Row (1982) . . . . Violet

Very Close Quarters (1984) . . . . Irina
• 0:36—Brief buns in panties, when mooning Alex.

Brighton Beach Memoirs (1986) . . . . Mrs. Laski
Silence Like Glass (1989) . . . . Mrs. Jacoby
Brain Donors (1992) . . . . Nurse
Body Snatchers (1994) . . . . Mrs. Platt
Mighty Aphrodite (1995) . . . . Ex-Landlord's Wife
Montana (1998) . . . . Mrs. Presser
No Looking Back (1998) . . . . Mrs. Ryan

Drake, Gabrielle

Films:

The Man Outside (1968; British) . . . . B.E.A. Girl

There's a Girl in My Soup (1970) . . . . . Julia Halford-Smythe
• 0:09—In beige bra with Peter Sellers, brief left breast in bed with him. Don't see her face well, but it is her.

Connecting Rooms (1971; British). . . . . Jean

The Au Pair Girls (1972; British). . . . . Randi Lindstrom

TV:

UFO (1970). . . . . Lieutenant Gay Ellis

Drake, Judith

Films:

Tales of Ordinary Madness (1983; Italian) . . . . . Fat Woman
• 0:49—Buns, in bra and panties in her bedroom with Ben Gazzara, then left breast when he fondles her.

The Sex O'Clock News (1986). . . . . Mary Ferrdip
Angel Heart (1987) . . . . Izzy's Wife
(Original Unedited Version reviewed.)
Necronomicon: Book of the Dead (1993) . . . . . . Mrs. Benedict
The Stoned Age (1994) . . . . Mrs. Hankey
A Little Princess (1995) . . . . Bakery Woman
Rumpelstiltskin (1995). Woman Deputy
White Man's Burden (1995) . . . . Dorothy

Made for Cable Movies:

If These Walls Could Talk (1996; HBO). . . . . Angry Woman

Drake, Marciee

Films:

Jackson County Jail (1976) . . . . . . Candy (David's Girlfriend)
• 0:04—Brief breasts wrapping towel around herself, in front of Howard Hesseman. Long shot.

Jokes My Folks Never Told Me (1976) . . . . n.a.

The Toolbox Murders (1978) . . . . Debbie
•• 0:09—In wet blouse, then breasts taking it off and putting a dry one on.

Drake, Michele *

Films:

American Gigolo (1980) . . . . 1st Girl on Balcony
• 0:03—Breasts on the balcony while Richard Gere and Lauren Hutton talk.

The Hollywood Knights (1980): . . . . Cheerleader
• 0:28—Brief lower nudity in raised cheerleader outfit doing cheers in front of school assembly.

History of the World, Part I (1981) . . . . Vestal Virgin

Drescher, Fran

Films:

Saturday Night Fever (1977) . . . . Connie
(R-rated version reviewed.)
The Hollywood Knights (1980) . . . . Sally
Doctor Detroit (1983) . . . . Karen Blittstein
This is Spinal Tap (1984) . . . . Bobbi Flekman
The Rosebud Beach Hotel (1985). Linda
The Big Picture (1989). . . . . Polo Habel
UHF (1989) . . . . Pamela Finklestein

Cadillac Man (1990) . . . . Joy Munchack
• 0:07—Very brief right breast several times while in bed with Robin Williams.

We're Talkin' Serious Money (1991). . . . . Valerie
Car 54, Where are You? (1993) . . . . Velma Velour
Jack (1996) . . . . Dolores Durante
The Beautician and the Beast (1997) . . . . Joy Miller

Made for Cable TV:

Dream On: The Second Greatest Story Ever Told (1991; HBO) . . . . Kathleen

TV:

Princesses (1991). . . . . Melissa
The Nanny (1993-). . . . . Fran Fine

Drew, Griffin *

a.k.a. Raquel Cristal.

Films:

Dinosaur Island (1993). . . . . May
••• 0:20—Breasts (she has dark necklaces on), while bathing in a stream with April and June, then bathing the guys.
••• 0:22—More breasts, while bathing the guys.
••• 0:30—Breasts, while helping Wayne's arm feel better in prehistoric spa.
••• 0:31—Breasts and buns, while making love with Wayne in spa.
• 1:15—Side of left breast during end credits.

The Perfect Gift (1993) . . . . Pajama Party Guest
Forbidden Games (1995). . . . . Model
(Unrated version reviewed.)

Friend of the Family (1995) . . . . Linda
a.k.a. Elke's Erotic Nights
(Unrated version reviewed.)
••• 0:05—Breasts, while making love with Montana's boyfriend in bed in dream.
••• 0:10—In sheer white nightgown, then breasts on balcony with her husband in flashback.
••• 0:44—Nude, while making love with Elke in bathtub. Nice, long scene.
••• 1:19—Nude, while making love with her husband in bed.

Indecent Behavior 3 (1995). . . . . Janet Colby
••• 0:01—Nude, taking off robe and going for a swim.
•• 0:49—Breasts, while joining Rosa and Billy in bed.

Masseuse (1995) . . . . Kristy
(Unrated version reviewed.)
• 0:23—Buns, in lingerie in bedroom.
••• 0:24—Breasts, while making love in bed with Jack.

••• 0:50—Breasts, while in bathtub with Connor during her dream.

Midnight Tease 2 (1995) . . . . Desiree
• 0:04—Brief breasts, while dancing on stage.
• 0:07—Buns in T-back, while in dressing room.
• 0:20—Breasts while in dressing room.
••• 0:37—Doing strip routine on stage, buns in T-back then breasts.
•• 1:05—Buns in T-back and breasts, while dancing on stage with Debra Beatty.

Over the Wire (1995). . . . . Sally
••• 0:51—Nude, while making love in office with Roy.

Sinful Intrigue (1995) . . . . Cindy
••• 0:20—Breasts and buns in office, while making love with Adam.
•• 0:39—Breasts, while making love with Chona Jason and Adam.

Busted (1996) . . . . Bambi
• 0:07—Breasts, while sunbathing outdoors.
••• 0:16—Stripping in jail cell in front of Dr. Kaplan. In lingerie, then buns and breasts.
• 0:40—Brief breasts, while lying in bed with Todd Bridges.
• 0:41—Brief breasts, while lying in bed with Bridges again.

Dinosaur Valley Girls (1996). . . . . Daphne Adrian
(Director's Cut reviewed.)
• 0:02—Brief breasts, when waking up in bed next to Tony.
•• 0:04—Breasts, when getting out of the pool and drying herself off.

Bikini Hoe Down (1997) . . . . Missy Sue
•• 0:13—Nude, undressing then bathing in a stream.
••• 0:16—Breasts, while making love with the hippy artist guy in stream.
••• 0:53—Nude, while showering with the other three girls.
••• 1:00—Breasts, while making love with the hippy artist guy.

Kounterfeit (1997). . . . . Jeaneen
• 0:31—Very brief buns in T-back swimsuit, while dancing with Travis by the swimming pool.

Made for Cable Movies:

Subliminal Seduction (1996; Showtime). . . . . Kim
•• 0:09—Breasts and buns in T-back, while a guy undoes her dress when she's hypnotized.
• 1:04—Very, very brief right breast in flashback.

Made for Cable TV:

Erotic Confessions: Games People Play (1995; Cinemax) . . . . Suzanne
• 0:02—Brief side of right breast, then breasts after taking off her bra during strip poker game.
•• 0:05—Breasts and buns in T-back, leaving the game.
••• 0:09—Breasts, while making love with Richard in the bedroom.
•• 0:13—Breasts, while making love with Richard.

Erotic Confessions: Coming Clean (1996; Cinemax) . . . . Carrie
(Available on video tape in *Erotic Confessions, Volume 1: Desire.*)
••• 0:20—Breasts after undressing in laundry room with Eric, then making love with him. Long scene.

Erotic Confessions: Judy and the Beast (1997; Cinemax) . . . . Judy
•• 0:05—Breasts, while making love with the football player in her dream.
••• 0:13—Full frontal nudity, while making love with the football player in bed.

Intimate Sessions: Lucy (1998; Cinemax). . . . . Lucy
••• 0:04—Breasts, while making love in bed with David.
••• 0:14—Breasts, while caressing herself when watching Missy and a guy make love in bed.
•• 0:20—Breasts, while putting on lingerie in bedroom.
•• 0:23—Breasts, while making love in bed with David.

Video Tapes:

Playboy's Erotic Fantasies II (1993). . . . . Cast Member

Playboy's Secret Confessions (1993) . . . . Dream Boy/Elaine
••• 0:04—Full frontal nudity, while making love with Barry in cabin.

Playboy's Real Couples: Sex in Dangerous Places (1995) . . . . Mile High Club/Woman
••• 0:32—Nude, while making love with Bobby in airplane restroom.

Penthouse: The Art of Massage (1996). . . . . Model
••• 0:18—In bra, then full frontal nudity, while making love on desk in office.

Drew, Linzi

Former Editor of the British edition of *Penthouse* magazine.

Adult Films:

An American Buttman in London (1991) . . . . Hair Salon Owner

Buttman's Bouncin' British Babes (1994) . . . . Hair Salon Owner

Films:

An American Werewolf in London (1981) . . . . Brenda Bristols
• 1:26—Side view of left breast in porno movie while David Naughton talks to his friend, Jack.
• 1:27—Brief breasts in movie talking on the phone.

Emmanuelle in Soho (1981) . . . . Showgirl

Aria (1987; U.S./British) . . . . Girl
• 1:09—Breasts on operating table after car accident. Hair is all covered with bandages.
•• 1:10—Breasts getting shocked to start her heart.

Salome's Last Dance (1987) . . . . 1st Slave
(Appears with 2 other slaves–can't tell who is who.)
•• 0:08—Breasts in black costume around a cage.
•• 0:52—Breasts during dance number.

The Lair of the White Worm (1988; British) . . . . .Maid/Nun

*Driggs, Deborah **

Films:

Total Exposure (1991) . . . . Kathy
••• 0:08—Breasts dancing in front of Jeff Conaway, then making love in bed with him. Long scene.
• 0:22—Brief side view breasts in B&W photos that Conaway looks at.
• 0:24—Brief buns in black G-string and side of right breast changing clothes in locker room.
•• 0:25—Breasts and buns, trying to beat up Season Hubley.

Martial Law II: Undercover (1992). . . . . .Tiffany
• 0:59—Side of left breast, while taking off lingerie and getting into bed with Billy Drago.
• 1:00—Breasts, rolling off Drago after he passes out.

Night Rhythms (1992). .Cinnamon
(Unrated version reviewed.)
••• 1:15—Left breast, then breasts and lower frontal nudity, making love with Martin Hewitt in bed.
••• 1:19—Breasts, sitting on bed and talking to Hewitt.

Twogether (1992). . . . . .Beach Babe/Melissa
(Unrated version reviewed.)
• 1:29—Brief right breast, while lying in bed with Nick Cassavetes.

Video Tapes:

Playboy Video Calendar 1991 (1990) .... October
••• 0:40—Nude.
Playboy Video Centerfold: Deborah Driggs & Karen Foster (1990)..............................Playmate
••• 0:02—Doing a strip tease, other dancing, some in bed. Nude.
Sexy Lingerie II (1990)..........................Model
Wet & Wild II (1990)..........................Model
Sexy Lingerie III (1991)........................Model
Wet & Wild III (1991)..........................Model
The Best of Sexy Lingerie (1992)................Model
The Best of Wet and Wild (1992)................Model
Playboy Playmates in Paradise (1992).........Playmate
Sexy Lingerie IV (1992).........................Model
Playboy's Sexy, Steamy, Sultry (1993)..........Playmate

Drinkwater, Carol

Films:

A Clockwork Orange (1971) ....Nurse Feeley
The Shout (1979; British) .... Wife
Father (1992; Australian)....................Anne Winton
An Awfully Big Adventure (1995; British) ... Dawn Allenby
•• 0:38—Full frontal nudity, while standing in dressing room when Stella opens the door.

Dubin, Alexis

See: Ross, Gaylen.

Dubois, Nicole

See: Yager, Missy.

*Ducati, Kristie **

a.k.a. Kristi Scott.

Films:

The Bikini Carwash Company (1992) .... Melissa
(Unrated version reviewed.)
• 0:13—Buns in G-string, while at the beach.
••• 0:20—Breasts, taking off her bikini top in shack with Jack.
•• 0:26—Nude, changing clothes in car wash.
•• 0:30—Breasts during water fight.
• 0:32—Brief breasts in Jack's fantasy.
• 0:45—Brief left breast and buns, dressing.
••• 0:47—Breasts and buns, dancing inside car wash.
••• 1:02—Nude, soaped up in car wash with Rita and Sunny.
••• 1:07—Breasts and buns, making love in shack with Jack. Wow!
••• 1:12—Breasts, posing for photos.
Intimate Obsession (1992) ....Laura
(Unrated version reviewed.)
••• 0:15—Breasts while making love with Rick while Rachel watches from outside. Long scene.
••• 0:17—More breasts, while making love on top of Rick.
••• 0:18—Buns and more breasts while making love.
••• 0:19—Brief partial lower frontal nudity and more breasts while making love with Rick.
•• 0:21—Breasts during Rachel's recollections.
Meatballs 4 (1992)............................Kristi
• 0:05—Very, very brief buns, getting her light blue robe pulled up by Neriah while walking to the showers. Long shot.
• 0:06—Brief side of left breast, while taking a shower with three other girls. (She's on the far right in the first shot.)
•• 0:37—Breasts, four times, while playing strip charades.
• 0:54—Left breast, while riding behind a guy on a four wheel motorcycle. (She's the one closest to the camera.)
The Bikini Carwash Company II (1993).......... Melissa
(Unrated version reviewed.)
•• 0:00—Breasts in back of limousine with a guy.
••• 0:09—Breasts with the other three girls, celebrating in office during music video number.
•• 0:16—Breasts at carwash during music video number. (Wearing orange bikini bottoms.)
••• 1:20—Breasts and buns while making love with Derek in the TV studio.
•• 1:29—Breasts and buns in bikini bottom during music video number at the carwash.
Sorceress (1994) .... Kathy
••• 1:12—Nude, while taking a shower. Long scene.
• 1:19—Breasts behind shower door. Buns and right breast, while lying unconscious on the shower floor.
• 1:20—Right breast, while lying unconscious on floor again.

Duce, Sharon

Films:

The Tamarind Seed (1974; British)........... Sandy Mitchell
Absolution (1978; British) .... Louella
Outland (1981) .... Prostitute
• 0:30—Right breast, whle lying down in room with drug crazed guy.
• 0:32—Breasts, while entering medical scanning device.

• *Duez, Sophie*

Films:

Eye of the Wolf (1995; Canadian/French) .... Jo

Made for Cable TV:

Strangers: Crash (1996; HBO) .... Claire
• 0:17—Lower frontal nudity and buns, in black bra, while starting to make love with David Keith. Messy with broken eggs.
• 0:18—Brief lower frontal nudity when putting skirt back on.

Duff, Denice

Films:

Bloodstone: Subspecies II (1992) .... Michelle Morgan
• 0:10—Very, very brief left breast under sheer part of dress while taking it off. Back side of right breast while putting on sweater.
•• 0:16—Breasts, while crying in the shower.
Martial Law II: Undercover (1992) .... Nancy Borelli
Return to Frogtown (1992) ....Dr. Spangle
a.k.a. Frogtown II
Warlords 3000 (1992) .... Anani
••• 0:50—Breasts, after taking off blouse in front of Nova, then making love and sleeping after.
Bloodfist V: Human Target (1993) .... Candy/Michelle
Bloodlust: Subspecies III (1993)........... Michelle Morgan
Phoenix (1995) .... Seline
•• 0:59—In black bra, then breasts, while making love with McClain in hospital bed.

Made for Cable TV:

Dream On: The Second Greatest Story Ever Told (1991; HBO) .... Sorority Girl
•• 0:20—Breasts in bed taking her sweater off, in bed with her boyfriend.

Made for TV Movies:

Robin Cook's "Invasion" (1997)................... Denise

Duffek, Patty *

Films:

Hard Ticket to Hawaii (1987)................ Patticakes
•• 0:48—Breasts talking to Michelle after swimming.

Picasso Trigger (1989)........................ Patticakes
•• 1:04—Breasts taking a Jacuzzi bath.

Savage Beach (1989)........................... Patticakes
• 0:06—Breasts in spa with Lisa London, Dona Speir and Hope Marie Carlton.
•• 0:50—Breasts changing clothes.

Video Tapes:

Playmate Playoffs .... Playmate

Duffy, Julia

Films:

Battle Beyond the Stars (1980) .... Mol
Cutter's Way (1981) .... Young Girl
a.k.a. Cutter and Bone

Night Warning (1982)..................... Julie Linden
• 0:44—Upper half of breasts after Jimmy McNichol gets out of bed.
• 0:46—Brief breasts when McNichol pulls the sheets down.
•• 0:47—Brief breasts when Susan Tyrrell opens the bedroom door.

Wacko (1983)............................ Mary Graves

Made for Cable TV:

Sex, Shock and Censorship in the 90's (1993; Showtime) .... Politically-Correct Mom

Miniseries:

Blue and the Gray (1982) .... Mary Hale

Made for TV Movies:

Menu for Murder (1990).................. Susan Henshaw

TV:

Love of Life (1972) .... Gerry Brayley
The Doctors (1973-77) .... Penny Davis
Newhart (1983-90)............... Stephanie Vanderkellen
Wizards and Warriors (1983).................. Princess Ariel
Baby Talk (1991)..................... Maggie Campbell
Designing Women (1991-92) .... Allison Sugarbaker
The Mommies (1993-94) .... Barb Ballantine
Social Studies (1997).................... Frances Harmon

Dukakis, Olympia

Cousin of politician Michael Dukakis.

Films:

Lilith (1964) .... Patient
Twice a Man (1964) .... Young Woman/Commentator
John and Mary (1969)..................... John's Mother
Made For Each Other (1971)................. Gig's Mother
Rich Kids (1979) .... Lawyer
The Wanderers (1979)...................... Joey's Mom
The Idolmaker (1980) .... Mrs. Vacarri
National Lampoon Goes to the Movies (1982) .... Helena
a.k.a. Movie Madness
Flanagan (1985) .... Mary
Moonstruck (1987)...................... Rose Castorini
(Academy Award for Best Supporting Actress.)
Dad (1989)............................ Bette Tremont
Look Who's Talking (1989) .... Rosie
Steel Magnolias (1989).................. Clairee Belcher
Working Girl (1989) .... Personnel Director
In the Spirit (1990) .... Sue
Look Who's Talking Too (1990) .... Rosie

Over the Hill (1991; Australian) .... Alma
•• 0:56—Breasts, while getting them painted for tribal ceremony.

The Cemetery Club (1993) .... Doris Silverman
Look Who's Talking Now! (1993)..................... Rosie
Dead Badge (1994)...................... Dr. Doris Rice
Digger (1994) .... Bea
I Love Trouble (1994) .... Jeannie
Mother (1994) .... Mrs. Jay
Jeffrey (1995) .... Mrs. Marcangelo
Mighty Aphrodite (1995) .... Jocasta
Mr. Holland's Opus (1995) .... Principal Jacobs

Made for Cable Movies:

A Century of Women (1994; TBS) .... Family Member
More Tales of the City (1998; Canadian/U.S.; Showtime) .... Anna Madrigal
The Pentagon Wars (1998; HBO)...... Madame Chairwoman

Made for TV Movies:

Sinatra (1992)............................ Dolly Sinatra
Tales of the City (1994).................. Anna Madrigal
Young at Heart (1995).................. Rose Garaventi
A Match Made in Heaven (1997)............. Helen Rosner
Scattering Dad (1998)......................... Dotty

Duke, Patty

a.k.a. Patty Duke Astin.

Ex-wife of actor John Astin.

Mother of actors Sean and Mackenzie Astin.

Films:

4D Man (1959)....................... Marjorie Sullivan
The Miracle Worker (1962) .... Helen Keller
(Academy Award for Best Supporting Actress.)
Valley of the Dolls (1967) .... Neely O'Hara
Me, Natalie (1969) .... Natalie Miller

By Design (1982; Canadian) .... Helen
•• 0:49—Left breast, lying in bed.
•• 1:05—Brief left breast sitting on bed.
• 1:06—Brief left breast, then brief right breast lying in bed with the photographer.

Something Special (1987)............ Mrs. Doris Niceman
Prelude to a Kiss (1992)..................... Mrs. Boyle

Made for Cable Movies:

When the Vows Break (1995; Lifetime) .... Barbara Parker

Miniseries:

Captains and the Kings (1976) .... Bernadette Hennessey Armagh

Made for TV Movies:

My Sweet Charlie (1970)............... Marlene Chambers
The Miracle Worker (1979) .... Anne Sullivan
Perry Mason: The Case of the Avenging Ace (1988) .... Althea Sloan
Everybody's Baby: The Rescue of Jessica McClure (1989) .... Carolyn Henry
Always Remember I Love You (1990).......... Ruth Monroe
Call Me Anna (1990)...................... Patty Duke
Absolute Strangers (1991)................... Judge Ray
Grave Secrets: The Legacy of Hilltop Drive (1992) .... Jean Williams
A Killer Among Friends (1992)............... Jean Monroe
Last Wish (1992) .... Betty Rollin
Family of Strangers (1993) .... Beth
A Matter of Justice (1993) .... Mary Brown
No Child of Mine (1993)................... Carolyn Henry
One Woman's Courage (1994) .... Grace McKenna
Harvest of Fire (1996) .... Annie Beiler
To Face Her Past (1996).................. Beth Bradfield

TV:

The Brighter Day .... Ellen Dennis
The Patty Duke Show (1963-66) .... Patty & Cathy Lane

It Takes Two (1982-83) . . . . Molly Quinn
Hail to the Chief (1985). . . . . President Julia Mansfield
Amazing Grace (1995) . . . . Hannah Miller

Dulany, Caitlin

Films:

Class of 1999 II: The Substitute (1993). . . . Jenna McKensie
•• 1:01—Breasts, while making love in bed with Emmett.
••• 1:02—More breasts while making love. Intercut with John shooting a machine gun.

Maniac Cop 3: Badge of Silence (1993). . . . . . Dr. Susan Fowler

Made for Cable TV:

Red Shoe Diaries: Auto Erotica (1993; Showtime) . . . . Claudia
(Available on the video tape *Red Shoe Diaries 4: Auto Erotica.*)
• 0:10—Very brief breasts in clips during car race.
• 0:12—Very brief right breast.
• 0:18—Very brief lower frontal nudity.
• 0:20—Very brief nipple.
• 0:22—Brief breasts.
• 0:24—Very briefly nude, several times in quick cuts.

Made for TV Movies:

Trouble Shooters: Trapped Beneath the Earth (1993). . . Claudia

Dumas, Sandrine

a.k.a. Sandra Dumas.

Films:

Twice a Woman (1979) . . . . Sylvia
• 0:06—Breasts, kneeling on the bed, then more brief breasts in bed with Bibi Andersson.
••• 0:47—Brief right breast, then breasts in bed with Andersson. Long scene.
• 1:15—Left breast, lying in bed with Anthony Perkins. Long shot.
••• 1:23—Breasts with Andersson.

Aria (1987; U.S./British). . . . . n.a.
Beyond Therapy (1987). . . . . Cindy
Valmont (1989). . . . . Martine
The Double Life of Veronique (1991; French) . . . . . . Catherine

Dunaway, Faye

Films:

Bonnie and Clyde (1967) . . . . Bonnie Parker
The Thomas Crown Affair (1968) . . . . Vicki Anderson
The Arrangement (1969) . . . . Gwen
• 0:25—Brief buns in various scenes while at the beach with Kirk Douglas.

Little Big Man (1970) . . . . Mrs. Pendrake
The Three Musketeers (1973; British) . . . . Milady
Chinatown (1974) . . . . Evelyn
• 1:26—Very brief right breast, in bed talking to Jack Nicholson.
• 1:28—Very brief right breast in bed talking to Nicholson. Very brief flash of right breast under robe when she gets up to leave the bedroom.

The Towering Inferno (1974). . . . . Susan Franklin
The Four Musketeers (1975) . . . . Milady
Three Days of the Condor (1975) . . . . Kathy Hale
Network (1976) . . . . Diana Christensen
(Academy Award for Best Actress.)
• 1:10—Brief left breast twice, taking off clothes in room with William Holden.

Voyage of the Damned (1976; British). . . . . Denise Kreisler
Eyes of Laura Mars (1978) . . . . Laura Mars
The Champ (1979) . . . . Annie
The First Deadly Sin (1980) . . . . Barbara Delaney
Mommie Dearest (1981) . . . . Joan Crawford
The Wicked Lady (1983; British) . . . . Barbara Skelton
Ordeal by Innocence (1984) . . . . Rachel Argyle
Supergirl (1984; British). . . . . Selena
Barfly (1987) . . . . Wanda Wilcox
• 0:58—Brief upper half of breasts in bathtub talking to Mickey Rourke.

Casanova (1987) . . . . Countess
Midnight Crossing (1988) . . . . Helen Barton
Wait Until Spring, Bandini (1989; Belgian/French/Italian) . . . . Mrs. Hildegarde
The Handmaid's Tale (1990) . . . . Serena Joy
The Two Jakes (1990) . . . . Evelyn Mulwray
Scorchers (1992) . . . . Thais
The Temp (1993). . . . . Charlene Towne
Arizona Dream (1994). . . . . Elaine
Don Juan DeMarco (1994). . . . . Marilyn Mickler
Dunston Checks In (1995). . . . . Mrs. Dubrow
Unzipped (1995) . . . . Herself
Albino Alligator (1996) . . . . Janet Boudreaux
The Chamber (1996). . . . . Lee Bowen

Made for Cable Movies:

Drunks (1995; Showtime) . . . . Becky
Twilight of the Golds (1997; HBO). . . . . Phyllis
Gia (1998; HBO) . . . . Wilhelmina Cooper

Miniseries:

Christopher Columbus (1985) . . . . Queen Isabella

Made for TV Movies:

Columbo: It's All in the Game (1993). . . . . Lauren Staton
A Family Divided (1995) . . . . Karen Billingsley
The People Next Door (1996) . . . . Ellen Morse

TV:

Ladies of the Night (1986). . . . . Lil Hutton
It Had To Be You (1993). Laura Scofield

• Duncan, Lindsay

Films:

Prick Up Your Ears (1987; British). . . . . Althea Lehr
The Reflecting Skin (1990; British) . . . . Dolphin Blue
Body Parts (1991) . . . . Dr. Agatha Webb
City Hall (1996). . . . . Sydney Pappas

Made for Cable Movies:

Tom Jones: Part 2 (1998; A&E) . . . . Lady Bellaston
•• 1:41—Brief breasts, after opening the door to show herself to Tom Jones. You can't see her face clearly, because she's wearing a mask, so it's probably a body double. (The body double's shoulders look wider than Duncan's.)

Dunlap, Dawn

Films:

Laura (1979) . . . . Laura
a.k.a. Shattered Innocence
• 0:20—Brief side view of left breast and buns talking to Maud Adams, then brief side view of right breast putting on robe.
••• 0:23—Nude, dancing while being photographed.
••• 1:15—Nude, letting Paul feel her so he can sculpt her, then making love with him.
• 1:22—Buns, putting on panties talking to Maud Adams.

Forbidden World (1982) . . . . Tracy Baxter
• 0:27—Brief breasts getting ready for bed.
••• 0:37—Nude in steam bath.
•• 0:54—Breasts in shower with June Chadwick.

Night Shift (1982) . . . . Maxine
Heartbreaker (1983) . . . . Kim
• 0:49—Breasts putting on dress in bedroom.

• 0:51—Very, very brief right breast in open dress during rape attempt. Dark.
•• 1:02—Left breast, lying on bed with her boyfriend. Long scene.

Barbarian Queen (1985) . . . . Taramis
• 0:00—Breasts, in the woods getting raped.

Dunsheath, Lisa

Films:

The Prowler (1981) . . . . Sherry
• 0:20—Very brief breasts in the shower (overhead view).
•• 0:21—More breasts and buns in shower, then breasts when Carl opens the door.
• 0:22—More breasts from overhead.
•• 0:23—Breasts, getting killed by the prowler with a pitchfork.
• 1:23—Breasts, dead in the bathtub when Pam discovers her.

They All Laughed (1981). . . . . Tulips
A Little Sex (1982) . . . . .Lucy (Down-On Girl)
Eddie Macon's Run (1983) . . . . Kay

• *Duplaix, Daphnee Lynn* *

Films:

Striptease (1996) . . . . Uncredited Dancer
(R-rated version reviewed.)
• 0:03—Breasts, while dancing in the background.
• 0:34—Brief breasts, while putting her dress on as she walks by Demi Moore, who is talking on the phone.

Video Tapes:

Playboy's Women Behaving Badly (1997) . . . . .Body Paint
••• 0:10—Nude, while in apartment with her girlfriend, then painting each other.

Playboy's Girls Next Door: Naughty and Nice (1998) . . . . .Naughty Neighbors
••• 0:51—Nude, while stripping with her girlfriend in their neighbor's apartment.

Dupree, Christine *

Films:

Armed and Dangerous (1986) . . . . Peep Show Girl
• 0:58—Very, very brief breasts shots behind glass dancing in front of John Candy and Eugene Levy.

Deathstalker II (1987) . . . . .Uncredited Body Double for Toni Naples
• 0:55—Brief breasts in strobe lights making love with the bad guy. Hard to see because of blinking lights.

• *Durant, Nicole*

Films:

Tender Loving Care (1993) . . . . .Tough Beach Girl
Evil Obsession (1996). . . . . Suzi
•• 1:23—Breasts, while posing for photos.

Durell, Marina

Films:

Badge 373 (1972). . . . . .Rita Garcia
a.k.a. The Police Connection
• 0:33—Brief breasts, while lying dead in bed, covered with blood. Don't see her face.
• 1:51—Brief breasts, while lying dead in bed, covered with blood in flashback.

Up the Sandbox (1972) . . . . Dr. Lopez
Innocent Blood (1992) . . . . Nurse
I Like It Like That (1994) . . . . Cookie

Durkin, Shevonne

Films:

Rage and Honor (1992). . . . . Groupie
Ghost in the Machine (1993) . . . . .Carol
The Liars' Club (1993) . . . . Marla
• 0:13—Very, very brief tip of right breast when standing up when Pat sees her. Left breast when he opens her dress top. Brief lower frontal nudity (dark) when he undoes her panties. Very, very brief left breast when she starts to fall backward.
•• 0:15—Right breast, then both breasts, when getting raped. (Don't see her face in close-ups.)

Magic Kid 2 (1993) . . . . Venus
Leprechaun 2 (1994). . . . . Bridget/William's Daughter
0:31—Breasts while in garage luring Ian to his death. Obvious body double.

Tammy and the T-Rex (1994) . . . . Wendy

Dusenberry, Ann

Films:

Goodbye Franklin High (1978) . . . . .n.a.
Jaws II (1978) . . . . .Tina Wilcox
Heart Beat (1979). . . . . Stevie
•• 0:41—Full frontal nudity frolicking in bathtub with Nick Nolte.

Cutter's Way (1981) . . . . Valerie Duran
a.k.a. Cutter and Bone

National Lampoon Goes to the Movies (1982) . . . . Dominique
a.k.a. Movie Madness

Basic Training (1984). . . . . Melinda Griffin
••• 1:13—Breasts in Russian guy's bedroom.

Lies (1984; British) . . . . Robyn Wallace
•• 0:10—Breasts opening the shower curtain in front of her boyfriend.
• 0:11—Right breast while kissing her boyfriend.

The Men's Club (1986). . . . . Page
•• 1:04—Breasts while lying in bed after making love with Roy Scheider.

Play Nice (1992) . . . . .Pam Crichmore
(Unrated version reviewed.)

Made for TV Movies:

The Secret War of Jackie's Girls (1980). . . . . Donna

TV:

Little Women (1979) . . . . Amy March Laurence
The Family Tree (1983) . . . . Molly Nichols Tanner
Life With Lucy (1986-87). . . . . .Margo McGibbon

Dutch, Deborah

a.k.a. Debra Dare.

Films:

Jokes My Folks Never Told Me (1976) . . . . Girl on Bed/Confessional Girl
•• 0:33—Left breast, while sitting on bed (on the right) talking to the sweater girl.

Bruce Lee Fights Back From the Grave (1981) . . . . Debbie
D.C. Cab (1983) . . . . .n.a.
The Man Who Wasn't There (1983). . . . . .Miss Dawson
Protocol (1984). . . . . Safari Girl
Torchlight (1984) . . . . Sydney's Girlfriend
Action Jackson (1988) . . . . .n.a.
The Haunting of Morella (1989) . . . . .Serving Girl
••• 0:14—Breasts and buns, taking off pink tap pants and getting into bath.
• 0:15—Buns, lying dead on the floor, covered with blood.

Hard to Die (1990) . . . . .Jackie Webster
a.k.a. Tower of Terror
•• 0:25—Breasts and buns, while taking a shower.

Sorority Girls and the Creature from Hell (1990) . . . . Mary Anne
• 0:08—Very brief, side of left breast while changing clothes in background.
• 0:32—Lower half of left breast, while dancing in cabin.

976-EVIL II: The Astral Factor (1991) . . . . Commerical Wife

Death Dancers (1992) . . . . Shannon
• 0:02—Briefly nude, while putting bathrobe on in B&W flashback.
• 0:30—Brief breasts in open robe, very brief buns, when crawling away.
• 0:31—Brief right breast in open robe outside.
• 0:37—Right breast in montage.
• 0:40—Brief breasts several times.
• 0:43—Brief breasts, while playing with a knife.
• 0:46—Buns in costume in hotel room with a guy.
• 0:49—Brief breasts in flashbacks.
• 0:56—Brief breasts in B&W flashback.
• 0:57—Breasts in stabbing scene.
•• 1:05—Breasts while making love with a guy.

Mind Twister (1992) . . . . Sheila Harrison
(Unrated version reviewed.)
•• 0:01—Brief breasts, after smashing her head through window to scream for help. Left breast, while dead on the floor.
•• 0:04—Breasts, while dead on the floor when photographed by police.
•• 0:05—More brief left breast shots while on the floor. Breasts, while getting put in body bag.
•• 1:22—In bra, then breasts on TV monitor during video playback that Heather watches.

Roadside Justice (1992) . . . . .Mom
Swingers (1992) . . . . Debra
Dinosaur Island (1993) . . . . .Cave Girl
Tender Loving Care (1993) . . . . .Tough Beach Girl/Party Girl
•• 1:07—Breasts, while in spa with a blonde party girl.

Saturday Night Special (1994). . . . . Uncredited Singer
(Unrated version reviewed.)
Vice Academy, Part 4 (1994) . . . . Bar Hooker
Attack of the 60 Foot Centerfold (1995) . . . . . . Nurse Williams
Bikini Drive-In (1995) . . . . Sorority Sister
(Unrated version reviewed.)
• 0:23—Very brief right breast, when her white polka dot top gets pulled down during water fight while cleaning up the drive-in. Very brief breasts, while running around afterwards.
• 0:58—Brief buns in black and gold swimsuit.
• 0:59—Breasts while collecting money at drive-in entrance.

TV:
Capitol (1985). . . . . .n.a.
The Young and the Restless (1987) . . . . n.a.
General Hospital (1988) . . . . .n.a.

Video Tapes:
Scream Queen Hot Tub Party (1991). . . . . . .Jackie Webster
•• 0:19—Breasts, taking off towel and getting into shower from *Hard to Die*.

Dutton, Melissa

Films:
Midnight Tease (1994). . . . . Satchi
•• 0:00—Breasts and buns during opening credits.
••• 0:04—Breasts and buns in silver T-back while stripping and dancing on stage.

Criminal Hearts (1995) . . . . .Amy Locane's Body Double
• 0:19—Breasts, while in bed with Kevin Dillon.
• 0:51—Breasts, several times, while in bed with Dillon. Upper half of buns while sitting on him.

Forbidden Games (1995). . . . . .Model
(Unrated version reviewed.)

• DuVall, Clea

Films:
Little Witches (1996) . . . . Kelsey
• 0:35—In bra, then brief buns and breasts with the other girls during ceremony.
• 1:25—Brief partial breasts and brief buns, with the other girls, during ceremony. Leaves get in the way.

Made for Cable Movies:
The Defenders: Payback (1997; Showtime) . . . . . . .Jessica Lane

Duvall, Shelley *

Producer.

Films:
Brewster McCloud (1970) . . . . Suzanne
McCabe and Mrs. Miller (1971). . . . . Ida Coyle
Thieves Like Us (1974) . . . . .Keechie
• 1:16—Brief upper half of left breast, several times, while in bathtub.
•• 1:17—Brief breasts and partial lower frontal nudity, then buns, standing up, getting out of tub and drying herself off.
•• 1:18—Brief back side of right breast, while putting on nightgown.

Nashville (1975) . . . . L.A. Jane
Buffalo Bill and the Indians (1976). . . . . Mrs. Cleveland
Annie Hall (1977) . . . . Pam
Three Women (1977) . . . . Millie
Popeye (1980). . . . . Olive Oyl
The Shining (1980) . . . . Wendy Torrance
Time Bandits (1981; British). . . . . Pansy
Frankenweenie (1984). . . . . Susan Frankenstein
Roxanne (1987). . . . . .Dixie
Suburban Commando (1991) . . . . .Jenny Wilcox
The Underneath (1994) . . . . Nurse
The Portrait of a Lady (1996; British/U.S.) . . . Countess Gemini

Made for Cable Movies:
Frogs! (1992; Disney) . . . . Annie
Alone (1997; Showtime) . . . . Estelle

Made for TV Movies:
Aliens for Breakfast (1995) . . . . .n.a.

• Dwyer, Karyn

Films:
The Paperboy (1994) . . . . Brenda
• 0:24—Breasts, while making out with her boyfriend on couch when Johnny peeks in the house.

Lethal Tender (1996) . . . . Sparky

Made for Cable Movies:
End of Summer (1995; Showtime) . . . . Jenny
••• 0:41—Breasts, while making love in bed with Julian Sands.

The Fixer (1997) . . . . .Irene
Thanks of a Grateful Nation (1998; Showtime) . . . . Deeni

Made for TV Movies:
JFK: Reckless Youth (1993). . . . . Sadie

Dziubinska, Anulka *

a.k.a. Anulka.

Films:

Vampyres (1974; British). . . . . Miriam
- 0:00—Brief full frontal nudity in bed with Fran, kissing each other before getting shot.
- 0:43—Breasts taking a shower with Fran.
- ••• 0:58—Breasts and buns in bed with Fran, drinking Ted's blood. Brief lower frontal nudity.

Lisztomania (1975; British). . . . . Lola Montez
- •• 0:08—Breasts sitting on Roger Daltrey's lap, kissing him. Nice close up.
- 0:21—Breasts, backstage with Daltrey after the concert.
- 0:39—Breasts, wearing pasties, during Daltrey's nightmare/song and dance number.

TV:

Bare Essence (1983) . . . . .Natasha

Eagger, Victoria

Films:

Man of Flowers (1984; Australian) . . . . .Angela
- •• 1:08—Breasts, when lying on the floor, then full frontal nudity while putting on her blouse.

A Woman's Tale (1991; Australian) . . . . .Nurse 1

Easterbrook, Leslie

Films:

Just Tell Me What You Want (1980). . . . . .Hospital Nurse

Police Academy (1984) . . . . Callahan

Private Resort (1985) . . . . Bobbie Sue
- •• 0:14—Very brief buns taking off swimsuit, then breasts and buns under sheer white nightgown.

Police Academy III: Back in Training (1986) . . . . Callahan

Police Academy 4: Citizens on Patrol (1987) . . . . Callahan

Police Academy 5: Assignment Miami Beach (1988) . . Callahan

Police Academy 6: City Under Siege (1989) . . . . Callahan

Police Academy: Mission to Moscow (1994) . . . Capt. Callahan

Made for Cable Movies:

Two Voices (1997; Lifetime) . . . . n.a.

Made for TV Movies:

The Taking of Flight 847: The Uli Derickson Story (1988) . . . . Audrey

TV:

Ryan's Hope . . . . Devlin Kowalski

Laverne & Shirley (1980-83) . . . . Rhonda Lee

Easton, Jackie

Films:

Hardbodies (1984) . . . . Girl in Dressing Room
- •• 0:27—Breasts taking off dress to try on swimsuit.
- •• 0:40—Breasts with other topless girls posing for photographs taken by Rounder. She's wearing a white skirt.

School Spirit (1985) . . . . .Hogette

Eastwood, Jayne

Films:

My Pleasure is My Business (1974) . . . . Isabella
- 1:16—Breasts in bed trying to get His Excellency's attention.
- •• 1:28—Breasts sitting up in bed with blonde guy.

One Man (1979; Canadian) . . . . Alicia Brady

Finders Keepers (1983) . . . . .Anna-Marie Biddlecoff

Night Friend (1987; Canadian) . . . . Rita the Bag Lady

Candy Mountain (1988; Swiss/Canadian/French) . . . . . . Lucille

Cold Comfort (1988) . . . . Mrs. Brocket

Hostile Takeover (1988; Canadian) . . . . Mrs. Talmage

a.k.a. Office Party

The Santa Clause (1994) . . . . Waitress

That Old Feeling (1997) . . . . Aunt Iris

Made for Cable Movies:

Harrison Bergeron (1995; Showtime) . . . . .Ms. Newbound

Made for TV Movies:

Anne of Green Gables (1985; Canadian) . . . . . Mrs. Hammond

Against Their Will: Women in Prison (1994). . . . . .Marge

Eccles, Aimée *

Films:

Little Big Man (1970) . . . . .Sunshine

Pretty Maids All in a Row (1971). . . . . .Hilda
- 1:06—Partial buns while sitting on desk in Rock Hudson's office. Her hair covers most of her right breast.

Group Marriage (1972) . . . . Chris
- 0:15—Buns, while getting into bed.
- 1:15—Brief side view of left breast and buns getting into the shower.

Ulzana's Raid (1972) . . . . .McIntosh's Indian Woman

Paradise Alley (1978). . . . . Susan

The Concrete Jungle (1982) . . . . .Spider

Lovelines (1984) . . . . Nisei

Eckert, Shari *

Films:

Nighttime Lover (1995). . . . . Frightened Young Woman

a.k.a. Call Girl
- •• 0:31—Breasts, when blindfolded and tied to a post while being caressed by a guy.

Kissing a Dream (1996) . . . . .Nicole
- •• 0:15—Breasts and buns, while making love with Peter.
- •• 0:49—Breasts, while trying to seduce Peter in office.

Bikini Traffic School (1997) . . . . .Vicky
- ••• 0:05—Breasts and buns in T-back, while dancing on stage with Marcie and Traci.
- •• 0:18—Breasts, while frolicking in the pool with Marcie and Vicki.
- •• 0:21—Breasts, while sunbathing.
- ••• 0:51—Breasts and very brief lower frontal nudity, while making love with the tennis instructor on tennis court.
- ••• 0:58—Breasts, while making love with the pool guy in spa.

Made for Cable TV:

Erotic Confessions: At the Tone (1997; Cinemax). . . . . Waitress

Compromising Situations: Single Love Missy (1998; Showtime) . . . . Lucy
- •• 0:18—Buns in panties and breasts, while making love with Renny in supply closet.

Video Tapes:

Playboy's Cheerleaders (1996). . . . . Cheerleader

Eden, Simone *

Video Tapes:

Playboy Video Calendar 1990 (1989) . . . . August
- ••• 0:40—Nude.

Wet & Wild (1989) . . . . .Model

Playmates at Play (1990) . . . . Gotta Dance

Playboy's 21 Playmates: Volume II (1996) . . . . . .Playmate
- ••• 0:36—Nude in still photos.
- ••• 0:37—Nude at the beach.

Edmondson, Donna *

Video Tapes:

Playboy Video Centerfold: Lynne Austin. . . . . . .Playmate

Playboy Video Calendar 1988 (1987) . . . . .Playmate

Playboy Video Centerfold: Donna Edmondson (1987) . . . . Playmate of the Year 1987
••• 0:00—Nude, behind shower door, in photo session, on sofa in house, in empty house and in the rain.
Playboy Video Magazine, Volume 12 (1987) . . . . Playmate
••• 0:08—Nude in clips from her Playmate video.
Playboy's Playmates of the Year: The '80s (1989) . . . . Playmate of the Year 1987
••• 0:21—Modeling swimsuits and lingerie. Nude on couch.
••• 0:22—In bra, garter belt and stockings, dancing in strobe light. Lower frontal nudity. Nude seen through open window.
••• 0:23—Nude, taking off her clothes in empty house. Nude in bed.
•• 0:26—Breasts, in the rain.
•• 0:52—Full frontal nudity in bed.
Wet & Wild (1989) . . . . Model
Playmates at Play (1990) . . . . Gotta Dance
The Best of Video Playmate Calendars (1992) . . Playmate
••• 0:30—In lingerie, then nude during music video segment with a chair.
••• 0:32—In lingerie, then nude in bed and in still photos.

*Edwards, Barbara **

Films:
Malibu Express (1984) . . . . May
•• 0:10—Breasts taking a shower with Kimberly McArthur on the boat.
•• 1:05—Breasts serving Cody coffee while he talks on the telephone.
Terminal Entry (1986) . . . . Lady Electric
••• 0:05—Breasts taking a shower and getting a towel during video game scene.
Another Chance (1989) . . . . Diana the Temptress
••• 0:38—Breasts in trailer with Johnny.
Video Tapes:
Playboy Video Magazine, Volume 4 (1983) . . . . . Playmate
•• 0:20—Breasts on sailboat.
••• 0:22—Nude, posing for centerfold photograph.
••• 0:24—Full frontal nudity on bed by herself.
••• 0:29—Nude, dancing in laser light show.
Playboy's Playmate Review 3 (1985) . . . . Playmate
Playboy Video Calendar 1987 (1986) . . . . Playmate
Playboy's Fantasies (1987) . . . . Fashion
•• 0:00—Full frontal nudity during modeling session.
Sexy Lingerie (1988) . . . . Model
Playboy's Playmates of the Year: The '80s (1989) . . . . Playmate of the Year 1984
••• 0:13—Nude in still photos.
••• 0:14—Full frontal nudity in centerfold photo session. More in bed.
•• 0:52—Full frontal nudity in bed.
Wet & Wild (1989) . . . . Model
Playboy Video Centerfold: Kerri Kendall (1990) . . . . Playmate
••• 0:37—Nude.
Playboy's Fantasies II (1990). . The Game/The Secret Garden
••• 0:07—Nude, walking around in garden while a guy watches her.
••• 0:30—Full frontal nudity while trying on different clothes for her lover.
Playboy's Playmates Revisited (1998) . . . . Playmate
••• 0:56—Nude in old footage and still photos.
••• 1:00—Nude in new footage.

Edwards, Elaine

Films:
Dancing in the Dark (1949) . . . . Girl
Old Oklahoma Plains (1952) . . . . Terry Ramsey
The Harder They Fall (1956) . . . . Vince's Girlfriend
Curse of the Faceless Man (1958) . . . . Tina Enright
The Bat (1959) . . . . Dale Dailey
The Purple Gang (1960) . . . . Gladys Harley
You Have to Run Fast (1961) . . . . Laurie Maitland
The Curious Female (1969) . . . . Mrs. Wilde
• 0:56—Breasts in bed with a young man before Joan walks in the room.
Fiddler on the Roof (1971). Shprintze

Edwards, Ella

Films:
Sweet Sugar (1972) . . . . Simone
a.k.a. Hellfire on Ice
• 0:58—Breasts in bed with Mojo.
Detroit 9000 (1973) . . . . Helen
Mr. Ricco (1975) . . . . Sally
Famous T & A (1982) . . . . Simone
(No longer available for purchase, check your video store for rental.)
•• 1:07—Buns and breasts in outtakes from *Sweet Sugar.*

Ege, Julie

Films:
On Her Majesty's Secret Sevice (1969; British) . . . . Scandanavian Girl
Think Dirty (1970; British) . . . . Inga
a.k.a. Every Home Should Have One
• 0:43—Brief full frontal nudity, twice, in photo that Marty Feldman looks at.
•• 0:44—Brief breasts in another photo. Breasts and buns, while running around in a "documentary" about Sweden with Marty Feldman, then in a "Swedish" film.
Creatures the World Forgot (1971; British) . . Nala, The Girl
• 0:56—Very brief breasts several times (it looks like a stunt double) fighting in cave with The Dumb Girl. Hard to see.
• 1:32—Very, very brief half of right breast when fighting a snake that is wrapped around her face.
Up Pompeii (1971; British) . . . . Voluptua
• 0:45—Partial right breast, while she thinks she seducing Ludicrus. There is some kind of jewelry covering her right nipple.
The Mutations (1973; British). Hedi
a.k.a. Freakmaker
1:19—Partial right breast, while in bathtub.
•• 1:26—Right breast, then breasts, while lying on table in Donald Pleasance's laboratory.
The Legend of the 7 Golden Vampires (1974; British/Chinese) . . . . Vanessa Buren

Eggar, Samantha

Films:
The Collector (1965) . . . . Miranda Grey
• 1:38—Brief back side of left breast after taking off gown in front of Stamp, just before she unbuttons his shirt.
Doctor Dolittle (1967) . . . . Emma
A Name for Evil (1973). Joanna Blake
• 0:42—Very brief breasts turning over in bed with Robert Culp. Dark, hard to see.
Battle Force (1976) . . . . Annelise Ackerman
The Uncanny (1977; British) . . . . Edina
The Brood (1979; Canadian) . . . . Nola Carveth

The Executioner (1980). . . . . Dr. Megan Stewart
Curtains (1983; Canadian) . . . . Samantha Sherwood
Round Numbers (1990) . . . . Anne
Dark Horse (1992). . . . . Mrs. Curtis
The Phantom (1996). . . . . Lily Palmer

Made for Cable Movies:
A Ghost in Monte Carlo (1990). Jeanne

Miniseries:
Secrets of Lake Success (1993) . . . . Diana

Made for TV Movies:
All the Kind Strangers (1974) . . . . Carol Ann
Barbara Taylor Bradford's "Everything to Gain" (1996)
. . . . Diana Keswick

TV:
Anna and the King (1972). . . . . Anna Owens

*Egger, Jolanda **

Video Tapes:
Playmates at Play (1990) . . . . Bareback, Making Waves

Eggert, Nicole

Films:
Clan of the Cave Bear (1985) . . . . Middle Ayla
Omega Syndrome (1986) . . . . Jessie Corbett
The Haunting of Morella (1989) . . . . Morella/Lenora
(Nude scenes are an obvious body double. Note different color hair and skin.)
Kinjite (1989) . . . . Dee Dee
Blown Away (1992) . . . . Megan
(Unrated version reviewed. Not to be confused with *Blown Away* (1994) with Jeff Bridges.)
••• 0:12—Right breast then breasts and buns, while standing in bedroom, making out with Corey Haim.
•• 0:15—Breasts and buns, getting out of bed with Haim.
•• 0:24—Breasts, while making love in bed with Haim.
• 0:26—Left breast, while in shower with Haim.
••• 0:46—Breasts, while making love, sitting on Haim's lap in front of fire.
• 1:00—Upper half of buns, in bed with Haim.
• 1:10—Brief breasts and buns, while getting out of bed.
• 1:26—Very brief half of right breast and buns in T-back under sheer nightgown, while making love in bed on top of Corey Feldman.
• 1:28—Very brief right breast, while getting shot by policeman.
The Double O Kid (1992) . . . . Melinda
Just One of the Girls (1992). . . . . Marie Stark
a.k.a. Anything For Love
Amanda and the Alien (1995). Amanda
The Demolitionist (1996) . . . . Alyssa/The Demolitionist

TV:
T.J. Hooker (1982-87) . . . . Chrissie
Charles in Charge (1987-90). . . . . Jamie Powell
Baywatch (1992-94) . . . . Summer Quinn
Home Fires (1992) . . . . Libby

*Egler, Kimberly **

Video Tapes:
Playboy's Girls of Radio: Talk, Rock and Shock (1995)
. . . . Herself
••• 0:00—In yellow bra and panties, then nude with three other women.

Eichhorn, Lisa

Films:
The Europeans (1979; British) . . . . Gertrude Wentworth
Yanks (1979) . . . . Jean Moreton
• 1:48—Brief breasts in bed when Richard Gere rolls off her.
Why Would I Lie? (1980). . . . . Kay
Cutter's Way (1981) . . . . Maureen "Mo" Cutter
a.k.a. Cutter and Bone
• 1:07—Brief right breast, wearing bathrobe, lying on lounge chair while Jeff Bridges looks at her.
The Weather in the Streets (1983; British) . . . . Olivia
Wild Rose (1984). . . . . June Lorich
Opposing Force (1986) . . . . Lieutenant Casey
a.k.a. Hell Camp
• 0:17—Wet T-shirt after going through river.
••• 0:33—Breasts getting sprayed with water and dusted with white powder.
•• 1:03—Breasts after getting raped by Anthony Zerbe in his office, while another officer watches.
••• 1:05—Breasts and buns, getting dressed.
Grim Prairie Tales (1990) . . . . Maureen
Moon 44 (1990; West German). . . . . Terry Morgan
King of the Hill (1993). . . . . Mrs. Kurlander
The Vanishing (1993) . . . . Helene
First Kid (1996) . . . . Linda Davenport

Made for Cable Movies:
Devlin (1991; Showtime). . . . . Anita Brennan

Made for TV Movies:
A Woman Named Jackie (1991). . . . . Dr. Jordan

TV:
All My Children . . . . Elizabeth Carlyle

Eilbacher, Lisa

Films:
An Officer and a Gentleman (1982). . . . . Casey Seeger
10 to Midnight (1983) . . . . Laurie Kessler
Beverly Hills Cop (1984) . . . . Jenny Summers
Live Wire (1992) . . . . Terry O'Neill
(Unrated version reviewed.)
••• 1:01—Brief breasts several times and partial buns, in bath tub and in bed with Pierce Brosnan. Some of the love making scenes in bed were cut for the R-rated version.

Made for Cable Movies:
Blind Man's Bluff (1992; USA) . . . . Dr. Herz

Miniseries:
Wheels (1978). . . . . Jody Horton
The Winds of War (1983). . . . . Madeline Henry

Made for TV Movies:
Ordeal of Patty Hearst (1979) . . . . Patty Hearst
Deadly Deception (1987) . . . . Anne
Manhunt: Search for the Night Stalker (1989). . . . . Ann
Joshua's Heart (1990) . . . . Kit
Judith Krantz's "Dazzle" (1995) . . . . Fernanda
The Return of Hunter (1995) . . . . Sally Vogel

TV:
The Texas Wheelers (1974-75). . . . . Sally
The Hardy Boys Mysteries (1977) . . . . Callie Shaw
Ryan's Four (1983) . . . . Dr. Ingrid Sorenson
Me and Mom (1985). . . . . Kate Morgan
Midnight Caller (1990-91). . . . . Nicolette "Nicky" Molloy

Eilber, Janet

Films:
Whose Life Is It, Anyway? (1981) . . . . Patty
•• 0:30—Nude, ballet dancing during B&W dream sequence.
• 1:13—Very brief side of left breast when her back is turned while changing clothes.
Romantic Comedy (1983) . . . . Allison
Hard to Hold (1984) . . . . Diana Lawson

The Craft (1996) . . . . Sarah's Mother
Made for Cable Movies:
Not Like Us (1995; Showtime). . . . . Mrs. Bower
Made for TV Movies:
Confessions: Two Faces of Evil (1994) . . . . Anne Watson
TV:
Two Marriages (1983-84) . . . . Nancy Armstrong
The Best Times (1985). . . . . Joanne Braithwaite

*Ekland, Britt **

Ex-wife of the late actor Peter Sellers.
Ex-wife of Stray Cats drummer Jim McDonnell.
Films:
After the Fox (1966) . . . . Gina Romantiea
The Bobo (1967). . . . . Olimpia Segura
The Night They Raided Minsky's (1968)
. . . . Rachel Schpitendavel
• 1:34—Brief breasts, when her dress accidentally falls down during strip tease routine on stage. Probably a body double because you don't see her face. (A reader has a letter from the director who says it's a body double.)
The Cannibals (1969) . . . . Antigone
Stiletto (1969). . . . . Illeana
Get Carter (1971; British) . . . . Anna
•• 0:39—Breasts, after taking off bra, and caressing herself while having phone sex with Michael Caine.
What the Peeper Saw (1971; British) . . . . Elise
a.k.a. Night Hair Child
• 0:38—Sort of side view of left breast in bed. Don't really see anything.
The Wicker Man (1973; British) . . . . Willow
••• 0:58—Breasts in bed knocking on the wall, then more breasts and buns getting up and walking around the bedroom. Long scene. Body double used when you don't see her face when pounding on the wall. (Britt's hair is shorter than the body double's.)
The Man with the Golden Gun (1974; British)
. . . . Mary Goodnight
The Ultimate Thrill (1974) . . . . Michele
Endless Night (1977) . . . . Greta
• 1:21—Brief breasts several times with Michael.
Slavers (1977) . . . . Anna
• 0:40—Breasts undressing in front of Ron Ely.
Sex on the Run (1979; German/French/Italian)
. . . . Countess Trivulsi
a.k.a. Some Like It Cool
a.k.a. Casanova and Co.
• 0:44—Left breast while making love in bed with Tony Curtis (don't see her face).
Demon Rage (1981) . . . . Ann-Marie
a.k.a. Dark Eyes
a.k.a. Demon Seed
The Monster Club (1981; British) . . . . Lintom's Mother
Erotic Images (1983) . . . . Julie Todd
• 0:16—Brief side view of left breast in bed with Glenn.
••• 0:29—In bra, then breasts in bed with Glenn.
Love Scenes (1984) . . . . Annie
a.k.a. Ecstacy
Moon in Scorpio (1987) . . . . Linda
Beverly Hills Vamp (1989) . . . . Madam Cassandra
Scandal (1989) . . . . Mariella Novotny
(Unrated version reviewed.)
•• 0:31—Breasts, while lying on table with John Hurt.
• 0:51—Right breast, while talking with Hurt and Joanne Whalley.
The Children (1990; British/German). . . . . Zinnia Wrench
Cold Heat (1991). . . . . Jackie Mallon

*Eleniak, Erika **

Films:
E.T. The Extraterrestrial (1982). . . . . Pretty Girl
The Blob (1988) . . . . Vicki De Soto
Under Siege (1992). . . . . Jordan Tate
•• 0:43—Buns in T-back, then brief breasts in open coat, while popping out of cake.
The Beverly Hillbillies (1993) . . . . Elly May
Chasers (1994). . . . . Toni Johnson
••• 1:03—In bra, then breasts and buns, while making love in bed with William McNamara.
Girl in the Cadillac (1995) . . . . Mandy
A Pyromaniac's Love Story (1995) . . . . Stephanie
Bordello of Blood (1996) . . . . Katherine Verdoux
Made for TV Movies:
Baywatch (1989). . . . . Shauni McLain
TV:
Charles in Charge (1988-89) . . . . Stephanie Curtis
Baywatch (1989-90) . . . . Shauni McLain
Baywatch (1991-94) . . . . Shauni McLain
Video Tapes:
Playboy Video Centerfold: Fawna MacLaren (1988)
. . . . Playmate
••• 0:07—In studio, nude.
Playboy Video Calendar 1991 (1990) . . . . May
••• 0:18—Nude.

Elian, Yona

Films:
The Jerusalem File (1972; U.S./Israel). . . . . Raschel
The Last Winter (1983; Israeli). Maya
•• 0:48—Breasts taking off her robe to get into pool.
• 0:49—Buns, while lying on marble slab with Kathleen Quinlan.

Elise, Esther

See: Alise, Esther.

• *Elkin, Karen*

Films:
Sci-Fighters (1996; Canadian). . . . . Zombie Woman
• 0:57—Breasts, while lying on bed in Billy Drago's room. Eye pattern artwork is drawn on her breasts.
• 0:59—Brief breasts, while lying on the bed. Brief buns, when the bed is tipped over and she rolls over on the floor.
Made for Cable TV:
The Hunger: Bridal Suite (1997; Canadian; Showtime)
. . . . Jenny
••• 0:07—In bra and panties, then breasts, while making love with Peter in the Bridal Suite.
The Hunger: But At My Back I Always Hear
(1997; Showtime) . . . . Samantha Perry
• 0:07—In bra, then breasts with Michael Gross during his dream.

Elliott, Alison

Films:
Monkey Trouble (1993). . . . . Tessa
The Underneath (1994) . . . . Rachel
• 0:39—Very brief buns, while rolling over with Peter Gallagher. Dark.
Wyatt Earp (1994) . . . . Lou Earp
The Spitfire Grill (1996) . . . . Percy Talbot

The Wings of the Dove (1997; British). . . . . .Milly Theale

Made for Cable Movies:

Indictment: The McMartin Trial (1995; HBO) . . . . .Peggy Ann Burkey

Miniseries:

The Buccaneers (1995; U.S./British) . . . . . . Virginia St. George

• *Ellison, Tara*

Films:

Poison Ivy 2: Lily (1995) . . . . Catherine
- • 0:01—Left breast, while making love with Xander Berkeley on couch.

Power 98 (1996). . . . . Poker Woman

Elvira

a.k.a. Cassandra Peterson.

Films:

The Working Girls (1973) . . . . .Katya
- ••• 0:20—Breasts, dancing on stage.

Cheech & Chong's Next Movie (1980) . . . . .Hostage

The Best of Sex and Violence (1981). . . . . .Katya
- •• 0:40—Brief breasts dancing on stage in scene from *Working Girls.*

Famous T & A (1982) . . . . .Katya

(No longer available for purchase, check your video store for rental.)
- ••• 0:28—Breasts scene from *Working Girls.*

Jekyll & Hyde... Together Again (1982) . . . . . .Busty Nurse
- • 0:56—Brief right breast, peeking out from smock in operating room. (She's wearing a surgical mask.)

Stroker Ace (1983) . . . . .Woman with Lugs

Pee Wee's Big Adventure (1985) . . . . .Biker Mama

Echo Park (1986). . . . . Sheri

Allan Quatermain and the Lost City of Gold (1987). . . . . Sorais

Elvira, Mistress of the Dark (1988). . . . . .Elvira

Ted & Venus (1991) . . . . Lisa

Ring of the Musketeers (1992) . . . . Jennifer

Made for Cable Movies:

Acting on Impulse (1993; Showtime) . . . . Roxy

England, Audie

Films:

Delta of Venus (1995) . . . . .Elena

(Unrated version reviewed.)
- ••• 0:21—Breasts, while making love with Costas Mandylor on cupboard counter top.
- ••• 0:29—Full frontal nudity, after dropping her blanket to let Mandylor look at her, then making love.
- •• 0:43—Nude, while posing with a male model for an art class.
- • 1:00—Side view of left breast and buns, while posing with male model in art class again.
- •• 1:01—Breasts, while posing and talking with the model.
- • 1:02—Brief buns, twice, when a guy feels her up her dress.
- •• 1:03—Breasts, while making love with a guy in back of car.
- •• 1:16—Full frontal nudity, taking off her clothes then making love with two other women in opium den.
- ••• 1:33—Breasts, while making love with Mandylor on stairs inside church.

One Good Turn (1995). . . . . .Kristen
- •• 0:49—Breasts, while making love with James Remar on roof of building.

Venus Rising (1995) . . . . Eve
- • 0:20—Very brief partial right breast while taking a bath.
- • 1:00—Breasts, while making love on bed with Billy Wirth.

Made for Cable Movies:

Miami Hustle (1996; Showtime). . . . . Jean Ivers
- • 0:26—Partial buns in panties while starting to do a strip routine for a customer in bar.
- • 0:41—Partial buns in panties in outfit in bar again.
- • 0:43—Partial buns in panties in upstairs room with a customer.

Made for Cable TV:

Red Shoe Diaries: Jake's Story (1993; Showtime) . . . . . Waitress

(Available on the video tape *Red Shoe Diaries 4: Auto Erotica.*)

Red Shoe Diaries: Hotline (1994; Showtime) . . Tess Thomas
- ••• 0:09—Breasts and brief buns, after taking off dress and making love with Adam on kitchen table.
- •• 0:13—Breasts under sheer blouse, while pretending to be a hooker for Adam. Lower half of buns, under leather jacket.
- • 0:15—Breasts under sheer blouse and partial buns, after taking off jacket.
- •• 0:28—Buns and breasts, while making love with Adam on bed.

Red Shoe Diaries: Liar's Tale (1994; Showtime) . . . . . .Paula
- ••• 0:04—In lingerie when dancing in room, then breasts, then making love with Jack while Erika Anderson takes photos from outside.
- • 0:08—Breasts and buns in still photos.
- •• 0:10—Breasts in flashbacks after Anderson gets into car accident.
- • 0:12—Breasts in B&W photos and in flashbacks.
- ••• 0:18—Breasts in flashbacks intercut with Anderson's nude scenes.

Red Shoe Diaries: Divorce, Divorce (1996; Showtime) . . . . Lily
- ••• 0:14—Breasts, while lying on table in open robe, then making love with her husband.
- •• 0:19—Breasts, while making love with her husband on the floor.
- ••• 0:20—Breasts and buns, while making love in bed.
- • 0:22—Brief left breast, while sitting up in bed.

Red Shoe Diaries: Laundrymat (1997; Showtime) . . . . The Woman
- • 0:01—Breasts and buns, while making love with a guy on bed.
- •• 0:19—In bra and panties, then breasts and buns while making love with the guy in a motel room.

Made for TV Movies:

W.E.I.R.D. World (1995) . . . . Diane

• *Erbe, Kathryn*

Films:

What About Bob? (1991). Anna Martin

Rich in Love (1992) . . . . Lucille Odom

D2: The Mighty Ducks (1994) . . . . .Michele

Kiss of Death (1994) . . . . .Rosie

The Addiction (1995) . . . . Anthropology Student

Dream with the Fishes (1997) . . . . .Liz
- •• 0:01—Breasts, while talking with Nick in room. (She has a tattoo on her right breast.)
- • 0:53—Brief breasts, while swinging on a swing in a barn. Long shot. Brief breasts in closer shot when she gets off the swing.

Made for TV Movies:

Breathing Lessons (1994) . . . . Fiona

TV:

Chicken Soup (1989). . . . . Patricia Reece

• Erickson, Amber

See: Marconi, Mason.

• Ericsson, Ulrika *

Video Tapes:

Playboy Video Calendar 1998 (1997) .... October
- •• 0:40—Nude, while posing in front of some antiques.
- ••• 0:41—Nude, while posing in a dark bedroom.

Errickson, Krista

Films:

Little Darlings (1980) .... Cinder
The First Time (1981) .... Dana
a.k.a. Doin' It
Jekyll & Hyde... Together Again (1982) .... Ivy
Mortal Passions (1989) .... Emily
- •• 0:08—Brief breasts in bed with Darcy, while tied to the bed. Breasts getting untied and rolling over.
- • 0:11—Very brief right breast, rolling back on top of Darcy.
- ••• 0:40—Breasts after dropping her sheet for Burke, then making love with him.
- •• 0:46—Breasts getting into bed with her husband.

Killer Image (1991) .... Shelley
Jailbait (1993) .... Merci Cooper
a.k.a. Streetwise
- 0:11—In black bra, panties, garter belt and stockings in room with Tommy.
- •• 0:12—Breasts, while in bed handcuffing Tommy to the bed.
- 0:19—In black bra in motel room.
- 1:11—Back half of left breast, while making love with a guy.

Martial Outlaw (1993) .... Lori White
The Paperboy (1994) .... Diana

Made for TV Movies:

Deadly Lessons (1983) .... Tember

TV:

Hello, Larry (1979-80) .... Diane Adler

Eskra, Donna

Films:

Child's Play 3 (1991) .... Ivers
Twisted Love (1994) .... Penny
- •• 0:04—Breasts, several times, while making out with Mark Paul Gosselar in a room during a party. Breasts, during introduction to Beau.

Estores, Lourdes *

Video Tapes:

Playmate Playoffs .... Playmate
Playboy's Playmate Review (1982) .... Playmate
- ••• 0:56—Nude at the beach, then under water, then outside near river.

Estrin, Patricia

Films:

Act of Vengeance (1974) .... Angie
a.k.a. The Rape Squad
(Not to be confused with the film with the same name starring Charles Bronson.)
- • 0:37—Brief full frontal nudity, several times, under water in spa. (She's third from the right.)

Baby Boom (1987) .... Secretary

Eubank, Shari *

Films:

Supervixens (1973) .... SuperAngel/SuperVixen
Chesty Anderson, U.S. Navy (1975) .... Chesty
- • 0:58—Brief right breast, while making love with Fred Willard.

Evans, Linda *

Ex-wife of the late photographer/director/actor John Derek.

Films:

Beach Blanket Bingo (1965) .... Sugar Kane
Those Calloways (1965) .... Bridie Mellot
The Klansman (1974) .... Nancy Poteet
Mitchell (1975) .... Greta
The Avalanche Express (1979) .... Elsa Lang
Tom Horn (1980) .... Glendoline Kimmel

Miniseries:

North and South, Book II (1986) .... Rose Sinclair
Dynasty: The Reunion (1991) .... Krystle Jennings Carrington

Made for TV Movies:

The Last Frontier (1986) .... Kate
The Gambler Returns: The Luck of the Draw (1991) .... Kate Muldoon

TV:

Big Valley (1965-69) .... Audra Barkley
Hunter (1977) .... Marty Shaw
Dynasty (1981-89) .... Krystle Jennings Carrington

Video Tapes:

Playboy Video Magazine, Volume 1 (1982) .... Herself
- •• 0:58—Breasts and side view of buns, in still photos from *Playboy* layout.

Evens, Candie

See: Poremba, Jean.

Evenson, Kim *

Films:

The Big Bet (1985) .... Beth
- •• 0:36—Right breast, sitting on couch with Chris.
- •• 0:45—Brief breasts, twice, taking off swimsuit top.
- •• 0:54—Brief breasts three times in elevator when Chris pulls her sweater up.
- •• 1:06—Nude when Chris fantasizes about her being in the video tape that he's watching. Long shot.
- ••• 1:19—In white bra and panties, then nude while undressing for Chris.

Porky's Revenge (1985; Canadian) .... Inga
- •• 0:02—Right breast, while opening her graduation gown during Pee Wee's dream.
- •• 1:27—Breasts showing Pee Wee that she doesn't have any clothes under her graduation gown.

Kidnapped (1986) .... Debbie
- • 0:25—Right breast in bed talking on the phone. Long shot, hard to see.
- ••• 1:28—Breasts getting her arm prepared for a drug injection. Long scene.
- ••• 1:30—Breasts acting in a movie. Long shot, then close up. Wearing a G-string.

Kandyland (1987) .... Joni
- ••• 0:31—Breasts doing first dance routine.
- •• 0:45—Brief breasts during another routine with bubbles floating around.

Video Tapes:

Playmate Playoffs .... Playmate
Wet & Wild (1989) .... Model
Playboy Video Centerfold: Kerri Kendall (1990) .... Playmate
- ••• 0:35—Nude.

Playmates at Play (1990) .... Flights of Fancy

Playboy's 21 Playmates (1996) .... Playmate
••• 0:55—Nude in still photos.
••• 0:56—Full frontal nudity in bedroom.

Everhard, Nancy

Films:
Double Revenge (1988) .... Susie Taylor
Deepstar Six (1989) .... Joyce Collins
The Punisher (1989) .... Sam Leary
Another 48 Hrs. (1990) .... Female Doctor
Demonstone (1990) .... Sharon Gale
• 0:47—Very, very brief backside view of tip of left breast after bending over to pick up robe off the floor.
Made for Cable Movies:
This Gun for Hire (1990; USA) .... Anne
•• 1:03—Buns and breasts, after taking off panties and sitting down in bathtub.
• 1:07—Buns, when walking toward Robert Wagner.
Made for TV Movies:
An Eight is Enough Wedding (1989) .... Mike
TV:
Houston Knights (1987-88)......................... Carol
The Family Man (1991)......................... Jill Nichols
Reasonable Doubts (1991-93)................ Kay Lockman

• Everhart, Angie *

Supermodel.
Ex-wife of actor Ashley Hamilton.
Films:
Last Action Hero (1993) .... Video Babe
Jade (1995)................................ Patrice Jacinto
Another 9 1/2 Weeks (1996) .... Lea
• 0:47—Brief buns in panties and side view of right breast, when checking out Mickey Rourke's closet.
• 0:48—Brief left breast in reflection in mirror. Brief buns in panties when dancing.
• 0:49—Brief left breast, when it slips out of her shirt, after getting a necktie.
• 1:15—Very brief left breast, when sitting up in bathtub.
•• 1:17—Brief side of right breast, then breasts and buns, while lying in bed when Rourke plays with her using flower petals, wine and honey.
• 1:34—Brief top of right breast, popping out of her top, when jerk guy rolls her over on the floor.
Bordello of Blood (1996).......................... Lilith
Executive Target (1996) ....Lacey
Mad Dog Time (1996) .... Gabriella
Video Tapes:
Sports Illustrated: 1994 Swimsuit Issue Video (1994).... Model
(Unedited Version reviewed.)

Evridge, Melissa *

Video Tapes:
Playboy Video Calendar 1992 (1991) .... April
••• 0:13—Nude outside in garden.
••• 0:15—Nude in action-movie fantasy in the desert.

Fabian, Ava *

a.k.a. Katherine Campbell.
Films:
Dragnet (1987)............................... Baitmate
Terminal Exposure (1988) .... Bruce's Girl
To Die For (1988) ....Franny
Limit Up (1989) .... Sasha
Ski School (1990) ....Victoria
••• 0:53—In white bra and panties, then breasts making love with Johnny.
Welcome Home Roxy Carmichael (1990)
.... Roxy Carmichael
• 0:10—Buns under the water in swimming pool, then more buns when getting out.
Auntie Lee's Meat Pies (1991) .... Magnolia
• 1:29—Buns, while swimming in one piece swimsuit under water.
Mobsters (1991) ....Cute Girl
a.k.a. Mobsters—The Evil Empire
Last Man Standing (1994)........................Lucretia
Midnight Temptations (1995) .... Raya
• 0:12—Brief buns, while making love with a guy in storage area while Wendy Hamilton watches.
•• 1:14—Breasts, while making love with Jonathon.
Busted (1996) .... Lacey
•• 0:05—Breasts and buns, while taking a shower with Devin De Vasquez in the police shower room. Sometimes with Corey Feldman.
• 1:08—Breasts and buns, while fooling around in bed with Martin and Devin.
Made for Cable TV:
Erotic Confessions: Chalk It Up (1995; Cinemax)
.... Jacqueline Stone
• 0:00—Breasts, while reading letter.
Erotic Confessions: Games People Play (1995; Cinemax)
.... Jacqueline Stone
• 0:01—Breasts, walking into house and reading letter.
Erotic Confessions: Watching Vanessa (1995; Cinemax)
.... Jacqueline Stone
• 0:01—Nude in steam room, while reading a letter.
Erotic Confessions: Arresting Developments (1996; Cinemax)....................... Jacqueline Stone
• 0:00—Breasts and buns, while reading letter in pool.
Erotic Confessions: Boss's Orders (1996; Cinemax)
.... Jacqueline Stone
(Available on video tape in *Erotic Confessions, Volume 2: Intrigue.*)
• 0:01—Brief breasts in open robe, while sitting in chair, reading letter.
Erotic Confessions: Coming Clean (1996; Cinemax)
.... Jacqueline Stone
(Available on video tape in *Erotic Confessions, Volume 1: Desire.*)
• 0:00—Breasts, when coming in from outside into the house.
Erotic Confessions: Elevation (1996; Cinemax)
.... Jacqueline Stone
• 0:01—In sheer white dress, while reading letter.
Erotic Confessions: Friends and Lovers (1996; Cinemax)
.... Jacqueline Stone
(Available on video tape in *Erotic Confessions, Volume 2: Intrigue.*)
• 0:00—Breasts, while reading letter on balcony.
Erotic Confessions: Gifts (1996; Cinemax)
.... Jacqueline Stone
(Available on video tape in *Erotic Confessions, Volume 2: Intrigue.*)
•• 0:00—Breasts, while taking off dress and putting on lingerie.

Erotic Confessions: Lap Dance (1996; Cinemax) . . . . Jacqueline Stone
(Available on video tape in *Erotic Confessions, Volume 4: Pleasure.*)
• 0:01—Partial right breast, while reading letter on balcony.
Erotic Confessions: Lessons (1996; Cinemax) . . . . Jacqueline Stone
(Available on video tape in *Erotic Confessions, Volume 2: Intrigue.*)
Erotic Confessions: Locked Up (1996; Cinemax) . . . . Jacqueline Stone
(Available on video tape in *Erotic Confessions, Volume 3: Passion.*)
Erotic Confessions: Love Calling (1996; Cinemax) . . . . Jacqueline Stone
(Available on video tape in *Erotic Confessions, Volume 3: Passion.*)
Erotic Confessions: Madelyn's Laundry (1996; Cinemax) . . . . Jacqueline Stone
(Available on video tape in *Erotic Confessions, Volume 4: Pleasure.*)
• 0:00—Breasts, while reading letter overlooking horse corral.
Erotic Confessions: Messy (1996; Cinemax) . . . . Jacqueline Stone
(Available on video tape in *Erotic Confessions, Volume 2: Intrigue.*)
• 0:00—Breasts, while reading letter on the floor next to fireplace.
Erotic Confessions: Model Situation (1996; Cinemax) . . . . Jacqueline Stone
• 0:00—Partial breasts in open robe when reading letter.
Erotic Confessions: The Address (1996; Cinemax) . . . . Jacqueline Stone
• 0:01—Breasts, while reading letter on the beach.
Erotic Confessions: The Business Trip (1996; Cinemax) . . . . Jacqueline Stone
(Available on video tape in *Erotic Confessions, Volume 4: Pleasure.*)
•• 0:01—Breasts, while reading letter by swimming pool.
Erotic Confessions: The Driver (1996; Cinemax) . . . . Jacqueline Stone
• 0:01—Breasts, while walking in house and leaning against the wall to read a letter.
Erotic Confessions: The Painting (1996; Cinemax) . . . . Jacqueline Stone
(Available on video tape in *Erotic Confessions, Volume 3: Passion.*)
•• 0:01—Breasts, while walking in panties and robe in garden.
Erotic Confessions: The Workout (1996; Cinemax) . . . . Jacqueline Stone
• 0:00—Brief full frontal nudity, after working out, while reading letter.
Erotic Confessions: At the Tone (1997; Cinemax) . . . . Jacqueline Stone
• 0:00—Breasts, while reading letter next to window.
Erotic Confessions: Finders Keepers (1997; Cinemax) . . . . Jacqueline Stone
•• 0:00—Breasts, while reading letter in chair.
Erotic Confessions: Midnight Showing (1997; Cinemax) . . . . Jacqueline Stone
Erotic Confessions: Opening Lines (1997; Cinemax) . . . . Jacqueline Stone
Erotic Confessions: Southern Hospitality (1997; Cinemax) . . . . Jacqueline Stone
• 0:00—Breasts, while reading letter in dining room.
Erotic Confessions: The Hat Check Boy (1997; Cinemax) . . . . Jacqueline Stone
•• 0:00—Nude, while reading letter by the pool.
Erotic Confessions: The Partners (1997; Showtime) . . . . Jacqueline Stone
•• 0:01—Nude, while reading letter in steam room.
Erotic Confessions: Through an Open Window (1997; Cinemax) . . . . Jacqueline Stone
Erotic Confessions: Trapped (1997; Cinemax) . . . . Jacqueline Stone

Video Tapes:
Playmate Playoffs . . . . Playmate
Playboy Video Magazine, Volume 12 (1987) . . . . Playmate
••• 1:08—Nude, in bed, in still photos, in rainy scene, dancing like Kim Basinger in *9 1/2 Weeks.*
Sexy Lingerie (1988) . . . . Model
Playboy Video Calendar 1990 (1989) . . . . July
••• 0:34—Nude.
Wet & Wild (1989) . . . . Model
Playmates at Play (1990) . . . . Gotta Dance
Sexy Lingerie II (1990) . . . . Model
Wet & Wild II (1990) . . . . Model
Sexy Lingerie III (1991) . . . . Model
Wet & Wild III (1991) . . . . Model
The Best of Sexy Lingerie (1992) . . . . Model
The Best of Wet and Wild (1992) . . . . Model
Playboy Playmates in Paradise (1992) . . . . Playmate
Playboy's Sexy, Steamy, Sultry (1993) . . . . Playmate
Playboy's Playmates Revisited (1998) . . . . Playmate
••• 0:39—Nude in old footage and still photos.
••• 0:44—Full frontal nudity in new footage.

Faillace, Mimi *

Films:
Uninhibited (1993) . . . . Rocco Gambino's Wife
• 0:18—Right breast, while making out with Gambino.

Video Tapes:
Penthouse Forum Letters: Volume 1 (1993) . . . . The Paint Job/Gina
••• 0:01—Full frontal nudity in bedroom, rubbing lotion on herself and masturbating.
••• 0:05—Nude while making love in kitchen with Mario.
•• 0:09—Left breast, while making love with Mario on the sofa.
••• 0:13—Breasts and buns, while making love in bed with the painter.

Fairchild, June *

Films:
Pretty Maids All in a Row (1971) . . Sonya "Sonny" Swingle
• 1:10—Brief breasts and lower frontal nudity, taking Polaroid photos of herself in Rock Hudson's office.
Drive, He Said (1972) . . . . Sylvie
• 0:16—Buns, brief breasts and lower frontal nudity, while walking around in the dark while Gabriel shines a flashlight on her.
• 1:01—Breasts, then briefly nude getting dressed while Gabriel goes crazy and starts trashing a house.
Top of the Heap (1972) . . . . Balloon Thrower
Detroit 9000 (1973) . . . . Barbara
Your Three Minutes Are Up (1973) . . . . Sandi

Thunderbolt and Lightfoot (1974) .... Gloria
- 0:20—Very brief right breast and buns, while getting dressed in the bathroom after making love with Clint Eastwood.

The Student Body (1975) .... Mitzi Mashall
- 0:15—Brief breasts and buns, running and jumping into the pool during party. Brief long shot breasts, while in the pool.
- •• 0:21—Breasts getting into bed.

Up in Smoke (1978) .... Ajax Lady

Fairchild, Morgan *

Films:

The Seduction (1982) .... Jamie
- 0:02—Brief breasts under water, swimming in pool.
- 0:05—Very brief left breast, getting out of the pool to answer the telephone.
- •• 0:51—Breasts pinning her hair up for her bath, then brief left breast in bathtub covered with bubbles.
- 1:21—Breasts getting into bed. Kind of dark, hard to see anything.

Terror in the Aisles (1984) .... Jamie
- •• 1:06—Breasts in mirror in scene from *The Seduction.*
- 1:08—Brief left breast, getting out of pool from *The Seduction.*

Pee Wee's Big Adventure (1985) .... "Dottie"

Red-Headed Stranger (1986) .... Kaysha
- 0:03—Bathing in stream in wet white dress. Long shot, then closer shot.

Campus Man (1987)................. Katherine Van Buren
Deadly Illusion (1987).......... Jane Mallory/Sharon Burton
Midnight Cop (1988; Italian) .... Lisa
Phantom of the Mall: Eric's Revenge (1988) ..... Karen Wilton
Mob Boss (1990) .... Gina
Body Chemistry 3: Point of Seduction (1993) .... Beth Clancey
Freaked (1993) .... Stewardess
Test Tube Teens From the Year 2000 (1993) ... Camella Swales
a.k.a. Virgin Hunters
Criminal Hearts (1995) .... D.A.
Venus Rising (1995) ....Peyton

Made for Cable Movies:

The Haunting of Sarah Hardy (1989; USA) .... n.a.
Writers Block (1991; USA)........................... n.a.

Miniseries:

North and South (1985) .... Burdetta Halloran
North and South, Book II (1986).......... Burdetta Halloran

Made for TV Movies:

The Initiation of Sarah (1978) .... Jennifer
How to Murder a Millionaire (1990) .... Loretta
Menu for Murder (1990).................... Paula Preston
Based on an Untrue Story (1993) .... Satin Chau

TV:

Search for Tomorrow (1973-77) .... Jennifer Pace Phillips
Dallas (1978) ....Jenna Wade
Flamingo Road (1981-82).........Constance Weldon Carlyle
Paper Dolls (1984) ....Racine
Falcon Crest (1985-86)....................Jordan Roberts
The City (1995-96) .... Sydney Chase

Video Tapes:

Playboy Video Magazine, Volume 5 (1983) ....The Seduction
- 0:43—Brief breasts in scenes from *The Seduction* in pool and bubble bath.

Morgan Fairchild Stress Management (1991) ....Herself

CD-ROM:

Celebrity Poker (1994)................................n.a.

Faithfull, Marianne

Singer.

Former girlfriend of *Rolling Stones* singer Mick Jagger.

Films:

Girl on a Motorcycle (1968; French/British)....... Rebecca
a.k.a. Naked Under Leather
- •• 0:05—Nude, getting out of bed and walking to the door.
- 0:38—Brief side view of left breast putting nightgown on.
- 1:23—Brief breasts while lying down and talking with Alain Delon.
- 1:30—Very brief right breast a couple of times making love with Delon.

Hamlet (1969; British)..........................Ophelia
Madhouse Mansion (1974; British) ....Sophy
Assault on Agathon (1976) .... Helen Rochefort
The Turn of the Screw (1992; British) .... Narrator
Shopping (1993; British)............................ Bev
Crimetime (1996; U.S./British).................Club Singer

Falana, Lola

Singer.

Films:

The Liberation of L. B. Jones (1970) .... Emma Jones
- 0:19—Very brief breasts walking by the doorway in the bathroom. Very long shot, don't really see anything.

The Klansman (1974) ....Loretta Sykes

Lady Cocoa (1974) ....Coco
- 0:45—Left breast lying on bed, pulling up yellow towel. Long shot, hard to see.
- ••• 1:23—Breasts on boat with a guy.

Mad About You (1990) ....Casey's Secretary

TV:

The New Bill Cosby Show (1972-73)...............Regular
Ben Vereen... Comin' At Ya (1975) ....Regular

Falbo, Catrina *

Video Tapes:

Playboy's College Girls (1994) .... Herself
- ••• 0:31—In two piece swimsuit at the beach, then nude.

Falchi, Anna *

Italian model.

Films:

Cemetery Man (1993; Italian)....................... She
a.k.a. Dellamorte Dellamore
- •• 0:19—Breasts several times, while making love with Rupert Everett at cemetery and after getting bitten by her zombie husband.
- 0:26—Breasts, when falling back onto table after Everett shoots her.
- •• 1:20—Back side of right breast after undressing. Left breast, while lying on bed after making love with Ruppert Everett.

Falcone, Lisa *

Films:

In the Kingdom of the Blind: The Man With One Eye is King (1995) .... Micky's Girlfriend
- 0:09—Breasts, while dancing on stage in club. Brief buns in T-back, after walking off stage.
- 0:11—Buns, while walking around in the club.

The Corporate Ladder (1996) ....Contestant #1

Made for Cable Movies:
Breast Men (1997; HBO) . . . . Savannah
•• 0:57—Breasts, while lap dancing on David Schwimmer in club.

Fallender, Deborah

Films:
Jabberwocky (1977) . . . . The Princess
• 0:56—Buns and brief full frontal nudity in bath when Michael Palin accidentally enters the room.
• 0:57—Breasts under sheer white robe.
Best Defense (1984) . . . . Tony
Stitches (1985) . . . . Nurse #1

Fanaro, Mary

Films:
Till the End of the Night (1994) . . . . Faith
• 0:16—Brief breasts, while making love in bed with Drew.
Made for Cable Movies:
Love, Cheat & Steal (1993; Showtime) . . . . Darlene
•• 0:09—Breasts, making love with Eric Roberts on hood of car.

Farentino, Debrah *

Ex-wife of actor James Farentino.
Real name is Deborah Mullowney.
Films:
Cellar Dweller (1987) . . . . Whitney
Capone (1989) . . . . Jennie
a.k.a. Revenge of Al Capone
(Originally a Made for TV Movie.)
• 1:01—Breasts, while making love in bed with Keith Carradine.
Mortal Sins (1989) . . . . Laura Rollins
Bugsy (1991) . . . . Girl in Elevator
Malice (1993) . . . . Tanya
• 0:25—Very brief upper half of right breast, while in bed with Alec Baldwin.
• 0:26—Brief buns and breasts, while running into the bathroom. Medium long shot.
Son of the Pink Panther (1993) . . . . Princess Yasmin
Made for Cable Movies:
Dead Air (1994; USA) . . . . Karen/Laura
Made for Cable TV:
The Outer Limits: Mind Over Matter (1996; Showtime) . . . . Dr. Rachel Carter
Made for TV Movies:
The Whereabouts of Jenny (1991) . . . . Liz
Back to the Streets of San Francisco (1992) . . . . Sarah Burns
A Mother's Instinct (1996) . . . . Holly
Sisters and Other Strangers (1997) . . . . n.a.
TV:
Capitol . . . . Sloane Denning
Hooperman . . . . n.a.
Equal Justice (1990-91) . . . . Julie Janovich
Earth 2 (1994-95) . . . . Devon Adair
NYPD Blue (1994) . . . . Robin Wirkus
XXX's & OOO's (1994) . . . . Pam Randall
NYPD Blue: Rockin' Robin (May 17, 1994) . . . . Robin Wirkus
• 0:56—Partial breast and partial buns, while making love with Kelly in bed.
EZ Streets (1996-97) . . . . Theresa Conners
Total Security (1997) . . . . Jody Kiplinger

Faria, Betty

Films:
Bye Bye Brazil (1980; Brazilian) . . . . Salomé
•• 0:28—Breasts, wearing red panties, backstage with Cigano.
• 0:29—Left breast while sitting in a chair.
•• 0:38—Breasts backstage with Ciço.
• 1:24—Buns, under a mosquito net with a customer.
The Story of Fausta (1988; Brazilian) . . . . Fausta
• 1:10—Left breast, while leaning out of the shower to talk to Lourdes.

• Farina, Kimberli

Films:
Lap Dancing (1995) . . . . Lapdancer
Made for Cable TV:
Erotic Confessions: At the Tone (1997; Cinemax) . . . Fiona
•• 0:06—Buns in G-string and breasts, while dancing in club.
••• 0:11—Buns in G-string and breasts, while dancing in club then dancing for Scott.
••• 0:15—Nude with Scott, then making love with him.
Video Tapes:
Playboy Celebrity Centerfold: Jessica Hahn (1993) . . . . Extra

Farinelli, Patty *

Video Tapes:
Playboy's Playmate Review (1982) . . . . Playmate
••• 0:11—Full frontal nudity during library photo shoot and then by swimming pool.

Farmer, Marva

Films:
Video Vixens (1973) . . . . Girl
•• 0:59—Full frontal nudity in the swimming pool with three other women during commercial.
The Candy Tangerine Man (1975) . . . . n.a.

Farmer, Mimsy

Films:
More (1969; Luxemburg) . . . . Estelle
Road to Salina (1969; French/Italian) . . . . Billie
••• 0:23—Breasts and buns, undressing and running to beach with Jonas. Nude, while swimming under water.
•• 0:24—Buns and breasts, while lying on the beach with Jonas.
• 0:40—Buns and brief right breast while taking a shower. Seen through lattice work.
•• 0:41—Nude in bed with Jonas.
• 0:42—Breasts, while making love with Jonas in tent.
• 0:44—Breasts and buns, while running out of the tent into the water. Nude in the water.
• 0:56—Brief right breast in bed with Jonas.
• 1:28—Buns and brief breasts after taking a shower outside and wrapping a towel around herself.
• 1:29—Briefly nude, while rolling over in bed.
Allonsanfan (1974; Italian) . . . . Mirella
•• 1:14—Buns, while lying in bed with Marcello Mastroianni. Breasts, sitting up in bed. (Subtitles get in the way.)
• 1:15—Buns, while standing up with Mastroianni.
• 1:34—Very brief part of right breast, under her arm while kneeling on bed.
The Black Cat (1984) . . . . Jill
Codename Wildgeese (1985; Italian/German) . . . . Kathy
The Death of Mario Ricci (1985; French/Swiss) . . . Cathy Burns
Poisons (1987; French/Swiss) . . . . Ann

Faro, Caroline

Films:

Rendez-Vous (1986; French). .Juliette
- 0:22—Buns, walking up stairs, then full frontal nudity on second floor during play. Buns, while hugging Romeo and falling back into a net.

Sincerely Charlotte (1986; French) . . . . . . Irene the Baby Sitter

Farr, La Joy

Made for Cable Movies:

The Hit List (1993; Showtime). . . . . .Linda

Made for Cable TV:

Dream On: I'm With Stupid (1994; HBO) . . . . Laylee
- •• 0:01—Breasts, while doing puzzle in bed and talking to Martin.

Love Street: Brownstone (1994; Showtime). . . . . .Julie
- ••• 0:06—Nude, while making love in bed with Vince.
- ••• 0:15—Nude, while taking a shower.
- •• 0:17—Breasts, while making love in bed with Vince.
- •• 0:22—Breasts, while making love in bed with Vince.

Farrell, Belinda

Films:

Cabin Fever (1992). Lenore Hoffman
- • 0:00—Brief right breast in gaping nightie when bending over.
- ••• 0:07—Breasts on the floor with Jack during her fantasy. Long scene.
- ••• 0:16—Breasts, sitting on floor, while playing with herself and fantasizing about Jack.
- ••• 0:20—Breasts and buns, undressing and getting into bathtub.
- • 0:23—Brief lower frontal nudity and right breast in open robe.
- •• 0:27—Nude in bed with Jack and rolling over and getting out of bed.
- • 0:30—Brief breasts opening her blouse in front of Jack.
- ••• 0:32—Nude, making love in bed with Jack. Nice, long scene.
- • 0:41—Right breast, while sitting in bed and putting on a blouse.

The Voyeur (1994) . . . . Aunt Helen

The Hottest Bid (1995) . . . . Angelique
- ••• 0:21—Breasts and buns in leather and chain outfit while seducing Marty.
- •• 0:50—Breasts while making love with Marty on the floor.

Made for TV Movies:

It Takes a Thief (1987). . . . . Opera Guest

Farrell, Sharon

Films:

Marlowe (1969) . . . . Orfamay Quest

It's Alive (1974). . . . . Lenore Davies

The Premonition (1976) . . . . Sheri Bennett

The Fifth Floor (1978) . . . . .Melanie

Out of the Blue (1982) . . . . Kathy
- • 1:18—Left breast, when Don Gordon pulls it out of her nightgown and fondles it.

Sweet Sixteen (1982) . . . . Kathy

Can't Buy Me Love (1987) . . . . .Mrs. Mancini

One Man Force (1989) . . . . .Shirley

Lonely Hearts (1991) . . . . Louise
- •• 0:52—Breasts, while lying back on bed in room with Eric Roberts.

Arcade (1993). . . . . .Alex's Mom

Beyond Desire (1994) . . . . .Shirley

Made for TV Movies:

Sworn to Vengeance (1993) . . . . Sylvia Haskell

TV:

The Young and the Restless . . . . .n.a.

Saints & Sinners (1962-63) . . . . Polly

Hawaii Five-O (1979-80) . . . . Lori Wilson

Rituals (1984-85). . . . . Cherry Lane

Farrow, Mia

Sister of actress Tisa Farrow.

Daughter of the late actress Maureen O'Sullivan and the late screenwriter/director John Farrow.

Ex-wife of actor/singer Frank Sinatra.

Films:

A Dandy in Aspic (1968) . . . . Caroline

Rosemary's Baby (1968) . . . . .Rosemary Woodhouse
- • 0:10—Brief left breast in room in new apartment on floor with John Cassavetes. Hard to see anything.
- • 0:43—Brief close up of her breasts while she's sitting on a boat during a nightmare.
- •• 0:44—Buns walking on boat, then breasts during impregnation scene with the devil.

Secret Ceremony (1968) . . . . Cenci

John and Mary (1969) . . . . .Mary
- • 0:03—Buns and brief tip of left breast, while standing at the window after getting out of bed.
- • 0:04—Brief buns, while walking to bathroom.

See No Evil (1971). . . . . Sarah

High Heels (1972; French). . . . . Christine Du Pont
a.k.a. Docteur Popaul

The Great Gatsby (1974). . . . . Daisy Buchanan

Avalanche (1978) . . . . .Caroline Brace

Death on the Nile (1978; British). . . . . . .Jacqueline de Bellefort

A Wedding (1978) . . . . Buffy Brenner
- ••• 1:10—Breasts posing in front of a painting, while wearing a wedding veil.

Hurricane (1979) . . . . Charlotte Bruckner
- • 0:39—Brief left breast in open dress top while crawling under bushes at the beach.

A Midsummer Night's Sex Comedy (1982) . . . . Ariel

Broadway Danny Rose (1984) . . . . .Tina Vitale

Supergirl (1984; British). . . . . .Alura

Zelig (1984) . . . . .Dr. Fletcher

The Purple Rose of Cairo (1985) . . . . Cecelia

Hannah and Her Sisters (1986) .Hannah

Radio Days (1987). . . . . Sally White

September (1987). . . . . Lane

Another Woman (1988) . . . . Hope

Crimes and Misdemeanors (1989). . . . . .Halley Reed

New York Stories (1989) . . . . Lisa

Alice (1990). . . . . Alice

Shadows and Fog (1991) . . . . Irmy

Husbands and Wives (1992) . . . . Judy Roth

Miami Rhapsody (1994) . . . . Nina

Widow's Peak (1994). . . . . Miss O'Hare

Reckless (1995) . . . . .Rachel

TV:

Peyton Place (1964-66) . . . . .Allison MacKenzie/Harrington

*Farrow, Tisa **

Sister of actress Mia Farrow.

Daughter of actress Maureen O'Sullivan.

Films:

Some Call It Loving (1972) . . . . .Jennifer
- ••• 1:17—Breasts, while in bed with Troy.

Strange Shadows in an Empty Room (1976) . . . . .n.a.

Fingers (1978). . . . . .Carol
Winter Kills (1979). . . . . Nurse Two
Zombie (1980) . . . . Anne Bolles
Search and Destroy (1981) . . . . Kate

Faulkner, Sally *

Films:

Vampyres (1974; British). . . . . Harriet
- 1:14—Side of left breast, partial buns, then right breast while making love with John in the trailer.
- •• 1:22—Full frontal nudity getting her clothes ripped off by Fran and Miriam in the wine cellar before being killed.

Whose Child Am I? (1974; British). n.a.
Alien Prey (1984; British) . . . . Josephine
- 0:32—Very, very brief left breast taking off top.
- 0:36—Buns, while in bed with Glory Annen.
- 0:37—Breasts on her back in bed with Annen.

Favier, Sophie

Films:

Frank and I (1983) . . . . Maud
- 0:16—Nude, undressing then breasts lying in bed with Charles.
- 0:40—Brief breasts in bed with Charles.

Cheech & Chong's The Corsican Brothers (1984) . . . . Lovely II

Fawcett, Farrah *

Ex-wife of actor Lee Majors.
Significant Other of actor Ryan O'Neal.

Films:

Myra Breckinridge (1970). . . . . Mary Ann
- 1:16—Very brief tip of a breast, when Raquel Welch helps put pajama top on her.
- 1:28—Brief tip of left breast, peeking out of nightgown, while lying in bed after Welch turns over.

Logan's Run (1976). . . . . .Holly
Sunburn (1979). . . . . .Ellie
Saturn 3 (1980). . . . . Alex
- •• 0:17—Brief right breast taking off towel and running to Kirk Douglas after taking a shower.

The Cannonball Run (1981) . . . . Pamela
Extremities (1986) . . . . Marjorie
- 0:37—Brief side view of right breast when Joe pulls down her top in the kitchen. Can't see her face, but reportedly her.

Double Exposure: The Story of Margaret Bourke-White (1989) . . . . .Margaret Bourke-White
See You in the Morning (1989) . . . . Jo Livingston
The Apostle (1997) . . . . n.a.

Made for TV Movies:

The Burning Bed (1984) . . . . Francine Hughes
The Red Light Sting (1984) . . . . .Kathy Dunne
Between Two Women (1986) . . . . Val Petherton
Poor Little Rich Girl: The Barbara Hutton Story (1987) . . . . Barbara Hutton
Small Sacrifices (1989) . . . . Diane Downs
Criminal Behavior (1992) . . . . Jessie Lee Stubbs
The Substitute Wife (1994) . . . . Pearl
Children of the Dust (1995) . . . . Nora
Dalva (1996). . . . . Dalva

TV:

Harry-O (1974-76) . . . . Next door neighbor
Charlie's Angels (1976-77) . . . . Jill Munroe
Good Sports (1991) . . . . Gayle Roberts

Video Tapes:

Farrah Fawcett: All of Me (1997) . . . . Herself
- 0:00—Briefly nude during introduction.
- ••• 0:15—Breasts and buns in still photos and in motion during photo shoot (some in B&W) from her first pictorial.
- ••• 0:30—Nude while working on a clay sculpture (also covering herself with clay).
- ••• 0:38—In beige slip, then nude, while painting with brushes, then her body.
- ••• 0:50—Nude during photo shoots.
- •• 1:03—Full frontal nudity, while playing an actress in a stage play.

Featherstone, Angela

Films:

Dark Angel: The Ascent (1994) . . . . Veronica
- •• 0:12—Buns, while standing in alley after first arriving from hell. Breasts, after turning around and running down the street.
- 1:05—Breasts in open blouse after Max stitches up cut on her stomach.
- 1:06—Brief breasts while making love in bed with Max.

The Pompatus of Love (1996) . . . . Times Square Kisser
Con Air (1997) . . . . Ginny
The Wedding Singer (1997). . . . . Linda
Zero Effect (1997) . . . . Jess

Made for TV Movies:

A Family of Cops (1995) . . . . Jackie
Breach of Faith: A Family of Cops II (1997) . . . . Jackie

• Feeney, Kim

Made for Cable TV:

The Hunger: Room 17 (1997; Showtime) . . . . .Carla
- •• 0:06—Breasts and buns in T-back, after taking off her lingerie on TV. Slightly distorted.
- 0:10—Breasts on TV again.
- ••• 0:14—In black lingerie, then breasts and buns in T-back on TV and after appearing in motel room and having sex with Curtis Armstrong.

The Hunger: Fly-By-Night (1998; Showtime) . . . . Sonia
- ••• 0:20—Nude, while having sex with Giancarlo Esposito in basement.

Fellner, Ursulla

See: Buchfellner, Ursula.

Fenech, Edwige

Films:

You've Got to Have Heart. . . . . Valentina
a.k.a. At Last, At Last
- ••• 0:10—Breasts and buns, while taking off nightgown for Giovanni.
- 0:11—Brief side view of left breast, while sitting up on the floor with Giovanni.
- ••• 0:20—Nude in bedroom with Giovanni.
- ••• 0:26—Right breast, when Giovanni gets out of bed.
- •• 0:43—Left breast, while entertaining herself and fantasizing.
- ••• 0:47—Breasts, while on boat getting lotion rubbed on her by Brigitte.
- ••• 0:53—Breasts and buns in G-string when Giovanni takes off her body suit.
- 0:58—Right breast, while getting molested by Uncle Frederico.
- •• 1:20—Breasts while getting out of her wet dress in tent.
- •• 1:24—Breasts in tent while making love with another man.

•• 1:25—Right breast while making love.
• 1:32—Brief full frontal nudity in bedroom during argument.

The Seducers (1970) . . . . Ulla
a.k.a. Sensation
a.k.a. Top Sensation
• 0:10—Very brief side of right breast, after Tony pulls her top down.
• 0:11—Brief buns, under towel while walking in hallway.
••• 0:13—Breasts, after taking off her top and rubbing suntan lotion on Paula.
• 0:22—Brief left breast, after opening her robe to let a goat lick her while Aldo takes pictures.
•• 1:10—Breasts, while on boat deck with Andrew.
•• 1:12—Breasts, a couple of more times with Andrew.

Sex with a Smile (1976; Italian). . . . . Dream Girl
•• 0:03—Breasts tied to bed with two holes cut in her red dress top.
• 0:09—Buns, in jail cell in court when the guy pulls her panties down with his sword.
•• 0:13—Brief breasts in bed with Dracula taking off her top and hugging him.
• 0:16—Breasts in bathtub. Long shot.

Phantom of Death (1987; Italian) . . . . Helene

Fenn, Sherilyn *

Films:

Out of Control (1984). . . . . Katie
The Wild Life (1984) . . . . Penny Hallin
Just One of the Guys (1986) . . . . Sandy
Thrashin' (1986). . . . . Velvet

The Wraith (1986) . . . . Keri
• 0:13—Very brief breasts when Packard's gang catches her in bed with Jamie.
• 1:02—Brief breasts during flashback when caught in bed by Packard's gang.
• 1:03—Very brief right breast, pulling her swimsuit top off in pond with Charlie Sheen.

Zombie High (1987) . . . . Suzi
a.k.a. The School That Ate My Brain

Two Moon Junction (1988). . . . . April
(Blonde hair throughout the film.)
••• 0:07—Breasts and brief buns, while taking a shower in the country club shower room.
•• 0:27—Brief breasts on the floor kissing Perry.
•• 0:42—Breasts in gas station restroom changing camisole tops with Kristy McNichol.
• 0:54—Brief breasts making love with Perry in a motel room.
••• 1:24—Nude at Two Moon Junction making love with Perry. Very hot!
• 1:40—Brief left breast, brief lower frontal nudity and buns in the shower with Perry.

Crime Zone (1989). . . . . Helen
•• 0:23—Breasts wearing black panties making love with Bone. Dark, long shot.

Meridian (1989) . . . . Catherine
a.k.a. Kiss of the Beast
a.k.a. Phantoms
•• 0:23—White bra and panties, getting clothes taken off by Lawrence, then breasts.
••• 0:28—Breasts in bed with Oliver.
•• 0:51—Breasts getting her blouse ripped open lying in bed.

True Blood (1989) . . . . .Jennifer Scott
• 1:22—Very brief right breast, while in closet trying to stab Spider with a piece of mirror.

Backstreet Dreams (1990). . . . . Lucy
• 0:00—Right breast while sleeping in bed with Dean. Medium long shot.

Desire and Hell at Sunset Motel (1990) . . . . Bridey
Wild at Heart (1990) . . . . Girl in Accident
Diary of a Hitman (1992). . . . . Jain
Of Mice and Men (1992). Curley's Wife
Ruby (1992) . . . . Candy Cane

Boxing Helena (1993) . . . . Helena
••• 0:13—Right breast, then breasts, while making love.
• 0:17—Very, very brief left breast when rolling over in bed.
• 0:18—Breasts, while getting out of bed after getting interrupted by a phone call.

Fatal Instinct (1993) . . . . Laura
Three of Hearts (1993) . . . . Ellen
The Assassination File (1996). . . . . Lauren Jacobs
LoveLife (1997) . . . . n.a.

Made for Cable Movies:

Slave of Dreams (1995; Showtime) . . . . Zulaikha
• 0:26—Almost buns, then brief left breast, while making love on the ground with Joseph in a dream.
• 0:40—Brief buns, while standing before getting a bath.
1:31—Partial left breast, while breast feeding her baby.

Made for Cable TV:

Tales From the Crypt: You, Murderer (1995; HBO) . . . . . . Erica

Made for TV Movies:

Silence of the Heart (1984) . . . . n.a.
Dillinger (1991). . . . . Billie Frechette
Liz: The Elizabeth Taylor Story (1995) . . . . Elizabeth Taylor

TV:

TV 101 (1988-89) . . . . n.a.
Twin Peaks (1990-91) . . . . Audrey Horne

Ferguson, Kate

Films:

Break of Day (1977; Australian) . . . . Jean

Spaced Out (1980; British) . . . . Skipper
a.k.a. Outer Touch
• 1:07—Brief breasts making love with Willy in bed. Lit with red light.

The Pirate Movie (1982; Australian). . . . . Edith

• Ferguson, Sharon

Films:

Malcolm X (1992). . . . . Hooker

Made for Cable TV:

Red Shoe Diaries: Forbidden Zone (1996; Showtime) . . . Zoner

Women: Stories of Passion-The Diamond Merchant (1997; Showtime) . . . . Fatima
•• 0:06—Buns and breasts, while having sex with Balthazar (a woman masquerading as a man).
•• 0:17—Breasts and buns in panties, while having sex with Phillips and two other women.

Fernandez, Evelina

Films:

Flatliners (1990) . . . . Latin Woman
Postcards from the Edge (1990) . . . . Airline Employee

American Me (1992) . . . . Julie
• 1:14—Brief right breast, while making love with Edward James Olmos in bed.
• 1:15—Brief buns, while moving away from him.

A Million to Juan (1993) . . . . Mrs. Gonzales

Ferrare, Ashley

Films:

Revenge of the Ninja (1983). Cathy

• 0:48—Brief breasts getting attacked by the Sumo Servant in the bedroom.

Cyclone (1986) . . . . Carla Hastings

Ferrare, Cristina

Former model.
Ex-wife of ex-car maker John De Lorean.
Spokeswoman for *Ultra Slim-Fast.*

Films:

J.W. Coop (1971) . . . . Bean

Mary, Mary, Bloody Mary (1975) . . . . Mary

•• 0:07—Brief breasts making love with some guy on the couch just before she kills him.

••• 0:41—Breasts when Greta helps pull down Ferrare's top to take a bath.

• 1:12—Bun and brief silhouette of left breast getting out of bed and getting dressed.

Made for Cable TV:

Dream On: Nightmare on Bleecker Street (1992; HBO). . .Laura

Home & Family (1996- ; Family) . . . . Co-Host

Made for TV Movies:

Perry Mason: The Case of the Telltale Talk Show Host (1993) . . . . Judith Jansen

TV:

Incredible Sunday (1988-89). . . . . Co-Host

Shame On You! (1993-95). . . . . Hostess

Ferraro, Simona

Films:

Straight Talk (1992). . . . . Waitress

Only You (1994) . . . . Alitalia Gate Attendant

Made for Cable TV:

Strangers: Visit (1996; HBO) . . . . .Corinne

•• 0:08—Right breast when Mark Harmon opens her blouse and caresses her.

•• 0:12—Nude, taking off nightgown and climbing into bed with John Wesley Shipp, then making love.

• 0:23—Brief breasts, while standing at the window with Shipp.

Ferratti, Rebecca *

Films:

Three Amigos (1986). . . . . Hot Señorita

Beverly Hills Cop II (1987) . . . . Playboy Playmate

Cheerleader Camp (1987). . . . . Theresa Salazar
a.k.a. Bloody Pom Poms

Outlaw of Gor (1987) . . . . Talana

Silent Assassins (1988). . . . . Miss Amy

Gor (1989) . . . . Talena

How I Got Into College (1989) . . . . Game Show Hostess

Small Kill (1991) . . . . Diana Conti

Ace Ventura: Pet Detective (1993). . . . . .Sexy Woman

Embrace of the Vampire (1994). . . . . Princess
(Unrated version reviewed.)

Hard Vice (1994). . . . . Christine

••• 0:02—Buns and breasts, getting out of bubble bath and making love on top of a customer in bed. Breasts while taking a shower.

••• 0:21—Breasts, while making love in bed with another customer.

•• 0:22—Breasts and buns, while taking a shower.

• 1:04—Buns in panties, while standing in bedroom. Long shot.

California Heat (1995) . . . . Alice

• 0:00—Breasts under sheer white lingerie, while modeling for Jack.

• 0:03—Partial buns and breasts under sheer white body suit.

Cyborg 3: The Recycler (1995) . . . . Elexia

• 0:14—Breasts, while dancing on stage in bar and kicking a customer (medium long shot). Breasts, while dancing in front of Richard Lynch (closer shot).

• 0:18—Breasts, while taking off her blouse in back room with Lynch.

Indecent Behavior 3 (1995) . . . . Morenika

To the Limit (1995) . . . . Lupe

Made for Cable TV:

Erotic Confessions: Arresting Developments (1996; Cinemax) . . . . Rebecca/Ms. Mary

• 0:05—Breasts on table in interrogation room in fantasy.

•• 0:07—In bra, then buns, left breast and lower frontal nudity, while stripping and dancing out side of jail cell in fantasy.

••• 0:11—In black bra and panties, after stripping out of her police officer uniform in bedroom with Andrew. Nude, while making love on top of him.

Made for TV Movies:

Op Center (1995) . . . . Maynard

Video Tapes:

Playboy Video Calendar 1989 (1988) . . . . June

••• 0:21—Nude.

Wet & Wild (1989) . . . . Model

Playmates at Play (1990). . . . . Gotta Dance

Wet & Wild III (1991). . . . . Model

The Best of Video Playmate Calendars (1992). . .Playmate

•• 0:15—Brief breasts and buns during dancing segment.

••• 0:16—Breasts and buns in B&W segment.

••• 0:17—Full frontal nudity in bathtub in warehouse.

••• 0:18—Nude, doing more dancing.

The Best of Wet and Wild (1992). . . . . .Model

Wet & Wild IV (1992). . . . . Model

Playboy's 21 Playmates (1996). . . . . Playmate

••• 0:10—Nude in still photos.

••• 0:11—Nude in numerous scenes.

• Ferrell, Jami *

Video Tapes:

Playboy Video Calendar 1998 (1997) . . . . January

••• 0:01—In lingerie and nude while shooting hoops in a warehouse and posing.

••• 0:03—In lingerie and nude while posing on a sofa.

Playboy's Fast Women (1997). . . . . Playmate

Playboy's Voluptuous Vixens (1997). . . . . .Playmate

Playboy's Women Behaving Badly (1997) . . . . Tie Me Tease Me/Lisa

••• 0:37—Nude, while her husband is tied to the bed

Ferréol, Andrea

Films:

La Grande Bouffe (1973; French/Italian) . . . . Andrea

The Infernal Trio (1974; French). . . . . Noemie

Submission (1976; Italian). . . . . Juliet

•• 0:43—Breasts in room with Franco Nero and Elaine.

Despair (1978; German/French) . . . . Lydia

• 0:07—Long shot of right breast and very brief lower frontal nudity and buns, while crawling into bed. Left breast in closer shot, while lying in bed with Dirk Bogarde.

•• 0:24—Long shot of right breast and buns, while crawling into bed again. Breasts and buns in closer shot in bed.

•• 1:21—Nude, after Bogarde takes off her clothes in the hallway.
• 1:24—Brief breasts when Bogarde walks by her.
••• 1:25—Nude in hall and bedroom while talking to Bogarde. Long shot of buns. Full frontal nudity while sitting on bed, then following Bogarde around until he leaves.

Mysteries (1978; Dutch) .... Kamma
Sex on the Run (1979; German/French/Italian) .... Beatrice
a.k.a. Some Like It Cool
a.k.a. Casanova and Co.
The Tin Drum (1979; German) .... Lina Greff
La Nuit de Varennes (1983; French/Italian)
.... Madame Adelaide Gagnon
Letters to an Unknown Lover (1985) .... Julia
A Zed and Two Noughts (1985; British) .... Alba Bewick
Wings of Fame (1990; Dutch) .... Theresa
The Sleazy Uncle (1991; Italian) .... Teresa
Street of No Return (1991; U.S./French) .... Rhoda
Stroke of Midnight (1991; U.S./French). .... Wanda
a.k.a. If the Shoe Fits
Sweet Killing (1992; Canadian/French) .... Louise Cross
Francesco (1994; Italian/German) .... Pica

Ferrer, Leilani

See: Sarelle, Leilani.

Ferris, Irena

Films:

Covergirl (1982; Canadian). .... Kit Paget
•• 0:19—Brief breasts taking off robe and getting into bathtub with Dee.
• 0:43—Very brief right breast sticking out of nightgown.
• 0:46—Upper half of left breast during modeling session.
• 0:47—Breasts in mirror in dressing room.
• 0:49—Brief breasts, while getting attacked by Joel.
• 0:53—Brief left breast, putting another blouse on.
• 0:53—Brief left breast, putting on blouse.

TV:

Cover Up (1984-85) .... Billie
Dallas (1989) .... Tammy

Feuer, Debra

Films:

Moment by Moment (1978). .... Stacie
The Hollywood Knights (1980) .... Cheetah
To Live and Die in L.A. (1985) .... Bianca Torres
• 0:58—Side view of buns, while lying on bed, watching Willem Dafoe burn the counterfeit money. Long shot.
• 1:47—Brief breasts on video tape being played back on TV in empty house, hard to see anything.

Homeboy (1988) .... Ruby
Night Angel (1989) .... Kirstie
• 0:46—Brief side of left breast. Dark.

Ficatier, Carol *

Video Tapes:

Playboy Video Calendar 1987 (1986) .... Playmate
Playmates at Play (1990) .... Making Waves
Playboy's 21 Playmates (1996) .... Playmate
••• 0:22—Nude in still photos.
••• 0:23—Nude on sailboat.

Fidler, Cindy

Films:

Loose Screws (1986; Canadian). .... Bath Tub Girl
Fireballs (1988; Canadian) .... Debbie Carlson
•• 0:46—In bra and panties, then breasts, while dancing on stage in bar.

Red Blooded American Girl (1988) .... Nurse
Speaking Parts (1989; Canadian). .... Woman at Party

Fiedler, Bea *

Films:

Island of 1000 Delights .... Julia
•• 0:25—Full frontal nudity washing herself in bathtub, then nude taking off her towel for Michael.
•• 0:27—Breasts lying on floor after making love, then buns walking to chair.
•• 0:46—Full frontal nudity, after taking off her dress and kissing Howard.
•• 0:50—Breasts in white bikini bottoms coming out of the water to greet Howard.
••• 1:06—Breasts sitting in the sand near the beach, then nude talking with Sylvia.
••• 1:17—Right breast (great close up) making love with Sylvia.
••• 1:18—Breasts above Sylvia.

Popcorn and Ice Cream (1978; West German)
.... Policewoman
a.k.a. Sex and Ice Cream
••• 0:47—Full frontal nudity getting dressed.
••• 1:13—Right breast, then breasts in bed with a lover.
••• 1:14—Full frontal nudity in bed some more.

Private Popsicle (1982) .... Eva
•• 0:04—In black bra with Bobby. Upper half of left breast, very brief side of right breast, then breasts.
••• 0:06—Full frontal nudity with Bobby in bed.
•• 0:07—More breasts with Bobby.
••• 0:08—Breasts on bed with Hughie.
•• 0:09—More breasts when her husband gets into bed.

Hot Chili (1985) .... The Music Teacher
•• 0:08—Breasts, while playing the cello and being fondled by Ricky.
• 0:29—Buns, while playing the violin.
•• 0:34—Nude during fight in restaurant with Chi Chi. Hard to see because of the flashing light.
••• 0:36—Breasts lying on inflatable lounge in pool, playing a flute.
••• 0:43—Left breast, while playing a tuba.
••• 1:01—Breasts and buns, while dancing in front of Mr. Lieberman.
• 1:07—Buns, then right breast while dancing with Stanley.

Up Your Anchor (1985) .... n.a.

Field, Angela

Films:

Psycho From Texas (1981). .... Wheeler's Mother
•• 0:09—Breasts and buns, while making love in bed with the salesman.

Hollywood High Part II (1984). .... n.a.

Field, Chelsea

Was a dancer on the TV show *Solid Gold* for two years.

Films:

Commando (1985) .... Stewardess
Perfect (1985) .... Randy
Death Spa (1987) .... Darla
Masters of the Universe (1987) .... Teela
Prison (1987). .... Katherine Walker
Skin Deep (1989) .... Amy

Harley Davidson and The Marlboro Man (1991) .... Virginia Slim
- 0:40—Side of left breast, sitting up in bed. Very brief buns standing up. Don't see her face very well.

The Last Boy Scout (1991).............. Sarah Hollenbeck
Dust Devil (1992; British) ....Wendy Robinson
- 0:22—Very, very brief partial left breast, when standing up in bathtub.

The Dark Half (1993)................... Annie Pangburn
Snapdragon (1993).........................Peckham
Andre (1994)................................. Whitney
I'll Do Anything (1994) .... Screentest Actress
A Passion to Kill (1994)......................... Diana
- 0:16—Buns and side of left breast, while reaching for a towel in bathroom when Scott Bakula sees her.
- 0:35—In sheer black polka dot blouse in Bakula's office.
- 0:37—Buns and side of right breast, while in office with Bakula.
- ••• 0:55—Right breast, then breasts, while making love with Bakula in garage, then inside car.

The Wrong Woman (1995) ....n.a.

Made for Cable Movies:

Extreme Justice (1993; HBO)............... Kelly Daniels
- 0:18—In white bra, then brief left breast on sofa with Lou Diamond Phillips.

The Birds II: Land's End (1994; Showtime)............. May
Royce (1994; Showtime).................. Marnie Paymer
Indictment: The McMartin Trial (1995; HBO) .... Christine Johnson

Made for Cable TV:

Dream On: A Midsummer Night's Dream On (1993; HBO) .... Allison Knowland

Miniseries:

James A. Michener's "Texas" (1994) .... Mattie Quimper

Made for TV Movies:

Murder C.O.D. (1990).............................Ellie
An Inconvenient Woman (1991) .... Camilla Ebury
Complex of Fear (1993) .... Michelle Dolan
The Bachelor's Baby (1996).......................... Jamie

TV:

Bronx Zoo (1988) .... Chris Barnes
Nightingales (1989) .... Samantha "Sam" Sullivan
Capital News (1990).......................Cassy Swann
Angel Falls (1993) .... Rae Dawn Snow

Field, Sally

Films:

Stay Hungry (1976) .... Mary Kay Farnsworth
- 0:27—Buns, then very, very brief side view of left breast jumping back into bed. Very fast, everything is a blur, hard to see anything.

Heroes (1977)...................................Carol
Smokey and the Bandit (1977) .... Carrie
The End (1978)............................Mary Ellen
- 0:26—Most of right breast, while wearing nightgown and lying in bed with Burt Reynolds.

Hooper (1978) .... Gwen
Beyond the Poseidon Adventure (1979) .....Celeste Whitman
Norma Rae (1979).......................... Norma Rae
(Academy Award for Best Actress.)
Absence of Malice (1981) .... Megan Carter
Back Roads (1981)............................ Amy Post
Kiss Me Goodbye (1982)..................... Kay Villano
Places in the Heart (1984)..................Edna Spalding
(Academy Award for Best Actress.)
Murphy's Romance (1985) .... Emma Moriarity
Surrender (1987)........................Daisy Morgan
Punchline (1988)...........................Lilah Krytsick
Steel Magnolias (1989) .... M'Lynn Eatenton
Not Without My Daughter (1991)......... Betty Mahmoody
Soapdish (1991) .... Celeste Talbert
Mrs. Doubtfire (1993) ....Miranda Hillard
Forrest Gump (1994)........................Mrs. Gump
Eye For an Eye (1995) .... Karen McCann

Miniseries:

A Woman of Independent Means (1995)......... Bess Alcott

Made for TV Movies:

Sybil (1976)..Sybil
(Emmy Award for Best Actress in a Drama Special.)

TV:

Gidget (1965-66) ....Francine "Gidget" Lawrence
The Flying Nun (1967-70).................. Sister Bertrille
Alias Smith and Jones (1971-73) ....Clementine Hale
Girl with Something Extra (1973-74)........... Sally Burton

• *Fielding, Anastasia*

Films:

A Night in the Life of Jimmy Reardon (1987).......... Elaine
Slipping into Darkness (1988) ....Genevieve
- 0:38—Brief breasts, after taking off her lingerie in graveyard with Otis.
- 0:43—Breasts, while lying dead on grave and being carried to another grave. Fairly long scene.

TV:

One Big Family (1986-87) .... Mairanne Hatton

Fiery, Alexa

Films:

Midnight Confessions (1993) ....Nikki
(Unrated version reviewed.)
- 0:03—In red bra, then breasts, while undressing in the back seat of a car.

Made for Cable TV:

Compromising Situations: First Time Caller (1994; Showtime) .... Ernie

Figura, Kasia

Films:

Near Mrs. (1990).................................. Sasha
The Player (1992) .... Cameo
Fatal Past (1993)......................Jennifer Lawrence
- •• 0:07—Brief breasts, while making love with Preston in flashback during interview.
- 0:53—Brief breasts and buns by the pool with Costas Mandylor.
- 0:55—Brief breasts, while in the pool with Mandylor.
- 0:56—Partial breasts, while making love with Mandylor.
- 0:58—Breasts, while getting up and walking by pool. Medium long shot.
- 1:05—Breasts, while getting her clothes ripped off by bad guys.
- 1:06—Right breast seen through sheer curtains over bed while tied by wrists to bed posts.
- 1:07—Breasts, when getting raped while tied to bed posts.
- 1:11—Very, very brief breasts, while getting pulled out of bed.

Ready to Wear (1994) .... Vivienne
a.k.a. Prêt-à-porter
- 1:13—Brief buns, while trying on red dress in background.

Too Fast, Too Young (1995)................ Kaddy Havel
- 0:10—Buns in panties and bra after taking off robe and walking around indoors.

- 0:42—Brief buns, while lying in bed with Dalton.
- 0:44—Very brief buns and breasts, while lying in bed with Dalton and after he gets out.

Finney, Carolyn

Films:

The Nutt House (1992) . . . . Ceremony Assistant

Video Tapes:

Inside Out 4 (1992) . . . . Faye/The Thief

(Unrated version reviewed.)

- ••• 0:41—Breasts in bed, making love with the burglar.

Finocchiaro, Angela

Films:

Man On Fire (1987; Italian/French) . . . . Foot Race Pro

Volere Volare (1991; Italian) . . . . Martina

0:05—Very, very brief nipple, while rolling over in bed.

- ••• 0:06—Nude, after getting out of bed and carrying two cups of coffee around, then in bathroom while two identical twin guys watch her.
- •• 0:10—Buns, while lying on table in kitchen getting chocolate poured over her by a chef.
- • 0:52—Side of left breast and buns, while kneeling on the bed.
- • 1:09—Buns, while taking a shower. Subtitles get in the way.
- •• 1:11—Brief left breast, while bending over to peek under covers of the bed. Subtitles get in the way. Right breast while sitting in bed with Maurizio.
- • 1:15—Very, very brief breasts in open blouse, while running out of the bedroom.
- • 1:25—Brief breasts, while getting into bed with the animated Maurizio. Subtitles get in the way.
- • 1:26—Right breast, in bed with animated Maurizio.
- •• 1:27—Nude, while frolicking in bed with animated Maurizio. Medium long shot.

Finzi, Lydia

Films:

Alien Warrior (1985) . . . . Beverly

a.k.a. King of the Streets

My Man Adam (1986) . . . . Sunbather

- • 0:32—Brief breasts sunbathing by the swimming pool when Adam jumps into the pool and angers her.

Fiorentino, Linda *

Films:

After Hours (1985) . . . . Kiki

- •• 0:19—Breasts taking off bra in doorway while Griffin Dunne watches.

Gotcha! (1985) . . . . Sasha

- •• 0:53—Brief breasts getting searched at customs.

Visionquest (1985) . . . . Carla

The Moderns (1988) . . . . Rachel Stone

- • 0:40—Breasts sitting in bathtub while John Lone shaves her armpits.
- • 0:41—Right breast while turning over onto stomach in bathtub.
- •• 1:18—Breasts getting out of tub while covered with bubbles to kiss Keith Carradine.

Wildfire (1988) . . . . Kay

Queens Logic (1991) . . . . Carla

Shout (1991) . . . . Molly

Chain of Desire (1992) . . . . Alma D'Angeli

- • 0:09—Very brief left breast, while rolling over in bed.

The Last Seduction (1994) . . . . Bridget Gregory

- •• 0:31—Breasts, while walking around the house, gathering her clothes and getting dressed.
- • 0:37—Brief side view of buns during pan shot from her feet to her head, while she's lying in bed.
- •• 0:50—Very brief breasts, buns, then left breast while making love in bed with Peter Berg.
- • 0:53—Very brief partial buns and very, very brief left breast, while getting out of bed.

Jade (1995) . . . . Trina Gavin

- •• 0:25—Buns, while sitting on chair and talking on the phone.
- • 0:49—Breasts in lingerie on B&W grainy video playback.
- • 1:06—Breasts and brief partial buns, when falling out of bed seen in B&W video playback.
- • 1:29—Breasts in several B&W photos.

Unforgettable (1995) . . . . Martha Briggs

Men In Black (1997) . . . . Dr. Laurel Weaver

Made for Cable Movies:

The Neon Empire (1989) . . . . Lucy

Beyond the Law (1992; HBO) . . . . Renee

- ••• 0:52—Breasts while making love with Charlie Sheen. Brief buns in T-back panties.

Acting on Impulse (1993; Showtime) . . . . Susan Gittes

The Desperate Trail (1994; TNT) . . . . Sarah O'Rourke

Convict Cowboy (1995) . . . . n.a.

Made for Cable TV:

Strangers: The Last Game (1992; HBO) . . . . Helen

(Available on the video tape *Strangers*.)

- • 0:07—Left breast, three times, making love with James Remar when Etienne walks by. Dark.

Fischer, Vera

Films:

I Love You (1982; Brazilian) . . . . Barbara Bergman

a.k.a. Eu Te Amo

- ••• 0:31—Left breast while in front of TV and in chair with Paulo.
- •• 0:46—Left breast sticking out of nightgown. Silhouette of breasts while getting up. Full frontal nudity after taking off nightgown.
- ••• 0:47—Nude in bed with Paulo.
- ••• 1:05—Breasts on couch with Paulo.
- • 1:09—Breasts, while opening her dress. (Seen on TV.)

Love Strange Love (1982; Brazilian) . . . . Anna

- •• 0:23—Brief breasts and lower frontal nudity in bathtub. Breasts and buns, getting out.
- •• 0:38—Breasts making love with Dr. Osmar.
- • 0:39—Brief buns, while lying in bed.
- •• 1:19—Breasts in bed with Dr. Osmar when Hugo watches.

The Fifth Monkey (1990) . . . . Mrs. Watts

Fisher, Frances

Films:

Can She Bake a Cherry Pie? (1983) . . . . Louise

Tough Guys Don't Dance (1987) . . . . Jessica Pond

Lost Angels (1989) . . . . Judith Loftis

Patty Hearst (1989) . . . . Yolanda

Pink Cadillac (1989) . . . . n.a.

Frame Up (1990) . . . . Jo Westlake

- •• 0:52—Breasts, lying back in bed with Wings Hauser.
- •• 0:54—Left breast, while lying in bed with Hauser.

Welcome Home Roxy Carmichael (1990) . . . . Rochelle Bossetti

Frame Up II (1991) . . . . Jo

a.k.a. Deadly Conspiracy

L.A. Story (1991) . . . . June

Unforgiven (1992). . . . . Strawberry Alice
Molly & Gina (1993) . . . . Molly
Praying Mantis (1993). . . . . Betty
Babyfever (1994). . . . . Rosie
Striptease (1996). . . . . Donna Garcia
Female Perversions (1997) . . . . Annunciata
• 1:06—Very brief back side of right breast, while posing for photos. Medium long shot. Brief partial breasts under open blue robe.
• 1:09—Buns in panties, while dancing in living room.
Wild America (1997) . . . . Agnes
Made for Cable Movies:
Devlin (1991; Showtime). . . . . Maryellen
Attack of the 50 ft. Woman (1993; HBO). . . . . .Dr. Cushing
Made for TV Movies:
Lucy & Desi: Before the Laughter (1991). . . . . .Lucille Ball
The Other Mother (1995) . . . . .Carol Schaefer
TV:
The Edge of Night . . . . .Deborah Saxon
Strange Luck (1995-96). . . . . .n.a.

Fisher, Jodie

Films:
Intimate Obsession (1992) . . . . .Rachel Taylor
(Unrated version reviewed.)
• 0:07—Full frontal nudity, swimming under water during her nightmare.
• 0:22—Partial breasts in bubble bath. Brief left breast, while rinsing herself off.
•• 0:30—Breasts, while taking off her bra in front of mirror.
••• 0:47—Breasts while making love with Rick on sofa. Long scene.
• 0:53—Breasts under water during nightmare.
•• 0:58—Buns, while lying in bed with Rick.
••• 0:59—Breasts and brief lower frontal nudity, while sitting up in bed when Rick gets out.
• 1:06—Brief breasts on TV during video playback.
Little Big League (1994) . . . . 1st Night Nurse
Body of Influence 2 (1995) . . . . Leza Watkins
• 0:19—Right breast, while making out with dream stranger on couch.
••• 0:32—Breasts and buns, while making love with Thomas.
••• 0:43—Breasts and buns, while making love with Thomas in bed.
• 0:48—Breasts, while getting out of bed.
•• 1:24—Breasts, while making love with Thomas in flashbacks.

Fisher, Tricia Leigh

Films:
Stick (1985). . . . . Katie
Pretty Smart (1986). . . . . .Daphne Ziegler
C.H.U.D. II (1989) . . . . Katie
The Book of Love (1991). . . . . .Gina Gabooch
Hostile Intentions (1994) . . . . Maureen
• 0:34—Brief breasts, three times, while being raped in jail cell by Mexican police captain.
I'll Do Anything (1994) . . . . .Airline Passenger

• *Fitzgerald, Annie*

Films:
Fatally Yours (1995) . . . . Patti
•• 0:36—Breasts and buns, while making love in bed with Rick Rossovich.
• 1:12—Breasts, while making love with Rossovich.
Phoenix (1998) . . . . Heist Stripper

FitzGerald, Helen *

Films:
Nuns on the Run (1990; British) . . . . .Tracey
Close My Eyes (1991; British) . . . . Scottish Girl
•• 0:08—Nude, lying down, then getting up in room with Richard.

Fitzgerald, Tara

Great-niece of actress Geraldine Fitzgerald.
Films:
Hear My Song (1991; British) . . . . .Nancy Doyle
•• 0:07—Brief breasts in bed, then nude, getting out of bed and getting dressed while angry at Micky.
A Man of No Importance (1994; Irish/British). . . .Adele Rice
• 1:09—Brief partial breasts, while making love with her boyfriend when Albert Finney sees her.
Sirens (1994; Australian) . . . . Estella Campion
• 0:19—Brief breasts, while changing behind divider.
•• 1:00—Brief breasts, while running outside. Brief full frontal nudity in church during daydream.
• 1:11—Right breast and brief lower frontal nudity in studio with Devlin.
• 1:30—Brief full frontal nudity on rock formation. Medium long shot. She's the fifth from the left.
The Englishman Who Went Up A Hill But Came Down A Mountain (1995; British) . . . . .n.a.
Made for TV Movies:
Fall From Grace (1994) . . . . Catherine Pradler

Fitzpatrick, Sharon *

Video Tapes:
The Girls of Penthouse, Volume 3 (1995). . . . . Pet
•• 0:37—Full frontal nudity while telling a little bit about herself.
••• 0:39—Nude in still photos. Nude while posing outside on a ranch.
••• 0:42—Nude, while posing in a studio.
••• 0:44—Full frontal nudity, outside in a field with cows. Filmed in duo-tone color.
••• 0:46—Nude, doing various things around a ranch, swinging on a swing, straddling a fence in the rain.

Flaherty, Maureen

Films:
Shadowzone (1989) . . . . Jenna
•• 0:13—Breasts, while lying under plastic cover.
• 0:18—Breasts, while lying on table during operation.
•• 1:11—Breasts again under plastic cover several times.
•• 1:17—Brief breasts again, then full frontal nudity.
• 1:24—Breasts, after reviving under the plastic cover.
Rich Girl (1991) . . . . .Girl in Restroom #1
Bikini Summer 2 (1992). . . . . Bridget
•• 0:04—Breasts, when waking up in bed in the morning with William.
•• 0:29—Breasts while in bed with William.
The Naked Truth (1992) . . . . Miss Romania
Bikini Squad (1993) . . . . Summer
••• 0:56—Breasts, while making love in bed with Biff.
Bikini Hoe Down (1997). . . . . May
••• 0:47—In bra, then breasts and brief partial buns, while making love in barn with Jeb.
••• 0:53—Nude, while showering with the other three girls.
•• 1:19—Breasts, while dancing on stage during bikini hoe down.

Bikini Traffic School (1997) . . . . Traci
- ••• 0:03—Breasts and buns in T-back, while dancing on stage with Marcie and Vicky.
- ••• 0:13—Breasts and buns in T-back, while dancing on stage with Marcie.
- •• 0:18—Breasts and buns in swimsuit bottom, while frolicking in the pool with Vicky and Marcie.
- •• 0:21—Breasts, while sunbathing.
- ••• 0:25—Breasts, during fantasy with the pool guy.
- ••• 0:45—Breasts, after taking off her top during tennis match and playing tennis against Marcie.
- •• 1:15—Breasts and buns, while making love with the pool guy in workout room.
- •• 1:22—Breasts, while on stage during traffic school lessons.

Flanagan, Fionnula

Films:

Ulysses (1967; U.S./British) . . . . Gerty MacDowell
Sinful Davey (1969; British) . . . . Penelope
Crossover (1980; Canadian) . . . . Abadaba
a.k.a. Mr. Patman
- • 0:27—Brief breasts opening her robe and flashing James Coburn.

James Joyce's Women (1983) . . . . Molly Bloom
- • 0:48—Brief breasts getting out of bed.
- ••• 0:56—Breasts getting back into bed.
- ••• 1:02—Full frontal nudity masturbating in bed talking to herself. Very long scene—9 minutes!

Reflections (1984; British) . . . . Charlotte Lawless
Youngblood (1986) . . . . Miss McGill
P.K. and the Kid (1987) . . . . Flo
Mad at the Moon (1993) . . . . Mrs. Hill
Money for Nothing (1993) . . . . Mrs. Coyle
Some Mother's Son (1996) . . . . Annie Higgins

Made for Cable Movies:

While Mile (1994; HBO) . . . . Gena Karns

Miniseries:

Rich Man, Poor Man (1976) . . . . Clothilde

Made for TV Movies:

Nightmare in Badham County (1976) . . . . Dulce
(Nudity added for video tape.)
Mary White (1977) . . . . Sallie White
Young Love, First Love (1979) . . . . Audrey
The Ewok Adventure (1984) . . . . Catarine
A Winner Never Quits (1986) . . . . Mrs. Wyshner

TV:

How the West was Won (1978-79) . . . . . . Aunt Molly Culhane

Flannery, Erin

Films:

Incubus (1981; Canadian) . . . . Jenny Cordell
- • 0:08—Briefly nude, while getting out of the shower. Seen by John Cassavetes. Medium long shot.

The Amateur (1982) . . . . Waitress
Class of 1984 (1982; Canadian) . . . . Deneen Bowden
Sticky Fingers (1988) . . . . Moura

Flannigan, Maureen

Films:

National Lampoon's Last Resort (1993) . . . . Sonja
Teenage Bonnie and Klepto Clyde (1993) . . . . Bonnie
- • 0:26—Very brief breasts, while climbing into back seat of car.
- ••• 0:34—In black bra and panties, lying on bed when Clyde pours money all over her. Right breast after taking off bra. Breasts while making love.

Made for TV Movies:

She Fought Alone (1995) . . . . n.a.

TV:

Out of This World (1987-91) . . . . Evie
Push (1998-) . . . . Erin Galway

*Fleiss, Heidi **

Films:

The Doom Generation (1995) . . . . Liquor Store Clerk
Heidi Fleiss: Hollywood Madam (1995; British/Canadian) . . . . Herself
- •• 0:39—Breasts, when getting up and putting on blouse while talking on cordless telephone.
- • 0:40—Briefly nude, after dropping a sheet and running away from the camera.

Florance, Sheila

Films:

Jock Petersen (1974; Australian) . . . . n.a.
a.k.a. Petersen
End Play (1975; Australian) . . . . Mavis Lipton
A Woman's Tale (1991; Australian) . . . . Martha
- • 0:07—Breasts, after leaning back in the bathtub. Dark. Check this out if you like really old women.

Floria, Holly

Films:

Presumed Guilty (1990) . . . . Mary Austin
- • 1:02—Side view of left breast, very brief lower frontal nudity and buns, while making love with Jessie.

Bikini Island (1991) . . . . Annie Kelly
- • 0:03—Buns in panties, then breasts in shower (seen through plastic shower curtain). Don't see her face.
- • 0:28—Buns in one piece white swimsuit at the beach.
- • 0:35—Buns in the shower. Don't see her face.

Dark Rider (1991) . . . . Dani
Netherworld (1991) . . . . Diane Palmer
Private Wars (1993) . . . . Ronnie

TV:

Acapulco H.E.A.T. (1993-94) . . . . Krissie Valentine

*Fluegel, Darlanne **

Films:

Eyes of Laura Mars (1978) . . . . Lulu
Battle Beyond the Stars (1980) . . . . Nanelia
The Last Fight (1983) . . . . Sally
Once Upon a Time in America (1984) . . . . Eve
(Long version reviewed.)
To Live and Die in L.A. (1985) . . . . Ruth Lanier
- •• 0:44—Brief breasts and buns, in bed when William Petersen comes home.
- • 1:50—Very brief breasts on bed with Petersen in a flashback.

Running Scared (1986) . . . . Anna Costanzo
Tough Guys (1986) . . . . Skye Foster
- • 0:47—Very brief side view of right breast, leaning over to kiss Kirk Douglas.

Border Heat (1988) . . . . Peggy Martin
Bulletproof (1988) . . . . Devon Shepard
Freeway (1988) . . . . Sarah "Sunny" Harper
- • 0:27—In bra in bathroom taking a pill, then very, very brief right breast, getting into bed.
- • 0:28—Brief left breast putting on robe and getting out of bed.

Lock Up (1989) . . . . Melissa

Project: Alien (1990) . . . . "Bird" McNamara
- 0:18—Buns, getting out of bed and putting on a kimono.

Pet Sematary II (1992). . . . . Renee Hallow
- 1:04—Probably a body double wearing a dog mask, breasts on top of Anthony Edwards during nightmare, lit with blue light.

Scanner Cop (1993) . . . . .Dr. Joan Alden

Breaking Point (1994; Canadian) . . . . Dana Preston/Molly Carpenter
- •• 0:11—Breasts and buns in panties, while making love with Gary Busey on boat. Dark.
- • 0:46—Buns in T-back, after taking off dress and walking up stairs, then lying in bed.
- •• 1:27—Right breast in open blouse, while tied up to bed by Greg before getting killed.

Relative Fear (1994). . . . . .Linda

Darkman III: Die Darkman Die (1995) . . . . Bridget Thorne

Made for Cable Movies:

Slaughter of the Innocents (1993; HBO) . . . . . Susan Broderick

Made for TV Movies:

Come Die With Me: A Mickey Spillane's Mike Hammer Mystery (1994). . . . . Pat

TV:

Crime Story (1986-89) . . . . Julie Torello

Wiseguy (1989). . . . . Lacey

Hunter (1990-91) . . . . .Joanne Malinski

*Flynn, Joni **

Films:

Felicity (1978; Australian) . . . . Mei Ling
- ••• 0:38—Nude in bath with Glory Annen and two other girls, then getting massaged. Long scene.
- ••• 0:43—Breasts and buns, making love on boat with a guy.
- ••• 1:13—Nude, making love in bed with Glory. Long scene.

Octopussy (1983; British) . . . . Octopussy Girl

*Folta, Danelle **

Video Tapes:

Playboy Video Calendar 1996 (1995) . . . . August
- •• 0:31—Nude in house at night.
- ••• 0:33—Nude in studio with a space theme.

Wet & Wild VIII: Bottoms Up (1996). . . . . .Playmate

Fonda, Bridget

Daughter of actor Peter Fonda.

Granddaughter of actor Henry Fonda.

Films:

You Can't Hurry Love (1984). . . . . .Peggy

Aria (1987; U.S./British) . . . . Girl Lover
- ••• 0:59—Brief right breast, then buns and breasts lying down on bed in hotel room in Las Vegas.
- •• 1:02—Breasts in the bathtub with her boyfriend.

Scandal (1989) . . . . Mandy Rice-Davis

(Unrated version reviewed.)
- • 0:20—Brief breasts dressed as an Indian dancing while Joanne Whalley tries to upstage her.
- • 0:53—In white lingerie, then brief lower frontal nudity under sheer nightgown in room with a guy.
- • 1:05—Brief buns, while walking back into bedroom. Long shot.

Shag (1989) . . . . .Melaina Buller

Frankenstein Unbound (1990). . . . . .Mary

The Godfather, Part III (1990) . . . . .Grace Hamilton

Out of the Rain (1990) . . . . Jo

Strapless (1990; British). .Amy Hempel

Doc Hollywood (1991) . . . . .Nancy Lee

Drop Dead Fred (1991) . . . . Annabella

Iron Maze (1991). . . . . .Chris

Leather Jackets (1991) . . . . .Claudi
- • 0:15—Brief breasts on bed with Mickey.

Army of Darkness (1992) . . . . Linda

Single White Female (1992) . . . . Allie
- • 0:04—Very, very brief right breast, while getting out of bed with Sam. Very brief side view of right breast, then buns, while walking to turn off answering machine.
- • 0:05—Brief breasts, grabbing her clothes.
- • 0:34—Buns and brief breasts, getting out of bed. Dark.
- • 1:18—Brief right breast, in gaping nightgown while kneeling on bathroom floor after throwing up in the toilet.
- • 1:20—Brief silhouette of left breast, while changing clothes.

singles (1992) . . . . .Janet Livermore

Bodies, Rest & Motion (1993) . . . . Beth

Little Buddha (1993) . . . . Lisa Conrad

Point of No Return (1993). . . . . .Maggie
- • 0:49—Brief right breast, while making love with J.P.

Camilla (1994). . . . . Freda Lopez
- • 0:46—Nude, after taking off her swimsuit and joining Jessica Tandy in the lake. Medium long shot.

It Could Happen to You (1994) . . . . Yvonne Biasi

The Road to Wellville (1994) . . . . .Eleanor Lightbody
- • 0:23—Breasts, while bathing in milk bath.
- • 1:46—Right breast, while getting sexually manipulated by Dr. Spitzvogel in the woods.

City Hall (1996). . . . . Mary Beth Cogan

Grace of My Heart (1996) .Kelly Porter

Touch (1996) . . . . Lynn Faulkner
- • 0:54—Very brief, partial buns, while lying in bed with Skeet Ulrich.

Jackie Brown (1997) . . . . Melanie

Rough Magic (1997) . . . . .Myra

Made for Cable Movies:

In the Gloaming (1997; HBO) . . . . .Anne

Fonda, Jane

Daughter of actor Henry Fonda.

Sister of actor Peter Fonda.

Has done a lot of exercise video tapes.

Wife of television tycoon Ted Turner.

Films:

Period of Adjustment (1962) . . . . Isabel Haverstick

Joy House (1964). . . . . Melinda

Cat Ballou (1965) . . . . .Cat Ballou

The Chase (1966) . . . . Anna Reeves

The Game is Over (1966) . . . . Renee Saccard
- • 0:15—Very brief left breast, getting out of bed. Breasts in mirror when running to the door.
- • 0:16—Brief breasts, several times, while behind sheer white curtain.
- • 0:17—Very brief breasts, while falling onto bed.
- •• 0:18—Breasts, while lying in bed with the guy.

Barefoot in the Park (1967) . . . . Corrie Bratter

Barbarella (1968; French/Italian). . . . . Barbarella
- •• 0:03—Breasts, while getting out of space suit during opening credits in zero gravity. Easier to see in version with letterboxed credits.
- • 0:07—Back side of right breast, while opening clear plastic case to get bracelet.
- • 0:08—Very brief buns, when walking around corner after dumping stuff in closet.

They Shoot Horses, Don't They? (1969). . . . . Gloria

Klute (1971) . . . . Bree Daniel
(Academy Award for Best Actress.)
- 0:27—Side view of left and right breasts stripping in the old man's office.

A Doll's House (1973; British) . . . . Nora
Steelyard Blues (1973) . . . . Iris Caine
The Blue Bird (1976) . . . . Night
Fun with Dick and Jane (1977) . . . . Jane Harper
Julia (1977) . . . . Lillian Hellman
California Suite (1978) . . . . Hannah Warren
Comes a Horseman (1978) . . . . Ella
Coming Home (1978) . . . . Sally Hyde
(Academy Award for Best Actress.)
- •• 1:26—Making love in bed with Jon Voight. Breasts only when her face is visible. Buns and brief left breast when you don't see a face is a body double.

The China Syndrome (1979) . . . . Kimberly Wells
The Electric Horseman (1979) . . . . Hallie
9 to 5 (1980) . . . . Judy Bernly
On Golden Pond (1981) . . . . Chelsea Thayer Wayne
Rollover (1981) . . . . Lee Winters
Agnes of God (1985) . . . . Dr. Martha Livingston
The Morning After (1986) . . . . Alex Sternbergen
- • 1:08—Brief breasts making love with Jeff Bridges.

Old Gringo (1989) . . . . Harriet Winslow
- • 1:24—Side of left breast, while undressing in front of Jimmy Smits. Sort of brief right breast, while lying in bed and hugging him.

Stanley and Iris (1990) . . . . Iris King

Made for TV Movies:

The Dollmaker (1984) . . . . Gertie Nevels
(Emmy Award for Best Actress.)

*Fondren, Debra Jo **

Films:

Spitfire (1994) . . . . Amanda Case
- •• 0:00—Breasts, after taking off her top in front of Lance Henriksen.
- ••• 0:01—Breasts, while lying in bed with Henriksen after Sarah Douglas and her men burst into the room.
- •• 0:03—Breasts, after getting shot and talking to Henriksen.

Video Tapes:

Playboy Playmates in Paradise (1992) . . . . Playmate
Playboy's Sexy, Steamy, Sultry (1993) . . . . Playmate
Sexy Lingerie V (1993) . . . . Model
If I'm So Famous, How Come Nobody's Ever Heard of Me? (1996) . . . . Herself
- • 0:18—Breasts in Playboy magazine photos during convention.

*Fondue, Stephanie **

Films:

The Cheerleaders (1973) . . . . Jeannie
- ••• 0:18—Nude, in the boy's showers, then running around when trying to elude a group of boys during her initiation.
- •• 0:38—Breasts, then nude in bed with Jon.
- •• 0:45—Brief full frontal nudity, while sliding out through doors after water bed breaks.
- •• 0:51—Brief breasts, then full frontal nudity, while running through garden party.
- • 1:09—Breasts, while with quarterback.

Fontaine, Alisha

Films:

The Gang That Couldn't Shoot Straight (1971) . . . . . Jelly's Girl
The Gambler (1974) . . . . Howie's Girl

French Quarter (1978)
. . . . Gertrude "Trudy" Dix/Christine Delaplane
- • 0:12—Dancing on stage for the first time. Buns in G-string. Breasts in large black pasties.
- • 0:47—Brief left breast several times, posing for Mr. Beloq.
- • 0:49—Left breast again.
- •• 1:13—Breasts during auction.
- •• 1:18—Brief breasts, then buns making love with Bruce Davison, then breasts again.
- • 1:26—Brief breasts getting her top pulled down during party.
- • 1:31—Brief breasts getting tied down during voodoo ceremony.
- •• 1:32—More breasts tied down during ceremony.

Forbes, Michelle

Films:

The Playboys (1992) . . . . Maggie Rudden
Kalifornia (1993) . . . . Carrie Loughlin
(Unrated version reviewed.)
- • 0:34—Very, very brief upper half of lower frontal nudity while in bed with David Duchovny.

The Road Killers (1993) . . . . Helen
Black Day Blue Night (1995) . . . . Rinda Wooley
Swimming With Sharks (1995) . . . . Dawn Lockard
Escape From L.A. (1996) . . . . Brazen

Made for Cable TV:

The Outer Limits: A Stitch in Time (1996; Showtime)
. . . . Jamie Pratt

TV:

The Guiding Light . . . . Sonni Lewis
Star Trek: The Next Generation (1991-93) . . . . Ensign Ro Laren
Homicide: Life on the Street (1996-98) . . . . Julianna Cox

Ford, Anitra

Films:

The Big Bird Cage (1972) . . . . Terry
- • 0:15—Left breast and buns taking shower. Brief lower frontal nudity after putting shirt on when leaving.
- • 0:19—Brief lower frontal nudity while turning around.
- • 0:44—Brief left breast during gang rape.
- • 1:14—Brief left breast in gaping dress. Dark.

Invasion of the Bee Girls (1973) . . . . Dr. Susan Harris
- ••• 0:47—Breasts and buns undressing in front of a guy in front of a fire.

Stacey! (1973) . . . . Tish Chambers
a.k.a. Stacey and Her Gangbusters
- •• 0:13—Breasts in bed making love with Frank.

Dead People (1974) . . . . Laura
The Longest Yard (1974) . . . . Melissa
- • 0:01—Breasts under see-though red nightgown with Burt Reynolds.

*Ford, Maria **

Films:

Dance of the Damned (1988) . . . . Teacher
- • 0:11—Brief breasts during dance routine in club wearing black panties, garter belt and stockings.

Stripped to Kill II (1988) . . . . Shady
- •• 0:21—Breasts, dancing on table in front of the detective. Buns, walking away.
- • 0:40—Brief upper half of left breast in the alley with the detective.
- •• 0:52—Breasts and buns during dance routine.

The Haunting of Morella (1989) . . . . Diane
••• 1:00—Breasts taking off nightgown and swimming in pond, then walking to waterfall.
The Turn-On (1989) . . . . Maria
a.k.a. Le Clic
••• 0:21—Breasts, then nude while dancing on stage after getting turned on by the black box.
Deathstalker IV: Match of Titans (1990) . . . . .Dionara
•• 0:13—Brief buns, then breasts, getting dressed in cave.
• 0:19—Left breast, while kissing Deathstalker in bed.
Masque of the Red Death (1990). . . . . Isabella
Naked Obsession (1990) . . . . Lynne Hauser
(Unrated version reviewed.)
••• 0:18—Buns in G-string.
••• 0:20—Breasts and buns in G-string, dancing on stage in front of William Katt. Long scene.
••• 0:23—Nude, dancing with Katt's necktie.
•• 0:34—Nude, on stage at end of another dance routine.
•• 0:44—Breasts in her apartment with Katt.
••• 0:45—Breasts and buns on top of Katt in bed while he gently strangles her with his necktie for oxygen deprivation.
•• 0:47—Breasts in bed after making love with Katt.
The Rain Killer (1990) . . . . Satin
•• 0:29—Nude, dancing on stage in club. Backlit too much.
••• 0:37—Breasts in bedroom with Jordan, taking off her clothes, getting tied to bed. Long scene.
• 0:41—Breasts lying on her back on bed, dead.
• 0:48—Same scene from 0:41 when Rosewall looks at B&W police photo.
Slumber Party Massacre 3 (1990) . . . . Maria
(Unrated version reviewed.)
Body Chemistry 2: Voice of a Stranger (1991)
. . . . Uncredited Victim
•• 0:37—Breasts in bed during flashback. (This scene is from *Naked Obsession.*)
Future Kick (1991). . . . . Dancer
Ring of Fire (1991). . . . . .Julie
•• 1:12—In black lingerie, then breasts, making love with Don Wilson.
• 1:14—Brief left breast, lying in bed, while he undresses her.
••• 1:15—Breasts, several, lying on her back in bed while making love.
• 1:17—Brief breasts, sitting up in bed afterward.
Final Judgment (1992). . . . . Nicole
••• 0:20—Breasts and buns in G-string while stripping and dancing on stage. Nice bending over action.
••• 0:39—In red bra and panties, then breasts and buns while dancing on stage.
••• 0:52—Breasts and buns in G-string while dancing on stage.
• 0:56—Very, very brief breast, while putting a towel around herself after getting out of the shower.
•• 0:58—Breasts while making love with Brad Dourif in bed during daydream.
Mind Twister (1992) . . . . Melanie Duncan
(Unrated version reviewed.)
Ring of Fire II: Blood and Steel (1992) . . . . .Julie
The Unnameable II (1992). . . . . .Alyda Winthrop
•• 0:52—Buns, when her long hair moves out of the way. Partial tip of right breast when looking at the telephone.
• 0:53—Brief buns and side of right breast in bedroom.
•• 0:54—Buns and breasts while checking out the bed.
• 0:57—Brief buns, while getting out of bed.
•• 0:58—Buns and brief breasts in bedroom with Mary.
• 1:01—Right breast in gaping nightgown while kneeling on elevator floor.
• 1:22—Brief glimpses of right breast in gaping nightgown.
• 1:32—Very brief right breast in gaping nightgown while crawling on the floor.
Necronomicon: Book of the Dead (1993) . . . . Clara
Angel of Destruction (1994). . . . . Jo Alwood
••• 0:41—Breasts and buns in panties while using martial arts on the bad guys!
••• 0:45—Breasts, while making love with Aaron in bed.
••• 0:59—Breasts and buns in G-string after stripping and dancing on stage.
Dillinger and Capone (1994) . . . . Business Woman
Saturday Night Special (1994) . . . . .Darlene
(Unrated version reviewed.)
••• 0:37—Breasts, while making love with Travis in the woods.
••• 0:50—Breasts, while making love with Travis on bed. Buns, when lying down afterwards. Great!
Alien Terminator (1995). . . . . McKay
Machine Gun Blues (1995) . . . . Alba
• 0:53—Buns and breasts, while making love in bed with Nick Cassavetes.
Night Hunter (1995) . . . . Tournier
Showgirl Murders (1995) . . . . Jessica Cross
•• 0:01—Breasts and buns in T-back while dancing on stage.
••• 0:13—Buns and breasts in T-back while dancing on stage.
•• 0:21—Buns in T-back, while wearing a black wig, doing strip routine on stage.
•• 0:31—Buns in T-back and breasts under sheer top, then breasts while dancing on stage.
•• 0:37—Breasts and buns while wearing a S&M outfit and dancing on stage.
••• 0:47—In silver outfit, then breasts and buns in T-back, dancing on stage with Nikki Fritz. Dribbling hot wax on Fritz.
•• 0:50—Breasts while making love with Mitch in the kitchen.
•• 0:55—Breasts and buns in T-back on stage, pouring liquid on herself while writhing around in one of those large cup props.
• 1:03—Very brief partial left breast, while making love with Mitch.
•• 1:05—Breasts and buns in T-back, while dancing on stage in bridal outfit.
•• 1:07—Breasts and buns in T-back, covered with fluorescent paint, while dancing on stage with another woman and a man.
• 1:16—Brief breasts in flashbacks.
•• 1:19—Breasts, while dancing on stage.
Stripteasers (1995). . . . . Christina Loren
••• 0:00—In bra and panties, then breasts and buns in panties while doing strip routine on stage.
•• 0:04—In bridal gown, then breasts and buns in panties while doing strip routine on stage.
• 0:33—Brief breasts, after being forced to perform oral sex on Carey.
• 0:41—Brief breasts with Carey.
•• 0:53—Buns and breasts, while dancing on stage in patriotic outfit.
The Glass Cage (1996) . . . . Dianne
•• 0:35—Right breast, while lying in bed in open blouse, then breasts and buns, when making love with Marko.
• 0:53—Buns in T-back and breasts, while dancing on stage.
Mind Games (1996) . . . . Ivory/Tess
•• 0:00—Buns and breasts, while making love in bed with Brian Krause.
• 0:04—Brief side view of buns and breasts, while committing suicide in bathtub.

- 0:18—Brief partial right breast, while sitting in bathtub in flashback.
- 0:53—Brief breasts, while making love with Brian Krause.

Made for Cable Movies:

Bram Stoker's Burial of the Rats (1995; Showtime) . . . . Madeleine
- 0:18—Brief buns in outfit, while bringing food to Stoker in prison cell.
- 0:25—Buns, in outfit while getting up from den of sleeping women.
- 0:27—Brief buns, in front of prison cell.
- •• 0:30—Breasts and brief buns, while making love with Stoker.

Wasp Woman (1995; Sci-Fi) . . . . Caitlin
- 0:22—Buns in two piece swimsuit, while posing for photos on the beach.
- •• 0:25—Full frontal nudity, while making love on the beach with Alec.

Made for Cable TV:

Hot Line: Visions of Love (1994; Cinemax) . . . . Kristin
(Available on video tape in *Hot Line.*)
- •• 0:04—In bra, then breasts while wearing panties in front of sink in her apartment when she can't see Paul looking at her.
- ••• 0:15—Breasts, when sitting in front of sink while washing and caressing herself.
- •• 0:21—Breasts, when making love in bed with Paul. Buns while getting out of bed and getting dressed.

Ford, Patricia *

Video Tapes:

Playboy's How to Reawaken Your Sexual Powers (1992) . . . . Cast Member
- 0:01—Buns in one piece swimsuit while on the beach.
- ••• 0:04—Nude, while swimming under water, working out on rock and on beach, and massaging her lover.

Wet & Wild: Hot Holidays (1995) . . . . Cast Member

• Ford, Tamara

See: Leigh, Summer.

• Foreman, Amanda

Films:

Forever Young (1992) . . . . Debbie
Live Wire (1992) . . . . Molly
(Unrated version reviewed.)
The Opposite Sex ...and How to Live with Them (1992) . . . . Waitress
Future Shock (1993) . . . . Paula
Sliver (1993) . . . . Samantha Moore

Made for Cable Movies:

Directed By: The Gift (1994; Showtime) . . . . n.a.
Breast Men (1997; HBO) . . . . Lola
- 0:02—Breasts, when David Schwimmer watches her remove her breast pads and rub breast enlargement cream on herself.

Foreman, Deborah

Films:

I'm Dancing as Fast as I Can (1981) . . . . Cindy
Valley Girl (1983) . . . . Julie
Real Genius (1985) . . . . Susan
3:15—The Moment of Truth (1986) . . . . . Sherry Havilland
- 0:26—Very brief blurry buns and side view of left breast jumping out of bed when her parents come home. Long shot, hard to see anything.

April Fool's Day (1986) . . . . Muffy/Buffy
My Chauffeur (1986) . . . . Casey Meadows
Destroyer (1988) . . . . Susan Malone
Waxwork (1988) . . . . Sarah
The Experts (1989) . . . . Jill
Friends, Lovers & Lunatics (1989) . . . . Annie
Lobster Man From Mars (1989) . . . . Mary
Sundown: The Vampire in Retreat (1989) . . . . Sandy
Lunatics: A Love Story (1991) . . . . Nancy

Foreman, Michelle

Films:

Stripped to Kill (1987) . . . . Angel
- ••• 0:02—Breasts dancing on stage for Norman Fell.

Sunset Strip (1992) . . . . Heather
- •• 0:29—In black bra and G-string, while practicing her dance routine in her living room.
- •• 1:24—Buns in G-string, while dancing during contest.
- •• 1:28—Breasts while in the shower with Jeff Conaway. Don't see her face well, but it looks like her.
- ••• 1:30—Buns in G-string, while dancing on stage and breasts (finally!) at the end.

Made for Cable Movies:

Fear (1991; Showtime) . . . . Gale the Stripper
- 0:50—Breasts and buns dancing in bar. Hard to see because seen through the killer's eyes.

Forlani, Claire

Films:

CIA Trackdown (1993) . . . . Katarina
- 0:58—Side of right breast, while changing blouses in room with Harry.
- •• 1:07—Breasts and buns, while making love in bed with Harry.
- 1:11—Upper half of breasts, while getting out of water with Harry.

Police Academy: Mission to Moscow (1994) . . . . Katrina
Mallrats (1995) . . . . Brandi
Basquiat (1996) . . . . Gina Cardinale
The Last Time I Committed Suicide (1996) . . . . Joan
The Rock (1996) . . . . Jade

Made for Cable Movies:

Directed By: The Gift (1994; Showtime) . . . . Flirting Woman in Restaurant

Made for TV Movies:

JFK: Reckless Youth (1993) . . . . Ann Cannon

Forqué, Verónica

Films:

The Year of Awakening (1986; Spanish) . . . . Irene
Don Juan, My Love (1991; Spanish) . . . . . Señora de Marquina
Kika (1994; Spanish) . . . . Kika
- ••• 0:37—Breasts, while making love in bed with Ramon, photographing each other. Long scene.
- 0:48—Brief, partial buns, while lying in bed.

Forster Jones, Glenna

Films:

Joanna (1968; British) . . . . Beryl
- 0:17—Brief upper half of breasts, while sitting in bed, smoking, talking with Joanna. Slightly out of focus.

Leo the Last (1970; British) . . . . Salambo

The Human Factor (1979) . . . . Black Prostitute
Flash Gordon (1980) . . . . Sandmoon Girl

• Forté, Marlene

Films:

The Bronx War (1989) . . . . Alicia
•• 1:01—Breasts after taking off bra while dancing. Intercut with scene of gang violence.

Fresh Kill (1994) . . . . Pam Mandel

Made for Cable Movies:

Path to Paradise: The Untold Story of the World Trade Center Bombing (1997; HBO) . . . . Monica Smith

Forte, Valentina

Films:

Cut and Run (1985; Italian) . . . . Ana
••• 0:29—Brief left breast being made love to in bed. Then breasts sitting up in bed and left side view and buns taking a shower.

Inferno in Diretta (1985; Italian) . . . . n.a.

Fortea, Isabelle *

Films:

Affairs of the Heart (1992) . . . . Karen
••• 1:06—Breasts making love in cabin with Tom.

Marilyn Chambers' Bedtime Stories (1993) . . . . . . Tatiana
••• 0:18—Breasts and buns in red G-string, after taking off dress with Bart's help.
••• 0:25—Breasts and buns with Bart, then in shower. Squished breasts against the glass.
• 0:33—Breasts in open solid color robe in bathroom.
• 1:17—Breasts in out take with Bart.

Bikini Bistro (1995) . . . . Donna
(Unrated version reviewed.)
••• 0:12—Nude, while changing into a swimsuit in room with the two other girls.
• 0:37—Buns in swimsuit.
•• 0:48—Breasts, after taking off her swimsuit top in kitchen with Ron.
• 0:52—Full frontal nudity, while changing into swimsuit.
••• 1:14—Full frontal nudity, while making love in the kitchen with Ron.

• Fortier, Laurie

Films:

To Gillian on her 37th Birthday (1996). . . . . . Cindy Bayles
• 0:16—Brief buns, then buns in blue T-back swimsuit, while talking with Claire Danes in bedroom.
• 0:40—Brief buns in swimsuit, while walking on the beach next to Danes.
• 0:41—Buns, while standing in swimsuit at the beach.

TV:

Push (1998-) . . . . Cara Bradford

Foss, Shirlene

Films:

Impure Thoughts (1986) . . . . n.a.
Dead Aim (1987) . . . . B.J.
• 0:14—Buns in G-string and white top.
• 0:55—Brief buns in G-string while dancing on stage in bridal outfit.

Funland (1987) . . . . n.a.

Fossey, Brigitte

Films:

Forbidden Games (1953; French) . . . . Paulette
Honor Among Thieves (1968; French/Italian) . . . . .Dominque "Waterloo" Austerlitz
a.k.a. Farewell, Friend

Going Places (1974; French) . . . . Young Mother
••• 0:32—In bra, then breasts in open blouse on the train when she lets Patrick Dewaere suck the milk out of her breasts.

Blue Country (1977; French) . . . . Louise
The Man Who Loved Women (1977; French) . . . . Benevieve Bigey
Quintet (1979) . . . . Vivia
La Boum (1980; French) . . . . Francoise
Chanel Solitaire (1981) . . . . .Adrienne
Enigma (1982) . . . . Karen
• 0:39—Brief breasts after undressing in jail cell. Very brief lower frontal nudity and buns, shielding herself from the light.
•• 0:40—Breasts getting interrogated.

Cinema Paradiso (1988; Italian/French) . . . . Elena

Foster, Jodie

Films:

Kansas City Bomber (1972) . . . . .Rita
Napolean and Samantha (1972) . . . . Samantha
One Little Indian (1973) . . . . Martha
Tom Sawyer (1973) . . . . Becky Thatcher
Alice Doesn't Live Here Anymore (1975) . . . . Audrey
Bugsy Malone (1976) . . . . Tallulah
Echoes of Summer (1976) . . . . Deirdre Striden
The Little Girl Who Lives Down the Lane (1976; Canadian) . . . . .Rynn
Taxi Driver (1976) . . . . Iris Steensman
Candleshoe (1977) . . . . Casey
Freaky Friday (1977) . . . . Annabel Andrews
Carny (1980) . . . . Donna
Foxes (1980) . . . . Jeanie
O'Hara's Wife (1982) . . . . .Barbara O'Hara
The Hotel New Hampshire (1984) . . . . Franny
Siesta (1987) . . . . .Nancy
The Accused (1988) . . . . Sarah Tobias
(Academy Award for Best Actress.)
• 1:27—Brief breasts a few times during rape scene on pinball machine by Dan and Bob.

Five Corners (1988) . . . . Linda
Backtrack (1989) . . . . .Anne Benton
a.k.a. Catch Fire
• 0:50—Breasts behind textured shower door.
••• 0:51—Breasts, leaning out of the shower to get her towel. Very, very brief side of left breast and buns, while drying herself off in bedroom. Side of left breast and buns, while putting on slip.

Silence of the Lambs (1990) . . . . Clarice Starling
(Academy Award for Best Actress 1992.)
Little Man Tate (1991) . . . . .Dede Tate
Shadows and Fog (1991). . . . . Prostitute
Sommersby (1993) . . . . Laurel Sommersby
Maverick (1994) . . . . Annabelle Bransford
Nell (1994) . . . . Nell
• 0:40—Nude at night, taking off her dress and going for a swim in the lake.
• 0:42—Breasts and buns, climbing on rock and getting out of the lake.
•• 0:46—Buns and breasts, getting out of water at night while hearing music and starting to cry.
•• 0:53—Breasts, when leaning on rock, then swimming to talk with Natasha Richardson.

- 0:54—Right breast, under the water when Liam Neeson attempts to show her that all men aren't bad.
- •• 1:15—Breasts, when she raises her dress in bar when local kid manipulates her.

Contact (1997) . . . . Ellie Arroway

Made for Cable Movies:

The Blood of Others (1984; HBO) . . . . Helene Bertrand

Made for TV Movies:

Svengali (1983). . . . . Zoe Alexander

TV:

Bob & Carol & Ted & Alice (1973) . . . . . . Elizabeth Henderson

Paper Moon (1974-75) . . . . Addie Pray

Foster, Karen *

Video Tapes:

Playboy Video Calendar 1991 (1990) . . . . March

Playboy Video Centerfold: Deborah Driggs & Karen Foster (1990). . . . . Playmate

- ••• 0:24—Baton twirling, outside on bed, other miscellaneous things. Nude.

Sexy Lingerie II (1990). . . . . Model

Wet & Wild II (1990) . . . . Model

Sexy Lingerie III (1991) . . . . Model

Wet & Wild III (1991) . . . . Model

The Best of Sexy Lingerie (1992). . . . . Model

The Best of Wet and Wild (1992) . . . . Model

Playboy's Sexy, Steamy, Sultry (1993). . . . . Playmate

Foster, Kylie

Films:

Kitty and the Bagman (1983; Australian) . . . . . . Sarah Jones

- 0:57—Very brief side view of left breast, while jumping off bed to see if Cyril is all right.
- 1:34—Very brief breasts, when getting out of bed after being discovered by Kitty.
- 1:35—Very brief full frontal nudity, then buns when forced to walk outside naked with Cyril.

Quigley Down Under (1990). . . . . n.a.

Foster, Lisa Raines *

a.k.a. Lisa Foster or Lisa Raines.

Films:

Fanny Hill (1981; British). . . . . Fanny Hill

- •• 0:09—Nude, getting into bathtub, then drying herself off.
- 0:10—Full frontal nudity getting into bed.
- ••• 0:12—Full frontal nudity making love with Phoebe in bed.
- ••• 0:30—Nude, making love in bed with Charles.
- •• 0:49—Breasts, whipping her lover, Mr. H., in bed.
- •• 0:53—Nude getting into bed with William while Hannah watches through the keyhole.
- ••• 1:26—Nude, getting out of bed, then running down the stairs to open the door for Charles.

Spring Fever (1983; Canadian) . . . . Lena

The Blade Master (1984). . . . . Mila

a.k.a. Ator, The Invincible

Made for Cable TV:

The Hitchhiker: Killer (HBO) . . . . Patty

- 0:02—Very brief breasts standing in the bathtub just before getting shot.
- 0:23—Very brief breasts again in Jenny Seagrove's flashback.

Foster, Meg

Films:

The Todd Killings (1970) . . . . n.a.

Thumb Tripping (1972) . . . . Shay

- 1:19—Very, very brief breasts leaning back in field with Jack. Long shot.
- 1:20—Breasts at night. Face is turned away from the camera.

Welcome to Arrow Beach (1973). . . . . Robbin Stanley

a.k.a. Tender Flesh

- 0:12—Buns and brief side view of right breast getting undressed to skinny dip in the ocean. Don't see her face.
- •• 0:40—Breasts getting out of bed.

A Different Story (1979) . . . . Stella

(R-rated version reviewed.)

- •• 0:53—Breasts, while sitting on Perry King, rubbing cake all over each other on bed.
- 0:59—Brief buns and side view of right breast, while getting into bed with King.

Carny (1980). . . . . Greta

Ticket to Heaven (1981; Canadian) . . . . Ingrid

The Osterman Weekend (1983) . . . . Ali Tanner

- 0:14—Very, very brief tip of right breast after getting nightgown out of closet.

The Emerald Forest (1985) . . . . Jean Markham

Masters of the Universe (1987) . . . . Evil-Lyn

The Wind (1987). . . . . Sian Anderson

They Live (1988) . . . . Holly

Leviathan (1989). . . . . Martin

Relentless (1989). . . . . Carol Dietz

Stepfather 2 (1989). . . . . Carol Grayland

Tripwire (1989) . . . . Julia

Backstab (1990) . . . . Sara Rudnick

Blind Fury (1990) . . . . Lynn Devereaux

Jezebel's Kiss (1990) . . . . Amanda Faberson

Diplomatic Immunity (1991). . . . . Gerta Hermann

Future Kick (1991). . . . . Nancy Morgan

Relentless 2: Dead On (1991) . . . . Carol Dietz

Best of the Best 2 (1992). . . . . Sue MacCauley

Hidden Fears (1992) . . . . Maureen Dietz

Project: Shadowchaser (1992). . . . . Sarah

Immortal Combat (1993) . . . . Quinn

Lady in Waiting (1994) . . . . n.a.

(Unrated version reviewed.)

Oblivion (1994). . . . . Stell Barr

Shrunken Heads (1994). . . . . Big Moe

Space Marines (1995) . . . . Commodore Lasser

Undercover (1995) . . . . Mrs. V

(Unrated version reviewed.)

Made for Cable TV:

The Hitchhiker: The Martyr (1989; USA) . . . . n.a.

Made for TV Movies:

Betrayal of Silence (1989) . . . . Julie

To Catch a Killer (1992; Canadian) . . . . . City Attorney Carlson

TV:

Sunshine (1975) . . . . Nora

Cagney & Lacey (1982). Chris Cagney

Fowler, Diane

See: Thomas, Sunset.

Fox, Jerica

Adult Films:

Bobby Hollander's The Girls from Hootersville-Volume 2 (1993). . . . . Herself

Films:

Housewife From Hell (1993) . . . . Party Girl

- ••• 0:53—In red bra and panties, then breasts while dancing beside spa, then getting into spa and sitting in spa.

One Million Heels B.C. (1993). . . . . Savannah
- ••• 0:16—In lingerie, then nude while dancing in living room with Rose.
- ••• 0:21—Full frontal nudity, while soaping Rose and Bauer in the spa.
- • 0:25—Brief full frontal nudity, after taking off her towel in bedroom.
- ••• 0:26—Full frontal nudity, while getting dressed.

Fox, Kerry

Films:

An Angel at My Table (1990; Australian/New Zealand) . . . . Janet
- • 1:45—Brief breasts and partial lower frontal nudity while in bathtub.
- •• 2:06—Left breast while sitting on bed with her boyfriend.
- • 2:07—Nude, while swimming in the water.
- •• 2:09—Long shot of right breast, while lying on rock outside, then breasts in a closer shot.

The Last Days of Chez Nous (1991; Australian) . . . . Vicki

Shallow Grave (1994; British). . . . . Juliet Miller
- •• 0:10—Brief breasts, getting her mail from Ewan McGregor.

Country Life (1995; Australian) . . . . Sally Voysey

Welcome to Sarajevo (1997) . . . . .Jane Carson

The Hanging Garden (1998). Rosemary

Made for Cable Movies:

The Affair (1995; U.S./British; HBO). . . . . Maggie

Made for Cable TV:

Tales From the Crypt: Last Respects (1996; HBO) . . . . . Dolores

Fox, Marcia

Films:

Doctor in Trouble (1970; British). . . . . Jean

Creatures the World Forgot (1971; British) . . . . The Dumb Girl
- • 0:51—Right breast, then brief breasts turning around by the pool.
- • 0:58—Brief breasts fighting with Julie Ege.
- • 1:20—Very brief right breast when The Dark Boy gets his leg cut.

The Au Pair Girls (1972; British). . . . . Eve

Fox, Morgan *

Films:

Flesh Gordon 2 (1990; Canadian). . . . . Robunda Hooters
- •• 0:12—Breasts, while opening her top to get Flesh Gordon excited.
- • 1:07—Brief breasts when her top is opened by the Evil Presence to get Flesh aroused.

Video Tapes:

Playboy Video Calendar 1992 (1991) . . . . .December
- ••• 0:48—Nude in aqueduct shoot.
- ••• 0:49—Breasts and buns in G-string while singing and dancing on stage.

Playboy Video Centerfold: Morgan Fox (1991) . . Playmate
- ••• 0:02—Nude in aqueduct shoot.
- ••• 0:06—Nude in bedroom/factory fantasy.
- • 0:15—Brief silhouette of breasts and buns, several times while dancing.
- ••• 0:18—Nude, taking a bath.
- ••• 0:20—Breasts and buns in still photos.
- ••• 0:22—Breasts and buns in G-string, garter belt and stockings, dancing on stage.

Playboy's Erotic Fantasies (1992). . . . . Cast Member

Sexy Lingerie IV (1992) . . . . .Model

Wet & Wild IV (1992) . . . . .Model

Playboy's Erotic Fantasies II (1993) . . . . .Model

Playboy's Sexy, Steamy, Sultry (1993) . . . . .Playmate

Sexy Lingerie V (1993). . . . . .Model

Playboy's 21 Playmates (1996). . . . . .Playmate
- ••• 0:25—Nude in still photos.
- ••• 0:26—Nude in bed and in fantasy.

Fox, Samantha

Adult film actress.

Not to be confused with the British singer with the same name.

a.k.a. Stacia Micula, Stasha Bergoff.

Adult Films:

Babylon Pink (1979) . . . . .n.a.

Films:

I, the Jury (1982) . . . . Uncredited Orgy Woman

It's Called Murder Baby (1982). . . . . .Lisa Benson

(R-rated version of the adult film *Dixie Ray, Hollywood Star.*)
- ••• 1:10—In bra, then breasts in bedroom in front of Nick and Sherry.
- •• 1:11—Breasts, sleeping on bed, then waking up and getting out.
- • 1:18—Brief breasts in B&W flashback.

C.O.D. (1983) . . . . Female Reporter

In Love (1983) . . . . .n.a.

Simply Irresistible (1983) . . . . Arlene Brooks

(R-rated version. *Irresistible* is the X-rated version.)
- • 1:20—In see-through white nightgown, then brief peeks at right breast when nightgown gapes open.

Delivery Boys (1984) . . . . Woman in Tuxedo

Streetwalkin' (1985) . . . . Topless Dancer
- • 0:22—Breasts, dancing on stage in nightclub (She's the one wearing a head band).
- • 0:27—More breasts, dancing on stage.
- • 0:29—More breasts, dancing on stage.
- • 0:56—Breasts, giving Antonio Fargas a massage at the bar.

Sex Appeal (1986). . . . . Sheila
- ••• 1:14—In black lingerie, then breasts and buns in black G-string with Rhonda. Long scene.

Slammer Girls (1987) . . . . Mosquito
- •• 0:17—Breasts in the shower hassling Melody with Tank.

Violated (1987) . . . . Joan
- • 0:52—Breasts, while in bed with Marilyn on video playback.

Warrior Queen (1987) . . . . Philomena/Augusta
- ••• 0:31—Nude, doing a dance with a snake during orgy scene.
- • 1:03—Brief right breast after unsuccessfully trying to seduce Marcus.

Fox, Vivica A.

Films:

Born on the Fourth of July (1989) . . . . Hooker
- • 0:50—Brief right breast, while taking off bra on top of patient in hospital. Dark.

Don't Be a Menace to South Central While Drinking Your Juice in the Hood (1995) . . . . .Ashtray's Mother

Independence Day (1996) . . . . Jasmine Dubrow
- • 0:35—Brief side view of buns in T-back, while in dressing room in club.

Set It Off (1996) . . . . Frankie

Batman & Robin (1997) . . . . Ms. B Haven

Booty Call (1997) . . . . .Lysterine
- • 0:29—Very, very brief partial right breast, three times, while making love with Jamie Foxx in bed.

Made for Cable Movies:

The Tuskegee Airmen (1995; HBO) . . . . .Charlene

TV:
Generations (1990) . . . . .Maya Daniels
Out All Night (1992-93) . . . . Charisse Chamberlain
The Young and the Restless (1994-96) . . . .Stephanie Simmons
Arsenio (1997) . . . . .Vivan
The Way We Work (1998-) . . . . n.a.

Francis, Carol

Films:
Crawlspace (1986) . . . . Jess
Violated (1987). . . . . .Katy Carson
•• 0:22—Breasts, while taking off her outfit during party, then diving into pool.

Frank, Diana

Films:
Not Since Casanova (1988). . . . . Gina
Monster High (1990) . . . . .Candice Cain
Pale Blood (1990). . . . . .Jenny
•• 0:21—Breasts lying on the bed with Michael when he bites her.
• 0:36—Close up of left breast on TV monitor that Wings Hauser is editing with. Don't see face.
• 0:42—Brief left breast on TV monitor several times while Hauser examines the bite marks.
• 1:03—Very brief breasts when Hauser pulls her dress top down to look at her bite mark.
Eyes of the Serpent (1992) . . . . .Fiona
•• 1:05—Buns and breasts, several times while making love in bed with Galen.
TV:
High Tide (1994). . . . . .Fritz Boller

Frank, Joanna

Wife of actor Alan Rachins.
Films:
The Savage Seven . . . . Maria Little Hawk
America, America (1963). . . . . Vartuhi
Double Exposure (1983) . . . . Bartender's Ex-Wife
Always (1984) . . . . Lucy
• 0:57—Right breast, while taking a bath and covering herself with powdered hot chocolate mix.
• 1:00—Brief upper half of right breast, while in bathtub some more.
Say Anything (1989) . . . . .Mrs. Kerwin
TV:
L.A. Law (1986-88) . . . . Sheilal Brackman

Franklin, Diane

Films:
Amityville II: The Possession (1982) . . . . . Patricia Montelli
• 0:41—Half of right breast, while sitting on bed talking to her brother.
The Last American Virgin (1982). . . . . Karen
••• 1:06—Breasts in room above the bleachers with Jason.
•• 1:17—Breasts and almost lower frontal nudity taking off her panties in the clinic.
Better Off Dead (1985) . . . . Monique Junet
Second Time Lucky (1986) . . . . Eve
•• 0:13—Breasts a lot during first sequence in the Garden of Eden with Adam.
••• 0:28—Brief full frontal nudity running to Adam after trying an apple.
• 0:41—Left breast, while taking top of dress down.
••• 1:01—Breasts, opening her blouse in defiance, while standing in front of a firing squad

Terrorvision (1986) . . . . .Suzy Putterman
Bill and Ted's Excellent Adventure (1989) . . . . . Princess Joanna
How I Got Into College (1989) . . . . Sharon Browne
Made for TV Movies:
Deadly Lessons (1983). . . . . Stephanie

Franklin, Pamela

Films:
The Innocents (1961) . . . . Flora
The Lion (1962; British). . . . . Tina
The Nanny (1965; British) . . . . .Bobby
The Night of the Following Day (1969) . . . . Girl
• 1:30—Brief breasts, while being helped onto bed by Marlon Brando after she was bound and hung by her wrists.
The Prime of Miss Jean Brodie (1969). . . . . Sandy
•• 1:21—Breasts posing as a model for Teddy's painting. Brief right breast, while kissing him. Long shot of buns, while getting dressed.
The Legend of Hell House (1973; British) . . Florence Tanner
• 1:03—Silhouette of breasts while taking off nightgown and getting into bed.
Food of the Gods (1976). . . . . Lorna
The Witching (1983) . . . . .Lori
a.k.a. Necromancy
(Originally filmed in 1971 as *Necromancy*, additional scenes were added and re-released in 1983.)
•• 0:38—Breasts lying in bed during nightmare.
• 1:07—Brief breasts putting on black robe.
• 1:17—Brief breasts in several quick cuts.
Made for TV Movies:
Flipper's New Adventure (1964) . . . . Penny
See How They Run (1964). . . . . Tirza Green
David Copperfield (1970) . . . . .Dora Spentow
The Letters (1973). . . . . Karen Foster
Satan's School for Girls (1973). . . . . Elizabeth Sayres
Eleanor and Franklin (1976). Anna Hall

Frazier, Sheila

Films:
Superfly (1972) . . . . .Georgia
•• 0:40—Breasts and buns, making love in the bathtub with Superfly.
Three the Hard Way (1974). . . . . Wendy Kane
California Suite (1978). . . . . .Bettina Panama
The Hitter (1978) . . . . .Lola
• 0:30—Brief side view of left breast, while making love in bed with Ron O'Neal.
•• 0:31—Breasts, while sitting in bed after making love.
Two of a Kind (1983). . . . . Reporter
Made for TV Movies:
The Lazarus Syndrome (1976) . . . . .Gloria St. Clair

Frederick, Lynne

Films:
No Blade of Grass (1970; British). . . . . Mary Custance
Nicholas and Alexandra (1971; British) . . . . Tatiana
Henry VIII and His Six Wives (1972; British) . .Catherine Howard
Voyage of the Damned (1976; British). . . . . .Anna Rosen
Schizo (1977; British) . . . . Samantha
a.k.a. Amok
a.k.a. Blood of the Undead
0:26—In white bra and panties, while changing clothes in bedroom.
•• 0:29—Breasts and buns, while walking to and taking a shower.
• 0:56—Brief frontal nudity, while getting into bed.

The Prisoner of Zenda (1979) . . . . Princess Flavia

Frederick, Vicki

Films:

All That Jazz (1979) . . . . Menage Partner

...All the Marbles (1981) . . . . Iris

a.k.a. The California Dolls

• 1:03—Brief side view of left breast, while crying in the shower after fighting with Peter Falk.

Body Rock (1984) . . . . Claire

A Chorus Line (1985) . . . . Sheila

Stewardess School (1987) . . . . Miss Grummet

Chopper Chicks in Zombietown (1989) . . . . Jewel

Scissors (1990) . . . . Nancy Leahy

Chaplin (1992; British/U.S.) . . . . Party Guest

Made for Cable TV:

Dream On: Doing the Bossa Nova (1990; HBO) . . . . Valerie

Freed, Rona

See: De Ricci, Rona.

Freeman, Cyndi

Made for Cable TV:

Compromising Situations: First Time Caller (1994; Showtime) . . . . Karen

Compromising Situations: The Casting Couch (1994; Showtime) . . . . Betty Condom

•• 0:12—Breasts, when wearing panties, while getting dressed in hotel room.

••• 0:19—Buns and breasts, while on sofa, chair and table making love with Phil.

• 0:22—Partial buns, while under robe on sofa.

Compromising Situations: The Master (1994; Showtime) . . . . Secretary

Erotic Confessions: Inspiration (1995; Cinemax) . . Receptionist (Available on video tape in *Erotic Zone: Inspiration.*)

• Freeman, Kalani

a.k.a. Kalani.

Films:

Eve's Beach Fantasy (1997) . . . . Model 2

•• 0:45—Breasts, after taking off her bra during photo shoot on bed.

• 1:05—Buns in swimsuit during photo shoot.

Video Tapes:

Sex on the Saddle . . . . Kalani

Sex on the Strip . . . . Kalani

Hot Body Competition: Bikinis & Bikes Contest (1996) . . . . Kalani

•• 0:34—Breasts and buns, while dancing on stage.

Penthouse: The World of Philip Mond (1998) . . . . n.a.

Freeman, Lindsay

Films:

Young Lady Chatterley (1977) . . . . . Sybil, Light-Duty Maid

• 1:35—Brief left breast, while on the floor, covered with cake.

Fairytales (1979) . . . . Jill

•• 0:24—Nude on hill with Jack.

French, Paige

Films:

Meatballs 4 (1992) . . . . Jennifer Lipton

•• 0:27—Breasts outside with Wes.

• 0:29—Brief breasts, after being splashed with water.

Made for Cable Movies:

Intimate Strangers (1991; Showtime) . . . . Meg Wheeler

TV:

Freshman Dorm (1992) . . . . Lulu Abercrombie

George Carlin (1994-95) . . . . Sydney

Friedland, Alice

Films:

The Killing of a Chinese Bookie (1976) . . . . Sherry

• 0:32—Upper half of breasts, while flashing for the M.C. during show on stage.

• 0:33—Brief left breast, while flashing for the audience.

• 1:13—Breasts dancing on stage. Long shot.

• 1:35—Left breast, while sitting in dressing room during discussion.

• 1:38—Breasts with the other dancers in the dressing room.

The Great Texas Dynamite Chase (1977) . . . . Dancer

Fritz, Nikki *

Films:

Smokey and the Bandit III (1983) . . . . Uncredited S&M Hooker

Spring Break (1983; Canadian) . . . . Girl In Corvette

••• 0:24—Breasts taking off clothes in room with Stu and O.T.

The New Kids (1985) . . . . Body Double for Lori Loughlin

• 0:52—Brief buns, partially visible behind plastic shower curtain.

Bad Blood (1993) . . . . Uncredited Dancer

• 0:09—Breasts and buns when wearing T-back while dancing on stage, twice.

Beach Babes From Beyond (1993) . . . . Sally's Model

••• 0:20—Breasts, while posing in spa outside (she's on the right) during catalog photo session with two other models.

••• 0:22—Nude, in bedroom during Hassler's fantasy.

• 1:02—Brief breasts, twice, when swimsuit top flies off while dancing on stage during bikini contest (she's the last one).

Dinosaur Island (1993) . . . . High Priestess

•• 0:00—Breasts (painted blue) and buns in G-string, while dancing during sacrifice ceremony.

Indecent Behavior II (1994) . . . . Woman on Balcony (Unrated version reviewed.)

•• 0:03—Buns in panties, then breasts and lower frontal nudity when making love with man on balcony while Shoshana watches from inside the house.

• 0:06—More frontal nudity while making love on balcony.

A Low Down Dirty Shame (1994) . . . . Exotic Dancer

• 1:03—Brief buns in sexy swimsuit, while dancing in a club.

Saturday Night Special (1994) . . . . Uncredited Line Dancer (Unrated version reviewed.)

Where Evil Lies (1994) . . . . Alex

• 0:00—Buns in outfit, while posing for still photos.

• 0:02—Very brief peeks at breasts and buns in G-string, while posing for photos.

• 0:04—Buns, in outfit when fooling around with her friends.

••• 0:19—Nude, doing strip tease dance on stage.

••• 0:58—Breasts and buns in outfit, while dancing on stage.

••• 1:00—Breasts, while making love with Kurt.

Attack of the 60 Foot Centerfold (1995) . . . . Rosita

• 0:33—Breasts, while giving Jay Richardson a backrub.

Bikini Drive-In (1995) . . . . Susan (Unrated version reviewed.)

• 0:53—Buns in swimsuit, after changing into swimsuit in restroom.

••• 1:10—Nude, while making love with Tom in drive-in office.

Showgirl Murders (1995) . . . . Dancer

••• 0:47—In green outfit, then breasts and buns, while dancing on stage with Maria Ford. Then getting hot wax dribbled on her by Ford.

Stripteasers (1995) . . . . Sandra
••• 0:08—Buns then breasts, while doing strip tease dance on stage.
• 1:08—Brief buns in T-back, while leaping over the bar to get a shot gun.

Fugitive Rage (1996) . . . . Nurse Wendy
• 0:13—Brief buns in white lingerie outfit, after taking off nurse outfit in bedroom with Jay Richardson.
•• 0:34—Left breast, while in bathtub with Richardson. Brief breasts, when getting out of the bathtub and buns, while walking down the hall.

Made for Cable Movies:

Bram Stoker's Burial of the Rats (1995; Showtime) . . . . Rat Woman

Terminal Virus (1995; Showtime) . . . . Casandra
•• 0:04—Breasts, while running away from the bad guy.
• 0:05—Very brief breasts, while getting up off the ground.
• 0:06—Breasts, while running away from some more bad guys, then climbing into car.

Made for Cable TV:

Beverly Hills Bordello: Drawing the Line (1997; Showtime) . . . . Paige
••• 0:02—Breasts and bun, while making love with Doug in bed. Long scene.
••• 0:04—Breasts, while sitting in chair, smoking a cigar and talking with Doug.
••• 0:10—Full frontal nudity, while making love with Donna in room and in bathtub. Long, hot scene.
••• 0:19—Nude, when making love with Doug while he's standing blindfolded, then blindfolded and tied to bed. Long scene.

Intimate Sessions: Tamara (1998; Cinemax) . . . . Tamara/Stella
••• 0:10—Breasts and buns, while taking a bath and talking, then making love with Jack. B&W.
••• 0:21—In lingerie, then breasts and partial buns, while making love with Rick.

Frost, Sadie

Films:

Empire State (1987; British). . . . . Tracy

Dark Obsession (1989; British). . . . . Rebecca
a.k.a. Diamond Skulls
• 0:22—Very brief right breast in bed after she rolls off Jamie.
••• 0:33—Breasts several times while making love with Jamie when Gabriel Byrne interrupts them.

Bram Stoker's Dracula (1992) . . . . Lucy
• 0:41—Left breast, while making love with Dracula on bench outside at night during the rain.
•• 0:58—Breasts in bed, quite a few times, after getting bitten by Dracula and getting a blood transfusion.
• 1:12—Brief right breast in gaping nightgown.
• 1:19—Left breast, while lying in bed when Dracula pays a return visit.
• 1:20—Brief left breast, when the wolf Dracula jumps on the bed.

Paper Marriage (1993) . . . . . . Employment Agency Interviewer

Shopping (1993; British). . . . . Jo

Splitting Heirs (1993) . . . . Angela

A Pyromaniac's Love Story (1995) . . . . Hattie

Crimetime (1996; U.S./British) . . . . Val
• 0:31—Brief breasts, when flashing herself for Stephen Baldwin in a doorway at night.
•• 0:59—Left breast, while sleeping when Baldwin pulls back the covers and caresses her.
• 1:00—Brief breasts, after waking up and calling for Baldwin.

Made for Cable Movies:

The Cisco Kid (1994; TNT) . . . . n.a.

Froton, Sara Lee

Films:

Psycho Cop 2 (1992) . . . . Go Go Dancer #2
• 0:21—Breasts on film that the guys are watching at bachelor party. (She's the brunette.)
• 1:17—Breasts and buns in pink panties in film during end credits.

Skinner (1993) . . . . Young Woman

Fuller, Victoria *

Video Tapes:

Playboy Video Calendar 1997 (1996) . . . . January
••• 0:01—Nude, while posing outside.
••• 0:03—In lingerie, then nude, while posing indoors.

Wet & Wild VIII: Bottoms Up (1996). . . . . Playmate

Playboy's Fast Women (1997). . . . . Playmate

Fulton, Christina

Films:

The Doors (1991) . . . . Nico
•• 0:56—Breasts, after taking off her top in elevator with Val Kilmer.

Dangerous Game (1993). . . . . Blonde
(Unrated version reviewed.)

A Brilliant Disguise (1994) . . . . Marlene

The Girl with the Hungry Eyes (1994). . . . . Louise
• 0:19—Brief buns, while putting panties on.
• 0:20—Breasts, while posing for Carlos.
• 1:06—Right breast, while making love in bed with Carlos. Lit with blue light.
• 1:18—Left breast, while lying in bed with Carlos.

Hard Drive (1994). . . . . Dana/Delilah
(Unrated version reviewed.)
• 0:23—Brief lower frontal nudity, brief left breast and brief buns while getting attacked on bed by Will.
• 0:25—Buns, while lying on bed after getting shot.
• 0:26—Brief buns and left breast in Will's flashback.
•• 1:15—Left breast, while making love with Will on kitchen counter.

Made for Cable TV:

Red Shoe Diaries: Another Woman's Lipstick (1993; Showtime) . . . . The Other Woman
(Available on the video tape *Red Shoe Diaries 3: Another Woman's Lipstick.*)
••• 0:16—Breasts, while in corner of the room, then crawling on the floor.
•• 0:28—Brief right breast, then breasts, while stripping in front of Maryam D'Abo.
•• 0:29—Left breast, while in room with D'Abo.

Red Shoe Diaries: Luscious Lola (1995; Showtime). . . . The Boss

Furman, Rachel *

Identical twin sister of Rebecca Furman.

Video Tapes:

Playboy's Sisters (1995). . . . . Herself/Double Trouble
••• 0:33—Nude when washing the car with her identical twin sister.

Furman, Rebecca *
Identical twin sister of Rachel Furman.
Video Tapes:
Playboy's Sisters (1995). . . . . Herself/Double Trouble
••• 0:33—Nude when washing the car with her identical twin sister.

Gabrielle, Monique *
Adult Films:
Bad Girls IV (1982). . . . . Sandy
(Credits have her listed as Luana Chass.)
••• 0:15—Left breast, then breasts in bed masturbating while Ron Jeremy peeks from window.
••• 1:24—Nude, making love (non-explicitly) with Jerry Butler.
Films:
Airplane II: The Sequel (1982) . . . . School Girl
• 0:02—Brief breasts seen on monitor when walking through the video X-ray scanner at the airport while holding her mother's hand.
Night Shift (1982) . . . . Tessie
• 0:55—Brief breasts, while sitting on college guy's shoulders during party in the morgue.
Black Venus (1983). . . . . Ingrid
••• 0:03—Nude in Sailor Room at the bordello.
••• 1:01—Breasts and buns, taking off clothes for Madame Lili's customers.
Chained Heat (1983; U.S./German) . . . . Debbie
••• 0:08—Nude, stripping for the Warden in his office.
••• 0:09—Nude, getting into the spa with the Warden.
Flashdance (1983) . . . . .Uncredited Stripper
•• 1:27—Buns, in G-string, walking down walkway of stage in club. Brief breasts, accepting a bill in her red G-string.
Bachelor Party (1984) . . . . .Tracey
•• 1:11—Full frontal nudity in the hotel bedroom with Tom Hanks as his bachelor party gift.
Hard to Hold (1984) . . . . .Wife #1
Hot Moves (1984). . . . . Babs
• 0:29—Nude on the nude beach.
•• 1:07—Breasts on and behind the sofa with Barry trying to get her top off.
Love Scenes (1984). . . . . Uncredited
a.k.a. Ecstacy
••• 1:11—Full frontal nudity making love with Rick on bed.
The Big Bet (1985) . . . . Fantasy Girl in Elevator
••• 0:51—In purple bra, then eventually nude in elevator with Chris.
The Rosebud Beach Hotel (1985). . . . . Lisa
•• 0:22—Breasts and buns undressing in hotel room with two other girls. She's on the right.
•• 0:44—Breasts taking off her red top in basement with two other girls and two guys.
• 0:56—In black see-through nightie in hotel room with Peter Scolari.
Emmanuelle 5 (1986). . . . . Emmanuelle
••• 0:01—Breasts and buns with a guy on rocks near the ocean in a film.
••• 0:05—Nude on boat after escaping from the crowd at Cannes who rip her clothes off.
•• 0:09—Brief breasts taking off her jacket in restaurant. Breasts on boat with Charles.
••• 0:10—Full frontal nudity, making love on boat with Charles.
••• 0:17—In black lingerie, then full frontal nudity while posing for Phillip.
•• 0:26—Full frontal nudity while changing clothes in her room.
••• 0:38—Full frontal nudity while undressing in room with other harem girls.
•• 0:40—Breasts, getting fixed up by three harem girls.
••• 0:52—Buns and breasts while making love with Phillip outside.
••• 1:07—Breasts in bed with Charles.
• 1:09—Very brief right breast, in airplane cockpit with Charles.
Hollywood Erotic Film Festival (1986) . . . . He Believes
Screen Test (1986) . . . . Roxanne
•• 0:06—Breasts taking off clothes in back room in front of a young boy.
••• 0:42—Nude, with Michelle Bauer, seducing a boy in his day dream.
•• 1:20—Breasts taking off her top for a guy.
Weekend Warriors (1986). . . . . .Showgirl on plane
•• 0:51—Brief breasts taking off top with other showgirls.
Young Lady Chatterley II (1986). . . . Eunice, Maid in Woods
•• 0:15—Breasts in the woods with the Gardener.
••• 0:43—Breasts in bed with Virgil.
Amazon Women on the Moon (1987). . . . . . . Taryn Steele
••• 0:05—Nude during Penthouse Video sketch. Long sequence of her nude in unlikely places.
Deathstalker II (1987) . . . . Reena the Seer/Princess Evie
• 0:57—Brief breasts getting dress torn off by guards.
••• 1:01—Breasts making love with Deathstalker.
• 1:24—Breasts, laughing during the blooper scenes during the end credits.
Up 'n' Coming (1987). . . . . Boat Girl #1
(R-rated version reviewed, X-rated version available.)
• 0:39—Breasts wearing white shorts on boat. Long shot.
• 0:40—More brief nude shots on the boat.
Not of This Earth (1988) . . . . Agnes
The Return of the Swamp Thing (1988). . . . . . . Miss Poinsettia
Silk 2 (1989) . . . . .Jenny "Silk" Sleighton
••• 0:27—Breasts, then full frontal nudity taking a shower while killer stalks around outside.
• 0:28—Very, very brief blurry right breast in open robe when she's on the sofa during fight.
• 0:29—Brief breasts doing a round house kick on the bad guy. Right breast several times during the fight.
••• 0:55—Breasts taking off her blouse and making love on bed. Too much diffusion!
Hard to Die (1990) . . . . Fifi Latour
a.k.a. Tower of Terror
Transylvania Twist (1990). . . . . Patty (Patricia)
976-EVIL II: The Astral Factor (1991) . . . . .Miss Lawlor
Angel Eyes (1991). . . . . Angel
••• 0:18—Nude, in shower with Michelle.
• 0:32—Brief breasts in robe in her bedroom.
••• 0:45—Left breast and lower frontal nudity, while caressing herself while watching Steven and Michelle make love in bed.
••• 0:47—Right breast, then breasts in bed while fantasizing Steven is making love with her. Then breasts in open robe.
••• 0:54—Breasts and buns, while making love in bed with Michelle. Very nice!
••• 1:10—Nude, while making love with Nick on the floor. (This scene was really worn down on the video tape that I rented—I think I know why!)

Body Chemistry 2: Voice of a Stranger (1991) . . . . Brunette in Flashback
- • 0:19—Very brief buns and left breast in bed. (This is a scene from *Uncaged*.)

Evil Toons (1991) . . . . Megan
- ••• 0:25—In bra, then breasts undressing in front of mirror.

Miracle Beach (1991). . . . . Cindy Beatty
- •• 0:03—Breasts in bed with a guy when Scotty comes home. Breasts getting out of bed and getting dressed. (Note in first shot when she's lying in bed, she doesn't have a dress around her waist, then in the next shot when she stands up, she does.)

Uncaged (1991) . . . . Beautiful Hooker
a.k.a. Angel in Red

Fear of a Black Hat (1992) . . Uncredited Girl in Music Video
- • 0:34—Buns, while dancing with several girls in swimsuits in music video "Booty Juice."

Munchie (1992) . . . . Miss Laurel

Made for Cable TV:

Dream On: 555-HELL (1990; HBO) . . . . Scuba Lady
- •• 0:07—Breasts wearing a scuba mask and bikini bottom when she opens the door.

Made for TV Movies:

Problem Child 3: Junior in Love (1995) . . . . Blonde in Leopard Print Bustier

Video Tapes:

E. Nick: A Legend in His Own Mind (1984) . . . Charmaine
- • 0:08—Brief breasts, when stretching in video. Brief side of right breast while sunbathing.
- •• 0:30—Buns and breasts in shower, breasts when coughing on steam. Buns, while trying on clothes in mirror.
- ••• 0:35—Buns in G-string in front of mirror again. Breasts while sunbathing and playing with teddy bear.
- ••• 0:39—Breasts and buns in G-string while sunbathing outside with her family.

Red Hot Rock (1984) . . . . Lab Girl
a.k.a. Sexy Shorts (on laser disc)
- ••• 0:06—Breasts and brief buns dancing after throwing off lab coat during "Lovelite" by O'Bryan.

Penthouse Love Stories (1986). . Monique and AC/DC Lover
- ••• 0:01—Nude in bedroom entertaining herself. A must for Monique fans!
- ••• 0:18—Nude making love with another woman.

Playboy's Fantasies (1987) . . . . Grand Theft
- ••• 0:25—Nude, in house after stealing jewelry.

Scream Queen Hot Tub Party (1991) . . . . .Herself
- •• 0:07—Breasts, taking off blue outfit and putting on white teddy.
- • 0:12—Buns, while walking up the stairs.
- ••• 0:21—Breasts and buns making love with a guy from *Emmanuelle 5*.
- ••• 0:23—Breasts taking off bra in front of mirror from *Evil Toons*.
- ••• 0:25—Breasts in black panties demonstrating the Dance of the Vampires.
- ••• 0:44—Breasts taking off her swimsuit top and soaping up with the other girls.
- •• 0:46—Breasts in still shot during the end credits.

Fantasies 2 (1992) . . . . Model

Penthouse Ready to Ride (1992) . . . . Model

Penthouse Satin & Lace: An Erotic History of Lingerie (1992). . . . . Model
- ••• 0:06—Breasts and buns with a blonde woman.
- ••• 0:33—Nude in blonde wig, with lover.
- ••• 0:47—Nude in bed with another blonde.

Penthouse Forum Letters: Volume 1 (1993) . . . . Mystery Caller/Cindy
- ••• 0:27—Breasts and buns while making love with Brad on the floor in the office.
- •• 0:45—Full frontal nudity, taking off her clothes in the office with Tanya and Vicky in front of Brad.

Centerfold Treasures (1995). . . . . Herself

Scream Queen Private Party (1995) . . . . Herself

Penthouse: The Art of Massage (1996). . . . . .Model
- ••• 0:21—Breasts, while giving and receiving a massage from a guy.
- ••• 0:34—Full frontal nudity, while massaging a guy on table with another female model, then receiving a massage by her and two other guys.
- ••• 0:40—Breasts, while massaging herself.
- •• 0:45—Breasts, while massaging a guy on table.
- ••• 0:51—Nude, while making love with a guy on table.

Gainsbourg, Charlotte

Daughter of actress Jane Birkin.

Films:

Le Petit Amour (1988; French). . . . . Lucy
a.k.a. Kung Fu Master

The Little Thief (1989; French) . . . . Janine Castang
a.k.a. La Petite Voleuse
- •• 0:41—Breasts twice, taking off blouse in bedroom with Michel.

The Cement Garden (1992; German/French/British) . . . Julie
- •• 1:35—Breasts, after taking off her T-shirt while in bed with her brother.
- •• 1:39—Side view of left breast, while in bed with her brother, after being discovered by Derek.
- • 1:41—Left breast, when talking with her brother. Right breast, while sleeping in bed next to her brother.

Dead Tired (1995; French). . . . . Herself
a.k.a. Grosse Fatigue

Jane Eyre (1996) . . . . .Jane Eyre

Gajewskia, Barbara *

Films:

Killer Image (1991) . . . . .Stacey
- • 0:22—Very, very brief left breast, taking off bra at window with M. Emmet Walsh.

Galiena, Anna

Films:

Nothing Underneath (1985; Italian) . . . . .n.a.
a.k.a. Sotto Il Vestito Niente

Hotel Colonial (1988) . . . . .n.a.

The Hairdresser's Husband (1990; French). . . . . Mathilde
a.k.a. Le Mari de la Coiffeuse

Jamón, Jamón (1992; Spanish) . . . . .Carmen
- •• 0:35—Breasts out of the top of her dress, while in the back of the restaurant with José Luis.

Being Human (1994). . . . . .Beatrice

Galik, Denise

Films:

The Happy Hooker (1975). . . . . .Cynthia

Next Stop, Greenwich Village (1976). . . . . Ellen

California Suite (1978). . . . . .Bunny

Don't Answer the Phone (1979) . . . . Lisa

The Deadly Games (1980) . . . . .Mary
a.k.a. The Eliminator
- • 1:13—Left breast, twice, making love on top of Roger in bed.

Humanoids from the Deep (1980). . . . . Linda Beale
Melvin and Howard (1980) . . . . Lucy
Partners (1982) . . . . Clara
Get Crazy (1983). . . . . Nurse Gwen
Eye of the Tiger (1986) . . . . Christie
Career Opportunities (1991) . . . . Lorraine

Made for Cable TV:

The Hitchhiker: Dead Heat (1987; HBO) . . . . Arielle
•• 0:20—Breasts taking off blouse and standing up with Cal in the barn, then right breast lying down in the hay with him.

TV:

Knots Landing (1980-81) . . . . Linda Stiker
Flamingo Road (1981-82) . . . . Christie Kovacs

Galindo, Kelly

Films:

The Malibu Beach Vampires (1991)
. . . . Chairperson Malibu Vampires Inc.
Outside the Law (1994). . . . . Greta
a.k.a. Blood Run
(Unrated version reviewed.)
Caged Hearts (1995). . . . . Prison Inmate

Made for Cable TV:

Love Street: Ex-Girlfriend (1994; Showtime) . . . . Lisa
Women: Stories of Passion-Kat Tails (1996; Showtime)
. . . . Lovely
•• 0:20—Breasts, while masturbating on stage in peep show booth in front of Angela.
• 0:22—Side of right breast, while making love with Angela in peep show booth.

Gallagher, Kelly *

Video Tapes:

Playboy Video Calendar 1996 (1995) . . . . January
••• 0:01—In lingerie and nude in an outdoor country setting.
••• 0:03—In lingerie and nude in a house at night.

Gallardo, Silvana

Films:

Death Wish II (1982) . . . . Rosario
• 0:11—Buns, on bed getting raped by gang. Brief breasts on bed and floor.
• 0:13—Nude, trying to get to the phone. Very brief full frontal nudity, lying on her back on the floor after getting hit.
Out of the Dark (1988) . . . . McDonald
Solar Crisis (1992) . . . . T.C.

Made for Cable Movies:

Prison Stories, Women on the Inside (1990; HBO). . . Mercedes

Gallego, Gina

Films:

The Champ (1979) . . . . Cuban Girl
Deadly Force (1983) . . . . Maria
Lust in the Dust (1985) . . . . Ninta
The Men's Club (1986) . . . . Felicia
My Demon Lover (1987). . . . . Sonia

Made for Cable Movies:

Keeper of the City (1991; Showtime) . . . . Elena
• 0:19—Brief half of left breast, getting out of bed and putting on black bra. Wearing black panties.

TV:

Santa Barbara . . . . Santana Andrade
Flamingo Road (1981-82) . . . . Alicia Sanchez
Rituals (1984-85). . . . . Diandra Santiago Gallagher
Generations (1990) . . . . Melina
NYPD Blue: Boxer Rebellion (May 2, 1995) . . . . n.a.

Gallimore, Tova

Films:

Death Wish V: The Face of Death (1993) . . . . Model #1
Masala (1993; Canadian) . . . . Saraswati
•• 1:00—Full frontal nudity and very brief buns, while making love with Anil in his dream.

• Gallo, Kelly

See: Stevens, Tabitha.

• Gam, Rita

Films:

King of Kings (1961) . . . . Herodias
Klute (1971) . . . . Trina
Shoot Out (1971) . . . . Emma
• 0:13—Brief right breast, when sitting up in bed with Gregory Peck. Seen through bed post.
Such Good Friends (1971). . . . . Doria
(Not available on video tape.)
Seeds of Evil (1972) . . . . Helena Boardman
Midnight (1989) . . . . Heidi

Gamba, Veronica *

Films:

A Night in Heaven (1983) . . . . Tammy

Video Tapes:

Playboy's Playmate Review 2 (1984) . . . . Playmate

Gangel, Gig *

a.k.a. Gig Rauch.

Films:

The Killing Device (1993) . . . . Sara
• 1:06—In bra, then brief breasts, with Kyle in house.

Gannes, Gayle

Films:

The Prey (1980). . . . . Gail
• 0:36—Brief breasts putting T-shirt on before the creature attacks her.
Hot Moves (1984) . . . . Jamie
• 1:09—Breasts, taking off her white blouse and getting in bed with Joey.

Ganzel, Teresa

Films:

National Lampoon Goes to the Movies (1982). . . . . Diana
a.k.a. Movie Madness
••• 0:19—Breasts, while lying in bed with Peter Riegert. Nice, long scene.
The Toy (1982) . . . . Fancy Bates
C.O.D. (1983). . . . . Lisa Foster
• 0:46—Right breast hanging out of dress while dancing at disco with Zack.
• 1:25—Brief side view of left breast taking off purple robe in dressing room scene. Then in white bra talking to Albert.
Hexed (1993) . . . . 3rd Reporter
a.k.a. All Shook Up
The Granny (1995) . . . . Leanne

Made for TV Movies:

Rest In Peace, Mrs. Columbo (1990) . . . . Dede Perkins
Backfield in Motion (1991) . . . . Joanne
Summertime Switch (1994). . . . . Miss Sykes

TV:

Teachers Only (1983) . . . . Samantha "Sam" Keating
The Duck Factory (1984). . . . . Mrs. Shree Winkler

Garber, Terri

Films:

Toy Soldiers (1983) . . . . Amy
- 0:18—Brief right breast taking off her tank top when the army guys force her. Her head is down.

Key Exchange (1985) . . . . Amy

Miniseries:

North and South (1985) . . . . Ashton Main
North and South, Book II (1986). . . . . Ashton Main
North and South, Book III: Heaven and Hell (1994) . . . . Ashton Main

TV:

General Hospital . . . . Victoria
Santa Barbara . . . . n.a.
Texas (1982). . . . . Allison Linden
Mr. Smith (1983) . . . . Dr. Judy Tyson
Dynasty (1987-88) . . . . Leslie Carrington

Garcia, Cristina *

Films:

Surf Nazis Must Die (1986). .Waitress
- 0:21—Breasts pulling her top up for Wheels while sitting on his lap.

Garcia, Nicole

Films:

Mon Oncle d'Amerique (1980; French). . . . . Janine Garnier
Beau Pere (1981; French) . . . . Martine
Bolero (1982; French) . . . . Anne
A Man and a Woman: 20 Years Later (1986; French). . . . Herself
La Lumiere du Lac (1988) . . . . n.a.
Overseas (1991; French) . . . . Zon
- 0:12—Brief breasts behind mosquito net while in bed.
- 0:13—Brief breasts while playing with Paul in the bathroom. Very brief left breast, while reaching for towel.

Gardner, Ashley

Films:

he said, she said (1991). . . . . Susan
- 1:05—Brief upper half of right breast, when her breast pops out of her dress while talking to Kevin Bacon and Elizabeth Perkins at restaurant.

Johnny Suede (1992) . . . . Ellen

Made for Cable Movies:

Breast Men (1997; HBO). . . . . Paula (Voice Only)

Made for TV Movies:

Complex of Fear (1993) . . . . Doreen Wylie

Gardner, Betsy

Films:

Crystal Force II: Dark Angel (1995) . . . . Allison
- ••• 0:56—In black bra, then breasts, while making love with Jake.
- • 1:07—Brief breasts in reflection in mirror in Jake's vision.

Made for Cable TV:

Love Street: Uninhibited Island (1994; Showtime) . . Laurel
- ••• 0:05—Nude, while making love with Fantasy Man on table in restaurant.
- ••• 0:18—Nude, while making love with Apollo on boat. Long scene.
- ••• 0:21—Breasts and buns, while swimming in the water with Apollo.

Hot Line: Hannah's Surprise (1996; Cinemax) . . . . Hannah

Garner, Shay

Films:

Thumbelina (1970) . . . . n.a.
Humongous (1982; Canadian) . . . . Ida Parsons
- 0:05—Brief left breast and brief lower frontal nudity getting her clothes ripped off by a guy. Don't see her face.

Garnett, Gale

Films:

The Children (1980) . . . . Cathy Freeman
Tribute (1980; Canadian) . . . . Hilary
- ••• 1:39—Breasts, while taking off her nurse outfit in front of Jack Lemmon. (Pretty amazing for a PG movie!)
- • 1:42—Brief half of right breast, while standing up.

Overnight (1986) . . . . Del
Mr. & Mrs. Bridge (1990) . . . . Mabel Ong

Garr, Teri

Films:

Head (1968) . . . . Testy True
The Conversation (1974). . . . . Amy
Young Frankenstein (1974) . . . . Inga
Won Ton Ton, The Dog Who Saved Hollywood (1976) . . . . Fluffy Peters
Close Encounters of the Third Kind (1977) . . . . . Ronnie Neary
Oh God! (1977) . . . . Bobbie Landers
The Black Stallion (1979). Alec's Mother
Honky Tonk Freeway (1981) . . . . Ericka
The Escape Artist (1982) . . . . Arlene
One from the Heart (1982). . . . . Frannie
- •• 0:09—Brief breasts getting out of the shower.
- •• 0:40—Side view of right breast changing in. bedroom while Frederic Forrest watches.
- ••• 1:20—Brief breasts in bed when standing up after Forrest drops in though the roof while she's in bed with Raul Julia.

Tootsie (1982). . . . . Sandy
The Black Stallion Returns (1983) . . . . Alec's Mother
Mr. Mom (1983) . . . . Caroline
The Sting II (1983) . . . . Veronica
Firstborn (1984) . . . . Wendy
After Hours (1985) . . . . Julie
Miracles (1986). . . . . Jean Briggs
Full Moon in Blue Water (1988). . . . . Louise
Let It Ride (1989) . . . . Pam
Out Cold (1989) . . . . Sunny Cannald
Short Time (1990). . . . . Carolyn Simpson
Waiting for the Light (1991) . . . . n.a.
Mom and Dad Save the World (1992). . . . . Marge Nelson
The Player (1992) . . . . Cameo
Dumb & Dumber (1994). . . . . Helen Swanson
Perfect Alibi (1994) . . . . Laney Tolbert
Ready to Wear (1994) . . . . Louise Hamilton
a.k.a. Prêt-à-porter
Michael (1996) . . . . Judge Esther Newberg
A Simple Wish (1997) . . . . Rena

Made for Cable Movies:

To Catch a King (1984; HBO) . . . . Hannah Winter
Ronnie and Julie (1996; Showtime) . . . . Elizabeth

Made for Cable TV:

Tales From the Crypt: The Trap (1991; HBO). . . . . Irene Paloma
Dream On: And Bimbo Was His Name-O (1992; HBO) . . . . Sondra McCadden

Made for TV Movies:

Fresno (1986) . . . . Talon Kensington
Pack of Lies (1987) . . . . n.a.

Deliver Them from Evil: The Taking of Alta View (1992) . . . . Susan Woolley
Fugitive Nights: Danger in the Desert (1993) . . . Brita Burrows
Aliens for Breakfast (1995) . . . . Mrs. Bickerstaff
Double Jeopardy (1996) . . . . Cindy Dubroski
Nightscream (1997) . . . . n.a.

TV:

Burns and Schreiber Comedy Hour (1973) . . . . Regular
Girl with Something Extra (1973-74) . . . . Amber
The Sonny and Cher Comedy Hour (1973-74) . . . . Regular
The Sonny Comedy Revue (1974) . . . . Regular
Good & Evil (1991) . . . . Denise

• *Garrett, Kelly*

See: Stevens, Tabitha.

Garrick, Barbara

Films:

Eight Men Out (1988) . . . . Helen Weaver
Working Girl (1989) . . . . Phyllis Trask
Postcards from the Edge (1990) . . . . Carol
The Firm (1993) . . . . Kay Quinn
Sleepless in Seattle (1993) . . . . Victoria
Miami Rhapsody (1994) . . . . Terri
A Couch in New York (1996; French/U.S.) . . . . Lisbeth
a.k.a. Un Divan a New York

Made for Cable Movies:

More Tales of the City (1998; Canadian/U.S.; Showtime) . . . . DeDe Day

Made for Cable TV:

The Outer Limits: Afterlife (1996; Showtime) . . Dr. Ellen Kursaw

Made for TV Movies:

Tales of the City (1994) . . . . DeDe Halcyon Day
••• 0:38—(Into Part 3) Brief breasts and partial buns, while changing positions in bed. Then breasts while sitting in bed and talking on the phone. Very long scene for regular TV!

Gastoni, Lisa *

Films:

Female Friends (1958; British) . . . . Marny Friend
Three Men in a Boat (1958) . . . . Primrose Porterhouse
Gidget Goes to Rome (1963) . . . . Anna Cellini
Submission (1976; Italian) . . . . Elaine
• 0:28—Lower frontal nudity, while on the floor behind the counter with Franco Nero.
• 0:30—Left breast, while talking on the phone with her husband while Nero fondles her.
•• 0:32—Breasts and buns, making love on bed with Nero. Slightly out of focus.
•• 0:33—Breasts getting out of bed to talk to her daughter.
••• 0:43—Breasts in room with Juliet and Nero. Long scene.
••• 0:45—More breasts on the floor yelling at Nero.
• 0:54—Brief lower frontal nudity in slip, while sitting on floor with Nero.
••• 0:57—Left breast, while wearing slip, walking in front of pharmacy. Then full frontal nudity while wearing only stockings. Long scene.
•• 1:00—Breasts in pharmacy with Nero, singing and dancing.
•• 1:28—Breasts when Nero cuts her slip open. Nice close up.
•• 1:29—Breasts getting up out of bed.

Gatti, Jennifer

Films:

Mobsters (1991) . . . . Secretary
a.k.a. Mobsters—The Evil Empire
We're Talkin' Serious Money (1991) . . . . Sophia
Nemesis (1992) . . . . Rosaria/German National
Street Knight (1992) . . . . Rebecca
Double Exposure (1993) . . . . Maria Putnam
•• 0:06—Breasts in B&W, while making love with a guy.
• 0:25—In bra, then brief lower frontal nudity and brief buns in B&W.
•• 0:39—Breasts, while making love on top of a guy in B&W.
•• 0:40—Breasts again while on top of and below the guy in B&W.
• 1:22—Brief left breast in bed with Dedee Pfeiffer (in color).
• 1:23—Brief right breast while in bed with Pfeiffer.

TV:

Search for Tomorrow (1983-84) . . . . Angela Moreno
The Guiding Light (1986-87) . . . . Dinah Mahler
Days of Our Lives (1994) . . . . Rain
The Young and the Restless (1995-96) . . . . Keesha Monroe

Gauthier, Connie *

Films:

18 Again! (1988) . . . . Artist's Model
•• 0:29—Very brief breasts, then buns taking her robe off during art class.

Gava, Cassandra

a.k.a. Cassandra Gaviola.

Films:

Conan the Barbarian (1982) . . . . Witch
Night Shift (1982) . . . . J.J.
High Road to China (1983) . . . . Alessa
The Black Room (1984) . . . . Bridget
Dead Aim (1987) . . . . Amber
• 0:14—Buns, while sitting on chair on stage.
• 0:52—Very brief breasts, while making love with Ed Marinaro in bed. Very dark, hard to see.
Mortal Passions (1989) . . . . Cinda
Last Man Standing (1996) . . . . Barmaid

Made for Cable Movies:

State of Emergency (1993; HBO) . . . . Paramedic #5

Gavin, Erica

Films:

Vixen. (1968) . . . . Vixen Palmer
Caged Heat (1974) . . . . Jacqueline Wilson
a.k.a. Renegade Girls
• 0:08—Buns, getting strip searched before entering prison.
•• 0:25—Breasts in shower scene.
• 0:30—Brief side view of left breast in another shower scene.

Gavin, Mary

See: Samples, Candy.

Gaviola, Cassandra

See: Gava, Cassandra.

Gaybis, Annie *

Wife of actor/comedian John Byner.

Films:

Fairytales (1979) . . . . Snow White
••• 0:21—Nude in room with the seven little dwarfs singing and dancing.
Beyond Evil (1980) . . . . Harlot

10 Violent Women (1982) . . . . Vickie
The Best Little Whorehouse in Texas (1982)
. . . . Uncredited Chicken Ranch Girl
• 1:12—Brief breasts, twice, while smoking a joint in bed with a football player when Dom DeLuise busts in with his news crew.
Friday the 13th, Part III (1982) . . . . Cashier
The Lost Empire (1983) . . . . Prison Referee
• 0:30—Breasts when her top gets ripped off by Angelique Pettyjohn during cat fight.
Scarred (1983) . . . . Movie Girl
•• 0:32—Breasts, while straddling a guy in bed during filming of a movie.
The Witching (1983) . . . . Spirit
a.k.a. Necromancy
(Originally filmed in 1971 as *Necromancy*, additional scenes were added and re-released in 1983.)
(Annie's scenes were filmed in 1983.)
Bachelor Party (1984) . . . . Hooker
Hollywood Zap! (1986) . . . . Debbie
••• 0:54—Breasts while wearing gold bikini bottoms, in bedroom with Tucker.
Rescue Force (1989) . . . . Commando
Bugsy (1991) . . . . Uncredited Mambo Dancer
Death Dancers (1992) . . . . Michelle
Distinguished Gentleman (1992)
. . . . Uncredited 900 Phone Girl, Maria
Twin Peaks: Fire Walk With Me (1992)
. . . . Uncredited Dancer on Stage
• 1:15—Breasts, dancing on stage. Lit with red light.
• 1:16—More breasts and very brief buns, while on stage.
• 1:18—More breasts while on stage.
Showgirls (1995) . . . . Uncredited Cheetahs Dancer
(NC-17 version reviewed.)
Waterworld (1995) . . . . Uncredited Deacon Gang Member

Gazelle, Wendy

Films:
Remo Williams: The Adventure Begins (1985)
. . . . Linda/Soap Opera
Hot Pursuit (1987) . . . . Lori Cronenberg
Sammy and Rosie Get Laid (1987; British) . . . . Anna
•• 0:03—Buns, while lying in bed with Sammy.
• 1:10—Breasts, while lying under Sammy. Seen on the top of a three segment split screen. Don't see her face.
The In Crowd (1988) . . . . Gail
The Understudy: Graveyard Shift II (1988)
. . . . Camilla Turner/Patti Venus
Triumph of the Spirit (1989) . . . . Allegra
Crooked Hearts (1991) . . . . Eileen
Queens Logic (1991) . . . . Kate
The Net (1995) . . . . Imposter

Gee, Joanna

See: Wayne, Taylor.

Geeson, Judy

Films:
Berserk (1967; British) . . . . Angela Rivers
To Sir, with Love (1967; British) . . . . Pamela Dare
Hammerhead (1968) . . . . Sue Trenton
Here We Go Round the Mulberry Bush (1968; British)
. . . . Mary Gloucester
(Nude, while swimming.)
Three into Two Won't Go (1969; British) . . . . Ella Patterson
The Executioner (1970; British) . . . . Polly Bendel
10 Rillington Place (1971; British) . . . . Beryl Evans
Fear in the Night (1972; British) . . . . Peggy Heller
a.k.a. Dynasty of Fear
Brannigan (1975; British) . . . . Jennifer Thatcher
Carry On England (1976; British) . . . . Sgt. Tilly Willing
The Eagle Has Landed (1977; British) . . . . Pamela Verecker
Horror Planet (1980; British) . . . . Sandy
a.k.a. Inseminoid
•• 0:31—Brief breasts on the operating table.
• 0:32—Brief full frontal nudity on table.
• 0:37—Brief full frontal nudity during flashbacks.
Made for Cable TV:
Sherman Oaks: Season 1, Episode 5 (1995; Showtime)
. . . . Leni Lemoyne
Miniseries:
Danger UXB (1980; British) . . . . Susan Mount

Geffner, Deborah *

Films:
All That Jazz (1979) . . . . Victoria
• 0:16—Brief breasts taking off her blouse and walking up the stairs while Roy Scheider watches. A little out of focus.
Star 80 (1983) . . . . Billie
Exterminator 2 (1984) . . . . Caroline

Gemser, Laura *

a.k.a. Moira Chen.
Films:
Emmanuelle, The Joys of a Woman (1975) . . . Massage Woman
Black Emanuelle (1976) . . . . Emanuelle
• 0:00—Brief breasts daydreaming on airplane.
• 0:19—Left breast in car kissing a guy at night.
•• 0:27—Breasts in shower with a guy.
••• 0:30—Full frontal nudity making love with a guy in bed.
••• 0:37—Breasts taking pictures with Karin Schubert.
•• 0:41—Full frontal nudity lying on bed dreaming about the day's events while masturbating, then full frontal nudity walking around.
•• 0:49—Breasts in studio with Johnny.
••• 0:52—Brief right breast making love on the side of the road. Full frontal nudity by the pool kissing Gloria.
•• 1:00—Nude, taking a shower, then answering the phone.
•• 1:04—Breasts on boat after almost drowning.
•• 1:08—Full frontal nudity dancing with African tribe, then making love with the leader.
•• 1:14—Full frontal nudity taking off clothes by waterfall.
•• 1:23—Breasts making love with the field hockey team on a train.
Emanuelle in Bangkok (1976; Italian) . . . . Emanuelle
•• 0:07—Breasts making love with a Robert.
•• 0:12—Full frontal nudity, while changing in hotel room in front of the bellboy.
••• 0:17—Full frontal nudity getting a bath, then massaged by another woman.
• 0:22—Brief right breast, while rolling across the bed to talk with the bellboy.
•• 0:24—Breasts, while lying on the bed, getting massaged by the bellboy.
•• 0:35—Breasts, during orgy scene.
•• 0:37—Buns, while getting massaged by Roberto, then breasts, when massaging him.
•• 0:40—Breasts, while undressing in bedroom.
•• 0:46—Breasts, trying to get the immigration official to help her with her passport.
•• 0:53—Full frontal nudity in room with Debra, then taking a shower.

- •• 1:01—Breasts in tent while Roberto makes love with Janet.
- •• 1:08—Full frontal nudity, while joining the belly dance with Janet and the belly dancer.
- •• 1:15—Full frontal nudity taking a bath with Debra.
- •• 1:18—Breasts on bed making love with Roberto.

Emanuelle Around the World (1977; Italian) . . . . Emanuelle
Emanuelle in Egypt (1977) . . . . .Laura
Emanuelle's Amazon Adventure (1977) . . . . Emanuelle

- • 0:17—Brief left breast in flashback sequence in bed with a man.
- • 0:21—Brief breasts making love in bed.
- • 0:25—Brief breasts in the water with a blonde woman.
- •• 1:10—Full frontal nudity painting her body.
- • 1:11—Brief breasts in boat.
- • 1:13—Nude walking out of the water trying to save Isabelle.
- • 1:14—Brief breasts getting into the boat with Isabelle.

Two Super Cops (1978; Italian) . . . . Susy Lee
Bushido Blade (1979; British/U.S.) . . . . Tomoe

- • 1:08—Brief right breast taking off her top in bedroom with Captain Hawk.

Emanuelle the Seductress (1979; Greek) . . . . Emanuelle

- • 0:01—Full frontal nudity lying in bed with Mario.
- • 0:02—Brief breasts riding horse on the beach.
- •• 0:42—Breasts making love then full frontal nudity getting dressed with Tommy.
- ••• 0:48—Breasts undressing in bedroom, then in white panties, then nude talking to Alona.
- •• 0:54—Breasts walking around in a skirt.
- •• 1:02—Breasts outside taking a shower, then on lounge chair making love with Tommy.

Fear (1980; French/Italian) . . . . Beryl

- • 0:00—Breasts, while getting strangled in bed at night during filming of a movie.
- • 0:29—Breasts, while almost drowning in bathtub. Dark.
- • 0:50—Full frontal nudity, while making love outside with Michael, then full frontal nudity, lying dead covered with blood.
- • 1:06—Brief breasts, dead, covered with blood in flashback.
- • 1:18—Brief breasts, while getting killed by Glenda in flashback.

The Best of Sex and Violence (1981) . . . . Emanuelle

- • 0:23—Side of left breast while getting clothes taken off by a guy. Long shot. Scene from *Emanuelle Around the World.*

Ator, The Fighting Eagle (1982) . . . . Indun
Famous T & A (1982) . . . . .Emanuelle
(No longer available for purchase, check your video store for rental.)

- ••• 0:55—Breasts scenes from *Emanuelle Around the World.*

Endgame (1983) . . . . Lilith

- • 1:10—Brief breasts a couple of times getting blouse ripped open by a gross looking guy.

Caged Women (1984; French/Italian) . . . . Emanuelle/Laura
a.k.a. Emanuelle in Hell
Metamorphosis (1989) . . . . Prostitute

- • 0:37—Very brief breasts several times in Peter's flashback.
- • 0:43—Very brief breasts in flashback again.

Passionate Pleasures (1989) . . . . Haunani
Quest for the Mighty Sword (1989; Italian) . . . . Grimilde
Top Model (1989; Italian) . . . . Dorothy/Eve

- • 0:44—Brief right breast and buns, frolicking with the cowboy.

Eleven Days, Eleven Nights 2 (1990) . . . . .Jackie Forrest
Object of Desire (1991) . . . . Uncredited Photographer

Gentry, Jaki

Video Tapes:
Hot Body International: #3 Lingerie Special (1992) . . . . Contestant

- •• 0:46—Buns, in G-string and bra.
- ••• 0:53—Breasts, while posing for photo shoot.

Hot Body International: #5 Miss Acapulco (1992) . . Contestant

Genzel, Carrie

Films:
Caged Hearts (1995) . . . . Kate

- • 0:15—Right breast, while standing up when first entering prison.
- •• 0:25—Nude, when three other girls, beat her up in the shower.
- • 0:57—In black bra and panties in bedroom with a customer, then partial left breast.

Made for Cable Movies:
Virtual Seduction (1995; Showtime) . . . . Paris

- •• 0:46—Breasts and buns, while making love with Jeff Fahey in paint studio, rubbing rubs paint over each other.

TV:
All My Children (1996-) . . . . Skye "Toni" Chandler

George, Betsy Lynn

Films:
Point Break (1991) . . . . Girl at Party
The Magic Bubble (1992) . . . . Angel
In the Heat of Passion II: Unfaithful (1994) . . . . .Lisa
a.k.a. Behind Closed Doors
(Unrated version reviewed.)
Lurid Tales: The Castle Queen (1995) . . . . .Miranda Dorset

- •• 0:34—Breasts, while her and her sister make love with Tom.
- • 1:04—Brief right breast, while making love under Tom.
- • 1:12—Very, very brief breasts during flashbacks.

Petticoat Planet (1995) . . . . Lily

- • 1:11—Breasts, while making love with Steve in saloon.

Music Videos:
Cradle of Love/Billy Idol . . . . The Girl

*George, Susan **

Films:
The Looking Glass War (1970; British) . . . . Susan
Die Screaming Marianne (1972) . . . . Marianne
Straw Dogs (1972) . . . . Amy

- •• 0:32—Breasts taking off sweater, tossing it down to Dustin Hoffman, then looking out the door at the workers.
- ••• 1:00—Breasts on couch getting raped by one of the construction workers.

Dirty Mary, Crazy Larry (1974) . . . . .Mary
Mandingo (1975) . . . . Blanche

- • 1:36—Brief breasts in bed with Ken Norton.

Out of Season (1975; British) . . . . Joanna

- • 1:24—Nude, while walking in front of Cliff Robertson. Long shot.

Small Town in Texas (1976) . . . . Mary Lee
Tintorera (1977) . . . . .Gabriella

- • 0:42—Brief breasts waking up Steven in hammock.

Enter the Ninja (1981) . . . . Mary-Ann Landers
House Where Evil Dwells (1982) . . . . Laura

- ••• 0:21—Breasts in bed making love with Edward Albert.
- •• 0:59—Breasts making love again.

Venom (1982; British) . . . . .Louise
The Jigsaw Man (1984) . . . . Penny
Lightning, The White Stallion (1986) . . . . Madame Rene

Made for Cable Movies:
The House That Mary Bought (1994; Showtime). . . . . Mary
Made for TV Movies:
Jack the Ripper (1988). . . . . Catherine

• George, Tami-Adrian

Films:
Sgt. Bilko (1996) . . . . Janet
Starship Troopers (1996) . . . . .Djana'D
• 0:29—Very brief left breast, while in the co-ed showers.
• 0:30—Very brief left breast, when giving Casper Van Dien a quick spank when he leaves the co-ed showers.
Romy and Michele's High School Reunion (1997) . . . . Receptionist at "Singled Out"
Video Tapes:
The Darker Image Swimsuit Calendar: Behind the Scenes (1996). . . . . .Herself

• George, Tracy *

Video Tapes:
Playboy's Sorority Girls (1997). . . . . Wet & Wild
••• 0:22—Nude outdoors in and by pool with Sterling Dunn.

Georges-Picot, Olga *

Films:
Honor Among Thieves (1968; French/Italian) . . Isabelle Manue
a.k.a. Farewell, Friend
Connecting Rooms (1971; British). . . . . Claudia Fouchet
Day of the Jackal (1973) . . . . .Denise
• 0:55—Brief breasts and buns, getting out of bed to use the phone.
Persecution (1974; British) . . . . Monique Kalfon
Love and Death (1975) . . . . .Countess Alexandrovna
Goodbye Emmanuelle (1977) .Woman

Geraghty, Erin

Films:
Games Girls Play (1974; British). . . . . Ducky
a.k.a. The Bunny Caper
a.k.a. Sex Play
• 1:11—In bra and panties, then breasts running around outside.
That'll Be the Day (1974; British). . . . . Joan

Gerardi, Joan

Films:
Affairs of the Heart (1992). . . . . Miss Valentine's Day
••• 0:15—Breasts, posing for photos in red bottoms.
Marilyn Chambers' Bedtime Stories (1993) . . . . .Jane
Bikini Bistro (1995) . . . . Luanne
(Unrated version reviewed.)
••• 0:12—Full frontal nudity, while changing into a swimsuit in room with the two other girls.
••• 0:24—Nude, while making love with David in a car. Long scene.
• 0:32—Buns, while in swimsuit in restaurant.
•• 0:38—Full frontal nudity, while making love outside at night with David.
• 0:43—Buns in swimsuit.
• 0:52—Full frontal nudity, while changing into swimsuit.
• 1:05—Breasts, while on roof top with David.

Gere, Ashlyn *

Adult film actress.
a.k.a. Kim McKamy.
Films:
Evil Laugh (1986) . . . . Connie
Creepozoids (1987). . . . . Kate
Dreamaniac (1987) . . . . Pat
Angel III: The Final Chapter (1988) . . . . .Video Girl #1
Fatal Instinct (1991). . . . . Frank Stegner's Girlfriend
a.k.a. To Kill For
(Unrated version reviewed.)
•• 0:01—Breasts, opening her towel in front of Frank at night before he gets shot.
In the Flesh (1995) . . . . Dancer
Video Tapes:
High Society Centerspread Video #16: Ashlyn Gere (1990). . . . . Ashlyn Gere

Gerrish, Flo

Films:
Superchick (1978) . . . . Funky Jane
Don't Answer the Phone (1979) . . . . Dr. Lindsay Gale
• 1:05—Very brief breasts rolling over in bed with McCabe. Brief breasts when he pulls the covers down.
• 1:19—Side view of right breast, several times, while taking off blouse and putting nightgown on.
Schizoid (1980) . . . . Pat
Hot Chili (1985) . . . . .Mrs. Baxter
The Naked Cage (1985) . . . . Mother
Over the Top (1987) . . . . .Martha, the Waitress

Gersak, Savina

Films:
Iron Warrior (1987) . . . . Janna
(Breasts under sheer red or blue dress during practically every scene she has in the film.)
• 0:06—Brief buns in outfit while getting a blue sheet wrapped around her by her servants.
• 0:18—Brief left breast, while lying on ceremonial table.
Beyond the Door III (1989; Yugoslavian) . . . . Sava
Sonny Boy (1989) . . . . Sandy
Midnight Ride (1990) . . . . Lara

Gershon, Gina *

Films:
3:15—The Moment of Truth (1986) . . . . One of the Cobrettes
Sweet Revenge (1987) . . . . K.C.
• 0:41—Brief breasts in water under a waterfall with Lee.
Cocktail (1988) . . . . .Coral
• 0:31—Very, very brief right breast, while romping around in bed with Tom Cruise.
Red Heat (1988) . . . . .Cat Manzetti
Voodoo Dawn (1989) . . . . Tina
City of Hope (1991) . . . . Laurie
Out for Justice (1991) . . . . Patti Modono
Flinch (1992). . . . . .Daphne
The Player (1992) . . . . Whitney Gersh
Joey Breaker (1993) . . . . .Jenny Chaser
Best of the Best 3: No Turning Back (1994) . . . . Margo Preston
Showgirls (1995) . . . . Cristal
(NC-17 version reviewed.)
• 0:09—Brief buns in G-string in her dressing room.
••• 0:10—Breasts and buns in G-string, while dancing on stage.
••• 0:13—Breasts, while undressing and taking off her make-up in dressing room.
• 0:59—Brief breasts backstage with Kyle MacLachlan.
••• 1:00—Breasts and buns in T-back, during dance number on stage.
• 1:01—Breasts and buns in G-string, while walking down the stairs backstage.

- 1:18—Breasts, while dancing on stage in sheer bodysuit.
- ••• 1:39—Breasts and buns in G-string while dancing on stage.
- • 1:40—Brief breasts, while running down the stairs.

Bound (1996) . . . . Corky
- •• 0:19—Brief long shot of left breast, then left breast, while making love with Jennifer Tilly.

Touch (1996) . . . . Debra Lusanne
Face/Off (1997). . . . . Sasha Hassler
This World, then the Fireworks (1997). . . . . .Carol
- • 0:12—Right breast, sticking out of slip, while lying in bed and talking with Billy Zane.
- • 1:27—Brief right breast in flashback of 0:12 scene.

Palmetto (1998) . . . . Nina

Made for Cable Movies:

Love Matters (1993; Showtime) . . . . Heat
(Unrated version reviewed.)
- • 0:33—Brief left breast when Tony Goldwyn lays her down.
- ••• 0:34—Breasts, while on table with Goldwyn. More breasts while making love on kitchen island. Buns when running away.
- •• 0:44—Breasts, after turning over and lying under Goldwyn.
- • 0:53—Partial left breast, while in shower, talking to Goldwyn.

Made for TV Movies:

Miss Rose White (1992). . . . . Angie
Sinatra (1992) . . . . Nancy Barbato Sinatra

Gertz, Jami

Films:

Endless Love (1981) . . . . Patty
Alphabet City (1984). . . . . Sophia
Sixteen Candles (1984) . . . . Robin
Mischief (1985). . . . . Rosalie
Crossroads (1986) . . . . Frances
Quicksilver (1986) . . . . Terri
Solarbabies (1986) . . . . Terra
Less than Zero (1987) . . . . Blair
The Lost Boys (1987). . . . . Star
Listen to Me (1989). . . . . Monica Tomanski
Renegades (1989) . . . . Barbara
Silence Like Glass (1989). . . . . .Eva March
- • 1:31—Very brief left breast, during defibrillation on operating table. Possible body double. The Doctor's arm covers her face.

Don't Tell Her It's Me (1990) . . . . .Emily Pear
Sibling Rivalry (1990) . . . . Jeanine
Twister (1996). . . . . Melissa

Made for Cable TV:

Dream On: The Taking of Pablum 1-2-3, Part I (1994; HBO) . . . . Jane Harnick
Dream On: The Taking of Pablum 1-2-3, Part II (1994; HBO) . . . . Jane Harnick
Dream On: Take Two Tablets, And Get Me to Mt. Sinai (1995; HBO) . . . . Martin's Lover

Made for TV Movies:

Jersey Girl (1993). . . . . Toby Mastallone
This Can't Be Love (1994) . . . . Sarah

TV:

Square Pegs (1982-83) . . . . Muffy Tepperman
Sibs (1991-92). . . . . Lily

Video Tapes:

The Kathy Kaehler Fitness System (1992). . . . . Exercise Student

Ghigliotti, Marilyn

Films:

Clerks (1994). . . . . Veronica
Invasion For Flesh & Blood (1996) . . . . Rape Victim
- • 0:33—Brief partial buns, while lying dead on the ground, covered with blood.
- • 0:37—Breasts, while lying dead on the ground, covered with blood.

• Gian, Nicole

Films:

Tainted Love (1995) . . . . Pauline
- •• 0:06—In lingerie, then breasts while undressing in bedroom in front of a police officer.

Made for Cable TV:

Beverly Hills Bordello (1997- ; Showtime) . . . Veronica Winston
Beverly Hills Bordello: The Lieutenant (1997; Showtime) . . . . Veronica Winston
- ••• 0:18—Breasts and buns, while in bedroom with Harry, then having sex with him. Long scene.

Beverly Hills Bordello: The Assignment (1998; Showtime) . . . . Veronica Winston
- ••• 0:20—Breasts, while making love with David.

Gianetti, Gina

Adult film actress.
a.k.a. Cassie Blake.

Films:

Simply Irresistible (1983) .Sunshine
(R-rated version. *Irresistible* is the X-rated version.)
- •• 0:49—Breasts in motel room with Walter and Juliet.

Gibb, Cynthia

Films:

Salvador (1986). . . . . Cathy Moore
Youngblood (1986). Jessie Chadwick
- • 0:50—Brief breasts and buns making love with Rob Lowe in his room.

Jack's Back (1987) . . . . Chris Moscari
Malone (1987) . . . . Jo Barlow
Modern Girls (1987) . . . . .Cece
Short Circuit 2 (1988) . . . . .Sandy Banatoni
Death Warrant (1990) . . . . Amanda Beckett

Made for Cable Movies:

High Stakes (1997; Lifetime) . . . . .Annie Dwyer

Made for Cable TV:

Tales From the Crypt: Korman's Kalamity (1992; HBO) . . . . Lorelai

Made for TV Movies:

The Karen Carpenter Story (1989). . . . . Karen Carpenter
When We Were Young (1989) . . . . Ellen
Gypsy (1993). . . . . Gypsy Rose Lee/Rose Louise Hovick
A Twist of the Knife (1993) . . . . Amanda Bentley
The Woman Who Loved Elvis (1993) . . . . .n.a.
Fatal Vows: The Alexandra O'Hara Story (1994) . . . . Alexandra O'Hara
Sin and Redemption (1994). . . . . Billie Simms
Volcano: Fire on the Mountain (1997) . . . . .n.a.

TV:

Search for Tomorrow (1981-83). . . . . .Suzi Wyatt Martin
Fame (1983-86). . . . . Holly Laird
Madman of the People (1994-95) . . . . Meg
Deadly Games (1995-96). . . . . .Lauren Ashborne

Giblin, Belinda

Films:

Jock Petersen (1974; Australian). . . . . Moira Winton
a.k.a. Petersen
•• 0:21—Left breast several times, under a cover with Jock, then buns when cover is removed.

End Play (1975; Australian) . . . . Margret Gifford

Demolition (1977) . . . . n.a.

The Empty Beach (1985). . . . . Marion Singer

Gibney, Susan

Films:

And You Thought Your Parents Were Weird (1991) . . . . Alice Woods

The Waterdance (1991) . . . . Cheryl Lynn

The Great White Hype (1996). . . . . Vivian

Made for Cable TV:

Bedtime (1996; Showtime) . . . . Liz

Bedtime: Episode 10 (1996; Showtime) . . . . Liz
• 0:10—Breasts, twice, while sitting in bubble bath with Donna. Green facial cream on her face.

Made for TV Movies:

The Secret She Carried (1996) . . . . Judy

Gibson, Greta

Films:

Warlords (1988) . . . . Harem Girl
•• 1:05—Breasts in tent with the other harem girls. Holding a snake.
•• 1:09—Breasts again.

Beverly Hills Vamp (1989). . . . . Screen Test Starlet
•• 0:53—Breasts and brief buns in G-string lying on Mr. Pendleton's desk.

• Gibson, Kathleen

Made for Cable TV:

Compromising Situations: First Time Caller (1994; Showtime). . . . . Mrs. Henry
• 0:08—In black lingerie, then breasts and buns, while making love with Jonathon in her office.

Compromising Situations: Lost Letters (1997; Showtime) . . . . Aunt June

Compromising Situations: Reunited (1997; Showtime) . . . . Martha

Gidley, Pamela

Films:

Thrashin' (1986) . . . . Chrissy

The Blue Iguana (1988). . . . . Dakota

Cherry 2000 (1988) . . . . Cherry

Permanent Record (1988). . . . . Kim

Disturbed (1990) . . . . Sandy Ramirez

The Last of the Finest (1990). . . . . Haley

Highway to Hell (1991). . . . . Clara

Liebestraum (1991) . . . . Jane Kessler
(Unrated Director's cut reviewed.)
• 1:07—Buns, while taking a shower. Almost breasts, but her arm gets in the way.

Bad Love (1992) . . . . Eloise
a.k.a. Wild Angel

Cheatin' Hearts (1992) . . . . Samantha

Twin Peaks: Fire Walk With Me (1992). . . . . Teresa Banks

Freefall (1993). . . . . Katy Mazur
• 0:29—Brief back side of left breast and upper half of buns, while making love with Eric Roberts in bed. Almost breasts when Roberts lies back down. Breasts later on don't show her face.
• 0:40—Right breast with Roberts in flashback. Don't see her face again.

The Crew (1994) . . . . Jennifer

S.F.W. (1994). . . . . Janet Streeter

The Little Death (1995) . . . . Kelly Hannon
• 0:47—Brief buns, while being placed on edge of spa.

TV:

Angel Street (1992) . . . . Dorothy Paretsky

Strange Luck (1995-96). . . . . n.a.

The Pretender (1997-) . . . . Brigitte

Gielser, Regina

a.k.a. Adult film actress Kim Wylde.

Films:

The Other Woman (1992) . . . . Neighbor
(Unrated version reviewed.)
•• 0:49—Breasts and buns, while in bed with Jessica's mother during young Jessica's flashback.

The Pamela Principle (1992). . . . . Felicia
(Unrated version reviewed.)
••• 1:27—Buns and breasts, while in bed with Carl and Pamela.

Giftos, Elaine

Films:

Gas-s-s! (1970) . . . . Cilla

On a Clear Day You Can See Forever (1970) . . . . Muriel

The Student Nurses (1970) . . . . Sharon
a.k.a. Young LA Nurses
• 1:14—Brief breasts undressing and getting into bed with terminally ill boy. Dark, hard to see.

Everything You Wanted to Know About Sex, But Were Afraid to Ask (1972). . . . . Mrs. Ross

The Wrestler (1974). . . . . Debbie

Paternity (1981) . . . . Woman in Bar

Angel (1983). . . . . Patricia Allen

The Trouble with Dick (1986) . . . . Sheila

Body Chemistry 4: Full Exposure (1995) . . . . Charlotte Sanders
(Unrated version reviewed.)

Made for TV Movies:

The Secret Night Caller (1975) . . . . Chloe

TV:

The Interns (1970-71) . . . . Bobbe Marsh

Gil, Ariadna

Films:

Revolver (1992). . . . . Miria Castel

Belle Epoque (1993; Spanish) . . . . Violeta
a.k.a. The Age of Beauty
• 0:48—Brief breasts, then brief right breast while making love with Fernando in hay in a loft. He's dressed as a maid and she's dressed as a soldier.

Celestial Clockwork (1993; French/Portugese) . . . . Ana
a.k.a. Mecánicas celestes

Gilbert, Melissa

Sister of actress Sara Gilbert.
Wife of actor Bruce Boxleitner.
Ex-wife of actor/writer Bo Brinkman.

Films:

Sylvester (1985) .... Charlie
- • 0:23—Very, very brief breasts struggling with a guy in truck cab. Seen through a dirty windshield.
- •• 0:24—Very brief left breast after Richard Farnsworth runs down the stairs to help her. Seen from the open door of the truck.

Ice House (1988)................................. Kay
Babymaker: The Dr. Cecil Jacobson Story (1994)......... n.a.

Made for Cable Movies:

Dying to Remember (1993; USA) .... Lynn Matthews

Made for Cable TV:

The Outer Limits: Relativity Theory (1998; Showtime) .... Theresa Janovitch

Made for TV Movies:

The Miracle Worker (1979) ....Helen Keller
The Diary of Anne Frank (1980)................ Anne Frank
Donor (1990) ....n.a.
Joshua's Heart (1990) .... Claudia
Family of Strangers (1993) ....n.a.
House of Secrets (1993) .... Marion Ravinel
Shattered Trust: The Shari Karney Story (1993) ... Shari Karney
With Hostile Intent (1993)..........................n.a.
Against Her Will: The Carrie Buck Story (1994) .... Melissa Prentice
Danielle Steel's "Zoya" (1995)...................... Zoya
Childhood Sweetheart? (1997) ....n.a.
Seduction in a Small Town (1997)....................n.a.

TV:

Little House on the Prairie (1974-83)......Laura Ingalls Wilder
Stand by Your Man (1992) .... Rochelle
Sweet Justice (1994-95)..................... Kate Delcroy

Gilbert, Pamela

Films:

Cyclone (1986) ....Uncredited Shower Girl
- • 0:06—Buns and breasts (she's the brunette) in the showers. Long shot.

Evil Spawn (1987)........................ Elaine Talbot
- ••• 0:46—Nude taking off black lingerie and going swimming in pool. Hubba, hubba!
- ••• 0:49—Breasts in the pool, then full frontal nudity getting out.

Lust for Freedom (1987) .... Snuff Victim
- •• 0:52—Breasts, while sitting on bed, looking all drugged out before being shot.

Demonwarp (1988) ....Carrie Austin
- ••• 0:20—In bra, then breasts, while in bed with Jack.
- ••• 0:22—Right breast, then breasts, while lying in bed, making love with Jack.
- •• 1:23—Breasts, while strapped to table.
- • 1:24—Breasts several more times, while on the table.
- •• 1:25—Breasts, while getting off table and dressing.

The Alien Within (1990) .... Elaine Talbot
(Contains footage from *The Evil Spawn* woven together with new material.)
- ••• 0:48—Nude taking off black lingerie and going swimming in pool.
- ••• 0:55—Breasts in the pool, then full frontal nudity getting out.

Gildersleeve, Linda

Films:

Beach Bunnies (1977) ....n.a.
Cinderella (1977) .... Farm Girl (redhead)
- ••• 0:21—Breasts and buns with her brunette sister in their house making love with the guy who is looking for Cinderella.
- •• 1:24—Full frontal nudity with her sister again when the Prince goes around to try and find Cinderella.

The Happy Hooker Goes to Washington (1977) .... Honeymoon Wife
- • 0:35—Brief breasts in a diner during the filming of a commercial.

Gillies, Isabel

Films:

Metropolitan (1990) .... Cynthia McClean
Nadja (1995)................................. Waitress
One Way Out (1995)........................... Betsy
- • 1:26—Very brief right breast, while kissing Frank in bedroom.

I Shot Andy Warhol (1996) .... Alison

Made for Cable TV:

Sex and the City: Bay of the Married Pigs (1998; HBO) . . Elaine

Gillingham, Kim

Films:

Valet Girls (1987).................... Madonna Wannabe
Captain America (1990)............ Bernice Stewart/Sharon
Corporate Affairs (1990).............. Ginny Malmquist
- • 1:09—Breasts, climbing out of cubicle.

Gilmore-Capps, Teresa

Films:

The Arrogant (1987) .... Charlotte
- • 0:23—Brief breasts, making love in a barn.

The Marrying Man (1991)................ Bugsy's Blonde
a.k.a. Too Hot to Handle
Wild Bill (1995) .... Jessie Hazlitt

Made for Cable Movies:

Fever (1991; HBO)........................... Jeanine

Giorgi, Eleonora *

Films:

Diary of a Cloistered Nun (1973; Italian/German/French) .... Carmela
Appassionata (1979; Italian).....................Nicola
- • 0:14—Very brief left breast in open blouse with Emilio in his dentist office. Breasts several times.
- •• 0:41—Full frontal nudity in bedroom when Emilio comes in. Dark.
- ••• 0:54—Nude in office with Emilio in stockings and garter belt.
- • 1:35—Brief right breast in bed with Emilio. Dark.

Beyond Obsession (1982) .... Nina
- •• 0:01—Breasts, taking off her top and getting into the shower with Tom Berenger.
- • 0:59—Right breast in bed with Marcello Mastroianni, brief right breast after.

Nudo di Donna (1984; Italian) .... Laura
a.k.a. Portrait of a Woman, Nude
- • 0:11—Very brief left breast, while taking off robe. Subtitles get in the way.
- • 0:12—Right breast, while in the shower, getting consoled.
- • 0:13—Brief upper half breasts, getting into bed.
- •• 0:14—Breasts in bed.

•• 0:36—Nude, mostly buns, sleeping in bed when Sandro pulls back the covers.
• 1:12—Brief right breast, while in bed with Sandro.
• 1:13—Right breast under sheer dress.
Il Volpone (1988; Italian). The Mayor

• Giorgio, Vanessa Ann

Films:

Sexual Intent (1994) . . . . Chris
•• 0:32—In black bra, then breasts, while in bedroom with John.
The Last Days of Frankie the Fly (1997) . . . . Bathroom Girl

Giosa, Susan

Films:

America 3000 (1986) . . . . Morha
The First Power (1990) . . . . Carmen
• 0:22—Brief right breast, lying dead with a bloody pentagram cut into her stomach.

TV:

Reasonable Doubts (1992-93). . . . . Diedre

• Girard, Simone Élise

Films:

Scanners 2: The New Order (1991). . . . . . Degenerate Scanner

Made for Cable TV:

The Hunger: The Lighthouse (1998; Showtime)
. . . . Angelica
•• 0:23—Nude, while swimming under water and grabbing Bruce Davison. She has body makeup on to make her look like an undersea creature.

Girling, Cindy

Films:

Left for Dead (1978) . . . . Pauline Corte
•• 0:19—Nude, taking off shirt in bedroom.
Meatballs (1979; Canadian) . . . . Wendy
Daughter of Death (1982) . . . . Irene
a.k.a. Julie Darling
•• 0:12—Breasts in bathtub and getting out.
Hostile Takeover (1988; Canadian) . . . . Mrs. Gayford
a.k.a. Office Party
Someone to Die For (1995). . . . . Attacked Woman

Made for Cable TV:

The Outer Limits: Second Thoughts (1997; Showtime)
. . . . Saleswoman
Dead Man's Gun: Buryin' Sam (1997; Showtime)
. . . . Betty Vandermere

Giroux, Jackie

Films:

Cross and the Switchblade (1970). . . . . Rosa
Sweet Sugar (1972) . . . . Fara
a.k.a. Hellfire on Ice
•• 0:33—Breasts, skinny dipping in stream with Dolores.
This is a Hijack (1973) . . . . Scott's Girl
Drive-In Massacre (1974) . . . . n.a.
Slaughter's Big Rip-Off (1975). . . . . Mrs. Duncan
Jokes My Folks Never Told Me (1976) . . . . n.a.
Sex Through a Window (1977) . . . . Barbie
Trick or Treats (1982) . . . . Linda
To Live and Die in L.A. (1985) . . . . Claudia Leith

Givens, Robin *

Ex-wife of boxer Mike Tyson.

Films:

A Rage in Harlem (1991). . . . . Imabelle
••• 0:32—Buns, while lying in bed with Forest Whitaker.
Boomerang (1992) . . . . Jacqueline
• 0:50—Very brief half of left breast, while lying with her back on bed with Eddie Murphy when she first puts her arm under his arm.
•• 1:02—Very brief side view of right breast, while making love on top of Murphy in bed.
Blankman (1994). . . . . Kimberly Jons
Foreign Student (1994) . . . . April
• 0:50—Left breast several times and buns, while making love in building with Philippe.

Made for TV Movies:

The Penthouse (1989). . . . . n.a.
Dangerous Intentions (1995). . . . . Kaye

TV:

Head of the Class (1986-91) . . . . Darlene Merriman
Angel Street (1992). . . . . Anita King
CourtHouse (1995-96) . . . . n.a.
Sparks (1996-) . . . . Wilma Cuthbert

Glaser, Lisa

Films:

Humanoids from the Deep (1980). . . . . Becky
(Brunette colored hair.)
••• 0:34—Full frontal nudity, while undressing in tent with Billy and his ventriloquist dummy.
• 0:35—Nude, while running on the beach at night, trying to escape from the humanoids.
Stripped to Kill II (1988) . . . . Victoria
(Blonde colored hair.)
•• 0:01—Breasts and buns in G-string doing a strip dance routine during Shadey's nightmare.
Future Kick (1991) . . . . Dancer
• 0:36—Breasts, dancing on stage in white outfit. (Taken from *Stripped to Kill II.*)

Glasner, Christine

Films:

Julia (1974; German) . . . . Sylvanna
•• 0:21—Breasts on couch with Miriam getting messy with some whipped cream.
• 0:39—Brief right breast getting attacked by Patrick.
• 1:08—Brief breasts, while turning over and getting oil rubbed on her by Miriam.
The Fifth Musketeer (1977) . . . . n.a.

Glass, Leslie *

Adult Films:

Blonde Justice 3 (1994) . . . . n.a.
(Non-explicit nude scenes.)
Vagablonde (1994). . . . . n.a.
The Moment (1997) . . . . n.a.

Films:

Mannequin Two: On the Move (1991)
. . . . Uncredited Mannequin in Theater Scene
Vampire Vixens From Venus (1995). . . . . Omay
•• 0:20—Breasts in open dress top, behind a guy on the couch.
•• 0:31—Breasts, while putting on make-up in bathroom.
• 0:41—Breasts, while dancing on stage.
• 1:07—Breasts, while greeting policemen at the door.
Strip Search (1997; Canadian). . . . . Gun Woman

Video Tapes:

Penthouse Satin & Lace II: Hollywood Undercover (1992) . . . . . Pet

The Penthouse All-Pet Workout (1993) . . . . . Pet
- •• 0:00—Breasts during introduction.
- •• 0:03—Brief nude shots while getting undressed and suited up.
- ••• 0:38—Nude on chair outside and in pool.
- ••• 0:43—Nude with the other girls, exercising, working with equipment, in the pool and spa.

Penthouse Pet of the Year Playoff 1993 (1993) . . . . . Pet
- ••• 0:11—Nude in back seat of limousine, in TV station (sometimes wearing a blonde wig), in Central Park on horseback, in the desert.

Penthouse The Great Pet Hunt—Part II (1993) . . . . . Pet
- ••• 0:25—Nude after stripping out of maid outfit on stage.

Penthouse Pet of the Year Winners 1993: Mahalia & Julie (1994) . . . . . Sneak Preview of Pet of the Year Playoff
- ••• 0:28—Nude in and around Central Park in New York City.

Penthouse Pet of the Year Winners 1994: Sasha & Leslie (1994) . . . . . Runner-Up Pet
- ••• 0:30—Breasts then nude in boxing gloves and shorts.
- ••• 0:31—Nude, posing inside and outside a house in color and B&W segments.
- ••• 0:36—Nude in still photos.
- ••• 0:37—Nude while posing in a house.
- ••• 0:38—In lingerie and nude after playing cards with a blonde woman and a guy.
- ••• 0:42—Nude on rooftop in city.
- •• 0:44—Nude in end credits.

Penthouse Behind the Scenes (1995) . . . . . Pet
- ••• 0:17—Nude in interviews and behind the scenes footage.

Penthouse: The Ultimate Pet Games (1996) . . . . . Pet
- ••• 0:02—Nude during obstacle course segment.
- ••• 0:13—Nude during badminton segment.
- ••• 0:21—Nude during oil wrestling segment.
- ••• 0:29—Nude in tug-of-war segment.
- ••• 0:33—Nude, while making love with Tiffany Burlingame in cabin (includes the use of honey and chocolate syrup).
- ••• 0:36—Breasts during pool volleyball game.
- 0:42—Nude during squirt gun segment.

CD-ROM:

Penthouse Interactive Virtual Photo Shoot, Disc 2 (1993) . . . . . Pet

Glasser, Isabel

Films:

Death Ring (1992) . . . . . Lauren Sadler
- •• 0:11—Breasts, after taking off swimsuit top on chair outside with Mike Norris.

Forever Young (1992) . . . . . Helen

Pure Country (1992) . . . . . Harley Tucker

The Enemy Within (1994) . . . . . Sarah McCann

The Surgeon (1995; German/U.S.) . . . . . Dr. Theresa McCann

a.k.a. Exquisite Tenderness
- •• 0:55—Nude, while frolicking in the pool with James Remar, then getting out.

Made for Cable Movies:

Circumstances Unknown (1995; USA) . . . . . Deena

TV:

NYPD Blue: The Final Adjustment (Nov 22, 1994) . . . . . Christie

NYPD Blue: Double Abandando (Nov 29, 1994) . . . . . Christie

Crisis Center (1997) . . . . . Stephanie

Glendenning, Candace

Films:

Nicholas and Alexandra (1971; British) . . . . . Marie

Tower of Evil (1972; British) . . . . . Penny

a.k.a. Beyond the Fog
- • 0:07—Breasts, screaming and killing a fisherman with a knife.
- • 0:12—Brief buns, while running up steps.
- • 0:13—Brief breasts, lying down with Gary during flashback.
- • 0:14—Brief buns, after swim with Gary, then breasts drying off.
- •• 0:15—Breasts, lying down with Gary.
- • 0:39—Breasts and buns, getting up and walking with Gary. Breasts, stopping to kiss him.
- • 0:40—Buns and breasts when Gary gets killed. Very brief breasts several times, getting blood spattered on her.
- • 0:41—Breasts, running.

Glenn, Carrick

Films:

The Burning (1981) . . . . . Sally
- ••• 0:19—Breasts, taking a shower in the outdoor showers.
- • 0:20—Very brief breasts, putting her T-shirt back on.

Girls Nite Out (1982) . . . . . Kathy

a.k.a. Scared to Death

Glenn, Charisse *

Films:

Bad Influence (1990) . . . . . Stylish Eurasian Woman
- ••• 1:26—Breasts and partial lower frontal nudity making love on Rob Lowe.
- • 1:28—Very brief left breast in bed with the blonde woman.

Go, Jade

Films:

Model Behavior (1982) . . . . . Golden Girl

Big Trouble in Little China (1986) . . Chinese Girl in White Tiger

The Last Emperor (1987) . . . . . Ar Mo
- • 0:10—Right breast in open top after breast feeding the young Pu Yi.
- • 0:20—Right breast in open top telling Pu Yi a story.
- • 0:29—Right breast in open top breast feeding an older Pu Yi. Long shot.

Goddard, Anna-Marie *

Video Tapes:

Playboy Video Calendar 1995 (1994) . . . . . May
- ••• 0:17—Nude posing in studio. Nude in bayou fantasy.

Playboy Video Centerfold: Anna-Marie Goddard (1994) . . . . . 40th Anniversary Playmate
- • 0:00—Full frontal nudity during introduction.
- ••• 0:02—Nude during studio segment. Sometimes in fishnet body suit and some in B&W.
- ••• 0:09—Taking off stockings, then full frontal nudity while fantasizing about a man and woman. A little bit of rubbing lotion on herself.
- ••• 0:14—Nude, in bayou shack.
- ••• 0:18—Nude in still photos.
- ••• 0:20—Nude in house in dream wedding sequence.
- • 0:27—Nude in end segment.
- •• 0:45—Breasts in centerfold still.
- •• 0:46—Nude during end credits.

Playboy's Rising Stars and Sexy Starlets (1996) . . Herself
- •• 0:51—Breasts, during photo sessions.

- ••• 0:52—Brief breasts in still photos, then nude while posing some more.

Wet & Wild VIII: Bottoms Up (1996)........... Playmate

• Goines, Siena

Made for Cable TV:

Women: Stories of Passion-Grip Till It Hurts (1997; Showtime)............................. Maya

- ••• 0:14—Breasts and partial buns, during her fantasy with Alex.
- ••• 0:23—Breasts, while making love with Alex in bed.

Made for TV Movies:

Co-Ed Call Girl (1996)............................ Jody

Going, Joanna

Films:

Wyatt Earp (1994)...................... Josie Marcus

- • 1:53—(0:14 into tape 2) Brief breasts, in B&W photo that Mark Harmon is showing to everybody in the saloon.
- • 2:03—(0:24 into tape 2) Very brief right breast, while in bed, kissing Kevin Costner.

How to Make an American Quilt (1995) ...... Young Em

- • 0:48—Brief buns, while lying on sofa and posing for painting by Tim Guinee. Partial left breast when he comes over to the sofa.
- • 0:49—Partial left breast in bathtub. Don't see her face.
- • 0:50—Left breast, after kissing Guinee when she's in the tub.

Nixon (1995) .... Young Student

Keys to Tulsa (1996) .... Cherry

(Unrated version reviewed.)

- ••• 0:37—Buns in T-back and breasts, while stripping and dancing on stage.
- •• 0:44—Nude, while lying on the floor with Eric Stoltz.
- •• 1:07—Buns and breasts, taking off her clothes and getting into bed with Stoltz.
- • 1:08—Brief side view of breasts in revealing dress.
- • 1:30—Brief right breast when it falls out of her dress top while she's shaking hands with Billy.
- • 1:33—Breasts, when they fall out of her dress top while dancing during party.

The Commandments (1997)............. Karen Warner

- • 0:05—Very brief part of right breast, when putting on her swimsuit top.

Inventing the Abbotts (1997) .... Alice Abbott

Phantoms (1997) .... Jenny

Made for TV Movies:

Columbo: No Time To Die (1992).................. Melissa

Children of the Dust (1995) .... Rachel

TV:

Dark Shadows (1991) .... Victoria Winters/Josette DuPres

Going to Extremes (1992-93) .... Kathleen McDermott

Gold, Glori

Films:

Embrace of the Vampire (1994)............... Nymph I

(Unrated version reviewed.)

- • 0:03—Brief breasts, while walking up to Martin Kemp with the other two Nymphs. Then breasts and partial buns sitting near Kemp's feet before biting him along with the other two Nymphs.

Phat Beach (1996) .... Glori

Made for Cable TV:

Erotic Confessions: Coming Clean (1996; Cinemax) .... Miriam

(Available on video tape in *Erotic Confessions, Volume 1: Desire.*)

- • 0:10—Buns in short skirt, while standing on step ladder in library.
- ••• 0:11—In red bra, then breasts, while on table in library with Eric.
- •• 0:13—Brief full frontal nudity, while starting to make love on desk with Eric.

Erotic Confessions: The Business Trip (1996; Cinemax) .... Listener

(Available on video tape in *Erotic Confessions, Volume 4: Pleasure.*)

- ••• 0:22—Full frontal nudity, when masturbating in hotel room while listening to the threesome make love in the next room.

Hot Springs Hotel (1998- ; Showtime)............... Lacey

Golden, Annie

Films:

Hair (1979) .... Jeannie

Desperately Seeking Susan (1985)............. Band Singer

Key Exchange (1985) .... Val

Streetwalkin' (1985) .... Phoebe

National Lampoon's "Class of '86" (1986)...... Cast Member

Forever Lulu (1987)............................ Diana

Strictly Business (1991) .... Sheila

Prelude to a Kiss (1992)............... Tin Market Musician

This is My Life (1992) .... Marianne

12 Monkeys (1995)..................... Woman Clerk

One Way Out (1995) .... Eve

- • 1:31—Very brief left breast, in gaping blouse when bending over to help Frank. Slow motion.

TV:

True Blue (1989-90) .... Connie Tollin

Golden, Shana

Films:

State Park (1988; Canadian)............. Blond in Shower

- • 0:46—Breasts taking a shower outside while park ranger watches. Long shot.

The Baby Doll Murders (1992) .... Prostitute

Molly & Gina (1993)............................ Sherry

- •• 1:05—Breasts, while making love on top of Peter Fonda in bed.
- • 1:06—Brief right breast, after rolling over after Fonda leaves the room.
- • 1:08—Brief buns in G-string after tossing off her robe.

Goldsmith, Clio

Films:

Honey (1980; Italian)............................ Annie

- •• 0:05—Nude kneeling in a room.
- •• 0:20—Nude getting into the bathtub.
- •• 0:42—Nude getting changed.
- ••• 0:44—Nude while hiding under the bed.
- •• 0:58—Nude getting disciplined, taking off clothes, then kneeling.

The Gift (1982; French)........................ Barbara

- •• 0:39—Brief breasts several times in the bathroom, then right breast in bathtub.
- • 0:49—Breasts lying in bed sleeping.
- • 0:51—Very brief left breast, while turning over in bed.
- • 0:52—Brief right breast then buns, reaching for phone while lying in bed.

- 1:16—Very brief left breast, when getting out of bed. Dark, hard to see.

The Heat of Desire (1982; French). . . . . Carol
a.k.a. Plein Sud
- 0:09—Breasts and buns, getting out of bed in train to look out the window. Dark.
- 0:12—Brief breasts in bathroom mirror when Serge peeks in.
- •• 0:19—Full frontal nudity in the bathtub.
- •• 0:20—Nude, sitting on the floor with Serge's head in her lap.
- •• 0:21—Buns, lying face down on floor. Very brief breasts. A little dark. Then breasts sitting up and drinking out of bottle.
- 0:22—Right breast, in gaping robe sitting on floor with Serge.
- 0:24—Partial left breast consoling Serge in bed.
- 0:25—Breasts sitting on chair on balcony, then walking inside. Dark.
- 0:56—Breasts walking from bathroom and getting into bed. Dark.
- 0:57—Brief right breast, while on couch with Guy Marchand.
- •• 0:58—Breasts getting dressed while Serge is yelling.

La Cicala (The Cricket) (1983) . . . . Cicala
- •• 0:26—Nude when Wilma brings her in to get Anthony Franciosa excited again.
- •• 0:39—Nude swimming under waterfall with Barbara De Rossi.
- ••• 0:43—Full frontal nudity undressing in room with De Rossi.

Miss Right (1987; Italian). . . . . n.a.

Goldson, Delia *

Films:

The Finishing Touch (1991) . . . . Sorvino's Model
- •• 1:06—In lingerie outfit, then breasts while handcuffed to bed while getting video taped by Sorvino.

Golino, Valeria *

Films:

Blind Date (1984) . . . . Girl in Bikini
a.k.a. Deadly Seduction
(Not to be confused with *Blind Date* (1987) with Bruce Willis.)

Detective School Dropouts (1986). . . . . Caterina

Big Top Pee Wee (1988) . . . . Gina Piccolapupula

Rain Man (1988). . . . . Suzanna
- 0:35—Very brief left breast four times and very, very brief right breast once with open blouse fighting with Tom Cruise after getting out of the bathtub.

The King's Whore (1990; French/British) . . . Jeanne de Luyes
- •• 0:08—Right breast, while making out with Alexander.
- 1:01—Brief upper half of breasts, while lying in bed with Timothy Dalton.
- ••• 1:02—Breasts and buns when Dalton beats her up and throws her out of the room.
- •• 1:16—Right breast when Dalton helps her with her skin disease.
- 1:19—Brief right breast when Dalton takes off her bandages.
- 1:20—Upper half of breasts while in bathtub. (She still has the skin disease.)

Torrents of Spring (1990) . . . . Gemma

Hot Shots (1991). Ramada Thompson

The Indian Runner (1991) . . . . Maria

Year of the Gun (1991) . . . . Lia Spinelli
- ••• 0:17—Breasts, making love in bed with Andrew McCarthy.
- 0:25—Half of buns and side of right breast, lying in bed with McCarthy.

Hot Shots! Part Deux (1993) . . . . . . Ramada Rodham Hayman

Clean Slate (1994). . . . . Sarah Novak/Beth

Immortal Beloved (1994) . . . . Giuletta Guicciardi
- 0:18—In wet dress, when getting a bath. Then side of right breast while getting dressed by her servants.

Four Rooms (1995) . . . . Athena

Leaving Las Vegas (1995). . . . . Terri

Escape From L.A. (1996) . . . . Taslima

An Occasional Hell (1996) . . . . Elizabeth Laughton
- ••• 0:56—In black bra, then breasts, while making love with Tom Berenger at night.

Made for Cable TV:

Fallen Angels: Red Wind (1995; Showtime)
. . . . Eugenie Kolchenko

Golovine, Marina

Films:

Olivier Olivier (1993; French) . . . . Nadine
- 0:53—Very, very brief buns, when falling on her mom in bed while playing around. Very brief lower half of left breast, while adjusting the sheet.
- 1:32—Breasts, while in bed with her brother. Don't see her face.

The Stolen Children (1993; Italian/French) . . . . Nathalie

Queen Margot (1994; French). . . . . Lady in Waiting
a.k.a. La Reine Margot

Gonzalez, Cordelia

Films:

Homeboy (1988). . . . . Cuban Boxer's Wife

Born on the Fourth of July (1989) . . . . Maria Elena
- ••• 1:43—Breasts in black panties, then full frontal nudity in bed with Tom Cruise.

Good, Melanie *

a.k.a. Alexandra Lakewood.

Films:

Psycho Cop 2 (1992). . . . . Cindy
- ••• 0:22—Buns in T-back, then breasts under chain bra after stripping out of maid outfit.
- •• 0:25—Breasts and buns, while with the two other dancers and the guys.
- 0:33—Breasts, when the guys start worrying about Mike. Buns in outfit for the rest of the film.

Campus Hustle (1993). . . . . Veronica

Die Watching (1993) . . . . Sheila Walsh
- ••• 0:05—In white bodysuit dancing while Christopher Atkins video tapes her. Then breasts through bodysuit, then breasts after she rips the bodysuit open.
- ••• 0:07—Breasts in ripped bodysuit while taped down in chair before Atkins kills her.

Desire (1994). . . . . Kathleen Rodgers
- 0:40—Brief right breast, twice, while blindfolded and rubbing perfume on herself before getting killed.

Money to Burn (1994) . . . . Ann
- 0:40—Buns in fishnet body suit, breasts under the suit, while making love with Julie Strain on the floor.

One Good Turn (1995) . . . . Newton
- 0:36—Breasts in open blouse, while doing stuff in the kitchen at night.
- •• 0:37—Breasts, while making love with James Remar seen by Suzy Amis.

Private Parts (1997). . . . . Brittany Fairchild
- 0:28—Side view of breasts and buns, while getting ready for a bath.
- 0:30—Breasts covered with bubbles, while in bathtub with Howard Stern and Fred Norris.

Made for Cable TV:

Love Street: Ex-Girlfriend (1994; Showtime) . . . . Lori
- ••• 0:04—Breasts, buns and brief lower frontal nudity, while making love with Parker in sauna.
- 0:17—Brief buns in panties and brief breasts in wedding dream.

Video Tapes:

Fantasies 2 (1992) . . . . Model
Playboy's Secret Confessions (1993) . . . . . On the Air/Venus
- ••• 0:12—In bra and panties, then breasts, while making love in radio station with Tony.

Goodfellow, Joan

Films:

Lolly-Madonna XXX (1973). . . . . Sister Gutshall
Buster and Billie (1974) . . . . Billie
- 0:33—Brief breasts in truck with Jan-Michael Vincent. Dark, hard to see.
- 1:06—Buns, then brief breasts in the woods with Vincent.
- 1:25—Brief left breast getting raped by jerks.

Sunburn (1979) . . . . Joanna
A Flash of Green (1984) . . . . Mitchie

Gorcey, Elizabeth

Films:

Footloose (1984). . . . . Wendy Jo
Teen Wolf (1985) . . . . Tina
The Trouble with Dick (1986) . . . . Haley
- 0:13—Very brief left breast in gaping T-shirt while she lies on bed, plays with a toy and laughs.
- 0:26—Lower half of buns under robe on sofa with Dick.
- 0:27—Half of right breast on top of Dick in bed.

Iced (1988). . . . . Diane

Gorham, Mel

Films:

Awakenings (1991) . . . . Nurse Sara
Carlito's Way (1993) . . . . Pachanga's Date
Blue in the Face (1995) . . . . Violeta
- •• 1:04—Breasts, after taking off dress and putting another dress on while looking at herself in the mirror.

The Perez Family (1995) . . . . Vilma/Raauel
Curdled (1996). . . . . Elena

• Gowan, Jordana

Films:

Caged Hearts (1995). . . . . Ranch Inmate
Midnight Temptations (1995) . . . . Beach Model
- 1:01—Buns in T-back, after taking off her clothes and walking away on the beach.

Babe Watch: The Forbidden Parody (1996). . . . . Miss Woodrow

Gracen, Elizabeth *

Real name is Elizabeth Ward.

Miss Arkansas and Miss America 1982.

Films:

Lisa (1989) . . . . Mary
Sundown: The Vampire in Retreat (1989) . . . . Alice
Lower Level (1990). . . . . Hillary
- 0:11—Breasts in back seat of BMW making love with Craig. Long shot.
- 0:12—Very, very brief partial left breast afterwards.
- 0:13—Brief right breast and lower frontal nudity getting dressed. Then in black lingerie.
- •• 0:23—In black lingerie, then brief breasts changing in her office while Sam secretly watches.

Marked for Death (1990). . . . . Melissa
Discretion Assured (1993). . . . . Miranda
- 0:28—Brief buns when Michael York removes her panties.
- ••• 0:39—Breasts and buns, while making love with York.
- 1:09—Back side of right and buns, while rubbing lotion on herself. Brief left breast, while putting on robe. Medium long shots.
- 1:22—Brief breasts, when York rips her dress open during argument.

Final Mission (1993). . . . . Caitlin Cole
- ••• 0:28—Breasts, while making out with Billy Wirth.
- 0:53—Breasts, while making love on bed with Wirth at night.

The Expert (1995) . . . . Liz Pierce
Kounterfeit (1997). . . . . Bridgette

Made for TV Movies:

83 Hours 'til Dawn (1990). . . . . Maria

TV:

Highlander: The Series (1992-98) . . . . Amanda
Extreme (1995) . . . . Callie

Graham, Aimee

Films:

Amos & Andrew (1993) . . . . Stacy
Don't Do It (1994) . . . . Great Girl 1
From Dusk Till Dawn (1995) . . . . Blonde Hostage
Jackie Brown (1997) . . . . Amy, Billingsley Sales Girl

Made for Cable Movies:

Rebel Highway: Reform School Girl (1994; Showtime)
. . . . Donna Patterson
- 0:48—In white bra in shack with Carmen.
- 0:49—Breasts, while making out in shack with Carmen.
- 0:51—Brief breasts while in shower.

Made for Cable TV:

Fallen Angels: Since I Don't Have You (1993; Showtime)
. . . . Gretchen Rae Shoftel
(Available on the video tape *Fallen Angels One.*)
- 0:07—Right breast and most of left breast in B&W photo.
- 0:08—Same photo in closer shot.

Graham, Ashley

Films:

CIA Trackdown (1993). . . . . Embassy Secretary
- •• 0:48—Breasts, while making love in room with Shane.

Shadow Warriors (1995) . . . . Natalie

Made for Cable Movies:

The Hit List (1993; Showtime). . . . . Bartender

• Graham, Heather

Films:

License to Drive (1988) . . . . Mercedes
Drugstore Cowboy (1989). . . . . Nadine
I Love You to Death (1990) . . . . Bridget
Shout (1991). . . . . Sara Benedict
Diggstown (1992). . . . . Emily Forrester
a.k.a. Midnight Sting
Guilty as Charged (1992) . . . . Kimberly
Twin Peaks: Fire Walk With Me (1992). . . . . . . Annie Blackburn
The Ballad of Little Jo (1993) . . . . Mary Addie
Six Degrees of Separation (1993) . . . . Elizabeth
Don't Do It (1994) . . . . Suzanna

Even Cowgirls Get the Blues (1994). . . . . Cowgirl Heather
Mrs. Parker and the Vicious Circle (1994) . . . . Mary Kennedy Taylor
Terrified (1994) . . . . .Olive
Entertaining Angels: The Dorothy Day Story (1996) . . . . Maggie Bowen
Swingers (1996) . . . . Lorraine
Boogie Nights (1997). . . . . Rollergirl
- •• 0:24—Nude, while taking off her dress and jumping onto Mark Wahlberg on couch.

Scream 2 (1997) . . . . .Casey Becker
Lost in Space (1998) . . . . .Judy Robinson
Two Girls and a Guy (1998). . . . . .Carla

Made for Cable TV:

Fallen Angels: Tomorrow I Die (1995; Showtime) . . . . Carol Whalen
The Outer Limits: Resurrection (1996; Showtime) . . . . . . .Alicia

Made for TV Movies:

O Pioneers! (1992) . . . . Young Alexandra Bergson

TV:

Twin Peaks (1991). . . . . Annie

Graham, Julie

Films:

Wonderland (1989; British) . . . . .Hazel
- •• 1:11—Nude, taking off her clothes at the beach while talking to Eddie.

Nuns on the Run (1990; British) . . . . .Casino Waitress
The Big Man (1991; British) . . . . .Melanie
a.k.a. Crossing the Line
- •• 1:09—Breasts when Liam Neeson undresses her and starts to make love with her.

*Graham, Juliet **

Films:

The Serpents of the Pirate Moon (1973) . . . . .Woman
Alice in Wonderland (1977) . . . . The Queen
(R-rated version reviewed.)
- ••• 0:51—Full frontal nudity in garter belt and stockings while walking, then talking with Alice.
- ••• 0:54—Full frontal nudity during trial.
- • 0:58—Breasts in quick cuts.
- •• 1:05—Full frontal nudity, while running after Alice.
- •• 1:13—Breasts during the end credits.

Graham, Sherri

Films:

Bad Girls from Mars (1990) . . . . Swimmer
- •• 0:22—Very brief breasts diving into, then climbing out of pool.

Haunting Fear (1990). Visconti's Girl
- • 0:45—Buns in swimming pool. (Breasts seen under water.)
- • 0:47—Breasts, giving Visconti a massage while he talks on the phone.

Mob Boss (1990). . . . . Bar Girl
- •• 0:46—Breasts and buns, dancing on stage. Medium long shot.

Naked Obsession (1990). . . . . Waitress
(Unrated version reviewed.)
Carnal Crimes (1991) . . . . Party Girl #1
Cyberzone (1995). . . . . .Captive Dancer
- •• 0:21—Breasts, while dancing in belly dancer outfit.

Masseuse (1995) . . . . Sheila
(Unrated version reviewed.)
- •• 0:54—Breasts and buns in lingerie, while in hotel room with Jack.

Granath, Tiffany

Films:

The Immortals (1995) . . . . Strip Club Waitress

Made for Cable Movies:

Breast Men (1997; HBO). . . . . Sexy Patient
- •• 0:40—Breasts, while David Schwimmer demonstrates how to massage her breasts.

Video Tapes:

Playboy's Cheerleaders (1996) . . . . .Dancer 3
- •• 0:39—Brief breasts (she has straight, shoulder length blonde hair), several times during Carmen Elektra music video.

Grant, Faye

Films:

Internal Affairs (1990). . . . . Penny
- • 0:50—Right breast, while straddling Richard Gere while she talks on the telephone.

The Gun in Betty Lou's Handbag (1992) . . . . .Charleen
Traces of Red (1992) . . . . Beth Frayn
- • 0:52—Buns in T-back under sheer dress.

Vibrations (1994). . . . . Zina

Made for Cable TV:

Tales From the Crypt: Spoiled (1991; HBO) . . . . .Janet

Miniseries:

V (1983) . . . . Dr. Julie Parrish
V: The Final Battle (1984). . . . . Dr. Julie Parrish

Made for TV Movies:

Omen IV: The Awakening (1991). . . . . Karen York

TV:

Greatest American Hero (1981-83) . . . . Rhonda Blake
V: The Series (1984-85) . . . . Dr. Julie Parrish

Grant, Lee

Mother of actress Dinah Manoff.

Films:

In the Heat of the Night (1967). . . . . Mrs. Leslie Colbert
Valley of the Dolls (1967). . . . . Miriam
Buono Sera, Mrs. Campbell (1968) . . . . Fritzie Braddock
Marooned (1969) . . . . .Celia Pruett
The Landlord (1970) . . . . .Mrs. Enders
There Was a Crooked Man (1970) . . . . Mrs. Bullard
Plaza Suite (1971) . . . . Norma Hubley
Portnoy's Complaint (1972). . . . . .Sophie Portnoy
Shampoo (1975) . . . . Felicia
(Academy Award for Best Supporting Actress.)
- • 0:03—Brief breasts in bed sitting up and putting bra on talking to Warren Beatty. Long shot, hard to see.

Airport '77 (1977) . . . . .Karen Wallace
Damien, Omen II (1978) . . . . Ann Thorn
The Mafu Cage (1978) . . . . Ellen
a.k.a. My Sister, My Love
When Ya Comin' Back Red Ryder (1979) . . . . Clarisse Ethridge
(Not available on video tape.)
Little Miss Marker (1980). . . . . .The Judge
Charlie Chan & the Curse of the Dragon Queen (1981) . . . . .Mrs. Lupowitz
Visiting Hours (1982; Canadian) . . . . Deborah Ballin
Teachers (1984). . . . . Dr. Burke
The Big Town (1987). . . . . .Ferguson Edwards

Defending Your Life (1991) . . . . Lena Foster
It's My Party (1995). . . . . Amalia Stark
Made for Cable Movies:
Citizen Cohn (1992; HBO) . . . . Dora
Miniseries:
Backstairs at the White House (1979) . . . . Grace Coolidge
Made for TV Movies:
The Neon Ceiling (1971) . . . . Carrie Miller
She Said No (1990). . . . . Doris Cantore
Something to Live For: The Alison Gertz Story (1992) . . . . . n.a.
TV:
Search for Tomorrow. . . . . Rose Peabody
Peyton Place (1965-66). Stella Chernak
Fay (1975-76) . . . . Fay Stewart

Grant, Rainer

a.k.a. Liza Smith.
Films:
Married People, Single Sex 2: For Better or Worse (1994). . . . . Karen
• 0:01—Breasts, while making love in bed with Sam.
• 0:02—Brief buns and breasts, while lying in bed, getting spanked.
••• 0:32—Right breast several times, then breasts while making love in bed with David.
•• 0:53—Brief left breast, then breasts, while in doorway with David.
• 1:11—Very brief partial breasts and buns in bra and panties on bed during fight with Sam.
Relentless 4: Ashes to Ashes (1994) . . . . Hairdresser/Victim #1
•• 0:02—Breasts, while making love in bed on top of a guy before getting killed.
• 0:17—Breasts, while lying dead on coroner's table during exam.
Made for Cable Movies:
Not Like Us (1995; Showtime) . . . . Janet
•• 0:08—Breasts, opening her blouse in old truck in front of hitchhiker.
• 0:09—Brief breasts, while putting on blouse after stabbing the hitchhiker with a needle.
•• 0:26—Breasts, while outside at night with two guys she picked up from bar.
••• 0:54—Breasts, while talking to Peter Onorati in doorway.
•• 0:55—Breasts, after taking off her jacket to distract a policeman.
Subliminal Seduction (1996; Showtime). . . . . Angie
•• 0:32—Right breast and buns, while making love with Ian Ziering.
Made for Cable TV:
Love Street: Freudian Slip (1994; Showtime) . . . . Janice/Phoebe
• 0:07—Breasts, while on sofa with Jay Richardson.
• 0:19—Buns in T-back and right breast after taking off her clothes in front of Rolf in a room.
•• 0:20—Buns and breasts, while making love with Rolf on the sofa.
•• 0:22—Breasts, while making love with Rolf in the bathroom.

• *Grappini, Floriela*

Films:
Forbidden Zone: Alien Abduction (1996). . . . . Patron
a.k.a. Alien Abduction: Intimate Secrets
• 0:00—Brief full frontal nudity and breasts, several times, while swimming in pool.
•• 0:03—Brief full frontal nudity, then breasts, while looking at the other woman in dressing room.
Vampire Journals (1996) . . . . Serena
• 0:59—Breasts, while in bed with Zachary before biting him and turning him into a vampire.

Grassnick, Michelle

Films:
Bikini Summer (1991) . . . . Debbie
Miracle Beach (1991). . . . . Miss Great Britain
• 0:35—Brief buns in swimsuit bottom, then right breast, while lying in bed, talking with Lars.
••• 1:03—Breasts, while trying on swimsuits backstage.
Final Impact (1992). . . . . Foxy Boxer
Knockouts (1992) . . . . Margo
••• 0:04—Breasts while lifting weights.
••• 0:35—Breasts, several times in locker room with her girlfriends.
•• 0:59—Breasts, while putting swimsuit on (she's on the left).
• 1:10—Buns, in outfit during wrestling match.
• 1:12—Brief right breast, when it falls out of her top.

Gravatte, Marianne *

Video Tapes:
Playboy Video Magazine, Volume 3 (1983) . . . . Playboy's Playmate of the Year 1983
••• 1:04—Nude in still photos.
••• 1:08—Full frontal nudity in bed at beach scene.
••• 1:09—Nude at the beach during the day.
••• 1:16—Nude while sitting at vanity and in bed.
Playboy Video Magazine, Volume 5 (1983) . . . . Playmate
• 0:06—Full frontal nudity outside.
••• 0:09—Nude, posing at beach in a bed set.
Playboy's Playmate Review 2 (1984). . . . . Playmate
Playboy's Playmates of the Year: The '80s (1989) . . . . Playmate of the Year 1983
••• 0:32—Nude in still photos.
••• 0:33—Nude in bed at the beach during photo session.
•• 0:51—Breasts in bed scene.
Playboy Video Centerfold: Reneé Tenison (1990) . . . . Portrait of a Photographer: Richard Fegley
••• 0:32—Nude, in photo session at the beach.
Playboy's 21 Playmates: Volume II (1996) . . . . . . Playmate
••• 0:02—Nude in still photos.
••• 0:03—Nude on the beach and in bedroom.

Gray, Andee

Films:
Sno-Line (1984). . . . . Ruth Lyle
9 1/2 Ninjas (1990) . . . . Lisa Thorne
•• 1:02—Breasts, while making love with Joe in the rain.
• 1:19—Brief breasts during flashback.
Dead Men Don't Die (1991) . . . . Isadora

Gray, Casey *

Films:
Sinful Intrigue (1995) . . . . Dancer #2
• 0:47—Brief breasts, while walking by swimming pool (medium long shot), then breasts, when massaging another woman (closer shot).

Touch (1996) . . . . Stripper
Video Tapes:
Playboy's Hard Bodies (1995) . . . . Herself
••• 0:11—In lingerie, then nude, while posing outdoors.
••• 0:15—Nude, while posing with Holly Hart in wrestling ring.

Gray, Julie

Films:
Gimme an "F" (1981) . . . . Falcon Marsha
a.k.a. T & A Academy 2
Stryker (1983; Philippines) . . . . Laurenz
School Spirit (1985) . . . . Kendall
Dr. Alien (1989) . . . . Karla
a.k.a. I Was a Teenage Sex Mutant
••• 0:44—In white bra, then breasts in Janitor's room with Wesley.
The Naked Truth (1992) . . . . Miss Hungary
Video Tapes:
Inside Out 3 (1992) . . . . Actress/The Branding

Gray, Marcia

Films:
Terrorgram (1991) . . . . Biker Bitch
Housewife From Hell (1993) . . . . Elvina
•• 0:44—In black bra, then nude while John is handcuffed to the bed on the floor.
Virtual Desire (1995) . . . . Stranger
••• 1:13—In bra and panties outside in the woods with Brad, then breasts while making love. Long scene.

Gray, Nadia

Films:
La Dolce Vita (1960; Italian/French) . . . . Nadia
• 1:09—Brief breasts, while lying on the floor after doing a strip tease.
The Naked Runner (1967; British) . . . . Karen Gisevius
The Oldest Profession (1967) . . . . "Paris Today"
Two for the Road (1967; British) . . . . Francoise Dalbret

Grazioli, Irene *

Films:
Trena Di Panna (1988; Italian) . . . . Tina
Mediterraneo (1991; Italian) . . . . Pastorella
••• 0:36—Breasts with the Munaron brothers.
• 0:52—Brief breasts, swimming in water.

Green, Marika *

Films:
Pickpocket (1963; French) . . . . Jeanne
Singapore, Singapore (1969; French/Italian) . . . . Monica
Rider on the Rain (1970; French/Italian) . . . . Hostess at Tania's
Emmanuelle (1974; French) . . . . Bee
(R-rated version reviewed.)
• 0:46—Nude, undressing outside with Sylvia Kristel. Brief full frontal nudity, when leaving blanket.
•• 0:47—Breasts, getting dressed.
• 0:50—Upper half of buns, while lying down, talking to Kristel.
Until September (1984) . . . . Banker

Greenberg, Sandy *

Video Tapes:
Playmates at Play (1990) . . . . Easy Rider

Greene, Ellen

Films:
Next Stop, Greenwich Village (1976) . . . . Sarah
•• 0:15—In white bra, then very brief right breast, then left breast, while on couch on porch with Larry.
I'm Dancing as Fast as I Can (1981) . . . . Karen Mulligan
Little Shop of Horrors (1986) . . . . Audrey
Me & Him (1988; West German) . . . . Anette Uttanzi
Talk Radio (1988) . . . . Ellen
Pump Up the Volume (1990) . . . . Jan Emerson
Stepping Out (1991) . . . . Maxine
Fathers and Sons (1992) . . . . Judy
The Professional (1994) . . . . Mathilda's Mother
Wagons East! (1994) . . . . Belle
Killer: A Journal of Murder (1995) . . . . Elizabeth Wyatt
An Occasional Hell (1996) . . . . Della
One Fine Day (1996) . . . . Elaine Lieberman
Made for Cable Movies:
Glory! Glory! (1988; HBO) . . . . Ruthie

Greene, Melinda

See: Armstrong, Melinda.

Gregson Wagner, Natasha

Daughter of screenwriter Richard Gregson and late actress Natalie Wood.
Stepdaughter of actor Robert Wagner.
Films:
Buffy The Vampire Slayer (1992) . . . . Cassandra
Dark Horse (1992) . . . . Martha
Fathers and Sons (1992) . . . . Lisa
Molly & Gina (1993) . . . . Gina
Dead Beat (1994) . . . . Kristen
• 0:31—Brief right breast, in mirror, when she draws on it with lipstick.
S.F.W. (1994) . . . . Kristen
Wes Craven's Mind Ripper (1995) . . . . Wendy
High School High (1996) . . . . Julie
Lost Highway (1997) . . . . Sheila
• 1:10—Breasts, when taking off her blouse in car with Bathazar Getty.
Two Girls and a Guy (1998) . . . . Lou
Made for Cable Movies:
The Substitute (1993; USA) . . . . n.a.
Rebel Highway: Dragstrip Girl (1994; Showtime) . . . . Laura
Made for TV Movies:
Hart to Hart: Secrets of the Heart (1995) . . . . Tibby

Greiner, Nicole

See: Dial, Nikki.

• Greist, Kimberly

Films:
C.H.U.D. (1984) . . . . Lauren Daniels
Brazil (1985; British) . . . . Jill Layton
• 1:55—(0:18 into side 5) [This scene is only available on the Criterion CAV laser disc and in the European video version.] Partial buns, while kneeling on bed. Very brief back side of left breast after Jonathan Pryce takes off her ribbon.
Manhunter (1986) . . . . Molly Graham
Punchline (1988) . . . . Madeline Urie
Why Me? (1990) . . . . June Daley
Made for Cable Movies:
Payoff (1991; Showtime) . . . . Justine Bates
Roswell (1994; Showtime) . . . . Vy Marcel
Last Exit to Earth (1996; Showtime) . . . . Eve

Grey, Dahlia
See: Dion, Jami.

Grey, Jennifer
Daughter of actor/dancer/choreographer Joel Grey.

Films:

The Cotton Club (1984) .... Patsy Dwyer
Reckless (1984) .... Cathy Bennario
Red Dawn (1984) .... Toni
American Flyers (1985) .... Leslie
Ferris Bueller's Day Off (1986) .... Jeanie Bueller
Dirty Dancing (1987) .... Frances "Baby" Houseman
Bloodhounds of Broadway (1989) .... Lovey Lou
Stroke of Midnight (1991; U.S./French) .... Kelly Carter
a.k.a. If the Shoe Fits
Wind (1992) .... Kate Bass
Eyes of a Witness (1994) .... Christine Baxter
Lover's Knot (1995) .... Megan Forrester
- 0:29—Very, very brief upper half of right breast, after sitting up in bed and moving the sheets with Bill Campbell.
- 0:45—Very brief buns, while running through the house in front of Bill Campbell.

Portraits of a Killer (1996; Canadian) .... Elaine Taylor

Made for Cable Movies:

Criminal Justice (1990; HBO) .... Liz Carter
A Case for Murder (1993; USA) .... Kate Weldon

Made for Cable TV:

Fallen Angels: A Dime a Dance (1995; Showtime)
.... Ginger Allen

Made for TV Movies:

Outrage (1998) .... n.a.

Grey, Nicole *
a.k.a. Brittany Noelle.

Films:

Wildest Dreams (1987) .... Girl on Street
Malibu Summer (1991) .... Jill
Sexual Outlaws (1993) .... Rita
- ••• 0:09—Breasts, after taking off her top with Jeannie, then making love in hotel room.

Midnight Tease (1994) .... Dusty
- ••• 0:17—Breasts after stripping out of policewoman's uniform on stage.

Silk n' Sabotage (1994) .... Jerri
- 0:07—Buns, while in lingerie during lingerie sales party.

Made for Cable Movies:

Rebel Highway: Reform School Girl (1994; Showtime)
.... Uncredited Girl in Back of Car
- 0:29—Brief right breast while making out with a guy in back of a convertible car in parking lot.

Grier, Pam *
Cousin of actor/former football player Rosey Grier.

Films:

Beyond the Valley of the Dolls (1970) .... Black Party Goer
The Big Doll House (1971) .... Grear
- 0:28—Very brief most of right breast rolling over in bed.
- •• 0:32—Breasts getting her back washed by Collier. Arms in the way a little bit.
- 0:44—Left breast covered with mud sticking out of her top after wrestling with Alcott.

The Big Bird Cage (1972) .... Blossom
Cool Breeze (1972) .... Mona
Hit Man (1972) .... Gozelda
Twilight People (1972) .... The Panther Woman
Black Mama, White Mama (1973; U.S./Philippines) .... Lee
Coffy (1973) .... Coffy
- 0:05—Upper half of right breast in bed with a guy.
- 0:19—Buns, walking past the fireplace, seen through a fish tank.
- •• 0:25—Breasts in open dress getting attacked by two masked burglars.
- ••• 0:38—Buns and breasts undressing in bedroom. Wow!
- 0:42—Brief right breast when breast pops out of dress while she's leaning over. Dark, hard to see.

Naked Warriors (1973) .... Mamawi
a.k.a. The Arena
- •• 0:08—Brief left breast, then lower frontal nudity and side view of right breast getting washed down in court yard.
- ••• 0:52—Breasts getting oiled up for a battle. Wow!

Scream, Blacula, Scream (1973) .... Lisa Fortier
Foxy Brown (1974) .... Foxy Brown
- 0:05—Breasts, getting out of bed and taking off nightgown.
- 0:40—Brief left breast, while getting dressed.
- ••• 1:05—Right breast, then breasts rolling over in bed.

Bucktown (1975) .... Aretha
- ••• 0:29—Left breast, while in bed with Fred Williamson.

Friday Foster (1975) .... Friday Foster
- ••• 0:29—Breasts, several times, while taking a shower while Carl Weathers stalks around in her apartment.
- ••• 1:12—Upper half of breast, while in bubble bath with Blake. Breasts in bed with him.

Sheba, Baby (1975) .... Sheba Shayne
- 0:26—Side view of left breast, while lying in bed with Brick.

Drum (1976) .... Regine
- 0:58—Very brief breasts getting undressed and into bed with Maxwell.

Greased Lightning (1977) .... Mary Jones
Fort Apache, The Bronx (1981) .... Charlotte
Something Wicked this Way Comes (1983) .... Dust Witch
Tough Enough (1983) .... Myra
On the Edge (1985) .... Cora
(Unrated version reviewed.)
- •• 0:42—Breasts in the mirror, then full frontal nudity making love with Bruce Dern standing up. Then brief left breast. A little dark.

Stand Alone (1985) .... Catherine
Vindicator (1986; Canadian) .... Hunter
a.k.a. Frankenstein '88
The Allnighter (1987) .... Sgt. MacLeish
Above the Law (1988) .... Delores "Jacks" Jackson
Class of 1999 (1990) .... Ms. Connors
Bill and Ted's Bogus Journey (1991) .... Ms. Wardroe
Posse (1993) .... Phoebe
Serial Killer (1995) .... Capt. Maggie Davis
Escape From L.A. (1996) .... Hershe Las Palmas
Mars Attacks! (1996) .... Louise Williams
Original Gangstas (1996) .... Laurie Thompson
Jackie Brown (1997) .... Jackie Brown
Strip Search (1997; Canadian) .... Janette

Made for TV Movies:

A Mother's Right: The Elizabeth Morgan Story (1992)
.... Linda Holman

Griffeth, Simone
Films:

Death Race 2000 (1975) .... Annie Smith
- 0:32—Side view of left breast, while holding David Carradine. Dark, hard to see.
- ••• 0:56—Breasts and buns getting undressed and lying on bed with Carradine.

Hot Target (1985; New Zealand) . . . . Christine Webber
- •• 0:09—Breasts taking off top for shower, then breasts and brief frontal nudity taking shower.
- ••• 0:19—Breasts in bed after making love with Steve Marachuck.
- •• 0:21—Buns, getting out of bed and walking to bathroom.
- •• 0:23—Breasts in bed with Marachuck again.
- • 0:34—Breasts in the woods with Marachuck while cricket match goes on.

The Patriot (1986) . . . . Sean
- •• 0:49—Brief breasts lying in bed, making love with Ryder.

TV:

Ladies' Man (1980-81) . . . . .Gretchen
Bret Maverick (1982). . . . . Jasmine DuBois
Amanda's (1983). . . . . Arlene Cartwright

Griffin, Renee

See: Ammann, Renee.

Griffis, Rhoda

Films:

Love Field (1993) . . . . .Jacqueline Kennedy
The Program (1993) . . . . .Reporter #3
Cobb (1994). . . . . .Ty's Mother
- • 0:47—Very brief right breast, when undressing in bedroom. Brief full frontal nudity while reaching for shotgun under bed.
- • 1:39—Brief breasts in open robe. Very brief lower frontal nudity.
- • 1:40—Full frontal nudity, twice, when getting shotgun. Brief side of left breast while sitting on bed, crying. Very, very brief left breast after walking away from window (seen behind her lover).

Something to Talk About (1995) . . . . Edna
Midnight in the Garden of Good & Evil (1997) . . . . Card Club Woman #2

Made for Cable Movies:

The Sister-In-Law (1995; USA). . . . . Kelly Richards
From the Earth to the Moon: Apollo 1 (1998; HBO) . . . . .Martha Chaffee

*Griffith, Melanie **

Daughter of actress Tippi Hedren.
Wife of actor Antonio Banderas.
Ex-wife of actor Don Johnson.
Ex-wife of actor Steven Bauer.
Sister of actress Tracy Griffith.

Films:

Smile (1974) . . . . Karen Love
- • 0:34—Very, very brief side view of right breast in dressing room, just before passing behind a rack of clothes.
- • 0:47—Very brief side view of right breast, then side view of left breast when Little Bob is outside taking pictures.
- • 0:48—Very brief breasts as Polaroid photograph that Little Bob took develops.
- • 1:51—Breasts in the same Polaroid in the policeman's sun visor.

Night Moves (1975) . . . . Delly Grastner
- • 0:42—Brief breasts changing tops outside while talking with Gene Hackman.
- • 0:46—Nude, saying "hi" from under water beneath a glass bottom boat.
- • 0:47—Brief side view of right breast getting out of the water.

The Drowning Pool (1976) . . . . Schuuler Devereaux
Joyride (1977) . . . . .Susie
- • 0:05—Breasts in back of station wagon with Robert Carradine, hard to see anything.
- •• 0:59—Brief breasts in spa with everybody.
- • 1:11—Brief breasts in shower with Desi Arnaz, Jr.

One on One (1977). . . . . .Hitchhiker
Roar (1981) . . . . Melanie
Body Double (1984) . . . . Holly Body
- •• 0:20—Breasts, while wearing a brunette wig, dancing around in bedroom being watched through telescope by Craig Wasson.
- • 0:28—Breasts, while in bedroom, being watched by Wasson and the Indian.
- •• 1:12—Breasts and buns, seen on TV that Wasson is watching.
- •• 1:13—Breasts and buns, seen on TV after Wasson buys the video tape.
- • 1:19—Brief buns in black leather outfit in bathroom during filming of movie.
- • 1:20—Brief buns again in the black leather outfit.

Fear City (1984) . . . . Loretta
- • 0:04—Buns, in blue G-string, while dancing on stage.
- •• 0:07—Breasts, dancing on stage.
- ••• 0:23—Breasts dancing on stage wearing a red G-string.

Something Wild (1986) . . . . "Lulu"/Audrey Hankel
- ••• 0:16—Strips to breasts in bed with Jeff Daniels.
- • 0:24—Buns and brief breasts, while looking out the window.

Cherry 2000 (1988). . . . . E. Johnson
The Milagro Beanfield War (1988) . . . . .Flossie Devine
Stormy Monday (1988) . . . . Kate
- • 1:11—Very brief left breast, while making love in bed with Brendan.

Working Girl (1989). . . . . Tess McGill
- • 1:18—Very, very brief right breast turning over in bed with Ford.
- • 1:20—Breasts, vacuuming. Long shot seen from the other end of the hall.

The Bonfire of the Vanities (1990) . . . . .Maria Ruskin
In the Spirit (1990) . . . . Lureen
Pacific Heights (1990) . . . . Patty Parker
Paradise (1991) . . . . .Lily Reed
Shining Through (1992) . . . . .Linda Voss
- •• 0:22—Breasts, making love in bed on top of Michael Douglas.

Stranger Among Us (1992) . . . . Emily Eden
a.k.a. Close to Eden
Born Yesterday (1993) . . . . Billie Dawn
Milk Money (1994) V
Nobody's Fool (1994) . . . . .Toby Roebuck
- •• 0:53—Very brief breasts, after pulling up her sweatshirt to flash for Paul Newman in office.

Now and Then (1995). . . . . Tina Tercell
Two Much (1995) . . . . .Betty
Mulholland Falls (1996). . . . . Katherine

Made for Cable Movies:

Women & Men: Stories of Seduction (1990; HBO) . . . . Hadley

Miniseries:

Buffalo Girls (1995) . . . . .Dora DuFran

Made for TV Movies:

She's in the Army Now (1981). . . . . Sylvie Knoll

TV:

Once an Eagle (1976-77). . . . . Jinny Massengale
Carter Country (1978-79) . . . . Tracy Quinn

Griffith, Tracy

Sister of actress Melanie Griffith.

Films:

Fear City (1984) .... Sandra Cook

The Good Mother (1988) .... Babe

- 0:06—Brief breasts opening her blouse to show a young Anna what it's like being pregnant.

Fast Food (1989)............................. Samantha

Sleepaway Camp III: Teenage Wasteland (1989) .... Marcia Holland

The First Power (1990) .... Tess Seaton

The Finest Hour (1991) .... Barbara

- 0:21—In wet, braless, white dress, getting out of the water after canoe tips over.
- 1:02—Swimming with Mazzoli under water in ocean in a wet, braless, white dress.
- 1:03—Brief side view of right breast, while taking the wet dress off.

All Tied Up (1992)....................... Sharon Stevens

Skeeter (1994) ....Sarah

- 0:59—Brief breasts, while sitting on bed with Boone after making love. Medium long shot.

Made for Cable Movies:

Their Second Chance (1997; Lifetime) .... n.a.

TV:

Monroes (1995-96)................................. Ruby

Griffiths, Linda

Films:

Lianna (1982) ....Lianna

- •• 0:29—Breasts and buns, making love in bed with Ruth. Dark.
- •• 1:26—Right breast, then breasts while lying in bed with Cindy. Long, dark scene.
- •• 1:42—Left breast while lying in bed with Ruth.

Reno and the Doc (1984; Canadian).........Savannah Gates

Samuel Lount (1986; Canadian) .... Elizabeth Lount

Made for TV Movies:

A Town Torn Apart (1992)..........................Hallie

• Griffiths, Rachel

Films:

Muriel's Wedding (1994; Australian) .... Rhonda

Cosi (1996; Australian) .... Lucy

Jude (1996; British) ....Arabella

- ••• 0:59—Brief breasts, then left breast, while lying in bed with Jude after making love.

Children of the Revolution (1997) .... Anna

My Best Friend's Wedding (1997) ...... Samantha Newhouse

Griggs, Camila

Films:

Forced Vengeance (1982) .... Joy Paschal

- 1:14—Brief breasts, on the bed when the bad guy rips her blouse open.

Bar Girls (1995).................................. J.R.

Grigsby, Andrea

Video Tapes:

BabeWatch, Episode 3: Sex Kittens (1994) ....Herself

- ••• 0:46—Breasts and buns, while posing on lounge chair outdoors next to pool.

BabeWatch, Episode 4: Naughty But Nice (1995) ....Herself

- 0:34—Buns while dancing on stage in a club.

Grimaldi, Eva *

Films:

Intervista (1987; Italian) ....n.a.

Obsession: A Taste For Fear (1987) ....n.a.

Midnight Seduction (1988; Italian) .... Tea

A Family Matter (1990)........................ Brenda

- ••• 0:53—Nude, getting out of the bubble bath, then dressing herself.

Forever (1992) .... Berenice Rondi

Grindlay, Annie

Films:

Lurkers (1987)..........................Lulu (Model)

- 0:12—Undressing in sheer bra (on the left) with another model.
- •• 0:13—Breasts, while changing clothes with the other model.

K2 (1991) .... Lisa

Groff, Nancy

Films:

Deranged (1987).............................Teacher

Lurkers (1987)................................. Rita

- 1:07—Partial right breast in bathroom with another woman while Cathy talks.

Grossman, Liora

Films:

I Don't Give a Damn (1985; Israeli) .... Maya

a.k.a. Lo Sam Zayin

- 1:11—Brief right breast, while posing for Rafi in the kitchen.

Irith, Irith (1985) ....Irith Katz

Grubel, Ilona

Films:

Jonathan (1973; German) .... Eleanore

Target (1985) ....Carla

- 1:12—Brief breasts in bed with Matt Dillon.

Guerin, Florence

Films:

Black Venus (1983)............................Louise

- •• 0:45—Nude talking, then making love with Venus in bed.
- ••• 1:16—Nude frolicking on the beach with Venus.
- ••• 1:18—Nude in bedroom getting out of wet clothes with Venus.
- 1:21—Buns in bed with Jacques and Venus.

Bizarre (1986; Italian) .... Laurie

- •• 0:03—Breasts on bed with Guido. Lower frontal nudity while he molests her with a pistol.
- ••• 0:18—Nude after taking off her clothes in hotel room with a guy. Nice.
- ••• 0:30—Full frontal nudity making love with Edward in the water.
- 0:34—Brief side of right breast, taking off robe in bathroom with Edward. (He's made himself up to look like a woman.)
- ••• 0:36—Breasts in white panties making love with Edward.
- •• 0:40—Breasts and brief lower frontal nudity in Guido's office with him.
- ••• 0:45—Nude, playing outside with Edward, then making love with his toe.
- •• 0:47—Breasts getting out of bed and putting a blouse on.
- •• 0:49—Breasts with Edward when Guido comes in.
- 1:11—Breasts sitting in chair talking to Edward.
- 1:20—Lower frontal nudity, putting the phone down there.

• 1:28—Buns and lower frontal nudity on bed when Guido rips her clothes off and rapes her.

The Turn-On (1989) .... Claudia Christiani
a.k.a. Le Clic
•• 0:02—Buns and breasts in mirror.
••• 0:34—Breasts, while looking at herself in dressing room mirror and caressing herself.
•• 0:54—Breasts, while walking through the woods and taking off her clothes.
••• 0:56—Nude, while playing with herself in the woods, then getting tied up and carried away on a guy's shoulders. Long scene.
••• 1:07—Breasts and buns, while on the beach with Dr. Fez. Nude, fighting with her husband and running away into the house.

Guerra, Blanca

Films:

Falcon's Gold (1982).............................n.a.
a.k.a. Robbers of the Sacred Mountain
Erendira (1983; Brazilian) ....Ulysses' Mother
Separate Vacations (1985; Canadian)..............Alicia
• 0:56—Breasts on the bed with David Naughton when she turns out to be a hooker.
Walker (1988) .... Yrena
Santa Sangre (1989; Italian/Spanish) ....Concha
• 0:34—Half of buns, while wearing a sexy circus outfit.
Danzon (1992; Mexican).................... La Colorada
Clear and Present Danger (1994) .... Escobedo's Wife

Guerrero, Evelyn *

Wife of comedian/actor Noriyuki "Pat" Morita.

Films:

Wild Wheels (1969).............................. Sissy
Trackdown (1976)...................... Social Worker
The Toolbox Murders (1978)...................... Maria
Fairytales (1979).......................S & M Dancer
•• 0:38—Breasts wearing masks with two other blonde S&M Dancers.
•• 0:56—Full frontal nudity dancing with the other S&M Dancers again.
Cheech & Chong's Next Movie (1980) .... Donna
Cheech & Chong's Nice Dreams (1981).......... Donna
• 0:43—Brief left breast sticking out of her spandex outfit, sitting down at table in restaurant.
Things Are Tough All Over (1982)................. Donna
Blood In, Blood Out: Bound by Honor (1992) .... Luisa
a.k.a. Bound by Honor

TV:

I Married Dora (1987-88) ....Marisol Calderon
Dallas (1989-90) ....Nancy

Guerri, Ruth *

Video Tapes:

Playboy's Playmate Review 2 (1984)...........Playmate
Playmates at Play (1990) ....Thrill Seeker, Bareback

Gunden, Scarlett

Films:

Island of 1000 Delights .... Francine
••• 0:02—Breasts on beach dancing with Ching. Upper half of buns sitting down.
•• 0:44—Full frontal nudity getting tortured by Ming.
• 1:16—Breasts on beach after Ching rescues her.

Melody in Love (1978; German)................ Angela
••• 0:17—Full frontal nudity taking off dress and dancing in front of statue.
••• 0:50—Nude with a guy on a boat.
•• 0:53—Breasts on another boat with Octavio.
•• 0:59—Buns and breasts in bed talking to Rachel.
•• 1:12—Full frontal nudity getting a tan on boat with Rachel.
• 1:14—Breasts making love in bed with Rachel and Octavio.

Gunn, Janet

Films:

Night of the Running Man (1994).........Chris Altman
•• 1:09—Breasts, while making love with Andrew McCarthy.
The Sweeper (1995) .... Melissa
Carnosaur 3: Primal Species (1996)............. Dr. Hodges
The Nurse (1996) .... Karen Martin
The Quest (1996) .... Carrie

Made for Cable Movies:

Marquis de Sade (1996; Showtime)................ Justine

Made for Cable TV:

Dream On: What Women Want (1992; HBO) ..... Girl in Hall

TV:

Dark Justice (1992-93).................... Kelly Cochrane
Silk Stalkings (1996-) ....Sgt. Cassandra St. John

Gurnett, Jane

Films:

Drowning by Numbers (1988; British).............Nancy
••• 0:04—Nude, undressing inside and running outside, taking a bath with Jake. Long scene.
••• 0:06—More breasts and buns, in the bathtub next to Jake.
• 0:10—Left breast, passed out in bathtub.
• 0:11—More left breast in bathtub.
• 0:15—Left breast, while in wheelbarrow.
• 0:16—Full frontal nudity when the women pull her onto the bed.
Lorna Doone (1990; British)................... Annie Ridd

Gurwitch, Annabelle

Films:

Battle in the Erogenous Zone..................Garmento
Delivery Boys (1984) .... Woman with Big Hat
Kiss Daddy Goodnight (1987)........................ Sue
Bright Lights, Big City (1988) ....Barbara
Life With Mikey (1993) .... Debbie
Automatic (1994) .... Gloria Takamatsu
Three Wishes (1995) .... Leland's Mother
The Cable Guy (1996).............. Steven's Sister-In-Law
Intimate Betrayal (1996) .... Claire
One Night Stand (1997) .... Marie

Made for Cable Movies:

Not Like Us (1995; Showtime)..................... Vicki
• 0:49—Breasts, while lying on operating table.
•• 1:03—Breasts, after putting on her new skin (there's a bit of blood on her).

Made for Cable TV:

Tales From the Crypt: Spoiled (1991; HBO) ....Louise
Red Shoe Diaries: Another Woman's Lipstick (1993; Showtime) .... Annie
(Available on the video tape *Red Shoe Diaries 3: Another Woman's Lipstick.*)
Dream On: 'Tis a Pity She's a Neighbor (1994; HBO)... Jo
• 0:10—Left breast while sitting on sofa and talking to Jeremy.

Made for TV Movies:
Chance of a Lifetime (1991) . . . . Sherry
The Tower (1993) . . . . Sally
TV:
Eddie Dodd (1991) . . . . Billie

Guthrie, Lynne

Films:
Night Call Nurses (1972) . . . . Cynthia
a.k.a. Young LA Nurses 2
• 0:00—Breasts on hospital roof taking off robe and standing on edge just before jumping off.
The Working Girls (1973) . . . . Jill
••• 0:43—Breasts, dancing on stage at club.
•• 0:48—Breasts in swimming pool with Nick.
Tears of Happiness (1974) . . . . Lisa
Chesty Anderson, U.S. Navy (1975) . . . . Lt. Ambrose
The Witch Who Came From the Sea (1976) . . . . Carol

Gutteridge, Lucy

Films:
The Greek Tycoon (1978) . . . . Mia
Top Secret (1984) . . . . Hillary
The Trouble with Spies (1984) . . . . Mona Smith
Tusks (1990) . . . . Micah Hill
•• 0:23—Breasts in tub taking a bath.
Grief (1993) . . . . Paula
Made for Cable TV:
The Hitchhiker: In the Name of Love (1987; HBO)
. . . . Jackie
•• 0:08—Breasts on bed talking to herself about Billy after unzipping and opening the top of her dress.
• 0:16—Brief right breast, while pulling down her dress top in car with Greg Evigan.
•• 0:17—Breasts making love with Evigan in bed.
• 0:20—Breasts in B&W photos that accidentally fall out of envelope.
Miniseries:
Little Gloria...Happy At Last! (1982)
. . . . Gloria Morgan Vanderbilt
Till We Meet Again (1989) . . . . Eve
Made for TV Movies:
The Woman He Loved (1988) . . . . Thelma

Haas, Victoria

Films:
Prelude to a Kiss (1992) . . . . Bridesmaid #3
Poison Ivy 2: Lily (1995) . . . . Bridgette
• 0:11—Brief breasts, while making love in bed with a guy when seen by Alyssa Milano.
Made for Cable Movies:
Attack of the 50 ft. Woman (1993; HBO)
. . . . Deputy Charlie Spooner

Hackett, Joan

Films:
The Group (1966) . . . . Dottie Renfrew
Will Penny (1968) . . . . Catherine Allen
Support Your Local Sheriff! (1969) . . . . Prudy Perkins
The Terminal Man (1974) . . . . Dr. Janet Ross
One Trick Pony (1980) . . . . Lonnie Fox
••• 1:21—Nude getting out of bed and getting dressed while talking to Paul Simon.
Flicks (1981) . . . . Capt. Grace
Only When I Laugh (1981) . . . . Toby
The Escape Artist (1982) . . . . Aunt Sybil

Made for TV Movies:
Paper Dolls (1982) . . . . Julia Blake
TV:
Young Dr. Malone . . . . Gail Prentiss
The Defenders (1961-62) . . . . Joan Miller
Another Day (1978) . . . . Ginny Gardner

*Haddon, Dayle **

Model for Estée Lauder cosmetics.
Films:
Paperback Hero (1973; Canadian) . . . . Joanna
• 0:31—Lower half of buns, under T-shirt while standing behind a bar with Keir Dullea.
The World's Greatest Athlete (1973) . . . . Jane
Sex with a Smile (1976; Italian) . . . . The Girl
•• 0:23—Breasts, covered with bubbles in the bathtub.
• 0:43—Buns, taking off robe to take a shower, then brief breasts with Marty Feldman.
Spermula (1976) . . . . Spermula
The Last Romantic Lover (1978) . . . . n.a.
• 0:56—Breasts.
The French Woman (1979) . . . . Elizabeth
a.k.a. Madame Claude
• 0:15—Very, very brief breasts in dressing room.
•• 0:49—Breasts on bed with Madame Claude.
• 0:55—Breasts kissing Pierre, then buns while lying on the floor.
• 1:11—Left breast, then buns at the beach with Frederick.
North Dallas Forty (1979) . . . . Charlotte
Cyborg (1989) . . . . Pearl Prophet
Silence Like Glass (1989) . . . . Darlene Meyers
The Magic Bubble (1992) . . . . Susan
Bullets Over Broadway (1994) . . . . Backstage Well-Wisher
Made for Cable Movies:
Bedroom Eyes (1985; Canadian; HBO) . . . . Alixe
Made for Cable TV:
The Hitchhiker: Ghost Writer (1986; HBO) . . . Debby Hunt
(Available on *The Hitchhiker, Volume 3.*)
• 0:14—Breasts and buns, getting into hot tub with Willem DaFoe before trying to drown him.

*Hagemann, Tracy **

Films:
The Deadly Secret (1993) . . . . Sarah
• 0:37—Brief buns in panties.
• 1:22—Very brief right breast, several times, during rape on beach.

Hahn, Gisela

Producer.
Films:
They Call Me Trinity (1971; Italian) . . . . Sarah
Julia (1974; German) . . . . Miriam
•• 0:12—Breasts tanning herself outside.
• 1:14—Brief breasts sitting in the rain.
The Manhunters (1980; French/Spanish/German) . . . . n.a.

*Hahn, Jessica **

The woman in the TV evangelist Jim Bakker scandal.
Films:
Bikini Summer 2 (1992) . . . . Marilyn
• 0:03—In black bra in bed with Harry, then buns in black G-string, climbing on his back.
Amanda and the Alien (1995) . . . . T.V. Host

Made for Cable TV:
Dream On: And Bimbo Was His Name-O (1992; HBO) . . . . Reporter
Music Videos:
Wild Thing/Sam Kinison . . . . The Girl
Video Tapes:
Thunder and Mud (1989) . . . . Hostess
Playboy Celebrity Centerfold: Jessica Hahn (1993) . . . . Herself
•• 0:02—Breasts and buns in an old church by the beach.
••• 0:05—Nude and in lingerie in an old mansion.
••• 0:10—Nude outside with a guy.
•• 0:14—Breasts, in lingerie and swimsuits around town and at a beach.
••• 0:17—Nude in bedroom. Very nice!
••• 0:20—Nude in still photos.
•• 0:21—Nude in wigs in studio. Also wearing lingerie and other outfits.
••• 0:23—Nude, picking an apple off a tree, lying in bed with a snake.
••• 0:26—Nude, checking out different rooms in a hotel, then in a room with a man and a woman.
••• 0:32—In bra and panties on a Merry-Go-Round, then nude.

Haiduk, Stacy

Films:
Luther the Geek (1988) . . . . Beth
(Hard to find video tape, but worth it when you find it!)
••• 0:26—Breasts with Rob in the shower, then leaving. Wow!
••• 0:28—Breasts, after taking off her robe in bed, then making love with Rob.
Steel and Lace (1990) . . . . Alison
The Beneficiary (1996) . . . . Lena Girard
• 1:03—Brief breasts, while making love in bed with Jimmy.
•• 1:18—Brief breasts, several times, while making love with Jimmy in bed.
Made for Cable Movies:
Sketch Artist (1992; Showtime) . . . . Claire
Yesterday's Target (1996; Showtime) . . . . Jessica Harper
Made for TV Movies:
Danielle Steel's "A Perfect Stranger" (1994) . . Raphaella Phillips
TV:
Superboy (1988-91) . . . . Lana Lang
The Round Table (1992) . . . . Rhea McPherson
Seaquest DSV (1993-94) . . . . Lt. Katherine Hitchcock
Kindred: The Embraced (1996) . . . . Lillie

Haines, Patricia

Films:
The Last Shot You Hear (1969; British) . . . . Anne Nordeck
Virgin Witch (1971; British) . . . . Sybil Waite
•• 0:50—Breasts, during ceremony when Gerald makes love with Christine.
• 0:52—Brief left breast, while lying in bed after Christine gets out.

Hair, Connie

Films:
Nevada Heat (1982) . . . . Roberta
a.k.a. Fake-Out
• 0:13—Breasts in the shower scene.
• 0:14—Brief breasts in the shower again. Brief buns in shower (Long shot).
Teenage Bonnie and Klepto Clyde (1993) . . . . Waitress

Hale, Georgina *

Films:
The Boy Friend (1971; British) . . . . Fay
Mahler (1974; British) . . . . Alma Mahler
•• 1:00—Breasts during musical number.
The World is Full of Married Men (1979; British) . . . . Lori Grossman
McVicar (1980; British) . . . . Kate
The Watcher in the Woods (1981; British) . . . . Young Mrs. Aylwood
Castaway (1986) . . . . Sister Saint Margaret
Nightscare (1993; British) . . . . Sister Romulus

• *Haliwell, Geri* *

a.k.a. Ginger Spice from the singing group, The Spice Girls.
Films:
Spice World (1997; British) . . . . Ginger Spice
Video Tapes:
Spice Exposed (1997) . . . . Ginger Spice
•• 0:00—Nude in still photos throughout.

Hall, Daisy

Films:
I'm Dangerous Tonight (1990) . . . . n.a.
Made for Cable TV:
Women: Stories of Passion-Table Service (1996; Showtime) . . . . Diana
•• 0:06—Breasts, while making love with Ricardo in his office when Jo watches.
• 0:09—Brief breasts, while making love with Ricardo some more.
Made for TV Movies:
Another Midnight Run (1994) . . . . Hotel Clerk

• *Hall, Gabriella* *

Films:
Centerfold (1995) . . . . Gail
••• 0:06—Nude, after taking off her robe, dancing for Scott, then making love with him. A bit on the dark side.
• 0:18—Breasts, while asking Manny if she looks good enough to pose for a magazine.
••• 0:21—Full frontal nudity, while posing for photographs in Manny's studio.
Different Strokes (1996) . . . . Alicia
(Unrated version reviewed.)
••• 0:22—Full frontal nudity, while making love with another woman. (She's the brunette.)
• 0:35—Full frontal nudity, while sleeping in bed next to Katy.
Love Me Twice (1996) . . . . Andrea
Sexual Roulette (1996) . . . . Sally Wills
(Unrated version reviewed.)
•• 0:03—Full frontal nudity, while making love with her husband in the shower.
••• 0:15—In bra, then nude, while making love with her husband at home.
••• 0:29—Nude, while making love with her husband in hotel bathroom and bedroom.
•• 1:17—Breasts and buns, while making love with the other guy in bed.
Double Your Pleasure (1997) . . . . Melissa Lamb
••• 0:18—Breasts and buns in T-back, while making love with James in his fantasy.
••• 0:24—Breasts and partial buns, while making love in bed with James and Henry.

Made for Cable TV:

Erotic Confessions: The Bad Boy (1997; Cinemax) . . . . .Angela

••• 0:04—Breasts, when fantasizing about making love with Barry.

•• 0:06—Breasts, while fantasizing and caressing herself then making love with Barry next to photocopy machine

••• 0:10—Breasts, while making love Barry in office.

Beverly Hills Bordello: Inspiration (1998; Showtime) . . . . Candace

•• 0:01—Nude, while standing outside at night with Henry in his story.

• 0:12—Brief breasts and buns, with Henry in story some more.

•• 0:18—Nude, while tying Henry to a chain link fence.

•• 0:22—Nude, while making love with Henry in bedroom in "real life."

Intimate Sessions: Mary (1998; Cinemax) . . . . Jessie

• 0:01—Brief buns and breasts, taking off robe and lying on massage table.

•• 0:03—Very, very brief lower frontal nudity, then breasts, after turning over on her back.

••• 0:13—Full frontal nudity, while making love with Teddy in massage room.

Intimate Sessions: Tamara (1998; Cinemax) . . . . Didi

•• 0:05—In bra on desk with Chad, then breasts, while making love. B&W.

Hall, Jerry

Former model.

Significant Other of singer/actor Mick Jagger.

Films:

Urban Cowboy (1980) . . . . n.a.

Willie and Phil (1980) . . . . Karen

• 0:05—Brief breasts getting dressed in bedroom with Phil.

Running Out of Luck (1986) . . . . Herself

Batman (1989) . . . . Alicia

Freejack (1992) . . . . Newswoman

Princess Caraboo (1994) . . . . Lady Motley

Video Tapes:

Jerry Hall Yogasize with Vimla Lalvani (1993) . . . . Herself

Hall, Landon

Films:

Puppet Master III: Toulon's Revenge (1990) . . . . Uncredited Prostitute

• 0:15—Breasts (she's on right), giving the General a bath.

The Bikini Carwash Company (1992) . . . . Ms. Hawthorne (Unrated version reviewed.)

• 0:51—Buns in lingerie when her clothes get vacuumed off.

Body of Influence 2 (1995) . . . . Girl at Club

Forbidden Passions (1995) . . . . Cindy

•• 0:48—Breasts, while making love with Stephen in his office.

Over the Wire (1995) . . . . Susan

••• 0:11—In bra and panties, then nude, while making love in bed with Mark.

••• 0:30—Breasts and buns, while making love in bedroom with Bruce.

Stolen Hearts (1995) . . . . .Tess

• 0:51—Brief right breast during a dream.

••• 1:19—Breasts while making love with Justin.

Busted (1996) . . . . Lisa

Different Strokes (1996) . . . . Jill (Unrated version reviewed.)

••• 0:06—Breasts, while making love with Jack.

•• 0:17—Nude, while swimming in the pool with Dana Plato and getting out.

•• 0:20—Breasts, while taking a shower.

••• 0:25—Nude, while taking a shower with Dana Plato.

• 0:29—Brief breasts in flashbacks.

•• 0:32—Very brief breasts in flashback. Breasts, while making love in bed with Jack.

• 0:36—Brief buns, when getting up out of bed.

••• 0:55—Breasts, while making love with Dana Plato in bed.

• 1:13—Very brief breasts during Jack's flashbacks.

Little Witches (1996) . . . . Masked Girl

• 0:02—Partial breasts and brief breasts during ceremony.

The Escort (1997) . . . . Debra Gray (Unrated version reviewed.)

Maximum Revenge (1997) . . . . Tracy Quinn

••• 0:54—Buns and breasts, while making love with Mace.

Made for Cable Movies:

Ladykiller (1996; Showtime) . . . . Vicky Gallagher

Made for Cable TV:

Erotic Confessions: Games People Play (1995; Cinemax) . . . . Annie

•• 0:04—Breasts, after getting her bra unhooked during strip poker game.

••• 0:06—Breasts, then nude, proving to that she's blonde all over.

•• 0:07—Breasts, while sitting on Donovan's lap.

••• 0:12—Breasts, while making out with Laurel.

•• 0:14—Breasts, while making love with Annie and Donovan.

Erotic Confessions: Model Situation (1996; Cinemax) . . . . Bridgette

••• 0:00—Nude, after getting out of shower and checking herself out in mirrors.

• 0:02—Nude, while undressing for art class.

• 0:04—Buns in swimsuit, during fantasy.

•• 0:06—Breasts, while sitting in a chair during her fantasy.

•• 0:09—Full frontal nudity, while posing for art class.

••• 0:12—Nude, while making love with Jake in his studio.

Hot Line: Shutterbugs (1996; Cinemax) . . . . Susie

•• 0:03—In bra, then breasts, while starting to make love with Jack on kitchen table. Buns in panties when answering the phone.

••• 0:25—In black bra and panties, then breasts and buns, while making love with Jack.

Beverly Hills Bordello: The Lieutenant (1997; Showtime) . . . . Millicent

••• 0:09—Full frontal nudity, while having sex with Harry, standing up.

••• 0:13—Breasts, when having sex with Tess while Harry watches.

Erotic Confessions: Finders Keepers (1997; Cinemax) . . . . Annie

••• 0:07—Breasts and buns, while making love with Sam in her living room.

Intimate Sessions: Celeste (1998; Cinemax) . . . . Jan

••• 0:06—Breasts and buns, while making love with Michael on the sofa.

•• 0:23—Nude, while making love in bed with Michael and Celeste.

Intimate Sessions: Janine (1998; Cinemax) . . . . Janine

••• 0:04—Breasts and buns, while making love with Greg on couch.

••• 0:15—Nude, while making love with Greg again.

••• 0:21—Breasts and buns, while making love with Stuart on couch.

Hall, Leana

Films:

The Linguini Incident (1991) .... Tracy

Witchcraft III: The Kiss of Death (1991) .... Roxy

•• 1:08—Breasts on bed with William making love when Charlotte gets trapped in the room.

Made for Cable Movies:

Red Shoe Diaries (1992; Showtime) .... Ingrid
(Unrated video tape version reviewed.)

Hall, Susie

Films:

Forced Vengeance (1982) .... Dancer

• 0:57—Breasts, dancing in club with an Asian dancer.

A Killing Affair (1985) .... Blanche

Hallaren, Jane

Films:

Hero at Large (1980) .... Gloria Preston

Body Heat (1981) .... Stella

Modern Romance (1981) .... Ellen

Lianna (1982) .... Ruth

• 0:29—Brief left breast lying under Lianna during love making scene in bed. Dark.

Unfaithfully Yours (1984) .... Janet

Lost Angels (1989) .... Grace Willig

My Girl (1991) .... Nurse Randall

Hallier, Lori

Films:

My Bloody Valentine (1981; Canadian) .... Sarah

Warning Sign (1985) .... Reporter

Higher Education (1987; Canadian) .... Nicole Hubert

• 0:44—Right breast, twice, while making love with Andy in bed.

Blindside (1988; Canadian) .... Julie

Night of the Twisters (1995) .... n.a.

Made for Cable Movies:

Moonshine Highway (1995; Showtime) .... Rose

Made for Cable TV:

Poltergeist: The Legacy/Ransom (1997; Showtime) .... n.a.

Made for TV Movies:

A Woman Scorned: The Betty Broderick Story (1992) .... Joan

Incident in a Small Town (1994) .... Madeleine Harold

Buried Secrets (1996) .... Cynthia

Halligan, Erin

Films:

I'm Dancing as Fast as I Can (1981) .... Denise

Joysticks (1983) .... Sandy

•• 1:08—Right breast, then breasts and lower frontal nudity in bed with Jefferson surrounded by candles.

Halo, Debee *

Video Tapes:

Playboy's Hard Bodies (1995) .... Herself

••• 0:37—Nude, while posing in empty warehouse.

Halsey, Elizabeth

Films:

Cinderella (1977) .... Farm Girl (brunette)

••• 0:21—Nude with her redhead sister in their house making love with the guy who is looking for Cinderella.

•• 1:24—Breasts with her sister again when the Prince goes around to try and find Cinderella.

Cheerleaders Wild Weekend (1985) .... Susan/Pierce

••• 0:40—Breasts in red panties, in contest.

••• 0:41—Breasts with the other five girls during contest.

••• 0:43—Breasts, while getting measured with the other two girls.

Hamilton, Alana

See: Stewart, Alana.

Hamilton, Jane

a.k.a. Adult film actress Veronica Hart.

Films:

It's Called Murder Baby (1982) .... Sherry
(R-rated version of the adult film *Dixie Ray, Hollywood Star.*)

• 0:59—Buns, raising her skirt for Nick.

• 1:11—Left breast, sleeping in bed, then waking up and getting out.

Model Behavior (1982) ...... Uncredited Adult Film Actress

• 0:50—Breasts on TV monitors during playback of adult video.

Deathmask (1983) .... Victoria Howe

Delivery Boys (1984) .... Art Snob

R.S.V.P. (1984) .... Mrs. Ellen Edwards

Hollywood Erotic Film Festival (1986) .... Movie Buffs

•• 0:27—Breasts and buns, when making love with a guy in bed while two little stop motion creatures film them.

Sex Appeal (1986) .... Monica

••• 0:58—Breasts dancing on the bed with Tony in his apartment. Long scene.

Sexpot (1986) .... Beth

••• 0:28—In bra, then breasts with her two sisters when their bras pop off. (She's on the right.)

• 1:32—Breasts during outtakes of 0:28 scene.

Deranged (1987) .... Joyce

• 0:29—Buns, getting undressed to take a shower. Side of left breast.

• 0:37—Side view of left breast, taking off towel and putting blouse on. Long shot.

• 1:01—Breasts, changing blouses in her bedroom.

• 1:05—Breasts in bedroom, taking off her blouse with Jamie Gillis.

• 1:07—Breasts in bed when Jennifer wakes her up.

If Looks Could Kill (1987) .... Mary Beth

Slammer Girls (1987) .... Miss Crabapples

Student Affairs (1987) .... Veronica

•• 0:48—Breasts changing in dressing room, showing herself off to a guy.

• 0:51—Brief breasts in a school room during a movie.

•• 0:56—In black lingerie outfit, then breasts in bedroom while she tape records everything.

Wildest Dreams (1987) .... Ruth Delaney

Wimps (1987) .... Tracy

• 0:40—Lifting up her sweater and shaking her breasts in the back of the car with Francis. Too dark to see anything.

•• 0:44—Breasts and buns taking off sweater in a restaurant.

Young Nurses in Love (1987) .... Franchesca

•• 1:05—Breasts on top of a guy on a gurney.

New York's Finest (1988) .... Bunny

Sensations (1988) .... Tippy

Bedroom Eyes II (1989) .... JoBeth McKenna

• 0:50—Breasts knifing Linda Blair, then fighting with Wings Hauser.

Bloodsucking Pharaohs from Pittsburgh (1989) .... Grace

Cleo/Leo (1989) .... Cleo Clock

•• 0:13—Nude undressing in front of three guys.

• 0:21—Breasts changing in dressing room.

••• 0:22—Breasts changing in dressing room with the Store Clerk.
•• 1:07—Left breast and lower frontal nudity making love with Bob on bed.

Enrapture (1989). . . . . Annie
Party Incorporated (1989)
. . . . Uncredited Whipped Cream Wrestling Girl
a.k.a. Party Girls
Alien Intruder (1992) . . . . Turk's Mama
Ruby (1992) . . . . Telephone Trixie
Beauty School (1993). . . . . Countess Sophia Von Spatula
• 0:18—Left breast while leaning up while lying on massage table.
• 1:11—Partial left breast while lying in bed. Breasts, when sitting up.
••• 1:15—Breasts while lying in bed.

Boogie Nights (1997) . . . . Judge

Hamilton, Linda

Ex-wife of director James Cameron.

Films:

T.A.G.: The Assassination Game (1982) . . . . Susan Swayze
Children of the Corn (1984) . . . . Vicky Baxter
The Terminator (1984) . . . . Sarah Connor
•• 1:18—Brief breasts about four times making love on top of Michael Biehn in motel room.

Black Moon Rising (1986). . . . . Nina
• 0:50—Brief left breast, while making love in bed with Tommy Lee Jones.

King Kong Lives! (1986) . . . . Amy Franklin
• 0:47—Very, very brief right breast getting out of sleeping bag after camping out near King Kong.

Mr. Destiny (1990) . . . . Ellen Burrows
Terminator 2: Judgment Day (1991) . . . . Sarah Connor
Silent Fall (1994). . . . . Karen Rainer
Separate Lives (1995) . . . . Lauren Porter/Lena
•• 1:14—Brief right breast, when Jim Belushi kisses her breast on kitchen table.

Dante's Peak (1997) . . . . Mayor Rachel Wando
Shadow Conspiracy (1997). . . . . Amanda Givens

Made for Cable Movies:

A Mother's Prayer (1995; USA) . . . . Rosemary Holmstrom

Made for TV Movies:

Rape and Marriage: The Rideout Case (1980) . . . Greta Rideout
Secrets of a Mother and Daughter (1983). . . . . . .Susan Decker
Secret Weapons (1985). . . . . Elena Koslov
Club Med (1986) . . . . Kate
Go Toward the Light (1988) . . . . Claire Madison

TV:

Secrets of Midland Heights (1980-81). . . . . Lisa Rogers
King's Crossing (1982) . . . . Lauren Hollister
Beauty and the Beast (1987-90) . . . . .Catherine Chandler

Hamilton, Suzanna

Films:

Tess (1979; French/British) . . . . .Izz
Brimstone and Treacle (1982; British) . . . . . . .Patricia Bates
•• 0:47—Breasts in bed when Sting opens her blouse and fondles her.
•• 1:18—Breasts in bed when Sting fondles her again.
• 1:20—Brief lower frontal nudity writhing around on the bed after Denholm Elliott comes downstairs.

1984 (1984). . . . . .Julia
•• 0:38—Full frontal nudity taking off her clothes in the woods with John Hurt.
••• 0:52—Nude in secret room standing and drinking and talking to Hurt. Long scene.
• 1:11—Side view of left breast kneeling down.
•• 1:12—Breasts after picture falls off the view screen on the wall.

Out of Africa (1985) . . . . Felicity
Wetherby (1985; British) .Karen Creasy
Barbara Cartland's "Duel of Hearts" (1990; British)
. . . . Harriet Wantage
Tale of a Vampire (1992; Japanese/Chinese) . . . . Anne/Virginia

Hamilton, Wendy *

Films:

Warlock: The Armageddon (1993). . . . . .Model
The Dallas Connection (1994) . . . . Scorpion
• 0:26—Buns in outfit in bar.
••• 0:27—Breasts and buns in the shower.
• 0:38—Buns in outfit on stage in bar.
••• 0:40—Buns and breasts, while dancing on stage.
•• 0:56—Buns in wet suit, then breasts, while making love with Mark outside.

Play Time (1994). . . . . Brad's Secretary
(Unrated version reviewed.)
Ski School 2 (1994). . . . . .Lois Schnitzelbank
••• 0:23—Buns and breasts, when wearing ski boots, while doing a painting of a geeky guy out in the snow.
•• 0:55—Breasts while outside, doing a painting.
••• 0:56—In purple bra and panties, then breasts and buns, while making love with Alex.

Midnight Temptations (1995) . . . . April
•• 0:22—Breasts, while taking a shower.
••• 0:27—Breasts, while making love with Damon. Long scene.
•• 1:08—Breasts and buns in body suit, while making love with Danny.
• 1:20—Brief breasts in flashback.

Scoring (1995) . . . . Jill

Video Tapes:

The Best of Sexy Lingerie (1992) . . . . .Model
The Best of Wet and Wild (1992) . . . . .Model
Playboy Video Calendar 1993 (1992) . . . . October
••• 0:40—Nude, in auto garage setting. Sometimes covered with grease.
••• 0:42—Nude in fire escape setting.
••• 0:43—Nude with old movies projected on her and the walls.

Playboy Video Centerfold: Pamela Anderson (1992)
. . . . .Playmate
••• 0:26—Nude throughout.

Playboy's Playmate Review 1992 (1992) . . Miss December
••• 0:44—Nude in a house and then dancing next to a car.

Sexy Lingerie IV (1992) . . . . .Model
Wet & Wild IV (1992). . . . . .Model
Playboy's Sexy, Steamy, Sultry (1993) . . . . .Playmate
Sexy Lingerie V (1993). . . . . .Model
Sexy Lingerie: Dreams & Desire (1994) . . . . .Playmate
Wet & Wild: The Locker Room (1994) . . . . .Playmate
Playboy The Best of Jenny McCarthy (1996) . . . . . Herself
••• 0:24—Nude, while dancing with 3 other Playmates with fire and ice from *Wet & Wild: The Locker Room.*

Playboy's 21 Playmates: Volume II (1996) . . . . . .Playmate
••• 1:03—Nude in still photos.
••• 1:04—Nude in auto repair shop fantasy.

Hammond, Barbara

Films:

Angel III: The Final Chapter (1988) . . . . .Video Girl #2
- 0:34—Breasts (on the right) on video monitor during audition tape talking with her roommate.

Vampire at Midnight (1988). . . . . Kelly
- •• 0:07—Breasts and buns, getting out of the shower and drying herself off.
- 0:16—Left breast, dead, in Victor's car trunk. Blood on her.

Hampton, Demetra

Films:

National Lampoon's Last Resort (1993) . . . . Alex

Made for Cable TV:

Red Shoe Diaries: The Psychiatrist (1995; Showtime) . . . . .Linda
- •• 0:11—In black bra, then breasts when taking off dress while standing in front of window with a guy.
- ••• 0:12—Buns, after taking off panties. In stockings, while lifting up her dress then dropping it and caressing herself.
- 0:17—Brief breasts several times (distorted) in Denise Crosby's flashbacks.

Hancock, Lynn

Films:

Evilspeak (1981) . . . . Miss Friedemyer
- •• 0:56—In bra, then breasts taking off bra in front of fireplace. Buns in panties, walking up the stairs.
- ••• 0:57—Breasts and buns in the shower, then getting killed by pigs.

TV:

The Nashville Palace (1981-82) . . . . Regular

Hannah, Daryl *

Films:

The Final Terror (1981) . . . . Wendy

Blade Runner (1982) . . . . Pris

Summer Lovers (1982). . . . . .Cathy Featherstone
- 0:07—Very brief breasts getting out of bed.
- 0:54—Buns, while lying on rock with Valerie Quennessen watching Michael dive off a rock.
- 1:03—Brief right breast sweeping the balcony.

The Pope of Greenwich Village (1984). . . . . Diane

Reckless (1984). . . . . Tracey Prescott
- ••• 0:52—Breasts in furnace room of school making love with Johnny. Lit with red light.

Splash (1984) . . . . Madison
- 0:24—Partial buns, while running into the water at the beach. Looks like the bottom of her hair is taped to her buns.
- 0:27—Brief right breast, swimming under water, entering the sunken ship.
- 0:28—Buns, while walking around the Statue of Liberty.
- 1:26—Brief right, then left breast while in tank when Eugene Levy looks at her.
- 1:44—Brief right breast, under water when frogman grabs her from behind.

Clan of the Cave Bear (1985) . . . . Ayla

Legal Eagles (1986). .Chelsea Deardon

Roxanne (1987) . . . . Roxanne Kowalski

Wall Street (1987). . . . . .Darian Taylor

High Spirits (1988; U.S./British). . . . . Mary Plunkett

Steel Magnolias (1989) . . . . Annelle Dupuy Desoto

Crazy People (1990) . . . . Kathy

At Play in the Fields of the Lord (1991) . . . . . Andy Huben
- 2:09—(0:39 into tape 2) Brief buns, while swimming in the water.
- ••• 2:10—(0:40 into tape 2) Buns, getting out and resting by tree. Long shot, then breasts in (excellent!) closer shot. Very brief top of lower frontal nudity. (Skip tape 1 and fast forward to this!)
- •• 2:11—(0:41 into tape 2) Brief buns, running away after kissing Tom Berenger.

Memoirs of an Invisible Man (1992) . . . . Alice Monroe

Grumpy Old Men (1993). . . . . Melanie Gustafson

The Little Rascals (1994) . . . . Miss Crabtree

Grumpier Old Men (1995). . . . . Melanie Gustafson

The Tie That Binds (1995) . . . . .Leann Netherwood

Two Much (1995) . . . . Liz

The Last Days of Frankie the Fly (1997) . . . . Margaret
- 0:09—Partial buns in sexy outfit while talking with Kiefer Sutherland and Dennis Hopper.

The Gingerbread Man (1998) . . . . .n.a.

The Real Blonde (1998) . . . . Kelly

Made for Cable Movies:

Attack of the 50 ft. Woman (1993; HBO). . . . . . . Nancy Archer

Made for TV Movies:

Paper Dolls (1982). . . . . .Taryn Blake

The Last Don (1997) .Athena Aquitane

Hanson, Heather

Films:

Mask of Death (1994; Canadian). . . . . Danielle

New Eden (1994) . . . . Carmen

Bordello of Blood (1996) . . . . Babe

The Limbic Region (1996) . . . . Reporter #2

Profile for Murder (1996) . . . . .Julie Hollis
- 1:14—Breasts and buns, while playing around in the pool with Lance Henriksen.
- 1:15—Brief buns, while floating face down, dead, in the pool.

Exception to the Rule (1997) . . . . Woman in Strip Club

Made for Cable Movies:

Robin of Locksley (1995; Showtime) . . . . Secretary

Made for Cable TV:

Outer Limits: Paradise (1996; Showtime) . . . . .Young Helen
- •• 0:30—Breasts, taking off her nightgown for young Jerry.
- •• 0:31—Breasts, while making love with young Jerry in bed.

Poltergeist: The Legacy/The Inheritance (1996; Showtime) . . . . Rebecca

Outer Limits: Hearts and Minds (1997; Showtime). . . . . .Archer

Dead Man's Gun: The Fortune Teller (1997; Showtime) . . . . Irene Wilson

Harden, Marcia Gay

Films:

The Imagemaker (1985) . . . . Stage Manager

Miller's Crossing (1990). . . . . Verna

Late for Dinner (1991). . . . . .Joy Husband

Crush (1992; New Zealand) . . . . Lane
- 0:21—Very brief left breast while turning over in bed when her dad comes to look for her.
- 0:42—Most of breasts, while in bed with a guy.

Used People (1992). . . . . Norma

The Daytrippers (1995) . . . . Libby

Far Harbor (1996) . . . . Arabella

The First Wives Club (1996). . . . . .n.a.

The Spitfire Grill (1996) . . . . Shelby Goodard

Spy Hard (1996) . . . . Miss Cheevus

Desperate Measures (1997). . . . . .n.a.

Flubber (1997) . . . . Sara Jean Reynolds

Made for Cable Movies:

Fever (1991; HBO). . . . . Lacy

- 0:18—Brief breasts while making love in bed with Sam Neill.
- •• 1:31—In bra in bed with bad guy, then breasts when he opens her bra. Kind of dark.

Convict Cowboy (1995) . . . . Maggie Sinclair

Path to Paradise: The Untold Story of the World Trade Center Bombing (1997; HBO) . . . . Nancy Floyd

Made for Cable TV:

Fallen Angels: Good Housekeeping (1995; Showtime). . . Marie

Made for TV Movies:

Sinatra (1992). . . . . Ava Gardner

Hardin, Dana *

Films:

Beauty School (1993). . . . . Ashley

- 0:58—Breasts, dancing in cage in club.

Harding, Tonya *

Former Olympic ice skater.

Films:

Breakaway (1995) . . . . Gina Taylor

Video Tapes:

Tonya & Jeff's Wedding Night (1994) . . . . .Herself

- ••• 0:00—Nude, while making love with Jeff Gilloly on their wedding night. Long scene.

Hardy, Leslie

Films:

Sneakers (1992) . . . . Gregor's Date

The Mummy Lives (1993) . . . . Sandra/Kia

0:07—Partial breasts behind shower door. Probably a body double.

Night of the Archer (1994). . . . . Katherine Reggiani

- 1:15—Left breast and buns, while making love with Travis.

Hargitay, Mariska

Daughter of the late actress Jayne Mansfield and Mickey Hargitay.

Films:

Jocks (1986) . . . . Nicole

Welcome to 18 (1986). . . . . .Joey

- 0:26—Buns, while taking a shower when video camera is taping her.
- 0:43—Buns, while watching herself on the videotape playback.

The Perfect Weapon (1991) . . . . Jennifer

Bank Robber (1993) . . . . .Marissa Benoit

Leaving Las Vegas (1995) . . . . Hooker at Bar

Made for Cable Movies:

Blind Side (1993; HBO). . . . . .Melanie

Made for TV Movies:

The Gambler V: Playing for Keeps (1994) . . . . Etta Place

TV:

Falcon Crest (1988). . . . . Carly Fixx

Tequila and Bonetti (1992) . . . . Garcia

Key West (1993) . . . . Laurel

Can't Hurry Love (1995-96) . . . . .Didi

ER (1997-98). . . . . .Cynthia

Prince Street (1997) . . . . .Nina Echeverria

Hargreaves, Amy

Films:

Brainscan (1994). . . . . .Kimberly

- 0:06—Brief left breast, then brief breasts, while Edward Furlong video tapes her from his house.

Made for Cable TV:

Remember Me (1995; CBS). . . . . Amy Nelson

TV:

Matt Waters (1996). . . . . Chloe

Harlow, Jean *

Films:

Platinum Blonde (1931). .Anne Schuyler

The Public Enemy (1931) . . . . Gwen Allen

Red Dust (1932) . . . . Jantine

Red-Headed Woman (1932) . . . . Lil Andrews

- 0:17—Very, very brief right breast when Una Merkel passes over a pajama top and Harlow raises it over her head to put it on.

Bombshell (1933) . . . . .Lola

Dinner at Eight (1933). . . . . .Kitty Packard

Hold Your Man (1933). . . . . Ruby Adams

The Girl From Missouri (1934). . . . . .Eadie

China Seas (1935). . . . . .China Doll

Reckless (1935) . . . . .Mona Leslie

Libeled Lady (1936). . . . . Gladys Benton

Riff-Raff (1936) . . . . Hattie

Suzy (1936). . . . . .Suzy Trent

Wife vs. Secretary (1936). . . . . Helen "Whitney" Wilson

Personal Property (1937). . . . . Crystal Wetherby

Saratoga (1937) . . . . Carol Clayton

Video Tapes:

Hollywood Scandals and Tragedies (1988). . . . . . . Herself

- 0:24—Breasts in B&W still photo. Her head is turned toward the side.
- •• 0:26—Breasts in B&W still photos.

Harney, Corinna *

Films:

Vegas Vacation (1997). . . . . Girl at Blackjack Table

Made for Cable Movies:

Vampirella (1996; Showtime). . . . . Sallah

- •• 0:42—Breasts, while changing clothes in room.

Video Tapes:

Wet & Wild III (1991). . . . . .Model

The Best of Sexy Lingerie (1992) . . . . .Model

The Best of Wet and Wild (1992) . . . . .Model

Playboy Video Calendar 1993 (1992) . . . . June

- ••• 0:23—Nude, dancing in studio setting.
- ••• 0:25—Nude outside in the desert.

Playboy Video Centerfold: Corrina Harney (1992) . . . . Playmate of the Year 1992

Playboy's Playmate Bloopers & Practical Jokes (1992) . . . . .n.a.

Playboy's Playmate Review 1992 (1992) . . . . Miss August

- ••• 0:48—Nude posing in a house and then outside.

Sexy Lingerie IV (1992) . . . . .Model

Wet & Wild IV (1992). . . . . .Model

Playboy's Sexy, Steamy, Sultry (1993). . . . . .Playmate

Sexy Lingerie V (1993). . . . . .Model

Playboy Video Centerfold: Jenny McCarthy (1994) . . . . . Angel

Wet & Wild: The Locker Room (1994) . . . . .Playmate

Playboy's Sisters (1995). . . . . .Herself/Natural Woman

- ••• 0:22—Nude with her sister and four other sisters outdoors.

Playboy The Best of Jenny McCarthy (1996) . . . . . . Angel

- 0:31—Breasts in backstage scenes while being an angel.

Harnos, Christine

Films:

The Rescue (1988). . . . . Adrian Phillips
Forbidden Sun (1989) . . . . Steph
Denial (1991) . . . . Sid
Dazed and Confused (1993) . . . . Kaye
Judgment Night (1993). . . . . Linda Wyatt
Hellraiser: Bloodline (1996) . . . . Rimmer
The Girl Gets Moe (1997) . . . . Dotty

Made for Cable Movies:

Rebel Highway: Cool and the Crazy (1994; Showtime) . . . . Lorraine

- •• 0:43—Breasts, several times, while making love in bed with Michael.

TV:

ER (1994-) . . . . Jennifer Green

Harper, Jessica

Films:

Phantom of the Paradise (1974) . . . . Phoenix
Love and Death (1975) . . . . Natasha
Inserts (1976) . . . . Cathy Cake

- ••• 1:15—Breasts in garter belt and stockings, lying in bed for Richard Dreyfuss. Long scene.

Suspiria (1977; Italian). . . . . Susy Banyon
The Evictors (1979) . . . . Ruth
Stardust Memories (1980). . . . . Violinist
Pennies from Heaven (1981) . . . . Joan

- • 0:43—Brief breasts opening her nightgown for Steve Martin.

Shock Treatment (1981) . . . . Janet Majors
My Favorite Year (1982) . . . . K.C. Downing
The Imagemaker (1985) . . . . Cynthia
The Blue Iguana (1988). . . . . Cora
Big Man on Campus (1991) . . . . Dr. Fisk
Mr. Wonderful (1993) . . . . Funny Face
Safe (1995) . . . . Joyce

Made for Cable TV:

Tales From the Crypt: My Brother's Keeper (1990; HBO) . . . . Marie Hilton

Made for TV Movies:

On the Edge of Innocence (1997) . . . . Alice Walker

TV:

Aspen (1977) . . . . Kit Pepe
Little Women (1979) . . . . Jo March
Studs Lonigan (1979) . . . . Loretta

Harper, Samantha

Films:

I Never Promised You a Rose Garden (1977) . . . . Teacher in Ward D
I Ought to Be in Pictures (1982) . . . . Larane

- • 0:27—Breasts, while nonchalantly coming out to talk to Walter Matthau and Dinah Manoff.

Lookin' to Get Out (1982). . . . . Lillian

Harrel, Terri

Films:

The Dark Dancer (1994) . . . . Kitty
The House on Todville Road (1994). . . . . . Cornelia Todville

- • 0:22—Very brief side view of left breast (out of focus right breast in reflection in mirror), when taking off robe to get into bath.
- • 0:27—Upper half of breasts, while in bath.
- •• 1:06—Buns and right breast, while making love in bed with Adam.
- ••• 1:10—Breasts, while making love in bed with Adam. Brief lower frontal nudity.
- •• 1:12—Breasts, while sitting in bathtub.
- • 1:15—Brief partial breasts and lower frontal nudity, while sitting dead in bathtub.

Harrell, Georgia

Films:

Incoming Freshman (1979) . . . . Student
The First Turn-On! (1983) . . . . Michelle Farmer

- ••• 1:17—Breasts and brief buns in cave with everybody during orgy scene.

The Gig (1985) . . . . The Blonde

Harring, Laura

a.k.a. Laura Herring.

Miss U.S.A. 1985.

Films:

Silent Night, Deadly Night III: Better Watch Out! (1989) . . . . Jerri

- ••• 0:48—Breasts, while in bathtub with her boyfriend, Chris.

The Forbidden Dance (1990). . . . . Nisa
Dead Women In Lingerie (1991) . . . . Marcia
Exit to Eden (1994) . . . . M.C. Kindra/Trainer

Made for Cable Movies:

Black Scorpion 2—Aftershock (1996; Showtime) . . . . . . Babette

Made for TV Movies:

Rio Diablo (1993) . . . . Maria

TV:

General Hospital (1990-91) . . . . Carla Greco
Sunset Beach (1997-98). . . . . Paula Stevens

Harrington, Laura

Films:

The Adventures of Buckaroo Banzai, Across the 8th Dimension (1984) . . . . Mrs. Johnson
The City Girl (1984). . . . . Anne
The Joy of Sex (1984) . . . . Pretty Girl #2
Maximum Overdrive (1986) . . . . Brett
Midnight Cabaret (1988) . . . . Tanya Richards

- • 0:33—Very, very brief upper half of right breast while leaning back.
- • 0:34—Very, very brief left breast when a guy sticks his tongue out.
- • 0:43—Brief breasts when short guys rip her dress off.
- • 0:49—Very brief right breast in gaping nightgown, while bending over to put pants on.
- • 1:08—Brief breasts while making love with a guy.

Verne Miller (1988) . . . . Judge's Daughter
The Dream Team (1989) . . . . Nurse
Perfect Witness (1989). . . . . Jeanie Paxton
What's Eating Gilbert Grape (1993) . . . . Amy Grape
Devil's Advocate (1997). . . . . Melissa Black

Made for Cable Movies:

Linda (1993; USA) . . . . Stella Jeffries
Dead Air (1994; USA) . . . . Susan

Made for TV Movies:

The Secret (1992) . . . . Meredith Dunmore

Harrington, Tabitha

Films:

Crossover (1980; Canadian) . . . . Montgomery
a.k.a. Mr. Patman

- • 0:11—Brief right breast, then brief full frontal nudity lying in bed, then struggling with James Coburn in her room. Wearing white make-up on her face.

•• 0:29—Nude walking in to room to talk with Coburn, then breasts and brief buns leaving.

Star 80 (1983). . . . . Blonde

Harris, Christi

Films:

Rescue Me (1991). . . . . Cathy

Night of the Demons 2 (1994) . . . . Bibi

•• 0:39—In bra, while in bed with Johnny, then breasts.

•• 0:41—Right breast, then breasts, while making love in bed with Johnny. Intercut with distracting stuff.

Lurid Tales: The Castle Queen (1995) . . . . Amy

• 0:39—Brief right breast, while her and her sister make love with Tom.

•• 0:51—Breasts, while sitting and posing.

• 1:12—Very, very brief left breast during flashbacks.

Night of the Scarecrow (1995) . . . . Stephanie

• 0:37—Breasts, while making out in van with Danny.

Harris, Gail

a.k.a. Robyn Harris and Gail Thackray.

Films:

Party Favors (1987) . . . . Nicole

• 0:04—Breasts in dressing room with the other three girls changing into blue swimsuit.

• 0:11—Brief left breast in the swimsuit during dance practice.

• 0:12—Breasts during dance practice.

• 0:17—More breasts during dance practice.

•• 0:42—Breasts doing strip routine at anniversary party. Great buns in G-string shots.

••• 1:01—Breasts and buns in G-string after stripping from cheerleader outfit. Lots of bouncing breast shots. Mingling with the men afterwards.

• 1:16—Nude by the swimming pool during the final credits.

Takin' It All Off (1987) . . . . Hannah McCall

••• 0:03—Breasts in red leotard and head band, in dance studio.

••• 0:11—Full frontal nudity in the showers (she's in the back on the right.)

••• 0:28—Nude, doing strip routine outside.

•• 1:24—Nude, dancing with the other girls on stage.

• 1:29—Breasts in crate backstage with Hadem.

Angel III: The Final Chapter (1988) . . . . n.a.

Death Feud (1989) . . . . Harry's Girl Friend

•• 1:12—Breasts on bed with Harry.

The Haunting of Morella (1989) . . . . Ilsa

•• 0:38—Breasts in bed with Niles. Buns also when getting out and getting dressed.

Nudity Required (1989). . . . . Midge

•• 0:36—Breasts, asking Buddy a question. Brief breasts (tenth girl) standing in line.

••• 0:37—Breasts doing her song and tap dance audition.

• 0:44—Breasts while playing in pool.

Hard to Die (1990). . . . . Dawn Grant

a.k.a. Tower of Terror

••• 0:31—Breasts, while taking a shower.

Sorority House Massacre 2 (1990). . . . . Linda

•• 0:25—In bra and panties, then breasts while changing clothes.

Sins of Desire (1992) . . . . Monica Waldman

(Unrated version reviewed.)

• 0:00—Breasts in quick clips, while making love with Scott during nightmare.

Cellblock Sisters: Banished Behind Bars (1995) . . . . May

•• 0:43—Breasts and buns, while taking a shower.

• 1:05—In bra, then brief breasts, while making love with Detective Armand in prison conference room.

Forbidden Games (1995). . . . . Tonya

(Unrated version reviewed.)

••• 0:49—In bra and panties, then nude when taking a bath, letting Michael watch. Brief breasts in Michael's vision.

••• 1:12—Breasts and buns in pool with Michael, then in bathtub, then in bed.

• 1:18—Buns, while making love with in bed. Seen on TV.

• 1:21—Nude, while getting out of bed.

Galaxy Girls (1995). . . . . Cindy

••• 1:15—Breasts, while making love with Matt.

Masseuse (1995) . . . . Diane

(Unrated version reviewed.)

•• 0:08—In bra, then breasts and buns, while making out in office with Jack.

Virtual Desire (1995) . . . . Wendy

••• 0:54—Nude, after stripping out of her clothes in back yard in front of Brad and in swimming pool.

•• 1:01—Full frontal nudity after getting out of the pool.

••• 1:05—Full frontal nudity, when making love with Brad on the floor while he is blindfolded.

Made for Cable TV:

Dream On: Finale With a Vengeance (1996; HBO)
. . . . Catering Girl

•• 0:15—Breasts and buns, during party in Eddie's fantasy.

Video Tapes:

The Girls of Malibu (1986) . . . . Gail

••• 0:28—In two piece swimsuit. Nude taking a shower and drying herself off.

In Search of the Perfect 10 (1986) . . . . Perfect Girl #5

••• 0:31—Nude, while trying on all sorts of lingerie in dressing room.

Starlet Screen Test (1986). . . . . Susan

••• 0:31—In robe, on red sofa, then in bra and panties, then nude.

The Stripper of the Year (1986). . . . . Billy Jean

••• 0:32—Nude, stripping from red overalls and a hat.

•• 0:53—Breasts on stage with the other contestants.

Trashy Ladies Wrestling (1987) . . . . Fifi

•• 0:02—Buns in G-string, black bra, garter belt and stockings. Breasts getting oil dribbled on her.

Starlets Exposed! Volume II (1991) . . . . Gail

(Same as *The Girls of Malibu.*)

••• 0:07—Nude, taking off robe, taking a shower, then drying herself off.

Harris, Jo Ann

Films:

Mary Jane (1968) . . . . Jo Ann

The Gay Deceivers (1969) . . . . Leslie Devlin

•• 1:12—Breasts, after taking off her top in front of Elliott in his apartment.

• 1:14—Very brief accidental left breast, when Danny grabs her arm.

The Beguiled (1971). . . . . Carol

• 1:09—Right breast, while in bed under Clint Eastwood at night.

• 1:10—Brief left breast and side view of buns on top of Eastwood in bed. Brief buns, when discovered by Edwina.

• 1:11—Very brief right breast, covering herself up in bed. Very brief breasts shadow on the wall, then very, very brief right breast covering herself with a sheet and walking out the door.

The Sporting Club (1971) . . . . Lu
••• 0:55—Breasts (mostly right breast) while in the woods, talking to James.

Act of Vengeance (1974). . . . . .Linda
a.k.a. The Rape Squad
(Not to be confused with the film with the same name starring Charles Bronson.)
••• 0:06—Breasts, taking off blouse for rapist, getting fondled by him, running away, then getting hit.
• 0:09—Brief left breast, while getting her blouse afterwards. Dark.
• 0:37—Breasts under water with other women in spa. (She's the third from the left.)

The Deadly Games (1980). . . . . Keegan
a.k.a. The Eliminator
• 0:48—Breasts in the shower. Hard to see because of the pattern on the glass.

Miniseries:
Rich Man, Poor Man (1976) . . . . Gloria Bartley
TV:
B.J. and the Bear . . . . .Barbara Sue McCallister
Most Wanted (1976-77) . . . . Officer Kate Manners
Detective School (1979) .Teresa Cleary

Harris, Lara

Films:
Mannequin (1987) . . . . Mannequin in Photo Window
Blood Red (1988) . . . . Angelica
No Man's Land (1988) . . . . Ann Varrick
The Fourth War (1990) . . . . Elena Novotna
Too Much Sun (1990) . . . . Sister Ursula
The Fisher King (1991) . . . . Sondra
All Tied Up (1992). . . . . Kim Roach
Demolition Man (1993). . . . . Taco Bell Patron
The Dogfighters (1995). . . . . Mikaela/Mike
•• 1:03—Buns and breasts, while getting into and out of the shower.

Mercenary (1996) . . . . Joanna Ambler
Made for Cable Movies:
Inhumanoid (1996; Showtime). . . . . Katrina
a.k.a. Circuit Breaker
• 0:06—Brief half of right breast in nightgown, when leaning up in bed.
••• 0:08—Breasts and brief buns, after taking off nightgown after being instructed to do so and starting to make love with a guy on the floor.
• 0:12—Very brief left breast in flashback.
• 0:48—Brief left breast again in flashback. Also in bra, while struggling on bed with Richard Grieco and running from him in the ship.
•• 1:22—Breasts and buns, while making love with Grieco before killing him.

Made for TV Movies:
On Seventh Avenue (1996) . . . . Mary Ann

• Harris, Laura

Films:
Stay Tuned (1992). . . . . Girlfriend #1
Habitat (1996; Canadian) . . . . .Deborah Marlowe
•• 1:09—Breasts, taking off her blouse and going for a swim with Balthazar Getty, then getting dressed.
• 1:34—Very, very brief left breast before she falls into the water.

Made for Cable TV:
The Outer Limits: Feasibility Study (1997; Showtime) . . . Sarah
Poltergeist: The Legacy/Rough Beast (1997; Showtime) . . .n.a.

Harris, Lee Anne *

Identical twin sister of actress Lynette Harris.
a.k.a. Leigh Harris.
Films:
I, the Jury (1982). . . . . 1st twin
••• 0:48—Breasts on bed talking to Armand Assante.
• 0:52—Full frontal nudity on bed wearing red wig, talking to the maniac.
• 0:54—Brief breasts, dead on bed when discovered by Assante.

Sorceress (1982) . . . . Mira
a.k.a. The Devil's Advocate
••• 0:11—Breasts (on the left) greeting the creature with her sister. Upper half of buns, getting dressed.
•• 0:29—Breasts (she's the second one) undressing with her sister in front of Erlick and Baldar.

Harris, Lynette *

Identical twin sister of actress Leigh Harris.
Films:
I, the Jury (1982). . . . . .2nd twin
••• 0:48—Breasts on bed talking to Armand Assante.
• 0:52—Full frontal nudity on bed wearing red wig, talking to the maniac.
• 0:54—Brief breasts, dead on bed when discovered by Assante.

Sorceress (1982) . . . . .Mara
a.k.a. The Devil's Advocate
••• 0:11—Breasts (on the right) greeting the creature with her sister.
••• 0:29—Breasts (she's the first one) undressing with her sister in front of Erlick and Baldar.

Harris, Moira

Wife of actor Gary Sinise.
Films:
The Fanatasist (1986; Irish) . . . . Patricia Teeling
• 1:24—Brief breasts and buns climbing onto couch for the weird photographer.
• 1:28—Brief right breast leaning over to kiss the photographer.
• 1:31—Very brief side view of left breast in bathtub.

One More Saturday Night (1986) . . . . Peggy
Of Mice and Men (1992). . . . . Girl in Red Dress
Tall Tale: The Unbelievable Adventure (1994) . . . Sarah Hackett
Three Wishes (1995) .Katherine Holman
Made for TV Movies:
Between Love and Hate (1993) . . . . Katherine Templeton

Harris, Robyn

See: Harris, Gail.

Harrison, Cathryn

Films:
Images (1972; Irish). . . . . Susannah
The Pied Piper (1972; British). . . Burgermeister's Daughter, Lisa
Black Moon (1975; French) . . . . Lily
The Dresser (1983) . . . . .Irene
Duet for One (1987) .Penny Smallwood
Empire State (1987; British). . . . . Marion
A Handful of Dust (1988). . . . . Milly
Made for TV Movies:
Portrait of a Marriage (1992; British) . . . . . . Violet Trefusis
• 0:48—Left breast when Vita admires her.

Harrison, Jenilee

Films:

Tank (1984) . . . . Sarah

Curse III: Blood Sacrifice (1990). . . . . . Elizabeth Armstrong

••• 0:43—Breasts, while sitting in bathtub. Almost side of right breast when wrapping a towel around herself.

Illicit Behavior (1991) . . . . Charlene Lernoux
(Unrated version reviewed.)

Prime Target (1991) . . . . Kathy Bloodstone

••• 0:12—Breasts, while lying back in bed with David Heavener. Short, but sweet!

• 0:13—Partial right breast, visible under Heavener's arm.

Fists of Iron (1994). . . . . Julie

•• 1:03—Breasts, while making love in bed with Dale.

TV:

Three's Company (1980-82) . . . . Cindy Snow

Dallas (1984-86) . . . . Jamie Ewing Barnes

Harrold, Kathryn

Films:

Nightwing (1979) . . . . Anne Dillon

The Hunter (1980) . . . . Dotty

In Pursuit of D.B. Cooper (1981) . . . . Hannah

Modern Romance (1981) . . . . Mary Harvard

• 0:46—Very brief breasts and buns taking off robe and getting into bed with Albert Brooks.

Pursuit of D.B. Cooper (1981) . . . . Hannah

The Sender (1982) . . . . Gail Farmer

Yes, Giorgio (1982) . . . . Pamela Taylor

Heartbreakers (1984) . . . . Cyd

Into the Night (1985) . . . . Christie

Raw Deal (1986) . . . . Monique

Made for Cable Movies:

Best Legs in the 8th Grade (1984; HBO) . . . . . Leslie Applegate

Dead Solid Perfect (1988; HBO) . . . . Beverly T. Lee

Rainbow Drive (1990; Showtime) . . . . Christine

Deadly Desire (1991; USA) . . . . Angela

The Companion (1994; USA) . . . . Gillian Tanner

Made for TV Movies:

Man Against the Mob (1988) . . . . Marilyn Butler

The Rockford Files: Punishment and Crime (1996) . . . . n.a.

Outrage (1998) . . . . Deena

TV:

The Doctors . . . . Nola Dancy

MacGruder & Loud (1985) . . . . Jenny Loud McGruder

Bronx Zoo (1987-88) . . . . Sara Newhouse

Capital News (1990) . . . . Mary Ward

I'll Fly Away (1991-93) . . . . Christina LeKatzis

Harrow, Lisa

Films:

The Final Conflict (1981). . . . . Kate Reynolds
a.k.a. Omen III

• 1:28—Partial buns, then buns and side of left breast, getting out of bed and putting shirt on.

Shaker Run (1985; New Zealand) . . . . Dr. Christine Rubin

The Last Days of Chez Nous (1991; Australian) . . . . . . Beth

• 1:10—Brief breasts, while moving around in bed with Bruno Ganz.

Sunday (1997). . . . . Madeleine Vesey

Harry, Deborah

Lead singer of the rock group *Blondie.*

Films:

Union City (1980) . . . . Lillian

Videodrome (1983; Canadian) . . . . Nicki Brand

•• 0:16—Breasts rolling over on the floor when James Woods is piercing her ear with a pin.

Forever Lulu (1987) . . . . Lulu

Hairspray (1988) . . . . Velma

Satisfaction (1988) . . . . Tina
a.k.a. Girls of Summer

Tales From the Darkside, The Movie (1990) . . . . Betty

Dead Beat (1994) . . . . Mrs. Kurtz

Heavy (1996) . . . . Delores

Made for Cable Movies:

Intimate Strangers (1991; Showtime) . . . . Cory Wheeler

Made for Cable TV:

John Carpenter's Body Bags (1993; Showtime) . . . . Hair/The Nurse

Made for TV Movies:

L.A. Johns (1997) . . . . Madam Jack

CD-ROM:

Double Switch (1994) . . . . n.a.

Hart, Christina

Films:

Red Sky at Morning (1971) . . . . Velva Mae Cloyd

The Mad Bomber (1973) . . . . Fromley's Victim

The Roommates (1973) . . . . Paula

Games Girls Play (1974; British) . . . . Bunny O'Hara
a.k.a. The Bunny Caper
a.k.a. Sex Play

• 0:00—Brief lower frontal nudity and buns when her dress blows up from the wind.

•• 0:01—Full frontal nudity in slow motion, jumping into bed. Then nude, twirling around in another room.

••• 0:18—Nude, undressing with the other girls, then walking around the house to the pool, then swimming nude.

• 1:01—Brief breasts getting dressed.

Charley Varrick (1975) . . . . Jana

Johnny Firecloud (1975) . . . . June

•• 0:22—Breasts, lying in bed with Johnny.

••• 0:26—Breasts, opening her blouse in barn in front of Johnny.

Mean Dog Blues (1978) . . . . Gloria Kinsman

• 1:24—Brief breasts, in house with Gregg Henry.

The Check is in the Mail (1986) . . . . Janet

Hart, Diane Lee

Films:

The Giant Spider Invasion (1975) . . . . Terri

Cannonball (1976; U.S./Hong Kong) . . . . n.a.

The Pom Pom Girls (1976) . . . . Judy

• 1:02—Breasts, in locker room when asking Cheryl Smith to feel for a lump in her breast, then buns, after taking off her panties. Right breast and brief buns, while taking off panties.

Hart, La Gena

Films:

Million Dollar Mystery (1987) . . . . Hope

Born to Race (1988) . . . . Jenny

Made for Cable TV:

The Hitchhiker: The Last Scene (HBO) . . . . Leda
(Available on *The Hitchhiker, Volume 2.*)

•• 0:01—Breasts, while making love with a guy in bed.

Hart, Roxanne

Films:

The Bell Jar (1979) . . . . n.a.

The Verdict (1982) . . . . Sally Doneghy
Oh God, You Devil! (1984) . . . . Wendy Shelton
Old Enough (1984) . . . . Carla
The Tender Age (1984) . . . . Sara
Highlander (1986) . . . . Brenda Wyatt
• 1:30—Brief breasts making love with Christopher Lambert. Dark, hard to see.
The Pulse (1988) . . . . Ellen
Once Around (1990) . . . . Gail Bella
Made for Cable Movies:
The Last Innocent Man (1987; HBO) . . . . Jenny Stafford
••• 1:06—Breasts in bed making love, then sitting up and arguing with Ed Harris in his apartment.
Alone (1997; Showtime) . . . . Grace Ann
Made for Cable TV:
Dream On: Dance Ten, Sex Three (1992; HBO) . . . . Kate Gower
Dream On: The Undergraduate (1992; HBO) . . . . . Kate Gower
Dream On: Take Two Tablets, And Get Me to Mt. Sinai (1995; HBO) . . . . Martin's Lover
Made for TV Movies:
Samaritan: The Mitch Snyder Story (1986) . . . . . Carol Fennelly
Our Mother's Murder (1997) . . . . Anne
When Secrets Kill (1997) . . . . n.a.
TV:
Chicago Hope (1994-96) . . . . Nurse Camille Shutt
The Road Home (1994) . . . . Dr. Buerring

Hart, Veronica

See: Hamilton, Jane.

Harte, Christine

Films:
Cage II ...The Arena of Death (1994) . . . . Sexy Girl #2
Wish Me Luck (1995) . . . . Rachel
(Unrated version reviewed.)
•• 0:33—Breasts in fantasy with the Dream Man.

Hartman Black, Lisa

Wife of Country music singer Clint Black.
Films:
Deadly Blessing (1981) . . . . Faith
1:31—It looks like brief left breast after getting hit with a rock, but it's a special-effect appliance over her breasts. (She's supposed to be a man in the film.)
Where the Boys Are '84 (1984) . . . . Jennie
Made for Cable Movies:
Bodily Harm (1989) . . . . Laura
Bare Essentials (1991) . . . . Sydney Wayne
Made for TV Movies:
Just Tell Me You Love Me (1978) . . . . n.a.
Full Exposure: The Sex Tapes Scandal (1989) . . . . Sarah Dutton
The Return of Eliot Ness (1991) . . . . Madeline Whitfield
Without a Kiss Goodbye (1993) . . . . Laurie Samuels
Search for Grace (1994) . . . . Ivy
Someone Else's Child (1994) . . . . n.a.
Judith Krantz's "Dazzle" (1995) . . . . Juanita "Jazz" Kilkullen
Have You Seen My Son? (1996) . . . . n.a.
TV:
Tabitha (1977-78) . . . . Tabitha Stephens
Knots Landing (1982-83) . . . . Ciji Dunne
High Performance (1983) . . . . Kate Flannery
Knots Landing (1983-86) . . . . Cathy Geary
2000 Malibu Road (1992) . . . . Jade

Hartman, Valerie

Films:
Sleepaway Camp II: Unhappy Campers (1988) . . . . . . Ally
••• 0:06—Breasts waking up and stretching in bed, then standing next to bathroom.
• 0:33—Breasts in Polaroid photographs that Angela confiscates from the boys.
••• 0:39—In beige bra, then breasts in restroom stall with Rob.
••• 0:43—Breasts making love in the woods with Rob, then getting dressed. Nice!
Intimate Obsession (1992) . . . . Karen

Hartt, Cathryn

Films:
Pink Motel (1982) . . . . Charlene
••• 1:18—Breasts, dropping her sheet in room in front of Max and Skip.
The Seduction (1982) . . . . Teleprompter Girl
Open House (1987) . . . . Melody

Harvey, Susan

Films:
Caged Heat 2: Stripped of Freedom (1993) . . . . Lucy
• 1:00—Brief breasts, while in her cell, flashing to distract a guard.
Caroline at Midnight (1993) Lilli
•• 0:03—Breasts, while being held by Stan, while Judd Nelson tries to get information from Miguel.

Haslehurst, Lisa

Films:
Death Match (1994) . . . . Newspaper Receptionist
Killing For Love (1995) . . . . Barbara
••• 0:09—In bra and panties. Nude, after taking them off and making love with Jay Richardson.
• 0:15—Brief breasts, when flashing herself in car while RIchardson drives.
• 0:36—Partial right breast, with Richardson in bed.

Hassall, Imogen

Films:
The Long Duel (1967; British) . . . . n.a.
Bloodsuckers (1970; British) . . . . Chriseis
• 0:05—Right breast, while standing up at the beach and kissing Richard.
Take a Girl Like You (1970; British) . . . . Samantha
El Condor (1971) . . . . n.a.
When Dinosaurs Ruled the Earth (1971; British) . . . . n.a.

Hassett, Marilyn

Films:
The Other Side of the Mountain (1975) . . . . Jill Kinmont
Two-Minute Warning (1976) . . . . Lucy
The Other Side of the Mountain, Part II (1978) . . . . Jill Kinmont
The Bell Jar (1979) . . . . Esther Greenwood
• 0:10—In bra, then brief breasts in bed with Buddy. Dark, hard to see.
•• 1:09—Breasts taking off her clothes and throwing them out the window while yelling.
Gypsy Angels (1980) . . . . Jan
Massive Retaliation (1984) . . . . Louis Fredericks
Messenger of Death (1988) . . . . Josephine
Twenty Dollar Star (1991) . . . . n.a.
Made for Cable TV:
The Hitchhiker: Man of Her Dreams (HBO) . . . . . . Jill McGinnis

Video Tapes:
Inside Out 3 (1992). . . . . Cindy/The Houseguest

Hatcher, Teri

Wife of actor Jon Tenney.
Films:
The Big Picture (1989) . . . . .Gretchen
Tango & Cash (1989) . . . . Kiki
Soapdish (1991) . . . . Ariel Maloney
All Tied Up (1992). . . . . Linda Alissio
The Cool Surface (1992) . . . . Dani Payson
••• 0:20—Close-up of left breast, while lying in bed with Robert Patrick during daydream.
••• 0:27—Breasts, while standing in front of Patrick when he takes off her lingerie.
• 0:29—Brief right breast, when Patrick gets out of bed.
Straight Talk (1992) . . . . Janice
BrainSmasher... A Love Story (1993). . . . . Samantha Crain
Heaven's Prisoners (1995). . . . . Claudette Rocque
•• 0:40—Nude, while standing on balcony when Alec Baldwin first sees her, long shot at first, then closer shot.
2 Days in the Valley (1996) . . . . Becky Foxx
Tomorrow Never Dies (1997) . . . . Paris Carver
Made for Cable Movies:
Dead In the Water (1991) . . . . Laura Stewart
Made for Cable TV:
Tales From the Crypt: The Thing From the Grave (1991; HBO)
. . . . .Stacy
TV:
Capitol . . . . Angelica
MacGuyver . . . . .Penny Parker
The Love Boat (1985-86). . . . . Amy
Karen's Song (1987) . . . . Laura Matthews
Sunday Dinner (1991). . . . . .T.T. Fagori
Lois & Clark: The New Adventures of Superman (1993-97)
. . . . .Lois Lane

Hathaway, Amy

Films:
Kinjite (1989) . . . . Rita Crowe
The Client (1994) . . . . Karen
Courage Under Fire (1996) . . . . Annie
Joyride (1996). . . . . Tanya Baer
Made for Cable Movies:
Last Exit to Earth (1996; Showtime) . . . . Kali
• 0:00—Breasts (nipples are covered with a special-effect appliance), while in time travel contraption.
TV:
My Two Dads (1989-90). . . . . Shelby Haskell
Arresting Behavior (1992) . . . . Rhonda Ruskin

Hawn, Goldie *

Significant Other of actor Kurt Russell.
Films:
The One and Only, Genuine, Original Family Band (1967)
. . . . .Giggly Girl
Cactus Flower (1969) . . . . Toni Simmons
(Academy Award for Best Supporting Actress.)
There's a Girl in My Soup (1970) . . . . Marion
• 0:37—Buns and very brief right side view of her body getting out of bed and walking to a closet to get a robe. Long shot.
Butterflies Are Free (1972). . . . . Jill
Dollars (1972). . . . . Dawn Divine
• 0:04—Very brief partial buns, when Sarge slips some money under her nightie while she's lying in bed.
The Girl from Petrovka (1974). . . . . Oktyabrina
• 1:30—Very, very brief breasts in bed with Hal Holbrook. Don't really see anything—it lasts for about one frame.
The Sugarland Express (1974) . . . . Lou Jean Poplin
Shampoo (1975) . . . . Jill
The Duchess and the Dirtwater Fox (1976) . . . . Amanda Quaid
Foul Play (1978) . . . . Gloria Mundy
Lovers and Liars (1979; Italian) . . . . .Anita
Private Benjamin (1980) . . . . .Judy Benjamin
Seems Like Old Times (1980) . . . . Glenda
Best Friends (1982) .Paula McCullen
• 0:18—Very, very brief side view of right breast getting into the shower with Burt Reynolds.
• 1:14—Upper half of left breast in the shower, twice.
Protocol (1984). . . . . Sunny
Swing Shift (1984) . . . . Kay Walsh
Wildcats (1986) . . . . Molly
• 0:30—Brief breasts while in bathtub.
Overboard (1987) . . . . Joanna Slayton/Annie
Bird on a Wire (1990) . . . . .Marianne Graves
• 0:31—Buns, in open dress climbing up ladder with Mel Gibson.
• 1:18—Very brief top of right breast rolling over on top of Gibson in bed. Don't see her face.
Deceived (1991) . . . . Adrienne Saunders
Criss Cross (1992). . . . . Tracy Cross
•• 0:23—Buns and breasts in pasties, dancing on stage in club while her son watches.
Death Becomes Her (1992) . . . . Helen Sharp
Housesitter (1992). . . . . Gwen
Everyone Says I Love You (1996) . . . . Steffi
The First Wives Club (1996). . . . . Elise
TV:
Good Morning, World (1967-68) . . . . Sandy Kramer
Rowan And Martin's Laugh-In (1968-70). . . . . Regular

Hay, Alexandra *

Films:
Guess Who's Coming to Dinner? (1967) . . . . Car Hop
How Sweet It Is (1968) . . . . Gloria
Skidoo (1968) . . . . .Darlene Banks
The Model Shop (1969) . . . . Gloria
1,000 Convicts and a Woman (1971; British). . . Angela Thorne
The Love Machine (1971) . . . . Tina St. Claire
• 0:34—Brief breasts in bed with Robin.
• 0:38—Brief breasts coming around the corner putting blue bathrobe on.
How to Seduce a Woman (1973) . . . . .Nell Brinkman
• 1:05—Brief right breast in mirror taking off black dress.
••• 1:06—Breasts posing for pictures. Long scene.
• 1:47—Breasts during flashback. Lots of diffusion.
How Come Nobody's on our Side? (1976) . . . . Brigitte
One Man Jury (1978) . . . . Tessie

Hayden, Jane

Films:
Confessions of a Pop Performer (1975; British) . . . . .n.a.
Emily (1976; British). . . . . .Rachel
•• 1:09—Breasts in bed with Billy.

Hayden, Linda *

Films:
Baby Love (1969) . . . . .Luci
• 0:32—Buns, while standing in room when Nick sneaks in.
• 0:34—Very brief right breast, while throwing doll at Robert.

- 0:39—Breasts in mirror taking a bath. Long shot. Brief left breast hidden by steam.
- 0:52—Brief breasts taking off her top to show Nick while sunbathing.
- 1:25—Brief breasts, while calling Robert from window. Long shot.
- 1:27—Very brief breasts, while sitting up and talking to Robert.
- 1:28—Breasts in open robe struggling with Robert.

Taste the Blood of Dracula (1970) . . . . Alice Hargood
The Barcelona Kill (1971) . . . . .Linda
Blood on Satan's Claw (1971; British) . . . . Angel Blake
a.k.a. Satan's Skin
•• 0:40—Breasts, while undressing in front of priest to tempt him.
Confessions of a Window Cleaner (1974; British) . . . . Elizabeth
The House on Straw Hill (1976; British) . . . . Linda Hindstatt
a.k.a. Exposé
• 0:28—Breasts getting undressed in her room.
••• 0:47—Breasts, masturbating in bed.
•• 1:06—Right breast, in bed with Fiona Richmond.
Love Trap (1977). . . . . Gloria
a.k.a. Let's Get Laid
The Boys From Brazil (1978). Nancy
• 0:44—Very brief right breast, in mirror. Very, very brief left breast, twice, while in bed.
• 0:50—Very brief breasts, gagged, lying dead on bed.

Hayek, Salma

Films:
Mi Vida Loca (My Crazy Life) (1994) . . . . Gata
Desperado (1995). . . . . Carolina
• 1:10—Brief breasts in quick cuts, while making love with Antonio Banderas.
Fair Game (1995) . . . . .Rita
Four Rooms (1995) . . . . TV Dancing Girl
From Dusk Till Dawn (1995) . . . . Santamico Pandemonium
Fled (1996) . . . . Cora
Breaking Up (1997). . . . . Monica
Fools Rush In (1997) . . . . Isabel
Made for Cable Movies:
Rebel Highway: Roadracers (1994; Showtime). . . . . Donna
The Hunchback (1997; TNT). . . . . Esmeralda
Made for Cable TV:
Dream On: Domestic Bliss (1992; HBO) . . . . Carmela

• Hayes, Amy *

Video Tapes:
Playboy's The Girls of Hawaiian Tropic (1994) . . . . Wild Orchids
••• 0:22—Nude, while posing outdoors in the water.

Hayes, Julia *

Video Tapes:
Soft Bodies: Party Favors (1992) . . . . Herself
••• 0:22—Buns in sheer nightie, while posing on bed, then breasts during photo session.
••• 0:29—In bra and panties on couch, then breasts and buns.
••• 0:35—Breasts and buns, on floating bed in pool with Becky LeBeau.
Soft Bodies: Bathing Beauties (1996) . . . . Herself

Hayland, Lysa

Films:
Novel Desires (1991). . . . . .Linda
Made for Cable TV:
Dream On: Here Comes the Bribe (1992; HBO) . . Amanda
•• 0:01—Breasts, while making love with Martin on the floor.

Haynes, Linda *

Films:
Coffy (1973) . . . . Meg
The Drowning Pool (1976) . . . . Gretchen
Rolling Thunder (1977) . . . . Linda Forchet
Brubaker (1980) . . . . Carol
• 1:03—Breasts, while getting dressed with Huey in bedroom when Robert Redford comes in.
Human Experiments (1980). . . . . Rachel Foster

Hays, Lauren *

Films:
Alien Intruder (1992). . . . . Roni
Meatballs 4 (1992) . . . . Lauren
• 0:05—Brief breasts (she's on the far right), while taking off her black top in cabin with Miche and Hillary.
Ring of Fire II: Blood and Steel (1992) . .Bad Girl Gang Member
Round Trip to Heaven (1992). . . . . Contestant
California or Bust (1994) . . . . .n.a.
The Great Bikini Off-Road Adventure (1994). . . Lori Baker
• 1:06—Buns in swimsuit while giving a tour.
••• 1:11—In bra in house with her boyfriend, then breasts while making love with him.
Surf, Sand and Sex (1994). . . . . Hostess
1:04—Brief buns in two piece swimsuit during end credits.
Raven (1996) . . . . Brunette
•• 0:27—In bra, then breasts, when making out with the Senator in back of limousine.
Rebecca's Secret (1997). . . . . Gwen
••• 0:22—Breasts, while making love with Jonathan in kitchen.
••• 0:33—Breasts and buns in lingerie, while making love with a guy.
••• 0:55—Buns and breasts, while making love with Jonathan on couch.
•• 1:09—Breasts and buns, while making love with Max on table.
Video Tapes:
California Girl Fox Hunt Bikini Competition #6 . . . Laura
••• 0:03—Buns in two piece swimsuit.
• 0:48—Buns during review.
Hot Body International: #3 Lingerie Special (1992) . . . . Contestant
•• 0:48—Buns in white G-string and bra.
Hot Body International: #5 Miss Acapulco (1992) . . . . Contestant
• 0:13—Buns, under mini-skirt.
Buck Naked Line Dancing (1993). . . . . Dancer
••• 0:00—Breasts and buns throughout. She's in the front on the right, wearing a black wig.
BabeWatch, Episode 3: Sex Kittens (1994). . . . . . . Hostess
• 0:54—Brief buns in swimsuit, while dancing during end credits.
Raw Adventures (1994) . . . . Herself
BabeWatch, Episode 4: Naughty But Nice (1995) . . . . Hostess
• 0:09—Brief buns in swimsuit.
• 0:25—Brief buns in swimsuit.

Hayward, Rachel

Films:
Breaking All the Rules (1985; Canadian) . . . . Angie
••• 0:16—Breasts while changing in the bathroom.

• 0:43—Brief breasts after being felt up on roller coaster.
Xtro 2, The Second Encounter (1991) . . . . Dr. Myers
Just One of the Girls (1992). . . . . Ms. Glatt
a.k.a. Anything For Love
Knight Moves (1992) . . . . Last Victim
• 1:05—Very, very brief breasts screaming when the killer pulls the covers on the bed and flashes with a camera.
Time Runner (1992) . . . . Caroline Raynor
Suspicious Agenda (1994). . . . . Roxanne
•• 0:17—Left breast and side view of buns, while lying in bed.
• 0:18—Left breast (close-up) while kissing Richard Grieco in bed.
• 0:19—Breasts, when sitting up in bed.
•• 0:20—Breasts after Grieco leaves.
The Final Cut (1995). . . . . Barmaid
Made for Cable TV:
Stargate SG-1: Children of the Gods (1997; Showtime)
. . . . Guard #3

Hayward, Susan

Films:
Beau Geste (1939) . . . . Isobel Rivers
Adam Had Four Sons (1941). . . . . Hester
Reap the Wild Wind (1942). . . . . Drusilla Alston
Jack London (1943). . . . . Charmain Kittredge
Young and Willing (1943). . . . . Kate Benson
The Fighting Seebees (1944). . . . . Constance Chesley
Deadline at Dawn (1946) . . . . June Goff
Smash Up: The Story of a Woman (1947) . . . . Angie Evans
They Won't Believe Me (1947) . . . . Verna Carlson
House of Strangers (1949) . . . . Irene Bennett
Tulsa (1949) . . . . Cherokee Lansing
David and Bathsheba (1951). . . . . Bathsheba
Rawhide (1951) . . . . Vinnie Holt
The Lusty Men (1952). . . . . Louise Merritt
The Snows of Kilimanjaro (1952). . . . . Helen
With a Song in My Heart (1952) . . . . Jane Froman
• 0:48—Very brief upper half of left breast, when it pops out of the top of her strapless dress during song and dance number when she lifts her right arm over her dancing partner's head.
I'll Cry Tomorrow (1955). . . . . Lillian Roth
Soldier of Fortune (1955) . . . . Jane Hoyt
The Conqueror (1956) . . . . Bortai
I Want to Live! (1958) . . . . Barbara Graham
(Academy Award for Best Actress.)
Back Street (1961; British). . . . . Christine Allison
Stolen Hours (1963) . . . . Laura Pember
Where Love Has Gone (1964) . . . . Valerie Hayden Miller
The Honey Pot (1967; British)
. . . . Mrs. Lonestar Crockett Sheridan
Valley of the Dolls (1967) . . . . Helen Lawson

Hazelhurst, Liza

Films:
The Perfect Gift (1993) . . . . Pajama Party Guest
Video Tapes:
BabeWatch, Episode 1: Lingerie Fantasies (1994)
. . . . Herself
••• 0:10—Nude, while trying on lingerie on bed in house. Long scene.
••• 0:45—Nude, in bathroom, then taking a shower. Long scene.
••• 0:57—Nude, while posing on bed after end credits.

Headey, Lena

Films:
Waterland (1992; British/U.S.) . . . . Young Mary
• 0:16—In braless white undershirt, then brief breasts while making love with Tom in train.
••• 0:20—Breasts, while talking with Tom.
Century (1993; British) . . . . Miriam
The Remains of the Day (1993; British/U.S.) . . . . Lizzie
The Summer House (1993; British) . . . . Margaret
Jungle Book (1994) . . . . Kitty
Mrs. Dalloway (1998) . . . . Sally
Made for Cable TV:
The Hunger: Ménage À Trois (1997; Showtime)
. . . . Steph Reynolds
• 0:15—Full frontal nudity under sheer patterned dress, then making love with Jerry.
• 0:19—Brief breasts, while having sex with Jerry in stairwell.

Healy, Patricia

Films:
Sweet Poison (1991) . . . . Charlene
• 0:01—Breasts and buns, while straddling her husband in bed.
••• 1:05—Breasts, dropping her towel in front of Bauer in the bathroom.
•• 1:08—Side view breasts, straddling Bauer in bed.
The Bodyguard (1992) . . . . Sound Winner
Public Eye (1992) . . . . Vera
Ultraviolet (1992). . . . . Kristen Halsey
• 0:21—Brief breasts, after taking off blouse and posing for Esai Morales in motor home.
••• 0:50—In wet bra and panties, coming out of the pond. Side view of buns, then breasts while posing for Morales.
••• 0:52—More buns in panties and breasts in pond with Morales and struggling with him.
China Moon (1993) . . . . Adele
•• 0:02—Breasts, while in motel room with Charles Dance.
• 0:13—Brief breasts in B&W photos that Madeleine Stowe looks at.
Heat (1995). . . . . Bosko's Date
Theodore Rex (1995). . . . . Reporter #2
TV:
Bless This House (1995). . . . . n.a.
Love and Marriage (1996). April Nardini
NYPD Blue: Auntie Maimed (Apr 30, 1996) . . . . Ms. Archer

Heasley, Marla

Films:
Born to Race (1988). . . . . Andrea Lombardo
• 0:52—Buns, outside at night while kissing Joseph Bottoms.
The Marrying Man (1991). . . . . Sheila
a.k.a. Too Hot to Handle
Amore! (1993). . . . . Marge Apple

*Heatherton, Joey **

Singer.
Films:
Bluebeard (1972) . . . . Anne
• 0:25—Breasts under black see-through nightie while Richard Burton photographs her. Very brief right breast.
••• 1:46—Brief breasts opening her dress top to taunt Richard Burton.
The Happy Hooker Goes to Washington (1977)
. . . . Xaviera Hollander
Cry Baby (1990) . . . . Milton's Mother

TV:
Dean Martin Presents the Golddiggers (1968) . . . . Regular
Joey & Dad (1975) . . . . Co-Host

Heche, Anne

Films:
The Adventures of Huck Finn (1993) . . . . Mary Jane Wicks
I'll Do Anything (1994) . . . . Claire
Milk Money (1994) . . . . Betty
The Juror (1995) . . . . Juliet
•• 1:19—Brief breasts, while in bed with Alec Baldwin.
Wild Side (1995) . . . . Alex Lee
(Unrated version reviewed.)
••• 0:13—Breasts, while making love on top of Christopher Walken in bed.
••• 0:40—Breasts and buns, while making love in bed with Joan Chen.
•• 0:54—Breasts, while in dressing room with Chen.
•• 0:55—Breasts and partial buns, while putting on a bustier in dressing room.
Pie in the Sky (1996) . . . . Amy
• 0:24—Brief right breast, while making love with Josh Charles outdoors.
Walking and Talking (1996) . . . . Laura
Donnie Brasco (1997) . . . . Maggie
I Know What You Did Last Summer (1997) . . . . . . Melissa Egan
Volcano (1997) . . . . Dr. Amy Barnes
Wag the Dog (1997) . . . . Winifred Ames
Six Days, Seven Nights (1998) . . . . Robin Moore
Made for Cable Movies:
Against the Wall (1994; HBO) . . . . Sharon
Rebel Highway: Girls in Prison (1994; Showtime)
. . . . Jennifer
•• 1:02—Breasts, while walking in showers past the other girls, taking a shower and dropping a bar of soap.
Kingfish: A Story of Huey P. Long (1995; TNT)
. . . . Aileen Dumont
If These Walls Could Talk (1996; HBO) . . . Christine Cullen
• 1:14—Brief breasts, while sitting in bathtub and talking on cordless telephone.
Made for Cable TV:
Subway Stories (1997; HBO) . . . . Pregnant Girl
Made for TV Movies:
O Pioneers! (1992) . . . . Marie
TV:
Another World (1988-92) . . Victoria Hudson/Marley McKinnon

*Hefner, Lené **

Adult film actress.
Adult Films:
Zazel (1996) . . . . n.a.
Films:
Killer Looks (1994) . . . . Angela's Lover
(Unrated version reviewed.)
•• 0:22—In white dress, then breasts, while Janine Lindemulder makes out with her in parking lot of restaurant.
•• 1:11—In black dress, then breasts and buns, while making out with Lindemulder.
•• 1:18—Breasts, while sunbathing outside by pool with Lindemulder.
Video Tapes:
Fantasies 2 (1992) . . . . Model
BabeWatch, Episode 2: Show Offs (1994) . . . . Lene
•• 0:33—Breasts and buns, while stripping and dancing in patriotic outfit.

Heigl, Katherine

Films:
King of the Hill (1993) . . . . Christina Sebastian
My Father The Hero (1993) . . . . Nicole
• 0:14—Buns in white, T-back swimsuit, getting up of lounge chair and walking while Gérard Depardieu tries to cover her up.
That Night (1993) . . . . Kathryn
Under Siege 2: Dark Territory (1995) . . . . Sarah Ryback

Heilveil, Elayne

Films:
Payday (1972) . . . . Rosamond
• 1:21—Left breast while lying in bed after Rip Torn gets out of bed.
TV:
Family (1976) . . . . Nancy Lawrence Maitland

• *Heitmeyer, Jayne*

Films:
Sci-Fighters (1996; Canadian) . . . . Kirbie
• 1:23—Very brief upper half of left breast, when Billy Drago struggles with her on the floor and he yanks her bra up.
Made for Cable TV:
The Outer Limits: First Anniversary (1996; Showtime)
. . . . Barbara
The Hunger: The Face of Helene Bournouw (1998; Showtime)
. . . . n.a.
TV:
Sirens (1994) . . . . Jessy Jaworski

Held, Ingrid

Films:
Après l'amour (1992; French) . . . . Anne
Made for Cable Movies:
Spymaker—The Secret Life of Ian Flemming (1990)
. . . . Countess de Tubinville
• 0:59—Very brief side view of right breast, while getting knocked unconscious by Jason Connery.

Helfer, Britt

Films:
Raw Force (1981) . . . . Betty
• 0:39—Brief buns and lower frontal nudity when bad guy peeks in through window. Don't see her face.
Alley Cat (1982) . . . . Hooker
••• 1:00—Breasts, while handcuffed to the bed when Johnny searches her apartment.
Surf II (1984) . . . . Hot Potato #2
•• 0:25—Breasts taking off bikini top with her friend in lifeguard station at beach with Eric Stoltz and his friend.
•• 0:27—Brief breasts with her friend, after dropping towel when she raises her hands for the police.
The Princess Academy (1986; U.S./Yugoslavian/French)
. . . . Lulu Belle
TV:
Loving . . . . Lily Slater

Helgenberger, Marg

Films:
After Midnight (1989) . . . . Alex
Always (1989) . . . . Rachel
Blind Vengeance (1990) . . . . Virginia Whitelaw
Crooked Hearts (1991) . . . . Jennetta
Desperate Motive (1992) . . . . Connie
The Cowboy Way (1994) . . . . Margarette

Bad Boys (1995) . . . . Allison Sinclair
Species (1995). . . . . Laura
- 1:21—Very, very brief tip of right breast, when yanking off Michael Madsen's socks. Very brief left breast, getting up to pull his underwear down.

The Last Time I Committed Suicide (1996) . . . . Lizzy
Fire Down Below (1997) . . . . Sarah Kellogg
Species II (1998) . . . . Dr. Laura Baker

Made for Cable Movies:

Death Dreams (1991; Lifetime) . . . . Crista Westfield
Directed By: Partners (1994; Showtime) . . Georgeanne Bidwell
Lie Down with Lions (1994; Lifetime) . . . . Kate Neesen
Frame by Frame (1995; Canadian; Showtime) . . .Rose Ekberg
a.k.a. Conundrum
- ••• 0:38—Brief breasts, several times, while sitting in bathtub then standing up when startled by Michael Biehn.
- •• 0:53—Left breast, three times, while making love in bed with Biehn.

Gold Coast (1997; Showtime). . . . . Karen Dicilia
Thanks of a Grateful Nation (1998; Showtime) . . . Jerrilinn Folz

Made for Cable TV:

Tales From the Crypt: Deadline (1991; HBO) . . . . Vicki
- 0:08—Brief side of right breast putting on halter top in Richard Jordan's apartment. Don't see her face, but it looks like her.

Fallen Angels: I'll Be Waiting (1993; Showtime). . . . . Eve Cressy
(Available on the video tape *Fallen Angels Two*.)

Made for TV Movies:

In Sickness and in Health (1992) . . . . Mickey
Through the Eyes of a Killer (1992) . . . . Laurie
The Tommyknockers (1993) . . . . .Bobbi Anderson
When Love Kills: The Seduction of John Hearn (1993)
. . . . .Debbie Banister
Inflammable (1995) . . . . Lt. J.G. Kay Dolan

TV:

Ryan's Hope . . . . Siobhan Ryan
Shell Game (1987) . . . . .Natalie Thayer
China Beach (1988-91). . . . . . . .Karen Charlene "K.C." Koloski

Helmcamp, Charlotte J. *

a.k.a. Charlotte Kemp.

Films:

Posed for Murder (1988) . . . . Laura Shea
- 0:00—Breasts in photos during opening credits.
- ••• 0:22—Posing for photos in sheer green teddy, then breasts in sailor's cap, then great breasts shots wearing just a G-string.
- 0:31—Very brief right breast in photo on desk.
- ••• 0:52—Breasts in bed making love with her boyfriend.

Frankenhooker (1990). . . . . .Honey
- •• 0:26—Breasts yanking down her top outside of Jeffrey's car window.

Repossessed (1990). . . . . Incredible Girl

Video Tapes:

Playboy Video Magazine, Volume 3 (1983)
. . . . Video Playmate
- ••• 0:12—Nude in bubble bath.
- 0:14—Full frontal nudity in centerfold still photo.
- ••• 0:17—Nude in house and on bed while wearing a girdle.

Playboy Video Magazine, Volume 5 (1983) . . . . . Playmate
- 0:05—Briefly nude in bubble bath.

Playboy's Playmate Review 3 (1985). . . . . .Playmate
Playboy's 21 Playmates (1996) . . . . Playmate
- ••• 0:02—Full frontal nudity in still photos.
- ••• 0:03—Nude in bedroom.

Hemingway, Margaux *

Model.
Sister of actress Mariel Hemingway.
Granddaughter of writer Ernest Hemingway.

Films:

Lipstick (1976) . . . . Chris McCormick
- •• 0:10—Brief breasts opening the shower door to answer the telephone.
- •• 0:19—Brief breasts during rape attempt, including close-up of side view of left breast.
- 0:24—Buns, lying on bed while rapist runs a knife up her leg and back while she's tied to the bed.
- •• 0:25—Brief breasts getting out of bed.

Killer Fish (1979; Italian/Brazilian) . . . . .Gabrielle
They Call Me Bruce? (1982) . . . . .Karmen
Over the Brooklyn Bridge (1983). . . . . .Elizabeth
Frame Up II (1991) . . . . Jean
a.k.a. Deadly Conspiracy
Inner Sanctum (1991) . . . . Anna Rawlins
- 0:09—Brief buns and tip of left breast in office with Joseph Bottoms.
- ••• 0:23—In bra with Bottoms, then breasts, while in bed. (When you don't see her face, it's Michelle Bauer doing the body double work.)

Bad Love (1992) . . . . Jackie
a.k.a. Wild Angel
Deadly Rivals (1992) . . . . Agent Linda Howerton
Double Obsession (1992). . . . . Heather Dwyer
- •• 0:31—Right breast, while wearing Indian headdress and making love on top of Fredric Forrest in bed.

Inner Sanctum 2 (1994) . . . . Anna Rollins
(Unrated version reviewed.)

Hemingway, Mariel *

Younger sister of actress Margaux Hemingway.
Granddaughter of writer Ernest Hemingway.

Films:

Lipstick (1976). . . . . Kathy McCormick
Manhattan (1979). . . . . .Tracy
Personal Best (1982) . . . . Chris Cahill
(Before breast enlargement.)
- •• 0:18—Brief lower frontal nudity getting examined by Patrice Donnelly, then breasts after making love with her.
- •• 0:31—Full frontal nudity in the steam room talking with the other women.

Star 80 (1983) . . . . .Dorothy Stratten
(After breast enlargement.)
- •• 0:00—Breasts in still photos during opening credits.
- 0:02—Breasts lying on bed in Paul's flashbacks.
- ••• 0:22—Breasts during Polaroid photo session with Paul
- 0:25—Breasts during professional photography session. Long shot.
- 0:36—Brief breasts during photo session.
- 0:57—Right breast, in centerfold photo on wall.
- 1:04—Upper half of breasts, in bathtub.
- 1:05—Brief breasts in photo shoot flashback.
- 1:17—Brief breasts during layout flashbacks.
- 1:20—Very brief breasts in photos on the wall.
- •• 1:33—Breasts undressing before getting killed by Paul. More brief breasts layout flashbacks.

Creator (1985) . . . . Meli
- 0:38—Brief breasts cooling herself off by pulling up T-shirt in front of a fan.
- 1:10—Brief breasts flashing David Ogden Stiers during football game to distract him.

The Mean Season (1985) . . . . .Christine Connelly
•• 0:15—Breasts, while taking a shower.
Superman IV: The Quest for Peace (1987) . . . . . . Lacy Warfield
Suicide Club (1988) . . . . Sasha Michaels
Sunset (1988) . . . . .Cheryl King
Delirious (1991) . . . . Janet/Louise
Into the Badlands (1991). . . . . .Alma
Falling From Grace (1992). .Alice Parks
Deceptions II: Edge of Deception (1994; Canadian)
. . . . .Joan Branson
Bad Moon (1996) . . . . .Janet
Deconstructing Harry (1997). . . . . Beth Kramer

Made for Cable Movies:
Steal the Sky (1988; HBO). . . . . .Helen Mason
The Celluloid Closet (1996; HBO) . . . . Chris Cahill
• 1:21—Breasts and brief lower frontal nudity in a clip from *Personal Best.*
The Crying Child (1996; USA) . . . . .Madeline Jeffreys

Made for Cable TV:
Tales From the Crypt: Loved to Death (1991; HBO)
. . . . Miranda Singer
• 0:03—In black lingerie. Very brief buns.
•• 0:07—In bra, then side view of left breast several times in laundry room while Andrew McCarthy secretly watches.
• 0:21—More buns, while in lingerie.

Miniseries:
Amerika (1987) . . . . Kimberly Ballard

Made for TV Movies:
Desperate Rescue: The Cathy Mahone Story (1993)
. . . . Cathy Mahone

TV:
Civil Wars (1991-93) . . . . Sydney Guilford
On the 9/30/92 show, she had a well-hyped "nude" scene on network TV. You get to see very brief upper half of buns between gaps in some plastic and side view buns, while standing during photo shoot. Side view of buns later when looking at B&W photos. Forget the teasing and watch *Star 80.*
Central Park West (1995). . . . . .Stephanie Wells

Hempel, Anouska

Films:
On Her Majesty's Secret Sevice (1969; British). . . Australian Girl
Scars of Dracula (1970) . . . . .Tania
Sweet Suzy (1973) . . . . Lady Susan
Tiffany Jones (1973; British) . . . . Tiffany Jones
• 0:02—Brief breasts walking in from the surf in wet white dress.
•• 0:13—Breasts in bath. Buns also, getting out.
• 0:18—Brief left breast, taking off her top in front of bright light.
• 0:23—Breasts, several times, changing clothes in her bedroom.
•• 0:24—Breasts walking around her apartment in white panties.
• 0:31—Breasts in bubble bath.
• 0:32—Brief left breast, wrapping an orange towel around herself.
••• 0:39—Lying on table in black and red bra, then breasts. More right breast.
• 0:41—Side view breasts, covered with sweat.
•• 0:55—Breasts, partial lower frontal nudity, taking a shower.
• 1:26—Breasts, running outside in a field when guys rip off her dress.

TV:
UFO (1970). . . . . .SHADO Radio Operator

Hendrix, Elaine

Films:
Last Dance (1992). . . . . Kelly
•• 0:20—Breasts and buns of body double in bed with Jim. Don't see her face.
• 0:52—Buns in white lingerie outfit while dancing on stage during DTV contest.
Lover's Knot (1995) . . . . Robin
Romy and Michele's High School Reunion (1997) . . . Lisa Ludor

Made for Cable TV:
Fallen Angels: Since I Don't Have You (1993; Showtime)
. . . . Auditioning Blonde #1
(Available on the video tape *Fallen Angels One.*)

TV:
Get Smart (1995) . . . . Agent 66

Hendrix, Lori Jo *

Films:
Bikini Summer (1991) . . . . Smart Girl on Beach
A Sensuous Summer (1991) . . . . Dream Girl/Beach
••• 0:16—Nude on beach with dark haired girl in Jinx's dream.
•• 0:24—Breasts while kneeling on one knee in Jinx's dream.
•• 0:39—Breasts again while kneeling on one knee in Jinx's dream.
Prison Heat (1992) . . . . Bonnie
• 0:12—In bra, then brief breasts and buns, while undressing to enter prison.
•• 0:15—Breasts, while showering next to Michelle.
•• 0:28—Breasts, while getting raped by Hellena.
• 0:35—Breasts, while getting raped by the warden.
•• 0:36—Breasts, while showering, getting sick and throwing up.
••• 0:48—Full frontal nudity, after undressing in the shower room with the warden.
••• 0:51—Nude in the shower room after the warden leaves, slitting her wrist with a piece of the mirror.
• 1:13—In bra in open blouse, then left breast, while getting felt up by the warden.
• 1:15—Left breast, while getting molested on couch by Akim.
• 1:17—More left breast in bra, while getting molested by Akim.
Sunset Strip (1992). . . . . .Tammy
•• 0:54—Breasts, after taking off her swimsuit top for Crystal's video camera.
••• 1:12—Breasts and buns in G-string, while doing strip routine on stage.
• 1:16—Breasts in music video.
Stolen Hearts (1995) . . . . Sherrie
•• 0:23—In bra, then breasts and partial buns, while making love with David in storage room.
• 0:50—Brief buns in T-back, while starting her routine on stage.
• 0:57—Breasts, while making love with Brandon in spa.

Video Tapes:
Erotic Dreams 2 (1992) . . . . .n.a.
Playboy's Erotic Weekend Getaways (1992)
. . . . Escape: The Desert
•• 0:09—In white bra and panties in moving car. Breasts changing into dress.
••• 0:11—Full frontal nudity while making love in the back seat of the convertible.
••• 0:12—Nude, outside with her lover by the pool.
••• 0:14—Nude, bringing drinks out to the pool.

••• 0:15—Nude, swimming in pool. Some are under water shots.

Playboy's How to Reawaken Your Sexual Powers (1992) . . . . Cast Member

••• 0:12—Nude with her lover in the woods, a stream, a pond and under a waterfall.

••• 0:45—Nude, outside by beach with her lover. Also on air mattresses and snorkeling under water.

Starlet Screen Test III (1992) . . . . Sherry Miller

••• 0:09—In bra, then breasts while kneeling on table.

Intimate Secrets—How Women Love to be Loved (1993) . . . . Lori

••• 0:46—In white bra and panties, then nude in bed.

Playboy's Erotic Fantasies II (1993) . . . . Cast Member

Playboy's Secret Confessions (1993) . . . . Teacher's Pet/Ruth Ann and Twins/Cindy & Sandy

••• 0:26—In green lingerie, then breasts and buns, while making love in bedroom with Jay.

• 0:39—Breasts and buns in hallway and with Stuart.

••• 0:43—Nude in bedroom, then making love with Stuart on the living room floor.

BabeWatch, Episode 1: Lingerie Fantasies (1994) . . . . .Herself

••• 0:01—Nude, while trying on lingerie on steps in front of a house. Long scene.

••• 0:35—Nude, while taking a shower. Long scene.

••• 0:49—Full frontal nudity, while trying on lingerie again outside.

Hendry, Beverly

Films:

Rad (1986) . . . . Tiger

Hello Mary Lou: Prom Night II (1987). . . . . Monica Walters

• 1:03—Brief side view of buns and breasts, while getting undressed in locker room.

• 1:04—Nude in shower room with Vicki.

Made for TV Movies:

Laura Lansing Slept Here (1988) . . . . n.a.

Hendry, Gloria *

Films:

Black Caesar (1973). . . . . Helen

• 0:43—Very brief breasts when Fred Williamson rips her nightgown top off and struggles with her.

• 1:04—Brief partial back side of left breast and buns, while making love in bed with Williamson.

• 1:05—Brief full frontal nudity, while making love with Williamson in bed.

• 1:07—Brief right and left breasts, when getting out of bed.

Hell Up in Harlem (1973) . . . . Helen Bradley

Live and Let Die (1973; British) . . . . Rosie

Black Belt Jones (1974) . . . . Sidney

Savage Sisters (1974) . . . . Lynn Jackson

Slaughter's Big Rip-Off (1975). . . . . .Marcia

Bare Knuckles (1984) .Barbara Darrow

Pumpkinhead II: Blood Wings (1994) . . . . . . .Delilah Pettibone

Hengstler, Dee

Films:

Vice Academy, Part 2 (1990). . . . . Felatia

Vice Academy, Part 3 (1991). . . . . .Lulu

Good Girls Don't (1993) . . . . Rosie

It's Pat (1994) . . . . First Stripper

Junior (1994) . . . . Banquet Dancing Couple

TV:

NYPD Blue: The Bank Dick (May 16, 1995) . . . . Vera

• 0:49—Very, very brief buns in G-string when walking over to talk to Dennis Franz while on stage in strip club.

Henner, Marilu

Films:

Between the Lines (1977) . . . . Danielle

Bloodbrothers (1978) . . . . .Annette

Hammett (1982). . . . . .Kit Conger/Sue Alabama

The Man Who Loved Women (1983). . . . . Agnes Chapman

•• 0:18—Brief breasts in bed with Burt Reynolds.

Cannonball Run II (1984) . . . . .Betty

Johnny Dangerously (1984). Lil

Perfect (1985). . . . . Sally

Rustler's Rhapsody (1985) . . . . .Miss Tracy

L.A. Story (1991). . . . . .Trudi

Noises Off (1992) . . . . .Belinda Blair/Flavia Brent

Chasers (1994) . . . . Katie

Made for Cable Movies:

Love With a Perfect Stranger (1986; Showtime) . . . . .Victoria Ducane

Chains of Gold (1991; Showtime) . . . . Jackie

Made for TV Movies:

Dream House (1981). . . . . .Laura Griffith

Ladykillers (1988) . . . . n.a.

Fight for Justice: The Nancy Conn Story (1995). . . Nancy Conn

Titanic (1996) . . . . Molly Brown

TV:

Taxi (1978-83). . . . . Elaine Nardo

Evening Shade (1990-94) . . . . Ava Evans Newton

Marilu (1994) . . . . Host

Video Tapes:

Marilu Henner's Dancerobics (1992) . . . . Herself

Hennessy, Tess *

Video Tapes:

Playboy's Girls of the Internet (1996). . . . Girls of the Web

••• 0:19—In black lingerie, then nude while undressing and dancing in office.

Henninger, Corie

Films:

The Invisible Kid (1988). . . . . .Gung Ho Cheerleader

•• 0:38—Brief breasts (she's wearing a cheerleading skirt), while horsing around in the girl's locker room with a friend, then in bra, while talking to Chynna Phillips.

Copycat (1995) . . . . .Jogger

• 0:16—Brief left breast, while lying dead in bathtub.

Metro (1996) . . . . Jewelry Salesgirl 1

• Henry, Gloria L.

Films:

Phantasm III: Lord of the Dead (1994) . . . . Rocky

•• 0:52—Brief left breast, then breasts while making love in bed with Reggie.

Devil's Advocate (1997). . . . . .Tiffany

Henry, Laura

Films:

Heavenly Bodies (1985). . . . . Debbie

• 0:46—Brief breasts making love while her boyfriend, Jack, watches TV.

Separate Vacations (1985; Canadian) . . . . .Nancy

Hensley, Pamela *

Films:

There Was a Crooked Man (1970) . . . . Edwina
- 0:12—Very brief left breast lying on pool table with a guy.

Making It (1971) . . . . Bar Girl
Doc Savage: The Man of Bronze (1975) . . . . Mona
Rollerball (1975) . . . . Mackie
Buck Rogers in the 25th Century (1979) . . . . . . Princess Ardala
Double Exposure (1983) . . . . Sergeant Fontain

TV:

Marcus Welby, M.D. (1975-76) . . . . Janet Blake
Kingston: Confidential (1977) . . . . Beth Kelly
Buck Rogers (1979-80) . . . . Princess Ardala
240 Robert (1981). . . . . Deputy Sandy Harper
Matt Houston (1982-85) . . . . C. J. Parsons

Henstridge, Natasha *

Model.
Ex-wife of actor Damian Chapa.

Films:

Standoff . . . . n.a.
Species (1995) . . . . Sil
- 0:18—Brief breasts and very brief lower frontal nudity, after hatching from alien cocoon. Covered with gunk.
- •• 0:36—Breasts, while wearing white panties, getting dressed in motel room.
- 0:42—Brief breasts, after taking off bra in bathroom in front of Robby.
- 0:44—Brief breasts, while taking a shower to wash blood off herself. Hard to see through the door.
- •• 0:53—Breasts, while in the hot tub with John.
- 0:59—Brief breasts, when running outside, then brief breasts, while getting into car.
- •• 1:22—Breasts, after taking off dress in hotel room with Alfred Molina.
- •• 1:25—Left breast, while making love on top of Molina.

Maximum Risk (1996) . . . . Alex
- 0:45—Brief breasts and partial buns in panties, while changing clothes.
- •• 1:10—In black bra, then breasts and brief buns, while making love with Jean-Claude Van Damme in bathroom.

Species II (1998) . . . . Eve

Made for Cable TV:

The Outer Limits: Bits of Love (1997; Showtime) . . . Emma
0:20—Brief back part of right breast after taking off her dress in front of Tenney. Back side of left breast while posing.
- 0:22—Very, very brief right breast after posing.

0:25—Squished left breast, while lying next to Tenney in bed.

Herd, Carla

Films:

Deathstalker III: The Warriors From Hell (1988)
. . . . Carlisa/Elizena
- 0:20—Side view of right breast, while making love in tent when guard looks in.
- •• 0:46—Breasts taking a bath.

Wild Zone (1989) . . . . Nicole Laroche

Herred, Brandy

Films:

Some Call It Loving (1972) . . . . Cheerleader
- ••• 1:12—Nude dancing in a club doing a strip tease dance in a cheerleader outfit.

The Arousers (1973) . . . . n.a.

Herrin, Kymberly *

Films:

Ghostbusters (1984) . . . . Dream Ghost
Romancing the Stone (1984). . . . . Angelina
Moving Violations (1985) . . . . Queen
Beverly Hills Cop II (1987) . . . . Playboy Playmate
Roadhouse (1989) . . . . Party Girl
Money to Burn (1994). . . . . Linda

Music Videos:

Legs/Z.Z. Top . . . . Legs Girl

Video Tapes:

Playmate Playoffs. . . . . Playmate
Playboy Video Magazine, Volume 2 (1983)
. . . . Herself/Playboy Playoffs
- 0:33—Breasts in tug-of-war game.

Playboy Video Magazine, Volume 5 (1983) . . . . . Playmate
- 0:05—Brief full frontal nudity next to car.

Herring, Laura

See: Harring, Laura.

Hershey, Barbara *

a.k.a. Barbara Seagull.

Films:

Last Summer (1969) . . . . Sandy
- 0:19—Breasts after taking off her swimsuit top on sailboat with Richard Thomas. Hair is in the way.
- 1:30—Very brief right breast, after taking off her top in the woods.

The Baby Maker (1970) . . . . Tish
- 0:14—Side view of left breast, after taking off dress and diving into the pool. Long shot and dark. Buns in water.
- 0:23—Left breast (out of focus) under sheet in bed.

The Liberation of L. B. Jones (1970) . . . . Nella Mundine
Boxcar Bertha (1972). . . . . Bertha Thompson
- •• 0:10—Breasts, while making love with David Carradine in a railroad boxcar, then brief buns walking around when the train starts moving.
- 0:52—Nude, side view while in house with David Carradine.
- 0:54—Buns and breasts, while putting on dress after hearing a gun shot.

Diamonds (1975) . . . . Sally
The Stunt Man (1980) . . . . Nina
- 1:29—Buns and side view of left breast in bed in a movie within a movie while everybody is watching in a screening room.

Americana (1981) . . . . Girl
Take This Job and Shove It (1981) . . . . J. M. Halstead
The Entity (1983) . . . . Carla Moran
- 0:33—Breasts and buns, after getting undressed before taking a bath. Don't see her face.

0:59—"Breasts" during special-effect when The Entity fondles her breasts with invisible fingers while she sleeps.
- 1:32—"Breasts" again getting raped by The Entity while Alex Rocco watches helplessly.

The Right Stuff (1983) . . . . Glennis Yeager
The Natural (1984) . . . . Harriet Bird
Hannah and Her Sisters (1986) . . . . Lee
Tin Men (1986) . . . . Nora
Beaches (1988) . . . . Hillary Whitney Essex
The Last Temptation of Christ (1988) . . . Mary Magdelene
- 0:16—Brief buns behind curtain. Brief right breast making love, then brief breasts.
- 0:17—Buns, while sleeping.
- •• 0:20—Breasts, tempting Jesus.

• 2:12—Brief tip of left breast, lying on ground under Jesus.
• 2:13—Left breast while caressing her pregnant belly.
Shy People (1988). . . . . Ruth
A World Apart (1988; British) . . . . Diana Roth
Tune in Tomorrow (1990) . . . . Aunt Julia
a.k.a. Aunt Julia and the Scriptwriter
Defenseless (1991) . . . . T. K. Katwuller
Public Eye (1992) . . . . Kay Levitz
A Dangerous Woman (1993). . . . . Frances
Falling Down (1993) . . . . Beth
Splitting Heirs (1993) . . . . Duchess Lucinda
Swing Kids (1993). . . . . Frau Müller
The Pallbearer (1996) . . . . Ruth Abernathy
The Portrait of a Lady (1996; British/U.S.) . . . . Madame Serena
Made for Cable Movies:
Paris Trout (1991; Showtime) . . . . Hanna Trout
Made for Cable TV:
Abraham (1994; TNT). . . . . Sarah
Miniseries:
Return to Lonesome Dove (1993) . . . . Clara Allen
Made for TV Movies:
Flood! (1976) . . . . Mary Cutler
My Wicked Ways... The Legend of Errol Flynn (1985)
. . . . Lili Damita
A Killing in a Small Town (1990) . . . . Candy Morrison
Stay the Night (1992) . . . . Jimmie Sue Finger
TV:
The Monroes (1966-67) . . . . Kathy Monroe
From Here to Eternity (1980) . . . . Karen Holmes

*Hess, Michelle **

Films:
Sex and the Single Alien (1993). . . . . Meg
•• 0:04—Buns in sexy outfit, while walking to Olivia's house and talking with her.
Taxi Dancers (1993) . . . . Candy
Video Tapes:
Playboy's Erotic Weekend Getaways (1992)
. . . . Indulgence: The Spa

Hess, Sandra

Films:
Encino Man (1992). . . . . Cave Nug
Endangered (1994) . . . . Kate
•• 0:18—Very brief breasts, when jumping up and splashing water in the lake. Brief breasts while standing up in lake (closer shot).
•• 0:19—Buns, while getting out of the lake and getting blanket.
• 0:20—Brief breasts, while turning around and putting on blouse.
•• 0:38—Buns and back side of left breast while taking a bath outside. Breasts in long shot, then closer shot.
BeastMaster III: The Eye of Braxus (1995) . . . . Shada
Mortal Kombat: Annihilation (1997) . . . . Sonya Blade

Hetrick, Jennifer

a.k.a. Jenni Hetrick.
Films:
Squeeze Play (1979). . . . . Samantha
a.k.a. Jenni Hetrick.
•• 0:00—Breasts in bed after making love.
• 0:26—Right breast, brief breasts with Wes on the floor.
Made for Cable Movies:
And Then There Was One (1994; Lifetime) . . . . Janet
Made for Cable TV:
Perversions of Science: Snap Ending (1997; HBO)
. . . . Captain Kate Branch
Made for TV Movies:
Absolute Strangers (1991). Nancy Klein
TV:
L.A. Law (1989-94) . . . . Connie Hammond
UNSUB (1989) . . . . Ann Madison
Bodies of Evidence (1992-93) . . . . Det. Haughton

*Hey, Virginia **

Films:
The Road Warrior (1981). . . . . Warrior Woman
Norman Loves Rose (1982; Australian) . . . . The Girlfriend
Castaway (1986) . . . . Janice
The Living Daylights (1987)
. . . . Rubavitch (Colonel Pushkin's girlfriend)
• 1:10—Brief side view of left breast when James Bond uses her to distract bodyguard.
Obsession: A Taste For Fear (1987) . . . . Diane
• 0:02—Breasts, lying in sauna.
• 0:04—Buns and very brief side view of right breast dropping towel to take a shower.
•• 0:14—Brief right breast in bed when sheet falls down.
• 0:37—Most of left breast, while crying.
• 0:39—Breasts, lying in bed talking to Kim.
••• 1:03—Breasts waking up in bed.
• 1:05—Breasts, getting ready to get dressed. Long shot.
••• 1:17—Breasts in hallway with Valerie.
• 1:19—Brief lower frontal nudity and right breast in bed with Valerie, then buns in bed.
••• 1:20—Breasts getting dressed, walking and running around the house when Valerie gets killed.
• 1:26—Breasts tied up in chair while Paul torments her. Lit with red light.

*Heywood, Anne **

Films:
Checkpoint (1957; British). . . . . Gabriela
The Fox (1967) . . . . March
•• 0:10—Right breast seen in reflection in mirror. Long shot of buns, when standing in front of mirror. Breasts, while rubbing lotion on herself. More buns, after the lights go out. Very impressive for 1967!
• 1:28—Very brief, partial squished left breast, while making love with Kier Dullea.
The Lady of Monza (1970; Italian). . . . . Virginia de Leyva
Trader Horn (1973) . . . . Nicole
The Shaming (1979). Evelyn Wyckoff
a.k.a. Good Luck, Miss Wyckoff
a.k.a. The Sin
••• 0:49—Right breast, then breasts in open blouse after being raped by Rafe in her classroom.
• 0:52—Breasts, while making love with Rafe on classroom floor.
What Waits Below (1986) . . . . Frida Shelley

*• Hiatt, Shana **

Video Tapes:
Playboy's The Girls of Hawaiian Tropic (1994)
. . . . Volcano
••• 0:52—Nude, while outdoors in the surf at night.

Hickey, Marilyn Faith

Films:

Incoming Freshman (1979). . . . Sargeant Laverne Finterplay
- 0:06—Breasts and buns when Professor Bilbo fantasizes about her.
- 0:56—Breasts and buns during Bilbo's fantasy.
- 1:18—Breasts during end credits.

The Night the Lights Went Out in Georgia (1981) . . . . Woman on Bus

Hickland, Catherine

Wife of actor Michael Knight.

Ex-wife of actor David Hasselhoff.

Films:

The Last Married Couple in America (1980). . . . . Rebecca

Ghost Town (1988) . . . . Kate

Witchery (1988) . . . . Linda Sullivan

Millions (1990) . . . . Connie
- 0:36—Buns, getting out of bed to open safe. Don't see her face, probably a body double because the hair is too dark.
- 1:20—Buns, walking away from John Stockwell. Very brief back side of right breast, when she bends over to pick up blouse. Don't see her face.

Sweet Justice (1991) . . . . Chris Barnes
- 0:52—Brief buns and left breast, getting into spa. (You don't see her face clearly, it looks like a body double because her hair is different.)
- •• 0:53—Brief upper half of left breast, while sitting in spa. This is definitely her!

TV:

Capitol . . . . Julie Clegg

Loving . . . . .Tess

Texas (1980-82) .Dr. Courtney Marshall

The City (1995-97) . . . . .Tess Wilder Partou Huston

Hicks, Catherine

Films:

Death Valley (1982). . . . . Sally

Better Late Than Never (1983; British). . . . . .Sable

Garbo Talks (1984) . . . . Jane

The Razor's Edge (1984) . . . . Isabel
- 0:43—Brief upper half of left breast, in bed after seeing a cockroach.

Fever Pitch (1985) . . . . Flo
- 0:11—Brief left breast, while sitting on bed in hotel room talking with Ryan O'Neal.

Peggy Sue Got Married (1986) . . . . Carol Heath

Star Trek IV: The Voyage Home (1986) . . . . .Gillian Taylor

Like Father, Like Son (1987). . . . . Dr. Amy Larkin

Child's Play (1988) . . . . Karen Barclay

Souvenir (1988; British). . . . . .Tina Boyer

Daddy's Little Girl (1989) . . . . .n.a.

Running Against Time (1990) . . . . .n.a.

Liebestraum (1991). . . . . Mary Parker

(Unrated Director's cut reviewed.)

Dillinger and Capone (1994). . . . . Abigail

Turbulence (1996). . . . . .Maggie

Made for Cable Movies:

Laguna Heat (1987; HBO) . . . . Jane Algernon
- •• 0:50—Breasts and buns, running around the beach with Harry Hamlin.
- •• 1:05—Brief breasts in bed making love with Harry Hamlin, having her head hit the headboard.

Made for TV Movies:

Marilyn: The Untold Story (1980) . . . . Marilyn Monroe

Hi Honey—I'm Dead (1991) . . . . .Carol

Redwood Curtain (1995). Julia Riordan

TV:

Ryan's Hope. . . . . Dr. Faith Coleridge

The Bad News Bears (1979-80) . . . . Dr. Emily Rappant

Tucker's Witch (1982-83). . . . . .Amanda Tucker

Winnetaka Road (1994) . . . . Jeannie

7th Heaven (1996-) . . . . Annie Camden

Higgins, Clare

Films:

1919 (1984; British). . . . . Young Sophie

Hellraiser (1987) . . . . Julia
- 0:17—Very, very brief left breast and buns making love with Frank.

Hellraiser II—Hellbound (1988) . . . . Julia
- 0:20—Very, very brief right breast, lying in bed with Frank. Scene from *Hellraiser.*

Wonderland (1989; British) . . . . Eve

Bad Behaviour (1992; British) . . . . Jessica Kennedy

Small Faces (1996; British). . . . . Lorna

Made for Cable Movies:

Fatherland (1994; HBO). . . . . .Klara

Higginson, Jane

Films:

Danger Zone II: Reaper's Revenge (1988). . . . . Donna
- •• 0:17—Breasts, while unconscious on sofa while the bad guys take Polaroid photos.
- 0:18—Brief breasts seen in the photo that Wade looks at.
- 0:22—Brief left breast, while adjusting her blouse outside. Long shot.
- 0:34—Left breast seen in another Polaroid photograph.

Slaughterhouse (1988) . . . . Annie

Silent Night, Deadly Night 5: The Toy Maker (1991) . . . . Sarah Quinn

Object of Obsession (1994). . . . . .Vicky

T-Force (1994). . . . . Hostage

The Silencers (1995) . . . . Joan

Access Denied (1996). . . . . Dawn Able
- •• 0:42—In black bra, then breasts, while making love with Bill in office.
- •• 1:01—Breasts, while making love with Raymond at her house.

TV:

General Hospital . . . . Arielle Ashton

High, Angelina

Films:

The Perfect Gift (1993) . . . . .Pajama Party Guest

Made for Cable TV:

Love Street: Ex-Girlfriend (1994; Showtime) . . . . Dana
- ••• 0:07—Breasts and lower frontal nudity while making love with Parker in his office. Breasts in wedding dream.
- 0:17—Brief buns in panties and brief breasts in wedding dream.

Hight, Ahmo *

Video Tapes:

Playboy's Hard Bodies (1995). . . . . Herself
- ••• 0:46—Nude, while posing at the beach by herself and two other women.

Hill, Mariana

Films:

Paradise, Hawaiian Style (1966). . . . . Lani

Medium Cool (1969) .... Ruth
- 0:18—Close-up of breast in bed with John.
- •• 0:36—Nude, running around the house frolicking with John.

El Condor (1971) .... Claudine
Thumb Tripping (1972)........................ Lynn
- 1:14—In black bra, then very, very brief left breast when Jack comes to cover her up.
- 1:19—Breasts frolicking in the water with Gary.

High Plains Drifter (1973) .... Callie Travers
Dead People (1974) .... Arletty
The Godfather, Part II (1974) .... Deanna Corleone
The Last Porno Flick (1974)......................... n.a.
Schizoid (1980)................................ Julie
- 0:58—Left breast, while making love in bed with Klaus Kinski. Dark, hard to see.

Blood Beach (1981) .... Catherine

Hill, Teresa
Films:
Puppet Master 4 (1993) .... Lauren
In the Heat of Passion II: Unfaithful (1994)....... Casey
a.k.a. Behind Closed Doors
(Unrated version reviewed.)
(All other nude shots are a body double.)
- 0:20—Very, very brief left breast while in bed with Barry Bostwick. (Seen at bottom of screen.)
- 0:21—Very brief right breast with Bostwick.
- 0:22—Very brief left breast, while rolling over in bed on top of Bostwick.
- 1:18—Very brief left breast, while rolling over (from 0:22) in flashback.

Puppet Master 5 (1994) .... Lauren
Bio-Dome (1995) .... Jen
TV:
Models Inc. (1994-95) .... Linda Holden

Hills, Gillian
Films:
Beat Girl (1962; British)...................... Jennifer
Blow-Up (1966; British/Italian).................. Teenager
- 1:08—Brief breasts and very, very brief lower frontal nudity while frolicking with David Hemmings and Jane Birkin in the studio.

Three (1969; British)............................. Ann
A Clockwork Orange (1971) .... Sonietta
Demons of the Mind (1972; British) .... Elizabeth

Hilton, Robyn
Films:
Bloody Friday (1973)........................... Denise
a.k.a. Single Girls
Video Vixens (1973)........................... Inga
- •• 1:18—Breasts, opening her top in a room full of reporters.

Blazing Saddles (1974) .... Governor's Secretary
The Last Porno Flick (1974)......................... n.a.
Doc Savage: The Man of Bronze (1975) .... n.a.
Malibu Express (1984) .... Maid Marian

Hippe, Laura
Films:
Logan's Run (1976)............. New You Shop Customer
Stay Hungry (1976) .... May Ruth
- 1:19—Brief buns, hanging upside down in gym.

The Swinging Barmaids (1976)....................... n.a.
Mausoleum (1983) .... Aunt Cora

Hoak, Clare
Films:
Masque of the Red Death (1990)................. Julietta
Home Alone 2: Lost in New York (1992) .....Gangster 'Dame'
Knights (1992) .... Mother
The Terror Within II (1992)....................... Ariel
- 0:25—Brief side view of right breast, while in front of fire with Andrew Stevens.

Made for Cable Movies:
Directed By: The Gift (1994; Showtime) ... Joe's Lovely Blonde
Made for Cable TV:
Tales From the Crypt: Surprise Party (1994; HBO) .... Josie

Hodge, Kate
Films:
Leatherface: The Texas Chainsaw Massacre III (1990) .... Michelle
Love Kills (1991) .... Jill
Rapid Fire (1992) .... Karla Withers
- 1:06—Brief breasts, taking off her blouse in bed on top of Brandon Lee. Don't see her face well.

The Hidden 2 (1993)............................... Juliet
Desire (1994)............................ Lauren Allen
- ••• 1:02—In bra, then breasts while making love with Martin Kemp in bed.

Made for Cable TV:
Tales From the Crypt: Dead Right (1990; HBO) .... Sally
(Available on *Tales From the Crypt, Volume 3.*)

• Hoffman, Kelly
See: Ashley, Kaitlyn.

• Hoffman, Linda
Films:
Total Exposure (1991) .... Patty
Clifford (1994) .... Stewardess
The Dentist (1996)........................... Brooke
- 0:08—Very brief side of right breast, twice, while fooling around in the backyard with the pool boy while Corbin Bernsen watches.
- •• 0:30—Breasts, while sitting in dentist's chair when Bernsen imagines a patient is his wife.

Face/Off (1997).................................... Livia
Made for Cable Movies:
Black Scorpion 2—Aftershock (1996; Showtime)........ Jane
Made for TV Movies:
Green Dolphin Beat (1994) .... Ty Martin

Holcomb, Sarah
Films:
Animal House (1978) .... Clorette DePasto
- •• 0:56—Brief breasts lying on bed after passing out in Tom Hulce's bed during toga party.

Walk Proud (1979) .... Sarah Lassiter
Caddyshack (1980) .... Maggie O'Hooligan
Happy Birthday, Gemini (1980)............ Judith Hastings

Holden, Marjean
Films:
Glitch (1988)............................. Hopeful #1
Stripped to Kill II (1988) .... Something Else
- •• 0:17—Breasts during strip dance routine.

The Turn-On (1989) ....Voodoo Priestess
a.k.a. Le Clic
Silent Night, Deadly Night 4: Initiation (1990) .... Jane
Sweet Justice (1991) ....MJ

Nemesis (1992). . . . . San
Stop! Or My Mom Will Shoot (1992). . . . . Stewardess
Ballistic (1993) . . . . Jessie Gavin
a.k.a. Fists of Justice
- • 0:00—Buns and back side of left breast while in the shower. Nude, seen behind shower door.
- •• 0:30—Partial right breast, then breasts, while making love with Ray in bed.
- • 0:31—Left breast during argument. Very brief breasts and buns when getting out of bed and putting on T-shirt.

The Philadelphia Experiment 2 (1993). . . . . Jess
Renegade: Fighting Cage (1993). . . . . Tigress/Sharon Miller
(Nudity added for video release.)
Automatic (1994) . . . . Epsilon Leader
Bordello of Blood (1996). . . . . Stunts
Made for Cable TV:
Tales From the Crypt: The Pit (1994; HBO) . . . Andrea Johnson

• Holland, Kristen *

Video Tapes:
Playboy's The Girls of Hawaiian Tropic (1994) . . . . Beach Girls
0:39—Nude, while posing with another girl at the beach.

Hollander, Xaviera *

Author of "The Happy Hooker."
Films:
My Pleasure is My Business (1974) . . . . Gabriele
- •• 0:14—Full frontal nudity in everybody's daydream.
- •• 0:39—Breasts sitting up in bed and putting on a blouse.
- •• 0:40—Breasts getting back into bed.
- ••• 0:59—Breasts and buns taking off clothes to go swimming in the pool, swimming, then getting out.
- •• 1:09—Breasts, buns and very brief lower frontal nudity, underwater in indoor pool with Gus.
- • 1:31—Buns and very brief side view of right breast, undressing at party.

Video Tapes:
Penthouse Love Stories (1986) . . . . Herself

Holliday, Melissa *

Video Tapes:
Playboy Video Calendar 1996 (1995) . . . . October
- ••• 0:39—Full frontal nudity in magician act.
- •• 0:41—Nude in Casablanca style fantasy.

Wet & Wild: Hot Holidays (1995) . . . . Playmate
Playboy's Voluptuous Vixens (1997). . . . . Playmate

Hollimon, Tina

Films:
Cave Girl Island (1994) . . . . Sola
a.k.a. Beach Babes 2: Cave Girl Island
- ••• 0:31—Nude, while making love in hut with Rock. Long scene.
- •• 1:05—Nude, during party on spaceship.

Demon Knight (1994) . . . . Party Babe 7
- • 1:02—Very brief left breast with other Party Babes in Dick Miller's fantasy. She is sitting at the bar on the left and says, "Try mine."

Hollitt, Raye

American Gladiator "Zap."
Films:
Penitentiary III (1987) . . . . Female Boxer
Skin Deep (1989) . . . . Lonnie
(Check this out if you like muscular women.)
- • 0:26—Brief side view breasts and buns getting undressed and into bed with John Ritter.

Immortalizer (1990). . . . . Queenie
The Last Hour (1990). . . . . Adler
a.k.a. Concrete War
Hot Shots! Part Deux (1993) . . . . American Gladiator Zap
Cyborg 3: The Recycler (1995) . . . . Finola
Day of the Warrior (1997) . . . . Kym
TV:
American Gladiators (1989). . . . . Zap

Holloman, Bridget

Films:
Slumber Party '57 (1976) . . . . Bonnie May
- • 0:10—Breasts with her five girl friends during swimming pool scene. Hard to tell who is who.
- • 0:26—Left breast in truck with her cousin Cal.

Evils of the Night (1985) . . . . Heather
Stoogemania (1986) . . . . Sexy Nurse

Holloman, Laurel

Films:
The Incredibly True Adventure of Two Girls in Love (1995). . . . . Randy
- • 1:11—Brief left breast, while in bed with Evie.
- • 1:15—Brief breasts, while running around in the bedroom when Evie's mom comes home.

Boogie Nights (1997) . . . . Sheryl Lynn
Made for TV Movies:
The Price of Love (1995) . . . . Roxann
Dalva (1996) . . . . Karen

Holly, Lauren

Wife of actor Jim Carrey.
Films:
Seven Minutes in Heaven (1985). . . . . Lisa
Band of the Hand (1986). . . . . Nikki
The Adventures of Ford Fairlane (1991) . . . . Julie "Jazz"
Dragon: The Bruce Lee Story (1993) . . . . Linda Lee
- • 0:39—Very, very brief tip of left breast when making love with Jason Scott Lee (when she moves her hand from the front of his shoulder to the back).

Dumb & Dumber (1994) . . . . Mary
- • 0:30—Brief lower half of buns, when Jim Carrey pulls her dress up a bit during his fantasy.

Down Periscope (1995). . . . . Emily
Sabrina (1995). . . . . Elizabeth Tyson
Beautiful Girls (1996). . . . . Darian Smalls
Turbulence (1996). . . . . Teri Halloran
A Smile Like Yours (1997) . . . . Jennifer Roberts
No Looking Back (1998) . . . . Claudia
Made for Cable Movies:
Dangerous Heart (1994; USA) . . . . Carol
Made for TV Movies:
Fugitive Among Us (1992). . . . . Suzie Bryant
TV:
All My Children (1986-89). . . . . Julie Chandler
The Antagonists (1991) . . . . Kate Ward
Picket Fences (1992-96). . . . . Deputy Maxine Stewart

Holman, Ann-Marie

Films:

Where Evil Lies (1994). . . . . Uncredited Dancer

• 1:07—Brief breasts, while dancing on stage. (Clip is from *Stripteasers.*)

Stripteasers (1995) . . . . Kitten

••• 0:41—In black bra and panties, then nude doing strip tease in front of the gunman.

Holman, Clare

Films:

Let Him Have It (1991; British) . . . . Iris Bentley

Afraid of the Dark (1992; British/French) . . . . Rose

••• 0:38—Breasts, while wearing white panties, garter belt and stockings while posing for photographer in studio on a wooden horse. Long scene.

Tom & Viv (1994) . . . . Louise Purdon

Looking for Richard (1996) . . . . n.a.

Holmes, Jennifer

Films:

The Demon (1981; South African). . . . . Mary

•• 0:22—Breasts in dressing room.

• 1:18—Brief side of left breast, taking off robe to take a bath.

• 1:26—Breasts, crawling around in the rafters. Dark.

••• 1:29—Breasts climbing through a hole in the roof, then landing on the bed. More breasts in the bathroom.

Raw Force (1981) . . . . Ann Davis

Life on the Edge (1992). .Karen Nelson

Made for TV Movies:

Hobson's Choice (1983) .Alice Hobson

Sampson and Delilah (1984). . . . . .Varinia

TV:

Newhart (1982-83). . . . . Leslie Vanderkellen

Misfits of Science (1985-86) .Jane Miller

Holmes, Mai-Lis

Films:

Witchcraft 8: Salems Ghost (1994) . . . . Cathy

•• 1:09—Brief breasts, while making love with Sonny in the house.

Witchcraft 7: Judgement Hour (1995) . . . . Sally

(Unrated version reviewed.)

•• 1:02—Breasts and buns in leather outfit, while being a dominatrix to a guy, then during fight with police.

Holmes, Meredyth

Films:

Caged Hearts (1995). . . . . .Aerobic Girl

Forbidden Zone: Alien Abduction (1996). . . . . . . Veronica

a.k.a. Alien Abduction: Intimate Secrets

•• 0:06—Breasts, while caressing herself and fantasizing about making love with a guy.

• 0:20—Very brief buns, when getting lifted up after passing out.

•• 1:03—In black bra, then breasts, while making love with the alien guy on his ship.

Holt, Sandrine

Films:

Black Robe (1991; Canadian/Australian). . . . . Annuka

• 1:10—Breasts (mostly left breast) while exposing herself to the Iroquois guard. Don't see her face.

Dance Me Outside (1994; Canadian) . . . . Poppy

Rapa Nui (1994) . . . . Ramana

•• 0:10—Brief breasts, when dancing around fire in the Short Ear village. More breasts, while walking to meet Jason Scott Lee.

••• 0:12—Breasts, while outside with Lee, lying in the grass and talking.

• 0:19—Breasts, while getting hassled by the other Short Ear women in the river.

•• 0:20—Breasts, while walking and talking with Lee.

• 0:22—Breasts, while standing on rock during examination.

• 1:26—Breasts, after seeing iceberg. (Her skin is painted white and she's pregnant.)

Pocahontas, The Legend (1995). . . . . Pocahontas

•• 1:01—Breasts, while making love with Miles O'Keeffe.

Made for Cable TV:

Poltergeist: The Legacy/Premiere (1996; Showtime) . . . . . Ellen

The Outer Limits: Last Supper (1997). . . . . Jade

• 0:23—Brief breasts with Peter Onorati, during B&W flashback.

• 0:25—Brief left breast, taking off her nightgown to show Onorati her birthmark.

Made for TV Movies:

John Woo's "Once a Thief" (1996) . . . . Li Ann Tsei

Holvöe, Maria

Films:

Willow (1988) . . . . .Cherlindrea

The Last Warrior (1989) . . . . Katherine

•• 1:24—Right breast, after the Japanese warrior removes her dress.

Worth Winning (1989) . . . . .Erin Cooper

Holzbog, Arabella

Films:

Stone Cold (1991). . . . . .Nancy

Carnosaur 2 (1994) . . . . Sarah Rawlins

Hologram Man (1995) . . . . Natalie

Made for Cable TV:

Red Shoe Diaries: Tears (1995; Showtime). . . . . .n.a.

Women: Stories of Passion-As Always, Madelaine (1996; Showtime) . . . . Young Madelaine

••• 0:09—In bra, then breasts, while making love in bed with Faith.

• 0:23—Brief breasts, while making love in bed with Faith.

Hope, Amanda *

Video Tapes:

Wet & Wild IV (1992). . . . . .Model

Playboy Video Calendar 1994 (1993) . . . . August

••• 0:31—Nude, outside in garden, in gazebo and by a pond.

••• 0:33—Nude in a house with a clarinet.

Playboy's Playmate Review 1993 (1993) . . . . Miss July

••• 0:19—Nude in pool and in house.

••• 0:21—Nude in military style segment.

Hope, Erica

Films:

Bloody Birthday (1980) . . . . Annie

• 0:04—Brief breasts in cemetery, making out with Duke.

Graduation Day (1981) . . . . Diane

• 1:02—Brief breasts in open blouse, while running away from the killer.

TV:

The Young and the Restless (1978-79). . . . . .Nikki Reed

Hope, Leslie

Films:

Prep School (1981; Canadian)....................Penelope
Love Streams (1984)............................Joanie
It Takes Two (1988)....................Stephi Lawrence
Kansas (1988)..............................Lori Bayles
Talk Radio (1988)...............................Laura
Men at Work (1990).....................Susan Wilkins
The Big Slice (1991)......................Jenny Colter
Doppelganger: The Evil Within (1992)..............Elizabeth
Sweet Killing (1992; Canadian/French)........Eva Bishop

- •• 0:36—Right breast and partial left breast, while making love with Alan.

Caught in the Act (1993)........................Rachel
Fun (1993; Canadian)...........................Jane
Paris, France (1993; Canadian)....................Lucy

- • 0:00—Full frontal nudity, while making love with Minter in bed. B&W.
- • 0:12—Breasts, while making love in bed with Sloane.
- ••• 0:13—Nude, while getting back into bed.
- • 0:14—Breasts, while making love.
- •• 0:18—Right breast, while lying in bed, then nude getting out and getting dressed.
- • 0:20—Left breast, while wearing a wig and masturbating when her husband watches in a fantasy. B&W.
- •• 0:30—Left breast in mirror, while shaving her armpit with a straight razor.
- • 0:41—Breasts, when making love with Minter in bed while wearing a wig. B&W.
- • 0:45—Very brief frontal nudity, when Sloane pushes her away and she sits on sofa.
- ••• 0:46—Breasts, while making love on sofa with Sloane and talking on the phone with her dad.
- • 0:48—Frontal nudity in open dress, then brief buns, when she lifts up her dress.
- •• 0:58—Buns, when lying on Minter and writing on his chest. Partial breast when hog-tied and blindfolded while Minter drops hot wax on her. Breasts when he rolls her over. B&W.
- • 1:23—Lower frontal nudity, in open robe.
- ••• 1:24—Full frontal nudity in open robe, lying in bed.
- •• 1:26—Buns and left breast, while watching Sloane make love to her husband.
- •• 1:28—Nude, while lying in bed and getting out.

The Conspiracy of Fear (1994; Canadian)............Jimmy
First Degree (1995)......................Hadley Pyne

Made for Cable Movies:

The Avenging Angel (1994; TNT).....................n.a.

Made for TV Movies:

Working Trash (1990)..................Susan Fahnestock
Blackout Effect (1998).........................Karen

TV:

Berrengers (1985)....................Cammie Springer
Knots Landing (1985-86)..................Linda Martin

• Hopke, Holiday

Films:

Friction (1995)..............................Ophelia
a.k.a. Lap Dance
(Unrated version reviewed.)

- • 0:27—Brief breasts, while dancing on stage in club.
- ••• 0:35—Breasts and buns, while making love with Denise in bed while Mr. Franklin watches.
- •• 0:52—Breasts and buns in T-back, while dancing on stage.

Made for Cable TV:

Love Street: The Mechanics of Desire (1994; Showtime) ....Roxie

- •• 0:17—Buns in black T-back and bra, then breasts while undressing and walking into bathroom.
- •• 0:19—Breasts, making love with Lisa Boyle in bathroom, while Lisa's husband watches.

Hopkins, Kaitlin *

Daughter of actress Shirley Knight.

Films:

Turk 182 (1985)....................Reporter on Subway
Spirits (1991)....................Succubus/Mrs. Heron

- •• 0:36—Breasts, several times, in bed on top of Harry. Then in gross make-up.

As Good As It Gets (1997)..............Woman in Lobby

Made for Cable Movies:

Breast Men (1997; HBO)..............Becca (Voice Only)

TV:

Another World..........................Kelsey Harrison

Hopkins, Kim

Films:

Cheech & Chong's Next Movie (1980)........Wardrobe Girl
The Happy Hooker Goes Hollywood (1980)....Young Xaviera
The Hollywood Knights (1980)............Pom Pom Girl

- • 0:01—Breasts, sunbathing outside with her two girlfriends.

Hopkins, Rhonda Leigh

Films:

Cover Girl Models (1975)......................Pamela
Summer School Teachers (1975)..............Denise

- • 0:45—Breasts making love with a guy. Close up of a breast.

Tidal Wave (1975; U.S./Japanese)..................Fran

Horan, Barbra

Films:

My Favorite Year (1982)..........................n.a.
The Malibu Bikini Shop (1985)................Ronnie

- • 0:33—In wet tank top during Alan's fantasy.
- • 1:13—Most of side of left breast, while kissing Alan in the spa.

Delusion (1990).................................Carly

TV:

B.J. and the Bear (1981)......................Samantha

Horan, Leslie

Films:

Repo Jake (1990)..................................Lea
Widow's Kiss (1995)........................Kelly Givens

- •• 0:40—In white bra, then breasts and side view of buns with Mackenzie Astin.

Made for TV Movies:

Danielle Steel's "Family Album" (1994)..............Anne

TV:

General Hospital..........................Miranda Jax

Horne, Suzi

Films:

Hot Moves (1984).........................Hooker #1
Jungle Warriors (1985).....................Pam Ross
a.k.a. Captive Women 9

- • 0:51—Brief breasts twice during jail scene. Wearing a white blouse, with a yellow shirt underneath. Brief buns. Don't see her face.

Horrocks, Jane

Films:

The Dressmaker (1988; British) . . . . Rita
Getting It Right (1989) . . . . .Jenny
The Witches (1989). . . . . .Miss Irvine
Memphis Belle (1990). . . . . Faith
Life is Sweet (1991; British) . . . . Nicola

- • 0:50—Breasts in bed with David Thewlis. Hard to see because she has chocolate all over her chest.

Second Best (1994). . . . . Debbie

Made for Cable TV:

Tales From the Crypt: Cold War (1996; HBO) . . . . .Cami

TV:

Absolutely Fabulous (1992-95; British) . . . . Bubble

Horton, Susan

Made for Cable Movies:

Psychic (1992; USA) .Woman in Club

- •• 0:03—Breasts during opening credits. Very, very brief partial lower frontal nudity, while getting strangled.
- • 0:11—Very brief buns and partial left breast, dead, being covered with a sheet.
- • 1:17—Very, very brief right breast, being murdered in Zach Galligan's psychic vision.

Triplecross (1994; Showtime) . . . . Girl in Club

Hossack, Allison

Films:

White Light (1990) . . . . Rachel Rutledge

- • 1:22—Very, very brief lower half of left breast, while in front of the fireplace with Martin Cove.
- • 1:23—Brief buns and breasts several times, while making love on the floor with Cove.

Made for Cable TV:

The Outer Limits: Dark Matters (1995; Showtime) . . . . Erin
Poltergeist: The Legacy/Revelations (1996; Showtime)
. . . . Constance Merrick
Dead Man's Gun: The Healer (1997; Showtime) . . . Anna Butler
Poltergeist: The Legacy/Stolen Hearts (1998; Showtime)
. . . . .Demon Woman
Fast Track: Kat's Cradle (1998; Showtime). . . . . Kat Kiernan

TV:

Another World . . . . Vicki/Marley
Cobra (1993-94). . . . . n.a.
Profit (1996) . . . . Nora

Houlihan, Carolyn

Films:

The Burning (1981) . . . . Karen

- •• 0:45—Nude, going skinny dipping with Eddy in lake at night.
- ••• 0:46—Brief breasts several times in the lake with Eddy, then breasts and buns getting out. Nice buns shot.
- •• 0:47—Nude, walking around in the woods, looking for her clothes.

A Little Sex (1982) . . . . Bathing Suit Model

House, Joey

Films:

Fist of Honor (1993) . . . . Gina

- • 0:19—Side of right breast and buns, after undressing in front of Sam Jones.

Exit to Eden (1994). . . . . Velvet/Trainer

Made for Cable TV:

Dream On: Attack of the 59-Inch Woman (1994; HBO)
. . . . Amy

- •• 0:03—Breast, while trying different sexual positions from a sex manual book with Martin.

Howard, Barbara

Films:

Friday the 13th, Part IV—The Final Chapter (1984)
. . . . Sara

- • 1:01—Buns, through shower door.

Racing with the Moon (1984) . . . . Gatsby Girl
Running Mates (1985). . . . . .n.a.
Lucky Stiff (1988) . . . . Frances
White Palace (1990) . . . . Sherri Klugman
Amityville: A New Generation (1993) . . . . Jane Cutler

Made for Cable TV:

Fallen Angels: A Dime a Dance (1995; Showtime) . . . . . . Janice
Fallen Angels: Love and Blood (1995; Showtime) . . . . . . Nurse

Made for TV Movies:

Those Secrets (1992). . . . . Beth

TV:

Falcon Crest (1985-86) . . . . Robin Agretti

Howard, Brie

Films:

Android (1982) . . . . .Maggie

- • 0:25—Buns, then breasts in bedroom when Klaus Kinski watches her on video monitor.
- • 0:54—Brief side of right breast, while sitting on Max's lap and kissing him.
- • 0:59—Partial left breast, while lying dead in bed.
- • 1:09—Brief side view of left breast while lying dead in bed.

The Runnin' Kind (1988). . . . . Thunder

Howe, Lynette

Films:

Beach Beverly Hills (1992). . . . . Shannon
Conflict of Interest (1992) . . . . Shannon

- ••• 0:45—Breasts in bed with another girl, then getting out to call the police.
- • 0:53—Breasts on top of Jason, lit with different colored lights.
- • 1:04—Breasts during Jason's recollection.

Blue Flame (1993). . . . . .Stripper

Howell, Chéri

Films:

Bloody Friday (1973) . . . . Shannon
a.k.a. Single Girls

- • 1:01—Breasts and buns after "accidentally" dropping her towel in front of Bud.

Soylent Green (1973) . . . . Furniture Girl
Sisters of Death (1976) . . . . .n.a.

Howell, Margaret

Films:

Tightrope (1984) . . . . .Judy Harper

- • 0:44—Brief left breast viewed from above in a room with Clint Eastwood.

Girls Just Want to Have Fun (1985) . . . . Mrs. Glenn
Messenger of Death (1988). . . . . Naomi Beecham
Candyman: Farewell to the Flesh (1995) . . . . .Clara

Made for Cable Movies:

Humanoids From the Deep (1996) . . . . Nurse

Made for Cable TV:
Tales From the Crypt: Food For Thought (1993; HBO) . . . . Siamese Twin
•• 0:15—One breast, while joined with a special-effect breast to her twin sister, while standing in shower.

Hoyt, Carol

Films:
Illegal Entry (1992) . . . . Catherine Reese
••• 0:59—Buns and breasts, getting into bubble bath and washing herself while talking with C.A. Long scene.
Midnight Confessions (1993) . . . . .Vanessa
(Unrated version reviewed.)
••• 1:13—Buns in lingerie, then breasts and buns while making love. Don't see her face well.
••• 1:18—Breasts, while taking a shower behind glass door.
Hollywood Passions (1994) . . . . Marla
••• 0:00—Breasts, while making love with her boyfriend on the floor.
••• 0:42—Breasts and buns, while making love on sofa with Stan.
• 0:47—Brief breasts, while fooling around behind the set with Stan.
Made for Cable TV:
Love Street: It's Only Love (1994; Showtime) . . . . . . Claire
• 0:01—Brief tip of right breast and buns, while getting dressed.

Hubley, Season

Ex-wife of actor Kurt Russell.
Films:
Hardcore (1979) . . . . .Niki
• 0:27—Breasts acting in a porno movie.
••• 1:05—Full frontal nudity talking to George C. Scott in a booth. Panties mysteriously appear later on.
Escape from New York (1981) . . . . . . Girl in Chock Full O'Nuts
Vice Squad (1982) . . . . .Princess
•• 0:57—Brief left breast and buns, wearing garter belt and stockings, getting out of bed after making love with a John.
• 0:58—More buns, under sheer panties while fighting with the John.
Pretty Kill (1987) . . . . Heather Todd
Total Exposure (1991) . . . . .Andi Robinson
• 0:07—Buns, while getting into hot tub. Probably a body double.
Stepfather III: Father's Day (1992) . . . . Jennifer Ashley
Made for Cable Movies:
Humanoids From the Deep (1996) . . . . Timmy's Mother
Made for Cable TV:
The Hitchhiker: Cabin Fever (1987; HBO) . . . . Miranda
Made for TV Movies:
She Lives (1973) . . . . Pam Rainey
The Three Wishes of Billy Grier (1984) . . . . Phyllis
Shakedown on Sunset Strip (1988) . . . . Officer Audre Davis
Child in the Night (1990) . . . . Valerie Winfield
Vestige of Honor (1990) . . . . Marilyn
Steel Justice (1992) . . . . Gina Morelli
TV:
Kung Fu (1974-75) . . . . Margit McLean
Family (1976-77). . . . . Salina Magee
All My Children (1992-94). . . . . .Angelique Marrick

Hudson, Stephanie

Films:
Cave Girl Island (1994). . . . . .Luna
a.k.a. Beach Babes 2: Cave Girl Island
••• 0:37—Nude, while dancing in front of Dusty, then making love with him. Long scene.
•• 1:06—Breasts, during party on spaceship.
Femalien (1995) . . . . Danielle

Huffman, Felicity

Wife of actor William H. Macy.
Films:
Reversal of Fortune (1990). . . . . Minnie
Golden Years (1991) . . . . Terry Spann
Quicksand: No Escape (1991) . . . . .n.a.
Hackers (1995) . . . . .Attorney
Made for Cable Movies:
The Water Engine (1992; TNT) . . . . Dance Hall Girl
The Heart of Justice (1993; TNT) . . . . Annie
Made for Cable TV:
Bedtime (1996; Showtime) . . . . Donna
Bedtime: Episode 1 (1996; Showtime). . . . . Donna
• 0:06—Buns behind plastic curtain in shower. Very brief side of right breast.
Bedtime: Episode 3 (1996; Showtime). . . . . Donna
•• 0:01—Breasts, while changing clothes.
Bedtime: Episode 7 (1996; Showtime). . . . . Donna
• 0:18—Brief breasts, after getting out of bed with Liz.
Bedtime: Episode 10 (1996; Showtime). . . . . Donna
•• 0:10—Breasts, twice, while sitting in bubble bath with Liz.

Hughes, Ann Margaret

Films:
Transformations (1988). . . . . .Myra
• 0:42—Right breast, then breasts under Rex Smith in bed.
• 0:43—More breasts, dead in bed.
Blue Tornado (1990) . . . . .n.a.
Fatal Temptation (1991; Italian). . . . . .n.a.

Hughes, Julie

Films:
Exit to Eden (1994). .Julie/Club Eden
• 0:26—Breasts and buns in T-back while on runway during introductions.
Stormswept (1994). . . . . .Brianna
•• 0:54—Breasts, while making love in bed with Kelly.
••• 1:26—Breasts in open robe and panties, while on couch during hypnosis session.
•• 1:29—Breasts, while making love in pantry with Eugene.

Hughes, Sharon

Films:
Chained Heat (1983; U.S./German) . . . . Val
•• 0:30—Brief breasts in the shower with Linda Blair.
•• 0:51—Buns, in lingerie, stripping for a guy.
•• 1:04—Breasts in the spa with the Warden.
The Man Who Loved Women (1983). . . . . Nurse
Hard to Hold (1984) . . . . .Wife #2
The Last Horror Film (1984). . . . . Stripper
American Justice (1986). . . . . .Valerie
A Fine Mess (1986) . . . . Tina
Grotesque (1987) . . . . .n.a.

Hughes, Wendy

Films:

Jock Petersen (1974; Australian)............. Patricia Kent

a.k.a. Petersen

••• 0:12—Breasts in her office with Tony.

• 0:13—Breasts making love with Tony on the floor.

•• 0:44—Nude running around the beach with Tony.

•• 0:50—Nude in bed making love with Tony.

• 1:24—Full frontal nudity when Tony rapes her in her office.

Newsfront (1978; Australian) .... Amy McKenzie

My Brilliant Career (1979; Australian) .... Aunt Helen

Lonely Hearts (1983; Australian) .... Patricia

• 1:05—Brief breasts getting out of bed and putting a dress on. Dark, hard to see.

Careful, He Might Hear You (1984; Australian) .... Vanessa

An Indecent Obsession (1985) .... Honour Langtry

• 0:32—Possibly Wendy's breasts, could be Sue because Luce is fantasizing about Wendy while making love with Sue. Dark, long shot, hard to see.

•• 1:10—Left breast, while making love in bed with Wilson.

My First Wife (1985; Australian).................. Helen

• 1:00—Brief breasts and lower frontal nudity under water during husband's dream. Don't see her face.

•• 1:08—In bra, then breasts on the floor with her husband.

•• 1:10—Breasts in bed lying down, then fighting with her husband. A little dark.

Happy New Year (1987) ....Carolyn Benedict

Warm Nights on a Slow Moving Train (1987) ....The Girl

• 1:23—Very, very brief silhouette of right breast getting back into bed after killing a man.

Echoes in Paradise (1989) .... Maria

Wild Orchid II: Two Shades of Blue (1992) .... Elle

Princess Caraboo (1994) .... Mrs. Worrall

Made for Cable Movies:

The Heist (1989; HBO) .... Susan

• 0:52—Very brief side view of right breast making love in bed with Pierce Brosnan.

Miniseries:

Return to Eden (1983; Australian) .... Jilly Stewart

Amerika (1987)................................ Marion

Made for TV Movies:

Donor (1990) .... Dr. Farrell

A Woman Named Jackie (1991) ....Janet Lee Bouvier

TV:

Homicide: Life on the Street (1993-94) ....Dr. Carol Blythe

Hull, Dianne

Films:

The Arrangement (1969) .... Ellen

The Magic Garden of Stanley Sweetheart (1970) .... Cathy

Hot Summer Week (1973; Canadian) .... n.a.

Man on a Swing (1974) .... Maggie Dawson

Aloha, Bobby and Rose (1975) .... Rose

The Fifth Floor (1978) .... Kelly McIntyre

•• 0:29—Breasts and buns in shower while Carl watches, then brief full frontal nudity running out of the shower.

•• 1:09—Breasts in whirlpool bath getting visited by Carl again, then raped.

The Onion Field (1979).......................... Helen

You Better Watch Out (1980) ....Jackie Stadling

The New Adventures of Pippi Longstocking (1988) .... Mrs. Settigren

Humphrey, Renée

Films:

Fun (1993; Canadian)........................... Hillary

Jailbait (1993)........................... Kyle Bradley

a.k.a. Streetwise

0:54—Almost left breast while taking off bathrobe in front of C. Thomas Howell.

1:10—In black bra and panties with Howell. Back half of left breast.

• 1:13—Breasts, while taking a shower. Don't see her face.

The Cure (1995) .... Angle

Devil in a Blue Dress (1995)...................... Barbara

French Kiss (1995)................................ Lilly

Mallrats (1995) .... Tricia

Cadillac Ranch (1997)............. Mary Katherine Crowley

Made for TV Movies:

Fighting for My Daughter (1995) .... Jessie

Humphreys, Ellyn Dawn

Films:

House IV (1991) ....Body Double for Terri Treas

• 0:46—Breasts, when the shower water becomes blood. You don't see her face.

Almost Hollywood (1994) .... Dawn

Caged Heat 3000 (1995)............................ Ice

Hunt, Helen

Films:

Rollercoaster (1977) .... Tracy Calder

Girls Just Want to Have Fun (1985) .... Lynne Stone

Trancers (1985).................................. Lena

Peggy Sue Got Married (1986) .... Beth Bodell

Project X (1987) .... Teresa McDonald

Miles From Home (1988) .... Jennifer

Next of Kin (1989) .... Jessie

Into the Badlands (1991)....................... Blossom

Trancers II (1991) .... Lena Deth

The Waterdance (1991).......................... Anna

••• 0:51—Breasts in bed, making love with Eric Stoltz.

•• 0:52—Brief buns and brief right breast, coming back to the bed to clean up.

Bob Roberts (1992; U.S./British) .... Reporter Rose Pondell

Mr. Saturday Night (1992) .... Annie

Only You (1992) .... Clare Enfield

Trancers III (1993)................................ Lena

Kiss of Death (1994) .... Bev

Twister (1996)............................ Jo Harding

As Good As It Gets (1997)................ Carol Connelly

• 1:46—Side view of right breast, when getting ready for bath. Medium long shot.

Made for Cable Movies:

Sexual Healing (1993; Showtime) .... Rene

Made for TV Movies:

Bill: On His Own (1983) .... Jenny

Quarterback Princess (1983) .... Tami Maida

Murder in New Hampshire: The Pamela Smart Story (1991) .... Pamela Smart

In the Company of Darkness (1993) .... Gina Pulasky

TV:

Amy Prentiss (1974-75)....................... Jill Prentiss

Swiss Family Robinson (1975-76) .... Helga Wagner

The Fitzpatricks (1977-78).................. Kerry Gerardi

It Takes Two (1982-83) .... Lisa Quinn

Mad About You (1992-) .... Jamie Buchman

Hunt, Leslie J.

Films:

The Man Who Wasn't There (1983).............. Nymphet

Forbidden Games (1995) . . . . Model
(Unrated version reviewed.)
Made for Cable TV:
Compromising Situations: The Master (1994; Showtime) . . . . Dianne
- ••• 0:01—Full frontal nudity while making love on sofa on top of a guy. Long scene.

Erotic Confessions: Locked Up (1996; Cinemax) . . . . Hanna
(Available on video tape in *Erotic Confessions, Volume 3: Passion.*)

Hunt, Marsha A.

Films:
Britannia Hospital (1982). . . . . Nurse Persil
The Sender (1982) . . . . Nurse Jo
Howling II: Your Sister is a Werewolf (1984). . . . Mariana
- •• 0:33—Breasts in bedroom with Sybil Danning and a guy.

Hunter, Ciara

Miss Canada 1988.
Films:
Mask of Death (1994; Canadian). Rachel
Dangerous Prey (1995) . . . . Tanya
- • 0:53—Brief buns, in T-back, when standing up next to bed.
- •• 1:09—Breasts and buns in T-back, while undressing and getting into bed with Yuri. (She's wearing a brown wig.)

Bordello of Blood (1996). . . . . Tamara
- •• 0:43—Breasts, while in S&M dungeon room with Dennis Miller.

Hunter, Heather

Adult film actress.
Films:
Frankenhooker (1990). . . . . Chartreuse
- • 0:36—Brief breasts during introduction to Jeffrey.
- • 0:37—Brief breasts bending over behind Sugar.
- ••• 0:41—Brief breasts and buns, running in front of bed. A little blurry. Then breasts and buns dancing with the other girls.
- • 0:43—Breasts dodging flying leg with Sugar.
- •• 0:44—Breasts, crawling on the floor.

TV:
Soul Train . . . . Dancer

Hunter, Holly *

Films:
The Burning (1981). . . . . Sophie
Swing Shift (1984) . . . . Jeannie Sherman
Broadcast News (1987). . . . . Jane Craig
End of the Line (1987). . . . . Charlotte Haney
Raising Arizona (1987) . . . . Edwina
Always (1989) . . . . Dorinda Durston
Miss Firecracker (1989) . . . . Carnelle Scott
Animal Behavior (1990). . . . . Coral Grable
Once Around (1990). . . . . Renata Bella
The Firm (1993) . . . . Tammy Hemphill
The Piano (1993) . . . . Ada
(Academy Award for Best Actress.)
- ••• 1:02—Nude, while sitting on bed.
- ••• 1:18—Buns then breasts while lying next to Harvey Keitel in bed.
- • 1:19—Very brief left nipple when kissing. Close-up shot.

Copycat (1995). . . . . Detective M.J. Monahan
Home for the Holidays (1995). . . . . Claudia Larson

Crash (1996; Canadian) . . . . Dr. Helen Remington
(NC-17 version reviewed.)
- • 0:08—Left breast, in open jacket when trying to get out of car after accident.
- • 0:23—In bra, then brief left breast and panties, then partial left breast sticking out of bra, while having sex in car with James Spader.
- • 0:46—Lower frontal nudity, wearing a bra, while having sex with Spader in back seat of car.

Made for Cable Movies:
Crazy in Love (1992; TNT). . . . . Georgie Swift Symonds
Made for TV Movies:
Svengali (1983) . . . . Leslie

• Hunter, Josie

See: Pickett, Blake.

Hunter, Kaki

Films:
Roadie (1980) . . . . Lola Bouiliabase
Willie and Phil (1980) . . . . Patti Sutherland
Porky's (1981; Canadian). . . . . Wendy
- • 1:02—Brief full frontal nudity, then brief breasts in the shower scene.

Whose Life Is It, Anyway? (1981) . . . . Mary Jo
Porky's II: The Next Day (1983; Canadian). . . . . Wendy
Just the Way You Are (1984) . . . . Lisa
Porky's Revenge (1985; Canadian). . . . . Wendy

Hunter, Neith

Films:
Born in East L.A. (1987). . . . . Marcie
Less than Zero (1987) . . . . Alana
Near Dark (1987) . . . . Lady in Car
Fright Night, Part 2 (1988) . . . . Young Admirer
Silent Night, Deadly Night 4: Initiation (1990) . . . . . . Kim
- • 0:03—Brief breasts several times in bed with Hank.
- • 0:47—Brief breasts during occult ceremony when a worm comes out of her mouth.
- • 1:05—Right breast, while lying on floor. Long shot.
- • 1:06—Breasts, covered with gunk, when transforming into a worm.
- • 1:07—Very brief side of right breast, while sitting up.

Silent Night, Deadly Night 5: The Toy Maker (1991) . . . . . . Kim
Carnosaur 2 (1994) . . . . Joanne Galloway
Gentleman's Bet (1995). . . . . Lauren Bernard
- •• 0:09—Nude, while taking a shower.
- •• 0:12—Breasts and buns, while starting to make love with her husband in the bathroom.
- ••• 0:24—Nude, while making love with her husband in bed (then with Chris after a camera trick).
- •• 0:33—Breasts, after taking off towel to put her bra and panties on. Brief buns in panties.
- • 0:42—Brief frontal nudity, while in bed with Chris in Paul's imagination.
- • 0:43—Brief breasts, while making love on the couch with Chris in Paul's imagination.
- •• 1:04—Buns and breasts, while making love with Chris on boat.
- • 1:14—Brief buns, while on top of Chris on boat.
- ••• 1:18—Nude, while making love with Jodie on bed.

Made for Cable TV:
Red Shoe Diaries: How I Met My Husband (1993; Showtime) . . . . Alice/Eve
- ••• 0:29—Breasts and buns, making love with Giuseppe on the stage.

•• 0:30—Brief breasts again.

Red Shoe Diaries: Juarez (1996; Showtime) . . . . The Girl

•• 0:02—Brief lower frontal nudity after taking off panties. Brief buns, then breasts, while on bed with her boyfriend.

• 0:10—Brief buns and breasts in fishnet body suit in fantasy with a wrestler.

•• 0:16—Full frontal nudity in bedroom, wearing wrestling mask. Sometimes in fishnet body suit in flashback.

••• 0:26—Breasts, while making love with Miguel.

Made for TV Movies:

Jonathan Stone: Threat of Innocence (1994) . . . . . . Nora Walsh

TV:

One Life to Live . . . . Laura

Video Tapes:

Inside Out (1992) . . . . Angela/The Diaries

(Unrated version reviewed.)

• 1:03—Buns, in swimsuit, while standing up.

•• 1:04—Right breast, then brief breasts in spa with Richard.

••• 1:06—Breasts in bed, getting fondled by David.

•• 1:08—Breasts in the shower.

•• 1:10—Right breast, while in bed with Richard.

*Hunter, Rachel **

Wife of singer Rod Stewart.

Sports Illustrated swimsuit model.

Spokesmodel for Pantene shampoo.

Made for Cable TV:

Body by VH-1 (1993- ; VH-1) . . . . Hostess

Made for TV Movies:

Sports Illustated Swimsuit Special: Class of '95 (1995). . . Model

Video Tapes:

Sports Illustrated's 25th Anniversary Swimsuit Video (1989). . . . . Model

(The version shown on HBO left out two music video segments at the end. If you like buns, definitely watch the video tape!)

• 0:03—Right breast in see-through black swimsuit with white stars on it.

Sports Illustrated Super Shape-Up Program: Body Sculpting (1990). . . . . Herself

Sports Illustrated: The 1993 Swimsuit Video (1993) . . . . Model

Sports Illustrated: 1994 Swimsuit Issue Video (1994). . . . Model

(Unedited Version reviewed.)

Rachel Hunter: Take Charge Workout, Kickboxing Cardio Workout (1995) . . . . Herself

Rachel Hunter: Take Charge Workout, Power Conditioning (1995). . . . . Herself

Huntly, Leslie

Films:

The Naked Cage (1985) . . . . Peaches

Back to School (1986) . . . . Coed #1

•• 0:14—Brief breasts in the shower room when Rodney Dangerfield first arrives on campus.

Demon of Paradise (1987) . . . . Gobby

•• 0:51—Breasts taking off her top on a boat, then swimming in the ocean.

Stewardess School (1987). . . . . Alison Hanover

•• 0:46—Breasts, doing a strip tease on a table at a party at her house.

Satan's Princess (1989) . . . . Karen Rhodes

••• 0:27—Breasts sitting on bed and in bed with Nicole.

I Will Dance on Your Grave: Lethal Victims (1992) . . . . Melinda McGee

• 0:31—Breasts, while on bed after Don Swayze knocks her out with chloroform.

*Huppert, Isabelle **

Films:

Going Places (1974; French). . . . . Jacqueline

• 1:53—Brief upper half of left breast making love with Gérard Depardieu.

Rosebud (1975). . . . . Helene Nikolaos

• 0:19—Buns, while on deck of boat with the other girls and the terrorists (she's second in line).

• 1:40—Partial side view of right breast in gaping robe, while lying back in bed with Peter O'Toole.

The Lacemaker (1977; French). . . . . Beatrice

• 0:50—Briefly nude while getting into bed.

• 0:57—Breasts under shawl, then nude while getting into bed.

•• 0:58—Breasts, lying in bed.

• 1:04—Nude, in her apartment.

••• 1:22—Nude, in her apartment with François.

Heaven's Gate (1980). . . . . Ella

•• 1:10—Nude running around the house and in bed with Kris Kristofferson.

••• 1:18—Nude, taking a bath in the river and getting out.

• 2:24—Very brief left breast getting raped by three guys.

Loulou (1980; French) . . . . Nelly

• 0:06—Very, very brief breasts leaning over in bed.

• 0:18—Brief breasts getting out of bed.

• 0:27—Brief breasts turning over in bed.

•• 0:36—Breasts lying in bed talking on phone. Mostly right breast.

• 0:40—Lower frontal nudity and buns taking off panties and getting into bed.

•• 0:59—Left breast in bed with André, then breasts taking him to the bathroom.

Clean Slate (1981; French) . . . . Rosalie

a.k.a. Coup de Torchon

•• 0:50—Breasts and buns, after taking off her slip in bedroom in front of Lucien.

••• 1:13—Breasts, after sitting up in bed, then full frontal nudity, after getting out of bed.

La Truite (The Trout) (1982; French) . . . . Frederique

Entre Nous (1983; French) . . . . Helen Webber

a.k.a. Coup de Foudre

• 1:01—Brief breasts in shower room talking about her breasts with Miou-Miou.

My Best Friend's Girl (1984; French). . . . . . . Vivian Arthund

a.k.a. La Femme du Mon Ami

• 0:40—Brief left breast peeking out of bathrobe walking around in living room.

• 1:00—Buns, while making love with Thierry Lhermitte while his friend watches.

Sincerely Charlotte (1986; French) . . . . Charlotte

• 0:20—Brief breasts while in bathtub. Long shot, out of focus.

• 1:07—Very brief left breast, while changing into red dress in the back seat of the car.

•• 1:15—Breasts in bed with Mathieu. Kind of dark.

The Bedroom Window (1987) . . . . Sylvia Wentworth

•• 0:06—Briefly nude while looking out the window at attempted rape.

Story of Women (1988; French) . . . . Marie Latour

Madame Bovary (1991; French) . . . . Emma Bovary

Après l'amour (1992; French) . . . . Lola

Amateur (1995). . . . . Isabelle

La Cérémonie (1996). . . . . Jeanne

Hurley, Diane

See: Lauren, Dyanna.

Hurley, Elizabeth *

Girlfriend of actor Hugh Grant.
Model for Estée Lauder cosmetics.

Films:

Aria (1987; U.S./British) . . . . Marietta
- 0:46—Brief breasts, turning around while singing to a guy.
- 0:47—Buns while standing and hugging him.

Rowing with the Wind (1988) . . . . Clair Clairmont
Kill Cruise (1990; German) . . . . Lou
- 0:15—Very brief breasts during strip tease routine on stage.
- 1:09—Side of right breast, while making love with Jürgen Prochnow.
- 1:15—Very brief right breast in open blouse, several times when Prochnow throws Patsy Kensit overboard.
- 1:25—Most of side of right breast, while consoling Kensit.

Passenger 57 (1992) . . . . Sabrina Ritchie
Nightscare (1993; British) . . . . Stephanie Lyell
- 0:19—Right breast, while making love with a guy in bed.
  0:21—Brief partial buns, while in bed.

Shameless (1994; British) . . . . .Antonia Dyer
- ••• 0:35—Breasts, while making love with C. Thomas Howell in bed.

Austin Powers: International Man of Mystery (1997) . . . . .Vanessa Kensington
Dangerous Ground (1997) . . . . Karin

Made for Cable Movies:

Samson and Delilah (1996; TNT). . . . . Delilah

Hushaw, Katherine *

Video Tapes:

Playboy Video Calendar 1988 (1987) . . . . .Playmate
Wet & Wild (1989). . . . . .Model
Playboy's 21 Playmates: Volume II (1996) . . . . . .Playmate
- ••• 0:47—Nude in still photos.
- ••• 0:48—Nude while picking grapes and playing with them in a vat.

Hussey, Olivia

Films:

Battle of the Villa Fiorita (1965; British) . . . . Donna
Romeo and Juliet (1968; British/Italian) . . . . Juliet
- 1:37—Very brief breasts rolling over and getting out of bed with Romeo.

Black Christmas (1975; Canadian). . . . . Jess
a.k.a. Stranger in the House
a.k.a. Silent Night, Evil Night
The Man with Bogart's Face (1980). . . . . Elsa Borsht
Virus (1980; Japanese). . . . . .Marit
Escape 2000 (1981) . . . . Chris
Undeclared War (1990). . . . . n.a.
Save Me (1993). . . . . Gail
(Unrated version reviewed.)
Ice Cream Man (1994) . . . . Nurse Wharton

Made for Cable Movies:

Psycho IV: The Beginning (1990; Showtime) . . Norma Bates
- •• 0:49—Breasts in motel room mirror while young Norman, watches through peephole.

Made for TV Movies:

Jesus of Nazareth (1977). . . . . .Virgin Mary
Ivanhoe (1982) . . . . Rebecca
Stephen King's "It" (1990) . . . . Audra

Huston, Anjelica

Daughter of actor/director John Huston.

Films:

Hamlet (1969; British) . . . . Court Lady
A Walk with Love and Death (1969) . . . . .Lady Claudia
The Last Tycoon (1976). . . . . Edna
Swashbuckler (1976). . . . . Woman of Dark Visage
The Postman Always Rings Twice (1981) . . . . Madge
- 1:30—Brief side view left breast sitting in trailer with Jack Nicholson.

Frances (1982). . . . . Hospital Sequence: Mental Patient
Ice Pirates (1984). . . . . .Maida
This is Spinal Tap (1984) . . . . Polly Deutsch
Prizzi's Honor (1985) . . . . .Maerose Prizzi
(Academy Award for Best Supporting Actress.)
The Dead (1987). . . . . Gretta Conroy
Gardens of Stone (1987) . . . . Samantha Davis
Enemies, A Love Story (1989) . . . . Tamara
The Witches (1989) . . . . Grand High Witch/Eva Ernst
The Grifters (1990) . . . . .Lilly Dillon
The Addams Family (1991) . . . . Morticia Addams
The Player (1992) . . . . Cameo
Addams Family Values (1993) . . . . Morticia Addams
Manhattan Murder Mystery (1993) . . . . Marcia Fox
The Crossing Guard (1995) . . . . .Mary
The Perez Family (1995) . . . . .Carmela Perez
- 0:38—Very brief left breast, while sitting in bubble bath. Very, very brief breasts, when getting up out of bathtub when she's startled by workmen outside the window.

Phoenix (1998) . . . . Leila

Made for Cable Movies:

And the Band Played On (1992; HBO). . . . . . . .Dr. Betsy Reisz

Miniseries:

Lonesome Dove (1989) . . . . Clara Allen
Family Pictures (1993). . . . . Lainey Eberlin
Buffalo Girls (1995) . . . . Calamity Jane

• *Hutchinson, Michelle*

Films:

Fargo (1996) . . . . Escort
- 1:07—Brief buns, running down hallway after Shep beats up Steve Buscemi.

My Best Friend's Wedding (1997) . . . . . . Drunken Trashy Girl

• *Hutchinson, Sarah* *

Video Tapes:

Playboy's The Girls of Hawaiian Tropic (1994) . . . . Secret Island
- ••• 0:29—Nude, while doing various things around the beach.

Playboy's Sex on the Beach: Tropical Heat (1997) . . . . Bonfire Dance/Sarah
- ••• 0:07—In Polynesian-style outfit, then nude, while dancing on the sand at night.

Penthouse: Island Girls (1998) . . . . n.a.

Hutchinson, Tracey E.

Films:

The Wild Life (1984). . . . . .Poker Girl #2
- 1:23—Brief breasts in a room full of guys and girls playing strip poker when Lea Thompson looks in.

Into the Night (1985) . . . . Federal Agent
Masterblaster (1986) . . . . Lisa
- ••• 0:57—Breasts taking a shower (wearing panties).

Amazon Women on the Moon (1987) .... Floozie
- 1:18—Brief right breast, while hitting balloon while Carrie Fisher talks to a guy. This sketch is in B&W and appears after the first batch of credits.

Stone Cold (1991) ....Pool Playing Chick
- 0:25—Brief breasts, playing pool with the guys.

Hutton, Lauren *

Former model.

Films:

Little Fauss and Big Halsy (1970).......... Rita Nebraska
- 0:44—Nude, while running down a road, then running to hide by a truck.
- 0:45—Buns, while lying in the cab of the truck.
- 1:04—Brief buns, while lying on bed when Robert Redford walks by.

The Gambler (1974) .... Billie
Gator (1976)............................Aggie Maybank
Viva Knievel (1977)........................Kate Morgan

Welcome to L.A. (1977)................... Nora Bruce
- 0:56—Very brief, obscured glimpse of left breast under red light in photo darkroom.

A Wedding (1978) .... Florence Farmer

American Gigolo (1980) .... Michelle
- 0:37—Left breast, making love with Richard Gere in bed in his apartment.

Paternity (1981) .... Jenny Lufton
Zorro, The Gay Blade (1981)...................Charlotte

Lassiter (1984) .... Kari Von Fursten
- 0:18—Brief breasts over-the-shoulder shot making love with a guy on the bed just before killing him.

Once Bitten (1985)..........................Countess
Malone (1987) ....Jamie
Trade Secrets (1989; French)...................Marléne
Millions (1990) .... Christina
Missing Pieces (1991) .... Jennifer
Guilty as Charged (1992) ....Liz Stanford
My Father The Hero (1993)..................... Megan
A Rat's Tale (1997) ....n.a.

Made for Cable Movies:

Fear (1991; Showtime).................. Jessica Moreau

Made for TV Movies:

Scandal Sheet (1985) .... Meg North

TV:

The Rhinemann Exchange (1977).........Leslie Hawkewood
Paper Dolls (1984) .... Colette Ferrier
Central Park West (1995) ....Linda Fairchild Rush
CPW (1996) ....Linda Fairchild Rush

Hyde, Kimberly

Films:

The Last Picture Show (1971) ....Annie-Annie Martin
- •• 0:36—Full frontal nudity, getting out of pool to meet Randy Quaid and Cybill Shepherd.
- 0:37—Breasts several times, sitting at edge of pool with Bobby.
- 0:38—More breasts, sitting on edge of pool in background.

Video Vixens (1973) .... Claudine
Young Nurses (1973) .... Peppermint
Candy Stripe Nurses (1974) .... April
Foxy Brown (1974).......................... Jennifer

Hylton, Gloria

Films:

Sorority Girls and the Creature from Hell (1990) ...... Kristina

Exit to Eden (1994) .... Angry Girlfriend/Flashback
- 0:01—Brief buns in T-back and black bra, while walking back into the house after throwing eggs at Paul Mercurio. Medium long shot.

Hyser, Joyce

Ex-girlfriend of singer Bruce Springsteen.

Films:

The Hollywood Knights (1980) .... Brenda Weintraub
They All Laughed (1981).......................... Sylvia
Staying Alive (1983) .... Linda
Valley Girl (1983)................................Joyce
This is Spinal Tap (1984) .... Belinda

Just One of the Guys (1986) .... Terry Griffith
- •• 1:27—Brief breasts opening her blouse to prove that she is really a girl.

Wedding Band (1989).................. Karla Thompson
Greedy (1993)...................................Muriel

TV:

L.A. Law (1988-89) .... Alison Gottlieb

Ilica, Laura

Films:

Trancers 4—Jack of Swords (1993) ....Tunnel Rat

Forbidden Zone: Alien Abduction (1996)......Wild Child

a.k.a. Alien Abduction: Intimate Secrets
- 0:18—Brief buns in outfit, while running up the stairs.
- 0:44—Brief breasts, while wearing a mask and a saddle and acting wild.
- 0:47—Brief buns in outfit, while running up the stairs.

Illiers, Isabelle

Films:

The Story of "O" Continues (1981; French)........... O

a.k.a. Les Fruits de la Passion
- ••• 0:06—Breasts in chair, getting made up.
- •• 0:08—Breasts and buns, walking up stairs.
- 0:10—Breasts sitting in bed.
- •• 0:11—Breasts sitting in bed putting up Klaus Kinski's picture on the wall.
- •• 0:12—Breasts and buns getting out of bed and walking around the room.
- 0:13—Tip of right breast, while looking out the window.
- •• 0:18—Breasts looking out the window.
- 0:24—Brief left breast, under her dress.
- 0:26—Tips of breasts, sticking out of dress top.
- •• 0:27—Breasts and buns in chair, more in room with a customer.
- 0:35—Breasts, sitting while looking at Kinski.
- •• 0:36—Brief left breast, then full frontal nudity lying on bed during fantasy.
- •• 0:40—Full frontal nudity, while getting chained up by Kinski.
- •• 0:58—Full frontal nudity running in slow-motion during boy's fantasy.
- •• 1:02—Breasts in room with the boy.
- •• 1:04—Breasts making love with the boy.

Miranda (1985; Italian) ....n.a.
Luci Iontane (1988; Italian) ....n.a.

Iman *

Supermodel.

Wife of singer/actor David Bowie.

Films:

The Human Factor (1979)......................... Sarah
Exposed (1983)...................................Model

Out of Africa (1985) .... Mariammo
No Way Out (1987) .... Nina Beka
Surrender (1987).................................Hedy
House Party 2 (1991) ....Sheila Landreaux
L.A. Story (1991).................................Cynthia
The Linguini Incident (1991)....................Dali Guest
Star Trek VI: The Undiscovered Country (1991)........Martia
Exit to Eden (1994) ....Nina
• 1:21—Side view of left breast behind foggy shower door.
Made for Cable Movies:
Lies of the Twins (1991; USA) .... Elle
Heart of Darkness (1994; TNT) .... Black Beauty
Made for Cable TV:
Dream On: oral sex, lies and videotape (1993; HBO)
....TV Reporter
Music Videos:
Remember the Time/Michael Jackson (1992) ....Queen

• Imboden, Elizabeth

Films:
This World, then the Fireworks (1997)... Neighbor's Wife
• 0:00—Brief buns, very brief lower frontal nudity and very brief right breast, while making love with another man in bed and getting caught.
Made for Cable TV:
Love Street: Grading on a Curve (1995; Showtime)
.... Elizabeth Lupton

Imershein, Deirdre

Films:
Black Belt (1992) .... Shanna
••• 1:08—Breasts in bed, making love with Don "The Dragon" Wilson.
Scanner Cop (1993) .... Officer Parker
Private Lessons—Another Story (1994) .... Jennifer
Skyscraper (1996) .... Natasha
Made for Cable TV:
Dream On: Martin Gets Lucky (1990; HBO) .... Sheila
••• 0:06—Breasts in bed making love with Martin. Nice sweaty shot.
TV:
Dallas (1991).....................................Jory
Video Tapes:
Eden 4 (1993) .... Melissa
•• 0:04—Breasts and buns, while making love with a guy in front of window in hotel room.
• 0:07—Breasts again on video playback.
••• 0:14—Breasts while making love in bed with a man and a woman.
•• 0:25—Breasts in bed with B.D.
• 0:55—Tip of right breast in open dress while in bed with Rod. More left breast seen on TV.
•• 1:06—Breasts in bed when B.D. helps take her top off.
• 1:10—More breasts in video playback.
• 1:25—Brief left breast twice, while in bed with B.D.

Inch, Jennifer

Films:
Frank and I (1983) .... Frank/Frances
• 0:10—Brief buns, getting pants pulled down for a spanking.
••• 0:22—Nude getting undressed and walking to the bed.
• 0:24—Briefly nude when Charles pulls the sheets off her.
• 0:32—Brief buns, getting spanked by two older women.
••• 0:38—Full frontal nudity getting out of bed and walking to Charles at the piano.
•• 0:45—Full frontal nudity lying on her side by the fireplace. Dark, hard to see.
•• 1:09—Brief breasts making love with Charles on the floor.
••• 1:11—Nude taking off her clothes and walking toward Charles at the piano.
Higher Education (1987; Canadian)........... Gladys/Glitter
State Park (1988; Canadian)..................... Linnie
• 0:34—Brief right breast, undoing swimsuit top while sunbathing.
• 0:39—Brief breasts, taking off swimsuit top while cutting Raymond's hair.
Physical Evidence (1989)....................... Waitress
Made for Cable Movies:
Soft Touch (1987; Playboy)...............Tracy Anderson
(Shown on *The Playboy Channel* as *Birds in Paradise.*)
• 0:01—Full frontal nudity during the opening credits.
• 0:02—Breasts with her two girlfriends during the opening credits.
••• 0:17—Breasts exercising on the floor, walking around the room, then lying on bed. Long scene.
• 0:20—Full frontal nudity getting out of bed.
•• 0:23—Breasts in bed.
••• 0:50—Breasts sunbathing on boat with Carrie.
•• 1:01—Full frontal nudity, sitting on towel, watching Carrie.
• 1:02—Full frontal nudity, waving to a dolphin.
•• 1:04—Breasts at night by campfire with Carrie.
••• 1:05—Brief left breast, then breasts putting on skirt and walking around the island.
•• 1:13—Breasts in hut with island guy.
• 1:19—Breasts in stills during the end credits.
Soft Touch II (1987; Playboy) ....Tracy Anderson
(Shown on *The Playboy Channel* as *Birds in Paradise.*)
• 0:01—Breasts during opening credits.
• 0:02—Breasts with her two girlfriends during opening credits.
•• 0:14—Breasts dancing in Harry's bar by herself.
• 0:27—Full frontal nudity on stage at Harry's after robbers tell her to strip.
• 0:29—Side of left breast tied to Neill on bed.
• 0:31—Breasts tied up when Ashley and Carrie discover her.
•• 0:52—Full frontal nudity during strip poker game, then covered with whipped cream.
• 0:57—Full frontal nudity getting out of bed.
Made for TV Movies:
Anne of Green Gables (1985; Canadian) ....Ruby Gillis

Ingalls, Joyce

Films:
The Man Who Would Not Die (1975) .... Pat Reagan
Paradise Alley (1978).......................... Bunchie
Deadly Force (1983) .... Eddie Cooper
•• 0:48—Breasts, while making out with Wings Hauser on hammock.

Ingerman, Randi

Films:
Desperate Crimes (1991; Italian) ....Nina
Deadly Rivals (1992)................. Rachel Richmond
••• 0:18—Breasts, while in bed in open robe with Rudy.
• 0:20—Right breast in open robe before killing Rudy.
• 0:46—Brief buns in panties, while trying to kill strong bad guy.
Treacherous (1993).........................Lisa Rivers
• 0:01—Brief buns, when getting a massage from another woman. Brief breasts while C. Thomas Howell watches.
• 0:03—Very brief right breast, when Howell joins her in bed.

- • 0:34—Very, very brief breasts, in spa with Howell after she takes her swimsuit top off.
- • 0:49—Breasts and buns in T-back under sheer black patterned body suit in bathroom while getting dressed.
- ••• 0:53—Breasts and buns in T-back, while making love in bed with Damon.
- • 0:57—Very brief buns and left breast, while getting out of bed.

Miniseries:

Trade Winds (1993). August DeGaulle

Made for TV Movies:

Come Die With Me: A Mickey Spillane's Mike Hammer Mystery (1994). . . . . Trinity

Ingersoll, Amy

Films:

Knightriders (1981). . . . . Linet

- • 0:00—Very brief left breast, while lying down, then sitting up in woods next to Ed Harris.

Splash (1984) . . . . Reporter

Ingledew, Rosalind

See: Allen, Rosalind.

Innes, Alexandra

Films:

Perfect Timing (1984) . . . . Salina

- •• 1:06—Right breast and buns, posing for Harry.

Joshua Then and Now (1985; Canadian). . . . . .Joanna

Canvas (1992; Canadian/British) . . . . Anna Maxwell

Made for Cable Movies:

Down Came a Blackbird (1995; Showtime). . . . . Stunts

Inouye, Lisa

Films:

Final Judgment (1992). . . . . Lily

- •• 0:32—Breasts, walking up behind Rob in room, then making love. Brief buns in G-string, getting out of bed. Side view of breasts in mirror.
- • 1:01—Buns in lingerie in mirror.

Death Wish V: The Face of Death (1993). . . . . . . .Janine Omori

Ireland, Kylie

Adult film actress.

Films:

Strange Days (1995) . . . . Stoned Looking Girl

- • 0:07—Breasts, seen from her point of view during playback of clip.

Made for Cable TV:

Tales From the Crypt: The Bribe (1994; HBO) . . . . Dancer

- •• 0:03—Buns in T-back and breasts when wearing a devil costume while dancing on stage in club.

Irving, Amy

Ex-wife of director/producer Steven Spielberg.
Wife of director Bruno Barreto.

Films:

Carrie (1976) . . . . Sue Snell

The Fury (1978) . . . . .Gillian Bellaver

Voices (1979) . . . . Rosemarie Lemon

The Competition (1980) . . . . Heidi Schoonover

Honeysuckle Rose (1980) . . . . Lily

Yentl (1983) . . . . Hadass

Micki & Maude (1984) . . . . .Maude Salinger

Rumpelstiltskin (1987) . . . . Katie

Crossing Delancey (1988). . . . . Isabelle Grossman

She's Having a Baby (1988). . . . . Cameo

A Show of Force (1990). . . . . Kate

Benefit of the Doubt (1993; U.S./German) . . . . .Karen Braswell

Kleptomania (1993). . . . . Diana Allen

- ••• 0:50—Full frontal nudity, standing up in bathtub, getting out and putting on robe. Seen in mirror.

Carried Away (1996) . . . . .Rosealee Henson

- ••• 1:11—Nude, while in room with Dennis Hopper.

I'm Not Rappaport (1996). . . . . .Clara

Deconstructing Harry (1997). . . . . Jane

TV:

Once an Eagle (1976-77) . . . . Emily Massengale

Irwin, Andi Sue *

Video Tapes:

Penthouse: The Ultimate Pet Games (1996) . . . . Pet

- ••• 0:01—Nude during obstacle course segment.
- ••• 0:29—Nude in tug-of-war segment.
- ••• 0:39—Nude, while posing in house.
- ••• 0:42—Nude during squirt gun segment.

Irwin, Jennifer

See: Warner, Missy.

Isaacs, Susan

Films:

Deadly Passion (1985) . . . . .Trixie

- •• 0:02—Breasts sitting up in bed talking to Brent Huff.

She's Out of Control (1989) . . . . Receptionist

The War of the Roses (1989) . . . . Auctioneer's Assistant

Delirious (1991) . . . . Marie

Made for Cable Movies:

Breast Men (1997; HBO) . . . . Desperate Woman

• *Isbell, Tammy*

Made for Cable Movies:

Elvis Meets Nixon (1997; Showtime) . . . . . . .Stewardess Mindy

Made for Cable TV:

The Outer Limits: The New Breed (1995; Showtime) . . . . Judy

- • 0:13—Breasts, while making love on the floor next to the fire with Andy.
- • 0:20—Breasts, after making love in bed with Andy.

• *Italiano-Zaza, Nicole*

See: Nova, Nikki.

Ivins, Tracie

Video Tapes:

Hot Body Video Magazine #6: Southern Belle (1993) . . . . .n.a.

Hot Body Video Magazine #15: Wild Thing (1996) . . . . Covergirl Update/Tracie

- ••• 0:24—In lingerie, then nude, while stripping and dancing indoors.

• *Jackson, Gina*

Made for Cable TV:

Intimate Sessions: Melanie (1998; Cinemax) . . . . . .Melanie

- •• 0:04—Breasts, while starting to make out with Victor in art exhibit.
- ••• 0:07—Breasts and buns, while posing for, then making love with Victor in his art studio. Later, he applies body paint on her.
- ••• 0:15—Breasts and buns, while making love with Victor in her apartment.
- •• 0:21—Breasts and buns, while making love with Victor on the sofa.

Video Tapes:

Playboy's Cheerleaders (1996) . . . . Dancer 1/Gina
•• 0:39—Nude during Carmen Elektra music video.

Jackson, Glenda *

Films:

Negatives (1968; British) . . . . .Vivan
• 0:27—Brief breasts, putting on fur coat in front of mirror.
• 0:30—Very brief left breast, while covering herself with fur coat before sitting up.

The Music Lovers (1971; British) . . . . .Nina Milyukova
(Full frontal nudity after stripping in railway carriage.)

Sunday, Bloody Sunday (1971). . . . . Alex Greville
• 0:10—Brief breasts, taking off her nightshirt and getting into bed with a guy.
• 1:11—Brief right breast, when wrapping a shawl around herself before getting out of bed.
• 1:15—Very brief breasts, when getting off the floor and wrapping a shawl around herself.

Women in Love (1971) . . . . Gudrun Brangwen
(Academy Award for Best Actress.)
••• 1:20—Breasts taking off her blouse on the bed with Oliver Reed watching her, then making love.
•• 1:49—Brief left breast making love with Reed in bed again.

A Touch of Class (1972). . . . . Vicki Allessio
(Academy Award for Best Actress.)

The Nelson Affair (1973) . . . . Lady Emma Hamilton

The Triple Echo (1973; British). . . . . Alice

The Romantic Englishwoman (1975; British/French)
. . . . .Elizabeth
• 0:30—Brief full frontal nudity outside, taking robe off in front of Michael Caine.
• 0:31—Buns, walking back into the house.
• 1:08—Side view of right breast sitting at edge of pool talking to Thomas.
• 1:45—Very, very brief breasts while in bed talking with Thomas.

The Incredible Sarah (1976; British). . . . . Sarah Bernhardt

Nasty Habits (1977) . . . . Alexandra

The Class of Miss MacMichael (1978) . . . . . Conor MacMichael

House Calls (1978) . . . . Ann Atkinson

Stevie (1978). . . . . Stevie Smith

Lost and Found (1979) . . . . .Tricia

Hopscotch (1980) . . . . Isobel von Schmidt

Return of the Soldier (1983; British). . . . . .Margaret

Turtle Diary (1986; British) . . . . .Naerea Duncan

Beyond Therapy (1987). . . . . Charlotte

Salome's Last Dance (1987). . . . . .Herodias/Lady Alice

The Rainbow (1989) . . . . Anna Brangwen

Jackson, Jennifer Lyn *

Video Tapes:

Playboy Video Calendar 1990 (1989) . . . . September
••• 0:46—Nude.

Jackson, Kelly

See: Darrian, Racquel.

Jackson, Kelly (2)

See: Jaye, Kelly.

Jackson, La Toya *

Singer.

Member of the singing Jackson clan.

Video Tapes:

La Toya Jackson's International Club Tour (1993). . . . . . Hostess

Playboy Celebrity Centerfold: La Toya Jackson (1994)
. . . . Herself
•• 0:01—Breasts during introduction.
••• 0:04—Breasts and buns during fantasy bedroom segment.
••• 0:09—Breasts and buns in still photos.
••• 0:12—Breasts, while dancing and doing things around the house.
••• 0:15—Breasts and buns in dance number.
••• 0:19—Breasts in recording studio fantasy.
••• 0:29—In red lingerie, then breasts and buns while making love with a guy in vampire fantasy and playing with a snake.

Jackson, Pamela

Films:

Roadhouse (1989) . . . . Strip Joint Girl

Angel of Passion (1991). . . . . Eileen
••• 1:13—Breasts and upper half of buns while on bed with Eric making love.

Jackson, Victoria

Films:

Double Exposure (1983) . . . . Racetrack Model #1

Baby Boom (1987) . . . . Eve, the Nanny

Casual Sex? (1988) . . . . Melissa
• 0:30—Brief buns lying down with Lea Thompson at a nude beach.
• 0:33—Brief buns wrapping a towel around herself just before getting a massage. Long shot, hard to see.
• 1:06—Brief buns, when getting out of bed.

Family Business (1989) . . . . .Christine

UHF (1989) . . . . .Teri

I Love You to Death (1990) . . . . Lacey

Made for TV Movies:

Based on an Untrue Story (1993). . . . . Corduroy

TV:

Half Nelson (1985) . . . . Annie O'Hara

Saturday Night Live (1986-93). . . . . .Regular

Jacob, Irène

Films:

Au Revoir, Les Enfants (1987; French) . . . . Mlle. Davenne

The Double Life of Veronique (1991; French)
. . . . Veronika/Véronique
•• 0:04—Left breast, then breasts lying in bed with her boyfriend.
••• 0:28—Brief lower frontal nudity, then breasts while making love with her boyfriend.
• 0:41—Brief left breast, while sitting up in bed to answer the phone.

The Secret Garden (1993) . . . . Mary's Mother/Lilias Craven

Red (1994; French) . . . . Valentine Dussant

All Men are Mortal (1995; British/Dutch/French) . . . . . . Regina

Othello (1995; British) . . . . Desdemona
• 0:32—Brief breasts, taking off her dress (long shot) and getting onto bed behind sheer curtain. Right breast, while in bed with Larry Fishburne.

U.S. Marshals (1998) . . . . Marie

Jacobs, Emma

Films:

The Stud (1978; British). . . . . .Alexandra
•• 0:44—In bra, then breasts taking bra off in bedroom.
• 0:48—Close up of breasts making love with Tony in his dark apartment.
• 1:14—Breasts in bed with Tony, yelling at him.

Lifeforce (1985). . . . . .Crew Member

Jade, Jacqueline

Films:

L.A. Heat (1988) . . . . Hooker

Totally Exposed (1991) . . . . Eleanor

- ••• 0:05—Full frontal nudity, taking off towel and lying on tanning table.
- •• 0:08—Nude, on massage table, talking with Bill.
- •• 0:09—Brief breasts, turning over on table, trying to make the moves on Bill.
- •• 0:10—Brief breasts, sitting up.
- •• 0:57—Nude, taking off towel and getting on massage table.
- ••• 0:58—Full frontal nudity, turning over to talk to Bill.

California Hot Wax (1992). . . . . Bikini Girl

Pleasure in Paradise (1992) . . . . .Carol

- •• 0:01—Left breast, then breasts while making love in field with a guy at night.

Jaeger, Elizabeth A.

Films:

Barbarian Queen II: The Empress Strikes Back (1989) . . . . Noki

Video Tapes:

Inside Out 4 (1992) . . . . Marie/Jilted Lover

(Unrated version reviewed.)

- ••• 0:50—Breasts with her lover, making out on the floor.

Jaffe, Chapelle

Films:

The Kidnapping of the President (1980; Canadian) . . . . n.a.

Who Has Seen the Wind? (1980; Canadian) . . . . Maggie

Silence of the North (1981). . . . . .John's Girlfriend

The Amateur (1982) . . . . .Gretchen

- • 1:19—Breasts (mostly right breast), while lying on operating table when doctors try to revive her after John Savage poisons her.
- • 1:20—More right breast again.

The Dead Zone (1983) . . . . Nurse

Terminal Choice (1985; Canadian) . . . . Mrs. Dodson

Confidential (1986). . . . . .Amelia

Millenium (1990) . . . . Council Chamber

Made for Cable Movies:

Harrison Bergeron (1995; Showtime) . . . . . . Head House Lady

Made for Cable TV:

Poltergeist: The Legacy/Doppleganger (1996; Showtime) . . . . Miss Clark

Made for TV Movies:

Sin and Redemption (1994) . . . . Emma Simms

Jagger, Bianca *

Ex-wife of singer Mick Jagger.

Films:

The American Success Company (1979) . . . . .Corinne

- • 0:35—Breasts under see-through black top while sitting on bed.

The Cannonball Run (1981) . . . . Sheik's Sister

C.H.U.D. II (1989). . . . . n.a.

Blast 'Em (1992). . . . . .Herself

- • 0:58—Left breast in gaping dress while dancing in B&W still photo.

Jago, Alexa

Films:

Witchcraft III: The Kiss of Death (1991). . . . . Marlena

- • 0:04—Brief breasts in open dress in alley with Louis before he kills her.

The Puppet Masters (1994) . . . . Wendy Markham

Waterworld (1995) . . . . .Atoll Woman

Jahan, Marine

Films:

Flashdance (1983) . . . . Uncredited Dance Double for Jennifer Beals

Streets of Fire (1984). . . . . "Torchie's" Dancer

- • 0:28—Buns in G-string, while dancing in club.
- • 0:35—Very brief right breast under body stocking, then almost breasts under stocking when taking off T-shirt.

Video Tapes:

Freedanse with Marine Jahan. . . . . Herself

James, Courtney

Films:

Galactic Gigolo (1988) . . . . Lisa

a.k.a. Club Earth

Breakfast in Bed (1990). . . . . Mitzi

- ••• 0:36—Breasts, walking into the pool. Also seen from under water.
- ••• 0:37—Breasts and bun in G-string, getting out of pool.
- • 0:39—Breasts on the beach with Mr. Stewart.

James, Elizabeth

Films:

Born Losers (1967) . . . . Vicky Barrington

- • 1:44—Buns, while lying on floor after biker guys beat her up. Don't see her face.

Dirty Mary, Crazy Larry (1974) . . . . Dispatcher

James, Kelly *

Video Tapes:

Playboy International Playmates (1993) . . . . Kelly

- ••• 0:16—Full frontal nudity in still photos. Nude on the beach with sand, a thick rope and a net.
- ••• 0:30—Nude, walking around the woods with Teresa. Her body is partially painted with stripes.

James, Mikel *

Films:

Hangup (1974) . . . . .n.a.

I Spit on Your Corpse (1974) . . . . Laura

a.k.a. Girls for Rent

The Naughty Stewardesses (1978). . . . . Diane

a.k.a. Fresh Air

- •• 0:34—Breasts, while waiting in bed for Ben, then in bed with him.

James, Nia

Films:

Spy Hard (1996) . . . . .Rancor Terrorist

Made for Cable TV:

Hot Line: Mistaken Identity (1996; Cinemax) . . . . . . Celina

(Available on video tape in *Hot Line 4*.)

- ••• 0:04—Breasts, while making love in bed with Mickey.
- •• 0:24—Breasts, while making love with Mickey.

James, Pepita Full

Films:

Christina (1984; U.S./French) .... Brigitte
(Never released on video tape. Is shown occasionally on cable television.)

- • 0:24—Breasts, while doing strip tease with Jewel Shepard in front of their boyfriends.
- •• 0:25—Full frontal nudity, while in sauna with her friends.
- •• 0:27—Breasts, while making love on sofa with Max. Briefly nude, when joining Shepard on sofa.

Monster Dog (1986) .... Angela

• Jameson, Jenna *

Adult film actress.

Films:

Private Parts (1997) .... Mandy

- ••• 1:29—Nude in the radio station, while giving Howard Stern a massage.

• Jameson, Laurianne

a.k.a. Adult film actress Layla LaShell.

Films:

Dollman (1990) .... Hysterical Fat Lady

The Dark Backward (1991) .... Shirley

- • 0:44—Buns, in bed with Bill Paxton and two other fat women.

Janisse, Carrie

Films:

Ghoulies II (1988) .... Carol

Desert Passion (1992) .... Heather

- •• 0:04—In gold bra and panties, then breasts making love with an actor on bed.
- ••• 0:17—In white bra, then full frontal nudity, making love in the desert with Nick. Long scene.
- •• 0:43—Breasts in S&M outfit during bondage fantasy.
- •• 0:54—Nude (near window), while talking to Maggie in the shower room.
- ••• 1:01—Breasts during cowboy fantasy outside. Long scene.

Desire (1994) .... Female Model

- • 0:10—Brief breasts, while Deborah Shelton poses her for photographs.

Video Tapes:

Starlet Screen Test III (1992) .... Alexa Jones

- ••• 0:14—Breasts, while sitting on table, then full frontal nudity while getting dressed.

Intimate Secrets—How Women Love to be Loved (1993) .... Carrie

- ••• 0:34—In gold bra and white lingerie, then full frontal nudity posing on and in front of a grand piano.

Janssen, Marlene *

Films:

School Spirit (1985) .... Sleeping Princess

- •• 0:16—Breasts in shower room, shaving her legs.
- •• 0:42—Breasts and buns, sleeping when old guy goes invisible to peek at her.

Video Tapes:

Playboy Video Magazine, Volume 5 (1983) ..... Playmate

- • 0:05—Brief breasts with rose.

Playboy's Playmate Review 2 (1984) .... Playmate

Playmates at Play (1990) .... Flights of Fancy

Janssen, Nicolette *

Films:

Angel 4: Undercover (1993) .... Music Video Groupie

- • 1:00—Breasts, while backstage with the drummer and the other groupie.

Jarrett, Catherine

Films:

S.A.S. San Salvador (1982) .... Rosa

- ••• 0:28—Buns and breasts, taking off swimsuit in bathroom, then taking a shower.

A Fine Romance (1992; Italian) .... Marguerite

• Jarrett, Jennifer

See: Burton, Jennifer Leigh.

Jasaé *

Films:

Cave Girl (1985) .... Locker Room Student

- •• 0:05—Breasts with four other girls in the girls' locker room undressing, then running after Rex. She's sitting on a bench, wearing red and white panties.

Glitch (1988) .... Extra

Unexpected Encounters, Vol. 3 (1988) .... Neighbor

- ••• 0:32—Doing strip tease in front of guitar playing neighbor. Buns in G-string and breasts.

Roadhouse (1989) .... Strip Joint Girl

Bad Girls from Mars (1990) .... Terry

- ••• 0:03—Breasts taking off her top.
- •• 0:05—More breasts going into dressing room.

Mob Boss (1990) .... Bar Girl

- •• 0:46—Breasts serving drinks to the guys at the table.

Carnal Crimes (1991) .... Christa

- ••• 0:19—Full frontal nudity in lingerie, making love with a guy while Linda Carol secretly watches.

Roots of Evil (1991) .... Subway Hooker
(Unrated version reviewed.)

- ••• 1:05—Breasts taking off her top in subway stairwell, then getting killed by the bad guy.

The Swindle (1991) .... Nina

- ••• 0:28—Nude, posing for Tom while he video tapes her. Long scene.
- ••• 0:31—Nude, making love with Tom.
- ••• 0:36—Breasts in back of limousine with Dude.

Teenage Exorcist (1992) .... Dead Woman

- • 0:01—Brief breasts, dead with a slashed throat, on stairway when discovered by the maid.
- • 0:16—Brief breasts, several times, during nightmare while Brinke Stevens is sleeping.

Secret Games 3 (1994) .... Uncredited Lover
(Unrated version reviewed.)

- •• 0:21—Full frontal nudity, while making love in bed with a redhead woman.

Cellblock Sisters: Banished Behind Bars (1995) .... Marie

- • 0:44—Breasts, taking off her towel in the showers behind Manny, then holding onto Gail Harris so Manny can beat her up.

Video Tapes:

Candid Candid Camera, Volume 4 (1985) .... Model

- ••• 0:03—Full frontal nudity, talking on the phone.
- •• 0:18—Buns and lower frontal nudity, when her skirt is blown upwards like Marilyn Monroe.
- ••• 0:31—Nude, trying to get people to sign a petition against nudity on cable TV.

Becky Bubbles (1987) . . . . .Herself
•• 0:16—Breasts, taking off yellow swimsuit top and getting pushed on swing, then pushing Brandi.
••• 0:17—Breasts, playing with a ball on the grass with Brandi.
••• 0:19—Breasts, drinking wine and sitting on swing.

Wild Bikinis (1987) . . . . .Herself
••• 0:32—Breasts on swing, then pushing Brandi on swing from *Becky Bubbles*.
••• 0:35—Breasts playing with ball on the grass.
••• 0:37—Breasts on swing, drinking wine.
• 0:55—Breasts on swing, making a funny face.

Centerfold Screen Test, Take 3 (1988) . . . . .Herself
••• 0:42—Nude after undressing and posing on sofa. Long scene.

Starlet Screen Test II (1991) . . . . Jasae
••• 0:05—Nude on couch (same segment from *Centerfold Screen Test, Take 3.*)

Love Scenes: Volume 2 (1992) . . . . Cheryl Lynch
••• 0:16—Breasts, while helping to bathe Marc.
••• 0:18—Breasts and buns, while bathing Marc, then making love on the floor.
••• 0:21—Breasts, while typing in front of a computer, then on chair with Marc.

Penthouse Forum Letters: Volume 1 (1993)
. . . . .Three is Definitely Not a Crowd/Carmilla
•• 0:00—Nude in the shower during the opening credits.
••• 0:47—Buns in swimsuit, then breasts, getting lotion rubbed on her by Sandy.
••• 0:51—Nude, undressing in bathroom while Chuck peeks through the door, then taking a bath.
••• 0:54—Full frontal nudity in the shower with Sandy and Chuck.

*Jasmine **

Video Tapes:

The Girls of Penthouse, Volume 2 (1993). . . . . Pet
••• 0:00—Nude in pool, outside of house, on the beach and in house covering herself with shaving cream.

*Jason, Chona **

Films:

Summer Job (1989) . . . . Beautiful Lady

Knockouts (1992). . . . . .Ninja
••• 0:03—Breasts while doing sit-ups.
• 1:05—Wearing a sheer black body stocking during kick fighting match.

Dragon Fury (1995) . . . . .Regina
• 0:08—Brief buns, several times, while talking to bad guy in room.
• 0:20—Brief left breast in bed with David Heavener after transporting back in time. Brief breasts, while crawling out of bed and getting a jacket to wear.
••• 0:45—Nude, after taking off her blouse and making love with Mason in motel room.

Sinful Intrigue (1995) . . . . Mei-Ling
• 0:21—Buns and breasts (she's on the right), while in bathtub with Bianca Rocilili.
•• 0:39—Breasts, while making love with Adam and Griffin Drew.
• 0:47—Brief breasts (she's on the far left), while sipping a margarita in the backyard. Medium long shot, then closer shot.

Made for Cable TV:

Erotic Confessions: Lap Dance (1996; Cinemax)
. . . . Topless Dancer
(Available on video tape in *Erotic Confessions, Volume 4: Pleasure.*)
• 0:06—Brief breasts and buns in T-back, when dancing on stage in background while Dana gives Robert a lap dance.
• 0:10—Brief breasts, while dancing when Robert returns to the club.
• 0:12—Brief breasts, while dancing just before Robert goes through the curtains.

Erotic Confessions: Messy (1996; Cinemax) . . . . . Cassandra
(Available on video tape in *Erotic Confessions, Volume 2: Intrigue.*)
•• 0:06—Breasts and buns, while making love with Jeff.
•• 0:10—Breasts, with Alycia in the kitchen.

Erotic Confessions: The Workout (1996; Cinemax)
. . . . .Paula
• 0:00—Very brief partial lower frontal nudity and brief breasts, while lying in steam room.
• 0:01—Brief right breast, while crying in the steam room.
•• 0:02—Full frontal nudity, after making love in bed with Kenny. Breasts, while sitting in steam room, talking with Gina.
• 0:03—Brief full frontal nudity, while drying herself off.
••• 0:11—Nude, while making love with Tim in locker room, then on workout equipment, then in steam room.

Video Tapes:

Big Bust Casting Call (1992). . . . . Herself
••• 0:25—Breasts and buns in G-string during audition, undressing and trying on bra and panties in front of mirror.

Playboy's 101 Ways to Excite Your Lover (1992)
. . . . Touch/Woman
••• 0:15—Nude in bathtub with her lover.
••• 0:35—Nude in shower with her lover, then drying each other off and frolicking in bed.

Playboy's Real Couples: Sex in Dangerous Places (1995)
. . . . Steamy Encounter/Extra

Jay, Julie

Films:

Streets (1989) . . . . .Dawn's Tattooed Roommate
• 0:20—Brief breasts, twice, pulling her blouse closed when Christina Applegate talks to her.

Poison Ivy (1992) . . . . Nurse at Desk
(Unrated version reviewed.)

*Jaye, Kelly **

Adult film actress.

a.k.a. Kelly Jackson and Kelly Cook.

Films:

Anthony's Desire (1993) . . . . Dancer
•• 0:54—Left breast, while lying on her side in a group of women. She's near the top of the screen.
•• 1:02—Breasts, while playing the violin on stage.

Hollywood Dreams (1993) . . . . Veronica
a.k.a. L.A. Dreams
(Unrated version reviewed.)
•• 0:08—Nude, while making love with Steve on the floor.
• 0:14—In black lingerie, then left breast after undressing in office for audition in front of Lou.
• 0:25—Buns and breasts while in shower set during filming.
• 0:52—Breasts, while making love on couch with Steve.
••• 1:15—Nude, after taking off her dress in bedroom and making love with Robby.
• 1:19—Brief left breast while hugging Robby.

Uninhibited (1993). . . . . .Girl in Bed
• 0:00—Breasts, while getting out of bed and getting dressed.
Body Strokes (1995). . . . . .Aqua
•• 0:30—Breasts, while in pool, then making love with Claire in her flashback dream.
Video Tapes:
Beverly Hills Workout (1993). . . . . Herself
••• 0:18—Breasts and buns in T-back, while working out by swimming pool.
••• 0:36—Nude, while dancing and posing in backyard.
•• 0:54—Nude, while posing outdoors.
Love Scenes: Volume 3 (1993) . . . . .Julianne
•• 0:09—Nude, while taking a shower in motorhome.
•• 0:21—Breasts and buns, with Alan outside by camp fire.
••• 0:23—Nude, while in the shower in the motorhome and making love in bed with Alan.
Nude Daydreams (1993) . . . . .Daydream 8/13
••• 0:27—Breasts and partial buns and partial lower frontal nudity (she's on the left) while playing violin in a musical trio.
••• 0:40—In black dress, then buns in lingerie, then nude while posing on a stool. Long scene.
BabeWatch, Episode 1: Lingerie Fantasies (1994)
. . . . Herself
••• 0:08—Nude, while trying on lingerie outside by a chair. Long scene.

Jean, Stevie

See: O'Brien, Shauna.

Jeffers, Juliette

Films:
The Surgeon (1995; German/U.S.) . . . . Lisa Wilson
a.k.a. Exquisite Tenderness
• 0:51—Left breast, while making love with her boyfriend, Tommy, when she's in hospital bed.
Made for Cable TV:
Dream On: Home Sweet Homeboy (1993; HBO). . . . . . Clarice

*Jeinsen, Elke **

Video Tapes:
Playboy's Sexy, Steamy, Sultry (1993). . . . . .Playmate
Playboy Video Calendar 1995 (1994) . . . . April
••• 0:13—Nude riding on and posing with a horse. Nude in a house.

Jemison, Anna

See: Monticelli, Anna-Maria.

*Jenkin, Devon **

Films:
Slammer Girls (1987). . . . . Melody Campbell
• 0:12—Brief breasts getting lingerie ripped off by the prison matron.
• 0:16—Brief breasts getting blouse ripped off by Tank in the shower.
Twisted Nightmare (1987) . . . . .Julie
Slumber Party Massacre 3 (1990) . . . . Sarah
(Unrated version reviewed.)
Music Videos:
Free Fallin'/Tom Petty . . . . n.a.

Jenkins, Rebecca

Films:
Cowboys Don't Cry (1988; Canadian). . . . . .Lucy Morgan
Bye Bye Blues (1989; Canadian) . . . . Daisy Cooper
• 0:01—Brief breasts, getting out of bathtub. Very brief buns, while running outside and putting on robe to get away from snake.
• 0:42—Upper half of breasts, while in bathtub.
• 0:45—Very brief left breast under water in bathtub.
Till Death Do Us Part (1991) . . . . Sandra Stockton
Bob Roberts (1992; U.S./British) . . . . Delores Perrigrew
Clearcut (1992; Canadian). . . . . Female Reporter
Made for TV Movies:
Legend of Ruby Silver (1996). . . . . .Katie Rainie

Jenkins, Sam

Wife of actor Kevin Sorbo.
Films:
The Bonfire of the Vanities (1990) . . . . .Fox's Assistant
Night of the Warrior (1991). . . . . Hooker
Ed and His Dead Mother (1993). . . . . Storm Reynolds
• 0:16—Buns in bedroom when Ned Beatty spies on her through telescope.
• 0:52—Very brief right breast, while going up stairs.
Fortunes of War (1993) . . . . Johanna Pimmler
Twenty Bucks (1993). . . . . Anna Holiday
The Crew (1994). . . . . Catherine
TV:
Hercules: The Legendary Journeys (1996-)
. . . . Serena/Golden Hind

*Jennings, Claudia **

Films:
Jud (1971) . . . . Sunny
• 0:22—Brief breasts, while taking off her clothes at the beach with Jud.
The Love Machine (1971) . . . . .Darlene
The Stepmother (1971). . . . . .Redhead
Group Marriage (1972) . . . . Elaine
••• 1:02—Breasts under mosquito net in bed with Phil. Long scene.
Unholy Rollers (1972). Karen Walker
a.k.a. Leader of the Pack
••• 0:32—Breasts on pool table, getting gang stripped by the other girls, then walking around and yelling at them.
• 0:38—Buns on top of Nick, on table in the middle of the roller derby rink.
•• 1:15—Breasts, twice, while changing clothes in locker room, then in bra and panties.
40 Carats (1973) . . . . .Gabriella
Bloody Friday (1973) . . . . .Allison
a.k.a. Single Girls
• 0:40—Breasts, taking off her dress to sunbathe on rock at the beach. Long shot. Side view of right breast, putting dress back on when George talks to her.
•• 0:57—Breasts, drying herself off after shower.
Gator Bait (1973) . . . . .Desiree Tibidoe
• 0:06—Brief left and right breasts during boat chase sequence.
Truck Stop Women (1974) . . . . Rose
• 0:27—Brief breasts taking off blouse and getting into bed.
• 0:48—Brief side view of right breast in mirror, while getting dressed.
• 1:10—Brief breasts wrapping and unwrapping a towel around herself.

The Man Who Fell to Earth (1976; British) .... Uncredited Girl by the Pool
(Uncensored version reviewed.)
- • 1:42—Breasts, standing by the pool and kissing Bernie Casey.

Sisters of Death (1976) .... n.a.
The Great Texas Dynamite Chase (1977) ...... Candy Morgan
Moonshine County Express (1977) .... Betty Hammer
Death Sport (1978) .... Deneer
Impulsion (1978) .... n.a.
Fast Company (1979; Canadian) .... Sammy
The Best of Sex and Violence (1981) .... Rose
- •• 0:46—Breasts taking off her blouse in scene from *Truck Stop Women.*

Famous T & A (1982) .... Rose
(No longer available for purchase, check your video store for rental.)
- •• 0:26—Breasts scenes from *Single Girls* and *Truck Stop Women.*

• Jennings, Claudine *

Made for Cable TV:

Erotic Confessions: An Erotic Christmas Carol (1997; Cinemax) .... Theresa
- •• 0:07—In white lingerie outfit, then buns and breasts, while fooling around with Gary in his office.
- • 0:10—Brief breasts and buns in flashbacks.

Beverly Hills Bordello: Use Your Imagination (1998; Showtime) .... Amanda
- • 0:08—Right breast, while making love with Felix.
- ••• 0:18—Nude, while helping Felix get warmed up in bedroom.

Video Tapes:

Playboy's Girls of the Internet (1996) .... Herself
- ••• 0:01—Nude, while stripping and dancing in the Internet Café, wearing stockings and boots.

Penthouse: Lipstick Girls (1997) .... n.a.

Jennings, Julia

Films:

Teachers (1984) .... The Blonde
- •• 0:05—Brief left breast, while sitting up in bed with Nick Nolte.

Dragnet (1987) .... Sylvia Wiss

Jenrette, Rita *

Ex-wife of former U.S. Representative John Jenrette, who was convicted in 1980 in the FBI's Abscam probe.
Now using her maiden name of Rita Carpenter.

Films:

Zombie Island Massacre (1984) .... Sandy
- ••• 0:01—Breasts taking a shower while Joe sneaks up on her. Breasts in bed with Joe.
- •• 0:10—Brief right breast with open blouse, in boat with Joe. Left breast with him on the couch.

The Malibu Bikini Shop (1985) .... Aunt Ida
End of the Line (1987) .... Sharon

Made for Cable TV:

Dream On: And Bimbo Was His Name-O (1992; HBO) .... Jennifer Klarik

Jensen, Maren

Films:

Beyond the Reef (1981) .... Diana
(Not available on video tape.)

Deadly Blessing (1981) .... Martha
- •• 0:27—Breasts and buns, while changing into a nightgown while a creepy guy watches through the window.
- • 0:52—Buns, while getting into bathtub. Kind of steamy and hard to see.
- • 0:56—Brief breasts, while in bathtub with snake. (Notice that she gets into the tub naked, but is wearing black panties in the water).

TV:

Battlestar Galactica (1978-79) .... Athena

Jillson, Joyce

Astrologer.

Films:

Slumber Party '57 (1976) .... Gladys
The Happy Hooker Goes to Washington (1977) .... Herself
Superchick (1978) .... Tara B. True/Superchick
- • 0:03—Brief upper half of right breast leaning back in bathtub.
- •• 0:06—Breasts in bed throwing cards up.
- • 0:16—Brief breasts under net on boat with Johnny.
- • 0:29—Brief right breast several times in airplane restroom with a Marine.
- • 1:12—Buns, frolicking in the ocean with Johnny. Don't see her face.
- • 1:27—Close up of breasts (probably body double) when sweater pops open.

TV:

Peyton Place (1968) .... Jill Smith/Rossi

Jilot, Yolanda

Films:

Diving In (1990) .... Amanda Lansky
- • 0:55—Brief breasts, in open blouse, getting dressed while talking to Burt Young.

Waxwork II: Lost in Time (1991) .... Lady of the Night

Made for TV Movies:

JFK: Reckless Youth (1993) .... Inga Arvad

TV:

Reasonable Doubts (1992-93) .... Marta

Jisél

See: Ledford, Brandy.

Johansen, Linda *

Video Tapes:

Penthouse Paradise Revisited (1992) .... Pet

Johari, Azizi *

Films:

The Killing of a Chinese Bookie (1976) .... Rachel
- • 1:14—Brief breasts, while dancing on stage.
- •• 1:15—Breasts dancing in red light, then coming over to talk to Ben Gazzara.
- • 1:26—Brief side view of right breast, while taking a shower.

Body and Soul (1981) .... Pussy Willow
- ••• 0:31—Breasts sitting on bed with Leon Isaac Kennedy, then left breast, while lying in bed.

John, Tylyn *

a.k.a. Tylyn.

Films:

Rising Sun (1993) .... Redhead
- ••• 0:56—Breasts, while sitting next to Eddie and when he licks sake off her left breast.
- •• 0:58—Breasts and buns, while jumping onto and riding on Wesley Snipes' back.

Video Tapes:
Playboy Video Calendar 1993 (1992) . . . . .November
••• 0:45—Nude on motorcycle in studio and in the rain.
••• 0:47—Nude in house and on balcony.
Playboy Video Centerfold: Corrina Harney (1992) . . . . .Playmate
Playboy's Playmate Review 1993 (1993) . . . . . Miss March
••• 0:40—Nude, while doing things around a country home.
••• 0:42—Nude in white studio fantasy.
Playboy's Sexy, Steamy, Sultry (1993). . . . . .Playmate
Babes, Bikes & Beyond (1994) . . . . Herself
• 0:43—Buns, while dancing in panties.
Wet & Wild VIII: Bottoms Up (1996). . . . . .Playmate
Playboy's Hot Wheels & High Heels Biker Babes (1997) . . . . Biker Bash/Tylyn
••• 0:33—Buns in motorcycle leather clothing. Nude while Avalon video tapes her posing on motorcycle.

Johns, Tracy Camilla *

Films:
She's Gotta Have It (1987) . . . . Nola Darling
••• 0:05—Breasts, making love in bed with Jamie.
•• 0:25—Brief left breast taking off leotard with Greer. More breasts waiting for him to undress.
•• 0:27—Breasts and buns in bed with Greer.
• 0:38—Breasts, close up of breast, while making love with Spike Lee.
•• 0:41—Left breast, while lying in bed with Lee.
•• 1:05—Breasts, twice, in bed masturbating.
Mo' Better Blues (1990) . . . . .Club Patron
New Jack City (1991) . . . . Unigua
• 0:40—Buns, while dancing in red bra, panties, garter belt and stockings.
• 0:53—Buns and right breast in bed with Wesley Snipes.
TV:
Snoops (1989-90) . . . . .Yolanda

Johnson, Anne-Marie

Films:
Hollywood Shuffle (1987) . . . . .Lydia
I'm Gonna Git You Sucka (1988) . . . . Cherry
Robot Jox (1990) . . . . Athena
•• 0:35—Buns, while walking to the showers after talking with Achilles and Tex.
The Five Heartbeats (1991) . . . . .Sydney Todd
Strictly Business (1991) . . . . .Diedre
True Identity (1991) . . . . Kristi
Miniseries:
Jackie Collins' Lucky/Chances (1990). . . . . Carrie
TV:
Double Trouble (1984-85). Aileen Lewis
In the Heat of the Night (1988). . . . . Althea Tibbs
In Living Color (1993-94) . . . . Cast Member
Melrose Place (1995-96) . . . . Alycia Barnett

Johnson, Beverly

Model.
Films:
Ashanti, Land of No Mercy (1979). . . . Dr. Anansa Linderby
•• 0:07—Buns and brief side view of breasts, taking off clothes to go skinny dipping.
•• 0:08—Briefly nude, running to put her clothes back on.
• 1:15—Right breast in gaping dress while bending over to bury dead bad guy.
Loaded Weapon 1 (1993) . . . . Doris Luger
0:50—In gold, braless, semi-sheer blouse.
The Meteor Man (1993) . . . . Doctor
A Brilliant Disguise (1994) . . . . .Barbara
Crossworlds (1996) . . . . The Queen
True Vengeance (1996) . . . . .Lt. Kada Wilson
How To Be a Player (1997). . . . . Robin
Made for Cable TV:
Red Shoe Diaries: Forbidden Zone (1996; Showtime) . . . . The Woman
•• 0:18—Brief left breast, twice, while making love in bed with Jay Acovone.
Made for TV Movies:
Ray Alexander: A Menu for Murder (1995) . . . . . Alana Durand

Johnson, Cara

See: Johnson, Caroline Key.

Johnson, Caroline Key

a.k.a. Cara Johnson.
Films:
Showgirls (1995) . . . . Nadia
(NC-17 version reviewed.)
Tainted Love (1995). . . . . Chloe
Made for Cable Movies:
National Lampoon's Favorite Deadly Sins (1995; Showtime) . . . . Step Sister 2
Made for Cable TV:
Love Street: Trick or Treat (1995; Showtime) . . . . Julie
• 0:01—Breasts while making love with Alex in bed.
••• 0:11—Buns and breasts when fantasizing about making love with another guy.
••• 0:22—Buns in T-back then breasts and buns while making love with Alex in Sandi's house.
Erotic Confessions: Through an Open Window (1997; Cinemax) . . . . Grace
•• 0:01—Breasts, while fooling around with Cliff in bed.
Intimate Sessions: Celeste (1998; Cinemax). . . . . . . Celeste
•• 0:01—Breasts, while lying in bed, talking on the telephone.
••• 0:10—Full frontal nudity, while taking a bath and getting out while talking with Michael.
•• 0:13—Buns and breasts, while making love with Michael in bed.
••• 0:17—Breasts, while caressing herself in bed.
•• 0:23—Breasts, while making love in bed with Michael and Jan.

Johnson, Deborah Nicholle *

a.k.a. Debi Johnson.
Video Tapes:
Playmate Playoffs. . . . . .Playmate
Playmates at Play (1990). . . . . .Hardbodies
Playboy's 21 Playmates: Volume II (1996) . . . . . .Playmate
••• 0:17—Nude in still photos.
••• 0:18—Nude, while stretching and lying in bed after working out.

Johnson, Echo *

Video Tapes:
Playboy Celebrity Centerfold: Jessica Hahn (1993) . . . . .Playmate
••• 0:39—Nude, doing various modeling things.
••• 0:42—Nude in loft fantasy.
••• 0:45—Nude in still photos.
••• 0:46—Nude in a mansion.
Playboy Video Calendar 1994 (1993) . . . . September
••• 0:35—Nude while working out and exercising.
••• 0:37—Nude, undressing from a tuxedo.

Playboy's Sexy, Steamy, Sultry (1993). . . . . Playmate
Sexy Lingerie V (1993) . . . . Model
Wet & Wild VIII: Bottoms Up (1996). . . . . Playmate

Johnson, Jill

Films:

Party Favors (1987) . . . . Trixie
•• 0:04—Breasts in dressing room, taking off blue dress and putting on red swimsuit.
••• 0:35—Breasts in doctor's office taking off her clothes.
••• 1:03—Breasts doing strip routine in cowgirl costume. More breasts after.
• 1:16—Breasts taking off swimsuit next to pool during final credits.

Wildest Dreams (1987) . . . . Rachel Richards
•• 0:51—Breasts on bed underneath Bobby in a net.
• 1:10—Brief breasts during fight with two other women.

Party Plane (1988) . . . . Laurie
••• 0:06—Breasts and buns changing clothes and getting into spa with her two girlfriends. (She's wearing a black swimsuit bottom.)
••• 0:11—Breasts getting out of spa.
•• 0:16—Breasts in pool after being pushed in and her swimsuit top comes off.
•• 0:20—In bra and panties, then breasts on plane doing a strip tease.

Taking Care of Business (1990) . . . . Tennis Court Girl

*Johnson, Kimberly **

Video Tapes:

Hot Body International: #2 Miss Puerto Vallarta (1990) . . . . Contestant
•• 0:43—Buns in two piece swimsuit.

Hot Body International: #4 Spring Break (1992) . . . . Contestant
• 0:25—Buns in G-string during wet T-shirt contest.

Johnson, Laura

Ex-wife of actor Harry Hamlin.

Films:

Opening Night (1977) . . . . Nancy Stein

Fatal Instinct (1991) . . . . Catherine Merrims
a.k.a. To Kill For
(Unrated version reviewed.)
• 0:45—Brief left breast in open robe, getting out of bed.
••• 0:47—Breasts in bed talking with Michael Madsen, then making love.
••• 0:51—Breasts in the bathtub when Bill comes in. Partial lower frontal nudity when standing up.
•• 0:52—Brief buns and breasts getting dressed in bedroom.
• 0:59—In wet T-shirt in pool. Brief buns, underwater, more when getting out.

Murderous Vision (1991). . . . . Elizabeth Larwin
Cheatin' Hearts (1992) . . . . Patsy

Trauma (1992) . . . . Grace Harrington
• 0:38—Breast, while making love in bed with David and after he leaves.

Deadly Exposure (1993) . . . . Rita Sullivan
(Nude scenes are a body double.)

Judge & Jury (1996) . . . . Grace Silvano

Made for Cable TV:

Red Shoe Diaries: Double Dare (1992; Showtime) . . Diane
(Available on the video tape *Red Shoe Diaries 2: Double Dare.*)
••• 0:16—Breasts, taking off her bra in her office.
•• 0:17—More breasts, caressing herself.
• 0:18—Breasts in bed, making love with her husband, Sam.
•• 0:25—Breasts in the shower.
•• 1:28—Breasts in bed with her husband. (Additional footage added for video tape.)

Made for TV Movies:

Chiller (1985) . . . . Leigh
Nick Knight (1989) . . . . Alyce
Awake to Danger (1995) . . . . Renee McAdams

TV:

Falcon Crest (1983-86) . . . . Terry Hartford Ranson
Heartbeat (1988-89) . . . . Dr. Eve Autrey/Calvert

*Johnson, Lynn **

Video Tapes:

Penthouse Pet of the Year Playoff 1991 (1992) . . . . . Pet
••• 0:23—Nude in African-theme segment with a man and another woman. Muddy.
• 0:25—Breasts in still photos.
••• 0:26—Nude in B&W and color water-theme segment.
••• 0:28—Nude in mirrored area.
••• 0:30—Nude doing various poses on chair, behind tubular wire screen in studio.

Penthouse: Fast Cars/Fantasy Women (1992) . . . . Model

Penthouse DreamGirls (1994) . . . . Lynn
••• 0:45—Full frontal nudity in house.

Johnson, Michelle

Films:

Blame It on Rio (1984). Jennifer Lyons
•• 0:19—Breasts on the beach greeting Michael Caine and Joseph Bologna with Demi Moore, then brief breasts in the ocean.
• 0:26—Breasts taking her clothes off for Caine on the beach. Dark, hard to see.
•• 0:27—Breasts seducing Caine. Dark, hard to see.
••• 0:56—Full frontal nudity taking off robe and sitting on bed to take a Polaroid picture of herself.
• 0:57—Very brief breasts in the Polaroid photo showing it to Caine.
• 1:02—Brief breasts taking off her top in front of Caine while her dad rests on the sofa.

Gung Ho (1985) . . . . Heather

Beaks The Movie (1987) . . . . Vanessa
• 0:26—Brief breasts covered with bubbles after taking a bath. Don't see her face.
• 0:31—Brief breasts covered with bubbles after getting out of bathtub with Christopher Atkins. Don't see her face.

The Jigsaw Murders (1988) . . . . Kathy DaVonzo
Slipping into Darkness (1988) . . . . Carlyle
Waxwork (1988) . . . . China

Genuine Risk (1989). . . . . Girl
• 0:43—On bed in black bra and panties with Henry. Left breast peeking out of the top of her bra.

Blood Ties (1991) . . . . Celia
Driving Me Crazy (1991). . . . . Ricki
Death Becomes Her (1992) . . . . Anna
Dr. Giggles (1992). . . . . Tamara
Far and Away (1992) . . . . Grace

Body Shot (1993) . . . . Danielle Wilde
0:23—Brief buns in T-back under fishnet outfit.
• 0:28—Brief buns, when dropping robe.

The Donor (1994) . . . . Dr. Lucy Flynn
Illicit Dreams (1994) . . . . Melinda Ryan
Specimen (1995; Canadian) . . . . Sarah
The Glimmer Man (1996) . . . . Jessica
Moving Target (1996) . . . . Casey

Made for Cable Movies:
Incident at Deception Ridge (1994; USA) ...... Natalie Harris
When the Bullet Hits the Bone (1996; Showtime) .... Lisa
Made for Cable TV:
Tales From the Crypt: Split Second (1991; HBO) .... Liz Kelly-Dixon
••• 0:15—Breasts, offering her towel to Ted for him to dry her off.
The Outer Limits: First Anniversary (1996; Showtime) .... Ady Sutton
Arli$$: Where Do Clients Come From? (1998; HBO) ...... n.a.
Made for TV Movies:
Werewolf (1987) .... Kelly Nichols
A Woman Scorned: The Betty Broderick Story (1992) .... Linda
Dallas: War of the Ewings (1998) .... Jennifer

Johnson, Penny

Films:
Swing Shift (1984) .... Genevieve
The Hills Have Eyes, Part II (1989) .... Sue
• 0:49—Brief breasts in bus, trying to get Foster's attention.
Fear of a Black Hat (1992) .... Re-Re
Molly & Gina (1993) .... Maria
What's Love Got to Do With It (1993) .... Lorraine
Automatic (1994) .... Julia Rodriguez
Death Benefit (1996) .... Sylvia Guzman
Absolute Power (1997) .... Laura Simon
Made for Cable Movies:
The Road to Galveston (1996; USA) .... n.a.
Made for Cable TV:
The Larry Sanders Show (1992-98; HBO) .... Beverly
TV:
Paper Chase (1984-86) .... Vivian
Homeroom (1989) .... Virginia

Johnson, Sandy *

Films:
Jokes My Folks Never Told Me (1976) .... n.a.
Two-Minute Warning (1976) .... Button's Wife
Gas Pump Girls (1978) .... April
•• 0:05—Breasts, when her graduation gown gets torn off during ceremony.
• 0:06—Breasts, when changing clothes in locker room while talking with her girlfriends.
•• 0:30—Breasts, while in back seat of car on hydraulic lift, then in the front seat with Michael.
• 0:32—Brief right breast, when sitting up in car.
• 0:48—Brief breasts, three times, while walking back and forth past doorway to distract Bruno.
Halloween (1978) .... Judith Meyers
• 0:06—Very brief breasts covered with blood on floor after Michael stabs her to death.
H.O.T.S. (1979) .... Stephanie
a.k.a. T & A Academy
•• 0:27—Breasts on balcony in red bikini bottoms.
•• 1:34—Breasts during football game during huddle with all the other girls.
The Best Little Whorehouse in Texas (1982) .... Chicken Ranch Girl
Terror in the Aisles (1984) .... Judith Meyers
• 0:15—Brief breasts in scene from *Halloween.*

• *Johnson, Shánn* *

Films:
Blues Brothers 2000 (1997) .... Matara
• 0:19—Brief buns in G-string, while dancing on stage.

• *Johnson, Stacii Jae*

Films:
A Thin Line Between Love and Hate (1995) .... Peaches
How To Be a Player (1997) .... Sherri
• 0:00—Brief breasts, while in bed with Bill Bellamy.
• 0:01—Very brief left breast, while in bed with Bellamy.

Johnson, Sunny

Films:
Animal House (1978) .... Otter's Co-Ed
Dr. Heckyl and Mr. Hype (1980) .... Coral Careen
Where the Buffalo Roam (1980) .... n.a.
The Night the Lights Went Out in Georgia (1981) ..... Wendy
Flashdance (1983) .... Jennie Szabo
• 1:28—Breasts, while sitting on stage and moving her legs around.
• 1:29—Very brief left breast in open rain coat, outside the club with Jennifer Beals.
Made for TV Movies:
The Red Light Sting (1984) .... Sonia

Johnson, Terri

Films:
Class Reunion (1970) .... n.a.
Snow Bunnies (1970) .... n.a.
Pleasure Unlimited/Sensous Wife (1972) .... n.a.
a.k.a. Drop Out Wife
Video Vixens (1973) .... Anita
•• 0:43—Full frontal nudity, talking with her mother in bedroom during commercial.
The Cocktail Hostess (1976) .... n.a.

Johnson, Victoria Lynn *

Films:
Dressed to Kill (1980) .... Body Double for Angie Dickinson
•• 0:02—Frontal nudity in the shower body doubling for Angie Dickinson.
Terror in the Aisles (1984) .... Body Double for Angie Dickinson
• 1:07—Breasts in shower from Angie Dickinson's shower scene in *Dressed to Kill.*
Video Tapes:
The Girls of Penthouse (1984) .... Centerfold
••• 0:43—Nude during photo session with Bob Guccione.

Johnston, Michelle

Films:
A Chorus Line (1985) .... Bebe
Dick Tracy (1990) .... Dancer
Faith (1990) .... Audition Choreographer
Opportunity Knocks (1990) .... Club Singer
California Casanova (1991) .... Laura
• 0:12—Buns in black G-string, while dancing on stage.
• 0:18—Brief breasts under sheer black top, while dancing in front of a guy in pool house.
Shout (1991) .... Loretta
Showgirls (1995) .... Gay
(NC-17 version reviewed.)

Johnston-Ulrich, Kim

Films:

Blood Ties (1991) . . . . Loren
- • 1:21—Very brief breasts, while rolling over in bed with Harry.

Spellcaster (1992) . . . . Teri

Rumpelstiltskin (1995) . . . . Shelly Stewart
- • 0:23—Very brief back side of right breast, then buns, while getting out of bed. Don't see her face well.

Made for TV Movies:

Judith Krantz's "Dazzle" (1995) . . . . Valerie

TV:

As the World Turns . . . . Diana McColl

Nightingales (1989) . . . . Allyson Yates

Joi, Marilyn

a.k.a. Tracey Ann King.

Films:

Hammer (1972) . . . . The Black Magic Woman

Hit Man (1972) . . . . Nita

Ilsa, Harem Keeper of the Oil Sheiks (1976) . . . . . . Velvet

The Happy Hooker Goes to Washington (1977) . . . Sheila
- • 0:09—Left breast while on a couch.
- • 0:47—Brief breasts during car demonstration.
- •• 1:14—Breasts in military guy's office.

The Kentucky Fried Movie (1977) . . . . Cleopatra
- • 1:11—Breasts in bed with Schwartz.

The Naughty Stewardesses (1978) . . . . Barbara

a.k.a. Fresh Air
- •• 0:56—Breasts, while dancing by the pool in front of everybody.

Nurse Sherri (1978) . . . . n.a.

Galaxina (1980) . . . . Winged Girl

C.O.D. (1983) . . . . Debbie Winter
- •• 1:16—Breasts during photo session.
- • 1:25—Brief breasts taking off robe wearing red garter belt during dressing room scene.

Cheerleaders Wild Weekend (1985) . . . . LaSalle/Polk
- • 0:00—Brief breasts while tying her shoelace in locker room.
- • 0:33—Brief breasts in catfight with another girl in cabin.
- ••• 0:39—Breasts, taking off her yellow blouse during contest.
- ••• 0:41—Breasts with the other five girls during contest.
- • 0:42—Breasts, losing contest.

Satan's Princess (1989) . . . . Hooker

Jolie, Angelina

Daughter of actor Jon Voight.

Wife of actor Jonny Lee Miller.

Films:

Lookin' to Get Out (1982) . . . . Tosh

Cyborg 2: Glass Shadow (1993) . . . . Cash
- • 1:14—Left breast, while in bed with Elias Koteas. Slightly out of focus.
- •• 1:16—Breasts, while making love on top of Koteas in bed.

Hackers (1995) . . . . Kate
- • 0:43—Very brief half of left breast, after she unzips her jacket in Dade's dream.
- • 0:51—Brief breasts under sheer black blouse, while sitting at desk.

Foxfire (1996) . . . . Legs Sadovsky
- ••• 0:37—Breasts, taking off her T-shirt and giving herself and her girl friends tattoos.

Playing God (1997) . . . . Claire

Made for Cable Movies:

Gia (1998; HBO) . . . . Gia Marie Carangi
- •• 0:24—Breasts and buns in color and B&W while posing for photos in studio in front of a chain link fence.
- ••• 0:27—Buns and breasts, when talking with Linda in hallway.

Made for TV Movies:

True Women (1997) . . . . Georgia

Jolliff-Andoh, Lisa

Films:

The Return of the Superfly (1990) . . . . Eddie's Girl

Scarlet Letter (1995) . . . . Mituba
- • 0:50—Very brief left breast, when bending over before getting into tub. Partial left breast while sitting in the tub, holding a candle.

Jones, Amanda

Films:

Honky Tonk Nights (1978) . . . . Honey
- •• 0:41—Breasts outside by car with Dan.
- ••• 0:42—Breasts and buns, in the woods with Dan.

Winter Kills (1979) . . . . Beautiful Woman Seven

Jones, Catherine Zeta

Films:

Christopher Columbus: The Discovery (1992; U.S./Spanish) . . . . Beatrix

Splitting Heirs (1993) . . . . Kitty
- • 0:39—Swimming in lap pool (hard to see anything because of the water distortion.) Brief buns and back half of left breast, while getting out of the pool. Long shot.

Tunnel Vision (1995; Australian) . . . . Bunny

The Phantom (1996) . . . . Sala

Made for TV Movies:

The Return of the Native (1994) . . . . Eustacia Vye

Masterpiece Theatre: The Cinder Path (1995) . . . . Victoria

Titanic (1996) . . . . Isabella Paradine

Jones, Charlene

Films:

The Curious Female (1969) . . . . Pearl Lucomb/Girl #2
- • 0:14—Brief breasts, twice, while taking a shower.
- • 0:29—Buns, while running in slow motion to the pool.
- • 0:30—Buns, while lying down.
- • 1:08—Breasts while making love with a guy. Hard to see because of psychedelic light
- •• 1:09—Breasts while turning over on her back with Andre.

Unholy Rollers (1972) . . . . Beverly

a.k.a. Leader of the Pack

The Woman Hunt (1975; U.S./Philippines) . . . . n.a.

Hard to Hold (1984) . . . . Wife #3

Avenging Angel (1985) . . . . Hooker

Perfect (1985) . . . . Shotsy
- • 0:17—Breasts stripping on stage in a club. Buns in G-string.

Jones, Grace *

Films:

Conan the Destroyer (1984) . . . . Zula

Deadly Vengeance (1985) . . . . Slick's Girlfriend

(Although the copyright on the movie states 1985, it looks more like the 1970's.)
- ••• 0:06—Right breast, then breasts in bed with Slick.
- •• 0:13—Left breast, when Slick sits up in bed, then full frontal nudity after he gets up.

A View to a Kill (1985) . . . . May Day

Vamp (1986) . . . . Katrina
- 0:23—Breasts under wire bra, dancing on stage. Body is painted, so it's difficult to see.

Siesta (1987) . . . . Conchita
Straight to Hell (1987; British) . . . . Sonya
Boomerang (1992) . . . . Strangé
- 0:35—Brief buns, under stockings during conference room meeting.
- 1:19—Brief buns and back side of left breast, several times on TV monitor during editing of a commercial.
- 1:29—Very brief breasts ripping off dress during a commercial.

Cyber Bandits (1994) . . . . Mesoko
CD-ROM:
Hell: A Cyberpunk Thriller (1994) . . . . n.a.

Jones, Helen

Films:
Bliss (1985; Australian) . . . . Honey Barbara
- ••• 0:58—Breasts, lying on the floor with Harry. Brief part of lower frontal nudity. Long scene.
- • 1:01—Brief breasts on bed when Adrian runs to the bathroom.
- • 1:24—Left breast, while standing outside with arms outstretched.
- • 1:39—Buns, while swimming. Long shot of buns while walking up rocks.

The Good Wife (1987; Australian) . . . . Rosie Gibbs
a.k.a. The Umbrella Woman
Made for Cable Movies:
The Silver Strand (1995; Showtime) . . . . Rose Guttierez
Made for TV Movies:
The Girl From Tomorrow (1990; Australian) . . . . Tulista

Jones, Josephine Jaqueline

a.k.a. J. J. Jones.
Former Miss Bahamas.
Films:
Black Venus (1983) . . . . Venus
- •• 0:05—Breasts, while in Jungle Room.
- ••• 0:11—Nude, in bedroom, posing for Armand while he sketches.
- • 0:14—Breasts and buns, while making love with Armand in bed.
- •• 0:17—Nude, posing for Armand while he models in clay, then on the bed, kissing him.
- • 0:21—Briefly nude, while getting dressed.
- ••• 0:38—Nude, making love in bed with Karin Schubert.
- ••• 0:45—Nude, talking and then making love in bed with Louise.
- •• 0:50—Breasts when Pierre brings everybody in to see her.
- •• 0:57—Breasts in silhouette while Armand fantasizes about his statue coming to life.
- ••• 1:04—Nude.
- ••• 1:07—Nude with the two diplomats on the bed.
- ••• 1:16—Nude frolicking on the beach with Louise.
- ••• 1:18—Breasts, while in bedroom getting out of wet clothes with Louise.
- •• 1:21—Breasts, while in bed with Jacques.
- •• 1:24—Full frontal nudity, while getting out of bed.

Christina (1984; U.S./French) . . . . Antoinette
(Never released on video tape. Is shown occasionally on cable television.)
- •• 0:44—Breasts, after her blouse gets ripped off during fight with Marie.
- ••• 0:53—Breasts, after taking off blouse, then making love with Jewel Shepard.
- ••• 0:57—Breasts, while at the beach with Shepard.
- •• 1:00—Breasts, while on boat, during fight with smugglers.

Love Circles Around the World (1984) . . . . Brigid
a.k.a. Love Circles
- •• 0:18—Breasts, then nude running around her apartment chasing Jack.
- • 0:30—Breasts, making love with Count Crispa in his hotel room.

Warrior Queen (1987) . . . . Chloe
- ••• 0:20—Breasts, while making love with Vespa.

Jones, Marilyn

Films:
Support Your Local Sheriff! (1969) . . . . Bordello Girl
The Scenic Route (1978) . . . . Lena
Meteor (1979) . . . . Stunt
The Love Butcher (1982) . . . . Lena
The Men's Club (1986) . . . . Allison
- •• 1:21—Breasts, while in bedroom talking to Harvey Keitel, then putting on dress.

On the Block (1990) . . . . Libby
Made for TV Movies:
The Lakeside Killer (1979) . . . . Cindy Lee
TV:
Secrets of Midland Heights (1980-81) . . . . Holly Wheeler
King's Crossing (1982) . . . . Carey Hollister

Jones, Rachel

Films:
Dracula's Widow (1988) . . . . Jenny
- • 0:54—Brief left breast, then brief breasts, twice, lying in the bathtub, getting stabbed by Sylvia Kristel.

Fresh Horses (1988) . . . . Bobo
Lorenzo's Oil (1993) . . . . Special Child

Jones, Rebunkah

Films:
Frankenstein General Hospital (1988) . . . . . . Elizabeth Rice
- •• 1:05—Breasts in the office letting Mark Blankfield examine her back.

Hide and Go Shriek (1988) . . . . Bonnie Williams
- •• 0:27—Breasts taking off her blouse. More breasts sitting in bed.

Jones, Samantha

Films:
Wait Until Dark (1967) . . . . Lisa
Way We Live Now (1970) . . . . Samantha
Get to Know Your Rabbit (1972) . . . . Susan
- •• 0:27—Right breast, after taking the bra off.
- • 0:28—Right breast, while dancing with Smothers in the store.

Jones, Sharon Lee

Films:
9 1/2 Ninjas (1990) . . . . Zelda
- • 0:52—Breasts, while eating Chinese food in the shower with Joe.

Princess Warrior (1990) . . . . Ovule
- • 0:33—Very, very brief buns while jumping through glass. Don't see her face.
- • 0:58—Brief breasts a few times, while making love with Bob.
- • 1:07—Very brief lower half of buns, while hitting Curette.

- 1:10—Brief buns, while climbing up on back of truck.
  1:16—Very brief breasts, while taking off her T-shirt to get into portal. (Note that the image has been blurred so you can't see them clearly.)

Grand Canyon (1991) . . . . Studio Girl

Jones, Shelly *

Films:

Can It Be Love (1992) . . . . Wet T-shirt Contestant
a.k.a. Spring Break Sorority Babes

Video Tapes:

Making of the "Carousel Girls' Calendar" (1993) . . . . Miss October
- ••• 1:07—Breasts and buns during photo shoot.
- ••• 1:10—Nude during interview segment.

Playboy's Girls of Radio: Talk, Rock and Shock (1995) . . . . Herself
- ••• 0:40—Nude in and out of various outfits.

Playboy's Sorority Girls (1997). . . . . Wash & Dry
- ••• 0:24—Nude, while dancing by herself in a laundromat.

Jones, Susan

Films:

RollerBlade Warriors: Taken By Force (1988) . . . . Slave Girl #2
- •• 0:20—Breasts, while getting hassled by two guys.
- ••• 0:23—Breasts, while walking through the desert.

Wilding, The Children of Violence (1990) . . . . Alley Rape Victim
- • 1:16—Breasts outside struggling with Jason and Bobby on the ground.

Jones-Davies, Sue

Films:

Monty Python's Life of Brian (1979; British) . . . . Judith
- • 1:04—Brief full frontal nudity, then nude when Brian comes back after opening the window.

Radio On (1980; British/German) . . . . Girl
Elenya (1992; British) . . . . Maggie

Jordan, Deanna

Video Tapes:

Hot Body International: #2 Miss Puerto Vallarta (1990) . . . . Contestant

Hot Body International: #4 Spring Break (1992) . . . . Contestant
- • 0:13—Dancing in two piece swimsuit on stage. Brief partial right breast.
- • 0:49—Brief breasts several times when she rips her wet T-shirt open. Buns in G-string.

Jourard, Gina

Films:

Novel Desires (1991) . . . . Shari
- •• 0:00—Right breast, then breasts in bed with Brian.
- •• 0:03—Breasts while taking a shower.
- •• 0:04—Brief tip of left breast while putting on a stocking. Breasts while getting dressed.

A Sensuous Summer (1991) . . . . Tracy
- ••• 0:09—Breasts while making love in bed with Alex.

Pleasure in Paradise (1992) . . . . Woman
- ••• 0:06—Breasts, while making in love in bed with Hansen.
- • 0:39—Breasts on bed with Hansen.

Jourdan, Catherine

Films:

Girl on a Motorcycle (1968; French/British) . . . . Catherine
a.k.a. Naked Under Leather

The Godson (1972; Italian/French) . . . . Hatcheck Girl

Aphrodite (1982; German/French) . . . . Valerie
- • 0:34—Brief upper half of breasts in bathtub.

Jovovich, Milla *

Model.

Daughter of Soviet actress Galina Jovovich.

a.k.a. Milla (as a singer.)

Films:

Two Moon Junction (1988) . . . . Samantha

Return to the Blue Lagoon (1991). Lilli
- • 0:49—Brief upper half breasts in front of mirror.
- • 1:07—Very brief breasts under water with Richard. Brief breasts under waterfall with Richard.
- • 1:20—Briefly in wet beige blouse, standing up in pond.
- • 1:26—Side view of right breast three times, washing make-up off her face in the pond.
- •• 1:28—Side view of right breast again. Very brief left breast, while picking up her top off rock.
- • 1:30—Side of left breast, while lying on bed and held down.

Chaplin (1992; British/U.S.) . . . . Mildred Harris
- • 0:55—Top of left breast peeking over top of lingerie while sitting on bed talking to Chaplin.
- • 0:56—Buns, after taking off lingerie and standing in front of Chaplin.

Kuffs (1992) . . . . Maya Carlton
Dazed and Confused (1993) . . . . Michelle

The Fifth Element (1997) . . . . Leeloo
- • 0:26—Brief right breast, while lying in regeneration chamber. Brief right breast when straps go around her.
- • 0:47—Brief breasts, while changing clothes in the background. Slightly out of focus.
- • 1:06—Very, very brief lower half of breasts, when taking off wet blouse in background. Slightly out of focus.

He Got Game (1998) . . . . Dakota Burns

Made for Cable Movies:

Night Train to Kathmandu (1988; Disney). . . . . Lily

Joyner, Michelle

Films:

Grim Prairie Tales (1990) . . . . Jenny
- • 0:35—Very brief right breast, then left breast while making love with Marc McClure. Kind of dark.

I Love You to Death (1990) . . . . Donna Joy

Traces of Red (1992) . . . . Morgan Cassidy
- • 0:08—In black bra, in bedroom with James Belushi. Brief breasts making love.
- •• 0:24—Left breast, while lying dead in bed when Belushi sees her.

Cliffhanger (1993). . . . . Sarah
Outbreak (1995) . . . . Sherry Mauldin

Painted Hero (1995). . . . . Katelin
- • 1:24—In bra and panties, while undressing in bedroom. Breasts, after taking off bra (medium long shot, then closer shot.)

Made for TV Movies:

Baby of the Bride (1991) . . . . Judy
Bonnie and Clyde: The True Story (1992) . . . . . Blanche Barrow
A Passion for Justice: The Hazel Brannon Smith Story (1994) . . . . Ann Sinclair

TV:

Knots Landing . . . . Lynnette

Jubert, Alice

Films:

Friday Foster (1975) . . . . Senator Hart's Secretary

J.D.'s Revenge (1976) . . . . Roberta Bliss/Betty Jo

•• 0:59—Breasts in open blouse, while leaning back on sofa with Isaac.

*Judd, Ashley **

Daughter of country singer Naomi Judd and sister of country singer Wynonna Judd.

Films:

Till Death Do Us Part (1991) . . . . Gwen Fox

Kuffs (1992) . . . . Paint Store Owner's Wife

Ruby in Paradise (1993). . . . . Ruby Lee Gissing

Heat (1995). . . . . Charlene

Smoke (1995) . . . . Felicity

Normal Life (1996). . . . . Pam Anderson

• 0:21—Brief right breast several times and very, very brief left breast, while lying in bed and talking with Luke Perry.

• 0:38—Breasts in open blouse, while cutting herself with a knife.

• 0:39—Right breast, while lying in bed when Perry discovers her cuts.

• 0:54—Breasts, while sitting on the bed, holding a gun to her head.

•• 1:04—Right breast, then brief breasts after having sex in bed with Perry.

••• 1:14—Breasts, while making love with Perry in bedroom.

•• 1:20—Breasts, while depressed when alone in bedroom.

A Time to Kill (1996) . . . . Carla Brigance

Kiss the Girls (1997) . . . . Kate Mctiernan

The Locusts (1997) . . . . Kitty

Made for Cable Movies:

Norma Jean & Marilyn (1996; HBO)

. . . . Norma Jean Dougherty

••• 0:02—Breasts, while unclothed in church filled with clothed people during dream.

•• 0:05—Breasts, after taking off her swimsuit by swimming pool in front of Eddie.

••• 0:36—Nude, after taking off robe and posing for photos.

•• 0:40—Breasts, pulling up her blouse for Johnny.

• 1:54—Brief breasts, cutting her dress open and ripping it off.

TV:

Sisters (1991-94) . . . . Reed Halsey

*Julia Ann **

Adult film actress.

Films:

Sex & Money (1994). . . . . Julie

Video Tapes:

Penthouse's 25th Anniversary Swimsuit Video (1993)

. . . . Pet

Ginger Lynn Allen's Lingerie Gallery (1994) . . . . Julia Ann

Penthouse Forum Letters: Volume 2 (1994)

. . . . The Big Switch/Debbie

••• 0:32—Breasts and buns in beige panties while doing strip tease with Cindy in front of their husbands. Nude in hot tub, then nude making love with Dan on bench.

Penthouse Women In & Out of Uniform (1995) . . . . . Pet

••• 0:33—Nude as a firewoman, playing around with gushing hoses with Janine Lindemulder.

••• 0:38—Nude as a policewoman with Lindemulder and Tiffany Burlingame in squad room.

••• 0:41—Nude as a stenographer, in courthouse with Lindemulder and Burlingame.

Julian, Janet

a.k.a. Janet Louise Johnson.

Films:

Humongous (1982; Canadian) . . . . Sandy Ralston

Fear City (1984). . . . . Ruby

Choke Canyon (1986) . . . . Vanessa Pilgrim

King of New York (1990) . . . . Jennifer

• 0:26—Very brief left breast, standing in subway car kissing Christopher Walken. Don't see her face.

Heaven is a Playground (1991) . . . . Dalton Ellis

Made for Cable TV:

Swamp Thing (1991-93; USA) . . . . Dr. Ann Fisk

TV:

The Nancy Drew Mysteries (1978). . . . . Nancy Drew

B.J. and the Bear (1979-80) . . . . Tommy

Falcon Crest (1989) . . . . Cookie Nash

Justin, Melissa

Made for Cable TV:

Dream On: Blinded by the Cheese (1994; HBO) . . . . Jolie

Dream On: Felines... Nothing More than Felines (1994; HBO) . . . . Heather

••• 0:17—Breasts, while with Martin in his apartment.

Dream On: Stone Cold (1994; HBO) . . . . Heather

••• 0:01—Breasts, while on bed with Martin in his apartment, then getting dressed and leaving.

• *Kablan, Therese*

Films:

Encino Man (1992) . . . . Fresh Nug

Made for Cable Movies:

Pronto (1997; Showtime) . . . . Gloria

• 0:18—Buns in two piece swimsuit.

• 0:22—Brief breasts, three times, while sitting up outside.

• 1:14—Brief breasts, when getting out of the spa.

Made for Cable TV:

Dream On: Nightmare on Bleecker Street (1992; HBO) . . Dana

Dream On: Take Two Tablets, And Get Me to Mt. Sinai (1995; HBO) . . . . Martin's Lover

TV:

NYPD Blue: Good Time Charlie (May 3, 1994). . . . . n.a.

Kabo, Olga

Films:

The Ice Runner (1993) . . . . Lena

•• 0:59—Breasts, twice, while washing her blouse in stream when Edward Albert sees her. Medium long shot.

••• 1:02—Breasts, while making love in bed with Albert.

Made for Cable Movies:

Bram Stoker's Burial of the Rats (1995; Showtime)

. . . . Anna

•• 0:21—Nude, while putting on a dress in front of a mirror.

Kafkaloff, Kim

a.k.a Adult film actress Sheri St. Clair or Sheri St. Cloud.

Films:

Sex Appeal (1986). . . . . Stephanie

•• 0:29—Buns, in G-string in Tony's bachelor pad. Breasts dancing and on bed.

Slammer Girls (1987). . . . . Ginny
- 0:23—Brief breasts changing clothes under table in the prison cafeteria.

• *Kaiser, Suki*

Films:

Red Scorpion 2 (1994) . . . . .Donna
Dangerous Indiscretion (1995) . . . . Sally
The Final Cut (1995). . . . . Kate Amis
Virtual Assassin (1995). . . . . .Alex

Made for Cable Movies:

Payoff (1991; Showtime). . . . . Catherine Concion
Circumstances Unknown (1995; USA) . . . . .Leah Kinsey

Made for Cable TV:

Poltergeist: The Legacy/Sins of the Father (1996; Showtime) . . . . n.a.
The Outer Limits: Stream of Consciousness (1997; Showtime) . . . . .Cheryl
Dead Man's Gun: Death Warrant (1997; Showtime) . . . . Maria
- 0:27—Very brief right breast, while fooling around with Michael Moriarty.

Made for TV Movies:

Jack Reed: A Killer Among Us (1996) . . . . .Sara

Kaitan, Elizabeth

a.k.a. Elizabeth Cayton.

Films:

The Lonely Guy (1983) . . . . n.a.
The Flamingo Kid (1984) . . . . n.a.
Savage Dawn (1984) . . . . Becky Sue
- 0:17—Right breast, while getting mauled by the bad guys.

Silent Madness (1984) . . . . Barbara
Zelig (1984) . . . . German Girl
Silent Night, Deadly Night, Part 2 (1986) . . . . Jennifer
- 0:58—Most of right breast, then buns, while kissing Ricky.

Thunder Run (1986) . . . . n.a.
Slavegirls from Beyond Infinity (1987). . . . . .Daria
(Wearing skimpy two piece loincloth outfit during most of the movie.)
- ••• 0:38—Breasts undressing and jumping into bed with Rik.

Violated (1987). . . . . Liz Grant
- •• 0:03—Breasts and lower frontal nudity while Frank rapes her in bedroom.
- 0:53—Very brief right breast several times while getting raped by Frank. Seen on video playback.
- ••• 0:59—Breasts and buns, while in bed with a customer.

Assault of the Killer Bimbos (1988) . . . . .Lulu
- 0:11—Brief breasts, after taking off costume top in dressing room.
- •• 0:41—Brief breasts, three times, during desert musical sequence, opening her blouse, then taking off her shorts, then putting on a light blue dress. Don't see her face.

Friday the 13th, Part VII: The New Blood (1988) . . Robin
- 0:53—Brief right breast, while making love in bed with a guy.
- 0:55—Brief breasts, while sitting up in bed after making love when the sheet falls down.
- •• 1:00—Brief breasts again, while sitting up in bed and putting a shirt on over her head.

Necromancer (1988) . . . . Julie Johnson
- •• 0:41—Breasts in the shower with Carl.
- 0:45—Very brief side view of right breast, taking off dress in front of Paul.

Nightwish (1988) . . . . Donna
(Unedited version reviewed.)
- 0:04—In wet T-shirt, then brief breasts taking it off during experiment. Long shot.
- 1:10—Briefly in braless, see-through purple dress.

RollerBlade Warriors: Taken By Force (1988) . . . . Gretchen Hope
- 0:51—Breasts, while tied to large spool and getting raped by Marachek.
- 1:03—Very brief breasts, several times, while getting raped in B&W vision.

Twins (1988) . . . . .Secretary
Dr. Alien (1989). . . . . Waitress
a.k.a. I Was a Teenage Sex Mutant
Night Club (1989). . . . . .Beth/Liza
- •• 0:31—Left breast, while pulling down blouse and caressing herself.
- •• 0:33—Left breast in pulled down blouse on stairwell with Nick.
- ••• 0:36—Breasts on warehouse floor with Nick.
- ••• 0:46—Full frontal nudity, taking off her dress in front of Nick.
- ••• 1:03—Breasts, making love with another guy in front of Nick.

Under the Boardwalk (1989) . . . . Donna
Aftershock (1990) . . . . .Sabina
The Girl I Want (1990). . . . . Amy
Lockdown (1990) . . . . Monica Taylor
Desperate Crimes (1991; Italian) . . . . Jamie Lee
- 0:04—Brief right breast, when getting her jacket opened by a bad guy, then more right breast after getting shot.

Vice Academy, Part 3 (1991) . . . . .Candy
- ••• 0:12—Breasts in back of van with her boyfriend.

Hellroller (1992) . . . . Lizzy
Beretta's Island (1993) . . . . Linda
- •• 1:33—Breasts, while playing with Franco Columbu in the ocean at the end of the film, during the end credits and after.

Good Girls Don't (1993) .TV Announcer
Vice Academy, Part 4 (1994) .Candy
- •• 0:46—Breasts, after taking off her dress top, while trying to seduce Anvil in his garage.

Petticoat Planet (1995). . . . . .Delia
- 0:05—Brief buns in white lingerie, while making love with Sarah.
- •• 0:10—Breasts and partial buns, while making love with Sarah.
- 0:39—Breasts and partial buns, while making love with Steve in bathtub.
- 0:59—Buns in lingerie, while talking and making love with Steve.

Virtual Encounters (1995). . . . . Amy
(Unrated version reviewed.)
- •• 0:42—Nude, while in the shower, fantasizing about making love with Michael.
- ••• 1:15—In sheer white nightgown, then breasts, while making love with Michael.
- •• 1:22—Full frontal nudity, while making love with Michael in office.

Spy Hard (1996) . . . . .Helicopter Ticket Agent
South Beach Academy (1997). . . . . Shannon McSorley
- 1:21—Breasts, while making love with Harry at night.

Made for Cable TV:

Love Street: Ex-Girlfriend (1994; Showtime) . . . . Judy

•• 0:14—Breasts and buns, while making love with Parker. Quick cuts.

• 0:17—Brief buns in panties and brief breasts in wedding dream.

Video Tapes:

B-Movie Queens Revealed: The Making of "Vice Academy" (1993). . . . . Candy

• Kalani

See: Freeman, Kalani.

Kalem, Toni

Films:

The Wanderers (1979). Despie Galasso
Private Benjamin (1980) . . . . .Private Ganelli
I'm Dancing as Fast as I Can (1981). . . . . Debbie
Paternity (1981) . . . . .Diane Cassabello
Silent Rage (1982) . . . . .Alison Halman

•• 0:22—Side view of left breast, then breasts, while in bed with Chuck Norris.

•• 0:46—Right breast, while lying in bed with Norris.

Two of a Kind (1983) . . . . Terri
Reckless (1984) . . . . Donna
Billy Galvin (1986). . . . . .Nora
Eyes of the Beholder (1992) . . . . Doctor Gruber
Sister Act (1992) . . . . Connie LaRocca
American Strays (1996) . . . . Alice

Made for TV Movies:

The Odd Couple (1993) . . . . Edna

TV:

Another World. . . . . Angie Perini
Arresting Behavior (1992-93) . . . . Wendy

Kallianiotes, Helena

Films:

The Baby Maker (1970). . . . . Wanda

• 1:30—Brief breasts when Barbara Hershey sees her in bed with Tad.

Five Easy Pieces (1970) .Palm Apodaca
Kansas City Bomber (1972). . . . . Jackie Burdette
Shanks (1974). . . . . Mata Hari
The Drowning Pool (1976) . . . . .Elaine Reaves
The Passover Plot (1976; Israeli) . . . . Visionary Woman
Stay Hungry (1976). . . . . .Anita
Backtrack (1989). . . . . Grace Carelli

a.k.a. Catch Fire

Kaminski, Dana

Films:

Hot Resort (1984). . . . . .Melanie

•• 1:02—Breasts taking off her white dress in a boat.

Irreconcilable Differences (1984) . . . . . . .Woman in Dress Shop
Big (1988). . . . . Personnel Receptionist
Super Mario Bros. (1993) . . . . .Daniella
The Day My Parents Ran Away (1994). . . . . .n.a.
The New Age (1994). . . . . Andrea

TV:

B.L. Stryker (1989-90) . . . . Lyynda Lennox

Kanakaredes, Melina

Films:

The Long Kiss Goodnight (1996). . . . . Trin

TV:

The Guiding Light . . . . Eleni
NYPD Blue (1994-95) . . . . .Benita Alden
New York News (1995-96). . . . . Angela Villanova
NYPD Blue: Vishy-Vashy-Vinny (Jan 17, 1995)
. . . . .Benita Alden

• 0:57—Very brief side of left breast, while undressing in Jimmy Smits apartment. Medium long shot.

NYPD Blue: Large Mouth Bass (Feb 7, 1995) . . . . . Benita Alden
Leaving L.A. (1997-) . . . . Libby Gallante

Kane, Carol

Films:

Carnal Knowledge (1971) . . . . .Jennifer
Desperate Characters (1971) . . . . Young Girl
The Last Detail (1973) . . . . Young Whore

• 1:02—Brief breasts sitting on bed talking with Randy Quaid. Her hair is in the way, hard to see.

Dog Day Afternoon (1975) . . . . Jenny
Hester Street (1975) . . . . Gitl
Annie Hall (1977) . . . . .Allison
Valentino (1977; British) . . . . Fatty's Girl
The World's Greatest Lover (1977). . . . . Annie
The Mafu Cage (1978) . . . . .Cissy

a.k.a. My Sister, My Love

• 0:08—Very brief tip of left breast in the bathtub.

When a Stranger Calls (1979) . . . . Jill Johnson
Norman Loves Rose (1982; Australian). . . . . Rose
Over the Brooklyn Bridge (1983) . . . . .Cheryl
Racing with the Moon (1984) . . . . Annie
Transylvania 6-5000 (1985) . . . . Lupi
Jumpin' Jack Flash (1986) . . . . .Cynthia
Ishtar (1987) . . . . Carol
The Princess Bride (1987) . . . . .Valerie
License to Drive (1988) . . . . Mom
Scrooged (1988) . . . . The Ghost of Christmas Present
Sticky Fingers (1988). . . . . Kitty
The Lemon Sisters (1990) . . . . Franki D'Angelo
My Blue Heaven (1990). . . . . Shaldeen
Ted & Venus (1991). . . . . Colette/Colette's Twin Sister
Baby On Board (1992). . . . . Maria
In the Soup (1992) . . . . .Barbara
Addams Family Values (1993) . . . . .Granny
Even Cowgirls Get the Blues (1994). . . . . .Carla
Big Bully (1995). . . . . Faith
American Strays (1996) . . . . Helen
The Pallbearer (1996) . . . . Tom's Mom
Sunset Park (1996) . . . . Mona

Made for Cable Movies:

When a Stranger Calls Back (1993) . . . . Jill Johnson

Made for Cable TV:

Tales From the Crypt: Judy, You're Not Yourself Today (HBO)
. . . . Judy

Made for TV Movies:

Freaky Friday (1995) . . . . .n.a.

TV:

Taxi (1981-83). . . . . Simka Gravas
All Is Forgiven (1986). . . . . Nicolette Bingham
American Dreamer (1990) . . . . .Lillian Abernathy
Brooklyn Bridge (1991-92) . . . . Aunt Sylvia
Pearl (1996). . . . . Annie

Kane, Kathleen

Films:

Flesh Gordon 2 (1990; Canadian) . . . . .Girl in Car
Shock 'Em Dead (1990). . . . . Pizza Girl 2
Angel of Passion (1991). . . . . Suzette

•• 1:08—Breasts while posing for Marty in the house.

Babyfever (1994) . . . . Lissa
Dracula: Dead and Loving It (1995) . . . . Villager
The People vs. Larry Flynt (1996) . . . . 1st Stripper

Kane, Sharon

See: Cain, Sharon.

• Kane, Tamara

Films:

The Perfect Gift (1993) . . . . Pajama Party Guest
Love Me Twice (1996) . . . . Artist Model
Lovers, Liars and Thieves (1996) . . . . Miss Emerson
•• 0:25—Breasts, while making love in bedroom with Cowboy.

Kaniak, Aleksandra

Films:

Blindfold: Acts of Obsession (1993) . . . . Natalie
Three of Hearts (1993) . . . . Bride
Unconditional Love (1994) . . . . Mary Chambers
• 0:11—Breasts, while taking a shower outdoors, when spotted by Steve.
•• 0:38—Breasts, while making love with Steve in his studio.
•• 0:51—Full frontal nudity, while posing for Steve in his studio.
Forbidden Games (1995) . . . . Amber
(Unrated version reviewed.)
• 1:04—Breasts and buns, while making love with Shauna in bed.

Made for Cable TV:

Love Street: Much Madness (1993; Showtime) . . . . Maggie
••• 0:18—Nude, while making love with Wyatt in front of fireplace.
• 0:24—Brief right breast, when sitting up in bed. Brief right breast, while putting on blouse.
Hot Line: Hannah's Surprise (1996; Cinemax) . . . Angelique
••• 0:10—Brief side view of buns in and out of lingerie, taking off stockings, then breasts while Hannah watches.
••• 0:18—Breasts and buns, while making love in bed with Lisa.
Women: Stories of Passion-City of Men (1996; Showtime) . . . . Anna
•• 0:18—Nude, while making love with Eros.
• 0:21—Full frontal nudity under fishnet body suit in cage, then walking down hallway with Pascale.

Kaprisky, Valerie *

Films:

Aphrodite (1982; German/French) . . . . Pauline
••• 0:12—Nude, washing herself off in front of a two-way mirror while a man on the other side watches.
Breathless (1983) . . . . Monica Poiccard
• 0:23—Brief side view of left breast in her apartment. Long shot, hard to see anything.
••• 0:47—Breasts in her apartment with Richard Gere kissing.
•• 0:52—Brief full frontal nudity standing in the shower when Gere opens the door, afterwards, buns in bed.
•• 0:53—Breasts, holding up two dresses for Gere to pick from, then breasts putting the black dress on.
• 1:23—Breasts behind a movie screen with Gere. Lit with red light.
L'Année des Meduses (1987; French) . . . . Chris
•• 0:06—Breasts pulling down swimsuit at the beach.
••• 0:24—Full frontal nudity while taking off dress with older man.
••• 0:42—Breasts walking around the beach talking to everybody.
•• 0:46—Breasts on the beach taking a shower.
••• 1:02—Breasts on the beach with her mom.
••• 1:37—Nude dancing on the boat for Romain.
•• 1:42—Breasts walking from the beach to the bar.
•• 1:43—Breasts in swimming pool.

Kapture, Mitzi

Films:

Private Road (1987) . . . . Helen Milshaw
•• 1:29—Nude, while making love in bed with Greg Evigan.
Angel III: The Final Chapter (1988) . . . . Molly Stewart
Lethal Pursuit (1989) . . . . Debra J.
•• 0:32—Breasts in motel shower, then getting out. (You can see the top of her swimsuit bottom.)
Liberty & Bash (1989) . . . . Sarah
The Vagrant (1992) . . . . Edie Roberts

TV:

Silk Stalkings (1991-95) . . . . Rita Lee Lance

Karasun, May

Films:

Lake Consequence (1992) . . . . Grace
(Unrated version reviewed.)
• 0:24—Brief breasts, coming up for air from under water in lake.
•• 0:25—Breasts, getting out of the water to get Joan Severance.
••• 0:26—Breasts, lying on float in the middle of the lake with Severance.
••• 0:28—Full frontal nudity and brief buns, diving into the lake.
•• 0:29—Buns and breasts, greeting Billy Zane after getting out of the lake.
• 0:30—Full frontal nudity, drying herself off and getting dressed. Long shot.
• 0:47—Left breast, while making out with Xiao in bar.
••• 0:50—Breasts close-up getting acupuncture.
••• 0:53—Breasts, walking to spa.
•• 0:55—Breasts in spa with Severance and Zane.
•• 0:57—Right breast while making love with Zane in spa.
Secret Games 3 (1994) . . . . Gwen
(Unrated version reviewed.)
••• 0:17—Left breast, then breasts and buns in G-string, while making love in room with Peter. Sometimes seen on monitor.

Made for Cable TV:

Red Shoe Diaries: Billy Bar (1996; Showtime) . . . . Daphne Bar
• 0:03—Breasts, while making out with Billy next to the bed.
• 0:04—Brief breasts, when Billy stops kissing her.
• 0:14—Breasts, while making love with Billy in closet during party.
• 0:16—Brief breasts, getting dressed by Angel.
•• 0:25—Breasts and buns, while making love with Billy on bed.

Karin, Anna

Films:

Body of Influence (1992) . . . . Beth
(Unrated version reviewed.)
Wild Cactus (1992) . . . . Inga
(Unrated version reviewed.)
••• 0:09—In black lingerie, then breasts and buns after undressing and making love on bed with Randall.

••• 0:14—Breasts while tied by her wrists to the bed by Randall.

Martial Outlaw (1993). . . . . Waitress

The Fear (1994). . . . . Tanya

Sacred Cargo (1995) . . . . Sasha Rosanov

• 1:06—Very brief side view of left breast while making love with Chris Penn.

Shelter (1997). . . . . Rana

Made for Cable Movies:

Red Shoe Diaries (1992; Showtime). . . . . Heidi #1

(Unrated video tape version reviewed.)

••• 1:29—Breasts, three times, making love with Tom.

Karina, Anna

Films:

The Oldest Profession (1967). . . . . "Anticipation"

Justine (1969; Italian/Spanish). . . . . Melissa

•• 0:13—Half of right breast, while fooling around in bed with Michael York.

Cayenne Palace (1989; French) . . . . Lola

*Kârkkâinen, Kata **

Video Tapes:

Sexy Lingerie (1988) . . . . Model

Karlatos, Olga

Films:

Wifemistress (1977; Italian) . . . . . . .Miss Paula Pagano, M.D.

•• 0:42—Breasts undressing in room with Laura Antonelli. Right breast and part of left breast lying in bed with Marcello Mastroianni.

• 0:46—Brief breasts in bed with Mastroianni and Clara.

Zombie (1980) . . . . Mrs. Menard

• 0:40—Breasts and buns taking a shower.

Once Upon a Time in America (1984)

. . . . Woman in the Puppet Theatre

(Long version reviewed.)

•• 0:11—Right breast twice when bad guy pokes at her nipple with a gun.

Made for TV Movies:

The Scarlet and the Black (1983). . . . . Francesca Lombardo

Karman, Janice

Films:

Switchblade Sisters (1975) . . . . Bunnie

Slumber Party '57 (1976) . . . . Hank

•• 1:06—Breasts, sitting watching Smitty and David make love in the stable.

Karr, Marcia

Films:

The Concrete Jungle (1982) . . . . Marcy

Chained Heat (1983; U.S./German) . . . . Twinks

••• 0:30—Breasts, getting soaped up by Edy Williams in the shower.

• 0:37—Brief breasts, taking off her top in bed with Edy Williams at night.

•• 0:40—Breasts in cell getting raped by the guard.

Hardbodies (1984) . . . . .Hardbody On Stairs

Savage Streets (1984) . . . . Stevie

Real Genius (1985) . . . . Cornell's Girl At Party

Sex Appeal (1986) . . . . Christina

• 1:12—Brief left breast, then in bra and panties on bed with her boyfriend.

Killer Workout (1987) . . . . .Rhonda

a.k.a. Aerobi-Cide

• 1:03—Breasts, opening her jacket to show the policeman her scars. Unappealing.

• 1:12—Breasts in locker room, while killing a guy. Covered with the special-effect scars.

The Nightstalker (1987). . . . . H.J. Salters

Maniac Cop (1988) . . . . .Nancy

Night of the Kickfighters (1990) . . . . Kedesha

I Will Dance on Your Grave: Lethal Victims (1992) . . . . . Sophie

Karras, Christina

Films:

Caroline at Midnight (1993) . . . . .Party Dancer

Made for Cable TV:

Love Street: Bordello (1993; Showtime) . . . Madison Knight

•• 0:09—Breasts and buns, while making love in bed with Ray.

••• 0:17—In bra, then breasts after taking off top in front of Ray. Buns in panties, garter belt and stockings.

• 0:20—Breasts, when sitting in bed while applying make-up and talking to Ray. Breasts visible in reflection in window.

••• 0:22—In red bra, then breasts and buns while making love in bed with Mike.

Kascha

Adult film actress.

a.k.a. Alison Le Priol.

Films:

Caged Fury (1989) . . . . .Blonde Escapee

• 0:00—In bra and panties, then buns in G-string, then brief breasts while crawling on the floor.

Fortress of Amerikkka (1989). . . . . .Elizabeth

• 0:37—Breasts and buns, when waking up from tent.

•• 0:38—Brief breasts, while flashing her boyfriend in the woods and making out with him.

•• 0:59—Breasts, while making out with Mercenary in tent.

Kasdorf, Lenore

Films:

Dark Horse (1984). . . . . Alice

Missing in Action (1984) . . . . Ann

• 0:41—Very brief breasts when Chuck Norris sneaks back in room and jumps into bed with her.

L.A. Bounty (1989) . . . . .Kelly Rhodes

Kid (1990). . . . . Alice

Nervous Ticks (1991). . . . . .Katie

Amityville Dollhouse (1996). . . . . Aunt Marla

Starship Troopers (1996) . . . . Mrs. RIco

Made for Cable Movies:

Dinner At Eight (1989) . . . . Lucy

Made for TV Movies:

A Murderous Affair: The Carolyn Warmus Story (1992)

. . . . .Betty Jeanne Solomon

Revenge on the Highway (1992) . . . . Shirley

TV:

Days of Our Lives. . . . . Dr. Victoria Kimball

The Guiding Light . . . . Rita Stapleton

Santa Barbara . . . . .Caroline Wilson

NYPD Blue: Taillights's Last Gleaming (Feb 18, 1997) . . . . .n.a.

Kassel, Aline

Films:

Lap Dancing (1995). . . . . Jackie

Witchcraft 7: Judgement Hour (1995) . . . . Emily
(Unrated version reviewed.)
•• 1:05—Brief breasts, twice, while making love in bed with Jack.

Kassman, Aline

Films:
Silk n' Sabotage (1994) . . . . Tracy
• 0:53—In a black teddy, then breasts with Michael on boat.
Made for Cable TV:
Compromising Situations: The Casting Couch (1994; Showtime) . . . . Julie
•• 0:03—In bra, then breasts while on couch with Phil.

Kastner, Daphna

Films:
Eating (1990) . . . . Jennifer
Julia Has Two Lovers (1990) . . . . Julia
• 0:11—Brief breasts, changing blouses while talking on the telephone.
• 0:25—Partial left breast, while in bubble bath.
• 0:29—Right breast, while in bubble bath.
• 0:30—Breasts in mirror, getting out of bathtub.
• 0:53—Left breast, while lying in bed with David Duchovny. Long shot.
Venice/Venice (1992) . . . . Eve

Kates, Kimberly

a.k.a. Kimberly La Belle.
Films:
Winners Take All (1987) . . . . Party Girl #1
Dangerous Love (1988) . . . . Susan
Rescue Me (1991) . . . . Cindy
Bad Blood (1993) . . . . Lindee
••• 0:13—Breasts and buns, while making love with Lorenzo Lamas.
• 0:16—Breasts, while running out of trailer after Lamas leaves.
Chained Heat 2 (1993) . . . . Alexandra Morrison
••• 0:30—Full frontal nudity, while in the shower with Tina.
• 0:56—Buns, in G-string under sheer blue dress during casino party.
•• 1:04—Breasts, while sitting up in bed and getting out. Wearing panties and stockings.
The New Age (1994) . . . . Other Katherine
• 1:11—Breasts, in black fishnet lingerie, seen through water in swimming pool.
The Pornographer (1994) . . . . Bettina
a.k.a. Family Values
TV:
On Our Own (1994) . . . . Alana Michaels

Kath, Camelia

Ex-wife of actor Kiefer Sutherland.
Films:
Nevada Heat (1982) . . . . Voice #4
a.k.a. Fake-Out
The Killing Time (1987) . . . . Laura Winslow
• 0:32—Very brief right breast, while making love with Beau Bridges. Hard to see anything. Dark, lit with red light.
• 0:43—Brief breasts lying in bed getting photographed with Beau Bridges to frame Kiefer Sutherland for a murder.

*Katon, Rosanne **

Films:
The Swinging Cheerleaders (1974) . . . . Lisa
•• 0:25—Breasts taking off her blouse in her teacher's office. Half of right breast while he talks on the phone.
Chesty Anderson, U.S. Navy (1975) . . . . Cocoa
•• 0:40—Breasts when bra pops open during fight in barracks.
Fox Fire (1976) . . . . n.a.
a.k.a. Fox Force
a.k.a. She Devils in Chains
Coach (1978) . . . . Sue
• 0:10—Very brief breasts flashing her breasts along with three of her girlfriends for their four boyfriends.
Motel Hell (1980) . . . . Suzi
Body and Soul (1981) . . . . Melody
• 0:04—Left breast several times making love in restroom with Leon Isaac Kennedy.
Lunch Wagon (1981) . . . . Shannon
a.k.a. Lunch Wagon Girls
a.k.a. Come 'N' Get It
• 0:01—Brief breasts getting dressed.
• 0:04—Brief side view of left breast changing tops in room in gas station with Pamela Bryant while a guy watches through key hole.
•• 0:10—Breasts changing again in gas station.
Zapped! (1982) . . . . Donna
Bachelor Party (1984) . . . . Bridal Shower Hooker
Harem (1985; French) . . . . Judy

Kauffman, Cristen

Films:
The Joy of Sex (1984) . . . . Sharon
Back to the Future (1985) . . . . Betty
Mischief (1985) . . . . Carhop
Jailbait: Betrayed by Innocence (1986) . . . . Marisa
••• 0:24—Breasts, when lying down on bed, then sitting up. Buns, while standing up and calling to Barry Bostwick, then breasts while making love with him. Long scene.
•• 0:49—Very brief right breast while in bed with Bostwick. Breasts, when sitting up in bed when she hears a noise outside, then coming back into the bedroom.
Welcome to 18 (1986) . . . . Talia
Masquerade (1988) . . . . Holly
Slipping into Darkness (1988) . . . . Alex
• 0:39—Brief breasts, after T-bone rips her blouse open.

Kaye, Caren

Films:
Checkmate (1973) . . . . Alex
The Lords of Flatbush (1974) . . . . Wedding Guest
Looking for Mr. Goodbar (1977) . . . . Rhoda
Kill Castro (1978) . . . . Tracy
a.k.a. Cuba Crossing
Some Kind of Hero (1982) . . . . Sheila
My Tutor (1983) . . . . Terry Green
•• 0:25—Breasts, while walking into swimming pool.
•• 0:52—Breasts, while in the pool with Matt Lattanzi.
••• 0:55—Right breast, while making love in bed with Lattanzi.
Satan's Princess (1989) . . . . Leah
Teen Witch (1989) . . . . Margaret
Pumpkinhead II: Blood Wings (1994) . . . . Beth Braddock
Made for TV Movies:
Poison Ivy (1985) . . . . Margo
TV:
The Betty White Show (1977-78) . . . . Tracy Garrett

Blansky's Beauties (1977). . . . . Bambi Benton
Who's Watching the Kids? (1978) . . . . Stacy Turner
Empire (1984). . . . . .Meredith
It's Your Move (1984-85). . . . . Eileen Burton

*Kaye, Wendy **

Films:

Miracle Beach (1991). . . . . .Girl in Bed
• 0:14—Breasts, while lying in bed next to Scotty, then sitting up. (She's on the left.)

Video Tapes:

Playboy Video Centerfold: Morgan Fox (1991) . . Playmate
••• 0:27—Nude in different settings.
••• 0:30—Nude in American-theme song and dance number.
••• 0:31—Breasts and buns in G-string at the beach.
••• 0:33—Full frontal nudity in still photos.
••• 0:34—Nude while dancing.
Wet & Wild III (1991). . . . . .Model
The Best of Sexy Lingerie (1992). . . . . .Model
The Best of Wet and Wild (1992) . . . . .Model
Playboy Video Calendar 1993 (1992) . . . . July
••• 0:28—Nude at the beach.
••• 0:30—Nude in building with graffiti on the walls.
Playboy's Playmate Review 1992 (1992) . . . . Miss July
••• 0:36—Nude in patriotic scene and then in a surreal scene.
Sexy Lingerie IV (1992). . . . . .Model
Wet & Wild IV (1992) . . . . .Model
Playboy's Sexy, Steamy, Sultry (1993). . . . . .Playmate
Sexy Lingerie V (1993). . . . . .Model

Kaye-Mason, Clarissa

Wife of actor James Mason.

Films:

Age of Consent (1969; Australian) . . . . Meg
• 0:05—Brief breasts, crawling on the bed to watch TV.
Adam's Women (1972; Australian) . . . . Matron
The Good Wife (1987; Australian) . . . . Mrs. Jackson
a.k.a. The Umbrella Woman

Keaton, Camille

Great-niece of Buster Keaton.

Films:

I Spit on Your Grave (1978) .Jennifer
(Uncut, unrated version reviewed.)
• 0:05—Breasts undressing to go skinny dipping in lake.
•• 0:23—Left breast sticking out of bathing suit top, then breasts after top is ripped off. Right breast several times.
• 0:25—Breasts, getting raped by the jerks.
• 0:27—Buns and brief full frontal nudity, crawling away from the jerks.
• 0:29—Nude, walking through the woods.
• 0:32—Breasts, getting raped again.
• 0:36—Breasts and buns after rape.
• 0:38—Buns, walking to house.
• 0:40—Buns and lower frontal nudity in the house.
• 0:41—More breasts and buns on the floor.
• 0:45—Nude, very dirty after all she's gone through.
• 0:51—Full frontal nudity while lying on the floor.
• 0:52—Side of left breast while in bathtub.
•• 1:13—Full frontal nudity seducing Matthew before killing him.
••• 1:23—Full frontal nudity in front of mirror, then getting into bathtub. Long scene.
Raw Force (1981) . . . . Girl in Toilet
•• 0:28—Breasts, while in bathroom with a guy.
•• 0:29—Breasts in bathroom again with the guy.
• 0:31—Breasts in bathroom again when he rips her pants off.
The Concrete Jungle (1982) . . . . .Rita
• 0:41—In black bra, then breasts getting raped by Stone. Brief lower frontal nudity sitting up afterwards.

Keaton, Diane

Films:

Lovers and Other Strangers (1970) . . . . Joan
The Godfather (1972) . . . . Kay Adams
Play It Again, Sam (1972) . . . . Linda Christie
Sleeper (1973). . . . . .Luna
The Godfather, Part II (1974). . . . . Kay Adams
Love and Death (1975) . . . . Sonja
Harry and Walter Go to New York (1976) . . . . . .Lissa Chestnut
I Will, I Will... For Now (1976) . . . . Katie Bingham
Annie Hall (1977) . . . . .Annie Hall
(Academy Award for Best Actress.)
Looking for Mr. Goodbar (1977) . . . . .Theresa
•• 0:11—Right breast in bed making love with her teacher, Martin, then putting blouse on.
• 0:31—Brief left breast over the shoulder when the Doctor playfully kisses her breast.
•• 1:04—Brief breasts smoking in bed in the morning, then more breasts after Richard Gere leaves.
••• 1:17—Breasts making love with Gere after doing a lot of cocaine.
• 1:31—Brief breasts in the bathtub when James brings her a glass of wine.
•• 2:02—Breasts during rape by Tom Berenger, before he kills her. Hard to see because of strobe lights.
Interiors (1978) . . . . Renata
Manhattan (1979). . . . . Mary Wilke
Reds (1981) . . . . Louise Bryant
• 0:50—Buns, while standing in the water with Jack Nicholson at night. Very long shot.
Shoot the Moon (1982). .Faith Dunlap
The Little Drummer Girl (1984) . . . . Charlie
Mrs. Soffel (1984) . . . . Kate Soffel
Crimes of the Heart (1986) . . . . .Lenny Magrath
Baby Boom (1987) . . . . J.C. Wiatt
Radio Days (1987). . . . . New Year's Singer
The Good Mother (1988) . . . . .Anna
The Godfather, Part III (1990) . . . . Kay Adams
The Lemon Sisters (1990) .Eloise Hamer
Father of the Bride (1991) . . . . Nina Banks
Manhattan Murder Mystery (1993) . . . . Carol Lipton
Father of the Bride, Part II (1995). . . . . Nina Banks
The First Wives Club (1996). . . . . Annie
Marvin's Room (1996) . . . . Bessie

Made for Cable Movies:

Running Mates (1992; HBO) . . . . Aggie Snow
Amelia Earhart: The Final Flight (1994; TNT) . . . Amelia Earhart

Keats, Ele

Films:

Frankie & Johnny (1991) . . . . .Artemis
Liebestraum (1991) . . . . Actress on Soap Opera
The Rocketeer (1991) . . . . .Girl at Newstand
Alive (1992). . . . . .Susana Parrado
Newsies (1992) . . . . .Sarah Jacobs
Lipstick Camera (1993) . . . . Omy Clark
• 0:57—In bra, while making out with Flynn, then left breast while lying back with him.
Mother (1994). . . . . Audrey Simms
There Goes My Baby (1994) . . . . Emily

White Wolves II: Legend of the Wild (1995). . . . . Beri
Made for TV Movies:
White Dwarf (1995) . . . . Ariel

Kedes, Maureen

Films:
Captive Rage (1988) . . . . Jan
•• 0:31—Breasts, getting chained to bed and raped by guards.
Made for Cable TV:
Dream On: The Son Also Rises (1992; HBO) . . . . Celia
••• 0:03—Breasts in bed while Martin looks for a condom.

Keener, Catherine

Films:
About Last Night... (1986) . . . . Cocktail Waitress
Backtrack (1989). . . . . Trucker's Girl
a.k.a. Catch Fire
Survival Quest (1989) . . . . Cheryl
Switch (1991) . . . . Steve's Secretary
The Gun in Betty Lou's Handbag (1992) . . . . Suzanne
Johnny Suede (1992) . . . . Yvonne
Living in Oblivion (1995) . . . . Nicole Springer
• 0:28—Breasts, while lying in bed in motel room after James Le Gros leaves.
• 0:57—Breasts, when waking up in bed in the morning. Very, very brief left breast, when closing the shower curtain.

Boys (1996) . . . . Jilly
Walking and Talking (1996). . . . . Amelia
The Real Blonde (1998). . . . . Mary
Made for Cable Movies:
If These Walls Could Talk (1996; HBO) . . . . Becky
TV:
Ohara (1987) . . . . Lt. Cricket Sideris

Keisha

Adult film actress.
a.k.a. Raquel Rios.
Films:
Watchers II (1990). . . . . Woman at Hotel
The Sweeper (1995) . . . . Mall Mother
Video Tapes:
High Society Centerspread Video #11: Keisha (1990) . . . . Herself
Big Bust Casting Call (1992). . . . . Keisha
••• 0:40—In sexy swimsuit in spa, then breasts after taking off her top. (Wearing sunglasses.)
Penthouse Satin & Lace: An Erotic History of Lingerie (1992). . . . . Model

Keller, Marthe

Films:
And Now My Love (1974; French) . . . . Sarah/Her Mother/Her Grandmother
Marathon Man (1976). . . . . Elsa
•• 0:42—Breasts lying on the floor after Dustin Hoffman rolls off her.
Black Sunday (1977) . . . . Dahlia
Bobby Deerfield (1977). . . . . Lillian
• 0:47—Brief breasts, while getting into bed.
The Formula (1980) . . . . Lisa
The Amateur (1982) . . . . Elisabeth
Wagner (1983; British) . . . . Mathilde Wesedonck
Red Kiss (1985; French). . . . . Bronka
Femmes de Persone (1986; French) . . . . Cecile
Dark Eyes (1987; Italian/Russian). . . . . Tina
Made for Cable Movies:
The Nightmare Years (1989) . . . . Tess
Young Catherine (1991; TNT) . . . . Johanna

Kellerman, Sally *

Films:
The Boston Strangler (1968) . . . . Dianne Cluny
The April Fool's (1969) . . . . Phyllis Brubaker
Brewster McCloud (1970) . . . . Louise
•• 1:07—Breasts, playing in a fountain.
M*A*S*H (1970). . . . . Margaret "Hot Lips" Houlihan
• 0:42—Very, very brief left breast opening her blouse for Frank in her tent.
• 1:11—Very, very brief buns and side view of right breast during shower prank. Long shot, hard to see.
• 1:54—Very brief breasts in a slightly different angle of the shower prank during the credits.

Last of the Red Hot Lovers (1972) . . . . Elaine Navazio
Reflection of Fear (1973) . . . . Anne
Rafferty and the Gold Dust Twins (1975). . . . . Mac Beachwood
The Big Bus (1976) . . . . Sybil Crane
Welcome to L.A. (1977). . . . . Ann Goode
A Little Romance (1979; U.S./French) . . . . Kay King
Foxes (1980) . . . . Mary
Serial (1980) . . . . Martha
••• 0:03—Breasts sitting on the floor with a guy.
Fatal Attraction (1981; Canadian). . . . . Michelle Keys
a.k.a. Head On
• 0:46—Brief breasts in building making out with a guy. Dark, hard to see.
• 1:19—Brief half of left breast, after struggling with a guy.

You Can't Hurry Love (1984). . . . . Kelly Bones
Moving Violations (1985) . . . . Judge Nedra Henderson
Back to School (1986) . . . . Diane
That's Life! (1986) . . . . Holly Parrish
Meatballs III (1987) . . . . Roxy Du Jour
Three for the Road (1987) . . . . Blanche
Doppelganger: The Evil Within (1992). . . . . Sister Jan
The Player (1992) . . . . Cameo
Mirror Mirror 2: Raven Dance (1993) . . . . Roslyn
Ready to Wear (1994) . . . . Sissy Wanamaker
a.k.a. Prêt-à-porter
• 1:16—Brief breasts, while flashing them for Stephen Rea in hotel room.

Younger & Younger (1994) . . . . ZigZag Lilian
It's My Party (1995). . . . . Sara Hart
Made for Cable Movies:
Boris and Natasha (1992; Showtime). . . . . Natasha Fatale
Made for Cable TV:
Dream On: Blinded by the Cheese (1994; HBO) . . . . Tracy
Dream On: Take Two Tablets, And Get Me to Mt. Sinai (1995; HBO) . . . . Martin's Lover
Made for TV Movies:
Secret Weapons (1985) . . . . Vera Malevich
TV:
Centennial (1978-79) . . . . Lise Bockweiss

Kellermann, Barbara

Films:
Satan's Slave (1976; British). . . . . Frances
The Sea Wolves (1980; British) . . . . Mrs. Cromwell
• 0:32—Brief right breast, while holding champagne bottle, then brief right breast throwing it at gunman in room with Roger Moore.

The Monster Club (1981; British). . . . . Angela

Kelley, Kimberly

Films:

Hard Bounty (1995) .... Glory
•• 0:11—Breasts, while in bedroom with a customer.
•• 0:54—Breasts, while in room with Jess, helping Benjamin lose his virginity.

Midnight Tease 2 (1995) .... Jennifer Brennan
•• 0:01—Breasts, while dancing in front of killer before getting killed (she's playing the part of her sister, Amy).
•• 0:12—In bra, then breasts and buns in T-back while doing strip routine on stage.
• 0:15—Breasts under sheer black blouse, while getting dressed.
••• 0:17—Buns and breasts under sheer black bodysuit, then breasts when doing a lap dance for Paul.
•• 0:30—Buns in red bodysuit, then breasts when doing lap dance.
••• 0:52—Breasts while making love in bed.
••• 0:57—Breasts, while dancing on stage and doing strip routine.

Night Eyes 4 ...Fatal Passion (1995) .... Sara
•• 0:11—Buns and breasts, while sunbathing outside and making out with Roy.
••• 0:29—Breasts and buns, while making love in bed with Roy.
•• 0:33—In bra, then breasts, while seducing Steve.

Kelley, Sheila

Films:

Some Girls (1988) .... Irenka
a.k.a. Sisters
• 0:13—Breasts and buns, while getting something at the end of the hall while Patrick Dempsey watches. Long shot, hard to see.
• 1:01—Breasts in window while Dempsey watches from outside. Long shot, hard to see.

Breaking In (1989) .... Carrie
Mortal Passions (1989) .... Adele
Staying Together (1989) .... Beth Harper
Where the Heart Is (1990) .... Sheryl
Pure Luck (1991) .... Valerie Highsmith
Soapdish (1991) .... Fran
singles (1992) .... Debbie
Passion Fish (1993) .... Kim
A Passion to Kill (1994) .... Beth
The Secretary (1994) .... Deidre Bosnell
One Fine Day (1996) .... Kristen
Secrets & Lies (1996; British) .... Fertile Mother

Made for Cable Movies:

Deconstructing Sarah (1994; USA) .... Sarah

Made for TV Movies:

The Fulfillment of Mary Gray (1989) .... Kate

TV:

L.A. Law (1990-94) .... Gwen Taylor
Sisters (1995-96) .... Dr. Charlotte Bennett

Kelly, Jill

Adult film actress.

Films:

Virtual Encounters (1995) .... Cave Girl
(Unrated version reviewed.)
••• 1:00—Nude, while making love with a cave guy in cave.

Video Tapes:

Penthouse: The Art of Massage (1996) .... Model
••• 0:02—Nude, while giving a massage, then making love with Vince Voyeur.

• Kelly, Lisa Robin

Films:

Payback (1994) .... Teenage Girl
(Special director's cut reviewed.)
Relentless 4: Ashes to Ashes (1994) ... Sherry, Cory's Girlfriend

Amityville Dollhouse (1996) .... Dana
• 0:42—In black panties, then breasts, while starting to make love with Todd in the shed in the backyard.

Made for Cable Movies:

Alone (1997; Showtime) .... Mary Louise

Made for Cable TV:

Poltergeist: The Legacy/Hell Hath No Fury (1998; Showtime) .... Janine

Made for TV Movies:

Cries Unheard: The Donna Yaklich Story (1994) .... n.a.
Spring Fling! (1995) .... n.a.

Kelly, Moira

Films:

Billy Bathgate (1991) .... Rebecca

Chaplin (1992; British/U.S.) .... Hetty Kelly/Oona O'Neill
•• 0:20—Brief breasts, while changing in dressing room when surprised by Chaplin.

The Cutting Edge (1992) .... Kate Moseley

Twin Peaks: Fire Walk With Me (1992) ... Donna Hayward
•• 1:22—Breasts, while lying on table in cabin.

Little Odessa (1994) .... Alla Shustervich
•• 0:54—Breasts, while making love in bed with Tim Roth.

With Honors (1994) .... Courtney Blumenthal

The Tie That Binds (1995) .... Dana Clifton
• 0:23—Partial side of left breast while in bed with Vincent Spano. Very, very brief partial right breast when he rolls off the top of her.
• 0:24—Brief left breast as Spano works his way down her torso with kisses.

Entertaining Angels: The Dorothy Day Story (1996) .... Dorothy Day
Dangerous Beauty (1998) .... Beatrice Venier

Made for Cable Movies:

Daybreak (1993; HBO) .... Blue
••• 0:43—Right breast, then breasts while making out with Cuba Gooding Jr.
••• 1:14—Breasts when Gooding has to take her top off in front of a guard.

Made for TV Movies:

Love, Lies and Murder (1991) .... Cinnamon Brown

Kelly, Paula *

Films:

Sweet Charity (1969) .... Helene
The Andromeda Strain (1971) .... Nurse
Cool Breeze (1972) .... Martha Harris
Top of the Heap (1972) .... Singer
Trouble Man (1973) .... Cleo
Uptown Saturday Night (1974) .... Leggy Peggy
Drum (1976) .... Rachel
Jo Jo Dancer, Your Life Is Calling (1986) .... Satin Doll
Bank Robber (1993) .... Mother
Drop Squad (1994) .... Aunt Tilly

Made for Cable Movies:
Run for the Dream: The Gail Devers Story (1996; Showtime) . . . . .Mrs. Devers
Miniseries:
Chiefs (1983) . . . . Liz Watts
TV:
Night Court (1984). . . . . Liz Williams
Room For Two (1992-93) . . . . Diahnn Boudreau
South Central (1994-95). . . . . Sweets

Kelly, Robyn

Films:
Flesh Gordon 2 (1990; Canadian) . . . . .Dale Ardor
•• 0:24—Brief breasts in push-up bra when Dr. Jerkoff rips her jacket open.
• 0:49—Brief buns, while acting like a dog on all fours on the floor.
Ultimate Desires (1991). . . . . Streetgirl
a.k.a. Silhouette

Kelly, Sharon

a.k.a. Adult film actress Colleen Brennan.
Films:
The Beauties and the Beast (1973) . . . . n.a.
Nude, being carried into a cave by the beast.
Innocent Sally (1973). . . . . Sally
a.k.a. The Dirty Mind of Young Sally
••• 0:35—Breasts, undressing in back of van. Long scene.
••• 0:37—Full frontal nudity, on pillow in back of van while caressing herself. Another long scene.
••• 0:39—More full frontal nudity in van.
••• 0:47—Right breast, then full frontal nudity, making love with Toby in van. Long scene.
••• 1:05—Breasts, making love in bed with another guy. Long scene.
••• 1:10—Full frontal nudity, making more love. Long scene.
•• 1:19—Breasts, after making love.
••• 1:23—Full frontal nudity, while making love with a guy.
Supervixens (1973). . . . . SuperCherry
Delinquent School Girls (1974) . . . . .Greta
• 0:05—Left breast in mirror while practicing martial arts.
Alice Goodbody (1975) . . . . Alice Goodbody
• 0:01—Brief breasts in mirror, getting dressed.
••• 0:16—In bra, then full frontal nudity, undressing in Arnold's place. More breasts in the shower with him.
••• 0:17—Frontal nudity, while lying in bed and making out with Arnold.
• 0:27—Breasts with Roger while he eats all sorts of food off her body.
• 0:28—Breasts, lying in bed with Roger afterwards.
••• 0:37—Right breast, then frontal nudity while talking to Rex.
••• 0:38—Breasts when Rex carries her to bed and makes love with her, while admiring himself.
•• 0:47—Breasts with bandages on her face.
••• 0:51—Breasts, taking off her robe and getting into bed. (Bandages are still on her face.)
•• 1:09—Buns, undressing and getting into bed.
• 1:21—Brief breasts in mirror in bed with Rex during the end credits.
The Boob Tube (1975) . . . . Selma Carpenter
••• 0:06—Breasts and buns, trying to seduce Dr. Carstairs.
••• 0:10—Breasts and buns, having fun by herself on the bed while Dr. Carstairs watches. Nice close-ups.
••• 0:11—More breasts and buns in bed with Dr. Carstairs.
• 1:03—Breasts under sheer nightie while Harvey checks her sink.
•• 1:09—Breasts and buns, on sofa, then leaving the room.
•• 1:11—Breasts and buns, entering the room.
••• 1:12—Breasts during orgy on couch.
• 1:16—Brief breasts in hallway.
Carnal Madness (1975) . . . . .n.a.
Hustle (1975). . . . . .Gloria Hollinger
• 0:12—Brief breasts, several times when rolled out of freezer, dead.
• 1:03—In pasties, dancing behind curtain when Gloria's father imagines the dancer is Gloria.
• 1:42—In black lingerie, brief buns and side views of breast in bed in film.
Shampoo (1975) . . . . Painted Lady
• 1:17—Brief breasts covered with tattoos all over her body during party. Lit with strobe light.
Ilsa, Harem Keeper of the Oil Sheiks (1976) . . . . n.a.
Slammer Girls (1987). . . . . Professor
• 0:23—Brief breasts, while changing clothes under table in the prison cafeteria.
•• 0:34—Breasts, while squishing them against the window during prison visiting hours.
•• 0:36—Breasts with an inflatable male doll.

Kelsey, Tasmin

Films:
Who's Harry Crumb? (1989) . . . . Marie
Bingo (1991). . . . . .Bunny
Common Bonds (1991) . . . . Ginger
• 0:04—Breasts in hotel room with the cop when Michael Ironside bursts into the room. Long shot. More out of focus breasts shots in the mirror.
Harmony Cats (1993; Canadian) . . . . Sandra
Needful Things (1993) . . . . Sheila Ratcliff
Made for Cable TV:
The Outer Limits: Corner of the Eye (1995; Showtime) . . . . .Victorine
The Outer Limits: The Sentence (1996; Showtime) . . . Dr. Glass
Poltergeist: The Legacy/Silent Partner (1997; Showtime) . . . . .Margaret
Stargate SG-1: Thor's Hammer (1997; Showtime) . . . . Gariwym
Made for TV Movies:
Beyond Betrayal (1994). . . . . DA

Kemp, Charlotte

See: Helmcamp, Charlotte J.

Kemp, Elizabeth

Films:
He Knows You're Alone (1980). . . . . .Nancy
••• 1:12—Breasts, taking off robe and taking a shower.
Sticky Fingers (1988). . . . . .Nancy
Eating (1990) . . . . .Nancy
Venice/Venice (1992). . . . . .Interviewee

*Kendall, Kerri **

Video Tapes:
Playboy Video Centerfold: Kerri Kendall (1990) . . . . .Playmate
••• 0:00—Nude throughout.
Wet & Wild II (1990) . . . . .Model
Playboy Video Calendar 1992 (1991) . . . . .March
••• 0:09—Nude in photo studio.
••• 0:10—In bra, then nude in bedroom.
Sexy Lingerie III (1991) . . . . .Model

Wet & Wild III (1991). . . . . .Model
The Best of Sexy Lingerie (1992) . . . . .Model
The Best of Wet and Wild (1992) . . . . .Model
Playboy's Sexy, Steamy, Sultry (1993). . . . . .Playmate
Playboy's 21 Playmates (1996). . . . . .Playmate
••• 1:03—Full frontal nudity in still photos.
••• 1:04—Nude on sofa.

Kennedy, Heather

Video Tapes:
Hot Body International: #2 Miss Puerto Vallarta (1990) . . . . Contestant
•• 0:40—Buns and almost breasts in one piece swimsuit.
Hot Body International: #4 Spring Break (1992) . . . . Contestant
• 0:23—Buns in G-string during wet T-shirt contest.
Hot Body Video Magazine #6: Southern Belle (1993) . . . . n.a.
Nude Daydreams (1993) . . . . Daydream 12
••• 0:36—Buns in red bra and panties, then nude while dancing around (including splits). Long scene.
Hot Body Competition: The Best of Hot Body (1994) . . . . Herself
•• 0:15—Buns in swimsuits.
Soft Bodies: Beyond Blonde (1995). . . . . Herself
••• 0:15—Buns in sheer lingerie outfit, then nude on stairs.
••• 0:23—In dress, then nude, while outside in garden.
•• 0:29—In skimpy outfit, then breasts, during pillow fight in bed with Becky LeBeau.
••• 0:30—Buns in two piece swimsuit, then nude while posing on and around chair next to pool.

Kennedy, Meredith

Films:
Erotic Images (1983) . . . . Ginger
•• 1:04—Breasts on the couch with two guys.
Night Train to Terror (1985). . . . . Dead Redhead
• 0:16—Right breast, while strapped to gurney, before getting killed with a saw by Richard Moll.

Kennedy, Sheila *

Films:
The First Turn-On! (1983) .Dreamgirl
• 0:52—In red two piece swimsuit, then breasts when the top falls down during Danny's daydream.
• 0:59—Right breast, while in bed with Danny.
Spring Break (1983; Canadian) .Carla
•• 0:49—Breasts during wet T-shirt contest.
Ellie (1984) . . . . .Ellie May
•• 0:29—Full frontal nudity posing for Billy while he takes pictures of her just before he falls over a cliff.
• 1:16—In bra and panties taking off dress with Art. Breasts taking off bra and throwing them on antlers. Brief breasts many times while frolicking around.
Dead Boyz Can't Fly (1992). . . . . Lorraine
• 0:00—Breasts and buns in G-string, while dancing in smoke filled club.
•• 0:16—Buns in G-string and breasts, while dancing in club.

Kennell, Kari *

See: Whitman, Kari.

Kensit, Patsy

Was the lead singer in the British group *Eighth Wonder.*
Wife of Liam Gallagher, lead singer of the British rock group *Oasis.*

Films:
The Great Gatsby (1974) . . . . .Daisy's Daughter
Oh, Alfie! (1975; British) . . . . Penny
a.k.a. Alfie Darling
Hanover Street (1979) . . . . Sarah Sallinger
Absolute Beginners (1986; British) . . . . .Crepe Suzette
Chicago Joe and the Showgirl (1989; British). . . . . .Joyce Cook
Lethal Weapon 2 (1989) . . . . Rika Van Den Haas
•• 1:15—Right breast lying in bed with Mel Gibson.
•• 1:19—Breasts in bed with Gibson.
Blue Tornado (1990) . . . . .Christina
Bullseye! (1990). . . . . .Sick Lady on Train
Does This Mean We're Married? (1990; French/U.S.). . . .Deena
Kill Cruise (1990; German). . . . . .Su
Timebomb (1990). Dr. Anna Nolmar
•• 1:15—Breasts, mostly left breast, making love with Michael Biehn in bed. Partial buns also.
The Skipper (1991) . . . . .Sue
Twenty-One (1991; British) . . . . .Katie
••• 1:17—Breasts in reflection in bathroom mirror undressing, then dressing.
Blame It on the Bellboy (1992; British). . . . . . . Caroline Wright
The Turn of the Screw (1992; British). . . . . Jenny
Bitter Harvest (1993) . . . . Jolene Leder
••• 0:40—In black bodysuit, then left breast while making love with Stephen Baldwin in bed. Breasts in bathtub.
• 0:41—Left breast, while lying in bathtub with Baldwin.
•• 0:49—Brief breasts in bed with Baldwin and Jennifer Rubin.
Kleptomania (1993) . . . . Julie
•• 0:16—Breasts, taking a shower and drying herself off.
Dream Man (1995) . . . . Kris Anderson
Tunnel Vision (1995; Australian). . . . . Kelly Wheatstone
Angels & Insects (1996; British) . . . . Eugenia
•• 0:47—Breasts, while making love with Edgar on bed behind sheer netting.
• 0:49—Left breast, while lying in bed with Edgar, seen behind sheer netting.
•• 0:58—Full frontal nudity, while sitting on the bed, then making love with Edgar.
• 1:00—Brief partial right breast, while making love in bed with Edgar.
Grace of My Heart (1996) .Cheryl Steed

Made for Cable Movies:
Full Eclipse (1993; HBO) . . . . Casey Spencer

Made for Cable TV:
Tales From the Crypt: As Ye Sow (1993; HBO) . . . . Bridget

Made for TV Movies:
Silas Marner (1985; British) . . . . Eppie
Masterpiece Theatre: Adam Bede (1992). . . . . Hetty Sorrel
Fall From Grace (1994) . . . . Deidre
Love and Betrayal: The Mia Farrow Story (1995) . . . Mia Farrow

Kent, Elizabeth

Films:
Trapped Alive (1988) . . . . .Rachel
• 0:28—Brief left breast, then breasts, while making love on the floor with Billy.
Mindwarp (1990) . . . . Cornelia

Kenton, Linda *

Films:

Hot Resort (1984). . . . . .Mrs. Geraldine Miller

- 0:11—Very brief right breast, while in back of car with a guy.
- 0:16—Right breast, while passed out in closet with a bunch of guys.
- 0:24—Brief upper half of right breast, while on boat with a guy.
- 0:46—Brief breasts in Volkswagen.
- 0:51—Brief breasts in bathtub with Bronson Pinchot.
- 1:24—Brief breasts making love on a table while covered with food.

Kernohan, Roxanne *

Films:

Fatal Pulse (1987). . . . . .Ann

- 0:58—Brief breasts in pulled up yellow tank top before getting thrown out of the window.

Angel III: The Final Chapter (1988) . . . . White Hooker

Critters 2: The Main Course (1988). . . . . Lee

- •• 0:37—Brief breasts after transforming from an alien into a Playboy Playmate. Buns in G-sting when walking away.

Not of This Earth (1988) . . . . Lead Hooker

- ••• 0:41—Breasts in cellar with Paul just before getting killed with two other hookers. Wearing a blue top.

Phoenix the Warrior (1988) . . . . Meda

- ••• 0:15—Breasts in waterfall (she's the white girl).

Tango & Cash (1989) . . . . Dressing Room Girl

- 1:06—Brief breasts in dressing room with three other girls. She's the second one in the middle.

Video Tapes:

Scream Queen Hot Tub Party (1991) . . . . .Herself

- •• 0:07—Breasts, taking off black dress and putting on sheer black robe.
- 0:12—Buns, while walking up the stairs.
- •• 0:43—Breasts, struggling with a monster in basement.
- ••• 0:44—Breasts taking off her swimsuit top and soaping up with the other girls.
- •• 0:46—Breasts in still shot during the end credits.

Kerns, Joanna

Films:

Coma (1978) . . . . Diane
Cross My Heart (1987) . . . . .Nancy
Street Justice (1988) . . . . Katharine Watson
An American Summer (1990) . . . . .Aunt Sunny
The Nightman (1992) . . . . Eve Rhodes

- •• 0:47—Buns, while rolling over in bed and sitting up.

Miniseries:

V (1983) . . . . Marge Donovan

Made for TV Movies:

Mistress (1987). . . . . Stephanie
The Big One: The Great Los Angeles Earthquake (1990) . . . . .Dr. Winslow
Deadly Intentions...Again? (1991) . . . . Sally
Desperate Choices: To Save My Child (1992) . . . . n.a.
The Man with Three Wives (1993) . . . . Katy
Not in My Family (1993). . . . . Veronica Ricci
Shameful Secrets (1993) . . . . .Maryanne Walker-Tate
Robin Cook's "Mortal Fear" (1994) . . . . .Dr. Jennifer Kessler
See Jane Run (1995) . . . . .Jane Ravenson
Whose Daughter is She? (1995) . . . . Laura Eagerton
No One Could Protect Her (1996). . . . . n.a.
Mother Knows Best (1997) . . . . Celeste
Sisters and Other Strangers (1997) . . . . n.a.

TV:

Four Seasons (1984) . . . . .Pat Devon
Growing Pains (1985-92) . . . . Maggie Seaver

Kerr, Deborah

Films:

Courageous Mr. Penn (1941; British). . . . . Gugliema
Major Barbara (1941; British). Jenny Hill
The Life and Death of Colonel Blimp (1945; British) . . . . .Edith Hunter/Barbara Wynne/Johny Cannon
Love on the Dole (1945; British) . . . . .Sally Hardcastle
I See a Dark Stranger (1946; British) . . . . Dridie Quilty
Black Narcissus (1947; British) . . . . Sister Clodagh
The Hucksters (1947) . . . . Kay Dorrance
Quo Vadis (1951) . . . . .Lygia
The Prisoner of Zenda (1952) . . . . Princess Flavia
From Here to Eternity (1953). . . . . Karen Holmes
Julius Caesar (1953). . . . . Portia
The King and I (1956) . . . . Anna Leonowens
Tea and Sympathy (1956) . . . . Laura Reynolds
An Affair to Remember (1958). . . . . Terry McKay
Bonjour Tristesse (1958) . . . . Anne Larsen
The Grass Is Greener (1960) . . . . Hilary Rhyall
The Sundowners (1960) . . . . .Ida Carmody
The Naked Edge (1961) . . . . Martha Radcliffe
The Chalk Garden (1964) . . . . .Madrigal
The Night of the Iguana (1964). . . . . Hannah Jelkes
Casino Royale (1967; British). . . Agent Mimi/Lady Fiona McTarry
The Arrangement (1969) . . . . Florence

- 0:36—Buns, behind curtain, while taking off her night gown. Brief long shot of left breast, behind curtain, getting into bed.

The Gypsy Moths (1969) . . . . .Elizabeth Brandon

- ••• 0:52—Buns and left breast, while making love with Burt Lancaster on sofa.

Miniseries:

A Woman of Substance (1984) . . . . Emma Harte

Made for TV Movies:

Witness for the Prosecution (1982) . . . . Nurse Pimsoll

Kerr, E. Katherine

Films:

Tattoo (1981) . . . . Wife
Reuben, Reuben (1983). . . . . Lucille Haxby

- 0:51—Brief left breast in bedroom, undressing in front of Tom Conti.

Silkwood (1984) . . . . .Gilda Schultz
Children of a Lesser God (1986) . . . . Mary Lee Ochs
Devil's Advocate (1997). .Woman Judge

Miniseries:

The Buccaneers (1995; U.S./British). . . . . Mrs. Parmore

Kerridge, Linda *

Films:

Fade to Black (1980) . . . . .Marilyn

- 0:44—Breasts, while in the shower.

Strangers Kiss (1984). . . . . .Shirley
Surf II (1984). . . . . Sparkle
Down Twisted (1987) . . . . .Soames
Alien from L.A. (1988) . . . . Roeyis Freki/Auntie Pearl

Kerrington, K.C.

Films:

Wild Child (1991) . . . . .Linda

••• 0:16—Buns in lingerie, while bending over bathtub. Breasts and buns, while making love with Pete in bathtub. Long scene.

• 0:29—Breasts, while in the swimming pool.

Video Tapes:

Love Scenes: Volume 1 (1991) . . . . .Linda Whitney

••• 1:34—Nude, while making love with Tom.

Kersh, Kathy

Films:

Americanization of Emily (1964) . . . . Nameless Broad

Gemini Affair (1974) . . . . Jessica

•• 0:11—Nude getting into bed with Kristen.

• 0:12—Brief breasts turning over onto her stomach in bed.

•• 0:17—Nude, standing up in bed and jumping off.

••• 0:57—Nude in bed with Kristen.

•• 1:04—Left breast sitting up in bed after Kristen leaves.

Kerwin, Maureen

Films:

The Destructors (1974; British) . . . . Lucianne

Laura (1979) . . . . Martine

a.k.a. Shattered Innocence

• 0:03—Brief full frontal nudity getting out of bed and putting white bathrobe on.

Reunion (1989; French/German). . . . . . Lisa, Henry's Daughter

Kesner, Jillian

Films:

The Student Body (1975) . . . . Carrie Rafferty

•• 0:29—Left breast, making out with Carter in the car.

Starhops (1978) . . . . Angel

Firecracker (1981) . . . . Susanne Carter

••• 0:44—Breasts, while fighting bad guys after her bra comes off. Nice!

••• 0:58—In panties on bed, then buns as Darby Hinton cuts her clothes off with a knife. Breasts while making love with him in bed.

Raw Force (1981) . . . . Cookie Winchell

Trick or Treats (1982). . . . . Andrea

Moon in Scorpio (1987). . . . . Claire

•• 0:39—Breasts sitting on deck of boat with bathing suit top down.

Beverly Hills Vamp (1989) . . . . Claudia

Jaded (1989). . . . . Sara

Roots of Evil (1991) . . . . Brenda

(Unrated version reviewed.)

••• 0:27—Breasts, giving Alex Cord a back massage in bed.

• 0:30—Brief breasts, getting up out of bed.

Made for Cable Movies:

Subliminal Seduction (1996; Showtime) . . . . .Cheri

TV:

Co-ed Fever (1979) . . . . Melba

Kestelman, Sara

Films:

Zardoz (1974; British) . . . . May

• 1:04—Left breast, in open blouse, under sheet with Sean Connery.

• 1:05—Very brief breasts grabbing Connery from behind during struggle.

Lisztomania (1975; British) . . . . Princess Carolyn

Break of Day (1977; Australian) . . . . Alice

Lady Jane (1987; British) .Frances Grey

Made for Cable Movies:

Tom Jones: Part 1 (1998; A&E) . . . . Mrs. Wilkins

• Khanjian, Arsinée

Wife of director/actor Atom Egoyan.

Films:

Family Viewing (1987; Canadian) . . . . Aline

Speaking Parts (1989; Canadian). . . . . Lisa

The Adjuster (1991; Canadian) . . . . Hera

Calendar (1993; Canadian) . . . . Translator

Exotica (1994; Canadian) . . . . .Zoe

Irma Vep (1996; French) . . . . .American Woman

••• 0:53—Full frontal nudity, while talking on the phone in motel room, after Maggie Cheung sneaks in.

The Sweet Hereafter (1997; Canadian) . . . . Wanda Otto

Kidder, Margot *

Films:

Gaily, Gaily (1969). . . . . Adeline

Quackser Fortune has a Cousin in the Bronx (1970; Irish) . . . . .Zazel

•• 1:03—Breasts undressing on a chair, then brief right, then breasts when Gene Wilder kisses her.

• 1:05—Side view of left breast, then buns, getting out of bed.

Sisters (1973). . . . . Danielle Breton

• 0:11—Very brief left breast, undressing while walking down hallway. Long shot.

• 0:14—Breasts opening her robe on couch for her new boyfriend. Shadows make it hard to see.

Gravey Train (1974) . . . . Margie

92 in the Shade (1975) . . . . Goldsboro

Black Christmas (1975; Canadian). . . . . Barb

a.k.a. Stranger in the House

a.k.a. Silent Night, Evil Night

The Reincarnation of Peter Proud (1975) . . Marcia Curtis

• 1:29—Brief breasts sitting in bathtub masturbating while remembering getting raped by husband.

Superman (1978) . . . . Lois Lane

The Amityville Horror (1979) . . . . Kathleen Lutz

• 0:21—Brief right breast in reflection in mirror while doing dance stretching exercises in the bedroom. Hard to see because of the pattern on the mirror tiles.

• 0:22—Cleavage in open blouse while talking to James Brolin.

• 0:23—Very brief partial right breast, on the floor, kissing Brolin.

Superman II (1980) . . . . Lois Lane

Willie and Phil (1980) . . . . Jeanette Sutherland

• 0:36—Brief breasts in bed when Phil opens up her blouse. Long shot.

• 0:47—Brief breasts playing in a lake with Willie and Phil.

Heartaches (1981; Canadian). . . . . Rita Harris

Some Kind of Hero (1982). . . . . Toni

Trenchcoat (1983). . . . . Mickey Raymond

Little Treasure (1985). . . . . Margo

Miss Right (1987; Italian). . . . . .Juliet

Superman IV: The Quest for Peace (1987) . . . . Lois Lane

Keeping Track (1988) .Mickey Tremaine

The Pornographer (1994) . . . . .Irene

a.k.a. Family Values

Made for Cable Movies:

The Glitter Dome (1984; HBO) . . . . Willie

BloodKnot (1995; Showtime) . . . . .Evelyn

Made for Cable TV:
The Hitchhiker: Night Shift (1985; HBO) . . . Jane Reynolds
(Available on *The Hitchhiker, Volume 2.*)
• 0:13—In a white corset, then brief left breast over the shoulder shot.
Tales From the Crypt: Curiosity Killed (1992; HBO) . . . . Cynthia
Hunger: The Sloan Men (1997; Showtime) . . . Mrs. Helen Sloan
Made for TV Movies:
To Catch a Killer (1992; Canadian) . . . . Rachel Grayson
One Woman's Courage (1994) . . . . Stella Jenson
TV:
Nichols (1971-72). . . . . Ruth
Shell Game (1987) . . . . Jennie Jerome
CD-ROM:
Under a Killing Moon (1994). . . . . Bartender

Kidman, Nicole

Wife of actor Tom Cruise.
Films:
BMX Bandits (1984; Australian). . . . . Judy
Windrider (1986; Australian) . . . . .Jade
• 0:40—Brief breasts in the shower with Tom Burlinson.
•• 0:42—Brief buns and breasts in bed with Burlinson.
• 0:43—Brief left breast on top of Burlinson in bed. Dark.
••• 0:47—Buns and very brief back side of left and right breasts, getting out of bed and putting on robe.
Dead Calm (1989) . . . . Rae Ingram
• 1:00—Brief buns and breasts on the floor with Billy Zane.
Days of Thunder (1990) . . . . .Dr. Claire Lewicki
Billy Bathgate (1991) . . . . Drew Preston
•• 0:42—Briefly nude, throwing off towel in front of a vanity with three mirrors.
•• 0:52—Very brief full frontal nudity underwater. Brief full frontal nudity getting out of water and putting on dress.
Far and Away (1992). . . . . .Shannon Christie
Flirting (1992; Australian) . . . . Nicola Radcliffe
Malice (1993) . . . . .Tracy
•• 0:13—Very brief left breast then buns, when leaning over Bill Pullman in bed.
My Life (1993) . . . . Gail Jones
Batman Forever (1995) . . . . Dr. Chase Meridian
To Die For (1995) . . . . Suzanne Stone
• 0:54—Partial buns in purple bra and panties seen in reflection in the mirror.
The Portrait of a Lady (1996; British/U.S.) . . . . Isabel Archer
• 0:59—Brief buns and breasts in B&W fantasy sequence.
The Peacemaker (1997) . . . . .Julia Kelly
Made for Cable Movies:
Bangkok Hilton (1990) . . . . Katrina Stanton

Kiel, Sue

Films:
Repo Man (1984) . . . . Ms. Magruder
Red Heat (1987; U.S./German) .Hedda
• 0:56—Brief breasts in shower room scene (third girl behind Linda Blair). Long shot, hard to see.
Straight to Hell (1987; British). . . . . Leticia
Survivor (1987). . . . . The Woman
••• 0:33—Right breast, then breasts and buns making love with Survivor in hammock. Long scene.
Made for Cable TV:
Red Shoe Diaries: Bounty Hunter (1993; Showtime) . . Francine
(Available on the video tape *Red Shoe Diaries 5: Weekend Pass.*)
Red Shoe Diaries: How I Met My Husband (1993; Showtime)
. . . . .Mistress Miranda

Kiger, Susan Lynn *

First Playboy Playmate to do an adult film *before* she became a Playmate.
Adult Films:
Deadly Love (1974). . . . . .n.a.
a.k.a. Hot Nasties
(Nude with snake and nude performing fellatio.)
Films:
H.O.T.S. (1979) . . . . .Honey Shayne
a.k.a. T & A Academy
• 0:00—Breasts in shower room with the other girls.
•• 0:33—Breasts in pool making love with Doug.
• 1:33—Breasts in football game.
Seven (1979) . . . . Jennie
••• 0:58—Breasts, while sitting on bed, then getting up and walking around in the kitchen, making coffee, then putting her swimsuit top on.
• 1:15—Brief breasts, while taking off swimsuit top to change outside by car.
Angels Brigade (1980). .Michelle Wilson
Galaxina (1980). . . . . Blue Girl
The Happy Hooker Goes Hollywood (1980) . . . . Susie
• 0:42—Breasts, singing "Happy Birthday" to a guy tied up on the bed.
••• 0:43—Breasts, wearing a red garter belt playing pool with K.C. Winkler.
The Return (1980). . . . . .Joyce
House of Death (1981) . . . . Lily Carpenter

Kim, Karen

Films:
Cover Me (1995) . . . . Brandy
•• 0:32—Buns and breasts in white lingerie, while dancing on stage in club.
• 0:49—Brief breasts on magazine cover.
• 0:52—Breasts, while dancing on stage in club. Brief breasts in magazine cover flashback.
•• 0:53—Breasts, while in bubble bath, then talking on the phone.
Made for Cable TV:
Sherman Oaks (1996-97; Showtime). . . . . .Min
Sherman Oaks: Season 2, Episode 2 (1996; Showtime) . . . .Min
Sherman Oaks: Season 2, Episode 3 (1996; Showtime) . . . .Min
Sherman Oaks: Season 2, Episode 6 (1996; Showtime) . . . .Min
Sherman Oaks: Season 2, Episode 16 (1996; Showtime) . . .Min
TV:
On Our Own (1995) . . . . Suki

King, Chantel

Films:
Naked Souls (1995) .Woman in Bath
• 0:10—Brief breasts in bathtub before being strangled in B&W flashback.
• 1:02—Brief breasts, while sitting in bath and being strangled in B&W flashback.
Made for Cable TV:
Erotic Confessions: Inspiration (1995; Cinemax) . . . . . Lisa
(Available on video tape in *Erotic Zone: Inspiration.*)
•• 0:08—Left breast and buns, while making love in bed with Greg.
Compromising Situations: Real Woman
(1997; Showtime) . . . . Virtual Reality Woman
•• 0:09—In lingerie and breasts, while undressing in Phillip's virtual reality session.
Video Tapes:
Erotic Zone: The Ring (1995). . . . . Ring Girl #1

King, Cheryl

Films:

Sex Through a Window (1977) . . . . Nurse
- 0:19—In bra and panties, under sheer white pantyhose, then breasts after taking off bra, while John watches her through a telephoto lens.

Love Child (1982) . . . . Van Inmate

King, Rowena

Films:

London Kills Me (1991; British) . . . . .Melanie

Wide Sargasso Sea (1993). Amelie

(Unrated version reviewed.)
- 0:54—Briefly nude in open window, while showing off for Rochester.
- ••• 1:16—Breasts, while making love standing up outside with Rochester.
- ••• 1:17—Full frontal nudity in bed, then getting out and getting dressed.

Hamlet (1996). Attendant to Gertrude

Miniseries:

Masterpiece Theatre: To Play the King (1994) . . . . Chloe

King, Tracey Ann

See: Joi, Marilyn.

King, Victoria

See: Tuscany.

Kingsley, Danitza

Films:

You Can't Hurry Love (1984). . . . . .Tracey

Amazons (1986) . . . . Tshingi
- ••• 0:30—Breasts and buns quite a few times with Colungo out of and in bed.

Jack's Back (1987) . . . . Denise Johnson

South of Reno (1987) . . . . Louise

No Man's Land (1988) . . . . .Magot

Verne Miller (1988) .German Drink Girl

Kingsley, Gretchen

Films:

Blood Sisters (1986). . . . . Ellen
- •• 0:32—Breasts, changing clothes to go to sleep in bedroom.
- ••• 0:50—Breasts in bed with Jim.

If Looks Could Kill (1987) . . . . Elizabeth

Wimps (1987). . . . . Debbie

• Kingston, Alex

Ex-wife of actor Ralph Fiennes.

Made for Cable Movies:

Weapons of Mass Distraction (1997; HBO) . . . . .Verity Graham

Made for TV Movies:

Masterpiece Theatre: The Fortunes and Misfortunes of Moll Flanders (1996; British/U.S.). . . . . Moll Flanders
- • 0:34—Brief breasts, while making love with Roland in bed.
- •• 1:02—Left breast, while making love with Lemuel in his cabin on the boat.
- • 1:05—Very, very brief left breast, while making love with Lemuel in his cabin on the boat.
- ••• 1:14—Brief breasts, while lying in bed before making love with Lemuel.
- •• 1:24—Breasts, while washing herself and talking with Lemuel.
- ••• 1:57—(0:15 into tape 2) Brief breasts, while in bed with James.
- • 1:58—(0:16 into tape 2) Very brief left breast, when scrambling out of bed.
- ••• 2:50—(1:08 into tape 2) Breasts, while lying asleep in bed with Lucy.
- •• 2:55—(1:13 into tape 2) Breasts, while opening her dress top, when riding in a coach with Sir Gregory.
- • 3:09—(1:27 into tape 2) Brief left breast, while bribing the jailer.
- • 3:13—(1:31 into tape 2) Partial breasts, while sitting down with James.

TV:

ER (1997-) . . . . Dr. Elizabeth Corday

Kinkade, Amelia

Films:

Body Rock (1984) . . . . Little Freak

My Best Friend Is a Vampire (1987) . . . . Brunette in Bar

Night of the Demons (1987). Angela

(Unrated version reviewed.)
- • 0:47—Brief buns in panties, garter belt and stockings under dress while doing sexy dance in living room.

Night of the Demons 2 (1994) . . . . Angela

Kinmont, Kathleen *

Ex-wife of actor Lorenzo Lamas.

Daughter of actress Abby Dalton.

Films:

Hardbodies (1984) . . . . .Pretty Skater

Fraternity Vacation (1985) . . . . Marianne
- ••• 0:16—Breasts and buns, after taking off her swimsuit in bedroom with two guys.

Nightforce (1986) . . . . Cindy

Winners Take All (1987). . . . . Party Girl #5

Halloween 4: The Return of Michael Meyers (1988). . . . . . Kelly

Phoenix the Warrior (1988) . . . . Phoenix

RollerBlade Warriors: Taken By Force (1988). . . . . . Karin Crosse

Bride of Re-Animator (1989) . . . . Gloria/The Bride
- • 0:58—Brief breasts several times with her top pulled down to defibrillate her heart.
- • 1:17—Breasts under gauze. Her body has gruesome looking special-effect appliances all over it.
- • 1:22—More breasts under gauze.
- • 1:24—More breasts. Pretty unappealing.
- • 1:27—Brief buns, when turning around after ripping out her own heart.

Midnight (1989) . . . . .Party

Rush Week (1989). Julie Ann McGuffin
- • 0:07—Brief breasts several times during modeling session. Buns in G-string getting dressed. Long shot.

SnakeEater II: The Drug Buster (1990) . . Detective Lisa Forester

The Art of Dying (1991) . . . . .Holly
- • 0:28—Brief left breast, making love with Wings Hauser in the kitchen. Brief breasts when he pours milk on her.
- •• 0:33—Breasts in bathtub with Hauser. Intercut with Janet getting stabbed.

Night of the Warrior (1991) . . . . Katherine Pierce
- • 0:29—Very brief upper half of right breast, while leaning out of the shower to get a towel.
- • 1:10—Brief right breast, while making love with Lamas on motorcycle.

Sweet Justice (1991) . . . . Heather

CIA—Code Name: Alexa (1992) . . . . Alexa
- • 1:04—Very brief buns and very, very brief right breast and brief left breast while making love with Lorenzo Lamas in bed.

Final Impact (1992). . . . . .Maggie

CIA II: Target Alexa (1993) . . . . .Alexa
Final Round (1993). . . . . Jordan
••• 0:18—Breasts, while making love on the floor with Lamas.
Renegade: Fighting Cage (1993). . . . . Cheyenne
(Nudity added for video release.)
Stormswept (1994) . . . . .Missy
Texas Payback (1994) . . . . .Angela
The Corporate Ladder (1996). . . . . .Nicole Landon
••• 0:39—In bra, panties and stockings, then breasts and buns, while making love with Matt in the office.
• 1:14—Brief breasts, while making love with Matt in bed.
•• 1:29—In bra, then breasts and buns, while undressing in backyard and walking into pool before killing Ben Cross with a champagne bottle.
That Thing You Do! (1996) . . . . Koss' Secretary
TV:
Renegade (1993-94) . . . . Cheyenne

Kinnaman, Melanie

Films:
Friday the 13th, Part V—A New Beginning (1985)
. . . . Pam Roberts
Thunder Alley (1985). . . . . .Star
• 0:52—Brief breasts under water in pool talking to a Richie. Side view of right breast, talking to Donnie.
•• 1:14—Breasts and buns, making love on bed with Richie, then getting out.
Best of the Best (1990) . . . . The Woman

*Kinski, Nastassja **

Daughter of the late actor Klaus Kinski.
Real last name is Nakzsynski.
Films:
Boarding School (1976; German) . . . . Deborah Collins
a.k.a. Virgin Campus
a.k.a. The Passion Flower Hotel
• 0:15—Brief breasts in the shower with her roommates. Hard to tell who is who.
• 1:11—Left breast, then breasts in the shower (She's the second from the right) consoling Marie-Louise.
• 1:16—Breasts under sheer nightie.
••• 1:32—Breasts making love with Sinclair.
To the Devil, a Daughter (1976; British/German)
. . . . .Catherine Beddows
••• 1:24—Full frontal nudity, taking off her robe outside and walking towards Richard Widmark in slow motion.
Stay As You Are (1978; Italian). . . . . Francesca
English language version.
• 0:07—Left breast, while sleeping in bed.
• 1:00—Breasts, undressing and sitting in bed. Brief side of left breast, while lying in bed.
••• 1:02—Buns, while lying in bed, then full frontal nudity sitting up and covering herself with a sheet.
••• 1:27—Left breast, then breasts and brief buns in bed with Marcello Mastroianni. Long scene.
••• 1:28—Breasts, sitting up in bed, talking with Mastroianni.
••• 1:30—Nude, fooling around at the table with Mastroianni. Long scene. Nice bun shots.
•• 1:33—Breasts in bedroom at night. Mostly silhouette.
For Your Love Only (1979; German) . . . . Zena
•• 0:04—Breasts, twice, in the woods with her teacher, Victor, while Michael watches through the bushes.
• 0:15—Brief right breast, in the woods with Michael.
•• 0:58—Partial left breast, sitting up in bed with Victor. Breasts walking around and putting on robe.
Tess (1979; French/British) . . . . Tess Durbeyfield
• 0:47—Brief left breast, opening blouse in field to feed her baby.
Cat People (1982). . . . . Irena Gallier
••• 1:03—Nude at night, walking around outside chasing a rabbit.
•• 1:35—Breasts taking off blouse, walking up the stairs and getting into bed.
• 1:37—Brief right breast, lying in bed with John Heard.
•• 1:38—Breasts getting out of bed and walking to the bathroom.
•• 1:40—Brief buns, getting back into bed. Breasts in bed.
•• 1:47—Full frontal nudity, walking around in the cabin at night.
• 1:49—Breasts, tied to the bed by Heard.
One from the Heart (1982). . . . . Leila
• 1:13—Brief breasts in open blouse when she leans forward after walking on a ball.
Exposed (1983) . . . . Elizabeth Carlson
•• 0:54—Breasts in bed with Rudolf Nureyev.
The Moon in the Gutter (1983; French/Italian) . . . . Loretta
a.k.a. La Lune dans Le Caniveau
Spring Symphony (1983). . . . . .Clara
• 0:29—Brief left breast, when it pops out of her corset when she tries on a dress.
The Hotel New Hampshire (1984) . . . . Susie the Bear
• 1:42—Very, very brief tip of left breast, then very brief right breast in room with Rob Lowe after she takes off her bear suit.
Paris, Texas (1984; French/German) . . . . Jane
Unfaithfully Yours (1984) . . . . .Daniella Eastman
• 0:37—Breasts and buns in the shower.
Harem (1985; French) . . . . Diane
• 0:14—Breasts getting into swimming pool.
•• 1:04—Breasts in motel room with Ben Kingsley.
Maria's Lovers (1985). . . . . Maria Bosic
• 1:12—Brief right breast, while looking at herself in the mirror.
Revolution (1986) .Daisy McConnahay
Magdelena (1988). . . . . Magdalena
Torrents of Spring (1990) . . . . Maria
Faraway, So Close (1993; German) . . . . .Raphaela
a.k.a. In weiter Ferne, so nah!
Crackerjack (1994) . . . . K.C.
Terminal Velocity (1994) . . . . Chris Morrow
Father's Day (1997). . . . . .Collette Andrews
One Night Stand (1997) . . . . Karen
• 0:30—Brief right breast, while making love in bed with Wesley Snipes.
Made for TV Movies:
Danielle Steel's "The Ring" (1996). . . . . .Ariana
Bella Mafia (1997). . . . . Sophia

*Kirkland, Sally **

Films:
Blue (1968) . . . . .n.a.
Going Home (1971) . . . . .Ann Graham
Cinderella Liberty (1973). . . . . Fleet Chick
The Sting (1973) . . . . Crystal
The Way We Were (1973) . . . . .Pony Dunbar
Young Nurses (1973). . . . . Patient
Big Bad Mama (1974) . . . . Barney's Woman
•• 0:13—Breasts and buns waiting for Barney then throwing shoe at Billy Jean.
• 1:23—Brief breasts, covering herself up scene from 0:13 during end credits.

Candy Stripe Nurses (1974) . . . . Woman in Clinic
Crazy Mama (1975) . . . . Ella Mae
A Star is Born (1976) . . . . Photographer
Tracks (1977) . . . . Uncredited
Hometown, U.S.A. (1979) . . . . n.a.
Private Benjamin (1980) . . . . Helga
Talking Walls (1982) . . . . Hooker
Double Exposure (1983) . . . . Hooker
•• 0:26—Breasts in alley getting killed.
Fatal Games (1984) . . . . .Diane Paine
Love Letters (1984) . . . . .Hippie
a.k.a. Passion Play
Anna (1987) . . . . .Anna
•• 0:28—Breasts, while in the bathtub talking to Daniel.
White Hot (1988) . . . . Harriet
a.k.a. Crack In the Mirror
Cold Feet (1989) . . . . Maureen Linoleum
(In tight fitting spandex dresses throughout most of the film.)
• 0:56—In black bra and panties taking off her dress in bedroom with Keith Carradine. Brief right breast pulling bra down.
• 0:58—Brief side view of right breast sitting up in bed talking to Carradine.
High Stakes (1989). . . . . Melanie "Bambi" Rose
• 0:01—In two piece costume, doing a strip tease routine on stage. Buns in G-string, then very, very brief breasts while flashing.
Paint It Black (1989) . . . . .Marion Easton
Best of the Best (1990) .Kathevu Wade
Bullseye! (1990) . . . . .Willie
Revenge (1990). . . . . .Rock Star
In the Heat of Passion (1991). . . . . .Dr. Lee Adams
(Unrated version reviewed.)
••• 0:21—In black bra, then breasts making love with Charlie while her husband is downstairs.
• 0:23—Brief breasts in the shower when her husband opens the shower curtain.
•• 0:29—Breasts with Charlie in stall in women's restroom.
•• 0:42—Breasts teasing Charlie from the bathroom.
• 0:45—Right breast, then breasts in bed with Charlie.
• 1:11—Very brief buns, while on the couch with Charlie.
JFK (1991) . . . . Rose Cheramie
Two Evil Eyes (1991) . . . . Eleonora
Blast 'Em (1992) . . . . Herself
Cheatin' Hearts (1992) . . . . Jenny
•• 1:09—Nude, taking off her clothes outside after she gets angry with James Brolin.
Double Threat (1992) . . . . Monica Martel
(Unrated version reviewed.)
• 0:13—In lingerie outfit while playing with herself. Partial left breast.
•• 0:51—Brief left breast, then breasts while dressing in bathroom.
Eye of the Stranger (1992) . . . . Lori
•• 0:47—Breasts, while making love in bed with David Heavener.
Forever (1992). . . . . Angelica Farina
• 0:14—Breasts, while making love with Keith Coogan in bed. Right breast, when lying in bed with him afterwards.
•• 0:20—Breasts, while on sofa with Coogan.
•• 1:25—Breasts, while starting to make love on desk in Coogan's office.
Hit the Dutchman (1992) . . . . Emma Flegenheimer
(Unrated version reviewed.)
The Player (1992) . . . . Cameo
Primary Motive (1992). . . . . .Helen Poulas
Prime Time Murder (1992) . . . . Joan
a.k.a. Stringer
Gunmen (1993). . . . . .Bennett
Excess Baggage (1997) . . . . .Louise
Made for Cable Movies:
The Westing Game (1997; Showtime) . . . . Sydelle Pulaski
Made for Cable TV:
Picture Windows: Song of Songs (1995; Showtime)
. . . . Blossom
• 0:17—Brief right breast, while lying in bed with George Segal.
•• 0:22—Breasts, while lying in bed with Segal.
The Hunger: Bridal Suite (1997; Canadian; Showtime)
. . . . .Mrs. Darington
• 0:21—Partial breasts, then breasts, while making love in bed with spirit guys.
Made for TV Movies:
The Haunted (1991) . . . . .Janet
The Woman Who Loved Elvis (1993) . . . . Sandee
Brave New World (1998) . . . . Linda

Kirshner, Mia

Films:
Cadillac Girls (1993; Canadian) . . . . .Page
• 0:02—Back half of breast in mirror when Miles gets out of bed. Long shot.
Exotica (1994; Canadian). . . . . .Christina
• 0:33—Brief, lower half of buns, while dancing in schoolgirl outfit.
• 0:54—Breasts in open blouse, while dancing in front of Bruce Greenwood.
•• 1:11—Right breast, while dancing in front of Thomas.
Murder in the First (1994) . . . . Adult Rosetta Young
Love and Human Remains (1995; Canadian) . . . . . . .Benita
• 1:25—Brief right breast, when her bra is ripped off by Bernie.
• 1:27—Very brief, blurry right breast, when Bernie pushes her on the bed.
The Crow: City of Angels (1996) . . . . Sarah
The Grass Harp (1996). . . . . .Maude Riordan
Anna Karenina (1997) . . . . Kitty
Mad City (1997) . . . . Laurie
Made for TV Movies:
Johnny's Girl (1995). . . . . Amy
TV:
Dracula: The Series (1990). . . . . Sophie Metternich

Kitaen, Tawny

Ex-wife of singer David Coverdale of the rock group *Whitesnake*.
Films:
Bachelor Party (1984) . . . . Debbie Thompson
The Perils of Gwendoline in the Land of the Yik Yak
(1984; French). . . . . Gwendoline
••• 0:36—Breasts in the rain in the forest, taking off her top. More breasts with Willard.
•• 0:52—Buns, while walking around with Willard in costumes.
• 0:55—Buns, falling into jail cell, then in jail cell in costume.
• 0:57—Buns, while rescuing Beth in torture chamber.
•• 1:01—Breasts in S&M costume in front of mirrors.
• 1:04—Brief breasts escaping from chains.
• 1:07—Buns, in costume while riding chariot and next to wall.
• 1:09—Buns, while standing up.

- •• 1:11—Buns, in costume during fight. Wearing green ribbon.
- •• 1:18—Breasts making love with Willard.

Crystal Heart (1987) . . . . Alley Daniels
- •• 0:46—Breasts and buns, while "making love" with Lee Curreri through the glass.
- •• 0:50—Nude, crashing through glass shower door, covered with blood during her nightmare.
- • 1:14—Brief breasts making love with Curreri in and falling out of bed.

Happy Hour (1987). . . . . Misty Roberts
Instant Justice (1987) . . . . Virginia
Witchboard (1987) . . . . Linda
- • 1:26—Nude, stuck in the shower and breaking the glass doors to get out.

White Hot (1988). . . . . Vanessa
a.k.a. Crack In the Mirror
- • 1:04—Brief half of lower frontal nudity, when sitting up in bed.

Three of Hearts (1993) . . . . Woman in Bar
Playback (1995) . . . . Sara Burgess
- • 0:23—Brief left breast, with her husband in bed.
- •• 0:40—Breasts, while making love in bed with her husband.
- • 0:48—Brief breasts on video playback.
- • 0:51—Very brief breasts in video playback in George Hamilton's office.
- • 1:27—Brief buns in two piece swimsuit.

Dead Tides (1997) . . . . Nola
Made for Cable Movies:
The Glory Years (1987; HBO) . . . . n.a.
Made for TV Movies:
Hercules and the Circle of Fire (1994) . . . . .Deianeira
Hercules in the Maze of the Minotaur (1994) . . . . . . .Deianeira
Hercules in the Underworld (1994) . . . . .Deianeira
TV:
Santa Barbara (1989-90). . . . . Lisa
New WKRP in Cincinnati (1991-93). . . . . Mona Loveland
America's Funniest People (1992-94). . . . . .Co-Host
Video Tapes:
Whitesnake—Trilogy (1987). . . . . .The Girl
- • 0:10—(2 min., 17 sec. into "Here I Go Again.") Very brief right breast, leaning out of car.
- • 0:18—Most of her buns, while kissing David Coverdale in out-take from "Is This Love."

The Kathy Kaehler Fitness System (1992) . . . . Exercise Student

Klarwein, Eleonore

Films:
Peppermint Soda (1979; French). . . . . Anne Weber
Stroke of Midnight (1991; U.S./French). . . . . . . .Second Model
a.k.a. If the Shoe Fits
Road to Ruin (1992). . . . . .Girl Friend
- •• 0:03—Breasts and buns, getting out of bed and walking into bathroom.

Klein, Barbara Ann

Films:
Night Eyes (1990). .Sleeping Woman
(Unrated version reviewed.)
- • 0:02—Brief breasts, while struggling with burglar/rapist.

Relentless 2: Dead On (1991) . . . . Realtor
Death Becomes Her (1992) . . . . . . Goldie Hawn's Stunt Double
Rapid Fire (1992) . . . . Stunts
Straight Talk (1992) . . . . Stunts
Jason Goes to Hell—The Final Friday (1993) . . . . Stunts
(Unrated Director's Original Cut reviewed.)
Sleepless in Seattle (1993). . . . . Stunts
Assassins (1995) . . . . Cop #4

Klemme, Brenda Lynn

Films:
Cutting Class (1988) . . . . Colleen
- • 0:32—In bra in locker room. Very, very brief buns cheerleading without any panties on.
- • 0:37—More very brief buns, ducking under bleachers.

Stone Cold (1991). . . . . Marie
Patriot Games (1992) . . . . .Secretary

Klenck, Margaret

Films:
Hard Choices (1986). . . . . Laura
- •• 1:10—Left breast, then breasts making love with Bobby. Nice close up shot.
- • 1:11—Very brief half of left breast and lower frontal nudity getting back into bed. Long shot.

Loose Cannons (1990) . . . . Eva Braun
TV:
One Life to Live (1977-84). . . . . Edwina Lewis

• Knight, Kimberly

See: St. Clair, Taylor.

• Knight, Madeline

Adult film actress.
Films:
Vice Girls (1995) . . . . Michelle
- • 0:04—Buns in T-back under fishnet dress.
- • 0:08—Breasts, after taking off dress while being video taped.
- •• 0:11—Breasts, while being video taped in bedroom.

Knight, Shirley

Films:
The Couch (1962). . . . . .Terry
House of Women (1962) . . . . Erica
The Group (1966) . . . . Polly Andrews
Petulia (1968; U.S./British). . . . . Polo
The Rain People (1969) . . . . Natalie
- • 0:15—Breasts walking around in motel room and getting into bed. Long shot.
- • 1:36—Very brief buns, with sheet wrapped around her, trying to get out of trailer.

Secrets (1971). . . . . .Beatrice
Juggernaut (1974; British) . . . . Barbara Banister
Beyond the Poseidon Adventure (1979) . . . . Hannah Meredith
Endless Love (1981). . . . . .Anne
The Sender (1982) . . . . Jerolyn
Panther Squad (1986; French/Belgian) . . . . n.a.
Color of Night (1994) . . . . Edith Niedelmeyer
Stuart Saves His Family (1995). . . . . Mom
Diabolique (1996) . . . . Edie Danziger
As Good As It Gets (1997) . . . . Beverly
Made for Cable Movies:
Indictment: The McMartin Trial (1995; HBO)
. . . . Peggy Buckey
- • 0:53—Brief buns, three times while in jail during body cavity search.

If These Walls Could Talk (1996; HBO). . . . . .Mary Donnely
A Promise to Carolyn (1996; CBS) . . . . .Colleen Parker
Stolen Memories: Secrets From the Rose Garden (1996; Family)
. . . . .Sally Ann

Made for TV Movies:
The Outsider (1967) .... Peggy Leydon
Billionaire Boys Club (1987) .... n.a.
Mother's Revenge (1993) .... Bess Jordan
When Love Kills: The Seduction of John Hearn (1993) .... Edna Larson
Baby Brokers (1994) .... Sylvia
Children of the Dust (1995) .... Aunt Bertha
Dying to be Perfect: The Ellen Hart Peña Story (1996) .... Joan Hart
The Uninvited (1996) .... Della
TV:
Angel Falls (1993) .... Edie Wren Cox
NYPD Blue: Large Mouth Bass (Feb 7, 1995) ... Agnes Cantwell

Knight, Tuesday

Films:
A Nightmare on Elm Street 4: The Dream Master (1988) .... Kristen
Mistress (1991) .... Peggy Pauline
Calendar Girl (1993) .... Nude Woman
• 0:45—Very brief buns and partial left breast, while lying down on the beach when first seen by Jason Priestley and his friends. Long shot.
Cover Story (1993) .... Tracy/Reen
•• 0:22—Breasts in outfit with painted face, while on video playback that Matt watches.
•• 1:08—Right breast, then breasts, while making love with Matt.
Wes Craven's New Nightmare (1994) .... Herself
The Babysitter (1995) .... Waitress
• 0:08—Breasts, while making love with Mark on the floor in a flashback.
The Fan (1996) .... Nurse
Hindsight (1996) .... Karen
Made for Cable Movies:
Rebel Highway: Cool and the Crazy (1994; Showtime) .... Brenda
TV:
General Hospital .... n.a.
2000 Malibu Road (1992) .... Joy

*Knittle, Kristen **

Films:
Body Strokes (1995) .... Beth
•• 0:21—Breasts, while undressing to model for Leo.
••• 0:23—Nude in flashback with David and making love on boat.
•• 0:45—In bra, then breasts, while starting to make love with her teacher in flashback.
••• 0:57—Full frontal nudity while posing on sofa and teasing her boyfriend.
•• 1:19—Breasts, while posing outdoors with Claire and rubbing oil on her.
•• 1:22—Breasts, while posing in white panties with Claire.
• 1:32—Breasts, while posing with Claire and Karen.
Dream Master: The Erotic Invader (1995) .... Dani
• 0:32—Breasts, while making love with Scott in her dream.
•• 0:46—Breasts, while making love with Troy in his dream.
Showgirls (1995) .... Al Torres' Girl
(NC-17 version reviewed.)
Sinful Intrigue (1995) .... Jake's Wife
•• 0:06—Breasts, while making love with Jake in his flashback.
CD-ROM:
Heidi's House (1996) .... n.a.

*Knudsen, Vibeke **

Films:
The Story of "O" (1975; French) .... n.a.
The French Woman (1979) .... Anne-Marie
a.k.a. Madame Claude
• 0:04—Breasts in chair in office with Robert Webber.
• 0:09—Breasts walking on beach with Japanese Businessman.
••• 0:11—Breasts on bed with David while she talks on the telephone. Then hot scene making love with him in the shower.
• 1:19—Breasts in bed with a customer when David comes over.

Kober, Marta

Films:
Friday the 13th, Part II (1981) .... Sandra
Baby, It's You (1983) .... Debra
Neon Maniacs (1985) .... Lorraine
School Spirit (1985) .... Ursula
Rad (1986) .... Becky
Vendetta (1986) .... Sylvia
• 1:10—Very brief, dark, right breast in open blouse, in her prison cell with the guard.
Slumber Party Massacre 3 (1990) .... Pizza Girl
Made for TV Movies:
Second Sight: A Love Story (1984) .... Megan
A Touch of Scandal (1984) .... Toni Allenby
Children of the Night (1985) .... Linda
Video Tapes:
Inside Out (1992) .... The Girl/Doubletalk
(Unrated version reviewed.)
••• 0:26—Breasts in raised blouse, on top of Jack on sofa.

Kohnert, Mary

Films:
Valet Girls (1987) .... Carnation
Beyond the Door III (1989; Yugoslavian) .... Beverly
•• 0:03—Breasts taking a shower.
Mr. Baseball (1992) .... Player's Wife

Koizumi, Ariane

See: Ariane.

Komorowska, Liliana

Films:
War and Love (1985) .... Esther
Astonished (1988) .... Sonia Borges/Lucille
•• 0:30—Breasts, while making love on the floor with Charles S. Dutton. More breasts, when stabbing him repeatedly with a knife.
• 0:32—Very brief breasts, while putting dress top back on.
Her Alibi (1989) .... Laura
Scanners III: The Takeover (1992) .... Helena Monet
•• 0:32—Breasts in and out of spa, talking with her dad.
• 0:35—Brief right breast, while sitting up.
Martial Outlaw (1993) .... Marina
Screamers (1995) .... Landowska
Made for Cable TV:
Hunger: Red Light (1997; Showtime) .... Natasha
• 0:08—Breasts and buns, while making love with Rick in the elevator.
• 0:15—Buns, when sleeping on Rick's sofa, while he photographs her.
• 0:18—Brief left breast, while making love with Rick.

Kong, Venice *

Films:

Beverly Hills Cop II (1987) . . . . Playboy Playmate
Number One with a Bullet (1987) . . . . Asian Woman

Video Tapes:

Wet & Wild (1989) . . . . Model
Playboy Video Centerfold: Kerri Kendall (1990) . . . . Playmate
••• 0:41—Full frontal nudity.
Playmates at Play (1990) . . . . Making Waves
Playboy's Women of Color (1994) . . . . Playmate
••• 0:20—Nude, when frolicking in the water in Jamaica.
Playboy's 21 Playmates: Volume II (1996) . . . . . . Playmate
••• 0:21—Nude in still photos.
••• 0:22—Nude in a river and waterfall.

Konop, Kelli

Films:

Bikini Summer (1991) . . . . Rene
Totally Exposed (1991) . . . . Sue
• 0:18—Undressing to take a shower. Brief right breast, bending over to take off panties. Brief side view of left breast, while getting into the shower.
• 0:19—Sort of breasts, while washing herself in the shower. Her arms get in the way.

Konopski, Sharry *

Video Tapes:

Playboy Video Calendar 1989 (1988) . . . . April
••• 0:13—Nude.
Wet & Wild (1989) . . . . Model
Playboy's 21 Playmates (1996) . . . . Playmate
••• 0:59—Nude in still photos.
••• 1:00—Nude outside in old building and in studio.

Kopf, Kim

Films:

Stormswept (1994) . . . . Maria
Witchcraft 8: Salems Ghost (1994) . . . Mary Ann Dunaway
•• 0:10—Breasts, while playing with food and making love with her husband in the kitchen.
••• 0:38—Nude, while making love with her husband on the bed.
• 0:41—Left breast, while sitting on bed with McArthur during dream.
••• 0:48—Breasts, while caressing herself in the bathroom and then the bathtub. Very brief lower frontal nudity when going under the water in the bathtub.
• 1:03—Buns in T-back, while in bed with McArthur in dream.
Midnight Tease 2 (1995) . . . . Katlin Clark
•• 0:28—Buns in T-back and bra, then breasts.

Made for Cable TV:

Love Street: Hot Set (1994; Showtime) . . . . Kelly
•• 0:02—In lingerie outfit, then breasts and buns, while acting in a movie.
• 0:05—Breasts, while dressing in dressing room.
••• 0:19—Full frontal nudity, while making love with John on the bed on the set.

Korn, Sandy

See: Taylor, Sandra.

Korot, Alla

Films:

Night of the Cyclone (1990) . . . . Angelique
• 0:21—Right breast, then brief breasts getting out of the shower.

Made for Cable TV:

Red Shoe Diaries: Details (1998; Showtime). . . Anne Adams
•• 0:04—Brief breasts, several times, while making love with her boyfriend.
• 0:20—Brief buns and breasts, while making love with Carlo in bedroom.

TV:

All My Children . . . . Allie Doyle
Another World (1991-) . . . . Jenna Norris

Koscina, Sylva

Films:

Hercules (1959; Italian) . . . . Iole
Deadly Sanctuary (1968; British/Spanish) . . . . n.a.
The Secret War of Harry Frigg (1969) . . Countess di Montefiore
The House of Exorcism (1972; Italian/Spanish) . . . . . Sophia
a.k.a. Lisa and the Devil
••• 0:24—Breasts, while making love in bed with George the chauffeur.
The Slasher (1975) . . . . Barbara
•• 0:17—Left breast lying down getting a massage.
•• 1:18—Breasts undressing and putting a robe on at her lover's house. Left breast after getting stabbed.
Sex on the Run (1979; German/French/Italian) . . . Jelsamina
a.k.a. Some Like It Cool
a.k.a. Casanova and Co.
••• 0:28—Breasts and brief buns dropping her top for Tony Curtis, then walking around with the "other" Tony Curtis.
•• 1:20—Breasts talking to her husband.

Kossack, Christine

Films:

Three Men and a Baby (1987) . . . . One of Jack's Girls
The Brain (1988) . . . . Vivian
•• 0:24—Breasts on monitor, then breasts in person during Jim's fantasy.
•• 1:11—Breasts again in the basement during Jim's hallucination.

Kotero, Patty

See: Apollonia.

Kozak, Harley Jane

Sister of actress Heidi Kozak.

Films:

House on Sorority Row (1983) . . . . Diane
Clean and Sober (1988) . . . . Ralston Receptionist
Parenthood (1989) . . . . Susan
When Harry Met Sally... (1989) . . . . Helen
Arachnophobia (1990) . . . . Molly Jennings
Side Out (1990) . . . . Kate Jacobs
• 0:53—Brief left breast, then out of focus left breast, while in bed with Peter Horton.
All I Want for Christmas (1991) . . . . Catherine O'Fallon
The Favor (1991) . . . . Kathy
Necessary Roughness (1991) . . . . Suzanne Carter
The Taking of Beverly Hills (1991) . . . . Laura Sage
Magic in the Water (1995) . . . . Dr. Wanda Bell

Made for Cable Movies:

The Android Affair (1995; USA) . . . . Karen

Made for Cable TV:

Dream On: I'm With Stupid (1994; HBO) .... Jill Chadfield
- 0:05—Back side of left breast, while undressing Martin on the sofa. Don't see her face.

Dream On: Take Two Tablets, And Get Me to Mt. Sinai (1995; HBO) .... Martin's Lover
Strangers: Cinema Verite (1996; HBO)................Leslie
The Outer Limits: The Camp (1997; Showtime) .... Prisoner 98843
Stargate SG-1: Cold Lazarus (1997; Showtime) .... n.a.

Made for TV Movies:

The Amy Fisher Story (1993)................ Amy Pagnozzi

TV:

The Guiding Light....................... Annabelle Sims
Santa Barbara .... Mary Duvall
Texas (1980-82) .... Brett Wheeler
Knightwatch (1988-89)......................... Barbara
Harts of the West (1993-94) .... Alison Hart
You Wish (1997-) .... Gillian Apple

Kozak, Heidi

Sister of actress Harley Jane Kozak.

Films:

Cold Steel (1987) .... Gang Girl
Slumber Party Massacre II (1987) .... Sally
Friday the 13th, Part VII: The New Blood (1988) .... Sandra
- 0:36—Buns, while taking off clothes to go skinny dipping. Briefly nude, three times, under water just before getting killed by Jason.

Society (1989)................................ Shauna

TV:

Dr. Quinn, Medicine Woman (1993).................Emily

Kozlowski, Linda

Wife of actor Paul Hogan.

Films:

Crocodile Dundee (1986; Australian)......... Sue Charlton
- •• 0:31—Buns in black one piece swimsuit with thong back after she takes off her skirt to fill her canteen with water.

Crocodile Dundee II (1988).................. Sue Charlton
Pass the Ammo (1988) .... Claire
Target: Favorite Son (1988)...................Sally Crain
Almost an Angel (1990) .... Rose Garner
Backstreet Justice (1993) ....Kerri Finnegan
- ••• 0:31—Breasts in open dress and while making love in bedroom with John Shea.

The Neighbor (1993) .... Mary Westhill
Village of the Damned (1995).............. Jill McGowan

Krige, Alice

Films:

Chariots of Fire (1981) ....Sybil Gordon
Ghost Story (1981)..........................Alma/Eva
- • 0:41—Brief breasts making love in bedroom with Craig Wasson.
- •• 0:44—Breasts in bathtub with Wasson.
- •• 0:46—Breasts sitting up in bed.
- ••• 0:49—Buns, then breasts standing on balcony turning and walking to bedroom talking to Wasson.

King David (1985) ....Bathsheba
- •• 1:16—Full frontal nudity getting a bath outside at dusk while Richard Gere watches.

Barfly (1987)...................................... Tully
Haunted Summer (1988) .... Mary Godwin
See You in the Morning (1989) ....Beth Goodwin
Code Name: Chaos (1990) ....Isabelle
Stephen King's "Sleepwalkers" (1992)...........Mary Brady
Habitat (1996; Canadian) .... Clarissa Symes
- ••• 0:21—Breasts, when starting to make love with Tcheky Karyo.
- • 1:20—Breasts visible under sheer dress.

Star Trek: First Contact (1996)................ Borg Queen

Made for Cable Movies:

Baja Oklahoma (1988; HBO) .... Patsy Cline
Ladykiller (1992; USA).......................May Packard
Joseph (1995; TNT)...............................Rachel
Hidden in America (1996; Showtime) .... Dee

Made for Cable TV:

Iran: Days of Crisis (1991; TNT)........... Parveneh Limbert
Donor Unknown (1995; USA) .... Alice Stillman

Made for TV Movies:

Jack Reed: Badge of Honor (1993).............Joan Anatole
Judgment Day: The John List Story (1993)........ Jean Syfert

Krim, Viju

Films:

Bloodsucking Freaks (1982)..................... Natasha
Twelfth Night (1988; Italian) .... Maria
- •• 1:09—Breasts, dancing in tavern in open top.

Kriss, Katherine

Films:

American Flyers (1985) .... Vera
Hot Chili (1985)......................... Allison Baxter
- ••• 0:56—Breasts getting out of the pool and talking to Ricky.
- • 1:09—Buns and side view of left breast, while lying down and kissing Ricky.

Student Confidential (1987) ....Elaine's Friend

Kristel, Sylvia *

Films:

Because of the Cats (1973) ....n.a.
- • 1:09—Breasts and buns, under water with Case.

Emmanuelle (1974; French) .... Emmanuelle
(R-rated version reviewed.)
- • 0:00—Very brief left breast in robe, while sitting on bed.
- • 0:02—Breasts in B&W photos.
- • 0:10—Breasts and buns, making love in bed with her husband under a net.
- • 0:13—Brief breasts taking off bikini top by swimming pool.
- ••• 0:14—Breasts getting up from chair, then full frontal nudity while talking to Ariane.
- ••• 0:15—Nude, swimming under water. Nice.
- • 0:18—Partial left breast, while sleeping in bed.
- •• 0:24—Breasts, making love with a stranger on an airplane.
- •• 0:31—Breasts with Ariane in the squash court.

Julia (1974; German) .... Julia
- • 0:23—Brief breasts in the lake.
- •• 0:25—Breasts on deck in the lake.
- • 0:28—Brief breasts changing clothes at night. Long shot.
- •• 0:34—Breasts on boat with two boys.
- •• 0:42—Breasts taking off her towel.
- • 1:12—Breasts on tennis court with Patrick.

Emmanuelle, The Joys of a Woman (1975)... Emmanuelle
- • 0:18—Breasts making love with her husband in bedroom.
- •• 0:22—Breasts, then full frontal nudity, undressing in bedroom, then making love with her husband.
- ••• 0:32—Breasts with acupuncture needles stuck in her. More breasts masturbating while fantasizing about Christopher.
- • 0:53—Right breast, while making love with polo player in locker room.

••• 0:58—Nude, getting massaged by another woman.
••• 1:14—Right breast in bedroom in open dress, then breasts with Jean in bed. Flashback of her with three guys in a bordello.

Game of Seduction (1976) .... Madame Leroy
••• 0:43—Full frontal nudity, while making love with Charles.
• 0:46—Breasts, while making love on top of Charles.
••• 0:47—Breasts, after getting out of trunk and sitting on chair, talking to Charles. More breasts while on the bed.

The Fifth Musketeer (1977) .... Maria Theresa

Goodbye Emmanuelle (1977) .... Emmanuelle
•• 0:03—Full frontal nudity in bath and getting out.
•• 0:04—Full frontal nudity taking off dress.
••• 0:06—Full frontal nudity in bed with Angelique.
••• 0:26—Breasts with photographer in old house.
• 0:42—Brief side view of right breast, in bed with Jean.
••• 1:03—Full frontal nudity on beach with movie director.
•• 1:06—Full frontal nudity lying on beach sleeping.
•• 1:28—Side view of left breast lying on beach with Gregory while dreaming.

Mysteries (1978; Dutch) .... Dany Kielland
• 0:29—Partial right breast, while lying on bed, then right breast and lower frontal nudity while lying in bed with Rutger Hauer.

Airport '79: The Concorde (1979) .... Isabelle

Tigers in Lipstick (1979) .... The Girl
• 0:04—Breasts in photograph on the sand.
•• 0:09—Breasts lying in bed with The Arab.
•• 0:16—Lying in bed in red lingerie, then left breast for awhile.

Lady Chatterley's Lover (1981; French/British) .... Constance Chatterley
•• 0:25—Nude in front of mirror.
• 0:59—Brief breasts with the Gardener.
• 1:04—Brief breasts.
••• 1:16—Nude in bedroom with the Gardener.

Private Lessons (1981) .... Mallow
• 0:20—Very brief breasts sitting up next to the pool when the sprinklers go on.
•• 0:24—Breasts and buns, stripping for Billy. Some shots might be a body double.
•• 0:51—Breasts in bed when she "dies" with Howard Hesseman.
• 1:28—Breasts making love with Billy. Some shots might be a body double.

Private School (1983) .... Ms. Copuletta

Emmanuelle IV (1984) .... Sylvia
•• 0:00—Breasts in photos during opening credits.

The Big Bet (1985) .... Michelle
• 0:07—Left breast in open nightgown while Chris tries to fix her sink.
•• 0:20—Breasts dressing while Chris watches through binoculars.
•• 0:28—Breasts undressing while Chris watches through binoculars.
••• 0:40—Breasts getting out of the shower and drying herself off.
• 1:00—Breasts getting into bed while Chris watches through binoculars.
••• 1:13—Breasts in bedroom with Chris, then making love.

Mata Hari (1985) .... Mata Hari
••• 0:11—Breasts making love with a guy on a train.
•• 0:31—Breasts standing by window after making love with the soldier.
• 0:35—Breasts making love in empty house by the fireplace.
•• 0:52—Breasts masturbating in bed wearing black stockings.
•• 1:02—Breasts during sword fight with another topless woman.
•• 1:03—Breasts in bed smoking opium and making love with two women.

The Arrogant (1987) .... Julie
• 0:14—In wet blouse, in lake.
• 0:22—In wet blouse again, walking out of the lake.
• 0:44—Brief breasts several times, in gaping dress.

Casanova (1987) .... Maddalena

Red Heat (1987; U.S./German) .... Sofia
•• 0:56—Breasts in shower room scene.
• 1:01—Brief breasts raping Linda Blair.

Dracula's Widow (1988) .... Vanessa

Hot Blood (1989; Spanish) .... Sylvia
• 0:44—Buns, getting molested by Dom Luis.

Beauty School (1993) .... Sylvia
• 1:27—Brief breasts in bed with the private investigator.

Video Tapes:

Playboy Video Magazine, Volume 2 (1983) ...... Herself
••• 0:16—Breasts in various scenes from her films.

Kristen, Marta

Films:

Terminal Island (1973) .... Lee Phillips

Gemini Affair (1974) .... Julie
••• 0:32—Breasts wearing beige panties talking with Jessica in the bathroom.
• 0:56—Very, very brief left breast and lower frontal nudity standing next to bed with a guy. Very brief left breast in bed with him.
••• 0:59—Breasts and buns making love in bed with Jessica. Wowzers!

Once (1974) .... Humanity
(Not available on video tape.)

Battle Beyond the Stars (1980) .... Lux

Below Utopia (1997) .... Marilyn

Lost in Space (1998) .... Reporter

TV:

Lost in Space (1965-68) .... Judy Robinson

• *Krucker, Fides*

Films:

When Night is Falling (1995; Canadian) ..... Roaring Woman

The Sweet Hereafter (1997; Canadian) .... Klara
• 0:01—Brief upper half of right breast, while sleeping in bed next to her baby and her husband.

• *Kruis, Julie* *

a.k.a. Julie Skiru.

Films:

Silk n' Sabotage (1994) .... Jamie
• 0:33—Brief breasts and buns in B&W dream with Michael.
• 0:38—Breasts, while changing clothes in bathroom.
• 0:45—Brief breasts, while in the pool with Michael.
••• 0:46—Buns in swimsuit bottom, then breasts and lower frontal nudity while making love in bedroom with Michael.
•• 0:54—Breasts, while in the shower.
•• 1:07—Breasts, while making love in bedroom with Robert.

Double Your Pleasure (1997) .... Janice Hanson
••• 0:47—Full frontal nudity, while making love with the hypnotist.

Illicit Confessions (1997) .... Dancer 2
••• 0:53—Nude, after stripping and dancing on stage, while wearing a cowboy hat.

••• 1:02—Nude, while having sex with three guys.

Made for Cable TV:

Prime Bodies (1992; Sports Channel) . . . . Julie

Video Tapes:

BabeWatch, Episode 4: Naughty But Nice (1995) . . . . Julie Kruis

• 0:13—Buns in swimsuit, while posing around pool area.

Kruschke, Karman

Films:

Under the Gun (1989). . . . . Girl at Pool

Hot Under the Collar (1991) . . . . Sherry

Ironheart (1991). . . . . Kristi

•• 0:55—Buns and brief side of left breast, getting out of bed with John. Brief breasts in bathroom.

Loaded Weapon 1 (1993) . . . . One of the Cindys

Kudoh, Youki

Films:

The Crazy Family (1986; Japanese) . . . . Daughter

Typhoon Club (1986; Japanese) . . . . Rie

Mystery Train (1989) . . . . Mitzuko

•• 0:30—In black bra, in bed. Breasts making love with Jun in bed.

Picture Bride (1995) . . . . Riyo

La Belle, Kimberly

See: Kates, Kimberly.

La Vette, Maureen

Films:

Hardcase and Fist (1988). . . . . Nora Wilde

•• 0:24—Breasts, while getting out of spa when Tony starts shooting gun in the house.

Virgin High (1990) . . . . Mrs. Murphy

Labrador, Honey

Films:

Strange Days (1995) . . . . Beach Beauty

Made for Cable TV:

Red Shoe Diaries: Forbidden Zone (1996; Showtime) . . . . Angelica

• 0:13—Brief lower frontal nudity, while getting wrapped in cloth.

• 0:14—Brief breasts, when the Zoners take off the cloth that is wrapped around her.

• 0:18—Nude, while making love in cage on truck with Goucho.

• 0:19—Very brief buns, after jumping off truck.

• 0:21—Very brief buns again.

Red Shoe Diaries: The Art of Loneliness (1996; Showtime). . Cis

• Lacatus, Carmen

Films:

Spirit of the Night (1994) . . . . Cocktail Waitress/Lover in Study

• 1:09—Breasts, while making love with a man in study when seen by Tara.

Forbidden Zone: Alien Abduction (1996) . . . . Motorcycle Cop Girl

a.k.a. Alien Abduction: Intimate Secrets

Lace, Vanna *

Video Tapes:

Penthouse The Great Pet Hunt—Part I (1992) . . . . . . Pet

Venus' Playhouse (1994) . . . . Herself

CD-ROM:

Venus' Playhouse (1994) . . . . Herself

LaCroix, Kari *

Video Tapes:

Playboy's Girls of Spring Break (1991) . . . . Herself

••• 0:11—Nude, while posing outdoors next to motorcycle for magazine pictorial.

Lahaie, Brigitte *

Films:

Come Play with Me (1977; German) . . . . Julia

Friendly Favors (1983) . . . . Greta

a.k.a. Six Swedes on a Pump

•• 0:02—Full frontal nudity riding a guy in bed. (She's wearing a necklace.)

••• 0:39—Full frontal nudity having fun on "exercise bike."

••• 0:46—Full frontal nudity taking off clothes and running outside with the other girls. Nice slow motion shots.

•• 0:53—Breasts, making love with Kerstin.

••• 1:01—Full frontal nudity in room with the Italian.

••• 1:15—Full frontal nudity in room with guy from the band.

Joy: Chapter II (1985; French). . . . . Joy

a.k.a. Joy and Joan

• 0:01—Left breast in coat during photo session.

••• 0:11—Nude, getting into bubble bath and out with Bruce.

•• 0:20—Breasts, lying in bed after party.

•• 0:22—Breasts, talking on the phone.

••• 0:27—Nude, getting a massage from Milaka. Nice.

•• 0:32—Breasts changing clothes.

••• 0:45—In bra, then breasts changing clothes with Joanne.

•• 0:47—Full frontal nudity, masturbating in bed. Medium long shot.

••• 0:54—Nude, making love with Joanne on train. Nice, long scene!

• 1:03—Breasts in the water with Joanne.

•• 1:08—Breasts, getting molested by a bunch of guys in the shower.

• 1:10—Right breast, lying next to a pool.

•• 1:17—Nude in bubble bath with Joanne and getting out.

• 1:23—Buns, dancing with Joanne.

••• 1:27—Nude, making love with Joanne and Mark.

Henry & June (1990). Harry's Whore

•• 0:23—Brief buns and breasts under sheer white dress going up stairs with Fred Ward.

•• 1:22—Breasts in sheer white dress again. Nude under dress walking up stairs.

••• 1:23—Breasts and buns making love with another woman while Anais and Hugo watch.

• 1:31—Breasts in bed with Anais. Intercut with Uma Thurman, so hard to tell who is who.

Lain, Chasey *

Adult film actress.

a.k.a. Tiffany Anne.

Films:

Demon Knight (1994) . . . . Party Babe 5

• 1:02—Brief breasts, several times with other Party Babes in Dick Miller's fantasy. She's in orange bikini bottoms and says "Here you go Uncle Willy."

Video Tapes:

Playboy's Girls of the Internet (1996). . . . . Herself

••• 0:10—Nude, while stripping and dancing (wearing black gloves and boots) with another woman.

Laine, Karen

Films:

Pretty in Pink (1986) . . . . .Girl at Prom

Made for Cable Movies:

Baja Oklahoma (1988; HBO) . . . . .Girl at Drive-In

- 0:04—Left breast, while in truck with a jerk. Dark, hard to see anything.

Laine, Sandi

See: Comshaw, Lisa.

Lakewood, Alexandra

See: Good, Melanie.

Lala

See: Sloatman, Lala.

• Lamanna, Carmelina

Films:

Specimen (1995; Canadian) . . . . Carol Hillary

- • 0:19—Buns, after taking off nightgown and walking in the woods at night.
- •• 0:50—Very, very brief buns in flashback, then nude, walking into lake.
- • 0:52—Brief breasts, after turning around in the lake.

Joe's So Mean to Josephine (1996; Canadian) . . . . Body Double for Sarah Polley

Made for Cable TV:

Fast Track (1997- ; Showtime). . . . . Mona Black

Fast Track: Fighting Words (1998; Showtime) . . . . Mona Black

- • 0:26—Brief breasts, during cat fight with Wendy in beauty salon.

Fast Track: Deconstructing Eagle Ridge (1998; Showtime) . . . . Mona Black

- •• 0:31—Breasts in B&W fantasy sequence.

LaMarca, Gina *

Adult Films:

Breeders (1996) . . . . n.a.

Zazel (1996) . . . . n.a.

Films:

Exit (1995). . . . . Rita

- •• 0:16—Breasts, while dancing on stage in black and silver outfit.
- •• 0:22—Breasts, while dancing on stage in black short pants.
- •• 0:23—Breasts, while getting dressed in dressing room.

Video Tapes:

Penthouse Behind the Scenes (1995) . . . . Pet

- ••• 0:25—Nude in interviews and behind the scenes footage.

Penthouse Pet of the Year Winners 1994: Gina & Natalie (1995). . . . . .Pet of the Year

- ••• 0:01—Nude on bed in leopard print outfit.
- ••• 0:08—Nude on a motorcycle and with a guy in black leather and chain outfit.
- ••• 0:12—Nude outside by a pool, sometimes in the rain, sometimes not.
- ••• 0:17—Nude as a construction worker (including eating a banana).
- ••• 0:22—Nude after stripping out of clothes outside.

Penthouse Women In & Out of Uniform (1995) . . . . . Pet

- ••• 0:16—Nude as a football player with two other women in locker room, then putting on a black dress.
- ••• 0:29—Nude as a business woman, seducing the bellboy while a maid watches from outside the hotel room.

Nude Golf (1996) . . . . Model

CD-ROM:

Penthouse Interactive Virtual Photo Shoot, Disc 2 (1993). . . . . Pet

Lamarr, Hedy

First instance of celebrity nudity in film.

Films:

Ecstasy (1932) . . . . The Wife

- • 0:25—Brief breasts starting to run after a horse in a field.
- • 0:26—Long shot running through the woods, side view naked, then brief breasts hiding behind a tree.

Algiers (1938) . . . . .Gaby

Ziegfield Girl (1941) . . . . Sandra Kolter

Dishonored Lady (1947) . . . . Madeleine Damien

Samson and Delilah (1949) . . . . Delilah

Instant Karma (1990) . . . . Movie Goddess

Lamatsch, Andrea

Films:

Sudden Thunder (1990). . . . . .Patricia Merrill

- • 0:18—Right breast, while getting raped by jerks in the woods and brief breasts after escaping from them.
- ••• 0:27—Nude, while skinny dipping in pond (some body parts are visible under the water).

Blood Ring (1991). . . . . Susan Dalton

Lamb, Debra *

Films:

Stripped to Kill (1987). . . . . Amateur Dancer

B.O.R.N. (1988) . . . . Sue

- • 0:24—Breasts, while getting molested by a jerk.

Deathrow Game Show (1988) . . . . Shanna Shallow

- ••• 0:23—Breasts dancing in white G-string and garter belt during the show.

Glitch (1988). . . . . .Fire Eater

Hardcase and Fist (1988). . . . . Chieko

- • 1:08—Buns in G-string while dancing on stage in a club.
- ••• 1:09—Breasts while dancing on stage and doing some fire eating. Nice, long scene.
- •• 1:13—Breasts, three times, while peeking from behind curtain.

Midnight Cabaret (1988) . . . . Dancer

Stripped to Kill II (1988) . . . . Mantra

- •• 0:04—Breasts during strip dance routine.
- ••• 0:42—Breasts in black lingerie during strip dance routine.

W. B., Blue and the Bean (1988) . . . . .Motel Clerk

a.k.a. Bail Out

- • 0:42—Full frontal nudity opening door in motel to talk to David Hasselhoff.

Warlords (1988) . . . . Harem Girl

- ••• 0:14—Breasts, getting her blouse ripped off by a bad guy, then kidnapped.
- ••• 0:17—Breasts in harem pants while shackled to another girl.

Beverly Hills Vamp (1989). . . . . .Jessica

- ••• 0:36—Breasts and buns in red G-string posing for Russell while he photographs her.
- ••• 0:41—More breasts posing on bed.

Out Cold (1989) . . . . Panetti's Dancer

- • 1:04—Brief breasts dancing in G-string on stage. Don't see her face.

Satan's Princess (1989) . . . . Fire Eater/Dancer

- •• 0:23—Breasts in G-string doing a fire dance in club.
- • 0:25—Breasts, doing more dancing. Long shot.

The Turn-On (1989) . . . . Assistant in White Dress

a.k.a. Le Clic

Evil Spirits (1990) . . . . Tina
••• 0:22—Breasts, while dancing in her bedroom while Michael Berryman watches through peep hole. Most of her buns in underwear. Long scene.

The Invisible Maniac (1990) . . . . Betty
• 0:21—Buns and very brief side view of right breast in the shower with the other girls.
••• 0:43—In bra, then breasts and buns standing on the left in the locker room with the other girls.
• 0:44—Buns and brief breasts in the shower with the other girls.
•• 0:56—In bra, then breasts getting killed by Dr. Smith.
• 0:58—Brief breasts, dead, discovered by April and Joan.

Mob Boss (1990) . . . . Janise
Point Break (1991) . . . . Uncredited Flame Blower at Party

Made for Cable TV:
Dream On: And Your Little Dog, Too (1991; HBO) . . . . Snake Lady

Video Tapes:
Best Buns on the Beach (1987) . . . . Buns Model
••• 0:04—Buns, in G-string, bending over during "Ideal Buns" demonstration.

Trashy Ladies Wrestling (1987) . . . . n.a.
•• 0:48—In black and silver S&M costume. Buns in G-string.

Lambert, Elizabeth

Films:
Class of Nuke 'Em High (1986) . . . . Bake Sale Person

Made for Cable TV:
Love Street: The Pickup (1993; Showtime). . . . . Allison
• 0:01—Brief, long shot of breasts and buns, after tossing off robe after her husband leaves the house.
••• 0:10—Breasts, while making love with Eric.
•• 0:22—Breasts, while making love in bed with Eric again.

Video Tapes:
Eden (1992) . . . . Victoria
••• 0:12—Breasts and side view of buns, in bedroom, then in bed while starting to make love with Ian.
•• 0:23—Breasts, while making love in bed under Ian.
••• 0:25—Breasts, sitting up in bed and buns, getting out of bed.

Lambert, Locky

Films:
Relentless (1989) . . . . Rene
Witchboard: The Possession (1995) . . . . Julie
• 0:04—Left breast, while making love in bed with Brian.
•• 0:44—In black bra, panties and stockings with Brian in living room, then breasts while making love.
•• 0:46—Breasts, while sitting up in bed.
• 0:57—Breasts, while making love in bed with Brian.

Lamothe, Michelle

See: Brin, Michele.

• *Lande, Anita*

Made for Cable TV:
Erotic Confessions: The Painting (1996; Cinemax) . . . Kara
(Available on video tape in *Erotic Confessions, Volume 3: Passion.*)
••• 0:05—Nude, getting out of bath and rubbing oil on herself while sitting at vanity, then fantasizing about making love with Michael. Long scene.
••• 0:12—Nude, while making love with Michael in kitchen (he pours honey on her body).
•• 0:16—Nude, while making love with Michael in the living room (she pours red sauce on his body).
••• 0:17—Nude, while making love with Michael next to his painting. (Covering each other with paint.) Long scene.

Erotic Confessions: Fringe Benefits (1997; Cinemax) . . . . Alana
••• 0:11—In black bra, then breasts, while making love with Miguel in mail room.

Landgrebe, Gudrun

Films:
Woman in Flames (1984; German) . . . . Eva
The Berlin Affair (1985; Italian/German) . . . . Louise Von Hollendorf
• 0:23—Very brief inner half of left breast, twice, while making out with Mio.

Colonel Redl (1985; Hungarian) . . . . Katalin Kubinyi

Landon, Laurene

Girlfriend of Christian Brando (Marlon Brando's son).

Films:
...All the Marbles (1981) . . . . Molly
a.k.a. The California Dolls
Airplane II: The Sequel (1982) . . . . Testa
I, the Jury (1982) . . . . Velda
Hundra (1983) . . . . Hundra
• 0:29—Very brief breasts, several times, riding her horse in the surf. Partial buns. Blurry.

Yellow Hair and the Fortress of Gold (1984) . . . . Yellow Hair
America 3000 (1986) . . . . Vena
Armed Response (1986) . . . . Deborah
It's Alive III: Island of the Alive (1988) . . . . Sally
Maniac Cop (1988) . . . . Theresa
Wicked Stepmother (1989) . . . . Vanilla
The Ambulance (1990) . . . . Patty
Maniac Cop 2 (1990) . . . . Teresa Mallory

Landry, Karen

Films:
The Personals (1982) . . . . Adrienne
Patti Rocks (1988) . . . . Patti
• 0:48—Buns, walking from bathroom to bedroom and shutting the door. Long shot.
• 0:48—Very brief right breast in shower with Billy.
•• 1:04—Breasts in bed with Eddie while Billy is out in the living room.

Ambition (1991) . . . . Woman in Bookstore

Made for Cable Movies:
Rebel Highway: Roadracers (1994; Showtime) . . . Donna's Mom

Landry, Tamara

a.k.a. Shelby Lane.

Films:
R.S.V.P. (1984) . . . . Vicky
•• 0:43—Breasts sitting in van taking her top off.
•• 0:48—Breasts making love in the van with two guys.

Las Vegas Weekend (1986) . . . . Lea
Tango & Cash (1989) . . . . Girl in Bar
Delusion (1990) . . . . Arabella
Mob Boss (1990) . . . . n.a.
The Pamela Principle (1992) . . . . Anne Breeding
(Unrated version reviewed.)
••• 0:08—Buns, while lying in bed with Carl, then breasts and lower frontal nudity.
•• 0:28—Breasts, while sitting up in bed.

••• 0:48—Breasts, waking up in bed, then buns and lower frontal nudity getting out.
••• 0:57—Breasts, while making love with Carl in the kitchen, then buns in bed.
••• 1:03—Buns and breasts while in the shower.

Beach Babes From Beyond (1993) .... Luna
•• 0:02—Breasts, while taking off pink top, getting dressed and talking with Xena and Sola.
••• 0:34—Breast, while making love in back of van with Jerry.
•• 0:39—Buns, in swimsuit at the beach.
• 0:58—Buns, while dancing in swimsuits and boots on stage at beach during bikini contest.

Renegade: Fighting Cage (1993) .... Ellen
(Nudity added for video release.)
•• 1:06—Breasts and buns in panties, making love with a guy and another woman.

Strike a Pose (1993) .... Candy
••• 0:23—In black bra, panties and stockings, then nude with Carl. Long scene.
••• 1:01—Breasts, while making love on bed.

Married People, Single Sex 2: For Better or Worse (1994) .... Monica
••• 0:28—Breasts, while in office with John.
• 0:54—Breasts, while crawling on John's desk.
• 0:55—Breasts, while in office with John.
••• 1:17—Breasts, while making love on desk with John in his office.

Surf, Sand and Sex (1994) .... Fifth Woman
••• 0:44—In bra, then breasts and very brief partial buns, while making love with a policeman in her house. Long scene.

California Heat (1995) .... Stephanie
•• 0:34—Breasts, while making love with Jack in lifeguard station at night.
• 0:48—Breasts, while sitting in bathtub with Jack.

Obsessed with Lust (1995) .... Jennifer
a.k.a. Prelude to Love
•• 0:01—Breasts, while making love with a guy backstage during fashion show.
•• 0:38—Breasts, when taking off dress and putting on a blouse while talking with David.
••• 0:43—Buns in T-back, then breasts and buns, while making love with Carlton on sofa.

Made for Cable TV:

Dream On: Second Time Aground (1996; HBO) .... Woman #3
• 0:16—Brief breasts, after taking off her white bikini top in Martin's dream.

Video Tapes:

Fantasies 2 (1992) .... Model

Penthouse: Fast Cars/Fantasy Women (1992) .... Ferrari Testarossa
••• 0:19—In lingerie, then nude, while posing with car.

Beverly Hills Workout (1993) .... Herself
•• 0:11—Breasts and buns in T-back, while working out in backyard.
••• 0:30—Nude, while dancing and posing in backyard.
•• 0:49—Nude, while posing outdoors.

Playboy's Secret Confessions (1993) . . . Jailhouse Rock/Tina
••• 0:34—In red lingerie, then nude, while making love with Rick in jail cell.

Playboy's Erotic Fantasies III (1994) . . . Lube Job/Customer
••• 0:20—Buns in lingerie in car repair shop, then nude while making love with the mechanic.

American Sweethearts (1995) .... Herself
••• 0:05—Breasts and buns, while dancing in front of various images.
••• 0:09—Full frontal nudity, while posing on lounge chair.
•• 0:30—Breasts and buns, while dressing in bedroom.
•• 0:36—Breasts and buns in quick cuts of her dancing. Buns, while dancing in front of her images.

Lands, Wendy

Films:

One Night Only (1984; Canadian) .... Jane
a.k.a. For One Night Only
•• 0:36—Breasts taking a bath while Jamie watches through keyhole.
•• 0:38—Brief left breast in open robe.
• 1:15—Brief breasts in bed with policeman.

Busted Up (1986) .... Drayton's Date

Lane, Cory *

Films:

Body Strokes (1995) .... Rachel
•• 1:13—Breasts, with Karen and Leo.
• 1:19—Brief right breast, while posing with Karen.
• 1:20—Full frontal nudity, with Karen and Leo.

Dream Master: The Erotic Invader (1995) .... Troy's Dream Girl
•• 0:39—Breasts and buns, while next to and on bed in Troy's fantasy.
••• 0:55—Breasts, while making love with Troy in his dream.

Forbidden Games (1995) .... Model
(Unrated version reviewed.)

Sinful Intrigue (1995) .... Denise
•• 0:57—Breasts and buns, while in shower.

Maui Heat: Swimsuit Edition (1996) ...... Shawn Daniels
•• 0:11—Breasts, while changing clothes in bedroom.
••• 0:16—Nude, while making love with Mitch.

Eve's Beach Fantasy (1997) .... Model 3
• 0:59—Buns in swimsuit, while posing on a motorcycle during photo shoot.

Made for Cable TV:

Erotic Confessions: Lap Dance (1996; Cinemax) .... Topless Dancer
(Available on video tape in *Erotic Confessions, Volume 4: Pleasure.*)
• 0:05—Very brief breasts, swinging around pole on stage.

Erotic Confessions: Love Calling (1996; Cinemax) .... Blonde
(Available on video tape in *Erotic Confessions, Volume 3: Passion.*)
••• 0:05—Full frontal nudity, while making love with Doug on bed in fantasy.

Erotic Confessions: The Address (1996; Cinemax) .... Jock's Girl
•• 0:05—Breasts and buns, on video playback on monitor.
• 0:12—Brief breasts, seen on video monitor again.

Erotic Confessions: The Workout (1996; Cinemax) .... Nude Girl
• 0:05—Nude, in workout room in Paula's fantasy. (She's wearing a green headband.)

Video Tapes:

All Nude Glamour (1995) .... Teresa
••• 0:21—Nude, while posing indoors and outdoors. Some behind-the-scenes shots included. Long scene.
••• 0:24—Full frontal nudity, while talking dirty.

Nude Bowling Party (1995) .... Tina
••• 0:00—Nude throughout.

Body Language (1996)....................... Fire Place
••• 0:12—Nude, while caressing two other women in front of fire place.
Erotic Heat (1996) .... Dining Room
••• 0:20—Breasts and buns in garter belt and stockings after stripping and dancing in front of Stacy Moran.
Hot Body Video Magazine #15: Wild Thing (1996)
.... Southern Exposure/Feature Model
••• 0:15—In blue two piece swimsuit, then nude, while modeling outdoors by pool.
••• 0:32—In swimsuit, then nude, while dancing outdoors next to pool.
Malibu Canyon Nights #1 (1997).............. Herself
••• 0:21—In bra and panties, then full frontal nudity, while posing in the woods.
Playboy's Hot Wheels & High Heels Biker Babes (1997)
................................Tattoo Mistress/Cory
••• 0:21—Nude, while posing and applyng tattoos.

CD-ROM:
Crystal Fantasy (1995).......................... Teresa
Heidi's House (1996) ....n.a.

Lane, Diane

Ex-wife of actor Christopher Lambert.

Films:
A Little Romance (1979; U.S./French) .... Lauren
Cattle Annie and Little Britches (1980) .... Jenny
Touched by Love (1980) .... Karen
Ladies and Gentlemen, The Fabulous Stains (1982)
....Corinne Burns
(Not available on video tape.)
• 0:31—Brief breasts, under sheer red blouse on stage.
• 0:53—Brief buns and side of right breast, taking off her towel and getting into shower.
National Lampoon Goes to the Movies (1982) .... Lisa
a.k.a. Movie Madness
Six Pack (1982)................................Breezy
The Outsiders (1983) .... Cherry Valance
Rumble Fish (1983)............................. Patty
The Cotton Club (1984) .... Vera Cicero
Streets of Fire (1984).........................Ellen Aim
The Big Town (1987) .... Lorry Dane
• 0:50—Doing a strip routine in the club wearing a G-string and pasties while Matt Dillon watches.
••• 1:17—Breasts, while making love on bed with Dillon in hotel room.
• 1:20—Very brief partial left breast, when the sheet she's holding drops slightly while sitting in bed.
• 1:27—Brief left breast wearing pasties walking into dressing room while Dillon plays craps.
Lady Beware (1987).......................Katya Yarno
••• 0:46—Breasts in her apartment and in bed making love with Mack.
•• 0:52—Brief breasts during Jack's flashback when he is in the store.
•• 0:59—Brief side view breasts in bed with Mack again during another of Jack's flashbacks.
• 1:02—Very brief breasts in bed with Mack.
• 1:06—Brief breasts lying in bed behind thin curtain in another of Jack's flashbacks.
Priceless Beauty (1989; Italian) ....China/Anna
•• 0:34—Breasts in bed with Christopher Lambert.
• 0:35—Brief left breast, then side of right breast on top of Lambert.
Vital Signs (1989)......................... Gina Wyler
••• 1:11—In white bra, then breasts making love with Michael in the basement.
Chaplin (1992; British/U.S.) .... Paulette Goddard
• 1:33—Upper half of breasts, while lying in bed.
Knight Moves (1992) .... Kathy Sheppard
•• 0:45—Breasts while making love with Christopher Lambert in bed.
My New Gun (1992).................... Debbie Bender
Indian Summer (1993) ....Beth Warden/Claire Everett
Judge Dredd (1995)...................... Judge Hershey
Wild Bill (1995) ....Susannah Moore
Jack (1996) ....Karen Powell
Mad Dog Time (1996)........................... Grace
Murder at 1600 (1997) ....Nina Chance

Made for Cable Movies:
Descending Angel (1990; HBO).............. Irina Stroia
• 0:01—Brief right breast, while making love with Eric Roberts on train during opening credits.
•• 0:44—In white camisole top with Roberts, then breasts lying in bed with him.

Made for Cable TV:
Fallen Angels: Murder, Obliquely (1993; Showtime)
.... Bernette Stone
(Available on the video tape *Fallen Angels One.*)

Miniseries:
Lonesome Dove (1989).................... Lorena Wood

Made for TV Movies:
Oldest Living Confederate Widow Tells All (1994)
.... Lucy Marsden (young)
A Streetcar Named Desire (1995) .... Stella

Lane, Krista

See: Lynn, Rebecca.

Lane, Nikki

Films:
Death of a Soldier (1985; Australian).......Stripper in Bar
•• 0:49—Nude, dancing on stage.
The Big Hurt (1987; Australian) .... Tank Girl #1
• 1:26—Possible full frontal nudity standing in water filled tube. Can't recognize her because wearing a swim mask and breathing apparatus.

Lane, Shelby

See: Landry, Tamara.

*Lane, Trisha **

Films:
Down the Drain (1989)........................... Robin
Mardi Gras for the Devil (1993)................ Jackie
•• 0:03—Breasts, while in panties, while simulating sex in front of Michael Ironside.

*Lang, Helen **

Films:
Revenge of the Cheerleaders (1976)............ Leslie
• 0:00—Left breast, changing in back seat of car.
•• 0:07—Breasts in girl's restroom powdering herself.
••• 0:53—Nude with Gail and hiker guy frolicking in the woods.
•• 0:55—Nude some more making out with the hiker guy with Gail.
••• 0:57—Nude walking down road with Gail when stopped by a policeman.
••• 1:24—Breasts during Hawaiian party. Nice dancing.

lang, k.d.

Singer.

Real name is Katherine Dawn Lang.

Films:

Salmonberries (1991; German) . . . . Kotzebue
- ••• 0:13—Brief full frontal nudity while standing in the library.

Teresa's Tattoo (1993) . . . . Michelle

Made for TV Movies:

The Last Don (1997) . . . . Dita Tommey

Lang, Katherine Kelly

Films:

Evilspeak (1981) . . . . Suzie Baker

Jocks (1986) . . . . Julie

The Nightstalker (1987) . . . . Denise

Made in U.S.A. (1988) . . . . Kelly

Till the End of the Night (1994) . . . . Diana Davenport
- • 0:04—Very, very brief breast in mirror, while making love with her husband in bed.

Made for Cable Movies:

Subliminal Seduction (1996; Showtime). . . . Debbie Danver
- ••• 0:10—Nude, while making love with Ian Ziering in bathtub.
- ••• 0:22—Breasts and side view of buns, while making love with Ziering in shower.

TV:

The Bold and the Beautiful (1987-) . . . . Brooke Logan

Lange, Jessica *

Films:

King Kong (1976) . . . . Dwan

All That Jazz (1979) . . . . Angelique

How to Beat the High Cost of Living (1980) . . . . Louise

The Postman Always Rings Twice (1981) . . Cora Papadakis
- • 0:18—Pubic hair peeking out of right side of her panties when Nicholson grabs her crotch.
- • 1:03—Very, very brief breasts, then very, very brief right breast twice, when Nicholson rips her dress down to simulate a car accident.
- • 1:26—Brief lower frontal nudity when Nicholson starts crawling up over her in bed.

Frances (1982) . . . . Frances Farmer
- • 0:41—Very brief upper half of left breast, while lying on bed and throwing a newspaper.
- • 0:50—Brief full frontal nudity covered with bubbles standing up in bathtub and wrapping a towel around herself. Long shot, hard to see.
- • 1:01—Brief buns and right breast running into the bathroom when the police bust in. Very, very brief full frontal nudity, then buns closing the bathroom door. Reportedly her, even though you don't see her face clearly.

Tootsie (1982) . . . . Julie Nichols

(Academy Award for Best Supporting Actress.)

Country (1984) . . . . Jewell Ivy

Sweet Dreams (1985) . . . . Patsy Kline

Crimes of the Heart (1986) . . . . Meg Magrath

Everybody's All-American (1988) . . . . Babs
- • 0:32—Brief breasts under sheer nightgown in bedroom with Dennis Quaid.
- • 0:54—Buns and very, very brief side view of left breast by the campfire by the lake with Timothy Hutton at night. Might be a body double.

Far North (1988) . . . . Kate

Men Don't Leave (1989) . . . . Beth Macauley

Blue Sky (1991) . . . . Carly Marshall

(Academy Award for Best Actress.)
- • 0:01—Very, very brief, partial back side of right breast, when turning over, while sunbathing on the beach.
- • 0:03—Brief breasts, while standing in the water, waving to Tommy Lee Jones as his helicopter passes by. Medium long shot.

Cape Fear (1991) . . . . Leigh Bowden

Night and the City (1992) . . . . Helen Nosseros

Losing Isaiah (1994) . . . . Margaret Lewin

Rob Roy (1995) . . . . Mary

A Thousand Acres (1997) . . . . Ginny Cook Smith

Cousin Bette (1998) . . . . Bette Fisher

Hush (1998) . . . . Martha

Made for Cable Movies:

Cat on a Hot Tin Roof (1984; HBO) . . . . Maggie

Made for TV Movies:

The Best Little Girl in the World (1981) . . . . n.a.

O Pioneers! (1992) . . . . Adult Alexandra Bergson

A Streetcar Named Desire (1995) . . . . Blanche DuBois

Langencamp, Heather

Films:

Nickel Mountain (1985) . . . . Callie
- ••• 0:24—Breasts in bed lying with Willard.
- • 0:29—Side view of left breast and brief breasts falling on bed with Willard.

A Nightmare on Elm Street (1985) . . . . . Nancy Thompson
- • 0:32—Very brief right breast, twice, while struggling under water after Freddy pulls her under the water in the bathtub.

A Nightmare on Elm Street 3: The Dream Warriors (1987) . . . . Nancy Thompson

Shocker (1989) . . . . Victim

Wes Craven's New Nightmare (1994) . . . . Herself/Nancy

The Demolitionist (1996) . . . . Christy Carruthers

Made for Cable TV:

Perversions of Science: Ultimate Weapon (1997; HBO) . . . . Luanne

Made for TV Movies:

Tonya & Nancy: The Inside Story (1994) . . . . . . Nancy Kerrigan

TV:

Just the Ten of Us (1988-90) . . . . Marie Lubbock

Langenfeld, Sarah

Films:

Blood Link (1983) . . . . Christine
- •• 1:01—Breasts while taking her top off in bed with Craig.
- • 1:04—Breasts in bed with Keith.

The Act (1984) . . . . Leslie

Langlois, Lisa

Films:

Blood Relatives (1978; French/Canadian) . . . . Muriel

Violette (1978; French) . . . . Maddy

Happy Birthday to Me (1980; Canadian) . . . . Amelia

Klondike Fever (1980) . . . . Gertie

Phobia (1980; Canadian) . . . . Laura

Class of 1984 (1982; Canadian) . . . . Patsy

Deadly Eyes (1982; Canadian) . . . . Trudy

The Man Who Wasn't There (1983) . . . . Cindy Worth
- •• 0:58—Nude running away from two policemen after turning visible.
- ••• 1:08—Breasts in white panties dancing in her apartment with an invisible Steve Guttenberg.

• 1:47—Very, very brief upper half of left breast, while throwing bouquet at wedding.

The Joy of Sex (1984) . . . . Melanie
The Slugger's Wife (1985) . . . . Aline Cooper
The Nest (1987) . . . . Elizabeth Johnson
Transformations (1988) . . . . Miranda
Mind Field (1990) . . . . Sarah Paradis
The Final Cut (1995) . . . . Sara
White Tiger (1995) . . . . Joanne Grogan

Langner, Marina

Films:

Banana Joe (1981; Italian/German) . . . . Dorianne
I Hate Blondes (1981; Italian) . . . . Valerie
•• 0:12—Breasts, sitting up in steam room, yelling at Emilio.
• 1:02—Brief buns, when Emilio accidentally rips her dress off at party.
•• 1:10—Brief breasts when Emilio causes her top to fall off at party.
•• 1:16—Breasts and buns, taking off her dress to demonstrate how Emilio took it off.

Langrick, Margaret

Films:

My American Cousin (1985; Canadian) . . . . Sandy
Harry and the Hendersons (1987) . . . . Sarah Henderson
Cold Comfort (1988) . . . . Dolores
•• 0:16—In tank top and panties, then breasts undressing in front of Stephen.
• 0:19—Very brief side of left breast and buns getting robe.
•• 0:41—Doing strip tease in front of her dad and Stephen. In black bra and panties, then breasts.
• 0:42—Very brief breasts jumping into bed.
Martha, Ruth & Edie (1988; Canadian) . . . . Young Edie
Thunderground (1989) . . . . Casey
American Boyfriends (1990) . . . . Sandy Wilcox

Made for TV Movies:

A Friend to Die For (1994) . . . . Jill

TV:

Camp Wilder (1992-93) . . . . Beth

Lankford, Kim

Films:

Malibu Beach (1978) . . . . Dina
• 0:32—Buns, while running into the ocean.
• 0:34—Brief right breast getting out of the ocean.
• 1:16—Right breast on beach at night with boyfriend.
• 1:19—Brief breasts at top of the stairs.
•• 1:20—Brief breasts when her parents come home.
• 1:21—Breasts in bed with her boyfriend.
The Octagon (1980) . . . . Nancy
Cameron's Closet (1989) . . . . Dory Lansing
Missing Pieces (1991) . . . . Sally
Night of the Running Man (1994) . . . . Waitress
Street Corner Justice (1996) . . . . Jeanette Connors

Made for Cable TV:

The Hitchhiker: A Time for Rifles (1985; HBO) . . . . Rae Bridgeman
••• 0:03—Breasts on the pool table while making love with a guy.
Dream On: Premarital Ex (1990; HBO) . . . . Hannah

TV:

The Waverly Wonders (1978) . . . . Connie Rafkin
Knots Landing (1979-83) . . . . Ginger Ward
Murphy's Law (1988-89) . . . . Marissa Danforth

Lanko, Vivian

Films:

The Rejuvenator (1988) . . . . Elizabeth Warren
• 0:31—Brief breasts in bed with Dr. Ashton while making love. Don't see her face well.
Simple Men (1992; U.S./British) . . . . Nun

Lapenseé, Francine

Films:

Demon Wind (1990) . . . . Elaine
2002: The Rape of Eden (1992) . . . . The Virgin
•• 1:06—Breasts and buns, while making love in bed with the Bounty Hunter during his dream.
Fist of Honor (1993) . . . . Mrs. Bones

Lara, Joanne

Films:

The Baby Doll Murders (1992) . . . . Mrs. Jayson
••• 0:44—Breasts, while taking a shower, getting out, drying herself off, walking to bed and talking on the phone. Long scene.
•• 0:46—Breasts, on bed while getting killed and afterwards.
Molly & Gina (1993) . . . . Stripper
••• 0:00—Breasts and buns in G-string while dancing on stage during opening credits.

*Large, Bonnie **

Films:

The Happy Hooker Goes to Washington (1977) . . . . Carolyn (Model)
• 0:06—Breasts during photo shoot.

Larkin, Lauré

Films:

The Silencers (1995) . . . . Mary Sue

TV:

NYPD Blue: Curt Russell (Nov 28, 1995) . . . . Hooker
• 0:45—Brief buns, three times, while getting up after detectives bust into room to get Sergei.

Larsen, Annabelle

Films:

Hard Rock Zombies (1985) . . . . Groupie
Alligator Eyes (1990) . . . . Pauline
•• 0:42—Nude, getting up from bed and walking around.

*Lasseter, Vicki **

Video Tapes:

Playboy's Playmate Review (1982) . . . . Playmate
••• 0:43—Full frontal nudity in office, then in the woods.

Lassez, Sarah

Films:

Roosters (1993) . . . . Angela
Malicious (1995) . . . . Laura
• 0:36—Brief right breast, while making out in the library with Doug.

• *Laumeister, Shannah **

Films:

The Brady Bunch Movie (1994) . . . . Molly
Bullets Over Broadway (1994) . . . . Movie Theatre Victim
Nobody's Fool (1994) . . . . Didi
Vegas Vacation (1997) . . . . Mariah

Made for Cable TV:
Women: Stories of Passion-The Little Vampire (1997; Showtime) . . . . Angelica
- • 0:01—Buns, while making out with the vampire guy in the woods.
- •• 0:04—Breasts, while having sex with Tom in house.
- •• 0:09—Breasts and buns, while making love with Tom in the house.
- ••• 0:12—Breasts, when the vampire guy talks with her.
- •• 0:14—Breasts, when having sex with the vampire guy.

*Laure, Carole **

Films:
Sweet Movie (1975) . . . . Virgin Bride
Strange Shadows in an Empty Room (1976) . . . . . . Louise
- ••• 1:29—Brief breasts, while running around the house and frolicking with Mrs. Wilkinson and Fred. Breasts while in slow motion, when beating Mrs. Wilkinson to death.

Get Out Your Handkerchiefs (1978) . . . . Solange
- •• 0:21—Breasts sitting in bed listening to her boyfriend talk.
- •• 0:31—Breasts sitting in bed knitting.
- • 0:41—Upper half of left breast in bed.
- •• 0:47—Left breast, while sitting in bed and the three guys talk.
- • 1:08—Brief right breast when the little boy peeks at her while she sleeps.
- • 1:10—Lower frontal nudity while he looks at her some more.
- ••• 1:17—Full frontal nudity taking off nightgown while sitting on bed for the little boy.

Dirty Dishes (1979; French) . . . . Armelle
- •• 0:09—Brief right breast, while putting her blouse on when walking in hallway.

Victory (1981) . . . . Renee
Naked Massacre (1983) . . . . Amy
Heartbreakers (1984) . . . . Liliane
- • 0:56—Brief breasts making love in car with Nick Mancuso. Dark, hard to see.
- • 1:25—In sheer black dress, then brief right breast making love in art gallery with Peter Coyote.

The Surrogate (1984; Canadian) . . . . Anouk Vanderlin
- • 0:48—Very brief breasts when Frank rips her blouse open in his apartment.

Sweet Country (1985) . . . . Eva
- •• 0:31—Breasts changing in apartment while Randy Quaid watches.
- • 0:43—Nude in auditorium with other women prisoners.
- ••• 1:13—Nude in bed with Quaid.

Lauren, Ashley

Adult film actress.
Video Tapes:
The Art of Desire (1992) . . . . n.a.
Penthouse The Great Pet Hunt—Part II (1993) . . . . . . Pet
- ••• 0:18—Nude after stripping out of nurse's outfit.

*Lauren, Dyanna **

Adult film actress.
a.k.a. Diane Hurley.
Films:
Killer Looks (1994) . . . . Cynthia
(Unrated version reviewed.)
- •• 0:57—Nude, while trying to make out with Sara Suzanne Brown.
- ••• 0:59—Full frontal nudity while making love with Vince on sofa.

Video Tapes:
Venus' Playhouse (1994) . . . . Herself
Penthouse: Lipstick Girls (1997) . . . . n.a.
CD-ROM:
Venus' Playhouse (1994) . . . . Herself

Lauren, Honey

a.k.a. Honey Smax.
Films:
Totally Exposed (1991) . . . . Linda
- •• 0:41—Full frontal nudity, taking off towel in massage room.

Bram Stoker's Dracula (1992) . . . . Peep Show Girl
Pleasure in Paradise (1992) . . . . Sandra
- ••• 0:14—Breasts in lingerie, while making love in bed with Hansen. Long scene.
- ••• 0:57—Nude in pool, while making love with Hansen, then getting out. Long scene.

Good Girls Don't (1993) . . . . Lolita
The Hidden 2 (1993) . . . . Rave Girl
Vice Academy, Part 4 (1994) . . . . Tiffany Berkowitz
Fatally Yours (1995) . . . . Flapper
Babe Watch: The Forbidden Parody (1996) . . . . Lisa's Mom
Made for Cable TV:
Dream On: B.S. Elliot (1992; HBO) . . . . Bibi
- •• 0:11—Breasts, while dancing on counter in biker bar.

Compromising Situations: The Casting Couch (1994; Showtime) . . . . Sondra

Laurence, Ashley

Films:
Hellraiser (1987) . . . . Kirsty
The Secret of My Success (1987) . . . . Fletcher
Hellraiser II—Hellbound (1988) . . . . Kirsty
One Last Run (1990) . . . . Jane
Hellraiser III: Hell on Earth (1992) . . . . Kirsty
(Unrated version reviewed.)
Mikey (1992) . . . . Shawn Gilder
American Cop (1994) . . . . Gina
Felony (1994) . . . . Laura Bryant
The Fighter (1994) . . . . Mary Parker
a.k.a. Savate
Outside the Law (1994) . . . . Paige
a.k.a. Blood Run
(Unrated version reviewed.)
Cupid (1996) . . . . Jennifer
Made for Cable Movies:
Triplecross (1994; Showtime) . . . . Julia
- •• 0:41—Breasts, while making out with Paré.
- ••• 0:42—Breasts, while making out with Paré on bed.
- •• 0:43—Breasts and partial buns, while making love with Paré.
- • 0:48—Partial left breast, while in bubble bath with Paré.

*Laurin, Marie **

Films:
Talking Walls (1982) . . . . Jeanne
The Lonely Guy (1983) . . . . . . One of "The Seven Deadly Sins"
Creature (1985) . . . . Susan Delambre
- •• 0:41—Breasts and brief buns with blood on her shoulders, getting Jon to take his helmet off.

Made for Cable Movies:
Bram Stoker's Burial of the Rats (1995; Showtime). . Rat Woman
Made for Cable TV:
The Hitchhiker: Petty Thieves (HBO) . . . . Pearl
- •• 0:09—Breasts making love with Steve Railsback on the couch.

•• 0:15—Breasts playing with a doll in the bathtub, then buns, standing up and wrapping herself with a towel.
•• 0:18—In black bra, then breasts while undressing in front of John Colicos.

Lautner, Kathrin

Films:
Caged Fury (1989) .... Orchid
Zero Tolerance (1989) .... TV Announcer
Night of the Wilding (1990) .... Marion
The Last Riders (1991) .... Anna
Spirits (1991) .... Beth
Final Impact (1992) .... Kimber
Night of the Running Man (1994) .... Lady
•• 0:10—Buns and left breast while making love in bed with Scott Glenn.
•• 0:11—Nude, walking from bathroom and getting back into bed with Glenn.
Hologram Man (1995) .... Corporate Spokesperson
The Sweeper (1995) .... Amy
To the Limit (1995) .... Nurse Ellen
Two-Bits and Pepper (1995) .... Carla

Lavoie, Jennifer *

Video Tapes:
Playboy Celebrity Centerfold: Dian Parkinson (1993) .... Playmate
• 0:41—Full frontal nudity in B&W poster, posted on brick wall.
•• 0:42—Nude, while doing various things outside.
••• 0:44—Nude, while dancing and doing gymnastics.
••• 0:47—Nude in still photos.
••• 0:48—Nude with neighbor in hot night fantasy. Some food play.
••• 0:55—Nude in hammock in tropical setting.
Playboy Video Calendar 1995 (1994) .... August
••• 0:31—Nude dancing and doing gymnastics. Nude in a hammock and near palm trees.
Wet & Wild VIII: Bottoms Up (1996) .... Playmate

Law, Barbara

Films:
The Surrogate (1984; Canadian) .... Maggie Simpson
Made for Cable Movies:
Bedroom Eyes (1985; Canadian; HBO) .... Jobeth
• 0:02—Breasts, while undressing when watched by Harry through the window.
•• 0:07—Breasts and buns, while kissing a woman.
• 0:14—Breasts during Harry's flashback when he talks to the psychiatrist.
•• 0:23—Breasts and buns, while dancing in bedroom.
•• 0:57—Breasts, while kissing Mary on the floor.
• 1:23—Brief breasts, while on top of Harry.

• Lawrence, Juli

Films:
Hardbodies (1984) .... Nicki
• 0:38—Breasts in bathroom after taking off her dress to clean it.
Video Tapes:
E. Nick: A Legend in His Own Mind (1984) .... Nymphet

Lawrence, Mitte

Films:
Funny Girl (1968) .... Emma
The New Centurions (1972) .... Gloria
Night Call Nurses (1972) .... Sandra
a.k.a. Young LA Nurses 2
•• 0:49—Breasts, while in bed with a guy.

Lawrence, Sharon

Films:
Bloodfist V: Human Target (1993) .... Jewelry Store Clerk
Someone She Knows (1994) .... Sharon
Made for TV Movies:
The Shaggy Dog (1994) .... Beth
Degree of Guilt (1995) .... Mary Carelli
The Face on the Milk Carton (1995) .... Sada Sands
The Heidi Chronicles (1995) .... Jill
The Uninvited (1996) .... n.a.
Five Desperate Hours (1997) .... n.a.
TV:
Beverly Hills, 90210 (1991) .... n.a.
Civil Wars (1992) .... n.a.
Cheers (1993) .... Rachel
NYPD Blue (1993-) .... Sylvia Costas
NYPD Blue: Steroid Roy (Feb 8, 1994) .... Sylvia Costas
• 0:56—Back half of left breast, while standing in Sipowicz's bedroom.
NYPD Blue: The Final Adjustment (Nov 22, 1994) .... Sylvia Costas
•• 0:56—Buns, while in the shower with Sipowicz.
NYPD Blue: Moby Greg (Oct 15, 1996) .... Sylvia Costas
• 0:57—Upper half of buns and back side of right breast, while kneeling in bed with Andy.
Fired Up (1997-98) .... Gwen Leonard

Lawrence, Suzanne Remey

Films:
Delivery Boys (1984) .... Nurse
R.S.V.P. (1984) .... Stripper
•• 0:56—Breasts dancing in a radio station in front of a D.J.

Lawson, Cristina

Films:
American Yakuza (1993) .... Yuko
• 1:06—Right breast, while making love with Viggo Mortensen in bed.
Best of the Best 3: No Turning Back (1994) .... Karen Banning
The Shadow (1994) .... Concubine
Made for Cable TV:
Hot Line: Highest Bidder (1994; Cinemax) .... Courtney
(Available on video tape in *Hot Line 2*.)
• 0:06—Brief left breast in open blouse in office with Gordon.
•• 0:12—In bra, garter belt and stockings then breasts while making love with Gordon on his desk in office.
Dream On: Take Two Tablets, And Get Me to Mt. Sinai (1995; HBO) .... Martin's Lover

Layne, Janet *

Video Tapes:
Playboy's Girls of Radio: Talk, Rock and Shock (1995) .... Herself
••• 0:24—Nude, while posing in and on a red Corvette.

Layng, Lissa

Films:
Whose Life Is It, Anyway? (1981) .... 1st Nurse
Night of the Comet (1984) .... Davenport
Say Yes (1986) .... Annie
•• 1:06—Breasts, getting her dress ripped off.
• 1:07—More breasts, putting on jacket in restroom.

Lazar, Ava

Films:

Death Wish II (1982) . . . . Girl in TV Soap Opera
Fast Times at Ridgemont High (1982) . . . . Playmate
Night Shift (1982) . . . . Sharon
Diamond Run (1988; Indonesian) . . . . Samantha
a.k.a. Java Burn
•• 0:07—Brief breasts, several times, making love in bed with Nicky. Hard to see her face.
Forever Young (1992) . . . . Waitress at Diner ('92)
Nature of the Beast (1996) . . . . Blue

Made for TV Movies:

In the Deep Woods (1992) . . . . Cynthia Manning

TV:

Santa Barbara . . . . Santana Andrade

Lazure, Gabrielle

Films:

Enigma (1982) . . . . n.a.
Chaste and Pure (1984; Italian) . . . . n.a.
Joshua Then and Now (1985; Canadian) . . . . Pauline Shapiro
• 0:39—Buns and brief side of left breast, while in bed with James Woods.

Le Brock, Kelly

Spokeswoman for Pantene cosmetics.
Ex-wife of actor/martial arts expert Steven Seagal.

Films:

The Woman in Red (1984) . . . . Charlotte
• 1:13—Brief right breast, getting into bed. Too far to see anything.
• 1:15—Brief lower frontal nudity getting out of bed when her husband comes home. Very brief left breast, but it's blurry and hard to see.
Weird Science (1985) . . . . Lisa
Hard to Kill (1990) . . . . Andy Stewart
Betrayal of the Dove (1992) . . . . Una
Hard Bounty (1995) . . . . Donnie
Tracks of a Killer (1995) . . . . Claire Hawkner

Le Priol, Alison

See: Kascha.

Le Roux, Madeleine

Films:

Behind Locked Doors (1969) . . . . Woman at Party
• 0:07—Breasts after taking off bra while making out with guy in barn.
Cry Uncle (1971) . . . . Cora Merrill
••• 0:22—Breasts and buns, undressing in bathroom while talking to Jake.
••• 0:27—Nude, taking off her dress in front of Keith and making love with him on the sofa. Long scene.
• 0:42—Brief breasts, sitting up in bed when door is slammed in Jake's face.
• 0:59—Full frontal nudity, while standing in bedroom doorway.
• 1:11—Breasts under sheer red and black nightie, then making love with Jake. Long scene.
• 1:18—Brief buns, while taking off her panties.

Leachman, Cloris

Films:

Kiss Me Deadly (1955) . . . . Christina Dailey/Berga Torn
Butch Cassidy and the Sundance Kid (1969) . . . . Agnes
Lovers and Other Strangers (1970) . . . . Bernice
The People Next Door (1970) . . . . Tina
• 0:59—Buns and very brief side view of right breast, while getting up out of bed and putting on a robe.
The Last Picture Show (1971) . . . . Ruth Popper
(Academy Award for Best Supporting Actress.)
The Steagle (1971) . . . . Rita Weiss
Charley & the Angel (1973) . . . . Nettie Appleby
Daisy Miller (1974) . . . . Mrs. Ezra B. Miller
Young Frankenstein (1974) . . . . Frau Blucher
Crazy Mama (1975) . . . . Melba
• 0:53—Brief left breast under clear plastic blouse while washing Stuart Whitman's hair in the sink.
High Anxiety (1977) . . . . Nurse Diesel
The North Avenue Irregulars (1979) . . . . Claire
Scavenger Hunt (1979) . . . . Mildred Carrothers
Foolin' Around (1980) . . . . Samantha
Herbie Goes Bananas (1980) . . . . Aunt Louise
History of the World, Part I (1981) . . . . Madame de Farge
Shadow Play (1986) . . . . Millie Crown
Walk Like a Man (1987) . . . . Margaret Shand
Prancer (1990) . . . . Mrs. McFarland
Texasville (1990) . . . . Ruth Popper
Love Hurts (1991) . . . . Ruth Weaver
The Beverly Hillbillies (1993) . . . . Granny
My Boyfriend's Back (1993) . . . . Maggie
Now and Then (1995) . . . . Grandma Albertson

Made for Cable Movies:

Fade to Black (1993; USA) . . . . Ruth

Made for TV Movies:

Danielle Steel's "Fine Things" (1990) . . . . Ruth Fine
In Broad Daylight (1991) . . . . Ruth Westerman
Double, Double, Toil and Trouble (1993) . . . . n.a.
Miracle Child (1993) . . . . Doc Betty
Without a Kiss Goodbye (1993) . . . . Mrs. Samuels
Between Love and Honor (1995) . . . . Anna Collura

TV:

Lassie (1957-58) . . . . Ruth Martin
The Mary Tyler Moore Show (1970-75) . . . . . Phyllis Lindstrom
Phyllis (1975-77) . . . . Phyllis Lindstrom
The Facts of Life (1986) . . . . Beverly Ann Stickle
Walter and Emily (1991) . . . . Emily Collins

Leardini, Christina *

Films:

Dream Trap (1989) . . . . Sorority Sister
•• 1:18—Breasts, when emerging from swimming pool during party.

Video Tapes:

Playboy Video Calendar 1992 (1991) . . . . August
••• 0:32—Nude trying on various outfits.
••• 0:33—Nude in old building.
Sexy Lingerie III (1991) . . . . Model
The Best of Sexy Lingerie (1992) . . . . Model
Playboy Playmates in Paradise (1992) . . . . Playmate
Playboy's Playmate Bloopers & Practical Jokes (1992) . . Hostess
Playboy's Playmate Review 1992 (1992) . . . . . . Miss April
••• 0:32—Nude in a car, then in a bed, then inside an old building.
Sexy Lingerie IV (1992) . . . . Model
Playboy's Sexy, Steamy, Sultry (1993) . . . . Playmate
Sexy Lingerie V (1993) . . . . Model
Playboy's Sisters (1995) . . . . Herself/Cherished Moments
••• 0:27—Nude with her sister in clothing store fantasy.
Playboy's Fast Women (1997) . . . . Playmate

Leary, Laura Jane

Films:

The Best of Sex and Violence (1981). . . . . .Girl Victim
• 0:00—Getting clothes ripped off, then in bra and panties, then breasts.

Famous T & A (1982) . . . . .Motorcycle Rider
(No longer available for purchase, check your video store for rental.)
• 0:29—Lower nudity, riding a motorcycle with only a jacket on.

*LeBeau, Becky **

a.k.a. Sharona Bonner.

Films:

Carnival of Love (1983). . . . . .Nancy
a.k.a. Inside the Love House
• 0:29—Brief breasts in open robe, while putting on pants.
••• 0:56—Nude, while making love with a guy in a flower setting. Long scene.
• 1:05—Brief breasts.

Joysticks (1983). . . . . .Liza

Hollywood Hot Tubs (1984) . . . . Veronica
•• 0:49—Breasts changing in the locker room with other girl soccer players while Jeff watches.
• 0:54—Breasts in hot tub with the other girls and Shawn.

School Spirit (1985) . . . . Hogette
• 1:07—Breasts sliding down water slide at dance, wearing black and white swimsuit bottom.

Back to School (1986) . . . . Bubbles, the Hot Tub Girl

Off the Mark (1986). . . . . .Uncredited Shower Girl
• 0:52—Brief breasts, after taking off her pink T-shirt in locker room. Brief buns, while walking into showers (2nd to the last girl).

Takin' It All Off (1987) . . . . Becky
•• 0:03—Breasts in pink leotard in dance studio.
••• 0:11—Nude in the showers (she's in the back on the left).
•• 0:16—Breasts and brief full frontal nudity getting introduced to Allison.
••• 0:23—In black bra and panties, then nude doing a strip routine outside.
• 0:35—Brief full frontal nudity pushing Elliot into the pool.
• 0:36—Brief breasts in studio with Allison again.
• 0:36—Brief left breast in dance studio with Allison.
•• 1:23—Nude, dancing with the other girls on stage.

The Underachievers (1987). . . . . Ginger Bronsky
••• 0:40—Breasts in swimming pool playing with an inflatable alligator after her exercise class has left.

Not of This Earth (1988) . . . . .Happy Birthday Girl
••• 0:47—Breasts doing a Happy Birthday stripper-gram for the old guy.

Nudity Required (1989). . . . . .Melanie
•• 0:35—Breasts, after taking off pink swimsuit.
•• 0:36—Brief breasts (third girl) standing in line.
• 0:37—Breasts, standing behind Scammer.
• 0:39—Very brief breasts.
•• 0:41—Breasts while sitting next to Scammer by the pool.

Ninja Academy (1990) . . . . .Nudist
•• 0:26—Nude, carrying plate, then going to swing at nudist colony. Then playing volleyball (she's the first one to hit the ball).

Transylvania Twist (1990) . . . . .Rita

The Malibu Beach Vampires (1991). . . . . The Census Taker

Munchie (1992) . . . . Pizza Screamer

Sins of Desire (1992) . . . . Sandy
(Unrated version reviewed.)
••• 0:23—Nude, stripping and dancing (she's the blonde on the left) with Clarise in front of Mr. O'Connor. Long scene.

Body Chemistry 3: Point of Seduction (1993) . . Margaret
•• 0:04—Full frontal nudity, seen on TV monitor, while taking her clothes off on bed during call-in show.

Dinosaur Island (1993). . . . . Virgin Sacrifice
••• 0:00—Breasts, after getting her bikini top ripped off while tied by her wrists during sacrifice ceremony.

Munchie Strikes Back (1994) . . . . Chased Woman

Bikini Drive-In (1995). . . . . .Candy
(Unrated version reviewed.)
••• 0:51—In white bra and panties, then buns and breasts, while dancing in radio studio in front of Fred Olen Ray.

Music Videos:

California Girls/David Lee Roth
. . . . Girl Squeezing Suntan Lotion Bottle

Video Tapes:

Centerfold Screen Test (1985) . . . . Herself

Best Chest in the West II (1986). . . . . Herself
••• 0:46—Dancing in red two piece swimsuit. Buns, then breasts.
•• 0:55—Buns and breasts after winning semi-finals.

Becky Bubbles (1987). . . . . Herself
••• 0:00—Breasts, when waking up and getting out of bed.
••• 0:01—Breasts, going outside for a swim in white panties. Long scene.
••• 0:06—Breasts, while rubbing lotion on herself.
••• 0:08—Breasts outside on chair and in pool with her friends.
••• 0:12—Breasts while playing on pool float with Lorraine and Brandi.
••• 0:22—Breasts drying her hair outside with hair dryer.
••• 0:24—Breasts while putting on make-up and fingernail polish.
•• 0:25—Buns and breasts while taking off swimsuit then getting dressed.

Trashy Ladies Wrestling (1987) . . . . Round Girl

Soft Bodies (1988) . . . . Herself
••• 0:01—In two piece swimsuit, then breasts in swimming pool.
•• 0:08—On bed during photo session in various lingerie, then breasts and buns in G-string.
••• 0:16—In bra and panties, then breasts on bed.

Soft Bodies Invitational (1990) . . . . Herself
• 0:00—Buns, under short skirt playing tennis with Julia Parton.
••• 0:15—Breasts while posing with Parton in photo session.
•• 0:24—In two piece swimsuit, then breasts while arguing with Parton about who has better breasts.
••• 0:38—In red bra and panties outside on bridge, then breasts.
••• 0:44—Breasts and buns in G-string in spa.

Soft Bodies: Curves Ahead (1991) . . . . Herself
• 0:00—Buns in G-string, while playing Frisbee with Kylie Rose.
••• 0:32—Breasts in pool with Tamara. Buns and partial lower frontal nudity. Long scene.
••• 0:36—Breasts while posing for photographs in various outfits.
••• 0:41—On balcony in two piece swimsuit, then breasts and buns taking an outdoor shower. Long scene.
••• 0:45—Breasts and buns in G-string, posing on bed for photo session in various lingerie. Long scene.

••• 0:51—In two piece swimsuit outside at night in spa. Breasts and buns in G-string. Long scene.

Soft Bodies: Party Favors (1992) . . . . Herself

••• 0:35—Breasts and buns, on floating bed in pool with Julia Hayes.

••• 0:39—Breasts and buns posing in bed in various lingerie outfits.

••• 0:46—Breasts and buns on couch.

••• 0:52—On balcony taking off dress, then in white lingerie, then breasts and buns.

Soft Bodies: Squeeze Play (1993). . . . . Herself

••• 0:15—Breasts and partial buns in cut-offs, while washing windows with Tuscany.

••• 0:27—In lingerie, then breasts and buns on bed with Elayne Dahl.

••• 0:37—In bra and panties, then nude in front of and on bar.

••• 0:47—In a dress, then in bra and panties, then nude on sofa.

••• 0:51—In bra and panties, then nude on bed.

Soft Bodies: Double Exposure (1994) . . . . Herself

•• 0:27—Breasts and buns in panties, while rehearsing with Julia Parton outside.

••• 0:38—In lingerie, then nude, while posing on bed.

••• 0:46—In two piece swimsuit, then nude, while posing in spa.

••• 0:52—In two piece outfit, then full frontal nudity, while posing on swinging chair outside.

BabeWatch, Episode 4: Naughty But Nice (1995). . Herself

••• 0:19—Breasts, after waking up, then going outdoors and swimming in pool.

Soft Bodies: Beyond Blonde (1995). . . . . Herself

•• 0:01—Breasts and buns in swimsuit, while playing tetherball in pool with Rachel Love.

•• 0:11—Breasts, while posing in pool with Love.

•• 0:29—In skimpy outfit, then breasts, during pillow fight in bed with Heather Kennedy.

••• 0:37—In lingerie, then nude, while posing on bed.

••• 0:44—In two piece swimsuit, then nude in pool.

••• 0:49—In white lingerie, then nude on chair inside.

Soft Bodies: Show 'n Tell (1995) . . . . Herself

•• 0:13—Breasts, while in swimming pool with St. Clair.

•• 0:16—Breasts and buns in swimsuit while washing and posing next to car with St. Clair.

••• 0:33—In lingerie, then nude, while posing indoors near entry way.

••• 0:44—In dress, then nude, while posing outside.

••• 0:47—In lingerie, then nude, while posing in bedroom.

Soft Bodies: Bathing Beauties (1996) . . . . Herself

Soft Bodies: Pillow Talk (1996) . . . . Herself

•• 0:37—Breasts, after taking off her top and doing cheerleader moves outdoors with Danni Ashe.

••• 0:38—In bra and panties, then nude, while posing in dining area.

••• 0:43—In bra and panties, then nude, while posing on bed.

••• 0:48—In dress, then nude, while posing on sofa.

Soft Bodies: All American Girls (1997) . . . . Herself

•• 0:01—Breasts, while frolicking outside with Candace.

••• 0:39—In bra and panties, when nude, while posing on bed.

••• 0:43—In schoolgirl outfit, then nude, while posing outdoors.

••• 0:48—In bra and panties, then nude, while posing indoors.

••• 0:52—In swimsuit, then nude, while posing outdoors in the pool.

Perfect Bodies: Foreign Affairs (1998) . . . . Herself

• *Lechner, Geno*

Films:

Schindler's List (1993) . . . . Majola

Immortal Beloved (1994) . . . . Josephine Von Brunsvik

•• 0:17—Breasts, after opening her dress top in the woods with Gary Oldman.

Flirt (1995) . . . . Greta

Made for TV Movies:

Danielle Steel's "The Ring" (1996). . . . . Effie Zelt

Lechner, Melissa

Films:

Inside Monkey Zetterland (1993) . . . . Observation Psychiatrist

S.F.W. (1994) . . . . Sandy Hooten

• 0:46—Brief side of right breast, while in bathtub.

• 0:50—Brief breasts after dropping her towel after professing her love for Stephen Dorff.

• *Ledford, Brandy* *

a.k.a. Brandy, Jisél and Brandy Sanders.

Films:

Demolition Man (1993). . . . . Fiber Op Girl

• 1:13—Very brief breasts, after accidentally calling the wrong number on her video phone.

Indecent Behavior (1993) . . . . Elaine Croft

(Unrated version reviewed.)

••• 0:59—Breasts and side view of buns, while taking off her clothes in front of Jan-Michael Vincent.

••• 1:10—Breasts, taking off her top in front of Vincent.

National Lampoon's Last Resort (1993) . . . . Mermaid

Irresistible Impulse (1995) . . . . Heather McNeill

•• 1:15—In black bra, panties and stockings, then breasts while making love with Simon.

• 1:22—Brief partial breasts, while putting her bra on.

Killing For Love (1995) . . . . Celena

••• 0:46—Buns in panties, then breasts and buns while making love in bedroom with Max. Nice, long scene.

Made for Cable TV:

Fast Track (1997- ; Showtime) . . . . Mimi Chandler

Fast Track: Sweet Thunder (1997; Showtime)
. . . . Mimi Chandler

Fast Track: The Race Fan (1997; Showtime) . . . . Mimi Chandler

Video Tapes:

Penthouse Pet of the Year Playoff 1991 (1992) . . . . . Pet

••• 0:32—Nude in bubble bath.

••• 0:34—Nude doing different things in a house in various lingerie outfits, then in bath again, then covered with rose petals.

••• 0:39—Nude in still photos, then in motion while wearing sunglasses while posing in front of a wall.

••• 0:40—Nude in color and B&W while posing in country setting with different lingerie.

••• 0:43—Nude in science-fiction style segment.

••• 0:45—Buns in G-string and bra, then nude while posing on bed. B&W.

••• 0:50—Nude while posing in a field during end credits.

Penthouse Pet of the Year Winners 1992: Brandy & Amy (1992). . . . . Pet

Penthouse Satin & Lace II: Hollywood Undercover (1992) . . Pet

Penthouse Satin & Lace: An Erotic History of Lingerie (1992). . . . . Model

Penthouse: Fast Cars/Fantasy Women (1992)
. . . . Mercedes 300 SL

••• 0:15—Nude while washing and posing with car.

Penthouse DreamGirls (1994) . . . . Brandy
- ••• 0:10—Nude in a house, on a piano bench, on a sofa.

Lee Varga, Sazzy *

a.k.a. Sazzy Lee.

Films:

Angel Eyes (1991) . . . . Amy

Video Tapes:

All Nude Glamour (1995) . . . . Sazzy
- ••• 0:09—Nude, while posing indoors and outdoors. Some behind-the-scenes shots included. Long scene.
- •• 0:12—Nude, in bathroom, while talking dirty.

CD-ROM:

Crystal Fantasy (1995). . . . . Sazzy

Hollywood Body Double (1995) . . . . Beach/Gangster

Lee, Adriane

Films:

Breeders (1986) . . . . Alec
- •• 0:49—Breasts, undressing while talking on the phone.
- • 1:07—Brief breasts, covered with goop, in the alien nest.
- • 1:08—Brief breasts in nest behind Frances Raines.
- • 1:09—Brief breasts behind Raines again.
- • 1:11—Breasts, lying back in the goop, then long shot breasts.

Mutant Hunt (1987) . . . . .Amber Dawn

Necropolis (1987) . . . . Cult Member

Slammer Girls (1987) . . . . Dead Convict

Lee, Cynthia

Films:

New York Nights (1981) . . . . The Porn Star
- •• 1:15—Breasts in the steam room talking to the prostitute.
- ••• 1:26—Breasts in office with the financier and making love on his desk.

Hot Resort (1984). . . . . Alice
- • 1:08—Breasts in the bathtub.

Hired to Kill (1990) . . . . Armwrestler

Lee, Hyapatia

Adult film actress.

Films:

Hellroller (1992). . . . . Dancer
- ••• 0:43—Breasts, dancing in room by herself.
- ••• 0:45—Breasts and buns, while taking a shower.

Swingers (1992) . . . . Sydney X

Killing Obsession (1994) . . . . Annie Smith
- ••• 0:12—Breasts and buns in G-string, while dancing on bar.
- •• 0:15—Breasts, while changing clothes in bathroom, then walking to John Savage.
- • 0:18—Brief right breast, while lying dead on floor.

Video Tapes:

Hyapatia Lee Presents: Taking' It Off, Volume 1 (1993) . . . . Herself
- ••• 0:41—Nude, doing strip dance routine on stage in club. Long scene.

Lee, Jennifer

Films:

Act of Vengeance (1974). . . . . .Nancy

a.k.a. The Rape Squad

(Not to be confused with the film with the same name starring Charles Bronson.)
- • 0:38—Breasts looking up in spa while talking to another woman.

Sunshine Boys (1975) . . . . Helen

The Wild Party (1975) . . . . Madeline Tru

The Duchess and the Dirtwater Fox (1976) . . . . Trollop

Lee, Jessica *

Video Tapes:

Playboy's Girls of Radio: Talk, Rock and Shock (1995) . . . . Herself
- ••• 0:35—In white lingerie, then nude.

Wet & Wild VIII: Bottoms Up (1996) . . . . .Playmate

Playboy's Fast Women (1997). . . . . .Playmate

Playboy's Voluptuous Vixens (1997). . . . . .Playmate

Lee, Joie

Sister of actor/director Spike Lee.

Films:

She's Gotta Have It (1987). . . . . Clorinda Bradford

School Daze (1988). . . . . Lizzie Life

Bail Jumper (1989). . . . . Athena

Do the Right Thing (1989) . . . . Jade

Mo' Better Blues (1990). Indigo Downes
- •• 1:06—Right breast while in bed with Denzel Washington.
- • 1:08—Very, very brief right breast while pounding the bed and yelling at Denzel Washington.

A Kiss Before Dying (1991) . . . . Cathy

Fathers and Sons (1992) . . . . .Lois

Crooklyn (1994) . . . . .Aunt Maxine

Losing Isaiah (1994) . . . . Marie

Get on the Bus (1996). . . . . Jindai

Girl 6 (1996) . . . . Switchboard Operator

Lee, Kaaren

Films:

The Right Stuff (1983). .Young Widow

Roadhouse 66 (1984). . . . . .Jesse Duran
- •• 1:00—Breasts, taking off her top to go skinny dipping with Willem Dafoe. Dark.

St. Elmo's Fire (1985). . . . . Welfare Woman

Remote Control (1987) . . . . Patricia

Lee, Kelli

Films:

Slash Dance (1989) . . . . Dancer

Sorority Girls and the Creature from Hell (1990) . . . . Body Double for Dori Courtney
- • 0:23—Breasts, while in bedroom with J.J.
- • 0:36—Breasts, while pretending to be strangled by Skip in the spa. Buns, when getting out.

Lee, Luann *

Films:

Beverly Hills Cop II (1987) . . . . Playboy Playmate

Terminal Exposure (1988) . . . . Bruce's Girl

Video Tapes:

Playboy Video Centerfold: Luann Lee . . . . .Playmate

Playboy Video Calendar 1988 (1987) . . . . .Playmate

Wet & Wild (1989) . . . . .Model

Playboy's 21 Playmates (1996). . . . . .Playmate
- ••• 0:45—Full frontal nudity in still photos.
- ••• 0:46—Nude in bedroom.

Lee, Margareth

Films:

Casanova '70 (1965; Italian) . . . . Dolly Greenwater

Secret Agent Super Dragon (1966; French/Italian/German) . . . . Cynthia Fulton

Dorian Gray (1970; Italian/British/German) . . . . Gwendolyn Wotten

Venus in Furs (1970) . . . . Olga
(Original version reviewed.)
• 0:53—Buns, lying on floor with Maria.
• 0:54—Buns, while walking and holding candelabra.
Slaughter Hotel (1971; Italian) . . . . Luise
a.k.a. Asylum Erotica
The Rogue (1976) . . . . n.a.

Lee, Pamela *

a.k.a. Pamela Anderson.
Ex-wife of Mötley Crüe drummer Tommy Lee.
Films:
The Taking of Beverly Hills (1991) . . . . Cheerleader
Snapdragon (1993) . . . . Felicity
• 0:06—Brief side view of right breast, while making love on top of a guy in bed before killing him.
• 0:26—Right breast, while making love on top of another guy in bed before killing him.
••• 0:55—Breasts and buns, while making love in bed on top of Steven Bauer in his dream.
• 1:06—In white bra and panties, then left breast and buns while making love on top of Bauer on the floor.
••• 1:22—Breasts and buns, while making love with Bauer.
Raw Justice (1994) . . . . Sarah
a.k.a. Good Cop, Bad Cop
••• 0:40—Breasts, when making out with David Keith in building while standing up.
•• 0:58—Breasts, while making love with Robert Hayes in hotel room.
Barb Wire (1995) . . . . Barb Wire
(Unrated version reviewed.)
•• 0:00—Breasts in black dress, while dancing in water spray during opening credits.
• 0:33—Brief silhouette of breasts behind curtain while changing clothes.
• 0:57—Brief partial left breast under water and above water in bubble bath.
• 1:02—Brief right breast in open robe, while walking in office.
••• 1:40—Breasts in black dress, while on trapeze and getting sprayed with water. Long scene shown after the credits.
Naked Souls (1995) . . . . Britt
•• 0:04—Left breast, while kissing Brian Krause in back of art gallery.
•• 0:42—Left breast, then breasts, while making love with Krause in bed.
•• 1:18—Breasts, while making love with Krause in bed.
Made for TV Movies:
Come Die With Me: A Mickey Spillane's Mike Hammer Mystery (1994) . . . . Velma
TV:
Home Improvement (1991-93) . . . . . . Lisa the "Tool Time" Girl
Baywatch (1992-97) . . . . C.J. Parker
Video Tapes:
Playboy Video Calendar 1991 (1990) . . . . July
••• 0:26—Nude.
Sexy Lingerie II (1990) . . . . Model
Sexy Lingerie III (1991) . . . . Model
Wet & Wild III (1991) . . . . Model
The Best of Video Playmate Calendars (1992) . . Playmate
••• 0:34—Nude on spiral staircase, then on floor.
••• 0:36—In lingerie, then nude during modeling session with lots of sheets.
Playboy Video Centerfold: Pamela Anderson (1992) . . . . Playmate
••• 0:00—Nude throughout.
Playboy's Sexy, Steamy, Sultry (1993) . . . . Playmate
Baywatch: The Movie—Forbidden Paradise (1994) . . . . C. J. Parker
Playboy The Best of Pamela Anderson (1995) . . . . Herself
•• 0:00—Nude during introduction in lingerie.
• 0:03—In sheer white outfit, then full frontal nudity in winter fantasy.
••• 0:08—Nude in still photos.
••• 0:10—Nude and in lingerie in studio and on bed.
••• 0:14—Nude in studio. Some behind-the-scenes shots.
••• 0:18—Full frontal nudity in motion and in still photos. Some behind-the-scenes shots of her pictorial photos.
••• 0:23—Nude in studio and in a room.
•• 0:25—Buns in panties, then nude, while playing in a bedroom.
••• 0:27—Breasts and partial buns, in music video segment.
•• 0:29—Nude, doing various things around the house.
••• 0:31—Nude, in house, in various pieces of lingerie.
••• 0:33—Nude in water fantasy.
••• 0:36—Full frontal nudity in fantasy with a guy.
••• 0:39—Nude in still photos.
•• 0:42—Nude in lots of different segments.
••• 0:44—Nude in stopped elevator with a guy.
••• 0:46—Nude in and around old mansion.
• 0:49—Buns in still photo with Tommy Lee.
•• 0:51—Full frontal nudity in end segment.
CD-ROM:
Pamela Anderson Lee (1996) . . . . Herself

Lee, Pat

Films:
Porky's (1981; Canadian) . . . . Stripper
• 0:33—Brief breasts dancing on stage at Porky's showing her breasts to Pee Wee.
Starman (1984) . . . . Bracero Wife
And God Created Woman (1988) . . . . Inmate
(Unrated version.)
Young Guns (1988) . . . . Janey

Lee, Robin

a.k.a. Robbie Lee.
Films:
Big Bad Mama (1974) . . . . Polly McClatchie
• 0:08—Brief left breast in gaping dress when cops try to pull her car over.
• 0:22—In see-through dress on stage with her sister and a stripper.
• 0:32—Brief breasts running around the bedroom chasing her sister.
• 0:52—Buns, taking off her nightgown and getting into bed with Tom Skerritt.
Switchblade Sisters (1975) . . . . Lace
• 0:48—Breasts sitting up in bed to talk to Dominic. Dark.

Lee, Shayna *

Films:
Forbidden Passions (1995) . . . . Sandy
••• 0:42—Breasts and buns, while making love with Brett in bed.
Made for Cable TV:
Erotic Confessions: Coming Clean (1996; Cinemax) . . . Kia
(Available on video tape in *Erotic Confessions, Volume 1: Desire.*)
•• 0:04—Nude, after taking off robe and getting into tub with a guy.
••• 0:06—Nude, while soaping up Eric on table, first with a sponge, then with her body.

Video Tapes:
All Nude Glamour (1995) .... Shayna
••• 0:13—Nude, while posing indoors and outdoors. Some behind-the-scenes shots included. Long scene.
•• 0:16—Breasts, while talking dirty.
Playboy's Real Couples: Sex in Dangerous Places (1995) .... Up on the Roof/Voyeur
••• 0:48—In sheer panties, when caressing herself when watching someone through a telescope. Nude, while making love with Dixie and James.
CD-ROM:
Crystal Fantasy (1995)........................ Shayna

Lee, Sheryl *

Films:
The Pink Chiquitas (1986; Canadian).......... Pink Chiquita
Wild at Heart (1990) .... Good Witch
Twin Peaks: Fire Walk With Me (1992)...... Laura Palmer
• 0:37—Very brief breasts, letting her boyfriend feel her breast.
•• 1:18—Breasts when a guy takes off her dress in cabin.
••• 1:19—Breasts, while talking with Ronette at table.
••• 1:21—More breasts in cabin and while sitting at the table with Ronette. More breasts when getting up.
• 1:49—Side view of buns and upper half of right breast (wearing lingerie) while lying in bed and rolling over.
• 1:58—Brief upper half of left breast while dancing in lingerie in cabin.
•• 1:59—Breasts, while struggling on bed with big guy.
• 2:01—Brief breasts talking with her dad in the cabin.
Backbeat (1994) .... Astrid Kirchiner
•• 0:47—Breasts, after taking off her sweater and making love.
• 1:03—Very brief left breast, then breasts, while covered with paint.
•• 1:28—Nude, taking off sweater and putting on a dress.
Don't Do It (1994) .... Michelle
Fall Time (1994) .... Patty/Carol
Homage (1994).......................... Lucy Samuel
• 0:37—Very brief breasts seen on TV that Frank Whaley is masturbating to.
Bliss (1996) .... Maria
•• 0:38—Breasts, while lying in bed with Craig Schaeffer.
• 0:42—Brief breasts.
•• 0:57—Breasts, while lying in bed with Schaeffer. Lit with blue light.
•• 1:04—Breasts in gaping nightie, after tying up Schaeffer to bed and making love with him.
• 1:09—Brief left breast, while lying in bed with Schaeffer.
• 1:10—Brief right breast, while sitting on Schaeffer's lap.
•• 1:11—Breasts, while making love with Schaeffer.
• 1:12—Breasts, while lying in bed with Schaeffer.
• 1:18—Very brief partial left breast, when closing the shower door.
Mother Night (1996) .... Hela/Resi Noth
•• 0:11—Breasts, after taking off her nightgown and getting into bed with Nick Nolte.
This World, then the Fireworks (1997)............ Lois
•• 0:30—Breasts, while making love in bed with Billy Zane. Lit with blue light.
• 0:52—In lingerie, then brief breasts, while fooling around on bed. Very brief tip of right breast, while sitting in bathtub.
Made for Cable Movies:
David (1997; TNT) .... Bathsheba
Made for Cable TV:
Red Shoe Diaries: Jake's Story (1993; Showtime) .... Kate Lyons
(Available on the video tape *Red Shoe Diaries 4: Auto Erotica.)*
• 0:14—Brief breasts while making love with Jake in and out of truck.
•• 0:20—In black bra, then breasts, while making love with Jake on roof.
• 0:27—Brief left and right breasts, while making love with Jake in bed.
Made for TV Movies:
Love, Lies and Murder (1991) .... Patti Bailey
Jersey Girl (1993)................................. Tara
Follow the River (1995) .... Mary Ingles
TV:
Twin Peaks (1990-91) ..... Laura Palmer/Madeleine Ferguson

• Lee, Sung Hi *

Films:
Midnight Blue (1996) .... Streetwalker
Made for Cable Movies:
Weapons of Mass Distraction (1997; HBO) .... Kelly
Video Tapes:
Playboy's The Girls of Hawaiian Tropic (1994) .... Passion Fruit
••• 0:14—Nude, while posing in and by a stream.

Lee, Tamara

Former adult film actress.
Video Tapes:
Soft Bodies: Curves Ahead (1991) .... Herself
••• 0:23—In lingerie on chair, then breasts during photo session. Brief lower frontal nudity under sheer lingerie. Long scene.
••• 0:31—In chair by pool. Breasts and partial lower frontal nudity.

Lee-Hsu, Diana *

Films:
License to Kill (1989).............................. Loti
Snapdragon (1993)....................... Professor Huan
Made for Cable Movies:
Blind Side (1993; HBO) .... Mrs. Dance
Video Tapes:
Playboy Video Calendar 1989 (1988) .... February
••• 0:05—Nude.
Playmates at Play (1990)................. Gotta Dance
Wet & Wild III (1991).......................... Model
The Best of Wet and Wild (1992)................ Model
Playboy Video Playmate Six-Pack 1992 (1992) . .Playmate

Légerè, Phoebe *

Singer.
Films:
Mondo New York (1987) .... Singer
• 0:01—On stage, singing "Marilyn Monroe." Buns and most of lower frontal nudity while writhing on stage in a mini-skirt.
The Toxic Avenger: Part II (1988) .... Claire
• 0:31—Brief right breast, while caressing herself while making out with the Toxic Avenger.
The Toxic Avenger III: The Last Temptation of Toxie (1989) .... Claire
King of New York (1990)................ Bordello Woman

Leigh, Barbara *

Films:

The Student Nurses (1970) .... Priscilla
a.k.a. Young LA Nurses
••• 0:43—Breasts on the beach with Les. Long scene.

The Christian Licorice Store (1971) .... Starlet

Pretty Maids All in a Row (1971).......... Jean McDrew
• 0:30—Brief partial side view of right breast when she leans over chess board on bed to touch Rock Hudson.

Junior Bonner (1972) .... Charmagne

Terminal Island (1973) .... Bunny Campbell
••• 0:22—Breasts and buns undressing in room while Bobbie watches from the bed.

Boss (1974)................................ Miss Pruitt
a.k.a. Boss Nigger

Mistress of the Apes (1979; British) .... Laura
••• 0:44—Breasts, washing her blouse in river and putting it on. (Seen through binoculars.)
• 0:46—Breasts, getting her blouse ripped off by jerks.

Seven (1979) .... Alexa
0:17—Briefly in braless, semi-sheer yellow blouse.

Famous T & A (1982).................. Bunny Campbell
(No longer available for purchase, check your video store for rental.)
••• 0:45—Breasts scene from *Terminal Island.* Includes additional takes that weren't used.

TV:

Harry-O... n.a.

Leigh, Cassandra

See: Boyle, Lisa.

Leigh, Jennifer Jason *

Daughter of the late actor Vic Morrow.

Films:

Eyes of a Stranger (1981) .... Tracy
• 1:15—Very brief breasts lying in bed getting attacked by rapist.
•• 1:19—Left breast, while cleaning herself in bathroom.

Fast Times at Ridgemont High (1982) .... Stacy Hamilton
• 0:18—Left breast, while making out with Ron in a dugout.
••• 1:00—Breasts in poolside dressing room.

Wrong is Right (1982)........................ Young Girl

Easy Money (1983).................... Allison Capuletti

Grandview, U.S.A. (1984) .... Candy Webster

Flesh + Blood (1985) .... Agnes
• 0:45—Brief right breast, while being held down.
•• 1:05—Full frontal nudity getting into the bath with Rutger Hauer and making love.
••• 1:16—Full frontal nudity getting out of bed with Hauer and walking to the window.
•• 1:35—Full frontal nudity, while throwing clothes into the fire.
•• 1:36—Breasts, when Hauer removes sheet that covers her.
•• 1:37—Buns and long shot brief side view of right breast, while walking to the castle behind Hauer. Brief breasts when stopped on stairs while watching Tom Burlinson throw food into well.

The Hitcher (1986) .... Nash

The Men's Club (1986)......................... Teensy

Sister Sister (1987)..................... Lucy Bonnard
•• 0:01—Breasts making love during a dream.
•• 0:53—Left breast, while making love with Stoltz in her bedroom.
• 0:58—Breasts in bathtub surrounded by candles.

Under Cover (1987) .... Tanille Lareoux

Heart of Midnight (1988) .... Carol
• 0:27—Very brief side view of right breast, while reaching for soap in the shower.

The Big Picture (1989)................... Lydia Johnson

Last Exit to Brooklyn (1990)................... Tralala
•• 1:28—Breasts, opening her blouse in bar after getting drunk.
• 1:33—Breasts getting dragged out of car, placed on mattress, then basically raped by a long line of guys. Long, painful-to-watch scene.
• 1:35—Breasts lying on mattress when Spook comes to save her.

Miami Blues (1990) .... Susie Waggoner
• 0:07—Very brief upper half of right breast, while changing clothes behind Alec Baldwin.
••• 0:10—Breasts in panties, taking off red dress and getting into bed.
• 0:24—Very, very brief half of right breast while taking a bath. Long shot.
• 0:33—Breasts making love with Baldwin in the kitchen.

Backdraft (1991) .... Jennifer Vaitkus
• 1:16—Very, very brief left breast on back of fire truck with William Baldwin. (Right after someone knocks open a door with an axe.)

Crooked Hearts (1991) .... Harriet
•• 1:10—In black bra, then breasts in bathtub with Tom.

Rush (1991)......................... Kristen Cates
• 1:09—Brief buns, when Jason Patric takes off her pajama bottoms and forces himself on her.

Single White Female (1992) .... Hedy Carlson
••• 0:18—Breasts, changing clothes in her room in front of Bridget Fonda.
• 0:29—Upper half of breasts, while in bathtub.
•• 0:37—Breasts, masturbating in bed while Fonda peeks in bedroom.
••• 1:04—Breasts in the shower, then full frontal nudity, getting out.
•• 1:09—Breasts, getting into bed with Sam.
• 1:10—Breasts, while in bed with Sam.

Short Cuts (1993) .... Lois Kaiser

The Hudsucker Proxy (1994)................ Amy Archer

Mrs. Parker and the Vicious Circle (1994)
.... Dorothy Parker
• 0:56—Brief breasts, while turning over in bed with Matthew Broderick.
• 0:57—Brief left breast, while lying under Broderick and kissing him.

Dolores Claiborne (1995) .... Selena St. George

Georgia (1996) .... Sadie
•• 1:04—Upper half of buns and breasts, while making love in bed with her husband, Axel. Dark.

Kansas City (1996) .... Blondie O'Hara

A Thousand Acres (1997) .... Caroline Cook

Made for Cable Movies:

Buried Alive (1990; USA)...................... Joanna

Bastard Out of Carolina (1996; Showtime) .... Anney

Thanks of a Grateful Nation (1998; Showtime). . Teri Small
• 0:10—Brief breasts, while making love with Chris in bed.
• 0:38—Brief breasts, while lying in bed with Chris.

Made for TV Movies:

The Best Little Girl in the World (1981) .... Casey Powell

Girls of the White Orchid (1983) .... Carol Heath
a.k.a. Death Ride to Osaka

The Killing of Randy Webster (1985) .... n.a.

Leigh, Melissa *

Films:

Affairs of the Heart (1992). . . . . Jealous Woman
••• 0:38—Buns, then breasts with the Jealous Man.

Leigh, Summer *

a.k.a. Tamara Ford.

Films:

Femalien (1995) . . . . Wheel Girl
••• 0:52—Full frontal nudity, while strapped to wheel by wrists and ankles during stage show.

Video Tapes:

Hot Body Competition: Bikinis & Bikes Contest (1996) . . . . Summer Leigh
•• 0:39—Breasts and buns, while dancing on stage.
••• 0:40—Nude, while posing on bed outdoors.

Leigh-Hunt, Barbara

Films:

Frenzy (1972; British). . . . . Brenda Blaney
• 0:31—Left breast, while sitting in chair with the necktie killer. Don't see her face.
Henry VIII and His Six Wives (1972; British) . . . . . Catherine Parr
The Nelson Affair (1973) . . . . Catherine Matcham
Oh Heavenly Dog! (1980) . . . . Margaret
Wagner (1983; British) . . . . Queen Mother
Paper Mask (1991; British). . . . . Celia Mumford

Leighton, Roberta

Films:

Barracuda (1978) . . . . Liza Williams
Stripes (1981) . . . . Anita
• 0:07—Breasts, while wearing blue panties, then putting her shirt on and talking to Bill Murray.
Covergirl (1982; Canadian) . . . . Dee Anderson

TV:

General Hospital . . . . Shirley Pickett
The Young and the Restless (1978-86). . . . . Dr. Casey Reed
Days of Our Lives (1991-). . . . . Ginger

• Leitch, Megan

Films:

The Resurrected (1990; British) . . . . Eliza
Knight Moves (1992) . . . . Mother
Misbegotten (1997) . . . . Serena

Made for Cable Movies:

When the Vows Break (1995; Lifetime) . . . . n.a.
Breaking the Surface: The Greg Louganis Story (1997; USA) . . . . Megan

Made for Cable TV:

The Outer Limits: The Vaccine (1998; Showtime) . . . . n.a.
Dead Man's Gun: The Highwayman (1998; Showtime) . . . . Brenda Cosgrove
••• 0:31—Breasts, after her husband opens her nightgown top to prove that she's beautiful.

Made for TV Movies:

Stephen King's "It" (1990) . . . . Library Aide
Omen IV: The Awakening (1991). . . . . . . Sister Yvonne/Felicity
No Child of Mine (1993). . . . . n.a.

TV:

The Sentinel . . . . Kimberly Asche

LeMay, Dorothy

Adult film actress.

Films:

Simply Irresistible (1983) . . . . Hitchhiker
(R-rated version. *Irresistible* is the X-rated version.)
••• 0:09—Nude in office with Walter.

Lemmons, Kasi

Writer/Director.
Wife of actor Vondie Curtis-Hall.

Films:

School Daze (1988). . . . . Perry
Vampire's Kiss (1989). . . . . Jackie
•• 0:05—In black bra and panties, then breasts in living room with Nicolas Cage.
Silence of the Lambs (1990) . . . . Ardelia Mapp
The Five Heartbeats (1991) . . . . Cookie
Candyman (1992). . . . . Bernadette Walsh
Fear of a Black Hat (1992) . . . . Nina Blackburn
Hard Target (1993) . . . . Carmine
Drop Squad (1994) . . . . June
GRIDLOCK'd (1997) . . . . Madonna and Child

Made for Cable Movies:

The Court-Martial of Jackie Robinson (1990) . . . . Rachel
Afterburn (1992; HBO) . . . . Carol

Made for Cable TV:

Zooman (1995; Showtime) . . . . Grace

Made for TV Movies:

The Lakeside Killer (1979) . . . . Hostage

TV:

Under Cover (1991) . . . . Alex Robbins

Lemon, Genevieve

Films:

Sweetie (1989; Australian) . . . . Sweetie
•• 1:23—Breasts in tree house (she's covered with paint).
• 1:25—Brief buns, mooning her dad.
The Piano (1993). . . . . Nessie
Women From Down Under (1995; Australian/New Zealand) . . . . Excursion to the Bridge of Friendship/Grace

Lemper, Ute

Singer.

Films:

Prospero's Books (1991; Dutch/French/Italian). . . . . Ceres
Ready to Wear (1994) . . . . Albertine
a.k.a. Prêt-à-porter
• 2:02—Lower frontal nudity and buns, wearing a veil and carrying flowers, while on runway with the other models. (She's really pregnant.)
• 2:05—Lower frontal nudity while standing with the other models after the "Lo" curtain goes up.
Bogus (1996). . . . . Babette

Made for Cable TV:

Tales From the Crypt: Smoke Wrings (1996; HBO) . . . . Jacqueline Edwards

Lennox, Lisa

Video Tapes:

Hot Body International: #1 Miss Cancun (1990) . . . Contestant
Hot Body International: #2 Miss Puerto Vallarta (1990) . . . . Contestant

Hot Body International: #4 Spring Break (1992) . . . . Contestant
- 0:48—Brief left breast during wet T-shirt contest. Buns in G-string.

Lennox, Natalie *

"Lace" on *American Gladiators.*

Video Tapes:

The Penthouse All-Pet Workout (1993) . . . . Pet
- •• 0:00—Full frontal nudity during introduction.
- •• 0:03—Brief nude shots while getting undressed and suited up.
- ••• 0:35—In sheer white body suit, then nude on rocks and in waterfall.
- ••• 0:43—Nude with the other girls, exercising, working with equipment, in the pool and spa.

BabeWatch, Episode 2: Show Offs (1994) . . . . Natalie
- ••• 0:25—Breasts and buns, while stripping and dancing.

Penthouse Behind the Scenes (1995) . . . . Pet
- ••• 0:00—Nude in various segments throughout the video tape.

CD-ROM:

Penthouse Interactive Virtual Photo Shoot, Disc 1 (1993). . . . . Pet

Lenska, Rula

Films:

Confessions of a Pop Performer (1975; British) . . . Receptionist

Oh, Alfie! (1975; British) . . . . Louise

a.k.a. Alfie Darling
- •• 0:12—Breasts, then left breast in bed after making love with Alfie.

Undercovers Hero (1975) . . . . Grenier Girl

The Deadly Females (1976). . . . . Luisa

TV:

Take a Letter, Mr. Jones (British) . . . . Joan

Lentini, Susan

Films:

Action Jackson (1988). . . . . VW Driver

Roadhouse (1989). . . . . Bandstand Babe

The Runestone (1990). . . . . Wife #1

Ricochet (1991) . . . . Reporter

Demolition Man (1993) . . . . TV Reporter

Jury Duty (1995). . . . . Judge Swartz

Made for Cable Movies:

Love, Cheat & Steal (1993; Showtime) . . . . Nun

Made for Cable TV:

Dream On: Sex and the Single Parent (1990; HBO) . . . . Ms. Susan Brodsky
- •• 0:10—Brief breasts, twice, talking to Martin while he fantasizes about her.

Tales From the Crypt: Dead Right (1990; HBO). . . . . . . Leanne

(Available on *Tales From the Crypt, Volume 3.*)

Lenz, Kay *

Ex-wife of actor/singer David Cassidy.

Films:

Breezy (1974) . . . . Breezy
- •• 0:01—Breasts, while sitting up in bed and putting on blouse.
- •• 0:28—Breasts, undressing in shower while talking with William Holden.
- • 0:58—Breasts, lying back in bed at night with Holden. Brief side of right breast and buns, putting on robe and getting out of bed.
- ••• 1:15—Breasts and buns, undressing in front of Holden in room at night.

White Line Fever (1975) . . . . Jerri Hummer

The Great Scout and Cathouse Thursday (1976) . . . . .Thursday

Mean Dog Blues (1978) . . . . Linda Ramsey

Moving Violation (1979) . . . . Cam Johnson

The Passage (1979; British). . . . . Leah Bergson

Fast Walking (1981). . . . . Moke
- • 0:26—Brief breasts closing the door after pulling James Woods into the room.
- ••• 1:27—Right breast in store. Breasts getting hosed down and dried off outside by James Woods.
- • 1:32—Brief left breast, making love with Woods.

House (1986) . . . . Sandy Sinclair

Death Wish 4: The Crackdown (1987). . . . . Karen Sheldon

Stripped to Kill (1987). . . . . Cody Sheehan
- •• 0:23—Breasts dancing on stage.
- ••• 0:47—Breasts dancing in white lingerie.

Fear (1988) . . . . Sharon Haden

Headhunters (1988) . . . . Katherine Hall

Physical Evidence (1989). . . . . Deborah Quinn

Streets (1989) . . . . Sergeant

Falling From Grace (1992). . . . . P.J. Parks

Trapped in Space (1994) . . . . Gillings

Gunfighter's Moon (1995). Linda Yarzell

A Gun, a Car, a Blonde (1996). . . . . Peep/Madge

Made for Cable Movies:

Hitler's Daughter (1990) . . . . n.a.

Miniseries:

Rich Man, Poor Man (1976) . . . . Kate Jordache

Made for TV Movies:

The Initiation of Sarah (1978) . . . . Sarah

Sanctuary of Fear (1979). . . . . Carol Bain

Against Their Will: Women in Prison (1994). . . . . Lisa

TV:

Rich Man, Poor Man—Book II (1976-77). . . . . . . Kate Jordache

Midnight Caller (1988) . . . . n.a.

Reasonable Doubts (1992-93). . . . . Maggie Zombro

Leo, Melissa

Films:

Always (1984) . . . . Peggy
- • 1:33—Very, brief breasts and buns, jumping over inflatable lounge in pool. Long shot.

Streetwalkin' (1985) . . . . Cookie
- • 0:05—Brief breasts taking off red blouse in front of mirror.
- •• 0:15—Breasts, stripping and taking off her top for a customer.
- • 0:18—Brief right breast, having sex with her pimp on the floor.
- • 0:44—Breasts, taking off her top and sitting on bed with a customer (long shot seen in mirror).
- • 0:53—Buns in body suit, while in hotel room with customer.

A Time of Destiny (1988). . . . . Josie

Venice/Venice (1992). . . . . Peggy

The Ballad of Little Jo (1993) . . . . Mrs. Grey

Miniseries:

Scarlett (1994) . . . . Suellen

Made for TV Movies:

The Bride in Black (1990) . . . . Mary Margaret

In the Line of Duty: Hunt for Justice (1995) . . . . Carol Manning

TV:

All My Children . . . . Linda Warner

Young Riders (1989-90). . . . . Emma Shannon

Homicide: Life on the Street (1993-97) . . . . . .Det. Kay Howard

Leod, Shannon
See: McLeod, Shannon.

• Leonetti, Elisa
Films:
Pure Danger (1995) . . . . Stella
• 0:30—Dancing on stage in bar, then breasts covered with pasties and buns in T-back.
Diary of a Serial Killer (1996) . . . . Wendy

Leong, Page
Films:
White Phantom (1987) . . . . Mai Lin
Rented Lips (1988) . . . . Dancer
The Wizard of Speed & Time (1988) . . . . Dancer
Ghostbusters II (1989). . . . . Spengler's Assistant
Angel Town (1990) . . . . Mr. Park's Connection
Another 48 Hrs. (1990) . . . . Angel Lee
• 1:00—Brief breasts, while getting out of bed with Willie.

Lepage, Monique
Films:
In Praise of Older Women (1978; Canadian)
. . . . The Countess
• 0:03—Breasts and buns in the shower, then talking with a boy.
Paper Wedding (1991; Canadian) . . . . Gaby

Leprince, Catherine
Films:
Bilitis (1977; French) . . . . Helene
•• 0:13—Breasts taking off dress and getting into bed with Bilitis.
Vive Les Femmes (1984) . . . . Viviane
Escalier C (1985; French). . . . . Florence
Paulette (1986; French). Joseph, Female

Lerman, April
Films:
Sorority House Party (1992). . . . . Alex
••• 0:50—Breasts, while making love on bed with Jamie Z.
• 1:00—Right breast, while in bubble bath with Jamie.
TV:
Charles in Charge (1984-85) . . . . Zila Pembroke

LeRoy, Jennifer *
Video Tapes:
Playboy Video Calendar 1994 (1993) . . . . June
••• 0:23—Nude in circus setting.
••• 0:23—Nude outside in bathtub by a shack.
Playboy's Sexy, Steamy, Sultry (1993). . . . . Playmate
Sexy Lingerie V (1993). . . . . Model

• Leslie, Lorelei
Films:
Pulp Fiction (1994) . . . . Mamie Van Doren
Evil Obsession (1996) . . . . Debra
South Beach Academy (1997). Harley
• 1:21—Breasts and partial buns, while making love with Corey Feldman at the beach at night.

Lesniak, Emilia
See: Crow, Emilia.

Lesseos, Mimi *
Films:
The American Angels, Baptism of Blood (1989)
. . . . Magnificent Mimi
The Last Riders (1991) . . . . Feather
• 0:01—Buns, in yellow two piece swimsuit, while walking down the beach.
Pushed to the Limit (1991) . . . . Mimi
Final Impact (1992) . . . . Roxy
Beyond Fear (1993) . . . . Tipper Taylor
Streets of Rage (1993) . . . . Melody Sails
• 0:33—Buns and brief side view of breasts after taking off robe and getting into shower. Breasts, sort of visible behind shower door.

Lester, Eleese
Films:
Cloak and Dagger (1984) . . . . Woman on Boat
Confessions of a Serial Killer (1987) . . . . Karen Grimes
• 0:34—Buns, while gagged and tied to bed before being raped and killed.
Carried Away (1996) . . . . Marie
Made for TV Movies:
Shadows of Desire (1994) . . . . Kerry

Leventon, Annabel
Films:
Think Dirty (1970; British) . . . . Chandler's Secretary
a.k.a. Every Home Should Have One
Come Back Peter (1971; British) . . . . Hippie
Real Life (1984; British) . . . . Carla
Defense of the Realm (1986; British) . . . . Trudy Markham
A Business Affair (1993; British/French) . . . . Literary Guest
M. Butterfly (1993). . . . . Frau Baden
•• 0:50—Breasts, while sitting on bed and talking to Jeremy Irons.

Levin, Rachel
Films:
Gaby, A True Story (1987) . . . . Gaby
• 0:56—Right breast, then breasts on the floor making love with another handicapped boy, Fernando.
White Palace (1990) . . . . Rachel

Levine Thomson, Anna
See: Thomson, Anna.

Lewis, Charlotte *
Films:
The Golden Child (1986). . . . . Kee Nang
Pirates (1986; French) . . . . Dolores
Dial Help (1988) . . . . Jenny Cooper
•• 1:09—Brief right breast while rolling around in the bathtub.
Tripwire (1989) . . . . Trudy
Storyville (1992) . . . . Lee
•• 0:17—Buns, taking off martial arts outfit and getting into hot tub. Brief breasts, sitting down (medium long shot).
• 0:18—Brief upper half of breasts, in hot tub with James Spader.
Excessive Force (1993) . . . . Anna Gilmour
a.k.a. Men of War
••• 0:54—Brief right breast, then breasts while in bed with Thomas Ian Griffith.
Lipstick Camera (1993) . . . . Roberta Dailey

Embrace of the Vampire (1994). . . . . .Sarah
(Unrated version reviewed.)
Men of War (1994). . . . . .Loki
•• 0:44—Breasts, in pond under waterfall, while bathing with the other townspeople.
•• 0:53—Brief breasts, with Dolph Lundgren, outside at night. A bit dark.
Decoy (1995) . . . . .Katya
The Glass Cage (1996). . . . . Jacqueline
••• 0:42—Breasts, while making love in bed with Richard Tyson.
Made for Cable Movies:
Bare Essentials (1991) . . . . .Tarita
• 0:55—Upper half of buns, in G-string swimsuit, while talking to Mark Linn-Baker.
• 0:59—Buns in swimsuit, while giving Linn-Baker a massage. Her long hair gets in the way of her breasts.
• 1:31—Very brief side view of buns in swimsuit, while walking from the ocean onto the beach.
Sketch Artist (1992; Showtime). . . . . .Leese
••• 0:02—Breasts, while making love on sofa. Buns in G-string, side of right breast, while changing CD. (Does this woman have the most awesome waist-to-chest ratio or what?)
Made for Cable TV:
Red Shoe Diaries: Midnight Bells (1993; Showtime)
. . . . The Woman
• 0:10—Lots of cleavage, then brief breasts, while making love with Robert on bed.
•• 0:13—Brief breasts, quite a few times, while making love in nightclub with Robert.
• 0:16—Brief breasts, several times, while in the shower. Out of focus.
• 0:20—Brief breasts, three times, in flashbacks.
TV:
Broken Badges (1990-91) . . . . Priscilla Mather

Lewis, Denice D.

Films:
Necronomicon: Book of the Dead (1993) . . . . Emma DeLapoer
Made for Cable TV:
Red Shoe Diaries: Love at First Sight (1995; Showtime)
. . . . Precious
•• 0:26—Breasts, while on making love on bed with Harry and Cecilia. Many quick cuts.
Red Shoe Diaries: Divorce, Divorce (1996; Showtime). . . . Ester

*Lewis, Fiona **

Films:
The Fearless Vampire Killers (1967) . . . . Maid
Joanna (1968; British) . . . . Miranda De Hyde
Dr. Phibes Rises Again (1972) . . . . Diana
Lisztomania (1975; British). . . . . Countess Marie
•• 0:00—Breasts, while in bed, when Roger Daltrey kisses them to the beat of a metronome.
• 0:01—Brief breasts, while swinging a chandelier to Daltrey.
•• 0:03—Brief breasts and buns, while running from chair (long shot). Brief breasts when catching a candle on the bed.
•• 0:04—Brief left breast when her dress top is cut down. Left breast, while sitting inside a piano with Daltrey.
Drum (1976) . . . . .Augusta Chauvet
••• 0:57—Breasts taking a bath, getting out, then having Pam Grier dry her off.
Tintorera (1977). . . . . Patricia
• 0:20—Brief side view (silhouette) of left breast while in hallway. Breasts and buns, while walking to the ocean (long shot).
•• 0:22—Nude, while swimming under water just before getting eaten by a shark. Don't see her face.
The Fury (1978) . . . . Dr. Susan Charles
Dead Kids (1981; Australian/New Zealand) . . . Gwen Parkinson
a.k.a. Strange Behavior
Strange Invaders (1983) . . . . .Waitress/Avon Lady
Innerspace (1987) . . . . Dr. Margaret Canker
Made for TV Movies:
Dracula (1974) . . . . .Lucy Westerna

Lewis, Juliette

Daughter of actor Geoffrey Lewis.
Films:
My Stepmother Is An Alien (1988). . . . . .Lexie
The Runnin' Kind (1988) . . . . Amy Curtis
Too Young To Die (1990) . . . . .Amanda Sue Bradley
Cape Fear (1991) . . . . Danny Bowden
Crooked Hearts (1991) . . . . Cassie
Husbands and Wives (1992) . . . . Rain
Kalifornia (1993) . . . . Adele Corners
(Unrated version reviewed.)
•• 0:09—Left breast, after opening robe to say "good-bye" to Brad Pitt.
That Night (1993). . . . . Sheryl O'Conner
What's Eating Gilbert Grape (1993). . . . . Becky
Natural Born Killers (1994). . . . . .Mallory
• 0:28—Very, very brief left breast, a few times, in gaping purple slip after climbing on top of Woody Harrelson in bed.
Romeo Is Bleeding (1994) . . . . .Sheri
The Basketball Diaries (1995). . . . . Diane Moody
From Dusk Till Dawn (1995) .Kate Fuller
Strange Days (1995). . . . . Faith Justin
••• 0:15—Breasts, after taking off her top in her apartment with Ralph Fiennes, when he replays an old clip.
• 0:43—Singing on stage in chain top.
• 0:45—Very brief back side of left breast under gaping top when bending over sink, washing herself.
••• 0:46—Breasts, after taking off chain top backstage while talking to Fiennes.
The Evening Star (1996) . . . . .Melanie
TV:
I Married Dora (1987-88) . . . . Kate Farrell
A Family for Joe (1990) . . . . Holly Bankston

Lexington, Lucia

Films:
Fatal Beauty (1987) . . . . .Stripper
Stripped to Kill (1987). . . . . Brandy
•• 0:35—Breasts dancing on stage.

• *Lick, Jacklyn*

Adult film actress.
Adult Films:
Beautiful (1998) . . . . .n.a.
Made for Cable TV:
Beverly Hills Bordello: The Assignment (1998; Showtime)
. . . . Julia
•• 0:03—Breasts and buns, while having sex with a man when Veronica peeks in the room.

Lightstone, Marilyn

Films:

Lies My Father Told Me (1975; Canadian) . . . . . .Annie Herman

In Praise of Older Women (1978; Canadian) . . . . Klari

• 0:45—Left breast, twice, while on floor with Tom Berenger before being discovered by Karen Black.

Spasms (1983; Canadian) . . . . Dr. Rothman

The Surrogate (1984; Canadian) . . . . Dr. Harriet Forman

Iron Eagle IV (1995; Canadian) . . . . Dr. Francis Gully

Made for Cable Movies:

Disaster in Time (1992; Showtime) . . . . Madame Iovine

a.k.a. Timescape

Made for TV Movies:

Anne of Green Gables (1985; Canadian) . . . . Miss Stacey

Lind, Traci

a.k.a. Traci Lin.

Films:

Casanova (1987) . . . . Heidi

• 1:56—Very, very brief right breast while bending over to help Richard Chamberlain. Long, long shot.

My Little Girl (1987) . . . . Alice

Fright Night, Part 2 (1988) . . . . Alex

Moving (1988) . . . . Natalie

A Tiger's Tale (1988) . . . . Penny

Survival Quest (1989) . . . . Olivia

• 0:50—Breasts, while bathing in a stream while seen by Gray. Long shot.

Class of 1999 (1990) . . . . Christine Langford

The Handmaid's Tale (1990) . . . . Ofwarren/Janine

Bugsy (1991) . . . . .Natalie St. Clair

No Secrets (1991) . . . . Sam

Voyager (1991; German/French) . . . . Charlene

Spellcaster (1992) . . . . Yvette

My Boyfriend's Back (1993) . . . . Missy McCloud

Model By Day (1994) . . . . Jae Davis

(Shown on network TV without the nudity.)

The Road to Wellville (1994) . . . . Nurse Irene Graves

•• 0:15—Buns and side of left breast in elevator in Matthew Broderick's fantasy.

The End of Violence (1997; French/German/U.S.) . . . . Cat

TV:

Ryan's Hope . . . . Pru Shepherd

Lindemulder, Janine *

Started doing adult films in 1992. First adult film is *Hidden Obsessions.*

Adult Films:

Hidden Obsessions (1993) . . . . Various Parts

Films:

Spring Fever USA (1988) . . . . Heather Lipton

a.k.a. Lauderdale

•• 0:14—Taking off her stockings, then brief breasts undressing for bath, then taking a bath.

Caged Fury (1989) . . . . Lulu

• 0:15—Brief breasts dancing in front of Erik Estrada.

Killer Looks (1994) . . . . Angela

(Unrated version reviewed.)

••• 1:12—In white lingerie, then breasts while making out with Lené Hefner and Mickey's lover.

•• 1:18—Breasts, while sunbathing outside by pool with Hefner.

•• 1:23—Breasts while making out on stairway with Hefner and Sara Suzanne Brown.

Lady in Waiting (1994) . . . . Sharon Masters

(Unrated version reviewed.)

•• 0:00—Full frontal nudity, undressing in bedroom with Scott, then on bed.

The Price of Desire (1996) . . . . Lydia

• 0:35—Brief buns and left breast, while having sex with Stephanie Swift in restroom.

• 1:00—Partial breasts in open bra, while trying to seduce Kira Reed in restroom.

•• 1:32—Breasts, while making love outdoors with Kira Reed and Sinclair.

• 1:34—Full frontal nudity, when opening her robe at night and sitting next to spa.

Private Parts (1997) . . . . Camp Director's Wife

Video Tapes:

Penthouse Passport to Paradise/Hawaii (1991) . . . Model

••• 0:37—Stripping out of a dress and lingerie, then nude dancing during her fantasy.

Penthouse Ready to Ride (1992) . . . . Model

Penthouse Satin & Lace II: Hollywood Undercover (1992) . . . . Pet

Penthouse Satin & Lace: An Erotic History of Lingerie (1992) . . . . Model

The Girls of Penthouse, Volume 2 (1993) . . . . Pet

••• 0:20—Nude in a pool, working out and in bed.

Penthouse DreamGirls (1994) . . . . Janine

••• 0:23—Nude, with space/alien style silver body paint and costume.

Penthouse Women In & Out of Uniform (1995) . . . . . Pet

••• 0:33—Nude as a firewoman, playing around with gushing hoses with Julia Ann.

••• 0:38—Nude as a policewoman with Tiffany Burlingame and Julia Ann in squad room.

••• 0:41—Nude as a lawyer, in courthouse with Burlingame and Julia Ann.

••• 0:45—Nude, as a police detective, when interrogating a guy while he's handcuffed in a chair.

CD-ROM:

Penthouse Interactive Virtual Photo Shoot, Disc 3 (1993) . . . . Pet

Linden, Jennie

Films:

Nightmare (1963; British) . . . . Janet

Dr. Who and the Daleks (1965; British) . . . . Barbara

A Severed Head (1971; British) . . . . Georgie Hands

• 0:02—Buns, while rolling over on the floor with Ian Holm.

Women in Love (1971) . . . . Ursula Bragwen

• 0:38—Brief breasts skinny dipping in the river with Glenda Jackson.

• 1:11—Brief breasts in a field with Alan Bates. Scene is shown sideways.

Hedda (1975; British) . . . . Mrs. Elvsted

Old Dracula (1975; British) . . . . Angela

Valentino (1977; British) . . . . Agnes Ayres

A Deadly Game (1979; British) . . . . Edith

Lindley, Gisele

Films:

Forbidden Zone (1980) . . . . The Princess

••• 0:21—Breasts, while in jail cell.

••• 0:39—Breasts, while turning a table around.

•• 0:45—Breasts, while bending over, making love with a frog.

•• 0:51—Breasts, while in a cave.

•• 0:53—More breast scenes.

•• 1:06—Even more breast scenes.
S.O.B. (1981) . . . . n.a.

Lindsay, Amy

Films:

The Dark Dancer (1994) . . . . Teenage Margaret
• 0:08—Partial breasts behind plastic curtain, medium long shot, seen from outside. Silhouette of left breast in the shower. Brief breasts, under robe in bedroom.
• 0:09—Very brief left breast under robe when standing up.
•• 0:13—Very brief right breast, then breasts on bed, while in bedroom at night with Ramone.
The House on Todville Road (1994). . . . . Isadora

Made for Cable TV:

Women: Stories of Passion-Lover From Another Planet (1997; Showtime). . . . . Jenny
••• 0:02—In bra, then breasts, while making love with Billy in back seat of car.
•• 0:17—Breasts and buns, while making love with the alien guy and also in flashback with Billy.
••• 0:19—In bra, then breasts, while making love with the alien guy disguised as Billy and afterward.

• Lindsley, Blake

Films:

Getting In (1994) . . . . Tina
The Glimmer Man (1996) . . . . School Teacher
Starship Troopers (1996) . . . . Katrina
• 0:28—Brief side of left breast, five times, while in the co-ed showers.
• 0:30—Very brief buns, when mooning the camera next to Shujimi.
Swingers (1996) . . . . Girl with Cigar

Ling, Bai

Films:

The Crow (1993). . . . . Myca
• 0:23—Buns, while taking a shower.
Dead Funny (1994). . . . . Norriko
Red Corner (1997) . . . . Shen Yuelin

Made for Cable Movies:

Dead Weekend (1995; Showtime). . . . . Amelia A

Linn, Teri Ann

Films:

Aloha Summer (1988). . . . . Mary Jean
Pure Danger (1995) . . . . Becky
• 1:06—Brief partial buns, while in bed with C. Thomas Howell.

TV:

The Bold and the Beautiful (1987-90) . . . . Kristen Forrester
The Bold and the Beautiful (1992-94) . . . . Kristen Forrester

Linnane, Teresa *

Video Tapes:

Playboy International Playmates (1993) . . . . Teresa
••• 0:28—Full frontal nudity in still photos. Nude, taking off swimsuit and in pool.
••• 0:30—Nude, walking around the woods with Kelly. Her body is partially painted with spots.

Linné, Jeanette

Films:

The Beach Girls (1982) . . . . Redhead
•• 0:38—Brief breasts, while walking around the house.
Scarface (1983). . . . . Woman at the Babylon Club

Linssen, Saskia *

Video Tapes:

Playboy's Playmate Review 1992 (1992) . . . . . . Miss June
••• 0:27—Nude doing futuristic dance and then taking a bath.
Playboy's Sexy, Steamy, Sultry (1993). . . . . Playmate

Lippa, Christine

Films:

Just One of the Girls (1992). . . . . Cashier
a.k.a. Anything For Love
Intersection (1993) . . . . Step Magazine
Tomcat: Dangerous Desires (1993) . . . . Randi
• 0:56—Buns, while lying on bed and talking to Richard Grieco.

Made for Cable TV:

The Outer Limits: White Light Fever (1995; Showtime) . . . . Nurse Hendricks

Liszewski, Janie

Films:

Princess Warrior (1990). . . . . Wet T-Shirt Girl
• 0:10—Buns in swimsuits during contest.
From Dusk Till Dawn (1995) . . . . Bar Dancer

Little, Michele

Films:

Out of the Blue (1982) . . . . Girl in Car
Radioactive Dreams (1984) . . . . Rusty Mars
My Demon Lover (1987). . . . . Denny
Out of Bounds (1987) . . . . Crystal
Sweet Revenge (1987). . . . . Lee
• 0:41—Brief breasts in water under a waterfall with K.C.
Appointment with Fear (1988) . . . . Carol
Blood Clan (1990). . . . . Katy Bane
Mystery Date (1991) . . . . Stella
Apollo 13 (1995). . . . . Jane Conrad

Littlefeather, Sacheen *

At the 1973 Academy Awards, she announced Marlon Brando's rejection of Best Actor Award.

Films:

Freebie and the Bean (1974) . . . . n.a.
The Laughing Policeman (1974) . . . . n.a.
The Trial of Billy Jack (1974). . . . . Patsy Littlejohn
Johnny Firecloud (1975) . . . . Nenya
••• 0:55—Breasts, getting raped by jerks on desk in classroom.
Winterhawk (1976) . . . . Paleflower
Shoot the Sun Down (1981) . . . . n.a.

Liu, Carolyn *

Films:

Do or Die (1991) . . . . Silk
••• 0:14—Breasts, getting up off massage table and putting robe on.
•• 1:04—Breasts in bed with Pat Morita.
Fit To Kill (1993). . . . . Silk
• 0:09—Buns in body suit, while in room with Kane.
•• 0:11—Breasts while making love in bed with Kane.
••• 0:46—Breasts, while taking off lingerie on boat with Kane.
Hard Hunted (1993). . . . . Silk
• 0:02—Buns, while in lingerie on boat with Mr. Kane.
••• 0:08—Breasts, while taking off her dress top on boat in front of Mr. Kane, then in bed with him.
• 0:10—Brief breasts, while lying in bed when the plastic explosive on the safe blows up.

Video Tapes:
Sexy Lingerie III (1991) . . . . Model
Penthouse Satin & Lace: An Erotic History of Lingerie (1992). . . . . Model

• Liu, Lucy Alexis

Films:
Jerry Maguire (1996). . . . . Former Girlfriend
City of Industry (1997) .Cathi Rose
•• 0:48—Brief breasts and buns, while dancing in club.
GRIDLOCK'd (1997) . . . . Cee-Cee
Made for Cable Movies:
Riot (1997; Showtime) . . . . .Tiffany
TV:
Pearl (1996) . . . . n.a.

Lizer, Kari

Films:
Smokey Bites the Dust (1981) . . . . Cindy
Private School (1983) . . . . Rita
• 0:30—Very brief left breast popping out of cheerleader's outfit along with the Coach.
Gotcha! (1985) . . . . Muffy
Made for Cable Movies:
Breast Men (1997; HBO) . . . . Female Interviewer
Made for Cable TV:
Dream On: A Midsummer Night's Dream On (1993; HBO) . . . . Becca
Made for TV Movies:
Double Edge (1992) . . . . Sister Theresa
TV:
Matlock (1987-88) . . . . Cassie Phillips
Sunday Dinner (1991). . . . . Diana

Llinas, Veronica

Films:
The Plague (1992; French/British). . . . . Strip Teaser
• 1:22—Very brief side of right breast and side of buns. Long shot.
•• 1:26—Breasts, while on stage with a rat. Closer shot.
I Don't Want to Talk About It (1994) . . . . .Myrna
a.k.a. De Eso No Se Habla

Lloyd, Emily

Films:
Wish You Were Here (1987) . . . . Lynda
• 0:43—Buns, while singing in the alley and lifting up her skirt to moon an older neighbor woman.
Chicago Joe and the Showgirl (1989; British) . . . . . Betty Jones
Cookie (1989). . . . . Carmella "Cookie" Voltecki
In Country (1989). . . . . .Samantha Hughes
A River Runs Through It (1992) . . . . Jessie Burns
Scorchers (1992). . . . . Splendid
Under the Hula Moon (1995) . . . . Betty Wall
Made for Cable TV:
Strangers: Costumes (1996; HBO). . . . . Jennie

Lloyd, Sue

Films:
Happy Housewives (1975; British). . . . . The Blonde
Revenge of the Pink Panther (1978) . . . . Claude Russo/Claudine Russo
The Stud (1978; British). . . . . .Vanessa
• 1:04—Breasts in the swimming pool with Joan Collins and Tony.
The Bitch (1979; British) . . . . .Vanessa Grant
• 1:12—Side view of left breast and breasts in the swimming pool.
Rough Cut (1980; British) . . . . Female Guest

Locane, Amy

Films:
Lost Angels (1989). . . . . .Cheryl Anderson
Cry Baby (1990) . . . . .Allison
Blue Sky (1991) . . . . Alex Marshall
No Secrets (1991) . . . . .Jennifer
School Ties (1992). . . . . Sally Wheeler
Airheads (1994) . . . . Kayla
• 0:35—Brief buns in T-back swimsuit in photo that Brendan Fraser hands to Ernie Hudson.
Criminal Hearts (1995) . . . . Kell
Carried Away (1996) . . . . Catherline Wheeler
••• 0:24—Breasts, after taking off her sweater while in loft in barn with Dennis Hopper.
••• 0:25—Breasts, when Hopper returns to the loft.
•• 0:37—Breasts and buns, while riding a horse in barn. Some long shots, some closer shots.
• 0:46—Left breast in open dress while standing behind truck in the road to tempt Hopper.
••• 0:47—Left breast, while making love in loft in barn with Hopper.
•• 0:56—Breasts, after sitting up in barn after being discovered with Hopper by Hal Holbrook. Almost partial lower frontal nudity.
••• 1:18—Nude, in bedroom with Hopper.
Bram Stoker's The Mummy (1997) .n.a.
The Girl Gets Moe (1997) . . . . Beth
Made for Cable Movies:
End of Summer (1995; Showtime) . . . . Alice
••• 0:37—Breasts, while making love in barn with Peter Weller.
TV:
Spencer: For Hire (1985) . . . . Andrea Winger
Melrose Place (1992). . . . . Sandy Louise Harding

Locke, Sondra

Films:
The Heart is a Lonely Hunter (1968) . . . . Mick Kelley
Willard (1971) . . . . Joan
Suzanne (1973) . . . . Suzanne
a.k.a. The Second Coming of Suzanne
(*Suzanne* has nudity in it, *The Second Coming of Suzanne* has the nudity cut out.)
•• 0:27—Breasts sitting, looking at a guy. Brief left breast several times lying down.
••• 0:29—Breasts lying down.
The Outlaw Josey Wales (1976) . . . . Laura Lee
•• 1:20—Briefly nude in rape scene.
Death Game, The Seducers (1977). . . . . Jackson
a.k.a. Mrs. Manning's Weekend
• 0:16—Buns and brief right breast in spa with Colleen Camp trying to get George in with them.
• 0:48—Brief breasts running around the room trying to keep George away from the telephone.
The Gauntlet (1977). . . . . Gus Mally
•• 1:10—Brief right breast, then breasts getting raped by two biker guys in a box car while Clint Eastwood is tied up.
Every Which Way But Loose (1978) . . . . Lynn Halsey Taylor
Any Which Way You Can (1980) . . . . Lynne
Bronco Billy (1980) . . . . Antoinette
Sudden Impact (1983). Jennifer Spencer
Ratboy (1986) . . . . Nikki Morrison

Made for TV Movies:
Rosie: The Rosemary Clooney Story (1982) . . . . Rosemary Clooney

*Lockhart, Anne **
Daughter of actress June Lockhart.
Granddaughter of actor Gene Lockhart.
Films:
Joyride (1977) . . . . Cindy
•• 0:59—Brief breasts in the spa with everybody.
••• 1:00—Breasts, standing in the kitchen kissing Desi Arnaz Jr.
The Young Warriors (1983; U.S./Canadian) . . . . Lucy
•• 0:42—Breasts and buns making love with Kevin on the bed. Looks like a body double.
Troll (1986) . . . . Young Eunice St. Clair
Dark Tower (1987) . . . . Elaine
Big Bad John (1989) . . . . Lady Police Officer
Made for TV Movies:
Just Tell Me You Love Me (1978) . . . . Kris
TV:
Battlestar Galactica (1979) . . . . Sheeba

Locklin, Loryn
Films:
Catch Me... If You Can (1989) . . . . Melissa
• 1:32—In bra trying to get policeman's attention. Very, very brief side of right breast while turning around. Looks like she's wearing flesh-colored pasties.
Taking Care of Business (1990) . . . . Jewel
• 0:42—Buns and very brief side view, twice, seen through door, changing by the pool. Then in black two piece swimsuit.
Fortress (1993; U.S./Australian) . . . . Karen Brennick
• 0:18—Lower half of buns, under lingerie while making love on top of Christopher Lambert in bed.
Made for TV Movies:
Shoot First: A Cop's Vengeance (1991) . . . . Lea
Abducted: A Father's Love (1996) . . . . Andrea

Logan, Phyllis
Films:
Another Time, Another Place (1983; British) . . . . Janie
••• 0:31—Breasts, washing herself off after working in the fields. Nice close-up shot.
•• 0:53—Full frontal nudity, after undressing then getting into bed.
••• 1:08—Breasts in front of a group of men.
The Chain (1985; British) . . . . Alison
The Doctor and the Devils (1985) . . . . Elizabeth Rock
The McGuffin (1985; British) . . . . Anne
The Inquiry (1986; Italian) . . . . n.a.
The Kitchen Toto (1987; British) . . . . Janet Graham
Soft Top, Hard Shoulder (1992; British) . . . . Karla
Secrets & Lies (1996; British) . . . . Monica
Made for TV Movies:
Silent Cries (1993) . . . . Nancy Muir

Lomas, Caroline
Films:
Nudity Required (1989) . . . . Caroline
•• 0:36—Brief breasts (fifth girl) standing in line.
•• 0:37—Breasts doing puppet routine for audition.
•• 0:38—Breasts while yelling for not having a script.
• 0:39—Breasts.
• 0:44—Breasts while sitting on the edge of the pool.
Society (1989) . . . . Extra

*Lombard, Karina **
Model.
Films:
The Doors (1991) . . . . Warhol Actress
The Firm (1993) . . . . Woman On Beach
Wide Sargasso Sea (1993) . . . . Antoinette
(Unrated version reviewed.)
••• 0:31—Buns and breasts, with her new husband, Rochester.
•• 0:37—Breasts and partial frontal nudity while making love in bedroom with Rochester.
•• 0:42—Buns and partial breasts, in wet white clothes. Left breast and buns while in bed with Rochester.
••• 0:52—Breasts while in bed before making love and after.
• 0:55—Right breast, while sitting in bed.
• 1:13—Breasts, while sitting in bed.
Legends of the Fall (1994) . . . . Isabel Two
• 1:35—Brief left breast, while lying in bed with Brad Pitt after getting married.
• 1:36—Brief partial right breast, while lying in bed with her baby and Pitt.
Last Man Standing (1996) . . . . Felina
• 1:00—Very brief left breast, then brief partial breasts, while burning some paper in her room.
Kull the Conqueror (1997) . . . . Zareta

Lombardi, Leigh
Films:
The Wild Life (1984) . . . . Stewardess
Murphy's Law (1986) . . . . Stewardess
A Tiger's Tale (1988) . . . . Marcia
Moontrap (1989) . . . . Mera
•• 1:08—Breasts with Walter Koenig in moon tent.

Lomez, Céline
Films:
The Far Shore (1976) . . . . Eulalia Turner
Plague (1978; Canadian) . . . . Margo Simar
a.k.a. The Gemini Strain
The Silent Partner (1978) . . . . Elaine
• 1:05—Side view of left breast, then breasts, then buns with Elliott Gould.
The Kiss (1988) . . . . Aunt Irene

London, Lisa
Films:
H.O.T.S. (1979) . . . . Jennie O'Hara
a.k.a. T & A Academy
• 1:22—Breasts changing clothes by the closet while a crook watches her.
• 1:33—Breasts playing football.
The Happy Hooker Goes Hollywood (1980) . . . . Laurie
Sudden Impact (1983) . . . . Young Hooker
•• 1:04—Breasts in bathroom, walking to Nick in the bed.
The Naked Cage (1985) . . . . Abbey
•• 0:22—Breasts in S&M costume with Angel Tompkins.
•• 0:38—Left breast making out in bed with Angel Tompkins.
Private Resort (1985) . . . . Alice
Black Moon Rising (1986) . . . . Redhead
Dragnet (1987) . . . . 1982 Redhead
Savage Beach (1989) . . . . Rocky
• 0:06—Breasts in spa with Patty Duffek, Dona Speir and Hope Marie Carlton.
•• 0:50—Breasts changing clothes.
Guns (1990) . . . . Rocky

I Will Dance on Your Grave: Lethal Victims (1992) .... Jody Bower
- 0:01—Very, very brief right breast, after getting raped by two guys at the beach.

Death Match (1994) .... Big Man's Girlfriend
Xtro: Watch the Skies (1995)................ Melissa Meed

Made for Cable Movies:
Prey of the Chameleon (1992; Showtime)............. Alice

Made for Cable TV:
Dream On: The Charlotte Letter (1991; HBO) .... Candy Striper #2
- 0:06—Breasts several times, acting in adult film that Martin is watching on TV. (She's first to take her outfit off.)

Video Tapes:
Inside Out 2 (1992) .... June/The Right Number
(Unrated version reviewed.)
- •• 1:25—Breasts, lying on the floor having phone sex and in bed.
- •• 1:28—More breasts talking on the phone.

Long, Kathy

Films:
Knights (1992) .... Nea
Rage and Honor (1992)........................... Fros-T
The Stranger (1994)...................... The Stranger
- •• 1:14—Buns and breasts, while making love on bed with Eric Pierpoint.

Romy and Michele's High School Reunion (1997) .... Kick Boxing Instructor

Long, Nia

Films:
Edgar Allan Poe's "Buried Alive" (1989)............. Fingers
Boyz N the Hood (1991) .... Brandi
- 1:17—Left breast, while in bed with Cuba Gooding Jr. Don't see her face, but it is her.

Made in America (1993) .... Zora Mathews
Love Jones (1996)....................... Nina Mosley
- •• 0:31—Brief breasts, several times while making love in bed with Larnez Tate.

Butter (1997) .... Carmen Jones

TV:
The Fresh Prince of Bel-Air .... Lisa Wilkes
The Guiding Light (1991-94)................. Kat Speakes

Long, Shannon *

Video Tapes:
Playboy Video Calendar 1990 (1989) .... November
- ••• 0:57—Nude.

Playboy's 21 Playmates (1996)............... Playmate
- ••• 0:52—Full frontal nudity in still photos.
- ••• 0:53—Nude in swimming pool and in the house.

Long, Shelley

Films:
A Small Circle of Friends (1980)..................... Alice
Caveman (1981)................................... Tala
Losin' It (1982) .... Kathy
Night Shift (1982)...................... Belinda Keaton
Irreconcilable Differences (1984)..... Lucy Van Patten Brodsky
The Money Pit (1986)................... Anna Crowley
Hello Again! (1987) .... Lucy Chadman
- 0:58—Brief buns, in hospital gown, walking down hallway.

Outrageous Fortune (1987)................ Lauren Ames
Troop Beverly Hills (1989).................. Phyllis Nefler
Don't Tell Her It's Me (1990) .... Lizzie Potts
Frozen Assets (1992) .... Dr. Grace Murdock
The Brady Bunch Movie (1994)................ Carol Brady
A Very Brady Sequel (1996).................. Carol Brady

Made for Cable TV:
Sex, Shock and Censorship in the 90's (1993; Showtime) .... Fay Sommerfield

Made for TV Movies:
Fatal Memories (1992)............... Eileen Franklin Lipsker
A Message From Holly (1992) .... Kate Barnes
Freaky Friday (1995) .... Ellen Andrews
The Women of Spring Break (1995).................. Anne

TV:
Cheers (1982-87) .... Diane Chambers
Good Advice (1993-95).................. Susan DeRuzza
Kelly Kelly (1998-) .... Kelly Novak

• Longwell, Anya

Films:
Mobsters (1991) .... Showgirl
a.k.a. Mobsters—The Evil Empire
Death Becomes Her (1992) .... Chagall Receptionist
Scorned (1993) .... The Woman

Made for Cable TV:
Red Shoe Diaries: Temple of Flesh (1997; Showtime) .... Ruth O'Hara
- 0:02—Briefly nude, while making love with Jonathan.
- •• 0:22—Brief buns in T-back, then brief breasts, while dancing in a synagogue. B&W.

Lopert, Tanya

Films:
What's New, Pussycat? (1965; U.S./French)....... Miss Lewis
Fellini Satyricon (1969; French/Italian).............. Caesar
Providence (1977; French/Swiss)................ Miss Lister
Tales of Ordinary Madness (1983; Italian) .... Vicky
- 0:58—Buns, then breasts in bedroom with Pepito and Ben Gazzara.

A Man and a Woman: 20 Years Later (1986; French) . . . Herself
Petit Con (1986; French)..................... Psychiatrist
Wait Until Spring, Bandini (1989; Belgian/French/Italian) .... Sister Celia

Lopez, Jennifer

Films:
Money Train (1995) .... Grace Santiago
- 0:54—Very brief left breast, twice, then partial right breast, then very brief left breast when Wesley Snipes cups it. Intercut with Woody Harrelson getting beat up.

My Family (1995) .... Young Maria
Jack (1996) .... Miss Marquez
Anaconda (1997)......................... Terri Flores
Blood & Wine (1997)......................... Gabriela
Selena (1997) .... Selena Quintanilla
U Turn (1997) .... Grace McKenna
- 1:46—Very brief left breast, twice, while making love with Nick Nolte during flashback montage.

Out of Sight (1998)....................... Karen Sisco

Made for TV Movies:
Nurses on the Line: The Crash of Flight 7 (1993) .... Rosie Romero

TV:
In Living Color (1991)........................ Fly Girl
Second Chances (1993-94) .... Melinda Lopez
Hotel Malibu (1994) .... Melinda Lopez
South Central (1994-95) .... Lucille

Lopez, Maria Isabel

a.k.a. Isabel Lopez.

Films:

Joy: Chapter II (1985; French) .... Milaka

a.k.a. Joy and Joan

•• 0:10—Breasts, showing Joy her breasts at Bruce's request.

••• 0:27—Breasts, taking off her robe and massaging Joy.

Silip (1985; Philippines)........................... Tonya

a.k.a. Daughters of Eve

Mission Manila (1989).......................... Jessie

• 0:22—Brief right breast several times in bed while Harry threatens her with knife.

Dune Warriors (1990) .... Miranda

•• 0:25—Breasts in underground lake with Val.

••• 0:43—Breasts making love with a guy in bed.

• *Lopez, Mercy **

Video Tapes:

Playboy's Sex on the Beach: Tropical Heat (1997) .... Sun Charter/Mercy

••• 0:01—Nude on sailboat with two other women, then in the water by herself.

*Lords, Traci **

Infamous under age adult film actress. Unfortunately, all of the adult films she was in before she was 18 years old are now illegal. The only legal adult film she did is *Traci, I Love You.*

Real name is Nora Louise Kuzma.

Films:

Not of This Earth (1988)...................... Nadine

•• 0:25—Buns and side view of left breast drying herself off with a towel while talking to Jeremy.

•• 0:42—Breasts in bed making love with Harry.

Fast Food (1989)............................ Dixie Love

Cry Baby (1990) .... Wanda

Shock 'Em Dead (1990) .... Lindsay Roberts

Desperate Crimes (1991; Italian).................... Laura

Laser Moon (1991) .... Barbara Fleck

Raw Nerve (1991).......................... Gina Clayton

A Time to Die (1991) .... Jackie

Intent to Kill (1992)...................... Vickie Stewart

The Nutt House (1992)...................... Miss Tress

0:31—In lingerie outfit in bedroom with Philbert, then Nathan.

Circuitry Man II: Plughead Rewired (1993) .... Norma

Ice (1993).................................. Ellen Reed

Serial Mom (1993) .... Carl's Date

Skinner (1993) .... Heidi

Virtuosity (1995)..................... Media Zone Singer

Underworld (1996)............................. Anna

Extramarital (1998)......................... Elizabeth

Made for Cable Movies:

Rebel Highway: Dragstrip Girl (1994; Showtime) ..... Blanche

As Good As Dead (1995; USA) .... Nikki

Made for Cable TV:

Tales From the Crypt: Two for the Show (1993; HBO) .... Emma Conway

Made for TV Movies:

The Tommyknockers (1993) .... Nanci

Bandit: Bandit and the Silver Angel (1994) .... Angel

TV:

Melrose Place (1994) .... Rikki

Video Tapes:

Red Hot Rock (1984) .... Miss Georgia

a.k.a. Sexy Shorts (on laser disc)

•• 0:41—Breasts several times in open-front swimsuit during beauty pageant during "Gimme Gimme Good Lovin'" by Helix.

•• 0:42—Breasts on stage wearing black outfit with mask, smashing a large avocado during the same song.

Warm Up with Traci Lords (1989) .... Herself

Brinke Stevens Private Collection Volume 2 (1994) .... Miss Georgia

• 0:05—Breasts in music video by Helix from *Red Hot Rock.*

*Loren, Sophia **

Films:

Era Lui, Si, Si (1952).............................. n.a.

Two Nights with Cleopatra (1954; Italian).... Cleopatra/Nisca

(It seems that her nude scenes have been cut for the video tape version.)

Boy on a Dolphin (1957)....................... Phaedra

The Pride and the Passion (1957) .... Juana

Desire Under the Elms (1958) .... Anna Cabot

Houseboat (1958)....................... Cinzia Zaccardi

A Breath of Scandal (1960) .... Princess Olympia

Heller in Pink Tights (1960)................ Angela Rossini

Two Women (1960; Italian)....................... Cesira

(Academy Award for Best Actress.)

El Cid (1961; U.S./Italian) .... Chimene

Boccaccio 70 (1962; Italian) .... Zoe

The Fall of the Roman Empire (1964) .... Lucilla

Yesterday, Today and Tomorrow (1964; Italian)....... Adelina

Arabesque (1966) .... Yasmin Azir

Man of La Mancha (1972)............... Dulcinea/Aldonza

Angela (1977; Canadian)......................... Angela

The Cassandra Crossing (1977; British) .... Jennifer

A Special Day (1977)......................... Antonietta

Brass Target (1978) .... Mara

Blood Feud (1979; Italian)......................... n.a.

Firepower (1979)........................... Adele Tasca

Ready to Wear (1994) .... Isabella de la Fontaine

a.k.a. Prêt-à-porter

Grumpier Old Men (1995) .... Maria Ragetti

Lorenz, Veronica

Films:

Flinch (1992)............................... Jasmine

••• 0:07—Nude in background, while undressing and posing as a model.

•• 0:20—Full frontal nudity while posing some more in studio.

Made for TV Movies:

Born to Run (1993) .... Bride

*Loring, Jeana **

Films:

The Malibu Bikini Shop (1985).............. Margie Hill

•• 0:43—Breasts, dancing on stage during bikini contest (Contestant #4).

Loring, Lisa

Ex-wife of adult film actor Jerry Butler.

Films:

Blood Frenzy (1987) .... Dory

Iced (1988)................................ Jeanette

• 0:46—Brief left breast in bathtub.

• 0:53—Buns and brief right breast in bathtub with Alex.

•• 1:05—Brief lower frontal nudity and buns, while getting into hot tub. Breasts in hot tub just before getting electrocuted.
•• 1:13—Full frontal nudity lying dead in the hot tub.
• 1:18—Brief full frontal nudity lying dead in the hot tub again.

Death Feud (1989) .... Roxey

TV:

The Addams Family (1964-66) . .Wednesday Thursday Addams
As the World Turns (1981-83) .... Cricket Montgomery

• *Lorraine, Bethany* *

Video Tapes:

Playboy's Hot Wheels & High Heels Biker Babes (1997) .... Navy Seals/Agent 96
••• 0:03—Nude on boat with a brunette woman and a guy.

Playboy's Women Behaving Badly (1997) .... Ladies Night
••• 0:17—In lingerie, then nude, while dancing on stage in women's club after dancing with male stripper.

Lorraine, Nita

Films:

The Viking Queen (1967; British).......... Nubian Girl-Slave
All Neat in Black Stockings (1969).................. Jolasta
Happy Housewives (1975; British)........... Jenny Elgin
• 0:31—Brief side view of left breast and buns in barn chasing after Bob.
• 0:32—Brief breasts in open dress talking to policeman.

Louise, Helli

Films:

Confessions of a Pop Performer (1975; British) .... Eva
Happy Housewives (1975; British) . . . Newsagent's Daughter
•• 0:16—Breasts with Mrs. Wain and Bob in the bathtub.

Louise, Jeanine

Made for Cable Movies:

Soft Touch (1987; Playboy)............. Carrie Crawford
(Shown on *The Playboy Channel* as *Birds in Paradise.*)
• 0:00—Breasts during opening credits.
• 0:02—Breasts with her two girlfriends during the opening credits.
• 0:03—Brief breasts getting out of the shower.
• 0:17—Breasts seen in mirror, while taking a shower.
•• 0:19—Full frontal nudity during pillow fight on bed.
•• 0:23—Breasts in bed with the other two girls.
• 0:27—Breasts in T-shirt, leaning over to wash car.
• 0:32—Breasts with Neill in open dress.
••• 0:35—Dancing on stage in red lingerie, then breasts and buns in G-string.
•• 0:41—Full frontal nudity walking in water with a guy.
••• 0:50—Breasts sunbathing on the boat with Tracy.
• 1:01—Nude, swinging into water. Long shot.
• 1:02—Buns, waving to a dolphin.
• 1:04—Breasts at night by campfire with Tracy.
• 1:05—Brief left breast, while sleeping.
• 1:06—Breasts when Tracy wakes her up.
• 1:19—Breasts in stills during the end credits.

Soft Touch II (1987; Playboy) .... Carrie Crawford
(Shown on *The Playboy Channel* as *Birds in Paradise.*)
• 0:00—Breasts during opening credits.
• 0:02—Breasts with her two girlfriends during opening credits.
•• 0:24—Breasts in bed feeling herself.
•• 0:41—Full frontal nudity undressing and putting swimsuit on.
• 0:51—Breasts with her diving instructor.

Louise, Tina

Films:

God's Little Acre (1958)........................ Griselda
How To Commit Marriage (1969) .... LaVerne Baker
The Wrecking Crew (1969) .... Lola Medina
The Stepford Wives (1975) .... Charmaine
Mean Dog Blues (1978) .... Donna Lacey
• 1:16—Very brief side view of right breast, while getting up off massage table. Don't see her face very well.

Dog Day (1984; French) .... Noemie Blue
Evils of the Night (1985) .... Cora
Dixie Lanes (1987)............................... Violet
O.C. and Stiggs (1987) .... Florence Beaugereaux
Johnny Suede (1992)...................... Mrs. Fontaine

Made for TV Movies:

Nightmare in Badham County (1976) .... Greer
(Nudity added for video tape.)

TV:

Gilligan's Island (1964-67).................. Ginger Grant
Dallas (1978)................................ Julie Grey
Rituals (1984-85)............ Taylor Chapin Field Von Platen

• *Love, Courtney* *

Singer.
Wife of the late Nirvana band member Kurt Cobain.

Films:

Sid and Nancy (1986; British) .... Gretchen
Straight to Hell (1987; British)...................... Velma
Basquiat (1996)............................. Big Pink
Feeling Minnesota (1996) .... Waitress
The People vs. Larry Flynt (1996)......... Althea Leasure
• 0:09—Very brief right breast when pulling up her blouse while dancing on stage.
•• 0:24—Buns and breasts, getting into spa with two other girls.
•• 0:45—Brief breasts, while posing for photos.
• 1:20—Left breast in sheer bra, when waking up in bed.
• 1:44—Brief breasts under sheer net part of outfit.
• 1:49—Full frontal nudity, lying dead under water after drowning in bathtub. Brief left breast when cradled by Woody Harrelson.
•• 2:04—Breasts on television when Harrelson reminisces and watches old video tape.

Love, Lucretia

Films:

Battle of the Amazons (1973; Italian/Spanish) .... Eraglia
Naked Warriors (1973) .... Deidre
a.k.a. The Arena
• 0:07—Brief breasts, while getting clothes torn off by guards.
•• 0:08—Briefly nude, while getting washed down in court yard.
• 1:08—Brief buns, while bent over riding a horse.

The Tormented (1978; Italian)...................... n.a.
Dr. Heckyl and Mr. Hype (1980) .... Debra Kate
Affair (1984; French/Italian)..................... Helen
••• 0:33—In black bra when on couch with Mark, then breasts and buns, while making love with him on bed.
• 1:06—Brief breasts in B&W photo that Mark looks at.
•• 1:09—Right breast, then breasts and very brief lower frontal nudity, while in bed with Mark.

• 1:16—Side of left breast and buns, after taking off robe while kissing Don.

Love, Patti

Films:

Butley (1974; British). Female Student
That'll Be the Day (1974; British). . . . . Sandra's Friend
Terror (1979; British). . . . . n.a.
The Long Good Friday (1980; British) . . . . Carol
Steaming (1985; British) . . . . Josie

• 0:08—Frontal nudity, while getting undressed.
• 0:45—Brief breasts.
• 1:30—Breasts, while jumping around in the pool.

A Business Affair (1993; British/French) . . . . Prostitute
An Awfully Big Adventure (1995; British). . . . . Mary

Made for TV Movies:

Masterpiece Theatre: Middlemarch (1994; British) . . . . Mrs. Plymdale
Masterpiece Theatre: The Fortunes and Misfortunes of Moll Flanders (1996; British/U.S.) . . . . Mrs. Riordan

Love, Rachel

Adult film actress.

Video Tapes:

Soft Bodies: Beyond Blonde (1995). . . . . .Herself

•• 0:01—Breasts and buns in swimsuit, while playing tetherball in pool with Becky LeBeau.
••• 0:02—In bra and panties, then nude while posing in chair.
••• 0:09—In two piece swimsuit, then nude by and in pool with LeBeau.
••• 0:13—In robe, then full frontal nudity in the shower.

Love, Suzanna

Films:

Cocaine Cowboys (1979) . . . . Lucy
The Boogeyman (1980) . . . . .Lacey
Boogeyman II (1983) . . . . .Lacey
Brainwaves (1983) . . . . Kaylie Bedford
Devonsville Terror (1983) . . . . Jessica Scanlon

•• 0:30—Breasts as an apparition, getting Mr. Gibbs attention.
• 0:36—Brief breasts during flashback to 0:30 scene.
• 0:43—Brief right breast during Ralph's past-life recollection.

Olivia (1983) . . . . Olivia
a.k.a. A Taste of Sin

•• 0:34—Buns and breasts making love in bed with Mike.
•• 0:58—Breasts and buns making love with Mike in the shower.
• 1:08—Very brief full frontal nudity getting into bed with Richard. Dark, long shot.
•• 1:09—Buns, lying in bed. Dark. Full frontal nudity getting out of bed and going to the bathroom.

Lovell, Jacqueline *

a.k.a. Sara St. James.
Publisher of the men's magazine, *Babe.*

Films:

Animal Instincts: The Seductress (1995) . . . . Cleaning Woman
(Unrated version reviewed.)

• 1:01—Brief breasts, while cleaning Lolly Pop's leg. B&W. She's on the left with blonde hair.
••• 1:08—In bra, then breasts and buns, while undressing after seeing Joanna and Lolly Pop in bathtub. Making love with the brunette cleaning woman.

Femalien (1995) . . . . Sun

••• 0:22—Breasts, taking off coffee soaked blouse, then full frontal nudity while caressing herself on lounge chair.
••• 1:19—Nude, while making love with Kara in bed.

Hard Time (1995) . . . . Star

••• 0:29—Nude, while stripping and dancing in front of Michael on a table. Excellent!

Night Eyes 4 ...Fatal Passion (1995). . . . . Runaway
Virtual Encounters (1995). . . . . Kika
(Unrated version reviewed.)

••• 0:19—In bra and panties, then full frontal nudity, while making love with Tricia Yen.

Head of the Family (1996) . . . . Lorretta

• 0:33—Brief buns, after taking off her panties and getting into bed with Lance.
•• 0:39—Full frontal nudity, while lying in bed with Lance.
• 0:44—Left breast under open blouse, while making love with Lance in storage room.
• 0:49—Left breast in gaping nightgown, while sleeping in bed.
•• 0:57—Breasts, after lowering her nightgown and letting Myron lick her breast.
•• 1:08—Full frontal nudity, while tied by her wrists when Myron attempts to burn her.
• 1:14—Brief, partial buns, while being carried by Otis.

Hideous (1997) . . . . Sheila

•• 0:16—Breasts, while in car and outdoors (wearing a gorilla mask).

Made for Cable TV:

Red Shoe Diaries: Billy Bar (1996; Showtime) . . . . Uncredited Bordello Woman

• 0:19—Brief breasts, getting candle wax dripped on her by another woman during bordello scene.

Red Shoe Diaries: Caged Bird (1997; Showtime) . . . Dakota

••• 0:04—Nude, undressing and taking a shower with Carmen.
••• 0:09—Nude, while crawling to Charlie, sitting on his lap and talking with him.
• 0:14—Brief breasts, lifting her blouse to show Charlie.
•• 0:18—Nude, while talking with Charlie from inside her jail cell.

Red Shoe Diaries: The Teacher (1998; Showtime) . . . . The Wife

• 0:03—Brief full frontal nudity, while taking a shower.
•• 0:08—Breasts, while making love in the woods with Harry.
• 0:11—Brief breasts, several times in flashbacks.
•• 0:16—Breasts and buns, while outdoors, wearing a blindfold.
•• 0:18—Nude, while in bedroom with the teacher and Harry.

Video Tapes:

All Nude Glamour (1995) . . . . Jacqueline

• 0:00—Full frontal nudity during the opening credits.
••• 0:01—Nude, by swimming pool. Some behind-the-scenes shots included. Long scene.
• 0:04—Full frontal nudity, while talking dirty.

Nude Bowling Party (1995) . . . . Barbie

••• 0:00—Nude throughout.

Playboy's Hard Bodies (1995). . . . . Herself

••• 0:30—Nude while making love with Bobbie Marie on a hilltop.

Body Language (1996). . . . . Sun Bath

••• 0:29—Nude, while sunbathing outdoors with Noelle and Lorissa McComas.

Erotic Heat (1996) . . . . Work Out/Jacuzzi

••• 0:34—Nude, while working out with Noelle.

••• 0:40—Nude, with the other girls in the spa.

Hot Body Competition: Bikinis & Bikes Contest (1996) . . . . Sara St. James

•• 0:29—Breasts and buns, while dancing on stage.

••• 0:30—Nude, while posing outdoors.

Playboy's Girls of the Internet (1996). . . . . Herself

••• 0:40—Nude, while trying on lingerie (she has long hair) and bathing with another woman.

Playboy's Rising Stars and Sexy Starlets (1996) . . Cowgirl

••• 0:38—Nude, undressing out of cowgirl outfit in barn, then making love with another woman.

CD-ROM:

Crystal Fantasy (1995). . . . . Jacqui

Loving, Candy *

Films:

Play Time (1994). . . . . Herself

(Unrated version reviewed.)

• 1:32—Brief breasts on TV that's playing her video.

Video Tapes:

Playboy Video Magazine, Volume 2 (1983) . . . . . Playmate

••• 0:14—Full frontal nudity posing for her centerfold photograph.

Dorothy Stratten, The Untold Story (1985). . . . . . Herself

• 0:22—Brief left breast in centerfold photo.

Playboy Video Centerfold: Kimberley Conrad (1989) . . . . Playboy Update

••• 0:42—Nude in old still photos.

Playboy Video Centerfold: Anna-Marie Goddard (1994) . . . . Playmate

• 0:28—Brief breasts in retrospective.

Lowell, Carey

Model for Oil of Olay cosmetics.

Wife of actor Griffin Dunne.

Films:

Club Paradise (1986). . . . . Fashion Model

Dangerously Close (1986). . . . . Julie

Down Twisted (1987) . . . . Maxine

Me & Him (1988; West German) . . . . Janet Anderson

• 0:37—Very brief upper half of right breast sticking out of nightgown after turning over in bed with Griffin Dunne.

License to Kill (1989). . . . . Pam Bouvier

The Guardian (1990) . . . . Kate

•• 0:37—Right breast twice, in bed with Phil.

Road to Ruin (1992). . . . . Jessie Taylor

• 0:25—Lower half of buns, while sitting in bed with Peter Weller.

• 0:26—Very, very brief buns, when Weller pulls her onto the bed.

Sleepless in Seattle (1993). . . . . Maggie Baldwin

Love Affair (1994) . . . . Martha

Leaving Las Vegas (1995) . . . . Bank Teller

TV:

League of Their Own (1993) . . . . Dottie Hinson

Law & Order (1996-) . . . . Jamie Ross

Lowery, Carolyn

Films:

Candyman (1992). . . . . Stacey

Vicious Circles (1997). . . . . Andrea

(Unrated version reviewed.)

• 0:05—Brief breasts, while flashing herself to Paul Hipp.

•• 0:10—Breasts, while sitting in steam room with Helga.

• 0:17—Brief partial breasts during examination.

•• 0:31—Breasts and buns, while posing when wearing harness.

••• 0:42—In bra and panties, then breasts, while dancing in front of mirror. Sometimes difficult to see because of the hallucination effect.

• 0:47—Brief right breast, when sitting up during massage.

0:55—Partial breasts, while wearing harness

•• 1:09—Breasts in harness after taking off her blouse, while talking with Stan.

• 1:14—Brief breasts and partial lower frontal nudity, standing up out of bath.

• 1:15—Brief lower frontal nudity, with green pubic hair.

• 1:16—Very brief breast and lower frontal nudity, looking at herself in the mirror.

•• 1:17—Breasts and buns in harness, while posing for Ben Gazzara.

Made for Cable TV:

Dream On: And Your Little Dog, Too (1991; HBO) . . . . Ginger

••• 0:22—Breasts getting dressed in Eddie's dressing room with Martin and Eddie.

Made for TV Movies:

Tales of the City (1994) . . . . Hillary

•• 0:25—(Into Part 2) Breast, while sitting on bed and talking to Brian in bathhouse room.

Problem Child 3: Junior in Love (1995) . . . . Dr. Gray

Video Tapes:

Eden 3 (1993) . . . . Amy

••• 0:03—Breasts in bed, making love with Lyle. Buns, while getting out.

•• 0:06—Breasts and buns, making love in bed with Lyle after Eve leaves

••• 0:53—Breasts, while making love in bed with Lyle.

•• 1:16—Breasts while with Lyle in her room.

Lowry, Lynn *

Films:

I Drink Your Blood (1970) . . . . Mute Hippie

Score! (1973). . . . . Betsy

• 0:35—Left breast, sticking out of lingerie outfit.

• 0:38—Brief full frontal nudity, in lingerie outfit while dancing.

• 0:40—Breasts, in lingerie, while sitting on the floor with Eddie.

• 1:01—Brief lower frontal nudity while in bed with Elvira.

• 1:06—Brief left breast in reflection in mirror.

• 1:07—Breasts in lingerie in bed with Elvira.

•• 1:15—Brief right breast and lower frontal nudity in bed with Elvira.

•• 1:22—Full frontal nudity, while in bed, then talking to Eddie.

Sugar Cookies (1973). . . . . Alta/Julie

••• 0:03—Brief breasts falling out of hammock, then breasts on couch with Max, then nude. Long scene. (Brunette wig as Alta.)

• 0:13—Brief right breast in B & W photo.

• 0:14—Left breast while lying on autopsy table.

•• 0:20—Breasts in movie.

•• 0:52—Breasts taking off clothes for Mary Woronov. Breasts on bed. (Blonde as Julie.)

••• 1:00—Breasts and buns with Woronov in bedroom, nude while wrestling with her.

• 1:04—Breasts with Woronov in bathtub.

••• 1:06—Nude in bed with Woronov. Long scene.

•• 1:11—Right breast outside displaying herself to Max.

• 1:16—Right breast, then breasts making love with Woronov.
••• 1:20—Nude with Woronov and Max. Long scene.

They Came From Within (1975; Canadian) . . . . Nurse Forsythe
a.k.a. Shivers
Fighting Mad (1976). . . . . .Lorene
Cat People (1982). . . . . Ruthie
• 0:16—In black bra in Malcolm McDowell's hotel room, then brief breasts when bra pops open after crawling down the stairs.

Lukesová, Sárka *

Video Tapes:
Playboy International Playmates (1993) . . . . .Sharka
••• 0:23—Full frontal nudity in still photos.
•• 0:24—Full frontal nudity, while posing on the floor.
••• 0:25—Full frontal nudity outside in the woods at night.
••• 0:44—Full frontal nudity in old mansion and sitting on couch caressing herself.

Lumley, Joanna

Films:
On Her Majesty's Secret Sevice (1969; British). . . . . English Girl
Games That Lovers Play (1970) . . . . Fanny
•• 0:17—Nude, getting out of bed and putting on robe.
• 0:50—Right breast, while in bed with Jonathan.
•• 1:18—Breasts sitting in bed, talking on the phone.
•• 1:29—Brief breasts several times in bed with Constance and a guy. Breasts after and during the end credits.

The Satanic Rites of Dracula (1973). . . . . . . Jessica Van Helsing
The Trail of the Pink Panther (1982) . . . . Marie Juvet
Shirley Valentine (1989; British). . . . . Marjorie
Innocent Lies (1995) . . . . .Lady Helena Graves
Cold Comfort Farm (1996; British) . . . . Mrs. Smiling
James and the Giant Peach (1996) . . . . Aunt Spiker
Miniseries:
Mistral's Daughter (1984) . . . . Lally Longbridge
Made for TV Movies:
Absolutely Fabulous: The Last Shout (1996; British). . . . . .Patsy
TV:
The New Avengers (1976). . . . . Purdy
Absolutely Fabulous (1992-96; British) . . . . .Patsy

Lund, Deanna

Films:
Dr. Goldfoot and the Bikini Machine (1965) . . . . Robot
Johnny Tiger (1966) . . . . Louise
Sting of Death (1966). . . . . Jessica
Tony Rome (1967) . . . . Georgia McKay
Hardly Working (1981) . . . . .Millie
Stick (1985) . . . . Diane
Elves (1989) . . . . Kirsten's Mother
The Girl I Want (1990) . . . . Mrs. Andrews
Transylvania Twist (1990) . . . . .Teacher
Roots of Evil (1991) . . . . Marissa
(Unrated version reviewed.)
• 0:19—Most of left breast, then brief right breast, while making love in bed with Johnny.
•• 0:20—More right breast, while making love.
•• 0:21—Still more right breast.
••• 1:33—Right breast, then breasts while lying in bed with Brinke Stevens.

TV:
General Hospital . . . . .Peggy Lowell
Land of the Giants (1968-70) . . . . Valerie Scott

Lund, Zoe

See: Tamerlis, Zoe.

Luner, Jamie

Films:
Tryst (1994). . . . . .Mindy
• 0:41—In black bra and panties, then back side of left breast, while changing clothes when Danny peeks through hole in wall and photographs her.
• 1:12—Back side of right breast, while changing clothes in motel room.
•• 1:13—Breasts, while struggling with Danny and getting raped in hotel room.

Made for Cable Movies:
Rebel Highway: Confessions of a Sorority Girl (1994; Showtime) . . . . Sabrina
Made for TV Movies:
Moment of Truth: Why My Daughter? (1993) . . . .Diana Moffet
TV:
Just the Ten of Us (1988-90) . . . . Cindy Lubbock
Savannah (1996-97) . . . . Peyton Richards
Melrose Place (1997-). . . . . Lexi Sterling

Lunghi, Cherie

Films:
Excalibur (1981; British) . . . . Guenevere
• 1:25—Brief breasts in the forest kissing Lancelot.
King David (1985) . . . . Michal
•• 0:28—Breasts lying in bed with Richard Gere. (Her hair is in the way a little bit.)

Letters to an Unknown Lover (1985) . . . . Helene
Parker (1985; British). . . . . Jenny Parker
The Mission (1986; British) . . . . Carlotta
To Kill a Priest (1988). . . . . .Halina
Mary Shelley's Frankenstein (1994) . . . . Victor's Mother
Jack & Sarah (1996; British/French) . . . . .Anna
Made for Cable TV:
Strangers: The One You Love (1996; HBO) . . . . Joan
••• 0:18—In bra and panties, then nude while making love with Veronika.

Miniseries:
Master of the Game (1984). . . . . Margaret Van der Merwe
The Buccaneers (1995; U.S./British). . . . . .Laura Testvalley
Made for TV Movies:
Silent Cries (1993). . . . . Audrey
The Canterville Ghost (1996). . . . . Lucille
TV:
Covington Cross (1992-93) . . . . .Lady Elizabeth
Moloney (1996-97) . . . . Dr. Sarah Bateman

Lusader, Shawn

Films:
Body of Evidence (1992) . . . . . Body Double for Anne Archer
(Unrated version reviewed.)
•• 1:12—Nude, while running around bedroom during video playback. Hard to see because the camera is moving around.

A Low Down Dirty Shame (1994). . . . . . Female Lovemaker
• 0:02—Very brief buns, lower frontal nudity and right breast in hotel bed with a guy when surprised by Jada Pinkett.

Lusiak, Gloria

Films:
Blondes Have More Guns (1995) . . . . .Dakota Beaver
•• 0:00—Breasts and buns, while making love on top of a guy in bed. Don't see her face.

- 0:04—Brief breasts, seen in a Viewmaster.
•• 0:40—Breasts, while making love on top of a guy on a sofa.
• 0:50—Breasts, throwing off her jacket and straddling Harry.
•• 1:00—Breasts, while making love with Harry in bed at night. Playing with pizza.
••• 1:03—Breasts, while dripping hot candle wax on Harry, then being held a gunpoint by two police people.

Crystal Force II: Dark Angel (1995) . . . . Jill
•• 0:19—Breasts and buns in T-back while in spa with Walter.
••• 0:33—Full frontal nudity, while making love with Virgil.

CyberSex Kittens (1995) . . . . Sandy
•• 0:11—Breasts, while posing for photographs.
••• 0:39—Breasts, while talking to a stuffed doll in bedroom, then nude, when taking a shower.
• 0:45—Brief breasts, while sitting in chair, getting reprogrammed.
•• 0:48—Breasts, while posing for Christmas theme photos, then fighting with Courtney.

Made for Cable TV:

Compromising Situations: The Elevator (1998; Showtime) . . . . Mrs. Sprague
Compromising Situations: Vegas (1998; Showtime) . . . Martha

Lussier, Sheila

a.k.a. Dusty Rose.

Films:

The Big Bet (1985) . . . . n.a.
Bits and Pieces (1985) . . . . Tanya
•• 0:07—In bra, tied down by Arthur, then brief breasts as he cuts her bra off before he kills her. Brief right breast several times with blood on her.

My Chauffeur (1986) . . . . Party Girl
• 1:23—Brief breasts after taking off her blue blouse in the back of the limousine.

Reform School Girls (1986) . . . . n.a.
The Nightstalker (1987) . . . . n.a.
Run If You Can (1987) . . . . n.a.
Glitch (1988) . . . . Extra

Video Tapes:

Starlet Screen Test II (1991) . . . . Dusty Rose
••• 0:31—Breasts, posing on car (same segment from *Centerfold Screen Test*.)

Lutra, Mara

Films:

Fantasm (1976; Australian) . . . . Felicity
Auditions (1978) . . . . Jenny Marino
•• 0:58—Nude during her audition.
•• 1:07—Breasts and buns during orgy scene.

*Luu, Pam **

Video Tapes:

Playboy's Girls of the Internet (1996) . . . . Girls of the Web
••• 0:21—In lingerie, then nude while stripping and dancing.

Luu, Thuy Ann

Films:

Diva (1982; French) . . . . Alba
• 0:13—Breasts in B&W photos when record store clerk asks to see her portfolio.
• 0:15—More of the B&W photos on the wall.
• 1:27—Very brief upper half of left breast taking off top, seen through window. Long shot.

Off Limits (1988) . . . . Lanh
•• 0:48—Breasts dancing on stage in a nightclub.

Does This Mean We're Married? (1990; French/U.S.) . . . . Thuy Lan

*Lydon, Christine **

Video Tapes:

Playboy's Hard Bodies (1995) . . . . Herself
••• 0:47—Nude, while posing at the beach by herself and two other women.

*Lynch, Kelly **

Former model.
Wife of screenwriter Mitch Glazer.

Films:

Portfolio (1983) . . . . Elite Model
Light of Day (1987) . . . . Elaine
Cocktail (1988) . . . . Kerry Coughlin
• 0:45—Buns, wearing a two piece swimsuit at the beach.
• 1:01—Buns, in string bikini swimsuit on boat with Tom Cruise and Bryan Brown.

Drugstore Cowboy (1989) . . . . Dianne Hughes
Roadhouse (1989) . . . . Doc
•• 1:04—Breasts and buns getting out of bed with a sheet wrapped around her.

Warm Summer Rain (1989) . . . . Kate
• 0:03—Brief breasts and side view of buns in B&W lying on floor during suicide attempt. Quick cuts breasts getting shocked to start her heart.
•• 0:23—Full frontal nudity when Guy gets off her in bed.
•• 0:24—Side view of right breast in bed, then breasts.
••• 0:58—Buns then breasts, getting washed by Guy on the table.
••• 1:07—Brief buns making love. Quick cuts full frontal nudity spinning around. Side view of left breast with Guy.
••• 1:09—Nude picking up belongings and running out of burning house with Guy.

Desperate Hours (1990) . . . . Nancy Breyers
• 0:10—Brief breasts, walking on sidewalk with Mickey Rourke when her breasts pop out of her suit.
• 1:19—Brief breasts, getting wired with a hidden microphone in bathroom.

Curly Sue (1991) . . . . Grey Ellison
Three of Hearts (1993) . . . . Connie
Forbidden Choices (1994) . . . . Roberta Bean
a.k.a. The Beans of Egypt, Maine
Imaginary Crimes (1994) . . . . Valery
Princess Caraboo (1994) . . . . Amon McCarthy
Heaven's Prisoners (1995) . . . . Annie Robicheaux
Persons Unknown (1995) . . . . Amanda
• 0:05—Very brief breasts, when rolling over next to Joe Mantegna in bed to show her tattoo.

White Man's Burden (1995) . . . . Marsha Lynch
Mr. Magoo (1997) . . . . Luanne Le Seur

Made for Cable TV:

The Hitchhiker: The Joker (1987; HBO) . . . Theresa/Melissa
• 0:11—Very, very brief left breast, while in storage room with Alan getting tied up by Timothy Bottoms.

Fallen Angels: Red Wind (1995; Showtime) . . . . Lola

Lynley, Carol

Films:

The Light in the Forest (1958) . . . . Shenandoe Hastings
The Poseidon Adventure (1972) . . . . Nonny Parry
Son of Blob (1972) . . . . Leslie
a.k.a. Beware! The Blob
The Four Deuces (1975) . . . . Wendy

Bad Georgia Road (1977) . . . . Molly Golden
- • 1:02—Very brief upper half of right breast, after hitting the water in anger after her clothes are stolen.

The Cat and The Canary (1978; British) . . . . Anabelle West
Vigilante (1983) . . . . D.A. Fletcher
Dark Tower (1987) . . . . Tilly
Blackout (1989) . . . . Esther Boyle
- •• 1:01—Brief breasts leaning against the wall while someone touches her left breast.

Howling VI—The Freaks (1990). . . . . Miss Eddington
Spirits (1991) . . . . Sister Jillian

Made for TV Movies:

The Night Stalker (1971). . . . . Gail Foster
Flood! (1976) . . . . Abbie Adams

TV:

The Immortal (1970-71) . . . . Sylvia

Lynn, Amber

Adult film actress.

Films:

Evils of the Night (1985) . . . . Joyce
- • 0:14—Brief breasts, taking her pink swimsuit top off for Eddie.
- •• 0:17—Breasts with Eddie in deserted house. Dark.
- •• 0:19—Full frontal nudity when Eddie takes her shorts off. Dark.
- • 0:21—Right breast, while in bed with Eddie. Still dark.
- • 0:22—More right breast.
- •• 0:23—Full frontal nudity in bed when Eddie gets out.
- •• 0:24—Nude, while getting out of bed and getting dressed. Dark.

52 Pick-Up (1986). . . . . Party Goer
- • 0:23—Breasts opening her blouse while being video taped at party.
- • 0:24—Breasts and buns on TV. B&W.
- • 0:26—Left breast, then breasts being video taped with another woman.

Video Tapes:

The Art of Desire (1992) . . . . n.a.

Lynn, Amy

See: Baxter, Amy Lynn.

Lynn, Porsche

Adult film actress.

Video Tapes:

Hyapatia Lee Presents: Taking' It Off, Volume 1 (1993) . . . . Herself
- ••• 0:07—Nude, doing strip dance routine on stage in club. Long scene.

Lynn, Rebecca

a.k.a. Adult film actress Cameron or Krista Lane.

Films:

Free Ride (1986) . . . . Nude Girl #2
- • 0:25—Brief buns taking a shower with another girl.

Sensations (1988). . . . . Jenny Hunter
- • 0:11—Breasts, sleeping on couch.
- •• 0:23—Breasts talking on the telephone.
- •• 1:09—Breasts making love in bed with Brian.

Thrilled to Death (1988). . . . . Elaine Jackson
- • 0:01—Breasts twice when Baxter opens her blouse.
- •• 0:31—Breasts in locker room talking to Nan.

Video Tapes:

In Search of the Perfect 10 (1986) . . . Perfect Girl #7/Ellen
- ••• 0:37—Breasts (she's the redhead) playing Twister with Iris Condon. Buns in G-string.

High Society Centerspread Video #1: Krista Lane (1990) . . . . Krista Lane

*Lynn, Theresa **

Films:

Beauty School (1993) . . . . Countess's Girl
Marilyn Chambers' Bedtime Stories (1993) . . . . . . Melissa
- •• 0:07—Breasts and buns in G-string, while changing lingerie in bedroom in front of mirror.
- •• 0:22—Breasts, while on sofa, practicing her acting with Bart.
- •• 0:29—Breasts, while making love with Bart on sofa.
- •• 0:33—Breasts, while in bathroom with blue towel.
- •• 1:17—Breasts, while on couch with Bart in out take.

New York Cop (1993). . . . . Babes
- • 0:23—Brief buns and brief breasts, while making love in bed with bad guy when interrupted by Toshi.

Vampire Vixens From Venus (1995). . . . . Shirley
- • 0:05—Breasts after pulling down her blouse, to get some attention while hitchhiking.
- • 0:20—Breasts in pulled down blouse, while on the sofa with a guy.
- • 0:40—Brief breasts, while dancing on stage.
- • 1:07—Breasts, while greeting policemen at the door.

Private Parts (1997). . . . . Orgasm Woman
- •• 0:54—In bra, then breasts when sitting on a speaker while Howard Stern brings her to orgasm over the radio.

*Lynne, Heidi **

a.k.a. Heidi Staley.

Films:

Forbidden Games (1995). . . . . Model
(Unrated version reviewed.)
Leprechaun 3 (1995) . . . . Fantasy Girl
- •• 0:54—Breasts, after removing her top on TV while Mitch watches.
- •• 0:55—Breasts on TV some more, then after coming out of the TV. Buns in lingerie in room with Mitch.
- •• 0:58—Breasts and buns, while on top of Mitch in bed.

Video Tapes:

Hot Body Video Magazine #7: Naughty But Nice (1993) . . . . Herself
Hot Body Video Magazine #8: Hot Stuff (1994) . . Herself
Hot Body Hall of Fame: Traci Dali (1995) . . . . Herself
- •• 0:33—Nude, while posing outdoors on balcony.

Hot Body International: Dreamgirl II (1995). . . . . Herself
Hot Body International: Steamed Heat (1995) . . . Herself
- • 0:08—Buns in swimsuit at the beach.
- • 0:13—Buns in swimsuit, outdoors at the beach.
- •• 0:14—Buns and breasts, while changing swimsuits outdoors.
- •• 0:20—Buns in swimsuit, then buns and breasts, while changing swimsuits.

Penthouse Pet Rocks (1995) . . . . Pet

Lynskey, Melanie

Films:

Heavenly Creatures (1994; New Zealand) . . . . Pauline
- • 1:20—Tip of right breast, while sitting in bathtub talking to Kate Winslet.

The Frighteners (1996) . . . . Deputy

Lyon, Lisa *

Bodybuilder.

Films:

Hollywood Erotic Film Festival (1986) . . . . Lisa Lyon: A Portrait of Power
- ••• 0:17—Breasts and buns in G-string, while doing body building poses.
- ••• 0:21—Breasts and buns while posing on a rooftop, with a city in the background.

Vamp (1986). . . . . Cimmaron

Made for TV Movies:

Getting Physical (1984). . . . . Pilar Jones

Lyon, Wendy

Films:

Hello Mary Lou: Prom Night II (1987). . . . . Vicki Carpenter
- • 0:58—Very, very brief left breast, while turning around after getting sucked into the blackboard.
- ••• 1:04—Nude in shower with Monica. Nude a lot walking around shower room.
- ••• 1:06—Full frontal nudity, walking in locker room, stalking Monica.

Made for Cable TV:

Dead Man's Gun: Buryin' Sam (1997; Showtime) . . . . Erica Beacon

Made for TV Movies:

Anne of Green Gables (1985; Canadian) . . . . . . Prissy Andrews

Breach of Faith: A Family of Cops II (1997) . . . . Mrs. Baskin

Lyons, Laura *

Films:

Tintorera (1977). . . . . .Cynthia
- • 0:27—Buns and brief side of left breast, taking off her dress to swim to boat. She's the second one to take off her dress.
- • 0:28—Full frontal nudity, while dancing on boat deck.
- • 0:29—Left breast and brief buns, while getting into hammock with Steven.
- • 0:30—Brief buns, while swimming in water.

Lyons, Susan

Films:

The Good Wife (1987; Australian) . . . . .Mrs. Fielding

a.k.a. The Umbrella Woman
- • 1:22—Very brief breasts coming in from the balcony.

...Almost (1990; Australian). . . . . Caroline

Ebbtide (1994; Australian). . . . . Alison

MacColl, Catriona

Films:

Afraid of the Dark (1992; British/French) . . . . Blind Woman/Wedding Friend

Made for Cable TV:

Strangers: Touch (1996; Canadian/French; HBO) . . . . . . Eva
- •• 0:25—Full frontal nudity, standing in room in front of her husband.

MacDonald, Jennifer *

Films:

Bad Blood (1993) . . . . Ray Ann

Object of Obsession (1994). . . . . Amy
- •• 1:16—Full frontal nudity, after taking off dress while lying in bed on video playback.

T-Force (1994) . . . . Mandragora
- • 0:56—Breasts, while outside with Adam, finding out if she can procreate. Don't see her face.

Orion's Key (1996) . . . . .Corinne

Made for Cable Movies:

Dead Weekend (1995; Showtime) . . . . .Amelia D
- • 0:46—Brief breasts, while making love with Stephen Baldwin.
- • 0:47—Very brief breasts, while sitting up in bed. Seen through bed railing and mosquito net.

Made for Cable TV:

Dream On: I'm With Stupid (1994; HBO) . . . . Veronica
- •• 0:22—Left breast, then breasts, while in bed with Martin.

Red Shoe Diaries: The Cake (1995; Showtime) . . . . Juliet Sanders
- • 0:11—Brief breasts, while getting undressed. Don't see her face well.
- • 0:16—Brief breasts and buns, while getting decorated.
- • 0:17—Breasts under some kind of frosting decoration.
- • 0:19—Brief breasts under fishnet covering, while standing in back of truck.
- • 0:20—Breasts in outfit when arriving at home to surprise her husband.
- •• 0:22—Breasts, while making love with her husband afterwards.

• MacDonald, Kelly

Films:

Stella Does Tricks (1996; British) . . . . Stella

Trainspotting (1996; British) . . . . Diane
- • 0:25—Breasts, while undressing in her bedroom.
- •• 0:26—Brief breasts, several times while making love with Ewan McGregor. Very brief lower frontal nudity when getting dressed.

Cousin Bette (1998). . . . . Hortense Hulot

MacDonald, Wendy *

Films:

Blood Frenzy (1987) . . . . Dr. Shelley

Dark Side of the Moon (1989) . . . . Alex
- • 0:54—In bra, then brief breasts having it torn off. Don't see her face.

Living to Die (1990). . . . . .Rookie Policewoman

Naked Obsession (1990) . . . . Saundra Carlyle

(Unrated version reviewed.)
- ••• 0:28—In black bra, panties and stockings on the dining table during William Katt's fantasy, then breasts.

Sinners! (1990) . . . . Fran

Blood Money (1991) . . . . Susan

a.k.a. The Killer's Edge

Legal Tender (1991) . . . . Verna Wheeler
- • 0:22—Brief buns in lingerie, while in Morton Downey Jr.'s office. Don't see her face.
- •• 1:20—Long shot of buns and side of left breast taking off robe in front of Downey. Breasts on bed with him.

L.A. Goddess (1992) . . . . Diane
- •• 0:08—Side of left breast, then breasts while making love with the Sheriff actor in motor home.
- • 1:06—Brief buns, while flashing while dancing on table during party.

Wild Cactus (1992) . . . . .Abby

(Unrated version reviewed.)

Broken Trust (1993). Dr. Joyce Radley

Deadly Target (1994). . . . . Barmaid

Improper Conduct (1994) . . . . Gabby

(Unrated version reviewed.)

Irresistible Impulse (1995) . . . . .Carolyn Wetherby
- •• 0:27—Breasts, after taking robe off in front of Richard. Breasts and buns, while making love in bed with him.

- 0:31—Very, very brief left breast, when Richard turns her over in bed after discovering her unconscious.
- 0:32—Brief half of right breast, while lying unconscious in bed.

Twisted Passion (1995) . . . . Head Nurse
a.k.a. Shades of Gray

MacGraw, Ali *

Former model.
Ex-wife of the late actor Steve McQueen.
Films:

Goodbye, Columbus (1969) . . . . Brenda
- 0:50—Very brief side view of left breast, taking off dress before running and jumping into a swimming pool. Brief right breast jumping into pool.
- 1:11—Very brief side view of right breast in bed with Richard Benjamin. Brief buns, getting out of bed and walking to the bathroom.

Love Story (1970) . . . . Jenny Cavilleri
The Getaway (1972). . . . . Carol McCoy
- 0:19—Very brief left breast lying back in bed kissing McQueen.

Convoy (1978) . . . . Melissa
Players (1979) . . . . Nicole
Just Tell Me What You Want (1980) . . . . Bones Burton
- •• 0:16—Breasts getting dressed in her bedroom.
- •• 1:26—Brief breasts in bathroom getting ready to take a shower.

Blast 'Em (1992) . . . . Herself
- 0:55—Brief right breast in gaping blouse in a B&W still photo.

Natural Causes (1993) . . . . Fran Jakes
Made for TV Movies:
Survive the Savage Sea (1992) . . . . Claire Carpenter
Gunsmoke: The Long Ride (1993). . . . . Uncle Jane Merckel
TV:
Dynasty (1985) . . . . Lady Ashley Mitchell
Video Tapes:
Ali MacGraw/Yoga Mind & Body (1994). . . . . Herself

Machart, Maria

Films:
Blood Sisters (1986). . . . . Marnie
- •• 0:45—In bra, then brief breasts putting on nightgown and caressing herself.

Slammer Girls (1987). . . . . Hooker
- •• 0:06—Breasts, getting fondled by a cop.

Mack, Kerry

Films:
Fair Game (1982; Australian). . . . . Joanne
Savage Attraction (1983; Australian) . . . . Christine Maresch
- ••• 0:10—Breasts, getting out of shower and putting on robe.
- 0:11—Breasts behind shower door, making love with Walter.
- •• 0:17—Breasts sitting at the end of the bed.
- •• 0:59—Breasts undressing in bedroom, then in bathtub with Walter.
- ••• 1:04—Breasts getting her blouse unbuttoned, then breasts in bed with Walter.

The Custodian (1993). . . . . Policewoman

MacKenzie, Jan *

Films:
Gator Bait II—Cajun Justice (1988) . . . . Angelique
- •• 0:34—Buns and side view of left breast, taking a bath outside. Brief breasts a couple of times while the bad guys watch.
- 0:41—Brief side view of left breast taking off towel in front of the bad guys.
- 1:05—Brief buns occasionally when her blouse flips up during boat chase.

The American Angels, Baptism of Blood (1989)
. . . . Luscious Lisa
- 0:07—Buns in G-string on stage in club. More buns getting lathered up for wrestling match.
- 0:11—Breasts and buns when a customer takes her top off. She's covered with shaving cream.
- •• 0:12—Breasts taking a shower when Diamond Dave looks in to talk to her.
- 0:56—Right breast, while in wrestling ring with Dave.

Mackenzie, Patch

Films:
Goodbye, Norma Jean (1975) . . . . Ruth Latimer
Serial (1980) . . . . Stella
- 0:59—Brief breasts in mirror in swinger's club with Martin Mull.

Graduation Day (1981) . . . . Anne Ramstead
Fighting Back (1982). . . . . Lilly Morelli
It's Alive III: Island of the Alive (1988) . . . . Robbins

Mackie, Allison

Films:
Amos & Andrew (1993) . . . . Anchorwoman
Sliver (1993) . . . . Naomi Singer
- 1:36—Brief buns, while making love on top of William Baldwin on video playback. B&W.

Lurking Fear (1994). . . . . Ms. Marlowe
Made for Cable Movies:
Gia (1998; HBO) . . . . Red Dress Designer
Made for TV Movies:
Undue Influence (1996) . . . . Melanie
Video Tapes:
Eden 5 (1993) . . . . Liza
- ••• 0:22—Breasts, after taking off swimsuit top, then buns after taking off swimsuit bottom while on beach with Douglas.
- ••• 0:26—Breasts, after Douglas takes off her swimsuit top.

• *MacLachlan, Samantha*

Films:
Entertaining Angels: The Dorothy Day Story (1996)
. . . . Woman in Jail
Set It Off (1996) . . . . Ursula
- 0:53—Buns and brief side view of left breast in swimsuit while dancing in front of Queen Latifah.

TV:
NYPD Blue: Heavin' Can Wait (Nov 14, 1995) . . . . n.a.

MacLaine, Shirley *

Sister of actor Warren Beatty.
Films:
The Trouble with Harry (1955) . . . . Jennifer Rogers
Around the World in 80 Days (1956). . . . . Princess Houda
Hot Spell (1958) . . . . Virginia Duval
Some Came Running (1958). . . . . Ginny Moorhead
The Apartment (1960). . . . . Fran Kubelik
Can-Can (1960) . . . . Simone Pistache

All In a Night's Work (1961) . . . . Katie Robbins
Irma La Douce (1963) . . . . Irma La Douce
Gambit (1966) . . . . .Nicole
Woman Times Seven (1967) . . . . Paulette
Sweet Charity (1969) . . . . Charity Hope Valentine
Two Mules for Sister Sara (1970) . . . . Sara
Desperate Characters (1971) . . . . Sophie Bentwood
•• 1:21—Left breast, while standing with Kenneth Mars, when he takes off her blouse.
••• 1:22—Breasts, while on bed, reluctantly kissing Kenneth Mars.
The Possession of Joel Delaney (1972) . . . . Norah Benson
The Turning Point (1977) . . . . DeeDee
Being There (1979) . . . . Eve Rand
A Change of Seasons (1980) . . . . Karen Evans
Loving Couples (1980) . . . . Evelyn
Terms of Endearment (1983) . . . . Aurora Greenway
(Academy Award for Best Actress.)
• 1:00—Very, very brief right breast wrestling with Jack Nicholson in the ocean when she finally frees his hand from her breast. One frame. Hard to see, but for the sake of thoroughness....
Cannonball Run II (1984) . . . . Veronica
Madame Sousatzka (1988) . . . . Madame Sousatzka
Steel Magnolias (1989) . . . . Ouiser Boudreaux
Postcards from the Edge (1990) . . . . Doris Mann
Defending Your Life (1991) . . . . Shirley MacLaine
Waiting for the Light (1991) . . . . Aunt Zena
Used People (1992). . . . . Pearl
Guarding Tess (1993) . . . . Tess Carlisle
Wrestling Ernest Hemingway (1993) . . . . Helen
The Evening Star (1996) . . . . Aurora Greenway
Mrs. Winterbourne (1996). . . . . Grace Winterbourne
Video Tapes:
Shirley MacLaine's Inner Workout (1989). . . . . Herself

MacLaren, Fawna *

Films:
Dragonfight (1990). . . . . Dark Servant
Amore! (1993) . . . . Cherry Cream Pie
Lady in Waiting (1994) . . . . Roxie
(Unrated version reviewed.)
•• 0:01—Nude in room while making love with Mr. Bennett and another woman.
• 0:28—Left breast, then breasts while posing in bedroom.
• 0:38—Brief left breast, while lying dead on bed.
Lover's Leap (1995) . . . . Billie
•• 0:14—Full frontal nudity, while starting to have sex with Alex in his backyard at night.
•• 0:49—Full frontal nudity, while sunbathing out in pool with Rita.
••• 1:11—Full frontal nudity, while starting to make love with Nick in kitchen.
••• 1:21—Breasts, while playing with herself in bathtub.
Video Tapes:
Playboy Video Centerfold: Fawna MacLaren (1988)
. . . . 35th Anniversary Playmate
••• 0:11—In front of brick wall. In studio, in bed. Nude.
Playboy Video Calendar 1990 (1989) . . . . January
••• 0:01—Nude.
Playmates at Play (1990) . . . . Gotta Dance
Sexy Lingerie II (1990). . . . . Model
Playboy Video Centerfold: Anna-Marie Goddard (1994)
. . . . Playmate
• 0:29—Brief breasts during retrospective.
Wet & Wild: The Locker Room (1994) . . . . Playmate

MacLeod, Mary

Films:
if... (1969; British). . . . . Mrs. Kemp
•• 1:27—Buns and side of left breast while walking around deserted boy's dormitory (B&W).
O Lucky Man! (1973; British)
. . . . Mary Ball/Salvationist/Vicar's Wife
• 1:06—Very brief left breast (over the shoulder shot) while letting Malcolm McDowell suck on her breast, after she catches him trying to steal food in church.
Britannia Hospital (1982). . . . . Casualty Sister
Orlando (1993; British) . . . . First Woman
Restoration (1995). . . . . Midwife
Miniseries:
Scarlett (1994). . . . . Mrs. Boswell

Macpherson, Elle *

Sports Illustrated magazine swimsuit model.
Spokesmodel for *Biotherm* cosmetics.
Films:
Alice (1990). . . . . Model
Sirens (1994; Australian) . . . . Sheela
•• 0:25—Breasts and buns, while in pond with Pru.
••• 0:26—Breasts, while in pond with Pru talking to Devlin.
•• 0:30—Full frontal nudity, while posing.
•• 0:45—Buns and right breast, then breasts while posing.
•• 1:15—Breasts and partial lower frontal nudity while posing for painting.
••• 1:24—Breasts, in pond with Pru and Giddy during Estella's fantasy.
• 1:30—Brief full frontal nudity on rock formation. Medium long shot. She's the fourth from the left.
If Lucy Fell (1996) . . . . Jane Lindquist
The Mirror Has Two Faces (1996) . . . . Candy
Batman & Robin (1997) . . . . Julie Madison
The Edge (1997) . . . . Mickey Morse
Made for Cable TV:
Victoria's Secret: Dreams & Fantasies (1994; Showtime)
. . . . Herself
Video Tapes:
Sports Illustrated's 25th Anniversary Swimsuit Video (1989). . . . . Model
(The version shown on HBO left out two music video segments at the end. If you like buns, definitely watch the video tape!)
• 0:23—Very, very brief lower breasts, when readjusting her yellow tank top.
Sports Illustrated Super Shape-Up Program: Stretch and Strengthen (1990). . . . . Herself
Sports Illustrated: 1994 Swimsuit Issue Video (1994) . . . . Model
(Unedited Version reviewed.)
Your Personal Best Workout with Elle Macpherson (1994)
. . . . Instructor

MacRae, Elizabeth

Films:
Love in a Goldfish Bowl (1961) . . . . Jackie
The Wild Westerners (1962). . . . . Crystal Plummer
For Love or Money (1963). . . . . Marsha
Wild is My Love (1963) . . . . Queenie
The Conversation (1974). . . . . Meredith
• 1:14—Breasts and buns, getting undressed in work area with Gene Hackman. Long shot, dark.
TV:
Gomer Pyle, U.S.M.C. (1967-69) . . . . Lou Ann Poovie

Madigan, Amy

Wife of actor Ed Harris.

Films:

Love Child (1982) .... Terry Jean Moore
- • 0:08—Brief side view of right breast and buns taking a shower in jail while the guards watch.
- •• 0:53—Brief breasts and buns, making love with Beau Bridges in a room at the women's prison.

Love Letters (1984) .... Wendy
a.k.a. Passion Play
Places in the Heart (1984) .... Viola Kelsey
Streets of Fire (1984) .... McCoy
Alamo Bay (1985) .... Glory
- •• 0:28—Breasts while lying in motel bed with Ed Harris.
- •• 0:30—Breasts while sitting up in the bed.

Twice in a Lifetime (1985) .... Sunny Sobel
Nowhere to Hide (1987) .... Barbara Cutter
- • 1:04—Brief side view of right breast taking off towel to get dressed in cabin. Long shot, hard to see.

The Prince of Pennsylvania (1988) .... Carla Headlee
- • 0:37—Left breast and buns, while getting out of bed with Keanu Reeves and putting on a robe.

Field of Dreams (1989) .... Annie
Uncle Buck (1989) .... Chanice Kobolowski
The Dark Half (1993) .... Liz Beaumont
Female Perversions (1997) .... Madelyn Stephens
- •• 1:33—Breasts and brief buns, when undressing and getting into the bathtub with Tilda Swinton.

Made for Cable Movies:
And Then There Was One (1994; Lifetime) ...... Roxy Ventola
Riders of the Purple Sage (1996; TNT) .... Milly Eme
A Bright Shining Lie (1998; HBO) .... Mary Jane Vann
Miniseries:
The Day After (1983) .... Alison
Made for TV Movies:
Roe vs. Wade (1989) .... Sarah Weddington
Lucky Day (1991) .... Kari Campbell

Madison

see: Stone, Madison.

Madison, Lisa *

Films:

Beauty School (1993) .... Kristina
- •• 0:02—Breasts while making out with a guy in bedroom.
- ••• 1:23—Breasts while making out with a guy.

Madonna *

Full name is Madonna Louise Cicconi.
Singer.
Ex-wife of actor Sean Penn.
Nude in her book, *Sex* (1992).

Films:

A Certain Sacrifice (1981) .... Bruna
(Very grainy film, done before she became famous.)
- ••• 0:22—Breasts during weird rape/love scene with one guy and two girls.
- • 0:40—Brief right breast in open top lying on floor after getting attacked by guy in back of restaurant.
- • 0:57—Brief breasts during love making scene, then getting smeared with blood.

Desperately Seeking Susan (1985) .... Susan
Visionquest (1985) .... Nightclub Singer
Shanghai Surprise (1986; British) .... Gloria Tatlock
Who's That Girl? (1987) .... Nikki Finn
Bloodhounds of Broadway (1989) .... Hortense Hathaway
Dick Tracy (1990) .... Breathless Mahoney
Shadows and Fog (1991) .... Marie
Truth or Dare (1991) .... Herself
- ••• 0:44—Brief breasts changing clothes backstage. B&W.
- • 1:35—Very brief half of left breast, while wearing robe and jumping up. B&W.

Body of Evidence (1992) .... Rebecca Carlson
(Unrated version reviewed.)
- • 0:01—Breasts, while making love on TV during video playback.
- • 0:03—Breasts and buns some more on TV.
- • 0:20—Upper half of buns, getting acupuncture.
- ••• 0:41—Breasts on stairs and in bed with Willem Dafoe.
- •• 0:42—Breasts on bed behind curtains with Dafoe.
- • 0:43—Brief right breast, while licking champagne off Dafoe's chest.
- ••• 0:45—Full frontal nudity, while climbing on top of Dafoe and making love. Seen through curtains.
- • 0:55—Lower frontal nudity, while making love with Dafoe in parking garage.
- ••• 1:07—Very, very brief left breast when Dafoe grabs her arm. Breasts opening her robe and lying on the floor and playing with herself while Dafoe watches.
- •• 1:10—Buns, while lying on the floor when Dafoe rips her panties off.
- ••• 1:11—Full frontal nudity on TV during video playback.

A League of Their Own (1992) .... Mae Mordabito
Dangerous Game (1993) .... Sarah Jennings
(Unrated version reviewed.)
- • 0:45—Brief buns in G-string, falling over back of sofa on video playback.
- •• 0:53—Nude, while getting out of bed and getting dressed.
- • 1:00—Brief buns, when getting her panties ripped off by Russo.

Before the Rain (1995; U.S./French) .... Madonna
- • 0:36—Brief breasts in photo that the woman is looking at. Again after coffee is spilled on the photo.

Blue in the Face (1995) .... n.a.
Four Rooms (1995) .... Elspeth
Evita (1996) .... Eva Perón
Girl 6 (1996) .... Boss #3
Video Tapes:
Penthouse: On the Wild Side (1988) .... Madonna
- ••• 0:14—Full frontal nudity in B&W and color still photographs.

Madonna: The Immaculate Collection (1990) .... Herself
- • 0:18—(1 min., 36 sec. into "Papa Don't Preach.") Very, very brief upper half of right breast after first head throwback in black strapless outfit. Long shot.
- • 0:18—(2 min., 10 sec. into "Papa Don't Preach.") Very, very brief left breast in black strapless outfit when she throws her head back. (After the daughter character she plays walks up the subway stairs.)

Madsen, Virginia

Sister of actor Michael Madsen.

Films:

Class (1983) .... Lisa
- •• 0:20—Brief left breast when Andrew McCarthy accidentally rips her blouse open at the girl's school.

Dune (1984) .... Princess Irulan
Electric Dreams (1984) .... Madeline
Creator (1985) .... Barbara
- ••• 0:58—Breasts while in shower with Spano.

Modern Girls (1987) .... Kelly
Slam Dance (1987; U.S./British) .... Yolanda Caldwell

Zombie High (1987) . . . . Andrea
a.k.a. The School That Ate My Brain
Hot to Trot (1988). . . . . Allison Rowe
Heart of Dixie (1989). . . . . Delia
The Hot Spot (1990) .Dolly Harshaw
- 0:41—Side view of left breast while sitting on bed talking to Don Johnson.
- 0:47—Tip of right breast when Johnson kisses it.
- •• 1:16—Buns, while undressing for a swim outside at night. Breasts, while hanging on rope.
- 1:18—Buns, getting out of water with Johnson. Long shot.
- 1:21—Left breast when robe gapes open while sitting up.
- 1:23—Brief lower frontal nudity and buns in open robe after jumping off tower at night.
- 1:24—Breasts at bottom of hill with Johnson. Long shot.
- 1:45—Nude, very, very briefly running out of house. Very blurry, could be anybody.

Highlander 2: The Quickening (1991) . . . . Louise Marcus
Love Kills (1991) . . . . .Rebecca Bishop
Becoming Colette (1992; French/German/U.S.) . . . . .Polaire
- •• 0:48—Breasts in bed, with Mathilda May.
- •• 0:49—Side view of left breast in bed with May and Klaus Maria Brandauer.

Candyman (1992). . . . . Helen Lyle
- 0:47—In bloody bra, while undressing after she was arrested. Side of right breast, after taking off bra. Bloody.
- 0:54—Brief left breast, while in bathtub. Lower half of right breast, after sitting up.

Caroline at Midnight (1993) . . . . Susan Prince
Blue Tiger (1994) . . . . Gina Hayes
- 1:07—Sort of left breast, while making love in bed with Seiji.

The Prophecy (1995). . . . . Katherine
Whiskey Down (1996). . . . . .Kim
The Rainmaker (1997). . . . . Jackie Lemanczyk
Ambushed (1998) . . . . .Lucy Monroe
Made for Cable Movies:
Mussolini and I (1985; HBO) . . . . Claretta Petacci
Fire With Fire (1986; Showtime) . . . . Lisa
Long Gone (1987; HBO) . . . . Dixie Lee Boxx
- 0:04—Brief buns several times, while sleeping face down on bed when William Petersen talks with Dermot Mulroney.

Gotham (1988; Showtime) . . . . Rachel Carlyle
a.k.a. The Dead Can't Lie
- 0:50—Brief breasts in the shower when Tommy Lee Jones comes over to her apartment, then breasts while lying on the floor.
- •• 1:12—Breasts, while dead, in the freezer when Jones comes back to her apartment, then brief breasts on the bed.
- 1:18—Breasts while in the bathtub under water.

Third Degree Burn (1989; HBO) . . . . Anne Scholes
Ironclads (1991) . . . . .Betty Stuart
Linda (1993; USA). . . . . .Linda Crowley
Bitter Vengeance (1994; USA) . . . . Annie
Made for Cable TV:
The Hitchhiker: Perfect Order (1987; HBO) . . . . . Christina
- •• 0:14—Brief breasts changing clothes while Simon watches her on video monitor.
- 0:16—Breasts getting into water in Simon's studio. Her body is covered with white make-up.

Made for TV Movies:
A Murderous Affair: The Carolyn Warmus Story (1992)
. . . . Carolyn Warmus
The Apocalypse Watch (1997). . . . . Karin De Vries

Magnuson, Ann *

Films:
Vortex (1982) . . . . Pamela Fleming
The Hunger (1983) . . . . Young Woman from Disco
- 0:05—Brief breasts in kitchen with David Bowie just before he kills her.

Perfect Strangers (1984) . . . . Maida
Desperately Seeking Susan (1985) . . . . Cigarette Girl
Making Mr. Right (1987) . . . . Frankie Stone
Mondo New York (1987). Poetry Reader
A Night in the Life of Jimmy Reardon (1987) . . . . . Joyce Fickett
Tequila Sunrise (1988). . . . . .Shaleen
Checking Out (1989). . . . . Connie Hagen
Heavy Petting (1989). . . . . .Herself/Television Spokesmodel
Love at Large (1990) . . . . .Doris
Clear and Present Danger (1994). . . . . Moira Wolfson
Before and After (1995). . . . . .Terry Taverner
Cabin Boy (1995) . . . . Calli
Made for Cable Movies:
From the Earth to the Moon: We Have Cleared the Tower (1998; HBO) . . . . .Dee O'Hara
TV:
Anything but Love (1989-92) . . . . .Catherine Hughes

Mahalia

See: Maria, Mahalia.

Mahoney, Victoria

Films:
Switch (1991) . . . . .Felicia
Wild Obsession (1992; Italian) . . . . Veronica
- •• 0:06—Breasts and buns, while dancing on stage.
- 0:44—Brief side of right breast, after taking off bra in dressing room while talking with Victor.
- ••• 1:16—Breasts, after taking off her top. Buns in G-string panties getting into bed with Victor and talking with him.

Wild Orchid II: Two Shades of Blue (1992). . . . . .Mary
Back in Business (1996) . . . . Java
Made for Cable TV:
Red Shoe Diaries: Just Like That (1993; Showtime). . . . .Woman
(Available on the video tape *Red Shoe Diaries 3: Another Woman's Lipstick.*)

Maille, Claudette *

Films:
Like Water for Chocolate (1993; Mexican). . . . . . Gertrudis
a.k.a. Como Agua Para Chocolate
- •• 0:30—Breasts and buns while taking a shower. Nude, running out of shower house after it catches fire, running and jumping on horse with a guy.
- 1:36—Brief side view of left breast in shower flashback.

Maillé, Maïté

Films:
A Nos Amours (1984; French) . . . . .Martine
The Passion of Beatrice (1988; French) . . . . . . La Noiraude
- 1:24—Brief left breast, showing Béatrice how she was abused.

Henry & June (1990). .Frail Prostitute
- 1:22—In black see-through dress.
- ••• 1:23—Breasts making love with Brigitte Lahaie in front of Anais and Hugo.

Maize, Autumn

Made for Cable TV:

Erotic Confessions: Lap Dance (1996; Cinemax) . . . . . . Blonde (Available on video tape in *Erotic Confessions, Volume 4: Pleasure.*)

Erotic Confessions: The Workout (1996; Cinemax) . . . . Nude Girl

- 0:05—Brief breasts and buns, in workout room in Paula's fantasy. (She's the one without a headband.)

Malick, Wendie

Films:

A Little Sex (1982) . . . . .Philomena

- 0:39—Very, very brief side of left breast in gaping robe when she bends over to put her cigarette down.

Bugsy (1991) . . . . Woman on Train

The American President (1995) . . . . .Susan Sloan

Trojan War (1997) . . . . Beverly Kimble

Made for Cable Movies:

North Shore Fish (1997; Showtime) . . . . Shimma

Made for Cable TV:

Dream On (1990-96; HBO) . . . . Judith

Dream On: Hey Diddle Diddle (1996; HBO) . . . . Judith

Made for TV Movies:

Madonna: Innocence Lost (1994) . . . . Camille Barbone

Hart to Hart: Secrets of the Heart (1995) . . . . Sarah Powell

The Return of Hunter (1995) . . . . Lafferty

Perfect Body (1997) . . . . .Janet Bradley

TV:

Trauma Center (1983) . . . . Dr. Brigitte Blaine

NYPD Blue: Brown Appetit (Oct 5, 1993) . . . . . . Susan Wagner

NYPD Blue: True Confessions (Oct 12, 1993) . . . Susan Wagner

Just Shoot Me (1997-) . . . . Nina

Malin, Kym *

Films:

Joysticks (1983) . . . . .Lola

- 0:03—Breasts with Alva showing a nerd their breasts by pulling their blouses open.
- ••• 0:18—Breasts during strip-video game with Jefferson, then in bed with him.
- 0:57—Breasts during fantasy sequence, lit with red lights, hard to see anything.
- 1:02—Brief breasts in slide show in courtroom.

Mike's Murder (1984) . . . . Beautiful Girl #1

Weird Science (1985) . . . . Girl Playing Piano

- 0:55—Brief breasts several times as her clothes get torn off by the strong wind and she gets sucked up and out of the chimney.

Die Hard (1988) . . . . .Hostage

Picasso Trigger (1989) . . . . Kym

- •• 1:04—Breasts taking a shower.

Roadhouse (1989) . . . . .Party Girl

Guns (1990) . . . . Kym

- ••• 0:28—Showering (in back) while talking to Hugs (in front).

Enemy Gold (1993) . . . . Cowboy's Hostess

The Dallas Connection (1994) . . . . Cowboy's Hostess

Video Tapes:

Playboy's Playmate Review (1982) . . . . Playmate

- ••• 0:37—Nude in bar, then on empty stage.

Playboy Video Magazine, Volume 2 (1983) . . . . .Herself/Playboy Playoffs

• Malkrabova, Lucie

a.k.a. Lucy Malkra.

Films:

Supermodel Invasion (1996) . . . . Model 5

- ••• 0:31—In swimsuit, then nude, while posing by the pool.
- 0:48—Full frontal nudity, while standing and posing.

Midnight Temptations 2 (1997) . . . . French Woman

- •• 0:37—Breasts, while making love with the French Soldier.

Video Tapes:

Nude Models in Hollywood (1995) . . . . Sophia

- •• 0:19—Buns in lingerie, while posing for photographs.
- ••• 0:21—Nude, wearing stockings, while posing for photographs.
- ••• 0:29—Nude, wearing stockings, while dancing next to Natasha.
- ••• 0:38—Nude, while dancing by herself.

• Malone, Mandy

Twin sister of Mindy Malone.

Video Tapes:

Playboy's Sisters (1995) . . . . .Herself/Mirror Image

- ••• 0:15—In lingerie and nude in room and in bathroom with her twin sister.

Playboy's Twins & Sisters Too (1997) . . . . . Sea Goddesses

- ••• 0:22—Nude, while frolicking on the beach with her twin sister.

• Malone, Mindy

Twin sister of Mandy Malone.

Video Tapes:

Playboy's Sisters (1995) . . . . .Herself/Mirror Image

- ••• 0:15—In lingerie and nude in room and in bathroom with her twin sister.

Playboy's Twins & Sisters Too (1997) . . . . . Sea Goddesses

- ••• 0:22—Nude, while frolicking on the beach with her twin sister.

Maltby, Katrina *

Films:

Demon Keeper (1993) . . . . Hilary Jackson

- ••• 0:27—Breasts, several times, while in black panties, after taking off robe and getting massaged by Dorothy.

Mandel, Joyce

Films:

Chesty Anderson, U.S. Navy (1975) . . . . .Suzi

- •• 0:15—Buns and very brief back side of left breast, taking off towel and putting on robe.

The Baltimore Bullet (1980) . . . . Waitress

Mandel, Suzy

Adult Films:

Blonde Ambition (1980; British) . . . . Sugar Kane

Nude in hard core sex scenes.

Films:

Confessions of a Driving Instructor (1976; British) . . . . Mrs. Hargreaves

Playbirds (1978; British) . . . . Lena

- •• 0:12—Nude stripping in Playbird office.

Mistress of the Apes (1979; British) . . . . .Secretary

Mangh, Selina

Films:

Heatseeker (1994) . . . . Liu

Hong Kong '97 (1994) Li
- 0:06—Breasts, while making love with Robert Patrick in living room.
- •• 0:08—Nude, during shoot out.

Manheim, Camryn

Films:

The Bonfire of the Vanities (1990) . . . . Poe Picketer
The Road to Wellville (1994) . . . . .Virginia Cranchill
- 1:02—Buns, while lying down and talking with Bridget Fonda.

Jeffrey (1995) . . . . .Single Woman
Eraser (1996). . . . . Nurse
Romy and Michele's High School Reunion (1997) . . . . .Toby Walters

Made for TV Movies:

Deadly Whispers (1995) . . . . .Betty

TV:

The Practice (1997-). . . . . Ellenor Frutt

Mani, Karen

Films:

Alley Cat (1982) . . . . Billie
- 0:01—Brief breasts in panties taking night gown off during opening credits.
- ••• 0:38—Brief side view of right breast and buns getting into the shower. Full frontal nudity in the shower.
- ••• 0:48—Breasts during women's prison shower room scene. Long scene.

Avenging Angel (1985) . . . . Janie Soon Lee
- ••• 0:06—Nude taking a shower, right breast in mirror drying herself off, then in bra getting dressed.

Manion, Cindy

Films:

Blow Out (1981) . . . . .Dancing Coed
Preppies (1984). . . . . Jo
- 0:11—Brief breasts changing into waitress costumes with her two friends.
- 0:44—Breasts during party with the three preppie guys.

The Toxic Avenger (1985) . . . . .Julie
- ••• 0:15—Breasts, after untying her swimsuit top in front of Melvin.

Mannen, Monique

Films:

Playing For Keeps (1986). . . . . .Dancer (Silk's Fantasy)
Coming to America (1988) . . . . Boring Girl/Dancer
Rented Lips (1988) . . . . Dancer
School Daze (1988). . . . . Monique "Mo-Freak"
The Adventures of Ford Fairlane (1991) . . . . Pussycat
The Five Heartbeats (1991) . . . . Sandra Talman
Three of Hearts (1993) . . . . .Daphne
The Fear (1994). . . . . .Mindy
- 0:40—Very brief breasts, while in bubble bath when she slaps Joey for feeling her up.

Mansfield, Jayne *

Films:

Pete Kelly's Blues (1955) . . . . Cigarette Girl
The Girl Can't Help It (1957) . . . . Jerri Jordan
Promises, Promises (1963) . . . . Sandy Brooks
- ••• 0:04—Breasts drying herself off with a towel. Same shot also at 0:48.
- ••• 0:06—Breasts in bed. Same shot also at 0:08, 0:39 and 0:40.
- ••• 0:59—Buns, kneeling next to bathtub, right breast in bathtub, then breasts drying herself off.

A Guide for the Married Man (1967) . . . . Technical Advisor
Single Room Furnished (1968). . . . . Eileen
The Wild, Wild World of Jayne Mansfield (1968) . . . . Herself
Breasts.

TV:

Down You Go (1956) . . . . Regular Panelist

Video Tapes:

Hollywood Scandals and Tragedies (1988) . . . . Herself
- 1:11—Breasts in color still photographs from *Playboy* pictorial.

Playboy Video Centerfold: Dutch Twins (1989) . . . Herself
- ••• 0:39—Breasts in color and B&W shots from *Promises, Promises.*

Manson, Jean *

a.k.a. Jeane Manson.
Popular singer in France.

Films:

Young Nurses (1973). . . . . Kitty
Dirty O'Neil (1974) . . . . .Ruby
10 to Midnight (1983). . . . . Margo
- ••• 1:25—Breasts in hotel room with killer when he tries to elude Charles Bronson.
- 1:26—Brief right breast, lying in bed, covered with sheet.

Mantia, Julianne J.

a.k.a. J.J. Mantia.

Films:

Die Watching (1993) . . . . Girl #2
- 1:05—Brief breasts, while sitting up in bed with Christopher Atkins' father. (She's the blonde girl.)

Centerfold (1995) . . . . .Sandra
- ••• 0:43—Breasts and buns, while making love with Kelly in spa, then making love on lounge chair with the senator.

Lap Dancing (1995) . . . . .Monica
- 0:17—Brief breasts and buns in T-back, while lap dancing with a customer.
- ••• 0:41—Nude, while during strip routine on stage in club. Long scene.
- 0:55—Brief breasts, while lap dancing with a customer.

Masseuse (1995) . . . . Carol
(Unrated version reviewed.)
- ••• 0:56—Breasts, after taking off her bra, then making love with a guy.

Nighttime Lover (1995) . . . . Woman in Room 2
a.k.a. Call Girl
- ••• 0:56—Nude, when a guy rips her top off in room in front of her husband.

Human Desires (1996) . . . . .Woman
- ••• 0:02—Breasts and buns in panties, while making love with a man while another man takes photographs.

Intimate Betrayal (1996). . . . . Debbie
- 0:11—Breasts, while dancing at bachelor party wearing tasseled pasties.
- 0:13—Right breast after pastie comes off and buns in T-back.

Video Tapes:

Penthouse: The Art of Massage (1996). . . . . .Model
- ••• 0:29—Nude, while making love with Rob Lee in bathroom.
- ••• 0:35—Nude, with another woman and two guys by swimming pool.

Marceau, Sophie *

Films:

La Boum (1980; French) Vic
L'Amour Braque (1985; French). . . . . Mary
Police (1985; French). . . . . Noria
- 0:10—Brief left breast in window during police strip search.
- 1:36—Right and left breasts several times, while in bed with Gérard Depardieu

Pour Sacha (1992; French) . . . . Laura
Braveheart (1995). . . . . Princess Isabelle
Anna Karenina (1997). . . . . Anna Karenina

Marcel, Tammy

Films:

Bikini Summer 2 (1992) . . . . Sandy
- 0:15—Buns in two piece swimsuit, while walking with Sandra.
- •• 0:38—Breasts (she's the brunette), taking off her T-shirt and jumping into the pool with Sandra.
- 0:40—Very brief breasts, while running past some guys.
- •• 0:42—More breasts, while running around the backyard.
- •• 0:44—More breasts and buns in swimsuit, while running around some more.

Ring of Fire II: Blood and Steel (1992). . Bad Girl Gang Member

March, Jane *

Films:

The Lover (1992) . . . . The Girl
(Unrated version reviewed.)
(When you don't see her face, it's reportedly a body double.)
- •• 0:32—Full frontal nudity in bed with Tony Leung.
- ••• 0:40—Left breast, while making love under Leung.
- ••• 0:42—Full frontal nudity, while lying in bed. Long shot.
- •• 0:43—Buns, while standing in tub, getting washed by Leung.
- ••• 0:44—Breasts, while lying in bed, talking with Leung. Long scene.
- •• 0:47—Left breast, while making love in bed.
- •• 0:48—Full frontal nudity, while lying in bed.
- •• 0:54—Breasts while making love on the floor with Leung.
- ••• 0:56—More full frontal nudity on the floor.
- ••• 0:59—Nude, walking around and watering the plants, getting into bed, then making love.
- 1:02—Brief breasts while making love.
- 1:17—Breasts while washing herself with Leung. Hard to see because bars get in the way.

Color of Night (1994) . . . . Rose
- ••• 0:59—Nude, while in pool with Bruce Willis.
- •• 1:00—Nude, while making love with Willis in the house.
- ••• 1:02—Breasts and brief lower frontal nudity, when sitting at the table. Breasts, while making love in the shower with Willis.
- 1:04—Breasts, after taking off her clothes in Lesley Ann Warren's bedroom.
- 1:35—Nude under apron while in the kitchen with Willis.
- •• 1:38—Full frontal nudity while in the bathtub with Willis.
- •• 1:47—Breasts, with Warren.
- 1:49—Brief right breast.
- 1:55—Left breast and buns in photo that Willis finds in notebook.
- 2:14—Left breast in gaping blouse, while on top of tower.

Provocateur (1997) . . . . Sook Hee/Miya
Tarzan and the Lost City (1998) . . . . Jane

Marconi, Mason *

Films:

Showgirls (1995) . . . . Uncredited Cheetahs Dancer
(NC-17 version reviewed.)
- 0:25—Breasts and buns on stage when camera pans across the room. (She's the dancer closest to the camera.)

Video Tapes:

Hot Body Hall of Fame: Traci Dali (1995) . . . . Herself
- ••• 0:36—In lingerie, then nude after stripping out of business suit in an office.

Hot Body International: Dreamgirl II (1995) . . . . . Herself
Hot Body International: Steamed Heat (1995) . . . Herself
- 0:03—Buns in swimsuit, outdoors next to car at gas station.
- 0:06—Buns in swimsuit, outdoors at the beach.

Soft Bodies: Show 'n Tell (1995) . . . . Herself
- ••• 0:19—In lingerie and nude, while posing in bedroom.
- ••• 0:26—In schoolgirl outfit, then nude while posing outside.
- ••• 0:33—Nude, while posing by swimming pool.

Marcus, Trula

Films:

Man's Best Friend (1993). . . . . Annie
One Night Stand (1997) . . . . Party Guest

Made for Cable TV:

Dream On: Depth Be Not Proud (1993; HBO). . . . . . . Kelly
- •• 0:10—Nude with Eddie Charles after he loses his job and his wife.

Margolin, Janet

Films:

David and Lisa (1962) . . . . Lisa
Bus Riley's Back in Town (1965). . . . . Judy
Buono Sera, Mrs. Campbell (1968) . . . . Gia Campbell
Take the Money and Run (1969) . . . . Louise
The Last Embrace (1979). . . . . Ellie "Eva" Fabian
- 1:10—Brief breasts in bathtub with Bernie, before strangling him.
- •• 1:14—Right breast, while reaching for the phone in bed with Roy Scheider.
- 1:20—Left breast in photo that Scheider is looking at with a magnifying glass (it's supposed to be her grandmother).

Distant Thunder (1988). . . . . Barbara Lambert
Ghostbusters II (1989). . . . . The Prosecutor

TV:

Lanigan's Rabbi (1977) . . . . Miriam Small

Margot, Sandra

a.k.a. Adult film actress Tyffany Million.
Gorgeous Ladies of Wrestling (GLOW) wrestler from 1987-90 using the name Tiffany Mellon.

Films:

Caged Fury (1989) . . . . Crazy Daisy
- 1:10—Buns in G-string and bra dancing for some men.
- •• 1:11—Breasts after taking off bra.

Demon Wind (1990). . . . . Beautiful Demon
- •• 0:50—Breasts trying to tempt Stacy and Chuck out of the cabin.

The Sleeping Car (1990) . . . . 19-Year Old Girl
- •• 0:00—Brief breasts shots taking off clothes then making love with a guy. Left breast while making love.

Kill, Kill Overkill (1991) . . . . Hitchhiker
Prime Target (1991). . . . . Girl in Shower
- ••• 0:52—Side view of left breast and buns, taking a shower.
- 0:53—Buns, in hotel room after getting out of the shower.

Spirits (1991). . . . . Nun Demon

Body of Influence (1992). .Margaret
(Unrated version reviewed.)
••• 0:03—Breasts and buns in black G-string panties, while undressing for Jonathon.
Made for Cable TV:
Tales From the Crypt: Dead Right (1990; HBO)
. . . . Stripper #2
(Available on *Tales From the Crypt, Volume 3*.)
• 0:13—Dancing on stage wearing pasties.
Video Tapes:
Thunder and Mud (1989) . . . . .Tiffany

Mari, Gina *

Films:
The Slumber Party Massacre (1982) . . . . Diane
• 0:43—Close up of right breast while making out in car with Daryl. Don't see her face.
Dark Side of Genius (1994) . . . . Naomi
Fire Down Below (1997) . . . . .Darlene
Made for Cable Movies:
Rebel Highway: Roadracers (1994; Showtime). . . . . Wanda
Made for Cable TV:
Full Frontal Comedy (1995; Showtime)
. . . . .Woman of Full Frontal Comedy

Maria, Mahalia *

Video Tapes:
Penthouse Pet of the Year Playoff 1992 (1992) . . . . . Pet
••• 0:37—Nude, in the desert, outside around a house, in a wild west theme, in a house and wrestling with another woman, on a bed, in front of a house.
••• 0:57—Nude, outside during the end credits.
Penthouse Satin & Lace: An Erotic History of Lingerie (1992). . . . . .Model
Penthouse Pet of the Year Winners 1993: Mahalia & Julie (1994) . . . . Pet
• 0:01—Full frontal nudity during introduction.
••• 0:18—Full frontal nudity in dominatrix outfit, while dominating Nikki Dial.
••• 0:20—Nude in pool.
••• 0:22—Nude on grass by some flowers, then inside a house.
••• 0:23—More nude while in house wearing a dark wig.

Marie, Bobbie

Films:
Femalien (1995) . . . . Girl Toy, Meditation Woman
••• 0:52—Buns in white T-back, then nude, while on stage with another woman.
••• 1:07—Breasts, while making love with a guy during meditation orgy.
Video Tapes:
Playboy's Hard Bodies (1995). . . . . Herself
••• 0:30—Nude while making love with Sara St. James on a hilltop.

Marie, Connie Lisa *

Films:
The Van (1977) . . . . Sally
• 0:40—In wet T-shirt, while talking to Bobby.
• 1:00—Brief right breast when changing clothes in house while bobby watches her through binoculars.
•• 1:03—Breasts and partial buns after taking off robe, then making love with Bobby in back of van.
• 1:05—Brief breasts, while getting dressed.

Marie, Constance

Films:
My Family (1995) . . . . Toni
• 1:05—Very brief right breast, while making love with Scott Bakula in flashback.
Selena (1997) . . . . .Marcela Quintanilla
Made for TV Movies:
12:01 (1993). . . . . Joan Zevo
TV:
Santa Barbara . . . . .Nikki Alvarez
Dirty Dancing (1988-89) . . . . .Penny Rivera
Union Square (1997-). . . . . Gabriela Diaz

Marie, Jeanne

Films:
If Looks Could Kill (1987) . . . . Jeannie Burns
•• 0:06—Breasts taking off her robe and kissing George.
Prime Evil (1987) . . . . Judy
• 1:13—Breasts after removing her gown (she's on the right) with Cathy and Brett.
Student Affairs (1987). Robin Ready
• 0:35—Brief breasts wearing black panties in bed trying to seduce a guy.
••• 0:41—Breasts making love with another guy, while banging her back against the wall.
• 0:44—Very brief breasts in VW with a nerd.
• 1:09—Very brief breasts falling out of a trailer home filled with water.
Wildest Dreams (1987) . . . . Isabelle
•• 0:35—Breasts in panties in bedroom with Bobby.
Wimps (1987) . . . . Janice
•• 0:20—Breasts in bed taking off top with Charles.
Young Nurses in Love (1987) . . . . .Nurse Ellis Smith
• 0:31—Brief side view of left breast in mirror with Dr. Riley.
•• 1:09—Breasts in panties, getting into bed with Dr. Riley.

Marin, Rikki

Films:
Loose Shoes (1977) . . . . .Commie Lady
Gas Pump Girls (1978). . . . . .January
• 0:49—Brief breasts after opening her blouse, in doorway to distract Moiv.
Cheech & Chong's Next Movie (1980) . . . . Gloria
Cheech & Chong's Nice Dreams (1981) . . . . Blonde in Car
Cheech & Chong's The Corsican Brothers (1984) . . . Princess II

Marino, Bonnie *

Video Tapes:
Playboy Video Calendar 1991 (1990) . . . . June
••• 0:22—Nude.

Mark, Heidi *

Made for Cable Movies:
Weapons of Mass Distraction (1997; HBO) . . .Cricket Paige
• 0:12—In bra and panties, then brief breasts, while jumping on bed in hotel room with Marvel. Seen through B&W video camera hidden in stuffed dog.
Made for Cable TV:
Red Shoe Diaries: Mercy (1996; Showtime) . . . The Woman
• 0:11—Brief nude shots while making love. Some in B&W.
•• 0:15—Buns, with Joey in kitchen. Nude, when making love with him.
TV:
Thunder in Paradise (1993-94) . . . . Allison Wilson
Big Deal (1997) . . . . Co-Host

Video Tapes:
Baywatch: The Movie—Forbidden Paradise (1994) . . . . n.a.
Playboy Video Calendar 1997 (1996) . . . . August
••• 0:32—Nude, while posing in a studio.
••• 0:34—Nude, while undressing in bed and putting on a strap outfit.
Playboy's Girls of the Internet (1996) . . . . Herself
••• 0:10—Nude, while at the beach with two other women.

Markey, Zoli

Films:
The Demon (1981; South African). Jo
••• 1:03—Breasts and buns, in front of mirror, then getting dressed. Long scene.
No One Cries Forever (1984; South African) . . . . Suzy

Markham, Kika

Films:
Deep Cover (1980; British) . . . . Linda Cavendish
a.k.a. Blade on the Feather
• 1:07—Breasts, while lying on bed, dead, when Denholm Elliott covers her with a sheet.
Outland (1981). . . . . Carol
A Woman at War (1991) . . . . Regine

Markov, Margaret *

Films:
Pretty Maids All in a Row (1971) . . . . Polly
The Hot Box (1972) . . . . Lynn Forrest
• 0:12—Breasts when bad guy cuts her swimsuit top open.
•• 0:16—Breasts in stream consoling Bunny.
• 0:21—Breasts in the furthest hammock from camera. Long shot.
••• 0:45—Breasts bathing in stream with the other girls.
Black Mama, White Mama (1973; U.S./Philippines) . . . . Karen Brent
Naked Warriors (1973) . . . . Bodicia
a.k.a. The Arena
• 0:07—Brief breasts getting clothes torn off by guards.
• 0:13—Breasts getting her dress ripped off, then raped during party.
• 0:19—Brief left breast, on floor making love, then right breast and buns.
• 0:52—Brief breasts sitting down, listening to Cornelia.

• Marks, Bridget *

Films:
Circuitry Man II: Plughead Rewired (1993) . . . . Jeannie
Deadly Outbreak (1995) . . . . Elaine Starkov
Thinner (1996) . . . . Gianelli Bar Girl
Made for Cable TV:
Erotic Confessions: The Partners (1997; Showtime) . . . . Hilary
•••• 0:10—In bra, then full frontal nudity, while making love in hotel room with Mona.

Marks, Shae *

Films:
Cover Me (1995). . . . . Candy Jefferson
• 0:01—Brief buns, on magazine cover on computer screen.
• 0:03—Brief breasts in photo on wall.
• 0:04—Breasts in photo on wall again.
•• 0:06—Breasts, while in panties, tied up to bed, before getting killed.
• 0:52—Breasts in photo on wall, then buns in magazine cover flashbacks.
Scoring (1995) . . . . Phyllis
Day of the Warrior (1997) . . . . Tiger
Video Tapes:
Playboy Video Calendar 1995 (1994) . . . . October
••• 0:39—Nude outside. Nude in a house.
Sexy Lingerie: Dreams & Desire (1994) . . . . Playmate
Wet & Wild: The Locker Room (1994) . . . . Playmate
Playboy's Real Couples: Sex in Dangerous Places (1995) . . . . Touching Me, Touching You/Masseuse
••• 0:24—Nude while massaging Carrie Westcott.
Wet & Wild: Hot Holidays (1995) . . . . Playmate
Playboy's Voluptuous Vixens (1997). . . . . Playmate
Playboy's Blondes, Brunettes, Redheads (1998) . . . . Herself

Marlow, Lorrie

Films:
Reform School Girls (1986) . . . . Shelly
Hollywood Shuffle (1987) . . . . Hooker #2/Reporter
Number One with a Bullet (1987) . . . . Hooker
The Night Before (1988) . . . . Whore
The Borrower (1989) . . . . Nurse Wilson
• 0:57—Brief left breast and upper half of right breast, while making love with a doctor in operating room.
To Sleep with Anger (1990). . . . . Cherry Bell

Maroney, Kelli

Films:
Fast Times at Ridgemont High (1982) . . . . Cindy
Night of the Comet (1984) . . . . Samantha
Slayground (1984; British). . . . . Jolene
The Zero Boys (1985) . . . . Jamie
Chopping Mall (1986). . . . . Alison
a.k.a. Killbots
Big Bad Mama II (1987) . . . . Willie McClatchie
Not of This Earth (1988) . . . . Nurse Mary Oxford
Jaded (1989) . . . . Jennifer
Transylvania Twist (1990) . . . . Script Supervisor
Servants of Twilight (1991) . . . . Sherry Ordway
Midnight Witness (1992). . . . . Devon
Miniseries:
Celebrity (1984) . . . . Joanna
TV:
One Life to Live . . . . Tina Clayton
Ryan's Hope (1983). . . . . n.a.
Video Tapes:
Scream Queen Hot Tub Party (1991). . . . . Herself
•• 0:07—Breasts after taking off flower print blouse and putting on pink teddy.
• 0:12—Buns, while walking up the stairs.
••• 0:30—Breasts and buns after stripping out of cheerleader outfit, rubbing lotion on herself and demonstrating the proper Scream Queen way to pump iron.
••• 0:44—Breasts taking off her swimsuit top and soaping up with the other girls.
•• 0:46—Breasts in still shot during the end credits.

Marsac, Laure *

Films:
Interview With the Vampire: The Vampire Chronicles (1994). . . . . Mortal Woman on Stage
••• 1:15—Nude after being stripped of her clothes, then killed while on stage during play put on by the vampires. Long scene.

Made for Cable TV:

Strangers: My Ward, My Keeper (1996; Canadian/French; HBO) . . . . Juliet

- 0:07—Breasts and buns, while making love with Eric on scaffolding.
- 0:09—Brief side of right breast, while lying in bed.
- 0:17—Right breast, while lying in bed with Eric, then in bra, when getting dressed.
- 0:20—Brief right breast, during flashback on scaffolding.

Marsani, Claudia

Films:

Conversation Piece (1974; Italian/French) . . . . Lietta

- 1:13—Breasts, while with Konrad.
- 1:15—Breasts, while getting dressed in other room. Medium long shot.

Submission (1976; Italian) . . . . Justine

Marshall, Paula

Films:

Hellraiser III: Hell on Earth (1992) . . . . Terri
(Unrated version reviewed.)

- 0:47—Very, very brief left breast under gaping blouse, while spinning around to get up off the floor to run to the door.

Warlock: The Armageddon (1993) . . . . Samantha Ellison

The New Age (1994) . . . . Alison Gale

- •• 0:08—Right breast, when lying in bed with Peter Weller, while he makes love to her.
- 1:06—Breasts, while lying face down on massage table in health club. Brief breasts and partial lower frontal nudity, sitting up and putting on robe.

A Family Thing (1996) . . . . Karen

A Gun, a Car, a Blonde (1996) . . . . Deborah/Girl in Photograph

That Old Feeling (1997) . . . . Molly

Made for Cable Movies:

Full Eclipse (1993; HBO) . . . . Liza

Made for TV Movies:

Nurses on the Line: The Crash of Flight 7 (1993) . . . Jill Houston

TV:

Wild Oats (1994) . . . . Shelly

Chicago Sons (1997) . . . . Lindsay

Spin City (1997-) . . . . Laurie Parres

Marshall, Ruth

Films:

Dolores Claiborne (1995) . . . . Secretary

Love and Human Remains (1995; Canadian) . . . . Candy

- 0:45—Breasts, while making love with Jerri.
- •• 0:52—Breasts, while in bed with Jerri, then getting out.
- 1:02—Brief, partial breasts, while making love with Robert.

Marsillach, Blanca

Sister of actress Christina Marsillach.

Films:

Flesh + Blood (1985) . . . . Clara

- •• 0:11—Full frontal nudity on bed having convulsions after getting hit on the head with a sword.

Collector's Item (1988) . . . . Jacqueline
a.k.a. The Trap

- •• 0:52—In white bra cleaning up Tony Musante in bed, then breasts.
- 1:04—Lower frontal nudity while watching Musante and Laura Antonelli making love in bed.
- 1:18—Breasts getting dressed. A little dark.
- •• 1:22—Breasts changing clothes in bedroom while Antonelli talks to her.

Dangerous Obsession (1990; Italian) . . . . Jessica

- 0:02—Left breast, getting fondled by Johnny in recording studio. Lower frontal nudity when he pulls down her panties.
- •• 0:05—Breasts while opening her blouse when Johnny plays his saxophone.
- 0:17—Lower frontal nudity on the stairs with Johnny, then brief breasts.
- 0:29—Brief breasts in video tape on T.V.
- •• 0:40—Breasts while changing sweaters.
- ••• 0:56—Full frontal nudity masturbating while looking at pictures of Johnny. Buns, then more full frontal nudity getting video taped.
- ••• 0:58—Breasts in bed with a gun. Nude walking around the house. Long scene.
- 1:05—Brief breasts on beach taking off sweater and burying a dog.
- 1:06—Brief full frontal nudity during video taping session.
- •• 1:07—Breasts while cleaning up Dr. Simpson.
- ••• 1:13—Breasts, taking chains off Dr. Simpson, then lying in bed. Full frontal nudity making love with him.

Marsillach, Cristina

Sister of actress Blanca Marsillach.

Films:

Every Time We Say Goodbye (1986) . . . . Sarah

- •• 1:09—Right breast, then brief breasts lying in bed with Tom Hanks.

Collector's Item (1988) . . . . Young Marie
a.k.a. The Trap

- •• 0:12—Right breast in elevator with Tony Musante.
- •• 0:36—Breasts in open blouse, then full frontal nudity in hut with Musante.

Terror at the Opera (1989; Italian) . . . . Betty

- 0:23—Brief left breast during nightmare. Brief breasts, sitting up in bed and screaming.

Marsilo, Geraldina

Films:

Sorority House Party (1992) . . . . Party Guest (Streaker)

- 0:04—Breasts, while walking by pool during party. Medium long shot.

California or Bust (1994) . . . . n.a.

Marta, Lynne

Films:

Blood Beach (1981) . . . . Jo

- 0:30—Brief left breast in ripped open blouse, while struggling with rapist on beach at night.

Footloose (1984) . . . . Lulu

*Marteen, Rachel Jeàn **

Video Tapes:

Playboy Video Calendar 1997 (1996) . . . . October

- ••• 0:41—Nude, while posing outdoors.
- ••• 0:42—In lingerie and nude, while posing outdoors.

Wet & Wild VIII: Bottoms Up (1996) . . . . Playmate

*Martin, Danielle **

a.k.a. Adult film actress Danielle.

Adult Films:

The Blond Next Door . . . . n.a.

Films:

My Therapist (1983) . . . . Francine

•• 0:29—In bra, garter belt, stockings and panties, then breasts in room with Rip.

Video Tapes:

The Girls of Penthouse (1984) . . . . Bad to the Bone Woman

••• 0:07—Nude, taking off her leather outfit.

Martin, Mitch

Films:

Hog Wild (1980; Canadian). . . . . Polly

Incubus (1981; Canadian) . . . . Mandy Pullman

• 0:13—Very brief left breast, when waking up on operating table.

The Gunrunner (1989; Canadian) . . . . Rosalyn

Martin, Pamela Sue *

Films:

The Poseidon Adventure (1972) . . . . Susan Shelby

Buster and Billie (1974) . . . . Margie Hooks

The Lady in Red (1979) . . . . Polly Franklin

• 0:07—Right breast, while in bedroom with a guy clutching her clothes.

••• 0:20—Breasts in jail with a group of women prisoners waiting to be examined by a nurse.

Flicks (1981) . . . . Liz

Torchlight (1984) . . . . Lillian Gregory

Made for TV Movies:

Human Feelings (1978). . . . . Verna Gold

TV:

The Hardy Boys Mysteries (1977-78). . . . . Nancy Drew

The Nancy Drew Mysteries (1977-78). . . . . Nancy Drew

Dynasty (1981-84) . . . . Fallon Carrington Colby

Martin, Sandy

Films:

Scalpel (1976). . . . . Sandy

48 Hrs. (1982) . . . . Policewoman

Real Genius (1985) . . . . Mrs. Meredith

Extremities (1986). . . . . Officer Sudow

Vendetta (1986) . . . . Kay Butler

• 0:34—Brief left breast, while making love with her boyfriend. Don't see her face.

Barfly (1987). . . . . Janice

Defenseless (1991) . . . . Judge

China Moon (1993) . . . . Gun Saleswoman

Above Suspicion (1994) . . . . Waitress

Speed (1994) . . . . Bartender

Female Perversions (1997) . . . . Trudy

Made for Cable Movies:

Indictment: The McMartin Trial (1995; HBO) . . . Deputy Phyllis

Maryott, Kirsten

Films:

The Dark Dancer (1994) . . . . Cocktail Waitress

The House on Todville Road (1994). . . . . Amelia

• 0:22—Brief breasts and buns, taking off nightgown and going for a swim in pool at night.

• 0:23—Buns, while in the water and getting out.

• 0:29—Buns and back side of left breast, while sitting on shower floor with bloody whip marks on her back.

•• 0:59—Buns and breasts, while in the showers (whip marks still visible on her back).

•• 1:03—Breasts, while taking off shirt and putting on dress in bedroom.

Mason, Marsha

Ex-wife of playwright Neil Simon.

Films:

Blume in Love (1973). . . . . Arlene

• 0:22—Side view of right breast, then brief breasts while lying in bed with George Segal.

• 0:35—Very brief right breast while reaching over the bed.

•• 0:54—Brief breasts twice, reaching over to get a pillow while talking to Segal.

Cinderella Liberty (1973) . . . . Maggie Paul

•• 0:17—Side view of left breast in room with Caan. Brief right breast sitting down on bed.

••• 0:38—Breasts sitting up in bed, yelling at Caan.

• 0:54—Very brief left breast turning over in bed and sitting up.

Audrey Rose (1977). . . . . Janice Templeton

The Goodbye Girl (1977) . . . . Paula McFadden

The Cheap Detective (1978) . . . . Georgia Merkle

Chapter Two (1979) . . . . Jennie MacLaine

Promises in the Dark (1979) . . . . Dr. Alexandra Kenda

Only When I Laugh (1981) . . . . Georgia

Max Dugan Returns (1983) . . . . Nora

Heartbreak Ridge (1986) . . . . Aggie

Drop Dead Fred (1991). . . . . Polly

I Love Trouble (1994) . . . . Senator Gayle Robbins

Nick of Time (1995) . . . . Governor Eleanor Grant

2 Days in the Valley (1996) . . . . Audrey Hopper

Made for Cable Movies:

Dinner At Eight (1989) . . . . Millicent Jordan

The Image (1990; HBO) . . . . Jean Cromwell

• 0:08—Two brief side views of left breast standing in bathroom after Albert Finney gets out of the shower.

Broken Trust (1995; TNT) . . . . Ruth

TV:

Where the Heart Is. . . . . Laura Blackburn

Dark Shadows (1969) . . . . Vampire Girl

Love of Life (1972) . . . . Judith Cole

Sibs (1991-92). . . . . Nora Rucio

Massari, Léa

Films:

L'avventura (1959; Italian/French) . . . . Anna

Murmur of the Heart (1971; French/Italian/German) . . . . Clara Chevalier

•• 1:19—Brief back sides of breasts, while taking a bath, buns when getting out of bath.

Story of a Love Story (1973; French/Italian). . . . . Hipolita

a.k.a. Impossible Object

Allonsanfan (1974; Italian) . . . . Charlotte

• 0:32—Buns, while undressing in bedroom in front of Marcello Mastroianni.

Massey, Anna

Sister of actor Daniel Massey.

Daughter of actor Raymond Massey.

Films:

Peeping Tom (1960; British) . . . . Helen Stephens

Frenzy (1972; British). Babs Milligan

•• 0:45—Breasts getting out of bed and then buns, walking to the bathroom. Probably a body double.

Sweet William (1980; British). . . . . Edna

Five Days One Summer (1982) . . . . Jennifer Pierce

Foreign Body (1986; British) . . . . Miss Furze

Mountains of the Moon (1989). . . . . Mrs. Arundell

The Tall Guy (1990; British) . . . . Mary

Haunted (1995). . . . . Nanny Tess

Angels & Insects (1996; British)................ Miss Mead
Made for TV Movies:
Tears in the Rain (1988; British).......... Lady Emily Bredon

Massey, Athena

Films:
Out for Justice (1991) ....n.a.
Cyber Tracker 2 (1995) .... Kessel
Undercover (1995) ....Cindy Hanen
(Unrated version reviewed.)
• 0:00—Brief breast and buns, while getting dressed during opening credits. Don't see her face.
•• 0:13—Buns and left breast, while making love in bed with Hunt.
•• 0:21—Breasts, while undressing in front of Meg Foster for her audition.
•• 0:31—In black bra, then breasts in front of Mr. Ralston.
• 0:45—Breasts under sheer black blouse.
••• 0:55—Breasts and buns doing a strip routine in front of a customer, then making love with him. Very, very brief partial lower frontal nudity when she pulls her dress up.
0:59—Brief buns under sheer nightgown.
••• 1:04—Breasts and buns in black rubber outfit in room with a customer, then making love with him on a chair.
• 1:11—Buns in T-back in sheer black robe.
•• 1:15—Breasts with a customer and his wife.
••• 1:16—Breasts and buns while making love in bed with the customer and his wife.
••• 1:21—Breasts while in bathtub. Breasts and buns in flashbacks.
••• 1:32—Nude, while making love with Hunt in bed.
Virtual Combat (1995) ....Liana
• 0:15—Brief breasts in virtual reality program. Then in bra and panties in real life.
•• 0:51—Breasts, while making love with Don "The Dragon" Wilson.
The Nutty Professor (1996) .... Sexy Girl
Poison Ivy 3: The New Seduction (1996) .... Rebecca
••• 0:03—In black bra and panties, then breasts, while making love with the pool boy.
Star Portal (1997).................... Quad Rena/Sarah
• 0:17—Brief breasts, when taking off her hospital gown in front of Steven Bauer.
•• 0:24—Breasts, while in bedroom with her boyfriend, in flashbacks and when picking out a dress.
••• 0:46—Breasts and buns, while taking a shower.
• 0:49—Brief breasts, while sitting up in bed and talking with Bauer.
• 0:52—Brief full frontal nudity, when standing up in bed and walking out from behind bead curtain.
Made for Cable Movies:
The Unspeakable (1996) .... Alice Redmond
a.k.a. Shadow of a Scream
• 0:00—Breasts in quick cuts during opening credits.
• 0:18—Breasts, while having rough sex with Cyril O'Reilly in bedroom.
•• 0:47—Breasts, while taking a shower. Overhead shots, then normal shots, when Cyril O'Reilly scares her.
• 1:16—In bra, with David Chokachi. Brief partial buns in panties.
•• 1:19—Breasts, while being threatened by Chokachi. Very brief buns and lower frontal nudity, lying back on bed.
Made for Cable TV:
The Larry Sanders Show: Hank's Sex Tape (1995; HBO)
.... Woman #1
Red Shoe Diaries: Slow Train (1996; Showtime)
.... Edna Gains/Granddaughter
• 0:10—Buns and breasts, while getting undressed in background.
•• 0:12—Full frontal nudity, while modeling for photographer.
• 0:19—Breasts in flashbacks with the photographer.
••• 0:21—Breasts and buns, while making love with Mac on train.

Massey, Edith

Films:
Pink Flamingos (1972).................. Edy the Egg Lady
Female Trouble (1974)............................ Ida
• 0:20—Breasts, massaging her breasts in front of the mirror.
Desperate Living (1977) ....Queen Carlotta
Polyester (1981) .... Cuddles

*Masterman, Jenifer **

Video Tapes:
Playboy's Girls of Radio: Talk, Rock and Shock (1995)
.... Herself
••• 0:32—In red bra and panties, then nude while posing on a bar.

Masterson, Chase

Films:
In a Moment of Passion (1992) ....Tammy Brandon
• 0:36—Very brief side of left breast, when dancing in a restaurant with Maxwell Caulfield in front of a lot of people.
• 1:01—Brief left breast, while making love with Caulfield.
Married People, Single Sex (1993)................ Beth
• 0:30—Buns in lingerie, while trying on clothes with her girlfriends.
Robin Hood: Men in Tights (1993) ...... Giggling Court Lady
Digital Man (1995).............................Susie
•• 0:27—Breasts, while in bed with Don Swayze.
TV:
General Hospital .... Ivy Lief
Live Shot (1995-96)............................. Sheila
Star Trek: Deep Space Nine (1995-) .... Leeta

Masterson, Fay

Films:
The Man Without a Face (1993) .... Gloria
Cops and Robbersons (1994)............. Cindy Robberson
The Quick and the Dead (1994) .... Mattie Silk
Made for Cable Movies:
The Avenging Angel (1994; TNT) ....n.a.
Made for Cable TV:
Strangers: Touch (1996; Canadian/French; HBO).... Clarice
• 0:10—Breasts, when looking at herself in the mirror. Don't see her face.

Mastrantonio, Mary Elizabeth

Wife of film director Pat O'Connor.
Films:
Scarface (1983)................................Gina
• 2:36—(0:39 into tape 2) Very, very brief left breast when she gets shot and her nightgown opens up.
The Color of Money (1986).................. Carmen
• 0:41—Brief breasts in bathroom mirror drying herself off while Paul Newman talks to Tom Cruise. Long shot, hard to see.
Slam Dance (1987; U.S./British)...............Helen Drood

The January Man (1988) . . . . Bernadette Flynn
- 0:40—Breasts in bed with Kevin Kline. Side view of left breast squished against Kline.
- ••• 0:42—Breasts after Kline gets out of bed. Brief shot, but very nice!

The Abyss (1989) . . . . Lindsey Brigman
- 1:41—Breasts during C.P.R. scene.

Fools of Fortune (1990). . . . . Marianne
Class Action (1991) . . . . Margaret Ward
Robin Hood: Prince of Thieves (1991) . . . . Marian
Consenting Adults (1992) . . . . Priscilla Parker
White Sands (1992) . . . . Lane Bodine
- 1:11—Brief left breast in shower with Willem Dafoe. You see her face, so this shot is really her.

Three Wishes (1995) . . . . Jeanne Holman
Two Bits (1996). . . . . Luisa
Made for Cable Movies:
Mussolini and I (1985; HBO) . . . . Edda Mussolini Ciano

Mastrogiacomo, Gina

Films:
Alien Space Avenger (1988) . . . . Ginny
- ••• 0:19—Breasts in bed, making love with Matt. Breasts and buns, getting out and getting dressed.

GoodFellas (1990). . . . . Janice Rossi
Jungle Fever (1991). . . . . Louise
The Naked Gun 2 1/2: The Smell of Fear (1991) . . . . "Is this some kind of bust?"
Made for Cable Movies:
Rebel Highway: Motorcycle Gang (1994; Showtime) . .Waitress
TV:
NYPD Blue: A Sudden Fish (Feb 15, 1994). . . . . .Chicky

Mateyko, Kristina *

Films:
Sinful Intrigue (1995) . . . . .Girl #1
Video Tapes:
Playboy's Sisters (1995). . . . . .Herself/Natural Woman
- ••• 0:22—Nude with her sister and four other sisters outdoors.

Mathias, Darian

Films:
My Chauffeur (1986) . . . . .Dolly
Blue Movies (1988) . . . . Kathy
- 0:37—Very brief breasts twice acting for the first time in a porno film.
- 0:39—Breasts, seen from above during screening of movie. Hard to see.

Made for TV Movies:
My Wicked Ways... The Legend of Errol Flynn (1985) . . 1st Girl

Mathis, Samantha

Daughter of actress Bibi Besch.
Films:
Pump Up the Volume (1990) . . . . Nora Diniro
- •• 1:13—Breasts taking off sweater on patio with Christian Slater.

This is My Life (1992) . . . . Erica Ingels
Super Mario Bros. (1993) . . . . .Daisy
The Thing Called Love (1993). . . . . .Miranda Presley
Little Women (1994). . . . . .Amy as 16 Year Old
The American President (1995). . . . . .Janie Basdin
How to Make an American Quilt (1995) . . . . Young Sophia
Broken Arrow (1996). Terry Carmichael
Jack & Sarah (1996; British/French). . . . . Amy
Made for Cable TV:
Directed By: Museum of Love (1996; Showtime). . . . Stephanie
Made for TV Movies:
83 Hours 'til Dawn (1990) . . . . .Julie Burdock
Extreme Close-Up (1990) . . . . Laura
To My Daughter (1990). . . . . .Anne Carlston
TV:
Aaron's Way (1988). . . . . Roseanne Miller
Knightwatch (1988-89). . . . . .Jake

Matlin, Marlee

Films:
Children of a Lesser God (1986). . . . . Sarah
(Academy Award for Best Actress.)
- 0:44—Brief buns under water in swimming pool. Don't see her face.
- 0:47—Part of left breast while hugging William Hurt (seen from under water).

Walker (1988) . . . . Ellen Martin
The Linguini Incident (1991) . . . . Jeanette
The Player (1992) . . . . Cameo
Hear No Evil (1993) .Jillian Shananhan
- •• 0:30—Brief breasts, getting out of the bathtub.

It's My Party (1995). . . . . Daphne Stark
Made for Cable Movies:
Dead Silence (1996; HBO). . . . . Melanie Charrol
Made for Cable TV:
The Outer Limits: The Message (1995; Showtime). . . . . Jennifer
Made for TV Movies:
Bridge to Silence (1988) . . . . Peggy Lawrence
Against Her Will: The Carrie Buck Story (1994) . . . . Carrie Buck
TV:
Reasonable Doubts (1991-93) . . . . Tess Kaufman

Matthews, Lisa *

Films:
Hudson Hawk (1991) . . . . Girl in Car
Video Tapes:
Playboy Video Calendar 1991 (1990) . . . . September
Sexy Lingerie II (1990). . . . . .Model
Wet & Wild II (1990) . . . . .Model
Playboy Video Calendar 1992 (1991) . . . . July
- •• 0:27—Nude in fashion show fantasy.
- ••• 0:28—Nude in mansion doing various things.

Playboy Video Centerfold: Lisa Matthews (1991) . . . . Playmate of the Year 1991
- ••• 0:00—Nude in front of curtains, then in bed, then in medical segment, then at the beach and finally in a fantasy modeling session.

The Best of Sexy Lingerie (1992) . . . . .Model
The Best of Video Playmate Calendars (1992). . .Playmate
- •• 0:19—Breasts and buns, while in the desert.
- ••• 0:20—Nude in a house.

Playboy's Sexy, Steamy, Sultry (1993). . . . . .Playmate

Mattson, Robin

Films:
Namu, The Killer Whale (1966) . . . . Lisa Rand
Bonnie's Kids (1973) . . . . .Myra
- 0:05—Brief side view of right breast, changing in bedroom while two men watch from outside.
- ••• 0:07—Breasts washing herself in the bathroom.

Candy Stripe Nurses (1974) . . . . Dianne
- •• 0:22—Nude in gym with the basketball player.
- ••• 0:40—Nude in bed with the basketball player.

Return to Macon County (1975) . . . . Junell

Wolf Lake (1978) . . . . .Linda
a.k.a. Survive the Night at Wolf Lake
• 0:54—Brief full frontal nudity during rape in cabin. Dark.
• 0:55—Brief breasts afterwards.
Take Two (1988) . . . . Susan Bentley
•• 0:25—Brief breasts taking a shower.
••• 0:29—Breasts in bed with Goodeve.
••• 0:45—Right breast in shower, then breasts getting into bed.
• 0:47—Brief breasts getting out of bed and putting an overcoat on.
••• 1:28—Breasts taking a shower after shooting Goodeve in bed.
In Between (1991). . . . . .Margo
Made for TV Movies:
The Secret Night Caller (1975) . . . . Jan Durant
Are You in the House Alone? (1978) . . . . Allison Bremmer
False Witness (1989) . . . . Jody
TV:
The Guiding Light (1976-77). . . . . .Hope Bauer
General Hospital (1980-83) . . . . Heather Grant Webber
Ryan's Hope (1984) . . . . Delia Reid
Santa Barbara (1985-93) . . . . .Gina Capwell Timmons
All My Children (1994-) . . . . .Janet Green

Maur-Thorp, Sarah

Films:
Edge of Sanity (1988) . . . . Susannah
• 0:00—Left breast, while pulling down top to show the little boy in the barn.
•• 0:09—Breasts, while talking to the two doctors after they examine her back.
•• 0:50—Breasts in red room with Anthony Perkins and Johnny.
• 0:56—Very brief breasts in nun outfit.
• 1:10—Brief breasts in Perkins' hallucination at Flora's whorehouse.
Ten Little Indians (1989) . . . . Vera Claythorne
River of Death (1990) . . . . Anna Blakesley
• 0:14—Very brief left breast while in tent with Michael Dudikoff.

Maura, Carmen

Films:
Matador (1986; Spanish). . . . . .Julie
The Law of Desire (1987; Spanish) . . . . Tina Quintero
Baton Rouge (1988; Spanish) . . . . Isabel Harris
• 1:22—Breasts, visible under water under crooked nightgown while standing in pool.
• 1:23—Breasts, sticking out of nightgown after Antonio Banderas drowns her.
Women on the Verge of a Nervous Breakdown (1988; Spanish) . . . . Pepa Marcos
• 0:57—Inner half of breasts visible under sheer portion of black lingerie while changing clothes.
Ay, Carmela! (1991; Spanish) . . . . Carmela
•• 0:42—Showing her left breast to the Lieutenant to explain why she had a Republican flag. Subtitles get in the way.
•• 1:38—Breasts taking off flag on stage during play. Subtitles get in the way again.
High Heels (1991; Spanish) . . . . Tina
Pepi, Luci, Bom and Other Girls on the Heap (1992; Spanish) . . . . Pepi

Maxwell, Maggy

Films:
The Music Lovers (1971; British) . . . Queen in Swan Lake Ballet
Savage Messiah (1972; British) . . . . .Tart
•• 0:39—Nude, undressing in bedroom and posing for a guy doing sketches.
Sitting Target (1972; British) . . . . Irate Mother

May, Mathilda

a.k.a. Mathilda May Haim.
Daughter of French playwright Victor Haim.
Films:
Dream One (1984; British/French). . . . . Alice
Letters to an Unknown Lover (1985) . . . . Agnes
• 0:43—Upper half of breasts in bathtub when Gervais opens the door.
••• 0:58—Buns and breasts taking off her robe in Gervais' room.
Lifeforce (1985) . . . . Space Girl
• 0:08—Full frontal nudity (upside down) in glass case.
• 0:13—Breasts, lying down in space shuttle. Lit with blue light.
••• 0:16—Breasts while sitting up in lab to suck the life out of military guard. Brief full frontal nudity.
•• 0:17—Breasts again in the lab.
•• 0:19—Breasts while walking around, then buns.
••• 0:20—Breasts, while walking down the stairs. Briefly nude, while fighting with the guards.
•• 0:44—Breasts with Steve Railsback during his nightmare. Lit with red light.
• 1:10—Brief breasts, whle in space shuttle with Railsback.
Naked Tango (1990) . . . . Alba/Stephanie
Becoming Colette (1992; French/German/U.S.) . . . . .Gabrielle Colette
•• 0:01—Left breast, in open dress top, on stage during play.
•• 0:16—Breasts, sitting up in bed.
•• 0:48—Left breast, then breasts in bed with Virginia Madsen.
•• 0:49—Side view of right breast in bed with Madsen and Klaus Maria Brandauer.
•• 1:13—Upper half of buns and right breast, while making love in bed on top of Brandauer.
The Cry of the Owl (1992; French/Italian) . . . . Juliette
Dead Tired (1995; French). . . . . Herself
a.k.a. Grosse Fatigue
The Jackal (1997). . . . . Isabella

• *May, Tracie*

Films:
Double Your Pleasure (1997) . . . . Kathleen Connell
••• 0:04—Breasts, while making love with Jack in back room of bookstore.
The Game (1997) . . . . Restaurant Cashier
Hideous (1997) . . . . Belinda Yost
• 0:59—Very, very brief partial buns in panties after falling on the floor.

• *Maybach, Christiane*

Films:
Dollars (1972) . . . . Helga
Naughty Nymphs (1972; German) . . . . Lilly Mae
a.k.a. Passion Pill Swingers
a.k.a. Don't Tell Daddy
• 0:29—Breasts in field with Gilbert.
• 0:40—Breasts getting out of car after making love with Gilbert.

•• 0:44—Breasts walking in field with Gilbert.
• 1:03—Breasts talking on phone while sitting in bed.
Just a Gigolo (1979; German) . . . . Gilda

Mayenzet, Maria

Films:
Jagged Edge (1985) . . . . Page Forrester
• 0:02—Very brief breast, on bed when the killer rips her pajamas open. Long shot.
Messenger of Death (1988). . . . . Esther Beecham

Mayne, Belinda

Films:
Krull (1983). . . . . Vella
Don't Open Till Christmas (1984; British) . . . . Kate
Lassiter (1984) . . . . Helen Boardman
••• 0:06—In bra then breasts letting Tom Selleck undress her while her husband is in the other room.
White Fire (1985). . . . . Ingrid
•• 0:33—Nude, while swimming in pool.
••• 0:34—Nude, swimming in pool, then getting out and taking a shower.
•• 0:35—Nude, after Robert Ginty steals her towel.
•• 0:37—Nude, standing up in pool and getting out and going up stairs.
•• 1:16—Breasts, when taking off her dress while on boat with Ginty.
Fatal Beauty (1987). . . . . Traci
The Tigress (1992) . . . . Elsy

Mayo, Jennifer

Films:
Scarred (1983) . . . . Ruby
••• 0:18—Breasts, undressing in bedroom in front of a customer, lying in bed, then making love. Long scene.
• 0:21—Breasts, while lying in bed afterward.
• 0:27—Breasts in bathtub, getting red paint washed off by a friend.
• 0:29—Left breast, while sitting in bathtub.
Cherry 2000 (1988) . . . . Randa

*Mayo-Chandler, Karen **

Films:
Beverly Hills Cop (1984) . . . . Maitland Receptionist
Explorers (1986) . . . . Starkiller's Girl Friend
Hamburger—The Motion Picture (1986)
. . . . Dr. Victoria Gotbottom
• 0:03—Brief breasts in her office trying to help, then seduce Russell.
Out of the Dark (1988) . . . . Barbara
• 0:16—Brief breasts pulling red dress down wearing black stocking in Kevin's studio.
••• 0:17—Breasts and buns posing during photo shoot.
Party Line (1988) . . . . Sugar Lips
•• 0:58—Breasts, opening her blouse while sitting on Garrett's lap.
• 1:01—Brief breasts, while lying dead in field, covered with blood.
Stripped to Kill II (1988). Cassandra
•• 0:18—Breasts taking off her top for a customer.
Take Two (1988). . . . . Dorothy
•• 1:17—Brief breasts on bed when her gold dress is pulled down a bit.
Death Feud (1989) . . . . Anne
•• 0:36—In white lingerie, then breasts several times outside taking off robe.

Hard to Die (1990) . . . . Diana Farrow
a.k.a. Tower of Terror
•• 0:10—Breasts, putting on her dress in office with Mr. Plimpton.
976-EVIL II: The Astral Factor (1991) . . . . Laurie
•• 0:00—Breasts, while taking a shower in shower room, then putting on wet T-shirt.

Mayor, Cari

Films:
Spring Fever USA (1988) . . . . Girl on Campus
a.k.a. Lauderdale
Summer Job (1989) . . . . Donna
• 0:10—Brief breasts twice, taking off her top before and after Herman comes into the room.

Mayron, Melanie

Films:
Harry and Tonto (1974). . . . . Ginger
(She's a lot heavier in this film than she is now.)
• 0:57—Very brief breasts in motel room with Art Carney taking off her towel and putting on blouse. Long shot, hard to see.
Car Wash (1976). . . . . Marsha
Gable and Lombard (1976). . . . . Dixie
The Great Smokey Roadblock (1976). . . . . Lulu
You Light Up My Life (1977) . . . . Annie Gerrara
Girlfriends (1978). . . . . Susan Weinblatt
(She's still a bit overweight.)
• 0:14—Buns, very brief lower frontal nudity and brief left breast getting dressed in bathroom.
Heartbeeps (1981) . . . . Susan
Missing (1982) . . . . Terry Simon
The Boss' Wife (1986) . . . . Janet Keefer
Sticky Fingers (1988). . . . . Lolly
Checking Out (1989) . . . . Jenny Macklin
My Blue Heaven (1990). . . . . Crystal
Drop Zone (1994). . . . . Mrs. Willins
Made for TV Movies:
Hustling (1975). . . . . Dee Dee
Playing for Time (1980). . . . . Marianne
(Lost a lot of weight.)
The Best Little Girl in the World (1981) . . . . Carol Link
Ordeal in the Arctic (1993) . . . . Sue
TV:
thirtysomething (1987-91) . . . . Melissa Steadman

Mays, Brittany

See: Delahunty, Justine.

*Mays, Melinda **

Video Tapes:
Playboy Video Magazine, Volume 5 (1983) . . . . . Playmate
• 0:05—Brief breasts in hay.
Playboy's Playmate Review 3 (1985). . . . . Playmate

Mazar, Debi

Films:
GoodFellas (1990). . . . . Sandy
The Doors (1991) . . . . Whiskey Girl
Jungle Fever (1991). . . . . Denise
Little Man Tate (1991). . . . . Gina

Bad Love (1992) . . . . Delores
a.k.a. Wild Angel
• 1:02—Very brief side view of right breast, taking off her sheer black top, wearing pasties over her nipples. Buns visible under sheer black pants.
In the Soup (1992) . . . . Suzi
Malcolm X (1992) . . . . Peg
Toys (1992) . . . . Nurse Debbie
Beethoven's 2nd (1993) . . . . Regina
Inside Monkey Zetterland (1993) . . . . Daphne
Money for Nothing (1993) . . . . Monica Russo
•• 0:39—Breasts, while making love in bed with John Cusack while covered with money.
So, I Married an Axe Murderer (1993) . . Tony's Girlfriend Susan
Bullets Over Broadway (1994) Vi
Batman Forever (1995) . . . . Spice
Empire Records (1995) . . . . Jane
Girl 6 (1996) . . . . Girl #39
Meet Wally Sparks (1996) . . . . Sandy Galo
Red Ribbon Blues (1997) . . . . Darcy
She's So Lovely (1997) . . . . Georgie
Made for Cable Movies:
Witch Hunt (1995; HBO) . . . . Manicurist
Made for Cable TV:
Musical Shorts (1994; Comedy Central) . . . . Host
TV:
Civil Wars (1992-93) . . . . Denise Iannello
L.A. Law (1993-94) . . . . Denise Iannello
Temporarily Yours (1997) . . . . Deb DeAngelo
Music Videos:
True Blue/Madonna . . . . True Blue Dancer

Mazzotta, Kathleen

Films:
Femalien (1995) . . . . Jean
• 0:05—Lower frontal nudity, while caressing herself outside.
••• 0:07—Nude, while making love with her boyfriend in backyard. Long scene.
Sinful Intrigue (1995) . . . . Girl #3
• 0:47—Brief breasts (she's the redhead), while sipping a margarita in the backyard. Medium long shot, then closer shot.
Made for Cable TV:
Erotic Confessions: Chalk It Up (1995; Cinemax) . . . . . Kim
•• 0:03—Breasts, while giving Ronny a lap dance in pool hall.
••• 0:06—Breasts, while making love in back room with Max.
••• 0:09—Nude, while with Max in bedroom. Making love with him while he's blindfolded and tied to the bed.
Erotic Confessions: Gifts (1996; Cinemax) . . . . Trisha
(Available on video tape in *Erotic Confessions, Volume 2: Intrigue.*)
• 0:09—In red bra, then very brief partial lower frontal nudity while making love with Tom in his office at school.
Erotic Confessions: Through an Open Window (1997; Cinemax) . . . . Alicia
•• 0:06—Breasts, while lying in bed and talking on the phone.
•• 0:08—Breasts, while fooling around in her apartment with Rose.
• 0:14—Breasts, while fooling around with her boyfriend in bed.
••• 0:22—Breasts, while making love with Cliff in his apartment.

*McArthur, Kimberly **

Films:
Young Doctors in Love (1982) . . . . Jyll Omato
•• 0:58—Breasts in front of Dabney Coleman after taking off her Santa Claus outfit in his study.
Easy Money (1983) . . . . Ginger Jones
•• 0:47—Breasts sunbathing in the backyard when seen by Rodney Dangerfield.
Malibu Express (1984) . . . . Faye
•• 0:10—Breasts taking a shower on the boat with Barbara Edwards.
Slumber Party Massacre II (1987) . . . . Amy
TV:
Santa Barbara (1988-90) . . . . Kelly
Video Tapes:
Playmate Playoffs . . . . Playmate
Playboy's Playmate Review (1982) . . . . Playmate
••• 0:19—Nude in sauna, then taking a shower, then in front of fireplace.
Playboy Video Magazine, Volume 2 (1983) . . . . Herself/Playboy Playoffs
Playboy Video Magazine, Volume 5 (1983) . . . . . Playmate
• 0:06—Brief breasts in front of fire.
Playboy's 21 Playmates (1996) . . . . Playmate
••• 0:42—Nude in still photos.
••• 0:43—Nude while taking a shower and posing on sofa.

McAuley, Nichole

Films:
Beverly Hills Cop III (1994) . . . . Spider Rider
The Nutty Professor (1996) . . . . Fit Woman
Kiss the Girls (1997) . . . . Beautiful Girl
Made for Cable TV:
Beverly Hills Bordello: Use Your Imagination (1998; Showtime) . . . . Fiona
•• 0:01—Breasts, while making love with Felix in bed.
•• 0:03—Breasts, while in bed and talking with Felix afterward.
••• 0:07—Breasts, while caressing herself in front of a mirror.
••• 0:17—Breasts, while starting to make love with Jake in bed.
••• 0:23—Breasts and buns, while making love in bed with Felix.
Video Tapes:
Playboy's Cheerleaders (1996) . . . . Dancer 2/Nichole
•• 0:39—Nude during Carmen Elektra music video.

*McBride, Harlee **

Wife of comedian/actor Richard Belzer.
Films:
Young Lady Chatterley (1977) . . . . Cynthia Chatterley
•• 0:19—Nude masturbating in front of mirror.
• 0:28—Brief breasts with young boy.
••• 0:41—Nude in bathtub while maid washes her.
••• 0:52—Nude in back of car with the hitchhiker while the chauffeur is driving.
••• 1:03—Nude in the garden with the sprinklers on making love with the Gardener.
••• 1:31—Breasts and buns in bed with the gardener.
House Calls (1978) . . . . Nurse
Young Lady Chatterley II (1986) . . . . Cynthia Chatterley
•• 0:20—Breasts getting a massage with Eleanor.
•• 0:22—Full frontal nudity during flashback to the first time she made love with Robert.
••• 0:28—Breasts taking a bath with Jenny.
••• 0:35—Breasts in library seducing Virgil.
••• 0:50—Breasts in back of the car with the Count.

••• 0:58—Breasts in the garden with Robert.

McBride, Michelle

Films:

Edgar Allan Poe's "The Masque of the Red Death" (1989) . . . . Rebecca

Subspecies (1990). . . . . Lillian

• 0:34—Left breast, while sleeping in bed when the vampire comes to get her.

Made for Cable Movies:

Prey of the Chameleon (1992; Showtime). . . . . .Leslie

McBroom, Dirga

Films:

Flashdance (1983). . . . . .Heels

The Rosebud Beach Hotel (1985). . . . . Bellhop

• 0:49—Buns, then breasts, standing with the other bell hops, outfitted with military attire. (She's the one at the far end, furthest from the camera.)

Vendetta (1986) . . . . .Willow

In the Eye of the Snake (1994; Swiss) . . . . .Beatrice

McCarthy, Danté

Films:

Forrest Gump (1994) . . . . Topless Girl

• 0:36—Very, very brief left breast, while bending over to grab money out of customer's hands when Tom Hanks first enters club. Medium long shot.

Showgirls (1995) . . . . Carmi

(NC-17 version reviewed.)

•• 0:19—Breasts and buns in T-back, when asking Elizabeth Berkley if her breasts look bigger.

McCarthy, Jenny *

Films:

The Pompatus of Love (1996) . . . . .Alien Babe

The Stupids (1996) .Glamorous Actress

Things to Do in Denver When You're Dead (1996) . . . . Blonde Nurse

Made for Cable TV:

Singled Out (1995-97; MTV). . . . . Host

The Jenny McCarthy Show (1997- ; MTV). . . . . .Herself

TV:

Jenny (1997). . . . . .Jenny McMillan

Video Tapes:

Playboy Video Calendar 1995 (1994) . . . . June

••• 0:21—Nude at horse race track. Nude in bar and on pool table.

Playboy Video Centerfold: Jenny McCarthy (1994) . . . . Playmate of the Year

•• 0:00—Full frontal nudity during introduction.

••• 0:02—Full frontal nudity, while posing around a race track.

••• 0:05—Nude, in pool table/diner fantasy.

••• 0:12—Nude in school girl, cheerleader and graduation gown fantasy.

••• 0:15—Nude while posing around the house.

••• 0:19—Nude in still photos.

••• 0:23—Nude in desert town fantasy with a guy.

••• 0:28—Full frontal nudity in near-death fantasy.

Playboy's College Girls (1994) . . . . .Herself

••• 0:43—In bra, then nude, while posing for photos by Ty Erickson.

Wet & Wild: The Locker Room (1994) . . . . Playmate

Playboy The Best of Jenny McCarthy (1996) . . . . . .Herself

•• 0:00—Full frontal nudity (B&W) during introduction.

•• 0:02—Full frontal nudity, while posing around horse race track.

••• 0:08—Nude during schoolgirl, cheerleader, graduation gown segment.

••• 0:13—Full frontal nudity in still photos.

•• 0:14—Nude and in lingerie, while posing outdoors.

••• 0:16—In sheer red dress, then nude outdoors with a water pump.

•• 0:20—Breasts, while sitting in a chair and in lingerie.

••• 0:22—Nude in still photos.

••• 0:24—Nude, while dancing with 3 other Playmates with fire and ice from *Wet & Wild: The Locker Room.*

• 0:29—Brief breasts, while getting dressed.

••• 0:34—Full frontal nudity, in near-death fantasy with two angels.

••• 0:40—Nude on billiard table and dancing in soda fountain fantasy.

••• 0:46—Nude with a guy in old town fantasy.

••• 0:50—Nude, while posing around a house.

••• 0:53—Nude (B&W), while swinging on a swing and lying on some sheets.

McCartney, Kimberly

Video Tapes:

Hot Body International: #2 Miss Puerto Vallarta (1990) . . . . Contestant

•• 0:48—Buns in one piece swimsuit. Practically breasts wearing pasties.

Hot Body International: #4 Spring Break (1992) . . . Contestant

Hot Body Competition: The Best of Hot Body (1994) . . . . Herself

••• 0:46—Buns in swimsuits. Breasts when wearing pasties. Brief breasts while flashing.

McCauley, Nancy

Films:

Van Nuys Blvd. (1979) . . . . .Mooner/Flasher

• 0:11—Brief buns, while mooning Chooch out the window of her car.

• 0:13—Brief breasts, while opening her jacket to flash Chooch and the police man.

Galaxina (1980). . . . . Elexia

McClellan, Michelle

See: Bauer, Michelle.

• McClendon, Yvette *

Films:

Caged Heat 3000 (1995). . . . . Uncredited Inmate

California Heat (1995). . . . . Donna

• 1:03—Breasts, while sitting in bathtub with Tracy.

Galaxy Girls (1995). . . . . Shauna

••• 0:19—Breasts, while in the bathtub with Becky.

Made for Cable TV:

Compromising Situations: Love Suit (1998; Showtime) . . . . .Mindy

••• 0:10—In black bra, then breasts and buns, while making love with Frank.

Video Tapes:

Erotic Zone: The Ring (1995). . . . . Ring Girl #2

McClure, Tané

a.k.a. Tané.
Daughter of actor Doug McClure.

Films:

Crawlspace (1986) . . . . Sophie Fisher
- • 0:00—Nipples, sticking out of holes that she cuts in her red bra. Brief breasts in bed making love with Hank. Dark.

Commando Squad (1987). . . . . Sunny

Death Spa (1987) . . . . .Vicky
- •• 1:10—Breasts in sauna with Tom.
- • 1:19—Brief breasts during the fire.

Death House (1988) . . . . Tanya Kerrington
- • 1:08—Brief breasts in Dennis Cole's vision.

Hot Under the Collar (1991). . . . . .Rowena
- ••• 0:32—Breasts, while in bed with Max.

Assault of the Party Nerds II: The Heavy Petting Detective (1993). . . . . Headi

Married People, Single Sex 2: For Better or Worse (1994) . . . . House Buyer

Surf, Sand and Sex (1994). . . . . . Uncredited Fourth Woman
- ••• 0:34—Breasts, while making love with Nick in a restaurant. Very brief partial lower frontal nudity. Lit with red light. Long scene.
- •• 1:09—Breasts, during end credits.

Bikini Drive-In (1995) . . . . Mandy
(Unrated version reviewed.)
- • 0:55—Brief buns, in yellow swimsuit, while dancing next to drive-in sign.
- • 0:58—Brief buns in swimsuit, while dancing next to drive-in sign.
- ••• 1:07—Buns in swimsuit and breasts, while dancing on hood of car.

Caged Hearts (1995) . . . . Sharon
- •• 0:57—Breasts, while in bed with a customer.
- • 1:00—Brief left breast, while crying in a chair.
- •• 1:11—In bra and panties, then breasts and buns while undressing in bedroom, then lying in bed.

Lap Dancing (1995) . . . . Claudia
- • 0:09—Brief buns in T-back, while walking back to get her clothes.
- ••• 0:14—Nude, while doing a strip routine on stage in club. Long scene.
- • 0:21—Buns in T-back in dressing room.
- ••• 0:24—Buns in T-back and breasts, while lap dancing with a customer.
- • 0:45—Brief breasts in flashbacks.
- • 0:57—Brief buns in T-back, going into supply closet with her boyfriend.
- • 1:19—Brief buns in G-string in dressing room.
- ••• 1:23—Nude, while singing and doing a strip routine on stage in club. Long scene.

Midnight Tease 2 (1995). . . . . Lacy

Stripshow (1995) . . . . .Raquel
- • 0:00—Breasts and buns in quick cuts.
- •• 0:05—Breasts, while making love with Cowboy. Buns in T-back afterward.
- • 0:33—Breasts in flashbacks.
- ••• 0:37—Breasts and buns while making love with Monique Parent in shack.
- ••• 0:43—Breasts while making love with Cowboy in the back of his truck.
- • 1:11—Breasts and buns while dancing. Quick cuts.
- •• 1:15—Breasts, while dancing. Quick cuts. Intercut with another dancer.

Target of Seduction (1995). Lauren
- • 0:04—Breasts, while dressing in front of mirror.
- ••• 0:18—Breasts and buns in T-back, while checking herself out in the mirror.
- ••• 0:25—Breasts and buns, while making love in bed with her boyfriend.
- • 0:50—Breasts, while putting make up on in dressing room.
- • 1:05—Left breast, while sleeping in bed.

Babe Watch: The Forbidden Parody (1996) . . . . . Bodacia
- •• 0:38—Breasts, after swimsuit top falls off during mambo contest.
- •• 0:41—Breasts, while taking off her swimsuit top in dressing room with a customer after being tricked by Lucki.

Lovers, Liars and Thieves (1996) . . . . .Madam
- • 0:00—Breasts, while having sex with a customer in bed.

Scorned 2 (1996) . . . . .Amanda Foley

Sexual Roulette (1996) . . . . Sherry Landis
(Unrated version reviewed.)
- ••• 0:26—Nude, while making love with Jed in several locations.
- ••• 0:45—Breasts, while making love with Jed in her suite.
- • 0:50—Brief breasts, while sitting up in bed with Jed.
- • 1:07—Breasts, while sitting in bed with Jed.
- •• 1:08—Breasts and buns, while making love with Jed in bed.

Made for Cable TV:

Sherman Oaks (1996-97; Showtime). . . . . Verna

Sherman Oaks: Season 2, Episode 1 (1996; Showtime) . . . . Verna
- • 0:14—Brief buns in T-back and brief breasts with Sanford in motel room.

Sherman Oaks: Season 2, Episode 2 (1996; Showtime) . . . . Verna
- •• 0:11—Breasts, while in bed with Sanford.
- • 0:13—Breasts, while in car with.Sanford.

Sherman Oaks: Season 2, Episode 3 (1996; Showtime) . . . . Verna
- • 0:00—Breasts, while protesting at beach, then in bed with Sanford, then sunbathing at the beach.
- •• 0:12—Breasts, while making love with Sanford in motel room.

Sherman Oaks: Season 2, Episode 4 (1996; Showtime) . . . . Verna
- •• 0:13—Breasts, while making love with Sanford on bed in motel room.
- •• 0:21—Breasts, while in motel room with Sanford and two midget clowns.

Sherman Oaks: Season 2, Episode 5 (1996; Showtime) . . . . Verna
- •• 0:11—In black bra, then breasts, while trying to get Sanford's attention in motel room.

Sherman Oaks: Season 2, Episode 6 (1996; Showtime) . . . . Verna
- • 0:18—Breasts and partial buns, while making love in bed with Sanford.
- •• 0:20—Breasts, while sitting in bed, talking with Sanford.

Sherman Oaks: Season 2, Episode 7 (1996; Showtime) . . . . Verna
- •• 0:06—Breasts, while making love in bed with Sanford.
- • 0:13—Brief breasts, while making love in bed with Sanford.

Sherman Oaks: Season 2, Episode 8 (1996; Showtime) . . . . Verna
- • 0:08—Breasts, while on bed with Sanford.
- • 0:12—Brief breasts, opening her jacket while in parking lot.

Sherman Oaks: Season 2, Episode 9 (1996; Showtime) . . . . Verna
- • 0:15—Breasts, while trying to make love in bed with Sanford.

Sherman Oaks: Season 2, Episode 10 (1996; Showtime) . . . . Verna
- •• 0:16—Breasts, while sitting in bed with Sanford.

Sherman Oaks: Season 2, Episode 11 (1996; Showtime) . . . . Verna
- •• 0:04—Buns and breasts, while making love in bed with Sanford.
- • 0:05—Brief right breast, while lying in bed with Sanford.

Sherman Oaks: Season 2, Episode 12 (1996; Showtime) . . . . Verna
- • 0:08—Breasts, while sitting up in bed with Sanford in motel.
- •• 0:12—Buns and breasts, while talking with Sanford in motel room.
- • 0:21—Brief breasts, when tearing open jumpsuit while outside with Sanford.

Sherman Oaks: Season 2, Episode 13 (1996; Showtime) . . . . Verna
- •• 0:15—Breasts, while with Sanford in his office.

Sherman Oaks: Season 2, Episode 15 (1996; Showtime) . . . . Verna
- •• 0:11—Breasts, after taking off ninja top and fooling around with Sanford in motel room.
- • 0:19—Breasts, while sitting in bed, acting with Sanford.

Sherman Oaks: Season 2, Episode 16 (1996; Showtime) . . . . Verna
- •• 0:03—Breasts, while massaging Sanford on bed.
- •• 0:13—Breasts in open dress, while in Sanford's examination room, when she meets Dr.

Sherman Oaks: Season 2, Episode 17 (1996; Showtime) . . . . Verna
- • 0:15—Breasts, after pulling down her blouse while sitting in her convertible car, talking with Sanford in parking lot.

Sherman Oaks: Season 2, Episode 18 (1996; Showtime) . . . . Verna
- • 0:14—Breasts, while in motel room with Sanford.
- • 0:21—Brief breasts and buns, while fooling around in motel room with Sanford again.

Sherman Oaks: Season 2, Episode 20 (1997; Showtime) . . . . Verna
- •• 0:11—Breasts, while sitting in bed, talking with Sanford.
- •• 0:18—Buns and left breast, while lying in bed, talking with Sanford.
- •• 0:25—Breasts, while sitting in bed, talking with Sanford.

Sherman Oaks: Season 2, Episode 21 (1997; Showtime) . . . . Verna
- •• 0:13—Breasts, after pulling down the top of her dress in Sanford's office to surprise him.

Sherman Oaks: Season 2, Episode 22 (1997; Showtime) . . . . Verna
- ••• 0:06—Breasts, while attempting to make love with Sanford, then sitting next to him in bed.
- •• 0:18—Breasts, while standing in motel room, wearing chastity belt.

TV:

Days of Our Lives . . . . Tiffany

Video Tapes:

Inside Out 2 (1992) . . . . Melanie Moss/Mis-Apprehended
(Unrated version reviewed.)
- •• 0:09—Breasts, taking off her blouse outside for Tim.

McComas, Lorissa *

Films:

Can It Be Love (1992). . . . . Montana
a.k.a. Spring Break Sorority Babes
- ••• 0:55—Breasts and buns, changing into lingerie behind two way mirror while David watches.

Stormswept (1994) . . . . Kelly
- ••• 0:53—Breasts, while making love in bed with Brianna.
- ••• 1:33—Nude, after taking off her robe in room in front of Eugene.

Cyberzone (1995) . . . . Moria
- • 0:09—Breasts, in room with the other three pleasure droids. (She's the one with the diamond pendant necklace and black shawl.)
- • 0:13—Breasts after taking off her lingerie top with the other three pleasure droids.
- • 1:06—Breasts, after taking off her dress top for Marc Singer.

Lap Dancing (1995) . . . . Angie
- ••• 0:11—Nude, while making love with Michael on sofa.
- ••• 0:19—Buns in G-string, then breasts, while performing an audition lap dance for Manny.
- •• 0:23—Buns in T-back and breasts, while lap dancing with a customer.
- • 0:33—Brief upper half of left breast, while teasing a grocer in his store with Kim Dawson.
- • 0:45—Brief breasts in flashbacks.
- • 0:55—Buns in G-string while in dressing room.
- ••• 0:59—Buns and breasts, lap dancing with a customer's wife while he watches.
- ••• 1:03—Nude, while doing strip routine on stage. Long scene.
- ••• 1:12—Nude, taking off her dress in front of Sam, then making love with him.
- • 1:23—Buns in panties, during second audition.

Sinful Intrigue (1995) . . . . Jean

Virtual Desire (1995) . . . . Julie
- • 0:43—Brief buns in panties and breasts.
- ••• 0:57—Buns in panties and breasts after stripping by the dinner table in front of Brad, then making love with him. Also see brief partial lower frontal nudity. Long scene.

Wish Me Luck (1995) . . . . Heather
(Unrated version reviewed.)
- • 0:39—In white bra and buns in panties getting out of her clothes.
- •• 0:43—In bra and panties, then buns and breasts with Eddie on sofa.

Hindsight (1996) . . . . Chantel
- • 0:46—Brief breasts, when opening her sweater for Jason.

Tiger Heart (1996). . . . . Jill

Vamps: Deadly Dreamgirls (1996) . . . . The Vampire Queen

Made for Cable Movies:

Piranha (1995; Showtime). . . . . Barbara
- •• 0:03—In white bra and panties, undressing to go skinny dipping in water tank with Dave. Nude, after undressing and swimming.

Made for Cable TV:

Sherman Oaks: Season 2, Episode 5 (1996; Showtime) . . . . Kelly Sinatra
- •• 0:13—Breasts, while sunbathing in backyard with Tiffany.
- ••• 0:23—Breasts, while making love on top of a guy during the porno movie shoot, then nude, when fighting with Tiffany.

Video Tapes:

Babes, Bikes & Beyond (1994) . . . . Herself
- ••• 0:02—Breasts and buns.

BabeWatch, Episode 4: Naughty But Nice (1995) . . . . Herself
••• 0:25—Nude, while posing on bed.
Body Language (1996). . . . . Sun Bath
••• 0:31—Breasts and buns, while sunbathing outdoors with Sara St. James and Noelle.
Erotic Heat (1996) . . . . Construction/Jacuzzi
••• 0:09—Nude with Taylor St. Claire.
••• 0:40—Nude, with the other girls in the spa.
Penthouse: The Art of Massage (1996). . . . . Model
••• 0:47—In pink dress, then nude, while dancing and massaging another woman.

McCormack, Catherine

Films:
Braveheart (1995) . . . . Huffon
•• 0:37—Breasts, with Mel Gibson at night.
Loaded (1996). . . . . Rose
•• 0:36—Breasts, while getting out of her swimsuit.
• 0:40—Left breast, while in bed with Neil.
North Star (1996; French/British/Norwegian) . . . . Sarah
Dangerous Beauty (1998) . . . . Veronica Franco

McCormick, Maureen

Films:
Take Down (1978). . . . . Brooke Cooper
Skatetown, U.S.A. (1979) . . . . Susan
The Idolmaker (1980) . . . . Ellen Fields
Texas Lightning (1980) . . . . Fay
• 1:04—Very brief upper half of right breast popping out of slip while struggling on bed with two jerks. Long shot, hard to see.
Return to Horror High (1987) . . . . Officer Tyler
Made for TV Movies:
A Very Brady Christmas (1988) . . . . Marcia Brady
TV:
The Brady Bunch (1969-74) . . . . Marcia Brady
Teen Angel (1997). . . . . Judy Beauchamp

McCormick, Michelle

Films:
Fatal Pulse (1987) . . . . Lisa
Showdown (1991) . . . . Mickey
Sweet Justice (1991) . . . . Kim
• 0:44—Buns in sexy outfit while dancing on stage in club.

McCourt, Emer

Films:
London Kills Me (1991; British) . . . . Sylvie
• 1:02—Left breast in open blouse, while sleeping.
••• 1:05—Breasts, while sitting in bathtub with Clint. Long scene.
Made for TV Movies:
Parnell & The Englishwoman (1991) . . . . Eileen

*McCrena, Brittany **

Films:
A Sensuous Summer (1991) . . . . Jill
•• 0:00—Breasts while making love in bed with Bobby in flashback.
•• 0:11—Breasts while making love with Bobby in flashback. Buns in swimsuit.
••• 0:59—In black bra then breasts while making love with Bobby.
Taxi Dancers (1993) . . . . Billie
•• 0:16—Breasts, while changing clothes in room with Star.
••• 0:27—Breasts, while making love on billiard table with Bobby.
••• 0:44—Breasts (mostly left breast) while making love with Bobby in van.
0:45—Partial right breast, when waking up in the morning with Bobby.
The Last Word (1994) . . . . Massage Girl
• 1:06—In bra, then breasts, while giving Timothy Hutton a massage in the bathroom.

*McCullough, Julie **

Films:
Big Bad Mama II (1987). . . . . Polly McClatchie
•• 0:12—Breasts with Danielle Brisebois playing in a pond underneath a waterfall.
•• 0:36—In lingerie, then breasts sitting on Jordan who is tied up in bed.
The Blob (1988) . . . . Susie
The Baby Doll Murders (1992). . . . . Betty
Round Trip to Heaven (1992). . . . . Lucille
Top of the World (1997) . . . . Ginger
Made for Cable Movies:
Breast Men (1997; HBO) . . . . 1972's Head Receptionist
TV:
Growing Pains (1989-90). . . . . Julie
Robin's Hoods (1994-95). . . . . Stacey Wright
Video Tapes:
Playboy Video Calendar 1987 (1986) . . . . Playmate
Playboy Video Calendar 1988 (1987) . . . . Playmate
Playboy Video Centerfold: Peggy McIntagart (1989) . . . . Playmate
••• 0:35—Nude in still photos and videos.

McCullough, Shanna

Adult film actress.
Films:
Malibu Express (1984) . . . . Uncredited Massage Girl
•• 0:33—Breasts, several times while giving a guy a rub down.

McCurry, Natalie

Films:
Dead-End Drive-In (1986; Australian). . . . . Carmen
•• 0:19—Breasts in red car with Ned Manning.
Made for TV Movies:
Danger Down Under (1988) . . . . Katherine Dillingham

McDaniel, Donna

Singer.
Films:
Angel (1983) . . . . Crystal
• 0:19—Brief breasts, dead in bed when the killer pulls the covers down.
Frightmare (1983). . . . . Donna
Hollywood Hot Tubs (1984). . . . . Leslie Maynard

*McDaniel, Sonja **

Video Tapes:
The Girls of Penthouse, Volume 2 (1993). . . . Nightstalker
••• 0:41—Nude, while making love in alley.

McDermott, Colleen

Films:
Paradise Motel (1985) . . . . Debbie
•• 0:24—Breasts in motel room with Mic, when Sam lets them use a room.

Demonwarp (1988) . . . . Cindy
- •• 0:23—Breasts and buns drying herself off after taking a shower.
- • 0:24—Very brief lower frontal nudity, under her towel, trying to run up the stairs.

Access Denied (1996). . . . . Sherry Johannson
- • 0:15—Right breast, while making out with Harvey in prison classroom.
- ••• 0:23—Full frontal nudity, while making love in bedroom with Raymond.
- •• 0:56—Breasts and buns, while making love on the floor with Joe.
- •• 1:06—Breasts, while making love with Joe in a stream outdoors.
- • 1:08—Breasts, while making love with Joe on the floor.
- • 1:17—Brief buns and brief left breast while in spa with Raymond.

Made for Cable TV:

Dream On: Try Not to Remember (1995; HBO) . . . . . . Lois
- • 0:02—Breasts, while making love with Martin in bed.

Women: Stories of Passion-Warm Hands, Cold Heart (1996; Showtime). . . . . .Greta
- •• 0:07—Right breast, while making out with Jeff on a chair.
- ••• 0:09—Breasts and buns while making love with Jeff in bed.
- • 0:14—Brief breasts, while adjusting towel before massage.
- •• 0:17—Breasts and buns, while fantasizing during Victor's massage.
- • 0:22—Brief breasts, while putting on blouse after massage.
- • 0:24—Very brief left breast, while lying in bed with Jeff.

Video Tapes:

Eden 6 (1994) . . . . Amanda
- • 1:08—Breasts, while in bed after making love with B.D.
- ••• 1:18—Breasts, when joining B.D. in the shower.

McDormand, Frances

Wife of director/writer/editor Joel Coen.

Films:

Blood Simple (1984) . . . . .Abby
Crimewave (1986) . . . . Nun
Raising Arizona (1987) . . . . Dot
Mississippi Burning (1988) . . . . Mrs. Pell
Chattahoochee (1990) . . . . Mae Foley
Darkman (1990) . . . . .Julie Hastings
Hidden Agenda (1990; British) . . . . Ingrid
The Butcher's Wife (1991). . . . . Grace
Passed Away (1992) . . . . .Nora Scanlan
Short Cuts (1993). . . . . Betty Weathers
- • 0:46—Very brief left breast and partial lower frontal nudity, while walking past doorway. Brief left breast and lower frontal nudity, while peeking around doorway and wrapping a towel around herself.

Beyond Rangoon (1995). . . . . .Andy
Fargo (1996). . . . . Marge Gunderson
(Academy Award for Best Actress.)
Palookaville (1996) . . . . June
Primal Fear (1996). Dr. Molly Arrington
Johnny Skidmarks (1997) . . . . Alice
Paradise Road (1997) . . . . .Dr. Verstak
Madeline (1998). . . . . Miss Clavel

Made for Cable Movies:

The Good Old Boys (1995; TNT). . . . . Eve
Hidden in America (1996; Showtime) . . . . Gus

TV:

Leg Work (1987). . . . . .Willie Pipal

• *McDougal, Karen* *

Video Tapes:

Playboy's Girls Next Door: Naughty and Nice (1998) . . . . Naughty Neighbors
- ••• 0:51—Nude, while stripping with her girlfriend in their neighbor's apartment.

McEachin, Bianca

Films:

Coming to America (1988) . . . . Uncredited Miss Black Awareness
- • 0:37—Buns, wearing pink sequined, two piece swimsuit on stage during Black Awareness meeting.

Video Tapes:

Dream Babies (1989) . . . . Herself
- ••• 0:06—Dancing in red two-piece swimsuit, then breasts and buns in G-string. Nice!
- •• 0:40—Breasts, introducing her segment.
- ••• 0:41—More breasts, dancing in red two-piece swimsuit.

Hot Body International: #1 Miss Cancun (1990) . . . Contestant

• *McElhone, Natascha*

Films:

Surviving Picasso (1996) . . . . Francoise
- •• 0:20—Full frontal nudity, while posing for Anthony Hopkins in his studio.

The Devil's Own (1997). . . . . Megan Doherty
Mrs. Dalloway (1998) . . . . Clarissa
The Truman Show (1998) . . . . Lauren/Sylvia

McEnroe, Annie *

Films:

The Hand (1981). . . . . Stella Roche
- •• 0:51—Breasts undressing for Michael Caine.

Warlords of the 21st Century (1982) . . . . Carlie
a.k.a. Battletruck
The Survivors (1983) . . . . Doreen
Howling II: Your Sister is a Werewolf (1984). . . . . Jenny
Purple Hearts (1984) . . . . .Hallaway
- •• 1:23—Brief breasts coming out of the bathroom surprising Ken Wahl and Cheryl Ladd.

True Stories (1986) . . . . Kay Culver
Wall Street (1987) . . . . Muffie Livingston
Beetlejuice (1988) . . . . .Jane Butterfield
Cop (1988) . . . . .Amy Cranfield
The Doors (1991) . . . . .Secretary
Criss Cross (1992) . . . . .Mrs. Sivil
Dangerous Game (1993). . . . . Cameo
(Unrated version reviewed.)
Heaven and Earth (1993). . . . . Dinner Guest #1
Josh and S.A.M. (1993) . . . . .Woman at Laundromat
Mr. Jones (1993) . . . . Crying Woman
S.F.W. (1994). . . . . .Dolly

McGavin, Graem

Films:

Angel (1983) . . . . Lana
- •• 0:31—Breasts standing in hotel bathroom talking to her John.

My Tutor (1983) . . . . Sylvia
- ••• 0:21—In white bra, then breasts in back seat of a car in a parking lot with Matt Lattanzi.

Weekend Pass (1984) . . . . Tawny Ryatt

McGillis, Kelly

Films:

Reuben, Reuben (1983). . . . . Geneva Spofford
Witness (1985) . . . . Rachel
••• 1:18—Breasts taking off her top to take a bath while Harrison Ford watches.
Top Gun (1986) . . . . Charlie
Made in Heaven (1987). . . . . Annie Packert/Ally Chandler
Unsettled Land (1987). . . . . Anda
The Accused (1988) . . . . Kathryn Murphy
Cat Chaser (1988). . . . . Mary De Boya
••• 0:23—Breasts on the floor with Peter Weller. Long scene.
••• 1:04—Full frontal nudity taking off her slip and getting raped by her husband's pistol. Kind of dark.
•• 1:06—Brief buns, getting pushed around the house. Right breast while signing a paper.
The House on Carroll Street (1988). . . . . Emily
• 0:39—Brief breasts reclining into the water in the bathtub.
Winter People (1989) . . . . Collie Wright
Grand Isle (1991) . . . . Edna Pontellier
••• 1:08—Breasts while on the floor making love with Julian Sands.
••• 1:19—Breasts, twice, in open robe while sketching while lying on the floor.
••• 1:30—Buns and breasts after taking off clothes at the beach.
••• 1:31—Nude, quite a few times, while swimming under water. Seen from under water.
•• 1:32—Breasts, while doing the backstroke above water.
The Babe (1992) . . . . Claire Hodgeson-Ruth
North (1994). . . . . Amish Mom

Made for Cable TV:

Remember Me (1995; CBS). . . . . Menly

Made for TV Movies:

Code of Honor (1984). . . . . Katherine Dennison Breen
Original title: *Sweet Revenge.*
In the Best of Families, Marriage, Pride and Madness (1994) . . . . Susie Leary
The Third Twin (1997). . . . . Dr. Jeanne Ferrami

TV:

Dark Eyes (1995). . . . . Maria McGann

McGovern, Elizabeth

Films:

Ordinary People (1980). . . . . Jeanine
Ragtime (1981). . . . . Evelyn Nesbit
••• 0:52—Breasts in living room sitting on couch and arguing with a lawyer. Very long scene.
Lovesick (1983). . . . . Chloe Allen
Once Upon a Time in America (1984) . . . . Deborah
(Long version reviewed.)
• 2:33—(0:32 into tape 2) Brief glimpses of left breast when Robert De Niro tries to rape her in the back seat of a car.
Racing with the Moon (1984) . . . . Caddie Winger
• 0:45—Upper half of breast in pond with Sean Penn.
The Bedroom Window (1987). . . . . Denise
She's Having a Baby (1988). . . . . Kristy
Johnny Handsome (1989) . . . . Donna McCarty
•• 0:47—Right breast, while in bed with Mickey Rourke.
The Handmaid's Tale (1990) . . . . Moira
A Shock to the System (1990). . . . . Stella Anderson
Tune in Tomorrow (1990) . . . . Elena Quince
a.k.a. Aunt Julia and the Scriptwriter
The Favor (1991). . . . . Emily
Me and Veronica (1992) . . . . Fanny
King of the Hill (1993). . . . . Lydia

Made for Cable Movies:

Women & Men: Stories of Seduction (1990; HBO). . . Vicki
••• 0:22—Breasts when Bridges takes her top off when she lies back in bed.
Broken Trust (1995; TNT) . . . . Janice Dillon
Clover (1997; USA) . . . . Sara Kate

Made for Cable TV:

Tales From the Crypt: Horror in the Night (1996; HBO) . . . . Laura Kendall

Made for TV Movies:

Masterpiece Theatre: Broken Glass (1996) . . . Margaret Hyman

TV:

If Not For You (1995). . . . . Jessie Kent

McGowan, Rose

Films:

Encino Man (1992) . . . . Nora
Bio-Dome (1995). . . . . Denise
The Doom Generation (1995). . . . . Amy Blue
•• 0:14—Breasts, while sitting in bathtub by herself.
•• 0:16—Breasts, while sitting in bathtub, then getting up to kiss Jordan.
• 0:19—Brief right breast, while frolicking in bathtub with Jordan.
•• 0:27—Breasts, while making love in back seat of car with Xavier.
•• 0:42—Breasts while making love in bed with Jordan.
• 1:11—Very brief left breast, then breasts, while making love with Jordan and Xavier.
•• 1:12—Breasts, while lying in bed after making love with Jordan and Xavier. Brief buns under clear plastic rain coat, getting up out of bed.
Scream (1996). . . . . Tatum
Phantoms (1997). . . . . Lisa

McGregor, Angela Punch

Films:

The Island (1980) . . . . Beth
•• 0:45—Breasts taking off poncho to make love with Michael Caine in hut after rubbing stuff on him.
We of the Never Never (1983). Jeannie
A Test of Love (1984; Australian) . . . . Jessica Hathaway
Spotswood (1991; Australian) . . . . Caroline
The Efficiency Expert (1992; Australian). . . . . Caroline

McIntaggart, Peggy *

a.k.a. Peggy Sands and Peggy Sanders.

Films:

Into the Night (1985). . . . . Shameless Woman
• 0:43—Breasts putting dress on after coming out of men's restroom stall after a man leaves the stall first.
Beverly Hills Cop II (1987) . . . . Stripper
• 0:48—Very brief breasts, while dancing at the 385 North Club.
Phoenix the Warrior (1988) . . . . Keela
Far Out Man (1990) . . . . Misty
••• 0:50—Breasts and buns in black G-string, undressing and getting into bathtub with Tommy Chong.
Camp Fear (1991) . . . . n.a.
a.k.a. Millenium Countdown
Lady Avenger (1991) . . . . Maggie
(In braless tank top for most of the film.)
••• 0:18—Breasts in bed with Kevin.
Two Evil Eyes (1991) . . . . Young Policeman
Cyber Tracker 2 (1995) . . . . Agnes 3000

Video Tapes:
Playboy Video Centerfold: Peggy McIntagart (1989) . . . . . Playmate
••• 0:00—Nude throughout.
Playboy Video Calendar 1991 (1990) . . . . . February
••• 0:05—Nude.
Playmates at Play (1990) . . . . . Gotta Dance
Rock Video Girls 2 (1992) . . . . . Herself

McIntosh, Judy

Films:
Hot Target (1985; New Zealand). . . . . Clare
Ebbtide (1994; Australian). . . . . Ellen Fielding
• 0:47—Brief buns, when Harry Hamlin pulls her panties down at the beach.
• 0:49—Breasts, while behind clear plastic shower curtain.
•• 0:59—Breasts, while making love with Hamlin in the house.

McIntosh, Michelle

Films:
Secret Sins (1992) . . . . . Sara Jenson
• 0:29—Tip of right breast, sticking out of bubbles in bubble bath, then putting on bra in bedroom while wearing panties.
•• 0:43—Breasts, while making love with Johnny on sofa and in living room.
Venice/Venice (1992) . . . . . Guest at Party

McIntosh, Valerie

Films:
Gimme an "F" (1981) . . . . . One of the "Vikings"
a.k.a. T & A Academy 2
Weekend Pass (1984) . . . . . Etta
The Naked Cage (1985). . . . . Ruby
••• 0:24—Breasts and buns in infirmary, then getting attacked by Smiley. Brief lower frontal nudity.
• 0:28—Breasts, while hanging by rope, dead.
Quicksilver (1986). . . . . Hooker
Number One with a Bullet (1987). . . . . Woman
The Mambo Kings (1992) . . . . . Tracy Blair
•• 1:10—Breasts, getting her bathing suit after Armand Assante discovers her with Antonio Banderas.

McIssac, Marianne

Films:
In Praise of Older Women (1978; Canadian) . . . . . Julika
•• 0:23—Breasts and buns, getting into bed with Tom Berenger.
TV:
The Baxters (1980-81). . . . . Allison Baxter

McIver, Susan

Films:
I Spit on Your Corpse (1974) . . . . . Donna
a.k.a. Girls for Rent
••• 0:24—Breasts undressing for a guy. More breasts and buns making love in bed with him, then getting out of bed.
Policewomen (1974) . . . . . Laura
•• 0:42—Breasts and buns, taking off two piece swimsuit and getting into the shower with Doc.
••• 0:44—Breasts in the shower after Doc leaves.
Shampoo (1975). . . . . Customer
Smokey and the Bandit (1977) . . . . . Hot Pants
Thunder Alley (1985) . . . . . Redhead

McKamy, Kim

See: Gere, Ashlyn.

*McKee, Lonette **

Films:
Sparkle (1976). . . . . Sister
Which Way Is Up? (1977) . . . . . Vanetta
Cuba (1979) . . . . . Therese Mederos
The Cotton Club (1984) . . . . . Lila Rose Oliver
Brewster's Millions (1985) . . . . . Angela Drake
Round Midnight (1986; U.S./French) . . . . . Darcey Leigh
Gardens of Stone (1987). . . . . Betty Rae
Dangerous Passion (1990). . . . . Meg
••• 0:39—Right breast, while in back of car with Carl Weathers.
Jungle Fever (1991) . . . . . Drew
•• 0:04—Left breast while making love with Wesley Snipes in bed.
• 2:03—Brief left breast in bed with Snipes again.
Malcolm X (1992). . . . . Louise Little
He Got Game (1998). . . . . Martha
Made for Cable Movies:
Blind Faith (1998; Showtime) . . . . . Carol Williams
Miniseries:
Queen (1993) . . . . . Alice
Made for TV Movies:
To Dance With Olivia (1997) . . . . . n.a.

McKenzie, Jacqueline

Films:
Romper Stomper (1993; Australian). . . . . Gabe
•• 0:18—Breasts, while making love with Hando at the gang's hangout.
••• 1:11—Breasts, while making love with Davey in bed.
Traps (1995; Australian). . . . . Viola
Angel Baby (1996; Australian). . . . . Kate
•• 0:32—Nude, when surprising Harry when he comes home from work.
•• 0:45—Brief breast, while making love with Harry, then breasts, when sitting in his lap afterwards.

McLeod, Shannon

a.k.a. Shannon Leod.
Films:
Lightning, The White Stallion (1986). . . . . Daphne
Necromancer (1988). . . . . Edna
The Refrigerator (1992). . . . . East Village Girl
Animal Instincts 2 (1993) . . . . . Miss Geary
•• 0:14—In black bra, then breasts and buns in panties after taking off her top while trying to tease Steve.
••• 0:20—Breasts, after taking off bra and making love with a guy in bed.
Criminal Passion (1993) . . . . . Isabelle Sabatini
• 0:03—Brief breasts, while making love on bed.
Witchcraft 6: The Devil's Mistress (1993). . . . . Cat
(Unrated version reviewed.)
•• 0:17—In bra, then right breast, while making love with Jonathan in front seat of car.
• 0:42—Brief lower frontal nudity, while cutting a string off her mini skirt.
• 1:01—Left breast, while making love with Will in his office.
••• 1:13—Breasts, while making love with Jonathan on trunk of car.
Seduce Me: Pamela Principle 2 (1994) . . . . . Melinda
• 0:50—Very brief breasts, while in spa.

Video Tapes:

Playboy's Sensual Fantasy for Lovers (1993) . . Risk-Taking

• 0:43—In black bra and panties, then buns, while outside during party with her lover.

••• 0:44—Full frontal nudity while making love outside.

McLish, Rachel

Miss Olympia 1980 and 1982.

Films:

Pumping Iron II: The Women (1985). . . . . Herself

Aces: Iron Eagle III (1992) . . . . .Anna

Raven Hawk (1995) . . . . Rhyia Shadowfeather

• 0:53—Long shot of buns in loincloth, then brief back side of right breast, while performing ceremony in cave.

Made for TV Movies:

Getting Physical (1984). . . . . Tawny Runyon

Video Tapes:

In Shape with Rachel McLish (1995) . . . . Herself

• McMurtry, Erin

Films:

Fresh Kill (1994) . . . . .Claire Mayakovsky

•• 0:13—Very brief breasts, when falling back onto bed. Breasts, while lying in bed next to Sarita Choudhurry.

Whore 2 (1994) . . . . Lisa

• McNeal, Julia

See: Mueller, Julia.

McNeil, Kate

a.k.a. Kathryn McNeil.

Films:

Beach House (1981) . . . . Cindy

House on Sorority Row (1983). . . . . Katherine

Monkey Shines: An Experiment in Fear (1988) . . . . Melanie Parker

• 1:07—Brief upper half of right breast, while making love with Allan. Dark, hard to see anything.

I'll Do Anything (1994) . . . . .Stacy

Sudden Death (1995) . . . . Kathi

Made for Cable Movies:

Escape Clause (1996; Showtime). . . . . Sarah Ramsay

•• 0:00—Breasts, while making love with Andrew McCarthy in bed, then pulling up the covers when the daughter opens the bedroom door.

••• 0:20—In white bra and panties, then breasts, while standing with McCarthy, then making love in bed with him.

Miniseries:

North and South, Book II (1986) . . . . .Augusta Barclay

Made for TV Movies:

A Walton Wedding (1995). . . . . Janet

Sleeping with the Devil (1997) . . . . Liz

A Walton Easter (1997) . . . . Janet

TV:

As the World Turns . . . . Karen Haines-Stenbeck

Anything but Love (1989-90) . . . . Kelly

WIOU (1990-91). . . . . .Taylor Young

Bodies of Evidence (1993). . . . . Nora

McNichol, Kristy

Sister of actor Jimmy McNichol.

Films:

The End (1978). . . . . Julie Lawson

Little Darlings (1980). . . . . Angel

The Night the Lights Went Out in Georgia (1981) . . . . .Amanda Child

Only When I Laugh (1981) . . . . Polly

The Pirate Movie (1982; Australian). . . . . .Mabel

White Dog (1982). . . . . Julie Sawyer

• 1:25—Most of the inside of breasts in gaping tank top when bending over to help lift dog off Burl Ives.

Just the Way You Are (1984). Susan

• 0:50—Very brief left breast showing her friend that she's not too hot because there is nothing under her white coat. Medium long shot.

You Can't Hurry Love (1984) . . . . .Rhonda

Dream Lover (1986) . . . . Kathy Gardner

• 0:17—Very, very brief right breast getting out of bed, then walking around in a white top and underwear.

Two Moon Junction (1988) . . . . Patti Jean

•• 0:42—Breasts in gas station restroom changing camisole tops with Sherilyn Fenn.

The Forgotten One (1989). . . . . Barbara Stupple

Made for TV Movies:

Like Mom, Like Me (1978). . . . . Jennifer Gruen

My Old Man (1979) . . . . Jo Butler

Women of Valor (1986) . . . . T.J. Nolan

Baby of the Bride (1991) . . . . .Mary

Mother of the Bride (1993) . . . . .Mary

TV:

Apple's Way (1974-75) . . . . Patricia Apple

Family (1976-80). . . . . Letitia "Buddy" Lawrence

Empty Nest (1989-95). . . . . Barbara Weston

McQuade, Kris

Films:

Alvin Purple (1973; Australian) . . . . Samantha

••• 0:21—Breasts and buns, while painting Alvin's body.

Alvin Rides Again (1974; Australian) . . . . Mandy

••• 0:48—Full frontal nudity, taking off red dress and getting into bed with Alvin. More breasts lying in bed. Long scene.

Lonely Hearts (1983; Australian) . . . . .Rosemarie

The Coca-Cola Kid (1985; Australian) . . . . Juliana

McTague, Heather *

Films:

Beach Beverly Hills (1992) . . . . Michelle

Intimate Obsession (1992) . . . . Beth Thompson

(Unrated version reviewed.)

••• 0:38—Nude, while making love with Tom in bedroom. (She's wearing a dark wig and sunglasses.) Long scene.

• 1:04—Breasts on TV in video playback that Rachel watches.

• 1:10—Left breast, while sitting on couch and kissing Tom.

McTeer, Janet

Films:

Half Moon Street (1986) . . . . Van Arkady's Ambassador

a.k.a. Escort Girl

Hawks (1988; British). . . . . Hazel

Carrington (1995; British) . . . . Vanessa Bell

Made for Cable Movies:

Wuthering Heights (1994; TNT) . . . . Ellen

Made for TV Movies:

Portrait of a Marriage (1992; British) . . . Vita Sackville-West

• 0:47—Brief right breast, while lying in bed with Violet.

•• 2:28—(0:04 into Part 3) Left breast and buns, getting out of bed. Brief breasts and buns, putting robe on.

McVeigh, Rose

a.k.a. Rosemary McVeigh.

Films:

A Night in Heaven (1983) . . . . Alison

Porky's Revenge (1985; Canadian) .... Miss Webster
- ••• 0:39—In black bra, panties, garter belt and stockings then breasts in her apartment with Mr. Dobish while Pee Wee and his friends secretly watch.

Casanova (1987)........................ Captain's Wife

McWhirter, Jillian

Films:

After Midnight (1989)........................... Allison
Nowhere to Run (1989) .... Cynthia
Dune Warriors (1990) .... Val
- • 0:25—Brief right breast with Miranda in underground lake. (Her hair is in the way of her left breast.)

Beyond the Call of Duty (1991)............... Mary Jackson
Servants of Twilight (1991)................. Vera Lancaster
Where Sleeping Dogs Lie (1991).............. Dol Whitney
Last Man Standing (1994) .... Anabella
- •• 0:12—Breasts, while making love in bed with Jeff Wincott.
- • 1:01—Brief breasts, when getting out of bed.

Manhunt (1994)..................... Stephanie Williams
Stranglehold (1994)..................... Helen Filmore
- • 1:00—In bra, then breasts, while starting to make out with Richter. Don't see her face.

Rage (1995) .... Bobby T
Bloodfist VIII: Hard Way Out (1996) ..... Danielle Mendelsohn

Made for Cable TV:

Love Street: To Kill (1995; Showtime)............. Nicole
- •• 0:04—Breasts, while putting on tank top in bedroom.
- •• 0:10—Breasts, while sunbathing on lounge chair, talking to Max Parrish.
- ••• 0:16—Breasts and buns, while making love with Parrish outside at night.

Mechsner, Susan

Films:

Cheech & Chong's Next Movie (1980).......... Leaflet Lady
...All the Marbles (1981).................. Creature #1
a.k.a. The California Dolls
- • 0:42—Breasts while wrestling in the mud.

Lovely But Deadly (1981) .... Suzie
Stripes (1981)........................ Mud Wrestler
- • 0:56—Brief breasts, while kneeling on the ground to the left of John Candy. Brief breasts, when punching Candy in the stomach after the police arrive (she's in the front to the left). Covered with mud.

The Concrete Jungle (1982) .... Breaker
Chained Heat (1983; U.S./German) .... Gunderson
The Cotton Club (1984) .... Gypse
Private Resort (1985).................. Aerobics Instructor
The Linguini Incident (1991)........... Female Ventriloquist

Medak, Karen

Films:

A Girl to Kill For (1989)......................... Sue
- ••• 0:17—Breasts showering at the beach after surfing with Chuck.
- •• 1:08—Breasts in spa when Chuck takes her shirt off. Then miscellaneous shots making love.

The Marrying Man (1991)......................... Sherry
a.k.a. Too Hot to Handle
Switch (1991)........................... Saleswoman
Galaxies are Colliding (1996; Canadian/U.S.) .... Margo

Medway, Heather

Films:

Center of the Web (1992)....................... Sidney
The Fear (1994).............................. Ashley
- • 0:33—Very, very brief blurry left breast, when turning around in bed after getting scared by shadow on the wall. Blurry. Good shot of very brief right breast, after Richard swears and bends down to get his pants. Very, very brief right breast again, when he lifts up the sheets to get out.

Speechless (1994) .... Make-Up Girl
Vibrations (1994)............................. Raynee
Serpent's Lair (1995) .... Alex

TV:

Models Inc. (1994-95)....................... Stephanie
Monroes (1995-96)........................... Jennifer
Viper (1996-) .... Det. Cameron Westlake

Meiner, Melissa *

Video Tapes:

California Girl Fox Hunt Bikini Competition #6 .. Chanel
- ••• 0:19—Buns in two piece swimsuit.
- • 0:49—Buns during review.

Mejias, Isabelle *

Films:

Daughter of Death (1982)......................... Julie
a.k.a. Julie Darling
Bay Boy (1985; Canadian).................. Mary McNeil
- •• 1:28—Brief breasts in her bedroom with Kiefer Sutherland, then brief breasts in bed with him.

Higher Education (1987; Canadian)........... Carrie Hanson
Meatballs III (1987) .... Wendy
Fall From Innocence (1988)............... Marsa Cummins
State Park (1988; Canadian) .... Marsha
Scanners 2: The New Order (1991).......... Alice Leonardo

Made for TV Movies:

Special People (1984) .... Julie

Melato, Mariangela

Films:

Love and Anarchy (1974; Italian).................. Salome
The Nada Gang (1974; French/Italian) .... Cash
The Seduction of Mimi (1974; Italian)................ Fiore
Swept Away (1975; Italian).............. Raffaela Lenzetti
a.k.a. Swept Away...by an unusual destiny in the blue sea of august
- •• 1:10—Breasts on the sand when Giancarlo Giannini catches her and makes love with her.

Moses (1976; British/Italian) .... Princess Bithia
Flash Gordon (1980) .... Kala
So Fine (1981).................................. Lira
Summer Night (1987; Italian)............... Signora Bolk
- •• 0:26—Breasts behind gauze net over bed making love with a German guy.
- •• 1:02—Breasts while on the bed making love with the prisoner.
- •• 1:09—Breasts again.
- ••• 1:13—Buns, while walking out of the ocean, then breasts.

Meldrum, Wendel

Films:

Vamping (1984) .... Rita
K-9 (1989)......................... Pretty Girl with Dog
Why Me? (1990) .... n.a.
Diplomatic Immunity (1991).................. Kim Dades
Beautiful Dreamers (1992; Canadian)......... Jessie Bucke
- • 1:00—Very, very brief tip of left breast, while bathing herself.

••• 1:09—Full frontal nudity, after taking off her clothes to go swimming with her husband and Rip Torn.
Sodbusters (1994; Canadian) . . . . .Lilac Gentry
TV:
Knots Landing (1984-85) . . . . .P.K. Kelly
Pursuit of Happiness (1987). . . . . Margaret Callahan
Due South (1994) . . . . .Lee Anne

Melini, Angela *

Films:
Silk Degrees (1994) . . . . Bonnie
Video Tapes:
Playboy Video Calendar 1993 (1992) . . . . February
• 0:06—Brief full frontal nudity doing various things outdoors.
••• 0:08—Nude outdoors in Japanese garden.
Wet & Wild IV (1992) . . . . .Model
Playboy's Playmate Review 1993 (1993) . . . . . . Miss June
••• 0:44—Nude in fashion designer fantasy.
••• 0:46—Nude in bedroom while it rains outside.
Playboy's Sexy, Steamy, Sultry (1993). . . . . .Playmate

Mell, Marisa *

Films:
5 Sinners (1961) . . . . .Liliane
French Dressing (1964) . . . . Francoise Fayol
Casanova '70 (1965; Italian) . . . . Thelma
City of Fear (1965; British). . . . . Ilona
Masquerade (1965). . . . . Sophie
Objective 500 Million (1966). . . . . Yo
Secret Agent Super Dragon (1966; French/Italian/German) . . . . Charity Farrell
Anyone Can Play (1968; Italian) .Paola
Danger: Diabolik (1968) . . . . Eva Kant
Mahogany (1975) . . . . .Carlotta Gavin
Sex on the Run (1979; German/French/Italian) . . . Francesca
a.k.a. Some Like It Cool
a.k.a. Casanova and Co.
• 0:52—Very, very brief left breast, while getting out of bed with Tony Curtis.
No One Cries Forever (1984; South African) . . . . .n.a.
Quest for the Mighty Sword (1989; Italian) . . . . Nephele

Melson, Sara

Films:
Dr. Giggles (1992). . . . . Coreen
Malice (1993) . . . . .Girl on Bike
The Low Life (1995) . . . . .Suzie
Made for Cable TV:
Women: Stories of Passion-Sing, Sing Me the Blues (1996; Showtime) . . . . Jenny
•• 0:05—Breasts, while kissing Vincent in the greenhouse.
••• 0:06—Breasts, while making love with Vincent on the floor.
•• 0:07—Brief breasts, while bathing in a small tub and talking with Vincent.
• 0:11—Brief left breast, when taking off nightgown at night.
•• 0:13—Breasts, while making love in bed with Vincent.
• 0:20—Brief right breast while making love with Thomas.
• 0:21—Brief buns, while lying in bed with Thomas.
•• 0:23—Left breast, while making love with Vincent outdoors.
Made for TV Movies:
Roseanne: An Unauthorized Biography (1994) . . . . . Stephanie
TV:
Big Wave Dave's (1993). . . . . Cyndi

• *Mendez, Monica* *

Video Tapes:
Penthouse: Lipstick Girls (1997). . . . . .n.a.
Playboy's Women Behaving Badly (1997). . . . . All Wet
••• 0:01—Nude, while undressing in locker room with her two girlfriends in locker room, then taking a shower.

Meneghel, Xuxa

See: Xuxa.

Meneses, Alex

Films:
Kissing Miranda (1994) . . . . Miranda Castillo
• 1:00—Brief left breast, while making love with Gib.
Amanda and the Alien (1995) . . . . Connie Flores
•• 0:23—Breasts under bra that's been put on backward, then breasts and buns after Nicole Eggert helps take the bra off and into the shower.
•• 0:34—Breasts, while making love with Charlie.
The Immortals (1995) . . . . Cleopatra
Selena (1997) . . . . Sara
Made for Cable TV:
Hot Line: Payback (1994; Cinemax). . . . . Ellen
• 0:18—Buns and in a bra, while undressing in front of Lee.
•• 0:20—Breasts, after Lee takes her bra off.
••• 0:22—Nude, while making love in bed with Lee.
Sherman Oaks (1995; Showtime) . . . . Elena
Sherman Oaks: Season 1, Episode 3 (1995; Showtime) . . Elena
TV:
Dr. Quinn, Medicine Woman (1997) . . . . Teresa Morales

Menuez, Stephanie *

Films:
Clean and Sober (1988). . . . . Ticket Agent
Gremlins 2: The New Batch (1990) . . . . Clamp's Secretary
The Rapture (1991) . . . . Diane
••• 0:06—Breasts in furniture store with Mimi Rogers, Vic and David Duchovny.
Lawnmower Man 2 (1995) . . . . Female Lawyer
Made for Cable Movies:
Blindsided (1993; USA) .Racehorse Girl

Mercer, Mae

Films:
The Beguiled (1971). . . . . Hallie
• 1:28—Very brief breasts in ripped open dress during flashback.
Dirty Harry (1971). . . . . .Mrs. Russell
Frogs (1972) . . . . .Maybelle
Pretty Baby (1978). . . . . .Mama Mosebery

Mercure, Monique

Films:
My Uncle Antoine (1971; Canadian) . . . . Alexandrine
Quintet (1979) . . . . Redstone's Mate
Stone Cold Dead (1979; Canadian). . . . . Dr. Bouvier
Naked Lunch (1991). . . . . .Fadela
• 1:45—Brief breasts, when first opening her blouse and grabbing her breasts before a cut to her tearing off some special-effect skin to become Roy Scheider.

Meredith, Penny

Films:
The Flesh & Blood Show (1974; British). . . . . .n.a.

Happy Housewives (1975; British) . . . . Margaretta
- 0:02—Brief right breast, while talking on the telephone while Bob makes love with her.
- •• 0:19—Breasts while standing up in bathtub and talking to Bob.
- 0:34—In sheer black lingerie.
- 1:05—Brief breasts pulling her top down when interrupted by the policeman at the window.

Meril, Macha

Films:

The Married Woman (1964; French). . . . . Charlotte
- 0:07—Brief glimpses of breasts while walking around inside house.
- 0:08—Brief side of left breast, when climbing through window from outside.

The Defector (1966; German/French) . . . . Frieda Hoffman
Belle de Jour (1968; French) . . . . Renee
Deep Red Hatchet Murders (1976; Italian) . . . . . Helga Ulmann
Beau Pere (1981; French) . . . . Birthday Hostess
Bolero (1982; French) . . . . Magda
Vagabond (1985; French) . . . . Madame Landier
- •• 0:45—Breasts, while sitting in the bathtub and talking on the phone.

Duet for One (1987) . . . . Anya
Meeting Venus (1990; British) . . . . Miss Malikoff
Double Vision (1992; French/Canadian) . . . . Jimmy

Merkle, Tina

Films:

The Lost Empire (1983). . . . . Girl Recruit
The Rosebud Beach Hotel (1985). . . . . Bellhop
- 0:49—Breasts, standing in line. Closest to the camera.

• Merryman, Deanna *

Made for Cable TV:

Hot Springs Hotel: Money Trouble (1998; Showtime)
. . . . Telegram Girl
- ••• 0:02—Breasts and buns, while making love on sofa bed with Randy.

Meyer, Bess

Films:

One More Saturday Night (1986) . . . . Tobi
- 1:02—Brief breasts in bed with Tom Davis.

In the Mood (1987) . . . . Teenage Girl (Slapper)
She's Out of Control (1989) . . . . Cheryl
The Inner Circle (1991; Italian) . . . . Katya—Age 16
Necronomicon: Book of the Dead (1993)
. . . . Emily/Amy Osterman
- 0:38—Brief breasts, while taking a shower. Don't see her face, probably a body double.

Stuart Saves His Family (1995) . . . . Laurie

TV:

Parenthood (1990) . . . . Julie
Room For Two (1992-93) . . . . Naomi Dillon
The Boys Are Back (1994-95) . . . . Judy Hansen

• Meyer, Dina

Films:

Johnny Mnemonic (1995). . . . . Jane
Dragonheart (1996) . . . . Kara
Starship Troopers (1996) . . . . Dizzy Flores
- •• 0:29—Breasts, after taking off her blouse in co-ed showers.
- ••• 1:21—Breasts, while taking off her T-shirt with Casper Van Dien. Later, brief breasts when hiding under the covers.

TV:

Beverly Hills, 90210 (1994) . . . . Lucinda Nicholson

• Meyer, Michele *

Films:

Nail Gun Massacre (1988). . . . . Linda

Made for Cable TV:

Erotic Confessions: Love Calling (1996; Cinemax)
. . . . Lauren
(Available on video tape in *Erotic Confessions, Volume 3: Passion.*)
- 0:01—Breasts, while making love with Doug during his phone sex fantasy. Breasts, while changing into lingerie in bedroom.
- •• 0:10—Breasts, while making love with Doug in her phone sex fantasy.
- ••• 0:11—Full frontal nudity, while in bed, talking on the phone, then making love with Doug.

Erotic Confessions: The Business Trip (1996; Cinemax)
. . . . Stephanie
(Available on video tape in *Erotic Confessions, Volume 4: Pleasure.*)
- 0:06—Brief left breast and partial buns, when her husband, Jeff, takes her towel in hotel hallway.
- •• 0:18—Nude, while making love with Jeff.
- ••• 0:19—Nude, when making love with Jeff while Erica watches, then when Erica joins in.

Meyer, Mimi

See: Craven, Mimi.

Michael, Joy

Films:

Homework (1982)
. . . . Diane, Age 16/Body Double for Joan Collins
- •• 0:39—In bra, then breasts in car making out with her boyfriend.
- •• 1:18—Breasts, taking off her bra and making love with Tommy. (Supposed to be Joan Collins.)

Fear City (1984) . . . . Metropole Dancer
Johnny Dangerously (1984). . . . . Chorus Girl
Surf II (1984). . . . . Hot Potato #1
- •• 0:25—Breasts taking off bikini top with her friend in lifeguard station at beach with Eric Stoltz and his friend.
- •• 0:27—Brief breasts with her friend, after dropping towel when she raises her hands for the police.

Michaels, Julie

Films:

Roadhouse (1989). . . . . Denise
- ••• 1:18—Breasts dancing on stage in club in front of Patrick Swayze.

Point Break (1991). . . . . Freight Train
- 0:53—Brief breasts in the shower.
- 0:54—Nude, beating up Keanu Reeves in the bathroom during shoot-out. Full frontal nudity while stabbing an FBI agent.

Doctor Mordrid (1992) . . . . Irene
- ••• 0:00—Breasts and buns, while talking with Brian Thompson, then getting picked up and placed on table.

Jason Goes to Hell—The Final Friday (1993)
. . . . Elizabeth Marcus F.B.I.
(Unrated Director's Original Cut reviewed.)
- •• 0:03—In white bra and panties, then buns and breasts while starting to take a shower. More breasts after grabbing towel.

Witchboard 2: The Devil's Doorway (1993) . . . . Susan
• 1:17—Brief breasts, in B&W photos that Russel looks at.

*Michaels, Lorraine **

Films:

Star 80 (1983). . . . . Paul's Party Guest
Malibu Express (1984) . . . . Liza Chamberlin
••• 0:23—Breasts in the shower making love with Shane, while getting photographed by a camera.
B.O.R.N. (1988) . . . . Dr. Black

Michaels, Michele

Films:

The Slumber Party Massacre (1982) . . . . Trish
•• 0:01—Breasts, in white panties, while getting dressed.
•• 0:08—Buns, then brief breasts while passing the soap to Kim.
•• 0:29—Breasts, in white panties, while putting shirt on while two boys watch from outside.

Video Tapes:

Scream Queen Hot Tub Party (1991). . . . . Trish
•• 0:14—Breasts and buns in shower scene from *Slumber Party Massacre.*

*Michaels, Roxanna **

Films:

Emmanuelle 5 (1986). . . . . Girl No. 2
••• 0:42—Breasts, while talking with the two other girls.
••• 0:43—Breasts, talking to Eddie and Monique Gabrielle.
•• 0:48—Breasts, during rescue/escape.
Glitch (1988). . . . . Cold Reader #2
The Newlydeads (1988) . . . . Lynda
0:23—In lacy black bra and panties, while in bed.
•• 0:44—Breasts, while in the shower.
• 0:47—Brief breast, while dead on the shower floor after being stabbed.
Caged Fury (1989) . . . . Katherine "Kat" Collins
• 0:39—Breasts while getting searched upon entering prison with other topless women.
Baja (1995) . . . . Prostitute
•• 0:44—Buns in G-string, then breasts, while in hotel room with Lance Henriksen.
•• 0:45—Breasts, while making love with Henriksen and afterwards.

Video Tapes:

Inside Out 3 (1992) . . . . Laila/The Perfect Woman
••• 0:38—Breasts and buns in G-string, changing out of her wet clothes, while Joe watches.
• 0:43—Brief breasts, taking off clothes on talk show on TV.

*Michaelsen, Helle **

Films:

Beach Fever (1988). . . . . Virgin Beauty

Video Tapes:

Playboy Video Calendar 1991 (1990) . . . . April
••• 0:14—Nude.

Michan, Cherie

Films:

Wrong is Right (1982). . . . . Erika
Fever Pitch (1985). . . . . Rose O'Sharon
A Brilliant Disguise (1994) . . . . Selma

Made for Cable Movies:

Weapons of Mass Distraction (1997; HBO) . . . . . . Nanci Gross

Made for Cable TV:

Dream On: The Name of the Game is Five-Card Stud (1991; HBO) . . . . .Allison
••• 0:16—In black bra, then breasts, literally losing her shirt during poker game.
• 0:17—Very brief nipple seen through her folded arms.
Dream On: To the Moon, Alex (1992; HBO) . . . . .Allison
Dream On: Hack Like Me (1994; HBO) . . . . .Allison
Dream On: Where There's Smoke, You're Fired (1994; HBO) . . . . .Allison

Michel, Delaune

Films:

A Woman, Her Men and Her Futon (1992) . . . . .Gail
Dirty Money (1993) . . . . CeCe
•• 0:08—Breasts and buns, while making love with Sam in bedroom.
• 0:10—Brief breasts, while talking in bed with Sam.

Made for Cable TV:

Women: Stories of Passion-Wishful Thinking (1996; Showtime) . . . . Betsy
•• 0:09—In bra, then breasts, while making love with her girlfriend, Kelly, in movie theater.

Michelle, Ann

Sister of actress Vicki Michelle.

Films:

Virgin Witch (1971; British) .Christine
• 0:00—Brief right breast, during opening credits.
••• 0:06—Breasts and lower frontal nudity, after undressing and getting her body measured by Sybil.
•• 0:17—Breasts, undressing and standing by doorway, then prancing around outside for Peter the photographer.
••• 0:23—Brief breasts, while lying on car, then more breasts while standing next to it and posing.
••• 0:27—Full frontal nudity, while posing for photographer outside. Buns while making love with him.
•• 0:33—Nude, undressing and taking a shower.
••• 0:47—Nude, while standing, then lying on table during ceremony.
•• 0:52—Breasts, while getting out of bed with Sybil.
•• 1:20—Breasts, during ceremony.
• 1:23—Breasts, while getting dressed.
House of Whipcord (1974; British). . . . . Julia
The Haunted (1976) . . . . .Abanaki/Jennifer Baines
••• 0:03—Breasts while on horseback as Abanaki.
•• 0:06—Breasts, while riding on horseback in the desert.
•• 0:48—Breasts while lying on towel outside with Patrick at night.
•• 1:19—Breasts while riding the horse again.
Justine (1977; British) . . . . Pauline
a.k.a. Cruel Passion
Young Lady Chatterley (1977). . . . . .Gwen, Roommate
French Quarter (1978)
. . . . "Coke Eye" Laura/Policewoman in French Hotel
• 0:42—Right breast, when Josie wakes her up.
••• 0:43—Breasts in bed, caressing Josie's breasts.
•• 0:58—Breasts during voodoo ceremony. Close ups of breasts with snake.
• 1:19—Brief breasts, sitting in bed.
••• 1:20—More breasts sitting in bed, talking to a customer. Long scene.

*Michelle, Shelley **

Films:

My Stepmother Is An Alien (1988) ....Body Double for Kim Basinger

In the Cold of the Night (1989) .... Model 3

Overexposed (1990)... Body Double for Catherine Oxenberg

•• 0:54—Left breast several times, buns when taking off panties, lower frontal nudity while in bed with Hank. Wearing a wig with wavy hair.

Pretty Woman (1990) .... Body Double for Julia Roberts

(Body double for Julia Roberts only at the *beginning* of the film when she is getting dressed.)

Bikini Summer (1991) ....Jazz

•• 0:33—Breasts and buns in the shower while Max peeks through hole.

•• 0:49—Breasts and buns, trying on swimsuits, then having a water fight with Cheryl.

Double Impact (1991)................Uncredited Student

Final Analysis (1992)..........................Body Parts

Forever (1992) .... Marilyn

The Magic Bubble (1992) ....Body Double

The Naked Truth (1992) .... Miss Honduras

•• 0:18—Nude, changing into "something more comfortable" in front of the two Franks.

• 0:22—Buns, in pink sequined G-string two piece swimsuit.

Sunset Strip (1992)........................... Veronica

Hexed (1993) ....Body Double for Claudia Christian

a.k.a. All Shook Up

•• 0:31—Breasts, while making love on top of Matthew in bed.

• 0:32—Buns and right breast, getting out of bed.

• 0:57—Buns and brief left breast, while standing up in bed.

Married People, Single Sex (1993) ....Carol

••• 0:54—Breasts and buns in G-string, garter belt and stockings while dancing on stage.

••• 1:05—Breasts and buns in black G-string, after opening her bathrobe and giving Will a private dance in the kitchen.

Rising Sun (1993)............................ Blonde

• 0:44—Very, very brief buns in black G-string, when her dress flies up while spinning around during party.

•• 0:56—Breasts, while lying down on her back with sushi on her front. More breasts when police bust in.

Midnight Blue (1996) ....Body Double

• 1:12—Brief side of left breast and buns, while lying next to Damian Chapa in his fantasy.

Made for Cable Movies:

Nails (1992; Showtime) ....Body Double

•• 0:16—Breasts and buns, several times body double for Anne Archer during love scene with Dennis Hopper.

The Hit List (1993; Showtime).................... Dancer

Made for Cable TV:

Full Frontal Comedy (1996; Showtime) ....Woman of Full Frontal Comedy

CD-ROM:

Hollywood Body Double (1995).................Herself

Michelle, Vicki

Sister of actress Ann Michelle.

Films:

Virgin Witch (1971; British) ....Betty

• 0:00—Brief breasts, while sitting up during opening credits.

•• 0:31—Breasts, while sitting in bathtub. Nude, getting out. Seen through fish-eye lens.

•• 1:17—Buns, during witches' ceremony. Left breast, then breasts while lying on table.

• 1:23—Brief left breast, while on the ground with Johnny.

• 1:25—Left breast, when Johnny gets up off her.

Oh, Alfie! (1975; British) ....Bird

a.k.a. Alfie Darling

The Greek Tycoon (1978) .... Nico's Girlfriend

Micula, Stacia

See: Fox, Samantha.

Middleton, Francine

Films:

Joe (1970) ....Gail

•• 1:31—Nude with Bill.

The Love-Thrill Murders (1971) ....Faith

•• 0:02—Full frontal nudity, while lying on table during ceremony. Long scene.

• 0:32—Right breast, while in bed with Maggie.

• 0:57—Brief buns and partial breasts (seen in mirror), while in bedroom with Maggie.

•• 1:01—Buns, while standing next to bed as Maggie undresses. Breasts, while making love on bed with Maggie.

•• 1:09—Breasts, while in bed with Maggie.

• *Midori*

Adult film actress.

a.k.a. Michele Watley.

Sister of singer Jody Watley.

Films:

Coming to America (1988) ....Bather

• 0:04—Brief buns, while standing in bathtub in front of Eddie Murphy.

Mierisch, Susan

Films:

Cave Girl (1985) .... Locker Room Student

•• 0:05—Breasts with four other girls in the girls' locker room undressing, then running after Rex. She's blonde, wearing red panties and a necklace.

Neon Maniacs (1985).................... Young Lover

• 0:07—Very brief upper half of right breast while kissing her boyfriend at night.

*Milano, Alyssa **

Films:

Old Enough (1984)......................... Diane Sloan

Commando (1985)............................... Jenny

The Canterville Ghost (1986; British)..............Jennifer

Speed Zone (1989)......................... Truck Driver

Little Sister (1991)................................ Diana

At Home with the Webbers (1992) ....Fan

Conflict of Interest (1992)........................... Eve

Where The Day Takes You (1992) .... Kimmy

Deadly Sins (1994; Canadian).................. Cristina

• 1:20—In lingerie and brief right breast while making love with David Keith.

Double Dragon (1994) .... Marian Delario

Embrace of the Vampire (1994).............. Charlotte

(Unrated version reviewed.)

•• 0:15—Left breast and buns, when changing clothes in bedroom while talking with Chris.

••• 0:21—Breasts in open nightgown while lying in bed when Martin Kemp visits her.

••• 0:50—Breasts in open blouse while letting Charlotte Lewis photograph her. Nice long scene.

••• 0:59—Breasts, while lying in bed, then with Chris, Lewis and Kemp.
• 1:05—Very brief breasts in flashback from 0:21.
Glory Daze (1995) . . . . Chelsea
Poison Ivy 2: Lily (1995) . . . . Lily
•• 0:43—In black bra, then breasts, while making love with Gredin outside at night. (Some of his artwork gets in the way.)
• 0:51—Brief right breast in open blouse, then breasts while posing for Xander Berkeley.
• 0:53—Very brief left breast, while posing for Berkeley.
• 1:04—Buns and breasts behind patterned glass while making out with Gredin in room during party.
Public Enemy #1 (1995) . . . . Amaryllis
• 1:13—Very brief partial buns in short dress when Frank Stallone picks her up after killing her.
Fear (1996) . . . . Margo Masse
Below Utopia (1997) . . . . Susanne
• 0:27—Very, very brief blurry tip of left breast, twice, when sitting up on couch.
Hugo Pool (1997) . . . . Hugo Dugay
Made for Cable Movies:
Candles in the Dark (1993; Family) . . . . Syvlia Velliste
Rebel Highway: Confessions of a Sorority Girl (1994; Showtime) . . . . Rita
Made for Cable TV:
The Outer Limits: Caught in the Act (1995; Showtime) . . . . Hannah Valesic
••• 0:11—In black bra and panties, then breasts, while in her bedroom with Karl before absorbing him into her body (she has an alien life-form in her).
• 0:13—Right breast, three times, while lying in bed when Jay comes over to talk to her.
• 0:41—Brief right breast, while taking off her top to make love with Jay in operating room.
Made for TV Movies:
Crash Course (1988) . . . . Vanessa Crawford
Dance 'Til Dawn (1988) . . . . Shelley Sheridan
Casualties of Love: The "Long Island Lolita" Story (1993) . . . . Amy Fisher
The Surrogate (1995) . . . . Amy Winslow
To Brave Alaska (1996) . . . . Denise Harris
TV:
Who's the Boss? (1984-92) . . . . Samantha Micelli
Melrose Place (1997-98) . . . . Jennifer Mancini

Miles, Rosalind

Films:
Shaft's Big Score! (1972) . . . . Arna Ashby
I Spit on Your Corpse (1974) . . . . Erica
a.k.a. Girls for Rent
Friday Foster (1975) . . . . Clorils Boston
• 0:20—Brief side view of left breast, while changing clothes backstage. Slightly out of focus.

Miles, Sarah *

Films:
The Servant (1963) . . . . Vera
Those Magnificent Men in their Flying Machines (1965) . . . . Patricia Rawnsley
Blow-Up (1966; British/Italian) . . . . Patricia
Ryan's Daughter (1970) . . . . Rosy Ryan
• 1:32—Brief right breast, in open red blouse, while outside with Major Doryan.
• 1:36—Very brief right breast, when reaching up to hug Doryan while lying on the ground together.
Lady Caroline Lamb (1973) . . . . Lady Caroline Lamb
The Man Who Loved Cat Dancing (1973) . . . . Catherine Crocker
•• 1:04—Back of left breast, then breasts, after taking off her blouse, then washing herself in water.
• 1:20—Brief left breast, while in bed with Burt Reynolds.
The Sailor Who Fell From Grace with the Sea (1976) . . . . Anne Osborne
• 0:18—Breasts sitting at the vanity getting dressed while her son watches through peephole.
•• 0:23—Breasts, fantasizing about her husband.
•• 0:42—Breasts, then nude, while making love with Kris Kristofferson.
• 1:15—Brief right breast, while in bed with Kristofferson.
The Big Sleep (1978; British) . . . . Charlotte Sternwood
Priest of Love (1980) . . . . Film Star
Venom (1982; British) . . . . Dr. Marion Stowe
Ordeal by Innocence (1984) . . . . Mary Durrant
Steaming (1985; British) . . . . Sarah
•• 0:23—Breasts while getting into pool with Vanessa Redgrave.
•• 0:49—Breasts while getting undressed.
•• 1:31—Nude while lying down next to pool.
Hope and Glory (1987; British) . . . . Grace Rohan
Queenie (1987) . . . . Lady Sybil
White Mischief (1988) . . . . Alice
Made for Cable Movies:
A Ghost in Monte Carlo (1990) . . . . Emille/Madame Bluet
Made for TV Movies:
Masterpiece Theatre: Dandelion Dead (1994) . . . . n.a.

Miles, Sherry

Films:
The Todd Killings (1970) . . . . Amata
Making It (1971) . . . . Debbie
The Velvet Vampire (1971) . . . . Susan Ritter
• 0:08—Brief breasts in bed with Lee.
••• 0:18—Breasts sitting up in bed, then making love with Lee.
• 0:21—Breasts in bed in desert during dream scene.
••• 0:22—Breasts sitting up in bed and turning on the light.
• 0:42—Breasts in bed during desert dream scene, long shot.
• 0:55—Breasts in bed during desert dream scene.
••• 0:56—Breasts in bed in desert scene, closer shot with Diane.
• 1:19—Brief breasts in desert scene during flashback.
Your Three Minutes Are Up (1973) . . . . Debbie
The Harrad Summer (1974) . . . . Dee
a.k.a. Student Union
The Long Dark Night (1977) . . . . Lois
a.k.a. The Pack
TV:
Hee Haw (1971-72) . . . . Regular

Miles, Sylvia *

Films:
Midnight Cowboy (1969) . . . . Cass
• 0:20—Brief buns, running into bedroom and jumping onto bed with Jon Voight. More when changing the TV channel with the remote control. Most of her right breast in bed under Voight.
92 in the Shade (1975) . . . . Bella
The Sentinel (1977) . . . . Gerde
• 0:33—Brief left breast, three times, standing behind Beverly D'Angelo. Right breast, while ripping dress off Christina Raines. B&W dream.

- 1:23—Brief breasts, three times, with D'Angelo made up to look like zombies, munching on a dead Chris Sarandon.
- 1:27—Very brief right breast during big zombie scene.
- 1:28—Brief breasts when the zombies start dying.

The Funhouse (1981) .... Madame Zena
Wall Street (1987) .... Realtor
Crossing Delancey (1988) .... Hannah Mandelbaum
Spike of Bensonhurst (1988) .... Congresswoman
She-Devil (1989) .... Mrs. Fisher
Denise Calls Up (1995) .... Gale's Aunt Sharon

Milford, Penelope

Films:

Man on a Swing (1974) .... Evelyn Moore
Valentino (1977; British) .... Lorna Sinclair
- ••• 1:28—Nude, while making love with Rudolf Nureyev in bedroom. Long scene.

Coming Home (1978) .... Viola Munson
- • 1:19—Doing strip tease in room with Jane Fonda and two guys. Sort of right breast peeking out between her arms when she changes her mind.

The Last Word (1979) .... Denise Travis
Endless Love (1981) .... Ingrid
Take This Job and Shove It (1981) .... Lenore Meade
Blood Link (1983) .... Julie Warren
- •• 0:22—Breasts while in bed with Craig. Very brief left breast, when she grabs the pillow.
- •• 1:24—In black bra in greenhouse with Keith, then breasts.
- • 1:27—Brief buns, while on top of Keith. Long shot.
- •• 1:28—Right breast, when Keith tries to strangle her.
- ••• 1:35—Breasts, while in bedroom with Keith.

The Golden Seal (1983) .... Tania Lee
Heathers (1989) .... Pauline Fleming
Cold Justice (1992; British) .... Eileen
Normal Life (1996) .... Adele Anderson

Made for Cable TV:

The Hitchhiker: Man at the Window (1985; HBO) .... Diane Hampton
- •• 0:09—Breasts in white panties making love with her husband on the couch.

Made for TV Movies:

Rosie: The Rosemary Clooney Story (1982) .... Betty
The Burning Bed (1984) .... Gaby

Milhench, Ann

Films:

Blood Debts (1983) .... Lisa
Sloane (1984) .... Janice Thursby
- •• 0:02—Breasts and buns getting out of shower and being held by kidnappers.

Millar, Jeannie

Made for Cable Movies:

Black Scorpion 2—Aftershock (1996; Showtime) . . Giggles
- •• 0:12—Breasts, while dancing in funhouse in front of two guys.

Ladykiller (1996; Showtime) .... Nikki
- •• 0:07—Breasts and partial buns in panties, while dancing on stage.
- ••• 0:37—Buns in G-string and breasts, while dancing on stage.
- • 0:55—Brief partial buns in T-back, while lying dead on stage.

Millardet, Patricia

Films:

Petit Con (1986; French) .... Aurore
Hot Chocolate (1992) .... Grace
Covert Assassin (1994; Italian) .... Magda Altmann
- • 0:23—Very brief buns, after dropping her robe in bedroom in front of Roy Scheider. Medium long shot. Don't see her face.

Miller, Ginger *

Films:

Beach Beverly Hills (1992) .... Bikini Audition Girl 14

Video Tapes:

Wild Bikinis (1987) .... Herself
- • 0:23—Buns in white two piece swimsuit, while rubbing oil on herself.
- • 0:26—Buns, while on pool float with Beckie Mullen.

Boxing Babes (1991) .... Herself
Made for Man: Intimate Fantasy (1992) ..... Darling Nikki
- • 0:03—Buns in G-string, doing strip routine out of black outfit.
- • 0:11—Buns, during gelatin wrestling with Baby Driver.
- • 0:37—Stripping down to two piece silver swimsuit.
- • 0:47—Wrestling with Sugar Ray Rene in lettuce.
- • 0:55—Brief left breast, popping out of swimsuit top.

Miller, Jennifer

Films:

Hit the Dutchman (1992) .... Frances Ireland
(Unrated version reviewed.)
- • 0:35—Most of side of right breast, while in dressing room with Arthur.
- •• 0:36—Breasts, while running around the room with Arthur. More breasts and buns, while on the floor with him.
- • 0:55—Brief breasts, after taking off her dress top for Legs Diamond.

Wayne's World 2 (1993) .... Girl at Concert
Never Say Die (1994) .... Brooke
Cyborg Cop III (1995) .... Evelyn
a.k.a. Terminal Impact

Miller, Marjorie

See: Blondi.

Miller, Mindi

See: Randolph, Ty.

Miller, Penelope Ann

Films:

Adventures in Babysitting (1987) .... Brenda
Big Top Pee Wee (1988) .... Winnie
Biloxi Blues (1988) .... Daisy
Miles From Home (1988) .... Sally
Dead Bang (1989) .... Linda
Downtown (1990) .... Lori Mitchell
The Freshman (1990) .... Tina Sabatini
Kindergarten Cop (1990) .... Joyce
Awakenings (1991) .... Paula
Other People's Money (1991) .... Kate Sullivan
Chaplin (1992; British/U.S.) .... Edna Purviance
The Gun in Betty Lou's Handbag (1992) .... Betty Lou
Year of the Comet (1992) .... Margaret Harwood
Carlito's Way (1993) .... Gail
- ••• 0:59—Breasts, while dancing on stage in club in auburn wig.

••• 1:18—Breasts, after opening her robe and enticing Al Pacino in her apartment.
The Shadow (1994). . . . . Margo Lane
The Relic (1996) . . . . .Dr. Margo Green
Made for Cable Movies:
Witch Hunt (1995; HBO). Kim Hudson
Made for TV Movies:
The Last Don (1997) . . . . Nalene
TV:
The Closer (1998) . . . . .Erica Hewitt
Video Tapes:
The Kathy Kaehler Fitness System (1992). . . . . Exercise Student

Miller, Rebecca

Daughter of playwright Arthur Miller.
Films:
Regarding Henry (1991) . . . . .Linda
Consenting Adults (1992). Kay Otis
• 0:28—Buns and brief side view of left breast, while getting out of tub. Seen through shutters while Kevin Kline watches through the window.
The Pickle (1992) . . . . Carrie
Wind (1992) . . . . Abigail Weld
Love Affair (1994) . . . . Receptionist
Mrs. Parker and the Vicious Circle (1994) . . . . . Neyso McMein

Miller, Sherry

Films:
Goin' All the Way (1981). . . . . .Candy
• 0:47—Brief right breast, while getting out of bubble bath.
•• 0:49—Breasts with Artie during his fantasy.
Separate Vacations (1985; Canadian) . . . . Sandy
Johnny Mnemonic (1995) . . . . .Takahashi's Secretary
The Stupids (1996) . . . . Anchorwoman
Made for Cable Movies:
Rent-a-Kid (1995) . . . . .Valerie Syracuse
Shadow Zone: The Undead Express (1996; Showtime) . . .Mom
Made for Cable TV:
E.N.G. (1989-90; Lifetime; Canadian) . . . . Jane Oliver
TV:
F/X: The Series (1996-97) . . . . Colleen

Millian, Andra

Films:
Stacy's Knights (1983). . . . . .Stacy
Nightfall (1988) . . . . .Anna
• 0:12—Very brief breasts making love with David Birney.
• 0:41—Very brief breasts making love in front of a fire.
Love Potion No. 9 (1992) . . . . Matron
TV:
Paper Chase (1984-86) . . . . .Laura

Millington, Mary

Films:
Come Play with Me (1977; German). . . . . Nurse
Playbirds (1978; British) . . . . Lucy Sheridan
••• 0:55—White bra, black garter belt, panties and stockings then nude taking off her clothes during the policewoman audition.
• 1:00—Breasts giving an old man a massage in a massage parlor.
••• 1:05—Breasts making love with another woman from the massage parlor.
••• 1:14—Nude doing a photo session for *Playbird* magazine.

Million, Tyffany

See: Margot, Sandra.

Mills, Brooke

Films:
The Big Doll House (1971). . . . . Harrad
• 0:28—Side of right breast, while lying in bed before rolling over.
Legacy of Blood (1973) . . . . Leslie Dean
The Student Teachers (1973). . . . . .n.a.
Walking Tall, Part II (1975). . . . . Ruby Ann
Two-Minute Warning (1976) . . . . Tyler's Girlfriend
Freaky Friday (1977) . . . . Mrs. Gibbons
Condition Red (1995) . . . . TV Reporter

*Mills, Donna **

Films:
Play Misty for Me (1971). . . . . Tobie
• 1:10—Brief side view of right breast hugging Clint Eastwood in a pond near a waterfall. Long shot, hard to see.
Murph the Surf (1975) . . . . Ginny Eaton
Fire! (1977) . . . . Harriet Malone
False Arrest (1991). . . . . Joyce Lukezic
(Video tape version is shorter than the miniseries that aired on TV. It also has nude scenes added.)
Made for Cable TV:
Dream On: Martin Tupper in "Magnum Farce" (1994; HBO)
. . . . Ashlyn
Made for TV Movies:
Doctor's Private Lives (1978) . . . . .Dr. Beth Demery
The President's Child (1992) . . . . Elizabeth Hemming
My Name is Kate (1994) . . . . Kate
Dangerous Intentions (1995). . . . . Beth Williamson
An Element of Truth (1995) . . . . Vanessa Graves
Knots Landing: Back to the Cul-de-Sac (1997). . . Abby Fairgate
TV:
The Good Life (1971-72) . . . . Jane Miller
Knots Landing (1980-89). . . Abby Ewing Sumner Cunningham

Mills, Hayley

Daughter of actor Sir John Mills.
Sister of actress Juliet Mills.
Ex-wife of British director Roy Boulting.
Films:
Tiger Bay (1959; British) . . . . .Gillie
Pollyanna (1960) . . . . Pollyanna
Whistle Down the Wind (1961; British) . . . . .Kathy Bostock
In Search of the Castaways (1962). . . . . Mary grant
The Chalk Garden (1964) . . . . Laurel
The Moon-Spinners (1964) .Nikky Ferris
The Parent Trap (1964) . . . . . . Sharon McKendirck/Susan Evers
That Darn Cat (1965) . . . . Patti Randall
The Trouble with Angels (1966). . . . . Mary Clancy
The Family Way (1969; British). . . . . Jenny Piper
•• 0:49—Buns, three times, with a towel wrapped around her front, while standing up in bathtub, talking to Geoffrey.
Deadly Strangers (1974; British) . . . . Belle
• 1:02—Buns in bathtub when her uncle watches her.
••• 1:13—In white bra and panties while Steven watches through keyhole, then breasts after taking off bra and reading a newspaper.
Endless Night (1977). . . . . .Ellie
Appointment with Death (1988) . . . . Miss Quinton
Made for Cable Movies:
The Parent Trap II (1986; Disney). . . Sharon Ferris/Susan Corey

Miniseries:
The Flame Trees of Thika (1982) . . . . Tilly

*Mills, Juliet **

Daughter of actor Sir John Mills.
Sister of actress Hayley Mills.
Wife of actor Maxwell Caulfield.

Films:
The Rare Breed (1966) . . . . Hilary Price
Avanti! (1973). . . . . Pamela Piggott
•• 1:23—Buns and breasts, while climbing out of the water onto a rock. Medium long shot. Closer shot of right breast, while lying on the rock.
••• 1:26—Breasts, twice, while waving to fishermen on a passing boat.
• 2:07—Very brief partial buns and partial left breast in mirror in bed's headboard when she props herself up while Jack Lemmon talks on the phone.
• 2:08—Brief lower half of buns, while putting stuff away in closet. Partial breasts in open pajama top.
Beyond the Door (1975; Italian/U.S.) . . . . Jessica
Waxwork II: Lost in Time (1991) . . . . The Defense Lawyer

Miniseries:
Till We Meet Again (1989). . . . . Vivianne

Made for TV Movies:
Columbo: No Time To Die (1992). . . . . Elaine Hacker

TV:
Nanny and the Professor (1970-71) . . . . Phoebe Figalilly

• *Milmore, Doris*

Films:
Sci-Fighters (1996; Canadian) . . . . Hooker
Strip Search (1997; Canadian). . . . . Julie

Made for Cable TV:
The Hunger: Footsteps (1998; Cinemax). . . . . n.a.
The Hunger: Plain Brown Envelope (1998; Showtime)
. . . . Sophie
•• 0:14—Breasts, in Tunisian fantasy with Jesse Borrego. Don't see her face very well.
• 0:22—Brief side view of right breast, while lying on bed in back of truck.

Mimieux, Yvette

Films:
The Time Machine (1960). . . . . Weena
Where the Boys Are (1960) . . . . Melanie
Diamond Head (1962) . . . . Sloan Howland
The Four Horsemen of the Apocalypse (1962)
. . . . Chi-Chi Desnoyers
Three in the Attic (1968). . . . . Tobey Clinton
Skyjacked (1972). . . . . Angela Thacher
Jackson County Jail (1976) . . . . Dinah Hunter
• 0:39—Breasts in jail cell getting raped by policeman.
The Black Hole (1979). Dr. Kate McGraw
Brainwash (1982) . . . . Bianca Ray

Made for TV Movies:
Outside Chance (1978). . . . . Dinah Hunter
Perry Mason: The Case of the Desperate Deception (1990)
. . . . Danielle Altmann

TV:
The Most Deadly Game (1970-71) . . . . Vanessa Smith
Berrengers (1985) . . . . Shane Bradley

Minnick, Dani

Films:
Lena's Holiday (1990) . . . . Julie Eden
The Sleeping Car (1990) . . . . Joanne

Made for Cable TV:
Tales From the Crypt: The Man Who was Death
(1989; HBO) . . . . Cynthia Baldwin
• 0:17—Very brief side view of right breast in shower.

• *Minot-Payer, Grégoriane*

Films:
Strip Search (1997; Canadian). . . . . Ailoo

Made for Cable TV:
The Hunger: The Secret Shih-Tan (1997; Showtime)
. . . . Xanthippa
• 0:22—Brief breasts, several times, while making love with Jason Scott Lee in bed.

Minter, Kristin

Films:
Home Alone (1990). . . . . Heather
Cool As Ice (1991). . . . . Kathy
Passed Away (1992) . . . . Cousin Karen
Flashfire (1993). . . . . Lisa Cates
•• 0:18—In black bra, panties, garter belt and stockings, then breasts while in hotel room with Artie.
•• 0:20—Breasts while making love in bed with Artie.
•• 0:21—Breasts when hit men burst into the room and kill Artie.
• 0:49—Buns in panties and side of right breast while undressing when Billy Zane sees her.
••• 1:11—Breasts, while making love on bed in a boat with Zane.
There Goes My Baby (1994) . . . . Tracy
Lover's Knot (1995). . . . . Cheryl
Savage (1995) . . . . Marie Beloc
••• 0:18—Breasts and buns, when having sex in bed with a guy, then getting out and looking at a computer monitor, then talking on the telephone. A bit on the dark side.

Made for Cable TV:
Fallen Angels: Fly Paper (1995; Showtime) . . . . Sue Hambleton

Made for TV Movies:
Danielle Steel's "Family Album" (1994) . . . . Valerie

TV:
ER (1995) . . . . Randi Fronzack
University Hospital (1995) . . . . n.a.

*Miou-Miou **

Films:
Going Places (1974; French). . . . . Marie-Ange
••• 0:14—Breasts sitting in bed, filing her nails. Full frontal nudity standing up and getting dressed.
•• 0:48—Breasts in bed with Gérard Depardieu and Patrick Dewaere.
• 0:51—Left breast under Dewaere.
••• 0:52—Buns in bed when Depardieu rolls off her. Full frontal nudity sitting up with the two guys in bed.
•• 1:21—Brief breasts, while opening the door. Breasts and panties, while walking in after the two guys.
• 1:27—Partial left breast taking off dress and walking into house.
• 1:28—Very brief breasts while closing the shutters.
•• 1:31—Full frontal nudity in open dress running after the two guys. Long shot. Full frontal nudity putting her wet dress on.
• 1:41—Breasts while in back of car. Dark.
The Genius (1976; Italian/German/French) . . . . Lucy
Jonah—Who Will be 25 in the Year 2000 (1976; Swiss)
. . . . Marie

This Sweet Sickness (1977; French) . . . . Juliette
a.k.a. dites-lui que je l'aime
Memoirs of a French Whore (1979) . . . . Marie
My Other Husband (1981; French) . . . . Alice
Entre Nous (1983; French) .Madeleine
a.k.a. Coup de Foudre
Dog Day (1984; French) . . . . Jessica
La Lectrice (1989; French) . . . . .Constance/Marie
a.k.a. The Reader
- • 1:18—Full frontal nudity lying in bed. Close-up pan shot from lower frontal nudity, then left breast, then right breast.
- • 1:19—Side view of buns, while lying on the floor with the company president.
- • 1:20—Very brief right breast, then lower frontal nudity while getting dressed.

May Fools (1990; French) . . . . Camille
Germinal (1993; French) . . . . Maheude
Tango (1993; French) . . . . Marie

Miracle, Irene *

Films:
Midnight Express (1978; British) . . . . Susan
- •• 1:40—Breasts in prison visiting booth showing her breasts to Brad Davis so he can masturbate.

Inferno (1980; Italian) . . . . Rose Elliot
In the Shadow of Kilimanjaro (1985) . . . . Lee Ringtree
- • 0:18—Brief breasts in bed with Timothy Bottoms. Kind of hard to see anything because it's dark.

The Last Days of Philip Banter (1987) . . . . Elizabeth Banter
Puppet Master (1989) . . . . Dana Hadley
Watchers II (1990) . . . . Sarah Ferguson
- ••• 0:40—Side view in black bra, then breasts a few times in the bathtub.

Made for TV Movies:
Shattered Dreams (1990) . . . . Elaine

• *Miriam, Jennifer* *

Video Tapes:
Playboy Video Calendar 1998 (1997) . . . . February
- ••• 0:05—Nude, while posing outdoors.
- 0:07—Nude, while posing indoors in bedroom setting.

• *Mirosova, Karolina*

a.k.a. Caroline Miro.
Films:
Supermodel Invasion (1996). . . . . Model 3
- ••• 0:10—Breasts and buns, while posing in lingerie on balcony.
- ••• 0:42—Nude, while rolling on the floor, then standing and posing.

Midnight Temptations 2 (1997). . . . . Revolutionary Woman
- •• 1:03—Breasts, while making love with the revolutionary man.
- • 1:05—Breasts, while making love with the stable boy.

Video Tapes:
Nude Models in Hollywood (1995) . . . . Natasha
- •• 0:10—Buns in lingerie, while posing for photographs.
- ••• 0:13—Nude, while posing for photographs.
- ••• 0:29—Nude, while dancing next to Sophia.
- 0:36—Nude, while dancing by herself.

Mirren, Helen *

Films:
A Midsummer Night's Dream (1968; British) . . . . Hermia
Age of Consent (1969; Australian) . . . . Cora
- • 0:48—Breasts several times in the mirror. Brief lower frontal nudity, kneeling on the floor.
- •• 0:55—Brief breasts and buns quite a few time, snorkeling under water.
- ••• 1:20—Breasts and half of buns, posing in the water for James Mason. Then getting out.

Savage Messiah (1972; British) . . . . Gosh Smith-Boyle
- ••• 0:39—Full frontal nudity, posing for sketches while walking up and down stairs and around. Nice long scene.
- •• 1:15—Brief buns, while covering herself up.

O Lucky Man! (1973; British) . . . . .Patricia Burgess
Caligula (1980) . . . . .Caesonia
(X-rated, 147 minute version.)
- • 1:13—Brief breasts several times getting out of bed to run after McDowell. Dark.
- • 1:15—Very brief left breast, when taking off her dress to dry McDowell off.

The Fiendish Plot of Dr. Fu Manchu (1980) . . . . .Alice Rage
Hussy (1980; British). . . . . Beaty
- •• 0:22—Left breast, then side of right breast, while lying in bed with John Shea.
- ••• 0:29—Nude, making love in bed with Shea.
- •• 0:31—Full frontal nudity in bathtub.

The Long Good Friday (1980; British) . . . . Victoria
Excalibur (1981; British) . . . . .Morgana
- • 1:31—Side view of left breast under a fishnet outfit climbing into bed.

2010 (1984) . . . . .Tanya Kirbuk
Cal (1984; Irish) . . . . Marcella
- •• 1:20—Brief frontal nudity taking off clothes and getting into bed with Cal in his cottage, then right breast making love.

White Knights (1985) . . . . Galina Ivanova
The Mosquito Coast (1986). . . . . Mother
Pascali's Island (1988; British) . . . . Lydia Neuman
- • 1:00—Left breast, lying in bed with Charles Dance. Long shot.

The Cook, The Thief, His Wife & Her Lover
(1989; Dutch/French) . . . . Georgina Spica
- •• 0:32—In lingerie undressing, then lower frontal nudity, buns and left breast in kitchen with Michael.
- • 0:42—Buns and right breast, while making love with Michael again.
- •• 0:57—Breasts sitting and talking with Michael.
- • 1:01—Buns, while kneeling on table.
- • 1:05—Brief breasts, while leaning back on table with Michael.
- • 1:07—Lower frontal nudity opening her coat for Michael.
- • 1:11—Buns and breasts in kitchen.
- ••• 1:14—Buns, getting into meat truck. Full frontal nudity in truck and walking around with Michael.

Red King, White Knight (1989) . . . . .Anna
When the Whales Came (1989). . . . . Clemmie Jenkins
The Comfort of Strangers (1991). . . . . Caroline
The Hawk (1992; British) . . . . Annie Marsh
Where Angels Fear to Tread (1992) . . . . Lilia Herriton
Dr. Bethune (1993; Canadian/French) . .Frances Penny Bethune
The Madness of King George (1994) . . . . .Queen Charlotte
Some Mother's Son (1996) . . . . Kathleen Quigley
Critical Care (1997) . . . . Stella
Made for Cable Movies:
Losing Chase (1996; Showtime) . . . . Chase Philips

Made for TV Movies:

Mystery! Cause Célèbre (1991) .... Alma Rattenbury
•• 0:27—Breasts in bed when Bowman pulls down the sheets in bed.
• 0:28—Brief breasts and buns putting slip on.

Mystery! Prime Suspect (1992) .... Detective Chief Inspector Jane Tennison

Mystery! Prime Suspect 2 (1993) .... Detective Chief Inspector Jane Tennison

Mystery! Prime Suspect 3 (1994) .... Detective Chief Inspector Jane Tennison

Masterpiece Theatre: Prime Suspect: The Lost Child (1995) .... Detective Chief Inspector Jane Tennison

Mystery! Prime Suspect: Inner Circles (1996) .... Det. Supt. Jane Tennison

Masterpiece Theatre: Prime Suspect 5: Errors of Judgement (1997)...................... Det. Supt. Jane Tennison

Misch Owens, Laura *

Films:

The Great Balloon Race (1975) .... n.a.

French Quarter (1978)......... "Ice Box" Josie/Girl on Bus
• 0:41—Breasts under sheer white nightgown.
••• 0:43—Full frontal nudity taking off nightgown, wearing garter belt. Getting into bed with Laura.

Mardi Gras Massacre (1978) .... First Prostitute/Victim

• Mitchell, Elizabeth

Made for Cable Movies:

Gia (1998; HBO) .... Linda
• 0:25—In bra, then partial left breast, to pose with Angelina Jolie during photo session.
• 0:26—Brief right breast, then brief breasts, while making love with Jolie.
• 1:03—Brief buns, while standing in the shower with Jolie.

TV:

L.A. Firefighters (1996) .... Laura Malloy

Significant Others (1998-) .... Jane Merrill-Chasin

Mitchell, Shareen

Films:

Out for Justice (1991) .... Laurie Lupo

American Heart (1993) .... Diane
•• 1:09—Breasts and buns in sheer black panties while dancing in peep show with three other women.
• 1:10—Breasts, while in dressing room. Seen on B&W monitor.
• 1:11—Breasts under sheer top while in dressing room, putting on make-up and getting a drink.

TV:

Boy Meets World .... n.a.

Hudson Street (1995-96) .... Lucy

Moase, Robyn

Films:

Journey Among Women (1977; Australian) .... Moira

Midnight Dancer (1987; Australian) .... Brenda
a.k.a. Belinda
• 0:43—Brief breasts while putting on black top.

• Mobley, Stacey Leigh

Films:

Femalien (1995) .... Uncredited Female Model
••• 0:26—Nude, while making love with a male model during photo shoot.

Stripteaser 2 (1997)............................. Angie
••• 0:28—Breasts and buns in T-back.
••• 0:34—Breasts and buns in T-back, while dancing on stage.
•• 0:38—Left breast, then breasts, while listening to the goings on in the office.
• 0:48—Breasts, while getting shown around upstairs.
•• 0:51—Breasts and buns in T-back, while in S&M room with the police chief.
•• 1:00—Breasts and buns, while making love with Marty in bedroom at night.
• 1:03—Buns, while asleep on top of Marty in the morning.
• 1:12—Breasts, covered with blood.

Moen, Jackie

Films:

Shock 'Em Dead (1990) .... Groupie 4
•• 1:05—Breasts, taking off her top to tempt Martin.

Wilding, The Children of Violence (1990) .... Car Rape Victim
• 0:23—Very brief right breast in back of car with her boyfriend when the gang of kids terrorizes them.

Class of Nuke 'Em High Part II: Subhumanoid Meltdown (1991) .... Diane/Bald Subhumanoid

Kill, Kill Overkill (1991) .... Video Girl

Switch (1991) .... Girl at City Grille

Babyfever (1994)................................ Diane

Moffatt, Geraldine

Films:

The Man Who Had Power Over Women (1970; British) .... Lydia Blake

Get Carter (1971; British) .... Glenda
• 1:09—Brief buns and breast, while making love with Michael Caine.
•• 1:10—Left breast, while lying in bed, talking with Caine, then nude, getting out of bed and walking to the bathroom.
• 1:12—Brief breasts in B&W movie.
• 1:14—Brief breasts, while sitting in bathtub.
• 1:17—Breasts, when Caine pushes her under the water.

Moffett, Michelle

Films:

Hollywood Boulevard II (1989) .... Mary Randolf

Deathstalker IV: Match of Titans (1990) .... Kana
••• 0:52—Very brief left breast, then breasts sitting on bed while trying to seduce Vaniat.
••• 0:59—Breasts on bed, trying to seduce Vaniat. More breasts, getting out of bed and getting dressed.

Hired to Kill (1990) .... Ana
• 0:46—Left breast in dress, then breasts when Oliver Reed lowers her top.
•• 0:47—More breasts in open dress top.
•• 1:04—Very, very brief tip of right breast, lying on table when Brian Thompson rips her blouse open. More breasts, lying on the table. Dark.

Wild Cactus (1992)........................... Maggie
(Unrated version reviewed.)
•• 0:20—Breasts while making love with Randall on trunk of car outside at night.
••• 0:58—Nude, taking a shower and getting out to talk to Alex.
• 1:00—Brief buns, while walking into bedroom.
••• 1:14—Breasts, while sitting in bed with Alex, then buns in sheer black panties.

Indecent Behavior (1993) . . . . Carol Leiter
(Unrated version reviewed.)
•• 0:07—Breasts, while making love under Frederic behind 2-way glass.
•• 0:10—Breasts and buns, while making love on top of Frederic. The camera move around a lot, so it's kind of hard to see.
•• 0:24—In black bra and panties, then breasts and buns, while making love with Robert while being observed behind 2-way glass.
•• 1:06—Breasts while making love with Brenda and getting video taped.
Sins of the Night (1993) . . . . Kay
(Unrated version reviewed.)
••• 0:20—In black bra, then breasts and lower frontal nudity while making love in bed with Jack. Long scene.
•• 0:22—Breasts and very brief buns, getting out of bed.
Warlock: The Armageddon (1993). . . . . Celine
Almost Hollywood (1994) . . . . Desiree
Made for Cable TV:
The Hitchhiker: Best Shot (1987; HBO) . . . . Lorri Ann
TV:
NYPD Blue: The Final Adjustment (Nov 22, 1994)
. . . . Judith Kraski
• 0:46—Partial buns and partial right breast while on sofa with Walter, trying to get him to confess to his wife's murder.
Video Tapes:
Eden 6 (1994) . . . . Sissy Lunch
•• 0:18—Breasts, while making love with Brett outside.
••• 0:20—Breasts, while making love with Brett in bed.
• 0:29—In pink swimsuit, then right breast while making out with Brett on bed.
••• 0:36—Breasts, while sitting on edge and in bathtub.
• 0:39—Breasts while in bed with Brett.
••• 1:06—Breasts and buns while stripping in front of Brett outside, then making love.
•• 1:29—Right breast, while making love on beach with Brett.

Moir, Alison

Films:
Hot to Trot (1988). . . . . Party Person
Johnny Suede (1992). . . . . Darlette
Joey Breaker (1993). . . . . Sexy Girl
Exit to Eden (1994) . . . . Kitty/Club Eden
• 1:21—Brief breasts, while giving Omar a massage.
A Little Princess (1995) . . . . Princess Sita

Moiseiwitsch, Sacha

Films:
Crooked Hearts (1991) . . . . Bonita
• 0:19—Very brief partial side view of right breast when Charlie carries her into the kitchen. Most of right breast when spinning her around when leaving the kitchen.
Arctic Blue (1993) . . . . Whore

• Mol, Gretchen

Films:
The Funeral (1996) . . . . Helen
Girl 6 (1996). . . . . Girl #12
The Last Time I Committed Suicide (1996)
. . . . Mary Greenway
• 1:13—Very brief silhouette of breasts while in bathtub fooling around with Neal. Long shot.
Donnie Brasco (1997) . . . . Sonny's Girlfriend

Made for Cable TV:
Subway Stories (1997; HBO) . . . . Wife

Molina, Angela *

Films:
That Obscure Object of Desire (1977; French/Spanish)
. . . . Conchita
• 0:53—Brief breasts in bathroom.
•• 1:20—Nude dancing in front of a group of tourists.
• 1:29—Brief breasts behind a gate taunting Fernando Rey.
The Sabina (1979; Spanish/Swedish) . . . . Pepa
The Eyes, The Mouth (1983; Italian/French) . . . . Vanda
Demons in the Garden (1984; Spanish). . . . . Angela
Camorra (1986; Italian) . . . . Annunziata
Streets of Gold (1986) . . . . Elena
1492: Conquest of Paradise (1992; British/U.S./Spanish/French)
. . . . Beatrix
Live Flesh (1997; French/Spanish) . . . . Clara
a.k.a. Carne Trémula

Momaday, Jill Scott

Films:
Silent Tongue (1994). . . . . Prostitute
Made for Cable Movies:
The Desperate Trail (1994; TNT). . . . . Janie
•• 0:14—Breasts, while sitting up in bed and lighting a cigarette and talking with a Craig Sheffer.

• Monaco, Kelly *

Video Tapes:
Playboy Video Calendar 1998 (1997) . . . . September
••• 0:35—Nude, while posing in an auto repair shop.
••• 0:38—Nude, while posing on a bed, wearing angel wings.
Playboy's Girls Next Door: Naughty and Nice (1998)
. . . . Afternoon Delight/Katie
••• 0:21—Nude, while frolicking in the woods with Brooke and Josh.

Moncrieff, Karen

Films:
Midnight Witness (1992) . . . . Katy
• 1:08—Very brief buns, while making love with Paul in bed in motel (don't see her face). Very brief part of right nipple. Very brief right breast, when falling back onto bed (medium long shot).
Deathfight (1993) . . . . n.a.
Xtro: Watch the Skies (1995). Watkins
TV:
Days of Our Lives. . . . . Gabrielle Pascal
Santa Barbara . . . . Cassandra Benedict

Moncure, Lisa

Films:
Moving (1988) . . . . Nina Franklin
Lisa (1989) . . . . Sarah
Corporate Affairs (1990). . . . . Carolyn Bean
• 1:07—Very, very brief left breast, while kicking Douglas out of cubicle.
Carnosaur (1993) . . . . Mallard
Made for TV Movies:
Tales of the City (1994) . . . . Spa Attendant

• Mondey, Fawnia

Films:
Profile for Murder (1996) . . . . Diane Curtis
• 0:02—Breasts, while making love with Lance Henriksen in bed.

•• 0:29—Breasts and partial buns, while making love with Henriksen in flashback.

• 0:34—Very brief breasts, during Joan Severance's fantasy with Henriksen.

Made for Cable TV:

The Outer Limits: Resurrection (1996; Showtime) . . . . New Human

• 0:42—Brief buns and breasts, coming out of hiding place to greet Cain.

• Monroe, Betsy

Films:

Mrs. Doubtfire (1993). . . . . Stunning Woman
Cover Me (1995) . . . . Lakey Snow
Friend of the Family (1995) . . . . Nancy
a.k.a. Elke's Erotic Nights
(Unrated version reviewed.)

Gentleman's Bet (1995) . . . . Jodie

• 0:37—Brief breasts, while sunbathing in backyard when talking with Paul.

•• 0:47—Breasts and buns in panties, while in bedroom, waiting for Paul.

• 0:49—Brief left breast, when play acting with Paul in the kitchen.

••• 0:50—Breasts and buns, while making love with Paul on pool table.

• 1:08—Brief breasts under red plastic top after photo session.

•• 1:18—Buns and breasts, while making love with Lauren on bed.

• 1:20—Brief left breast in open robe while walking through house.

Nine Months (1995) . . . . Bobbie
The Dentist (1996) . . . . Young Female

Made for Cable Movies:

Breast Men (1997; HBO). . . . . 1970's Receptionist

Monroe, Kimber

a.k.a. Kimber Sissons.

Films:

You Can't Hurry Love (1984). . . . . Brenda

Master of Dragonard Hill (1987). . . . . Jane Abdee

•• 0:08—Breasts making love in bed with Richard.

Phantom of the Mall: Eric's Revenge (1988) . . . . Suzie
The Adventures of Ford Fairlane (1991). . . . . Pussycat
Martial Law II: Undercover (1992). . . . . Celeste
The Opposite Sex ...and How to Live with Them (1992). . Tracy
Silence of the Hams (1993). . . . . Push-up Lady
Empire Records (1995) . . . . Woman at Craps Table

Double Tap (1997) . . . . Stripper

•• 0:24—Breasts and brief buns in panties, while dancing in apartment in front of Ulysses and his girlfriend.

Made for Cable TV:

Dream On: The Charlotte Letter (1991; HBO) . . . . Candy Striper #3

•• 0:06—Breasts several times, getting examined by a doctor while acting in adult film that Martin is watching on TV. (She's the blonde one.)

Erotic Confessions: The Driver (1996; Cinemax) . . . . Madelyn Macy

•• 0:01—Breasts, with making love with an actor in bed, then stopping after acting.

•• 0:03—Brief buns, then breasts when taking off robe and getting dressed.

••• 0:06—Nude, while lying in bed, making love with the actor and with Marco, in his fantasy.

••• 0:12—Breasts, while making love with Marco in the back seat of limousine.

Hot Line: Mistaken Identity (1996; Cinemax) . . . . . Sabrina
(Available on video tape in *Hot Line 4.*)

•• 0:17—In red bra and panties, then breasts and buns, while making love in bed with Ricky.

Erotic Confessions: Southern Hospitality (1997; Cinemax). . . . . Claire

• 0:06—Buns in white lingerie outfit.

••• 0:09—Breasts and buns, while making love with Anthony in bedroom.

• 0:11—Brief breasts, when getting out of bed.

TV:

Sea Hunt (1987-88). . . . . Jennifer Nelson

Monroe, Lynn

See: Morrissey, Lori.

Monroe, Marilyn *

Films:

Love Happy (1949) . . . . Grunion's Client
All About Eve (1950) . . . . Miss Casswell
Gentlemen Prefer Blondes (1953) . . . . Lorelei
How to Marry a Millionaire (1953) . . . . Pola
There's no Business like Show Business (1954). . . . . Vicky
Bus Stop (1956) . . . . Cherie
The Prince and the Showgirl (1957) . . . . Elsie Marina
The Seven Year Itch (1957) . . . . The Girl
Some Like it Hot (1959). . . . . Sugar Kane Kowa
The Misfits (1961) . . . . Roslyn Taber

Myra Breckinridge (1970). . . . . Herself

• 1:08—Breasts in B&W version of Playboy centerfold photo.

Video Tapes:

Playboy Video Magazine, Volume 12 (1987) . . . . A Loving Tribute to Marilyn Monroe

•• 1:02—Buns and left breast in still photos by swimming pool from unreleased last film.

••• 1:03—Breasts in B&W reference photos for artist Earl Moran. Taken around 1946-50.

Hugh Hefner: Once Upon a Time (1992). . . . . Herself

•• 0:12—Brief breasts in first centerfold.

Playboy The Best of Anna Nicole Smith (1995) . . . Herself

•• 0:24—Breasts in B&W and color still photos.

Monroe, Tami

Adult film actress.

Video Tapes:

Big Bust Casting Call (1992). Jessica

••• 0:00—Nude, during her audition.

Intimate Secrets—How Women Love to be Loved (1993) . . . . Tami

••• 0:22—In white bra and panties, then breasts on couch.

How to Give Pleasure to a Woman by a Woman (1995). . . . n.a.

Montgomery, Belinda

Films:

The Todd Killings (1970). . . . . n.a.

• 0:43—Breasts in open nightgown while struggling with Skipper.

The Other Side of the Mountain (1975) . . . . Audra Jo
The Other Side of the Mountain, Part II (1978) . . . . . . Audra Jo
Stone Cold Dead (1979; Canadian). . . . . Sandy MacAuley
Silent Madness (1984). . . . . Joan Gillmore

Made for Cable TV:

The Hitchhiker: Man at the Window (1985; HBO) . . . . Carla Magnuson

TV:

The Man From Atlantis (1977-78) . . . . Dr. Elizabeth Merrill
Days of Our Lives (1986-87) . . . . Sylvie Gallagher
Aaron's Way (1988). . . . . .Sarah Miller
Doogie Howser, M.D. (1989-93) . . . . Katherine Howser

Montgomery, Julia

Films:

Girls Nite Out (1982) . . . . Lynn Connors
a.k.a. Scared to Death
Revenge of the Nerds (1984) .Betty
•• 0:49—Breasts, after taking off robe to take a shower.
• 1:10—Breasts in photo in pie pan.
Up the Creek (1984) . . . . Lisa
The Kindred (1987). . . . . .Cindy Russell
South of Reno (1987). . . . . Susan
• 1:22—Brief breasts, while kissing Martin. Dark, hard to see.
Stewardess School (1987) . . . . Pimmie Polk
Black Snow (1989) . . . . Lindsey Devereaux
Stop! Or My Mom Will Shoot (1992). . . . . .Secretary
Milk Money (1994) . . . . Stacy's Mom

Made for TV Movies:

Earth-Star Voyager (1988) . . . . Dr. Sally Arthur
Revenge of the Nerds III: The Next Generation (1992)
. . . . Betty Skolnick
Revenge of the Nerds IV: Nerds in Love (1994) . . . . .Betty

TV:

One Life to Live . . . . Samantha Vernon

Monti, Mary Elaine

Films:

Is There Sex After Death? (1975). . . . . Stag Film Scene/Sue
•• 0:53—Buns and right breast, while in bed with a guy during filming of stag film.
•• 1:00—Breasts and buns, while in bed with Fred.

TV:

Park Place (1981) . . . . Joel "Jo" Keene

Monticelli, Anna-Maria

a.k.a. Anna Jemison.

Films:

Smash Palace (1981; New Zealand) . . . . Jacqui Shaw
• 0:21—Silhouette of right breast changing while sitting on the edge of the bed.
••• 0:39—Breasts in bed after arguing, then making up with Bruno Lawrence.
Heatwave (1983; Australian) . . . . Victoria
My First Wife (1985; Australian). Hillary
Nomads (1986) . . . . .Niki
• 0:57—Left breast, making love in bed with Pierce Brosnan. Dark, hard to see anything.

Montone, Rita

Films:

The Children (1980). . . . . Dee Dee Shore
•• 0:20—Breasts, lying on chair by pool before talking to the Sheriff.
Maniac (1980) . . . . Hooker
Bloodsucking Freaks (1982). . . . . .n.a.

Montpetit, Pascale

Films:

Eclipse (1994; Canadian) . . . . Sylvie
• 0:13—Breasts after taking off her T-shirt to make love with Brian.
•• 0:16—Nude after hearing Brian's wife, then getting up and dressing.
•• 0:24—Breasts after taking off blouse in room with Gabriel and making love on the floor, then sitting up afterwards.
Eldorado (1995; Canadian) . . . . Henriette

Moody, Lynne

Films:

Scream, Blacula, Scream (1973). . . . . Denny
The Evil (1977) . . . . Felecia
White Dog (1982). . . . . Molly

Made for Cable Movies:

Last Light (1993; Showtime) . . . . Hope Whitmore

Miniseries:

Roots (1977) . . . . .Irene
Roots: The Next Generation (1979). . . . . Irene Harvey

Made for TV Movies:

Nightmare in Badham County (1976). . . . . . . Diane Emery
(Nudity added for video tape.)
• 0:16—Brief breasts close-up of her breasts when Chuck Connors rips her T-shirt off in jail cell. (Don't see her face.)
The Atlanta Child Murders (1985) . . . . Selena Cobb
Escape to Witch Mountain (1995) . . . . Lindsay Brown

TV:

That's My Mama (1974-75). . . . . Tracy Curtis Taylor
Soap (1979-81) . . . . Polly Dawson
E/R (1984-85) . . . . Nurse Julie Williams
Knots Landing (1988-90). . . . . Patricia Williams

Moon, Tonya

Films:

Eyes of the Serpent (1992) . . . . Suzette
• 0:24—Right breast, while standing next to Seemus.
Sunset Strip (1992). . . . . Amateur Dancer
•• 0:33—Breasts, while dancing on stage in black shorts.
Friction (1995). . . . . Glitter Dome Dancer
a.k.a. Lap Dance
(Unrated version reviewed.)

Moore, Barbara *

Films:

Cyber Bandits (1994) . . . . Hope
• 0:19—Brief buns in T-back seen on computer screen.
•• 0:20—Breasts, after taking off flower pasties while talking to Martin Kemp in virtual reality.
Temptress (1994) . . . . Champagne Glass Model
••• 0:18—Breasts, while posing in a large champagne glass during photo session.
Wild Malibu Weekend! (1994). . . . . Mary Johnson

Video Tapes:

Playboy Video Calendar 1994 (1993) . . . . July
••• 0:27—Nude in diner while dancing and posing.
••• 0:29—Nude on couch and in phone booth during fantasies while waiting at a bar.
Playboy's Playmate Review 1993 (1993). . . Miss December
••• 0:02—Nude with children's toys in studio.
••• 0:03—Nude, in a stable with a horse.
Playboy's Sexy, Steamy, Sultry (1993) . . . . .Playmate
Sexy Lingerie V (1993). . . . . .Model
Wet & Wild: The Locker Room (1994). . . . . .Playmate
Wet & Wild: Hot Holidays (1995). . . . . .Playmate
Playboy's 21 Playmates: Volume II (1996) . . . . . .Playmate
••• 1:18—Full frontal nudity in still photos.
••• 1:19—Nude, while doing various things around the house.

CD-ROM:
Fox Hunt (1995) . . . . n.a.

Moore, Candy

Films:
Tomboy and the Champ (1961) . . . . Tommy Joe
The Night of the Grizzly (1966). Meg
Lunch Wagon (1981) . . . . Diedra
a.k.a. Lunch Wagon Girls
a.k.a. Come 'N' Get It
•• 0:53—Breasts under sheer robe, then breasts while on couch with Arnie.

• Moore, Carmen

Made for Cable TV:
Stargate SG-1: Cold Lazarus (1997; Showtime) . . . Lab Assistant
Dead Man's Gun: Medicine Man (1997; Showtime) . . . . Winter Bird
• 0:23—Buns, while standing up next to a stream.
Made for TV Movies:
Rose Hill (1997). . . . . n.a.

Moore, Christine

Films:
Lurkers (1987) . . . . Cathy
••• 0:19—Breasts in bed, making love with her boyfriend.
• 0:42—Brief breasts in bubble bath during hallucination scene with her mother.
Prime Evil (1987). . . . . Alexandra Parkman
Alexa (1988) . . . . Alexa
•• 0:24—Breasts lying in bed with Anthony while reminiscing.
•• 1:08—Breasts in bed with Anthony again.
Thrilled to Death (1988). . . . . Nan Christie
••• 0:38—Breasts in office with Mr. Dance just before killing him.

*Moore, Demi **

Wife of actor Bruce Willis.
Films:
Parasite (1982) . . . . Patricia Welles
Blame It on Rio (1984) . . . . Nicole Hollis
• 0:19—Very brief right breast turning around to greet Michael Caine and Joseph Bologna.
No Small Affair (1984) . . . . Laura
• 1:34—Very, very brief side view of left breast in bed with Jon Cryer.
St. Elmo's Fire (1985) . . . . Jules
About Last Night... (1986) . . . . Debbie
• 0:34—Brief upper half of right breast in the bathtub with Rob Lowe.
• 0:50—Side view of right breast, then very brief breasts and brief buns, with Rob Lowe.
••• 0:51—Buns and breasts in bed with Lowe, arching her back, then lying in bed when he rolls off her.
•• 0:52—Breasts and buns in kitchen with Lowe.
One Crazy Summer (1986) . . . . Cassandra
Wisdom (1986). . . . . Karen
The Seventh Sign (1988). . . . . Abby Quinn
• 1:03—Brief breasts, taking off bathrobe to take a bath. Her pregnant belly is not real—it's a full body prosthetic. Brief breasts when sitting in bathtub.
• 1:04—Brief tip of left breast, while sitting in bathtub and rubbing her belly.
We're No Angels (1989) . . . . Molly
• 0:18—One long shot, then two brief side views of left breast when Robert De Niro watches from outside. Reflections in the window make it hard to see.
Ghost (1990). . . . . Molly Jensen
The Butcher's Wife (1991) . . . . Marina
Mortal Thoughts (1991) . . . . Cynthia Kellogg
Nothing But Trouble (1991) . . . . Diane Lightson
A Few Good Men (1992). . . Lt. Commander Jo-Anne Gallaway
Indecent Proposal (1993) . . . . Diana Murphy
•• 0:05—In black bra, brief buns and breasts while making out with Woody Harrelson on the kitchen floor.
• 0:37—Upper half of right breast, while lying in bed with Harrelson.
• 0:40—Upper half of right breast, while lying in bed and talking with Harrelson. Very brief right breast, when lifting sheet over her head.
Disclosure (1994) . . . . Meredith Johnson
The Juror (1995) . . . . Annie Laird
Now and Then (1995). . . . . Samantha Albertson
Scarlet Letter (1995) . . . . Hester Prynne
• 0:36—Brief breasts under dress while she bathes herself.
•• 0:37—Partial buns and side of left breast while standing in tub when spied on by Mituba.
Striptease (1996) . . . . Erin Grant
(R-rated version reviewed.)
• 0:10—Brief buns in G-string, while running off the stage.
•• 0:16—Buns in T-back and sheer black bra, while dancing on stage.
•• 0:43—Breasts, while dancing around and singing when drying her hair in her bedroom (towel around her neck gets in the way).
••• 0:56—Buns in T-back and breasts, while dancing on stage.
••• 1:15—Buns in T-back and in bra, then breasts while dancing on boat in front of Burt Reynolds.
Deconstructing Harry (1997). . . . . Helen
G.I. Jane (1997) . . . . Lt. Jordan O'Neil
• 1:00—Brief buns, while in the shower. Dark.
Made for Cable Movies:
If These Walls Could Talk (1996; HBO). . . . . Claire Donnely
Made for Cable TV:
Tales From the Crypt: Dead Right (1990; HBO) . . . . Cathy Fitch-Marno
TV:
General Hospital (1982-83) . . . . Jackie Templeton

Moore, Glenda

Video Tapes:
Nudes in Limbo (1983) . . . . Model
Hot Bodies (1988). . . . . Herself
••• 0:37—Breasts, dancing with a sword. Sort of buns, under skirt.
••• 0:40—Dancing without the sword. Buns in G-string.
••• 0:44—Breasts and buns dancing with sword again.

Moore, Jeanie

Films:
Vampire at Midnight (1988). . . . . Amalia
•• 0:32—Breasts getting up to run an errand.
Wild Man (1988). . . . . Lady at Pool
Dream Trap (1989) . . . . Blondee
After Dark, My Sweet (1990). . . . . Nanny
The Final Alliance (1990). . . . . Carrie
• 1:03—Brief breasts getting into bed with David Hasselhoff, then brief right breast twice in bed with him. A little dark.
We're Talkin' Serious Money (1991). . . . . Amelia

Moore, Jessica

Films:

Eleven Days, Eleven Nights (1988; Italian) . . .Sarah Asproon
- • 0:03—Breasts opening her raincoat on boat for Michael, then making love.
- • 0:11—Buns, taking off robe in front of Michael.
- •• 0:16—Right breast, on T.V., then side of breast.
- •• 0:29—Breasts with Michael, changing clothes with him in restroom.
- ••• 0:33—Breasts in motel room with Michael, then making love.
- • 0:44—Brief breasts and buns when leaving Michael all tied up.
- •• 0:51—Breasts and buns in recording studio with Michael.
- • 1:17—Breasts during flashbacks.
- ••• 1:19—Nude, making love with Michael on bed.

Top Model (1989; Italian) . . . . Sarah Asproon/Gloria
- ••• 0:03—Nude, posing for photographer customer in his loft with mannequins, then talking on the phone.
- • 0:08—Breasts in dressing room, when seen by Cliff.
- •• 0:23—Buns and brief side of right breast, undressing in front of a customer.
- •• 0:24—Breasts, rubbing oil on him.
- •• 0:30—Full frontal nudity, in her bedroom when Peter blackmails her.
- ••• 0:35—Nude in photographer customer's loft again.
- • 0:40—Brief buns, turning over in bed.
- •• 0:43—Breasts on couch, making love (disinterestedly) with cowboy.
- • 0:56—Buns and partial right breast, while getting dressed.
- ••• 1:00—Breasts making love with Cliff on sofa, then sleeping afterward.
- •• 1:04—Nude, undressing and walking down hallway.
- ••• 1:08—Nude, in hotel room, making love with Cliff.
- ••• 1:19—Buns, with Cliff in stairwell. Breasts and buns in bathroom with him.

Moore, Julianne

Ex-ife of actor John Gould Rubin.

Films:

Tales From the Darkside, The Movie (1990). . . . . Susan

Body of Evidence (1992) . . . . Sharon Dulaney
(Unrated version reviewed.)
- ••• 0:14—Breasts in bed, while making love with Willem Dafoe, then breasts and buns getting out of bed to take a shower.

The Gun in Betty Lou's Handbag (1992) . . . . Elinor
The Hand That Rocks the Cradle (1992) . . . . Marlene
Benny & Joon (1993) . . . . Ruthie
The Fugitive (1993). Dr. Anne Eastman

Short Cuts (1993). . . . . Marian Wyman
- ••• 2:22—(0:39 into Part 2) Buns and lower frontal nudity in top part of outfit, after having to take off the skirt to clean it. Long scene.

Roommates (1994) . . . . Beth
Vanya on 42nd Street (1994) . . . . .Yelena
Assassins (1995) . . . . .Electra
Nine Months (1995) . . . . Rebecca Taylor
Safe (1995) . . . . .Carol
Surviving Picasso (1996) . . . . Dora

Boogie Nights (1997). . . . . Amber Waves
- •• 0:51—Breasts, while kissing Mark Wahlberg during filming of porno movie.
- • 0:53—Brief close-up of right breast, while having sex with Wahlberg during filming.
- • 0:54—Very, very brief left breast while lying on desk with Wahlberg after filming. Long shot.

The Lost World: Jurassic Park (1997) . . . . Dr. Sarah Harding
The Big Lebowski (1998) . . . . Maude

Made for Cable Movies:

Cast a Deadly Spell (1991; HBO) . . . . Connie Stone

TV:

The Edge of Night . . . . Carmen Engler
As the World Turns (1985-88) . . . . Frannie/Sabrina Hughes

Moore, Lisa

Films:

A Dream of Kings (1969). . . . . Nurse
Hit Man (1972) . . . . Laural

Act of Vengeance (1974). . . . . Karen
a.k.a. The Rape Squad
(Not to be confused with the film with the same name starring Charles Bronson.)
- ••• 0:24—Breasts after rapist cuts her dress open and fondles her breasts while she has a cloth stuffed in her mouth.
- • 0:37—Buns and breasts, walking into the spa to join the other women.
- • 1:27—Brief breasts during fight while tied up in cage. Dark.

The Harrad Summer (1974). . . . . Arnae
a.k.a. Student Union
Slaughter's Big Rip-Off (1975) . . . . .n.a.
Swashbuckler (1976). . . . . Pirates' Lady

• Moore, Mary

Films:

Murder at 1600 (1997) . . . . Carla Town
- • 0:03—Very brief breasts, while making love in a room in the White House at night.
- • 0:20—Brief right breast (with blood on it), while lying dead on autopsy table.

Made for Cable TV:

Fast Track: Sweet Thunder (1997; Showtime)
. . . . .Mona Black
- •• 0:18—Brief breasts and partial buns in panties, while in examination room with Keith Carradine.

Moore, Melissa Anne *

Films:

Caged Fury (1989) . . . . Gloria
Fatal Skies (1989) . . . . Suzy

Scream Dream (1989) . . . . .Jamie Summers
- ••• 0:39—Breasts in black panties in room with Derrick. Then straddling him.
- •• 0:58—Breasts in dressing room pulling her top down during transformation into monster.

The Alien Within (1990) . . . . Monica Roarke
(Contains footage from *The Evil Spawn* woven together with new material.)
- •• 0:52—Left breast, taking off her purple dress.
- ••• 1:18—Breasts, lying on bed when the monster strangles her and pulls her top down.
- • 1:19—Left breast, while lying in bed, then getting up.

Hard to Die (1990) . . . . Tess Cochran
a.k.a. Tower of Terror
- ••• 0:21—Breasts, after taking off her top, then taking a shower. Long scene.

The Invisible Maniac (1990) .Bunny
- • 0:21—Buns in shower with the other girls.
- ••• 0:43—In bra, then breasts sitting with yellow towel in locker room with the other girls.
- • 0:44—Breasts in shower with the other girls.

••• 1:09—In bra, then breasts making out in Principal's Office with Chet. Long scene.

Repossessed (1990) .... Bimbo Student

•• 0:05—Breasts pulling her top down in classroom in front of Leslie Nielsen.

Sorority House Massacre 2 (1990)............... Jessica

••• 0:22—Breasts, talking to Kimberly, then taking a shower.

• 0:53—Buns, while going up the stairs.

Vampire Cop (1990).................. Melanie Roberts

••• 0:46—Breasts in bed with the Vampire Cop.

•• 0:51—Right breast, sitting in bed talking with Hans.

• 1:21—Right breast, in bed on the phone during end credits.

Vice Academy, Part 2 (1990).......................Glaze

Into the Sun (1991) .... Female Sergeant

The Killing Zone (1991) ....Tracy

Poker Night (1991) ....n.a.

Soul Mates (1991).................................n.a.

Angel Fist (1992) .... Lorda

•• 0:03—Breasts and buns, in the showers.

•• 0:35—Nude, behind Katara in the showers.

••• 1:03—Breasts when she gets a bad guy to open her blouse and untie her. Very brief breasts during fight scenes.

Consenting Adults (1992).................Trudy Seaton

(Melissa is also the reclining model draped with a sheet used in the advertising artwork. She was incorrectly credited as Michelle Moore.)

• 0:37—Buns, while lying in bed when Kevin Kline takes the place of the husband.

Da Vinci's War (1992) .... Fred

••• 0:14—Breasts and buns, with Michael Nouri in his workout room.

The Other Woman (1992)...................... Elysse

(Unrated version reviewed.)

•• 0:58—Breasts, taking off her blouse while taking pictures during photo shoot.

Savage Vengeance: I Will Dance on Your Grave (1992) .. Singer

One Man Army (1993).................. Natalie Pierce

a.k.a. Kick and Fury

••• 0:26—Breasts, while taking a shower and drying herself off.

••• 0:29—Breasts, while making love with Jerry Trimble in bed.

•• 0:33—Left breasts, while taking off her blouse to go for a swim. Breasts while in water after getting shot in the arm.

Stormswept (1994) .... Dottie

•• 0:33—Breasts, when her towel falls off while talking to Brianna.

• 0:40—Breasts in open robe, while sitting on bed.

••• 1:10—Breasts, while making love on table with Damon.

Bikini Drive-In (1995) ....Actress in Film

(Unrated version reviewed.)

• 0:59—Brief breasts on bed in film shown on drive-in screen.

Video Tapes:

Scream Queen Hot Tub Party (1991) .... Jessica

• 0:00—Breasts during opening credits.

••• 0:17—Breasts opening her towel, then in the shower from *Sorority House Massacre 2.*

Hot Body Video Magazine #1: Premiere Edition (1992) ....Herself

• 0:04—Brief breasts on the floor in a robe in front of a fireplace.

Sexy Lingerie IV (1992).......................Model

Moran, Sharon

Films:

If Looks Could Kill (1987).............. Madonna Maid

•• 0:17—Full frontal nudity after Laura leaves the apartment.

Young Nurses in Love (1987).................. Bambi/Bibi

*Moran, Stacy **

a.k.a. Pipi.

a.k.a. Sabrina Allen.

Films:

Embrace of the Vampire (1994).............. Nymph III

(Unrated version reviewed.)

•• 0:03—Brief breasts, while walking up to Martin Kemp with the other two Nymphs. Then breasts and partial buns sitting to the right of Kemp before biting him along with the other two Nymphs.

• 1:22—Brief breasts in Martin Kemp's flashback.

Made for Cable TV:

Erotic Confessions: Private Dance (1997)........ Camille

•• 0:05—Breasts and buns in T-back, while dancing on stage in club. (She's wearing several pearl necklaces.)

•• 0:08—Breasts and buns in T-back while giving Antonio a lap dance.

••• 0:15—Breasts, while showing Rosie how to dance.

••• 0:20—Breasts and buns in T-back, while dancing in club and giving Rosie a lap dance.

•• 0:26—Breasts after joining Rosie on stage.

Hot Springs Hotel: Money Trouble (1998; Showtime) ....Vicky

Hot Springs Hotel: Cheerleaders (1998; Showtime) . .Vicky

••• 0:10—Breasts and buns, while making love with Randy in bed.

Hot Springs Hotel: To Your Health (1998; Showtime) ....Vicky

Hot Springs Hotel: Bachelorette Party (1998; Showtime) ....Vicky

••• 0:01—Breasts, while making love in bed with Randy.

Video Tapes:

Penthouse Swimsuit Video 2 (1994) .... Pet

Penthouse Pet Rocks (1995)...................... Pet

Body Language (1996).................... Motorcycle

••• 0:44—Nude, while posing on motorcycle.

Erotic Heat (1996) .... Dining Room

••• 0:21—Breasts, while Cory Lane strips and dances in front of her.

Hot Body Competition: Lusty Lingerie Contest (1996) .... Stacy Moran

••• 0:38—Nude, dancing on stage during contest.

••• 0:49—Nude, while posing on bed after winning contest.

Morante, Laura

Films:

The Tragedy of a Ridiculous Man (1981; Italian).... Laura

••• 1:30—Breasts taking off her sweater in front of Primo because she's "uneasy."

Blow to the Heart (1985; Italian)......................n.a.

Distant Lights (1987; Italian)..................... Renata

Man On Fire (1987; Italian/French) .... Julia, David's Wife

Luci lontane (1988; Italian) ....n.a.

More, Camilla

Identical twin sister of actress Carey More.

Films:

Friday the 13th, Part IV—The Final Chapter (1984) .... Tina

• 0:26—Very brief breasts in the lake jumping up with her twin sister to show they are skinny dipping. Very brief buns, when diving under the water.

• 0:48—Left breast, in bed with Crispin Glover.

Dark Side of the Moon (1989)...................... Lesli

The Serpent of Death (1989) .... Rene

•• 0:15—Brief breasts in bed with Jeff Fahey.

•• 1:22—Brief left breast while in bed, then breasts and buns, getting out of bed (in mirror).

Dead Tides (1997) .... Lori

••• 0:23—Breasts and buns, while making love with Roddy Piper.

TV:

Days of Our Lives .... Gillian Forrester

More, Carey

Identical twin sister of actress Camilla More.

Films:

Friday the 13th, Part IV—The Final Chapter (1984) .... Terri

• 0:26—Very brief breasts in the lake jumping up with her twin sister to show they are skinny dipping. Very brief buns, when diving under the water.

Once Bitten (1985) .... Moll Flanders Vampire

TV:

Days of Our Lives (1987).................. Grace Forrester

Moreau, Jeanne *

Films:

The Lovers (1958).............................. Jeanne

Jules and Jim (1962; French) .... Catherine

Mademoiselle (1966; French/British) .... Mademoiselle

•• 1:17—Right breast, while opening her blouse in field in front of her lover. Don't see her face.

The Oldest Profession (1967).......... "Mademoiselle Mimi"

The Bride Wore Black (1968; French/Italian) ... Julie Kohler

• 1:24—Brief breasts, taking off her dress in front of a patterned mirror.

Alex in Wonderland (1970) .... Herself

Going Places (1974; French) .... Jeanne Pirolle

The Last Tycoon (1976)........................... Didi

La Femme Nikita (1991; French/Italian)............ Amande

a.k.a. Nikita

Until the End of the World (1991)............. Edith Farber

Map of the Human Heart (1992; Australian/Canadian) .... Sister Banville

The Summer House (1993; British) Lili

The Proprietor (1996) .... Adrienne Mark

Made for TV Movies:

A Foreign Field (1993)......................... Angelique

Morehart, Deborah

See: Tylo, Hunter.

• Moreland, Rosalind

See: Blake, Stephanie.

• Morell, Linda *

Films:

Hardcore (1979) .... "Les Girls" Woman

•• 1:04—Breasts, when taking George C. Scott's money in a bar.

Moreno, Rita

Singer.

Films:

Pagan Love Song (1950).......................... Terru

The Toast of New Orleans (1950) .... Tina

Singin' In the Rain (1952).................. Zelda Zanders

Latin Lovers (1953)........................... Christina

Seven Cities of Gold (1955)........................ Ula

The King and I (1956) .... Tuptim

Summer and Smoke (1961)......................... Rosa

West Side Story (1961) .... Anita

(Academy Award for Best Supporting Actress.)

Cry of Battle (1963)............................... Sisa

Marlowe (1969)...................... Dolores Gonzales

• 1:29—Buns in G-string, while doing fan dance/strip tease on stage. Brief breasts (with pasties) under jacket.

•• 1:32—Breasts (with pasties), after taking off jacket while dancing on stage before getting shot. Medium long shot at first, closer shot later.

The Night of the Following Day (1969).......... Blonde

• 0:32—Very, very brief tip of left breast, while sitting in bed, wrapping robe around herself.

Popi (1969) .... Lupe

Carnal Knowledge (1971) .... Louise

The Ritz (1976) .... Googie Gomez

The Boss' Son (1978)............................ Esther

Happy Birthday, Gemini (1980).............. Lucille Pompi

Four Seasons (1981) .... Claudia Zimmer

• 0:48—Brief buns, twice, in water while skinny dipping with Jack Weston.

Age Isn't Everything (1991) .... Rita

I Like It Like That (1994) .... Rosaria Linares

Angus (1995) .... Madame Rulenska

Made for Cable Movies:

The Wharf Rat (1995; Showtime).................... Mom

The Spree (1998; TMC)............................ n.a.

Made for Cable TV:

Oz (1997- ; HBO) .... Sister Peter Marie

TV:

9 to 5 (1982-83) .... Violet Newstead

B.L. Stryker (1989-90) .... Kimberly Baskin

Top of the Heap (1991).................. Alixandra Stone

The Cosby Mysteries (1994-95)...................... Angie

Morgan Greene, Kim

Films:

Immortal Combat (1993) .... Karen

Scorned (1993) .... Marina Weston

•• 0:42—Brief breasts, while sitting in bubble bath and getting out. Buns, when Shannon Tweed helps dry her off.

••• 1:09—Left breast, then breasts while in bed when Tweed makes love with her.

• 1:28—Breasts, while crying in shower after discovering her birds are dead.

Soft Kill (1994) .... Kimberly Lewis

••• 0:02—Right breast when lying in bed. Breasts, after sitting up with Jack and rearranging the covers. Long scene. Lower frontal nudity while opening the door.

Dr. Jekyll and Ms. Hyde (1995) ..... Paparazzi Lady/Party Lady

Made for Cable Movies:

Subliminal Seduction (1996; Showtime) .... Meg

TV:

Another World............................. Nicole Love

Days of Our Lives (1990)......... Sheila Salsbury/Kelly Parker

Morgan, Alexandra

Films:

The First Nudie Musical (1979)............. Mary La Rue

• 0:54—Breasts, singing and dancing during dancing dildo routine.

••• 1:04—Full frontal nudity in bed trying to do a take.

•• 1:07—Breasts, while in bed with a guy with a continuous erection.

•• 1:17—Breasts in bed in another scene.

The Deadly Games (1980) . . . . .Linda
a.k.a. The Eliminator
•• 0:03—In bra, standing in doorway at night, then breasts. Dark.
• 0:04—Very brief left breast and lots of cleavage in open blouse talking on the phone.
• 0:05—Most of right breast, when standing up.
The Happy Hooker Goes Hollywood (1980) . . . . Max
Erotic Images (1983) . . . . Emily Stewart
•• 0:57—In black lingerie, then breasts on the living room floor with Glenn.
• 1:05—Breasts in bed, making love with Glenn.
••• 1:12—Breasts in the kitchen with Glenn.
•• 1:21—Right breast, on couch with Glenn.
Spellbinder (1988) . . . . Pamela

Morgan, Brittany
Adult film actress.
Video Tapes:
High Society Centerspread Video #5: Brittany Morgan (1990). . . . . .Herself
High Society Centerspread Video #7: Nina Hartley (1990). . . . . .Herself

Morgan, Cindy
Films:
Up Yours . . . . Elaine
Caddyshack (1980). . . . . .Lacey Underall
• 0:50—Very, very brief side view of left breast sliding into the swimming pool. Very blurry.
•• 0:58—Breasts in bed with Danny three times.
Tron (1982). . . . . Lora/Yori
Amanda and the Alien (1995) . . . . Holly Hoedown
Galaxis (1995). . . . . Kelly
Made for Cable Movies:
Dead Weekend (1995; Showtime). . . . . Newscaster
Out There (1995; Showtime) . . . . .Judith Daws
TV:
Bring 'Em Back Alive (1982-83). . . . . Gloria Marlowe
Falcon Crest (1987-88) . . . . Gabrielle Short

• Morgan, Dawn
Films:
Miracle Beach (1991). . . . . Miss Chile
• 0:48—Brief breasts, when winning bingo game.
Back to Back (1996) . . . . Joe Snapper's Girl

Morgan, Debbi
Ex-wife of actor Charles S. Dutton.
Films:
Cry Uncle (1971). . . . . Olga Winter
••• 0:40—Breasts and buns, taking off her blouse and skirt in room with Jake. Long scene.
Mandingo (1975) . . . . .Dite
• 0:17—Breasts in bed talking to Perry King.
The Monkey Hustle (1976) Vi
Miniseries:
Roots: The Next Generation (1979). . . . . Elizabeth Harvey
Made for TV Movies:
The Jesse Owens Story (1984). . . . . Ruth Solomon Owens
TV:
Behind the Screen (1981-82) . . . . Lynette Porter
All My Children (1982-90) . . . . Angie Hubbard
Generations (1990). . . . . .Chantal Marshall
Loving (1993-95) . . . . Angie
The City (1995-97) . . . . .Angela
Port Charles (1997-) . . . . Dr. Ellen Burgess

Morgan, Mariana
Films:
Ring of the Musketeers (1992). Hostess
Exit to Eden (1994) . . . . Rachel/Los Angeles
Private Lessons—Another Story (1994) . . . . Lauren
•• 0:22—Breasts, while in shower reminiscing about Marissa.
•• 0:43—Breasts and buns, while making love with the chauffeur.
•• 1:12—Breasts, while making love on the beach during storm with Raul.
Busted (1996) . . . . Captain Mary Mae
••• 1:16—In black bra, then breasts, while making love with Corey Feldman
Dear God (1996). . . . . .Neighbor with Dog

Morgan, Penny
See: Ryan, Rachel.

Morgan, Shelly Taylor
Films:
The Sword and the Sorcerer (1982) . . . . Bar-Bra
• 0:54—Brief breasts when Lee Horsley crashes through the window and almost lands on her.
My Tutor (1983) . . . . .Louisa
Scarface (1983). . . . . .Woman at the Babylon Club
Malibu Express (1984) . . . . Anita Chamberlain
• 0:22—Breasts doing exercises on the floor.
•• 0:26—Breasts making love with Shane in bed while being video taped. Then right breast while standing by door.
Cross My Heart (1987) . . . . Woman in Restaurant
Made for Cable TV:
Tales From the Crypt: The Ventriloquist's Dummy (1990; HBO) . . . . Sally
TV:
Days of Our Lives. . . . . Anjelica Deveraux
General Hospital . . . . .Lorena Sharpe

• Morgenstern, Stephanie
Films:
Forbidden Love: The Unashamed Stories of Lesbian Lives (1992; Canadian) . . . . Laura
•• 1:17—In bra, then breasts and buns with another woman.
The Sweet Hereafter (1997; Canadian) . . . . .Allison

Moritz, Louisa *
Films:
Death Race 2000 (1975) . . . . .Myra
• 0:28—Breasts and buns getting a massage and talking to David Carradine.
One Flew Over the Cuckoo's Nest (1975) . . . . Rose
The Happy Hooker Goes to Washington (1977) . . . . .Natalie Naussbaum
• 0:39—Brief breasts and buns, lying down on top of Larry Storch in tennis court.
Loose Shoes (1977). . . . . Margie
Up in Smoke (1978) . . . . Officer Gloria
Cuba (1979) . . . . Miss Wonderly
• 0:55—Dancing on stage in pasties.
Lunch Wagon (1981) . . . . .Sunshine
a.k.a. Lunch Wagon Girls
a.k.a. Come 'N' Get It
• 0:37—Breasts in spa taking off her swimsuit top.
New Year's Evil (1981). . . . . Sally
True Confessions (1981) . . . . .Whore

The Last American Virgin (1982). . . . . Carmela
••• 0:42—Breasts and buns in her bedroom with Rick.
Chained Heat (1983; U.S./German). . . . . .Bubbles
Hot Chili (1985) . . . . Chi Chi
• 0:06—Brief buns, when turning around in white apron after talking with the boys.
•• 0:34—Nude during fight in restaurant with the Music Teacher. Hard to see because of the flashing light.
Jungle Warriors (1985) . . . . Laura McCashin
a.k.a. Captive Women 9
Galaxis (1995). . . . . Bar Lady

Morley, Grace

a.k.a. Bambi Mohrle when she was a stripper in Las Vegas.
Wife of television talk show host Montel Williams.
Films:
Sex Crimes (1991). . . . . .Cynthia
• 0:13—Buns in swimsuit in club. Very, very brief left breast, while taking off her swimsuit top in dressing room.
• 0:36—Buns in G-string and red pasties while dancing in club. More in dressing room.
American Me (1992) . . . . .JD's Friend

Moro, Alicia

Films:
The Exterminators of the Year 3000 (1985; Italian) . . . . . .Trash
Slugs (1988; Spanish) .Maureen Watson
Hot Blood (1989; Spanish) . . . . .Alicia
• 0:00—Buns and lower frontal nudity in stable with Ricardo. Long shot.
• 0:06—In bra and panties with Julio, then buns and breasts. Looks like a body double because hair doesn't match.
Velvet Dreams (1991; Italian). . . . . .n.a.
Golden Balls (1993; Spanish). Gil's Girl

Morrell, Carla *

Twin sister of Carmen Morrell.
Films:
Basket Case 3: The Progeny (1991). . . . . Twin #1
•• 0:41—Breasts in bed with her twin sister and Duane's brother.
• 1:29—Brief breast, lying in bed with her twin sister and Duane's brother after the end credits.
California Hot Wax (1992). . . . . Bikini Girl
Made for Cable TV:
Sessions: Episode 2 (1991; HBO) . . . . Twin #2
Full Frontal Comedy (1996; Showtime)
. . . . .Woman of Full Frontal Comedy

Morrell, Carmen *

Twin sister of Carla Morrell.
Films:
Basket Case 3: The Progeny (1991). . . . . Twin #2
•• 0:41—Breasts in bed with her twin sister and Duane's brother.
• 1:29—Brief breast, lying in bed with her twin sister and Duane's brother after the end credits.
California Hot Wax (1992). . . . . Bikini Girl
Made for Cable TV:
Sessions: Episode 2 (1991; HBO) . . . . Twin #1
Full Frontal Comedy (1996; Showtime)
. . . . .Woman of Full Frontal Comedy

Morris, Anita

Films:
The Happy Hooker (1975) . . . . .Linda Jo/Mary Smith
• 0:59—Breasts lying on table while a customer puts ice cream all over her.
• 1:24—Breasts covered with whipped cream getting it sprayed off with champagne by another customer.
So Fine (1981). . . . . So Fine Dancer
The Hotel New Hampshire (1984) . . . . Ronda Ray
Maria's Lovers (1985) . . . . Mrs. Wynic
Absolute Beginners (1986; British) . . . . .Dido Lament
Blue City (1986) . . . . Molvina Kerch
Ruthless People (1986) . . . . Carol
Aria (1987; U.S./British). . . . . .Phoebe
18 Again! (1988). . . . . Madeline
Bloodhounds of Broadway (1989) . . . . Missouri Martin
Radioland Murders (1994). . . . . Claudette
Made for Cable TV:
Tales From the Crypt: Spoiled (1991; HBO) . . . . Fuschia
Miniseries:
Trade Winds (1993). . . . . .Contessa
TV:
Berrengers (1985) . . . . Babs Berrenger

Morris, Kim *

Films:
The Sex and Violence Family Hour (1983; Canadian)
. . . . Body Flash Dancer
••• 0:57—Breasts, buns in T-back and lower frontal nudity, while dancing in a studio and on couch in interview.
Video Tapes:
E. Nick: A Legend in His Own Mind (1984) . . . . Nymphet
Playboy Video Calendar 1988 (1987) . . . . .Playmate
Wet & Wild (1989) . . . . .Model
Playboy's 21 Playmates: Volume II (1996) . . . . . .Playmate
••• 0:59—Nude in still photos.
••• 1:00—In lingerie and nude in restaurant fantasy.

Morris, Marianne

Films:
Percy's Progress (1974; British) . . . . Beauty Contestant
Vampyres (1974; British) . . . . Fran
•• 0:00—Breasts, then full frontal nudity in bed with Miriam, kissing each other before getting shot.
••• 0:20—Side of right breast, then breasts in bed with Ted, drinking wine, then making love.
• 0:23—Buns, lying in bed when Ted gets out.
••• 0:39—In black bra, panties, garter belt and stockings, then taking them off in front of Ted. Breasts and buns, then in bed.
••• 0:43—Breasts getting kissed by Miriam in the shower.
•• 0:56—Breasts taking off dress in front of Ted and getting into bed. Partial lower frontal nudity getting into bed.
•• 0:58—Breasts and brief lower frontal nudity in bed with Miriam, drinking Ted's blood.
• 1:00—Full frontal nudity getting dragged out of bed by Miriam.
• 1:18—Brief left breast, getting fondled by the Playboy guy in the wine cellar.

Morrison, Julie *

Video Tapes:
Love Scenes: Volume 2 (1992) . . . . Dr. Grace Wells
••• 0:50—Nude, while massaging Travis, then making love in her examination room.

Penthouse Forum Letters: Volume 2 (1994) . . . . The Window Washer/Lover
••• 0:46—Nude, making love with another woman on sofa, on kitchen counter and on bed.

Morrissey, Lori

a.k.a. Lynn Monroe.

Films:

Femme Fontaine Killer Babe for the C.I.A. (1993) . . . . . Bubbles
Tender Loving Care (1993) . . . . Candy
••• 0:15—Breasts, while running and sunbathing at the beach.
Virtual Encounters (1995) . . . . Candle Girl
(Unrated version reviewed.)
••• 0:15—Nude, when making love with the Candle Boy in bed surrounded by lit candles while Elizabeth Kaitan watches.

Made for Cable TV:

Erotic Confessions: Inspiration (1995; Cinemax) . . Sharon
(Available on video tape in *Erotic Zone: Inspiration.*)
•• 0:02—Breasts and buns, while in studio with Nick, then making love with him on the bed.
Compromising Situations: Singin' The Blues (1998; Showtime) . . . . Buxom Admirer
•• 0:02—Breasts and buns, while making love with Kid in his dressing room.
Hot Springs Hotel: Travels with Travis (1998; Showtime) . . . . Teddy

TV:

The Bold and the Beautiful . . . . Michelle

Video Tapes:

Soft Bodies: Pillow Talk (1996) . . . . Herself
••• 0:22—In lingerie, while posing in front of doors, then nude.
••• 0:26—In shirt and short pants, then lingerie, then nude outdoors.
••• 0:31—In a slip, then nude, while posing next to swimming pool.

Morrow, Deirdre

See: Simone, Dominique.

• *Morrow, Mari*

Films:

Children of the Corn III: Urban Harvest (1994) . . . . Maria
Undercover (1995) . . . . Victoria
(Unrated version reviewed.)
Virtuosity (1995) . . . . Linda Barnes
How To Be a Player (1997) . . . . Katrina
•• 1:26—Brief right breast, then breasts, while making love with Bill Bellamy.

Made for Cable TV:

Red Shoe Diaries: Emily's Dance (1993; Showtime) . . . . . . Emily

TV:

One Life to Live (1995-96) . . . . Rachel Gannon

Morrow, Sue

Made for Cable Movies:

Soft Touch (1987; Playboy) . . . . Ashley Keyes
(Shown on *The Playboy Channel* as *Birds in Paradise.*)
• 0:01—Breasts during opening credits.
• 0:02—Breasts with her two girlfriends during the opening credits.
•• 0:19—Breasts taking off her T-shirt in bed. More breasts sleeping, then waking up.
• 0:20—Breasts getting out of bed.
•• 0:22—Breasts making love with a guy.
• 0:23—Breasts in bed.
•• 0:53—Breasts on bed with Ensign Landers.
••• 0:59—Breasts and buns in play pool with Landers.
• 1:19—Breasts in stills during end credits.
Soft Touch II (1987; Playboy) . . . . Ashley Keyes
(Shown on *The Playboy Channel* as *Birds in Paradise.*)
• 0:01—Breasts during opening credits.
• 0:02—Breasts with her two girlfriends during the opening credits.
•• 0:26—Breasts while sunbathing on boat.
• 0:50—Brief breasts in the water.
• 0:52—Breasts during strip poker game, then covered with whipped cream.
•• 0:56—Full frontal nudity getting out of bed.

Morsell, Victoria

Films:

Savage (1995) . . . . Julie Verne

Made for Cable TV:

Hot Line: Sleepless Nights (1996; Cinemax) . . . Rachel Davis
(Available on video tape in *Hot Line 3.*)
•• 0:01—In white bra, then breasts while undressing in bathroom, then caressing herself.
••• 0:20—Nude, while making love with Neil on the floor.
• 0:26—Brief breasts, while lying back into bed next to Neil.
The Outer Limits: Falling Star (1996; Showtime) . . . . Candice
• 0:13—Brief breasts, when caught in bed with Xander Berkeley by Sheena Easton.
•• 0:18—Breasts, after time travel guy from the future enters her body.
•• 0:23—Breasts, while getting into position with Berkeley in bed.

Mortagua, Cristina *

Video Tapes:

Playboy International Playmates (1993) . . . . Cristina
••• 0:35—Full frontal nudity in still photos.
••• 0:36—Full frontal nudity on balcony, then taking an outdoor shower. Breasts during recollections of dancing with a guy.
••• 0:46—Nude with Cida, trying on clothing at the beach.
••• 0:48—Breasts taking off clothes and dancing.

Mosely, Melanie

Films:

Ironheart (1991) . . . . Pretty Girl
•• 0:18—Breasts, while getting her T-shirt ripped off by four jerks. Long shot and closer shots.
My Own Private Idaho (1991) . . . . Lounge Hostess

Moss, Carrie-Anne

Films:

Flashfire (1993) . . . . Meredith Neal
Soft Kill (1994) . . . . Jane Tanner
• 1:10—In white bra, then breasts while making love with Jack.
Terrified (1994) . . . . Tracy
Lethal Tender (1996) . . . . Melissa Wilkins
Sabotage (1996; Canadian) . . . . Louise "Lou" Castle

Made for Cable TV:

Matrix (1993; USA) . . . . Liz Teel

TV:

Dark Justice (1991-93) . . . . Tara McDonald
Models Inc. (1994-95) . . . . Carrie Spencer
F/X: The Series (1996-97) . . . . Lucinda Scott

Mounds, Melissa

Adult film actress.

Films:

Flesh Gordon 2 (1990; Canadian). . . . . .Bazonga Bomber
- ••• 0:46—Breasts standing by table with Flesh Gordon and Dr. Jerkoff.
- ••• 0:48—More breasts with Dr. Jerkoff.

Mountjoy, Andrea *

Video Tapes:

Penthouse: The Art of Massage (1996). . . . . .Model

Penthouse: The Ultimate Pet Games (1996) . . . . Pet
- ••• 0:13—Nude during badminton segment.
- ••• 0:21—Nude during oil wrestling segment.
- ••• 0:25—Nude, while giving a dog a bath, then bathing herself outdoors.
- ••• 0:36—Breasts during pool volleyball game.

Mucciante, Christie

Films:

Fatal Pulse (1987). . . . . Karen
- •• 0:51—Breasts, while getting dressed for bed.

Tango & Cash (1989) . . . . .Dressing Room Girl
- • 1:06—Brief breasts in dressing room. (She's the first topless blonde.)

• Mueller, Cookie

Films:

Pink Flamingos (1972). . . . . Cookie
- •• 0:28—Full frontal nudity, while having sex with Cracker and a chicken.

Female Trouble (1974) . . . . .Concetta

Desperate Living (1977) . . . . Flipper

Mulford, Nancy

Films:

Any Man's Death (1989) . . . . Tara

Act of Piracy (1990; South African/U.S.). . . . . . Laura Warner
- • 0:11—Very brief left breast under Gary Busey in bed. Dark, hard to see.
- • 0:34—Brief, upper half of left breast, in bed with Ray Sharkey.

Mullen, Beckie *

Films:

Glitch (1988). . . . . .Extra

Affairs of the Heart (1992). . . . . Pool Girl
- ••• 0:52—Breasts, after taking off her bikini top, then diving into pool.
- •• 0:53—Breasts, lying on towel on diving board, then turning over.

The Bikini Carwash Company II (1993) . . . . School Teacher
(Unrated version reviewed.)

Hard Hunted (1993). . . . . Becky
- •• 0:38—Breasts and buns in G-string in spa with Ava doing radio show.
- ••• 0:56—Breasts while getting out of spa and getting coffee.

Forbidden Games (1995). . . . . .Linda
(Unrated version reviewed.)
- ••• 0:04—Dancing in front of Michael in black bra and panties, then breasts while making love with him. Long scene.

Sinful Intrigue (1995) . . . . Steph
- • 0:02—Breasts, after getting her T-shirt ripped off in kitchen by Adam. Dark.
- ••• 0:03—Brief buns seen through open back of shirt, then breasts, while taking a bath.
- ••• 0:27—In white bra, then breasts and buns in T-back, in bedroom and bathroom with Adam. Long scene
- •• 0:29—Breasts in black leather and chain outfit, while standing in bathroom, looking at herself in the mirror.
- ••• 0:30—Breasts, when making love in bed on top of Adam while wearing the outfit.
- • 0:45—Side view of left breast and buns in T-back, taking off robe and putting on a bra.
- •• 0:52—Breasts, after taking off her robe in front of Jake
- ••• 1:03—In white bra, then breasts, while tied by her wrists to the bed.

Made for Cable Movies:

Cast a Deadly Spell (1991; HBO) . . . . .Drop Dead Babe

Made for Cable TV:

Sessions: Episode 2 (1991; HBO) . . . . Vicki

Video Tapes:

The Perfect Body Contest (1987). . . . . .Beckie

Wild Bikinis (1987). . . . . Herself

Bikini Blitz (1990) . . . . .Model

Rock Video Girls (1991) . . . . Herself

Fantasies 2 (1992). . . . . .Model

Marilyn Chambers: Wet & Wild Fantasies (1994)
. . . . .Pool Cleaner
- •• 0:32—In swimsuit, then breasts by and in the swimming pool.

Mullen, Patty *

Films:

Doom Asylum (1987) . . . . .Judy LaRue/Kiki LaRue
(In red two piece swimsuit a lot.)

Frankenhooker (1990). . . . . .Elizabeth
- •• 1:01—Breasts and buns in garter belt and stockings, in room with a customer.

Müller, Lillian *

a.k.a. Liliane Mueller or Yulis Ruvaal.

Films:

Rosemarie's Daughter (1975; German) . . . . .n.a.

Women's Clinic (1975; German) . . . . .n.a.

Sex on the Run (1979; German/French/Italian). . . . . Angela
a.k.a. Some Like It Cool
a.k.a. Casanova and Co.
- ••• 0:15—Second woman (blonde) to take off her clothes with the other two women, nude. Long scene.

Best Defense (1984) . . . . French Singer

Video Tapes:

Playboy's Playmates Revisited (1998) . . . . .Playmate
- ••• 1:03—Nude in old footage and still photos.
- ••• 1:09—Nude in new footage.

Munro, Caroline

Films:

Captain Kronos, Vampire Hunter (1972; British). . . . . .Carla

Dracula A.D. 1972 (1972; British) . . . . Laura
a.k.a. Dracula Today

The Golden Voyage of Sinbad (1974; British) . . . Margiana
- • 0:51—Very brief right nipple, sticking out of top when Sinbad carries her from the boat to the shore. Long shot.

The Devil Within Her (1976; British). . . . . Mandy

The Spy Who Loved Me (1977; British) . . . . Naomi

Starcrash (1979; Italian). . . . . Stella Star

Don't Open Till Christmas (1984; British). . . . . Herself

The Last Horror Film (1984). .Jana Bates

Slaughter High (1986). . . . . Carol

Night Owl (1993) . . . . Herself

Murakoshi, Suzen

Films:

Wall Street (1987) . . . . Girl in Bed
- 0:13—Brief full frontal nudity getting out of bed and walking past the camera in Charlie Sheen's bedroom (slightly out of focus).

Quick Change (1990) . . . . Hostage

Night Owl (1993) . . . . Woman at Bar
- 0:24—Breasts, while in bathroom after coming home from the bar, before getting killed by Jake.

Murdoch, Laura

Films:

The Raffle (1994) . . . . Dream Dancer

Timecop (1994) . . . . Virtual Reality Woman
- •• 0:38—Full frontal nudity, while in bed in virtual reality image that Ricky is experiencing.

Murgia, Antonella

Films:

Reborn (1978) . . . . Maria
- 0:35—Breasts in bed with Michael Moriarty.
- •• 0:37—More breasts in bed with Moriarty.
- ••• 0:38—Nude, getting out of bed.
- ••• 0:39—Nude, walking around in bedroom.

Anguish (1987; Spanish) . . . . Ticket Girl

Murphy, Barri

Films:

Action U.S.A. (1988) . . . . Carmen
- •• 0:03—Breasts, in house, making love with, then getting beaten up by a bad guy.

Armed for Action (1992) . . . . Sara

Murray, Beverley

Films:

Cathy's Curse (1976; Canadian) . . . . Vivian
- 1:13—Very, very brief left breast, while jumping around in bathtub, brushing leaches off her body.

The Last Straw (1987; Canadian) . . . . Nurse Thompson

Still Life (1990) . . . . Performance Space Lady

Muscarella, Lynn *

Hostess of Manhattan Cable TV "Voyeurvision" live call-in telefantasy show.

Made for Cable TV:

Real Sex 4 (1992; HBO) . . . . Voyeurvision
- 0:33—Buns, in lingerie doing her phone-in sex cable TV show.

Muti, Ornella *

Films:

Appassionata (1979; Italian) . . . . Virginia
- 0:32—Brief breasts in bathroom when her father rips open her T-shirt while looking for hickeys.
- 0:57—Partial left breast, while leaning over to tempt her father.
- 1:35—Buns, getting out of bed with her father. Brief side of left breast when leaving the room.

Summer Affair (1979) . . . . Lisa
- 0:44—Silhouette of breasts in cave by the water.
- 1:00—Brief breasts getting chased around in the grass and by the beach.

Flash Gordon (1980) . . . . Princess Aura

Love and Money (1980) . . . . Catherine Stockheinz

Famous T & A (1982) . . . . Lisa

(No longer available for purchase, check your video store for rental.)
- •• 0:07—Breasts in scenes from *Summer Affair.* Nude underwater and running around the beach.

Tales of Ordinary Madness (1983; Italian) . . . . Cass
- •• 0:37—Buns, four times, while standing at window in room with Ben Gazzara. Medium long shot.
- 1:06—Buns, while standing at the beach and feeding the seagulls. One medium long shot and one long shot.

Swann in Love (1984; French/German) . . . . Odette de Crêcy

a.k.a. Un Amour de Swann
- •• 1:15—Brief left breast, making love with Jeremy Irons.
- ••• 1:28—Breasts sitting on bed talking to Irons.

Casanova (1987) . . . . Henriette

Wait Until Spring, Bandini (1989; Belgian/French/Italian) . . . . Maria

Oscar (1991) . . . . Sofia Provolone

Once Upon A Crime (1992) . . . . Elena Morosco

Especially on Sunday (1993) . . . . Anna

Made for Cable TV:

The Hitchhiker: True Believer (HBO) . . . . n.a.

(Available on *The Hitchhiker, Volume 3.*)

Myers, T.J.

Films:

The Dallas Connection (1994) . . . . Dancer #2
- 1:11—Breasts (she's on the left), while on stage with another dancer. Medium long shot.

Seduction of Innocence (1994) . . . . Tammy
- 1:06—Buns in panties and bra in front of mirror.

Lebensborn (1996) . . . . Lorelei

Nail, Joanne

Films:

Switchblade Sisters (1975) . . . . Maggie
- 0:21—Very, very brief right breast in ripped blouse when she tries to rip Dominic's shirt off.

The Gumball Rally (1976) . . . . Jane

The Visitor (1980; Italian/U.S.) . . . . Barbara Collins

Nankervis, Debbie

Films:

Alvin Purple (1973; Australian) . . . . Girl in Blue Movie
- •• 1:04—Nude, running after Alvin in bedroom during showing of movie.

Libido (1973; Australian) . . . . First Girl

Alvin Rides Again (1974; Australian) . . . . Woman Cricketer

Nann, Erika

Films:

Beach Fever (1988) . . . . Girl Singer #1

Glitch (1988) . . . . Extra

Death Feud (1989) . . . . Hooker

Camp Fear (1991) . . . . n.a.

a.k.a. Millenium Countdown

Animal Instincts (1992) . . . . Dianne

(Unrated version reviewed.)

Final Impact (1992) . . . . Foxy Boxer

Mind Twister (1992) . . . . Lisa Strahten

(Unrated version reviewed.)
- ••• 0:28—Breasts, while making love in candlelit bathtub with a young stud.
- 0:33—In black lingerie in bedroom with Daniel.
- 0:37—Breasts, while in bed with Daniel.

0:42—In sheer black body suit in bathroom while talking to Daniel.
0:49—In black bra, panties, garter belt and stockings.
0:54—In black lingerie outfit.
••• 0:56—Breasts and buns, while making love with Heather while getting videotaped by Daniel.
• 1:22—In lingerie on TV monitor during video playback. Buns, while wrestling with Sheila.

Night Rhythms (1992) .... Alex
(Unrated version reviewed.)
••• 1:00—Buns in G-string and bra, then breasts, undressing in front of Martin Hewitt and making love with him.

Die Watching (1993) .... Gabrielle
•• 0:51—Right breast, while caressing with herself while Christopher Atkins videotapes her before killing her. Her right hand is handcuffed to shelves.

Made for Cable Movies:
Norma Jean & Marilyn (1996; HBO) .... Jane Russell

Nanty, Isabelle

Films:
Red Kiss (1985; French).......................... Jeanine
On a Volé Charlie Spencer! (1987)................. Suzette
The Passion of Beatrice (1988; French) .... La Nourrice
•• 1:53—Right breast, offering her breast milk to Arnaud.
Tatie Danielle (1991; French).................... Sandrine
Les Visiteurs (1993; French)............... Fabienne Morlot

Napaul, Neriah

See: Davis, Neriah.

Naples, Toni

a.k.a. Karen Chorak.
Films:
Doctor Detroit (1983) .... Dream Girl
Chopping Mall (1986).................. Bathing Beauty
a.k.a. Killbots
Deathstalker II (1987) .... Sultana
The Turn-On (1989) .... Harold's Wife
a.k.a. Le Clic
••• 0:31—Nude, during ceremony and after getting turned on by the black box.
Hard to Die (1990) .... Sgt. Shawlee
a.k.a. Tower of Terror
Sorority House Massacre 2 (1990)............. Sgt. Shawlee
Transylvania Twist (1990) .... Maxine
Final Judgment (1992)...................... Dancer #2
• 0:51—Breasts, while dancing on stage, wearing sunglasses.
Munchie (1992) .... Mrs. Blaylok
Prison Heat (1992)............................ Hellena
•• 0:43—Breasts, while in the shower with Colleen.
American Yakuza (1993) .... Mrs. Campaneia
Dinosaur Island (1993) .... Queen Morganna
• 0:37—Brief left breast, popping out of bikini top when June starts dragging her around by her hair.
Munchie Strikes Back (1994).................. Newscaster
Sorceress (1994) .... Maria
•• 0:17—Breasts under sheer black bodysuit. Breasts after taking off top and joining Larry and Julie Strain in bed.
• 0:36—Left breast in open blouse, after fighting in bed with Larry.
••• 0:53—Buns and breasts, while on bed with Julie Strain and Rochelle Swanson.
The Assault (1996) .... Jodi
Fugitive Rage (1996)............................ Helga

Napoli, Susan *

a.k.a. Stephanie Ryan.
Films:
Wildest Dreams (1987) .... Punk #4
• 0:21—Brief left breast, leaning backwards on couch with her boyfriend.
Party Incorporated (1989) .... Uncredited Party Girl
a.k.a. Party Girls
• 0:05—Brief breasts, while wearing a mask and dancing during party with two other girls.
• 0:08—Brief breasts again.
Frankenhooker (1990)......................... Anise
• 0:42—Brief left breast on bed with Amber, taking off her top. Brief breasts after Angel explodes.
• 0:43—Breasts, kneeling on bed screaming before exploding.
Street Hunter (1990) .... Eddie's Girl
•• 0:40—Breasts in bed with Eddie (she's on the left, wearing white panties).
Beauty School (1993)........................ Otis' Girl
•• 0:21—Breasts undoing her swimsuit top for Mr. Otis.
New York Nights (1994)......................... Vicki
•• 0:05—Full frontal nudity while in room with a guy.
•• 0:21—Breasts, while putting on lingerie for show.
••• 0:45—In bra and panties, then full frontal nudity, then making love with Kurt in apartment.
••• 1:03—Breasts and buns, while making love with Chris.
•• 1:25—Nude, while making love with a guy.
Marilyn Chambers: Bedtime Fantasies (1996) ....n.a.

Video Tapes:
Penthouse Satin & Lace II: Hollywood Undercover (1992).. Pet
The Penthouse All-Pet Workout (1993) .... Pet
•• 0:00—Full frontal nudity during introduction.
•• 0:03—Brief nude shots while getting undressed and suited up.
••• 0:14—Nude on couch inside.
••• 0:43—Nude with the other girls, exercising, working with equipment, in the pool and spa.
Penthouse Pet of the Year Winners 1994: Sasha & Leslie (1994) .... Pet

Naschak, Andrea

a.k.a. Adult film actress April Rayne.
Films:
Hold Me, Thrill Me, Kiss Me (1993) .... Sabra
(Unrated version reviewed.)
• 0:04—Buns in yellow and orange two piece swimsuit while dancing on stage.
• 0:08—Buns in G-string and out of it in trailer with Max.
• 0:09—Very brief left breast under sheer black blouse.
0:25—Buns, while on stage in black outfit.
• 0:46—Buns and most of breast, while dancing on stage in sexy outfit.

Nash, Jennifer

Films:
The Player (1992) .... Cameo
Invisible: The Chronicles of Benjamin Knight (1993) ....Zanna
• 0:15—Buns, while making love in bed with Wade. Don't see her face well.
Clifford (1994)................................ Wendy

Made for Cable TV:
Red Shoe Diaries: Hard Labor (1995; Showtime) .... Alex

Nassar, Deborah Ann

Films:

Stripped to Kill (1987) . . . . Dazzle
- ••• 0:07—Breasts wearing a G-string dancing on stage with a motorcycle prop.

Dance of the Damned (1988). . . . . La Donna
- • 0:07—Brief breasts during dance routine in club.

Nathenson, Zoë

Films:

Mona Lisa (1987; British) . . . . Jeannie

The Raggedy Rawney (1988; British) . . . . Jessie
- • 0:44—Buns, after taking off her dress and going skinny dipping while Dexter Fletcher watches.
- •• 0:56—Breasts, after sitting up while kissing Fletcher.

One Night Stand (1997). . . . . Mickey

Natividad, Francesca "Kitten" *

Adult Films:

Bodacious Ta-Tas. . . . . .n.a.

Bad Girls IV (1982). . . . . n.a.
- •• 0:26—Breasts in back of pizza truck.

Titillation (1982) . . . . n.a.

Breasts.

Films:

Up! (1976) . . . . Greek Chorus

Beneath the Valley of the Ultravixens (1979) . . . . Lavonia & Lola Langusta

The Lady in Red (1979) . . . . Uncredited Partygoer
- • 0:39—Brief breasts outside during party.

An Evening with Kitten (1983) . . . . Herself
- •• 0:02—Breasts busting out of her blouse.
- •• 0:09—Breasts while in miniature city scene.
- •• 0:11—Brief breasts while on stage.
- • 0:20—Left breast, in bed with a vampire.
- ••• 0:21—Breasts and buns in G-string during dance in large champagne glass prop. Long scene.
- ••• 0:24—Breasts on beach in mermaid costume with little shell pasties.
- ••• 0:25—Breasts while in the glass again.
- •• 0:28—Breasts while in and out of glass.
- •• 0:29—Brief breasts during end credits.

My Tutor (1983) . . . . Anna Maria
- ••• 0:10—Breasts in room with Matt Lattanzi, then lying in bed.

Doin' Time (1984). . . . . Tassle

Takin' It Off (1984) . . . . Betty Bigones
- •• 0:01—Breasts dancing on stage.
- ••• 0:04—Breasts and buns dancing on stage.
- •• 0:29—Breasts in the Doctor's office.
- ••• 0:32—Nude dancing in the Psychiatrist's office.
- ••• 0:39—Nude in bed with a guy during fantasy sequence playing with vegetables and fruits.
- •• 0:49—Breasts in bed covered with popcorn.
- • 0:51—Nude doing a dance routine in the library.
- ••• 1:09—Nude splashing around in a clear plastic bathtub on stage.
- •• 1:20—Nude at a fat farm dancing.
- •• 1:24—Nude running in the woods in slow motion.

The Wild Life (1984) . . . . Stripper #2
- ••• 0:50—Breasts doing strip routine in a bar just before a fight breaks out.

Night Patrol (1985) . . . . Hippie Woman
- •• 1:01—Breasts in kitchen with Pat Paulsen, the other police officer and her hippie boyfriend.

Takin' It All Off (1987). . . . . Betty Bigones
- ••• 0:12—Nude, washing herself in the shower.
- •• 0:39—Nude, on stage in a giant glass, then breasts backstage in her dressing room.
- •• 0:42—Breasts in flashbacks from *Takin' It Off.*
- •• 0:46—Breasts in group in the studio.
- ••• 0:53—Nude, dancing on the deck outside. Some nice slow motion shots.
- •• 1:16—Breasts on stage in club.
- ••• 1:23—Nude, dancing with the other girls on stage.

The Tomb (1987) . . . . Stripper
- ••• 0:19—Breasts and buns in G-string dancing on stage.
- • 0:21—Brief breasts again.

Another 48 Hrs. (1990) . . . . Girl in Movie
- • 1:04—Brief breasts on movie screen when two motorcycles crash through it.

The Girl I Want (1990). . . . . Miss Langusta

Buford's Beach Bunnies (1992) . . . . Madam #1

Video Tapes:

The Stripper of the Year (1986). . . . . Kitten
- ••• 0:51—Nude, stripping out of black outfit.
- •• 0:53—Breasts on stage with the other contestants.

Inside Out 2 (1992) . . . . Busty Dusty/Profiles in Cleavage

(Unrated version reviewed.)
- •• 0:56—Bouncing her breasts while wearing pasties.
- • 1:02—Dancing in disco wearing pasties. B&W.
- • 1:03—Brief breasts with pasties.

Neal, Billie

Films:

Down by Law (1986) . . . . Bobbie
- •• 0:11—Breasts lying in bed, talking to Jack. Medium long shot. Long scene.
- ••• 0:12—Side view of right breast, partial lower frontal nudity, lying in bed.
- •• 0:13—More breasts, medium long shot again, lying in bed.
- •• 0:14—Right breast when Jack covers her up with sheet.

The January Man (1988) . . . . Gwen

Born on the Fourth of July (1989) . . . . Nurse Washington

Internal Affairs (1990) . . . . Dorian's Wife

Jacob's Ladder (1990) . . . . Della

A Kiss Before Dying (1991) . . . . Nurse

Mortal Thoughts (1991) . . . . Linda Nealon

Consenting Adults (1992) . . . . Annie Duttonville

The Gun in Betty Lou's Handbag (1992) . . . . Gail

Sweet Nothing (1994). . . . . n.a.

Girl 6 (1996) . . . . Angela's Mother

GRIDLOCK'd (1997) . . . . Medicaid Woman #1

Neal, Christy

Films:

Coming Together (1978). . . . . Vicky Hughes

a.k.a. A Matter of Love
- • 0:30—Brief right breast in shower with Angie.
- • 0:37—Breasts and buns making love standing up in front of sliding glass door with Frank. Quick cuts.
- • 0:49—Brief breasts again during flashbacks.
- •• 0:57—Breasts with Angie and Richard.
- • 1:05—Breasts on beach with Angie. Long shot.

Take Down (1978). . . . . Suzette Smith

Neal, Siri

Films:

The Rachel Papers (1989; British). Suki

The Children (1990; British/German). . . . . Judith

Waterland (1992; British/U.S.) . . . . Helen Atkinson
- 0:40—Brief side view of breast in mirror while rubbing her legs. Long shot at far left of TV screen.

Nebout, Claire

Films:

Scene of the Crime (1987; French) . . . . Alice

The Conviction (1994; Italian) . . . . Sandra Celestini

a.k.a. La Condanna

- •• 0:22—Breasts, after taking off her dress in dark room with Lorenzo. Dark.

Ponette (1996; French) . . . . n.a.

Negoda, Natalya *

Films:

Little Vera (1988; U.S.S.R.) . . . . Vera
- • 0:15—Very brief breasts and buns getting dressed. Dark, hard to see.
- ••• 0:50—Breasts making love with Sergei.
- •• 1:05—Breasts taking off her dress in the kitchen.

Back In the U.S.S.R. (1992) . . . . Lena
- •• 0:46—Side view of left breast, making love with Sloan in the bathtub. Brief right breast when Dimitri comes into the bathroom.

Made for Cable Movies:

The Comrades of Summer (1992; HBO) . . . . Tanya

Neidhardt, Elke

Films:

Alvin Purple (1973; Australian). . . . . . .Woman in Blue Movie
- •• 1:07—In red bra, then full frontal nudity in bedroom with Alvin during showing of film.

Libido (1973; Australian) . . . . .Penelope

Inside Looking Out (1977; Australian) . . . . Marianne

Nelkin, Stacey

Films:

California Dreaming (1978). . . . . Marsha

Serial (1980) . . . . Marlene

Going Ape! (1981) . . . . .Cynthia

Up the Academy (1981) . . . . .Candy

Get Crazy (1983). . . . . Susie

Halloween III: Season of the Witch (1983) . . . . Ellie Grimbridge
- • 0:37—Brief right breast, behind shower door, when getting out of the shower.

Yellowbeard (1983) . . . . .Triola

Desperate Motive (1992). . . . . Bank Teller

Bullets Over Broadway (1994) . . . . Rita

Everything Relative (1996). . . . . Katie

Made for Cable TV:

Sex, Shock and Censorship in the 90's (1993; Showtime) . . . . Patty Turner

Miniseries:

The Last Convertible (1979) . . . . Sheilah Garrigan

TV:

The Chisholms (1979). . . . . Bonnie Sue Chisholm

Generations (1990) . . . . .Christy Russell

Nell, Nathalie

Films:

Rape of Love (1979; French). . . . . .Nicole

a.k.a. L'Amour Violé

- • 0:20—Breasts, while wearing her skirt when running in the woods, trying to get away from the guys.
- • 0:21—Breasts, while standing in white panties, after they take her skirt off. Full frontal nudity after they rip her panties off.
- •• 0:22—Nude, being held down and brutally raped by the four guys.
- • 0:28—Breasts, while being examined by a doctor.
- • 0:35—Brief full frontal nudity, while sitting in the bathtub.

Echoes (1983) . . . . .Christine

Man, Woman and Child (1983). . . . . Nicole Guerin

Nelligan, Kate

Films:

The Romantic Englishwoman (1975; British/French) . . . . Isabel

Dracula (1979) . . . . Lucy

Crossover (1980; Canadian) . . . . Peabody

a.k.a. Mr. Patman

Eye of the Needle (1981) . . . . Lucy
- •• 0:52—Brief left breast, while drying herself off in the bathroom when Donald Sutherland accidentally sees her.
- • 1:15—Top half of buns, making love in bed with Sutherland.
- • 1:26—Breasts making love in bed with Sutherland after he killed her husband. Dark, hard to see.

Without a Trace (1983) . . . . .Susan Selky

Eleni (1985). . . . . Eleni

Frankie & Johnny (1991) . . . . Cora

The Prince of Tides (1991). . . . . Lila Wingo

Shadows and Fog (1991). . . . . Eve

Fatal Instinct (1993). . . . . Lana Revine

Wolf (1994) . . . . Charlotte Randall

How to Make an American Quilt (1995) . . . . Constance

Up Close & Personal (1996). . . . . Joanna Kennelly

U.S. Marshals (1998) . . . . Walsh

Made for Cable Movies:

Control (1987; HBO) . . . . .n.a.

The Diamond Fleece (1992; USA) . . . . Holly Plum

Old Times (1993) . . . . Kate

A Mother's Prayer (1995; USA) . . . . Sheila Walker

Miniseries:

Million Dollar Babies (1994). . . . . Helena Reid

Made for TV Movies:

Therese Raquin (1981). . . . . .Therese

Kojak: The Price of Justice (1987). Kitty

Liar, Liar (1993) . . . . .Susan Miori

Shattered Trust: The Shari Karney Story (1993) . . . . Stephanie Chadford

Spoils of War (1994) . . . . Elise

• Nelson, Yvette

See: Stephens, Yvette.

Nemour, Stacey

Films:

Computer Beach Party (1988) . . . . .Allison

Hardcase and Fist (1988). . . . . Jill
- • 0:30—Right breast, while on desk with her boyfriend, talking on the phone with Sharon.

Neri, Francesca *

Daughter of actress Rosalba Neri.

Films:

Captain America (1990). . . . . Valentina de Santis

Flight of the Innocent (1993; Italian/French) . . . . . Marta Rienzi

Outrage (1993; Spanish) . . . . Giuditta/Anna Meltzer
a.k.a. Shoot
a.k.a. Dispara
•• 0:20—Breasts, after taking off robe and putting on blouse in her trailer.
•• 0:32—Full frontal nudity, while in bed with Antonio Banderas.
• 0:42—Nude, in her trailer at night, getting raped by three punks.
•• 0:45—Full frontal nudity, while in shower, washing herself off.
Live Flesh (1997; French/Spanish) . . . . Elena
a.k.a. Carne Trémula

Neri, Rosalba

a.k.a. Sara Bay.
Mother of actress Francesca Neri.
Films:
Esther and the King (1960; U.S./Italian) . . . . Keresh
Johnny Yuma (1967; Italian) . . . . Samantha Felton
A Long Ride From Hell (1970; Italian) . . . . Prostitute
The Seducers (1970) . . . . Paula
a.k.a. Sensation
a.k.a. Top Sensation
•• 0:06—Breasts, under lots of necklaces, in cabin with Mudy. Partial buns in panties.
••• 0:12—Buns, while sunbathing on boat, then brief left breast.
•• 0:13—Right breast with Ulla on boat deck.
• 0:35—Brief buns, pulling down her swimsuit bottom to show off her tan.
• 0:54—Brief breasts, while on boat deck with Andrew.
• 1:05—Upper half of buns, when Andrew pulls her swimsuit down.
The Devil's Wedding Night (1971; Italian) . . . . Countess
Lady Frankenstein (1971; Italian) . . . . Tanya
Slaughter Hotel (1971; Italian) . . . . Ann Palmer
a.k.a. Asylum Erotica
Maniac Mansion (1972; Italian) . . . . n.a.
Naked Warriors (1973) . . . . Cornelia
a.k.a. The Arena

Nero, Toni

Films:
Silent Night, Deadly Night (1984) . . . . Pamela
• 0:30—Brief right breast twice just before Billy gets stabbed during fantasy scene.
• 0:42—Breasts in stock room when Andy attacks her.
• 0:44—Breasts while in stock room struggling with Billy, then getting killed by him.
Silent Night, Deadly Night, Part 2 (1986) . . . . Pamela
•• 0:22—Breasts in back of toy store in flashback from *Silent Night, Deadly Night*.
Commando Squad (1987) . . . . Putita

Nesbitt, Victoria

Films:
Murder Weapon (1989) . . . . Vicki
••• 0:05—Breasts in bed with a guy after taking off her swimsuit top, then making love on top of him. Long scene.
The Girl I Want (1990) . . . . Cindy
Marked for Murder (1990) . . . . Girlfriend
•• 0:57—Breasts, while in backyard by pool with Wings Hauser.

Video Tapes:
Linnea Quigley's Horror Workout (1990) . . . . Missy

Neumann, Jenny

Writer.
Films:
Mistress of the Apes (1979; British) . . . . Susan Jamison
• 0:23—Brief side of right breast, getting ready for bed in her tent.
• 0:25—Brief half of right breast in open blouse. Very brief right breast, when pushing a guy away.
• 1:08—Back side of left breast and brief breasts while washing her blouse in river and putting it on.
Swim Team (1979) . . . . Erin
The Last Married Couple in America (1980) . . . . Nurse
Hell Night (1981) . . . . May
My Favorite Year (1982) . . . . Connie
Off the Wall (1982) . . . . Linda
Stagefright (1983; Australian) . . . . Helen Selleck
a.k.a. Nightmares
The Delos Adventure (1985) . . . . Deni
Stitches (1985) . . . . Joan
Miniseries:
V (1983) . . . . Barbara
Made for TV Movies:
The Girl in the Empty Grave (1977) . . . . Susie

• *Neuwirth, Bebe*

Films:
Say Anything (1989) . . . . Mrs. Evans
Green Card (1990) . . . . Lauren
Bugsy (1991) . . . . Countess di Frasso
The Paint Job (1992) . . . . Margaret
Malice (1993) . . . . Dana
Jumanji (1995) . . . . Aunt Nora
The Adventures of Pinocchio (1996) . . . . Felinet
The Associate (1996) . . . . Camille
• 0:37—Buns in black lingerie outfit. Seen in mirror.
• 1:16—Buns in lingerie while in hotel room with Whoopi Goldberg (who is made up like Robert Cutty.)
Miniseries:
Wild Palms (1993) . . . . Tabba Schwartzkopf
TV:
Cheers (1986-93) . . . . Dr. Lilith Sternin-Crane

Newman, Amber

Films:
Lap Dancing (1995) . . . . Lapdancer
Vamps: Deadly Dreamgirls (1996) . . . . Randi
Made for Cable TV:
Erotic Confessions: The Workout (1996; Cinemax) . . Gina
•• 0:03—Breasts, while sitting in steam room, talking with Paula. Full frontal nudity, while in the locker room.

*Newmar, Julie **

Films:
Mackenna's Gold (1969) . . . . Hesh-de
• 1:09—Brief breasts and buns under water. Long shots, hard to see anything. Not clear because of all the dirty water. Brief buns, getting out of the pond.
Hysterical (1983) . . . . Venetia
Love Scenes (1984) . . . . Belinda
a.k.a. Ecstacy
Evils of the Night (1985) . . . . Doctor Zarma
Streetwalkin' (1985) . . . . Queen Bee
Deep Space (1988) . . . . Lady Elaine

Ghosts Can't Do It (1989) . . . . Angel
Nudity Required (1989) . . . . Irina
• 0:57—Side of left breast and side view of buns behind textured shower door with Buddy.
Oblivion (1994) . . . . Miss Kitty
To Wong Foo, Thanks for Everything! Julie Newmar (1995) . . . . Herself
TV:
Batman (1966-67) . . . . The Catwoman

Newton, Thandie

Films:
Flirting (1992; Australian) . . . . Thandiwe Adjewa
•• 1:30—Brief breasts, getting out of bed and putting a coat on over herself after getting caught with Danny.
The Young Americans (1993; British) . . . . Rachael Stevens
Interview With the Vampire: The Vampire Chronicles (1994) . . . . Yvette
Jefferson in Paris (1995) . . . . Sally Hemings
The Journey of August King (1995) . . . . Annalees
Loaded (1996) . . . . Zita
GRIDLOCK'd (1997) . . . . Cookie
• 0:03—Brief breasts, when Tim Roth and Tupac Shakur drag her out of the bathtub to take her to the hospital.

Nicholas, Angela *

Films:
Psychos in Love (1987) . . . . Diane
•• 0:04—Breasts while taking a shower, before being killed.
Wildest Dreams (1987) . . . . Claudia
•• 1:01—Breasts typing on computer doing Bobby's book keeping.
Alien Space Avenger (1988) . . . . Doris
• 0:56—Brief breasts making whoopee with Jaimie Gillis.
••• 0:57—More breasts making love on top of Gillis while killing him.
Galactic Gigolo (1988) . . . . Peggy Sue Peggy
a.k.a. Club Earth
• 0:21—Brief right breast in open blouse leaving room with Eoj.
Affairs of the Heart (1992) . . . . Dreamgirl
•• 0:14—In bra, then left breast while in bed with the Geek.
Hand Gun (1994) . . . . Woman in Bed
• 0:04—Breasts, while sitting up in bed after police bust in.

Nicholas, Sky

Films:
Fatal Pulse (1987) . . . . Carol
• 0:16—Brief breasts, while looking at herself in the mirror in bedroom, then closer shot, while putting on tank top.
Campus Hustle (1993) . . . . Ellen
Hindsight (1996) . . . . Chateau
Video Tapes:
Hot Body Competition: Bikinis & Bikes Contest (1996) . . . . Sky
•• 0:05—Breasts and buns, while dancing on stage.
••• 0:06—Nude, while posing outdoors with motorcycle.

Nicholls, Phoebe

Films:
Deep Cover (1980; British) . . . . Christabel Cavendish
a.k.a. Blade on the Feather
• 0:39—Partial buns, while lying in bed and talking with Tom Conti, very brief right breast, when turning around to hit him.
The Elephant Man (1980; British) . . . . Merrick's Mother
The Missionary (1982; British) . . . . Deborah
Maurice (1987; British) . . . . Anne Durham
Persuasion (1995) . . . . Elizabeth Elliot
Made for Cable Movies:
Heart of Darkness (1994; TNT) . . . . The Intended
Miniseries:
Brideshead Revisited (1981; British) . . . . Cordelia Flyte
Made for TV Movies:
Gulliver's Travels (1996) . . . . Empress of Lilliput

Nichols, Kelly

Adult film actress.
a.k.a. Marianne Walter.
Films:
The Toolbox Murders (1978) . . . . Dee Ann
••• 0:22—Right breast, then breasts taking a bath and enjoying herself. Long scene. Nude, running around trying to get away from Cameron Mitchell.
• 0:32—Breasts, while dead in her apartment and later on the coroner's table.
It's Called Murder Baby (1982) . . . . Leslie
(R-rated version of the adult film *Dixie Ray, Hollywood Star.*)
Model Behavior (1982) . . . . Anne #2
••• 0:40—Breasts, while taking off her top before the other Anne in front of Dino.
Deathmask (1983) . . . . Lover Nurse
• 1:37—Very brief partial buns while making love on top of a guy in examination room. Very brief left breast, then very, very brief right breast when shot by Jane Hamilton.
In Love (1983) . . . . Jill Travis
Delivery Boys (1984) . . . . Elizabeth
• 0:44—Top half of right breast, while eating rolls with a young boy.
Sno-Line (1984) . . . . Ellen

Nicholson, Celia

Films:
An Angel at My Table (1990; Australian/New Zealand) . . Piona
Jack Be Nimble (1994; New Zealand) . . . . Motel Woman
• 0:02—Brief breasts, while making love with Clarrie in motel room bed.

Nicholson, Kathrin

Films:
Midnight Heat (1994) . . . . Vivian Grey
• 0:10—Very, very brief blurry right breast, getting up out of bed to answer the door. (She's in bed, caressing Mimi Craven.)
A Simple Twist of Fate (1994) . . . . TV Reporter
Made for Cable TV:
The Outer Limits: First Anniversary (1996; Showtime) . . Ady #1
Red Shoe Diaries: Cowboy, Cowboy (1997; Showtime) . . . . Susan
••• 0:15—Nude, while standing in front of a mirror with Johnny, then making love with him in bed.
Red Shoe Diaries: The Ex (1997; Showtime) . . . . Daisy
••• 0:02—Full frontal nudity, while making love in bedroom with Michael.
• 0:20—Breasts, while in bedroom with Michael.
TV:
Sleepwalkers (1997-) . . . . n.a.

Nickson, Julia

Films:
Rambo: First Blood, Part II (1985) . . . . Co
Glitch (1988) . . . . Michelle

The Chinatown Murders: Man Against the Mob (1989) . . . . Kei Lee
- 1:15—Breasts, while taking off her dress in bedroom in front of George Peppard. Very dark. It looks like she's wearing pasties when she gets into bed.
- 1:18—Very brief breasts getting out of bed. It looks like she's wearing the pastie things again.

K2 (1991). . . . . Cindy
- 0:26—Briefly nude, getting up out of bed and putting robe on.

Sidekicks (1992) . . . . Noreen Chan

Amityville: A New Generation (1993). . . . . Suki
- •• 0:28—Left breast, with David Naughton while taking off her coveralls.
- 0:29—Very brief back side of left breast, putting on her coverall strap.

Double Dragon (1994) . . . . Salori Imada

White Tiger (1995) . . . . Jade
- ••• 1:04—Breasts, while making love with Gary Daniels.

TV:

Babylon 5 (1994) . . . . Catherine Sakai

Nicoll, Kristina

Films:

Giant Steps (1992; Canadian). . . . . Tara Stewart
- 0:33—Left breast, while lying on grass with Arva.
- 0:34—Brief left breast, after Graeme wakes her up. Very brief right breast, while walking angrily away.

TV:

T and T (1990) . . . . Terri Taler

Nicolodi, Daria

Films:

Deep Red Hatchet Murders (1976; Italian) . . . . . Gianna Brezzi

Beyond the Door II (1977; Italian). . . . . Dora
- 0:30—Buns, in the shower.
- 0:47—Brief left breast in gaping nightgown, sitting up in bed.

Inferno (1980; Italian). . . . . Countess Elise

Unsane (1982) . . . . Anne
a.k.a. Tenebrae

Creepers (1985; Italian). . . . . School Director's Assistant

Macaroni (1985; Italian) . . . . Laura Di Falco

Terror at the Opera (1989; Italian). . . . . Mira

Nielsen, Barbara

Films:

L'Année des Meduses (1987; French) . . . . Barbara
- 0:37—Brief breasts taking off T-shirt at the beach.
- •• 0:40—Breasts at the beach with Valerie Kaprisky.
- •• 1:04—Breasts while sitting on Kaprisky at the beach.
- •• 1:08—Right breast, lying on the beach with Kaprisky.
- •• 1:41—Breasts on the beach taking off her top.
- ••• 1:43—Nude, in the swimming pool.

The Light in the Jungle (1990) . . . . Rachel

Nielsen, Brigitte *

Ex-wife of actor Sylvester Stallone.

Films:

Red Sonja (1985) . . . . Red Sonja
- 0:01—Half of right nipple through torn outfit, while sitting up.

Rocky IV (1985). . . . . Ludmilla

Cobra (1986) . . . . Ingrid

Beverly Hills Cop II (1987). . . . . Karla Fry

Bye Bye Baby (1989; Italian). . . . . Lisa
- 0:20—Brief side view of right breast, while lying on a guy in bed. Nice buns shot also.

Domino (1989) . . . . Domino
- 0:05—Right breast, lying down next to swimming pool, breasts getting out.
- ••• 1:04—Right breast, caressing herself in a white lingerie body suit, wearing a black wig.

976-EVIL II: The Astral Factor (1991) . . . . Agnes

The Double O Kid (1992) . . . . Rhonda

Mission of Justice (1992). . . . . Rachel K. Larkin

Chained Heat 2 (1993) . . . . Magda Kassar

Body Count (1995) . . . . Sybil

Galaxis (1995). . . . . Ladera

Made for TV Movies:

Murder by Moonlight (1989) . . . . Maggie Bartok

• Nielsen, Connie

Films:

Devil's Advocate (1997). Christabella
- 1:00—Very brief breasts, while kissing Keanu Reeves.
- 1:01—Brief breasts, while lying on the floor with Reeves.
- •• 2:10—Nude, after taking off her dress in office and making love with Reeves.

Made for Cable TV:

Voyage (1993; USA) . . . . Ronnie Freeland

Nielsen, Karen

Films:

Wildest Dreams (1987) . . . . Punk #2
- 0:21—Left breast, while sitting on couch.

Galactic Gigolo (1988). . . . . Kathy/Cheerleader
a.k.a. Club Earth
- •• 0:27—Breasts (she's on the left) while in hot tub with Eoj and Sandy.

New York's Finest (1988). . . . . Hooker #1

Sensations (1988) . . . . Scared Woman

Thrilled to Death (1988) . . . . n.a.

Party Incorporated (1989). . . . . Diane
a.k.a. Party Girls

Fright House (1990) . . . . Tracy

Niemi, Lisa

Wife of actor Patrick Swayze.

Films:

Slam Dance (1987; U.S./British) . . . . Ms. Schell
- ••• 0:54—Nude in Tom Hulce's apartment.
- 1:00—Breasts, dead, lying on the floor in Hulce's apartment.

She's Having a Baby (1988). . . . . Model

Steel Dawn (1988) . . . . Kasha

Younger & Younger (1994) . . . . Donna Weller

TV:

Super Force (1990) . . . . Carla Frost

• Nikaido, Miho

Films:

Tokyo Decadence (1992; Japanese) . . . . Ai
- ••• 0:00—Breasts, while strapped, bound and gagged in a chair for a customer.
- 0:11—Buns in lingerie, while talking on the phone.
- •• 0:13—Buns in and out of panties, while standing on window sill for Mr. Ishioka.
- •• 0:24—Buns in panties, then buns and breasts in bathroom.
- ••• 0:26—Buns and breasts, while crawling on the floor, then watching Yuko have sex with Mr. Ishioka.

•• 0:33—Breasts, while cleaning herself in the bathroom.
• 0:45—Partial buns, while in lingerie in hotel room with a customer.
••• 1:07—Breasts, while standing in front of mirror when Saki takes her dress off, then when having sex with Saki while Turtle Face guy watches.

Flirt (1995) .... Miho
• 0:46—Partial breasts, visible under clear plastic that is wrapped around her body while practicing for a play. Covered with white body paint.
• 1:14—Brief partial right breast in gaping blouse, while kneeling over her boyfriend in bed in flashback.

Nirvana, Yana

Films:

Cinderella (1977) .... Drucella
• 0:02—Breasts taking off clothes with her sister Maribella to let Cinderella wash.
• 0:06—Brief breasts sitting up in bed with Maribella.

Brewster's Millions (1985) .... Louise
Club Life (1987) .... Butchette
He's My Girl (1987)................................ Olga
Another 48 Hrs. (1990) .... CHP Officer

Made for TV Movies:

Getting Physical (1984).................... Astrid Anders

TV:

The Last Precinct (1986) .... Sgt. Martha Haggerty

Niven, Barbara

a.k.a. Barbara Lee Alexander.

Films:

Hired to Kill (1990) .... Sheila
Illegal Entry (1992) .... Pamela Raby
••• 1:02—Breasts, while making out with her boyfriend.
•• 1:15—Breasts, while making love on piano with her boyfriend.

Psycho Cop 2 (1992)........................... Sharon
Under Lock and Key (1994).......................... Tina
Foxfire (1996) .... Goldie's Stepmother

Made for Cable Movies:

The Sister-In-Law (1995; USA).............. Ashley Hawkins
Humanoids From the Deep (1996) .... Fran Taylor
Breast Men (1997; HBO)......................... Cindy

Nix, Stacey

See: Dare, Barbara.

Niznik, Stephanie

Films:

Exit to Eden (1994) .... Diana/Club Eden
•• 0:37—Full frontal nudity, after getting out of swimming pool and helping Dana Delany into a robe.

Dear God (1996)....................... Emanda Maine

Made for Cable Movies:

Twilight of the Golds (1997; HBO) .... Shauna

TV:

Vanishing Son (1995) .... Agent Judith Phillips

Nobis, Karen *

Video Tapes:

Playboy's Girls of Radio: Talk, Rock and Shock (1995) .... Herself
••• 0:29—Nude outside in country western theme.

Noel, Magali

Films:

La Dolce Vita (1960; Italian/French)................. Fanny
Fellini Satyricon (1969; French/Italian)............ Fortunata
Z (1969; French) .... Nick's Sister
The Man Who Had Power Over Women (1970; British) .... Mrs. Franchetti
Tropic of Cancer (1970)..................... The Princess
••• 0:17—In sheer bra, then breasts after taking off her bra while sitting in bed in front of a guy.

Amarcord (1974; Italian/French) .... Gradisca
The Death of Mario Ricci (1985; French/Swiss) ...... Solange

Noel, Monique *

Films:

Bert Rigby, You're a Fool (1989)........ Jim Shirley's Girlfriend
Roadhouse (1989) .... Uncredited Barfly
Mobsters (1991) .... Showgirl
a.k.a. Mobsters—The Evil Empire
Meatballs 4 (1992) .... Lovelie #1
I Like to Play Games (1994)...................... Valerie

Video Tapes:

Wet & Wild (1989) .... Model

• Noelle

Video Tapes:

Body Language (1996)..................... Fire Place
••• 0:12—Nude, while caressing two other women in front of fire place.

Erotic Heat (1996) .... Car Wash/Work Out/Jacuzzi
••• 0:02—Nude, while washing a car.
••• 0:33—Nude, while working out with Sara St. James.

Noelle, Brittany

See: Grey, Nicole.

Noonan, Christine

Films:

If... (1969; British)............................ The Girl
• 0:59—Very brief full frontal nudity with Malcolm McDowell on the floor (B&W).

O Lucky Man! (1973; British). . Coffee Trainee/Girl at Stag Party

Norris, Michele

Films:

Ginger (1970) .... n.a.
The Love-Thrill Murders (1971) .... Maggie's Girlfriend
•• 0:30—Nude, when getting out of bed with Maggie, then dressing.
•• 0:32—Full frontal nudity, while dressing.

North, J. J. *

Films:

Beauty School (1993) .... Renee
••• 0:44—Breasts while doing breast exercises, then buns in G-string going for a swim. (She's on the far left.)
• 0:46—Brief breasts, while standing in pool.
•• 0:57—Breasts and buns in G-string while undressing in locker room.

Attack of the 60 Foot Centerfold (1995) .... Angel
••• 0:05—Breasts and buns in panties with the other two girls in photo shoot.
• 0:09—In black bra, brief buns in black panties, while showing the doctor her body.
•• 0:25—Right breast, then breasts, while in bedroom with Mark.
• 0:30—Buns in yellow swimsuit, while posing for photos at the beach.
••• 0:31—Breasts and buns in swimsuit, while posing at the beach with the other two girls.

•• 0:33—Breasts, while at the beach after she grows to 60 feet tall.
•• 0:51—Right breast, sticking out of bikini top, while lying asleep, then waking up to talk with Wilson.
••• 1:03—Breasts and partial buns, when taking a bath in water tank while Mark takes photos.
•• 1:07—Breasts, while resting against a rock and talking to Mark and Richardson.

Vampire Vixens From Venus (1995) . . . . Arylai
• 0:18—Left breast, while on couch with a guy.
• 1:07—Left breast, while greeting policemen at the door.

Bikini Hotel (1996). Samantha Vance
•• 0:01—Breasts, while in bed with her boyfriend, Brad.
• 0:12—Brief buns in T-back, getting out of spa. Very, very brief right breast while putting on white blouse.
• 0:17—Brief breasts and buns in panties, while trying on different outfits.
• 0:28—Breasts, while changing clothes in room.
• 0:48—Brief breasts, while putting on swimsuit top in bedroom.

Video Tapes:

Marilyn Chambers: Wet & Wild Fantasies (1994) . . . . Exercising Girl 1
• 0:25—Breasts, while exercising and swimming in pool.

North, Noelle

Films:

Report to the Commissioner (1975) . . . . Samantha
Slumber Party '57 (1976) . . . . Angie
•• 0:37—Buns, then breasts in bed with a party guest of her parents.
Sweater Girls (1978) . . . . Bunnie
Blood Song (1982) . . . . Cathy
a.k.a. Dreamslayer
Jekyll & Hyde... Together Again (1982). . . . . Student

North, Sheree

Films:

Madigan (1968) . . . . Jonesy
The Gypsy Moths (1969) . . . . Waitress
•• 0:37—Breasts while dancing on stage in pink pasties and pink bikini bottoms.
• 0:53—Most of left breast, while lying in bed next to Gene Hackman.
The Trouble with Girls (1969) . . . . Nita Bisk
Lawman (1971). . . . . Laura Shelby
••• 1:19—Right breast, then breasts, while in bed with Burt Lancaster.
The Organization (1971). . . . . Gloria Morgan
Breakout (1975) . . . . Myrna
Charley Varrick (1975). . . . . Jewell Everett
Telefon (1977) . . . . Marie Wills
Rabbit Test (1978). . . . . Mystery Lady
Only Once in a Lifetime (1979) . . . . Sally
Maniac Cop (1988). . . . . Sally Noland
Defenseless (1991) . . . . Mrs. Bodeck

Made for TV Movies:

Key West (1973) . . . . Brandi
Snatched (1977). . . . . Kim Sutter
The Real American Hero (1978). . . . . n.a.
Portrait of a Stripper (1979) . . . . n.a.

TV:

I'm a Big Girl Now (1980-81) . . . . Edie McKendrick
Bay City Blues (1983) . . . . Lynn Holtz

Norton, Sara *

Video Tapes:

Penthouse The Great Pet Hunt—Part I (1992). . . . . . . Pet

Norton, Terri

Films:

Dust Devil (1992; British) . . . . Saartjie Haarhoff
• 0:06—Breasts and brief side view of buns, while making love in bed with Dust Devil before he breaks her neck.
Freefall (1993). . . . . Susan

Norton-Taylor, Judy *

Made for TV Movies:

A Walton Thanksgiving Reunion (1993). . . . . Mary Ellen
A Walton Wedding (1995). . . . . Mary Ellen

TV:

The Waltons (1972-81) . . . . Mary Ellen Walton Willard

Video Tapes:

Playboy Video Magazine, Volume 10 (1986) . . . . . Herself
••• 0:45—Nude in still photos.

Nottoli, Elizabeth *

Model for Bisou Bisou.

Films:

Waxwork II: Lost in Time (1991) . . . . Party Babe
Warlock: The Armageddon (1993) . . . . Model 3
• 0:29—Very brief breasts under sheer black blouse, while backstage during fashion show. (She's blowing a bubble with bubble gum.)
A Brilliant Disguise (1994) . . . . Janet/Fashion Model

Nova

Video Tapes:

Hot Body Video Magazine #3: Blonde Fever (1993) . . . . Fashion
•• 0:00—Breasts during introduction.
••• 0:30—Breasts, while changing clothes with Dottie and Samantha.
Hot Body Video Magazine #4: Extra Sexy (1993) . . . . Feature Girl
••• 0:00—Breasts during introduction.
••• 0:26—Breasts under sheer black top, then nude, while posing on balcony.

• Nova, Nikki

a.k.a. Nicole Italiano-Zaza.

Films:

Illicit Confessions (1997). . . . . Pamela
• 0:09—Very brief partial buns in lingerie, while walking up to the bar.
• 1:12—Brief buns in lingerie in dressing room.
••• 1:14—Nude, while stripping and dancing on stage.

Video Tapes:

Hot Body Competition: Beverly Hills Hot Legs Contest (1997). . . . . Herself
All Nude Nikki (1998) . . . . Herself
••• 0:00—Nude throughout.

Novak, Lenka *

a.k.a. Hana Byrbo.

Films:

The Kentucky Fried Movie (1977) . . . . Linda Chambers
• 0:09—Breasts sitting on a couch with two other girls.
Coach (1978). . . . . Marilyn
• 0:10—Very brief breasts flashing her breasts along with her girlfriends for their boyfriends.

Vampire Hookers (1979) . . . . Suzy
•• 0:51—Breasts in bed during the orgy with the guy and the other two Vampire Hookers.
Cheerleaders Wild Weekend (1985) . . . . . . Jeanne/Darwell
••• 0:40—Breasts during contest after taking off white skirt, then blouse.
••• 0:41—Breasts with the other five girls during contest.
••• 0:43—Breasts, while getting measured with the other two girls, then getting attacked by Big John.
••• 0:44—Breasts getting into bathtub and getting washed by Frankie.
Video Tapes:
Terror on Tape (1985) . . . . Suzy
• 0:00—Breasts in scene from *Vampire Hookers.*

Nychols, Darcy

Adult film actress.
Films:
Mugsy's Girls (1985) . . . . Madame Antoinette
Slammer Girls (1987) . . . . Tank
• 0:17—Breasts ripping blouse open while hassling Melody.

Nygren, Mia *

Films:
Emmanuelle IV (1984) . . . . Emmanuelle IV
• 0:13—Buns, while lying on table after plastic surgery.
••• 0:15—Full frontal nudity walking around looking at her new self in the mirror.
• 0:20—Brief breasts a couple of times making love on top of a guy getting coached by Sylvia Kristel in dream-like sequence.
•• 0:22—Full frontal nudity taking off blouse in front of Dona.
••• 0:30—Nude undressing in front of Maria.
•• 0:39—Full frontal nudity taking her dress off and getting covered with a white sheet.
••• 0:40—Full frontal nudity lying down and then putting dress back on.
•• 0:45—Full frontal nudity during levitation trick.
• 0:52—Brief breasts in stable.
••• 0:54—Breasts taking off black dress in chair. Brief lower frontal nudity.
• 0:57—Brief lower frontal nudity, while putting on white panties.
• 1:00—Brief breasts when Susanna takes her dress off.
• 1:03—Brief right breast, while making love on ground with a boy.
••• 1:07—Breasts while walking on beach.
• 1:09—Breasts with Dona. Dark.
Plaza Real (1988) . . . . n.a.

O'Brien, Mariah

Films:
Gas, Food, Lodging (1992) . . . . .Ivy
Halloween: The Curse of Michael Myers (1995) . . . . Beth
• 0:58—Breasts, when leaning up in bed after making love with Tim.

O'Brien, Maureen

Films:
She'll be Wearing Pink Pyjamas (1985; British) . . . . . Joan
• 0:46—Brief breasts making love in bed with Tom. Dark.
Zina (1985; British) . . . . n.a.

O'Brien, Shauna *

a.k.a. Stevie Jean.
Films:
Another 48 Hrs. (1990) . . . . Uncredited Waitress
Flatliners (1990). . . . . One of Joe's Women
Seduce Me: Pamela Principle 2 (1994) . . . . Michelle
••• 0:15—Breasts and buns in G-string, after taking off lingerie for photo session.
Wild Malibu Weekend! (1994) . . . . Natalie Woodman
Friend of the Family (1995) . . . . Elke
a.k.a. Elke's Erotic Nights
(Unrated version reviewed.)
••• 0:25—Breasts and buns in panties, when dancing next to swimming pool at night, while Jeff watches from the house.
••• 0:39—In red, two piece swimsuit, then breasts with Jeff in Linda's dream.
• 0:43—Brief breasts, while getting out of bed.
••• 0:44—Full frontal nudity, while making love with Linda in bathtub. Nice, long scene.
••• 0:53—In white two piece swimsuit while dancing next to pool, then breasts and buns.
• 0:56—Buns in swimsuit, while next to pool, talking to Jeff.
••• 1:04—Nude, while making love with Jeff in bed.
• 1:14—Brief breasts and buns in swimsuit on TV when Josh shows his video work to Laura.
Over the Wire (1995) . . . . .Rachel
••• 0:20—Nude, while making love in bed with Mark, when seen by Susan. Long scene.
• 0:47—Breasts, while changing clothes in dressing room.
••• 1:01—Nude, while making love with Bruce in living room, then bathtub.
Body Armor (1996). . . . . .Beautiful Girl
•• 0:07—Breasts and buns in black panties, while getting fondled by John Rhys-Davies.
• 0:09—Buns in panties and brief breasts, while in bed on top of Rhys-Davies.
Friend of the Family 2 (1996) . . . . Linda
a.k.a. Innocence Betrayed
••• 0:08—In bra and panties, then buns and breasts, while making love with Alex.
•• 0:13—Buns and breasts, while making love with Alex.
••• 0:49—Nude, while making love in bed with Alex.
• 0:52—Brief buns in panties, while standing in bedroom in front of Alex.
• 0:55—Buns in panties, in room with Byron.
••• 0:57—In bra and panties, then nude, while making love with Byron.
••• 1:14—In bra and panties, then breasts and buns, while making love with Mark in office.
Fugitive Rage (1996) . . . . Josie Williams
Midnight Blue (1996) . . . . Sandra
A Passion for Murder (1996). . . . . Kirsty
a.k.a. Deadlock
•• 0:31—Buns in T-back, then breasts, while making love with Nick.
••• 0:45—In bra, then breasts and buns , while making love with Nick in barn.
The Escort (1997) . . . . Suzanne Lane
(Unrated version reviewed.)
Made for Cable TV:
Beverly Hills Bordello: Silence is Golden (1997; Showtime) . . . . Lily
••• 0:01—Breasts and buns, while lying on sofa, then making love with Doug.

- ••• 0:05—Breasts and very brief lower frontal nudity, while sitting in steam room and caressing Casey.
- ••• 0:09—Nude, while undressing and making love with Doug.
- • 0:16—Partial buns and brief breasts, while lying in steam room and talking to Casey.
- ••• 0:18—Nude, while caressing Casey, while Doug is tied up, then making love with him. Long scene.

Video Tapes:

Penthouse Satin & Lace II: Hollywood Undercover (1992). . . . . Pet

Penthouse Satin & Lace: An Erotic History of Lingerie (1992). . . . . Model

Rock Video Girls 2 (1992) . . . . . Herself
- ••• 0:33—Breasts in shower during music video.

Beverly Hills Workout (1993). . . . . Herself
- •• 0:00—Breasts and buns in T-back, while working out in backyard.
- ••• 0:22—Nude, while dancing and posing in backyard.
- •• 0:39—Nude, while posing outdoors.

Penthouse Pet of the Year Playoff 1993 (1993) . . . . . Pet
- ••• 0:42—Nude at the beach, in a warehouse, in bathroom while rubbing shaving cream on herself.

Hot Body Video Magazine #8: Hot Stuff (1994) . . . . . n.a.

Penthouse Pet of the Year Winners 1993: Mahalia & Julie (1994) . . . . . Sneak Preview of Pet of the Year Playoff
- ••• 0:31—Nude on stairs in empty building.

The Girls of Penthouse, Volume 3 (1995). . . . . Pet
- ••• 0:29—Nude in still photos.
- ••• 0:30—In lingerie, then nude in a liquor store.
- ••• 0:31—Nude, while working out on an exercise machine.
- ••• 0:33—Nude, while posing in a house.
- ••• 0:36—Nude, while posing on yellow stairs.

Penthouse Behind the Scenes (1995) . . . . . Pet
- ••• 0:00—Nude in various segments throughout the video tape.

Playboy's Rising Stars and Sexy Starlets (1996) . . . Herself
- • 0:55—Brief breasts from *Over the Wire.*
- ••• 0:56—Nude, while dancing in studio.

O'Byrne, Kehli

See: Burns, Kelly.

O'Connell, Natalie

Films:

Breeders (1986) . . . . . Donna
- • 0:02—Very brief left breast, getting her blouse ripped by creature.
- •• 0:44—Breasts, sitting up in hospital bed, then buns, walking down the hall.
- ••• 0:47—More breasts and buns, walking around outside.
- • 1:10—Brief breasts, standing up in the alien nest.

I Was a Teenage T.V. Terrorist (1987) . . . . . Woman on Audition Line

O'Connell, Taaffe

Films:

Rocky II (1979) . . . . . Ring Girl

Galaxy of Terror (1981). . . . . Damelia
- •• 0:42—Breasts getting raped by a giant alien slug. Nice and slimy.
- • 0:46—Buns, covered with slime being discovered by her crew mates.

New Year's Evil (1981). . . . . Jane

Caged Fury (1984) . . . . . Honey
- •• 0:17—Breasts on bed with a guard. Mostly left breast.
- • 0:40—Very, very brief tip of left breast peeking out between arms in shower.
- • 1:06—Very brief breasts getting blouse ripped open by a guard in the train.

Hot Chili (1985) . . . . . Brigitte
- ••• 0:21—Breasts while lying on the bed. Shot with lots of diffusion.
- • 0:30—Brief breasts while playing the drums.
- • 1:11—Brief breasts in bed while making love with Ernie, next to her drunk husband.

Not of This Earth (1988) . . . . . Damelia
- • 0:04—Brief breasts and buns from *Galaxy of Terror* during the opening credits.

TV:

Blansky's Beauties (1977). . . . . Hillary S. Prentiss

O'Connor, Glynnis

Films:

Baby Blue Marine (1976). . . . . Rose

Ode to Billy Joe (1976) . . . . . Bobby Lee Hartley

California Dreaming (1978) . . . . . Corky
- •• 0:11—Breasts pulling her top over her head when T.T. is using the bathroom.
- ••• 1:14—Breasts in bed with T.T.

Those Lips, Those Eyes (1980) . . . . . Ramona
- • 0:37—Left breast in car with Tom Hulce. Dark, hard to see.
- •• 1:12—Breasts and buns on bed with Tom Hulce. Dark.

Night Crossing (1981). . . . . Petra Wetzel

Melanie (1982) . . . . . Melanie
- • 0:08—Very brief right breast, while turning over in bed next to Don Johnson.
- •• 0:09—Breasts, while sitting up and putting on a T-shirt, then getting out of bed.

Made for TV Movies:

The Boy in the Plastic Bubble (1976). . . . . Gina

Why Me? (1984). . . . . Leola Mae Harmon

Death in Small Doses (1995). . . . . n.a.

TV:

As the World Turns . . . . . Margo Hughes

Sons and Daughters (1974). . . . . Anita Cramer

O'Grady, Gail

Films:

Blackout (1989). . . . . Caroline Boyle

Nobody's Perfect (1990). . . . . Shelly

Spellcaster (1992). . . . . Jackie

That Old Feeling (1997) . . . . . Rowena

Made for Cable Movies:

Two Voices (1997; Lifetime). . . . . Kathleen Anneken

Made for TV Movies:

Parker Kane (1990) . . . . . Cindy Kane

Nothing Lasts Forever (1995) . . . . . Dr. Paige Taylor

She Stood Alone: The Tailhook Scandal (1995) . . . . . Lieutenant Paula Coughlin

Trial by Fire (1995) . . . . . n.a.

Medusa's Child (1997) . . . . . Vivan Henry

The Three Lives of Karen (1997) . . . . . Karen/Emily

TV:

NYPD Blue (1993-96) . . . . . Donna Abandando

NYPD Blue: Abandando Abandoned (Jan 11, 1994) . . . . . Donna Abandando
- • 0:03—Brief back side of left breast, after dropping her robe in front of Metavoy.

O'Grady, Lani

Films:

Baby Blue Marine (1976). . . . . Girl #2

Massacre at Central High (1976) . . . . Jane

••• 1:09—Breasts walking out of a tent and getting back into it with Rainbeaux Smith and Robert Carradine.

The Campus Corpse (1977). . . . . Campus Girl

TV:

The Headmaster (1970-71) . . . . Judy

Eight is Enough (1977-81). . . . . Mary Bradford

O'Mara, Kate

Films:

The Horror of Frankenstein (1970; British) . . . . Alys

Vampire Lovers (1970; British). . . . . Madame Perrodot

The Tamarind Seed (1974; British). . . . . Anna Skriabina

Whose Child Am I? (1974; British). . . . . Barbara Martin

••• 0:00—Breasts and buns, while making love with her husband in bed.

•• 0:06—Breasts, while reading the newspaper in bed next to her husband.

••• 0:25—In bra, then nude, while in hospital room with Michael, then starting to make love with him to get pregnant.

••• 0:32—Nude, while in bathroom, then in bed with Michael.

TV:

Dynasty (1986) . . . . Caress Morell

O'Neal, Tatum *

Ex-wife of tennis player John McEnroe.

Daughter of actor Ryan O'Neal and actress Joanna Moore.

Films:

Paper Moon (1973). . . . . Addie Loggins

(Academy Award for Best Supporting Actress.)

The Bad News Bears (1976). . . . . Manda Whurlizer

International Velvet (1978; British). . . . . Sarah Brown

Circle of Two (1980). . . . . Sarah Norton

•• 0:56—Breasts standing behind a chair in Richard Burton's studio talking to him.

Little Darlings (1980) . . . . Ferris

• 0:35—Very, very brief half of left nipple, sticking out of swimsuit top when she comes up for air after falling into the pool to get Armand Assante's attention.

Certain Fury (1985). . . . . Scarlet

Basquiat (1996). . . . . Cynthia Kruger

Made for TV Movies:

Woman on the Run: The Lawrencia Bembenek Story (1993) . . . . Lawrencia "Bambi" Bembenek

• O'Neil, Linda

Made for Cable TV:

Hot Springs Hotel: Travels with Travis (1998; Showtime) . . . . Molly

••• 0:01—Breasts and brief buns, while making love with Randy in bathttub, then the shower, then in bed.

Video Tapes:

Playboy's Hot Wheels & High Heels Biker Babes (1997) . . . . The Presentation

••• 0:30—Nude, while posing on motorcycle during sales presentation.

O'Neill, Maggie

Films:

Gorillas in the Mist (1988). . . . . Kim

Under Suspicion (1992) . . . . Hazel

• 0:02—Breasts and lower frontal nudity in shower with Liam Neeson.

• 0:03—Very brief right breast, while ducking to avoid shotgun blast.

All Men are Mortal (1995; British/Dutch/French) . . . . . Florence

O'Neill, Remy

Films:

Angel of H.E.A.T. (1981) . . . . Andrea Shockley

a.k.a. The Protectors, Book I

•• 0:43—Breasts, wearing a blue swimsuit, wrestling in the mud with Mary Woronov.

Erotic Images (1983) . . . . Vickie Coleman

••• 0:04—Breasts while sitting in chaise lounge talking to Britt Ekland about sex survey. Long scene.

• 0:06—Breasts while in bed with Marvin. Brief lower frontal nudity.

•• 0:07—Brief left breast while in spa with TV repairman, then brief breasts.

Hollywood Hot Tubs (1984) . . . . Pam Landers

• 1:00—Brief right breast in hot tub with Jeff.

Return to Horror High (1987) . . . . Esther Molvania

To Die For (1988) . . . . Jane

Hollywood Hot Tubs 2—Educating Crystal (1989) . . . . Pam Landers

The Forbidden Dance (1990). . . . . Robin

To Die For 2 (1991) . . . . Jane

a.k.a. Son of Darkness: To Die For II

O'Reilly, Erin

Films:

How Sweet It Is (1968) . . . . Tour Girl

Little Fauss and Big Halsy (1970). . . . . Sylvene McFall

• 0:11—Brief left breast, while sleeping in bed with the photographer.

T. R. Baskin (1971). . . . . Kathy

Blume in Love (1973). . . . . Cindy

•• 0:40—Breasts and buns, getting out of and back in bed with George Segal. Very brief buns, when crawling over the bed.

Busting (1974). . . . . Doris

O'Reilly, Kathryn

Films:

Jack's Back (1987) . . . . Hooker

Puppet Master (1989) . . . . Carissa Stamford

• 0:41—Left breast in bathtub, covered with bubbles.

• 0:43—Brief left breast getting out of tub. Nipple covered with bubbles.

• 1:11—Right breast under sheer black nightgown, dead sitting at the table. Blood on her face.

O'Shea, Missy

Films:

Blow Out (1981) . . . . Dancing Coed

New York Nights (1981). . . . . The Model

•• 0:37—in black bra, panties, garter belt and stockings then breasts taking off bra and getting into bed.

•• 0:40—Breasts while on the floor when the photographer throws her on the floor and rips her bra off.

••• 0:41—Full frontal nudity putting bathrobe on.

• 0:44—Breasts while standing in front of a mirror with short black hair and a mustache getting dressed to look like a guy.

Model Behavior (1982) . . . . Anne #1
••• 0:40—Breasts, while taking off her top after the other Anne in front of Dino.

O'Toole, Annette *

Films:

Smile (1974) . . . . Doria Houston
One on One (1977) . . . . Janet Hays
King of the Gypsies (1978) . . . . Sharon
Foolin' Around (1980) . . . . Susan
48 Hrs. (1982) . . . . Elaine
Cat People (1982) . . . . Alice Perrin
••• 1:30—In a bra, then breasts undressing in locker room.
• 1:31—Some breasts shots of her in the pool. Distorted because of the water.
• 1:33—Brief right breast, after getting out of the pool.
Superman III (1983) . . . . Lana Lang
Cross My Heart (1987) . . . . Kathy
•• 0:46—Left breast, in bed with Short.
•• 0:48—Breasts in bed when Short heads under the covers.
•• 0:49—Brief breasts again getting her purse.
• 1:05—Brief breasts and buns, dressing after Short finds out about her daughter.
Love at Large (1990) . . . . Mrs. King
Imaginary Crimes (1994) . . . . Ginny Rucklehaus

Made for Cable Movies:

Best Legs in the 8th Grade (1984; HBO) . . . . Rachel Blackstone
Love Matters (1993; Showtime) . . . . Julie
(Unrated version reviewed.)
Directed By: On Hope (1994; Showtime) . . . . Hope

Made for Cable TV:

Dream On: Bess You is Not My Woman Now (1995; HBO) . . . . Bess
The Outer Limits: Dark Matters (1995; Showtime) . . . . Commander Lydia Manning

Miniseries:

The Kennedys of Massachusetts (1990) . . . . Rose Fitzgerald

Made for TV Movies:

Love for Rent (1979) . . . . Carol Martin
Stand by Your Man (1981) . . . . Tammy Wynette
The Dreamer of Oz (1990) . . . . Maud
Stephen King's "It" (1990) . . . . Beverly Marsh
Danielle Steel's "Jewels" (1992) . . . . Sarah
Kiss of a Killer (1993) . . . . n.a.
Mother's Revenge (1993) . . . . Ellen Wells
The Christmas Box (1995) . . . . Keri Evans
Dead by Sunset (1995) . . . . Cheryl
My Brother's Keeper (1995) . . . . Joann
The Man Next Door (1996) . . . . Annie Hopkins
Keeping the Promise (1997) . . . . n.a.

TV:

Nash Bridges (1996-97) . . . . Lisa Bridges

Oberman, Claire

Films:

Goodbye Pork Pie (1980; New Zealand) . . . . Shirl
•• 0:46—Breasts while in freight car with Gerry.
Patriot Games (1992) . . . . Lady Holmes

Made for TV Movies:

To Be The Best (1992) . . . . Sarah

Obregon, Ana

Films:

Bolero (1984) . . . . Catalina Terry
• 1:32—Brief breasts making love with Robert.
Killing Machine (1986; Spanish/Mexican) . . . . Liza

Oddo, Lynn

Films:

Hero (1992) . . . . Buxom Woman
Dead On (1993) . . . . Lisa
(Unrated version reviewed.)
•• 1:00—Breasts, while getting dressed after spending the night in Matt McCoy's bed.

Made for Cable Movies:

Virtual Seduction (1995; Showtime) . . . . Woman at Restaurant

• Offner, Deborah

Films:

Ghost Story (1981) . . . . Helen
Soup for One (1982) . . . . Girl in Neon Bedroom
Key Exchange (1985) . . . . Chiropractor Woman
Streetwalkin' (1985) . . . . Heather
Project X (1987) . . . . Carol Lee
Crossing Delancey (1988) . . . . Karen
Immediate Family (1989) . . . . Kathy
True Believer (1989) . . . . Laura Gayley
Unlawful Entry (1992) . . . . Penny
Love Field (1993) . . . . Police Dispatcher

Made for Cable TV:

Women: Stories of Passion-Woman on a Train
(1997; Showtime) . . . . Carolyn
• 0:02—Brief right breast, seen in window of train during her fantasy.
• 0:04—Brief nipple flash in fantasy.
• 0:05—Breast, during fantasy while listening to headphones.
• 0:08—Very brief right breast, during fantasy.
•• 0:11—Breasts, while making love with Nicky in fantasy.
••• 0:18—Breasts and buns, while making love with Nicky on the floor in fantasy.
•• 0:21—Right breast and partial buns in panties, while making love with Nicky in restroom on train in fantasy.

Ogle, Natalie

Films:

Joseph Andrews (1977; British/French) . . . . Fanny
• 1:15—Very brief side of left breast, getting her blouse ripped off to get flogged.
•• 1:20—Breasts while hugging Joseph Andrews after he beats up the guy who was attacking her.
•• 1:21—Right breast while walking, then breasts after taking off her blouse in front of Joseph.
•• 1:35—Breasts, after undressing and getting into bed.
The Stud (1978; British) . . . . Maddy

Ohana, Claudia *

Films:

Luzia . . . . Luzia
• 1:11—Breasts, while swimming in the lake. Brief lower frontal nudity and brief buns, partially visible under water.
• 1:12—Nude, while getting out of the water when Tereza talks with her.
•• 1:26—Breasts, while squatting in corner of room and washing herself off with water from a bowl, then putting on blouse.
• 1:28—Brief left breast in open blouse with a guy.
Erendira (1983; Brazilian) . . . . Erendira
• 0:14—Breasts while getting fondled by a guy against her will.

- •• 0:26—Breasts while lying in bed sweating and crying after having to have sex with an army of men.
- ••• 1:04—Breasts while lying in bed sleeping.
- • 1:08—Brief breasts while getting out of bed. Long shot, hard to see.
- •• 1:24—Breasts and buns while on bed with Ulysses.

Priceless Beauty (1989; Italian) . . . . Lisa
Erotique (1993). . . . . .Final Call
- • 0:59—Brief partial breasts in bra and partial buns in panties, while tied by her wrists by a couple of bad guys.
- ••• 1:10—Breasts and buns, when carried to the bed, making love and sitting in bed afterwards.
- •• 1:20—Nude, while making love again.

Olin, Lena

Films:

Fanny and Alexander (1983; Swedish/French/German) . . . Rosa
After the Rehearsal (1984; Swedish) . . . . Anna Egerman
The Unbearable Lightness of Being (1988) . . . . . . .Sabina
- •• 0:03—Breasts in bed with Daniel Day Lewis, then while looking in a mirror.
- • 0:27—Brief back side of right breast and upper half of buns, while making love in bed with Lewis.
- •• 1:29—Breasts and buns while Juliette Binoche photographs her.
- • 1:43—Very brief left breast, in bed with Lewis.
- • 2:32—Brief breasts in B&W photo found in a drawer by Lewis.

Enemies, A Love Story (1989). . . . . .Masha
- •• 0:16—In white bra, then brief breasts several times in bed with Ron Silver. Breasts again after making love and starting to make love again.

Havana (1990) . . . . Bobby Duran
Mr. Jones (1993) . . . . Libbie
Romeo Is Bleeding (1994). . . . . Mona Demakov
- •• 1:20—Breasts under leather outfit with fake arm.
- •• 1:22—More breasts in the leather outfit.
- • 1:29—Buns in sexy black bodysuit.

The Night and the Moment (1997). . . . . .n.a.
Night Falls on Manhattan (1997) . . . . .Peggy Lindstrom

• *Olivan, Leslie*

Films:

Exposé (1997) . . . . .Bianca
- • 0:33—Brief breasts, while having sex with Shapiro on sofa in video playback.
- • 0:35—Full frontal nudity, while dancing with a guy. Seen on television during video playback.

Video Tapes:

Playboy's Twins & Sisters Too (1997) . . . . . . Special Touch
- ••• 0:13—Nude with her sister in bathtub segment.

Oliver, Anne Marie

Films:

Spring Fever USA (1988) . . . . .Rita Durango
a.k.a. Lauderdale
- •• 1:02—Breasts, during wet T-shirt contest.

Summer Job (1989). Kathy's Friend #2

Oliver, Leslie

Films:

The Student Teachers (1973). . . . . .n.a.
Thunderbolt and Lightfoot (1974) . . . . Teenage Girl
- •• 1:16—Brief breasts in bed when robbers break in and George Kennedy watches her.
- • 1:31—Brief buns, tied up with her boyfriend in bed.

Venice/Venice (1992). . . . . .Guest at Party

Oliver, Pita

Films:

Deadly Companion (1979; Canadian) . . . . Lorraine
- • 0:14—Very brief left breast, then very brief breasts sitting up in bed during Michael Sarrazin's daydream. Dark.
- • 1:32—Brief full frontal nudity, dead on bed when Susan Clark comes into the bedroom.

Prom Night (1980) . . . . Vicki
- •• 0:35—Brief buns, mooning Mr. Sykes outside of tennis court.

*Olivia, Lorraine **

Video Tapes:

Playboy Video Calendar 1992 (1991) . . . . May
- ••• 0:18—Full frontal nudity in the desert.
- ••• 0:19—Nude in Egyptian bed fantasy.

Playboy Video Centerfold: Lisa Matthews (1991)
. . . . .Playmate
- ••• 0:28—Nude in the desert, then washing an old car, then on an airplane, then in Egyptian style bedroom.

Playboy's Sexy, Steamy, Sultry (1993) . . . . .Playmate
Playboy's Women of Color (1994) . . . . .Playmate
- ••• 0:04—Nude in motion and in still photos in flight attendant in and out of uniform on airplane set.
- ••• 0:06—Nude out in the desert and washing an old car.
- ••• 0:08—Nude in lighted bed.

*Ono, Yoko **

Wife of the late singer John Lennon.

Films:

Imagine: John Lennon (1988). . . . . Herself
- • 0:43—Nude in B&W photos from John Lennon's "Two Virgins" album.
- • 0:57—Brief full frontal nudity from album cover again during an interview.

*Oreskovich, Alesha **

Video Tapes:

Playboy Video Calendar 1994 (1993) . . . . February
- ••• 0:06—Breasts and buns, posing in a big "O" prop.
- ••• 0:08—Nude, undressing and dancing in an alley.

Playboy's Sexy, Steamy, Sultry (1993) . . . . .Playmate
The Making of the 1995 Sport Magazine Swimsuit Issue (1994)
. . . . Herself
Playboy's Girls of the Internet (1996). . . . . Herself
- ••• 0:10—Nude, while at the beach (she's the brunette one) with two other women.

• *Orgolini, Lisa*

Films:

Trick or Treat (1986) . . . . .Leslie Graham
Born to Ride (1992). . . . . Claire Tate
Shining Through (1992) . . . . Girl in Canteen
Two Deaths (1994; British) . . . . Young Ana
- • 0:29—Brief breasts, when sitting up in bed when the young Daniel visits her at night.
- •• 1:09—Nude after undressing in young Daniel's medical office.

Made for Cable Movies:

Stalin (1992; HBO) . . . . .Anya Larina

Ormond, Julia
Films:
The Baby of Mâcon (1993; British/French) . . . . . . .Daughter
(Not available in the U.S. yet.)
••• 0:49—Breasts and buns, while starting to make love with Ralph Fiennes, then nude after bad things happen. Long scene. Sometimes has blood on her.
Nostradamus (1993) . . . . Marie
••• 0:34—Left breast, several times, while making love in bed with Tcheky Karyo.
Captives (1994; British). . . . . .Rachel Clifford
Legends of the Fall (1994) . . . . Susannah
• 0:56—Very brief right breast, while making love with Brad Pitt in bed.
First Knight (1995) . . . . Guinevere
Sabrina (1995) . . . . Sabrina Fairchild
Smilla's Sense of Snow (1997) . . . . .Smilla Jaspersen
• 1:06—Brief, partial buns, while lying on top of Gabriel Byrne.
Made for Cable Movies:
Young Catherine (1991; TNT). . . . . Catherine
Stalin (1992; HBO) . . . . .Nadya

Otis, Carré *
Model.
Ex-wife of actor Mickey Rourke.
Films:
Wild Orchid (1990) . . . . Emily Reed
•• 0:51—Left breast in mirror looking at herself while getting dressed.
••• 1:01—Breasts when a guy takes off her dress while Mickey Rourke watches.
••• 1:02—Right breast, then breasts while on the floor with Bruce Greenwood.
• 1:31—Brief breasts in flashback with Greenwood.
• 1:42—Breasts while opening her blouse for Rourke.
••• 1:44—Nude while making love with Rourke. Nice and sweaty.
Exit in Red (1996) . . . . Kate

Overbey, Kellie
Films:
Defenseless (1991). . . . . Janna Seldes
••• 0:58—Brief breasts, nonchalantly changing into swimsuit at the beach.
•• 1:22—Breasts, while posing on bed with her father in video playback.
Outbreak (1995). . . . . Alice
Miniseries:
Stephen King's "The Stand" (1994). . . . . .Dayna Jurgens
Made for TV Movies:
Wife, Mother, Murderer: The Marie Hilley Story (1991)
. . . . Carol Hilley
TV:
These Are the Days (1998-) . . . . .n.a.

• Overbye Roos, Camilla
Films:
White Squall (1995) . . . . Bregita
Vicious Circles (1997) . . . . Helga
(Unrated version reviewed.)
•• 0:10—Breasts, while sitting in steam room with Carolyn Lowry.

Owen, Rena
Films:
Once Were Warriors (1994; New Zealand) . . . . . . Beth Heke
• 0:29—Brief side view of left breast, while sitting up in bed.
Rapa Nui (1994) . . . . .Hitirenga
• 0:19—Breasts, while in the river with the other women.

Owens, Susie *
Films:
They Bite (1991) . . . . Kate
• 1:01—Right breast, while lying on the beach after getting attacked.
••• 1:02—Breasts and buns, while in bed on top of a guy before killing him.
Video Tapes:
Playboy Video Calendar 1989 (1988) . . . . August
••• 0:29—Nude.
Wet & Wild (1989) . . . . .Model
Playmates at Play (1990) . . . . Gotta Dance
If I'm So Famous, How Come Nobody's Ever Heard of Me? (1996) . . . . Herself
• 0:17—Breasts in still photo she shows during convention.
Playboy's 21 Playmates: Volume II (1996) . . . . . .Playmate
••• 0:14—Full frontal nudity in still photos.
••• 0:14—Nude, while dancing in various settings to country music.

Pace, Judy
Films:
The Fortune Cookie (1966) . . . . .Elvira
The Thomas Crown Affair (1968). . . . . Pretty Girl
Three in the Attic (1968) . . . . Eulice
Cotton Comes to Harlem (1970) . . . . Iris
•• 0:28—Buns and breasts, taking off dress and getting into shower.
••• 0:29—Breasts and buns while getting out of the shower.
• 0:30—Upper half of breasts in mirror while sitting at vanity.
••• 0:31—Brief breasts, unwrapping from towel and lying on bed. Breasts, when lying in bed. Breasts and buns while getting out of bed.
Cool Breeze (1972) . . . . .Obalese Eaton
Frogs (1972) . . . . Bella
TV:
The Young Lawyers (1970-71). . . . . Pat Walters

Pacula, Joanna
Films:
Gorky Park (1983) . . . . Irina
•• 1:20—Brief breasts in bed making love with William Hurt.
Not Quite Paradise (1986; British) . . . . .Gila
a.k.a. Not Quite Jerusalem
• 1:04—Left breast, lying in bed with Sam Robards.
Death Before Dishonor (1987). . . . . .Elli
The Kiss (1988) . . . . Felice
•• 0:49—Side view breasts making love with a guy. Inter cut with Meredith Salenger seeing a model of a body spurt blood.
• 0:57—Breasts covered with body paint doing a ceremony in a hotel room.
•• 1:24—Brief right breast, while making love with a guy on bed while Salenger is asleep in the other room.
Sweet Lies (1989) . . . . .Joëlle
Marked for Death (1990). . . . . .Leslie

Husbands and Lovers (1991; Italian) . . . . Helena
(Unrated version reviewed.)
••• 0:03—Breasts, making love on top of Julian Sands in bed. Left breast, while lying in bed after.
••• 0:10—Nude, walking around and getting into bed with Sands.
••• 0:18—Breasts in bathroom, brushing her teeth, then getting dressed.
••• 0:32—Buns and breasts, getting into the shower with Sands.
• 0:35—Brief breasts getting into bed.
•• 0:37—Breasts in white panties, putting on stockings.
•• 0:59—Buns, getting spanked by Paolo.
••• 1:17—Buns, then breasts making love in bed with Sands. Nude getting out of bed.
• 1:19—Brief breasts, putting on stockings, then white bra and panties.
• 1:21—Buns, in greenhouse with Paolo when he beats her.
Black Ice (1992; U.S./Canadian) . . . . Vanessa
(Nude scenes are a body double.)
Body Puzzle (1992) . . . . Tracy
Every Breath (1992) . . . . Lauren
• 0:21—Very, very brief right breast in jacket while kissing Judd Nelson in bedroom.
••• 0:36—Brief back side of right breast, then breasts while kissing Nelson outside by pool.
0:43—In black bra and panties in bedroom with Bob.
••• 1:10—Breasts and buns while in the shower.
Eyes of the Beholder (1992) . . . . Diana Carlyle
Private Lessons II (1993; Japanese) . . . . Sophie Morgan
•• 0:26—Buns, when getting out of swimming pool.
• 0:55—Buns, while lying in bed next to Ken.
Silence of the Hams (1993) . . . . Lily
Tombstone (1993) . . . . Kate
Warlock: The Armageddon (1993) . . . . Paula Darc
Deep Red (1994) . . . . Monica Qwik
Demolition Day (1995) . . . . Brenda Franelli
Last Gasp (1995) . . . . Nora Weeks
• 0:20—Brief right breast, twice, during dream while making love with her husband.
TimeMaster (1995) . . . . Evelyn
Captain Nuke and the Bomber Kids (1996) . . . . Brenda Franelli
Made for Cable Movies:
36 Hours (1989) . . . . n.a.
Breaking Point (1989) . . . . Nurse
Not Like Us (1995; Showtime) . . . . Anita
Made for TV Movies:
Condition: Critical (1992) . . . . Dr. Lena Poole
TV:
E.A.R.T.H. Force (1990) . . . . Diana Randall

• Padilla Sánchez, Marisol

Films:
The End of Violence (1997; French/German/U.S.) . . . . Mathilda
L.A. Confidential (1997) . . . . Inez Soto (Rape Victim)
• 0:57—Brief breasts, while gagged and tied to bed. She's bruised and bloodied, so it's not a pretty sight.

Paes, Dira *

Films:
The Emerald Forest (1985) . . . . Kachiri
•• 0:24—Brief buns while running from waterfall and diving into the pond.
• 0:33—Breasts while in water talking to Tommy.
• 0:56—Left breast in courtyard when Tommy proposes marriage to her.
• 0:57—Left breast in forest with Tommy. Long shot.
•• 1:01—Breasts, by the river.
•• 1:04—Breasts and buns during wedding ceremony.
•• 1:16—Breasts with the other tribe women after being captured by the fierce people.
• 1:18—Breasts with the other girls being herded into the building.
•• 1:38—Breasts, in forest taking off clothes.
• 1:40—Buns, returning to the forest.
• 1:48—Breasts while in the river.

Page, Amy

See: Ager, Suzanne.

Pai, Sue Francis *

a.k.a. Suzie Pai.
Films:
Sharky's Machine (1981) . . . . Siakwan
Big Trouble in Little China (1986) . . . . Miao Yin
Jakarta (1988) . . . . Esha
• 1:01—Brief right breast, while making love in the courtyard with Falco.
• 1:13—Brief side of right breast while kissing Falco.
•• 1:13—Side view of right breast, then brief breasts twice, making love under a mosquito net with Falco. Hard to see her face clearly.
TV:
Tattingers (1988-89) . . . . Billie Low

Paige, Kym *

Films:
Beverly Hills Cop II (1987) . . . . Playboy Playmate
Mortuary Academy (1988) . . . . Nurse
Video Tapes:
Playboy Video Calendar 1988 (1987) . . . . Playmate
Playboy Video Magazine, Volume 12 (1987)
. . . . Music Video
••• 0:55—Full frontal nudity.
Playmates at Play (1990) . . . . Hoops
The Best of Video Playmate Calendars (1992) . . . Playmate
•• 0:14—In lingerie during bedroom fantasy, then breasts and buns.
Playboy's 21 Playmates: Volume II (1996) . . . . . . Playmate
••• 1:10—Nude in still photos.
••• 1:11—Nude, while doing various things in studio loft.

• Pailhas, Géraldine

Films:
IP5 (1992; French) . . . . Gloria
Don Juan DeMarco (1994) . . . . Doña Ana
Suite 16 (1996) . . . . Helen
• 1:20—Brief right breast when Chris caresses her while Pete Postlethwaite watches.

Paine, Bonnie

Films:
Ninja Academy (1990) . . . . Nudist
• 0:26—Brief buns and breasts playing volleyball. (She's the second blonde on the far side of the net who misses the ball.)
Repo Jake (1990) . . . . R.V. Girl
•• 0:28—Breasts (mostly left breast) while in R.V. with her boyfriend.
•• 0:29—More breasts, while making love with him.

Twisted Justice (1990). . . . . Hooker
•• 0:11—Breasts, wearing black panties and stockings, while getting photographed.

Paine, Heidi

Films:

Emmanuelle 5 (1986). . . . . Girl No. 1
••• 0:42—Breasts, while talking with the two other girls. Wearing a red turban.
•• 0:44—Breasts, while drinking champagne with the other harem girls.

Wildest Dreams (1987) . . . . Dancee
• 0:23—Breasts, while being held in the arms of a gladiator in Bobby's bedroom.

Glitch (1988) . . . . Cake Lady

New York's Finest (1988). . . . . Carley Pointer
• 0:04—Brief breasts with a bunch of hookers.
• 0:36—Breasts with her two friends doing push-ups on the floor.

Nudity Required (1989) . . . . .Jane

Roadhouse (1989). . . . . Party Girl

Skin Deep (1989) . . . . .Tina
• 0:01—Brief side view breasts sitting on John Ritter's lap while Denise Crosby watches.

Wizards of the Demon Sword (1990) . . . . .Melina
a.k.a. Demon Sword
• 0:39—Left breast, while lying with Thane, then trying to stab him with a knife.

Alien Seed (1991) . . . . n.a.

Video Tapes:

In Search of the Perfect 10 (1986) . . . . Perfect Girl #8
••• 0:45—Brief breasts pulling down her top outside of car.

Palance, Holly

Daughter of actor Jack Palance.

Films:

Tuxedo Warrior (1970) . . . . Sally
•• 0:32—Breasts, while making love in bed with Cliff.
• 0:40—Brief breasts, while putting on a robe.
•• 0:55—Breasts, while in bed with Cliff.

The Omen (1976). . . . . .Nanny

Under Fire (1983) . . . . .Journalist

The Best of Times (1986) .Elly Dundee

Miniseries:

The Thorn Birds (1983). . . . . Miss Carmichael

Made for TV Movies:

Cast the First Stone (1989) . . . . .Ellen Armstrong

TV:

Ripley's Believe It or Not (1983-85) . . . . .Co-Host

Pallenberg, Anita

Films:

A Degree of Murder (1967). . . . . Marie

Barbarella (1968; French/Italian) . . . . .The Black Queen

Candy (1968) . . . . Nurse Bullock

Performance (1970). . . . . Pherber
• 0:44—Side view of left breast, while in bed with Mick Jagger.
••• 0:47—Breasts and buns, while in bathtub with Lucy and Jagger.
• 0:50—Buns, injecting herself with drugs.
•• 1:20—Right breast, while lying on the floor. Then breasts and buns, in bed with Chas.

Pallett, Lori Deann *

Films:

Summer's Games (1987) . . . . .Torch Carrier
• 0:00—Half breasts running in short T-shirt carrying torch.
•• 0:04—Breasts opening her swimsuit top after contest. (2nd place winner.)

Screwball Hotel (1988) . . . . .Candy
••• 0:26—Breasts in the shower while Herbie is accidentally in there with her.

Video Tapes:

Mermaid's Illustrated. . . . . .n.a.

How to Fill a Wild Wet T-shirt (1986) . . . . .Lori from Dallas
••• 0:16—Breasts while dancing on stage, then being interviewed backstage with two other topless girls.
•• 0:28—Breasts during quiz time.
••• 0:43—Breasts dancing during semi-finals.
••• 0:45—Breasts dancing during finals.
••• 0:46—Breasts dancing as the winner.
•• 0:48—Breasts during final credits "report card."

Daydreams (1988) . . . . Lori
••• 0:01—Breasts cleaning sail boat. Long scene.
••• 0:03—Breasts on sail boat during daydream.
• 0:09—Brief breasts, sitting up on lounge chair when beer is spilled on her back.
•• 0:10—Breasts, while sitting on a bar during beer daydream.
••• 0:13—Breasts in kitchen after spilling whipped cream on herself.
••• 0:14—Breasts and buns, getting into bathtub.
••• 0:16—Nude, in bathtub during daydream.
••• 0:20—Breasts in open tuxedo jacket during dance number.
••• 0:21—More breasts during end credits.

The Best of the Mermaids (1992) . . . . . The Snakecharmer
••• 1:05—Breasts while scuba diving, posing on boat and at the beach. Buns in swimsuit.

Hot Body International: #3 Lingerie Special (1992)
. . . . Contestant
•• 0:21—Buns in G-string and black top.

Hot Body International: #5 Miss Acapulco (1992)
. . . . Contestant
•• 0:26—Buns, while dancing in two piece swimsuit.

Mermaids of the Aztec Empire (1992) . . . . . Carla Monroe
•• 0:01—Breasts scuba diving under water during the opening credits.
••• 0:04—Breasts, wearing swimsuit bottom, posing for photographer outside by pool.
•• 0:06—Breasts outside by pool and under water.
••• 0:13—Breasts on boat.
••• 0:15—Breasts and buns in swimsuit bottom while scuba diving under water.
•• 0:19—Full frontal nudity during disco fantasy.
••• 0:23—Breasts and buns at the beach. Long scene.
••• 0:33—Breasts, while snorkeling under water.
••• 0:37—Breasts and buns at the beach again.
••• 0:41—Breasts, while scuba diving.
••• 0:45—Breasts in spa by herself, then with a girlfriend.
••• 0:49—Breasts and buns, wearing swimsuit bottom, undressing at the beach during the end credits.

BabeWatch, Episode 3: Sex Kittens (1994)
. . . . Lori Deann Pallett
•• 0:09—Breasts, while on sailboat.
••• 0:49—Breasts and buns, while in bubble bath.

Palme, Beatrice

Films:

Foxtrap (1986; U.S./Italian) . . . . Marianna
•• 0:41—Brief breasts and buns in bed with Fred Williamson, then more breasts making love.

Cinema Paradiso (1988; Italian/French) . . . . n.a.

The Sleazy Uncle (1991; Italian) . . . . Singer

Palmer, Gretchen

One of the three Diet Pepsi Uh-huh! Girls (1992-1995).

Films:

The Malibu Bikini Shop (1985) . . . . Woman

Crossroads (1986) . . . . Beautiful Girl/Dancer

Red Heat (1988) . . . . Hooker
• 1:20—Breasts and buns in hotel during shoot out.

Chopper Chicks in Zombietown (1989) . . . . Rusty

When Harry Met Sally... (1989) . . . . Stewardess

I Got The Hook Up (1998) . . . . Lorraine

Made for Cable Movies:

Alien Avengers (1996; Showtime) . . . . Melissa Rose
a.k.a. Welcome to Planet Earth

Made for Cable TV:

Bedtime (1996; Showtime) . . . . Nikki

Dream On: The Way We War (1996; HBO) . . . . . Foxy Lady #2

Tales From the Crypt: Ear Today... Gone Tomorrow (1996; HBO) . . . . Kate
••• 0:13—Breasts and buns, trying to seduce Glenn.

Bedtime: Episode 1 (1996; Showtime) . . . . Nikki
• 0:19—Brief breasts in gaping blouse.
• 0:27—Very brief side view of right breast, turning around to talk to Mark.

Bedtime: Episode 2 (1996; Showtime) . . . . Nikki
•• 0:19—Partial buns in T-back and breasts, while kneeling on top of Mark on bed.

Bedtime: Episode 3 (1996; Showtime) . . . . Nikki
• 0:20—Partial buns, while straddling Mark in bed.

Bedtime: Episode 4 (1996; Showtime) . . . . Nikki
• 0:23—Side of right breast, after dropping her towel.

Bedtime: Episode 6 (1996; Showtime) . . . . Nikki
•• 0:14—Brief breasts, after taking off her top in front of Mark.

Bedtime: Episode 7 (1996; Showtime) . . . . Nikki
••• 0:11—Brief left breast, while in bed (dark), then breasts and buns walking around after smoke alarm goes off. Long scene.

Bedtime: Episode 8 (1996; Showtime) . . . . Nikki

Bedtime: Episode 10 (1996; Showtime) . . . . Nikki
• 0:08—Very brief lower half of buns, under short nightie, while running to greet Mark.

Bedtime: Episode 12 (1996; Showtime) . . . . Nikki
••• 0:12—Breasts, while making love in bed, talking on the phone. Long scene.

Bedtime: Episode 13 (1996; Showtime) . . . . Nikki
••• 0:27—Breasts, while lying in bed after making love with Mark.

Perversions of Science: Dream of Doom (1997; HBO) . . . . Various Personalities
• 0:07—Brief breasts, when getting out of the shower. Brief breasts, when flashing David Carradine.
• 0:15—Buns and breasts, while dancing on stage in bar. More in background.

TV:

Robin's Hoods (1994-95) . . . . K.T.

Palmer, Jacqueline

Films:

Glitch (1988) . . . . Extra

Party Plane (1988) . . . . Suzie
••• 0:06—Breasts and buns changing clothes and getting into spa with her two girlfriends. (She's the dark haired one.)
••• 0:11—Breasts again, getting out of spa.
••• 0:23—In bra, then breasts doing strip tease routine on plane.
•• 0:35—Breasts doing another routine on the plane.

Sensations (1988) . . . . Tess

Roadhouse (1989) . . . . Party Girl

Repo Jake (1990) . . . . Porn Gal
••• 0:47—Breasts and buns, while on bed, acting in a movie.

Camp Fear (1991) . . . . n.a.
a.k.a. Millenium Countdown

Legal Tender (1991) . . . . Mal's Girl
• 0:24—Breasts in bubble bath with blonde girl and Morton Downey Jr.
•• 0:31—Breasts outside by the swimming pool.

Paltrow, Gwyneth *

Daughter of actress Blythe Danner and producer/director Bruce Paltrow.

Films:

Hook (1991) . . . . Wendy

Shout (1991) . . . . Rebecca

Flesh and Bone (1993) . . . . Ginnie
•• 1:09—Left breast, while in motel room, talking with Meg Ryan.

Malice (1993) . . . . Paula Bell

Mrs. Parker and the Vicious Circle (1994) . . . . Paula Hunt
• 1:02—Breasts, while sitting in bed when she's discovered by Jennifer Jason Leigh in Matthew Broderick's apartment.

Jefferson in Paris (1995) . . . . Patsy Jefferson

Moonlight and Valentino (1995) . . . . Lucy Trager
• 1:15—Right half of buns, after dropping robe in front of her sister because she's insecure about how her body looks. Very, very brief back part of right breast when bending down to pick up her robe. Don't see her face.

Seven (1995) . . . . Tracy

Emma (1996; British/U.S.) . . . . Emma Woodhouse

Hard Eight (1996) . . . . Clementine

The Pallbearer (1996) . . . . Julie Demarco

Great Expectations (1997) . . . . Estella

Hush (1998) . . . . Helen

A Perfect Murder (1998) . . . . Emily Taylor

Made for TV Movies:

Cruel Doubt (1992) . . . . Angela Pritchard

Deadly Relations (1993) . . . . Carol

Paluzzi, Luciana

Films:

Muscle Beach Party (1964) . . . . Julie

Thunderball (1965; British) . . . . Fiona Volpe

99 Women (1969) . . . . Nathalie

Black Gunn (1972) . . . . Toni

Manhunt (1973) . . . . Eva
a.k.a. The Italian Connection.

The Klansman (1974) . . . . Trixie

The Sensuous Nurse (1975; Italian) . . . . Jole Carpa
•• 0:20—Breasts in room, ripping off her clothes and reluctantly making love with Benito.

The Greek Tycoon (1978) . . . . Paola Scotti

Papanicolas, Tanya

Films:

Vamp (1986) . . . . Waitress

Blood Diner (1987). . . . . Sheetar & Bitsy
- 0:15—Brief breasts, while taking photos during topless aerobics photo shoot.
- 0:24—Breasts, while lying dead on operating table, then standing up.

Papas, Irene

Films:

Attila (1958; Italian) . . . . Grune
The Guns of Navarone (1961). . . . . Maria
Electra (1962; German). . . . . Electra
Zorba the Greek (1963) . . . . The Widow
The Brotherhood (1968) . . . . Ida Ginetta
Anne of the Thousand Days (1969; British) . . . . Ajmi
A Dream of Kings (1969). . . . . Caliope
Z (1969; French). . . . . Helene
The Trojan Women (1972; British) . . . . Helen
- 1:11—Very brief breasts, kneeling down to bathe in a pan of water. Seen between slats in wall. Long shot.
- 1:12—Brief breasts and very brief side view of buns, standing up and moving away from the slat wall when the women start throwing stones.

Moses (1976; British/Italian) . . . . Zipporah
Bloodline (1979) . . . . Simonetta Palazza
Lion of the Desert (1981; Libyan/British) . . . . Mabrouka
Erendira (1983; Brazilian) . . . . The Grandmother
The Assisi Underground (1985). . . . . Mother Giuseppina
Into the Night (1985) . . . . Shaheen Parvizi
Sweet Country (1985). . . . . Mrs. Araya
High Season (1988; British). . . . . Penelope

Papusha

See: Demitro, Papusha.

Parent, Monique

Films:

Secret Games (1991) . . . . Robin
(Unrated version reviewed.)
- 0:33—Right breast, buns and crotch, while in bed with Julianne.

Body of Influence (1992) . . . . Chic Woman
(Unrated version reviewed.)
- •• 0:57—Buns in lingerie and breasts undressing in front of Jonathan and Lana at gun point.

Buford's Beach Bunnies (1992) . . . . Amber Dexterous
- •• 0:09—Breasts, fooling around with a customer in the restroom.
- 0:11—More breasts, with the customer.
- 0:42—Left breast in gaping vest, trying to get into Jeeter's pants.
- ••• 1:14—Breasts in bedroom with a customer.

Sins of Desire (1992) . . . . Clarise
(Unrated version reviewed.)
- ••• 0:23—Nude, stripping and dancing (she's the redhead on the right) with Sandy in front of Mr. O'Connor. Long scene.

Dangerous Touch (1993). . . . . Nicole
- •• 0:47—Full frontal nudity, while in the shower when surprised by Kate Vernon.
- ••• 0:49—Full frontal nudity, after dropping towel to join Lou Diamond Phillips and Vernon in bed.
- ••• 0:51—Breasts, while handcuffed in bed with Vernon.

Dragon Fire (1993). . . . . Dancer 6
- •• 0:57—Breasts and buns in T-back, while dancing on stage painted with fluorescent paint. Lit with blacklight.

Midnight Confessions (1993) . . . . Joni
(Unrated version reviewed.)
- ••• 0:31—Full frontal nudity, while making love with Lisa Comshaw.

Night Eyes 3 (1993) . . . . Brandy
- ••• 0:09—Breasts and buns in G-string, stripping out of her clothes in Zoe's house in front of Dan.

The Perfect Gift (1993) . . . . Lori
Sex and the Single Alien (1993). Jennifer
Sexual Outlaws (1993). . . . . Uncredited Annie
- ••• 0:31—In green bra, while sitting on bed and posing for John, then breasts while making love with him.

...And God Spoke (1994) . . . . Nude Ninja
- 0:02—Brief breasts, while putting her sword away. (She's on the left, the third one to talk.)

Blonde Heaven (1994) . . . . Viva
- 0:33—Buns in panties, while surrounded by several admiring guys during party.
- •• 0:36—Breasts, while dancing on table in front of four guys with Jospehina at party.
- •• 1:01—Full frontal nudity, after turning into a vampire in movie theater in front of Kyle.

Married People, Single Sex 2: For Better or Worse (1994). . . . . Valerie
- 0:00—Brief right breast, while making love in bed with David.
- 0:13—Brief breasts, behind sliding glass door, showing off her body for John.
- ••• 0:14—Breasts, while wearing panties, in the house with John.
- •• 0:16—Breasts, when John ties her wrists up with drapery cord and makes love while standing up.
- ••• 0:18—Breasts, while standing in bedroom and talking with John afterward.
- •• 0:35—In slip, then breasts when wearing panties, while talking with John.
- •• 0:59—Breasts while wearing panties, taking off her dress in living room in front of David.

Play Time (1994). . . . . Geena
(Unrated version reviewed.)
- •• 0:02—Breasts, when lying in bed, enjoying herself, while listening to Lindsey and Joe make love.
- •• 0:07—Breasts while on lounge chair, rubbing lotion on herself next to Lindsey.
- •• 0:09—Brief left breast in gaping nightie, then partial buns and breasts in fantasy.
- •• 0:11—Breasts, while running into the house with Lindsey to hide from the pool man.
- ••• 0:13—Breasts, when masturbating on sofa while Lindsey dances (and masturbates) in front of her. Steamy!
- ••• 0:16—Breasts, while on patio and talking with Lindsey in the pool.
- ••• 0:19—Full frontal nudity, while making love with Brad in bed.
- •• 0:26—Breasts, when undressing in office and caressing Lindsey while masturbating.
- ••• 0:36—Breasts, masturbating and caressing Lindsey on bed, while Joe watches from closet.
- •• 0:41—Full frontal nudity, while sitting in spa and talking with Lindsey and Joe.
- ••• 0:48—Breasts and buns, while making love with Lindsey and Joe in spa.
- •• 1:07—Left breast, while in bed, talking on the phone with Joe.

- • 1:10—Brief buns, when getting caught making love in the bushes with Joe.
- • 1:17—Brief breasts in open robe during argument.
- ••• 1:35—Full frontal nudity, after taking off her swimsuit and rubbing lotion on Lindsey while the guys watch.

Dark Secrets (1995) .... Claire Reynolds
- • 0:33—Buns in black panties, while trying on dress in bedroom.
- • 0:45—Brief breasts, while in the shower.
- ••• 0:51—In white bra and panties, then full frontal nudity while making love with Justin Carroll.
- • 0:55—Brief buns, twice, while trying on different outfits in store.
- •• 1:16—Breasts, while getting tortured by Julie Strain at the Midnight Club. Breasts and buns, after running out of the room.
- ••• 1:17—Nude, while outdoors in the rain, having sex with Strain.

Galaxy Girls (1995)............................ Janet
- •• 0:01—Buns and breasts, while taking a shower, then dressing.

Masseuse (1995)................................. J.J.
(Unrated version reviewed.)
- ••• 0:16—Nude, while standing in pool, tempting the pool guy.

Scoring (1995) .... Marsha

Stripshow (1995) .... Kara
- • 0:12—Buns in swimsuit bottom outside, getting ready to sunbathe.
- ••• 0:37—Buns and lower frontal nudity, while making love with Tané McClure in shack.
- • 0:46—Buns, while lying in bed.
- ••• 0:52—Nude, stripping in motel room in front of McClure and Cowboy, then playing with herself.
- • 1:02—Buns and breasts, bending over in bed, while having sex with Cowboy.
- •• 1:13—Breasts, while on stage, reluctantly taking off her dress.

Busted (1996) .... Carrie
- • 0:07—Brief breasts, while sunbathing outdoors.
- •• 0:31—Breasts, while showering with Howe in the showers. Buns and very brief lower frontal nudity while getting out of the showers.

Lebensborn (1996)...................... Jocelyn Speer
- • 0:08—Very brief breasts, when Kyle spots her painting in her studio.
- • 0:28—Breasts, while painting nude in her studio when seen by Kyle.
- •• 0:30—Breasts and buns, while seducing Kyle in his bedroom.
- •• 0:33—Nude, when getting out of bed with Kyle
- ••• 0:51—Nude, while making love with Kyle.

Love Me Twice (1996) .... Jessica/Julie

Lovers, Liars and Thieves (1996) .... The Teacher
- • 0:44—Breasts, while taking a shower, seen through peephole. Very brief lower frontal nudity and partial left breast, when reaching for a towel.
- •• 1:09—Breasts and buns, while making love with Cowboy in bed.

Mirror Mirror III (1996)..................... Cassandra
- •• 0:03—Nude, while making love with Billy Drago.
- •• 0:16—Breasts, while making love with Drago some more.
- ••• 0:32—Breasts and buns, while making love in bed with Drago and getting out.
- •• 0:40—Breasts, while making love with Drago on the floor.
- • 0:47—Brief breasts, during flashback.

Maximum Revenge (1997) .... Katya

Made for Cable Movies:

Ladykiller (1996; Showtime).................... Debbie
- • 0:01—Breasts, while tied by her wrists and killed by killer.

Made for Cable TV:

Love Street: I Dreamed of Angels Crying (1994; Showtime) .... Rebecca Heartstrings
- ••• 0:08—Nude, after taking off dress in her apartment in front of Detective Kowalski.
- • 0:09—Breasts and buns, while making love with the Detective on sofa.
- ••• 0:10—Breasts, while bent over back of chair while making love. Buns seen, while on shelf.
- •• 0:14—Breasts, while in front of closet and the Detective pulls her dress top down.

Erotic Confessions: The Business Trip (1996; Cinemax) .... Erica
(Available on video tape in *Erotic Confessions, Volume 4: Pleasure.*)
- •• 0:02—Nude, while unpacking her suitcase in hotel room.
- ••• 0:04—Full frontal nudity, when masturbating while listening to Stephanie and her husband make love in the next room.
- ••• 0:15—Nude, when bathing, getting dressed in panties, then masturbating while listening to the couple make love in the next room.
- ••• 0:19—Nude, while watching the couple make love, then joining in.

Hot Line: Shutterbugs (1996; Cinemax) .... Sheila
- ••• 0:14—Nude while posing on bed when Jack photographs her.
- ••• 0:20—Breasts and buns, while posing on bed with Peggy Trentini when Jack photographs them.

Beverly Hills Bordello: Wish List (1997; Showtime) .... Michelle Abbott
- •• 0:09—In bra, then breasts, when caressing herself while watching Dan have sex with Sarah.
- • 0:11—In lingerie, while lying next to Dan and talking with him in bed.
- • 0:13—Lower frontal nudity, in lingerie, when trying to seduce Dan.
- ••• 0:14—Breasts and buns, while making love with Dan in bed, then getting out of bed and dressing.
- ••• 0:21—In bra, then nude, when having sex with Jacques while her husband watches.

Erotic Confessions: Behind the Lens (1997; Cinemax) .... Joely Adams
- • 0:09—Breasts, when joining the photo shoot with Lisa Comshaw and Robert.
- •• 0:11—Breasts, while sitting up in bed.

Intimate Sessions: Laura (1998; Cinemax) .... Laura
- ••• 0:05—Breasts and buns, while making love with the bartender in the empty bar.
- ••• 0:15—Breast and buns, while making love with Alex in bedroom.
- ••• 0:22—In bra and panties, then breasts and buns, while making love with the professor in his office.

Video Tapes:

Playboy's Erotic Fantasies (1992).......... Cast Member

Nude Daydreams (1993) .... Daydream 4
- ••• 0:12—In black lingerie, then nude while caressing Ashlie Rhey on sofa. Long scene.

Playboy Night Dreams (1993) . . . . Intimate Strangers
••• 0:12—Lower nudity in sheer black nightgown with guy from restaurant. Nude, while making love in hotel room.
Playboy's Sensual Fantasy for Lovers (1993) . . . . Secret Desires
0:30—In green bra and panties, while talking on the phone with her lover.
••• 0:32—Full frontal nudity after taking off bra and making love in bed.
Playboy Celebrity Centerfold: Patti Davis (1994) . . . . Donna
••• 0:36—Breasts in sexy outfit, then nude in futuristic dial-a-date fantasy with Patti Davis and Greg.
Playboy's Erotic Fantasies III (1994) . . . . Midnight Madness/Vampiress
••• 0:00—Nude, while making love with a guy and the other vampiress. (She's wearing solid arm bands.)
Sexy Lingerie: Dreams & Desire (1994) . . . . Victorian Secret/Maid
••• 0:40—Breasts, with gardener and the woman who owns the house.
American Sweethearts (1995) . . . . Herself
••• 0:01—Nude, while dancing in TV fantasy.
••• 0:21—Ballet dancing in clothes, then nude, while making love with Ashlie Rhey.
••• 0:32—Nude, while dancing and stripping out of a man's suit.
••• 0:41—In wet clothes, then nude, while dancing with Ashlie.
•• 0:46—Nude, while dancing during the end credits.
Playboy's Rising Stars and Sexy Starlets (1996) . . . Herself
•• 0:30—Breasts in clips from some of her films.
••• 0:32—Nude, while making love with a guy in bed.

Parillaud, Anne

Films:
Patricia (1984) . . . . Patricia Cook
•• 0:25—Breasts, opening her jumpsuit top to get attention while trying to hitchhike.
•• 0:30—Breasts in white panties, running around at a seminary, trying to get away from a group of guys.
•• 0:31—Breasts in confessional booth.
• 0:32—Running around some more.
•• 0:37—Nude making love with Priscilla on bed.
••• 0:49—Dancing in two piece swimsuit, then breasts.
•• 0:50—Breasts while lying on her stomach.
• 0:52—Brief breasts running into the ocean.
• 0:53—Brief breasts under water.
• 0:55—More brief breasts shots under the water.
••• 0:56—Nude, getting out of the ocean and lying down on the beach.
•• 1:09—Breasts taking off her dress and playing bullfight with Harry.
•• 1:10—Nude, dancing in her room. Hard to see because the curtains get in the way.
• 1:24—Brief buns while making love with Harry.
• 1:26—Brief breasts while making love with Harry.
••• 1:27—Full frontal nudity making love on top of Harry in bed.
Juillet en Septembre (1988; French) . . . . Marie
La Femme Nikita (1991; French/Italian) . . . . Nikita
a.k.a. Nikita
• 0:59—Very brief right nipple, peeking out of her top when she sits up in bed.
Innocent Blood (1992) . . . . Marie
••• 0:03—Nude in her apartment.
• 1:17—Brief buns, taking off coat and getting into bed.
•• 1:24—Breasts, taking off sheet and kneeling over in bed to get handcuffs put on.
••• 1:25—Breasts and buns, while making love in bed with Anthony LaPaglia.
Map of the Human Heart (1992; Australian/Canadian) . . . . Albertine
• 1:14—Partial left breast (close-up), then right breast, while making love with Avik on top of blimp.
Frankie Starlight (1995; Irish/British) . . . . Bernadette
The Man in The Iron Mask (1998) . . . . Queen Mother, Anne d'Autriche

Paris, Cheryl

Films:
Liberty & Bash (1989) . . . . Melissa
Rescue Me (1991) . . . . Hannah
Sweet Justice (1991) . . . . Suzanne
•• 0:12—Brief breasts while making love with Singer standing up by tree.
Made for TV Movies:
From the Files of Joseph Wambaugh: A Jury of One (1992) . . . . Rita Mulick

Parker, Mary-Louise

Films:
Longtime Companion (1990) . . . . Lisa
Fried Green Tomatoes (1991) . . . . Ruth
a.k.a. Fried Green Tomatoes at the Whistle Stop Café
Grand Canyon (1991) . . . . Dee
• 1:00—Breasts, pulling sheet down, while lying in bed during dream sequence.
Mr. Wonderful (1993) . . . . Rita
Naked in New York (1993) . . . . Joanne
• 0:21—Brief left breast, while making love in bed with Eric Stoltz.
Boys on the Side (1994) . . . . Robin
Bullets Over Broadway (1994) . . . . Ellen
The Client (1994) . . . . Dianne Sway
The Portrait of a Lady (1996; British/U.S.) . . Henrietta Stackpole
The Marker (1997) . . . . Officer Emily Peck
Made for Cable Movies:
Sugartime (1995; HBO) . . . . Phyllis McGuire
Made for TV Movies:
A Place for Annie (1994) . . . . Linda

*Parker, Mim **

Films:
Demon Knight (1994) . . . . Party Babe
Made for Cable Movies:
Body Language (1995; HBO) . . . . Tera the Dancer
•• 0:28—Breasts and buns in T-back, while dancing on stage in club. Lit with red light.

Parker, Nicole Ari

Films:
The Incredibly True Adventure of Two Girls in Love (1995) . . . . Evie
• 1:12—Breasts and brief side view of buns, while making love in bed with Randy.
• 1:15—Brief breasts, while running around in the bedroom when her mom comes home.
Boogie Nights (1997) . . . . Becky Barnett
• 0:58—Brief breasts, while acting in a porno movie with Reed.
The End of Violence (1997; French/German/U.S.) . . . . . . Kenya

Excess Baggage (1997) . . . . Waitress at Knotty Pines

Made for Cable Movies:

Divas (1995) . . . . Stephanie

Made for Cable TV:

Subway Stories (1997; HBO) . . . . Sharon

Parker, Sage

Films:

Songwriter (1984) . . . . Pattie McLeish
- 1:01—Brief breasts, in bed when Rip Torn catches her in bed with Sam.

The Legend of Billie Jean (1985) . . . . TV Reporter

The Dirt Bike Kid (1986) . . . . Miss Clavell

Parkhurst, Heather-Elizabeth *

Films:

Conflict of Interest (1992) . . . . Francesca

Silence of the Hams (1993) . . . . Beautiful Woman

Beverly Hills Cop III (1994) . . . . Annihilator Girl

The Granny (1995) . . . . Antoinette
- 0:47—Brief breasts, after opening her blouse to show David that he would be satisfied with her breasts.
- •• 0:58—In bra and panties, when undressing in her room, then breasts, while dancing and looking at herself in the mirror.

Bikini Summer 3 (1997) . . . . Jamie
- ••• 0:10—In bra and panties, then breasts and buns, while trying on swimsuits.
- ••• 0:22—Nude, with her two girlfriends in the shower, then getting dressed.
- ••• 0:40—Breasts, while trying on clothes in pro shop with her two girlfriends.
- ••• 1:01—Breasts, while trying on swimsuits.

Made for Cable TV:

Sherman Oaks (1995-97; Showtime). . . . . Tiffany

Sherman Oaks: Season 1, Episode 1 (1995; Showtime) . . . . Tiffany
- 0:04—Breasts underwater, while sitting in hot tub. Brief partial breasts.

Sherman Oaks: Season 1, Episode 2 (1995; Showtime) . . . . Tiffany

Sherman Oaks: Season 1, Episode 3 (1995; Showtime) . . . . Tiffany
- 0:21—Breasts, when raising her T-shirt to show Mr. Duckworth for his birthday.

Sherman Oaks: Season 1, Episode 4 (1995; Showtime) . . . . Tiffany
- 0:15—Partial breasts, under water in hot tub.
- •• 0:22—Breasts when swimsuit top pops off while shackled at neighbor's house for satanic ritual.

Sherman Oaks: Season 1, Episode 5 (1995; Showtime) . . . . Tiffany

0:11—Brief partial buns in swimsuit while lying down in backyard, getting a tan.

Sherman Oaks: Season 1, Episode 6 (1995; Showtime) . . . . Tiffany
- 0:15—Buns in swimsuit, while in hot tub, talking to E.W.

Sherman Oaks: Season 1, Episode 7 (1995; Showtime) . . . . Tiffany
- 0:04—Partial breasts, while sitting in hot tub, talking to the camera.

Sherman Oaks: Season 1, Episode 8 (1995; Showtime) . . . . Tiffany

Sherman Oaks: Season 1, Episode 10 (1995; Showtime) . . . . Tiffany
- 0:10—Brief breast, while sitting down in hot tub.

Sherman Oaks: Season 1, Episode 12 (1995; Showtime) . . . . Tiffany
- 0:07—Buns (seen in mirror) while in bedroom in black panties and bra. Lying on bed and moaning as a phone sex operator.

Sherman Oaks: Season 1, Episode 13 (1995; Showtime) . . . . Tiffany

Sherman Oaks: Season 2, Episode 1 (1996; Showtime) . . . . Tiffany
- 0:07—Brief breasts while getting dressed.
- 0:21—Buns in dominatrix outfit while flogging her boyfriend, seen in mirror.
- 0:24—Brief buns in dominatrix outfit again.
- 0:27—Upper half of left breast and very brief right breast, during end credits.

Sherman Oaks: Season 2, Episode 2 (1996; Showtime) . . . . Tiffany
- •• 0:14—Breasts, while sitting and talking in bathtub.

Sherman Oaks: Season 2, Episode 3 (1996; Showtime) . . . . Tiffany
- 0:00—Breasts, while protesting, then sunbathing at the beach.
- •• 0:08—Breasts, while sitting in the spa and talking to the camera.
- 0:18—Brief breasts, while sitting in chair at the beach.

Sherman Oaks: Season 2, Episode 4 (1996; Showtime) . . . . Tiffany
- •• 0:08—Breasts, while E.W. interviews her in the spa.

Sherman Oaks: Season 2, Episode 5 (1996; Showtime) . . . . Tiffany
- •• 0:07—Breasts, while sitting in candle-lit bubble bath, talking with E.W.
- 0:11—Brief breasts, while sunbathing in backyard with Kelly.
- •• 0:13—Breasts, while sunbathing in the backyard with Kelly.

Sherman Oaks: Season 2, Episode 7 (1996; Showtime) . . . . Tiffany
- 0:10—Breasts, while talking and standing in spa.

Sherman Oaks: Season 2, Episode 8 (1996; Showtime) . . . . Tiffany
- 0:01—Breasts under water, while in spa talking with E.W.

Sherman Oaks: Season 2, Episode 9 (1996; Showtime) . . . . Tiffany
- •• 0:04—Breasts, while sitting in bathtub, talking with E.W.

Sherman Oaks: Season 2, Episode 10 (1996; Showtime) . . . . Tiffany
- 0:08—Partial upper breasts, while sitting in spa and talking with E.W.

Sherman Oaks: Season 2, Episode 11 (1996; Showtime) . . . . Tiffany
- •• 0:03—Brief breasts, when taking off her swimsuit top in her bedroom. Breasts, while sitting in spa and talking with E.W.

Sherman Oaks: Season 2, Episode 12 (1996; Showtime) . . . . Tiffany
- •• 0:14—Breasts, while sitting in bathtub.

Sherman Oaks: Season 2, Episode 13 (1996; Showtime) . . . . Tiffany
- •• 0:05—Breasts, while talking with E.W. in spa.

Sherman Oaks: Season 2, Episode 14 (1996; Showtime) . . . . Tiffany
- 0:22—Upper half of breasts, then brief breasts, while in the spa, talking to the camera.

Sherman Oaks: Season 2, Episode 15 (1996; Showtime) . . . . Tiffany
- •• 0:06—Breasts, while sitting in spa and talking with E.W.
- • 0:18—Breasts, while sitting in bubble bath, talking with E.W.

Sherman Oaks: Season 2, Episode 16 (1996; Showtime) . . . . Tiffany
- •• 0:06—Breasts, while talking with E.W. when in the spa.

Sherman Oaks: Season 2, Episode 17 (1996; Showtime) . . . . Tiffany
- • 0:02—Breasts, while in the spa, talking with E.W.
- • 0:03—Breasts, while in the spa, talking with E.W.

Sherman Oaks: Season 2, Episode 18 (1996; Showtime) . . . . Tiffany
- •• 0:13—Breasts, while sitting in spa, talking with E.W. (seen from under the water.)
- • 0:20—Brief breasts under water in spa again.

Sherman Oaks: Season 2, Episode 19 (1996; Showtime) . . . . Tiffany
- •• 0:15—Breasts, while sitting in bubble bath and talking with E.W.
- •• 0:23—Breasts, while lying in bed after making love with her boyfriend, Father Gene.

Perversions of Science: Boxed In (1997; HBO) . . . . . Emmy
- 0:02—Most of breasts under flimsy, small top with Kevin Pollak.
- • 0:05—Left breast, when falling to the floor after Pollak turns her off.
- •• 0:12—Breasts, when making love with Pollak. (There are times when it's fairly obvious her body is a substitute dummy.)
- • 0:15—Brief side of left breast and buns, just before Pollak begins dismantling her.

Sherman Oaks: Season 2, Episode 20 (1997; Showtime) . . . . Tiffany
- •• 0:09—Breasts, while talking with E.W. in spa.

Sherman Oaks: Season 2, Episode 21 (1997; Showtime) . . . . Tiffany
- • 0:14—Breasts, while sitting in bubble bath, talking with E.W.
- •• 0:16—Breasts, while sitting in bubble bath, talking with E.W.
- • 0:22—Partial buns in blue lingerie, while sitting on top of Edward in bed.

Sherman Oaks: Season 2, Episode 22 (1997; Showtime) . . . . Tiffany
- •• 0:09—Breasts, while sitting in spa, talking with E.W. (sometimes seen under water.)
- •• 0:12—Breasts, while posing for art class.
- • 0:16—Breasts, while posing for all-male art class.
- • 0:17—Right breast, while posing for Archelino.
- •• 0:19—Breasts, while dancing for all-male art class.

Video Tapes:

Hot Body International: #1 Miss Cancun (1990) . . . . Contestant
- •• 0:26—Buns, in two piece swimsuit.
- •• 0:52—Winner. Buns, in two piece swimsuit during photo session after the contest.

Inside Out 2 (1992) . . . . Woman/I've Got a Crush on You
(Unrated version reviewed.)
- •• 0:14—Brief buns, in swimsuit, suntanning. Breasts, trying to prevent guy from jumping.
- • 0:15—More breasts and buns shots when she's flattened during the rest of the segment.

Hot Body Competition: The Best of Hot Body (1994) . . . Herself

Parkins, Barbara *

Films:

Valley of the Dolls (1967) . . . . Anne Welles
- • 0:28—Very brief silhouette of a breast, when taking off nightgown and getting into bed.

The Mephisto Waltz (1971) . . . . Roxanne
- • 1:26—Left breast, while kissing Alan Alda during witchcraft sequence.

Asylum (1972; British) . . . . Bonnie
Christina (1974) . . . . Christina
Shout at the Devil (1976; British) . . . . Rosa
Bear Island (1980; British/Canadian) . . . . Judith Ruben

Breakfast in Paris (1981) . . . . Jackie Wyatt
- ••• 0:41—Right breast, while rolling over in bed. Breasts when sitting up in bed.

Made for Cable Movies:

To Catch a King (1984; HBO) . . . . Dutchess of Windsor

Made for TV Movies:

Snatched (1977) . . . . Barbara Maxvill
Calendar Girl Murders (1984) . . . . Cleo

TV:

Peyton Place (1964-69) . . . . . Betty Anderson/Harrington/Cord
Captains and the Kings (1976) . . . . Martinique

Parkinson, Dian *

TV:

The Price is Right (1975-93) . . . . Hostess

Video Tapes:

Playboy Celebrity Centerfold: Dian Parkinson (1993) . . . . Herself
- •• 0:00—Breasts during introduction.
- ••• 0:05—Nude, after stripping out of a man's business suit in studio.
- ••• 0:12—In white, bra, garter belt and stockings, then nude while making love with a guy in art gallery fantasy.
- ••• 0:17—Nude in still photos.
- ••• 0:20—Nude in desert fantasy.
- ••• 0:23—Nude in dress while dancing in music video.
- ••• 0:27—In lingerie, then nude in bedroom fantasy.
- • 0:32—Brief breasts while changing clothes by car.
- ••• 0:35—In white bra in hotel room, then nude making love in robbery fantasy.

Parks, Tammy

Films:

The Perfect Gift (1993) . . . . Pajama Party Guest

Illegal in Blue (1994) . . . . Jennifer
- • 0:30—Buns in G-string (she's on the left) when leaving the sofa after sitting next to Mickey.
- •• 0:31—Left breast (she's on the right), while making love with another woman on sofa.

Play Time (1994) . . . . Michelle
(Unrated version reviewed.)
- •• 1:32—In bra, while undressing in bedroom, then nude with Julie Strain. B&W.

Secret Games 3 (1994) . . . . Uncredited Lover
(Unrated version reviewed.)
- • 0:21—Buns and partial breasts, while making love with a brunette woman on bed.

Attack of the 60 Foot Centerfold (1995) . . . . Betty
- ••• 0:05—Breasts and buns in panties with the other two girls in photo shoot.
- • 0:27—Brief buns in red swimsuit while posing for photos at the beach.
- ••• 0:31—Breasts and buns in swimsuit, while posing at the beach with the other two girls.

- 0:53—Buns in lingerie, while walking around the house.
- 1:06—Buns, while snooping around in Angels' bedroom.
- 1:10—Right breast, when it pops out of her bikini top during fight with Angel.

Cyberzone (1995) . . . . Runaway Wife
- •• 0:29—Breasts and brief buns, while making love on top of a guy in a room.

Deadly Currency (1995). . . . . Nicole (Dancer)
- •• 0:00—Breasts, while dancing on stage after stripping out of black outfit.

Forbidden Games II (1995) . . . . Hooker

Midnight Tease 2 (1995) . . . . .Misty
- ••• 0:06—Breasts and buns in T-back while doing strip routine on stage.
- •• 0:09—Breasts and buns in T-back while in dressing room.
- • 0:27—Breasts, while dancing in front of the killer before getting killed.

Scoring (1995) . . . . Masseuse

Stolen Hearts (1995) . . . . Diana
- •• 0:37—In lingerie, then buns in T-back, then breasts while dancing on stage.
- • 0:38—Breasts and buns in T-back, while backstage.
- • 0:49—Breasts and buns in T-back, while dancing on stage.

Virtual Desire (1995) . . . . Susan
- ••• 0:11—Left breast, then breasts, while making love on the sofa with Brad.
- ••• 0:17—Stripping outside by hot tub in front of Brad. In white lingerie outfit, then nude while making love with him in the hot tub. Long scene.
- •• 0:36—Breasts and buns, while making love on the sofa with Brad.

Day of the Warrior (1997) . . . . Scorpion

Made for Cable TV:

Compromising Situations: The Casting Couch (1994; Showtime) . . . . Girl
- •• 0:18—Buns in lingerie, then breasts after taking off bra in B&W on video monitor.

Compromising Situations: The Surprise (1994; Showtime) . . . . Nurse
- • 0:09—Brief partial buns in short nurse's outfit.

Erotic Confessions: Coming Clean (1996; Cinemax) . . . . Diana/Red-Alicia

(Available on video tape in *Erotic Confessions, Volume 1: Desire.*)
- ••• 0:16—Breasts, while making love with the other woman in the tattoo parlor in front of Eric.
- ••• 0:17—Breasts and buns, while making love with Julie and Eric on motorcycle.

Video Tapes:

Nude Bowling Party (1995) . . . . Bambi
- ••• 0:00—Nude throughout.

Penthouse Women In & Out of Uniform (1995) . . . . Cast Member
- ••• 0:08—Nude as a dentist assistant, with Tiffany Burlingame in dental office.
- ••• 0:22—Nude as a paramedic, with Parks, while the guy watches from gurney inside ambulance. Wears a leather strap outfit.

Penthouse: Lipstick Girls (1997). . . . . n.a.

CD-ROM:

Hollywood Body Double (1995) . . . . .Jungle/Space

Parton, Julia

a.k.a. Adult film actress Nina Alexander.

Cousin of singer/actress Dolly Parton.

Films:

Erotic Images (1983) . . . . Marvin's Nurse
- • 0:08—Brief breasts in office with Marvin. Dark, hard to see.

The Rosebud Beach Hotel (1985). . . . . Bellhop
- •• 0:49—Buns, then breasts, standing in line. Second from the camera.

Reform School Girls (1986) . . . . .Uncredited Shower Girl

Vice Academy, Part 3 (1991). . . . . Melanie/Malathion
- •• 0:44—Breasts, opening her blouse after seeing all the money.

Good Girls Don't (1993). . . . . Betina
- •• 0:05—Buns in T-back then breasts, while doing strip routine on stage.
- • 0:13—Breasts, in front of a guy in office.
- • 0:52—Brief buns in outfit.
- • 1:06—Brief partial buns in panties and bra, while changing into her jail clothing.

New York Nights (1994). . . . . .Jessie
- • 0:00—Buns in swimsuit on beach.
- •• 0:02—Breasts, while making out with a guy on the beach.
- •• 0:03—Breasts, while making love with a guy in bed.
- • 0:06—Breasts, while making out with a guy. Kind of misty.
- ••• 0:17—Full frontal nudity in apartment with a guy.
- • 0:31—In bra and panties, then buns, while trying on clothes.
- •• 0:43—Breasts, in open robe.
- • 0:56—Brief breasts, while in storage room with Gene.
- • 1:02—Buns, when in panties, while trying to put pants on.
- ••• 1:23—Nude, after taking off lingerie with Eric.

Vice Academy, Part 4 (1994). . . . . .Malathion
- • 0:06—Buns in two piece swimsuit, getting clothes from Debbie Dutch in club.
- •• 0:08—Breasts, while stripping out of dress in garage in front of Anvil.

Marilyn Chambers: Bedtime Fantasies (1996) . . . . .n.a.

Video Tapes:

Love Skills: A Guide to the Pleasures of Sex (1984) . . . . .Model
- ••• 0:49—Nude in bed with Barbara Peckinpaugh while a guy watches.

Penthouse Love Stories (1986). . . . . Loveboat Woman
- ••• 0:51—In white bra and panties in bed. Nude masturbating while the other girls watch. Nice, long, sweaty scene.

Penthouse: On the Wild Side (1988) . . . . Punk or Bust Customer
- ••• 0:34—Nude while wearing black leather outfit, making love with Michelle Bauer.

High Society Centerspread Video #15: Julia Parton (1990). . . . . Herself
- ••• 0:01—Breasts and buns taking off her clothes.
- ••• 0:04—Full frontal nudity in bathtub making love with a girl friend. Nice, long scene.
- ••• 0:09—Nude, doing a strip tease dance.
- ••• 0:17—Nude, relaxing on the floor and masturbating.
- ••• 0:18—Nude on bed, making love with the maid during fantasy.

Soft Bodies Invitational (1990) . . . . .Nina Alexander
- • 0:00—Buns, under short skirt, playing tennis with Becky LeBeau.
- ••• 0:03—In lingerie during photo session, then breasts and buns in G-string. Long scene.
- ••• 0:15—Breasts posing with LeBeau.

••• 0:18—Outside in dress, then undressing to two piece swimsuit, then breasts. Long scene.
•• 0:24—In two piece swimsuit, then breasts arguing with LeBeau about who has better breasts.
••• 0:28—In two piece swimsuit, then breasts by the pool.
The Art of Desire (1992) .... n.a.
B-Movie Queens Revealed: The Making of "Vice Academy" (1993) .... Melanie/Malathion
• 0:00—Brief breasts, opening her blouse from *Vice Academy 3.*
BabeWatch, Episode 1: Lingerie Fantasies (1994) .... Herself
••• 0:20—Nude, taking a shower. Long scene.
••• 0:57—Nude, in shower after end credits.
Marilyn Chambers: Wet & Wild Fantasies (1994) .... Girl at the Beach/Shower Girl
••• 0:21—Breasts, while making love with her boyfriend at the beach.
••• 0:28—Full frontal nudity, while taking a shower.
Soft Bodies: Double Exposure (1994) .... Herself
••• 0:18—In purple lingerie, then nude on sofa.
•• 0:27—Breasts and buns in panties, while rehearsing with Becky LeBeau outside.
••• 0:28—In dress, then nude, while posing on chair outside.
••• 0:33—In lingerie, then nude, while posing on chair inside.
Venus' Playhouse (1994) .... Herself
CD-ROM:
Venus' Playhouse (1994) .... Herself

Pascal, Olivia *

Films:
Island of 1000 Delights .... Peggy
•• 0:16—Breasts, tied up while being tortured by two guys. Upper half lower frontal nudity.
•• 0:23—Full frontal nudity lying in bed, then buns running out the door. Full frontal nudity running up stairs, nude hiding in bedroom.
••• 0:57—Nude, taking off her clothes in shower with Michael.
• 1:26—Brief breasts running on the beach with Michael.
Vanessa (1977; West German) .... Vanessa
••• 0:08—Nude undressing, taking a bath and getting washed by Jackie. Long scene.
••• 0:16—Buns, then full frontal nudity getting a massage.
• 0:26—Breasts, while getting fitted for new clothes.
• 0:47—Full frontal nudity when Adrian rips her clothes off.
••• 0:56—Full frontal nudity on beach with Jackie.
••• 1:05—Nude making love with Jackie in bed. Nice close up of left breast.
•• 1:19—Full frontal nudity lying on the table.
•• 1:27—Breasts, wearing white panties, garter belt and stockings shackled up by Kenneth.
Popcorn and Ice Cream (1978; West German) Vivi
a.k.a. Sex and Ice Cream
• 0:26—Full frontal nudity (she's on the right), covered with soap, taking a shower with Bea.
The Joy of Flying (1979) .... Maria
a.k.a. Erotic Ways
•• 0:39—Breasts wearing panties, in bedroom with George, then nude.
•• 0:46—Nude with George in bathroom.
Sex on the Run (1979; German/French/Italian) .... Convent Girl
a.k.a. Some Like It Cool
a.k.a. Casanova and Co.
••• 0:15—First woman (brunette) to take off her clothes with the other two women, full frontal nudity. Long scene.

Bloody Moon (1980; West German) .... Angela
C.O.D. (1983) .... Holly Fox

Pasco, Isabelle *

Films:
Ave Maria (1984; French) .... Ursula
Hors La Loi (1985; French) .... Sissi
High Frequency (1988; Italian) .... Anna
Prospero's Books (1991; Dutch/French/Italian) .... Miranda
• 0:13—Tip of left breast, when it peeks out between an opening in her blouse, while lying in bed as John Gielgud sits beside her on the bed.

Pasmore, Kathy

Films:
Beach Beverly Hills (1992) .... Marilyn
Hollywood Dreams (1993) .... Tiffany
a.k.a. L.A. Dreams
(Unrated version reviewed.)
••• 0:15—Breasts and buns, while sitting on desk.
••• 0:27—Getting a massage while wearing a sexy suit, then breasts and buns in T-back when making out with Natasha.
•• 0:28—Breasts and buns, while making love with Natasha and Robby.
• 1:06—Breasts in background while getting dressed.
Wild Malibu Weekend! (1994) .... Kelly Johnson
Video Tapes:
Beverly Hills Workout (1993) .... Herself
•• 0:14—Breasts and buns in T-back, while working out in backyard.
••• 0:33—Nude, while dancing and posing in backyard.
•• 0:51—Nude, while posing outdoors.

Pass, Cyndi *

Films:
Bikini Island (1991) .... Kari
• 0:47—Brief upper half of right breast, while changing swimsuit tops at the beach.
• 0:55—Side of left breast, while taking off her top on bed with Jack.
• 0:59—Buns, in black bra and panties after Max disappears.
Bounty Tracker (1992) .... Jewels
Deadbolt (1992) .... Diana
Desperate Motive (1992) .... Ms. Simms
Mission of Justice (1992) .... Erin Miller
Round Trip to Heaven (1992) .... Cindy
Scanner Cop (1993) .... Sara Kopek
The Force (1994) .... Erin
Serial Killer (1995) .... Marianne Capriato
Hindsight (1996) .... Cassandra Bennett
•• 0:21—Breasts, while making love in bed with Jason.
• 0:23—Brief right breast, while talking with Jason.
•• 0:25—Full frontal nudity, while making love with Jason.
•• 0:37—Breasts and brief buns, while making love with Jason.
• 1:17—Brief buns, getting into bathtub.
TV:
NYPD Blue: Sheedy Dealings (Nov 18, 1997) .... n.a.

Patitz, Tatjana

Supermodel.
Films:
Rising Sun (1993) .... Cheryl Lynn Austin
• 0:06—Upper half of buns and side of right breast, while sitting in front of vanity in her apartment.

•• 0:10—Very brief lower frontal nudity and breasts, getting her dress ripped open while on board room table.
• 0:52—Very brief right breast, on video monitor during playback of murder surveillance video.
• 1:44—Brief half of right breast in open dress during Wesley Snipes' daydream after being shot. Out of focus.

Ready to Wear (1994) .... Herself
a.k.a. Prêt-à-porter

Patrick, Barbara

Films:

Zero Tolerance (1989) .... Wendy
Body Shot (1993) .... Candy
•• 0:06—Breasts, while sitting on couch in Robert Patrick's studio.

Lord of Illusions (1995) .... Lead Female Cultist
(Unrated version reviewed.)

Within the Rock (1997) .... Samantha Rogers

Paul, Alexandra

Films:

American Nightmare (1981; Canadian)
.... Isabelle Blake/Tanya Kelly
••• 0:02—Left breast while smoking in bed. Breasts before getting killed. Long scene.

Christine (1983) .... Leigh
Just the Way You Are (1984) .... Bobbie
American Flyers (1985) .... Becky
• 0:50—Very brief right breast, then very brief half of left breast changing tops with David Grant. Brief side view of right breast. Dark.
•• 1:13—Brief breasts in white panties getting into bed with David Grant.

8 Million Ways to Die (1986) .... Sunny
•• 0:24—Full frontal nudity, standing in bathroom while Jeff Bridges watches.

Dragnet (1987) .... Connie Swail
Harlequin Romance: Out of the Shadows (1988)... Jan Lindsey
Millions (1990) .... Julia
••• 0:44—Breasts while making love in bed with Billy Zane.
• 0:59—Breasts in bed with Zane.

In Between (1991) .... Amy
Kuffs (1992) .... Uncredited Police Chief's Wife
Sunset Grill (1992) .... Anita
••• 1:14—Breasts and upper half of buns, while on top of Peter Weller in bed. Nice.
•• 1:15—Very brief buns, while rolling over on her back, then right breast.

Cyber Bandits (1994) .... Rebecca
Nothing to Lose (1994) .... Natasha
The Paperboy (1994) .... Melissa
Spy Hard (1996) .... Woman in Murphy Bed

Made for Cable Movies:

Prey of the Chameleon (1992; Showtime) .... Carrie
Death Train (1993; USA) .... Sabrina Carver
Alistair MacLean's Night Watch (1995; USA) ... Sabrina Carver
Piranha (1995; Showtime) .... Maggie McNamara
House of the Damned (1996; Showtime) .... Maura South
a.k.a. Spectre

Made for Cable TV:

The Hitchhiker: Minuteman (HBO) .... Julie
•• 0:04—Brief left breast in car with husband, then brief breasts flashing the couple on the motorcycle.

Made for TV Movies:

Paper Dolls (1982) .... Laurie
Getting Physical (1984) .... Kendall Gibley
Perry Mason: The Case of the Lethal Lesson (1988) ...... Amy
The Laker Girls (1990) .... Heidi/Jenny
Danielle Steel's "Mixed Blessings" (1995) .... Beth
Echo (1997) .... Olivia

TV:

Baywatch (1992-96) .... Lt. Stephanie Holden

Video Tapes:

Baywatch: The Movie—Forbidden Paradise (1994)
.... Lt. Stephanie Holden

• Paul, Meilani

One of the three Diet Pepsi Uh-huh! Girls (1992).
Ex-wife of actor Adrian Paul.

Films:

Hard Time (1995) .... Angel Woods
•• 0:06—In lingerie, then breasts, while undressing in front of Michael during his dream.
•• 0:11—In lingerie, then breasts, while making love with Kelly (a guy) in Michael's dream.
••• 1:03—In white body suit, then nude, while making love with Michael in bed.
• 1:09—Buns and breasts, while making love with Michael.
•• 1:26—Buns and breasts, while making love in bed with Michael and Devin De Vasquez.

Back in Business (1996) .... Mrs. Royce
The Corporate Ladder (1996) .... Bianca
• 0:21—Very brief right breast during photo shoot.
••• 0:42—Breasts, after taking off her dress in backyard, then in swimming pool with Ben Cross.
••• 1:11—Breasts and buns in T-back, after taking off her dress in bedroom, while trying to seduce Matt.

Paul, Nancy

Films:

Sheena (1984) .... Betsy Ames
Gulag (1985) .... Susan
•• 0:42—Buns, then breasts taking a shower while David Keith daydreams while he's on a train.

V. I. Warshawski (1991) .... Paige

TV:

Space Precinct (1994-95) .... Sally Brogan

Paul, Sue *

Films:

All That Jazz (1979) .... Stacy
• 1:18—Brief right breast in bed with Roy Scheider at the hospital.

• Paulsen, Tiffany

Films:

Fortress of Amerikkka (1989) .... Photographer's Assistant
Friday the 13th, Part VIII—Jason Takes Manhattan (1989) .... Suzi
• 0:03—Side view of left breast and upper half of buns in boat with Jim.

Pavis, Bobbi

Films:

The Malibu Bikini Shop (1985) .... Stunning Girl
•• 0:19—Breasts trying on bikini behind two-way glass.

Mortuary Academy (1988) .... Sexy Dancer

Pavlova, Natasha

Films:

The Naked Truth (1992) .... Miss Bolivia
Martial Outlaw (1993) .... Mia
Son of the Pink Panther (1993) .... Rima

Made for Cable TV:

Dream On: The Guilty Party (1992; HBO) . . . . Joy

••• 0:10—In black bra, panties and stockings, stripping at Eddie's bachelor party. Breasts and buns in G-string.

Payne, Julie

Films:

The Lonely Guy (1983) . . . . Rental Agent

Private School (1983) . . . . .Coach Whelan

• 0:30—Very, very brief left breast popping out of cheerleader's outfit along with Rita.

Fraternity Vacation (1985). . . . . .Naomi Tvedt

Jumpin' Jack Flash (1986) . . . . . Receptionist at Elizabeth Arden

Just Between Friends (1986) . . . . Karen

Misery (1990) . . . . .Reporter #1

Monkey Trouble (1993). . . . . Librarian

The Brady Bunch Movie (1994). . . . . .Mrs. Simmons

Spy Hard (1996) . . . . Mother Superior

TV:

Wizards and Warriors (1983). . . . . .Queen Lattinia

Leo and Liz in Beverly Hills (1986). . . . . Lucille Trumbley

Pays, Amanda

Wife of actor Corbin Bernsen.

Films:

The Cold Room (1984) . . . . .Carla Martin/Christa Bruchner

Oxford Blues (1984) . . . . Lady Victoria

The Kindred (1987). Melissa Leftridge

Off Limits (1988). . . . . Nicole

Leviathan (1989). . . . . Elizabeth Williams

Exposure (1991) . . . . Marie

Solitaire for 2 (1995; British) . . . . Katie

• 0:57—Right breast, while making love in bed with Daniel.

Made for Cable Movies:

Dead on the Money (1991). . . . . .Jennifer Ashford

Made for TV Movies:

Parker Kane (1990) . . . . .Sarah

I Know My Son Is Alive (1994) . . . . Katherine

TV:

Max Headroom (1987) . . . . Theora Jones

The Flash (1990-91) . . . . Christina McGee

Peabody, Dixie Lee

Films:

Bury Me an Angel (1972) . . . . .Dag

• 0:13—Very brief right breast, while getting back into bed.

••• 0:41—Nude, skinny dipping in river and getting out.

• 1:16—Breasts making love in bed with Dan Haggerty. Lit with red light.

Night Call Nurses (1972). . . . . Robin

a.k.a. Young LA Nurses 2

•• 0:35—Breasts taking off clothes in encounter group.

• 0:39—Brief breasts in Barbara's flashback.

Peace, Jennifer

a.k.a. Adult film actress Devon Shire.

Films:

Death Dancers (1992). Shower Demon

Housewife From Hell (1993). . . . . Sue

•• 0:27—Breasts, while undoing her dress in John's office.

Secret Games 2—The Escort (1993). . . . . Darci

(Unrated version reviewed.)

••• 0:47—Full frontal nudity, while making love with Martin Hewitt in bed.

• 1:05—Breasts, in flashbacks.

Sexual Outlaws (1993). . . . . .Betty

••• 0:10—Breasts, in lingerie and after taking it off with Frank while acting for a video.

••• 0:13—Breasts with Frank and Harriet for video.

Peake, Teri Lynn *

Films:

Boys Night Out (1987). . . . . .Maid

••• 0:25—Buns in G-string, then breasts doing a strip routine. Long scene.

Summer's Games (1987). . . . . Penthouse Girl

Video Tapes:

The Girls of Malibu (1986) . . . . Lenee

••• 0:51—Nude outside and in a hot tub.

In Search of the Perfect 10 (1986) . . . . .Perfect Girl #9

••• 0:47—Buns and breasts taking a shower.

The Stripper of the Year (1986). . . . . Lenee

••• 0:47—Nude, stripping out of red sequined dress.

•• 0:53—Breasts, on stage with the other contestants.

•• 0:54—Breasts, as a finalist.

••• 0:55—Breasts, as a finalist, then in dance-off.

Night of the Living Babes (1987). . . . . Vesuvia

••• 0:25—Breasts and buns in G-string, dancing in front of Chuck and Buck. Long scene.

Wet Water T's (1987). . . . . Herself

••• 0:13—Breasts and buns, dancing on stage in white G-string, in a contest.

•• 0:36—Breasts again during judging.

•• 0:39—Breasts during semi-finals.

••• 0:40—Breasts dancing with the other women.

••• 0:43—Breasts dancing during finals.

•• 0:46—Breasts during final judging.

Starlets Exposed! Volume II (1991) . . . . Lenee

(Same as *The Girls of Malibu.*)

••• 0:52—Nude outside and in a hot tub.

Peaker, E.J.

Films:

Hello, Dolly! (1969). . . . . Minnie Fay

The All-American Boy (1973) . . . . Janelle Sharkey

••• 0:37—Breasts and buns, while in bathroom with Jon Voight.

The Four Deuces (1975) . . . . Lory

Graduation Day (1981) . . . . Blondie

The Banker (1989). . . . . Renee

TV:

That's Life (1968-69) . . . . Gloria Quigly Dickson

Peaks, Pandora *

a.k.a. Schick, Stephanie.

Adult Films:

Score Busty Covergirls, Volume 2: Pandora & LA Bust (1995). . . . . .Pandora Peaks

Films:

Do or Die (1991) . . . . Atlanta Lee

••• 1:09—Breasts making love with Shane outside at night.

• 1:15—Brief breasts in background, getting dressed. Out of focus.

Striptease (1996) . . . . Urbana Sprawl

(R-rated version reviewed.)

• 0:03—Breasts, while dancing on stage. Medium long shot.

Pearce, Adrienne

Films:

Lethal Woman (1988) . . . . Trudy

Out on Bail (1988) . . . . .Maggie

Purgatory (1988) . . . . Janine
•• 0:51—Brief breasts in shower scene with Kirsten.
American Ninja 3: Blood Hunt (1989) . . . . . Minister's Secretary
Demon Keeper (1993). . . . . Dia Gregory
0:51—Very brief right breast under wet nightgown, while being carried back into the house.

Pearce, Jacqueline

Films:
The Plague of the Zombies (1966; British). . . . Alice Thompson
The Reptile (1966; British). . . . . Anna Franklyn
Don't Raise the Bridge, Lower the River (1968) . . Pamela Lester
How to Get Ahead in Advertising (1988; British) . . . . Maud
White Mischief (1988). . . . . Idina
•• 0:07—Buns, then breasts several times while standing up in the bathtub and talking with her male and female friends.
Princess Caraboo (1994) . . . . Lady Apthorpe
Made for TV Movies:
Doctor Who: The Two Doctors (1985; British). . . . . . Chessene
TV:
Blake's 7 (British). . . . . Servalan

• Pearce, Mary Vivian

Films:
Pink Flamingos (1972). . . . . Cotton
• 1:39—(Note this scene is only available on the Criterion laser disc version. 0:40 into side B of the laser disc.) Breasts, when running from her bed to talk with Divine.
Female Trouble (1974) . . . . Donna
Desperate Living (1977) . . . . Princess Coo-Coo
Serial Mom (1993) . . . . Book Buyer

• Pearcy, Patricia

Films:
Cockfighter (1974). . . . . Mary Elizabeth
••• 0:28—Breasts, while talking with Warren Oates outdoors, next to lake. Long scene.
The Goodbye Girl (1977) . . . . Rhonda
TV:
One Life to Live (1973-74). . . . . Melinda Cramer

Pease, Patsy

Films:
He Knows You're Alone (1980). . . . . Joyce
• 0:42—Very, very brief left breast in open blouse when she turns around to turn off the lights.
Space Raiders (1983). . . . . Amanda
Improper Conduct (1994). . . . . Jo Ann
(Unrated version reviewed.)
TV:
Days of Our Lives . . . . Kimberly Brady Donovan
Search for Tomorrow. . . . . Cissy Mitchell

Peckinpaugh, Barbara

a.k.a. Adult film actress Susanna Britton.
Films:
Shadows Run Black (1981) . . . . Sandy
••• 0:57—Full frontal nudity, undressing in bedroom.
•• 0:58—Buns and very, very brief breasts getting into the shower.
••• 0:59—Full frontal nudity, drying herself off. Nude, walking around the house. Long scene.
•• 1:01—Nude, in the bathroom, trying to avoid the killer.
Homework (1982) . . . . Uncredited Magazine Model
••• 0:01—Brief breasts in magazine layout. In lingerie, then breasts in Tommy's photo session fantasy.
Erotic Images (1983) . . . . Cheerleader
• 0:07—Breasts dancing in an office with another cheerleader.
The Witching (1983) . . . . Jennie
a.k.a. Necromancy
(Originally filmed in 1971 as *Necromancy*, additional scenes were added and re-released in 1983.)
••• 0:02—Breasts and buns in open gown during occult ceremony. Brief full frontal nudity holding a doll up.
Basic Training (1984) . . . . Salesgirl 1
• 0:00—Breasts, while on desk.
Body Double (1984) . . . . Girl #2 (Holly Does Hollywood)
• 1:12—Brief breasts in orgy scene in adult film preview that Craig Wasson watches on TV. (Lettering gets in the way.)
Roller Blade (1986). . . . . Bod Sister
•• 0:33—Breasts during ceremony. Cut on her throat is unappealing.
••• 0:35—Full frontal nudity after dip in hot tub with the other two Bod Sisters. (She's the first to leave.)
•• 0:40—Nude, on skates with the other two Bod Sisters. (She's in the middle.)
Video Tapes:
Nudes in Limbo (1983) . . . . Model
Best Chest in the West (1984) . . . . Chrissy
••• 0:28—In two piece swimsuit, then breasts and buns.
Love Skills: A Guide to the Pleasures of Sex (1984)
. . . . Model
•• 0:02—Breasts, falling back into bed.
••• 0:09—Nude outside in field, making love with her lover.
••• 0:36—Nude, making love in bed with her lover.
••• 0:49—Nude in bed with Julie Parton while a guy watches.
Penthouse Love Stories (1986) . . . . Therapist's Assistant
••• 0:45—Nude, making love in Therapist's office, with the patient.

Pedriana, Lesa *

Video Tapes:
Playmates at Play (1990). . . . . Thrill Seeker, Flights of Fancy

Pelikan, Lisa

Wife of actor Bruce Davison.
Films:
Julia (1977) . . . . Young Julia
Jennifer (1978) . . . . Jennifer
• 0:45—Back side of right breast, in the showers by herself.
• 0:49—Full frontal nudity, falling into the pool from ladder. (Possibly a stunt double.)
The House of God (1984) . . . . Jo Miller
(Not available on video tape.)
Swing Shift (1984). . . . . Violet Mulligan
Ghoulies (1985). . . . . Rebecca
Lionheart (1990) . . . . Helena
Into the Badlands (1991). . . . . Sarah
Return to the Blue Lagoon (1991) . . . . Sarah
Made for Cable Movies:
The Color of Justice (1997; Showtime). . . . . Betty
Made for Cable TV:
Directed By: Present Tense, Past Perfect (1995; Showtime)
. . . . Lisa
Made for TV Movies:
The Best Little Girl in the World (1981) . . . . Gail Powell
TV:
Studs Lonigan (1979) . . . . Lucy Scanlon

Pelletier, Michèle Barbara

Films:

The Lotus Eaters (1993; Canadian) . . . . Anne-Marie Andrews
- 0:58—Side of left breast, when in cabin with Zoe's dad, Hal, while Zoe peeks in with her friend through the window.

Brainscan (1994) . . . . Stacie
Love and Human Remains (1995; Canadian) . . . . n.a.

Peluso, Felicia *

Films:

Enrapture (1989) . . . . Ingenue
Lunch Box (1991) . . . . Annie
- ••• 0:12—In sheer red bra, then nude, while doing strip routine on forklift truck in C.C.'s fantasy. Nice long scene.
- •• 0:40—Partial buns in swimsuit by pool in C.C.'s fantasy.
- •• 1:13—Breasts after taking off sheer red bra in front of C.C. in his room.

Peña, Elizabeth

Films:

Times Square (1980) . . . . Disco Hostess
They All Laughed (1981) . . . . Rita
Crossover Dreams (1985) . . . . Liz
Down and Out in Beverly Hills (1986) . . . . Carmen
La Bamba (1987) . . . . Rosie Morales
- 0:06—Brief side view of right breast taking a shower outside when two young boys watch her from a water tower. Long shot, hard to see.

*batteries not included (1987) . . . . Marisa
Blue Steel (1989) . . . . Tracy Perez
Jacob's Ladder (1990) . . . . Jezzie
- 0:14—Side view of right breast taking off robe and getting into shower with Tim Robbins.
- ••• 0:16—Breasts several times opening dress and putting pants on, then in black bra.
- •• 0:31—Very, very brief breasts in bed with Robbins, then left breast a lot. Dark.

The Waterdance (1991) . . . . Rosa
Across the Moon (1994) . . . . Carmen
- 0:46—Left breast, while hugging James Remar in hot spring pool after people on off-road vehicles leave.

Dead Funny (1994) Viv
- 1:07—Left breast in gaping kimono (her face is painted white like a Japanese Kabuki dancer.)

It Came From Outer Space II (1996) . . . . Ellen Fields
Lone Star (1996) . . . . Pilar Cruz
GRIDLOCK'd (1997) . . . . Uncredited

Made for Cable Movies:

The Second Civil War (1997; HBO) . . . . Christina Fernandez

Made for Cable TV:

Dream On: Super Freak (1993; HBO) . . . . Debra
The Outer Limits: Living Hell (1995; Showtime) . . . . Dr. Jennifer Martinez
Dead Man's Gun: The Fortune Teller (1997; Showtime) . . . . Gisella

Made for TV Movies:

Shannon's Deal (1989) . . . . Lucy
Fugitive Among Us (1992) . . . . Flo Martin
Roommates (1994) . . . . Lisa
The Invaders (1995) . . . . Ellen

TV:

Tough Cookies (1986) . . . . Officer Connie Rivera
I Married Dora (1987-88) . . . . Dora
Shannon's Deal (1991) . . . . Lucy

Pencheva, Anya

Films:

Time of Violence (1988; Bulgarian) . . . . Sevda
a.k.a. Vreme Razdelno
Deathstalker IV: Match of Titans (1990) . . . . Janeris
- 0:16—Brief left breast in open top, while wrestling with Maria Ford in the water.
- 0:36—Brief left breast, while kissing her lover slave girl during brief orgy scene.

Pendlebury, Anne

Films:

Alvin Purple (1973; Australian) . . . . Woman with Pin
- •• 0:48—Right breast and lower frontal nudity, while lying in bed, talking with Alvin.

Jock Petersen (1974; Australian) . . . . Peggy
a.k.a. Petersen

Penhaligon, Susan

Films:

The Land That Time Forgot (1975; British) . . . . Lisa
Soldier of Orange (1977; Dutch) . . . . Susan
- 1:34—Brief breasts kissing her boyfriend when Rutger Hauer sees them through the window. Medium long shot.
- ••• 1:36—Breasts in bed with her boyfriend and Hauer.

The Uncanny (1977; British) . . . . Janet

Made for TV Movies:

Count Dracula (1977; British) . . . . Lucy

Penotti, Bernadette

Films:

Regarding Henry (1991) . . . . Lawyer
Kiss of Death (1994) . . . . Molested Dancer
- 0:52—Brief breasts on stage.

Pensler Gabrielli, Elisa

Films:

Alien Space Avenger (1988) . . . . Red Riding Hood
Naked Gun 33 1/3: The Final Insult (1993) . . . . Mourner
The Brady Bunch Movie (1994) . . . . Miss Lynley

Made for Cable Movies:

Rebel Highway: Reform School Girl (1994; Showtime) . . . . Velmont Girl

Video Tapes:

Eden 2 (1992) . . . . Celine
- ••• 0:06—Breasts in sauna talking with Randi.
- ••• 0:25—Breasts in bed with Randi.
- 1:16—Breasts while frolicking in the ocean with Randi.
- ••• 1:24—Breasts while making love in bed with Greg.
- •• 1:27—Left breast, while lying in bed and talking with Greg.

Perez, Rosie *

Dancer/Choreographer.

Films:

Do the Right Thing (1989) . . . . Tina
- •• 1:22—Breasts when Spike Lee rubs ice all over her. Don't see her face, but it's her.

Night on Earth (1992) . . . . Angela
a.k.a. Une Nuit Sur Terre
White Men Can't Jump (1992) . . . . Gloria Clemente
- •• 0:36—Breasts in shower and making love in bed with Woody Harrelson.
- 0:39—Brief right breast, while sitting up in bed.
- 0:40—Very brief side of right breast, three times, while getting out of bed quickly.

Fearless (1993) . . . . Carla Rodrigo

Untamed Heart (1993) . . . . Cindy
It Could Happen to You (1994) . . . . Muriel Lang
Made for Cable Movies:
Criminal Justice (1990; HBO). . . . . Denise Moore
Made for Cable TV:
Subway Stories (1997; HBO) .The Girl

Perkins, Elizabeth

Films:
About Last Night... (1986) . . . . Joan
From the Hip (1987) . . . . .Jo Ann
Big (1988). . . . . Susan
Sweet Hearts Dance (1988). . . . . .Adie Nims
Avalon (1990) . . . . .Ann
Love at Large (1990) .Stella Wynkowski
The Doctor (1991) . . . . June Ellis
he said, she said (1991). Lorie Bryer
- 1:15—Brief breasts getting into the shower with Kevin Bacon.

Over Her Dead Body (1992) . . . . June
a.k.a. Enid Is Sleeping
Indian Summer (1993) . . . . .Jennifer Morton
The Flintstones (1994). . . . . Wilma Flintstone
Miracle on 34th Street (1994) . . . . Dorey Walker
Moonlight and Valentino (1995) . . . . . Rebecca Trager Lott
- 0:27—Brief tip of right breast, while sitting in bathtub. Brief partial right breast when starting to clean the tiles.
- 0:48—Brief buns, while lying in steam room.

Made for Cable Movies:
Rescuers, Stories of Courage: Two Women (1997; Showtime) . . . . .Gertrude Babilinska
Made for TV Movies:
For Their Own Good (1993) . . . . Sally Wheeler

Perkins, Millie

Films:
The Diary of Anne Frank (1959). . . . . Anne Frank
Ensign Pulver (1964) . . . . Scotty
Ride in the Whirlwind (1965) . . . . .Abby
The Shooting (1967). . . . . .Woman
Wild in the Streets (1968) . . . . Mary Fergus
Cockfighter (1974) . . . . Frances Mansfield
The Witch Who Came From the Sea (1976). . . . . . . Molly
- 0:14—Brief left breast, while talking with two guy who smoke drugs.
- •• 0:16—Breasts, when putting on blouse in bedroom while talking to the two guys and tying them up.
- 0:17—Right breast in open blouse while guy in bed plays with her left breast using his foot.
- 0:30—Breasts, while lying back in bed and talking with a guy.
- •• 0:41—Breasts, while lying on her back, getting a tattoo.
- •• 1:00—Breasts, while lying on her back with a guy.
- 1:01—Very, very brief left breast, when getting out of bed, upper half of breasts, when walking to the bathroom.
- •• 1:02—Breasts, after killing guy with razor in bathroom.

Table for Five (1983) . . . . Kathleen
At Close Range (1986). . . . . Julie Whitewood
Jake Speed (1986) . . . . Mrs. Winston
Slam Dance (1987; U.S./British) . . . . .Bobbie Nye
Wall Street (1987) . . . . Mrs. Fox
Two Moon Junction (1988) . . . . .Mrs. Delongpre
Necronomicon: Book of the Dead (1993) . . . . Lena
The Chamber (1996). . . . . Ruth Kramer
Made for TV Movies:
Broken Angel (1988) . . . . .n.a.
Call Me Anna (1990) . . . . Frances Duke
Murder of Innocence (1993) . . . . Edna Webber
TV:
Knots Landing (1983-84). .Jane Sumner

Perle, Rebecca

Films:
Bachelor Party (1984) . . . . Screaming Woman
Savage Streets (1984) . . . . .Cindy Clark
- •• 0:53—Brief breasts in biology class getting her top torn off by Linda Blair.

Tightrope (1984). . . . . .Becky Jacklin
Stitches (1985) . . . . .Bambi Belinka
- ••• 0:33—Breasts during female medical student's class where they examine each other.
- 1:00—Brief breasts on bed with Parker Stevenson when discovered by Nancy.

Heartbreak Ridge (1986). . . . . Student in Shower
- 1:48—Very brief breasts getting out of shower when the Marines rescue the students.

Not of This Earth (1988) . . . . .Alien Girl
Made for TV Movies:
His Mistress (1984) . . . . Megan

Perrier, Mireille

Films:
Bad Blood (1987; French) . . . . The Young Mother
Love Without Pity (1991; French) . . . . Nathalie
Toto the Hero (1991; French). . . . . Adult Evelyne
- ••• 1:04—Breasts, while sitting up in bed and turning around after making love with Thomas.

*Perrine, Valerie **

Films:
Slaughterhouse Five (1972). . . . . Montana Wildhack
- 0:39—Breasts in *Playboy* magazine as a Playmate.
- 0:43—Breasts getting into the bathtub.
- ••• 1:27—Breasts in a dome with Michael Sacks.

The Last American Hero (1973) .Marge
a.k.a. Hard Driver
Lenny (1974) . . . . .Honey Bruce
- ••• 0:14—Breasts in bed when Dustin Hoffman pulls the sheet off her then makes love.
- •• 0:17—Breasts sitting on the floor in a room full of flowers when Hoffman comes in.
- 0:24—Left breast wearing pastie doing dance in flashback.
- 0:43—Right breast with Kathryn Witt.

Mr. Billion (1977). . . . . Rosi Jones
Superman (1978) . . . . Eve
The Electric Horseman (1979) . . . . Charlotta Steele
The Magician of Lublin (1979). . . . . Zeftel
Can't Stop the Music (1980) . . . . .Samantha Simpson
- 1:12—Brief breasts, while splashing around in the spa with The Village People.

Agency (1981; Canadian) . . . . Brenda Wilcox
The Border (1982). . . . . .Marcy
Water (1986; British) . . . . Pamela
Maid to Order (1987) . . . . .Georgette Starkey
Bright Angel (1990). . . . . Alleen
Boiling Point (1992; U.S./French). Mona
The Break ...Is All You Need (1994) . . . . .Delores Smith
Girl in the Cadillac (1995) . . . . Tilly
Miniseries:
Secrets of Lake Success (1993). . . . . Honey Potts Atkins

TV:

Leo and Liz in Beverly Hills (1986) . . . . Liz Green

Perry, Donna *

Video Tapes:

Wet & Wild: Hot Holidays (1995) . . . . Playmate

Playboy Video Calendar 1997 (1996) . . . . March

••• 0:10—In lingerie and nude, while posing in a studio, sometimes with a seal.

••• 0:11—In lingerie and nude, while posing indoors and making love with a fantasy guy in bed.

Playboy's 21 Playmates (1996) . . . . Playmate

••• 0:06—Nude in still photos.

••• 0:07—Nude in outdoor pool scenes.

Persaud, Jenna *

Films:

The Other Woman (1992) . . . . Traci Collins

(Unrated version reviewed.)

•• 0:21—Breasts under sheer black top in her apartment with her boyfriend.

••• 0:22—Breasts taking off her top and getting milk poured on her.

••• 0:23—Breasts and buns, making love in kitchen while Jessica secretly watches.

•• 0:31—Breasts posing with Sheila at the beach for Elysse.

••• 0:32—Full frontal nudity at the beach some more.

• 0:33—Breasts and buns, running in the surf. Long shot.

•• 0:40—Breasts, during Jessica's flashbacks.

••• 0:53—Nude, taking a shower, drying herself off and putting on robe.

••• 0:57—Breasts posing with Carl during photo shoot.

•• 0:59—More breasts during photo shoot.

••• 1:09—Breasts and buns, on the floor making love with Jessica. Interesting camera angles.

• 1:23—Breasts, while on the floor with Jessica during video playback on TV.

Video Tapes:

Penthouse The Great Pet Hunt—Part I (1992) . . . . . . Pet

Persson, Carina *

Video Tapes:

Playboy's Playmate Review 2 (1984) . . . . Playmate

Playmates at Play (1990) . . . . . . Thrill Seeker, Free Wheeling

Pescia, Lisa

Films:

Tough Guys (1986) . . . . Customer #1

Body Chemistry (1990) . . . . Claire

••• 0:18—Breasts making love with Marc Singer standing up, then at foot of bed.

• 0:55—Buns, standing in hallway. Long shot.

Body Chemistry 2: Voice of a Stranger (1991) . . . . Claire Archer

• 0:42—Brief buns and side of left breast, making love on stairs with Dan.

••• 0:52—Breasts and buns, in bathtub, standing up, sitting back down while talking with Dan.

• 1:07—Buns, in leather outfit in radio control booth with Morton Downey Jr.

• 1:18—Very brief buns and left breast on the stairs in flashback.

The Dark Dancer (1994) . . . . Carla Simpson

• 0:00—Brief buns in G-string, while dancing on stage.

The New Age (1994) . . . . Nova Trainee

Peters, Lorraine

Films:

More Deadly than the Male (1961) . . . . Rita

The Wicker Man (1973; British) . . . . Girl on Grave

• 0:22—Side view of right breast sitting on grave, crying. Dark, long shot, hard to see.

The Innocent (1985; British) . . . . n.a.

Peters, Luan

Films:

Freelance (1970; British) . . . . Rosemary

a.k.a. Con Man

• 0:25—Right breast and buns, while making love with Gary and Mitch.

• 0:26—Left breast, twice, while making love with Gary and Mitch.

Lust for a Vampire (1970; British) . . . . Trudi

Man of Violence (1970; British) . . . . Angel

a.k.a. The Sex Racketeers

Not Tonight Darling (1971; British) . . . . Karen

•• 0:04—Breasts and buns, taking off nightie and getting into bathtub.

• 0:05—Most of right breast, while sitting in tub, wishing her husband would look at her.

•• 0:20—Breasts, while in bathroom, taking off her nightie while Eddie watches through binoculars.

•• 0:26—Right breast, while sitting in bathtub. Brief full frontal nudity when getting out.

••• 0:38—In white bra, then breasts, while undressing in room with Alex.

••• 0:39—Right breast, while making love in bed with Alex. Brief breasts in close-up.

• 0:42—Breasts under sheer top.

• 0:58—Buns, while getting massaged by Joan at the health club.

Twins of Evil (1971; British) . . . . Gerta

The Flesh & Blood Show (1974; British) . . . . Carol

Land of the Minotaur (1976) . . . . Laurie Gordon

Pacific Banana (1980; Australian) . . . . Candy Bubbles

•• 1:00—Breasts several times flashing her breasts for Martin.

Peters, Vicki *

Films:

Blood Mania (1970) . . . . Gail

•• 1:04—Breasts, while making love with Dr. Cooper in front of the fire. Seen through flames. Intercut with a rape scene.

• 1:10—Brief breasts in bathroom. More brief breasts, while getting beaten to death by Victoria and dragged through the house.

• 1:15—Very brief breasts, while dead, covered with blood when discovered by Craig.

• 1:17—Brief breasts while being placed in car. Covered with blood.

Peterson, Cassandra

See: Elvira.

Peterson, Julie *

Video Tapes:

Playboy Video Calendar 1988 (1987) . . . . Playmate

Sensual Pleasures of Oriental Massage (1990) . . . . . . n.a.

Playboy's 21 Playmates: Volume II (1996) . . . . . . Playmate

••• 1:07—Full frontal nudity in still photos.

••• 1:07—Nude in fire fantasy sequence.

Peterson, Marion *

Films:

Aria (1987; U.S./British) . . . . Young Girl in Pink
- • 0:22—Brief breasts with another girl in a weight lifting room walking around with muscular guys.
- • 0:25—Brief breasts again.
- •• 0:27—Nude in front of a weight lifter.
- • 0:29—More nude, posing while the guys walk by.

Les Expoits d'un Jeune Don Juan (1987; French/Italian) . . . Kate

Made for Cable TV:

Strangers: Windows (1992; HBO) . . . . n.a.
(Available on the video tape *Strangers.*)

Peterson, Monica

Films:

M*A*S*H (1970) . . . . Pretty WAC

Antony and Cleopatra (1972) . . . . Iras
- • 0:33—Brief buns, when another woman playfully spanks her and covers her with a towel.

The Dark (1979) . . . . Mrs. Lydell

Petruno, Lisa

Films:

Galactic Gigolo (1988) . . . . Sandy
a.k.a. Club Earth
- •• 0:27—Breasts (she's on the right) while in hot tub with Eoj and Kathy.

Angel of Passion (1991) . . . . Sheryl Diamond
- •• 0:00—Making love with the husband on the stairs.

Pettet, Joanna

Films:

The Group (1966) . . . . Kay Strong
Casino Royale (1967; British) . . . . Mata Bond
The Night of the Generals (1967; British/French) . . . . Ulrike
Robbery (1967; British) . . . . Kate Clifton
Blue (1968) . . . . Joanne Morton
The Best House in London (1969; British)
. . . . Josephine Pacefoot
Welcome to Arrow Beach (1973) . . . . Grace Henry
a.k.a. Tender Flesh
A Killer in Every Corner (1974; British) . . . . Sylvia
The Evil (1977) . . . . Caroline
Double Exposure (1983) . . . . Mindy Jordache
- •• 0:55—Breasts, making love in bed with Adrian.

Sweet Country (1985) . . . . Monica

Miniseries:

Captains and the Kings (1976) . . . . Katherine Hennessey

TV:

Knots Landing (1983) . . . . Janet Baines

Petty, Danielle

Films:

Seduction of Innocence (1994) . . . . Star
- •• 0:15—Breasts, while dancing with a customer.
- • 0:16—Breasts, while in office.

Surf, Sand and Sex (1994) . . . . Sixth Woman
- ••• 0:54—In bra, then breasts, buns and very, very brief partial lower frontal nudity, when making love with a guy she met while hiking in the mountains.
- • 1:10—Breasts, during end credits.

Made for Cable TV:

Erotic Confessions: Trapped (1997; Cinemax) . . . . Reba
- ••• 0:09—Nude, while trying on lingerie in store with Beverly, then making love with her.

Petty, Lori *

Films:

Cadillac Man (1990) . . . . Lila

Point Break (1991) . . . . Tyler
- • 1:14—Very brief buns, running out of Keanu Reeves' bedroom.

A League of Their Own (1992) . . . . Kit Keller
Free Willy (1993) . . . . Rae Lindley
Poetic Justice (1993) . . . . Penelope
The Glass Shield (1994) . . . . Deputy Deborah Fields
In the Army Now (1994) . . . . Christine Jones
Tank Girl (1995) . . . . Rebecca Buck/Tank Girl

TV:

The Thorns (1988) . . . . Cricket
Booker (1990) . . . . Suzanne Dunne
Lush Life (1996) . . . . Georgette Sanders

Petty, Rhonda

a.k.a. Adult film actress Rhonda Jo Petty.

Films:

Auditions (1978) . . . . Patty Rhodes
- •• 0:26—Breasts during audition.
- •• 0:30—Breasts, standing next to Larry and full frontal nudity straddling him on the table.

Pettyjohn, Angelique

a.k.a. Heaven St. John.

Adult Films:

Body Talk (1982) . . . . Cassie
Breasts and more!

Titillation (1982) . . . . Brenda Weeks
Breasts and more!

Films:

Clambake (1967) . . . . Gloria
Childish Things (1969) . . . . Angelique

The Curious Female (1969) . . . . Susan Rome/Girl #1
- ••• 0:29—Buns, while running in slow motion to the pool, then putting on towel. Breasts on diving board.
- ••• 0:30—Breasts and buns, while on inflatable mattress in pool.
- •• 0:52—Breasts while talking on the phone.
- • 0:55—Breasts while making love in bed with a guy.
- • 1:01—Brief breasts, while jumping into pool. Long shot.

Heaven with a Gun (1969) . . . . Emily
The Mad Doctor of Blood Island (1969; Philippines/U.S.)
. . . . Sheila Willard
Tell Me That You Love Me, Junie Moon (1970) . . . . Melissa

The G.I. Executioner (1971) . . . . Bonnie
a.k.a. Wit's End
a.k.a. Dragon Lady
- •• 0:16—Doing a strip routine on stage. Buns in G-string, very brief side view of right breast, then breasts at end.
- •• 0:40—Breasts, lying asleep in bed.
- ••• 0:58—Breasts and buns, undressing in front of Dave, getting into bed, fighting an attacker and getting shot. Long scene.
- • 1:14—Breasts, lying shot in rope net.

The Lost Empire (1983) . . . . Whiplash

Bio-Hazard (1984) . . . . Lisa Martyn
- •• 0:30—Partial left breast on couch with Mitchell. In beige bra and panties talking on telephone, breast almost falling out of bra.
- ••• 1:15—Left breast, on couch with Mitchell, in out-take scene during the end credits.
- • 1:16—Upper half of left breast on couch again during a different take.

Repo Man (1984) .... Repo Wife #2
Takin' It Off (1984) .... Anita Little
The Wizard of Speed & Time (1988) .... Dora Belair
TV:
Star Trek: The Gamesters of Triskelion .... Shahna

Pfeiffer, Dedee

Sister of actress Michelle Pfeiffer.
Films:
Into the Night (1985) .... Hooker
Moving Violations (1985) .... Cissy
Dangerously Close (1986) .... Nicki
Vamp (1986) .... Amaretto
The Allnighter (1987) .... Val
The Horror Show (1989) .... Bonnie McCarthy
- • 1:06—Brief breasts and buns from above, shampooing her hair in the shower. Breasts, seen through shower curtain. Probably a body double.

Red Surf (1989) .... Rebecca
A Climate for Killing (1990) .... Donna
Tune in Tomorrow (1990) .... Nellie
a.k.a. Aunt Julia and the Scriptwriter
Frankie & Johnny (1991) .... Frankie's Cousin
Shoot (1991) .... Catherine
Double Exposure (1993) .... Linda Mack
- • 1:22—Brief left breast while in bed with Jennifer Gatti.
- •• 1:23—Left breast, quite a few times, while lying on her back.

Falling Down (1993) .... Sheila (Whammyburger)
Running Cool (1993) .... Michele
Deadly Past (1994) .... Kirsten
- • 0:38—Brief breasts, while making love with Luke in the kitchen.

My Family (1995) .... Karen Gillespie
Up Close & Personal (1996) .... Luanne Atwater
Made for Cable TV:
Dream On: ...And Sheep Are Nervous (1990) .... Mary
Made for TV Movies:
Toughlove (1985) .... Kristen March
Highway Heartbreaker (1992) .... Emily
A Kiss So Deadly (1996) .... Katherine Deese
TV:
Cybill (1995-98) .... Rachel Blanders
For Your Love (1998-) .... n.a.

Pfeiffer, Michelle

Sister of actress DeDee Pfeiffer.
Ex-wife of actor Peter Horton.
Films:
Falling in Love Again (1980) .... Sue Wellington
The Hollywood Knights (1980) .... Suzi Q.
Charlie Chan & the Curse of the Dragon Queen (1981)
.... Cordella Farrington III
Grease 2 (1982) .... Stephanie Zinone
Scarface (1983) .... Elvira
Into the Night (1985) .... Diana
- •• 0:27—Brief buns while in bathroom.
- • 0:28—Brief side nudity, twice, walking past doorway. Medium long shot.

Ladyhawke (1985) .... Isabeau
Sweet Liberty (1986) .... Faith Healey
Amazon Women on the Moon (1987) .... Brenda Landers
The Witches of Eastwick (1987) .... Sukie Ridgemont
Dangerous Liaisons (1988) .... Madame de Tourvel
Married to the Mob (1988) .... Angela de Marco
Tequila Sunrise (1988) .... Jo Ann
The Fabulous Baker Boys (1989) .... Susie Diamond
The Russia House (1990) .... Katya
Frankie & Johnny (1991) .... Frankie
Batman Returns (1992) .... Selina Kyle/Catwoman
The Age of Innocence (1993) .... Countess Ellen Olenska
Love Field (1993) .... Lurene Hallett
Wolf (1994) .... Laura Alden
Dangerous Minds (1995) .... LouAnne Johnson
One Fine Day (1996) .... Melanie Parker
To Gillian on her 37th Birthday (1996) .... Gillian Lewis
Up Close & Personal (1996) .... Tally Atwater
A Thousand Acres (1997) .... Rose Cook Lewis
- • 0:16—Brief right breast (with left breast covered with a prosthetic appliance to make it appear she has lost a breast to surgery) while lying down during medical exam. (The entire chest area below her neck is probably a prosthetic appliance, I haven't been able to get positive verification yet.)

Made for TV Movies:
The Children Nobody Wanted (1980) .... Jennifer Williams
Natica Jackson (1987) .... Natica Jackson
TV:
Delta House (1979) .... Bombshell

*Pflanzer, Krista **

Films:
Cheerleader Camp (1987) .... Suzy
a.k.a. Bloody Pom Poms
- •• 0:11—Breasts several times sunbathing on the rocks.
- • 0:14—Brief breasts in flashback.
- • 0:17—Breasts on TV in Timmy's video tape of sunbathing on the rocks.

*Pham, Linh Dan **

Films:
Indochine (1992; French) .... Camille
- •• 0:46—Right breast, when getting blood wiped off after a prisoner is shot and falls on her.
- •• 1:05—Brief breasts, while sitting in front of a mirror.

• *Phillips, Ashley*

Video Tapes:
Body Language (1996) .... Bath Tub
- ••• 0:34—Nude, while caressing herself and taking a bath.

Hot Body Competition: Lusty Lingerie Contest (1996)
.... Ashley Phillips
- ••• 0:29—Nude, dancing on stage during contest. Including playing with fire.
- ••• 0:44—Nude, while posing on balcony.

Phillips, Bobbie

Films:
Body of Influence (1992) .... First Woman
(Unrated version reviewed.)
Animal Instincts 2 (1993) .... Waitress
Hail Caesar (1993) .... Buffer
TC 2000 (1993) .... Zoey Kinsella/TC 2000 X
Back in Action (1994) .... Helen
Ring of Fire 3: Lion Strike (1994) .... Kelly
Showgirls (1995) .... Dee
(NC-17 version reviewed.)
- •• 0:19—Breasts, while standing behind Carmi and holding a snake.
- • 0:31—Breasts under sheer purple bodysuit backstage after Elizabeth Berkley's lap dance.

• 0:49—Breasts and buns in G-string, while sitting down (wearing sunglasses), then standing up.

Made for Cable TV:

Red Shoe Diaries: Luscious Lola (1995; Showtime) .... Mimi Johnson

• 0:15—Breasts, under sheer blouse.

••• 0:21—Breasts, while making love in bed with Michael.

Stargate SG-1: Brief Candle (1997; Showtime) .... Kynthia

TV:

The Bold and the Beautiful (1994)................. Rhonda

Murder One (1995)........................ Julie Costello

Pointman (1995)............................. Brenner

The Watcher (1995) .... Lori Danforth

The Cape (1996-97) .... Barbara De Santos

*Phillips, Michelle **

Former singer with the group the Mamas and the Papas.

Mother of actress/singer Chynna Phillips.

Ex-wife of actor Dennis Hopper.

Films:

The Last Movie (1971) .... Banker's Daughter

Dillinger (1973)........................ Billie Frechette

Valentino (1977; British)............... Natasha Rambova

• 0:53—Brief buns, enticing Rudolf Nureyev into tent.

• 0:54—Brief lower frontal nudity, when sitting up in bed.

••• 0:55—Brief left breast when Nureyev moves her hair out of the way. Breasts, while getting up and out of bed.

•• 1:39—Brief right breast, after Nureyev rolls off her.

Bloodline (1979) .... Vivian Nichols

The Man with Bogart's Face (1980)........... Gena Anastas

Savage Harvest (1981) .... Maggie

American Anthem (1987) .... Linda Tevere

Let It Ride (1989) .... Mrs. Davis

Rubdown (1990)................................. n.a.

Scissors (1990) .... Ann Carter

Army of One (1993) .... Esther

Made for TV Movies:

The Users (1978)......................... Marina Brent

Assault & Matrimony (1987)..................... Madge

Pretty Poison (1996) .... Mrs. Stepanek

Knots Landing: Back to the Cul-de-Sac (1997).......... Anne

TV:

Search for Tomorrow...................... Ruby Ashford

Hotel (1986) .... Elizabeth Bradshaw Cabot

Knots Landing (1987) .... Anne Matheson

Knots Landing (1990-93) .... Anne Matheson

Second Chances (1993-94)....................... Joanna

Malibu Shores (1996) .... Suki Walker

*Phillips, Sam **

Not to be confused with the Sam Phillips (formerly known as Leslie Phillips) in *Die Hard with a Vengeance.*

Films:

Phantasm II (1988)......................... Alchemy

•• 1:00—Breasts making love in bed with Lance.

Deceit (1989)......................... Eve Bendibuckle

• 0:25—In bra and panties after Bailey forces her to strip. Buns in panties. Dressed like this until 1:22.

Sonny Boy (1989) .... Wife

Dollman (1990)................................... Tina

Rescue Me (1991) .... Cherie

Angel 4: Undercover (1993) .... Jade

• 0:18—Breasts in open robe, while sitting on dressing room counter in front of Piston.

Sexual Malice (1993) .... Nicole

(Unrated version reviewed.)

••• 1:30—Brief buns in raised skirt, then breasts, while making love with Edward Albert on sofa.

Weekend at Bernie's II (1993) .... Pretty Young Thing

The Dallas Connection (1994)........... Samantha Maxx

• 0:21—Breasts, while getting out of sweaty workout clothes.

0:36—Breasts, while making love with Mark on couch.

•• 0:51—Buns in lingerie then breasts in Antonio's daydream.

Phantasm III: Lord of the Dead (1994)............. Alchemy

Butter (1997)................................... Dina

• 0:47—Brief breasts, while dancing with another girl.

Made for Cable TV:

Hot Springs Hotel (1998- ; Showtime).................. Kat

Hot Springs Hotel: Travels with Travis (1998; Showtime) .... Kat

••• 0:20—Breasts, while making love with Travis in bed.

Hot Springs Hotel: Cheerleaders (1998; Showtime) . . . Kat

••• 0:20—Breasts, while making love with Kevin.

Hot Springs Hotel: To Your Health (1998; Showtime) .... Kat

• 0:17—Partial buns in panties, while watching TV.

Video Tapes:

Rock Video Girls (1991) .... Herself

•• 0:47—Brief breasts and buns quite a few times, while wearing a G-string.

Playboy's 101 Ways to Excite Your Lover (1992) .... Hearing/Woman

•• 0:24—In lingerie, then nude with her lover.

Playboy's How to Reawaken Your Sexual Powers (1992) .... Cast Member

••• 0:17—Full frontal nudity while making love with her lover by lava flow.

••• 0:37—Nude while writing love letter, making love by campfire and kissing by waterfall.

Making of the "Carousel Girls' Calendar" (1993) .... Miss September

••• 1:00—Breasts and brief buns during photo shoot.

••• 1:03—Nude during interview segment.

Penthouse's 25th Anniversary Swimsuit Video (1993) .... Pet

Penthouse Party with the Pets (1994) .... n.a.

Penthouse Behind the Scenes (1995) .... Pet

••• 0:00—Nude in various segments throughout the video tape.

CD-ROM:

Penthouse Interactive Virtual Photo Shoot, Disc 3 (1993)... Pet

Phoenix, Rainbow

Sister of the late actor River Phoenix and actor Joaquin Phoenix.

Films:

Maid to Order (1987) .... Brie Starkey

Even Cowgirls Get the Blues (1994)..... Bonanza Jellybean

• 0:49—Very brief lower frontal nudity, after pulling down her pants with the other cowgirls.

Picard, Nicole

Films:

Deadtime Stories (1985) .... Rachel (Red Riding Hood)

• 0:48—Very brief right breast in shack with boyfriend.

Dangerous Love (1988)............................ Jane

Ghoulies III, Ghoulies Go To College (1991)........ Party Girl

A Time to Die (1991)............................ Patti

*Picasso, Paloma **

Daughter of the late painter Pablo Picasso.
Sells her own perfume.

Films:

Immoral Tales (1975; French) . . . Countess Erzsebet Bathory
- ••• 0:59—Nude, getting her clothes ripped off by a bunch of women in a room.
- • 1:00—Briefly nude, while walking away from the women.
- •• 1:02—Nude, while bathing in blood.
- ••• 1:05—Nude, walking down stairs. Then in bed with another woman.
- ••• 1:08—Nude in bed and sitting up.

• Piccolini, Joli

Films:

Wish Me Luck (1995). . . . . Dream Girl
(Unrated version reviewed.)
- ••• 0:08—Full frontal nudity (she's the redhead), while frolicking in bed and making love with a blonde Dream Girl.

A Passion for Murder (1996) .Waitress
a.k.a. Deadlock

• Piccolo, Ottavia

Films:

The 13 Chairs (1969; French/Italian/British) . . . . . . Stefanella
- • 1:18—Very brief buns while running up the stairs, while wearing an apron during chase through the garden. Long shot.
- • 1:21—Brief buns, twice, wearing apron during chase.
- • 1:23—Very brief blurry right breast, while getting into bed with Mario and Sharon Tate.

Zorro (1974; French/Italian) .Hortensia
Mado (1976; French) . . . . Mdo
The Family (1987; Italian/French) . . . . n.a.

Pick, Amelie

Films:

Souvenir (1988; British). . . . . Janni
Reunion (1989; French/German). . . . . Young Lover
- • 0:47—Brief breasts, twice, while making out in the woods with her boyfriend while two boys watch.

Pickett, Blake

Former hostess on the Nashville Network game show *Top Card.*
a.k.a. Josie Hunter.

Films:

Hauntedween (1991). . . . . n.a.
They Bite (1991). . . . . Model
- ••• 0:03—Left breast, then breasts and buns, taking off swimsuit for the photographer. More breasts in the water, struggling with the monster.

Traces of Blood (1991) . . . . Stunts
Vampire Trailer Park (1991) . . . . Jana Wisher
Can It Be Love (1992) . . . . Dyanne
a.k.a. Spring Break Sorority Babes
Dark Universe (1993). . . . . Kim Masters
- ••• 0:45—Breasts, in open blouse, while outside in the woods with Jack.

Hourglass (1995) . . . . Model
Double Your Pleasure (1997) . . . . Uncredited Judy
- ••• 1:13—Breasts and buns, while making love in bed with Robert.

Illicit Confessions (1997). . . . . Erica
- •• 0:00—Breasts and buns in T-back, while dancing in club.
- ••• 0:02—Nude, while having sex with a customer in bed.
- ••• 0:13—Buns in T-back and breasts, while having sex with Karl in bedroom.
- ••• 0:23—Nude, while stripping and dancing on stage.
- ••• 0:33—Nude, when having sex with Andrea, while her husband watches.
- ••• 0:43—Breasts, while starting to have sex with a customer.
- ••• 1:00—Nude, while having sex with another customer.
- ••• 1:09—Breasts and buns, while bathing, showering, then making love in bed with Ron.
- • 1:13—Breasts, while starting to lap dancer for a customer.
- ••• 1:24—Nude, while dancing on stage with another woman.
- •• 1:27—Breasts and buns in lingerie, while giving a customer a lap dance.

*Pickett, Cindy **

Wife of actor Lyman Ward.

Films:

Night Games (1980). Valerie St. John
- •• 0:05—Brief breasts, while getting scared by her husband in the shower.
- • 0:45—Buns and breasts by and in the swimming pool with Joanna Cassidy.
- • 0:46—Breasts under sheer blue dress during fantasy sequence with Cassidy.
- •• 0:48—Brief full frontal nudity getting out of the pool, then breasts lying down with Cassidy.
- ••• 1:14—Full frontal nudity standing up in bathtub, then breasts during fantasy with a guy in gold.
- •• 1:18—Breasts, while getting out of pool at night.
- ••• 1:24—Breasts, while sitting up in bed and stretching.

Brainwash (1982) . . . . Lyn Nilsson
Hysterical (1983). . . . . Kate
Ferris Bueller's Day Off (1986) . . . . Katie Bueller
The Men's Club (1986) . . . . .Hannah
Hot to Trot (1988). . . . . Victoria Peyton
Deepstar Six (1989). . . . . Diane Norris
Crooked Hearts (1991) . . . . Jill
Original Intent (1992) . . . . Marguerite
Stephen King's "Sleepwalkers" (1992). . . . . Mrs. Robertson
Son-In-Law (1993). . . . . Connie
Evolver (1994). . . . . Melanie Baxter
Coyote Summer (1995). . . . . .n.a.
Painted Hero (1995) . . . . .Sadie

Made for Cable Movies:

Wild Card (1992; USA) . . . . .Dana

Miniseries:

Amerika (1987) . . . . Amanda Bradford

Made for TV Movies:

Into the Homeland (1987). Rye Swallow
Plymouth (1991). . . . . .Addy
Her Hidden Truth (1995). . . . . .Laney Devereaux
Not Our Son (1995) . . . . Margaret Keller

TV:

The Guiding Light (1976-80). . . . . Jackie Scott Marler
Call to Glory (1984-85). Vanessa Sarnac
St. Elsewhere (1986-88) . . . . .Dr. Carol Novino

• Picot, Genevieve

Films:

Proof (1991; Australian). . . . . Celia
- •• 0:58—Breasts, in open blouse with Martin.
- • 0:59—Brief breasts, while turning around when Martin leaves.

Muriel's Wedding (1994; Australian) . . . . Store Detective

*Pierce, Jill **

Films:

Dance with Death (1991) . . . . Lola
- •• 0:07—Breasts and buns, dancing in wedding outfit on stage.
- • 0:11—Breasts and buns in G-string, dancing on stage. Long shot, seen in mirror. Buns while getting tips.
- • 0:28—Buns, while dancing on stage in the background.
- • 0:42—Buns in G-string dancing with Sherilyn on stage.
- • 0:56—Brief breasts on stage when Kelly talks to her.
- • 1:11—Buns, while dancing on stage.

Ring of the Musketeers (1992). . . . . Woman Fencer

Kickboxer 4—The Aggressor (1993) . . . . Darcy Cove
- •• 0:44—Breasts, while in room with Lando after taking off her dress.
- • 1:04—Left breast, after sitting up in bed.
- • 1:05—Brief breasts while lying back down on bed.

The Unborn II (1993) . . . . Young Mother
Cyborg Cop II (1994) . . . . Liz McDowell
Omega Doom (1995) . . . . Zinc
Mean Guns (1996) . . . . Mambo Woman

Made for Cable Movies:

Suspect Device (1995; Showtime) . . . . Operator

Witch Hunt (1995; HBO) . . . . Marie
- • 1:29—Breasts, while in bathtub when Eric Bogosian keeps putting her head under the water.

Video Tapes:

Eden (1992). . . . . Lacey
- ••• 0:20—In pink bra, then breasts and buns, while making love with B.D. in bedroom.
- ••• 1:05—Breasts undressing in bedroom with B.D.
- ••• 1:06—Breasts and buns, while making love in bed with B.D.
- ••• 1:32—Breasts in room with Marnie, while getting even with B.D.

Pigg, Alexandra

Films:

Letter to Brezhnev (1986; British). . . . . Elaine
- •• 0:57—Brief breasts in bed with a guy.

Chicago Joe and the Showgirl (1989; British) . . . . Violet
Bullseye! (1990) . . . . Car Hire Girl
Immortal Beloved (1994) . . . . Therese Obermayer

Pinkett, Jada

Wife of rapper/actor Will Smith.

Films:

The Inkwell (1993) . . . . Lauren Kelly
Menace II Society (1993). . . . . Ronnie
Demon Knight (1994). . . . . Jeryline
Jason's Lyric (1994) . . . . Lyric
(Unrated version reviewed.)
- 1:02—Nudity in the woods with Allen Payne was done by a body double.
- • 1:15—Brief buns in hiked up dress, while making love with Allen Payne in store.

A Low Down Dirty Shame (1994) . . . . Peaches
The Nutty Professor (1996) . . . . Carla Purty
Set It Off (1996) . . . . Stony
Scream 2 (1997) . . . . Maureen Evans
Woo (1998). . . . . Darlene "Woo" Bates

Made for Cable Movies:

If These Walls Could Talk (1996; HBO). . . . . Patti

TV:

A Different World (1991) . . . . Lena James

Piper, Lara

Films:

The Courtyard (1995). . . . . Kimberly
- • 0:01—Brief left and right breast, in close-up shot. You don't see her face.

TV:

Head of the Class (1989-91) . . . . Viki Amory
Key West (1993) . . . . Rikki

Pisier, Marie-France

Films:

Love at Twenty (1963; French/Italian/Japan) . . . . Colette
Trans-Europ-Express (1968; French). . . . . Eva
Stolen Kisses (1969; French) . . . . Colette Tazzi
Cousin, Cousine (1975; French). Karine
Other Side of Midnight (1977). . . . . Noëlle Page
- • 0:10—Very brief breasts in bed with Lanchon.
- • 0:28—Buns, in bed with John Beck. Medium long shot.
- • 0:50—Breasts in bathtub, while giving herself an abortion with a coat hanger. Painful to watch!
- •• 1:11—Breasts wearing white slip in room getting dressed in front of Henri.
- ••• 1:17—Full frontal nudity in front of fireplace with Armand, rubbing herself with oil, then making love with ice cubes. Very nice!
- • 1:35—Full frontal nudity taking off dress for Constantin in his room.

The Bronte Sisters (1979; French) . . . . Charlotte
French Postcards (1979) . . . . Madame Tessier
- •• 0:16—In white bra, then breasts in dressing room while a guy watches without her knowing.

Love on the Run (1979). . . . . Colette
a.k.a. L'Amour en Fuite
(French version with English subtitles.)
Chanel Solitaire (1981) . . . . Gabrielle Chanel
Miss Right (1987; Italian) . . . . Bebe
- •• 0:07—Breasts in open top dress when the reporter discovers her in a dressing room behind a curtain.

Miniseries:

Scruples (1980) . . . . Valentine O'Neill

• *Pitman Quinn, Patrice*

Films:

A Family Thing (1996) . . . . Willa Mae
- • 1:31—Brief buns, while lying on bed before giving birth in flashback. B&W.

TV:

NYPD Blue: Taillights's Last Gleaming (Feb 18, 1997) . . . . . n.a.

Pitt, Ingrid

Films:

Where Eagles Dare (1969; British) . . . . Heidi
The House That Dripped Blood (1970; British). . . . . Carla
Vampire Lovers (1970; British) . . . . Marcilla/Carmilla
- •• 0:32—Breasts and buns in the bathtub and reflection in the mirror talking to Emma.

Countess Dracula (1972; British) . . Countess Elizabeth Nadasdy
The Wicker Man (1973; British) . . . . Librarian
- •• 1:11—Brief breasts in bathtub seen by Edward Woodward.

The Final Option (1982; British). Helga
a.k.a. Who Dares Win
Wild Geese II (1985; British). . . . . The Hooker

Transmutations (1986) . . . . Pepperdine
a.k.a. Underworld
Hanna's War (1988) . . . . Margit

Place, Mary Kay

Films:
Starting Over (1979) . . . . Marie
The Big Chill (1983) . . . . Meg
Smooth Talk (1985) . . . . Katherine
A New Life (1988) . . . . Donna
Bright Angel (1990) . . . . Judy
Samantha (1991) . . . . Marilyn
Bed of Lies (1992) . . . . Jean Daniel Murph
Captain Ron (1992) . . . . Katherine Harvey
- 0:32—Brief right breast, then brief breasts in shower in boat with Martin Short. Overhead view. Hard to see her face, but it is her.

0:34—Buns, seen through shower door is a stunt double.
Teresa's Tattoo (1993) . . . . Nora
Citizen Ruth (1996) . . . . Gail Stoney
Manny and Lo (1996) . . . . Elaine
The Rainmaker (1997) . . . . Dot Black
Made for Cable Movies:
Directed By: Leslie's Folly (1994; Showtime) . . . . Susan
Directed By: The Gift (1994; Showtime) . . . . n.a.
Made for TV Movies:
Just My Imagination (1992) . . . . Sheila Hawk
Telling Secrets (1993) . . . . Shelley
In the Line of Duty: The Price of Vengeance (1994)
. . . . Norma Williams
Tales of the City (1994) . . . . Prue Giroux
For My Daughter's Honor (1996) . . . . Betty Ann Dustin
My Very Best Friend (1996) . . . . Molly
Love in Another Town (1997) . . . . Sam
TV:
Mary Hartman, Mary Hartman (1976-78) . . . . . Loretta Haggers

• *Plato, Dana* *

Films:
Return to Boggy Creek (1977) . . . . n.a.
The Sex Puppets (1992) . . . . J. D.
Different Strokes (1996) . . . . Jill Martin
(Unrated version reviewed.)
- 0:16—Briefly nude, taking off her robe and going for a swim. Long shot.
- •• 0:17—Very brief buns, when going under the water after talking with Jill. Nude, while swimming in the pool.
- •• 0:25—Nude, while taking a shower with Jill.
- 0:31—Breasts, while taking a shower when Jack peeks in the window.
- 0:32—Very brief left breast in flashback.
- 0:35—Brief breasts, taking off sweater before going to sleep.
- •• 0:54—Breasts, while making love with Jill in bed.
- 0:59—Buns, while lying in bed next to Jill.
- ••• 1:19—Breasts, while making love with Jill in bed.

TV:
Diff'rent Strokes (1978-84) . . . . Kimberly Drummond
CD-ROM:
Night Trap (1993) . . . . n.a.

Player Jarreau, Susan

Films:
Invasion of the Bee Girls (1973) . . . . Girl
The Pom Pom Girls (1976) . . . . Sue Ann
- 0:14—Breasts, when making out with Jesse in the back of his van while parked at burger joint.
- 0:47—Breasts, when making out with Jesse in the back of his van while parked at school.
- 1:02—Brief buns, taking off her panties in locker room with the other girls.

Malibu Beach (1978) . . . . Sally
- 0:28—Side view of left breast with boyfriend at night on the beach. Long shot.
- 0:32—Buns, when running into the ocean with her two male friends.
- 0:33—Brief side view of left breast in water. Long shot.
- 0:34—Brief breasts while in the ocean, then breasts while getting dressed by the fire.

Plimpton, Martha

Daughter of actor Keith Carradine and actress Shelley Plimpton.
Films:
Rollover (1981) . . . . Fewster's Older Daughter
The River Rat (1984) . . . . Jonsy
The Goonies (1985) . . . . Stef
The Mosquito Coast (1986) . . . . Emily Spellgood
Another Woman (1988) . . . . Laura Post
Running on Empty (1988) . . . . Lorna Phillips
Shy People (1988) . . . . Grace
Stars and Bars (1988) . . . . Bryant
Parenthood (1989) . . . . Julie
Silence Like Glass (1989) . . . . Claudia Jacoby
Stanley and Iris (1990) . . . . Kelly King
Samantha (1991) . . . . Samantha
A Woman at War (1991) . . . . Hélène
Inside Monkey Zetterland (1993) . . . . Sofie
Josh and S.A.M. (1993) . . . . Alison
My Life's In Turnaround (1993) . . . . Herself
Forbidden Choices (1994) . . . . Earlene Pomerleau
a.k.a. The Beans of Egypt, Maine
Mrs. Parker and the Vicious Circle (1994) . . . . Jane Grant
Last Summer in the Hamptons (1995) . . . . Chloe Garfield
Beautiful Girls (1996) . . . . Jan
I Shot Andy Warhol (1996) . . . . Stevie
- 0:16—Breasts, when having sex with Lili Taylor on bed while a customer watches and masturbates.

I'm Not Rappaport (1996) . . . . Laurie
Eye of God (1997) . . . . Ainsley DuPree
Made for Cable Movies:
Chantilly Lace (1993; Showtime) . . . . Ann
Daybreak (1993; HBO) . . . . Laurie
The Defenders: Payback (1997; Showtime) . . Mary Jane Preston
The Defenders: Choice of Evils (1998; Showtime)
. . . . Mary Jane Preston

Plimpton, Shelley

Mother of actress Martha Plimpton.
Films:
Alice's Restaurant (1969) . . . . Reenie
- •• 0:21—Breasts, taking off her blouse while sitting on bed and talking to Arlo Guthrie.

Putney Swope (1969) . . . . Face-Off Girl
Glen and Randa (1971) . . . . Randa
- ••• 0:01—Nude in the woods with Glen. Long scene.
- 0:40—Lower nudity, while lying on the ground when Glen tickles her.

Plummer, Amanda *

Daughter of actor Christopher Plummer and actress Tammy Grimes.

Films:

Cattle Annie and Little Britches (1980) .... Annie
- 0:39—Breasts visible under braless, wet long johns while standing in lake.

World According to Garp (1982)............... Ellen James
Daniel (1983) .... Susan Isaacson
The Hotel New Hampshire (1984).......... Miss Miscarriage
Made in Heaven (1987)..................... Wiley Foxx
Joe vs. the Volcano (1990)..................... Dagmar
The Fisher King (1991) ....Lydia
Freejack (1992)................................ Nun
Needful Things (1993) .... Nettie Cobb
Nostradamus (1993).................Catherine De Medici
So, I Married an Axe Murderer (1993)......... Rose Michaels
Pulp Fiction (1994) .... Honey Bunny
The Final Cut (1995)..........................Rothstein
The Prophecy (1995)............................Rachel

Butterfly Kiss (1996; British) ....Eunice
- 0:10—Breasts, after taking off her blouse and showing off her body piercing, chains and tattoos.
- •• 0:14—Breasts and buns, after taking off her blouse and getting into bed with Saskia Reeves. (Still wearing her body piercing, chains and tattoos.)
- 0:18—Brief breasts, when showing her chains and piercings to truck driver.
- 0:20—Partial buns, while having sex with the truck driver in the back of his truck.
- 1:05—Brief breasts, showing Mr. McDermott her chains and piercings in car.
- 1:09—Breasts, when taking off her clothes in room with Mr. McDermott.
- 1:11—Breasts, while in the shower when Reeves beats Mr. McDermott to death.
- ••• 1:15—Full frontal nudity, outdoors at night, when she takes her chains off with help from Reeves.

Freeway (1996)............................. Ramona
A Simple Wish (1997) .... Boots

Made for Cable Movies:

Last Light (1993; Showtime)................. Lillian Burke
Drunks (1995; Showtime)...................... Shelley
The Right to Remain Silent (1995; Showtime) . . Paulina Marcos
Don't Look Back (1996; HBO)................... Bridget

Made for Cable TV:

The Outer Limits: A Stitch in Time (1996; Showtime)
.... Dr. Theresa Givens

Made for TV Movies:

Miss Rose White (1992)..........................Luisa
Whose Child Is This? The War for Baby Jessica (1993)
............................Cara Clausen Schmidt

Podewell, Cathy

Films:

Night of the Demons (1987)...................... Judy
(Unrated version reviewed.)
- 0:06—Brief buns, while changing clothes and talking on the phone.

Beverly Hills Brats (1989).........................Tiffany

Made for TV Movies:

Earth Angel (1991) .... Angela

TV:

Dallas (1988-91) .... Cally Harper Ewing

Pohlkotte, Tanya

Films:

The New Age (1994)......................... Bettina
- •• 1:10—Breasts, while wearing black swimsuit bottom, walking into swimming pool. Tattoos on her arm and chest.
- 1:11—Breasts and buns in swimsuit, under the water in the swimming pool while talking with Peter Weller.

Search and Destroy (1995) .... Kim's Secretary

Made for Cable Movies:

National Lampoon's Favorite Deadly Sins (1995; Showtime)
.... Sara

Polo, Teri

Films:

Mystery Date (1991) .... Geena Matthews
Born to Ride (1992).......................... Beryl Ann
Passed Away (1992)...................... Rachel Scanlan
Aspen Extreme (1993)...................... Robin Hand

The House of Spirits (1993)....................... Rosa
- 0:09—Very, very brief upper half of left breast, while lying dead when Cora peeks in doorway to watch autopsy. Very brief breasts, while lying on table with cut open chest when Rosa peeks in the window. Probably not her real body.

Quick (1993) .... Quick
- 0:14—Brief buns, while lying face down, handcuffed to bed by Jeff Fahey.
- •• 0:42—Breasts, taking off her blouse in front of mirror, then putting on black bra.
- •• 1:06—In black bra, then breasts (mostly right breast) while making love in car with Herschel.

Golden Gate (1994) ....Cynthia
The Arrival (1996) .... Char

Made for Cable Movies:

A Prayer in the Dark (1997; USA)..................Janet

Made for Cable TV:

Tales From the Crypt: Revenge Is the Nuts (1994; HBO)
.... Sheila
Outer Limits: Identity Crisis (1998; Showtime). . . . Sally McCoy

Made for TV Movies:

Danielle Steel's "Full Circle" (1996) ....Tana Roberts
House of Frankenstein 1997 (1997)................. Grace

TV:

Loving .... Kristen Larsen
TV 101 (1988-89) .... Amanda Hampton
Northern Exposure (1994-95) .... Michelle Capra

Pond, Pamela

See: Runo, Pamela.

Pons, Joy *

Video Tapes:

Playboy's Girls of Radio: Talk, Rock and Shock (1995)
.... Herself
- ••• 0:37—Nude in airplane fantasy.

Poole, Tonya *

Films:

The Bikini Carwash Company II (1993)
.... Uncredited Bikini Girl Blonde
(Unrated version reviewed.)
- •• 0:16—Breasts at carwash during music video number. (Wearing black bikini bottoms.)
- •• 0:35—Breasts, when vacuum sucks her bikini top off at the carwash.

••• 0:40—In black lingerie, then buns in T-back and breasts in motorcycle cop commercial.
••• 0:42—Breasts and buns in T-back in "Rock Me" music video number.
••• 0:57—Breasts, while on kitchen table during commercial.
•• 1:29—Breasts during music video number at the carwash.
Seduce Me: Pamela Principle 2 (1994) .... Eve
••• 0:58—Breasts, while posing during photo shoot in studio.
Made for Cable Movies:
Attack of the 5' 2" Women (1994; Showtime)........ Cookie
Video Tapes:
Playboy's Erotic Fantasies (1992) .... Cast Member
Playboy's Secret Confessions (1993).. Wash & Wax/Jogger
••• 0:17—In wet leotard top, while washing the car. Full frontal nudity while making love with Dennis.

• *Poon, Alice*

Films:
Crash (1996; Canadian).....................Camera Girl
(NC-17 version reviewed.)
• 0:05—Left breast, then brief breasts, while making love with James Spader in camera room.
Half Baked (1997)......................... Supply Clerk
Made for Cable Movies:
Mistrial (1996; HBO).........................Linda Woo

Poremba, Jean

a.k.a. Adult film actress Candie Evens.
Films:
You Can't Hurry Love (1984) .... Model in Back
• 0:05—Breasts posing in the backyard getting photographed.
•• 0:48—Nude in backyard again getting photographed.
Takin' It All Off (1987) ....Allison
• 0:36—Buns in G-string and in pink bra.
••• 0:49—In white lingerie, then breasts, then nude dancing.
••• 0:58—Breasts and buns in G-string, dancing outside when she hears the music.
••• 0:59—Nude dancing in a park.
•• 1:01—Nude dancing in a laundromat.
••• 1:03—Nude dancing in a restaurant.
••• 1:07—Nude in shower with Adam.
•• 1:13—Breasts dancing for the music in a studio.
••• 1:23—Nude, dancing with the other girls on stage.

Porizkova, Paulina

Supermodel.
Wife of singer Rick Ocasek.
Films:
Anna (1987)............................... Krystyna
Her Alibi (1989) .... Nina
• 1:00—Very brief right nipple when pulling herself up out of the water in the swimming pool.
Arizona Dream (1994)............................Millie
Female Perversions (1997) .... Langley Flynn

Posey, Parker

Films:
Coneheads (1993) .... Stephanie
Dazed and Confused (1993)..........................Darla
Dead Connection (1993) ....Denise
Joey Breaker (1993)..........................Irene Kidare
Mixed Nuts (1994).........................Rollerblader
Sleep With Me (1994) .... Athena
• 0:56—Breasts, after taking off her blouse while straddling Eric Stoltz on sofa.
• 0:58—Brief breasts, while getting up off the floor after Stoltz changes his mind. Slightly out of focus.
Amateur (1995).......................... Girl Squatter
The Daytrippers (1995) .... Jo
The Doom Generation (1995)......................Brandl
Flirt (1995) ....Emily
Kicking and Screaming (1995)......................Miami
Party Girl (1995)..................................Mary
• 0:58—Very brief side of left breast, while getting into the shower with Leo.
Basquiat (1996)......................... Mary Boone
SubUrbia (1996) .... Erica
Waiting for Guffman (1996) .... Libby Mae Brown
The House of Yes (1997) .... Jackie-O
Made for Cable Movies:
Drunks (1995; Showtime) .... Debbie
More Tales of the City (1998; Canadian/U.S.; Showtime)
.... Connie Bradshaw
Made for TV Movies:
Tales of the City (1994) .... Connie Bradshaw
TV:
As the World Turns (1991-92) .... Tess Shelby

Potter, Madeleine

Films:
The Bostonians (1984)...................Verena Tarrant
Suicide Club (1988)............................Nancy
Bloodhounds of Broadway (1989)............Widow Mary
Slaves of New York (1989) ....Daria
• 1:14—Breasts making love with Stash on chair. Mostly see left breast. Dark.
Two Evil Eyes (1991) .... Annabelle
Made for TV Movies:
Svengali (1983).............................Antonia

Potts, Annie

Films:
Corvette Summer (1978).....................Vanessa
• 0:51—Silhouette of right breast in van with Mark Hamill. Out of focus breasts washing herself in the van while talking to him. Don't really see anything.
King of the Gypsies (1978) ....Persa
Heartaches (1981; Canadian) .... Bonnie Howard
Crimes of Passion (1984).................... Amy Grady
(Unrated version reviewed.)
Ghostbusters (1984) ....Janine Melnitz
Jumpin' Jack Flash (1986) .... Liz Carlson
Pretty in Pink (1986) .... Iona
Pass the Ammo (1988) .... Darla Potter
Ghostbusters II (1989)...................Janine Melnitz
Who's Harry Crumb? (1989) ....Helen Downing
Texasville (1990) ....Karla Jackson
Breaking the Rules (1992) .... Mary Klingsmith
Made for TV Movies:
Her Deadly Rival (1995)...................Kris Lanford
TV:
Goodtime Girls (1980) .... Edith Bedelmeyer
Designing Women (1986-93) ....Mary Jo Shively
Love & War (1993-95)..................Dana Paladino
Dangerous Minds (1996)............... Louanne Johnson
Over the Top (1997-) ....n.a.

Pouget, Ely

Films:
Endless Descent (1989)....................Ana Rivera

Cool Blue (1990) . . . . Christiane
•• 0:18—Side view of right breast, then breasts with Woody Harrelson.
Curly Sue (1991) . . . . Dinah Tompkins
Silent Victim (1992) . . . . Lauren McKinley
Death Machine (1994) . . . . Hayden Cale
Lawnmower Man 2 (1995) . . . . Dr. Cori Platt
Made for Cable TV:
Red Shoe Diaries: Weekend Pass (1993; Showtime) . . . . Private Jane Chandler
(Available on the video tape *Red Shoe Diaries 5: Weekend Pass.*)
••• 0:07—Breasts while making love in barracks with Eddie. Long scene.
••• 0:09—Buns and left breast while playing with camouflage paint.
••• 0:11—Breasts, when waking up in the morning and getting dressed.
• 0:12—Breasts in flashbacks.
••• 0:23—Breasts in bed with Eddie again.
TV:
Dark Shadows (1991) . . . . Maggie Evans

*Powell, Brittney **
a.k.a. Brittney Raché.
Films:
Round Trip to Heaven (1992) . . . . Contestant
• 0:36—Brief breasts, while putting on dark gray, one piece swimsuit in dressing room.
Airborne (1993) . . . . Nikki
To Be The Best (1993) . . . . Cheryl
The Unborn II (1993) . . . . Sally Anne Philips
Dragonworld (1994) . . . . Beth Armstrong
Fled (1996) . . . . Faith/Cindy
• 0:48—Brief beasts, while crawling on stage in club to kiss Stephen Baldwin, then standing up afterward.
That Thing You Do! (1996) . . . . Shades Fan
Made for TV Movies:
L.A. Johns (1997) . . . . Liz
TV:
High Sierra Search and Rescue (1995) . . . . Kaja
Pacific Palisades (1997) . . . . Beth Hooper
Video Tapes:
Playboy's Girls of Spring Break (1991) . . . . Herself
•• 0:26—Full frontal nudity in still photos.
•• 0:27—Full frontal nudity while posing for photos in studio.
••• 0:30—Breasts and buns in panties, while dancing in Western theme segment with Tina Bockrath.
Babes, Bikes & Beyond (1994) . . . . Biker Girl
••• 0:36—Breasts and buns in T-back.

Powell, Renato
Films:
Out of Sync (1995) . . . . Debra B. Collins
• 1:21—Brief right breast, while lying dead in bathtub when discovered by LL Cool J.
Made for Cable Movies:
Inhumanoid (1996; Showtime) . . . . Nurse
a.k.a. Circuit Breaker

Power, Deanne
Films:
24 Hours to Midnight (1991) . . . . Chan's Girlfriend/Woman in Ninja Suit
• 0:14—Breasts, while getting dressed in black ninja suit.
Knockouts (1992) . . . . Julie the Secretary
Assault of the Party Nerds II: The Heavy Petting Detective (1993) . . . . Stripper
• 0:51—Breasts and buns in G-string, while dancing during party.
Midnight Confessions (1993) . . . . Mrs. Parker
(Unrated version reviewed.)
••• 0:14—Breasts and buns, while making love in her house with Ryan.
Naked Instinct (1993) . . . . Joanne
••• 0:19—Breasts, in open robe and red panties, watching the pool man masturbate while she plays with herself.
••• 0:28—Nude, taking off robe and getting into tub, then making love with the Hot Tub Repairman.
••• 0:32—More nude, while making love with him. Long scene.
••• 0:36—Full frontal nudity, standing in tub with him.
••• 0:54—Nude, making love with the Military Recruit. Long scene.
••• 0:59—Nude, making love with the Football Jock.
Sex and the Single Alien (1993) . . . . Rachel
••• 0:00—Breasts and buns in G-string, while dancing on stage during opening credits.
•• 0:12—Breasts, while dancing on stage in black panties.
• 1:13—Breasts, while dancing on stage.
Tender Loving Care (1993) . . . . Veronica
••• 0:53—Breasts, while sitting on Julio's lap.
••• 0:55—Buns and breasts, while dancing and stripping in front of the doctor in his office.
Hard Drive (1994) . . . . Candle Dream Girl
(Unrated version reviewed.)
•• 0:03—Left breast, then breasts, while making love with Will on the floor surrounded by lit candles.
• 0:05—Brief breasts on the floor again.
Hindsight (1996) . . . . Lori
A Passion for Murder (1996) . . . . Lisa
a.k.a. Deadlock
••• 0:24—Breasts and buns, wearing chaps, while posing outdoors for photos.
•• 1:16—Brief buns, while lying in bed. Breasts, while in bedroom with Evan.
Maximum Revenge (1997) . . . . Wife
••• 0:11—Breasts, while making love with Richard.
Made for Cable TV:
Beverly Hills Bordello: Forbidden Fruit (1997; Showtime) . . . . Carol Richards
••• 0:02—Breasts, while making love with Brian on sofa.
••• 0:14—Nude, while having sex with Robin in bedroom.
••• 0:22—Breasts and buns, while having sex with Robin in bedroom.
Beverly Hills Bordello: Better Than the Couch (1998; Showtime) . . . . Linda
••• 0:16—Breasts, while making love with John in his office.
• 0:21—Full frontal nudity, while standing next to Muriel.
••• 0:22—Breasts, while making love with Muriel in bed while John watches.

Power, Deborah
Films:
Emmanuelle IV (1984) . . . . Dona
• 1:09—Buns, while lying down and getting a massage from Mia Nygren.
Glamour (1985; French) . . . . n.a.

Power, Robin
Films:
Graffiti Bridge (1990) . . . . Robin

Video Tapes:

Playboy's Erotic Weekend Getaways (1992) .... Anticipation: The Mountains

- ••• 0:03—Breasts in cabin with her lover. Buns in G-string.
- ••• 0:04—Nude in front of fireplace with her lover.
- ••• 0:06—Breasts in bathtub with her lover, playing with honey and other food.

Playboy's How to Reawaken Your Sexual Powers (1992) .... Cast Member

- ••• 0:26—Nude at the beach while standing and touching her lover.
- ••• 0:43—Nude outside by stream and on blanket with her lover.

Playboy's Women of Color (1994) .... Weekend Getaway/Sexual Power

- ••• 0:25—Nude, while making love with a guy in cabin.
- •• 0:27—Breasts, while playing with food with a guy in bathtub.
- ••• 0:38—Nude at the beach with a guy.

Power, Taryn

Daughter of actor Tyrone Power.

Films:

Sinbad and the Eye of the Tiger (1977; U.S./British) .... Dione

- • 1:16—Very brief buns, skinny dipping in pond with Jane Seymour. Long shot, but still pretty amazing for a G-rated film.
- • 1:18—Very brief partial side view of right breast, running away from the troglodyte.

Tracks (1977) .... Stephanie

- • 0:32—Brief side view of right breast changing in her room on the train. Don't see her face.
- • 1:15—Brief left breast making love with Dennis Hopper in a field.

Eating (1990) .... Anita

Made for TV Movies:

The Count of Monte Cristo (1975) ...... Valentine De Villefort

Powers, Beverly

Films:

Kissin' Cousins (1964) .... Trudy
More Dead than Alive (1968) .... Sheree
Angel in My Pocket (1969) .... Charlene de Gaulle
J.W. Coop (1971) .... Dora Mae
Invasion of the Bee Girls (1973) .... Harriet Williams

- • 1:14—In white bra and panties, then right breast and buns, taking off her clothes for her husband.

Powers, Stefanie

Films:

Crescendo (1972; British) .... Susan
(Not available on video tape.)
Little Moon & Jud McGraw (1976) .... Little Moon
a.k.a. Gone with the West

- • 0:29—Buns, taking a bath outside. At first, hidden behind a bush, then not. Long shot, Don't see her face. Partial right breast, but her hair gets in the way.

Prather, Joan

Films:

Bloody Friday (1973) .... Lola
a.k.a. Single Girls

- •• 1:06—Breasts, acting out her fantasy with Blue just before getting killed. Dark.

Big Bad Mama (1974) .... Jane Kingston

- •• 1:15—Breasts and buns in the bathroom with Tom Skerritt.

Smile (1974) .... Robin

- • 0:47—Brief buns in dressing room, while taking off pants while Little Bob is outside taking pictures. (She's wearing a pink ribbon in her hair.)

The Devil's Rain (1975; U.S./Mexican) .... Julie Preston
Rabbit Test (1978) .... Segoynia
The Best of Sex and Violence (1981) .... Herself

- •• 0:38—Breasts getting her breasts squeezed by an attacker. Dark.

Famous T & A (1982) .... Herself
(No longer available for purchase, check your video store for rental.)

- •• 0:49—Brief breasts in scene from *Bloody Friday.*

Made for TV Movies:

The Deerslayer (1978) .... Judith Hutter

TV:

Executive Suite (1976-77) .... Glory Dalessio
Eight is Enough (1979-81) .... Janet Bradford

Prati, Pamela

Films:

Monsignor (1982) .... 1st Roman Girl

- • 1:22—Brief breasts (on the left, wearing necklaces) next to a guy sitting in a chair, with another Roman girl on the right.

Hercules II (1985) .... Aracne
Man Spricht Deutsh (1988; West German) .... Violetta
Transformations (1988) .... Woman Succubus

- ••• 0:05—Breasts and buns making love on top of Rex Smith in bed. She starts transforming into a creature.
- • 0:21—Brief breasts again during Smith's flashback.
- • 0:24—Brief breasts again, while transforming.
- • 0:26—Brief breasts again, while transforming.

Prentiss, Paula *

Films:

Where the Boys Are (1960) .... Tuggle Carpenter
Man's Favorite Sport? (1964) .... Abigail Page
The World of Henry Orient (1964) .... Stella
In Harm's Way (1965) .... Bev
What's New, Pussycat? (1965; U.S./French) .... Liz
Catch-22 (1970) .... Nurse Duckett

- • 0:22—Full frontal nudity on platform in the water, throwing her dress to Alan Arkin during his dream. Long shot, over exposed, hard to see.

Move (1970) .... Dolly Jaffe
Last of the Red Hot Lovers (1972) .... Bobbi Michele
The Parallax View (1974) .... Lee Carter
The Stepford Wives (1975) .... Bobby
The Black Marble (1980) .... Sgt. Natalie Zimmerman
Buddy Buddy (1981) .... Celia Clooney
Saturday the 14th (1981) .... Mary

TV:

He & She (1967-68) .... Paula Hollister

Presley, Theresa *

Video Tapes:

Penthouse Pet of the Year Playoff 1992 (1992) ..... Pet

- ••• 0:01—Nude in helicopter, in office, tearing off her clothes in house, fantasy photo shoot, in a car and jumping on a trampoline.

The Girls of Penthouse, Volume 2 (1993) .... Pet

- ••• 0:11—Nude on bed, in tub, in kitchen, getting dressed, in milk bath and in a bar.
- ••• 0:33—Nude on bed, walking and posing in the house.

Penthouse The Great Pet Hunt—Part II (1993) . . . . . . Pet
••• 0:41—Nude after stripping out of red dress with white polka dots.

Penthouse DreamGirls (1994) . . . . Theresa
••• 0:01—Nude by waterfall by pool, in a mansion, on a bed, in a shower/bath.

• Pressly, Jaime *

Films:

Poison Ivy 3: The New Seduction (1996) . . . . Violet
•• 0:12—Buns and breasts, getting into bathtub and taking a bath.
• 0:27—Brief buns in panties, while putting on her slip.
••• 0:30—Breasts and buns in swimsuit bottom, while going for a swim.
• 0:43—Buns, getting out of swimming pool after going for a swim.
••• 0:45—Breasts, while making love with Michael outside at night.
• 0:57—Brief breasts, while starting to make love with Ivan.
••• 0:59—Breasts and buns, while making love with Ivan in bedroom.
• 1:16—Brief breasts, when caught with Ivan by Joy.

TV:

Push (1998-) . . . . Nikki Lang

Prester, Meaghan

Films:

Cyberzone (1995) . . . . Pleasure Droid #2
• 0:09—Breasts, in room with the other three pleasure droids. (she's the tall one with a diamond choker.)
• 0:13—Breasts after taking off her lingerie top with the other three pleasure droids.

Masseuse (1995) . . . . Michelle
(Unrated version reviewed.)
••• 1:17—Buns and breasts, while in bedroom with a customer.

Preston, Cyndy

Films:

The Dark Side (1987) . . . . Laura
The Brain (1988) . . . . Janet
Pin (1988) . . . . Ursula
Prom Night III (1989) . . . . Sarah
If Looks Could Kill (1991) . . . . Melissa Tyler
a.k.a. Teen Agent

Made for Cable TV:

The Outer Limits: I Robot (1995; Showtime) . . . . Mina Link
Picture Windows: Armed Response (1995; Showtime) . . . . Paula
•• 0:03—Brief breasts in the bathtub, while talking to her brother.

Made for TV Movies:

To Catch a Killer (1992; Canadian) . . . . Cindy Beck
Madonna: Innocence Lost (1994) . . . . Jude O'Mally
Black Fox (1995) . . . . Delores Holtz
Black Fox: The Prince of Peace (1995) . . . . Delores Holtz

Preston, Kelly

a.k.a. Kelly Palzis.
Wife of actor John Travolta.

Films:

10 to Midnight (1983) . . . . Doreen
Christine (1983) . . . . Roseanne
Metalstorm: The Destruction of Jared-Syn (1983) . . . . . Dhyana
Mischief (1985) . . . . Marilyn McCauley
••• 0:56—In a bra, then breasts, brief buns and brief partial lower frontal nudity, while seducing and making love with Doug McKeon in her bedroom.

Secret Admirer (1985) . . . . Deborah Anne Fimple
•• 0:53—Brief breasts in car with C. Thomas Howell.
• 1:17—Very brief breasts in and out of bed.

52 Pick-Up (1986) . . . . Cini
• 0:09—Brief buns in video tape made by blackmailers.
• 0:36—Breasts, tied to chair on video tape made by blackmailers.
• 0:39—Very brief breasts covered with blood after being shot.

SpaceCamp (1986) . . . . Tish
Amazon Women on the Moon (1987) . . . . Violet
Love at Stake (1988) . . . . Sara Lee
Spellbinder (1988) . . . . Miranda Reed
••• 0:19—Breasts in bed making love with Timothy Daly.

A Tiger's Tale (1988) . . . . Shirley
•• 0:03—Breasts in the car, letting C. Thomas Howell open her blouse and look at her breasts.

Twins (1988) . . . . Marnie Mason
The Experts (1989) . . . . Bonnie
Run (1990) . . . . Karen Landers
Only You (1992) . . . . Amanda Hughes
Cheyenne Warrior (1994) . . . . Rebecca Carver
Double Cross (1994) . . . . Vera Blanchard
• 0:08—In bra, panties, garter belt and stockings in hotel room with Patrick Bergin. Buns and partial left breast, when he rips off her panties. Don't see her face.
• 0:24—Buns, while getting into the shower. Don't see her face.

Love is a Gun (1994) . . . . Jean Starr
From Dusk Till Dawn (1995) . . . . Newscaster Kelly Houge
Citizen Ruth (1996) . . . . Rachel
Curdled (1996) . . . . Kelly
Jerry Maguire (1996) . . . . Avery Bishop
Addicted to Love (1997) . . . . Linda Green
Nothing to Lose (1997) . . . . Ann Beam

Made for Cable Movies:

The Perfect Bride (1991) . . . . Laura
Mrs. Munck (1995; Showtime) . . . . Young Rose
• 0:51—Partial buns, while making love on top of Bruce Dern in bed.

Made for Cable TV:

Tales From the Crypt: The Switch (1990; HBO) . . . . Linda
(Available on *Tales From the Crypt, Volume 3.*)

TV:

For Love and Honor (1983) . . . . Mary Lee

Price, Sue

Films:

Nemesis 2: Nebula (1995) . . . . Alex
• 0:13—Brief buns under grass skirt.
• 0:19—Brief buns under grass skirt during fight with Zumi.
• 0:27—Brief buns under grass skirt, when running around.
• 0:29—Brief buns in G-string after getting rid of her grass skirt.
• 0:37—Buns in G-string and back side of left breast, while changing clothes.

Nemesis 3: Time Lapse (1995) . . . . Alex
• 1:04—Buns in G-string, while getting dressed outside. Great if you like muscular women!

Primeaux, Suzanne

Films:

Stripper (1985) .... Herself

•• 0:03—Breasts dancing on stage, kneeling on her left knee. Very brief buns in G-string.

Traxx (1988) .... Hooker #1

•• 0:37—Breasts, dancing on stage while wearing a mask.

Darkman III: Die Darkman Die (1995) .... Mother

Made for TV Movies:

Betrayal of Silence (1989) .... Bartender

Principal, Victoria *

Films:

The Life and Times of Judge Roy Bean (1972) ..... Marie Elena

The Naked Ape (1972) .... Cathy

(Not available on video tape.)

Breasts.

Earthquake (1974) .... Rosa

I Will, I Will... For Now (1976) .... Jackie Martin

Vigilante Force (1976) .... Linda

Made for Cable Movies:

Dancing in the Dark (1995; Lifetime) .... Anna Forbes

Miniseries:

The Burden of Proof (1992) .... Margy Allison

Made for TV Movies:

Mistress (1987) .... Rae Colton

Naked Lie (1989) .... Joanne Dawson

Don't Touch My Daughter (1991) .... n.a.

Nightmare (1991) .... Linda

Seduction: Three Tales from "The Inner Sanctum" (1992) .... Sylvia/Lisa/Joan

River of Rage: The Taking of Maggie Keene (1993) .... Maggie Keene

Beyond Obsession (1994) .... Eleonor

Love in Another Town (1997) .... Maggie Sorrell

TV:

Dallas (1978-89) .... Pamela Barnes Ewing

Pringle, Joan

Films:

J.D.'s Revenge (1976) .... Christella

•• 0:27—Breasts, while making love with Isaac.

•• 1:05—Breasts, in open blouse while struggling on the floor with Isaac.

Made for Cable Movies:

Gia (1998; HBO) .... Therapist at Rehab

Made for TV Movies:

Visions of Murder (1993) .... Gwen

Eyes of Terror (1994) .... Gwen Singleton

Greyhounds (1994) .... Ann Smith

TV:

Ironside (1974-75) .... Diana Sanger

That's My Mama (1975) .... Tracy Curtis Taylor

Rafferty (1977) .... Nurse Keynes

The White Shadow (1978-81) .... Sybil Buchanan

• Procter, Emily

Films:

Crosscut (1995) .... Counter Girl

Leaving Las Vegas (1995) .... Debbie

Jerry Maguire (1996) .... Former Girlfriend

The Girl Gets Moe (1997) .... Tammy

Made for Cable Movies:

Breast Men (1997; HBO) .... Laura Pierson

•• 0:42—Breasts, while in office with David Schwimmer before her implant operation.

0:44—Breasts scene after Laura's operation is her head placed onto a body double's torso using special-effects.

Made for TV Movies:

Fast Company (1995) .... Roz Epstein

Prophet, Melissa *

Films:

Players (1979) .... Ann

Van Nuys Blvd. (1979) .... Camille

Looker (1981) .... Commercial Script Girl

Blame It on the Night (1984) .... Charlotte

Fatal Games (1984) .... Nancy Wilson

• 0:14—Buns and side view of left breast in shower with other girls. Long shot. (She's wearing a white towel on her head.)

Invasion U.S.A. (1985) .... McGuirre

Action Jackson (1988) .... Newscaster

GoodFellas (1990) .... Angie

Casino (1995) .... Jennifer Santoro

Props, Renée

a.k.a. Babette Props.

Films:

Weird Science (1985) .... One of The Weenies

Free Ride (1986) .... Kathy

• 0:13—Brief breasts in the shower while Dan watches.

Get Shorty (1995) .... Nicki

The Pompatus of Love (1996) .... Flynn

TV:

As the World Turns .... Ellie Snyder

Pryor, Gloria

Films:

The Swindle (1991) .... Claudia

•• 1:15—Breasts with Tom.

Beach Beverly Hills (1992) .... Roxanne

Silk n' Sabotage (1994) .... TV Interviewer

Wish Me Luck (1995) .... Tierra

(Unrated version reviewed.)

Pryor, Mowava

Daughter of comedian/actor Richard Pryor.

Films:

SnakeEater (1988) .... Chloe

••• 0:07—In bra and panties, then breasts and buns, while undressing in room with Lorenzo Lamas to prove each other is not a cop.

• 0:10—Breasts, while lying down, then getting up.

Across the Moon (1994) .... Public Defender

Purl, Linda

Ex-wife of actor Desi Arnaz Jr.

Films:

Crazy Mama (1975) .... Cheryl

• 0:52—Very brief buns, then brief breasts when Snake and Donny Most keep opening the door after she has taken a shower. Long shot, hard to see.

The High Country (1980; Canadian) .... Kathy

• 1:03—Brief buns, while taking a shower in the waterfall.

Visiting Hours (1982; Canadian) .... Sheila Munroe

Viper (1988) .... Laura Macalla

Web of Deceit (1991) .... n.a.

Natural Causes (1993) .... Jessie MacCarthy

Made for Cable Movies:

Body Language (1992; USA) .... Norma

Incident at Deception Ridge (1994; USA) .... Helen Davis

Made for TV Movies:
Outrage! (1986) . . . . Arlene Robbins
Pleasures (1986) . . . . Eve Harper
Danielle Steel's "Secrets" (1992) . . . . Jane Adams
TV:
Happy Days (1974-75) . . . . Gloria
Happy Days (1982-83) . . . . Ashley Pfister
Matlock (1986-89) . . . . Charlene Matlock
Under Cover (1991) . . . . Kate Del'Amico
Robin's Hoods (1994-95). . . . . Brett Robin

Q, Stacey

Real name is Stacey Swain.
Pop singer.
Formerly with the group SSQ.
Films:
One Man Force (1989) . . . . Lea
Video Tapes:
Red Hot Rock (1984) . . . . Singer
a.k.a. Sexy Shorts (on laser disc)
•• 0:18—Full frontal nudity while in bed with a guy, then a woman during "Screaming in My Pillow" song.

Quennessen, Valerie

Films:
French Postcards (1979) . . . . Toni
Like a Turtle on Its Back (1981; French) . . . . Nietzsche
Conan the Barbarian (1982) . . . . The Princess
Summer Lovers (1982). . . . . Lina
• 0:12—Breasts, while on balcony.
••• 0:19—Nude on the beach with Michael.
• 0:23—Brief breasts in a cave with Michael.
•• 0:30—Breasts, while lying on the floor with Michael.
• 0:54—Buns, while lying on a rock with Daryl Hannah watching Michael dive off a rock.
• 1:03—Left breast, while in bed.
•• 1:05—Breasts while dancing on the balcony.
•• 1:09—Breasts while on the beach.

Quick, Diana

Films:
The Big Sleep (1978; British) . . . . Mona Grant
1919 (1984; British) . . . . Anna
Ordeal by Innocence (1984) . . . . Gwenda Vaughn
The Misadventures of Mr. Wilt (1990) . . . . Sally
Nostradamus (1993) . . . . Diane De Portier
1:28—Back side of right breast, while getting dressed after sitting for painting.
Made for Cable Movies:
Rasputin (1996; HBO) . . . . Grand Duchess Ella
Miniseries:
Brideshead Revisited (1981; British) . . . . Julia Flyte
• 0:18—(Part 10 on TV or Book 5 on video tape.) Several quick peeks at partial right breast in mirror, while lying under Jeremy Irons in bed.
•• 0:19—Left breast, while lying on top of Jeremy Irons after making love with him.
Made for TV Movies:
Mystery! Absolute Conviction (1995) . . . . Mrs. Stevens

Quigley, Linnea *

Adult Films:
Sweethearts (1986). . . . . Cupid's Corner Hostess
(Appears fully clothed, only as a hostess to introduce the explicit segments.)
Films:
Auditions (1978). . . . . Sally Webster
••• 0:06—Breasts and buns, undressing and dancing during her audition.
••• 0:26—Full frontal nudity, acting with two guys.
Don't Go Near the Park (1979). . . . . Bondi's Mother
• 0:08—Full frontal nudity, behind shower door.
• 0:09—Brief left breast, while wrapping a towel around herself.
••• 0:19—Left breast, while lying in bed with Mark.
Fairytales (1979) . . . . Dream Girl
•• 1:07—Breasts waking up after being kissed by The Prince.
Nightstalker (1979) . . . . Bondi's Mother
Stone Cold Dead (1979; Canadian) . . . . First Victim
• 0:03—Very brief right breast after getting shot through shower door. Buns after falling to the floor.
Summer Camp (1979). . . . . n.a.
Cheech & Chong's Nice Dreams (1981) . . . . Blondie Group #2
Graduation Day (1981) . . . . Dolores
•• 0:36—Breasts by the piano in classroom with Mr. Roberts unbuttoning her blouse.
Psycho From Texas (1981). Barmaid
••• 1:16—Nude, after taking off her dress and dancing in front of Wheeler. (He pours beer on her.) Long scene.
Cheech & Chong's Still Smokin' (1983)
. . . . Uncredited Spa Girl
•• 0:42—Breasts, looking into two-way mirror. (She's the last girl.)
• 0:53—Breasts, walking in front of Cheech in the shower room.
•• 1:00—Breasts, sitting on the floor with five other naked girls with Cheech.
The Young Warriors (1983; U.S./Canadian). . . . . Ginger
• 0:05—Nude in and getting out of bed in bedroom.
The Black Room (1984) . . . . Milly
Fatal Games (1984) . . . . Athelete
Savage Streets (1984) . . . . Heather
• 0:28—Breasts getting raped by the jerks.
Silent Night, Deadly Night (1984) . . . . Denise
••• 0:52—Breasts while on pool table with Tommy, then putting on shorts and walking around the house. More breasts, while impaled on antlers.
The Return of the Living Dead (1985). . . . . Trash
••• 0:19—Breasts and buns, strip tease and dancing in cemetery. (Lower frontal nudity is covered with some kind of make-up appliance).
•• 0:25—Breasts and buns, while in cemetery with her boyfriend.
• 0:37—Breasts and buns, while running around in cemetery when it starts to rain.
• 0:38—Breasts, while running to the car in the rain (very long shot). Brief breasts while in back seat of car.
• 0:42—Breasts, while in back seat of car.
• 0:44—Breasts, while in back seat of car, trying to hold the convertible top closed.
• 0:46—Brief buns, while running up stairs.
• 0:49—Buns, while running into the cemetery.
1:04—Brief right breast, while in cemetery after seeing a zombie.
• 1:05—Brief breasts, while walking from the cemetery on the street to catch a streetperson.
• 1:21—Brief breasts, while running to munch on a policeman in blockade.
• 1:25—Brief breasts in still photo.

- 1:27—Breasts, during end credits in cemetery with her boyfriend.

Silent Night, Deadly Night, Part 2 (1986) . . . . .Denise
- ••• 0:26—Breasts on pool table and getting dressed flashback from *Silent Night, Deadly Night.*

Creepozoids (1987) . . . . .Blanca
- •• 0:15—Breasts taking off her top to take a shower.
- •• 0:16—Right breast, while standing in shower with Butch.
- • 0:24—Right breast several times while sleeping in bed with Butch.

Night of the Demons (1987) . . . . Suzanne
(Unrated version reviewed.)
- 0:10—Buns in panties under short skirt, while bending over to distract the convenience store clerks.
- •• 0:52—Breasts twice, opening her dress top while acting weird. Pushes a tube of lipstick into her left breast. (Don't try this at home kids!)
- • 0:56—Lower frontal nudity, lifting her skirt up for Jay.

Nightmare Sisters (1987) . . . . Melody
- ••• 0:39—Breasts, wearing panties, while standing with Mickey and Marci after transforming from nerds to sexy women.
- ••• 0:40—Breasts in the kitchen with Mickey and Marci.
- ••• 0:44—Breasts in the bathtub with Mickey and Marci. Excellent, long scene.
- ••• 0:46—Breasts, while in the bathtub. Nice close up.
- ••• 0:48—Still more breasts, while in the bathtub.
- ••• 0:55—Breasts, while dancing and singing in front of Kevin. Long scene.
- •• 0:57—Breasts while on the couch with Bud.

Treasure of the Moon Goddess (1987) . . . . Lu De Belle
American Rampage (1988) . . . . .n.a.
Hollywood Chainsaw Hookers (1988) . . . . Samantha
- •• 0:32—Breasts, dancing on stage.
- • 1:02—Breasts, (but her body is painted) dancing in a ceremony.

A Nightmare on Elm Street 4: The Dream Master (1988)
. . . . .Soul from Freddy's Chest
- • 1:23—Brief breasts twice, trying to get out of Freddy's body. Don't see her face clearly.

Sorority Babes in the Slimeball Bowl-O-Rama (1988). . . . Spider
Vice Academy (1988). . . . . .Didi
- ••• 0:45—Breasts making love with Chuck while he's handcuffed.

Assault of the Party Nerds (1989). . . . . Bambi
- ••• 0:25—Breasts straddling Cliff in bed.

Deadly Embrace (1989). . . . . Michelle Arno
- •• 0:15—In white lingerie, then breasts and buns during Chris' fantasy.
- •• 0:34—Breasts and buns caressing herself.
- •• 0:43—Breasts again.
- • 0:46—Brief breasts.
- •• 0:50—Breasts and buns undressing.
- ••• 0:58—Breasts in bed on top of Chris, then making love.
- • 1:02—Breasts and buns on top of Chris while Charlotte watches on T.V.
- • 1:11—Breasts in Chris' fantasy.
- • 1:12—Breasts and buns in playback of video tape.

Dr. Alien (1989) . . . . Rocker Chick #2
a.k.a. I Was a Teenage Sex Mutant
- ••• 0:21—Breasts in white outfit during dream sequence with two other rocker chicks.

Murder Weapon (1989). . . . . Dawn
- • 0:08—Buns and very brief side of left breast walking into shower. Long shot.
- •• 0:40—Breasts taking off her top in car.
- •• 0:48—Breasts and buns taking off her top in bedroom.
- ••• 0:50—Breasts in bed on top of a guy. Excellent long scene. Brief buns, getting out of bed.

Robot Ninja (1989) . . . . Miss Barbeau
Witchtrap (1989) . . . . .Ginger Kowoski
- ••• 0:34—Nude taking off robe and getting into the shower.
- •• 0:36—Breasts just before getting killed when the shower head goes into her neck.

The Girl I Want (1990). . . . . .Teri
Vice Academy, Part 2 (1990) . . . . Didi
- •• 1:04—Buns in G-string, then breasts dancing with Ginger Lynn Allen on stage at club.

Virgin High (1990) . . . . .Kathleen
- •• 0:24—Breasts, nonchalantly making love on top of Derrick.
- •• 0:55—Brief breasts several times on top of Derrick, then breasts.
- • 1:21—Breasts in photo during party.

Blood Church (1991). . . . . .n.a.
Freddy's Dead: The Final Nightmare (1991)
. . . . Soul from Freddy's Chest
- • 1:25—Brief breasts, struggling in Freddy's stomach during the end credits special-effects review.

The Guyver (1991) . . . . Scream Queen
Sex Bomb (1991) . . . . .n.a.
Innocent Blood (1992) . . . . Nurse
Assault of the Party Nerds II: The Heavy Petting Detective (1993). . . . . .Bambi
- • 0:32—Breasts, when making love on top of a guy in bed, while using an adding machine.
- •• 0:33—More, breasts, while making love on top of a guy in bed.
- •• 0:45—Breasts, while making love on top of banker guy in bed.

Beach Babes From Beyond (1993). . . . . Sally
Pumpkinhead II: Blood Wings (1994) . . . . Nadine
- •• 0:41—Breasts, while making love on top of a guy in bed.

Jack-O (1995). . . . . Carolyn Miller
a.k.a. Jacko Lantern
- •• 0:23—Breasts and buns, while taking a shower.

Stripteasers (1995) . . . . Uncredited Waitress

Made for Cable Movies:

Bram Stoker's Burial of the Rats (1995; Showtime)
. . . . .Rat Woman

Video Tapes:

Nudes in Limbo (1983) . . . . .Model
Playboy Video Magazine, Volume 4 (1983) . . .Flashdancer
- • 0:15—Full frontal nudity.
- •• 0:16—Nude, fighting with Brinke Stevens in the shower.

Linnea Quigley's Horror Workout (1990) . . . . Herself
- ••• 0:00—Breasts and buns, taking a shower and drying herself off. Nice.
- ••• 0:09—Breasts in scene from *Assault of the Party Nerds*, making love on top of a guy in bed.
- • 0:19—Breasts in still photo from *Return of the Living Dead.*
- •• 0:34—Breasts, while singing and dancing in living room, in scene from *Nightmare Sisters.*
- • 0:54—Breasts, while screaming.
- • 0:57—Breasts in still photos during end credits.

Scream Queen Hot Tub Party (1991). . . . . Samantha
- • 0:01—Breasts during opening credits.
- •• 0:36—Breasts with painted body, doing double chainsaw dance from *Hollywood Chainsaw Hookers.*

B-Movie Queens Revealed: The Making of "Vice Academy" (1993) . . . . .Didi
- ••• 0:33—Breasts with Chuck while he's handcuffed to sink from *Vice Academy 1*.
- • 0:34—Buns in T-back, dancing on stage with Ginger Lynn Allen from *Vice Academy 2*.
- •• 0:38—Breasts, dancing on stage with Ginger Lynn Allen from *Vice Academy 2*.

Quinlan, Kathleen

Films:

Lifeguard (1975) . . . . Wendy
I Never Promised You a Rose Garden (1977) . . . . Deborah
- • 0:27—Breasts changing in a mental hospital room with the orderly.
- • 0:52—Brief breasts riding a horse in a hallucination sequence. Blurry, hard to see. Then close up of left breast (could be anyone's).

The Promise (1979). . . . . .Nancy/Marie
The Runner Stumbles (1979). . . . . Sister Rita
Hanky Panky (1982) . . . . Janet Dunn
Independence Day (1983). . . . . Mary Ann Taylor
The Last Winter (1983; Israeli). . . . . .Joyce
- •• 0:48—Brief side view of left breast taking off her robe and diving into pool Very brief buns.
- • 0:49—Buns, while lying on marble slab, talking with Maya.
- • 0:50—Very brief right breast, when sitting up. Long shot, hard to see.

Twilight Zone—The Movie (1983). . . . . Helen
Warning Sign (1985). . . . . .Joanie Morse
Man Outside (1987) . . . . Grace Freemont
Wild Thing (1987; U.S./Canadian). . . . . Jane
Clara's Heart (1988) . . . . Leona Hart
Sunset (1988) . . . . .Nancy Shoemaker
The Doors (1991) . . . . .Patricia Kennealy
- ••• 1:00—Brief left breast, while in bed with Val Kilmer, breasts (while wearing glasses) out of bed.
- • 1:02—Left breast, while crawling on the floor.
- ••• 1:03—Nude, dancing around her apartment with Kilmer.

Perfect Alibi (1994) . . . . Melanie Bauers
Trial By Jury (1994) . . . . Wanda
- • 0:04—Brief buns, while dancing in room wearing black bra, panties, garter belt and stockings (in a blonde wig) in front of Limpy.

Apollo 13 (1995). . . . . Marilyn Lovell
Zeus and Roxanne (1996) . . . . .Mary Beth
Breakdown (1997). . . . . Amy Taylor
Event Horizon (1997) . . . . Peters
Lawn Dogs (1997). . . . . .Clare
My Giant (1998) . . . . .Serena

Made for Cable Movies:

Blackout (1985; HBO) . . . . .Chris
- • 0:26—Brief side view of left breast while making love in bed. Dark, hard to see.

Bodily Harm (1989). . . . . Dr. Virginia Betters
Trapped (1989). . . . . Mary Ann
Strays (1991; USA) . . . . .Lindsay Jarrett
Last Light (1993; Showtime) . . . . Kathy Rubicek
Stolen Babies (1993; Lifetime). . . . . Bekka

Made for Cable TV:

Picture Windows: Lightning (1995; Showtime) . . . . Mollie

Made for TV Movies:

She's in the Army Now (1981) . . . . Cass Donner
Children of the Night (1985). . . . . .Lois Lee
An American Story (1992). Hope Tyler

Quinn, Alexandria

See: Colazzo, Dianne.

Quinn, Patricia

Films:

The Rocky Horror Picture Show (1975; British). . . . . . .Magenta
Shock Treatment (1981) . . . . .Nation McKinley
Monty Python's the Meaning of Life (1983; British) . . . . Professor's Wife
- •• 0:25—Breasts, while undressing to give a real sex education demonstration with John Cleese for a classroom full of boys.

Miniseries:

I, Claudius—Episode 4, What Shall We Do About Claudius? (1976; British) . . . . Livilla
(Available on video tape in *I, Claudius—Volume 2*.)
- • 1:28—(0:39 into episode 4) Brief right breast, while climbing back onto bed after framing Postumus for rape.

I, Claudius—Episode 7, Queen of Heaven (1976; British) . . . . Livilla
(Available on video tape in *I, Claudius—Volume 4*.)
- • 0:20—Very brief tip of right breast under arm of Patrick Stewart in bed.

Quintard, Mika

Films:

Candyman (1992). . . . . .T.V. Reporter
Hard Hunted (1993) . . . . .Mika
- ••• 0:11—In two piece swimsuit on boat. Breasts, while taking a shower outside.

• Rabe, Pamela

Films:

Sirens (1994; Australian) . . . . .Rose Lindsay
- •• 0:52—Nude, undressing to pose for Sam Neill.
- • 1:15—Breasts, while posing for painting.
- • 1:30—Brief full frontal nudity on rock formation. Medium long shot. She's the third from the left.

Cosi (1996; Australian) . . . . Ruth
Paradise Road (1997). . . . . Mrs. Tippler

Rabett, Catherine

Films:

Real Life (1984; British) . . . . Kate
The Living Daylights (1987). . . . . Liz
Maurice (1987; British) . . . . Pippa Durham
Frankenstein Unbound (1990) . . . . .Elizabeth
1:10—Very brief left breast, while lying dead after getting shot by Frankenstein. Unappealing looking because of all the gruesome make-up.

Raché, Brittney

See: Powell, Brittney.

Racimo, Victoria

Films:

The Magic Garden of Stanley Sweetheart (1970). . . . . . Andrea
The G.I. Executioner (1971) . . . . .Foon Mae Lee
a.k.a. Wit's End
a.k.a. Dragon Lady
- • 0:12—Nude in bathroom mirror getting dressed.
- • 0:54—Brief breasts undressing and getting into bed. (See reflection in glass on headboard.)
- • 1:15—Sort of buns, lying in Dave's lap. Then left breast.
- • 1:18—Buns, while tied up by wrists. Sort of breasts being turned around (hair is in the way).

Red Sky at Morning (1971) . . . . Viola Lopez
The Day of the Dolphin (1973) . . . . Lana
Prophecy (1979) . . . . Ramona
The Mountain Men (1980) . . . . Running Moon
Choke Canyon (1986) . . . . Rachel
Ernest Goes to Camp (1987) . . . . Nurse St. Cloud
White Fang 2: Myth of the White Wolf (1994) . . . . Katria

TV:

The Chisholms (1979-80) . . . . Kewedinok
Falcon Crest (1983-84) . . . . Corene Powers

Radford, Natalie

Films:

Tomcat: Dangerous Desires (1993) . . . . Imogen
- ••• 1:04—Brief left breast, then breasts and lower frontal nudity in bed with Richard Grieco.
- •• 1:08—Brief buns and breasts in bed some more.
- •• 1:09—More breasts while sitting in bed and watching video tape on TV.

Operation Golden Phoenix (1994) . . . . Anne
Sodbusters (1994; Canadian) . . . . Young Becky
Synapse (1995) . . . . Alice
a.k.a. Memory Run

Made for Cable Movies:

Spencer: The Judas Goat (1994; Lifetime) . . . . . Cloris Caldwell
The Android Affair (1995; USA) . . . . Rachel Tyler
Harrison Bergeron (1995; Showtime) . . . . Alma Starbuck

Made for Cable TV:

TekWar (1995; USA) . . . . Nika

Made for TV Movies:

JFK: Reckless Youth (1993) . . . . Rosemary Kennedy
Danielle Steel's "Rememberance" (1996) . . . . Greg's Wife

Rae, Taija

Adult film actress.

Films:

Delivery Boys (1984) . . . . Nurse
Sex Appeal (1986) . . . . Rhonda
- •• 1:14—In black lingerie, then breasts in black push-up teddy with Sheila.

*Ragnarsson, Carina **

Films:

Beauty School (1993) . . . . Heather
- •• 0:40—Breasts, dancing with her top down on stage in club.

Video Tapes:

Penthouse: On the Wild Side (1988) . . . . Car Wash
- ••• 0:16—Breasts and buns in car wash with another woman. Nice and wet.

Rain, Jeramie

Films:

The Abductors (1971) . . . . Jane
- • 0:02—Breasts, while getting wrists tied.
- •• 0:08—Breasts, while standing, gagged and with hands tied behind her back.
- •• 0:10—Full frontal nudity (she's the brunette), while taking off her panties with the two other girls.

Last House on the Left (1972) . . . . Sadie

*Raines, Cristina **

a.k.a. Tina Herazo.

Films:

Hex (1973) . . . . Oriole
Stacey! (1973) . . . . Pamela Chambers
a.k.a. Stacey and Her Gangbusters

Nashville (1975) . . . . Mary
Russian Roulette (1975) . . . . Bogna Kirchoff
The Duellists (1977; British) . . . . Adele
The Sentinel (1977) . . . . Alison Parker
- • 0:18—Briefly in sheer beige bra, putting her blouse on.
- • 0:33—Very, very brief left breast immediately after Sylvia Miles rips her dress off. B&W dream sequence.

Touched by Love (1980) . . . . Amy
Real Life (1984; British) . . . . Laurel
North Shore (1987) . . . . Rick's Mother

TV:

Centennial (1978-79) . . . . Lucinda
Flamingo Road (1981-82) . . . . Lane Ballou

Raines, Frances

Films:

Model Behavior (1982) . . . . Lily White Girl
The Mutilator (1983) . . . . Linda
- •• 0:35—Breasts, while in swimming pool, just before getting killed.

Breeders (1986) . . . . Karinsa Marshall
- ••• 0:12—Nude stretching and exercising in photo studio.
- • 0:16—Brief full frontal nudity, getting attacked by the creature.
- ••• 0:53—Breasts and buns, taking off her blouse and walking down the hall and into the basement. Long scene.
- • 1:07—Very brief right breast in the alien nest with the other women.
- • 1:10—Brief breasts standing up.

Raines, Lisa

See: Foster, Lisa Raines.

Rains, Gianna

Films:

Firehouse (1987) . . . . Barrett Hopkins
- ••• 0:33—Breasts taking a shower, then drying herself after the fire alarm goes off.
- •• 0:56—Breasts making love with the reporter on the roof of a building.

Homeboy (1988) . . . . Phyllis

Ramish, Trish

Made for Cable TV:

Dream On: Super Freak (1993; HBO) . . . . Joanne
- ••• 0:17—Breasts in shower with Martin and after getting shampoo in their eyes.

Video Tapes:

Cher Fitness: Body Confidence (1992) . . . . Cast Member

*Rampling, Charlotte **

Films:

Rotten to the Core (1965; British) . . . . Sara
Georgy Girl (1966; British) . . . . Meredith
The Long Duel (1967; British) . . . . Jane Stafford
The Damned (1969; German) . . . . Elizabeth Thallman
Three (1969; British) . . . . Marty
Asylum (1972; British) . . . . Barbara
Corky (1972) . . . . Corky's Wife
Henry VIII and His Six Wives (1972; British) . . . . . . Anne Boleyn
'Tis Pity She's a Whore (1972; Italian) . . . . Annabella
Breasts.

Caravan to Vaccares (1974; British/French) . . . . Lila
Brief buns standing at window, then brief full frontal nudity getting back into bed.

The Night Porter (1974; Italian/U.S.) . . . . Lucia
•• 0:11—Side nudity being filmed with a movie camera in the concentration camp line.
• 0:13—Nude running around a room while a Nazi taunts her by shooting his gun near her.
••• 1:12—Breasts doing a song and dance number wearing pants, suspenders and a Nazi hat. Long scene.
Zardoz (1974; British) . . . . Consuella
• 0:29—Breasts under yellow net blouse.
• 1:05—Very brief left breast, when Sean Connery grabs her during struggle.
• 1:26—Wearing yellow blouse, trying to kill Connery.
• 1:44—Very brief right breast feeding her baby in time lapse scene at the end of the film.
Farewell, My Lovely (1975; British) . . . . Velma
Foxtrot (1976; Mexican/Swiss) . . . . Julia
Orca, The Killer Whale (1977) . . . . Rachel Bedford
The Purple Taxi (1977; French/Italian/Irish) . . . . Sharon
Stardust Memories (1980) . . . . Dorrie
The Verdict (1982) . . . . Laura
Angel Heart (1987) . . . . Margaret Krusemark
(Original Unedited Version reviewed.)
• 1:10—Brief left breast, lying dead on the floor, covered with blood.
• 1:46—Very brief left breast during flashback of the dead-on-the-floor-covered-with-blood scene.
Mascara (1987; French/Belgian) . . . . Gaby Hart
• 1:03—Brief breasts putting on sweater when Michael Sarrazin watches through binoculars.
• 1:18—Right breast, while making love with Chris.
D.O.A. (1988) . . . . Mrs. Fitzwaring
Invasion of Privacy (1995) . . . . Deidre Stiles
The Wings of the Dove (1997; British) . . . . Aunt Maud

*Ranay, Chrissy **

Video Tapes:
Playboy's Cheerleaders (1996) . . . . Cheerleader
••• 0:32—Nude (she's the second to take her bra off) outside during car wash with two other cheerleaders.

*Randall, Anne **

Films:
The Split (1968) . . . . Negli's Girl
The Model Shop (1969) . . . . 2nd Model
Hell's Bloody Devils (1970) . . . . Amanda
The Christian Licorice Store (1971) . . . . Texas Girl
A Time for Dying (1971) . . . . Nellie Winters
Get to Know Your Rabbit (1972) . . . . Stewardess
Stacey! (1973) . . . . Stacey Hansen
a.k.a. Stacey and Her Gangbusters
••• 0:01—Breasts taking off her driving jump suit.
••• 0:12—Breasts changing clothes.
••• 0:39—Breasts in bed with Bob.
Westworld (1973) . . . . Servant Girl
Made for TV Movies:
The Night Strangler (1973) . . . . Policewoman Sheila
TV:
Hee Haw (1972-73) . . . . Regular

Randle, Theresa

Films:
Maid to Order (1987) . . . . Doni
Near Dark (1987) . . . . Lady in Car
Easy Wheels (1989) . . . . Ace
The Guardian (1990) . . . . Arlene Russell
Heart Condition (1990) . . . . Ciao Chow Club Maitre D'
King of New York (1990) . . . . Raye
The Five Heartbeats (1991) . . . . Brenda
Jungle Fever (1991) . . . . Inez
Malcolm X (1992) . . . . Laura
CB4 (1993) . . . . Eve
Sugar Hill (1993) . . . . Melissa
Beverly Hills Cop III (1994) . . . . Janice
Bad Boys (1995) . . . . Theresa Burnett
Girl 6 (1996) . . . . Girl 6
••• 0:06—Breasts, after taking off her dress top during audition interview.
Space Jam (1996) . . . . Juanita Jordan
Spawn (1997) . . . . Wanda Blake

Randolph, Randi

Films:
Blood Games (1989) . . . . Ingrid
••• 0:13—Breasts taking off bra, buns in shower with Stoney.
Hollywood Boulevard II (1989) . . . . Doreen
Malibu Summer (1991) . . . . n.a.

Randolph, Ty

a.k.a. Windsor Taylor Randolph.
a.k.a. Mindi Miller.
Films:
That Man Bolt (1973) . . . . n.a.
Westworld (1973) . . . . n.a.
Airport 1975 (1974) . . . . n.a.
Funny Lady (1975) . . . . Chorus Girl
Take a Hard Ride (1975; U.S./Italian) . . . . n.a.
1900 (1976; Italian) . . . . n.a.
(NC-17 version reviewed.)
The Big Bus (1976) . . . . n.a.
Paternity (1981) . . . . n.a.
Body Double (1984) . . . . Mindi
••• 1:50—Breasts in the shower during filming of movie with Craig Wasson made up as a vampire.
Ice Pirates (1984) . . . . n.a.
Sacred Ground (1984) . . . . Wannetta
Amazons (1986) . . . . Dyala
•• 0:22—Breasts skinny dipping then getting dressed with Tashi.
•• 0:24—Brief breasts getting her top opened by bad guys then fighting them.
Penitentiary III (1987) . . . . Sugar
Turnaround (1987) . . . . n.a.
Caged Fury (1989) . . . . Warden Sybil Thorn
•• 0:53—Breasts and buns undressing for bath, then in the bathtub.
Deadly Embrace (1989) . . . . Charlotte Morland
•• 0:28—Breasts taking off her top. Mostly side view of left breast.
• 0:29—More left breast, while in bed with Chris.
••• 0:30—Breasts,while making love in bed with Chris.
• 1:10—Brief right breast, on T.V. when she replays video tape for Linnea Quigley.
Hollywood Boulevard II (1989)
. . . . Amazon Warrior from Brooklyn
Nudity Required (1989) . . . . Brenda
Batman Returns (1992) . . . . Uncredited Penguin Crony
Warlords 3000 (1992) . . . . Bull Woman
TV:
Switch (1976-77) . . . . Revel

• Rappaport, Sheeri

Films:

Little Witches (1996). . . . . .Jamie

- 0:09—In bra, then left breast, while caressing herself in confessional when talking with Father Michael.
- •• 0:17—Breasts and panties, while stripping out of her school girl uniform in front of window for construction workers.
- •• 0:34—In bra, then breasts and side view of buns and side view of lower frontal nudity with the other girls during ceremony.
- •• 0:58—Breasts and buns, while in her room with Daniel.
- 1:05—Brief, partial breasts, while kneeling on the floor by herself during ceremony.
- •• 1:25—Right breast, brief buns and brief lower frontal nudity, with the other girls during ceremony.

Made for Cable Movies:

Two Voices (1997; Lifetime) . . . . Amy

Rattray, Heather

Films:

Across the Great Divide (1976) . . . . Holly

The Further Adventures of the Wilderness Family (1978) . . . . Jenny Robinson

The Sea Gypsies (1978). . . . . .Courtney

Mountain Family Robinson (1979) . . . . .Jenny

Basket Case 2 (1989) . . . . Susan

- 1:20—Brief right breast twice, when white blouse gapes open in bedroom with Duane. Special-effect scar on her stomach makes it a little unappealing looking.

Basket Case 3: The Progeny (1991) . . . . Susan

TV:

As the World Turns (1990-) . . . . Lily Walsh

Rau, Andrea

Films:

Daughters of Darkness (1971; Belgian/French/German/Italian). . . . . Ilona

- 0:39—Buns and side of right breast, kneeling on floor while bending over the toilet.
- 0:56—Brief breasts on top of Stefan in bed.
- ••• 1:00—Left breast, while standing in bathroom watching Stefan take a shower.
- ••• 1:01—Breasts when Stefan tries to drag her into the shower.
- 1:02—Breasts, lying dead on the floor.
- 1:03—Breasts, lying dead on the floor. Long shot.

Beyond Erotica (1973). . . . . .Lola

- 0:26—Breasts, undressing in her bedroom.
- •• 0:30—Nude, undressing, then lying in bed, then trying on bunny costume.
- 0:47—Left breast, while lying on the floor.
- 0:56—Brief buns, running around in her cell.
- 0:57—Briefly nude, behind wall with holes in it.
- 0:59—Left breast, seen though hole in the wall.
- •• 1:10—Breasts in her bedroom.
- 1:23—Left breast, in flashback to 0:47 scene.

Rauch, Gig

See: Gangel, Gig.

Ravera, Gina

Films:

Illegal in Blue (1994). . . . . Alexis

Showgirls (1995) . . . . Molly Abrams
(NC-17 version reviewed.)

- 1:50—Brief buns, while getting raped by Carver and his goons.

Get on the Bus (1996). . . . . Gina

Kiss the Girls (1997) . . . . .Naomi Cross

Made for Cable Movies:

While Mile (1994; HBO) . . . . .Alma

Soul of the Game (1996; HBO) . . . . Grace

Made for TV Movies:

W.E.I.R.D. World (1995) . . . . .n.a.

Ray, Diane *

Video Tapes:

Playboy's Girls of Radio: Talk, Rock and Shock (1995) . . . . Herself

- ••• 0:16—In white slip, then nude with four other women.

Ray, Ola *

Films:

Body and Soul (1981). . . . . .Hooker #1

- 0:54—Brief breasts sitting on top of Leon Isaac Kennedy in bed with two other hookers.

48 Hrs. (1982). . . . . Vroman's Dancers

Night Shift (1982). . . . . Dawn

10 to Midnight (1983). . . . . Ola

- 1:30—Very brief buns and very brief left breast, taking off robe and getting into the shower.
- •• 1:31—Breasts in the shower.
- •• 1:32—More breasts in the shower.
- 1:39—Very brief breasts, dead, covered with blood in the shower.

Fear City (1984) . . . . .Honey Powers

Beverly Hills Cop II (1987). . . . . Playboy Playmate

The Nightstalker (1987) . . . . Sable Fox

Music Videos:

Thriller/Michael Jackson (1983). . . . . .His Girlfriend

• Ray, Tantala

Adult film actress.

Films:

Assault of the Party Nerds (1989) . . . . Vanna

- •• 1:10—Breasts dancing during party with her breasts sticking out of red dress, then covering herself with whipped cream.

Ray, Tracey *

Video Tapes:

Playboy's Girls of Radio: Talk, Rock and Shock (1995) . . . . Herself

- ••• 0:11—Nude while working out with various exercise equipment and in sauna.

Raymond, Candy

Films:

Alvin Rides Again (1974; Australian) . . . . Girl in Office

- 0:05—Lower frontal nudity and buns, in office with Alvin.

Don's Party (1976; Australian) . . . . .Kerry

Monkey Grip (1983; Australian). Lillian

Raymond, Cathleen *

a.k.a. Adult flim actress Gabrielle Scream.

Films:

The Perfect Gift (1993) . . . . Pajama Party Guest

Seduce Me: Pamela Principle 2 (1994) . . . . Cindy

- 0:03—Breast, while in background, changing clothes. Out of focus.

- ••• 0:04—Breasts and buns in G-string, after taking off lingerie during photo session. Long scene.

Virtual Encounters (1995). . . . . Rain Dancer 1
(Unrated version reviewed.)

- ••• 0:50—In pink dress, then nude after stripping and making love with another woman in the rain (wearing sunglasses the entire time). Long scene.

Video Tapes:

Penthouse Pet Rocks (1995). . . . . Pet
Hot Body Competition: Bikinis & Bikes Contest (1996) . . . . Noelle

- •• 0:07—Breasts and buns, while dancing on stage.

Rayne, April

See: Naschak, Andrea.

Redden, Leslie

Films:

Caged Heat 3000 (1995). . . . . Eden
Boogie Nights (1997) . . . . KC Sunshine

Made for Cable TV:

Hot Line: e-mail (1996; Cinemax) . . . . Linda

- • 0:24—In white bra, then breasts while making love with Gabe in stopped freight elevator.

Redgate, Sheila

Films:

Death Match (1994) . . . . Venik's Massage Girl
California Heat (1995). . . . . Boudoir Bikini Girl

- • 0:01—Breasts, while posing for Jack.

Watch Me (1995) . . . . Sherry

- • 0:04—Full frontal nudity, while posing for Paul, the photographer. (She has blonde hair.)

Hindsight (1996). . . . . Swing Club

Redgrave, Lynn *

Daughter of actor Sir Michael Redgrave.
Sister of actress Vanessa Redgrave.
Spokeswoman for *Weight Watchers* products.

Films:

Georgy Girl (1966; British) . . . . Georgy
The Virgin Soldiers (1969). . . . . Phillipa Raskin
Everything You Wanted to Know About Sex, But Were Afraid to Ask (1972). . . . . The Queen
The Happy Hooker (1975). . . . . Xaviera Hollander
(Before Weight Watchers.)
Morgan Stewart's Coming Home (1987). . . . . . Nancy Stewart
Getting It Right (1989) . . . . Joan

- •• 0:46—Brief right breast, then brief breasts on couch seducing Gavin. More right breast shot when wrestling with him.

Midnight (1989) . . . . Midnight
Shine (1996; Australian). . . . . Gillian

- • 1:36—Brief left breasts (dark) while lying under Geoffrey Rush in bed.

Made for TV Movies:

The Seduction of Miss Leona (1980) . . . . Leona DeVos
The Great American Sex Scandal (1989) . . . . Abby
What Ever Happened to Baby Jane? (1991) . . . . . . Jane Hudson

TV:

Centennial (1978-79) . . . . Charlotte Buckland Lloyd Seccombe
House Calls (1979-81). . . . . Ann Anderson
Teachers Only (1982-83). . . . . Diana Swanson
Chicken Soup (1989) . . . . Maddie

Redgrave, Vanessa

Daughter of actor Sir Michael Redgrave.
Sister of actress Lynn Redgrave.

Films:

Blow-Up (1966; British/Italian). . . . . Jane
Camelot (1967). . . . . Guenevere
Isadora (1968; British) . . . . Isadora Duncan

- • 0:47—Brief glimpses of breasts and buns dancing around in her boyfriend's house at night. Hard to see anything.
- • 2:19—Very brief breasts dancing on stage after coming back from Russia.

The Sea Gull (1968; U.S./British) . . . . Nina
The Trojan Women (1972; British) . . . . Andromache
Murder on the Orient Express (1974; British). . . . . Mary
Out of Season (1975; British) . . . . Ann

- • 0:35—Breasts, while putting on slip in bedroom.
- • 0:53—Full frontal nudity, after throwing open bed covers for Cliff Robertson. Don't see her face.

The Seven-Per-Cent Solution (1976) . . . . Lola Deveraux
Julia (1977) . . . . Julia
(Academy Award for Best Supporting Actress.)
Agatha (1979; British) . . . . Agatha Christie

- • 0:38—Buns, while lying face down and getting a massage. Then wearing a wet gown in bathtub.

Yanks (1979) . . . . Helen

- • 1:25—Brief side of left breast and buns, taking off robe and getting into bed.

Bear Island (1980; British/Canadian) . . . . Hedi Lindquist
Wagner (1983; British). . . . . Cosima
The Bostonians (1984). . . . . Olive Chancellor
Steaming (1985; British) . . . . Nancy

- • 1:32—Buns and brief side view of right breast getting into pool.

Wetherby (1985; British) . . . . Jean Travers
Prick Up Your Ears (1987; British). . . . . Peggy Ramsay
Consuming Passions (1988; U.S./British) . . . . Mrs. Garza
Orpheus Descending (1990) . . . . Lady Torrance

- •• 1:18—Buns, after taking off her robe and opening curtains to see Kevin Anderson. Shadow of left breast on curtain.

The Ballad of the Sad Cafe (1991) . . . . Miss Amelia
Howards End (1992) . . . . Ruth Wilcox
The House of Spirits (1993) . . . . Nivea
Little Odessa (1994) . . . . Irina Shapira
Mother's Boys (1994) . . . . Lydia
Looking for Richard (1996) . . . . Herself
Mission: Impossible (1996) . . . . Max
Smilla's Sense of Snow (1997) . . . . Elsa Lübing
Deep Impact (1998) . . . . Robin
Déjà Vu (1998) . . . . Skelly
Mrs. Dalloway (1998) . . . . Clarissa Dalloway
Wilde (1998) . . . . Lady Speranza Wilde

Made for Cable Movies:

Young Catherine (1991; TNT) . . . . Empress
They (1993; Showtime). . . . . Florence Latimer
Down Came a Blackbird (1995; Showtime) . . . . Anna Lenke

Made for TV Movies:

Playing for Time (1980). Fania Fenelon
A Man for All Seasons (1988). . . . . Lady Alice
What Ever Happened to Baby Jane? (1991) . . . Blanche Hudson
Two Mothers for Zachary (1996). . . . . Nancy Shaffell
Bella Mafia (1997) . . . . Graziella Luciano

Redman, Amanda

Films:

Richard's Things (1980; British) . . . . Josie
•• 0:51—Breasts, while lying in bed talking to Liv Ullman.

Give My Regards to Broad Street (1984; British) . . . . Office Receptionist

For Queen and Country (1989; British) . . . . Stacey

Made for TV Movies:

Masterpiece Theatre: Body & Soul (1994). . . . . Lynn

Reed, Kira *

a.k.a. Kaitlin Brennan.

Films:

Live Wire (1992) . . . . n.a.
(Unrated version reviewed.)

Mr. Saturday Night (1992) . . . . n.a.

Maui Heat: Swimsuit Edition (1996) . . . . Sara
••• 0:44—Nude, while making love with Mitch.
• 0:54—Buns in swimsuit while walking by the pool.
••• 0:58—Nude, while making love on the beach with Mitch and Karlie.
••• 1:02—Nude, while making love indoors with Mitch and Karlie.

The Price of Desire (1996) . . . . Monica
•• 0:08—In bra, then breasts, while making love with Mac on car parked on freeway overpass.
••• 0:09—Breasts, while making love with Mac in bed.
• 0:25—Brief left breast, while making out with a guy in the parking lot.
• 0:26—Brief left breast, when the guy slams her against the hood of the car.
• 0:41—Buns in panties.
•• 0:42—Breasts, while talking to her husband.
•• 0:53—Breasts and buns in panties, while changing clothes.
••• 1:10—In bra and panties, then nude, while making love with Sinclair.
•• 1:16—Breasts and partial buns, while making love with Sinclair out of the rocks by the ocean.
•• 1:23—Breasts, while sunbathing and reading.
•• 1:32—In bra, then breasts while making love outdoors with Janine Lindemulder and Sinclair.
• 1:35—Brief buns, when getting out of spa.
•• 1:37—Briefly nude, while getting dressed in bedroom.

Made for Cable TV:

Women: Stories of Passion-For the Sake of Science (1996; Showtime) . . . . .Marlene
••• 0:08—In bra and panties, then breasts, while lying on table to get hooked up to orgasm meter. Good moaning.
•• 0:13—Breasts, while lying on table after experiment ends.

Beverly Hills Bordello: All Night Long (1997; Showtime) . . . . Jenny Cochran
•• 0:01—In a dress, then a bra and panties, then nude, while doing a strip routine in front of Carol in bedroom.
• 0:03—Very brief lower frontal nudity when Carol flips her dress up.
••• 0:23—In bra, then nude, while having sex with Tommy in lobby area.

Erotic Confessions: Behind the Lens (1997; Cinemax) . . . . Tracy
• 0:02—Brief breasts, twice, in B&W photo.
••• 0:04—Breasts and buns, while posing for photographs in Monique Parent's studio.

Perversions of Science: Panic (1997; HBO) . . . . Vampiress

Red Shoe Diaries: Picnic (1997; Showtime) . . . . Rita
•• 0:01—Buns and breasts, while making love with Buddy outdoors at night on hood of a car.
••• 0:08—Breasts, while wearing black panties in open dress while fooling around outdoors with Kit.
••• 0:15—Nude, while sitting in back of truck then making love with Kit.

Intimate Sessions: Renee (1998; Cinemax) . . . . Renee
•• 0:04—In bra, then breasts, while making love with Brad in the office during her fantasy.
•• 0:11—In bra, then breasts, while making love with Brad in his photo studio.
••• 0:18—In bra and panties, then breasts and buns, while making love with Brad in bed.

Video Tapes:

Soft Bodies: All American Girls (1997) . . . . Herself
••• 0:02—In lingerie, then nude, while posing indoors on sofa.
••• 0:06—In dress, then nude, while posing outdoors.
••• 0:10—In lingerie, then nude, while posing indoors.

Reed, Pamela

Films:

The Long Riders (1980) . . . . Belle Starr
• 0:18—Buns, while standing up in bathtub to hug David Carradine. (Don't see her face.)

Melvin and Howard (1980) . . . . Bonnie Dummar
Eyewitness (1981) . . . . Linda
Young Doctors in Love (1982). . . . . .Norine Sprockett
The Right Stuff (1983). . . . . Trudy Cooper
Clan of the Cave Bear (1985) . . . . .Iza
The Best of Times (1986). . . . . Gigi Hightower
Rachel River (1989) . . . . Mary Graving
Cadillac Man (1990) . . . . Tina
Chattahoochee (1990) . . . . Earlene
Kindergarten Cop (1990) . . . . Phoebe
Bob Roberts (1992; U.S./British) . . . . Carol Cruise
Passed Away (1992) . . . . Terry Scanlan
Junior (1994). . . . . Angela

Made for Cable Movies:

Critical Choices (1996; Showtime). . . . . Arlene

Made for TV Movies:

Scandal Sheet (1985) . . . . Helen Grant
Woman with a Past (1992) . . . . Dee Johnson
Born Too Soon (1993). . . . . Elizabeth Mehren
Deadly Whispers (1995) . . . . .Carol Acton
The Man Next Door (1996). . . . . Wanda Gilmore

TV:

The Andros Targets (1977) . . . . Sandi Farrell
Grand (1990) . . . . .Janice Pasetti
Family Album (1993). . . . . Denise Lerner
The Home Court (1995-96). . . . . Judge Sydney J. Solomon

Reed, Penelope

Films:

Amazons (1986) . . . . Tashi
•• 0:22—Breasts and buns undressing to go skinny dipping. More breasts getting dressed.
• 0:24—Brief breasts getting top opened by bad guys.

Hollywood Boulevard II (1989) . . .Amazon Warrior with Crystal
Far Out Man (1990) . . . . Stewardess
Hired to Kill (1990) . . . . Katrina

Reed, Tracy

Films:

Dr. Strangelove (1963) . . . . Miss Scott

...All the Marbles (1981) . . . . Diane
a.k.a. The California Dolls
Running Scared (1986) . . . . Maryann
• 0:18—Brief buns.
• 1:30—Very brief breasts in bed with Gregory Hines.
Made for TV Movies:
Death of a Centerfold: The Dorothy Stratten Story (1981) . . . . Mindy
TV:
Love, American Style (1969-70). . . . . Repertory Player
Barefoot in the Park (1970-71) . . . . Corie Bratter
Love, American Style (1972-74). . . . . Repertory Player
Knots Landing (1990-93) . . . . Charlotte Anderson

Rees, Donogh
Films:
Starlight Hotel (1987; New Zealand). . . . . Helen
Crush (1992; New Zealand). Christina
• 0:42—Right breast in pulled up hospital gown.

Reeves, Lisa
Films:
The Pom Pom Girls (1976) . . . . Sally
• 1:02—Brief breasts, pulling black T-shirt over her head.
The Chicken Chronicles (1977) . . . . Margaret
You Light Up My Life (1977) . . . . Carla Wright
TV:
The San Diego Beach Bums (1977) . . . . Margie

Reeves, Perrey
Films:
Child's Play 3 (1991) . . . . DeSilva
Kicking and Screaming (1995). Amy
•• 0:32—In bra, then breasts while in dorm room with Josh Hamilton.
Made for Cable TV:
Red Shoe Diaries: The Last Motel (1996; Showtime) . . . . Joey
••• 0:08—Breasts, while motel room with her boyfriend.
••• 0:17—Partial buns, while getting up off her boyfriend and taking off her panties. In black bra, then breasts.
• 0:19—Breasts, while on bed with her boyfriend.
Made for TV Movies:
Mothers, Daughters and Lovers (1989) . . . . Laura
Plymouth (1991). . . . . Hannah
An Element of Truth (1995). . . . . Maizie
Escape to Witch Mountain (1995) . . . . Zoe Moon

*Reeves, Saskia **
Films:
Antonia & Jane (1991; British) . . . . Antonia McGill
•• 0:42—Brief partial left breast, while lying in bed on top of her lover. Breasts, turning over on her back.
• 0:44—Breasts, leaning over her lover while she is tied and blindfolded in bed.
Close My Eyes (1991; British) . . . . Natalie Gillespie
•• 0:29—Very brief right breast, twice, then breasts twice in room with Richard.
••• 0:31—Full frontal nudity, getting up and getting dressed.
••• 0:45—In white bra, then breasts standing, then lying on the floor with Richard.
•• 0:46—Buns, while lying in bed with Richard. Nude, getting out of bed and putting on robe.
• 0:56—Right breast, while lying in bed.
December Bride (1994; British) . . . . Sarah
Traps (1995; Australian). . . . . Louise Duffield

Butterfly Kiss (1996; British). Miriam
•• 0:15—Left breast, while making love in bed with Amanda Plummer.

Regan, Linda
Films:
The Adventures of a Private Eye (1974; British) . . . Clarissa
• 0:34—Full frontal nudity in boat with Scott.
• 0:36—Very brief side view of left breast, getting up and diving off boat.
Confessions of a Pop Performer (1975; British) . Brenda Climax
Carry On England (1976; British). . . . . Pvt. Taylor
Fiona (1978; British) . . . . Secretary

Regan, Mary
Films:
Heart of the Stag (1983; New Zealand). . . . . . Cathy Jackson
• 0:03—Brief right breast twice, very brief lower frontal nudity in bed with her father.
•• 1:06—Breasts in bed, ripping her blouse open while yelling at her father.
Midnight Dancer (1987; Australian). . . . . Crystal
a.k.a. Belinda
•• 0:29—Breasts in dressing room, undressing and rubbing make-up on herself.
•• 0:56—In bra, then breasts in panties, changing clothes and getting into bed.
The Year My Voice Broke (1987; Australian) . . . . . . Miss McColl
Out of the Body (1988; Australian) . . . . Marry Mason
Fever (1989; Australian). Leanne Welles
Women From Down Under (1995; Australian/New Zealand) . . . . Excursion to the Bridge of Friendship/Shelly

Regan, Misty
Adult film actress.
Films:
Nudity Required (1989) . . . . Featured Dancer
• 0:02—Breasts dancing on stage in club.
• 0:04—Breasts and buns, on stage in G-string.

Regard, Suzanne M.
Films:
48 Hrs. (1982) . . . . Cowgirl Dancer
Malibu Express (1984) . . . . Sexy Sally
• 0:50—Brief breasts, while talking on the telephone.
•• 1:06—Breasts, while talking on the telephone.

*Register, Meg **
Films:
Ministry of Vengeance (1989) . . . . Gail Miller
Backstreet Dreams (1990) . . . . Candy
Lena's Holiday (1990) . . . . Bridgette
Boxing Helena (1993) . . . . Marion Cavanaugh
•• 0:06—Right breast in open dress in Julian Sand's flashback.

*Reid, Tanya **
Films:
Exit to Eden (1994). . . . . Naomi/Citizen
• 0:26—Breasts while on runway during introductions.
Listen (1996; Canadian). . . . . Krista's Double
Phat Beach (1996) . . . . Ulga
• 0:30—Very brief, partial lower half of buns, while in dancing in hotel room with Durrel.

Reidy, Gabrielle
Films:
Educating Rita (1983; British). . . . . Barbara

The Fanatasist (1986; Irish) . . . . Kathy O'Malley
- 0:03—Breasts, while getting attacked in a room.

The Baby of Mâcon (1993; British/French) . . . . Midwife
(Not available in the U.S. yet.)
December Bride (1994; British) . . . . Birdie
The Devil's Own (1997) . . . . Frankie's Mother

Reinhardt, Sandra

Films:

Illegal in Blue (1994) . . . . Joanne
- ••• 0:07—Breasts, while making love with Chris.

Made for Cable TV:

Hot Line: Voyeur (1994; Cinemax) . . . . Stephanie
(Available on video tape in *Hot Line*.)
- ••• 0:08—Nude, while making love on the floor with her husband.
- • 0:11—Left breast while watching Val make love with the masseuse.
- 0:19—In wet white slip, while outside in the rain.
- •• 0:25—Right breast, when making love with Val while her husband watches.

Dream On: Long Distance Turnaround (1995; HBO) . . . . Ann
- •• 0:01—Breasts, while making love on the floor with Martin.

Relph, Emma

Films:

Eureka (1983; British) . . . . Mary (blue dress)
- • 1:17—Brief breasts during African voodoo ceremony.

The Witches (1989) . . . . Millie

Remberg, Erika

Films:

Circus of Horrors (1960; British) . . . . Elissa
Saturday Night Out (1963; British) . . . . Wanda
Cave of the Living Dead (1966; Yugoslavian) . . . . Maria
The Lickerish Quartet (1970; Italian) . . . . Wife
a.k.a. Erotic Illusion
- •• 1:14—Nude, getting up off sofa and sitting back down, then in B&W film.
- •• 1:15—Breasts, while the girl feels her up. Close-up shot.
- • 1:26—Right breast, while in bed in film.

Rene, Sugar Ray

See: Rome, Cindy.

*Renée, Mallesia **

Video Tapes:

Hot Body Competition: Lusty Lingerie Contest (1996) . . . . Mallesia Renee
- ••• 0:34—Nude, dancing on stage during contest.
- ••• 0:35—Nude, while posing outdoors.

*Rener, Shawna **

Video Tapes:

The Best of the Mermaids (1992) . . Jus' Catchin' Some Rays
- ••• 0:20—Breasts and buns, while scuba diving.

Renet, Sinitta

Singer in England.

Films:

Shock Treatment (1981) . . . . Frankie
Foreign Body (1986; British) . . . . Lovely Indian Girl
- • 0:06—Buns, then breasts in bedroom.

Renn, Grace C.

Films:

Beauty School (1993) . . . . Betty
- •• 0:56—In white bra, then breasts while on stage, practicing her talent routine.

Jurassic Women (1995) . . . . Koo

Renney, Janice

Films:

Crimes of Passion (1984) . . . . Stripper
(Unrated version reviewed.)
- ••• 0:06—Breasts and buns dancing while Anthony Perkins watches.
- • 1:00—Buns again.

Savage Dawn (1984) . . . . Susan

Renshaw, Jeannine

Films:

Hook (1991) . . . . Drama Teacher

Made for Cable TV:

Dream On: Death Takes a Coffee Break (1990; HBO) . . . . Robin
- •• 0:10—Breasts in kitchen after taking off her top with Martin, then on sofa.

Dream On: Take Two Tablets, And Get Me to Mt. Sinai (1995; HBO) . . . . Martin's Lover

*Reuben, Gloria **

Films:

Immediate Family (1989) . . . . Maternity Nurse
ShadowHunter (1992) . . . . Cayla
- • 0:07—Buns, lifting up her skirt to tempt Scott Glenn. Don't see her face and slightly out of focus.

Wild Orchid II: Two Shades of Blue (1992) . . . . Celeste
- •• 0:32—Breasts on floor in front of fire when Mona and Blue peek in the rooms. (She's wearing a blonde wig.)

Timecop (1994) . . . . Sarah Fielding

Made for Cable Movies:

Dead Air (1994; USA) . . . . Judy

Made for TV Movies:

Confessions: Two Faces of Evil (1994) . . . . Tanya Blackmon
Johnny's Girl (1995) . . . . Monica

TV:

ER (1995-) . . . . Dr. Jeanie Boulet

Reve'e, Paula

Films:

Angel Eyes (1991) . . . . Julie
- •• 0:13—Breasts, while standing in yellow bikini bottoms and rubbing lotion on herself.
- • 0:23—Breasts, while lying on pool float in the pool.
- • 0:25—More breasts while on pool float.

Knockouts (1992) . . . . Candy
- •• 0:04—Breasts, going to look in the guys' locker room.
- •• 0:23—Breasts during strip poker game.
- •• 0:27—Breasts while sitting on chest of drawers.
- ••• 0:43—In lingerie, then breasts while posing for photographs.
- •• 0:59—Breasts while working out (seen mostly in silhouette).

Video Tapes:

Love Scenes: Volume 1 (1991) . . . . Madilyn Jones
- ••• 0:20—Nude, while in the room and in the shower with Christopher.

Inside Out 4 (1992) .... Lola/My Cyberian Rhapsody
(Unrated version reviewed.)
••• 1:30—Breasts in cybersex machine.
••• 1:31—Breasts several times when cybersex machine starts malfunctioning.

Reyes, Pia *

Films:

Auntie Lee's Meat Pies (1991) .... Sky
•• 1:10—Breasts in basement with her rock star boyfriend.
•• 1:15—Breasts in basement with her pot smoking boyfriend.

On Deadly Ground (1993) .... Dancer

Return of the Living Dead 3 (1993) .... Alicia

Indecent Behavior 3 (1995) .... Rosa Venezuela
•• 0:34—In black bra, then breasts while in room with Mr. Cowen.
•• 0:45—Breasts, while wearing a mask and making love in bed with Billy (also wearing a mask).

Nighttime Lover (1995) .... Tracy
a.k.a. Call Girl
•• 0:01—Breasts and buns, while posing for photographs with another model.
• 0:05—Left breast in B&W still photo. Brief breasts in another B&W photo.
• 1:07—Brief buns in panties in outfit while getting photographed.
• 1:09—Brief breasts in B&W photo.

Sinful Intrigue (1995) .... Yvette
• 0:18—Breasts, quite a few times, under sheer body suit while talking with Beckie Mullen.

Forbidden Zone: Alien Abduction (1996) .... Tedra
a.k.a. Alien Abduction: Intimate Secrets
• 0:17—Very, very brief breasts while lying on the floor in arena dream.
• 0:40—Brief breasts, while making love with the foreign exchange student in flashback.
• 0:41—Brief breasts, while on top of frat boy in flashback.
•• 0:42—Breasts, while making love with the runner guy, then very brief breasts in arena dream.
• 0:50—Very, very brief breasts, when getting out of pool, then left breast in arena dream.
• 0:53—Breasts during arena dream.

Made for Cable TV:

Hot Line: Voyeur (1994; Cinemax) .... Masseuse
(Available on video tape in *Hot Line.*)
•• 0:11—Breasts, when making love with Val while Stephanie watches.

Video Tapes:

Sexy Lingerie (1988) .... Model

Playboy Video Calendar 1990 (1989) .... June
••• 0:28—Nude.

Sensual Pleasures of Oriental Massage (1990) ...... n.a.

Playboy's 21 Playmates (1996) .... Playmate
••• 0:16—Nude in still photos.
••• 0:17—Nude outdoors in a park.

Rhey, Ashlie *

Films:

Body of Influence (1992) .... Dominatrix
(Unrated version reviewed.)

Ring of Fire II: Blood and Steel (1992) . . Bad Girl Gang Member

Anthony's Desire (1993) .... Dancer
• 0:22—Breasts, while lying on her back under another woman on stage.
• 0:54—Left breast and brief lower frontal nudity, while lying down with other women. She's at the bottom of the screen.

The Perfect Gift (1993) .... Carol

Renegade: Fighting Cage (1993) .... Redhead
(Nudity added for video release.)
••• 1:14—Breasts and buns, while in a room with a guy, then making love with him on a small table.

Save Me (1993) .... Customer
(Unrated version reviewed.)
••• 0:21—Nude, while trying on lingerie after Lysette Anthony shows Harry Hamlin secret one-way mirror in dressing room in lingerie store.

...And God Spoke (1994) .... Nude Ninja
• 0:02—Brief breasts, while putting her sword away. (She's in the middle, the second one to talk.)

Inner Sanctum 2 (1994) .... Uncredited Body Double
(Unrated version reviewed.)
• 0:12—Left breast and buns, then breasts while making love in bed. Body double for Jennifer Ciesar.
•• 0:13—Buns and right breast, then breasts while making love. Body double for Jennifer Ciesar.
• 0:50—Breasts, while in bed with Michael Nouri. Body double for Tracy Brooks Swope.
••• 0:56—Breasts and buns, while making love in bedroom. Body double for Jennifer Ciesar.

Midnight Tease (1994) .... Mantra
•• 0:00—Breasts and buns during opening credits.
••• 0:42—Buns and breasts in black dominatrix outfit while dancing on stage with Samantha.
•• 0:47—Breasts while talking with Samantha in dressing room.
• 0:50—Breasts, when whipping Samantha's stepfather in dream while Samantha kills her.

Money to Burn (1994) .... Gina
• 1:02—Nude in bathtub with Don Swayze.

The Mosaic Project (1994) .... Stewardess

Play Time (1994) .... Connie
(Unrated version reviewed.)
•• 0:45—Breasts and buns in panties in bedroom while caressing Lindsey in front of Joe.

Bikini Drive-In (1995) .... Kim Taylor
(Unrated version reviewed.)
••• 0:05—Breasts after opening her red swimsuit top and rubbing suntan lotion on herself.
• 0:24—Breasts under white T-shirt, when wiping her face off after water fight while cleaning the drive-in.
••• 0:34—Breasts and buns, while making love in bed with Richard Gabai.
• 0:54—Brief right breast, after Gabai takes of her bikini top in office.

Forbidden Games (1995) .... Trish
(Unrated version reviewed.)
• 0:18—Buns in blue swimsuit, greeting Michael at the door and taking him to meet Shauna.
••• 0:39—Breasts and buns, while making love with Michael in bedroom.
•• 1:00—Breasts, while in bed with Shauna, tying and blindfolding Michael in bed.

Obsessed with Lust (1995) .... Lanie
a.k.a. Prelude to Love
••• 0:21—Full frontal nudity, while making love with Steve in bed.
• 0:25—Brief breasts, while sitting up in bed when Steve leaves.

••• 1:12—Breasts, while making love with Eric on pool table.

Witchcraft 7: Judgement Hour (1995) . . . . Rachel

(Unrated version reviewed.)

•• 0:03—Breasts and brief partial lower frontal nudity, while making love with Martin. Extreme close-ups of nipples.

••• 0:08—Breasts, while on operating table in hospital, when they defibrillate her several times to get her heart started.

•• 0:21—Buns in open back of hospital gown, while running away from hospital.

••• 0:23—Buns, then breasts, while making love with jogger outside, then during fight with police.

•• 0:52—Full frontal nudity on video monitor that the policemen watch, while she makes love with the invisible vampire.

Babe Watch: The Forbidden Parody (1996). . . . . . . Ty-Dy

••• 0:54—Breasts, while undressing in dressing room with Brock, then making love.

• 1:14—Brief buns in swimsuit at the beach.

A Passion for Murder (1996) . . . . Debbie

a.k.a. Deadlock

• 0:09—Very brief breasts, while sitting in lounge chairs by the pool.

••• 0:13—Breasts, while posing for photos with Allison.

••• 0:56—Breasts and buns, while making love with Evan in bath.

• 1:03—Brief beasts, while making love, seen on TV.

• 1:10—Brief breasts, twice, while making love, seen on TV.

Bikini Hoe Down (1997) . . . . April

• 0:07—Brief buns in swimsuit bottom.

• 0:40—Brief buns in panties and brief breasts while changing clothes.

••• 0:53—Nude, while showering with the other three girls.

1:10—Nude, while making love in hot tub with David.

•• 1:19—Breasts, while dancing on stage during bikini hoe down.

Made for Cable TV:

Erotic Confessions: Trapped (1997; Cinemax). . . . . Beverly

• 0:02—In bra, then breasts, while starting to make love with Patrick on table.

••• 0:10—In bra, then nude, while trying on lingerie in store with Reba, then making love with her.

••• 0:14—In bra, then breasts and partial buns, while making love with Patrick in bed.

Beverly Hills Bordello: Teach Me (1998; Showtime) . . . . Sandra

•• 0:08—Full frontal nudity, while in bedroom while talking with Elaine.

••• 0:10—Breasts, while making love with a customer.

•• 0:21—Breasts and buns, when making love with Elaine while her husband watches.

Video Tapes:

Fantasies 2 (1992) . . . . Model

Nude Daydreams (1993) . . . . Daydream 5

••• 0:12—In black and white lingerie, then nude while caressing Monique Parent on sofa. Long scene.

Playboy's Sensual Fantasy for Lovers (1993) . . . . Film Fantasies

••• 0:25—In bra and panties, then nude while making love, in "sheik" fantasy with her lover.

• 0:47—Breasts during review.

Playboy's Erotic Fantasies III (1994) . . . Final Exam/Teacher

••• 0:39—In white bra, panties and stockings, then full frontal nudity while making love with the student.

Sexy Lingerie: Dreams & Desire (1994). . . . . Cast Member

American Sweethearts (1995) . . . . Herself

••• 0:13—In lingerie, then nude, while posing on bed in front of a video camera by herself, then with a guy.

••• 0:23—Full frontal nudity, while making love with Monique Parent.

••• 0:41—In wet clothes, then nude, while dancing with Monique.

Playboy's Girls of the Internet (1996). . . . . Herself

••• 0:31—Nude in virtual reality segment.

Playboy's Rising Stars and Sexy Starlets (1996) . . Herself

••• 0:26—In lingerie, then nude, while dancing for her boyfriend.

Rialson, Candice

Films:

The Gay Deceivers (1969) . . . . Uncredited Girl in Bikini

Candy Stripe Nurses (1974) . . . . Sandy

•• 0:05—Breasts in hospital linen closet with a guy.

•• 0:08—Breasts smoking and writing in bathtub.

• 0:14—Breasts in hospital bed.

Mama's Dirty Girls (1974) . . . . .n.a.

Pets (1974) . . . . Bonnie

•• 0:26—Breasts dancing in field while Dan is watching her while he's tied up.

••• 0:33—Breasts making love on top of Dan while he's still tied up.

•• 0:40—Breasts getting into bath at Geraldine's house.

• 0:45—Breasts posing for Geraldine.

••• 1:02—Breasts taking off lingerie in bed with Ron, then making love with him.

The Eiger Sanction (1975). Art Student

Summer School Teachers (1975) . . . . Conklin T.

• 0:14—Breasts and buns when Mr. Lacey fantasizes about what she looks like. Don't see her face, but it looks like her.

••• 0:38—Breasts outside with other teacher, kissing on the ground.

Hollywood Boulevard (1976) . . . . Candy Wednesday

•• 0:29—Breasts getting her blouse ripped off by actors during a film.

••• 0:32—Breasts sunbathing with Bobbi and Jill.

•• 0:45—Brief breasts in the films she's watching at the drive-in. Same as 0:29.

Logan's Run (1976) . . . . . . Uncredited Girl with Richard Jordan

Silent Movie (1976). . . . . Uncredited Club Patron

Chatterbox (1977) . . . . Penny

•• 0:01—Left breast, in bed with Ted, then breasts getting out of bed.

••• 0:15—Side view of right breast then breasts during demonstration on stage.

••• 0:26—Breasts in bed talking on phone.

•• 0:35—Breasts during photo shoot.

•• 0:38—Breasts again for more photos while opening a red coat.

•• 0:43—Breasts in bed with Ted.

••• 0:55—Breasts taking off white dress, walking up the stairs and opening the door.

•• 1:09—Breasts opening her raincoat for Ted.

Moonshine County Express (1977) . . . . Mayella

Stunts (1977) . . . . Judy Blake

Winter Kills (1979). Second Blonde Girl

Riave, Andrea

Films:

The Perfect Gift (1993) . . . . Nicole

Desire (1994) . . . . Nicole's Roommate

Object of Obsession (1994). . . . . Francine
•• 1:18—Full frontal nudity, while on bed with Scott Valentine in video playback.
Lover's Leap (1995). . . . . Clarine
Made for Cable TV:
Red Shoe Diaries: How I Met My Husband (1993; Showtime) . . . . Wealthy Woman
•• 0:15—Breasts, while making love with Gusipe in car while Neith Hunter watches.
Red Shoe Diaries: Runway (1994; Showtime). . . . . Jana
•• 0:17—Breasts and buns in panties, several times while posing for photos with Miguel.
• 0:21—Brief breasts (she's on the left) while watching Alia and Miguel making love.

Rich, Cindy *
Films:
Can It Be Love (1992) . . . . Megan
a.k.a. Spring Break Sorority Babes
Video Tapes:
Fantasies (1992) . . . . Cast
Playboy's Cheerleaders (1996) . . . . Cheerleader/Cindy
••• 0:32—Nude (she's the third to take her bra off) outside during car wash with two other cheerleaders.

Richarde, Tessa
Films:
The Beach Girls (1982) . . . . Doreen
Cat People (1982). . . . . Billie
•• 1:00—Breasts in bed with Malcolm McDowell trying to get him excited.
The Last American Virgin (1982). . . . . Brenda
•• 0:15—Brief breasts walking into the living room when Gary's parents come home.
Young Doctors in Love (1982). . . . . Rocco's Wife
National Lampoon's Vacation (1983). . . . . Motel Guest

Richards, Elise
Films:
Trick or Treat (1986) . . . . Genie Wooster
•• 0:39—In black bra, then breasts in back seat of car when taken over by evil spirits.
•• 0:41—Very brief breasts, getting attacked by monster, then breasts when unconscious and found by Tim.
Valet Girls (1987). . . . . Cindy

Richards, Kim
Films:
Escape to Witch Mountain (1975) . . . . Tia
Assault on Precinct 13 (1976) . . . . Kathy
No Deposit, No Return (1976) . . . . .Tracy
Special Delivery (1976) . . . . Juliette
The Car (1977) . . . . Lynn Marie
Return from Witch Mountain (1978) . . . . Tia
Meatballs, Part II (1984) . . . . .Cheryl
Tuff Turf (1984) . . . . Frankie Croyden
• 1:29—Brief breasts supposedly of a body double (Fiona Morris) in bedroom with James Spader but I have heard from a very reliable source that it really was her.
Escape (1988) . . . . Brooke Howser
TV:
Nanny and the Professor (1970-71). . . . . Prudence Everett
Here We Go Again (1973) . . . . Jan
James at 15 (1977-78). . . . . Sandy Hunter
Hello, Larry (1979-80) . . . . Ruthie Adler

Richards, Lisa
Films:
House of Dark Shadows (1970) . . . . Daphne Rudd
Rolling Thunder (1977) . . . . .Janet
Heaven Can Wait (1978) . . . . Reporter
Return (1985) . . . . Ann Stoving
The Beat (1986). . . . . .Amy Kahn
Eating (1990). . . . . Helene
• 0:12—Brief right breast, while putting a sweater over her head.
Venice/Venice (1992). . . . . .Guest at Party

Richardson, Joely *
Daughter of actress Vanessa Redgrave and director Tony Richardson.
Sister of actress Natasha Richardson.
Films:
The Hotel New Hampshire (1984) . . . . Waitress
Wetherby (1985; British). . . . . Young Jean Travers
•• 1:10—Breasts in room with Jim when he takes off her coat.
Drowning by Numbers (1988; British). . . . . . Cisse Colpitts 3
• 0:28—Breasts, taking off swimsuit and drying herself off. Long shot.
••• 0:43—Breasts and buns, making love on couch with Bellamy.
• 1:23—Breasts under water in pool with Bellamy.
•• 1:24—Breasts getting out of pool.
••• 1:25—Breasts standing up and putting swimsuit back on.
•• 1:37—Left breast, while in car with Madgett.
King Ralph (1991) . . . . Princess Anna
Shining Through (1992) . . . . .Margrete von Eberstien
I'll Do Anything (1994) . . . . .Cathy Breslow
• 1:03—Very brief frontal nudity, while walking past hallway when surprised by Nick Nolte.
Sister My Sister (1995; British). . . . . .Christine
101 Dalmatians (1996) . . . . .Anita
Event Horizon (1997). . . . . Starck
Hollow Reed (1997; British). . . . . Hannah Wyatt
Made for TV Movies:
Loch Ness (1996; British). . . . . Laura MacFeteridge

Richardson, Miranda
Films:
Dance with a Stranger (1985; British). . . . . Ruth Ellis
• 0:08—Very brief upper half of left breast, twice, while in bed making love with David.
• 0:18—Very brief tip of left breast, while getting into bed with David. Dark.
• 0:20—Very, very brief side view of left breast, putting robe on in bed.
The Innocent (1985; British) . . . . Mary Turner
Underworld (1985; British) . . . . Oriel
The Death of the Heart (1986; British). . . . . Daphne
Transmutations (1986). . . . . Oriel
a.k.a. Underworld
Empire of the Sun (1987) . . . . Mrs. Victor
Twisted Obsession (1990) . . . . .Marilyn
The Bachelor (1991) . . . . Frederica/Widow
Enchanted April (1991; British) . . . . Rose
The Crying Game (1992). . . . . Jude
Damage (1992; French/British) . . . . Ingrid
(Unrated Director's cut reviewed.)
••• 1:40—Breasts, while standing in front of Jeremy Irons in the bedroom.
Century (1993; British). . . . . .Clara
••• 0:51—Breasts, while making love with Clive Owen.

- 1:06—Partial right breast, while talking with Owen in bed.
- 1:07—Breasts, while lying on top of Owen, then right breast, after getting off him.

Tom & Viv (1994) .... Vivienne Haigh-Wood
The Evening Star (1996) .... Patsy Carpenter
Kansas City (1996) .... Carolyn Stilton
The Apostle (1997) .... Toosie
The Night and the Moment (1997). .... Julie

Made for Cable Movies:
Old Times (1993) .... Anna
Fatherland (1994; HBO) .... Charlie Maguire

Made for TV Movies:
Mystery! Die Kinder (1991). .... Sidonie Reiger
Merlin (1998) .... Queen Mab

Richardson, Natasha

Daughter of actress Vanessa Redgrave and director Tony Richardson.
Sister of actress Joely Richardson.
Wife of actor Liam Neeson.

Films:
Gothic (1986; British) .... Mary
A Month in the Country (1988; British). .... Alice Keach
Fat Man and Little Boy (1989). .... Jean Tatlock
Patty Hearst (1989) .... Patricia Hearst
- •• 0:13—Breasts, blindfolded in the bathtub while talking to a woman member of the S.L.A.

The Handmaid's Tale (1990). .... Kate
- •• 0:30—Breasts twice at the window getting some fresh air.
- • 0:59—Breasts making love with Aidan Quinn.
- ••• 1:00—Breasts after Quinn rolls off her.

The Comfort of Strangers (1991) .... Mary
- ••• 0:45—Breasts sleeping in bed. Long shot. Then closer breasts after waking up. Long scene.
- •• 1:05—Breasts making love with Colin. Lit with blue light.
- •• 1:06—Right breast, lying in bed with Colin. Lit with blue light.

The Favor, the Watch and the Very Big Fish (1991; French/British) .... Sybil
a.k.a. Rue Saint-Sulpice
Nell (1994) .... Paula Olsen
Widow's Peak (1994). .... Edwina Broome

Made for Cable Movies:
Past Midnight (1992; USA) .... Laura Matthews
- ••• 0:48—Breasts while making love in bed with Rutger Hauer.
- • 1:10—Very brief side of left breast, while getting into the shower.

Hostages (1993; HBO) .... Jill Morrell
Zelda (1993; TNT) .... Zelda Sayre-Fitzgerald

Made for Cable TV:
Tales From the Crypt: Fatal Caper (1996; HBO) .... Fiona Havisham

Richardson, Rickey

Films:
Bloody Trail (1972) .... Miriam
- • 1:01—Peek at left breast in torn blouse.
- • 1:05—Right breast while sleeping, dark, hard to see.

The Hot Box (1972) .... Ellie St. George
- •• 0:16—Breasts cleaning herself off in stream and getting out.
- • 0:21—Breasts sleeping in hammocks. (She's the second one from the front.)
- • 0:26—Breasts getting accosted by the People's Army guys.
- ••• 0:43—Full frontal nudity making love with Flavio.
- ••• 0:45—Breasts in stream bathing with the other three girls.
- • 1:01—Breasts taking off top in front of soldiers.

Richardson, Salli

Films:
Mo' Money (1992) .... Pretty Customer
Prelude to a Kiss (1992). .... Bridesmaid #2
How U Like Me Now (1993) .... Valerie
Posse (1993) .... Lana
- • 1:10—Brief buns, while taking off her dress in front of Mario Van Peebles, then brief breasts (don't see her face, but it's her).
- •• 1:11—Breasts, while making love with Van Peebles in bed.

A Low Down Dirty Shame (1994) .... Angela
Sioux City (1994) .... Jolene Buckley
The Great White Hype (1996) .... Bambi
Butter (1997) .... Blusette Ford

Made for Cable Movies:
Soul of the Game (1996; HBO) .... Lahoma

Made for Cable TV:
Stargate SG-1: Bloodlines (1997; Showtime) .... Dreya'c

Made for TV Movies:
I Spy Returns (1994) .... Nicole

Richmond, Fiona

Films:
Barry McKenzie Holds His Own... (1974; Australian) .... French Stripper
The House on Straw Hill (1976; British) .... Suzanne
a.k.a. Exposé
- ••• 0:05—Buns and breasts undressing and getting into bed and making love with Udo Kier.
- •• 0:56—In black bra, then breasts undressing in front of Kier.
- ••• 1:00—Breasts in bedroom, then making love with Kier.
- • 1:03—Brief buns, while lying on Linda's bed.
- • 1:05—Buns, while lying on Linda's bed.
- •• 1:06—Right breast, in bed with Linda.
- •• 1:07—Breasts in bed with Linda.
- • 1:09—Buns and side of left breast getting up from bed.
- • 1:11—Full frontal nudity, getting stabbed in the bathroom. Covered with blood.

Love Trap (1977). .... Maxine Lupercal
a.k.a. Let's Get Laid
- •• 0:10—Nude, while in the shower/tub.
- • 0:21—Brief left breast when her lingerie is torn off in Gordon's hand.
- ••• 0:24—Nude, while doing strip routine on stage (wearing a big blonde wig).
- 0:26—Breasts, with a guy in bedroom.
- • 0:27—Breasts and buns in bed with him.
- •• 0:56—Nude, after stripping out of Nazi uniform, then bra and panties, then making love with two girls.
- •• 1:09—Breasts, while in bubble bath, talking to Gordon, then standing up.
- • 1:34—Brief breasts when Gordon pulls her dress top down during filming.

Fiona (1978; British). .... Fiona Richmond
- •• 0:23—Breasts on boat with a blonde woman rubbing oil on her.
- •• 0:27—In a bra, then frontal nudity stripping in a guy's office for an audition.
- •• 0:35—Breasts, then frontal nudity lying down during photo session.
- • 0:51—Breasts walking around her apartment in boots.
- •• 1:00—Breasts with old guy ripping each other's clothes off.
- •• 1:08—Frontal nudity taking off clothes for a shower.

History of the World, Part I (1981). . . . . .Queen

Richmond, Laura *

Video Tapes:

Sexy Lingerie (1988) . . . . .Model
Playboy Video Calendar 1990 (1989) . . . . February
••• 0:07—Nude.
Playboy Video Centerfold: Kerri Kendall (1990) . . . . .Playmate
••• 0:39—Nude.
Playboy Video Playmate Six-Pack 1992 (1992) . . . . .Playmate

Richter, Debi

Miss California 1975.

Films:

Hometown, U.S.A. (1979) . . . . .Dolly
Swap Meet (1979) . . . . Susan
Gorp (1980) . . . . .Barbara
Midnight Madness (1980). . . . . .Candy
Hot Moves (1984). . . . . .Heidi
• 0:29—Breasts on nude beach.
••• 1:09—Breasts, taking off her red dress in bed with Michael.
Square Dance (1987) . . . . Gwen
a.k.a. Home is Where the Heart Is
Winners Take All (1987). Cindy Wickes
Promised Land (1988). . . . . Pammie
The Banker (1989). . . . . .Melanie
Cyborg (1989). . . . . Nady Simmons
• 0:28—Buns, after taking off clothes and running into the ocean.
• 0:30—Brief left breast by the fire showing herself to Jean-Claude Van Damme.

Made for TV Movies:

My Wicked Ways... The Legend of Errol Flynn (1985) . . . . Lucille Hartley

TV:

Aspen (1977) . . . . .Angela Morelli
All Is Forgiven (1986) . . . . Sherry Levy

Richters, Christine *

Video Tapes:

Playmates at Play (1990) . . . . .Free Wheeling

Richwine, Maria

Films:

The Buddy Holly Story (1978) . . . . Maria Elena Holly
Hamburger—The Motion Picture (1986) . . . . . . .Conchita
•• 0:49—Breasts trying to seduce Russell in a room.
Ministry of Vengeance (1989) . . . . .Fatima
Sex Crimes (1991). . . . . Rosanna
• 0:09—Very brief tip of right breast, while sitting in bathtub, covered with bruises and cuts after getting raped.
• 1:19—Brief breast in mirror, while taking a shower.

TV:

a.k.a. Pablo (1984) . . . . Carmen Rivera

Rickter, Alicia *

Video Tapes:

Playboy Video Calendar 1997 (1996) . . . . September
••• 0:36—In lingerie and nude while posing in apartment.
••• 0:38—Nude, while posing and dancing in bedroom.

Rief, Tammy *

Video Tapes:

Hot Body International: #3 Lingerie Special (1992) . . . . Contestant
•• 0:20—Buns in black bra and G-string.
Hot Body International: #5 Miss Acapulco (1992) . . . . Contestant
•• 0:52—Buns in one piece swimsuit during photo shoot.

Riffel, Rena

Films:

Satan's Princess (1989) . . . . Erica Dunn
•• 0:16—Breasts getting white dress torn open, then killed with a knife.
Gunmen (1993). . . . . Loomis' Bride
Showgirls (1995). . . . . .Penny
(NC-17 version reviewed.)
• 0:24—Nude on stage.
• 0:26—Breasts and buns in G-string, after taking off robe and stepping onto stage.
• 0:27—Breasts and buns in G-string as Elizabeth Berkley walks into the lap dance room.
•• 0:35—Nude, while on stage dancing with Berkley.
• 0:51—Brief buns (long shot) at James' place when seen by Berkley. Very brief partial left breast under robe, then breasts when James caresses her.
Undercover (1995) . . . . Rain
(Unrated version reviewed.)
• 0:37—Brief full frontal nudity while in bathtub with another blonde woman on TV monitor.
•• 0:39—Breasts and brief buns, while in bathtub with the other blonde.
••• 0:43—In black lingerie, then breasts and buns while doing strip routine in front of Cindy.
•• 0:46—Breasts and buns after undressing out of purple outfit.
• 0:48—Left breast, then breasts while making love with mystery guy.
Striptease (1996) . . . . Tiffany Glass
(R-rated version reviewed.)
• 0:02—Breasts and buns in T-back while dancing on stage during opening credits.

Made for Cable Movies:

Breast Men (1997; HBO). . . . . Swimming Pool Girl
•• 0:14—Breasts, while letting David Schwimmer make a plaster mold of her breasts for his research.

Riley, Colleen

Films:

Deadly Blessing (1981) . . . . Melissa
The Hills Have Eyes, Part II (1989) . . . . Jane
• 0:55—Very brief left breast, twice, while taking a shower outside when Foster talks to her.

Ringstrom, Erica *

Films:

Last Dance (1992). . . . . Heather
• 0:48—Buns in G-string outfit, while dancing on stage during DTV contest.

Ringwald, Molly

Films:

The Tempest (1982) . . . . Miranda
Spacehunter: Adventures in the Forbidden Zone (1983) . . .Niki
Sixteen Candles (1984) . . . . Samantha
The Breakfast Club (1985) . . . . Claire Standish

Pretty in Pink (1986) . . . . Andie Walsh
P.K. and the Kid (1987) . . . . P.K.
The Pick-Up Artist (1987) . . . . .Randy Jensen
For Keeps (1988). . . . . Darcy
Fresh Horses (1988) . . . . Jewel
King Lear (1988) . . . . Cordelia
Betsy's Wedding (1990) . . . . Betsy Hopper
Strike it Rich (1990). . . . . Cary Porter
Face the Music (1993). . . . . Lisa Hunter
Baja (1995) . . . . Bebe
Malicious (1995). . . . . Melissa Nelson
0:23—Very, very brief silhouette of breasts seen through sweater.
••• 0:24—Breasts, when making love on top of Doug while his wrists are tied up. Excellent!

Made for Cable Movies:
Women & Men: Stories of Seduction (1990; HBO) . . . . Kit

Miniseries:
Stephen King's "The Stand" (1994). . . . . Fran Goldsmith

Made for TV Movies:
Something to Live For: The Alison Gertz Story (1992)
. . . . .Alison Gertz

TV:
Townies (1996-97) . . . . Carrie

Rio, Nicole

Films:
The Zero Boys (1985) . . . . Sue
Sorority House Massacre (1987) . . . . .Tracy
•• 0:20—In a sheer bra changing clothes with two other girls in a bedroom.
•• 0:49—Breasts in a tepee with her boyfriend, Craig, just before getting killed.
The Visitants (1987) . . . . Ellen
Terminal Exposure (1988) . . . . Hostage Girl

Rios, Raquel

See: Keisha.

Rive, Patricia

Films:
The Arrival (1990) . . . . .Parking Lot Woman
Demolition Man (1993) . . . . .Police Officer
The Dogfighters (1995). . . . . Louise
• 0:12—Brief breasts, when sitting up in bed with Robert Davi before getting shot by Ben Gazzara.

*Rivera, Janice **

Films:
Blame It on the Vodka (1992) . . . . Karen
• 0:37—Buns in one piece swimsuit, making out with Robert while Herman and Annette watch.
•• 0:39—Breasts, while making out with Robert some more.
• 0:55—Buns and brief breasts, while making love with Herman and Annette in bed.
Bulletproof (1996). . . . . .Señorita
Mars Attacks! (1996). . . . . Cindy

• *Rivers, Tanya*

See: Ashland, Brittany.

*Rivet, Catherine **

Films:
Emmanuelle, The Joys of a Woman (1975) . . . Anna-Maria
••• 0:58—Nude, while getting massaged by Laura Gemser.
••• 1:25—Nude making love with Sylvia Kristel and Jean.

*Rixon, Cheryl **

Films:
Swap Meet (1979). . . . . Annie
Used Cars (1980). . . . . .Margaret
•• 0:29—Breasts after getting her dress torn off during a used car commercial.
I Like to Play Games (1994) . . . . Sean
Dark Secrets (1995) . . . . .Philipa

Robbins, Deanna

Films:
Final Exam (1981). . . . . Lisa
•• 1:13—Buns and breasts, after taking off dress and covering herself with a sheet in studio.

Made for TV Movies:
Return of the Rebels (1981) . . . . Amy Allen
A Day for Thanks on Walton's Mountain (1982)
. . . . .Aimee Godsey
Mother's Day on Walton's Mountain (1982) . . . .Aimee Godsey
A Wedding on Walton's Mountain (1982) . . . . . .Aimee Godsey

TV:
Days of Our Lives. . . . . Diane Parker
The Young and the Restless (1982-83). . . . . Cindy Lake

*Robért, Jeanine **

Films:
Anthony's Desire (1993) . . . . Dancer
0:04—Inner half of breasts, while sitting in the background on stage. She's on the right.
•• 0:22—Full frontal nudity, while sitting in the background on stage. She's in the middle.
• 0:54—Buns, while lying down with a group of women. She's on the bottom of the screen.
• 1:02—Right breast, while playing the cello on stage.

Video Tapes:
Nude Daydreams (1993) . . . . Daydream 9
•• 0:27—Right breast (she's in the middle) while playing cello in a musical trio.

Roberts, Julia

Ex-wife of singer/actor Lyle Lovett.
Sister of actor Eric Roberts.

Films:
Blood Red (1988) . . . . Maria Collogero
Mystic Pizza (1988) . . . . Daisy Araujo
Satisfaction (1988) . . . . Daryle Shane
a.k.a. Girls of Summer
Steel Magnolias (1989) . . . . .Shelby Eatenton Latcherio
Flatliners (1990) . . . . Rachel Mannus
Pretty Woman (1990) . . . . .Vivian Ward
(Shelley Michelle, the body double for Julia Roberts, only did the *opening* scenes when Roberts is supposed to be getting dressed in her sexy outfit—*not* for the nude scene at 1:30.)
• 1:30—Very, very brief tip of left breast, then right breast, then left breast seen through head board, in bed with Richard Gere. It's her—look especially at the vertical vein that pops out in the middle of her forehead whenever her blood pressure goes up.
Dying Young (1991) . . . . .Hilary O'Neil
Hook (1991) . . . . Tinkerbell
Sleeping with the Enemy (1991) . . . . Sara/Laura Burney
The Player (1992) . . . . Cameo
The Pelican Brief (1993) . . . . Darby Shaw
I Love Trouble (1994) . . . . Sabrina Peterson
Ready to Wear (1994) . . . . Anne Eisenhower
a.k.a. Prêt-à-porter

Mary Reilly (1995). . . . . Mary Reilly
Something to Talk About (1995) . . . . Grace
Everyone Says I Love You (1996) . . . . .Von
Michael Collins (1996; British/U.S.) . . . . Kitty Kiernan
Conspiracy Theory (1997). . . . . Alice Sutton
My Best Friend's Wedding (1997) . . . . Julianne Potter
Made for Cable Movies:
Baja Oklahoma (1988; HBO) . . . . .Candy

• *Roberts, Layla* *

Video Tapes:
Playboy's Women Behaving Badly (1997) . . . . . . .Wanted
••• 0:32—Nude, while bathing, then rubbing oil on herself in old west style segment.

Roberts, Luanne

Films:
The Dark Side of Tomorrow (1970) . . . . Producer's Wife
Weekend with the Babysitter (1970) . . . . Mona Carlton
Welcome Home, Soldier Boys (1972). . . . . Charlene
Thunderbolt and Lightfoot (1974) . . . Suburban Housewife
• 0:57—Brief full frontal nudity standing behind a sliding glass door tempting Jeff Bridges.

Roberts, Mariwin *

Adult Films:
Pet of the Month (1977). . . . . .n.a.
Films:
Jokes My Folks Never Told Me (1976) . . . . n.a.
Cinderella (1977) . . . . Trapper's Daughter
••• 0:11—Frontal nudity getting a bath outside by her blonde sister. Long scene.
Jailbait Babysitter (1978) . . . . Trisha
•• 0:08—Breasts and buns, taking off her dress and getting into van with Cal.
•• 0:18—Breasts and buns in shower with Marion while Mike and Cal help them.
Fairytales (1979). . . . . Elevator Operator
• 0:20—Brief full frontal nudity in the elevator.
•• 0:23—Breasts again, closer shot.

Roberts, Tanya *

Films:
Forced Entry (1975) . . . . Nancy Ulman
The Yum-Yum Girls (1976) . . . . April
California Dreaming (1978). Stephanie
Fingers (1978). . . . . .Julie
Racquet (1979) . . . . Bambi
The Tourist Trap (1979). . . . . Becky
The Beastmaster (1982) . . . . Kiri
••• 0:35—Breasts in a pond while Marc Singer watches, then breasts getting out of the water when his pet ferrets steal her towel.
Hearts and Armour (1983) . . . . Angelica
Sheena (1984). . . . . Sheena
•• 0:18—Breasts and buns taking a shower under a waterfall. Full frontal nudity (long shot), diving into the water.
••• 0:54—Nude taking a bath in a pond while Ted Wass watches.
A View to a Kill (1985). . . . . Stacey Sutton
Purgatory (1988) . . . . Carly Arnold
• 0:29—Nude, getting into the shower.
• 0:42—Very brief breasts in bed with the Warden.
•• 0:57—Left breast, then brief breasts in bed talking to Tommy.
Night Eyes (1990) . . . . .Nikki
(Unrated version reviewed.)
• 0:20—Side view of left breast, while getting dressed while sitting on bed.
••• 1:09—Breasts giving Stevens a massage, then making love. Nice! Buns and left breast, while in the shower making love.
• 1:27—Buns, making love with Stevens in a chair.
Twisted Justice (1990) . . . . Secretary
Inner Sanctum (1991) . . . . .Lynn Foster
• 0:35—Right breast, several times, while looking out the window.
••• 0:40—Buns in lingerie on sofa with Joseph Bottoms, then breasts while making love.
••• 0:57—In black lingerie under trench coat, stripping for Bret Clark. Buns, then breasts making love.
Legal Tender (1991) . . . . .Rikki Rennick
• 0:41—Buns and breasts making love with Robert Davi. Don't see her face.
Almost Pregnant (1992) . . . . Linda Alderson
(Unrated version reviewed.)
••• 0:04—Breasts and buns, in bed with a guy.
• 0:10—Brief right breast, while under Conaway in bed.
• 0:18—In white lingerie, then brief left breast, while in bed with another guy during Conaway's dream.
• 0:40—Very brief side view of buns, in lingerie, while walking down stairs.
• 1:08—Buns, while lying in bed when Gordon writes.
• 1:10—Very brief buns, while in bed with Gordon.
•• 1:11—Breasts and buns in bed, sometimes playing with whipped cream.
•• 1:12—Nude in bed with Gordon and Conaway.
Sins of Desire (1992) . . . . Kay Egan
(Unrated version reviewed.)
• 0:50—Buns, while in panties in bed with Barry.
••• 0:51—Nude, while making love in bed with Barry. Long scene.
• 1:06—Breasts under patterned black body suit with Jessica.
• 1:10—Brief left breast, under body suit.
Deep Down (1993) . . . . Charlotte
(Unrated version reviewed.)
• 0:16—In wet top and panties, getting out of pool while talking to Andy.
• 0:20—Briefly nude, getting out of pool at night while Andy peeks from the bushes.
•• 0:35—Full frontal nudity, while making love with Andy in bed. Quick cuts. Very brief buns, getting into the shower.
••• 0:51—In bra, after dancing in front of Andy. Left breast, then breasts, while making love with him.
Made for Cable Movies:
Body Slam (1989; HBO). . . . . Candace Vandervagen
National Lampoon's Favorite Deadly Sins (1995; Showtime)
. . . . Herself
Made for Cable TV:
Hot Line (1996-97; Cinemax) . . . . Rebecca
TV:
Charlie's Angels (1980-81). . . . . .Julie Rogers

Roberts, Teal

Films:
Fatal Games (1984). . . . . .Lynn Fox
••• 0:08—Breasts on bed and floor when Frank takes her clothes off, more breasts in shower.
•• 0:21—Breasts in sauna with Sue.

Hardbodies (1984) . . . . Kristi Kelly
•• 0:02—Breasts in bed after making love with Scotty, then putting her sweater on.
••• 0:48—Breasts standing in front of closet mirrors talking about breasts with Kimberly.
••• 0:56—Breasts making love with Scotty on the beach.
•• 1:23—Breasts, while on fancy car bed with Scotty.
Beverly Hills Cop II (1987). . . . . Stripper
•• 0:45—Breasts and buns several times, while wearing G-string and dancing at the 385 North Club.
The Last Boy Scout (1991) . . . . Dancer
Night of the Warrior (1991) . . . . Still Model
Video Tapes:
The Perfect Body Contest (1987) . . . . Judge

Robertson, Jenny

Films:
Bull Durham (1988) . . . . Millie
Heart of Dixie (1989) . . . . Sister
The Nightman (1992) . . . . Dr. Margaret Rhodes
• 1:25—Very brief right breast in gaping dress when she looks at old things hidden under floor boards.
Made for Cable Movies:
Notorious (1992; Lifetime) . . . . Alicia Velorus
Made for TV Movies:
Call Me Anna (1990). . . . . Patty (as a young adult)
The Danger of Love (1992). . . . . Carolyn Warmus
Danielle Steel's "Message from Nam" (1993)
. . . . Paxton Andrews
Kansas (1995). . . . . Betsy

Robertson, Kimmy

Films:
Battle in the Erogenous Zone . . . . Tammy
The Last American Virgin (1982) . . . . Rose
Bad Manners (1989) . . . . Sarah Fitzpatrick
•• 0:38—Breasts and buns taking off robe and getting into the shower when Mouse takes a picture of her.
Honey, I Shrunk the Kids (1989) . . . . Gloria Forrester
Trust Me (1989) . . . . Party Gal
Don't Tell Mom the Babysitter's Dead (1991) . . . . Cathy
Leprechaun 2 (1994). . . . . Tourist's Girlfriend
Speed 2: Cruise Control (1997). . . . . Liza (Cruise Director)
Made for Cable TV:
Tales From the Crypt: Top Billing (1991; HBO) . . . . Lisa
TV:
Twin Peaks (1990-91) . . . . Lucy

Robey

Real name is Darian O'Toole.
Talk show host at KBGG radio in San Francisco, California.
Singer.
Films:
Bay Boy (1985; Canadian). . . . . n.a.
The Money Pit (1986). Female Vocalist
Raw Deal (1986) . . . . Lamanski's Girl
Play Nice (1992) . . . . Jill/Rapunzel
(Unrated version reviewed.)
• 0:28—Side view of right breast, while sitting on top of a victim in bed. Don't see her face.
••• 0:35—Breasts, making love in bed with Jack. Nice, long scene.
•• 0:46—Breasts, making love on the floor with Jack.
••• 1:09—Breasts in bed on top of Jack, then getting out of bed and getting dressed.

TV:
Friday the 13th: The Series (1987-90) . . . . Micki Foster

Robins, Laila

Films:
Planes, Trains and Automobiles (1987) . . . . Susan Page
An Innocent Man (1989). . . . . Kate Rainwood
Welcome Home Roxy Carmichael (1990) . . . . . . Elizabeth Zaks
Live Nude Girls (1996) . . . . Rachel
• 0:17—Brief side view of right breast and buns, while sitting at table in neighbor boy's fantasy.
• 1:34—Very brief side view of right breast, while sitting at the table.
Female Perversions (1997). . . . . Emma
Made for TV Movies:
Trial: The Price of Passion (1992) . . . . Charm Blackburn
TV:
Gabriel's Fire (1990-91). Victoria Heller

Robinson, Betsy Julia

Films:
Return of the Secaucus Seven (1980). . . . . Amy
Lianna (1982) . . . . Cindy
•• 1:26—Breasts, while in bed with Lianna.

Robinson, Serina

See: Ryan, Rachel.

*Rochelle, Amy **

a.k.a. Amy Rochelle Weiss.
Films:
Round Trip to Heaven (1992) . . . . Yvette
••• 0:19—In black bra and G-string in bedroom with Corey Feldman, then breasts and buns on top of him in bed.
Midnight Confessions (1993) . . . . Renee
(Unrated version reviewed.)
••• 0:49—In black leather outfit, then full frontal nudity undressing and then dressing back up.
Possessed by the Night (1993) . . . . Bikini Woman/Tina
••• 0:16—Breasts, while giving Scott a back rub, then leaving the room.
Secret Games 2—The Escort (1993). . . . . Stacey
(Unrated version reviewed.)
••• 0:09—Full frontal nudity, while making love with Martin Hewitt in front of fireplace.
••• 0:16—Nude, while in bedroom then making love with Hewitt on dining room table.
•• 0:19—Breasts, while sitting in bed with Hewitt and talking.
••• 0:21—Breasts in video playback and in bed while talking with Hewitt on the phone.
••• 0:24—Nude, after taking off coat, covering Hewitt with birthday cake and in the shower with him and Lisa.
•• 0:26—Breasts and buns while making love in bed with Lisa and Hewitt.
• 0:37—Breasts, several times in flashback.
• 0:38—Breasts on video playback.
••• 0:41—Breasts, while making love with Hector in bed while Hewitt watches.
••• 0:54—Breasts, while modeling clothes for Hewitt in bedroom.
••• 0:57—Breasts, while making love with Hewitt in newlywed fantasy.
•• 1:04—Breasts and buns, while making love on top of Hewitt in flashbacks.
•• 1:11—Breasts, while in bed with Hector while talking on the phone.

- •• 1:13—Breasts on video playback.
- • 1:16—Brief breasts on video playback.

California or Bust (1994) . . . . n.a.
Masseuse (1995) . . . . Rosa
(Unrated version reviewed.)
- ••• 0:32—Breasts and buns, while making love in bed with Jack when seen by Griffin Drew.

Rebecca's Secret (1997). . . . . Rebecca
- •• 0:00—Nude, while swimming in a pool.
- ••• 0:02—Nude, getting up out of bed and taking a bath.
- ••• 0:05—Nude, while making love with Jonathan in the bathroom.
- •• 0:37—Nude, while taking a shower.
- •• 0:39—Breasts and buns, while getting information out of Max.
- ••• 0:46—Nude, while making love with Max in bed.
- ••• 0:58—Nude, while making love with Max in the basement.
- • 1:12—Nude, while getting out of bathtub.
- • 1:16—Breasts during struggle in swimming pool.

Made for Cable Movies:
The Hit List (1993; Showtime) . Body Double for Yancy Butler
- • 0:31—Buns, taking off swimsuit in front of Jeff Fahey. Long shot, don't see her face.
- • 1:00—Brief left breast in bed while making love with Fahey. Don't see her face very well.

Music Videos:
What Comes Naturally/Sheena Easton
. . . . Body Double for Sheena
Video Tapes:
Playboy's Secrets of EuroMassage (1989)
. . . . .No. 1 Late Night Passion
- ••• 0:01—Nude, during massage session on bed.

Sexy Lingerie III (1991) . . . . .Model
Fantasies 2 (1992) . . . . .Model
Intimate Workout For Lovers (1992) . . . . . Water Workout
- ••• 0:21—Nude, outside by swimming pool and in pool.

Playboy's Erotic Fantasies (1992). . . . . Cast Member
Babes, Bikes & Beyond (1994) . . . . Herself
- ••• 0:29—Breasts.

Playboy's Erotic Fantasies III (1994)
. . . . Morning Splendor/Horserider
- ••• 0:14—Breasts in push-up bra, buns in G-string panties, garter belt and lingerie. Then nude while making love in the stable with a guy.

Rochon, Debbie

Films:
Ladies and Gentlemen, The Fabulous Stains (1982)
. . . . Uncredited Skunkette
(Not available on video tape.)
Lurkers (1987). . . . . Uncredited Evil Host
Cleo/Leo (1989) . . . . Reporter
Party Incorporated (1989). . . . . .Trixie
a.k.a. Party Girls
Lonely in America (1990) . . . . .Woman at Museum (Jenny)
Abducted II: The Reunion (1994). . . . . .Sharon Baker
- • 1:15—Breasts, while waving her sweater to try and get helicopter pilot's attention.

Regenerated Man (1994) . . . . Kelley
- • 0:37—Breasts in ripped open blouse while being hassled by three biker guys.

Broadcast Bombshells (1995). . . . . Amanda
- ••• 0:16—In black bra, then breasts, while making love in with Gordon in editing room. Long scene.
- ••• 0:24—In black bra, then full frontal nudity, while undressing in room, then buns after putting on a black dominatrix outfit.
- • 0:32—Brief buns in black outfit in dressing room with Brian.
- ••• 0:43—Breasts, while changing clothes in room with the other two girls.
- • 0:45—Brief full frontal nudity, while opening her robe for peeper.
- •• 0:47—In purple bra, then breasts while in room with Frank.
- •• 0:48—Brief left breast, while in bed with Frank.

Tromeo & Juliet (1995) . . . . Ness
(Unrated director's cut reviewed.)
- •• 0:17—Right breast, while making out with Juliet on bed.

Santa Claws (1996). . . . . .Raven Quinn
Scream Queens Naked Christmas (1996) . . . . .n.a.
Made for Cable Movies:
That's Tromatainment (1994; Showtime). . . . . .Tromette

• *Rochon, Lela*

Films:
Foxtrap (1986; U.S./Italian) . . . . Lindy
The Wild Pair (1988) . . . . Debby
Harlem Nights (1989) . . . . .Sunshine
Boomerang (1992) . . . . .Christie
The Meteor Man (1993) . . . . .Vanessa
Waiting to Exhale (1995) . . . . Robin
The Chamber (1996). . . . . Nora Stark
Gang Related (1997) . . . . .Cynthia
- • 0:00—Buns in T-back, while dancing on stage.
- • 0:21—Buns in T-back, while dancing on stage. Nice moves!
- • 1:38—Brief buns in T-back, while dancing on stage.

Made for Cable Movies:
Mr. and Mrs. Loving (1996; Showtime)
. . . . Mildred "Bean" Loving
Made for Cable TV:
Tales From the Crypt: Werewolf Concerto (1992; HBO) . . . .n.a.
The Outer Limits: The Awakening (1997; Showtime)
. . . . .Beth Carter
Made for TV Movies:
A Bunny's Tale (1985) . . . . Charlotte
Into the Homeland (1987). . . . . Exquisite Woman
TV:
The Wayans Bros. (1995) . . . . .Lisa

Rocilili, Bianca *

Films:
Where Evil Lies (1994) . . . . Dancer
- ••• 0:09—In bra and buns in G-string, then breasts while doing strip routine on stage in club. Very good, well photographed, long scene.
- • 0:46—Buns in G-string, while dancing on stage.
- • 0:48—Breasts, while dancing on stage.

Cyberzone (1995) . . . . Pleasure Droid #3
- • 0:09—Breasts, in room with the other three pleasure droids. (She's the one with the gold necklace and the blue shawl.)
- • 0:13—Breasts after taking off her lingerie top with the other three pleasure droids.

Gentleman's Bet (1995). . . . . .Uncredited Model
- • 1:05—Brief breasts, several times, under clear plastic top during photo session. (she's the only brunette.)

Masseuse (1995) . . . . Gina
(Unrated version reviewed.)
- •• 1:19—Breasts, while making out with a customer on bed.

Sinful Intrigue (1995) . . . . Hispanic Girl
- 0:21—Brief buns and breasts (she's on the left) while in bathtub.
- 0:38—Breasts, while sitting in bathtub.

Stripteasers (1995) . . . . Housewife
- 0:22—Buns in lingerie, seen in phony porno film seen on TV at Arnie's apartment.
- 0:23—Breasts, squished against shower door on TV.
- 0:25—More breasts on TV in the background.
- 0:27—More brief breasts on TV.

Bikini Hotel (1996). . . . . Tiki Hotel Maid
- 0:41—Brief breasts when her bikini top pops off.
- 1:08—Buns in white lingerie.

Made for Cable Movies:

Terminal Virus (1995; Showtime)
. . . . Uncredited Woman on TV
- •• 0:40—Breasts, while making love on phony porno video tape seen on TV.

Made for Cable TV:

Love Street: Grading on a Curve (1995; Showtime)
. . . . Librarian Girl
- 0:05—Brief breasts, when taking off sweater and glasses.

Video Tapes:

Hot Body International: Steamed Heat (1995) . . . .Herself
- 0:13—Buns in swimsuit, while posing on stairs.
- 0:35—Breasts and buns under sheer pink dress.
- ••• 0:48—Buns in sheer white body suit, then breasts while posing on bed.

Hot Body Video Magazine #15: Wild Thing (1996)
. . . . Bianca
- ••• 0:01—In black lingerie, then nude, while dancing and stripping on a stairwell.

Rodger, Kate *

Films:

Poison Ivy 2: Lily (1995) . . . . Isabel
- 0:05—Brief breasts, while posing as an artist's model for art class.
- 0:17—Brief right breast, while posing in a chair for art class.
- 0:19—Brief right breast again.

Made for Cable TV:

Women: Stories of Passion-Wishful Thinking (1996; Showtime). . . . . Kelly
- •• 0:05—In bra, then buns in panties, while making love with the milk man.
- •• 0:09—Breasts, while making love with her girlfriend, Betsy, in movie theater.
- 0:15—Brief breasts, while in the shower with Sam, her sister's husband.
- 0:18—In bra, then brief breasts, while making love with Kurt and the female manager in art gallery.
- ••• 0:22—In bra, then breasts and buns, while making love with Mark.

Video Tapes:

Playboy's Rising Stars and Sexy Starlets (1996) . . .Herself
- 0:37—Right breast in a scene from *Walnut Creek*.
- ••• 0:38—Breasts, while in barn, then making love with a cowgirl.

• Rodriguez, Arlene

Films:

The Takeover (1994) . . . . Brandi
- •• 0:00—Buns in two piece outfit, then breasts, while dancing on stage in club.

Video Tapes:

Playboy's Hard Bodies (1995). . . . . Herself
- ••• 0:20—Breasts, while swimming under water as a mermaid. In lingerie and nude while dancing and posing on land.

Roe, Karen

Films:

Dracula: Dead and Loving It (1995). . . . . Blond Vampire
The Corporate Ladder (1996) . . . . Katrina
The Last Days of Frankie the Fly (1997) . . . . Sal's Girl

Made for Cable Movies:

Body Language (1995; HBO). . . . . Katrina Hostegg

Made for Cable TV:

Dream On: Am I Blue (1995; HBO) . . . . .Tawny
- •• 0:20—Breasts, after opening her blouse and jacket during script reading session at Martin's apartment.

Rogers, Mimi *

Ex-wife of actor Tom Cruise.

Films:

Gung Ho (1985) . . . . Audrey
Someone to Watch Over Me (1987) . . . . Claire Gregory
Street Smart (1987). . . . . .Alison Parker
Hider in the House (1989). .Julie Dreyer
The Mighty Quinn (1989) . . . . Hadley
The Palermo Connection (1989; Italian) . . . . Carrie
Desperate Hours (1990) .Nora Cornell
The Doors (1991) . . . . Magazine Photographer

The Rapture (1991) . . . . Sharon
- 0:08—Most of her left breast, while lying in bed with David Duchovny.
- •• 0:36—Very brief side view of right breast, dropping nightgown and walking into closet.

Dark Horse (1992). . . . . .Dr. Susan Hadley
The Player (1992) . . . . Cameo
Shooting Elizabeth (1992; French). . . . . Elizabeth Pigeon
White Sands (1992). . . . . Uncredited Molly Dolezal
Monkey Trouble (1993). . . . . Amy

Bulletproof Heart (1994). . . . . Fiona
a.k.a. Killer
- ••• 0:39—Breasts, while making love in bed with Anthony LaPaglia.

Reflections in the Dark (1995) . . . . Regina
- 0:26—Buns and breasts, while making love with her husband. Some shots are a body double. Note the body double's moles on her back when you don't see her face.
- 1:00—Buns and breasts, while making love with her husband in bed. Some shots are done by a body double. Note the body double's breasts are smaller than Rogers'.

The Mirror Has Two Faces (1996) . . . . Claire
Austin Powers: International Man of Mystery (1997)
. . . . Mrs. Kensington
Lost in Space (1998) . . . . Maureen Robinson

Made for Cable Movies:

The Fourth Story (1990; Showtime) . . . . . .Valerie McCoughlin
Dead Lock (1991; HBO) . . . . Tracy Riggs
Ladykiller (1992; USA). . . . . Michael Madison

Full Body Massage (1995; Showtime) . . . . Nina
- •• 0:07—Buns in panties, then breasts, while looking at herself in the mirror. Buns, taking off towel and stepping into hot tub.
- 0:12—Brief buns, while lying outside in flashback.
- 0:26—Brief buns, while lying on table, getting massaged by Douglas in flashback.
- 0:44—Very brief, partial left breast, while rolling over onto her stomach.

- •• 0:47—Right breast and most of left breast, while lying on her back on table.
- • 0:50—Buns, while lying on table.
- ••• 0:52—Buns, while lying on table, getting massaged by Brown.
- • 0:54—Buns, while walking to get her robe.
- •• 0:58—Breasts, while getting massaged by Brown.
- ••• 1:01—Breasts, while sitting and getting massaged by Brown.
- • 1:08—Brief buns, while lying on the table.
- ••• 1:12—Buns, when getting massaged. Breasts, while getting massaged by Douglas, then Brown. Oh my!
- • 1:15—Very brief right breast, then buns, getting up off the table.

Tricks (1997) . . . . Jackie
- • 1:09—Brief breasts, while making love with Adam in bed. (Don't see her face.)

Weapons of Mass Distraction (1997; HBO) . . . . . . Ariel Powers

Made for Cable TV:

Dream On: The Second Greatest Story Ever Told (1991; HBO) . . . . Julia Montana

Dream On: And Bimbo Was His Name-O (1992; HBO) . . . . Julia Montana

Tales From the Crypt: Beauty Rest (1992; HBO). . . . . Helen

Miniseries:

Bloodlines: Murder in the Family (1993) . . . Melody Woodman

Made for TV Movies:

A Kiss to Die For (1993). . . . . n.a.

TV:

The Rousters (1983-84). . . . . Ellen Slade

Paper Dolls (1984) . . . . Blair Harper-Fenton

Rohm, Maria

Films:

City of Fear (1965; British). . . . . Maid

Deadly Sanctuary (1968; British/Spanish) . . . . n.a.

Against All Odds (1969) . . . . Ursula

(Breasts in still photo on the back of the video box cover—not in the film.)

Dorian Gray (1970; Italian/British/German). . . . . Alice

Venus in Furs (1970) . . . . Wanda Reed

(Original version reviewed.)
- • 0:05—Breasts, while dead on the beach.
- • 0:08—Breasts in stockings and panties, getting whipped by Olga.
- •• 0:10—Breasts before getting stabbed by Klaus Kinski.
- • 0:11—More breasts on beach, dead.
- • 0:17—Brief breasts.
- • 0:21—Right breast several times, making love in bed with a guy.
- ••• 0:22—Breasts, lying in bed with the guy afterwards.
- • 0:23—Brief breasts on beach again.
- • 0:32—Breasts, dead on the beach with two cuts.
- • 0:43—Breasts on couch when Olga opens her blouse.
- •• 0:45—Breasts in bed.
- •• 0:52—Breasts posing for Olga.
- • 0:54—Breasts, dead.
- •• 0:56—Breasts walking down stairs, wearing panties.
- • 0:59—Breasts in bed again.
- • 1:02—Brief side view of right breast, hugging Jimmy.
- • 1:05—Left breast while acting as a slave girl.
- • 1:06—Brief breasts seen through sheer curtain.
- • 1:09—Very brief right breast, dead.
- •• 1:10—Left breast, with Klaus Kinski.
- • 1:12—Buns, whlie lying on couch.

Black Beauty (1971; British/German). . . . . Anne

Count Dracula (1971; Spanish/Italian) . . . . Mina Harker

Treasure Island (1972; British/Spanish). . . . . Mrs. Hawkins

Ten Little Indians (1975) . . . . Elsa

Rohmer, Patrice

Films:

The Harrad Summer (1974) . . . . Marcia

a.k.a. Student Union
- • 0:33—Brief breasts, starting to take off her blouse in motel room with Harry.

Hustle (1975). . . . . Linda (Dancer)
- • 1:03—In pasties, dancing on stage behind beaded curtain. Buns in G-string.

Jackson County Jail (1976). . . . . Cassie Anne

Revenge of the Cheerleaders (1976) . . . . Sesame
- • 0:28—Brief breasts and buns in the boys' shower room.

Small Town in Texas (1976). . . . . Trudy

Rojo, Helena

Films:

Aguirre, The Wrath of God (1972; West German) . . . . Inez

Mary, Mary, Bloody Mary (1975) . . . . Greta
- • 0:42—Buns and brief breasts getting into bathtub with Cristina Ferrare.

Foxtrot (1976; Mexican/Swiss) . . . . Alexandra

Rojo, Maria

Films:

Candy Stripe Nurses (1974). Marisa
- •• 0:29—Breasts making love with convict.
- • 0:52—Brief breasts during attempted rape in kitchen pantry.

Danzon (1992; Mexican). . . . . Julia

Rollins, Brittany

Films:

Cyberzone (1995) . . . . Pleasure Droid #1
- • 0:09—Breasts, in room with the other three pleasure droids. (She's the redhead with a pearl necklace.)
- • 0:13—Breasts after taking off her lingerie top with the other three pleasure droids.

Masseuse (1995) . . . . Suzy

(Unrated version reviewed.)
- •• 1:20—Breasts, while in bedroom with a customer.

Roman, Candice

Films:

The Big Bird Cage (1972) . . . . Carla
- • 0:16—Buns, while in the shower.

Unholy Rollers (1972). . . . . Donna

a.k.a. Leader of the Pack
- ••• 0:06—Breasts in bed with Greg when Karen comes home.
- •• 0:12—Breasts, dancing on stage in club next to a brunette dancer.
- • 0:13—More breasts in background.
- • 0:14—More breasts in background.

Roman, Leticia

Films:

G.I. Blues (1960) . . . . Tina

The Evil Eye (1964; Italian). . . . . Nora Dralston

Fanny Hill: Memoirs of a Woman of Pleasure (1964) . . . . Fanny Hill
- • 0:13—Very brief right breast, while turning over in tub and talking with Phoebe.

*Romanelli, Carla **

Films:

Steppenwolf (1974) . . . . Maria

••• 0:59—Breasts sitting on bed with Max von Sydow. Long scene.

The Sensuous Nurse (1975; Italian) . . . . Tosca

•• 0:06—Breasts, then nude standing in the winery, then running around.

•• 0:41—Nude, in basement, playing army, then making love with bearded guy.

Sex on the Run (1979; German/French/Italian) . . . . Dice Girl

a.k.a. Some Like It Cool

a.k.a. Casanova and Co.

•• 0:58—Breasts and buns with two other women, losing their clothes during dice game.

The Lonely Lady (1983) . . . . Carla Maria Peroni

•• 1:10—Brief breasts taking off her top to make love with Pia Zadora while a guy watches.

A Very Moral Night (1985; Hungarian) . . . . n.a.

Romay, Lina

Wife of Spanish director Jess Franco.

Films:

Erotikill (1973) . . . . Irina

a.k.a. La Comtesse Noire

a.k.a. The Loves of Irina

•• 0:00—Full frontal nudity, wearing a belt and cape walking towards the camera during the opening credits.

•• 0:08—Full frontal nudity on bed, then walking around while wearing a cape. Out of focus.

••• 0:17—Full frontal nudity, lying in bed and drinking.

• 0:31—Very brief right breast during struggle with another woman on bed.

•• 0:32—Full frontal nudity, while walking through the woods with a cape and belt.

• 0:33—Breasts, flapping her cape.

• 0:43—Breasts under sheer black nightgown.

••• 0:45—Full frontal nudity when the other woman takes her nightgown off.

••• 0:47—Full frontal nudity biting another woman and sucking her blood.

•• 1:05—Full frontal nudity sitting down in bath filled with red water.

••• 1:07—More breasts and brief buns doing pelvic thrusts in bathtub. Out of focus sometimes.

••• 1:08—Nude in bathtub.

Demoniac (1974; French/Spanish) . . . . Anne

• 1:02—Brief lower frontal nudity, while Jess Franco drags her into the bedroom.

•• 1:04—Full frontal nudity, while lying on the bed with Franco.

Ilsa, The Wicked Warden (1980) . . . . n.a.

a.k.a. Ilsa—Absolute Power

a.k.a. Greta, The Mad Butcher.

Ilsa—Absolute Power is about 4 minutes shorter.

Rome, Cindy

a.k.a. Sugar Ray Rene.

Films:

Banzai Runner (1986) . . . . Sweet Young Thing

Summer's Games (1987) . . . . Boxer

Knockouts (1992) . . . . Vicki

• 0:04—Breasts while putting on make-up in front of mirror. Long shot. Breasts walking in front of Brooke in pink G-string and white tights when Garth peeks in the locker room.

• 0:14—Buns in G-string swimsuit. Brief breasts while lying down in lounge chair.

• 0:25—Brief breasts, after losing her tennis shoe during strip poker game.

• 0:28—Breasts while in bedroom.

••• 0:37—In red, white and blue swimsuit, then breasts and buns while posing for photographs.

••• 0:45—Breasts and buns in G-string, while posing for October photograph.

•• 0:59—Breasts while talking on the phone, combing her hair and doing her nails. Seen mostly in silhouette.

Video Tapes:

Battling Beauties (1983) . . . . Foxy Boxer

The Perfect Body Contest (1987) . . . . Sugar Ray Rene

Made for Man: Intimate Fantasy (1992) . . . Sugar Ray Rene

• 0:23—Stripping out of cave girl outfit down to purple two piece swimsuit.

•• 0:40—Buns, stripping to leopard print two piece swimsuit and wrestling with Ginger Miller.

*Rome, Sydne **

Films:

Diary of Forbidden Dreams (1973; Italian) . . . . The Girl

••• 0:06—Brief breasts taking off torn T-shirt in a room, then breasts sitting on edge of bed.

••• 0:09—Nude getting out of shower, drying herself off and getting dressed.

• 0:20—Brief side view of right breast, while talking to Marcello Mastroianni in her room.

•• 0:22—Brief breasts putting shirt on.

•• 1:28—Breasts outside on stairs fighting for her shirt.

• 1:30—Brief buns and breasts climbing onto truck.

The Raw Edge (1975; Italian/German/French) . . . . Ann

a.k.a. La Baby Sitter

Sex with a Smile (1976; Italian) . . . . . . "A Dog's Day" segment

The Twist (1976) . . . . Nathalie

Just a Gigolo (1979; German) . . . . Cilly

Looping (1981) . . . . Tanja

• *Romero, Joanelle Nadine*

Films:

Parasite (1982) . . . . Bo

City Limits (1984) . . . . Woman in Desert

• 0:03—Almost breasts, then buns, while swimming in water tower with John Stockwell.

Vendetta (1986) . . . . Elena

Powwow Highway (1988; U.S./British) . . . . . . Bonnie Red Bow

Made for Cable Movies:

Miracle in the Wilderness (1991; TNT) . . . . Little Deer

Rone, Doria

Films:

Dark Secrets (1995) . . . . Leona

• 1:04—Breasts and buns in panties, after Justin Carroll takes her dress off in front of a group of men in a vacant lot.

• 1:07—Brief left breast, while walking back to the car.

Obsessed with Lust (1995) . . . . Carrie

a.k.a. Prelude to Love

••• 0:27—Breasts and buns, while making love on the floor with David. Long scene.

••• 0:58—Breasts and partial lower frontal nudity, while making love with Eric in bed. Long scene.

A Passion for Murder (1996) . . . . Allison

a.k.a. Deadlock

• 0:09—Very brief breasts, while sitting in lounge chairs by the pool.

••• 0:13—Nude, while posing for photos with Debbie.
••• 1:05—Buns and breasts, while making love with the detective in kitchen.

Rose, Dusty

See: Lussier, Sheila.

Rose, Gabrielle

Films:

The Journey of Natty Gann (1985) . . . . Exercise Matron
Family Viewing (1987; Canadian) . . . . Sandra
• 0:27—Brief left breast, lying down with Stan. Seen on TV that Van watches.
• 0:29—Same 0:27 scene again.
The Stepfather (1987) . . . . Dorothy
Speaking Parts (1989; Canadian) . . . . Clara
•• 0:41—Right breast, on TV monitor, masturbating with Lance, then breasts, while getting dressed.
The Adjuster (1991; Canadian) . . . . Mimi
Sleeping with Strangers (1992) . . . . Claire
Timecop (1994) . . . . Judge Marshall
The Sweet Hereafter (1997; Canadian) . . . . Dolores Driscoll

Made for Cable Movies:

Devlin (1991; Showtime) . . . . Sister Anne Elizabeth

Made for Cable TV:

Poltergeist: The Legacy/Town Without Pity (1996; Showtime) . . . . Esther

Rose, Jamie

Films:

Just Before Dawn (1980) . . . . Megan
• 0:33—Breasts in pond. Long shot.
• 0:34—Brief breasts in pond, closer shot.
•• 0:36—Brief upper half of left breast, then brief breasts several times splashing in the water.
• 0:37—Breasts getting out of the water.
Heartbreakers (1984) . . . . Libby
••• 0:09—Breasts in bed talking with Nick Mancuso and Peter Coyote.
Tightrope (1984) . . . . Melanie Silber
• 0:07—Buns, lying face down on bed, dead.
Rebel Love (1985) . . . . Columbine Cromwell
• 0:43—Very, very brief tip of right breast, while making love in bed under Terence Knox.
Chopper Chicks in Zombietown (1989) . . . . Dede
Playroom (1989) . . . . Marcy
a.k.a. Schizo
Crack Down (1990) . . . . Constance Bigelow
The Chain (1996) . . . . Ellen Morrisey

Made for TV Movies:

Voices Within: The Lives of Truddi Chase (1990) . . . . Truddi's Mother
Death Hits the Jackpot (1991) . . . . Nancy Brower

TV:

Falcon Crest (1981-83) . . . . Victoria Gioberti Hogan
Lady Blue (1985-86) . . . . Detective Katy Mahoney
St. Elsewhere (1986-88) . . . . Dr. Susan Birch

Rose, Kristine *

Films:

Eleven Days, Eleven Nights 2 (1990) . . . . Sarah Asproon
•• 0:18—Breasts, while getting undressed and into bathtub.
••• 0:20—Breasts and buns while washing herself in bathtub while being secretly videotaped.
0:32—In lingerie with panties, garter belt and stockings after hopping on stage in club and dancing and stripping, showing off to Sonny.
•• 0:38—Left breast, while making love in kitchen with Bob, while being watched on video monitor.
0:57—In black bra, panties, garter belt and stockings after taking off dress with George.
• 1:09—Breasts, with Sonny. Left breast afterwards.
Auntie Lee's Meat Pies (1991) . . . . Fawn
•• 1:12—Breasts in Stonehedge bedroom with her rock star boyfriend. More breasts in silhouette.
• 1:28—Buns, in G-string in swimming pool.
Demonic Toys (1991) . . . . Miss July
• 0:25—Breasts in centerfold photo in magazine.
•• 0:59—Breasts in warehouse as a ghost in front of Mark.
Total Exposure (1991) . . . . Rita
Night Rhythms (1992) . . . . Marilyn
(Unrated version reviewed.)
••• 0:17—Taking off her blouse at bar with Martin Hewitt, then nude, making love on the bar with him.
Round Trip to Heaven (1992) . . . . Tina
To Sleep with a Vampire (1992) . . . . Prom Queen
Save Me (1993) . . . . Cheryl
(Unrated version reviewed.)

Video Tapes:

Playboy's Erotic Fantasies (1992) . . . . Cast Member

Rose, Laurie

Films:

The Hot Box (1972) . . . . Sue
•• 0:16—Breasts cleaning herself off in stream and getting out.
•• 0:21—Breasts sleeping in hammocks. (She's the first one from the front.)
• 0:26—Breasts getting accosted by the People's Army guys.
••• 0:45—Breasts in stream bathing with the other three girls.
• 0:58—Full frontal nudity getting raped by Major Dubay.
The Roommates (1973) . . . . Brea
The Working Girls (1973) . . . . Denise
Policewomen (1974) . . . . Janette
• 0:02—Brief side of left breast, changing clothes during prison break.
The Woman Hunt (1975; U.S./Philippines) . . . . n.a.
The Wizard of Speed & Time (1988) . . . . Bellydancer

Rose, Sherrie *

Films:

After School (1987) . . . . First Tribe Member
Cat Chaser (1988) . . . . Uncredited Waitress
Spring Fever USA (1988) . . . . Vinyl Vixen #1
a.k.a. Lauderdale
American Tiger (1989; Italian) . . . . Mary Jo
a.k.a. American Rickshaw
Summer Job (1989) . . . . Kathy Shields
• 0:52—Buns, while walking around in swimsuit and jacket.
•• 0:53—Breasts taking off swimsuit top kneeling by the phone, then brief buns standing up.
•• 1:24—Brief breasts taking off her yellow top on the beach talking to Bruce.
A Climate for Killing (1990) . . . . Rita Paris
•• 1:30—Breasts in bed while Wayne recollects his crime to John Beck.
King of the Kickboxers (1990) . . . . Molly
• 1:05—Very brief buns in G-string and partial side of left breast, while getting into tub with Jake.
Body Waves (1991) . . . . Suzanne

In Gold We Trust (1991) . . . . Debbie
Deadly Bet (1992). . . . . Doris
Double Threat (1992) . . . . Lisa Shane
(Unrated version reviewed.)
- • 0:09—Buns in lingerie, while sleeping in bed.
- • 0:23—Buns in white lingerie while acting in movie with Andrew Stevens.
- ••• 0:47—Right breast, then breasts while making love with Stevens in bed.

Final Judgment (1992) . . . . Amanda Peterson
Martial Law II: Undercover (1992). . . . . Bree
Maximum Force (1992). . . . . Cody Randal
- • 0:59—Breasts, while in bed with Sam Jones.

Unlawful Entry (1992). Girl in Jeep
- •• 0:42—Breasts, making love with Ray Liotta in police car, then getting thrown out.

Demon Knight (1994). . . . . Wanda
New Crime City: Los Angeles 2020 (1994) . . . . Darla
- •• 0:52—Nude, taking off robe and starting to make love with Rick Rossovich.

Markus 4 (1996) . . . . Dancer
The Nurse (1996) . . . . Brooke Martin

Made for Cable Movies:

Black Scorpion 2—Aftershock (1996; Showtime)
. . . . Ursula/Aftershock

Made for Cable TV:

Dream On: Terms of Employment (1992; HBO) . . . . .Tasha
- •• 0:03—Breasts, while making love with Martin in his office.

Tales From the Crypt: On a Dead Man's Chest (1992; HBO) . . . . Danny's Girlfriend
- ••• 0:06—Breasts, opening her blouse to show Danny her new snake tattoo. Breasts, then full frontal nudity, under Danny in bed.
- ••• 0:08—Left breast, then breasts, getting dressed.
- • 0:18—Brief buns in G-string, showing Danny her tattoo scar.

Tales From the Crypt: Only Skin Deep (1994; HBO)
. . . . Molly
- • 0:10—Breasts, while making love under Peter Onorati. Medium long shot.

Red Shoe Diaries: The Boxer (1997; Showtime). . . . . Laurie

Video Tapes:

Wet & Wild II (1990) . . . . Model
Inside Out (1992) . . . . Bethany/The Leda
(Unrated version reviewed.)
- • 0:35—Right breast, while making love with the other criminal. Dark.
- • 0:40—Upper half of right breast while making love with him again after he's connected to the computer.

Inside Out 2 (1992) . . . . Marina/The Freak
(Unrated version reviewed.)
- • 0:29—Breasts, getting her clothes and mask taken off in front of other masked people. B&W.
- •• 0:35—Breasts in bed with alien guy. B&W.

Playboy's Erotic Weekend Getaways (1992)
. . . . Adventure: The Beach
- ••• 0:43—Nude, while making love on sofa with her lover.
- ••• 0:46—Nude, taking off swimsuit with him, frolicking at the beach, running home, taking an outdoor shower.
- ••• 0:50—Breasts and very brief buns in pool with her lover.

Ross, Annie

Films:

Straight on Till Morning (1974). . . . . Liza
Oh, Alfie! (1975; British) . . . . Claire
a.k.a. Alfie Darling
- •• 1:34—Breasts on top of Alfie in open black dress while he's lying injured in bed.

Yanks (1979) . . . . Red Cross Lady
Superman III (1983) . . . . .Vera Webster
Witchery (1988) . . . . Rose Brooks
Basket Case 2 (1989). . . . . Granny Ruth
Basket Case 3: The Progeny (1991) . . . . Granny Ruth
Blue Sky (1991). . . . . .Lydia
The Player (1992) . . . . Cameo
Short Cuts (1993) . . . . Tess Trainer

• Ross, Diana

Singer with The Supremes and on her own.

Films:

Lady Sings the Blues (1972). . . . . Billie Holliday
Mahogany (1975) . . . . .Tracy
- •• 1:25—Very, very brief side view of left breast in gaping white dress, just before taking it off. Very, very brief right breast, while putting on striped robe.

The Wiz (1978) . . . . Dorothy

Made for TV Movies:

Out of Darkness (1994). Paulie Cooper

Ross, Gaylen

a.k.a. Alexis Dubin.

Films:

Dawn of the Dead (1979) . . . . Francine
(Director's cut reviewed.)
- • 1:44—(0:22 into tape 2) Brief left breast, while sitting in bed with the guy.

Creepshow (1982). . . . . Becky
Madman (1982) . . . . .Betsy
- • 0:24—Very brief full frontal nudity, getting into hot tub with T.P.

Ross, Katharine *

Wife of actor Sam Elliott.

Films:

The Graduate (1967). .Elaine Robinson
Butch Cassidy and the Sundance Kid (1969) . . . . Etta Place
Tell Them Willie Boy is Here (1969) . . . . .Lola
Get to Know Your Rabbit (1972) . . . . .Terrific-Looking Girl
They Only Kill Their Masters (1972) . . . . Kate
- • 1:00—Very brief upper half of buns and very, very brief back side of right breast, when getting out of bed.

The Stepford Wives (1975) . . . . Joanna
(Her breasts are a prosthetic cover.)
1:49—Prosthetic breasts under sheer nightgown of robotic Katharine Ross.
The Betsy (1978). . . . . .Sally Hardeman
- • 1:02—Very brief upper half of left breast, while breast feeding baby in front of Laurence Olivier.

The Legacy (1979; British). . . . . .Maggie Walsh
a.k.a. The Legacy of Maggie Walsh
The Final Countdown (1980). . . . . . Laurel Scott/Mrs. Tideman
Wrong is Right (1982). . . . . .Sally Blake
Red-Headed Stranger (1986). . . . . Laurie
A Climate for Killing (1990) . . . . Grace Hines

Made for TV Movies:

The Shadow Riders (1982). . . . . Kate Connery
Secrets of a Mother and Daughter (1983) . . . . Ava Pryce

TV:

The Colbys (1985-87) . . . . .Francesca Scott Colby

Ross, Mary Ella

Films:

Leather Jackets (1991) . . . . Student Girl #2

Bound and Gagged: A Love Story (1993) . . . . .Lida

•• 0:05—Partial right breast, when getting caught making love in bed. Breasts, while in bed afterwards.

• 0:54—Right breast, while in bed with Chris Mulkey and Cliff during Cliff's dream.

• 0:58—Brief breasts, while making love with her lover when Cliff looks through skylight.

Ross, Ruthy *

Films:

The Centerfold Girls (1974) . . . . Glory

••• 0:49—Breasts and buns posing for photographer outside with Charly.

Ross, Shana *

Video Tapes:

Penthouse Love Stories (1986). . . . . .AC/DC Lover

••• 0:17—Full frontal nudity in bedroom with Monique Gabrielle.

Rossellini, Isabella

Daughter of actress Ingrid Bergman.

Spokesmodel for *Lancôme* cosmetics.

Films:

A Matter of Time (1976; Italian/U.S.). . . . . Sister Pia

White Nights (1985) . . . . .Darya Greenwood

Blue Velvet (1986) . . . . Dorothy

• 0:36—Buns, after taking off panties in her bathroom. Long shot.

• 1:08—Brief full frontal nudity, while frolicking with MacLachlan in bed.

• 1:27—Very, very brief lower frontal nudity, while rolling over in bed in MacLachlan's flashback.

• 1:40—Nude, while standing on porch, bruised.

• 1:41—Briefly nude, while sitting in car. Long shot. Brief right breast, while getting covered up.

•• 1:42—Brief breasts at Laura Dern's house.

Siesta (1987). . . . . Marie

Tough Guys Don't Dance (1987). . . . . .Madeleine

Cousins (1989) . . . . Maria Hardy

Wild at Heart (1990) . . . . Perdita

Death Becomes Her (1992) . . . . Lisle Von Rhuman

The Pickle (1992) . . . . .Actress in Film

Fearless (1993) . . . . Laura Klein

Immortal Beloved (1994) . . . . Anna Marie Erdody

Wyatt Earp (1994). . . . . Big Nose Kate

Big Night (1996). . . . . Gabriella

The Funeral (1996) . . . . .Clara

Made for Cable Movies:

Lies of the Twins (1991; USA) . . . . .Rachel Marks

• 0:44—Very brief lower half of buns, while putting blouse on.

Directed By: The Gift (1994; Showtime) . . . . n.a.

Crime of the Century (1996; HBO) . . . . Anna Hauptmann

Made for Cable TV:

Fallen Angels: The Frightening Frammis (1993). . .Babe Lonsdale

(Available on the video tape *Fallen Angels One.*)

Tales From the Crypt: You, Murderer (1995; HBO) . . . . . . Betty

Made for TV Movies:

The Odyssey (1997) . . . . Athena

Merlin (1998) . . . . Nimue

Rossini, Bianca

Films:

Moon Over Parador (1988) . . . . Tilde

Mobsters (1991) . . . . Rosalie Luciano

a.k.a. Mobsters—The Evil Empire

Video Tapes:

Inside Out 3 (1992). . . . . Ollala/The Branding

••• 0:23—Breasts, making love in bed with Mike.

Roth, Andrea

Films:

Princess in Exile (1991; Canadian) . . . . .Marlene Lancaster

Seedpeople (1992) . . . . Heidi Tucker

The Club (1993) . . . . Amy

Crossworlds (1996) . . . . Laura

Divided by Hate (1996) . . . . Carol Gibbs

Sunchaser (1996) . . . . Head Nurse

Made for Cable Movies:

Psychic (1992; USA). . . . . .April Morris

• 1:01—Brief buns, partially covered with leaves, lying dead in park.

Made for Cable TV:

The Outer Limits: The Sentence (1996; Showtime)
. . . . Dr. Dana Elwin

Miniseries:

A Woman of Independent Means (1995). . Eleanor (as an adult)

Made for TV Movies:

Spoils of War (1994) . . . . Penny

TV:

RoboCop (1994-95) . . . . Diana Powers

• Rothberg, Elise

Films:

Crosscut (1995). . . . . Angie

• 0:01—Brief left breast, when pulling sheet on top of her after Costas Mandylor takes the sheet away while she lies on the sofa. Medium long shot.

Asylum (1996). . . . . .Davis Receptionist

Roussel, Myriem

Films:

First Name: Carmen (1983; French). . . . . Claire

Hail, Mary (1985; French) . . . . .Mary

a.k.a. Je Vous Salve, Marie

• 0:56—Brief full frontal nudity in bathroom.

••• 0:57—Full frontal nudity in bathtub, washing herself while kneeling.

••• 1:13—Nude, undressing and putting on nightgown in bedroom.

• 1:17—Brief breasts, while moving around under sheets in bed.

••• 1:18—Breasts, while sitting on bed.

• 1:19—Lower frontal nudity and tops of breasts while undressing and bending over in gaping top.

•• 1:22—Close-up of lower frontal nudity, while in bedroom with Joseph.

•• 1:23—Lower frontal nudity and buns, after lifting up her blouse.

• 1:30—Very, very brief right breast, while rolling around in bed under the sheets.

••• 1:31—Lower frontal nudity, then breasts, while in bed. Nice close-ups.

••• 1:33—Lower frontal nudity and breasts, while lying in bed on her back.

Sacrilege (1986) . . . . Sister Virginia Maria di Leva
••• 0:50—Full frontal nudity, when making love with a guy, while two other sisters watch.

Routledge, Alison

Films:

The Quiet Earth (1985; New Zealand) . . . . Joanne
• 0:49—Brief buns, after making breakfast for Zac.
•• 1:24—Breasts in guard tower making love with Api.

Bridge to Nowhere (1986; New Zealand) . . . . Lise

Rowan, Gay

Films:

The Girl in Blue (1973; Canadian) . . . . Bonnie
a.k.a. U-turn
• 0:06—Left breast, in bed with Scott.
• 0:31—Brief breasts in bathtub.
• 0:48—Right breast, while in shower talking to Scott. Brief breasts (long shot) on balcony throwing water down at him.
• 1:21—Brief right breast and buns getting out of bed and running out of the room.

Sudden Fury (1975) . . . . Janet
S.O.B. (1981) . . . . n.a.
Second Thoughts (1983). . . . . Annie

*Rowe, Kimberly **

Films:

Wild Malibu Weekend! (1994). . . . . Teri Anderson

Maui Heat: Swimsuit Edition (1996) . . . . Dakota
• 0:39—Partial buns in swimsuit, while posing during photo shoot.
•• 0:51—Breasts under sheer red swimsuit. Full frontal nudity, while changing swimsuits.
• 0:54—Breasts, while sunbathing on lounge chair, holding an umbrella.
••• 1:06—Nude, while with Jake at the beach and waterfalls.

Made for Cable Movies:

Black Scorpion 2—Aftershock (1996; Showtime) . . . Divine
•• 0:20—Breasts in open coat while posing for photographs by police men.

Made for Cable TV:

Women: Stories of Passion-For the Sake of Science (1996; Showtime) . . . . Josie
•• 0:01—Right breast, while making love with some people in her dream.
• 0:02—Left breast, after making love in bed with John.
•• 0:03—Breasts and buns in the shower.
• 0:04—Right breast, during fantasy with Dr. Luck in the lab.
• 0:13—Left breast while taking a shower. Breasts during daydream.
• 0:14—Brief breasts after making love in bed with John.
••• 0:18—Breasts, while sitting in chair to measure her orgasm, with help from her fellow students. Good moaning.
••• 0:23—Breasts and buns, while John is hooked up to orgasm measuring machine.

*Rowe, Misty **

Films:

The Hitchhikers (1971) . . . . Maggie
• 0:00—Brief side view of left breast getting dressed.
• 0:17—Very brief breasts getting dress ripped open, then raped in van.
• 0:48—Brief right breast while getting dressed.
• 1:09—Left breast, making love with Benson.
• 1:10—Brief breasts taking a bath in tub.
• 1:13—Very brief right breast in car with another victim.

Goodbye, Norma Jean (1975) . . . . Norma Jean Baker
•• 0:08—In white bra and panties, then breasts.
• 0:14—Brief breasts in bed getting raped.
• 0:31—Very, very brief silhouette of right breast, in bed with Rob.
••• 0:59—Breasts during shooting of stag film, then in B&W when some people watch the film.

Loose Shoes (1977). . . . . Louise
A Pleasure Doing Business (1978) . . . . Ronnie
The Man with Bogart's Face (1980). . . . . Duchess

National Lampoon's Class Reunion (1982) . . . Cindy Shears
• 0:37—Very brief breasts running around school stage in Hawaiian hula dance outfit.

Double Exposure (1983) . . . . Bambi
Meatballs, Part II (1984) . . . . Fanny

Made for TV Movies:

When Things Were Rotten (1975) . . . . Maid Marion

TV:

Hee Haw (1972-91). . . . . Regular
Happy Days (1974-75) . . . . Wendy
When Things Were Rotten (1975) . . . . Maid Marion
Hee Haw Honeys (1978-79) . . . . Misty Honey
Joe's World (1979-80) . . . . Judy Wilson

Rowland, Leesa

Films:

The Book of Love (1991) . . . . Honeymoon

Class of Nuke 'Em High Part II: Subhumanoid Meltdown (1991). . . . . Victoria
•• 0:24—Breasts in room with Roger. Special-effect mouth in her stomach.
• 0:25—Most of side of left breast, while making love on top of Roger.

Royce, Roselyn

Films:

Cheech & Chong's Nice Dreams (1981) . . . . . Beach Girl #3
• 0:29—Brief breasts on the beach with two other girls. Long shot, unsteady, hard to see.
• 0:32—More brief breasts again.
• 0:33—More brief breasts again.

Malibu Hot Summer (1981) . . . . Cheryl Rielly
a.k.a. Sizzle Beach
(*Sizzle Beach* is the re-released version with Kevin Costner featured on the cover. It is missing all the nude scenes during the opening credits before 0:06.)
•• 0:15—On exercise bike, then breasts getting into bed.
••• 0:16—Breasts sitting up in bed, buns going to closet to get dressed to go jogging.
•• 0:52—Breasts on boat with Brent.

Off the Wall (1982) . . . . Buxom Blonde
• 0:35—Left breast, while kissing an inmate in visiting room while the guards watch.
•• 0:51—Left breast again, while kissing inmate through bars while the guards watch.

Stay Tuned (1992). . . . . Three's Company Spoof

Royle, Carol

Films:

Tuxedo Warrior (1970) . . . . Lisa
•• 0:35—Breasts, while lying in bed and talking with Cliff.

The Greek Tycoon (1978) . . . . Nico's Girlfriend

• *Rubanoff, Annie*

See: Wood, Annie.

Rubens, Mary Elizabeth

Films:

Prom Night (1980) . . . . Kelly
- 0:59—Very brief right breast making out with Drew in the locker room.
- 1:02—Brief upper half of breasts, standing up to put dress on. Dark.

Firebird 2015 AD (1981) . . . . Jill

Perfect Timing (1984) . . . . Judy
- • 0:04—In a bra, then breasts in bedroom with Joe.
- •• 0:05—Nude, walking to kitchen, then talking with Harry.
- • 0:08—Left breast seen through the camera's view finder.
- • 0:10—Nude, getting dressed in bedroom.
- •• 0:50—Nude, in bed with Joe.
- ••• 1:00—Nude, discovering Joe's hidden video camera, then going downstairs.

Made for Cable TV:

E.N.G. (1989-90; Lifetime; Canadian) . . . . Bobbi Katz

The Outer Limits: Unnatural Selection (1996; Showtime) . . . . Fran

Rubin, Jennifer

Films:

A Nightmare on Elm Street 3: The Dream Warriors (1987) . . . . Taryn

1969 (1988) . . . . Wife

Bad Dreams (1988) . . . . Cynthia

Permanent Record (1988) . . . . Lauren

Delusion (1990) . . . . Patti
- • 0:34—Brief buns, pulling her panties down to moon the guys before entering the lake.
- ••• 1:07—Breasts in motel bathroom, drying her hair. More breasts in the motel room with George.
- • 1:12—Right breast, in open blouse, while sitting on the bed, talking with George.

Too Much Sun (1990) . . . . Gracia

The Doors (1991) . . . . Edie

A Woman, Her Men and Her Futon (1992) . . . . Helen
- •• 0:22—Breasts, making love in bed with Randy.
- ••• 0:31—Breasts, lying in bed with Donald.
- • 0:35—Brief breasts, while making love in bed with Randy.
- •• 1:04—Breasts, lying in bed and starting to make love with Donald.

Bitter Harvest (1993) . . . . Kelly Ann Walsh
- • 0:21—Brief breasts while wearing panties, trying on clothes in front of closet mirror.
- •• 0:28—Brief breasts, then left breast while adjusting her robe so Stephen Baldwin can give her a massage.
- ••• 0:30—Breasts, after taking off robe, walking to bedroom with Baldwin and making love.

The Crush (1993) . . . . Amy

The Coriolis Effect (1994) . . . . Ruby

Deceptions II: Edge of Deception (1994; Canadian) . . . . Irene Stadler
- • 0:11—Very brief right breast, twice, while adjusting her robe when Steve Shellen watches.
- • 0:30—Breasts, while making love with Shellen.
- • 0:48—Left breast, while making love with Shellen.
- 0:55—Side view of buns, while lying in bed with Shellen.
- • 0:58—Brief left breast, while in the shower. Right breast, seen in the mirror.

Playmaker (1994) . . . . Jamie Harris
- ••• 0:37—Nude, while lying on piano after Colin Firth cuts her dress off with scissors.
- • 0:39—Breasts, after getting out of bed and putting on robe at night.

Red Scorpion 2 (1994) . . . . Sam Guiness
- • 0:53—In white slip in bedroom, then breasts while in shower. Seen on B&W monitor.

Saints and Sinners (1994) . . . . Eva
- • 0:03—Buns in short nightie, after kicking the covers off herself while lying in bed.
- ••• 0:31—In black bra and panties, then breasts, while making love with Damian Chapa.
- • 0:42—Breasts, while making love with Chapa and Scott Plank at the same time.
- •• 0:43—Breasts, while lying in bed and talking with Chapa and Plank, then getting out of bed and putting on blouse.
- • 0:45—Brief breasts, taking off her blouse and going into the bathroom.
- • 0:57—Breasts, while making love in bed with Chapa and Plank again.

Stranger By Night (1994) . . . . Anne Richmond
- ••• 0:57—Breasts, while making love in bed with Steven Bauer.

Screamers (1995) . . . . Jessica

Little Witches (1996) . . . . Sherilyn

Made for Cable Movies:

The Fear Inside (1992; Showtime) . . . . Jane Caswell
- • 0:26—Breasts with Peter. Hard to see because of the strobe light effect.
- • 0:53—Buns and partial left breast visible under water while skinny dipping in pool.
- • 0:55—Full frontal nudity under water. Hard to see because of the distortion.

Full Eclipse (1993; HBO) . . . . Helen

Wasp Woman (1995; Sci-Fi) . . . . Janice

Made for Cable TV:

Tales From the Crypt: Beauty Rest (1992; HBO) . . . . . . Druscilla

The Outer Limits: Second Thoughts (1997; Showtime) . . . . Rose Ciotti

Ruddell, Shanae *

Video Tapes:

Hot Body International: #2 Miss Puerto Vallarta (1990) . . . . Contestant
- •• 0:33—Buns, in one piece swimsuit.

Hot Body International: #4 Spring Break (1992) . . . . Contestant

Ruiz, Mia M.

Films:

Witchcraft II: The Temptress (1989) . . . . Michelle
- • 0:27—Brief breasts several times making love with a guy on the floor during William's hallucination.

Demon Wind (1990) . . . . Reana

Wild at Heart (1990) . . . . . . Mr. Reindeer's Resident Valet #1
- •• 0:32—Breasts standing next to Mr. Reindeer on the right, holding a tray. Long scene.

Black Belt (1992) . . . . Hooker
- ••• 0:04—Breasts, while sitting on bed.
- • 0:16—Breasts, while dead on bed, covered with blood.

Runacre, Jenny

Films:

Joseph Andrews (1977; British/French) . . . . The Gypsy

Jubilee (1977) . . . . Queen Elizabeth I/Bod
- •• 0:36—Breasts then lower frontal nudity, while eating food from a bowl.
- •• 1:14—Breasts, after taking off her jacket in bed next to Mad.

Restoration (1995) . . . . Painted Lady

Runo, Pamela *

a.k.a. Pamela Pond.

Films:

Munchie (1992) . . . . Female Celebrity

Sins of Desire (1992) . . . . Rachel

(Unrated version reviewed.)

••• 0:12—Right breast while in bubble bath, covered with bubbles, then rinsed off. Breasts and buns, getting out and walking down hall.

Campus Hustle (1993) . . . . Susan

Dragon Fire (1993). . . . . Marta

••• 0:25—Breasts and buns in T-back, while doing strip routine on stage. Lit with strobe lights.

•• 0:29—Breasts and buns in T-back, while dancing on stage.

••• 0:49—Breasts, while making love in bed with Powers.

Future Shock (1993) . . . . Model

Concealed Weapon (1994) . . . . Victim

Runyon, Jennifer

Films:

To All a Goodnight (1980) . . . . Nancy

Ghostbusters (1984) . . . . Female Student

Up the Creek (1984) . . . . Heather Merriweather

The Falcon and the Snowman (1985) . . . . Carole

Flight of the Spruce Goose (1986). . . . . Terry

18 Again! (1988). . . . . Robin

The In Crowd (1988) . . . . Vicky

A Man Called Serge (1990) . . . . Fifi

Killing Streets (1991) . . . . Sandra Ross

• 1:00—In white lingerie then brief breasts taking off lingerie in bed with Michael Paré. Hard to see.

Till Death Do Us Part (1991) . . . . Judy

• 1:02—Breasts and buns in T-back, undressing in bathroom. Don't see her face.

Carnosaur (1993) . . . . Thrush

Miniseries:

Space (1987) . . . . Marcia Grant

Made for TV Movies:

A Very Brady Christmas (1988) . . . . Cindy Brady

TV:

Another World . . . . Sally Spencer

Charles in Charge (1984-85). . . . . Gwendolyn Pierce

Rushmore, Karen

Films:

Coast to Coast (1980). Callahan's Wife

Too Scared to Scream (1985) . . . . Nadine

••• 0:51—Breasts in sauna, rubbing oil on herself.

••• 0:52—Breasts, lying in sauna.

••• 0:53—Buns and breasts in spa.

TV:

13 Queens Boulevard (1979) . . . . Camille

Russell, Andaluz

Films:

The Assassin (1989) . . . . Amanda Portales

• 0:21—Brief breasts while changing clothes in room with the other assassins.

Pure Luck (1991). . . . . Reception Manager

Gunmen (1993) . . . . Guzman's Wife

Russell, Betsy

Films:

Private School (1983). . . . . Jordan Leigh-Jensen

(Blonde hair.)

• 0:04—Very, very brief right breast and buns when Bubba takes her towel off through window.

••• 0:19—Breasts riding a horse after Kathleen Wilhoite steals her blouse.

• 1:24—Upper half of buns flashing with the rest of the girls during graduation ceremony.

Out of Control (1984) . . . . Chrissie

(Brunette hair.)

•• 0:29—Breasts taking off her top while playing Strip Spin the Bottle.

• 0:30—Buns, taking off her panties.

Avenging Angel (1985) . . . . Angel/Molly Stewart

Tomboy (1985) . . . . Tomasina "Tommy" Boyd

•• 0:44—In wet T-shirt, then brief breasts after landing in the water with her motorcycle.

•• 0:59—Breasts making love with the race car driver in an exercise room.

Cheerleader Camp (1987). . . . . Alison Wentworth

a.k.a. Bloody Pom Poms

Trapper County War (1989). . . . . Lacey Luddigger

Camp Fear (1991) . . . . n.a.

a.k.a. Millenium Countdown

Delta Heat (1992) . . . . Vicki

• 0:54—Brief buns and partial side of right breast, walking from bed, past two guys. (More buns seen in mirror.)

Amore! (1993). . . . . Cheryl Schwartz

The Break ...Is All You Need (1994) . . . . Candy

Made for TV Movies:

Roxanne: The Prize Pulitzer (1989) . . . . Liza Pulitzer

Russell, Karen

Films:

Vice Academy (1988) . . . . Shawnee

•• 0:09—Breasts exposing herself to Dwayne to disarm him.

•• 1:13—Breasts pulling her top down to distract a bad guy.

Dr. Alien (1989). . . . . Coed #2

a.k.a. I Was a Teenage Sex Mutant

••• 0:53—Breasts taking off her top (she's on the right) in the women's locker room before another coed takes hers off in front of Wesley.

Easy Wheels (1989) . . . . Candy

Hell High (1989) . . . . Teen Girl

•• 0:04—Breasts in shack with Teen Boy while little girl watches through a hole in the wall.

Murder Weapon (1989). . . . . Amy

• 0:34—Brief breasts in shower.

Dick Tracy (1990) . . . . Dancer

The Girl I Want (1990). . . . . Lisa

Havana (1990) . . . . Dancer #2

Mob Boss (1990). . . . . Mary

Shock 'Em Dead (1990) . . . . Michelle

•• 0:16—In lingerie, then breasts twice with Martin.

Wilding, The Children of Violence (1990) . . . . Cathy

•• 0:20—Breasts in bedroom when Wings Hauser pulls her lingerie down.

Bugsy (1991). . . . . Dancer

Mobsters (1991) . . . . Showgirl

a.k.a. Mobsters—The Evil Empire

Murder Blues (1991) . . . . Isabella

Made for Cable TV:
Dream On: Hey Diddle Diddle (1996; HBO). . . . Woman #1
•• 0:05—Breasts, when joining Martin in the shower.
Video Tapes:
B-Movie Queens Revealed: The Making of "Vice Academy" (1993) . . . . Shawnee
• 0:00—Very brief breasts, pulling down her top from *Vice Academy 1.*
•• 0:27—Same shot as 0:00.

Russell, Theresa *

Wife of director Nicholas Roeg.
Films:
The Last Tycoon (1976). . . . . Cecilia Brady
Straight Time (1978) . . . . Jenny Mercer
••• 1:00—Left breast, while in bed with Dustin Hoffman. Don't see her face.
Bad Timing: A Sensual Obsession (1980) . . Milena Flaherty
• 0:14—Buns and breasts under short, sheer blouse.
• 0:17—Almost brief right breast in bed during Art Garfunkel's flashback. Very brief left breast, while kneeling on bed with him.
• 0:31—Full frontal nudity in bed with Garfunkel. Intercut with tracheotomy footage. Kind of gross.
•• 0:32—Right breast, while sitting in bed talking to Garfunkel.
• 0:41—Brief breasts several times on operating table.
• 0:55—Full frontal nudity making love on stairwell with Garfunkel. Quick cuts.
• 0:56—Brief breasts twice after stairwell episode while throwing a fit.
•• 1:45—In bra, then breasts passed out on bed while Garfunkel cuts her clothes off. Brief full frontal nudity.
•• 1:48—More breasts cuts while Garfunkel makes love to her while she's unconscious from an overdose of drugs.
Eureka (1983; British) . . . . Tracy
• 0:40—Right breast, lying in bed with Hauer.
• 1:04—Very brief left breast in bed with Hauer, then brief lower frontal nudity and brief buns when Gene Hackman bursts into the room.
•• 1:09—Breasts on a boat with Hauer.
• 1:41—Left breast peeking out from under black top while lying in bed.
••• 1:59—Full frontal nudity kicking off sheets in the bed.
The Razor's Edge (1984) . . . . Sophie
Insignificance (1985). . . . . Actress
Aria (1987; U.S./British). . . . . .King Zog
Black Widow (1987). . . . . Catherine
• 0:28—Briefly nude, making love in cabin.
•• 1:18—Nude in pool with Paul.
Track 29 (1988; British) . . . . Linda Henry
Impulse (1989) . . . . Lottie
•• 0:37—Left breast, while making love with Stan in bed.
Physical Evidence (1989). Jenny Hudson
Cold Heaven (1990) . . . . Marie Davenport
• 0:09—Very brief upper half of right breast, when it pops out of her swimsuit top when struggling to get Mark Harmon onto boat.
• 0:18—Side of left breast while washing herself at the sink.
• 1:14—Brief breasts several times, making love in bed with James Russo.
Whore (1991) . . . . Liz
a.k.a. If you're afraid to say it... Just see it
•• 0:13—Breasts and buns in G-string outfit, taking off her coat.
••• 0:25—In black bra, doing sit-ups. Breasts making love in spa with Blake.
• 1:18—Brief buns, in open skirt in back of car with a customer.
Kafka (1992; U.S./French) . . . . Gabriela
Being Human (1994). . . . . The Storyteller
The Spy Within (1994). . . . . .Alex Canis
a.k.a. Flight of the Dove
••• 0:19—In black bra, then breasts, while making love with Scott Glenn inside.
• 0:47—Partial left breast and brief partial right breast when taking a shower and talking to Glenn.
• 1:07—Brief partial buns and brief partial side of right breast, while making love in bed with Glenn.
Public Enemy #1 (1995). . . . . Kate "Ma" Barker
•• 0:58—Left breast while making love in bed with Eric Roberts.
••• 1:00—Breasts while taking off dress in front of mirror and getting into bed with Roberts.
Wild Things (1998) . . . . Sandra
Made for Cable Movies:
Trade-Off (1994) . . . . Jackie Daniels
• 0:18—Breasts, while making love in bed with Adam Baldwin.
• 0:40—Brief breasts in the bathtub with Baldwin. Covered with bubbles.
Made for TV Movies:
Thicker Than Water (1993; British). . . . . Jo/Debbie
Once You Meet a Stranger (1996) . . . . Margo Anthony

Ruval, Yulis

See: Müller, Lillian.

• *Ruymen, Ayn*

Films:
Private Parts (1972) . . . . Cheryl Stratton
••• 0:57—Breasts and buns, while undressing and getting into bathtub wearing a blindfold, then breasts, seen through peephole.
Made for TV Movies:
Firestorm: 72 Hours in Oakland (1993) . . . . Mavis
TV:
The McLean Stevenson Show (1976-77) . . . . Janet

• *Ryan, Amanda*

Films:
Jude (1996; British) . . . . Gypsy Saleswoman
Made for Cable TV:
The Hunger: The Swords (1997; Showtime) . . . . . Musidora
••• 0:14—Breasts and partial buns, wearing panties, garter belt and stockings, while in bedroom with Balthazar Getty.
• 0:18—Brief breasts, while making love with Getty in bed and fooling around afterwards.
• 0:21—Breasts, while making love with Balthazar Getty in bed. Camera movement makes you a bit dizzy.

Ryan, Leslie

Films:
Night of the Creeps (1986) . . Sorority Girl with Hairbrush 1959
976-EVIL II: The Astral Factor (1991) . . . . Paula
Pontiac Moon (1994) . . . . Auburn
Body Chemistry 4: Full Exposure (1995) . . . . Amy Mitchell
(Unrated version reviewed.)
••• 0:09—Breasts, while making love in bed with Simon.
Cover Me (1995). . . . . Hostess
The Assault (1996). . . . . Lisa Wilks

Ryan, Lisa Dean

Films:

At Home with the Webbers (1992) .... Annabelle Nelson
Hostile Intentions (1994)........................ Caroline
Twisted Love (1994)............................Janna
• 0:48—Buns in T-back, taking off slip and getting into bed with Beau. Dark.

Made for Cable TV:

Dead at 21 (1994-95; MTV) .... Maria

TV:

Doogie Howser, M.D. (1989) ....Wanda Plenn
Class of '96 (1993) .... Jessica Cohen

Ryan, Meg

Wife of actor Dennis Quaid.

Films:

Rich and Famous (1981)............... Debbie at 18 years
Amityville 3-D (1983) .... Lisa
Armed and Dangerous (1986)...........Maggie Cavanaugh
Top Gun (1986) ....Carole
Innerspace (1987)................................Lydia
D.O.A. (1988) ....Sydney Fuller
• 0:44—Brief back side of right breast, dropping a towel that was wrapped around her to put a slip on over her head.
The Presidio (1988)............................Donna
Promised Land (1988) .... Beverly
• 0:22—Very brief side view of left breast in bed with Kiefer Sutherland.
When Harry Met Sally... (1989)...............Sally Albright
Joe vs. the Volcano (1990).......... DeDe/Angelica/Patricia
The Doors (1991) .... Pamela Courson
•• 1:06—Right breast, while lying in bed with Val Kilmer.
Prelude to a Kiss (1992) .... Rita Boyle
Flesh and Bone (1993).....................Kay Davies
•• 0:59—Right breast, several times, while making love with Dennis Quaid in bed.
Sleepless in Seattle (1993).................... Annie Reed
When a Man Loves a Woman (1993) .... Alice Green
I.Q. (1994) ....Catherine Boyd
French Kiss (1995) .... Kate
Restoration (1995) .... Katharine
Courage Under Fire (1996)........... Capt. Karen Walden
Addicted to Love (1997)........................Maggie
City of Angels (1998) .... Maggie Rice

TV:

As the World Turns (1982-84) ..... Betsy Stewart Montgomery
One of the Boys (1982)...........................Jane
Wildside (1985)..............................Cally Oaks

Ryan, Rachel

Adult film actress.
a.k.a. Serina Robinson and Penny Morgan.
Ex-wife of actor Richard Mulligan.

Films:

Clean and Sober (1988)........ Uncredited Dead Girlfriend
• 0:02—Buns, lying dead in Michael Keaton's bed. Don't see her face, but it's her.

Video Tapes:

Secrets of Making Love... To the Same Person Forever (1991)............................... Blonde Girl/Boat
••• 0:04—Breasts in boat and on river bank with her lover.
•• 0:47—Breasts in boat again.
Inside Out (1992) .... Love the One You're With
(Unrated version reviewed.)
•• 1:13—Left breast, in bed with a guy.
•• 1:14—Right breast and buns, climbing on top of him in bed.
•• 1:15—Breasts and buns, making love on top of him. More breasts after making love.

Ryan, Seana *

Films:

Return to Two Moon Junction (1993) ....Gena
Embrace of the Vampire (1994).............. Nymph II
(Unrated version reviewed.)
•• 0:03—Brief breasts, while walking up to Martin Kemp with the other two Nymphs. Then breasts and partial buns sitting to the left of Kemp before biting him along with the other two Nymphs.
• 1:22—Brief right breast in Martin Kemp's flashback.
Naked Souls (1995) ....Woman in Pool
• 0:10—Full frontal nudity in and out of pool in B&W flashback.
• 0:12—Brief breasts, while floating dead in pool in B&W flashback.
• 0:36—Nude, while walking next to pool in B&W flashback.
• 0:49—Full frontal nudity, while walking into pool in B&W flashback.
• 1:00—Brief full frontal nudity, while floating dead in pool in B&W flashback.
• 1:02—Nude, while getting out of, then floating dead in pool in B&W flashback.
• 1:16—Full frontal nudity, while floating dead in pool in B&W flashback.

Video Tapes:

Penthouse Satin & Lace II: Hollywood Undercover (1992)....................................... Pet
Penthouse's 25th Anniversary Swimsuit Video (1993) .... Pet
The Girls of Penthouse, Volume 3 (1995)........... Pet
••• 0:16—Nude on stage, doing a strip routine.
••• 0:20—Breasts and lower frontal nudity, in open swim suit, when sunbathing next to a swimming pool while a guy watches her with binoculars.
••• 0:23—Breasts and buns under sheer red outfit while playing pool. Breasts and buns through openings in it.
Penthouse Pet Rocks (1995)......................... Pet
Penthouse: The Ultimate Pet Games (1996) .... Pet
••• 0:02—Nude during obstacle course segment.
••• 0:05—Nude while posing outdoors.
••• 0:29—Nude in tug-of-war segment.
••• 0:42—Nude during squirt gun segment.

CD-ROM:

Penthouse Interactive Virtual Photo Shoot, Disc 4 (1995).. Pet

• Ryan, Shayna

Films:

Bikini Hoe Down (1997) .... June
•• 0:01—In black bra, then breasts, while making love in bed with Jeffrey.
• 0:07—Brief buns in swimsuit bottom.
••• 0:23—Breasts, while making love in bed with Jeffrey.
• 0:40—In lingerie, brief buns in panties and breasts while changing clothes.
••• 0:53—Nude, while showering with the other three girls.
•• 1:19—Breasts, while dancing on stage during bikini hoe down.
Bikini Traffic School (1997) .... Marcie
•• 0:01—Breasts, while in kitchen and in bedroom with Skipper.

••• 0:03—Breasts, while dancing on stage with Traci and Vicky.
•• 0:11—Breasts, while making love in back seat of car with .
••• 0:13—Breasts, while dancing on stage with Traci.
•• 0:18—Breasts and buns in swimsuit bottom, while frolicking in the pool with Vicky and Traci.
•• 0:21—Breasts, while sunbathing.
••• 0:39—Breasts, while making love with the pool guy during her fantasy.
•• 0:42—Breasts, while making love with Skippy on the floor.
• 0:45—Very brief breasts, while flashing Traci on miniature gold course.
••• 0:45—Breasts, after taking off her top during tennis match and playing tennis against Traci.
••• 1:02—Breasts and parital buns, while making love on top of a table.
•• 1:22—Breasts, while on stage during traffic school lessons.

The Escort (1997) . . . . .Lianne
(Unrated version reviewed.)

Ryan, Stephanie

See: Napoli, Susan.

Ryusaki, Kimberly

Films:

Punchline (1988). Gas Station Waitress
Da Vinci's War (1992) . . . . Cocktail Waitress #3

Video Tapes:

Inside Out (1992) . . . . Linda/Life Is For the Taking
(Unrated version reviewed.)
••• 0:52—Breasts in bedroom, undressing while Charlie has an out of body experience.
•• 0:53—Left breast, while lying on bed.

Saalman, Raelyn

Films:

Blonde Heaven (1994) . . . . Angie
• 0:17—In bra, then breasts, while making love with Kyle on bed. Medium long shot.
•• 0:21—In bra and panties, then breasts, while changing clothes. Seen from behind a 2-way mirror.
• 0:44—Buns in lingerie, while dancing and modeling in front of Julie Strain.
•• 0:47—Full frontal nudity, several times, while holding spot light on Josephina and Al.
• 0:58—Breasts, while making love with Kyle on table.
•• 0:59—Breasts, while lying in bed with Strain.
• 1:00—Brief buns, after taking off her dress in movie theater in front of Kyle.
••• 1:02—Breasts and buns in panties, while making love in bed with Strain.
•• 1:05—Nude, while taking a shower, getting out and running down the hall.
• 1:12—Brief buns in panties, while getting out of bed.

The Affair (1995) . . . . Jennifer
•• 0:01—Breasts, while making love in bed with Greg.
• 0:12—Breasts, while sitting at piano when fondled by Greg.
••• 0:16—Full frontal nudity while undressing in her imagination, then making love with Mark when watched by Alexis.
• 0:18—Breasts, while making love with Mark in her imagination.
••• 0:29—Buns in panties, then breasts and lower frontal nudity, while making love with Mark. Very nice, long scene.
•• 0:39—Nude, while drying herself off in bathroom.
••• 1:16—In lingerie, then nude, while making love with Greg in bedroom.

Attack of the 60 Foot Centerfold (1995) . . . . Inga
••• 0:05—Breasts and buns in panties with the other two girls in photo shoot.
••• 0:31—Breasts and buns in swimsuit, while posing at the beach with the other two girls.
••• 1:05—Breasts, while sunbathing outside and talking with Betty.
• 1:13—Partial buns, while helping Jay Richardson.

Friend of the Family (1995) . . . . Laura
a.k.a. Elke's Erotic Nights
(Unrated version reviewed.)
•• 1:15—Buns in swimsuit bottom and brief breasts, while dancing around for Josh and his video camera.
••• 1:35—Nude, while in bedroom, making love with Josh.

Galaxy Girls (1995). . . . . Ginnie
•• 0:22—Nude, while bathing in a stream by herself.

Killing For Love (1995). . . . . Amber
•• 0:31—Breasts, while lying in bed and talking with Ken.
••• 0:44—Nude, while making love with Ken in bathroom. Nice, long scene.

Babe Watch: The Forbidden Parody (1996) . . . . .Lucki
•• 0:10—Breasts, while in backyard with Dek.
•• 1:11—Breasts, while making love with her boyfriend in spa.

Made for Cable TV:

Erotic Confessions: Locked Up (1996; Cinemax) . . . . Cindy
(Available on video tape in *Erotic Confessions, Volume 3: Passion.*)
••• 0:03—Nude, while undressing outside of jail cell with a dream lover.
•• 0:09—In black lingerie, then breasts, while making love with Martin in jail cell.
•• 0:15—Full frontal nudity, while making love with Martin.

*Sachs, Adrianne **

Films:

Cat Chaser (1988) . . . . .Anita De Boya

Two to Tango (1988) . . . . Cecilia Lorca
•• 0:29—Side of left breast and buns in bedroom with Lucky Lara. More left breast while Dan Stroud watches through camera.
•• 0:59—Breasts and buns in bed with Dan Stroud.

In the Cold of the Night (1989) . . . . Kimberly Shawn
••• 0:52—Buns and breasts in shower, then making love with Scott. Long, erotic scene.
• 0:59—Brief breasts in outdoor spa.
•• 1:06—Breasts making love on Scott's lap in bed.

Best of the Best (1990) . . . . Kelly
Alien Intruder (1992). . . . . Yvonne

• *Sachs, Leslie*

Films:

At Home with the Webbers (1992) . . . . Billy
Hard Promises (1992) . . . . .Mail Woman
Night Eyes 3 (1993). . . . . Karen
Scorned (1993) . . . . .Alex's Secretary
Dracula: Dead and Loving It (1995). . . . . Usherette

Made for Cable Movies:

Running Mates (1992; HBO) . . . . Photographer

Made for Cable TV:

Women: Stories of Passion-Hat Trick (1997; Showtime)
. . . . Miranda
•• 0:05—Breasts, several times, and brief partial buns, while making love with J.T. and his sister in bed.
••• 0:12—Breasts and buns, while making love with a guy on a stairwell at a party.

••• 0:19—Buns and breasts, while making love with a guy in bed during fantasy.

• *Sage, Wendy*

Films:

Target of Seduction (1995). . . . . .Alex

• 0:59—Breasts and buns, while taking a shower. Don't see her face.

Made for Cable TV:

Compromising Situations: Real Woman (1997; Showtime) . . . . .Susan Whitman

•• 0:22—Breasts, while making love with Phillips on bed.

Sägebrecht, Marianne *

Films:

Sugarbaby (1985; German) . . . . Marianne

a.k.a. Zuckerbaby

•• 0:44—Breasts, while undressing with Huber.

0:48—Partial right breast, under bubbles in bubble bath with Huber.

• 0:59—Breasts, while sitting in bubble bath with Huber.

The Bagdad Café (1988) . . . . .Jasmin

(Check this out if you like full-figured women.)

•• 1:09—Right breast slowly lowering her top, posing while Jack Palance paints.

•• 1:12—More breasts posing for Palance.

Moon Over Parador (1988). . . . . .Magor

The War of the Roses (1989) . . . . Susan

Rosalie Goes Shopping (1990) . . . . Rosalie Greenspace

Dust Devil (1992; British) . . . . Dr. Leidzinger

Erotique (1993). . . . . Taboo Parlor/Hilde

All Men are Mortal (1995; British/Dutch/French). . . . . . . Annie

Martha and I (1995) . . . . Martha

Sahagun, Elena *

Films:

Caged Fury (1989) . . . . Tracy Collins

•• 0:58—Left breast while taking a shower.

Corporate Affairs (1990) . . . . .Stacy

Marked for Death (1990) . . . . .Carmen

• 0:06—Breasts in room, when shooting Steven Seagal's partner.

Naked Obsession (1990) . . . . Becky

(Unrated version reviewed.)

••• 1:10—In white bra, panties, garter belt and stockings while wearing the mask. Breasts and buns in G-string.

Sunset Heat (1991) . . . . .Brandon's Model

a.k.a. Midnight Heat

(Unrated version reviewed.)

Uncaged (1991) . . . . .Joey

a.k.a. Angel in Red

Intent to Kill (1992). . . . . Mia

Ring of Fire II: Blood and Steel (1992) . . . . Teez

Teenage Exorcist (1992) . . . . Sally

• 0:09—Brief side view of right breast and buns in panties, while putting robe on.

• 0:31—Buns and brief side of right breast, while getting into the shower.

•• 0:32—Buns and right breast, while getting soaped up by creature's hand. Sort of frontal nudity behind fabric shower curtain.

Tiger Heart (1996) . . . . Chi-Chi

Made for Cable Movies:

Terminal Virus (1995; Showtime). . . . . .Blanca

• 0:32—Very brief side of right breast, then buns, while undressing and joining two other nude women in the bath outside.

•• 1:09—Breasts, after taking off top during strip poker game.

Saint, Bonita *

Video Tapes:

Penthouse Forum Letters: Volume 2 (1994) . . . . The Big Switch/Cindy

••• 0:32—Breasts and buns in white panties while doing strip tease with Debbie in front of their husbands. Nude in hot tub, then nude making love with Steve on lounge chair.

Penthouse Behind the Scenes (1995) . . . . Pet

••• 0:31—Nude in interviews and behind the scenes footage.

CD-ROM:

Penthouse Interactive Virtual Photo Shoot, Disc 4 (1995) . . . . Pet

• *Sakelaris, Anastasia*

Films:

Austin Powers: International Man of Mystery (1997) . . . . '60s Model

Made for Cable Movies:

Alien Avengers (1996; Showtime) . . . . .Daphne

a.k.a. Welcome to Planet Earth

• 0:40—Brief side view of left breast, while pushing Joseph onto the bed.

•• 0:51—Brief breasts, twice, and buns in T-back after taking off her dress in police station to get some attention.

Sal, Jeanne

Films:

Corporate Affairs (1990). . . . . Sandy

• 0:38—Left breast in open dress while sneaking around the office with Buster.

Dead Women In Lingerie (1991) . . . . Bing

Saldivar, Laura

Made for Cable Movies:

Full Body Massage (1995; Showtime) . . . . .Young Nina

•• 0:48—Nude, while standing in room with a guy. Don't see her face.

Made for Cable TV:

Erotic Confessions: Boss's Orders (1996; Cinemax) . Laura

(Available on video tape in *Erotic Confessions, Volume 2: Intrigue.*)

••• 0:07—Nude, while making love with Billy in her uncle's office.

• 0:12—Breasts, while making out with Billy in his office.

• 0:14—Breasts, while making love with Billy behind drapes during party.

Salem, Pamela

Films:

The Bitch (1979; British) . . . . Lynn

•• 0:46—Breasts in bed making love with a guy after playing at a casino.

Never Say Never Again (1983) . . . . .Miss Moneypenny

After Darkness (1985) . . . . Elizabeth Huninger

Salomé (1986; Italian) . . . . Herodias

• 0:05—Brief left breast, when her top gets ripped off.

• 0:26—Left breast when servant girl helps take her dress off.

• 0:27—Left breast and lower frontal nudity while standing in front of pool. Medium long shot.

Salerno, Tiffany

Films:

The Pickle (1992) . . . . Elegant Woman
Forrest Gump (1994). . . . . .Carla
The Whispering (1994) . . . . Jenna
- 0:09—Breasts, while making love in bed with Leif Garrett. Don't see her face.

Lover's Knot (1995). . . . . Juliet

Salin, Kari

See: Wührer, Kari.

Salinger, Diane

Films:

Battle in the Erogenous Zone . . . . Datemaster 2000
Creature (1985) . . . . Melanie Bryce
Pee Wee's Big Adventure (1985) . . . . Simone
The Morning After (1986). . . . . Isabel Harding
Bird (1988) . . . . Baroness Nica
Verne Miller (1988) . . . . Mortician's Wife
Alice (1990). . . . . .Carol
The Butcher's Wife (1991) . . . . Trendoid
Batman Returns (1992) . . . . Penguin's Mother
The Magic Bubble (1992) . . . . .Julia
- 0:11—Very, very brief breasts after whipping off towel in front of her husband. Very, very brief buns, walking away. Back side of right breast, while pulling back curtain in front of her husband while he sits on the toilet.
- 1:21—Very brief side of left breast while putting on night-gown.

Venice/Venice (1992) . . . . Stephanie
One Night Stand (1994) . . . . Barbara Joslyn
a.k.a. Before the Night
Scarlet Letter (1995) . . . . Margaret Bellingham

Made for Cable TV:

Women: Stories of Passion-As Always, Madelaine (1996; Showtime) . . . . .Madelaine

Made for TV Movies:

Stormy Weathers (1992) . . . . Bogey

TV:

NYPD Blue: The Bank Dick (May 16, 1995) . . . . . . Mrs. Snyder

Salmon, Nancy

Films:

Cry Uncle (1971). . . . . Connie
- 0:16—Breasts and buns in bed with two other girls while spanking Dominic. Hard to see because the negative image is projected.
- 0:26—Full frontal nudity in B&W photo that Keith shows Cora.
- 0:45—Brief breasts in the same B&W photo.
- 0:46—Brief right breast with Lena when Jake peeks in the window.
- •• 0:48—Breasts, fixing drugs while sitting on bed.
- ••• 0:51—Breasts, while sitting on bed, then full frontal nudity getting out of bed.
- 1:04—Buns, while lying on bed.
- •• 1:06—Full frontal nudity, rolling off bed and onto the floor, when Jake discovers she's dead.

Okay Bill (1971) . . . . .Nancy Thornberry
Injun Fender (1973) . . . . Girl

Salt, Jennifer

Films:

Midnight Cowboy (1969) . . . . Annie
- 0:31—Very brief buns, while running away from some bad guys in flashback.
- 0:42—Brief left breast on bed with Voight in flashback.
- 0:49—Very brief breasts in car in B&W flashback. More brief breasts and buns in car and running on porch.

The Wedding Party (1969). . . . . Phoebe
Brewster McCloud (1970) . . . . Hope
Hi, Mom! (1971) . . . . .Judy Bishop
Play It Again, Sam (1972) . . . . Sharon
Sisters (1973). . . . . .Grace Collier
It's My Turn (1980) . . . . .Maisie

TV:

Soap (1977-81) . . . . Eunice Tate
The Marshall Chronicles (1990). . . . . Cynthia Brightman

Salvatore, Donna *

Films:

Marilyn Chambers' Bedtime Stories (1993) . . . . Letitia
- 0:01—Brief breasts in shower through hole in wall during opening credits.
- •• 0:11—Breasts, getting out of shower when Bart peeks through hole in wall.
- •• 0:32—Buns in T-back and breasts, while dancing with Bart.
- 0:33—Breasts in open polka dot robe.
- 1:17—Brief breasts in shower out take.

New York Nights (1994) . . . . Lingerie Girl #1

Samples, Candy

Adult film actress.
a.k.a. Mary Gavin.

Films:

Pleasure Unlimited/Sensous Wife (1972) . . . . .n.a.
a.k.a. Drop Out Wife
Fantasm (1976; Australian) . . . . Belle
Up! (1976). . . . . The Headsperson
Superchick (1978). . . . . Lady on Boat
- ••• 0:08—Breasts in bed with Johnny on boat.

Beneath the Valley of the Ultravixens (1979) . . . . The Very Big Blonde

Video Tapes:

Best Chest in the West (1984) . . . . Herself
- ••• 0:54—Breasts dancing on stripping and dancing on stage with Pat McCormick.

Sanches, Kim *

Sister of Playmate Stacy Sanches.

Video Tapes:

Playboy's Sisters (1995) . . . . Herself/Loving Competition
- ••• 0:01—Nude with her sister in boxing workout fantasy.

Playboy Video Centerfold: Stacy Sanches (1996) . . . . .Special Appearance
- ••• 0:16—Nude, while posing in a house, by herself and with her sister, Stacy.

Wet & Wild VIII: Bottoms Up (1996) . . . . Featured Model
Playboy's Fast Women (1997) . . . . Cast
Playboy's Voluptuous Vixens (1997). . . . . .Featured

Sanches, Stacy *

Video Tapes:

Playboy Video Calendar 1996 (1995) . . . . April
- ••• 0:14—In lingerie and nude while posing outdoors and in-doors.
- ••• 0:16—Nude, while posing in studio.

Playboy's Hot Latin Ladies (1995)
. . . . Stacy/Spanish American
••• 0:20—Nude in office and on the roof.
Playboy's Sisters (1995). . . . . . . .Herself/Loving Competition
••• 0:01—Nude with her sister in boxing workout fantasy.
Playboy Video Calendar 1997 (1996) . . . . December
••• 0:49—Nude, while dancing and posing in music video segment.
••• 0:52—In lingerie and nude, while posing indoors during a rainy day.
Playboy Video Centerfold: Stacy Sanches (1996)
. . . . Playmate of the Year
• 0:00—Breasts during introduction.
••• 0:01—Nude, while posing in various outfits outdoors.
••• 0:07—Nude, while dancing in studio with two guys.
••• 0:10—In lingerie, while undressing in house, then nude.
••• 0:15—Nude, while posing in a house, by herself and with her sister, Kim.
••• 0:24—In bra and panties, while bathing a guy, then nude.
••• 0:28—Nude in still photos.
••• 0:31—Nude, while lying on bed and dreaming.
•• 0:34—Full frontal nudity during ending.
Wet & Wild VIII: Bottoms Up (1996). . . . . Playmate
Playboy's Voluptuous Vixens (1997) . . . . Playmate
Playboy's Girls Next Door: Naughty and Nice (1998)
. . . . Summer Job/Toni
••• 0:36—Nude, while making love with John in auto repair shop.

• *Sánchez-Gijón, Aitana*

Films:
Casanova (1987). . . . . Therese
The Monk (1990; British/Spanish). . . . . Sister Ines
The Perfect Husband (1995; Spanish) . . . . Klara
A Walk in the Clouds (1995) . . . . Victoria Aragón
Mouth to Mouth (1996; Spanish) . . . . Amanda
a.k.a. Boca a Boca
Love Walked In (1997) . . . . Vicki Rivas
• 0:05—Brief left breast, while making love with Denis Leary.
• 0:26—Partial right breast visible in nightgown, while lying in bed.

Sand, Shauna *

Wife of actor Lorenzo Lamas.
Films:
The Chosen One (1997) . . . . Emma
Video Tapes:
Playboy Video Calendar 1997 (1996) . . . . February
••• 0:05—In lingerie and nude, while posing indoors.
••• 0:07—In lingerie and nude, while posing outdoors.
Playboy Video Centerfold: Victoria Silvstedt (1997)
. . . . Playmate
••• 0:42—In lingerie and nude, while posing in house.
••• 0:46—Nude and in lingerie in B&W fantasy segment at the beach.
••• 0:50—Nude and in leather outfits while posing with a motorcycle.
••• 0:52—Nude in still photos.
••• 0:54—Nude while posing in bed.
Playboy's Girls Next Door: Naughty and Nice (1998)
. . . . Virtual Girl/Virtual Girl
••• 0:29—Nude, taking off her clothes, then dancing and giving herself a rubdown.
Playboy's Playmates Revisited (1998). . . . . .Herself
• 0:25—Brief breasts in still photo.

Sanda, Dominique *

Films:
The Conformist (1970; Italian/French) . . . . Anna Quadri
•• 1:01—Breasts, taking off leotard for Jean-Louis Trintignant.
First Love (1970; German/Swiss). . . . . Sinaida
The Garden of the Finzi-Continis (1971; Italian/German)
. . . . Micol
• 1:12—Breasts, while sitting on a bed after turning a light on so the guy standing outside can see her.
Without Apparent Motive (1972; French) . . . . . . Sandra Forest
The Makintosh Man (1973; British) . . . . Mrs. Smith
Story of a Love Story (1973; French/Italian) . . . . . . Nathalie
a.k.a. Impossible Object
0:13—Briefly in wet dress in the surf.
• 0:21—Breasts, after taking off nightgown in bathroom while talking to Georges.
• 0:26—Breasts in open blouse, with Georges in his office.
• 1:11—Breasts, while undressing in front of Alan Bates.
• 1:13—Brief left breast, while turning over in bed.
•• 1:23—Breasts while pregnant and brushing her hair.
• 1:24—Brief breasts, while lying on sofa in Bates' lap.
• 1:27—Partial left breast while breast feeding a baby.
• 1:28—Breasts while making love in bed with Bates.
• 1:31—Brief left breast, when moving her hair away to breast feed her baby.
Conversation Piece (1974; Italian/French) . . . . Mother
Steppenwolf (1974) . . . . Hermine
• 1:40—Brief lower frontal nudity, while sleeping with a guy.
• 1:41—Very brief left breast, waking up and rolling over to hug Max Von Sydow.
1900 (1976; Italian) . . . . .Ada
(NC-17 version reviewed.)
••• 2:30—Left breast, then breasts in hay with Robert De Niro. Long shot of full frontal nudity while lying in the hay.
••• 2:48—(0:08 into tape 2.) Nude under thin fabric dancing with De Niro for photographer.
Beyond Good and Evil (1977; Italian/German/French)
. . . . Lou-Andreas-Salome
Damnation Alley (1977) . . . . Janice
The Inheritance (1978; Italian). .Irene
•• 0:18—Full frontal nudity getting undressed and lying on the bed with her new husband.
••• 0:37—Full frontal nudity lying in bed with her lover.
• 1:19—Very brief right breast, while undoing top for Anthony Quinn.
••• 1:22—Left breast, lying in bed. Full frontal nudity jumping out of bed after realizing that Quinn is dead.
Cabo Blanco (1982) . . . . Marie Claire Allesandri
• 1:27—Buns, swimming in pool. Long shot.
Made for Cable Movies:
Nobody's Children (1994; USA). . . . . Stephanie Vaugier
Made for TV Movies:
Voyage of Terror: The Achillie Largo Affair (1990) . . . . .n.a.

Sanders, Brandy

See: Ledford, Brandy.

Sandifer, Elizabeth

a.k.a. Erika West.
Films:
Animal Instincts 2 (1993) . . . . Catherine
••• 0:23—In white bra and panties, then breasts and brief buns, while making love with Steve in bed.
• 1:16—Brief breasts, while undressing in her room when Steve sees her from outside. Long shot.

••• 1:18—Breasts, while in bedroom with Steve, then making love on bed.

Sexual Outlaws (1993). . . . . Lisa Bauer

• 0:39—Partial buns in G-string in bedroom.

••• 0:41—Breasts, after taking off bra and posing for John for ad. Also putting on stockings.

• 0:46—Upper half of breasts while in bathtub.

••• 0:47—In black lingerie, then breasts, while posing for photos.

•• 1:25—Breasts while making love with Mitch Gaylord.

Illicit Dreams (1994) . . . . Vicky

Indecent Behavior II (1994) . . . . Shoshona Reed

(Unrated version reviewed.)

Seduce Me: Pamela Principle 2 (1994) . . . . Jill

• 1:13—Buns and breasts, while walking to spa, then in spa. Medium long shot.

Forbidden Games (1995) . . . . Rachel

(Unrated version reviewed.)

Sandlund, Debra

Films:

Tough Guys Don't Dance (1987) . . . . Patty Lareine

•• 1:24—Breasts ripping her blouse off to kiss the policeman after they have killed and buried another woman.

• 1:24—Very brief left breast, twice, in bed with Ryan O'Neal. Long shot.

Murder by Numbers (1990) . . . . Leslie

Gladiator (1992) . . . . Charlene

TV:

Full House (1990) . . . . Cindy

Sandrelli, Stefania

Films:

Seduced and Abandoned (1964; Italian) . . . . . Agnese Ascalone

The Conformist (1970; Italian/French) . . . . Giulia

• 0:41—Right breast, while in train with Jean-Louis Trintignant.

• 1:07—Very brief, upper half of buns, while turning around.

1900 (1976; Italian) . . . . Anita Foschi

(NC-17 version reviewed.)

The Key (1985; Italian) . . . . Teresa Rolfe

a.k.a. La Chiave

(Nude a lot. Only the best are listed.)

••• 0:31—Nude when Nino examines her while she's passed out. Long scene.

•• 0:42—Full frontal nudity in bathtub while Nino peeks in over the door.

•• 1:04—In lingerie, then breasts and buns, undressing sexily in front of Nino.

•• 1:16—Left breast, sticking out of nightgown so Nino can suck on it.

••• 1:19—Breasts and buns making love in bed with Laszlo.

•• 1:21—Breasts and buns getting up and cleaning herself.

•• 1:28—Breasts sitting in bed talking to Nino.

••• 1:30—Nude, getting on top of Nino in bed.

The Family (1987; Italian/French) . . . . Beatrice

The Sleazy Uncle (1991; Italian). . . . . Isabella

Jamón, Jamón (1992; Spanish) . . . . Conchita

Of Love and Shadows (1995) . . . . Beatriz

Stealing Beauty (1996) . . . . Noemi

Sands, Peggy

See: McIntaggart, Peggy.

Santana, Susie

Made for Cable TV:

Erotic Confessions: Model Situation (1996; Cinemax) . . . . Art Student

Video Tapes:

The Perfect Body Contest (1987). . . . . Susie Santana

••• 0:38—In black garter belt, stockings, panties and bra. Brief buns and breasts.

• 0:50—Breasts on stage with the other contestants.

Santangelo, Melody

Films:

Death Wish II (1982) . . . . Tourist's Wife

• 0:37—Breasts, while being held as a shield by a gang member in parking garage.

Newsies (1992) . . . . Nun

Sara, Mia

Wife of actor Jason Connery.

Films:

Ferris Bueller's Day Off (1986) . . . . Slone Peterson

Legend (1986). Lili

Apprentice to Murder (1987) . . . . Alice

• 0:29—Left side view breasts making love with Chad Lowe.

Queenie (1987). . . . . Queenie Kelly/Dawn Avalon

Shadows in the Storm (1988) . . . . Melanie

Any Man's Death (1989) . . . . Gerlind

• 0:50—Brief right nipple when John Savage undoes her top. Don't see her face.

Daughters of Darkness (1989) . . . . Cathy Thatcher

a.k.a. Bloodlines

A Climate for Killing (1990) . . . . Elise Shipp

By the Sword (1991) . . . . Clavelli

Stranger Among Us (1992) . . . . Leah

a.k.a. Close to Eden

Caroline at Midnight (1993). . . . . Victoria

••• 0:24—Breasts, while making love with Jack.

•• 0:30—Left breast, in open robe in bedroom with Tim Daly.

••• 0:51—Breasts, while making love on top and under Jack in bed. Nice!

Timecop (1994). . . . . Melissa

•• 0:10—Brief breasts, while making love in bed with Jean-Claude Van Damme.

Black Day Blue Night (1995). . . . . Hallie Schrag

••• 0:48—In lingerie, then nude, after undressing outside in desert and going for a swim at night.

••• 0:50—Breasts, when standing up and kissing Gil Bellows then making love. Great!

•• 1:01—Buns and right breast, while lying next to the water, talking with Bellows.

• 1:03—Partial buns, when a scorpion starts crawling on the small of her back.

•• 1:19—Breasts, while lying in bed with Bellows.

• 1:23—Breasts, while in the shower. Seen through plastic shower curtain.

The Maddening (1995) . . . . Cassie Osborne

• 0:42—Partial left breast, twice, while sitting in bathtub, talking with Angie Dickinson.

• 0:47—Very, very brief side view of left breast, while struggling on the floor with Burt Reynolds when he rips her dress open.

Undertow (1995) . . . . Willie Yates

••• 0:51—Breasts, while taking a shower, then making out with Lou Diamond Phillips.

The Pompatus of Love (1996) . . . . Cynthia

Made for Cable Movies:

Blindsided (1993; USA). . . . . Chandler Strange

• 0:16—Very brief right breast while making love under Jeff Fahey.

The Set-Up (1995; Showtime). . . . . Gina Sands

• 0:23—Brief breasts, several times, while making love in bed with Billy Zane.

• 1:10—Breasts, while making love in office with James Russo. Quick cuts.

Made for Cable TV:

Strangers: Stone Heart (1996; HBO) . . . . Ginny

•• 0:15—Right breast, while making love with Mila.

Miniseries:

Till We Meet Again (1989). . . . . Delphine

Made for TV Movies:

Call of the Wild (1993) . . . . Jessie Gosselin

20,000 Leagues Under the Sea (1997) . . . . Mara

*Sarandon, Susan **

Significant Other of actor Tim Robbins.

Ex-wife of actor Chris Sarandon.

Films:

Joe (1970) . . . . Melissa Compton

• 0:02—Breasts and very brief lower frontal nudity taking off clothes and getting into bathtub with Frank.

Lady Liberty (1972; Italian/French) . . . . Sally

The Front Page (1974) . . . . Peggy

The Great Waldo Pepper (1975) . . . . Mary Beth

The Rocky Horror Picture Show (1975; British) . . . . Janet Weiss

The Great Smokey Roadblock (1976) . . . . Ginny

Other Side of Midnight (1977) . . . . Catherine Douglas

• 1:10—Breasts in bedroom with John Beck. Long shot, then right breast while lying in bed.

King of the Gypsies (1978) . . . . Rose

• 0:49—Brief right breast during fight with Judd Hirsch.

Pretty Baby (1978). . . . . Hattie

• 0:12—Feeding a baby with her left breast, while sitting by the window in the kitchen.

• 0:24—Brief side view, taking a bath.

••• 0:39—Breasts on the couch when Keith Carradine photographs her.

Something Short of Paradise (1979) . . . . Madeleine Ross

Loving Couples (1980) . . . . Stephanie

Atlantic City (1981; French/Canadian). . . . . Sally

•• 0:50—Left breast cleaning herself with lemon juice while Burt Lancaster watches through window.

The Tempest (1982). . . . . Aretha

• 1:57—Brief right, then left breasts in open T-shirt saving someone in the water.

The Hunger (1983). . . . . Sarah Roberts

••• 0:59—In a wine stained white T-shirt, then breasts during love scene with Catherine Deneuve.

The Buddy System (1984). . . . . Emily

Compromising Positions (1985) . . . . Judith Singer

The Witches of Eastwick (1987). . . . . Jane Spofford

Bull Durham (1988) . . . . Annie Savoy

• 1:37—Very brief right breast, when turning over in the bathtub under Kevin Costner.

• 1:39—Brief right breast peeking out from under her dress after crawling on the kitchen floor to get a match.

The January Man (1988) . . . . Christine Starkey

Sweet Hearts Dance (1988) . . . . Sandra Boon

• 1:25—Very, very brief left breast, then very brief right breast, under white bathrobe arguing with Don Johnson in the bathroom.

White Palace (1990). . . . . Nora Baker

••• 0:28—Breasts on top of James Spader. Great shots of right breast.

• 0:38—Breasts on bed with Spader.

Thelma and Louise (1991). . . . . Louise

Bob Roberts (1992; U.S./British) . . . . Tawna Titan

Light Sleeper (1992) . . . . .Ann

The Player (1992) . . . . Cameo

Lorenzo's Oil (1993) . . . . Michaela Odone

The Client (1994) . . . . Reggie Love

Little Women (1994) . . . . Marmee March

Dead Man Walking (1995) . . . . .Sister Helen Prejean

(Academy Award for Best Actress.)

Twilight (1998) . . . . Catherine Ames

Made for Cable Movies:

Mussolini and I (1985; HBO) . . . . Edda Ciano

The Celluloid Closet (1996; HBO) . . . . Sarah Roberts

• 1:24—Breasts in clips from *The Hunger.*

Made for TV Movies:

Women of Valor (1986) . . . . Colonel Margaret Ann Jessup

TV:

Search for Tomorrow. . . . . Sarah

A World Apart . . . . Patrice Kahlman

Sarelle, Leilani

a.k.a. Leilani Ferrer.

Wife of actor Miguel Ferrer.

Films:

Neon Maniacs (1985) . . . . Natalie

Shag (1989) . . . . Suette

Days of Thunder (1990) . . . . . . Female Highway Patrol Officer

Little Sister (1991). . . . . Catherine

Till Death Do Us Part (1991) . . . . Gloria

Basic Instinct (1992) . . . . Roxy

(Unrated Director's cut reviewed.)

The Harvest (1992). . . . . Natalie Caldwell

•• 1:13—Side view of buns, then breasts, while in car with Miguel Ferrer. Don't see her face very well.

••• 1:19—Full frontal nudity, while making love with Ferrer in bed.

Breach of Trust (1995). . . . . .Madeline

•• 0:58—Breasts, while making love with Michael Biehn.

Made for Cable Movies:

Barbarians at the Gate (1993; HBO) . . . . . . Laurie Johnson

• 0:59—Side view of right breast, twice, while taking off bra and putting on T-shirt.

Sketch Artist II: Hands That See (1994; Showtime) . . . . Vicki Rosenthal

Sarrasin, Donna

Films:

Dr. Jekyll and Ms. Hyde (1995) . . . . .Mintz's Secretary

Witchboard: The Possession (1995) . . . . Lisa

• 1:03—Brief breasts in white panties, when Brian comes to get her. Brief breasts, while crawling across the bed.

•• 1:04—Right breast, then breasts in bathroom, just before Brian kills her with broken glass.

Marked Man (1996; Canadian) . . . . Mercedes Lady

Sci-Fighters (1996; Canadian). . . . . .Tricia

• 0:45—Brief breasts, while convulsing on laboratory table. Covered with unappealing makeup on her body.

• 0:46—Brief left breast, after dying on the table.

Sassaman, Nicole

Films:

Bikini Summer (1991) . . . . .Band Member

Desert Passion (1992) . . . . .Linda
•• 0:34—Breasts in spa with Maggie. In the background while Maggie makes love with Mr. Sasso.
• 0:37—Brief left breast and buns in the spa. Breasts in spa in the background.
••• 0:55—Nude, getting out of the pool.
Knockouts (1992) . . . . Hallie
Sorority House Party (1992). . . . . Topless Sorority Girl
•• 0:39—Breasts, opening Alex's bedroom door to ask for a bra.
Hold Me, Thrill Me, Kiss Me (1993). . . . . Girl on a Leash
(Unrated version reviewed.)
Witchcraft V: Dance with the Devil (1993) . . . . Marta
• 0:03—Brief breasts in open bra, just before the customer gets killed.
••• 0:30—Breasts in bed, while making love with Bill while Keli is asleep.
• 0:51—Breasts under sheer black blouse.
••• 0:55—Breasts with Bill at the top of the stairs.
Money to Burn (1994). . . . . .Rich Girl #1

Sassoon, Catya *

Daughter of hair guy Vidal Sassoon and actress Beverly Adams.
Films:
Tuff Turf (1984). . . . . Feather
Dance with Death (1991) . . . . Jodie
••• 0:29—Breasts and buns in G-string, while dancing on stage.
••• 0:37—Breasts and buns, dancing on stage. Her body is painted gold.
••• 0:38—More breasts and buns.
Secret Games (1991) . . . . Sandra
(Unrated version reviewed.)
••• 0:21—Breasts during modeling session with the other girls. (She's the only brunette.)
••• 0:26—Breasts, making love in bed with Emil.
•• 0:34—Breasts in yellow bikini bottoms, sunbathing with the other girls.
••• 0:40—Breasts, getting out of the swimming pool and lying on lounge chair.
Angel Fist (1992) . . . . Katara/Kat Lang
• 0:19—Brief breasts, dropping towel and putting on shirt in front of Alcatraz.
•• 0:31—Right breast, while in the shower.
••• 0:32—Breasts in red panties, doing martial arts on a couple of bad guys in her apartment.
••• 0:35—Full frontal nudity in the showers.
••• 0:49—Breasts, while making love on bed with Alcatraz. Long scene.
Bloodfist IV: Die Trying (1992). . . . . Lisa
Bloodfist VI: Ground Zero (1994) . . . . Teri
• 0:02—Breasts in bathroom and bedroom with Steve Garvery.
Made for Cable Movies:
The Alien Within (1995; Showtime) . . . . .Woman on TV
• 0:18—Breasts, during fight on TV that Wyatt is watching. The scenes are from *Angel Fist*.
Video Tapes:
Inside Out 4 (1992) . . . . .Pauline/Natalie Would
(Unrated version reviewed.)
••• 0:08—Breasts in bed with Ted, then getting out and getting dressed.

Satana, Tura *

Films:
Irma La Douce (1963) . . . . Suzette Wong
Who's Been Sleeping in My Bed (1963) . . . Uncredited Stripper
Faster Pussycat, Kill! Kill! (1966). . . . . .Varla
Doll Squad (1973). . . . . Lavelle Sumara
• 0:23—Buns in outfit on stage in club. Breasts, but wearing pasties.
• 0:24—Breasts wearing pasties, while changing clothes in dressing room.

• *Saunders, Jennifer*

Wife of actor Adrian Edmondson.
Films:
The Supergrass (1985; British) . . . . Lesley
•• 0:44—In white bra and black panties, then side of right breast when changing into her pajamas in hotel room.
Muppet Treasure Island (1996) . . . . Mrs. Bluverdige
Spice World (1997; British) . . . . Fashionable Woman
Made for TV Movies:
Absolutely Fabulous: The Last Shout (1996; British)
. . . . Edina Monsoon
TV:
Absolutely Fabulous (1992-96; British). . . . . . . Edina Monsoon

Saunders, Loni *

Adult film actress.
Films:
Up 'n' Coming (1987). . . . . Dixanne
(R-rated version reviewed, X-rated version available.)
• 0:19—Breasts, while kissing a guy on the bus.

Saunders, Pamela *

Video Tapes:
Playboy Video Calendar 1987 (1986) . . . . .Playmate
Playboy Video Magazine, Volume 11 (1986) . . . .Playmate
••• 0:52—Nude, undressing after party, in still photos and at the beach.
Playmates at Play (1990). .Bareback

Saura, Marina

Films:
Flesh + Blood (1985). . . . . Polly
• 0:59—Brief left breast during feast in the castle.
• 1:09—Breasts on balcony of the castle with everybody during the day.
Crystal Heart (1987) . . . . Justine
The Monk (1990; British/Spanish) . . . . Jacinta

Savage, Tracy

Used to be a reporter for WHIO in Dayton, Ohio. Now a reporter for KNBC in Los Angeles, California.
Films:
The Devil & Max Devlin (1981) . . . . .Pammy
Friday the 13th, Part III (1982) . . . . Debbie
• 0:59—Brief breasts, while getting back into the shower after shutting the door.
• 1:00—Very brief right breast, while getting towel.
Made for TV Movies:
Hurricane (1974). . . . . Liz Damon
Friendly Persuasion (1975). . . . . .Mattie Birdwell
The Legend of Lizzie Borden (1975). . . . . Young Lizzie
TV:
Little House on the Prairie (1974-76) . . . . Christy

Savannah

Adult film actress.

a.k.a. Shannon Wilsey.

Films:

The Invisible Maniac (1990) . . . . Vicky
- • 0:21—Buns and very, very brief side of left breast in the shower with the other girls.
- • 0:33—Right breast covered with bubbles.
- ••• 0:43—In bra, then breasts and lots of buns in locker room with the other girls.
- •• 0:44—Buns and left breast in the shower with the other girls.
- ••• 1:04—Undressing in locker room in white bra and panties, then breasts. More breasts taking a shower and getting electrocuted.

Sorority House Massacre 2 (1990) . . . . Satana
- •• 0:43—Breasts and buns in G-string, dancing in club.

Camp Fear (1991) . . . . n.a.

a.k.a. Millenium Countdown

Legal Tender (1991) . . . . Mal's Girl
- •• 0:24—Breasts in bubble bath with brunette girl and Morton Downey Jr.
- •• 0:31—Breasts and buns in G-string bringing phone to Downey.

Video Tapes:

The Art of Desire (1992) . . . . n.a.

• Savenkoff, Elizabeth Carol

Films:

Someone to Die For (1995) . . . . Sandra Davis

Made for Cable Movies:

Robin of Locksley (1995; Showtime) . . . . Janet McAllister

Tricks (1997) . . . . Daria
- •• 0:49—Breasts, during strip tease dance in front of Adam during party.

Savoy, Teresa Ann *

Films:

La Bambina (1976; Italian) . . . . Clotilde

Caligula (1980) . . . . Druscilla

(X-rated, 147 minute version.)
- •• 0:01—Nude, running around in the forest with Malcolm McDowell.
- • 0:05—Buns, rolling in bed with McDowell. Very brief breasts getting out of bed.
- • 0:26—Left breast several times in bed.
- • 0:46—Brief right breast in bed with McDowell again.
- • 1:15—Left breast with McDowell and Helen Mirren.
- • 1:22—Very brief left breast getting up in open dress.
- •• 1:45—Full frontal nudity, then buns when dead and McDowell tries to revive her.

Video Tapes:

Penthouse: On the Wild Side (1988) . . . . Druscilla
- • 0:51—Breasts in scenes from *Caligula.*

Sawyer-Young, Kathi

Films:

Pink Motel (1982) . . . . Lola
- • 0:36—Brief breasts, after opening her bra and falling onto bed with Mark.
- ••• 0:41—Breasts and buns in panties, trying to coax Mark out of the bathroom. Long scene.
- •• 1:13—Breasts, while lying in bed with Mark.

Talking Walls (1982) . . . . n.a.

Life on the Edge (1992) . . . . Tovah Torrence

The Unborn II (1993) . . . . Mrs. Sanchez

Made for Cable TV:

Hot Line: Fountain of Youth (1994; Cinemax) . . . . Claudia

(Available on video tape in *Hot Line.*)

Saxton, Lisa *

Films:

Night Eyes 2 (1991) . . . . Car Rental Girl
- ••• 0:05—Breasts and buns, making love in bed with Jesse.
- • 0:09—Buns, on TV when video tape is played back.

Ring of Fire (1991) . . . . Linda
- •• 0:10—Breasts and buns in several times, making love with Brad. Intercut with martial arts fight.
- •• 0:18—Brief buns, in G-string swimsuit, getting into spa with Brad. Breasts in spa.
- ••• 0:22—Breasts and buns in bathroom, while talking to Maria Ford.

Twogether (1992) . . . . Naked Lady in Bed

(Unrated version reviewed.)
- • 0:01—Brief buns, while turning over in bed next to Nick Cassavetes.

Made for Cable TV:

Dream On: The Second Greatest Story Ever Told (1991; HBO) . . . . Coed #2
- •• 0:08—(She's the brunette one.) Breasts taking off her purple sweater in bedroom set with Coed #1 (redhead). More breasts opening the closet door and falling back onto the bed.
- • 0:34—Brief breasts (on the right) with swamp creature and Coed #1 (on the left) during Martin's daydream.

Video Tapes:

Bikini Blitz (1990) . . . . Model

Intimate Workout For Lovers (1992) . . . . Intimate Harmony
- ••• 0:39—Nude, in dance studio and in the showers. Excellent!

Playboy's 101 Ways to Excite Your Lover (1992) . . . . Cast Member

Playboy's Fast Women (1997) . . . . Cast

Scacchi, Greta *

Films:

Heat and Dust (1982) . . . . Olivia Rivers
- •• 1:25—Buns, lying in bed under a mosquito net with Douglas, then breasts rolling over.

Burke and Wills (1985; Australian) . . . . Julia Matthews

The Coca-Cola Kid (1985; Australian) . . . . Terri
- ••• 0:49—Nude, while taking a shower with her daughter.
- •• 1:20—Brief breasts, while wearing a Santa Claus outfit, then brief breasts and brief buns in bed with Eric Roberts.
- • 1:23—Brief buns and breasts, while in bed with Roberts.
- • 1:24—Brief breasts and very brief full frontal nudity (medium long shot), then brief buns and breasts when getting dressed, after getting out of bed.

The Ebony Tower (1985) . . . . Mouse
- • 0:37—Full frontal nudity, undressing and going skinny dipping in lake. Long shot.
- • 0:41—Brief lower half of left breast, while lying down next to Toyah Wilcox.
- • 0:43—Brief nude walking into the lake.

Good Morning, Babylon (1987; Italian/French) . . . . Edna
- •• 1:05—Breasts in the woods making love with Vincent Spano.

A Man in Love (1987) . . . . Jane Steiner
- ••• 0:31—Breasts with Peter Coyote.
- •• 1:04—Buns and left breast in bed with Coyote.
- • 1:10—Brief side view breasts, when putting black dress on.
- • 1:24—Brief breasts in bed.

White Mischief (1988). . . . . Diana Broughton
- •• 0:16—Breasts taking a bath while an old man watches through a peephole in the wall.
- •• 0:24—Brief breasts in bedroom with her husband.
- •• 0:29—Brief breasts taking off bathing suit top in the ocean in front of Charles Dance.
- •• 0:30—Breasts while lying in bed, then talking to Dance.
- •• 0:49—Breasts while sitting in bed and talking to Dance.

Presumed Innocent (1990) . . . . Carolyn Polhemus
- • 0:46—Left breast, while making love on desk with Harrison Ford.
- • 0:53—Buns, lying in bed on top of Ford.

Fires Within (1991) . . . . Isabel
- • 0:18—Upper half of buns, very brief breasts in bed.
- • 0:38—Very brief breasts in bed.

Shattered (1991) . . . . Judith Merrick
- •• 0:14—Breasts, turning over in bed.
- • 0:16—Breasts in a strip of B&W photos that Tom Berenger looks at.
- • 0:36—Breasts in B&W photos in Bob Hoskins' office. Brief breasts in flashback.
- •• 1:24—Breasts during love-making flashback.

The Player (1992) . . . . June Gudmundsdottir

Turtle Beach (1992; Australian). . . . . Judith
a.k.a. The Killing Beach
- • 0:44—Upper half of buns and almost breasts, making love.

The Browning Version (1994) . . . . Laura Crocker-Harris
Country Life (1995; Australian) . . . . Deborah Voysey
Jefferson in Paris (1995). Maria Cosway
Emma (1996; British/U.S.). . . . . Mrs. Weston

Made for Cable Movies:
Rasputin (1996; HBO) . . . . Alexandra

Made for TV Movies:
The Odyssey (1997) . . . . Penelope

Scarabelli, Michele

Films:
Covergirl (1982; Canadian) . . . . Snow Queen
The Hotel New Hampshire (1984). . . . . . . Chip Dove Girlfriend

Perfect Timing (1984) . . . . Charlotte
- •• 1:11—Brief buns, then breasts in bed with Harry.
- • 1:18—Breasts in bed with Harry during the music video.

SnakeEater II: The Drug Buster (1990). . . . . Dr. Pierce
Deadbolt (1992) . . . . Theresa Levez
I Don't Buy Kisses Anymore (1992) . . . . Connie Klinger
The Wrong Woman (1995) . . . . Christine Henley

Made for Cable Movies:
Age-Old Friends (1989; HBO) . . . . Nurse Wilson

Made for Cable TV:
The Hitchhiker: Face to Face (1984; HBO). . . . . Dr. Ensman
(Available on *The Hitchhiker, Volume 4.*)
- ••• 0:07—Breasts in Robert Vaughn's office.

Made for TV Movies:
Alien Nation: Dark Horizon (1994) . . . . Susan
Alien Nation: The Udara Legacy (1997). . . . . Susan

TV:
Airwolf (1987-88) . . . . Jo Santini
Alien Nation (1989-91) . . . . Susan Francisco

• *Scelfo, Leonora*

Films:
Power 98 (1996). . . . . Cynthia Berkley
- • 0:47—Buns in panties and breasts, while making love with Jason Gedrick.

Scream (1996) . . . . Cheerleader in Bathroom

Schanz, Heidi

Films:
Seven (1995). . . . . Beautiful Woman (Sin of Pride)
Virtuosity (1995) . . . . Sheila 3.2

Underworld (1996). . . . . Simone/Joyce Alt
- •• 0:01—In red lingerie, then breasts, while modeling lingerie during show.

Kiss the Girls (1997). . . . . Megan Murphy
The Truman Show (1998) . . . . Vivien

Made for Cable Movies:
Body Language (1995; HBO) . . . . Dora Circe
- • 0:13—Brief breasts in B&W photos that Tom Berenger looks at.
- • 0:15—Brief breasts, while putting on dress when seen by Berenger.
- •• 0:21—Breasts, while kissing Berenger in the kitchen.
- •• 0:22—Breasts and buns, while making love on bed with Berenger, then when smoking in the kitchen.
- ••• 0:23—Nude, while walking back to bed and talking with Berenger in bed.
- •• 0:29—Breasts in push-up bra and buns in lingerie while doing strip routine on stage in club.
- •• 0:31—Breasts and buns in G-string, while kidding Berenger in dressing room.
- • 1:08—Breasts in push-up bra, while dancing on stage.

Schick, Stephanie

See: Peaks, Pandora.

• *Schieler, Nikki* *

Wife of actor Ian Ziering.

Video Tapes:
Playboy's Hot Wheels & High Heels Biker Babes (1997)
. . . . Pool Hall
- ••• 0:00—Nude, while in pool hall.

• *Schild, Tonja*

Video Tapes:
Playboy's Girls of Radio: Talk, Rock and Shock (1995)
. . . . Herself
- ••• 0:34—In black lingerie, then nude.

Hot Body Competition: Bikinis & Bikes Contest (1996)
. . . . Felicia
- ••• 0:04—Breasts and buns, while dancing on stage.

Schmidtmer, Christiane

Films:
Fanny Hill: Memoirs of a Woman of Pleasure (1964) . . . . Fiona
The Big Doll House (1971). . . . . Miss Dietrich

The Specialist (1975) . . . . Nude Model
- ••• 0:12—Breasts, while posing for artist, then buns when she gets up to leave.

Schneider, Maria *

Films:
Last Tango In Paris (1972). . . . . Jeanne
(X-rated, letterbox version.)
- • 0:15—Lower frontal nudity and very brief buns, rolling on the floor.
- • 0:44—Breasts in jeans, walking around the apartment.
- •• 0:53—Left breast, while lying down, then walking to Marlon Brando, then breasts.
- ••• 0:55—Breasts, kneeling while talking to Brando.
- • 0:56—Side of left breast.
- • 0:57—Breasts, rolling off the bed, onto the floor.
- •• 1:01—Right breast, in bathroom. Breasts in mirror.

• 1:03—Brief breasts in bathroom with Brando while she puts on make-up.
••• 1:04—Nude, in bathroom with Brando, then sitting on counter.
• 1:27—Brief lower frontal nudity, pulling up her dress in elevator.
• 1:30—Breasts in bathtub with Brando.
••• 1:32—Nude, standing up in bathtub while Brando washes her. More breasts, getting out. Long scene.
The Passenger (1975; Italian)....................... Girl
The Raw Edge (1975; Italian/German/French)........ Michele
a.k.a. La Baby Sitter
Memoirs of a French Whore (1979) .... Maloup
A Woman Called Eva (1979).................... Liliane
a.k.a. A Woman Like Eve
Mamma Dracula (1980; Belgian/French)....... Nancy Hawaii
Savage Nights (1992; French)...................... Noria
a.k.a. Les Nuits Fauves
Jane Eyre (1996) .... n.a.

Schneider, Romy *

Films:
Vengeance... One by One......................... n.a.
• 0:28—Very brief left breast when a soldier rips her bra open during struggle.
Boccaccio 70 (1962; Italian) .... "The Job" Segment
What's New, Pussycat? (1965; U.S./French)..... Carole Werner
The Infernal Trio (1974; French) .... Philomene Schmidt
• 0:32—Brief side of left breast, while standing in front of open window. Brief breasts, during struggle with a guy.
Dirty Hands (1975; French) .... Julie
• 0:01—Buns and right breast getting a tan, lying on the grass after a man's kite lands on her.
•• 0:09—Side view of right breast, while lying in bed with a man, then breasts.
• 1:04—Breasts lying on floor, then brief breasts sitting up and looking at something on the table.
Mado (1976; French) .... Helene
Bloodline (1979)....................... Helene Martin

Schoelen, Jill

Films:
D.C. Cab (1983) .... Claudette
Hot Moves (1984)............................ Julie Ann
That Was Then... This Is Now (1985).........Angela Shepard
Thunder Alley (1985)........................... Beth
• 0:55—Very, very brief left breast and side view of buns, when Richie sits up while she's lying on her stomach on rocks.
The Stepfather (1987)................. Stephanie Maine
•• 1:16—Buns and brief side of right breast, while getting into the shower. Breasts in the shower.
Curse II: The Bite (1988) .... Lisa Snipes
Cutting Class (1988) .... Paula Carson
• 1:00—Very, very brief breasts in mirror when Gary helps put her robe on. (Out of focus.)
Phantom of the Opera (1989)................... Christine
Operation Lookout (1991) .... Julie Converse
Popcorn (1991)................................. Maggie
Rich Girl (1991)............................... Courtney
Adventures in Spying (1992)................ Julie Converse
There Goes My Baby (1994) .... Babette
Made for Cable Movies:
When a Stranger Calls Back (1993) .... Julia
• 1:21—Breasts in Polaroid photos, supposedly of her, but it could be anybody.

Made for TV Movies:
Chiller (1985) .... Stacey
Shattered Spirits (1986)......................... Allison
Billionaire Boys Club (1987)....................... n.a.

Schofield, Annabel

Films:
Blood Tide (1982) .... Vicki
Dragonard (1988)............................. Honore
• 0:26—Brief side view of left breast, brief breasts lying down, then left breast again in stable with Abdee.
Solar Crisis (1992) .... Alex Noffe
•• 0:34—Breasts in the shower.
•• 0:35—Breasts, sitting in chair, getting her mind probed.
•• 0:54—Brief breasts during recollection of shower scene. Slightly distorted and out of focus.
Clifford (1994) .... Woman at Party
Body Armor (1996) .... Marisa
Exit in Red (1996) .... Ally Mercer
Midnight Blue (1996)................. Martine/Georgina
••• 0:11—In bra and panties, then breasts, while making love in hotel room with Chapa.
• 0:15—Breasts, when sitting up in bed and getting out to look at painting.
• 0:46—Brief breasts and buns, in bed during flashbacks.
• 0:55—In bra and panties, then brief right breast, when undressing inside when Chapa watches from outside.
•• 1:11—Breasts, while making love with Chapa in bed.
TV:
Dallas (1988)............................... Laurel Ellis

• Schrader, Maria

Films:
Nobody Loves Me (1994; German/French)...... Fanny Fink
a.k.a. Keiner Liebt Mich
• 1:20—Breasts, while bathing with Orfeo in bathtub.
Flirt (1995) .... Woman at Phone Booth

Schreiner, Alexis

Films:
Scarred (1983) .... Movie Girl
• 0:32—Breasts, while dancing during filming of a movie. (She's the auburn hair girl wearing a gold necklace.)
Hollywood Hot Tubs (1984) .... Soccer Girl

Schubert, Karin

Has done a lot of adult films in Europe.
Films:
Companeros (1971) .... Zaira
Bluebeard (1972) .... Greta
• 1:43—Brief breasts, spinning around, unwrapping herself from a red towel for Richard Burton.
Till Marriage Do Us Part (1974; Italian) .... Evelyn
Black Emanuelle (1976).................. Anne Danielli
• 0:06—Brief breasts adjusting a guy's tie.
••• 0:14—Breasts making love in gas station with the gas station attendant.
••• 0:37—Nude, running in the jungle while Laura Gemser takes pictures of her.
• 0:40—Breasts, kissing Gemser.
• 0:44—Right breast, making love with Johnny in bed.
Emanuelle Around the World (1977; Italian) .... n.a.
Black Venus (1983)............................ Marie
•• 0:38—Nude in bed with Venus, making love.

Christina (1984; U.S./French) . . . . Rosa
(Never released on video tape. Is shown occasionally on cable television.)
Panther Squad (1986; French/Belgian) . . . . Barbara

Schumacher, Wendy

a.k.a. Alexander Keith.
Films:
Animal Instincts: The Seductress (1995) . . . . Joanna Coles
(Unrated version reviewed.)
•• 0:00—Breasts, while dancing with two knives during opening credits. B&W.
•• 0:04—Breasts, while making love on pool table in a bar with Orlando in front of a group of people.
• 0:09—Brief breasts on pool table.
•• 0:12—Breasts, after taking off top of one piece swimsuit and oiling herself up.
•• 0:14—Breasts and buns, while taking a shower.
• 0:20—Breasts and upper part of lower frontal nudity. B&W.
••• 0:27—Full frontal nudity, after taking off her dress in front of Savage, then making love with him while she's blindfolded. Long scene.
• 0:35—Buns in T-back, while pulling up her dress when dancing outside in a garden nursery.
• 0:39—Brief side view of right breast, twice. B&W.
••• 0:40—Breasts, after opening her robe at table and caressing herself.
•• 0:45—In black bra, buns in T-back, then breasts, while dancing in recording studio in front of Trick Willy.
••• 0:48—In black bra, then nude, when making love with Willy while "blind" Savage plays the piano.
• 0:50—Full frontal nudity, while acting like a puppet. B&W.
• 0:51—Full frontal nudity. B&W.
••• 0:54—In green bra and buns in T-back, then breasts, while in kitchen with Shane Hooligan.
••• 1:04—In bra and panties, then full frontal nudity, undressing while Savage caresses Lolly Pop. Nude getting into bathtub with her.
• 1:23—Breasts, pulling her dress top open for Chill.
••• 1:24—Breasts and buns, while making out with Chill's bodyguard.
•• 1:27—Nude, while Chill writes stuff on her body.
•• 1:30—Nude after Savage throws a knife at Chill.
Diary of a Serial Killer (1996) . . . . Boookstore Cashier
Fugitive Rage (1996) . . . . Tara McCormick
•• 0:11—Breasts, during search.
••• 1:03—Nude, while taking a shower with James, then making love on bed with him.
Scorned 2 (1996) . . . . Cynthia Meadows

Schygulla, Hanna

Films:
Beware of a Holy Whore (1971; German) . . . . Woman
a.k.a. Warnung Vo Einer Heiligen Nutte
• 1:15—Breasts, when sitting on bed, buns, while walking to the bathroom. Very brief right breast, while leaning out of the bathroom to talk.
The Bitter Tears of Petra von Kant (1972; German)
. . . . Karin Thimm
The Marriage of Maria Braun (1979; German)
. . . . Maria Braun
• 0:22—Brief upper half of right breast, when peeking from behind divider in doctor's office.
• 0:33—Buns, while lying in bed with her lover.
• 0:34—Brief buns and left breast, while standing up in doctor's office. Subtitles get in the way.
•• 1:15—Buns, while dropping sheet in room with her boss.
Circle of Deceit (1982; French/German) . . . . . . Arianna Nassar
Berlin Alexanderplatz (1983; West German). . . . . Eva
La Nuit de Varennes (1983; French/Italian)
. . . . Countess Sophie de la Borde
A Love in Germany (1984; French/German). . . . . Pauline Kropp
The Delta Force (1986) . . . . Ingrid
Casanova (1987) . . . . Casanova's Mother
Forever Lulu (1987) . . . . Elaine
• 1:03—Brief breasts in and getting out of bubble bath.
Dead Again (1991) . . . . Inge

Sciorra, Annabella

Films:
True Love (1989) . . . . Donna
Cadillac Man (1990) . . . . Donna
Reversal of Fortune (1990). . . . . Sarah
The Hard Way (1991) . . . . Susan
Jungle Fever (1991) . . . . Angie Tucci
The Hand That Rocks the Cradle (1992). . . . . Claire Bartel
• 0:08—Brief side of right breast in open gown, while lying on Dr. Mott's examination table.
Whispers in the Dark (1992) . . . . Ann Hecker
• 1:25—Buns in mirror in front of closet (don't see her face). Partial left breast.
Mr. Wonderful (1993) . . . . Lee
The Night We Never Met (1993) . . . . Ellen Holder
Romeo Is Bleeding (1994) . . . . Natalie
The Addiction (1995) . . . . Casanova
The Cure (1995) . . . . Linda
The Funeral (1996) . . . . Jean
Underworld (1996) . . . . Dr. Leah
Made for Cable Movies:
Prison Stories, Women on the Inside (1990; HBO) . . . . . . Nicole
National Lampoon's Favorite Deadly Sins (1995; Showtime)
. . . . Brenda
Made for TV Movies:
Asteroid (1997) . . . . Lily McKee

Scoggins, Tracy

Films:
Toy Soldiers (1983) . . . . Monique
In Dangerous Company (1988). . . . . Evelyn
• 0:42—Very, very brief half of left breast in bed with Blake. Then, very, very brief left breast getting out of bed. Blurry, hard to see.
• 0:58—Brief upper half of left breast taking a bath. Long shot, hard to see.
The Gumshoe Kid (1990). . . . . Rita Benson
• 0:33—In two piece white swimsuit. Nice buns shot while Jay Underwood hides in the closet.
••• 1:10—Side view of left breast in the shower with Underwood. Excellent slow motion breasts shot while turning around. Brief side view of right breast in bed afterwards.
One Last Run (1990) . . . . Cindy
The Raven Red Kiss-Off (1990). . . . . Vala Vuvalle
Timebomb (1990) . . . . Ms. Blue
Watchers II (1990) . . . . Barbara White
Demonic Toys (1991) . . . . Judith Gray
Play Murder For Me (1991) . . . . Tricia Merritt
•• 0:37—Right breast, then breasts when her husband sexually attacks her.
Ultimate Desires (1991). . . . . Samantha Stewart
a.k.a. Silhouette
• 0:59—Very brief buns and side of left breast taking off her dress and walking out of the room.

••• 1:10—Breasts, several times, in bed with Singer.

Alien Intruder (1992) .... Ariel
• 0:54—Breasts and buns (mostly silhouette) while straddling Caulfield on bed.

Dead On (1993) .... Marla Beaumont
(Unrated version reviewed.)
• 0:00—Partial breasts in shower during opening credits. Brief breasts when getting out of shower.
• 0:19—Brief left breast while in bathtub when she reaches up to turn off the speaker phone.

Dollman vs. the Demonic Toys (1993)........... Judith Grey

Made for Cable TV:

Babylon 5 (1998- ; TNT)............ Capt. Elizabeth Lochley

Made for TV Movies:

The Great American Sex Scandal (1989)..... Hope Hathaway
Jake Lassiter: Justice on the Bayou (1995) ... Melanie Corrigan
Dallas: J.R. Returns (1996)..................Anita Smithfield

TV:

Renegades (1983).............................Tracy
Hawaiian Heat (1984).................... Irene Gorley
The Colbys (1985-87)..................... Monica Colby
Dynasty (1989)........................... Monica Colby
Lois & Clark: The New Adventures of Superman (1993-94) .... Cat
Lonesome Dove: The Outlaw Years (1995-96) .... Amanda Carpenter

Video Tapes:

Tracy Scoggins: Mind Your Body (1993) ....Herself

*Scorsese, Nicolette **

Films:

Perfect Victims (1988)......................Melissa Cody
National Lampoon's Christmas Vacation (1989) .... Mary
Aspen Extreme (1993)............................Tina

Boxing Helena (1993) .... Fantasy Lover/Nurse
••• 1:22—In black bra, panties and stockings then buns and breasts while making love with Julian Sands while Sherilyn Fenn watches.

Made for Cable Movies:

Rebel Highway: Girls in Prison (1994; Showtime) .... Suzy

Scott, Adrian

Films:

Lust for Freedom (1987)......................... Karen
•• 0:40—Full frontal nudity, after her boyfriend forces her to take off her clothes.
• 0:41—Brief lower frontal nudity with her boyfriend in prison cell.

The Doors (1991) .... New York Journalist

Scott, Anneliza

a.k.a. Anneliza Wolf.

Films:

Demolition Man (1993) ....Police Officer
The Unborn II (1993) .... Officer Craig
Disclosure (1994) .... Secretary #2
Manhunt (1994)................................ Cop #1
Dead Cold (1995)............................ Susan
Hologram Man (1995) .... Carradine

Made for Cable TV:

Love Street: Most Pleasurable Death (1994; Showtime) .... Marian

Women: Stories of Passion-Gun Shy (1996; Showtime) .... Officer Penny Cox
•• 0:02—Breasts, while taking off blouse and putting on bra in front of mirror.

• 0:07—Brief partial right breast, while dreaming about Billy.
••• 0:13—Breasts, while making love with Billy in bed.
•• 0:21—Breasts, while making love with Billy in bed.

*Scott, Kathleen **

Films:

The Affair (1995) .... Linda
•• 0:33—Breasts, while caressing herself after watching Jennifer make love with Mark.
•• 0:39—Brief buns under short nightie, then nude, while talking with Jennifer in bathroom.
••• 0:51—In lingerie, then breasts and buns in panties, while in the house with Mark.
• 0:55—Breasts and buns in panties, in the house with Mark some more.
•• 0:59—Breasts and buns in panties, while dancing in front of Mark and Alexis.
••• 1:03—Nude, while making love with Alexis in bedroom.
•• 1:08—Breasts, while making love with Mark in bedroom.

Made for Cable TV:

Hot Line: Voyeur (1994; Cinemax)................. Toni
(Available on video tape in *Hot Line.*)
• 0:06—Breasts, when making love with the neighbor guy while Stephanie watches.

Love Street: Celibates Anonymous (1995; Showtime) . .Daphne

Scott, Kristi

See: Ducati, Kristi.

Scott, Leonette

Films:

Boyz N the Hood (1991) ....Tisha
• 0:42—Side view of left breast, while in bed with Cuba Gooding Jr. Don't see her face.

TV:

Soul Train .... Dancer

Scott, Linda Gaye

Films:

Psych-Out (1968) .... Lynn

Little Fauss and Big Halsy (1970)...............Moneth
• 0:37—Brief left breast, while sleeping in bed with another girl.
• 1:23—Buns, while holding a sheet and talking with Michael J. Pollard.

Westworld (1973) .... Arielle

*Scott, Lisa Marie **

Films:

The Corporate Ladder (1996).................... Kyoko
•• 0:15—In bra, then breasts and buns in backyard and in swimming pool with Ben Cross.

The Glass Cage (1996) .... Kiko
•• 0:30—In sheer white dress, then breasts and buns in panties, while dancing on stage.

Ringer (1996) .... Shimeka
•• 0:30—Buns and breasts in panties, garter belt and stockings while dressing being assisted by Shannon Whirry.
•• 0:38—Nude, undressing and joining Shannon Whirry and Malcolm McDowell in hot tub.

Video Tapes:

Playboy Video Calendar 1996 (1995) .... May
••• 0:18—Nude, while ballet dancing in house.
••• 0:20—Nude in bedroom fantasy.

Wet & Wild: Hot Holidays (1995)..............Playmate

Playboy's Rising Stars and Sexy Starlets (1996) . . Herself
•• 0:09—Full frontal nudity in still photos.
•• 0:10—Brief breasts and buns in panties from *The Glass Cage.*
••• 0:12—Nude, while dancing alone, then with a guy in ballet studio.

Scott, Susie *

Films:
Student Confidential (1987). . . . . Susan Bishop
• 0:02—Lying in bed covered with a gold sheet. Sort of right breast through her hair.
•• 1:26—Full frontal nudity standing in front of Greg.
Video Tapes:
Playboy Video Magazine, Volume 5 (1983) . . . . . Playmate
• 0:05—Brief breasts, while stroking her hair.
Playboy's Playmate Review 3 (1985). . . . . Playmate
Playmates at Play (1990) . . . . Making Waves
Playboy's Playmates Revisited (1998). . . . . Playmate
••• 0:30—Nude in old footage and still photos.
••• 0:36—Nude in new footage.

Scott-Thomas, Kristin

Films:
Under the Cherry Moon (1986). . . . . Mary
Secret Life of Ian Fleming (1990; British) . . . . Leda
Bitter Moon (1994) . . . . Fiona
• 2:14—Very, very brief breasts, while sitting up in bed after Peter Coyote shoots Emmanuelle Seinger.
Four Weddings and a Funeral (1994; British) . . . . Fiona
Richard III (1995; British). . . . . Lady Anne
Angels & Insects (1996; British). Molly
The English Patient (1996) . . . . Katharine Clifton
• 1:12—(0:06 into Tape 2) Very brief right breast, when Ralph Fiennes rips open her dress.
•• 1:14—(0:08 into Tape 2) Full frontal nudity, taking off her robe and getting into bathtub with Fiennes.
••• 1:15—(0:09 into Tape 2) Full frontal nudity when getting out of the bathtub.
••• 1:27—(0:21 into Tape 2) Breasts, while rolling over in bed with Fiennes.
Mission: Impossible (1996) . . . . Sarah Davies
The Pompatus of Love (1996) . . . . Caroline
The Horse Whisperer (1998) . . . . Annie
Made for Cable Movies:
The Endless Game (1990; Showtime) . . . . Caroline
Miniseries:
Mistral's Daughter (1984) . . . . Nancy
Made for TV Movies:
Masterpiece Theatre: Body & Soul (1994) . . . Sister Gabriel
••• 1:46—(0:24 into Part 2) Full frontal nudity, taking off nightgown in front of mirror.
• 1:50—(0:28 into Part 2) Full frontal nudity in flashback.
••• 3:42—(0:34 into Part 4) Nude in bedroom with Hal.
Gulliver's Travels (1996). . . . . Immortal Gatekeeper

Seagrove, Jenny

Films:
Local Hero (1983; British) . . . . Marina
Nate and Hayes (1983) . . . . Sophia
Appointment with Death (1988). . . . . Dr. Sarah King
Harlequin Romance: Magic Moments (1989) . . . Melanie James
Bullseye! (1990) . . . . Health Club Receptionist
The Guardian (1990) . . . . Camilla
••• 0:21—Side view of left breast, while in bathtub with the baby. Right breast, then breasts.
• 0:23—Buns, while drying herself off. Long shot.
•• 0:38—Breasts, mostly left breast on top of Phil. Don't see her face, probably a body double.
• 0:46—Buns, while skinny dipping. Long shot.
•• 0:47—Breasts healing her wound by a tree. Side view of right breast.
• 1:18—Very brief breasts under sheer gown in forest just before getting hit by a Jeep.
• 1:24—Very briefly breasts, while scaring Carey Lowell. Body is painted all over.
Made for Cable TV:
The Hitchhiker: Killer (HBO). . . . . Meg
Miniseries:
A Woman of Substance (1984) . . . . Young Emma Hart
Made for TV Movies:
In Like Flynn (1985). . . . . Terri McLane
Sherlock Holmes and the Incident at Victoria Falls (1991)
. . . . Lillie Langtry

Seberg, Jean

Films:
Saint Joan (1957). . . . . Joan of Arc
Bonjour Tristesse (1958) . . . . Cecile
Breathless (1959; French) . . . . Patricia Franchini
The Mouse That Roared (1959; British) . . . . Helen
Time Out for Love (1961) . . . . Michele
Lilith (1964). . . . . Lilith Arthur
A Fine Madness (1966) . . . . Lydia West
Paint Your Wagon (1969). . . . . Elizabeth
Pendulum (1969) . . . . Adele Matthews
Airport (1970) . . . . Tanya Livingston
Macho Callahan (1970) . . . . Alexandra
• 0:36—Brief buns and partial breast in mirror. (Don't see her face clearly.)
• 1:01—Very brief left breast when David Janssen rips her blouse open. Brief breasts during struggle with him before he rapes her. Brief left breast during rape. (Never see face with body.)
Kill (1971; French/Spanish/German). . . . . Emily
a.k.a. Kill! Kill! Kill!
• 0:42—Side view of right breast and buns. Don't see her face.
• 0:45—More right breast a couple of times. Still don't see her face.

Sedgwick, Kyra

Wife of actor Kevin Bacon.
Films:
War and Love (1985). . . . . Halina
Tai-Pan (1986). . . . . Tess
Kansas (1988) . . . . Prostitute Drifter
Born on the Fourth of July (1989) . . . . Donna
Mr. & Mrs. Bridge (1990) . . . . Ruth Bridge
Pyrates (1991). . . . . Sam
••• 0:19—In sheer lingerie on top of Kevin Bacon in bed, then breasts.
• 0:22—Brief buns, while lying on top of Bacon.
• 0:26—Breasts under water in hot tub with Bacon.
singles (1992) . . . . Linda Powell
Heart and Souls (1993) . . . . Julia
Murder in the First (1994) . . . . Blanche
The Low Life (1995). . . . . Bevan
Something to Talk About (1995) . . . . Emma Rae
Phenomenon (1996) . . . . Lace Pennamin
Critical Care (1997) . . . . Felicia Potter
Montana (1998) . . . . Claire

Made for Cable Movies:
Women & Men 2: Three Short Stories (1991; HBO) ....Arlene Megaffin
Losing Chase (1996; Showtime) ....Elizabeth Cole
Miniseries:
Family Pictures (1993)............................ Nina
Made for TV Movies:
Miss Rose White (1992)............ Rose White/Reyzel Weiss
TV:
Another World (1982-83) .... Julia Shearer

*Seigner, Emmanuelle **

Wife of director Roman Polanski.
Films:
Detective (1985; French/Swiss)................. Grace Kelly
Frantic (1988)............................... Michelle
• 1:02—Brief side view of right breast, while changing blouses in bedroom.
Bitter Moon (1994) ....Mimi
•• 0:25—Breasts, while in front of fire with Peter Coyote.
•• 0:26—Breasts, when sitting up in bed. Buns, while standing at window.
•• 0:30—Nude, dancing in white dress in front of Coyote.
••• 0:31—Breasts in open robe, drooling milk over her breasts, then rubbing them.
•• 0:46—Buns in garter belt and stockings.
• 1:03—Side view of buns, when sleeping in bed, then brief right breast while putting on red dress.

Seka

Adult film actress.
Films:
Men Don't Leave (1989).................. Adult Film Star
Video Tapes:
Playboy's Girls of Radio: Talk, Rock and Shock (1995) ....Herself
•• 0:43—Left breast, while talking into microphone.

*Sellers, Victoria **

Daughter of the late actor Peter Sellers and actress Britt Ekland.
Films:
Warlords (1988)...........................Desert Girl
• 0:06—Getting out of car and running into the desert while wearing the sheer white top.

• *Selway, Laura **

Video Tapes:
Playboy's Women Behaving Badly (1997) .....Body Paint
••• 0:11—Nude, while in apartment with her girlfriend, then painting each other.

Senatore, Paola

Films:
Zig-Zag (1975; French)...................Madame Bruyer
Women in Cell Block 7 (1977; Italian/U.S.) ....Musumeci
Affair (1984; French/Italian) ....Beatrice
••• 0:00—Full frontal nudity, while lying in bed, caressing herself, then making love with Mark.
• 0:05—Very brief right breast in open top, while reaching for a book.
•• 0:07—Very brief right breast in mirror when Mark puts a necklace on her. Breasts when he opens her blouse and she kneels down next to him.
••• 0:15—Breasts, while making love in bed with Mark.
• 0:17—Breasts in open fur coat, while in front of Mark.
••• 0:28—Very brief lower frontal nudity, when Don rips off her panties, then breasts, while making out on the couch with him.
••• 0:43—Breasts, while making love with Norma on bed (later, Mark joins in also).
••• 1:16—Nude, while making love in bed with Mark.
Doomed to Die (1985; Italian)................Diana Morris

Senit, Laurie

Films:
Body and Soul (1981).......................Hooker #3
• 0:54—Brief breasts lying next to Leon Isaac Kennedy in bed with two other hookers.
Doctor Detroit (1983) .... Dream Girl
The Witching (1983)..................... Witches Coven
a.k.a. Necromancy
(Originally filmed in 1971 as *Necromancy*, additional scenes were added and re-released in 1983.)
R.S.V.P. (1984)......................... Sherry Worth
•• 1:00—Breasts in the shower with Harry Reems.
•• 1:06—Breasts again.

Sennet, Susan

Films:
Big Bad Mama (1974) ....Billy Jean
• 0:50—Breasts and buns getting onto bed with Tom Skerritt.
•• 0:51—Breasts and buns, getting out of bed with Skerritt.
• 0:52—Brief buns, getting back into bed with Skerritt along with Polly.
Tidal Wave (1975; U.S./Japanese) ....n.a.
TV:
Ozzie's Girls (1973) .... Susie Hamilton

*Serena **

Adult film actress.
Films:
Fantasm (1976; Australian) ....n.a.
Honky Tonk Nights (1978) .... Dolly Pop
• 0:04—Breasts in open blouse, getting restrained after getting in a fight with a guy who tries to molest her.
••• 0:10—Breasts in bed with Bobby, then putting on a robe.
••• 0:38—Breasts standing in doorway, then in kitchen with Bill.

*Serna, Assumpta **

Films:
Lola (1986) ....Silvia
Matador (1986; Spanish)................. Maria Cardinal
• 0:03—Breasts taking off wrap and making love with a guy just before she kills him.
••• 1:38—Breasts on floor with Diego. Long shot, hard to see. Breasts in front of the fire.
• 1:41—Brief breasts making love with Diego.
• 1:43—Breasts lying on floor dead.
Wild Orchid (1990)............................Hanna
••• 0:39—Breasts at the beach and in the limousine. Very erotic.
Chain of Desire (1992) .... Cleo
Revolver (1992).................Countess Angela Rosetta
Nostradamus (1993) ....Anne
• 1:13—Right breast, while standing and kissing Tcheky Karyo.
Hidden Assassin (1994) .... Marta
The Craft (1996) .... Lirio

Made for TV Movies:
Day of Reckoning (1994). . . . . Marissa
TV:
Falcon Crest (1989). . . . . Anna Cellini

*Severance, Joan **

Films:
No Holds Barred (1989) . . . . Samantha Moore
See No Evil, Hear No Evil (1989). . . . . Eve
•• 1:08—Breasts in and leaning out of the shower while Gene Wilder tries to get her bag.
Worth Winning (1989) . . . . .Lizbette
Bird on a Wire (1990) . . . . Rachel Varnay
The Runestone (1990). . . . . Marla Stewart
Write to Kill (1990) . . . . Belle Washburn
••• 1:01—Breasts, making love in bed with Valentine.
• 1:04—Very brief, blurry breasts when Valentine tosses her a blouse.
Illicit Behavior (1991) . . . . .Melissa Yarnell
(Unrated version reviewed.)
(Nude scenes where you don't see her face are body doubles.)
•• 1:10—Breasts and buns in car with Davi. (Sometimes you see her face with her breasts, sometimes not.)
•• 1:16—Right breast, while lying in bed and talking to Davi.
Almost Pregnant (1992) . . . . .Maureen Mallory
(Unrated version reviewed.)
•• 0:58—In belly dancer outfit in bedroom with Jeff Conaway, then breasts.
•• 1:06—In black leather outfit, then breasts and buns in G-string in bedroom with Conaway. Her hair gets in the way a lot.
• 1:09—Brief breasts and buns in various sexual positions in bed with Conaway.
• 1:12—Brief breasts, while playing with whipped cream in bed with Conaway.
Lake Consequence (1992) . . . . Irene
(Unrated version reviewed.)
• 0:02—Left breast, while lying in bed.
• 0:41—Brief breasts several times while making love with Billy Zane.
••• 0:50—Full frontal nudity in spa in bathhouse, while making love with Zane.
••• 0:54—Breasts in spa making out with Zane and Grace.
• 1:06—Brief glimpses of right breast in open coat, while struggling in a field with Zane.
••• 1:07—Breasts in field with Zane. Oh yeah!
•• 1:19—Brief side view breasts and buns in bedroom with Zane.
Criminal Passion (1993) . . . . Melanie Hudson
•• 0:57—Breasts and buns, while making love with Ashcroft in swimming pool.
•• 1:20—Buns and partial breasts, after getting out of the pool and drying herself off.
••• 1:23—Breasts, while in room with Ashcroft. Long scene.
Hard Evidence (1994) .Madelyn Turner
Payback (1994). . . . . Rose
(Special director's cut reviewed.)
•• 0:49—Breasts and partial lower frontal nudity, while making love with C. Thomas Howell in diner kitchen.
••• 0:55—Breasts and brief top of lower frontal nudity while making love with Howell on hood of car.
• 1:05—Brief half of left breast, in open robe.
Dangerous Indiscretion (1995) . . . . Caroline Everett
• 0:08—In lingerie in house with C. Thomas Howell. Then brief breasts and buns, while crawling on the floor with him.
• 0:25—Brief partial breasts, while making love with Howell in bed. Hard to see.
Profile for Murder (1996) . . . . Hanna Carras
•• 0:33—Brief breasts, several times, while playing with herself in bathtub when fantasizing.
• 1:03—Brief partial right breast, while making love with Lance Henriksen in boat.
Made for Cable Movies:
Another Pair of Aces (1991) . . . . Susan Davis
(Video tape includes nude scenes not shown on cable TV.)
•• 1:00—Brief breasts several times, making love with Kris Kristofferson in bed.
Black Scorpion (1995; Showtime) . . . . Darcy
Black Scorpion 2—Aftershock (1996; Showtime)
. . . . Darcy/Black Scorpion
Made for Cable TV:
Red Shoe Diaries: Safe Sex (1992; Showtime)
. . . . The Woman
(Available on the video tape *Red Shoe Diaries 2: Double Dare.*)
• 0:11—Breasts, standing up, then lying on the floor. Medium long shot.
••• 0:12—Breasts, lying on the floor, then making love with Steven Bauer.
• 0:13—Brief breasts, gathering her clothes.
•• 0:16—Nude, in front of mirror when Bauer takes her dress off.
••• 0:17—More nude in bed and in front of mirror.
• 0:19—Breasts during flashback.
••• 0:32—Nude in bed. Nice close-up shots. (Additional footage added for video tape.)
Tales From the Crypt: The New Arrival (1992; HBO) . . . . .Rona
TV:
Wiseguy (1988). . . . . Susan Profitt

Severeid, Suzanne

Films:
Hollywood High (1976) . . . . Jan
• 0:07—Breasts under sheer white swimsuit while frolicking in the surf with her girlfriends.
• 0:09—Breasts under sheer white swimsuit top while talking on the beach with Frasier.
•• 0:29—Breasts, while lifting up her blouse to distract the class brain so every one else in class can copy his answers.
• 0:43—Very brief right breast, when leaving the pool after washing her clothes.
• 0:51—Brief buns, while mooning her friends in passing van.
•• 1:14—Breasts, while in swimming pool with her friends and running around outside and in house.
Don't Answer the Phone (1979). . . . . Hooker
• 0:43—Very brief right breast in open blouse after the killer strangles her.
Van Nuys Blvd. (1979) . . . . Jo
••• 0:02—Breasts and buns, bringing a beer to Bobby, then sitting and watching TV.
Howling IV: The Original Nightmare (1988) . . . . Janice

*Seymour, Jane **

Wife of actor/director/producer James Keach.
Films:
Young Winston (1972; British) . . . . Pamela Plowden
Live and Let Die (1973; British) . . . . Solitaire
Sinbad and the Eye of the Tiger (1977; U.S./British). . . . . Farah
• 1:16—Very brief buns, skinny dipping in pond with Taryn Power. Long shot, but still pretty amazing for a G-rated film.

• 1:17—Very brief partial right breast (arm covers most of it) screaming when scared by the troglodyte.
Oh Heavenly Dog! (1980) .... Jackie Howard
Somewhere in Time (1980) .... Elise McKenna
Lassiter (1984) .... Sara
• 0:10—Buns and brief side view of right breast lying on stomach on bed with Tom Selleck.
Head Office (1986) .... Jane
The Tunnel (1987; Spanish) .... Maria
• 0:29—Very brief left breast, while in bed with Peter Weller when the sheet is pulled down.
•• 0:44—Brief right breast, while getting dressed, throwing off her robe.
• 0:48—Very brief, buns in pulled up skirt while struggling with Weller on the floor.
• 1:43—Brief buns behind textured glass divider, while changing clothes.
Sunstroke (1992) .... Theresa
Praying Mantis (1993) .... Linda Crandell
Made for Cable Movies:
Jamaica Inn (1982) .... Mary Yellan
Matters of the Heart (1990) .... Hadley Norman
Miniseries:
Captains and the Kings (1976) .... Chisholm Armagh
Seventh Avenue (1977) .... Eva Meyers
East of Eden (1981) .... Cathy/Kate Ames
War and Remembrance (1988) .... Natalie Jastrow
Made for TV Movies:
The Story of David (1976) .... Bathsheba
Battlestar Gallactica (1978) .... Serina
The Dallas Cowboy Cheerleaders (1979) .... Laura Cole
The Scarlet Pimpernel (1982) .... Marguerite St. Just
The Sun Also Rises (1984) .... Lady Brett
Jack the Ripper (1988) .... Emma
The Richest Man in the World: The Story of Aristotle Onassis (1988) .... Maria Callas
The Woman He Loved (1988) .... Wallis Simpson
Dr. Quinn, Medicine Woman (1992) ...... Dr. Michaela Quinn
A Passion for Justice: The Hazel Brannon Smith Story (1994) .... Hazel Brannon Smith
TV:
Dr. Quinn, Medicine Woman (1992-) ..... Dr. Michaela Quinn

Seynhaeve, Ingrid *

Video Tapes:
Sports Illustrated: The 1993 Swimsuit Video (1993) .... Model
Sports Illustrated: 1994 Swimsuit Issue Video (1994) .... Model
(Unedited Version reviewed.)
• 0:00—Very, very brief right breast when adjusting fishnet top.

Seyrig, Delphine

Films:
Muriel (1963) .... Helene
Accident (1967; British) .... Francesca
Daughters of Darkness (1971; Belgian/French/German/Italian) .... Countess Elisabeth Bathory
Day of the Jackal (1973) .... Colette
• 1:25—Side view of right breast while lying in bed with the Jackal. Dark.
• 1:40—Very brief side view of left breast, when she rolls on her back. Brief side view of left breast after the Jackal kills her.
The Black Windmill (1974; British) .... Ceil Burrows
•• 0:34—Right breast and buns, undressing and getting into bed to pose for a photo taken by John Vernon.
Golden Eighties (1987; French/Belgian) .... Jeanne

Shaffer, Stacey

Films:
The Naked Cage (1985) .... Amy
••• 1:03—Nude in shower room getting hassled by the other girls.
Blood Screams (1986; U.S./Mexican) .... Karen

Shannon, Moriah

Films:
Alley Cat (1982) .... Sam
••• 0:48—Full frontal nudity, while taking a shower and talking with Billie.
D.C. Cab (1983) .... Venus Club Passenger
•• 0:16—In bra, then breasts, undressing in back seat of cab.
•• 0:17—Breasts when Albert tries to get his fare.
• 0:18—Breasts, then buns when Gary Busey takes her money. Buns and very brief lower frontal nudity running out of the club after him.

Shannon, Polly

Films:
No Contest (1994) .... Candy
Love and Human Remains (1995; Canadian) .... The Second Victim
• 0:36—Very brief breasts, while in bed, struggling with the killer. Dark.
Made for Cable Movies:
End of Summer (1995; Showtime) .... Maid

Shapiro, Hilary

See: Shepard, Hilary.

Sharkey, Rebecca

See: Wood-Sharkey, Rebecca.

Sharpe, Becky

Films:
The Boob Tube (1975) .... Massage Girl
•• 0:20—Right breast, then breasts, while getting massaged by Sid on the table.
If You Don't Stop It You'll Go Blind (1979) .... n.a.

Sharpe, Cornelia *

Films:
Kansas City Bomber (1972) .... Tammy O'Brien
Serpico (1973) .... Leslie
•• 0:41—Breasts in bathtub with Al Pacino.
Busting (1974) .... Jackie
Open Season (1974; U.S./Spanish) .... Nancy
The Reincarnation of Peter Proud (1975) .... Nora Hayes
•• 0:03—Breasts in bed with Michael Sarrazin, then buns when getting out of bed.
The Next Man (1976) .... Nicole Scott
a.k.a. Double Hit
Venom (1982; British) .... Ruth Hopkins
Made for TV Movies:
S.H.E. (1979) .... Lavinia Kean

Shatner, Melanie

Daughter of actor William Shatner.
Films:
Star Trek V: The Final Frontier (1989) ...... Enterprise Yeoman

The First Power (1990) . . . . Shopgirl

Bloodstone: Subspecies II (1992) . . . . Rebecca Morgan
- • 0:34—Upper half of buns and breasts behind translucent plastic shower door. Hard to see.

Cthulhu Mansion (1992) . . . . Eva

Bloodlust: Subspecies III (1993) . . . . Rebecca Morgan
- • 0:04—Very brief left breast and buns, while taking off blood-stained dress and putting on a coat. Long shot.

Made for Cable Movies:

The Alien Within (1995; Showtime) . . . . Catherine Harding

Made for Cable TV:

Perversions of Science: Boxed In (1997; HBO) . . . . Delcine

Shattuck, Shari

Wife of actor Ronn Moss.

Films:

Tainted . . . . Cathy
- •• 0:09—Buns, while lying on top of Frank.
- ••• 0:27—Breasts in bubble bath, getting up, drying herself off, then putting on white bra while wearing panties.
- ••• 0:49—Breasts taking a shower.
- • 0:51—Brief side view of left breast in the shower again.

Portfolio (1983) . . . . Elite Model

The Naked Cage (1985) . . . . Michelle
- •• 0:42—Buns and breasts in shower, then getting slashed by Rita during a dream.
- •• 1:00—Left breast getting attacked by Smiley in jail cell, then fighting back.

Death Spa (1987) . . . . Catherine

Hot Child in the City (1987) . . . . Abby

Number One with a Bullet (1987) . . . . Regina

Arena (1988) . . . . Jade
- • 1:06—Upper half of buns, while sitting up in bed. Brief half of right breast, getting up while wearing robe.

Desert Warrior (1988) . . . . Racela
- • 0:45—Brief breasts, when the bad guy rips open her jumpsuit to see if she has radiation sickness.

The Uninvited (1988) . . . . Suzanne

A Man of Passion (1989) . . . . Teresa
- •• 0:18—Left breast, while posing for Anthony Quinn. Breasts under sheer blouse when leaving the room.
- • 0:20—Brief partial right breast, when caught in bed with Quinn by George.
- • 0:22—Tip of left breast, while sitting on edge of bed.
- • 1:12—Brief breasts, while turning over in bed with Quinn.

The Spring (1989) . . . . Dyanne
- • 0:00—Nude, several times, swimming under the water. Shot from under water.
- • 0:50—Breasts and buns, swimming under water.
- •• 0:51—Breasts, getting out of the water.
- •• 0:59—Brief breasts, turning over in bed with Dack Rambo.
- • 1:05—Standing up in wet lingerie, then swimming under water.

Lower Level (1990) . . . . Dawn Simms

Mad About You (1990) . . . . Renee

Immortal Sins (1992; Spanish) . . . . Diana
- • 0:13—Very brief breasts during Mike's dream.
- • 0:32—Breasts several times, while making love with Mike.
- •• 0:44—Left breast while making love with Mike.
- ••• 1:09—Breasts making love with Mike.
- ••• 1:18—Still more breasts making love with Mike.
- • 1:20—Almost full frontal nudity, while standing in doorway. (Hard to see because of shadows.)

Out for Blood (1992) . . . . Joanna Montague

Body Chemistry 3: Point of Seduction (1993)
. . . . Dr. Claire Archer
- •• 0:15—Breasts, while making love on bed with Andrew Stevens at night during storm.
- ••• 0:28—Side view of buns and breasts, while making love with Stevens on bed.
- ••• 0:57—Breasts, taking off robe in front of Stevens. More breasts and buns while making love with him.

Dead On (1993) . . . . Erin Davenport
(Unrated version reviewed.)
- ••• 0:15—Breasts and buns in panties, while making out with Matt McCoy in doorway, then making love on the floor. Wow!
- ••• 0:29—Breasts, while making love with McCoy in her studio. Shot almost in silhouette.
- • 0:49—Brief breasts, while rolling over in bed to answer the phone.

On Deadly Ground (1993) . . . . Liles

Spy Hard (1996) . . . . Stewardess

Made for TV Movies:

The Laker Girls (1990) . . . . Libby

TV:

The Young and the Restless . . . . Ashley

Dallas (1991) . . . . Kit

Shaver, Helen *

Films:

Shoot (1976; Canadian) . . . . Paula Lissitzen

The Supreme Kid (1976; Canadian) . . . . Girl

Outrageous! (1977; Canadian) . . . . Jo

High-Ballin' (1978; Canadian) . . . . Pickup

In Praise of Older Women (1978; Canadian)
. . . . Ann MacDonald
- ••• 1:40—Blue bra and panties, then breasts with Tom Berenger.
- ••• 1:42—Nude lying in bed with Berenger, then getting out and getting dressed.

Starship Invasions (1978; Canadian) . . . . Betty

The Amityville Horror (1979) . . . . Carolyn

Gas (1981; Canadian) . . . . Rhonda

Harry Tracy (1982; Canadian) . . . . Catherine

The Osterman Weekend (1983) . . . . Virginia Tremayne
- •• 0:24—Breasts in an open blouse yelling at her husband in the bedroom.
- • 0:41—Breasts in the swimming pool when everyone watches on the TV.

Best Defense (1984) . . . . Claire Lewis

The Color of Money (1986) . . . . Janelle

Desert Hearts (1986) . . . . Vivian Bell
- •• 1:09—Breasts when robe is taken off by Patricia Charboneau in motel room.
- ••• 1:10—Breasts making love in bed with Patricia Charboneau.

The Men's Club (1986) . . . . Sarah (uncredited)
- •• 0:13—Breasts under Roy Scheider in bed, then breasts again, getting back into bed.

The Believers (1987) . . . . Jessica Halliday
- • 0:38—Brief glimpse of right breast while lying in bed with Martin Sheen.
- • 1:17—Buns, getting out of bed.

Innocent Victim (1988) . . . . Benet Archdale
- • 1:05—Very brief side of left breast on top of a guy in bed.

Zebrahead (1992) . . . . Diane

Murder So Sweet (1993) . . . . Edie Ballew

That Night (1993) . . . . Ann O'Conner

Born to be Wild (1995) . . . . Margaret Heller

Tremors 2: Aftershocks (1995). . . . . Kate White
The Craft (1996) . . . . Grace
Open Season (1996) . . . . Rachel Rowen
Made for Cable Movies:
The Park is Mine (1985; HBO). . . . . Valery Weaver
• 0:46—Very brief breasts undressing then very, very brief left breast, while catching clothes from Tommy Lee Jones.
Survive the Night (1993; USA) .Stacy
Made for Cable TV:
The Outer Limits: Sandkings (1995; Showtime). . . . Cathy Kress
Poltergeist: The Legacy (1996- ; Showtime) . . .Rachel Corrigan
Poltergeist: The Legacy/Premiere (1996; Showtime) . . . . .Rachel Corrigan
• 0:45—In sheer lingerie, the left breast, while making love with William Sadler.
• 0:46—Left breast while lying on bed.
Poltergeist: The Legacy/Town Without Pity (1996; Showtime) . . . . .Rachel Corrigan
Poltergeist: The Legacy/The Choice (1997; Showtime) . . . . .Rachel Corrigan
Dead Man's Gun: Next of Kin (1997; Showtime) . . . . Dianna McKinney
Made for TV Movies:
Mothers, Daughters and Lovers (1989) . . . . Claire Nichols
Rest In Peace, Mrs. Columbo (1990) . . . . Vivian Dimitri
Fatal Memories (1992) . . . . Elaine Tipton
Poisoned by Love: The Kern County Murders (1993) . . . . Edie Ballew
Ride with the Wind (1994) . . . . Katherine Barnes
TV:
United States (1980). . . . . .Libby Chapin
Jessica Novak (1981). . . . . .Jessica Novak
WIOU (1990-91). . . . . Kelby Robinson

Shaw, Alonna

Films:
Double Impact (1991) . . . . Danielle Shaw
•• 1:09—Breasts, in white panties, changing out of her wet clothes on boat.
•• 1:10—Breasts and buns several times, making love with Chad during Alex's jealous fantasy.
• 1:11—More breasts and buns in fantasy.
• 1:12—More breasts.
Cyborg Cop (1993). . . . . Cathy
••• 0:58—Breasts, while making love with Jack.

Shaw, Crystal

Films:
American Drive-In (1984) . . . . .Featuring
Hardbodies (1984) . . . . .Candy
Hard Rock Zombies (1985) . . . . Mrs. Buff
The Alien Within (1990) . . . . .Secretary
(Contains footage from *The Evil Spawn* woven together with new material.)
Laser Moon (1991). . . . . Jacelyn
• 0:11—Breasts, while making love in bed on top of Cruz.

Shaw, Fiona

Films:
Mountains of the Moon (1989) . . . . Isabel
•• 0:33—Breasts and very brief lower frontal nudity letting Patrick Bergin wax the hair off her legs.
•• 1:43—Breasts in bed after Bergin returns from Africa.
My Left Foot (1989; British). . . . . .Dr. Eileen Cole
Three Men and a Little Lady (1990) . . . . Miss Lomax
London Kills Me (1991; British) . . . . .Headley
Super Mario Bros. (1993) . . . . Lena
Undercover Blues (1993). . . . . Novacek
Anna Karenina (1997) . . . . .Lydia
Made for TV Movies:
Hedda Gabler (1993). . . . . Hedda Gabler

Shaw, Linda

Adult film actress.
Films:
Body Double (1984) . . . . Linda Shaw
• 1:11—Left breast on monitor while Craig Wasson watches TV.

Shaw, Tina

Films:
The Secrets of Love—Three Rakish Tales (1986) . . . . The Weaver's Wife
••• 0:10—Breasts in bed with Luke.
••• 0:17—Breasts in the barn.
Salome's Last Dance (1987) . . . . 2nd Slave
(Appears with 2 other slaves–can't tell who is who.)
•• 0:08—Breasts in black costume around a cage.
•• 0:52—Breasts during dance number.
The Lair of the White Worm (1988; British) . . . . Maid/Nun
Taffin (1988; U.S./British) . . . . Lola the Stripper
•• 1:04—Breasts doing routine in a club.
Split Second (1992) . . . . Nightclub Stripper
•• 0:07—Breasts, dancing in club in black S&M outfit, wearing a mask over her head.

Shayne, Linda

Films:
Humanoids from the Deep (1980). . . . . Miss Salmon
• 1:06—Breasts after getting bathing suit ripped off by a humanoid.
Graduation Day (1981) . . . . .Uncredited Paula
Lovely But Deadly (1981) . . . . Barb
The Lost Empire (1983). . . . . .Cindy Blake
Screwballs (1983). Bootsie Goodhead
••• 0:43—Right breast, while in back of van at drive-in theater, then breasts.
Big Bad Mama II (1987) . . . . Bank Teller
Out of Bounds (1987) . . . . Chris Cage
Daddy's Boys (1988) . . . . Nanette
No Man's Land (1988) . . . . Peggy
Munchie (1992) . . . . .Band Member
Leprechaun 3 (1995). . . . . Nurse
Made for TV Movies:
My Wicked Ways... The Legend of Errol Flynn (1985) . . . . Girl on 1st Train

Shé, Elizabeth

Films:
Howling V (1989) . . . . .Mary Lou Summers
• 0:33—Buns and side view of right breast getting into pool with Donovan.
• 0:36—Very brief full frontal nudity climbing out of pool with Donovan.
Howling VI—The Freaks (1990) . . . . .Mary Lou Summers
The Howling: New Moon Rising (1995). . . . . Mary Lou

Shea, Cherilyn *

Films:
Beverly Hills Cop III (1994) . . . . Girl at Counter
Silk n' Sabotage (1994) . . . . .Dagny
•• 0:02—Breasts, while making love in bed with Tyler.

•• 0:03—Breasts, while making love some more.
••• 0:12—Breasts, while making love in bed with Tyler.

Shea, Katt

a.k.a. Kathleen M. Shea or Katt Shea Ruben.
Actress turned Director.

Films:

The Cannonball Run (1981) .... Starting Girl
My Tutor (1983) .... Mud Wrestler
• 0:48—Brief breasts when a guy rips her dress off.
Scarface (1983)............... Woman at the Babylon Club
Cannonball Run II (1984) ....n.a.
Hollywood Hot Tubs (1984) .... Dee-Dee
• 0:21—Breasts with her boyfriend while Shawn is working on the hot tub.
Preppies (1984)............................. Margot
••• 0:20—Breasts teasing Richard through the glass door of her house.
• 1:07—Brief breasts after taking off bra in bed.
R.S.V.P. (1984).......................... Rhonda Rivers
• 0:31—Side view of left breast, making love in bed with Jonathan.
Barbarian Queen (1985) .... Estrild
• 0:31—Brief breasts, when her top gets torn off by guards.
The Destroyers (1985)......................... Audrey
Psycho III (1986) ....Patsy

Made for Cable Movies:

Last Exit to Earth (1996; Showtime)......... Surgeon Athena

Shear, Rhonda *

Films:

J.D.'s Revenge (1976) .... 1942 Girl
Galaxina (1980) .... Mime/Robot
Basic Training (1984)......................... Debbie
•• 0:07—Breasts making love with Mark.
Doin' Time (1984)............................Adrianne
Spaceballs (1987) .... Woman in Diner
Return to Frogtown (1992) .... Fuzzy
a.k.a. Frogtown II
Assault of the Party Nerds II: The Heavy Petting Detective (1993).. Tina
Tender Loving Care (1993) ....Gretchen

Made for Cable TV:

Up All Night (1991- ; USA) .... Host

Sheedy, Ally

Wife of actor David Lansbury.

Films:

Bad Boys (1983) .... J. C. Walenski
• 0:12—Very, very brief left breast, while kneeling on floor next to bed when Sean Penn leaves. A little blurry and a long shot.
Wargames (1983) ....Jennifer
The Breakfast Club (1985)................ Allison Reynolds
St. Elmo's Fire (1985) ....Leslie
Blue City (1986) .... Annie Rayford
Short Circuit (1986) .... Stephanie Speck
Maid to Order (1987) .... Jessie Montgomery
Heart of Dixie (1989)......................... Maggie
Betsy's Wedding (1990).................. Connie Hopper
Only the Lonely (1991) ....Theresa Luna
Home Alone 2: Lost in New York (1992) ..... NY Ticket Agent
The Pickle (1992) .... Molly-Girl
Man's Best Friend (1993).................... Lori Tanner
The Haunting of Seacliff Inn (1994)........... Susan Enright
One Night Stand (1994)...............Mickey Sanderson
a.k.a. Before the Night
• 0:59—Very brief right breast, while making love under A Martinez in flashback.
The Tin Soldier (1995).......................Billy's Mom

Made for Cable Movies:

The Lost Capone (1990) ....Kathleen
Fear (1991; Showtime) ....Cayce Bridges
Chantilly Lace (1993; Showtime)................Elizabeth
Parallel Lives (1994; Showtime)....................Louise
Buried Alive II (1997; USA)...................Laura Riskin

Made for Cable TV:

Kurt Vonnegut's Monkey House: Epicac (Showtime; Canadian) ....Lisa
Red Shoe Diaries: Accidents Happen (1993; Showtime). . Karen
(Available on the video tape *Red Shoe Diaries 4: Auto Erotica.*)
The Outer Limits: I Hear You Calling (1996; Showtime) .... Carter Jones

Made for TV Movies:

The Best Little Girl in the World (1981) ....n.a.
The Violation of Sarah McDavid (1981) ....n.a.
Deadly Lessons (1983).................. Marita Armstrong
Lethal Exposure (1993) .... Chris Cassidy
Ultimate Betrayal (1994) ....Mary
Hijacked: Flight 285 (1996) .... Denny

Sheehan, Patti

Films:

Bar Girls (1995)..............................Destiny
•• 0:18—Breasts, while sitting in a spa and talking on the phone.

Video Tapes:

The Making of Bar Girls (1995) ....Destiny
• 0:19—Breasts, while sitting down in spa and talking on the phone. Shot from different angles than shown in the film.

Sheen, Jacqueline *

Films:

Blue Chips (1994) .... Uncredited Girl at Party

Video Tapes:

Playboy Video Calendar 1991 (1990) ....December
••• 0:49—Nude.
Playboy Video Centerfold: Tawnni Cable (1990) ....Playmate
••• 0:14—Nude in Hawaii with Tawnni Cable and Pamela Stein.
Wet & Wild III (1991)..........................Model
Playboy Playmates in Paradise (1992) ....Playmate

Shelton, Deborah *

Miss USA in the 1970-71 Miss Universe Pageant.

Films:

Blood TIde (1982) .... Madeline
Body Double (1984) .... Gloria
Hunk (1987) ....O'Brien
Perfect Victims (1988) .... Liz Winters
Blind Vision (1990)................... Leanne Dunaway
••• 0:25—Breasts, making love with her boyfriend on the floor. Some shots are a body double.
Nemesis (1992) .... Julian
• 0:30—Buns, while lying on bed.
•• 0:31—Buns, while standing up and hugging Billy.
• 0:36—Buns, while standing at window. Side view of left breast.

••• 0:37—Full frontal nudity, punching Billy and getting dressed. Looking good! Very buff—she worked out for three and a half hours a day.

Circuitry Man II: Plughead Rewired (1993) . . . . .Kyle
•• 1:00—Breasts, after taking off blouse on horseback with Danner, then making love in a field.

Sins of the Night (1993) . . . . Roxanne Flowers
(Unrated version reviewed.)
••• 0:48—Breasts, while making love with Jack. Some nice close-ups! Great, long scene.
•• 0:58—Breasts during Jack's recollections.
••• 1:03—Breasts and buns, while making love with Jack. Long scene.

Desire (1994) . . . . Grace Lantel

Silk Degrees (1994) . . . . Alex Ramsey
• 0:49—Full frontal nudity behind plastic shower curtain.
•• 0:56—Breasts, while making love with Marc Singer in cabin.

TV:

The Yellow Rose (1983-84) . . . . Juliette Hollister
Dallas (1984-87) . . . . Mandy Winger

Shepard, Hilary

a.k.a. Hilary Shapiro and Hilary Shepard Turner.

Films:

Soup for One (1982). . . . . .Girl #4
Radioactive Dreams (1984) . . . . Biker Leader

Weekend Pass (1984) . . . . Cindy Hazard
•• 1:05—In red bra, then breasts taking off bra.
• 1:07—Buns and breasts getting into bathtub.

Private Resort (1985) . . . . .Shirley
••• 0:36—Breasts, then buns, taking off her dress in front of Rob Morrow.

Tough Guys (1986). . . . . Sandy
Hunk (1987) . . . . Alexis Cash
Lucky Stiff (1988) . . . . Cissy

Peace Maker (1990). . . . . Dori Caisson
• 1:08—Brief upper half of buns, taking off shirt and getting into shower. Brief side view of upper half of left breast, twice while making love with Townsend.

I Don't Buy Kisses Anymore (1992) . . . . Ada Fishbine
Scanner Cop (1993) . . . . Zena
Theodore Rex (1995) . . . . Sarah Jiminez
Turbo: A Power Rangers Movie (1997) . . . . Divatox

Made for Cable Movies:

Attack of the 50 ft. Woman (1993; HBO) . . . . Nurse
Last Exit to Earth (1996; Showtime) . . . . Lilith

Made for Cable TV:

Dream On: The First Episode (1990; HBO) . . . . .Date 2

TV:

Mighty Morphin Power Rangers (1997-) . . . . Divatox

Shepard, Jewel

Films:

Raw Force (1981) . . . . Drunk Sexpot
• 0:31—Breasts in black swimsuit, when a guy adjusts her straps and it falls open.

The Junkman (1982) . . . . Credit Girl

Zapped! (1982). . . . . Uncredited Girl in Car
• 0:39—Brief breasts after red and white top pops off when Scott Baio uses his Telekinesis on her.

My Tutor (1983) .Girl in Phone Booth
• 0:40—Brief left breast in car when Matt Lattanzi fantasizes about making love with her.

The Sex and Violence Family Hour (1983; Canadian)
. . . . Body Flash Dancer
••• 1:09—Buns and partial lower frontal nudity in T-back, breasts under short black top, while dancing in studio. Nude during interview.

Christina (1984; U.S./French) . . . . Christina
(Never released on video tape. Is shown occasionally on cable television.)
• 0:00—Cleavage and brief glimpses of breasts, while dancing in disco in open jacket.
• 0:04—Breasts, while wearing swimsuit bottom on sailboat.
• 0:05—Brief breasts, while flashing.
• 0:12—Silhouette of breasts, while making love on the beach with Patrick.
••• 0:17—Nude, while undressing in bathroom, taking a shower, then getting kidnapped by a masked woman.
•• 0:23—Breasts doing strip tease in front of her friends in living room.
•• 0:25—Full frontal nudity, while in sauna with her friends.
• 0:26—Breasts and buns, while making love with Patrick on sofa.
• 0:27—Full frontal nudity, while resting on Patrick's lap.
•• 0:28—Nude, while getting out of bed and opening the curtains.
•• 0:33—Breasts in nightmare, then waking up, while tied by her wrists.
• 0:36—Breasts in nightmare, while blindfolded and tied up.
• 0:43—Left breast in torn T-shirt.
••• 0:45—Nude, while getting out of bathtub.
••• 0:46—Nude, while making love with Marie on bed.
• 0:52—Breasts under sheer nightie.
•• 0:53—Full frontal nudity, while tied to table, then making love with Antoinette.
•• 0:55—Full frontal nudity in a dream.
• 0:56—Breasts in field after getting her blouse ripped open by Antoinette.
•• 1:01—Breasts, while making love with a sailor in a dream.
••• 1:06—Full frontal nudity, while making love with Alain on boat.
• 1:20—Breasts, while making love with Pablo.
•• 1:29—Nude, while dancing in a disco.
•• 1:30—Full frontal nudity, while typing on a computer.

Hollywood Hot Tubs (1984) . . . . Crystal Landers
(No breasts, but bouncing around a lot in short, braless T-shirts.)

Operation Overkill (1984) . . . . .n.a.
The Return of the Living Dead (1985) . . . . Casey

Party Camp (1987). . . . . Dyanne Stein
••• 0:57—In white bra and panties, then breasts playing strip poker with the boys.

Scenes from the Goldmine (1987). . . . . .Dana

The Underachievers (1987). . . . . Sci-Fi Teacher
• 0:27—Breasts ripping off her Star Trek uniform when someone enters her classroom. Dark, hard to see.

Going Undercover (1988; British) . . . . .Peaches

Hollywood Hot Tubs 2—Educating Crystal (1989)
. . . . Crystal Landers
• 1:12—Brief left breast, while lying down, kissing Gary.

Roots of Evil (1991) . . . . Wanda
(Unrated version reviewed.)
• 1:31—Brief right breast, a couple of times, when it pops out of her blouse while she's in police station.

Caged Heat 2: Stripped of Freedom (1993) . . . . . Amanda
•• 0:15—In bra and panties, then breasts, while undressing for strip search in the warden's office.

•• 0:49—Breasts, after getting her prison shirt ripped open, then whipped in front of the other prisoners.
Scanners: The Showdown (1994) .... Nurse
Video Tapes:
Jewel Naked Around the World (1995).......... Herself
• 0:00—Brief breasts (wearing a mask) while on stage with another woman and a guy wearing a mask.
• 0:05—Brief breasts, while opening her fur coat to flash the camera.
••• 0:05—Nude, undressing and taking a shower in clip from *Christina.*
•• 0:07—Brief breasts, while wrists are tied from *Christina.*
•• 0:08—Full frontal nudity, in clips from *Christina.*
••• 0:10—More full frontal nudity, in clips from *Christina.*
•• 0:19—In sheer black lingerie, then breasts, while dancing in video tape.
• 0:31—Brief breasts, while in car with Matt Lattanzi in clip from *My Tutor.*
••• 0:32—Nude while dancing in clip from *The Sex and Violence Family Hour.*
• 0:38—Brief breasts after her top gets popped of by Scott Baio in clip from *Zapped!.*
••• 0:39—Nude in several clips from *In the Flesh.*
If I'm So Famous, How Come Nobody's Ever Heard of Me? (1996)...................................... Herself

Shepherd, Cybill *

Former model.
Films:
The Last Picture Show (1971) .... Jacy Farrow
•• 0:37—Undressing on diving board. Very brief left breast falling onto diving board. Brief breasts tossing bra aside.
• 0:38—Brief left breast jumping into the water.
••• 1:05—Breasts and buns in motel room with Jeff Bridges.
The Heartbreak Kid (1972) .... Kelly Corcoran
Daisy Miller (1974) .... Annie P. "Daisy" Miller
Special Delivery (1976) .... Mary Jane
Taxi Driver (1976)................................Betsy
The Lady Vanishes (1979; British) .... Amanda Kelly
The Return (1980)........................... Daughter
Chances Are (1989)...................... Corrine Jeffries
Alice (1990)............................... Nancy Brill
Texasville (1990) .... Jacy Farrow
Once Upon A Crime (1992)............... Marilyn Schwary
Married to It (1993) .... Claire Laurent
The Last Word (1994) .... Kiki Taylor
Made for Cable Movies:
Memphis (1991; TNT)..................... Reeny Perdew
Which Way Home (1991) .... Karen Parsons
Made for TV Movies:
The Long Hot Summer (1985)................. Eula Varner
Moonlighting (1985)...................... Maddie Hayes
Stormy Weathers (1992) .... Samantha "Sam" Weathers
Telling Secrets (1993) ....Faith Kelsey
There Was a Little Boy (1993) ....Julie
Baby Brokers (1994) .... Debbie
While Justice Sleeps (1994) .... Jody Stokes
Journey of the Heart (1997)................ Janice Johnston
TV:
The Yellow Rose (1983-84) .... Colleen Champion
Moonlighting (1985-89).................. Maddie Hayes
Cybill (1995-98) .... Cybill Sheridan

Sheppard, Delia *

Films:
Witchcraft II: The Temptress (1989) ....Dolores
•• 1:20—Brief breasts several times with William.
Haunting Fear (1990)............................Lisa
••• 0:13—Breasts on desk, making love with Terry.
••• 1:10—Full frontal nudity, making love in bed with Terry. Long scene.
Rocky V (1990) .... Karen
The Adventures of Ford Fairlane (1991)............ Pussycat
Mirror Images (1991).................. Kaitlin/Shauna
•• 0:07—Right breast, while undressing in front of vanity mirror.
•• 0:08—More breasts as Shauna in bed.
• 0:12—Buns, while dancing on stage with a band, wearing a sexy outfit.
••• 0:14—Breasts in bed with Georgio.
••• 0:27—Breasts and buns in G-string, making love with Joey. Long scene.
••• 0:33—Buns in black bra and panties, walking around her sister's apartment. Long scene.
•• 0:39—Right breast, while with a guy with a mask.
••• 0:41—Nude, taking a shower. Great!
••• 0:43—Breasts in bedroom after her shower.
•• 0:48—Left breast, while making love in bed with Julie Strain.
••• 1:29—Breasts in bed in lingerie with the policeman.
Roots of Evil (1991) ....Monica
(Unrated version reviewed.)
••• 0:04—Breasts and buns in G-string, dancing on stage.
• 0:07—Breasts and buns, while on stage when wounded guy disturbs her act.
••• 0:38—Buns in outfit, then breasts dancing on stage.
••• 0:41—More buns and breasts in bed, making love with Johnny. Long scene.
Secret Games (1991) .... Celeste
(Unrated version reviewed.)
• 0:38—Breasts under sheer black body suit.
• 0:45—Buns, under sheer robe.
•• 0:48—Breasts with her lover, while watching Julianne and Eric on TV.
Sex Bomb (1991) ....n.a.
Animal Instincts (1992)........................ Ingrid
(Unrated version reviewed.)
•• 0:50—Breasts, while in bed with her lover and Joanne.
••• 0:54—Breasts, while in bed with only Joanne.
Dead Boyz Can't Fly (1992)..................... Angie
•• 1:01—In white bra and panties, then breasts in doctor's office when bad guy pretends to be a doctor and examines her.
Night Rhythms (1992)........................ Bridget
(Unrated version reviewed.)
••• 1:25—Full frontal nudity, making love with Kit in bed. Long scene.
Sins of Desire (1992) .... Jessica Callister
(Unrated version reviewed.)
••• 0:10—Full frontal nudity, while tied by her wrists in bed with Scott.
••• 0:45—Breasts and buns, while making love on the floor with Scott. Nice close-ups.
Body Chemistry 3: Point of Seduction (1993) ..... Wilhemina

Sheridan, Leisa *

Films:
Red Sun Rising (1993)...........................Katie

Video Tapes:
Playboy's 21 Playmates (1996) .... Playmate
••• 1:07—Nude in still photos.
••• 1:08—Nude outdoors in swimming pool.

Sheridan, Millicent

Films:
Sex Crimes (1992) .... Demon Lover
•• 0:23—Buns, then breasts, while making love with J.J. in his nightmare. (She's wearing deformed face make-up.)
• 0:32—Breasts, while in bed with J.J.—ugly make-up still on.
Casino (1995) .... Senator's Hooker
• 0:18—Brief buns and out of focus breasts, while undressing in room with Senator.
The Crossing Guard (1995)...................... Dancer

Sheridan, Nicollette *

Ex-wife of actor Harry Hamlin.
Films:
The Sure Thing (1985) .... The Sure Thing
Noises Off (1992) .... Brooke Ashton/Vicki
Beverly Hills Ninja (1996) .... Alison
Spy Hard (1996) .... Veronique Ukrinsky
Made for Cable Movies:
Deceptions (1990; Showtime) .... Adrienne Erickson
• 0:35—Very, very brief silhouette of breasts, while hugging Harry Hamlin when the camera tilts down from her head to her buns.
The Silver Strand (1995; Showtime) ...... Michelle Hughes
• 0:44—Very, very brief side of right breast, while in bunker with Del Piso. Partial buns when he takes off her panties.
• 0:49—Brief buns and breasts, while swimming under water in pool with Del Piso. (Mostly seen in silhouette.)
Miniseries:
Jackie Collins' Lucky/Chances (1990)....... Lucky Santangelo
Made for TV Movies:
Shadows of Desire (1994).................. Rowena Ekland
A Time to Heal (1994)...................... Jenny Barton
Robin Cook's "Virus" (1995) .... Dr. Harbuck
The People Next Door (1996)................. Anna Morse
Murder in My Mind (1997)......................... n.a.
TV:
Paper Dolls (1984) .... Taryn Blake
Knots Landing (1986-93) .... Paige Matheson

Sheridan, Robin

Films:
Vice Academy, Part 4 (1994) .... Scabia
• 0:14—Brief partial right breast poking out of bra during struggle on sofa with Amber.
Made for Cable TV:
Love Street: Ex-Girlfriend (1994; Showtime)
.... Dr. Anderson
• 0:10—Brief breasts, putting on lab coat after making love with Parker in one of her exam rooms.
• 0:11—Brief left breast in wedding dream.
• 0:17—Brief buns in panties and brief breasts in wedding dream.

Sherman, Geraldine

Films:
Interlude (1968; British) .... Natalie
Poor Cow (1968) .... Trixie
Take a Girl Like You (1970; British) .... Anna
There's a Girl in My Soup (1970) .... Caroline
•• 0:43—Breasts in bed, then getting out after Goldie Hawn splashes water on her.
Get Carter (1971; British) .... Girl in Cafe
Cry of the Penguins (1972; British) .... Penny

Sherwood, Robin

Films:
Loose Shoes (1977)...................... Biker Chic #2
The Tourist Trap (1979).......................... Eileen
Hero at Large (1980)................ Laboratory Assistant
Serial (1980) .... Woman
Blow Out (1981)............................ Screamer
Death Wish II (1982) .... Carol Kersey
• 0:15—Breasts after getting raped by gang member in their hideout.
The Love Butcher (1982)...................... Sheila
• 0:39—Very brief buns, while putting on swimsuit bottom.
• 0:40—Brief breasts several times, while struggling in pool with killer when he kills her with garden hose.
• 0:41—Buns, while getting carried out of pool by killer. Breasts under water in bathtub, dead.
• 0:43—Brief breasts, while throwing bikini top while in pool.
Made for TV Movies:
Outside Chance (1978)......................... Tootsie

Shields, Brooke *

Wife of tennis player Andre Agassi.
Films:
Alice, Sweet Alice (1977)......................... Karen
King of the Gypsies (1978) .... Tita
Pretty Baby (1978)........................... Violet
(She was only 11–12 years old at this time so there isn't really a whole lot to see here!)
• 0:57—Breasts and buns taking a bath.
• 1:26—Breasts posing on couch for Keith Carradine.
• 1:28—Buns, getting thrown out of the room, then trying to get back in.
Tilt (1978)...................................... Tilt
Just You and Me, Kid (1979) .... Kate
• 0:07—Brief buns, running down stairs after her towel gets caught in fence.
Wanda Nevada (1979) .... Wanda Nevada
Blue Lagoon (1980).......................... Emmeline
(Nudity is a body double, Kathy Trout.)
• 0:27—Nude swimming underwater after growing up from being little children.
• 0:43—More underwater swimming.
Endless Love (1981)............................. Jade
Sahara (1984) .... Dale
Brenda Starr (1986)...................... Brenda Starr
(Finally released in 1992.)
Speed Zone (1989) .... Stewardess
Backstreet Dreams (1990) .... Stephanie "Stevie" Bloom
Freaked (1993) .... Skye Daley
The Seventh Floor (1993; Australian)................. Kate
Freeway (1996) .... Mimi
Made for Cable TV:
Tales From the Crypt: Came the Dawn (1993)......."Norma"
Made for TV Movies:
Wet Gold (1984)............................. Laura
I Can Make You Love Me: The Stalking of Laura Black (1993)
.... Laura Black
Nothing Lasts Forever (1995) .... Honey Beth Taft

TV:
Suddenly Susan (1996-) . . . . Susan Keane

• Shimizu, Jenny *
Model.
Films:
Foxfire (1996) . . . . Goldie Goldman
••• 0:42—Breasts, while sitting and getting a tattoo, then watching Rita get a tattoo.

Shimkus, Joanna
Films:
Six in Paris (1968; French) . . . . Monica
Virgin and the Gypsy (1970; British) . . . . Yvette
The Marriage of a Young Stockbroker (1971) . . Lisa Alren
• 1:27—Very, very brief silhouette of left breast, while going into towel closet with Richard Benjamin.

Shinas, Sofia
Singer.
Films:
The Crow (1993) . . . . Shelly Webster
Terminal Velocity (1994) . . . . Broken Legs
Hourglass (1995) . . . . Dara
Hostile Intent (1997) . . . . Gina
Made for Cable TV:
Red Shoe Diaries: Borders of Salt (1994; Showtime) . . . . The Girl
(Some shots are a body double.)
• 0:08—Brief breasts, while on her back in flash forward scene in bed.
• 0:14—Brief left breast, brief breasts while on her back. You can see face with body.
•• 0:21—Breasts, while making love with the guy. Intercut with shots of the body double.
The Outer Limits: Valerie 23 (1995; Showtime) . . . . . Valerie
••• 0:21—Nude in bedroom, after taking off her nightgown to show William Sadler that she's fully functional.
The Hunger: Footsteps (1998; Cinemax) . . . . Claire
• 0:05—Back side of left breast, while taking off robe and putting on dress.
• 0:14—Brief breasts, while starting to make love with the second victim.
•• 0:21—Breasts and buns in panties while making love with a guy.
The Outer Limits: Mary 25 (1998; Showtime) . . . . Mary 25
•• 0:16—Breasts, while in the bathroom with Charlie.
• 0:26—Brief buns and very brief side of right breast, when walking into the shower.

Shire, Devon
See: Peace, Jennifer.

Shirkani, Kym
Made for Cable TV:
Dream On: The Undergraduate (1992; HBO) . . . . Julie
••• 0:03—In bra, then breasts, while making love with Martin.
Dream On: The French Conception (1993; HBO) . . . . Julie
Dream On: Take Two Tablets, And Get Me to Mt. Sinai (1995; HBO) . . . . Martin's Lover

Shirley, Aleisa
Films:
Sweet Sixteen (1982) . . . . Melissa Morgan
• 0:16—Side view of body, nude, taking a shower.
• 1:11—Breasts undressing to go skinny dipping with Hank. Dark, hard to see.
• 1:13—Breasts, getting out of the water.
Spacehunter: Adventures in the Forbidden Zone (1983) . . . . Reena
Ballistic (1993) . . . . Hooker
a.k.a. Fists of Justice
Made for Cable TV:
The Hitchhiker: Shattered Vows (1983; HBO) . . . . Pamela
• 0:08—Breasts and buns in bathroom with Jeff.
•• 0:18—In bed wearing black bra, panties, garter belt and stockings, then breasts.
Video Tapes:
Rock Video Girls (1991) . . . . Herself

Shoop, Pamela Susan
Films:
Empire of the Ants (1977) . . . . Coreen Bradford
One Man Jury (1978) . . . . Wendy
Halloween II (1981) . . . . Karen
••• 0:48—Breasts getting into the whirlpool bath with Budd in the hospital.
Made for TV Movies:
The Dallas Cowboy Cheerleaders (1979) . . . . Betty Denton

Shower, Kathy *
Films:
Double Exposure (1983) . . . . Mudwrestler #1
Commando Squad (1987) . . . . Kat Withers
The Further Adventures of Tennessee Buck (1987) . . . . Barbara Manchester
••• 0:57—Breasts getting rubbed with oil by the cannibal women. Nice close up shots.
•• 1:02—Breasts in a hut with the Chief of the tribe.
Frankenstein General Hospital (1988) . . Dr. Alice Singleton
• 1:15—Brief breasts running out of her office after the monster, putting her lab coat on.
Out on Bail (1988) . . . . Sally Anne
• 1:01—Brief breasts in shower with Robert Ginty.
Bedroom Eyes II (1989) . . . . Carolyn Ross
•• 0:22—Breasts in the artist's studio fighting with her lover while Wings Hauser watches through the window.
Robo C.H.I.C. (1990) . . . . Robo C.H.I.C.
a.k.a. Cyber C.H.I.C.
Velvet Dreams (1991; Italian) . . . . Laura
•• 0:15—Left breast, while making love with Paul in the dressing room.
• 0:35—Brief buns, while getting a massage.
•• 0:42—Breasts, tied to a tree during her writing fantasy.
American Kickboxer II (1992) . . . . Lilian
a.k.a. To the Death
L.A. Goddess (1992) . . . . Lisa Moore
•• 0:00—Full frontal nudity, getting out of the shower.
•• 0:45—Side view of buns and breasts, getting into and in bathtub.
••• 0:53—Nude in spa with Damian.
• 0:56—Left breast, while lying in park with Damian.
•• 0:58—Breasts while making love in bed with Damian.
• 1:20—Brief breasts in spa with Damian in flashback.
Wild Cactus (1992) . . . . Celeste
(Unrated version reviewed.)
•• 0:52—Breasts, while lying in bed.
•• 1:16—Breasts in bed with bullet through her head, when discovered by Philip.
Sexual Malice (1993) . . . . Laura Altman
(Unrated version reviewed.)
••• 0:10—Breasts, while making love on pool table with a guy when Christine peeks in room.

A Brilliant Disguise (1994) . . . . Lila Foster

Improper Conduct (1994). . . . . .Emily
(Unrated version reviewed.)
- •• 0:19—Breasts, while getting into bed with John Loughlin, then making love.

Married People, Single Sex 2: For Better or Worse (1994). . . . . .Carol
- ••• 0:47—Breasts, after getting out of shower in bathroom with John.
- ••• 1:14—Breasts, while lying in bed with John.

Irresistible Impulse (1995) . . . . Tina Lovejoy
- • 1:30—Brief breasts, while lying in bed with Richard.
- • 1:31—Brief breasts, while sitting up in bed.

To the Limit (1995) . . . . Vinnie
- • 0:30—Breasts and partial buns, while making love with a guy in bed.

Twisted Passion (1995) . . . . Joyce Walker
a.k.a. Shades of Gray

Hindsight (1996) . . . . Joanne Lehman
- • 0:08—Breasts, while making love with Jason.

Made for Cable TV:

Hot Line: Fountain of Youth (1994; Cinemax). . . . . . . Judy
(Available on video tape in *Hot Line.*)
- •• 0:23—Breasts, while making love with Kurt on the beach. Sometimes in silhouette.

Love Street: Radio (1995; Showtime) . . . . Shannon

TV:

Santa Barbara (1987-90). . . . . Janice Harrison

Video Tapes:

Playboy Video Magazine, Volume 9. . . . . Playmate

Playboy Video Calendar 1987 (1986) . . . . Playmate

Playboy's Playmates of the Year: The '80s (1989) . . . . .Playmate of the Year 1986
- ••• 0:17—Full frontal nudity outside by spa.
- ••• 0:19—Breasts in still photos. Full frontal nudity, posing in bed.

The Best of Sexy Lingerie (1992). . . . . .Model

The Best of Video Playmate Calendars (1992) . . Playmate
- •• 0:04—Full frontal nudity in still photos. In lingerie in bedroom.
- ••• 0:05—Full frontal nudity on bed.

Playboy's Playmates Revisited (1998). . . . . Playmate
- ••• 0:02—Nude in old footage and still photos.
- ••• 0:08—Nude in new footage.

Shue, Elisabeth

Sister of actor Andrew Shue.

Films:

The Karate Kid (1984) . . . . Ali

Link (1986) . . . . Jane Chase
- • 0:50—Brief right breast and buns, side view of a body double, standing in bathroom getting ready to take a bath while Link watches.

Adventures in Babysitting (1987) . . . . .Chris Parker

Cocktail (1988). . . . . Jordan Mooney

Back to the Future, Part II (1989). . . . . Jennifer

Back to the Future, Part III (1990) . . . . Jennifer

The Marrying Man (1991). . . . . .Adele Horner
a.k.a. Too Hot to Handle

Soapdish (1991) . . . . Lori Craven

Heart and Souls (1993) . . . . .Anne

Twenty Bucks (1993). . . . . Emily Adams

Radio Inside (1994) . . . . Natalie
- •• 0:40—Brief left breast in mirror in dressing room.

The Underneath (1994) . . . . Susan

Leaving Las Vegas (1995) . . . . Sera
- •• 1:19—Breasts, while making out with Nicolas Cage outside by the pool.

The Trigger Effect (1996) . . . . Annie
- • 0:11—Very brief, left nipple when she fondles herself while talking with Kyle MacLachlan.

Deconstructing Harry (1997). . . . . Fay

The Saint (1997) . . . . Dr. Emma Russell

Palmetto (1998) . . . . .Mrs. Donnelly/Rhea Malroux

Made for Cable Movies:

Blind Justice (1994; HBO). . . . . Caroline
- • 0:36—Very, very brief right breast in gaping dress after getting up slightly after Armand Assante falls over.
- • 0:39—Brief upper half of right breast with part of nipple sticking out of camisole top while sitting on bed.

Made for Cable TV:

Dream On: oral sex, lies and videotape (1993; HBO). . . .Maura

Made for TV Movies:

Call to Glory (1984) . . . . .Jackie Sarnac

TV:

Call to Glory (1984-85) . . . . .Jackie Sarnac

Shugart, Reneé

Films:

Screwball Hotel (1988) . . . . Blue Bell

Spring Fever USA (1988) . . . . Beach Beauty
a.k.a. Lauderdale

Summer Job (1989) . . . . Karen
- • 0:42—Breasts taking off her top. Long shot, dark.
- • 0:45—In white lingerie, standing on stairs, then very brief left breast flashing.

Siani, Sabrina

Films:

Ator, The Fighting Eagle (1982). .Roon

2020 Texas Gladiators (1983; Italian) . . . . Maida
- •• 0:07—Left breast, in open white dress after gang rape.
- • 0:34—Breasts during rape.

The Throne of Fire (1983; Italian) . . . . .Princess Belkaren

Sidney, Ann

Films:

Sebastian (1968; British) . . . . Naomi

Performance (1970). . . . . .Dana
- • 0:01—Very brief breasts and buns.
- • 0:24—Brief breasts with Chas in flashbacks.

The Treasure of the Amazon (1985; Mexican) . . . . Barbara

Siemaszko, Nina

Sister of actor Casey Siemaszko.

Films:

One More Saturday Night (1986) . . . . .Karen Lundahl

License to Drive (1988) . . . . Natalie

Tucker: The Man and His Dream (1988) . . . Marilyn Lee Tucker

Lost Angels (1989) . . . . Merilee
- • 0:38—Brief breasts and buns, running through courtyard. Long shot, don't really see anything.
- • 0:45—Buns, sitting at table outside, undressing and rubbing feces (yuck!) on herself.

Bed & Breakfast (1992) . . . . Cassie

Wild Orchid II: Two Shades of Blue (1992). . . . . Blue
- ••• 0:27—Breasts and buns, getting undressed in front of Wendy Hughes.
- •• 0:43—Breasts and buns in steam room with a customer.
- •• 0:58—Breasts in panties, garter belt and stockings while undressing for Josh.

••• 1:06—Breasts while humiliating J. J. in front of everyone at a party.

Twenty Bucks (1993) . . . . Bank Teller
Airheads (1994) . . . . Suzzi
Floundering (1994) . . . . Gal
The American President (1995) . . . . Beth Wade

Made for Cable Movies:

Power of Attorney (1995) . . . . Maria
Sawbones (1995; Showtime) . . . . Jenny Sloan
More Tales of the City (1998; Canadian/U.S.; Showtime) . . . . Mona Ramsey

•• 1:26—(0:37 into Part 2) Breasts, while changing clothes.

Made for Cable TV:

Red Shoe Diaries: Just Like That (1993; Showtime) . Trudy
(Available on the video tape *Red Shoe Diaries 3: Another Woman's Lipstick.*)

• 0:09—In white bra, while making out in the elevator with Kyle. Very, very brief lower frontal nudity when he rips her panties off.
••• 0:14—In white bra, then breasts in bed with Phillip.
••• 0:16—Breasts, while making love on top of Phillip in bed. Full frontal nudity, while lying in bed.
•• 0:17—Briefly in black body suit, then breasts making love on top of Phillip in bed.

Tales From the Crypt: Creep Course (1993; HBO) . . . . Stella Bishop

Made for TV Movies:

Sinatra (1992) . . . . Mia Farrow
Baby Brokers (1994) . . . . Leeanne
Runaway Car (1997) . . . . n.a.

Siewkumar, Asha

Films:

Tropical Heat (1993) . . . . Kamala

•• 0:45—Brief breasts, while opening her blouse in front of Rick Rossovich.
••• 1:09—Breasts and buns, undressing in front of mirror and walking into bathroom.
••• 1:10—Breasts and buns, while getting out of the shower, drying herself off and walking out of the bathroom.
••• 1:16—Buns and breasts while making love in bed with Rossovich.

Uninhibited (1993) . . . . Cassandra

•• 1:12—Breasts, while making love with Jugginson.

Sillas, Karen

Films:

Trust (1991; British/U.S.) . . . . Nurse Paine
Simple Men (1992; U.S./British) . . . . Kate
Risk (1993) . . . . Maya

•• 0:04—Breasts and buns, while sitting as an artist's model then getting up. Medium long shot.
• 0:05—Left breast, while changing tops in her apartment.
• 0:11—Very brief partial right breast, while getting into bathtub with Joe.
••• 0:19—Breasts, after taking off robe in art classroom and posing in a chair.
• 0:21—Brief breasts, getting up from chair, when Joe gets caught starting to take off his clothes.

What Happened Was... (1994) . . . . Jackie
Flirt (1995) . . . . Doctor Clint
Female Perversions (1997) . . . . Renee

••• 0:53—Breasts (mostly left), when Tilda Swinton kisses her, while lying in hammock.
•• 0:55—More breasts, while in hammock with Swinton.

Sour Grapes (1998) . . . . Joan

Made for TV Movies:

The Beast (1996) . . . . Kathryn Marcus
Lies He Told (1997) . . . . n.a.
Night Sins (1997) . . . . Hannah Garrison

TV:

Under Suspicion (1994-95) . . . . . Detective Rose "Phil" Phillips

Silver, Cindy

Films:

Gimme an "F" (1981) . . . . One of the "Ducks"
a.k.a. T & A Academy 2
Hardbodies (1984) . . . . Kimberly

•• 0:07—Brief breasts on beach when a dog steals her bikini top.
••• 0:47—Breasts standing in front of closet mirrors talking about breasts with Kristi.

• *Silvstedt, Victoria* *

Video Tapes:

Playboy Video Calendar 1998 (1997) . . . . December

•• 0:49—Nude, while posing outdoors.
••• 0:50—Nude, while posing during modeling session.

Playboy Video Centerfold: Victoria Silvstedt (1997) . . . . Playmate of the Year

•• 0:00—Nude during introduction.
•• 0:02—In lingerie and nude, while dancing and posing outdoors.
••• 0:05—Nude while dancing and posing in a studio.
•• 0:13—Nude when dancing and posing with her (clothed) sister.
••• 0:16—Nude, while making love with her boyfriend in a barn.
••• 0:23—Nude in still photos.
••• 0:25—In lingerie and nude, while posing for photos with a white feather boa.
••• 0:28—Nude, while posing in a house.
••• 0:32—Nude, while posing in rain segment.
••• 0:34—Nude, during Cinderella style fantasy.
•• 0:40—Full frontal nudity, while lying on bed.

Simmons, Allene

Films:

Porky's (1981; Canadian) . . . . Jackie

• 1:02—Breasts in the shower scene.

R.S.V.P. (1984) . . . . Patty De Fois Gras

•• 0:13—Breasts taking off red top behind the bar with the bartender.
•• 0:38—Breasts in bed with Mr. Edwards, then buns running to hide in the closet.
•• 0:41—Frontal nudity in room with Mr. Anderson.
••• 0:51—Breasts talking to Toby in the hallway trying to get help for the Governor.

The Malibu Bikini Shop (1985) . . . . Milinda Riley
Young Lady Chatterley II (1986) . . . . Marta, Maid in Bed

Simon, Tania

Films:

Rapa Nui (1994) . . . . Koreto

• 0:19—Breasts, while in the river with the other women.
• 0:24—Left breast, while arguing about small rations.
• 0:24—Brief left breast, while arguing for more food.

Women From Down Under (1995; Australian/New Zealand) . . . . Peach/Sal

Simone, Domonique

Adult film actress.
a.k.a. Deirdre Morrow.
Films:
Carnal Crimes (1991)....................... Leggy Girl
• 1:22—Buns, in G-string, leaning over to talk to Renny and Stanley.
Mirror Images (1991) .... Slave Girl
••• 0:58—Buns in G-string, then breasts with masked guy.
••• 1:00—Breasts on bed with masked guy and Julie Strain.
Uninhibited (1993) .... Detective Jordan's Wife
•• 0:02—Breasts, while in bed by herself, then making love with Detective Jordan.
Nighttime Lover (1995)..................... Prostitute
a.k.a. Call Girl
•• 1:12—Breasts, while getting dressed for photo session, then breasts and buns in G-string during photo session with another prostitute.
• 1:16—Brief left breast in B&W photo and breasts in photo session.
• 1:17—Brief breasts in another photo session and in B&W photos.

Simonsen, Renee

Films:
Nothing Underneath (1985; Italian) .... Barbara
a.k.a. Sotto Il Vestito Niente
• 0:51—Brief side view of left breast, changing backstage during fashion show.
Via Montenapoleone (1987; Italian) .... Elena

Simpson, Danone

a.k.a. Danone Camden.
Films:
Can't Stop the Music (1980)...... Stewardess in Record Store
Texas Lightning (1980)............................. n.a.
Hard Country (1981) .... Cowgirl
The Killer Instinct (1982; Canadian)................ Amy
a.k.a. Trapped
• 0:12—Nude, when Henry Silva catches her in bed with another man.
• 0:13—Very brief left breast in open robe on porch.
• 0:14—Very brief breasts in open robe when Silva beats her on the bed.
•• 0:43—Breasts, while drying herself off with a towel, then sitting in front of a mirror, covering up bruises with make-up.
TV:
Dallas (1989-91).............................. Kendall

Simpson, Suzi *

Films:
Enemy Gold (1993)...................... Becky Midnite
••• 0:09—Breasts, while undressing and changing clothes in bathroom.
••• 0:33—Breasts and buns, while making love with Chris.
••• 1:05—Breasts and buns while taking a shower outside.
• 1:11—Buns in panties, while standing outside when the boys return.
The Last Road (1997)........................... Katie
• 0:09—Breasts, while making out in a car with a guy, then getting out.
Video Tapes:
Eden (1992) ....Uncredited Girl in Exercise Room
Playboy Video Calendar 1993 (1992) .... September
••• 0:37—Nude in cave woman studio setting.
••• 0:39—Nude in haunted house setting.
Playboy's Playmate Review 1993 (1993) .... Miss January
••• 0:37—Nude while playing billiards.
••• 0:38—Nude in a cabin.
Playboy's Sexy, Steamy, Sultry (1993).......... Playmate

• Sims, Clare

Films:
Marked Man (1996; Canadian) .... Lisa Elkins
Made for Cable TV:
Hunger: The Sloan Men (1997; Showtime)......... Judith
•• 0:14—Breasts, while making love with Herman on the floor of a museum with other people watching.

Sinclair, Annette

Ex-wife of singer Bob Seger.
Films:
Thief of Hearts (1984) .... College Girl #1
(Special Home Video Version reviewed.)
Weekend Pass (1984) .... Maxine
Hide and Go Shriek (1988) .... Kim Downs
• 0:51—Brief breasts and buns, undressing and getting into bed. Long shot.
•• 0:57—Breasts, getting up and out of bed, then getting dressed.
• 1:02—Breasts and buns, tied up on top of freight elevator.
• 1:05—Breasts on top of elevator.
• 1:17—Breasts on top of elevator fighting with the killer. Lit with red light.
Listen to Me (1989)........................ Fountain Girl
Instant Karma (1990) .... Amy
Lunatics: A Love Story (1991) .... Blonde

Singer, Linda

Films:
Zombie Nightmare (1987) .... Maggie
Whispers (1989) .... Prostitute
Return to Frogtown (1992)................. Nurse Cloris
a.k.a. Frogtown II
• 0:48—Buns, in sexy outfit in room with Robert D'Zar.
• 0:50—Brief top of breasts, sticking out of her top while she's on top of D'Zar.
Relative Fear (1994)......................... K-9 Cop
Stalked (1994; Canadian/Australian) .... Strip Dancer
Video Tapes:
Ultimate Sensual Massage (1991) .... Awakening
••• 0:02—Breasts and buns, during massage session in bed.

Singer, Lori

Sister of actor Marc Singer.
Films:
Footloose (1984).......................... Ariel Moore
The Falcon and the Snowman (1985) .... Lana
The Man With One Red Shoe (1985)............... Maddy
Trouble in Mind (1986) .... Georgia
• 1:01—Very brief left breast, in bed with Kris Kristofferson.
Summer Heat (1987) .... Roxy
•• 0:36—Breasts in bed with Jack. Kind of dark and hard to see.
Made in U.S.A. (1988) .... Annie
• 0:26—Brief left breast and very brief lower frontal nudity in the back of a convertible with Dar at night.
Warlock (1990) .... Kassandra
Equinox (1992) .... Sharon Ace
Sunset Grill (1992) .... Loren
•• 0:57—Breasts, taking off bra and putting on robe.

- 0:58—Brief full frontal nudity sitting down in open robe. Left breast, while sitting down in tub.
- ••• 0:59—Breasts and buns, with Peter Weller in bathtub.
- ••• 1:15—Breasts, sitting up in bed after making love with Weller. Covered with sweat.

Short Cuts (1993) . . . . Zoe Trainer
- •• 0:48—Nude, stripping out of her clothes, then jumping in pool and floating. Seen through a fence.

The Last Ride (1994) . . . . Scarlett Stuart
- • 0:34—Side of right breast, while taking off towel in front of Mickey Rourke.
- •• 0:46—Breasts, while bathing and making love with Rourke in pond outside.
- •• 1:04—Brief side view of left breast, then left breast while making love in bed with Rourke. Quick cuts.

Made for TV Movies:

Storm and Sorrow (1990) . . . . Molly Higgins

TV:

Fame (1982-83) . . . . Julie Miller

VR.5 (1995). . . . . Sydney Bloom

Sirtis, Marina

Films:

The Wicked Lady (1983; British) . . . . Jackson's Girl
- ••• 1:06—Full frontal nudity in and getting out of bed when Faye Dunaway discovers her in bed with Alan Bates.
- ••• 1:20—Breasts getting whipped by Dunaway during their fight during Bates' hanging.

Blind Date (1984) . . . . Hooker

a.k.a. Deadly Seduction

(Not to be confused with *Blind Date* (1987) with Bruce Willis.)
- ••• 0:21—Breasts walking to and lying in bed just before taxi driver kills her.

Death Wish III (1985). . . . . Maria
- • 0:42—Breasts getting blouse ripped open next to a car by the bad guys.
- • 0:43—More breasts on mattress at the bad guys' hangout.

Waxwork II: Lost in Time (1991) . . . . Gloria

Star Trek Generations (1994). . . . . Counselor Deanna Troi

Star Trek: First Contact (1996). . . . Lt. Commander Deanna Troi

TV:

Star Trek: The Next Generation (1987-95) . . . . Counselor Deanna Troi

Sissons, Kimber

See: Monroe, Kimber.

• Skeriotis, Patricia

Films:

Backstreet Justice (1993) . . . . Cele
- •• 0:28—Left breast, getting out of shower and wrapping towel around herself.

Dream Master: The Erotic Invader (1995) . . . . Devora
- •• 0:14—Buns in lingerie, then right breasts, while making love with Grant while he's handcuffed to a park bench.
- • 0:27—Brief breasts, when Grant is making love with her.
- • 1:12—Buns in lingerie in Grant's dream.
- •• 1:18—Breasts and buns in lingerie, while talking with September.

Diary of a Serial Killer (1996). . . . . Marla

Mercenary (1996). . . . . Kurdish Woman
- • 0:57—Very brief nude, several times, during fight and after getting killed.

Skinner, Anita

Films:

Girlfriends (1978) . . . . Anne Munroe

Sole Survivor (1982). Denise Watson
- • 0:29—Very, very brief right breast in bed with Dr. Richardson. Brief side view of right breast when he jumps out of bed.

Skinner, Rainee

Films:

Rebel (1985; Australian) . . . . Prostitute in bed
- • 0:37—Brief breasts sitting up in bed.

Kiss the Night (1988; Australian) . . . . n.a.

Pandemonium (1988) . . . . First Twin

Skiru, Julie

See: Kruis, Julie.

Skobline, Irene

Films:

Clean Slate (1981; French) . . . . Anne

a.k.a. Coup de Torchon
- •• 1:07—Breasts, while taking a shower and getting spied on by Nono.

Summer (1986; French). . . . . In Paris

a.k.a. Le Rayon Vert

a.k.a. The Green Ray

Skorohodove, Elena

Films:

Svidanie Na Mlechnom Puti (1987; U.S.S.R.) . . . . n.a.

Hit the Dutchman (1992) . . . . Anastasia

(Unrated version reviewed.)
- •• 1:17—Breasts, while making love with Arthur in bedroom.
- ••• 1:19—Nude, making love in bed with Arthur and afterwards.
- •• 1:23—Breasts in bed with Arthur.

Killer Instinct (1992) . . . . Baby

a.k.a. Mad Dog Coll

Skriver, Ina

Films:

Emily (1976; British). . . . . Augustine
- ••• 0:43—Breasts getting into the shower with Koo Stark to give her a massage.

Victor/Victoria (1982) . . . . Simone Kallisto

• Sky

See: Solari, Sky.

Skye, Gabriella

Made for Cable TV:

Erotic Confessions: Madelyn's Laundry (1996; Cinemax) . . . . Madelyn

(Available on video tape in *Erotic Confessions, Volume 4: Pleasure.*)
- • 0:02—Brief breasts and buns, while modeling lingerie in front of mirror.
- ••• 0:06—Nude, while making love with Luke in clothing store.
- ••• 0:12—Breasts, while making love with Luke in meeting room.

Video Tapes:

Playboy's Girls of the Internet (1996). . . . . Herself
- ••• 0:36—In lingerie, then nude, while taking off her clothes and dancing for a voyeuristic neighbor.

Skye, Ione

a.k.a. Ione Skye Leitch.
Daughter of '60s singer Donovan Leitch.
Wife of Beastie Boy Adam Horovitz.

Films:

A Night in the Life of Jimmy Reardon (1987).... Denise Hunter
River's Edge (1987)........................... Clarissa
Stranded (1987)........................... Deirdre Clark
The Rachel Papers (1989; British).......... Rachel Noyce
•• 0:58—Breasts getting undressed and into bed with Charles. Long shot, then breasts in bed.
••• 1:03—Brief breasts in three scenes. From above in bathtub, in bed and in bathtub again.
•• 1:04—Left breast, making love sitting up with Charles.
• 1:06—Brief breasts sitting up in bathtub.
• 1:08—Brief breasts long shot getting dressed in Charles' room.
• 1:28—Brief breasts kissing Charles in bed during his flashback.

Say Anything (1989)...................... Diane Court
Mindwalk (1991)............................... Kit
Samantha (1991)............................ Elaine
Gas, Food, Lodging (1992).................... Trudi
••• 0:38—Breasts, taking off her blouse in a cave with her boyfriend, then making love.
• 0:40—Brief right breast, while sitting up.

Wayne's World (1992)........................ Elyse
Dream for an Insomniac (1995)............... Frankie
Four Rooms (1995)............................ Eva
••• 0:10—Breasts, after taking off her top during witch ceremony.
••• 0:13—Breasts, when she's about to pour her part of the ceremony into the cauldron.
•• 0:14—Breasts, while alone in hotel room with Tim Roth.
••• 0:18—Breasts, after taking off jacket and seducing Roth using witchcraft.

One Night Stand (1997).................. Charlie's Friend

Made for Cable Movies:

Guncrazy (1992; Showtime)........................ Joy
Rebel Highway: Girls in Prison (1994; Showtime).... Carol
• 0:23—Right breast, while in the showers with Melba.
• 1:02—Very, very brief breasts, while washing Melba's back in the showers.

Made for Cable TV:

Nightmare Classics: Carmilla (1989; HBO).......... Marie

TV:

Covington Cross (1992-93)..................... Eleanor

Slater, Helen

Films:

Supergirl (1984; British)............... Linda Lee/Supergirl
The Legend of Billie Jean (1985)................. Billie Jean
Ruthless People (1986).................... Sandy Kessler
The Secret of My Success (1987)................. Christy
Happy Together (1988)........... Alexandra "Alex" Page
•• 0:17—Brief right breast changing clothes while talking to Patrick Dempsey. Unfortunately, she has a goofy expression on her face.

Sticky Fingers (1988).......................... Hattie
City Slickers (1991).................... Bonnie Rayburn
Betrayal of the Dove (1992)...................... Ellie
• 0:29—Brief tip of right breast while in bed with Billy Zane.
•• 0:30—Brief right breast, while in pool with Zane. Brief breasts in bed, then left breast.
••• 0:31—Very, very brief breasts, then more breasts while in bed with Zane.

A House in the Hills (1993)............... Alex Weaver
••• 0:15—Breasts, while in bedroom in front of mirror, trying on various lingerie. Very nice!
0:36—Sort of breasts, in shower when Michael Madsen brings her a dress. Shower door is too fogged up to see anything.

Lassie (1994).............................. Laura Turner
No Way Back (1996)............................ Mary

Made for Cable Movies:

Chantilly Lace (1993; Showtime).................. Hannah
Parallel Lives (1994; Showtime).............. Elsa Freedman

Made for Cable TV:

Dream On: Theory of Relativity (1992; HBO).......... Sarah

Made for TV Movies:

The Great Air Race (1990; Australian).... Jacqueline Cochrane
12:01 (1993).................................... Lisa

TV:

Capital News (1990).................... Anne McKenna

Slater, Suzanne *

a.k.a. Suzee Slater.

Films:

Savage Streets (1984).................... Uncredited
•• 0:09—Breasts being held by jerks when they yank her tube top down.

Chopping Mall (1986)......................... Leslie
a.k.a. Killbots
•• 0:28—Brief breasts in bed showing breasts to Mike.

Real Men (1987)..................... Woman in Bed
• 0:07—Brief left breast, in bed with James Belushi.

Take Two (1988)............................ Sherrie
•• 0:11—Breasts in office talking with Grant Goodeve, wearing panties, garter belt and stockings.
• 1:00—Breasts undressing to get into hot tub wearing black underwear bottom.

The Big Picture (1989).................... Stewardess
Cartel (1990)................................ Nancy
• 0:36—Breasts during brutal rape/murder scene.

Mind Twister (1992).................... Heather Black
(Unrated version reviewed.)
••• 0:17—Breasts and partial buns, while making love on sofa with Roy. Long scene.
• 0:39—Inside half of left breast in open robe when pizza delivery guy sees her.
••• 0:56—Breasts and buns, while in bed with Lisa while getting videotaped by Daniel. A little bit of fluorescent paint added to her breasts for color. Great!

Slavens, Darla

Films:

Class of Nuke 'Em High Part II: Subhumanoid Meltdown (1991)
.... Plain White Rapper
Married People, Single Sex (1993)................ Fran
•• 0:03—In white bra and buns in panties while undressing in bedroom. Full frontal nudity, walking to closet.
•• 0:10—In white bra, then breasts while undressing in bedroom.
••• 0:53—Left breast in mirror, while trying out vibrator.

Sloan, Tiffany *

Video Tapes:

Playboy Video Centerfold: Tiffany Sloan (1992)
.... Playmate
••• 0:00—Nude in the desert.

•• 0:02—Buns, in aqueduct.
••• 0:03—Nude in factory with fire and ice.
••• 0:09—Nude in warehouse gymnastics and dance routine. Nice.
••• 0:12—Nude in still photos.
••• 0:15—Nude in warehouse song and dance routine.
••• 0:18—Nude in bed in fantasy scene with a guy.
••• 0:23—Nude in the desert.

Playboy Video Calendar 1994 (1993) . . . . May
••• 0:19—Nude in bathtub in the desert.
••• 0:20—Nude in ballet/dance number in warehouse.

Playboy's Erotic Fantasies II (1993) . . . . .Model
Playboy's Playmate Review 1993 (1993) . . . Miss October
•• 0:48—Lower nudity, while in aqueduct.
••• 0:50—Nude in fire and ice fantasy segment.

Playboy's Sexy, Steamy, Sultry (1993). . . . . .Playmate
Sexy Lingerie V (1993). . . . . .Model
Playboy Video Centerfold: Jenny McCarthy (1994) . . . . Angel/Nurse
Sexy Lingerie: Dreams & Desire (1994) . . . . .Playmate
Wet & Wild: The Locker Room (1994) . . . . .Playmate
Playboy The Best of Jenny McCarthy (1996) . . . . . Angel/Nurse

Sloatman, Lala

a.k.a. Lala.

Films:

Watchers (1988) . . . . .Tracey
Joe vs. the Volcano (1990). . . . . Waitress
The Adventures of Ford Fairlane (1991). . . . . Sorority Girl
Amityville: A New Generation (1993) . . . . Lianie
•• 0:14—Breasts, undressing and making love with Keyes.

Dragon: The Bruce Lee Story (1993) . . . . Sherry Schnell

Small, Marya

Films:

Sleeper (1973). . . . . Dr. Nero
One Flew Over the Cuckoo's Nest (1975) . . . . .Candy
• 1:00—Very brief side view of left breast, bending over to pick up her clothes on boat.

The Wild Party (1975) . . . . .Bertha
The Great Smokey Roadblock (1976) . . . . Alice
The World's Greatest Lover (1977) . . . . Slave Girl #2
Thank God It's Friday (1978) . . . . Jackie
Fade to Black (1980) . . . . Doreen
National Lampoon's Class Reunion (1982). . . . . Iris Augen
Zapped! (1982). . . . . Mrs. Springboro

• Smart, Dee

Films:

'Blackwater Trail (1995; Australian) . . . . Cathy
Back of Beyond (1996; Australian) . . . . Charlie
• 0:58—Brief breasts, while lying on table when Connor tries to force himself on her.

Smax, Honey

See: Lauren, Honey.

Smith Bouchér, Savannah

Films:

Five Days from Home (1978). . . . . Georgie Haskin
North Dallas Forty (1979) . . . . Joanne
• 0:27—Very brief breasts in bed tossing around with Nick Nolte.

The Long Riders (1980) . . . . Zee
Meet the Applegates (1989) . . . . Dottie
Eating (1990) . . . . Eloise
Relentless 3 (1992). . . . . Marianne
• 0:10—Very brief breast when Walter starts to kiss it.
0:36—In black bra, then in white bra, while sitting in chair, getting photographed by Walter.

Scanner Cop (1993) . . . . Margaret Harrigan

Smith, Amanda

Films:

Dancing In the Dark (1986; Canadian) . . . . Neighbor
Fall From Innocence (1988). . . . . Janis Cummins
• 0:05—Brief right breast while lying in bed when Bob gets out.
• 0:48—Left breast, in open nightie top, while walking down hallway.

The Freshman (1990) . . . . .Mall Patron

Made for Cable Movies:

Down Came a Blackbird (1995; Showtime) . . . . .Professor's Wife
• 1:41—Very brief left breast, then breasts, twice, while strapped down and tortured on a table during Raul Julia's flashback.

Smith, Amber *

Films:

The Funeral (1996). . . . . Bridgette
••• 0:31—Breasts, while having sex in bed with Paul Hipp, while Vincent Gallo talks to him.

The Mirror Has Two Faces (1996) . . . . .Felicia (Video)
How To Be a Player (1997) . . . . Amber
• 0:04—Brief side of right breast, while lying on top of Bill Bellamy in bed.
• 0:42—In white lingerie, then buns and breasts, while fooling around with Bellamy.

L.A. Confidential (1997) . . . . Susan Lefferts
• 0:34—Very brief left breast, twice, dead, when sheet is pulled up so that her mother can identify her.

Private Parts (1997) . . . . Julie

Made for Cable TV:

Red Shoe Diaries: Runway (1994; Showtime). . . . . .Alia
•• 0:02—Brief breasts, while sitting in front of mirror with her lover.
••• 0:20—Breasts, buns and brief lower frontal nudity while making love with Miguel while two hookers watch. Great!
• 0:23—Breasts, while lying on top of Miguel.

Red Shoe Diaries: As She Wishes (1998; Showtime) . . . . .Woman
•• 0:01—Full frontal nudity, while floating in the surf and rescued by the guy.
••• 0:06—Breasts, while making love with the guy in shipwrecked boat.
• 0:09—In braless wet T-shirt, then breasts and buns, while changing clothes.
•• 0:13—Nude, while making love with the guy at night by the fire.
••• 0:18—Breasts and buns, while making love with the guy in the surf, then running and swimming to the boat.

Video Tapes:

Sports Illustrated: The 1993 Swimsuit Video (1993). . . . .Model

Smith, Anna Nicole *

a.k.a. Vickie Smith.
Model for *Guess?* jeans.

Films:

Naked Gun 33 1/3: The Final Insult (1993) . . . . Tanya
The Hudsucker Proxy (1994) . . . . Za-Za

To the Limit (1995) .... Colette
••• 0:06—Breasts, while taking a bath and enjoying herself. Very brief lower frontal nudity when standing up to get out.
••• 0:11—Breasts, while making love in bed with Michael Nouri.
••• 1:13—Full frontal nudity, while taking a shower and enjoying herself.
•• 1:17—Breasts, while making love with Frank in bed.
• 1:22—Breasts and brief buns in T-back, while getting out of bed.
Skyscraper (1996) .... Carrie Wink
•• 0:10—Breasts and buns, while taking a shower.
••• 0:11—Breasts, while making love in bed with her husband.
••• 0:52—Breasts in open dress top, while making love with her husband outdoors.
•• 1:15—Breasts, while getting raped in office by bad guy.
Music Videos:
Will You Love Me Tomorrow/Bryan Ferry................ n.a.
Video Tapes:
Playboy Video Calendar 1993 (1992) .... January
•• 0:02—Breasts and buns during Country music number.
••• 0:03—Nude in outdoor Western setting by campfire.
Playboy Video Centerfold: Tiffany Sloan (1992) ....Playmate Profile
••• 0:26—Nude in country bar.
••• 0:28—Nude at the beach.
••• 0:29—Nude in still photos.
••• 0:30—Nude in bed in Victorian fantasy.
••• 0:32—Nude, dancing in front of male body builders.
••• 0:34—Nude in campfire setting.
Playboy Video Calendar 1994 (1993) .... January
••• 0:04—Full frontal nudity, in country setting, washing herself and rolling around in the hay. B&W.
Playboy's Playmate Review 1993 (1993) ....Miss May
••• 0:23—Breasts and buns, while at the beach.
••• 0:25—Nude, posing with male bodybuilders.
••• 0:26—Nude in Victorian style fantasy.
Playboy's Sexy, Steamy, Sultry (1993).......... Playmate
Playboy The Best of Anna Nicole Smith (1995).... Herself
•• 0:00—Breasts, during opening credits.
•• 0:05—Breasts, while dancing in western style bar.
••• 0:07—Nude in still photos.
••• 0:08—Nude, while posing on bed.
• 0:10—Breasts in still photos.
••• 0:12—Nude in B&W country segment.
• 0:15—Buns, while posing for photos.
••• 0:18—Nude, while posing on bed and around the house.
••• 0:25—Nude, while in bubble bath.
••• 0:32—Nude, while making love with a guy in a diner fantasy.
••• 0:37—Nude, while posing on the beach.
••• 0:44—Nude in B&W casino/hotel fantasy with a guy.
•• 0:49—Breasts and buns in still photos.
•• 0:50—Nude, while dancing in front of some muscular guys.
•• 0:52—Nude in still photos.
•• 0:53—Nude in quick cuts of behind-the-camera shots.
•• 0:55—Nude, while posing in bed in B&W.

*Smith, Carolyn R. **

Films:
Broadcast Bombshells (1995)................ Aerobicette
••• 1:00—Breasts and buns in panties, while changing clothes with two other women. (She's wearing a blue dress.)
Bushwacked (1995) .... Uncredited Reporter
Tromeo & Juliet (1995) .... Pauline
(Unrated director's cut reviewed.)
Executive Target (1996) .... Dancer
• 0:17—Brief partial buns, while dancing on stage in skimpy maid outfit in front of Bela.

*Smith, Cheryl **

a.k.a. Rainbeaux Smith.
Films:
Evel Knievel (1972) ....n.a.
Video Vixens (1973)................ Twinkle Twat Girl
••• 0:24—Full frontal nudity doing a commercial, sitting next to pool.
Caged Heat (1974) .... Lavelle
a.k.a. Renegade Girls
• 0:04—Brief left breast, dreaming in her jail cell that a guy is caressing her through the bars.
•• 0:25—Breasts in the shower scene.
•• 0:50—Brief nude in the solitary cell.
The Swinging Cheerleaders (1974) .... Andrea
•• 0:12—Breasts taking off her bra and putting sheer blouse on.
• 0:17—Left breast, several times, sitting in bed with Ross.
Farewell, My Lovely (1975; British) ....Doris
• 0:56—Frontal nudity in bedroom in a bordello with Sylvester Stallone before getting beaten by the madam.
Drum (1976) .... Sophie Maxwell
•• 0:54—Breasts in the stable trying to get Yaphet Kotto to make love with her.
Massacre at Central High (1976) ....Mary
• 0:27—Brief breasts in a classroom getting attacked by some guys.
••• 1:09—Nude walking around on a mountain side with Robert Carradine and Lani O'Grady.
The Pom Pom Girls (1976) .... Roxanne
• 1:02—Very brief breasts, taking off her dress in locker room while talking to Judy.
• 1:03—Brief breasts, while putting her cheerleader top on.
Revenge of the Cheerleaders (1976)............Heather
• 0:00—Brief breasts changing tops in back of car. (Blonde on the far right.)
• 0:28—Buns, in shower room scene.
• 0:36—Full frontal nudity, but covered with bubbles.
Slumber Party '57 (1976) .... Sherry
The Choirboys (1977) .... Tammy
Cinderella (1977) .... Cinderella
•• 0:03—Breasts dancing and singing.
••• 0:30—Frontal nudity getting "washed" by her sisters for the Royal Ball.
•• 0:34—Breasts in the forest during a dream.
••• 0:41—Breasts taking a bath. Frontal nudity drying herself off.
• 1:16—Brief breasts with the Prince.
• 1:30—Brief left breast after making love with the Prince to prove it was her.
• 1:34—Brief side view of left breast making love in the Prince's carriage.
The Incredible Melting Man (1977).................Model
Laserblast (1978).................................. Kathy
Up in Smoke (1978) .... Laughing Lady
The Best of Sex and Violence (1981).......... Cinderella
• 0:14—Breasts taking a bath in scene from *Cinderella*.
Cheech & Chong's Nice Dreams (1981) .... Blondie Group #1
Parasite (1982) ....Captive Girl
•• 0:08—Breasts tied by wrists in kitchen.

•• 0:12—Breasts knocking gun out of guy's hands standing behind fence.

Vice Squad (1982). . . . . White Prostitute

Smith, Crystal *

Films:

Hot Dog... The Movie (1984) . . . . Motel Clerk

•• 0:10—Nude getting out of spa and going to the front desk to sign people in.

Smith, Donna *

Video Tapes:

Playmate Playoffs. . . . . Playmate

Playboy Video Calendar 1987 (1986) . . . . Playmate

Playmates at Play (1990) . . . . Hoops

Playboy's 21 Playmates: Volume II (1996) . . . . . . Playmate

••• 0:43—Nude in still photos.

••• 0:44—Nude, while swimming in pool and bathing in bathtub.

Smith, Eileen *

Films:

The Perfect Gift (1993) . . . . Pajama Party Guest

Made for Cable TV:

Compromising Situations: First Time Caller (1994; Showtime) . . . . Miss Lewis

• 0:01—Buns in G-string and breasts, while making love with Jonathon in back room.

Compromising Situations: Let Your Fingers Do the Walking (1995; Showtime) . . . . Nancy

••• 0:06—Breasts and buns, while making love with Matt on sofa.

Video Tapes:

Love Scenes: Volume 3 (1993) . . . . Laura

••• 1:47—Buns in panties and full frontal nudity, while making love with Tom on bed.

BabeWatch, Episode 1: Lingerie Fantasies (1994) . . . . Herself

••• 0:24—Nude, while trying on lingerie outside on steps. Long scene.

••• 0:56—Lower frontal nudity, outside after end credits.

Hot Body Competition: Bikinis & Bikes Contest (1996) . . . . Danielle

•• 0:16—Breasts and buns, while dancing on stage.

••• 0:17—Nude, while posing outdoors.

Smith, Julie Kristen *

Films:

Pretty Smart (1986). . . . . Samantha Falconwright

•• 0:20—Nude in her room when Daphne sees her.

•• 0:26—Breasts in bed talking to Jennifer.

•• 0:40—Breasts in bed.

•• 0:52—Breasts sitting in lounge by the pool.

• 0:57—Brief left breast, while brushing teeth.

• 1:10—Brief right breast, while making love with boyfriend in bed.

• 1:13—More brief right breast.

••• 1:14—Nude, sitting on pillow on top of her boyfriend in bed.

Disorderlies (1987). Skinny Dipper #2

• 0:56—Brief breasts and buns walking around near pool. Long shot.

Mankillers (1987) . . . . High School Girl

Angel III: The Final Chapter (1988) . . . . Darlene

••• 0:40—Breasts during caveman shoot with a brunette girl.

••• 0:44—Breasts again dancing in caveman shoot.

The Dallas Connection (1994). . . . . Cobra

• 0:26—Buns in outfit in bar.

••• 0:27—Breasts and buns in the shower.

• 0:38—Buns in outfit on stage in bar doing splits.

••• 0:40—Buns and breasts, while dancing on stage.

••• 0:53—Breasts and buns, while making love with Chris in spa.

Midnight Tease 2 (1995) . . . . Cherry

••• 0:02—Buns in outfit while dancing on stage in club. In black bra, panties, garter belt and stockings, then breasts.

••• 0:10—Breasts and buns in T-back while dancing on stage.

• 0:20—Breasts, while in dressing room.

• 0:45—Brief breasts, while dancing on stage.

•• 0:47—Breasts and buns in T-back while doing dance for killer before getting killed.

Day of the Warrior (1997) . . . . Cobra

Made for Cable Movies:

Wasp Woman (1995; Sci-Fi). . . . . Carla

Made for Cable TV:

Full Frontal Comedy (1995; Showtime) . . . . Woman of Full Frontal Comedy

Erotic Confessions: Lap Dance (1996; Cinemax) . . . . Dana

(Available on video tape in *Erotic Confessions, Volume 4: Pleasure.*)

• 0:02—Buns in T-back and breasts, while dancing on stage.

•• 0:05—Buns in T-back and breasts, while dancing for a customer, then for Robert.

• 0:07—Side of left breast in Robert's fantasy.

••• 0:13—Nude, while doing a private dance for Robert in back room of club.

Erotic Confessions: Opening Lines (1997; Cinemax) . . . . Monica

•• 0:01—Breasts and buns, while getting dressed in her bedroom.

••• 0:08—In lingerie, then breasts and buns, while stripping and dancing in Edward's fantasy.

••• 0:15—In bra, then breasts and buns, while having sex with Pete in alley.

••• 0:20—In bra, then breasts and buns, while making love with the bartender in the bar.

Erotic Confessions: Virtual Vixen (1997; Cinemax) . . . . Vixen

• 0:05—Most of breasts in leather strap outfit.

••• 0:07—Breasts, after outfit comes off and she tangles with the bad guy.

• 0:11—Most of breasts and buns in leather strap outfit in bedroom.

••• 0:16—Most of breasts in leather strap outfit, then breasts with Herbert.

Video Tapes:

Penthouse Ready to Ride (1992) . . . . Model

Score with Chicks (1992). . . . . Cast Member

Making of the "Carousel Girls' Calendar" (1993) . . . . Miss February

••• 0:16—Breasts during photo shoot.

••• 0:19—Nude during interview segment.

Penthouse's 25th Anniversary Swimsuit Video (1993) . . . . Pet

Penthouse Behind the Scenes (1995) . . . . Pet

••• 0:00—Nude in various segments throughout the video tape.

Penthouse Pet Rocks (1995) . . . . Pet

CD-ROM:

Penthouse Interactive Virtual Photo Shoot, Disc 2 (1993) . . . . Pet

Smith, Laurie

Adult film actress.

Films:

Paradise Motel (1985). . . . . Honeymoon Wife

••• 0:02—Left breast, then breasts in Honeymoon Suite with her new husband, then making love in bed.

Video Tapes:

Nudes in Limbo (1983). . . . . Model

Smith, Linda

Films:

Hardcore (1979) . . . . .Hope (Mistress Victoria)

The Beastmaster (1982) . . . . Kiri's Friend

• 0:35—Breasts in a pond with Tanya Roberts.

Smith, Liza

See: Grant, Rainer.

Smith, Madeline

Films:

The Killing of Sister George (1968) . . . . Nun

Taste the Blood of Dracula (1970). . . . . Dolly

Vampire Lovers (1970; British). . . . . Emma

•• 0:32—Breasts trying on a dress in the bedroom after Carmilla has taken a bath.

• 0:49—Breasts in bed, getting her top pulled down by Carmilla.

Carry On Matron (1971). . . . . .Mrs. Pullitt

Up Pompeii (1971; British) . . . . .Erotica

• 0:35—Breasts while in bubble bath.

Frankenstein and The Monster From Hell (1973). . . . . . . .Sarah

Live and Let Die (1973; British) . . . . .Miss Caruso

The Bawdy Adventures of Tom Jones (1976; British) . . . .Sophia

TV:

Doctor in the House (1970-73). Nurse

Smith, Maggie

Films:

The Prime of Miss Jean Brodie (1969) . . . . Jean Brodie

(Academy Award for Best Actress.)

California Suite (1978) . . . . Diana Barrie

(Academy Award for Best Supporting Actress.)

• 1:05—Very brief side of left breast, putting nightgown on over her head.

Clash of the Titans (1981). . . . . Thetis

Quartet (1981; British/French) . . . . Lois

Better Late Than Never (1983; British). . . . . Anderson

Lily in Love (1985) . . . . Lily Wynn

A Private Function (1985; British) . . . . Joyce Chilvers

A Room with a View (1986; British). . . . . .Charlotte Bartlett

The Lonely Passion of Judith Hearne (1988) . . . . Judith Hearne

Hook (1991) . . . . Granny Wendy

Sister Act (1992) . . . . Mother Superior

The Secret Garden (1993). . . . . Mrs. Medlock

Sister Act 2: Back in the Habit (1993) . . . . Mother Superior

Richard III (1995; British). . . . . .Duchess of York

The First Wives Club (1996) . . . . Gunila Garson Goldberg

Smith, Martha *

Films:

Animal House (1978) . . . . .Babs Jansen

Blood Link (1983). . . . . .Hedwig

•• 0:41—Breasts, wearing black panties while in bed with Keith.

•• 0:43—Brief breasts, while kneeling on bed, talking to Keith.

• 0:48—Right breast, while sitting in bed and talking. Shadow and scarf get in the way. Brief breasts.

• 0:49—Breasts, while getting slapped around by Keith.

••• 0:51—Breasts sitting up in bed when Craig and Keith meet each other for the first time.

• 1:13—Breasts, wearing red panties, with Keith before he kills her.

• 1:14—Brief buns, covered with blood when discovered by policemen.

TV:

Days of Our Lives. . . . . Sandy Horton

Scarecrow and Mrs. King (1983-87) . . . . . . Francine Desmond

Smith, Melanie

Films:

The Baby Doll Murders (1992) . . . . Peggy Davis

••• 0:09—Breasts, while taking off her blouse and getting into hot tub with Jeff Kober.

•• 0:10—Breasts in hot tub with Kober. Fence gets in the way.

•• 0:11—Breasts, getting out of the hot tub.

•• 0:56—Breasts in hot tub with Kober while making out.

Molly & Gina (1993) . . . . .Dixie

Trancers III (1993) . . . . R.J.

Night Hunter (1995) . . . . Raimy Baker

Made for TV Movies:

Green Dolphin Beat (1994) . . . . Linda Rodriguez

TV:

As the World Turns . . . . Emily Stewart

Smith, Natalie *

Video Tapes:

Penthouse Behind the Scenes (1995) . . . . Pet

••• 0:37—Nude in interviews and behind the scenes footage.

Penthouse Pet of the Year Winners 1994: Gina & Natalie (1995). . . . . .Pet of the Year Runner-Up

••• 0:29—Nude, in western theme segment.

••• 0:33—Nude in pearl outfit outside in bed.

••• 0:37—Nude outside by pool, soaping herself up.

••• 0:40—Nude outside in white western outfit.

Penthouse Women In & Out of Uniform (1995) . . . . . Pet

••• 0:13—Nude as a painter, while painting on herself outside.

••• 0:16—Nude as a football player with two other women in locker room, then putting on a white dress.

Smith, Rainbeaux

See: Smith, Cheryl.

Smith, Stephanie Ann

Films:

Under Lock and Key (1994). . . . . Sarah

• 0:02—Breasts, while getting up out of bed in cell.

• 0:05—Breasts, while getting menaced by Zelda and her two friends.

••• 0:13—Nude in the showers with Danielle.

•• 0:14—Nude, while getting hassled by Wincott.

••• 0:25—Nude, while getting examined by the doctor.

Caged Hearts (1995). . . . . .Guard Lynn

Smith, Vickie

See: Smith, Anna Nicole.

Smith, Yeardley

Films:

Heaven Help Us (1985) . . . . .Cathleen

The Legend of Billie Jean (1985) . . . . Putter

Maximum Overdrive (1986) . . . . Connie

Ginger Ale Afternoon (1989) . . . . Bonnie Cleator
• 0:53—Brief upper half of left breast, taking off top in trailer with Hank.
Listen to Me (1989). . . . . Cootz
City Slickers (1991) . . . . Nancy
Toys (1992). . . . . Researcher
As Good As It Gets (1997). . . . . Jackie
TV:
The Simpsons (1989-) . . . . Voice of Lisa Simpson
Herman's Head (1991) . . . . Louise Fitzer

• Snelgrove, Lisha

Films:
Just One of the Girls (1992) . . . . First Shower Girl
a.k.a. Anything For Love
••• 0:27—Beasts, while taking a shower. Slow motion.
••• 0:27—Full frontal nudity, in shower room while Corey Haim (in drag) is mopping the floor.
• 0:50—Very brief breasts, while giving Haim her towel in the shower room.
Made for TV Movies:
Fighting for My Daughter (1995) . . . . Sheila

Snodgress, Carrie

Films:
Diary of a Mad Housewife (1970) . . . . Tina Balser
••• 0:01—Breasts taking off nightgown and getting dressed, putting on white bra while Richard Benjamin talks to her.
• 0:36—Buns and brief side view of left breast, while kissing Frank Langella.
• 0:41—Very brief breasts lying on floor when Langella pulls the blanket up.
• 0:54—Breasts lying in bed with Langella.
••• 1:21—Breasts in the shower with Langella, then drying herself off.
The Fury (1978) . . . . Hester
Homework (1982). . . . . Dr. Delingua
Trick or Treats (1982). . . . . Joan
A Night in Heaven (1983) . . . . Mrs. Johnson
Pale Rider (1985). . . . . .Sarah Wheeler
Murphy's Law (1986) . . . . Joan Freeman
Across the Tracks (1990) . . . . Rosemary Maloney
Blue Sky (1991). . . . . .Vera Johnson
Mission of the Shark (1991). . . . . Louise McVay
8 Seconds (1993) . . . . Elsie Frost
The Ballad of Little Jo (1993). . . . . Ruth Badger
White Man's Burden (1995) . . . . Josine
Death Benefit (1996). . . . . Virginia McGinnis
Made for TV Movies:
Woman with a Past (1992) . . . . Florence

Snow, Raven

Films:
Delta of Venus (1995) . . . . Leila
(Unrated version reviewed.)
Made for Cable TV:
Red Shoe Diaries: Naked in the Moonlight (1994; Showtime) . . . . Camille des Champs
••• 0:13—Breasts, after undressing and joining James in the shower.
••• 0:16—Breasts, while lying in bed.
••• 0:21—Breasts, while making love with James on bed.
Red Shoe Diaries: The Art of Loneliness (1996; Showtime) . . . . Elizabeth
• 0:09—Brief left breast while in bathtub, seen under the water and above, when talking with Frances.
• 0:11—Brief left breast, above the water.

Snyder, Susan Marie

Films:
Jailbait: Betrayed by Innocence (1986). . . . . Andrea
Sleepaway Camp II: Unhappy Campers (1988) . . . . .Mare
• 0:08—Brief breasts lifting up her T-shirt.
• 0:24—Brief breasts flashing in boys' cabin.
• 0:33—Breasts in Polaroid photograph that Angela confiscates from the boys.
TV:
As the World Turns . . . . .Julie Wendall
Santa Barbara . . . . Laken Capwell

Snyder, Suzanne

Films:
The Oasis (1984) . . . . .Jennifer
Remo Williams: The Adventure Begins (1985) . . . . Nurse/Soap Opera
Weird Science (1985). . . . . Deb
Night of the Creeps (1986) . . . . Lisa
Pretty Kill (1987) . . . . Franci/Stella/Paul
Killer Klowns from Outer Space (1988) . . . . Debbie
The Night Before (1988) . . . . Lisa
Retribution (1988). . . . . Angel
The Return of the Living Dead II (1988). . . . . Brenda
Femme Fatale (1990) . . . . Andrea
••• 0:08—Breasts, nonchalantly taking off her top and posing for Billy Zane's painting. (She sometimes has a bag over her head.)
•• 0:46—Breasts posing again with the bag on and off her head.
Fools Rush In (1997) . . . . .Cathy Stewart

Soares, Alana *

Films:
Beverly Hills Cop II (1987) . . . . Playboy Playmate
Video Tapes:
Playboy Video Magazine, Volume 5 (1983) . . . . .Playmate
• 0:06—Brief breasts on chair.

Socas, Maria

Films:
The Warrior and the Sorceress (1984) . . . . Naja
(Breasts in every scene she's in.)
••• 0:15—Breasts wearing robe and bikini bottoms in room with Zeg. Sort of brief buns, leaving the room.
•• 0:22—Breasts standing by a wagon at night.
•• 0:27—Breasts in room with David Carradine. Dark. Most of buns when leaving the room.
•• 0:31—Breasts and buns climbing down wall.
• 0:34—Brief breasts, then left breast with rope around her neck at the well.
• 0:44—Breasts when Carradine rescues her.
• 0:47—Breasts walking around outside.
• 0:57—More breasts outside.
• 1:00—Breasts watching a guy pound a sword.
• 1:05—Breasts under a tent after Carradine uses the sword. Long shot.
• 1:09—Breasts during big fight scene.
• 1:14—Breasts next to well. Long shot.
Soldier's Revenge (1986) . . . . Baetriz
Deathstalker II (1987) .Amazon Queen
Hollywood Boulevard II (1989) . . . . .Amazon Queen

Søeberg, Camilla

Films:

Twist & Shout (1986; Danish) . . . . Anna

Manifesto (1988) . . . . Svetlana

a.k.a. A Night of Love

••• 0:15—Nude, in bathtub and bedroom with Emile. Long scene.

• 0:19—Brief left breast when Emile cuts off her hair.

•• 1:04—Left breast, several times when Emile is in her room. More left breast cleaning up after Emile accidentally dies.

• 1:15—Brief side of left breast, while making love with Eric Stoltz. Dark. Buns, getting out of bed.

•• 1:16—Breasts and buns unrolling Emile in the rug.

•• 1:23—Breasts sitting in bed with puppies.

Erotique (1993) . . . . Taboo Parlor/Jukia

•• 0:29—Breasts, while in bed with Priscilla Barnes.

• 0:51—Partial buns in panties, while lying on the bed.

Solari, Sky

a.k.a. Sky.

Made for Cable TV:

Compromising Situations: Reunion '76 (1994; Showtime) . . . . Jane

•• 0:17—Buns in panties and left breast, while standing in motel room with Jake.

••• 0:18—Breasts and buns, while making love in bed with Jake.

Compromising Situations: Let Your Fingers Do the Walking (1995; Showtime) . . . . Terry

••• 0:12—In bra, then breasts, while making love with Matt. Brief buns in panties.

Compromising Situations: The Elevator (1998; Showtime) . . . . Julie Anthony

•• 0:19—In white lingerie, then breasts and buns, while making love with Jeff in stopped elevator.

*Solari, Suzanne **

Films:

Roller Blade (1986) . . . . Sister Sharon Cross

• 0:04—Buns, in G-string, while lying in bed.

• 1:21—Brief upper half of right breast, taking off suit. Buns in G-string.

Hell Comes to Frogtown (1987) . . . . Runaway Girl

RollerBlade Warriors: Taken By Force (1988) . . . . Sharon Crosse

Class of Nuke 'Em High Part II: Subhumanoid Meltdown (1991) . . . . Toxie Squirrel Gang Member

Kill, Kill Overkill (1991) . . . . Roxanne

Number One Fan (1994) . . . . Gabrielle

•• 0:36—Right breast, twice, while making love in bed with Chad McQueen during filming of a movie.

• 1:11—Buns and breasts, dressing in the background (slightly out of focus) while McQueen does his lines.

Mulholland Falls (1996) . . . . Perino's Girl

*Soles, P.J. **

P.J. stands for Pamela Jane.

Ex-wife of actor Dennis Quaid.

Films:

Carrie (1976) . . . . Norma

Halloween (1978) . . . . Lynda

• 1:04—Brief right breast, sitting up in bed after making love in bed with Bob.

• 1:07—Brief breasts getting strangled by Michael in the bedroom.

Breaking Away (1979) . . . . Suzy

Old Boyfriends (1979) . . . . Sandy

Rock 'n' Roll High School (1979) . . . . Riff Randell

Private Benjamin (1980) . . . . Private Wanda Winter

Stripes (1981) . . . . Stella

Terror in the Aisles (1984) . . . . Lynda

• 0:24—Brief breasts in scene from *Halloween.*

Sweet Dreams (1985) . . . . Wanda

B.O.R.N. (1988) . . . . Liz

Alienator (1989) . . . . Tara

Soldier's Fortune (1991) . . . . Debra

Made for Cable Movies:

Rebel Highway: Shake, Rattle and Rock! (1994; Showtime) . . . . Evelyn Randall

Out There (1995; Showtime) . . . . Religious Nut

Somers, Gwen

Films:

Faith (1990) . . . . Kate Davis

Alien Intruder (1992) . . . . Annie

••• 0:19—Breasts, taking off her top in front of Lloyd while he sits in bathtub.

Anthony's Desire (1993) . . . . Jessica

••• 0:29—Nude, while lying on bed and talking. Long scene.

••• 1:09—Full frontal nudity, while on bed with Anthony and Desiree sitting next to her.

Good Girls Don't (1993) . . . . Bimbo Betina

• 0:42—Brief buns in outfit.

Renegade: Fighting Cage (1993) . . . . Lena

(Nudity added for video release.)

• 1:07—Breasts, while making love with a guy and a blonde woman in bed.

Surf, Sand and Sex (1994) . . . . Suzanne

••• 0:27—Breasts while making love with Kato Kaelin on hood of car. Wearing sunglasses the entire time.

The Voyeur (1994) . . . . Woman at Poolside

••• 0:52—Full frontal nudity, while the pool guy rubs lotion on her in Brenda's fantasy.

The Hottest Bid (1995) . . . . Jessica

•• 0:01—Nude while taking a bubble bath and getting out and drying herself off.

•• 0:03—Breasts, when powdering her body in front of mirror and putting on lingerie. Partial buns in lingerie while putting on stockings.

• 0:07—Breasts, while fantasizing a lover is caressing her.

• 0:39—Brief buns under lingerie outfit outside in Don's fantasy.

• 0:40—Lower frontal nudity, when she raises her lingerie skirt to get on top of Don.

•• 0:41—Left breasts, then breasts, while making love.

•• 0:50—Nude, taking off towel and getting into shower and taking a shower behind plastic shower curtain.

••• 1:05—Breasts, after taking off her blouse and making love with Don in bed. Nice, long scene.

• 1:15—Brief breasts, while getting out of bed. Brief breasts in open window.

• 1:16—Brief right breast, while sitting in bed, crying.

••• 1:26—In black bra, then nude, while making love with Don in a Jeep.

Video Tapes:

Playboy's How to Reawaken Your Sexual Powers (1992) . . . . Cast Member

••• 0:21—Full frontal nudity in the forest with her lover.

••• 0:29—Nude on hammock on sailboat with her lover.

Buck Naked Line Dancing (1993) . . . . Dancer

••• 0:00—Breasts throughout. She's usually in the back in the right, with a bandana in her pocket.

Playboy's Secret Confessions (1993)
. . . . Teacher's Pet/Marilyn
•• 0:27—Breasts, while making love in bed with Warren. Full frontal nudity and brief buns, while standing on stairs with Jay.

Playboy's Real Couples: Sex in Dangerous Places (1995)
. . . . The Show Room/Woman
•• 0:42—Full frontal nudity, while making love with George in a furniture store.

Somers, Kristi

Films:

Carnival of Love (1983) . . . . Kristi
a.k.a. Inside the Love House
•• 0:50—Breasts and buns, while making love with a guy in the clouds.
••• 1:01—Breasts and buns, while making love with a guy in the clouds. Long scene.

Rumble Fish (1983) . . . . Lake Girl

Hardbodies (1984) . . . . Michelle
•• 0:53—Nude, dancing on the beach while Ashley plays the guitar and sings.

Savage Streets (1984) . . . . .Valerie

Girls Just Want to Have Fun (1985) . . . . Rikki

Mugsy's Girls (1985). . . . . Laurie
• 0:15—Brief breasts several times while mud wrestling.
•• 0:29—Breasts and buns in bathtub on bus.
• 0:34—Brief breasts holding up sign to get truck driver to stop.

Tomboy (1985) . . . . Seville Ritz
•• 0:14—Breasts taking a shower while talking to Betsy Russell.
• 0:53—Brief breasts stripping at a party.

Hell Comes to Frogtown (1987) . . . . .Arabella

Return to Horror High (1987) . . . . Ginny McCall

Somers, Suzanne *

Films:

American Graffiti (1973) . . . . The Blonde in the T-bird

Magnum Force (1973) . . . . Uncredited Pool Girl
•• 0:26—In blue swimsuit getting into a swimming pool, brief breasts a couple of times before getting shot, brief breasts floating dead.

Yesterday's Hero (1979; British) . . . . .Cloudy Martin

Nothing Personal (1980; Canadian) . . . . Abigail

Serial Mom (1993) . . . . Herself

Made for Cable Movies:

Seduced by Evil (1994; USA) . . . . Lee Lindsay

Miniseries:

Hollywood Wives (1988) . . . . Gina Germaine

Made for TV Movies:

Keeping Secrets (1991) . . . . Suzanne Somers

TV:

Three's Company (1977-81) . . . . Chrissy Snow

She's the Sheriff (1987-89) . . . . .Sheriff Hildy Granger

Step by Step (1991-96) . . . . Carol Foster

Step by Step (1997-) . . . . Carol Foster

Sommer, Elke *

Films:

Sweet Ecstasy (1962). . . . . Elke
Nude.

A Shot in the Dark (1964) . . . . Maria Gambrelli

Boy, Did I Get a Wrong Number (1966) . . . . .Didi

The Corrupt Ones (1966) . . . . Lily

The Oscar (1966) . . . . .Kay Bergdahl

The Invincible Six (1969). . . . . .Zari
• 0:44—Right breast under wet, skin-colored outfit after fight in pool.
•• 1:09—Right breast, while tending to her wound.
•• 1:10—Breasts, while making love in the dark.

The House of Exorcism (1972; Italian/Spanish) . . Lisa Reiner
a.k.a. Lisa and the Devil
••• 1:10—Breasts, lying on floor when Maximillian opens her blouse.

Ten Little Indians (1975) . . . . Vera

Left for Dead (1978) . . . . Magdalene Krushcen
•• 0:38—Left breast, while posing for photographer.
• 0:39—Very brief left breast in B&W photo.
• 0:58—Buns and breasts when police officers lift her up to put plastic under her. Covered with blood, can't see her face.
• 1:09—Very brief left breast in B&W photo.

The Prisoner of Zenda (1979) . . . . The Countess

No One Cries Forever (1984; South African) . . . . . . Lou Parker

Lily in Love (1985). . . . . Alicia Brown

Severed Ties (1992) . . . . Helena Harrison

Sommerfield, Diane

Films:

Love in a Taxi (1980) . . . . .Carine

Back Roads (1981). . . . . Liz

The Nightstalker (1987) . . . . Lonnie Roberts
• 0:35—Side view of right breast lying dead in morgue.

Song, Cheryl

Films:

Weekend Pass (1984). . . . . .Chop Suzi
• 0:26—Breasts while giving a guy a massage.

TV:

Soul Train . . . . Dancer

Songer, Melinda

Films:

Showgirls (1995). . . . . Nicky
(NC-17 version reviewed.)
• 1:11—Breasts, while standing in front of Elizabeth Berkley backstage.
• 1:13—Breasts, while sitting at make-up table, talking with Berkley.
• 1:29—Buns in G-string during audition.
• 1:40—Brief breasts, while running down the stairs.

The Glass Cage (1996) . . . . Dancer

Made for Cable TV:

Hot Line: Sexual Chemistry (1996; Cinemax)
. . . . Barbara Prescott
(Available on video tape in *Hot Line 4*.)
••• 0:01—Breasts, while making love with her husband in bed, then talking with him afterwards. Good moaning!
•• 0:12—In lingerie, then breasts and buns, while making love with her husband around the house.
• 0:19—Buns in dominatrix outfit, while in the house with her husband.
••• 0:23—Breasts and buns, while making love on top of her blindfolded husband in bed. Good moaning!

Sorenson, Heidi *

Films:

History of the World, Part I (1981). . . . . Vestal Virgin

Fever Pitch (1985) . . . . Airport Attendant

Fright Night (1985). . . . . Hooker

Spies Like Us (1985). . . . . Fitz-Hume's Supervisor

Roxanne (1987) . . . . Trudy
For the Boys (1991). . . . . Showgirl
Made for Cable Movies:
Suspect Device (1995; Showtime) . . . . .Kristen
•• 0:05—Breasts and buns, after taking off nightgown then making love in bed with C. Thomas Howell.
Made for Cable TV:
Dream On: Martin Tupper in "Magnum Farce" (1994; HBO) . . . . Jodi
••• 0:01—Buns in G-string panties, then breasts, while making love on top of and under Martin.
••• 0:16—In white bra, then breasts and buns, while making love on sofa with Mack to get even with Martin. More breasts after getting caught and getting dressed.
Dream On: Take Two Tablets, And Get Me to Mt. Sinai (1995; HBO) . . . . Martin's Lover
Video Tapes:
Playboy Video Magazine, Volume 5 (1983) . . . . . Playmate
• 0:06—Brief breasts in library.

Sorvino, Mira

Daughter of actor Paul Sorvino.
Films:
Amongst Friends (1993) . . . . .Laura
New York Cop (1993) . . . . Maria
Barcelona (1994). . . . . Marta
Quiz Show (1994). . . . . Sandra Goodwin
Sweet Nothing (1994) . . . . Monika
Blue in the Face (1995). . . . . The Young Lady
Mighty Aphrodite (1995) . . . . Linda Ash
(Academy Award for Best Supporting Actress.)
Tales of Erotica (1995). . . . . Teresa
Beautiful Girls (1996) . . . . Sharon Cassidy
Mimic (1997) . . . . Susan
The Replacement Killers (1997). . . . . Meg Coburn
Romy and Michele's High School Reunion (1997) . . . . Romy White
Made for Cable Movies:
Parallel Lives (1994; Showtime). . . . . Matty Derosa
Norma Jean & Marilyn (1996; HBO) . . . . . . Marilyn Monroe
• 1:00—Brief lower half of buns under sweater, when getting orange juice out of the refrigerator.
•• 2:01—Brief breasts, pulling open her dress in front of Eddie.
Miniseries:
The Buccaneers (1995; U.S./British) . . . . Conchita Closson

Soto, Talisa *

Wife of actor Costas Mandylor.
Films:
Spike of Bensonhurst (1988) . . . . India
License to Kill (1989). . . . . Lupe Lamora
Hostage (1992). . . . . .Joanna
• 0:56—Very brief out-of-focus breasts, while leaning back when making love with Sam Neill.
• 1:16—Out-of-focus breasts again.
The Mambo Kings (1992) . . . . Maria Rivera
Don Juan DeMarco (1994). Doña Julia
• 0:35—Very brief right breast, in gaping dress top, while sitting on Johnny Depp.
Mortal Kombat (1995) . . . . Princess Kitana
The Corporate Ladder (1996) . . . . Susan Taylor
Sunchaser (1996) . . . . Navajo Woman
Mortal Kombat: Annihilation (1997) . . . . Kitana
Made for Cable Movies:
Prison Stories, Women on the Inside (1990; HBO). . . . . . Rosina
Vampirella (1996; Showtime) . . . . .Vampirella
TV:
Harts of the West (1993-94) . . . . Cassie Velasquez

Sotres, Sherry

Video Tapes:
Hot Body Video Magazine #2: Double Trouble (1992) . . . . Street Scene/Model/Sherry
•• 0:01—Breasts and buns during opening credits.
••• 0:26—Breasts, taking off black swimsuit and putting another on.
••• 0:33—Breasts and buns, while posing in front of a red Ferrari.
•• 0:58—Breasts in outtake during the end credits.
Hot Body Video Magazine #4: Extra Sexy (1993) . . . . .Interview
•• 0:01—Breasts during introduction.
••• 0:36—Left breast, in wet top, while posing in shower for her husband, photographer Craig X. Sotres.

Soutendijk, Reneé

Films:
Spetters (1980; Dutch) . . . . .Fientje
•• 1:12—Breasts making love in trailer with Jeff.
The Girl with the Red Hair (1983; Dutch) . . . . Hannie
The Cold Room (1984) Lili
The Fourth Man (1984; Dutch) . . . . Christine
••• 0:27—Full frontal nudity removing robe, brief buns in bed, side view left breast, then breasts in bed with Gerard.
• 0:32—Brief left breast in bed with Gerard after he hallucinates and she cuts his penis off.
••• 0:53—Left breast, then right breast in red dress when Gerard opens her dress.
• 1:11—Breasts making love with Herman while Gerard watches through keyhole.
Grave Secrets (1990). . . . . .Iris Norwood
Eve of Destruction (1991) . . . . Dr. Eve Simmons/Eve VIII
• 0:17—Left breast, while on table as a robot, with half her skin removed. Possibly a special-effect body.
• 0:22—Brief breasts in bathroom (as a robot), fixing her wound. Breasts while sitting on bed, putting a large bandage over the wound.
Made for Cable Movies:
Murderers Among Us: The Simon Wiesenthal Story (1989; HBO) . . . . Cyla
Keeper of the City (1991; Showtime). . . . . Vickie Benedetto
Made for Cable TV:
The Hitchhiker: Murderous Feelings (HBO) . . . Sara Kendal
••• 0:04—In bra, then breasts with stockings and a garter belt on couch with a guy.
• 0:18—Right breast when mysterious attacker surprises her from behind.

• *South, Robin*

Films:
Cellblock Sisters: Banished Behind Bars (1995) . . . . Inmate
Little Witches (1996) . . . . Illuminati Girl
Made for Cable TV:
Beverly Hills Bordello: The Boyfriend (1997; Showtime) . . . . .Heather
••• 0:17—Nude, while undressing, then having sex in bedroom with Frank.

Spacek, Sissy *

Cousin of actor Rip Torn.

Films:

Prime Cut (1972) . . . . Poppy
- • 0:25—Brief side view of left breast lying in hay, then buns when Gene Hackman lifts her up to show to Lee Marvin.
- ••• 0:30—Breasts sitting in bed, then getting up to try on a dress while Marvin watches.
- • 0:32—Close up of breasts though sheer black dress in a restaurant.

Badlands (1973) . . . . Holly
Ginger in the Morning (1973) . . . . Ginger
Carrie (1976) . . . . Carrie White
- •• 0:02—Nude, taking a shower, then having her first menstrual period in the girls' locker room.
- • 1:25—Brief breasts taking a bath to wash all the pig blood off her after the dance.

Three Women (1977) . . . . Pinky Rose
Welcome to L.A. (1977) . . . . Linda Murray
- •• 0:51—Brief breasts after bringing presents into Keith Carradine's bedroom.

Heart Beat (1979) . . . . Carolyn Cassady
Coal Miner's Daughter (1980) . . . . Loretta Lynn
(Academy Award for Best Actress.)
Raggedy Man (1981) . . . . Nita
Missing (1982) . . . . Beth Horman
The River (1984) . . . . Mae Garvey
Marie (1986) . . . . Marie Ragghianti
'night Mother (1986) . . . . Jessie Cates
Violets Are Blue (1986) . . . . Gussie Sawyer
The Long Walk Home (1990) . . . . Miriam Thompson
JFK (1991) . . . . Liz Garrison
Hard Promises (1992) . . . . Chris Coalter
Trading Mom (1994) . . . . . Mrs. Martin/Maman/Mom/Natasha
The Grass Harp (1996) . . . . Verena Talbo

Made for Cable Movies:

A Private Matter (1992; HBO) . . . . Sherri Finkbine
The Good Old Boys (1995; TNT) . . . . Spring Renfro
Beyond the Call (1996; Showtime) . . . . Pam O'Brien
If These Walls Could Talk (1996; HBO) . . . . Barbara Barrows

Made for TV Movies:

A Place for Annie (1994) . . . . Susan Lansing
Streets of Laredo (1995) . . . . Lorena

Spangler, Donna *

Films:

Glitch (1988) . . . . Extra
Another Chance (1989) . . . . Cynthia
Guns (1990) . . . . Hugs Huggins
Virgin High (1990) . . . . Uncredited Car Wash Girl
Carnal Crimes (1991) . . . . Esther
Roots of Evil (1991) . . . . Scarlett
(Unrated version reviewed.)
- •• 0:04—Breasts, getting attacked by the crazy guy, then killed.
- • 0:07—Brief breasts, dead, covered with blood when Alex Cord discovers her.

Hollywood Passions (1994) . . . . Dancer #1
- •• 1:04—Breasts (she has the red boa), while dancing with two other girls.

Dinosaur Valley Girls (1996) . . . . Mee-Shell
(Director's Cut reviewed.)
- • 0:08—Brief breasts, while dancing in Tony's vision.
- • 0:40—Brief breasts, while running in slow motion in Big-Mac's vision.
- • 0:54—Brief breasts, while running in slow motion in Big-Mac's vision.
- •• 0:55—Breasts, while dancing outside.
- •• 0:57—Breasts, while dancing in cave.
- • 1:01—Breasts, while making love outdoors with Tony.
- • 1:14—Breasts, while fighting in cave with the cave men.

Made for Cable TV:

Compromising Situations: Let Your Fingers Do the Walking (1995; Showtime) . . . . Delores
- ••• 0:19—Breasts, while making love with Matt on the wet kitchen floor.

Compromising Situations: Jim and Jane (1998; Showtime) . . . . Carol
- •• 0:09—Buns and breasts, while making love with Jim.

Video Tapes:

Sexy Lingerie II (1990) . . . . Model
Wet & Wild II (1990) . . . . Model
Sexy Lingerie III (1991) . . . . Model

Sparrow, Sharolyn

Films:

Skullduggery (1983; Canadian) . . . . Carmen
The Pink Chiquitas (1986; Canadian)
. . . . Cast Member of Zombie Beach Party III
Higher Education (1987; Canadian) . . . . Helen Dobish
Three Men and a Baby (1987) . . . . Vanessa
Death Wish V: The Face of Death (1993) . . . . Dawn
- •• 1:01—Left breast, while in bathtub with Freddie.
- • 1:03—Brief breasts, getting out of bathtub after soccer ball explodes outside.

Made for TV Movies:

Courage (1986) . . . . Bikini Girl
Many Happy Returns (1986) . . . . 1st Hooker

Spaulding, Tracy

Films:

Armed for Action (1992) . . . . Lori
- • 0:10—Brief breasts, while in back room of restaurant with her boyfriend, Jake.

The Deadly Secret (1993) . . . . Reyna Vaught
- •• 0:00—Breasts, several times during opening credits.
- ••• 0:25—Breasts, with Joe Estevez in study.
- • 0:35—Brief breasts.
- • 0:38—Brief breasts several times in B&W.
- •• 0:41—Buns in G-string and breasts while making love with Estevez in bed.
- • 0:44—Brief breasts, while getting out of bed and putting robe on.
- • 1:10—Brief breasts when Estevez comes up behind her and feels her breasts.
- •• 1:11—Breasts, while making love with Estevez on bed.
- •• 1:17—Breasts and brief buns in B&W day dream.
- • 1:27—Brief right breast, while making love in flashback.

Striking Point (1994) . . . . Tina Wells
- ••• 0:22—Buns and breasts, when dancing on stage in a black T-back, then in black bra while talking to the two policemen.

The Nurse (1996) . . . . Susan Lang

Made for Cable TV:

Erotic Confessions: Behind the Lens (1997; Cinemax) . . . Leslie
Erotic Confessions: The Partners (1997; Showtime)
. . . . Annette
- ••• 0:21—Full frontal nudity, while undressing in bathroom with Frank, then making love with him in the shower.
- • 0:26—Brief side of right breast in flashback.

Speed, Carol

Films:

The Big Bird Cage (1972) . . . . Mickie
The New Centurions (1972) . . . . Martha
The Mack (1973) . . . . .Lulu
•• 0:23—Breasts, while lying in bed with Goldie.
Abby (1974) . . . . Abby Williams

*Speir, Dona **

Films:

Doin' Time (1984). . . . . Card Holder
Dragnet (1987). . . . . Baitmate
Hard Ticket to Hawaii (1987). . . . . .Donna
• 0:01—Breasts on boat kissing her boyfriend, Rowdy.
••• 0:23—Breasts in the spa with Hope Marie Carlton looking at diamonds they found.
••• 1:04—Breasts and buns with Rowdy after watching a video tape.
•• 1:33—Breasts during the end credits.
Mortuary Academy (1988) . . . . Nurse
Click: Calendar Girl Killer (1989). . . . . Nancy
• 0:11—Brief glimpses of breasts during photo session. Buns and breasts under sheer fabric.
•• 0:12—Brief buns, dropping the piece of fabric.
Picasso Trigger (1989). . . . . .Donna
••• 0:49—Breasts and buns standing, then making love in bed.
Savage Beach (1989) . . . . .Dona
• 0:32—Breasts changing clothes in airplane with Hope Marie Carlton.
•• 0:48—Nude, going for a swim on the beach with Carlton.
Guns (1990). . . . . Donna Hamilton
••• 1:00—Breasts and buns in black G-string getting dressed in locker room. Then in black lingerie.
Do or Die (1991). . . . . Donna Hamilton
• 0:06—Brief breasts taking off towel and getting into spa.
•• 0:32—Breasts, mostly right breast, changing clothes in back of airplane.
••• 1:21—Breasts and buns, in swimming pool with Erik Estrada.
Fit To Kill (1993). . . . . Donna Hamilton
•• 0:21—Breasts and buns in G-string, while undressing and putting dresses on with Vasquez.
••• 1:18—Buns in two piece swimsuit, then breasts during Kane's fantasy.
Hard Hunted (1993). . . . . Donna Hamilton
•• 1:22—Left breast, then breasts on beach with the bad guy, while making love and resting afterwards.

Video Tapes:

Playmate Playoffs . . . . Playmate
Playboy Video Calendar 1987 (1986) . . . . Playmate
Playboy Video Centerfold: Teri Weigel (1986) . . Playmate
Glamour Through Your Lens—Outdoor Techniques (1989) . . . . .Herself
Wet & Wild (1989). . . . . Model
Sexy Lingerie III (1991) . . . . Model

Speiss, Kimberly

Films:

Night of the Wilding (1990) . . . . Doris
California Hot Wax (1992). Bikini Girl
Last Dance (1992). . . . . Meryll
• 1:03—Partial buns, while dancing on stage during DTV contest.
Psycho Cop 2 (1992) . . . . Chloe
• 0:37—Buns, while falling off of desk with Tony, then standing up and talking to Sharon.

*Spelvin, Georgina **

Adult film actress.

Films:

I Spit on Your Corpse (1974). . . . . Sandra
a.k.a. Girls for Rent
• 0:38—Flashing her left breast to get three guys to stop their car.
••• 0:39—Breasts, fighting with the three guys.
• 0:47—Brief right breast in gaping blouse.
••• 0:53—Breasts outside, de-virginizing the backwoods kid.
•• 1:08—Breasts, close-up view, showing her breasts to him.
• 1:10—Buns, in lowered pants and left breast in open blouse.
Honky Tonk Nights (1978) .Georgia
• 0:06—Breasts, lying with her head in a guy's lap.
Police Academy III: Back in Training (1986) . . . . . . .The Hooker

Made for Cable TV:

Dream On: Am I Blue (1995; HBO) . . . . .Mrs. Bono

Spencer, Holly

Films:

Beach Beverly Hills (1992) . . . . Bikini Audition Girl 1
Secret Games 2—The Escort (1993). . . . . Lisa
(Unrated version reviewed.)
••• 0:24—Nude, after taking off coat, covering Hewitt with birthday cake and in the shower with him and Stacey.
•• 0:26—Breasts and buns while making love in bed with Stacey and Hewitt.
•• 1:05—Breasts in flashbacks.

• *Spencer-Nairn, Tara*

Made for Cable TV:

The Outer Limits: Double Helix (1997; Showtime) .Heather
• 0:24—In bra, then brief breasts and brief buns, when disrobing during Professor Nodel's class.
Poltergeist: The Legacy/The Enlightened One (1998; Showtime) . . . . Cindy

Spiro, Alyson

Films:

She'll be Wearing Pink Pyjamas (1985; British). . . . . .Anita
•• 0:07—Nude talking to Julie Walters in the shower.
•• 0:58—Nude, undressing and going skinny dipping in mountain lake with Julie Walters, then getting out. Nice buns shot while walking into the lake.

Made for TV Movies:

Mystery! Prime Suspect 3 (1994). . . . . Margaret Speel

Sportolaro, Tina

Films:

Sincerely Charlotte (1986; French) .n.a.
Frantic (1988) . . . . .TWA Clerk
The Passion of Beatrice (1988; French) . . . . Mère de François Enfant
• 0:06—Brief breasts when the young François discovers her in bed with another man and kills him.
Paris By Night (1989; British). . . . . Violet

Spradling, Charlie

a.k.a. Charlie.

Films:

The Blob (1988) . . . . Co-ed

Unexpected Encounters, Vol. 3 (1988) . . Woman in House
••• 0:50—In lingerie, then breasts on sofa with the gardener.
Meridian (1989) . . . . Gina
a.k.a. Kiss of the Beast
a.k.a. Phantoms
•• 0:22—Breasts getting her blouse torn off by Lawrence while lying on the table.
••• 0:28—Breasts standing next to fireplace, then breasts on the couch. Hot!
Twice Dead (1989) . . . . Tina
•• 1:11—Breasts taking off jacket next to bed.
••• 1:14—Breasts making love with her boyfriend in bed.
• 1:18—Brief breasts dead in bed.
Mirror Mirror (1990) . . . . Charleen Kane
• 1:05—Very, very brief side of left breast, after taking of swimsuit in locker room.
• 1:06—Buns, taking a shower. Brief breasts a couple of times when the hot water pipes break.
• 1:09—Buns, while lying on the floor, dead, covered with blisters.
Puppet Master II (1990) . . . . Wanda
•• 1:04—Breasts getting out of bed and adjusting her panties.
Ski School (1990) . . . . Paulette
Wild at Heart (1990) . . . . Irma
•• 0:40—Brief breasts in bed during flashback.
The Doors (1991) . . . . CBS Girl Backstage
Bad Channels (1992). . . . . Cookie
Caged Fear (1992) . . . . Joy
To Sleep with a Vampire (1992). . . . . Nina
• 0:04—On stage in black lingerie, then buns in T-back.
••• 0:05—Breasts and buns in push up bra and T-back while dancing on stage.
••• 0:59—In red top and red T-back on stage, breasts and buns. Excellent close up of breasts.
••• 1:03—Breasts while making love on stage with Scott Valentine.
Test Tube Teens From the Year 2000 (1993) . . . Girl on TV
a.k.a. Virgin Hunters
• 0:23—Breasts in scenes from *Meridian: Kiss of the Beast* being shown on TV.
Angel of Destruction (1994) . . . . Brit Alwood
Johnny Skidmarks (1997) . . . . Lorraine
• 0:10—Brief breasts, when caught in bed with John Lithgow during setup.
• 0:46—Very brief breast in B&W flashback.
• 0:57—Very, very brief partial right breast in B&W flashback.
TV:
Twin Peaks (1990-91) . . . . Swabbie

Springsteen, Pamela

Sister of singer Bruce Springsteen.
Films:
Fast Times at Ridgemont High (1982) . . . . Dina Phillips
Reckless (1984) . . . . Karen Sybern
My Science Project (1985). . . . . Hall Monitor/Ellie's Friend
Dixie Lanes (1987) . . . . Judy
•• 1:00—Breasts, while turning around in pond, talking to Everett at night.
Modern Girls (1987) . . . . Tanya
Scenes from the Goldmine (1987). . . . . Stephanie
Sleepaway Camp II: Unhappy Campers (1988) . . . . Angela
Fast Food (1989). . . . . Mary Beth Bensen
Sleepaway Camp III: Teenage Wasteland (1989) . . Angela Baker
The Gumshoe Kid (1990) . . . . Mona Krause

Made for TV Movies:
My Mother's Secret Life (1984) . . . . Kelly

Sprinkle, Annie

Adult film actress.
Films:
Mondo New York (1987) . . . . Model/Performer
• 0:17—Nude, painted body with other models during "Rapping & Rocking" segment.
Wimps (1987) . . . . Head Stripper
•• 1:12—Breasts on stage with two other strippers, teasing Francis.
Young Nurses in Love (1987) . . . . Twin Falls
•• 0:23—Breasts getting measured by Dr. Spencer.
Shadows in the City (1991) . . . . Ex-Girlfriend
Made for Cable TV:
Real Sex 2 (1991; HBO) . . . . Herself
Real Sex 4 (1992; HBO). . Annie Sprinkle's One Woman Show
•• 0:00—Brief breasts during opening credits.
•• 0:01—Breasts several times during her show.
••• 0:09—Breasts with vibrator during a ceremonial sex routine in her show.
Wild Cards (1996; HBO) . . . . Herself
•• 0:00—Breasts, while taking pasties off.
•• 0:02—Breasts, while taking photos of herself.
•• 0:21—Breasts, with frosting on her breasts on stage, then playing with squirt gun.
• 0:56—Brief breasts during finale.

Spurrier, Linda

Films:
Jubilee (1977) Viv
•• 0:42—Breasts, while sitting up in bed with Angel and Sphinx. Nude getting out of bed.
Prick Up Your Ears (1987; British). . . . . RADA Instructor
War Requiem (1988; British) . . . . .Nurse 3
Tom & Viv (1994) . . . . Edith Sitwell

Spybey, Dina

Films:
Big Night (1996). . . . . Natalie
The First Wives Club (1996). . . . . .Young Elise
Striptease (1996) . . . . .Monique Jr.
(R-rated version reviewed.)
•• 0:05—Buns in T-back and breasts, while dancing on stage.
• 0:36—Breasts, while dancing on stage in background, when Demi Moore talks with Armand Assante.
SubUrbia (1996) . . . . Bee-Bee
Made for Cable TV:
Remember WENN (1996- ; AMC) . . . . Celia Mellon

Squire, Janie

Films:
Piranha (1978) . . . . .Barbara
•• 0:02—Breasts taking off her top to go swimming with her boyfriend.
Cheerleaders Wild Weekend (1985) . . . . . . Donna/Darwell
••• 0:39—Breasts and brief buns, taking off her white blouse during contest.
••• 0:41—Breasts with the other five girls during contest.
••• 0:43—Breasts, while getting measured with the other two girls.

St. Claire, Jacqueline

a.k.a. Adult film actress Jacqueline.
a.k.a. Adult film actress Claire Tyler.

Films:

Hollywood Dreams (1993) .... Stripper
a.k.a. L.A. Dreams
(Unrated version reviewed.)
•• 0:57—Breasts and buns in T-back, after stripping out of outfit while dancing in bar set.

Housewife From Hell (1993)................. Mary-Lou
••• 0:12—Breasts, while taking off blouse on bed with John, then making love.
• 0:15—Brief frontal nudity while in bathroom with John.
•• 0:16—Buns and breasts, while getting dressed in bedroom while talking to John.
••• 0:40—In purple bra and panties, then buns and breasts while in office with John.
• 1:01—Brief buns in bodysuit, while getting up out of bed.

Video Tapes:

Love Scenes: Volume 3 (1993) .... Diana
••• 1:25—Breasts and buns, while playing with food with four guys.
••• 1:29—Nude, while with the four guys.

St. Claire, Taylor *

a.k.a. Kimberly Knight, Linsey Taylor.
Adult film actress.

Adult Films:

Infinite Bliss (1998) .... n.a.

Films:

Femalien (1995) .... Gena, Meditation Woman
••• 0:34—In lingerie, while modeling for Kara in lingerie store. Nude, while making love with Angel.
••• 1:07—Full frontal nudity (she's brunette), while making love with a guy during meditation orgy.

Virtual Desire (1995) .... Taylor
••• 0:46—Stripping down to black bra, panties, garter belt and stockings, then breasts and buns in panties.

Virtual Encounters (1995)......... Maggie/Rain Dancer 2
(Unrated version reviewed.)
•• 0:00—Breasts, when caressing herself while wearing VR helmet.
••• 0:50—In blue dress, then nude after stripping and making love with another woman in the rain (wearing sunglasses the entire time). Long scene.

Stripteaser 2 (1997).................... Junior Samples
•• 0:03—Breasts and buns in panties, while dancing on stage with Sylvia.
• 0:09—Breasts and buns in black T-back, while in dressing room.
••• 0:10—Breasts and buns in T-back, while dancing on stage.
•• 0:47—Breasts and brief buns in T-back, while talking with Bronson.
••• 1:01—Breasts and buns in panties on stage with Sindy in dream.
•• 1:08—Breasts and buns, while dancing for customers in upstairs room (wearing mask).

Video Tapes:

Soft Bodies: Show 'n Tell (1995) .... Herself
••• 0:02—In lingerie, then nude while posing on sofa.
••• 0:08—Nude in swimming pool, by herself and with LeBeau.
••• 0:16—Nude, while washing and posing next to car with LeBeau.

Body Language (1996)........................ Elevator
••• 0:03—Nude in garter belt and stockngs, while standing in an elevator and playing with a pistol.

Erotic Heat (1996) .... Construction/Jacuzzi
••• 0:11—Nude with Lorissa McComas.
••• 0:40—Nude, with the other girls in the spa.

Malibu Canyon Nights #1 (1997)............... Herself
••• 0:31—Nude (wearing a black corset), while posing on bed.

CD-ROM:

Hollywood Body Double (1995) .... Receptionist/Girl

St. Croix, Dominique *

Films:

Recruits (1986; Canadian) .... n.a.

Video Tapes:

Penthouse Ready to Ride (1992) .... Model

Penthouse Satin & Lace II: Hollywood Undercover (1992).. Pet

Penthouse The Great Pet Hunt—Part II (1993)...... Pet
••• 0:10—Breasts and buns in T-back, then nude while stripping out of dominatrix outfit on stage.

CD-ROM:

Penthouse Interactive Virtual Photo Shoot, Disc 1 (1993).. Pet

St. George, Cathy *

Films:

Star 80 (1983).................... Playboy Mansion Guest

Beverly Hills Brats (1989)........................... Sally

Video Tapes:

Playboy's Playmate Review 2 (1984)........... Playmate

Wet & Wild (1989)............................ Model

Playboy's 21 Playmates (1996)................ Playmate
••• 0:35—Full frontal nudity in still photos.
••• 0:36—Nude during photo session.

Playboy's Playmates Revisited (1998).......... Playmate
••• 0:12—Nude in old footage and still photos.
••• 0:17—Full frontal nudity in new footage.

St. James, Sara

See: Lovell, Jacqueline.

St. Jon, Ashley

Adult Films:

Centerfold Celebrities 3 .... Herself/Nurse
Having sex with Paul Thomas.

Films:

Takin' It Off (1984) .... Sin
••• 0:20—Breasts and buns doing two dance routines on stage.
•• 0:53—Nude, stripping and dancing in the library.

Weekend Pass (1984)..................... Xylene B-12
•• 0:13—Breasts dancing on stage.

The Wild Life (1984) .... Stripper #1
••• 0:47—Breasts and brief buns doing strip tease routine in front of Christopher Penn and his friends.

Sorority Girls and the Creature from Hell (1990) .... Bar Patron

Video Tapes:

Centerfold Screen Test (1985) .... Herself
••• 0:32—Breasts and buns in G-string, taking off her fur coat while auditioning in a car.

The Stripper of the Year (1986) .... Judge

St. Onge, Korrine

Films:

Bordello of Blood (1996)................ Bordello Vampire

Listen (1996; Canadian) . . . . Sarah's Double

Made for Cable Movies:

Deathgame (1996; Showtime) . . . . Felicia

•• 0:42—Breasts, while making love with Hawk just before trying to kill him.

Stafford, Jamie

a.k.a. Adult film actress Jamie Summers.

Films:

Night Rhythms (1992). . . . . Kit

(Unrated version reviewed.)

•• 0:40—Breasts in push-up bra in dressing room.

••• 0:51—Nude, in bed, making love with Lila and Martin Hewitt.

• 0:54—Buns, while watching TV while lying in bed.

••• 0:55—Nude, undressing to take a shower with Lila.

•• 1:23—In sheer black blouse, talking to Delia Sheppard in the radio station.

••• 1:25—Nude, in bed with Sheppard, then getting dressed. Long scene.

Stagno, Lisa Marie

See: Breeze, Crystal.

Stahl, Jennifer

Films:

Dirty Dancing (1987) . . . . Dirty Dancer

Firehouse (1987). . . . . Mindy

•• 0:25—Breasts while dancing in club.

Necropolis (1987) . . . . Cat

Stakis, Anastassia

Films:

Nevada Heat (1982) . . . . Wooly

a.k.a. Fake-Out

• 0:13—Breasts in the shower room scene.

Siesta (1987). . . . . Desdra

Staley, Heidi

See: Lynne, Heidi.

Staley, Lora

Films:

American Nightmare (1981; Canadian) . . . . Louise Harmon

•• 0:44—Breasts and buns in G-string dancing on stage.

••• 0:54—Breasts making love in bed with Eric.

• 0:59—Brief right breast, then breasts auditioning in TV studio.

Thief (1981) . . . . Paula

Risky Business (1983). . . . . Call Girl

Deadly Weapon (1989) . . . . Leslie

Samantha (1991) . . . . TV Reporter

*Staller, Ilona **

a.k.a. Italian adult film actress Cicciolina.

Was a member of the Italian Parliament from 1987-92.

Adult Films:

Maiden Italy, Part 1 (1994). Herself

Maiden Italy, Part 2 (1994). Herself

Films:

Inhibition (1984; Italian). . . . . Anna

••• 0:08—Nude taking a shower with Carol.

• 0:43—Brief full frontal nudity getting out of swimming pool.

••• 0:55—Breasts making love in the water with Robert.

••• 1:00—Full frontal nudity getting disciplined by Carol.

Replikator (1994) . . . . Tina

• 0:28—Breasts, in virtual reality visor display.

•• 1:05—Breasts and bun in G-string, while dancing on stage.

••• 1:07—Nude in room and walking to bathtub with Ludo.

•• 1:08—Breasts, while sitting in bathtub.

Made for Cable TV:

Real Sex 3 (1992; HBO). . . . . Ciccolina

•• 0:00—Breasts several times during the opening credits.

• 0:16—Breasts several times.

• 0:17—Brief lower frontal nudity and buns. More breasts in clips.

••• 0:20—More breasts clips.

• 0:24—More breasts shots.

• *Stanford, Michelle **

Video Tapes:

Playboy's The Girls of Hawaiian Tropic (1994)

. . . . White Sand Beach

••• 0:26—Nude, while posing at the beach during the day.

Stansfield, Claire

Films:

The Doors (1991) . . . . Warhol Eurosnob

The Favor (1991). . . . . Miranda/Lamaze Class

Nervous Ticks (1991). . . . . Lu

Best of the Best 2 (1992) . . . . Greta

The Swordsman (1992) . . . . Julie

Drop Zone (1994) . . . . Kara

Gladiator Cop: The Swordsman II (1994) . . . . Julie

• 0:40—In white bra and panties, then very brief right breast while making love with Lorenzo Lamas.

Sensation (1994). . . . . Paula

••• 1:03—In black bra, panties, garter belt and stockings, then buns and breasts, while making love on sofa with Eric Roberts.

Wes Craven's Mind Ripper (1995) . . . . Joanne

• 0:04—Brief buns, when getting into, then in the shower.

Steel (1997). . . . . Duvray

Made for Cable TV:

Red Shoe Diaries: Bounty Hunter (1993; Showtime)

. . . . The Bounty Hunter

(Available on the video tape *Red Shoe Diaries 5: Weekend Pass.*)

• 0:16—Buns, in black G-string. Don't see her face.

• 0:19—Brief breasts several times, making love outside in the rain with Oliver. Hard to see because of the lightning effect.

••• 0:25—Breasts several times, making love with Oliver on the floor in the cafe.

Starbuck, Cheryl

Films:

Angel III: The Final Chapter (1988) . . . . Video Girl #3

Mortuary Academy (1988) . . . . Linda Hollyhead

• 1:08—Breasts, dead, in morgue when Paul Bartel tries to make love with her.

Shy People (1988) . . . . Stewardess

Stark, Kimberleigh

Films:

Crime Lords (1990) . . . . Lieutenant Sylvestri

Night of the Cyclone (1990) . . . . Venna

• 0:01—Brief left breast while posing for the painter.

• 0:40—Breasts on the boat, fighting with the businessman. Breasts on the floor, dead.

Eliminator Woman (1992) . . . . Lianna
- • 0:33—Very brief buns in panties, viewed up her dress as she climbs down the stairs.

Lethal Ninja (1992) . . . . Farida
- •• 1:01—Buns and breasts, while getting out of bath and putting on robe.

Cyborg Cop (1993). . . . . Woman Hostage
Woman of Desire (1993). . . . . Nurse Vivian Donner
(Unrated version reviewed.)
Cyborg Cop II (1994) . . . . Gloria Alvarez
Fleshtone (1994). . . . . Detective #3
Project Shadowchaser II (1994). . . . . Carla
a.k.a. Armed and Deadly
Danger Zone (1995). . . . . Mercenary 6
Made for TV Movies:
Bridge of Time (1997). . . . . Keza

Stark, Koo

Former girlfriend of Prince Andrew of England in 1982, before he met and married "Fergie."
Special Stills Photographer in the film *Aria*.
Films:
The Rocky Horror Picture Show (1975; British) . . . . Bridesmaid
Emily (1976; British) . . . . .Emily
- •• 0:08—Breasts, lying in bed caressing herself while fantasizing about James.
- ••• 0:30—Breasts in studio posing for Augustine, then kissing her.
- ••• 0:42—Buns and breasts taking a shower after posing for Augustine.
- •• 0:56—Left breast, under a tree with James.
- • 1:16—Breasts in the woods seducing Rupert.

Justine (1977; British) . . . . .Justine
a.k.a. Cruel Passion
- •• 0:09—Breasts getting fondled by a nun.
- • 0:16—Breasts getting attacked by a nun.
- • 0:57—Breasts in open dress getting attacked by old guy.
- ••• 1:00—Breasts getting bathed, then lower frontal nudity.
- • 1:28—Right breast and buns taking off clothes, then brief full frontal nudity getting dressed again.
- • 1:32—Breasts getting thrown in to the water.

Electric Dreams (1984) . . . . .Girl in Soap Opera

Stark, Melody *

Films:
Crackerjack (1994). . . . . .Newlywed
- • 0:33—Brief side view of left breast, while undressing in room with her husband.
- ••• 0:34—Breasts, when her husband plays with an ice cube on her breasts. Buns when the terrorists break into the room.

Staunton, Imelda

Films:
Comrades (1986; British) . . . . Betsy Loveless
Antonia & Jane (1991; British) . . . . Jane Hartman
- • 0:08—Right breast, while lying in bed with Norman, reading a book to get him turned on.

Much Ado About Nothing (1993; British) . . . . .Margaret
Peter's Friends (1993; British/U.S.). . . . . Mary
Sense and Sensibility (1995) . . . . Charlotte Palmer
Twelfth Night (1996; British). . . . . Maria
Made for Cable Movies:
Citizen X (1995; HBO) .Mrs. Burakov
Made for Cable TV:
Tales From the Crypt: About Face (1996; HBO). . . . . n.a.

Stavin, Mary

Films:
Octopussy (1983; British) . . . . Octopussy Girl
A View to a Kill (1985). . . . . Kimberley Jones
House (1986) . . . . Tanya
Open House (1987). . . . . .Katie Thatcher
Howling V (1989) . . . . .Anna
- •• 1:09—Breasts three times drying herself off while Richard watches in the mirror. Possible body double.

Desire (1994) . . . . .Adrienne
TV:
Twin Peaks (1990-91) . . . . .Heba

Steafel, Sheila

Films:
Baby Love (1969) . . . . .Tessa
Goodbye Mr. Chips (1969; British) .Tilly
Tropic of Cancer (1970). . . . . .Tania
- •• 0:25—Breasts, while ballet dancing in studio while wearing only a tutu.

Bloodbath at the House of Death (1985; British) . . .Sheila Finch

Steel, Pippa

Films:
Cop-Out (1967; British). . . . . Sue Phillips
Lust for a Vampire (1970; British). . . . . Susan Pelley
Take a Girl Like You (1970; British). Ted
Vampire Lovers (1970; British). . . . . Laura
- • 0:24—Left breast in bed when the doctor pulls her top down to listen to her heart beat.

Young Winston (1972; British). . . . . Clementine Hozier

Steele, Vanessa

Films:
Wet and Wild Summer! (1992; Australian) . . . . . . .Charlene
a.k.a. Exchange Lifeguards
- •• 1:25—Breasts, opening her leather jacket to distract the other lifeguard boat.

Sniper (1993) . . . . Mrs. Alvarez
Tunnel Vision (1995; Australian). . . . . Rachel Kossinger
- • 0:41—Very, very brief left breast when girl dressed in bunny suit discovers her. Lit with flashlight.

Steenburgen, Mary

Ex-wife of actor Malcolm McDowell.
Wife of actor Ted Danson.
Films:
Goin' South (1978) . . . . .Julia Tate
Time After Time (1979; British) . . . . .Amy Robbins
Melvin and Howard (1980) . . . . .Lynda Dummar
(Academy Award for Best Supporting Actress.)
- •• 0:31—Breasts and buns, ripping off barmaid outfit and walking out the door.

Ragtime (1981). . . . . Mother
A Midsummer Night's Sex Comedy (1982) . . . . .Adrian
Cross Creek (1983) . . . . Marjorie Kinnan Rawlings
Romantic Comedy (1983) . . . . Phoebe
Dead of Winter (1987) . . . . .Julie Rose/Katie McGovern/Evelyn
End of the Line (1987). . . . . .Rose Pickett
Miss Firecracker (1989) . . . . Elain
Parenthood (1989) . . . . .Karen Buckman
Back to the Future, Part III (1990) . . . . Clara Clayton
The Butcher's Wife (1991) . . . . .Stella
Philadelphia (1993). . . . . Belinda Conine
What's Eating Gilbert Grape (1993). . . . . Betty Carver
Clifford (1994) . . . . .Sarah Davis

My Summer Story (1994) . . . . Mom
Pontiac Moon (1994) . . . . Katherine Bellamy
My Family (1995) . . . . Gloria
Nixon (1995) . . . . Hannah Nixon
Powder (1995) . . . . Jessie Caldwell
The Grass Harp (1996) . . . . Sister Ida
Made for Cable Movies:
Directed By: The Gift (1994; Showtime) . . . . n.a.
Made for TV Movies:
One Magic Christmas (1985; U.S./Canadian) . . Ginny Grainger
The Attic—The Hiding of Anne Frank (1988) . . . . Miep Gies
Gulliver's Travels (1996) . . . . Mary Gulliver
TV:
Ink (1996-97) . . . . Kate Montgomery

*Stefanelli, Simonetta **

Films:
The Godfather (1972) . . . . Apollonia
•• 1:50—Breasts in bedroom on honeymoon night.
Three Brothers (1982; Italian) . . . . Young Donato's Wife

Stegers, Bernice

Films:
City of Women (1980; Italian/French) . . . . Woman on Train
Frozen Terror (1980; Italian) . . . . Jane Baker
a.k.a. Macabro
•• 0:08—Breasts, while taking off her slip in bedroom and putting on night gown.
• 0:10—Brief right breast, while making love in bed with Fred.
• 0:40—Briefly nude, while getting up out of bathtub.
Quartet (1981; British/French) . . . . Miss Nicholson
Xtro (1982) . . . . Rachel Phillips
The Girl (1987; British) . . . . Eva Berg
Four Weddings and a Funeral (1994; British) . . . . Shop Assistant
Made for Cable TV:
The Garden of Redemption (1997; Showtime) . . . . Renata

*Stein, Pamela J. **

Video Tapes:
Playboy Video Calendar 1989 (1988) . . . . September
••• 0:33—Nude.
Playboy Video Centerfold: Tawnni Cable (1990) . . . . Playmate
••• 0:14—Nude in Hawaii with Tawnni Cable and Jacqueline Sheen.
Playboy Playmates in Paradise (1992) . . . . Playmate

Steiner, Riley

Films:
Beginner's Luck (1983) . . . . Tech
• 0:05—Brief side view of right breast, while in bathtub with Aris.
Made for TV Movies:
In the Line of Duty: The Price of Vengeance (1994) . . . . Press Person
TV:
General Hospital . . . . Page Bowen

Stenberg, Brigitta

Films:
Queens Logic (1991) . . . . Girl in Club Bathroom
Homicidal Impulse (1992) . . . . Receptionist
a.k.a. Killer Instinct
(Unrated version reviewed.)
Raiders of the Sun (1992) . . . . Vera
Rapid Fire (1992) . . . . Rosalyn
• 0:10—Brief side view of right breast, posing in art class. Don't see her face. Long shot breasts, getting up and putting on robe.
Stop! Or My Mom Will Shoot (1992) . . . . Stewardess
Made for TV Movies:
Siringo (1994) . . . . Bella

Stensgaard, Yutte

Real name is Jytte Stensgaard.
Films:
Lust for a Vampire (1970; British) . . . . Mircalla
••• 0:19—Breasts, three times, getting a massage from another school girl.
•• 0:53—Breasts outside with Lestrange. Left breast when lying down.
• 0:58—Breasts during Lestrange's dream.
Scream and Scream Again (1970; British) . . . . Erika
The Buttercup Chain (1971; British) . . . . Ullah

Stephen, Karen

Films:
Pick-Up Summer (1979; Canadian) . . . . Donna
• 0:25—Very brief lower half of breast, pulling her T-shirt up to distract someone.
• 0:34—Very, very brief breasts when the boys spray her and she jumps up.
Happy Birthday to Me (1980; Canadian) . . . . Miss Calhoun
Hog Wild (1980; Canadian) . . . . Brenda

*Stephens, Yvette **

a.k.a. Yvette Nelson.
Frederick's of Hollywood catalog model.
Wife of singer Matthew Nelson of Nelson.
Films:
Carnal Crimes (1991) . . . . Mia
•• 0:25—Left breast, when Renny makes out with her.
••• 0:28—Brief left breast, then breasts posing with Linda.
••• 0:29—Full frontal nudity making love with Linda Carol and Renny.
• 0:48—Breasts and brief buns on TV.
• 0:50—Brief breasts in flashback.

Stephenson, Pamela

Films:
Stand Up Virgin Soldiers (1976) . . . . Nurse
Breasts and brief buns after removing clothes and getting into bed.
History of the World, Part I (1981) . . . . Mademoiselle Rimbaud
The Secret Policeman's Other Ball (1982; British) . . . . . . Herself
Finders Keepers (1983) . . . . Georgiana Latimer
Scandalous (1983) . . . . Fiona Maxwell Sayle
Superman III (1983) . . . . Lorelei Ambrosia
Bloodbath at the House of Death (1985; British) . . . . Barbara Coyle
• 0:50—Very brief breasts getting clothes ripped off by an unseen being.
TV:
Saturday Night Live (1984-85) . . . . Regular

Sterling, Alicyn

See: Bittner, Carrie.

Sterling, Gayle

Adult film actress.

Films:

Simply Irresistible (1983) . . . . Juliet
(R-rated version. *Irresistible* is the X-rated version.)
•• 0:40—Breasts and buns in bed with Walter.

*Sterling, Lesli Kay **

Films:

Forbidden Games (1995) . . . . Shannon
(Unrated version reviewed.)

Forbidden Passions (1995) . . . . .Jana

Galaxy Girls (1995) . . . . Laticia
••• 0:11—Breasts, while sunbathing outdoors and talking to the girls.
• 0:21—Brief breasts, while sitting and chanting.

Petticoat Planet (1995). . . . . Sheriff Sarah Parker
•• 0:10—Breasts, while making love with Delia.
••• 0:26—Breasts, while dancing in jail cell in front of Steve.

Made for Cable TV:

Hot Line: The Gardener (1996; Cinemax). . . . . . . Samantha
(Available on video tape in *Hot Line 4*.)
•• 0:01—Breasts, taking off robe and lying down on chair outside, then rubbing lotion on herself.
••• 0:11—Full frontal nudity, while making love with J.M. Shown in annoying quick cuts.
••• 0:15—Nude, after walking out of the pool at night, then making love with J.M. in the back yard. Quick cuts again.
• 0:18—Full frontal nudity, while making love with J.M. in flashbacks.
•• 0:25—Breasts and buns, while making love with J.M. in bed.

Women: Stories of Passion-Table Service
(1996; Showtime). . . . . Jo
• 0:08—Breasts, while fantasizing that Ricardo is making love with her in his office.
• 0:20—Right breast in open dress, several times, while making love with Ricardo in a restaurant.
••• 0:22—Buns and breasts, while making love with Ricardo in her house.

TV:

As the World Turns (1997-) . . . . Molly Conlan

Sterling, Nici

Adult film actress.

Films:

Tainted Love (1995). . . . . Carol Spencer
• 0:17—Full frontal nudity, while lying dead in bed with her wrists tied to bed. More in photos.

Stern, Ellen

Films:

The Duchess and the Dirtwater Fox (1976) . . . . Bride

Jessi's Girls (1976) . . . . Kana
••• 1:10—Left breast, then breasts in bed with a guy.

• *Stern, Gilya*

Films:

The Finest Hour (1991) . . . . Diane

The Human Shield (1991) . . . . Stewardess

Prison Heat (1992). . . . . Michelle
•• 0:11—In bra, then breasts, while undressing to enter prison.
•• 0:15—Breasts and very brief buns, while showering next to Bonnie.
• 1:01—In bra, then breasts, while tricking guard.
• 1:03—Brief breasts, while dressing after tricking guard.

*Stevens, Brinke **

Ex-wife of *The Rocketeer* comic book creator David Stevens.

Films:

The Slumber Party Massacre (1982) . . . . Linda
•• 0:07—Buns, then breasts taking a shower during girls' locker room scene.

Sole Survivor (1982). . . . . .Jennifer
•• 0:45—Breasts after taking off bra while playing strip poker.

The Man Who Wasn't There (1983) . . . . Nymphet
• 0:45—Buns and brief breasts in the girls' shower, when she gets shampoo from an invisible Steve Guttenberg.

Private School (1983). . . . . Uncredited School Girl
•• 0:42—Brief breasts and buns in shower room scene. She's the brunette wearing a pony tail who passes in front of the chalkboard.

The Witching (1983) . . . . Black Sabbath Member
a.k.a. Necromancy
(Originally filmed in 1971 as *Necromancy*, additional scenes were added and re-released in 1983.)

Body Double (1984) . . . . Girl in Bathroom #3
• 1:12—Breasts sitting in chair in adult film preview that Craig Wasson watches on TV.

Emmanuelle IV (1984) . . . . Uncredited Dream Girl
••• 0:19—Breasts, getting coached by Sylvia Kristel during dream-like sequence on how to get a guy aroused.

Fatal Games (1984) . . . . .Uncredited Shower Girl
• 0:14—Brief, out of focus side of left breast and upper half of buns, taking a shower in the background while two girls talk. (She's wearing a light blue towel around her hair.)

Psycho III (1986) . . . . Body Double for Diana Scarwid
•• 0:30—Brief breasts and buns getting ready to take a shower, body doubling for Diana Scarwid.

Nightmare Sisters (1987) . . . . Marci
••• 0:39—Breasts wearing panties, while standing with Melody and Mickey after transforming from nerds to sexy women.
••• 0:40—Breasts while in the kitchen with Melody and Mickey.
••• 0:44—Nude in the bathtub with Melody and Mickey. Excellent, long scene.
••• 0:47—Breasts while in the bathtub. Nice close up.
••• 0:48—Still more buns and breasts in the bathtub.

Slavegirls from Beyond Infinity (1987). . . . . .Shala
• 0:29—Chained up wearing black lingerie. Brief right breast.
• 0:31—Brief side view of left breast on table. Nice pan from her feet to her head while she's lying on her back.

Grandmother's House (1988) . . . . .Woman

The Jigsaw Murders (1988). . . . . Stripper #1
• 0:28—Very, very brief breasts posing for photographer in white bra and panties when camera passes between her and the other stripper.

Phantom of the Mall: Eric's Revenge (1988)
. . . . Girl in Dressing Room
• 0:14—Breasts in dressing room and on B&W monitor several times (second room from the left).

Sorority Babes in the Slimeball Bowl-O-Rama (1988)
. . . . Taffy
••• 0:12—Nude, while showering off whipped cream in bathtub when talking to Michelle Bauer. Excellent long scene!

Warlords (1988) . . . . Dow's Wife

Murder Weapon (1989). . . . . .Girl in Shower on TV
• 1:00—Brief left breast on TV that the guys are watching. Scene from *Nightmare Sisters*.

Bad Girls from Mars (1990) . . . . Myra
- 0:11—Brief side of left breast, then breasts getting massaged on diving board.

Haunting Fear (1990). . . . . Victoria
- ••• 0:10—Full frontal nudity, taking a bath and getting out.
- •• 0:22—Breasts, while changing into nightgown in bedroom.
- ••• 0:32—Breasts while lying on Coroner's table.

Mob Boss (1990). . . . . Sara
Transylvania Twist (1990) . . . . Betty Lou
Roots of Evil (1991) . . . . .Candy
(Unrated version reviewed.)
- •• 1:33—Right breast, then breasts while sitting on bed talking to Deanna Lund.

Shadows in the City (1991). . . . . Fortune Teller
Spirits (1991) . . . . .Amy Goldwyn
Munchie (1992) . . . . .Band Member
Teenage Exorcist (1992) . . . . Dianne
- 1:03—Brief partial buns in sexy, skimpy outfit, while walking down stairs with Eddie Deezen.
- 1:06—More brief partial buns.
- 1:13—Partial buns, during struggle with Elena Sahagan.
- 1:13—More partial buns, while bending over Jay Richardson.
- 1:16—Partial buns under fishnet stockings with Deezen.

Mommy (1994). . . . . Beth
Cyberzone (1995). . . . . Kitten
- ••• 0:04—Breasts and buns in T-back, while doing strip routine on stage. She's made up to look like an alien kitten.
- 0:52—Brief buns in T-back, while dancing on stage.

Jack-O (1995) . . . . Witch
a.k.a. Jacko Lantern
Masseuse (1995). . . . . Hotel Manager
(Unrated version reviewed.)
Over the Wire (1995) . . . . Jenny

Made for Cable Movies:
Acting on Impulse (1993; Showtime) . . . . Waitress

Video Tapes:
Playboy Video Magazine, Volume 1 (1982)
. . . . Marie/Ribald Classic
- 0:01—Full frontal nudity.
- •• 0:46—Breasts on the bed with Jean-Pierre.
- ••• 0:47—Breasts in bathtub. Full frontal nudity in front of fire.
- •• 0:49—Breasts outside in the garden.

More Candid Candid Camera (1983). Horseriding Student 1
- ••• 0:00—Buns and lower frontal nudity, learning how to ride a horse "bareback" style.

Playboy Video Magazine, Volume 4 (1983)
. . . . Flashdancer/Dream Lover
- 0:15—Very brief lower frontal nudity and buns in orange lingerie.
- ••• 0:16—Nude, fighting over blue towel with Linnea Quigley in the shower.
- ••• 0:43—Nude in a sheet covered chair during fantasy sequence. Best for Brinke fans!

Playboy Video Magazine, Volume 5 (1983)
. . . . Candid Camera Girl
- •• 0:18—Lots of buns shots, during prank learning how to ride a horse "bare back."

The Girls of Penthouse (1984). . . . . Ghost Town Woman
Red Hot Rock (1984) . . . . Miss Utah
a.k.a. Sexy Shorts (on laser disc)
- 0:41—Brief breasts several times in open-front swimsuit during beauty pageant during "Gimme Gimme Good Lovin'" by Helix.

Dark Romances: Volume I and II (1987) . . . . . Various Parts
- 3:26—(1:39 into Volume II) Partial breasts in B&W segment while wearing a blonde wig.

Scream Queen Hot Tub Party (1991). . . . . Herself
- •• 0:07—Breasts, taking off white outfit and putting on black teddy.
- 0:12—Buns, while walking up the stairs.
- •• 0:14—Buns and breasts in shower scene from *Slumber Party Massacre.*
- ••• 0:19—Breasts and buns, demonstrating the proper Scream Queen way to take a shower.
- ••• 0:44—Breasts taking off her swimsuit top and soaping up with the other girls.
- •• 0:46—Breasts in still shot during the end credits.

Brinke Stevens Private Collection Volume 1 (1992)
. . . . Herself
- •• 0:16—Breasts in *Flashdancers* segment from *Playboy* video magazine.
- •• 0:19—Nude in still photo sequence in shower with Linnea Quigley.
- 0:22—Brief breasts lying on slab from *Slavegirls from Beyond Infinity.*
- 0:30—Breasts scenes from *Nightmare Sisters.*
- ••• 0:41—Breasts, in scenes from that were cut from the U.S. version of *Bad Girls From Mars.*
- 0:43—Buns, in G-string outfit posing for photo session.

Brinke Stevens Private Collection Volume 2 (1994)
. . . . Herself
- 0:01—Buns in gynecology-at-home sketch from *Playboy.*
- •• 0:03—Breasts, while in garden as Marie, from *Ribald Classics.*
- 0:05—Breasts and partial buns in music video by Helix from *Red Hot Rock.*
- •• 0:09—Breasts, after taking off bra in strip-poker scene from *Sole Survivor.*
- ••• 0:10—Breasts with Sylvia Kristel from *Emmanuelle IV.*
- ••• 0:12—Breasts and buns, in screen tests for *The Girls of Penthouse.*
- ••• 0:16—Full frontal nudity, in screen tests for *The Girls of Penthouse.*

• Stevens, Carrie *

Films:
Sins of Desire (1992) . . . . Pam
(Unrated version reviewed.)
Body Chemistry 3: Point of Seduction (1993) . . . . Leslie

Video Tapes:
Playboy Video Calendar 1998 (1997) . . . . July
- ••• 0:27—Nude, while posing outdoors while fishing.
- ••• 0:29—Nude, while posing in a dressing room.

Playboy's Voluptuous Vixens (1997). . . . . .Playmate
Playboy's Girls Next Door: Naughty and Nice (1998)
. . . . Picture This/Cindy
- ••• 0:42—Nude, while undressing and posing by the window, on the bed and giving herself a sponge bath.

Stevens, Connie

Films:
Scorchy (1971) . . . . Jackie Parker
- •• 0:23—Open blouse, revealing left bra cup while talking on the telephone. Brief breasts swimming in the water after taking off bathing suit top.
- •• 0:52—Side view left breast, taking a shower.
- ••• 0:56—Brief right breast making love in bed with Greg Evigan. Breasts getting tied to the bed by the thieves. Kind of a long shot and a little dark and hard to see.

- 1:00—Brief breasts getting covered with a sheet by the good guy.

Grease 2 (1982) . . . . Miss Mason
Back to the Beach (1987) . . . . Connie
Tapeheads (1988) . . . . June Tager
Miniseries:
Scruples (1980) . . . . Maggie McGregor
Made for TV Movies:
The Littlest Angel (1969) . . . . Flying Mistress
Playmates (1972) . . . . Patti Holvey
Love's Savage Fury (1979) . . . . Dolby
TV:
Hawaiian Eye (1959-63) . . . . Cricket Blake
Wendy and Me (1964-65) . . . . Wendy Conway
Head Over Heels (1997-) . . . . Roxanne

Stevens, Deborah *

Films:
Illegal Entry (1992) . . . . Swimming Pool Party Girl #2
Sex Crimes (1992) . . . . Hooker
Femme Fontaine Killer Babe for the C.I.A. (1993)
. . . . Mile's Girlfriend
Video Tapes:
Love Scenes: Volume 2 (1992) . . . . Pamela Carey

- ••• 1:09—Full frontal nudity, while working out with Chuck, then working with pottery wheel and covering each other with clay.
- •• 1:14—Breasts and partial buns in bath with Chuck.
- ••• 1:17—Nude, while making love in bed with Chuck.

• Stevens, Janet

Made for Cable TV:
Compromising Situations: First Time Caller (1994; Showtime) . . . . Woman/Transexual

- • 0:24—Breasts, while making out on couch with Jonathon.

Compromising Situations: Jim and Jane (1998; Showtime)
. . . . Bartender

Stevens, Stella *

Mother of actor Andrew Stevens.
Films:
Li'l Abner (1959) . . . . Appasionata von Climax
Girls! Girls! Girls! (1962) . . . . Robin Gantner
The Nutty Professor (1963) . . . . Stella Purdy
The Ballad of Cable Hogue (1970) . . . . Hildy

- • 1:12—Buns, while changing into nightgown in bedroom.
- • 1:14—Brief top half of breasts in outdoor tub, then buns running into cabin when stagecoach arrives.

The Poseidon Adventure (1972) . . . . Linda Rogo
Slaughter (1972) . . . . Ann

- •• 0:47—Left breast, several times in bed with Jim Brown.
- • 0:55—Left breast, making love in bed with Brown again. Dark.
- • 0:57—Brief right breast, in bed afterwards. Close up shot.
- ••• 1:14—Buns and breasts taking a shower and getting out. This is her best nude scene.

Stand Up and Be Counted (1972) . . . . Yvonne Kellerman
Arnold (1973) . . . . Karen
The Manitou (1977) . . . . Amelia Crusoe
Chained Heat (1983; U.S./German) . . . . Taylor
The Longshot (1986) . . . . Nicki
Down the Drain (1989) . . . . Sophia
Mom (1989) . . . . Beverly Hills
Last Call (1990) . . . . Betty

- • 0:52—Very brief left nipple popping out of black lingerie top while making love with Jason on a pool table.

Eye of the Stranger (1992) . . . . Doc
The Nutt House (1992) . . . . Mrs. Robinson
South Beach (1992) . . . . Nancy
a.k.a. Night Caller
The Terror Within II (1992) . . . . Kara
Body Chemistry 3: Point of Seduction (1993) . . . Frannie Sibley
Molly & Gina (1993) . . . . Mrs. Sweeny
Hard Drive (1994) . . . . Susan
(Unrated version reviewed.)
Illicit Dreams (1994) . . . . Cicily
Body Chemistry 4: Full Exposure (1995) . . . . Fran Sibley
(Unrated version reviewed.)
The Granny (1995) . . . . Granny
Virtual Combat (1995) . . . . Mary
Bikini Hotel (1996) . . . . Gail Regent
Made for Cable Movies:
Attack of the 5' 2" Women (1994; Showtime) . . . . Lawanda
Subliminal Seduction (1996; Showtime) . . . . Mrs. Beecham
Made for Cable TV:
Dream On: Over Your Dead Body (1990; HBO) . . . Lyla Murphy
Made for TV Movies:
Amazons (1984) . . . . Kathryn Lundquist
Man Against the Mob (1988) . . . . Joey Day
Dukes of Hazzard: Reunion! (1997) . . . . Mama Max
TV:
Santa Barbara . . . . Phyllis Blake
Ben Casey (1965) . . . . Jane Hancock
Flamingo Road (1981-82) . . . . Lute-Mae Sanders

Stevens, Tabitha

Adult film actress.
Films:
Eve's Beach Fantasy (1997) . . . . Model 1

- • 0:40—Breasts under sheer fabric during photo shoot.

Video Tapes:
BabeWatch, Episode 3: Sex Kittens (1994)
. . . . Tabitha Stevens

- •• 0:21—Breasts and buns, while playing outdoors in a mud puddle.

Stevenson, Cynthia

Films:
The Player (1992) . . . . Bonnie Sherow

- •• 0:19—Breasts, sitting in spa with Tim Robbins.

Watch It (1993) . . . . Ellen
Home for the Holidays (1995) . . . . Joanne Wedman
Live Nude Girls (1996) . . . . Marcy

- • 1:34—Brief left breast, when sitting at the table.

Made for Cable TV:
Dream On: Off-Off Broadway Bound (1994; HBO)
. . . . Abby Kaplow
TV:
Cheers (1989) . . . . Doris
My Talk Show (1990) . . . . Jennifer Bass
Bob (1992-93) . . . . Tricia
Hope & Gloria (1995-96) . . . . Hope

Stevenson, Judy

Films:
Alvin Rides Again (1974; Australian) . . . . Housewife

- •• 0:01—Full frontal nudity, dropping her towel while Alvin washes her window.

Cathy's Child (1979; Australian) Lil

Stevenson, Juliet

Films:

Drowning by Numbers (1988; British) ..... Cisse Colpitts 2
- • 0:57—Lower frontal nudity and left breast, while trying to entice Hardy. Long shot.

The March (1990; British) .... Uare Fitzgerald
Truly, Madly, Deeply (1991) .... Nina
- • 0:46—Very, very brief, blurry tip of left breast, when Alan Rickman pushes her out of the bedroom.

The Secret Rapture (1994; British) .... Isobel Coleridge
- ••• 0:23—Full frontal nudity, taking off blouse and getting into bed with a guy.
- •• 0:24—Breasts, while making love with him in bed.
- •• 0:29—Brief side of right breast, when standing up with him, then breasts, while making love on desk.
- •• 0:48—Left breast, then breasts, while in bed with him.
- • 1:04—Brief right breast, while taking shower. Overhead view.
- •• 1:07—Brief full frontal nudity, while walking to bed in flashback.
- • 1:09—Brief breasts, while getting into bed in flashback.
- 1:24—Brief side of right breast, while washing herself off.

The Trial (1994; British) .... Fraulein Burstner
Emma (1996; British/U.S.) .... Mrs. Elton

Made for TV Movies:

Masterpiece Theatre: A Doll's House (1992) .... Nora
Masterpiece Theatre: The Politician's Wife (1996) .... Flora Matlock

Stewart, Alana *

a.k.a. Alana Hamilton or Alana Collins.
Ex-wife of singer Rod Stewart.
Ex-wife of actor George Hamilton.

Films:

Evel Knievel (1972) .... Nurse
Night Call Nurses (1972) .... Janis
a.k.a. Young LA Nurses 2
- •• 0:12—Breasts in bed with Zach.
- •• 0:28—Breasts and buns on bed with Kyle.
- • 0:52—Brief right breast twice in shower with Kyle.

The Ravagers (1979) .... Miriam
Swing Shift (1984) .... Frankie Parker
- • 0:11—Buns in B&W photo that Christine Lahti shows to Fred Ward. Possible photo composite.

Where the Boys Are '84 (1984) .... Maggie

TV:

The George & Alana Show (1995-96) .... Co-Host

Stewart, Alexandra *

Films:

The Bride Wore Black (1968; French/Italian) ...... Miss Becker
Kemek (1970) .... Marisa
- • 0:26—Brief right breast while sitting up in bed.
- • 0:49—Right breast while kneeling in bed. Out of focus.
- • 0:51—Very, very brief tip of right breast while crying in bed and talking to David Henison.
- • 0:52—Brief breasts lying in bed with Henison.

The Man Who Had Power Over Women (1970; British) .... Frances
Because of the Cats (1973) .... Theodora
- • 0:16—Breasts under sheer black blouse.
- •• 0:43—Breasts, sitting up and covering herself while sunbathing outside.

Goodbye Emmanuelle (1977) .... Dorothee
The Uncanny (1977; British) .... Mrs. Blake
In Praise of Older Women (1978; Canadian) .... Paula
- •• 1:21—Breasts in bed with Tom Berenger.
- •• 1:23—Nude, in and out of bed with Berenger.

The Last Chase (1980) .... Eudora
Phobia (1980; Canadian) .... Barbara
Agency (1981; Canadian) .... Mimi
Chanel Solitaire (1981) .... n.a.
Final Assignment (1981) .... Sam O'Donnell
Under the Cherry Moon (1986) .... Mrs. Sharon
Frantic (1988) .... Edie

Made for Cable TV:

The Hitchhiker: Shattered Vows (1983; HBO) .... Jackie Winslow
- • 0:04—In white bra and panties, then side view breasts making love in bed with Jeff.

Miniseries:

Mistral's Daughter (1984) .... Mary Jane Kilkullen

Stewart, Catherine Mary

Films:

Nighthawks (1981) .... Salesgirl
The Beach Girls (1982) .... Surfer Girl
The Last Starfighter (1984) .... Maggie Gordon
Night of the Comet (1984) .... Regina
Mischief (1985) .... Bunny
Dudes (1987) .... Jessie, Gas Station Owner
Nightflyers (1987) .... Miranda
Scenes from the Goldmine (1987) .... Debi D'Angelo
World Gone Wild (1988) .... Angie
Weekend at Bernie's (1989) .... Gwen Saunders
a.k.a. Hot and Cold
Cafe Romeo (1991) .... Lia
Samurai Cowboy (1993) .... n.a.
Number One Fan (1994) .... Holly Newman

Made for Cable Movies:

Psychic (1992; USA) .... Laurel
- • 0:45—Very brief right breast, twice, at the end of love making scene with Zach Galligan.

The Sea Wolf (1993; TNT) .... Flaxen Brewster
Out of Annie's Past (1995; USA) .... Annie Carver

Made for Cable TV:

The Outer Limits: Unnatural Selection (1996; Showtime) .... Joanne Sharp

Made for TV Movies:

Ordeal in the Arctic (1993) .... Wilma

TV:

Days of Our Lives .... Kayla Brady
Hearts are Wild (1991) .... Kyle Hubbard

Stewart, Liz *

Video Tapes:

Playmate Playoffs .... Playmate
Playboy Video Magazine, Volume 10 (1986) .... The Goldner Girls
- •• 0:17—Breasts during modeling session for photographer David Goldner.

Wet & Wild (1989) .... Model
Playboy's 21 Playmates: Volume II (1996) ...... Playmate
- ••• 0:10—Nude in still photos.
- ••• 0:11—Nude at the beach.

Steyn, Jennifer

Films:

Curse III: Blood Sacrifice (1990). . . . . Cindy
- • 0:35—Side of left breast, kissing Roger while at the beach inside a tent. Upper half of left breast when blade tears through tent.
- • 0:40—Breasts, covered with blood when Geoff looks in the tent.

Night of the Cyclone (1990). . . . . Celeste

Demon Keeper (1993). Ruth Stanley
- • 0:31—Very brief right breast, while lying dead in bed next to Howard.
- •• 0:37—Breasts after taking off robe in front of mirror.
- • 0:39—Breasts, while caressed by devil creature. Close-up, don't see face.

Freefall (1993). . . . . .Secretary

Stiles, Shannon

Films:

Bikini Island (1991) . . . . Nikki
- • 0:35—Breasts in bed with Jack taking off her top while someone watches through keyhole.

Video Tapes:

Rock Video Girls 2 (1992) . . . . .Herself

Stillo, Janine

Films:

To Protect and Serve (1992) . . . . Counter Girl

Blonde Heaven (1994). . . . . Megan
- • 0:52—Nude, while taking a shower behind two-way glass when Kyle is sneaking around in room. Long shot.

Deadly Currency (1995) . . . . .Bar Dancer 2
- •• 0:00—Breasts and buns, while dancing.

Where Truth Lies (1995). . . . Body Double for Candice Daly
- • 0:45—Very brief breasts, three times, while making love with Eric Pierpoint, seen in John Savage's vision.
- • 1:00—Breasts, while making love with Pierpoint when seen by Savage.

Double Your Pleasure (1997) . . . . Debora
- ••• 0:54—Breasts, while making love in bed with her husband.

Made for Cable TV:

Red Shoe Diaries: The Game (1994; Showtime). . . . . . .Tara
- • 0:14—Brief breasts, while arching her back while making love with Marty while Lily and John make love nearby.

Red Shoe Diaries: The Cake (1995; Showtime) . . . Lady in Cake

Erotic Confessions: Midnight Showing (1997; Cinemax) . . . . Gina
- ••• 0:04—Breasts, while making love with Dominic in movie theater projection booth.
- •• 0:21—Breasts, while making love with Dominic in movie theater projection booth.
- •• 0:25—Breasts and buns, while making love with Jasmine and Dominic in movie theater projection booth.

Intimate Sessions: Janine (1998; Cinemax) . . . . Suzy

Stoicov, Mihaella

Films:

Anthony's Desire (1993) . . . . Desiree
- ••• 0:17—Full frontal nudity, while making love in bed with Anthony and afterwards.
- ••• 0:24—Breasts and buns, while making love in bed with Anthony.
- • 0:45—Left breast, while making love at the beach with Anthony.
- ••• 0:46—Full frontal nudity while making love in bed with Anthony.
- •• 1:16—Nude while lying in bed.

Sex and the Single Alien (1993). . . . . .Thousand Ways
- ••• 0:19—Breasts and buns in T-back, dancing while wearing a mask.
- • 0:23—Brief buns in T-back, while talking backstage with Sam.
- ••• 1:10—Breasts and buns, while dancing on stage, wearing a mask.
- • 1:25—Brief breasts and buns, while dancing on stage, wearing a mask.

Made for Cable TV:

Love Street: Brownstone (1994; Showtime). . . . . . Breanna
- •• 0:16—Nude, undressing and talking with Vince, before she takes a shower.
- ••• 0:19—Breasts, after taking off blouse when she gets paint on it. Buns in T-back after taking off her clothes and playing with paint. Full frontal nudity while making love on the floor with Vince.
- •• 0:24—Nude, after taking off robe in studio with Vince, then getting caught by Julie.

• Stole, Mink

Films:

Pink Flamingos (1972). . . . . Connie Marble
- ••• 0:35—Full frontal nudity, while making out and talking with Raymond in bed. Long scene.

Female Trouble (1974) . . . . Taffy

Desperate Living (1977) . . . . Peggy Gravel

Liquid Dreams (1992) . . . . Felix
(Unrated version reviewed.)

Serial Mom (1993) . . . . .Dottie Hinkle

Lost Highway (1997). . . . . .Forewoman

Made for Cable Movies:

A Bucket of Blood (1995; Showtime). . . . . Older Woman

Stolze, Lena

Films:

Man Under Suspicion (1985). . . . . .Jessica

Maschenka (1987; British/German) . . . . Klara

The Nasty Girl (1989; German) . . . . Sonja
- • 1:27—Brief breasts and lower frontal nudity, while swimming in water.

• Stone, Brett

Made for Cable TV:

The Outer Limits: Bits of Love (1997; Showtime) . . . . Michelle
- • 0:34—Very brief buns, while lying dead on the floor with a knife stuck in her back.

Dead Man's Gun: The Photographer (1998; Showtime) . . . . Mimi Shaw

Stone, Brittany

See: Conrad, Stevi.

Stone, Dee Wallace

See: Wallace Stone, Dee.

Stone, Madison

a.k.a. Adult film actress Madison.

Films:

Naked Obsession (1990) . . . . Jezebel
(Unrated version reviewed.)
- •• 0:35—In black leather outfit. Buns in G-string and breasts.
- •• 0:37—More breasts and buns.
- • 0:38—More.
- •• 0:39—Brief full frontal nudity.

Evil Toons (1991) . . . . Roxanne
- ••• 0:20—Buns in G-string, then breasts doing a strip routine in front of her girlfriends.
- ••• 0:33—Breasts, taking off blouse and putting on bra and panties. Buns in sheer panties.
- •• 0:36—Breasts on the floor, getting attacked by the monster.
- ••• 0:38—Breasts walking around, covered with blood, talking with Megan.
- •• 0:41—Breasts putting blouse on.
- • 0:42—Breasts on couch with Biff.
- • 0:55—Left breast in open blouse, seducing Burt.
- • 0:59—Brief breasts several times, dead, when the other girls discover her.

Stone, Sharon *

Wife of San Francisco Examiner executive editor Phil Bronstein.

Films:

Stardust Memories (1980). . . . . Blonde on Passing Train
Deadly Blessing (1981) . . . . Lana
Irreconcilable Differences (1984) . . . . Blake Chandler
- •• 0:56—Breasts lowering her blouse in front of Ryan O'Neal during film test.

King Solomon's Mines (1985) . . . . Jessica
Allan Quatermain and the Lost City of Gold (1987) . . . . Jesse Huston
- • 0:20—Very brief lower frontal nudity, seen under loose panties, when she stands up in back of car and pulls her dress off over her head. (Don't really see much, but for the sake of completeness...)

Cold Steel (1987) . . . . Kathy Conners
- • 0:33—Brief left breast making love in bed with Brad Davis. Dark, hard to see. Brief breasts turning over after making love.

Police Academy 4: Citizens on Patrol (1987) . . . . Claire Matson
Above the Law (1988). . . . . Sara Toscani
Action Jackson (1988) . . . . Patrice Dellaplane
- •• 0:34—Breasts, while in a steam room. Hard to see because of all the steam.
- • 0:56—Brief right breast, dead, on the bed when police view her body.

Blood and Sand (1989; Spanish) . . . . Doña Sol
- • 0:57—Very brief upper half of right breast, while making love on table with Juan.
- •• 0:58—Left breast, making love in bed with Juan. Don't see her face well.
- ••• 1:04—Breasts quite a few times, making love with Juan in the woods.

Scissors (1990) . . . . Angela Anderson
- • 0:04—Upper half of left breast, while sitting up after attack in elevator.
- •• 0:12—Breasts changing clothes.

Total Recall (1990) . . . . Lori
- • 0:04—Brief right breast in gaping lingerie when leaning over Arnold Schwarzenegger in bed.

he said, she said (1991). . . . . Linda
Where Sleeping Dogs Lie (1991) . . . . Serena Black
Year of the Gun (1991) . . . . Alison King
- • 1:00—Brief left breast, while standing against the door, with Andrew McCarthy. Long shot.
- • 1:01—Side of left breast, while making love on bed.

Basic Instinct (1992) . . . . Catherine Trammel
(Unrated Director's cut reviewed.)
- ••• 0:02—Buns and breasts while making love on top of Johnny in bed, then killing him.
- •• 0:21—Buns and left breast in mirror in her bedroom while Michael Douglas watches while waiting for her.
- • 0:26—Two brief crotch shots while crossing and uncrossing her legs during interrogation.
- •• 0:44—Nude, undressing in her house, while Douglas watches from outside. Medium long shot.
- ••• 1:10—Breasts while in bed with Douglas.
- ••• 1:13—Breasts and buns, tying Douglas up in bed and on top of him.
- •• 1:15—Buns, while sitting on top of Douglas.
- • 1:32—Very brief right breast, with Douglas in front of fireplace.
- ••• 1:43—Breasts, while taking off her blouse in Douglas' apartment.
- ••• 2:00—Breasts, while in bed on top of Douglas.

Diary of a Hitman (1992). . . . . Kiki
Intersection (1993). . . . . Sally Eastman
- • 0:18—Right breast behind glass blocks in shower, then very brief left breast in mirror when she adjusts her robe.

Last Action Hero (1993). . . . . Herself
Sliver (1993) . . . . Carly Norris
- • 0:14—Brief left breast, while in bathtub.
- • 0:43—Buns, in black bra, while making love on William Baldwin's lap.
- • 0:44—Half of right breast, while under Baldwin.
- •• 0:45—Brief left breast, while getting up out of bed. Side view breasts and buns, while getting dressed.
- •• 0:46—Buns and breasts, while taking off her top again.

The Quick and the Dead (1994) . . . . Ellen
- • 0:21—Brief right breast in gaping blouse, when bending over after sitting up in bed.

The Specialist (1994) . . . . May Munro
- • 0:29—Left breast and buns in panties in her house.
- •• 1:14—Breasts and buns, in the shower with Sylvester Stallone.

Casino (1995) . . . . Ginger McKenna
Diabolique (1996) . . . . Nicole Horner
Last Dance (1996) . . . . Cindy Liggett
Sphere (1997) . . . . Beth Halperin

Miniseries:

War and Remembrance (1988) . . . . Janice Henry

Made for TV Movies:

Calendar Girl Murders (1984) . . . . Cassie
Tears in the Rain (1988; British) . . . . Casey Cantrell

TV:

Bay City Blues (1983). Cathy St. Marie

Stoner, Sherri

Story editor for Steven Spielberg.

She was Disney's animator's model for Ariel in *The Little Mermaid* and Belle in *Beauty and the Beast.*

Films:

Impulse (1984) . . . . Young Girl
Lovelines (1984) . . . . Suzy
Reform School Girls (1986) . . . . Lisa
- • 1:03—Very brief breasts and buns, lying on stomach in the restroom, getting branded by bad girls.

Made for TV Movies:

My Mother's Secret Life (1984) . . . . Laura Sievers

Stones, Tammy

Films:

Neurotic Cabaret (1991) . . . . Terri
a.k.a. Good Girl, Bad Girl

Death Ring (1992) . . . . Cindy Maddin
••• 0:53—Breasts in open lingerie top in Skylord's apartment.

Stowe, Madeleine *

Wife of actor Brian Benben.

Films:

Stakeout (1987) . . . . Maira McGuire
• 0:43—Buns and brief side view of right breast getting a towel after taking a shower while Richard Dreyfuss watches her.

Tropical Snow (1989). . . . . Marina
• 0:05—Very brief side view of left breast putting red dress on.
• 0:11—Buns, lying in bed. Very brief right breast sitting up. (I wish they could have panned the camera to the right!)
•• 0:24—Breasts in mirror putting red dress on.
• 0:32—Buns, while lying on top of Tavo in bed.
• 0:54—Brief breasts making love in the water with Tavo. Then buns, lying on the beach (long shot.)
• 1:22—Long shot side view of right breast in water with Tavo.

Worth Winning (1989) . . . . Veronica Briskow
Closet Land (1990) . . . . The Author

Revenge (1990). . . . . .Miryea
• 0:44—Side view of buns when Kevin Costner pulls up her dress to make love with her.
• 1:00—Buns, making love with Costner in jeep. Very brief breasts coming out of the water.
• 1:07—Very brief breasts when Costner is getting beat up.

The Two Jakes (1990) . . . . .Lillian Bodine
• 0:23—Very brief buns, when Jack Nicholson lifts her slip up in bed.

The Last of the Mohicans (1992). . . . . Cora Munro

Unlawful Entry (1992). . . . . .Karen Carr
••• 0:56—Breasts and partial buns, while making love on top of Kurt Russell in bed.

Another Stakeout (1993). . . . . Maria

Blink (1993) . . . . Emma Brody
• 1:04—Side of left breast while walking to look at roses.
•• 1:06—Breasts, after taking off top and making love with Aidan Quinn.

China Moon (1993) . . . . Rachel Munro
••• 0:22—Full frontal nudity after taking off dress and panties and jumping into lake from boat.

Short Cuts (1993). . . . . .Sherri Shepard
•• 1:20—Left breast, while posing for painting by Julianne Moore.
• 2:07—(0:24 into Part 2) Brief left breast, while turning over in bed.

Bad Girls (1994) . . . . Cody Zamora
(Extended version reviewed.)

12 Monkeys (1995). . . . . Kathryn Reilly

Made for TV Movies:

Amazons (1984) . . . . Dr. Sharon Fields

TV:

The Gangster Chronicles (1981) . . . . Ruth Lasker

Strain, Julie *

Films:

Carnal Crimes (1991). . . . . Ingrid
••• 0:55—Breasts and partial buns, wearing black garter belt and stockings, making love with Renny in restroom. Long scene.

Double Impact (1991) . . . . .Student
• 0:09—Brief buns, while lying on floor in pink leotard in exercise class.

Mirror Images (1991). . . . . Gina
•• 0:48—Buns and right breast, making love in bed with Kaitlin.
•• 0:49—Buns in black bra and panties.
• 0:57—Buns in black body suit.
••• 0:58—Breasts lying on bed, watching the slave girl and guy with the mask make love.

Out for Justice (1991) . . . . Roxanne Ford
• 0:53—Brief side view of right breast in Polaroid photograph that Steven Seagal looks at.
• 1:06—Brief side view of right breast in Polaroid again.
• 1:11—Brief right breast, twice, dead in bed when discovered by Seagal.
• 1:12—Briefly in Polaroid again.

Sunset Heat (1991). . . . . . Carl's Breakfast Girl/Party Statuette
a.k.a. Midnight Heat
(Unrated version reviewed.)
•• 0:51—Breasts, covered with silver paint, made up to look like a statue at the party.

Bad Love (1992) . . . . Amber
a.k.a. Wild Angel
• 0:57—Brief breasts, seen on video monitor, while Jack makes love on top of her during filming of a movie.
• 1:02—Very brief partial right breast, seen behind Debi Mazar after she throws off her shawl. Very, very brief tip of right breast, seen on video monitor.
• 1:04—Brief breasts, while straddling a guy on bed on a movie set. Medium long shot.

Kuffs (1992) . . . . .Kane's Girl

Night Rhythms (1992). . . . . Linda
(Unrated version reviewed.)
••• 0:03—In white bra, then left breast, while talking on the phone and playing with herself.

Psycho Cop 2 (1992) . . . . Stephanie
• 0:19—Brief buns, when elevator door opens.
••• 0:21—Buns in cowboy outfit, then breasts with red star pasties while doing dance routine.
•• 0:25—Breasts and buns, while with the two other dancers and the guys.
• 0:31—Breasts and buns, when Mike comes back.
• 0:33—Breasts, when the guys start worrying about Mike.
• 0:38—Breasts, when putting them in Brian's face.
• 0:41—Breasts, when with Brian. Buns in cowboy outfit for the rest of the film.

The Unnameable II (1992). . . . . Creature

Witchcraft IV: Virgin Heart (1992) . . . . Belladonna
• 0:25—Buns, while dancing on stage in a red bra and red G-string.
••• 0:27—Breasts, dancing on stage.
•• 0:46—Breasts on the floor with Santara.
• 0:49—Brief breasts in open dress on couch with Will.
• 1:15—Breasts, lying on couch in her dressing room while Will tries to talk to her.

Bikini Squad (1993) . . . . Actress
• 0:10—Partial buns in swimsuit when leaving the casting office.
•• 0:21—Breasts, while making love with the casting guy.

Enemy Gold (1993). . . . . Jewel Panther
••• 1:03—Breasts and buns in leather outfit while dancing with a sword in front of a fire.

Fit To Kill (1993). . . . . Blu Steele
•• 0:10—Buns in swimsuit while doing stretching exercises.
•• 0:11—Breasts, undoing her swimsuit top.
•• 0:47—Breasts and buns in G-string, while making love in the kitchen with Brett Clark.

Future Shock (1993). Female Dancer
- 0:03—Brief buns in sexy black G-string outfit with black top, while dancing in front of guy sitting in electric chair.

Midnight Confessions (1993) . . . . Mariana
(Unrated version reviewed.)
- •• 0:04—In bra and panties, then breasts and buns, while talking on the phone to the radio talk show host.
- •• 0:07—Breasts and buns, while caressing herself and talking on the phone some more.

Naked Gun 33 1/3: The Final Insult (1993) . . . . Dominatrix
Beverly Hills Cop III (1994) . . . . Annihilator Girl
Blonde Heaven (1994) . . . . Illyana
- •• 0:00—Breasts, while making love with a guy during the opening credits.
- • 0:13—Brief breasts, while straddling a guy on bed.
- •• 1:03—Breasts and buns in panties, while making love with Angie in bed.
- • 1:12—Breasts, while fighting with the other vampire girl in bed.

The Dallas Connection (1994) . . . . Black Widow
- •• 0:03—Buns in lingerie on bed with Mr. Lesarge, then breasts, while making love.
- • 0:38—Buns in western outfits on stage.
- •• 1:00—Breasts and buns, under sexy leather and chain outfit in office with Nicholas.

Married People, Single Sex 2: For Better or Worse (1994). . . . . S&M Woman
- •• 1:21—Breasts and buns in panties in motel room bed with David when Karen watches helplessly while tied by her wrists to doorway.

Money to Burn (1994) . . . . Jill
- • 0:38—Brief buns in G-string under hiked up dress, several times, while dancing in club.
- •• 0:39—Stripping out of her dress down to red bra, panties, garter belt and stockings, then breasts and buns. More when making love with Ann on the floor.
- ••• 0:42—Nude, waking up and getting dressed.

The Mosaic Project (1994) . . . . .Tess
- • 0:47—Brief buns in panties, doing a sexy dance during party to distract everybody.

Play Time (1994). . . . . Sheraton
(Unrated version reviewed.)
- ••• 1:31—Full frontal nudity, while in bed with a young Brad. B&W.
- •• 1:32—Nude, in bed with Michelle.

Sorceress (1994) . . . . Erica
- ••• 0:00—Breasts under sheer black robe, then breasts while rubbing oil on herself.
- ••• 0:16—Breasts in red push-up bra, while making love on top of Larry in bed.
- • 0:19—Buns, while lying on top of Larry in front of fire in flashback.
- ••• 0:53—Breasts, while on bed with Toni Naples and Rochelle Swanson.

Victim of Desire (1994) . . . . Linda Hammond
- •• 0:10—Nude, taking a shower.
- ••• 0:12—Breasts and buns in red panties, while making love with Wings Hauser on the floor at night. Nice finger sucking!

Dark Secrets (1995) . . . . Mauri
- • 0:00—Brief breasts and buns while wearing lingerie in quick cuts during photo shoot. Her face is painted white.
- •• 0:18—Breasts and buns, while having sex with Dennis.
- •• 1:14—Breasts, while whipping a woman at the Midnight Club.
- •• 1:16—Breasts, while torturing Monique Parent at the Midnight Club.
- ••• 1:17—Breasts, while outside in the rain, having sex with Parent.

Red Line (1995). . . . . Crystal
- • 0:19—Nude, taking off robe and walking into swimming pool.
- • 0:23—Breasts, while making love with Corey Feldman in darkened garage.

Virtual Desire (1995) . . . . Sascha
- ••• 0:25—Nude, while taking a shower when Brad peeks in the window.
- ••• 0:30—Full frontal nudity, while making love with Brad in the living room. Long scene.

Bikini Hotel (1996) . . . . Raquel
- •• 0:36—Breasts and buns during interview.
- • 0:49—Breasts in hallway, while walking past Japanese guy.
- • 0:54—Breasts, after taking off robe.
- • 1:00—Buns in swimsuit.

Busted (1996) . . . . Annette
- • 0:37—Briefly nude when her towel falls off in police station.
- • 0:38—Brief breasts when her towel falls off again.

Big Sister 2000 (1997). . . . . .n.a.
Day of the Warrior (1997) . . . . Willow Black
The Last Road (1997) . . . . .Maggie
- ••• 0:24—In bra and panties, then breasts and buns, while making love with Harry in bed.
- ••• 0:57—In wet white top, then nude, while fooling around with Harry outdoors under spraying water.

Video Tapes:

Penthouse Centerfold—Julie Strain (1991). . . . . Pet
- ••• 0:00—Nude.

Sexy Lingerie III (1991) . . . . .Model
Penthouse Pet of the Year Playoff 1992 (1992) . . . . . Pet
- ••• 0:16—Nude at the beach, in the house, in the bathtub, outside, at a desk on a bed.

Penthouse Ready to Ride (1992) . . . . .Model
Penthouse Satin & Lace II: Hollywood Undercover (1992) . . . . Pet
Penthouse Satin & Lace: An Erotic History of Lingerie (1992) . . . . .Model
- ••• 0:01—Nude with blonde woman.
- ••• 0:09—Nude with blonde woman in elevator.
- ••• 0:29—Nude outside.
- ••• 0:46—Full frontal nudity with three guys.
- ••• 0:49—Full frontal nudity with two blonde women.

Penthouse: Fast Cars/Fantasy Women (1992) . . . . .Mercedes 500 SL/Police Officer
- •• 0:27—Breasts, while making love with the driver.

Sexy Lingerie IV (1992) . . . . .Model
Buck Naked Line Dancing (1993). . . . . Dancer
- ••• 0:00—Breasts and buns throughout. Sometimes wearing pasties with tassels. If you are a faithful reader of this book, you should be able to recognize who she is!

The Penthouse All-Pet Workout (1993) . . . . Pet
- • 0:00—Breasts during introduction.
- •• 0:03—Brief nude shots while getting undressed and suited up.
- ••• 0:06—Nude while posing outside.
- ••• 0:43—Nude with the other girls, exercising, working with equipment, in the pool and spa.

Penthouse Forum Letters: Volume 1 (1993) . . . . Reach Out and Touch Someone/Wife
- ••• 1:09—Breasts on couch having phone sex with her husband. Great if you also like to hear women talk dirty.

Hot Body Video Magazine #8: Hot Stuff (1994) . . . . . n.a.
Penthouse Pet of the Year Winners 1993: Mahalia & Julie (1994) . . . . Pet
- • 0:00—Brief lower frontal nudity during introduction.
- ••• 0:01—Nude in bed.
- ••• 0:04—Nude in chair and making love with a guy.
- ••• 0:06—Nude, while touching herself while a trio of women work on a film.
- ••• 0:10—Full frontal nudity, while making love with a guy in a B&W movie.
- ••• 0:12—Nude in house in a bodysuit, then after ripping it off.
- ••• 0:16—Nude, while wearing a garter belt and stockings outside and in pool.
- •• 0:34—Nude during end credits.

Penthouse Behind the Scenes (1995) . . . . Pet
- ••• 0:00—Nude in various segments throughout the video tape.

Playboy's Rising Stars and Sexy Starlets (1996) . . .Herself
- •• 0:17—Full frontal nudity in clips from different films.
- ••• 0:20—Buns in swimsuit in movie, then nude while posing in a theater.

CD-ROM:
Penthouse Interactive Virtual Photo Shoot, Disc 1 (1993). . . . . Pet
Heidi's House (1996) . . . . n.a.

Strasberg, Susan

Daughter of acting teacher Lee Strasberg.
Films:
The Trip (1967). . . . . .Sally Groves
- • 0:17—Very brief left breast, while making love with Peter Fonda in bed. Very difficult to see because it's lit with psychedelic lights.

The Brotherhood (1968) . . . . .Emma Ginetta
Psych-Out (1968) . . . . .Jennie Davis
Psycho Sisters (1974) . . . . Brenda
The Manitou (1977). . . . . Karen Tandy
- • 1:33—Breasts, while fighting the creature in bed. Really bad special-effects. Too dark to see anything.

Rollercoaster (1977) . . . . Fran
In Praise of Older Women (1978; Canadian) . . . . . . Bobbie
- •• 1:03—Left breast, while making love in bed with Tom Berenger.
- ••• 1:04—Breasts in bed after Berenger rolls off her.

Bloody Birthday (1980). . . . . Miss Davis
Sweet Sixteen (1982) . . . . Joanne Morgan
The Delta Force (1986) . . . . .Debra Levine
The Runnin' Kind (1988). . . . . .Carol Curtis
The Light in the Jungle (1990) . . . . .Helene Schweitzer
TV:
The Marriage (1954). . . . . Emily Marriott
Toma (1973-74) . . . . Patty Toma

*Stratten, Dorothy **

Films:
Americathon (1979) . . . . Playboy Bunny
Autumn Born (1979) . . . . .Tara
- •• 0:26—Left breast taking bath, then right breast getting up, then breasts dressing.
- • 0:30—Side view of left breast, then breasts climbing back into bed.
- ••• 0:46—In white bra and panties, side view of left breast and buns, then breasts in bathtub. Long scene.
- • 0:50—Side view of left breast and buns getting undressed. Nice buns shot. Right breast lying down in chair.
- • 1:03—Brief breasts shots during flashbacks.

Skatetown, U.S.A. (1979) . . . . Girl who orders Pizza
Galaxina (1980). . . . . Galaxina
They All Laughed (1981) . . . . Dolores Martin
Video Tapes:
Playboy Video Magazine, Volume 4 (1983) . . . . .Playmate
- • 1:09—Brief breasts in black lingerie during photo shoot.
- •• 1:13—Breasts and buns in bubble bath.
- •• 1:19—Breasts posing in dance studio.
- • 1:22—More brief breasts shots from photo shoot.

Dorothy Stratten, The Untold Story (1985) . . . . . . Herself
- •• 0:02—Breasts during photo session on sofa.
- •• 0:03—Left breast in mirror before falling off sofa, breasts after.
- ••• 0:06—Breasts outside in a field.
- ••• 0:14—Breasts and buns in still photos.
- ••• 0:17—Full frontal nudity while posing in front of mirrored wall with a ballet rail
- •• 0:26—Breasts in still photos.
- ••• 0:39—Breasts in bathtub for Playmate of the Year pictorial.
- ••• 1:02—Nude in classic pin-up girl poses.
- ••• 1:05—Breasts in bathtub and on sofa.

Playboy's Playmates of the Year: The '80s (1989) . . . . Playmate of the Year 1980
- ••• 0:27—Breasts and buns in various settings during photo session.
- •• 0:32—Brief breasts holding flowers in a field.
- •• 0:51—Breasts in field.

Hugh Hefner: Once Upon a Time (1992). . . . . Herself
- • 1:08—Right breast in bathtub.

Streep, Meryl

Films:
Julia (1977) . . . . Anne Marie
The Deer Hunter (1978) . . . . Linda
Kramer vs. Kramer (1979) . . . . Joanna Kramer
(Academy Award for Best Supporting Actress.)
Manhattan (1979). . . . . Jill
The Seduction of Joe Tynan (1979) . . . . Karen Traynor
The French Lieutenant's Woman (1981) . . . . .Sarah/Anna
Sophie's Choice (1982) . . . . Sophie
(Academy Award for Best Actress.)
Still of the Night (1982) . . . . Brooke Reynolds
- • 0:22—Side view of right breast and buns taking off robe for the massage guy. Long shot, don't see her face.

Falling In Love (1984) . . . . .Molly Gilmore
Silkwood (1984) . . . . Karen Silkwood
- • 0:24—Very brief glimpse of upper half of left breast when she flashes it in nuclear reactor office.

Out of Africa (1985) . . . . Karen Blixen
Plenty (1985) . . . . Susan
Heartburn (1986) . . . . .Rachel
Ironweed (1987) . . . . Helen
A Cry in the Dark (1988) . . . . Lindy Chamberlain
- • 1:44—Brief side view of right breast in jail being examined by two female guards. Don't see her face, probably a body double.

She-Devil (1989) . . . . .Mary Fisher
Postcards from the Edge (1990) . . . . .Suzanne Vale
Defending Your Life (1991) . . . . Julia
Death Becomes Her (1992) . . . . .Madeline Ashton
The House of Spirits (1993) . . . . .Clara
- • 0:32—Brief buns, while in bed with Jeremy Irons. Probably a body double.

The River Wild (1994) . . . . .Gail
Before and After (1995). . . . . Carolyn Ryan
The Bridges of Madison County (1995) . . . . Robert Kincaid

Marvin's Room (1996). . . . . Lee
Miniseries:
Holocaust (1978) . . . . Inga Helms Weiss
Made for TV Movies:
First Do No Harm (1997). . . . . Lori Reimuller

Street, Rebecca

Films:
Lonely Hearts (1991) . . . . .Jane Ericson
• 1:12—Brief side of right breast, while making love on top of Eric Roberts on couch.
Warlock: The Armageddon (1993). . . . . Kate

Strickland, Connie

Films:
The Roommates (1973). . . . . Alice
Act of Vengeance (1974). . . . . Teresa
a.k.a. The Rape Squad
(Not to be confused with the film with the same name starring Charles Bronson.)
• 0:37—Brief full frontal nudity under water, several times, sitting in spa with other women. (She's the blonde on the far right.)
The Centerfold Girls (1974) . . . . .Patsy
•• 1:07—Breasts in bathroom washing her halter top just before getting killed.

Strindberg, Anita

Films:
Women in Cell Block 7 (1977; Italian/U.S.) . . . . .Hilda
Fear (1980; French/Italian). . . . . Glenda
• 1:10—Breast, during flashback struggle on bed with Oliver.
• 1:15—Brief, out of focus breasts in reflection in the mirror, then very brief breasts when pulling up the sheets while in bed with Oliver.
The Salamander (1981). . . . . .Princess Faubiani

Stringfield, Sherry

TV:
The Guiding Light (1990-93). . . . . .Blake
NYPD Blue (1993-94) . . . . Laura Hughes Kelly
NYPD Blue: True Confessions (Oct 12, 1993)
. . . . Laura Hughes Kelly
•• 0:22—Very brief partial right breast while in the shower with David Caruso (seen between his left arm and torso). Brief buns and back side of right breast, twice, getting out of bed and walking to get her robe.
ER (1994-96). . . . . .Dr. Susan Lewis

Strohmeier, Tara

Films:
Candy Stripe Nurses (1974) . . . . .Irene
Truck Turner (1974). . . . . Turnpike
Cover Girl Models (1975) . . . . Mandy
• 0:04—Climbing out of swimming pool in braless wet T-shirt.
• 0:11—Breasts, after taking off swimsuit to and putting on T-shirt.
••• 0:23—Breasts, while posing for photographs with Mark.
••• 0:40—Breasts, while in hotel room with Mark.
•• 0:54—Breasts, while posing outdoors for photographs with Mark.
Hollywood Boulevard (1976) . . . . .Jill McBain
•• 0:00—Breasts getting out of van and standing with film crew.
• 0:31—Silhouette of breasts, while making love with P.G.
••• 0:32—Breasts sunbathing with Bobbi and Candy.
••• 0:33—Breasts acting for film on hammock. Long scene.
The Great Texas Dynamite Chase (1977). . . . . Pam
The Kentucky Fried Movie (1977) . . . . Girl
•• 1:16—In bra, then breasts making love on couch with her boyfriend while people on the TV news watch them.
Malibu Beach (1978) . . . . Glorianna
• 0:08—Breasts kissing her boyfriend at the beach when someone steals her towel.
Van Nuys Blvd. (1979) . . . . Wanda
•• 0:21—Breasts, while playing around with food with Bobby in the back of his van.
• 0:51—Brief breasts, flashing while hitchhiking to get a ride.
Made for TV Movies:
The Lakeside Killer (1979) . . . . Janie

Strong, Brenda

Films:
Weekend Warriors (1986). . . . . Danny El Dubois
• 0:44—Breasts, lit from the side, standing in the dark.
Spaceballs (1987) . . . . Nurse
Stepfather III: Father's Day (1992) . . . . . Crime Search Reporter
Malice (1993) . . . . .Claudia
My Life (1993). . . . . Laura
The Craft (1996) . . . . Doctor
Starship Troopers (1996) . . . . .Captain Deladier
Black Dog (1998). . . . . Melanie
Made for TV Movies:
Island City (1994) . . . . Dr. Sammy Helding
TV:
Twin Peaks (1990-91) . . . . Jones

Struthers, Sally

Films:
Five Easy Pieces (1970). . . . . .Betty
•• 0:34—Brief breasts a couple of times making love with Nicholson. Lots of great moaning, but hard to see anything.
The Getaway (1972) . . . . Fran Clinton
Made for TV Movies:
Hey, I'm Alive (1975). . . . . Helen Klaben
Intimate Strangers (1977) . . . . .Janis Halston
In the Best Interest of the Children (1992). . . . . . .Patty Pepper
TV:
The Summer Smother's Show (1970) . . . . .Regular
The Tim Conway Comedy Hour (1970). . . . . .Regular
All In the Family (1971-78) . . . . .Gloria Bunker Stivic
Gloria (1982-83) . . . . .Gloria Bunker Stivic
9 to 5 (1986-88) . . . . Marsha Shrimpton

Stuart, Cassie

Films:
Ordeal by Innocence (1984) . . . . .Maureen Clegg
•• 1:14—Breasts in bed talking to Donald Sutherland.
Secret Places (1984; British) . . . . Nina
• 0:07—Brief breasts, after pulling up her blouse to show off her breasts to her girlfriends.
• 1:15—Brief left breast, getting into bathtub with the help of her girlfriends. (She's drunk.)
Slayground (1984; British). . . . . Fran
Stealing Heaven (1988; British/Yugoslavian) . . . . Petronilla
Afraid of the Dark (1992; British/French) . . . .Woman Neighbor

Stuart, Wendy

Films:

Incoming Freshman (1979). . . . . Miss Seymour
••• 0:25—In purple bra and panties, then breasts and buns stripping during Professor Bilbo's fantasy.
• 0:55—Buns and side of right breast in Bilbo's fantasy.
• 1:18—Breasts during end credits.

Model Behavior (1982) . . . . Lily White Girl

Stubbs, Imogen

Films:

Deadline (1988) . . . . .Lady Romy-Burton
• 0:44—Brief left breast, while getting out of bed with John Hurt. Full frontal nudity turning toward bed, brief breasts getting back into bed.

A Summer Story (1988). . . . . Megan David
•• 0:36—Left breast several times, then right breast while making love with Frank in barn.
• 0:41—Very, very brief buns, while frolicking in pond at night with Frank.
• 1:03—Very brief silhouette of left breast during Frank's flashback sequence.

Erik the Viking (1989; British) . . . . Aud
True Colors (1991) . . . . Diana Stiles
Sense and Sensibility (1995) . . . . Lucy Steele
Jack & Sarah (1996; British/French). . . . . .Sarah
Twelfth Night (1996; British). . . . . Viola

Made for Cable Movies:

Fellow Traveller (1989; HBO) . . . . Sarah Aitchison
• 0:54—Breasts in bed with Asa. Very, very brief right breast when he rolls off her.

Anna Lee: Diversion (1994; A&E) . . . . .Anna Lee
Anna Lee: Dupe (1994; A&E) .Anna Lee
Anna Lee: Headcase (1994; A&E) . . . . .Anna Lee
Anna Lee: Stalker (1994; A&E) . . . . .Anna Lee

Styler, Trudie

Wife of singer/actor Sting.

Films:

Fair Game (1988; Italian) . . . . Eva
• 0:14—Very, very brief blurry top of right breast in gaping blouse, while standing up after changing clothes.
• 0:37—Brief buns, kneeling in bathtub. Very brief buns in the mirror several times putting on robe and getting out of the bathtub.

Sucharetza, Marla

Films:

Forrest Gump (1994) . . . . .Lenore
Whore 2 (1994) . . . . Lori
•• 0:33—Breasts and buns in panties in bathroom.
• 0:59—Breasts while dancing on stage in club.
•• 1:07—Breasts and buns in panties, after taking off her dress for Nico.

Lover's Knot (1995). . . . . Erin
The Fan (1996). . . . . Angie
The First Wives Club (1996) . . . . The Exercising Woman
For Richer or Poorer (1997). . . . . .Stacy

Made for Cable Movies:

Virtual Seduction (1995; Showtime) . . . . Coat Girl

Sugg, Catherine *

Films:

Wish Me Luck (1995) . . . . Dream Girl
(Unrated version reviewed.)
••• 0:08—Breasts (she's the blonde), while frolicking in bed and making love with a redhead Dream Girl.

Sukowa, Barbara

Films:

Berlin Alexanderplatz (1983; West German) . . . . Mieze
The Sicilian (1987) . . . . Camilia Duchess of Crotone
(Director's uncut version reviewed.)
•• 0:05—Buns and brief breasts taking a bath, three times.
• 0:07—Brief right breast reading Time magazine. Full frontal nudity in the mirror standing up in the tub.
• 0:08—Brief right breast standing at the window watching Christopher Lambert steal a horse.
••• 1:01—In bra, then breasts in bedroom with Lambert. More breasts, then nude. Long scene.

Voyager (1991; German/French) . . . . .Hannah
Zentropa (1991; Danish). . . . . Katharina Hartmann
(Subtitled.)
M. Butterfly (1993) . . . . .Jeanne Gallimard
Johnny Mnemonic (1995) . . . . Anna K

Miniseries:

Space (1987). . . . . Liesl Kolff

Sullivan, Dail

Films:

Map of the Human Heart (1992; Australian/Canadian)
. . . . Barrage Balloon WAAC
Century (1993; British) . . . . Theo's Girl
• 0:13—Brief buns and right breast, while making love with Theo, when seen by Clive Owen through a gap in the curtains.
• 0:14—Full frontal nudity, after opening the curtains.

• Sullivan, Kelly

Films:

Death By Dialogue (1988). . . . . Shelly
Caged Fury (1989) . . . . Lip Service
Cover Me (1995). . . . . Dimitri's Mother

Made for Cable TV:

Erotic Confessions: The Hat Check Boy (1997; Cinemax)
. . . . Katherine
• 0:04—Breasts, while playing with herself of bed.
••• 0:12—Full frontal nudity, while making love with Skip in the hat check room of the restaurant.
•• 0:17—Breasts and buns, while making love with Skip in the hat check room.
••• 0:22—Breasts and buns while making love in apartment with Skip and Tracy.

Sullivan, Sheila *

Films:

Hickey and Boggs (1972) . . . . Edith Boggs
A Name for Evil (1973) . . . . .Luanna Baxter
• 0:51—Full frontal nudity dancing in the bar with everybody.
• 0:54—Breasts while Robert Culp makes love with her.
• 0:56—Breasts getting dressed.
• 1:17—Nude, skinny dipping with Culp.

Sumers, Stephanie

Films:

Anthony's Desire (1993) . . . . Dancer
•• 0:22—Breasts, while on stage, lying in the lap of another woman. (She's wearing a choker.)

Midnight Tease (1994). . . . . .Tiffany
•• 0:00—Breasts and buns, while dancing during opening credits.
••• 0:07—Breasts and buns in T-back, while dancing on stage.
••• 0:09—Breasts, while dressing and talking to Samantha in dressing room.
••• 0:12—Nude, while making love on top of Samantha's step-father, then getting killed in dream.
0:14—Breasts while tied to pole in club with a slit throat and covered with blood.
• 0:50—Breasts with slit throat and blood in dream.

Video Tapes:

Hot Body Video Magazine #7: Naughty But Nice (1993) . . . . Herself
Hot Body Video Magazine #8: Hot Stuff (1994) . . Herself
Hot Body International: Dreamgirl II (1995). . . . . Herself
Hot Body International: Steamed Heat (1995) . . . Herself
• 0:06—Buns in swimsuit at the beach.
• 0:10—Buns in swimsuit at the beach.
••• 0:14—Buns and breasts, while changing swimsuits outdoors.
••• 0:21—Buns and breasts, while changing swimsuits outdoors.
• 0:42—Buns in black outfit outdoors.
• 0:43—Buns in swimsuit in bedroom.
• 0:47—Buns in swimsuit in bedroom.

Summer, Jamie

See: Stafford, Jamie.

Summers, Sylvia

Films:

Goin' All the Way (1981). . . . . Wendy
••• 0:12—Breasts in the girl's locker room shower. Standing on the right.

Dreamaniac (1987). . . . . Lily
• 0:35—Brief side view of left breast, when taking off her blue dress in front of Ace.

Sunare

See: Cornell, Angela.

Sutton, Lisa

See: Comshaw, Lisa.

Sutton, Lori

Films:

History of the World, Part I (1981). . . . . Vestal Virgin
Looker (1981) . . . . Reston Girl
Fast Times at Ridgemont High (1982) . . . . .Playmate
Malibu Express (1984). . . . . Beverly McAfee
••• 0:54—Breasts and buns, making love in bed with Cody.

Up the Creek (1984). . . . . .Cute Girl
• 0:40—Brief breasts, twice, after ripping open her blouse to get a crowd excited while cheerleading.

Night Patrol (1985) . . . . Edith Hutton
••• 0:47—In white bra, panties, garter belt and stockings, then breasts three times taking off bra in bedroom with the Police officer.

Swafford, Jody

Adult film actress.

Films:

Evils of the Night (1985) . . . . Lotion Girl
•• 0:12—Breasts while rubbing lotion on another girl.
•• 0:13—More breasts with the other girl.
• 0:14—Brief breasts when Eddie watches her and her friend.

Video Tapes:

The Girls of Penthouse (1984) . . . . Ghost Town Woman
••• 0:29—In black lingerie, then full frontal nudity making love with cowboy.

Swanson, Brenda

Films:

Dangerous Love (1988). . . . . Felicity
Skin Deep (1989). . . . . Emily
Steel and Lace (1990). . . . . .Miss Fairweather
•• 0:58—Breasts in lunchroom, opening her blouse in front of one of the bad guys on the table.

Prototype X29A (1992) . . . . Dr. Alexis Zalazny
Dead Connection (1993). . . . . Susan
Indecent Behavior (1993) . . . . Judith Miller
(Unrated version reviewed.)
••• 1:05—In white bra, then breasts, while making love with Carol in observation room.

Open Fire (1994). . . . . Kesack
Scanners: The Showdown (1994) . . . . Glory Avionis
Secret Games 3 (1994) . . . . .Ruthie
(Unrated version reviewed.)

Video Tapes:

Inside Out 2 (1992)
. . . . Mrs. Jenkins/There's This Traveling Salesman, See
(Unrated version reviewed.)
•• 0:43—Breasts, taking off her top in barn.

Swanson, Jackie

Films:

Lethal Weapon (1987) . . . . .Amanda Hunsacker
•• 0:01—Brief breasts standing on balcony rail getting ready to jump.

It's Alive III: Island of the Alive (1988) . . . . Tenant
Perfect Victims (1988). Carrie Marks
•• 0:13—In bra, then left breast, while changing clothes by closet.
• 0:23—Brief left breast, while lying on sofa when Brandon opens her robe while she's drugged out. Brief right breast and lower frontal nudity when he rips off her panties.
• 0:25—Right breast several more times, while lying on sofa when Brandon torments her.
••• 1:15—Left breast and buns, seen through clear shower door. Nice shot for bun lovers!
• 1:16—Brief buns in the shower, seen from above.

Oblivion (1994). . . . . Mattie Chase

TV:

Cheers (1989-93) . . . . Kelly Gaines

Swanson, Rochelle

Films:

Rubdown (1990) . . . . Librarian
Dead On (1993) . . . . Woman at Party
(Unrated version reviewed.)
Illicit Dreams (1994). . . . . .Beverly Keen
••• 0:05—Breasts, while making love with Joe Cortese in his house.
• 1:12—Left breast, then breasts, when Cortese threatens her at his house.

Indecent Behavior II (1994) . . . . Jordan Mueller
(Unrated version reviewed.)
• 0:44—Left breast, while making love in an alley.
•• 0:46—More left breast, then breasts, while in the alley.
••• 1:06—In black bra and panties, when nude, while making love in bed with Tom, then getting out.
•• 1:15—Breasts and buns, while making love with Chad McQueen in recall of a "dream."
Night Fire (1994) . . . . Gwen
• 0:10—Brief breasts and brief buns in T-back, lifting up her top to flash passing cars while standing up in convertible car.
• 0:21—Brief buns in T-back while fooling around on the bed with Martin Hewitt.
•• 0:29—In black bra, panties and stockings while in bedroom with Hewitt, then breasts and brief partial buns.
• 0:32—Breasts, while in bathtub with Hewitt.
•• 0:36—In red bra and panties, then breasts while in room with Hewitt.
• 0:41—Brief buns in red swimsuit.
•• 0:43—Breasts, when her swimsuit top comes off in spa with Hewitt.
• 0:47—Brief side view of buns, while walking by the spa. Brief buns in swimsuit, when walking back to the house.
• 0:50—Buns in swimsuit, while walking around the house.
•• 0:53—Breasts, when making love outside by fence with Hewitt, while Shannon Tweed watches from inside the house.
• 1:03—Brief breasts, with Hewitt in the spa at night. Medium long shots, then closer shots.
• 1:23—Left breast, while lying in front of Hewitt and talking with Tweed and John Laughlin.
Secret Games 3 (1994) . . . . Diana Larson
(Unrated version reviewed.)
• 0:00—Breasts, while in bathtub.
•• 0:02—Breasts, while in bathtub, then making love with a fantasy guy.
•• 0:07—Breasts and buns, while making love with Terrell in daydream.
• 0:09—Brief buns in daydream.
••• 0:28—In white bra and panties, then breasts in room and on monitor while making love on bed with Jack.
•• 0:32—In white bra and panties, then breasts and buns, undressing and getting into bathtub.
••• 0:40—Breasts and buns in black panties in bedroom with Terrell.
•• 0:43—Buns, getting into bathtub. Breasts, while sitting in tub and getting out.
•• 0:50—Breasts, while making love on bed with Terrell.
• 0:56—Brief breasts on TV monitor while making love with Terrell.
••• 0:58—In white bra, then breasts and buns, while making love with Terrell in bed.
• 1:01—Brief breasts in bathtub while talking to her husband.
•• 1:03—Right breast, then breasts while making love in front of the fire with her husband.
• 1:27—Brief right breast, while in bathtub.
Sorceress (1994) . . . . Carol
••• 0:23—Breasts and buns (wearing a blonde wig), while making love in bed with Larry.
••• 0:51—Buns and breasts (wearing blonde wig) while making love in bed in her dream with Julie Strain and Toni Naples.
1:01—In sexy black lingerie in bedroom with Larry (no more wig).
•• 1:16—Breasts, while undressing in sauna.
•• 1:19—Breasts in panties after taking off towel and putting on bra.
T-Force (1994) . . . . Cocktail Waitress
Cyberzone (1995) . . . . Beth
Deadly Outbreak (1995) . . . . Dr. Allie Levin
Hard Bounty (1995) . . . . Jess
•• 0:13—Breasts, after taking off lingerie top and almost getting into bed with a customer.
••• 0:36—Breasts and side view of buns, while making love in bed with a customer. Long scene.
•• 0:54—Breasts, while in room with Glory, helping Benjamin lose his virginity.
Hungry For You (1996) . . . . Viva
••• 0:06—Breasts and buns, while making love in bed with Joe.
••• 0:26—In black lingerie, then breasts and buns, while making love with Jack.
•• 0:36—Buns in black leather outfit, then breasts and buns, while making love with Arnold.
• 0:45—Very, very brief breasts in quick cuts.
• 0:48—Breasts, while talking with Rodney.
•• 0:58—In bra, then breasts, while making love in bed with Rodney.
••• 1:09—Breasts and brief buns, while bathing with Rodney.
Made for Cable TV:
Love Street: Radio (1995; Showtime) . . . . Michelle
••• 0:06—Breasts and buns, while making love on top of her husband in bed.
•• 0:11—Breasts, while making love in bed.
• 0:15—Breasts, while on the floor with her husband.
Sherman Oaks (1995; Showtime) . . . . Sheila Silver
Sherman Oaks: Season 1, Episode 1 (1995; Showtime) . . . . Sheila Silver
• 0:09—Brief breast while making love with Sherman in his medical office. B&W.
Sherman Oaks: Season 1, Episode 2 (1995; Showtime) . . . . Sheila Silver
•• 0:20—Breasts, while making love with the Dr. Baker in bed, then getting out. B&W.
Sherman Oaks: Season 1, Episode 8 (1995; Showtime) . . . . Sheila Silver
Made for TV Movies:
In the Deep Woods (1992) . . . . Allison Cox
TV:
NYPD Blue: Assistant DA Sipowicz (May 23, 1995) . . . . Sabrina
• 0:37—Brief buns in G-string, in bar when Martinez gets up to talk on microphone.

Swift, Sally

a.k.a. Adult film actress Jennifer West.
Films:
Auditions (1978). . . . . Melinda Sale
••• 0:21—Full frontal nudity, undressing and masturbating during her audition.
•• 0:30—Breasts and buns, whipping Harry.
Hell Squad (1986) . . . . Ann

• *Swift, Stephanie*

Adult film actress.
a.k.a. Darrian Mayfair.
Adult Films:
Beautiful (1998) . . . . n.a.

Films:

The Price of Desire (1996) . . . . Girl in Bathroom

• 0:37—Brief full frontal nudity, when stall door opens in restroom with Janine Lindemulder.

• 0:41—Brief right breast, then brief left breast in B&W flashback.

Made for Cable TV:

Beverly Hills Bordello: The Assignment (1998; Showtime) . . . . Mysterious Person

••• 0:12—Breasts, while having sex with the blonde woman in bedroom.

Swinn, Monica

Films:

Erotikill (1973) . . . . Princess de Rochefort

a.k.a. La Comtesse Noire

a.k.a. The Loves of Irina

•• 0:47—Breasts, getting her dress taken off and blood sucked.

•• 0:55—Breasts, lying on table in doctor's office.

Demoniac (1974; French/Spanish) . . . . The Count's Sadistic Partner

• 0:51—Brief breast in open gown, in bedroom with The Count.

Swinney, Stephanie

Films:

Witchcraft 6: The Devil's Mistress (1993) . . . . Mary

(Unrated version reviewed.)

••• 0:13—Breasts, while making love in the kitchen with Jonathan.

• 0:25—Full frontal nudity, dead, while lying on table in morgue and also in flashbacks.

Outside the Law (1994). . . . . Billy

a.k.a. Blood Run

(Unrated version reviewed.)

••• 0:02—Breasts after taking off swimsuit top, then buns and breasts, in bathtub and getting out. Very, very brief partial lower frontal nudity behind towel.

Swinton, Tilda

Films:

Caravaggio (1986; British). . . . . Lena

Aria (1987; U.S./British). . . . . Young Girl

The Last of England (1987; British) . . . . n.a.

War Requiem (1988; British) . . . . Nurse

Edward II (1992; British) . . . . Isabella

Orlando (1993; British) . . . . Orlando

••• 0:56—Full frontal nudity while looking at herself in mirror.

Female Perversions (1997) . . . . Evelyn Stephens

• 0:01—Brief breasts and buns during her fantasy.

•• 0:03—Full frontal nudity, while making love in bed with Clancy Brown, then getting out of bed.

•• 0:11—Most of her buns, while walking around in lingerie store, wearing a sheer body suit.

• 0:28—Brief lower frontal nudity when Brown rips her pantyhose open to shave her down there in his office.

• 0:54—Breasts during fantasy sequences.

• 0:58—Very brief buns, when getting up out of hammock.

•• 1:29—Breasts, while sitting in bathroom and cutting her breast with a razor blade.

• 1:32—Brief lower frontal nudity, while sitting on edge of bathtub.

• 1:39—Very brief right breast, during dream. Dark.

Sykes, Brenda *

Films:

The Baby Maker (1970) . . . . Francis

Getting Straight (1970). . . . . Luan

•• 0:53—Brief left breast, when scooting up in bed with Elliott Gould, then breasts, while getting back in bed.

The Liberation of L. B. Jones (1970) . . . . Jelly

Honky (1971). . . . . Sheila Smith

••• 0:42—Breasts with her boyfriend, making love on the floor.

• 1:22—Brief breasts several times getting raped by two guys.

Pretty Maids All in a Row (1971) . . . . Pamela Wilcox

Skin Game (1971) . . . . Naomi

Black Gunn (1972) . . . . Judith

• 0:45—Brief side view of right breast, while getting out of bed with Jim Brown.

Cleopatra Jones (1973) . . . . Tiffany

Mandingo (1975) . . . . Ellen

• 0:58—Breasts in bed with Perry King.

Drum (1976) . . . . Calinda

• 0:19—Breasts standing next to bed with Ken Norton.

TV:

Ozzie's Girls (1973) . . . . Brenda (Jennifer) MacKenzie

Executive Suite (1976-77) . . . . Summer Johnson

Szapolowska, Grazyna

Films:

Hanussen (1989; Hungarian) . . . . Valery de la Meer

Kill Cruise (1990; German). . . . . Mona

Wild Obsession (1992; Italian) . . . . Caroline

• 1:29—Very, very brief partial left breast in gaping blouse when she wipes her hands on towel in bathroom.

The Conviction (1994; Italian) . . . . Monica

a.k.a. La Condanna

• 0:45—Buns, while lying asleep in bed. Dark.

• Taarud, Shellani *

Video Tapes:

Playboy's The Girls of Hawaiian Tropic (1994) . . . . Lagoon

0:43—Nude, while posing in and beside a lagoon.

Playboy's Sex on the Beach: Tropical Heat (1997) . . . . Massage/Shellani

••• 0:16—Nude, while getting massaged by another woman.

Tabrizi, Tera *

Films:

Cool As Ice (1991). . . . . Club Dancer

Showdown in Little Tokyo (1991) . . . . Pool Girl

• 0:13—Brief breasts, walking into pool during party.

White Sands (1992) . . . . Body Double for Mary Elizabeth Mastrontonio

•• 1:10—Left breast and upper half of buns in the shower undressing in the shower with Willem Dafoe. Don't see face, so it's probably Tera.

Carlito's Way (1993) . . . . Club Date

The Shadow (1994). . . . . Concubine

Made for Cable Movies:

Red Shoe Diaries (1992; Showtime). . . . . Alex's Friend

(Unrated video tape version reviewed.)

Taggart, Sharon

Films:

The Last Picture Show (1971). . . . . Charlene Duggs

•• 0:11—In bra, then breasts making out in truck with Timothy Bottoms.

The Harrad Experiment (1973) . . . . Barbara

Tallman, Patricia

Films:

Knightriders (1981) . . . . Julie

- 0:46—Brief breasts in the bushes in moonlight talking to her boyfriend while a truck driver watches.

Stuck on You (1982) . . . . Queen Guenevere

Monkey Shines: An Experiment in Fear (1988) . . . . Party Guest and Stunts

After Midnight (1989) . . . . Stunt Player

Roadhouse (1989) . . . . Bandstand Babe

Night of the Living Dead (1990) . . . . Barbara

Sweet Justice (1991) . . . . Josie

Army of Darkness (1992) . . . . Possessed Witch

Me and Veronica (1992) . . . . Stunt Player

Ring of the Musketeers (1992) . . . . Stunts

Benefit of the Doubt (1993; U.S./German) . . . . Karen's Mother

Criminal Passion (1993) . . . . Stunts

Kalifornia (1993) . . . . Stunts
(Unrated version reviewed.)

Cobb (1994) . . . . Stunts

Made for Cable Movies:

Attack of the 50 ft. Woman (1993; HBO) . . . . Stunts

Made for Cable TV:

Red Shoe Diaries: Double or Nothing (1993; Showtime) . . . . Stunts
(Available on the video tape *Red Shoe Diaries 5: Weekend Pass.*)

TV:

Babylon 5 (1996-97) . . . . Lyta Alexander

Tamerlis, Zoe

a.k.a. Zoë Tamerlaine and Zoe Lund.

Films:

Ms. 45 (1980) . . . . Thana

Special Effects (1984) . . . . Amelia/Elaine

- 0:01—Side view of right breast, wearing pasties during photo session.
- 0:16—Brief breasts sitting by pool with Eric Bogosian.
- •• 0:19—Breasts getting into bed and in bed with Bogosian.
- 0:22—Breasts, dead in spa while Bogosian washes her off.
- 0:44—Brief breasts in moviola that Bogosian watches.
- •• 1:12—Breasts making love on bed with Keefe.
- 1:17—Breasts getting into bed during filming of movie. Brief breasts during Bogosian's flashbacks.
- 1:20—More left breast shots on moviola getting strangled.
- ••• 1:33—Breasts with Bogosian when he takes her dress off.
- 1:35—Breasts sitting on bed kissing Bogosian. More breasts and more flashbacks.
- 1:40—Brief breasts during struggle. Dark.

Heavy Petting (1989) . . . . Herself/Writer, Actress

Bad Lieutenant (1992) . . . . Zoe

• Tamu

Films:

Claudine (1974) . . . . Charlene

- 1:14—Brief breasts, when fighting with Diahann Carroll.

Super Cops (1974) . . . . Girl

Tandy, Jessica

Late wife of actor Hume Cronyn.

Films:

Forever Amber (1947) . . . . Nan Britton

The Desert Fox (1951) . . . . Frau Rommel

The Birds (1963) . . . . Lydia Brenner

Honky Tonk Freeway (1981) . . . . Carol

Best Friends (1982) . . . . Eleanor McCullen

Still of the Night (1982) . . . . Grace Rice

World According to Garp (1982) . . . . Mrs. Fields

The Bostonians (1984) . . . . Miss Birdseye

Cocoon (1985) . . . . Alma Finley

*batteries not included (1987) . . . . Faye Riley

Cocoon, The Return (1988) . . . . Alma Finley

The House on Carroll Street (1988) . . . . Miss Venable

Driving Miss Daisy (1989) . . . . Miss Daisy Werthan
(Academy Award for Best Actress.)

Fried Green Tomatoes (1991) . . . . Ninny Threadgoode
a.k.a. Fried Green Tomatoes at the Whistle Stop Café

Used People (1992) . . . . Frieda

Camilla (1994) . . . . Camilla Cara

- 0:46—Brief buns and partial back side or right breast, while walking into the water in front of Bridget Fonda.

Nobody's Fool (1994) . . . . Miss Beryl

Made for TV Movies:

To Dance with the White Dog (1993) . . . . Cora Samuel

Tané

See: McClure, Tané.

Tanner, Joy

Films:

Liar's Edge (1991) . . . . Ruth

Prom Night IV: Deliver Us From Evil (1991) . . . . Laura
(All nude scenes look like a body double.)

- 0:58—Buns, lying in bed with Jeff. Don't see her face.
- 0:59—Very brief right breast, while making love with Jeff, standing up. Don't see her face.
- 1:00—Buns and back half of right breast, getting out of bed. Don't see her face.
- •• 1:01—Breasts in shower. Don't see her face. It looks like a body double because the double's breasts are bigger than Joy's.

Tasker, Barbara

Films:

J.D.'s Revenge (1976) . . . . Sheryl

- 1:11—Very brief left breast, while lying on her stomach on bed. Brief breasts, while getting up and out of bed with Isaac.

Hard Target (1993) . . . . Waitress

Tate, Laura

Films:

Dead Space (1990) . . . . Marissa Salinger

- •• 0:33—Breasts in bed with Marc Singer during her dream.

Subspecies (1990) . . . . Michelle

Tate, Sharon *

Late wife of director Roman Polanski.

Victim of the Manson Family murders on August 9, 1969.

Films:

The Fearless Vampire Killers (1967) . . . . Sarah Shagal

- 0:24—Very, very brief breasts struggling in bathtub with vampire. Hard to see.

Valley of the Dolls (1967) . . . . Jennifer North

- 1:21—In bra, acting in a movie. Very, very brief left breast in bed with a guy (curtain gets in the way).
- 1:23—Very brief side view of right breast, while sitting up in bed.

The 13 Chairs (1969; French/Italian/British) . . . . Pat

- 0:14—In bra, then very brief left breast, while in struggle in bedroom with Mario.

•• 1:20—Breasts clearly visible under sheer wet blouse after getting out of the pool.
• 1:24—Left breast, while in bed with Mario and Stefanella.
Ciao Frederico! (1971). . . . . n.a.
TV:
The Beverly Hillbillies (1963-65) . . . . Janet Trego
Petticoat Junction (1963). . . . . Billie Jo Bradley

Tatum, Judy
Films:
Witchboard (1987) . . . . Dr. Gelineau
Witchtrap (1989) . . . . Agnes Goldberg
•• 0:05—Breasts in the bathtub.

• *Taub, Melissa*
Films:
My Boyfriend's Back (1993). . . . . Beefy Girl in Library
Little Witches (1996) . . . . Erica
• 0:35—In bra, then brief buns and breasts with the other girls during ceremony.

• *Tavarez, Jacqueline* *
Films:
Tromeo & Juliet (1995) . . . . Rosy
(Unrated director's cut reviewed.)
••• 0:10—Breasts, while making love with a guy and talking on the phone.

Taye-Loren, Carolyn *
Films:
Scanner Cop (1993) . . . . Nurse in Emergency Room
Witchcraft V: Dance with the Devil (1993) . . . . Keli
••• 1:01—Breasts while making love with Bill under leaky water pipes in the basement.

• *Taylor Allen, Lee*
Films:
Alone in the Dark (1982). . . . . Toni Potter
Very Close Quarters (1984). . . . . Vera
•• 0:12—Right breast, while in bathtub with Luda in Vadik's imagination. Breasts in bathtub when old guy peeks through keyhole.
Stargate (1994). . . . . Jenny
Made for TV Movies:
Casualties of Love: The "Long Island Lolita" Story (1993)
. . . . Nurse

Taylor, Alex *
Video Tapes:
Penthouse Pet Rocks (1995). . . . . Pet
Penthouse: The Ultimate Pet Games (1996) . . . . Pet
••• 0:01—Nude during obstacle course segment.
••• 0:09—Nude, while posing in stagecoach outdoors.
••• 0:29—Nude in tug-of-war segment.
••• 0:42—Nude during squirt gun segment.

Taylor, Courtney
Films:
Prom Night III (1989) . . . . Mary Lou Maloney
Sins of the Night (1993) . . . . Danielle
(Unrated version reviewed.)
• 1:20—In black bra and panties, then breasts in room with Deborah Shelton and Miles O'Keeffe. Medium long shot. Side of right breast in closer shot.
Cover Me (1995). . . . . Holly Jacobsen
• 0:07—Breasts, while making love in bed with Rick Rossovich.
••• 0:28—Breasts and buns in T-backs, during photo session.
•• 0:30—Breasts during another photo session.
• 0:36—Breasts in photo CD pictures that she looks at with Rossovich on TV.
• 0:38—Brief buns in T-back and right breast in still photos in portfolio.
•• 0:46—Breasts, while making love in bed with Rossovich.
•• 0:52—Breasts and buns in yellow T-back, while dancing in club in a shower.
•• 1:04—Breasts and buns in T-back, while dancing on stage.
• 1:10—Breasts and buns in panties, under sheer nightie in booth.
Tracks of a Killer (1995) . . . . Bella
• 0:07—Left breast, while taking off her clothes in office with Patrick.
•• 0:17—Breasts, while in bed when Patrick rips off her lingerie and makes love in bed.
Made for Cable Movies:
The Companion (1994; USA). . . . . Shelley

• *Taylor, Devyn*
Made for Cable TV:
Intimate Sessions: Mary (1998; Cinemax) . . . . Mary
•• 0:07—Breasts, while making love with Teddy next to hot tub.
••• 0:21—Breasts and buns, taking off robe and making love with Teddy in hot tub.
Intimate Sessions: Renee (1998; Cinemax). . . . . Kim

Taylor, Elizabeth
Films:
Cleopatra (1963). . . . . Cleopatra
• 0:28—Half of buns, lying face down, while getting a massage.
Reflections in a Golden Eye (1970). . . . . Leonora Penderton
(She used a body double for the nude scenes in this film.)
X, Y and Zee (1972) . . . . Zee
• 1:11—Brief right breast, in bloody bathtub water, trying to commit suicide. Probably a body double—Don't see her face.
Ash Wednesday (1973) . . . . Barbara
• 0:10—Long shot breasts, closer shot of buns, getting prepared for plastic surgery in hospital. Don't see her face, probably a body double.
Psychotic (1975; Italian) . . . . Lise
a.k.a. Driver's Seat

Taylor, Femi
Films:
The Return of the Jedi (1983). Oola
• 0:13—Very, very brief blurry right breast, twice, popping out of skimpy outfit, just before falling into pit after dancing for Jabba the Hutt. She's covered with green body paint.
Flirting (1992; Australian) . . . . Letitia Adjewa

Taylor, Karin *
Video Tapes:
Playboy Video Calendar 1997 (1996) . . . . May
••• 0:19—Nude, while swimming underwater.
••• 0:21—Nude, while posing in bedroom for fantasy guy.
Playboy's Hot Wheels & High Heels Biker Babes (1997)
. . . . Space Age Speed
••• 0:12—Nude, while posing on a motorcycle in a studio.

*Taylor, Kimberly **

Films:

Bedroom Eyes II (1989). . . . . Michelle

Cleo/Leo (1989) . . . . Store Clerk

••• 0:22—Breasts in white panties, changing in dressing room with Jane Hamilton. Very nice!

Party Incorporated (1989) . . . . Felicia

a.k.a. Party Girls

•• 0:26—Breasts shaking her breasts trying an outfit on.

••• 0:39—Breasts and buns in G-string in the bar with the guys.

Frankenhooker (1990). . . . . .Amber

• 0:36—Brief left breast in green top during introduction to Jeffrey.

•• 0:37—Brief breasts during exam by Jeffrey. Then breasts getting breasts measured with calipers.

• 0:41—Brief right breast, twice, enjoying drugs.

•• 0:42—Breasts, getting off bed and onto another bed with Anise.

• 0:43—Breasts kneeling in bed screaming before exploding.

Beauty School (1993). . . . . Kimberly

• 0:43—Buns in white lingerie on balcony. Long shot.

••• 0:44—Breasts doing breast exercises, then buns in G-string going for a swim. (She's on the far right.)

••• 0:45—Buns and breasts, getting out of the swimming pool.

••• 0:51—Breasts while making love with Quincy outside.

••• 1:22—Breasts, taking off her dress and making love with Quincy.

Marilyn Chambers: Bedtime Fantasies (1996) . . . . n.a.

Taylor, Lili

Films:

Mystic Pizza (1988). . . . . Jojo Barboza

Born on the Fourth of July (1989) . . . . Jamie Wilson

Say Anything (1989). . . . . Corey

Bright Angel (1990). . . . . Lucy

• 0:26—Brief top of breasts under water, taking a bath in a pond.

••• 0:27—Breasts, while walking out of the pond.

Dogfight (1991) . . . . Rose

Household Saints (1992). . . . . Teresa

•• 1:35—Breasts while in her bedroom, after undressing in front of Leonard.

Rudy (1993) . . . . Sherry

Short Cuts (1993). . . . . .Honey Bush

Watch It (1993). . . . . Brenda

Arizona Dream (1994). . . . . Grace

Mrs. Parker and the Vicious Circle (1994) . . . . .Edna Ferber

Ready to Wear (1994). . . . . .Fiona Ulrich

a.k.a. Prêt-à-porter

The Addiction (1995) . . . . .Kathleen Conklin

Four Rooms (1995). . . . . Raven

Killer: A Journal of Murder (1995) . . . . Uncredited Sally

Girls Town (1996). . . . . Patti Lucci

I Shot Andy Warhol (1996). . . . . .Valerie Solanas

• 1:33—Brief breasts, while sitting in shower.

Ransom (1996) . . . . Maris Connor

Made for Cable TV:

Subway Stories (1997; HBO). Belinda

Taylor, Lindsay

See: Mayo-Chandler, Karen.

• *Taylor, Linsey*

See: St. Claire, Taylor.

Taylor, Lisa

Films:

Love Trap (1977). . . . . Eleanor

a.k.a. Let's Get Laid

•• 0:37—Breasts, while answering and talking on the phone.

• 0:53—Partial lower frontal nudity when talking on the phone to Gordon. Brief breasts, while hanging up the phone.

• 1:33—Brief left breast while making love on bed with two guys.

Eyes of Laura Mars (1978). .Michele

• 0:59—Very brief right breast, while on table just before getting killed.

Where the Buffalo Roam (1980) . . . . Ruthie

Windy City (1984). . . . . Sherry

Taylor, Marianne

Films:

Vendetta (1986) . . . . .Star

Bloodmatch (1991) . . . . Max Manduke

• 0:13—Breasts and buns, making love in bed on top of Caldwell.

TV:

NYPD Blue: Bombs Away (Feb 28, 1995). . . . . Mrs. Loftus

• *Taylor, Priscilla **

Video Tapes:

Playboy Video Calendar 1998 (1997) . . . . March

••• 0:10—Nude, while posing indoors and outdoors with a water theme.

••• 0:12—Nude, while posing indoors.

Playboy's Fast Women (1997). . . . . .Playmate

Playboy's Playmates Revisited (1998) . . . . Herself

• 0:25—Brief breasts in still photo.

*Taylor, Sandra **

a.k.a. Sandy Korn.

Films:

Possessed by the Night (1993)

. . . . Uncredited Body Double for Shannon Tweed

••• 1:05—Breasts and buns in panties, while caressing herself. Did this because the film makers didn't need to have Tweed come back to shoot only this one insert scene.

Exit to Eden (1994) .Riba/Club Eden

• 0:26—Breasts while on runway during introductions.

Lady in Waiting (1994) .Lady in Red

(Unrated version reviewed.)

•• 0:09—Breasts, when undressing and rolling her stockings down. Nude while blindfolded and tied by her wrists to the bed.

Under Siege 2: Dark Territory (1995). . . . . Kelly

Batman & Robin (1997) . . . . Debutante

L.A. Confidential (1997) . . . . . Mickey Cohen's Mambo Partner

Phoenix (1998) . . . . .Video Game Stripper

Video Tapes:

Penthouse Passport to Paradise/Hawaii (1991) . . . Model

•• 0:25—Breasts, taking off her top and going down into an underground cave.

••• 0:27—Nude, taking an outdoor shower to wash the dirt off herself.

Penthouse The Great Pet Hunt—Part II (1993) . . . . . . Pet

••• 0:50—Breasts and buns in T-back after stripping out of motorcycle mama outfit.

*Taylor, Vanessa **

a.k.a. Vanessa Tendler.

Films:

Femalien (1995) . . . . Collector/Kara
- •• 0:02—Breasts and buns in T-back, in bedroom after arriving on earth.
- • 0:04—Breasts, while watching a man and woman in backyard.
- ••• 0:07—Breasts, while caressing herself when watching the man and woman make love.
- •• 0:15—Breasts, while dressing in bedroom.
- •• 0:30—Left breast, while caressing herself when watching a guy and girl model make love.
- ••• 0:45—Nude, while making love with Drew in bed.
- ••• 0:59—Nude, while in massage room with MJ, then getting massaged, then massaging him.
- ••• 1:19—Nude, while making love with Sun in bed.

Sinful Intrigue (1995) . . . . Laurie
- •• 0:11—Breasts, while making out with Mr. Dorsey on his lap in his office.

Video Tapes:

Playboy Strip (1996) . . . . Dancer
- ••• 0:05—Nude, after stripping out of maid costume on stage, to the surprise of her boyfriend.
- ••• 0:08—Nude, while getting shaved with a straight razor by another dancer on stage.
- ••• 0:36—Nude, while dancing by herself and sometime with Raquel.

Taylor, Vida

Films:

God Told Me To (1976) . . . . Mrs. Mulling as a Child

Clash of the Titans (1981) . . . . Danae
- • 0:11—Right breast while breast feeding her baby. Buns, walking on beach.

Taylor-Gordon, Hannah

Films:

The House of Spirits (1993) . . . . Blanca (Child)
- • 0:43—Nude, while in pond with young Pedro.

Mary Shelley's Frankenstein (1994) . . . . Young Elizabeth

Taylor-Young, Leigh

Films:

I Love You, Alice B. Toklas (1968) . . . . Nancy

The Big Bounce (1969) . . . . Nancy Barker

(Not available on video tape.)

The Adventurers (1970). . . . . Amparo

The Buttercup Chain (1971; British) . . . . Manny

The Gang That Couldn't Shoot Straight (1971) . . . . Angela Palumbo

The Horsemen (1971) . . . . Zereh

Soylent Green (1973) . . . . Shirl

Can't Stop the Music (1980) . . . . Claudia Walters

Looker (1981) . . . . Jennifer Long

Jagged Edge (1985) . . . . Virginia Howell

Secret Admirer (1985). . . . . Elizabeth Fimple

Accidents (1988). . . . . Beryl Chambers

Honeymoon Academy (1990) . . . . Mrs. Doris Kent

Bliss (1996) . . . . Redhead
- • 0:08—Brief partial breasts, visible through sheer curtains.

Made for TV Movies:

Moment of Truth: Murder or Memory? (1994) . . . . n.a.

TV:

The Devlin Connection (1982) . . . . Lauren Dane

Dallas (1987-88) . . . . Kimberly Cryder

Picket Fences (1993-96). . . . . Rachel

Sunset Beach (1997-) . . . . Elaine Stevens

Tedesco, Paola

Films:

The Gospel According to St. Matthew (1966; French/Italian) . . . . Salome

Battle of the Amazons (1973; Italian/Spanish) . . . . Valeria

Crime Boss (1976; Italian) . . . . n.a.

I Hate Blondes (1981; Italian) . . . . Teresa
- ••• 0:06—Breasts, sitting up in bed at night and turning on the light. Buns, while walking around the room.

Telek, April

Films:

Deadly Sins (1994; Canadian) . . . . Gwen

Deadlock 2 (1995). . . . . Blonde Singer

Made for Cable Movies:

When Danger Follows You Home (1997; USA). . . . . Pam

Made for Cable TV:

Outer Limits: Paradise (1996; Showtime) . . . . . . Young Lucy
- • 0:01—Breasts, while making love with Jimmy. Very brief buns and almost lower frontal nudity when she straddles him.

Dead Man's Gun: The Great McDonacle (1997) . . . . . . Brittany

*Tempest **

Films:

Affairs of the Heart (1992) . . . . Miss September
- ••• 0:54—Breasts posing in skirt during photo session.
- ••• 1:00—More breasts during photo session.

Video Tapes:

Playboy's Girls of Radio: Talk, Rock and Shock (1995) . . . . Herself
- ••• 0:06—Nude, while taking a shower, then bathing with Amy Lynn Baxter.

Tendler, Vanessa

See: Taylor, Vanessa.

*Tenison, Reneé **

Films:

Shout (1991). . . . . Girl in Bar

CB4 (1993) . . . . Twin

Video Tapes:

Playboy Video Calendar 1991 (1990) . . . . August
- ••• 0:31—Nude.

Playboy Video Centerfold: Reneé Tenison (1990) . . . . Playmate of the Year 1990
- ••• 0:00—Nude throughout.

Wet & Wild III (1991). . . . . Model

The Best of Video Playmate Calendars (1992). . . Playmate
- ••• 0:06—Nude in the desert.
- ••• 0:08—Nude working out in warehouse gym.
- ••• 0:10—Nude, taking a milk bath.
- ••• 0:11—Nude in bedroom.

Playboy's Sexy, Steamy, Sultry (1993) . . . . Playmate

Playboy's Women of Color (1994) . . . . . . Playmate/Hostess
- ••• 0:01—Breasts and buns, while working out in warehouse.
- ••• 0:02—Nude in still photos.
- ••• 0:41—Nude in house, while taking a milk bath.
- ••• 0:43—Nude in bed and in house.
- ••• 0:45—Nude in dance/music number.

Tennant, Victoria

Ex-wife of comedian/actor Steve Martin.

Films:

The Ragman's Daughter (1974; British) . . . . Doris Randall
Horror Planet (1980; British) . . . . Barbara
a.k.a. Inseminoid
All of Me (1984) . . . . Terry Hoskins
The Holcroft Covenant (1985) . . . . Helden Tennyson
Flowers in the Attic (1987) . . . . Mother
Best Seller (1988) . . . . Roberta Gillian
Whispers (1989) . . . . Hilary Thomas
• 0:42—Brief partial left breast, while in bed with Chris Sarandon. The later scenes in bathtub and on stairs look like a body double.
The Handmaid's Tale (1990) . . . . Aunt Lydia
L.A. Story (1991) . . . . Sara
The Plague (1992; French/British) . . . . Alice Rieux
Edie & Pen (1996) . . . . Blonde with Dog

Ter Steege, Johanna

Films:

Vanishing (1988) . . . . Saskia Wagner
Vincent and Theo (1990; British/French/U.S.) . . . . . . Jo Bonger
Immortal Beloved (1994) . . . . Johanna Reiss
• 0:39—Brief left breast and lower frontal nudity while sitting up after Gary Oldman whips the sheets off the bed she's sleeping in with his brother.
Paradise Road (1997) . . . . Sister Wilhelminia

Terashita, Jill *

Films:

The Big Bet (1985) . . . . Koko
Terminal Entry (1986) . . . . Gwen
Dirty Laundry (1987) . . . . n.a.
Night of the Demons (1987) . . . . Frannie
(Unrated version reviewed.)
•• 0:57—Breasts while making love with her boyfriend in a coffin.
Sleepaway Camp III: Teenage Wasteland (1989) . . . Arab
•• 0:16—Breasts putting sweatshirt on.
Why Me? (1990) . . . . Hostess
Rapid Fire (1992) . . . . Stunts

Texter, Gilda

Films:

Angels Hard as They Come (1971) . . . . Astrid
• 0:26—Brief breasts several times when bad guys try to rape her. Dark.
Vanishing Point (1971) . . . . Nude Rider
• 1:17—Breasts while riding motorcycle outside.
••• 1:19—Breasts riding motorcycle and walking around without wearing any clothes. Long scene.

Thackray, Gail

See: Harris, Gail.

Theel, Lynn

Films:

Fyre (1979) . . . . Fyre
Humanoids from the Deep (1980) . . . . Peggy Larsen
• 0:22—Very, very brief half of right breast, when fight in parking lot startles her and her boyfriend in back of truck.
• 0:30—Brief breasts getting raped on the beach by a humanoid.
• 0:51—Brief breasts, dead, lying on the beach all covered with seaweed.
Without Warning (1980) . . . . Beth
Hollywood Boulevard II (1989) . . . . Ann Gregory

Thelen, Jodi

Films:

Four Friends (1981) . . . . Georgia
•• 0:17—Left breast in open blouse three times with her three male friends.
The Black Stallion Returns (1983) . . . . Tabari
Twilight Time (1983) . . . . Lena
One Night Stand (1994) . . . . Janice
a.k.a. Before the Night
Playback (1995) . . . . Mary

Made for TV Movies:

Follow Your Heart (1990) . . . . Cecile

TV:

Duet (1987-89) . . . . Jane Kelly

Theodore, Sondra *

Video Tapes:

Wet & Wild (1989) . . . . Model

• Thériault, Janine

Made for Cable Movies:

More Tales of the City (1998; Canadian/U.S.; Showtime) . . . . Bobby

Made for Cable TV:

Hunger: A Matter of Style (1997; Showtime) . . . . . . Sondra
• 0:20—Left breast, while with Chad Lowe in his apartment.
• 0:21—Right breast, while lying in bed before he starts to get her blood.

• Theron, Charlize

Films:

2 Days in the Valley (1996) . . . . Helga Svelgen
• 0:11—Brief breasts, while lying "dead" in a photograph with blood on her left breast.
••• 0:37—Breasts, while making love with James Spader.
That Thing You Do! (1996) . . . . Tina
Devil's Advocate (1997) . . . . Mary Ann Lomax
•• 1:01—Breasts, while making love with Keanu Reeves.
• 1:41—Brief full frontal nudity, taking off blanket and standing up in church. (She has bloody cut marks all over her body.)
Trial and Error (1997) . . . . Billie

Thom, Cristy *

Films:

Best of the Best 2 (1992) . . . . Girl at Restaurant
Meatballs 4 (1992) . . . . Hillary
••• 0:38—Breasts, taking off her blouse and washing herself off.

Video Tapes:

Playboy Video Calendar 1992 (1991) . . . . September
••• 0:35—Full frontal nudity walking and posing around the house.
••• 0:37—Nude in room of mirrors.
••• 0:38—Nude in bathtub.
Playboy's Playmate Review 1992 (1992) . . . Miss February
••• 0:22—Nude on motorcycle, then with a snake and then in a house.
Wet & Wild IV (1992) . . . . Model
Playboy's Sexy, Steamy, Sultry (1993) . . . . Playmate

Thomas, Ali

Films:

Hangin' with the Homeboys (1991) . . . . Disco Woman

Night Owl (1993) . . . . Anne
- 0:37—In bra, then left breast while on the floor with Jake.
- 0:38—Left breast, when sleeping, then breasts, while getting up off the floor.
- 0:51—Very brief right breast when Jake lifts his head up and dribbles blood on her after biting her neck.

Rain Without Thunder (1995) . . . . Allison Goldring

Thomas, Betty

Films:

Chesty Anderson, U.S. Navy (1975). . . . . Party Guest #1
Jackson County Jail (1976). . . . . Waitress
Tunnelvision (1976) . . . . Brigit Bert Richards
- 0:19—Breasts in pasties, during game show. Long scene. (She jumps up and down a lot.)

Loose Shoes (1977). . . . . Biker Chick #1
- 0:02—Brief right breast dancing on the table during the *Skateboarders from Hell* sketch.

Used Cars (1980). . . . . Bunny
- 0:37—Dancing on top of a car next to Kurt Russell wearing pasties to attract customers (wearing a brunette wig).

Homework (1982). Reddog's Secretary
Troop Beverly Hills (1989) . . . . Velda Plendor

Made for TV Movies:

Outside Chance (1978). . . . . Katherine

TV:

Hill Street Blues (1981-87). . . . . Lucy Bates

Thomas, Heather

Films:

Zapped! (1982). . . . . Jane Mitchell
1:29—Body double brief breasts when Scott Baio drops her dress during the dance.

Cyclone (1986) . . . . Teri Marshall
Deathstone (1986; German) . . . . Merryl Davis
Red Blooded American Girl (1988) . . . . Paula Bukowsky
Hidden Obsession (1992) . . . . Ellen Carlyle
1:01—Squished breast, against Vincent while on the floor.

TV:

Co-ed Fever (1979). . . . . Sandi
The Fall Guy (1981-86) . . . . Jodi Banks
The Ultimate Challenge (1991) . . . . Co-Host

Thomas, Heidi

Films:

Crack House (1989) . . . . Annie
- 1:09—Brief left breast and buns in a G string, on table getting raped by a gang.
- 1:14—Breasts in bathtub, dead.

Ricochet (1991). . . . . Reporter
Night of the Running Man (1994). . . . . Stewardess

Made for Cable TV:

Tales From the Crypt: Split Personality (1992; HBO)
. . . . Prostitute
- •• 0:06—Breasts, lying in bed with Joe Pesci.

• Thomas, Lynn *

Video Tapes:

Playboy Video Calendar 1998 (1997) . . . . August
- ••• 0:31—Nude, while during still photography session.
- ••• 0:33—In lingerie and nude, while posing in a Japanese style house.

Thomas, Serena Scott

Films:

Let Him Have It (1991; British) . . . . Stella

Made for Cable Movies:

Harnessing Peacocks (1995; British; A&E) . . . . Hebe
- •• 0:52—Brief buns, then breasts, while in bedroom, talking with Rory. (Frontal nudity in reflection in the mirror is blurred out in the U.S. version shown on TV.)

Made for TV Movies:

Diana: Her True Story (1993) . . . . Princess Diana
Bermuda Grace (1994) . . . . Kathy Madeira
Masterpiece Theatre: Nostromo (1997) . . . . Emilia

TV:

Nash Bridges (1996-) . . . . Kelly Weld

Thomas, Sunset *

Adult film actress.
a.k.a. Diane Fowler.

Films:

Death Dancers (1992) . . . . Itsani
- •• 0:16—Breasts in open blouse with Will and a nude dancer in club.
- •• 0:35—Breasts in bedroom with Ruben.

Witchcraft IV: Virgin Heart (1992) . . . . Nora Breckenridge
- 0:02—Brief tip of right breast, outside with Pete at night when he tries to make some moves on her.
- 0:11—Very brief breasts, twice, lying with blood covering her chest.

Thompson, Alina *

Films:

Trapped (1993) . . . . Monica
a.k.a. The Killing Jar
- 0:16—In sheer white lingerie outfit in bedroom with Alan.
- 0:26—Right breast while in bed with Alan in Laura's imagination.
- ••• 0:33—In two piece swimsuit, then nude, while making love with Alan outside by pool.
- •• 0:37—Nude, undressing and going for a swim in the pool, then getting killed.

Seduce Me: Pamela Principle 2 (1994) . . . . Pamela
- ••• 0:23—Buns in sexy swimsuit, then breasts during photo session.
- 0:33—Brief lower half of buns, while walking up stairs in short dress.
- ••• 0:35—Breasts and buns, opening towel, then getting dressed.
- ••• 0:37—Nude, changing clothes then posing for photos outside. Some in B&W. Long scene.
- •• 0:44—Buns in G-string and left breast while making love with Charles in kitchen.
- 0:49—Brief right breast and buns in swimsuit bottom while getting out of spa.
- ••• 1:16—Breasts and buns, while making love in bed with Charles.

Dead Cold (1995) . . . . Sarah
- •• 0:15—Breasts, while making love with Peter Dobson in pickup truck.

Marked Man (1996; Canadian) . . . . Sylvia Elkins
The Fiancé (1997) . . . . Veronica Lang

Made for Cable TV:

Women: Stories of Passion-Wishful Thinking
(1996; Showtime) . . . . Art Gallery Manager
- •• 0:18—Breasts, while making love with Kelly and Kurt in art gallery.

• Thompson, Andrea

Ex-wife of actor Jerry Doyle.

Films:

Wall Street (1987) .... Hooker
Doin' Time on Planet Earth (1988) .... Lisa Winston
Delirious (1991) .... Nurse Helen Caldwell
A Gun, a Car, a Blonde (1996) .... The Blonde/Jade
••• 1:08—Nude, when walking in the garden to greet and kiss Rick during B&W segment.

Made for Cable TV:

ArliSS: Visionary For A New Millennium (1997; HBO) ....Giselle Jaynes
• 0:05—Brief breasts, while in bed after making love with Robert Wuhl.
•• 0:07—Brief breasts, when getting up out of bed, then in black lingerie while talking with Wuhl.
• 0:21—In black lingerie and very brief right breast, while having sex with Wuhl on his desk.

TV:

Falcon Crest (1989-90) ....Genele Ericson
Baywatch (1991-92) ....Devon
Babylon 5 (1993) .... Talia Winters
JAG (1995) .... Commander Allison Krennick
NYPD Blue (1996-) .... Det. Jill Kirkendall
NYPD Blue: As Flies to Careless Boys Are We to the Gods or This Bud's For You (Sep 30, 1997) . . . Det. Jill Kirkendall
• 0:29—Brief back side of left breast while starting to make out with Leo on the sofa.

Thompson, Brooke

Video Tapes:

Hot Body International: #1 Miss Cancun (1990) .... Contestant
•• 0:40—Buns, in one piece swimsuit.
Hot Body International: #2 Miss Puerto Vallarta (1990) .... Contestant
•• 0:26—Buns in red one piece swimsuit. Brief left breast a couple of times when it accidentally falls out.
Hot Body International: #4 Spring Break (1992) . . . Contestant
• 0:38—Buns in G-string during wet T-shirt contest.

Thompson, Cynthia Ann

Films:

Cave Girl (1985) .... Eba
• 0:41—Buns, standing in stream while bathing. Long shot.
•• 1:04—Breasts making love with Rex.
Tomboy (1985) .... Amanda
• 0:23—Brief right breast getting out of car in auto repair shop.
•• 1:02—Breasts delivering drinks to two guys in the swimming pool.
Not of This Earth (1988) ....Third Hooker (black dress)
Rescue Force (1989) .... Angel
•• 1:17—Breasts, after taking off robe and getting into bubble bath with two other girls.

Thompson, Emma

Wife of actor/director Kenneth Branagh.
Sister of actress Sophie Thompson.

Films:

Henry V (1989) .... Princess Katherine
The Tall Guy (1990; British) .... Kate
••• 0:33—Very brief right breast, brief buns, then breasts during funny love making scene with Jeff Goldblum.
Dead Again (1991) .... Margaret Strauss/Jane Doe
Impromptu (1991) .... Duchess d'Antan
Howards End (1992) .... Margaret Schlegel
(Academy Award for Best Actress.)
In the Name of the Father (1993; British/U.S.) . . . Gareth Peirce
Much Ado About Nothing (1993; British) ....Beatrice
My Father The Hero (1993) .... Uncredited Isabelle
Peter's Friends (1993; British/U.S.) ....Maggie
The Remains of the Day (1993; British/U.S.) ..... Miss Kenton
Junior (1994) ....Dr. Diana Reddin
Carrington (1995; British) .... Dora Carrington
• 0:29—Brief back side of right breast while putting pajamas on.
• 1:29—Most of right breast, while making love on a boat with a guy.
Sense and Sensibility (1995) ....Elinor Dashwood
The Winter Guest (1997; British/U.S.) .... Frances
Primary Colors (1998) .... Susan

Made for TV Movies:

Masterpiece Theatre: The Blue Boy (1994; British) .... Marie Bonnar

Thompson, Lea

Wife of director Howard Deutsch.

Films:

All The Right Moves (1983) .... Lisa
••• 1:00—Breasts and brief buns and lower frontal nudity, getting undressed and into bed with Tom Cruise in his bedroom.
Jaws 3 (1983) ....Kelly Ann Bukowski
Red Dawn (1984) .... Erica
The Wild Life (1984) ....Anita
Back to the Future (1985) .... Lorraine Baines-McFly
Howard the Duck (1986) ....Beverly Switzler
SpaceCamp (1986) ....Kathryn
Some Kind of Wonderful (1987) ....Amanda Jones
Casual Sex? (1988) ....Stacy
• 0:27—Buns, while lying down at nude beach with Victoria Jackson.
• 0:30—Buns at the beach. Pan shot from her feet to her head.
Going Undercover (1988; British) ...... Marigold De La Hunt
The Wizard of Loneliness (1988) .... Sybil
Back to the Future, Part II (1989) .... Lorraine Baines-McFly
Back to the Future, Part III (1990) ....Maggie McFly/Lorraine McFly
Article 99 (1992) ....Dr. Robin Van Dorn
The Beverly Hillbillies (1993) .... Laura
Dennis the Menace (1993) .... Alice Mitchell
The Little Rascals (1994) ....Ms. Roberts

Made for Cable Movies:

Nightbreaker (1989) .... Sally Matthews
Stolen Babies (1993; Lifetime) .... Annie Beales
The Right to Remain Silent (1995; Showtime) . . Christine Paley

Made for Cable TV:

Tales From the Crypt: Only Sin Deep (1989; HBO) .... Sylvia Vane

Made for TV Movies:

Montana (1990) .... Peg Guthrie
The Substitute Wife (1994) ....Amy Hightower
The Unspoken Truth (1995) .... Brianne Hawkins

TV:

Caroline in the City (1995-) .... Caroline

Thompson, Teri

Films:

Almost Dead (1993) ....Restaurant Woman #2

Married People, Single Sex (1993)................ Meg
- • 0:33—Right breast after having phone sex with Artie.
- • 0:55—Nude, while talking with Artie on the phone.
- •• 1:18—Breasts and buns when Artie pushes her off him and she puts on robe.

Breakaway (1995) .... Myra Styles
- •• 0:34—Brief breasts, while sitting down in bathtub.
- •• 1:19—Buns and breasts while making love with Dan.

Thompson, Victoria

Films:

The Harrad Experiment (1973) .... Beth Hillyer
- • 0:08—Buns, in the bathroom while talking to Harry.
- • 0:10—Brief breasts getting into bed.
- •• 0:21—Breasts in nude encounter group.
- • 0:41—Breasts getting into the swimming pool with Don Johnson and Laurie Walters.
- • 0:49—Buns, getting dressed after making love with Johnson.

The Harrad Summer (1974) .... Beth Hillyer
a.k.a. Student Union
- •• 0:57—Buns and brief breasts running down hallway and jumping into bed, pretending to be asleep.
- • 1:03—Buns, lying on inflatable lounge in the pool.
- • 1:04—Buns, lying face down on lounge chair.

Famous T & A (1982) .... Beth Hillyer
(No longer available for purchase, check your video store for rental.)
- • 1:07—Brief breasts and bun scene from *The Harrad Experiment.*
- • 1:12—Brief nude, getting up from the floor with Don Johnson.

Thomsen, Martha *

Video Tapes:

Centerfold (1980)............................ Herself
- • 0:00—Full frontal nudity in still photos.
- • 0:06—Breasts, after taking off sweater in make-up room.
- •• 0:11—Breasts, while walking to get some lingerie.
- ••• 0:12—Full frontal nudity, while getting dressed in sheer white panties, garter belt, stockings and sheer white robe in make-up room.
- ••• 0:16—In lingerie, then full frontal nudity, while posing in studio for photos.
- ••• 0:25—Nude, while posing for photos in studio. Long scene.
- ••• 0:33—Nude, while posing some more.
- ••• 0:38—Breasts, while getting made up.
- •• 0:42—Full frontal nudity after taking off her pants and putting on a robe.
- ••• 0:44—Nude, while posing with for photos with Kathleen Sands. Very long scene.

Thomson, Anna

a.k.a. Anna Levine Thomson.

Films:

The Pope of Greenwich Village (1984)
............................Waitress at Country Inn
Desperately Seeking Susan (1985)................. Crystal
Maria's Lovers (1985) .... Kathy
Murphy's Romance (1985) .... Wanda
At Close Range (1986)................. Barroom Dancer
Something Wild (1986)...................... The Girl in 3F
Bird (1988) .... Audrey
Leonard, Part 6 (1988) .... Nurse Carvalho
Talk Radio (1988) ....Woman at Basketball Game

White Hot (1988) .... Heather
a.k.a. Crack In the Mirror
- ••• 0:04—In bra, then breasts when undressing for drug dealer in exchange for cocaine.

Warlock (1990) .... Pastor's Wife
Criss Cross (1992) .... Monica
Unforgiven (1992).................... Delilah Fitzgerald
The Crow (1993)................................ Darla
True Romance (1993) .... Lucy
(Unrated version reviewed.)

Hand Gun (1994) .... Laura
- •• 0:48—Upper half of left breast, while lying in bed after Seymour Cassel gets up out of bed.

Outside the Law (1994)........................ Tanya
a.k.a. Blood Run
(Unrated version reviewed.)
- • 0:32—Buns under water in pool and getting out. Partial breasts while putting on robe in front of David Bradley.
- ••• 0:33—Breasts, while making love with Bradley on counter of bar. Nice, but some of it is her, and some is a body double.
- • 0:49—In white bra, then breasts and buns, while making love with Bradley. Don't see her face, it looks like a body double.

Angus (1995) .... April Thomas
Bad Boys (1995) .... Francine

I Shot Andy Warhol (1996)........................ Iris
- • 0:39—Breasts in B&W film.

Made for Cable Movies:

Dead In the Water (1991) .... Edie Meyers
Cafe Society (1995; Showtime) .... Erica Steele

Drunks (1995; Showtime) .... Tanya
- ••• 0:47—In bra and panties, then breasts, while making out with Richard Lewis in bedroom.

Thomson, Kim

Films:

The Lords of Discipline (1983)................. Girlfriend
Party Party (1983; British) .... Brenda

Stealing Heaven (1988; British/Yugoslavian)........ Heloise
- • 0:42—Side of left breast kneeling on floor with steam. Long shot.
- •• 0:43—Closer view of left breast.
- ••• 0:47—Breasts and very brief lower frontal nudity lying in bed with Abelard. More left breast afterwards.
- • 1:07—Nude, left side view on top of Abelard in bed. Long shot.

Thorn, Frankie

Films:

Lisa (1989) .... Judy

Bad Lieutenant (1992)........................... Nun
- • 0:17—Very brief lower frontal nudity, while getting raped by two guys in church.
- •• 0:26—Full frontal nudity while lying on hospital bed during examination.

Liquid Dreams (1992) .... Paula
(Unrated version reviewed.)

Bad Blood (1993) .... Rhonda
- •• 0:52—Breasts, while making love with Lorenzo Lamas.

Thorne, Dyanne

Films:

Point of Terror (1971) .... Andrea

Ilsa, She Wolf of the S.S. (1974)................... Ilsa
- •• 0:00—Buns, then breasts making love in bed.

••• 0:01—Breasts taking a shower.
••• 0:29—Buns and breasts in bed with Wolfe.
•• 0:32—Right breast several times in bed with Wolfe.
••• 0:48—In white bra, then breasts undressing for Wolfe.
•• 0:50—Right breast, while lying in bed.

Chesty Anderson, U.S. Navy (1975) . . . . Nurse
Ilsa, Harem Keeper of the Oil Sheiks (1976) . . . . Ilsa
Ilsa, The Wicked Warden (1980) . . . . Ilsa
a.k.a. Ilsa—Absolute Power
a.k.a. Greta, The Mad Butcher.
Ilsa—Absolute Power is about 4 minutes shorter.
Hellhole (1985) . . . . Chrysta
Real Men (1987) . . . . Dad

Thornton, Ann

Films:
Eureka (1983; British) . . . . Jane (red dress)
• 1:17—Brief breasts during African voodoo ceremony.
Hope and Glory (1987; British) . . . . Honeymoon Wife

Thornton, Sigrid

Films:
The Day After Halloween (1978; Australian) . . . . Angela
a.k.a. Snapshot
• 0:04—Very brief breasts in ad photos on wall.
•• 0:19—Breasts during modeling session at the beach.
••• 0:21—More breasts at the beach.
•• 0:37—Breasts in magazine ad several times.
• 0:43—Brief right breast in magazine ad.
• 0:46—Breasts in ad again.
• 1:18—Entering room covered with the ad.
The Man from Snowy River (1982; Australian). . . . . Jessica
Great Expectations (1987; Australian) . . . . Bridget
Slate, Wyn & Me (1987; Australian) . . . . Blanche/Max
The Lighthorsemen (1988; Australian). . . . . Anne
Return to Snowy River (1988) . . . . Jessica
Over the Hill (1991; Australian) . . . . Elizabeth
Trapped in Space (1994) . . . . Isaacs
Made for Cable Movies:
All the Rivers Run (1984; HBO) . . . . Philadelphia
TV:
Paradise (1989-90) . . . . Amelia Lawson
Guns of Paradise (1991) . . . . Amelia Lawson

Thorsen, Laura

See: Hays, Lauren.

Thorson, Linda

Films:
Valentino (1977; British). . . . . Billie Streeter
• 0:14—Brief left breast, under a guy in bed.
The Greek Tycoon (1978) . . . . Angela
Curtains (1983; Canadian) . . . . Brooke Parsons
Flanagan (1985) . . . . Andrea
Sweet Liberty (1986). . . . . Grace
TV:
One Life to Live . . . . Julia Medina
The Avengers (1968-69) . . . . Tara King
Marblehead Manor (1987-88). . . . . Hilary Stonehill

• Throw, Lisa M.

Films:
Tender Loving Care (1993). . . . . Stacy
••• 0:06—Breasts, sleeping, waking up, then taking a shower.
Video Tapes:
Playboy's Real Couples 2: Best Sex Ever (1997)
. . . . Photography

Thulin, Ingrid

Films:
Brink of Life (1957; Swedish). . . . . Cecila
Wild Strawberries (1957; Swedish) . . . . Marianne Borg
The Magician (1959). . . . . Manda Aman
The Four Horsemen of the Apocalypse (1962)
. . . . Marquerite Laurier
The Winter Light (1963; Swedish) . . . . Marta Lundberg
Hour of the Wolf (1968; Swedish) . . . . Veronica Vogler
The Damned (1969; German). . . . . Sophie Von Essenbeck
•• 1:23—Breasts in bed with Dirk Bogarde. Long scene for a 1969 film.
• 2:03—Left breast in bed with Martin (her son in the film).
Cries and Whispers (1972; Swedish) . . . . Karin
a.k.a. Viskingar Och Rop
•• 0:57—Breasts and buns, undressing and getting ready for bed. Something covers lower frontal nudity.
Moses (1976; British/Italian) . . . . Miriam
After the Rehearsal (1984; Swedish). . . . . Rakel
• 0:33—Brief breasts, when pulling up her sweater to show Henrik how beautiful her breasts still look.

Thurman, Uma *

Ex-wife of actor Gary Oldman.
Films:
Kiss Daddy Goodnight (1987). . . . . Laura
Dangerous Liaisons (1988) . . . . Cécile de Volanges
••• 0:59—Breasts taking off her nightgown in her bedroom with John Malkovich.
Johnny Be Good (1988). Georgia Elkans
The Adventures of Baron Munchausen (1989; British/German)
. . . . Venus/Rose
• 1:14—Brief upper half of right breast when the flying ladies wrap her with the flowing cloth.
Henry & June (1990). . . . . June Miller
Where the Heart Is (1990) . . . . Daphne McBain
• 0:08—Breasts during art film, but her entire body is artfully painted to match the background paintings. The second segment.
• 0:40—More breasts with body painted posing for her sister. Long shot.
• 1:16—In slide of painting taken at 0:40.
• 1:43—Same painting from 0:40 during the end credits.
Final Analysis (1992) . . . . Diana Baylor
Jennifer 8 (1992). . . . . Helena
0:50—Body double did nude scene in bathroom.
Mad Dog and Glory (1993) . . . . Glory
•• 0:56—Left breast, while in bed with Robert De Niro.
• 0:58—Very brief breasts when De Niro gets off her.
Even Cowgirls Get the Blues (1994). . . . . Sissy Hankshaw
Pulp Fiction (1994) . . . . Mia Wallace
Beautiful Girls (1996). . . . . Andera
The Truth About Cats and Dogs (1996). . . . . Noelle
Batman & Robin (1997) . . . . Poison Ivy/Dr. Pamela Isley
Gattaca (1997) . . . . Irene Cassini
Les Miserables (1998) . . . . Fantine
Made for TV Movies:
Robin Hood (1991) . . . . Maid Marian

Tia

Video Tapes:
Mermaid's Illustrated . . . . n.a.

The Best of the Mermaids (1992) . . . . Sand and Lace
- ••• 1:12—Breasts and buns in G-string on boat, at the beach and while scuba diving.

Mermaids of the Aztec Empire (1992) . . . . . . Mona Brock
- •• 0:01—Breasts during opening credits.
- ••• 0:02—Breasts and buns in G-string at the beach during opening credits.
- •• 0:06—Breasts outside with Lori Pallett by pool and under water.
- •• 0:10—In bra and panties, then breasts in jewelry store fantasy.
- • 0:11—Buns, in swimsuit, by the pool.
- • 0:13—Brief buns, while turning over in the spa.
- ••• 0:14—Breasts and buns in G-string bottom on boat.
- ••• 0:23—Breasts and buns at the beach. Long scene.
- ••• 0:31—Breasts and buns in G-string while snorkeling under water.
- ••• 0:37—Breasts and buns at the beach again.
- ••• 0:49—Breasts and buns in swimsuit bottoms undressing at the beach during the end credits.

Mermaids of Sand, Sea and Surf (1993) . . . . n.a.

Ticotin, Rachel

Ex-wife of actor David Caruso.

Films:

Fort Apache, The Bronx (1981) . . . . Isabelle
- • 1:25—Brief upper half of breasts in bathtub while Paul Newman pours bubble bath in.

Critical Condition (1987). . . . . Rachel
Total Recall (1990) . . . . Melina
FX 2 (1991). . . . . Kim Brandon
One Good Cop (1991) . . . . Grace
Where The Day Takes You (1992) . . . . Officer Landers
Criminal Passion (1993). . . . . Uncredited Tracy Perry
Falling Down (1993) . . . . Sandra
Don Juan DeMarco (1994) . . . . Doña Inez
- 0:21—Buns, when standing in bathroom while brushing her hair looks like a body double.

Steal Big, Steal Little (1995). . . . . Laura Martinez
Turbulence (1996). . . . . Rachel Taper
Con Air (1997) . . . . Sally Bishop

Made for Cable Movies:

Prison Stories, Women on the Inside (1990; HBO). . . . . Iris
- 0:07—Brief buns, squatting while getting strip searched in jail. Don't see her face.

Keep the Change (1992; TNT) . . . . Astrid
Deconstructing Sarah (1994; USA) . . . . Elizabeth Davis
The Wharf Rat (1995; Showtime) . . . . Dexter Ireland
First Time Felon (1997; HBO) . . . . McBride

Made for TV Movies:

Spies, Lies & Naked Thighs (1988) . . . . Sonia
From the Files of Joseph Wambaugh: A Jury of One (1992) . . . . Christine Avila
Thicker Than Blood: The Larry McLinden Story (1994) . . . . n.a.

TV:

For Love and Honor (1983) . . . . Cpl. Grace Pavlik
Ohara (1987-88). . . . . Teresa Storm
Crime & Punishment (1993) . . . . Annette Rey

Tierney, Maura

Films:

Dead Women In Lingerie (1991) . . . . Molly Field
- • 1:03—Brief left breast while sleeping in bed.
- • 1:09—Very brief left breast, while rolling over in bed on top of Nick.
- • 1:20—Very brief lower half of right breast when falling back onto bed with Nick. Slightly different take from 1:09.

The Linguini Incident (1991) . . . . Cecelia
Fly By Night (1992) . . . . Denise
White Sands (1992) . . . . Noreen
The Temp (1993). . . . . Sharon Derns
Mercy (1995). . . . . Simonet
Primal Fear (1996) . . . . Naomi Chance
Liar, Liar (1997) . . . . Audrey Reede
Primary Colors (1998) . . . . Daisy

Made for TV Movies:

Crossing the Mob (1988) . . . . Michelle
Out of Darkness (1994) . . . . Meg

TV:

The Van Dyke Show (1988) . . . . Jillian Ryan
704 Hauser (1993-94) . . . . Cherlyn
NewsRadio (1995-). . . . . Lisa

Tilly, Jennifer *

Sister of actress Meg Tilly.

Films:

No Small Affair (1984). . . . . Mona
Moving Violations (1985) . . . . Amy Hopkins
He's My Girl (1987) . . . . Lisa
Remote Control (1987) . . . . Allegra
High Spirits (1988; U.S./British) . . . . Miranda
Johnny Be Good (1988). Connie Hisler
Rented Lips (1988) . . . . Mona Lisa
The Fabulous Baker Boys (1989) . . . . Monica Moran
Far From Home (1989) . . . . Amy
Let It Ride (1989). . . . . Vicki
At Home with the Webbers (1992) . . . . Miranda Webber
Scorchers (1992) . . . . Talbot

Shadow of the Wolf (1992). . . . . Iglyook
- • 0:21—Very brief right breast under Lou Diamond Phillips.
- • 0:22—Very, very brief left breast when Phillips is on top of her and holds her arms down.
- •• 1:27—Very brief breasts, after taking off her clothes, then making love with Phillips.

The Getaway (1993). . . . . Fran Carvey
(Unrated version reviewed.)
- •• 1:12—Breasts and buns while making love on top of Michael Madsen in bed while her husband is tied to chair in bathroom.

Heads (1993). . . . . Tina Abbot

Made in America (1993) . . . . Stacy
- • 0:13—Very, very brief back side of left breast, when jumping up out of bed. Brief buns and very, very brief back side of left breast while doing cartwheels into the bathroom. Possible body double.

Bullets Over Broadway (1994) . . . . Olive Neal
Double Cross (1994) . . . . Melissa
Embrace of the Vampire (1994). . . . . Marika
(Unrated version reviewed.)
Man With a Gun (1994) . . . . Rena Rushton/Kathy Payne
Bird of Prey (1995) . . . . Kily Griffith
American Strays (1996) . . . . Patty Mae

Bound (1996). . . . . Violet
- •• 0:19—Brief buns and brief right breast, while making love with Gina Gershon.

Edie & Pen (1996) . . . . Edie
House Arrest (1996). . . . . Cindy Figler
The Pompatus of Love (1996) . . . . Tarzaan
Liar, Liar (1997) . . . . Samantha Cole

Made for Cable TV:

Dream On: What Women Want (1992; HBO) . . . . Ryan

Made for TV Movies:
Bella Mafia (1997)............................Moyra
TV:
Shaping Up (1984)....................Shannon Winters
Key West (1993)............................ Savannah

Tilly, Meg

Sister of actress Jennifer Tilly.
Films:
Fame (1980)........................... Principal Dancer
Tex (1982)...............................Jamie Collins
The Big Chill (1983)........................... Chloé
One Dark Night (1983)............................Julie
Psycho II (1983)..................................Mary
Impulse (1984)....................................Jenny
Agnes of God (1985)......................Sister Agnes
Off Beat (1986).........................Rachel Wareham
Masquerade (1988)......................Olivia Lawrence
The Girl in a Swing (1989; U.S./British)........Karin Foster
•• 0:44—In white bra, then breasts and buns.
•• 0:50—Nude, while swimming under water.
••• 1:14—Breasts while sitting on swing, then making love.
••• 1:44—Breasts while at the beach.
Valmont (1989)................................ Tourvel
The Two Jakes (1990)....................Kitty Berman
Leaving Normal (1992)...................... Marianne
Body Snatchers (1994)................... Carol Malone
Sleep With Me (1994)............................Sarah
Made for Cable Movies:
Primal Secrets (1994)....................Faith Crowell
Made for Cable TV:
Nightmare Classics: Carmilla (1989; HBO) .... Carmilla
Fallen Angels: Dead-End for Delia (1993; Showtime)
.... Lois Weldon
(Available on the video tape *Fallen Angels Two.*)
Made for TV Movies:
In the Best Interest of the Child (1990) .... Jennifer Colton
Journey (1995).....................................Min
TV:
Winnetaka Road (1994)......................... George

Timmins, Cali

Films:
Spacehunter: Adventures in the Forbidden Zone (1983) . . Nova
The Hotel New Hampshire (1984)............... Bitty Tuck
Hard Evidence (1994) ....Dina Davis
• 0:07—In lingerie, then breasts while making love with Gregory Harrison.
•• 0:20—In lingerie, while posing for Harrison when he takes photos of her, then breasts, when making love in bed.
The Takeover (1994) .... Kathy
• 1:12—Brief left breast, several times, while making love in bed with Jonathan.
The Heist (1996).......................Janice Simmons
Made for Cable TV:
Rin Tin Tin K-9 Cop (1988-89; Family) .... Maggie Davenport
Fast Track: Combustion (1997; Showtime) ...Samantha Cleary

*Ting, Chan **

Video Tapes:
Playboy International Playmates (1993) .... Ting
••• 0:00—Full frontal nudity, on sofa, caressing herself.
••• 0:02—Breasts in still photos.
••• 0:03—Full frontal nudity outside with statue.
•• 0:22—Breasts in restaurant with another woman during food fight.
••• 0:53—Nude, stripping and dancing in basement during interrogation fantasy.

Tippo, Patti

Films:
10 to Midnight (1983).........................Party Girl
•• 0:52—Breasts, making love with a guy in the laundry room at a party.
Omega Syndrome (1986)........................... Sally
Sid and Nancy (1986; British) ......Tanned and Sultry Blonde
Brain Dead (1989)............................. Resident
Roadside Prophets (1992).................. Casino Cashier
Freaked (1993)........................ Rosie the Pinhead
Ed Wood (1994)..................................... Nurse
Ace Ventura: When Nature Calls (1995)......... Mom Tourist
Barb Wire (1995)...................................... Mom
(Unrated version reviewed.)
Made for Cable Movies:
Dangerous Heart (1994; USA)............... Policewoman
TV:
Sledge Hammer! (1987-88)..................Officer Daley

Todd, Trisha

Films:
Claire of the Moon (1992).............. Claire Jabrowski
•• 0:21—Side of right breast, while making love in bed on top of a guy she picked up in a bar.
••• 0:24—Breasts, while getting a cigarette when in bed after making love with the guy.
•• 0:28—Breasts, after taking off top in kitchen in front of Noel.
••• 1:39—Breasts, while making love in bed with Noel. Long scene.
Moments... The Making of Claire of the Moon (1992)
.... Claire Jabrowski
•• 0:28—Breasts, while straddling Noel in bed.
•• 0:44—Breasts, several times in outtakes not seen in the film, taking off her sweater after bumping into Noel.

Tolan, Kathleen

Films:
Death Wish (1974)........................ Carol Toby
• 0:09—Brief breasts and buns getting raped by three punks.
The Line (1982)..Janie
The Rosary Murders (1987)............... Sister Ann Vania

*Tolo, Marilu **

Films:
The Oldest Profession (1967)............"Anticipation"
• 1:23—Brief side view of left breast, while walking to the bathroom. Shown as a negative image, so it's hard to see.
Confessions of a Police Captain (1971) .... Serena Li Puma
Bluebeard (1972)..................................Brigitt
• 1:25—Breasts in sheer blue blouse arguing with Richard Burton.
•• 1:27—Breasts getting whipped by Burton.
Beyond Fear (1975)................................Nicole
The Greek Tycoon (1978) .... Sophia Matalas
•• 0:26—Nude, getting out of bed and fighting with Anthony Quinn.

*Tomasina, Jeana **

Films:
History of the World, Part I (1981)............. Vestal Virgin
Looker (1981).. Suzy
Lovely But Deadly (1981) ....Woman with Stuck Zipper

The Beach Girls (1982) . . . . Ducky
•• 0:12—Breasts and buns, lying on the beach with Ginger, while a guy looks through a telescope.
••• 0:54—Breasts on a sailboat with a guy.
• 0:55—Brief breasts on the beach after being "saved" after falling off the boat.
•• 1:12—Breasts in sauna with Ginger and an older guy.
Off the Wall (1982) . . . . Mrs. Buck Banner
Six Pack (1982) . . . . .Lonnie
10 to Midnight (1983) . . . . Karen
Double Exposure (1983) . . . . Renee
• 0:20—Very brief glimpse of left breast under water in swimming pool.
Up the Creek (1984) . . . . Molly
Music Videos:
Gimme All Your Loving/Z.Z. Top . . . . Girl
Legs/Z.Z. Top . . . . Legs Girl
Sharp Dressed Man/Z.Z. Top. . . . . Girl in White
Video Tapes:
Playboy's Playmate Workout . . . . .Playmate
Playboy Video Magazine, Volume 2 (1983)
. . . . .Herself/Playboy Playoffs
Playboy Video Magazine, Volume 5 (1983) . . . . .Playmate
• 0:06—Brief breasts on piano.
• 0:12—Breasts, then full frontal nudity posing on piano.
Playboy Video Centerfold: Reneé Tenison (1990)
. . . . Portrait of a Photographer: Richard Fegley
•• 0:34—Full frontal nudity, posing on piano for centerfold photo.

• Tomita, Tamlyn

Films:
The Karate Kid, Part II (1986) . . . . Kumiko
Come See the Paradise (1990). . . . . Lily Kawamura
The Joy Luck Club (1993) . . . . .Waverly
Four Rooms (1995) . . . . Wife
Picture Bride (1995) . . . . Kana
The Killing Jar (1996). . . . . Diane Sanford
•• 0:29—Brief buns, then breasts, while lying in bed, then making love with her husband.
Touch (1996) . . . . .Prosecutor
Made for TV Movies:
Hiroshima: Out of the Ashes (1990). . . . . Sally
Babylon 5 (1993) . . . . .Laurel Takashima
Vanishing Son II (1994) . . . . .Lanchi
Vanishing Son IV (1994) . . . . .Lanchi
TV:
Santa Barbara (1984) . . . . .Ming Li
Sisters (1995-96). . . . . .Kiri Adams
The Burning Zone (1996-97). . . . . Dr. Kimberly Shiroma

Tomlin, Melanie

Films:
Rich Girl (1991). . . . . Diana
• 0:03—Half of left breast, while in bed with Jeffrey.
• 0:04—Almost side of left breast again, while looking for her keys.
Traces of Red (1992) . . . . Amanda

Tompkins, Angel *

Films:
Hang Your Hat on the Wind (1969). . . . . .Fran Harper
I Love My Wife (1970) . . . . Helene Donnelly
Prime Cut (1972) . . . . Clarabelle
• 1:03—Very brief left breast sitting up in bed to talk to Lee Marvin.
• 1:04—Very brief back side view of left breast, while jumping out of bed.
The Don is Dead (1973) . . . . .Ruby
How to Seduce a Woman (1973). . . . . Pamela
The Teacher (1974). . . . . Diane Marshall
••• 0:09—Breasts on a boat taking off her swimsuit.
••• 0:12—More breasts on the boat getting a suntan.
••• 0:36—Breasts taking off her top in bedroom, then buns and breasts taking a shower.
• 0:41—Brief right breast lying back on bed.
•• 0:43—Brief breasts opening her bathrobe for Jay North.
•• 0:47—Side view of right breast lying on bed, then right breast from above.
•• 0:52—Breasts in boat after making love.
Walking Tall, Part II (1975). . . . . Marganne Stilson
The Farmer (1977). . . . . .Betty
The Bees (1978) . . . . Sandra Miller
One Man Jury (1978). . . . . Kitty
Alligator (1980) . . . . News Reporter
The Naked Cage (1985) . . . . .Diane Wallace
•• 0:22—In lingerie, then breasts with Abbey.
• 0:38—Brief right breast, in bed with Abbey.
Dangerously Close (1986) . . . . Mrs. Waters
Murphy's Law (1986) . . . . Jan
• 0:19—Breasts doing a strip routine on stage while Charles Bronson watches.
• 0:27—Brief breasts doing another routine.
Amazon Women on the Moon (1987) . . . . First Lady
A Tiger's Tale (1988) . . . . La Vonne
Crack House (1989). . . . . .Mother
Relentless (1989) . . . . Carmen
Made for Cable TV:
The Hitchhiker: Homebodies (HBO) . . . . Janet O'Mell
TV:
Search (1972-73). . . . . Gloria Harding

Toothman, Lisa

Films:
American Drive-In (1984) . . . . Featuring
Hard Rock Zombies (1985) . . . . .Elsa
• 0:01—Buns, undressing to go skinny dipping. Breasts long shot.
••• 0:32—Buns, while getting into the shower. Breasts and buns in the shower behind clear plastic curtain.
RollerBlade Warriors: Taken By Force (1988)
. . . . Slave Girl #1
•• 0:21—Breasts after getting her top ripped off by two guys.
••• 0:23—Breasts, while walking through the desert.
The Girl I Want (1990). . . . . Girl 2
Witchcraft III: The Kiss of Death (1991) . . . . Charlotte
•• 1:02—Buns and breasts in shower with Louis while William has a bad dream.
•• 1:12—Left breast, while on bed with Louis, against her will.
Eyes of the Serpent (1992). . . . . Neema

Torday, Terry

Films:
Julia (1974; German) . . . . Yvonne
• 0:08—Brief right breast, while making love in train restroom.
•• 0:18—Breasts, while in bed with Ralph. Dark, hard to see.
• 0:37—Breasts, while getting up to put swimsuit on.
• 0:41—Brief breasts, while getting dressed in bedroom with Ralph.
•• 0:57—Full frontal nudity in bedroom seducing Patrick.

•• 1:01—Breasts, while sitting up in bed eating breakfast with Patrick.

Hanna's War (1988) .... Baroness Hatvany

Torek, Denise

Films:

New York's Finest (1988)...................... Hooker #2

Sensations (1988)...................... Phone Girl #2

• 0:23—Breasts talking on the phone sex line.

Torena, Lyllah

Films:

Fly Me (1973)................................ Sherry

The Boob Tube (1975)................... Natalie Nolan

••• 0:28—Breasts, putting on her blouse.

• 0:42—Breasts, getting raped by three Hell's Angel guys outside during flashback.

•• 0:45—Breasts and buns, on bed, taking off her clothes with Dr. Carstairs.

••• 0:46—Breasts and buns, while making love with Dr. Carstairs in bed. Nice buns shot. More breasts after making love.

•• 0:48—Breasts and buns, while making love in bed with Gretchen.

•• 1:08—Left breast, while in front of Sid when her robe is pulled down by Gretchen.

• 1:10—Breasts on sofa with Gretchen.

••• 1:12—Breasts during orgy on couch.

• 1:16—Brief breasts in hallway.

Torres, Samantha *

Made for Cable Movies:

Gia (1998; HBO)........................ Patty (Model)

Video Tapes:

Playboy's Hot Latin Ladies (1995)....... Samantha/Spain

••• 0:15—Nude, while posing in a living room.

Playboy Video Calendar 1997 (1996) .... April

••• 0:15—Nude, while posing outdoors.

••• 0:16—In lingerie and nude, while posing in bedroom.

Toscano, Gabriela

Films:

South (1988; Argentinian/French).................. Blondi

Satanic Attraction (1991; Italian) ....Fernanda

• 0:43—Partial left breast, making love with Lionel. Brief side view of left breast, eating fruit afterwards.

Totschek, Jasmine

Films:

Puppet Master III: Toulon's Revenge (1990) ... Prostitute

• 0:15—Breasts (she's on left), giving the General a bath.

Wild Child (1991)............................ Katrina

••• 0:51—Breasts, while making love with Johnny in bed. Nice, long scene.

Tough, Kelly *

Video Tapes:

Playboy's Playmate Review (1982) ....Playmate

••• 0:27—Nude, camping, then in bedroom setting.

Playmates at Play (1990) ....Making Waves

Playboy's 21 Playmates (1996) ....Playmate

••• 0:29—Nude in still photos.

••• 0:30—Nude in bedroom.

Toussaint, Beth

Films:

Berserker (1987)............................... Shelly

•• 0:40—Breasts, while making love on top of Mike in the woods. Nice close-up. Kind of foggy and dark.

•• 0:41—Side view of breasts, while making love on top of Mark.

•• 0:43—Nude, while getting up and getting dressed.

Blackmail (1991)............................Charlene

The Presence (1992)............................ Karen

Project Shadowchaser II (1994)..............Laurie Webber

a.k.a. Armed and Deadly

Made for Cable Movies:

Breach of Conduct (1994; USA)................Paula Waite

Made for TV Movies:

Jackie Collins' Lady Boss (1992)............... Venus Maria

TV:

Dallas (1988-89) .... Tracy Lawton

Savannah (1996-97) .... Veronica Koslowski

Townsend, K.C.

Films:

Husbands (1970)............................. Barmaid

Is There Sex After Death? (1975)

................Round Table Discussion/Woman on Table

•• 1:25—Full frontal nudity, while making love on table with a guy in front of a discussion group of men.

All That Jazz (1979) ....Stripper

• 0:20—Breasts backstage getting Joey excited before he goes on stage. Lit by red light.

Below the Belt (1980) .... Thalia

The Burning (1981)............................ Hooker

Townsend, Patrice

Films:

Sitting Ducks (1978) .... Jenny

••• 0:55—Breasts, taking off her blouse in room with Sid.

•• 0:58—Buns and brief left breast, sitting up in bed with Simon after getting seen by Leona.

Always (1984)................................... Judy

Tracy

See: Williams, K.C.

Trainor, Saxon

Films:

Scorchers (1992)............................... Renee

The Legend of Wolf Mountain (1993) .... Helen

Skeeter (1994).........................Dr. Jill Wylde

Made for Cable TV:

Dream On: Home Sweet Homeboy (1993; HBO)........Carol

Red Shoe Diaries: The Cake (1995; Showtime).......Abby

• 0:05—Brief breasts, in pulled up blouse in back of bakery. One long shot, two close ups.

• 0:18—Breasts, covered with frosting, while making love on table in bakery with Leonardo.

TV:

NYPD Blue: Head Case (Feb 27, 1996) ....n.a.

NYPD Blue: He's Not Guilty, He's My Brother (May 21, 1996)

....n.a.

Video Tapes:

Inside Out 2 (1992) .... The Doctor

(Unrated version reviewed.)

• 0:52—Breasts in bed on top of Drake. B&W.

Tranelli, Deborah

Films:

Naked Vengeance (1985) .... Carla Harris
- • 0:25—In black bra, then breasts during gang rape.
- ••• 0:43—Nude, while walking into the water to seduce a guy before killing him.

Made for TV Movies:

Mistress (1987) .... Clerk

TV:

Dallas (1989-90) .... Phyllis

Trapp, Robin

Films:

Look Who's Talking Too (1990) .... Cool Chick

South Beach (1992) .... Casey

a.k.a. Night Caller
- ••• 0:59—Buns, while making love with Fred Williamson. Nice close-up of breasts.

Exit (1995) .... News Reporter

Travis, Kylie

Films:

Eyes of the Beholder (1992) .... Holly Brandon
- •• 1:08—Left breast, then breasts after taking her dress top down in front of Janice.

Retroactive (1997) .... Karen

Sanctuary (1997) .... Rachel Malcolm

Made for Cable Movies:

Gia (1998; HBO) .... Stephanie

TV:

Models Inc. (1994-95) .... Julie Dante

Central Park West (1995) .... Rachel Dennis

CPW (1996) .... Rachel Dennis

Travis, Lara

Films:

Empire Records (1995) .... Veronica

Made for Cable TV:

Love Street: See Me (1995; Showtime) .... Marsha
- • 0:01—Buns while wearing panties, doing stuff around the house.
- • 0:05—In red bra, panties and stockings. Buns in panties.
- ••• 0:21—Breasts, while making love with Michael in bed.

Travis, Nancy

Films:

Three Men and a Baby (1987) .... Sylvia

Married to the Mob (1988) .... Karen Lutnick
- •• 0:15—Very brief breasts, when getting out of bed. Buns and brief side view of right breast, with Dean Stockwell in hotel room. Breasts in the bathtub.

Air America (1990) .... Corinne Landreaux

Internal Affairs (1990) .... Kathleen Avila
- • 0:38—Side view of left breast when Raymond opens the shower door to talk to her.

Loose Cannons (1990) .... Riva

Three Men and a Little Lady (1990) .... Sylvia

Chaplin (1992; British/U.S.) .... Joan Barry

Passed Away (1992) .... Cassie Slocombe

Greedy (1993) .... Robin

So, I Married an Axe Murderer (1993) .... Harriet Michaels

The Vanishing (1993) .... Rita Baker

Fluke (1994) .... Carol Johnson

Destiny Turns on the Radio (1995) .... Lucille

Bogus (1996) .... Lorraine

Made for Cable Movies:

Body Language (1995; HBO) .... T.J. Harlow

Made for Cable TV:

Fallen Angels: The Frightening Frammis (1993) . . . Bette Allison (Available on the video tape *Fallen Angels One.*)

Directed By: Lieberman in Love (1995; Showtime) .... Kate

Made for TV Movies:

Malice in Wonderland (1985) .... n.a.

TV:

Almost Perfect (1995-96) .... Kim Cooper

Travis, Stacey

Films:

Deadly Dreams (1988) .... Librarian

Phantasm II (1988) .... Jeri

Dr. Hackenstein (1989) .... Melanie Victor

Earth Girls are Easy (1989) .... Tammy

Hardware (1990) .... Jill
- • 0:21—Almost breasts in shower. Brief left breast in bed with Moses. Lit with blue light.
- • 0:38—Brief breasts in bedroom seen by a guy through telescope. Infrared-looking effect.

The Super (1991) .... Heather

Dracula Rising (1992) .... Theresa
- •• 0:44—Breasts, while on rocks in front of waterfall with Christopher Atkins. Long shot, then closer shot. Nude under water, sometimes with another woman, sometimes with Atkins.

Caroline at Midnight (1993) .... Christine Jenkins

Only the Strong (1993) .... Dianna

Playing God (1997) .... Nurse

Made for Cable Movies:

Attack of the 5' 2" Women (1994; Showtime) .... Christy

Suspect Device (1995; Showtime) .... Jessica

Made for Cable TV:

Dream On: Home is Where the Cart Is (1995; HBO) . . . Lisbett

Traylor, Susan

Films:

Bright Lights, Big City (1988) .... Leather Lady

Bail Jumper (1989) .... Lawyer

The Bodyguard (1992) .... Dress Designer

A River Runs Through It (1992) .... Rawhide
- • 1:17—Buns, sleeping in the woods with Neal. Don't see her face.

The New Age (1994) .... Ellen Saltonstall

Sleep With Me (1994) .... Deborah

Heat (1995) .... Elaine Cheritto

Lord of Illusions (1995) .... Marueen Pimm (Unrated version reviewed.)

To Die For (1995) .... Faye Stone

Father's Day (1997) .... Flight Attendant

Made for Cable Movies:

Bastard Out of Carolina (1996; Showtime) .... Alma

Don't Look Back (1996; HBO) .... Open Door Girl

Treas, Terri

Films:

All That Jazz (1979) .... Fan Dancer

The Best Little Whorehouse in Texas (1982) .... Chicken Ranch Girl

The Nest (1987) .... Dr. Morgan Hubbard

Deathstalker III: The Warriors From Hell (1988) .... Camlearde

The Terror Within (1988) .... Linda

The Fabulous Baker Boys (1989) . . . . Girl in Bed
• 0:00—Brief upper half of right breast when sheet falls down when she leans over in bed.
Frankenstein Unbound (1990). . . . . Computer Voice
House IV (1991) . . . . Kelly Cobb
Rage and Honor (1992) . . . . Rita Carlson
Yankee Zulu (1993). . . . . Rowena
Made for Cable Movies:
Ladykiller (1996; Showtime) . . . . Capt. Lorraine Hanover
Made for TV Movies:
Alien Nation: Dark Horizon (1994) . . . . Cathy Frankel
Alien Nation: Body and Soul (1995) . . . . Cathy Frankel
Alien Nation: The Enemy Within (1996) . . . . Cathy Frankel
Alien Nation: The Udara Legacy (1997). . . . . Cathy Frankel
TV:
Seven Brides for Seven Brothers (1982-83)
. . . . Hannah McFadden
Alien Nation (1989-91). . . . . Cathy Frankel
D.E.A. (1991) . . . . Ellen Brunner

Trego, Lisa

See: De Leeuw, Lisa.

• Trentham, Barbara

Films:
The Possession of Joel Delaney (1972) . . . . . . Sherry Talbot
• 0:32—Brief right breast, several times, while making love under Perry King.
Made for TV Movies:
Deathmoon (1978). . . . . Diane May

Trentini, Peggy *

Films:
Young Doctors in Love (1982) . . . . Christmas Elf
•• 0:55—Brief breasts greeting visitors to the party.
• 0:57—Breasts again sitting on couch.
Up the Creek (1984) . . . . Co-Ed
• 1:25—Left breast, in cabin with James B. Sikking.
• 1:27—Breasts, while in room with Sikking before mud slide hits the cabin.
Ghoulies IV (1993) . . . . Monica
Demon Knight (1994) . . . . Amanda
• 0:01—Brief buns in black bra and panties.
•• 0:02—Breasts, while in the bathtub in film within a film.
Demolition High (1995) . . . . Blonde Reporter
Vice Girls (1995). . . . . Top Popper
• 0:41—Brief breasts, when taking off her black dress top while talking with a guy at party.
Virtual Combat (1995) . . . . Debbie
•• 0:09—Full frontal nudity getting out of bubble bath during a guy's virtual reality session.
Virtual Desire (1995) . . . . Beth
••• 0:41—Stripping on office table, in black lingerie outfit, then breasts and buns in panties.
The Assault (1996) . . . . Bambi
Human Desires (1996). . . . . Julia
•• 0:11—Breasts and buns, while in bed with Zoe.
• 0:16—Brief buns, while floating dead in pool.
•• 0:37—Breasts and buns, while in bed with Peter.
•• 0:57—Breasts and buns, while making love in bed with Miles.
Made for Cable Movies:
Vampirella (1996; Showtime). . . . . Vampire Girl #1
• 0:51—Breasts, while lying on sofa and pulling her top down to distract Adam.

Made for Cable TV:
Erotic Confessions: Lessons (1996; Cinemax) . . . . Cora
(Available on video tape in *Erotic Confessions, Volume 2: Intrigue.*)
• 0:00—Brief full frontal nudity, while sunbathing on lounge chair.
• 0:04—Buns in swimsuit, while learning how to swim.
••• 0:06—Breasts, while making love with Jimmy in swimming pool.
••• 0:08—Nude, while in spa by herself and being "rescued" by Jimmy.
••• 0:10—Breasts, while making love with Jimmy in swimming pool.
Hot Line: Shutterbugs (1996; Cinemax) . . . . Kelly
• 0:18—Brief buns in black outfit.
••• 0:20—Nude, while posing on bed with Monique Parent when Jack photographs them.
Beverly Hills Bordello: Teach Me (1998; Showtime)
. . . . Elaine Robbins
••• 0:00—Full frontal nudity, while rubbing lotion on herself and masturbating.
•• 0:03—Breasts, while attempting to make love in bed with her husband.
••• 0:19—Breasts and buns, while making love with Ashlie Rhey, then her husband.

Trickey, Paula

Films:
Maniac Cop 2 (1990) . . . . Cheryl
•• 0:41—In orange two piece swimsuit on stage, then breasts and buns in G-string.
Carnal Crimes (1991) . . . . Jasmine
A Kiss Goodnight (1994). . . . . Natalie Collins
• 0:37—Brief breasts and buns in T-back under sheer nightgown.
Made for Cable Movies:
Black Scorpion (1995; Showtime) . . . . Leslie Vance
Made for Cable TV:
Dream On: Futile Attraction (1991; HBO). . . . . Janice
•• 0:02—Breasts sitting in bed with Martin.
Sessions: Episode 3 (1991; HBO) . . . . Fantasy Woman
Pacific Blue (1996- ; USA) . . . . Cory McNamara
Miniseries:
Trade Winds (1993). . . . . Lisa Topping

Trigger, Sarah

Films:
Kid (1990). . . . . Kate
Bill and Ted's Bogus Journey (1991). . . . . Joanna
Grand Canyon (1991) . . . . Vanessa
Paradise (1991). . . . . Darlene
• 0:14—Brief breasts ironing her clothes in open window while Willard and Billie watch from their tree house. Long shot after. Hard to see her face.
Pet Sematary II (1992). . . . . Marjorie Hargrove
Deadfall (1993). . . . . Diane
••• 0:42—In white bra and panties, after taking off dress in motel room with Michael Biehn. Breasts, while making love with him.
• 0:44—Right breast, while lying in bed with Biehn when he changes positions and the covers move.
•• 0:45—Breasts, while wearing white panties, leaving bed and getting dressed.

Don't Do It (1994) . . . . .Alicia
- 0:12—Very brief buns in swimsuit bottom, when her dress flies up when she rolls over on top of James Marshall at the beach.
- 1:02—Very, very brief left breast in gaping blouse when sitting up after leaning on Marshall.

PCU (1994) . . . . Samantha
Destiny Turns on the Radio (1995) . . . . Francine
Good Luck (1996) . . . . .Heidi
Things to Do in Denver When You're Dead (1996) . . . . . . Meg
Made for Cable Movies:
Fellow Traveller (1989; HBO). . . . . Gloria
- •• 0:02—Breasts, when sitting up in bed, stretching, then getting out.

Made for TV Movies:
Original Sins (1995) . . . . .Laura
Too Close to Home (1997) . . . . .Abby
TV:
EZ Streets (1996-97) . . . . Elli Rooney

Trilling, Zoe

a.k.a. Geri Betzler.
Films:
Fear (1988) . . . . Jennifer Haden
The Borrower (1989). . . . . Astrid
Nervous Ticks (1991) . . . . Marci
- •• 0:24—Brief breasts in shower when Bill Pullman opens the shower curtains.

Dr. Giggles (1992). . . . . .Normi
To Protect and Serve (1992). . . . . Beverly
- 0:24—Breasts in bed with a guy. Lit with strobe light.

Hellbound (1993) . . . . Hooker
- 0:18—Very brief back half of left breast while in the shower.

Tobe Hooper's Night Terrors (1993) . . . . Genie
- ••• 0:35—Buns and breasts, while making love with Mahmoud.
- •• 0:37—In bra, then breasts, when Mahmoud makes love with her on bed.
- 1:04—Buns, several times, while lying in bed with Sabina.

Night of the Demons 2 (1994) .Shirley
Leprechaun 3 (1995). . . . . .Uncredited Shirley
Sunchaser (1996) . . . . Mini-Mart Cashier
Made for Cable Movies:
Last Exit to Earth (1996; Showtime). . . . . Goldfinger
Made for TV Movies:
Children of the Night (1985). . . . . Melody

• *Trintignant, Marie*

Daughter of actor Jean-Louis Trintignant.
Films:
Story of Women (1988; French) . . . . Lulu/Lucie
Wings of Fame (1990; Dutch) . . . . .Bianca
- 1:10—Very brief partial buns, while making love in Colin Firth's lap.
- •• 1:11—Buns and lower frontal nudity, while walking around the room and talking with Firth.

Ponette (1996; French) . . . . Mother

Tripoldi, Idy

Films:
Auditions (1978). . . . . Bonnie Tirol
- ••• 1:01—Full frontal nudity, taking off sweater.
- •• 1:07—Breasts and buns during orgy scene.

Fairytales (1979). . . . . Naked Girl
- ••• 0:06—Nude, dancing in bedroom and getting in and out of bed with The Prince.

Famous T & A (1982) . . . . Bonnie Tirol
(No longer available for purchase, check your video store for rental.)
- ••• 0:35—Full frontal nude scene from *Auditions.*

Tripplehorn, Jeanne

Films:
Basic Instinct (1992). Dr. Beth Garner
(Unrated Director's cut reviewed.)
- ••• 0:35—Briefly in bra, then breasts with Michael Douglas in her apartment. Buns when he rips her panties off.
- ••• 0:37—Breasts, sitting up, then getting up off the floor.

The Firm (1993) . . . . Abby McDeere
The Night We Never Met (1993). Pastel
Reality Bites (1994) . . . . Uncredited
Waterworld (1995) . . . . Helen
(Buns scene is done by a body double.)
'Til There was You (1997) .Gwen Moss
Made for TV Movies:
The Perfect Tribute (1991). . . . . Julia
William Faulkner's Old Man (1997) . . . . Addie

Tristan, Dorothy

Films:
End of the Road (1969) . . . . Renny Morgan
Klute (1971) . . . . Arlyn Page
Scarecrow (1973) . . . . Coley
Man on a Swing (1974). . . . . .Janet
Swashbuckler (1976) . . . . Alice
California Dreaming (1978) . . . . Fay
- 0:20—Brief breasts changing clothes while a group of boys peek through a hole in the wall.

Truchon, Isabelle

Films:
Backstab (1990) . . . . .Jennifer
- •• 0:08—In bra, then breasts in back seat of car with James Brolin. Don't see her face very well.
- 0:16—Buns, black panties and stockings while on the floor with Brolin. Brief right breast.
- 0:18—Brief buns in front of fireplace. Side view of right breast. Buns, while walking into the other room.

Jesus of Montreal (1990; French/Canadian)
. . . . Richard's Girlfriend
If Looks Could Kill (1991). . . . . 1st Class Stewardess
a.k.a. Teen Agent
Deadbolt (1992) . . . . Linda

Trucksess, Kristen

Films:
Alien from L.A. (1988) . . . . .n.a.
Checking Out (1989). . . . . Stewardess
Peephole (1994) . . . . Sheena
- 0:16—Partial buns in panties, bra and garter belt while undressing in room in front of the Doctor.
- 0:17—Brief upper half of right breast, when raising her hands to wrap a shawl around herself.
- 0:40—Brief partial buns in panties in hiked up T-shirt.
- 0:45—Partial buns, while making out with a guy on the bed. Medium long shot.
- ••• 0:56—Buns and breasts, after getting out of bed and talking to the Doctor.

Theodore Rex (1995). . . . . Reporter #3
Made for TV Movies:
Murder Between Friends (1994) . . . . .n.a.

Truesdale, Teresa

Films:

Killer Workout (1987) . . . . Rachel

a.k.a. Aerobi-Cide

- 0:12—Brief left breast, dead, sliding down in shower. Covered with blood.
- 0:16—Very brief left breast, when she falls out of locker. Breasts, while getting zipped into a body bag.

Made for Cable Movies:

Bitter Vengeance (1994; USA) . . . . Kate

As Good As Dead (1995; USA) . . . . Young Nurse

Trumbo, Karen

Films:

Claire of the Moon (1992) . . . . Dr. Noel Benedict

- 1:22—Very brief left breast, twice, in open jacket in restroom with her fantasy woman, then Claire.
- ••• 1:39—Breasts, while making love on bed with Claire. Long scene.

Moments... The Making of Claire of the Moon (1992) . . . . Dr. Noel Benedict

- 0:28—Breasts, with Claire in bed.

Hear No Evil (1993). . . . . Nadine Brock

Made for Cable Movies:

The Last Innocent Man (1987; HBO). . . . Officer Marge Hersch

Body Language (1992; USA) . . . . Optician's Assistant

Made for TV Movies:

Child in the Night (1990) . . . . Julia Florl

Trzepiechinska, Joanna

Films:

Paper Marriage (1993) . . . . Alicja Straikowska

- 0:41—Very brief breasts, under short top when she raises her arms to hold up tipping armoire. Very brief underside of right breast, while kneeling on the floor to prop up the armoire.

Beyond Forgiveness (1994). . . . . Anna

a.k.a. Blood of the Innocent

- •• 1:09—In white bra, then right breast, while making love with Thomas Ian Griffith.

Tsopei, Corinna

Films:

Valley of the Dolls (1967) . . . . Telephone Girl

The Sweet Ride (1968) . . . . Tennis Girl

(Not available on video tape.)

A Man Called Horse (1970). . . . . Running Deer

- 1:03—Long shot of buns, before entering sweat house. Side view of left breast kneeling inside the sweat house.
- 1:15—Very brief breasts when startled by Richard Harris' screaming.
- 1:22—Left nipple while in tepee with Harris.
- 1:23—Side of left breast and right breast in tepee with Harris.

Tucek, Sarabeth

Films:

Flatliners (1990) . . . . One of Joe's Women

Midnight Edition (1993) . . . . Becky Gallagher

- 0:15—Breasts, after Darryl pushes her back onto the bed and points a gun at her.

Tucker, Kendra

Films:

Danger Zone III: Steel Horse War (1991) . . . . n.a.

Trained to Fight (1992) . . . . Kimberly

The Surgeon (1995; German/U.S.) . . . . TV Nurse (Soap Opera)

a.k.a. Exquisite Tenderness

Made for Cable TV:

Love Street: Grading on a Curve (1995; Showtime) . . . . Amelia Stratford

- 0:01—Breasts and buns, while bathing and getting dressed.
- ••• 0:15—Nude, while making love with Lloyd in the shower, then on the bed.
- •• 0:16—Brief breasts while making love with Lloyd on kitchen table and in front of fireplace.
- ••• 0:20—Nude while bathing Lloyd in bathroom, then making love on bed.

• Tunie, Tamara

Films:

Sweet Lorraine (1987) . . . . Julie

Wall Street (1987) . . . . Carolyn

Bloodhounds of Broadway (1989) . . . . Cynthia Harris

Rising Sun (1993) . . . . Lauren

City Hall (1996). . . . . Leslie Christos

Spirit Lost (1996). . . . . Anne

Devil's Advocate (1997). . . . . Jackie Heath

- ••• 0:56—In black bra, then breasts while changing clothes in a store.

The Peacemaker (1997). . . . . Jody

Made for Cable Movies:

Rebound (1996; HBO). . . . . Miss Marcus

TV:

NYPD Blue (1994-) . . . . Lillian Fancy

Tunney, Robin

Films:

Encino Man (1992) . . . . Ella

Empire Records (1995) . . . . Debra

The Craft (1996) . . . . Sarah

Montana (1998) . . . . Kitty

Niagara, Niagara (1998) . . . . Marcy

Made for Cable Movies:

Frogs! (1992; Disney) . . . . Hannah

Riders of the Purple Sage (1996; TNT). . . . . Bess

Made for Cable TV:

Dream On: Silent Night, Holy Cow (1993; HBO) . . . . Marybeth

- 0:35—Very, very brief right breast, while lying down on the floor next to Jeremy.

Made for TV Movies:

JFK: Reckless Youth (1993). . . . . Kathleen Kennedy

TV:

Class of '96 (1993) . . . . Linda Miller

Cutters (1993). . . . . Deborah Hart

• Turner, Guinevere

Films:

Go Fish (1994). . . . . Max

- 1:09—Very, very brief partial buns, while sleeping, when Ely covers her with a blanket.
- 1:19—Very, very brief partial right breast, while lying on top of Ely, during the end credits.

Chasing Amy (1997) . . . . Singer

Turner, Janine

Films:

Young Doctors in Love (1982). Cameo

Tai-Pan (1986). . . . . Shevaun

Monkey Shines: An Experiment in Fear (1988) . . . . Linda Aikman
- 0:01—Side view of buns, while lying in bed when Jason Beghe wakes up. Don't really see anything.

Steel Magnolias (1989) . . . . Nancy Beth Marmillion
The Ambulance (1990) . . . . Cheryl
Cliffhanger (1993). . . . . Jessie Deighan
Leave It to Beaver (1997). . . . . June Cleaver

Made for TV Movies:
Stolen Women, Captured Hearts (1997) . . . . Anna Morgan

TV:
Behind the Screen (1981) . . . . Janie-Claire Willow
General Hospital (1982-83) . . . . Laura Templeton
Northern Exposure (1990-95) . . . . Maggie O'Connell

Turner, Kathleen

Films:

Body Heat (1981) . . . . Maddy Walker
- 0:22—Brief side view of left breast in bed with William Hurt.
- •• 0:24—Breasts in a shack with Hurt.
- 0:32—Buns, while getting dressed. Long shot, hard to see.
- 0:54—Brief left breast in bathtub. Long shot, hard to see.

The Man with Two Brains (1983). . . . . Dolores Benedict
- 0:08—Right breast when Steve Martin is operating on her in the operating room.
- 0:36—Buns, in hotel room with a guy about to squeeze her buns when Steve Martin walks in.

Crimes of Passion (1984). . . . . Joanna Crane/China Blue
(Unrated version reviewed.)
- ••• 0:45—Breasts, wearing black panties and stockings, in bed with Bobby. Shadows of them making love on the wall.
- 1:00—Right breast in back of a limousine with a rich couple.
- 1:27—Right breast in bed with Bobby.

Romancing the Stone (1984) . . . . Joan Wilder
The Jewel of the Nile (1985) . . . . Joan Wilder

Prizzi's Honor (1985) . . . . Irene Walker
- 0:30—Very brief left breast making love with Jack Nicholson on bed.

Peggy Sue Got Married (1986) . . . . Peggy Sue

Julia and Julia (1987; Italian) . . . . Julia
(This movie was shot using a high-definition video system and then transferred to film.)
- ••• 0:32—Breasts making love in bed with her husband.
- ••• 1:08—Breasts, then right breast making love in bed with Sting.

The Accidental Tourist (1988) . . . . Sarah
Switching Channels (1988) . . . . Christy

The War of the Roses (1989) . . . . Barbara Rose
- 0:08—Very brief left breast, while lying in bed with Douglas and she moves the sheets.
- 0:33—Very, very brief lower frontal nudity, after squeezing Douglas' waist with her legs in bed.

V. I. Warshawski (1991) Vic
House of Cards (1993) . . . . Ruth Matthews
Naked in New York (1993) . . . . Dana
Serial Mom (1993) . . . . Mom
Undercover Blues (1993). . . . . Jane Blue
Moonlight and Valentino (1995) . . . . Alberta Russell
A Simple Wish (1997) . . . . Claudia
The Real Blonde (1998). . . . . Dee Dee

Made for Cable Movies:

A Breed Apart (1984; HBO) . . . . Stella Clayton
- •• 1:12—Breasts in bed with Rutger Hauer, then left breast.

Made for TV Movies:
Friends at Last (1995) . . . . Fanny Conlon

TV:
The Doctors (1978-79) . . . . Nola Aldrich Dancy

• Turner, Sharon

Films:

Sinful Intrigue (1995) . . . . Gorgeous Girl
- 0:37—Brief breasts in mirror, while applying lip gloss on another girl's lips. Buns in black T-back and breasts, while walking to, then sitting on the edge of bathtub.

Made for Cable TV:

Compromising Situations: The Elevator (1998; Showtime) . . . . Maid of Honor
- •• 0:07—Breasts and brief buns, while making love in bed with Emerson.

• Turner, Tiffany

Films:

Striptease (1996) . . . . Uncredited Dancer
(R-rated version reviewed.)

Bikini Summer 3 (1997). . . . . Devereaux
- ••• 0:22—Nude, with her two girlfriends in the shower, then getting dressed.
- •• 0:34—Breasts and buns in panties, while making out with her new boyfriend on the beach at night.
- ••• 0:40—Breasts, while trying on clothes in pro shop with her two girlfriends.
- ••• 0:58—Breasts, while making love in bed with Peter.

Video Tapes:

Playboy's Sorority Girls (1997) . . . . Yoga
- ••• 0:14—Nude, while doing yoga by herself.

Turpin, Bahni

Films:
Daughters of the Dust (1991) . . . . Iona Peazant
Malcolm X (1992) . . . . Follower at Temple #7
Getting In (1994) . . . . Valerie Bookbinder
Rain Without Thunder (1995) . . . . "Baby Bomb" Prisoner

Made for Cable Movies:

Rebel Highway: Girls in Prison (1994; Showtime) . . . Melba
- 0:23—Back side of left breast, while in the showers with Ione Skye.

Made for Cable TV:
Women: Stories of Passion-Grip Till It Hurts (1997; Showtime) . . . . n.a.

Tuscany *

a.k.a. Heather Tuscany, Christina Tuscany and Victoria King.

Films:

Angel of Passion (1991). . . . . Ellen
- ••• 0:36—Buns and breasts making love with a guy on a boat.

The Baby Doll Murders (1992) . . . . Young Woman
- ••• 0:34—Breasts in bedroom with the suspected killer, then on bed.

Real Fantasies (1992) . . . . The Woman
- •• 0:02—Breasts, while putting on lingerie.
- ••• 0:07—Breasts and buns in black stockings, garter belt and panties, while on piano with Jonathan during fantasy. Long scene.
- ••• 0:11—Breasts and buns in white bodysuit while on chair in another fantasy with Jonathan. Long scene.
- ••• 0:15—Breasts and buns, while making love with Jonathan outside in the spa. Long scene.

Video Tapes:
Bikini Blitz (1990) . . . . Model

Love Scenes: Volume 2 (1992) . . . . Suzanne Coooper
1:21—Sitting in lingerie in hotel room with Lisa.

•• 1:36—Nude, while swimming under water with David, Tom and Lisa.
••• 1:38—Full frontal nudity, while on boat with David and Tom, then during food fight with ice cream and chocolate.
••• 1:45—Nude, during orgy on boat with David, Tom and Lisa.

Soft Bodies: Squeeze Play (1993). . . . . Victoria King
••• 0:03—In bra and panties, then nude on bed.
••• 0:09—Breasts and buns in bathtub.
••• 0:15—Breasts and partial buns in cut-offs, while washing windows with Becky LeBeau.
••• 0:19—In T-shirt and cut-offs, then breasts and partial buns, while posing outside on stepladder.

Tweed, Shannon *

Sister of model/actress Tracy Tweed.
Significant other of Kiss singer/actor Gene Simmons.

Films:

Of Unknown Origin (1983; Canadian) . . . . Meg Hughes
• 0:00—Brief side view of right breast taking a shower.

Hot Dog... The Movie (1984) . . . . Sylvia Fonda
••• 0:42—Nude, while undressing, then making love in bed and in spa with Harkin.

The Surrogate (1984; Canadian) . . . . Lee Wake
••• 0:03—Breasts taking a Jacuzzi bath.
• 0:42—Brief breasts changing in bedroom, then in bra getting dressed. Long shot.
••• 1:02—Breasts in sauna talking with Frank. Long scene.

Meatballs III (1987). The Love Goddess

Steele Justice (1987) . . . . Angela

Cannibal Women in the Avocado Jungle of Death (1988) . . . . Dr. Margot Hunt

Lethal Woman (1988) . . . . Tory
••• 1:01—Breasts at the beach with Derek. Brief buns in white bikini bottom.

Code Name: Vengeance (1989) . . . . Sam

In the Cold of the Night (1989). . . . . Lena
• 0:02—Right breast while making love with Scott.

Night Visitor (1989) . . . . Lisa Grace

Last Call (1990). . . . . Cindy/Audrey
• 0:12—In black body stocking, dancing on stage. Breasts and buns in G-string underneath.
•• 0:29—Right breast, on the floor with William Katt.
•• 0:39—Brief buns, rotating in chair with Katt. Breasts leaning against column.
• 0:40—Breasts on stair railing.
• 1:01—Left breast, while leaning against column and kissing Katt.
• 1:02—Left breast in bed with Katt.
••• 1:05—Breasts making love on roof with Katt.

The Last Hour (1990). . . . . Susan
a.k.a. Concrete War
•• 0:05—Breasts in bed, making love with Eric.
• 0:07—Brief buns and side of left breast, in the shower.

Twisted Justice (1990). . . . . Hinkle

Firing Line (1991). . . . . Sandra Spencer
• 0:49—Sort of buns and breasts, seen through water while she's skinny dipping in water.
• 0:59—Very, very brief side view of right breast, when turning over onto Reb Brown while on rocks. Medium long shot.

Liar's Edge (1991) . . . . Heather Burnz

Night Eyes 2 (1991) . . . . Marilyn Mejenes
••• 0:49—Buns and breasts making love with Andrew Stevens in bed.
••• 1:06—Breasts, making love with Stevens (nice use of raspberries).

The Naked Truth (1992) . . . . First Class Stewardess

Sexual Response (1992). . . . . Eve
(Unrated version reviewed.)
••• 0:25—Breasts in studio with Edge, while he checks her out.
••• 0:29—Breasts, making love with him. Long scene.
••• 0:31—Full frontal nudity, lying in bed, then sitting up.
••• 0:43—Breasts, while making love in her house with Edge.
•• 0:51—Breasts in pool at night with Edge.
•• 0:52—Full frontal nudity, getting up out of bed and putting robe on.
•• 0:55—Breasts in study with Edge.
••• 1:07—Breasts and buns, while taking a shower. Nude, getting out and drying herself off.

Cold Sweat (1993) . . . . Beth Moore
••• 0:14—Breasts squished against the glass shower door while making out with Sean. More breasts and buns.
0:15—In bra, while sitting on bed.
•• 0:17—Breasts and buns while playing with fluorescent paints with Adam Baldwin in bathtub. Kind of dark.
••• 0:43—Breasts and very brief lower frontal nudity while on bed with Sean.
•• 0:53—Buns and back side of left breast getting into bathtub. More breasts, twice, while in bathtub.

Indecent Behavior (1993) . . . . Rebecca Mathis
(Unrated version reviewed.)
• 0:12—Breasts seen through water in spa. Brief buns, getting out of spa.
•• 0:56—Breasts while making love with Gary Hudson.
••• 1:24—In bra and panties, then breasts and buns, while making love in observation room with Nick.
• 1:26—Breasts, while getting out of bed.

Night Eyes 3 (1993) . . . . Zoe Clairmont
•• 0:16—Breasts, while getting her clothes ripped off by Dan, then sitting up in bed.
• 0:23—Brief full frontal nudity in shower behind the door.
••• 0:51—Breasts and buns, while making love in bed with Andrew Stevens.
• 0:53—Buns, while lying in bed afterwards.
••• 0:56—Nude, while getting into the shower and in the shower.
••• 1:01—Full frontal nudity, while taking off her robe in front of fireplace.
•• 1:02—Partial buns and breasts, while on top of Stevens.
• 1:15—Brief breasts in B&W photo from security video tape.

Possessed by the Night (1993) . . . . Carol McKay
•• 0:42—Breasts, while wiping off her sweat with the tank top.
••• 0:45—In bra on bed with Ted Prior, then breasts and brief lower frontal nudity, while making love with him.

Scorned (1993) . . . . Patricia Langley/Amanda Chessfield
•• 0:50—Breasts, after taking off bra with Robey, then in bed.
•• 0:59—Left breast and buns, while making love on top of Robey in bed.
•• 1:19—In bra, then breasts, while making love on bed with Robey.

The Dark Dancer (1994) . . . . Dr. Margaret Simpson
••• 0:25—Breasts, while dancing on stage in club wearing a mask.
• 0:28—Left breast, after making love in bed with her boyfriend.
• 0:56—Breasts and buns, after taking off robe and getting into bed with Ron. Long shot, dark.
• 1:00—Left breast, while getting into the shower with Ron.

• 1:18—Breasts and buns, while in bedroom with Ron. Dark.

Hard Vice (1994). . . . . Andrea

•• 0:44—Breasts after taking off her top in front of Sam Jones.

Illicit Dreams (1994) . . . . .Moira Davis

•• 0:11—Breasts, while making love with Andrews Stevens in dream.

•• 0:34—Breasts, while in dream with Stevens. Lit with red light.

••• 0:46—Breasts and buns, while making love with Stevens in a dream.

••• 1:01—Breasts and buns, while making love with Stevens in "real life."

• 1:07—Breasts, when tied by her wrists to the bed, while getting punished by Joe Cortese.

Indecent Behavior II (1994) . . . . Dr. Rebecca Mathis

(Unrated version reviewed.)

••• 0:24—Breasts, after taking off her bra, then taking a shower.

•• 0:55—Breasts and buns, while making love in bed with James Brolin.

•• 1:12—Side of right breast, then breasts, while in the shower.

• 1:13—Breasts, while in bed with Brolin.

Model By Day (1994) . . . . Shannon

(Shown on network TV without the nudity.)

• 0:42—Breasts, while letting the club owner feel her up before she beats him up.

Night Fire (1994) . . . . .Lydia

•• 0:16—Breasts, while tied and blindfolded on bed.

• 0:36—Breasts, while making love with John Laughlin.

• 1:27—Brief breasts in Polaroid photo. Brief breasts, while in the shower.

• 1:32—Brief breasts in gaping blouse after falling down.

No Contest (1994) . . . . Sharon Bell

Victim of Desire (1994) . . . . Carla Duvall

•• 0:21—In black lingerie outfit, then breasts, when changing clothes in bedroom while talking to Marc Singer.

••• 0:41—In white bra, then breasts and buns, while making love with Singer.

••• 0:52—Breasts and buns, while lying in bed after Singer sneaks back in the house, then making love.

Body Chemistry 4: Full Exposure (1995). . . . . Claire Archer

(Unrated version reviewed.)

• 0:21—Left breast on video tape playback.

•• 0:23—In bra, then left breast, then breasts while making love with Simon in parking garage.

••• 0:37—In blue bra, then nude, while making love with Simon next to and on top of pool table.

Electra (1995) . . . . Lorna Duncan/Electra

• 0:16—Breasts, while in bathtub after taking off her top.

Indecent Behavior 3 (1995) . . . . Dr. Rebecca Mathis

•• 0:56—Breasts, while making love with Frank in bed.

Human Desires (1996) . . . . Alicia Royale

••• 1:07—Breasts and buns, while in bedroom with Dean.

Made for Cable TV:

Hitchhiker: Videodate (HBO) . . . . .Monique

(Available on *The Hitchhiker, Volume 4.*)

The Hitchhiker: Doctor's Orders (1987; HBO) . . Dr. Rita de Roy

Hot Line (1994; Cinemax). . . . . Talk Show Host

Pacific Blue (1996; USA) . . . . .Sheila Silver

TV:

Falcon Crest (1982-83) . . . . Diana Hunter

Days of Our Lives (1985-86) . . . . Savannah Wilder

Fly By Night (1991). . . . . Sally "Slick" Monroe

The Tom Show (1997). . . . . .Maggie

Video Tapes:

Playboy Video Magazine, Volume 1 (1982)

. . . . Playmate of the Year

•• 0:02—Full frontal nudity, posing by bathtub for photo session.

••• 1:13—Nude, posing in bed.

••• 1:15—Full frontal nudity in photo session.

••• 1:21—Full frontal nudity in front of piano, in bathtub and in bed.

Playboy's Playmate Review (1982). . . . . .Playmate

••• 0:47—Nude in bed, then in photo shoot by a table, then by a piano, then in bathtub.

Playboy Video Magazine, Volume 5 (1983) . . . . .Playmate

• 0:05—Brief breasts in bathtub.

••• 0:13—Full frontal nudity in bedroom set.

Playboy's Playmates of the Year: The '80s (1989)

. . . . Playmate of the Year 1982

••• 0:36—Full frontal nudity in photo session in a house.

••• 0:37—Nude in still photos. Nude posing by piano, in bathtub, in bed.

•• 0:51—Full frontal nudity standing by bed.

Playboy Video Centerfold: Reneé Tenison (1990)

. . . . Portrait of a Photographer: Richard Fegley

••• 0:36—Full frontal nudity, posing by bed for centerfold photo.

Playboy's 21 Playmates (1996). . . . . .Playmate

••• 0:14—Nude in still photos.

••• 0:15—Nude in centerfold photo session.

Tweed, Tracy *

Sister of *Playboy* Playmate/actress Shannon Tweed.

Films:

Sunset Heat (1991). . . . . Lena

a.k.a. Midnight Heat

(Unrated version reviewed.)

••• 0:19—Breasts making love with Michael Paré. Nice, long scene.

••• 0:22—Breasts and buns, making love with Paré on stairs, sofa and the floor.

••• 0:24—Breasts, lying on the floor when the bad guys come in. Brief partial right breast, standing up and covering herself with a jacket.

Live Wire (1992) . . . . Rolls Royce Girl

(Unrated version reviewed.)

Night Rhythms (1992) . . . . .Honey

(Unrated version reviewed.)

••• 0:28—Breasts making love with Martin Hewitt in radio station. Nice, long scene.

••• 0:31—Nude, getting up after changing positions.

•• 0:33—Breasts, lying dead on the floor.

Night Eyes 3 (1993) . . . . Dana Gray

•• 0:25—Left breast, then breasts while in bed with Edgar.

••• 0:40—Breasts and side view of buns, while wearing black G-string panties in dressing room while nonchalantly talking to Andrew Stevens.

Johnny Mnemonic (1995) . . . . Pretty

Twiggy

Famous '60s model.

Real name is Lesley Hornby.

Wife of British actor Leigh Lawson.

Films:

The Boy Friend (1971; British) . . . . .Polly Browne

The Doctor and the Devils (1985) . . . . Jenny Bailey

Madame Sousatzka (1988) . . . . Jenny

Istanbul (1990) . . . . Maud

Made for Cable TV:

Tales From the Crypt: The New Arrival (1992; HBO) . . . Bonnie

John Carpenter's Body Bags (1993; Showtime) . . Eye/Cathy

• 1:20—Two very brief peeks of her crotch between Mark Hamill's legs while he is on top of her in bed. When she pushes him off her, she quickly pulls her nightgown down.

Made for TV Movies:

Something Borrowed, Something Blue (1997) . . . . n.a.

TV:

Princesses (1991) . . . . Georgy

Twomey, Anne

Films:

Refuge (1981) . . . . n.a.

The Imagemaker (1985) . . . . Molly Grainger

• 0:11—Very, very brief breasts, while reading newspaper in bedroom (wearing flesh colored tape over her nipples). Then in white bra and panties talking to a guy in bed.

Deadly Friend (1986) . . . . Jeannie Conway

Last Rites (1988) . . . . Zena Pace

Orpheus Descending (1990) . . . . Carol Cutrere

The Scout (1994) . . . . Jennifer

Made for TV Movies:

Bump in the Night (1991) . . . . Sarah

The Secret (1992) . . . . Dr. Meyers

Tydings, Alexandra

Films:

Sunchaser (1996) . . . . Victoria Reynolds

Made for Cable TV:

Red Shoe Diaries: Burning Up (1994; Showtime) . . . . Lynn

• 0:01—Brief breasts, twice, while floating on water during introduction.

• 0:06—Breasts, while floating on water again.

•• 0:07—Breasts and buns, during fantasy with the fireman.

••• 0:11—Breasts, while sleeping in bed, talking on the phone, then doing some deep breathing.

• 0:24—Breasts, while floating on the water.

• 0:25—In wet lingerie in water in her fantasy.

••• 0:26—Breasts and buns, during fantasy while making love with the fireman.

Red Shoe Diaries: Love at First Sight (1995; Showtime) . . . . Cecilia

• 0:02—Lower half of buns, while bending over to take her panties off in front of policeman outside.

• 0:03—Brief buns, when the policeman throws her against the fence and lifts her skirt.

•• 0:05—Breasts, while making love with Harry in the car. Breasts, after getting out of the car.

• 0:07—Brief glimpses of breasts under suit while dancing in the desert with Harry.

• 0:08—Buns and partial breast, while making love with Harry.

•• 0:10—Breasts, while making love again.

• 0:26—Breasts, while in bed with Harry and Precious. Many quick cuts.

TV:

Hercules: The Legendary Journeys (1996-) . . . . Aphrodite

Tyler, Liv

Model.

Daughter of Aerosmith's Steven Tyler and model/Playmate Bebe Buell (November 1974).

Films:

Silent Fall (1994) . . . . Sylvie Warden

Empire Records (1995) . . . . Corey

Heavy (1996) . . . . Callie

Stealing Beauty (1996) . . . . Lucy

•• 0:48—Brief right breast while reaching up in bathtub.

•• 1:02—Left breast, after pulling her dress aside, sitting next to tree.

• 1:48—Partial breasts, while making love with a guy.

• 1:51—Very brief partial crotch, while making love on the ground with the guy.

That Thing You Do! (1996) . . . . Faye Dolan

Inventing the Abbotts (1997) . . . . Pamela Abbott

U Turn (1997) . . . . Girl in Bus Station

Armageddon (1998) . . . . n.a.

Music Videos:

Crazy/Aerosmith (1994) . . . . n.a.

Tyler, Trixie

Adult film actress.

Video Tapes:

Hyapatia Lee Presents: Taking' It Off, Volume 1 (1993) . . . . Herself

•• 0:19—Partial buns, then breasts, while getting dressed in dressing room and talking to Hyapatia Lee.

••• 0:23—Nude, doing strip dance routine on stage in club. Long scene.

Tylo, Hunter

a.k.a. Deborah Morehart.

Spokesmodel for Pantene shampoo.

Wife of actor Michael Tylo.

Films:

The Initiation (1984) . . . . Alison

••• 0:33—Frontal nudity in shower, then getting out and drying herself off.

••• 0:57—Breasts, changing tops in sporting goods store in mall.

Final Cut (1986) . . . . Annie

TV:

All My Children (1985-87) . . . . Robin McCall

The Bold and the Beautiful (1990-) . . . . Taylor Hayes

Tylyn

See: John, Tylyn.

Tyrrell, Susan

Films:

Shoot Out (1971) . . . . Alma

• 0:13—Right breast, while in bed with Bobby Jay.

The Steagle (1971) . . . . Louise

• 0:48—Brief left breast twice, lying on bed with Richard Benjamin.

Fat City (1972) . . . . Oma

Zandy's Bride (1974) . . . . Maria Cordova

The Killer Inside Me (1975) . . . . Joyce Lakeland

•• 1:27—Very brief left breast, then very brief breasts (both breasts!) in bed with Stacy Keach during flashback scene.

Andy Warhol's Bad (1977; Italian) . . . . Mary Aiken

I Never Promised You a Rose Garden (1977) . . . . Lee

Islands in the Stream (1977) Lil

Loose Shoes (1977) . . . . Boobies

Forbidden Zone (1980) . . . . Queen Doris

•• 0:19—Left breast sticking out of dress, sitting on big dice with Herve Villechaize.

•• 1:02—Left breast sticking out of dress after fighting with the Ex-Queen.

Fast Walking (1981) . . . . Evie

Night Warning (1982) .... Cheryl Roberts
- • 0:17—Left breast, sticking out of dress just before she stabs the TV repairman.

Angel (1983) .... Solly Mosler
Tales of Ordinary Madness (1983; Italian) .... Vera
- • 0:19—Right nipple, seen in between strings in bra when she's lying on the floor.
- • 0:20—Upper half of breasts, in between strings in bra. Lower frontal nudity.
- •• 0:22—Lower frontal nudity and upper half of breasts in bra, while standing by the door. Brief buns, while getting carried to bed by Ben Gazzara.
- •• 0:23—Upper half of breasts, buns and lower frontal nudity while lying in bed.

Avenging Angel (1985) .... Solly Mosler
Flesh + Blood (1985) .... Celine
- • 1:35—Right breast sticking out of her dress when everybody throws their clothes into the fire.

The Offspring (1986) .... Beth Chandler
The Underachievers (1987) .... Mrs. Grant
Big Top Pee Wee (1988) .... Midge Montana
Far From Home (1989) .... Agnes Reed
- • 0:29—Very, very brief right breast in bathtub getting electrocuted.

Cry Baby (1990) .... Ramona
Rockula (1990) .... Chuck the Bartender
Motorama (1991) .... Bartender
Digital Man (1995) .... Town Woman
Powder (1995) .... Maxine
The Demolitionist (1996) .... Mayor Grimbaum
Poison Ivy 3: The New Seduction (1996) .... Mrs. B

Made for Cable TV:
The Hitchhiker: In the Name of Love (1987; HBO) .... Doris

Made for TV Movies:
Sidney Sheldon's Windmill of the Gods (1988) .... Neusa

TV:
Open All Night (1981-82) .... Gretchen Feester

Tyson, Cathy

Films:
Mona Lisa (1987; British) .... Simone
Business as Usual (1988; British) .... Josie Patterson
The Serpent and the Rainbow (1988)
.... Dr. Marielle Duchamp
- • 0:41—Brief breasts making love with Dennis. Probably a body double, don't see her face.

Made for Cable Movies:
Band of Gold: Parts 1 & 2 (1995; British; HBO)
.... Carol Johnson
- •• 0:19—Breasts, while bathing in bathtub, talking to Gina. In black bra and panties, while getting dressed.
- 1:22—Lower half of buns in lingerie, in hotel room with a customer.
- • 1:31—In black bra and panties in bathroom, brief buns in panties.
- • 1:32—Brief breasts, while in bathtub and jumping up when startled by the detective.

Udenio, Fabiana

Films:
Boarding School (1976; German) .... Gina
a.k.a. Virgin Campus
a.k.a. The Passion Flower Hotel
Hardbodies 2 (1986) .... Cleo/Princess
Summer School (1987) .... Anna-Maria
Bride of Re-Animator (1989) .... Francesca Danelli
Robocop 2 (1990) .... Sunblock Woman
Diplomatic Immunity (1991) .... Teresa
- •• 1:06—Breasts in panties, on the floor with her hands tied behind her back when Klaus rips her blouse open to photograph her.

In the Army Now (1994) .... Gabriella
Austin Powers: International Man of Mystery (1997)
.... Alotta Fagina

Made for TV Movies:
The Scarlet and the Black (1983) .... Guilia Lombardo
Journey to the Center of the Earth (1993) .... Sandy Miller

TV:
One Life to Live (1985-86) .... Gulietta
NYPD Blue: Don We Now Our Gay Apparel (Jan 3, 1995)
.... Ramona

Udy, Claudia

Films:
American Nightmare (1981; Canadian) .... Andrea
- ••• 0:08—Buns, then breasts dancing on stage.
- • 0:22—Buns getting into bathtub. Breasts during struggle with killer.

Joy (1983; French/Canadian) .... Joy
- •• 0:11—Nude, undressing, getting into bath then into and out of bed.
- ••• 0:14—Nude in bed with Marc.
- ••• 0:31—In swimsuits, posing for photos, then full frontal nudity.
- •• 0:54—Breasts sitting with Bruce at encounter group.
- • 1:04—Buns and breasts getting into bathtub.

Skullduggery (1983; Canadian) .... Dolly
Out of Control (1984) .... Tina
- • 0:28—In leopard bra and panties playing Strip Spin the Bottle, then very brief breasts taking off her top. Long shot.
- • 0:47—Brief left breast getting raped by bad guy on the boat.
- • 0:54—Brief left breast, then right breast making love with Cowboy.

Savage Dawn (1984) .... Katie Rand
Nightforce (1986) .... Christy Hanson
- •• 0:07—Breasts making love in the stable with Steve during her engagement party.
- ••• 0:10—Nude, fantasizing in the shower.

The Pink Chiquitas (1986; Canadian) .... Helen Walkman
Master of Dragonard Hill (1987) .... Arabella
- ••• 0:11—Nude, undressing to seduce Calabar. More breasts and buns while kissing him.
- •• 0:14—Silhouette of breasts while making love with Calabar, then breasts.
- • 0:58—Brief buns and side of right breast during flash back. Brief right breast when she gets out of bed.

Captive Rage (1988) .... Chiga
Dragonard (1988) .... Arabella
- •• 1:11—Breasts dressed as Cleopatra dancing a routine in front of a bunch of guys.

Edge of Sanity (1988) .... Liza
Any Man's Death (1989) .... Laura
Thieves of Fortune (1989) .... Marissa
To the Death (1991) .... Carol Quinn

Udy, Helene

Films:
Pick-Up Summer (1979; Canadian) .... Suzy
- • 0:34—Very, very brief breasts when the boys spray her and she jumps up.

Incubus (1981; Canadian) .... Sally Harper

My Bloody Valentine (1981; Canadian) . . . . Sylvia
One Night Only (1984; Canadian) . . . . Suzanne
a.k.a. For One Night Only
- 0:50—Buns and right breast in bed talking with a guy.
- 1:12—Over the shoulder, brief left breast on top of a guy in bed.

Nightflyers (1987). . . . . Lilly
Pin (1988) . . . . Marcia Bateman
- ••• 1:03—Breasts in bedroom with Leon.

Sweet Murder (1990). . . . . Lisa Smith
- •• 0:44—Brief buns, twice, while standing in doorway in Dell's apartment.
- •• 0:47—Breasts in bed while talking to Dell, then nude, getting out of bed while he's asleep.
- 0:48—Brief nude while stabbing Dell with a knife.
- 0:49—Buns and right breast while dragging Dell out of the bedroom.

Made for TV Movies:
Children of the Night (1985) . . . . Dallas
Toughlove (1985) . . . . Randa
The Hollywood Detective (1989). . . . . .Lois Wednesday
TV:
As the World Turns (1983). . . . . Frannie Hughes
Dr. Quinn, Medicine Woman (1993-). . . . . Myra Bing

Ullman, Tracey

Films:
Give My Regards to Broad Street (1984; British) . . . . . . Sandra
Plenty (1985) . . . . Alice Park
Jumpin' Jack Flash (1986) . . . . Fiona
I Love You to Death (1990) . . . . .Rosalie
Household Saints (1992). . . . . Catherine Falconetti
- 0:33—Brief left breast, while making love in bed with Vincent D'Onofrio. Don't see her face. Probably a body double.

Robin Hood: Men in Tights (1993) . . . . .Latrine
Bullets Over Broadway (1994). . . . . Eden Brent
I'll Do Anything (1994) . . . . Beth Hobbs
Ready to Wear (1994) . . . . Nina Scant
a.k.a. Prêt-à-porter
- 1:32—Brief buns in G-string panties, while leaving bedroom when Stephen Rea tries to take a photograph of her.

Made for Cable TV:
Tracey Takes On (1996; HBO) . . . . .Various Characters
TV:
The Tracey Ullman Show (1987-90) . . . . Host

Ullmann, Liv

Films:
Persona (1966; Swedish). . . . . .Elisabeth Vogler
Hour of the Wolf (1968; Swedish) . . . . .Alma Borg
Shame (1968; Swedish) .Eva Rosenberg
The Passion of Anna (1969; Swedish) . . . . .Anna Fromm
Cold Sweat (1970; Italian/French). . . . . Fabienne
The Night Visitor (1970; U.S./Swedish) . . . . Esther Jenks
Cries and Whispers (1972; Swedish) . . . . Maria
a.k.a. Viskingar Och Rop
40 Carats (1973). . . . . .Ann Stanley
Scenes from a Marriage (1973; Swedish). . . . . Marianne
Zandy's Bride (1974). . . . . Hannah Lund
A Bridge Too Far (1977; British). . . . . Kate ter Horst
The Serpent's Egg (1977; U.S./German) . . .Manuela Rosenberg
Autumn Sonata (1978; Swedish). . . . . Eva
Richard's Things (1980; British). Kate
- 0:12—Very, very brief left breast, while wrapping a towel around herself.

The Wild Duck (1983; Australian) . . . . Gina
Bay Boy (1985; Canadian). . . . . Jennie Campbell
Dangerous Moves (1985; Swiss) . . . . Marina
Gaby, A True Story (1987). . . . . Sari Brimmer
Mosca Addio (1987; Italian) . . . . Ida Nudel
The Rose Garden (1989; West German/U.S.)
. . . . Gabriele Schlueter-Freund
Mindwalk (1991). . . . . Sonia Hoffman

Ulrich, Kim

See: Johnston-Ulrich, Kim.

Unger, Deborah

Films:
Prisoners of the Sun (1990; Australian) . . . . Sister Littell
Till There Was You (1990; Australian). . . . . .Anna
Whispers in the Dark (1992) . . . . .Eve Abergray
- 0:14—Breasts during dream visualizations. Don't see her face.
- 0:24—Brief breasts during visualization by Sciorra. Don't see her face.
- 0:37—Brief breasts during Sciorra's dream.
- 0:38—Buns and side view of left breast, dead, while hanging by her neck.

Highlander III: The Final Dimension (1994) . . . Alex/Sarah
- •• 1:14—In black bra and panties, then nude while making love in bed with Christopher Lambert. Don't see her face very well. Nice buns shots.

Crash (1996; Canadian) . . . . Catherine Ballard
(NC-17 version reviewed.)
- 0:03—In bra, then partial right breast, brief partial lower frontal nudity and side of buns, while having sex with a guy in airplane hanger.
- 0:05—Brief buns through slit in dress, while on balcony, seen by James Spader.
- 0:13—Brief, partial lower frontal nudity under skirt when Spader touches her in hospital room.
- •• 0:43—Lower frontal nudity, while making love with Spader in bed. Long scene.
- •• 1:05—In bra, then right breast, while sitting in back of car with Elias Koteas while Spader is in the front seat.
- 1:07—Lower frontal nudity, while having rough sex with Koteas in back of car as it goes through a car wash with Spader in the front seat.
- •• 1:09—Lower frontal nudity, then partial right breast, when Spader examines her bruises.
- 1:35—Partial lower frontal nudity, when making love with Spader after her car crash. Medium long shot.

Keys to Tulsa (1996). . . . . Vicky Michaeels Stover
(Unrated version reviewed.)
- •• 1:16—In black bra and panties, then buns and lower frontal nudity while in bedroom with Eric Stoltz.

The Game (1997) . . . . Christine
Made for Cable Movies:
Hotel Room (1993; HBO) . . . . Getting Rid of Robert
State of Emergency (1993; HBO). . . . . Sue Payton

*Unverzagt, Tamara **

Video Tapes:
Playboy's College Girls (1994) . . . . Herself
- ••• 0:06—Nude while dancing in a deserted building and on a Harley.

Vaccaro, Brenda

Films:

Midnight Cowboy (1969) . . . . .Shirley
- • 1:30—Very, very brief out of focus left breast in open fur coat, lying down with Jon Voight.
- • 1:31—Very brief left breast when falling back onto bed with Voight.
- •• 1:32—Brief right breast, while rolling in bed with Voight.

I Love My Wife (1970). . . . . .Jody Burrows
Once is Not Enough (1975). . . . . .Linda
Airport '77 (1977). . . . . .Eve Clayton
House by the Lake (1977; Canadian). . . . . Diane
Breasts.
The First Deadly Sin (1980) . . . . Monica Gilbert
Chanel Solitaire (1981) . . . . .n.a.
Zorro, The Gay Blade (1981). Florinda
Supergirl (1984; British) . . . . .Bianca
Water (1986; British). . . . . .Bianca
Heart of Midnight (1988) . . . . Betty
Edgar Allan Poe's "The Masque of the Red Death" (1989) . . . . Elaina
Ten Little Indians (1989) . . . . Marion Marshall
Love Affair (1994) . . . . Nora Stillman
The Mirror Has Two Faces (1996) . . . . .Doris

Made for Cable Movies:

Red Shoe Diaries (1992; Showtime). . . . . Martha
(Unrated video tape version reviewed.)

Made for TV Movies:

Paper Dolls (1982) . . . . Julia Blake

TV:

Sara (1976) . . . . Sara Yarnell
Dear Detective (1979). . . . . . . Detective Sergeant Kate Hudson
Paper Dolls (1984) . . . . Julia Blake

Vaccaro, Tracy *

Films:

The Man Who Loved Women (1983) . . . . Legs
Candy The Stripper (1993) . . . . .Candy
- • 0:01—Very brief left breast, opening her blouse to flash a guy on the street.
- ••• 0:26—Breasts and buns in G-string, doing strip tease routine on stage.
- ••• 0:28—Breasts, while hiding behind bar with David after fight breaks out.
- •• 0:38—Breasts in open blouse, showing her breasts to David.
- ••• 0:46—Breasts, while wearing panties, while in bedroom with Larry.
- • 0:50—Wearing pasties, buns in G-string while posing for photographer.
- • 0:56—Left breast in open robe in bedroom with Larry.
- • 0:57—Breasts, while in bedroom, kissing Larry.
- • 1:01—Breasts and buns in flashback on the bar.
- ••• 1:11—Breasts, while making out with David.
- ••• 1:13—Breasts, while making out with David on the floor.
- •• 1:15—More breasts, while on the floor with David.
- ••• 1:28—Breasts and buns in G-string doing strip tease routine out of dress and lingerie.

Vail, Justina

Films:

Naked Souls (1995) . . . . Amelia
- •• 0:27—Breasts, after taking off robe in front of Brian Krause, then climbing into bed with him.

Carnosaur 3: Primal Species (1996) . . . . Proudfoot
Jerry Maguire (1996). . . . . Former Girlfriend
Kiss the Girls (1997). . . . . .Beautiful Girl

Made for TV Movies:

Journey to the Center of the Earth (1993) . . . . .n.a.

Vail, Lorin Jean

Films:

The Patriot (1986) . . . . Howard's Girl
Rest in Pieces (1987) . . . . .Helen Hewitt
- •• 0:15—Breasts in the bubble bath.
- • 0:17—Breasts hanging onto outside of tub after struggle.
- • 0:25—Brief breasts making love in bed with Bob during concert. Dark.
- • 0:26—Brief breasts lying under Bob in bed. Dark.
- • 0:30—Brief left breast, getting out of bed and putting on robe.
- • 0:58—Brief right breast, reaching around to put her right arm into sleeve of robe. Dark.
- •• 1:00—Breasts, getting robe taking off and pushed into swimming pool. More breasts under the water.
- • 1:01—More breasts in the swimming pool.
- • 1:05—Brief side view of left breast getting out of bed and putting on robe.

Valandrey, Charlotte

Films:

Red Kiss (1985; French). . . . . Nadia
- • 0:52—Very brief right breast, in bed with the photographer. Very dark.
- •• 1:21—Very brief right breast, then breasts with the photographer.

Orlando (1993; British) . . . . Sasha

Made for Cable Movies:

The House That Mary Bought (1994; Showtime). . Claire Benoit

Vale, Suzanne

Films:

Dreams of Desire (1981) . . . . Dress Shopgirl
Sex Appeal (1986). . . . . Audrey
- •• 0:00—Breasts, while on the couch making out with Tony.

Valen, Nancy

Films:

The Heavenly Kid (1985) . . . . Melissa
Porky's Revenge (1985; Canadian). . . . . Ginger
The Big Picture (1989). .Young Sharon
Listen to Me (1989) . . . . .Mia
- • 0:06—Very, very brief left breast in bed with Garson when Kirk Cameron first meets him.

Loverboy (1989) . . . . .Jenny Gordon
Final Embrace (1991). . . . . Candy Vale/Laurel Parrish

Made for TV Movies:

Perry Mason: The Case of the Fatal Framing (1992) . . . . .Mala Sikorski

TV:

Ryan's Hope. . . . . Melinda Weaver
Hull High (1990) . . . . Donna Breedlove
Baywatch (1996-97) . . . . .Capt. Samantha Thomas

Valk, Blair

Films:

Spirit of the Night (1994) . . . . Michelle
- • 0:20—In bra, then breasts, while making love with Alek on sofa while Tara watches.
- • 0:37—Full frontal nudity, after taking off her towel and climbing onto piano.

Executive Decision (1995) . . . . Yugoslavian Girl

Made for Cable Movies:

Dead Weekend (1995; Showtime) . . . . Amelia C
- • 0:28—Buns in T-back, then brief breasts, while making love in hotel room with Stephen Baldwin.
- 0:31—Very brief buns in T-back under skirt, while straddling Baldwin in bed.

*van Breeschooten, Karin **

Identical twin sister of Miryam van Breeschooten.

Video Tapes:

Playboy Video Calendar 1990 (1989) . . . . October
- ••• 0:51—Nude.

Playboy Video Centerfold: Dutch Twins (1989) . Playmate
- ••• 0:00—Nude throughout.

The Best of Video Playmate Calendars (1992) . . Playmate
- •• 0:27—In lingerie and nude in modeling session, then running around house with her twin sister. Quick cuts.
- ••• 0:28—Nude, in a house with her twin sister, posing, bathing and dressing.

*van Breeschooten, Miryam **

Identical twin sister of Karin van Breeschooten.

Video Tapes:

Playboy Video Calendar 1990 (1989) . . . . October
- ••• 0:51—Nude.

Playboy Video Centerfold: Dutch Twins (1989) . Playmate
- ••• 0:00—Nude throughout.

The Best of Video Playmate Calendars (1992) . . Playmate
- •• 0:27—In lingerie and nude in modeling session, then running around house with her twin sister. Quick cuts.
- ••• 0:28—Nude, in a house with her twin sister, posing, bathing and dressing.

Van De Ven, Monique

Films:

Turkish Delight (1974; Dutch). Olga
- •• 0:24—Breasts when Rutger Hauer opens her blouse, then nude on the bed.
- •• 0:27—Breasts, waking up in bed.
- ••• 0:33—Breasts on bed with Hauer, then nude getting up to fix flowers.
- • 0:42—Buns, with Hauer at the beach.
- •• 0:46—Breasts modeling for Hauer, then brief nude running around outside.
- •• 0:54—Breasts in bed with open blouse with flowers.
- • 1:04—In wet T-shirt in the rain with Hauer, then brief breasts coming down the stairs.

Keetje Tippel (1978; Dutch). . . . . Katie
a.k.a. Katie's Passion
(Dutch with English subtitles.)
- • 0:37—Brief buns when guy rips her panties off.
- •• 0:43—Breasts in hospital when a group of doctors examine her.
- • 0:48—Left breast a couple of times talking to a doctor. Brief buns sitting down.
- • 1:09—Brief buns, while getting into bed.
- • 1:11—Very brief left breast in bed with Rutger Hauer when he catches her eating his chocolate.
- ••• 1:15—Nude burning all her old clothes and getting into bathtub.

The Assault (1986; Dutch). . . . . . Truus Coster/Saskia de Graaff
Amsterdamned (1988; Dutch) . . . . .Laura
Lily Was Here (1989; Dutch) .Midwife
Paint It Black (1989) . . . . Kyla Leif

Van Kamp, Merete

Films:

The Osterman Weekend (1983) . . . . Zuna Brickman
- •• 0:01—Breasts and brief buns in bed on a TV monitor, then breasts getting injected by two intruders.
- • 0:35—Brief breasts on video again while Rutger Hauer watches in the kitchen on TV.
- • 1:30—Breasts again on video during TV show.

You Can't Hurry Love (1984). . . . . .Monique
Lethal Woman (1988) . . . . .Diana/Christine
- • 1:23—Very brief side view of left breast, reaching for towel after bath. Hard to see.

Poison Ivy 3: The New Seduction (1996). . . . . Catherine

Miniseries:

Princess Daisy (1983). . . . . Princess Daisy

TV:

Dallas (1985-86) . . . . Grace

*Van Laar, Diana **

Video Tapes:

Playboy International Playmates (1993) . . . . Diana
- ••• 0:08—Breasts in still photos.
- ••• 0:09—Nude, in S&M style segment.
- ••• 0:26—In white lingerie, then nude in schoolgirl fantasy.
- ••• 0:40—Breasts, while taking a bath.
- ••• 0:51—Breasts, taking off dress.

Van Patten, Joyce

Sister of actor Dick Van Patten.

Films:

I Love You, Alice B. Toklas (1968). . . . . .Joyce
Making It (1971) . . . . Betty Fuller
Housewife (1972) . . . . Bernadette
- • 0:46—Breasts and buns on pool table getting attacked by Yaphet Kotto. Probably a body double, don't see her face.
- • 1:05—Brief side of right breast under Kotto's arm several times after she falls on the floor with him.

Thumb Tripping (1972). . . . . Mother
Mame (1974) . . . . Sally Cato
The Bad News Bears (1976). Cleveland
The Falcon and the Snowman (1985) . . . . Mrs. Boyce
St. Elmo's Fire (1985). . . . . Mrs. Beamish
Billy Galvin (1986). . . . . Mae
Blind Date (1987) . . . . .Nadia's Mother
Monkey Shines: An Experiment in Fear (1988). . Dorothy Mann
Trust Me (1989) . . . . Nettie Brown

Made for TV Movies:

Breathing Lessons (1994) . . . . Serena
The Gift of Love (1994) . . . . .Erika Magnussen

TV:

As the World Turns (1956-57) . . . . Janice Turner Hughes
The Good Guys (1968-70). . . . . Claudia Gramus
Unhappily Ever After (1995-96). . . . . .Maureen

• *Van Tassel, Sabrina*

Films:

One Night Stand (1997) . . . . .Armani Model

Made for Cable TV:

Women: Stories of Passion-The Diamond Merchant (1997; Showtime) . . . . .Balthazar
- ••• 0:01—Breasts, undressing in front of a mirror and smearing paint on her lips and nipples.
- •• 0:16—Breasts, while dancing in front of Phillipe.
- •• 0:17—Breasts and buns in panties, while having sex with Phillips and two other women.

Van Tilborgh, Guusje

Films:

A Zed and Two Noughts (1985; British) . . . . Caterina Bolnes

• 0:42—Brief lower frontal nudity when Oliver lifts her skirt up in restroom to check to see what kind of panties she's wearing.

• 0:51—Lower frontal nudity, then very brief breasts while posing for photo by Van Meegeren.

Zjoek (1987; Dutch) . . . . Olga

Van Vooren, Monique

Films:

Tarzan and the She-Devil (1953) . . . . Lyra

Gigi (1958) . . . . Showgirl

Ash Wednesday (1973) . . . . German Woman

Sugar Cookies (1973) . . . . Helene

Andy Warhol's Frankenstein (1974; Italian/German/French) . . . . Katherine

•• 0:47—Breasts in bed with Nicholas. Brief lower frontal nudity twice when he rolls on top of her.

• 1:21—Left breast letting Sascha, the creature, caress her breast

• 1:26—Breasts, dead, when her breasts pop out of her blouse.

Wall Street (1987) . . . . Woman at "21"

Vander Woude, Teresa

Films:

Killer Workout (1987) . . . . Jaimy

a.k.a. Aerobi-Cide

•• 0:43—Breasts in locker room with Tommy during his nightmare.

Night Visitor (1989) . . . . Kelly Fremont

Vandernoot, Alexandra

Films:

Mascara (1987; French/Belgian) . . . . Euridice

Blood of the Hunter (1994) . . . . Marie Thoreau

• 1:03—Very brief back side of right breast, then brief side view of left breast while bathing herself when seen by Michael Biehn through hole he cuts in curtain.

Ready to Wear (1994) . . . . Sky TV Reporter

a.k.a. Prêt-à-porter

Made for Cable Movies:

Doomsday Gun (1994; HBO) . . . . Marie

Made for Cable TV:

Strangers: Windows (1992; HBO) . . . . The Woman

(Available on the video tape *Strangers.*)

•• 0:10—Breasts, making love with her lover while Timothy Hutton watches from across the street.

• 0:12—Right breast, while in bed struggling with her lover.

• 0:13—Right breast, while tied to bed when Hutton comes to rescue her.

• 0:14—Brief breasts while sitting on toilet.

TV:

Highlander: The Series (1992-93) . . . . Tessa Noel

• Vanickova, Darina *

Films:

Supermodel Invasion (1996) . . . . Model 2

•• 0:09—Brief breasts, while posing.

•• 0:34—Breasts, while lying by the pool.

Vanity *

Singer.

a.k.a. D. D. Winters.

Real name is Denise Matthews.

Sister of model Patricia Matthews.

Films:

Tanya's Island (1980; Canadian) . . . . Tanya

• 0:04—Very brief breasts and buns covered with paint during B&W segment.

••• 0:07—Nude caressing herself and dancing during the opening credits.

•• 0:09—Nude making love on the beach.

• 0:11—Brief right breast, while talking to Lobo.

•• 0:19—Brief breasts on the beach with Lobo, then more breasts while yelling at him.

• 0:28—Mostly breasts in flimsy halter top exploring a cave.

• 0:33—Full frontal nudity undressing in tent.

• 0:35—Left breast sleeping. Dark, hard to see.

• 0:37—Buns while sleeping.

• 0:40—Breasts superimposed over another scene.

• 0:48—Brief buns swimming in the ocean.

•• 0:51—Full frontal nudity walking out of the ocean and getting dressed.

• 0:53—Brief breasts in open blouse.

•• 1:08—Breasts in middle of compound when Lobo rapes her in front of Blue.

• 1:16—Full frontal nudity running through the jungle in slow motion. Brief buns.

Terror Train (1980; Canadian) . . . . Merry

The Best of Sex and Violence (1981) . . . . Tanya

• 0:24—Buns and breasts in various scenes from *Tanya's Island.*

Famous T & A (1982) . . . . Tanya

(No longer available for purchase, check your video store for rental.)

• 1:02—Breasts scenes from *Tanya's Island.*

The Last Dragon (1985) . . . . Laura

52 Pick-Up (1986) . . . . Doreen

••• 0:47—Breasts, stripping in room while Roy Scheider takes Polaroid pictures.

• 0:52—Breasts under sheer purple nightgown. Partial buns in G-string underneath also.

Never Too Young to Die (1986) . . . . Donja Deering

• 1:04—Wearing a bikini swimsuit, putting on suntan lotion. Brief breasts in quick cuts making love with John in a cabin bedroom.

Deadly Illusion (1987) . . . . Rina

Action Jackson (1988) . . . . Sydney Ash

•• 0:29—Breasts, while in bed with Craig T. Nelson.

Neon City (1991) . . . . Reno

Da Vinci's War (1992) . . . . Lupe

South Beach (1992) . . . . Jennifer Derringer

a.k.a. Night Caller

Made for Cable Movies:

Memories of Murder (1990; Lifetime) . . . . Carmen

Made for Cable TV:

Tales From the Crypt: Dead Wait (1991; HBO) . . . Catarine

• 0:15—Brief breasts and buns several times in and out of bed with James Remar.

Made for TV Movies:

Jackie Collins' Lady Boss (1992) . . . . Mary Lou Morley

Vannicola, Joanne

Films:

Toby McTeague (1986; Canadian) . . . . Girl Punker

Love and Murder (1988) . . . . . Hooker
Iron Eagle IV (1995; Canadian) . . . . . Wheeler
Love and Human Remains (1995; Canadian) . . . . . Jenni
• 0:45—Brief buns and back side of left breast, while making love with Candy.
• 0:52—Right breast, while lying in bed next to Candy.

Made for TV Movies:
Betrayal of Silence (1989) . . . . . Karen
To Save the Children (1994) . . . . . Melanie Young
Ultimate Betrayal (1994) . . . . . Karla
Derby (1995) . . . . . Kate Woods

Varga, Sazzy Lee

See: Lee Varga, Sazzy.

Vargas, Valentina

Films:
The Name of the Rose (1986) . . . . . The Girl
••• 0:45—Breasts and buns making love with Christian Slater in the monastery kitchen.
The Big Blue (1988) . . . . . Bonita
Street of No Return (1991; U.S./French) . . . . . Celia
The Tigress (1992) . . . . . Tigress/Pauline
•• 0:06—Nude, undressing in room and lying in bed with James Remar.
•• 0:10—Nude, sitting up in bed, then getting out and leaving the room.
•• 0:18—Nude, getting out of bed and getting dressed.
•• 0:45—Right breast, while in room when Remar pulls her dress down.
•• 0:48—Buns, while in bed with Remar.
• 0:52—Brief breasts, while changing clothes in room.
••• 0:53—Breasts when Remar opens her blouse and massages her breasts.
• 1:03—Half of left breast while primping herself in front of mirror.
Hellraiser: Bloodline (1996) . . . . . Angelique
•• 0:40—Breasts and brief partial buns, while making love with John in his dream.

Varsi, Diane

Films:
Peyton Place (1957) . . . . . Allison MacKenzie
Compulsion (1959) . . . . . Ruth Evans
Sweet Love, Bitter (1967) . . . . . Della
Killers Three (1968) . . . . . Carol Ward
Wild in the Streets (1968) . . . . . Sally Leroy
Bloody Mama (1970) . . . . . Mona Gibson
••• 0:16—Breasts, sitting up in bed with Dan Stroud. Buns, when getting out of bed. Long scene.
Johnny Got His Gun (1971) . . . . . 4th Nurse
I Never Promised You a Rose Garden (1977) . . . . . Sylvia

Vasil, Nadia

Films:
Erotique (1969) . . . . . Solange
Tropic of Cancer (1970) . . . . . Madame Hamilton's Girl
•• 0:32—Full frontal nudity in open dresses with other girls in room.

Made for Cable TV:
Strangers: Windows (1992; HBO) . . . . . n.a.
(Available on the video tape *Strangers.*)

Vasilopoulos, Nicole

Films:
Class of Nuke 'Em High Part II: Subhumanoid Meltdown (1991) . . . . . Bald Subhumanoid
Warlords 3000 (1992) . . . . . Ox's Wife
•• 0:23—Breasts, in open blouse in bedroom with Ox.

*Vasquez, Roberta **

Films:
Easy Wheels (1989) . . . . . Tondalco
Picasso Trigger (1989) . . . . . Pantera
Street Asylum (1989) . . . . . Kristen
Guns (1990) . . . . . Nicole Justin
•• 0:50—Right breast while making love on motorcycle with her boyfriend.
The Rookie (1990) . . . . . Heather Torres
Do or Die (1991) . . . . . Nicole Justin
•• 0:56—Breasts, making love with Bruce, outside.
Final Judgment (1992) . . . . . Whitney
Out for Blood (1992) . . . . . Detective Price
Sins of Desire (1992) . . . . . Motel Girl
(Unrated version reviewed.)
Fit To Kill (1993) . . . . . Nicole Justin
•• 0:21—Breasts and buns in G-string, while undressing and putting dresses on with Speir.
••• 0:52—Breasts and buns, while making love with her boyfriend in bed.
Hard Hunted (1993) . . . . . Nicole Justin
•• 1:20—Breasts while making out with Bruce in the ocean.

Video Tapes:
Playmate Playoffs . . . . . Playmate
Playboy Video Calendar 1987 (1986) . . . . . Playmate
Wet & Wild (1989) . . . . . Model
Playmates at Play (1990) . . . . . Hardbodies
Playboy's 21 Playmates: Volume II (1996) . . . . . Playmate
••• 1:14—Full frontal nudity in still photos.
••• 1:15—Full frontal nudity while undressing in locker room and relaxing in spa.

*Vaughn, Linda Rhys **

Video Tapes:
Playboy's Playmate Workout . . . . . Playmate
Playboy's Playmate Review (1982) . . . . . Playmate
••• 1:06—Nude on horseback, then next to stream.
Playmates at Play (1990) . . . . . Bareback

*Vega, Isela **

Films:
Bring Me the Head of Alfredo Garcia (1974) . . . . . Elita
• 0:25—Brief right breast a couple of times, then brief breasts in bed with Warren Oaks.
••• 0:44—Breasts when Kris Kristofferson rips her top off. Long scene.
•• 0:52—Breasts sitting in shower with wet hair.
•• 1:49—Still from shower scene during credits.
Drum (1976) . . . . . Marianna
• 0:04—Breasts in bed with the maid, Rachel.
•• 0:22—Brief breasts standing next to the bed with Maxwell.
The Streets of L.A. (1979) . . . . . n.a.
Barbarosa (1982) . . . . . Josephina
Blood Screams (1986; U.S./Mexican) . . . . . n.a.

Vela, Rosie

Films:
The Two Jakes (1990) . . . . . n.a.

Inside Edge (1991) . . . . Lisa Zamora
••• 1:06—Breasts, while making love with Michael Madsen in bed.

*Velasquez, Necole **

Made for Cable TV:
Full Frontal Comedy (1995; Showtime) . . . . .Woman of Full Frontal Comedy
Video Tapes:
Playboy Strip (1996) . . . . Dancer
••• 0:41—Nude, while dancing and stripping on stage in warehouse for a guy.
Wet & Wild VIII: Bottoms Up (1996) . . . . .Featured Model

*Velasquez, Patricia **

Model.
Films:
Unzipped (1995). . . . . Herself
Video Tapes:
Sports Illustrated: 1994 Swimsuit Issue Video (1994) . . . . .Model
(Unedited Version reviewed.)
• 0:34—Brief breasts under sheer white swimsuit. Buns in other swimsuit.
• 0:36—Very, very brief right breast, when covering her breast while holding a fan while posing for photos in Bali.

*Velez, Karen **

Ex-wife of actor Lee Majors.
Video Tapes:
Playboy Video Magazine, Volume 7 (1985) . . . . .Playmate
••• 1:01—Breasts and buns on lounge chair, rubbing oil on herself.
••• 1:04—Nude, undressing outside in gazebo and on porch.
••• 1:09—Full frontal nudity undressing in living room.
Playboy's Playmates of the Year: The '80s (1989) . . . . Playmate of the Year 1985
••• 0:39—Breasts and buns, in lounge chair, rubbing oil on herself.
••• 0:42—Nude, in a gazebo.
•• 0:52—Right breast in open dress.
Wet & Wild (1989). . . . . .Model

Venora, Diane

Films:
Wolfen (1981). . . . . .Rebecca Neff
The Cotton Club (1984) . . . . .Gloria Swanson
Terminal Choice (1985; Canadian). . . . . .Anna
• 0:48—Brief left breast, making love in bed with Frank. Don't see her face.
F/X (1986) . . . . Ellen
Bird (1988) . . . . Chan Richardson Parker
Heat (1995). . . . . .Justine
Three Wishes (1995) . . . . .Joyce
The Substitute (1996) . . . . .Jane Hetzko
Surviving Picasso (1996) . . . . .Jacqueline
William Shakespeare's Romeo & Juliet (1996) . . .Gloria Capulet
The Jackal (1997) . . . . Valentina Koslova
TV:
Chicago Hope (1994-95). . . . . Dr. Geri Infante
Thunder Alley (1994) . . . . .Bobbi Turner

Venturelli, Silvana

Films:
Macabre . . . . Annie
• 1:03—Very, very brief right breast, while wrapping a robe around herself.
• 1:05—Brief right breast while lying on bed when Gert checks her out.
Camille 2000 (1969). . . . . Olympe
The Lickerish Quartet (1970; Italian) . . . . The Woman
a.k.a. Erotic Illusion
• 0:01—Brief right breast under a guy in B&W porno film.
•• 0:03—Breasts, after taking off her top in film.
•• 0:05—Breasts while sitting on bed in film.
•• 0:06—Breasts, while in bed with another woman.
• 0:30—Breasts, while on couch with a guy in film.
• 0:32—Breasts, while on bed with guy in film.
• 0:47—Lower half of buns under mini-skirt while in library with the father.
••• 0:49—Nude, while in library on table and the floor with the father.
••• 1:00—Nude, while undressing outside with the son and making love.
•• 1:10—Breasts, while tied by wrists to bed in film.
A Long Ride From Hell (1970; Italian) . . . . Ruth

*Venus, Brenda **

Films:
Foxy Brown (1974) . . . . Arabella
The Eiger Sanction (1975). .George
• 0:50—Very brief breasts opening her blouse to get Clint Eastwood to climb up a hill.
• 1:06—Breasts taking off her clothes in Eastwood's room, just before she tries to kill him. Dark, hard to see.
Swashbuckler (1976) . . . . Bath Attendant
48 Hrs. (1982). . . . . Hooker

Vera, Victoria

Films:
Monster Dog (1986) . . . . Sandra
A Man of Passion (1989) . . . . Nuria
•• 1:10—Breasts, after taking off her dress at table in front of Anthony Quinn.

• *Verdu, Jodi*

Made for Cable Movies:
The Second Civil War (1997; HBO) . . . NewsNet Technician #1
Made for Cable TV:
Women: Stories of Passion-Astral Eros (1996; Showtime) . . . . .Claudia
• 0:05—Buns and partial breasts with Lloyd. Quick cuts.
•• 0:07—Breasts, while making love with Lloyd on table, then kissing Marguerite.
• 0:21—Brief breasts, in flashbacks while talking with Marguerite.
Compromising Situations: Singin' The Blues (1998; Showtime) . . . . Shannon
•• 0:19—Breasts, while making love with Kid.

Verdú, Maribel

Films:
The Year of Awakening (1986; Spanish). . . . . Maria Jesus
Lovers (1992; Spanish). . . . . Trini
a.k.a. Amantes
• 0:49—Lower frontal nudity, while lying in bed for Paco.
Belle Epoque (1993; Spanish) . . . . Rocio
a.k.a. The Age of Beauty

Golden Balls (1993; Spanish). . . Claudia (the mistress, 52 kilos)

Verkaik, Petra *

Films:

Auntie Lee's Meat Pies (1991) . . . . Baby
Pyrates (1991). . . . . Basia
The Last Road (1997). . . . . Angel
• 0:07—Breasts in open vest, when signaling start of road race.
••• 0:18—Buns and breasts, while making love in bed with Billy.

Video Tapes:

Playboy Video Calendar 1991 (1990) . . . . .November
••• 0:45—Nude.
Sexy Lingerie II (1990). . . . . Model
Wet & Wild II (1990) . . . . Model
Sexy Lingerie III (1991) . . . . Model
Wet & Wild III (1991) . . . . Model
The Best of Wet and Wild (1992) . . . . Model
Playboy Playmates in Paradise (1992) . . . . Playmate
Playboy's 21 Playmates: Volume II (1996) . . . . . . Playmate
••• 0:55—Nude in still photos.
••• 0:56—Nude outdoors in field, then in studio.
Centerfold Fantasies (1997) .Herself
••• 0:08—Nude, while posing near a stairwell.
••• 0:39—Nude, while cavorting around pool with the other girls.
••• 0:44—Nude, while posing outdoors on stairs.
••• 0:51—Nude, while walking around outdoors by the pool.

Vernon, Kate

Daughter of actor John Vernon.

Films:

Chained Heat (1983; U.S./German) . . . . Cellmate
Alphabet City (1984). . . . . Angie
• 0:54—Breasts, while making love with Vincent Spano.
Roadhouse 66 (1984). Melissa Duran
• 1:03—Brief breasts in back of car with Judge Reinhold. Dark.
Pretty in Pink (1986) . . . . Benny
The Last Days of Philip Banter (1987) . . . . .Brent
Hostile Takeover (1988; Canadian) . . . . Sally
a.k.a. Office Party
• 0:35—Very brief, left breast undressing in office with John Warner. Dark.
•• 0:39—Right breast, turning over in her sleep, then playing with the chain.
Malcolm X (1992). . . . . .Sophia
Dangerous Touch (1993). . . . . Amanda Grace
••• 0:29—Breasts, while making love with Phillips in convertible car in the woods.
••• 0:36—In black leotard, garter belt and stockings, then breasts while undressing in front of Phillips.
••• 0:38—More breasts when Phillips ties her hands to the headboard.
••• 0:51—Breasts, while making love in bed with Nicole while Phillips video tapes everything.
• 0:53—Breasts, on video monitor when she looks at video tape of her with Nicole.
Soft Deceit (1994) . . . . Anne Fowler
• 0:43—Right breast in pulled down blouse when making love with Patrick Bergin in the woods.
•• 0:58—Side view of right breast, while making love with Bergin on staircase railing in her house.
Downdraft (1996). . . . . .Alexa

Made for Cable Movies:

Probable Cause (1994; Showtime). . . . . Lynn Reilly
BloodKnot (1995; Showtime) . . . . Kaye
• 0:23—Brief breast, when Arthur accidentally opens the bathroom door.
•• 0:54—Breasts and very brief lower frontal nudity, while making love in back room of store with Patrick Dempsey.
• 1:05—Breasts, while making love outside with Craig Shefer.
The Sister-In-Law (1995; USA) . . . . Sarah Preston

Made for Cable TV:

Tales From the Crypt: Till Death Do We Part (1994; HBO) . . . . Lucille
The Outer Limits: Blood Brothers (1995; Showtime) . . . . .Tricia Lange
The Outer Limits: Josh (1998; Showtime) . . . . Judy Warren

Made for TV Movies:

Daughters of Privilege (1990) . . . . Diana
House of Secrets (1993) . . . . Laura Morrell

TV:

Falcon Crest (1984-85) . . . . .Lorraine Prescott
Who's the Boss? (1990). . . . . Kathleen Sawyer
Kindred: The Embraced (1996) . . . . Alexandra
Nash Bridges (1996-97) . . . . .Whitney Thomas

Veronica, Christina

a.k.a. Christina Veronique.

Films:

Sexpot (1986) . . . . Betty
••• 0:28—In bra, then breasts with her two sisters when their bras pop off. (She's on the left.)
•• 0:46—Breasts taking off her top in boat with Gorilla.
• 0:54—Breasts lying on the grass with Gorilla.
• 1:28—Breasts during outtakes of 0:28 scene.
Assault of the Killer Bimbos (1988) . . . . Dancer
Thrilled to Death (1988) . . . . Satin
•• 0:33—Breasts talking to Cliff during porno film shoot.
Girlfriend from Hell (1989). Dancer
••• 1:17—Breasts dancing on stage in club.
Party Incorporated (1989) . . . . .Christina
a.k.a. Party Girls
••• 0:52—Buns and breasts dancing in front of everybody at party.
Roadhouse (1989). . . . . Strip Joint Girl
A Woman Obsessed (1989). . . . . Crystal the Maid
Corporate Affairs (1990) . . . . Tanning Woman
They Bite (1991) . . . . Tammy
••• 0:20—Breasts in bed during porno movie shoot.
••• 0:55—Breasts, sunbathing on the beach while a guy rubs suntan lotion on her.
• 1:03—Breasts on the beach during playback of film.
•• 1:08—Breasts on boat, getting attacked by monster.
• 1:09—Breasts in water, struggling with the monster.
• 1:10—Brief breasts on beach during playback of film.
Dragon Fire (1993) . . . . Dancer

Verran, Michelle

a.k.a. Adult film actress Barbii.

Films:

Sorority House Massacre 2 (1990). . . . . Suzanne
••• 0:23—Buns in panties, then breasts changing clothes.

Verrell, Cec

Films:

Runaway (1984) . . . . Hooker
•• 0:44—Breasts in hotel bathroom while Tom Selleck sneaks into her room.

Hollywood Vice Squad (1986) . . . . Judy

Silk (1986). . . . . Jenny Sleighton

Hell Comes to Frogtown (1987). . . . . Centinella
•• 0:19—Breasts taking off her blouse and getting into sleeping bag with Roddy Piper. Brief breasts again after he throws her off him.

Transformations (1988) . . . . Antonia

Three of Hearts (1993) . . . . Allison

TV:

Supercarrier (1988) . . . . . . Lt. Cmdr. Ruth "Beebee" Rutkowski

NYPD Blue: Girl Talk (Mar 19, 1996) . . . . Gym Teacher

Video Tapes:

Inside Out (1992) . . . . The Psychiatrist/Shrink Wrap
(Unrated version reviewed.)
••• 0:18—In red bra, then breasts making love with the guy she picked up in the bar.

Inside Out 3 (1992). . . . . Susan/Tango

Veruschka *

Model.

Films:

Blow-Up (1966; British/Italian) . . . . Veruschka

The Bride (1985) . . . . Countess

Vetri, Victoria *

a.k.a. *Playboy* Playmate Angela Dorian.

Films:

Rosemary's Baby (1968) . . . . Terry Fionoffrio

Group Marriage (1972) . . . . Jan
••• 0:28—Buns and breasts getting into bed with Dennis, Sander and Chris. More breasts sitting in bed. Long scene.
• 1:19—Brief side view of right breast in lifeguard booth.

Invasion of the Bee Girls (1973). . . . . Julie Zorn
• 0:30—Brief breasts getting molested by jerks.
••• 1:19—Breasts in the bee transformer, then brief buns getting rescued.

Made for TV Movies:

Night Chase (1970). . . . . Beverly Dorn

Vickers, Vicki

a.k.a. Adult film actress Raven.

a.k.a. Rachel Vickers and Nellie Marie Vickers.

Films:

Angel Eyes (1991). . . . . Michelle
••• 0:02—Breasts and buns, while making love with Steven in bed. Long scene.
••• 0:18—Buns and breasts in shower. Partial lower frontal nudity.
••• 0:25—Right breast, then breasts while making love with Steven in bed while Angel watches. Long scene.
•• 0:32—Breasts, while rolling over in bed.
••• 0:40—Breasts, getting into shower, washing herself and getting out.
••• 0:44—Buns and breasts while making love in bed with Steven.
• 0:51—Brief left breast, while adjusting the covers in bed.
••• 0:53—Breasts in bed while making love in bed with Angel. Buns in G-string when getting out of bed.
•• 0:55—Breasts, while bending over sink to wash her face. Right breast, while peeking around the door.

Masquerade (1992) . . . . Linda

Video Tapes:

The Girls of Penthouse (1984) . . . . The Locket
••• 0:17—Breasts, then nude, making love.

Penthouse Love Stories (1986)
. . . . Snapshot and Loveboat Woman
••• 0:37—Nude, taking pictures of herself.
•• 0:51—Breasts on hammock watching Julie Parton.
•• 0:55—Left breast, twice while lying on hammock.

Villalobos, Candi

See: Rocilili, Bianca.

Villiegas, Cristina *

Made for Cable Movies:

Terminal Virus (1995; Showtime). . . . . Cristina
• 0:32—Nude, while bathing outside when joined by Elena Sahagun. (She's the one furthest from Sahagun.)

Vinni, Sasha *

Adult Films:

Zazel (1996) . . . . n.a.

Video Tapes:

Making of the "Carousel Girls' Calendar" (1993)
. . . . Miss November
••• 1:13—Full frontal nudity during photo shoot.
••• 1:16—Nude during interview segment.

Penthouse Pet of the Year Playoff 1993 (1993) . . . . . Pet
••• 0:20—Nude, outside with a car, in a dance studio, in the back seat of a limousine, in a house, in the shower.

Penthouse Pet of the Year Winners 1994: Sasha & Leslie (1994). . . . . Pet of the Year
••• 0:00—Breasts, outside of trailer.
••• 0:03—Nude on bed.
••• 0:08—Breasts, outside with tigers and nude while painted like a tiger.
••• 0:14—In lingerie and nude in room.
••• 0:19—Sunbathing nude outside.
••• 0:23—Nude in front of some seats.

Viva

Films:

Midnight Cowboy (1969) . . . . Gretel McAlbertson

Cisco Pike (1971). . . . . Merna

Play It Again, Sam (1972) . . . . Jennifer

Forbidden Zone (1980) . . . . Ex-Queen

Superstar: The Life and Times of Andy Warhol (1990)
. . . . Herself
• 0:26—Very brief right breast, while raising blouse to breast feed a baby.
• 0:49—Brief breasts, while lying in bed on right side of split screen in a clip from another film.

The Man Without a Face (1993) . . . . Mrs. Cooper

Vives, Vivianne

Films:

Hot Blood (1989; Spanish) . . . . Connie
• 1:19—Buns and very brief side view of left breast in bed with Julio.
•• 1:21—Breasts in bed several times, then lower frontal nudity with Julio.

All Tied Up (1992). . . . . Carmen

TV:

Dark Justice (1991) . . . . Maria Marti

Vogel, Darlene

Films:

Back to the Future, Part II (1989). . . . . Spike

Ski School (1990) . . . . Lori
- 1:03—Breasts in bed with Johnny.

Angel 4: Undercover (1993) . . . . Molly
Ring of Steel (1994). . . . . Elena Carter
- •• 0:15—Left breast, then breasts, while making love with Alex.

Decoy (1995) . . . . Diana
Made for Cable TV:
Pacific Blue (1996- ; USA) . . . . Chris Kelly

• Vogel, Victoria *

Made for Cable TV:
Hot Springs Hotel: Money Trouble (1998; Showtime) . . . Donna
Hot Springs Hotel: Travels with Travis (1998; Showtime) . . . . Donna
Hot Springs Hotel: To Your Health (1998; Showtime) . . . Donna
Video Tapes:
Playboy Strip (1996) . . . . Dancer
- ••• 0:23—Nude, while dancing and stripping for a customer.

Vold, Ingrid

Films:
Side Roads (1988). . . . . Bonnie Velasco
- 0:29—Brief breasts in motel room, getting undressed and carried into bed by Joe.
- 1:45—Brief breasts in mirror, getting out of bed.

Communion (1989) . . . . Uncredited Magician's Assistant
Time Barbarians (1990). . . . . Wizard
- 0:45—Breasts visible under sheer white gown.

Angel of Passion (1991) . . . . Vanessa
- 1:01—Brief breasts posing on the couch for the photographer.

To Sleep with a Vampire (1992). . . . . Stripper #1
- ••• 0:06—Breasts, while dancing on stage. (Wearing a wig.)
- 0:07—Brief breasts on stage (seen in B&W through the vampire's eyes.)

Good Girls Don't (1993) . . . . Prison Guard

von Bergen, Raven

Video Tapes:
Encounters (1987) . . . . Spa Encounter
- ••• 0:06—Breasts taking off her top in spa, then masturbating.

The Lover's Guide to Sexual Ecstasy: A Sensual Guide to Lovemaking (1992) . . . . Overture
- ••• 0:05—Breasts, while in black panties, garter belt and stockings.
- •• 0:12—Breasts while modeling jewelry and lingerie.

Von Glatz, Ilse

Films:
The Understudy: Graveyard Shift II (1988) . . . . Ash
- 0:49—Very brief side view of right breast and several very, very brief and brief breasts shots in bed with Baisez.

Made for TV Movies:
Danielle Steel's "Kaleidoscope" (1990) . . . . Marjorie
TV:
War of the Worlds (1988-89). . . . . Advocate #2

Von Palleske, Heidi

Films:
Dead Ringers (1988) . . . . Cary
- 0:45—Brief left breast sticking out of bathrobe, while talking to Jeremy Irons in the bathroom.

Blind Fear (1989; Canadian) . . . . Marla
Renegades (1989). . . . . Hooker in Bar
White Light (1990) . . . . Debra Halifax

Deceived (1991) . . . . Mrs. Peabody
Ramona (1992) . . . . Ramona Soco
- 0:04—Brief breasts, while making love with Henry.
- •• 0:06—Brief breasts, several times, while rolling over in bed.
- 1:13—Breasts, after taking off blouse in hotel room with Henry.

Sabotage (1996; Canadian). Susan Trent
Strip Search (1997; Canadian). . . . . Sheila
Made for Cable TV:
Fast Track: Combustion (1997; Showtime) . . . . . . Jenny Marsh

• von Weitershausen, Gila

Films:
Murmur of the Heart (1971; French/Italian/German) . . . . Freda
- •• 0:44—Breasts, while in bedroom, making love with Laurent, when helping him lose his virginity.
- 0:46—Brief breasts, while hitting Laurent's friend.

Circle of Deceit (1982; French/German) . . . . Greta Laschen

Voorhees, Deborah

a.k.a. Debisue Voorhees.
Films:
Avenging Angel (1985) . . . . Roxie
Friday the 13th, Part V—A New Beginning (1985) . . Tina
- ••• 0:41—Breasts after making love with Eddie, then lying down and relaxing just before getting killed.
- 0:43—Buns and brief left breast when Eddie turns her over and discovers her dead.

Appointment with Fear (1988) . . . . Ruth
- 0:21—Very, very brief side view of left breast taking off bra to go swimming, then very brief breasts getting out of the pool.

Vorgan, Gigi *

Films:
Jaws II (1978) . . . . Brook
Hardcore (1979) . . . . Teenage Girl
- 0:32—Breasts on sofa in Peter Boyle's apartment.

Caveman (1981) . . . . Folg's Daughter
Children of a Lesser God (1986) . . . . Announcer
Rain Man (1988) . . . . Voice-Over Actress
Red Heat (1988) . . . . Audrey
Vital Signs (1989) . . . . Nell
TV:
Knots Landing (1984) . . . . Carol

Vuletic, Jenny

Films:
Howling III: The Marsupials (1987) . . . . Goolah
Women From Down Under (1995; Australian/New Zealand) . . . . Jumping the Gun/Host
- 0:42—Breasts, while waking up next to another woman in the morning.

Waddell, Karen

Films:
The Donor (1994) . . . . Talia Green
Half Baked (1997) . . . . Record Store Employee
Made for Cable Movies:
Frame by Frame (1995; Canadian; Showtime) . . . Julie Horak
a.k.a. Conundrum
- 0:33—Brief buns, while hanging dead, upside down in room, when discovered by Michael Biehn. Probably a stunt woman.

• 1:23—Brief breasts in B&W photos (face has been scratched off) that Marg Helgenberger looks at.

Wagner, Lindsay

Films:

Two People (1973) . . . . Deidre McCluskey
(Not available on video tape.)

Wagner, Lori *

Films:

Caligula (1980) . . . . Agrippina
(X-rated, 147 minute version.)
••• 1:16—Nude, making love with Anneka Di Lorenzo. Long scene.

Trained to Kill (1988). Ace Duran's Girl

UHF (1989) . . . . Mud Wrestler

Dark Secrets (1995) . . . . Woman with Senator
••• 0:18—Breasts and buns, while having sex with the Senator in bedroom.

Video Tapes:

Penthouse: On the Wild Side (1988) . . . . Lover
• 0:54—Nude with Anneka de Lorenzo during scenes from *The Making of Caligula.*

Wagner, Natasha

See: Gregson Wagner, Natasha.

Wagner, Rachel *

Films:

Universal Soldier (1992) . . . . Girl in Motel

My Girl 2 (1994) . . . . Nancy

Kingpin (1996) . . . . n.a.

Made for Cable TV:

Hot Line: Fountain of Youth (1994; Cinemax) . . . . Amanda
(Available on video tape in *Hot Line.*)
•• 0:05—Breasts and very brief buns, while making love in bed with Kurt.

Video Tapes:

Playboy Video Centerfold: Jenny McCarthy (1994)
. . . . Cast Member

Wahl, Corinne

See: Alphen, Corrine.

Waite, Genevieve *

Films:

Joanna (1968; British) . . . . Joanna
• 0:18—Very brief buns, while walking into pond. Brief buns and back side of right breast, when getting out.
• 0:57—Brief side of left breast, when getting out of bed.
• 1:22—Breasts in large B&W photo on the wall.
• 1:28—Left breast, while putting on blouse. Another view of left breast in mirror on the wall.

Move (1970) . . . . The Girl

Myra Breckinridge (1970) . . . . Dental Patient

Walden, Lynette

Films:

Split Image (1982) . . . . Sexy Girl

Mobsters (1991) . . . . Cute Debutante
a.k.a. Mobsters—The Evil Empire
•• 0:32—Breasts when Richard Grieco undoes her dress.

Almost Blue (1992) . . . . Jasmine
••• 0:34—Breasts in bed on top of Michael Madsen.
• 0:35—Brief breasts, while walking to the bed and lying down while wearing panties.
••• 1:08—In black bra, then breasts and brief partial buns, while making love with Madsen on the sofa.
•• 1:10—Buns, while lying on sofa asleep with Madsen.

The Silencer (1992). . . . . Angel
••• 0:09—Breasts and buns, taking off clothes and getting into bathtub with her boyfriend.
•• 0:10—More breasts, while making love with him in the bathtub.

Benny & Joon (1993). . . . . Female Customer

Corrina, Corrina (1994) . . . . Annie

Made for Cable TV:

Fallen Angels (1993; Showtime). . . . . .Your Host "Fay Friendly"

Fallen Angels: Murder, Obliquely (1993; Showtime)
. . . . .Your Host "Fay Friendly"
(Available on the video tape *Fallen Angels One.*)

Red Shoe Diaries: Gina (1994; Showtime). . . . . Gina
• 0:18—Buns and breasts, while making love with Antonio.

Made for TV Movies:

A Matter of Justice (1993) . . . . .Patty

Saved by the Light (1995) . . . . Casey

In the Line of Duty: Smoke Jumpers (1996) . . . . .Lori

TV:

Orleans (1997) . . . . Rene Doucette

Walker, Arnetia

Films:

The Best Little Whorehouse in Texas (1982). . . . . Dogette

The Wizard of Speed & Time (1988)
. . . . Tina Dreem/Running Girl

Scenes from the Class Struggle in Beverly Hills (1989)
. . . . To-Bel
• 0:37—Breasts making love with Ray Sharkey on the sofa.
•• 1:10—Breasts in bed waking up with Wallace Shawn.
••• 1:23—Breasts making love on top of Ed Begley, Jr. on the floor.

Love Crimes (1991) . . . . Maria Johnson
(Unrated version reviewed.)

Made for Cable Movies:

Cast a Deadly Spell (1991; HBO) . . . . .Hipolite Kropolkin

The Cherokee Kid (1996; HBO) . . . . Jenny

TV:

Nurses (1991-94) . . . . Annie Roland

NYPD Blue: Ted and Carey's Bogus Adventure (Dec 3, 1996)
. . . . .n.a.

Walker, Christina

Films:

The Banker (1989) . . . . .Girl
• 0:18—Breasts on bed with Jeff Conaway

The Malibu Beach Vampires (1991)
. . . . Vice President Vampire Affairs

Walker, Kathryn

Films:

The Fringe Dwellers (1986; Australian). . . . . Eva

Midnight Dancer (1987; Australian). . . . . Kathy
a.k.a. Belinda

Dangerous Game (1988; Australian). . . . . Kathryn
• 1:19—Very, very brief breasts when her black top is pulled up while struggling with Murphy.

Walker, Liza

Films:

Twisted Obsession (1990) . . . . Jenny Greene
• 1:12—Lower frontal nudity while lying down. (Don't see her face.)

- 1:35—Brief breasts in blue light when Jeff Goldblum sees her.

Buddy's Song (1993; British) .... Elaine
Century (1993; British) .... Katie
Jungle Book (1994) .... Alice
E=mc² (1995) .... Lucy Amore
a.k.a. Wavelength
- 0:33—Brief right breast, after taking off her dress outside in front of Paul.

Hackers (1995) .... Laura
Solitaire for 2 (1995; British) .... Lucy

Walker, Melanie

Films:
Cyborg Cop II (1994) .... Pretty Co-worker
- 0:29—Left breast, while making out with guy in laboratory.
- 0:31—Brief breasts, while stumbling out of the laboratory after being shot in the back.

Fleshtone (1994) .... Mrs. Peale
- •• 0:21—Buns and breasts in photos that Matthew looks at. Partial left breast behind steering wheel of car.
- •• 0:37—Breasts, while lying in bed before Matthew discovers she's dead.

Project Shadowchaser II (1994) .... Stewardess
a.k.a. Armed and Deadly

Walker, Tracy

Films:
The Invisible Maniac (1990) .... Telescope Gal
- •• 0:01—Nude, taking off clothes during opening credits. Nice dancing.

Video Tapes:
Bikini Blitz (1990) .... Model

Wallace Stone, Dee

a.k.a. Dee Wallace.
Wife of actor Christopher Stone.
Films:
The Stepford Wives (1975) .... Nettie the Maid
The Hills Have Eyes (1977) .... Lynne Wood
10 (1979) .... Mary Lewis
- 1:09—Brief side view of buns, while on the floor.
- 1:10—Brief upper half of buns, going into bathroom and dropping her sheet.

The Howling (1981) .... Karen White
E.T. The Extraterrestrial (1982) .... Mary
Cujo (1983) .... Donna
Secret Admirer (1985) .... Connie Ryan
Critters (1986) .... Helen Brown
Shadow Play (1986) .... Morgan Hanna
- 1:06—Brief breasts making love with Ron Kuhlman. Kind of dark and hard to see.

The Christmas Visitor (1987) .... Elizabeth
Club Life (1987) .... Tilly Francesca
I'm Dangerous Tonight (1990) .... Wanda
Alligator II: The Mutation (1991) .... Christine Hodges
Popcorn (1991) .... Suzanne
Rescue Me (1991) .... Sarah Sweeney
Discretion Assured (1993) .... Kitten
Best of the Best 3: No Turning Back (1994) .... Georgia
Temptress (1994) .... Allison Mackie
The Frighteners (1996) .... Patricia Bradley
Skeletons (1996) .... Heather Crane
Made for Cable Movies:
Rebel Highway: Runaway Daughters (1994; Showtime) .... Mrs. Gordon
Subliminal Seduction (1996; Showtime) .... Sissy Bonner
Made for TV Movies:
The Secret War of Jackie's Girls (1980) .... Maxine
Sins of Innocence (1986) .... Vicki McGary
Addicted to his Love (1988) .... Betty Ann Brennan
Stranger on My Land (1988) .... Annie
Moment of Truth: Cradle of Conspiracy (1994) .... Suzanne Guthrie
Vanishing Son IV (1994) .... Megan
Witness to the Execution (1994) .... Emily Dawson
Love's Deadly Triangle: The Texas Cadet Murder (1997) .... Adrianne's Mother
TV:
Together We Stand (1986) .... Lori Randall
High Sierra Search and Rescue (1995) .... Morgan

Wallace, Julie T.

Films:
The Living Daylights (1987) .... n.a.
Hawks (1988; British) .... Ward Sister
The Lunatic (1992) .... Inga
Anchoress (1993; British) .... Bertha
The Fifth Element (1997) .... Major Iceborg
Made for Cable Movies:
The Life and Loves of a She-Devil (1991; British; A&E) .... Ruth
- 0:54—(With commercials.) Brief buns, while walking down hallway.
- 1:05—(Into part 2 with commercials.) brief side view of buns while tied up in bed before getting spanked by the judge.
- 1:06—(With commercials.) Brief buns again.

Walsh, Gwynyth

Films:
The Challenger (1989) .... Angie Daniels
Soft Deceit (1994) .... Captain Brock
Star Trek Generations (1994) .... B'Etor
The Girl From Mars (1996; Canadian/New Zealand) .... n.a.
The Limbic Region (1996) .... Ann Lucca
- 0:33—Very brief right breast, while starting to make love with Edward James Olmos.
- 1:01—Brief lower half of left breast under blouse, when Olmos stops making love with her.

Made for TV Movies:
My Son Johnny (1991) .... Janet David
Darkness Before Dawn (1993) .... Sandra
Without a Kiss Goodbye (1993) .... Jenine
Falling From the Sky! Flight 174 (1995) .... Pearl Dion
The Other Mother (1995) .... Barbara

• Walsh, Susan

Films:
Pink Flamingos (1972) .... Suzie, Blonde in Basement
- 0:15—Very brief upper half of right breast in gaping nightgown in pit when Chan hits her.
- 0:35—Brief right nipple sticking out of nightgown when she throws up in pit, after watching Chan inseminate unconscious woman.

Female Trouble (1974) .... Chiclett

Walter, Harriet

Films:
The French Lieutenant's Woman (1981) .... n.a.
Reflections (1984; British) .... Ottilie Granger
The Good Father (1986; British) .... Emmy Hooper

Turtle Diary (1986; British) . . . . Harriet
May Fools (1990; French) . . . . Lily
The Advocate (1993; British/French) . . . . Jeannine
a.k.a. The Hour of the Pig
- 0:06—Briefly nude, while running in a field, being hunted.

Sense and Sensibility (1995) . . . . Fanny Dashwood

Walter, Jessica

Films:

Lilith (1964) . . . . Laura
Grand Prix (1966) . . . . Pat
The Group (1966) . . . . Libby MacAusland
Play Misty for Me (1971) . . . . Evelyn
- 0:13—Very brief right breast in bed with Clint Eastwood. Lit with blue light. Hard to see anything.

The Flamingo Kid (1984) . . . . Phyllis Brody
Ghost in the Machine (1993) . . . . Elaine
PCU (1994) . . . . President Garcia-Thompson
Temptress (1994) . . . . Dr. Phyllis Evergreen

Made for Cable TV:

Poltergeist: The Legacy/The Light (1998; Showtime) . . . . Suzanne Barnard

Miniseries:

Wheels (1978) . . . . Ursula
Bare Essence (1983) . . . . Ava Marshall

Made for TV Movies:

Leave of Absence (1994) . . . . Bess
Mother Knows Best (1997) . . . . Joan

TV:

Love of Life . . . . Julie Murano
For the People (1965) . . . . Phyllis Koster
Amy Prentiss (1974-75) . . . . Amy Prentiss
All That Glitters (1977) . . . . Joan Hamlyn
The Round Table (1992) . . . . Anne McPherson

Walter, Marianne

See: Nichols, Kelly.

Walters, Julie

Films:

Educating Rita (1983; British) . . . . Rita
She'll be Wearing Pink Pyjamas (1985; British) . . . . . Fran
- ••• 0:07—Full frontal nudity taking a shower with the other women. Long scene.
- •• 0:58—Nude, undressing and going skinny dipping in mountain lake, then getting out. Nice bun shot walking into the lake.

Personal Services (1987) . . . . Cynthia Payne
- 0:21—Very brief side view of left breast, while reaching to turn off radio in the bathtub. Her face is covered with cream.

Prick Up Your Ears (1987; British) . . . . Elise Orton
Buster (1988) . . . . June
Stepping Out (1991) . . . . Vera
Just Like a Woman (1992; British) . . . . Monica
The Summer House (1993; British) . . . . Monica
Sister My Sister (1995; British) . . . . Madame Danzard

Walters, Laurie

Films:

The Harrad Experiment (1973) . . . . Sheila Grove
- 0:29—Breasts, wearing white panties, while with Don Johnson.
- 0:40—Nude taking off blue dress and getting into the swimming pool with Johnson.

The Harrad Summer (1974) . . . . Sheila Grove
a.k.a. Student Union
- 0:02—Breasts, while undressing in bathroom. Long shot, out of focus.
- •• 1:04—Breasts, while lying on lounge chair, then buns and more breasts getting up and pushing Harry into the pool.

Famous T & A (1982) . . . . Sheila Grove
(No longer available for purchase, check your video store for rental.)
- 1:08—Breasts scene from *The Harrad Experiment.*
- •• 1:11—Nude pool scene from *The Harrad Experiment.*

Made for TV Movies:

Eight is Enough: A Family Reunion (1987) . . . . Joannie Bradford

TV:

Eight is Enough (1977-81) . . . . Joannie Bradford

Walters, Melora

Films:

All Tied Up (1992) . . . . Bliss
Beethoven (1992) . . . . Pet Shop Owner
Twenty Bucks (1993) . . . . Stripper
- •• 0:14—Buns and breasts, while getting ready for bachelor party in bathroom.
- •• 0:15—Buns in G-string, then breasts, while dancing during bachelor party.
- 0:18—Brief breasts, getting dressed in bathroom.
- 0:20—Brief breasts, while on fire escape.

Ed Wood (1994) . . . . Secretary #2
America's Deadliest Home Video (1995) . . . . Gloria
- 0:52—Breasts, after Clint cuts her bra off.

Cabin Boy (1995) . . . . Trina
American Strays (1996) . . . . Cindy
Eraser (1996) . . . . Darleen
Hard Eight (1996) . . . . Jimmy's Girl
Boogie Nights (1997) . . . . Jessie St. Vincent

Made for Cable Movies:

Los Locos: Posse Rides Again (1997) . . . . Allison
- 0:20—Brief side of right breast, while skinny dipping in pond.
- 0:21—Breasts and buns, while in pond and walking out.
- 0:56—Lower frontal nudity in bedroom with Mario Van Peebles.
- •• 0:57—Nude, after taking off robe and getting into bathtub with Van Peebles.

Made for Cable TV:

Dream On: Little Orphan Eddie (1995; HBO) . . . . Dina
- 0:02—Left breast, while lying in bed, talking with Martin.

TV:

NYPD Blue: The Bank Dick (May 16, 1995) . . . . . . Holly Snyder
NYPD Blue: Dirty Laundry (Nov 21, 1995) . . . . Holly Snyder

Walthall, Romy

a.k.a. Romy Windsor.

Films:

Thief of Hearts (1984) . . . . Nicole
(Special Home Video Version reviewed.)
- ••• 0:12—Full frontal nudity with Steven Bauer getting dressed.

Up the Creek (1984) . . . . Corky
Howling IV: The Original Nightmare (1988) . . . . Marie
Big Bad John (1989) . . . . Marie Mitchelle
Edgar Allan Poe's "The House of Usher" (1990) . . . . Molly
Surf Ninjas (1993) . . . . Miss Robertson
Camp Nowhere (1994) . . . . Nancy Himmel
The Howling: New Moon Rising (1995) . . . . Marie Adams
Face/Off (1997) . . . . Kimberly

Made for TV Movies:
Family Reunion: A Relative Nightmare (1995) . . . . Grace
TV:
Man of the People (1991) . . . . Rita
Hotel Malibu (1994) . . . . Nancy Radzimski Salvucci

Waltrip, Kim

Films:
Pretty Smart (1986) . . . . Sara Gentry (the teacher)
•• 0:53—Breasts, while sunbathing with her students.
Nights in White Satin (1987) . . . . Stevie Hughes
• 0:53—Breasts in bathtub with Walker. Out of focus, hard to see.

Waltz, Lisa

Films:
Brighton Beach Memoirs (1986) . . . . Nora
The Opposite Sex ...and How to Live with Them (1992) . . . . Lizbeth
Pet Sematary II (1992) . . . . Amanda Gilbert
• 0:53—Very brief right breast, while in bed when Clancy Brown rips her nightgown off.
Red Ribbon Blues (1997) . . . . Barnes
Made for Cable Movies:
Roswell (1994; Showtime) . . . . Janet Foss
Made for TV Movies:
Lifepod (1993) . . . . n.a.
TV:
Ask Harriet (1998-) . . . . Melissa

• *Wan, Ai*

Made for Cable TV:
Erotic Confessions: Midnight Showing (1997; Cinemax) . . . . Jasmine
•• 0:10—Breasts and buns, while making love with Dominic in projection booth.
• 0:13—Partial breasts, while fooling around with Fernando in bedroom.
••• 0:14—Breasts and buns, while making love with a blind-folded Fernando while Dominic video tapes them.
• 0:17—Brief breasts and buns, while seen on video tape playback.
• 0:19—Brief breasts on video playback again.
•• 0:20—Breasts, while making love with Fernando in movie theater.
•• 0:26—Breasts and buns, while making love with Gina and Dominic in movie theater projection booth.
CD-ROM:
Heidi's House (1996) . . . . n.a.

• *Ward, Heather*

Films:
Sinful Intrigue (1995) . . . . Rebecca
Vice Girls (1995) . . . . Dominique Star
• 0:32—Brief breasts, three times, while pulling down her dress top during autograph session at video store.

Ward, Lalla

Films:
Vampire Circus (1972; British) . . . . Helga
Rosebud (1975) . . . . Margaret Carter
• 0:19—Buns, while on deck of boat with the other girls and the terrorists (she's third in line).
Crossed Swords (1978; Panamanian) . . . . . . Princess Elizabeth
TV:
Dr. Who: Destiny of the Daleks . . . . Romana

Ward, Mary B.

Films:
Playing For Keeps (1986) . . . . Chloe
•• 0:49—Breasts, after taking off her sweatshirt outside at night in front of Danny.
Hangin' with the Homeboys (1991) . . . . Luna
Smoke (1995) . . . . April Lee
TV:
TV 101 (1988-89) . . . . Penny Lipton
Michael Hayes (1997-) . . . . Caitlin Hayes

Ward, Pamela

Films:
Hellhole (1985) . . . . Tina
School Spirit (1985) . . . . Girl in Sorority Room
••• 0:15—Buns, then breasts in her room while Billy is invisible.
••• 0:16—More breasts and buns with other women in shower room.
The Women's Club (1987) . . . . Fashion Show Woman
Knockouts (1992) . . . . n.a.
Video Tapes:
Battling Beauties (1983) . . . . Foxy Boxer/Valley Girl

*Ward, Rachel **

Wife of actor Bryan Brown.
Films:
Night School (1980) . . . . Eleanor
• 0:25—In sheer white bra and panties, taking off clothes to take a shower. Breasts after taking off bra. Hard to see because she's behind a shower curtain. Brief buns and back side of left breast.
• 0:27—Very brief upper half of right breast, when opening the shower curtain.
•• 0:29—Brief upper half of breasts, and then buns, when her boyfriend rubs red paint all over her in the shower.
The Final Terror (1981) . . . . Margaret
Sharky's Machine (1981) . . . . Dominoe
Dead Men Don't Wear Plaid (1982) . . . . Juliet Forrest
Against All Odds (1984) . . . . Jessie Wyler
• 0:49—Very brief buns, while lying down with Jeff Bridges.
The Good Wife (1987; Australian) . . . . Marge Hills
a.k.a. The Umbrella Woman
Hotel Colonial (1988) . . . . Irene Costa
How to Get Ahead in Advertising (1988; British) . . . . Julia
After Dark, My Sweet (1990) . . . . Fay Anderson
• 1:22—Very, very brief half of right breast under Jason Patric in bed when he moves slightly.
Christopher Columbus: The Discovery (1992; U.S./Spanish) . . . . Queen Isabella
Double Obsession (1992) . . . . Grandmother
Wide Sargasso Sea (1993) . . . . Annette Cosway
(Unrated version reviewed.)
Made for Cable Movies:
Fortress (1985; HBO) . . . . Sally Jones
Black Magic (1992; Showtime) . . . . Lillian Blatman
Double Jeopardy (1992; Showtime) . . . . Lisa Burns
• 0:21—Very brief left breast, in the shower with Boxleitner. Hard to see because of the shadows. Also steam on glass obscures her face.
• 0:23—Very brief right breast, when Eddie opens her robe to rip her panties off. Hard to see because of the beveled glass in the door. Very, very brief right breast while getting attacked by Eddie when she reaches back to get a knife. Don't see her face clearly.
My Stepson, My Lover (1997; USA) . . . . n.a.

Miniseries:
The Thorn Birds (1983) .... Meggie Cleary
Made for TV Movies:
And the Sea Will Tell (1991) .... Jennifer Jenkins

• Warfel, Stacy *
Films:
Beauty School (1993)......................Amanda Alps
••• 0:14—Breasts with the other three girls in the showers.
•• 1:00—Breasts in the shower with Stephanie and a guy.
Sexual Roulette (1996) ....Laura
(Unrated version reviewed.)
••• 1:01—Partial buns under short skirt, then breasts, while making love with Jed in suite, while Tané McClure watches.
• 1:07—Full frontal nudity, while sitting in bed and after getting out.

Warncke, Margaret
Films:
Children's Games (1969)............................. Jo
Shaft (1971) ....Linda
• 1:04—Very brief breasts while getting into the shower with Richard Roundtree.

Warner, Julie
Films:
Flatliners (1990) .... One of Joe's Women
Doc Hollywood (1991)........................... Lou
• 0:15—Silhouette of right breast while standing in lake during Michael J. Fox's dream. Possible lower frontal nudity since she is facing the camera, but since it is shot in silhouette, you can't see anything.
••• 0:16—Breasts several times, skinny dipping in lake, then getting out while Fox watches.
Mr. Saturday Night (1992) .... Elaine
Indian Summer (1993) ....Kelly Berman
The Puppet Masters (1994).................. Mary Sefton
Tommy Boy (1995)...................... Michelle Brock
TV:
Pride and Joy (1995).....................Amy Sherman

Warner, Missy
Adult film actress.
a.k.a. Jennifer Irwin.
Films:
The Gate (1988; Canadian)........... Linda Lee, Lori's Sister
Bikini Summer (1991) ....Mindy
Wild Child (1991)............................ Laurie
•• 0:01—Breasts, while sitting on chair on balcony.
••• 0:04—Breasts and buns, while making love with Jon in the pool, then talking afterward. Long scene.
•• 0:29—Breasts while in swimming pool after her top comes off, then getting out.
••• 1:10—In white bra and panties, then breasts, while making love on bed with Todd.
The Bikini Carwash Company (1992) . Awesome Beach Girl
(Unrated version reviewed.)
• 0:00—Buns, on beach in a very small swimsuit.
•• 0:02—Brief right breast, turning over, then breasts while yelling at Jack.
Made for TV Movies:
Anne of Green Gables (1985; Canadian) ....Student

Video Tapes:
Big Bust Casting Call (1992).................... Herself
••• 0:31—In bra and G-string, undressing for audition, then nude in front of mirror.
L.A. Strippers (1992) .... Missy Warner
••• 0:01—Breasts dancing on stage during introduction.
••• 0:18—In raincoat, then lingerie, then nude dancing on stage. Long scene.

Warner, T.C.
Films:
The Art of Dying (1991) ....Janet
• 0:14—Buns, while shackled up in S&M chamber with a customer.
••• 0:32—Breasts in the shower. Buns and side of right breast, before getting stabbed to death.
Made for TV Movies:
Overkill: The Aileen Wuornos Story (1992)............. Amy
Lies of the Heart: The Story of Laurie Kellogg (1994)
....Nicole Pappas

Warner, Vanessa
Films:
Beauty School (1993).................. Becky Bustin'
• 0:13—Breasts, taking off her bra on stage.
••• 0:14—Breasts with the other three girls in the showers.
The Last Party (1993).......................... Herself

Warren, Jennifer *
Films:
Night Moves (1975) .... Paula
•• 0:56—Breasts in bed with Gene Hackman.
• 0:57—Right breast after making love in bed with Hackman.
Another Man, Another Chance (1977; U.S./French)......Mary
Slap Shot (1977) .... Francine Dunlop
Ice Castles (1979) ....Deborah Macland
Forbidden Choices (1994) ....Cop #1
a.k.a. The Beans of Egypt, Maine
Made for TV Movies:
Amazons (1984) ....Dr. Diane Cosgrove
TV:
Paper Dolls (1984)......................Dinah Caswell

Warren, Judette
Films:
Stephen King's "Sleepwalkers" (1992).............. Carrie
Showgirls (1995)...................... Spelling Dancer
(NC-17 version reviewed.)
Made for Cable TV:
Women: Stories of Passion-The Boxer (1996; Showtime)
.... Lorraine
••• 0:11—Breasts and buns, after joining Ajax in the showers.
• 0:17—Buns in panties, while kissing Ajax in boxing ring.
••• 0:22—In bra, then breasts and buns, while making love with Ajax in boxing ring.
Video Tapes:
Rock Video Girls (1991)......................... Herself

• Warren, Kiersten
Films:
Painted Hero (1995)..........................Teresa
•• 0:22—Breasts, when flashing herself for Dwight Yokam while in the front seat of a car.
Independence Day (1996)....................... Tiffany
Made for TV Movies:
Fugitive Among Us (1992)................... Sherry Nash

Grave Secrets: The Legacy of Hilltop Drive (1992) . . . . .Tina
Saved by the Bell: Wedding in Las Vegas (1994) . . . . Alex Taber
TV:
Life Goes On (1992-93). . . . . Goodman
Saved by the Bell: The College Years (1993-94). . . . . Alex Taber

Warren, Sandra

a.k.a. Sandee Currie.
Films:
Terror Train (1980; Canadian) . . . . Mitchy
Gas (1981; Canadian) . . . . .Sarah Marshall
Curtains (1983; Canadian) . . . . Tara Demillo
• 0:58—Side view of left breast practicing a scene in the play with Summers.
Terminal Choice (1985; Canadian) . . . . Nurse Tipton

Wasa, Maxine *

Films:
L.A. Bounty (1989) . . . . Model
• 0:07—Right breast while posing for Wings Hauser while he paints. Left breast, getting up. Long shot.
• 0:26—Left breast while posing on couch for Hauser.
•• 0:38—Breasts lying on couch again.
Savage Beach (1989) . . . . .Sexy Beauty
••• 0:08—Side view of left breast, in pool with Shane, then breasts getting out of pool.
••• 0:10—Breasts while Shane talks on the phone.
Made for Cable TV:
Dream On: The First Episode (1990; HBO) . . . . . . Andrea Kelly
Video Tapes:
Wet & Wild (1989) . . . . Model

Waters, Cheryl

Films:
Act of Vengeance (1974). . . . . Tamara
a.k.a. The Rape Squad
(Not to be confused with the film with the same name starring Charles Bronson.)
Macon County Line (1974) . . . . .Jenny
• 0:57—Buns and brief back side of right breast, while undressing in barn.
• 0:58—Buns and lower frontal nudity while in tub with Chris. Very brief right breast, when he dries her off.
Messenger of Death (1988). . . . . Magda Beecham

Watkins, Michelle

Films:
Terms of Endearment (1983). . . . . .Woman
The Outing (1987) . . . . Faylene
•• 0:12—Breasts taking off her top, standing by the edge of the swimming pool, then running breasts through the house with panties on.

• Watley, Michele

See: Midori.

Watson, Alberta

Films:
In Praise of Older Women (1978; Canadian) . . . . Mitzi
•• 0:51—Breasts, while sitting in chair talking with Tom Berenger, then more breasts when lying in bed. Long scene.
Power Play (1978; Canadian) .Donna
• 0:21—Brief breasts, while lying on table getting shocked through her nipples.
Stone Cold Dead (1979; Canadian). . . . . Olivia Page
The Soldier (1982) . . . . Susan Goodman
The Keep (1983) . . . . Eva Cuza
• 0:59—Very brief breasts, while making love with Scott Glenn, then brief lower frontal nudity.
Best Revenge (1984) . . . . Dinah
White of the Eye (1988) . . . . Ann Mason
The Hitman (1991) . . . . Christine De Vera
Zebrahead (1992) . . . . .Phyliss
Spanking the Monkey (1994) . . . . Susan Aibelli
• 0:12—Full frontal nudity, when getting into the shower. Brief right breast, while in the shower, assisted by her son.
Hackers (1995) . . . . .Lauren Murphy
The Sweet Hereafter (1997; Canadian). . . . . Risa Walker
• 0:45—Brief breasts, after turning away from the window then lying on the bed, while talking with Bruce Greenwood.
•• 0:46—Brief full frontal nudity, while putting her panties on.
Made for Cable Movies:
Gotti (1996; HBO). . . . . Victoria Gotti
Made for Cable TV:
Outer Limits: If These Walls Could Talk (1995; Showtime) . . . . Linda Tillman
Made for TV Movies:
Women of Valor (1986). . . . . Helen
Relentless: Mind of a Killer (1993) . . . . Ellen Giancola
Jonathan Stone: Threat of Innocence (1994) . . . . .Deborah Walsh Bradford
A Child is Missing (1995). . . . . Agent Lynette Graham
TV:
Fortune Dane (1986). . . . . Amy Steiner
Buck James (1987-88) . . . . Dr. Rebecca Meyer
Island Son (1990) . . . . Nina Delaney
La Femme Nikita (1997-) . . . . .Madeline

• Watson, Emily *

Films:
Breaking the Waves (1996; Danish) . . . . Bess McNeill
•• 0:19—Breasts, while standing in bedroom with her husband, Jan.
•• 1:22—Full frontal nudity, while lying on bed, trying to get Dr. Richardson to make love with her.
• 2:14—Brief breasts, while in hospital. (She's cut and covered with blood.)
The Boxer (1997) . . . . Maggie Hamill
Metroland (1997) . . . . .n.a.

Watson, Virginia

Films:
The Spring (1989). . . . . Pafinya
•• 0:45—Breasts taking off her top in front of Dack Rambo in his hotel room.
Dead On (1993) . . . . Dorian
(Unrated version reviewed.)
Don't Be a Menace to South Central While Drinking Your Juice in the Hood (1995) . . . . Loc Dog's Mom
Virtuosity (1995) . . . . Anchorwoman
Made for Cable Movies:
Running Mates (1992; HBO) . . . . .TV Anchorwoman
Made for TV Movies:
Another Midnight Run (1994). . . . . Woman Guard

Way, Renee

Films:
The Newlydeads (1988) . . . . Brenda
• 0:19—Buns and side of right breast, while in spa with her boyfriend.

Party Plane (1988) . . . . .Andy
••• 0:01—Breasts, while taking off her blouse to fix the plane.
••• 0:06—Breasts, while sitting on edge of spa.
••• 0:11—Breasts again, when getting out of spa.
• 0:12—Brief breasts after dropping her towel while talking to Tim.

Waymouth, Belinda

Films:

Hard Drive (1994). . . . . .Laura
(Unrated version reviewed.)
• 0:56—Very brief right breast, while in shower with Matt McCoy.

Playmaker (1994) . . . . Angie

Wayne, April

Former model for Ujena Swimwear (*Swimwear Illustrated* magazine).

Films:

Moon in Scorpio (1987). . . . . Isabel
• 0:32—Brief right breast in bed with a guy.
• 0:35—Brief breasts putting bathing suit on in a bathroom on a boat when a guy opens the door.

Party Camp (1987) . . . . Nurse Brenda
A Cop for the Killing (1990) . . . . Hooker

Video Tapes:

Swimwear Illustrated: On Location (1986). . . . Swimsuit Model

Wayne, Carol *

Films:

The Party (1968) . . . . June Warren
Scavenger Hunt (1979) . . . . Nurse
Gypsy Angels (1980) . . . . Waitress
Savannah Smiles (1983) . . . . Doreen
Heartbreakers (1984) . . . . .Candy
••• 0:41—In white bra and panties, then brief breasts in the mirror stripping in front of Coyote and Nick Mancuso. Brief breasts, while lying in bed with Coyote.

Surf II (1984). . . . . Mrs. O'Finlay

TV:

The Tonight Show. . . . . Regular

Video Tapes:

E. Nick: A Legend in His Own Mind (1984) . . . . Regine

Wayne, Taylor *

Adult film actress.
Former "Page 3 Girl" from England.
a.k.a. Joanna Gee and Joanna Wolfman.

Films:

Secret Sins (1992). . . . . Blonde Temptress
• 0:13—Right breast while in porno film.

Weatherly, Shawn

Miss South Carolina 1980.
Miss U.S.A. 1980.
Miss Universe 1980.

Films:

Cannonball Run II (1984) . . . . Dean's Girl
Police Academy III: Back in Training (1986) . . . . . Cadet Adams
Party Line (1988). . . . . Asst. D.A. Stacy Sloane
Shadowzone (1989) . . . . Dr. Kidwell
Thieves of Fortune (1989). . . . . Peter
• 1:09—Brief breasts several times, taking a shower (while wearing beard and mustache disguise).
••• 1:21—Breasts in white panties distracting tribe so she can get away.

Amityville 1992: It's About Time (1992). . . . . Andra
••• 0:07—Breasts, making love in bed on top of her husband. Nice and sweaty!

TV:

Shaping Up (1984) . . . . Melissa McDonald
Oceanquest (1985) . . . . Host
J.J. Starbuck (1987-88). . . . . .Jill Starbuck
Baywatch (1988-90) . . . . .Jill Riley

Weaver, Jacki

Films:

Alvin Purple (1973; Australian) . . . . .Second Sugar Girl
•• 0:33—Brief full frontal nudity, lying in bean bag chair.

Jock Petersen (1974; Australian). . . . . .Susie Petersen
a.k.a. Petersen
••• 0:01—Full frontal nudity lying in bed with Jock.

Picnic at Hanging Rock (1975). Minnie
The Removalists (1975) . . . . Marilyn Carter
Caddie (1976) . . . . Josie
Squizzy Taylor (1984) . . . . .Dolly
Cosi (1996; Australian) . . . . Cherry

Weaver, Sigourney *

Films:

Annie Hall (1977) . . . . Alvy's Date Outside Theatre
Alien (1979) . . . . Lt. Ellen Ripley
Eyewitness (1981) . . . . Tony Sokolow
Deal of the Century (1983) . . . . Mrs. De Voto
The Year of Living Dangerously (1983; Australian) . . . Jill Bryant
Ghostbusters (1984) . . . . Dana Barrett
Aliens (1986) . . . . Lt. Ellen Ripley
Half Moon Street (1986) . . . . Lauren Slaughter
a.k.a. Escort Girl
• 0:05—Brief breasts in the bathtub.
•• 0:11—Brief breasts in the bathtub again.
• 0:18—Brief buns and side view of right breast while putting on make-up in front of the mirror. Wearing a black garter belt and stockings.
••• 0:39—Breasts, while riding exercise bike while being photographed, then brief breasts getting out of the shower.
• 0:46—Very, very brief breasts wearing a sheer black blouse with no bra during daydream sequence.
• 0:50—Brief breasts, while in bed with Michael Caine, then left breast.

One Woman or Two (1986; French) . . . . .Jessica
a.k.a. Une Femme Ou Deux
•• 1:31—Very brief side view of left breast in bed with Gerard Depardieu.

Gorillas in the Mist (1988) . . . . Dian Fossey
Ghostbusters II (1989). . . . . Dana Barrett
Working Girl (1989). . . . . Katherine Parker
1492: Conquest of Paradise (1992; British/U.S./Spanish/French) . . . . Queen Isabella
Alien 3 (1992) . . . . Lt. Ellen Ripley
Dave (1993) . . . . Ellen Mitchell
Copycat (1995) . . . . .Helen Hudson
Death and the Maiden (1995) . . . . .Paulina Escobar
•• 0:11—Brief side of right breast, then breasts in bathroom.
•• 0:12—Breasts, while dressing in front of closet.
•• 0:14—Left breast, while making love in bed.

Jeffrey (1995). . . . . .Debra Moorhouse
Alien Resurrection (1997) . . . . Ellen Ripley
The Ice Storm (1997). . . . . .n.a.

Made for Cable Movies:

Snow White: A Tale of Terror (1997; Showtime) . . . . .Claudia Hoffman

TV:

Somerset. . . . . .Avis Ryan

Webb, Chloe

Films:

Sid and Nancy (1986; British). Nancy

• 0:21—Left breast, under Sid's arm in bed with him. Covered up, hard to see.

•• 0:44—Breasts in bed after making love, then arguing with Sid.

The Belly of an Architect (1987; British/Italian)
. . . . Louisa Kracklite

•• 0:01—Very brief right breast, making love on train with Brian Dennehy. Brief side view of right breast sitting up and putting camisole top on.

• 0:56—Brief buns in room with Lambert Wilson.

• 1:07—Brief buns, lying in bed with Wilson.

• 1:27—Breasts in B&W photos of a pregnant woman. Supposedly her, but probably not.

Twins (1988). . . . . Linda Mason

Heart Condition (1990). Crystal Gerrity

Queens Logic (1991). . . . . Patricia

A Dangerous Woman (1993). . . . . Birdy

Twenty Bucks (1993). . . . . Uncredited Convenience Store Clerk

Love Affair (1994) . . . . Tina Wilson

Made for TV Movies:

Lucky Day (1991) . . . . Allison Campbell

Silent Cries (1993) . . . . Dinki Denk

Tales of the City (1994). . . . . Mona Ramsey

•• 0:15—(Into Part 1) Breasts, while nonchalantly changing clothes in front of Mary Ann.

TV:

Thicke of the Night (1983) . . . . Regular

China Beach (1988) . . . . Laurette Barber

*Weber, Amy **

Films:

Forbidden Games (1995). . . . . Shauna

(Unrated version reviewed.)

•• 0:19—Breasts and buns, while talking with Michael outside.

• 0:23—Breasts in Michael's vision.

•• 1:00—Breasts, while in bed with Trish, tying and blindfolding Michael in bed.

••• 1:04—Breasts, while making love with Amber in bathtub.

*Weber, Catherine **

Films:

Body Strokes (1995) . . . . Claire

••• 0:30—Breasts, while posing by pool, then making love with Aqua in flashback dream.

•• 0:36—Full frontal nudity, while taking a bath.

••• 0:53—Nude, while posing, then making love with two guys in a fantasy.

••• 1:03—Nude while dressed as a geisha girl, making love with Mark.

•• 1:19—Breasts, while posing outdoors with Beth and rubbing oil on her. Brief buns in T-back.

•• 1:22—Breasts and brief buns, while posing in black panties with Beth.

• 1:32—Breasts, while posing with Beth and Karen.

To the Limit (1995) . . . . Mona

• 0:21—Brief breasts, while getting strangled for failing to kill Frank.

Virtual Desire (1995) . . . . Molly

• 0:43—Brief breasts, while making out with Brad on tennis court.

Weber, Sharon Clark

See: Clark, Sharon.

*Weeks, Kathe **

Made for Cable TV:

Tales From the Crypt: Death of Some Salesman (1993; HBO) . . . . .Stella

••• 0:02—Breasts, while making love in bed with Ed Begley Jr.

••• 0:03—Breasts, while sitting in bed and talking with Begley.

• *Weeks, Perdita*

Films:

The Cold Light of Day (1995; German). . . . . . . Anna Tatour

• 1:22—Brief partial buns, while being carried by her mother in the rain in Richard E. Grant's nightmare.

Hamlet (1996). . . . . Player

Spice World (1997; British) . . . . Evie

Weickgenant, Blair

Films:

Smooth Talker (1990) . . . . Lisa Charles

• 0:33—Breasts, lying in bed and sitting up during Carl's B&W fantasy.

Double Obsession (1992) . . . . Lillian Robinson

*Weigel, Teri **

The first *Playboy* Playmate to star in adult films *after* she became a Playmate.

Adult Films:

The Barlow Affairs (1991). . . . . n.a.

Lingerie Busters (1991) . . . . n.a.

Starr (1991). . . . . n.a.

Wicked (1991). . . . . n.a.

Films:

Cheerleader Camp (1987) . . . . Pam Bently

a.k.a. Bloody Pom Poms

•• 0:12—Breasts taking off her swimsuit top while sunbathing.

Glitch (1988) . . . . Lydia

• 0:41—Brief buns in pink bathing suit, while talking to Bo.

• 0:54—Buns in swisuit bottom and brief right breast in bathtub with Todd.

Return of the Killer Tomatoes (1988) . . . . Matt's Playmate

The Banker (1989) . . . . Jaynie

••• 0:02—Taking off dress, then in lingerie, then breasts making love with Osbourne in bed. More breasts after.

Far From Home (1989). . . . . .Woman in Trailer

•• 0:16—Breasts making love when Drew Barrymore peeks in window.

Night Visitor (1989). Victim in Cellar

• 0:50—Brief out of focus breasts changing tops in the cellar.

• 0:55—Right breast, during ceremony. Very brief breasts just before being stabbed.

Savage Beach (1989) . . . . .Anjelica

••• 0:33—Breasts taking off black teddy and getting into bed to make love.

•• 0:47—Breasts making love in the back seat of car.

Marked for Death (1990) . . . . Sexy Girl #2

• 0:39—Brief breasts on bed with Jimmy when Steven Seagal bursts into the room. (She's the brunette.)

Predator 2 (1990). . . . . Columbian Girl
- 0:22—Brief breasts making love on bed. More breasts several times being held on the floor, brief full frontal nudity getting up when the Predator starts his attack.

Auntie Lee's Meat Pies (1991) . . . . .Coral
- 1:23—Breasts under sheer outfit.
- 1:29—Buns, while swimming in one piece swimsuit under water.

Innocent Blood (1992). . . . . .Melody Lounge Dancer
- •• 1:32—Breasts (holding a red and white boa, in the middle of two other dancers), dancing in front of Robert Loggia.

Masquerade (1992) . . . . .n.a.

Video Tapes:

Playboy Video Centerfold: Teri Weigel (1986) . .Playmate
- ••• 0:00—Nude, in shower, taking a bath, in bedroom.
- ••• 0:15—Nude outside in spa, and modeling lingerie with Dona Speir and Hope Marie Carlton.
- ••• 0:18—Nude in bed taking off black lingerie outfit.

Playboy Video Calendar 1988 (1987) . . . . .Playmate

Playboy's Fantasies (1987) . . . . The Mannequin
- ••• 0:21—Nude, after coming to life from being a mannequin.

Playboy's Secrets of EuroMassage (1989) . . . . .No. 4 Sensual Power of Water
- ••• 0:23—Nude (including breasts squished against glass), during massage session in the shower, then in spa and on wooden platform. Long scene.

Wet & Wild (1989) . . . . .Model

Playboy's Fantasies II (1990). . . . . Grand Illusions
- ••• 0:31—Nude outside in the woods during a surveyor's fantasy.

Sexy Lingerie II (1990). . . . . .Model

Wet & Wild II (1990) . . . . .Model

Secrets of Making Love... To the Same Person Forever (1991). . . . . .Mirror, Spa & Bed
- ••• 0:33—Breasts and buns in front of mirror, in spa and tied up in bed.
- 0:48—Breasts and lower frontal nudity in spa and in bed.

Sexy Lingerie III (1991) . . . . .Model

Inside Out 3 (1992) . . . . Woman/The Portal
- •• 0:27—Brief breasts, standing up in the water.

Penthouse: Fast Cars/Fantasy Women (1992). . Jaguar XK
- ••• 0:42—Nude, while making love with a guy in several different locations.

Weiss, Amy Rochelle

See: Rochelle, Amy.

Weiss, Roberta

Films:

Autumn Born (1979). . . . . Melissa
- 0:07—Buns, wearing panties and bending over desk to get whipped.

Cross Country (1983; Canadian) . . . . Alma Jean
- •• 0:59—Breasts on bed with two other people.

The Dead Zone (1983). . . . . Alma Frechette
- 0:49—Briefly in beige bra, then brief breasts when the killer rips her blouse open during Christopher Walken's vision.

Abducted (1986; Canadian) . . . . Renee

Made for Cable TV:

The Hitchhiker: And If We Dream (1987; HBO) . . . . .Rosanne Lucas

(Available on *The Hitchhiker, Volume 3.*)
- •• 0:11—Breasts and buns in barn making love with Stephen Collins.
- •• 0:17—Breasts in dream classroom with Collins.
- 0:23—Brief breasts in bed after second dream with Collins.

Weisz, Rachel

Films:

Death Machine (1994) . . . . Junior Executive

Chain Reaction (1996). Dr. Lily Sinclair

Stealing Beauty (1996) . . . . Miranda
- •• 0:11—Left breast and brief upper half of lower frontal nudity, while lying on a cot next to pool.

Swept From the Sea (1998). . . . . Amy Foster

*Welch, Tahnee **

Daughter of actress Raquel Welch.

Films:

Cocoon (1985). . . . . Kitty
- 1:01—Brief buns, while walking into swimming pool.

Lethal Obsession (1987; German) . . . . Daniela Santini

a.k.a. The Joker
- 0:14—Buns, putting on robe after talking to John on the phone.
- 0:15—Half of left breast, taking off coat to hug John in the kitchen.
- 0:16—Sort of left breast, while in bed with John. Too dark to see anything.
- 1:16—Buns, when getting an injection.

Cocoon, The Return (1988). . . . . Kitty

The Criminal Mind (1993). . . . . Gabrielle Dupre
- •• 0:57—Left breast, while making love in bed with Nick.

Night Train to Venice (1993) . . . . Vera
- 0:48—Silhouette of right breast, while in room on train with Hugh Grant. Don't see her face, but it looks like her.
- •• 1:18—Very brief breast, twice, while in bed with Hugh Grant, then breasts.
- •• 1:33—Brief left breast, then breasts, while kissing Hugh Grant in bed at end of film. The darn credits get in the way!

Improper Conduct (1994) . . . . .Ashley

(Unrated version reviewed.)

0:10—Right breast, then breasts, while in office supply room with Adrian Zmed. Don't see her face.

Search and Destroy (1995) . . . . Dead World Girl

I Shot Andy Warhol (1996) . . . . Viva

TV:

Falcon Crest (1987-89) . . . . .Shannon

Weldon, Cirsten

Films:

Hard to Die (1990) . . . . Agent's Girlfriend

a.k.a. Tower of Terror
- 0:19—Breasts in bedroom with Tess's agent. Medium long shot.

The Doors (1991) . . . . .Girl in Car

Weller, Mary Louise

Films:

The Evil (1977) . . . . Laurie Belden

Animal House (1978) . . . . Mandy Pepperidge
- ••• 0:38—In white bra, then breasts in bedroom while John Belushi watches on a ladder through the window.

The Bell Jar (1979). . . . . .Doreen

Blood Tide (1982) . . . . .Sherry

Forced Vengeance (1982) . . . . Claire Bonner
- 1:04—Brief breasts, struggling with the bad guy.
- 1:08—Very brief right breast then left breast, while lying dead on the floor.

Q (1982) . . . . .Mrs. Pauley

Welles, Gwen *

Films:

A Safe Place (1971) . . . . Bari

Hit! (1973) . . . . Sherry Nielson

••• 2:03—Breasts, taking off her clothes in front of a woman before killing her.

California Split (1974) . . . . Susan Peters

Nashville (1975) . . . . Sueleen Gay

•• 2:09—In bra singing to a room full of men, then breasts doing a strip tease, buns walking up the steps and out of the room.

Between the Lines (1977) . . . . Laura

•• 0:32—Buns and breasts drying off with a towel in front of a mirror.

Desert Hearts (1986) . . . . Gwen

The Men's Club (1986) . . . . Redhead

Sticky Fingers (1988) . . . . Marcie

New Year's Day (1989) . . . . n.a.

Eating (1990) . . . . Sophie

Boys Life (1994) . . . . Melissa

Welles, Jennifer *

Films:

Sugar Cookies (1973) . . . . Max's Secretary

• 0:28—Breasts in red panties in Max's office while he talks on the phone, then lower frontal nudity.

•• 0:56—Full frontal nudity getting dressed.

The Groove Tube (1974) . . . . The Geritan Girl

•• 0:21—Dancing nude around her husband, Chevy Chase.

Is There Sex After Death? (1975)

. . . . Magic Act/Merkin's Assistant

•• 0:41—Brief left breast and buns, while helping Merkin, then full frontal nudity.

Welles, Terri *

Films:

Looker (1981) . . . . Lisa

• 0:02—Brief breasts getting photographed for operation. In black bra and panties in her apartment a lot.

The Firm (1993) . . . . Woman Dancing With Avery

Video Tapes:

Playboy's Playmates of the Year: The '80s (1989)

. . . . Playmate of the Year 1981

••• 0:08—Nude in still photos.

••• 0:10—Nude at the beach.

••• 0:11—Nude in still photos.

•• 0:51—Breasts coming out of the water.

Wells, Aarika

Films:

Sharky's Machine (1981) . . . . Tiffany

• 0:52—Brief side view breasts (mostly silhouette) in Rachel Ward's apartment.

Walking the Edge (1985) . . . . Julia

TV:

Supertrain (1979) . . . . Gilda

Wells, Victoria

Films:

Cheech & Chong's Next Movie (1980) . . . . Massage Girl

Cheech & Chong's Nice Dreams (1981) . . . . . Beach Girl #1

• 0:29—Brief breasts on the beach with two other girls. Long shot, unsteady, hard to see.

• 0:32—More brief breasts again.

• 0:33—More brief breasts again.

The Best Little Whorehouse in Texas (1982) . . . . . Washing Girl

Losin' It (1982) . . . . Dave's Whore

• 0:39—Breasts, after taking off sheer top in room with Dave. Seen in mirror.

• Welsh, Dawnya

Films:

The Pompatus of Love (1996) . . . . Leonard's Stripper

• 0:17—Brief side of right breast and buns in T-back while dancing in front of Roscoe Lee Browne in club.

• 0:19—Breasts and buns in T-back, when dancing while Browne talks with Runyon.

• 0:20—Breasts and buns in T-back, when snatching bills from Browne. More breasts in background while getting dressed.

Video Tapes:

Making of the "Carousel Girls' Calendar" (1993)

. . . . Miss April

••• 0:29—Nude during photo shoot.

••• 0:32—Nude during interview segment.

• Wen, Ming-Na

Films:

The Joy Luck Club (1993) . . . . June

Hong Kong '97 (1994) . . . . Katie Chun

Street Fighter (1994) . . . . Chun-Li

Rain Without Thunder (1995) . . . . "Uudie" Prisoner

Starquest (1995) . . . . Han

One Night Stand (1997) . . . . Mimi

••• 1:04—Breasts, while sleeping in bed next to Wesley Snipes before he covers her up.

Made for TV Movies:

Vanishing Son II (1994) . . . . Mai

Vanishing Son IV (1994) . . . . Mai

TV:

As the World Turns (1989-91) . . . . Lien Hughes

ER (1995) . . . . Dr. Deborah Chen

The Single Guy (1995) . . . . Trudy Sloan

Wendel, Lara *

Films:

Desire, The Interior Life (1980; Italian/German) . . . . . . Desideria

Unsane (1982) . . . . Maria

a.k.a. Tenebrae

Identification of a Woman (1983; Italian) . . . . n.a.

Intervista (1987; Italian) . . . . La Sposa

Ghosthouse (1989; Italian) . . . . Martha

Husbands and Lovers (1991; Italian) . . . . Louisa

(Unrated version reviewed.)

••• 0:47—In bra and panties with Julian Sands, then breasts, while making love with him.

Werchan, Bonnie

Films:

Auditions (1978) . . . . Tracy Matthews

••• 0:02—Breasts, then full frontal nudity, undressing for her audition.

••• 0:31—Nude, undressing herself and Van.

•• 0:33—Buns and side of right breast, making love with Van.

•• 1:07—Breasts and buns during orgy scene.

Summer Camp (1979) . . . . n.a.

• West, Erika

See: Sandifer, Elizabeth

West, Jennifer

See: Swift, Sally.

• West, Kimber *

Video Tapes:

Playboy Video Calendar 1998 (1997) . . . . Mary
••• 0:19—Nude, while moving furniture into a house.
••• 0:20—Nude, while posing indoors in the dark.
Playboy's Fast Women (1997) . . . . Playmate
Playboy's Voluptuous Vixens (1997). . . . . Playmate
Playboy's Blondes, Brunettes, Redheads (1998) . . . . Herself

Westbrook, Wendi

Films:

Blame It on the Vodka (1992) . . . . Roxanne
0:18—In bra and panties, while in the kitchen.
••• 0:20—Buns and breasts, while in the bathroom with Barry, then making love with him in the shower. Long scene.
Married People, Single Sex (1993). . . . . Shelley
••• 0:16—Breasts, in bed with her husband, then getting out and back in bed.
• 0:31—Buns while in purple lingerie with her girlfriends.
0:45—In sheer blue lingerie with Richard.
••• 0:48—Right breast under Will, making love while wearing mask. Breasts and very, very brief lower frontal nudity, while getting out of bed and putting on bra.
• 1:03—Right breast, while kneeling on floor in front of Richard.
Almost Hollywood (1994) . . . . Girl 1
Under Lock and Key (1994) . . . . Danielle Peters
• 0:11—Breasts, when changing clothes while sitting on bed in cell.
••• 0:13—Nude, with Sarah in the showers.
• 0:18—Nude while getting undressed for "conjugal visit."
• 0:19—Partial left breast, while in bed during "conjugal visit."
•• 0:50—Nude, getting undressed, taking a shower, and getting out.

Made for Cable TV:

Hot Line: Highest Bidder (1994; Cinemax)
. . . . Elizabeth Willman
(Available on video tape in *Hot Line 2.*)
• 0:19—In bra, then breasts, while in bedroom with Scott.
••• 0:22—Breasts and buns while making love on bed with Scott.

Westcott, Carrie *

Films:

Ring of Fire II: Blood and Steel (1992) . . Bad Girl Gang Member
Lover's Leap (1995) . . . . Johanna
• 0:00—Brief right breast, while on boat with Nick.
••• 0:02—Nude, while making love in the woods with Nick.
• 0:05—Brief breasts, while walking in the woods.
••• 0:36—Breasts and buns, while making love with Alex in living room.
•• 0:38—Nude, while standing on the balcony, then getting dressed inside.
••• 0:55—Nude, while dancing in room, making love with Alex, then in bathroom afterwards.
•• 1:08—Buns and breasts, while making love with Alex on balcony at night.
• 1:17—Brief buns in panties, while lying on the bed, talking on the phone.

Made for Cable TV:

Erotic Confessions: Virtual Vixen (1997; Cinemax)
. . . . Mary Ann
•• 0:04—Breasts, when Alec starts feeling her up in comic book store.
•• 0:13—Breasts, while in bedroom with Herbert.
••• 0:20—Full frontal nudity, while making love with Herbert in comic book store.

Video Tapes:

Playboy Night Dreams (1993). . . . . Detour
••• 0:04—Nude after stripping out of bra, panties, garter belt and stockings, after picking up a guy and making love in house.
Playboy Video Calendar 1995 (1994) . . . . December
••• 0:49—Nude in a greenhouse with water. Nude on different colored beds.
Sexy Lingerie: Dreams & Desire (1994) . . . . Playmate
Wet & Wild: The Locker Room (1994). . . . . Playmate
Playboy's Real Couples: Sex in Dangerous Places (1995)
. . . . Touching Me, Touching You/Masseuse
••• 0:24—Nude while massaging Shae Marks.
Wet & Wild: Hot Holidays (1995). . . . . Playmate
Playboy The Best of Jenny McCarthy (1996) . . . . . Herself
••• 0:24—Nude, while dancing with 3 other Playmates with fire and ice from *Wet & Wild: The Locker Room.*
Centerfold Fantasies (1997) . . . . Herself
••• 0:02—Nude, while posing in dining room.
••• 0:18—Nude, while posing outdoors on stairs.
••• 0:39—Nude, while cavorting around pool with the other girls.
••• 0:50—Nude, while walking around outdoors by the pool.
Playboy's Voluptuous Vixens (1997). . . . . Playmate

Weston, Whitney

Films:

Professional Affair (1994). . . . . Belinda
• 0:05—Brief side of right breast, while making love on top of Michael in bed.

Video Tapes:

Inside Out 3 (1992). . . . . Debbie/The Perfect Woman
•• 0:30—Breasts, while talking on talk show seen on TV.
• 0:43—Brief breasts, after taking off clothes on talk show on TV.

Wexler, Karen

Films:

The Refrigerator (1992) . . . . Nikki
Night Owl (1993) . . . . Zohra
• 0:12—Breasts, while making love with Jake in kitchen.
0:14—Breasts, dead, while covered with blood on the floor after Jake bites her neck.
• 0:15—Brief breasts when Jake wipes the blood off her and stuffs her into a garbage bag.

• Whaley, Rachelle

Films:

Kounterfeit (1997). . . . . Rachelle

Video Tapes:

Playboy Strip (1996). . . . . Dancer
••• 0:06—Nude, after joining another dancer on stage in club.

Wharton, Wally Anne *

Films:

Up in Smoke (1978) . . . . Debbie
Heartbeeps (1981). . . . . Party House Interior Decorator
Cheerleaders Wild Weekend (1985) . . . . Lisa/Darwell
•• 0:06—Breasts in back of school bus, flashing a guy in pickup truck, then pressing her breasts against the window.
••• 0:37—Breasts, opening her white blouse during contest.
••• 0:39—Breasts and brief buns, in white skirt during contest.
Last Resort (1985) . . . . Wanda

Video Tapes:
Thunder and Mud (1989) . . . . Wanda Wallinsky

Whirry, Shannon

Films:
Out for Justice (1991) . . . . Terry Malloy

Animal Instincts (1992). . . . . .Joanne Cole
(Unrated version reviewed.)
- ••• 0:18—In white bra and panties in bed then full frontal nudity during her fantasies with several guys.
- •• 0:23—Breasts and buns, in various lingerie outfits, in front of mirror.
- •• 0:26—Full frontal nudity under sheer white body suit, trying to get Maxwell Caulfield interested in her.
- •• 0:28—Breasts while taking a bath.
- ••• 0:30—Nude in bed, making love with the Cable TV guy.
- ••• 0:43—In bra and panties, then nude while in bed with the Assistant DA while Caulfield watches on TV.
- ••• 0:46—Breasts, while sitting in bed with Caulfield.
- •• 0:50—Breasts with Delia Sheppard and a guy.
- ••• 0:51—In black bra and panties on TV after undressing as a businessman. Breasts in bed with a guy.
- ••• 0:54—Breasts in bedroom and on bed with Delia.
- ••• 0:59—In black bra and panties, then breasts and buns with Mitch Gaylord in bedroom while making love.
- • 1:16—Buns in G-string and side of left breast, while in bed with Jan-Michael Vincent.

Body of Influence (1992) . . . . Laura/Lana
(Unrated version reviewed.)
- ••• 0:08—Breasts on bed with her lover during recollection for Jonathon.
- • 0:16—Left breast, while on bed, tied by wrists and getting raped during recollection.
- •• 0:26—In black bra, undressing in office. Right breast, while lying on desk. Buns in panties.
- ••• 0:44—In burgundy bra and panties with Jonathon in his house. Then nude, while making love in living room. Long scene.
- ••• 1:05—In black bra, then breasts and buns, while making love on top of Jonathon.
- ••• 1:08—Breasts, while sitting up in bed and talking to Jonathon.

Animal Instincts 2 (1993) . . . . .Joanna
- ••• 0:11—Breasts, in bed with a fantasy lover while she imagines another guy watching them make love.
- ••• 0:30—Breasts, while rubbing lotion on herself in the backyard while Steve watches from his backyard.
- • 0:38—Brief breasts, while in her bedroom. Seen on video monitor.
- ••• 0:47—Full frontal nudity while making love with a guy she picks up in a bar while Steve watches on video monitor.
- ••• 0:49—Nude, while making love in bedroom with a woman she picks up in a bar.
- •• 0:53—Left breast, while opening her robe and talking on the phone.
- ••• 1:01—Nude, while posing for Eric in his studio.
- •• 1:04—Breasts, while taking a shower.
- • 1:05—Brief left breast in photos that Eric shows her.
- •• 1:07—In white bra and panties, then breasts and buns while making love with Eric.

Mirror Images II (1993). . . . . Carrie/Terrie
- ••• 0:03—Nude, while taking a shower during the opening credits. Then breasts, while making love on top of her twin sister's boyfriend in bed.
- • 0:19—Buns in panties and bra while trying on lingerie in front of mirror.
- ••• 0:25—Full frontal nudity while making love with her female psychologist, Dr. Rubin. Long scene.
- ••• 0:31—Nude, while making love outside in pool with Dan before getting caught by Phyllis
- ••• 0:39—In black bra, then full frontal nudity while making love on bed with Clete. She gives him a hot wax treatment. Long scene.
- • 0:49—Breasts, while making love in bed with a customer while Jake watches from outside the window. Long shot.
- ••• 0:56—In black bra and panties, the full frontal nudity while making love in bedroom with a customer.
- •• 1:01—In white bra, then breasts and buns in G-string with another woman in hotel room.
- ••• 1:10—Breasts, while making love in bed with Jake. Long scene.
- • 1:27—Breasts while making love with Jake (in B&W).

Lady in Waiting (1994) . . . . Lori
(Unrated version reviewed.)
- • 0:16—Left breast while making out in car with Michael Nouri.
- ••• 0:30—Breasts, while sitting in bathtub and talking on the phone.
- •• 0:36—Buns and breasts while making love in bed with Nouri.
- •• 0:47—Full frontal nudity in mirror, while putting a shirt on.
- ••• 0:49—Nude, after taking off shirt and taking a shower with her lover and making love while Nouri watches from outside the house.

Private Obsession (1994). . . . . Emanuelle Griffith
- • 0:09—Buns and breasts, while getting dressed in motor home.
- • 0:27—Brief breasts, after Richard rips her top off after she tries to squeeze through the pet door.
- •• 0:28—Breasts, when Richard rubs butter on her breasts, to help her slip back through.
- ••• 0:30—Breasts, when in the bathroom, to clean herself off. Nude while in the shower. Sometimes seen on TV monitor.
- ••• 0:56—In black lingerie, after taking off gold dress, for Richard. Nude after taking off bra and panties, and dancing for Richard in only stockings.
- ••• 1:02—Breasts, while making love with Richard in living room.
- • 1:07—Breasts, after Richard takes her dress off after her escape attempt.
- • 1:08—Buns, while sleeping on the bed, then breasts, sitting up to watch monitor.
- •• 1:12—Breasts and buns, going into bathroom to get glass out of toilet tank.
- • 1:14—Nude by the door, listening to Richard yelling.
- • 1:25—Breasts, while making love with Richard in bed.
- • 1:34—Buns in panties and white bra after undressing in her room.

Dangerous Prey (1995) . . . . Robin
- ••• 0:06—Nude, while making love in bed on top of her boyfriend.
- • 0:20—Brief breasts in flashbacks.
- •• 0:24—Nude, while taking a shower, then knocking a guy unconscious.
- • 0:30—Brief full frontal nudity in flashbacks.

Exit (1995) . . . . Diane
- ••• 0:08—Nude, while making love with Kyle.
- •• 0:29—Breasts, during strip routine on stage, before being interrupted by gunmen.

The Granny (1995) .... Kelly
•• 0:55—Breasts while wearing panties and walking around in her room after taking a shower.
Omega Doom (1995) .... Zed
Playback (1995) .... Karen Stone
• 0:02—Partial buns, while getting dressed in black lingerie.
Ringer (1996) .... Kristin/Tracy
• 0:02—Brief buns in panties. Don't see her face.
• 0:05—Breasts, while making love with her husband on the floor.
•• 0:37—Nude, getting in and out of hot tub with Malcolm McDowell.
•• 1:28—Breasts and brief partial buns, while making love with Timothy Bottoms in bed.
Retroactive (1997)............................ Rayanne
Made for Cable Movies:
Directed By: The Gift (1994; Showtime) ...... Sitting Woman
Video Tapes:
Eden 6 (1994)......................... Lauren's Friend

Whitaker, Christina

Films:
The Naked Cage (1985)........................... Rita
••• 0:08—Breasts in bed with Willy.
• 0:55—Brief breasts in gaping sweatshirt during fight with Sheila.
• 1:29—Sort of left breast in gaping dress.
Assault of the Killer Bimbos (1988) ....Peaches
Midnight Cabaret (1988) .... Dancer
Stormquest (1988) .... Asha
Vampire at Midnight (1988) .... Ingrid
Made for Cable TV:
Love Street: Seven Fifteen (1993; Showtime).... Eve Sutter
0:08—In bra in motel room with Jack.
••• 0:09—Breasts and buns, while making love in bed with Jack.
0:14—In white bra, panties, garter belt and stockings while in motel room with Jack.
• 0:15—Brief breasts while tied to the bed by her wrists.
0:18—In black bra, panties, garter belt and stocking in motel room with Jack.
•• 0:19—Brief breasts, while dropping her towel.
••• 0:20—Breasts, while making love in bed with Jack.
••• 0:22—Breasts, while making love in bed.

Whitcraft, Elizabeth

Films:
Birdy (1985) .... Rosanne
Angel Heart (1987) .... Connie
(Original Unedited Version reviewed.)
(Blonde hair.)
•• 0:33—Breasts, while in bed talking with Mickey Rourke and taking off her clothes.
Working Girl (1989)................... Doreen DiMucci
(Brunette hair.)
•• 0:29—Breasts, while on bed on Alec Baldwin when Melanie Griffith opens the door.
GoodFellas (1990)..............Tommy's Girlfriend at Copa
Where Sleeping Dogs Lie (1991).......... Serena's Secretary
Object of Obsession (1994)..................... Christy
Video Tapes:
Inside Out 2 (1992) .... Sarah/Some Guys Have All the Luck
(Unrated version reviewed.)
••• 1:10—Breasts, while taking off her top in bed. More breasts while in bed. Brief partial buns.

Eden 3 (1993) .... Val
•• 0:15—Left breast, while lying in bed under Lyle.
••• 0:29—Breasts while in room, then making love with Lyle.
••• 1:03—Breasts while taking off her swimsuit top outside in front of Lyle.

White, April Daisy

Films:
Silent Madness (1984) .... Susan
• 0:06—Breasts, while changing tops at back of van.
Violated (1987)........................... Lisa Robb
••• 0:16—Breasts, while wearing panties while getting dressed in bedroom while talking to her little brother.
•• 0:22—Breasts, after taking off her dress and diving into pool.
•• 0:25—Full frontal nudity while getting raped in bedroom by Jack while Marilyn and Frank help.
• 0:28—Breasts and lower frontal nudity while washing herself off in bathtub.
•• 0:40—Breasts in flashback of rape scene.
• 0:53—Full frontal nudity in flashback of rape scene.
• 1:08—Breasts on video playback of taking her dress off by pool.

• White, Carla

Made for Cable TV:
Outer Limits: The Revelations of 'Becka Paulson (1997; Showtime) .... Actress
Poltergeist: The Legacy/Black Widow (1997; Showtime) .... Isabelle
• 0:36—Brief left breast, while lowering her nightgown when trying to seduce Derek in his bedroom.

White, Carol *

Films:
Never Let Go (1960; British) .... Jackie
Daddy's Gone A-Hunting (1969) .... Cathy Palmer
The Man Who Had Power Over Women (1970; British) .... Jody Pringle
Something Big (1971; British) .... Dover MacBride
Some Call It Loving (1972) .... Scarlett
Up the Sandbox (1972)............... Miss Spittlemeister
The Squeeze (1977; British)......................... Jill
••• 0:58—Nude, after taking off her clothes in front of the three bad guys. Long scene.

White, Sheila

Films:
Cop-Out (1967; British)......................... Hazel
Here We Go Round the Mulberry Bush (1968; British) ... Paula
Oliver! (1968; British) .... Bet
Confessions of a Window Cleaner (1974; British)........Rosie
Confessions of a Pop Performer (1975; British) ....Rosie
Oh, Alfie! (1975; British) .... Norma
a.k.a. Alfie Darling
Miniseries:
I, Claudius—Episode 12, A God in Colchester (1976; British) .... Lady Messalina
(Available on video tape in *I, Claudius—Volume 6.*)
•• 0:00—Left breast, in bed with Mnester.
• 0:02—Buns, getting out of bed and putting on a sheer dress.
• 0:18—Right breast, in bed with Silius.
••• 0:29—Breasts in bed with Silius.

White, Vanna *

Films:

Gypsy Angels (1980) . . . . Mickey

• 0:46—Partial right breast, while making out with Jeff outside by a fire.

Graduation Day (1981) . . . . Doris

Looker (1981) . . . . Reston Girl

Naked Gun 33 1/3: The Final Insult (1993) . . . . Herself

Double Dragon (1994) . . . . Herself

Made for TV Movies:

The Goddess of Love (1988) . . . . Venus

TV:

Wheel of Fortune (1982-) . . . . Hostess

Video Tapes:

Vanna White—Get Slim, Stay Slim . . . . Herself

CD-ROM:

Wheel of Fortune (1994) . . . . Herself

• Whitely, Arkie

Films:

Razorback (1984; Australian) . . . . Sarah Cameron

• 0:50—Brief right breast, while showering outdoors when seen by Gregory Harrison.

Scandal (1989) . . . . Vicky

(Unrated version reviewed.)

Princess Caraboo (1994) . . . . Betty

Made for TV Movies:

Mystery! Gallowglass (1995; British) . . . . Nina

Whitfield, Lynn *

Films:

Doctor Detroit (1983) . . . . Thelma Cleland

Silverado (1985) . . . . Ray

The Slugger's Wife (1985) . . . . Tina Alvarado

Dead Aim (1987) . . . . Sheila Freeman

Jaws: The Revenge (1987) . . . . Louisa

Taking the Heat (1993) . . . . Carolyn

In the Army Now (1994) . . . . Sergeant Ladd

A Thin Line Between Love and Hate (1995) . . . . Brandi

•• 0:53—Brief right breast, then brief left breast, while making love in bed with Martin Lawrence.

Gone Fishin' (1997) . . . . Angie

Made for Cable Movies:

The Josephine Baker Story (1991; HBO) . . . Josephine Baker

• 0:00—Breasts while dancing during opening credits. Slow motion.

•• 0:13—Breasts after taking off her dress top for the French painter.

••• 0:14—Breasts in the mirror and while dancing with the painter after making love. Nice. Dancer doing splits looks like a body double.

• 0:16—Brief buns, in wet dress, getting out of swimming pool.

••• 0:31—Breasts while on stage doing the Banana Dance.

••• 0:33—Breasts, while doing the Banana Dance.

• 2:02—Brief breasts while dancing in flashback.

State of Emergency (1993; HBO) . . . . Dehlia Johnson

Sophie & The Moonhanger (1996; Lifetime) . . . . Sophie

Miniseries:

Women of Brewster Place (1989) . . . . Ciel

Made for TV Movies:

Triumph of the Heart: The Ricky Bell Story (1991) . . . . . . Natala

The Cosby Mysteries (1994) . . . . Barbara Lorenz

Thicker Than Blood: The Larry McLinden Story (1994) . . . . Bobbie Mallory

TV:

Heartbeat (1988-89) . . . . Dr. Cory Banks

Equal Justice (1991) . . . . Maggie Mayfield

The Cosby Mysteries (1994-95) . . . . Barbara Lorenz

Whitlow, Jill

Films:

Porky's (1981; Canadian) . . . . Mindy

Mask (1985) . . . . Annie Marie

Weird Science (1985) . . . . Perfume Salesgirl

Night of the Creeps (1986) . . . . Cynthia Cronenberg

• 0:33—Brief breasts putting nightgown on over her head in her bedroom.

Thunder Run (1986) . . . . Kim

Twice Dead (1989) . . . . Robin/Myrna

TV:

Baby Boom (1988-89) . . . . J.C. Wiatt as a Teenager

Whitman, Kari *

a.k.a. Kari Kennel.

Films:

Masterblaster (1986) . . . . Jennifer

Beverly Hills Cop II (1987) . . . . Playboy Model

Phantom of the Mall: Eric's Revenge (1988) . . . . . Melody Austin

Men at Work (1990) . . . . Judy

Chained Heat 2 (1993) . . . . Suzanne Morrison

Forced to Kill (1993) . . . . Heather

Made for TV Movies:

Deadly Medicine (1991) . . . . n.a.

Video Tapes:

Rock Video Girls (1991) . . . . Small Town Girl

• 0:31—Breasts under sheer white nightie.

Playboy Playmates in Paradise (1992) . . . . Playmate

Whitting, Robyn

Films:

Innocent Sally (1973) . . . . n.a.

a.k.a. The Dirty Mind of Young Sally

Video Vixens (1973) . . . . Patient and Virginia

•• 0:40—Breasts, then nude on couch in psychiatrist's office. In B&W.

•• 0:52—Full frontal nudity acting in bed with Rex for a film. In B&W.

Whitton, Margaret

Films:

Love Child (1982) . . . . Jacki Steinberg

National Lampoon Goes to the Movies (1982) . . . . . First Lady

a.k.a. Movie Madness

9 1/2 Weeks (1986) . . . . Molly

The Best of Times (1986) . . . . Darla

Ironweed (1987) . . . . Katrina

•• 1:19—Full frontal nudity leaving the house and walking down steps while young Francis brushes a horse.

The Secret of My Success (1987) . . . . Vera Prescott

• 0:31—Very brief breasts taking off swimsuit top in swimming pool with Michael J. Fox.

Little Monsters (1989) . . . . Holly Stevenson

Major League (1989) . . . . Rachel Phelps

Big Girls Don't Cry... They Get Even (1991) . . . . Melinda

The Man Without a Face (1993) . . . . Catherine

Major League II (1994) . . . . Rachel Phelps

Trial By Jury (1994) . . . . Jane Lyle

Made for TV Movies:

The Summer My Father Grew Up (1991) . . . . Naomi

Menendez: A Killing in Beverly Hills (1994) . . . Leslie Abramson

TV:

Hometown (1985) .... Barbara Donnelly
Fine Romance (1989) .... Louisa
Good & Evil (1991) .... Genny
Cutters (1993) .... Adrienne St. John

Wiesmeier, Lynda *

Films:

Joysticks (1983) .... Candy
Private School (1983) .... School Girl
- ••• 0:42—Nude in shower room scene. First blonde in shower on the left.

Malibu Express (1984) .... June Khnockers
- •• 0:04—Breasts in locker room taking jumpsuit off.
- • 1:16—Breasts leaning out of racing car window while a helicopter chases her and Cody.

Preppies (1984) .... Trini
- ••• 1:06—Breasts on bed with Mark.

R.S.V.P. (1984) .... Jennifer Edwards
- •• 0:11—Breasts diving into the pool while Toby fantasizes about her being nude.
- • 0:19—Breasts in kitchen when Toby fantasizes about her again.
- ••• 1:21—Nude getting out of the pool and kissing Toby, when she really is nude.

Touch and Go (1984) .... Girl in Bar
Wheels of Fire (1984) .... Arlie
a.k.a. Desert Warrior
- ••• 0:18—Breasts on the ground, being held down by two bad guys, then getting tied to hood of car.
- •• 0:20—More breasts, long shot, tied to hood of car.
- • 0:22—More breasts while tied to the hood of the car.
- •• 0:23—Breasts, being brought into tent.
- ••• 0:34—Breasts, chained up in tent and trying to escape. Long scene.
- •• 0:45—Left breast, while lying on cot.
- •• 0:47—Breasts outside, fighting off crowd of guys.

Avenging Angel (1985) .... Debbie
Real Genius (1985) .... Chris' Girl at Party
Teen Wolf (1985) .... n.a.
Evil Town (1987) .... Dianne
- ••• 0:09—Breasts, while on top of Tony outside while camping.
- •• 0:11—Right breast while making out with boyfriend outside. Breasts when getting up.
- • 0:13—Breasts in open blouse, while running from bad guy. Nice bouncing action.
- •• 0:15—Breasts, while getting captured by bad guys.
- •• 0:17—Breasts, when getting out of car and brought into the house.
- •• 0:23—Breasts while tied up in chair.

Going Undercover (1988; British) .... Beach Girl

Video Tapes:

Playboy's Playmate Workout .... Playmate
Playboy's Playmate Review (1982) .... Playmate
- ••• 1:17—Nude undressing and taking a shower. Wow! Then in ballet studio.

Playboy Video Magazine, Volume 2 (1983) ..... Playmate
- ••• 1:12—In bra, stockings and garter belt. Undressing then full frontal nudity taking a shower.
- ••• 1:18—Nude, working out in dance studio.

Playboy Video Magazine, Volume 5 (1983) ..... Playmate
- • 0:06—Brief breasts in shower.

Red Hot Rock (1984) .... Girl in Shower
a.k.a. Sexy Shorts (on laser disc)
- • 0:01—Brief upper half of buns, then breasts taking off bra while a guy peeks into the locker room during "Girls" by Dwight Tilley.
- • 0:02—Brief full frontal nudity in the shower. (On the left.)

Wet & Wild (1989) .... Model
Playmates at Play (1990) .... Hardbodies

Wilbur, Claire

Films:

Score! (1973) .... Elvira
- • 0:01—Brief breasts, while making love with Jack.
- • 0:04—Brief buns, after taking off overcoat.
- • 0:13—Left breast, while on bed in open blouse, lying on bed for Lynn Lowry to take a picture.
- ••• 0:20—Full frontal nudity after taking off her robe in front of Mike. Buns, while making love.
- • 0:33—Brief breasts, while taking off bra.
- • 0:53—Brief right breast while sitting back in bed.
- •• 0:59—Breasts, after taking off her dress to go to sleep with Betsy.
- • 1:02—Brief left breast, while in bed with Betsy.
- ••• 1:09—Full frontal nudity while standing up in bed, making love with Betsy.
- ••• 1:12—Breasts, while making love with Lynn.
- • 1:15—Breasts, while waking up in bed.
- • 1:22—Right breast, while in bed with everybody.
- • 1:24—Breasts, while in bed.

Teenage Hitchikers (1975) .... n.a.

Wilcox, Mary *

Films:

Marlowe (1969) .... YWCA Clerk
Willie Dynamite (1973) .... Scatback
Lepke (1975; U.S./Israeli) .... Marion
- • 1:17—Breasts, while in apartment with Tony Curtis.

The Big Bus (1976) .... Mary Jane Beth Sue
Black Oak Conspiracy (1977) .... Beulah

Wilcox, Toyah

British singer.

Films:

Jubilee (1977) .... Mad
Quadrophenia (1979; British) .... Monkey
The Tempest (1979; British) .... Miranda
The Ebony Tower (1985) .... Freak
- • 0:37—Full frontal nudity, undressing and going skinny dipping in lake. Long shot.
- • 0:38—Buns and side of right breast, kneeling during picnic after swimming.
- • 0:39—Buns, while lying down next to Lawrence Olivier.
- •• 0:40—Buns, while lying next to Greta Scacchi and talking to David.
- •• 0:44—More buns, while talking to David and watching him go swimming.

Anchoress (1993; British) .... Pauline Carpenter

Wild, Kelley *

Video Tapes:

The Best of the Mermaids (1992) .... Heartstrings
- ••• 0:35—Nude, while playing harp.

Hot Body International: #3 Lingerie Special (1992) .... Contestant
- •• 0:22—Buns in purple and black bra and G-string.

••• 0:55—Breasts, when getting out of bed. Buns, in G-string. Breasts in bathtub.
••• 0:57—Buns and breasts, getting a massage.
Hot Body International: #5 Miss Acapulco (1992) . . . . Contestant
•• 0:01—Brief breasts while saying "Hi Mom!"
••• 0:39—Breasts, taking off her bikini top.
•• 0:40—Buns, dancing in green two piece swimsuit.
Mermaids of Sand, Sea and Surf (1993) . . . . n.a.
Vixens of Bandelero (1993) . . . . n.a.
Mermaids at War (1994) . . . . n.a.

Wild, Sándra *

Films:
Body Waves (1991) . . . . Anita
••• 0:39—Breasts under sheer white robe, then breasts with Larry on chair.
••• 1:12—Breasts in bedroom with Larry.
California Hot Wax (1992) . . . . Bikini Girl
Sunset Grill (1992) . . . . Mrs. Pietrowski
• 0:03—Out-of-focus breasts, while making love. Seen through telephoto camera lens.
••• 0:04—Breasts in bed with her lover, then nude while struggling in bedroom with her husband.
Fit To Kill (1993) . . . . Sandy
••• 0:07—Breasts, while talking on phone while standing in spa. Buns in gold swimsuit bottom, while getting out. Breasts while pouring coffee.
••• 0:21—Breasts in spa in long shot. More breasts in closer shot while putting swimsuit on.
• 1:11—Buns, while wearing a sexy black swimsuit/lingerie outfit.
Made for Cable TV:
Sessions: Episode 2 (1991; HBO) . . . . Amber
Video Tapes:
Wet & Wild (1989) . . . . Model
Sexy Lingerie II (1990) . . . . Model
Fantasies 2 (1992) . . . . Model
Inside Out 4 (1992) . . . . Blonde Woman/The Thief
(Unrated version reviewed.)
••• 0:44—Breasts, sitting up in bed and getting out.
Playboy's 101 Ways to Excite Your Lover (1992) . . . . Smell/Woman
••• 0:08—Nude in green robe in bedroom.
Rock Video Girls 2 (1992) . . . . Herself
••• 0:21—Breasts taking off her tank top by water pump in music video.

Wilde, Cecilia

Films:
Psychos in Love (1987) . . . . Nikki
•• 0:08—Breasts, dancing on stage in a bar.
••• 0:14—Buns, in G-string while dancing on stage, then breasts.
•• 0:45—Breasts, dancing on stage with a fluorescent light.
Pledge Night (1988) . . . . Connie

Wildman, Valerie

Films:
Splash (1984) . . . . Wedding Guest
The Falcon and the Snowman (1985) . . . . U.S. Embassy Official
A Fine Mess (1986) . . . . Anchorwoman
Salvador (1986) . . . . Pauline Axelrod
Inner Sanctum (1991) . . . . Jennifer Reed
•• 0:11—Right breast, while sitting on bed with Joseph Bottoms.
Neon City (1991) . . . . Sandy
Josh and S.A.M. (1993) . . . . Dallas Airline Officer
My Family (1995) . . . . Sunny, Gloria's Friend
Rumpelstiltskin (1995) . . . . Nedda
Dear God (1996) . . . . Southern Tourist
Mars Attacks! (1996) . . . . GNN Reporter
Skeletons (1996) . . . . Belinda
Made for Cable Movies:
Indictment: The McMartin Trial (1995; HBO) . . . . Diana Sullivan
Made for Cable TV:
Tales From the Crypt: Came the Dawn (1993) . . . . Woman in Restaurant
TV:
Beverly Hills, 90210 (1993-94) . . . . Christine Pettit
CD-ROM:
Jedi Knight: Dark Forces II (1997) . . . . Sariss

Wildsmith, Dawn

Films:
Armed Response (1986) . . . . Thug
Cyclone (1986) . . . . Henna
Star Slammer—The Escape (1986) . . . . Muffin
Surf Nazis Must Die (1986) . . . . Eva
• 0:25—Breasts being fondled at the beach wearing a wet suit by Adolf. Mostly right breast.
Commando Squad (1987) . . . . Consuela
Evil Spawn (1987) . . . . Evelyn Avery
Phantom Empire (1987) . . . . Eddy Colchilde
The Tomb (1987) . . . . Anna Conda
••• 0:54—Breasts taking off robe in room with Michelle Bauer, then getting pushed onto a bed full of snakes.
B.O.R.N. (1988) . . . . Singer
Deep Space (1988) . . . . Janice
Hollywood Chainsaw Hookers (1988) . . . . Lori
It's Alive III: Island of the Alive (1988) . . . . Uncredited Dancer in Club
Warlords (1988) . . . . Danny
Alienator (1989) . . . . Caroline
Beverly Hills Vamp (1989) . . . . Sherry Santa Monica
Nerds of a Feather (1989) . . . . Fortune Telling Client
The Alien Within (1990) . . . . Evelyn Avery
(Contains footage from *The Evil Spawn* woven together with new material.)
Wizards of the Demon Sword (1990) . . . . Selena
a.k.a. Demon Sword
Jack-O (1995) . . . . Sorceress
a.k.a. Jacko Lantern

Wiley, Laurel *

Films:
Shock 'Em Dead (1990) . . . . Monique
• 0:26—Brief breasts, pulling her top down to show Martin her scar. Don't see her face.
Test Tube Teens From the Year 2000 (1993) . . . . . . Annie
a.k.a. Virgin Hunters
••• 0:30—Breasts, taking off towel and in the showers (she's on the right) with Victoria while Vin and Naldo watch.
Made for Cable TV:
Red Shoe Diaries: The Last Motel (1996; Showtime) . . . . Mrs. Betsy Fremont
• 0:02—Brief left breast with Bruno.
• 0:06—Breasts, after taking off her top.
• 0:07—Brief breasts, after taking off her top.
•• 0:19—Breasts, after taking off her top and dancing with Bruno.

Wilkening, Catherine

Films:

Contrainte Par Corps (1988; French) .... Lola
Deux Minutes de Soleil en Plus (1988; French) .... Aina
Jesus of Montreal (1990; French/Canadian) .... Mireille Fontaine
- • 1:08—Brief breasts starting to take off her sweatshirt during an audition.

Made for Cable TV:

Strangers: Going Without (1996; HBO) .... Julie
- •• 0:12—Breasts, while making love in bed with Julian Sands. Seen on camcorder LCD screen, on TV and in real life.

Wilkes, Donna

Films:

Almost Summer (1978) .... Meredith
Jaws II (1978) .... Jackie
Fyre (1979) .... Carol
Hard Knocks (1979) .... Chrissy
a.k.a. Hollywood Knight
Schizoid (1980) .... Allison Foles
- • 0:12—Breasts taking off her bra in bathroom while Klaus Kinski watches. Buns, getting into the shower. Out of focus shots.
- •• 0:13—Side view breasts getting into the shower.

Blood Song (1982) .... Marion
a.k.a. Dreamslayer
Angel (1983) .... Angel/Molly
Grotesque (1987) .... Kathy

Made for TV Movies:

The Courage and the Passion (1978) .... Tracy
Born to Be Sold (1981) .... Cindy Carlson

TV:

Hello, Larry (1979) .... Diane Adler
Days of Our Lives (1982-83) .... Pamela Prentiss

Wilkinson, June *

Films:

The Immoral Mr. Teas (1959) .... Uncredited torso
Talking Walls (1982) .... Blonde
- • 0:13—Brief left breast, in car room, getting green towel yanked off.
- • 0:14—Very, very brief left breast in car room again. Dark.
- •• 1:08—Brief breasts, getting green towel taken off.

Sno-Line (1984) .... Audrey
Keaton's Cop (1990) .... Archie "Big Mama" Gish

Willets, Kathy *

Wife of a policeman who ran a prostitution ring with her in Florida. She claimed Prozac made her a nymphomaniac.

Adult Films:

Naked Scandal (1996) .... n.a.
Naked Scandal 2 (1996) .... n.a.

Williams, Barbara

Films:

Thief of Hearts (1984) .... Mickey Davis
(Special Home Video Version reviewed.)
- • 0:46—Right breast in bathtub when her husband comes in and tries to read her diary.
- ••• 0:53—Breasts, while making love with Steven Bauer in his condo. Very brief lower frontal nudity when Bauer picks her up.

Jo Jo Dancer, Your Life Is Calling (1986) .... Dawn
Tiger Warsaw (1988) .... Karen
Watchers (1988) .... Nora
City of Hope (1991) .... Angela
Indecency (1992) .... Marie
Oh, What a Night (1992) .... Vera
- •• 0:21—Very brief right breast, then very brief breasts, while undressing to go for a swim while Corey Haim watches without her knowledge. Brief breasts in the water and getting out.
- • 0:46—Breasts, while swimming the backstroke in the water while Haim watches again.
- ••• 0:59—Breasts, while swimming the backstroke again and getting out. (This time she knows that Haim is watching.) Nice slow motion shot for a PG-13 film! Very brief wet panties.
- •• 1:15—Left breast, while lying down on her back with Haim in a barn.

Inventing the Abbotts (1997) .... Joan Abbott
Bone Daddy (1998) .... Sharon

Made for Cable Movies:

Keeper of the City (1991; Showtime) .... Grace
Spencer: Ceremony (1993) .... Susan
Joe Torre: Curveballs Along the Way (1997; Showtime) .... Ali Torre

Made for Cable TV:

The Outer Limits: Under the Bed (1995; Showtime) .... Detective Kaitlin Doyle

Made for TV Movies:

Quiet Killer (1992) .... Charlene
A Family of Cops (1995) .... Kate Fein
In the Line of Duty: Kidnapped (1995) .... Beth Honeycutt
Breach of Faith: A Family of Cops II (1997) .... Kate

Williams, Carol Ann

Films:

1941 (1979) .... USO Girl
Butch and Sundance: The Early Days (1979) .... Lilly
The Hollywood Knights (1980) .... Jane
- • 0:51—Very brief breasts, opening her blouse to distract Dudley. Don't see her face.

Williams, Cynda

Ex-wife of actor/director Billy Bob Thornton.

Films:

Mo' Better Blues (1990) .... Clarke Betancourt
- •• 0:24—Breasts, then left breast after kissing Denzel Washington.
- ••• 1:07—Breasts on bed when Denzel Washington accidentally calls her "Indigo."
- •• 1:28—Left breast while making love in bed with Wesley Snipes.

The Killing Box (1992) .... Rebecca
One False Move (1992) .... Fantasia
Ghost Brigade (1994) .... n.a.
Condition Red (1995) .... Gidell
- • 0:42—Brief breasts, when James Russo stops making love with her.

Machine Gun Blues (1995) .... Georgia
- • 0:18—Very brief left breast, while lying in bed with Nick Cassavetes.
- • 0:34—Side of left breast, while sitting in Cassavetes' lap and kissing him.
- ••• 0:38—In bra, then breasts, while making love in bed with Cassavetes.

The Sweeper (1995) .... Diane
Tales of Erotica (1995) .... Davida Urked
- •• 1:30—Breasts and buns, getting out of bubble bath and walking to the front door. Covered with bubbles.

- 1:31—Brief breasts, getting back into the bathtub.
- 1:32—Brief breasts, moving back in bathtub. Upper half of breasts, while sitting in bathtub.
- 1:34—Brief breasts, while turning around in bathtub.
- 1:36—Buns, while standing up in bathtub. Brief close up shot of buns.
- 1:38—Brief buns in video playback.

The Tie That Binds (1995) . . . . Lisa-Marie Chandler
Spirit Lost (1996) . . . . Arabella
- •• 0:32—Side of left breast, then left and right breasts, while making love with Leon on the floor.
- •• 0:41—Breasts, while making love with Leon in bed.
- • 1:00—Brief left breast, when covering herself with the comforter.
- • 1:22—Brief breasts, while making love on top of Leon in bed when confronted by his wife.

Caught Up (1998). . . . . n.a.

Made for Cable Movies:

Gang in Blue (1996; Showtime) . . . . Anita Bayard

Made for Cable TV:

Fallen Angels: Fearless (1995; Showtime). . . . . Deletha
- •• 0:09—Right breast, while lying in bed with Giancarlo Esposito, then putting on dress.

Made for TV Movies:

Tales of the City (1994). . . . . D'orothea Wilson

Williams, Edy *

Ex-wife of director Russ Meyer.

Films:

The Secret Life of an American Wife (1968). . . . Susie Steinberg
Beyond the Valley of the Dolls (1970) . . . . Ashley St. Ives
The Seven Minutes (1971) . . . . Faye Osborn
Dr. Minx (1975) . . . . Carol Evans
Breasts.
An Almost Perfect Affair (1979) . . . . Herself
- • 0:18—Breasts and buns, while showing off during Cannes Film Festival.
- • 0:38—Brief breasts in a photo of herself that she holds up.

The Best of Sex and Violence (1981). . . . . Herself
- •• 0:46—Breasts in various scenes from *Dr. Minx.*

Famous T & A (1982). . . . . Herself
(No longer available for purchase, check your video store for rental.)
- •• 0:39—Breasts and bun scenes from *Dr. Minx.*

Chained Heat (1983; U.S./German) . . . . Paula
- •• 0:30—Full frontal nudity in the shower, soaping up Twinks.
- •• 0:36—Breasts at night in bed with Twinks.

Hollywood Hot Tubs (1984) . . . . Desiree
- ••• 0:26—Breasts, trying to seduce Shawn while he works on a hot tub.
- • 1:30—Partial breasts with breasts sticking out of her bra while she sits by hot tub with Jeff.
- •• 1:32—Breasts in hot tub room with Shawn.
- • 1:36—Brief breasts while running around.
- • 1:38—Breasts again in the hot tub lobby.

Hellhole (1985). . . . . Vera
- ••• 0:22—Breasts on bed posing for Ray Sharkey.
- ••• 0:24—Breasts in white panties in shower, then fighting with another woman.
- ••• 1:03—Breasts in mud bath with another woman. Long scene.

Mankillers (1987) . . . . Sergeant Roberts
Rented Lips (1988). . . . . Heather Darling
- • 0:15—Breasts in bed, under Robert Downey, Jr. during playback of porno movie.

Bad Manners (1989) . . . . Mrs. Slatt
Dr. Alien (1989). . . . . Buckmeister
a.k.a. I Was a Teenage Sex Mutant
- ••• 0:54—Breasts taking off her top in the women's locker room in front of Wesley.

Nudity Required (1989) . . . . Isabella
- ••• 1:05—Breasts, with whip, while acting in movie.
- •• 1:07—More breasts in movie.
- •• 1:09—More right breast.
- •• 1:13—Breasts, during screening of the movie.

Bad Girls from Mars (1990) . . . . Emanuelle
- •• 0:17—Breasts, several times changing in back of convertible car.
- ••• 0:23—Breasts, changing out of wet dress in bathroom.
- ••• 0:30—Breasts taking off blouse to get into spa.
- • 0:32—Breasts in back of Porsche and getting out.
- ••• 0:35—Breasts in store, signing autograph for robber.
- • 0:46—Buns in G-string, then breasts taking off her top again.
- ••• 0:58—Breasts in T.J.'s office. More breasts when wrestling with Martine.
- • 1:05—Breasts while tied up.
- • 1:07—Breasts again.
- •• 1:17—Breasts while taking off her outfit during outtakes.

Williams, JoBeth

Films:

Kramer vs. Kramer (1979). . . . . Phyllis Bernard
- • 0:45—Buns and brief breasts in the hallway meeting Dustin Hoffman's son.

The Dogs of War (1980; British). . . . . Jessie
Stir Crazy (1980) . . . . Meredith
Endangered Species (1982) . . . . Harriet Purdue
Poltergeist (1982) . . . . Diane Freeling
The Big Chill (1983) . . . . Karen
American Dreamer (1984). . . . . Cathy Palmer
Teachers (1984) . . . . Lisa
- • 1:39—Brief breasts taking off clothes and running down school hallway yelling at Nick Nolte.

Desert Bloom (1986). . . . . Lily
Poltergeist II: The Other Side (1986) . . . . Diane Freeling
Memories of Me (1988). Lisa McConnell
Welcome Home (1989) . . . . Sarah
Dutch (1991) . . . . Natalie
a.k.a. Driving Me Crazy
Switch (1991) . . . . Margo Brofman
Stop! Or My Mom Will Shoot (1992). . . . . Gwen Harper
Wyatt Earp (1994). . . . . Bessie Earp
Jungle 2 Jungle (1997). . . . . Patricia

Made for Cable Movies:

Chantilly Lace (1993; Showtime) . . . . Natalie
- • 0:59—Brief breasts, taking off her blouse in bedroom with the pizza boy.

Sex, Love and Cold Hard Cash (1993; USA). . . . . n.a.
Parallel Lives (1994; Showtime) . . . . Win Winslow
Ruby Jean and Joe (1996; Showtime). . . . . Rose
When Danger Follows You Home (1997; USA). . . Anne Werden

Made for Cable TV:

Dead Man's Gun: Stage Coach Marty (1998; Showtime)
. . . . Marty

Miniseries:

The Day After (1983). . . . . Nancy

Made for TV Movies:

Adam (1983). . . . . Reve Walsh
Baby M (1988) . . . . Mary Beth Whitehead
My Name is Bill W. (1989). . . . . Lois Wilson
Child in the Night (1990) . . . . Dr. Jackie Hollis

Jonathan: The Boy Nobody Wanted (1992)..... Ginny Moore
Final Appeal (1993)................................n.a.
Voices From Within (1994) .... Nancy Parkhurst
A Season of Hope (1995)................ Elizabeth Hackett
Breaking Through (1996) .... Pam
TV:
Somerset (1975) .... Carrie Wheeler
The Guiding Light (1977-81)...............Brandy Shelooe
The Client (1995-96)....................... Reggie Love

Williams, K.C. *

a.k.a. Tracy Wolf and Tracy.
Adult film actress.
Films:
The Pamela Principle (1992) .... Shannon
(Unrated version reviewed.)
• 0:05—Very brief left breast in open blouse with Steve.
••• 0:06—Breasts and partial buns, while in hot tub with Steve.
Uninhibited (1993)................. Detective Jugginson
•• 0:58—Right breast, while lying in bed, talking on the phone with Detective Gunn.
•• 1:08—Breasts and buns, while in bathtub. Buns in sheer white outfit.
• 1:10—In sheer white outfit again. Buns, while talking with Cassandra.
•• 1:11—Breasts, while making love with Cassandra.
•• 1:24—Buns in G-string, while putting on make-up and in bed with Gunn.
••• 1:27—Breasts, while making love in bed with Gunn.
Video Tapes:
Penthouse Pet of the Year Playoff 1993 (1993) ..... Pet
••• 0:31—Nude on bed, in front of mirror while making herself up and getting dressed, in a house (sometimes wearing a black wig).
Penthouse Pet of the Year Winners 1993: Mahalia & Julie (1994) .... Sneak Preview of Pet of the Year Playoff
••• 0:25—In lingerie, then nude on bed and couch.
The Girls of Penthouse, Volume 3 (1995)........... Pet
•• 0:09—Left breast, while telling a little bit about herself.
••• 0:10—Nude in still photos.
••• 0:11—Nude, posing on white sheet.
••• 0:12—Nude at the beach.
••• 0:13—Nude, while posing in a house with another blonde woman.

• *Williams, Kelli*

Films:
Zapped Again! (1989)............................ Lucy
Mr. Jones (1993).................................Kelli
There Goes My Baby (1994) ....Sunshine
E=mc² (1995).......................... Claire Higgins
a.k.a. Wavelength
• 0:54—Brief right breast, while lying in bed with Jeremy Plven when he starts to make love with her. Very dark.
Made for TV Movies:
The Case of the Hillside Strangler (1989)..... Margaret Wilson
Switched at Birth (1991)..........................Irisa
A Woman Scorned: The Betty Broderick Story (1992) ....Kate Broderick
For Their Own Good (1993) ....Erma
Her Final Fury: Betty Broderick, the Last Chapter (1993) ....Kate Broderick
Lifepod (1993) .... Rena
Snowbound: The Jim and Jennifer Stolpa Story (1994) ....Jennifer Stolpa
TV:
New York News (1995-96)..........................Ellie
The Practice (1997-)......................Lindsay Dole

Williams, Meadow

Films:
Beverly Hills Cop III (1994).................. Spider Rider
The Mask (1994)...............................Pebbles
Apollo 13 (1995)..................................Kim
Made for Cable Movies:
Virtual Seduction (1995; Showtime) ....Hostess
Made for Cable TV:
Dream On: Try Not to Remember (1995; HBO) ..... Tina
• 0:21—In black bra, then brief breasts, while making out with Martin on sofa.
The Larry Sanders Show: Hank's Sex Tape (1995; HBO) ....Woman #2
• 0:06—Buns, while lying in bed when Jeffrey Tambor gets up out of bed.

Williams, Melissa

Films:
Showgirls (1995)............................... Julie
(NC-17 version reviewed.)
• 1:11—Brief breasts, while sitting at her make-up table backstage. Brief buns in T-back when she carries her daughter away.
• 1:40—Brief breasts, while running down the stairs.
Made for Cable TV:
Red Shoe Diaries: Forbidden Zone (1996; Showtime) . . . Zoner
Red Shoe Diaries: Banished (1998; Showtime). . . .Dancer 2
• 0:16—Buns, while lying on platform.

Williams, Wendy O. *

Lead singer of *The Plasmatics.*
Adult Films:
800 Fantasy Lane (1979).........................n.a.
Candy Goes to Hollywood (1979)....................n.a.
Films:
Reform School Girls (1986).................... Charlie
•• 0:26—Breasts talking to two girls in the shower.
Pucker Up and Bark Like a Dog (1989)............... Butch

• *Williamson, Kirsten*

Made for Cable TV:
The Outer Limits: Double Helix (1997; Showtime)..... Sharon
The Outer Limits: Lithia (1998; Showtime).......... Pele
•• 0:11—Breasts and buns, while taking a shower with and kissing Miranda.

• *Willis, Cher*

Films:
Animal Instincts: The Seductress (1995)........ Party Waitress
(Unrated version reviewed.)
Video Tapes:
Malibu Canyon Nights #1 (1997)............... Herself
••• 0:11—In lingerie, then nude, while posing in bathtub.

• *Willis, Dawn* *

Twin sister of Deanna Willis.
Video Tapes:
Playboy's Twins & Sisters Too (1997) ....Curtain Calls
••• 0:34—In lingerie, then nude, while posing with her twin sister.

• Willis, Deanna *

Twin sister of Dawn Willis.

Video Tapes:

Playboy's Twins & Sisters Too (1997) . . . . Curtain Calls
- ••• 0:34—In lingerie, then nude, while posing with her twin sister.

Wilsey, Shannon

See: Savannah.

Wilson, Ajita

Transexual (she used to be a he).

Films:

Love Lust and Ecstasy (1978) . . . . .Sara
- •• 0:02—Nude taking a shower and getting into bed with an old guy.
- •• 0:04—Nude making love with a young guy.
- •• 0:17—Breasts in bathtub, then making love on bed.
- •• 0:22—Breasts making love in a swimming pool, in a river, by a tree.
- •• 0:26—Nude getting undressed and taking a shower.
- •• 0:35—Full frontal nudity changing clothes.
- ••• 0:54—Full frontal nudity making love in bed.

The Joy of Flying (1979) . . . . Madame Gaballi

a.k.a. Erotic Ways
- •• 1:20—Full frontal nudity undressing for George.
- •• 1:23—Breasts, making love on top of George.
- • 1:25—Left breast, while in bed with George.

Catherine Cherie (1982) . . . . Dancer/Miss Ajita
- • 0:23—Breasts and buns dancing in club. Covered with paint. Long shot.
- • 0:24—Brief buns, while greeting Carlo after the show.
- •• 0:43—Full frontal nudity in room with Carlo.

A Man for Sale (1982) . . . . .Dancer/Model
- • 0:02—Breasts several times posing for photographer with another model.
- • 0:26—Breasts and buns, dancing in an erotic ballet show.

Savage Island (1985). . . . . Marie

Twelfth Night (1988; Italian) . . . . .Antonia
- •• 0:50—Buns, taking off her dress and walking into stream with a guy.
- • 0:51—Very brief breasts, making love with him in the stream.
- •• 1:11—Right breast, hanging out of black dress, dancing in tavern.

Wilson, Alisa

Films:

The Terror on Alcatraz (1986) . . . . Clarissa
- • 1:14—Brief breasts opening her blouse to distract Frank, so she can get away from him.

Loverboy (1989) . . . . Nurse Darlene

Psycho Cop 2 (1992) . . . . Anchorwoman

Wilson, Cheryl-Ann

Films:

Terminal Choice (1985; Canadian) . . . . .Nurse Fields

Cellar Dweller (1987). . . . . Lisa
- • 0:58—Brief left breast, in gaping blouse, while bending over exercising.
- •• 0:59—Brief right breast, then breasts while taking a shower.
- • 1:01—Partial left breast, then brief breasts, before getting killed by the cellar dweller.

TV:

Days of Our Lives. . . . . Megan Hathaway

Wilson, Janie

Films:

Mirror Images (1991). . . . . 1st Girl in Commercial
- •• 0:17—Breasts (she's on the right) on a guy's shoulders in pool, wrestling with another couple.

Video Tapes:

Fantasies 2 (1992) . . . . .Model

• Wilson, Peta

Films:

Loser (1996) . . . . Alyssha Rourke
- •• 0:34—Brief right breast, several times, while making love with Erica in bed.

Made for Cable Movies:

Woman Undone (1996; Showtime). . . . . Receptionist

Made for Cable TV:

Strangers: Going Without (1996; HBO). . . . . Martha
- • 0:22—Brief lower half of buns and very brief lower frontal nudity in black slip on video playback. Breasts partially visible under the slip.

La Femme Nikita: Choice (1997; USA) . . . . Nikita
- • 0:07—Brief side of left breast, sitting up in bed on top of her boyfriend and putting on her blouse.

La Femme Nikita: Hard Landing (1998; USA) . . . . . . Nikita
- • 0:33—Brief buns and very brief back side of right breast, when walking up to Michael in boat. (This is reportedly a body double.)

TV:

La Femme Nikita (1997-) . . . . Nikita

Wilson, Reagan *

Films:

Blood Mania (1970) . . . . .Cheryl
- •• 0:07—Breasts and buns, while in bubble bath.
- • 0:17—In bra, while undressing in bedroom. Very brief side of right breast, when putting on robe.
- • 0:21—Very brief side of left breast, while leaning over to kiss Craig in bed.
- • 0:34—Partial right breast, while on couch with the blackmailer.

Wilson, Seretta

Films:

Our Miss Fred (1972; British). . . . . .Elvira

Tower of Evil (1972; British) . . . . Mae

a.k.a. Beyond the Fog
- • 0:34—Very, very brief breasts, lying in bed in flashbacks. Then breasts, sleeping in bed.
- •• 0:35—Breasts, while sleeping in bed.
- • 0:38—More breasts, while sleeping in bed.
- • 0:39—Very, very brief breasts, getting the covers taken off before getting killed.
- • 0:41—Very brief breasts, dead, covered with blood.

Wilson, Sheree

Films:

Fraternity Vacation (1985) . . . . .Ashley Taylor
- • 0:47—Breasts and buns of body double (Roberta Whitewood), while in the bedroom when the guys photograph her with a telephoto lens.

Crimewave (1986). . . . . .Nancy

Hellbound (1993) . . . . .Leslie

Made for Cable Movies:

Past Tense (1994; Showtime) . . . . Emily Talbert

•• 1:00—Left breast and most of right breast in open vest in front of Scott Glenn. Definitely not a body double!

Miniseries:

Kane & Abel (1985) . . . . Melanie LeRoy

TV:

Our Family Honor (1985-86). . . . . Rita Danzig

Dallas (1987-91) . . . . April

Walker, Texas Ranger (1993-) . . . . .Alex Cahill

Winchester, Maude

Films:

Birdy (1985) . . . . Doris Robinson

•• 1:32—Breasts in car letting Mathew Modine feel her.

Brain Dead (1989). . . . . Crazy Anna

The Spirit of '76 (1991). . . . . Cyndi the Waitress

Bram Stoker's Dracula (1992) . . . . .Downstairs Maid

A Few Good Men (1992). . . . . Aunt Ginny

Carnosaur (1993) . . . . Downey

Roosters (1993). . . . . Waitress

Corrina, Corrina (1994). .Mrs. Rodgers

North (1994). . . . . Stewart's Mom

The American President (1995) . . . . White House Aide

Dracula: Dead and Loving It (1995). . . . . Ballroom Guest

Made for Cable Movies:

Attack of the 50 ft. Woman (1993; HBO). . . . . Donna

Windsor, Romy

See: Walthall, Romy.

Winger, Debra

Ex-wife of actor Timothy Hutton.

Films:

Slumber Party '57 (1976) . . . . Debbie

• 0:10—Breasts with her five girl friends during swimming pool scene. Hard to tell who is who.

••• 0:53—Breasts three times, lying down, making out with Bud.

Thank God It's Friday (1978) . . . . .Jennifer

French Postcards (1979) . . . . .Melanie

Urban Cowboy (1980) . . . . Sissy

Cannery Row (1982). . . . . Suzy

An Officer and a Gentleman (1982) . . . . .Paula Pokrifki

••• 1:05—Brief side view of right breast, then breasts making love with Richard Gere in a motel.

Terms of Endearment (1983). . . . . . . .Emma Greenway Horton

Mike's Murder (1984) . . . . .Betty

• 0:26—Brief left breast in bathtub.

Legal Eagles (1986). . . . . Laura Kelly

Black Widow (1987) . . . . Alexandra

Made in Heaven (1987). . . . . .Emmett

Betrayed (1988) . . . . .Katie Phillips/Cathy Weaver

Everybody Wins (1990) . . . . Angela Crispini

The Sheltering Sky (1990). . . . . Kit Moresby

• 0:13—Upper half of lower frontal nudity in open robe when John Malkovich caresses her stomach.

• 0:24—Buns, when getting out of bed.

• 0:41—Very brief breasts grabbing sheets and getting out of bed with Tunner.

• 1:58—Lower frontal nudity and sort of buns, while getting undressed with Belqassim.

Leap of Faith (1992) . . . . Jane

A Dangerous Woman (1993). . . . . .Martha Horgan

• 0:42—Very, very brief lower frontal nudity, then buns, while masturbating in bed. Don't see her face. Medium long shot.

Shadowlands (1993; British) . . . . .Joy Gresham

Wilder Napalm (1993) . . . . Vida

• 0:09—Left breast, after falling into bed with Arliss Howard.

Forget Paris (1995) . . . . .n.a.

TV:

Wonder Woman (1976-77) . . . . Drusilla/Wonder Girl

Winkler, Angela

Films:

The Lost Honor of Katharina Blum (1975; German) . . . . .Katharina Blum

•• 0:15—Full frontal nudity, while in bathroom, getting strip searched by policewoman.

• 0:43—Brief right breast, after getting out of the shower.

The Tin Drum (1979; German) . . . . Agnes Matzerath

•• 0:38—Very brief right breast after taking off clothes in room with Jan. Buns and side view of left breast in bed with him.

Benny's Video (1992). . . . . Mother

Winkler, K.C. *

Films:

H.O.T.S. (1979) . . . . .Cynthia

a.k.a. T & A Academy

• 0:27—Breasts in blue bikini bottom on balcony.

•• 0:31—Breasts in van making love, then arguing with John.

The Happy Hooker Goes Hollywood (1980) . . . . . . Amber

•• 0:41—Breasts in cowboy outfit on bed with a guy.

••• 0:43—Breasts, wearing a blue garter belt playing pool with Susan Kiger.

Night Shift (1982) . . . . .Cheryl

They Call Me Bruce? (1982). . . . . .n.a.

Armed and Dangerous (1986) . . . . Vicki

TV:

High Rollers . . . . .Hostess

Winn, Kitty

Films:

The Panic in Needle Park (1971) . . . . Helen

• 0:33—Brief side view of right breast, when reaching over to hug and kiss Al Pacino.

••• 0:42—Breasts, while sitting up in bed next to Pacino, then putting on T-shirt.

The Exorcist (1973) . . . . Sharon

Peepers (1975) . . . . Mianne Prendergast

Exorcist II: The Heretic (1977) . . . . Sharon

Mirrors (1978). . . . . Marianne

Miniseries:

Beacon Hill (1975). Rosamond Lassiter

Winningham, Mare *

Ex-wife of actor A Martinez.

Films:

One Trick Pony (1980) . . . . McDeena Dandridge

•• 0:14—Breasts, while in the bathtub with Paul Simon, smoking a cigarette. Long scene.

Threshold (1983; Canadian) . . . . Carol Severance

• 0:56—Brief full frontal nudity, lying on operating table, then side view of left breast getting prepped for surgery.

St. Elmo's Fire (1985). . . . . Wendy

Nobody's Fool (1986) . . . . Pat

Made in Heaven (1987). . . . . Brenda Carlucci

Shy People (1988)................................Candy
Miracle Mile (1989)...........................Julie Peters
Turner & Hooch (1989).......................Emily Carson
Hard Promises (1992)..............................Dawn
Teresa's Tattoo (1993)...........................Singer
The War (1994)............................Lois Simmons
Wyatt Earp (1994)......................Mattie Blaylock
Georgia (1996)..................................Georgia

Made for Cable Movies:
Better Off Dead (1992; Lifetime)........................n.a.
Sexual Healing (1993; Showtime)................... Marla
Letter to My Killer (1995; USA)...................... Judy

Miniseries:
The Thorn Birds (1983)....................Justine O'Neill

Made for TV Movies:
Helen Keller: The Miracle Continues (1984).......Helen Keller
Who is Julia? (1986) ....Mary Frances
A Winner Never Quits (1986) .... Annie
Crossing to Freedom (1990)...............Nicole Rougeron
Love & Lies (1990)..........................Kim Paris
She Stood Alone (1991)................Prudence Crandall
Intruders (1992)...........................Mary Wilkes
Those Secrets (1992)................................Faye
Betrayed by Love (1994)............................Dana
The Boys Next Door (1996) ....Sheila

Winslet, Kate

Films:
Heavenly Creatures (1994; New Zealand)........... Juliet
• 1:01—Breasts, sort of visible under water while sitting in bathtub talking to Melanie Lynskey
A Kid in King Arthur's Court (1995)...................n.a.
Sense and Sensibility (1995) ....Marianne Dashwood
Hamlet (1996) ....Ophelia
Jude (1996; British) ....Sue Bridehead
••• 1:21—Full frontal nudity, after taking off her nightgown and lying on bed with Jude.
Titanic (1997)....................................Rose

Winters, D.D.

See: Vanity.

Winters, Deborah

Films:
Hail, Hero! (1969)................................ Becky
Me, Natalie (1969) .... Betty Simon
The People Next Door (1970)..................... Maxie
•• 0:39—Brief left breast and buns, getting out of bed and walking toward her father.
•• 0:57—Nude, walking down the stairs and outside the house while on drugs.
Kotch (1971)........................... Erica Herzenstiel
Class of '44 (1973) ....Julie

*Witt, Holly **

Video Tapes:
Playboy Video Calendar 1997 (1996) .... June
••• 0:23—Nude, while posing outdoors after mountain climbing.
••• 0:25—In lingerie, then nude when posing in a house while a guy watches through a telescope.

Witt, Kathryn

Films:
Freebie and the Bean (1974) ....Whitey's Girl
•• 0:16—Buns, while tied up in bed when James Caan tries to get Whitey to talk.
Lenny (1974)......................................Girl
• 0:43—Right breast with Valerie Perrine while Dustin Hoffman watches.
Looker (1981) .... Tina Cassidy
Star 80 (1983).....................................Robin
Cocaine Wars (1986) ....Janet
a.k.a. Vice Wars
• 0:36—Brief breasts and buns making love in bed with John Schneider.
Demon of Paradise (1987)........................ Annie
Philadelphia (1993)..................... Melissa Benedict

TV:
Flying High (1978-79).....................Pam Bellagio

*Witter, Cherie **

Video Tapes:
Playboy Video Calendar 1987 (1986) ....Playmate

*Witter, Karen **

Films:
Dangerously Close (1986)..........................Betsy
The Perfect Match (1987) .... Tammy
Hero and the Terror (1988) .... Ginger
Mortuary Academy (1988) .... Christie Doll
Out of the Dark (1988) ....Jo Ann
Paramedics (1988) ....Danger Girl
Silent Assassins (1988)..................... Sushi Bar Girl
The Vineyard (1988) .... Rebecca Fairchild
Another Chance (1989).................. Nancy Burton
• 0:44—Brief side view of right breast and buns getting out of bed.
Edgar Allan Poe's "Buried Alive" (1989)...............Janet
Midnight (1989) .... Missy Angel
• 0:32—In bed with Mickey. Nice squished breasts against him, but only a very brief side view of left breast.
Popcorn (1991)...................................... Joy

Made for Cable TV:
Dream On: Home is Where the Cart Is (1995; HBO) .....Lydia
Bedtime (1996; Showtime) .... Kathy
Bedtime: Episode 4 (1996; Showtime)................ Kathy
Bedtime: Episode 6 (1996; Showtime)............. Kathy
• 0:17—Very, very brief side of left breast, while in the shower with Rick.
Bedtime: Episode 11 (1996; Showtime) .... Kathy
• 0:23—Very brief partial buns, while maneuvering into sexual positions on the floor with Rick.
Bedtime: Episode 13 (1996; Showtime) .... Kathy
• 0:09—Very brief right breast, while lying in bed next to Rick
• 0:10—Half of right breast, while lying in bed, talking with Rick.

Made for TV Movies:
I Married a Centerfold (1984) ....Ms. February

TV:
One Life to Live (1990-94)............... Tina Lord Roberts

Video Tapes:
Playboy's Playmate Workout ....Playmate
Playboy's Playmate Review (1982) ....Playmate
••• 0:00—Nude deep sea fishing, then sunbathing on sailboat.
Playmates at Play (1990) ....Making Waves
Playboy's 21 Playmates: Volume II (1996) ......Playmate
••• 0:51—Nude in still photos.

••• 0:52—Full frontal nudity on sailboat.

Wolf, Anneliza

See: Scott, Anneliza.

Wolf, Lynn *

Films:

Obsessed with Lust (1995) . . . . Chloe

a.k.a. Prelude to Love

••• 0:08—Breasts, while making love with Eric in his apartment.

Watch Me (1995) . . . . Nadia

•• 0:06—Breasts, while posing on sofa and talking with Paul.

•• 0:13—Breasts, while posing on table in studio for Paul.

••• 0:21—Nude, after taking off her sweater and looking out window while Paul photographs her.

Wolf, Rita

Films:

My Beautiful Laundrette (1985; British) . . . . Tania

•• 0:15—Breasts holding blouse up, showing off her breasts outside window to Omar.

Slipstream (1990) . . . . Maya

Covert Assassin (1994; Italian) . . . . Vritra

Girl 6 (1996) . . . . Wife of Indian Shopkeeper

Wolfe, Nancy Allison

Films:

Bar Girls (1995) . . . . Loretta

•• 1:12—In bra, when in hallway with J.R. Breasts, while in the bedroom with her.

Video Tapes:

The Making of Bar Girls (1995) . . . . Loretta

•• 0:29—In bra, when in hallway with J.R. Breasts, while in the bedroom with her. These are the same scenes that are seen in the film itself.

Wolfe, Tracy

See: Williams, K.C.

Wolfman, Joanna

See: Wayne, Taylor.

Wolter, Sherilyn

Films:

Eyewitness to Murder (1989) . . . . Suzanne

• 1:00—Very, very brief lower half of right breast while making love with Andrew Stevens. Don't see her face.

TV:

General Hospital . . . . Celia Quartermaine

The Guiding Light . . . . n.a.

Santa Barbara . . . . Elena Nikolas

B.J. and the Bear (1981) . . . . Cindy Grant

Wood, Annie

a.k.a. Annie Rubanoff.

Films:

Breathing Fire (1990) . . . . April

Caged Hearts (1995) . . . . Marzy

Cellblock Sisters: Banished Behind Bars (1995) . . . . April

•• 0:15—Breasts, while making love with Wreck in bedroom.

• 0:19—Brief breast, when taking off her tank top to try on a dress.

Made for Cable TV:

Love Street: Second Chance (1995; Showtime)

. . . . Laura/Tara

•• 0:02—Nude, while making love with Marc in bed.

•• 0:12—Breasts, while making love with Morgan on the floor.

••• 0:22—Breasts, while making love with Marc in the house and in the swimming pool.

Made for TV Movies:

Fall From Grace (1990) . . . . Jessica Hahn

TV:

Bzzz! (1997) . . . . Host

Video Tapes:

Inside Out 4 (1992) . . . . Ms. Morely/Save the Wetlands

(Unrated version reviewed.)

•• 0:32—Left breast, while playing with herself during interviewed.

• 0:33—Partial buns, while bending over to pick up photo off the floor.

Wood, Cyndi *

Films:

Apocalypse Now (1979) . . . . Playmate of the Year

Van Nuys Blvd. (1979) . . . . Moon

•• 0:57—Left breast outside on boat with Bobby, then breasts, while making love in bed with him.

Video Tapes:

Playboy Video Centerfold: Teri Weigel (1986)

. . . . Playmate Update

••• 0:25—Nude in still photos.

Wood, Jane

Films:

The Ragman's Daughter (1974; British) . . . . . Older Tony's Wife

Lassiter (1984) . . . . Mary Becker

She'll be Wearing Pink Pyjamas (1985; British) . . . . . . Jude

• 0:07—Nude, shaving her legs in the women's shower room.

Blood Red Roses (1986; Scottish) . . . . n.a.

The Raggedy Rawney (1988; British) . . . . Vie

Wood, Janet

Films:

Angels Hard as They Come (1971) . . . . Vicki

•• 1:09—Breasts taking off her top, dancing with Clean Sheila at the bikers' party.

•• 1:16—Breasts outside when the General rips her blouse open.

The G.I. Executioner (1971) . . . . Cynthia Jordan

a.k.a. Wit's End

a.k.a. Dragon Lady

•• 0:29—Breasts and buns in bed with Dave.

Terror House (1972) . . . . Pamela

The Centerfold Girls (1974) . . . . Linda

•• 0:14—Breasts putting on robe and getting out of bed.

Slumber Party '57 (1976) . . . . Smitty

• 0:10—Breasts with her five girl friends during swimming pool scene. Hard to tell who is who.

•• 1:06—Left breast, then breasts in stable with David while his sister watches.

Ice Cream Man (1994) . . . . Mrs. Spodak

Twisted Love (1994) . . . . Nurse

Wood, Lana *

Sister of the late actress Natalie Wood.

Films:

The Searchers (1956) . . . . Debbie as a Child

Diamonds are Forever (1971; British) . . . . Plenty O'Toole

A Place Called Today (1972) . . . . Carolyn Scheider

••• 0:40—Side view of left breast, then breasts lying down talking to Ron.

Demon Rage (1981) . . . . Lisa
a.k.a. Dark Eyes
a.k.a. Demon Seed
• 0:00—Breasts when breasts pop out of nightgown while running from someone at the beach.
••• 0:09—Breasts and very brief partial lower frontal nudity in bed when sheets get pulled off her.
••• 0:19—Breasts, while taking a shower when she sees the spirit.
••• 0:26—Breasts and very brief lower frontal nudity while lying in bed when the spirit visits her and makes love.
••• 0:38—Breasts in bed, while making love with the spirit.
• 0:53—Brief breasts with the spirit, while making love in bed.
• 1:22—Brief full frontal nudity getting her nightgown torn off.
Made for TV Movies:
Nightmare in Badham County (1976). . . . . Smitty
(Nudity added for video tape.)
TV:
The Long Hot Summer (1965-66) . . . . Eula Harker
Peyton Place (1966-67). . . . . .Sandy Webber
Capitol (1983) . . . . .Fran Bruke

Wood, Laurie *
Video Tapes:
Playboy Video Calendar 1990 (1989) . . . . April
••• 0:18—Nude.

Wood, Nicole *
Video Tapes:
Playboy Video Calendar 1994 (1993) . . . . October
••• 0:39—Nude while running around a house and posing.
••• 0:40—Nude while posing in water-theme backdrops in color and B&W.
Playboy's Sexy, Steamy, Sultry (1993). . . . . Playmate
Playboy's 21 Playmates (1996) . . . . Playmate
••• 0:48—Nude in still photos.
••• 0:49—Nude in hotel lobby fantasy.

Wood, Rebecca
a.k.a. Rebecca Sharkey.
Ex-wife of the late actor Ray Sharkey.
Films:
Friday the 13th, Part V—A New Beginning (1985). . Lana
• 0:33—Brief breasts opening her dress while changing to go out with Billy.
Mask (1985) . . . . Angel
Barbarian Queen II: The Empress Strikes Back (1989) . . . . Ziela
The Forgotten One (1989) . . . . Barmaid
Switch (1991) . . . . Gay Club Patron

Woodell, Pat
Films:
The Big Doll House (1971) . . . . Bodine
• 0:27—Brief breasts hung by wrists and whipped by a guard. Hair covers most of her breasts.
The Roommates (1973). . . . . .Heather
The Woman Hunt (1975; U.S./Philippines) . . . . n.a.
TV:
Petticoat Junction (1963-65) . . . . Bobby Jo Bradley

Woods, Barbara Alyn *
Films:
Circuitry Man (1990) . . . . Yoyo
Delusion (1990) . . . . .Julie
Dance with Death (1991) . . . . Kelly
••• 0:16—In black bra, panties and stockings, doing strip tease on stage. Breasts and buns in G-string.
•• 0:24—Breasts, dancing in red bra and panties.
••• 0:46—Breasts and buns in G-string, dancing on stage.
• 0:47—Brief side view of left breast, while changing back stage. Buns seen in mirror.
••• 0:59—Breasts and buns, doing strip tease routine in Marilyn Monroe outfit.
••• 1:01—Breasts, making love in bed with Maxwell Caulfield.
The Waterdance (1991). . . . . Annabelle Lee
• 1:24—Buns, in G-string, while on stage in a strip club.
We're Talkin' Serious Money (1991). . . . . Baggage Claim Agent
The Terror Within II (1992). Sharon
•• 0:28—Buns and breasts while in bed with Jamie.
Flesh and Bone (1993) . . . . Cindy
• 0:16—Partial buns, while lying on her stomach on bed.
Ghoulies IV (1993) . . . . Kate
Frankie Starlight (1995; Irish/British) . . . . Marcia
Striptease (1996) . . . . .Lorelei
(R-rated version reviewed.)
•• 0:38—Breasts and buns in T-back, while dancing on stage with a snake.
Made for Cable Movies:
Dead Weekend (1995; Showtime) . . . . Amelia E
•• 0:58—Right breast, then breasts, while making love with Stephen Baldwin in bed.
Made for Cable TV:
Dream On: It Came From Beneath the Sink (1992; HBO)
. . . . Linda
•• 0:01—Breasts, kneeling on bed in Martin's office in his dream. Brief buns, on top of him in bed.
•• 0:02—Brief left breast with Martin in his dream.
• 0:03—Brief breasts in flashback/daydream.
•• 0:09—Breasts and buns in bed with Martin in more of his dreams.
• 0:11—Breasts in flashback.
• 0:13—Buns, several times in G-string at Martin's apartment.
Dream On: 9 1/2 Days (1995; HBO) . . . . Phoebe
•• 0:06—Brief right breast, opening her jacket in hallway in front of Martin's apartment. Breasts in milk bath with Martin.
Dream On: Take Two Tablets, And Get Me to Mt. Sinai (1995; HBO) . . . . Martin's Lover
Video Tapes:
Eden (1992) . . . . Eve Sinclair
• 0:09—Buns and breasts, while kissing Grant outside during her fantasy.
••• 0:10—Breasts in pool and on beach, making love with Grant during more fantasy.
• 0:24—Brief breasts, putting on lingerie.
••• 0:30—Breasts, while making love on table with Grant during another fantasy.
• 0:54—Buns in maroon bra and T-back in her bedroom.
••• 0:55—Breasts and buns in the shower making love with Grant during her fantasy.
• 1:18—Buns in lingerie in fantasy with Grant.
••• 1:19—Left breast, while on couch with Grant/Josh in her fantasy.
Eden 2 (1992) . . . . Eve Sinclair
• 0:20—Brief breasts on boat in fantasy with Grant.
• 0:43—In bra, then brief breasts in hay in a stable with Grant during a fantasy.
• 1:01—Brief breasts in bubble bath. Don't see her face.

- • 1:02—Breasts under sheer nightgown.
- ••• 1:04—Breasts with Grant outside by pool, then in bathtub.
- •• 1:19—Breasts and buns in the shower with Steve then Grant during a fantasy.

Inside Out (1992) . . . . Terri/Brush Strokes
(Unrated version reviewed.)
- ••• 0:07—Breasts and buns in G-string, undressing for Jack.
- ••• 0:08—Close-up of breasts as Jack paints on her with his paintbrush.
- ••• 0:09—Full frontal nudity, getting paint poured all over her body.
- • 0:11—Brief breasts, while holding onto chair while making love.

Eden 3 (1993) . . . . Eve Sinclair
- •• 0:10—Breasts, fantasizing about Grant during her massage.
- ••• 0:35—In white bra, then breasts during her fantasy while making love outside with Grant.
- • 0:47—In black bra and panties, then left breast while making love with Josh in bedroom.
- •• 0:49—Breasts, while crying in the shower.
- • 0:59—In wet nightgown, then buns and brief right breast while out in the rain with Grant.
- •• 1:26—Breasts while making love on the hood of a car with Grant.

Eden 4 (1993) . . . . Eve Sinclair

Eden 5 (1993) . . . . Eve Sinclair
- •• 0:37—Buns and breasts, while making love on beach with Grant in flashback.
- •• 0:48—Breasts, while making love on beach at night with Paul.
- •• 0:50—Brief buns in panties while frolicking in the surf with Paul. Breasts while making love.
- • 1:01—Breasts, while making love with Grant.
- • 1:28—In pink bra, then left breast with Grant in bed.

Eden 6 (1994) . . . . Eve Sinclair
- • 0:54—Brief breasts, while fooling around in bed with Paul.
- •• 1:34—Brief buns and breasts while making love with Paul in bed.
- •• 2:01—Breasts, while making love with Paul. Half of right breast when Paul makes out with her.
- • 2:04—Right breast, while making love with Paul.
- •• 2:17—Breasts, while making love on table with Paul.

Woods, Connie

Films:

The Forbidden Dance (1990) . . . . Trish

Made for Cable TV:

Dream On: Futile Attraction (1991; HBO). . . . . Darlene
- •• 0:03—Breasts dressed as a cheerleader on top of Martin in bed.

Dream On: Take Two Tablets, And Get Me to Mt. Sinai (1995; HBO) . . . . Martin's Lover

Video Tapes:

Night of the Living Babes (1987). . . . . Lulu
- • 0:46—Breasts and buns in lingerie, in a cell with Buck.
- ••• 0:48—More breasts in cell with Buck.
- • 0:50—Breasts getting rescued with Michelle Bauer.

Woods, Jerii

Films:

Switchblade Sisters (1975) . . . . Toby

Revenge of the Cheerleaders (1976). . . . . Gail
- • 0:00—Breasts, while changing clothes in front left seat of car.
- • 0:05—Lower frontal nudity taking off cheerleader skirt in girls' restroom and putting on panties.
- • 0:26—Brief right breast, while sitting in bleachers with the other cheerleaders.
- ••• 0:28—Nude in boys' shower room scene.
- •• 0:37—Breasts, while sitting up in sleeping bag.
- • 0:44—Brief breasts in front seat of car with David Hasselhoff.
- ••• 0:53—Nude with Leslie and hiker guy while frolicking in the woods.
- •• 0:55—Nude some more making out with the hiker guy with Leslie.
- ••• 0:57—Nude, walking down road with Leslie when stopped by a policeman.
- ••• 1:23—Breasts during Hawaiian party.

Woodville, Kate

Films:

Black Gunn (1972). . . . . Louella

Sex Through a Window (1977). . . . . Sally Norman
- •• 0:29—Left breast, after sitting up in bed after John sits up, then brief breasts while turning over in bed.
- ••• 1:15—Breasts, while making love in bed and after with John.

Woronov, Mary

Films:

Kemek (1970) . . . . Mary

Seizure (1973). . . . . Mikki

Sugar Cookies (1973). . . . . Camila
- ••• 0:10—Breasts in bathtub, then wearing white panties exercising breasts on the floor. Long scene.
- • 1:04—Breasts with Julie in the bathtub.
- • 1:07—Brief breasts, then left breast, making love with Julie.
- • 1:17—Brief right breast when Lynn Lowry yanks her dress up.

Silent Night, Bloody Night (1974). . . . . Diane

Cover Girl Models (1975) . . . . Diane

Death Race 2000 (1975) . . . . Calamity Jane
- • 0:27—Brief breasts arguing with Matilda the Hun.

Hollywood Boulevard (1976). . . . . Mary McQueen

Jackson County Jail (1976). . . . . Pearl

Bad Georgia Road (1977) . . . . Hackett

Mr. Billion (1977). . . . . Actress

The Lady in Red (1979) . . . . Woman Bankrobber

Rock 'n' Roll High School (1979) . . . . Evelyn Togar

Angel of H.E.A.T. (1981) . . . . Samantha Vitesse
a.k.a. The Protectors, Book I
- ••• 0:11—Frontal nudity changing clothes on a boat dock after getting out of the lake.
- •• 0:43—Breasts wrestling in the mud after wearing white bathing suit.

Heartbeeps (1981). Party House Owner

Eating Raoul (1982) . . . . Mary Bland
- ••• 0:46—Breasts, while struggling with Ed Begley Jr. on the couch. More breasts while Raoul counts money on her stomach. Long scene.
- • 0:53—Buns and side view of right breast, while in hospital room with Raoul. A little dark.

National Lampoon Goes to the Movies (1982). . . . . Secretary
a.k.a. Movie Madness

Get Crazy (1983). . . . . Violetta

Night of the Comet (1984) . . . . Carol

Hellhole (1985) . . . . Dr. Fletcher

Chopping Mall (1986). . . . . Mary Bland
a.k.a. Killbots

Nomads (1986). . . . . Dancing Mary
Terrorvision (1986) . . . . Raquel
Mortuary Academy (1988) . . . . Mary Purcell
Let It Ride (1989) . . . . Quinella
Scenes from the Class Struggle in Beverly Hills (1989)
. . . . Lizabeth
- ••• 1:06—In black lingerie, then breasts in bedroom, then in bed with Robert Beltran.

Club Fed (1990) . . . . Jezebel
Dick Tracy (1990) . . . . Welfare Person
Rock 'n' Roll High School Forever (1990). . . . . . . .Doctor Vadar
Warlock (1990) . . . . Channeller
Watchers II (1990). . . . . Dr. Glatman
Motorama (1991) . . . . Kidnapping Wife
Where Sleeping Dogs Lie (1991). . . . . Woman Tourist
Good Girls Don't (1993) . . . . Wilemena
Grief (1993) . . . . Attorney
Number One Fan (1994). . . . . Wedding Coordinator
Glory Daze (1995) . . . . Joanie's Mom
Made for Cable Movies:
Acting on Impulse (1993; Showtime) . . . . Receptionist
Rebel Highway: Shake, Rattle and Rock! (1994; Showtime)
. . . . E. Joyce Togar
Made for TV Movies:
A Bunny's Tale (1985) . . . . Miss Renfroe

Worthington, Jennifer

Films:
New York Nights (1994) . . . . Delivery Woman
- •• 0:23—Full frontal nudity, while in closet with the doorman.
- • 0:25—Brief right breast and buns, while leaving the apartment.

Video Tapes:
Marilyn Chambers: Wet & Wild Fantasies (1994). . . . . n.a.

Wray, Fay

Films:
Doctor X (1932) . . . . Joan
The Most Dangerous Game (1932). . . . . Eve Trowbridge
King Kong (1933). . . . . Ann Darrow
- • 1:12—Right breast, after surfacing from the water after jumping off cliff with Bruce Cabot.

Mystery of the Wax Museum (1933). . . . . . . Charlotte Duncan
The Vampire Bat (1933) . . . . Ruth Bertin
Viva Villa! (1934). . . . . Teresa
The Evil Mind (1935; British). . . . . Rene
a.k.a. The Clairvoyant
Melody for Three (1941). Mary Stanley
Small Town Girl (1953) . . . . Mrs. Gordon Kimbell
Hell on Frisco Bay (1956) . . . . Kay Stanley
Rock, Pretty Baby (1956). . . . . Beth Daley
Crime of Passion (1957) . . . . Alice Pope
Tammy and the Bachelor (1957). . . . . Mrs. Brent

Wren, Clare

Films:
Extremities (1986). . . . . Racquetball Player
No Man's Land (1988) . . . . Deborah
Season of Fear (1989) . . . . Sarah Drummond
- • 0:22—Brief, partial left breast, while in bed with Mick. Long shot, hard to see.
- • 0:25—Brief full frontal nudity, seen behind shower door.
- • 0:42—Side view of left breast, while making love on top of Mick. Very, very brief left breast, when turning over after hearing a noise outside.

Steel and Lace (1990) . . . . Gally

Midnight Edition (1993) . . . . Sarah Travers
TV:
Young Riders (1990-92). . . . . Rachel Dunn

Wright, Amy

Films:
The Deer Hunter (1978) . . . . Bridesmaid
Girlfriends (1978). . . . . Ceil
- • 0:42—Brief breasts, while getting out of bed to talk to Melanie Mayron.

The Amityville Horror (1979). . . . . Jackie
Breaking Away (1979) . . . . Nancy
Wise Blood (1979; U.S./German). . . . . Sabbath Lilly
Heartland (1980). . . . . Clara
Inside Moves (1980) . . . . Ann
Stardust Memories (1980). . . . . Shelley
The Accidental Tourist (1988) . . . . Rose Leary
Crossing Delancey (1988) . . . . Ricki
Deceived (1991) . . . . Evelyn Wade
Love Hurts (1991) . . . . Karen Weaver
Hard Promises (1992) . . . . Shelley
Josh and S.A.M. (1993) . . . . Waitress
Robot in the Family (1993) . . . . n.a.
Where the River Flows North (1994) . . . . Loose Woman
Scarlet Letter (1995) . . . . Goody Gotwick
Made for TV Movies:
Settle the Score (1989) . . . . Becky
To Dance with the White Dog (1993) . . . . Carrie

Wright, Angela

Films:
Enemy Gold (1993). . . . . Dancer #2
- • 0:22—Buns in G-string lingerie, while dancing on stage.
- •• 0:26—Breasts and buns in the shower with the other dancer and Santiago.
- • 0:35—Buns in T-back, while dancing on stage.
- ••• 0:37—Breasts and buns in T-back, while dancing on stage.

Seduction of Innocence (1994) . . . . Gretchen

Wright, Jenny

Films:
The Executioner's Song (1982) . . . . April Baker
(European Version reviewed.)
Pink Floyd The Wall (1982). . . . . American Groupie
- ••• 0:41—Breasts, while doing strip tease dance, in back of a truck while it's parked backstage.

World According to Garp (1982). . . . . Curbie
- •• 0:33—Brief breasts behind the bushes with Robin Williams giving him "something to write about."

The Wild Life (1984) . . . . Eileen
- •• 0:22—In bra and panties, then breasts changing in her bedroom while Christopher Penn watches from the window.

St. Elmo's Fire (1985). . . . . Felicia
Near Dark (1987) . . . . Mae
Out of Bounds (1987) . . . . Dizz
The Chocolate War (1988) . . . . Lisa
Valentino Returns (1988). . . . . Sylvia Fuller
I, Madman (1989). . . . . Virginia
A Shock to the System (1990) . . . . Melanie O'Connor
Young Guns II (1990) . . . . Jane Greathouse
- • 1:07—Buns, taking off her clothes, getting on a horse and riding away. Hair covers breasts.
- • 1:38—Buns, while walking down stairs during epilogue.

Queens Logic (1991). . . . . Asha

The Lawnmower Man (1992) . . . . Marnie Burke
(Unrated Director's cut reviewed.)
- •• 1:04—Right breast, while in bed with Jeff Fahey.
- • 1:15—Brief right breast, while in bed under Fahey.

TV:
Capital News (1990) . . . . Doreen Duncan
NYPD Blue: (Jan 21, 1997) . . . . Trish Taylor

Wright, Maggie

Films:
What's New, Pussycat? (1965; U.S./French) . . . . . . Striptease #2
Hammerhead (1968) . . . . Roselle
Twins of Evil (1971; British) . . . . Aleta
Suburban Wives (1973; British) . . . . Irene
Confessions of a Pop Performer (1975; British) . . . . n.a.
Joseph Andrews (1977; British/French) . . . . First Nun
- • 1:03—Breasts under sheer area of habit.

Wright, Robin

Significant other of actor/director Sean Penn.
Films:
Hollywood Vice Squad (1986) . . . . Lori
The Princess Bride (1987) . . . . Buttercup
State of Grace (1990) . . . . Kathleen
- •• 0:38—Breasts making love standing up with Sean Penn in the hall. Dark.
- • 1:58—Brief side of right breast taking off towel and putting on blouse.

Denial (1991) . . . . Sarah
- • 0:37—Side view of buns, while lying on top of Jason Patric.

The Playboys (1992) . . . . Tara Maguire
Toys (1992) . . . . Gwen Tyler
Forrest Gump (1994) . . . . Jenny Curran
- • 0:36—Brief upper half of buns, while sitting on stage, playing a guitar in a club.
- • 0:37—Very brief buns and side view of breasts, after pushing guitar into Tom Hanks and walking off the stage.

The Crossing Guard (1995) . . . . Jojo
Moll Flanders (1996) . . . . Moll Flanders
- •• 1:00—Right breast, several times, while sitting on couch and posing for paintings.
- •• 1:27—Brief right breast in mirror, then left breast while pregnant and reclining on sofa. Left breast, while lying on bed.

She's So Lovely (1997) . . . . Maureen
TV:
Santa Barbara . . . . Kelly Capwell

Wright, Sylvia

Films:
Bloody Birthday (1980) . . . . Girl in Van
- ••• 0:45—Breasts undressing in a van and making out with a guy.

Terror on Tour (1980) . . . . Carol
Malibu Hot Summer (1981) . . . . Actress at Party
a.k.a. Sizzle Beach
(*Sizzle Beach* is the re-released version with Kevin Costner featured on the cover. It is missing all the nude scenes during the opening credits before 0:06.)
- •• 0:01—Nude, standing up during opening credits.
- ••• 1:07—Breasts fixing her hair in front of mirror, then full frontal nudity talking to Howard.
- • 1:09—Breasts on top of Howard.

• *Wu, Vivian*

Films:
The Last Emperor (1987) . . . . Wen Hsiu
The Guyver (1991) . . . . Misky Segawa
Shadow of China (1991; U.S./Japanese) . . . . Moo-Ling
Heaven and Earth (1993) . . . . Madame Lien
The Joy Luck Club (1993) . . . . An Mei's Mother
Teenage Mutant Ninja Turtles III (1993) . . . . Mitsu
The Pillow Book (1995) . . . . Nagiko
- •• 0:17—Breasts, with Chinese characters painted on her body, then standing in the rain, as it washes off.
- •• 0:33—Breasts, while Chinese characters are painted on her body.
- •• 0:36—Nude, while a guy paints Chinese characters on her body.
- • 0:43—Brief back side of right breast, while sitting in bathtub.
- •• 0:46—Nude, while lying in bed next to a guy.
- •• 0:55—Nude, while standing next to Ewan McGregor, then in bed with him.
- ••• 0:58—Breasts, while sitting in bed as Chinese characters are painted on her.
- •• 1:00—Full frontal nudity, standing up in bathtub.

Made for Cable Movies:
A Bright Shining Lie (1998; HBO) . . . . Lee
Made for TV Movies:
Danielle Steel's "Message from Nam" (1993) . . . . France
Vanishing Son (1994) Lili
Vanishing Son II (1994) Lili
Vanishing Son III (1994) Lili
Vanishing Son IV (1994) Lili

Wührer, Kari *

Former Video Jockey on MTV.
Former co-host on MTV's Remote Control.
a.k.a. Kari Salin.
Films:
Beastmaster 2: Through the Portal of Time (1990) . . . . . . Jackie
The Adventures of Ford Fairlane (1991) . . . . Melodi
Beyond Desire (1994) . . . . Rita
- • 0:06—Very brief buns in panties, while starting to make love with William Forsythe.
- •• 0:07—Left breast, while lying in bed next to Forsythe, then breasts, when getting out of bed and putting on dress.
- • 0:09—Brief left breast, when getting back into bed with Forsythe.
- •• 0:10—Breasts, while in bed with Forsythe.
- •• 0:32—Breasts, while lying in bed with Forsythe.
- • 0:33—Brief breasts, while standing up in Corvette and showing her breasts, when riding through the streets of Las Vegas.
- • 0:43—Brief, partial buns under short dress, while bending over desk to talk to Leo Rossi.
- • 0:51—Breasts, while sitting in bathtub with Forsythe.
- • 1:02—Very brief buns under short dress when getting slapped by Rossi.

Boulevard (1994) . . . . Jennefer
- •• 0:14—Breasts and buns in bathroom, getting into the shower and in the shower.
- ••• 0:41—Breasts, while making love in bed with Lou Diamond Phillips. Brief buns, when running out of the room when she changes her mind.
- •• 1:10—Breasts, while making love with Rae Dawn Chong.
- • 1:13—Partial buns, while dancing in club.
- • 1:15—Brief breasts in the shower and getting out.

•• 1:23—Nude, while taking a shower and getting out.
Higher Learning (1994). . . . . Claudia
Sensation (1994) . . . . Lila Reed
• 0:01—Brief buns in G-string while getting out of bed. Long shot.
• 0:23—Breasts under overalls while painting in her studio.
•• 0:33—Brief breasts, quite a few times on cafeteria table with Eric Roberts in her vision. Lit with blue light.
•• 0:39—Breasts and buns, after taking off robe and putting on slip. Kind of dark.
••• 0:41—Breasts and buns in T-back, while dancing in her living room at night.
• 0:53—Brief breasts and buns in the shower and getting out. Seen from above.
•• 0:55—Right breast, while in bed with Roberts when she imagines Carrie is her.
••• 1:08—Full frontal nudity, while making love in bed with Roberts.
•• 1:14—Breasts, while on bed, making love with Roberts, when she imagines him strangling her.
• 1:32—Very brief partial right breast while in bed with Roberts.
The Crossing Guard (1995). . . . . Mia
• 0:05—Brief breasts, going into bathroom after talking with Jack Nicholson.
• 1:11—Buns in T-back, while dancing on stage by herself, then with Nicholson.
• 1:13—Brief breasts in open blouse, while fooling around with Nicholson in room.
Terminal Justice (1995) . . . . Pamela
•• 0:47—Brief breasts, while in the bathroom when Lorenzo Lamas talks with her.
••• 1:04—Breasts, while making love with Lamas in bed.
An Occasional Hell (1996). . . . . Jeri Gillen
• 0:00—Very, very brief right breast, while making love in car with Alex. Then brief breasts, covered with blood after he gets shot.
••• 0:34—Breasts, while wearing shorts, then panties, when taking photographs outdoors with Alex in Tom Berenger's fantasy.
• 1:25—Brief breasts in car again when Alex is shot, then when she runs through the woods.
Sex and the Other Man (1996) . . . . Jessica
• 0:27—Breasts, while making love with Ron Eldard in bed when Stanley Tucci is forced to watch.
••• 0:50—Full frontal nudity and side view of buns, while making love with Eldard again when Tucci has to watch.
Thinner (1996) . . . . Gina Lempke
Anaconda (1997) . . . . Denise Kalberg
Kissing a Fool (1998). . . . . Dara
Phoenix (1998) . . . . Katie Shuster
• 1:31—Brief partial buns and very brief left breast, when caught in bed with Xander Berkeley by Ray Liotta.
• 1:33—Brief upper half of breasts, when trying to get Liotta to stop burning the money.
• 1:35—Brief breasts, when getting out of bed.
Made for Cable TV:
Swamp Thing (1991-93; USA). .Abigail
TV:
Class of '96 (1993) . . . . Robin Farr
Sliders (1997-) . . . . Maggie Beckett

Wyhl, Jennifer
Made for Cable Movies:
Soft Touch (1987; Playboy). . . . . Nancy
(Shown on *The Playboy Channel* as *Birds in Paradise.*)
• 0:00—Breasts during opening credits.
Soft Touch II (1987; Playboy) . . . . Nancy
(Shown on *The Playboy Channel* as *Birds in Paradise.*)
• 0:01—Breasts during opening credits.
• 0:05—Breasts in bed with Neill.
• 0:18—Breasts undressing for robbers. Brief full frontal nudity.
•• 0:57—Breasts in bed with Neill.
•• 1:01—Full frontal nudity in bed with Neill.

Wylde, Kim
See: Gielser, Regina.

• *Wynter, Sarah*
Made for Cable TV:
Sex and the City: Premiere Episode (1998; HBO)
. . . . Elizabeth
• 0:02—Brief silhouette of breasts, while making love with a guy in bed.
Made for TV Movies:
Masterpiece Theatre: The Politician's Wife (1996)
. . . . Lib Dem Committee Member
TV:
The City (1997). . . . . Catherine

Wyss, Amanda
Films:
Fast Times at Ridgemont High (1982) . . . . Lisa
Better Off Dead (1985) . . . . Beth Truss
A Nightmare on Elm Street (1985) . . . . Tina Gray
Silverado (1985) . . . . Phoebe
Deadly Innocents (1988) . . . . Andy/Angela
•• 0:12—Breasts, taking off T-shirt and putting on lingerie.
••• 1:29—Right breast, twice, with Andrew Stevens.
Powwow Highway (1988; U.S./British) . . . . Rabbit Layton
To Die For (1988) . . . . Celia Kett
Black Magic Woman (1990) . . . . Diane Abbott
Shakma (1990) . . . . Tracy
To Die For 2 (1991). . . . . Celia
a.k.a. Son of Darkness: To Die For II
Bloodfist IV: Die Trying (1992). . . . . Shannon
Digital Man (1995) . . . . .Uncredited Lt. Fredericks
Made for TV Movies:
My Mother's Secret Life (1984) . . . . Tobi Jensen
TV:
Highlander: The Series (1992-93) . . . . Randi McFarland
NYPD Blue: Sorry, Wrong Suspect (Jan 9, 1996) . . . . Ellen

Xuxa
Real name is Maria da Garca Meneghel.
Brazilian children's television show host.
Films:
Love Strange Love (1982; Brazilian). . . . . Tamara
•• 0:26—Breasts standing on table, getting measured for outfit.
••• 0:29—Breasts again when Hugo watches. Long scene.
•• 0:58—Right breast when she lets Hugo caress it. (Film is reversed since mole above her right breast appears over the left.)
• 1:00—More right breast.
•• 1:09—Breasts, stripping out of bear costume during party.

- ••• 1:13—Breasts several times undressing in room. Long scene.
- •• 1:27—Side view of left breast in bed with Hugo.

TV:

Xuxa! (1994-) . . . . Hostess

Yager, Missy

a.k.a. Nicole Dubois.

Films:

Interview With the Vampire: The Vampire Chronicles (1994) . . . . Creole Woman

- • 0:49—Full frontal nudity, then left breast, while washing herself when seen by Kirsten Dunst through open doorway.

Dead Man Walking (1995) . . . . Hope Percy

- • 1:49—Partial buns, while crawling on the ground during rape/murder flashback. Buns, while lying dead on the ground in overhead shot.

Yarbrough, Staci

Video Tapes:

Wet & Wild II (1990) . . . . Model

The Best of Wet and Wild (1992) . . . . Model

Hot Body International: #3 Lingerie Special (1992) . . . . Contestant

- •• 0:45—Buns, in white G-string.

Hot Body International: #5 Miss Acapulco (1992) . . . . Contestant

- •• 0:31—Buns, in two piece swimsuit.
- •• 0:55—Buns in pink two piece swimsuit during photo session.

Hot Body Competition: The Best of Hot Body (1994) . . . . Herself

- •• 1:13—Buns in swimsuits.

Yarnell, Celeste

Films:

The Nutty Professor (1963) . . . . College Student

Bob & Carol & Ted & Alice (1969) . . . . Susan

The Velvet Vampire (1971) . . . . Diane Le Fanu

- • 0:32—Brief breasts, while zipping up her blouse after trying to seduce Lee.
- •• 0:42—Breasts in desert scene when Lee pulls her blouse down.
- ••• 0:45—Breasts, while on the floor, making love with Lee.
- •• 0:55—Breasts in desert scene with Lee.
- • 0:57—Side view of buns, lying on top of someone in a coffin.
- •• 1:02—Breasts, while in bed with Lee.

The Mechanic (1972) . . . . The Mark's Girl

Scorpio (1973) . . . . Helen Thomas

Fatal Beauty (1987) . . . . Laura

Funny About Love (1990) . . . . Delta Gamma

Ambition (1991) . . . . Beverly Hills Shopper

Driving Me Crazy (1991) . . . . Volvo Boss

Midnight Kiss (1992) . . . . Sheila

Born Yesterday (1993) . . . . Mrs. Hedges

Yates, Cassie

Films:

The Evil (1977) . . . . Mary

Rolling Thunder (1977) . . . . Candy

- ••• 1:31—Breasts while undressing in bedroom with Tommy Lee Jones.
- • 1:32—Right breast, while sitting on bed with Jones.
- • 1:33—Right breast, when Jones sits up in bed.

Convoy (1978) . . . . Violet

- • 0:21—Very brief left breast, while in truck sleeper with Kris Kristofferson.

F.I.S.T. (1978) . . . . Molly

FM (1978) . . . . Laura Coe

The Osterman Weekend (1983) . . . . Betty Cardone

- •• 0:48—Breasts getting into bed with Chris Sarandon while Rutger Hauer watches on TV.
- • 0:51—Right breast, making love with Sarandon.

Unfaithfully Yours (1984) . . . . Carla Robbins

Made for TV Movies:

Having Babies II (1977) . . . . Paula Plotkin

Who'll Save Our Children? (1978) . . . . Lurene Garver

Of Mice and Men (1981) . . . . Mae

Listen To Your Heart (1983) . . . . Stacey

Moment of Truth: Stalking Back (1993) . . . . Sandi Boyer

TV:

Rich Man, Poor Man—Book II (1976-77) . . . . Annie Adams

Nobody's Perfect (1980) . . . . Detective Jennifer Dempsey

Detective in the House (1985) . . . . Diane Wyman

Dynasty (1987) . . . . Sarah Curtis

Yates, Kim

Films:

Maui Heat: Swimsuit Edition (1996) . . . . Karlie

- ••• 0:18—Breasts and buns, while joining Jake in the spa.
- • 0:23—Brief left breast, when taking off her swimsuit top.
- • 0:24—Buns in swimsuit during photo session.
- • 0:33—Buns in swimsuits during photo session.
- ••• 0:35—Nude, while video taping herself on the bed.
- •• 0:52—Breasts, taking off her robe and joining Dakota in pool.
- • 0:54—Breasts, while sunbathing on lounge chair.
- ••• 0:58—Nude, while making love on the beach with Mitch and Sara.
- ••• 1:02—Nude, while making love indoors with Mitch and Sara.

The Price of Desire (1996) . . . . Hazel

- • 0:14—Breasts and buns in T-back, while in yoga position, then getting her outfit.
- •• 0:19—Breasts, while undressing in room when talking with Kira Reed.
- ••• 0:33—Breasts, buns and partial lower frontal nudity, while making love with her boyfriend.
- • 1:24—Buns in panties while modeling.

Made for Cable TV:

Erotic Confessions: Elevation (1996; Cinemax) . . . . . Karen

- • 0:03—In bra, then breasts, while changing clothes in elevator. Seen on B&W security monitor and in color.
- • 0:06—In bra and brief breasts when Ray watches B&W monitor again.
- ••• 0:08—In lingerie, then breasts, while undressing on table for Ray, then making love.
- ••• 0:13—Nude, while making love in elevator with Ray. Long scene.

Erotic Confessions: Friends and Lovers (1996; Cinemax) . . . . Carol

(Available on video tape in *Erotic Confessions, Volume 2: Intrigue.*)

- •• 0:05—Breasts, while starting to make love with Mike.

Erotic Confessions: Lap Dance (1996; Cinemax) . . . . Topless Dancer
(Available on video tape in *Erotic Confessions, Volume 4: Pleasure.*)
• 0:06—Very brief partial buns, while lifting her leg when holding onto pole, then brief left breast, when Dana starts Robert's lap dance.
Beverly Hills Bordello: The Boyfriend (1997; Showtime) . . . . .Linda
••• 0:00—Nude, when undressing and making love with her boyfriend, Frank, in bedroom. Long scene.
••• 0:05—Full frontal nudity, while having sex with a business man in bedroom. Long scene.
••• 0:23—Breasts, while making love with Frank in bedroom.
Erotic Confessions: Private Dance (1997). . . . . Rosie
•• 0:03—Breasts and buns, while making love with her blindfolded boyfriend, Antonio, on the sofa.
••• 0:09—Nude, while making love with Antonio in the living room after returning from the strip club.
••• 0:15—Breasts and buns in T-back, while learning how to dance from Camille
••• 0:24—Breasts and buns in T-back, while dancing on stage in club.

Yazel, Carrie Jean *

Films:
Death Becomes Her (1992). . . . . Girl at Dakota's
• 0:27—Brief buns in mirror, hiding from Meryl Streep at Dakota's.
Mr. Baseball (1992) . . . . Coed in Bed
• 0:03—Very, very brief upper half of right breast, while sleeping when Tom Selleck gets out of bed.
Made for Cable TV:
Compromising Situations: Reunion '76 (1994; Showtime) . . . . Kathy
••• 0:00—Breasts and partial buns, while making love with Jake in bed.
••• 0:02—Left breast, then breasts, while lying in bed, talking with Jake. Long scene.
• 0:06—Very brief, almost right breast in gaping lingerie, while bending over to pick up something.
Video Tapes:
Playboy Video Calendar 1992 (1991) . . . . June
••• 0:22—Breasts and buns in kitchen shoot. More when pouring honey on her body.
••• 0:25—Nude, dancing in bar fantasy.
Sexy Lingerie III (1991) . . . . .Model
The Best of Sexy Lingerie (1992). . . . . .Model
Playboy's Playmate Review 1992 (1992) . . . . . . .Miss May
••• 0:14—Nude outside with piano, then outside in doorway and then in a house.
Playboy's Sexy, Steamy, Sultry (1993). . . . . Playmate

Yen, Tricia

Adult film actress.
Films:
Virtual Encounters (1995). . . . . Miko
(Unrated version reviewed.)
••• 0:19—In bra and panties, then breasts, while making love with Sara St. James.

York, Brittany *

a.k.a. Alison Armitage.
Films:
I Posed for Playboy (1991) . . . . Herself
a.k.a. Posing: Inspired by Three Real Stories
(Shown on network TV without the nudity.)
(Nude scenes added for video tape.)
••• 0:20—Right breast, then breasts on motorcycle during photo shoot.
••• 0:22—In T-shirt, then breasts during second photo shoot.
Miracle Beach (1991) . . . . .Girl in Bed
•• 0:14—Breasts, lying in bed next to Scotty, then sitting up. She's on the right.
Secret Games (1991). . . . . Nun
(Unrated version reviewed.)
Jerry Maguire (1996). . . . . Former Girlfriend
TV:
Acapulco H.E.A.T. (1993-94) . . . . "Cat" Pascal
Beach Clash (1995-96) . . . . .Hostess
Video Tapes:
Playboy Video Calendar 1992 (1991) . . . . November
••• 0:43—Breasts in lingerie. Nude in studio shoot.
••• 0:45—In black body stocking and nude in oriental style shoot.
Wet & Wild III (1991). . . . . .Model
The Best of Video Playmate Calendars (1992). . .Playmate
••• 0:23—Nude in studio.
••• 0:25—In lingerie and nude in Asian-style studio setting.
The Best of Wet and Wild (1992) . . . . .Model
Sexy Lingerie IV (1992) . . . . .Model
Wet & Wild IV (1992). . . . . .Model
Playboy's Sexy, Steamy, Sultry (1993). . . . . .Playmate

York, Linda

Films:
Chain Gang Women (1972) . . . . n.a.
Video Vixens (1973). . . . . Dial-A-Snatch Girl
•• 0:34—Nude on a turntable during a commercial, getting felt by four blindfolded guys.

York, Rachel

Films:
Billy Bathgate (1991). . . . . .Embassy Club Singer
Killer Instinct (1992) . . . . .Lotti Coll
a.k.a. Mad Dog Coll
Dead Center (1993) . . . . .Mary
Taking the Heat (1993). . . . . Susan
•• 0:19—Left breast, while enthusiastically making love in bed on top of George Segal. Very, very brief breasts when changing positions to under the sheets.
One Fine Day (1996). . . . . .Liza

York, Susannah *

Films:
Tunes of Glory (1960) . . . . .Morag Sinclair
Tom Jones (1963) . . . . Sophie
A Man for All Seasons (1966). . . . . Margaret More
The Killing of Sister George (1968) . . . . . . Alice McNaught
• 0:19—Breasts under sheer blue nightgown.
•• 2:07—(0:09 into tape 2) Breasts lying in bed with another woman.
Happy Birthday, Wanda June (1971) . . . . Penelope Ryan
Images (1972; Irish). . . . . Cathryn
• 0:59—Brief lower frontal nudity, then right breast lying on the bed.
• 1:38—Brief buns in the shower.

X, Y and Zee (1972) . . . . .Stella
That Lucky Touch (1975). . . . . .Julia Richardson
The Adventures of Eliza Fraser (1976; Australian)
. . . . , . Elisa Fraser
- 1:10—Brief breasts twice during ceremony. Paint on her face while running from hut.
- 1:30—Brief, upper half of left beast, while bathing in river with Bracefell.

The Silent Partner (1978) . . . . .Julie
- 0:38—Very brief right breast pulling her dress back up with Elliott Gould.

Superman (1978) . . . . Lara
The Shout (1979; British) . . . . Rachel Fielding
- •• 0:53—Brief breasts changing from a bathrobe to a blouse in bedroom.
- 1:02—Briefly nude, in upstairs room getting ready to make love with Alan Bates.
- 1:05—Brief buns, standing at end of hallway.
- 1:11—Breasts in bathtub with John Hurt.
- 1:18—Brief breasts getting up from bed with Bates. Long shot, hard to see anything.

The Awakening (1980) . . . . Jane Turner
Falling in Love Again (1980) . . . . Sue Lewis
Pretty Kill (1987). . . . . Toni
A Summer Story (1988). . . . . .Mrs. Narracrombe
Illusions (1992) . . . . Dr. Sinclair

Young, Dey

Films:

Rock 'n' Roll High School (1979) . . . . .Kate Rambeau
Dead Kids (1981; Australian/New Zealand) . . . . Caroline
a.k.a. Strange Behavior
Strange Invaders (1983) . . . . .Teen Girl
Doin' Time (1984). . . . . Vicki Norris
The Running Man (1987) . . . . Amy
Spaceballs (1987) . . . . Waitress
The Serpent and the Rainbow (1988) . . . . .Mrs. Cassedy
Spontaneous Combustion (1989) . . . . .Rachel
Pretty Woman (1990) . . . . Snobby Saleswoman
Frankie & Johnny (1991) . . . . Johnny's Ex-Wife
No Place to Hide (1991) . . . . Karen
Back In the U.S.S.R. (1992) . . . . .Claudia
Conflict of Interest (1992) . . . . Vera
- 0:31—Brief right breast, while turning over on her back in bed with Mick.
- •• 0:32—Left breast, while in bed, getting kissed by Mick.

Executive Decision (1995) . . . . .Gail
Pie in the Sky (1996) . . . . .Mrs. Tarnell

Made for Cable Movies:

Rebel Highway: Shake, Rattle and Rock! (1994; Showtime)
. . . . .Kate Rambeau Jr.
The Right to Remain Silent (1995; Showtime)
. . . . School Board Member

Made for Cable TV:

The Outer Limits: Last Supper (1997) . . . . Carol Martin

Made for TV Movies:

In the Shadows, Someone's Watching (1993) . . . Lydia Holroyd

TV:

Extreme (1995). . . . . Marnie Shepard

*Young, Gabriela **

Video Tapes:

Intimate Workout For Lovers (1992)
. . . . Romantic Relaxation
- ••• 0:01—Nude, in bedroom, in bathtub and in bed.

Playboy's 101 Ways to Excite Your Lover (1992)
. . . . Cast Member

*Young, Julianna **

Video Tapes:

Playboy Video Calendar 1995 (1994) . . . . .March
- ••• 0:09—Nude in photo session. Nude outside on rocks.

Young, Karen

Wife of actor/director Tom Noonan.

Films:

Deep in the Heart (1983; British). . . . . Kathleen Sullivan
a.k.a. Handgun
- 0:35—Buns and brief breasts undressing and getting forced into bed with Larry. (Her hair gets in the way.)
- •• 0:36—Brief breasts and buns, getting out of bed. Brief right breast when putting her dress on.

Almost You (1984). . . . . Lisa Willoughby
Birdy (1985) . . . . .Hannah Rourke
9 1/2 Weeks (1986). . . . . Sue
Heat (1987). . . . . .Holly
Jaws: The Revenge (1987) .Carla Brody
Torch Song Trilogy (1988) . . . . Laurel
Criminal Law (1989). . . . . Ellen Falkner
- 1:21—Very brief buns, then brief breasts in bed with Ben.

Night Game (1989). . . . . Roxy
- 0:06—Right breast, while in bed with Scheider after he answers the phone.

Love and Human Remains (1995; Canadian) . . . . . . The Singer
Daylight (1996) . . . . Sarah Crighton

Made for TV Movies:

The Summer My Father Grew Up (1991) . . . . .Chandelle

Young, Sean

Films:

Jane Austen in Manhattan (1980) . . . . .Ariadne
Stripes (1981) . . . . Louise Cooper
Blade Runner (1982) . . . . .Rachael
Young Doctors in Love (1982) . . . . Dr. Stephanie Brody
Dune (1984) . . . . Chani
(On the back of the laser disc cover, there is a small photo of her in a sheer black blouse lying down with Kyle MacLachlan.)
Baby... Secret of the Lost Legend (1985)
. . . . .Susan Matthew-Loomis
No Way Out (1987). . . . . Susan Atwell
- ••• 0:13—Side view of left breast, then brief right breast, going into Nina's apartment with Costner.

Wall Street (1987) . . . . Kate Gekko
The Boost (1989) . . . . Linda Brown
- 0:16—Very, very brief breasts jumping into the swimming pool with James Woods. Very, very brief side view of right breast and buns, twice, getting out of the pool, sitting on edge, then getting pulled back in by James Woods.
- •• 0:17—Left breast, while in pool talking to Woods. Right breast visible under water.
- 0:48—Brief breasts under water in spa with Woods.

Cousins (1989) . . . . Tish Kozinski
Fire Birds (1990) . . . . .Billie Lee Guthrie
a.k.a. Wings of the Apache
- 0:52—Very, very brief right breast twice in bed with Nicolas Cage.

A Kiss Before Dying (1991) . . . . Ellen/Dorothy Carlsson
- •• 0:31—Brief breasts making love in bed with Matt Dillon. Kind of dark.
- 0:35—Brief side view or right breast in shower with Dillon. Don't see her face.

- 1:11—Very brief partial left breast in gaping pajama top when she leans over to turn off the light.

Love Crimes (1991) . . . . Dana Greenway
(Unrated version reviewed.)
- •• 0:20—Almost left breast, getting out of bathtub. Buns and partial lower frontal nudity, getting dressed.
- •• 0:55—Breasts in open blouse, yelling at Patrick Bergin.
- • 0:57—Brief right breast, on bed in open blouse.
- ••• 0:59—Nude in bathtub.
- ••• 1:01—Breasts, making love with Bergin. Lit with red light.
- ••• 1:03—Full frontal nudity, getting covered with a towel.
- • 1:08—Full frontal nudity, in Polaroid that Maria looks at.
- • 1:11—More full frontal nudity in Polaroid.
- • 1:21—Partial right breast, while taking a shower.
- • 1:23—Brief breasts in the shower.
- • 1:25—Very brief right breast in gaping robe.
- • 1:27—Full frontal nudity in burning Polaroid photograph.

Forever (1992) . . . . Mary Miles Minter
- • 1:09—Breasts while in bathtub and making love in bed with Keith Coogan.
- •• 1:26—Breasts, while making love in bed with Coogan.

Once Upon A Crime (1992) . . . . Phoebe
Ace Ventura: Pet Detective (1993). . . . . Lois
Fatal Instinct (1993) . . . . .Lola Cain
Hold Me, Thrill Me, Kiss Me (1993). . . . . Twinkle
(Unrated version reviewed.)

Even Cowgirls Get the Blues (1994) . . . . .Marie Garth
- • 0:21—Brief breasts, while making love with Crispin Glover in front of Uma Thurman.

Model By Day (1994) . . . . Mercedes
(Shown on network TV without the nudity.)

Dr. Jekyll and Ms. Hyde (1995). . . . . Helen Hyde
- • 0:41—Very brief real breasts, opening her lingerie top in front of Stephen Tobolowsky, then special-effect as her right breast shrinks.

Mirage (1995). . . . . Jennifer Gale
- • 0:15—Buns in sexy outfit, while dancing on stage in bar.
- • 0:19—Nude, getting out of a steamy shower.
- • 1:04—Brief breasts, while lying in bed, opening the covers for Edward James Olmos.
- • 1:05—Brief partial buns and side of left breast, while making love in bed with Olmos.

Evil Has a Face (1996) . . . . Gwen
The Proprietor (1996) . . . . Virginia Kelly
Exception to the Rule (1997). . . . . .Angela Bayer
The Invader (1997) . . . . Annie

Made for Cable Movies:

Blue Ice (1992; Showtime) . . . . Stacy Mansdorf
- • 0:17—Brief breasts and buns, while making love with Michael Caine.
- • 0:18—Brief buns and partial back side of left breast, while sitting up in bed.

Sketch Artist (1992; Showtime). . . . . Rayanne
- •• 0:52—Right breast, several times while making love in bed with Fahey.

Made for TV Movies:

Witness to the Execution (1994) . . . . .Jessica Traynor
Barbara Taylor Bradford's "Everything to Gain" (1996) . . . . n.a.

Young, Sheila

Films:

Time Barbarians (1990). . . . . Minomo
- •• 0:19—Breasts, (she's the blonde one) while bathing with a brunette woman in the water.

Timebomb (1990). . . . . Nude Film Star
- • 0:50—Brief breasts, several times (mostly out of focus) in adult theater during shoot out.

Zabou

Films:

The Perils of Gwendoline in the Land of the Yik Yak
(1984; French) . . . . Beth
- •• 0:36—Breasts, after taking off her blouse in the rain in the forest.
- •• 0:57—Breasts while in torture chamber, getting rescued by Tawny Kitaen.
- •• 1:04—Breasts after Kitaen escapes.
- • 1:11—Buns, in costume during fight.

One Woman or Two (1986; French) . . . . .Constance
a.k.a. Une Femme Ou Deux
- •• 0:28—Brief breasts pulling up her blouse for Gerard Depardieu.

C'est La Vie (1990; French) . . . . Bella

Zadora, Pia *

Singer.

Films:

Santa Claus Conquers the Martians (1964) . . . . Girmar
Butterfly (1982) . . . . .Kady
- •• 0:33—Breasts and buns getting into the bath.
- ••• 0:35—Breasts in bathtub when Keach is giving her a bath.

Nevada Heat (1982) . . . . Bobbi
a.k.a. Fake-Out
- • 0:14—Very brief partial right breast and brief buns, in the showers.
- • 0:47—Side of left breast, while in bubble bath with Desi Arnaz, Jr.

The Lonely Lady (1983) . . . . JeniLee Randall
- • 0:12—Brief breasts getting raped by Ray Liotta, after getting out of the pool.
- •• 0:22—Brief breasts, then left breast, while making love with Walter.
- •• 0:28—Side view breasts lying in bed with Walter.
- •• 0:44—Buns and side view of left breast taking a shower.
- • 0:46—Very brief right breast, in bed with George.
- •• 1:05—Left breast, then brief breasts making love with Vinnie.

Voyage of the Rock Aliens (1985) . . . . .DeeDee
a.k.a. When the Rains Begin to Fall
Hairspray (1988) . . . . The Beatnik Chick
Naked Gun 33 1/3: The Final Insult (1993) . . . . Herself

Made for Cable Movies:

National Lampoon's Favorite Deadly Sins (1995; Showtime)
. . . . Herself

Zakovich, Denise *

Films:

Round Trip to Heaven (1992) . . . . Miss Moscow
- •• 1:06—Buns and upper half breasts, undressing in bedroom.
- ••• 1:07—Breasts, opening her towel for Zach Galligan.
- • 1:12—Very brief right breast, while in bed with Galligan.

Video Tapes:

Inside Sports: Beauties on the Beach (1992) . . . . .Model

• *Zal, Roxana*

Films:

Table for Five (1983) . . . . Tilde
Testament (1983) . . . . Mary Liz Wetherly
Under the Boardwalk (1989) . . . . Gitch

Red Line (1995). . . . . Gem
••• 0:50—Breasts, while wearing black panties, talking with Chad McQueen in motel room.
Daddy's Girl (1996). . . . . Karen Conners
Markus 4 (1996) . . . . Lara
Made for TV Movies:
Something About Amelia (1984). . . . . Amelia Bennett
Shattered Spirits (1986). . . . . Lesley Mollencamp
Everybody's Baby: The Rescue of Jessica McClure (1989) . . . . Cissy
Something to Live For: The Alison Gertz Story (1992) . . . .Tracy
Deadly Relations (1993) . . . . Marty

Zambelli, Zaira

Films:
Bye Bye Brazil (1980; Brazilian) . . . . Dasdô
•• 1:11—Buns, then breasts outside by a boat with Cigano.
Fulaninha (1986; Brazilian) . . . . Sulamita

Zane, Lisa

Sister of actor Billy Zane.
Films:
Gross Anatomy (1989) . . . . Luann
Pucker Up and Bark Like a Dog (1989). . . . . Taylor Phillips
•• 0:52—Breasts in shower with Max. Left breast, while in bed.
Bad Influence (1990) . . . . Claire
• 0:39—Brief breasts on video tape seen on TV at party.
Femme Fatale (1990) . . . . .Cynthia
Freddy's Dead: The Final Nightmare (1991) . . . . Maggie Burroughs
Unveiled (1993) . . . . Stephania Montgomery
• 1:06—Very, very brief left breast in gaping gown, while bending over to pick stuff up off the floor.
Floundering (1994) . . . . .Jessica
Terrified (1994) . . . . Pearl
The Nurse (1996) . . . . Laura Harriman
Made for TV Movies:
Dark Reflection (1994) . . . . .Elizabeth
Her Deadly Rival (1995). . . . . Lynne
TV:
ER (1994-95). . . . . Diane Leeds
Profit (1996) . . . . Joanne Meltzer
Roar (1997). . . . . .Queen Diana

Zane, Lora

Films:
Men Don't Leave (1989) . . . . .Nina Simon
Live Nude Girls (1996) . . . . .Georgina
• 0:03—Very brief side view of left breast and buns, while in the shower. Very brief breasts in the shower (closer shot).
••• 0:05—Breasts, while lying on table in kitchen, getting covered with flour during fantasy.
• 0:17—Brief side view of left breast, while sitting at table in neighbor boy's fantasy.
•• 0:45—Brief breasts, taking off her blouse and getting into bed with Olivia D'Abo.
•• 0:46—Breasts, while in bed with D'Abo. B&W.

Zann, Lenore *

Films:
Black Mirror (1980; Canadian). . . . . n.a.
Happy Birthday to Me (1980; Canadian) . . . . Maggie
The Hounds of Notre Dame (1980; Canadian) . . . . . Lila Petrie
American Nightmare (1981; Canadian) . . . . Tina
••• 0:25—Breasts and buns while dancing on stage.
•• 1:05—Breasts and buns while dancing on stage again.
Visiting Hours (1982; Canadian) . . . . Lisa
Murder By Phone (1983; Canadian). . . . . Connie Lawson
a.k.a. Bells
One Night Only (1984; Canadian) . . . . .Anne
a.k.a. For One Night Only
•• 0:20—Breasts while getting dressed in bedroom with Jamie.
• 1:04—Right breast in bedroom with Jamie.
••• 1:19—Breasts and buns while making love with Jamie.
Def-Con 4 (1985) . . . . J. J.
Return (1985) . . . . Susan
Mania (1986; Canadian) . . . .The Good Samaritan/Julie Somers
The Girl (1987; British) . . . . .Viveca
Pretty Kill (1987) . . . . Carrie
Geeks in Love (1992; Canadian) . . . . .n.a.
Cold Sweat (1993) . . . . Catherine Wicker
•• 0:04—Brief buns in panties, then partial lower frontal nudity in bra, panties, garter belt and stockings. Brief breasts while making love in office with David.
•• 0:46—Breasts in bubble bath while talking to Ben Cross.
••• 0:50—Breasts, while lying on bed and talking to Cross.
Natural Enemy (1996) . . . . Gina
• 0:14—Brief buns, several times, after William McNamara takes her pants off while she's tied to the bed.
• 0:20—Brief breasts, several times, in mirror, while making love with McNamara. Brief buns, when he burns her with a cigarette.
Made for TV Movies:
Love and Hate (1989) . . . . Lynne
Tom Alone (1989) . . . . Lily Manse
Ed McBain's 87th Precinct: Ice (1996) . . . . Angie
TV:
On Thin Ice: The Tai Babilonia Story . . . . .n.a.

Zdrok, Victoria *

Video Tapes:
Playboy Celebrity Centerfold: Patti Davis (1994) . . . . .Playmate
• 0:44—Full frontal nudity in introduction.
••• 0:46—Nude while posing outside.
••• 0:49—Nude in schoolgirl in library fantasy.
••• 0:52—Nude in still photos.
••• 0:53—Nude in various lingerie outfits.
••• 0:56—Nude in mansion fantasy.
Sexy Lingerie: Dreams & Desire (1994) . . . . .Playmate
Playboy Video Calendar 1996 (1995) . . . . November
••• 0:44—Nude in library fantasy.
••• 0:46—Nude in mansion.

Zee, Ona *

Adult film actress.
a.k.a. Ona Simms Wiegers.
Films:
Enrapture (1989) . . . . Chase Webb
•• 0:13—In red bra, panties, garter belt and stockings. Buns in G-string, then breasts undressing when she doesn't know Keith is watching.
•• 0:17—Breasts when Keith fantasizes about her while he's making love with Martha.
•• 0:21—Breasts in back of limousine with a lucky guy.
••• 1:08—Full frontal nudity making love on top of Keith in bed.
The Art of Dying (1991). . . . . Frances Warner

Made for Cable TV:

Real Sex 5 (1993; HBO) . . . . Of Human Bondage
- • 0:00—Brief left breast during opening credits.
- ••• 0:12—Breasts, leading Frank Zee up stairs and in bed. More breasts while spanking him.
- ••• 0:15—Breasts, getting clips put on her nipples. Buns in T-back while getting spanked.

Zenor, Suzanne

Films:

Get to Know Your Rabbit (1972). . . . . Paula
- • 0:06—Very brief buns, getting out of bed.

Play It Again, Sam (1972) . . . . Discotheque Girl
Lucky Lady (1973). . . . . Brunette
The Way We Were (1973) . . . . Dumb Blonde
The Choirboys (1977) . . . . Blonde at Party
Rabbit Test (1978). . . . . Mother of Triplets

Zentout, Delphine

Films:

36 Fillette (1988; French). Lili
- • 1:15—Breasts, while in bed with Maurice.
- • 1:19—Left breast, while crying under the covers in bed.
- • 1:20—Brief breasts several times, then buns, while getting out of bed and getting dressed.
- • 1:23—Left breast, then breasts, while making love with Bertrand in bed.

Farinelli (1995; Swiss/French/Belgian). . . . The Young Admirer
a.k.a. Farinelli: il castrato
- • 0:24—Breasts, while making love in bed with Farinelli.

Zhivago, Stacia

Films:

Sorority House Massacre 2 (1990). . . . . Kimberly
- ••• 0:21—Nude, taking a shower.
- • 0:53—Buns, while going up the stairs.
- • 0:55—Brief buns, while going up the stairs.
- • 1:00—Brief breasts, sitting up in bathtub filled with bloody water to strangle Linda.

Video Tapes:

Scream Queen Hot Tub Party (1991) . . . . Kimberly
- ••• 0:16—Nude, in shower scene from *Sorority House Massacre 2.*

Zimmie, Elizabeth

Films:

Sorority House Party (1992) . . . . Screaming Sorority Girl
Killing Obsession (1994) . . . . Babs
- • 0:43—Brief left breast, several times, while posing with Randy during photo shoot.

*Zinszer, Pamela **

Films:

The Happy Hooker Goes to Washington (1977) . . . . Linda
- • 1:19—Brief breasts in raincoat flashing in front of congressional panel.

Video Tapes:

Playboy Video Magazine, Volume 2 (1983)
. . . . Herself/Playboy Playoffs

Zucker, Miriam

Films:

Prime Evil (1987) . . . . Nancy Deans
- •• 0:03—Breasts several times, during sacrificial ceremony.

Senior Week (1987) . . . . Princeton Dream Girl
- •• 0:42—Breasts during dream.

Wildest Dreams (1987) . . . . Customer
Alien Space Avenger (1988). . . . . Bordello Reporter
New York's Finest (1988) . . . . Mrs. Rush
Sensations (1988). . . . . Cookie Woman
- • 0:06—Breasts on couch making love with a guy while Jenny and Brian watch.

A Woman Obsessed (1989) . . . . Betsy

*Zuniga, Daphne **

Films:

The Initiation (1984) . . . . Kelly Terry
The Sure Thing (1985) . . . . Alison Bradbury
Visionquest (1985) . . . . Margie Epstein
Modern Girls (1987) . . . . Margo
Spaceballs (1987) . . . . Princess Vespa
Last Rites (1988). . . . . Angela
- • 0:04—Very brief breasts running into the bathroom to escape from being shot. Covered with blood, don't see her face. Very brief right breast reaching for a bathrobe. Don't really see anything.
- • 0:40—Buns, behind a shower door.
- • 0:50—Buns, getting out of bed and standing in front of Tom Berenger.

The Fly II (1989) . . . . Beth
Gross Anatomy (1989) . . . . Laurie Rorbach
Staying Together (1989) . . . . Beverly Young
- •• 0:56—Buns, lying in bed with Kit. Nice, long buns scene.

Mad at the Moon (1993). . . . Jenny's Mom as a Young Woman

Made for Cable Movies:

Prey of the Chameleon (1992; Showtime) . . . Elizabeth Burrows

Made for Cable TV:

Dead Man's Gun: Black Widow (1997; Showtime)
. . . . Tanya/Lillian

Made for TV Movies:

Quarterback Princess (1983) . . . . Kim Maida
Degree of Guilt (1995) . . . . Terri Peralta
Pandora's Clock (1996) . . . . Dr. Roni Sanders

TV:

Melrose Place (1992-96) . . . . Jo Reynolds

*Zylberstein, Elsa **

Films:

Van Gogh (1992; French) . . . . Cathy
Farinelli (1995; Swiss/French/Belgian). . . . . . Alexandra Lerris
a.k.a. Farinelli: il castrato
- •• 1:45—Breasts, while making love in bed with Carlo, then Riccardo.

Jefferson in Paris (1995). . . . . Adrienne de Lafayette

Titles

10 *(1979)*

Julie Andrews. . . . . Sam
Bo Derek . . . . Jennifer Hanley
- • 1:29—Brief buns and breasts taking off towel and putting on robe when Moore visits her. Long shot, hard to see.
- • 1:36—Brief breasts taking off dress trying to seduce Moore. Dark, hard to see.
- • 1:37—Breasts, lying in bed. Dark, hard to see.
- •• 1:41—Breasts, going to fix the skipping record. Long shot, hard to see. Buns, while jumping back into bed.
- • 1:43—Breasts and buns, while sitting up in bed.
- • 1:44—Breasts and buns in bed when Moore gets out.

Dee Wallace Stone . . . . Mary Lewis
- • 1:09—Brief side view of buns, while on the floor.
- • 1:10—Brief upper half of buns, going into bathroom and dropping her sheet.

10 to Midnight *(1983)*

Lisa Eilbacher. . . . . Laurie Kessler
Jean Manson . . . . .Margo
- ••• 1:25—Breasts in hotel room with killer when he tries to elude Charles Bronson.
- • 1:26—Brief right breast, lying in bed, covered with sheet.

Kelly Preston . . . . Doreen
Ola Ray . . . . Ola
- • 1:30—Very brief buns and very brief left breast, taking off robe and getting into the shower.
- •• 1:31—Breasts in the shower.
- •• 1:32—More breasts in the shower.
- • 1:39—Very brief breasts, dead, covered with blood in the shower.

Patti Tippo . . . . .Party Girl
- •• 0:52—Breasts, making love with a guy in the laundry room at a party.

Jeana Tomasina . . . . Karen

• ***The 13 Chairs*** *(1969; French/Italian/British)*

Ottavia Piccolo . . . . Stefanella
- • 1:18—Very brief buns while running up the stairs, while wearing an apron during chase through the garden. Long shot.
- • 1:21—Brief buns, twice, wearing apron during chase.
- • 1:23—Very brief blurry right breast, while getting into bed with Mario and Sharon Tate.

Sharon Tate. . . . . Pat
- • 0:14—In bra, then very brief left breast, while in struggle in bedroom with Mario.
- •• 1:20—Breasts clearly visible under sheer wet blouse after getting out of the pool.
- • 1:24—Left breast, while in bed with Mario and Stefanella.

18 Again! *(1988)*

Connie Gauthier . . . . Artist's Model
- •• 0:29—Very brief breasts, then buns taking her robe off during art class.

Anita Morris . . . . .Madeline
Jennifer Runyon. . . . . Robin

• ***187*** *(1997)*

Karina Arroyave . . . . Rita
- • 0:19—Very, very brief left breast, while putting her bra back on in shed after getting discovered by John Heard.
- • 0:52—Brief right breast, while lying nude on Samuel L. Jackson's couch.

1900 *(1976; Italian)*

(NC-17 version reviewed.)

Stefania Casini . . . . Epileptic Girl
- •• 2:02—Breasts taking off her top, more breasts in bed with Robert De Niro and Gerard Depardieu.
- ••• 2:04—Breasts sitting up in bed, then nude while having a seizure.

Ty Randolph . . . . .n.a.
Dominique Sanda . . . . .Ada
- ••• 2:30—Left breast, then breasts in hay with Robert De Niro. Long shot of full frontal nudity while lying in the hay.
- ••• 2:48—(0:08 into tape 2.) Nude under thin fabric dancing with De Niro for photographer.

Stefania Sandrelli . . . . Anita Foschi

1941 *(1979)*

Nancy Allen . . . . Donna
Susan Backlinie . . . . .Polar Bear Girl
- • 0:02—Brief breasts and buns, while taking off robe and running into the ocean. Dark, hard to see. This is a parody of her part in *Jaws*.
- • 0:05—Buns, while hanging on submarine periscope.
- • 0:06—Very, very brief left breast when getting back into the water.

Carol Ann Williams . . . . USO Girl

1984 *(1984)*

Suzanna Hamilton . . . . Julia
- •• 0:38—Full frontal nudity taking off her clothes in the woods with John Hurt.
- ••• 0:52—Nude in secret room standing and drinking and talking to Hurt. Long scene.
- • 1:11—Side view of left breast kneeling down.
- •• 1:12—Breasts after picture falls off the view screen on the wall.

• ***2 Days in the Valley*** *(1996)*

Teri Hatcher. . . . . Becky Foxx
Marsha Mason. . . . . Audrey Hopper
Charlize Theron . . . . Helga Svelgen
- • 0:11—Brief breasts, while lying "dead" in a photograph with blood on her left breast.
- ••• 0:37—Breasts, while making love with James Spader.

2002: The Rape of Eden *(1992)*

Francine Lapenseé . . . . The Virgin
- •• 1:06—Breasts and buns, while making love in bed with the Bounty Hunter during his dream.

2020 Texas Gladiators *(1983; Italian)*

Sabrina Siani . . . . Maida
- •• 0:07—Left breast, in open white dress after gang rape.
- • 0:34—Breasts during rape.

24 Hours to Midnight *(1991)*

Deanne Power. . . . . Chan's Girlfriend/Woman in Ninja Suit
- • 0:14—Breasts, while getting dressed in black ninja suit.

36 Fillette *(1988; French)*

Delphine Zentout Lili
- • 1:15—Breasts, while in bed with Maurice.
- • 1:19—Left breast, while crying under the covers in bed.
- • 1:20—Brief breasts several times, then buns, while getting out of bed and getting dressed.
- • 1:23—Left breast, then breasts, while making love with Bertrand in bed.

3:15—The Moment of Truth *(1986)*

Wendy Barry . . . . Lora
Deborah Foreman . . . . Sherry Havilland
- 0:26—Very brief blurry buns and side view of left breast jumping out of bed when her parents come home. Long shot, hard to see anything.

Gina Gershon . . . . One of the Cobrettes

48 Hrs. *(1982)*

Greta Blackburn . . . . Lisa
- •• 0:13—Breasts and buns in bathroom in hotel room with James Remar.

Denise Crosby . . . . Sally
- 0:47—Very, very brief side view of half of left breast, while swinging baseball bat at Eddie Murphy.
- 1:24—Very brief side view of right breast when James Remar pushes her onto bed.
- 1:25—Very brief breasts, then very brief side view of right breast while attacking Nick Nolte.

Sandy Martin . . . . Policewoman
Annette O'Toole . . . . Elaine
Ola Ray . . . . Vroman's Dancers
Suzanne M. Regard . . . . Cowgirl Dancer
Brenda Venus . . . . Hooker

52 Pick-Up *(1986)*

Ann-Margret . . . . Barbara Mitchell
Vanity . . . . Doreen
- ••• 0:47—Breasts, stripping in room while Roy Scheider takes Polaroid pictures.
- 0:52—Breasts under sheer purple nightgown. Partial buns in G-string underneath also.

Amber Lynn . . . . Party Goer
- 0:23—Breasts opening her blouse while being video taped at party.
- 0:24—Breasts and buns on TV. B&W.
- 0:26—Left breast, then breasts being video taped with another woman.

Kelly Preston . . . . Cini
- 0:09—Brief buns in video tape made by blackmailers.
- 0:36—Breasts, tied to chair on video tape made by blackmailers.
- 0:39—Very brief breasts covered with blood after being shot.

8 Million Ways to Die *(1986)*

Rosalind Allen . . . . Tote Lady
Rosanna Arquette . . . . Sarah
Alexandra Paul . . . . Sunny
- •• 0:24—Full frontal nudity, standing in bathroom while Jeff Bridges watches.

9 1/2 Ninjas *(1990)*

Andee Gray . . . . Lisa Thorne
- •• 1:02—Breasts, while making love with Joe in the rain.
- 1:19—Brief breasts during flashback.

Sharon Lee Jones . . . . Zelda
- 0:52—Breasts, while eating Chinese food in the shower with Joe.

9 1/2 Weeks *(1986)*

Kim Basinger . . . . Elizabeth
- 0:27—Blindfolded while Mickey Rourke plays with an ice cube on her. Brief right breast.
- 0:54—Very brief left breast, while rolling over in bed.
- ••• 1:11—In wet lingerie, then breasts making love in a wet stairwell with Rourke.
- 1:19—Doing a sexy dance for Rourke in a white slip.
- 1:22—Buns, showing off to Rourke on building.
- 1:44—Brief buns, putting on pants and getting out of bed.

Margaret Whitton . . . . Molly
Karen Young . . . . Sue

976-EVIL *(1988)*

Lezlie Deane . . . . Suzie
- 0:34—Brief right breast in open leather jacket, making love on top of Spike. Brief breasts several times getting off him.
- •• 0:37—Brief breasts opening jacket after putting on underwear.

976-EVIL II: The Astral Factor *(1991)*

Joy Ballard . . . . Stripper
Deborah Dutch . . . . Commerical Wife
Monique Gabrielle . . . . Miss Lawlor
Karen Mayo-Chandler . . . . Laurie
- •• 0:00—Breasts, while taking a shower in shower room, then putting on wet T-shirt.

Brigitte Nielsen . . . . Agnes
Leslie Ryan . . . . Paula

à la mode *(1994; French)*

a.k.a. In Fashion
a.k.a. Fausto

Florence Darel . . . . Tonie
- •• 1:05—Full frontal nudity, while lying in bed with Fausto.

A Nos Amours *(1984; French)*

Sandrine Bonnaire . . . . Suzanne
- 0:17—Brief breasts, pulling dress top down to put on nightgown.
- •• 0:34—Breasts sitting up in bed talking to Bernard. Brief side view of buns.
- 0:42—Very brief side view of left breast while waking up in bed.
- 0:57—Very brief lower frontal nudity, while getting out of bed with Martine and her boyfriend. Long shot of buns, while hugging Bernard in the background (out of focus).

Maïté Maillé . . . . Martine

Abducted II: The Reunion *(1994)*

Raquel Bianca . . . . Maria Marcolini
- •• 0:57—Breasts, after taking off her wet blouse in Vern's cave.
- ••• 1:04—Breasts, while making love with a good looking guy.
- 1:17—Breasts, while on cliff with Vern.

Debbie Rochon . . . . Sharon Baker
- 1:15—Breasts, while waving her sweater to try and get helicopter pilot's attention.

Abduction *(1975)*

Judith-Marie Bergan . . . . Patricia
- 0:08—Very brief buns and very brief lower frontal nudity on sofa when terrorists break into her apartment and kidnap her.
- 0:19—Lower frontal nudity several times, when blindfolded and raped on bed by one of the terrorists.
- •• 0:41—Breasts, after taking off T-shirt while sitting on chair in front of Carol.
- 0:49—Breasts on B&W video monitors in playback of scene at 0:41.
- •• 1:10—Full frontal nudity, after taking off her clothes in bedroom in front of Dory and Frank.
- 1:24—Brief breasts, while making love in bed with Dory.

The Abductors (1971)

Cheri Caffaro . . . . Ginger
- • 0:23—Breasts under sheer green blouse while talking with Ken Stanton.
- ••• 0:52—Nude, while making love with Stanton on the floor.
- •• 1:01—Breasts, when getting molested by a bad guy while she's tied to a pole.
- • 1:05—Breasts in open blouse outside after escaping.
- •• 1:20—Breasts, after taking off blouse and washing Stanton in the shower while he's tied up.

Jeramie Rain . . . . Jane
- • 0:02—Breasts, while getting wrists tied.
- •• 0:08—Breasts, while standing, gagged and with hands tied behind her back.
- •• 0:10—Full frontal nudity (she's the brunette), while taking off her panties with the two other girls.

About Last Night... (1986)

Catherine Keener. . . . . .Cocktail Waitress
Demi Moore . . . . Debbie
- • 0:34—Brief upper half of right breast in the bathtub with Rob Lowe.
- • 0:50—Side view of right breast, then very brief breasts and brief buns, with Rob Lowe.
- ••• 0:51—Buns and breasts in bed with Lowe, arching her back, then lying in bed when he rolls off her.
- •• 0:52—Breasts and buns in kitchen with Lowe.

Elizabeth Perkins . . . . Joan

Above Suspicion (1994)

Kim Cattrall . . . . .Gail
- •• 0:02—Breasts, while making love in bed with Nick and after getting interrupted by his beeper.
- • 0:19—Brief breasts, while getting out of the shower after making love with Nick.
- • 0:20—Brief buns and very brief side view of right breast, while taking off robe and getting into nightgown.
- • 0:22—Brief left breast in gaping nightgown in bed with Christopher Reeve.

Holley Chant . . . . .Nancy
Sandy Martin. . . . . Waitress

The Abyss (1989)

Mary Elizabeth Mastrantonio. . . . . Lindsey Brigman
- • 1:41—Breasts during C.P.R. scene.

• *Access Denied* (1996)

Jordana Capra . . . . Martha Riley
Jane Higginson . . . . Dawn Able
- •• 0:42—In black bra, then breasts, while making love with Bill in office.
- •• 1:01—Breasts, while making love with Raymond at her house.

Colleen McDermott. Sherry Johannson
- • 0:15—Right breast, while making out with Harvey in prison classroom.
- ••• 0:23—Full frontal nudity, while making love in bedroom with Raymond.
- •• 0:56—Breasts and buns, while making love on the floor with Joe.
- •• 1:06—Breasts, while making love with Joe in a stream outdoors.
- • 1:08—Breasts, while making love with Joe on the floor.
- • 1:17—Brief buns and brief left breast while in spa with Raymond.

The Accused (1988)

Jodie Foster . . . . .Sarah Tobias
- • 1:27—Brief breasts a few times during rape scene on pinball machine by Dan and Bob.

Kelly McGillis . . . . Kathryn Murphy

Across the Moon (1994)

Christina Applegate . . . . Kathy
Elizabeth Peña . . . . Carmen
- • 0:46—Left breast, while hugging James Remar in hot spring pool after people on off-road vehicles leave.

Mowava Pryor . . . . Public Defender

Act of Piracy (1990; South African/U.S.)

Belinda Bauer. . . . . .Sandy Andrews
Nancy Mulford . . . . Laura Warner
- • 0:11—Very brief left breast under Gary Busey in bed. Dark, hard to see.
- • 0:34—Brief, upper half of left breast, in bed with Ray Sharkey.

Act of Vengeance (1974)

a.k.a. The Rape Squad
(Not to be confused with the film with the same name starring Charles Bronson.)

Anneka di Lorenzo . . . . .Chris
- ••• 1:07—Buns and breasts, getting dressed in house. Seen from outside through simulated camera viewfinder.

Patricia Estrin . . . . Angie
- • 0:37—Brief full frontal nudity, several times, under water in spa. (She's third from the right.)

Jo Ann Harris . . . . Linda
- ••• 0:06—Breasts, taking off blouse for rapist, getting fondled by him, running away, then getting hit.
- • 0:09—Brief left breast, while getting her blouse afterwards. Dark.
- • 0:37—Breasts under water with other women in spa. (She's the third from the left.)

Jennifer Lee . . . . .Nancy
- • 0:38—Breasts looking up in spa while talking to another woman.

Lisa Moore. . . . . Karen
- ••• 0:24—Breasts after rapist cuts her dress open and fondles her breasts while she has a cloth stuffed in her mouth.
- • 0:37—Buns and breasts, walking into the spa to join the other women.
- • 1:27—Brief breasts during fight while tied up in cage. Dark.

Connie Strickland . . . . .Teresa
- • 0:37—Brief full frontal nudity under water, several times, sitting in spa with other women. (She's the blonde on the far right.)

Cheryl Waters . . . . .Tamara

Action Jackson (1988)

Vanity . . . . .Sydney Ash
- •• 0:29—Breasts, while in bed with Craig T. Nelson.

Deborah Dutch . . . . .n.a.
Susan Lentini . . . . .VW Driver
Melissa Prophet . . . . .Newscaster
Sharon Stone. . . . . .Patrice Dellaplane
- •• 0:34—Breasts, while in a steam room. Hard to see because of all the steam.
- • 0:56—Brief right breast, dead, on the bed when police view her body.

Action U.S.A. *(1988)*

Barri Murphy . . . . Carmen

•• 0:03—Breasts, in house, making love with, then getting beaten up by a bad guy.

The Adjuster *(1991; Canadian)*

Jennifer Dale . . . . Arianne

••• 0:46—Breasts, while making love on top of Elias Koteas and discussing her insurance adjustments. Dark but nice.

Arsinée Khanjian . . . . Hera

Gabrielle Rose . . . . Mimi

The Adultress *(1973)*

Tyne Daly . . . . Inez

• 0:21—Brief side view of right breast, while in room with Carl. Brief out of focus breasts in bed.

•• 0:51—Breasts, while outside with Hank.

••• 0:53—Breasts, while on a horse with Hank.

The Adventures of a Private Eye *(1974; British)*

Nicola Austine . . . . Wife in Bed

•• 0:00—Breasts and buns, getting out of bed to take a shower.

Linda Regan . . . . Clarissa

• 0:34—Full frontal nudity in boat with Scott.

• 0:36—Very brief side view of left breast, getting up and diving off boat.

The Adventures of Eliza Fraser *(1976; Australian)*

Abigail . . . . Buxom Girl

• 0:01—Breasts when Martin pulls the sheets off her.

Susannah York . . . . Elisa Fraser

• 1:10—Brief breasts twice during ceremony. Paint on her face while running from hut.

• 1:30—Brief, upper half of left beast, while bathing in river with Bracefell.

The Advocate *(1993; British/French)*

a.k.a. The Hour of the Pig

Amina Annabi . . . . Samira

• 0:42—Brief breasts, while talking with Colin Firth.

•• 1:07—Left breast, while making love with Firth.

Lysette Anthony . . . . Filette d'Auferre

• 1:03—Brief full frontal nudity, after dropping her dress for Colin Firth.

Sophie Dix . . . . Maria

••• 0:32—In nightgown, then nude, after taking it off and making love on top of Colin Firth in bed.

Harriet Walter . . . . Jeannine

• 0:06—Briefly nude, while running in a field, being hunted.

Affair *(1984; French/Italian)*

Lucretia Love . . . . Helen

••• 0:33—In black bra when on couch with Mark, then breasts and buns, while making love with him on bed.

• 1:06—Brief breasts in B&W photo that Mark looks at.

•• 1:09—Right breast, then breasts and very brief lower frontal nudity, while in bed with Mark.

• 1:16—Side of left breast and buns, after taking off robe while kissing Don.

Paola Senatore . . . . Beatrice

••• 0:00—Full frontal nudity, while lying in bed, caressing herself, then making love with Mark.

• 0:05—Very brief right breast in open top, while reaching for a book.

•• 0:07—Very brief right breast in mirror when Mark puts a necklace on her. Breasts when he opens her blouse and she kneels down next to him.

••• 0:15—Breasts, while making love in bed with Mark.

• 0:17—Breasts in open fur coat, while in front of Mark.

••• 0:28—Very brief lower frontal nudity, when Don rips off her panties, then breasts, while making out on the couch with him.

••• 0:43—Breasts, while making love with Norma on bed (later, Mark joins in also).

••• 1:16—Nude, while making love in bed with Mark.

The Affair *(1995)*

Kimberly Blair . . . . Bobbie Pins

Jenna Bodnar . . . . Alexis

•• 0:06—Full frontal nudity, after dropping towel in her bedroom.

••• 1:03—Full frontal nudity, while making love with Linda in bedroom.

Raelyn Saalman . . . . Jennifer

•• 0:01—Breasts, while making love in bed with Greg.

• 0:12—Breasts, while sitting at piano when fondled by Greg.

••• 0:16—Full frontal nudity while undressing in her imagination, then making love with Mark when watched by Alexis.

• 0:18—Breasts, while making love with Mark in her imagination.

••• 0:29—Buns in panties, then breasts and lower frontal nudity, while making love with Mark. Very nice, long scene.

•• 0:39—Nude, while drying herself off in bathroom.

••• 1:16—In lingerie, then nude, while making love with Greg in bedroom.

Kathleen Scott . . . . Linda

•• 0:33—Breasts, while caressing herself after watching Jennifer make love with Mark.

•• 0:39—Brief buns under short nightie, then nude, while talking with Jennifer in bathroom.

••• 0:51—In lingerie, then breasts and buns in panties, while in the house with Mark.

• 0:55—Breasts and buns in panties, in the house with Mark some more.

•• 0:59—Breasts and buns in panties, while dancing in front of Mark and Alexis.

••• 1:03—Nude, while making love with Alexis in bedroom.

•• 1:08—Breasts, while making love with Mark in bedroom.

Affairs of the Heart *(1992)*

Tempest . . . . Miss September

••• 0:54—Breasts posing in skirt during photo session.

••• 1:00—More breasts during photo session.

Amy Lynn Baxter . . . . Josie Hart

•• 0:00—Breasts during opening credits.

•• 0:02—Breasts and buns in G-string, while posing for photos.

••• 1:09—Breasts posing in Santa cap during photo session.

•• 1:13—Breasts with Richard during smoky dream scene.

Cody Carmack . . . . Itchy

••• 0:45—Breasts taking off her bikini top with her husband.

Lorna Courtney . . . . Jane

••• 1:04—Breasts, making love in front of a fire in sleeping bag with Dick.

Isabelle Fortea . . . . Karen

••• 1:06—Breasts making love in cabin with Tom.

Joan Gerardi . . . . Miss Valentine's Day

••• 0:15—Breasts, posing for photos in red bottoms.

Melissa Leigh. . . . . Jealous Woman
••• 0:38—Buns, then breasts with the Jealous Man.
Beckie Mullen . . . . Pool Girl
••• 0:52—Breasts, after taking off her bikini top, then diving into pool.
•• 0:53—Breasts, lying on towel on diving board, then turning over.
Angela Nicholas . . . . Dreamgirl
•• 0:14—In bra, then left breast while in bed with the Geek.

Afraid of the Dark *(1992; British/French)*

Fanny Ardant. . . . . Miriam
Clare Holman . . . . Rose
••• 0:38—Breasts, while wearing white panties, garter belt and stockings while posing for photographer in studio on a wooden horse. Long scene.
Catriona MacColl . . . . Blind Woman/Wedding Friend
Cassie Stuart . . . . Woman Neighbor

After Dark, My Sweet *(1990)*

Jeanie Moore. . . . . Nanny
Rachel Ward . . . . Fay Anderson
• 1:22—Very, very brief half of right breast under Jason Patric in bed when he moves slightly.

After Hours *(1985)*

Rosanna Arquette . . . . Marcy
Linda Fiorentino . . . . Kiki
•• 0:19—Breasts taking off bra in doorway while Griffin Dunne watches.
Teri Garr . . . . Julie

After School *(1987)*

Renee Coleman. . . . . September Lane
•• 0:35—Breasts and buns getting into bathtub. Almost lower frontal nudity.
Sherrie Rose . . . . First Tribe Member

After the Rehearsal *(1984; Swedish)*

Lena Olin . . . . Anna Egerman
Ingrid Thulin . . . . Rakel
• 0:33—Brief breasts, when pulling up her sweater to show Henrik how beautiful her breasts still look.

Agatha *(1979; British)*

Vanessa Redgrave . . . . Agatha Christie
• 0:38—Buns, while lying face down and getting a massage. Then wearing a wet gown in bathtub.

Age of Consent *(1969; Australian)*

Clarissa Kaye-Mason . . . . Meg
• 0:05—Brief breasts, crawling on the bed to watch TV.
Helen Mirren. . . . . Cora
• 0:48—Breasts several times in the mirror. Brief lower frontal nudity, kneeling on the floor.
•• 0:55—Brief breasts and buns quite a few time, snorkeling under water.
••• 1:20—Breasts and half of buns, posing in the water for James Mason. Then getting out.

Agony of Love *(1966)*

Pat Barringer . . . . Barbara Thomas
•• 0:10—Breasts, after taking off bra, then on bed with the customer. Upper half of buns in pulled down panties.
••• 0:16—Breasts and buns, standing in front of bathroom mirror, then taking a bath and drying herself off.
•• 0:19—Breasts, while making love with the Beatnik and his girlfriend.
• 0:29—Brief breasts several times during nightmare with money.
• 0:38—Brief breasts while wearing panties, in bed with a Conventioneer.
••• 0:42—Breasts, while lying on bed and getting out of bed after making love with the Conventioneer.
• 0:43—Breasts, while sitting up after making love with the other Conventioneer.
• 0:54—In white bra and panties on bed, then breasts several times with a customer.
•• 1:02—In white bra, taking off her clothes in front of a customer. Then breasts while wearing panties while she poses and he messily eats a lot of food.
• 1:16—Brief breasts, while turning over in bed before seeing her husband.

Airheads *(1994)*

Amy Locane. . . . . Kayla
• 0:35—Brief buns in T-back swimsuit in photo that Brendan Fraser hands to Ernie Hudson.
Nina Siemaszko . . . . Suzzi

Airplane II: The Sequel *(1982)*

Sandahl Bergman . . . . Officer #1
Monique Gabrielle. . . . . School Girl
• 0:02—Brief breasts seen on monitor when walking through the video X-ray scanner at the airport while holding her mother's hand.
Laurene Landon. . . . . Testa

Alamo Bay *(1985)*

Amy Madigan . . . . Glory
•• 0:28—Breasts while lying in motel bed with Ed Harris.
•• 0:30—Breasts while sitting up in the bed.

Albino *(1976)*

a.k.a. Night of the Askari
Sybil Danning . . . . Sally
• 0:19—Breasts, then full frontal nudity getting raped by the Albino and his buddies.

Alex in Wonderland *(1970)*

Ellen Burstyn . . . . Beth
• 1:19—Breasts, while sitting in bed, then putting her nightgown on.
Jeanne Moreau . . . . Herself

Alexa *(1988)*

Ruth Corrine Collins. . . . . Marshall
• 0:01—Breasts a couple of times taking blue dress off and putting it on again. Long shot.
Jennifer Delora. . . . . Woman 2
• 0:42—Breasts undressing behind shelves.
Christine Moore. . . . . Alexa
•• 0:24—Breasts lying in bed with Anthony while reminiscing.
•• 1:08—Breasts in bed with Anthony again.

Alice Goodbody *(1975)*

Angela Carnon. . . . . Harmonica Girl
••• 1:07—Buns and lower frontal nudity playing a harmonica without her mouth. (Never see her face.)
• 1:20—Buns, during end credits.
Sharon Kelly . . . . Alice Goodbody
• 0:01—Brief breasts in mirror, getting dressed.

- ••• 0:16—In bra, then full frontal nudity, undressing in Arnold's place. More breasts in the shower with him.
- ••• 0:17—Frontal nudity, while lying in bed and making out with Arnold.
- • 0:27—Breasts with Roger while he eats all sorts of food off her body.
- • 0:28—Breasts, lying in bed with Roger afterwards.
- ••• 0:37—Right breast, then frontal nudity while talking to Rex.
- ••• 0:38—Breasts when Rex carries her to bed and makes love with her, while admiring himself.
- •• 0:47—Breasts with bandages on her face.
- ••• 0:51—Breasts, taking off her robe and getting into bed. (Bandages are still on her face.)
- •• 1:09—Buns, undressing and getting into bed.
- • 1:21—Brief breasts in mirror in bed with Rex during the end credits.

Alice in Wonderland (1977)

(R-rated version reviewed.)

Kristine DeBell. . . . . Alice
- • 0:10—Brief left breast, several times after shrinking.
- • 0:12—In braless wet sheet, after getting out of the water.
- • 0:14—Brief lower frontal nudity in open sheet during song and dance number.
- •• 0:16—Lower frontal nudity and breasts while getting licked by her new friends.
- •• 0:18—Full frontal nudity while putting new dress on.
- • 0:19—Left breast in gaping dress when sitting down on rock.
- ••• 0:22—Breasts, after taking off dress and playing with herself.
- • 0:40—Brief right breast, while lying on the ground with Tweedledum and Tweedledee.
- • 0:42—Brief breasts under dress while singing and dancing.
- •• 0:51—Full frontal nudity on bed with the king.
- ••• 0:59—Full frontal nudity getting bathed and primped by two women, then making love with them, then with the Queen. Brief buns, when getting up.
- • 1:05—Right breast in dress, while running from the Queen.
- •• 1:07—Nude while making love with her boyfriend after returning from Wonderland.
- ••• 1:10—Breasts, while running around in field in white dress, then riding a horse. Full frontal nudity in waterfall.
- •• 1:15—Nude during end credits.

Juliet Graham . . . . The Queen
- ••• 0:51—Full frontal nudity in garter belt and stockings while walking, then talking with Alice.
- ••• 0:54—Full frontal nudity during trial.
- • 0:58—Breasts in quick cuts.
- •• 1:05—Full frontal nudity, while running after Alice.
- •• 1:13—Breasts during the end credits.

Alice's Restaurant (1969)

Shelley Plimpton . . . . Reenie
- •• 0:21—Breasts, taking off her blouse while sitting on bed and talking to Arlo Guthrie.

• *Alien Avengers* (1996; Made for Cable Movie)

a.k.a. Welcome to Planet Earth

Gretchen Palmer . . . . Melissa Rose

Anastasia Sakelaris . . . . Daphne
- • 0:40—Brief side view of left breast, while pushing Joseph onto the bed.
- •• 0:51—Brief breasts, twice, and buns in T-back after taking off her dress in police station to get some attention.

Alien Intruder (1992)

Melinda Armstrong . . . . Tammy
- •• 0:29—In two piece swimsuit, then nude in shower during Maxwell Caulfield's virtual reality experience.
- • 0:30—Very, very brief right breast, while putting on robe while walking on balcony.
- • 0:54—Breasts, while lying dead on beach.

Jane Hamilton . . . . Turk's Mama

Lauren Hays. . . . . Roni

Adrianne Sachs . . . . Yvonne

Tracy Scoggins . . . . Ariel
- • 0:54—Breasts and buns (mostly silhouette) while straddling Caulfield on bed.

Gwen Somers . . . . Annie
- ••• 0:19—Breasts, taking off her top in front of Lloyd while he sits in bathtub.

Alien Prey (1984; British)

Glory Annen . . . . Jessica
- • 0:22—Breasts unbuttoning blouse to sunbathe.
- •• 0:34—Breasts taking off top, getting into bed with Josephine, then making love with her.
- • 0:36—Buns, while rolling on top of Josephine.
- ••• 0:38—More breasts when Josephine is playing with her.
- • 0:39—More buns in bed. Long shot.
- • 0:46—Left breast and buns standing up in bathtub.
- •• 1:05—Breasts getting out of bed and putting a dress on.
- •• 1:19—Breasts in bed with Anders. Brief buns when he rips her panties off.

Sally Faulkner . . . . Josephine
- • 0:32—Very, very brief left breast taking off top.
- • 0:36—Buns, while in bed with Glory Annen.
- • 0:37—Breasts on her back in bed with Annen.

Alien Space Avenger (1988)

Vicki Darnell . . . . Bordello Lady

Gina Mastrogiacomo. . . . . Ginny
- ••• 0:19—Breasts in bed, making love with Matt. Breasts and buns, getting out and getting dressed.

Angela Nicholas. . . . . Doris
- • 0:56—Brief breasts making whoopee with Jaimie Gillis.
- ••• 0:57—More breasts making love on top of Gillis while killing him.

Elisa Pensler Gabrielli . . . . Red Riding Hood

Miriam Zucker. . . . . Bordello Reporter

Alien Terminator (1995)

Lisa Boyle . . . . Rachel
- •• 0:18—Breasts, while making out with Pete in maintenance tunnel.
- ••• 0:19—More breasts, while making out some more.
- •• 0:31—Breasts, while taking a shower, then putting on T-shirt.

Maria Ford. . . . . McKay

Alien Warrior (1985)

a.k.a. King of the Streets

Tally Chanel . . . . Barbara
- •• 0:46—In white lingerie, then breasts and buns while undressing in room with the Police Captain.
- • 1:03—Brief breasts and buns in flashback of 0:46 scene.

Lydia Finzi . . . . Beverly

The Alien Within *(1990)*

(Contains footage from *The Evil Spawn* woven together with new material.)

Suzanne Ager . . . . Erin West

Bobbie Bresee . . . . Lynn Roman

• 0:12—Very brief half of right breast in bed with a guy.

••• 0:37—Breasts and side view of buns in bathroom looking at herself in the mirror, then taking a shower.

Pamela Gilbert. . . . . Elaine Talbot

••• 0:48—Nude taking off black lingerie and going swimming in pool.

••• 0:55—Breasts in the pool, then full frontal nudity getting out.

Melissa Anne Moore . . . . Monica Roarke

•• 0:52—Left breast, taking off her purple dress.

••• 1:18—Breasts, lying on bed when the monster strangles her and pulls her top down.

• 1:19—Left breast, while lying in bed, then getting up.

Crystal Shaw . . . . Secretary

Dawn Wildsmith . . . . Evelyn Avery

The Alien Within *(1995; Made for Cable Movie)*

Catya Sassoon . . . . Woman on TV

• 0:18—Breasts, during fight on TV that Wyatt is watching. The scenes are from *Angel Fist*.

Melanie Shatner . . . . Catherine Harding

• ***All Nude Glamour*** *(1995; Video Tape)*

Danni Ashe . . . . Danni

••• 0:05—Nude, while posing indoors. Some behind-the-scenes shots included. Long scene.

•• 0:09—Full frontal nudity, while talking dirty.

Cory Lane . . . . Teresa

••• 0:21—Nude, while posing indoors and outdoors. Some behind-the-scenes shots included. Long scene.

••• 0:24—Full frontal nudity, while talking dirty.

Shayna Lee . . . . Shayna

••• 0:13—Nude, while posing indoors and outdoors. Some behind-the-scenes shots included. Long scene.

•• 0:16—Breasts, while talking dirty.

Sazzy Lee Varga. . . . . Sazzy

••• 0:09—Nude, while posing indoors and outdoors. Some behind-the-scenes shots included. Long scene.

•• 0:12—Nude, in bathroom, while talking dirty.

Jacqueline Lovell . . . . Jacqueline

• 0:00—Full frontal nudity during the opening credits.

••• 0:01—Nude, by swimming pool. Some behind-the-scenes shots included. Long scene.

•• 0:04—Full frontal nudity, while talking dirty.

• ***All Nude Nikki*** *(1998; Video Tape)*

Nikki Nova . . . . Herself

••• 0:00—Nude throughout.

All That Jazz *(1979)*

Leah Ayres-Hamilton . . . . Nurse Capobianco

Sandahl Bergman . . . . Sandra

•• 0:51—Breasts and buns in T-back while dancing on scaffolding during a dance routine.

Vicki Frederick . . . . Menage Partner

Deborah Geffner . . . . Victoria

• 0:16—Brief breasts taking off her blouse and walking up the stairs while Roy Scheider watches. A little out of focus.

Jessica Lange . . . . Angelique

Sue Paul. . . . . Stacy

• 1:18—Brief right breast in bed with Roy Scheider at the hospital.

K.C. Townsend . . . . Stripper

• 0:20—Breasts backstage getting Joey excited before he goes on stage. Lit by red light.

Terri Treas . . . . Fan Dancer

...All the Marbles *(1981)*

a.k.a. The California Dolls

Angela Aames . . . . Louise

•• 0:21—Breasts, when caught in Peter Falk's motel room by Iris, then sitting on the bed, while talking with Falk.

Vicki Frederick . . . . Iris

• 1:03—Brief side view of left breast, while crying in the shower after fighting with Peter Falk.

Laurene Landon. . . . . Molly

Susan Mechsner . . . . Creature #1

• 0:42—Breasts while wrestling in the mud.

Tracy Reed. . . . . Diane

All the Mornings of the World *(1992; French)*

a.k.a. Tout Les Matins Du Monde

Anne Brochet. . . . . Madeleine

• 0:46—Nude by river bank while running to hide behind tree when seen by Marin. Long shot.

•• 0:56—Left breast, while opening her dress and letting Marin feel and kiss her breast.

• 1:06—Brief breasts, after opening her blouse for Marin in the hallway.

• 1:08—Brief upper half of right breast while holding Marin's hand.

•• 1:20—Lower frontal nudity under nightgown, while getting out of bed.

All The Right Moves *(1983)*

Lea Thompson. . . . . Lisa

••• 1:00—Breasts and brief buns and lower frontal nudity, getting undressed and into bed with Tom Cruise in his bedroom.

The All-American Boy *(1973)*

Anne Archer . . . . Drenna Valentine

Rosalind Cash . . . . Poppy

Jeanne Cooper. . . . . Nola Bealer

E.J. Peaker . . . . Janelle Sharkey

••• 0:37—Breasts and buns, while in bathroom with Jon Voight.

All-American Murder *(1991)*

Josie Bissett . . . . Tally Fuller

• 1:01—Brief breasts in Polaroid photographs that Charlie Schlatter looks at. Hard to see.

• 1:07—Very brief breasts several times during B&W flashbacks.

• 1:12—Breasts on top of the Dean during Joanna Cassidy's B&W flashbacks. Quick cuts.

Joanna Cassidy. . . . . Erica Darby

Allan Quatermain and the Lost City of Gold *(1987)*

Elvira . . . . Sorais

Sharon Stone. . . . . Jesse Huston

• 0:20—Very brief lower frontal nudity, seen under loose panties, when she stands up in back of car and pulls her dress off over her head. (Don't really see much, but for the sake of completeness...)

Alley Cat *(1982)*

Britt Helfer . . . . Hooker
- ••• 1:00—Breasts, while handcuffed to the bed when Johnny searches her apartment.

Karen Mani . . . . Billie
- • 0:01—Brief breasts in panties taking night gown off during opening credits.
- ••• 0:38—Brief side view of right breast and buns getting into the shower. Full frontal nudity in the shower.
- ••• 0:48—Breasts during women's prison shower room scene. Long scene.

Moriah Shannon . . . . Sam
- ••• 0:48—Full frontal nudity, while taking a shower and talking with Billie.

Alligator Eyes *(1990)*

Annabelle Larsen . . . . Pauline
- •• 0:42—Nude, getting up from bed and walking around.

Allonsanfan *(1974; Italian)*

Mimsy Farmer . . . . Mirella
- •• 1:14—Buns, while lying in bed with Marcello Mastroianni. Breasts, sitting up in bed. (Subtitles get in the way.)
- • 1:15—Buns, while standing up with Mastroianni.
- • 1:34—Very brief part of right breast, under her arm while kneeling on bed.

Léa Massari . . . . Charlotte
- • 0:32—Buns, while undressing in bedroom in front of Marcello Mastroianni.

Almost Blue *(1992)*

Lynette Walden . . . . Jasmine
- ••• 0:34—Breasts in bed on top of Michael Madsen.
- • 0:35—Brief breasts, while walking to the bed and lying down while wearing panties.
- ••• 1:08—In black bra, then breasts and brief partial buns, while making love with Madsen on the sofa.
- •• 1:10—Buns, while lying on sofa asleep with Madsen.

Almost Hollywood *(1994)*

India Allen . . . . Herself
- •• 0:55—Left breast, then breasts, while in bed with Dirk.
- • 1:02—Brief buns, while wearing lingerie on the set.

Ellyn Dawn Humphreys . . . . Dawn

Michelle Moffett . . . . Desiree

Wendi Westbrook . . . . Girl 1

An Almost Perfect Affair *(1979)*

Edy Williams . . . . Herself
- • 0:18—Breasts and buns, while showing off during Cannes Film Festival.
- • 0:38—Brief breasts in a photo of herself that she holds up.

Almost Pregnant *(1992)*

(Unrated version reviewed.)

Lisa Comshaw . . . . Body Double for Tanya Roberts
- • 1:11—Close up shots of brief buns with a feather duster and getting bitten.
- • 1:12—Brief breasts and buns, with sentences projected on them.
- • 1:13— Close up of breasts, getting cupped by Gordon.

Lezlie Deane . . . . Party Girl

Tanya Roberts . . . . Linda Alderson
- ••• 0:04—Breasts and buns, in bed with a guy.
- • 0:10—Brief right breast, while under Conaway in bed.
- • 0:18—In white lingerie, then brief left breast, while in bed with another guy during Conaway's dream.
- • 0:40—Very brief side view of buns, in lingerie, while walking down stairs.
- • 1:08—Buns, while lying in bed when Gordon writes.
- • 1:10—Very brief buns, while in bed with Gordon.
- •• 1:11—Breasts and buns in bed, sometimes playing with whipped cream.
- •• 1:12—Nude in bed with Gordon and Conaway.

Joan Severance . . . . Maureen Mallory
- •• 0:58—In belly dancer outfit in bedroom with Jeff Conaway, then breasts.
- •• 1:06—In black leather outfit, then breasts and buns in G-string in bedroom with Conaway. Her hair gets in the way a lot.
- • 1:09—Brief breasts and buns in various sexual positions in bed with Conaway.
- • 1:12—Brief breasts, while playing with whipped cream in bed with Conaway.

Alphabet City *(1984)*

Jami Gertz . . . . Sophia

Kate Vernon . . . . Angie
- • 0:54—Breasts, while making love with Vincent Spano.

Altered States *(1980)*

Drew Barrymore . . . . Margaret Jessup

Blair Brown . . . . Emily Jessup
- • 0:10—Brief left breast making love with William Hurt in red light from an electric heater.
- •• 0:34—Breasts lying on her stomach during Hurt's mushroom induced hallucination.
- • 1:39—Buns, sitting in hallway with Hurt after the transformations go away.

Alvin Purple *(1973; Australian)*

Abigail . . . . Girl in See-Through

Lynette Curran . . . . First Sugar Girl
- •• 0:02—Brief full frontal nudity when Alvin opens the door.

Kris McQuade . . . . Samantha
- ••• 0:21—Breasts and buns, while painting Alvin's body.

Debbie Nankervis . . . . Girl in Blue Movie
- •• 1:04—Nude, running after Alvin in bedroom during showing of movie.

Elke Neidhardt . . . . Woman in Blue Movie
- •• 1:07—In red bra, then full frontal nudity in bedroom with Alvin during showing of film.

Anne Pendlebury . . . . Woman with Pin
- •• 0:48—Right breast and lower frontal nudity, while lying in bed, talking with Alvin.

Jacki Weaver . . . . Second Sugar Girl
- •• 0:33—Brief full frontal nudity, lying in bean bag chair.

Alvin Rides Again *(1974; Australian)*

Abigail . . . . Mae
- ••• 0:12—Breasts in store with Alvin.

Chantal Contouri . . . . Boobs La Touche
- • 1:15—Very brief lower frontal nudity, putting panties on in the car. Brief breasts, putting red dress on.

Kris McQuade . . . . Mandy
- ••• 0:48—Full frontal nudity, taking off red dress and getting into bed with Alvin. More breasts lying in bed. Long scene.

Debbie Nankervis . . . . Woman Cricketer

Candy Raymond . . . . Girl in Office
- • 0:05—Lower frontal nudity and buns, in office with Alvin.

Judy Stevenson . . . . Housewife
•• 0:01—Full frontal nudity, dropping her towel while Alvin washes her window.

Always (1984)

Joanna Frank . . . . Lucy
• 0:57—Right breast, while taking a bath and covering herself with powdered hot chocolate mix.
• 1:00—Brief upper half of right breast, while in bathtub some more.

Melissa Leo . . . . Peggy
• 1:33—Very, brief breasts and buns, jumping over inflatable lounge in pool. Long shot.

Patrice Townsend . . . . Judy

Amanda and the Alien (1995)

Nicole Eggert . . . . Amanda
Jessica Hahn . . . . T.V. Host
Alex Meneses . . . . Connie Flores
•• 0:23—Breasts under bra that's been put on backward, then breasts and buns after Nicole Eggert helps take the bra off and into the shower.
•• 0:34—Breasts, while making love with Charlie.

Cindy Morgan . . . . Holly Hoedown

The Amateur (1982)

Erin Flannery . . . . Waitress
Chapelle Jaffe . . . . Gretchen
• 1:19—Breasts (mostly right breast), while lying on operating table when doctors try to revive her after John Savage poisons her.
• 1:20—More right breast again.

Marthe Keller . . . . Elisabeth

Amazon Women on the Moon (1987)

Corinne Alphen . . . . Shari
••• 1:13—In black bra, then breasts on TV while Ray watches.

Rosanna Arquette . . . . Karen
Belinda Balaski . . . . Bernice Pitnik
Lana Clarkson . . . . Alpha Beta
Sybil Danning . . . . Queen Lara
Monique Gabrielle . . . . Taryn Steele
••• 0:05—Nude during Penthouse Video sketch. Long sequence of her nude in unlikely places.

Tracey E. Hutchinson . . . . Floozie
• 1:18—Brief right breast, while hitting balloon while Carrie Fisher talks to a guy. This sketch is in B&W and appears after the first batch of credits.

Michelle Pfeiffer . . . . Brenda Landers
Kelly Preston . . . . Violet
Angel Tompkins . . . . First Lady

Amazons (1986)

Danitza Kingsley . . . . Tshingi
••• 0:30—Breasts and buns quite a few times with Colungo out of and in bed.

Ty Randolph . . . . Dyala
•• 0:22—Breasts skinny dipping then getting dressed with Tashi.
•• 0:24—Brief breasts getting her top opened by bad guys then fighting them.

Penelope Reed . . . . Tashi
•• 0:22—Breasts and buns undressing to go skinny dipping. More breasts getting dressed.
• 0:24—Brief breasts getting top opened by bad guys.

The Ambassador (1984)

Ellen Burstyn . . . . Alex Hacker
••• 0:06—Breasts opening her robe to greet her lover.
••• 0:07—Brief breasts making love in bed.
••• 0:29—Breasts in a movie while her husband, Robert Mitchum, watches.

Ambition (1991)

Katherine Armstrong . . . . Roseanne
••• 1:13—Buns in G-string, then breasts in Clancy Brown's apartment.

Karen Landry . . . . Woman in Bookstore
Celeste Yarnell . . . . Beverly Hills Shopper

America's Deadliest Home Video (1995)

Melora Walters . . . . Gloria
• 0:52—Breasts, after Clint cuts her bra off.

The American Angels, Baptism of Blood (1989)

Mimi Lesseos . . . . Magnificent Mimi
Jan MacKenzie . . . . Luscious Lisa
• 0:07—Buns in G-string on stage in club. More buns getting lathered up for wrestling match.
• 0:11—Breasts and buns when a customer takes her top off. She's covered with shaving cream.
•• 0:12—Breasts taking a shower when Diamond Dave looks in to talk to her.
• 0:56—Right breast, while in wrestling ring with Dave.

American Flyers (1985)

Rae Dawn Chong . . . . Sarah
Jennifer Grey . . . . Leslie
Katherine Kriss . . . . Vera
Alexandra Paul . . . . Becky
• 0:50—Very brief right breast, then very brief half of left breast changing tops with David Grant. Brief side view of right breast. Dark.
•• 1:13—Brief breasts in white panties getting into bed with David Grant.

American Gigolo (1980)

Michele Drake . . . . 1st Girl on Balcony
• 0:03—Breasts on the balcony while Richard Gere and Lauren Hutton talk.

Lauren Hutton . . . . Michelle
• 0:37—Left breast, making love with Richard Gere in bed in his apartment.

American Heart (1993)

Shareen Mitchell . . . . Diane
•• 1:09—Breasts and buns in sheer black panties while dancing in peep show with three other women.
• 1:10—Breasts, while in dressing room. Seen on B&W monitor.
• 1:11—Breasts under sheer top while in dressing room, putting on make-up and getting a drink.

American Me (1992)

Evelina Fernandez . . . . Julie
• 1:14—Brief right breast, while making love with Edward James Olmos in bed.
• 1:15—Brief buns, while moving away from him.

Grace Morley . . . . JD's Friend

American Nightmare *(1981; Canadian)*

Alexandra Paul . . . . Isabelle Blake/Tanya Kelly
••• 0:02—Left breast while smoking in bed. Breasts before getting killed. Long scene.
Lora Staley . . . . Louise Harmon
•• 0:44—Breasts and buns in G-string dancing on stage.
••• 0:54—Breasts making love in bed with Eric.
• 0:59—Brief right breast, then breasts auditioning in TV studio.
Claudia Udy . . . . Andrea
••• 0:08—Buns, then breasts dancing on stage.
• 0:22—Buns getting into bathtub. Breasts during struggle with killer.
Lenore Zann . . . . .Tina
••• 0:25—Breasts and buns while dancing on stage.
•• 1:05—Breasts and buns while dancing on stage again.

The American Success Company *(1979)*

Belinda Bauer . . . . .Sarah
Judy Brown . . . . n.a.
Bianca Jagger . . . . .Corinne
• 0:35—Breasts under see-through black top while sitting on bed.

• American Sweethearts *(1995; Video Tape)*

Tamara Landry . . . . .Herself
••• 0:05—Breasts and buns, while dancing in front of various images.
••• 0:09—Full frontal nudity, while posing on lounge chair.
•• 0:30—Breasts and buns, while dressing in bedroom.
•• 0:36—Breasts and buns in quick cuts of her dancing. Buns, while dancing in front of her images.
Monique Parent . . . . .Herself
••• 0:01—Nude, while dancing in TV fantasy.
••• 0:21—Ballet dancing in clothes, then nude, while making love with Ashlie Rhey.
••• 0:32—Nude, while dancing and stripping out of a man's suit.
••• 0:41—In wet clothes, then nude, while dancing with Ashlie.
•• 0:46—Nude, while dancing during the end credits.
Ashlie Rhey . . . . .Herself
••• 0:13—In lingerie, then nude, while posing on bed in front of a video camera by herself, then with a guy.
••• 0:23—Full frontal nudity, while making love with Monique Parent.
••• 0:41—In wet clothes, then nude, while dancing with Monique.

An American Werewolf in London *(1981)*

Jenny Agutter . . . . Alex Price
• 0:41—Brief right breast in bed with David Naughton. Dark, hard to see.
Linzi Drew. . . . . Brenda Bristols
• 1:26—Side view of left breast in porno movie while David Naughton talks to his friend, Jack.
• 1:27—Brief breasts in movie talking on the phone.

American Yakuza *(1993)*

Cristina Lawson. . . . . Yuko
• 1:06—Right breast, while making love with Viggo Mortensen in bed.
Toni Naples. . . . . Mrs. Campaneia

Amityville 1992: It's About Time *(1992)*

Shawn Weatherly . . . . Andra
••• 0:07—Breasts, making love in bed on top of her husband. Nice and sweaty!

• Amityville Dollhouse *(1996)*

Starr Andreeff . . . . Claire
Lenore Kasdorf . . . . Aunt Marla
Lisa Robin Kelly . . . . .Dana
• 0:42—In black panties, then breasts, while starting to make love with Todd in the shed in the backyard.

The Amityville Horror *(1979)*

Margot Kidder. . . . . Kathleen Lutz
• 0:21—Brief right breast in reflection in mirror while doing dance stretching exercises in the bedroom. Hard to see because of the pattern on the mirror tiles.
• 0:22—Cleavage in open blouse while talking to James Brolin.
• 0:23—Very brief partial right breast, on the floor, kissing Brolin.
Helen Shaver . . . . .Carolyn
Amy Wright. . . . . Jackie

Amityville II: The Possession *(1982)*

Rutanya Alda . . . . Deloris Montelli
Diane Franklin . . . . Patricia Montelli
• 0:41—Half of right breast, while sitting on bed talking to her brother.

Amityville: A New Generation *(1993)*

Barbara Howard . . . . Jane Cutler
Julia Nickson . . . . Suki
•• 0:28—Left breast, with David Naughton while taking off her coveralls.
• 0:29—Very brief back side of left breast, putting on her coverall strap.
Lala Sloatman . . . . Lianie
•• 0:14—Breasts, undressing and making love with Keyes.

Amor Ciego *(1980; Mexican)*

Apollonia. . . . . .Patty
• 0:32—Breasts, while getting out of hammock.
••• 0:52—Right breast, when standing up, then breasts while kissing Daniel. More breasts while in bed.
••• 0:59—Buns, while making love in bed, then breasts afterwards.
•• 1:11—Breasts, after taking off her towel and putting Daniel's hand on her left breast.
•• 1:15—Breasts, while turning over, then lying in bed.

And God Created Woman *(1988)*

(Unrated version.)
Rebecca De Mornay . . . . Robin
•• 0:06—Brief Left breast and buns in gymnasium with Vincent Spano. Brief right breast making love.
• 0:53—Brief buns and breasts in the shower when Spano sees her.
•• 1:02—Brief left breast with Langella on the floor.
••• 1:12—Breasts making love with Spano in a museum.
Pat Lee . . . . Inmate

...and God created woman *(1957; French)*

Brigitte Bardot. . . . . Juliette
• 0:40—Very brief side view of right breast getting out of bed.

...And God Spoke (1994)

Lisa Comshaw . . . . Nude Ninja
- 0:02—Brief breasts, while putting her sword away. (She's on the right, the first one to talk.)

Monique Parent . . . . Nude Ninja
- 0:02—Brief breasts, while putting her sword away. (She's on the left, the third one to talk.)

Ashlie Rhey . . . . Nude Ninja
- 0:02—Brief breasts, while putting her sword away. (She's in the middle, the second one to talk.)

Android (1982)

Brie Howard . . . . Maggie
- 0:25—Buns, then breasts in bedroom when Klaus Kinski watches her on video monitor.
- 0:54—Brief side of right breast, while sitting on Max's lap and kissing him.
- 0:59—Partial left breast, while lying dead in bed.
- 1:09—Brief side view of left breast while lying dead in bed.

Andy Warhol's Frankenstein (1974; Italian/German/French)

Dalila Di'Lazzaro . . . . The Girl
- •• 0:09—Breasts lying on platform in the lab.
- • 0:37—Close up of left breast while the Count cuts her stitches. (Pretty bloody.)
- • 0:43—Breasts, while strapped to table, covered with blood.
- • 0:49—Breasts, while on table, all wired up.
- • 1:03—Right breast lying on table. Long shot.
- • 1:05—More right breast, long shot.
- •• 1:06—More breasts on table, then standing in the lab.
- •• 1:20—Brief right breast when Otto pulls her top down.
- •• 1:23—Breasts on table again, then walking around. (Scar on chest.) Lower frontal nudity when Otto pulls her bandage down, then gross breasts when he removes her guts.

Monique Van Vooren . . . . Katherine
- •• 0:47—Breasts in bed with Nicholas. Brief lower frontal nudity twice when he rolls on top of her.
- • 1:21—Left breast letting Sascha, the creature, caress her breast
- • 1:26—Breasts, dead, when her breasts pop out of her blouse.

Angel (1983)

Elaine Giftos . . . . Patricia Allen

Donna McDaniel . . . . Crystal
- • 0:19—Brief breasts, dead in bed when the killer pulls the covers down.

Graem McGavin . . . . Lana
- •• 0:31—Breasts standing in hotel bathroom talking to her John.

Susan Tyrrell . . . . Solly Mosler

Donna Wilkes . . . . Angel/Molly

Angel 4: Undercover (1993)

Rebekka Armstrong . . . . Catfight Groupie
- • 0:41—Brief breasts, while with a band member and another woman in dressing room.

Kerrie Clark . . . . Paula
- ••• 0:26—Breasts, while making love with Piston in bedroom.
- •• 0:28—Very briefly nude, getting up out of bed. Breasts, while taking a shower.

Nicolette Janssen . . . . Music Video Groupie
- • 1:00—Breasts, while backstage with the drummer and the other groupie.

Sam Phillips . . . . Jade
- • 0:18—Breasts in open robe, while sitting on dressing room counter in front of Piston.

Darlene Vogel . . . . Molly

An Angel at My Table (1990; Australian/New Zealand)

Kerry Fox . . . . Janet
- • 1:45—Brief breasts and partial lower frontal nudity while in bathtub.
- •• 2:06—Left breast while sitting on bed with her boyfriend.
- • 2:07—Nude, while swimming in the water.
- •• 2:09—Long shot of right breast, while lying on rock outside, then breasts in a closer shot.

Celia Nicholson . . . . Piona

• Angel Baby (1996; Australian)

Jacqueline McKenzie . . . . Kate
- •• 0:32—Nude, when surprising Harry when he comes home from work.
- •• 0:45—Brief breast, while making love with Harry, then breasts, when sitting in his lap afterwards.

Angel Eyes (1991)

Suzanne Ager . . . . Nurse Stewart

Monique Gabrielle . . . . Angel
- ••• 0:18—Nude, in shower with Michelle.
- • 0:32—Brief breasts in robe in her bedroom.
- ••• 0:45—Left breast and lower frontal nudity, while caressing herself while watching Steven and Michelle make love in bed.
- ••• 0:47—Right breast, then breasts in bed while fantasizing Steven is making love with her. Then breasts in open robe.
- ••• 0:54—Breasts and buns, while making love in bed with Michelle. Very nice!
- ••• 1:10—Nude, while making love with Nick on the floor. (This scene was really worn down on the video tape that I rented—I think I know why!)

Sazzy Lee Varga . . . . Amy

Paula Reve'e . . . . Julie
- •• 0:13—Breasts, while standing in yellow bikini bottoms and rubbing lotion on herself.
- • 0:23—Breasts, while lying on pool float in the pool.
- • 0:25—More breasts while on pool float.

Vicki Vickers . . . . Michelle
- ••• 0:02—Breasts and buns, while making love with Steven in bed. Long scene.
- ••• 0:18—Buns and breasts in shower. Partial lower frontal nudity.
- ••• 0:25—Right breast, then breasts while making love with Steven in bed while Angel watches. Long scene.
- •• 0:32—Breasts, while rolling over in bed.
- ••• 0:40—Breasts, getting into shower, washing herself and getting out.
- ••• 0:44—Buns and breasts while making love in bed with Steven.
- • 0:51—Brief left breast, while adjusting the covers in bed.
- ••• 0:53—Breasts in bed while making love in bed with Angel. Buns in G-string when getting out of bed.
- •• 0:55—Breasts, while bending over sink to wash her face. Right breast, while peeking around the door.

Angel Fist (1992)

Melissa Anne Moore . . . . Lorda
- •• 0:03—Breasts and buns, in the showers.
- •• 0:35—Nude, behind Katara in the showers.

••• 1:03—Breasts when she gets a bad guy to open her blouse and untie her. Very brief breasts during fight scenes.

Catya Sassoon . . . . Katara/Kat Lang

• 0:19—Brief breasts, dropping towel and putting on shirt in front of Alcatraz.

•• 0:31—Right breast, while in the shower.

••• 0:32—Breasts in red panties, doing martial arts on a couple of bad guys in her apartment.

••• 0:35—Full frontal nudity in the showers.

••• 0:49—Breasts, while making love on bed with Alcatraz. Long scene.

Angel Heart *(1987)*

(Original Unedited Version reviewed.)

Lisa Bonet . . . . Epiphany Proudfoot

• 1:01—Brief left breast, twice, in open dress during voodoo ceremony.

••• 1:27—Breasts in bed with Rourke. It gets kind of bloody.

• 1:32—Breasts in bathtub.

• 1:48—Breasts in bed, dead. Covered with a bloody sheet.

Judith Drake . . . . Izzy's Wife

Charlotte Rampling . . . . Margaret Krusemark

• 1:10—Brief left breast, lying dead on the floor, covered with blood.

• 1:46—Very brief left breast during flashback of the dead-on-the-floor-covered-with-blood scene.

Elizabeth Whitcraft . . . . Connie

•• 0:33—Breasts, while in bed talking with Mickey Rourke and taking off her clothes.

Angel III: The Final Chapter *(1988)*

Maud Adams . . . . Nadine

Laura Albert . . . . Nude Dancer

• 0:00—Brief breasts dancing in a casino. Wearing red G-string.

• 0:01—Brief breasts dancing in background.

• 0:06—Side view of left breast and buns, while yelling at Molly for taking her picture.

Toni Basil . . . . Hillary

Ashlyn Gere . . . . Video Girl #1

Barbara Hammond . . . . Video Girl #2

• 0:34—Breasts (on the right) on video monitor during audition tape talking with her roommate.

Gail Harris . . . . n.a.

Mitzi Kapture . . . . Molly Stewart

Roxanne Kernohan . . . . White Hooker

Julie Kristen Smith . . . . Darlene

••• 0:40—Breasts during caveman shoot with a brunette girl.

••• 0:44—Breasts again dancing in caveman shoot.

Cheryl Starbuck . . . . Video Girl #3

Angel of Destruction *(1994)*

Chanda . . . . Reena Jacobs

••• 0:09—Buns in lingerie, then breasts, while dancing on stage with Delilah.

••• 0:36—Breasts and buns in lingerie, while performing for music video with Delilah.

Maria Ford . . . . Jo Alwood

••• 0:41—Breasts and buns in panties while using martial arts on the bad guys!

••• 0:45—Breasts, while making love with Aaron in bed.

••• 0:59—Breasts and buns in G-string after stripping and dancing on stage.

Charlie Spradling . . . . Brit Alwood

Angel of H.E.A.T. *(1981)*

a.k.a. The Protectors, Book I

Marilyn Chambers . . . . Angel Harmony

•• 0:15—Full frontal nudity making love with an intruder on the bed.

• 0:17—Breasts in a bathtub.

•• 0:40—Breasts in a hotel room with a short guy.

• 0:52—Breasts getting out of a wet suit.

•• 1:01—Breasts sitting on floor with some robots.

• 1:29—Breasts in bed with Mark.

Remy O'Neill . . . . Andrea Shockley

•• 0:43—Breasts, wearing a blue swimsuit, wrestling in the mud with Mary Woronov.

Mary Woronov . . . . Samantha Vitesse

••• 0:11—Frontal nudity changing clothes on a boat dock after getting out of the lake.

•• 0:43—Breasts wrestling in the mud after wearing white bathing suit.

Angel of Passion *(1991)*

Tuscany . . . . Ellen

••• 0:36—Buns and breasts making love with a guy on a boat.

Venus De Light . . . . Carol

•• 0:15—Breasts taking a shower.

••• 0:19—Breasts and buns in G-string dancing outside next to pool at a birthday party.

••• 0:23—Breasts and buns in red lingerie in camper, then breasts while making love on top of Will.

Pamela Jackson . . . . Eileen

••• 1:13—Breasts and upper half of buns while on bed with Eric making love.

Kathleen Kane . . . . Suzette

•• 1:08—Breasts while posing for Marty in the house.

Lisa Petruno . . . . Sheryl Diamond

•• 0:00—Making love with the husband on the stairs.

Ingrid Vold . . . . Vanessa

• 1:01—Brief breasts posing on the couch for the photographer.

Angels & Insects *(1996; British)*

Patsy Kensit . . . . Eugenia

•• 0:47—Breasts, while making love with Edgar on bed behind sheer netting.

• 0:49—Left breast, while lying in bed with Edgar, seen behind sheer netting.

•• 0:58—Full frontal nudity, while sitting on the bed, then making love with Edgar.

• 1:00—Brief partial right breast, while making love in bed with Edgar.

Anna Massey . . . . Miss Mead

Kristin Scott-Thomas . . . . Molly

Angels Hard as They Come *(1971)*

Gilda Texter . . . . Astrid

• 0:26—Brief breasts several times when bad guys try to rape her. Dark.

Janet Wood . . . . Vicki

•• 1:09—Breasts taking off her top, dancing with Clean Sheila at the bikers' party.

•• 1:16—Breasts outside when the General rips her blouse open.

Animal House *(1978)*

Karen Allen . . . . Katherine "Katy" Fuller

• 1:21—Brief buns putting on shirt when Boone visits her at her house.

Sarah Holcomb . . . . Clorette DePasto
•• 0:56—Brief breasts lying on bed after passing out in Tom Hulce's bed during toga party.
Sunny Johnson . . . . Otter's Co-Ed
Martha Smith . . . . Babs Jansen
Mary Louise Weller . . . . Mandy Pepperidge
••• 0:38—In white bra, then breasts in bedroom while John Belushi watches on a ladder through the window.

Animal Instincts *(1992)*

(Unrated version reviewed.)
Erika Nann . . . . Dianne
Delia Sheppard . . . . Ingrid
•• 0:50—Breasts, while in bed with her lover and Joanne.
••• 0:54—Breasts, while in bed with only Joanne.
Shannon Whirry . . . . Joanne Cole
••• 0:18—In white bra and panties in bed then full frontal nudity during her fantasies with several guys.
•• 0:23—Breasts and buns, in various lingerie outfits, in front of mirror.
•• 0:26—Full frontal nudity under sheer white body suit, trying to get Maxwell Caulfield interested in her.
•• 0:28—Breasts while taking a bath.
••• 0:30—Nude in bed, making love with the Cable TV guy.
••• 0:43—In bra and panties, then nude while in bed with the Assistant DA while Caulfield watches on TV.
••• 0:46—Breasts, while sitting in bed with Caulfield.
•• 0:50—Breasts with Delia Sheppard and a guy.
••• 0:51—In black bra and panties on TV after undressing as a businessman. Breasts in bed with a guy.
••• 0:54—Breasts in bedroom and on bed with Delia.
••• 0:59—In black bra and panties, then breasts and buns with Mitch Gaylord in bedroom while making love.
• 1:16—Buns in G-string and side of left breast, while in bed with Jan-Michael Vincent.

Animal Instincts 2 *(1993)*

Debra Beatty . . . . Cindy
•• 0:24—Full frontal nudity, while posing for Eric in his studio and putting a robe on.
Jennifer Campbell . . . . Mary
Shannon McLeod . . . . Miss Geary
•• 0:14—In black bra, then breasts and buns in panties after taking off her top while trying to tease Steve.
••• 0:20—Breasts, after taking off bra and making love with a guy in bed.
Bobbie Phillips . . . . Waitress
Elizabeth Sandifer . . . . Catherine
••• 0:23—In white bra and panties, then breasts and brief buns, while making love with Steve in bed.
• 1:16—Brief breasts, while undressing in her room when Steve sees her from outside. Long shot.
••• 1:18—Breasts, while in bedroom with Steve, then making love on bed.
Shannon Whirry . . . . Joanna
••• 0:11—Breasts, in bed with a fantasy lover while she imagines another guy watching them make love.
••• 0:30—Breasts, while rubbing lotion on herself in the backyard while Steve watches from his backyard.
• 0:38—Brief breasts, while in her bedroom. Seen on video monitor.
••• 0:47—Full frontal nudity while making love with a guy she picks up in a bar while Steve watches on video monitor.
••• 0:49—Nude, while making love in bedroom with a woman she picks up in a bar.
•• 0:53—Left breast, while opening her robe and talking on the phone.
••• 1:01—Nude, while posing for Eric in his studio.
•• 1:04—Breasts, while taking a shower.
• 1:05—Brief left breast in photos that Eric shows her.
•• 1:07—In white bra and panties, then breasts and buns while making love with Eric.

Animal Instincts: The Seductress *(1995)*

(Unrated version reviewed.)
Jacqueline Lovell . . . . Cleaning Woman
• 1:01—Brief breasts, while cleaning Lolly Pop's leg. B&W. She's on the left with blonde hair.
••• 1:08—In bra, then breasts and buns, while undressing after seeing Joanna and Lolly Pop in bathtub. Making love with the brunette cleaning woman.
Wendy Schumacher. . . . . Joanna Coles
•• 0:00—Breasts, while dancing with two knives during opening credits. B&W.
•• 0:04—Breasts, while making love on pool table in a bar with Orlando in front of a group of people.
• 0:09—Brief breasts on pool table.
•• 0:12—Breasts, after taking off top of one piece swimsuit and oiling herself up.
•• 0:14—Breasts and buns, while taking a shower.
• 0:20—Breasts and upper part of lower frontal nudity. B&W.
••• 0:27—Full frontal nudity, after taking off her dress in front of Savage, then making love with him while she's blindfolded. Long scene.
• 0:35—Buns in T-back, while pulling up her dress when dancing outside in a garden nursery.
• 0:39—Brief side view of right breast, twice. B&W.
••• 0:40—Breasts, after opening her robe at table and caressing herself.
•• 0:45—In black bra, buns in T-back, then breasts, while dancing in recording studio in front of Trick Willy.
••• 0:48—In black bra, then nude, when making love with Willy while "blind" Savage plays the piano.
• 0:50—Full frontal nudity, while acting like a puppet. B&W.
• 0:51—Full frontal nudity. B&W.
••• 0:54—In green bra and buns in T-back, then breasts, while in kitchen with Shane Hooligan.
••• 1:04—In bra and panties, then full frontal nudity, undressing while Savage caresses Lolly Pop. Nude getting into bathtub with her.
• 1:23—Breasts, pulling her dress top open for Chill.
••• 1:24—Breasts and buns, while making out with Chill's bodyguard.
•• 1:27—Nude, while Chill writes stuff on her body.
•• 1:30—Nude after Savage throws a knife at Chill.
Cher Willis . . . . Party Waitress

Anna *(1987)*

Sally Kirkland . . . . Anna
•• 0:28—Breasts, while in the bathtub talking to Daniel.
Paulina Porizkova . . . . Krystyna

L'Année des Meduses *(1987; French)*

Caroline Cellier . . . . Claude, Chris' Mother
•• 0:02—Breasts taking off top at the beach.
•• 0:56—Breasts on boat at night with Romain.
•• 1:06—Breasts on the beach with Valerie Kaprisky.
• 1:14—Left breast, lying on beach with Romain at night.
Valerie Kaprisky . . . . Chris
•• 0:06—Breasts pulling down swimsuit at the beach.

••• 0:24—Full frontal nudity while taking off dress with older man.
••• 0:42—Breasts walking around the beach talking to everybody.
•• 0:46—Breasts on the beach taking a shower.
••• 1:02—Breasts on the beach with her mom.
••• 1:37—Nude dancing on the boat for Romain.
•• 1:42—Breasts walking from the beach to the bar.
•• 1:43—Breasts in swimming pool.

Barbara Nielsen . . . . Barbara
• 0:37—Brief breasts taking off T-shirt at the beach.
•• 0:40—Breasts at the beach with Valerie Kaprisky.
•• 1:04—Breasts while sitting on Kaprisky at the beach.
•• 1:08—Right breast, lying on the beach with Kaprisky.
•• 1:41—Breasts on the beach taking off her top.
••• 1:43—Nude, in the swimming pool.

Another 48 Hrs. *(1990)*

Nancy Everhard. . . . . .Female Doctor
Page Leong. . . . . Angel Lee
• 1:00—Brief breasts, while getting out of bed with Willie.
Francesca "Kitten" Natividad. . . . . Girl in Movie
• 1:04—Brief breasts on movie screen when two motorcycles crash through it.
Yana Nirvana. . . . . CHP Officer
Shauna O'Brien. . . . . Uncredited Waitress

• Another 9 1/2 Weeks *(1996)*

Lana Clarkson .Woman at Fashion Show
Angie Everhart. . . . . Lea
• 0:47—Brief buns in panties and side view of right breast, when checking out Mickey Rourke's closet.
• 0:48—Brief left breast in reflection in mirror. Brief buns in panties when dancing.
• 0:49—Brief left breast, when it slips out of her shirt, after getting a necktie.
• 1:15—Very brief left breast, when sitting up in bathtub.
•• 1:17—Brief side of right breast, then breasts and buns, while lying in bed when Rourke plays with her using flower petals, wine and honey.
• 1:34—Brief top of right breast, popping out of her top, when jerk guy rolls her over on the floor.

Another Chance *(1989)*

Vanessa Angel. . . . . .Jacky Johanssen
• 0:26—Sort of breasts under water in spa. Hard to see because of the bubbles.
Leslee Bremmer. . . . . Girl in Womanizer's Meeting
Barbara Edwards . . . . Diana the Temptress
••• 0:38—Breasts in trailer with Johnny.
Donna Spangler . . . . .Cynthia
Karen Witter . . . . Nancy Burton
• 0:44—Brief side view of right breast and buns getting out of bed.

Another Pair of Aces *(1991; Made for Cable Movie)*

(Video tape includes nude scenes not shown on cable TV.)
Joan Severance . . . . .Susan Davis
•• 1:00—Brief breasts several times, making love with Kris Kristofferson in bed.

Another Time, Another Place *(1983; British)*

Phyllis Logan. . . . . Janie
••• 0:31—Breasts, washing herself off after working in the fields. Nice close-up shot.
•• 0:53—Full frontal nudity, after undressing then getting into bed.
••• 1:08—Breasts in front of a group of men.

Anthony's Desire *(1993)*

Annastasia Alexander. . . . . Dancer
••• 0:04—Nude, on stage stripping out of black dress. Wearing gloves.
•• 0:22—Full frontal nudity, while stretching in the background on the left.
•• 0:54—Breasts while lying on her back in the middle of the group of women.
• 1:02—Breasts, while sitting in the background on the left.
Debra Beatty . . . . Dancer
••• 0:04—Full frontal nudity, while stripping out of green dress on stage with other women.
•• 0:22—Breasts, while sitting on stage on the right.
• 1:02—Left breast, while sitting behind Annastasia Alexander on the left side of the stage.
Nicole Broderson. . . . . Dancer
• 0:54—Buns, while sitting on her stomach in the middle of the group of women. Tattoo on her right butt cheek.
Kelly Jaye. . . . . Dancer
•• 0:54—Left breast, while lying on her side in a group of women. She's near the top of the screen.
•• 1:02—Breasts, while playing the violin on stage.
Ashlie Rhey . . . . Dancer
• 0:22—Breasts, while lying on her back under another woman on stage.
• 0:54—Left breast and brief lower frontal nudity, while lying down with other women. She's at the bottom of the screen.
Jeanine Robért. . . . . Dancer
0:04—Inner half of breasts, while sitting in the background on stage. She's on the right.
•• 0:22—Full frontal nudity, while sitting in the background on stage. She's in the middle.
• 0:54—Buns, while lying down with a group of women. She's on the bottom of the screen.
• 1:02—Right breast, while playing the cello on stage.
Gwen Somers . . . . .Jessica
••• 0:29—Nude, while lying on bed and talking. Long scene.
••• 1:09—Full frontal nudity, while on bed with Anthony and Desiree sitting next to her.
Mihaella Stoicov . . . . Desiree
••• 0:17—Full frontal nudity, while making love in bed with Anthony and afterwards.
••• 0:24—Breasts and buns, while making love in bed with Anthony.
• 0:45—Left breast, while making love at the beach with Anthony.
••• 0:46—Full frontal nudity while making love in bed with Anthony.
•• 1:16—Nude while lying in bed.
Stephanie Sumers . . . . Dancer
•• 0:22—Breasts, while on stage, lying in the lap of another woman. (She's wearing a choker.)

Antonia & Jane *(1991; British)*

Saskia Reeves. . . . . Antonia McGill
•• 0:42—Brief partial left breast, while lying in bed on top of her lover. Breasts, turning over on her back.
• 0:44—Breasts, leaning over her lover while she is tied and blindfolded in bed.

Imelda Staunton . . . . Jane Hartman
- 0:08—Right breast, while lying in bed with Norman, reading a book to get him turned on.

Antony and Cleopatra (1972)

Monica Peterson . . . . Iras
- 0:33—Brief buns, when another woman playfully spanks her and covers her with a towel.

Any Man's Death (1989)

Nancy Mulford . . . . Tara
Mia Sara . . . . Gerlind
- 0:50—Brief right nipple when John Savage undoes her top. Don't see her face.

Claudia Udy . . . . Laura

Any Time, Any Play (1989)

Ruth Corrine Collins . . . . Kelly
- •• 0:16—In black bra, then breasts after taking it off and walking into bathroom. Breasts under sheer white nightgown.
- ••• 0:32—Nude, while pouring drinks in bedroom, then making love with Vince in bed.
- ••• 0:41—Breasts, while wearing black panties, garter belt and stockings in dressing room with a friendly female saleswoman.
- ••• 0:52—Breasts, while making love in bed with Michael.

Aphrodite (1982; German/French)

Catherine Jourdan . . . . Valerie
- 0:34—Brief upper half of breasts in bathtub.

Valerie Kaprisky . . . . Pauline
- ••• 0:12—Nude, washing herself off in front of a two-way mirror while a man on the other side watches.

Apocalypse Now (1979)

Colleen Camp . . . . Playmate
Linda Carpenter . . . . Playmate
- 1:01—Breasts in centerfold photo, hung up for display. Long shot.

Cyndi Wood . . . . Playmate of the Year

Appassionata (1979; Italian)

Eleonora Giorgi . . . . Nicola
- 0:14—Very brief left breast in open blouse with Emilio in his dentist office. Breasts several times.
- •• 0:41—Full frontal nudity in bedroom when Emilio comes in. Dark.
- ••• 0:54—Nude in office with Emilio in stockings and garter belt.
- 1:35—Brief right breast in bed with Emilio. Dark.

Ornella Muti . . . . Virginia
- 0:32—Brief breasts in bathroom when her father rips open her T-shirt while looking for hickeys.
- 0:57—Partial left breast, while leaning over to tempt her father.
- 1:35—Buns, getting out of bed with her father. Brief side of left breast when leaving the room.

Appointment with Fear (1988)

Pamela Bach . . . . Samantha
- 0:56—Breasts getting into the spa. Long shot, hard to see.

Michele Little . . . . Carol
Deborah Voorhees . . . . Ruth
- 0:21—Very, very brief side view of left breast taking off bra to go swimming, then very brief breasts getting out of the pool.

Apprentice to Murder (1987)

Rutanya Alda . . . . Elma Kelly
Mia Sara . . . . Alice
- 0:29—Left side view breasts making love with Chad Lowe.

• *Arena (1988)*

Claudia Christian . . . . Quinn
Shari Shattuck . . . . Jade
- 1:06—Upper half of buns, while sitting up in bed. Brief half of right breast, getting up while wearing robe.

Aria (1987; U.S./British)

Valerie Allain . . . . Young Girl in Blue
- 0:22—Brief breasts with another girl in a weight lifting room walking around with muscular guys.
- 0:25—Brief breasts again.
- •• 0:27—Nude in front of a weight lifter.
- 0:29—More nude, posing while the guys walk by.

Beverly D'Angelo . . . . Gilda
Linzi Drew . . . . Girl
- 1:09—Breasts on operating table after car accident. Hair is all covered with bandages.
- •• 1:10—Breasts getting shocked to start her heart.

Sandrine Dumas . . . . n.a.
Bridget Fonda . . . . Girl Lover
- ••• 0:59—Brief right breast, then buns and breasts lying down on bed in hotel room in Las Vegas.
- •• 1:02—Breasts in the bathtub with her boyfriend.

Elizabeth Hurley . . . . Marietta
- 0:46—Brief breasts, turning around while singing to a guy.
- 0:47—Buns while standing and hugging him.

Anita Morris . . . . Phoebe
Marion Peterson . . . . Young Girl in Pink
- 0:22—Brief breasts with another girl in a weight lifting room walking around with muscular guys.
- 0:25—Brief breasts again.
- •• 0:27—Nude in front of a weight lifter.
- 0:29—More nude, posing while the guys walk by.

Theresa Russell . . . . King Zog
Tilda Swinton . . . . Young Girl

Arizona Heat (1988)

Denise Crosby . . . . Jill Andrews
- 1:13—Brief upper half of left breast in shower with Larry.

Armed and Dangerous (1986)

Teagan Clive . . . . Staff Member
Christine Dupree . . . . Peep Show Girl
- 0:58—Very, very brief breasts shots behind glass dancing in front of John Candy and Eugene Levy.

Meg Ryan . . . . Maggie Cavanaugh
K.C. Winkler . . . . Vicki

Armed for Action (1992)

Barri Murphy . . . . Sara
Tracy Spaulding . . . . Lori
- 0:10—Brief breasts, while in back room of restaurant with her boyfriend, Jake.

Armed Response (1986)

Kai Baker . . . . Pam
Michelle Bauer . . . . Stripper
- 0:41—Breasts, dancing on stage.

Bobbie Bresee . . . . Anna
Laurene Landon . . . . Deborah
Dawn Wildsmith . . . . Thug

Army Brats (1984; Dutch)

Akkemay . . . . Madeline Gisberts
- •• 0:22—Breasts in the shower with her boyfriend.
- • 0:26—Brief breasts, taking off towel and putting on robe while arguing with her mother.
- • 0:32—Brief breasts while changing tops.
- • 0:47—Brief breasts while sunbathing outside (seen through binoculars).
- • 1:24—Breasts in bed with her boyfriend.

Army of One (1993)

Khandi Alexander . . . . Maralena

Crystal Breeze . . . . Body Double for Kristian Alfonso
- •• 0:34—Breasts and buns, while undressing and getting into shower. Body double for Kristian Alfonso.

Michelle Phillips . . . . Esther

The Arrangement (1969)

Faye Dunaway. . . . . Gwen
- • 0:25—Brief buns in various scenes while at the beach with Kirk Douglas.

Dianne Hull. . . . . Ellen

Deborah Kerr . . . . Florence
- • 0:36—Buns, behind curtain, while taking off her night gown. Brief long shot of left breast, behind curtain, getting into bed.

The Arrogant (1987)

Teresa Gilmore-Capps. . . . . .Charlotte
- • 0:23—Brief breasts, making love in a barn.

Sylvia Kristel . . . . .Julie
- • 0:14—In wet blouse, in lake.
- • 0:22—In wet blouse again, walking out of the lake.
- • 0:44—Brief breasts several times, in gaping dress.

The Art of Dying (1991)

Kathleen Kinmont. . . . . Holly
- • 0:28—Brief left breast, making love with Wings Hauser in the kitchen. Brief breasts when he pours milk on her.
- •• 0:33—Breasts in bathtub with Hauser. Intercut with Janet getting stabbed.

T.C. Warner . . . . Janet
- • 0:14—Buns, while shackled up in S&M chamber with a customer.
- ••• 0:32—Breasts in the shower. Buns and side of right breast, before getting stabbed to death.

Ona Zee . . . . Frances Warner

• *As Good As It Gets* (1997)

Danielle Brisebois . . . . Singer

Kaitlin Hopkins . . . . .Woman in Lobby

Helen Hunt . . . . Carol Connelly
- • 1:46—Side view of right breast, when getting ready for bath. Medium long shot.

Shirley Knight . . . . Beverly

Yeardley Smith . . . . Jackie

• *Ash Wednesday* (1973)

Margaret Blye . . . . Kate

Elizabeth Taylor. . . . . Barbara
- • 0:10—Long shot breasts, closer shot of buns, getting prepared for plastic surgery in hospital. Don't see her face, probably a body double.

Monique Van Vooren . . . . German Woman

Ashanti, Land of No Mercy (1979)

Beverly Johnson. . . . . Dr. Anansa Linderby
- •• 0:07—Buns and brief side view of breasts, taking off clothes to go skinny dipping.
- •• 0:08—Briefly nude, running to put her clothes back on.
- • 1:15—Right breast in gaping dress while bending over to bury dead bad guy.

The Assassin (1989)

Elpidia Carrillo . . . . .Elena

Andaluz Russell . . . . .Amanda Portales
- • 0:21—Brief breasts while changing clothes in room with the other assassins.

Assault of the Killer Bimbos (1988)

Elizabeth Kaitan. . . . . Lulu
- • 0:11—Brief breasts, after taking off costume top in dressing room.
- •• 0:41—Brief breasts, three times, during desert musical sequence, opening her blouse, then taking off her shorts, then putting on a light blue dress. Don't see her face.

Christina Veronica . . . . Dancer

Christina Whitaker. . . . . .Peaches

Assault of the Party Nerds (1989)

Michelle Bauer. . . . . .Muffin
- • 0:16—Side view of left breast kissing Bud.
- ••• 0:20—Breasts lying in bed seen from Bud's point of view, then sitting up by herself.
- • 1:15—Brief right breast, then breasts in bed with Scott.

Linnea Quigley . . . . Bambi
- ••• 0:25—Breasts straddling Cliff in bed.

Tantala Ray . . . . Vanna
- •• 1:10—Breasts dancing during party with her breasts sticking out of red dress, then covering herself with whipped cream.

Assault of the Party Nerds II: The Heavy Petting Detective (1993)

Melinda Armstrong . . . . Babe #1

Michelle Bauer. . . . . .Muffin
- •• 0:47—Breasts, while making love with Bud in bed.

Tané McClure . . . . Headi

Deanne Power. . . . . .Stripper
- • 0:51—Breasts and buns in G-string, while dancing during party.

Linnea Quigley . . . . .Bambi
- • 0:32—Breasts, when making love on top of a guy in bed, while using an adding machine.
- •• 0:33—More, breasts, while making love on top of a guy in bed.
- •• 0:45—Breasts, while making love on top of banker guy in bed.

Rhonda Shear . . . . Tina

• *The Associate* (1996)

Colleen Camp . . . . Detective Jones

Bebe Neuwirth . . . . Camille
- • 0:37—Buns in black lingerie outfit. Seen in mirror.
- • 1:16—Buns in lingerie while in hotel room with Whoopi Goldberg (who is made up like Robert Cutty.)

Astonished (1988)

Liliana Komorowska. . . . . Sonia Borges/Lucille
- •• 0:30—Breasts, while making love on the floor with Charles S. Dutton. More breasts, when stabbing him repeatedly with a knife.
- • 0:32—Very brief breasts, while putting dress top back on.

At Play in the Fields of the Lord (1991)

Kathy Bates . . . . .Hazel Quarrier
- • 2:22—(0:52 into tape 2) Nude, covered with mud and leaves, going crazy outside after her son dies.

Daryl Hannah . . . . Andy Huben
- • 2:09—(0:39 into tape 2) Brief buns, while swimming in the water.
- ••• 2:10—(0:40 into tape 2) Buns, getting out and resting by tree. Long shot, then breasts in (excellent!) closer shot. Very brief top of lower frontal nudity. (Skip tape 1 and fast forward to this!)
- •• 2:11—(0:41 into tape 2) Brief buns, running away after kissing Tom Berenger.

Atlantic City (1981; French/Canadian)

Susan Sarandon. . . . . Sally
- •• 0:50—Left breast cleaning herself with lemon juice while Burt Lancaster watches through window.

Attack of the 50 ft. Woman (1993; Made for Cable Movie)

Cristi Conaway . . . . .Honey
- • 0:16—Very brief buns and back side of left breast, after getting out of bed and walking to the bathroom.

Frances Fisher . . . . Dr. Cushing

Victoria Haas . . . . Deputy Charlie Spooner

Daryl Hannah . . . . Nancy Archer

Hilary Shepard. . . . . Nurse

Patricia Tallman. . . . . Stunts

Maude Winchester . . . . Donna

Attack of the 60 Foot Centerfold (1995)

Michelle Bauer. . . . . .Dr. Joyce Mann

Deborah Dutch . . . . Nurse Williams

Nikki Fritz . . . . Rosita
- • 0:33—Breasts, while giving Jay Richardson a backrub.

J. J. North . . . . Angel
- ••• 0:05—Breasts and buns in panties with the other two girls in photo shoot.
- • 0:09—In black bra, brief buns in black panties, while showing the doctor her body.
- •• 0:25—Right breast, then breasts, while in bedroom with Mark.
- • 0:30—Buns in yellow swimsuit, while posing for photos at the beach.
- ••• 0:31—Breasts and buns in swimsuit, while posing at the beach with the other two girls.
- •• 0:33—Breasts, while at the beach after she grows to 60 feet tall.
- •• 0:51—Right breast, sticking out of bikini top, while lying asleep, then waking up to talk with Wilson.
- ••• 1:03—Breasts and partial buns, when taking a bath in water tank while Mark takes photos.
- •• 1:07—Breasts, while resting against a rock and talking to Mark and Richardson.

Tammy Parks. . . . . .Betty
- ••• 0:05—Breasts and buns in panties with the other two girls in photo shoot.
- • 0:27—Brief buns in red swimsuit while posing for photos at the beach.
- ••• 0:31—Breasts and buns in swimsuit, while posing at the beach with the other two girls.
- • 0:53—Buns in lingerie, while walking around the house.
- • 1:06—Buns, while snooping around in Angels' bedroom.
- • 1:10—Right breast, when it pops out of her bikini top during fight with Angel.

Raelyn Saalman . . . . Inga
- ••• 0:05—Breasts and buns in panties with the other two girls in photo shoot.
- ••• 0:31—Breasts and buns in swimsuit, while posing at the beach with the other two girls.
- ••• 1:05—Breasts, while sunbathing outside and talking with Betty.
- • 1:13—Partial buns, while helping Jay Richardson.

Auditions (1978)

Marita Ditmar . . . . .Frieda Volker
- •• 1:05—Breasts and partial buns with another woman and a guy.

Mara Lutra. . . . . Jenny Marino
- •• 0:58—Nude during her audition.
- •• 1:07—Breasts and buns during orgy scene.

Rhonda Petty. . . . . .Patty Rhodes
- •• 0:26—Breasts during audition.
- •• 0:30—Breasts, standing next to Larry and full frontal nudity straddling him on the table.

Linnea Quigley . . . . Sally Webster
- ••• 0:06—Breasts and buns, undressing and dancing during her audition.
- ••• 0:26—Full frontal nudity, acting with two guys.

Sally Swift . . . . .Melinda Sale
- ••• 0:21—Full frontal nudity, undressing and masturbating during her audition.
- •• 0:30—Breasts and buns, whipping Harry.

Idy Tripoldi . . . . Bonnie Tirol
- ••• 1:01—Full frontal nudity, taking off sweater.
- •• 1:07—Breasts and buns during orgy scene.

Bonnie Werchan . . . . Tracy Matthews
- ••• 0:02—Breasts, then full frontal nudity, undressing for her audition.
- ••• 0:31—Nude, undressing herself and Van.
- •• 0:33—Buns and side of right breast, making love with Van.
- •• 1:07—Breasts and buns during orgy scene.

Auntie Lee's Meat Pies (1991)

Karen Black . . . . Auntie Lee

Ava Fabian. . . . . Magnolia
- • 1:29—Buns, while swimming in one piece swimsuit under water.

Pia Reyes . . . . Sky
- •• 1:10—Breasts in basement with her rock star boyfriend.
- •• 1:15—Breasts in basement with her pot smoking boyfriend.

Kristine Rose . . . . Fawn
- •• 1:12—Breasts in Stonehedge bedroom with her rock star boyfriend. More breasts in silhouette.
- • 1:28—Buns, in G-string in swimming pool.

Petra Verkaik . . . . .Baby

Teri Weigel . . . . Coral
- • 1:23—Breasts under sheer outfit.
- • 1:29—Buns, while swimming in one piece swimsuit under water.

Autumn Born (1979)

Dorothy Stratten . . . . Tara
•• 0:26—Left breast taking bath, then right breast getting up, then breasts dressing.
• 0:30—Side view of left breast, then breasts climbing back into bed.
••• 0:46—In white bra and panties, side view of left breast and buns, then breasts in bathtub. Long scene.
• 0:50—Side view of left breast and buns getting undressed. Nice buns shot. Right breast lying down in chair.
• 1:03—Brief breasts shots during flashbacks.

Roberta Weiss . . . . Melissa
• 0:07—Buns, wearing panties and bending over desk to get whipped.

Avanti! (1973)

Juliet Mills . . . . Pamela Piggott
•• 1:23—Buns and breasts, while climbing out of the water onto a rock. Medium long shot. Closer shot of right breast, while lying on the rock.
••• 1:26—Breasts, twice, while waving to fishermen on a passing boat.
• 2:07—Very brief partial buns and partial left breast in mirror in bed's headboard when she props herself up while Jack Lemmon talks on the phone.
• 2:08—Brief lower half of buns, while putting stuff away in closet. Partial breasts in open pajama top.

Avenging Angel (1985)

Laura Burkett . . . . Blonde Hooker
Charlene Jones . . . . Hooker
Karen Mani . . . . Janie Soon Lee
••• 0:06—Nude taking a shower, right breast in mirror drying herself off, then in bra getting dressed.

Betsy Russell . . . . Angel/Molly Stewart
Susan Tyrrell . . . . Solly Mosler
Deborah Voorhees . . . . Roxie
Lynda Wiesmeier . . . . Debbie

• An Awfully Big Adventure (1995; British)

Georgina Cates . . . . Stella Bradshaw
•• 1:12—Breasts, when sitting up in bed and putting her bra on after making love with Alan Rickman.
• 1:22—Very brief right breast, while making love in bed with Rickman.
• 1:25—Partial left breast, while sitting in bed with Rickman.

Carol Drinkwater . . . . Dawn Allenby
•• 0:38—Full frontal nudity, while standing in dressing room when Stella opens the door.

Patti Love . . . . Mary

Ay, Carmela! (1991; Spanish)

Carmen Maura . . . . Carmela
•• 0:42—Showing her left breast to the Lieutenant to explain why she had a Republican flag. Subtitles get in the way.
•• 1:38—Breasts taking off flag on stage during play. Subtitles get in the way again.

• B-Movie Queens Revealed: The Making of "Vice Academy" (1993; Video Tape)

Ginger Lynn Allen . . . . Holly
• 0:35—Buns in T-back, dancing on stage with Linnea Quigley from *Vice Academy 2.*
•• 0:38—Breasts, dancing on stage with Quigley from *Vice Academy 2.*

Elizabeth Kaitan . . . . Candy

Julia Parton . . . . Melanie/Malathion
• 0:00—Brief breasts, opening her blouse from *Vice Academy 3.*

Linnea Quigley . . . . Didi
••• 0:33—Breasts with Chuck while he's handcuffed to sink from *Vice Academy 1.*
• 0:34—Buns in T-back, dancing on stage with Ginger Lynn Allen from *Vice Academy 2.*
•• 0:38—Breasts, dancing on stage with Ginger Lynn Allen from *Vice Academy 2.*

Karen Russell . . . . Shawnee
• 0:00—Very brief breasts, pulling down her top from *Vice Academy 1.*
•• 0:27—Same shot as 0:00.

B.O.R.N. (1988)

Debra Lamb . . . . Sue
• 0:24—Breasts, while getting molested by a jerk.

Lorraine Michaels . . . . Dr. Black
P.J. Soles . . . . Liz
Dawn Wildsmith . . . . Singer

Babe Watch: The Forbidden Parody (1996)

Kaitlyn Ashley . . . . Bambi
•• 0:07—Breasts, while trying on swimsuit in dressing room.
• 0:20—Buns in swimsuit, while skating in parking lot. Brief breasts, when her swimsuit top comes off after falling on Derek.
• 1:01—Brief buns, after being rescued at the beach.
• 1:15—Buns in pink swimsuit, then brief breasts, while dancing on stage.

Jordana Gowan . . . . Miss Woodrow
Honey Lauren . . . . Lisa's Mom
Tané McClure . . . . Bodacia
•• 0:38—Breasts, after swimsuit top falls off during mambo contest.
•• 0:41—Breasts, while taking off her swimsuit top in dressing room with a customer after being tricked by Lucki.

Ashlie Rhey . . . . Ty-Dy
••• 0:54—Breasts, while undressing in dressing room with Brock, then making love.
• 1:14—Brief buns in swimsuit at the beach.

Raelyn Saalman . . . . Lucki
•• 0:10—Breasts, while in backyard with Dek.
•• 1:11—Breasts, while making love with her boyfriend in spa.

• Babes, Bikes & Beyond (1994; Video Tape)

Alex Andrea . . . . Herself
••• 0:09—Breasts and buns in T-back.

Lisa Comshaw . . . . Elaine
••• 0:04—Nude.

Tylyn John . . . . Herself
• 0:43—Buns, while dancing in panties.

Lorissa McComas . . . . Herself
••• 0:02—Breasts and buns.

Brittney Powell . . . . Biker Girl
••• 0:36—Breasts and buns in T-back.

Amy Rochelle . . . . Herself
••• 0:29—Breasts.

• BabeWatch, Episode 1: Lingerie Fantasies (1994; Video Tape)

Joy Ballard . . . . Herself
••• 0:05—Nude, while trying on lingerie in a bathroom. Long scene.
••• 0:51—Nude, while posing on chair outside. Long scene.

••• 0:55—Nude, after end credits.

Liza Hazelhurst . . . . Herself

••• 0:10—Nude, while trying on lingerie on bed in house. Long scene.

••• 0:45—Nude, in bathroom, then taking a shower. Long scene.

••• 0:57—Nude, while posing on bed after end credits.

Lori Jo Hendrix . . . . Herself

••• 0:01—Nude, while trying on lingerie on steps in front of a house. Long scene.

••• 0:35—Nude, while taking a shower. Long scene.

••• 0:49—Full frontal nudity, while trying on lingerie again outside.

Kelly Jaye. . . . . Herself

••• 0:08—Nude, while trying on lingerie outside by a chair. Long scene.

Julia Parton . . . . Herself

••• 0:20—Nude, taking a shower. Long scene.

••• 0:57—Nude, in shower after end credits.

Eileen Smith . . . . Herself

••• 0:24—Nude, while trying on lingerie outside on steps. Long scene.

••• 0:56—Lower frontal nudity, outside after end credits.

• *BabeWatch, Episode 2: Show Offs* *(1994; Video Tape)*

Lené Hefner. . . . . Lene

•• 0:33—Breasts and buns, while stripping and dancing in patriotic outfit.

Natalie Lennox . . . . Natalie

••• 0:25—Breasts and buns, while stripping and dancing.

• *BabeWatch, Episode 3: Sex Kittens* *(1994; Video Tape)*

Bobbi Brown . . . . Bobbi Brown

••• 0:07—Breasts, wearing a skirt, while dancing in house with her girlfriend.

••• 0:28—Nude, while taking a shower, then joined by her girlfriend.

Andrea Grigsby . . . . Herself

••• 0:46—Breasts and buns, while posing on lounge chair outdoors next to pool.

Lauren Hays . . . . Hostess

• 0:54—Brief buns in swimsuit, while dancing during end credits.

Lori Deann Pallett . . . . Lori Deann Pallett

•• 0:09—Breasts, while on sailboat.

••• 0:49—Breasts and buns, while in bubble bath.

Tabitha Stevens. . . . . Tabitha Stevens

•• 0:21—Breasts and buns, while playing outdoors in a mud puddle.

• *BabeWatch, Episode 4: Naughty But Nice* *(1995; Video Tape)*

Andrea Grigsby . . . . Herself

• 0:34—Buns while dancing on stage in a club.

Lauren Hays . . . . Hostess

• 0:09—Brief buns in swimsuit.

• 0:25—Brief buns in swimsuit.

Julie Kruis . . . . Julie Kruis

• 0:13—Buns in swimsuit, while posing around pool area.

Becky LeBeau . . . . Herself

••• 0:19—Breasts, after waking up, then going outdoors and swimming in pool.

Lorissa McComas. . . . . Herself

••• 0:25—Nude, while posing on bed.

The Baby Doll Murders *(1992)*

Tuscany. . . . . Young Woman

••• 0:34—Breasts in bedroom with the suspected killer, then on bed.

Alretha Baker. . . . . Rhodes Receptionist

Shana Golden . . . . Prostitute

Joanne Lara . . . . Mrs. Jayson

••• 0:44—Breasts, while taking a shower, getting out, drying herself off, walking to bed and talking on the phone. Long scene.

•• 0:46—Breasts, on bed while getting killed and afterwards.

Julie McCullough. . . . . Betty

Melanie Smith . . . . Peggy Davis

••• 0:09—Breasts, while taking off her blouse and getting into hot tub with Jeff Kober.

•• 0:10—Breasts in hot tub with Kober. Fence gets in the way.

•• 0:11—Breasts, getting out of the hot tub.

•• 0:56—Breasts in hot tub with Kober while making out.

Baby Love *(1969)*

Linda Hayden . . . . Luci

• 0:32—Buns, while standing in room when Nick sneaks in.

• 0:34—Very brief right breast, while throwing doll at Robert.

• 0:39—Breasts in mirror taking a bath. Long shot. Brief left breast hidden by steam.

• 0:52—Brief breasts taking off her top to show Nick while sunbathing.

• 1:25—Brief breasts, while calling Robert from window. Long shot.

• 1:27—Very brief breasts, while sitting up and talking to Robert.

• 1:28—Breasts in open robe struggling with Robert.

Sheila Steafel . . . . Tessa

The Baby Maker *(1970)*

Barbara Hershey . . . . Tish

• 0:14—Side view of left breast, after taking off dress and diving into the pool. Long shot and dark. Buns in water.

• 0:23—Left breast (out of focus) under sheet in bed.

Helena Kallianiotes. . . . . Wanda

• 1:30—Brief breasts when Barbara Hershey sees her in bed with Tad.

Brenda Sykes . . . . Francis

The Baby of Mâcon *(1993; British/French)*

(Not available in the U.S. yet.)

Julia Ormond. . . . . Daughter

••• 0:49—Breasts and buns, while starting to make love with Ralph Fiennes, then nude after bad things happen. Long scene. Sometimes has blood on her.

Gabrielle Reidy. . . . . Midwife

Baby, It's You *(1983)*

Rosanna Arquette . . . . Jill

•• 1:17—Left breast, making love in bed with Vincent Spano.

Marta Kober . . . . Debra

The Babysitter *(1995)*

Lois Chiles . . . . Bernice Holsten

Tuesday Knight . . . . Waitress

• 0:08—Breasts, while making love with Mark on the floor in a flashback.

Bachelor Party *(1984)*

Angela Aames . . . . Mrs. Klupner
Toni Alessandrini . . . . . . Desiree, Woman Dancing with Donkey
• 1:24—Buns, in G-string, while dancing with donkey during party.
Monique Gabrielle . . . . Tracey
•• 1:11—Full frontal nudity in the hotel bedroom with Tom Hanks as his bachelor party gift.
Annie Gaybis . . . . Hooker
Rosanne Katon . . . . Bridal Shower Hooker
Tawny Kitaen . . . . Debbie Thompson
Rebecca Perle . . . . Screaming Woman

Back In the U.S.S.R. *(1992)*

Natalya Negoda . . . . Lena
•• 0:46—Side view of left breast, making love with Sloan in the bathtub. Brief right breast when Dimitri comes into the bathroom.
Dey Young . . . . Claudia

• ***Back of Beyond*** *(1996; Australian)*

Dee Smart . . . . Charlie
• 0:58—Brief breasts, while lying on table when Connor tries to force himself on her.

Back to School *(1986)*

Adrienne Barbeau . . . . Vanessa
Leslie Huntly . . . . Coed #1
•• 0:14—Brief breasts in the shower room when Rodney Dangerfield first arrives on campus.
Sally Kellerman . . . . Diane
Becky LeBeau . . . . Bubbles, the Hot Tub Girl

Backbeat *(1994)*

Sheryl Lee . . . . Astrid Kirchiner
•• 0:47—Breasts, after taking off her sweater and making love.
• 1:03—Very brief left breast, then breasts, while covered with paint.
•• 1:28—Nude, taking off sweater and putting on a dress.

Backdraft *(1991)*

Rebecca De Mornay . . . . Helen McCaffrey
Jennifer Jason Leigh . . . . Jennifer Vaitkus
• 1:16—Very, very brief left breast on back of fire truck with William Baldwin. (Right after someone knocks open a door with an axe.)

Backfire *(1987)*

Karen Allen . . . . Mara
• 0:48—Lots of buns, then brief breasts with Keith Carradine in the bedroom.
• 1:00—Brief breasts in the shower.

Backstab *(1990)*

June Chadwick . . . . Mrs. Caroline Chambers
Meg Foster . . . . Sara Rudnick
Isabelle Truchon . . . . Jennifer
•• 0:08—In bra, then breasts in back seat of car with James Brolin. Don't see her face very well.
• 0:16—Buns, black panties and stockings while on the floor with Brolin. Brief right breast.
• 0:18—Brief buns in front of fireplace. Side view of right breast. Buns, while walking into the other room.

Backstreet Dreams *(1990)*

Maria Celedonio . . . . Maria M.
Sherilyn Fenn . . . . Lucy
• 0:00—Right breast while sleeping in bed with Dean. Medium long shot.
Meg Register . . . . Candy
Brooke Shields . . . . Stephanie "Stevie" Bloom

Backstreet Justice *(1993)*

Linda Kozlowski . . . . Kerri Finnegan
••• 0:31—Breasts in open dress and while making love in bedroom with John Shea.
Patricia Skeriotis . . . . Cele
•• 0:28—Left breast, getting out of shower and wrapping towel around herself.

Backtrack *(1989)*

a.k.a. Catch Fire

Jodie Foster . . . . Anne Benton
• 0:50—Breasts behind textured shower door.
••• 0:51—Breasts, leaning out of the shower to get her towel. Very, very brief side of left breast and buns, while drying herself off in bedroom. Side of left breast and buns, while putting on slip.
Helena Kallianiotes . . . . Grace Carelli
Catherine Keener . . . . Trucker's Girl

Bad Blood *(1993)*

Kim Dawson . . . . Chang's Girl
• 0:16—Breasts and brief partial lower frontal nudity while in bed with Chang.
Nikki Fritz . . . . Uncredited Dancer
• 0:09—Breasts and buns when wearing T-back while dancing on stage, twice.
Kimberly Kates . . . . Lindee
••• 0:13—Breasts and buns, while making love with Lorenzo Lamas.
• 0:16—Breasts, while running out of trailer after Lamas leaves.
Jennifer MacDonald . . . . Ray Ann
Frankie Thorn . . . . Rhonda
•• 0:52—Breasts, while making love with Lorenzo Lamas.

Bad Boys *(1983)*

Ally Sheedy . . . . J. C. Walenski
• 0:12—Very, very brief left breast, while kneeling on floor next to bed when Sean Penn leaves. A little blurry and a long shot.

Bad Company *(1994)*

Ellen Barkin . . . . Margaret Wells
Michelle Beaudoin . . . . Wanda
• 0:11—Brief right breast in bed with John.
Gia Carides . . . . Julie Amis

Bad Georgia Road *(1977)*

Carol Lynley . . . . Molly Golden
• 1:02—Very brief upper half of right breast, after hitting the water in anger after her clothes are stolen.
Mary Woronov . . . . Hackett

Bad Girls *(1994)*

(Extended version reviewed.)

Drew Barrymore . . . . Lilly Laronette
• 0:15—Brief right breast while frolicking in the water with the other women.
• 1:15—Left breast in mirror while putting on dress in front of bad buy.
Madeleine Stowe . . . . Cody Zamora

Bad Girls from Mars *(1990)*

Jasaé . . . . Terry
- ••• 0:03—Breasts taking off her top.
- •• 0:05—More breasts going into dressing room.

Dana Bentley Konkel . . . . Martine
- •• 0:28—Breasts taking off her blouse in office.
- •• 0:59—Breasts several times wrestling with Edy Williams.

Sherri Graham . . . . Swimmer
- •• 0:22—Very brief breasts diving into, then climbing out of pool.

Brinke Stevens . . . . Myra
- • 0:11—Brief side of left breast, then breasts getting massaged on diving board.

Edy Williams . . . . Emanuelle
- •• 0:17—Breasts, several times changing in back of convertible car.
- ••• 0:23—Breasts, changing out of wet dress in bathroom.
- ••• 0:30—Breasts taking off blouse to get into spa.
- • 0:32—Breasts in back of Porsche and getting out.
- ••• 0:35—Breasts in store, signing autograph for robber.
- • 0:46—Buns in G-string, then breasts taking off her top again.
- ••• 0:58—Breasts in T.J.'s office. More breasts when wrestling with Martine.
- • 1:05—Breasts while tied up.
- • 1:07—Breasts again.
- •• 1:17—Breasts while taking off her outfit during outtakes.

Bad Influence *(1990)*

Marcia Cross . . . . Ruth Fielding

Charisse Glenn . . . . Stylish Eurasian Woman
- ••• 1:26—Breasts and partial lower frontal nudity making love on Rob Lowe.
- • 1:28—Very brief left breast in bed with the blonde woman.

Lisa Zane . . . . Claire
- • 0:39—Brief breasts on video tape seen on TV at party.

Bad Lieutenant *(1992)*

Victoria Bastell . . . . Bowtay
- •• 0:10—Breasts and brief side view of buns in bed with another woman. Brief side view of right breast, while dancing with Harvey Keitel.

Zoe Tamerlis . . . . Zoe

Frankie Thorn . . . . Nun
- • 0:17—Very brief lower frontal nudity, while getting raped by two guys in church.
- •• 0:26—Full frontal nudity while lying on hospital bed during examination.

Bad Love *(1992)*

a.k.a. Wild Angel

Kim Bolin . . . . Porn Actress #1

Alisa Christensen . . . . Felicia

Pamela Gidley . . . . Eloise

Margaux Hemingway . . . . Jackie

Debi Mazar . . . . Delores
- • 1:02—Very brief side view of right breast, taking off her sheer black top, wearing pasties over her nipples. Buns visible under sheer black pants.

Julie Strain . . . . Amber
- • 0:57—Brief breasts, seen on video monitor, while Jack makes love on top of her during filming of a movie.
- • 1:02—Very brief partial right breast, seen behind Debi Mazar after she throws off her shawl. Very, very brief tip of right breast, seen on video monitor.
- • 1:04—Brief breasts, while straddling a guy on bed on a movie set. Medium long shot.

Bad Manners *(1989)*

Karen Black . . . . Mrs. Fitzpatrick

Kimmy Robertson . . . . Sarah Fitzpatrick
- •• 0:38—Breasts and buns taking off robe and getting into the shower when Mouse takes a picture of her.

Edy Williams . . . . Mrs. Slatt

Bad Timing: A Sensual Obsession *(1980)*

Theresa Russell. . . . . Milena Flaherty
- • 0:14—Buns and breasts under short, sheer blouse.
- • 0:17—Almost brief right breast in bed during Art Garfunkel's flashback. Very brief left breast, while kneeling on bed with him.
- • 0:31—Full frontal nudity in bed with Garfunkel. Intercut with tracheotomy footage. Kind of gross.
- •• 0:32—Right breast, while sitting in bed talking to Garfunkel.
- • 0:41—Brief breasts several times on operating table.
- • 0:55—Full frontal nudity making love on stairwell with Garfunkel. Quick cuts.
- • 0:56—Brief breasts twice after stairwell episode while throwing a fit.
- •• 1:45—In bra, then breasts passed out on bed while Garfunkel cuts her clothes off. Brief full frontal nudity.
- •• 1:48—More breasts cuts while Garfunkel makes love to her while she's unconscious from an overdose of drugs.

Badge 373 *(1972)*

a.k.a. The Police Connection

Marina Durell. . . . . Rita Garcia
- • 0:33—Brief breasts, while lying dead in bed, covered with blood. Don't see her face.
- • 1:51—Brief breasts, while lying dead in bed, covered with blood in flashback.

The Bagdad Café *(1988)*

Marianne Sägebrecht. . . . . Jasmin
- •• 1:09—Right breast slowly lowering her top, posing while Jack Palance paints.
- •• 1:12—More breasts posing for Palance.

Baja *(1995)*

Roxanna Michaels . . . . Prostitute
- •• 0:44—Buns in G-string, then breasts, while in hotel room with Lance Henriksen.
- •• 0:45—Breasts, while making love with Henriksen and afterwards.

Molly Ringwald . . . . Bebe

Baja Oklahoma *(1988; Made for Cable Movie)*

Alice Krige . . . . Patsy Cline

Karen Laine . . . . Girl at Drive-In
- • 0:04—Left breast, while in truck with a jerk. Dark, hard to see anything.

Julia Roberts. . . . . Candy

The Ballad of Cable Hogue *(1970)*

Stella Stevens. . . . . Hildy
- • 1:12—Buns, while changing into nightgown in bedroom.
- • 1:14—Brief top half of breasts in outdoor tub, then buns running into cabin when stagecoach arrives.

***The Ballad of Little Jo** (1993)*

Suzy Amis . . . . Jo Monaghan
- • 0:12—Buns and left breast in reflection in mirror. Hard to see her face clearly.
- ••• 1:16—Breasts, while on bed with Tinman.

Heather Graham . . . . Mary Addie
Melissa Leo . . . . Mrs. Grey
Carrie Snodgress . . . . Ruth Badger

***Ballistic** (1993)*

a.k.a. Fists of Justice

Marjean Holden . . . . Jessie Gavin
- • 0:00—Buns and back side of left breast while in the shower. Nude, seen behind shower door.
- •• 0:30—Partial right breast, then breasts, while making love with Ray in bed.
- • 0:31—Left breast during argument. Very brief breasts and buns when getting out of bed and putting on T-shirt.

Aleisa Shirley . . . . Hooker

***The Baltimore Bullet** (1980)*

Cissie Colpitts-Cameron . . . . Sugar
- • 0:09—Breasts behind shower door after James Coburn gets out.

Joyce Mandel . . . . Waitress

***La Bamba** (1987)*

Elizabeth Peña . . . . Rosie Morales
- • 0:06—Brief side view of right breast taking a shower outside when two young boys watch her from a water tower. Long shot, hard to see.

***Band of Gold: Parts 1 & 2** (1995; Made for Cable Movie; British)*

Cathy Tyson . . . . Carol Johnson
- •• 0:19—Breasts, while bathing in bathtub, talking to Gina. In black bra and panties, while getting dressed.
- 1:22—Lower half of buns in lingerie, in hotel room with a customer.
- • 1:31—In black bra and panties in bathroom, brief buns in panties.
- • 1:32—Brief breasts, while in bathtub and jumping up when startled by the detective.

***Bank Robber** (1993)*

Lisa Bonet . . . . Priscilla
- •• 0:36—Buns, while lying on bed, waiting for Patrick Dempsey.
- •• 0:37—Breasts, while making love in bed with Dempsey.
- •• 1:05—Brief breasts while making love in bed with Dempsey.

Olivia D'Abo . . . . Selina
- • 0:03—Very, very brief right breast, when pulling the sheets over herself in bed. Brief breasts, while getting out of bed.
- • 0:04—Brief, upper half of left breast at doorway, then brief partial left breast in mirror.
- • 0:21—Brief side of right breast, while making love in bed with Chris.
- • 1:10—Brief breasts, while turning over in bed after making love with Andy.

Mariska Hargitay . . . . Marissa Benoit
Paula Kelly . . . . Mother

***The Banker** (1989)*

E.J. Peaker . . . . Renee
Debi Richter . . . . Melanie
Christina Walker . . . . Girl
- • 0:18—Breasts on bed with Jeff Conaway

Teri Weigel . . . . Jaynie
- ••• 0:02—Taking off dress, then in lingerie, then breasts making love with Osbourne in bed. More breasts after.

***Bar Girls** (1995)*

Camila Griggs . . . . J.R.
Patti Sheehan . . . . Destiny
- •• 0:18—Breasts, while sitting in a spa and talking on the phone.

Nancy Allison Wolfe . . . . Loretta
- •• 1:12—In bra, when in hallway with J.R. Breasts, while in the bedroom with her.

***Barb Wire** (1995)*

(Unrated version reviewed.)

Adriana Alexander . . . . Redhead
Tina Coté . . . . Woman in Bar
Pamela Lee . . . . Barb Wire
- •• 0:00—Breasts in black dress, while dancing in water spray during opening credits.
- • 0:33—Brief silhouette of breasts behind curtain while changing clothes.
- • 0:57—Brief partial left breast under water and above water in bubble bath.
- • 1:02—Brief right breast in open robe, while walking in office.
- ••• 1:40—Breasts in black dress, while on trapeze and getting sprayed with water. Long scene shown after the credits.

Patti Tippo . . . . Mom

***Barbarella** (1968; French/Italian)*

Catherine Chevalier . . . . n.a.
Jane Fonda . . . . Barbarella
- •• 0:03—Breasts, while getting out of space suit during opening credits in zero gravity. Easier to see in version with letterboxed credits.
- • 0:07—Back side of right breast, while opening clear plastic case to get bracelet.
- • 0:08—Very brief buns, when walking around corner after dumping stuff in closet.

Anita Pallenberg . . . . The Black Queen

***Barbarian Queen** (1985)*

Lana Clarkson . . . . Amethea
- •• 0:38—Brief breasts during attempted rape.
- ••• 0:48—Breasts being tortured with metal hand then raped by torturer.

Dawn Dunlap . . . . Taramis
- • 0:00—Breasts, in the woods getting raped.

Katt Shea . . . . Estrild
- • 0:31—Brief breasts, when her top gets torn off by guards.

***Barbarian Queen II: The Empress Strikes Back** (1989)*

Orietta Aguilar . . . . Erigina
- •• 0:14—Breasts during fight in mud with Lana Clarkson.

Lana Clarkson . . . . Athelia
- ••• 0:14—Breasts during fight with Erigina in mud. More breasts afterwards.
- ••• 0:31—Left breast, while making love with Aurion outside.
- ••• 0:43—Breasts, tied up to torture rack.
- ••• 0:49—More breasts, tied up to torture rack.
- •• 0:51—Brief right breast then breasts several times, while lying down, tied to the rack.

• 0:54—Very brief breasts when Aurion covers her up.
Elizabeth A. Jaeger . . . . Noki
Rebecca Wood . . . . Ziela

Barbarians at the Gate (1993; Made for Cable Movie)

Joanna Cassidy . . . . Linda Robinson
Leilani Sarelle . . . . Laurie Johnson
• 0:59—Side view of right breast, twice, while taking off bra and putting on T-shirt.

Barfly (1987)

Faye Dunaway . . . . Wanda Wilcox
• 0:58—Brief upper half of breasts in bathtub talking to Mickey Rourke.
Alice Krige . . . . Tully
Sandy Martin . . . . Janice

• *Barry McKenzie Holds His Own...* (1974; Australian)

Nell Campbell . . . . Narida Breeley
• 0:15—Brief buns, while sitting on a chair on stage, talking with Barry in the audience. Brief buns and breasts, when Barry gets up on stage.
Chantal Contouri . . . . Zizi
Fiona Richmond . . . . French Stripper

Basic Instinct (1992)

(Unrated Director's cut reviewed.)
Leilani Sarelle . . . . Roxy
Sharon Stone . . . . Catherine Trammel
••• 0:02—Buns and breasts while making love on top of Johnny in bed, then killing him.
•• 0:21—Buns and left breast in mirror in her bedroom while Michael Douglas watches while waiting for her.
• 0:26—Two brief crotch shots while crossing and uncrossing her legs during interrogation.
•• 0:44—Nude, undressing in her house, while Douglas watches from outside. Medium long shot.
••• 1:10—Breasts while in bed with Douglas.
••• 1:13—Breasts and buns, tying Douglas up in bed and on top of him.
•• 1:15—Buns, while sitting on top of Douglas.
• 1:32—Very brief right breast, with Douglas in front of fireplace.
••• 1:43—Breasts, while taking off her blouse in Douglas' apartment.
••• 2:00—Breasts, while in bed on top of Douglas.
Jeanne Tripplehorn . . . . Dr. Beth Garner
••• 0:35—Briefly in bra, then breasts with Michael Douglas in her apartment. Buns when he rips her panties off.
••• 0:37—Breasts, sitting up, then getting up off the floor.

Basic Training (1984)

Angela Aames . . . . Cheryl
• 0:19—Brief breasts in bathtub.
Erika Dockery . . . . Salesgirl 2
• 0:00—Brief breasts, whlie standing behind the desk.
Ann Dusenberry . . . . Melinda Griffin
••• 1:13—Breasts in Russian guy's bedroom.
Barbara Peckinpaugh . . . . Salesgirl 1
• 0:00—Breasts, while on desk.
Rhonda Shear . . . . Debbie
•• 0:07—Breasts making love with Mark.

Basket Case 2 (1989)

Heather Rattray . . . . Susan
• 1:20—Brief right breast twice, when white blouse gapes open in bedroom with Duane. Special-effect scar on her stomach makes it a little unappealing looking.
Annie Ross . . . . Granny Ruth

Basket Case 3: The Progeny (1991)

Carla Morrell . . . . Twin #1
•• 0:41—Breasts in bed with her twin sister and Duane's brother.
• 1:29—Brief breast, lying in bed with her twin sister and Duane's brother after the end credits.
Carmen Morrell . . . . Twin #2
•• 0:41—Breasts in bed with her twin sister and Duane's brother.
• 1:29—Brief breast, lying in bed with her twin sister and Duane's brother after the end credits.
Heather Rattray . . . . Susan
Annie Ross . . . . Granny Ruth

Baton Rouge (1988; Spanish)

Victoria Abril . . . . Dr. Ana Alonso
• 0:41—Brief buns, when sitting on her office desk, before making love with Antonio Banderas.
• 0:48—Right breast, while sitting in bed after stabbing Leon.
Carmen Maura . . . . Isabel Harris
• 1:22—Breasts, visible under water under crooked nightgown while standing in pool.
• 1:23—Breasts, sticking out of nightgown after Antonio Banderas drowns her.

The Bawdy Adventures of Tom Jones (1976; British)

Judy Buxton . . . . Lizzy
• 0:39—Brief breasts in bed several times, helping to keep Tom Jones and Prudence hidden.
Joan Collins . . . . Black Bess
Madeline Smith . . . . Sophia

Bay Boy (1985; Canadian)

Robey . . . . n.a.
Isabelle Mejias . . . . Mary McNeil
•• 1:28—Brief breasts in her bedroom with Kiefer Sutherland, then brief breasts in bed with him.
Liv Ullmann . . . . Jennie Campbell

Beach Babes From Beyond (1993)

Sara Bellomo . . . . Xena
••• 0:01—Breasts and very brief lower frontal nudity while in shower and getting dressed with Luna and Sola during opening credits.
•• 0:32—Buns, in swimsuit at the beach.
• 0:58—Buns, while dancing in swimsuits and boots on stage at beach during bikini contest.
Katie Colburn . . . . Sally's Model
••• 0:20—Breasts, while posing in spa outside (she's in the middle) during catalog photo session with two other models.
• 1:02—Brief breasts, when swimsuit top flies off while dancing on stage during bikini contest (she's the first one).
Angela Cornell . . . . Sally's Model
••• 0:20—Breasts, while posing in spa outside (she's on the left) during catalog photo session with two other models.
• 1:02—Brief breasts, when swimsuit top flies off while dancing on stage during bikini contest (she's the second one).

Nikki Fritz . . . . Sally's Model
- ••• 0:20—Breasts, while posing in spa outside (she's on the right) during catalog photo session with two other models.
- ••• 0:22—Nude, in bedroom during Hassler's fantasy.
- • 1:02—Brief breasts, twice, when swimsuit top flies off while dancing on stage during bikini contest (she's the last one).

Tamara Landry . . . . Luna
- •• 0:02—Breasts, while taking off pink top, getting dressed and talking with Xena and Sola.
- ••• 0:34—Breast, while making love in back of van with Jerry.
- •• 0:39—Buns, in swimsuit at the beach.
- • 0:58—Buns, while dancing in swimsuits and boots on stage at beach during bikini contest.

Linnea Quigley . . . . Sally

Beach Balls *(1988)*

Leslie Danon . . . . Kathleen
- • 1:06—In bra, then brief breasts in car with Doug.

The Beach Girls *(1982)*

Debra Blee . . . . .Sarah
- ••• 1:22—Brief breasts opening her swimsuit top on the beach.

Corinne Bohrer . . . . Champagne Girl

Jeanette Linné . . . . Redhead
- •• 0:38—Brief breasts, while walking around the house.

Tessa Richarde. . . . . Doreen

Catherine Mary Stewart . . . . Surfer Girl

Jeana Tomasina . . . . Ducky
- •• 0:12—Breasts and buns, lying on the beach with Ginger, while a guy looks through a telescope.
- ••• 0:54—Breasts on a sailboat with a guy.
- • 0:55—Brief breasts on the beach after being "saved" after falling off the boat.
- •• 1:12—Breasts in sauna with Ginger and an older guy.

Beaks The Movie *(1987)*

Michelle Johnson. . . . . .Vanessa
- • 0:26—Brief breasts covered with bubbles after taking a bath. Don't see her face.
- • 0:31—Brief breasts covered with bubbles after getting out of bathtub with Christopher Atkins. Don't see her face.

The Beast Within *(1982)*

Bibi Besch . . . . .Caroline MacCleary
- •• 0:06—Breasts, getting her blouse torn off by the beast while she is unconscious. Dark, hard to see her face.

The Beastmaster *(1982)*

Tanya Roberts . . . . Kiri
- ••• 0:35—Breasts in a pond while Marc Singer watches, then breasts getting out of the water when his pet ferrets steal her towel.

Linda Smith. . . . . Kiri's Friend
- • 0:35—Breasts in a pond with Tanya Roberts.

Beautiful Dreamers *(1992; Canadian)*

Wendel Meldrum . . . . .Jessie Bucke
- • 1:00—Very, very brief tip of left breast, while bathing herself.
- ••• 1:09—Full frontal nudity, after taking off her clothes to go swimming with her husband and Rip Torn.

Beauty Investigators *(1992; Hong Kong)*

Sophia Crawford . . . . .Brother Bee's Assistant
- •• 0:39—Breasts and buns, while taking a shower.
- • 0:40—Breasts under sheer white nightie.

Beauty School *(1993)*

Jane Hamilton . . . . Countess Sophia Von Spatula
- • 0:18—Left breast while leaning up while lying on massage table.
- • 1:11—Partial left breast while lying in bed. Breasts, when sitting up.
- ••• 1:15—Breasts while lying in bed.

Dana Hardin . . . . .Ashley
- • 0:58—Breasts, dancing in cage in club.

Sylvia Kristel . . . . Sylvia
- • 1:27—Brief breasts in bed with the private investigator.

Theresa Lynn . . . . Countess's Girl

Lisa Madison . . . . Kristina
- •• 0:02—Breasts while making out with a guy in bedroom.
- ••• 1:23—Breasts while making out with a guy.

Susan Napoli . . . . .Otis' Girl
- •• 0:21—Breasts undoing her swimsuit top for Mr. Otis.

J. J. North . . . . Renee
- ••• 0:44—Breasts while doing breast exercises, then buns in G-string going for a swim. (She's on the far left.)
- • 0:46—Brief breasts, while standing in pool.
- •• 0:57—Breasts and buns in G-string while undressing in locker room.

Carina Ragnarsson. . . . . .Heather
- •• 0:40—Breasts, dancing with her top down on stage in club.

Grace C. Renn . . . . .Betty
- •• 0:56—In white bra, then breasts while on stage, practicing her talent routine.

Kimberly Taylor . . . . Kimberly
- • 0:43—Buns in white lingerie on balcony. Long shot.
- ••• 0:44—Breasts doing breast exercises, then buns in G-string going for a swim. (She's on the far right.)
- ••• 0:45—Buns and breasts, getting out of the swimming pool.
- ••• 0:51—Breasts while making love with Quincy outside.
- ••• 1:22—Breasts, taking off her dress and making love with Quincy.

Stacy Warfel . . . . .Amanda Alps
- ••• 0:14—Breasts with the other three girls in the showers.
- •• 1:00—Breasts in the shower with Stephanie and a guy.

Vanessa Warner. . . . . .Becky Bustin'
- • 0:13—Breasts, taking off her bra on stage.
- ••• 0:14—Breasts with the other three girls in the showers.

Because of the Cats *(1973)*

Sylvia Kristel . . . . .n.a.
- • 1:09—Breasts and buns, under water with Case.

Alexandra Stewart . . . . Theodora
- • 0:16—Breasts under sheer black blouse.
- •• 0:43—Breasts, sitting up and covering herself while sunbathing outside.

• ***Becky Bubbles*** *(1987; Video Tape)*

Jasaé . . . . Herself
- •• 0:16—Breasts, taking off yellow swimsuit top and getting pushed on swing, then pushing Brandi.
- ••• 0:17—Breasts, playing with a ball on the grass with Brandi.
- ••• 0:19—Breasts, drinking wine and sitting on swing.

Lorraine Dorado . . . . Herself
- ••• 0:09—Brief right breast and buns in black and white swimsuit, then breasts in pool.
- ••• 0:12—Breasts while playing on pool float with Becky and Brandi.
- ••• 0:14—Breasts getting in and out of pool, then rubbing lotion on herself.
- ••• 0:18—Breasts while playing on the grass in open swimsuit top.

Brandi Downs . . . . Herself
- •• 0:11—Breasts in pool after Lorraine pushes her off the pool float.
- ••• 0:12—Breasts while playing on pool float with Lorraine and Becky.
- ••• 0:14—Breasts sunbathing on chair and putting her swimsuit back on.

Becky LeBeau . . . . Herself
- ••• 0:00—Breasts, when waking up and getting out of bed.
- ••• 0:01—Breasts, going outside for a swim in white panties. Long scene.
- ••• 0:06—Breasts, while rubbing lotion on herself.
- ••• 0:08—Breasts outside on chair and in pool with her friends.
- ••• 0:12—Breasts while playing on pool float with Lorraine and Brandi.
- ••• 0:22—Breasts drying her hair outside with hair dryer.
- ••• 0:24—Breasts while putting on make-up and fingernail polish.
- •• 0:25—Buns and breasts while taking off swimsuit then getting dressed.

Becoming Colette (1992; French/German/U.S.)

Virginia Madsen . . . . Polaire
- •• 0:48—Breasts in bed, with Mathilda May.
- •• 0:49—Side view of left breast in bed with May and Klaus Maria Brandauer.

Mathilda May . . . . Gabrielle Colette
- •• 0:01—Left breast, in open dress top, on stage during play.
- •• 0:16—Breasts, sitting up in bed.
- •• 0:48—Left breast, then breasts in bed with Virginia Madsen.
- •• 0:49—Side view of right breast in bed with Madsen and Klaus Maria Brandauer.
- •• 1:13—Upper half of buns and right breast, while making love in bed on top of Brandauer.

Bedroom Eyes
(1985; Made for Cable Movie; Canadian)

Dayle Haddon . . . . Alixe

Barbara Law . . . . Jobeth
- • 0:02—Breasts, while undressing when watched by Harry through the window.
- •• 0:07—Breasts and buns, while kissing a woman.
- • 0:14—Breasts during Harry's flashback when he talks to the psychiatrist.
- •• 0:23—Breasts and buns, while dancing in bedroom.
- •• 0:57—Breasts, while kissing Mary on the floor.
- • 1:23—Brief breasts, while on top of Harry.

Bedroom Eyes II (1989)

Linda Blair . . . . Sophie Stevens
- • 0:31—Buns, in bed with Wings Hauser.
- • 0:33—Brief left breast under bubbles in the bathtub. Don't see her face.

Jennifer Delora . . . . Gwendolyn
- •• 0:04—Undressing in hotel room with Vinnie. Breasts, then making love.

Jane Hamilton . . . . JoBeth McKenna
- • 0:50—Breasts knifing Linda Blair, then fighting with Wings Hauser.

Kathy Shower . . . . Carolyn Ross
- •• 0:22—Breasts in the artist's studio fighting with her lover while Wings Hauser watches through the window.

Kimberly Taylor . . . . Michelle

The Bedroom Window (1987)

Isabelle Huppert . . . . Sylvia Wentworth
- •• 0:06—Briefly nude while looking out the window at attempted rape.

Elizabeth McGovern . . . . Denise

• *Before the Rain* (1995; U.S./French)

Madonna . . . . Madonna
- • 0:36—Brief breasts in photo that the woman is looking at. Again after coffee is spilled on the photo.

Katrin Cartlidge . . . . Anne
- • 0:35—Breasts, seen behind shower door, while taking a shower.

Beginner's Luck (1983)

Riley Steiner . . . . Tech
- • 0:05—Brief side view of right breast, while in bathtub with Aris.

The Beguiled (1971)

Jo Ann Harris . . . . Carol
- • 1:09—Right breast, while in bed under Clint Eastwood at night.
- • 1:10—Brief left breast and side view of buns on top of Eastwood in bed. Brief buns, when discovered by Edwina.
- • 1:11—Very brief right breast, covering herself up in bed. Very brief breasts shadow on the wall, then very, very brief right breast covering herself with a sheet and walking out the door.

Mae Mercer . . . . Hallie
- • 1:28—Very brief breasts in ripped open dress during flashback.

Behind Locked Doors (1969)

Madeleine Le Roux . . . . Woman at Party
- • 0:07—Breasts after taking off bra while making out with guy in barn.

The Believers (1987)

Helen Shaver . . . . Jessica Halliday
- • 0:38—Brief glimpse of right breast while lying in bed with Martin Sheen.
- • 1:17—Buns, getting out of bed.

The Bell Jar (1979)

Roxanne Hart . . . . n.a.

Marilyn Hassett . . . . Esther Greenwood
- • 0:10—In bra, then brief breasts in bed with Buddy. Dark, hard to see.
- •• 1:09—Breasts taking off her clothes and throwing them out the window while yelling.

Mary Louise Weller . . . . Doreen

Belle de Jour (1968; French)

Catherine Deneuve . . . . Séverine
- • 0:52—Very brief partial left breast, then buns under sheer black fabric, while walking around in house.
- 1:05—Brief partial right breast, while sitting on bed. Subtitles get in the way.

Macha Meril . . . . Renee

Belle Epoque (1993; Spanish)

a.k.a. The Age of Beauty

Penelope Cruz . . . . Luz

Ariadna Gil . . . . Violeta
- 0:48—Brief breasts, then brief right breast while making love with Fernando in hay in a loft. He's dressed as a maid and she's dressed as a soldier.

Maribel Verdú . . . . Rocio

La Belle Noiseuse (1992; French)

Emmanuelle Béart . . . . Marianne
- •• 1:11—Full frontal nudity, after taking off robe and posing in studio.
- •• 1:24—Left breast and lower frontal nudity while posing.
- •• 1:27—Full frontal nudity after finishing posing and putting on robe.
- •• 1:34—Nude, after taking off robe and getting ready to pose.
- ••• 1:38—Nude, after taking off robe and getting ready to pose while leaning on stool.
- ••• 1:43—Nude, after taking off robe and posing while sitting on chair.
- •• 1:49—Nude, lying on chair after taking off robe.
- •• 1:51—Nude, after taking off robe and posing on floor.
- ••• 1:53—Nude, while kneeling on bench while posing.
- ••• 1:57—Full frontal nudity while posing on stool, then sitting on chairs and sitting on floor. Long scene.
- • 2:03—(0:00 into tape 2) Full frontal nudity while posing on bench.
- •• 2:06—(0:03 into tape 2) Nude, while getting off bench and putting on robe.
- •• 2:10—(0:07 into tape 2) Breasts and buns, after taking off robe and sitting on bench.
- ••• 2:16—(0:13 into tape 2) Breasts, while posing on stool, then full frontal nudity, getting up off stool and putting on robe.
- ••• 2:33—(0:30 into tape 2) Nude, after taking off robe, and posing on mattress on the floor.
- ••• 2:42—(0:39 into tape 2) Nude, while walking around the studio, looking at the paintings, then sitting on mattress on the floor. Long scene.
- •• 2:57—(0:54 into tape 2) Buns and breasts, when sitting on mattress on the floor. Full frontal nudity while lying down, then getting up, putting on robe and walking away.
- •• 3:17—(1:14 into tape 2) Breasts and buns, while standing and posing.
- •• 3:20—(1:17 into tape 2) Right beast, while standing and posing. Long shot at first, then closer shot.

Jane Birkin . . . . Liz

Marianne Denicourt . . . . Julienne

The Belly of an Architect (1987; British/Italian)

Stefania Casini . . . . Flavia Speckler
- ••• 1:15—Lower frontal nudity, in open robe with Brian Dennehy. Then buns and breasts on couch. Kind of a long shot.

Chloe Webb . . . . Louisa Kracklite
- •• 0:01—Very brief right breast, making love on train with Brian Dennehy. Brief side view of right breast sitting up and putting camisole top on.
- • 0:56—Brief buns in room with Lambert Wilson.
- • 1:07—Brief buns, lying in bed with Wilson.
- • 1:27—Breasts in B&W photos of a pregnant woman. Supposedly her, but probably not.

• *Below Utopia* (1997)

Marta Kristen . . . . Marilyn

Alyssa Milano . . . . Susanne
- • 0:27—Very, very brief blurry tip of left breast, twice, when sitting up on couch.

• *The Beneficiary* (1996)

Suzy Amis . . . . Connie Roos

Corey Anne Chang . . . . Lauren Powers
- • 0:01—In braless blouse and panties, then very brief buns after ripping off her panties in B&W underwear commercial.
- •• 0:04—Breasts, opening her blouse in office in front of Ron Silver.

Colleen Coffey . . . . Commercial Voice

Stacy Haiduk . . . . Lena Girard
- • 1:03—Brief breasts, while making love in bed with Jimmy.
- •• 1:18—Brief breasts, several times, while making love with Jimmy in bed.

Beretta's Island (1993)

Jo Champa . . . . Celeste

Elizabeth Kaitan . . . . Linda
- •• 1:33—Breasts, while playing with Franco Columbu in the ocean at the end of the film, during the end credits and after.

The Berlin Affair (1985; Italian/German)

Gudrun Landgrebe . . . . Louise Von Hollendorf
- • 0:23—Very brief inner half of left breast, twice, while making out with Mio.

Berserker (1987)

Beth Toussaint . . . . Shelly
- •• 0:40—Breasts, while making love on top of Mike in the woods. Nice close-up. Kind of foggy and dark.
- •• 0:41—Side view of breasts, while making love on top of Mark.
- •• 0:43—Nude, while getting up and getting dressed.

• *Best Buns on the Beach* (1987; Video Tape)

Blondi . . . . Blondi
- ••• 0:06—Breasts, stripping on stage during dance routine. Buns, in G-string.
- •• 0:52—Breasts and buns with all the contestants during review.
- ••• 0:53—Breasts and buns in final pose-off.
- •• 0:57—Breasts and buns winning the contest.
- ••• 0:58—More slow motion breasts and bun shots during the final credits.

Debra Lamb . . . . Buns Model
- ••• 0:04—Buns, in G-string, bending over during "Ideal Buns" demonstration.

• *Best Chest in the U.S.* (1987; Video Tape)

Leslee Bremmer . . . . Bernadette
- • 0:25—Buns in G-string.

Brandi Downs . . . . Charlene
- ••• 0:48—Breasts and buns, dancing in two piece swimsuit.
- ••• 0:54—Breasts on stage with the other finalists.
- ••• 0:57—Breasts winning.

• *Best Chest in the West* (1984; Video Tape)

Michelle Bauer . . . . Michelle
- ••• 0:24—In two piece swimsuit, then breasts and buns.

Leslee Bremmer . . . . Leslee
- ••• 0:29—In black, two piece swimsuit, then breasts and buns.
- • 0:32—More breasts during judging and winning the 2nd round.

Raven De La Croix . . . . Herself
••• 0:34—Breasts doing strip tease routine on stage.
Barbara Peckinpaugh . . . . Chrissy
••• 0:28—In two piece swimsuit, then breasts and buns.
Candy Samples . . . . Herself
••• 0:54—Breasts dancing on stripping and dancing on stage with Pat McCormick.

• *Best Chest in the West II* *(1986; Video Tape)*

Leslee Bremmer . . . . Herself
• 0:49—Dancing in pink top. Buns, in G-string.
Becky LeBeau . . . . Herself
••• 0:46—Dancing in red two piece swimsuit. Buns, then breasts.
•• 0:55—Buns and breasts after winning semi-finals.

Best Friends *(1982)*

Goldie Hawn . . . . Paula McCullen
• 0:18—Very, very brief side view of right breast getting into the shower with Burt Reynolds.
• 1:14—Upper half of left breast in the shower, twice.
Jessica Tandy . . . . Eleanor McCullen

The Best Little Whorehouse in Texas *(1982)*

Annie Gaybis . . . . Uncredited Chicken Ranch Girl
• 1:12—Brief breasts, twice, while smoking a joint in bed with a football player when Dom DeLuise busts in with his news crew.
Sandy Johnson . . . . Chicken Ranch Girl
Terri Treas . . . . Chicken Ranch Girl
Arnetia Walker . . . . Dogette
Victoria Wells . . . . Washing Girl

The Best of Sex and Violence *(1981)*

Elvira . . . . Katya
•• 0:40—Brief breasts dancing on stage in scene from *Working Girls.*
Vanity . . . . Tanya
• 0:24—Buns and breasts in various scenes from *Tanya's Island.*
Angela Aames . . . . Little Bo Peep
• 0:18—Brief breasts in scene from *Fairytales.*
• 0:20—Brief right breast in scene from *Fairytales.*
Phyllis Davis . . . . Sugar/Joy
•• 0:56—Breasts after bath and in bed in scenes from *Sweet Sugar.*
••• 0:59—Breasts and buns walking out of lake in scene from *Terminal Island.*
Uschi Digard . . . . Truck Stop Woman
• 0:47—Breasts getting chased by policeman in parking lot in scene from *Truck Stop Women.*
Laura Gemser . . . . Emanuelle
• 0:23—Side of left breast while getting clothes taken off by a guy. Long shot. Scene from *Emanuelle Around the World.*
Claudia Jennings . . . . Rose
•• 0:46—Breasts taking off her blouse in scene from *Truck Stop Women.*
Laura Jane Leary . . . . Girl Victim
• 0:00—Getting clothes ripped off, then in bra and panties, then breasts.
Joan Prather . . . . Herself
•• 0:38—Breasts getting her breasts squeezed by an attacker. Dark.
Cheryl Smith . . . . Cinderella
• 0:14—Breasts taking a bath in scene from *Cinderella.*

Edy Williams . . . . Herself
•• 0:46—Breasts in various scenes from *Dr. Minx.*

• *The Best of the Mermaids* *(1992; Video Tape)*

Tia . . . . Sand and Lace
••• 1:12—Breasts and buns in G-string on boat, at the beach and while scuba diving.
Lori Deann Pallett . . . . The Snakecharmer
••• 1:05—Breasts while scuba diving, posing on boat and at the beach. Buns in swimsuit.
Shawna Rener . . . . Jus' Catchin' Some Rays
••• 0:20—Breasts and buns, while scuba diving.
Kelley Wild . . . . Heartstrings
••• 0:35—Nude, while playing harp.

• *The Best of Video Playmate Calendars* *(1992; Video Tape)*

India Allen . . . . Playmate
•• 0:39—Breasts and buns in B&W music video.
••• 0:40—Nude in bed.
••• 0:41—Nude in more B&W and color music video segments.
••• 0:42—Nude in bed.
Kimberley Conrad . . . . Playmate
••• 0:43—Breasts and buns in over exposed music video segment. Breasts while dancing in silk pajamas.
•• 0:44—In lingerie.
••• 0:45—Nude in outdoor fountain in slow motion.
•• 0:46—Nude in house, lit with a sliver of light.
Devin De Vasquez . . . . Playmate
••• 0:02—Nude during fantasy photo session.
Donna Edmondson . . . . Playmate
••• 0:30—In lingerie, then nude during music video segment with a chair.
••• 0:32—In lingerie, then nude in bed and in still photos.
Rebecca Ferratti . . . . Playmate
•• 0:15—Brief breasts and buns during dancing segment.
••• 0:16—Breasts and buns in B&W segment.
••• 0:17—Full frontal nudity in bathtub in warehouse.
••• 0:18—Nude, doing more dancing.
Pamela Lee . . . . Playmate
••• 0:34—Nude on spiral staircase, then on floor.
••• 0:36—In lingerie, then nude during modeling session with lots of sheets.
Lisa Matthews . . . . Playmate
•• 0:19—Breasts and buns, while in the desert.
••• 0:20—Nude in a house.
Kym Paige . . . . Playmate
•• 0:14—In lingerie during bedroom fantasy, then breasts and buns.
Kathy Shower . . . . Playmate
•• 0:04—Full frontal nudity in still photos. In lingerie in bedroom.
••• 0:05—Full frontal nudity on bed.
Reneé Tenison . . . . Playmate
••• 0:06—Nude in the desert.
••• 0:08—Nude working out in warehouse gym.
••• 0:10—Nude, taking a milk bath.
••• 0:11—Nude in bedroom.
Karin van Breeschooten . . . . Playmate
•• 0:27—In lingerie and nude in modeling session, then running around house with her twin sister. Quick cuts.
••• 0:28—Nude, in a house with her twin sister, posing, bathing and dressing.

Miryam van Breeschooten....................... Playmate
•• 0:27—In lingerie and nude in modeling session, then running around house with her twin sister. Quick cuts.
••• 0:28—Nude, in a house with her twin sister, posing, bathing and dressing.

Brittany York................................ Playmate
••• 0:23—Nude in studio.
••• 0:25—In lingerie and nude in Asian-style studio setting.

Betrayal of the Dove (1992)

Bobbi Brown................................ Dancer
•• 1:03—Buns in outfit, then breasts while dancing on stage in club.

Kelly Le Brock................................Una

Helen Slater................................Ellie
• 0:29—Brief tip of right breast while in bed with Billy Zane.
•• 0:30—Brief right breast, while in pool with Zane. Brief breasts in bed, then left breast.
••• 0:31—Very, very brief breasts, then more breasts while in bed with Zane.

The Betsy (1978)

Jane Alexander .... Alicia Hardeman

Kathleen Beller .... Betsy Hardeman
••• 0:12—Nude getting into swimming pool.
•• 1:14—Breasts lying under Tommy Lee Jones.

Lesley-Anne Down .... Lady Bobby Ayres
• 0:38—Brief left breast and upper half of buns, while with Tommy Lee Jones.
• 0:57—Very brief left breast in bed with Jones.

Katharine Ross......................... Sally Hardeman
• 1:02—Very brief upper half of left breast, while breast feeding baby in front of Laurence Olivier.

Betty Blue (1986; French)

Béatrice Dalle ....Betty
••• 0:01—Breasts making love in bed with Zorg. Long sequence.
••• 0:30—Nude on bed having sex with boyfriend.
••• 1:03—Nude trying to sleep in living room.
••• 1:21—Breasts in white tap pants in hallway.
••• 1:29—Breasts lying down with Zorg.
••• 1:39—Breasts sitting on bathtub crying & talking.

Consuela de Haviland .... Lisa

Between the Lines (1977)

Allison Argo................................ Dancer
• 0:28—Breasts dancing on stage.

Lindsay Crouse .... Abbie
• 0:52—Brief side view of right breast, lying in bed with John Heard.

Marilu Henner................................Danielle

Gwen Welles................................Laura
•• 0:32—Buns and breasts drying off with a towel in front of a mirror.

Beverly Hills Cop II (1987)

Rebecca Ferratti .... Playboy Playmate

Kymberly Herrin .... Playboy Playmate

Venice Kong .... Playboy Playmate

Luann Lee........................... Playboy Playmate

Peggy McIntaggart...........................Stripper
• 0:48—Very brief breasts, while dancing at the 385 North Club.

Brigitte Nielsen .... Karla Fry

Kym Paige.......................... Playboy Playmate

Ola Ray .... Playboy Playmate

Teal Roberts ....Stripper
•• 0:45—Breasts and buns several times, while wearing G-string and dancing at the 385 North Club.

Alana Soares .... Playboy Playmate

Kari Whitman .... Playboy Model

Beverly Hills Vamp (1989)

Michelle Bauer................................Kristina
• 0:12—Buns and brief side view of right breast in bed biting a guy.
•• 0:38—Breasts trying to get into Kyle's pants.

Britt Ekland .... Madam Cassandra

Greta Gibson....................... Screen Test Starlet
•• 0:53—Breasts and brief buns in G-string lying on Mr. Pendleton's desk.

Jillian Kesner ....Claudia

Debra Lamb ....Jessica
••• 0:36—Breasts and buns in red G-string posing for Russell while he photographs her.
••• 0:41—More breasts posing on bed.

Dawn Wildsmith ....Sherry Santa Monica

• *Beverly Hills Workout (1993; Video Tape)*

Tamara Carrera .... Herself
•• 0:08—Breasts and buns in T-back, while working out in backyard.
••• 0:27—Nude, while dancing and posing in backyard.
••• 0:45—Nude, while posing outdoors.

Angela Cornell................................ Herself
•• 0:04—Breasts, while working out on balcony with weights.
••• 0:24—Nude, while dancing and posing in backyard.
•• 0:42—Nude, while posing outdoors.

Kelly Jaye................................ Herself
••• 0:18—Breasts and buns in T-back, while working out by swimming pool.
••• 0:36—Nude, while dancing and posing in backyard.
•• 0:54—Nude, while posing outdoors.

Tamara Landry .... Herself
•• 0:11—Breasts and buns in T-back, while working out in backyard.
••• 0:30—Nude, while dancing and posing in backyard.
•• 0:49—Nude, while posing outdoors.

Shauna O'Brien .... Herself
•• 0:00—Breasts and buns in T-back, while working out in backyard.
••• 0:22—Nude, while dancing and posing in backyard.
•• 0:39—Nude, while posing outdoors.

Kathy Pasmore .... Herself
•• 0:14—Breasts and buns in T-back, while working out in backyard.
••• 0:33—Nude, while dancing and posing in backyard.
•• 0:51—Nude, while posing outdoors.

Beware of a Holy Whore (1971; German)

a.k.a. Warnung Vo Einer Heiligen Nutte

Hanna Schygulla ....Woman
• 1:15—Breasts, when sitting on bed, buns, while walking to the bathroom. Very brief right breast, while leaning out of the bathroom to talk.

Beyond Desire (1994)

Sharon Farrell ....Shirley

Kari Wührer................................Rita
• 0:06—Very brief buns in panties, while starting to make love with William Forsythe.

- •• 0:07—Left breast, while lying in bed next to Forsythe, then breasts, when getting out of bed and putting on dress.
- • 0:09—Brief left breast, when getting back into bed with Forsythe.
- •• 0:10—Breasts, while in bed with Forsythe.
- •• 0:32—Breasts, while lying in bed with Forsythe.
- • 0:33—Brief breasts, while standing up in Corvette and showing her breasts, when riding through the streets of Las Vegas.
- • 0:43—Brief, partial buns under short dress, while bending over desk to talk to Leo Rossi.
- • 0:51—Breasts, while sitting in bathtub with Forsythe.
- • 1:02—Very brief buns under short dress when getting slapped by Rossi.

Beyond Erotica *(1973)*

Andrea Rau . . . . Lola
- • 0:26—Breasts, undressing in her bedroom.
- •• 0:30—Nude, undressing, then lying in bed, then trying on bunny costume.
- • 0:47—Left breast, while lying on the floor.
- • 0:56—Brief buns, running around in her cell.
- • 0:57—Briefly nude, behind wall with holes in it.
- • 0:59—Left breast, seen though hole in the wall.
- •• 1:10—Breasts in her bedroom.
- • 1:23—Left breast, in flashback to 0:47 scene.

Beyond Forgiveness *(1994)*

a.k.a. Blood of the Innocent

Joanna Trzepiechinska . . . . Anna
- •• 1:09—In white bra, then right breast, while making love with Thomas Ian Griffith.

Beyond Innocence *(1988)*

Katia Caballero . . . . Marthe Foscari
- •• 0:29—Breasts, after taking off nightgown in bed with Paul, then making love.
- •• 0:31—Buns, brief lower frontal nudity and side view of right breast, while looking out the window.
- • 0:32—Very brief right breast, while putting on robe.
- • 0:37—Breasts, while in bed with Paul after he moves the covers down.
- •• 1:08—Left breast, while lying in bed with Paul.

Beyond Obsession *(1982)*

Eleonora Giorgi . . . . Nina
- •• 0:01—Breasts, taking off her top and getting into the shower with Tom Berenger.
- • 0:59—Right breast in bed with Marcello Mastroianni, brief right breast after.

Beyond the Door II *(1977; Italian)*

Daria Nicolodi . . . . Dora
- • 0:30—Buns, in the shower.
- • 0:47—Brief left breast in gaping nightgown, sitting up in bed.

Beyond the Door III *(1989; Yugoslavian)*

Savina Gersak . . . . Sava

Mary Kohnert . . . . Beverly
- •• 0:03—Breasts taking a shower.

Beyond the Law *(1992; Made for Cable Movie)*

Linda Fiorentino . . . . Renee
- ••• 0:52—Breasts while making love with Charlie Sheen. Brief buns in T-back panties.

Beyond the Limit *(1983)*

Elpidia Carrillo . . . . Clara
- •• 0:31—Breasts making love with Richard Gere. Long scene.
- •• 1:08—Breasts talking to Gere. Another long scene.

Big Bad Mama *(1974)*

Angie Dickinson. . . . . Wilma McClatchie
- • 0:38—Buns, getting into bed with Tom Skerritt. Brief right breast, while on top of him.
- ••• 0:48—Breasts in bed with William Shatner.
- • 1:00—Very brief breasts, pulling the sheets up while lying in bed with Shatner.
- ••• 1:18—Breasts and brief full frontal nudity putting a shawl and then a dress on.

Sally Kirkland . . . . Barney's Woman
- •• 0:13—Breasts and buns waiting for Barney then throwing shoe at Billy Jean.
- • 1:23—Brief breasts, covering herself up scene from 0:13 during end credits.

Robin Lee . . . . Polly McClatchie
- • 0:08—Brief left breast in gaping dress when cops try to pull her car over.
- • 0:22—In see-through dress on stage with her sister and a stripper.
- • 0:32—Brief breasts running around the bedroom chasing her sister.
- • 0:52—Buns, taking off her nightgown and getting into bed with Tom Skerritt.

Joan Prather. . . . . Jane Kingston
- •• 1:15—Breasts and buns in the bathroom with Tom Skerritt.

Susan Sennet . . . . Billy Jean
- • 0:50—Breasts and buns getting onto bed with Tom Skerritt.
- •• 0:51—Breasts and buns, getting out of bed with Skerritt.
- • 0:52—Brief buns, getting back into bed with Skerritt along with Polly.

Big Bad Mama II *(1987)*

Danielle Brisebois. . . . . Billy Jean McClatchie
- ••• 0:12—Breasts with Julie McCullough playing in a pond underneath a waterfall.

Angie Dickinson. . . . . Wilma McClatchie
- • 0:48—Very brief full frontal nudity putting on her shawl scene from *Big Bad Mama* superimposed over a car chase scene.
- •• 0:52—Breasts and brief buns (probably a body double) in bed with Robert Culp. You don't see her face with the body.

Kelli Maroney . . . . Willie McClatchie

Julie McCullough . . . . Polly McClatchie
- •• 0:12—Breasts with Danielle Brisebois playing in a pond underneath a waterfall.
- •• 0:36—In lingerie, then breasts sitting on Jordan who is tied up in bed.

Linda Shayne . . . . Bank Teller

The Big Bet *(1985)*

Stephanie Blake . . . . Mrs. Roberts
- ••• 0:04—Breasts sitting on bed, then making love with Chris.
- •• 0:37—Nude on bed with Chris. Shot at fast speed, he runs between bedrooms.
- •• 0:59—Full frontal nudity in bed again. Shot at fast speed.

Elizabeth Cochrell . . . . Sister in Stag Film
- ••• 1:05—Breasts and buns, undressing and getting into bathtub in a video tape that Chris is watching.

•• 1:08—Breasts again on video tape, when Chris watches it on TV at home.

Kim Evenson . . . . Beth

•• 0:36—Right breast, sitting on couch with Chris.

•• 0:45—Brief breasts, twice, taking off swimsuit top.

•• 0:54—Brief breasts three times in elevator when Chris pulls her sweater up.

•• 1:06—Nude when Chris fantasizes about her being in the video tape that he's watching. Long shot.

••• 1:19—In white bra and panties, then nude while undressing for Chris.

Monique Gabrielle . . . . Fantasy Girl in Elevator

••• 0:51—In purple bra, then eventually nude in elevator with Chris.

Sylvia Kristel . . . . Michelle

• 0:07—Left breast in open nightgown while Chris tries to fix her sink.

•• 0:20—Breasts dressing while Chris watches through binoculars.

•• 0:28—Breasts undressing while Chris watches through binoculars.

••• 0:40—Breasts getting out of the shower and drying herself off.

• 1:00—Breasts getting into bed while Chris watches through binoculars.

••• 1:13—Breasts in bedroom with Chris, then making love.

Sheila Lussier . . . . n.a.

Jill Terashita . . . . Koko

The Big Bird Cage (1972)

Teda Bracci . . . . Bull Jones

•• 0:15—Breasts in front of the guard, Rocco.

• 0:51—Very brief right breast, then left breast during fight with Pam Grier. Brief left breast standing up in rice paddy.

Anitra Ford . . . . Terry

• 0:15—Left breast and buns taking shower. Brief lower frontal nudity after putting shirt on when leaving.

• 0:19—Brief lower frontal nudity while turning around.

• 0:44—Brief left breast during gang rape.

• 1:14—Brief left breast in gaping dress. Dark.

Pam Grier . . . . Blossom

Candice Roman . . . . Carla

• 0:16—Buns, while in the shower.

Carol Speed . . . . Mickie

• *Big Bust Casting Call (1992; Video Tape)*

Keisha . . . . Keisha

••• 0:40—In sexy swimsuit in spa, then breasts after taking off her top. (Wearing sunglasses.)

Nikki Dial . . . . Roxanne

••• 0:09—In bra and panties, then nude during her audition.

Chona Jason . . . . Herself

••• 0:25—Breasts and buns in G-string during audition, undressing and trying on bra and panties in front of mirror.

Tami Monroe . . . . Jessica

••• 0:00—Nude, during her audition.

Missy Warner . . . . Herself

••• 0:31—In bra and G-string, undressing for audition, then nude in front of mirror.

The Big Chill (1983)

Glenn Close . . . . Sara

• 0:27—Breasts sitting down in the shower crying.

Mary Kay Place . . . . Meg

Meg Tilly . . . . Chloé

JoBeth Williams . . . . Karen

The Big Doll House (1971)

Judy Brown . . . . Marnie Collier

• 0:03—Very brief breasts while getting blouse taken off and searched before going to jail.

•• 0:04—Right breast getting examined by the doctor. Brief left breast. Long scene.

•• 0:32—Breasts after Pam Grief leaves shower room.

••• 1:06—Breasts a lot while tied down on table by the guard. Mostly left breast. Long scene.

• 1:42—Breasts while changing blouse while riding in back of truck.

Roberta Collins . . . . Alcott

••• 0:33—Breasts in shower. Seen through blurry window by prison worker, Fred. Blurry, but nice.

• 0:34—Brief left breast, while opening her blouse for Fred.

Pam Grier . . . . Grear

• 0:28—Very brief most of right breast rolling over in bed.

•• 0:32—Breasts getting her back washed by Collier. Arms in the way a little bit.

• 0:44—Left breast covered with mud sticking out of her top after wrestling with Alcott.

Brooke Mills . . . . Harrad

• 0:28—Side of right breast, while lying in bed before rolling over.

Christiane Schmidtmer . . . . Miss Dietrich

Pat Woodell . . . . Bodine

• 0:27—Brief breasts hung by wrists and whipped by a guard. Hair covers most of her breasts.

The Big Easy (1987)

Ellen Barkin . . . . Anne Osborne

• 0:32—Brief buns, when jumping up in kitchen after pinching a guy who she thinks is Quaid.

The Big Hurt (1987; Australian)

Nikki Lane . . . . Tank Girl #1

• 1:26—Possible full frontal nudity standing in water filled tube. Can't recognize her because wearing a swim mask and breathing apparatus.

The Big Man (1991; British)

a.k.a. Crossing the Line

Julie Graham . . . . Melanie

•• 1:09—Breasts when Liam Neeson undresses her and starts to make love with her.

The Big Sleep (1978; British)

Candy Clark . . . . Camilla Sternwood

••• 0:18—Breasts, sitting in a chair when Robert Mitchum comes in after a guy is murdered.

• 0:30—Brief breasts in a photograph that Mitchum is looking at.

• 0:38—Breasts in the photos again. Out of focus.

•• 0:39—Breasts sitting in chair during recollection of the murder.

•• 1:03—Very brief full frontal nudity in bed, throwing open the sheets for Mitchum.

• 1:05—Very, very brief buns, while getting up out of bed.

Joan Collins . . . . Agnes Lozelle

Sarah Miles . . . . Charlotte Sternwood

Diana Quick . . . . Mona Grant

The Big Town (1987)

Suzy Amis . . . . Aggie Donaldson

• 0:56—Very brief lower half of right breast, when falling back onto bed with Matt Dillon.

Lolita Davidovich. Black Lace Stripper
Lee Grant . . . . .Ferguson Edwards
Diane Lane . . . . Lorry Dane
- • 0:50—Doing a strip routine in the club wearing a G-string and pasties while Matt Dillon watches.
- ••• 1:17—Breasts, while making love on bed with Dillon in hotel room.
- • 1:20—Very brief partial left breast, when the sheet she's holding drops slightly while sitting in bed.
- • 1:27—Brief left breast wearing pasties walking into dressing room while Dillon plays craps.

Bikini Bistro *(1995)*

(Unrated version reviewed.)

Amy Lynn Baxter. . . . . Judy
- ••• 0:12—Nude, while changing into a swimsuit in room with the two other girls.
- • 0:53—Nude, while changing into swimsuit.
- ••• 0:56—Breasts and buns, while making love in back room with Russel.

Marilyn Chambers. . . . . Marilyn
- ••• 1:17—Nude, after opening her bra for Colin, then making love.

Isabelle Fortea . . . . Donna
- ••• 0:12—Nude, while changing into a swimsuit in room with the two other girls.
- • 0:37—Buns in swimsuit.
- •• 0:48—Breasts, after taking off her swimsuit top in kitchen with Ron.
- • 0:52—Full frontal nudity, while changing into swimsuit.
- ••• 1:14—Full frontal nudity, while making love in the kitchen with Ron.

Joan Gerardi . . . . Luanne
- ••• 0:12—Full frontal nudity, while changing into a swimsuit in room with the two other girls.
- ••• 0:24—Nude, while making love with David in a car. Long scene.
- • 0:32—Buns, while in swimsuit in restaurant.
- •• 0:38—Full frontal nudity, while making love outside at night with David.
- • 0:43—Buns in swimsuit.
- • 0:52—Full frontal nudity, while changing into swimsuit.
- • 1:05—Breasts, while on roof top with David.

The Bikini Carwash Company *(1992)*

(Unrated version reviewed.)

Suzanne Ager . . . . Foxy
- • 0:59—Buns in G-string, doing strip routine.

Rikki Brando . . . . Amy
- • 0:15—Brief breasts when Stanley steals her bikini top.
- • 0:30—Brief breasts during water fight.
- • 0:31—Brief breasts at car wash.
- • 0:43—Brief right breast, while making love with Donovan.
- •• 0:44—Buns and breasts, making love with Donovan.
- •• 0:59—Breasts, making out in car with Donovan.
- ••• 1:00—More breasts in car with Donovan.
- • 1:02—Brief breasts in car wash.
- •• 1:12—Breasts posing for photos.

Sara Suzanne Brown . . . . Sunny
- • 0:15—Brief breasts when Stanley steals her bikini top.
- •• 0:25—Breasts, washing windshield and side window.
- ••• 0:26—More breasts while window washing.
- •• 0:30—Breasts during water fight.
- •• 0:31—Breasts at car wash.
- •• 0:35—Breasts running after a guy who stole her bikini top.
- ••• 0:46—Breasts and buns in G-string, hand washing a customer with Rita.
- ••• 0:47—Breasts and buns, dancing inside car wash.
- •• 0:53—Breasts outside at car wash.
- ••• 1:02—Nude, soaped up in car wash with Melissa and Rita.
- ••• 1:12—Breasts, posing for photos.
- •• 1:15—Breasts when Stanley takes her top off.

Neriah Davis . . . . .Rita
- ••• 0:15—Breasts taking off her bikini top so Stanley can "catch some fish" with it.
- ••• 0:18—Breasts and buns, making love with Big Bruce.
- •• 0:43—Breasts and buns, making love with Big Bruce. (same as 0:18)
- ••• 0:45—Brief left breast, getting dressed. Then buns, after forgetting to put on her bikini bottoms.
- ••• 0:46—Breasts and buns in G-string, hand washing a customer with Sunny.
- ••• 0:47—Buns, bending over while wearing a cowboy outfit.
- ••• 0:48—Breasts and buns, dancing inside car wash with Sunny and Melissa.
- ••• 1:02—Nude, soaped up in car wash with Sunny and Melissa.
- •• 1:11—Buns, posing while wearing cowboy outfit.
- ••• 1:13—Breasts and buns.

Kristie Ducati . . . . Melissa
- • 0:13—Buns in G-string, while at the beach.
- ••• 0:20—Breasts, taking off her bikini top in shack with Jack.
- •• 0:26—Nude, changing clothes in car wash.
- •• 0:30—Breasts during water fight.
- • 0:32—Brief breasts in Jack's fantasy.
- • 0:45—Brief left breast and buns, dressing.
- ••• 0:47—Breasts and buns, dancing inside car wash.
- ••• 1:02—Nude, soaped up in car wash with Rita and Sunny.
- ••• 1:07—Breasts and buns, making love in shack with Jack. Wow!
- ••• 1:12—Breasts, posing for photos.

Landon Hall. . . . . .Ms. Hawthorne
- • 0:51—Buns in lingerie when her clothes get vacuumed off.

Missy Warner. . . . . .Awesome Beach Girl
- • 0:00—Buns, on beach in a very small swimsuit.
- •• 0:02—Brief right breast, turning over, then breasts while yelling at Jack.

The Bikini Carwash Company II *(1993)*

(Unrated version reviewed.)

Melissa Barrick. . . . . Cyndi
- ••• 0:38—In black lingerie, then breasts during kitchen commercial.
- ••• 0:42—Breasts and buns under black body stocking in "Rock Me" music video number.
- ••• 0:46—In lingerie, then breasts during repairman commercial.
- • 0:52—Brief breasts, while making out on kitchen table.
- • 1:28—Breasts during music video number at the carwash.

Rikki Brando. . . . . Amy
- ••• 0:09—Breasts with the other three girls, celebrating in office during music video number.
- •• 1:09—Buns in lingerie, then breasts in dressing room with Marshall.

Sara Suzanne Brown . . . . Sunny
- ••• 0:09—Breasts with the other three girls, celebrating in office during music video number.
- •• 0:16—Breasts at carwash during music video number. (Wearing yellow bikini bottoms.)
- • 0:24—Buns in lingerie in offices of The Miracle Network with Rita.

- • 0:27—Brief breasts, twice, while flashing her breasts in office.
- ••• 1:16—In black lingerie, then breasts in office fantasy.
- •• 1:29—Breasts and buns in bikini bottoms during music video number at the carwash.

Carrie Chambers . . . . Chairwoman
- • 0:26—Brief back side of left breast in her office with Derek.

Neriah Davis . . . . Rita
- ••• 0:09—Breasts with the other three girls, celebrating in office during music video number.
- ••• 0:16—Breasts at carwash during music video number. (Wearing pink bikini bottoms.)
- • 0:24—Buns in lingerie in offices of The Miracle Network with Sunny.
- • 0:27—Brief breasts while flashing her breasts in office.
- ••• 0:35—Breasts and buns in studio when she's caught without her clothes on.
- • 1:15—Brief breasts and buns during clean up at the studio.
- •• 1:29—Breasts and buns in swimsuit during music video number at the carwash.

Kristie Ducati. . . . . Melissa
- •• 0:00—Breasts in back of limousine with a guy.
- ••• 0:09—Breasts with the other three girls, celebrating in office during music video number.
- •• 0:16—Breasts at carwash during music video number. (Wearing orange bikini bottoms.)
- ••• 1:20—Breasts and buns while making love with Derek in the TV studio.
- •• 1:29—Breasts and buns in bikini bottom during music video number at the carwash.

Beckie Mullen . . . . School Teacher

Tonya Poole . . . . .Uncredited Bikini Girl Blonde
- •• 0:16—Breasts at carwash during music video number. (Wearing black bikini bottoms.)
- •• 0:35—Breasts, when vacuum sucks her bikini top off at the carwash.
- ••• 0:40—In black lingerie, then buns in T-back and breasts in motorcycle cop commercial.
- ••• 0:42—Breasts and buns in T-back in "Rock Me" music video number.
- ••• 0:57—Breasts, while on kitchen table during commercial.
- •• 1:29—Breasts during music video number at the carwash.

Bikini Drive-In (1995)

(Unrated version reviewed.)

Michelle Bauer . . . . .Dyanne Lynn
- ••• 0:40—Breasts and buns in swimsuit relaxing by the pool and swimming. Some under water shots.
- ••• 0:43—Breasts, after getting out of the pool after talking on the phone, then getting oil rubbed on her breasts by her servant.

Sara Bellomo. . . . . Carrie
- ••• 0:05—Breasts, after taking off her purple swimsuit top at the beach and rubbing suntan lotion on herself.
- ••• 0:15—Buns and breasts, while making love in bathtub with her boyfriend.
- • 0:24—Breasts under red top, when wiping her face off after water fight while cleaning the drive-in.

Robin Chaney . . . . Snack Bar A-Go-Go Girl
- • 0:58—Brief buns in black lingerie outfit while dancing in the snack bar.
- • 1:01—Brief buns in black lingerie in closer shot.
- • 1:02—More brief buns.

Deborah Dutch . . . . Sorority Sister
- • 0:23—Very brief right breast, when her white polka dot top gets pulled down during water fight while cleaning up the drive-in. Very brief breasts, while running around afterwards.
- • 0:58—Brief buns in black and gold swimsuit.
- • 0:59—Breasts while collecting money at drive-in entrance.

Nikki Fritz . . . . Susan
- • 0:53—Buns in swimsuit, after changing into swimsuit in restroom.
- ••• 1:10—Nude, while making love with Tom in drive-in office.

Becky LeBeau. . . . . .Candy
- ••• 0:51—In white bra and panties, then buns and breasts, while dancing in radio studio in front of Fred Olen Ray.

Tané McClure . . . . Mandy
- • 0:55—Brief buns, in yellow swimsuit, while dancing next to drive-in sign.
- • 0:58—Brief buns in swimsuit, while dancing next to drive-in sign.
- ••• 1:07—Buns in swimsuit and breasts, while dancing on hood of car.

Melissa Anne Moore . . . . .Actress in Film
- • 0:59—Brief breasts on bed in film shown on drive-in screen.

Ashlie Rhey . . . . Kim Taylor
- ••• 0:05—Breasts after opening her red swimsuit top and rubbing suntan lotion on herself.
- • 0:24—Breasts under white T-shirt, when wiping her face off after water fight while cleaning the drive-in.
- ••• 0:34—Breasts and buns, while making love in bed with Richard Gabai.
- • 0:54—Brief right breast, after Gabai takes of her bikini top in office.

• *Bikini Hoe Down* (1997)

Griffin Drew . . . . Missy Sue
- •• 0:13—Nude, undressing then bathing in a stream.
- ••• 0:16—Breasts, while making love with the hippy artist guy in stream.
- ••• 0:53—Nude, while showering with the other three girls.
- ••• 1:00—Breasts, while making love with the hippy artist guy.

Maureen Flaherty . . . . May
- ••• 0:47—In bra, then breasts and brief partial buns, while making love in barn with Jeb.
- ••• 0:53—Nude, while showering with the other three girls.
- •• 1:19—Breasts, while dancing on stage during bikini hoe down.

Ashlie Rhey . . . . April
- • 0:07—Brief buns in swimsuit bottom.
- • 0:40—Brief buns in panties and brief breasts while changing clothes.
- ••• 0:53—Nude, while showering with the other three girls.
- 1:10—Nude, while making love in hot tub with David.
- •• 1:19—Breasts, while dancing on stage during bikini hoe down.

Shayna Ryan . . . . June
- •• 0:01—In black bra, then breasts, while making love in bed with Jeffrey.
- • 0:07—Brief buns in swimsuit bottom.
- ••• 0:23—Breasts, while making love in bed with Jeffrey.
- • 0:40—In lingerie, brief buns in panties and breasts while changing clothes.
- ••• 0:53—Nude, while showering with the other three girls.
- •• 1:19—Breasts, while dancing on stage during bikini hoe down.

• *Bikini Hotel* (1996)

Katie Colburn . . . . Eunice
- 0:32—Brief breasts, while taking off bikini top in front of registration desk.
- 0:38—Buns in T-back while making bed and vacuuming.
- 0:40—Buns in T-back while vacuuming.
- 0:47—Breasts, after taking off her bikini top during card game.
- 0:48—Buns in swimsuit, while gathering clothes.
- 0:51—Brief buns in T-back.
- 0:56—Breasts during card game.

J. J. North . . . . Samantha Vance
- •• 0:01—Breasts, while in bed with her boyfriend, Brad.
- 0:12—Brief buns in T-back, getting out of spa. Very, very brief right breast while putting on white blouse.
- 0:17—Brief breasts and buns in panties, while trying on different outfits.
- 0:28—Breasts, while changing clothes in room.
- 0:48—Brief breasts, while putting on swimsuit top in bedroom.

Bianca Rocilili . . . . Tiki Hotel Maid
- 0:41—Brief breasts when her bikini top pops off.
- 1:08—Buns in white lingerie.

Stella Stevens . . . . Gail Regent

Julie Strain . . . . Raquel
- •• 0:36—Breasts and buns during interview.
- 0:49—Breasts in hallway, while walking past Japanese guy.
- 0:54—Breasts, after taking off robe.
- 1:00—Buns in swimsuit.

Bikini Island (1991)

Holly Floria . . . . Annie Kelly
- 0:03—Buns in panties, then breasts in shower (seen through plastic shower curtain). Don't see her face.
- 0:28—Buns in one piece white swimsuit at the beach.
- 0:35—Buns in the shower. Don't see her face.

Cyndi Pass . . . . Kari
- 0:47—Brief upper half of right breast, while changing swimsuit tops at the beach.
- 0:55—Side of left breast, while taking off her top on bed with Jack.
- 0:59—Buns, in black bra and panties after Max disappears.

Shannon Stiles . . . . Nikki
- 0:35—Breasts in bed with Jack taking off her top while someone watches through keyhole.

Bikini Squad (1993)

Donna Baltron . . . . Muffy
- •• 0:38—Breasts, while on sofa with David after taking off her bra.

Maureen Flaherty . . . . Summer
- ••• 0:56—Breasts, while making love in bed with Biff.

Julie Strain . . . . Actress
- 0:10—Partial buns in swimsuit when leaving the casting office.
- •• 0:21—Breasts, while making love with the casting guy.

Bikini Summer (1991)

Rebekah Alfred . . . . D.A. Rachel Green
- •• 1:20—In bra, then breasts and buns in dressing room, trying on swimsuit after everyone has left.

Melinda Armstrong . . . . Cheryl
- 0:07—Very brief breasts and partial buns, in bathroom when Chet interrupts her.
- 0:25—Close-up of buns in swimsuit, while bending over.
- ••• 0:35—Nude in swimming pool and talking to Burt. Nice, long scene.
- •• 0:49—Breasts and buns, trying on swimsuits, then having a water fight with Shelley Michelle.
- 0:51—Buns in swimsuit, while at the beach.
- ••• 1:17—Full frontal nudity in swimming pool flashback.

Michelle Grassnick . . . . Debbie

Lori Jo Hendrix . . . . Smart Girl on Beach

Kelli Konop . . . . Rene

Shelley Michelle . . . . Jazz
- •• 0:33—Breasts and buns in the shower while Max peeks through hole.
- •• 0:49—Breasts and buns, trying on swimsuits, then having a water fight with Cheryl.

Nicole Sassaman . . . . Band Member

Missy Warner . . . . Mindy

Bikini Summer 2 (1992)

Avalon Anders . . . . Clarice
- ••• 0:11—Breasts in sexy outfit, acting as a dominatrix with Harry in his office.
- •• 0:13—More breasts, while spanking Harry in his office.
- 0:33—Buns and brief left breast, while teasing Harry.
- •• 0:37—In black body stocking, then breasts with Harry in his office.
- ••• 0:41—More breasts in white corset with Harry.

Melinda Armstrong . . . . Venessa
- ••• 0:05—Breasts and buns, while taking a shower.
- ••• 0:52—Breasts, taking off swimsuit top in bedroom. Breasts and buns, taking a shower.
- •• 0:54—Breasts and buns in T-back panties, taking off robe and getting into bed, then sitting up to eat breakfast.

Carrie Bittner . . . . Sandra
- 0:15—Buns in two piece swimsuit, while walking with Sandy.
- •• 0:38—Breasts (she's the blonde), taking off her T-shirt and jumping into the pool with Sandy.
- 0:40—Very brief breasts, while running past some guys.
- •• 0:42—More breasts, while running around the backyard.
- •• 0:44—More breasts and buns in swimsuit, while running around some more.

Tracy Dali . . . . Anita
- 0:42—Brief buns, while bending over in maid outfit by the pool.
- 0:49—Buns, in black lingerie after taking off her maid outfit in front of Harry.
- •• 0:51—Breasts in back seat of limousine, while making love with Harry.
- 0:55—Brief buns, while bending over in maid outfit.
- 1:00—Brief buns, while bending over in maid outfit.

Maureen Flaherty . . . . Bridget
- •• 0:04—Breasts, when waking up in bed in the morning with William.
- •• 0:29—Breasts while in bed with William.

Jessica Hahn . . . . Marilyn
- 0:03—In black bra in bed with Harry, then buns in black G-string, climbing on his back.

Tammy Marcel . . . . Sandy
- 0:15—Buns in two piece swimsuit, while walking with Sandra.
- •• 0:38—Breasts (she's the brunette), taking off her T-shirt and jumping into the pool with Sandra.
- 0:40—Very brief breasts, while running past some guys.
- •• 0:42—More breasts, while running around the backyard.
- •• 0:44—More breasts and buns in swimsuit, while running around some more.

• *Bikini Summer 3* *(1997)*

Heather-Elizabeth Parkhurst. . . . . Jamie
- ••• 0:10—In bra and panties, then breasts and buns, while trying on swimsuits.
- ••• 0:22—Nude, with her two girlfriends in the shower, then getting dressed.
- 0:40—Breasts, while trying on clothes in pro shop with her two girlfriends.
- 1:01—Breasts, while trying on swimsuits.

Tiffany Turner . . . . Devereaux
- ••• 0:22—Nude, with her two girlfriends in the shower, then getting dressed.
- •• 0:34—Breasts and buns in panties, while making out with her new boyfriend on the beach at night.
- ••• 0:40—Breasts, while trying on clothes in pro shop with her two girlfriends.
- ••• 0:58—Breasts, while making love in bed with Peter.

• *Bikini Traffic School* *(1997)*

Shari Eckert . . . . Vicky
- ••• 0:05—Breasts and buns in T-back, while dancing on stage with Marcie and Traci.
- •• 0:18—Breasts, while frolicking in the pool with Marcie and Vicki.
- •• 0:21—Breasts, while sunbathing.
- ••• 0:51—Breasts and very brief lower frontal nudity, while making love with the tennis instructor on tennis court.
- ••• 0:58—Breasts, while making love with the pool guy in spa.

Maureen Flaherty . . . . Traci
- ••• 0:03—Breasts and buns in T-back, while dancing on stage with Marcie and Vicky.
- ••• 0:13—Breasts and buns in T-back, while dancing on stage with Marcie.
- •• 0:18—Breasts and buns in swimsuit bottom, while frolicking in the pool with Vicky and Marcie.
- •• 0:21—Breasts, while sunbathing.
- ••• 0:25—Breasts, during fantasy with the pool guy.
- ••• 0:45—Breasts, after taking off her top during tennis match and playing tennis against Marcie.
- •• 1:15—Breasts and buns, while making love with the pool guy in workout room.
- •• 1:22—Breasts, while on stage during traffic school lessons.

Shayna Ryan . . . . Marcie
- •• 0:01—Breasts, while in kitchen and in bedroom with Skipper.
- ••• 0:03—Breasts, while dancing on stage with Traci and Vicky.
- •• 0:11—Breasts, while making love in back seat of car with .
- ••• 0:13—Breasts, while dancing on stage with Traci.
- •• 0:18—Breasts and buns in swimsuit bottom, while frolicking in the pool with Vicky and Traci.
- •• 0:21—Breasts, while sunbathing.
- ••• 0:39—Breasts, while making love with the pool guy during her fantasy.
- •• 0:42—Breasts, while making love with Skippy on the floor.
- • 0:45—Very brief breasts, while flashing Traci on miniature gold course.
- ••• 0:45—Breasts, after taking off her top during tennis match and playing tennis against Traci.
- ••• 1:02—Breasts and parital buns, while making love on top of a table.
- •• 1:22—Breasts, while on stage during traffic school lessons.

Bilitis *(1977; French)*

Patti D'Arbanville . . . . Bilitis
- •• 0:25—Breasts, while copying Melissa undressing.
- •• 0:27—Breasts, while on tree.
- ••• 0:31—Full frontal nudity, after taking off swimsuit with Melissa.
- • 0:36—Buns, while cleaning herself in the bathroom.
- •• 0:59—Breasts and buns, while making love with Melissa.

Catherine Leprince . . . . Helene
- •• 0:13—Breasts taking off dress and getting into bed with Bilitis.

Billy Bathgate *(1991)*

Moira Kelly . . . . Rebecca

Nicole Kidman. . . . . Drew Preston
- •• 0:42—Briefly nude, throwing off towel in front of a vanity with three mirrors.
- •• 0:52—Very brief full frontal nudity underwater. Brief full frontal nudity getting out of water and putting on dress.

Rachel York . . . . Embassy Club Singer

Bio-Hazard *(1984)*

Angelique Pettyjohn . . . . Lisa Martyn
- •• 0:30—Partial left breast on couch with Mitchell. In beige bra and panties talking on telephone, breast almost falling out of bra.
- ••• 1:15—Left breast, on couch with Mitchell, in out-take scene during the end credits.
- • 1:16—Upper half of left breast on couch again during a different take.

Biohazard The Alien Force *(1994)*

Katheryn Culliver Pierce. . . . . Shana Alexander
- ••• 0:50—Breasts and buns, while making love on top of her boyfriend on the floor. Long scene.
- •• 0:59—Breasts, while sitting up in bed during nightmare when her boyfriend morphs into creature.

Bird on a Wire *(1990)*

Goldie Hawn . . . . Marianne Graves
- • 0:31—Buns, in open dress climbing up ladder with Mel Gibson.
- • 1:18—Very brief top of right breast rolling over on top of Gibson in bed. Don't see her face.

Joan Severance . . . . Rachel Varnay

Birdy *(1985)*

Sandra Beall . . . . Shirley

Elizabeth Whitcraft . . . . Rosanne

Maude Winchester . . . . Doris Robinson
- •• 1:32—Breasts in car letting Mathew Modine feel her.

Karen Young . . . . Hannah Rourke

The Bitch *(1979; British)*

Joan Collins . . . . Fontaine Khaled
- • 0:03—Brief breasts in the shower with a guy.
- •• 0:24—Brief breasts taking black corset off for the chauffeur in the bedroom, then buns getting out of bed and walking to the bathroom.
- • 1:01—Left breast after making love in bed.

Sue Lloyd . . . . Vanessa Grant
- • 1:12—Side view of left breast and breasts in the swimming pool.

Pamela Salem . . . . Lynn
- •• 0:46—Breasts in bed making love with a guy after playing at a casino.

Bits and Pieces *(1985)*

Sandy Brooke . . . . Mrs. Talbot
- ••• 1:03—Breasts in bathtub washing herself before the killer drowns her. Very brief right breast when struggling.

• 1:09—Brief breasts under water in bathtub, dead.

Tally Chanel . . . . Jennifer

Sheila Lussier . . . . Tanya

•• 0:07—In bra, tied down by Arthur, then brief breasts as he cuts her bra off before he kills her. Brief right breast several times with blood on her.

Bitter Harvest *(1993)*

Patsy Kensit . . . . Jolene Leder

••• 0:40—In black bodysuit, then left breast while making love with Stephen Baldwin in bed. Breasts in bathtub.

• 0:41—Left breast, while lying in bathtub with Baldwin.

•• 0:49—Brief breasts in bed with Baldwin and Jennifer Rubin.

Jennifer Rubin . . . . Kelly Ann Walsh

• 0:21—Brief breasts while wearing panties, trying on clothes in front of closet mirror.

•• 0:28—Brief breasts, then left breast while adjusting her robe so Stephen Baldwin can give her a massage.

••• 0:30—Breasts, after taking off robe, walking to bedroom with Baldwin and making love.

Bitter Moon *(1994)*

Olivia Brunaux . . . . Cindy

Kristin Scott-Thomas . . . . Fiona

• 2:14—Very, very brief breasts, while sitting up in bed after Peter Coyote shoots Emmanuelle Seinger.

Emmanuelle Seigner . . . . Mimi

•• 0:25—Breasts, while in front of fire with Peter Coyote.

•• 0:26—Breasts, when sitting up in bed. Buns, while standing at window.

•• 0:30—Nude, dancing in white dress in front of Coyote.

••• 0:31—Breasts in open robe, drooling milk over her breasts, then rubbing them.

•• 0:46—Buns in garter belt and stockings.

• 1:03—Side view of buns, when sleeping in bed, then brief right breast while putting on red dress.

Bizarre *(1986; Italian)*

Florence Guerin . . . . Laurie

•• 0:03—Breasts on bed with Guido. Lower frontal nudity while he molests her with a pistol.

••• 0:18—Nude after taking off her clothes in hotel room with a guy. Nice.

••• 0:30—Full frontal nudity making love with Edward in the water.

• 0:34—Brief side of right breast, taking off robe in bathroom with Edward. (He's made himself up to look like a woman.)

••• 0:36—Breasts in white panties making love with Edward.

•• 0:40—Breasts and brief lower frontal nudity in Guido's office with him.

••• 0:45—Nude, playing outside with Edward, then making love with his toe.

•• 0:47—Breasts getting out of bed and putting a blouse on.

•• 0:49—Breasts with Edward when Guido comes in.

• 1:11—Breasts sitting in chair talking to Edward.

• 1:20—Lower frontal nudity, putting the phone down there.

• 1:28—Buns and lower frontal nudity on bed when Guido rips her clothes off and rapes her.

Black Belt *(1992)*

Sean'a Arthur . . . . Reporter

Deirdre Imershein . . . . Shanna

••• 1:08—Breasts in bed, making love with Don "The Dragon" Wilson.

Mia M. Ruiz . . . . Hooker

••• 0:04—Breasts, while sitting on bed.

• 0:16—Breasts, while dead on bed, covered with blood.

• ***Black Caesar*** *(1973)*

Gloria Hendry . . . . Helen

• 0:43—Very brief breasts when Fred Williamson rips her nightgown top off and struggles with her.

• 1:04—Brief partial back side of left breast and buns, while making love in bed with Williamson.

• 1:05—Brief full frontal nudity, while making love with Williamson in bed.

• 1:07—Brief right and left breasts, when getting out of bed.

Black Day Blue Night *(1995)*

Michelle Forbes . . . . Rinda Wooley

Mia Sara . . . . Hallie Schrag

••• 0:48—In lingerie, then nude, after undressing outside in desert and going for a swim at night.

••• 0:50—Breasts, when standing up and kissing Gil Bellows then making love. Great!

•• 1:01—Buns and right breast, while lying next to the water, talking with Bellows.

• 1:03—Partial buns, when a scorpion starts crawling on the small of her back.

•• 1:19—Breasts, while lying in bed with Bellows.

• 1:23—Breasts, while in the shower. Seen through plastic shower curtain.

Black Emanuelle *(1976)*

Laura Gemser . . . . Emanuelle

• 0:00—Brief breasts daydreaming on airplane.

• 0:19—Left breast in car kissing a guy at night.

•• 0:27—Breasts in shower with a guy.

••• 0:30—Full frontal nudity making love with a guy in bed.

••• 0:37—Breasts taking pictures with Karin Schubert.

•• 0:41—Full frontal nudity lying on bed dreaming about the day's events while masturbating, then full frontal nudity walking around.

•• 0:49—Breasts in studio with Johnny.

••• 0:52—Brief right breast making love on the side of the road. Full frontal nudity by the pool kissing Gloria.

•• 1:00—Nude, taking a shower, then answering the phone.

•• 1:04—Breasts on boat after almost drowning.

•• 1:08—Full frontal nudity dancing with African tribe, then making love with the leader.

•• 1:14—Full frontal nudity taking off clothes by waterfall with Johnny.

•• 1:23—Breasts making love with the field hockey team on a train.

Karin Schubert . . . . Anne Danielli

• 0:06—Brief breasts adjusting a guy's tie.

••• 0:14—Breasts making love in gas station with the gas station attendant.

••• 0:37—Nude, running in the jungle while Laura Gemser takes pictures of her.

• 0:40—Breasts, kissing Gemser.

• 0:44—Right breast, making love with Johnny in bed.

Black Gunn *(1972)*

Jeannie Bell . . . . Lisa

Luciana Paluzzi . . . . Toni

Brenda Sykes . . . . Judith

• 0:45—Brief side view of right breast, while getting out of bed with Jim Brown.

Kate Woodville . . . . Louella

• ***Black Magic Woman*** *(1990)*

Apollonia . . . . .Cassandra Perry

- 0:18—Brief side of left breast with Mark Hamill. Don't see her face.
- 0:25—Very brief upper half of left breast, while in shower with Hamill.

Amanda Wyss . . . . Diane Abbott

Black Moon Rising *(1986)*

Linda Hamilton . . . . Nina

- 0:50—Brief left breast, while making love in bed with Tommy Lee Jones.

Lisa London. . . . . Redhead

Black Rainbow *(1989; British)*

Rosanna Arquette . . . . Martha Travis

••• 0:50—Breasts in bed with Hulce, then walking to bathroom.

Black Robe *(1991; Canadian/Australian)*

Sandrine Holt . . . . Annuka

- 1:10—Breasts (mostly left breast) while exposing herself to the Iroquois guard. Don't see her face.

• ***Black Scorpion 2—Aftershock*** *(1996; Made for Cable Movie)*

Laura Harring . . . . Babette

Linda Hoffman . . . . .Jane

Jeannie Millar . . . . Giggles

•• 0:12—Breasts, while dancing in funhouse in front of two guys.

Sherrie Rose . . . . Ursula/Aftershock

Kimberly Rowe . . . . Divine

•• 0:20—Breasts in open coat while posing for photographs by police men.

Joan Severance . . . . Darcy/Black Scorpion

Black Venus *(1983)*

Monique Gabrielle . . . . Ingrid

••• 0:03—Nude in Sailor Room at the bordello.

••• 1:01—Breasts and buns, taking off clothes for Madame Lilli's customers.

Florence Guerin. . . . . Louise

•• 0:45—Nude talking, then making love with Venus in bed.

••• 1:16—Nude frolicking on the beach with Venus.

••• 1:18—Nude in bedroom getting out of wet clothes with Venus.

- 1:21—Buns in bed with Jacques and Venus.

Josephine Jaqueline Jones . . . . Venus

•• 0:05—Breasts, while in Jungle Room.

••• 0:11—Nude, in bedroom, posing for Armand while he sketches.

- 0:14—Breasts and buns, while making love with Armand in bed.

•• 0:17—Nude, posing for Armand while he models in clay, then on the bed, kissing him.

- 0:21—Briefly nude, while getting dressed.

••• 0:38—Nude, making love in bed with Karin Schubert.

••• 0:45—Nude, talking and then making love in bed with Louise.

•• 0:50—Breasts when Pierre brings everybody in to see her.

•• 0:57—Breasts in silhouette while Armand fantasizes about his statue coming to life.

••• 1:04—Nude.

••• 1:07—Nude with the two diplomats on the bed.

••• 1:16—Nude frolicking on the beach with Louise.

••• 1:18—Breasts, while in bedroom getting out of wet clothes with Louise.

•• 1:21—Breasts, while in bed with Jacques.

•• 1:24—Full frontal nudity, while getting out of bed.

Karin Schubert. . . . . Marie

•• 0:38—Nude in bed with Venus, making love.

Black Widow *(1987)*

Rutanya Alda . . . . .Irene

Theresa Russell . . . . Catherine

- 0:28—Briefly nude, making love in cabin.

•• 1:18—Nude in pool with Paul.

Debra Winger . . . . Alexandra

The Black Windmill *(1974; British)*

Delphine Seyrig. . . . . Ceil Burrows

•• 0:34—Right breast and buns, undressing and getting into bed to pose for a photo taken by John Vernon.

Blackout *(1989)*

Carol Lynley . . . . Esther Boyle

•• 1:01—Brief breasts leaning against the wall while someone touches her left breast.

Gail O'Grady . . . . .Caroline Boyle

• ***Blackout*** *(1995)*

Marie Barrientos . . . . Cindy

Azalea Davila. . . . . Mystery Woman

- 0:10—Brief breasts, while making love on top of Brian Bosworth. Don't see her face.

Blackwater *(1989)*

Denise Crosby . . . . Sally

Stacey Dash. . . . . Minnie

- 0:37—Upper half of buns and back side of right breast, while walking to and sitting on edge of bed.
- 0:44—Very brief side view of left breast, while propping herself up while lying on couch.
- 0:59—Brief right breast, while in bed on top of Julian Sands.

Blade Runner *(1982)*

Joanna Cassidy . . . . Zhora

•• 0:54—Breasts getting dressed after taking a shower while talking with Harrison Ford.

Daryl Hannah . . . . Pris

Sean Young. . . . . Rachael

Blame It on Rio *(1984)*

Michelle Johnson. . . . . Jennifer Lyons

•• 0:19—Breasts on the beach greeting Michael Caine and Joseph Bologna with Demi Moore, then brief breasts in the ocean.

- 0:26—Breasts taking her clothes off for Caine on the beach. Dark, hard to see.

•• 0:27—Breasts seducing Caine. Dark, hard to see.

••• 0:56—Full frontal nudity taking off robe and sitting on bed to take a Polaroid picture of herself.

- 0:57—Very brief breasts in the Polaroid photo showing it to Caine.
- 1:02—Brief breasts taking off her top in front of Caine while her dad rests on the sofa.

Demi Moore . . . . Nicole Hollis

- 0:19—Very brief right breast turning around to greet Michael Caine and Joseph Bologna.

Blame It on the Vodka (1992)

Cie Allman. . . . . Annette Robertson

- • 0:30—Brief right breast, while making love in bed with Christopher.
- •• 0:55—Breasts, while making love in bed with Herman and Karen.
- ••• 1:08—Breasts, while making love in a car with Greg. Long scene.

Janice Rivera . . . . Karen

- • 0:37—Buns in one piece swimsuit, making out with Robert while Herman and Annette watch.
- •• 0:39—Breasts, while making out with Robert some more.
- • 0:55—Buns and brief breasts, while making love with Herman and Annette in bed.

Wendi Westbrook . . . . Roxanne

- 0:18—In bra and panties, while in the kitchen.
- ••• 0:20—Buns and breasts, while in the bathroom with Barry, then making love with him in the shower. Long scene.

• *Blast 'Em (1992)*

Bianca Jagger . . . . Herself

- • 0:58—Left breast in gaping dress while dancing in B&W still photo.

Sally Kirkland. . . . . Herself

Ali MacGraw . . . . Herself

- • 0:55—Brief right breast in gaping blouse in a B&W still photo.

Blaze (1989)

Lolita Davidovich. . . . . .Blaze Starr

- • 0:09—In bra doing her first strip routine. Very brief side views of left breast under hat.
- • 0:15—Strip tease routine in front of Paul Newman. At the end, she takes off bra to reveal pasties.
- •• 0:48—Breasts on top of Newman, then side view of left breast.

Blind Date (1984)

a.k.a. Deadly Seduction

(Not to be confused with *Blind Date* (1987) with Bruce Willis.)

Kirstie Alley . . . . Claire Simpson

- • 0:12—Brief breasts making love in bed with Joseph Bottoms. Dark, hard to see anything.

Lana Clarkson . . . . .Rachel

- • 0:52—Brief breasts rolling over in bed when Joseph Bottoms sneaks in. Dark, hard to see.

Valeria Golino . . . . Girl in Bikini

Marina Sirtis . . . . Hooker

- ••• 0:21—Breasts walking to and lying in bed just before taxi driver kills her.

Blind Justice (1994; Made for Cable Movie)

Elisabeth Shue. . . . . Caroline

- • 0:36—Very, very brief right breast in gaping dress after getting up slightly after Armand Assante falls over.
- • 0:39—Brief upper half of right breast with part of nipple sticking out of camisole top while sitting on bed.

Blind Side (1993; Made for Cable Movie)

Tamara Clatterbuck. . . . . Barbara Hall

- •• 1:13—In bra and panties, outside with Rutger Hauer by the spa. Then breasts several times.

Rebecca De Mornay . . . . .Lynn Kaines

Mariska Hargitay . . . . .Melanie

Diana Lee-Hsu . . . . Mrs. Dance

Blind Vision (1990)

Deborah Shelton . . . . Leanne Dunaway

- ••• 0:25—Breasts, making love with her boyfriend on the floor. Some shots are a body double.

Blindfold: Acts of Obsession (1993)

Tara Buckman . . . . Barmaid

Shannen Doherty. . . . . Madeleine Dalton

- ••• 0:07—Breasts, while making love.
- •• 0:08—Breasts while making love in the shower with Mike.
- ••• 0:21—Breasts, in bed, while making love with Mike.
- •• 0:39—Breasts, during photo session with pillows while posing for Mike. More breast flashes while in bed.
- 1:06—In black bra on desk in Judd Nelson's office. Brief, partial right breast, when he caresses it.

Aleksandra Kaniak . . . . Natalie

Blindside (1988; Canadian)

Lolita Davidovich. . . . . Adele

- •• 0:32—Breasts dancing on stage.

Lori Hallier. . . . . Julie

Blindsided (1993; Made for Cable Movie)

Stephanie Menuez. . . . . .Racehorse Girl

Mia Sara . . . . Chandler Strange

- • 0:16—Very brief right breast while making love under Jeff Fahey.

Blink (1993)

Madeleine Stowe. . . . . .Emma Brody

- • 1:04—Side of left breast while walking to look at roses.
- •• 1:06—Breasts, after taking off top and making love with Aidan Quinn.

Bliss (1985; Australian)

Gia Carides . . . . Lucy Joy

- • 1:25—Brief breasts during nightmare. Cockroaches crawl out of cut between her breasts. Pretty gross. (The cockroaches—not her.)

Lynette Curran. . . . . Bettina Joy

Helen Jones . . . . Honey Barbara

- ••• 0:58—Breasts, lying on the floor with Harry. Brief part of lower frontal nudity. Long scene.
- • 1:01—Brief breasts on bed when Adrian runs to the bathroom.
- • 1:24—Left breast, while standing outside with arms outstretched.
- • 1:39—Buns, while swimming. Long shot of buns while walking up rocks.

• *Bliss (1996)*

Lois Chiles . . . . Eva

Sheryl Lee . . . . Maria

- •• 0:38—Breasts, while lying in bed with Craig Schaeffer.
- • 0:42—Brief breasts.
- •• 0:57—Breasts, while lying in bed with Schaeffer. Lit with blue light.
- •• 1:04—Breasts in gaping nightie, after tying up Schaeffer to bed and making love with him.
- • 1:09—Brief left breast, while lying in bed with Schaeffer.
- • 1:10—Brief right breast, while sitting on Schaeffer's lap.
- •• 1:11—Breasts, while making love with Schaeffer.
- • 1:12—Breasts, while lying in bed with Schaeffer.
- • 1:18—Very brief partial left breast, when closing the shower door.

Leigh Taylor-Young . . . . Redhead
- 0:08—Brief partial breasts, visible through sheer curtains.

Blonde Heaven *(1994)*

Michelle Bauer . . . . Amanda Blackwell
- ••• 1:08—Nude, while making love with Pluto.

Tamara Carrera . . . . Dee
- •• 0:05—Breasts, after taking off dress top while being video taped.
- • 0:06—Breasts, while taking a shower.
- •• 0:09—Breasts, while making love in the shower with a guy.

Monique Parent . . . . Viva
- • 0:33—Buns in panties, while surrounded by several admiring guys during party.
- •• 0:36—Breasts, while dancing on table in front of four guys with Jospehina at party.
- •• 1:01—Full frontal nudity, after turning into a vampire in movie theater in front of Kyle.

Raelyn Saalman . . . . Angie
- • 0:17—In bra, then breasts, while making love with Kyle on bed. Medium long shot.
- •• 0:21—In bra and panties, then breasts, while changing clothes. Seen from behind a 2-way mirror.
- • 0:44—Buns in lingerie, while dancing and modeling in front of Julie Strain.
- •• 0:47—Full frontal nudity, several times, while holding spot light on Josephina and Al.
- • 0:58—Breasts, while making love with Kyle on table.
- •• 0:59—Breasts, while lying in bed with Strain.
- • 1:00—Brief buns, after taking off her dress in movie theater in front of Kyle.
- ••• 1:02—Breasts and buns in panties, while making love in bed with Strain.
- •• 1:05—Nude, while taking a shower, getting out and running down the hall.
- • 1:12—Brief buns in panties, while getting out of bed.

Janine Stillo . . . . Megan
- • 0:52—Nude, while taking a shower behind two-way glass when Kyle is sneaking around in room. Long shot.

Julie Strain . . . . Illyana
- •• 0:00—Breasts, while making love with a guy during the opening credits.
- • 0:13—Brief breasts, while straddling a guy on bed.
- •• 1:03—Breasts and buns in panties, while making love with Angie in bed.
- • 1:12—Breasts, while fighting with the other vampire girl in bed.

Blondes Have More Guns *(1995)*

Gloria Lusiak . . . . Dakota Beaver
- •• 0:00—Breasts and buns, while making love on top of a guy in bed. Don't see her face.
- • 0:04—Brief breasts, seen in a Viewmaster.
- •• 0:40—Breasts, while making love on top of a guy on a sofa.
- • 0:50—Breasts, throwing off her jacket and straddling Harry.
- •• 1:00—Breasts, while making love with Harry in bed at night. Playing with pizza.
- ••• 1:03—Breasts, while dripping hot candle wax on Harry, then being held a gunpoint by two police people.

Blood & Concrete: A Love Story *(1991)*

Jennifer Beals. . . . . Mona
- • 0:10—Buns, in pulled up slip on bed with Billy Zane. Brief, out-of-focus shot of her left breast. Don't see her face.

Blood and Sand *(1989; Spanish)*

Sharon Stone. . . . . Doña Sol
- • 0:57—Very brief upper half of right breast, while making love on table with Juan.
- •• 0:58—Left breast, making love in bed with Juan. Don't see her face well.
- ••• 1:04—Breasts quite a few times, making love with Juan in the woods.

Blood Beach *(1981)*

Laura Burkett. . . . . Girl in Sand

Mariana Hill. . . . . Catherine

Lynne Marta . . . . Jo
- • 0:30—Brief left breast in ripped open blouse, while struggling with rapist on beach at night.

Blood Diner *(1987)*

Cynthia Baker . . . . Cindy
- ••• 0:44—Nude outside by fire with her boyfriend, then fighting a guy with an axe.

Tanya Papanicolas . . . . Sheetar & Bitsy
- • 0:15—Brief breasts, while taking photos during topless aerobics photo shoot.
- • 0:24—Breasts, while lying dead on operating table, then standing up.

Blood Games *(1989)*

Laura Albert. . . . . Babe

Randi Randolph. . . . . Ingrid
- ••• 0:13—Breasts taking off bra, buns in shower with Stoney.

Blood Link *(1983)*

Sarah Langenfeld. . . . . Christine
- •• 1:01—Breasts while taking her top off in bed with Craig.
- • 1:04—Breasts in bed with Keith.

Penelope Milford . . . . Julie Warren
- •• 0:22—Breasts while in bed with Craig. Very brief left breast, when she grabs the pillow.
- •• 1:24—In black bra in greenhouse with Keith, then breasts.
- • 1:27—Brief buns, while on top of Keith. Long shot.
- •• 1:28—Right breast, when Keith tries to strangle her.
- ••• 1:35—Breasts, while in bedroom with Keith.

Martha Smith . . . . Hedwig
- •• 0:41—Breasts, wearing black panties while in bed with Keith.
- •• 0:43—Brief breasts, while kneeling on bed, talking to Keith.
- • 0:48—Right breast, while sitting in bed and talking. Shadow and scarf get in the way. Brief breasts.
- • 0:49—Breasts, while getting slapped around by Keith.
- ••• 0:51—Breasts sitting up in bed when Craig and Keith meet each other for the first time.
- • 1:13—Breasts, wearing red panties, with Keith before he kills her.
- • 1:14—Brief buns, covered with blood when discovered by policemen.

Blood Mania *(1970)*

Maria de Aragon . . . . Victoria
- ••• 0:11—Breasts while wearing panties and taking off her dress and getting into pool with the pool boy, then getting out.
- • 0:26—Right breast, while doing amyl nitrate in bed with Dr. Cooper. Brief upper half of buns.
- • 0:27—Breasts during the drug-induced visions.
- •• 0:37—Breasts in front of mirror, after taking off nightgown. Seen from below.

••• 0:46—Breasts and buns, taking off her dress in front of Dr. Cooper.

Vicki Peters . . . . Gail

•• 1:04—Breasts, while making love with Dr. Cooper in front of the fire. Seen through flames. Intercut with a rape scene.

• 1:10—Brief breasts in bathroom. More brief breasts, while getting beaten to death by Victoria and dragged through the house.

• 1:15—Very brief breasts, while dead, covered with blood when discovered by Craig.

• 1:17—Brief breasts while being placed in car. Covered with blood.

Reagan Wilson. . . . . Cheryl

•• 0:07—Breasts and buns, while in bubble bath.

• 0:17—In bra, while undressing in bedroom. Very brief side of right breast, when putting on robe.

• 0:21—Very brief side of left breast, while leaning over to kiss Craig in bed.

• 0:34—Partial right breast, while on couch with the blackmailer.

Blood of the Hunter *(1994)*

Alexandra Vandernoot. Marie Thoreau

• 1:03—Very brief back side of right breast, then brief side view of left breast while bathing herself when seen by Michael Biehn through hole he cuts in curtain.

Blood on Satan's Claw *(1971; British)*

a.k.a. Satan's Skin

Linda Hayden . . . . Angel Blake

•• 0:40—Breasts, while undressing in front of priest to tempt him.

Blood Relations *(1989; Canadian)*

Lynne Adams. . . . . Sharon Hamilton

Lydie Denier . . . . Marie

•• 0:07—Left breast making love with Thomas on stairway.

• 0:44—Brief left breast in bed with Thomas' father. Very brief cuts of her breasts in B&W.

••• 0:54—Full frontal nudity undressing for the Grandfather.

Blood Sisters *(1986)*

Amy Brentano . . . . Linda

••• 0:12—Breasts, getting out of bed.

•• 0:14—Breasts, walking around. Right breast, in bed with Russ. Brief upper half of buns.

Ruth Corrine Collins . . . . Prostitute

Gretchen Kingsley . . . . Ellen

•• 0:32—Breasts, changing clothes to go to sleep in bedroom.

••• 0:50—Breasts in bed with Jim.

Maria Machart. . . . . Marnie

•• 0:45—In bra, then brief breasts putting on nightgown and caressing herself.

Blood Ties *(1986; Made for Cable Movie; Italian)*

Maria Conchita Alonso . . . . Caterina

•• 0:35—Brief breasts when Vincent Spano rips her dress off.

Barbara De Rossi . . . . Luisa

• 0:58—Brief breasts on couch when bad guy rips her clothes off.

Blood Ties *(1991)*

Michelle Johnson. . . . . Celia

Kim Johnston-Ulrich . . . . Loren

• 1:21—Very brief breasts, while rolling over in bed with Harry.

Bloodbath *(1976)*

a.k.a. The Sky is Falling

Carroll Baker . . . . Treasure

• 0:16—Outline of left breast in see-through blouse when kneeling in the ocean to urinate.

• 0:50—Very brief buns, while mooning her mute lover.

Bloodbath at the House of Death *(1985; British)*

Sheila Steafel . . . . Sheila Finch

Pamela Stephenson . . . . Barbara Coyle

• 0:50—Very brief breasts getting clothes ripped off by an unseen being.

Bloodfist III: Forced to Fight *(1991)*

Pat Anderson . . . . Elaine

• 0:55—Buns and breasts in clip from movie *TNT Jackson* that the inmates watch while Diddler gets stabbed to death.

Jeannie Bell . . . . Diana "TNT" Jackson

•• 0:55—Breasts several times in movie *TNT Jackson* that the inmates watch while Diddler gets stabbed to death.

Bloodfist VI: Ground Zero *(1994)*

Catya Sassoon . . . . Teri

• 0:02—Breasts in bathroom and bedroom with Steve Garvery.

BloodKnot *(1995; Made for Cable Movie)*

Krista Bridges. . . . . Julie

Nancy Cser . . . . Connie

Margot Kidder. . . . . Evelyn

Kate Vernon. . . . . Kaye

• 0:23—Brief breast, when Arthur accidentally opens the bathroom door.

•• 0:54—Breasts and very brief lower frontal nudity, while making love in back room of store with Patrick Dempsey.

• 1:05—Breasts, while making love outside with Craig Shefer.

Bloodlust: Subspecies III *(1993)*

Elvira Deatcu . . . . Woman Victim

•• 0:18—Breasts, after her blouse is lowered so vampires can feast on her. More breasts, while on the floor.

Denice Duff . . . . Michelle Morgan

Melanie Shatner . . . . Rebecca Morgan

• 0:04—Very brief left breast and buns, while taking off blood-stained dress and putting on a coat. Long shot.

Bloodmatch *(1991)*

Hope Marie Carlton. . . . . Connie Angel

Marianne Taylor . . . . Max Manduke

• 0:13—Breasts and buns, making love in bed on top of Caldwell.

Bloodstone *(1988)*

Laura Albert. . . . . Kim Chi

• 0:05—Very brief side view of left breast turning around in pool to look at a guy.

Bloodstone: Subspecies II *(1992)*

Denice Duff . . . . Michelle Morgan

• 0:10—Very, very brief left breast under sheer part of dress while taking it off. Back side of right breast while putting on sweater.

•• 0:16—Breasts, while crying in the shower.

Melanie Shatner . . . . Rebecca Morgan

• 0:34—Upper half of buns and breasts behind translucent plastic shower door. Hard to see.

Bloodsuckers *(1970; British)*

Imogen Hassall . . . . Chriseis

- 0:05—Right breast, while standing up at the beach and kissing Richard.

Bloody Birthday *(1980)*

Julie Brown . . . . Beverly

••• 0:13—Dancing in red bra, then breasts while two boys peek through hole in the wall, then buns. Nice, long scene.

Erica Hope . . . . Annie

- 0:04—Brief breasts in cemetery, making out with Duke.

Susan Strasberg. . . . . Miss Davis

Sylvia Wright. . . . . Girl in Van

••• 0:45—Breasts undressing in a van and making out with a guy.

Bloody Friday *(1973)*

a.k.a. Single Girls

Robyn Hilton. . . . . .Denise

Chéri Howell . . . . Shannon

- 1:01—Breasts and buns after "accidentally" dropping her towel in front of Bud.

Claudia Jennings . . . . Allison

- 0:40—Breasts, taking off her dress to sunbathe on rock at the beach. Long shot. Side view of right breast, putting dress back on when George talks to her.

•• 0:57—Breasts, drying herself off after shower.

Joan Prather . . . . .Lola

•• 1:06—Breasts, acting out her fantasy with Blue just before getting killed. Dark.

Bloody Mama *(1970)*

Diane Varsi . . . . Mona Gibson

••• 0:16—Breasts, sitting up in bed with Dan Stroud. Buns, when getting out of bed. Long scene.

Bloody Trail *(1972)*

Rickey Richardson . . . . Miriam

- 1:01—Peek at left breast in torn blouse.
- 1:05—Right breast while sleeping, dark, hard to see.

Blow Out *(1981)*

Nancy Allen . . . . Sally

- 0:58—Brief upper half of right breast with the sheet pulled up in B&W photograph that John Travolta examines.

Amanda Cleveland . . . . Coed Lover/Shower Victim

- 0:01—Left breast in room while someone watches from the outside.
- 0:02—Breasts in shower and on TV monitor while killer stalks outside.

Cindy Manion. . . . . .Dancing Coed

Missy O'Shea . . . . .Dancing Coed

Robin Sherwood . . . . .Screamer

Blow-Up *(1966; British/Italian)*

Veruschka . . . . Veruschka

Jane Birkin. . . . . .Teenager

- 1:06—Breasts, while changing clothes in David Hemming's studio.
- 1:08—Brief breasts while frolicking with Hemmings and the other teenage girl in the studio. Very, very brief lower frontal nudity under Hemmings.

Gillian Hills . . . . .Teenager

- 1:08—Brief breasts and very, very brief lower frontal nudity while frolicking with David Hemmings and Jane Birkin in the studio.

Sarah Miles . . . . Patricia

Vanessa Redgrave . . . . Jane

Blown Away *(1992)*

(Unrated version reviewed. Not to be confused with *Blown Away* (1994) with Jeff Bridges.)

Nicole Eggert . . . . Megan

••• 0:12—Right breast then breasts and buns, while standing in bedroom, making out with Corey Haim.

•• 0:15—Breasts and buns, getting out of bed with Haim.

•• 0:24—Breasts, while making love in bed with Haim.

- 0:26—Left breast, while in shower with Haim.

••• 0:46—Breasts, while making love, sitting on Haim's lap in front of fire.

- 1:00—Upper half of buns, in bed with Haim.
- 1:10—Brief breasts and buns, while getting out of bed.
- 1:26—Very brief half of right breast and buns in T-back under sheer nightgown, while making love in bed on top of Corey Feldman.
- 1:28—Very brief right breast, while getting shot by policeman.

• **Blue Collar** *(1978)*

Gloria Delaney. . . . . Party Girl 1

- 0:33—Brief breasts, while standing in doorway, then hugging Yaphet Kotto.

Blue Desert *(1990)*

Vali Ashton . . . . Young Woman

Courteney Cox . . . . .Lisa Roberts

- 0:52—Silhouette of right breast, while standing up with Steve. Probably a body double. Very, very brief right nipple between Steve's arms lying in bed. Dark, hard to see.

•• 0:53—Left breast, lying in bed under Steve. A little hard to see her face, but it sure looks like her to me!

Blue Flame *(1993)*

Melissa Behr . . . . .Jack

- 0:49—Brief side view of left breast, then brief partial glimpses of breasts as she circles Brian Wimmer. Partial upper half of right breast, when held by Wimmer.

Amanda de Cadenet . . . . .Hooker #2

Lynette Howe . . . . .Stripper

Blue Ice *(1992; Made for Cable Movie)*

Sean Young. . . . . .Stacy Mansdorf

- 0:17—Brief breasts and buns, while making love with Michael Caine.
- 0:18—Brief buns and partial back side of left breast, while sitting up in bed.

Blue in the Face *(1995)*

Madonna . . . . n.a.

Mel Gorham . . . . Violeta

•• 1:04—Breasts, after taking off dress and putting another dress on while looking at herself in the mirror.

Mira Sorvino . . . . The Young Lady

The Blue Max *(1966)*

Ursula Andress. . . . . Countess Kasti

- 1:26—Very, very brief half of left breast, lying on her back in bed.
- 1:47—(0:04 into tape 2) Very brief half of right breast, while kneeling down in front of Peppard in hotel room. Very, very brief breasts under towel around her neck when she stands up.

- 1:48—(0:05 into tape 2) Very, very brief silhouette of right breast, while lying back down in bed with George Peppard in bedroom.

Blue Movies *(1988)*

Vickie Benson . . . . Andrea

Lucinda Crosby . . . . Randy Moon

- • 0:10—Breasts, while in a spa in a movie.
- •• 0:11—Breasts, while kneeling on a table, shooting a porno movie.
- ••• 0:32—Breasts, while auditioning for Buzz.
- • 1:02—Breasts, while on desk in a movie.

Darian Mathias . . . . Kathy

- • 0:37—Very brief breasts twice acting for the first time in a porno film.
- • 0:39—Breasts, seen from above during screening of movie. Hard to see.

Blue Sky *(1991)*

Jessica Lange . . . . Carly Marshall

- • 0:01—Very, very brief, partial back side of right breast, when turning over, while sunbathing on the beach.
- • 0:03—Brief breasts, while standing in the water, waving to Tommy Lee Jones as his helicopter passes by. Medium long shot.

Amy Locane . . . . Alex Marshall

Annie Ross. . . . . Lydia

Carrie Snodgress . . . . Vera Johnson

Blue Tiger *(1994)*

Virginia Madsen . . . . Gina Hayes

- • 1:07—Sort of left breast, while making love in bed with Seiji.

Blue Velvet *(1986)*

Laura Dern . . . . Sandy Williams

Isabella Rossellini . . . . Dorothy

- • 0:36—Buns, after taking off panties in her bathroom. Long shot.
- • 1:08—Brief full frontal nudity, while frolicking with MacLachlan in bed.
- • 1:27—Very, very brief lower frontal nudity, while rolling over in bed in MacLachlan's flashback.
- • 1:40—Nude, while standing on porch, bruised.
- • 1:41—Briefly nude, while sitting in car. Long shot. Brief right breast, while getting covered up.
- •• 1:42—Brief breasts at Laura Dern's house.

Bluebeard *(1972)*

Agostina Belli. . . . . Caroline

- • 1:31—Brief left breast lying on grass getting a tan.
- •• 1:32—Breasts taking off clothes and lying on the couch.

Sybil Danning . . . . The Prostitute

- • 1:08—Brief breasts kissing Nathalie Delon showing her how to make love to her husband.
- • 1:09—Brief left breast, lying on the floor with Delon just before Richard Burton kills both of them.

Nathalie Delon . . . . Erika

- • 1:03—Breasts in bed, showing Richard Burton her breasts.
- • 1:09—Brief right breast lying on the floor with Sybil Danning just before Richard Burton kills both of them.

Joey Heatherton . . . . Anne

- • 0:25—Breasts under black see-through nightie while Richard Burton photographs her. Very brief right breast.
- ••• 1:46—Brief breasts opening her dress top to taunt Richard Burton.

Karin Schubert. . . . . Greta

- • 1:43—Brief breasts, spinning around, unwrapping herself from a red towel for Richard Burton.

Marilu Tolo . . . . Brigitt

- • 1:25—Breasts in sheer blue blouse arguing with Richard Burton.
- •• 1:27—Breasts getting whipped by Burton.

• ***Blues Brothers 2000*** *(1997)*

Shánn Johnson . . . . Matara

- • 0:19—Brief buns in G-string, while dancing on stage.

Blume in Love *(1973)*

Susan Anspach. . . . . .Nina Blume

Marsha Mason. . . . . .Arlene

- • 0:22—Side view of right breast, then brief breasts while lying in bed with George Segal.
- • 0:35—Very brief right breast while reaching over the bed.
- •• 0:54—Brief breasts twice, reaching over to get a pillow while talking to Segal.

Erin O'Reilly . . . . Cindy

- •• 0:40—Breasts and buns, getting out of and back in bed with George Segal. Very brief buns, when crawling over the bed.

Boarding School *(1976; German)*

a.k.a. Virgin Campus

a.k.a. The Passion Flower Hotel

Nastassja Kinski . . . . Deborah Collins

- • 0:15—Brief breasts in the shower with her roommates. Hard to tell who is who.
- • 1:11—Left breast, then breasts in the shower (She's the second from the right) consoling Marie-Louise.
- • 1:16—Breasts under sheer nightie.
- ••• 1:32—Breasts making love with Sinclair.

Fabiana Udenio . . . . Gina

Bobbie Jo and the Outlaw *(1976)*

Belinda Balaski. . . . . Essie Beaumont

- ••• 0:29—Breasts in pond with Marjoe Gortner and Lynda Carter.
- • 0:43—Very brief breasts, when Gortner pushes her into a pond.

Lynda Carter . . . . Bobbie Jo Baker

- • 0:10—Partial side of left breast, while changing blouses in her bedroom.
- ••• 0:17—Left breast, several times, while making love with Marjoe Gortner.
- •• 0:27—Brief left breast, making love with Gortner again at night.
- • 0:31—Very brief left breast, then very brief breasts in pond with Gortner experimenting with mushrooms.

Bobby Deerfield *(1977)*

Marthe Keller. . . . . Lillian

- • 0:47—Brief breasts, while getting into bed.

Boca *(1994)*

Rae Dawn Chong . . . . .JJ

- •• 0:25—Brief breasts, when Boca plays with Moema.
- ••• 0:29—Breasts, then nude while making love with Martin Kemp. Long scene.
- ••• 0:55—Brief breasts, after dancer pulls her up, then dancing after doing drugs.
- • 1:09—Very brief right breast in gaping jacket when getting up off bed.
- • 1:18—Brief right breast, then left breast in flashback.

Luma De Oliveira . . . . Celeste
- 0:35—Breasts, after taking off her top at junk yard in a contest to win drugs from Boca. (She's wearing a pink dress.)
•• 0:38—Breasts while making love on table with Boca.

The Body (1980)

Zeudi Araya. . . . . .Princess
- 0:26—Silhouette of right breast, then breasts and buns, while running in the dark at the beach.
•• 0:27—Full frontal nudity, while lying down at the beach with Alan.
•• 0:38—Breasts, while opening her dress top to tease Alan, then on bed making love.
- 1:00—Right breast in open dress, while playing in the surf with Alan.
- 1:13—Brief breasts while on the beach, making love with Alan.

Carroll Baker . . . . Madeliene
- 1:19—Brief left breast, twice, while making love with Alan. Close-up shot.
- 1:20—Buns, when getting letter out of drawer. Brief left breast when sitting on bed.

Body and Soul (1981)

Azizi Johari . . . . Pussy Willow
••• 0:31—Breasts sitting on bed with Leon Isaac Kennedy, then left breast, while lying in bed.

Rosanne Katon . . . . Melody
- 0:04—Left breast several times making love in restroom with Leon Isaac Kennedy.

Ola Ray . . . . Hooker #1
- 0:54—Brief breasts sitting on top of Leon Isaac Kennedy in bed with two other hookers.

Laurie Senit . . . . Hooker #3
- 0:54—Brief breasts lying next to Leon Isaac Kennedy in bed with two other hookers.

• *Body Armor* (1996)

Carol Alt . . . . Agent Monica McBride

Shauna O'Brien . . . . Beautiful Girl
•• 0:07—Breasts and buns in black panties, while getting fondled by John Rhys-Davies.
- 0:09—Buns in panties and brief breasts, while in bed on top of Rhys-Davies.

Annabel Schofield . . . . .Marisa

Body Chemistry (1990)

Mary Crosby . . . . .Marlee

Lisa Pescia . . . . Claire
••• 0:18—Breasts making love with Marc Singer standing up, then at foot of bed.
- 0:55—Buns, standing in hallway. Long shot.

Body Chemistry 2: Voice of a Stranger (1991)

Maria Ford . . . . Uncredited Victim
•• 0:37—Breasts in bed during flashback. (This scene is from *Naked Obsession.*)

Monique Gabrielle . . . . Brunette in Flashback
- 0:19—Very brief buns and left breast in bed. (This is a scene from *Uncaged.*)

Lisa Pescia . . . . Claire Archer
- 0:42—Brief buns and side of left breast, making love on stairs with Dan.
••• 0:52—Breasts and buns, in bathtub, standing up, sitting back down while talking with Dan.
- 1:07—Buns, in leather outfit in radio control booth with Morton Downey Jr.
- 1:18—Very brief buns and left breast on the stairs in flashback.

Body Chemistry 3: Point of Seduction (1993)

Elayne Dahl . . . . Brunette in Room
- 0:00—Breasts, while in room with a Krissy and Robert Forster.

Antonia Dorian . . . . Krissy
- 0:00—Breasts, while in room with a brunette woman and Robert Forster.

Morgan Fairchild . . . . .Beth Clancey

Becky LeBeau. . . . . .Margaret
•• 0:04—Full frontal nudity, seen on TV monitor, while taking her clothes off on bed during call-in show.

Shari Shattuck . . . . Dr. Claire Archer
•• 0:15—Breasts, while making love on bed with Andrew Stevens at night during storm.
••• 0:28—Side view of buns and breasts, while making love with Stevens on bed.
••• 0:57—Breasts, taking off robe in front of Stevens. More breasts and buns while making love with him.

Delia Sheppard . . . . Wilhemina

Carrie Stevens . . . . .Leslie

Stella Stevens . . . . Frannie Sibley

Body Chemistry 4: Full Exposure (1995)

(Unrated version reviewed.)

Elaine Giftos . . . . Charlotte Sanders

Leslie Ryan. . . . . Amy Mitchell
••• 0:09—Breasts, while making love in bed with Simon.

Stella Stevens . . . . Fran Sibley

Shannon Tweed . . . . .Claire Archer
- 0:21—Left breast on video tape playback.
•• 0:23—In bra, then left breast, then breasts while making love with Simon in parking garage.
••• 0:37—In blue bra, then nude, while making love with Simon next to and on top of pool table.

Body Count (1995)

Cindy Ambuehl . . . . Janet Hood
- 0:34—Brief close-up of buns, when bending over in sauna and Robert Davi sees her tattoo. Don't see her face.

Brigitte Nielsen . . . . Sybil

Body Double (1984)

Barbara Crampton. . . . . .Carol Sculley
•• 0:04—Breasts, while making love in bed with another man when her husband walks in.

Alexandra Day. . . . . Girl in Bathroom #1

Melanie Griffith . . . . Holly Body
•• 0:20—Breasts, while wearing a brunette wig, dancing around in bedroom being watched through telescope by Craig Wasson.
- 0:28—Breasts, while in bedroom, being watched by Wasson and the Indian.
•• 1:12—Breasts and buns, seen on TV that Wasson is watching.
•• 1:13—Breasts and buns, seen on TV after Wasson buys the video tape.
- 1:19—Brief buns in black leather outfit in bathroom during filming of movie.
- 1:20—Brief buns again in the black leather outfit.

Barbara Peckinpaugh. . . . . Girl #2 (Holly Does Hollywood)
• 1:12—Brief breasts in orgy scene in adult film preview that Craig Wasson watches on TV. (Lettering gets in the way.)

Ty Randolph . . . . Mindi
••• 1:50—Breasts in the shower during filming of movie with Craig Wasson made up as a vampire.

Linda Shaw . . . . Linda Shaw
• 1:11—Left breast on monitor while Craig Wasson watches TV.

Deborah Shelton . . . . Gloria

Brinke Stevens. . . . . Girl in Bathroom #3
• 1:12—Breasts sitting in chair in adult film preview that Craig Wasson watches on TV.

Body Heat (1981)

Jane Hallaren . . . . .Stella

Kathleen Turner. . . . . .Maddy Walker
• 0:22—Brief side view of left breast in bed with William Hurt.
•• 0:24—Breasts in a shack with Hurt.
• 0:32—Buns, while getting dressed. Long shot, hard to see.
• 0:54—Brief left breast in bathtub. Long shot, hard to see.

Body Language (1995; Made for Cable Movie)

Mim Parker . . . . Tera the Dancer
•• 0:28—Breasts and buns in T-back, while dancing on stage in club. Lit with red light.

Karen Roe . . . . Katrina Hostegg

Heidi Schanz . . . . Dora Circe
• 0:13—Brief breasts in B&W photos that Tom Berenger looks at.
• 0:15—Brief breasts, while putting on dress when seen by Berenger.
•• 0:21—Breasts, while kissing Berenger in the kitchen.
•• 0:22—Breasts and buns, while making love on bed with Berenger, then when smoking in the kitchen.
••• 0:23—Nude, while walking back to bed and talking with Berenger in bed.
•• 0:29—Breasts in push-up bra and buns in lingerie while doing strip routine on stage in club.
•• 0:31—Breasts and buns in G-string, while kidding Berenger in dressing room.
• 1:08—Breasts in push-up bra, while dancing on stage.

Nancy Travis . . . . T.J. Harlow

• *Body Language* (1996; Video Tape)

Noelle . . . . Fire Place
••• 0:12—Nude, while caressing two other women in front of fire place.

Stevi Conrad . . . . Fire Place/Sun Bath
••• 0:17—Nude, while caressing two other women in front of fire place.
••• 0:28—Nude, while sunbathing outdoors with Sara St. James and Lorissa McComas.

Cory Lane . . . . Fire Place
••• 0:12—Nude, while caressing two other women in front of fire place.

Jacqueline Lovell . . . . Sun Bath
••• 0:29—Nude, while sunbathing outdoors with Noelle and Lorissa McComas.

Lorissa McComas. . . . . Sun Bath
••• 0:31—Breasts and buns, while sunbathing outdoors with Sara St. James and Noelle.

Stacy Moran . . . . Motorcycle
••• 0:44—Nude, while posing on motorcycle.

Ashley Phillips . . . . Bath Tub
••• 0:34—Nude, while caressing herself and taking a bath.

Taylor St. Claire . . . . Elevator
••• 0:03—Nude in garter belt and stockngs, while standing in an elevator and playing with a pistol.

Body of Evidence (1992)

(Unrated version reviewed.)

Madonna. . . . . Rebecca Carlson
• 0:01—Breasts, while making love on TV during video playback.
• 0:03—Breasts and buns some more on TV.
• 0:20—Upper half of buns, getting acupuncture.
••• 0:41—Breasts on stairs and in bed with Willem Dafoe.
•• 0:42—Breasts on bed behind curtains with Dafoe.
• 0:43—Brief right breast, while licking champagne off Dafoe's chest.
••• 0:45—Full frontal nudity, while climbing on top of Dafoe and making love. Seen through curtains.
• 0:55—Lower frontal nudity, while making love with Dafoe in parking garage.
••• 1:07—Very, very brief left breast when Dafoe grabs her arm. Breasts opening her robe and lying on the floor and playing with herself while Dafoe watches.
•• 1:10—Buns, while lying on the floor when Dafoe rips her panties off.
••• 1:11—Full frontal nudity on TV during video playback.

Anne Archer . . . . Joanne Braslow
1:12—Nude scene on video playback is body double Shawn Lusader.

Shawn Lusader . . . . Body Double for Anne Archer
•• 1:12—Nude, while running around bedroom during video playback. Hard to see because the camera is moving around.

Julianne Moore . . . . Sharon Dulaney
••• 0:14—Breasts in bed, while making love with Willem Dafoe, then breasts and buns getting out of bed to take a shower.

Body of Influence (1992)

(Unrated version reviewed.)

Diana Barton . . . . Jennifer

Sandahl Bergman . . . . Clarissa

Anna Karin. . . . . Beth

Sandra Margot . . . . Margaret
••• 0:03—Breasts and buns in black G-string panties, while undressing for Jonathon.

Monique Parent. . . . . Chic Woman
•• 0:57—Buns in lingerie and breasts undressing in front of Jonathan and Lana at gun point.

Bobbie Phillips . . . . First Woman

Ashlie Rhey . . . . Dominatrix

Shannon Whirry. . . . . Laura/Lana
••• 0:08—Breasts on bed with her lover during recollection for Jonathon.
• 0:16—Left breast, while on bed, tied by wrists and getting raped during recollection.
•• 0:26—In black bra, undressing in office. Right breast, while lying on desk. Buns in panties.
••• 0:44—In burgundy bra and panties with Jonathon in his house. Then nude, while making love in living room. Long scene.
••• 1:05—In black bra, then breasts and buns, while making love on top of Jonathon.
••• 1:08—Breasts, while sitting up in bed and talking to Jonathon.

Body of Influence 2 (1995)

Jodie Fisher . . . . Leza Watkins
- • 0:19—Right breast, while making out with dream stranger on couch.
- ••• 0:32—Breasts and buns, while making love with Thomas.
- ••• 0:43—Breasts and buns, while making love with Thomas in bed.
- • 0:48—Breasts, while getting out of bed.
- •• 1:24—Breasts, while making love with Thomas in flashbacks.

Landon Hall. . . . . Girl at Club

Body Shot (1993)

Viveka Davis . . . . Rita

Michelle Johnson. . . . . Danielle Wilde
- 0:23—Brief buns in T-back under fishnet outfit.
- • 0:28—Brief buns, when dropping robe.

Barbara Patrick . . . . Candy
- •• 0:06—Breasts, while sitting on couch in Robert Patrick's studio.

Body Snatchers (1994)

Gabrielle Anwar . . . . Marti Malone
- • 0:49—Very, very brief breast while in bathtub when pod creature falls on top of her.
- ••• 1:13—Several brief breast shots, while sitting up, looking at Tim and writhing around on bed in infirmary.

Kathleen Doyle . . . . Mrs. Platt

Meg Tilly. . . . . Carol Malone

Body Strokes (1995)

Dixie Beck. . . . . Karen
- •• 0:14—Breasts, while making love with Leo.
- •• 0:50—Full frontal nudity, while making love with Leo.
- •• 1:13—Breasts, with Rachel and Leo.
- • 1:19—Brief right breast, while posing with Rachel.
- • 1:20—Brief right breast, while posing with Rachel.
- ••• 1:25—Breasts and buns, while making love with Leo.
- •• 1:29—Breasts, while posing for Leo.
- • 1:32—Breasts, while posing with Beth and Claire.

Kelly Jaye. . . . . Aqua
- •• 0:30—Breasts, while in pool, then making love with Claire in her flashback dream.

Kristen Knittle . . . . Beth
- •• 0:21—Breasts, while undressing to model for Leo.
- ••• 0:23—Nude in flashback with David and making love on boat.
- •• 0:45—In bra, then breasts, while starting to make love with her teacher in flashback.
- ••• 0:57—Full frontal nudity while posing on sofa and teasing her boyfriend.
- •• 1:19—Breasts, while posing outdoors with Claire and rubbing oil on her.
- •• 1:22—Breasts, while posing in white panties with Claire.
- • 1:32—Breasts, while posing with Claire and Karen.

Cory Lane . . . . Rachel
- •• 1:13—Breasts, with Karen and Leo.
- • 1:19—Brief right breast, while posing with Karen.
- • 1:20—Full frontal nudity, with Karen and Leo.

Catherine Weber. . . . . Claire
- ••• 0:30—Breasts, while posing by pool, then making love with Aqua in flashback dream.
- •• 0:36—Full frontal nudity, while taking a bath.
- ••• 0:53—Nude, while posing, then making love with two guys in a fantasy.
- ••• 1:03—Nude while dressed as a geisha girl, making love with Mark.
- •• 1:19—Breasts, while posing outdoors with Beth and rubbing oil on her. Brief buns in T-back.
- •• 1:22—Breasts and brief buns, while posing in black panties with Beth.
- • 1:32—Breasts, while posing with Beth and Karen.

Body Waves (1991)

Pat Anderson. . . . . Elaine
- • 0:41—Breasts, getting out of the shower in drive-in movie from *TNT Jackson.*

Sean'a Arthur . . . . Dream Girl
- •• 0:02—Brief buns in swimsuit, walking into office.
- ••• 0:03—Breasts, taking off her bathing suit top during Rick's dream.
- •• 0:07—Breasts and side view of buns in swimsuit bottom, during Dooner's fantasy.

Jeannie Bell . . . . Diana "TNT" Jackson
- •• 0:43—Breasts in open top in drive-in movie from *TNT Jackson.*

Sherrie Rose. . . . . Suzanne

Sándra Wild. . . . . Anita
- ••• 0:39—Breasts under sheer white robe, then breasts with Larry on chair.
- ••• 1:12—Breasts in bedroom with Larry.

Bolero (1984)

Olivia D'Abo . . . . Paloma
- • 0:38—Nude covered with bubbles taking a bath.
- • 1:05—Brief breasts in the steam room with Bo.
- • 1:32—Breasts in the steam room talking with Bo. Hard to see because it's so steamy.

Bo Derek . . . . Ayre McGillvary
- • 0:04—Brief breasts, stripping to panties, outside after graduating from school.
- ••• 0:19—Breasts making love with Arabian guy covered with honey, messy.
- ••• 0:58—Breasts making love in bed with Angel.
- ••• 1:38—Breasts during fantasy love making session with Angel in fog.

Ana Obregon . . . . Catalina Terry
- • 1:32—Brief breasts making love with Robert.

Bonnie's Kids (1973)

Tiffany Bolling . . . . Ellie
- •• 0:21—Breasts, modeling in office.
- • 1:16—Brief right breast making love in bed.

Robin Mattson. . . . . Myra
- • 0:05—Brief side view of right breast, changing in bedroom while two men watch from outside.
- ••• 0:07—Breasts washing herself in the bathroom.

The Boob Tube (1975)

Elana Casey . . . . Greta Van Allen
- • 0:27—Buns, while lying in bed with Dr. Carstens.
- ••• 0:48—Breasts, taking off her blouse in bed, then making love with Natalie.
- • 1:01—Buns and side of left breast on sofa.
- ••• 1:11—Nude, opening the door.
- ••• 1:12—Breasts during orgy on the couch.
- • 1:16—Brief breasts in hallway.

Sharon Kelly . . . . Selma Carpenter
- ••• 0:06—Breasts and buns, trying to seduce Dr. Carstairs.
- ••• 0:10—Breasts and buns, having fun by herself on the bed while Dr. Carstairs watches. Nice close-ups.

- ••• 0:11—More breasts and buns in bed with Dr. Carstairs.
- • 1:03—Breasts under sheer nightie while Harvey checks her sink.
- •• 1:09—Breasts and buns, on sofa, then leaving the room.
- •• 1:11—Breasts and buns, entering the room.
- ••• 1:12—Breasts during orgy on couch.
- • 1:16—Brief breasts in hallway.

Becky Sharpe. . . . . Massage Girl
- •• 0:20—Right breast, then breasts, while getting massaged by Sid on the table.

Lyllah Torena. . . . . Natalie Nolan
- ••• 0:28—Breasts, putting on her blouse.
- • 0:42—Breasts, getting raped by three Hell's Angel guys outside during flashback.
- •• 0:45—Breasts and buns, on bed, taking off her clothes with Dr. Carstairs.
- ••• 0:46—Breasts and buns, while making love with Dr. Carstairs in bed. Nice buns shot. More breasts after making love.
- •• 0:48—Breasts and buns, while making love in bed with Gretchen.
- •• 1:08—Left breast, while in front of Sid when her robe is pulled down by Gretchen.
- • 1:10—Breasts on sofa with Gretchen.
- ••• 1:12—Breasts during orgy on couch.
- • 1:16—Brief breasts in hallway.

The Boogens *(1981)*

(Not available on videotape.)

Rebecca Balding . . . . Trish Michaels
- • 0:31—Buns, twice, while getting caught in the hallway with a towel wrapped halfway around herself.
- •• 0:55—Breasts, while making love with Mark on the floor of the cabin.

• ***Boogie Nights*** *(1997)*

Skye Blue. . . . . Uncredited Actress in Hot Tub 2
- • 1:42—Buns and breasts while in hot tub with another actress during filming of a movie. (She's the blonde.)

Summer Cummings . . . . Uncredited Actress in Hot Tub 1
- • 1:42—Buns and breasts while in hot tub with another actress during filming of a movie. (She's the brunette.)

Heather Graham . . . . Rollergirl
- •• 0:24—Nude, while taking off her dress and jumping onto Mark Wahlberg on couch.

Jane Hamilton . . . . Judge

Laurel Holloman . . . . Sheryl Lynn

Julianne Moore . . . . Amber Waves
- •• 0:51—Breasts, while kissing Mark Wahlberg during filming of porno movie.
- • 0:53—Brief close-up of right breast, while having sex with Wahlberg during filming.
- • 0:54—Very, very brief left breast while lying on desk with Wahlberg after filming. Long shot.

Nicole Ari Parker . . . . Becky Barnett
- • 0:58—Brief breasts, while acting in a porno movie with Reed.

Leslie Redden . . . . KC Sunshine

Melora Walters . . . . Jessie St. Vincent

Boomerang *(1992)*

Robin Givens. . . . . Jacqueline
- • 0:50—Very brief half of left breast, while lying with her back on bed with Eddie Murphy when she first puts her arm under his arm.
- •• 1:02—Very brief side view of right breast, while making love on top of Murphy in bed.

Grace Jones . . . . Strangé
- • 0:35—Brief buns, under stockings during conference room meeting.
- • 1:19—Brief buns and back side of left breast, several times on TV monitor during editing of a commercial.
- • 1:29—Very brief breasts ripping off dress during a commercial.

Lela Rochon. . . . . Christie

The Boost *(1989)*

Sean Young . . . . Linda Brown
- • 0:16—Very, very brief breasts jumping into the swimming pool with James Woods. Very, very brief side view of right breast and buns, twice, getting out of the pool, sitting on edge, then getting pulled back in by James Woods.
- •• 0:17—Left breast, while in pool talking to Woods. Right breast visible under water.
- • 0:48—Brief breasts under water in spa with Woods.

• ***Booty Call*** *(1997)*

Vivica A. Fox . . . . Lysterine
- • 0:29—Very, very brief partial right breast, three times, while making love with Jamie Foxx in bed.

Bordello of Blood *(1996)*

Erika Eleniak. . . . . Katherine Verdoux

Angie Everhart. . . . . Lilith

Heather Hanson. . . . . Babe

Marjean Holden. . . . . Stunts

Ciara Hunter . . . . Tamara
- •• 0:43—Breasts, while in S&M dungeon room with Dennis Miller.

Korrine St. Onge . . . . Bordello Vampire

The Border *(1982)*

Elpidia Carrillo . . . . Maria
- • 1:19—Half of right breast and half of left breast, after opening her blouse in shack with Jack Nicholson.

Valerie Perrine . . . . Marcy

Born Losers *(1967)*

Elizabeth James . . . . Vicky Barrington
- • 1:44—Buns, while lying on floor after biker guys beat her up. Don't see her face.

Born on the Fourth of July *(1989)*

Holly Marie Combs . . . . Jenny

Vivica A. Fox . . . . Hooker
- • 0:50—Brief right breast, while taking off bra on top of patient in hospital. Dark.

Cordelia Gonzalez . . . . Maria Elena
- ••• 1:43—Breasts in black panties, then full frontal nudity in bed with Tom Cruise.

Billie Neal . . . . Nurse Washington

Kyra Sedgwick . . . . Donna

Lili Taylor. . . . . Jamie Wilson

Born to Race *(1988)*

La Gena Hart . . . . Jenny

Marla Heasley . . . . Andrea Lombardo
- • 0:52—Buns, outside at night while kissing Joseph Bottoms.

The Borrower *(1989)*

Mädchen Amick. . . . . Megan

Rae Dawn Chong . . . . Diana Pierce

Tamara Clatterbuck. . . . . Michele Chodiss
Lorrie Marlow . . . . Nurse Wilson
• 0:57—Brief left breast and upper half of right breast, while making love with a doctor in operating room.
Zoe Trilling . . . . Astrid

The Boss' Wife (1986)

Arielle Dombasle . . . . Mrs. Louise Roalvang
• 1:01—Brief breasts getting a massage by the swimming pool.
••• 1:07—Breasts trying to seduce Daniel Stern at her place.
•• 1:14—Brief breasts in Stern's shower.
Melanie Mayron . . . . Janet Keefer

Boulevard (1994)

Rae Dawn Chong . . . . Ola
• 0:05—Breasts, while making love with a customer on bed.
• 0:30—Left breast then breasts, while sitting in bathtub, talking and smoking a joint with Kari Wüher.
• 0:45—Right breast, while taking a shower.
• 1:08—Breasts, while getting a massage from Wüher.
• 1:13—Partial buns, while dancing in club.
Kari Wührer. . . . . Jennefer
•• 0:14—Breasts and buns in bathroom, getting into the shower and in the shower.
••• 0:41—Breasts, while making love in bed with Lou Diamond Phillips. Brief buns, when running out of the room when she changes her mind.
•• 1:10—Breasts, while making love with Rae Dawn Chong.
• 1:13—Partial buns, while dancing in club.
• 1:15—Brief breasts in the shower and getting out.
•• 1:23—Nude, while taking a shower and getting out.

• *Bound (1996)*

Gina Gershon . . . . Corky
•• 0:19—Brief long shot of left breast, then left breast, while making love with Jennifer Tilly.
Jennifer Tilly . . . . Violet
•• 0:19—Brief buns and brief right breast, while making love with Gina Gershon.

Bound and Gagged: A Love Story (1993)

Ginger Lynn Allen . . . . Leslie
••• 0:13—Breasts, while making love on kitchen counter with Chris Mulkey, then on the floor.
0:43—Very, very brief inner half of right breast, when her blouse is opened by Elizabeth.
• 0:48—Breasts, in back seat of car when a guy tries to "help" her.
Karen Black . . . . Carla
Mary Ella Ross . . . . Lida
•• 0:05—Partial right breast, when getting caught making love in bed. Breasts, while in bed afterwards.
• 0:54—Right breast, while in bed with Chris Mulkey and Cliff during Cliff's dream.
• 0:58—Brief breasts, while making love with her lover when Cliff looks through skylight.

Boxcar Bertha (1972)

Barbara Hershey . . . . Bertha Thompson
•• 0:10—Breasts, while making love with David Carradine in a railroad boxcar, then brief buns walking around when the train starts moving.
• 0:52—Nude, side view while in house with David Carradine.
• 0:54—Buns and breasts, while putting on dress after hearing a gun shot.

Boxing Helena (1993)

Sherilyn Fenn. . . . . Helena
••• 0:13—Right breast, then breasts, while making love.
• 0:17—Very, very brief left breast when rolling over in bed.
• 0:18—Breasts, while getting out of bed after getting interrupted by a phone call.
Meg Register. . . . . Marion Cavanaugh
•• 0:06—Right breast in open dress in Julian Sand's flashback.
Nicolette Scorsese . . . . Fantasy Lover/Nurse
••• 1:22—In black bra, panties and stockings then buns and breasts while making love with Julian Sands while Sherilyn Fenn watches.

A Boy and His Dog (1976)

Suzanne Benton . . . . Quilla June
•• 0:29—Nude, getting dressed while Don Johnson watches.
• 0:45—Right breast lying down with Johnson after making love with him.

The Boy in Blue (1986; Canadian)

Melody Anderson . . . . Dulcie
• 0:07—Brief cleavage while making love with Nicolas Cage, then very brief top half of right breast when a policeman scares her.
Cynthia Dale . . . . Margaret
••• 1:15—Breasts standing in a loft kissing Nicolas Cage.

The Boys From Brazil (1978)

Linda Hayden . . . . Nancy
• 0:44—Very brief right breast, in mirror. Very, very brief left breast, twice, while in bed.
• 0:50—Very brief breasts, gagged, lying dead on bed.

Boys Night Out (1987)

Teri Lynn Peake . . . . Maid
••• 0:25—Buns in G-string, then breasts doing a strip routine. Long scene.

Boys on the Side (1994)

Drew Barrymore . . . . Holly
• 0:22—Very brief breasts, twice, when pulling up her blouse to tease Billy Wirth while he's tied up in a chair.
• 1:10—Brief breasts, while fooling around in bed with Matthew McConaughey.
Mary-Louise Parker . . . . Robin

Boyz N the Hood (1991)

Angela Bassett. . . . . Reva Styles
Nia Long . . . . Brandi
• 1:17—Left breast, while in bed with Cuba Gooding Jr. Don't see her face, but it is her.
Leonette Scott. . . . . Tisha
• 0:42—Side view of left breast, while in bed with Cuba Gooding Jr. Don't see her face.

The Brain (1988)

Christine Kossack. . . . . Vivian
•• 0:24—Breasts on monitor, then breasts in person during Jim's fantasy.
•• 1:11—Breasts again in the basement during Jim's hallucination.
Cyndy Preston. . . . . Janet

• *Brainscan* (1994)

Amy Hargreaves . . . . Kimberly

0:05—In bra, while sitting in front of mirror in her bedroom.

• 0:06—Brief left breast, then brief breasts, while Edward Furlong video tapes her from his house.

Michèle Barbara Pelletier . . . . Stacie

Brainwaves (1983)

Corinne Alphen . . . . Lelia Adams

• 0:03—Brief side of right breast, reaching out to turn off the water faucets in the bathtub.

• 0:05—Full frontal nudity, getting electrocuted in the bubble bath.

• 0:50—Brief right breast, during Kaylie's vision.

Suzanna Love . . . . Kaylie Bedford

Bram Stoker's Burial of the Rats (1995; Made for Cable Movie)

Adrienne Barbeau . . . . The Queen

Maria Ford . . . . Madeleine

• 0:18—Brief buns in outfit, while bringing food to Stoker in prison cell.

• 0:25—Buns, in outfit while getting up from den of sleeping women.

• 0:27—Brief buns, in front of prison cell.

•• 0:30—Breasts and brief buns, while making love with Stoker.

Nikki Fritz . . . . Rat Woman

Olga Kabo . . . . Anna

•• 0:21—Nude, while putting on a dress in front of a mirror.

Marie Laurin . . . . Rat Woman

Linnea Quigley . . . . Rat Woman

Bram Stoker's Dracula (1992)

Sadie Frost . . . . Lucy

• 0:41—Left breast, while making love with Dracula on bench outside at night during the rain.

•• 0:58—Breasts in bed, quite a few times, after getting bitten by Dracula and getting a blood transfusion.

• 1:12—Brief right breast in gaping nightgown.

• 1:19—Left breast, while lying in bed when Dracula pays a return visit.

• 1:20—Brief left breast, when the wolf Dracula jumps on the bed.

Honey Lauren . . . . Peep Show Girl

Maude Winchester . . . . Downstairs Maid

Braveheart (1995)

Sophie Marceau . . . . Princess Isabelle

Catherine McCormack . . . . Huffon

•• 0:37—Breasts, with Mel Gibson at night.

• *Brazil* (1985; British)

Kimberly Greist . . . . Jill Layton

• 1:55—(0:18 into side 5) [This scene is only available on the Criterion CAV laser disc and in the European video version.] Partial buns, while kneeling on bed. Very brief back side of left breast after Jonathan Pryce takes off her ribbon.

Breach of Trust (1995)

Leilani Sarelle . . . . Madeline

•• 0:58—Breasts, while making love with Michael Biehn.

• *Breakaway* (1995)

Tonya Harding . . . . Gina Taylor

Teri Thompson . . . . Myra Styles

•• 0:34—Brief breasts, while sitting down in bathtub.

•• 1:19—Buns and breasts while making love with Dan.

Breakfast in Bed (1990)

Marilyn Chambers . . . . Marilyn Valentine

•• 0:04—Full frontal nudity, getting out of bubble bath and drying herself off while talking to her manager.

••• 0:21—Breasts, taking off swimsuit top and sunbathing. Nude, swimming underwater.

•• 0:53—In bra, then breasts making love.

•• 1:16—Full frontal nudity, getting out of bed, putting on robe, then getting back in with Jonathan.

Courtney James . . . . Mitzi

••• 0:36—Breasts, walking into the pool. Also seen from under water.

••• 0:37—Breasts and bun in G-string, getting out of pool.

• 0:39—Breasts on the beach with Mr. Stewart.

Breakfast in Paris (1981)

Barbara Parkins . . . . Jackie Wyatt

••• 0:41—Right breast, while rolling over in bed. Breasts when sitting up in bed.

Breaking All the Rules (1985; Canadian)

Papusha Demitro . . . . Patty

Rachel Hayward . . . . Angie

••• 0:16—Breasts while changing in the bathroom.

• 0:43—Brief breasts after being felt up on roller coaster.

Breaking Point (1994; Canadian)

Kim Cattrall . . . . Allison Meadows

• 0:41—Buns in T-back, then breasts, while making love with Busey. Don't see her face well.

Darlanne Fluegel . . . . Dana Preston/Molly Carpenter

•• 0:11—Breasts and buns in panties, while making love with Gary Busey on boat. Dark.

• 0:46—Buns in T-back, after taking off dress and walking up stairs, then lying in bed.

•• 1:27—Right breast in open blouse, while tied up to bed by Greg before getting killed.

• *Breaking the Waves* (1996; Danish)

Katrin Cartlidge . . . . Dodo

Emily Watson . . . . Bess McNeill

•• 0:19—Breasts, while standing in bedroom with her husband, Jan.

•• 1:22—Full frontal nudity, while lying on bed, trying to get Dr. Richardson to make love with her.

• 2:14—Brief breasts, while in hospital. (She's cut and covered with blood.)

• *Breast Men* (1997; Made for Cable Movie)

Starr Andreeff . . . . Scrub Nurse

Jenna Bodnar . . . . Capsulotomy Patient

Beth Broderick . . . . Terri (Voice Only)

Mari Deno . . . . Pleased First-Op Girl

• 0:40—Slightly bruised breasts, when examining them for the first time after her implant operation.

Lisa Falcone . . . . Savannah

•• 0:57—Breasts, while lap dancing on David Schwimmer in club.

Amanda Foreman . . . . Lola

• 0:02—Breasts, when David Schwimmer watches her remove her breast pads and rub breast enlargement cream on herself.

Ashley Gardner . . . . Paula (Voice Only)

Tiffany Granath . . . . Sexy Patient
•• 0:40—Breasts, while David Schwimmer demonstrates how to massage her breasts.
Kaitlin Hopkins . . . . Becca (Voice Only)
Susan Isaacs . . . . .Desperate Woman
Kari Lizer . . . . Female Interviewer
Julie McCullough. . . . . 1972's Head Receptionist
Betsy Monroe . . . . 1970's Receptionist
Barbara Niven . . . . Cindy
Emily Procter. . . . . .Laura Pierson
•• 0:42—Breasts, while in office with David Schwimmer before her implant operation.
0:44—Breasts scene after Laura's operation is her head placed onto a body double's torso using special-effects.
Rena Riffel . . . . Swimming Pool Girl
•• 0:14—Breasts, while letting David Schwimmer make a plaster mold of her breasts for his research.

Breathless (1983)

Valerie Kaprisky . . . . Monica Poiccard
• 0:23—Brief side view of left breast in her apartment. Long shot, hard to see anything.
••• 0:47—Breasts in her apartment with Richard Gere kissing.
•• 0:52—Brief full frontal nudity standing in the shower when Gere opens the door, afterwards, buns in bed.
•• 0:53—Breasts, holding up two dresses for Gere to pick from, then breasts putting the black dress on.
• 1:23—Breasts behind a movie screen with Gere. Lit with red light.

A Breed Apart (1984; Made for Cable Movie)

Jane Bentzen . . . . Reporter
••• 0:55—Left breast in bed with Powers Booth, then full frontal nudity getting out of bed and putting her clothes on.
Kathleen Turner . . . . Stella Clayton
•• 1:12—Breasts in bed with Rutger Hauer, then left breast.

Breeders (1986)

LeeAnne Baker . . . . Kathleen
••• 0:28—Nude, undressing from her nurse outfit in the kitchen, then taking a shower.
• 0:59—Brief breasts in alien nest. (She's the blonde in front.)
•• 1:08—Breasts in alien nest.
•• 1:09—Breasts in alien nest again. (Behind Alec.)
• 1:11—Breasts behind Alec again. Then long shot when nest is electrocuted. (On the left.)
Amy Brentano . . . . Gail
• 0:59—Long shot of buns, getting into the nest.
• 1:07—Breasts in nest, throwing her head back.
•• 1:08—Brief breasts, writhing around in the nest, then breasts, arching her back.
• 1:11—Breasts, long shot, just before the nest is destroyed.
Adriane Lee . . . . .Alec
•• 0:49—Breasts, undressing while talking on the phone.
• 1:07—Brief breasts, covered with goop, in the alien nest.
• 1:08—Brief breasts in nest behind Frances Raines.
• 1:09—Brief breasts behind Raines again.
• 1:11—Breasts, lying back in the goop, then long shot breasts.
Natalie O'Connell . . . . .Donna
• 0:02—Very brief left breast, getting her blouse ripped by creature.
•• 0:44—Breasts, sitting up in hospital bed, then buns, walking down the hall.
••• 0:47—More breasts and buns, walking around outside.
• 1:10—Brief breasts, standing up in the alien nest.
Frances Raines . . . . Karinsa Marshall
••• 0:12—Nude stretching and exercising in photo studio.
• 0:16—Brief full frontal nudity, getting attacked by the creature.
••• 0:53—Breasts and buns, taking off her blouse and walking down the hall and into the basement. Long scene.
• 1:07—Very brief right breast in the alien nest with the other women.
• 1:10—Brief breasts standing up.

Breezy (1974)

Kay Lenz . . . . .Breezy
•• 0:01—Breasts, while sitting up in bed and putting on blouse.
•• 0:28—Breasts, undressing in shower while talking with William Holden.
• 0:58—Breasts, lying back in bed at night with Holden. Brief side of right breast and buns, putting on robe and getting out of bed.
••• 1:15—Breasts and buns, undressing in front of Holden in room at night.

Brewster McCloud (1970)

Shelley Duvall . . . . Suzanne
Sally Kellerman . . . . Louise
•• 1:07—Breasts, playing in a fountain.
Jennifer Salt . . . . Hope

Bride of Re-Animator (1989)

Kathleen Kinmont . . . . Gloria/The Bride
• 0:58—Brief breasts several times with her top pulled down to defibrillate her heart.
• 1:17—Breasts under gauze. Her body has gruesome looking special-effect appliances all over it.
• 1:22—More breasts under gauze.
• 1:24—More breasts. Pretty unappealing.
• 1:27—Brief buns, when turning around after ripping out her own heart.
Fabiana Udenio . . . . Francesca Danelli

The Bride Wore Black (1968; French/Italian)

Jeanne Moreau . . . . Julie Kohler
• 1:24—Brief breasts, taking off her dress in front of a patterned mirror.
Alexandra Stewart . . . . .Miss Becker

Bright Angel (1990)

Valerie Perrine . . . . Alleen
Mary Kay Place . . . . Judy
Lili Taylor. . . . . Lucy
• 0:26—Brief top of breasts under water, taking a bath in a pond.
••• 0:27—Breasts, while walking out of the pond.

A Brilliant Disguise (1994)

Lysette Anthony . . . . Michele Ramsey
•• 0:44—Breasts and buns, while making love with Andy.
Dawn Ann Billings . . . . Brunette in French Restaurant
Devin De Vasquez . . . . Gianna
Christina Fulton. . . . . Marlene
Beverly Johnson. . . . . .Barbara
Cherie Michan. . . . . Selma
Elizabeth Nottoli . . . . .Janet/Fashion Model
Kathy Shower . . . . Lila Foster

Brimstone and Treacle (1982; British)

Suzanna Hamilton . . . . Patricia Bates
•• 0:47—Breasts in bed when Sting opens her blouse and fondles her.
•• 1:18—Breasts in bed when Sting fondles her again.
• 1:20—Brief lower frontal nudity writhing around on the bed after Denholm Elliott comes downstairs.

Bring Me the Head of Alfredo Garcia (1974)

Isela Vega . . . . Elita
• 0:25—Brief right breast a couple of times, then brief breasts in bed with Warren Oaks.
••• 0:44—Breasts when Kris Kristofferson rips her top off. Long scene.
•• 0:52—Breasts sitting in shower with wet hair.
•• 1:49—Still from shower scene during credits.

• *Brinke Stevens Private Collection Volume 1* (1992; Video Tape)

Brinke Stevens . . . . Herself
•• 0:16—Breasts in *Flashdancers* segment from *Playboy* video magazine.
•• 0:19—Nude in still photo sequence in shower with Linnea Quigley.
• 0:22—Brief breasts lying on slab from *Slavegirls from Beyond Infinity.*
• 0:30—Breasts scenes from *Nightmare Sisters.*
••• 0:41—Breasts, in scenes from that were cut from the U.S. version of *Bad Girls From Mars.*
• 0:43—Buns, in G-string outfit posing for photo session.

• *Brinke Stevens Private Collection Volume 2* (1994; Video Tape)

Traci Lords . . . . Miss Georgia
• 0:05—Breasts in music video by Helix from *Red Hot Rock.*
Brinke Stevens . . . . Herself
• 0:01—Buns in gynecology-at-home sketch from *Playboy.*
•• 0:03—Breasts, while in garden as Marie, from *Ribald Classics.*
• 0:05—Breasts and partial buns in music video by Helix from *Red Hot Rock.*
•• 0:09—Breasts, after taking off bra in strip-poker scene from *Sole Survivor.*
••• 0:10—Breasts with Sylvia Kristel from *Emmanuelle IV.*
••• 0:12—Breasts and buns, in screen tests for *The Girls of Penthouse.*
••• 0:16—Full frontal nudity, in screen tests for *The Girls of Penthouse.*

Broadcast Bombshells (1995)

Amy Lynn Baxter . . . . Kendall Saranski
•• 0:05—Breasts, while wearing black panties, changing clothes in dressing room.
••• 0:43—Full frontal nudity, while changing clothes in room with the other two girls.
••• 0:55—In white bra, then nude, while making love with Neil. Long scene.
••• 1:14—Full frontal nudity, while making love with Neil backstage.
Debbie Rochon . . . . Amanda
••• 0:16—In black bra, then breasts, while making love in with Gordon in editing room. Long scene.
••• 0:24—In black bra, then full frontal nudity, while undressing in room, then buns after putting on a black dominatrix outfit.
• 0:32—Brief buns in black outfit in dressing room with Brian.
••• 0:43—Breasts, while changing clothes in room with the other two girls.
• 0:45—Brief full frontal nudity, while opening her robe for peeper.
•• 0:47—In purple bra, then breasts while in room with Frank.
•• 0:48—Brief left breast, while in bed with Frank.
Carolyn R. Smith . . . . Aerobicette
••• 1:00—Breasts and buns in panties, while changing clothes with two other women. (She's wearing a blue dress.)

The Bronx War (1989)

Marlene Forté . . . . Alicia
•• 1:01—Breasts after taking off bra while dancing. Intercut with scene of gang violence.

Brubaker (1980)

Jane Alexander . . . . Lillian
Linda Haynes . . . . Carol
• 1:03—Breasts, while getting dressed with Huey in bedroom when Robert Redford comes in.

• *Buck Naked Line Dancing* (1993; Video Tape)

Lisa Comshaw . . . . Dancer
••• 0:00—Breasts throughout. She's usually in the front in the left, wearing a choker.
Kim Dawson . . . . Dancer
••• 0:00—Breasts throughout. She's in the back in the left.
Lauren Hays . . . . Dancer
••• 0:00—Breasts and buns throughout. She's in the front on the right, wearing a black wig.
Gwen Somers . . . . Dancer
••• 0:00—Breasts throughout. She's usually in the back in the right, with a bandana in her pocket.
Julie Strain . . . . Dancer
••• 0:00—Breasts and buns throughout. Sometimes wearing pasties with tassels. If you are a faithful reader of this book, you should be able to recognize who she is!

A Bucket of Blood (1995; Made for Cable Movie)

Darcy De Moss . . . . Alice
••• 0:55—Breasts, buns and very, very brief lower frontal nudity, after taking off her red dress to pose for Anthony Michael Hall, before he kills her. Long scene.
Mink Stole . . . . Older Woman

Bucktown (1975)

Pam Grier . . . . Aretha
••• 0:29—Left breast, while in bed with Fred Williamson.

Buford's Beach Bunnies (1992)

Suzanne Ager . . . . Boopsie Underall
•• 0:19—Breasts in the shower.
• 0:20—Brief breasts when her towel falls off in front of telegram guy.
• 0:36—Buns, in red two piece swimsuit at the beach.
• 0:37—Buns, while walking up the stairs.
Avalon Anders . . . . Santa's Helper
Stephanie Anderson . . . . Marilyn
Rikki Brando . . . . Lauren Beatty
•• 0:54—Breasts in bed with Jeeter.
Francesca "Kitten" Natividad . . . . Madam #1
Monique Parent . . . . Amber Dexterous
•• 0:09—Breasts, fooling around with a customer in the restroom.
• 0:11—More breasts, with the customer.

• 0:42—Left breast in gaping vest, trying to get into Jeeter's pants.
••• 1:14—Breasts in bedroom with a customer.

Bull Durham *(1988)*

Jenny Robertson . . . . Millie
Susan Sarandon . . . . Annie Savoy
• 1:37—Very brief right breast, when turning over in the bathtub under Kevin Costner.
• 1:39—Brief right breast peeking out from under her dress after crawling on the kitchen floor to get a match.

Bulletproof *(1988)*

Lydie Denier . . . . Tracy
•• 0:14—Breasts in Gary Busey's bathtub.
• 0:20—Brief buns, putting on shirt after getting out of bed. Very, very brief side view of left breast.
Darlanne Fluegel . . . . Devon Shepard

Bulletproof Heart *(1994)*

a.k.a. Killer
Mimi Rogers . . . . Fiona
••• 0:39—Breasts, while making love in bed with Anthony LaPaglia.

Bullies *(1985)*

Olivia D'Abo . . . . Becky Cullen
•• 0:39—In wet white T-shirt swimming in river while Matt watches.

The Burning *(1981)*

Leah Ayres-Hamilton . . . . Michelle
Carrick Glenn . . . . Sally
••• 0:19—Breasts, taking a shower in the outdoor showers.
• 0:20—Very brief breasts, putting her T-shirt back on.
Carolyn Houlihan . . . . Karen
•• 0:45—Nude, going skinny dipping with Eddy in lake at night.
••• 0:46—Brief breasts several times in the lake with Eddy, then breasts and buns getting out. Nice buns shot.
•• 0:47—Nude, walking around in the woods, looking for her clothes.
Holly Hunter . . . . Sophie
K.C. Townsend . . . . Hooker

Bury Me an Angel *(1972)*

Dixie Lee Peabody. . . . . Dag
• 0:13—Very brief right breast, while getting back into bed.
••• 0:41—Nude, skinny dipping in river and getting out.
• 1:16—Breasts making love in bed with Dan Haggerty. Lit with red light.

Bushido Blade *(1979; British/U.S.)*

Laura Gemser . . . . Tomoe
• 1:08—Brief right breast taking off her top in bedroom with Captain Hawk.

A Business Affair *(1993; British/French)*

Carole Bouquet . . . . Kate Swallow
• 0:37—Buns and right breast, while lying in bed next to Christopher Walken.
• 1:11—Buns, while lying on tanning bed.
Annabel Leventon . . . . Literary Guest
Patti Love . . . . Prostitute

• ***Busted*** *(1996)*

Devin De Vasquez . . . . Casey
• 0:05—Breasts and buns, while showering with Ava Fabian in the police showers. Sometimes with Corey Feldman.
• 1:08—Breasts and buns while fooling around in bed with Ava and Martin.
Griffin Drew . . . . Bambi
• 0:07—Breasts, while sunbathing outdoors.
••• 0:16—Stripping in jail cell in front of Dr. Kaplan. In lingerie, then buns and breasts.
• 0:40—Brief breasts, while lying in bed with Todd Bridges.
• 0:41—Brief breasts, while lying in bed with Bridges again.
Ava Fabian. . . . . Lacey
•• 0:05—Breasts and buns, while taking a shower with Devin De Vasquez in the police shower room. Sometimes with Corey Feldman.
• 1:08—Breasts and buns, while fooling around in bed with Martin and Devin.
Landon Hall. . . . . Lisa
Mariana Morgan . . . . Captain Mary Mae
••• 1:16—In black bra, then breasts, while making love with Corey Feldman
Monique Parent. . . . . Carrie
• 0:07—Brief breasts, while sunbathing outdoors.
•• 0:31—Breasts, while showering with Howe in the showers. Buns and very brief lower frontal nudity while getting out of the showers.
Julie Strain . . . . Annette
• 0:37—Briefly nude when her towel falls off in police station.
• 0:38—Brief breasts when her towel falls off again.

Buster and Billie *(1974)*

Joan Goodfellow . . . . Billie
• 0:33—Brief breasts in truck with Jan-Michael Vincent. Dark, hard to see.
• 1:06—Buns, then brief breasts in the woods with Vincent.
• 1:25—Brief left breast getting raped by jerks.
Pamela Sue Martin . . . . Margie Hooks

Butterfly *(1982)*

Pia Zadora. . . . . Kady
•• 0:33—Breasts and buns getting into the bath.
••• 0:35—Breasts in bathtub when Keach is giving her a bath.

• ***Butterfly Kiss*** *(1996; British)*

Amanda Plummer . . . . Eunice
• 0:10—Breasts, after taking off her blouse and showing off her body piercing, chains and tattoos.
•• 0:14—Breasts and buns, after taking off her blouse and getting into bed with Saskia Reeves. (Still wearing her body piercing, chains and tattoos.)
• 0:18—Brief breasts, when showing her chains and piercings to truck driver.
• 0:20—Partial buns, while having sex with the truck driver in the back of his truck.
• 1:05—Brief breasts, showing Mr. McDermott her chains and piercings in car.
• 1:09—Breasts, when taking off her clothes in room with Mr. McDermott.
• 1:11—Breasts, while in the shower when Reeves beats Mr. McDermott to death.
••• 1:15—Full frontal nudity, outdoors at night, when she takes her chains off with help from Reeves.
Saskia Reeves. . . . . Miriam
•• 0:15—Left breast, while making love in bed with Amanda Plummer.

Buying Time *(1987)*

Laura Cruikshank . . . . Jessica

•• 0:52—Breasts several times making love with Ron on pool table.

By Design *(1982; Canadian)*

Sara Botsford . . . . Angie

• 0:23—Full frontal nudity in the ocean. Long shot, hard to see anything.

• 1:08—Brief side view of left breast making love in bed while talking on the phone.

Patty Duke . . . . Helen

•• 0:49—Left breast, lying in bed.

•• 1:05—Brief left breast sitting on bed.

• 1:06—Brief left breast, then brief right breast lying in bed with the photographer.

Bye Bye Baby *(1989; Italian)*

Carol Alt . . . . Sandra

• 0:09—Part of right breast, while in the shower.

Brigitte Nielsen . . . . Lisa

• 0:20—Brief side view of right breast, while lying on a guy in bed. Nice buns shot also.

Bye Bye Blues *(1989; Canadian)*

Rebecca Jenkins . . . . Daisy Cooper

• 0:01—Brief breasts, getting out of bathtub. Very brief buns, while running outside and putting on robe to get away from snake.

• 0:42—Upper half of breasts, while in bathtub.

• 0:45—Very brief left breast under water in bathtub.

Bye Bye Brazil *(1980; Brazilian)*

Betty Faria . . . . Salomé

•• 0:28—Breasts, wearing red panties, backstage with Cigano.

• 0:29—Left breast while sitting in a chair.

•• 0:38—Breasts backstage with Ciço.

• 1:24—Buns, under a mosquito net with a customer.

Zaira Zambelli . . . . Dasdô

•• 1:11—Buns, then breasts outside by a boat with Cigano.

C.C. & Company *(1970)*

Ann-Margret . . . . Ann

• 1:01—Buns and breasts, while making love with Joe Namath.

Jennifer Billingsley . . . . Pom Pom

•• 0:14—Breasts, when her biker friends cheer her on while she's bathing in a pond.

• 0:54—Breasts in pulled up blouse, while struggling on the ground with Joe Namath.

Teda Bracci . . . . Pig

C.O.D. *(1983)*

Corinne Alphen . . . . Cheryl Westwood

• 0:21—Brief breasts changing clothes in dressing room while talking to Zacks.

• 1:25—Brief breasts taking off her blouse in dressing room scene.

Carole Davis . . . . Contessa Bazzini

• 1:25—Brief breasts in dressing room scene in black panties, garter belt and stockings when she takes off her robe.

Samantha Fox . . . . Female Reporter

Teresa Ganzel . . . . Lisa Foster

• 0:46—Right breast hanging out of dress while dancing at disco with Zack.

• 1:25—Brief side view of left breast taking off purple robe in dressing room scene. Then in white bra talking to Albert.

Marilyn Joi . . . . Debbie Winter

•• 1:16—Breasts during photo session.

• 1:25—Brief breasts taking off robe wearing red garter belt during dressing room scene.

Olivia Pascal . . . . Holly Fox

Cabin Fever *(1992)*

Belinda Farrell . . . . Lenore Hoffman

• 0:00—Brief right breast in gaping nightie when bending over.

••• 0:07—Breasts on the floor with Jack during her fantasy. Long scene.

••• 0:16—Breasts, sitting on floor, while playing with herself and fantasizing about Jack.

••• 0:20—Breasts and buns, undressing and getting into bathtub.

• 0:23—Brief lower frontal nudity and right breast in open robe.

•• 0:27—Nude in bed with Jack and rolling over and getting out of bed.

• 0:30—Brief breasts opening her blouse in front of Jack.

••• 0:32—Nude, making love in bed with Jack. Nice, long scene.

• 0:41—Right breast, while sitting in bed and putting on a blouse.

Cabo Blanco *(1982)*

Ana de Sade . . . . Rosa

• 0:34—Brief breasts, lying in bed and talking to a guy.

• 0:36—Brief right breast, twice, when he gets out of bed to look out the window.

Dominique Sanda . . . . Marie Claire Allesandri

• 1:27—Buns, swimming in pool. Long shot.

Caddyshack *(1980)*

Sarah Holcomb . . . . Maggie O'Hooligan

Cindy Morgan . . . . Lacey Underall

• 0:50—Very, very brief side view of left breast sliding into the swimming pool. Very blurry.

•• 0:58—Breasts in bed with Danny three times.

Cadillac Girls *(1993; Canadian)*

Jennifer Dale . . . . Sally

••• 0:41—In bra, then breasts while making love in bedroom with Gregory Harrison.

Mia Kirshner . . . . Page

• 0:02—Back half of breast in mirror when Miles gets out of bed. Long shot.

Cadillac Man *(1990)*

Fran Drescher . . . . Joy Munchack

• 0:07—Very brief right breast several times while in bed with Robin Williams.

Lori Petty . . . . Lila

Pamela Reed . . . . Tina

Annabella Sciorra . . . . Donna

Cafe Society *(1995; Made for Cable Movie)*

Lara Flynn Boyle . . . . Pat Ward

• 0:18—Brief side view of right breast, while making love with Frank Whaley. Don't see her face.

Anna Thomson . . . . Erica Steele

Caged Fury (1984)

Taaffe O'Connell . . . . Honey
- •• 0:17—Breasts on bed with a guard. Mostly left breast.
- • 0:40—Very, very brief tip of left breast peeking out between arms in shower.
- • 1:06—Very brief breasts getting blouse ripped open by a guard in the train.

Caged Fury (1989)

Kascha . . . . Blonde Escapee
- • 0:00—In bra and panties, then buns in G-string, then brief breasts while crawling on the floor.

April Dawn Dollarhide . . . . Rhonda Wallace
- • 0:54—Briefly nude, after dropping towel and joining Kat in the showers.

Kathrin Lautner . . . . Orchid

Janine Lindemulder . . . . Lulu
- • 0:15—Brief breasts dancing in front of Erik Estrada.

Sandra Margot . . . . Crazy Daisy
- • 1:10—Buns in G-string and bra dancing for some men.
- •• 1:11—Breasts after taking off bra.

Roxanna Michaels . . . . Katherine "Kat" Collins
- • 0:39—Breasts while getting searched upon entering prison with other topless women.

Melissa Anne Moore . . . . Gloria

Ty Randolph . . . . Warden Sybil Thorn
- •• 0:53—Breasts and buns undressing for bath, then in the bathtub.

Elena Sahagun . . . . Tracy Collins
- •• 0:58—Left breast while taking a shower.

Kelly Sullivan . . . . Lip Service

Caged Hearts (1995)

Trisha Berdot . . . . Lisa

Jennifer Leigh Burton . . . . Ranch Inmate

Kelly Galindo . . . . Prison Inmate

Carrie Genzel . . . . Kate
- • 0:15—Right breast, while standing up when first entering prison.
- •• 0:25—Nude, when three other girls, beat her up in the shower.
- • 0:57—In black bra and panties in bedroom with a customer, then partial left breast.

Jordana Gowan . . . . Ranch Inmate

Meredyth Holmes . . . . Aerobic Girl

Tané McClure . . . . Sharon
- •• 0:57—Breasts, while in bed with a customer.
- • 1:00—Brief left breast, while crying in a chair.
- •• 1:11—In bra and panties, then breasts and buns while undressing in bedroom, then lying in bed.

Stephanie Ann Smith . . . . Guard Lynn

Annie Wood . . . . Marzy

Caged Heat (1974)

a.k.a. Renegade Girls

Juanita Brown . . . . Maggie
- • 0:25—Breasts in shower scene.

Roberta Collins . . . . Belle
- • 0:11—Very brief breasts getting blouse ripped open by Juanita.
- ••• 1:01—Breasts while the prison doctor has her drugged so he can take pictures of her.

Erica Gavin . . . . Jacqueline Wilson
- • 0:08—Buns, getting strip searched before entering prison.
- •• 0:25—Breasts in shower scene.
- • 0:30—Brief side view of left breast in another shower scene.

Cheryl Smith . . . . Lavelle
- • 0:04—Brief left breast, dreaming in her jail cell that a guy is caressing her through the bars.
- •• 0:25—Breasts in the shower scene.
- •• 0:50—Brief nude in the solitary cell.

Caged Heat 2: Stripped of Freedom (1993)

Pamella D'Pella . . . . Paula
- ••• 0:13—Breasts, while making love with the warden on sofa in his office.
- ••• 0:42—Brief buns in T-back and breasts, while dancing for the warden in his office.

Susan Harvey . . . . Lucy
- • 1:00—Brief breasts, while in her cell, flashing to distract a guard.

Jewel Shepard . . . . Amanda
- •• 0:15—In bra and panties, then breasts, while undressing for strip search in the warden's office.
- •• 0:49—Breasts, after getting her prison shirt ripped open, then whipped in front of the other prisoners.

Caged Heat 3000 (1995)

Debra Beatty . . . . Billie
- •• 0:14—Breasts, while in showers, throwing sponge at Kira.
- •• 0:28—Brief breasts, while standing in the showers, then whipping a guy.

Lisa Boyle . . . . Kira
- •• 0:14—Breasts and buns in shower scene.
- ••• 0:34—Breasts, while being fondled by a guy when she's asleep.

Ellyn Dawn Humphreys . . . . Ice

Yvette McClendon . . . . Uncredited Inmate

Leslie Redden . . . . Eden

Cal (1984; Irish)

Helen Mirren . . . . Marcella
- •• 1:20—Brief frontal nudity taking off clothes and getting into bed with Cal in his cottage, then right breast making love.

Calendar Girl (1993)

Stephanie Anderson . . . . Marilyn Monroe
- • 0:46—Buns and very brief back side of rght breast, while standing at the beach, taking off her wig behind the two bad guys.

Tuesday Knight . . . . Nude Woman
- • 0:45—Very brief buns and partial left breast, while lying down on the beach when first seen by Jason Priestley and his friends. Long shot.

California Casanova (1991)

Michelle Johnston . . . . Laura
- • 0:12—Buns in black G-string, while dancing on stage.
- • 0:18—Brief breasts under sheer black top, while dancing in front of a guy in pool house.

California Dreaming (1978)

Kirsten Baker . . . . Karen

Stacey Nelkin . . . . Marsha

Glynnis O'Connor . . . . Corky
- •• 0:11—Breasts pulling her top over her head when T.T. is using the bathroom.
- ••• 1:14—Breasts in bed with T.T.

Tanya Roberts . . . . Stephanie

Dorothy Tristan . . . . Fay
- • 0:20—Brief breasts changing clothes while a group of boys peek through a hole in the wall.

• California Girl Fox Hunt Bikini Competition #6 *(Video Tape)*

Avalon Anders . . . . Avalon
••• 0:02—Buns in sexy one piece swimsuit.
• 0:47—Buns during review.
Lauren Hays . . . . Laura
••• 0:03—Buns in two piece swimsuit.
• 0:48—Buns during review.
Melissa Meiner . . . . Chanel
••• 0:19—Buns in two piece swimsuit.
• 0:49—Buns during review.

• California Heat *(1995)*

Leigh Betchley . . . . Boudoir Bikini Girl
• 0:01—Very brief buns in black body suit, while posing for Jack.
Rebecca Ferratti . . . . Alice
• 0:00—Breasts under sheer white lingerie, while modeling for Jack.
• 0:03—Partial buns and breasts under sheer white body suit.
Tamara Landry . . . . Stephanie
•• 0:34—Breasts, while making love with Jack in lifeguard station at night.
• 0:48—Breasts, while sitting in bathtub with Jack.
Yvette McClendon . . . . Donna
• 1:03—Breasts, while sitting in bathtub with Tracy.
Sheila Redgate . . . . Boudoir Bikini Girl
• 0:01—Breasts, while posing for Jack.

California Hot Wax *(1992)*

Sharon Cain . . . . Loretta
•• 0:55—Breasts, changing in car wash maintenance room in front of Scott.
•• 0:59—Breasts in and out of swimming pool with Scott.
Jacqueline Jade . . . . Bikini Girl
Carla Morrell . . . . Bikini Girl
Carmen Morrell . . . . Bikini Girl
Kimberly Speiss . . . . Bikini Girl
Sándra Wild . . . . Bikini Girl

California Suite *(1978)*

Jane Fonda . . . . Hannah Warren
Sheila Frazier . . . . Bettina Panama
Denise Galik . . . . Bunny
Maggie Smith . . . . Diana Barrie
• 1:05—Very brief side of left breast, putting nightgown on over her head.

Caligula *(1980)*

(X-rated, 147 minute version.)
Adrianna Asti . . . . Ennia
• 0:27—Breasts at side of bed with Malcolm McDowell when he feels her breasts.
•• 0:54—Breasts lying down surrounded by slaves. Mostly her right breast.
Mirella D'Angelo . . . . Livia
•• 1:08—Buns and breasts in kitchen with Malcolm McDowell. Full frontal nudity on table when he rapes her in front of her husband-to-be.
Anneka di Lorenzo . . . . Messalina
••• 1:16—Nude, making love with Lori Wagner. Long scene.
Helen Mirren . . . . Caesonia
• 1:13—Brief breasts several times getting out of bed to run after McDowell. Dark.
• 1:15—Very brief left breast, when taking off her dress to dry McDowell off.
Teresa Ann Savoy . . . . Druscilla
•• 0:01—Nude, running around in the forest with Malcolm McDowell.
• 0:05—Buns, rolling in bed with McDowell. Very brief breasts getting out of bed.
• 0:26—Left breast several times in bed.
• 0:46—Brief right breast in bed with McDowell again.
• 1:15—Left breast with McDowell and Helen Mirren.
• 1:22—Very brief left breast getting up in open dress.
•• 1:45—Full frontal nudity, then buns when dead and McDowell tries to revive her.
Lori Wagner . . . . Agrippina
••• 1:16—Nude, making love with Anneka Di Lorenzo. Long scene.

Call Me *(1988)*

Patricia Charbonneau . . . . Anna
•• 1:18—Brief left breast making love in bed with a guy, then breasts putting blouse on and getting out of bed.
Patti D'Arbanville . . . . Cori

Camilla *(1994)*

Bridget Fonda . . . . Freda Lopez
• 0:46—Nude, after taking off her swimsuit and joining Jessica Tandy in the lake. Medium long shot.
Jessica Tandy . . . . Camilla Cara
• 0:46—Brief buns and partial back side or right breast, while walking into the water in front of Bridget Fonda.

Can It Be Love *(1992)*

a.k.a. Spring Break Sorority Babes
Julie Clarke . . . . Crystal
Shelly Jones . . . . Wet T-shirt Contestant
Lorissa McComas . . . . Montana
••• 0:55—Breasts and buns, changing into lingerie behind two way mirror while David watches.
Blake Pickett . . . . Dyanne
Cindy Rich . . . . Megan

Can She Bake a Cherry Pie? *(1983)*

Karen Black . . . . Zee
• 1:02—Very brief upper half of left breast in bed when she reaches up to touch her hair.
Frances Fisher . . . . Louise

Can't Stop the Music *(1980)*

Valerie Perrine . . . . Samantha Simpson
• 1:12—Brief breasts, while splashing around in the spa with The Village People.
Danone Simpson . . . . Stewardess in Record Store
Leigh Taylor-Young . . . . Claudia Walters

• Candid Candid Camera, Volume 4 *(1985; Video Tape)*

Jasaé . . . . Model
••• 0:03—Full frontal nudity, talking on the phone.
•• 0:18—Buns and lower frontal nudity, when her skirt is blown upwards like Marilyn Monroe.
••• 0:31—Nude, trying to get people to sign a petition against nudity on cable TV.
Michelle Bauer . . . . Model
••• 0:08—Full frontal nudity, undressing while complaining about a bad tan from a tanning salon.
••• 0:50—Nude, posing in front of a guy, asking his opinion on her poses. Long scene.

• ***Candid Candid Camera, Volume 5***
(1986; Video Tape)
Michelle Bauer . . . . Debbie White
••• 0:34—Buns, pulling down her pants while a guy rubs purple paint on her rear.

Candy Stripe Nurses *(1974)*
Elana Casey . . . . Zouzou
Kimberly Hyde . . . . April
Sally Kirkland . . . . Woman in Clinic
Robin Mattson . . . . Dianne
•• 0:22—Nude in gym with the basketball player.
••• 0:40—Nude in bed with the basketball player.
Candice Rialson . . . . Sandy
•• 0:05—Breasts in hospital linen closet with a guy.
•• 0:08—Breasts smoking and writing in bathtub.
• 0:14—Breasts in hospital bed.
Maria Rojo . . . . Marisa
•• 0:29—Breasts making love with convict.
• 0:52—Brief breasts during attempted rape in kitchen pantry.
Tara Strohmeier . . . . Irene

Candy The Stripper *(1993)*
Tracy Vaccaro . . . . Candy
• 0:01—Very brief left breast, opening her blouse to flash a guy on the street.
••• 0:26—Breasts and buns in G-string, doing strip tease routine on stage.
••• 0:28—Breasts, while hiding behind bar with David after fight breaks out.
•• 0:38—Breasts in open blouse, showing her breasts to David.
••• 0:46—Breasts, while wearing panties, while in bedroom with Larry.
• 0:50—Wearing pasties, buns in G-string while posing for photographer.
• 0:56—Left breast in open robe in bedroom with Larry.
• 0:57—Breasts, while in bedroom, kissing Larry.
• 1:01—Breasts and buns in flashback on the bar.
••• 1:11—Breasts, while making out with David.
••• 1:13—Breasts, while making out with David on the floor.
•• 1:15—More breasts, while on the floor with David.
••• 1:28—Breasts and buns in G-string doing strip tease routine out of dress and lingerie.

Candyman *(1992)*
Kasi Lemmons . . . . Bernadette Walsh
Carolyn Lowery . . . . Stacey
Virginia Madsen . . . . Helen Lyle
• 0:47—In bloody bra, while undressing after she was arrested. Side of right breast, after taking off bra. Bloody.
• 0:54—Brief left breast, while in bathtub. Lower half of right breast, after sitting up.
Mika Quintard . . . . T.V. Reporter

Capone *(1975)*
Susan Blakely . . . . Iris Crawford
•• 1:13—Breasts, taking off her clothes outside in front of Ben Gazzara.
• 1:22—Left breast, while lying in bed with Gazzara.
••• 1:23—Nude, getting out of bed and getting dressed, then more breasts while fooling around with Gazzara.

Capone *(1989)*
a.k.a. Revenge of Al Capone
(Originally a Made for TV Movie.)
Debrah Farentino . . . . Jennie
• 1:01—Breasts, while making love in bed with Keith Carradine.

Captain Ron *(1992)*
Mary Kay Place . . . . Katherine Harvey
• 0:32—Brief right breast, then brief breasts in shower in boat with Martin Short. Overhead view. Hard to see her face, but it is her.
0:34—Buns, seen through shower door is a stunt double.

Captive Rage *(1988)*
Maureen Kedes . . . . Jan
•• 0:31—Breasts, getting chained to bed and raped by guards.
Claudia Udy . . . . Chiga

Carlito's Way *(1993)*
Mel Gorham . . . . Pachanga's Date
Penelope Ann Miller . . . . Gail
••• 0:59—Breasts, while dancing on stage in club in auburn wig.
••• 1:18—Breasts, after opening her robe and enticing Al Pacino in her apartment.
Tera Tabrizi . . . . Club Date

Carmen *(1983; Spanish)*
Laura Del Sol . . . . Carmen
• 1:14—Left breast, while lying in bed with Antonio.
• 1:27—Brief partial left breast, standing up when Antonio catches her in wardrobe room with another dancer.

Carnal Crimes *(1991)*
Jasaé . . . . Christa
••• 0:19—Full frontal nudity in lingerie, making love with a guy while Linda Carol secretly watches.
Linda Carol . . . . Elise
• 0:01—Very brief left breast, while rolling over in bed.
• 0:05—In wet lingerie and very brief side view of right breast in shower fantasy.
• 0:07—Breasts in B&W photo collage.
• 0:09—Full frontal nudity under sheer nightie, trying to get Stanley into bed.
• 0:11—Breasts in B&W photo again.
• 0:24—Brief right breast outside window opening her top while watching Renny & Mia make out.
• 0:26—Brief upper half of right breast when bum molests her.
••• 0:28—Breasts posing for Renny with Mia.
••• 0:29—Full frontal nudity making love with Renny and Mia.
• 0:30—Brief buns, sleeping in bed.
••• 0:38—Breasts making love with the baker. Long scene.
• 0:49—Breasts in B&W photo again.
• 1:02—Brief side view of right breast in gaping blouse.
• 1:33—Side view of buns in dominatrix outfit.
Sherri Graham . . . . Party Girl #1
Domonique Simone . . . . Leggy Girl
• 1:22—Buns, in G-string, leaning over to talk to Renny and Stanley.
Donna Spangler . . . . Esther
Yvette Stephens . . . . Mia
•• 0:25—Left breast, when Renny makes out with her.
••• 0:28—Brief left breast, then breasts posing with Linda.

••• 0:29—Full frontal nudity making love with Linda Carol and Renny.
• 0:48—Breasts and brief buns on TV.
• 0:50—Brief breasts in flashback.

Julie Strain . . . . Ingrid
••• 0:55—Breasts and partial buns, wearing black garter belt and stockings, making love with Renny in restroom. Long scene.

Paula Trickey . . . . Jasmine

Carnal Knowledge *(1971)*

Ann-Margret . . . . Bobbie
• 0:48—Breasts and buns, while making love in bed with Jack Nicholson. Dark.
•• 0:49—Buns and brief breasts, lying in bed, then getting out and into shower with Nicholson.
• 1:07—Brief side view of left breast putting a bra on in the bedroom.
1:08—In black bra and panties, while sitting in bed talking with Nicholson.

Candice Bergen . . . . Susan
Carol Kane . . . . Jennifer
Rita Moreno . . . . Louise

Carnival of Love *(1983)*

a.k.a. Inside the Love House

Becky LeBeau . . . . Nancy
• 0:29—Brief breasts in open robe, while putting on pants.
••• 0:56—Nude, while making love with a guy in a flower setting. Long scene.
• 1:05—Brief breasts.

Kristi Somers . . . . Kristi
•• 0:50—Breasts and buns, while making love with a guy in the clouds.
••• 1:01—Breasts and buns, while making love with a guy in the clouds. Long scene.

Caroline at Midnight *(1993)*

Julie Baltay . . . . Dream Lover
• 0:31—Right breast, while in bed during Jack's dream. Don't see her face.

Susan Harvey Lilli
•• 0:03—Breasts, while being held by Stan, while Judd Nelson tries to get information from Miguel.

Christina Karras . . . . Party Dancer
Virginia Madsen . . . . Susan Prince
Mia Sara . . . . Victoria
••• 0:24—Breasts, while making love with Jack.
•• 0:30—Left breast, in open robe in bedroom with Tim Daly.
••• 0:51—Breasts, while making love on top and under Jack in bed. Nice!

Stacey Travis . . . . Christine Jenkins

Carrie *(1976)*

Nancy Allen . . . . Chris Hargenson
•• 0:01—Nude, in slow motion in girls' locker room behind Amy Irving.

Amy Irving . . . . Sue Snell
P.J. Soles . . . . Norma
Sissy Spacek . . . . Carrie White
•• 0:02—Nude, taking a shower, then having her first menstrual period in the girls' locker room.
• 1:25—Brief breasts taking a bath to wash all the pig blood off her after the dance.

Carried Away *(1996)*

Amy Irving . . . . Rosealee Henson
••• 1:11—Nude, while in room with Dennis Hopper.

Eleese Lester . . . . Marie
Amy Locane . . . . Catherline Wheeler
••• 0:24—Breasts, after taking off her sweater while in loft in barn with Dennis Hopper.
••• 0:25—Breasts, when Hopper returns to the loft.
•• 0:37—Breasts and buns, while riding a horse in barn. Some long shots, some closer shots.
• 0:46—Left breast in open dress while standing behind truck in the road to tempt Hopper.
••• 0:47—Left breast, while making love in loft in barn with Hopper.
•• 0:56—Breasts, after sitting up in barn after being discovered with Hopper by Hal Holbrook. Almost partial lower frontal nudity.
••• 1:18—Nude, in bedroom with Hopper.

Carrington *(1995; British)*

Janet McTeer . . . . Vanessa Bell
Emma Thompson . . . . Dora Carrington
• 0:29—Brief back side of right breast while putting pajamas on.
• 1:29—Most of right breast, while making love on a boat with a guy.

Cartel *(1990)*

Suzanne Slater . . . . Nancy
• 0:36—Breasts during brutal rape/murder scene.

Casanova *(1987)*

Marina Baker . . . . Lucretia
Faye Dunaway . . . . Countess
Sylvia Kristel . . . . Maddalena
Traci Lind . . . . Heidi
• 1:56—Very, very brief right breast while bending over to help Richard Chamberlain. Long, long shot.

Rose McVeigh . . . . Captain's Wife
Ornella Muti . . . . Henriette
Aitana Sánchez-Gijón . . . . Therese
Hanna Schygulla . . . . Casanova's Mother

Casino *(1995)*

Melissa Prophet . . . . Jennifer Santoro
Millicent Sheridan . . . . Senator's Hooker
• 0:18—Brief buns and out of focus breasts, while undressing in room with Senator.

Sharon Stone . . . . Ginger McKenna

Castaway *(1986)*

Frances Barber . . . . Sister Saint Winifred
Amanda Donohoe . . . . Lucy Irvine
••• 0:22—Breasts talking to Reed.
•• 0:32—Nude on beach after helicopter leaves.
•• 0:48—Full frontal nudity lying on her back on the rocks at the beach.
••• 0:51—Breasts on rock when Reed takes a blue sheet off her, then catching a shark.
••• 0:54—Nude yelling at Reed at the campsite, then walking around looking for him.
••• 1:01—Breasts getting seafood out of a tide pool.
•• 1:03—Breasts lying down at night talking with Reed in the moonlight.
••• 1:18—Breasts taking off bathing suit top after the visitors leave, then arguing with Reed.

Georgina Hale . . . . Sister Saint Margaret
Virginia Hey . . . . Janice

Casual Sex? (1988)

Melinda Armstrong . . . . Uncredited Exercise Instructor
Victoria Jackson . . . . Melissa
- 0:30—Brief buns lying down with Lea Thompson at a nude beach.
- 0:33—Brief buns wrapping a towel around herself just before getting a massage. Long shot, hard to see.
- 1:06—Brief buns, when getting out of bed.

Lea Thompson . . . . Stacy
- 0:27—Buns, while lying down at nude beach with Victoria Jackson.
- 0:30—Buns at the beach. Pan shot from her feet to her head.

Cat Chaser (1988)

Brooke Becker . . . . Philly
Kelly McGillis. . . . . Mary De Boya
- ••• 0:23—Breasts on the floor with Peter Weller. Long scene.
- ••• 1:04—Full frontal nudity taking off her slip and getting raped by her husband's pistol. Kind of dark.
- •• 1:06—Brief buns, getting pushed around the house. Right breast while signing a paper.

Sherrie Rose . . . . Uncredited Waitress
Adrianne Sachs . . . . Anita De Boya

Cat in the Cage (1978)

Colleen Camp . . . . Gilda Riener
- 0:36—Very brief left breast twice, while making love in bed with Bruce.

Sybil Danning . . . . Susan Khan
- 0:24—Brief breasts getting slapped around by Ralph.
- 0:25—Brief left breast several times smoking and talking to Ralph, brief left breast getting up.
- •• 0:30—Full frontal nudity getting out of the pool.
- 0:52—Black bra and panties undressing and getting into bed with Ralph. Brief left breast and buns.
- 1:18—Very brief right breast several times, struggling with an attacker on the floor.

Cat People (1982)

Nastassja Kinski . . . . Irena Gallier
- ••• 1:03—Nude at night, walking around outside chasing a rabbit.
- •• 1:35—Breasts taking off blouse, walking up the stairs and getting into bed.
- 1:37—Brief right breast, lying in bed with John Heard.
- •• 1:38—Breasts getting out of bed and walking to the bathroom.
- •• 1:40—Brief buns, getting back into bed. Breasts in bed.
- •• 1:47—Full frontal nudity, walking around in the cabin at night.
- 1:49—Breasts, tied to the bed by Heard.

Lynn Lowry . . . . Ruthie
- 0:16—In black bra in Malcolm McDowell's hotel room, then brief breasts when bra pops open after crawling down the stairs.

Annette O'Toole . . . . Alice Perrin
- ••• 1:30—In a bra, then breasts undressing in locker room.
- 1:31—Some breasts shots of her in the pool. Distorted because of the water.
- 1:33—Brief right breast, after getting out of the pool.

Tessa Richarde . . . . Billie
- •• 1:00—Breasts in bed with Malcolm McDowell trying to get him excited.

• *Catch Me... If You Can* (1989)

Loryn Locklin . . . . Melissa
- 1:32—In bra trying to get policeman's attention. Very, very brief side of right breast while turning around. Looks like she's wearing flesh-colored pasties.

Catch the Heat (1987)

Tiana Alexandra. . . . . Checkers Goldberg
- 0:20—Left breast, several times, while in the shower.

Catch-22 (1970)

Suzanne Benton . . . . Dreedle's WAC
Olimpia Carlisi . . . . Luciana
- 1:04—Breasts lying in bed talking with Alan Arkin.

Paula Prentiss . . . . Nurse Duckett
- 0:22—Full frontal nudity on platform in the water, throwing her dress to Alan Arkin during his dream. Long shot, over exposed, hard to see.

Catherine & Co. (1975; French)

Jane Birkin . . . . Catherine
- 0:07—Breasts, standing up in the bathtub to open the door for another woman.
- •• 0:09—Side view of left breast, while taking off her blouse in bed.
- ••• 0:10—Breasts, sitting up and turning the light on, smoking a cigarette.
- •• 0:17—Right breast, while making love in bed.
- •• 0:24—Breasts taking off her dress, then buns jumping into bed.
- •• 0:36—Buns and left breast posing for a painter.
- 0:45—Breasts taking off dress, walking around the house. Left breast, inviting the neighbor in.

Catherine Cherie (1982)

Ajita Wilson . . . . Dancer/Miss Ajita
- 0:23—Breasts and buns dancing in club. Covered with paint. Long shot.
- 0:24—Brief buns, while greeting Carlo after the show.
- •• 0:43—Full frontal nudity in room with Carlo.

Cathy's Curse (1976; Canadian)

Beverley Murray . . . . Vivian
- 1:13—Very, very brief left breast, while jumping around in bathtub, brushing leaches off her body.

Cattle Annie and Little Britches (1980)

Diane Lane . . . . Jenny
Amanda Plummer . . . . Annie
- 0:39—Breasts visible under braless, wet long johns while standing in lake.

• *Caught* (1996)

Maria Conchita Alonso . . . . Betty
- 0:31—Brief breasts in mirror tiles when seen by Nick and before closing the door.
- •• 0:44—Breasts, while making love with Nick.
- 1:00—Buns, when in the shower with Nick, when almost caught by Edward James Olmos.

Cave Girl *(1985)*

Jasaé . . . . Locker Room Student
- •• 0:05—Breasts with four other girls in the girls' locker room undressing, then running after Rex. She's sitting on a bench, wearing red and white panties.

Michelle Bauer. Locker Room Student
- •• 0:05—Breasts with four other girls in the girls' locker room undressing, then running after Rex. She's the first to take her top off, wearing white panties, running and carrying a tennis racket.

Susan Mierisch . . . . Locker Room Student
- •• 0:05—Breasts with four other girls in the girls' locker room undressing, then running after Rex. She's blonde, wearing red panties and a necklace.

Cynthia Ann Thompson . . . . Eba
- • 0:41—Buns, standing in stream while bathing. Long shot.
- •• 1:04—Breasts making love with Rex.

Cave Girl Island *(1994)*

a.k.a. Beach Babes 2: Cave Girl Island

Sara Bellomo . . . . Xena
- •• 0:02—Breasts, when meeting Moon and kissing him.
- ••• 0:05—Nude, while making love with Moon. Long scene.
- •• 0:17—Breasts, while sexily playing with a banana.
- ••• 0:22—Breasts, while making love with Moon some more.
- •• 1:05—Nude, during party on spaceship.

Tina Hollimon . . . . Sola
- ••• 0:31—Nude, while making love in hut with Rock. Long scene.
- •• 1:05—Nude, during party on spaceship.

Stephanie Hudson. . . . . Luna
- ••• 0:37—Nude, while dancing in front of Dusty, then making love with him. Long scene.
- •• 1:06—Breasts, during party on spaceship.

CB4 *(1993)*

Khandi Alexander . . . . Sissy
- • 0:51—In bra and brief partial buns in panties on bed on top of Chris Rock. Side view of right breast, twice, while letting Allen Payne and Chris Rock poke it (Don't see her face, probably a body double).

Theresa Randle . . . . Eve

Reneé Tenison. . . . . Twin

Cellar Dweller *(1987)*

Debrah Farentino . . . . Whitney

Cheryl-Ann Wilson. . . . . Lisa
- • 0:58—Brief left breast, in gaping blouse, while bending over exercising.
- •• 0:59—Brief right breast, then breasts while taking a shower.
- • 1:01—Partial left breast, then brief breasts, before getting killed by the cellar dweller.

Cellblock Sisters: Banished Behind Bars *(1995)*

Jasaé . . . . Marie
- • 0:44—Breasts, taking off her towel in the showers behind Manny, then holding onto Gail Harris so Manny can beat her up.

Jenna Bodnar. . . . . Manny
- •• 0:30—Buns and breasts, while sitting on bench with other inmates when first entering prison.
- •• 0:44—Full frontal nudity, while in the showers with her girl gang, giving Gail Harris a hard time.

Gail Harris . . . . May
- •• 0:43—Breasts and buns, while taking a shower.
- • 1:05—In bra, then brief breasts, while making love with Detective Armand in prison conference room.

Robin South. . . . . Inmate

Annie Wood . . . . April
- •• 0:15—Breasts, while making love with Wreck in bedroom.
- • 0:19—Brief breast, when taking off her tank top to try on a dress.

• *The Celluloid Closet* *(1996; Made for Cable Movie)*

Patrice Donnelly . . . . Tory Skinner
- • 1:20—Brief buns, then breasts in clips from *Personal Best.*

Mariel Hemingway . . . . Chris Cahill
- • 1:21—Breasts and brief lower frontal nudity in a clip from *Personal Best.*

Susan Sarandon. . . . . Sarah Roberts
- • 1:24—Breasts in clips from *The Hunger.*

The Cement Garden *(1992; German/French/British)*

Charlotte Gainsbourg . . . . Julie
- •• 1:35—Breasts, after taking off her T-shirt while in bed with her brother.
- •• 1:39—Side view of left breast, while in bed with her brother, after being discovered by Derek.
- • 1:41—Left breast, when talking with her brother. Right breast, while sleeping in bed next to her brother.

Cemetery Man *(1993; Italian)*

a.k.a. Dellamorte Dellamore

Barbara Cupisti . . . . n.a.

Anna Falchi . . . . She
- •• 0:19—Breasts several times, while making love with Rupert Everett at cemetery and after getting bitten by her zombie husband.
- • 0:26—Breasts, when falling back onto table after Everett shoots her.
- •• 1:20—Back side of right breast after undressing. Left breast, while lying on bed after making love with Ruppert Everett.

• *Centerfold* *(1980; Video Tape)*

Martha Thomsen. . . . . Herself
- • 0:00—Full frontal nudity in still photos.
- • 0:06—Breasts, after taking off sweater in make-up room.
- •• 0:11—Breasts, while walking to get some lingerie.
- ••• 0:12—Full frontal nudity, while getting dressed in sheer white panties, garter belt, stockings and sheer white robe in make-up room.
- ••• 0:16—In lingerie, then full frontal nudity, while posing in studio for photos.
- ••• 0:25—Nude, while posing for photos in studio. Long scene.
- ••• 0:33—Nude, while posing some more.
- ••• 0:38—Breasts, while getting made up.
- •• 0:42—Full frontal nudity after taking off her pants and putting on a robe.
- ••• 0:44—Nude, while posing with for photos with Kathleen Sands. Very long scene.

• *Centerfold* *(1995)*

Cheryl Bartel . . . . Billie
- •• 0:28—Breasts, while talking with Gail outside by pool.
- ••• 0:33—Breasts and buns, while making love with a guy in the massage room.
- •• 0:56—Nude, while undressing on diving board and diving into the pool during a party.
- • 0:59—Breasts, while starting to make love with the senator in the stable.

•• 1:11—Breasts and buns, while tied by her wrists, having sex with the senator in the stable.

Gabriella Hall. . . . . Gail

••• 0:06—Nude, after taking off her robe, dancing for Scott, then making love with him. A bit on the dark side.

• 0:18—Breasts, while asking Manny if she looks good enough to pose for a magazine.

••• 0:21—Full frontal nudity, while posing for photographs in Manny's studio.

Julianne J. Mantia . . . . Sandra

••• 0:43—Breasts and buns, while making love with Kelly in spa, then making love on lounge chair with the senator.

• *Centerfold Fantasies* (*1997; Video Tape*)

Tawnni Cable . . . . .Herself

• 0:31—Brief buns in swimsuit.

Lisa Comshaw. . . . . .Herself

••• 0:13—Nude, while posing in dining room.

••• 0:35—Nude, while posing outdoors on stairs.

••• 0:39—Nude, while cavorting around pool with the other girls.

••• 0:49—Nude, while walking around outdoors by the pool.

Petra Verkaik . . . . .Herself

••• 0:08—Nude, while posing near a stairwell.

••• 0:39—Nude, while cavorting around pool with the other girls.

••• 0:44—Nude, while posing outdoors on stairs.

••• 0:51—Nude, while walking around outdoors by the pool.

Carrie Westcott . . . . .Herself

••• 0:02—Nude, while posing in dining room.

••• 0:18—Nude, while posing outdoors on stairs.

••• 0:39—Nude, while cavorting around pool with the other girls.

••• 0:50—Nude, while walking around outdoors by the pool.

The Centerfold Girls (*1974*)

Jennifer Ashley . . . . .Charly

• 0:34—Breasts taking off blouse while changing clothes.

•• 0:49—Breasts and buns posing for photographer outside with Glory.

Jaime Lyn Bauer . . . . Jackie

•• 0:04—Breasts getting out of bed and walking around the house.

••• 0:14—Breasts getting undressed in the bathroom.

•• 0:15—Brief breasts and buns putting on robe and getting out of bed, three times.

Tiffany Bolling. . . . . Vera

• 1:02—Brief breasts in photograph.

••• 1:12—Breasts in the shower.

• 1:21—Brief breasts in motel bed getting raped by two guys after they drug her beer.

Teda Bracci . . . . Rita

• 0:18—Breasts taking off her clothes in the living room in front of everybody.

Kitty Carl. . . . . .Sandi

•• 0:45—Breasts taking off her top while sitting on the bed with Perry.

• 0:51—Breasts while on the beach, dead. Long shot, hard to see.

Talie Cochrane . . . . .Donna

Anneka di Lorenzo . . . . Pam

Ruthy Ross . . . . .Glory

••• 0:49—Breasts and buns posing for photographer outside with Charly.

Connie Strickland . . . . .Patsy

•• 1:07—Breasts in bathroom washing her halter top just before getting killed.

Janet Wood . . . . Linda

•• 0:14—Breasts putting on robe and getting out of bed.

• *Centerfold Screen Test* (*1985; Video Tape*)

Leslee Bremmer. . . . . Herself

• 0:22—Breasts under fishnet top. (Practically see-through top.)

•• 0:24—Dancing, wearing the fishnet top and black G-string.

••• 0:28—Closer shot, dancing, while wearing the top.

Becky LeBeau. . . . . Herself

Ashley St. Jon . . . . Herself

••• 0:32—Breasts and buns in G-string, taking off her fur coat while auditioning in a car.

• *Centerfold Screen Test, Take 2* (*1986; Video Tape*)

Michelle Bauer. . . . . Marsha

••• 0:12—Breasts taking off her dress for Mr. Johnson. Then full frontal nudity. Nice, long scene.

• *Centerfold Screen Test, Take 3* (*1988; Video Tape*)

Jasaé . . . . Herself

••• 0:42—Nude after undressing and posing on sofa. Long scene.

Sylvia Baker . . . . Herself

••• 0:38—Nude after taking off dress during audition.

Century (*1993; British*)

Lena Headey . . . . Miriam

Miranda Richardson. . . . . .Clara

••• 0:51—Breasts, while making love with Clive Owen.

• 1:06—Partial right breast, while talking with Owen in bed.

• 1:07—Breasts, while lying on top of Owen, then right breast, after getting off him.

Dail Sullivan. . . . . Theo's Girl

• 0:13—Brief buns and right breast, while making love with Theo, when seen by Clive Owen through a gap in the curtains.

• 0:14—Full frontal nudity, after opening the curtains.

Liza Walker . . . . .Katie

Certain Fury (*1985*)

Irene Cara . . . . Tracy

• 0:32—Getting undressed to take a shower. Very brief side views of left breast.

• 0:35—Very brief breasts in shower after Tatum O'Neal turns on the kitchen faucet. Hard to see because of the shower door.

•• 0:36—Frontal nudity and side view of buns, behind shower door while Sniffer comes into the bathroom.

•• 0:39—Breasts several times when Sniffer tries to rape her and she fights back.

• 0:41—Buns, kneeling on floor. Overhead view.

Tatum O'Neal . . . . .Scarlet

A Certain Sacrifice (*1981*)

Madonna . . . . Bruna

••• 0:22—Breasts during weird rape/love scene with one guy and two girls.

• 0:40—Brief right breast in open top lying on floor after getting attacked by guy in back of restaurant.

• 0:57—Brief breasts during love making scene, then getting smeared with blood.

Chain of Desire (1992)

Angel Aviles. . . . . Isa
- 0:14—In bra in bed with Jesus, then breasts. Dark.

Holly Marie Combs . . . . Diana
Linda Fiorentino . . . . Alma D'Angeli
- 0:09—Very brief left breast, while rolling over in bed.

Assumpta Serna. . . . . Cleo

Chained Heat (1983; U.S./German)

Jennifer Ashley. . . . . Grinder
Greta Blackburn . . . . Lulu
Linda Blair . . . . Carol
- ••• 0:30—Breasts in the shower.
- •• 0:56—In bra, then breasts in the Warden's office when he rapes her.

Christina Cardan . . . . Miss King
Sybil Danning . . . . Erika
- ••• 0:30—Breasts in the shower with Linda Blair.

Monique Gabrielle. . . . . Debbie
- ••• 0:08—Nude, stripping for the Warden in his office.
- ••• 0:09—Nude, getting into the spa with the Warden.

Sharon Hughes . . . . Val
- •• 0:30—Brief breasts in the shower with Linda Blair.
- •• 0:51—Buns, in lingerie, stripping for a guy.
- •• 1:04—Breasts in the spa with the Warden.

Marcia Karr . . . . Twinks
- ••• 0:30—Breasts, getting soaped up by Edy Williams in the shower.
- • 0:37—Brief breasts, taking off her top in bed with Edy Williams at night.
- •• 0:40—Breasts in cell getting raped by the guard.

Susan Mechsner . . . . Gunderson
Louisa Moritz. . . . . Bubbles
Stella Stevens . . . . Taylor
Kate Vernon . . . . Cellmate
Edy Williams . . . . Paula
- •• 0:30—Full frontal nudity in the shower, soaping up Twinks.
- •• 0:36—Breasts at night in bed with Twinks.

Chained Heat 2 (1993)

Kimberly Kates . . . . Alexandra Morrison
- ••• 0:30—Full frontal nudity, while in the shower with Tina.
- • 0:56—Buns, in G-string under sheer blue dress during casino party.
- •• 1:04—Breasts, while sitting up in bed and getting out. Wearing panties and stockings.

Brigitte Nielsen . . . . Magda Kassar
Kari Whitman . . . . Suzanne Morrison

The Challenge (1982)

Donna Kei Benz. . . . . Akiko
- • 1:23—Breasts making love with Scott Glenn in motel room. Could be a body double. Dark, hard to see anything.

A Change of Seasons (1980)

Bo Derek . . . . Lindsey Routledge
- •• 0:00—Breasts in hot tub during the opening credits.
- • 0:25—Side view of left breast in the shower talking to Anthony Hopkins.

Shirley MacLaine . . . . Karen Evans

Chantilly Lace (1993; Made for Cable Movie)

Lindsay Crouse . . . . Rheza
Martha Plimpton . . . . Ann
Ally Sheedy . . . . Elizabeth
Helen Slater. . . . . Hannah
JoBeth Williams . . . . Natalie
- • 0:59—Brief breasts, taking off her blouse in bedroom with the pizza boy.

Chaplin (1992; British/U.S.)

Geraldine Chaplin . . . . Hannah Chaplin
Vicki Frederick . . . . Party Guest
Milla Jovovich . . . . Mildred Harris
- • 0:55—Top of left breast peeking over top of lingerie while sitting on bed talking to Chaplin.
- • 0:56—Buns, after taking off lingerie and standing in front of Chaplin.

Moira Kelly . . . . Hetty Kelly/Oona O'Neill
- •• 0:20—Brief breasts, while changing in dressing room when surprised by Chaplin.

Diane Lane . . . . Paulette Goddard
- • 1:33—Upper half of breasts, while lying in bed.

Penelope Ann Miller . . . . Edna Purviance
Nancy Travis . . . . Joan Barry

Chasers (1994)

Erika Eleniak. . . . . Toni Johnson
- ••• 1:03—In bra, then breasts and buns, while making love in bed with William McNamara.

Marilu Henner . . . . Katie

Chaste and Pure (1984; Italian)

Laura Antonelli . . . . Rosa
- • 0:35—Breasts and brief partial lower frontal nudity, while lying in bed and undressing, posing for Fernanado's Polaroid photos.
- • 0:58—Brief breasts, twice, falling out of her dress, while running through the woods at night.

Gabrielle Lazure . . . . n.a.

Chatterbox (1977)

Candice Rialson . . . . Penny
- •• 0:01—Left breast, in bed with Ted, then breasts getting out of bed.
- ••• 0:15—Side view of right breast then breasts during demonstration on stage.
- ••• 0:26—Breasts in bed talking on phone.
- •• 0:35—Breasts during photo shoot.
- •• 0:38—Breasts again for more photos while opening a red coat.
- •• 0:43—Breasts in bed with Ted.
- ••• 0:55—Breasts taking off white dress, walking up the stairs and opening the door.
- •• 1:09—Breasts opening her raincoat for Ted.

• *Cheatin' Hearts* (1992)

Pamela Gidley . . . . Samantha
Laura Johnson . . . . Patsy
Sally Kirkland . . . . Jenny
- •• 1:09—Nude, taking off her clothes outside after she gets angry with James Brolin.

Cheech & Chong's Nice Dreams (1981)

Sandra Bernhard . . . . Girl Nut
Shelby Chong . . . . Body Builder
Evelyn Guerrero. . . . . Donna
- • 0:43—Brief left breast sticking out of her spandex outfit, sitting down at table in restaurant.

Rikki Marin. . . . . Blonde in Car
Linnea Quigley . . . . Blondie Group #2

Roselyn Royce . . . . Beach Girl #3
- 0:29—Brief breasts on the beach with two other girls. Long shot, unsteady, hard to see.
- 0:32—More brief breasts again.
- 0:33—More brief breasts again.

Cheryl Smith . . . . Blondie Group #1
Victoria Wells . . . . Beach Girl #1
- 0:29—Brief breasts on the beach with two other girls. Long shot, unsteady, hard to see.
- 0:32—More brief breasts again.
- 0:33—More brief breasts again.

Cheech & Chong's Still Smokin' *(1983)*
Linnea Quigley . . . . Uncredited Spa Girl
- •• 0:42—Breasts, looking into two-way mirror. (She's the last girl.)
- • 0:53—Breasts, walking in front of Cheech in the shower room.
- •• 1:00—Breasts, sitting on the floor with five other naked girls with Cheech.

Cheerleader Camp *(1987)*
a.k.a. Bloody Pom Poms

Vickie Benson . . . . Miss Tipton
- • 0:27—Brief breasts undressing in her bedroom.

Rebecca Ferratti . . . . Theresa Salazar
Krista Pflanzer . . . . Suzy
- •• 0:11—Breasts several times sunbathing on the rocks.
- • 0:14—Brief breasts in flashback.
- • 0:17—Breasts on TV in Timmy's video tape of sunbathing on the rocks.

Betsy Russell . . . . Alison Wentworth
Teri Weigel . . . . Pam Bently
- •• 0:12—Breasts taking off her swimsuit top while sunbathing.

The Cheerleaders *(1973)*
Jovita Bush . . . . Bonnie
- • 0:02—Brief breasts, while taking off blouse in the locker room.
- •• 0:28—Brief breasts with the other cheerleaders in locker room.
- •• 0:54—Side view of right breast, while at slumber party.
- ••• 0:58—Nude, while running around at slumber party/orgy.
- • 1:00—Brief buns and left breast, when football player lifts her up.
- • 1:13—Breasts, with the other cheerleaders in back seat at carwash.

Denise Dillaway. . . . . Claudia
- • 0:08—Brief right breast, while in the car wash with Jon.
- ••• 0:23—Breasts and buns, while fooling around with Coach Gannon.
- •• 0:28—Brief breasts with the other cheerleaders in locker room.
- •• 0:49—Nude, while struggling on the ground with Sal outside.
- • 0:56—Partial buns and partial breasts under sheer nightie.
- • 1:13—Breasts, with the other cheerleaders in back seat at carwash.

Stephanie Fondue . . . . Jeannie
- ••• 0:18—Nude, in the boy's showers, then running around when trying to elude a group of boys during her initiation.
- •• 0:38—Breasts, then nude in bed with Jon.
- •• 0:45—Brief full frontal nudity, while sliding out through doors after water bed breaks.
- •• 0:51—Brief breasts, then full frontal nudity, while running through garden party.
- • 1:09—Breasts, while with quarterback.

Cheerleaders Wild Weekend *(1985)*
Kristine DeBell . . . . Debbie/Pierce
Elizabeth Halsey. . . . . Susan/Pierce
- ••• 0:40—Breasts in red panties, in contest.
- ••• 0:41—Breasts with the other five girls during contest.
- ••• 0:43—Breasts, while getting measured with the other two girls.

Marilyn Joi . . . . LaSalle/Polk
- • 0:00—Brief breasts while tying her shoelace in locker room.
- • 0:33—Brief breasts in catfight with another girl in cabin.
- ••• 0:39—Breasts, taking off her yellow blouse during contest.
- ••• 0:41—Breasts with the other five girls during contest.
- • 0:42—Breasts, losing contest.

Lenka Novak . . . . Jeanne/Darwell
- ••• 0:40—Breasts during contest after taking off white skirt, then blouse.
- ••• 0:41—Breasts with the other five girls during contest.
- ••• 0:43—Breasts, while getting measured with the other two girls, then getting attacked by Big John.
- ••• 0:44—Breasts getting into bathtub and getting washed by Frankie.

Janie Squire . . . . Donna/Darwell
- ••• 0:39—Breasts and brief buns, taking off her white blouse during contest.
- ••• 0:41—Breasts with the other five girls during contest.
- ••• 0:43—Breasts, while getting measured with the other two girls.

Wally Anne Wharton . . . . Lisa/Darwell
- •• 0:06—Breasts in back of school bus, flashing a guy in pick-up truck, then pressing her breasts against the window.
- ••• 0:37—Breasts, opening her white blouse during contest.
- ••• 0:39—Breasts and brief buns, in white skirt during contest.

Chesty Anderson, U.S. Navy *(1975)*
Marcie Barkin . . . . Pucker
Uschi Digard . . . . Baron's Girlfriend #1
Shari Eubank . . . . Chesty
- • 0:58—Brief right breast, while making love with Fred Willard.

Lynne Guthrie . . . . Lt. Ambrose
Rosanne Katon . . . . Cocoa
- •• 0:40—Breasts when bra pops open during fight in barracks.

Joyce Mandel . . . . Suzi
- •• 0:15—Buns and very brief back side of left breast, taking off towel and putting on robe.

Betty Thomas . . . . Party Guest #1
Dyanne Thorne . . . . Nurse

Chickboxer *(1992)*
Michelle Bauer. . . . . Greta "Chickboxer" Holtz
- ••• 0:57—Full frontal nudity, making love with a guy in bed.

The Children *(1980)*
Gale Garnett . . . . Cathy Freeman
Rita Montone . . . . Dee Dee Shore
- •• 0:20—Breasts, lying on chair by pool before talking to the Sheriff.

Children of a Lesser God *(1986)*
E. Katherine Kerr . . . . Mary Lee Ochs

Marlee Matlin . . . . Sarah
- 0:44—Brief buns under water in swimming pool. Don't see her face.
- 0:47—Part of left breast while hugging William Hurt (seen from under water).

Gigi Vorgan. . . . . Announcer

• China 9, Liberty 37 *(1978; Italian)*

a.k.a. Gunfire

(Hard to find this video tape. *Gunfire* has the nude scenes cut out.)

Jenny Agutter . . . . Catherine
- •• 0:06—Full frontal nudity (long shot), while undressing to bathe in a stream. Close up shot of breasts partially under the water when she is sitting in the stream.
- •• 0:35—Breasts, after taking off her dress outdoors with Clayton.
- •• 0:47—Brief buns and side of right breast, when standing up in bathtub. Brief breasts, while getting dried off.
- •• 1:09—Breasts and partial buns, while making love in bed with Clayton.

China Moon *(1993)*

Patricia Healy. . . . . Adele
- •• 0:02—Breasts, while in motel room with Charles Dance.
- • 0:13—Brief breasts in B&W photos that Madeleine Stowe looks at.

Sandy Martin. . . . . Gun Saleswoman

Madeleine Stowe. . . . . Rachel Munro
- ••• 0:22—Full frontal nudity after taking off dress and panties and jumping into lake from boat.

Chinatown *(1974)*

Faye Dunaway. . . . . Evelyn
- • 1:26—Very brief right breast, in bed talking to Jack Nicholson.
- • 1:28—Very brief right breast in bed talking to Nicholson. Very brief flash of right breast under robe when she gets up to leave the bedroom.

• The Chinatown Murders: Man Against the Mob *(1989)*

Ursula Andress. . . . . Betty Starr

Julia Nickson . . . . Kei Lee
- • 1:15—Breasts, while taking off her dress in bedroom in front of George Peppard. Very dark. It looks like she's wearing pasties when she gets into bed.
- • 1:18—Very brief breasts getting out of bed. It looks like she's wearing the pastie things again.

The Choirboys *(1977)*

Jeannie Bell . . . . Fanny Forbes

Blair Brown . . . . Kimberly Lyles

Phyllis Davis. . . . . Foxy/Gina
- •• 0:29—Breasts wearing pasties, under sheer pink robe.

Cheryl Smith . . . . Tammy

Suzanne Zenor . . . . Blonde at Party

Chopping Mall *(1986)*

a.k.a. Killbots

Angela Aames . . . . Miss Vanders

Barbara Crampton. . . . . Suzie
- •• 0:22—Brief breasts taking off top in furniture store in front of her boyfriend on the couch.

Kelli Maroney . . . . Alison

Toni Naples. . . . . Bathing Beauty

Suzanne Slater. . . . . Leslie
- •• 0:28—Brief breasts in bed showing breasts to Mike.

Mary Woronov . . . . Mary Bland

Christina *(1984; U.S./French)*

(Never released on video tape. Is shown occasionally on cable television.)

Pepita Full James . . . . Brigitte
- • 0:24—Breasts, while doing strip tease with Jewel Shepard in front of their boyfriends.
- •• 0:25—Full frontal nudity, while in sauna with her friends.
- •• 0:27—Breasts, while making love on sofa with Max. Briefly nude, when joining Shepard on sofa.

Josephine Jaqueline Jones. . . . . Antoinette
- •• 0:44—Breasts, after her blouse gets ripped off during fight with Marie.
- ••• 0:53—Breasts, after taking off blouse, then making love with Jewel Shepard.
- ••• 0:57—Breasts, while at the beach with Shepard.
- •• 1:00—Breasts, while on boat, during fight with smugglers.

Karin Schubert. . . . . Rosa

Jewel Shepard . . . . Christina
- • 0:00—Cleavage and brief glimpses of breasts, while dancing in disco in open jacket.
- • 0:04—Breasts, while wearing swimsuit bottom on sailboat.
- • 0:05—Brief breasts, while flashing.
- • 0:12—Silhouette of breasts, while making love on the beach with Patrick.
- ••• 0:17—Nude, while undressing in bathroom, taking a shower, then getting kidnapped by a masked woman.
- •• 0:23—Breasts doing strip tease in front of her friends in living room.
- •• 0:25—Full frontal nudity, while in sauna with her friends.
- • 0:26—Breasts and buns, while making love with Patrick on sofa.
- • 0:27—Full frontal nudity, while resting on Patrick's lap.
- •• 0:28—Nude, while getting out of bed and opening the curtains.
- •• 0:33—Breasts in nightmare, then waking up, while tied by her wrists.
- • 0:36—Breasts in nightmare, while blindfolded and tied up.
- • 0:43—Left breast in torn T-shirt.
- ••• 0:45—Nude, while getting out of bathtub.
- ••• 0:46—Nude, while making love with Marie on bed.
- • 0:52—Breasts under sheer nightie.
- •• 0:53—Full frontal nudity, while tied to table, then making love with Antoinette.
- •• 0:55—Full frontal nudity in a dream.
- • 0:56—Breasts in field after getting her blouse ripped open by Antoinette.
- •• 1:01—Breasts, while making love with a sailor in a dream.
- ••• 1:06—Full frontal nudity, while making love with Alain on boat.
- • 1:20—Breasts, while making love with Pablo.
- •• 1:29—Nude, while dancing in a disco.
- •• 1:30—Full frontal nudity, while typing on a computer.

The Church *(1991; Italian)*

a.k.a. La Chiesa

Asia Argento . . . . Lotte

Barbara Cupisti . . . . Lisa
- • 0:28—Very brief back side of right breast, while sitting up in bed. Side of right breast, while scooting over on bed while talking to Evald.

- 0:48—Very brief left breast in gaping nightgown, while scrambling for the phone. Very brief right breast in gaping nightgown when getting up off ground after jumping through window.
- 1:25—Breasts, while lying on slab and getting painted.
- 1:31—Breasts, while getting raped by beast.

CIA Trackdown *(1993)*

Claire Forlani . . . . Katarina
- 0:58—Side of right breast, while changing blouses in room with Harry.
- •• 1:07—Breasts and buns, while making love in bed with Harry.
- 1:11—Upper half of breasts, while getting out of water with Harry.

Ashley Graham . . . . Embassy Secretary
- •• 0:48—Breasts, while making love in room with Shane.

CIA—Code Name: Alexa *(1992)*

Kathleen Kinmont . . . . Alexa
- 1:04—Very brief buns and very, very brief right breast and brief left breast while making love with Lorenzo Lamas in bed.

La Cicala (The Cricket) *(1983)*

Barbara De Rossi . . . . Saveria
- •• 0:39—Nude swimming under waterfall with Clio Goldsmith.
- •• 0:43—Breasts undressing in room with Goldsmith.
- 0:57—Brief right breast changing into dress in room.
- 1:05—In wet white lingerie in waterfall with a guy, then in a wet dress.
- 1:26—Very brief buns in bed with Anthony Franciosa.
- •• 1:28—Breasts in bathroom with Franciosa.
- 1:36—Brief right breast making love with trucker.

Clio Goldsmith . . . . Cicala
- •• 0:26—Nude when Wilma brings her in to get Anthony Franciosa excited again.
- •• 0:39—Nude swimming under waterfall with Barbara De Rossi.
- ••• 0:43—Full frontal nudity undressing in room with De Rossi.

Cinderella *(1977)*

Linda Gildersleeve . . . . Farm Girl (redhead)
- ••• 0:21—Breasts and buns with her brunette sister in their house making love with the guy who is looking for Cinderella.
- •• 1:24—Full frontal nudity with her sister again when the Prince goes around to try and find Cinderella.

Elizabeth Halsey . . . . Farm Girl (brunette)
- ••• 0:21—Nude with her redhead sister in their house making love with the guy who is looking for Cinderella.
- •• 1:24—Breasts with her sister again when the Prince goes around to try and find Cinderella.

Yana Nirvana . . . . Drucella
- 0:02—Breasts taking off clothes with her sister Maribella to let Cinderella wash.
- 0:06—Brief breasts sitting up in bed with Maribella.

Mariwin Roberts . . . . Trapper's Daughter
- ••• 0:11—Frontal nudity getting a bath outside by her blonde sister. Long scene.

Cheryl Smith . . . . Cinderella
- •• 0:03—Breasts dancing and singing.
- ••• 0:30—Frontal nudity getting "washed" by her sisters for the Royal Ball.
- •• 0:34—Breasts in the forest during a dream.
- ••• 0:41—Breasts taking a bath. Frontal nudity drying herself off.
- 1:16—Brief breasts with the Prince.
- 1:30—Brief left breast after making love with the Prince to prove it was her.
- 1:34—Brief side view of left breast making love in the Prince's carriage.

Cinderella Liberty *(1973)*

Sally Kirkland . . . . Fleet Chick

Marsha Mason . . . . Maggie Paul
- •• 0:17—Side view of left breast in room with Caan. Brief right breast sitting down on bed.
- ••• 0:38—Breasts sitting up in bed, yelling at Caan.
- 0:54—Very brief left breast turning over in bed and sitting up.

Circle of Two *(1980)*

Tatum O'Neal . . . . Sarah Norton
- •• 0:56—Breasts standing behind a chair in Richard Burton's studio talking to him.

Circuitry Man II: Plughead Rewired *(1993)*

Traci Lords . . . . Norma

Bridget Marks . . . . Jeannie

Deborah Shelton . . . . Kyle
- •• 1:00—Breasts, after taking off blouse on horseback with Danner, then making love in a field.

Cisco Pike *(1971)*

Viva . . . . Merna

Joy Bang . . . . Lynn
- 0:45—Very, very brief right breast, seen under Kris Kristofferson's arm at the beginning of the scene in bed with Merna.

Karen Black . . . . Sue
- •• 0:47—Breasts, getting dressed in bedroom.

City Limits *(1984)*

Kim Cattrall . . . . Wickings
- •• 1:02—Right breast, while sitting up in bed with a piece of paper stuck to her.

Rae Dawn Chong . . . . Yogi

Joanelle Nadine Romero . . . . Woman in Desert
- 0:03—Almost breasts, then buns, while swimming in water tower with John Stockwell.

City of Hope *(1991)*

Angela Bassett . . . . Reesha
- •• 1:20—Breasts in bed with Joe Morton.

Gina Gershon . . . . Laurie

Barbara Williams . . . . Angela

• *City of Industry* *(1997)*

Tamara Clatterbuck . . . . Sunny

Lucy Alexis Liu . . . . Cathi Rose
- •• 0:48—Brief breasts and buns, while dancing in club.

Claire of the Moon *(1992)*

Trisha Todd . . . . Claire Jabrowski
- •• 0:21—Side of right breast, while making love in bed on top of a guy she picked up in a bar.
- ••• 0:24—Breasts, while getting a cigarette when in bed after making love with the guy.
- •• 0:28—Breasts, after taking off top in kitchen in front of Noel.

••• 1:39—Breasts, while making love in bed with Noel. Long scene.

Karen Trumbo . . . . Dr. Noel Benedict

• 1:22—Very brief left breast, twice, in open jacket in restroom with her fantasy woman, then Claire.

••• 1:39—Breasts, while making love on bed with Claire. Long scene.

Clash of the Titans *(1981)*

Ursula Andress. . . . . Aphrodite
Claire Bloom . . . . Hera
Judi Bowker. . . . . .Andromeda

• 1:41—Buns and partial side view of right breast getting out of bath. Don't see her face.

Maggie Smith . . . . Thetis
Vida Taylor . . . . .Danae

• 0:11—Right breast while breast feeding her baby. Buns, walking on beach.

Class *(1983)*

Jacqueline Bisset . . . . Ellen
Lolita Davidovich. . . . . 1st Girl (motel)
Virginia Madsen . . . . Lisa

•• 0:20—Brief left breast when Andrew McCarthy accidentally rips her blouse open at the girl's school.

Class of 1999 II: The Substitute *(1993)*

Caitlin Dulany . . . . .Jenna McKensie

•• 1:01—Breasts, while making love in bed with Emmett.

••• 1:02—More breasts while making love. Intercut with John shooting a machine gun.

Class of Nuke 'Em High *(1986)*

Janelle Brady . . . . Chrissy

•• 0:26—Breasts sitting on bed in the attic with Warren.

• 0:31—Brief breasts scene from 0:26 superimposed over Warren's nightmare.

Elizabeth Lambert . . . . Bake Sale Person

Class of Nuke 'Em High Part II: Subhumanoid Meltdown *(1991)*

Jackie Moen. Diane/Bald Subhumanoid
Leesa Rowland. . . . . Victoria

•• 0:24—Breasts in room with Roger. Special-effect mouth in her stomach.

• 0:25—Most of side of left breast, while making love on top of Roger.

Darla Slavens. . . . . Plain White Rapper
Suzanne Solari. . . . . Toxie Squirrel Gang Member
Nicole Vasilopoulos . . . . Bald Subhumanoid

• Claudine *(1974)*

Tamu . . . . Charlene

• 1:14—Brief breasts, when fighting with Diahann Carroll.

Diahann Carroll . . . . Claudine

• 0:17—Very brief tip of left breast, while sitting up in bubble bath.

•• 0:18—Brief partial left breast, while sitting in bubble bath after she puts hand towel down when she's talking with James Earl Jones.

Clean and Sober *(1988)*

Claudia Christian. . . . . .Iris
Harley Jane Kozak . . . . Ralston Receptionist
Stephanie Menuez. . . . . Ticket Agent
Rachel Ryan . . . . Uncredited Dead Girlfriend

• 0:02—Buns, lying dead in Michael Keaton's bed. Don't see her face, but it's her.

Clean Slate *(1981; French)*

a.k.a. Coup de Torchon

Isabelle Huppert . . . . Rosalie

•• 0:50—Breasts and buns, after taking off her slip in bedroom in front of Lucien.

••• 1:13—Breasts, after sitting up in bed, then full frontal nudity, after getting out of bed.

Irene Skobline . . . . .Anne

•• 1:07—Breasts, while taking a shower and getting spied on by Nono.

Cleo/Leo *(1989)*

Ginger Lynn Allen . . . . Karen

••• 0:39—Full frontal nudity getting out of the shower, getting dried with a towel by Jane Hamilton, then in nightgown.

••• 0:57—Full frontal nudity getting out of the shower and dried off again.

Ruth Corrine Collins. . . . . Sally

••• 0:08—Breasts getting dress pulled off by Leo.

Jennifer Delora. . . . . Bernice
Jane Hamilton . . . . Cleo Clock

•• 0:13—Nude undressing in front of three guys.

• 0:21—Breasts changing in dressing room.

••• 0:22—Breasts changing in dressing room with the Store Clerk.

•• 1:07—Left breast and lower frontal nudity making love with Bob on bed.

Debbie Rochon . . . . Reporter
Kimberly Taylor . . . . Store Clerk

••• 0:22—Breasts in white panties, changing in dressing room with Jane Hamilton. Very nice!

Cleopatra *(1963)*

Elizabeth Taylor . . . . Cleopatra

• 0:28—Half of buns, lying face down, while getting a massage.

Click: Calendar Girl Killer *(1989)*

Lisa Axelrod . . . . .Jennifer

•• 0:58—Breasts, while on bed in photography studio with Andy.

• 0:59—Breasts, while making love in bed with Andy. Hard to see because of the strobe lights.

• 1:00—Brief breasts and buns in G-string getting killed. Still lit with strobe lights.

• 1:01—Brief breasts, dead, covered with blood, after crashing through glass in door.

Juliette Cummins . . . . .Uncredited Model

••• 0:44—Buns in G-string, while undressing, then breasts and buns, dancing around in bathroom.

• 0:46—Partial breasts, while in bubble bath.

0:47—Slashed breasts, while in bathtub, after struggle with killer.

Tracy Dali . . . . June
Dona Speir . . . . .Nancy

• 0:11—Brief glimpses of breasts during photo session. Buns and breasts under sheer fabric.

•• 0:12—Brief buns, dropping the piece of fabric.

A Climate for Killing *(1990)*

Dedee Pfeiffer . . . . Donna

Sherrie Rose . . . . Rita Paris
- •• 1:30—Breasts in bed while Wayne recollects his crime to John Beck.

Katharine Ross. . . . . Grace Hines
Mia Sara . . . . Elise Shipp

A Clockwork Orange *(1971)*

Adrienne Corri . . . . Mrs. Alexander
- •• 0:11—Breasts through cut-outs in her top, then full frontal nudity getting raped by Malcolm McDowell and his friends.

Carol Drinkwater. . . . . Nurse Feeley
Gillian Hills . . . . Sonietta

Close My Eyes *(1991; British)*

Helen FitzGerald . . . . Scottish Girl
- •• 0:08—Nude, lying down, then getting up in room with Richard.

Saskia Reeves. . . . . Natalie Gillespie
- •• 0:29—Very brief right breast, twice, then breasts twice in room with Richard.
- ••• 0:31—Full frontal nudity, getting up and getting dressed.
- ••• 0:45—In white bra, then breasts standing, then lying on the floor with Richard.
- •• 0:46—Buns, while lying in bed with Richard. Nude, getting out of bed and putting on robe.
- • 0:56—Right breast, while lying in bed.

Club Extinction *(1990)*

a.k.a. Doctor M

Jennifer Beals. . . . . Sonja Vogler
- • 1:16—Brief side of left breast rolling over in bed with Hartmann. Don't see her face, but probably her.
- •• 1:17—Brief breasts in bed with Hartmann when he kisses her right breast, then brief right breast.

Coach *(1978)*

Meridith Baer . . . . Janet
Cathy Lee Crosby . . . . Randy
- • 0:31—Very brief side view of left breast when Michael Biehn opens the door while she's putting on her top.
- • 1:11—Very, very brief breasts in shower room with Biehn. Blurry, hard to see anything.

Rosanne Katon . . . . Sue
- • 0:10—Very brief breasts flashing her breasts along with three of her girlfriends for their four boyfriends.

Lenka Novak . . . . Marilyn
- • 0:10—Very brief breasts flashing her breasts along with her girlfriends for their boyfriends.

Cobb *(1994)*

Lolita Davidovich. . . . . Ramona
- • 1:04—Brief breasts, while kneeling on bed with Tommy Lee Jones.

Rhoda Griffis . . . . Ty's Mother
- • 0:47—Very brief right breast, when undressing in bedroom. Brief full frontal nudity while reaching for shotgun under bed.
- • 1:39—Brief breasts in open robe. Very brief lower frontal nudity.
- • 1:40—Full frontal nudity, twice, when getting shotgun. Brief side of left breast while sitting on bed, crying. Very, very brief left breast after walking away from window (seen behind her lover).

Patricia Tallman. . . . . Stunts

The Coca-Cola Kid *(1985; Australian)*

Gia Carides . . . . Chambermaid
Kris McQuade . . . . Juliana
Greta Scacchi . . . . Terri
- ••• 0:49—Nude, while taking a shower with her daughter.
- •• 1:20—Brief breasts, while wearing a Santa Claus outfit, then brief breasts and brief buns in bed with Eric Roberts.
- • 1:23—Brief buns and breasts, while in bed with Roberts.
- • 1:24—Brief breasts and very brief full frontal nudity (medium long shot), then brief buns and breasts when getting dressed, after getting out of bed.

Cocaine Wars *(1986)*

a.k.a. Vice Wars

Kathryn Witt . . . . Janet
- • 0:36—Brief breasts and buns making love in bed with John Schneider.

• ***Cockfighter*** *(1974)*

Patricia Pearcy . . . . Mary Elizabeth
- ••• 0:28—Breasts, while talking with Warren Oates outdoors, next to lake. Long scene.

Millie Perkins . . . . Frances Mansfield

Cocktail *(1988)*

Gina Gershon . . . . Coral
- • 0:31—Very, very brief right breast, while romping around in bed with Tom Cruise.

Kelly Lynch . . . . Kerry Coughlin
- • 0:45—Buns, wearing a two piece swimsuit at the beach.
- • 1:01—Buns, in string bikini swimsuit on boat with Tom Cruise and Bryan Brown.

Elisabeth Shue . . . . Jordan Mooney

• ***Cocoon*** *(1985)*

Jessica Tandy . . . . Alma Finley
Tahnee Welch . . . . Kitty
- • 1:01—Brief buns, while walking into swimming pool.

Coffy *(1973)*

Pam Grier . . . . Coffy
- • 0:05—Upper half of right breast in bed with a guy.
- • 0:19—Buns, walking past the fireplace, seen through a fish tank.
- •• 0:25—Breasts in open dress getting attacked by two masked burglars.
- ••• 0:38—Buns and breasts undressing in bedroom. Wow!
- • 0:42—Brief right breast when breast pops out of dress while she's leaning over. Dark, hard to see.

Linda Haynes. . . . . Meg

Cold Comfort *(1988)*

Jayne Eastwood . . . . Mrs. Brocket
Margaret Langrick . . . . Dolores
- •• 0:16—In tank top and panties, then breasts undressing in front of Stephen.
- • 0:19—Very brief side of left breast and buns getting robe.
- •• 0:41—Doing strip tease in front of her dad and Stephen. In black bra and panties, then breasts.
- • 0:42—Very brief breasts jumping into bed.

Cold Feet *(1989)*

Sally Kirkland. . . . . Maureen Linoleum
- • 0:56—In black bra and panties taking off her dress in bedroom with Keith Carradine. Brief right breast pulling bra down.

- 0:58—Brief side view of right breast sitting up in bed talking to Carradine.

Cold Heaven *(1990)*

Theresa Russell . . . . Marie Davenport

- 0:09—Very brief upper half of right breast, when it pops out of her swimsuit top when struggling to get Mark Harmon onto boat.
- 0:18—Side of left breast while washing herself at the sink.
- 1:14—Brief breasts several times, making love in bed with James Russo.

The Cold Light of Day *(1995; German)*

Lynsey Baxter . . . . Milena Tatour

- 1:17—Side view of left breast, while making love in bed with Richard E. Grant. Kind of dark.

Perdita Weeks . . . . Anna Tatour

- 1:22—Brief partial buns, while being carried by her mother in the rain in Richard E. Grant's nightmare.

Cold Steel *(1987)*

Heidi Kozak . . . . Gang Girl

Sharon Stone . . . . Kathy Conners

- 0:33—Brief left breast making love in bed with Brad Davis. Dark, hard to see. Brief breasts turning over after making love.

Cold Sweat *(1993)*

Maria Del Mar . . . . Joanne

- 0:35—Brief breasts, opening her robe to get Ben Cross' attention. Brief breasts when he gets off of her.

Shannon Tweed . . . . Beth Moore

- ••• 0:14—Breasts squished against the glass shower door while making out with Sean. More breasts and buns.
  0:15—In bra, while sitting on bed.
- •• 0:17—Breasts and buns while playing with fluorescent paints with Adam Baldwin in bathtub. Kind of dark.
- ••• 0:43—Breasts and very brief lower frontal nudity while on bed with Sean.
- •• 0:53—Buns and back side of left breast getting into bathtub. More breasts, twice, while in bathtub.

Lenore Zann . . . . Catherine Wicker

- •• 0:04—Brief buns in panties, then partial lower frontal nudity in bra, panties, garter belt and stockings. Brief breasts while making love in office with David.
- •• 0:46—Breasts in bubble bath while talking to Ben Cross.
- ••• 0:50—Breasts, while lying on bed and talking to Cross.

Coldfire *(1990)*

Lisa Axelrod . . . . Dancer

- •• 0:11—Breasts, twice, dancing on stage.
- 0:13—Brief breasts, getting pushed off the stage.

Darcy De Moss . . . . Maria

- ••• 0:27—Partial right breast and buns, lying in bed with Nick. Left breast, then breasts making love with him.
- •• 0:30—Breasts in bathtub with Nick.

The Collector *(1965)*

Samantha Eggar . . . . Miranda Grey

- 1:38—Brief back side of left breast after taking off gown in front of Stamp, just before she unbuttons his shirt.

Collector's Item *(1988)*

a.k.a. The Trap

Laura Antonelli . . . . Marie Colbert

- 0:20—Lower frontal nudity, then right breast while making love with Musante. Dark.

Blanca Marsillach . . . . Jacqueline

- •• 0:52—In white bra cleaning up Tony Musante in bed, then breasts.
- 1:04—Lower frontal nudity while watching Musante and Laura Antonelli making love in bed.
- 1:18—Breasts getting dressed. A little dark.
- •• 1:22—Breasts changing clothes in bedroom while Antonelli talks to her.

Cristina Marsillach . . . . Young Marie

- •• 0:12—Right breast in elevator with Tony Musante.
- •• 0:36—Breasts in open blouse, then full frontal nudity in hut with Musante.

The Color of Money *(1986)*

Mary Elizabeth Mastrantonio . . . . Carmen

- 0:41—Brief breasts in bathroom mirror drying herself off while Paul Newman talks to Tom Cruise. Long shot, hard to see.

Helen Shaver . . . . Janelle

Color of Night *(1994)*

Shirley Knight . . . . Edith Niedelmeyer

Jane March . . . . Rose

- ••• 0:59—Nude, while in pool with Bruce Willis.
- •• 1:00—Nude, while making love with Willis in the house.
- ••• 1:02—Breasts and brief lower frontal nudity, when sitting at the table. Breasts, while making love in the shower with Willis.
- 1:04—Breasts, after taking off her clothes in Lesley Ann Warren's bedroom.
- 1:35—Nude under apron while in the kitchen with Willis.
- •• 1:38—Full frontal nudity while in the bathtub with Willis.
- •• 1:47—Breasts, with Warren.
- 1:49—Brief right breast.
- 1:55—Left breast and buns in photo that Willis finds in notebook.
- 2:14—Left breast in gaping blouse, while on top of tower.

Colors *(1988)*

Maria Conchita Alonso . . . . Louisa Gomez

- ••• 0:48—Breasts making love in bed with Sean Penn.

The Comfort of Strangers *(1991)*

Helen Mirren . . . . Caroline

Natasha Richardson . . . . Mary

- ••• 0:45—Breasts sleeping in bed. Long shot. Then closer breasts after waking up. Long scene.
- •• 1:05—Breasts making love with Colin. Lit with blue light.
- •• 1:06—Right breast, lying in bed with Colin. Lit with blue light.

Coming Home *(1978)*

Jane Fonda . . . . Sally Hyde

- •• 1:26—Making love in bed with Jon Voight. Breasts only when her face is visible. Buns and brief left breast when you don't see a face is a body double.

Penelope Milford . . . . Viola Munson

- 1:19—Doing strip tease in room with Jane Fonda and two guys. Sort of right breast peeking out between her arms when she changes her mind.

Coming to America *(1988)*

Midori . . . . Bather

- 0:04—Brief buns, while standing in bathtub in front of Eddie Murphy.

Victoria Dillard . . . . Bather
•• 0:04—Breasts, standing up in royal bathtub to announce "The royal penis is clean, Your Highness."
Monique Mannen . . . . Boring Girl/Dancer
Bianca McEachin . . . . Uncredited Miss Black Awareness
• 0:37—Buns, wearing pink sequined, two piece swimsuit on stage during Black Awareness meeting.

Coming Together *(1978)*

a.k.a. A Matter of Love

Christy Neal . . . . Vicky Hughes
• 0:30—Brief right breast in shower with Angie.
• 0:37—Breasts and buns making love standing up in front of sliding glass door with Frank. Quick cuts.
• 0:49—Brief breasts again during flashbacks.
•• 0:57—Breasts with Angie and Richard.
• 1:05—Breasts on beach with Angie. Long shot.

• ***The Commandments*** *(1997)*

Courteney Cox . . . . Rachel Luce
• 0:52—Very brief upper half of left breast, while making love in bed with Aidan Quinn.
Joanna Going . . . . Karen Warner
• 0:05—Very brief part of right breast, when putting on her swimsuit top.

Commando *(1985)*

Ava Cadell . . . . Girl in Bed
• 0:46—Very brief breasts three times in bed when Arnold Schwarzenegger knocks a guy through the motel door into her room.
Rae Dawn Chong . . . . Cindy
Chelsea Field . . . . Stewardess
Alyssa Milano . . . . Jenny

Common Bonds *(1991)*

Rae Dawn Chong . . . . Ilene Curtis
Tasmin Kelsey . . . . Ginger
• 0:04—Breasts in hotel room with the cop when Michael Ironside bursts into the room. Long shot. More out of focus breasts shots in the mirror.

The Company of Wolves *(1985)*

Danielle Dax . . . . Wolfgirl
• 1:26—Brief buns and breasts running around outside. Her hair is in the way a lot.

Con el Corazón en la Mano *(1988; Mexican)*

Maria Conchita Alonso . . . . n.a.
• 0:38—Very, very brief right breast, while turning over in bed with her husband.
• 0:39—Breasts several times, taking a bath.
•• 1:15—Breasts while ripping off her dress. Long shot, side view, standing while kissing a guy.

Conan the Barbarian *(1982)*

Sandahl Bergman . . . . Valeria
•• 0:49—Brief left breast making love with Arnold Schwarzenegger.
Cassandra Gava. . . . . Witch
Valerie Quennessen . . . . The Princess

Concealed Weapon *(1994)*

Lisa Boyle . . . . Polish Emigree
•• 0:07—Breasts in ripped open dress top, while getting molested by the American guy.
•• 0:10—Breasts in open dress top when the American guy caresses her breasts with gun before killing her.
Pamela Runo . . . . Victim

The Concrete Jungle *(1982)*

Greta Blackburn. . . . . Lady in Bar
Sondra Currie . . . . Katherine
Aimée Eccles . . . . Spider
Marcia Karr . . . . Marcy
Camille Keaton . . . . Rita
• 0:41—In black bra, then breasts getting raped by Stone. Brief lower frontal nudity sitting up afterwards.
Susan Mechsner . . . . Breaker

Condition Red *(1995)*

Brooke Mills. . . . . TV Reporter
Cynda Williams . . . . Gidell
• 0:42—Brief breasts, when James Russo stops making love with her.

Confessions of a Serial Killer *(1987)*

Eleese Lester . . . . Karen Grimes
• 0:34—Buns, while gagged and tied to bed before being raped and killed.

Conflict of Interest *(1992)*

Lynette Howe . . . . Shannon
••• 0:45—Breasts in bed with another girl, then getting out to call the police.
• 0:53—Breasts on top of Jason, lit with different colored lights.
• 1:04—Breasts during Jason's recollection.
Alyssa Milano . . . . Eve
Heather-Elizabeth Parkhurst. Francesca
Dey Young . . . . Vera
• 0:31—Brief right breast, while turning over on her back in bed with Mick.
•• 0:32—Left breast, while in bed, getting kissed by Mick.

The Conformist *(1970; Italian/French)*

Dominique Sanda . . . . Anna Quadri
•• 1:01—Breasts, taking off leotard for Jean-Louis Trintignant.
Stefania Sandrelli . . . . Giulia
• 0:41—Right breast, while in train with Jean-Louis Trintignant.
• 1:07—Very brief, upper half of buns, while turning around.

Consenting Adults *(1992)*

Mary Elizabeth Mastrantonio . . . . Priscilla Parker
Rebecca Miller. . . . . Kay Otis
• 0:28—Buns and brief side view of left breast, while getting out of tub. Seen through shutters while Kevin Kline watches through the window.
Melissa Anne Moore . . . . Trudy Seaton
• 0:37—Buns, while lying in bed when Kevin Kline takes the place of the husband.
Billie Neal . . . . Annie Duttonville

Contempt *(1963; French/Italian)*

Brigitte Bardot . . . . Camille Javal
• 0:04—Buns.
• 0:54—Buns, while lying on rug.
• 1:30—Buns, while lying on beach. Long shot.

The Conversation *(1974)*

Teri Garr . . . . Amy

Elizabeth MacRae . . . . .Meredith
- 1:14—Breasts and buns, getting undressed in work area with Gene Hackman. Long shot, dark.

Conversation Piece (1974; Italian/French)

Claudia Marsani . . . . Lietta
- 1:13—Breasts, while with Konrad.
- 1:15—Breasts, while getting dressed in other room. Medium long shot.

Dominique Sanda . . . . Mother

The Conviction (1994; Italian)

a.k.a. La Condanna

Claire Nebout . . . . Sandra Celestini
- •• 0:22—Breasts, after taking off her dress in dark room with Lorenzo. Dark.

Grazyna Szapolowska . . . . Monica
- 0:45—Buns, while lying asleep in bed. Dark.

Convoy (1978)

Ali MacGraw . . . . Melissa

Cassie Yates . . . . Violet
- 0:21—Very brief left breast, while in truck sleeper with Kris Kristofferson.

The Cook, The Thief, His Wife & Her Lover (1989; Dutch/French)

Helen Mirren . . . . Georgina Spica
- •• 0:32—In lingerie undressing, then lower frontal nudity, buns and left breast in kitchen with Michael.
- 0:42—Buns and right breast, while making love with Michael again.
- •• 0:57—Breasts sitting and talking with Michael.
- 1:01—Buns, while kneeling on table.
- 1:05—Brief breasts, while leaning back on table with Michael.
- 1:07—Lower frontal nudity opening her coat for Michael.
- 1:11—Buns and breasts in kitchen.
- ••• 1:14—Buns, getting into meat truck. Full frontal nudity in truck and walking around with Michael.

Cool Blue (1990)

Judie Aronson . . . . Cathy
- •• 1:03—Breasts in bed on top of Woody Harrelson.

Ely Pouget . . . . Christiane
- •• 0:18—Side view of right breast, then breasts with Woody Harrelson.

The Cool Surface (1992)

Elizabeth Barondes . . . . Actress

Teri Hatcher . . . . Dani Payson
- ••• 0:20—Close-up of left breast, while lying in bed with Robert Patrick during daydream.
- ••• 0:27—Breasts, while standing in front of Patrick when he takes off her lingerie.
- 0:29—Brief right breast, when Patrick gets out of bed.

Copycat (1995)

Corie Henninger . . . . .Jogger
- 0:16—Brief left breast, while lying dead in bathtub.

Holly Hunter . . . . Detective M.J. Monahan

Sigourney Weaver . . . . Helen Hudson

The Coriolis Effect (1994)

Corinne Bohrer . . . . Suzy
- 0:01—Partial breasts, while making love with Dana Ashbrook on kitchen table.

Jennifer Rubin . . . . .Ruby

Corporate Affairs (1990)

Ria Coyne . . . . Mistress
- •• 0:10—Left breast several times in back of car with Arthur.

Mary Crosby . . . . .Jessica Pierce

Kim Gillingham . . . . Ginny Malmquist
- 1:09—Breasts, climbing out of cubicle.

Lisa Moncure . . . . Carolyn Bean
- 1:07—Very, very brief left breast, while kicking Douglas out of cubicle.

Elena Sahagun . . . . Stacy

Jeanne Sal . . . . Sandy
- 0:38—Left breast in open dress while sneaking around the office with Buster.

Christina Veronica . . . . .Tanning Woman

• The Corporate Ladder (1996)

Lisa Falcone . . . . .Contestant #1

Kathleen Kinmont . . . . Nicole Landon
- ••• 0:39—In bra, panties and stockings, then breasts and buns, while making love with Matt in the office.
- 1:14—Brief breasts, while making love with Matt in bed.
- •• 1:29—In bra, then breasts and buns, while undressing in backyard and walking into pool before killing Ben Cross with a champagne bottle.

Meilani Paul . . . . .Bianca
- 0:21—Very brief right breast during photo shoot.
- ••• 0:42—Breasts, after taking off her dress in backyard, then in swimming pool with Ben Cross.
- ••• 1:11—Breasts and buns in T-back, after taking off her dress in bedroom, while trying to seduce Matt.

Karen Roe . . . . Katrina

Lisa Marie Scott . . . . .Kyoko
- •• 0:15—In bra, then breasts and buns in backyard and in swimming pool with Ben Cross.

Talisa Soto . . . . Susan Taylor

Corvette Summer (1978)

Annie Potts . . . . Vanessa
- 0:51—Silhouette of right breast in van with Mark Hamill. Out of focus breasts washing herself in the van while talking to him. Don't really see anything.

Cotton Comes to Harlem (1970)

Judy Pace . . . . Iris
- •• 0:28—Buns and breasts, taking off dress and getting into shower.
- ••• 0:29—Breasts and buns while getting out of the shower.
- 0:30—Upper half of breasts in mirror while sitting at vanity.
- ••• 0:31—Brief breasts, unwrapping from towel and lying on bed. Breasts, when lying in bed. Breasts and buns while getting out of bed.

• The Courtyard (1995)

Mädchen Amick . . . . Lauren

Lara Piper . . . . .Kimberly
- 0:01—Brief left and right breast, in close-up shot. You don't see her face.

Cousin, Cousine (1975; French)

Marie-Christine Barrault . . . . Marthe
- •• 1:05—Breasts in bed with her lover, cutting his nails.
- 1:07—Brief side view of right breast, while giving him a bath.
- ••• 1:16—Breasts with penciled tattoos all over her body.

• 1:33—Braless in see-through white blouse saying "good-bye" to everybody.

Marie-France Pisier . . . . Karine

Cover Girl Models (1975)

Pat Anderson. . . . . Barbara

• 0:12—Very brief breasts, taking off dress during fitting session.
• 0:22—Right breast, while making love in bed with a guy.
•• 0:24—Breasts, when getting out of bed.
• 1:02—Brief breasts, after undoing her halter top to get the attention of policeman.

Lindsay Bloom. . . . . Claire

• 0:11—Brief right breast, after taking off swimsuit top during photo session.
• 0:32—Brief left breast, while putting on robe in bathroom.
•• 0:57—Brief breasts, while struggling with bad guy.

Rhonda Leigh Hopkins . . . . Pamela

Tara Strohmeier . . . . Mandy

• 0:04—Climbing out of swimming pool in braless wet T-shirt.
• 0:11—Breasts, after taking off swimsuit to and putting on T-shirt.
••• 0:23—Breasts, while posing for photographs with Mark.
••• 0:40—Breasts, while in hotel room with Mark.
•• 0:54—Breasts, while posing outdoors for photographs with Mark.

Mary Woronov . . . . Diane

Cover Me (1995)

Julie Cialini . . . . Waitress

Karen Kim. . . . . Brandy

•• 0:32—Buns and breasts in white lingerie, while dancing on stage in club.
• 0:49—Brief breasts on magazine cover.
• 0:52—Breasts, while dancing on stage in club. Brief breasts in magazine cover flashback.
•• 0:53—Breasts, while in bubble bath, then talking on the phone.

Shae Marks . . . . Candy Jefferson

• 0:01—Brief buns, on magazine cover on computer screen.
• 0:03—Brief breasts in photo on wall.
• 0:04—Breasts in photo on wall again.
•• 0:06—Breasts, while in panties, tied up to bed, before getting killed.
• 0:52—Breasts in photo on wall, then buns in magazine cover flashbacks.

Betsy Monroe . . . . Lakey Snow

Leslie Ryan . . . . Hostess

Kelly Sullivan. . . . . Dimitri's Mother

Courtney Taylor . . . . Holly Jacobsen

• 0:07—Breasts, while making love in bed with Rick Rossovich.
••• 0:28—Breasts and buns in T-backs, during photo session.
•• 0:30—Breasts during another photo session.
• 0:36—Breasts in photo CD pictures that she looks at with Rossovich on TV.
• 0:38—Brief buns in T-back and right breast in still photos in portfolio.
•• 0:46—Breasts, while making love in bed with Rossovich.
•• 0:52—Breasts and buns in yellow T-back, while dancing in club in a shower.
•• 1:04—Breasts and buns in T-back, while dancing on stage.
• 1:10—Breasts and buns in panties, under sheer nightie in booth.

Cover Story (1993)

Marissa Cody. . . . . Allison

•• 0:02—Breasts, while making love with Matt in bed.
• 0:10—Brief breasts, while making love in B&W flashback.
• 0:12—Left breast, while reading a letter and making love with Matt, then dead in B&W flashbacks.
• 0:34—Very, very brief breasts in B&W flashback.
• 0:53—Very brief breasts, in B&W flashback.

Tuesday Knight . . . . Tracy/Reen

•• 0:22—Breasts in outfit with painted face, while on video playback that Matt watches.
•• 1:08—Right breast, then breasts, while making love with Matt.

Covergirl (1982; Canadian)

Irena Ferris. . . . . Kit Paget

•• 0:19—Brief breasts taking off robe and getting into bathtub with Dee.
• 0:43—Very brief right breast sticking out of nightgown.
• 0:46—Upper half of left breast during modeling session.
• 0:47—Breasts in mirror in dressing room.
• 0:49—Brief breasts, while getting attacked by Joel.
• 0:53—Brief left breast, putting another blouse on.
• 0:53—Brief left breast, putting on blouse.

Roberta Leighton. . . . . Dee Anderson

Michele Scarabelli . . . . Snow Queen

Covert Assassin (1994; Italian)

Patricia Millardet . . . . Magda Altmann

• 0:23—Very brief buns, after dropping her robe in bedroom in front of Roy Scheider. Medium long shot. Don't see her face.

Rita Wolf . . . . Vritra

Crack House (1989)

Heidi Thomas . . . . Annie

• 1:09—Brief left breast and buns in a G string, on table getting raped by a gang.
• 1:14—Breasts in bathtub, dead.

Angel Tompkins . . . . Mother

Crackerjack (1994)

Nastassja Kinski . . . . K.C.

Melody Stark. . . . . Newlywed

• 0:33—Brief side view of left breast, while undressing in room with her husband.
••• 0:34—Breasts, when her husband plays with an ice cube on her breasts. Buns when the terrorists break into the room.

• Crash (1996; Canadian)

(NC-17 version reviewed.)

Rosanna Arquette . . . . Gabrielle

•• 1:14—Left breast, while having sex in Mercedes with James Spader.

Holly Hunter . . . . Dr. Helen Remington

• 0:08—Left breast, in open jacket when trying to get out of car after accident.
• 0:23—In bra, then brief left breast and panties, then partial left breast sticking out of bra, while having sex in car with James Spader.
• 0:46—Lower frontal nudity, wearing a bra, while having sex with Spader in back seat of car.

Alice Poon . . . . Camera Girl

• 0:05—Left breast, then brief breasts, while making love with James Spader in camera room.

Deborah Unger . . . . Catherine Ballard
- 0:03—In bra, then partial right breast, brief partial lower frontal nudity and side of buns, while having sex with a guy in airplane hanger.
- 0:05—Brief buns through slit in dress, while on balcony, seen by James Spader.
- 0:13—Brief, partial lower frontal nudity under skirt when Spader touches her in hospital room.
- •• 0:43—Lower frontal nudity, while making love with Spader in bed. Long scene.
- •• 1:05—In bra, then right breast, while sitting in back of car with Elias Koteas while Spader is in the front seat.
- 1:07—Lower frontal nudity, while having rough sex with Koteas in back of car as it goes through a car wash with Spader in the front seat.
- •• 1:09—Lower frontal nudity, then partial right breast, when Spader examines her bruises.
- 1:35—Partial lower frontal nudity, when making love with Spader after her car crash. Medium long shot.

Crash and Burn *(1990)*
Katherine Armstrong . . . . Christine
- ••• 1:00—Breasts taking a shower before being killed.

Crawlspace *(1986)*
Carol Francis . . . . Jess
Tané McClure . . . . Sophie Fisher
- 0:00—Nipples, sticking out of holes that she cuts in her red bra. Brief breasts in bed making love with Hank. Dark.

Crazy Mama *(1975)*
Sally Kirkland . . . . Ella Mae
Cloris Leachman . . . . Melba
- 0:53—Brief left breast under clear plastic blouse while washing Stuart Whitman's hair in the sink.

Linda Purl . . . . Cheryl
- 0:52—Very brief buns, then brief breasts when Snake and Donny Most keep opening the door after she has taken a shower. Long shot, hard to see.

Creator *(1985)*
Mariel Hemingway . . . . Meli
- 0:38—Brief breasts cooling herself off by pulling up T-shirt in front of a fan.
- 1:10—Brief breasts flashing David Ogden Stiers during football game to distract him.

Virginia Madsen . . . . Barbara
- ••• 0:58—Breasts while in shower with Spano.

Creature *(1985)*
Marie Laurin . . . . Susan Delambre
- •• 0:41—Breasts and brief buns with blood on her shoulders, getting Jon to take his helmet off.

Diane Salinger . . . . Melanie Bryce

Creatures the World Forgot *(1971; British)*
Julie Ege . . . . Nala, The Girl
- 0:56—Very brief breasts several times (it looks like a stunt double) fighting in cave with The Dumb Girl. Hard to see.
- 1:32—Very, very brief half of right breast when fighting a snake that is wrapped around her face.

Marcia Fox . . . . The Dumb Girl
- 0:51—Right breast, then brief breasts turning around by the pool.
- 0:58—Brief breasts fighting with Julie Ege.
- 1:20—Very brief right breast when The Dark Boy gets his leg cut.

Creepozoids *(1987)*
Ashlyn Gere . . . . Kate
Linnea Quigley . . . . Blanca
- •• 0:15—Breasts taking off her top to take a shower.
- •• 0:16—Right breast, while standing in shower with Butch.
- 0:24—Right breast several times while sleeping in bed with Butch.

Creepshow 2 *(1987)*
Lois Chiles . . . . Annie Lansing
- •• 0:59—Brief breasts getting out of boyfriend's bed, then getting dressed.

Cries and Whispers *(1972; Swedish)*
a.k.a. Viskingar Och Rop

Harriet Andersson . . . . Agnes
Ingrid Thulin . . . . Karin
- •• 0:57—Breasts and buns, undressing and getting ready for bed. Something covers lower frontal nudity.

Liv Ullmann . . . . Maria

Crime Lords *(1990)*
Susan Byun . . . . Monahan
- •• 1:06—Left breast, then right breast, while making out with Wayne Crawford on the couch.

Kimberleigh Stark . . . . Lieutenant Sylvestri

Crime Zone *(1989)*
Sherilyn Fenn . . . . Helen
- •• 0:23—Breasts wearing black panties making love with Bone. Dark, long shot.

Crimes of Passion *(1984)*
(Unrated version reviewed.)

Annie Potts . . . . Amy Grady
Janice Renney . . . . Stripper
- ••• 0:06—Breasts and buns dancing while Anthony Perkins watches.
- 1:00—Buns again.

Kathleen Turner. Joanna Crane/China Blue
- ••• 0:45—Breasts, wearing black panties and stockings, in bed with Bobby. Shadows of them making love on the wall.
- 1:00—Right breast in back of a limousine with a rich couple.
- 1:27—Right breast in bed with Bobby.

• ***Crimetime*** *(1996; U.S./British)*
Karen Black . . . . Millicent Hargreave
Geraldine Chaplin . . . . Thelma
Marianne Faithfull . . . . Club Singer
Sadie Frost . . . . Val
- 0:31—Brief breasts, when flashing herself for Stephen Baldwin in a doorway at night.
- •• 0:59—Left breast, while sleeping when Baldwin pulls back the covers and caresses her.
- 1:00—Brief breasts, after waking up and calling for Baldwin.

• ***Criminal Hearts*** *(1995)*
Lisa Boyle . . . . Claire
Melissa Dutton . . . . Amy Locane's Body Double
- 0:19—Breasts, while in bed with Kevin Dillon.
- 0:51—Breasts, several times, while in bed with Dillon. Upper half of buns while sitting on him.

Morgan Fairchild . . . . D.A.
Amy Locane . . . . Kell

Criminal Law *(1989)*

Karen Young . . . . Ellen Falkner

- 1:21—Very brief buns, then brief breasts in bed with Ben.

The Criminal Mind *(1993)*

Tahnee Welch . . . . Gabrielle Dupre

•• 0:57—Left breast, while making love in bed with Nick.

Criminal Passion *(1993)*

Shannon McLeod . . . . Isabelle Sabatini

- 0:03—Brief breasts, while making love on bed.

Joan Severance . . . . Melanie Hudson

•• 0:57—Breasts and buns, while making love with Ashcroft in swimming pool.

•• 1:20—Buns and partial breasts, after getting out of the pool and drying herself off.

••• 1:23—Breasts, while in room with Ashcroft. Long scene.

Patricia Tallman. . . . . Stunts

Rachel Ticotin . . . . Uncredited Tracy Perry

Criss Cross *(1992)*

Cathryn De Prume . . . . Oakley

Goldie Hawn. . . . . Tracy Cross

•• 0:23—Buns and breasts in pasties, dancing on stage in club while her son watches.

Annie McEnroe . . . . Mrs. Sivil

Anna Thomson . . . . Monica

Critters 2: The Main Course *(1988)*

Roxanne Kernohan . . . . Lee

•• 0:37—Brief breasts after transforming from an alien into a Playboy Playmate. Buns in G-sting when walking away.

Critters 4: They're Invading Your Space *(1992)*

Angela Bassett. . . . . Fran

•• 0:25—Buns in nice, tilt-up shot with partial back side view of right breast, but you don't see her face.

Crocodile Dundee *(1986; Australian)*

Linda Kozlowski. . . . . Sue Charlton

•• 0:31—Buns in black one piece swimsuit with thong back after she takes off her skirt to fill her canteen with water.

Crooked Hearts *(1991)*

Wendy Gazelle . . . . Eileen

Marg Helgenberger. . . . . Jennetta

Jennifer Jason Leigh. . . . . Harriet

•• 1:10—In black bra, then breasts in bathtub with Tom.

Juliette Lewis . . . . Cassie

Sacha Moiseiwitsch . . . . Bonita

- 0:19—Very brief partial side view of right breast when Charlie carries her into the kitchen. Most of right breast when spinning her around when leaving the kitchen.

Cindy Pickett. . . . . Jill

Cross Country *(1983; Canadian)*

Nina Axelrod. . . . . Lois Hayes

- 0:28—Brief buns and sort of breasts, getting fondled by Richard.
- 1:05—Very, very brief breasts, while fighting outside the motel in the rain with Johnny.

Roberta Weiss . . . . Alma Jean

•• 0:59—Breasts on bed with two other people.

Cross My Heart *(1987)*

Corinne Bohrer . . . . Susan

Joanna Kerns. . . . . Nancy

Shelly Taylor Morgan. . . . . Woman in Restaurant

Annette O'Toole . . . . Kathy

•• 0:46—Left breast, in bed with Short.

•• 0:48—Breasts in bed when Short heads under the covers.

•• 0:49—Brief breasts again getting her purse.

- 1:05—Brief breasts and buns, dressing after Short finds out about her daughter.

Cross of Iron *(1977)*

Senta Berger . . . . Eva

- 0:55—Brief buns, while taking off her nightgown in bedroom.

• *Crosscut* *(1995)*

Emily Procter. . . . . Counter Girl

Elise Rothberg . . . . Angie

- 0:01—Brief left breast, when pulling sheet on top of her after Costas Mandylor takes the sheet away while she lies on the sofa. Medium long shot.

The Crossing Guard *(1995)*

Priscilla Barnes. . . . . Verna

••• 0:37—Breasts while walking backstage into dressing room and talking with Jack Nicholson.

Anjelica Huston . . . . Mary

Millicent Sheridan . . . . Dancer

Robin Wright. . . . . Jojo

Kari Wührer. . . . . Mia

- 0:05—Brief breasts, going into bathroom after talking with Jack Nicholson.
- 1:11—Buns in T-back, while dancing on stage by herself, then with Nicholson.
- 1:13—Brief breasts in open blouse, while fooling around with Nicholson in room.

Crossover *(1980; Canadian)*

a.k.a. Mr. Patman

Fionnula Flanagan . . . . Abadaba

- 0:27—Brief breasts opening her robe and flashing James Coburn.

Tabitha Harrington . . . . Montgomery

- 0:11—Brief right breast, then brief full frontal nudity lying in bed, then struggling with James Coburn in her room. Wearing white make-up on her face.

•• 0:29—Nude walking in to room to talk with Coburn, then breasts and brief buns leaving.

Kate Nelligan. . . . . Peabody

• *The Crow* *(1993)*

Bai Ling. . . . . Myca

- 0:23—Buns, while taking a shower.

Sofia Shinas. . . . . Shelly Webster

Anna Thomson . . . . Darla

Crush *(1992; New Zealand)*

Marcia Gay Harden . . . . Lane

- 0:21—Very brief left breast while turning over in bed when her dad comes to look for her.
- 0:42—Most of breasts, while in bed with a guy.

Donogh Rees. . . . . Christina

- 0:42—Right breast in pulled up hospital gown.

Cry of a Prostitute: Love Kills *(1975; Italian)*

Barbara Bouchet . . . . Margie

- 0:30—Brief left breast, lying in bed with Rico.
- 0:31—Brief breasts in bed, with Rico when he starts making love with her.

•• 0:50—Breasts in panties and robe, walking angrily around her room.

Cry Uncle (1971)

Maureen Byrnes ....Lena Right

• 0:16—Breasts and buns in bed with two other girls while spanking Dominic. Hard to see because the negative image is projected.

••• 0:46—Brief breasts with Connie when Jake peeks in the window. Full frontal nudity, talking with Jake at the doorway.

• 0:48—Breasts, making love with Jake in bed.

• 0:49—Nude, getting out of bed after knocking out Jake.

••• 0:50—Full frontal nudity, while interrogating Jake.

•• 0:53—Breasts, in room with gun while covering Jake.

•• 0:54—Full frontal nudity, while shooting gun and leaving.

Madeleine Le Roux ....Cora Merrill

••• 0:22—Breasts and buns, undressing in bathroom while talking to Jake.

••• 0:27—Nude, taking off her dress in front of Keith and making love with him on the sofa. Long scene.

• 0:42—Brief breasts, sitting up in bed when door is slammed in Jake's face.

• 0:59—Full frontal nudity, while standing in bedroom doorway.

• 1:11—Breasts under sheer red and black nightie, then making love with Jake. Long scene.

• 1:18—Brief buns, while taking off her panties.

Debbi Morgan.......................... Olga Winter

••• 0:40—Breasts and buns, taking off her blouse and skirt in room with Jake. Long scene.

Nancy Salmon................................ Connie

• 0:16—Breasts and buns in bed with two other girls while spanking Dominic. Hard to see because the negative image is projected.

• 0:26—Full frontal nudity in B&W photo that Keith shows Cora.

• 0:45—Brief breasts in the same B&W photo.

• 0:46—Brief right breast with Lena when Jake peeks in the window.

•• 0:48—Breasts, fixing drugs while sitting on bed.

••• 0:51—Breasts, while sitting on bed, then full frontal nudity getting out of bed.

• 1:04—Buns, while lying on bed.

•• 1:06—Full frontal nudity, rolling off bed and onto the floor, when Jake discovers she's dead.

Crystal Force II: Dark Angel (1995)

Betsy Gardner................................Allison

••• 0:56—In black bra, then breasts, while making love with Jake.

• 1:07—Brief breasts in reflection in mirror in Jake's vision.

Gloria Lusiak .... Jill

•• 0:19—Breasts and buns in T-back while in spa with Walter.

••• 0:33—Full frontal nudity, while making love with Virgil.

Crystal Heart (1987)

Tawny Kitaen .... Alley Daniels

•• 0:46—Breasts and buns, while "making love" with Lee Curreri through the glass.

•• 0:50—Nude, crashing through glass shower door, covered with blood during her nightmare.

• 1:14—Brief breasts making love with Curreri in and falling out of bed.

Marina Saura................................. Justine

The Curious Female (1969)

Julie Conners....................... Andre Lewis/Girl #3

•• 1:12—Breasts while giving Pearl a back rub.

Elaine Edwards............................ Mrs. Wilde

• 0:56—Breasts in bed with a young man before Joan walks in the room.

Charlene Jones.................... Pearl Lucomb/Girl #2

• 0:14—Brief breasts, twice, while taking a shower.

• 0:29—Buns, while running in slow motion to the pool.

• 0:30—Buns, while lying down.

• 1:08—Breasts while making love with a guy. Hard to see because of psychedelic light

•• 1:09—Breasts while turning over on her back with Andre.

Angelique Pettyjohn .... Susan Rome/Girl #1

••• 0:29—Buns, while running in slow motion to the pool, then putting on towel. Breasts on diving board.

••• 0:30—Breasts and buns, while on inflatable mattress in pool.

•• 0:52—Breasts while talking on the phone.

• 0:55—Breasts while making love in bed with a guy.

• 1:01—Brief breasts, while jumping into pool. Long shot.

Curse III: Blood Sacrifice (1990)

Jenilee Harrison .... Elizabeth Armstrong

••• 0:43—Breasts, while sitting in bathtub. Almost side of right breast when wrapping a towel around herself.

Jennifer Steyn .... Cindy

• 0:35—Side of left breast, kissing Roger while at the beach inside a tent. Upper half of left breast when blade tears through tent.

• 0:40—Breasts, covered with blood when Geoff looks in the tent.

Curtains (1983; Canadian)

Samantha Eggar .... Samantha Sherwood

Linda Thorson .... Brooke Parsons

Sandra Warren............................Tara Demillo

• 0:58—Side view of left breast practicing a scene in the play with Summers.

Cut and Run (1985; Italian)

Karen Black .... Karin

Lisa Blount.............................. Fran Hudson

Valentina Forte ....Ana

••• 0:29—Brief left breast being made love to in bed. Then breasts sitting up in bed and left side view and buns taking a shower.

Cutter's Way (1981)

a.k.a. Cutter and Bone

Julia Duffy .... Young Girl

Ann Dusenberry......................... Valerie Duran

Lisa Eichhorn .... Maureen "Mo" Cutter

• 1:07—Brief right breast, wearing bathrobe, lying on lounge chair while Jeff Bridges looks at her.

Cutting Class (1988)

Brenda Lynn Klemme.......................... Colleen

• 0:32—In bra in locker room. Very, very brief buns cheerleading without any panties on.

• 0:37—More very brief buns, ducking under bleachers.

Jill Schoelen ....Paula Carson

• 1:00—Very, very brief breasts in mirror when Gary helps put her robe on. (Out of focus.)

• *Cyber Bandits* (1994)

Grace Jones . . . . Mesoko
Barbara Moore . . . . Hope
• 0:19—Brief buns in T-back seen on computer screen.
•• 0:20—Breasts, after taking off flower pasties while talking to Martin Kemp in virtual reality.
Alexandra Paul . . . . Rebecca

***CyberSex Kittens* (1995)**

Gloria Lusiak . . . . Sandy
•• 0:11—Breasts, while posing for photographs.
••• 0:39—Breasts, while talking to a stuffed doll in bedroom, then nude, when taking a shower.
• 0:45—Brief breasts, while sitting in chair, getting reprogrammed.
•• 0:48—Breasts, while posing for Christmas theme photos, then fighting with Courtney.

***Cyberzone* (1995)**

Sherri Graham . . . . Captive Dancer
•• 0:21—Breasts, while dancing in belly dancer outfit.
Lorissa McComas . . . . Moria
• 0:09—Breasts, in room with the other three pleasure droids. (She's the one with the diamond pendant necklace and black shawl.)
• 0:13—Breasts after taking off her lingerie top with the other three pleasure droids.
• 1:06—Breasts, after taking off her dress top for Marc Singer.
Tammy Parks . . . . Runaway Wife
•• 0:29—Breasts and brief buns, while making love on top of a guy in a room.
Meaghan Prester . . . . Pleasure Droid #2
• 0:09—Breasts, in room with the other three pleasure droids. (she's the tall one with a diamond choker.)
• 0:13—Breasts after taking off her lingerie top with the other three pleasure droids.
Bianca Rocilili . . . . Pleasure Droid #3
• 0:09—Breasts, in room with the other three pleasure droids. (She's the one with the gold necklace and the blue shawl.)
• 0:13—Breasts after taking off her lingerie top with the other three pleasure droids.
Brittany Rollins . . . . Pleasure Droid #1
• 0:09—Breasts, in room with the other three pleasure droids. (She's the redhead with a pearl necklace.)
• 0:13—Breasts after taking off her lingerie top with the other three pleasure droids.
Brinke Stevens . . . . Kitten
••• 0:04—Breasts and buns in T-back, while doing strip routine on stage. She's made up to look like an alien kitten.
• 0:52—Brief buns in T-back, while dancing on stage.
Rochelle Swanson . . . . Beth

***Cyborg* (1989)**

Dayle Haddon . . . . Pearl Prophet
Debi Richter . . . . Nady Simmons
• 0:28—Buns, after taking off clothes and running into the ocean.
• 0:30—Brief left breast by the fire showing herself to Jean-Claude Van Damme.

***Cyborg 2: Glass Shadow* (1993)**

Renee Ammann . . . . Davena
• 0:04—Brief breasts, several times, while making love with a guy before she blows up.
Angelina Jolie . . . . Cash
• 1:14—Left breast, while in bed with Elias Koteas. Slightly out of focus.
•• 1:16—Breasts, while making love on top of Koteas in bed.

***Cyborg 3: The Recycler* (1995)**

Margaret Avery . . . . Doc Edford
Debra Beatty . . . . Pleasure Unit #2
Rebecca Ferratti . . . . Elexia
• 0:14—Breasts, while dancing on stage in bar and kicking a customer (medium long shot). Breasts, while dancing in front of Richard Lynch (closer shot).
• 0:18—Breasts, while taking off her blouse in back room with Lynch.
Raye Hollitt . . . . Finola

***Cyborg Cop* (1993)**

Alonna Shaw . . . . Cathy
••• 0:58—Breasts, while making love with Jack.
Kimberleigh Stark . . . . Woman Hostage

• *Cyborg Cop II* (1994)

Jill Pierce . . . . Liz McDowell
Kimberleigh Stark . . . . Gloria Alvarez
Melanie Walker . . . . Pretty Co-worker
• 0:29—Left breast, while making out with guy in laboratory.
• 0:31—Brief breasts, while stumbling out of the laboratory after being shot in the back.

***Cyclone* (1986)**

Michelle Bauer . . . . Uncredited Shower Girl
• 0:06—Very brief buns and side of left breast walking around in locker room. (Passes several times in front of camera.)
Martine Beswicke . . . . Waters
Ashley Ferrare . . . . Carla Hastings
Pamela Gilbert . . . . Uncredited Shower Girl
• 0:06—Buns and breasts (she's the brunette) in the showers. Long shot.
Heather Thomas . . . . Teri Marshall
Dawn Wildsmith . . . . Henna

***D.C. Cab* (1983)**

Irene Cara . . . . Herself
Deborah Dutch . . . . n.a.
Jill Schoelen . . . . Claudette
Moriah Shannon . . . . Venus Club Passenger
•• 0:16—In bra, then breasts, undressing in back seat of cab.
•• 0:17—Breasts when Albert tries to get his fare.
• 0:18—Breasts, then buns when Gary Busey takes her money. Buns and very brief lower frontal nudity running out of the club after him.

***D.O.A.* (1988)**

Charlotte Rampling . . . . Mrs. Fitzwaring
Meg Ryan . . . . Sydney Fuller
• 0:44—Brief back side of right breast, dropping a towel that was wrapped around her to put a slip on over her head.

***Da Vinci's War* (1992)**

Vanity . . . . Lupe
Kim Burnette . . . . Monique
••• 0:49—Breasts, kneeling by herself, while putting on a show for the bad guy.
Melissa Anne Moore . . . . Fred
••• 0:14—Breasts and buns, with Michael Nouri in his workout room.

Kimberly Ryusaki . . . . Cocktail Waitress #3

Daddy's Boys (1988)

Laura Burkett. . . . . Christie
- ••• 0:17—Breasts in room with Jimmy.
- •• 0:20—Left breast, while making love with Jimmy in bed again.
- • 0:21—Brief breasts during Jimmy's nightmare.
- • 0:43—Brief breasts in bed again, then getting dressed.
- • 0:53—Brief breasts in bed consoling Jimmy.
- • 1:11—Left breast, while in bed with Jimmy.

Linda Shayne. . . . . Nanette

The Dallas Connection (1994)

Wendy Hamilton . . . . Scorpion
- • 0:26—Buns in outfit in bar.
- ••• 0:27—Breasts and buns in the shower.
- • 0:38—Buns in outfit on stage in bar.
- ••• 0:40—Buns and breasts, while dancing on stage.
- •• 0:56—Buns in wet suit, then breasts, while making love with Mark outside.

Kym Malin. . . . . Cowboy's Hostess

T.J. Myers . . . . .Dancer #2
- • 1:11—Breasts (she's on the left), while on stage with another dancer. Medium long shot.

Sam Phillips. . . . . Samantha Maxx
- • 0:21—Breasts, while getting out of sweaty workout clothes.
- 0:36—Breasts, while making love with Mark on couch.
- •• 0:51—Buns in lingerie then breasts in Antonio's daydream.

Julie Kristen Smith . . . . Cobra
- • 0:26—Buns in outfit in bar.
- ••• 0:27—Breasts and buns in the shower.
- • 0:38—Buns in outfit on stage in bar doing splits.
- ••• 0:40—Buns and breasts, while dancing on stage.
- ••• 0:53—Breasts and buns, while making love with Chris in spa.

Julie Strain. . . . . Black Widow
- •• 0:03—Buns in lingerie on bed with Mr. Lesarge, then breasts, while making love.
- • 0:38—Buns in western outfits on stage.
- •• 1:00—Breasts and buns, under sexy leather and chain outfit in office with Nicholas.

Damage (1992; French/British)

(Unrated Director's cut reviewed.)

Juliette Binoche . . . . .Anna
- • 0:52—Brief breasts while sitting on floor and making love with Jeremy Irons.
- •• 1:31—Breasts on bed after getting caught by Iron's son.

Leslie Caron. . . . . .Elizabeth Prideaux

Miranda Richardson . . . . Ingrid
- ••• 1:40—Breasts, while standing in front of Jeremy Irons in the bedroom.

The Damned (1969; German)

Charlotte Rampling . . . . Elizabeth Thallman

Ingrid Thulin . . . . .Sophie Von Essenbeck
- •• 1:23—Breasts in bed with Dirk Bogarde. Long scene for a 1969 film.
- • 2:03—Left breast in bed with Martin (her son in the film).

Damned River (1990)

Lisa Aliff. . . . . .Anne
- • 0:32—Very, very brief top of right breast in open blouse, then half of right breast in wet blouse washing her hair.
- • 0:50—Very brief breasts struggling with Ray when he rips her top open. Don't see her face.

Dance of the Damned (1988)

Starr Andreeff . . . . .Jodi
- •• 0:03—Breasts dancing in black bikini bottoms on stage in a club.
- •• 1:08—Breasts in the bar with the vampire.

Maria Ford. . . . . Teacher
- • 0:11—Brief breasts during dance routine in club wearing black panties, garter belt and stockings.

Deborah Ann Nassar . . . . La Donna
- • 0:07—Brief breasts during dance routine in club.

Dance with a Stranger (1985; British)

Miranda Richardson. . . . . .Ruth Ellis
- • 0:08—Very brief upper half of left breast, twice, while in bed making love with David.
- • 0:18—Very brief tip of left breast, while getting into bed with David. Dark.
- • 0:20—Very, very brief side view of left breast, putting robe on in bed.

Dance with Death (1991)

Sean'a Arthur. . . . . Sherilyn
- • 0:42—Buns, while dancing on stage with Lola.

Alretha Baker . . . . .Sunny
- ••• 0:23—Breasts and buns in G-string, dancing on stage and falling off because she's on drugs.

Tracey Burch . . . . Whitney
- ••• 0:03—Breasts and buns in G-string, dancing on stage.
- ••• 0:05—More breasts and buns while dancing.

Jill Pierce . . . . Lola
- •• 0:07—Breasts and buns, dancing in wedding outfit on stage.
- • 0:11—Breasts and buns in G-string, dancing on stage. Long shot, seen in mirror. Buns while getting tips.
- • 0:28—Buns, while dancing on stage in the background.
- • 0:42—Buns in G-string dancing with Sherilyn on stage.
- • 0:56—Brief breasts on stage when Kelly talks to her.
- • 1:11—Buns, while dancing on stage.

Catya Sassoon . . . . .Jodie
- ••• 0:29—Breasts and buns in G-string, while dancing on stage.
- ••• 0:37—Breasts and buns, dancing on stage. Her body is painted gold.
- ••• 0:38—More breasts and buns.

Barbara Alyn Woods . . . . Kelly
- ••• 0:16—In black bra, panties and stockings, doing strip tease on stage. Breasts and buns in G-string.
- •• 0:24—Breasts, dancing in red bra and panties.
- ••• 0:46—Breasts and buns in G-string, dancing on stage.
- • 0:47—Brief side view of left breast, while changing back stage. Buns seen in mirror.
- ••• 0:59—Breasts and buns, doing strip tease routine in Marilyn Monroe outfit.
- ••• 1:01—Breasts, making love in bed with Maxwell Caulfield.

Danger Zone II: Reaper's Revenge (1988)

Stephanie Blake . . . . Tattooed Topless Dancer
- ••• 0:47—Breasts, dancing on stage in bikini bottoms.

Alisha Das . . . . Francine

Jane Higginson . . . . Donna
- •• 0:17—Breasts, while unconscious on sofa while the bad guys take Polaroid photos.
- • 0:18—Brief breasts seen in the photo that Wade looks at.

- • 0:22—Brief left breast, while adjusting her blouse outside. Long shot.
- • 0:34—Left breast seen in another Polaroid photograph.

***Dangerous Game** (1988; Australian)*

Kathryn Walker . . . . Kathryn

- • 1:19—Very, very brief breasts when her black top is pulled up while struggling with Murphy.

***Dangerous Game** (1993)*

(Unrated version reviewed.)

Madonna . . . . Sarah Jennings

- • 0:45—Brief buns in G-string, falling over back of sofa on video playback.
- •• 0:53—Nude, while getting out of bed and getting dressed.
- • 1:00—Brief buns, when getting her panties ripped off by Russo.

Christina Fulton. . . . . Blonde

Annie McEnroe . . . . Cameo

***Dangerous Indiscretion** (1995)*

Suki Kaiser. . . . . Sally

Joan Severance . . . . Caroline Everett

- • 0:08—In lingerie in house with C. Thomas Howell. Then brief breasts and buns, while crawling on the floor with him.
- • 0:25—Brief partial breasts, while making love with Howell in bed. Hard to see.

***Dangerous Liaisons** (1988)*

Glenn Close . . . . Marquise de Merteuil

Michelle Pfeiffer . . . . Madame de Tourvel

Uma Thurman. . . . . Cécile de Volanges

- ••• 0:59—Breasts taking off her nightgown in her bedroom with John Malkovich.

***Dangerous Love** (1988)*

Teri Austin. . . . . Dominique

Brenda Bakke . . . . Chris

Eloise Broady. . . . . Bree

- ••• 0:06—Breasts changing into lingerie in the mirror.

Kimberly Kates . . . . Susan

Nicole Picard. . . . . Jane

Brenda Swanson . . . . Felicity

***Dangerous Obsession** (1990; Italian)*

Corrine Clery. . . . . Carol Simpson

- • 0:14—Right breast sticking out of lingerie while lying in bed.
- •• 0:36—Full frontal nudity lying in bed waiting for her husband, then with him, then getting out of bed.

Blanca Marsillach . . . . Jessica

- • 0:02—Left breast, getting fondled by Johnny in recording studio. Lower frontal nudity when he pulls down her panties.
- •• 0:05—Breasts while opening her blouse when Johnny plays his saxophone.
- • 0:17—Lower frontal nudity on the stairs with Johnny, then brief breasts.
- • 0:29—Brief breasts in video tape on T.V.
- •• 0:40—Breasts while changing sweaters.
- ••• 0:56—Full frontal nudity masturbating while looking at pictures of Johnny. Buns, then more full frontal nudity getting video taped.
- ••• 0:58—Breasts in bed with a gun. Nude walking around the house. Long scene.
- • 1:05—Brief breasts on beach taking off sweater and burying a dog.
- • 1:06—Brief full frontal nudity during video taping session.
- •• 1:07—Breasts while cleaning up Dr. Simpson.
- ••• 1:13—Breasts, taking chains off Dr. Simpson, then lying in bed. Full frontal nudity making love with him.

***Dangerous Passion** (1990)*

Elpidia Carrillo . . . . Angela

Lonette McKee . . . . Meg

- ••• 0:39—Right breast, while in back of car with Carl Weathers.

• ***Dangerous Prey** (1995)*

Ciara Hunter . . . . Tanya

- • 0:53—Brief buns, in T-back, when standing up next to bed.
- •• 1:09—Breasts and buns in T-back, while undressing and getting into bed with Yuri. (She's wearing a brown wig.)

Shannon Whirry . . . . Robin

- ••• 0:06—Nude, while making love in bed on top of her boyfriend.
- • 0:20—Brief breasts in flashbacks.
- •• 0:24—Nude, while taking a shower, then knocking a guy unconscious.
- • 0:30—Brief full frontal nudity in flashbacks.

***Dangerous Touch** (1993)*

Monique Parent. . . . . Nicole

- •• 0:47—Full frontal nudity, while in the shower when surprised by Kate Vernon.
- ••• 0:49—Full frontal nudity, after dropping towel to join Lou Diamond Phillips and Vernon in bed.
- ••• 0:51—Breasts, while handcuffed in bed with Vernon.

Kate Vernon . . . . Amanda Grace

- ••• 0:29—Breasts, while making love with Phillips in convertible car in the woods.
- ••• 0:36—In black leotard, garter belt and stockings, then breasts while undressing in front of Phillips.
- ••• 0:38—More breasts when Phillips ties her hands to the headboard.
- ••• 0:51—Breasts, while making love in bed with Nicole while Phillips video tapes everything.
- • 0:53—Breasts, on video monitor when she looks at video tape of her with Nicole.

***A Dangerous Woman** (1993)*

Viveka Davis . . . . Mercy

Barbara Hershey . . . . Frances

Chloe Webb . . . . Birdy

Debra Winger . . . . Martha Horgan

- • 0:42—Very, very brief lower frontal nudity, then buns, while masturbating in bed. Don't see her face. Medium long shot.

***The Dark** (1993)*

Cynthia Belliveau. . . . . Tracy

- •• 0:29—In slip, then bra, then breasts, while making love on bed in motel with Hunter.

Neve Campbell . . . . Jesse

• ***Dark Angel: The Ascent** (1994)*

Kelly Burns . . . . Angel

Angela Featherstone . . . . Veronica

- •• 0:12—Buns, while standing in alley after first arriving from hell. Breasts, after turning around and running down the street.
- • 1:05—Breasts in open blouse after Max stitches up cut on her stomach.

- 1:06—Brief breasts while making love in bed with Max.

The Dark Backward (1991)

Lara Flynn Boyle . . . . Rosarita
Claudia Christian . . . . Kitty
Laurianne Jameson . . . . Shirley
- 0:44—Buns, in bed with Bill Paxton and two other fat women.

The Dark Dancer (1994)

Terri Harrel . . . . Kitty
Amy Lindsay . . . . Teenage Margaret
- 0:08—Partial breasts behind plastic curtain, medium long shot, seen from outside. Silhouette of left breast in the shower. Brief breasts, under robe in bedroom.
- 0:09—Very brief left breast under robe when standing up.
- •• 0:13—Very brief right breast, then breasts on bed, while in bedroom at night with Ramone.

Kirsten Maryott . . . . Cocktail Waitress
Lisa Pescia . . . . Carla Simpson
- 0:00—Brief buns in G-string, while dancing on stage.

Shannon Tweed . . . . Dr. Margaret Simpson
- ••• 0:25—Breasts, while dancing on stage in club wearing a mask.
- 0:28—Left breast, after making love in bed with her boyfriend.
- 0:56—Breasts and buns, after taking off robe and getting into bed with Ron. Long shot, dark.
- 1:00—Left breast, while getting into the shower with Ron.
- 1:18—Breasts and buns, while in bedroom with Ron. Dark.

Dark Obsession (1989; British)

a.k.a. Diamond Skulls

Amanda Donohoe . . . . Ginny
- •• 0:01—Breasts getting felt by a pair of hands.
- ••• 0:41—Left breast, breasts, brief lower frontal nudity while making love with Gabriel Byrne.
- 0:47—In black bra and panties, then full frontal nudity getting into tub. Right breast while sitting in the tub.

Sadie Frost . . . . Rebecca
- 0:22—Very brief right breast in bed after she rolls off Jamie.
- ••• 0:33—Breasts several times while making love with Jamie when Gabriel Byrne interrupts them.

• *Dark Romances: Volume I and II* (1987; Video Tape)

Brinke Stevens . . . . Various Parts
- 3:26—(1:39 into Volume II) Partial breasts in B&W segment while wearing a blonde wig.

Dark Secrets (1995)

Chanda . . . . Nancy Boyer
Skye Blue . . . . Dominatrix
Summer Cummings . . . . . Uncredited Woman with Dominatrix
- ••• 0:03—Breasts and buns in strap outfit, while getting whipped, candle wax dripped on her, wrapped up in cellophane and hit with thorny roses. Long scene.

Monique Parent . . . . Claire Reynolds
- 0:33—Buns in black panties, while trying on dress in bedroom.
- 0:45—Brief breasts, while in the shower.
- ••• 0:51—In white bra and panties, then full frontal nudity while making love with Justin Carroll.
- 0:55—Brief buns, twice, while trying on different outfits in store.
- •• 1:16—Breasts, while getting tortured by Julie Strain at the Midnight Club. Breasts and buns, after running out of the room.
- ••• 1:17—Nude, while outdoors in the rain, having sex with Strain.

Cheryl Rixon . . . . Philipa
Doria Rone . . . . Leona
- 1:04—Breasts and buns in panties, after Justin Carroll takes her dress off in front of a group of men in a vacant lot.
- 1:07—Brief left breast, while walking back to the car.

Julie Strain . . . . Mauri
- 0:00—Brief breasts and buns while wearing lingerie in quick cuts during photo shoot. Her face is painted white.
- •• 0:18—Breasts and buns, while having sex with Dennis.
- •• 1:14—Breasts, while whipping a woman at the Midnight Club.
- •• 1:16—Breasts, while torturing Monique Parent at the Midnight Club.
- ••• 1:17—Breasts, while outside in the rain, having sex with Parent.

Lori Wagner . . . . Woman with Senator
- ••• 0:18—Breasts and buns, while having sex with the Senator in bedroom.

Dark Side of Genius (1994)

Tina Coté . . . . Anna/Kristi
- •• 0:01—Breasts, while posing for painting, then getting killed during opening credits.
- 0:17—Brief breasts, while lying dead on sofa in a flashback.
- 0:22—Breasts and buns in G-string in Julian's studio (wearing a wig), then brief breasts (with blonde hair) in flashback.
- 0:32—Brief buns in G-string while posing on pedestal.
- 0:58—Breasts (blonde hair), while posing for paintings. Brief breasts (in wig) after Julian pushes her off the pedestal.
- ••• 1:02—Brief lower half of buns in long sweater, then breasts and upper half of buns, while making love with Julian in bed.

Gina Mari . . . . Naomi

Dark Side of the Moon (1989)

Wendy MacDonald . . . . Alex
- 0:54—In bra, then brief breasts having it torn off. Don't see her face.

Camilla More . . . . Lesli

Dark Tide (1993)

Adriana Agcaoili . . . . Lia
- 1:14—Very, very brief right breast, while getting her blouse ripped open on table by Richard Tyson.

Brigitte Bako . . . . Andi
- 0:26—Very brief tip of left breasts in bathtub. Brief breasts, while covering up when Richard Tyson looks at her.
- 0:27—Right breast, under water after Tyson leaves.
- ••• 0:43—Breasts, while making love with Tyson in underground pool. Great!
- ••• 1:05—Breasts, while sitting in bathtub, with a snake crawling up her chest.

Dark Universe (1993)

Blake Pickett . . . . Kim Masters
- ••• 0:45—Breasts, in open blouse, while outside in the woods with Jack.

• *The Darker Image Swimsuit Calendar: Behind the Scenes* *(1996; Video Tape)*

Traci Bingham . . . . Herself

• 0:16—Brief buns in two piece swimsuit in B&W.

Tami-Adrian George . . . . Herself

Darling Lili *(1970)*

Julie Andrews . . . . Lili Smith

• 1:12—Very, very brief left breast, when doing strip tease and tossing aside yellow outfit to duck behind curtain.

Date with an Angel *(1987)*

Emmanuelle Béart . . . . Angel

• 1:14—Breasts, when bathing in pond in forest while Michael E. Knight watches from the bushes. Long shot, don't really see anything. In a closer shot, her hair covers breasts.

Bibi Besch . . . . Grace Sanders

Phoebe Cates . . . . Patty Winston

Daughter of Death *(1982)*

a.k.a. Julie Darling

Sybil Danning . . . . Susan

•• 0:36—Breasts in bed with Anthony Franciosa.

• 0:38—Brief right breast under Franciosa.

Cindy Girling . . . . Irene

•• 0:12—Breasts in bathtub and getting out.

Isabelle Mejias . . . . Julie

Daughters of Darkness

(1971; Belgian/French/German/Italian)

Andrea Rau . . . . Ilona

• 0:39—Buns and side of right breast, kneeling on floor while bending over the toilet.

• 0:56—Brief breasts on top of Stefan in bed.

••• 1:00—Left breast, while standing in bathroom watching Stefan take a shower.

••• 1:01—Breasts when Stefan tries to drag her into the shower.

• 1:02—Breasts, lying dead on the floor.

• 1:03—Breasts, lying dead on the floor. Long shot.

Delphine Seyrig . . . . Countess Elisabeth Bathory

• *Dawn of the Dead* *(1979)*

(Director's cut reviewed.)

Gaylen Ross . . . . Francine

• 1:44—(0:22 into tape 2) Brief left breast, while sitting in bed with the guy.

The Day After Halloween *(1978; Australian)*

a.k.a. Snapshot

Chantal Contouri . . . . Madeline

Sigrid Thornton . . . . Angela

• 0:04—Very brief breasts in ad photos on wall.

•• 0:19—Breasts during modeling session at the beach.

••• 0:21—More breasts at the beach.

•• 0:37—Breasts in magazine ad several times.

• 0:43—Brief right breast in magazine ad.

• 0:46—Breasts in ad again.

• 1:18—Entering room covered with the ad.

The Day of the Cobra *(1980)*

Sybil Danning . . . . Brenda

• 0:41—Buns and side view of right breast getting out of bed and putting robe on with Lou. Long shot.

Day of the Jackal *(1973)*

Olga Georges-Picot . . . . Denise

• 0:55—Brief breasts and buns, getting out of bed to use the phone.

Delphine Seyrig . . . . Colette

• 1:25—Side view of right breast while lying in bed with the Jackal. Dark.

• 1:40—Very brief side view of left breast, when she rolls on her back. Brief side view of left breast after the Jackal kills her.

Daybreak *(1993; Made for Cable Movie)*

Moira Kelly . . . . Blue

••• 0:43—Right breast, then breasts while making out with Cuba Gooding Jr.

••• 1:14—Breasts when Gooding has to take her top off in front of a guard.

Martha Plimpton . . . . Laurie

• *Daydreams* *(1988; Video Tape)*

Lori Deann Pallett . . . . Lori

••• 0:01—Breasts cleaning sail boat. Long scene.

••• 0:03—Breasts on sail boat during daydream.

• 0:09—Brief breasts, sitting up on lounge chair when beer is spilled on her back.

•• 0:10—Breasts, while sitting on a bar during beer daydream.

••• 0:13—Breasts in kitchen after spilling whipped cream on herself.

••• 0:14—Breasts and buns, getting into bathtub.

••• 0:16—Nude, in bathtub during daydream.

••• 0:20—Breasts in open tuxedo jacket during dance number.

••• 0:21—More breasts during end credits.

Dead Aim *(1987)*

Sandi Brannon . . . . Misty

• 0:05—Buns in G-string, while dancing on stage during opening credits.

• 0:09—Breasts, while dancing on stage with the other girls (wearing a white bottom).

••• 1:02—Breasts and buns in G-string doing dance routine.

• 1:14—Very brief right breast, several times, while covered with blood, lying dead on bed.

Carol Chambers . . . . Nicole

• 0:15—Buns in G-string.

Shirlene Foss . . . . B.J.

• 0:14—Buns in G-string and white top.

• 0:55—Brief buns in G-string while dancing on stage in bridal outfit.

Cassandra Gava . . . . Amber

• 0:14—Buns, while sitting on chair on stage.

• 0:52—Very brief breasts, while making love with Ed Marinaro in bed. Very dark, hard to see.

Lynn Whitfield . . . . Sheila Freeman

Dead and Buried *(1981)*

Melody Anderson . . . . Janet

Lisa Blount . . . . Girl on the Beach

• 0:06—Brief breasts on the beach getting her picture taken by a photographer.

Dead Beat *(1994)*

Natasha Gregson Wagner . . . . Kristen

• 0:31—Brief right breast, in mirror, when she draws on it with lipstick.

Deborah Harry . . . . Mrs. Kurtz

Dead Boyz Can't Fly (1992)

Ruth Corrine Collins .... Myra Kandinsky
- 0:14—Brief breasts while getting raped by Buzz in elevator.

Jennifer Delora .... Helen
Sheila Kennedy .... Lorraine
- 0:00—Breasts and buns in G-string, while dancing in smoke filled club.
- •• 0:16—Buns in G-string and breasts, while dancing in club.

Delia Sheppard .... Angie
- •• 1:01—In white bra and panties, then breasts in doctor's office when bad guy pretends to be a doctor and examines her.

Dead Calm (1989)

Nicole Kidman............................ Rae Ingram
- 1:00—Brief buns and breasts on the floor with Billy Zane.

Dead Cold (1995)

Lysette Anthony ....Alicia
Anneliza Scott .... Susan
Alina Thompson .... Sarah
- •• 0:15—Breasts, while making love with Peter Dobson in pickup truck.

Dead Connection (1993)

Lisa Bonet .... Catherine Briggs
- 0:58—Breasts, while making love in bed with Michael Madsen.

Susan Byun .... Sarah
- 0:50—Very, very brief left breast while catching shirt that Michael Madsen throws to her.

Parker Posey ....Denise
Brenda Swanson .... Susan

Dead Funny (1994)

Bai Ling.................................... Norriko
Elizabeth Peña.................................. Viv
- 1:07—Left breast in gaping kimono (her face is painted white like a Japanese Kabuki dancer.)

• *Dead Man Walking* (1995)

Susan Sarandon..................... Sister Helen Prejean
Missy Yager.............................. Hope Percy
- 1:49—Partial buns, while crawling on the ground during rape/murder flashback. Buns, while lying dead on the ground in overhead shot.

Dead On (1993)

(Unrated version reviewed.)

Lynn Oddo .... Lisa
- •• 1:00—Breasts, while getting dressed after spending the night in Matt McCoy's bed.

Tracy Scoggins .... Marla Beaumont
- 0:00—Partial breasts in shower during opening credits. Brief breasts when getting out of shower.
- 0:19—Brief left breast while in bathtub when she reaches up to turn off the speaker phone.

Shari Shattuck .... Erin Davenport
- ••• 0:15—Breasts and buns in panties, while making out with Matt McCoy in doorway, then making love on the floor. Wow!
- ••• 0:29—Breasts, while making love with McCoy in her studio. Shot almost in silhouette.
- 0:49—Brief breasts, while rolling over in bed to answer the phone.

Rochelle Swanson .... Woman at Party
Virginia Watson .... Dorian

Dead Ringers (1988)

Genevieve Bujold......................... Claire Niveau
- •• 0:49—Very brief right breast in bed with Jeremy Irons, then brief breasts reaching for pills and water. Dark, hard to see.

Heidi Von Palleske .... Cary
- 0:45—Brief left breast sticking out of bathrobe, while talking to Jeremy Irons in the bathroom.

Dead Solid Perfect (1988; Made for Cable Movie)

Bibi Besch ....Rita
Corinne Bohrer .... Janie Rimmer
- ••• 0:31—Nude, getting out of bed to get some ice for Randy Quaid. Nice scene!

Linda Doná .... Blonde
Kathryn Harrold......................... Beverly T. Lee

Dead Space (1990)

Laura Tate .... Marissa Salinger
- •• 0:33—Breasts in bed with Marc Singer during her dream.

• *Dead Tides* (1997)

Debra Beatty .... Body Double for Tawny Kitaen
- 0:43—Brief buns, while making out with Roddy Piper. Don't see her face.
- 0:55—Brief buns, while making love with Piper. Don't see her face.

Tawny Kitaen.................................... Nola
Camilla More......................................Lori
- ••• 0:23—Breasts and buns, while making love with Roddy Piper.

Dead Weekend (1995; Made for Cable Movie)

Afifi Alaouie .... Amelia B
- •• 0:15—Breasts, while making love with Stephen Baldwin in barn.

Bai Ling .... Amelia A
Jennifer MacDonald......................... Amelia D
- 0:46—Brief breasts, while making love with Stephen Baldwin.
- 0:47—Very brief breasts, while sitting up in bed. Seen through bed railing and mosquito net.

Cindy Morgan .... Newscaster
Blair Valk .... Amelia C
- 0:28—Buns in T-back, then brief breasts, while making love in hotel room with Stephen Baldwin.
- 0:31—Very brief buns in T-back under skirt, while straddling Baldwin in bed.

Barbara Alyn Woods .... Amelia E
- •• 0:58—Right breast, then breasts, while making love with Stephen Baldwin in bed.

Dead Women In Lingerie (1991)

Laura Harring.................................. Marcia
Jeanne Sal .... Bing
Maura Tierney .... Molly Field
- 1:03—Brief left breast while sleeping in bed.
- 1:09—Very brief left breast, while rolling over in bed on top of Nick.
- 1:20—Very brief lower half of right breast when falling back onto bed with Nick. Slightly different take from 1:09.

The Dead Zone (1983)

Brooke Adams .... Sarah Bracknell
Chapelle Jaffe.................................. Nurse

Roberta Weiss . . . . Alma Frechette
- 0:49—Briefly in beige bra, then brief breasts when the killer rips her blouse open during Christopher Walken's vision.

Dead-End Drive-In *(1986; Australian)*

Natalie McCurry . . . . Carmen
- •• 0:19—Breasts in red car with Ned Manning.

Deadfall *(1993)*

Sarah Trigger . . . . Diane
- ••• 0:42—In white bra and panties, after taking off dress in motel room with Michael Biehn. Breasts, while making love with him.
- • 0:44—Right breast, while lying in bed with Biehn when he changes positions and the covers move.
- •• 0:45—Breasts, while wearing white panties, leaving bed and getting dressed.

Deadline *(1988)*

Imogen Stubbs . . . . Lady Romy-Burton
- • 0:44—Brief left breast, while getting out of bed with John Hurt. Full frontal nudity turning toward bed, brief breasts getting back into bed.

Deadly Blessing *(1981)*

Lisa Hartman Black . . . . Faith
- 1:31—It looks like brief left breast after getting hit with a rock, but it's a special-effect appliance over her breasts. (She's supposed to be a man in the film.)

Maren Jensen . . . . Martha
- •• 0:27—Breasts and buns, while changing into a nightgown while a creepy guy watches through the window.
- • 0:52—Buns, while getting into bathtub. Kind of steamy and hard to see.
- • 0:56—Brief breasts, while in bathtub with snake. (Notice that she gets into the tub naked, but is wearing black panties in the water).

Colleen Riley . . . . Melissa
Sharon Stone . . . . Lana

Deadly Companion *(1979; Canadian)*

Susan Clark . . . . Paula West
- • 0:19—Brief left breast, while consoling Michael Sarrazin in bed, then brief side view of left breast.
- • 0:20—Brief breasts sitting up in bed.

Pita Oliver . . . . Lorraine
- • 0:14—Very brief left breast, then very brief breasts sitting up in bed during Michael Sarrazin's daydream. Dark.
- • 1:32—Brief full frontal nudity, dead on bed when Susan Clark comes into the bedroom.

Deadly Dreams *(1988)*

Juliette Cummins. . . . . Maggie Kallir
- • 0:25—Breasts on bed, taking off her blouse and kissing Alex.
- ••• 0:55—Breasts and brief buns, making love with Jack in bed.

Stacey Travis . . . . Librarian

Deadly Embrace *(1989)*

Michelle Bauer . . . . Female Spirit of Sex
- •• 0:22—Breasts caressing herself during fantasy sequence.
- ••• 0:28—Breasts taking off tube top and caressing herself.
- ••• 0:40—Breasts and buns kissing blonde guy. Nice close up of him kissing her breasts.
- • 0:42—Side of left breast lying down with the guy.
- • 1:03—Buns and side of right breast with the guy.

Ruth Corrine Collins . . . . Dede Magnolia

Linnea Quigley . . . . Michelle Arno
- •• 0:15—In white lingerie, then breasts and buns during Chris' fantasy.
- •• 0:34—Breasts and buns caressing herself.
- •• 0:43—Breasts again.
- • 0:46—Brief breasts.
- •• 0:50—Breasts and buns undressing.
- ••• 0:58—Breasts in bed on top of Chris, then making love.
- • 1:02—Breasts and buns on top of Chris while Charlotte watches on T.V.
- • 1:11—Breasts in Chris' fantasy.
- • 1:12—Breasts and buns in playback of video tape.

Ty Randolph . . . . Charlotte Morland
- •• 0:28—Breasts taking off her top. Mostly side view of left breast.
- • 0:29—More left breast, while in bed with Chris.
- ••• 0:30—Breasts,while making love in bed with Chris.
- • 1:10—Brief right breast, on T.V. when she replays video tape for Linnea Quigley.

Deadly Eyes *(1982; Canadian)*

Sara Botsford. . . . . Kelly Leonard
- • 0:42—Breasts several times, making love with Paul.

Lisa Langlois . . . . Trudy

Deadly Force *(1983)*

Marilyn Chambers. . . . . Actress in Video Tape
- • 0:25—Breasts in adult video tape on projection TV.

Gina Gallego . . . . Maria
Joyce Ingalls . . . . Eddie Cooper
- •• 0:48—Breasts, while making out with Wings Hauser on hammock.

The Deadly Games *(1980)*

a.k.a. The Eliminator

Colleen Camp . . . . Randy
Denise Galik . . . . Mary
- • 1:13—Left breast, twice, making love on top of Roger in bed.

Jo Ann Harris . . . . Keegan
- • 0:48—Breasts in the shower. Hard to see because of the pattern on the glass.

Alexandra Morgan. . . . . Linda
- •• 0:03—In bra, standing in doorway at night, then breasts. Dark.
- • 0:04—Very brief left breast and lots of cleavage in open blouse talking on the phone.
- • 0:05—Most of right breast, when standing up.

Deadly Innocents *(1988)*

Mary Crosby . . . . Beth/Cathy
- • 0:00—Very, very brief right breast in gaping nightgown when her husband grabs her wrist.
- • 0:38—Brief upper back half of left breast in bathroom mirror after taking off her nightgown.

Amanda Wyss . . . . Andy/Angela
- •• 0:12—Breasts, taking off T-shirt and putting on lingerie.
- ••• 1:29—Right breast, twice, with Andrew Stevens.

Deadly Passion *(1985)*

Ingrid Boulting . . . . Martha Greenwood
- • 0:46—Brief buns taking off clothes and jumping into pool. Long shot.
- •• 0:47—Breasts getting out of pool and kissing Brent Huff. Right breast in bed.
- • 0:54—Breasts in whirlpool bath with Huff.

••• 1:02—Breasts, wearing white panties and massaging herself in front of a mirror.
•• 1:31—Breasts taking off clothes and jumping into bed with Huff.

Susan Isaacs . . . . Trixie
•• 0:02—Breasts sitting up in bed talking to Brent Huff.

Deadly Past *(1994)*

Carol Alt . . . . Saundra
Dedee Pfeiffer . . . . Kirsten
• 0:38—Brief breasts, while making love with Luke in the kitchen.

Deadly Rivals *(1992)*

Brooke Becker . . . . Shallie Kittle
• 0:14—Breasts visible under sheer white blouse while talking to Andrew Stevens in auditorium.

Margaux Hemingway . . . . Agent Linda Howerton
Randi Ingerman . . . . Rachel Richmond
••• 0:18—Breasts, while in bed in open robe with Rudy.
• 0:20—Right breast in open robe before killing Rudy.
• 0:46—Brief buns in panties, while trying to kill strong bad guy.

The Deadly Secret *(1993)*

Tracy Hagemann . . . . Sarah
• 0:37—Brief buns in panties.
• 1:22—Very brief right breast, several times, during rape on beach.

Tracy Spaulding . . . . Reyna Vaught
•• 0:00—Breasts, several times during opening credits.
••• 0:25—Breasts, with Joe Estevez in study.
• 0:35—Brief breasts.
• 0:38—Brief breasts several times in B&W.
•• 0:41—Buns in G-string and breasts while making love with Estevez in bed.
• 0:44—Brief breasts, while getting out of bed and putting robe on.
• 1:10—Brief breasts when Estevez comes up behind her and feels her breasts.
•• 1:11—Breasts, while making love with Estevez on bed.
•• 1:17—Breasts and brief buns in B&W day dream.
• 1:27—Brief right breast, while making love in flashback.

Deadly Sins *(1994; Canadian)*

Jo Anne Bates . . . . Rita
Corrie Clark . . . . Beth
•• 0:25—In white bra, then breasts, while making love with Eric.
•• 0:54—In black bra and panties, then breasts, while making love with Eric on bed.

Alyssa Milano . . . . Cristina
• 1:20—In lingerie and brief right breast while making love with David Keith.

April Telek . . . . Gwen

Deadly Strangers *(1974; British)*

Hayley Mills . . . . Belle
• 1:02—Buns in bathtub when her uncle watches her.
••• 1:13—In white bra and panties while Steven watches through keyhole, then breasts after taking off bra and reading a newspaper.

Deadly Surveillance *(1991; Made for Cable Movie)*

Susan Almgren . . . . Rachel
• 0:00—Very, very brief right breast, while getting dressed. Don't see her face. B&W.
• 0:12—Breasts in the shower. Long shot.
•• 0:34—Breasts in the shower with Nickels.
••• 0:54—Buns, in black panties and bra, then breasts in room with Michael Ironside.

Deadly Vengeance *(1985)*

(Although the copyright on the movie states 1985, it looks more like the 1970's.)

Grace Jones . . . . Slick's Girlfriend
••• 0:06—Right breast, then breasts in bed with Slick.
•• 0:13—Left breast, when Slick sits up in bed, then full frontal nudity after he gets up.

Deadtime Stories *(1985)*

Cathryn De Prume . . . . Goldi-lox
•• 1:08—Breasts taking a shower, quick cuts.

Nicole Picard . . . . Rachel (Red Riding Hood)
• 0:48—Very brief right breast in shack with boyfriend.

Death and the Maiden *(1995)*

Sigourney Weaver . . . . Paulina Escobar
•• 0:11—Brief side of right breast, then breasts in bathroom.
•• 0:12—Breasts, while dressing in front of closet.
•• 0:14—Left breast, while making love in bed.

Death Becomes Her *(1992)*

Stephanie Anderson . . . . Marilyn Monroe
Donna Baltron . . . . Madeline Body Double
Catherine Bell . . . . Lisle Body Double
•• 1:19—Buns, while getting out of swimming pool and drying herself off. (2 long shots and 1 close-up.)

Goldie Hawn . . . . Helen Sharp
Michelle Johnson . . . . Anna
Barbara Ann Klein . . . . Goldie Hawn's Stunt Double
Anya Longwell . . . . Chagall Receptionist
Isabella Rossellini . . . . Lisle Von Rhuman
Meryl Streep . . . . Madeline Ashton
Carrie Jean Yazel . . . . Girl at Dakota's
• 0:27—Brief buns in mirror, hiding from Meryl Streep at Dakota's.

Death By Dialogue *(1988)*

Laura Albert . . . . Linda
••• 0:29—Breasts in white panties, while making love on top of her boyfriend.
•• 0:57—Breasts after pulling her dress top down in nightmare, then yanking her boyfriend's head off.

Kelly Sullivan . . . . Shelly

Death Dancers *(1992)*

Deborah Dutch . . . . Shannon
• 0:02—Briefly nude, while putting bathrobe on in B&W flashback.
• 0:30—Brief breasts in open robe, very brief buns, when crawling away.
• 0:31—Brief right breast in open robe outside.
• 0:37—Right breast in montage.
• 0:40—Brief breasts several times.
• 0:43—Brief breasts, while playing with a knife.
• 0:46—Buns in costume in hotel room with a guy.
• 0:49—Brief breasts in flashbacks.
• 0:56—Brief breasts in B&W flashback.
• 0:57—Breasts in stabbing scene.
•• 1:05—Breasts while making love with a guy.

Annie Gaybis . . . . Michelle
Jennifer Peace . . . . Shower Demon

Sunset Thomas . . . . Itsani
•• 0:16—Breasts in open blouse with Will and a nude dancer in club.
•• 0:35—Breasts in bedroom with Ruben.

Death Feud (1989)

Greta Blackburn . . . . Jenny
Gail Harris . . . . Harry's Girl Friend
•• 1:12—Breasts on bed with Harry.
Lisa Loring . . . . Roxey
Karen Mayo-Chandler . . . . Anne
•• 0:36—In white lingerie, then breasts several times outside taking off robe.
Erika Nann . . . . Hooker

Death Game, The Seducers (1977)

a.k.a. Mrs. Manning's Weekend
Colleen Camp . . . . Donna
• 0:16—Buns, in spa with Sondra Locke trying to get George in with them.
• 0:47—Brief breasts jumping up and down on the bed while George is tied up.
•• 1:16—Breasts behind stained glass door taunting George. Hard to see.
Sondra Locke . . . . Jackson
• 0:16—Buns and brief right breast in spa with Colleen Camp trying to get George in with them.
• 0:48—Brief breasts running around the room trying to keep George away from the telephone.

Death House (1988)

Tané McClure . . . . Tanya Kerrington
• 1:08—Brief breasts in Dennis Cole's vision.

Death in Brunswick (1990; Australian)

Zoë Carides . . . . Sophie Papafagos
• 0:28—Side of left breast, while on top of Neill.
• 0:29—Right breast, while lying in bed with Neill.

Death Match (1994)

Renee Ammann . . . . Danielle Richardson
•• 1:07—Breasts, when getting into shower with John. Breasts and partial buns, while making love in bed.
Lisa Haslehurst . . . . Newspaper Receptionist
Lisa London . . . . Big Man's Girlfriend
Sheila Redgate . . . . Venik's Massage Girl

Death Merchant (1990)

Dana Bentley Konkel . . . . Jason's Girlfriend
• 0:35—Brief breasts undressing for shower during dream.
Martina Castel . . . . Martina

Death of a Soldier (1985; Australian)

Nikki Lane . . . . Stripper in Bar
•• 0:49—Nude, dancing on stage.

Death Race 2000 (1975)

Roberta Collins . . . . Matilda the Hun
•• 0:27—Breasts being interviewed and arguing with Calamity Jane.
Simone Griffeth . . . . Annie Smith
• 0:32—Side view of left breast, while holding David Carradine. Dark, hard to see.
••• 0:56—Breasts and buns getting undressed and lying on bed with Carradine.
Louisa Moritz . . . . Myra
• 0:28—Breasts and buns getting a massage and talking to David Carradine.
Mary Woronov . . . . Calamity Jane
• 0:27—Brief breasts arguing with Matilda the Hun.

Death Ring (1992)

Isabel Glasser . . . . Lauren Sadler
•• 0:11—Breasts, after taking off swimsuit top on chair outside with Mike Norris.
Tammy Stones . . . . Cindy Maddin
••• 0:53—Breasts in open lingerie top in Skylord's apartment.

Death Spa (1987)

Brenda Bakke . . . . Laura
••• 0:05—Very brief lower frontal nudity, while taking off pants in locker room. Don't see her face. Then nude, in steam room.
Rosalind Cash . . . . Sgt. Stone
Cindi Dietrich . . . . Linda
Chelsea Field . . . . Darla
Tané McClure . . . . Vicky
•• 1:10—Breasts in sauna with Tom.
• 1:19—Brief breasts during the fire.
Shari Shattuck . . . . Catherine

Death Wish (1974)

Kathleen Tolan . . . . Carol Toby
• 0:09—Brief breasts and buns getting raped by three punks.

Death Wish II (1982)

Roberta Collins . . . . Woman at Party
Silvana Gallardo . . . . Rosario
• 0:11—Buns, on bed getting raped by gang. Brief breasts on bed and floor.
• 0:13—Nude, trying to get to the phone. Very brief full frontal nudity, lying on her back on the floor after getting hit.
Ava Lazar . . . . Girl in TV Soap Opera
Melody Santangelo . . . . Tourist's Wife
• 0:37—Breasts, while being held as a shield by a gang member in parking garage.
Robin Sherwood . . . . Carol Kersey
• 0:15—Breasts after getting raped by gang member in their hideout.

Death Wish III (1985)

Marina Sirtis . . . . Maria
• 0:42—Breasts getting blouse ripped open next to a car by the bad guys.
• 0:43—More breasts on mattress at the bad guys' hangout.

Death Wish V: The Face of Death (1993)

Lesley-Anne Down . . . . Olivia Regent
Tova Gallimore . . . . Model #1
Lisa Inouye . . . . Janine Omori
Sharolyn Sparrow . . . . Dawn
•• 1:01—Left breast, while in bathtub with Freddie.
• 1:03—Brief breasts, getting out of bathtub after soccer ball explodes outside.

• *Deathgame* (1996; Made for Cable Movie)

Korrine St. Onge . . . . Felicia
•• 0:42—Breasts, while making love with Hawk just before trying to kill him.

Deathmask (1983)

Jane Hamilton . . . . Victoria Howe

Kelly Nichols . . . . Lover Nurse
- 1:37—Very brief partial buns while making love on top of a guy in examination room. Very brief left breast, then very, very brief right breast when shot by Jane Hamilton.

Deathrow Game Show *(1988)*
Esther Alise . . . . Groupie
- •• 0:08—Breasts in bed with Chuck.

Debra Lamb . . . . Shanna Shallow
- ••• 0:23—Breasts dancing in white G-string and garter belt during the show.

Deathstalker *(1983)*
Barbi Benton . . . . Codille
- •• 0:39—Breasts struggling while chained up and everybody is fighting.
- • 0:47—Right breast, struggling on the bed with Deathstalker.

Lana Clarkson . . . . Kaira
- •• 0:26—Breasts when her cape opens, while talking to Deathstalker and Oghris.
- ••• 0:29—Breasts lying down by the fire when Deathstalker comes to make love with her.
- • 0:49—Brief breasts with gaping cape, sword fighting with a guard.

Deathstalker II *(1987)*
Christine Dupree . . . . Uncredited Body Double for Toni Naples
- • 0:55—Brief breasts in strobe lights making love with the bad guy. Hard to see because of blinking lights.

Monique Gabrielle. . . . . Reena the Seer/Princess Evie
- • 0:57—Brief breasts getting dress torn off by guards.
- ••• 1:01—Breasts making love with Deathstalker.
- • 1:24—Breasts, laughing during the blooper scenes during the end credits.

Toni Naples. . . . . Sultana
Maria Socas. . . . . .Amazon Queen

Deathstalker III: The Warriors From Hell *(1988)*
Carla Herd. . . . . .Carlisa/Elizena
- • 0:20—Side view of right breast, while making love in tent when guard looks in.
- •• 0:46—Breasts taking a bath.

Terri Treas . . . . Camlearde

Deathstalker IV: Match of Titans *(1990)*
Maria Ford . . . . .Dionara
- •• 0:13—Brief buns, then breasts, getting dressed in cave.
- • 0:19—Left breast, while kissing Deathstalker in bed.

Michelle Moffett . . . . Kana
- ••• 0:52—Very brief left breast, then breasts sitting on bed while trying to seduce Vaniat.
- ••• 0:59—Breasts on bed, trying to seduce Vaniat. More breasts, getting out of bed and getting dressed.

Anya Pencheva . . . . .Janeris
- • 0:16—Brief left breast in open top, while wrestling with Maria Ford in the water.
- • 0:36—Brief left breast, while kissing her lover slave girl during brief orgy scene.

Deceit *(1989)*
Sam Phillips. . . . . Eve Bendibuckle
- • 0:25—In bra and panties after Bailey forces her to strip. Buns in panties. Dressed like this until 1:22.

Deceptions *(1990; Made for Cable Movie)*
Nicollette Sheridan . . . . Adrienne Erickson
- • 0:35—Very, very brief silhouette of breasts, while hugging Harry Hamlin when the camera tilts down from her head to her buns.

Deceptions II: Edge of Deception *(1994; Canadian)*
Mariel Hemingway . . . . Joan Branson
Jennifer Rubin . . . . .Irene Stadler
- • 0:11—Very brief right breast, twice, while adjusting her robe when Steve Shellen watches.
- • 0:30—Breasts, while making love with Shellen.
- • 0:48—Left breast, while making love with Shellen.
- 0:55—Side view of buns, while lying in bed with Shellen.
- • 0:58—Brief left breast, while in the shower. Right breast, seen in the mirror.

The Deep *(1977)*
Jacqueline Bisset . . . . .Gail Berke
- ••• 0:01—Scuba diving underwater in a wet T-shirt.
- • 0:08—More wet T-shirt, getting out of water, onto boat.

Deep Cover *(1980; British)*
a.k.a. Blade on the Feather

Kika Markham . . . . Linda Cavendish
- • 1:07—Breasts, while lying on bed, dead, when Denholm Elliott covers her with a sheet.

Phoebe Nicholls. Christabel Cavendish
- • 0:39—Partial buns, while lying in bed and talking with Tom Conti, very brief right breast, when turning around to hit him.

Deep Cover *(1992)*
Alisa Christensen . . . . Ivy's Driver
Victoria Dillard. . . . . .Betty
- • 0:52—Brief breasts, taking off her blouse to make love with Larry Fishburne.

Deep Down *(1993)*
(Unrated version reviewed.)

Melinda Armstrong . . . . .Holly
- •• 0:08—Left breast in open blouse, while making love with a boy.
- •• 0:21—Full frontal nudity, while making love with a boy in Andy's dream.
- •• 0:26—Breasts, while on bed with a boy in Andy's daydream.

Kathryn Atwood . . . . .Waitress #2
- • 0:07—Brief right breast in gaping dress top while cleaning table when Andy sees her.

Tanya Roberts . . . . Charlotte
- • 0:16—In wet top and panties, getting out of pool while talking to Andy.
- • 0:20—Briefly nude, getting out of pool at night while Andy peeks from the bushes.
- •• 0:35—Full frontal nudity, while making love with Andy in bed. Quick cuts. Very brief buns, getting into the shower.
- ••• 0:51—In bra, after dancing in front of Andy. Left breast, then breasts, while making love with him.

Deep in the Heart *(1983; British)*
a.k.a. Handgun

Karen Young . . . . Kathleen Sullivan
- • 0:35—Buns and brief breasts undressing and getting forced into bed with Larry. (Her hair gets in the way.)

•• 0:36—Brief breasts and buns, getting out of bed. Brief right breast when putting her dress on.

Defenseless *(1991)*

Barbara Hershey . . . . T. K. Katwuller
Sandy Martin . . . . Judge
Sheree North . . . . Mrs. Bodeck
Kellie Overbey . . . . Janna Seldes
••• 0:58—Brief breasts, nonchalantly changing into swimsuit at the beach.
•• 1:22—Breasts, while posing on bed with her father in video playback.

Delinquent School Girls *(1974)*

Sharon Kelly . . . . Greta
• 0:05—Left breast in mirror while practicing martial arts.

Delivery Boys *(1984)*

Samantha Fox . . . . Woman in Tuxedo
Annabelle Gurwitch . . . . Woman with Big Hat
Jane Hamilton . . . . Art Snob
Suzanne Remey Lawrence . . . . Nurse
Kelly Nichols . . . . Elizabeth
• 0:44—Top half of right breast, while eating rolls with a young boy.
Taija Rae . . . . Nurse

Delta Fox *(1977)*

Priscilla Barnes . . . . Karen
• 0:36—Left breast undressing in room for David. Very dark, hard to see.
• 0:38—Very brief breasts struggling with a bad guy and getting slammed against the wall.
• 0:39—Very brief blurry left breast, while running in front of the fireplace.
• 0:40—Breasts sneaking out of house. Brief breasts getting into Porsche.
• 0:49—Brief right breast reclining onto bed with David. Side view of left breast several times while making love.
• 1:29—Very brief side view of left breast in David's flashback.

Delta Heat *(1992)*

Linda Doná . . . . Tine Tulane
Betsy Russell . . . . Vicki
• 0:54—Brief buns and partial side of right breast, walking from bed, past two guys. (More buns seen in mirror.)

Delta of Venus *(1995)*

(Unrated version reviewed.)
Audie England . . . . Elena
••• 0:21—Breasts, while making love with Costas Mandylor on cupboard counter top.
••• 0:29—Full frontal nudity, after dropping her blanket to let Mandylor look at her, then making love.
•• 0:43—Nude, while posing with a male model for an art class.
• 1:00—Side view of left breast and buns, while posing with male model in art class again.
•• 1:01—Breasts, while posing and talking with the model.
• 1:02—Brief buns, twice, when a guy feels her up her dress.
•• 1:03—Breasts, while making love with a guy in back of car.
•• 1:16—Full frontal nudity, taking off her clothes then making love with two other women in opium den.
••• 1:33—Breasts, while making love with Mandylor on stairs inside church.
Raven Snow . . . . Leila

Delusion *(1990)*

Barbra Horan . . . . Carly
Tamara Landry . . . . Arabella
Jennifer Rubin . . . . Patti
• 0:34—Brief buns, pulling her panties down to moon the guys before entering the lake.
••• 1:07—Breasts in motel bathroom, drying her hair. More breasts in the motel room with George.
• 1:12—Right breast, in open blouse, while sitting on the bed, talking with George.
Barbara Alyn Woods . . . . Julie

Demolition Man *(1993)*

Lara Harris . . . . Taco Bell Patron
Brandy Ledford . . . . Fiber Op Girl
• 1:13—Very brief breasts, after accidentally calling the wrong number on her video phone.
Susan Lentini . . . . TV Reporter
Patricia Rive . . . . Police Officer
Anneliza Scott . . . . Police Officer

The Demon *(1981; South African)*

Jennifer Holmes . . . . Mary
•• 0:22—Breasts in dressing room.
• 1:18—Brief side of left breast, taking off robe to take a bath.
• 1:26—Breasts, crawling around in the rafters. Dark.
••• 1:29—Breasts climbing through a hole in the roof, then landing on the bed. More breasts in the bathroom.
Zoli Markey . . . . Jo
••• 1:03—Breasts and buns, in front of mirror, then getting dressed. Long scene.

Demon Keeper *(1993)*

Katrina Maltby . . . . Hilary Jackson
••• 0:27—Breasts, several times, while in black panties, after taking off robe and getting massaged by Dorothy.
Adrienne Pearce . . . . Dia Gregory
0:51—Very brief right breast under wet nightgown, while being carried back into the house.
Jennifer Steyn . . . . Ruth Stanley
• 0:31—Very brief right breast, while lying dead in bed next to Howard.
•• 0:37—Breasts after taking off robe in front of mirror.
• 0:39—Breasts, while caressed by devil creature. Close-up, don't see face.

Demon Knight *(1994)*

Brenda Bakke . . . . Cordelia
• 0:21—Brief partial breasts, while sitting on Thomas Haden Church's lap in bed.
Te-See Bender . . . . Party Babe 6
• 1:02—Very brief left breast with other Party Babes in Dick Miller's fantasy. She licks the tip of a long neck beer bottle.
Traci Bingham . . . . Party Babe 2
• 1:02—Brief breasts, several times with other Party Babes in Dick Miller's fantasy. She's in yellow bikini bottoms and says "You've had a long, hard day Uncle Willy."
Tina Hollimon . . . . Party Babe 7
• 1:02—Very brief left breast with other Party Babes in Dick Miller's fantasy. She is sitting at the bar on the left and says, "Try mine."
Chasey Lain . . . . Party Babe 5
• 1:02—Brief breasts, several times with other Party Babes in Dick Miller's fantasy. She's in orange bikini bottoms and says "Here you go Uncle Willy."
Mim Parker . . . . Party Babe

Jada Pinkett . . . . Jeryline
Sherrie Rose . . . . Wanda
Peggy Trentini . . . . Amanda
- 0:01—Brief buns in black bra and panties.
•• 0:02—Breasts, while in the bathtub in film within a film.

Demon of Paradise (1987)

Laura Banks . . . . Cahill
Leslie Huntly . . . . Gobby
•• 0:51—Breasts taking off her top on a boat, then swimming in the ocean.
Kathryn Witt . . . . Annie

Demon Rage (1981)

a.k.a. Dark Eyes
a.k.a. Demon Seed
Britt Ekland . . . . Ann-Marie
Lana Wood . . . . Lisa
- 0:00—Breasts when breasts pop out of nightgown while running from someone at the beach.
••• 0:09—Breasts and very brief partial lower frontal nudity in bed when sheets get pulled off her.
••• 0:19—Breasts, while taking a shower when she sees the spirit.
••• 0:26—Breasts and very brief lower frontal nudity while lying in bed when the spirit visits her and makes love.
••• 0:38—Breasts in bed, while making love with the spirit.
- 0:53—Brief breasts with the spirit, while making love in bed.
- 1:22—Brief full frontal nudity getting her nightgown torn off.

Demon Seed (1977)

Julie Christie . . . . Susan Harris
- 0:25—Side view of left breast, getting out of bed.
•• 0:30—Breasts and buns getting out of the shower while the computer watches with its camera.

Demon Wind (1990)

Francine Lapenseé . . . . Elaine
Sandra Margot . . . . Beautiful Demon
•• 0:50—Breasts trying to tempt Stacy and Chuck out of the cabin.
Mia M. Ruiz . . . . Reana

Demoniac (1974; French/Spanish)

Lina Romay . . . . Anne
- 1:02—Brief lower frontal nudity, while Jess Franco drags her into the bedroom.
•• 1:04—Full frontal nudity, while lying on the bed with Franco.
Monica Swinn . . . . The Count's Sadistic Partner
- 0:51—Brief breast in open gown, in bedroom with The Count.

Demonic Toys (1991)

Kristine Rose . . . . Miss July
- 0:25—Breasts in centerfold photo in magazine.
•• 0:59—Breasts in warehouse as a ghost in front of Mark.
Tracy Scoggins . . . . Judith Gray

Demonstone (1990)

Nancy Everhard . . . . Sharon Gale
- 0:47—Very, very brief backside view of tip of left breast after bending over to pick up robe off the floor.

Demonwarp (1988)

Michelle Bauer . . . . Betsy
•• 0:41—Breasts, after taking off her T-shirt to get a tan in the woods.
•• 0:43—Left breast, while lying down, then brief breasts getting up when the creature attacks.
•• 0:47—Breasts, while putting blood-stained T-shirt back on.
•• 1:19—Breasts, while strapped to table, getting ready to be sacrificed.
- 1:22—Breasts, while lying on stretcher, dead.
Pamela Gilbert . . . . Carrie Austin
••• 0:20—In bra, then breasts, while in bed with Jack.
••• 0:22—Right breast, then breasts, while lying in bed, making love with Jack.
•• 1:23—Breasts, while strapped to table.
- 1:24—Breasts several more times, while on the table.
•• 1:25—Breasts, while getting off table and dressing.
Colleen McDermott . . . . Cindy
•• 0:23—Breasts and buns drying herself off after taking a shower.
- 0:24—Very brief lower frontal nudity, under her towel, trying to run up the stairs.

Denial (1991)

Rae Dawn Chong . . . . Julie
Christine Harnos . . . . Sid
Robin Wright . . . . Sarah
- 0:37—Side view of buns, while lying on top of Jason Patric.

• *The Dentist* (1996)

Linda Hoffman . . . . Brooke
- 0:08—Very brief side of right breast, twice, while fooling around in the backyard with the pool boy while Corbin Bernsen watches.
•• 0:30—Breasts, while sitting in dentist's chair when Bernsen imagines a patient is his wife.
Betsy Monroe . . . . Young Female

Deranged (1987)

Jennifer Delora . . . . Maryann
- 1:09—Breasts in bed with Frank. Long shot.
Nancy Groff . . . . Teacher
Jane Hamilton . . . . Joyce
- 0:29—Buns, getting undressed to take a shower. Side of left breast.
- 0:37—Side view of left breast, taking off towel and putting blouse on. Long shot.
- 1:01—Breasts, changing blouses in her bedroom.
- 1:05—Breasts in bedroom, taking off her blouse with Jamie Gillis.
- 1:07—Breasts in bed when Jennifer wakes her up.

Descending Angel (1990; Made for Cable Movie)

Diane Lane . . . . Irina Stroia
- 0:01—Brief right breast, while making love with Eric Roberts on train during opening credits.
•• 0:44—In white camisole top with Roberts, then breasts lying in bed with him.

Desert Hearts (1986)

Andra Akers . . . . Silver
- 1:16—Left breast, while sitting in windowsill with Patricia Charboneau.
Patricia Charbonneau . . . . Cay Rivvers
- 1:05—Breasts, while sitting on the bed, waiting for Helen Shaver.

- • 1:06—Right breast, while talking to Shaver.
- • 1:08—Breasts, while kissing Shaver.
- ••• 1:10—Breasts, while making love in bed with Shaver.

Denise Crosby . . . . Pat
Helen Shaver . . . . Vivian Bell
- •• 1:09—Breasts when robe is taken off by Patricia Charboneau in motel room.
- ••• 1:10—Breasts making love in bed with Patricia Charboneau.

Gwen Welles . . . . Gwen

Desert Passion (1992)

Carrie Janisse . . . . Heather
- •• 0:04—In gold bra and panties, then breasts making love with an actor on bed.
- ••• 0:17—In white bra, then full frontal nudity, making love in the desert with Nick. Long scene.
- •• 0:43—Breasts in S&M outfit during bondage fantasy.
- •• 0:54—Nude (near window), while talking to Maggie in the shower room.
- ••• 1:01—Breasts during cowboy fantasy outside. Long scene.

Nicole Sassaman . . . . Linda
- •• 0:34—Breasts in spa with Maggie. In the background while Maggie makes love with Mr. Sasso.
- • 0:37—Brief left breast and buns in the spa. Breasts in spa in the background.
- ••• 0:55—Nude, getting out of the pool.

Desert Warrior (1988)

Shari Shattuck . . . . Racela
- • 0:45—Brief breasts, when the bad guy rips open her jumpsuit to see if she has radiation sickness.

Desire (1989; Italian)

Josie Bissett . . . . Jessica Harrison
- ••• 0:28—Breasts and buns, while making love in bed with her boyfriend. Long scene.
- •• 0:32—Brief breasts, getting out of bed and getting dressed.
- ••• 0:45—Breasts, while making love with the taxi boy.
- ••• 0:51—Breasts, playing the piano while getting caressed and kissed.
- ••• 0:55—Breasts, while lying in bed.
- •• 1:16—Breasts in bed with an older man.
- • 1:17—Brief breasts in bed while wearing a brunette wig (she's supposed to be her mother).
- • 1:20—Side view of left breast on top of a guy in bed in slow motion. (Wearing a wig).
- • 1:21—More left breast (still wearing wig).
- • 1:27—Left breast, while in bed in flashbacks.

Desire (1994)

Jennifer Leigh Burton . . . . Cynthia Hoffman
- • 0:18—Brief partial breasts, while blindfolded and rubbing perfume on herself before getting killed.

Carrie Chambers . . . . Nicole Meyers
- •• 0:01—Breasts, while blindfolded and putting on perfume before getting killed.

Melanie Good . . . . Kathleen Rodgers
- • 0:40—Brief right breast, twice, while blindfolded and rubbing perfume on herself before getting killed.

Kate Hodge . . . . Lauren Allen
- ••• 1:02—In bra, then breasts while making love with Martin Kemp in bed.

Carrie Janisse . . . . Female Model
- • 0:10—Brief breasts, while Deborah Shelton poses her for photographs.

Andrea Riave . . . . Nicole's Roommate
Deborah Shelton . . . . Grace Lantel
Mary Stavin . . . . Adrienne

Despair (1978; German/French)

Andrea Ferréol . . . . Lydia
- • 0:07—Long shot of right breast and very brief lower frontal nudity and buns, while crawling into bed. Left breast in closer shot, while lying in bed with Dirk Bogarde.
- •• 0:24—Long shot of right breast and buns, while crawling into bed again. Breasts and buns in closer shot in bed.
- •• 1:21—Nude, after Bogarde takes off her clothes in the hallway.
- • 1:24—Brief breasts when Bogarde walks by her.
- ••• 1:25—Nude in hall and bedroom while talking to Bogarde. Long shot of buns. Full frontal nudity while sitting on bed, then following Bogarde around until he leaves.

Desperado (1995)

Angel Aviles . . . . Zamira
Salma Hayek . . . . Carolina
- • 1:10—Brief breasts in quick cuts, while making love with Antonio Banderas.

Desperate Characters (1971)

Carol Kane . . . . Young Girl
Shirley MacLaine . . . . Sophie Bentwood
- •• 1:21—Left breast, while standing with Kenneth Mars, when he takes off her blouse.
- ••• 1:22—Breasts, while on bed, reluctantly kissing Kenneth Mars.

Desperate Crimes (1991; Italian)

Denise Crosby . . . . Bella Blu
Randi Ingerman . . . . Nina
Elizabeth Kaitan . . . . Jamie Lee
- • 0:04—Brief right breast, when getting her jacket opened by a bad guy, then more right breast after getting shot.

Traci Lords . . . . Laura

Desperate Hours (1990)

Lindsay Crouse . . . . Chandler
Kelly Lynch . . . . Nancy Breyers
- • 0:10—Brief breasts, walking on sidewalk with Mickey Rourke when her breasts pop out of her suit.
- • 1:19—Brief breasts, getting wired with a hidden microphone in bathroom.

Mimi Rogers . . . . Nora Cornell

• *The Desperate Trail* (1994; Made for Cable Movie)

Linda Fiorentino . . . . Sarah O'Rourke
Jill Scott Momaday . . . . Janie
- •• 0:14—Breasts, while sitting up in bed and lighting a cigarette and talking with a Craig Sheffer.

Desperately Seeking Susan (1985)

Madonna . . . . Susan
Rosanna Arquette . . . . Roberta Glass
- • 0:24—Upper half of breasts in bubble bath.
- • 0:46—Breasts while getting dressed when Aidan Quinn sees her through the fish tank. Long shot, hard to see.
- • 1:22—Very, very brief left breast, when getting up after lying down with Quinn.

Anne Carlisle . . . . Victoria
Annie Golden . . . . Band Singer
Ann Magnuson . . . . Cigarette Girl
Anna Thomson . . . . Crystal

Devil in the Flesh *(1986; French/Italian)*

Maruschka Detmers. . . . . Giulia Dozza

- 0:20—Very brief side view of left breast and buns going past open door way to get a robe.
- ••• 0:27—Nude, talking to Andrea's dad in his office.
- • 0:55—Breasts putting a robe on. Dark.
- •• 0:57—Breasts and buns in bedroom with Andrea.
- •• 1:09—Breasts in hallway with Andrea.
- ••• 1:22—Full frontal nudity holding keys for Andrea to see, brief buns.
- • 1:42—Lower frontal nudity, while dancing in living room in red robe.

• Devil's Advocate *(1997)*

Laura Harrington. . . . . Melissa Black

Gloria L. Henry . . . . Tiffany

E. Katherine Kerr . . . . Woman Judge

Connie Nielsen . . . . Christabella

- • 1:00—Very brief breasts, while kissing Keanu Reeves.
- • 1:01—Brief breasts, while lying on the floor with Reeves.
- •• 2:10—Nude, after taking off her dress in office and making love with Reeves.

Charlize Theron. . . . . Mary Ann Lomax

- •• 1:01—Breasts, while making love with Keanu Reeves.
- • 1:41—Brief full frontal nudity, taking off blanket and standing up in church. (She has bloody cut marks all over her body.)

Tamara Tunie . . . . Jackie Heath

- ••• 0:56—In black bra, then breasts while changing clothes in a store.

Devonsville Terror *(1983)*

Suzanna Love . . . . Jessica Scanlon

- •• 0:30—Breasts as an apparition, getting Mr. Gibbs attention.
- • 0:36—Brief breasts during flashback to 0:30 scene.
- • 0:43—Brief right breast during Ralph's past-life recollection.

Diabolique *(1996)*

Isabelle Adjani . . . . Mia Baran

- • 0:03—Nude in bathroom.
- • 0:05—Very, very brief right breast, while lying on the floor.

Kathy Bates . . . . Shirley Vogel

Shirley Knight . . . . Edie Danziger

Sharon Stone. . . . . Nicole Horner

Dial Help *(1988)*

Charlotte Lewis . . . . Jenny Cooper

- •• 1:09—Brief right breast while rolling around in the bathtub.

Diamond Run *(1988; Indonesian)*

a.k.a. Java Burn

Ayu Azhari. . . . . Aileen

Ava Lazar. . . . . Samantha

- •• 0:07—Brief breasts, several times, making love in bed with Nicky. Hard to see her face.

Diary of a Mad Housewife *(1970)*

Carrie Snodgress . . . . Tina Balser

- ••• 0:01—Breasts taking off nightgown and getting dressed, putting on white bra while Richard Benjamin talks to her.
- • 0:36—Buns and brief side view of left breast, while kissing Frank Langella.
- • 0:41—Very brief breasts lying on floor when Langella pulls the blanket up.
- • 0:54—Breasts lying in bed with Langella.
- ••• 1:21—Breasts in the shower with Langella, then drying herself off.

Diary of Forbidden Dreams *(1973; Italian)*

Sydne Rome . . . . The Girl

- ••• 0:06—Brief breasts taking off torn T-shirt in a room, then breasts sitting on edge of bed.
- ••• 0:09—Nude getting out of shower, drying herself off and getting dressed.
- • 0:20—Brief side view of right breast, while talking to Marcello Mastroianni in her room.
- •• 0:22—Brief breasts putting shirt on.
- •• 1:28—Breasts outside on stairs fighting for her shirt.
- • 1:30—Brief buns and breasts climbing onto truck.

Die Hard *(1988)*

Cheryl Baker . . . . Woman with Man

- • 0:22—Brief breasts in office with a guy when the terrorists first break into the building.

Bonnie Bedelia. . . . . Holly McClane

Terri Lynn Doss . . . . Girl at Airport

Kym Malin. . . . . Hostage

Die Watching *(1993)*

Avalon Anders . . . . Marie

- ••• 0:40—In pink outfit doing strip tease while getting videotaped by Christopher Atkins, then breasts. Long scene.
- • 0:52—Brief breasts, seen on TV monitor.

Vali Ashton . . . . Nola Carlisle

- • 1:00—Buns in white panties and right breast while making love with Atkins.

Melanie Good . . . . Sheila Walsh

- ••• 0:05—In white bodysuit dancing while Christopher Atkins video tapes her. Then breasts through bodysuit, then breasts after she rips the bodysuit open.
- ••• 0:07—Breasts in ripped bodysuit while taped down in chair before Atkins kills her.

Julianne J. Mantia. . . . . Girl #2

- • 1:05—Brief breasts, while sitting up in bed with Christopher Atkins' father. (She's the blonde girl.)

Erika Nann. . . . . Gabrielle

- •• 0:51—Right breast, while caressing with herself while Christopher Atkins videotapes her before killing her. Her right hand is handcuffed to shelves.

A Different Story *(1979)*

(R-rated version reviewed.)

Linda Carpenter. . . . . Chastity

- • 1:33—Very brief breasts in shower, shutting the door when Meg Foster discovers her with Perry King.

Meg Foster . . . . Stella

- •• 0:53—Breasts, while sitting on Perry King, rubbing cake all over each other on bed.
- • 0:59—Brief buns and side view of right breast, while getting into bed with King.

• Different Strokes *(1996)*

(Unrated version reviewed.)

Gabriella Hall . . . . Alicia

- ••• 0:22—Full frontal nudity, while making love with another woman. (She's the brunette.)
- • 0:35—Full frontal nudity, while sleeping in bed next to Katy.

Landon Hall. . . . . Jill
- ••• 0:06—Breasts, while making love with Jack.
- •• 0:17—Nude, while swimming in the pool with Dana Plato and getting out.
- •• 0:20—Breasts, while taking a shower.
- ••• 0:25—Nude, while taking a shower with Dana Plato.
- • 0:29—Brief breasts in flashbacks.
- •• 0:32—Very brief breasts in flashback. Breasts, while making love in bed with Jack.
- • 0:36—Brief buns, when getting up out of bed.
- ••• 0:55—Breasts, while making love with Dana Plato in bed.
- • 1:13—Very brief breasts during Jack's flashbacks.

Dana Plato . . . . Jill Martin
- • 0:16—Briefly nude, taking off her robe and going for a swim. Long shot.
- •• 0:17—Very brief buns, when going under the water after talking with Jill. Nude, while swimming in the pool.
- •• 0:25—Nude, while taking a shower with Jill.
- • 0:31—Breasts, while taking a shower when Jack peeks in the window.
- • 0:32—Very brief left breast in flashback.
- • 0:35—Brief breasts, taking off sweater before going to sleep.
- •• 0:54—Breasts, while making love with Jill in bed.
- • 0:59—Buns, while lying in bed next to Jill.
- ••• 1:19—Breasts, while making love with Jill in bed.

Digital Man *(1995)*

Megan Blake. . . . . Lt. Thompson
Kristen Dalton. . . . . Gena
Chase Masterson. . . . . Susie
- •• 0:27—Breasts, while in bed with Don Swayze.

Susan Tyrrell . . . . Town Woman
Amanda Wyss . . . . Uncredited Lt. Fredericks

Dinosaur Island *(1993)*

Julie Baltay . . . . Cave Girl
Michelle Bauer . . . . June
- ••• 0:20—Breasts (she has white necklaces on), while bathing in a stream with April and May, then bathing the guys.
- ••• 0:22—More breasts, while bathing the guys.
- • 0:38—Brief upper half of left breast, popping out of bikini top after winning fight with the Queen.
- ••• 1:07—Breasts, while making love outside at night with Turbo.

Robin Chaney . . . . Tara
Antonia Dorian . . . . April
- ••• 0:20—Breasts (she has white head band on), while bathing in a stream with May and June, then bathing the guys.
- ••• 0:22—More breasts, while bathing the guys.
- ••• 0:53—Breasts, while making love outside with Skeemer.

Griffin Drew . . . . May
- ••• 0:20—Breasts (she has dark necklaces on), while bathing in a stream with April and June, then bathing the guys.
- ••• 0:22—More breasts, while bathing the guys.
- ••• 0:30—Breasts, while helping Wayne's arm feel better in prehistoric spa.
- ••• 0:31—Breasts and buns, while making love with Wayne in spa.
- • 1:15—Side of left breast during end credits.

Deborah Dutch. . . . . Cave Girl
Nikki Fritz . . . . High Priestess
- •• 0:00—Breasts (painted blue) and buns in G-string, while dancing during sacrifice ceremony.

Becky LeBeau. . . . . Virgin Sacrifice
- ••• 0:00—Breasts, after getting her bikini top ripped off while tied by her wrists during sacrifice ceremony.

Toni Naples. . . . . Queen Morganna
- • 0:37—Brief left breast, popping out of bikini top when June starts dragging her around by her hair.

• ***Dinosaur Valley Girls*** *(1996)*

(Director's Cut reviewed.)

Denise Ames . . . . Hea-Thor
- • 0:25—Brief breasts, when the dinosaur takes her top off and Tony carries her away.
- •• 0:46—Breasts and partial buns, while making love with Tony in cave.
- •• 1:27—Breasts, while sitting on lounge chair by the pool.

Karen Black . . . . Ro-Kell
Griffin Drew . . . . Daphne Adrian
- • 0:02—Brief breasts, when waking up in bed next to Tony.
- •• 0:04—Breasts, when getting out of the pool and drying herself off.

Donna Spangler . . . . Mee-Shell
- • 0:08—Brief breasts, while dancing in Tony's vision.
- • 0:40—Brief breasts, while running in slow motion in Big-Mac's vision.
- • 0:54—Brief breasts, while running in slow motion in Big-Mac's vision.
- •• 0:55—Breasts, while dancing outside.
- •• 0:57—Breasts, while dancing in cave.
- • 1:01—Breasts, while making love outdoors with Tony.
- • 1:14—Breasts, while fighting in cave with the cave men.

Diplomatic Immunity *(1991)*

Meg Foster . . . . Gerta Hermann
Wendel Meldrum . . . . Kim Dades
Fabiana Udenio . . . . Teresa
- •• 1:06—Breasts in panties, on the floor with her hands tied behind her back when Klaus rips her blouse open to photograph her.

• ***Dirty Dishes*** *(1979; French)*

Carole Laure . . . . Armelle
- •• 0:09—Brief right breast, while putting her blouse on when walking in hallway.

Dirty Hands *(1975; French)*

Romy Schneider . . . . Julie
- • 0:01—Buns and right breast getting a tan, lying on the grass after a man's kite lands on her.
- •• 0:09—Side view of right breast, while lying in bed with a man, then breasts.
- • 1:04—Breasts lying on floor, then brief breasts sitting up and looking at something on the table.

• ***Dirty Money*** *(1993)*

Delaune Michel . . . . CeCe
- •• 0:08—Breasts and buns, while making love with Sam in bedroom.
- • 0:10—Brief breasts, while talking in bed with Sam.

Disaster in Time *(1992; Made for Cable Movie)*

a.k.a. Timescape

Mimi Craven . . . . Carolyn
Emilia Crow. . . . . Reeve
- • 0:18—Side view of left breast, sitting in front of vanity while Jeff Daniels watches. Long shot.

Marilyn Lightstone . . . . Madame Iovine

Discretion Assured (1993)

Elizabeth Gracen . . . . Miranda
- 0:28—Brief buns when Michael York removes her panties.
- ••• 0:39—Breasts and buns, while making love with York.
- 1:09—Back side of right and buns, while rubbing lotion on herself. Brief left breast, while putting on robe. Medium long shots.
- 1:22—Brief breasts, when York rips her dress open during argument.

Dee Wallace Stone . . . . Kitten

Disorderlies (1987)

Julie Kristen Smith . . . . Skinny Dipper #2
- 0:56—Brief breasts and buns walking around near pool. Long shot.

Diva (1982; French)

Thuy Ann Luu . . . . Alba
- 0:13—Breasts in B&W photos when record store clerk asks to see her portfolio.
- 0:15—More of the B&W photos on the wall.
- 1:27—Very brief upper half of left breast taking off top, seen through window. Long shot.

The Divine Enforcer (1991)

Carrie Chambers . . . . Kim
- 1:21—Upper half of right breast in bra, while strapped into a chair by Dan Stroud.

The Divine Nymph (1977; Italian)

Laura Antonelli . . . . Manoela Roderighi
- •• 0:10—Full frontal nudity reclining in chair.
- 0:18—Right breast in open blouse sitting in bed. Lower frontal nudity while getting up.

Diving In (1990)

Yolanda Jilot . . . . Amanda Lansky
- 0:55—Brief breasts, in open blouse, getting dressed while talking to Burt Young.

Dixie Lanes (1987)

Karen Black . . . . Zelma
Tina Louise . . . . Violet
Pamela Springsteen . . . . Judy
- •• 1:00—Breasts, while turning around in pond, talking to Everett at night.

Do or Die (1991)

Cynthia Brimhall . . . . Edy Stark
- 0:31—Most of buns, wearing white lingerie outfit, singing and dancing at night.
- ••• 0:36—Breasts and buns, making love with Lucas on floor in front of fire.

Ava Cadell . . . . Ava
- •• 0:20—Buns and brief breasts, getting dressed in motor home. Lots of buns shots, wearing swimsuit.

Carolyn Liu . . . . Silk
- ••• 0:14—Breasts, getting up off massage table and putting robe on.
- •• 1:04—Breasts in bed with Pat Morita.

Pandora Peaks . . . . Atlanta Lee
- ••• 1:09—Breasts making love with Shane outside at night.
- 1:15—Brief breasts in background, getting dressed. Out of focus.

Dona Speir . . . . Donna Hamilton
- 0:06—Brief breasts taking off towel and getting into spa.
- •• 0:32—Breasts, mostly right breast, changing clothes in back of airplane.
- ••• 1:21—Breasts and buns, in swimming pool with Erik Estrada.

Roberta Vasquez . . . . Nicole Justin
- •• 0:56—Breasts, making love with Bruce, outside.

Do the Right Thing (1989)

Joie Lee . . . . Jade
Rosie Perez . . . . Tina
- •• 1:22—Breasts when Spike Lee rubs ice all over her. Don't see her face, but it's her.

Doc Hollywood (1991)

Cristi Conaway . . . . Receptionist
Bridget Fonda . . . . Nancy Lee
Julie Warner . . . . Lou
- 0:15—Silhouette of right breast while standing in lake during Michael J. Fox's dream. Possible lower frontal nudity since she is facing the camera, but since it is shot in silhouette, you can't see anything.
- ••• 0:16—Breasts several times, skinny dipping in lake, then getting out while Fox watches.

Doctor Mordrid (1992)

Julie Michaels . . . . Irene
- ••• 0:00—Breasts and buns, while talking with Brian Thompson, then getting picked up and placed on table.

The Dogfighters (1995)

Lara Harris . . . . Mikaela/Mike
- •• 1:03—Buns and breasts, while getting into and out of the shower.

Patricia Rive . . . . Louise
- 0:12—Brief breasts, when sitting up in bed with Robert Davi before getting shot by Ben Gazzara.

• Dogwatch (1996)

Mimi Craven . . . . Janet
- •• 0:07—Breasts and buns in T-back, while dancing on stage.

La Dolce Vita (1960; Italian/French)

Anouk Aimee . . . . Maddalena
Nadia Gray . . . . Nadia
- 1:09—Brief breasts, while lying on the floor after doing a strip tease.

Magali Noel . . . . Fanny

Doll Squad (1973)

Tura Satana . . . . Lavelle Sumara
- 0:23—Buns in outfit on stage in club. Breasts, but wearing pasties.
- 0:24—Breasts wearing pasties, while changing clothes in dressing room.

Dollars (1972)

Goldie Hawn . . . . Dawn Divine
- 0:04—Very brief partial buns, when Sarge slips some money under her nightie while she's lying in bed.

Christiane Maybach . . . . Helga

The Dolls (1984; German)

a.k.a. The Story of the Dolls

Tetchie Agbayani . . . . Lee
- 0:12—Brief right breast, several times, while fighting with Pedro on the beach.

••• 0:24—Breasts and buns, while undressing and taking a bubble bath with the other models.
•• 0:39—Buns and right breast, then full frontal nudity while posing on beach for Tom.
••• 0:41—Full frontal nudity, while making love on the beach with Tom.
•• 0:57—Buns, while making love with Tom.
• 0:58—Breasts in magazine photos.
• 1:01—Brief breasts in magazine photos.
• 1:03—Nude in magazine photos.
•• 1:04—Nude, while running on beach in flashback.
• 1:10—Very brief right breast, during tribal ceremony.
••• 1:12—Breasts, getting paint taken off her in bed, then sitting up.
• 1:24—Brief buns, while on the ground with Tom.

Domino (1989)

Brigitte Nielsen . . . . .Domino
• 0:05—Right breast, lying down next to swimming pool, breasts getting out.
••• 1:04—Right breast, caressing herself in a white lingerie body suit, wearing a black wig.

Don Juan DeMarco (1994)

Jo Champa . . . . .Sultana Gulbeta
Lisa Comshaw. . . . . Body Double for Woman in Restaurant
• 0:05—Very, very brief partial right breast, while making love in bed.
Faye Dunaway. . . . . Marilyn Mickler
Géraldine Pailhas. . . . . Doña Ana
Talisa Soto. . . . . Doña Julia
• 0:35—Very brief right breast, in gaping dress top, while sitting on Johnny Depp.
Rachel Ticotin . . . . Doña Inez
0:21—Buns, when standing in bathroom while brushing her hair looks like a body double.

Don't Answer the Phone (1979)

Pamela Bryant. . . . . Sue Ellen
•• 0:28—Breasts in the killer's photo studio when he rips her jacket off and kills her.
Denise Galik . . . . Lisa
Flo Gerrish . . . . Dr. Lindsay Gale
• 1:05—Very brief breasts rolling over in bed with McCabe. Brief breasts when he pulls the covers down.
• 1:19—Side view of right breast, several times, while taking off blouse and putting nightgown on.
Suzanne Severeid . . . . Hooker
• 0:43—Very brief right breast in open blouse after the killer strangles her.

Don't Do It (1994)

Elizabeth Barondes .Waitress/Phone Sex
Aimee Graham . . . . .Great Girl 1
Heather Graham . . . . Suzanna
Sheryl Lee . . . . Michelle
Sarah Trigger . . . . .Alicia
• 0:12—Very brief buns in swimsuit bottom, when her dress flies up when she rolls over on top of James Marshall at the beach.
• 1:02—Very, very brief left breast in gaping blouse when sitting up after leaning on Marshall.

Don't Go Near the Park (1979)

Linnea Quigley . . . . Bondi's Mother
• 0:08—Full frontal nudity, behind shower door.
• 0:09—Brief left breast, while wrapping a towel around herself.
••• 0:19—Left breast, while lying in bed with Mark.

Don't Look Now (1973)

Julie Christie . . . . Laura Baxter
• 0:27—Brief breasts and lower frontal nudity, while sitting in bathtub and in front of mirror, talking with Donald Sutherland.
••• 0:30—Breasts, brief buns and brief partial lower frontal nudity, while making love with Sutherland in bed.

Don't Open Till Christmas (1984; British)

Pat Astley . . . . Sharon
••• 0:19—Breasts in sexy gold outfit while posing for photo session. Nice, long scene.
•• 0:22—Breasts flashing while wearing a Santa outfit for Cliff.
•• 0:24—Breasts in Santa outfit when the killer checks her out while holding a razor.
•• 0:26—Breasts, sitting on bed opening her robe for policemen.
Belinda Mayne . . . . Kate
Caroline Munro. . . . . Herself

Dona Flor and Her Two Husbands (1978; Brazilian)

Sonia Braga . . . . .Flor
• 0:13—Buns and brief breasts with her husband, Vadinho.
•• 0:15—Breasts, while lying on the bed.
• 0:17—Brief buns, twice, when getting out of bed.
•• 0:54—Breasts, while making love on the bed with Vadinho.
•• 0:57—Breasts, while lying on the bed.
••• 1:41—Breasts, while kissing Vadinho.

The Donor (1994)

Christina Cox . . . . Angel
•• 0:07—Buns, after taking off white dress in bedroom with Jeff Wincott.
Michelle Johnson. . . . . .Dr. Lucy Flynn
Karen Waddell. . . . . Talia Green

Doom Asylum (1987)

Ruth Corrine Collins . . . . Tina
•• 0:19—Breasts pulling up her top while yelling at kids below.
Patty Mullen . . . . .Judy LaRue/Kiki LaRue

The Doom Generation (1995)

Heidi Fleiss. . . . . Liquor Store Clerk
Rose McGowan . . . . Amy Blue
•• 0:14—Breasts, while sitting in bathtub by herself.
•• 0:16—Breasts, while sitting in bathtub, then getting up to kiss Jordan.
• 0:19—Brief right breast, while frolicking in bathtub with Jordan.
•• 0:27—Breasts, while making love in back seat of car with Xavier.
•• 0:42—Breasts while making love in bed with Jordan.
• 1:11—Very brief left breast, then breasts, while making love with Jordan and Xavier.
•• 1:12—Breasts, while lying in bed after making love with Jordan and Xavier. Brief buns under clear plastic rain coat, getting up out of bed.
Parker Posey . . . . .Brandl

The Doors (1991)

Josie Bissett . . . . Robby Krieger's Girlfriend

Christina Fulton . . . . Nico
•• 0:56—Breasts, after taking off her top in elevator with Val Kilmer.
Karina Lombard . . . . Warhol Actress
Debi Mazar . . . . Whiskey Girl
Annie McEnroe . . . . Secretary
Kathleen Quinlan . . . . Patricia Kennealy
••• 1:00—Brief left breast, while in bed with Val Kilmer, breasts (while wearing glasses) out of bed.
• 1:02—Left breast, while crawling on the floor.
••• 1:03—Nude, dancing around her apartment with Kilmer.
Mimi Rogers . . . . Magazine Photographer
Jennifer Rubin . . . . Edie
Meg Ryan . . . . Pamela Courson
•• 1:06—Right breast, while lying in bed with Val Kilmer.
Adrian Scott . . . . New York Journalist
Charlie Spradling . . . . CBS Girl Backstage
Claire Stansfield . . . . Warhol Eurosnob
Cirsten Weldon . . . . Girl in Car

Doppelganger: The Evil Within *(1992)*

Drew Barrymore . . . . Holly Gooding
•• 0:23—Breasts in shower when water turns blood red. Great shot, but ruined by the red water.
• 0:26—Brief side of left breast in kitchen with Patrick.
Leslie Hope . . . . Elizabeth
Sally Kellerman . . . . Sister Jan

• ***Dorothy Stratten, The Untold Story*** *(1985; Video Tape)*

Candy Loving . . . . Herself
• 0:22—Brief left breast in centerfold photo.
Dorothy Stratten . . . . Herself
•• 0:02—Breasts during photo session on sofa.
•• 0:03—Left breast in mirror before falling off sofa, breasts after.
••• 0:06—Breasts outside in a field.
••• 0:14—Breasts and buns in still photos.
••• 0:17—Full frontal nudity while posing in front of mirrored wall with a ballet rail
•• 0:26—Breasts in still photos.
••• 0:39—Breasts in bathtub for Playmate of the Year pictorial.
••• 1:02—Nude in classic pin-up girl poses.
••• 1:05—Breasts in bathtub and on sofa.

Double Cross *(1994)*

Kelly Preston . . . . Vera Blanchard
• 0:08—In bra, panties, garter belt and stockings in hotel room with Patrick Bergin. Buns and partial left breast, when he rips off her panties. Don't see her face.
• 0:24—Buns, while getting into the shower. Don't see her face.
Jennifer Tilly . . . . Melissa

Double Exposure *(1983)*

Joanna Frank . . . . Bartender's Ex-Wife
Pamela Hensley . . . . Sergeant Fontain
Victoria Jackson . . . . Racetrack Model #1
Sally Kirkland . . . . Hooker
•• 0:26—Breasts in alley getting killed.
Joanna Pettet . . . . Mindy Jordache
•• 0:55—Breasts, making love in bed with Adrian.
Misty Rowe . . . . Bambi
Kathy Shower . . . . Mudwrestler #1
Jeana Tomasina . . . . Renee
• 0:20—Very brief glimpse of left breast under water in swimming pool.

Double Exposure *(1993)*

Jennifer Gatti . . . . Maria Putnam
•• 0:06—Breasts in B&W, while making love with a guy.
• 0:25—In bra, then brief lower frontal nudity and brief buns in B&W.
•• 0:39—Breasts, while making love on top of a guy in B&W.
•• 0:40—Breasts again while on top of and below the guy in B&W.
• 1:22—Brief left breast in bed with Dedee Pfeiffer (in color).
• 1:23—Brief right breast while in bed with Pfeiffer.
Dedee Pfeiffer . . . . Linda Mack
• 1:22—Brief left breast while in bed with Jennifer Gatti.
•• 1:23—Left breast, quite a few times, while lying on her back.

Double Impact *(1991)*

Shelley Michelle . . . . Uncredited Student
Alonna Shaw . . . . Danielle Shaw
•• 1:09—Breasts, in white panties, changing out of her wet clothes on boat.
•• 1:10—Breasts and buns several times, making love with Chad during Alex's jealous fantasy.
• 1:11—More breasts and buns in fantasy.
• 1:12—More breasts.
Julie Strain . . . . Student
• 0:09—Brief buns, while lying on floor in pink leotard in exercise class.

Double Jeopardy *(1992; Made for Cable Movie)*

Rachel Ward . . . . Lisa Burns
• 0:21—Very brief left breast, in the shower with Boxleitner. Hard to see because of the shadows. Also steam on glass obscures her face.
• 0:23—Very brief right breast, when Eddie opens her robe to rip her panties off. Hard to see because of the beveled glass in the door. Very, very brief right breast while getting attacked by Eddie when she reaches back to get a knife. Don't see her face clearly.

The Double Life of Veronique *(1991; French)*

Sandrine Dumas . . . . Catherine
Irène Jacob . . . . Veronika/Véronique
•• 0:04—Left breast, then breasts lying in bed with her boyfriend.
••• 0:28—Brief lower frontal nudity, then breasts while making love with her boyfriend.
• 0:41—Brief left breast, while sitting up in bed to answer the phone.

Double Obsession *(1992)*

Maryam D'Abo . . . . Claire Burke
• 0:34—Breasts, while taking a shower. Seen behind plastic shower curtain.
Margaux Hemingway . . . . Heather Dwyer
•• 0:31—Right breast, while wearing Indian headdress and making love on top of Fredric Forrest in bed.
Rachel Ward . . . . Grandmother
Blair Weickgenant . . . . Lillian Robinson

• ***Double Tap*** *(1997)*

Kimber Monroe . . . . Stripper
•• 0:24—Breasts and brief buns in panties, while dancing in apartment in front of Ulysses and his girlfriend.

Double Threat (1992)
(Unrated version reviewed.)
Sally Kirkland. . . . . .Monica Martel
- • 0:13—In lingerie outfit while playing with herself. Partial left breast.
- •• 0:51—Brief left breast, then breasts while dressing in bathroom.

Sherrie Rose . . . . Lisa Shane
- • 0:09—Buns in lingerie, while sleeping in bed.
- • 0:23—Buns in white lingerie while acting in movie with Andrew Stevens.
- ••• 0:47—Right breast, then breasts while making love with Stevens in bed.

• *Double Your Pleasure* (1997)
Gabriella Hall. . . . . Melissa Lamb
- ••• 0:18—Breasts and buns in T-back, while making love with James in his fantasy.
- ••• 0:24—Breasts and partial buns, while making love in bed with James and Henry.

Julie Kruis . . . . Janice Hanson
- ••• 0:47—Full frontal nudity, while making love with the hypnotist.

Tracie May . . . . .Kathleen Connell
- ••• 0:04—Breasts, while making love with Jack in back room of bookstore.

Blake Pickett . . . . Uncredited Judy
- ••• 1:13—Breasts and buns, while making love in bed with Robert.

Janine Stillo . . . . Debora
- ••• 0:54—Breasts, while making love in bed with her husband.

Down by Law (1986)
Ellen Barkin . . . . .Laurette
Billie Neal . . . . Bobbie
- •• 0:11—Breasts lying in bed, talking to Jack. Medium long shot. Long scene.
- ••• 0:12—Side view of right breast, partial lower frontal nudity, lying in bed.
- •• 0:13—More breasts, medium long shot again, lying in bed.
- •• 0:14—Right breast when Jack covers her up with sheet.

Down Came a Blackbird (1995; Made for Cable Movie)
Sarita Choudhury . . . . .Myrna
Laura Dern . . . . Helen McNulty
- • 0:40—Very, very brief partial left breast, while under water in a pool in flashback. B&W.
- • 1:21—Very brief breasts, while being pushed into a swimming pool, blindfolded and tied by wrists.
- • 1:23—Very, very brief breasts, while diving under the water to get Jan.

Alexandra Innes . . . . Stunts
Vanessa Redgrave . . . . Anna Lenke
Amanda Smith . . . . .Professor's Wife
- • 1:41—Very brief left breast, then breasts, twice, while strapped down and tortured on a table during Raul Julia's flashback.

Down the Drain (1989)
Teri Copley . . . . .Kathy Miller
- • 0:04—Full frontal nudity making love on couch with Andrew Stevens. Looks like a body double.

Trisha Lane . . . . Robin
Stella Stevens . . . . .Sophia

Dr. Alien (1989)
a.k.a. I Was a Teenage Sex Mutant
Laura Albert. . . . . Rocker Chick #3
- ••• 0:21—Breasts in black outfit during dream sequence with two other rocker chicks.

Ginger Lynn Allen . . . . Rocker Chick #1
- ••• 0:21—Breasts in red panties during dream sequence with two other rocker chicks.

Michelle Bauer. . . . . Coed #1
- ••• 0:53—Breasts taking off her top (she's on the left) in the women's locker room after another coed takes hers off in front of Wesley.

Julie Gray. . . . . .Karla
- ••• 0:44—In white bra, then breasts in Janitor's room with Wesley.

Elizabeth Kaitan. . . . . Waitress
Linnea Quigley . . . . Rocker Chick #2
- ••• 0:21—Breasts in white outfit during dream sequence with two other rocker chicks.

Karen Russell . . . . Coed #2
- ••• 0:53—Breasts taking off her top (she's on the right) in the women's locker room before another coed takes hers off in front of Wesley.

Edy Williams . . . . Buckmeister
- ••• 0:54—Breasts taking off her top in the women's locker room in front of Wesley.

Dr. Caligari (1989)
Laura Albert. . . . . .Mrs. Van Houten
- ••• 0:05—Breasts taking off yellow towel, then sitting in bathtub.
- •• 0:07—Lying down, making love with guy wearing a mask.
- ••• 0:10—Breasts taking orange bra off, then lying back and playing with herself.
- •• 0:11—More breasts, lying on the floor.
- •• 0:12—More breasts, lying on the floor again.
- • 0:30—Brief left breast with big tongue.

Catherine Case . . . . .Patient with Extra Hormones
Debra De Liso . . . . Grace Butter

Dr. Jekyll and Ms. Hyde (1995)
Lysette Anthony . . . . Sarah Carver
Kim Morgan Greene . . . . .Paparazzi Lady/Party Lady
Donna Sarrasin . . . . Mintz's Secretary
Sean Young. . . . . .Helen Hyde
- • 0:41—Very brief real breasts, opening her lingerie top in front of Stephen Tobolowsky, then special-effect as her right breast shrinks.

Dr. Jekyll and Sister Hyde (1971)
Martine Beswicke . . . . Sister Hyde
- • 0:25—Breasts, opening her blouse and examining her breasts after transforming from a man.
- • 0:27—Left breast, feeling herself.
- • 0:44—Brief buns, taking off coat to put on a dress.

Dracula Rising (1992)
Stacey Travis . . . . .Theresa
- •• 0:44—Breasts, while on rocks in front of waterfall with Christopher Atkins. Long shot, then closer shot. Nude under water, sometimes with another woman, sometimes with Atkins.

Dracula's Widow (1988)

Rachel Jones . . . . Jenny
- • 0:54—Brief left breast, then brief breasts, twice, lying in the bathtub, getting stabbed by Sylvia Kristel.

Sylvia Kristel . . . . Vanessa

Dragon Fire (1993)

Monique Parent . . . . Dancer 6
- •• 0:57—Breasts and buns in T-back, while dancing on stage painted with fluorescent paint. Lit with blacklight.

Pamela Runo . . . . Marta
- ••• 0:25—Breasts and buns in T-back, while doing strip routine on stage. Lit with strobe lights.
- •• 0:29—Breasts and buns in T-back, while dancing on stage.
- ••• 0:49—Breasts, while making love in bed with Powers.

Christina Veronica . . . . Dancer

Dragon Fury (1995)

Trisha Berdot . . . . Dixie Dancer

Chona Jason . . . . Regina
- • 0:08—Brief buns, several times, while talking to bad guy in room.
- • 0:20—Brief left breast in bed with David Heavener after transporting back in time. Brief breasts, while crawling out of bed and getting a jacket to wear.
- ••• 0:45—Nude, after taking off her blouse and making love with Mason in motel room.

Dragon: The Bruce Lee Story (1993)

Lauren Holly . . . . Linda Lee
- • 0:39—Very, very brief tip of left breast when making love with Jason Scott Lee (when she moves her hand from the front of his shoulder to the back).

Lala Sloatman . . . . Sherry Schnell

Dragonard (1988)

Annabel Schofield . . . . Honore
- • 0:26—Brief side view of left breast, brief breasts lying down, then left breast again in stable with Abdee.

Claudia Udy . . . . Arabella
- •• 1:11—Breasts dressed as Cleopatra dancing a routine in front of a bunch of guys.

Draw! (1984; Made for Cable Movie)

Alexandra Bastedo . . . . Bess
- • 0:52—Silhouette of right breast, leaning over Kirk Douglas while making love in bed.

• *Dream Babies* (1989; Video Tape)

Bianca McEachin . . . . Herself
- ••• 0:06—Dancing in red two-piece swimsuit, then breasts and buns in G-string. Nice!
- •• 0:40—Breasts, introducing her segment.
- ••• 0:41—More breasts, dancing in red two-piece swimsuit.

Dream Lover (1986)

Kristy McNichol . . . . Kathy Gardner
- • 0:17—Very, very brief right breast getting out of bed, then walking around in a white top and underwear.

Dream Lover (1994)

(Unrated version reviewed.)

Mädchen Amick . . . . Lena Reardon
- •• 0:24—Breasts and buns, while making love with James Spader.
- • 0:26—Brief buns and left breast while making love in dining room with Spader.
- ••• 0:29—Right breast, while lying in bed. Nude getting out of bed and walking to bathroom.

Bess Armstrong . . . . Elaine

Dream Man (1995)

Megan Blake . . . . Ballet Mistress

Denise Crosby . . . . Barbara
- •• 0:01—Breasts while blindfolded during opening credits. Slightly distorted.
- • 1:25—Brief breasts on video monitor.

Patsy Kensit . . . . Kris Anderson

• *Dream Master: The Erotic Invader* (1995)

Lisa Boyle . . . . September
- •• 1:17—Breasts, while tied to a bed by Devora.
- ••• 1:20—Buns and breasts, while making love on top of Grant in bed.

Kristen Knittle . . . . Dani
- • 0:32—Breasts, while making love with Scott in her dream.
- •• 0:46—Breasts, while making love with Troy in his dream.

Cory Lane . . . . Troy's Dream Girl
- •• 0:39—Breasts and buns, while next to and on bed in Troy's fantasy.
- ••• 0:55—Breasts, while making love with Troy in his dream.

Patricia Skeriotis . . . . Devora
- •• 0:14—Buns in lingerie, then right breasts, while making love with Grant while he's handcuffed to a park bench.
- • 0:27—Brief breasts, when Grant is making love with her.
- • 1:12—Buns in lingerie in Grant's dream.
- •• 1:18—Breasts and buns in lingerie, while talking with September.

• *Dream Trap* (1989)

Christina Leardini . . . . Sorority Sister
- •• 1:18—Breasts, when emerging from swimming pool during party.

Jeanie Moore . . . . Blondee

• *Dream with the Fishes* (1997)

Kathryn Erbe . . . . Liz
- •• 0:01—Breasts, while talking with Nick in room. (She has a tattoo on her right breast.)
- • 0:53—Brief breasts, while swinging on a swing in a barn. Long shot. Brief breasts in closer shot when she gets off the swing.

• *Dreamaniac* (1987)

Ashlyn Gere . . . . Pat

Sylvia Summers . . . . Lily
- • 0:35—Brief side view of left breast, when taking off her blue dress in front of Ace.

Dressed to Kill (1980)

Nancy Allen . . . . Liz Blake
- • 1:36—Breasts (from above), buns and brief right breast in shower.

Angie Dickinson . . . . Kate Miller
- • 0:01—Brief side view behind shower door. Long shot, hard to see.
- 0:02—Frontal nude scene in shower is a body double, Victoria Lynn Johnson.
- • 0:24—Brief buns getting out of bed after coming home from museum with a stranger.

Victoria Lynn Johnson . . . . . Body Double for Angie Dickinson
- •• 0:02—Frontal nudity in the shower body doubling for Angie Dickinson.

The Drifter (1988)

Kim Delaney . . . . Julia Robbins
- • 0:11—Brief breasts making love with Miles O'Keeffe on motel floor.
- •• 0:21—Breasts in bed talking with Timothy Bottoms.

Drive, He Said (1972)

Karen Black . . . . Olive
- • 1:15—Brief breasts screaming in the bathtub when she gets scared when a bird flies in.
- • 1:19—Brief lower frontal nudity running out of the house in her bathrobe.

June Fairchild . . . . Sylvie
- • 0:16—Buns, brief breasts and lower frontal nudity, while walking around in the dark while Gabriel shines a flashlight on her.
- • 1:01—Breasts, then briefly nude getting dressed while Gabriel goes crazy and starts trashing a house.

Drowning by Numbers (1988; British)

Jane Gurnett . . . . Nancy
- ••• 0:04—Nude, undressing inside and running outside, taking a bath with Jake. Long scene.
- ••• 0:06—More breasts and buns, in the bathtub next to Jake.
- • 0:10—Left breast, passed out in bathtub.
- • 0:11—More left breast in bathtub.
- • 0:15—Left breast, while in wheelbarrow.
- • 0:16—Full frontal nudity when the women pull her onto the bed.

Joely Richardson . . . . Cisse Colpitts 3
- • 0:28—Breasts, taking off swimsuit and drying herself off. Long shot.
- ••• 0:43—Breasts and buns, making love on couch with Bellamy.
- • 1:23—Breasts under water in pool with Bellamy.
- •• 1:24—Breasts getting out of pool.
- ••• 1:25—Breasts standing up and putting swimsuit back on.
- •• 1:37—Left breast, while in car with Madgett.

Juliet Stevenson. . . . . Cisse Colpitts 2
- • 0:57—Lower frontal nudity and left breast, while trying to entice Hardy. Long shot.

Drum (1976)

Pam Grier . . . . Regine
- • 0:58—Very brief breasts getting undressed and into bed with Maxwell.

Paula Kelly. . . . . Rachel

Fiona Lewis . . . . Augusta Chauvet
- ••• 0:57—Breasts taking a bath, getting out, then having Pam Grier dry her off.

Cheryl Smith. . . . . Sophie Maxwell
- •• 0:54—Breasts in the stable trying to get Yaphet Kotto to make love with her.

Brenda Sykes. . . . . Calinda
- • 0:19—Breasts standing next to bed with Ken Norton.

Isela Vega . . . . Marianna
- • 0:04—Breasts in bed with the maid, Rachel.
- •• 0:22—Brief breasts standing next to the bed with Maxwell.

• *Drunks (1995; Made for Cable Movie)*

Faye Dunaway. . . . . Becky

Amanda Plummer . . . . Shelley

Parker Posey . . . . Debbie

Anna Thomson . . . . Tanya
- ••• 0:47—In bra and panties, then breasts, while making out with Richard Lewis in bedroom.

Duet for One (1987)

Julie Andrews. . . . . Stephanie Anderson
- • 0:28—Very brief left breast in gaping blouse in bathroom splashing water on her face because she feels sick, then wet T-shirt.
- ••• 1:06—Breasts stretching, lying in bed.
- • 1:07—Very brief buns and very brief right breast, when she rolls off the bed onto the floor.

Cathryn Harrison . . . . Penny Smallwood

Macha Meril . . . . Anya

Dumb & Dumber (1994)

Traci Adell . . . . Sexy Woman

Teri Garr . . . . Helen Swanson

Lauren Holly . . . . Mary
- • 0:30—Brief lower half of buns, when Jim Carrey pulls her dress up a bit during his fantasy.

Dune Warriors (1990)

Maria Isabel Lopez. . . . . Miranda
- •• 0:25—Breasts in underground lake with Val.
- ••• 0:43—Breasts making love with a guy in bed.

Jillian McWhirter . . . . Val
- • 0:25—Brief right breast with Miranda in underground lake. (Her hair is in the way of her left breast.)

Dust (1985; French/Belgian)

Jane Birkin . . . . Magda
- • 1:17—Brief breasts and buns, taking off robe and pounding the wall. Very dark.

Dust Devil (1992; British)

Chelsea Field . . . . Wendy Robinson
- • 0:22—Very, very brief partial left breast, when standing up in bathtub.

Terri Norton . . . . Saartjie Haarhoff
- • 0:06—Breasts and brief side view of buns, while making love in bed with Dust Devil before he breaks her neck.

Marianne Sägebrecht . . . . Dr. Leidzinger

• *E. Nick: A Legend in His Own Mind (1984; Video Tape)*

Andra Akers. . . . . Aunt Mona

Leslee Bremmer. Nymphet/Announcer
- • 0:03—Breasts, while getting dressed in bunny costume with other nymphets.
- • 0:09—Partial buns, in lingerie on video tape.
- • 0:38—Breasts under wet, white T-shirt, while playing volleyball in pool with other Nymphets.

Monique Gabrielle. . . . . Charmaine
- • 0:08—Brief breasts, when stretching in video. Brief side of right breast while sunbathing.
- •• 0:30—Buns and breasts in shower, breasts when coughing on steam. Buns, while trying on clothes in mirror.
- ••• 0:35—Buns in G-string in front of mirror again. Breasts while sunbathing and playing with teddy bear.
- ••• 0:39—Breasts and buns in G-string while sunbathing outside with her family.

Juli Lawrence . . . . Nymphet

Kim Morris . . . . Nymphet

Betty Thomas . . . . Herself

Carol Wayne . . . . Regine

• *E=mc²* *(1995)*

a.k.a. Wavelength

Liza Walker . . . . .Lucy Amore

• 0:33—Brief right breast, after taking off her dress outside in front of Paul.

Kelli Williams . . . . Claire Higgins

• 0:54—Brief right breast, while lying in bed with Jeremy Plven when he starts to make love with her. Very dark.

Easy Kill *(1989)*

Jane Badler . . . . Jade

• 0:35—Brief breasts, while sitting in spa with slit wrists. Brief crotch shot when Frank Stallone carries her out of the spa.

• 0:43—Brief right breast, while making love in bed with Stallone.

• 1:07—Left breast, while making love in bed with Stallone. Don't see her face.

Easy Money *(1983)*

Sandra Beall . . . . Maid of Honor

Jennifer Jason Leigh . . . . Allison Capuletti

Kimberly McArthur . . . . Ginger Jones

•• 0:47—Breasts sunbathing in the backyard when seen by Rodney Dangerfield.

Easy Rider *(1969)*

Toni Basil . . . . Mary

• 1:24—Brief right breast (her hair gets in the way) and very, very brief buns, taking off clothes in graveyard during hallucination sequence.

• 1:26—Very brief buns, when climbing on something (seen through fish-eye lens).

• 1:27—Buns, while lying down (seen through fish-eye lens).

Karen Black . . . . Karen

Eating *(1990)*

Nelly Alard . . . . .Martine

••• 0:06—Breasts, several times while sunbathing, then getting up and walking by pool, sitting down and tying a blouse around her waist.

Toni Basil . . . . Jackie

Rachelle Carson . . . . Cathy

Mary Crosby . . . . Kate

Daphna Kastner . . . . Jennifer

Elizabeth Kemp . . . . Nancy

Taryn Power . . . . Anita

Lisa Richards . . . . Helene

• 0:12—Brief right breast, while putting a sweater over her head.

Savannah Smith Bouchér . . . . Eloise

Gwen Welles . . . . Sophie

Eating Raoul *(1982)*

Mary Woronov . . . . Mary Bland

••• 0:46—Breasts, while struggling with Ed Begley Jr. on the couch. More breasts while Raoul counts money on her stomach. Long scene.

• 0:53—Buns and side view of right breast, while in hospital room with Raoul. A little dark.

• *Ebbtide* *(1994; Australian)*

Susan Lyons . . . . Alison

Judy McIntosh . . . . .Ellen Fielding

• 0:47—Brief buns, when Harry Hamlin pulls her panties down at the beach.

• 0:49—Breasts, while behind clear plastic shower curtain.

•• 0:59—Breasts, while making love with Hamlin in the house.

The Ebony Tower *(1985)*

Greta Scacchi . . . . Mouse

• 0:37—Full frontal nudity, undressing and going skinny dipping in lake. Long shot.

• 0:41—Brief lower half of left breast, while lying down next to Toyah Wilcox.

• 0:43—Brief nude walking into the lake.

Toyah Wilcox . . . . Freak

• 0:37—Full frontal nudity, undressing and going skinny dipping in lake. Long shot.

• 0:38—Buns and side of right breast, kneeling during picnic after swimming.

• 0:39—Buns, while lying down next to Lawrence Olivier.

•• 0:40—Buns, while lying next to Greta Scacchi and talking to David.

•• 0:44—More buns, while talking to David and watching him go swimming.

Echo Park *(1986)*

Elvira . . . . Sheri

Susan Dey . . . . .Meg "May" Greer

• 1:17—Brief glimpse of right breast, while doing a strip tease at a party.

Eclipse *(1994; Canadian)*

Maria Del Mar . . . . Sarah

Pascale Montpetit . . . . Sylvie

• 0:13—Breasts after taking off her T-shirt to make love with Brian.

•• 0:16—Nude after hearing Brian's wife, then getting up and dressing.

•• 0:24—Breasts after taking off blouse in room with Gabriel and making love on the floor, then sitting up afterwards.

Ecstasy *(1932)*

Hedy Lamarr . . . . .The Wife

• 0:25—Brief breasts starting to run after a horse in a field.

• 0:26—Long shot running through the woods, side view naked, then brief breasts hiding behind a tree.

Ed and His Dead Mother *(1993)*

Sam Jenkins . . . . Storm Reynolds

• 0:16—Buns in bedroom when Ned Beatty spies on her through telescope.

• 0:52—Very brief right breast, while going up stairs.

• *Eden* *(1992; Video Tape)*

Diana Barton . . . . Andrea

••• 0:05—Breasts, undressing, making love, then getting dressed in locker room with Ian. Long scene.

••• 0:37—Breasts, taking off her swimsuit top to tease Ian. More breasts and buns while making love with him on the sofa.

Tawnni Cable . . . . Uncredited Girl in Exercise Room

Darcy De Moss . . . . Randi

•• 1:21—Breasts, getting out of the water and putting on T-shirt.

••• 1:22—Breasts on beach, while making love with Abe.

•• 1:30—Brief breasts in bathroom.

Elizabeth Lambert . . . . Victoria

••• 0:12—Breasts and side view of buns, in bedroom, then in bed while starting to make love with Ian.

•• 0:23—Breasts, while making love in bed under Ian.

••• 0:25—Breasts, sitting up in bed and buns, getting out of bed.

Jill Pierce . . . . .Lacey
- ••• 0:20—In pink bra, then breasts and buns, while making love with B.D. in bedroom.
- ••• 1:05—Breasts undressing in bedroom with B.D.
- ••• 1:06—Breasts and buns, while making love in bed with B.D.
- ••• 1:32—Breasts in room with Marnie, while getting even with B.D.

Suzi Simpson. . . . . .Uncredited Girl in Exercise Room

Barbara Alyn Woods . . . . Eve Sinclair
- • 0:09—Buns and breasts, while kissing Grant outside during her fantasy.
- ••• 0:10—Breasts in pool and on beach, making love with Grant during more fantasy.
- • 0:24—Brief breasts, putting on lingerie.
- ••• 0:30—Breasts, while making love on table with Grant during another fantasy.
- • 0:54—Buns in maroon bra and T-back in her bedroom.
- ••• 0:55—Breasts and buns in the shower making love with Grant during her fantasy.
- • 1:18—Buns in lingerie in fantasy with Grant.
- ••• 1:19—Left breast, while on couch with Grant/Josh in her fantasy.

• *Eden 2* *(1992; Video Tape)*

Darcy De Moss . . . . Randi
- ••• 0:06—Breasts in sauna, while talking with Celine.
- ••• 0:25—Breasts, after waking up in bed with Celine.
- ••• 0:28—Breasts, taking off robe and putting on dress.
- • 1:00—Brief breast, while making love with Celine.
- ••• 1:11—Breasts, in black panties, taking off her dress and diving into pool.
- • 1:16—Breasts while frolicking in the ocean with Celine.

Terry Donahoe . . . . Juliet
- ••• 0:57—Breasts in bed making love with Paul and after getting interrupted.

Elisa Pensler Gabrielli. . . . . Celine
- ••• 0:06—Breasts in sauna talking with Randi.
- ••• 0:25—Breasts in bed with Randi.
- • 1:16—Breasts while frolicking in the ocean with Randi.
- ••• 1:24—Breasts while making love in bed with Greg.
- •• 1:27—Left breast, while lying in bed and talking with Greg.

Barbara Alyn Woods . . . . Eve Sinclair
- • 0:20—Brief breasts on boat in fantasy with Grant.
- • 0:43—In bra, then brief breasts in hay in a stable with Grant during a fantasy.
- • 1:01—Brief breasts in bubble bath. Don't see her face.
- • 1:02—Breasts under sheer nightgown.
- ••• 1:04—Breasts with Grant outside by pool, then in bathtub.
- •• 1:19—Breasts and buns in the shower with Steve then Grant during a fantasy.

• *Eden 3* *(1993; Video Tape)*

Darcy De Moss . . . . Randi
- ••• 1:36—In white bra and panties, then breasts while making love in bed with Josh.

Carolyn Lowery . . . . Amy
- ••• 0:03—Breasts in bed, making love with Lyle. Buns, while getting out.
- •• 0:06—Breasts and buns, making love in bed with Lyle after Eve leaves
- ••• 0:53—Breasts, while making love in bed with Lyle.
- •• 1:16—Breasts while with Lyle in her room.

Elizabeth Whitcraft . . . . Val
- •• 0:15—Left breast, while lying in bed under Lyle.
- ••• 0:29—Breasts while in room, then making love with Lyle.
- ••• 1:03—Breasts while taking off her swimsuit top outside in front of Lyle.

Barbara Alyn Woods . . . . Eve Sinclair
- •• 0:10—Breasts, fantasizing about Grant during her massage.
- ••• 0:35—In white bra, then breasts during her fantasy while making love outside with Grant.
- • 0:47—In black bra and panties, then left breast while making love with Josh in bedroom.
- •• 0:49—Breasts, while crying in the shower.
- • 0:59—In wet nightgown, then buns and brief right breast while out in the rain with Grant.
- •• 1:26—Breasts while making love on the hood of a car with Grant.

• *Eden 4* *(1993; Video Tape)*

Darcy De Moss . . . . Randi
- • 0:27—Right breast, while in bed talking to Josh.

Deirdre Imershein . . . . Melissa
- •• 0:04—Breasts and buns, while making love with a guy in front of window in hotel room.
- • 0:07—Breasts again on video playback.
- ••• 0:14—Breasts while making love in bed with a man and a woman.
- •• 0:25—Breasts in bed with B.D.
- • 0:55—Tip of right breast in open dress while in bed with Rod. More left breast seen on TV.
- •• 1:06—Breasts in bed when B.D. helps take her top off.
- • 1:10—More breasts in video playback.
- • 1:25—Brief left breast twice, while in bed with B.D.

Barbara Alyn Woods . . . . Eve Sinclair

• *Eden 5* *(1993; Video Tape)*

Mimi Craven . . . . Marla Burke
- •• 0:06—Breasts and brief buns in bubble bath with Douglas.

Darcy De Moss . . . . Randi
- • 0:02—Brief left breast, while in bed with Josh.
- • 0:20—Very brief tip of breast, while lying in bed with Josh.
- • 0:44—Very brief left breast when Gabe tries to put the moves on her.
- •• 1:03—In white bra, then breasts in bedroom with Gabe.
- ••• 1:15—Breasts, while making love on bed with Josh.

Allison Mackie . . . . .Liza
- ••• 0:22—Breasts, after taking off swimsuit top, then buns after taking off swimsuit bottom while on beach with Douglas.
- ••• 0:26—Breasts, after Douglas takes off her swimsuit top.

Barbara Alyn Woods . . . . Eve Sinclair
- •• 0:37—Buns and breasts, while making love on beach with Grant in flashback.
- •• 0:48—Breasts, while making love on beach at night with Paul.
- •• 0:50—Brief buns in panties while frolicking in the surf with Paul. Breasts while making love.
- • 1:01—Breasts, while making love with Grant.
- • 1:28—In pink bra, then left breast with Grant in bed.

• *Eden 6* *(1994; Video Tape)*

Michele Brin . . . . Ginny Lynch

Darcy De Moss . . . . Randi
- •• 0:06—Breasts and buns while making love in bed with Josh.
- ••• 1:09—Breasts, while taking off her top in front of mirror, then making love with Josh in bed. Nice close-up of Josh putting lotion on her breast.
- ••• 1:40—Breasts, with Josh. Seen in mirror.
- • 2:00—Very, very brief side of right breast when Josh takes her dress off.

••• 2:01—Breasts and buns with Josh.
••• 2:14—Breast, while in bed with George.

Colleen McDermott. . . . . Amanda
• 1:08—Breasts, while in bed after making love with B.D.
••• 1:18—Breasts, when joining B.D. in the shower.

Michelle Moffett . . . . Sissy Lunch
•• 0:18—Breasts, while making love with Brett outside.
••• 0:20—Breasts, while making love with Brett in bed.
• 0:29—In pink swimsuit, then right breast while making out with Brett on bed.
••• 0:36—Breasts, while sitting on edge and in bathtub.
• 0:39—Breasts while in bed with Brett.
••• 1:06—Breasts and buns while stripping in front of Brett outside, then making love.
•• 1:29—Right breast, while making love on beach with Brett.

Shannon Whirry . . . . Lauren's Friend

Barbara Alyn Woods . . . . Eve Sinclair
• 0:54—Brief breasts, while fooling around in bed with Paul.
•• 1:34—Brief buns and breasts while making love with Paul in bed.
•• 2:01—Breasts, while making love with Paul. Half of right breast when Paul makes out with her.
• 2:04—Right breast, while making love with Paul.
•• 2:17—Breasts, while making love on table with Paul.

Edgar Allan Poe's "Buried Alive" *(1989)*

Ginger Lynn Allen . . . . Debbie
• 0:12—Very, very brief left breast, while struggling with the other girls in the kitchen.

Nia Long . . . . Fingers

Karen Witter . . . . Janet

Edge of Sanity *(1988)*

Glynnis Barber. . . . . .Elisabeth Jekyll

Sarah Maur-Thorp . . . . Susannah
• 0:00—Left breast, while pulling down top to show the little boy in the barn.
•• 0:09—Breasts, while talking to the two doctors after they examine her back.
•• 0:50—Breasts in red room with Anthony Perkins and Johnny.
• 0:56—Very brief breasts in nun outfit.
• 1:10—Brief breasts in Perkins' hallucination at Flora's whorehouse.

Claudia Udy . . . . Liza

The Eiger Sanction *(1975)*

Candice Rialson. . . . . Art Student

Brenda Venus . . . . George
• 0:50—Very brief breasts opening her blouse to get Clint Eastwood to climb up a hill.
• 1:06—Breasts taking off her clothes in Eastwood's room, just before she tries to kill him. Dark, hard to see.

Electra *(1995)*

Lara Daans . . . . Karen
• 0:03—Buns in T-back, while dancing on stage.
•• 0:58—Breasts and buns in outfit, after taking off her top to entice Billy.

Shannon Tweed . . . . Lorna Duncan/Electra
• 0:16—Breasts, while in bathtub after taking off her top.

Eleven Days, Eleven Nights *(1988; Italian)*

Jessica Moore . . . . .Sarah Asproon
• 0:03—Breasts opening her raincoat on boat for Michael, then making love.
• 0:11—Buns, taking off robe in front of Michael.
•• 0:16—Right breast, on T.V., then side of breast.
•• 0:29—Breasts with Michael, changing clothes with him in restroom.
••• 0:33—Breasts in motel room with Michael, then making love.
• 0:44—Brief breasts and buns when leaving Michael all tied up.
•• 0:51—Breasts and buns in recording studio with Michael.
• 1:17—Breasts during flashbacks.
••• 1:19—Nude, making love with Michael on bed.

Eleven Days, Eleven Nights 2 *(1990)*

Ruth Corrine Collins. Dana Durrington
••• 0:14—Breasts while wearing stockings and making out with George on bed.

Laura Gemser . . . . .Jackie Forrest

Kristine Rose . . . . Sarah Asproon
•• 0:18—Breasts, while getting undressed and into bathtub.
••• 0:20—Breasts and buns while washing herself in bathtub while being secretly videotaped.
0:32—In lingerie with panties, garter belt and stockings after hopping on stage in club and dancing and stripping, showing off to Sonny.
•• 0:38—Left breast, while making love in kitchen with Bob, while being watched on video monitor.
0:57—In black bra, panties, garter belt and stockings after taking off dress with George.
• 1:09—Breasts, with Sonny. Left breast afterwards.

Eliminator Woman *(1992)*

Kimberleigh Stark . . . . Lianna
• 0:33—Very brief buns in panties, viewed up her dress as she climbs down the stairs.

Ellie *(1984)*

Sheila Kennedy . . . . .Ellie May
•• 0:29—Full frontal nudity posing for Billy while he takes pictures of her just before he falls over a cliff.
• 1:16—In bra and panties taking off dress with Art. Breasts taking off bra and throwing them on antlers. Brief breasts many times while frolicking around.

Emanuelle in Bangkok *(1976; Italian)*

Debra Berger. . . . . Debra
•• 1:15—Full frontal nudity, while taking a bath with Laura Gemser.
• 1:21—Breasts, while making love in bed with Gemser.

Laura Gemser . . . . .Emanuelle
•• 0:07—Breasts making love with a Robert.
•• 0:12—Full frontal nudity, while changing in hotel room in front of the bellboy.
••• 0:17—Full frontal nudity getting a bath, then massaged by another woman.
• 0:22—Brief right breast, while rolling across the bed to talk with the bellboy.
•• 0:24—Breasts, while lying on the bed, getting massaged by the bellboy.
•• 0:35—Breasts, during orgy scene.
•• 0:37—Buns, while getting massaged by Roberto, then breasts, when massaging him.
•• 0:40—Breasts, while undressing in bedroom.
•• 0:46—Breasts, trying to get the immigration official to help her with her passport.
•• 0:53—Full frontal nudity in room with Debra, then taking a shower.

- •• 1:01—Breasts in tent while Roberto makes love with Janet.
- •• 1:08—Full frontal nudity, while joining the belly dance with Janet and the belly dancer.
- •• 1:15—Full frontal nudity taking a bath with Debra.
- •• 1:18—Breasts on bed making love with Roberto.

Emanuelle the Seductress *(1979; Greek)*

Laura Gemser . . . . Emanuelle

- • 0:01—Full frontal nudity lying in bed with Mario.
- • 0:02—Brief breasts riding horse on the beach.
- •• 0:42—Breasts making love then full frontal nudity getting dressed with Tommy.
- ••• 0:48—Breasts undressing in bedroom, then in white panties, then nude talking to Alona.
- •• 0:54—Breasts walking around in a skirt.
- •• 1:02—Breasts outside taking a shower, then on lounge chair making love with Tommy.

Emanuelle's Amazon Adventure *(1977)*

Laura Gemser . . . . Emanuelle

- • 0:17—Brief left breast in flashback sequence in bed with a man.
- • 0:21—Brief breasts making love in bed.
- • 0:25—Brief breasts in the water with a blonde woman.
- •• 1:10—Full frontal nudity painting her body.
- • 1:11—Brief breasts in boat.
- • 1:13—Nude walking out of the water trying to save Isabelle.
- • 1:14—Brief breasts getting into the boat with Isabelle.

Embrace of the Vampire *(1994)*

(Unrated version reviewed.)

Rebecca Ferratti . . . . Princess

Glori Gold . . . . Nymph I

- • 0:03—Brief breasts, while walking up to Martin Kemp with the other two Nymphs. Then breasts and partial buns sitting near Kemp's feet before biting him along with the other two Nymphs.

Charlotte Lewis . . . . Sarah

Alyssa Milano . . . . Charlotte

- •• 0:15—Left breast and buns, when changing clothes in bedroom while talking with Chris.
- ••• 0:21—Breasts in open nightgown while lying in bed when Martin Kemp visits her.
- ••• 0:50—Breasts in open blouse while letting Charlotte Lewis photograph her. Nice long scene.
- ••• 0:59—Breasts, while lying in bed, then with Chris, Lewis and Kemp.
- • 1:05—Very brief breasts in flashback from 0:21.

Stacy Moran . . . . Nymph III

- •• 0:03—Brief breasts, while walking up to Martin Kemp with the other two Nymphs. Then breasts and partial buns sitting to the right of Kemp before biting him along with the other two Nymphs.
- • 1:22—Brief breasts in Martin Kemp's flashback.

Seana Ryan . . . . Nymph II

- •• 0:03—Brief breasts, while walking up to Martin Kemp with the other two Nymphs. Then breasts and partial buns sitting to the left of Kemp before biting him along with the other two Nymphs.
- • 1:22—Brief right breast in Martin Kemp's flashback.

Jennifer Tilly . . . . Marika

Embryo *(1976)*

Barbara Carrera . . . . Victoria

- •• 1:10—Brief buns and breasts in the mirror after making love with Hudson.
- • 1:11—Left breast sticking out of bathrobe.

The Emerald Forest *(1985)*

Tetchie Agbayani . . . . Caya

- • 1:48—Breasts in the river when Kachiri is match making all the couples together.

Meg Foster . . . . Jean Markham

Dira Paes . . . . Kachiri

- •• 0:24—Brief buns while running from waterfall and diving into the pond.
- • 0:33—Breasts while in water talking to Tommy.
- • 0:56—Left breast in courtyard when Tommy proposes marriage to her.
- • 0:57—Left breast in forest with Tommy. Long shot.
- •• 1:01—Breasts, by the river.
- •• 1:04—Breasts and buns during wedding ceremony.
- •• 1:16—Breasts with the other tribe women after being captured by the fierce people.
- • 1:18—Breasts with the other girls being herded into the building.
- •• 1:38—Breasts, in forest taking off clothes.
- • 1:40—Buns, returning to the forest.
- • 1:48—Breasts while in the river.

Emily *(1976; British)*

Sarah Brackett . . . . Margaret

- • 0:09—Buns, while looking out the window at Koo Stark.

Jeannie Collings . . . . Rosalind

- • 1:05—Brief breasts on the couch with Gerald while Richard watches.

Jane Hayden . . . . Rachel

- •• 1:09—Breasts in bed with Billy.

Ina Skriver . . . . Augustine

- ••• 0:43—Breasts getting into the shower with Koo Stark to give her a massage.

Koo Stark . . . . Emily

- •• 0:08—Breasts, lying in bed caressing herself while fantasizing about James.
- ••• 0:30—Breasts in studio posing for Augustine, then kissing her.
- ••• 0:42—Buns and breasts taking a shower after posing for Augustine.
- •• 0:56—Left breast, under a tree with James.
- • 1:16—Breasts in the woods seducing Rupert.

Emmanuelle *(1974; French)*

(R-rated version reviewed.)

Christine Boisson . . . . Marie-Ange

- •• 0:16—Full frontal nudity diving into swimming pool. Also buns, under water.
- ••• 0:19—Breasts outside in hanging chair with Sylvia Kristel.

Marika Green . . . . Bee

- • 0:46—Nude, undressing outside with Sylvia Kristel. Brief full frontal nudity, when leaving blanket.
- •• 0:47—Breasts, getting dressed.
- • 0:50—Upper half of buns, while lying down, talking to Kristel.

Sylvia Kristel . . . . Emmanuelle

- • 0:00—Very brief left breast in robe, while sitting on bed.
- • 0:02—Breasts in B&W photos.
- • 0:10—Breasts and buns, making love in bed with her husband under a net.

- 0:13—Brief breasts taking off bikini top by swimming pool.
- ••• 0:14—Breasts getting up from chair, then full frontal nudity while talking to Ariane.
- ••• 0:15—Nude, swimming under water. Nice.
- • 0:18—Partial left breast, while sleeping in bed.
- •• 0:24—Breasts, making love with a stranger on an airplane.
- •• 0:31—Breasts with Ariane in the squash court.

Emmanuelle 5 *(1986)*

Michele Burger . . . . Girl No. 3
- ••• 0:42—Breasts, while talking with the two other girls. Wearing a blue head band.
- •• 0:44—Breasts, while drinking champagne with the other harem girls.

Monique Gabrielle. . . . . Emmanuelle
- ••• 0:01—Breasts and buns with a guy on rocks near the ocean in a film.
- ••• 0:05—Nude on boat after escaping from the crowd at Cannes who rip her clothes off.
- •• 0:09—Brief breasts taking off her jacket in restaurant. Breasts on boat with Charles.
- ••• 0:10—Full frontal nudity, making love on boat with Charles.
- ••• 0:17—In black lingerie, then full frontal nudity while posing for Phillip.
- •• 0:26—Full frontal nudity while changing clothes in her room.
- ••• 0:38—Full frontal nudity while undressing in room with other harem girls.
- •• 0:40—Breasts, getting fixed up by three harem girls.
- ••• 0:52—Buns and breasts while making love with Phillip outside.
- ••• 1:07—Breasts in bed with Charles.
- • 1:09—Very brief right breast, in airplane cockpit with Charles.

Roxanna Michaels . . . . Girl No. 2
- ••• 0:42—Breasts, while talking with the two other girls.
- ••• 0:43—Breasts, talking to Eddie and Monique Gabrielle.
- •• 0:48—Breasts, during rescue/escape.

Heidi Paine . . . . Girl No. 1
- ••• 0:42—Breasts, while talking with the two other girls. Wearing a red turban.
- •• 0:44—Breasts, while drinking champagne with the other harem girls.

Emmanuelle IV *(1984)*

Sophie Berger . . . . Maria
- •• 0:46—Full frontal nudity putting on robe.
- • 0:49—Buns, taking off robe in front of Mia Nygren.

Sylvia Kristel . . . . Sylvia
- •• 0:00—Breasts in photos during opening credits.

Mia Nygren. . . . . Emmanuelle IV
- • 0:13—Buns, while lying on table after plastic surgery.
- ••• 0:15—Full frontal nudity walking around looking at her new self in the mirror.
- • 0:20—Brief breasts a couple of times making love on top of a guy getting coached by Sylvia Kristel in dream-like sequence.
- •• 0:22—Full frontal nudity taking off blouse in front of Dona.
- ••• 0:30—Nude undressing in front of Maria.
- •• 0:39—Full frontal nudity taking her dress off and getting covered with a white sheet.
- ••• 0:40—Full frontal nudity lying down and then putting dress back on.
- •• 0:45—Full frontal nudity during levitation trick.
- • 0:52—Brief breasts in stable.
- ••• 0:54—Breasts taking off black dress in chair. Brief lower frontal nudity.
- • 0:57—Brief lower frontal nudity, while putting on white panties.
- • 1:00—Brief breasts when Susanna takes her dress off.
- • 1:03—Brief right breast, while making love on ground with a boy.
- ••• 1:07—Breasts while walking on beach.
- • 1:09—Breasts with Dona. Dark.

Deborah Power . . . . Dona
- • 1:09—Buns, while lying down and getting a massage from Mia Nygren.

Brinke Stevens . . . . Uncredited Dream Girl
- ••• 0:19—Breasts, getting coached by Sylvia Kristel during dream-like sequence on how to get a guy aroused.

Emmanuelle, The Joys of a Woman *(1975)*

Laura Gemser . . . . Massage Woman

Sylvia Kristel. . . . . Emmanuelle
- • 0:18—Breasts making love with her husband in bedroom.
- •• 0:22—Breasts, then full frontal nudity, undressing in bedroom, then making love with her husband.
- ••• 0:32—Breasts with acupuncture needles stuck in her. More breasts masturbating while fantasizing about Christopher.
- • 0:53—Right breast, while making love with polo player in locker room.
- ••• 0:58—Nude, getting massaged by another woman.
- ••• 1:14—Right breast in bedroom in open dress, then breasts with Jean in bed. Flashback of her with three guys in a bordello.

Catherine Rivet . . . . .Anna-Maria
- ••• 0:58—Nude, while getting massaged by Laura Gemser.
- ••• 1:25—Nude making love with Sylvia Kristel and Jean.

• ***Encounters*** *(1987; Video Tape)*

Raven von Bergen . . . . Spa Encounter
- ••• 0:06—Breasts taking off her top in spa, then masturbating.

• ***End of Summer*** *(1995; Made for Cable Movie)*

Jacqueline Bisset . . . . .Christine

Karyn Dwyer . . . . Jenny
- ••• 0:41—Breasts, while making love in bed with Julian Sands.

Amy Locane. . . . . Alice
- ••• 0:37—Breasts, while making love in barn with Peter Weller.

Polly Shannon . . . . .Maid

Endangered *(1994)*

Sandra Hess. . . . . Kate
- •• 0:18—Very brief breasts, when jumping up and splashing water in the lake. Brief breasts while standing up in lake (closer shot).
- •• 0:19—Buns, while getting out of the lake and getting blanket.
- • 0:20—Brief breasts, while turning around and putting on blouse.
- •• 0:38—Buns and back side of left breast while taking a bath outside. Breasts in long shot, then closer shot.

Endgame *(1983)*

Laura Gemser . . . . Lilith
- • 1:10—Brief breasts a couple of times getting blouse ripped open by a gross looking guy.

Endless Night *(1977)*

Britt Ekland . . . . Greta
- • 1:21—Brief breasts several times with Michael.

Hayley Mills . . . . .Ellie

Enemies, A Love Story (1989)

Anjelica Huston . . . . Tamara
Lena Olin . . . . Masha
•• 0:16—In white bra, then brief breasts several times in bed with Ron Silver. Breasts again after making love and starting to make love again.

Enemy Gold (1993)

Tai Collins . . . . Ava Noble
••• 0:20—Breasts and very brief lower frontal nudity in sauna. Breasts and buns, getting out of the sauna and into the shower.
••• 1:26—Breasts, while making love with Mark.
Kym Malin . . . . Cowboy's Hostess
Suzi Simpson. . . . . Becky Midnite
••• 0:09—Breasts, while undressing and changing clothes in bathroom.
••• 0:33—Breasts and buns, while making love with Chris.
••• 1:05—Breasts and buns while taking a shower outside.
• 1:11—Buns in panties, while standing outside when the boys return.
Julie Strain. . . . . Jewel Panther
••• 1:03—Breasts and buns in leather outfit while dancing with a sword in front of a fire.
Angela Wright. . . . . Dancer #2
• 0:22—Buns in G-string lingerie, while dancing on stage.
•• 0:26—Breasts and buns in the shower with the other dancer and Santiago.
• 0:35—Buns in T-back, while dancing on stage.
••• 0:37—Breasts and buns in T-back, while dancing on stage.

• *The English Patient (1996)*

Juliette Binoche. . . . . Hana
••• 1:54—(0:48 into Tape 2) Right breast, while lying in bed.
Kristin Scott-Thomas . . . . Katharine Clifton
• 1:12—(0:06 into Tape 2) Very brief right breast, when Ralph Fiennes rips open her dress.
•• 1:14—(0:08 into Tape 2) Full frontal nudity, taking off her robe and getting into bathtub with Fiennes.
••• 1:15—(0:09 into Tape 2) Full frontal nudity when getting out of the bathtub.
••• 1:27—(0:21 into Tape 2) Breasts, while rolling over in bed with Fiennes.

Enigma (1982)

Brigitte Fossey. . . . . Karen
• 0:39—Brief breasts after undressing in jail cell. Very brief lower frontal nudity and buns, shielding herself from the light.
•• 0:40—Breasts getting interrogated.
Gabrielle Lazure . . . . n.a.

Enrapture (1989)

Deborah Blaisdell . . . . Martha
••• 0:10—Breasts undressing in her apartment with Keith.
•• 0:17—Left breast, in bed with Keith, then brief breasts.
Jane Hamilton . . . . Annie
Felicia Peluso. . . . . Ingenue
Ona Zee . . . . Chase Webb
•• 0:13—In red bra, panties, garter belt and stockings. Buns in G-string, then breasts undressing when she doesn't know Keith is watching.
•• 0:17—Breasts when Keith fantasizes about her while he's making love with Martha.
•• 0:21—Breasts in back of limousine with a lucky guy.
••• 1:08—Full frontal nudity making love on top of Keith in bed.

Enter the Dragon (1973)

Ahna Capri . . . . Tania
• 0:47—Very brief left breast three times in open blouse in bed with John Saxon.

The Entity (1983)

Margaret Blye . . . . Cindy Nash
Barbara Hershey . . . . Carla Moran
• 0:33—Breasts and buns, after getting undressed before taking a bath. Don't see her face.
0:59—"Breasts" during special-effect when The Entity fondles her breasts with invisible fingers while she sleeps.
• 1:32—"Breasts" again getting raped by The Entity while Alex Rocco watches helplessly.

Entre Nous (1983; French)

a.k.a. Coup de Foudre
Miou-Miou . . . . Madeleine
Isabelle Huppert . . . . Helen Webber
• 1:01—Brief breasts in shower room talking about her breasts with Miou-Miou.

Equus (1977; British)

Jenny Agutter . . . . Jill Mason
••• 2:00—Nude in loft above the horses in orange light, then making love with Alan.

Erendira (1983; Brazilian)

Blanca Guerra . . . . Ulysses' Mother
Claudia Ohana . . . . Erendira
• 0:14—Breasts while getting fondled by a guy against her will.
•• 0:26—Breasts while lying in bed sweating and crying after having to have sex with an army of men.
••• 1:04—Breasts while lying in bed sleeping.
• 1:08—Brief breasts while getting out of bed. Long shot, hard to see.
•• 1:24—Breasts and buns while on bed with Ulysses.
Irene Papas . . . . The Grandmother

• *Erotic Heat (1996; Video Tape)*

Noelle . . . . Car Wash/Work Out/Jacuzzi
••• 0:02—Nude, while washing a car.
••• 0:33—Nude, while working out with Sara St. James.
Stevi Conrad . . . . Dining Room/Jacuzzi
••• 0:29—Nude, after stripping in kitchen and rubbing whipped cream all over herself.
••• 0:40—Nude, with the other girls in the spa.
Cory Lane . . . . Dining Room
••• 0:20—Breasts and buns in garter belt and stockings after stripping and dancing in front of Stacy Moran.
Jacqueline Lovell . . . . Work Out/Jacuzzi
••• 0:34—Nude, while working out with Noelle.
••• 0:40—Nude, with the other girls in the spa.
Lorissa McComas. Construction/Jacuzzi
••• 0:09—Nude with Taylor St. Claire.
••• 0:40—Nude, with the other girls in the spa.
Stacy Moran . . . . Dining Room
••• 0:21—Breasts, while Cory Lane strips and dances in front of her.
Taylor St. Claire. . . . . Construction/Jacuzzi
••• 0:11—Nude with Lorissa McComas.
••• 0:40—Nude, with the other girls in the spa.

Erotic Images (1983)

Alexandra Day. . . . . Logan's Girlfriend
- •• 0:37—Breasts getting out of bed while Logan talks on the phone to Britt Ekland.

Britt Ekland . . . . Julie Todd
- • 0:16—Brief side view of left breast in bed with Glenn.
- ••• 0:29—In bra, then breasts in bed with Glenn.

Meredith Kennedy. . . . . Ginger
- •• 1:04—Breasts on the couch with two guys.

Alexandra Morgan. . . . . Emily Stewart
- •• 0:57—In black lingerie, then breasts on the living room floor with Glenn.
- • 1:05—Breasts in bed, making love with Glenn.
- ••• 1:12—Breasts in the kitchen with Glenn.
- •• 1:21—Right breast, on couch with Glenn.

Remy O'Neill. . . . . Vickie Coleman
- ••• 0:04—Breasts while sitting in chaise lounge talking to Britt Ekland about sex survey. Long scene.
- • 0:06—Breasts while in bed with Marvin. Brief lower frontal nudity.
- •• 0:07—Brief left breast while in spa with TV repairman, then brief breasts.

Julia Parton . . . . Marvin's Nurse
- • 0:08—Brief breasts in office with Marvin. Dark, hard to see.

Barbara Peckinpaugh. . . . . Cheerleader
- • 0:07—Breasts dancing in an office with another cheerleader.

Erotikill (1973)

a.k.a. La Comtesse Noire
a.k.a. The Loves of Irina

Lina Romay . . . . Irina
- •• 0:00—Full frontal nudity, wearing a belt and cape walking towards the camera during the opening credits.
- •• 0:08—Full frontal nudity on bed, then walking around while wearing a cape. Out of focus.
- ••• 0:17—Full frontal nudity, lying in bed and drinking.
- • 0:31—Very brief right breast during struggle with another woman on bed.
- •• 0:32—Full frontal nudity, while walking through the woods with a cape and belt.
- • 0:33—Breasts, flapping her cape.
- • 0:43—Breasts under sheer black nightgown.
- ••• 0:45—Full frontal nudity when the other woman takes her nightgown off.
- ••• 0:47—Full frontal nudity biting another woman and sucking her blood.
- •• 1:05—Full frontal nudity sitting down in bath filled with red water.
- ••• 1:07—More breasts and brief buns doing pelvic thrusts in bathtub. Out of focus sometimes.
- ••• 1:08—Nude in bathtub.

Monica Swinn . . . . Princess de Rochefort
- •• 0:47—Breasts, getting her dress taken off and blood sucked.
- •• 0:55—Breasts, lying on table in doctor's office.

• *Erotique* (1993)

Priscilla Barnes. . . . . Taboo Parlor/Claire
- •• 0:30—Breasts and brief partial buns, while in bed with Camilla Søeberg.

Michelle Clunie . . . . Let's Talk About Sex

Claudia Ohana . . . . .Final Call
- • 0:59—Brief partial breasts in bra and partial buns in panties, while tied by her wrists by a couple of bad guys.
- ••• 1:10—Breasts and buns, when carried to the bed, making love and sitting in bed afterwards.
- •• 1:20—Nude, while making love again.

Marianne Sägebrecht. . . . . Taboo Parlor/Hilde

Camilla Søeberg . . . . Taboo Parlor/Jukia
- •• 0:29—Breasts, while in bed with Priscilla Barnes.
- • 0:51—Partial buns in panties, while lying on the bed.

Escape Clause (1996; Made for Cable Movie)

Laura Catalano . . . . Dark Haired Hooker
- • 1:00—Breasts, with wrists tied behind her back in bedroom with Abe, when Andrew McCarthy comes in to save her.

Kate McNeil. . . . . Sarah Ramsay
- •• 0:00—Breasts, while making love with Andrew McCarthy in bed, then pulling up the covers when the daughter opens the bedroom door.
- ••• 0:20—In white bra and panties, then breasts, while standing with McCarthy, then making love in bed with him.

Escape From Brothel (1991; Hong Kong)

Sophia Crawford . . . . Blackmail Girl
- • 0:12—Left breast, while making love in bed with a guy. Brief full frontal nudity, while sitting up in bed.
- •• 0:13—Nude, while martial arts fighting the guy. Sometimes in slow motion. It looks like some frames were cut.
- ••• 0:14—Nude, while fighting some more, sometimes in slow motion (again, some frames are missing, especially when she does high kicks), before the guy gets even with her.

Eternity (1989)

Eileen Davidson . . . . Dahlia/Valerie
- • 0:33—In black bra and panties in dressing room. Brief buns standing in bathtub during Jon Voight's flashback.
- • 0:52—Brief left breast, then breasts, in bed with Voight. Don't see face.

Eureka (1983; British)

Emma Relph . . . . Mary (blue dress)
- • 1:17—Brief breasts during African voodoo ceremony.

Theresa Russell. . . . . Tracy
- • 0:40—Right breast, lying in bed with Hauer.
- • 1:04—Very brief left breast in bed with Hauer, then brief lower frontal nudity and brief buns when Gene Hackman bursts into the room.
- •• 1:09—Breasts on a boat with Hauer.
- • 1:41—Left breast peeking out from under black top while lying in bed.
- ••• 1:59—Full frontal nudity kicking off sheets in the bed.

Ann Thornton . . . . .Jane (red dress)
- • 1:17—Brief breasts during African voodoo ceremony.

Eve of Destruction (1991)

Reneé Soutendijk. . . . . Dr. Eve Simmons/Eve VIII
- • 0:17—Left breast, while on table as a robot, with half her skin removed. Possibly a special-effect body.
- • 0:22—Brief breasts in bathroom (as a robot), fixing her wound. Breasts while sitting on bed, putting a large bandage over the wound.

• *Eve's Beach Fantasy* (1997)

April Adams . . . . Eve
- • 0:01—Breasts and buns during fantasy.
- • 0:23—Very brief left breast, popping out of her bra, when turning over in bed.
- •• 0:30—Breasts, while in back seat of limousine during fantasy with a guy.

• 0:36—Brief left breast, when standing up in restaurant in dream.
• 0:38—Very brief left breast, popping out of her bra, when turning over in bed.
••• 0:47—Nude, while trying on different swimsuits and clothes in bathroom.
••• 0:55—Nude, when taking off robe and taking a shower.
• 1:02—Brief breasts and buns in flashback of 0:47 scenes.
• 1:05—Buns in swimsuit during photo shoot.
• 1:09—Buns in lingerie, while posing during photo session.
••• 1:15—Nude, while making love with the photographer.

Brittany Andrews . . . . Jamie
••• 0:22—Breasts and buns, while making love with Roland.

Kalani Freeman . . . . Model 2
•• 0:45—Breasts, after taking off her bra during photo shoot on bed.
• 1:05—Buns in swimsuit during photo shoot.

Cory Lane . . . . Model 3
• 0:59—Buns in swimsuit, while posing on a motorcycle during photo shoot.

Tabitha Stevens . . . . Model 1
• 0:40—Breasts under sheer fabric during photo shoot.

Even Cowgirls Get the Blues (1994)

Lorraine Bracco . . . . Delores Del Ruby
• 0:49—Brief lower frontal nudity, after pulling down her pants with the other cowgirls.

Angie Dickinson . . . . Miss Adrian
Heather Graham . . . . Cowgirl Heather
Carol Kane . . . . Carla
Rainbow Phoenix . . . . Bonanza Jellybean
• 0:49—Very brief lower frontal nudity, after pulling down her pants with the other cowgirls.

Uma Thurman . . . . Sissy Hankshaw
Sean Young . . . . Marie Garth
• 0:21—Brief breasts, while making love with Crispin Glover in front of Uma Thurman.

An Evening with Kitten (1983)

Francesca "Kitten" Natividad . . . . Herself
•• 0:02—Breasts busting out of her blouse.
•• 0:09—Breasts while in miniature city scene.
• 0:11—Brief breasts while on stage.
• 0:20—Left breast, in bed with a vampire.
••• 0:21—Breasts and buns in G-string during dance in large champagne glass prop. Long scene.
••• 0:24—Breasts on beach in mermaid costume with little shell pasties.
••• 0:25—Breasts while in the glass again.
•• 0:28—Breasts while in and out of glass.
•• 0:29—Brief breasts during end credits.

• *Event Horizon* (1997)

Holley Chant . . . . Claire
• 0:10—Very brief right breast, when Sam Neill starts to turn her around in chair.
• 1:08—Breasts, while sitting in bathtub and committing suicide in Neill's hallucination and later, when standing next to him.

Kathleen Quinlan . . . . Peters
Joely Richardson . . . . Starck

Every Breath (1992)

Cynthia Brimhall . . . . Kris

Joanna Pacula . . . . Lauren
• 0:21—Very, very brief right breast in jacket while kissing Judd Nelson in bedroom.
••• 0:36—Brief back side of right breast, then breasts while kissing Nelson outside by pool.
0:43—In black bra and panties in bedroom with Bob.
••• 1:10—Breasts and buns while in the shower.

Every Time We Say Goodbye (1986)

Cristina Marsillach . . . . Sarah
•• 1:09—Right breast, then brief breasts lying in bed with Tom Hanks.

Everybody's All-American (1988)

Jessica Lange . . . . Babs
• 0:32—Brief breasts under sheer nightgown in bedroom with Dennis Quaid.
• 0:54—Buns and very, very brief side view of left breast by the campfire by the lake with Timothy Hutton at night. Might be a body double.

Everybody's Fine (1991; Italian)

a.k.a. Stanno Tutti Bene

Valeria Cavalli . . . . Tosca
• 0:54—Brief glimpses of left breast, after taking off her dress backstage at fashion show. Left breast, while breast feeding her baby.

The Evil Below (1991)

Sheri Able . . . . Tracy
• 0:10—Buns, in two piece swimsuit on boat.
• 0:21—Right breast, with Max behind curtain. Hard to see.

June Chadwick . . . . Sarah Livingston
• 0:08—Very, very brief left breast, while on the floor with Max after he takes off her bra.
• 0:45—Very brief left breast, while on the floor with Max. Different angle from 0:08.

• *Evil Obsession* (1996)

Nicole Durant . . . . Suzi
•• 1:23—Breasts, while posing for photos.

Lorelei Leslie . . . . Debra

Evil Spawn (1987)

Bobbie Bresee . . . . Lynn Roman
• 0:14—Very brief half of right breast in bed with a guy.
••• 0:36—Breasts and side view of buns in bathroom looking at herself in the mirror, then taking a shower.

Pamela Gilbert . . . . Elaine Talbot
••• 0:46—Nude taking off black lingerie and going swimming in pool. Hubba, hubba!
••• 0:49—Breasts in the pool, then full frontal nudity getting out.

Dawn Wildsmith . . . . Evelyn Avery

Evil Spirits (1990)

Martine Beswicke . . . . Vanya
Karen Black . . . . Ella Purdy
Dori Courtney . . . . Bank Teller
Debra Lamb . . . . Tina
••• 0:22—Breasts, while dancing in her bedroom while Michael Berryman watches through peep hole. Most of her buns in underwear. Long scene.

Evil Toons (1991)

Suzanne Ager . . . . Terry
- ••• 0:31—Breasts and buns in G-string, taking off clothes to put on her pajamas.
- •• 1:09—Right breast, while on the floor getting her pajamas ripped open by Roxanne.
- •• 1:10—Brief breasts when Roxanne rips the pajamas all the way down.

Michelle Bauer. . . . . Mrs. Burt
- •• 0:48—Breasts opening her lingerie for Burt. Buns, while walking away in G-string.

Barbara Dare . . . . Jan
- ••• 0:30—Breasts, taking off robe and putting on red nightgown.
- •• 1:06—Breasts when her top is pulled down by Roxanne.

Monique Gabrielle. . . . . Megan
- ••• 0:25—In bra, then breasts undressing in front of mirror.

Madison Stone . . . . Roxanne
- ••• 0:20—Buns in G-string, then breasts doing a strip routine in front of her girlfriends.
- ••• 0:33—Breasts, taking off blouse and putting on bra and panties. Buns in sheer panties.
- •• 0:36—Breasts on the floor, getting attacked by the monster.
- ••• 0:38—Breasts walking around, covered with blood, talking with Megan.
- •• 0:41—Breasts putting blouse on.
- • 0:42—Breasts on couch with Biff.
- • 0:55—Left breast in open blouse, seducing Burt.
- • 0:59—Brief breasts several times, dead, when the other girls discover her.

Evil Town (1987)

Lynda Wiesmeier. . . . . Dianne
- ••• 0:09—Breasts, while on top of Tony outside while camping.
- •• 0:11—Right breast while making out with boyfriend outside. Breasts when getting up.
- • 0:13—Breasts in open blouse, while running from bad guy. Nice bouncing action.
- •• 0:15—Breasts, while getting captured by bad guys.
- •• 0:17—Breasts, when getting out of car and brought into the house.
- •• 0:23—Breasts while tied up in chair.

Evils of the Night (1985)

Bridget Holloman . . . . Heather

Tina Louise . . . . Cora

Amber Lynn . . . . Joyce
- • 0:14—Brief breasts, taking her pink swimsuit top off for Eddie.
- •• 0:17—Breasts with Eddie in deserted house. Dark.
- •• 0:19—Full frontal nudity when Eddie takes her shorts off. Dark.
- • 0:21—Right breast, while in bed with Eddie. Still dark.
- • 0:22—More right breast.
- •• 0:23—Full frontal nudity in bed when Eddie gets out.
- •• 0:24—Nude, while getting out of bed and getting dressed. Dark.

Julie Newmar. . . . . Doctor Zarma

Jody Swafford . . . . Lotion Girl
- •• 0:12—Breasts while rubbing lotion on another girl.
- •• 0:13—More breasts with the other girl.
- • 0:14—Brief breasts when Eddie watches her and her friend.

Evilspeak (1981)

Lynn Hancock . . . . Miss Friedemyer
- •• 0:56—In bra, then breasts taking off bra in front of fireplace. Buns in panties, walking up the stairs.
- ••• 0:57—Breasts and buns in the shower, then getting killed by pigs.

Katherine Kelly Lang . . . . Suzie Baker

• *The Ex (1996)*

Suzy Amis . . . . Molly Kenyon
- • 0:22—Very brief upper part of left breast, when Nick Mancuso is on top of her in bed.

Yancy Butler . . . . Deidre Kenyon
- • 0:11—Brief back side of right breast, while getting into bathtub with Frank, then drowning him.
- • 1:02—Brief buns and partial back side of right breast, when taking off her dress in her apartment with Nick Mancuso, so that Suzy Amis can see. Medium long shot.

Excalibur (1981; British)

Katrine Boorman . . . . Igrayne
- • 0:14—Right breast, then breasts in front of the fire when Uther tricks her into thinking that he is her husband and makes love to her.

Cherie Lunghi . . . . Guenevere
- • 1:25—Brief breasts in the forest kissing Lancelot.

Helen Mirren . . . . Morgana
- • 1:31—Side view of left breast under a fishnet outfit climbing into bed.

Excessive Force (1993)

a.k.a. Men of War

Liza Cruzat. . . . . Hooker

Charlotte Lewis . . . . Anna Gilmour
- ••• 0:54—Brief right breast, then breasts while in bed with Thomas Ian Griffith.

The Executioner's Song (1982)

(European Version reviewed.)

Rosanna Arquette . . . . Nicole Baker
- ••• 0:30—Brief breasts in bed, then getting out of bed. Buns, walking to kitchen.
- ••• 0:41—Breasts in bed with Tommy Lee Jones.
- ••• 0:48—Breasts on top of Jones making love.
- •• 1:36—Right breast and buns, standing up getting strip searched before visiting Jones in prison.

Jenny Wright . . . . April Baker

• *Executive Target (1996)*

Angie Everhart. . . . . Lacey

Carolyn R. Smith . . . . Dancer
- • 0:17—Brief partial buns, while dancing on stage in skimpy maid outfit in front of Bela.

Exit (1995)

Angel Boris . . . . Dancer 2
- ••• 0:15—Breasts and buns in green T-back, while dancing on stage with another dancer.

Gina LaMarca . . . . Rita
- •• 0:16—Breasts, while dancing on stage in black and silver outfit.
- •• 0:22—Breasts, while dancing on stage in black short pants.
- •• 0:23—Breasts, while getting dressed in dressing room.

Robin Trapp. . . . . News Reporter

Shannon Whirry. . . . . Diane
- ••• 0:08—Nude, while making love with Kyle.

•• 0:29—Breasts, during strip routine on stage, before being interrupted by gunmen.

Exit to Eden *(1994)*

Iman . . . . Nina
- • 1:21—Side view of left breast behind foggy shower door.

Judith Baldwin. . . . . .Priscilla/Los Angeles
Lucinda Crosby . . . . Claudia/Trainer
Dana Delany . . . . Lisa
- ••• 0:37—Full frontal nudity, when getting out of the pool. Brief buns, while using Paul Mercurio as a chair.
- •• 0:54—Brief right breast, when in bubble bath while talking with Mercurio. Buns, when standing up.
- • 1:01—Buns in G-string, under sheer nightgown.
- • 1:20—Left breast, when Mercurio rubs butter and sprinkles cinnamon on it.
- •• 1:32—Partial buns, then breasts while making love with Mercurio in bed behind sheer curtain.

Laura Harring . . . . M.C. Kindra/Trainer
Joey House . . . . Velvet/Trainer
Julie Hughes . . . . Julie/Club Eden
- • 0:26—Breasts and buns in T-back while on runway during introductions.

Gloria Hylton. . . . . Angry Girlfriend/Flashback
- • 0:01—Brief buns in T-back and black bra, while walking back into the house after throwing eggs at Paul Mercurio. Medium long shot.

Alison Moir . . . . .Kitty/Club Eden
- • 1:21—Brief breasts, while giving Omar a massage.

Mariana Morgan . . . . Rachel/Los Angeles
Stephanie Niznik. . . . . .Diana/Club Eden
- •• 0:37—Full frontal nudity, after getting out of swimming pool and helping Dana Delany into a robe.

Tanya Reid . . . . .Naomi/Citizen
- • 0:26—Breasts while on runway during introductions.

Sandra Taylor . . . . Riba/Club Eden
- • 0:26—Breasts while on runway during introductions.

Exotica *(1994; Canadian)*

Arsinée Khanjian . . . . Zoe
Mia Kirshner . . . . Christina
- • 0:33—Brief, lower half of buns, while dancing in schoolgirl outfit.
- • 0:54—Breasts in open blouse, while dancing in front of Bruce Greenwood.
- •• 1:11—Right breast, while dancing in front of Thomas.

• ***Exposé*** *(1997)*

Kim Dawson . . . . Mrs. Holmes
Leslie Olivan . . . . .Bianca
- • 0:33—Brief breasts, while having sex with Shapiro on sofa in video playback.
- • 0:35—Full frontal nudity, while dancing with a guy. Seen on television during video playback.

Exposed *(1983)*

Iman . . . . .Model
Bibi Andersson . . . . .Margaret
Nastassja Kinski. . . . . .Elizabeth Carlson
- •• 0:54—Breasts in bed with Rudolf Nureyev.

• ***Extramarital*** *(1998)*

Susan Byun . . . . .Masseuse
Maria Diaz. . . . . .Ann
- •• 0:13—Brief back side of left breast after taking off bra. Breasts and partial buns, while making love with Bob (wearing a mask) in bed.
- • 0:15—Brief full frontal nudity, when talking to Bob in bed afterwards.
- • 0:28—Buns in lingerie.

Traci Lords. . . . . .Elizabeth

Extreme Justice *(1993; Made for Cable Movie)*

Julie Austin . . . . Cindy
Chelsea Field . . . . Kelly Daniels
- • 0:18—In white bra, then brief left breast on sofa with Lou Diamond Phillips.

Extreme Prejudice *(1987)*

Maria Conchita Alonso . . . . Sarita Cisneros
- •• 0:27—Brief breasts in the shower while Nick Nolte is in the bathroom talking to her.

Extremities *(1986)*

Farrah Fawcett. . . . . Marjorie
- • 0:37—Brief side view of right breast when Joe pulls down her top in the kitchen. Can't see her face, but reportedly her.

Sandy Martin. . . . . .Officer Sudow
Clare Wren . . . . .Racquetball Player

Eye of the Needle *(1981)*

Kate Nelligan. . . . . Lucy
- •• 0:52—Brief left breast, while drying herself off in the bathroom when Donald Sutherland accidentally sees her.
- • 1:15—Top half of buns, making love in bed with Sutherland.
- • 1:26—Breasts making love in bed with Sutherland after he killed her husband. Dark, hard to see.

Eye of the Stranger *(1992)*

Sally Kirkland. . . . . .Lori
- •• 0:47—Breasts, while making love in bed with David Heavener.

Stella Stevens . . . . .Doc

Eyes of a Stranger *(1981)*

Jennifer Jason Leigh . . . . Tracy
- • 1:15—Very brief breasts lying in bed getting attacked by rapist.
- •• 1:19—Left breast, while cleaning herself in bathroom.

Eyes of Fire *(1983)*

Karlene Crockett . . . . Leah
- • 0:44—Brief breasts sitting up in the water and scaring Mr. Dalton.
- • 1:16—Breasts talking to Dalton who is trapped in a tree. Brief breasts again when he pulls the creature out of the tree.

Eyes of Laura Mars *(1978)*

Faye Dunaway. . . . . Laura Mars
Darlanne Fluegel . . . . Lulu
Lisa Taylor . . . . .Michele
- • 0:59—Very brief right breast, while on table just before getting killed.

Eyes of the Beholder *(1992)*

Toni Kalem . . . . Doctor Gruber
Joanna Pacula . . . . Diana Carlyle

Kylie Travis . . . . Holly Brandon
•• 1:08—Left breast, then breasts after taking her dress top down in front of Janice.

Eyes of the Serpent (1992)

Diana Frank . . . . Fiona
•• 1:05—Buns and breasts, several times while making love in bed with Galen.

Tonya Moon . . . . Suzette
• 0:24—Right breast, while standing next to Seemus.

Lisa Toothman . . . . Neema

Eyewitness to Murder (1989)

Sherilyn Wolter . . . . Suzanne
• 1:00—Very, very brief lower half of right breast while making love with Andrew Stevens. Don't see her face.

The Fabulous Baker Boys (1989)

Michelle Pfeiffer . . . . Susie Diamond
Jennifer Tilly . . . . Monica Moran
Terri Treas . . . . Girl in Bed
• 0:00—Brief upper half of right breast when sheet falls down when she leans over in bed.

Fade to Black (1980)

Linda Kerridge . . . . Marilyn
• 0:44—Breasts, while in the shower.

Marya Small . . . . Doreen

Fair Game (1985; Australian)

Cassandra Delaney . . . . Jessica
• 0:15—Buns and brief side of left breast, taking off her outfit and lying on bed.
• 0:16—Breasts rolling over in bed.
• 0:32—Brief left breast, taking off outfit to take a shower.
•• 0:48—Brief breasts when the bad guys cut her blouse open. Breasts several times, while tied to front of truck.
• 0:49—Brief left breast while getting up off the ground.
• 0:50—Half of right breast, while sitting in the shower. Dark.

Fair Game (1988; Italian)

Trudie Styler . . . . Eva
• 0:14—Very, very brief blurry top of right breast in gaping blouse, while standing up after changing clothes.
• 0:37—Brief buns, kneeling in bathtub. Very brief buns in the mirror several times putting on robe and getting out of the bathtub.

Fair Game (1995)

Cindy Crawford . . . . Kate McQuean
• 0:57—Back side of left breast, while changing clothes next to truck.
•• 1:09—Brief breasts, while making love with William Baldwin in the train. Brief breasts, when shooting the bad guy.

Salma Hayek . . . . Rita

Fairytales (1979)

Angela Aames . . . . Little Bo Peep
••• 0:14—Nude with The Prince in the woods.

Nai Bonet . . . . Sheherazade
• 0:29—Buns and very brief left breast doing a belly dance and rubbing oil on herself.

Marita Ditmar . . . . S & M Dancer
• 0:38—Breasts wearing masks with two other S&M Dancers.

Lindsay Freeman . . . . Jill
•• 0:24—Nude on hill with Jack.

Annie Gaybis . . . . Snow White
••• 0:21—Nude in room with the seven little dwarfs singing and dancing.

Evelyn Guerrero . . . . S & M Dancer
•• 0:38—Breasts wearing masks with two other blonde S&M Dancers.
•• 0:56—Full frontal nudity dancing with the other S&M Dancers again.

Linnea Quigley . . . . Dream Girl
•• 1:07—Breasts waking up after being kissed by The Prince.

Mariwin Roberts . . . . Elevator Operator
• 0:20—Brief full frontal nudity in the elevator.
•• 0:23—Breasts again, closer shot.

Idy Tripoldi . . . . Naked Girl
••• 0:06—Nude, dancing in bedroom and getting in and out of bed with The Prince.

• *Fall* (1997)

Amanda de Cadenet . . . . Sarah Easton
• 0:50—Partial left breast, while lying under Michael.

Fall From Innocence (1988)

Isabelle Mejias . . . . Marsa Cummins
Amanda Smith . . . . Janis Cummins
• 0:05—Brief right breast while lying in bed when Bob gets out.
• 0:48—Left breast, in open nightie top, while walking down hallway.

Fame (1980)

Irene Cara . . . . Coco
• 1:57—Brief breasts during "audition" on a B&W TV monitor.

Meg Tilly . . . . Principal Dancer

A Family Matter (1990)

Carol Alt . . . . Nancy
•• 1:08—Buns, in panties. Brief side view of left breast with Eric Roberts.

Josie Bell . . . . Cissy
Eva Grimaldi . . . . Brenda
••• 0:53—Nude, getting out of the bubble bath, then dressing herself.

• *A Family Thing* (1996)

Paula Marshall . . . . Karen
Patrice Pitman Quinn . . . . Willa Mae
• 1:31—Brief buns, while lying on bed before giving birth in flashback. B&W.

Family Viewing (1987; Canadian)

Arsinée Khanjian . . . . Aline
Gabrielle Rose . . . . Sandra
• 0:27—Brief left breast, lying down with Stan. Seen on TV that Van watches.
• 0:29—Same 0:27 scene again.

The Family Way (1969; British)

Hayley Mills . . . . Jenny Piper
•• 0:49—Buns, three times, with a towel wrapped around her front, while standing up in bathtub, talking to Geoffrey.

Famous T & A (1982)

(No longer available for purchase, check your video store for rental.)

Elvira . . . . Katya
••• 0:28—Breasts scene from *Working Girls*.

Vanity . . . . Tanya
• 1:02—Breasts scenes from *Tanya's Island.*
Angela Aames . . . . Little Bo Peep
•• 0:50—Breasts scene from *Fairytales.*
Ursula Andress . . . . Herself
••• 0:15—Full frontal nudity scenes from *Slave of the Cannibal God.*
Brigitte Bardot . . . . Joan
• 0:25—Buns, then brief breasts in scene from *Ms. Don Juan.*
Jacqueline Bisset . . . . Jenny
••• 0:31—Breasts scene from *Secrets.*
Pamela Collins . . . . Dolores
••• 1:05—Breasts in scenes and outtakes from *Sweet Sugar.*
Sybil Danning . . . . Hostess
• 0:00—Brief side view of buns and partial left breast, getting dressed.
Phyllis Davis . . . . Sugar/Joy
••• 0:02—Nude in lots of great out-takes from *Terminal Island.* Check this out if you are a Phyllis Davis fan!
••• 0:51—Breasts in scenes from *Sweet Sugar.* Includes more out-takes.
••• 1:04—More out-takes from *Sweet Sugar.*
Uschi Digard . . . . Truck Stop Woman
•• 0:44—Breasts scenes from *Cherry, Harry & Raquel* and *Truck Stop Women.*
Ella Edwards . . . . Simone
•• 1:07—Buns and breasts in outtakes from *Sweet Sugar.*
Laura Gemser . . . . Emanuelle
••• 0:55—Breasts scenes from *Emanuelle Around the World.*
Claudia Jennings . . . . Rose
•• 0:26—Breasts scenes from *Single Girls* and *Truck Stop Women.*
Laura Jane Leary . . . . Motorcycle Rider
• 0:29—Lower nudity, riding a motorcycle with only a jacket on.
Barbara Leigh . . . . Bunny Campbell
••• 0:45—Breasts scene from *Terminal Island.* Includes additional takes that weren't used.
Ornella Muti . . . . Lisa
•• 0:07—Breasts in scenes from *Summer Affair.* Nude underwater and running around the beach.
Joan Prather . . . . Herself
•• 0:49—Brief breasts in scene from *Bloody Friday.*
Victoria Thompson . . . . Beth Hillyer
• 1:07—Brief breasts and bun scene from *The Harrad Experiment.*
• 1:12—Brief nude, getting up from the floor with Don Johnson.
Idy Tripoldi . . . . Bonnie Tirol
••• 0:35—Full frontal nude scene from *Auditions.*
Laurie Walters . . . . Sheila Grove
• 1:08—Breasts scene from *The Harrad Experiment.*
•• 1:11—Nude pool scene from *The Harrad Experiment.*
Edy Williams . . . . Herself
•• 0:39—Breasts and bun scenes from *Dr. Minx.*

The Fanatasist *(1986; Irish)*

Moira Harris . . . . Patricia Teeling
• 1:24—Brief breasts and buns climbing onto couch for the weird photographer.
• 1:28—Brief right breast leaning over to kiss the photographer.
• 1:31—Very brief side view of left breast in bathtub.
Gabrielle Reidy . . . . Kathy O'Malley
• 0:03—Breasts, while getting attacked in a room.

Fanny Hill *(1981; British)*

Lisa Raines Foster . . . . Fanny Hill
•• 0:09—Nude, getting into bathtub, then drying herself off.
• 0:10—Full frontal nudity getting into bed.
••• 0:12—Full frontal nudity making love with Phoebe in bed.
••• 0:30—Nude, making love in bed with Charles.
•• 0:49—Breasts, whipping her lover, Mr. H., in bed.
•• 0:53—Nude getting into bed with William while Hannah watches through the keyhole.
••• 1:26—Nude, getting out of bed, then running down the stairs to open the door for Charles.

Fanny Hill: Memoirs of a Woman of Pleasure *(1964)*

Leticia Roman . . . . Fanny Hill
• 0:13—Very brief right breast, while turning over in tub and talking with Phoebe.
Christiane Schmidtmer . . . . Fiona

Fantasies *(1974)*

a.k.a. Once Upon a Love
Bo Derek . . . . Anastasia
• 0:03—Left breast, in bathtub.
•• 0:15—Breasts taking off top, then right breast, in bathtub.
• 0:43—Breasts getting her dress top pulled down.
• 0:59—Brief breasts in the water. Very brief full frontal nudity walking back into the house.
• 1:00—Buns and left breast several times outside the window.
• 1:17—Upper left breast, in bathtub again.

Far From Home *(1989)*

Drew Barrymore . . . . Joleen Cox
Jennifer Tilly . . . . Amy
Susan Tyrrell . . . . Agnes Reed
• 0:29—Very, very brief right breast in bathtub getting electrocuted.
Teri Weigel . . . . Woman in Trailer
•• 0:16—Breasts making love when Drew Barrymore peeks in window.

• ***Far Harbor*** *(1996)*

Jennifer Connelly . . . . Ellie
• 0:34—Partial right breast under water, while sitting in bathtub.
Marcia Gay Harden . . . . Arabella

Far Out Man *(1990)*

Rae Dawn Chong . . . . Rae Dawn Chong
Robbi Chong . . . . Dancer
Shelby Chong . . . . Tree
• 0:11—Very brief side view of left breast, in gaping blouse when she leans over to light a joint.
Peggy McIntaggart . . . . Misty
••• 0:50—Breasts and buns in black G-string, undressing and getting into bathtub with Tommy Chong.
Penelope Reed . . . . Stewardess

Farewell, My Lovely *(1975; British)*

Charlotte Rampling . . . . Velma
Cheryl Smith . . . . Doris
• 0:56—Frontal nudity in bedroom in a bordello with Sylvester Stallone before getting beaten by the madam.

• Fargo (1996)

Michelle Hutchinson . . . . Escort
- • 1:07—Brief buns, running down hallway after Shep beats up Steve Buscemi.

Frances McDormand . . . . Marge Gunderson

Farinelli (1995; Swiss/French/Belgian)

a.k.a. Farinelli: il castrato

Marianne Basler. . . . . Countess Mauer
Caroline Cellier . . . . Margaret Hunter
Delphine Zentout . . . . The Young Admirer
- • 0:24—Breasts, while making love in bed with Farinelli.

Elsa Zylberstein . . . . Alexandra Lerris
- •• 1:45—Breasts, while making love in bed with Carlo, then Riccardo.

• Farmer & Chase (1994)

Lara Flynn Boyle . . . . Hillary
- • 0:52—Very brief side right breast, when rolling over underneath Todd Field in bed.

• Farrah Fawcett: All of Me (1997; Video Tape)

Farrah Fawcett. . . . . Herself
- • 0:00—Briefly nude during introduction.
- ••• 0:15—Breasts and buns in still photos and in motion during photo shoot (some in B&W) from her first pictorial.
- ••• 0:30—Nude while working on a clay sculpture (also covering herself with clay).
- ••• 0:38—In beige slip, then nude, while painting with brushes, then her body.
- ••• 0:50—Nude during photo shoots.
- •• 1:03—Full frontal nudity, while playing an actress in a stage play.

Fast Times at Ridgemont High (1982)

Phoebe Cates . . . . Linda Barrett
- ••• 0:50—Breasts getting out of swimming pool during Judge Reinhold's fantasy.

Lana Clarkson . . . . Mrs. Vargas
Ava Lazar. . . . . Playmate
Jennifer Jason Leigh . . . . Stacy Hamilton
- • 0:18—Left breast, while making out with Ron in a dugout.
- ••• 1:00—Breasts in poolside dressing room.

Kelli Maroney . . . . Cindy
Pamela Springsteen. . . . . Dina Phillips
Lori Sutton . . . . Playmate
Amanda Wyss . . . . Lisa

Fast Walking (1981)

Kay Lenz . . . . Moke
- • 0:26—Brief breasts closing the door after pulling James Woods into the room.
- ••• 1:27—Right breast in store. Breasts getting hosed down and dried off outside by James Woods.
- • 1:32—Brief left breast, making love with Woods.

Susan Tyrrell . . . . Evie

Fatal Attraction (1981; Canadian)

a.k.a. Head On

Sally Kellerman . . . . Michelle Keys
- • 0:46—Brief breasts in building making out with a guy. Dark, hard to see.
- • 1:19—Brief half of left breast, after struggling with a guy.

Fatal Attraction (1987)

Anne Archer . . . . Ellen Gallagher
Glenn Close. . . . . Alex Forrest
- •• 0:17—Left breast when she opens her top to let Michael Douglas kiss her. Then very brief buns, falling into bed with him.
- • 0:20—Brief right breast in freight elevator with Douglas.
- ••• 0:32—Breasts in bed talking to Douglas. Long scene, sheet keeps changing positions between cuts.

Fatal Bond (1991; Australian)

Linda Blair . . . . Leonie
- •• 0:25—Brief right breast out of her slip, while making love on top of Joe in bed.

Fatal Charm (1991; Made for Cable Movie)

Tracy Dali . . . . Dream Girl
- •• 0:11—Breasts in van with Christopher Atkins. Lots of diffusion.
- • 0:20—Brief breasts in van during Amanda Peterson's fantasy.

Fatal Games (1984)

Angela Bennett . . . . Sue Allen Baines
- •• 0:21—Full frontal nudity in the sauna with Teal Roberts.
- • 0:23—Nude, running around the school, trying to get away from the killer. Dark.

Sally Kirkland . . . . Diane Paine
Melissa Prophet . . . . Nancy Wilson
- • 0:14—Buns and side view of left breast in shower with other girls. Long shot. (She's wearing a white towel on her head.)

Linnea Quigley . . . . Athelete
Teal Roberts. . . . . Lynn Fox
- ••• 0:08—Breasts on bed and floor when Frank takes her clothes off, more breasts in shower.
- •• 0:21—Breasts in sauna with Sue.

Brinke Stevens . . . . Uncredited Shower Girl
- • 0:14—Brief, out of focus side of left breast and upper half of buns, taking a shower in the background while two girls talk. (She's wearing a light blue towel around her hair.)

Fatal Instinct (1991)

a.k.a. To Kill For

(Unrated version reviewed.)

Ashlyn Gere . . . . Frank Stegner's Girlfriend
- •• 0:01—Breasts, opening her towel in front of Frank at night before he gets shot.

Laura Johnson . . . . Catherine Merrims
- • 0:45—Brief left breast in open robe, getting out of bed.
- ••• 0:47—Breasts in bed talking with Michael Madsen, then making love.
- ••• 0:51—Breasts in the bathtub when Bill comes in. Partial lower frontal nudity when standing up.
- •• 0:52—Brief buns and breasts getting dressed in bedroom.
- • 0:59—In wet T-shirt in pool. Brief buns, underwater, more when getting out.

Fatal Justice (1992)

Suzanne Ager . . . . Diana
- ••• 0:12—In black body suit, then breasts and buns in G-string while making love with her boyfriend.
- • 0:36—Breasts while changing clothes behind room divider. Hard to see.

Fatal Mission (1990)

Tia Carrere. . . . . Mai Chang
- • 0:22—Side view of right breast while changing tops. Dark, hard to see, but it is her.

Fatal Past *(1993)*

Kasia Figura. . . . . Jennifer Lawrence

•• 0:07—Brief breasts, while making love with Preston in flashback during interview.
• 0:53—Brief breasts and buns by the pool with Costas Mandylor.
• 0:55—Brief breasts, while in the pool with Mandylor.
• 0:56—Partial breasts, while making love with Mandylor.
• 0:58—Breasts, while getting up and walking by pool. Medium long shot.
• 1:05—Breasts, while getting her clothes ripped off by bad guys.
• 1:06—Right breast seen through sheer curtains over bed while tied by wrists to bed posts.
• 1:07—Breasts, when getting raped while tied to bed posts.
• 1:11—Very, very brief breasts, while getting pulled out of bed.

Fatal Pulse *(1987)*

Roxanne Kernohan . . . . Ann

• 0:58—Brief breasts in pulled up yellow tank top before getting thrown out of the window.

Michelle McCormick . . . . Lisa

Christie Mucciante . . . . Karen

•• 0:51—Breasts, while getting dressed for bed.

Sky Nicholas . . . . Carol

• 0:16—Brief breasts, while looking at herself in the mirror in bedroom, then closer shot, while putting on tank top.

Fatal Skies *(1989)*

Kim Anderson . . . . Cindy

• 0:48—Buns in lingerie, while posing for Lance in his office.

Veronica Carothers . . . . Toni

•• 0:31—Buns, while putting on swimsuit bottom.
•• 0:32—Breasts, while putting on swimsuit top.

Melissa Anne Moore . . . . Suzy

• **Fatally Yours** *(1995)*

Robbi Chong. . . . . Bobbi

Annie Fitzgerald . . . . Patti

•• 0:36—Breasts and buns, while making love in bed with Rick Rossovich.
• 1:12—Breasts, while making love with Rossovich.

Honey Lauren . . . . Flapper

Fear *(1980; French/Italian)*

Silvia Dionisio . . . . Deborah

• 0:18—Brief breasts, while making out with Michael on the sofa.
• 0:32—Left breast in open sheer robe, while running from a hooded figure.
• 0:35—Breasts in open robe outside in the woods.
•• 0:38—Breasts, after her gown is ripped off while she's tied by her wrists.

Laura Gemser . . . . Beryl

• 0:00—Breasts, while getting strangled in bed at night during filming of a movie.
• 0:29—Breasts, while almost drowning in bathtub. Dark.
• 0:50—Full frontal nudity, while making love outside with Michael, then full frontal nudity, lying dead covered with blood.
• 1:06—Brief breasts, dead, covered with blood in flashback.
• 1:18—Brief breasts, while getting killed by Glenda in flashback.

Anita Strindberg . . . . Glenda

• 1:10—Breast, during flashback struggle on bed with Oliver.
• 1:15—Brief, out of focus breasts in reflection in the mirror, then very brief breasts when pulling up the sheets while in bed with Oliver.

Fear *(1991; Made for Cable Movie)*

Michelle Foreman . . . . .Gale the Stripper

• 0:50—Breasts and buns dancing in bar. Hard to see because seen through the killer's eyes.

Lauren Hutton. . . . . Jessica Moreau

Ally Sheedy . . . . Cayce Bridges

The Fear *(1994)*

Anna Karin . . . . Tanya

Monique Mannen . . . . Mindy

• 0:40—Very brief breasts, while in bubble bath when she slaps Joey for feeling her up.

Heather Medway. . . . . Ashley

• 0:33—Very, very brief blurry left breast, when turning around in bed after getting scared by shadow on the wall. Blurry. Good shot of very brief right breast, after Richard swears and bends down to get his pants. Very, very brief right breast again, when he lifts up the sheets to get out.

Fear City *(1984)*

Maria Conchita Alonso . . . . Silver Chavez

Rae Dawn Chong . . . . Leila

••• 0:26—Breasts and buns, dancing on stage.
• 0:50—Brief breasts in the hospital getting defibrillated to get her heart started.

Emilia Crow. . . . . Bibi

•• 0:16—Breasts, dancing at the Metropole club.
•• 1:00—Breasts, dancing on the stage.

Melanie Griffith . . . . Loretta

• 0:04—Buns, in blue G-string, while dancing on stage.
•• 0:07—Breasts, dancing on stage.
••• 0:23—Breasts dancing on stage wearing a red G-string.

Tracy Griffith . . . . Sandra Cook

Janet Julian . . . . Ruby

Joy Michael . . . . .Metropole Dancer

Ola Ray . . . . Honey Powers

The Fear Inside *(1992; Made for Cable Movie)*

Maria Diaz. . . . . Reporter

Jennifer Rubin . . . . Jane Caswell

• 0:26—Breasts with Peter. Hard to see because of the strobe light effect.
• 0:53—Buns and partial left breast visible under water while skinny dipping in pool.
• 0:55—Full frontal nudity under water. Hard to see because of the distortion.

Fear of a Black Hat *(1992)*

Monique Gabrielle. . . . . Uncredited Girl in Music Video

• 0:34—Buns, while dancing with several girls in swimsuits in music video "Booty Juice."

Penny Johnson . . . . Re-Re

Kasi Lemmons . . . . Nina Blackburn

Fear of Scandal *(1992; Italian)*

Linda Carol . . . . Anna

• 0:21—Brief left breast, while making love with a guy in bed.
•• 0:42—Left breast, while making love in bed.
•• 0:43—Breasts, while covering herself with the bed covers.

Fearless (1978)

Joan Collins . . . . Bridgitte
- • 0:01—In bra and panties, then brief right breast during opening credits.
- •• 0:41—Breasts after doing a strip tease routine on stage.
- • 1:17—Undressing in front of Wally in white bra and panties, then right breast.
- • 1:20—Brief right breast lying dead on couch.

The Fearless Vampire Killers (1967)

Fiona Lewis . . . . Maid
Sharon Tate . . . . Sarah Shagal
- • 0:24—Very, very brief breasts struggling in bathtub with vampire. Hard to see.

Felicity (1978; Australian)

Glory Annen . . . . Felicity
- •• 0:02—Breasts taking off leotard in girl's shower room, then nude taking a shower.
- • 0:05—Buns, then left breast, then right breast undressing to go skinny dipping.
- •• 0:10—Breasts and buns at night at the girl's dormitory with Jenny.
- •• 0:15—Breasts undressing in room in front of Christine.
- • 0:16—Left breast, while touching herself in bed.
- ••• 0:20—Lots of lower frontal nudity trying on clothes, bras and panties in dressing room. Brief breasts and buns.
- ••• 0:25—Buns and breasts taking a bath. Full frontal nudity when Steve peeks in at her.
- • 0:31—Brief full frontal nudity losing her virginity on car with Andrew.
- ••• 0:38—Full frontal nudity in bath with Mei Ling and two other girls, then getting massaged. Long scene.
- ••• 0:58—Full frontal nudity in bed with Miles.
- ••• 1:13—Full frontal nudity with Mei Ling making love on bed. Long scene.
- • 1:20—Left breast, while making love standing up.
- •• 1:21—Breasts and buns making love with Miles.
- •• 1:27—Nude making love again with Miles.
- • 1:29—Buns, while in the water with Miles.

Joni Flynn . . . . Mei Ling
- ••• 0:38—Nude in bath with Glory Annen and two other girls, then getting massaged. Long scene.
- ••• 0:43—Breasts and buns, making love on boat with a guy.
- ••• 1:13—Nude, making love in bed with Glory. Long scene.

Fellow Traveller (1989; Made for Cable Movie)

Imogen Stubbs . . . . Sarah Aitchison
- • 0:54—Breasts in bed with Asa. Very, very brief right breast when he rolls off her.

Sarah Trigger . . . . Gloria
- •• 0:02—Breasts, when sitting up in bed, stretching, then getting out.

• *Female Perversions* (1997)

Marcia Cross . . . . Eve's Mother
- • 0:48—Very, very brief breast, while falling to the floor.
- • 1:04—Very, very brief tip of right breast, just before being pushed back.
- •• 1:11—Breasts, while tracing her right breast with a pen while straddling her husband.
- ••• 1:36—Brief right breast, then breasts, while opening her dress and tracing circles around her breasts with a pen, then being pushed onto the floor.

Azalea Davila . . . . Queen
- • 0:56—Brief breasts, in open blouse while wearing a mask.

Frances Fisher . . . . Annunciata
- • 1:06—Very brief back side of right breast, while posing for photos. Medium long shot. Brief partial breasts under open blue robe.
- • 1:09—Buns in panties, while dancing in living room.

Amy Madigan . . . . Madelyn Stephens
- •• 1:33—Breasts and brief buns, when undressing and getting into the bathtub with Tilda Swinton.

Sandy Martin . . . . Trudy
Paulina Porizkova . . . . Langley Flynn
Laila Robins . . . . Emma
Karen Sillas . . . . Renee
- ••• 0:53—Breasts (mostly left), when Tilda Swinton kisses her, while lying in hammock.
- •• 0:55—More breasts, while in hammock with Swinton.

Tilda Swinton . . . . Evelyn Stephens
- • 0:01—Brief breasts and buns during her fantasy.
- •• 0:03—Full frontal nudity, while making love in bed with Clancy Brown, then getting out of bed.
- •• 0:11—Most of her buns, while walking around in lingerie store, wearing a sheer body suit.
- • 0:28—Brief lower frontal nudity when Brown rips her pantyhose open to shave her down there in his office.
- • 0:54—Breasts during fantasy sequences.
- • 0:58—Very brief buns, when getting up out of hammock.
- •• 1:29—Breasts, while sitting in bathroom and cutting her breast with a razor blade.
- • 1:32—Brief lower frontal nudity, while sitting on edge of bathtub.
- • 1:39—Very brief right breast, during dream. Dark.

Female Trouble (1974)

Elizabeth Coffey . . . . Ernestine
- • 1:24—Right breast, while lying on cot in jail cell with Divine.
- • 1:25—More right breast.
- • 1:26—Brief lower frontal nudity when kissing Divine.

Edith Massey . . . . Ida
- • 0:20—Breasts, massaging her breasts in front of the mirror.

Cookie Mueller . . . . Concetta
Mary Vivian Pearce . . . . Donna
Mink Stole . . . . Taffy
Susan Walsh . . . . Chiclett

Femalien (1995)

Michelle Barry . . . . Girl Cop, Theatre Woman
Stevi Conrad . . . . Angel
- ••• 0:34—In lingerie, while modeling for Kara in lingerie store. Nude, while making love with Gena.

Stephanie Hudson . . . . Danielle
Summer Leigh . . . . Wheel Girl
- ••• 0:52—Full frontal nudity, while strapped to wheel by wrists and ankles during stage show.

Jacqueline Lovell . . . . Sun
- ••• 0:22—Breasts, taking off coffee soaked blouse, then full frontal nudity while caressing herself on lounge chair.
- ••• 1:19—Nude, while making love with Kara in bed.

Bobbie Marie . . . . Girl Toy, Meditation Woman
- ••• 0:52—Buns in white T-back, then nude, while on stage with another woman.
- ••• 1:07—Breasts, while making love with a guy during meditation orgy.

Kathleen Mazzotta . . . . Jean
- • 0:05—Lower frontal nudity, while caressing herself outside.
- ••• 0:07—Nude, while making love with her boyfriend in backyard. Long scene.

Stacey Leigh Mobley . . . . Uncredited Female Model
••• 0:26—Nude, while making love with a male model during photo shoot.
Taylor St. Claire . . . . Gena, Meditation Woman
••• 0:34—In lingerie, while modeling for Kara in lingerie store. Nude, while making love with Angel.
••• 1:07—Full frontal nudity (she's brunette), while making love with a guy during meditation orgy.
Vanessa Taylor . . . . Collector/Kara
•• 0:02—Breasts and buns in T-back, in bedroom after arriving on earth.
• 0:04—Breasts, while watching a man and woman in backyard.
••• 0:07—Breasts, while caressing herself when watching the man and woman make love.
•• 0:15—Breasts, while dressing in bedroom.
•• 0:30—Left breast, while caressing herself when watching a guy and girl model make love.
••• 0:45—Nude, while making love with Drew in bed.
••• 0:59—Nude, while in massage room with MJ, then getting massaged, then massaging him.
••• 1:19—Nude, while making love with Sun in bed.

Femme Fatale (1990)

Lisa Blount . . . . Jenny
Suzanne Snyder . . . . Andrea
••• 0:08—Breasts, nonchalantly taking off her top and posing for Billy Zane's painting. (She sometimes has a bag over her head.)
•• 0:46—Breasts posing again with the bag on and off her head.
Lisa Zane . . . . Cynthia

La Femme Nikita (1991; French/Italian)

a.k.a. Nikita
Jeanne Moreau . . . . Amande
Anne Parillaud . . . . Nikita
• 0:59—Very brief right nipple, peeking out of her top when she sits up in bed.

Fever (1991; Made for Cable Movie)

Teresa Gilmore-Capps . . . . Jeanine
Marcia Gay Harden . . . . Lacy
• 0:18—Brief breasts while making love in bed with Sam Neill.
•• 1:31—In bra in bed with bad guy, then breasts when he opens her bra. Kind of dark.

Fever Pitch (1985)

Catherine Hicks . . . . Flo
• 0:11—Brief left breast, while sitting on bed in hotel room talking with Ryan O'Neal.
Cherie Michan . . . . Rose O'Sharon
Heidi Sorenson . . . . Airport Attendant

• *The Fifth Element* (1997)

Milla Jovovich . . . . Leeloo
• 0:26—Brief right breast, while lying in regeneration chamber. Brief right breast when straps go around her.
• 0:47—Brief breasts, while changing clothes in the background. Slightly out of focus.
• 1:06—Very, very brief lower half of breasts, when taking off wet blouse in background. Slightly out of focus.
Julie T. Wallace . . . . Major Iceborg

The Fifth Floor (1978)

Patti D'Arbanville . . . . Cathy Burke
Sharon Farrell . . . . Melanie
Dianne Hull . . . . Kelly McIntyre
•• 0:29—Breasts and buns in shower while Carl watches, then brief full frontal nudity running out of the shower.
•• 1:09—Breasts in whirlpool bath getting visited by Carl again, then raped.

The Final Alliance (1990)

Jeanie Moore . . . . Carrie
• 1:03—Brief breasts getting into bed with David Hasselhoff, then brief right breast twice in bed with him. A little dark.

Final Analysis (1992)

Kim Basinger . . . . Heather Evans
•• 0:21—Brief breasts, while making love in bed under Richard Gere. Dark.
Shelley Michelle . . . . Body Parts
Uma Thurman . . . . Diana Baylor

The Final Conflict (1981)

a.k.a. Omen III
Lisa Harrow . . . . Kate Reynolds
• 1:28—Partial buns, then buns and side of left breast, getting out of bed and putting shirt on.

• *Final Equinox* (1995)

Robin Joi Brown . . . . Piper
•• 0:45—Nude, while making love in bed with a guy.

Final Exam (1981)

Deanna Robbins . . . . Lisa
•• 1:13—Buns and breasts, after taking off dress and covering herself with a sheet in studio.

Final Judgment (1992)

Karen Black . . . . Mrs. Sorrel
Maria Ford . . . . Nicole
••• 0:20—Breasts and buns in G-string while stripping and dancing on stage. Nice bending over action.
••• 0:39—In red bra and panties, then breasts and buns while dancing on stage.
••• 0:52—Breasts and buns in G-string while dancing on stage.
• 0:56—Very, very brief breast, while putting a towel around herself after getting out of the shower.
•• 0:58—Breasts while making love with Brad Dourif in bed during daydream.
Lisa Inouye . . . . Lily
•• 0:32—Breasts, walking up behind Rob in room, then making love. Brief buns in G-string, getting out of bed. Side view of breasts in mirror.
• 1:01—Buns in lingerie in mirror.
Toni Naples . . . . Dancer #2
• 0:51—Breasts, while dancing on stage, wearing sunglasses.
Sherrie Rose . . . . Amanda Peterson
Roberta Vasquez . . . . Whitney

Final Mission (1993)

Elizabeth Gracen . . . . Caitlin Cole
••• 0:28—Breasts, while making out with Billy Wirth.
• 0:53—Breasts, while making love on bed with Wirth at night.

Final Round (1993)

Kathleen Kinmont . . . . Jordan
••• 0:18—Breasts, while making love on the floor with Lamas.

The Finest Hour (1991)

Tracy Griffith . . . . Barbara
- 0:21—In wet, braless, white dress, getting out of the water after canoe tips over.
- 1:02—Swimming with Mazzoli under water in ocean in a wet, braless, white dress.
- 1:03—Brief side view of right breast, while taking the wet dress off.

Gilya Stern . . . . Diane

The Finishing Touch (1991)

Delia Goldson . . . . Sorvino's Model
- •• 1:06—In lingerie outfit, then breasts while handcuffed to bed while getting video taped by Sorvino.

Fiona (1978; British)

Linda Regan . . . . Secretary

Fiona Richmond . . . . Fiona Richmond
- •• 0:23—Breasts on boat with a blonde woman rubbing oil on her.
- •• 0:27—In a bra, then frontal nudity stripping in a guy's office for an audition.
- •• 0:35—Breasts, then frontal nudity lying down during photo session.
- • 0:51—Breasts walking around her apartment in boots.
- •• 1:00—Breasts with old guy ripping each other's clothes off.
- •• 1:08—Frontal nudity taking off clothes for a shower.

Fire Birds (1990)

a.k.a. Wings of the Apache

Sean Young . . . . Billie Lee Guthrie
- 0:52—Very, very brief right breast twice in bed with Nicolas Cage.

• *Fireballs* (1988; Canadian)

Lara Daans . . . . Bikini Contestant

Cindy Fidler. . . . . Debbie Carlson
- •• 0:46—In bra and panties, then breasts, while dancing on stage in bar.

Firecracker (1981)

Jillian Kesner . . . . Susanne Carter
- ••• 0:44—Breasts, while fighting bad guys after her bra comes off. Nice!
- ••• 0:58—In panties on bed, then buns as Darby Hinton cuts her clothes off with a knife. Breasts while making love with him in bed.

Firehouse (1987)

Ruth Corrine Collins . . . . Bubbles

Gianna Rains . . . . Barrett Hopkins
- ••• 0:33—Breasts taking a shower, then drying herself after the fire alarm goes off.
- •• 0:56—Breasts making love with the reporter on the roof of a building.

Jennifer Stahl. . . . . Mindy
- •• 0:25—Breasts while dancing in club.

Fires Within (1991)

Greta Scacchi . . . . Isabel
- 0:18—Upper half of buns, very brief breasts in bed.
- 0:38—Very brief breasts in bed.

Firing Line (1991)

Shannon Tweed . . . . Sandra Spencer
- 0:49—Sort of buns and breasts, seen through water while she's skinny dipping in water.
- 0:59—Very, very brief side view of right breast, when turning over onto Reb Brown while on rocks. Medium long shot.

First Love (1977)

Beverly D'Angelo . . . . Shelley
- 0:05—Very, very brief half of left breast when her jacket opens up while talking to William Katt.
- 1:10—Brief breasts taking off her top in bedroom with Katt.

Susan Dey . . . . Caroline Hedges
- ••• 0:31—Breasts making love in bed with William Katt. Long scene.
- • 0:51—Breasts taking off her top in her bedroom with Katt.

First Name: Carmen (1983; French)

Maruschka Detmers. . . . . Carmen
- ••• 0:36—Breasts while standing by window with a guy.
- •• 0:40—Breasts several times while in bedroom with Joseph.
- • 0:42—Lower frontal nudity (out of focus) while talking to Joseph. Long scene.
- • 0:44—Brief lower frontal nudity with Joseph.
- • 0:46—More lower frontal nudity.
- •• 0:58—Nude, after Joseph takes off her robe.
- •• 1:07—Breasts while undressing in bedroom.
- ••• 1:08—Breasts in red panties, getting out of bed and walking through the house, sitting on couch and lying on bed. Long scene.
- •• 1:13—Brief full frontal nudity in bathroom and in shower.

Myriem Roussel . . . . Claire

The First Nudie Musical (1979)

Leslie Ackerman . . . . Susie

Alexandra Morgan . . . . Mary La Rue
- • 0:54—Breasts, singing and dancing during dancing dildo routine.
- ••• 1:04—Full frontal nudity in bed trying to do a take.
- •• 1:07—Breasts, while in bed with a guy with a continuous erection.
- •• 1:17—Breasts in bed in another scene.

The First Power (1990)

Susan Giosa . . . . Carmen
- • 0:22—Brief right breast, lying dead with a bloody pentagram cut into her stomach.

Tracy Griffith . . . . Tess Seaton

Melanie Shatner . . . . Shopgirl

The First Turn-On! (1983)

Georgia Harrell . . . . Michelle Farmer
- ••• 1:17—Breasts and brief buns in cave with everybody during orgy scene.

Sheila Kennedy . . . . Dreamgirl
- • 0:52—In red two piece swimsuit, then breasts when the top falls down during Danny's daydream.
- • 0:59—Right breast, while in bed with Danny.

Fist of Honor (1993)

Joey House. . . . . Gina
- • 0:19—Side of right breast and buns, after undressing in front of Sam Jones.

Francine Lapenseé . . . . Mrs. Bones

Fists of Iron (1994)

Maria Diaz. . . . . Michelle

Jenilee Harrison . . . . Julie
- •• 1:03—Breasts, while making love in bed with Dale.

Fit To Kill (1993)

Cynthia Brimhall . . . . Edy Stark
- •• 1:00—Breasts under sheer white body suit while posing for her boyfriend while he photographs her.

Ava Cadell . . . . Ava
- •• 1:13—Half of right breast, sticking out of bra. Buns in G-string.
- •• 1:14—Left breast, while making love with Petrov in radio station while still talking on the air.
- ••• 1:17—Breasts in spa with Petrov.

Carolyn Liu . . . . Silk
- • 0:09—Buns in body suit, while in room with Kane.
- •• 0:11—Breasts while making love in bed with Kane.
- ••• 0:46—Breasts, while taking off lingerie on boat with Kane.

Dona Speir . . . . Donna Hamilton
- •• 0:21—Breasts and buns in G-string, while undressing and putting dresses on with Vasquez.
- ••• 1:18—Buns in two piece swimsuit, then breasts during Kane's fantasy.

Julie Strain . . . . Blu Steele
- •• 0:10—Buns in swimsuit while doing stretching exercises.
- •• 0:11—Breasts, undoing her swimsuit top.
- •• 0:47—Breasts and buns in G-string, while making love in the kitchen with Brett Clark.

Roberta Vasquez . . . . Nicole Justin
- •• 0:21—Breasts and buns in G-string, while undressing and putting dresses on with Speir.
- ••• 0:52—Breasts and buns, while making love with her boyfriend in bed.

Sándra Wild . . . . Sandy
- ••• 0:07—Breasts, while talking on phone while standing in spa. Buns in gold swimsuit bottom, while getting out. Breasts while pouring coffee.
- ••• 0:21—Breasts in spa in long shot. More breasts in closer shot while putting swimsuit on.
- • 1:11—Buns, while wearing a sexy black swimsuit/lingerie outfit.

Five Easy Pieces (1970)

Susan Anspach . . . . Catherine Van Oost
Toni Basil . . . . Terry Grouse
Karen Black . . . . Rayette Dipesto
Helena Kallianiotes . . . . Palm Apodaca
Sally Struthers . . . . Betty
- •• 0:34—Brief breasts a couple of times making love with Nicholson. Lots of great moaning, but hard to see anything.

• The Fixer (1997; Made for Cable Movie)

Brenda Bakke . . . . CJ
- • 0:12—Very, very brief left breast, while making love with Jon Voight in bed.

Sara Botsford . . . . Bonnie
Karyn Dwyer . . . . Irene

A Flash of Green (1984)

Blair Brown . . . . Catherine "Kat" Hubble
- • 1:30—Very brief right breast moving around in bed with Ed Harris.

Joan Goodfellow . . . . Mitchie

Flashdance (1983)

Belinda Bauer . . . . Katie Hurley
Jennifer Beals . . . . Alex
Monique Gabrielle . . . . Uncredited Stripper
- •• 1:27—Buns, in G-string, walking down walkway of stage in club. Brief breasts, accepting a bill in her red G-string.

Marine Jahan . . . . . Uncredited Dance Double for Jennifer Beals
Sunny Johnson . . . . Jennie Szabo
- • 1:28—Breasts, while sitting on stage and moving her legs around.
- • 1:29—Very brief left breast in open rain coat, outside the club with Jennifer Beals.

Dirga McBroom . . . . Heels

Flashfire (1993)

Kristin Minter . . . . Lisa Cates
- •• 0:18—In black bra, panties, garter belt and stockings, then breasts while in hotel room with Artie.
- •• 0:20—Breasts while making love in bed with Artie.
- •• 0:21—Breasts when hit men burst into the room and kill Artie.
- • 0:49—Buns in panties and side of right breast while undressing when Billy Zane sees her.
- ••• 1:11—Breasts, while making love on bed in a boat with Zane.

Carrie-Anne Moss . . . . Meredith Neal

Fled (1996)

Salma Hayek . . . . Cora
Brittney Powell . . . . Faith/Cindy
- • 0:48—Brief beasts, while crawling on stage in club to kiss Stephen Baldwin, then standing up afterward.

Flesh + Blood (1985)

Nancy Cartwright . . . . Kathleen
- • 0:28—Brief breasts showing Jennifer Jason Leigh how to make love. Long shot.

Jennifer Jason Leigh . . . . Agnes
- • 0:45—Brief right breast, while being held down.
- •• 1:05—Full frontal nudity getting into the bath with Rutger Hauer and making love.
- ••• 1:16—Full frontal nudity getting out of bed with Hauer and walking to the window.
- •• 1:35—Full frontal nudity, while throwing clothes into the fire.
- •• 1:36—Breasts, when Hauer removes sheet that covers her.
- •• 1:37—Buns and long shot brief side view of right breast, while walking to the castle behind Hauer. Brief breasts when stopped on stairs while watching Tom Burlinson throw food into well.

Blanca Marsillach . . . . Clara
- •• 0:11—Full frontal nudity on bed having convulsions after getting hit on the head with a sword.

Marina Saura . . . . Polly
- • 0:59—Brief left breast during feast in the castle.
- • 1:09—Breasts on balcony of the castle with everybody during the day.

Susan Tyrrell . . . . Celine
- • 1:35—Right breast sticking out of her dress when everybody throws their clothes into the fire.

Flesh and Bone (1993)

Gwyneth Paltrow . . . . Ginnie
- •• 1:09—Left breast, while in motel room, talking with Meg Ryan.

Meg Ryan . . . . Kay Davies
- •• 0:59—Right breast, several times, while making love with Dennis Quaid in bed.

Barbara Alyn Woods . . . . Cindy
- 0:16—Partial buns, while lying on her stomach on bed.

Flesh Gordon 2 (1990; Canadian)

Morgan Fox . . . . Robunda Hooters
- •• 0:12—Breasts, while opening her top to get Flesh Gordon excited.
- • 1:07—Brief breasts when her top is opened by the Evil Presence to get Flesh aroused.

Kathleen Kane . . . . Girl in Car
Robyn Kelly . . . . Dale Ardor
- •• 0:24—Brief breasts in push-up bra when Dr. Jerkoff rips her jacket open.
- • 0:49—Brief buns, while acting like a dog on all fours on the floor.

Melissa Mounds . . . . Bazonga Bomber
- ••• 0:46—Breasts standing by table with Flesh Gordon and Dr. Jerkoff.
- ••• 0:48—More breasts with Dr. Jerkoff.

Fleshtone (1994)

Lise Cutter. . . . . Jennifer Womak
- ••• 0:56—In black bra, then breasts while making love with Matthew in bathroom and on bed.
- ••• 0:58—Right breast, while lying on bed talking to Matthew. Brief partial left breast. Long scene.
- ••• 1:03—Buns and left breast while lying on bed, posing for Matthew.

Kimberleigh Stark . . . . Detective #3
Melanie Walker . . . . Mrs. Peale
- •• 0:21—Buns and breasts in photos that Matthew looks at. Partial left breast behind steering wheel of car.
- •• 0:37—Breasts, while lying in bed before Matthew discovers she's dead.

Flinch (1992)

Gina Gershon . . . . Daphne
Veronica Lorenz. . . . . Jasmine
- ••• 0:07—Nude in background, while undressing and posing as a model.
- •• 0:20—Full frontal nudity while posing some more in studio.

• Flirt (1995)

Susie Bick . . . . Model
- •• 0:28—Full frontal nudity, while standing, then putting on dress.

Geno Lechner . . . . Greta
Miho Nikaido . . . . Miho
- • 0:46—Partial breasts, visible under clear plastic that is wrapped around her body while practicing for a play. Covered with white body paint.
- • 1:14—Brief partial right breast in gaping blouse, while kneeling over her boyfriend in bed in flashback.

Parker Posey . . . . Emily
Maria Schrader . . . . Woman at Phone Booth
Karen Sillas . . . . Doctor Clint

Flirting (1992; Australian)

Nicole Kidman. . . . . Nicola Radcliffe
Thandie Newton . . . . Thandiwe Adjewa
- •• 1:30—Brief breasts, getting out of bed and putting a coat on over herself after getting caught with Danny.

Femi Taylor . . . . Letitia Adjewa

The Fly (1986)

Joy Boushel . . . . Tawny
- • 0:54—Very brief breasts viewed from below when Jeff Goldblum pulls her by the arm to get her out of bed.

Geena Davis . . . . Veronica Quaife

• The Folds of the Flesh (1970; Italian)

Pier Angeli . . . . Falesse/Ester
- • 0:16—Upper half of left breast, sticking out of nightgown, twice, while leaning over Michael after stabbing him.
- • 0:45—Right breast, when Pascal pulls down her nightgown. Don't see her face.

For Your Love Only (1979; German)

Nastassja Kinski . . . . Zena
- •• 0:04—Breasts, twice, in the woods with her teacher, Victor, while Michael watches through the bushes.
- • 0:15—Brief right breast, in the woods with Michael.
- •• 0:58—Partial left breast, sitting up in bed with Victor. Breasts walking around and putting on robe.

Forbidden Games (1995)

(Unrated version reviewed.)

Griffin Drew. . . . . Model
Melissa Dutton . . . . Model
Gail Harris . . . . Tonya
- ••• 0:49—In bra and panties, then nude when taking a bath, letting Michael watch. Brief breasts in Michael's vision.
- ••• 1:12—Breasts and buns in pool with Michael, then in bathtub, then in bed.
- • 1:18—Buns, while making love with in bed. Seen on TV.
- • 1:21—Nude, while getting out of bed.

Leslie J. Hunt . . . . Model
Aleksandra Kaniak . . . . Amber
- • 1:04—Breasts and buns, while making love with Shauna in bed.

Cory Lane . . . . Model
Heidi Lynne . . . . Model
Beckie Mullen . . . . Linda
- ••• 0:04—Dancing in front of Michael in black bra and panties, then breasts while making love with him. Long scene.

Ashlie Rhey . . . . Trish
- • 0:18—Buns in blue swimsuit, greeting Michael at the door and taking him to meet Shauna.
- ••• 0:39—Breasts and buns, while making love with Michael in bedroom.
- •• 1:00—Breasts, while in bed with Shauna, tying and blindfolding Michael in bed.

Elizabeth Sandifer . . . . Rachel
Lesli Kay Sterling . . . . Shannon
Amy Weber . . . . Shauna
- •• 0:19—Breasts and buns, while talking with Michael outside.
- • 0:23—Breasts in Michael's vision.
- •• 1:00—Breasts, while in bed with Trish, tying and blindfolding Michael in bed.
- ••• 1:04—Breasts, while making love with Amber in bathtub.

• Forbidden Love: The Unashamed Stories of Lesbian Lives (1992; Canadian)

Lynne Adams. . . . . Mitch
- • 1:17—Breasts, while with another woman.

Stephanie Morgenstern . . . . Laura
- •• 1:17—In bra, then breasts and buns with another woman.

• *Forbidden Passions* (1995)

Debra Beatty . . . . Mara
- ••• 0:07—Breasts, while making love with her husband, Stephen.
- • 0:12—Brief breasts when standing up and talking with Stephen, then sitting back in bed.
- •• 0:14—Nude, while by herself in a beach like setting.
- ••• 0:26—Full frontal nudity while posing for the painter, then letting him paint on her, then making love with him.
- ••• 1:02—Breasts, while making love with Amy.
- •• 1:14—Breasts, while making love with Bob.

Landon Hall. . . . . Cindy
- •• 0:48—Breasts, while making love with Stephen in his office.

Shayna Lee . . . . Sandy
- ••• 0:42—Breasts and buns, while making love with Brett in bed.

Lesli Kay Sterling . . . . Jana

Forbidden World (1982)

June Chadwick . . . . Dr. Barbara Glaser
- •• 0:29—Breasts in bed making love with Jesse Vint.
- •• 0:54—Breasts taking a shower with Dawn Dunlap.

Dawn Dunlap . . . . Tracy Baxter
- • 0:27—Brief breasts getting ready for bed.
- ••• 0:37—Nude in steam bath.
- •• 0:54—Breasts in shower with June Chadwick.

Forbidden Zone (1980)

Viva. . . . . Ex-Queen

Gisele Lindley . . . . The Princess
- ••• 0:21—Breasts, while in jail cell.
- ••• 0:39—Breasts, while turning a table around.
- •• 0:45—Breasts, while bending over, making love with a frog.
- •• 0:51—Breasts, while in a cave.
- •• 0:53—More breast scenes.
- •• 1:06—Even more breast scenes.

Susan Tyrrell . . . . Queen Doris
- •• 0:19—Left breast sticking out of dress, sitting on big dice with Herve Villechaize.
- •• 1:02—Left breast sticking out of dress after fighting with the Ex-Queen.

Forbidden Zone: Alien Abduction (1996)

a.k.a. Alien Abduction: Intimate Secrets

Darcy De Moss . . . . Sheri
- • 0:07—Brief breasts, taking off her red towel by pool.
- • 0:19—Brief breasts, while talking about her experience with another woman.
- • 0:20—Very brief breasts, while getting splashed with water in flashback.
- •• 0:33—In bra, with the vet, then breasts when he soaps her up.
- • 0:43—Breasts, when getting splashed with water again.
- • 0:47—Brief partial right breast, while lying in bed.
- • 0:58—Breasts during flashback with the vet.

Floriela Grappini . . . . Patron
- • 0:00—Brief full frontal nudity and breasts, several times, while swimming in pool.
- •• 0:03—Brief full frontal nudity, then breasts, while looking at the other woman in dressing room.

Meredyth Holmes . . . . Veronica
- •• 0:06—Breasts, while caressing herself and fantasizing about making love with a guy.
- • 0:20—Very brief buns, when getting lifted up after passing out.
- •• 1:03—In black bra, then breasts, while making love with the alien guy on his ship.

Laura Ilica . . . . Wild Child
- • 0:18—Brief buns in outfit, while running up the stairs.
- • 0:44—Brief breasts, while wearing a mask and a saddle and acting wild.
- • 0:47—Brief buns in outfit, while running up the stairs.

Carmen Lacatus. . . . . Motorcycle Cop Girl

Pia Reyes . . . . Tedra
- • 0:17—Very, very brief breasts while lying on the floor in arena dream.
- • 0:40—Brief breasts, while making love with the foreign exchange student in flashback.
- • 0:41—Brief breasts, while on top of frat boy in flashback.
- •• 0:42—Breasts, while making love with the runner guy, then very brief breasts in arena dream.
- • 0:50—Very, very brief breasts, when getting out of pool, then left breast in arena dream.
- • 0:53—Breasts during arena dream.

Force Ten from Navarone (1978)

Barbara Bach . . . . Maritza
- • 0:32—Brief breasts, while taking a bath in the German officer's room.

Forced Vengeance (1982)

Camila Griggs . . . . Joy Paschal
- • 1:14—Brief breasts, on the bed when the bad guy rips her blouse open.

Susie Hall. . . . . Dancer
- • 0:57—Breasts, dancing in club with an Asian dancer.

Mary Louise Weller . . . . Claire Bonner
- • 1:04—Brief breasts, struggling with the bad guy.
- • 1:08—Very brief right breast then left breast, while lying dead on the floor.

Foreign Body (1986; British)

Amanda Donohoe. . . . . Susan
- • 0:37—Undressing in her bedroom down to lingerie. Very brief side view of right breast, then brief left breast putting blouse on.
- •• 0:40—Breasts opening her blouse for Ram.

Anna Massey . . . . Miss Furze

Sinitta Renet . . . . Lovely Indian Girl
- • 0:06—Buns, then breasts in bedroom.

Foreign Student (1994)

Robin Givens . . . . April
- • 0:50—Left breast several times and buns, while making love in building with Philippe.

Forever (1992)

Sally Kirkland. . . . . Angelica Farina
- • 0:14—Breasts, while making love with Keith Coogan in bed. Right breast, when lying in bed with him afterwards.
- •• 0:20—Breasts, while on sofa with Coogan.
- •• 1:25—Breasts, while starting to make love on desk in Coogan's office.

Shelley Michelle. . . . . Marilyn

Sean Young. . . . . Mary Miles Minter
- • 1:09—Breasts while in bathtub and making love in bed with Keith Coogan.
- •• 1:26—Breasts, while making love in bed with Coogan.

Forever Lulu (1987)

Annie Golden . . . . Diana

Deborah Harry. . . . . Lulu

Hanna Schygulla . . . . Elaine
- 1:03—Brief breasts in and getting out of bubble bath.

Forrest Gump *(1994)*

Sally Field . . . . Mrs. Gump
Danté McCarthy . . . . Topless Girl
- 0:36—Very, very brief left breast, while bending over to grab money out of customer's hands when Tom Hanks first enters club. Medium long shot.

Tiffany Salerno . . . . Carla
Marla Sucharetza. . . . . Lenore
Robin Wright. . . . . Jenny Curran
- 0:36—Brief upper half of buns, while sitting on stage, playing a guitar in a club.
- 0:37—Very brief buns and side view of breasts, after pushing guitar into Tom Hanks and walking off the stage.

Fort Apache, The Bronx *(1981)*

Kathleen Beller . . . . Theresa
Pam Grier . . . . Charlotte
Rachel Ticotin . . . . Isabelle
- 1:25—Brief upper half of breasts in bathtub while Paul Newman pours bubble bath in.

Fortress *(1993; U.S./Australian)*

Loryn Locklin. . . . . Karen Brennick
- 0:18—Lower half of buns, under lingerie while making love on top of Christopher Lambert in bed.

• **Fortress of Amerikkka** *(1989)*

Kascha. . . . . Elizabeth
- 0:37—Breasts and buns, when waking up from tent.
- •• 0:38—Brief breasts, while flashing her boyfriend in the woods and making out with him.
- •• 0:59—Breasts, while making out with Mercenary in tent.

Tiffany Paulsen . . . . Photographer's Assistant

Four Friends *(1981)*

Jodi Thelen . . . . Georgia
- •• 0:17—Left breast in open blouse three times with her three male friends.

Four Rooms *(1995)*

Madonna . . . . Elspeth
Jennifer Beals. . . . . Angela
Sammi Davis-Voss . . . . Jezebel
- ••• 0:10—Breasts, after taking off her top during witch ceremony.
- ••• 0:12—Breasts, while pouring sweat into cauldron and watching Ione Skye do her part.

Amanda de Cadenet . . . . Diana
Valeria Golino . . . . Athena
Salma Hayek . . . . TV Dancing Girl
Ione Skye. . . . . Eva
- ••• 0:10—Breasts, after taking off her top during witch ceremony.
- ••• 0:13—Breasts, when she's about to pour her part of the ceremony into the cauldron.
- •• 0:14—Breasts, while alone in hotel room with Tim Roth.
- ••• 0:18—Breasts, after taking off jacket and seducing Roth using witchcraft.

Lili Taylor. . . . . Raven
Tamlyn Tomita . . . . Wife

Four Seasons *(1981)*

Bess Armstrong . . . . Ginny Newley
- 0:38—Brief buns, twice, while skinny dipping in the water with Nick.

Rita Moreno. . . . . Claudia Zimmer
- 0:48—Brief buns, twice, in water while skinny dipping with Jack Weston.

The Fourth Man *(1984; Dutch)*

Reneé Soutendijk. . . . . Christine
- ••• 0:27—Full frontal nudity removing robe, brief buns in bed, side view left breast, then breasts in bed with Gerard.
- 0:32—Brief left breast in bed with Gerard after he hallucinates and she cuts his penis off.
- ••• 0:53—Left breast, then right breast in red dress when Gerard opens her dress.
- 1:11—Breasts making love with Herman while Gerard watches through keyhole.

The Fourth Protocol *(1987; British)*

Joanna Cassidy. . . . . Vassilieva
- 1:39—Brief left breast. She's lying dead in Pierce Brosnan's bathtub.
- 1:49—Same thing, different angle.

The Fox *(1967)*

Anne Heywood . . . . March
- •• 0:10—Right breast seen in reflection in mirror. Long shot of buns, when standing in front of mirror. Breasts, while rubbing lotion on herself. More buns, after the lights go out. Very impressive for 1967!
- 1:28—Very brief, partial squished left breast, while making love with Kier Dullea.

Fox Style *(1974)*

Jovita Bush. . . . . Bonnie
- 1:02—Brief right breast while in dressing room, changing clothes.

Denise Denise . . . . Cindy
- 0:42—Brief breasts rolling over on her stomach on river bank with A. J.
- 1:21—Most of right breast, while in bed with A.J.

• **Foxfire** *(1996)*

Maria Celedonio . . . . Zoe
Angelina Jolie. . . . . Legs Sadovsky
- ••• 0:37—Breasts, taking off her T-shirt and giving herself and her girl friends tattoos.

Barbara Niven . . . . Goldie's Stepmother
Jenny Shimizu . . . . Goldie Goldman
- ••• 0:42—Breasts, while sitting and getting a tattoo, then watching Rita get a tattoo.

Foxtrap *(1986; U.S./Italian)*

Beatrice Palme. . . . . Marianna
- •• 0:41—Brief breasts and buns in bed with Fred Williamson, then more breasts making love.

Lela Rochon. . . . . Lindy

Foxy Brown *(1974)*

Juanita Brown . . . . Claudia
Pam Grier . . . . Foxy Brown
- 0:05—Breasts, getting out of bed and taking off nightgown.
- 0:40—Brief left breast, while getting dressed.
- ••• 1:05—Right breast, then breasts rolling over in bed.

Kimberly Hyde. . . . . Jennifer

Brenda Venus . . . . .Arabella

Frame by Frame
(1995; Made for Cable Movie; Canadian)
a.k.a. Conundrum

Marg Helgenberger. . . . . .Rose Ekberg
- ••• 0:38—Brief breasts, several times, while sitting in bathtub then standing up when startled by Michael Biehn.
- •• 0:53—Left breast, three times, while making love in bed with Biehn.

Karen Waddell. . . . . .Julie Horak
- • 0:33—Brief buns, while hanging dead, upside down in room, when discovered by Michael Biehn. Probably a stunt woman.
- • 1:23—Brief breasts in B&W photos (face has been scratched off) that Marg Helgenberger looks at.

Frame Up (1990)

Frances Fisher . . . . Jo Westlake
- •• 0:52—Breasts, lying back in bed with Wings Hauser.
- •• 0:54—Left breast, while lying in bed with Hauser.

Frances (1982)

Anjelica Huston . . . . Hospital Sequence: Mental Patient

Jessica Lange . . . . Frances Farmer
- • 0:41—Very brief upper half of left breast, while lying on bed and throwing a newspaper.
- • 0:50—Brief full frontal nudity covered with bubbles standing up in bathtub and wrapping a towel around herself. Long shot, hard to see.
- • 1:01—Brief buns and right breast running into the bathroom when the police bust in. Very, very brief full frontal nudity, then buns closing the bathroom door. Reportedly her, even though you don't see her face clearly.

Frank and I (1983)

Sophie Favier. . . . . Maud
- • 0:16—Nude, undressing then breasts lying in bed with Charles.
- • 0:40—Brief breasts in bed with Charles.

Jennifer Inch . . . . Frank/Frances
- • 0:10—Brief buns, getting pants pulled down for a spanking.
- ••• 0:22—Nude getting undressed and walking to the bed.
- • 0:24—Briefly nude when Charles pulls the sheets off her.
- • 0:32—Brief buns, getting spanked by two older women.
- ••• 0:38—Full frontal nudity getting out of bed and walking to Charles at the piano.
- •• 0:45—Full frontal nudity lying on her side by the fireplace. Dark, hard to see.
- •• 1:09—Brief breasts making love with Charles on the floor.
- ••• 1:11—Nude taking off her clothes and walking toward Charles at the piano.

Frankenhooker (1990)

Lia Chang . . . . .Crystal
- • 0:38—Buns, when Jeffrey draws a check mark on her.
- • 0:40—Brief buns, fighting with the other girls over the drugs.

Vicki Darnell . . . . Sugar
- • 0:36—Brief middle part of each breast through slit bra during introduction to Jeffrey.
- •• 0:37—Breasts, sticking out of black lingerie while getting legs measured.
- • 0:38—Right breast, while sitting in chair.
- • 0:39—Breasts through slit lingerie three times while folding clothes.
- • 0:40—Buns, when fighting over drugs.
- ••• 0:41—Very brief right breast, sitting on bed (on the right) enjoying drugs. Breasts dancing with the other girls.

Jennifer Delora. . . . . Angel
- • 0:36—Brief breasts during introduction to Jeffrey.
- ••• 0:41—Breasts dancing in room with the other hookers. (Nice tattoos!)

Charlotte J. Helmcamp . . . . .Honey
- •• 0:26—Breasts yanking down her top outside of Jeffrey's car window.

Heather Hunter . . . . Chartreuse
- • 0:36—Brief breasts during introduction to Jeffrey.
- • 0:37—Brief breasts bending over behind Sugar.
- ••• 0:41—Brief breasts and buns, running in front of bed. A little blurry. Then breasts and buns dancing with the other girls.
- • 0:43—Breasts dodging flying leg with Sugar.
- •• 0:44—Breasts, crawling on the floor.

Patty Mullen . . . . .Elizabeth
- •• 1:01—Breasts and buns in garter belt and stockings, in room with a customer.

Susan Napoli . . . . .Anise
- • 0:42—Brief left breast on bed with Amber, taking off her top. Brief breasts after Angel explodes.
- • 0:43—Breasts, kneeling on bed screaming before exploding.

Kimberly Taylor . . . . Amber
- • 0:36—Brief left breast in green top during introduction to Jeffrey.
- •• 0:37—Brief breasts during exam by Jeffrey. Then breasts getting breasts measured with calipers.
- • 0:41—Brief right breast, twice, enjoying drugs.
- •• 0:42—Breasts, getting off bed and onto another bed with Anise.
- • 0:43—Breasts kneeling in bed screaming before exploding.

Frankenstein General Hospital (1988)

Rebunkah Jones. . . . . Elizabeth Rice
- •• 1:05—Breasts in the office letting Mark Blankfield examine her back.

Kathy Shower . . . . Dr. Alice Singleton
- • 1:15—Brief breasts running out of her office after the monster, putting her lab coat on.

Frankenstein Unbound (1990)

Myriam Cyr . . . . Information Officer

Bridget Fonda . . . . .Mary

Catherine Rabett . . . . .Elizabeth

1:10—Very brief left breast, while lying dead after getting shot by Frankenstein. Unappealing looking because of all the gruesome make-up.

Terri Treas . . . . Computer Voice

Frankie Starlight (1995; Irish/British)

Georgina Cates . . . . Young Emma
- • 0:42—Side view of right breast, while bathing herself.

Anne Parillaud . . . . Bernadette

Barbara Alyn Woods . . . . Marcia

Frantic (1988)

Emmanuelle Seigner . . . . Michelle
- • 1:02—Brief side view of right breast, while changing blouses in bedroom.

Tina Sportolaro . . . . .TWA Clerk

Alexandra Stewart . . . . Edie

Fraternity Vacation (1985)

Barbara Crampton . . . . Chrissie

••• 0:16—Breasts and buns in bedroom with two guys taking off her swimsuit.

Kathleen Kinmont . . . . Marianne

••• 0:16—Breasts and buns, after taking off her swimsuit in bedroom with two guys.

Julie Payne . . . . Naomi Tvedt

Sheree Wilson . . . . Ashley Taylor

• 0:47—Breasts and buns of body double (Roberta Whitewood), while in the bedroom when the guys photograph her with a telephoto lens.

Freddy's Dead: The Final Nightmare (1991)

Lezlie Deane . . . . Tracy

Linnea Quigley . . . . Soul from Freddy's Chest

• 1:25—Brief breasts, struggling in Freddy's stomach during the end credits special-effects review.

Lisa Zane . . . . Maggie Burroughs

Free Ride (1986)

Tally Chanel . . . . Candy

• 0:53—Brief buns, wearing G-string, taking off her clothes on porch. Long shot.

• 0:57—Brief breasts in bedroom with Dan.

Elizabeth Cochrell . . . . Nude Girl #1

• 0:25—Brief buns taking a shower with another girl.

Rebecca Lynn . . . . Nude Girl #2

• 0:25—Brief buns taking a shower with another girl.

Renée Props . . . . Kathy

• 0:13—Brief breasts in the shower while Dan watches.

Freebie and the Bean (1974)

Sacheen Littlefeather . . . . n.a.

Kathryn Witt . . . . Whitey's Girl

•• 0:16—Buns, while tied up in bed when James Caan tries to get Whitey to talk.

Freefall (1993)

Pamela Gidley . . . . Katy Mazur

• 0:29—Brief back side of left breast and upper half of buns, while making love with Eric Roberts in bed. Almost breasts when Roberts lies back down. Breasts later on don't show her face.

• 0:40—Right breast with Roberts in flashback. Don't see her face again.

Terri Norton . . . . Susan

Jennifer Steyn . . . . Secretary

Freelance (1970; British)

a.k.a. Con Man

Luan Peters . . . . Rosemary

• 0:25—Right breast and buns, while making love with Gary and Mitch.

• 0:26—Left breast, twice, while making love with Gary and Mitch.

Freeway (1988)

Darlanne Fluegel . . . . Sarah "Sunny" Harper

• 0:27—In bra in bathroom taking a pill, then very, very brief right breast, getting into bed.

• 0:28—Brief left breast putting on robe and getting out of bed.

French Postcards (1979)

Marie-France Pisier . . . . Madame Tessier

•• 0:16—In white bra, then breasts in dressing room while a guy watches without her knowing.

Valerie Quennessen . . . . Toni

Debra Winger . . . . Melanie

French Quarter (1978)

Lindsay Bloom . . . . "Big Butt" Annie/Policewoman in Bar

Susan Clark . . . . Bag Stealer/Sue

Alisha Fontaine . . . . Gertrude "Trudy" Dix/Christine Delaplane

• 0:12—Dancing on stage for the first time. Buns in G-string. Breasts in large black pasties.

• 0:47—Brief left breast several times, posing for Mr. Beloq.

• 0:49—Left breast again.

•• 1:13—Breasts during auction.

•• 1:18—Brief breasts, then buns making love with Bruce Davison, then breasts again.

• 1:26—Brief breasts getting her top pulled down during party.

• 1:31—Brief breasts getting tied down during voodoo ceremony.

•• 1:32—More breasts tied down during ceremony.

Ann Michelle . . "Coke Eye" Laura/Policewoman in French Hotel

• 0:42—Right breast, when Josie wakes her up.

••• 0:43—Breasts in bed, caressing Josie's breasts.

•• 0:58—Breasts during voodoo ceremony. Close ups of breasts with snake.

• 1:19—Brief breasts, sitting in bed.

••• 1:20—More breasts sitting in bed, talking to a customer. Long scene.

Laura Misch Owens . . . . "Ice Box" Josie/Girl on Bus

• 0:41—Breasts under sheer white nightgown.

••• 0:43—Full frontal nudity taking off nightgown, wearing garter belt. Getting into bed with Laura.

• *French Twist* (1996; French)

Victoria Abril . . . . Loli

•• 0:19—Full frontal nudity, while in bed with her husband.

• 0:23—Very brief left breast, when getting back into bed.

• 0:45—Left breast, while sitting in bathtub with Marijo.

•• 0:58—Brief buns and very, very brief side of right breast, when leaving the room.

• 1:00—Very brief buns, when standing up to make love with her husband.

•• 1:01—Nude, getting out of bed and walking around the house.

• 1:04—Buns visible through opening in apron.

• 1:06—Brief buns, when turning over on couch with her husband. Long shot. Very, very brief partial breasts, when sitting up.

Josiane Balasko . . . . Marijo

• 0:46—Partial right breast, while sitting in bathtub with Victoria Abril.

Katrine Boorman . . . . Emily Crumble

The French Woman (1979)

a.k.a. Madame Claude

Marie-Christine Deshayes . . . . Florence

•• 0:45—Breasts on bed dressed as a guy with a man dressed as a woman.

Dayle Haddon . . . . Elizabeth

• 0:15—Very, very brief breasts in dressing room.

•• 0:49—Breasts on bed with Madame Claude.

• 0:55—Breasts kissing Pierre, then buns while lying on the floor.

- 1:11—Left breast, then buns at the beach with Frederick.

Vibeke Knudsen . . . . Anne-Marie
- 0:04—Breasts in chair in office with Robert Webber.
- 0:09—Breasts walking on beach with Japanese Businessman.
- ••• 0:11—Breasts on bed with David while she talks on the telephone. Then hot scene making love with him in the shower.
- 1:19—Breasts in bed with a customer when David comes over.

Frenzy (1972; British)

Barbara Leigh-Hunt. . . . . Brenda Blaney
- 0:31—Left breast, while sitting in chair with the necktie killer. Don't see her face.

Anna Massey. . . . . .Babs Milligan
- •• 0:45—Breasts getting out of bed and then buns, walking to the bathroom. Probably a body double.

• *Fresh Kill (1994)*

Sarita Choudhury . . . . Shareen Lightfoot
Marlene Forté . . . . Pam Mandel
Erin McMurtry. . . . . .Claire Mayakovsky
- •• 0:13—Very brief breasts, when falling back onto bed. Breasts, while lying in bed next to Sarita Choudhurry.

• *Friction (1995)*

a.k.a. Lap Dance
(Unrated version reviewed.)

Holiday Hopke . . . . .Ophelia
- 0:27—Brief breasts, while dancing on stage in club.
- ••• 0:35—Breasts and buns, while making love with Denise in bed while Mr. Franklin watches.
- •• 0:52—Breasts and buns in T-back, while dancing on stage.

Tonya Moon . . . . Glitter Dome Dancer

Friday Foster (1975)

Pam Grier . . . . Friday Foster
- ••• 0:29—Breasts, several times, while taking a shower while Carl Weathers stalks around in her apartment.
- ••• 1:12—Upper half of breast, while in bubble bath with Blake. Breasts in bed with him.

Alice Jubert . . . . Senator Hart's Secretary
Rosalind Miles . . . . Clorils Boston
- 0:20—Brief side view of left breast, while changing clothes backstage. Slightly out of focus.

Friday the 13th, Part II (1981)

Kirsten Baker . . . . Terry
- •• 0:45—Breasts and buns taking off clothes to go skinny dipping.
- 0:47—Very brief breasts jumping up in the water.
- 0:48—Full frontal nudity and buns getting out of the water. Long shot.

Marta Kober . . . . Sandra

Friday the 13th, Part III (1982)

Annie Gaybis. . . . . Cashier
Tracy Savage. . . . . Debbie
- 0:59—Brief breasts, while getting back into the shower after shutting the door.
- 1:00—Very brief right breast, while getting towel.

Friday the 13th, Part IV—The Final Chapter (1984)

Judie Aronson . . . . Samantha
- 0:26—Brief breasts and very brief buns taking clothes off to go skinny dipping.
- 0:29—Brief breasts under water pretending to be dead.
- •• 0:39—Breasts and brief buns taking off her T-shirt to go skinny dipping at night.

Kimberly Beck . . . . Trish
Barbara Howard . . . . Sara
- 1:01—Buns, through shower door.

Camilla More. . . . . Tina
- 0:26—Very brief breasts in the lake jumping up with her twin sister to show they are skinny dipping. Very brief buns, when diving under the water.
- 0:48—Left breast, in bed with Crispin Glover.

Carey More . . . . Terri
- 0:26—Very brief breasts in the lake jumping up with her twin sister to show they are skinny dipping. Very brief buns, when diving under the water.

Friday the 13th, Part VII: The New Blood (1988)

Kimberly Beck . . . . Tricia/Prologue
Darcy De Moss . . . . Nikki/Prologue
Elizabeth Kaitan. . . . . Robin
- 0:53—Brief right breast, while making love in bed with a guy.
- 0:55—Brief breasts, while sitting up in bed after making love when the sheet falls down.
- •• 1:00—Brief breasts again, while sitting up in bed and putting a shirt on over her head.

Heidi Kozak . . . . Sandra
- 0:36—Buns, while taking off clothes to go skinny dipping. Briefly nude, three times, under water just before getting killed by Jason.

• *Friday the 13th, Part VIII—Jason Takes Manhattan (1989)*

Tiffany Paulsen . . . . .Suzi
- 0:03—Side view of left breast and upper half of buns in boat with Jim.

Friday the 13th, Part V—A New Beginning (1985)

Juliette Cummins. . . . . Robin
- ••• 1:01—Breasts, wearing panties getting undressed and climbing into bed just before getting killed.
- 1:05—Very brief breasts, covered with blood when Reggie discovers her dead.

Melanie Kinnaman . . . . Pam Roberts
Deborah Voorhees. . . . . Tina
- ••• 0:41—Breasts after making love with Eddie, then lying down and relaxing just before getting killed.
- 0:43—Buns and brief left breast when Eddie turns her over and discovers her dead.

Rebecca Wood . . . . Lana
- 0:33—Brief breasts opening her dress while changing to go out with Billy.

Friend of the Family (1995)

a.k.a. Elke's Erotic Nights
(Unrated version reviewed.)

Lisa Boyle . . . . .Montana
- •• 0:02—Breasts, while making out with a guy in the pool at night, then during argument with Linda.
- ••• 0:23—Breasts and buns, while making love outside on the grass at night with another guy.
- ••• 0:35—Breasts, while making love in the back seat of a convertible car with a guy.

Griffin Drew . . . . Linda
- ••• 0:05—Breasts, while making love with Montana's boyfriend in bed in dream.

- ••• 0:10—In sheer white nightgown, then breasts on balcony with her husband in flashback.
- ••• 0:44—Nude, while making love with Elke in bathtub. Nice, long scene.
- ••• 1:19—Nude, while making love with her husband in bed.

Betsy Monroe . . . . Nancy

Shauna O'Brien . . . . Elke

- ••• 0:25—Breasts and buns in panties, when dancing next to swimming pool at night, while Jeff watches from the house.
- ••• 0:39—In red, two piece swimsuit, then breasts with Jeff in Linda's dream.
- • 0:43—Brief breasts, while getting out of bed.
- ••• 0:44—Full frontal nudity, while making love with Linda in bathtub. Nice, long scene.
- ••• 0:53—In white two piece swimsuit while dancing next to pool, then breasts and buns.
- • 0:56—Buns in swimsuit, while next to pool, talking to Jeff.
- ••• 1:04—Nude, while making love with Jeff in bed.
- • 1:14—Brief breasts and buns in swimsuit on TV when Josh shows his video work to Laura.

Raelyn Saalman . . . . Laura

- •• 1:15—Buns in swimsuit bottom and brief breasts, while dancing around for Josh and his video camera.
- ••• 1:35—Nude, while in bedroom, making love with Josh.

• Friend of the Family 2 *(1996)*

a.k.a. Innocence Betrayed

Jenna Bodnar. . . . . Maddy

- • 0:21—Left breast when starting to make love with Alex in bed.
- ••• 0:30—In lingerie, then breasts and buns, while making love with Alex in bed.

Shauna O'Brien . . . . Linda

- ••• 0:08—In bra and panties, then buns and breasts, while making love with Alex.
- •• 0:13—Buns and breasts, while making love with Alex.
- ••• 0:49—Nude, while making love in bed with Alex.
- • 0:52—Brief buns in panties, while standing in bedroom in front of Alex.
- • 0:55—Buns in panties, in room with Byron.
- ••• 0:57—In bra and panties, then nude, while making love with Byron.
- ••• 1:14—In bra and panties, then breasts and buns, while making love with Mark in office.

Friendly Favors *(1983)*

a.k.a. Six Swedes on a Pump

Brigitte Lahaie . . . . Greta

- •• 0:02—Full frontal nudity riding a guy in bed. (She's wearing a necklace.)
- ••• 0:39—Full frontal nudity having fun on "exercise bike."
- ••• 0:46—Full frontal nudity taking off clothes and running outside with the other girls. Nice slow motion shots.
- •• 0:53—Breasts, making love with Kerstin.
- ••• 1:01—Full frontal nudity in room with the Italian.
- ••• 1:15—Full frontal nudity in room with guy from the band.

From Beyond *(1986)*

Barbara Crampton. . . . . Dr. Katherine McMichaels

- •• 0:44—Brief breasts after getting blouse torn off by the creature in the laboratory.
- • 0:51—Buns, while getting on top of Jeffrey Combs in black leather outfit.

Frozen Terror *(1980; Italian)*

a.k.a. Macabro

Bernice Stegers . . . . Jane Baker

- •• 0:08—Breasts, while taking off her slip in bedroom and putting on night gown.
- • 0:10—Brief right breast, while making love in bed with Fred.
- • 0:40—Briefly nude, while getting up out of bathtub.

• Fugitive Rage *(1996)*

Nikki Fritz . . . . Nurse Wendy

- • 0:13—Brief buns in white lingerie outfit, after taking off nurse outfit in bedroom with Jay Richardson.
- •• 0:34—Left breast, while in bathtub with Richardson. Brief breasts, when getting out of the bathtub and buns, while walking down the hall.

Toni Naples . . . . Helga

Shauna O'Brien . . . . Josie Williams

Wendy Schumacher. . . . . Tara McCormick

- •• 0:11—Breasts, during search.
- ••• 1:03—Nude, while taking a shower with James, then making love on bed with him.

Full Body Massage *(1995; Made for Cable Movie)*

Elizabeth Barondes. . . . . Alice

- • 0:22—Brief breasts, while sitting in pond with Bryan Brown. Medium long shot.
- • 0:36—Nude, taking off towel, and lying on ground for Hopi Medicine Man. Medium long shot.
- •• 0:51—Breasts, while making love with Bryan Brown in bed.
- •• 0:58—Breasts, while in pond with Brown.

Mimi Rogers . . . . Nina

- •• 0:07—Buns in panties, then breasts, while looking at herself in the mirror. Buns, taking off towel and stepping into hot tub.
- • 0:12—Brief buns, while lying outside in flashback.
- • 0:26—Brief buns, while lying on table, getting massaged by Douglas in flashback.
- • 0:44—Very brief, partial left breast, while rolling over onto her stomach.
- •• 0:47—Right breast and most of left breast, while lying on her back on table.
- • 0:50—Buns, while lying on table.
- ••• 0:52—Buns, while lying on table, getting massaged by Brown.
- • 0:54—Buns, while walking to get her robe.
- •• 0:58—Breasts, while getting massaged by Brown.
- ••• 1:01—Breasts, while sitting and getting massaged by Brown.
- • 1:08—Brief buns, while lying on the table.
- ••• 1:12—Buns, when getting massaged. Breasts, while getting massaged by Douglas, then Brown. Oh my!
- • 1:15—Very brief right breast, then buns, getting up off the table.

Laura Saldivar . . . . Young Nina

- •• 0:48—Nude, while standing in room with a guy. Don't see her face.

Full Contact *(1992)*

Denise Buick . . . . Tori

- ••• 0:31—Buns in T-back, then in bra, then breasts, while doing strip routine on stage.
- •• 0:39—Buns in T-back and breasts while dancing on stage.
- •• 1:02—Breasts and buns, while making love with Luke.

• *The Funeral* (1996)
Gretchen Mol . . . . Helen
Isabella Rossellini . . . . Clara
Annabella Sciorra . . . . Jean
Amber Smith . . . . Bridgette
••• 0:31—Breasts, while having sex in bed with Paul Hipp, while Vincent Gallo talks to him.

The Funhouse (1981)
Elizabeth Berridge . . . . Amy Harper
•• 0:03—Brief breasts taking off robe to get into the shower, then very brief breasts getting out to chase Joey.
Sylvia Miles . . . . Madame Zena

The Further Adventures of Tennessee Buck (1987)
Kathy Shower . . . . Barbara Manchester
••• 0:57—Breasts getting rubbed with oil by the cannibal women. Nice close up shots.
•• 1:02—Breasts in a hut with the Chief of the tribe.

Future Hunters (1987)
Linda Carol . . . . Michelle
• 0:35—Very brief right breast and lower frontal nudity, stepping through doorway and wrapping robe around herself.
•• 0:36—Breasts in open robe in hotel room with the bad guys.

Future Kick (1991)
Linda Doná . . . . Tye
Maria Ford . . . . Dancer
Meg Foster . . . . Nancy Morgan
Lisa Glaser . . . . Dancer
• 0:36—Breasts, dancing on stage in white outfit. (Taken from *Stripped to Kill II*.)

Future Shock (1993)
Amanda Foreman . . . . Paula
Pamela Runo . . . . Model
Julie Strain . . . . Female Dancer
• 0:03—Brief buns in sexy black G-string outfit with black top, while dancing in front of guy sitting in electric chair.

The G.I. Executioner (1971)
a.k.a. Wit's End
a.k.a. Dragon Lady
Angelique Pettyjohn . . . . Bonnie
•• 0:16—Doing a strip routine on stage. Buns in G-string, very brief side view of right breast, then breasts at end.
•• 0:40—Breasts, lying asleep in bed.
••• 0:58—Breasts and buns, undressing in front of Dave, getting into bed, fighting an attacker and getting shot. Long scene.
• 1:14—Breasts, lying shot in rope net.
Victoria Racimo . . . . Foon Mae Lee
• 0:12—Nude in bathroom mirror getting dressed.
• 0:54—Brief breasts undressing and getting into bed. (See reflection in glass on headboard.)
• 1:15—Sort of buns, lying in Dave's lap. Then left breast.
• 1:18—Buns, while tied up by wrists. Sort of breasts being turned around (hair is in the way).
Janet Wood . . . . Cynthia Jordan
•• 0:29—Breasts and buns in bed with Dave.

• *G.I. Jane* (1997)
Demi Moore . . . . Lt. Jordan O'Neil
• 1:00—Brief buns, while in the shower. Dark.

Gabriela (1984; Brazilian)
Sonia Braga . . . . Gabriela
•• 0:26—Breasts leaning back out the window making love on a table with Marcello Mastroianni.
••• 0:27—Nude, taking a shower outside and cleaning herself up.
• 0:32—Right breast in bed.
•• 0:38—Nude, making love with Mastroianni on the kitchen table.
•• 0:45—Nude, getting in bed with Mastroianni.
• 1:13—Full frontal nudity, on bed with another man, then getting beaten up by Mastroianni.
••• 1:17—Nude, changing clothes in the bedroom.
•• 1:32—Breasts and buns making love outside with Mastroianni. Lots of passion!

Gaby, A True Story (1987)
Rachel Levin . . . . Gaby
• 0:56—Right breast, then breasts on the floor making love with another handicapped boy, Fernando.
Liv Ullmann . . . . Sari Brimmer

Galactic Gigolo (1988)
a.k.a. Club Earth
LeeAnne Baker . . . . Lucy
• 0:08—Breasts in hot tub behind Eoj.
Ruth Corrine Collins . . . . Dr. Ruth Pepper
•• 0:47—Breasts, while stripping in front of Eoj.
• 0:49—Breasts, while getting tied up by Sammy.
• 0:53—Breasts in open cape while in the Goldberg's family room.
•• 0:55—Breasts, while getting rescued.
Courtney James . . . . Lisa
Angela Nicholas . . . . Peggy Sue Peggy
• 0:21—Brief right breast in open blouse leaving room with Eoj.
Karen Nielsen . . . . Kathy/Cheerleader
•• 0:27—Breasts (she's on the left) while in hot tub with Eoj and Sandy.
Lisa Petruno . . . . Sandy
•• 0:27—Breasts (she's on the right) while in hot tub with Eoj and Kathy.

• *Galaxy Girls* (1995)
Gail Harris . . . . Cindy
••• 1:15—Breasts, while making love with Matt.
Yvette McClendon . . . . Shauna
••• 0:19—Breasts, while in the bathtub with Becky.
Monique Parent . . . . Janet
•• 0:01—Buns and breasts, while taking a shower, then dressing.
Raelyn Saalman . . . . Ginnie
•• 0:22—Nude, while bathing in a stream by herself.
Lesli Kay Sterling . . . . Laticia
••• 0:11—Breasts, while sunbathing outdoors and talking to the girls.
• 0:21—Brief breasts, while sitting and chanting.

Galaxy of Terror (1981)
Taaffe O'Connell . . . . Damelia
•• 0:42—Breasts getting raped by a giant alien slug. Nice and slimy.
• 0:46—Buns, covered with slime being discovered by her crew mates.

The Game is Over (1966)

Jane Fonda . . . . Renee Saccard
- • 0:15—Very brief left breast, getting out of bed. Breasts in mirror when running to the door.
- • 0:16—Brief breasts, several times, while behind sheer white curtain.
- • 0:17—Very brief breasts, while falling onto bed.
- •• 0:18—Breasts, while lying in bed with the guy.

Game of Seduction (1976)

Nathalie Delon . . . . Countess Flora De Saint Gilles
Sylvia Kristel . . . . Madame Leroy
- ••• 0:43—Full frontal nudity, while making love with Charles.
- • 0:46—Breasts, while making love on top of Charles.
- ••• 0:47—Breasts, after getting out of trunk and sitting on chair, talking to Charles. More breasts while on the bed.

Games Girls Play (1974; British)

a.k.a. The Bunny Caper
a.k.a. Sex Play

Erin Geraghty . . . . Ducky
- • 1:11—In bra and panties, then breasts running around outside.

Christina Hart . . . . Bunny O'Hara
- • 0:00—Brief lower frontal nudity and buns when her dress blows up from the wind.
- •• 0:01—Full frontal nudity in slow motion, jumping into bed. Then nude, twirling around in another room.
- ••• 0:18—Nude, undressing with the other girls, then walking around the house to the pool, then swimming nude.
- • 1:01—Brief breasts getting dressed.

Games That Lovers Play (1970)

Penny Brahms . . . . Constance
- •• 0:08—Breasts outside with a customer.
- •• 0:10—Breasts again putting dress back on.

Joanna Lumley. . . . . Fanny
- •• 0:17—Nude, getting out of bed and putting on robe.
- • 0:50—Right breast, while in bed with Jonathan.
- •• 1:18—Breasts sitting in bed, talking on the phone.
- •• 1:29—Brief breasts several times in bed with Constance and a guy. Breasts after and during the end credits.

• *Gang Related* (1997)

Lela Rochon . . . . Cynthia
- • 0:00—Buns in T-back, while dancing on stage.
- • 0:21—Buns in T-back, while dancing on stage. Nice moves!
- • 1:38—Brief buns in T-back, while dancing on stage.

The Garden of the Finzi-Continis (1971; Italian/German)

Dominique Sanda . . . . Micol
- • 1:12—Breasts, while sitting on a bed after turning a light on so the guy standing outside can see her.

Gas Pump Girls (1978)

Kirsten Baker . . . . June
- • 0:05—Breasts, when her graduation gown gets torn off during ceremony, after April's.
- • 0:32—Brief right breast, when sitting up in car.
- • 0:48—Brief breasts, three times, while walking back and forth past doorway to distract Bruno.

Sandy Johnson . . . . April
- •• 0:05—Breasts, when her graduation gown gets torn off during ceremony.
- • 0:06—Breasts, when changing clothes in locker room while talking with her girlfriends.
- •• 0:30—Breasts, while in back seat of car on hydraulic lift, then in the front seat with Michael.

Rikki Marin. . . . . January
- • 0:49—Brief breasts after opening her blouse, in doorway to distract Moiv.

Gas, Food, Lodging (1992)

Brooke Adams . . . . Nora
Fairuza Balk . . . . Shade
Mariah O'Brien . . . . Ivy
Ione Skye. . . . . Trudi
- ••• 0:38—Breasts, taking off her blouse in a cave with her boyfriend, then making love.
- • 0:40—Brief right breast, while sitting up.

Gator Bait (1973)

Janit Baldwin . . . . Julie
- •• 0:27—Breasts and buns walking into a pond, then getting out and getting dressed.
- • 0:35—Very brief right breast, twice, popping out of her dress when the bad guys hold her.
- • 0:40—Brief left breast struggling against two guys on the bed.

Claudia Jennings . . . . Desiree Tibidoe
- • 0:06—Brief left and right breasts during boat chase sequence.

Gator Bait II—Cajun Justice (1988)

Jan MacKenzie. . . . . Angelique
- •• 0:34—Buns and side view of left breast, taking a bath outside. Brief breasts a couple of times while the bad guys watch.
- • 0:41—Brief side view of left breast taking off towel in front of the bad guys.
- • 1:05—Brief buns occasionally when her blouse flips up during boat chase.

The Gauntlet (1977)

Sondra Locke. . . . . Gus Mally
- •• 1:10—Brief right breast, then breasts getting raped by two biker guys in a box car while Clint Eastwood is tied up.

The Gay Deceivers (1969)

Jeanne Baird . . . . Mrs. Conway
- • 0:51—Very brief buns, coming out of the bathroom and going back in when Danny shows up.

Jo Ann Harris . . . . Leslie Devlin
- •• 1:12—Breasts, after taking off her top in front of Elliott in his apartment.
- • 1:14—Very brief accidental left breast, when Danny grabs her arm.

Candice Rialson . . . . Uncredited Girl in Bikini

Gemini Affair (1974)

Kathy Kersh . . . . Jessica
- •• 0:11—Nude getting into bed with Kristen.
- • 0:12—Brief breasts turning over onto her stomach in bed.
- •• 0:17—Nude, standing up in bed and jumping off.
- ••• 0:57—Nude in bed with Kristen.
- •• 1:04—Left breast sitting up in bed after Kristen leaves.

Marta Kristen. . . . . Julie
- ••• 0:32—Breasts wearing beige panties talking with Jessica in the bathroom.
- • 0:56—Very, very brief left breast and lower frontal nudity standing next to bed with a guy. Very brief left breast in bed with him.

••• 0:59—Breasts and buns making love in bed with Jessica. Wowzers!

• Gentle Into the Night (1996)

Vittoria Belvedere . . . . .Serena
- • 1:03—Very brief right breast, while photographed in bed with a guy.
- • 1:15—Very brief right breast in B&W photo.

• Gentleman's Bet (1995)

Neith Hunter. . . . . Lauren Bernard
- •• 0:09—Nude, while taking a shower.
- •• 0:12—Breasts and buns, while starting to make love with her husband in the bathroom.
- ••• 0:24—Nude, while making love with her husband in bed (then with Chris after a camera trick).
- •• 0:33—Breasts, after taking off towel to put her bra and panties on. Brief buns in panties.
- • 0:42—Brief frontal nudity, while in bed with Chris in Paul's imagination.
- • 0:43—Brief breasts, while making love on the couch with Chris in Paul's imagination.
- •• 1:04—Buns and breasts, while making love with Chris on boat.
- • 1:14—Brief buns, while on top of Chris on boat.
- ••• 1:18—Nude, while making love with Jodie on bed.

Betsy Monroe . . . . Jodie
- • 0:37—Brief breasts, while sunbathing in backyard when talking with Paul.
- •• 0:47—Breasts and buns in panties, while in bedroom, waiting for Paul.
- • 0:49—Brief left breast, when play acting with Paul in the kitchen.
- ••• 0:50—Breasts and buns, while making love with Paul on pool table.
- • 1:08—Brief breasts under red plastic top after photo session.
- •• 1:18—Buns and breasts, while making love with Lauren on bed.
- • 1:20—Brief left breast in open robe while walking through house.

Bianca Rocilili . . . . .Uncredited Model
- • 1:05—Brief breasts, several times, under clear plastic top during photo session. (she's the only brunette.)

Genuine Risk (1989)

Michelle Johnson. . . . . Girl
- • 0:43—On bed in black bra and panties with Henry. Left breast peeking out of the top of her bra.

Georgia (1996)

Jennifer Jason Leigh. . . . . .Sadie
- •• 1:04—Upper half of buns and breasts, while making love in bed with her husband, Axel. Dark.

Mare Winningham . . . . .Georgia

Get Carter (1971; British)

Britt Ekland . . . . .Anna
- •• 0:39—Breasts, after taking off bra, and caressing herself while having phone sex with Michael Caine.

Geraldine Moffatt . . . . Glenda
- • 1:09—Brief buns and breast, while making love with Michael Caine.
- •• 1:10—Left breast, while lying in bed, talking with Caine, then nude, getting out of bed and walking to the bathroom.
- • 1:12—Brief breasts in B&W movie.
- • 1:14—Brief breasts, while sitting in bathtub.
- • 1:17—Breasts, when Caine pushes her under the water.

Geraldine Sherman . . . . Girl in Cafe

Get Out Your Handkerchiefs (1978)

Carole Laure . . . . .Solange
- •• 0:21—Breasts sitting in bed listening to her boyfriend talk.
- •• 0:31—Breasts sitting in bed knitting.
- • 0:41—Upper half of left breast in bed.
- •• 0:47—Left breast, while sitting in bed and the three guys talk.
- • 1:08—Brief right breast when the little boy peeks at her while she sleeps.
- • 1:10—Lower frontal nudity while he looks at her some more.
- ••• 1:17—Full frontal nudity taking off nightgown while sitting on bed for the little boy.

Get to Know Your Rabbit (1972)

Samantha Jones. . . . . Susan
- •• 0:27—Right breast, after taking the bra off.
- • 0:28—Right breast, while dancing with Smothers in the store.

Anne Randall . . . . Stewardess

Katharine Ross. . . . . Terrific-Looking Girl

Suzanne Zenor . . . . .Paula
- • 0:06—Very brief buns, getting out of bed.

The Getaway (1972)

Ali MacGraw . . . . .Carol McCoy
- • 0:19—Very brief left breast lying back in bed kissing McQueen.

Sally Struthers . . . . Fran Clinton

The Getaway (1993)

(Unrated version reviewed.)

Kim Basinger . . . . .Carol McCoy
- •• 0:18—In bra and panties in bedroom with Alec Baldwin, then nude (kind of silhouette).
- • 0:25—Very brief left breast and lower frontal nudity while pulling down towel behind steamy shower door. Hard to see.
- • 1:29—Side view of buns in the shower.
- ••• 1:30—Breasts and buns, while making love with Baldwin. Nice. Very, very brief lower frontal nudity.

Jennifer Tilly. . . . . .Fran Carvey
- •• 1:12—Breasts and buns while making love on top of Michael Madsen in bed while her husband is tied to chair in bathroom.

Getting It Right (1989)

Helena Bonham Carter . . . . Minerva Munday
- •• 0:18—Breasts a couple of times in bed talking to Gavin. It's hard to recognize her because she has lots of make-up on her face.

Jane Horrocks . . . . Jenny

Lynn Redgrave. . . . . Joan
- •• 0:46—Brief right breast, then brief breasts on couch seducing Gavin. More right breast shot when wrestling with him.

Getting Straight (1970)

Candice Bergen. . . . . Jan

Brenda Sykes . . . . Luan
- •• 0:53—Brief left breast, when scooting up in bed with Elliott Gould, then breasts, while getting back in bed.

Ghost Story (1981)

Alice Krige . . . . Alma/Eva
- • 0:41—Brief breasts making love in bedroom with Craig Wasson.
- •• 0:44—Breasts in bathtub with Wasson.
- •• 0:46—Breasts sitting up in bed.
- ••• 0:49—Buns, then breasts standing on balcony turning and walking to bedroom talking to Wasson.

Deborah Offner . . . . Helen

Ghosts Can't Do It (1989)

Bo Derek . . . . Kate
- ••• 0:26—In one piece swimsuit on beach, then full frontal nudity taking it off. Brief buns covered with sand on her back. Long scene.
- ••• 0:32—Breasts, sitting and washing herself. Very brief buns, jumping into tub.
- •• 0:48—Full frontal nudity taking a shower.
- • 0:49—Very, very brief breasts and buns jumping into pool. Long shot. Full frontal nudity under water.
- • 0:52—Very, very brief partial breasts pulling a guy into the pool
- •• 1:12—Breasts behind mosquito net with her boyfriend.

Julie Newmar . . . . Angel

• *Ghoulies III, Ghoulies Go To College* (1991)

Hope Marie Carlton . . . . Veronica
- • 0:25—Brief right breast, while lying in bed with her boyfriend.
- • 0:53—Buns in black panties, bra and stockings while dancing around in her bedroom. Almost breasts, after taking off her bra.
- • 0:55—Brief breasts, while dancing in her bedroom.
- • 0:57—Brief buns and breasts, while taking a shower.

Nicole Picard . . . . Party Girl

• *Gia* (1998; Made for Cable Movie)

Faye Dunaway . . . . Wilhelmina Cooper

Angelina Jolie . . . . Gia Marie Carangi
- •• 0:24—Breasts and buns in color and B&W while posing for photos in studio in front of a chain link fence.
- ••• 0:27—Buns and breasts, when talking with Linda in hallway.

Allison Mackie . . . . Red Dress Designer

Elizabeth Mitchell . . . . Linda
- • 0:25—In bra, then partial left breast, to pose with Angelina Jolie during photo session.
- • 0:26—Brief right breast, then brief breasts, while making love with Jolie.
- • 1:03—Brief buns, while standing in the shower with Jolie.

Joan Pringle . . . . Therapist at Rehab

Samantha Torres . . . . Patty (Model)

Kylie Travis . . . . Stephanie

Giant Steps (1992; Canadian)

Kristina Nicoll . . . . Tara Stewart
- • 0:33—Left breast, while lying on grass with Arva.
- • 0:34—Brief left breast, after Graeme wakes her up. Very brief right breast, while walking angrily away.

The Gift (1982; French)

Clio Goldsmith . . . . Barbara
- •• 0:39—Brief breasts several times in the bathroom, then right breast in bathtub.
- • 0:49—Breasts lying in bed sleeping.
- • 0:51—Very brief left breast, while turning over in bed.
- • 0:52—Brief right breast then buns, reaching for phone while lying in bed.
- • 1:16—Very brief left breast, when getting out of bed. Dark, hard to see.

Ginger (1970)

Cheri Caffaro . . . . Ginger
- ••• 1:06—Breasts, taking off her top in front of Rodney and lying on top of him in bed.
- •• 1:10—Full frontal nudity, getting up off the bed.
- • 1:22—Sort of breasts during recollection of her rape. Hard to see.
- • 1:23—Breasts, taking off her towel in front of Jimmy.
- ••• 1:32—Nude, on bed handcuffed behind her back by Rex, then getting molested by him. Long scene.

Michele Norris . . . . n.a.

Ginger Ale Afternoon (1989)

Yeardley Smith . . . . Bonnie Cleator
- • 0:53—Brief upper half of left breast, taking off top in trailer with Hank.

Girl 6 (1996)

Madonna . . . . Boss #3

Joie Lee . . . . Switchboard Operator

Debi Mazar . . . . Girl #39

Gretchen Mol . . . . Girl #12

Billie Neal . . . . Angela's Mother

Theresa Randle . . . . Girl 6
- ••• 0:06—Breasts, after taking off her dress top during audition interview.

Rita Wolf . . . . Wife of Indian Shopkeeper

The Girl from Petrovka (1974)

Goldie Hawn . . . . Oktyabrina
- • 1:30—Very, very brief breasts in bed with Hal Holbrook. Don't really see anything—it lasts for about one frame.

• *The Girl Gets Moe* (1997)

Elizabeth Barondes . . . . Monica
- • 0:41—Very brief left breast, while making love with Tony Danza. Don't see her face.

Christine Harnos . . . . Dotty

Amy Locane . . . . Beth

Emily Procter . . . . Tammy

The Girl in a Swing (1989; U.S./British)

Lynsey Baxter . . . . Barbara

Meg Tilly . . . . Karin Foster
- •• 0:44—In white bra, then breasts and buns.
- •• 0:50—Nude, while swimming under water.
- ••• 1:14—Breasts while sitting on swing, then making love.
- ••• 1:44—Breasts while at the beach.

The Girl in Blue (1973; Canadian)

a.k.a. U-turn

Maud Adams . . . . Paula/Tracy
- • 1:16—Side view of right breast, while sitting on bed with Scott.

Gay Rowan . . . . Bonnie
- • 0:06—Left breast, in bed with Scott.
- • 0:31—Brief breasts in bathtub.
- • 0:48—Right breast, while in shower talking to Scott. Brief breasts (long shot) on balcony throwing water down at him.
- • 1:21—Brief right breast and buns getting out of bed and running out of the room.

Girl on a Motorcycle (1968; French/British)

a.k.a. Naked Under Leather

Marianne Faithfull . . . . Rebecca
•• 0:05—Nude, getting out of bed and walking to the door.
• 0:38—Brief side view of left breast putting nightgown on.
• 1:23—Brief breasts while lying down and talking with Alain Delon.
• 1:30—Very brief right breast a couple of times making love with Delon.

Catherine Jourdan . . . . Catherine

A Girl to Kill For (1989)

Karen Medak . . . . Sue
••• 0:17—Breasts showering at the beach after surfing with Chuck.
•• 1:08—Breasts in spa when Chuck takes her shirt off. Then miscellaneous shots making love.

The Girl with the Hungry Eyes (1994)

Christina Fulton . . . . Louise
• 0:19—Brief buns, while putting panties on.
• 0:20—Breasts, while posing for Carlos.
• 1:06—Right breast, while making love in bed with Carlos. Lit with blue light.
• 1:18—Left breast, while lying in bed with Carlos.

Girlfriend from Hell (1989)

Lezlie Deane . . . . Diane
Christina Veronica . . . . Dancer
••• 1:17—Breasts dancing on stage in club.

Girlfriends (1978)

Melanie Mayron . . . . Susan Weinblatt
• 0:14—Buns, very brief lower frontal nudity and brief left breast getting dressed in bathroom.

Anita Skinner . . . . Anne Munroe
Amy Wright . . . . Ceil
• 0:42—Brief breasts, while getting out of bed to talk to Melanie Mayron.

Girls Are For Loving (1973)

Cheri Caffaro . . . . Ginger
• 0:02—Breasts under sheer pink nightie.
• 0:04—Buns, while lying on bed with her boyfriend.
• 0:18—Full frontal nudity, after taking off towel and getting into pool with Ronnie St. Clair.
•• 0:19—Breasts in front of mirror, putting on make-up while talking to Clay.
•• 0:26—Buns and breasts in pasties after song and dance number on stage.
••• 0:29—In sheer black nightie, then breasts while making love with Jim Whitney.
•• 0:32—Breasts in black nightie during martial arts fight.
••• 0:44—Buns and breasts at beach with bad guy, then fighting with him.
•• 1:07—Nude on table, while held down by bad guys.
••• 1:08—Full frontal nudity, when tied by wrists and ankles to the bed, talking to Ronnie, then making love with William while Ronnie watches.
•• 1:16—Buns and breasts, while getting untied by Clay during rescue.

• *The Girls of Malibu* (1986; Video Tape)

Blondi . . . . Marjorie
••• 0:06—In two piece swimsuit. Breasts riding a motorcycle. Full frontal nudity posing on it. Nude outside.

Leslee Bremmer . . . . Leslee
••• 0:01—In two piece swimsuit, then nude, posing outside.

Gail Harris . . . . Gail
••• 0:28—In two piece swimsuit. Nude taking a shower and drying herself off.

Teri Lynn Peake . . . . Lenee
••• 0:51—Nude outside and in a hot tub.

• *The Girls of Penthouse* (1984; Video Tape)

Alexandra Day . . . . Tattoo Woman & Use Me Woman
••• 0:34—Nude, getting tattooed by another woman, then making love with her.
••• 0:40—Nude, dancing and stripping off her clothes down to stockings and garter belt, then on bed. Quick cuts and strobe light make it hard to see.

Victoria Lynn Johnson . . . . Centerfold
••• 0:43—Nude during photo session with Bob Guccione.

Danielle Martin . . . . Bad to the Bone Woman
••• 0:07—Nude, taking off her leather outfit.

Brinke Stevens . . . . Ghost Town Woman
Jody Swafford . . . . Ghost Town Woman
••• 0:29—In black lingerie, then full frontal nudity making love with cowboy.

Vicki Vickers . . . . The Locket
••• 0:17—Breasts, then nude, making love.

• *The Girls of Penthouse, Volume 2* (1993; Video Tape)

Jasmine . . . . Pet
••• 0:00—Nude in pool, outside of house, on the beach and in house covering herself with shaving cream.

Janine Lindemulder . . . . Pet
••• 0:20—Nude in a pool, working out and in bed.

Sonja McDaniel . . . . Nightstalker
••• 0:41—Nude, while making love in alley.

Theresa Presley . . . . Pet
••• 0:11—Nude on bed, in tub, in kitchen, getting dressed, in milk bath and in a bar.
••• 0:33—Nude on bed, walking and posing in the house.

• *The Girls of Penthouse, Volume 3* (1995; Video Tape)

Jami Dion . . . . Pet
••• 0:01—Nude in still photos.
••• 0:02—Nude in motel.
••• 0:05—Nude outside and in a studio.

Sharon Fitzpatrick . . . . Pet
•• 0:37—Full frontal nudity while telling a little bit about herself.
••• 0:39—Nude in still photos. Nude while posing outside on a ranch.
••• 0:42—Nude, while posing in a studio.
••• 0:44—Full frontal nudity, outside in a field with cows. Filmed in duo-tone color.
••• 0:46—Nude, doing various things around a ranch, swinging on a swing, straddling a fence in the rain.

Shauna O'Brien . . . . Pet
••• 0:29—Nude in still photos.
••• 0:30—In lingerie, then nude in a liquor store.
••• 0:31—Nude, while working out on an exercise machine.
••• 0:33—Nude, while posing in a house.
••• 0:36—Nude, while posing on yellow stairs.

Seana Ryan . . . . Pet
••• 0:16—Nude on stage, doing a strip routine.

••• 0:20—Breasts and lower frontal nudity, in open swim suit, when sunbathing next to a swimming pool while a guy watches her with binoculars.
••• 0:23—Breasts and buns under sheer red outfit while playing pool. Breasts and buns through openings in it.

K.C. Williams . . . . Pet
•• 0:09—Left breast, while telling a little bit about herself.
••• 0:10—Nude in still photos.
••• 0:11—Nude, posing on white sheet.
••• 0:12—Nude at the beach.
••• 0:13—Nude, while posing in a house with another blonde woman.

Gladiator Cop: The Swordsman II (1994)

Claire Stansfield . . . . Julie
• 0:40—In white bra and panties, then very brief right breast while making love with Lorenzo Lamas.

The Glass Cage (1996)

Maria Ford . . . . Dianne
•• 0:35—Right breast, while lying in bed in open blouse, then breasts and buns, when making love with Marko.
• 0:53—Buns in T-back and breasts, while dancing on stage.

Charlotte Lewis . . . . Jacqueline
••• 0:42—Breasts, while making love in bed with Richard Tyson.

Lisa Marie Scott . . . . Kiko
•• 0:30—In sheer white dress, then breasts and buns in panties, while dancing on stage.

Melinda Songer . . . . Dancer

Glen and Randa (1971)

Shelley Plimpton . . . . Randa
••• 0:01—Nude in the woods with Glen. Long scene.
• 0:40—Lower nudity, while lying on the ground when Glen tickles her.

Glitch (1988)

Jasaé . . . . Extra

Laura Albert . . . . Topless
• 0:33—Brief breasts auditioning for Todd and Bo by taking off her top.

Christina Cardan . . . . Non SAG
• 0:47—Brief breasts in spa taking off her swimsuit top.

Marjean Holden . . . . Hopeful #1

Debra Lamb . . . . Fire Eater

Sheila Lussier . . . . Extra

Roxanna Michaels . . . . Cold Reader #2

Beckie Mullen . . . . Extra

Erika Nann . . . . Extra

Julia Nickson . . . . Michelle

Heidi Paine . . . . Cake Lady

Jacqueline Palmer . . . . Extra

Donna Spangler . . . . Extra

Teri Weigel . . . . Lydia
• 0:41—Brief buns in pink bathing suit, while talking to Bo.
• 0:54—Buns in swisuit bottom and brief right breast in bathtub with Todd.

• *Glory Daze* (1995)

Kristin Bauer . . . . Dina
•• 0:20—Breasts, in sexy black rubber outfit, then breasts while in Ben Affleck's bedroom.

Alyssa Milano . . . . Chelsea

Mary Woronov . . . . Joanie's Mom

• *Go Fish* (1994)

Guinevere Turner . . . . Max
• 1:09—Very, very brief partial buns, while sleeping, when Ely covers her with a blanket.
• 1:19—Very, very brief partial right breast, while lying on top of Ely, during the end credits.

God's Gun (1977)

a.k.a. A Bullet from God

Sybil Danning . . . . Jenny
• 1:09—Right breast popping out of dress with a guy in the barn during flashback.

The Godfather (1972)

Diane Keaton . . . . Kay Adams

Simonetta Stefanelli . . . . Apollonia
•• 1:50—Breasts in bedroom on honeymoon night.

Goin' All the Way (1981)

Gina Calabrese . . . . n.a.
•• 0:12—Left breast, in the girls' locker room shower. Standing on the left.

Eileen Davidson . . . . BJ
••• 0:12—Breasts in the girls' locker room shower. Standing next to Monica.
••• 0:22—Exercising in her bedroom in braless pink T-shirt, then breasts talking on the phone to Monica.

Sherry Miller . . . . Candy
• 0:47—Brief right breast, while getting out of bubble bath.
•• 0:49—Breasts with Artie during his fantasy.

Sylvia Summers . . . . Wendy
••• 0:12—Breasts in the girl's locker room shower. Standing on the right.

Going Places (1974; French)

Miou-Miou . . . . Marie-Ange
••• 0:14—Breasts sitting in bed, filing her nails. Full frontal nudity standing up and getting dressed.
•• 0:48—Breasts in bed with Gérard Depardieu and Patrick Dewaere.
• 0:51—Left breast under Dewaere.
••• 0:52—Buns in bed when Depardieu rolls off her. Full frontal nudity sitting up with the two guys in bed.
•• 1:21—Brief breasts, while opening the door. Breasts and panties, while walking in after the two guys.
• 1:27—Partial left breast taking off dress and walking into house.
• 1:28—Very brief breasts while closing the shutters.
•• 1:31—Full frontal nudity in open dress running after the two guys. Long shot. Full frontal nudity putting her wet dress on.
• 1:41—Breasts while in back of car. Dark.

Brigitte Fossey . . . . Young Mother
••• 0:32—In bra, then breasts in open blouse on the train when she lets Patrick Dewaere suck the milk out of her breasts.

Isabelle Huppert . . . . Jacqueline
• 1:53—Brief upper half of left breast making love with Gérard Depardieu.

Jeanne Moreau . . . . Jeanne Pirolle

The Golden Voyage of Sinbad (1974; British)

Caroline Munro . . . . Margiana
• 0:51—Very brief right nipple, sticking out of top when Sinbad carries her from the boat to the shore. Long shot.

Good Girls Don't *(1993)*

Veronica Carothers . . . . Bimbo Jeannie
Dee Hengstler . . . . Rosie
Elizabeth Kaitan . . . . TV Announcer
Honey Lauren . . . . Lolita
Julia Parton . . . . Betina
•• 0:05—Buns in T-back then breasts, while doing strip routine on stage.
• 0:13—Breasts, in front of a guy in office.
• 0:52—Brief buns in outfit.
• 1:06—Brief partial buns in panties and bra, while changing into her jail clothing.
Gwen Somers . . . . Bimbo Betina
• 0:42—Brief buns in outfit.
Ingrid Vold . . . . Prison Guard
Mary Woronov . . . . Wilemena

Good Morning, Babylon *(1987; Italian/French)*

Desiree Becker . . . . Mabel
• 1:06—Brief breasts in the woods making love.
Berangere Bonvoisin . . . . Mrs. Moglie Griffith
Greta Scacchi . . . . Edna
•• 1:05—Breasts in the woods making love with Vincent Spano.

The Good Mother *(1988)*

Tracy Griffith . . . . Babe
• 0:06—Brief breasts opening her blouse to show a young Anna what it's like being pregnant.
Diane Keaton . . . . Anna

The Good Wife *(1987; Australian)*

a.k.a. The Umbrella Woman
Helen Jones . . . . Rosie Gibbs
Clarissa Kaye-Mason . . . . Mrs. Jackson
Susan Lyons . . . . Mrs. Fielding
• 1:22—Very brief breasts coming in from the balcony.
Rachel Ward . . . . Marge Hills

Goodbye Emmanuelle *(1977)*

Charlotte Alexandra . . . . Chloe
••• 0:17—Breasts and brief lower frontal nudity with another girl.
••• 0:20—Nude, walking around the house while everybody is eating breakfast.
Olga Georges-Picot . . . . Woman
Sylvia Kristel . . . . Emmanuelle
•• 0:03—Full frontal nudity in bath and getting out.
•• 0:04—Full frontal nudity taking off dress.
••• 0:06—Full frontal nudity in bed with Angelique.
••• 0:26—Breasts with photographer in old house.
• 0:42—Brief side view of right breast, in bed with Jean.
••• 1:03—Full frontal nudity on beach with movie director.
•• 1:06—Full frontal nudity lying on beach sleeping.
•• 1:28—Side view of left breast lying on beach with Gregory while dreaming.
Alexandra Stewart . . . . Dorothee

Goodbye Pork Pie *(1980; New Zealand)*

Claire Oberman . . . . Shirl
•• 0:46—Breasts while in freight car with Gerry.

Goodbye, Columbus *(1969)*

Ali MacGraw . . . . Brenda
• 0:50—Very brief side view of left breast, taking off dress before running and jumping into a swimming pool. Brief right breast jumping into pool.
• 1:11—Very brief side view of right breast in bed with Richard Benjamin. Brief buns, getting out of bed and walking to the bathroom.

Goodbye, Norma Jean *(1975)*

Patch Mackenzie . . . . Ruth Latimer
Misty Rowe . . . . Norma Jean Baker
•• 0:08—In white bra and panties, then breasts.
• 0:14—Brief breasts in bed getting raped.
• 0:31—Very, very brief silhouette of right breast, in bed with Rob.
••• 0:59—Breasts during shooting of stag film, then in B&W when some people watch the film.

Gorky Park *(1983)*

Joanna Pacula . . . . Irina
•• 1:20—Brief breasts in bed making love with William Hurt.

Gotcha! *(1985)*

Linda Fiorentino . . . . Sasha
•• 0:53—Brief breasts getting searched at customs.
Kari Lizer . . . . Muffy

Gotham *(1988; Made for Cable Movie)*

a.k.a. The Dead Can't Lie
Virginia Madsen . . . . Rachel Carlyle
• 0:50—Brief breasts in the shower when Tommy Lee Jones comes over to her apartment, then breasts while lying on the floor.
•• 1:12—Breasts, while dead, in the freezer when Jones comes back to her apartment, then brief breasts on the bed.
• 1:18—Breasts while in the bathtub under water.

Gothic *(1986; British)*

Myriam Cyr . . . . Claire
•• 0:53—Left breast, then breasts while lying in bed with Gabriel Byrne.
• 0:55—Brief left breast lying in bed. Long shot.
• 1:02—Breasts, while sitting on pool table opening her top for Julian Sands. Special-effect with eyes in her nipples.
• 1:12—Buns and brief breasts covered with mud.
Natasha Richardson . . . . Mary

Graduation Day *(1981)*

Erica Hope . . . . Diane
• 1:02—Brief breasts in open blouse, while running away from the killer.
Patch Mackenzie . . . . Anne Ramstead
E.J. Peaker . . . . Blondie
Linnea Quigley . . . . Dolores
•• 0:36—Breasts by the piano in classroom with Mr. Roberts unbuttoning her blouse.
Linda Shayne . . . . Uncredited Paula
Vanna White . . . . Doris

Grand Avenue *(1996; Made for Cable Movie)*

Deenie Dakota . . . . Justine
• 0:00—Very brief breasts, several times, while making love with her boyfriend in car.

Grand Canyon *(1991)*

Sharon Lee Jones . . . . Studio Girl

Mary-Louise Parker . . . . Dee
- 1:00—Breasts, pulling sheet down, while lying in bed during dream sequence.

Sarah Trigger . . . . Vanessa

Grand Isle (1991)

Ellen Burstyn . . . . Mademoiselle Reisa
Kelly McGillis . . . . Edna Pontellier
- ••• 1:08—Breasts while on the floor making love with Julian Sands.
- ••• 1:19—Breasts, twice, in open robe while sketching while lying on the floor.
- ••• 1:30—Buns and breasts after taking off clothes at the beach.
- ••• 1:31—Nude, quite a few times, while swimming under water. Seen from under water.
- •• 1:32—Breasts, while doing the backstroke above water.

Grandview, U.S.A. (1984)

Jamie Lee Curtis . . . . Michelle "Mike" Cody
- ••• 1:00—Left breast, lying in bed with C. Thomas Howell.

Jennifer Jason Leigh . . . . Candy Webster

The Granny (1995)

Teresa Ganzel . . . . Leanne
Heather-Elizabeth Parkhurst . . . . Antoinette
- • 0:47—Brief breasts, after opening her blouse to show David that he would be satisfied with her breasts.
- •• 0:58—In bra and panties, when undressing in her room, then breasts, while dancing and looking at herself in the mirror.

Stella Stevens . . . . Granny
Shannon Whirry . . . . Kelly
- •• 0:55—Breasts while wearing panties and walking around in her room after taking a shower.

Graveyard Shift (1987)

Sugar Bouche . . . . Fabulous Frannie
- ••• 0:12—Breasts doing a stripper routine on stage.
- • 0:24—Brief breasts in the shower.

Kim Cayer . . . . Suzy
- •• 0:06—In black bra, then brief left breast when vampire rips the bra off.
- • 0:53—Brief breasts in junk yard with garter belt, black panties and stockings.

The Great Bikini Off-Road Adventure (1994)

Avalon Anders . . . . Paulina Smalls
- •• 0:01—Breasts, while sunbathing and lying on ground and spraying herself with water.
- •• 0:16—Breasts, while sunbathing outside on the rocks with Tisha.
- ••• 0:21—Breasts, while undoing her swimsuit top in front of two guys out in the desert.
- • 0:31—Brief buns, while in swimsuit.
- ••• 0:44—Breasts, while posing on a jeep for a customer with a camera.
- ••• 0:50—Breasts and buns, while posing outside for a customer.
- ••• 1:02—Breasts and buns during water fight.

Lauren Hays . . . . Lori Baker
- • 1:06—Buns in swimsuit while giving a tour.
- ••• 1:11—In bra in house with her boyfriend, then breasts while making love with him.

• *The Greek Tycoon* (1978)

Jacqueline Bisset . . . . Liz Cassidy
Lucy Gutteridge . . . . Mia
Vicki Michelle . . . . Nico's Girlfriend
Luciana Paluzzi . . . . Paola Scotti
Carol Royle . . . . Nico's Girlfriend
Linda Thorson . . . . Angela
Marilu Tolo . . . . Sophia Matalas
- •• 0:26—Nude, getting out of bed and fighting with Anthony Quinn.

Greetings (1968)

Ruth Alda . . . . Linda (Shoplifter)
- • 0:59—Undressing on bed in sheer bra while Robert De Niro films her.

• *GRIDLOCK'd* (1997)

Kasi Lemmons . . . . Madonna and Child
Lucy Alexis Liu . . . . Cee-Cee
Billie Neal . . . . Medicaid Woman #1
Thandie Newton . . . . Cookie
- • 0:03—Brief breasts, when Tim Roth and Tupac Shakur drag her out of the bathtub to take her to the hospital.

Elizabeth Peña . . . . Uncredited

The Grifters (1990)

Annette Bening . . . . Myra Langtry
- •• 0:36—In bra and panties in her apartment, then breasts lying in bed "paying" her rent. Kind of dark.
- ••• 1:06—Nude, walking down the hall to the bedroom and into bed.
- • 1:30—Very brief right breast, dead in morgue. Long shot.

Anjelica Huston . . . . Lilly Dillon

Grim Prairie Tales (1990)

Lisa Eichhorn . . . . Maureen
Michelle Joyner . . . . Jenny
- • 0:35—Very brief right breast, then left breast while making love with Marc McClure. Kind of dark.

The Groove Tube (1974)

Jennifer Welles . . . . The Geritan Girl
- •• 0:21—Dancing nude around her husband, Chevy Chase.

Group Marriage (1972)

Aimée Eccles . . . . Chris
- • 0:15—Buns, while getting into bed.
- • 1:15—Brief side view of left breast and buns getting into the shower.

Claudia Jennings . . . . Elaine
- ••• 1:02—Breasts under mosquito net in bed with Phil. Long scene.

Victoria Vetri . . . . Jan
- ••• 0:28—Buns and breasts getting into bed with Dennis, Sander and Chris. More breasts sitting in bed. Long scene.
- • 1:19—Brief side view of right breast in lifeguard booth.

The Guardian (1990)

Carey Lowell . . . . Kate
- •• 0:37—Right breast twice, in bed with Phil.

Theresa Randle . . . . Arlene Russell
Jenny Seagrove . . . . Camilla
- ••• 0:21—Side view of left breast, while in bathtub with the baby. Right breast, then breasts.
- • 0:23—Buns, while drying herself off. Long shot.
- •• 0:38—Breasts, mostly left breast on top of Phil. Don't see her face, probably a body double.
- • 0:46—Buns, while skinny dipping. Long shot.

- •• 0:47—Breasts healing her wound by a tree. Side view of right breast.
- • 1:18—Very brief breasts under sheer gown in forest just before getting hit by a Jeep.
- • 1:24—Very briefly breasts, while scaring Carey Lowell. Body is painted all over.

Gulag *(1985)*

Nancy Paul . . . . Susan
- •• 0:42—Buns, then breasts taking a shower while David Keith daydreams while he's on a train.

The Gumshoe Kid *(1990)*

Tracy Scoggins . . . . Rita Benson
- • 0:33—In two piece white swimsuit. Nice buns shot while Jay Underwood hides in the closet.
- ••• 1:10—Side view of left breast in the shower with Underwood. Excellent slow motion breasts shot while turning around. Brief side view of right breast in bed afterwards.

Pamela Springsteen. . . . . Mona Krause

• ***A Gun, a Car, a Blonde*** *(1996)*

Kay Lenz . . . . Peep/Madge
Paula Marshall. . . . . Deborah/Girl in Photograph
Andrea Thompson . . . . The Blonde/Jade
- ••• 1:08—Nude, when walking in the garden to greet and kiss Rick during B&W segment.

Guncrazy *(1992; Made for Cable Movie)*

Drew Barrymore . . . . Anita
- • 1:24—Brief buns, while in bed on top of her boyfriend. Don't see her face.

Ione Skye . . . . Joy

Guns *(1990)*

Cynthia Brimhall . . . . Edy Stark
- • 0:26—Buns in G-string, while singing and dancing at club.
- •• 0:27—Breasts in dressing room.
- • 0:53—Buns, in black one piece outfit and stockings, while singing in club. Nice legs!

Phyllis Davis . . . . Kathryn Hamilton
Devin De Vasquez . . . . Cash
- • 1:12—Brief side of right breast and buns undressing for bath.

Lisa London. . . . . Rocky
Kym Malin . . . . Kym
- ••• 0:28—Showering (in back) while talking to Hugs (in front).

Donna Spangler . . . . Hugs Huggins
Dona Speir . . . . Donna Hamilton
- ••• 1:00—Breasts and buns in black G-string getting dressed in locker room. Then in black lingerie.

Roberta Vasquez . . . . Nicole Justin
- •• 0:50—Right breast while making love on motorcycle with her boyfriend.

Gypsy Angels *(1980)*

Marilyn Hassett . . . . Jan
Carol Wayne . . . . Waitress
Vanna White . . . . Mickey
- • 0:46—Partial right breast, while making out with Jeff outside by a fire.

The Gypsy Moths *(1969)*

Bonnie Bedelia . . . . Annie Burke
- • 0:28—Very, very brief right breast, while opening and folding her robe together while walking up the stairs. Partially hidden by shadow.

Deborah Kerr. . . . . Elizabeth Brandon
- ••• 0:52—Buns and left breast, while making love with Burt Lancaster on sofa.

Sheree North. . . . . Waitress
- •• 0:37—Breasts while dancing on stage in pink pasties and pink bikini bottoms.
- • 0:53—Most of left breast, while lying in bed next to Gene Hackman.

H.O.T.S. *(1979)*

a.k.a. T & A Academy

Angela Aames . . . . Boom-Boom Bangs
- • 0:21—Breasts parachuting into pool.
- • 0:39—Breasts in bathtub playing with a seal.
- • 1:33—Breasts while playing football.

Lindsay Bloom. . . . . Melody Ragmore
- • 0:28—Very brief right breast on balcony.
- • 1:34—Brief breasts, while throwing football. (She's the quarterback.)

Pamela Bryant . . . . Teri Lynn
- • 1:33—Breasts during football game.

Sandy Johnson . . . . Stephanie
- •• 0:27—Breasts on balcony in red bikini bottoms.
- •• 1:34—Breasts during football game during huddle with all the other girls.

Susan Lynn Kiger. . . . . Honey Shayne
- • 0:00—Breasts in shower room with the other girls.
- •• 0:33—Breasts in pool making love with Doug.
- • 1:33—Breasts in football game.

Lisa London. . . . . Jennie O'Hara
- • 1:22—Breasts changing clothes by the closet while a crook watches her.
- • 1:33—Breasts playing football.

K.C. Winkler . . . . Cynthia
- • 0:27—Breasts in blue bikini bottom on balcony.
- •• 0:31—Breasts in van making love, then arguing with John.

• ***Habitat*** *(1996; Canadian)*

Lynne Adams. . . . . Tara Fisher
- • 1:30—Brief breasts in torn outfit after explosion.

Laura Harris. . . . . Deborah Marlowe
- •• 1:09—Breasts, taking off her blouse and going for a swim with Balthazar Getty, then getting dressed.
- • 1:34—Very, very brief left breast before she falls into the water.

Alice Krige . . . . Clarissa Symes
- ••• 0:21—Breasts, when starting to make love with Tcheky Karyo.
- • 1:20—Breasts visible under sheer dress.

Hack-O-Lantern *(1987)*

a.k.a. Halloween Night

Carla Baron . . . . Vera
- • 0:16—Breasts, while in bubble bath. Breasts and buns, getting out of bathtub after getting scared by a rubber spider.
- • 0:44—Brief breasts, while in bed with Brian when caught by Joey.

Hackers *(1995)*

Lorraine Bracco . . . . Margo
Felicity Huffman . . . . Attorney
Angelina Jolie . . . . Kate
- • 0:43—Very brief half of left breast, after she unzips her jacket in Dade's dream.
- • 0:51—Brief breasts under sheer black blouse, while sitting at desk.

Liza Walker . . . . .Laura
Alberta Watson . . . . Lauren Murphy

Hail, Mary *(1985; French)*
a.k.a. Je Vous Salve, Marie
Juliette Binoche . . . . Juliette
Myriem Roussel . . . . .Mary
• 0:56—Brief full frontal nudity in bathroom.
••• 0:57—Full frontal nudity in bathtub, washing herself while kneeling.
••• 1:13—Nude, undressing and putting on nightgown in bedroom.
• 1:17—Brief breasts, while moving around under sheets in bed.
••• 1:18—Breasts, while sitting on bed.
• 1:19—Lower frontal nudity and tops of breasts while undressing and bending over in gaping top.
•• 1:22—Close-up of lower frontal nudity, while in bedroom with Joseph.
•• 1:23—Lower frontal nudity and buns, after lifting up her blouse.
• 1:30—Very, very brief right breast, while rolling around in bed under the sheets.
••• 1:31—Lower frontal nudity, then breasts, while in bed. Nice close-ups.
••• 1:33—Lower frontal nudity and breasts, while lying in bed on her back.

Hair *(1979)*
Beverly D'Angelo . . . . Sheila
• 0:59—In white bra and panties, then breasts on rock near pond. Medium long shot.
••• 1:01—Breasts in panties getting out of the pond.
• 1:38—Side view of right breast changing clothes in car with George.
Annie Golden . . . . Jeannie

Half Moon Street *(1986)*
a.k.a. Escort Girl
Janet McTeer . . . . Van Arkady's Ambassador
Sigourney Weaver . . . . .Lauren Slaughter
• 0:05—Brief breasts in the bathtub.
•• 0:11—Brief breasts in the bathtub again.
• 0:18—Brief buns and side view of right breast while putting on make-up in front of the mirror. Wearing a black garter belt and stockings.
••• 0:39—Breasts, while riding exercise bike while being photographed, then brief breasts getting out of the shower.
• 0:46—Very, very brief breasts wearing a sheer black blouse with no bra during daydream sequence.
• 0:50—Brief breasts, while in bed with Michael Caine, then left breast.

Halloween *(1978)*
Jamie Lee Curtis . . . . Laurie
Sandy Johnson . . . . Judith Meyers
• 0:06—Very brief breasts covered with blood on floor after Michael stabs her to death.
P.J. Soles . . . . Lynda
• 1:04—Brief right breast, sitting up in bed after making love in bed with Bob.
• 1:07—Brief breasts getting strangled by Michael in the bedroom.

Halloween II *(1981)*
Jamie Lee Curtis . . . . Laurie
Pamela Susan Shoop . . . . Karen
••• 0:48—Breasts getting into the whirlpool bath with Budd in the hospital.

Halloween III: Season of the Witch *(1983)*
Stacey Nelkin . . . . Ellie Grimbridge
• 0:37—Brief right breast, behind shower door, when getting out of the shower.

Halloween: The Curse of Michael Myers *(1995)*
Mariah O'Brien . . . . Beth
• 0:58—Breasts, when leaning up in bed after making love with Tim.

Hamburger—The Motion Picture *(1986)*
Debra Blee . . . . Mia Vunk
Randi Brooks . . . . .Mrs. Vunk
•• 0:52—Brief breasts in helicopter with a guy.
Karen Mayo-Chandler . . . . .Dr. Victoria Gotbottom
• 0:03—Brief breasts in her office trying to help, then seduce Russell.
Maria Richwine . . . . .Conchita
•• 0:49—Breasts trying to seduce Russell in a room.

The Hand *(1981)*
Annie McEnroe . . . . Stella Roche
•• 0:51—Breasts undressing for Michael Caine.

Hand Gun *(1994)*
Angela Nicholas . . . . Woman in Bed
• 0:04—Breasts, while sitting up in bed after police bust in.
Anna Thomson . . . . Laura
•• 0:48—Upper half of left breast, while lying in bed after Seymour Cassel gets up out of bed.

The Hand That Rocks the Cradle *(1992)*
Rebecca De Mornay . . . . Peyton
• 0:29—Upper half of right breast, breast feeding Claire's baby.
Julianne Moore . . . . Marlene
Annabella Sciorra . . . . Claire Bartel
• 0:08—Brief side of right breast in open gown, while lying on Dr. Mott's examination table.

The Handmaid's Tale *(1990)*
Faye Dunaway . . . . .Serena Joy
Traci Lind . . . . Ofwarren/Janine
Elizabeth McGovern . . . . Moira
Natasha Richardson . . . . Kate
•• 0:30—Breasts twice at the window getting some fresh air.
• 0:59—Breasts making love with Aidan Quinn.
••• 1:00—Breasts after Quinn rolls off her.
Victoria Tennant . . . . Aunt Lydia

Hanover Street *(1979)*
Lesley-Anne Down . . . . Margaret Sallinger
• 0:22—In bra and slip, then brief breasts in bedroom with Harrison Ford.
Patsy Kensit . . . . Sarah Sallinger

The Happy Hooker *(1975)*
Denise Galik . . . . .Cynthia
Anita Morris . . . . .Linda Jo/Mary Smith
• 0:59—Breasts lying on table while a customer puts ice cream all over her.
• 1:24—Breasts covered with whipped cream getting it sprayed off with champagne by another customer.

Lynn Redgrave . . . . Xaviera Hollander

The Happy Hooker Goes Hollywood (1980)

Martine Beswicke . . . . Xaviera Hollander
•• 0:05—Brief breasts in bedroom with Dick Miller.
••• 0:22—Brief buns, jumping into the swimming pool, then breasts next to the pool with Adam West.
• 0:27—Breasts in bed with West, then breasts waking up.
Lindsay Bloom. . . . . Chris
Tanya Boyd . . . . Sylvie
• 0:39—Brief breasts in jungle room when an older customer accidentally comes in.
Kim Hopkins . . . . .Young Xaviera
Susan Lynn Kiger. . . . . Susie
• 0:42—Breasts, singing "Happy Birthday" to a guy tied up on the bed.
••• 0:43—Breasts, wearing a red garter belt playing pool with K.C. Winkler.
Lisa London. . . . . Laurie
Alexandra Morgan . . . . Max
K.C. Winkler . . . . .Amber
•• 0:41—Breasts in cowboy outfit on bed with a guy.
••• 0:43—Breasts, wearing a blue garter belt playing pool with Susan Kiger.

The Happy Hooker Goes to Washington (1977)

Dawn Clark. . . . . Candy
• 1:18—Breasts, covered with spaghetti in a restaurant.
Cissie Colpitts-Cameron . . . . Miss Goodbody
• 0:29—Very brief breasts when her top pops open during the senate hearing.
Raven De La Croix. . . . . Uncredited Ice Cream Girl
• 0:31—Brief breasts, while lying on table, getting her rear end covered with ice cream.
Linda Gildersleeve . . . . Honeymoon Wife
• 0:35—Brief breasts in a diner during the filming of a commercial.
Joey Heatherton . . . . Xaviera Hollander
Joyce Jillson. . . . . .Herself
Marilyn Joi. . . . . Sheila
• 0:09—Left breast while on a couch.
• 0:47—Brief breasts during car demonstration.
•• 1:14—Breasts in military guy's office.
Bonnie Large. . . . . Carolyn (Model)
• 0:06—Breasts during photo shoot.
Louisa Moritz . . . . Natalie Naussbaum
• 0:39—Brief breasts and buns, lying down on top of Larry Storch in tennis court.
Pamela Zinszer . . . . .Linda
• 1:19—Brief breasts in raincoat flashing in front of congressional panel.

Happy Housewives (1975; British)

Ava Cadell. . . . . Schoolgirl
• 0:39—Buns, when caught by the Squire and getting spanked.
Jeannie Collings . . . . Mrs. Wain
• 0:16—Very, very brief right breast with the Newsagent's Daughter and Bob in the bathtub.
Sue Lloyd . . . . The Blonde
Nita Lorraine. . . . . Jenny Elgin
• 0:31—Brief side view of left breast and buns in barn chasing after Bob.
• 0:32—Brief breasts in open dress talking to policeman.
Helli Louise . . . . Newsagent's Daughter
•• 0:16—Breasts with Mrs. Wain and Bob in the bathtub.
Penny Meredith. . . . . Margaretta
• 0:02—Brief right breast, while talking on the telephone while Bob makes love with her.
•• 0:19—Breasts while standing up in bathtub and talking to Bob.
• 0:34—In sheer black lingerie.
• 1:05—Brief breasts pulling her top down when interrupted by the policeman at the window.

Happy Together (1988)

Helen Slater. . . . . Alexandra "Alex" Page
•• 0:17—Brief right breast changing clothes while talking to Patrick Dempsey. Unfortunately, she has a goofy expression on her face.

Hard Bounty (1995)

Antonia Dorian . . . . .Junie Ray
Kimberly Kelley . . . . Glory
•• 0:11—Breasts, while in bedroom with a customer.
•• 0:54—Breasts, while in room with Jess, helping Benjamin lose his virginity.
Kelly Le Brock . . . . Donnie
Rochelle Swanson . . . . Jess
•• 0:13—Breasts, after taking off lingerie top and almost getting into bed with a customer.
••• 0:36—Breasts and side view of buns, while making love in bed with a customer. Long scene.
•• 0:54—Breasts, while in room with Glory, helping Benjamin lose his virginity.

Hard Choices (1986)

Margaret Klenck . . . . Laura
•• 1:10—Left breast, then breasts making love with Bobby. Nice close up shot.
• 1:11—Very brief half of left breast and lower frontal nudity getting back into bed. Long shot.

Hard Drive (1994)

(Unrated version reviewed.)
Robin Joi Brown. . . . . Assistant Examiner
Christina Fulton. . . . . .Dana/Delilah
• 0:23—Brief lower frontal nudity, brief left breast and brief buns while getting attacked on bed by Will.
• 0:25—Buns, while lying on bed after getting shot.
• 0:26—Brief buns and left breast in Will's flashback.
•• 1:15—Left breast, while making love with Will on kitchen counter.
Deanne Power. . . . . Candle Dream Girl
•• 0:03—Left breast, then breasts, while making love with Will on the floor surrounded by lit candles.
• 0:05—Brief breasts on the floor again.
Stella Stevens . . . . Susan
Belinda Waymouth . . . . Laura
• 0:56—Very brief right breast, while in shower with Matt McCoy.

Hard Evidence (1994)

Joan Severance . . . . Madelyn Turner
Cali Timmins . . . . Dina Davis
• 0:07—In lingerie, then breasts while making love with Gregory Harrison.
•• 0:20—In lingerie, while posing for Harrison when he takes photos of her, then breasts, when making love in bed.

Hard Hunted (1993)

Cynthia Brimhall . . . . .Edy Stark
••• 0:50—Breasts in bedroom while making love with Lucas.

•• 1:18—Left breast, then breasts in bed with Lucas.

Ava Cadell . . . . Ava
••• 0:38—Breasts in spa with Becky while doing radio show.

Carolyn Liu . . . . Silk
• 0:02—Buns, while in lingerie on boat with Mr. Kane.
••• 0:08—Breasts, while taking off her dress top on boat in front of Mr. Kane, then in bed with him.
• 0:10—Brief breasts, while lying in bed when the plastic explosive on the safe blows up.

Beckie Mullen . . . . Becky
•• 0:38—Breasts and buns in G-string in spa with Ava doing radio show.
••• 0:56—Breasts while getting out of spa and getting coffee.

Mika Quintard. . . . . Mika
••• 0:11—In two piece swimsuit on boat. Breasts, while taking a shower outside.

Dona Speir . . . . Donna Hamilton
•• 1:22—Left breast, then breasts on beach with the bad guy, while making love and resting afterwards.

Roberta Vasquez . . . . Nicole Justin
•• 1:20—Breasts while making out with Bruce in the ocean.

Hard Rock Zombies (1985)

Annabelle Larsen. . . . . Groupie
Crystal Shaw . . . . Mrs. Buff
Lisa Toothman. . . . . Elsa
• 0:01—Buns, undressing to go skinny dipping. Breasts long shot.
••• 0:32—Buns, while getting into the shower. Breasts and buns in the shower behind clear plastic curtain.

Hard Ticket to Hawaii (1987)

Cynthia Brimhall . . . . Edy
•• 0:47—Breasts changing out of a dress into a blouse and pants.
•• 1:33—Breasts during the end credits.

Hope Marie Carlton. . . . . Taryn
•• 0:07—Breasts taking a shower outside while talking to Dona Speir.
••• 0:23—Breasts in the spa with Speir looking at diamonds they found.
••• 0:40—Breasts and buns on the beach making love with her boyfriend, Jimmy John.
•• 1:33—Breasts during the end credits.

Patty Duffek . . . . Patticakes
•• 0:48—Breasts talking to Michelle after swimming.

Dona Speir . . . . Donna
• 0:01—Breasts on boat kissing her boyfriend, Rowdy.
••• 0:23—Breasts in the spa with Hope Marie Carlton looking at diamonds they found.
••• 1:04—Breasts and buns with Rowdy after watching a video tape.
•• 1:33—Breasts during the end credits.

• *Hard Time* (1995)

Devin De Vasquez . . . . .Linda
••• 0:42—In body suit, then breasts and buns, while making love with Michael in bed.
• 1:16—Breasts, while sitting in bubble bath.
• 1:21—Brief partial right breast, while sitting in bubble bath.
•• 1:26—Buns and breasts, while making love in bed with Michael and Angel.

Jacqueline Lovell . . . . Star
••• 0:29—Nude, while stripping and dancing in front of Michael on a table. Excellent!

Meilani Paul. . . . . Angel Woods
•• 0:06—In lingerie, then breasts, while undressing in front of Michael during his dream.
•• 0:11—In lingerie, then breasts, while making love with Kelly (a guy) in Michael's dream.
••• 1:03—In white body suit, then nude, while making love with Michael in bed.
• 1:09—Buns and breasts, while making love with Michael.
•• 1:26—Buns and breasts, while making love in bed with Michael and Devin De Vasquez.

Hard to Die (1990)

a.k.a. Tower of Terror

Bridget Carney . . . . Shayne Hobbie
••• 0:24—Breasts and buns while taking a shower. Long scene.

Deborah Dutch . . . . Jackie Webster
•• 0:25—Breasts and buns, while taking a shower.

Monique Gabrielle. . . . . Fifi Latour

Gail Harris . . . . Dawn Grant
••• 0:31—Breasts, while taking a shower.

Karen Mayo-Chandler . . . . Diana Farrow
•• 0:10—Breasts, putting on her dress in office with Mr. Plimpton.

Melissa Anne Moore . . . . Tess Cochran
••• 0:21—Breasts, after taking off her top, then taking a shower. Long scene.

Toni Naples . . . . .Sgt. Shawlee

Cirsten Weldon . . . . Agent's Girlfriend
• 0:19—Breasts in bedroom with Tess's agent. Medium long shot.

The Hard Truth (1994)

Lysette Anthony. . . . . Lisa Kantrell
0:04—In black bra and panties.
0:22—In black bra in office with Jonah.
••• 0:39—In black bra, then breasts, while making love with Jonah.

Loretta Devine. . . . . .Nichols' Secretary

Hard Vice (1994)

Rebecca Ferratti. . . . . .Christine
••• 0:02—Buns and breasts, getting out of bubble bath and making love on top of a customer in bed. Breasts while taking a shower.
••• 0:21—Breasts, while making love in bed with another customer.
•• 0:22—Breasts and buns, while taking a shower.
• 1:04—Buns in panties, while standing in bedroom. Long shot.

Shannon Tweed. . . . . Andrea
•• 0:44—Breasts after taking off her top in front of Sam Jones.

Hardbodies (1984)

Julie Always . . . . Photo Session Hardbody
•• 0:40—Breasts with other girls posing breasts getting pictures taken by Rounder. She's wearing blue dress with a white belt.

Leslee Bremmer. . . . . Photo Session Hardbody
• 0:02—Breasts in the surf when her friends take off her swimsuit top during the opening credits.
•• 0:40—Breasts with other topless girls posing for photographs taken by Rounder. She takes off her dress and is wearing a black G-string.

Roberta Collins . . . . Lana

Darcy De Moss . . . . Dede
••• 0:54—Breasts, while in the back seat of the limousine with Rounder.
Erika Dockery . . . . Hardbody in Car
Jackie Easton . . . . Girl in Dressing Room
•• 0:27—Breasts taking off dress to try on swimsuit.
•• 0:40—Breasts with other topless girls posing for photographs taken by Rounder. She's wearing a white skirt.
Marcia Karr . . . . Hardbody On Stairs
Kathleen Kinmont . . . . Pretty Skater
Juli Lawrence . . . . Nicki
• 0:38—Breasts in bathroom after taking off her dress to clean it.
Teal Roberts . . . . Kristi Kelly
•• 0:02—Breasts in bed after making love with Scotty, then putting her sweater on.
••• 0:48—Breasts standing in front of closet mirrors talking about breasts with Kimberly.
••• 0:56—Breasts making love with Scotty on the beach.
•• 1:23—Breasts, while on fancy car bed with Scotty.
Crystal Shaw . . . . Candy
Cindy Silver . . . . Kimberly
•• 0:07—Brief breasts on beach when a dog steals her bikini top.
••• 0:47—Breasts standing in front of closet mirrors talking about breasts with Kristi.
Kristi Somers . . . . Michelle
•• 0:53—Nude, dancing on the beach while Ashley plays the guitar and sings.

Hardbodies 2 *(1986)*

Brenda Bakke . . . . Morgan
•• 0:34—Buns, getting into bathtub, then breasts, taking a bath.
Roberta Collins . . . . Lana Logan
Fabiana Udenio . . . . Cleo/Princess

Hardcase and Fist *(1988)*

Maureen La Vette . . . . Nora Wilde
•• 0:24—Breasts, while getting out of spa when Tony starts shooting gun in the house.
Debra Lamb . . . . Chieko
• 1:08—Buns in G-string while dancing on stage in a club.
••• 1:09—Breasts while dancing on stage and doing some fire eating. Nice, long scene.
•• 1:13—Breasts, three times, while peeking from behind curtain.
Stacey Nemour . . . . Jill
• 0:30—Right breast, while on desk with her boyfriend, talking on the phone with Sharon.

Hardcore *(1979)*

Leslie Ackerman . . . . Felice
• 0:44—Breasts in porno house with George C. Scott.
Bibi Besch . . . . Mary
Season Hubley . . . . Niki
• 0:27—Breasts acting in a porno movie.
••• 1:05—Full frontal nudity talking to George C. Scott in a booth. Panties mysteriously appear later on.
Linda Morell . . . . "Les Girls" Woman
•• 1:04—Breasts, when taking George C. Scott's money in a bar.
Linda Smith. . . . . Hope (Mistress Victoria)
Gigi Vorgan. . . . . Teenage Girl
• 0:32—Breasts on sofa in Peter Boyle's apartment.

Hardware *(1990)*

Stacey Travis . . . . Jill
• 0:21—Almost breasts in shower. Brief left breast in bed with Moses. Lit with blue light.
• 0:38—Brief breasts in bedroom seen by a guy through telescope. Infrared-looking effect.

Harem *(1985; French)*

Rosanne Katon . . . . Judy
Nastassja Kinski . . . . Diane
• 0:14—Breasts getting into swimming pool.
•• 1:04—Breasts in motel room with Ben Kingsley.

Harley Davidson and The Marlboro Man *(1991)*

Tia Carrere . . . . Kimiko
Chelsea Field . . . . Virginia Slim
• 0:40—Side of left breast, sitting up in bed. Very brief buns standing up. Don't see her face very well.

Harnessing Peacocks
(1995; Made for Cable Movie; British)

Elizabeth Ashley. . . . . Grandmother
Serena Scott Thomas. . . . . Hebe
•• 0:52—Brief buns, then breasts, while in bedroom, talking with Rory. (Frontal nudity in reflection in the mirror is blurred out in the U.S. version shown on TV.)

The Harrad Experiment *(1973)*

Sharon Taggart . . . . Barbara
Victoria Thompson . . . . Beth Hillyer
• 0:08—Buns, in the bathroom while talking to Harry.
• 0:10—Brief breasts getting into bed.
•• 0:21—Breasts in nude encounter group.
• 0:41—Breasts getting into the swimming pool with Don Johnson and Laurie Walters.
• 0:49—Buns, getting dressed after making love with Johnson.
Laurie Walters . . . . Sheila Grove
• 0:29—Breasts, wearing white panties, while with Don Johnson.
• 0:40—Nude taking off blue dress and getting into the swimming pool with Johnson.

The Harrad Summer *(1974)*

a.k.a. Student Union

Sherry Miles. . . . . Dee
Lisa Moore . . . . Arnae
Patrice Rohmer . . . . Marcia
• 0:33—Brief breasts, starting to take off her blouse in motel room with Harry.
Victoria Thompson . . . . Beth Hillyer
•• 0:57—Buns and brief breasts running down hallway and jumping into bed, pretending to be asleep.
• 1:03—Buns, lying on inflatable lounge in the pool.
• 1:04—Buns, lying face down on lounge chair.
Laurie Walters . . . . Sheila Grove
• 0:02—Breasts, while undressing in bathroom. Long shot, out of focus.
•• 1:04—Breasts, while lying on lounge chair, then buns and more breasts getting up and pushing Harry into the pool.

Harry and Tonto *(1974)*

Ellen Burstyn . . . . Shirley

Melanie Mayron . . . . Ginger
- 0:57—Very brief breasts in motel room with Art Carney taking off her towel and putting on blouse. Long shot, hard to see.

The Harvest (1992)

Leilani Sarelle. . . . . Natalie Caldwell
- •• 1:13—Side view of buns, then breasts, while in car with Miguel Ferrer. Don't see her face very well.
- ••• 1:19—Full frontal nudity, while making love with Ferrer in bed.

The Haunted (1976)

Ann Michelle. .Abanaki/Jennifer Baines
- ••• 0:03—Breasts while on horseback as Abanaki.
- •• 0:06—Breasts, while riding on horseback in the desert.
- •• 0:48—Breasts while lying on towel outside with Patrick at night.
- •• 1:19—Breasts while riding the horse again.

Haunting Fear (1990)

Karen Black . . . . Dr. Julia Harcourt

Sherri Graham. . . . . Visconti's Girl
- • 0:45—Buns in swimming pool. (Breasts seen under water.)
- • 0:47—Breasts, giving Visconti a massage while he talks on the phone.

Delia Sheppard . . . . Lisa
- ••• 0:13—Breasts on desk, making love with Terry.
- ••• 1:10—Full frontal nudity, making love in bed with Terry. Long scene.

Brinke Stevens. . . . . Victoria
- ••• 0:10—Full frontal nudity, taking a bath and getting out.
- •• 0:22—Breasts, while changing into nightgown in bedroom.
- ••• 0:32—Breasts while lying on Coroner's table.

The Haunting of Morella (1989)

Lana Clarkson . . . . Coel Deveroux
- ••• 0:17—Breasts, taking a bath, then getting out and wrapping a towel around herself.
- ••• 1:00—Breasts in white panties, standing under a waterfall.

Deborah Dutch . . . . .Serving Girl
- ••• 0:14—Breasts and buns, taking off pink tap pants and getting into bath.
- • 0:15—Buns, lying dead on the floor, covered with blood.

Nicole Eggert . . . . Morella/Lenora

Maria Ford . . . . Diane
- ••• 1:00—Breasts taking off nightgown and swimming in pond, then walking to waterfall.

Gail Harris . . . . Ilsa
- •• 0:38—Breasts in bed with Niles. Buns also when getting out and getting dressed.

Havana (1990)

Lise Cutter. . . . . .Patty
- • 0:44—Most of side of left breast with Robert Redford. Very, very brief part of right breast while he turns her around. Very brief left breast when Redford puts a cold glass on her chest. Dark, hard to see.

Lena Olin . . . . Bobby Duran

Karen Russell . . . . .Dancer #2

He Knows You're Alone (1980)

Elizabeth Kemp . . . . .Nancy
- ••• 1:12—Breasts, taking off robe and taking a shower.

Patsy Pease . . . . Joyce
- • 0:42—Very, very brief left breast in open blouse when she turns around to turn off the lights.

he said, she said (1991)

Ashley Gardner . . . . Susan
- • 1:05—Brief upper half of right breast, when her breast pops out of her dress while talking to Kevin Bacon and Elizabeth Perkins at restaurant.

Elizabeth Perkins . . . . Lorie Bryer
- • 1:15—Brief breasts getting into the shower with Kevin Bacon.

Sharon Stone. . . . . Linda

The Head of the Family (1967; Italian/French)

Claudine Auger . . . . .Adriana
- • 1:18—Very brief side of right breast, while putting Marco's shirt on.

Leslie Caron. . . . . Paola
- • 0:22—Very brief upper half of left breast while sitting at drafting table and breast feeding her baby.

Head of the Family (1996)

Dianne Colazzo . . . . .Ernestina
- •• 0:48—Breasts, while in bedroom, then making love with Lance.

Jacqueline Lovell . . . . .Lorretta
- • 0:33—Brief buns, after taking off her panties and getting into bed with Lance.
- •• 0:39—Full frontal nudity, while lying in bed with Lance.
- • 0:44—Left breast under open blouse, while making love with Lance in storage room.
- • 0:49—Left breast in gaping nightgown, while sleeping in bed.
- •• 0:57—Breasts, after lowering her nightgown and letting Myron lick her breast.
- •• 1:08—Full frontal nudity, while tied by her wrists when Myron attempts to burn her.
- • 1:14—Brief, partial buns, while being carried by Otis.

Hear My Song (1991; British)

Tara Fitzgerald. . . . . .Nancy Doyle
- •• 0:07—Brief breasts in bed, then nude, getting out of bed and getting dressed while angry at Micky.

Hear No Evil (1993)

Marlee Matlin . . . . Jillian Shananhan
- •• 0:30—Brief breasts, getting out of the bathtub.

Karen Trumbo . . . . Nadine Brock

Heart Beat (1979)

Ann Dusenberry. . . . . Stevie
- •• 0:41—Full frontal nudity frolicking in bathtub with Nick Nolte.

Sissy Spacek. . . . . Carolyn Cassady

Heart of Midnight (1988)

Jennifer Jason Leigh . . . . Carol
- • 0:27—Very brief side view of right breast, while reaching for soap in the shower.

Brenda Vaccaro . . . . .Betty

Heart of the Stag (1983; New Zealand)

Mary Regan. . . . . Cathy Jackson
- • 0:03—Brief right breast twice, very brief lower frontal nudity in bed with her father.

•• 1:06—Breasts in bed, ripping her blouse open while yelling at her father.

Heartbreak Ridge (1986)

Marsha Mason . . . . Aggie
Rebecca Perle . . . . Student in Shower
- 1:48—Very brief breasts getting out of shower when the Marines rescue the students.

Heartbreaker (1983)

Apollonia . . . . Rose
Dawn Dunlap . . . . Kim
- 0:49—Breasts putting on dress in bedroom.
- 0:51—Very, very brief right breast in open dress during rape attempt. Dark.

•• 1:02—Left breast, lying on bed with her boyfriend. Long scene.

Heartbreakers (1984)

Kathryn Harrold . . . . Cyd
Carole Laure . . . . Liliane
- 0:56—Brief breasts making love in car with Nick Mancuso. Dark, hard to see.
- 1:25—In sheer black dress, then brief right breast making love in art gallery with Peter Coyote.

Jamie Rose. . . . . Libby
••• 0:09—Breasts in bed talking with Nick Mancuso and Peter Coyote.

Carol Wayne . . . . Candy
••• 0:41—In white bra and panties, then brief breasts in the mirror stripping in front of Coyote and Nick Mancuso. Brief breasts, while lying in bed with Coyote.

Hearts and Armour (1983)

Zeudi Araya. . . . . Marfisa
Barbara De Rossi . . . . Bradamante
•• 1:05—Breasts while sleeping with Ruggero.
Tanya Roberts . . . . Angelica

Heat and Dust (1982)

Julie Christie . . . . Anne
Greta Scacchi . . . . Olivia Rivers
•• 1:25—Buns, lying in bed under a mosquito net with Douglas, then breasts rolling over.

The Heat of Desire (1982; French)

a.k.a. Plein Sud

Clio Goldsmith . . . . Carol
- 0:09—Breasts and buns, getting out of bed in train to look out the window. Dark.
- 0:12—Brief breasts in bathroom mirror when Serge peeks in.

•• 0:19—Full frontal nudity in the bathtub.
•• 0:20—Nude, sitting on the floor with Serge's head in her lap.
•• 0:21—Buns, lying face down on floor. Very brief breasts. A little dark. Then breasts sitting up and drinking out of bottle.
- 0:22—Right breast, in gaping robe sitting on floor with Serge.
- 0:24—Partial left breast consoling Serge in bed.
- 0:25—Breasts sitting on chair on balcony, then walking inside. Dark.
- 0:56—Breasts walking from bathroom and getting into bed. Dark.
- 0:57—Brief right breast, while on couch with Guy Marchand.

•• 0:58—Breasts getting dressed while Serge is yelling.

Heatseeker (1994)

Tina Coté . . . . Jo
- 0:48—Breasts, while rolling on the floor in pain. Seen on TV monitor.
- 0:50—Breasts, while making love with Tung in Chance's bad dream.

Selina Mangh . . . . Liu

Heaven's Gate (1980)

Isabelle Huppert . . . . Ella
•• 1:10—Nude running around the house and in bed with Kris Kristofferson.
••• 1:18—Nude, taking a bath in the river and getting out.
- 2:24—Very brief left breast getting raped by three guys.

Heaven's Prisoners (1995)

Teri Hatcher . . . . Claudette Rocque
•• 0:40—Nude, while standing on balcony when Alec Baldwin first sees her, long shot at first, then closer shot.
Kelly Lynch . . . . Annie Robicheaux

Heavenly Bodies (1985)

Jo Anne Bates . . . . Girl in Locker Room
Sugar Bouche . . . . Stripper
- 0:16—Breasts doing stripper-gram for Steve.

Cynthia Dale . . . . Samantha Blair
- 0:30—Brief breasts fantasizing about making love with Steve while doing aerobic exercises.

Laura Henry. . . . . Debbie
- 0:46—Brief breasts making love while her boyfriend, Jack, watches TV.

Heavenly Creatures (1994; New Zealand)

Melanie Lynskey . . . . Pauline
- 1:20—Tip of right breast, while sitting in bathtub talking to Kate Winslet.

Kate Winslet . . . . Juliet
- 1:01—Breasts, sort of visible under water while sitting in bathtub talking to Melanie Lynskey

Heidi Fleiss: Hollywood Madam (1995; British/Canadian)

Corinne Bohrer . . . . Actor
Heidi Fleiss. . . . . Herself
•• 0:39—Breasts, when getting up and putting on blouse while talking on cordless telephone.
- 0:40—Briefly nude, after dropping a sheet and running away from the camera.

The Heist (1989; Made for Cable Movie)

Wendy Hughes . . . . Susan
- 0:52—Very brief side view of right breast making love in bed with Pierce Brosnan.

Hell Comes to Frogtown (1987)

Sandahl Bergman . . . . Spangle
Suzanne Solari. . . . . Runaway Girl
Kristi Somers . . . . Arabella
Cec Verrell. . . . . Centinella
•• 0:19—Breasts taking off her blouse and getting into sleeping bag with Roddy Piper. Brief breasts again after he throws her off him.

Hell High (1989)

Karen Russell . . . . .Teen Girl

•• 0:04—Breasts in shack with Teen Boy while little girl watches through a hole in the wall.

Hell Up in Harlem (1973)

Margaret Avery . . . . Sister Jennifer

••• 0:42—Breasts in bed, while making love with Fred Williamson.

Gloria Hendry . . . . Helen Bradley

Hellbound (1993)

Zoe Trilling . . . . Hooker

• 0:18—Very brief back half of left breast while in the shower.

Sheree Wilson . . . . .Leslie

Hellhole (1985)

Lamya Derval . . . . Jacuzzi Girl

••• 1:08—Breasts (she's on the right) sniffing glue in closet with another woman.

••• 1:12—Full frontal nudity in Jacuzzi room with Mary Woronov.

Dyanne Thorne . . . . .Chrysta

Pamela Ward. . . . . Tina

Edy Williams . . . . Vera

••• 0:22—Breasts on bed posing for Ray Sharkey.

••• 0:24—Breasts in white panties in shower, then fighting with another woman.

••• 1:03—Breasts in mud bath with another woman. Long scene.

Mary Woronov . . . . .Dr. Fletcher

Hello Again! (1987)

Shelley Long . . . . Lucy Chadman

• 0:58—Brief buns, in hospital gown, walking down hallway.

Hello Mary Lou: Prom Night II (1987)

Beverly Hendry . . . . .Monica Walters

• 1:03—Brief side view of buns and breasts, while getting undressed in locker room.

• 1:04—Nude in shower room with Vicki.

Wendy Lyon . . . . Vicki Carpenter

• 0:58—Very, very brief left breast, while turning around after getting sucked into the blackboard.

••• 1:04—Nude in shower with Monica. Nude a lot walking around shower room.

••• 1:06—Full frontal nudity, walking in locker room, stalking Monica.

Hellraiser (1987)

Clare Higgins. . . . . .Julia

• 0:17—Very, very brief left breast and buns making love with Frank.

Ashley Laurence . . . . Kirsty

Hellraiser III: Hell on Earth (1992)

(Unrated version reviewed.)

Ashley Laurence . . . . Kirsty

Paula Marshall. . . . . Terri

• 0:47—Very, very brief left breast under gaping blouse, while spinning around to get up off the floor to run to the door.

Hellraiser II—Hellbound (1988)

Catherine Chevalier. . . . . Tiffany's Mother

Clare Higgins . . . . Julia

• 0:20—Very, very brief right breast, lying in bed with Frank. Scene from *Hellraiser.*

Ashley Laurence. . . . . Kirsty

• *Hellraiser: Bloodline* (1996)

Laura Albert. . . . . Stunt Double Rimmer

Christine Harnos . . . . .Rimmer

Valentina Vargas . . . . .Angelique

•• 0:40—Breasts and brief partial buns, while making love with John in his dream.

Hellroller (1992)

Michelle Bauer. . . . . .Michelle Novak

••• 0:30—Breasts taking a bath.

Ruth Corrine Collins. . . . . Eugene's Mother

Elizabeth Kaitan . . . . Lizzy

Hyapatia Lee . . . . Dancer

••• 0:43—Breasts, dancing in room by herself.

••• 0:45—Breasts and buns, while taking a shower.

Henry & June (1990)

Maria de Medeiros. . . . . Anais Nin

• 0:50—Brief right breast, popping out of dress top.

•• 0:52—Breasts lying in bed with Richard E. Grant.

•• 1:13—Breasts in bed with Fred Ward, buns getting out. Right breast standing by the window.

••• 1:31—Breasts in bed with Brigitte Lahaie.

• 1:37—Nude under sheer black patterned dress.

•• 1:43—Close up of right breast as Ward plays with her.

•• 2:01—Left breast, then breasts after taking off her top in bed with Uma Thurman.

Brigitte Lahaie . . . . .Harry's Whore

•• 0:23—Brief buns and breasts under sheer white dress going up stairs with Fred Ward.

•• 1:22—Breasts in sheer white dress again. Nude under dress walking up stairs.

••• 1:23—Breasts and buns making love with another woman while Anais and Hugo watch.

• 1:31—Breasts in bed with Anais. Intercut with Uma Thurman, so hard to tell who is who.

Maïté Maillé. . . . . .Frail Prostitute

• 1:22—In black see-through dress.

••• 1:23—Breasts making love with Brigitte Lahaie in front of Anais and Hugo.

Uma Thurman . . . . June Miller

Her Alibi (1989)

Liliana Komorowska. . . . . Laura

Paulina Porizkova. . . . . Nina

• 1:00—Very brief right nipple when pulling herself up out of the water in the swimming pool.

Hexed (1993)

a.k.a. All Shook Up

Laura Banks . . . . 1st Reporter

Claudia Christian . . . . Hexina

• 0:30—Tip of right breast, several times, while lying on her back in bed. (You can tell when the body double is used because of the bad wig.)

•• 0:31—Brief right breast, several times, while making love in bed.

• 0:34—Very brief inside of right breast in gaping coat, while raising knife. Brief buns, while getting pushed off bed.

Teresa Ganzel . . . . 3rd Reporter

Shelley Michelle . . . . .Body Double for Claudia Christian
- •• 0:31—Breasts, while making love on top of Matthew in bed.
- • 0:32—Buns and right breast, getting out of bed.
- • 0:57—Buns and brief left breast, while standing up in bed.

Hidden Assassin *(1994)*

Maruschka Detmers . . . . .Simone Rosset
- •• 0:48—In black bra and panties, then breasts, getting into bathtub in front of Dolph Lundgren.

Assumpta Serna . . . . Marta

Hide and Go Shriek *(1988)*

Donna Baltron. . . . . Judy Ramerize
- •• 0:56—In white bra and panties, then breasts after undressing seductively in front of her boyfriend.

Rebunkah Jones. . . . . .Bonnie Williams
- •• 0:27—Breasts taking off her blouse. More breasts sitting in bed.

Annette Sinclair. . . . . Kim Downs
- • 0:51—Brief breasts and buns, undressing and getting into bed. Long shot.
- •• 0:57—Breasts, getting up and out of bed, then getting dressed.
- • 1:02—Breasts and buns, tied up on top of freight elevator.
- • 1:05—Breasts on top of elevator.
- • 1:17—Breasts on top of elevator fighting with the killer. Lit with red light.

• ***Hideous*** *(1997)*

Jacqueline Lovell . . . . Sheila
- •• 0:16—Breasts, while in car and outdoors (wearing a gorilla mask).

Tracie May . . . . Belinda Yost
- • 0:59—Very, very brief partial buns in panties after falling on the floor.

Hider in the House *(1989)*

Rebekka Armstrong. . . . . .Attractive Woman
- • 0:47—Brief breasts in bed with Mimi Roger's husband when she surprises them.

Mimi Rogers . . . . Julie Dreyer

The High Country *(1980; Canadian)*

Linda Purl . . . . Kathy
- • 1:03—Brief buns, while taking a shower in the waterfall.

High Heels *(1972; French)*

a.k.a. Docteur Popaul

Laura Antonelli . . . . .Martine
- • 0:35—Breasts, while undressing and Jean-Paul Belmondo watches. Long, long shot.
- • 0:36—Briefly nude when Belmondo watches through opera glasses.
- ••• 0:53—Breasts and buns, getting out of bed and walking around.
- • 0:55—Buns, getting a shot while lying on examination table.
- •• 0:56—Breasts, twice, sitting naked on examination table.
- • 1:30—Brief side of right breast during flashback of 0:56 scene.
- • 1:31—Brief full frontal nudity, while running around her house and Mia Farrow watches. Long shot.

Mia Farrow . . . . Christine Du Pont

High Heels *(1991; Spanish)*

Victoria Abril . . . . .Rebecca Giner
- • 0:31—Breasts, when her dress falls down slightly while hanging on a pole and making love with Lethal.

Bibi Andersen . . . . Chon

Carmen Maura . . . . Tina

High Season *(1988; British)*

Jacqueline Bisset . . . . .Katherine Shaw
- • 0:56—Brief breasts doing the backstroke in the water with Kenneth Branagh, then left breast while lying down. Hard to see, everything is lit with blue light.

Irene Papas . . . . .Penelope

• ***High Society Centerspread Video #10: Barbara Dare*** *(1990; Video Tape)*

Barbara Dare . . . . Herself
- •• 0:01—Breasts undressing.
- ••• 0:03—Nude on bed with a guy video taping, then making love with her. Nice, long scene.
- ••• 0:08—Full frontal nudity during photo shoot and interview.
- ••• 0:13—Nude, on lounge chair, masturbating.
- •• 0:18—Breasts, sitting in chair during interview.

• ***High Society Centerspread Video #15: Julia Parton*** *(1990; Video Tape)*

Julia Parton . . . . Herself
- ••• 0:01—Breasts and buns taking off her clothes.
- ••• 0:04—Full frontal nudity in bathtub making love with a girl friend. Nice, long scene.
- ••• 0:09—Nude, doing a strip tease dance.
- ••• 0:17—Nude, relaxing on the floor and masturbating.
- ••• 0:18—Nude on bed, making love with the maid during fantasy.

High Stakes *(1989)*

Kathy Bates . . . . Jill

Maia Danziger. . . . . Veronica

Sally Kirkland. . . . . Melanie "Bambi" Rose
- • 0:01—In two piece costume, doing a strip tease routine on stage. Buns in G-string, then very, very brief breasts while flashing.

Higher Education *(1987; Canadian)*

Lori Hallier. . . . . .Nicole Hubert
- • 0:44—Right breast, twice, while making love with Andy in bed.

Jennifer Inch . . . . Gladys/Glitter

Isabelle Mejias. . . . . .Carrie Hanson

Sharolyn Sparrow . . . . Helen Dobish

Highlander *(1986)*

Roxanne Hart . . . . Brenda Wyatt
- • 1:30—Brief breasts making love with Christopher Lambert. Dark, hard to see.

Highlander III: The Final Dimension *(1994)*

Deborah Unger . . . . Alex/Sarah
- •• 1:14—In black bra and panties, then nude while making love in bed with Christopher Lambert. Don't see her face very well. Nice buns shots.

The Hills Have Eyes, Part II *(1989)*

Penny Johnson . . . . Sue
- • 0:49—Brief breasts in bus, trying to get Foster's attention.

Colleen Riley . . . . Jane
- 0:55—Very brief left breast, twice, while taking a shower outside when Foster talks to her.

• *Hindsight* (1996)

Tuesday Knight . . . . Karen
Lorissa McComas. . . . . Chantel
- 0:46—Brief breasts, when opening her sweater for Jason.

Sky Nicholas . . . . Chateau
Cyndi Pass. . . . . Cassandra Bennett
- •• 0:21—Breasts, while making love in bed with Jason.
- • 0:23—Brief right breast, while talking with Jason.
- •• 0:25—Full frontal nudity, while making love with Jason.
- •• 0:37—Breasts and brief buns, while making love with Jason.
- • 1:17—Brief buns, getting into bathtub.

Deanne Power. . . . . Lori
Sheila Redgate. . . . . Swing Club
Kathy Shower . . . . Joanne Lehman
- 0:08—Breasts, while making love with Jason.

Hired to Kill (1990)

Jordana Capra . . . . Joanna
Cynthia Lee. . . . . Armwrestler
Michelle Moffett . . . . Ana
- • 0:46—Left breast in dress, then breasts when Oliver Reed lowers her top.
- •• 0:47—More breasts in open dress top.
- •• 1:04—Very, very brief tip of right breast, lying on table when Brian Thompson rips her blouse open. More breasts, lying on the table. Dark.

Barbara Niven . . . . Sheila
Penelope Reed. . . . . Katrina

The Hit List (1993; Made for Cable Movie)

Yancy Butler . . . . Jordan Henning
La Joy Farr . . . . Linda
Ashley Graham . . . . Bartender
Shelley Michelle . . . . Dancer
Amy Rochelle . . . . Body Double for Yancy Butler
- • 0:31—Buns, taking off swimsuit in front of Jeff Fahey. Long shot, don't see her face.
- • 1:00—Brief left breast in bed while making love with Fahey. Don't see her face very well.

Hit the Dutchman (1992)

(Unrated version reviewed.)
Sally Kirkland. . . . . Emma Flegenheimer
Jennifer Miller . . . . Frances Ireland
- • 0:35—Most of side of right breast, while in dressing room with Arthur.
- •• 0:36—Breasts, while running around the room with Arthur. More breasts and buns, while on the floor with him.
- • 0:55—Brief breasts, after taking off her dress top for Legs Diamond.

Elena Skorohodove . . . . Anastasia
- •• 1:17—Breasts, while making love with Arthur in bedroom.
- ••• 1:19—Nude, making love in bed with Arthur and afterwards.
- •• 1:23—Breasts in bed with Arthur.

Hit! (1973)

Gwen Welles . . . . Sherry Nielson
- ••• 2:03—Breasts, taking off her clothes in front of a woman before killing her.

The Hitchhikers (1971)

Misty Rowe . . . . Maggie
- • 0:00—Brief side view of left breast getting dressed.
- • 0:17—Very brief breasts getting dress ripped open, then raped in van.
- • 0:48—Brief right breast while getting dressed.
- • 1:09—Left breast, making love with Benson.
- • 1:10—Brief breasts taking a bath in tub.
- • 1:13—Very brief right breast in car with another victim.

The Hitter (1978)

Sheila Frazier . . . . Lola
- • 0:30—Brief side view of left breast, while making love in bed with Ron O'Neal.
- •• 0:31—Breasts, while sitting in bed after making love.

Hitz (1992)

a.k.a. Judgment
Karen Black . . . . Tiffany Powers
Emilia Crow . . . . Chelsea Walker
- ••• 0:27—Breasts and very brief upper half of lower frontal nudity, making love in bed with Jimmy. Lit with red light.

Hold Me, Thrill Me, Kiss Me (1993)

(Unrated version reviewed.)
Andrea Naschak. . . . . Sabra
- • 0:04—Buns in yellow and orange two piece swimsuit while dancing on stage.
- • 0:08—Buns in G-string and out of it in trailer with Max.
- • 0:09—Very brief left breast under sheer black blouse.
- 0:25—Buns, while on stage in black outfit.
- • 0:46—Buns and most of breast, while dancing on stage in sexy outfit.

Nicole Sassaman . . . . Girl on a Leash
Sean Young . . . . Twinkle

Hollywood Boulevard (1976)

Candice Rialson . . . . Candy Wednesday
- •• 0:29—Breasts getting her blouse ripped off by actors during a film.
- ••• 0:32—Breasts sunbathing with Bobbi and Jill.
- •• 0:45—Brief breasts in the films she's watching at the drive-in. Same as 0:29.

Tara Strohmeier. . . . . Jill McBain
- •• 0:00—Breasts getting out of van and standing with film crew.
- • 0:31—Silhouette of breasts, while making love with P.G.
- ••• 0:32—Breasts sunbathing with Bobbi and Candy.
- ••• 0:33—Breasts acting for film on hammock. Long scene.

Mary Woronov . . . . Mary McQueen

Hollywood Boulevard II (1989)

Ginger Lynn Allen . . . . Candy Chandler
- •• 0:33—Breasts in screening room with Woody, the writer.

Michelle Moffett . . . . Mary Randolf
Randi Randolph. . . . . Doreen
Ty Randolph . . . . Amazon Warrior from Brooklyn
Penelope Reed. . . . . Amazon Warrior with Crystal
Maria Socas . . . . Amazon Queen
Lynn Theel. . . . . Ann Gregory

Hollywood Chainsaw Hookers (1988)

Esther Alise . . . . Lisa
- ••• 0:25—Breasts playing with a baseball bat while a John photographs her.

Michelle Bauer . . . . Mercedes
••• 0:09—Nude in motel room with a John just before chain-sawing him to pieces.

Tricia Brown . . . . Ilsa
•• 0:37—Breasts while Jack is tied up in bed.

Linnea Quigley . . . . Samantha
•• 0:32—Breasts, dancing on stage.
• 1:02—Breasts, (but her body is painted) dancing in a ceremony.

Dawn Wildsmith . . . . Lori

Hollywood Dreams *(1993)*

a.k.a. L.A. Dreams

(Unrated version reviewed.)

Debra Beatty . . . . Sara
••• 0:11—Breasts after taking off her top in office for audition in front of Lou.
••• 0:19—Nude, diving into pool and getting out, then making love at Lou's.
•• 0:24—Left breast and partial lower frontal nudity while lying on bed on a set.
•• 0:39—Breasts while making love with Robby on bed in bedroom set.
• 1:06—Side of right breast while getting made up.

Kelly Jaye . . . . Veronica
•• 0:08—Nude, while making love with Steve on the floor.
• 0:14—In black lingerie, then left breast after undressing in office for audition in front of Lou.
• 0:25—Buns and breasts while in shower set during filming.
• 0:52—Breasts, while making love on couch with Steve.
••• 1:15—Nude, after taking off her dress in bedroom and making love with Robby.
• 1:19—Brief left breast while hugging Robby.

Kathy Pasmore . . . . Tiffany
••• 0:15—Breasts and buns, while sitting on desk in Lou's office.
••• 0:27—Getting a massage while wearing a sexy suit, then breasts and buns in T-back when making out with Natasha.
•• 0:28—Breasts and buns, while making love with Natasha and Robby.
• 1:06—Breasts in background while getting dressed.

Jacqueline St. Claire . . . . Stripper
•• 0:57—Breasts and buns in T-back, after stripping out of outfit while dancing in bar set.

Hollywood Erotic Film Festival *(1986)*

Vickie Benson . . . . Thin Walls/Yvette

Monique Gabrielle . . . . He Believes

Jane Hamilton . . . . Movie Buffs
•• 0:27—Breasts and buns, when making love with a guy in bed while two little stop motion creatures film them.

Lisa Lyon . . . . Lisa Lyon: A Portrait of Power
••• 0:17—Breasts and buns in G-string, while doing body building poses.
••• 0:21—Breasts and buns while posing on a rooftop, with a city in the background.

Hollywood High *(1976)*

Suzanne Severeid . . . . Jan
• 0:07—Breasts under sheer white swimsuit while frolicking in the surf with her girlfriends.
• 0:09—Breasts under sheer white swimsuit top while talking on the beach with Frasier.
•• 0:29—Breasts, while lifting up her blouse to distract the class brain so every one else in class can copy his answers.
• 0:43—Very brief right breast, when leaving the pool after washing her clothes.
• 0:51—Brief buns, while mooning her friends in passing van.
•• 1:14—Breasts, while in swimming pool with her friends and running around outside and in house.

Hollywood Hot Tubs *(1984)*

Becky LeBeau . . . . Veronica
•• 0:49—Breasts changing in the locker room with other girl soccer players while Jeff watches.
• 0:54—Breasts in hot tub with the other girls and Shawn.

Donna McDaniel . . . . Leslie Maynard

Remy O'Neill . . . . Pam Landers
• 1:00—Brief right breast in hot tub with Jeff.

Alexis Schreiner . . . . Soccer Girl

Katt Shea . . . . Dee-Dee
• 0:21—Breasts with her boyfriend while Shawn is working on the hot tub.

Jewel Shepard . . . . Crystal Landers

Edy Williams . . . . Desiree
••• 0:26—Breasts, trying to seduce Shawn while he works on a hot tub.
• 1:30—Partial breasts with breasts sticking out of her bra while she sits by hot tub with Jeff.
•• 1:32—Breasts in hot tub room with Shawn.
• 1:36—Brief breasts while running around.
• 1:38—Breasts again in the hot tub lobby.

Hollywood Hot Tubs 2—Educating Crystal *(1989)*

Martina Castel . . . . Hardie

Tally Chanel . . . . Mindy Wright

Dori Courtney . . . . Hot Tub Girl
•• 1:00—Breasts stuck in the spa and getting her hair freed.

Remy O'Neill . . . . Pam Landers

Jewel Shepard . . . . Crystal Landers
• 1:12—Brief left breast, while lying down, kissing Gary.

The Hollywood Knights *(1980)*

Dawn Clark . . . . Pom Pom Girl
•• 0:01—Breasts sunbathing outside with Fran Drescher and another Pom Pom Girl.
• 0:11—In bra, then brief breasts, changing clothes at night.
• 0:20—Breasts in B&W Polaroid photograph. Long shot.

Michele Drake . . . . Cheerleader
• 0:28—Brief lower nudity in raised cheerleader outfit doing cheers in front of school assembly.

Fran Drescher . . . . Sally

Debra Feuer . . . . Cheetah

Kim Hopkins . . . . Pom Pom Girl
• 0:01—Breasts, sunbathing outside with her two girlfriends.

Joyce Hyser . . . . Brenda Weintraub

Michelle Pfeiffer . . . . Suzi Q.

Carol Ann Williams . . . . Jane
• 0:51—Very brief breasts, opening her blouse to distract Dudley. Don't see her face.

Hollywood Passions *(1994)*

Leigh Betchley . . . . Connie
• 0:33—Brief breasts, while dressing.

Diana Cuevas . . . . Denise
•• 0:07—In bra, then breasts, after undressing and making out with Lou.

Carol Hoyt . . . . Marla
••• 0:00—Breasts, while making love with her boyfriend on the floor.

••• 0:42—Breasts and buns, while making love on sofa with Stan.
• 0:47—Brief breasts, while fooling around behind the set with Stan.

Donna Spangler . . . . Dancer #1
•• 1:04—Breasts (she has the red boa), while dancing with two other girls.

• Hollywood Scandals and Tragedies *(1988; Video Tape)*

Jean Harlow. . . . . Herself
• 0:24—Breasts in B&W still photo. Her head is turned toward the side.
•• 0:26—Breasts in B&W still photos.

Jayne Mansfield. . . . . Herself
• 1:11—Breasts in color still photographs from *Playboy* pictorial.

Hollywood Zap! *(1986)*

Annie Gaybis. . . . . Debbie
••• 0:54—Breasts while wearing gold bikini bottoms, in bedroom with Tucker.

Holocaust 2000 *(1978)*

Agostina Belli. . . . . Sara Golen
•• 0:50—Breasts in bed making love with Kirk Douglas.

• Homage *(1994)*

Blythe Danner . . . . Katherine Samuel
Sheryl Lee . . . . Lucy Samuel
• 0:37—Very brief breasts seen on TV that Frank Whaley is masturbating to.

Home Movies *(1980)*

Nancy Allen. . . . . Kristina
• 1:14—Very brief left breast when bending over while sitting on bed and again when reaching up to touch Keith Gordon's face.

Homework *(1982)*

Michelle Bauer. . . . . Uncredited Dream Groupie
••• 1:01—Breasts with two other groupies, groping Tommy while he sings. (She has a flower in her hair and is the only brunette.)

Joan Collins . . . . Diane
Joy Michael . . . . . . Diane, Age 16/Body Double for Joan Collins
•• 0:39—In bra, then breasts in car making out with her boyfriend.
•• 1:18—Breasts, taking off her bra and making love with Tommy. (Supposed to be Joan Collins.)

Barbara Peckinpaugh. . . . . Uncredited Magazine Model
••• 0:01—Brief breasts in magazine layout. In lingerie, then breasts in Tommy's photo session fantasy.

Carrie Snodgress . . . . Dr. Delingua
Betty Thomas . . . . Reddog's Secretary

Homicidal Impulse *(1992)*

a.k.a. Killer Instinct
(Unrated version reviewed.)

Vanessa Angel . . . . Deborah
•• 0:13—In bra, then breasts making love with Scott Valentine in his office on top of the photocopier (Don't see her face).
•• 0:24—Breasts and buns, while making love in bed (you can see her face a little bit).
••• 0:30—In black bra, then breasts while making love (don't see her face).
• 0:39—Very brief breasts in flashes during Valentine's drug induced visions.

Brigitta Stenberg . . . . Receptionist

Honey *(1980; Italian)*

Donatella Damiani. . . . . The Landlady
• 0:24—Very, very brief right breast dodging Clio Goldsmith's hand while playfully drying her off with a towel.

Clio Goldsmith . . . . Annie
•• 0:05—Nude kneeling in a room.
•• 0:20—Nude getting into the bathtub.
•• 0:42—Nude getting changed.
••• 0:44—Nude while hiding under the bed.
•• 0:58—Nude getting disciplined, taking off clothes, then kneeling.

Honeymoon *(1985; French/Canadian)*

Nathalie Baye . . . . Cécile
• 1:00—Brief breasts, while sitting on bed with John Shea.

Hong Kong '97 *(1994)*

Selina Mangh Li
• 0:06—Breasts, while making love with Robert Patrick in living room.
•• 0:08—Nude, during shoot out.

Ming-Na Wen . . . . Katie Chun

Honky *(1971)*

Maia Danziger . . . . Sharon
Brenda Sykes . . . . Sheila Smith
••• 0:42—Breasts with her boyfriend, making love on the floor.
• 1:22—Brief breasts several times getting raped by two guys.

Honky Tonk Nights *(1978)*

Serena . . . . Dolly Pop
• 0:04—Breasts in open blouse, getting restrained after getting in a fight with a guy who tries to molest her.
••• 0:10—Breasts in bed with Bobby, then putting on a robe.
••• 0:38—Breasts standing in doorway, then in kitchen with Bill.

Carol Doda . . . . Belle Barnette
••• 0:17—Breasts changing blouses in bedroom with Doris Ann.
• 0:28—Left breast several times while making out with a guy.
••• 1:11—Breasts in bedroom with Doris Ann during flashback. (Different camera angle than 0:17.)

Amanda Jones . . . . .Honey
•• 0:41—Breasts outside by car with Dan.
••• 0:42—Breasts and buns, in the woods with Dan.

Georgina Spelvin . . . . Georgia
• 0:06—Breasts, lying with her head in a guy's lap.

Horror Planet *(1980; British)*

a.k.a. Inseminoid

Jennifer Ashley . . . . .Holly
Stephanie Beacham . . . . Kate
Judy Geeson . . . . Sandy
•• 0:31—Brief breasts on the operating table.
• 0:32—Brief full frontal nudity on table.
• 0:37—Brief full frontal nudity during flashbacks.

Victoria Tennant . . . . Barbara

• *The Horror Show* *(1989)*

Dedee Pfeiffer . . . . Bonnie McCarthy

• 1:06—Brief breasts and buns from above, shampooing her hair in the shower. Breasts, seen through shower curtain. Probably a body double.

• *The Horseman on the Roof* *(1995; French)*

Juliette Binoche . . . . Pauline

• 1:48—Breasts, while Angelo rubs her down with alcohol to help her over her bout with cholera. Don't see her face with her body.

Hospital Massacre *(1982)*

a.k.a. X-Ray

Barbi Benton . . . . Susan Jeremy

••• 0:31—Breasts getting examined by the Doctor. First sitting up, then lying down.

••• 0:34—Great close up shot of breasts while the Doctor uses stethoscope on her.

• *Hostage* *(1992)*

Talisa Soto. . . . . Joanna

• 0:56—Very brief out-of-focus breasts, while leaning back when making love with Sam Neill.

• 1:16—Out-of-focus breasts again.

Hostile Intentions *(1994)*

Tia Carrere . . . . Nora

Tricia Leigh Fisher . . . . Maureen

• 0:34—Brief breasts, three times, while being raped in jail cell by Mexican police captain.

Lisa Dean Ryan . . . . Caroline

Hostile Takeover *(1988; Canadian)*

a.k.a. Office Party

Jayne Eastwood. . . . . Mrs. Talmage

Cindy Girling. . . . . Mrs. Gayford

Kate Vernon . . . . Sally

• 0:35—Very brief, left breast undressing in office with John Warner. Dark.

•• 0:39—Right breast, turning over in her sleep, then playing with the chain.

Hot Blood *(1989; Spanish)*

Sylvia Kristel . . . . Sylvia

• 0:44—Buns, getting molested by Dom Luis.

Alicia Moro . . . . Alicia

• 0:00—Buns and lower frontal nudity in stable with Ricardo. Long shot.

• 0:06—In bra and panties with Julio, then buns and breasts. Looks like a body double because hair doesn't match.

Vivianne Vives . . . . Connie

• 1:19—Buns and very brief side view of left breast in bed with Julio.

•• 1:21—Breasts in bed several times, then lower frontal nudity with Julio.

• *Hot Bodies* *(1988; Video Tape)*

Sara Costa. . . . . Herself

••• 0:00—Nude, dancing on stage. Long scene. Dancing with a big boa snake.

••• 0:04—Breasts and buns in G-string.

Venus De Light . . . . Herself

•• 0:22—Breasts, dancing and taking off dress.

••• 0:24—Nude in large champagne glass prop.

••• 0:27—Nude dancing on stage.

••• 0:47—Breasts and buns in G-string stripping in nurse uniform.

••• 0:49—Breasts and buns, while on hospital gurney.

••• 0:52—Breasts and buns dancing with a life-size dummy prop.

Glenda Moore . . . . Herself

••• 0:37—Breasts, dancing with a sword. Sort of buns, under skirt.

••• 0:40—Dancing without the sword. Buns in G-string.

••• 0:44—Breasts and buns dancing with sword again.

• *Hot Body Competition: Bikinis & Bikes Contest* *(1996; Video Tape)*

Stevi Conrad . . . . Stevi Conrad

•• 0:35—Breasts and buns, while dancing on stage.

••• 0:36—Nude, while posing outdoors by pool.

Kalani Freeman . . . . Kalani

•• 0:34—Breasts and buns, while dancing on stage.

Summer Leigh. . . . . Summer Leigh

•• 0:39—Breasts and buns, while dancing on stage.

••• 0:40—Nude, while posing on bed outdoors.

Jacqueline Lovell . . . . Sara St. James

•• 0:29—Breasts and buns, while dancing on stage.

••• 0:30—Nude, while posing outdoors.

Sky Nicholas . . . . Sky

•• 0:05—Breasts and buns, while dancing on stage.

••• 0:06—Nude, while posing outdoors with motorcycle.

Cathleen Raymond . . . . Noelle

•• 0:07—Breasts and buns, while dancing on stage.

Tonja Schild . . . . Felicia

••• 0:04—Breasts and buns, while dancing on stage.

Eileen Smith . . . . Danielle

•• 0:16—Breasts and buns, while dancing on stage.

••• 0:17—Nude, while posing outdoors.

• *Hot Body Competition: Lusty Lingerie Contest* *(1996; Video Tape)*

Stacy Moran . . . . Stacy Moran

••• 0:38—Nude, dancing on stage during contest.

••• 0:49—Nude, while posing on bed after winning contest.

Ashley Phillips . . . . Ashley Phillips

••• 0:29—Nude, dancing on stage during contest. Including playing with fire.

••• 0:44—Nude, while posing on balcony.

Mallesia Renée. . . . . Mallesia Renee

••• 0:34—Nude, dancing on stage during contest.

••• 0:35—Nude, while posing outdoors.

• *Hot Body Competition: The Best of Hot Body* *(1994; Video Tape)*

Tiffany Ann . . . . Herself

••• 0:58—Buns in swimsuits. Breasts under pasties.

Melinda Armstrong . . . . Herself

••• 0:11—Buns in swimsuits. Breasts while trying on lingerie.

Janell Burns . . . . Herself

••• 0:08—Breasts and buns in swimsuit.

Tanya Carr. . . . . Herself

••• 0:42—Buns in swimsuits. Breasts while wearing pasties.

Tracy Dali . . . . Herself

••• 0:33—Buns in lingerie and swimsuits. Breasts while trying on lingerie.

Angela Dawn. . . . . Herself

•• 0:50—Buns in swimsuits.

Heather Kennedy. . . . . Herself

•• 0:15—Buns in swimsuits.

Kimberly McCartney . . . . Herself
••• 0:46—Buns in swimsuits. Breasts when wearing pasties. Brief breasts while flashing.
Heather-Elizabeth Parkhurst. . . . . Herself
Staci Yarbrough. . . . . Herself
•• 1:13—Buns in swimsuits.

• ***Hot Body Hall of Fame: Traci Dali***

(1995; Video Tape)

Avalon Anders . . . . Herself
•• 0:51—Nude in various clips.
Tracy Dali . . . . Herself
••• 0:01—Stripping out of black outfit on balcony, then nude.
••• 0:06—Nude on the snow and in a spa.
••• 0:09—Nude, while stripping out of swimsuit in front of window.
•• 0:10—Nude, while posing next to swimming pool.
••• 0:11—Nude, while dancing in front of a black Testarossa.
••• 0:17—Nude, while posing and changing clothes during lingerie shoot.
••• 0:23—In lingerie, then nude, while posing on the floor in front of fireplace.
•• 0:27—In swimsuit, then nude, while posing out by pool.
Heidi Lynne. . . . . Herself
•• 0:33—Nude, while posing outdoors on balcony.
Mason Marconi . . . . Herself
••• 0:36—In lingerie, then nude after stripping out of business suit in an office.

• ***Hot Body International: #1 Miss Cancun***

(1990; Video Tape)

Leslee Bremmer. . . . . Contestant
•• 0:25—Buns in two piece swimsuit.
Lisa Lennox . . . . Contestant
Bianca McEachin . . . . Contestant
Heather-Elizabeth Parkhurst. . . . . Contestant
•• 0:26—Buns, in two piece swimsuit.
•• 0:52—Winner. Buns, in two piece swimsuit during photo session after the contest.
Brooke Thompson . . . . Contestant
•• 0:40—Buns, in one piece swimsuit.

• ***Hot Body International: #2 Miss Puerto Vallarta***

(1990; Video Tape)

Tiffany Ann . . . . Contestant
•• 0:29—Breasts wearing pasties and buns, in G-string.
•• 0:58—Buns, posing in wet, green two piece swimsuit.
Tanya Carr . . . . Contestant
• 0:15—Very, very brief breasts, while flashing.
•• 0:24—Buns, in two piece swimsuit, then breasts wearing pasties.
•• 0:56—Wearing pasties.
Tamara Carrera . . . . Contestant
Kimberly Johnson . . . . Contestant
•• 0:43—Buns in two piece swimsuit.
Deanna Jordan . . . . Contestant
Heather Kennedy. . . . . Contestant
•• 0:40—Buns and almost breasts in one piece swimsuit.
Lisa Lennox . . . . Contestant
Kimberly McCartney . . . . Contestant
•• 0:48—Buns in one piece swimsuit. Practically breasts wearing pasties.
Shanae Ruddell . . . . Contestant
•• 0:33—Buns, in one piece swimsuit.

Brooke Thompson . . . . Contestant
•• 0:26—Buns in red one piece swimsuit. Brief left breast a couple of times when it accidentally falls out.

• ***Hot Body International: #3 Lingerie Special***

(1992; Video Tape)

Janell Burns . . . . Contestant
•• 0:31—Buns in one piece body suit.
Angela Dawn . . . . Contestant
•• 0:13—Buns in body suit.
Jaki Gentry . . . . Contestant
•• 0:46—Buns, in G-string and bra.
••• 0:53—Breasts, while posing for photo shoot.
Lauren Hays . . . . Contestant
•• 0:48—Buns in white G-string and bra.
Lori Deann Pallett . . . . Contestant
•• 0:21—Buns in G-string and black top.
Tammy Rief . . . . Contestant
•• 0:20—Buns in black bra and G-string.
Kelley Wild . . . . Contestant
•• 0:22—Buns in purple and black bra and G-string.
••• 0:55—Breasts, when getting out of bed. Buns, in G-string. Breasts in bathtub.
••• 0:57—Buns and breasts, getting a massage.
Staci Yarbrough . . . . Contestant
•• 0:45—Buns, in white G-string.

• ***Hot Body International: #4 Spring Break***

(1992; Video Tape)

Tiffany Ann . . . . Contestant
• 0:36—Barely there wet T-shirt. Brief right breast, when bending over.
Tanya Carr. . . . . Contestant
••• 0:42—Breasts popping out of wet T-shirt, quite a few times. Buns in G-string.
• 0:58—Brief breasts several times winning 3rd place in wet T-shirt contest.
Tamara Carrera . . . . Contestant
Kimberly Johnson . . . . Contestant
• 0:25—Buns in G-string during wet T-shirt contest.
Deanna Jordan. . . . . Contestant
• 0:13—Dancing in two piece swimsuit on stage. Brief partial right breast.
• 0:49—Brief breasts several times when she rips her wet T-shirt open. Buns in G-string.
Heather Kennedy. . . . . Contestant
• 0:23—Buns in G-string during wet T-shirt contest.
Lisa Lennox . . . . Contestant
• 0:48—Brief left breast during wet T-shirt contest. Buns in G-string.
Kimberly McCartney . . . . Contestant
Shanae Ruddell . . . . Contestant
Brooke Thompson . . . . Contestant
• 0:38—Buns in G-string during wet T-shirt contest.

• ***Hot Body International: #5 Miss Acapulco***

(1992; Video Tape)

Janell Burns . . . . Contestant
••• 0:14—Breasts and buns in swimsuit in pool. Breasts applying flowers to her breasts, then taking them off.
•• 0:16—Breasts taking off bikini top outside next to pool.
Angela Dawn. . . . . Contestant
•• 0:46—Buns, while dancing in orange two piece swimsuit.
Jaki Gentry. . . . . Contestant

Lauren Hays . . . . Contestant
• 0:13—Buns, under mini-skirt.
Lori Deann Pallett . . . . Contestant
•• 0:26—Buns, while dancing in two piece swimsuit.
Tammy Rief . . . . Contestant
•• 0:52—Buns in one piece swimsuit during photo shoot.
Kelley Wild . . . . Contestant
•• 0:01—Brief breasts while saying "Hi Mom!"
••• 0:39—Breasts, taking off her bikini top.
•• 0:40—Buns, dancing in green two piece swimsuit.
Staci Yarbrough . . . . Contestant
•• 0:31—Buns, in two piece swimsuit.
•• 0:55—Buns in pink two piece swimsuit during photo session.

• *Hot Body International: Steamed Heat*
(1995; Video Tape)

Dottie Bittle . . . . Herself
• 0:11—Buns in swimsuit, while posing outdoors with two other models.
Christy Carrera . . . . Herself
• 0:32—Brief breasts, after taking off her black top.
Tracy Dali . . . . Herself
• 0:10—Buns in swimsuit, while posing outdoors with another model.
• 0:18—Buns in swimsuit, while posing outdoors with another model.
Heidi Lynne . . . . Herself
• 0:08—Buns in swimsuit at the beach.
• 0:13—Buns in swimsuit, outdoors at the beach.
•• 0:14—Buns and breasts, while changing swimsuits outdoors.
•• 0:20—Buns in swimsuit, then buns and breasts, while changing swimsuits.
Mason Marconi . . . . Herself
• 0:03—Buns in swimsuit, outdoors next to car at gas station.
• 0:06—Buns in swimsuit, outdoors at the beach.
Bianca Rocilili . . . . Herself
• 0:13—Buns in swimsuit, while posing on stairs.
• 0:35—Breasts and buns under sheer pink dress.
••• 0:48—Buns in sheer white body suit, then breasts while posing on bed.
Stephanie Sumers . . . . Herself
• 0:06—Buns in swimsuit at the beach.
• 0:10—Buns in swimsuit at the beach.
••• 0:14—Buns and breasts, while changing swimsuits outdoors.
••• 0:21—Buns and breasts, while changing swimsuits outdoors.
• 0:42—Buns in black outfit outdoors.
• 0:43—Buns in swimsuit in bedroom.
• 0:47—Buns in swimsuit in bedroom.

• *Hot Body Video Magazine #15: Wild Thing*
(1996; Video Tape)

Tracie Ivins . . . . Covergirl Update/Tracie
••• 0:24—In lingerie, then nude, while stripping and dancing indoors.
Cory Lane . . . . Southern Exposure/Feature Model
••• 0:15—In blue two piece swimsuit, then nude, while modeling outdoors by pool.
••• 0:32—In swimsuit, then nude, while dancing outdoors next to pool.
Bianca Rocilili . . . . Bianca
••• 0:01—In black lingerie, then nude, while dancing and stripping on a stairwell.

• *Hot Body Video Magazine #1: Premiere Edition*
(1992; Video Tape)

Avalon Anders . . . . Model
••• 0:41—Buns and breasts modeling, sunbathing and dancing. Great, long scenes.
Sara Costa . . . . Lingerie Model/Sara
••• 0:26—Breasts and buns in room with three other models, trying on lingerie.
Angela Dawn . . . . Street Scene/Model
••• 0:34—Buns in G-string and breasts during photo session on a Harley.
Melissa Anne Moore . . . . Herself
• 0:04—Brief breasts on the floor in a robe in front of a fireplace.

• *Hot Body Video Magazine #2: Double Trouble*
(1992; Video Tape)

Melinda Armstrong . . . . Model
•• 0:00—Breasts during opening credits.
••• 0:03—In white bra, then breasts, buns in panties, posing outside.
••• 0:25—Breasts and buns (on the left), changing swimsuits.
Angela Dawn . . . . Feature Girl/Model
•• 0:01—Breasts during opening credits.
••• 0:28—Nude, taking off a red swimsuit and putting on a hot pink one.
••• 0:30—Outside on hay, in white bra and panties, then breasts and buns.
Sherry Sotres . . . . Street Scene/Model/Sherry
•• 0:01—Breasts and buns during opening credits.
••• 0:26—Breasts, taking off black swimsuit and putting another on.
••• 0:33—Breasts and buns, while posing in front of a red Ferrari.
•• 0:58—Breasts in outtake during the end credits.

• *Hot Body Video Magazine #3: Blonde Fever*
(1993; Video Tape)

Nova . . . . Fashion
•• 0:00—Breasts during introduction.
••• 0:30—Breasts, while changing clothes with Dottie and Samantha.
Bobbi Baird . . . . Coming Attractions
•• 0:55—Breasts.
Dottie Bittle . . . . Covergirl/Fashion
•• 0:00—Breasts during introduction.
••• 0:30—Full frontal nudity, while changing clothes with Nova and Samantha.
••• 0:40—Buns in two piece swimsuit, then nude by and in swimming pool.
••• 0:45—Nude, while stripping out of one of her sexy outfits.
••• 0:51—Nude, while posing on bed.

• *Hot Body Video Magazine #4: Extra Sexy*
(1993; Video Tape)

Nova . . . . Feature Girl
••• 0:00—Breasts during introduction.
••• 0:26—Breasts under sheer black top, then nude, while posing on balcony.
Bobbi Baird . . . . Covergirl
•• 0:02—Breasts during introduction.

••• 0:43—Breasts and side of buns, while posing on pool table.
•• 0:49—Breasts under sheer purple bodysuit, then breasts after taking it off.
••• 0:51—In sexy swimsuit in spa, then breasts and buns.
Angela Dawn. . . . . Street Scene
•• 0:01—Breasts and buns during introduction.
••• 0:38—In two piece swimsuit, then breasts and buns while posing on a Harley-Davidson motorcycle.
Sherry Sotres . . . . .Interview
•• 0:01—Breasts during introduction.
••• 0:36—Left breast, in wet top, while posing in shower for her husband, photographer Craig X. Sotres.

The Hot Box *(1972)*

Andrea Cagan . . . . Bunny
•• 0:16—Breasts cleaning herself off in stream behind Ellie and getting out.
• 0:21—Breasts sleeping in hammock. (She's the third girl from the front, stretching.)
••• 0:45—Breasts in stream while bathing with the other three girls.
Margaret Markov . . . . Lynn Forrest
• 0:12—Breasts when bad guy cuts her swimsuit top open.
•• 0:16—Breasts in stream consoling Bunny.
• 0:21—Breasts in the furthest hammock from camera. Long shot.
••• 0:45—Breasts bathing in stream with the other girls.
Rickey Richardson . . . . Ellie St. George
•• 0:16—Breasts cleaning herself off in stream and getting out.
• 0:21—Breasts sleeping in hammocks. (She's the second one from the front.)
• 0:26—Breasts getting accosted by the People's Army guys.
••• 0:43—Full frontal nudity making love with Flavio.
••• 0:45—Breasts in stream bathing with the other three girls.
• 1:01—Breasts taking off top in front of soldiers.
Laurie Rose . . . . Sue
•• 0:16—Breasts cleaning herself off in stream and getting out.
•• 0:21—Breasts sleeping in hammocks. (She's the first one from the front.)
• 0:26—Breasts getting accosted by the People's Army guys.
••• 0:45—Breasts in stream bathing with the other three girls.
• 0:58—Full frontal nudity getting raped by Major Dubay.

Hot Child in the City *(1987)*

Leah Ayres-Hamilton . . . . Rachel
• 1:12—Very brief breasts in the shower with a guy. Long shot, hard to see anything.
Shari Shattuck . . . . Abby

Hot Chili *(1985)*

Victoria Barrett . . . . .Victoria Stevenson
• 0:55—Very brief close up shot of right breast when it pops out of her dress. Don't see her face.
Bea Fiedler. . . . . The Music Teacher
•• 0:08—Breasts, while playing the cello and being fondled by Ricky.
• 0:29—Buns, while playing the violin.
•• 0:34—Nude during fight in restaurant with Chi Chi. Hard to see because of the flashing light.
••• 0:36—Breasts lying on inflatable lounge in pool, playing a flute.
••• 0:43—Left breast, while playing a tuba.
••• 1:01—Breasts and buns, while dancing in front of Mr. Lieberman.
• 1:07—Buns, then right breast while dancing with Stanley.
Flo Gerrish. . . . . Mrs. Baxter
Katherine Kriss . . . . Allison Baxter
••• 0:56—Breasts getting out of the pool and talking to Ricky.
• 1:09—Buns and side view of left breast, while lying down and kissing Ricky.
Louisa Moritz. . . . . Chi Chi
• 0:06—Brief buns, when turning around in white apron after talking with the boys.
•• 0:34—Nude during fight in restaurant with the Music Teacher. Hard to see because of the flashing light.
Taaffe O'Connell . . . . Brigitte
••• 0:21—Breasts while lying on the bed. Shot with lots of diffusion.
• 0:30—Brief breasts while playing the drums.
• 1:11—Brief breasts in bed while making love with Ernie, next to her drunk husband.

Hot Chocolate *(1992)*

Bo Derek . . . . B.J. Cassidy
• 0:30—Brief side view of right breast, while pulling sheets up on herself in bed.
Patricia Millardet . . . . Grace

Hot Dog... The Movie *(1984)*

Crystal Smith. . . . . .Motel Clerk
•• 0:10—Nude getting out of spa and going to the front desk to sign people in.
Shannon Tweed. . . . . Sylvia Fonda
••• 0:42—Nude, while undressing, then making love in bed and in spa with Harkin.

Hot Moves *(1984)*

Monique Gabrielle. . . . . Babs
• 0:29—Nude on the nude beach.
•• 1:07—Breasts on and behind the sofa with Barry trying to get her top off.
Gayle Gannes . . . . Jamie
• 1:09—Breasts, taking off her white blouse and getting in bed with Joey.
Suzi Horne. . . . . Hooker #1
Debi Richter. . . . . .Heidi
• 0:29—Breasts on nude beach.
••• 1:09—Breasts, taking off her red dress in bed with Michael.
Jill Schoelen . . . . .Julie Ann

Hot Resort *(1984)*

Victoria Barrett. . . . . Jane
Dana Kaminski. . . . . Melanie
•• 1:02—Breasts taking off her white dress in a boat.
Linda Kenton . . . . Mrs. Geraldine Miller
• 0:11—Very brief right breast, while in back of car with a guy.
• 0:16—Right breast, while passed out in closet with a bunch of guys.
• 0:24—Brief upper half of right breast, while on boat with a guy.
• 0:46—Brief breasts in Volkswagen.
• 0:51—Brief breasts in bathtub with Bronson Pinchot.
• 1:24—Brief breasts making love on a table while covered with food.
Cynthia Lee . . . . Alice
• 1:08—Breasts in the bathtub.

The Hot Spot *(1990)*

Debra Cole . . . . Irene Davey
- • 1:26—Breasts sunbathing next to Jennifer Connelly at side of lake. Long shot.
- •• 1:27—Breasts talking with Connelly some more.

Jennifer Connelly. . . . . Gloria Harper
- • 1:26—Buns, while lying next to Irene next to lake. Long shot.
- ••• 1:27—Breasts, while talking to Irene next to lake. Wow!

Virginia Madsen . . . . Dolly Harshaw
- • 0:41—Side view of left breast while sitting on bed talking to Don Johnson.
- • 0:47—Tip of right breast when Johnson kisses it.
- •• 1:16—Buns, while undressing for a swim outside at night. Breasts, while hanging on rope.
- • 1:18—Buns, getting out of water with Johnson. Long shot.
- • 1:21—Left breast when robe gapes open while sitting up.
- • 1:23—Brief lower frontal nudity and buns in open robe after jumping off tower at night.
- • 1:24—Breasts at bottom of hill with Johnson. Long shot.
- • 1:45—Nude, very, very briefly running out of house. Very blurry, could be anybody.

Hot T-Shirts *(1980)*

Corinne Alphen. . . . . Judy
- • 1:10—In yellow outfit dancing in wet T-shirt contest. Brief breasts while flashing the crowd.

Hot Target *(1985; New Zealand)*

Simone Griffeth. . . . . Christine Webber
- •• 0:09—Breasts taking off top for shower, then breasts and brief frontal nudity taking shower.
- ••• 0:19—Breasts in bed after making love with Steve Marachuck.
- •• 0:21—Buns, getting out of bed and walking to bathroom.
- •• 0:23—Breasts in bed with Marachuck again.
- • 0:34—Breasts in the woods with Marachuck while cricket match goes on.

Judy McIntosh. . . . . Clare

Hot Under the Collar *(1991)*

Melinda Clarke . . . . Monica

Karman Kruschke . . . . Sherry

Tané McClure . . . . Rowena
- ••• 0:32—Breasts, while in bed with Max.

The Hotel New Hampshire *(1984)*

Jodie Foster . . . . Franny

Nastassja Kinski . . . . Susie the Bear
- • 1:42—Very, very brief tip of left breast, then very brief right breast in room with Rob Lowe after she takes off her bear suit.

Anita Morris . . . . Ronda Ray

Amanda Plummer . . . . Miss Miscarriage

Joely Richardson . . . . Waitress

Michele Scarabelli . . . . Chip Dove Girlfriend

Cali Timmins. . . . . Bitty Tuck

The Hottest Bid *(1995)*

Belinda Farrell . . . . Angelique
- ••• 0:21—Breasts and buns in leather and chain outfit while seducing Marty.
- •• 0:50—Breasts while making love with Marty on the floor.

Gwen Somers . . . . Jessica
- •• 0:01—Nude while taking a bubble bath and getting out and drying herself off.
- •• 0:03—Breasts, when powdering her body in front of mirror and putting on lingerie. Partial buns in lingerie while putting on stockings.
- • 0:07—Breasts, while fantasizing a lover is caressing her.
- • 0:39—Brief buns under lingerie outfit outside in Don's fantasy.
- • 0:40—Lower frontal nudity, when she raises her lingerie skirt to get on top of Don.
- •• 0:41—Left breasts, then breasts, while making love.
- •• 0:50—Nude, taking off towel and getting into shower and taking a shower behind plastic shower curtain.
- ••• 1:05—Breasts, after taking off her blouse and making love with Don in bed. Nice, long scene.
- • 1:15—Brief breasts, while getting out of bed. Brief breasts in open window.
- • 1:16—Brief right breast, while sitting in bed, crying.
- ••• 1:26—In black bra, then nude, while making love with Don in a Jeep.

A House in the Hills *(1993)*

Helen Slater. . . . . Alex Weaver
- ••• 0:15—Breasts, while in bedroom in front of mirror, trying on various lingerie. Very nice!
- 0:36—Sort of breasts, in shower when Michael Madsen brings her a dress. Shower door is too fogged up to see anything.

House IV *(1991)*

Ellyn Dawn Humphreys . . . . Body Double for Terri Treas
- • 0:46—Breasts, when the shower water becomes blood. You don't see her face.

Terri Treas . . . . Kelly Cobb

House of Angels *(1993; Swedish)*

Helena Bergstrom . . . . Fanny Zander
- • 1:13—Nude, standing with her friends near the water. Medium long shot.

Ing-Marie Carlsson . . . . Eva Agren

The House of Exorcism *(1972; Italian/Spanish)*

a.k.a. Lisa and the Devil

Sylva Koscina. . . . . Sophia
- ••• 0:24—Breasts, while making love in bed with George the chauffeur.

Elke Sommer . . . . Lisa Reiner
- ••• 1:10—Breasts, lying on floor when Maximillian opens her blouse.

The House of Spirits *(1993)*

Maria Conchita Alonso . . . . Transito
- •• 0:18—Breasts and buns, undressing and starting to make love with Jeremy Irons.

Sarita Choudhury . . . . Pancha
- • 0:17—Brief breasts when Jeremy Irons rips open her blouse and rapes her.

Glenn Close. . . . . Ferula

Teri Polo . . . . Rosa
- • 0:09—Very, very brief upper half of left breast, while lying dead when Cora peeks in doorway to watch autopsy. Very brief breasts, while lying on table with cut open chest when Rosa peeks in the window. Probably not her real body.

Vanessa Redgrave . . . . Nivea

Meryl Streep . . . . Clara
- • 0:32—Brief buns, while in bed with Jeremy Irons. Probably a body double.

Hannah Taylor-Gordon . . . . Blanca (Child)
• 0:43—Nude, while in pond with young Pedro.

• House of the Damned *(1996; Made for Cable Movie)*

a.k.a. Spectre

Elizabeth Costello . . . . Woman in Bed
•• 0:30—Full frontal nudity while sleeping in bed in B&W vision, with a hand crawling up her body.

Alexandra Paul . . . . .Maura South

House of the Rising Sun *(1987)*

Jamie Barrett . . . . Janet
• 1:04—Very brief breasts making love with Louis.

The House on Carroll Street *(1988)*

Kelly McGillis. . . . . .Emily
• 0:39—Brief breasts reclining into the water in the bathtub.

Jessica Tandy . . . . .Miss Venable

House on Sorority Row *(1983)*

Eileen Davidson. . . . . Vicki
•• 0:16—Breasts and buns in room making love with her boyfriend.

Harley Jane Kozak . . . . Diane

Kate McNeil . . . . Katherine

The House on Straw Hill *(1976; British)*

a.k.a. Exposé

Linda Hayden . . . . Linda Hindstatt
• 0:28—Breasts getting undressed in her room.
••• 0:47—Breasts, masturbating in bed.
•• 1:06—Right breast, in bed with Fiona Richmond.

Fiona Richmond . . . . Suzanne
••• 0:05—Buns and breasts undressing and getting into bed and making love with Udo Kier.
•• 0:56—In black bra, then breasts undressing in front of Kier.
••• 1:00—Breasts in bedroom, then making love with Kier.
• 1:03—Brief buns, while lying on Linda's bed.
• 1:05—Buns, while lying on Linda's bed.
•• 1:06—Right breast, in bed with Linda.
•• 1:07—Breasts in bed with Linda.
• 1:09—Buns and side of left breast getting up from bed.
• 1:11—Full frontal nudity, getting stabbed in the bathroom. Covered with blood.

The House on Todville Road *(1994)*

Terri Harrel . . . . .Cornelia Todville
• 0:22—Very brief side view of left breast (out of focus right breast in reflection in mirror), when taking off robe to get into bath.
• 0:27—Upper half of breasts, while in bath.
•• 1:06—Buns and right breast, while making love in bed with Adam.
••• 1:10—Breasts, while making love in bed with Adam. Brief lower frontal nudity.
•• 1:12—Breasts, while sitting in bathtub.
• 1:15—Brief partial breasts and lower frontal nudity, while sitting dead in bathtub.

Amy Lindsay . . . . Isadora

Kirsten Maryott . . . . Amelia
• 0:22—Brief breasts and buns, taking off nightgown and going for a swim in pool at night.
• 0:23—Buns, while in the water and getting out.
• 0:29—Buns and back side of left breast, while sitting on shower floor with bloody whip marks on her back.
•• 0:59—Buns and breasts, while in the showers (whip marks still visible on her back).
•• 1:03—Breasts, while taking off shirt and putting on dress in bedroom.

House Where Evil Dwells *(1982)*

Susan George . . . . Laura
••• 0:21—Breasts in bed making love with Edward Albert.
•• 0:59—Breasts making love again.

Household Saints *(1992)*

Lili Taylor. . . . . .Teresa
•• 1:35—Breasts while in her bedroom, after undressing in front of Leonard.

Tracey Ullman . . . . Catherine Falconetti
• 0:33—Brief left breast, while making love in bed with Vincent D'Onofrio. Don't see her face. Probably a body double.

Housewife *(1972)*

Joyce Van Patten . . . . Bernadette
• 0:46—Breasts and buns on pool table getting attacked by Yaphet Kotto. Probably a body double, don't see her face.
• 1:05—Brief side of right breast under Kotto's arm several times after she falls on the floor with him.

Housewife From Hell *(1993)*

Lisa Comshaw . . . . Melissa
•• 0:03—Nude, after taking off robe in front of bathroom mirror (while wearing glasses), then getting into shower.
•• 0:04—Breasts, while sitting in bathtub and talking to John.
••• 0:36—Breasts, while sitting in bubble bath and talking to John.
• 0:48—In bra, buns in T-back while dancing in garage in between two other dancers.
• 1:00—Breasts under white bodysuit.

Jerica Fox. . . . . Party Girl
••• 0:53—In red bra and panties, then breasts while dancing beside spa, then getting into spa and sitting in spa.

Marcia Gray. . . . . Elvina
•• 0:44—In black bra, then nude while John is handcuffed to the bed on the floor.

Jennifer Peace . . . . Sue
•• 0:27—Breasts, while undoing her dress in John's office.

Jacqueline St. Claire . . . . Mary-Lou
••• 0:12—Breasts, while taking off blouse on bed with John, then making love.
• 0:15—Brief frontal nudity while in bathroom with John.
•• 0:16—Buns and breasts, while getting dressed in bedroom while talking to John.
••• 0:40—In purple bra and panties, then buns and breasts while in office with John.
• 1:01—Brief buns in bodysuit, while getting up out of bed.

How Funny Can Sex Be? *(1973)*

Laura Antonelli . . . . Miscellaneous Personalities
• 0:01—Brief breasts taking off swimsuit.
• 0:04—Brief breasts in bathtub covered with bubbles.
• 0:26—Breasts getting into bed.
• 0:36—Breasts making love in elevator behind frosted glass. Shot at fast speed.
• 1:08—In sheer white nun's outfit during fantasy sequence. Brief breasts and buns. Nice slow motion.
• 1:24—In black bra and panties, then breasts while changing clothes.

• How To Be a Player *(1997)*

Beverly Johnson . . . . Robin

Stacii Jae Johnson . . . . Sherri
- 0:00—Brief breasts, while in bed with Bill Bellamy.
- 0:01—Very brief left breast, while in bed with Bellamy.

Mari Morrow. . . . . Katrina
- •• 1:26—Brief right breast, then breasts, while making love with Bill Bellamy.

Amber Smith. . . . . .Amber
- 0:04—Brief side of right breast, while lying on top of Bill Bellamy in bed.
- 0:42—In white lingerie, then buns and breasts, while fooling around with Bellamy.

How to Beat the High Cost of Living (1980)

Jane Curtin . . . . Elaine
- 1:29—Close up breasts, taking off her bra. Probably a body double.

Sybil Danning . . . . .Charlotte

Jessica Lange . . . . Louise

• *How to Fill a Wild Wet T-shirt* (1986; Video Tape)

Lori Deann Pallett . . . . .Lori from Dallas
- ••• 0:16—Breasts while dancing on stage, then being interviewed backstage with two other topless girls.
- •• 0:28—Breasts during quiz time.
- ••• 0:43—Breasts dancing during semi-finals.
- ••• 0:45—Breasts dancing during finals.
- ••• 0:46—Breasts dancing as the winner.
- •• 0:48—Breasts during final credits "report card."

How to Make an American Quilt (1995)

Ellen Burstyn . . . . .Hy

Kate Capshaw . . . . Sally

Maria Celedonio . . . . Young Anna

Claire Danes . . . . .Young Geady Joe

Melinda Dillon . . . . Mrs. Darling

Joanna Going . . . . .Young Em
- 0:48—Brief buns, while lying on sofa and posing for painting by Tim Guinee. Partial left breast when he comes over to the sofa.
- 0:49—Partial left breast in bathtub. Don't see her face.
- 0:50—Left breast, after kissing Guinee when she's in the tub.

Samantha Mathis . . . . Young Sophia

Kate Nelligan . . . . .Constance

How to Seduce a Woman (1973)

Alexandra Hay. . . . . .Nell Brinkman
- 1:05—Brief right breast in mirror taking off black dress.
- ••• 1:06—Breasts posing for pictures. Long scene.
- 1:47—Breasts during flashback. Lots of diffusion.

Angel Tompkins . . . . Pamela

The Howling (1981)

Belinda Balaski. . . . . Terry Fisher

Elisabeth Brooks . . . . Marsha
- •• 0:46—Full frontal nudity taking off her robe in front of a campfire.
- 0:48—Breasts sitting on Bill by the fire.

Dee Wallace Stone . . . . Karen White

Howling II: Your Sister is a Werewolf (1984)

Sybil Danning . . . . Stirba
- 0:35—Left breast, then breasts with Mariana in bedroom about to have sex with a guy.
- 1:20—Very brief breasts during short clips during the end credits. Same shot repeated about 10 times.

Marsha A. Hunt . . . . Mariana
- •• 0:33—Breasts in bedroom with Sybil Danning and a guy.

Annie McEnroe . . . . Jenny

Howling III: The Marsupials (1987)

Imogen Annesley. . . . . .Jerboa
- 0:42—Very brief breasts taking off dress in barn to give birth. Breasts are covered with make-up.

Jenny Vuletic . . . . Goolah

Howling IV: The Original Nightmare (1988)

Lamya Derval . . . . Elanor
- •• 0:32—Brief left breast, then breasts making love with Richard. Nice silhouette on the wall.

Suzanne Severeid . . . . Janice

Romy Walthall . . . . Marie

Howling V (1989)

Elizabeth Shé. . . . . .Mary Lou Summers
- 0:33—Buns and side view of right breast getting into pool with Donovan.
- 0:36—Very brief full frontal nudity climbing out of pool with Donovan.

Mary Stavin . . . . .Anna
- •• 1:09—Breasts three times drying herself off while Richard watches in the mirror. Possible body double.

• *Hugh Hefner: Once Upon a Time* (1992; Video Tape)

Marilyn Monroe . . . . Herself
- •• 0:12—Brief breasts in first centerfold.

Dorothy Stratten . . . . Herself
- 1:08—Right breast in bathtub.

• *Human Desires* (1996)

Dawn Ann Billings . . . . .Zoe
- •• 0:11—Breasts, while making love in bed with Julia in bed.
- ••• 0:49—In bra and panties, then breasts and buns, while making love with Dean on sofa.

Julianne J. Mantia . . . . .Woman
- ••• 0:02—Breasts and buns in panties, while making love with a man while another man takes photographs.

Peggy Trentini . . . . Julia
- •• 0:11—Breasts and buns, while in bed with Zoe.
- 0:16—Brief buns, while floating dead in pool.
- •• 0:37—Breasts and buns, while in bed with Peter.
- •• 0:57—Breasts and buns, while making love in bed with Miles.

Shannon Tweed . . . . Alicia Royale
- ••• 1:07—Breasts and buns, while in bedroom with Dean.

The Human Tornado (1976)

Gloria Delaney. . . . . Hurricane Annie
- ••• 0:35—Full frontal nudity, taking off dress, exercising on bed, then making love with Rudy Ray Moore.

Humanoids from the Deep (1980)

Denise Galik . . . . Linda Beale

Lisa Glaser . . . . Becky
- ••• 0:34—Full frontal nudity, while undressing in tent with Billy and his ventriloquist dummy.
- 0:35—Nude, while running on the beach at night, trying to escape from the humanoids.

Linda Shayne. . . . . Miss Salmon
- 1:06—Breasts after getting bathing suit ripped off by a humanoid.

Lynn Theel . . . . Peggy Larsen
- 0:22—Very, very brief half of right breast, when fight in parking lot startles her and her boyfriend in back of truck.
- 0:30—Brief breasts getting raped on the beach by a humanoid.
- 0:51—Brief breasts, dead, lying on the beach all covered with seaweed.

Humongous *(1982; Canadian)*

Janit Baldwin . . . . Carla Simmons
Joy Boushel . . . . Donna Blake
- •• 0:09—Breasts looking out the window. More breasts in the room in the mirror.
- • 0:48—Breasts undoing her top to warm up Bert.

Shay Garner . . . . Ida Parsons
- • 0:05—Brief left breast and brief lower frontal nudity getting her clothes ripped off by a guy. Don't see her face.

Janet Julian . . . . Sandy Ralston

Hundra *(1983)*

Laurene Landon . . . . Hundra
- • 0:29—Very brief breasts, several times, riding her horse in the surf. Partial buns. Blurry.

The Hunger *(1983)*

Catherine Deneuve . . . . Miriam
- • 0:08—Brief breasts taking a shower with David Bowie. Probably a body double, you don't see her face.

Ann Magnuson . . . . Young Woman from Disco
- • 0:05—Brief breasts in kitchen with David Bowie just before he kills her.

Susan Sarandon. . . . . Sarah Roberts
- ••• 0:59—In a wine stained white T-shirt, then breasts during love scene with Catherine Deneuve.

• ***Hungry For You*** *(1996)*

Rochelle Swanson . . . . .Viva
- ••• 0:06—Breasts and buns, while making love in bed with Joe.
- ••• 0:26—In black lingerie, then breasts and buns, while making love with Jack.
- •• 0:36—Buns in black leather outfit, then breasts and buns, while making love with Arnold.
- • 0:45—Very, very brief breasts in quick cuts.
- • 0:48—Breasts, while talking with Rodney.
- •• 0:58—In bra, then breasts, while making love in bed with Rodney.
- ••• 1:09—Breasts and brief buns, while bathing with Rodney.

The Hunted *(1994)*

Joan Chen . . . . Kirina
- • 0:10—Very brief half of right breast, then back half of right breast, while in hot tub in front of Christopher Lambert.

Hunting *(1990; Australian)*

Kerry Armstrong . . . . Michelle Harris
- • 0:29—Side view of left breast in steamy shower.
- •• 0:35—Breasts, making love with John Savage in bed. Seen on video monitors.
- • 1:00—Breasts and upper half of buns, making love with Savage.
- • 1:02—Brief buns, turning over in bed.
- • 1:26—Very, very brief breasts, getting her dress top yanked down. Breasts, long shot, getting raped on dining table. Left breast, lying on the floor afterwards.

Hurricane *(1979)*

Mia Farrow . . . . Charlotte Bruckner
- • 0:39—Brief left breast in open dress top while crawling under bushes at the beach.

Hurricane Smith *(1990)*

Cassandra Delaney . . . . Julie
- •• 0:45—Breasts, while making love with Carl Weathers in bed.

Husbands and Lovers *(1991; Italian)*

(Unrated version reviewed.)

Joanna Pacula . . . . Helena
- ••• 0:03—Breasts, making love on top of Julian Sands in bed. Left breast, while lying in bed after.
- ••• 0:10—Nude, walking around and getting into bed with Sands.
- ••• 0:18—Breasts in bathroom, brushing her teeth, then getting dressed.
- ••• 0:32—Buns and breasts, getting into the shower with Sands.
- • 0:35—Brief breasts getting into bed.
- •• 0:37—Breasts in white panties, putting on stockings.
- •• 0:59—Buns, getting spanked by Paolo.
- ••• 1:17—Buns, then breasts making love in bed with Sands. Nude getting out of bed.
- • 1:19—Brief breasts, putting on stockings, then white bra and panties.
- • 1:21—Buns, in greenhouse with Paolo when he beats her.

Lara Wendel . . . . Louisa
- ••• 0:47—In bra and panties with Julian Sands, then breasts, while making love with him.

Husbands and Wives *(1992)*

Lysette Anthony. . . . . Sam
Cristi Conaway . . . . Shawn Grainger
Blythe Danner . . . . Rain's Mother
Judy Davis . . . . Sally
- • 1:07—Brief breasts, then brief left breast, while making love in bed with Liam Neeson.

Mia Farrow . . . . Judy Roth
Juliette Lewis . . . . Rain

Hussy *(1980; British)*

Helen Mirren . . . . Beaty
- •• 0:22—Left breast, then side of right breast, while lying in bed with John Shea.
- ••• 0:29—Nude, making love in bed with Shea.
- •• 0:31—Full frontal nudity in bathtub.

Hustle *(1975)*

Catherine Bach . . . . Peggy Summers
Eileen Brennan. . . . . Paula Hollinger
Catherine Deneuve . . . . Nicole Britton
Sharon Kelly . . . . Gloria Hollinger
- • 0:12—Brief breasts, several times when rolled out of freezer, dead.
- • 1:03—In pasties, dancing behind curtain when Gloria's father imagines the dancer is Gloria.
- • 1:42—In black lingerie, brief buns and side views of breast in bed in film.

Patrice Rohmer . . . . Linda (Dancer)
- • 1:03—In pasties, dancing on stage behind beaded curtain. Buns in G-string.

• Hyapatia Lee Presents: Taking' It Off, Volume 1 *(1993; Video Tape)*

Hyapatia Lee . . . . .Herself
••• 0:41—Nude, doing strip dance routine on stage in club. Long scene.

Porsche Lynn. . . . . .Herself
••• 0:07—Nude, doing strip dance routine on stage in club. Long scene.

Trixie Tyler . . . . .Herself
•• 0:19—Partial buns, then breasts, while getting dressed in dressing room and talking to Hyapatia Lee.
••• 0:23—Nude, doing strip dance routine on stage in club. Long scene.

I Don't Give a Damn *(1985; Israeli)*

a.k.a. Lo Sam Zayin

Liora Grossman . . . . .Maya
• 1:11—Brief right breast, while posing for Rafi in the kitchen.

I Hate Blondes *(1981; Italian)*

Corrine Clery. . . . . Angelica
• 1:17—Left breast and upper half of buns, in bedroom with a guy when he tries to seduce her.

Marina Langner. . . . . .Valerie
•• 0:12—Breasts, sitting up in steam room, yelling at Emilio.
• 1:02—Brief buns, when Emilio accidentally rips her dress off at party.
•• 1:10—Brief breasts when Emilio causes her top to fall off at party.
•• 1:16—Breasts and buns, taking off her dress to demonstrate how Emilio took it off.

Paola Tedesco . . . . Teresa
••• 0:06—Breasts, sitting up in bed at night and turning on the light. Buns, while walking around the room.

I Like to Play Games *(1994)*

Lisa Boyle . . . . Suzanne
•• 0:13—Breasts, while making out with Michael in alley.
••• 0:15—In black bra and panties in bed, then breasts and partial lower frontal nudity.
• 0:24—In white lingerie, then wet white lingerie while in bathtub with Michael.
••• 0:25—Full frontal nudity while in bed with Michael.
•• 0:32—Breasts and partial lower frontal nudity in black leather strap outfit in Michael's office.
••• 0:35—Breasts and buns in leather strap outfit in motel room with Michael (including dropping hot wax on him).
••• 0:40—Breasts and lower frontal nudity, while making love.
• 0:44—Left breast, while playing with an ice cube in limousine.
••• 0:52—Breasts and buns, while watching Michael make love with Tiffany.
••• 0:54—Breasts and buns, while joining in and making love with Michael and Tiffany.
• 1:02—Left breast, while making love with Michael in punk club.
••• 1:06—Nude, while making love outside with Michael next to the pool.
• 1:16—Brief right breast in ripped blouse, during fight with Michael.
• 1:21—Breasts, while in bed, when Michael wakes her up.
• 1:25—Left breast, in pulled down blouse in pool during struggle with Michael.

Jennifer Leigh Burton. . . . . Tiffany
•• 0:53—Nude, when rubbing oil on Michael while Lisa Boyle watches.
•• 0:57—Breasts and buns, while making love with Michael and Boyle in bed.

Pamela Dickerson . . . . Melody
• 0:00—Partial left breast, when getting fondled by Michael while playing chess.
0:01—Breasts, while on bed after taking off her dress for Michael.

Monique Noel. . . . . .Valerie
Cheryl Rixon . . . . Sean

I Love You *(1982; Brazilian)*

a.k.a. Eu Te Amo

Sonia Braga . . . . Maria
••• 0:34—Full frontal nudity making love with Paulo.
•• 0:36—Breasts sitting on the edge of the bed.
• 0:49—Breasts running around the house teasing Paulo.
•• 0:50—Briefly nude in blinking light. Don't see her face.
• 0:53—Breasts eating fruit with Paulo.
••• 0:54—Breasts wearing white panties in front of windows with Paulo. Long scene.
• 1:03—Left breast standing talking to Paulo.
• 1:10—Left breast talking to Paulo.
• 1:15—Very brief full frontal nudity, several times, in Paulo's flashback in blinking light scene.
••• 1:23—Breasts with Paulo during an argument. Dark, but long scene.
•• 1:28—Breasts walking around Paulo's place with a gun. Dark.
•• 1:33—Various breasts scenes.

Vera Fischer. . . . . Barbara Bergman
••• 0:31—Left breast while in front of TV and in chair with Paulo.
•• 0:46—Left breast sticking out of nightgown. Silhouette of breasts while getting up. Full frontal nudity after taking off nightgown.
••• 0:47—Nude in bed with Paulo.
••• 1:05—Breasts on couch with Paulo.
• 1:09—Breasts, while opening her dress. (Seen on TV.)

I Never Promised You a Rose Garden *(1977)*

Bibi Andersson. . . . . Dr. Fried
Samantha Harper . . . . Teacher in Ward D
Kathleen Quinlan. . . . . Deborah
• 0:27—Breasts changing in a mental hospital room with the orderly.
• 0:52—Brief breasts riding a horse in a hallucination sequence. Blurry, hard to see. Then close up of left breast (could be anyone's).

Susan Tyrrell . . . . Lee
Diane Varsi . . . . Sylvia

I Ought to Be in Pictures *(1982)*

Ann-Margret . . . . Stephanie
Samantha Harper . . . . .Larane
• 0:27—Breasts, while nonchalantly coming out to talk to Walter Matthau and Dinah Manoff.

I Posed for Playboy *(1991)*

a.k.a. Posing: Inspired by Three Real Stories

(Shown on network TV without the nudity.)

Josie Bissett . . . . .Claire Baywood
Lynda Carter . . . . .Meredith Lanahan

Brittany York . . . . Herself
••• 0:20—Right breast, then breasts on motorcycle during photo shoot.
••• 0:22—In T-shirt, then breasts during second photo shoot.

I Shot Andy Warhol (1996)

Myriam Cyr . . . . Ultra Violet
Isabel Gillies . . . . Alison
Martha Plimpton . . . . Stevie
• 0:16—Breasts, when having sex with Lili Taylor on bed while a customer watches and masturbates.
Lili Taylor . . . . Valerie Solanas
• 1:33—Brief breasts, while sitting in shower.
Anna Thomson . . . . Iris
• 0:39—Breasts in B&W film.
Tahnee Welch . . . . Viva

I Spit on Your Corpse (1974)

a.k.a. Girls for Rent
Talie Cochrane . . . . Hitchhiker
• 0:47—Brief right breast, then breasts getting shot. More breasts, dead, covered with blood.
Mikel James . . . . Laura
Susan McIver . . . . Donna
••• 0:24—Breasts undressing for a guy. More breasts and buns making love in bed with him, then getting out of bed.
Rosalind Miles . . . . Erica
Georgina Spelvin . . . . Sandra
• 0:38—Flashing her left breast to get three guys to stop their car.
••• 0:39—Breasts, fighting with the three guys.
• 0:47—Brief right breast in gaping blouse.
••• 0:53—Breasts outside, de-virginizing the backwoods kid.
•• 1:08—Breasts, close-up view, showing her breasts to him.
• 1:10—Buns, in lowered pants and left breast in open blouse.

I Spit on Your Grave (1978)

(Uncut, unrated version reviewed.)
Camille Keaton . . . . Jennifer
• 0:05—Breasts undressing to go skinny dipping in lake.
•• 0:23—Left breast sticking out of bathing suit top, then breasts after top is ripped off. Right breast several times.
• 0:25—Breasts, getting raped by the jerks.
• 0:27—Buns and brief full frontal nudity, crawling away from the jerks.
• 0:29—Nude, walking through the woods.
• 0:32—Breasts, getting raped again.
• 0:36—Breasts and buns after rape.
• 0:38—Buns, walking to house.
• 0:40—Buns and lower frontal nudity in the house.
• 0:41—More breasts and buns on the floor.
• 0:45—Nude, very dirty after all she's gone through.
• 0:51—Full frontal nudity while lying on the floor.
• 0:52—Side of left breast while in bathtub.
•• 1:13—Full frontal nudity seducing Matthew before killing him.
••• 1:23—Full frontal nudity in front of mirror, then getting into bathtub. Long scene.

I Will Dance on Your Grave: Lethal Victims (1992)

Georgette Baker . . . . Lupe
Leslie Huntly . . . . Melinda McGee
• 0:31—Breasts, while on bed after Don Swayze knocks her out with chloroform.
Marcia Karr . . . . Sophie
Lisa London . . . . Jody Bower
• 0:01—Very, very brief right breast, after getting raped by two guys at the beach.

I'll Do Anything (1994)

Chelsea Field . . . . Screentest Actress
Tricia Leigh Fisher . . . . Airline Passenger
Anne Heche . . . . Claire
Kate McNeil . . . . Stacy
Joely Richardson . . . . Cathy Breslow
• 1:03—Very brief frontal nudity, while walking past hallway when surprised by Nick Nolte.
Tracey Ullman . . . . Beth Hobbs

I, the Jury (1982)

Corinne Bohrer . . . . Soap Opera Actress
Bobbi Burns . . . . Sheila Kyle
• 0:01—Brief side view of right breast, while in bed with Armand Assante.
Barbara Carrera . . . . Dr. Charolette Bennett
••• 1:02—Nude on bed making love with Armand Assante. Very sexy.
• 1:45—Brief breasts, while in hallway kissing Assante.
• 1:46—Brief left breast, while falling to the floor. Breasts while lying on the floor wounded.
Samantha Fox . . . . Uncredited Orgy Woman
Lee Anne Harris . . . . 1st twin
••• 0:48—Breasts on bed talking to Armand Assante.
• 0:52—Full frontal nudity on bed wearing red wig, talking to the maniac.
• 0:54—Brief breasts, dead on bed when discovered by Assante.
Lynette Harris . . . . 2nd twin
••• 0:48—Breasts on bed talking to Armand Assante.
• 0:52—Full frontal nudity on bed wearing red wig, talking to the maniac.
• 0:54—Brief breasts, dead on bed when discovered by Assante.
Laurene Landon . . . . Velda

The Ice Runner (1993)

Olga Kabo . . . . Lena
•• 0:59—Breasts, twice, while washing her blouse in stream when Edward Albert sees her. Medium long shot.
••• 1:02—Breasts, while making love in bed with Albert.

Iced (1988)

Debra De Liso . . . . Trina
• 0:11—In a bra, then briefly nude while making love with Cory in hotel room.
Elizabeth Gorcey . . . . Diane
Lisa Loring . . . . Jeanette
• 0:46—Brief left breast in bathtub.
• 0:53—Buns and brief right breast in bathtub with Alex.
•• 1:05—Brief lower frontal nudity and buns, while getting into hot tub. Breasts in hot tub just before getting electrocuted.
•• 1:13—Full frontal nudity lying dead in the hot tub.
• 1:18—Brief full frontal nudity lying dead in the hot tub again.

• *If I'm So Famous, How Come Nobody's Ever Heard of Me?* (1996; Video Tape)

Michelle Bauer . . . . Herself
• 0:16—Brief breasts in still photo on table during convention.

Debra Jo Fondren . . . . Herself
- • 0:18—Breasts in Playboy magazine photos during convention.

Susie Owens . . . . Herself
- • 0:17—Breasts in still photo she shows during convention.

Jewel Shepard . . . . Herself

If Looks Could Kill (1987)

Beth Broderick. . . . . Newswoman
Jane Hamilton . . . . Mary Beth
Gretchen Kingsley . . . . Elizabeth
Jeanne Marie. . . . . Jeannie Burns
- •• 0:06—Breasts taking off her robe and kissing George.

Sharon Moran. . . . . Madonna Maid
- •• 0:17—Full frontal nudity after Laura leaves the apartment.

• *If These Walls Could Talk (1996; Made for Cable Movie)*

Eileen Brennan . . . . Tessie
Lindsay Crouse . . . . Frances White
Judith Drake . . . . Angry Woman
Anne Heche . . . . Christine Cullen
- • 1:14—Brief breasts, while sitting in bathtub and talking on cordless telephone.

Catherine Keener . . . . Becky
Shirley Knight . . . . Mary Donnely
Demi Moore . . . . Claire Donnely
Jada Pinkett. . . . . Patti
Sissy Spacek . . . . Barbara Barrows

If You Don't Stop It You'll Go Blind (1979)

Talie Cochrane . . . . n.a.
Sandra Dempsey. . . . . n.a.
Uschi Digard . . . . Various Characters
- •• 0:02—Breasts in bed and closets during opening credits.
- • 0:03—Breasts, pulling up her T-shirt during beginning credits.
- • 0:23—Brief breasts raising her hand in classroom.
- ••• 0:26—Breasts, while showing them to a guy and letting him feel them.
- • 0:36—Brief upper half of left breast, when it sticks out of her dress.
- ••• 0:52—Full frontal nudity (Contestant #1) on bed, waiting for Omar.
- •• 1:17—Breasts in class during end credits.

Becky Sharpe . . . . n.a.

if... (1969; British)

Mary MacLeod . . . . Mrs. Kemp
- •• 1:27—Buns and side of left breast while walking around deserted boy's dormitory (B&W).

Christine Noonan . . . . The Girl
- • 0:59—Very brief full frontal nudity with Malcolm McDowell on the floor (B&W).

Illegal Entry (1992)

Carol Hoyt . . . . Catherine Reese
- ••• 0:59—Buns and breasts, getting into bubble bath and washing herself while talking with C.A. Long scene.

Barbara Niven . . . . Pamela Raby
- ••• 1:02—Breasts, while making out with her boyfriend.
- •• 1:15—Breasts, while making love on piano with her boyfriend.

Deborah Stevens. . . . . Swimming Pool Party Girl #2

Illegal in Blue (1994)

Stacey Dash. . . . . Kari Truitt
- ••• 0:46—Breasts, while making love with Chris.
- ••• 1:08—Breasts, while making love with Chris in bed.

Tammy Parks. . . . . Jennifer
- • 0:30—Buns in G-string (she's on the left) when leaving the sofa after sitting next to Mickey.
- •• 0:31—Left breast (she's on the right), while making love with another woman on sofa.

Gina Ravera . . . . Alexis
Sandra Reinhardt. . . . . Joanne
- ••• 0:07—Breasts, while making love with Chris.

Illicit Behavior (1991)

(Unrated version reviewed.)

Sondra Currie . . . . Yolanda
Pamella D'Pella . . . . Marilyn
Jenilee Harrison . . . . Charlene Lernoux
Joan Severance . . . . Melissa Yarnell
- •• 1:10—Breasts and buns in car with Davi. (Sometimes you see her face with her breasts, sometimes not.)
- •• 1:16—Right breast, while lying in bed and talking to Davi.

• *Illicit Confessions (1997)*

Lindsay Blair . . . . Jo
- ••• 0:51—Breasts and buns, while making love with Mark on the floor in front of the fireplace.

Lisa Comshaw . . . . Andrea
- ••• 0:33—In black bra and panties, then full frontal nudity, while blindfolded and tied to fireplace, when having sex with Erica as her husband watches.

Julie Kruis . . . . Dancer 2
- ••• 0:53—Nude, after stripping and dancing on stage, while wearing a cowboy hat.
- ••• 1:02—Nude, while having sex with three guys.

Nikki Nova . . . . Pamela
- • 0:09—Very brief partial buns in lingerie, while walking up to the bar.
- • 1:12—Brief buns in lingerie in dressing room.
- ••• 1:14—Nude, while stripping and dancing on stage.

Blake Pickett . . . . Erica
- •• 0:00—Breasts and buns in T-back, while dancing in club.
- ••• 0:02—Nude, while having sex with a customer in bed.
- ••• 0:13—Buns in T-back and breasts, while having sex with Karl in bedroom.
- ••• 0:23—Nude, while stripping and dancing on stage.
- ••• 0:33—Nude, when having sex with Andrea, while her husband watches.
- ••• 0:43—Breasts, while starting to have sex with a customer.
- ••• 1:00—Nude, while having sex with another customer.
- ••• 1:09—Breasts and buns, while bathing, showering, then making love in bed with Ron.
- • 1:13—Breasts, while starting to lap dancer for a customer.
- ••• 1:24—Nude, while dancing on stage with another woman.
- •• 1:27—Breasts and buns in lingerie, while giving a customer a lap dance.

Illicit Dreams (1994)

Michelle Johnson. . . . . Melinda Ryan
Elizabeth Sandifer . . . . Vicky
Stella Stevens . . . . Cicily
Rochelle Swanson . . . . Beverly Keen
- ••• 0:05—Breasts, while making love with Joe Cortese in his house.
- • 1:12—Left breast, then breasts, when Cortese threatens her at his house.

Shannon Tweed . . . . Moira Davis
- •• 0:11—Breasts, while making love with Andrews Stevens in dream.
- •• 0:34—Breasts, while in dream with Stevens. Lit with red light.
- ••• 0:46—Breasts and buns, while making love with Stevens in a dream.
- ••• 1:01—Breasts and buns, while making love with Stevens in "real life."
- • 1:07—Breasts, when tied by her wrists to the bed, while getting punished by Joe Cortese.

Ilsa, She Wolf of the S.S. *(1974)*

Dyanne Thorne . . . . Ilsa
- •• 0:00—Buns, then breasts making love in bed.
- ••• 0:01—Breasts taking a shower.
- ••• 0:29—Buns and breasts in bed with Wolfe.
- •• 0:32—Right breast several times in bed with Wolfe.
- ••• 0:48—In white bra, then breasts undressing for Wolfe.
- •• 0:50—Right breast, while lying in bed.

The Image *(1990; Made for Cable Movie)*

Marsha Mason . . . . Jean Cromwell
- • 0:08—Two brief side views of left breast standing in bathroom after Albert Finney gets out of the shower.

• ***The Imagemaker*** *(1985)*

Marcia Gay Harden . . . . Stage Manager
Jessica Harper . . . . Cynthia
Anne Twomey . . . . Molly Grainger
- • 0:11—Very, very brief breasts, while reading newspaper in bedroom (wearing flesh colored tape over her nipples). Then in white bra and panties talking to a guy in bed.

Images *(1972; Irish)*

Cathryn Harrison . . . . Susannah
Susannah York . . . . Cathryn
- • 0:59—Brief lower frontal nudity, then right breast lying on the bed.
- • 1:38—Brief buns in the shower.

Imagine: John Lennon *(1988)*

Yoko Ono . . . . Herself
- • 0:43—Nude in B&W photos from John Lennon's "Two Virgins" album.
- • 0:57—Brief full frontal nudity from album cover again during an interview.

Immoral Tales *(1975; French)*

Charlotte Alexandra . . . . Therese the Philosopher
- •• 0:32—Breasts, undressing by herself in room.
- •• 0:34—Breasts and buns, in bed while playing with a cucumber.
- ••• 0:36—Breasts and buns.
- •• 0:38—Buns and breasts while lying in bed.

Paloma Picasso . . . . Countess Erzsebet Bathory
- ••• 0:59—Nude, getting her clothes ripped off by a bunch of women in a room.
- • 1:00—Briefly nude, while walking away from the women.
- •• 1:02—Nude, while bathing in blood.
- ••• 1:05—Nude, walking down stairs. Then in bed with another woman.
- ••• 1:08—Nude in bed and sitting up.

Immortal Beloved *(1994)*

Valeria Golino . . . . Giuletta Guicciardi
- • 0:18—In wet dress, when getting a bath. Then side of right breast while getting dressed by her servants.

Geno Lechner . . . . Josephine Von Brunsvik
- •• 0:17—Breasts, after opening her dress top in the woods with Gary Oldman.

Alexandra Pigg . . . . Therese Obermayer
Isabella Rossellini . . . . Anna Marie Erdody
Johanna Ter Steege . . . . Johanna Reiss
- • 0:39—Brief left breast and lower frontal nudity while sitting up after Gary Oldman whips the sheets off the bed she's sleeping in with his brother.

Immortal Sins *(1992; Spanish)*

Maryam D'Abo . . . . Susan
Shari Shattuck . . . . Diana
- • 0:13—Very brief breasts during Mike's dream.
- • 0:32—Breasts several times, while making love with Mike.
- •• 0:44—Left breast while making love with Mike.
- ••• 1:09—Breasts making love with Mike.
- ••• 1:18—Still more breasts making love with Mike.
- • 1:20—Almost full frontal nudity, while standing in doorway. (Hard to see because of shadows.)

Immortalizer *(1990)*

Rebekka Armstrong . . . . June
- • 0:16—Breasts getting blouse taken off by nurse.
- ••• 0:29—Breasts when a worker fondles her while she's asleep.

Raye Hollitt . . . . Queenie

The Immortals *(1995)*

Tia Carrere . . . . Gina
Alisa Christensen . . . . Stripper Shooter
- • 0:17—Very brief breasts, twice, while shooting a shot gun in strip club office during robbery.

Tiffany Granath . . . . Strip Club Waitress
Alex Meneses . . . . Cleopatra

Improper Conduct *(1994)*

(Unrated version reviewed.)

Lee Anne Beaman . . . . Kay
- •• 0:12—Full frontal nudity while in the shower.
- •• 1:02—Breasts while in photocopy room with John Loughlin.
- ••• 1:07—In red bra and panties, then buns and breasts while making love with John Loughlin in motel room.
- •• 1:16—In black bra and panties, then breasts while in office with Steven Bauer.

Wendy MacDonald . . . . Gabby
Patsy Pease . . . . Jo Ann
Kathy Shower . . . . Emily
- •• 0:19—Breasts, while getting into bed with John Loughlin, then making love.

Tahnee Welch . . . . Ashley
- 0:10—Right breast, then breasts, while in office supply room with Adrian Zmed. Don't see her face.

Impulse *(1989)*

Theresa Russell . . . . Lottie
- •• 0:37—Left breast, while making love with Stan in bed.

In a Moment of Passion (1992)

Chase Masterson. . . . . Tammy Brandon
- • 0:36—Very brief side of left breast, when dancing in a restaurant with Maxwell Caulfield in front of a lot of people.
- • 1:01—Brief left breast, while making love with Caulfield.

• *In Dangerous Company* (1988)

Tracy Scoggins . . . . Evelyn
- • 0:42—Very, very brief half of left breast in bed with Blake. Then, very, very brief left breast getting out of bed. Blurry, hard to see.
- • 0:58—Brief upper half of left breast taking a bath. Long shot, hard to see.

In Harm's Way (1965)

Barbara Bouchet . . . . Liz Eddington
- • 0:05—Very, very brief right breast, while waving to Hugh O'Brian from the water (B&W).

Paula Prentiss . . . . Bev

In Praise of Older Women (1978; Canadian)

Karen Black . . . . .Maya
- •• 0:35—Breasts in bed with Tom Berenger.

Monique Lepage. . . . . The Countess
- • 0:03—Breasts and buns in the shower, then talking with a boy.

Marilyn Lightstone . . . . Klari
- • 0:45—Left breast, twice, while on floor with Tom Berenger before being discovered by Karen Black.

Marianne McIssac . . . . Julika
- •• 0:23—Breasts and buns, getting into bed with Tom Berenger.

Helen Shaver. . . . . Ann MacDonald
- ••• 1:40—Blue bra and panties, then breasts with Tom Berenger.
- ••• 1:42—Nude lying in bed with Berenger, then getting out and getting dressed.

Alexandra Stewart. . . . . .Paula
- •• 1:21—Breasts in bed with Tom Berenger.
- •• 1:23—Nude, in and out of bed with Berenger.

Susan Strasberg. . . . . Bobbie
- •• 1:03—Left breast, while making love in bed with Tom Berenger.
- ••• 1:04—Breasts in bed after Berenger rolls off her.

Alberta Watson . . . . Mitzi
- •• 0:51—Breasts, while sitting in chair talking with Tom Berenger, then more breasts when lying in bed. Long scene.

• *In Search of the Perfect 10* (1986; Video Tape)

Blondi . . . . .Perfect Girl #3
- ••• 0:14—Breasts in back of car.

Lois Ayer . . . . .Perfect Girl #2
- ••• 0:08—In swimsuit, then breasts exercising by the pool.

Michelle Bauer . . . . Perfect Girl #10
- ••• 0:53—In yellow outfit stripping in office. Breasts and buns in G-string bottom.

Iris Condon . . . . Perfect Girl #6/Jackie
- ••• 0:37—Breasts (she's the blonde) playing Twister with Rebecca Lynn. Buns in G-string.

Venus De Light . . . . Perfect Girl #4
- ••• 0:18—Breasts talking on the phone and buns in G-string seen through the Nude-Cam.
- ••• 0:21—In two piece swimsuit, then breasts taking it off in the doorway.

Gail Harris . . . . .Perfect Girl #5
- ••• 0:31—Nude, while trying on all sorts of lingerie in dressing room.

Rebecca Lynn . . . . Perfect Girl #7/Ellen
- ••• 0:37—Breasts (she's the redhead) playing Twister with Iris Condon. Buns in G-string.

Heidi Paine . . . . .Perfect Girl #8
- ••• 0:45—Brief breasts pulling down her top outside of car.

Teri Lynn Peake . . . . .Perfect Girl #9
- ••• 0:47—Buns and breasts taking a shower.

In the Cold of the Night (1989)

Melinda Armstrong . . . . Laser Model 2

Shelley Michelle. . . . . Model 3

Adrianne Sachs . . . . Kimberly Shawn
- ••• 0:52—Buns and breasts in shower, then making love with Scott. Long, erotic scene.
- • 0:59—Brief breasts in outdoor spa.
- •• 1:06—Breasts making love on Scott's lap in bed.

Shannon Tweed . . . . Lena
- • 0:02—Right breast while making love with Scott.

In the Heat of Passion (1991)

(Unrated version reviewed.)

Sally Kirkland. . . . . Dr. Lee Adams
- ••• 0:21—In black bra, then breasts making love with Charlie while her husband is downstairs.
- • 0:23—Brief breasts in the shower when her husband opens the shower curtain.
- •• 0:29—Breasts with Charlie in stall in women's restroom.
- •• 0:42—Breasts teasing Charlie from the bathroom.
- • 0:45—Right breast, then breasts in bed with Charlie.
- • 1:11—Very brief buns, while on the couch with Charlie.

In the Heat of Passion II: Unfaithful (1994)

a.k.a. Behind Closed Doors

(Unrated version reviewed.)

Linda Doná . . . . .Bartender #2

Lesley-Anne Down. . . . . Jean

Betsy Lynn George . . . . .Lisa

Teresa Hill . . . . Casey
- • 0:20—Very, very brief left breast while in bed with Barry Bostwick. (Seen at bottom of screen.)
- • 0:21—Very brief right breast with Bostwick.
- • 0:22—Very brief left breast, while rolling over in bed on top of Bostwick.
- • 1:18—Very brief left breast, while rolling over (from 0:22) in flashback.

In the Kingdom of the Blind: The Man With One Eye is King (1995)

Lisa Falcone. . . . . Micky's Girlfriend
- • 0:09—Breasts, while dancing on stage in club. Brief buns in T-back, after walking off stage.
- • 0:11—Buns, while walking around in the club.

In the Shadow of Kilimanjaro (1985)

Irene Miracle . . . . Lee Ringtree
- • 0:18—Brief breasts in bed with Timothy Bottoms. Kind of hard to see anything because it's dark.

Incoming Freshman (1979)

Alice Barrett. . . . . Boxing Student
- •• 0:43—Breasts answering a question during Professor Bilbo's fantasy.
- • 0:55—Breasts in another of Bilbo's fantasies.

• 1:18—Breasts during end credits.
Georgia Harrell . . . . Student
Marilyn Faith Hickey . . . . Sargeant Laverne Finterplay
• 0:06—Breasts and buns when Professor Bilbo fantasizes about her.
• 0:56—Breasts and buns during Bilbo's fantasy.
• 1:18—Breasts during end credits.
Wendy Stuart . . . . Miss Seymour
••• 0:25—In purple bra and panties, then breasts and buns stripping during Professor Bilbo's fantasy.
• 0:55—Buns and side of right breast in Bilbo's fantasy.
• 1:18—Breasts during end credits.

The Incredibly True Adventure of Two Girls in Love (1995)

Laurel Holloman . . . . Randy
• 1:11—Brief left breast, while in bed with Evie.
• 1:15—Brief breasts, while running around in the bedroom when Evie's mom comes home.
Nicole Ari Parker . . . . Evie
• 1:12—Breasts and brief side view of buns, while making love in bed with Randy.
• 1:15—Brief breasts, while running around in the bedroom when her mom comes home.

Incubus (1981; Canadian)

Erin Flannery . . . . Jenny Cordell
• 0:08—Briefly nude, while getting out of the shower. Seen by John Cassavetes. Medium long shot.
Mitch Martin. . . . . Mandy Pullman
• 0:13—Very brief left breast, when waking up on operating table.
Helene Udy . . . . Sally Harper

Indecent Behavior (1993)

(Unrated version reviewed.)
Brandy Ledford . . . . Elaine Croft
••• 0:59—Breasts and side view of buns, while taking off her clothes in front of Jan-Michael Vincent.
••• 1:10—Breasts, taking off her top in front of Vincent.
Michelle Moffett . . . . Carol Leiter
•• 0:07—Breasts, while making love under Frederic behind 2-way glass.
•• 0:10—Breasts and buns, while making love on top of Frederic. The camera move around a lot, so it's kind of hard to see.
•• 0:24—In black bra and panties, then breasts and buns, while making love with Robert while being observed behind 2-way glass.
•• 1:06—Breasts while making love with Brenda and getting video taped.
Brenda Swanson . . . . Judith Miller
••• 1:05—In white bra, then breasts, while making love with Carol in observation room.
Shannon Tweed . . . . Rebecca Mathis
• 0:12—Breasts seen through water in spa. Brief buns, getting out of spa.
•• 0:56—Breasts while making love with Gary Hudson.
••• 1:24—In bra and panties, then breasts and buns, while making love in observation room with Nick.
• 1:26—Breasts, while getting out of bed.

Indecent Behavior 3 (1995)

Kaitlyn Ashley . . . . Candy
•• 0:02—Nude, while in bedroom with Mr. Cowens.
Colleen Coffey . . . . Ellie Maddox
••• 0:24—Breasts and buns, while making love in office with Billy.
Griffin Drew. . . . . Janet Colby
••• 0:01—Nude, taking off robe and going for a swim.
•• 0:49—Breasts, while joining Rosa and Billy in bed.
Rebecca Ferratti . . . . Morenika
Pia Reyes . . . . Rosa Venezuela
•• 0:34—In black bra, then breasts while in room with Mr. Cowen.
•• 0:45—Breasts, while wearing a mask and making love in bed with Billy (also wearing a mask).
Shannon Tweed. . . . . Dr. Rebecca Mathis
•• 0:56—Breasts, while making love with Frank in bed.

Indecent Behavior II (1994)

(Unrated version reviewed.)
Nikki Fritz . . . . Woman on Balcony
•• 0:03—Buns in panties, then breasts and lower frontal nudity when making love with man on balcony while Shoshana watches from inside the house.
• 0:06—More frontal nudity while making love on balcony.
Elizabeth Sandifer . . . . Shoshona Reed
Rochelle Swanson . . . . Jordan Mueller
• 0:44—Left breast, while making love in an alley.
•• 0:46—More left breast, then breasts, while in the alley.
••• 1:06—In black bra and panties, when nude, while making love in bed with Tom, then getting out.
•• 1:15—Breasts and buns, while making love with Chad McQueen in recall of a "dream."
Shannon Tweed. . . . . Dr. Rebecca Mathis
••• 0:24—Breasts, after taking off her bra, then taking a shower.
•• 0:55—Breasts and buns, while making love in bed with James Brolin.
•• 1:12—Side of right breast, then breasts, while in the shower.
• 1:13—Breasts, while in bed with Brolin.

An Indecent Obsession (1985)

Wendy Hughes . . . . Honour Langtry
• 0:32—Possibly Wendy's breasts, could be Sue because Luce is fantasizing about Wendy while making love with Sue. Dark, long shot, hard to see.
•• 1:10—Left breast, while making love in bed with Wilson.

Indecent Proposal (1993)

Catlyn Day. . . . . Wine Goddess
Demi Moore . . . . Diana Murphy
•• 0:05—In black bra, brief buns and breasts while making out with Woody Harrelson on the kitchen floor.
• 0:37—Upper half of right breast, while lying in bed with Harrelson.
• 0:40—Upper half of right breast, while lying in bed and talking with Harrelson. Very brief right breast, when lifting sheet over her head.

Independence Day (1996)

Kimberly Beck . . . . Housewife
Vivica A. Fox . . . . Jasmine Dubrow
• 0:35—Brief side view of buns in T-back, while in dressing room in club.
Kiersten Warren . . . . Tiffany

Indictment: The McMartin Trial
(1995; Made for Cable Movie)

Lolita Davidovich. . . . . .Kee McFarlane
Alison Elliott . . . . Peggy Ann Burkey
Chelsea Field. . . . . Christine Johnson
Shirley Knight . . . . Peggy Buckey
- • 0:53—Brief buns, three times while in jail during body cavity search.

Sandy Martin . . . . Deputy Phyllis
Valerie Wildman . . . . Diana Sullivan

Indochine *(1992; French)*

Catherine Deneuve . . . . Eliane
Linh Dan Pham . . . . Camille
- •• 0:46—Right breast, when getting blood wiped off after a prisoner is shot and falls on her.
- •• 1:05—Brief breasts, while sitting in front of a mirror.

• The Infernal Trio *(1974; French)*

Andrea Ferréol. . . . . .Noemie
Romy Schneider . . . . Philomene Schmidt
- • 0:32—Brief side of left breast, while standing in front of open window. Brief breasts, during struggle with a guy.

Infinity *(1989)*

Megan Blake . . . . Karen
- • 0:40—Very brief breasts, while bathing in pond.
- • 1:20—Brief buns and side of right breast, while being carried by the guy. (It looks like there is tape over her nipples.)

• The Informant *(1996; Irish/U.S.)*

Simone Bendix . . . . Samantha
- • 1:19—Breasts, while lying in bed after making love with her boyfriend.
- ••• 1:20—Breasts and buns, getting out of the bed, answering the phone, then sitting in bed, then nude when dressing with Cary Elwes.

The Inheritance *(1978; Italian)*

Adrianna Asti. . . . . .Teta Ferramonti
Dominique Sanda . . . . Irene
- •• 0:18—Full frontal nudity getting undressed and lying on the bed with her new husband.
- ••• 0:37—Full frontal nudity lying in bed with her lover.
- • 1:19—Very brief right breast, while undoing top for Anthony Quinn.
- ••• 1:22—Left breast, lying in bed. Full frontal nudity jumping out of bed after realizing that Quinn is dead.

Inhibition *(1984; Italian)*

Claudine Beccarie . . . . .Carol
- • 0:11—Brief lower frontal nudity in open nightgown walking into bedroom.
- • 0:23—Brief buns and left breast in dressing room.
- • 0:51—Brief lower frontal nudity, while sitting on a swing.
- ••• 0:57—Nude masturbating in bed.
- ••• 1:00—Nude sitting, then being mean to Anna in a bathtub.
- • 1:10—Full frontal nudity under sheer black nightgown greeting Robert.
- ••• 1:11—Nude, making love in bed with Robert.
- •• 1:29—Breasts, making love in bed with Peter.
- • 1:32—Brief breasts waking up in bed in the morning.

Ilona Staller. . . . . .Anna
- ••• 0:08—Nude taking a shower with Carol.
- • 0:43—Brief full frontal nudity getting out of swimming pool.
- ••• 0:55—Breasts making love in the water with Robert.
- ••• 1:00—Full frontal nudity getting disciplined by Carol.

• Inhumanoid *(1996; Made for Cable Movie)*

a.k.a. Circuit Breaker

Lara Harris . . . . Katrina
- • 0:06—Brief half of right breast in nightgown, when leaning up in bed.
- ••• 0:08—Breasts and brief buns, after taking off nightgown after being instructed to do so and starting to make love with a guy on the floor.
- • 0:12—Very brief left breast in flashback.
- • 0:48—Brief left breast again in flashback. Also in bra, while struggling on bed with Richard Grieco and running from him in the ship.
- •• 1:22—Breasts and buns, while making love with Grieco before killing him.

Renato Powell . . . . Nurse

The Initiation *(1984)*

Hunter Tylo . . . . Alison
- ••• 0:33—Frontal nudity in shower, then getting out and drying herself off.
- ••• 0:57—Breasts, changing tops in sporting goods store in mall.

Daphne Zuniga . . . . .Kelly Terry

Inner Sanctum *(1991)*

Suzanne Ager . . . . Maureen
Michelle Bauer. . . . . Body Double for Margaux Hemingway
- • 0:09—Left breast, body double in office for Margaux Hemingway.
- •• 0:23—Breasts body double for Hemingway, while in bed with Joseph Bottoms.

Margaux Hemingway . . . . Anna Rawlins
- • 0:09—Brief buns and tip of left breast in office with Joseph Bottoms.
- ••• 0:23—In bra with Bottoms, then breasts, while in bed. (When you don't see her face, it's Michelle Bauer doing the body double work.)

Tanya Roberts . . . . Lynn Foster
- • 0:35—Right breast, several times, while looking out the window.
- ••• 0:40—Buns in lingerie on sofa with Joseph Bottoms, then breasts while making love.
- ••• 0:57—In black lingerie under trench coat, stripping for Bret Clark. Buns, then breasts making love.

Valerie Wildman . . . . .Jennifer Reed
- •• 0:11—Right breast, while sitting on bed with Joseph Bottoms.

Inner Sanctum 2 *(1994)*

(Unrated version reviewed.)

Suzanne Ager . . . . Maureen
Sandahl Bergman . . . . Sharon Reed
Jennifer Ciesar . . . . Jane
Margaux Hemingway . . . . Anna Rollins
Ashlie Rhey . . . . .Uncredited Body Double
- • 0:12—Left breast and buns, then breasts while making love in bed. Body double for Jennifer Ciesar.
- •• 0:13—Buns and right breast, then breasts while making love. Body double for Jennifer Ciesar.
- • 0:50—Breasts, while in bed with Michael Nouri. Body double for Tracy Brooks Swope.
- ••• 0:56—Breasts and buns, while making love in bedroom. Body double for Jennifer Ciesar.

The Innocent (1976; Italian)

Laura Antonelli . . . . .Julianna

••• 0:41—Breasts in bed with her husband.

••• 0:53—Full frontal nudity in bed when her husband lifts her dress up.

Innocent Blood (1992)

Angela Bassett. . . . . U.S. Attorney Sinclair

Marina Durell . . . . Nurse

Anne Parillaud. . . . . Marie

••• 0:03—Nude in her apartment.

• 1:17—Brief buns, taking off coat and getting into bed.

•• 1:24—Breasts, taking off sheet and kneeling over in bed to get handcuffs put on.

••• 1:25—Breasts and buns, while making love in bed with Anthony LaPaglia.

Linnea Quigley . . . . Nurse

Teri Weigel . . . . .Melody Lounge Dancer

•• 1:32—Breasts (holding a red and white boa, in the middle of two other dancers), dancing in front of Robert Loggia.

Innocent Lies (1995)

Gabrielle Anwar. . . . . Celia Graves

• 1:21—Partial buns in hiked up dress in office with Stephen Dorff.

Marianne Denicourt . . . . Maud Graves

Joanna Lumley. . . . . .Lady Helena Graves

Innocent Sally (1973)

a.k.a. The Dirty Mind of Young Sally

Angela Carnon . . . . .n.a.

Sharon Kelly . . . . Sally

••• 0:35—Breasts, undressing in back of van. Long scene.

••• 0:37—Full frontal nudity, on pillow in back of van while caressing herself. Another long scene.

••• 0:39—More full frontal nudity in van.

••• 0:47—Right breast, then full frontal nudity, making love with Toby in van. Long scene.

••• 1:05—Breasts, making love in bed with another guy. Long scene.

••• 1:10—Full frontal nudity, making more love. Long scene.

•• 1:19—Breasts, after making love.

••• 1:23—Full frontal nudity, while making love with a guy.

Robyn Whitting. . . . . .n.a.

Innocent Victim (1988)

Helen Shaver. . . . . Benet Archdale

• 1:05—Very brief side of left breast on top of a guy in bed.

Inserts (1976)

Veronica Cartwright . . . . .Harlene

•• 0:16—Breasts sitting on bed with Richard Dreyfuss.

••• 0:31—Nude on bed with Stephen Davies making a porno movie for Dreyfuss. Long scene.

Jessica Harper . . . . .Cathy Cake

••• 1:15—Breasts in garter belt and stockings, lying in bed for Richard Dreyfuss. Long scene.

Inside Edge (1991)

Rosie Vela . . . . Lisa Zamora

••• 1:06—Breasts, while making love with Michael Madsen in bed.

• Inside Out (1992; Video Tape)

(Unrated version reviewed.)

Marie Chambers . . . . Terry's Female Half/My Better Half

•• 1:20—Breasts, while lying on couch with open robe.

• 1:21—Brief left breast in open robe, while standing up.

• 1:22—Brief right breast.

••• 1:24—Breasts, while kissing Terry and rolling around on the couch and on the floor.

Chana Jael Chiesa . . . . My Secret Moments

••• 0:42—Breasts, rubbing lotion on them, then joined by a large cast of people during her fantasy as the camera pulls back.

•• 0:44—Full frontal nudity, still in bed. Long shot.

Neith Hunter . . . . Angela/The Diaries

• 1:03—Buns, in swimsuit, while standing up.

•• 1:04—Right breast, then brief breasts in spa with Richard.

••• 1:06—Breasts in bed, getting fondled by David.

•• 1:08—Breasts in the shower.

•• 1:10—Right breast, while in bed with Richard.

Marta Kober . . . . The Girl/Doubletalk

••• 0:26—Breasts in raised blouse, on top of Jack on sofa.

Sherrie Rose. . . . . .Bethany/The Leda

• 0:35—Right breast, while making love with the other criminal. Dark.

• 0:40—Upper half of right breast while making love with him again after he's connected to the computer.

Rachel Ryan .Love the One You're With

•• 1:13—Left breast, in bed with a guy.

•• 1:14—Right breast and buns, climbing on top of him in bed.

•• 1:15—Breasts and buns, making love on top of him. More breasts after making love.

Kimberly Ryusaki . . . . Linda/Life Is For the Taking

••• 0:52—Breasts in bedroom, undressing while Charlie has an out of body experience.

•• 0:53—Left breast, while lying on bed.

Cec Verrell. . . . . .The Psychiatrist/Shrink Wrap

••• 0:18—In red bra, then breasts making love with the guy she picked up in the bar.

Barbara Alyn Woods . . . . Terri/Brush Strokes

••• 0:07—Breasts and buns in G-string, undressing for Jack.

••• 0:08—Close-up of breasts as Jack paints on her with his paintbrush.

••• 0:09—Full frontal nudity, getting paint poured all over her body.

• 0:11—Brief breasts, while holding onto chair while making love.

• Inside Out 2 (1992; Video Tape)

(Unrated version reviewed.)

Linda Carol . . . . The Hitchhiker/The Hitchhiker

••• 1:17—Breasts undressing in room, while a guy watches from across the way. Long scene. B&W.

Lisa London . . . . June/The Right Number

•• 1:25—Breasts, lying on the floor having phone sex and in bed.

•• 1:28—More breasts talking on the phone.

Tané McClure . . . . Melanie Moss/Mis-Apprehended

•• 0:09—Breasts, taking off her blouse outside for Tim.

Francesca "Kitten" Natividad . . Busty Dusty/Profiles in Cleavage

•• 0:56—Bouncing her breasts while wearing pasties.

• 1:02—Dancing in disco wearing pasties. B&W.

• 1:03—Brief breasts with pasties.

Heather-Elizabeth Parkhurst . . Woman/I've Got a Crush on You

•• 0:14—Brief buns, in swimsuit, suntanning. Breasts, trying to prevent guy from jumping.

• 0:15—More breasts and buns shots when she's flattened during the rest of the segment.

Sherrie Rose . . . . Marina/The Freak
• 0:29—Breasts, getting her clothes and mask taken off in front of other masked people. B&W.
•• 0:35—Breasts in bed with alien guy. B&W.

Brenda Swanson . . . . Mrs. Jenkins/There's This Traveling Salesman, See
•• 0:43—Breasts, taking off her top in barn.

Saxon Trainor . . . . The Doctor
• 0:52—Breasts in bed on top of Drake. B&W.

Elizabeth Whitcraft . . . . . . Sarah/Some Guys Have All the Luck
••• 1:10—Breasts, while taking off her top in bed. More breasts while in bed. Brief partial buns.

• *Inside Out 3* (1992; Video Tape)

Alex Datcher . . . . .Annie/The Wet Dream
••• 1:24—Breasts, taking off her blouse in front of the fish tank.
•• 1:25—Breasts, getting up when Dennis leaves.
• 1:26—Breasts, getting into bathtub. Long shot.
• 1:28—Breasts in bathtub.
• 1:29—Breasts in bathtub with Greg Louganis.

Julie Gray . . . . Actress/The Branding

Marilyn Hassett . . . . Cindy/The Houseguest

Roxanna Michaels . . . . .Laila/The Perfect Woman
••• 0:38—Breasts and buns in G-string, changing out of her wet clothes, while Joe watches.
• 0:43—Brief breasts, taking off clothes on talk show on TV.

Bianca Rossini . . . . Ollala/The Branding
••• 0:23—Breasts, making love in bed with Mike.

Cec Verrell . . . . .Susan/Tango

Teri Weigel . . . . Woman/The Portal
•• 0:27—Brief breasts, standing up in the water.

Whitney Weston . . . . Debbie/The Perfect Woman
•• 0:30—Breasts, while talking on talk show seen on TV.
• 0:43—Brief breasts, after taking off clothes on talk show on TV.

• *Inside Out 4* (1992; Video Tape)

(Unrated version reviewed.)

Denise Buick . . . . .Claudia/What Anna Wants...
••• 1:08—Nude in bed with William while Anna takes photos.

Susan Byun . . . . Lee Anne/Three on a Match
••• 0:58—Breasts, changing blouse in the bathroom.

Sharon Cain . . . . Video Mate
•• 1:14—Breasts on TV.
••• 1:16—Breasts in Dave's living room.
• 1:17—Nude, making love with Dave in fast speed.
••• 1:18—Breasts and buns, on sofa with Dave.
• 1:19—More breasts in fast speed.
••• 1:20—Nude in Dave's living room.
• 1:22—Nude on TV again.

Chana Jael Chiesa . . . . Actress/Motivation
• 0:13—Lower frontal nudity, dropping her shorts to show Dick her haircut.
••• 0:14—Nude, out in the desert with Dick, shooting a scene.
• 0:16—Breasts, while opening her blouse to show Dick her breasts, brief full frontal nudity, running to get into truck.
•• 0:17—Brief full frontal nudity, out in the desert with Dick again.

Mimi Craven . . . . Dolores/Put Asunder
• 0:18—Left breast in bed with her husband.
••• 0:22—Breasts, lying in bed after making love with her husband.

Carolyn Finney . . . . Faye/The Thief
••• 0:41—Breasts in bed, making love with the burglar.

Elizabeth A. Jaeger. Marie/Jilted Lover
••• 0:50—Breasts with her lover, making out on the floor.

Paula Reve'e . . . . Lola/My Cyberian Rhapsody
••• 1:30—Breasts in cybersex machine.
••• 1:31—Breasts several times when cybersex machine starts malfunctioning.

Catya Sassoon . . . . Pauline/Natalie Would
••• 0:08—Breasts in bed with Ted, then getting out and getting dressed.

Sándra Wild. . . . . Blonde Woman/The Thief
••• 0:44—Breasts, sitting up in bed and getting out.

Annie Wood . . . . Ms. Morely/Save the Wetlands
•• 0:32—Left breast, while playing with herself during interviewed.
• 0:33—Partial buns, while bending over to pick up photo off the floor.

Internal Affairs (1990)

Pamella D'Pella . . . . .Cheryl

Victoria Dillard. . . . . Kee

Faye Grant. . . . . Penny
• 0:50—Right breast, while straddling Richard Gere while she talks on the telephone.

Billie Neal . . . . Dorian's Wife

Nancy Travis . . . . Kathleen Avila
• 0:38—Side view of left breast when Raymond opens the shower door to talk to her.

Intersection (1993)

Lolita Davidovich. . . . . Olivia Marshak
• 0:01—Breasts during Richard Gere's flashback. Don't see her face.
• 0:04—Very brief right breast while rolling over in bed.
•• 1:15—Brief breasts while pulling up her pajama tops during game of charades.

Christine Lippa . . . . Step Magazine

Sharon Stone. . . . . Sally Eastman
• 0:18—Right breast behind glass blocks in shower, then very brief left breast in mirror when she adjusts her robe.

Interview With the Vampire: The Vampire Chronicles (1994)

Katia Caballero . . . . Woman in Audience

Laure Marsac. .Mortal Woman on Stage
••• 1:15—Nude after being stripped of her clothes, then killed while on stage during play put on by the vampires. Long scene.

Thandie Newton . . . . Yvette

Missy Yager . . . . Creole Woman
• 0:49—Full frontal nudity, then left breast, while washing herself when seen by Kirsten Dunst through open doorway.

• *Intimate Betrayal* (1996)

Cristi Conaway . . . . Shelley

Annabelle Gurwitch. . . . . Claire

Julianne J. Mantia . . . . Debbie
• 0:11—Breasts, while dancing at bachelor party wearing tasseled pasties.
• 0:13—Right breast after pastie comes off and buns in T-back.

Intimate Obsession (1992)

(Unrated version reviewed.)

Kristie Ducati . . . . Laura
••• 0:15—Breasts while making love with Rick while Rachel watches from outside. Long scene.
••• 0:17—More breasts, while making love on top of Rick.

••• 0:18—Buns and more breasts while making love.
••• 0:19—Brief partial lower frontal nudity and more breasts while making love with Rick.
•• 0:21—Breasts during Rachel's recollections.

Jodie Fisher . . . . Rachel Taylor
• 0:07—Full frontal nudity, swimming under water during her nightmare.
• 0:22—Partial breasts in bubble bath. Brief left breast, while rinsing herself off.
•• 0:30—Breasts, while taking off her bra in front of mirror.
••• 0:47—Breasts while making love with Rick on sofa. Long scene.
• 0:53—Breasts under water during nightmare.
•• 0:58—Buns, while lying in bed with Rick.
••• 0:59—Breasts and brief lower frontal nudity, while sitting up in bed when Rick gets out.
• 1:06—Brief breasts on TV during video playback.

Valerie Hartman . . . . Karen
Heather McTague . . . . Beth Thompson
••• 0:38—Nude, while making love with Tom in bedroom. (She's wearing a dark wig and sunglasses.) Long scene.
• 1:04—Breasts on TV in video playback that Rachel watches.
• 1:10—Left breast, while sitting on couch and kissing Tom.

• ***Intimate Secrets—How Women Love to be Loved*** *(1993; Video Tape)*

Nikki Dial. . . . . Nicole
••• 0:13—In white bra and red panties, then full frontal nudity on couch.

Lori Jo Hendrix . . . . Lori
••• 0:46—In white bra and panties, then nude in bed.

Carrie Janisse. . . . . Carrie
••• 0:34—In gold bra and white lingerie, then full frontal nudity posing on and in front of a grand piano.

Tami Monroe . . . . Tami
••• 0:22—In white bra and panties, then breasts on couch.

Intimate Strangers *(1991; Made for Cable Movie)*

Tia Carrere . . . . Mino
• 0:34—In black lingerie in Nick's apartment. Very brief side of right breast in bed with him.

Paige French . . . . Meg Wheeler
Deborah Harry . . . . Cory Wheeler

• ***Intimate Workout For Lovers*** *(1992; Video Tape)*

Rebekka Armstrong . . . . Sensual Exercise
••• 0:11—Nude, exercising in living room and exercise room.

Amy Rochelle . . . . Water Workout
••• 0:21—Nude, outside by swimming pool and in pool.

Lisa Saxton . . . . Intimate Harmony
••• 0:39—Nude, in dance studio and in the showers. Excellent!

Gabriela Young . . . . Romantic Relaxation
••• 0:01—Nude, in bedroom, in bathtub and in bed.

Into the Fire *(1988)*

a.k.a. Legend of Lone Wolf

Susan Anspach . . . . Rosalind Winfield
•• 0:22—Left breast, under trench coat when she first comes into the house, briefly again in the kitchen.
•• 0:31—Breasts in bedroom standing up with Wade.

Olivia D'Abo . . . . Liette
• 0:07—Very, very brief silhouette of left breast in bed with Wade.
•• 0:32—Breasts on bed with Wade. A little bit dark and hard to see.
•• 1:10—Breasts in the bathtub. (Note her panties when she gets up.)

Into the Night *(1985)*

Sue Bowser . . . . Girl on Boat
•• 0:24—Breasts taking off blouse with Jake on his boat after Michelle Pfeiffer leaves.

Kathryn Harrold. . . . . Christie
Tracey E. Hutchinson. . . . . Federal Agent
Peggy McIntaggart . . . . Shameless Woman
• 0:43—Breasts putting dress on after coming out of men's restroom stall after a man leaves the stall first.

Irene Papas . . . . Shaheen Parvizi
Dedee Pfeiffer . . . . Hooker
Michelle Pfeiffer. . . . . Diana
•• 0:27—Brief buns while in bathroom.
• 0:28—Brief side nudity, twice, walking past doorway. Medium long shot.

• ***Intruso*** *(1993; Spanish)*

Victoria Abril . . . . Luisa
• 0:53—Partial breasts behind glass shower door. Partial right breast and buns while making love with Angel in the shower.
• 1:03—Brief breasts, taking off her nightgown and getting into bed with Angel.
• 1:04—Partial buns, while making love in bed with Angel. Dark.
• 1:06—Brief right breast, while making love with her husband in bed. Brief buns, when getting out of bed.

Invasion For Flesh & Blood *(1996)*

Marilyn Ghigliotti . . . . Rape Victim
• 0:33—Brief partial buns, while lying dead on the ground, covered with blood.
• 0:37—Breasts, while lying dead on the ground, covered with blood.

Invasion of Privacy *(1992)*

(Unrated version reviewed.)

Diana Cuevas. . . . . Alex's Mother
•• 0:01—Left breast, while in bedroom with her lover, while young Alex watches from closet.

Lydie Denier . . . . Vicky
• 0:54—Brief breasts in her apartment dancing in front of Robby Benson while he video tapes her.
••• 1:19—Breasts on top of Benson in bed.

Invasion of the Bee Girls *(1973)*

Anna Aries . . . . Cora Kline
•• 0:55—Buns and breasts getting transformed into a Bee Girl.
••• 1:00—Breasts getting out of the bee transformer.

Anitra Ford . . . . Dr. Susan Harris
••• 0:47—Breasts and buns undressing in front of a guy in front of a fire.

Susan Player Jarreau. . . . . Girl
Beverly Powers. . . . . Harriet Williams
• 1:14—In white bra and panties, then right breast and buns, taking off her clothes for her husband.

Victoria Vetri . . . . Julie Zorn
• 0:30—Brief breasts getting molested by jerks.
••• 1:19—Breasts in the bee transformer, then brief buns getting rescued.

Invasion of the Body Snatchers (1978)

Brooke Adams . . . . Elizabeth Driscoll

•• 1:43—Brief breasts behind plants when Sutherland sees her change into a pod person. Hard to see because plants are in the way.

• 1:48—Breasts walking through the pod factory pointing out Sutherland to everybody. Long shot, hard to see.

Veronica Cartwright . . . . Nancy Bellicec

• *Inventing the Abbotts (1997)*

Jennifer Connelly. . . . . Eleanor Abbott

•• 0:17—Brief left breast several times, while making love with Billy Crudup in garage when seen by Joaquin Phoenix.

• 0:28—Very brief right breast, while making love with Crudup on the ground.

Joanna Going . . . . Alice Abbott

Liv Tyler . . . . Pamela Abbott

Barbara Williams . . . . Joan Abbott

The Invincible Six (1969)

Elke Sommer. . . . . Zari

• 0:44—Right breast under wet, skin-colored outfit after fight in pool.

•• 1:09—Right breast, while tending to her wound.

•• 1:10—Breasts, while making love in the dark.

The Invisible Kid (1988)

Karen Black . . . . Mom

Corie Henninger . . . . Gung Ho Cheerleader

•• 0:38—Brief breasts (she's wearing a cheerleading skirt), while horsing around in the girl's locker room with a friend, then in bra, while talking to Chynna Phillips.

The Invisible Maniac (1990)

Savannah . . . . Vicky

• 0:21—Buns and very, very brief side of left breast in the shower with the other girls.

• 0:33—Right breast covered with bubbles.

••• 0:43—In bra, then breasts and lots of buns in locker room with the other girls.

•• 0:44—Buns and left breast in the shower with the other girls.

••• 1:04—Undressing in locker room in white bra and panties, then breasts. More breasts taking a shower and getting electrocuted.

Dana Bentley Konkel . . . . Newscaster

• 1:22—Brief breasts on monitor doing the news.

Stephanie Blake. . . . . Mrs. Cello

•• 0:42—Breasts opening her blouse for Chet.

•• 0:52—Breasts in her office trying to seduce Dr. Smith. Nice close up of right breast.

Debra Lamb . . . . Betty

• 0:21—Buns and very brief side view of right breast in the shower with the other girls.

••• 0:43—In bra, then breasts and buns standing on the left in the locker room with the other girls.

• 0:44—Buns and brief breasts in the shower with the other girls.

•• 0:56—In bra, then breasts getting killed by Dr. Smith.

• 0:58—Brief breasts, dead, discovered by April and Joan.

Melissa Anne Moore . . . . Bunny

• 0:21—Buns in shower with the other girls.

••• 0:43—In bra, then breasts sitting with yellow towel in locker room with the other girls.

• 0:44—Breasts in shower with the other girls.

••• 1:09—In bra, then breasts making out in Principal's Office with Chet. Long scene.

Tracy Walker . . . . Telescope Gal

•• 0:01—Nude, taking off clothes during opening credits. Nice dancing.

Invisible: The Chronicles of Benjamin Knight (1993)

Jennifer Nash. . . . . Zanna

• 0:15—Buns, while making love in bed with Wade. Don't see her face well.

• *Irma Vep (1996; French)*

Arsinée Khanjian . . . . American Woman

••• 0:53—Full frontal nudity, while talking on the phone in motel room, after Maggie Cheung sneaks in.

Iron Warrior (1987)

Savina Gersak . . . . Janna

• 0:06—Brief buns in outfit while getting a blue sheet wrapped around her by her servants.

• 0:18—Brief left breast, while lying on ceremonial table.

Ironheart (1991)

Karman Kruschke. . . . . Kristi

•• 0:55—Buns and brief side of left breast, getting out of bed with John. Brief breasts in bathroom.

Melanie Mosely . . . . Pretty Girl

•• 0:18—Breasts, while getting her T-shirt ripped off by four jerks. Long shot and closer shots.

Ironweed (1987)

Carroll Baker . . . . Annie Phelan

Meryl Streep . . . . Helen

Margaret Whitton . . . . Katrina

•• 1:19—Full frontal nudity leaving the house and walking down steps while young Francis brushes a horse.

Irreconcilable Differences (1984)

Drew Barrymore . . . . Casey Brodsky

Dana Kaminski. . . . . Woman in Dress Shop

Shelley Long . . . . Lucy Van Patten Brodsky

Sharon Stone. . . . . Blake Chandler

•• 0:56—Breasts lowering her blouse in front of Ryan O'Neal during film test.

Irresistible Impulse (1995)

Lee Anne Beaman . . . . Jeannine Miller

•• 0:47—Breasts, while lying in hammock, then in sheer black robe when talking with Richard.

• 1:03—Buns in panties, while walking away and on the beach.

••• 1:05—Buns and breasts, while making love with Richard on the beach, then on a hammock, then inside the house.

•• 1:07—Breasts and buns in spa, then getting out.

•• 1:31—Breasts, while making love with Simon in bed, then sitting up in bed afterwards.

Brandy Ledford . . . . Heather McNeill

•• 1:15—In black bra, panties and stockings, then breasts while making love with Simon.

• 1:22—Brief partial breasts, while putting her bra on.

Wendy MacDonald . . . . Carolyn Wetherby

•• 0:27—Breasts, after taking robe off in front of Richard. Breasts and buns, while making love in bed with him.

• 0:31—Very, very brief left breast, when Richard turns her over in bed after discovering her unconscious.

• 0:32—Brief half of right breast, while lying unconscious in bed.

Kathy Shower . . . . Tina Lovejoy

• 1:30—Brief breasts, while lying in bed with Richard.

• 1:31—Brief breasts, while sitting up in bed.

Is There Sex After Death? (1975)

Iris Brooks . . . . Breast Development Student

••• 1:18—Breasts in open blouse with Buck Henry.

Mary Elaine Monti . . . . Stag Film Scene/Sue

•• 0:53—Buns and right breast, while in bed with a guy during filming of stag film.

•• 1:00—Breasts and buns, while in bed with Fred.

K.C. Townsend . . . . .Round Table Discussion/Woman on Table

•• 1:25—Full frontal nudity, while making love on table with a guy in front of a discussion group of men.

Jennifer Welles . . . . Magic Act/Merkin's Assistant

•• 0:41—Brief left breast and buns, while helping Merkin, then full frontal nudity.

Isadora (1968; British)

Vanessa Redgrave . . . . Isadora Duncan

• 0:47—Brief glimpses of breasts and buns dancing around in her boyfriend's house at night. Hard to see anything.

• 2:19—Very brief breasts dancing on stage after coming back from Russia.

Ishtar (1987)

Isabelle Adjani . . . . Shirra Assel

• 0:27—Very brief left breast flashing herself to Dustin Hoffman at the airport while wearing sunglasses.

Carol Kane . . . . Carol

The Island (1980)

Angela Punch McGregor . . . . Beth

•• 0:45—Breasts taking off poncho to make love with Michael Caine in hut after rubbing stuff on him.

Island of 1000 Delights (German)

Bea Fiedler . . . . Julia

•• 0:25—Full frontal nudity washing herself in bathtub, then nude taking off her towel for Michael.

•• 0:27—Breasts lying on floor after making love, then buns walking to chair.

•• 0:46—Full frontal nudity, after taking off her dress and kissing Howard.

•• 0:50—Breasts in white bikini bottoms coming out of the water to greet Howard.

••• 1:06—Breasts sitting in the sand near the beach, then nude talking with Sylvia.

••• 1:17—Right breast (great close up) making love with Sylvia.

••• 1:18—Breasts above Sylvia.

Scarlett Gunden . . . . Francine

••• 0:02—Breasts on beach dancing with Ching. Upper half of buns sitting down.

•• 0:44—Full frontal nudity getting tortured by Ming.

• 1:16—Breasts on beach after Ching rescues her.

Olivia Pascal . . . . Peggy

•• 0:16—Breasts, tied up while being tortured by two guys. Upper half lower frontal nudity.

•• 0:23—Full frontal nudity lying in bed, then buns running out the door. Full frontal nudity running up stairs, nude hiding in bedroom.

••• 0:57—Nude, taking off her clothes in shower with Michael.

• 1:26—Brief breasts running on the beach with Michael.

It's Called Murder Baby (1982)

(R-rated version of the adult film *Dixie Ray, Hollywood Star.*)

Judy Carr . . . . Adrian Ross

• 1:21—Brief breasts, sitting up on bed in background.

Lisa De Leeuw . . . . Dixie Ray

• 0:26—Lower frontal nudity, raising her dress at the beach to prove to Nick that she never wears panties.

••• 0:42—Nude on table, getting massaged by Adrian.

•• 0:49—Full frontal nudity when Nick leaves the room.

•• 1:21—Breasts, getting up to get dressed.

• 1:22—Brief lower frontal nudity in open robe, while walking around the house.

••• 1:24—Breasts, opening her nightgown in front of Nick.

Samantha Fox . . . . Lisa Benson

••• 1:10—In bra, then breasts in bedroom in front of Nick and Sherry.

•• 1:11—Breasts, sleeping on bed, then waking up and getting out.

• 1:18—Brief breasts in B&W flashback.

Jane Hamilton . . . . Sherry

• 0:59—Buns, raising her skirt for Nick.

• 1:11—Left breast, sleeping in bed, then waking up and getting out.

Kelly Nichols . . . . Leslie

It's My Turn (1980)

Jill Clayburgh . . . . Kate Gunzinger

• 1:10—Brief upper half of left breast in bed with Michael Douglas after making love.

Jennifer Salt . . . . Maisie

J.D.'s Revenge (1976)

Alice Jubert . . . . Roberta Bliss/Betty Jo

•• 0:59—Breasts in open blouse, while leaning back on sofa with Isaac.

Joan Pringle . . . . Christella

•• 0:27—Breasts, while making love with Isaac.

•• 1:05—Breasts, in open blouse while struggling on the floor with Isaac.

Rhonda Shear . . . . 1942 Girl

Barbara Tasker . . . . Sheryl

• 1:11—Very brief left breast, while lying on her stomach on bed. Brief breasts, while getting up and out of bed with Isaac.

Jabberwocky (1977)

Deborah Fallender . . . . The Princess

• 0:56—Buns and brief full frontal nudity in bath when Michael Palin accidentally enters the room.

• 0:57—Breasts under sheer white robe.

Jack Be Nimble (1994; New Zealand)

Celia Nicholson . . . . Motel Woman

• 0:02—Brief breasts, while making love with Clarrie in motel room bed.

Jack-O (1995)

a.k.a. Jacko Lantern

Linnea Quigley . . . . Carolyn Miller

•• 0:23—Breasts and buns, while taking a shower.

Brinke Stevens . . . . Witch

Dawn Wildsmith . . . . Sorceress

Jackson County Jail (1976)

Marciee Drake . . . . Candy (David's Girlfriend)
- 0:04—Brief breasts wrapping towel around herself, in front of Howard Hesseman. Long shot.

Yvette Mimieux . . . . Dinah Hunter
- 0:39—Breasts in jail cell getting raped by policeman.

Patrice Rohmer . . . . Cassie Anne
Betty Thomas . . . . Waitress
Mary Woronov . . . . Pearl

Jacob's Ladder (1990)

Billie Neal . . . . Della
Elizabeth Peña . . . . Jezzie
- 0:14—Side view of right breast taking off robe and getting into shower with Tim Robbins.
- ••• 0:16—Breasts several times opening dress and putting pants on, then in black bra.
- •• 0:31—Very, very brief breasts in bed with Robbins, then left breast a lot. Dark.

Jade (1995)

Angie Everhart . . . . Patrice Jacinto
Linda Fiorentino . . . . Trina Gavin
- •• 0:25—Buns, while sitting on chair and talking on the phone.
- • 0:49—Breasts in lingerie on B&W grainy video playback.
- • 1:06—Breasts and brief partial buns, when falling out of bed seen in B&W video playback.
- • 1:29—Breasts in several B&W photos.

Jagged Edge (1985)

Glenn Close . . . . Teddy Barnes
- • 0:46—Side view of left breast, making love in bed with Jeff Bridges.
- • 1:38—Very brief side view of right breast running down the hall taking off her blouse. Back is toward camera. Blurry shot.

Maria Mayenzet . . . . Page Forrester
- • 0:02—Very brief breast, on bed when the killer rips her pajamas open. Long shot.

Leigh Taylor-Young . . . . Virginia Howell

Jailbait (1993)

a.k.a. Streetwise

Melinda Armstrong . . . . Dawn
- • 0:43—Brief buns in G-string, then breasts, while talking to C. Thomas Howell in room in sex club.

Angel Aviles . . . . Pizza Girl
Krista Errickson . . . . Merci Cooper
- 0:11—In black bra, panties, garter belt and stockings in room with Tommy.
- •• 0:12—Breasts, while in bed handcuffing Tommy to the bed.
- 0:19—In black bra in motel room.
- 1:11—Back half of left breast, while making love with a guy.

Renée Humphrey . . . . Kyle Bradley
- 0:54—Almost left breast while taking off bathrobe in front of C. Thomas Howell.
- 1:10—In black bra and panties with Howell. Back half of left breast.
- • 1:13—Breasts, while taking a shower. Don't see her face.

Jailbait Babysitter (1978)

Mariwin Roberts . . . . Trisha
- •• 0:08—Breasts and buns, taking off her dress and getting into van with Cal.
- •• 0:18—Breasts and buns in shower with Marion while Mike and Cal help them.

Jailbait: Betrayed by Innocence (1986)

Cristen Kauffman . . . . Marisa
- ••• 0:24—Breasts, when lying down on bed, then sitting up. Buns, while standing up and calling to Barry Bostwick, then breasts while making love with him. Long scene.
- •• 0:49—Very brief right breast while in bed with Bostwick. Breasts, when sitting up in bed when she hears a noise outside, then coming back into the bedroom.

Susan Marie Snyder . . . . Andrea

Jakarta (1988)

Sue Francis Pai . . . . Esha
- • 1:01—Brief right breast, while making love in the courtyard with Falco.
- • 1:13—Brief side of right breast while kissing Falco.
- •• 1:13—Side view of right breast, then brief breasts twice, making love under a mosquito net with Falco. Hard to see her face clearly.

James Joyce's Women (1983)

Fionnula Flanagan . . . . Molly Bloom
- • 0:48—Brief breasts getting out of bed.
- ••• 0:56—Breasts getting back into bed.
- ••• 1:02—Full frontal nudity masturbating in bed talking to herself. Very long scene—9 minutes!

Jamón, Jamón (1992; Spanish)

Penelope Cruz . . . . Silvia
- ••• 0:11—Right breast, then breasts, while making out with José Luis.
- • 0:46—Breasts, while kneeling on ground in dream sequence.
- • 1:02—Left breast sticking out of dress while José Luis has a temper tantrum.
- 1:03—In braless, wet white dress.
- 1:05—Partial buns, while kissing Raul.
- ••• 1:09—Breasts, while making love with Raul.

Anna Galiena . . . . Carmen
- •• 0:35—Breasts out of the top of her dress, while in the back of the restaurant with José Luis.

Stefania Sandrelli . . . . Conchita

The January Man (1988)

Mary Elizabeth Mastrantonio . . . . Bernadette Flynn
- • 0:40—Breasts in bed with Kevin Kline. Side view of left breast squished against Kline.
- ••• 0:42—Breasts after Kline gets out of bed. Brief shot, but very nice!

Billie Neal . . . . Gwen
Susan Sarandon . . . . Christine Starkey

Jason Goes to Hell—The Final Friday (1993)

(Unrated Director's Original Cut reviewed.)

Kathryn Atwood . . . . Alexis, the blonde camper
- •• 0:26—Breasts, after taking off wet blouse after skinny dipping with her friends.

Michelle Clunie . . . . Deborah, the dark-haired camper
- • 0:29—Brief right breast, while on top of Luke in tent.
- ••• 0:31—Breasts, while making love with Luke in tent before getting killed.

Barbara Ann Klein . . . . Stunts

Julie Michaels . . . . Elizabeth Marcus F.B.I.
•• 0:03—In white bra and panties, then buns and breasts while starting to take a shower. More breasts after grabbing towel.

Jason's Lyric *(1994)*
(Unrated version reviewed.)
Jada Pinkett . . . . Lyric
1:02—Nudity in the woods with Allen Payne was done by a body double.
• 1:15—Brief buns in hiked up dress, while making love with Allen Payne in store.

Jaws *(1975)*
Susan Backlinie . . . . Chrissie Watkins
• 0:02—Brief back side of right breast, while taking off her clothes and running on the beach. Seen mostly in silhouette.
• 0:03—Brief left breast (seen from the shark's point-of-view from underneath), while swimming in the water. Dark.

Jekyll & Hyde... Together Again *(1982)*
Elvira . . . . Busty Nurse
• 0:56—Brief right breast, peeking out from smock in operating room. (She's wearing a surgical mask.)
Bess Armstrong . . . . Mary
Krista Errickson . . . . Ivy
Noelle North . . . . Student

Jennifer *(1978)*
Lisa Pelikan . . . . Jennifer
• 0:45—Back side of right breast, in the showers by herself.
• 0:49—Full frontal nudity, falling into the pool from ladder. (Possibly a stunt double.)

Jessi's Girls *(1976)*
Regina Carroll . . . . Claire
•• 0:58—Breasts and buns in hay with Indian guy. Don't see her face.
Sondra Currie . . . . Jessica
• 0:02—Nude in water cleaning up, then brief left breast getting dressed.
• 0:07—Breasts getting raped by four guys. Fairly long scene.
• 0:37—Breasts kissing Clay under a tree. Hard to see because of the shadows.
Ellen Stern . . . . Kana
••• 1:10—Left breast, then breasts in bed with a guy.

Jesus of Montreal *(1990; French/Canadian)*
Isabelle Truchon . . . . Richard's Girlfriend
Catherine Wilkening . . . . Mireille Fontaine
• 1:08—Brief breasts starting to take off her sweatshirt during an audition.

• ***Jewel Naked Around the World*** *(1995; Video Tape)*
Michelle Bauer . . . . Herself
• 0:39—Brief breasts and buns in several clips from *In the Flesh.*
Jewel Shepard . . . . Herself
• 0:00—Brief breasts (wearing a mask) while on stage with another woman and a guy wearing a mask.
• 0:05—Brief breasts, while opening her fur coat to flash the camera.
••• 0:05—Nude, undressing and taking a shower in clip from *Christina.*
•• 0:07—Brief breasts, while wrists are tied from *Christina.*
•• 0:08—Full frontal nudity, in clips from *Christina.*
••• 0:10—More full frontal nudity, in clips from *Christina.*
•• 0:19—In sheer black lingerie, then breasts, while dancing in video tape.
• 0:31—Brief breasts, while in car with Matt Lattanzi in clip from *My Tutor.*
••• 0:32—Nude while dancing in clip from *The Sex and Violence Family Hour.*
• 0:38—Brief breasts after her top gets popped of by Scott Baio in clip from *Zapped!.*
••• 0:39—Nude in several clips from *In the Flesh.*

Jezebel's Kiss *(1990)*
Katherine Barrese . . . . Jezebel
•• 0:36—Full frontal nudity washing herself off in kitchen after having sex with the sheriff.
• 0:42—Brief buns, going for a swim in the ocean. Dark.
••• 0:48—Breasts taking off her robe in front of Hunt, then making love with him.
• 0:58—Brief right breast and buns while Malcolm McDowell watches through slit in curtain. Long shot.
• 1:09—Right breast and buns getting undressed. Long shot. Closer shot of buns, putting robe on.
••• 1:12—Breasts making love with McDowell. More breasts after.
Meredith Baxter . . . . Virginia De Leo
Meg Foster . . . . Amanda Faberson

The Jigsaw Murders *(1988)*
Laura Albert . . . . Blonde Stripper
••• 0:19—Breasts and buns in black G-string, stripping during bachelor party in front of a group of policemen.
Carla Baron . . . . Script Girl
Michelle Bauer . . . . Cindy Jakulski
• 0:20—Brief buns on cover of puzzle box during bachelor party.
• 0:21—Brief breasts in puzzle on underside of glass table after the policemen put the puzzle together.
• 0:29—Very brief breasts when the police officers show the photographer the puzzle picture.
• 0:43—Very brief breasts long shots in some pictures that the photographer is watching on a screen.
Catherine Case . . . . Stripper #2
• 0:27—Brief breasts in black peek-a-boo bra posing for photographer.
Michelle Johnson . . . . Kathy DaVonzo
Brinke Stevens . . . . Stripper #1
• 0:28—Very, very brief breasts posing for photographer in white bra and panties when camera passes between her and the other stripper.

• ***Joanna*** *(1968; British)*
Glenna Forster Jones . . . . Beryl
• 0:17—Brief upper half of breasts, while sitting in bed, smoking, talking with Joanna. Slightly out of focus.
Fiona Lewis . . . . Miranda De Hyde
Genevieve Waite . . . . Joanna
• 0:18—Very brief buns, while walking into pond. Brief buns and back side of right breast, when getting out.
• 0:57—Brief side of left breast, when getting out of bed.
• 1:22—Breasts in large B&W photo on the wall.
• 1:28—Left breast, while putting on blouse. Another view of left breast in mirror on the wall.

Jock Petersen *(1974; Australian)*
a.k.a. Petersen
Sheila Florance . . . . n.a.

Belinda Giblin . . . . Moira Winton
•• 0:21—Left breast several times, under a cover with Jock, then buns when cover is removed.
Wendy Hughes . . . . Patricia Kent
••• 0:12—Breasts in her office with Tony.
• 0:13—Breasts making love with Tony on the floor.
•• 0:44—Nude running around the beach with Tony.
•• 0:50—Nude in bed making love with Tony.
• 1:24—Full frontal nudity when Tony rapes her in her office.
Anne Pendlebury. . . . . Peggy
Jacki Weaver . . . . Susie Petersen
••• 0:01—Full frontal nudity lying in bed with Jock.

Joe *(1970)*

Francine Middleton. . . . . Gail
•• 1:31—Nude with Bill.
Susan Sarandon . . . . Melissa Compton
• 0:02—Breasts and very brief lower frontal nudity taking off clothes and getting into bathtub with Frank.

John and Mary *(1969)*

Tyne Daly . . . . Hilary
Olympia Dukakis. . . . . John's Mother
Mia Farrow . . . . Mary
• 0:03—Buns and brief tip of left breast, while standing at the window after getting out of bed.
• 0:04—Brief buns, while walking to bathroom.

Johnny Firecloud *(1975)*

Christina Hart . . . . June
•• 0:22—Breasts, lying in bed with Johnny.
••• 0:26—Breasts, opening her blouse in barn in front of Johnny.
Sacheen Littlefeather. . . . . Nenya
••• 0:55—Breasts, getting raped by jerks on desk in classroom.

Johnny Handsome *(1989)*

Ellen Barkin . . . . Sunny Boyd
Elizabeth McGovern . . . . Donna McCarty
•• 0:47—Right breast, while in bed with Mickey Rourke.

• ***Johnny Skidmarks*** *(1997)*

Frances McDormand. . . . . Alice
Charlie Spradling . . . . Lorraine
• 0:10—Brief breasts, when caught in bed with John Lithgow during setup.
• 0:46—Very brief breast in B&W flashback.
• 0:57—Very, very brief partial right breast in B&W flashback.

Jokes My Folks Never Told Me *(1976)*

Raven De La Croix. . . . . n.a.
Marciee Drake. . . . . n.a.
Deborah Dutch . . . . Girl on Bed/Confessional Girl
•• 0:33—Left breast, while sitting on bed (on the right) talking to the sweater girl.
Jackie Giroux. . . . . n.a.
Sandy Johnson . . . . n.a.
Mariwin Roberts . . . . n.a.

Joseph Andrews *(1977; British/French)*

Ann-Margret . . . . Lady Boaby
Natalie Ogle . . . . Fanny
• 1:15—Very brief side of left breast, getting her blouse ripped off to get flogged.
•• 1:20—Breasts while hugging Joseph Andrews after he beats up the guy who was attacking her.
•• 1:21—Right breast while walking, then breasts after taking off her blouse in front of Joseph.
•• 1:35—Breasts, after undressing and getting into bed.
Jenny Runacre . . . . The Gypsy
Maggie Wright . . . . First Nun
• 1:03—Breasts under sheer area of habit.

The Josephine Baker Story *(1991; Made for Cable Movie)*

Lynn Whitfield. . . . . Josephine Baker
• 0:00—Breasts while dancing during opening credits. Slow motion.
•• 0:13—Breasts after taking off her dress top for the French painter.
••• 0:14—Breasts in the mirror and while dancing with the painter after making love. Nice. Dancer doing splits looks like a body double.
• 0:16—Brief buns, in wet dress, getting out of swimming pool.
••• 0:31—Breasts while on stage doing the Banana Dance.
••• 0:33—Breasts, while doing the Banana Dance.
• 2:02—Brief breasts while dancing in flashback.

Joshua Then and Now *(1985; Canadian)*

Alexandra Innes. . . . . Joanna
Gabrielle Lazure. . . . . Pauline Shapiro
• 0:39—Buns and brief side of left breast, while in bed with James Woods.

Joy *(1983; French/Canadian)*

Nancy Cser . . . . Unidentified
Claudia Udy . . . . Joy
•• 0:11—Nude, undressing, getting into bath then into and out of bed.
••• 0:14—Nude in bed with Marc.
••• 0:31—In swimsuits, posing for photos, then full frontal nudity.
•• 0:54—Breasts sitting with Bruce at encounter group.
• 1:04—Buns and breasts getting into bathtub.

The Joy of Flying *(1979)*

a.k.a. Erotic Ways
Olivia Pascal . . . . Maria
•• 0:39—Breasts wearing panties, in bedroom with George, then nude.
•• 0:46—Nude with George in bathroom.
Ajita Wilson . . . . Madame Gaballi
•• 1:20—Full frontal nudity undressing for George.
•• 1:23—Breasts, making love on top of George.
• 1:25—Left breast, while in bed with George.

Joy: Chapter II *(1985; French)*

a.k.a. Joy and Joan
Brigitte Lahaie . . . . Joy
• 0:01—Left breast in coat during photo session.
••• 0:11—Nude, getting into bubble bath and out with Bruce.
•• 0:20—Breasts, lying in bed after party.
•• 0:22—Breasts, talking on the phone.
••• 0:27—Nude, getting a massage from Milaka. Nice.
•• 0:32—Breasts changing clothes.
••• 0:45—In bra, then breasts changing clothes with Joanne.
•• 0:47—Full frontal nudity, masturbating in bed. Medium long shot.
••• 0:54—Nude, making love with Joanne on train. Nice, long scene!
• 1:03—Breasts in the water with Joanne.

•• 1:08—Breasts, getting molested by a bunch of guys in the shower.
• 1:10—Right breast, lying next to a pool.
•• 1:17—Nude in bubble bath with Joanne and getting out.
• 1:23—Buns, dancing with Joanne.
••• 1:27—Nude, making love with Joanne and Mark.

Maria Isabel Lopez. . . . . .Milaka
•• 0:10—Breasts, showing Joy her breasts at Bruce's request.
••• 0:27—Breasts, taking off her robe and massaging Joy.

Joyride (1977)

Melanie Griffith . . . . Susie
• 0:05—Breasts in back of station wagon with Robert Carradine, hard to see anything.
•• 0:59—Brief breasts in spa with everybody.
• 1:11—Brief breasts in shower with Desi Arnaz, Jr.

Anne Lockhart . . . . Cindy
•• 0:59—Brief breasts in the spa with everybody.
••• 1:00—Breasts, standing in the kitchen kissing Desi Arnaz Jr.

Joysticks (1983)

Corinne Bohrer . . . . .Patsy Rutter

Erin Halligan . . . . Sandy
•• 1:08—Right breast, then breasts and lower frontal nudity in bed with Jefferson surrounded by candles.

Becky LeBeau . . . . .Liza

Kym Malin. . . . . .Lola
• 0:03—Breasts with Alva showing a nerd their breasts by pulling their blouses open.
••• 0:18—Breasts during strip-video game with Jefferson, then in bed with him.
• 0:57—Breasts during fantasy sequence, lit with red lights, hard to see anything.
• 1:02—Brief breasts in slide show in courtroom.

Lynda Wiesmeier. . . . . .Candy

Jubilee (1977)

Nell Campbell . . . . Crabs
• 0:37—Brief breasts in bed with a new lover, Happy Days.
••• 1:31—Breasts, after taking off her T-shirt in laundromat while talking with the policeman. Buns, when making love with him in bed.

Jenny Runacre . . . . Queen Elizabeth I/Bod
•• 0:36—Breasts then lower frontal nudity, while eating food from a bowl.
•• 1:14—Breasts, after taking off her jacket in bed next to Mad.

Linda Spurrier Viv
•• 0:42—Breasts, while sitting up in bed with Angel and Sphinx. Nude getting out of bed.

Toyah Wilcox . . . . Mad

• *Jud* (1971)

Claudia Jennings . . . . Sunny
• 0:22—Brief breasts, while taking off her clothes at the beach with Jud.

• *Jude* (1996; British)

Rachel Griffiths . . . . .Arabella
••• 0:59—Brief breasts, then left breast, while lying in bed with Jude after making love.

Amanda Ryan . . . . Gypsy Saleswoman

Kate Winslet . . . . .Sue Bridehead
••• 1:21—Full frontal nudity, after taking off her nightgown and lying on bed with Jude.

Judicial Consent (1994)

Bonnie Bedelia . . . . Gwen
• 0:24—Brief left breast while making love with Billy Wirth at his place. Don't see her face.

Lisa Blount. . . . . Theresa Lewis

Julia (1974; German)

Christine Glasner . . . . .Sylvanna
•• 0:21—Breasts on couch with Miriam getting messy with some whipped cream.
• 0:39—Brief right breast getting attacked by Patrick.
• 1:08—Brief breasts, while turning over and getting oil rubbed on her by Miriam.

Gisela Hahn . . . . Miriam
•• 0:12—Breasts tanning herself outside.
• 1:14—Brief breasts sitting in the rain.

Sylvia Kristel. . . . . Julia
• 0:23—Brief breasts in the lake.
•• 0:25—Breasts on deck in the lake.
• 0:28—Brief breasts changing clothes at night. Long shot.
•• 0:34—Breasts on boat with two boys.
•• 0:42—Breasts taking off her towel.
• 1:12—Breasts on tennis court with Patrick.

Terry Torday . . . . .Yvonne
• 0:08—Brief right breast, while making love in train restroom.
•• 0:18—Breasts, while in bed with Ralph. Dark, hard to see.
• 0:37—Breasts, while getting up to put swimsuit on.
• 0:41—Brief breasts, while getting dressed in bedroom with Ralph.
•• 0:57—Full frontal nudity in bedroom seducing Patrick.
•• 1:01—Breasts, while sitting up in bed eating breakfast with Patrick.

Julia and Julia (1987; Italian)

(This movie was shot using a high-definition video system and then transferred to film.)

Kathleen Turner. . . . . Julia
••• 0:32—Breasts making love in bed with her husband.
••• 1:08—Breasts, then right breast making love in bed with Sting.

Julia Has Two Lovers (1990)

Daphna Kastner. . . . . Julia
• 0:11—Brief breasts, changing blouses while talking on the telephone.
• 0:25—Partial left breast, while in bubble bath.
• 0:29—Right breast, while in bubble bath.
• 0:30—Breasts in mirror, getting out of bathtub.
• 0:53—Left breast, while lying in bed with David Duchovny. Long shot.

Jungle Fever (1991)

Gina Mastrogiacomo. . . . . .Louise

Debi Mazar . . . . Denise

Lonette McKee . . . . Drew
•• 0:04—Left breast while making love with Wesley Snipes in bed.
• 2:03—Brief left breast in bed with Snipes again.

Theresa Randle . . . . Inez

Annabella Sciorra. . . . . .Angie Tucci

Jungle Warriors *(1985)*

a.k.a. Captive Women 9

Ava Cadell . . . . Didi Belair
- 0:50—Brief breasts getting yellow top ripped open by Sybil Danning.

Sybil Danning . . . . Angel
- 0:53—Buns, while getting a massage.

Suzi Horne . . . . Pam Ross
- 0:51—Brief breasts twice during jail scene. Wearing a white blouse, with a yellow shirt underneath. Brief buns. Don't see her face.

Louisa Moritz . . . . Laura McCashin

The Juror *(1995)*

Lindsay Crouse . . . . Tallow
Anne Heche . . . . Juliet
- •• 1:19—Brief breasts, while in bed with Alec Baldwin.

Demi Moore . . . . Annie Laird

Just Before Dawn *(1980)*

Jamie Rose . . . . Megan
- 0:33—Breasts in pond. Long shot.
- 0:34—Brief breasts in pond, closer shot.
- •• 0:36—Brief upper half of left breast, then brief breasts several times splashing in the water.
- 0:37—Breasts getting out of the water.

• ***Just One of the Girls*** *(1992)*

a.k.a. Anything For Love

Nicole Eggert . . . . Marie Stark
Rachel Hayward . . . . Ms. Glatt
Christine Lippa . . . . Cashier
Lisha Snelgrove . . . . First Shower Girl
- ••• 0:27—Beasts, while taking a shower. Slow motion.
- ••• 0:27—Full frontal nudity, in shower room while Corey Haim (in drag) is mopping the floor.
- 0:50—Very brief breasts, while giving Haim her towel in the shower room.

Just One of the Guys *(1986)*

Sherilyn Fenn . . . . Sandy
Joyce Hyser . . . . Terry Griffith
- •• 1:27—Brief breasts opening her blouse to prove that she is really a girl.

Just Tell Me What You Want *(1980)*

Leslie Easterbrook . . . . Hospital Nurse
Ali MacGraw . . . . Bones Burton
- •• 0:16—Breasts getting dressed in her bedroom.
- •• 1:26—Brief breasts in bathroom getting ready to take a shower.

Just the Way You Are *(1984)*

Kaki Hunter . . . . Lisa
Kristy McNichol . . . . Susan
- 0:50—Very brief left breast showing her friend that she's not too hot because there is nothing under her white coat. Medium long shot.

Alexandra Paul . . . . Bobbie

Just You and Me, Kid *(1979)*

Brooke Shields . . . . Kate
- 0:07—Brief buns, running down stairs after her towel gets caught in fence.

Justine *(1969; Italian/Spanish)*

Anouk Aimee . . . . Justine
- •• 0:36—Nude, while frolicking in the ocean.

Anna Karina . . . . Melissa
- •• 0:13—Half of right breast, while fooling around in bed with Michael York.

Justine *(1977; British)*

a.k.a. Cruel Passion

Glory Annen . . . . Prostitute
Jeannie Collings . . . . Prostitute
Ann Michelle . . . . Pauline
Koo Stark . . . . Justine
- •• 0:09—Breasts getting fondled by a nun.
- 0:16—Breasts getting attacked by a nun.
- 0:57—Breasts in open dress getting attacked by old guy.
- ••• 1:00—Breasts getting bathed, then lower frontal nudity.
- 1:28—Right breast and buns taking off clothes, then brief full frontal nudity getting dressed again.
- 1:32—Breasts getting thrown in to the water.

K2 *(1991)*

Kelly Burns . . . . Pam
Patricia Charbonneau . . . . Jacki Metcalfe
Annie Grindlay . . . . Lisa
Julia Nickson . . . . Cindy
- 0:26—Briefly nude, getting up out of bed and putting robe on.

Kalifornia *(1993)*

(Unrated version reviewed.)

Michelle Forbes . . . . Carrie Loughlin
- 0:34—Very, very brief upper half of lower frontal nudity while in bed with David Duchovny.

Juliette Lewis . . . . Adele Corners
- •• 0:09—Left breast, after opening robe to say "good-bye" to Brad Pitt.

Patricia Tallman . . . . Stunts

• ***Kama Sutra: A Tale of Love*** *(1996)*

(Unrated version reviewed.)

Sarita Choudhury . . . . Tara
- •• 0:25—Breasts, while starting to make love with Singh.
- 1:19—Left breast, while being examined by a doctor under a sheet.
- ••• 1:33—Full frontal nudity, when starting to make love with Maya.

Kandyland *(1987)*

Sandahl Bergman . . . . Harlow Divine
Catlyn Day . . . . Diva
- ••• 0:50—Breasts wearing pasties doing strip routine.
- 1:06—Brief breasts talking on the telephone in dressing room.
- 1:12—Brief breasts during dance routine with the other girls.

Kim Evenson . . . . Joni
- ••• 0:31—Breasts doing first dance routine.
- •• 0:45—Brief breasts during another routine with bubbles floating around.

The Keep *(1983)*

Alberta Watson . . . . Eva Cuza
- 0:59—Very brief breasts, while making love with Scott Glenn, then brief lower frontal nudity.

Keeper of the City (1991; Made for Cable Movie)

Gina Gallego . . . . Elena
- 0:19—Brief half of left breast, getting out of bed and putting on black bra. Wearing black panties.

Reneé Soutendijk. . . . . Vickie Benedetto
Barbara Williams . . . . Grace

Keetje Tippel (1978; Dutch)

a.k.a. Katie's Passion
(Dutch with English subtitles.)
Monique Van De Ven . . . . Katie
- 0:37—Brief buns when guy rips her panties off.
- •• 0:43—Breasts in hospital when a group of doctors examine her.
- 0:48—Left breast a couple of times talking to a doctor. Brief buns sitting down.
- 1:09—Brief buns, while getting into bed.
- 1:11—Very brief left breast in bed with Rutger Hauer when he catches her eating his chocolate.
- ••• 1:15—Nude burning all her old clothes and getting into bathtub.

Kemek (1970)

Alexandra Stewart . . . . Marisa
- 0:26—Brief right breast while sitting up in bed.
- 0:49—Right breast while kneeling in bed. Out of focus.
- 0:51—Very, very brief tip of right breast while crying in bed and talking to David Henison.
- 0:52—Brief breasts lying in bed with Henison.

Mary Woronov . . . . Mary

The Kentucky Fried Movie (1977)

Uschi Digard . . . . Woman in Shower
- •• 0:09—Breasts while getting them massaged in the shower, then squished breasts against the shower door.

Marilyn Joi. . . . . Cleopatra
- 1:11—Breasts in bed with Schwartz.

Lenka Novak . . . . Linda Chambers
- 0:09—Breasts sitting on a couch with two other girls.

Tara Strohmeier. . . . . Girl
- •• 1:16—In bra, then breasts making love on couch with her boyfriend while people on the TV news watch them.

The Key (1985; Italian)

a.k.a. La Chiave
Barbara Cupisti . . . . Lisa Rolfe
Stefania Sandrelli. . . . . Teresa Rolfe
- ••• 0:31—Nude when Nino examines her while she's passed out. Long scene.
- •• 0:42—Full frontal nudity in bathtub while Nino peeks in over the door.
- •• 1:04—In lingerie, then breasts and buns, undressing sexily in front of Nino.
- •• 1:16—Left breast, sticking out of nightgown so Nino can suck on it.
- ••• 1:19—Breasts and buns making love in bed with Laszlo.
- •• 1:21—Breasts and buns getting up and cleaning herself.
- •• 1:28—Breasts sitting in bed talking to Nino.
- ••• 1:30—Nude, getting on top of Nino in bed.

Key Exchange (1985)

Brooke Adams . . . . Lisa
- 0:45—Very brief right breast getting into the shower with her boyfriend, then hard to see behind the shower curtain.

Kerry Armstrong . . . . The Beauty
Sandra Beall. . . . . Marcy
- ••• 1:14—Breasts on bed taking off her clothes and talking to Daniel Stern.

Terri Garber . . . . Amy
Annie Golden . . . . Val
Deborah Offner . . . . Chiropractor Woman

• Keys to Tulsa (1996)

(Unrated version reviewed.)
Joanna Going . . . . Cherry
- ••• 0:37—Buns in T-back and breasts, while stripping and dancing on stage.
- •• 0:44—Nude, while lying on the floor with Eric Stoltz.
- •• 1:07—Buns and breasts, taking off her clothes and getting into bed with Stoltz.
- 1:08—Brief side view of breasts in revealing dress.
- 1:30—Brief right breast when it falls out of her dress top while she's shaking hands with Billy.
- 1:33—Breasts, when they fall out of her dress top while dancing during party.

Deborah Unger . . . . Vicky Michaeels Stover
- •• 1:16—In black bra and panties, then buns and lower frontal nudity while in bedroom with Eric Stoltz.

Kickboxer 4—The Aggressor (1993)

Jill Pierce . . . . Darcy Cove
- •• 0:44—Breasts, while in room with Lando after taking off her dress.
- 1:04—Left breast, after sitting up in bed.
- 1:05—Brief breasts while lying back down on bed.

Kicking and Screaming (1995)

Cara Buono . . . . Kate
Olivia D'Abo . . . . Jane
Kaela Dobkin . . . . Audra
- 1:04—Breasts, while sitting on bed, listening to a guy in dorm room. Medium long shot.
- 1:05—Brief breasts, while walking around in the dorm room.

Parker Posey . . . . Miami
Perrey Reeves. . . . . Amy
- •• 0:32—In bra, then breasts while in dorm room with Josh Hamilton.

Kidnapped (1986)

Barbara Crampton. . . . . Bonnie
- ••• 0:37—Breasts getting tormented by a bad guy in bed.
- •• 1:12—Breasts after opening her pajamas for David Naughton.
- •• 1:14—Breasts in white panties getting dressed.

Kim Evenson . . . . Debbie
- 0:25—Right breast in bed talking on the phone. Long shot, hard to see.
- ••• 1:28—Breasts getting her arm prepared for a drug injection. Long scene.
- ••• 1:30—Breasts acting in a movie. Long shot, then close up. Wearing a G-string.

Kika (1994; Spanish)

Victoria Abril . . . . Andrea Caracortada (Scarface)
Bibi Andersen . . . . Susana
- ••• 0:40—Nude, while standing on balcony and singing, then inside apartment with Peter Coyote.
- 1:15—Brief buns, with Coyote on TV monitor.
- 1:23—Nude, on balcony and inside apartment on TV monitor.

- 1:24—Nude, while lying on floor dead, getting wrapped in a blanket by Coyote.
- 1:30—Brief breasts, while lying dead in bathtub when discovered by Ramon.

Rossy de Palma . . . . Juana
Verónica Forqué . . . . Kika
- ••• 0:37—Breasts, while making love in bed with Ramon, photographing each other. Long scene.
- • 0:48—Brief, partial buns, while lying in bed.

Kill *(1971; French/Spanish/German)*
a.k.a. Kill! Kill! Kill!
Jean Seberg . . . . Emily
- • 0:42—Side view of right breast and buns. Don't see her face.
- • 0:45—More right breast a couple of times. Still don't see her face.

Kill Crazy *(1989)*
Danielle Brisebois . . . . Libby
- •• 0:39—Breasts taking off top to go skinny dipping with Rachel.
- • 0:46—Very brief right breast, while lying on ground with a bad guy while getting raped. Buns, getting turned over before being shot.

Rachelle Carson . . . . Rachel
- •• 0:39—Breasts taking off top to go skinny dipping with Libby.

Kill Cruise *(1990; German)*
Elizabeth Hurley . . . . Lou
- • 0:15—Very brief breasts during strip tease routine on stage.
- • 1:09—Side of right breast, while making love with Jürgen Prochnow.
- • 1:15—Very brief right breast in open blouse, several times when Prochnow throws Patsy Kensit overboard.
- • 1:25—Most of side of right breast, while consoling Kensit.

Patsy Kensit . . . . Su
Grazyna Szapolowska . . . . Mona

The Killer Elite *(1975)*
Tiana Alexandra . . . . Tommie
Uschi Digard . . . . Uncredited Party Girl
- • 0:00—Brief right breast, while sitting in front of Robert Duvall at a party. Long shot. Continuity error: Note the next time you see her, the blouse is closed!

Killer Image *(1991)*
Krista Errickson . . . . Shelley
Barbara Gajewskia . . . . Stacey
- • 0:22—Very, very brief left breast, taking off bra at window with M. Emmet Walsh.

The Killer Inside Me *(1975)*
Susan Tyrrell . . . . Joyce Lakeland
- •• 1:27—Very brief left breast, then very brief breasts (both breasts!) in bed with Stacy Keach during flashback scene.

The Killer Instinct *(1982; Canadian)*
a.k.a. Trapped
Gina Dick . . . . Diana
- •• 1:15—Breasts, after Henry Silva rips her blouse open to taunt Nicholas Campbell.

Danone Simpson . . . . Amy
- • 0:12—Nude, when Henry Silva catches her in bed with another man.
- • 0:13—Very brief left breast in open robe on porch.
- • 0:14—Very brief breasts in open robe when Silva beats her on the bed.
- •• 0:43—Breasts, while drying herself off with a towel, then sitting in front of a mirror, covering up bruises with make-up.

Killer Looks *(1994)*
(Unrated version reviewed.)
Sara Suzanne Brown . . . . Diane
- • 0:01—Buns, while in two piece swimsuit in pool.
- • 0:02—Buns and breasts after getting out of pool and taking off swimsuit top.
- ••• 0:04—Full frontal nudity while making love with the plumber.
- ••• 0:26—Breasts, while making love in spa with her husband.
- • 0:30—Breasts, while putting bra on in bedroom.
- ••• 0:41—Nude while making love with Mickey in bed.
- • 0:47—Briefly nude, while getting into bed.
- • 0:50—Full frontal nudity in flashbacks while on bed with Mickey.
- • 0:59—Breasts in open dress top, while trying to get back away from Cynthia's advances.
- •• 1:23—In bra and panties, then breasts, while blindfolded and making out with Janine Lindemulder and Lené Hefner on stairway.
- ••• 1:25—Nude, while in the shower.

Lené Hefner . . . . Angela's Lover
- •• 0:22—In white dress, then breasts, while Janine Lindemulder makes out with her in parking lot of restaurant.
- •• 1:11—In black dress, then breasts and buns, while making out with Lindemulder.
- •• 1:18—Breasts, while sunbathing outside by pool with Lindemulder.

Dyanna Lauren . . . . Cynthia
- •• 0:57—Nude, while trying to make out with Sara Suzanne Brown.
- ••• 0:59—Full frontal nudity while making love with Vince on sofa.

Janine Lindemulder . . . . Angela
- ••• 1:12—In white lingerie, then breasts while making out with Lené Hefner and Mickey's lover.
- •• 1:18—Breasts, while sunbathing outside by pool with Hefner.
- •• 1:23—Breasts while making out on stairway with Hefner and Sara Suzanne Brown.

Killer Workout *(1987)*
a.k.a. Aerobi-Cide
Marcia Karr . . . . Rhonda
- • 1:03—Breasts, opening her jacket to show the policeman her scars. Unappealing.
- • 1:12—Breasts in locker room, while killing a guy. Covered with the special-effect scars.

Teresa Truesdale . . . . Rachel
- • 0:12—Brief left breast, dead, sliding down in shower. Covered with blood.
- • 0:16—Very brief left breast, when she falls out of locker. Breasts, while getting zipped into a body bag.

Teresa Vander Woude . . . . Jaimy
- •• 0:43—Breasts in locker room with Tommy during his nightmare.

A Killing Affair *(1985)*
Sandi Brannon . . . . Sara
- •• 0:08—Breasts, sitting up in bed, then kissing Pink.

Susie Hall . . . . Blanche

The Killing Device (1993)

Gig Gangel . . . . Sara
- 1:06—In bra, then brief breasts, with Kyle in house.

Killing For Love (1995)

Jennifer Leigh Burton. . . . . .Zoe
- ••• 0:33—Full frontal nudity, while making love with Paul in bed.
- •• 1:01—Full frontal nudity, while making love with Paul in the kitchen, then getting dressed.
- •• 1:08—Breasts, while trying to seduce Jay Richardson on sofa.

Lisa Haslehurst. . . . . Barbara
- ••• 0:09—In bra and panties. Nude, after taking them off and making love with Jay Richardson.
- • 0:15—Brief breasts, when flashing herself in car while Richardson drives.
- • 0:36—Partial right breast, with Richardson in bed.

Brandy Ledford . . . . Celena
- ••• 0:46—Buns in panties, then breasts and buns while making love in bedroom with Max. Nice, long scene.

Raelyn Saalman . . . . .Amber
- •• 0:31—Breasts, while lying in bed and talking with Ken.
- ••• 0:44—Nude, while making love with Ken in bathroom. Nice, long scene.

Killing Heat (1981)

Karen Black . . . . Mary Turner
- •• 0:41—Full frontal nudity giving herself a shower in the bedroom.

• *The Killing Jar (1996)*

Holley Chant . . . . .Katie

Tamlyn Tomita . . . . .Diane Sanford
- •• 0:29—Brief buns, then breasts, while lying in bed, then making love with her husband.

The Killing Kind (1973)

Sue Bernard. . . . . Tina
- • 0:00—Breasts during gang rape.
- • 0:19—Breasts again during flashback.
- • 1:12—Brief breasts again several times during flashbacks.

Killing Obsession (1994)

Kimberly Chase . . . . Annie Smith
- •• 0:31—Right breast, then breasts, while making love with Randy in photo studio.
- • 0:51—Breasts after Randy pulls her robe off.
- •• 1:09—Breasts and buns in panties, while undressing and changing into lingerie in bedroom.

Victoria Dillard. . . . . .Jean Wilson

Hyapatia Lee . . . . Annie Smith
- ••• 0:12—Breasts and buns in G-string, while dancing on bar.
- •• 0:15—Breasts, while changing clothes in bathroom, then walking to John Savage.
- • 0:18—Brief right breast, while lying dead on floor.

Elizabeth Zimmie. . . . . Babs
- • 0:43—Brief left breast, several times, while posing with Randy during photo shoot.

The Killing of a Chinese Bookie (1976)

Alice Friedland. . . . . .Sherry
- • 0:32—Upper half of breasts, while flashing for the M.C. during show on stage.
- • 0:33—Brief left breast, while flashing for the audience.
- • 1:13—Breasts dancing on stage. Long shot.
- • 1:35—Left breast, while sitting in dressing room during discussion.
- • 1:38—Breasts with the other dancers in the dressing room.

Azizi Johari. . . . . .Rachel
- • 1:14—Brief breasts, while dancing on stage.
- •• 1:15—Breasts dancing in red light, then coming over to talk to Ben Gazzara.
- • 1:26—Brief side view of right breast, while taking a shower.

The Killing of Sister George (1968)

Madeline Smith . . . . Nun

Susannah York. . . . . Alice McNaught
- • 0:19—Breasts under sheer blue nightgown.
- •• 2:07—(0:09 into tape 2) Breasts lying in bed with another woman.

Killing Streets (1991)

Jennifer Runyon . . . . Sandra Ross
- • 1:00—In white lingerie then brief breasts taking off lingerie in bed with Michael Paré. Hard to see.

The Killing Time (1987)

Camelia Kath . . . . Laura Winslow
- • 0:32—Very brief right breast, while making love with Beau Bridges. Hard to see anything. Dark, lit with red light.
- • 0:43—Brief breasts lying in bed getting photographed with Beau Bridges to frame Kiefer Sutherland for a murder.

Killing Zoe (1994)

Kimberly Beck . . . . Woman Customer

Julie Delpy . . . . .Zoe
- •• 0:09—In black bra, then breasts, while in motel room with Eric Stoltz.
- •• 0:10—Breasts, while making love on top of Stoltz in slow motion. Intercut with old B&W films.
- • 0:12—Brief breasts, while lying in bed next to Stoltz.
- • 0:18—Brief breasts in the shower, while struggling with Jean-Hughes Anglade, then outside hotel room.

King David (1985)

Alice Krige . . . . .Bathsheba
- •• 1:16—Full frontal nudity getting a bath outside at dusk while Richard Gere watches.

Cherie Lunghi . . . . Michal
- •• 0:28—Breasts lying in bed with Richard Gere. (Her hair is in the way a little bit.)

King Kong (1933)

Fay Wray . . . . Ann Darrow
- • 1:12—Right breast, after surfacing from the water after jumping off cliff with Bruce Cabot.

King Kong Lives! (1986)

Linda Hamilton . . . . .Amy Franklin
- • 0:47—Very, very brief right breast getting out of sleeping bag after camping out near King Kong.

King of Marvin Gardens (1972)

Ellen Burstyn . . . . Sally
- • 0:50—Brief breasts, while kneeling on the floor and turning around to shoot squirt guns.

King of New York (1990)

Ariane . . . . Dinner Guest

Vanessa Angel . . . . British Female

Janet Julian . . . . Jennifer
• 0:26—Very brief left breast, standing in subway car kissing Christopher Walken. Don't see her face.
Phoebe Légerè . . . . Bordello Woman
Theresa Randle . . . . Raye

King of the Gypsies (1978)
Danielle Brisebois . . . . Young Tita
Annette O'Toole . . . . Sharon
Annie Potts . . . . Persa
Susan Sarandon . . . . Rose
• 0:49—Brief right breast during fight with Judd Hirsch.
Brooke Shields . . . . Tita

King of the Kickboxers (1990)
Sherrie Rose . . . . Molly
• 1:05—Very brief buns in G-string and partial side of left breast, while getting into tub with Jake.

The King's Whore (1990; French/British)
Valeria Golino . . . . Jeanne de Luyes
•• 0:08—Right breast, while making out with Alexander.
• 1:01—Brief upper half of breasts, while lying in bed with Timothy Dalton.
••• 1:02—Breasts and buns when Dalton beats her up and throws her out of the room.
•• 1:16—Right breast when Dalton helps her with her skin disease.
• 1:19—Brief right breast when Dalton takes off her bandages.
• 1:20—Upper half of breasts while in bathtub. (She still has the skin disease.)

The Kiss (1988)
Céline Lomez . . . . Aunt Irene
Joanna Pacula . . . . Felice
•• 0:49—Side view breasts making love with a guy. Inter cut with Meredith Salenger seeing a model of a body spurt blood.
• 0:57—Breasts covered with body paint doing a ceremony in a hotel room.
•• 1:24—Brief right breast, while making love with a guy on bed while Salenger is asleep in the other room.

A Kiss Before Dying (1991)
Lia Chang . . . . Shoe Saleslady
Joie Lee . . . . Cathy
Billie Neal . . . . Nurse
Sean Young . . . . Ellen/Dorothy Carlsson
•• 0:31—Brief breasts making love in bed with Matt Dillon. Kind of dark.
• 0:35—Brief side view or right breast in shower with Dillon. Don't see her face.
• 1:11—Very brief partial left breast in gaping pajama top when she leans over to turn off the light.

A Kiss Goodnight (1994)
Paula Trickey . . . . Natalie Collins
• 0:37—Brief breasts and buns in T-back under sheer nightgown.

• *Kiss of Death* (1994)
Kathryn Erbe . . . . Rosie
Helen Hunt . . . . Bev
Bernadette Penotti . . . . Molested Dancer
• 0:52—Brief breasts on stage.

• *Kissing a Dream* (1996)
Tracy Dali . . . . Laura
••• 0:51—Breasts and partial buns, while making love with Peter in office.
••• 1:04—Buns and breasts, while making love with Marc on lounge chair.
Shari Eckert . . . . Nicole
•• 0:15—Breasts and buns, while making love with Peter.
•• 0:49—Breasts, while trying to seduce Peter in office.

Kissing Miranda (1994)
Alex Meneses . . . . Miranda Castillo
• 1:00—Brief left breast, while making love with Gib.

Kitty and the Bagman (1983; Australian)
Liddy Clark . . . . Kitty O'Rourke
• 0:28—Very brief side view of right breast in pulled-down dress during fight with Big Lil. Very brief upper half of breasts when Big Lil drags her across the floor. Very, very brief upper half of right breast, just before grabbing Big Lil's hair.
Kylie Foster . . . . Sarah Jones
• 0:57—Very brief side view of left breast, while jumping off bed to see if Cyril is all right.
• 1:34—Very brief breasts, when getting out of bed after being discovered by Kitty.
• 1:35—Very brief full frontal nudity, then buns when forced to walk outside naked with Cyril.

Kleptomania (1993)
Amy Irving . . . . Diana Allen
••• 0:50—Full frontal nudity, standing up in bathtub, getting out and putting on robe. Seen in mirror.
Patsy Kensit . . . . Julie
•• 0:16—Breasts, taking a shower and drying herself off.

Klute (1971)
Rosalind Cash . . . . Pat
Jane Fonda . . . . Bree Daniel
• 0:27—Side view of left and right breasts stripping in the old man's office.
Rita Gam . . . . Trina
Dorothy Tristan . . . . Arlyn Page

Knight Moves (1992)
Elizabeth Baldwin . . . . Christine Eastman
Kelly Burns . . . . Debi Rutledge
•• 0:08—Breasts and partial lower frontal nudity, while making love in bed with Christopher Lambert.
Holly Chester . . . . Officer No. 2
Rachel Hayward . . . . Last Victim
• 1:05—Very, very brief breasts screaming when the killer pulls the covers on the bed and flashes with a camera.
Diane Lane . . . . Kathy Sheppard
•• 0:45—Breasts while making love with Christopher Lambert in bed.
Megan Leitch . . . . Mother

Knightriders (1981)
Amy Ingersoll . . . . Linet
• 0:00—Very brief left breast, while lying down, then sitting up in woods next to Ed Harris.
Patricia Tallman . . . . Julie
• 0:46—Brief breasts in the bushes in moonlight talking to her boyfriend while a truck driver watches.

Knockouts (1992)

Leigh Betchley. . . . . Brooke
- 0:04—Brief breasts while putting on white bra in dressing room.
- 0:26—Very brief left breast after winning strip poker game.
- ••• 0:41—Breasts while taking off lingerie, while wearing blue panties.
- ••• 0:44—Breasts while posing in space costume for photographs.
- 0:46—Brief right breast while posing in front of blinds.

Tally Chanel . . . . Samantha Peters
- •• 0:15—Breasts taking off swimsuit top and getting ready for a bath.
- ••• 0:16—Breasts and buns, while undressing and getting into bathtub while Garth peeks in.
- ••• 0:25—Breasts during strip poker game.
- •• 0:26—Breasts and buns in G-string while walking to her bedroom.
- 0:29—Breasts while sitting on the bed.
- ••• 0:39—In white lingerie, then breasts while posing for photographs.
- •• 0:42—Breasts while Wesley helps put her top on.
- •• 0:43—Breasts while taking a shower (seen on TV monitor).
- ••• 0:47—Breasts while making love with Wesley.
- 0:59—Brief breasts while punching a bag (seen in mostly silhouette).
- 1:16—Breasts in shower in video playback.

Michelle Grassnick. . . . . .Margo
- ••• 0:04—Breasts while lifting weights.
- ••• 0:35—Breasts, several times in locker room with her girlfriends.
- •• 0:59—Breasts, while putting swimsuit on (she's on the left).
- 1:10—Buns, in outfit during wrestling match.
- 1:12—Brief right breast, when it falls out of her top.

Chona Jason . . . . .Ninja
- ••• 0:03—Breasts while doing sit-ups.
- 1:05—Wearing a sheer black body stocking during kick fighting match.

Deanne Power. . . . . Julie the Secretary
Paula Reve'e . . . . .Candy
- •• 0:04—Breasts, going to look in the guys' locker room.
- •• 0:23—Breasts during strip poker game.
- •• 0:27—Breasts while sitting on chest of drawers.
- ••• 0:43—In lingerie, then breasts while posing for photographs.
- •• 0:59—Breasts while working out (seen mostly in silhouette).

Cindy Rome . . . . Vicki
- 0:04—Breasts while putting on make-up in front of mirror. Long shot. Breasts walking in front of Brooke in pink G-string and white tights when Garth peeks in the locker room.
- 0:14—Buns in G-string swimsuit. Brief breasts while lying down in lounge chair.
- 0:25—Brief breasts, after losing her tennis shoe during strip poker game.
- 0:28—Breasts while in bedroom.
- ••• 0:37—In red, white and blue swimsuit, then breasts and buns while posing for photographs.
- ••• 0:45—Breasts and buns in G-string, while posing for October photograph.
- •• 0:59—Breasts while talking on the phone, combing her hair and doing her nails. Seen mostly in silhouette.

Nicole Sassaman . . . . Hallie
Pamela Ward. . . . . .n.a.

• *Kounterfeit* (1997)

Griffin Drew. . . . . Jeaneen
- 0:31—Very brief buns in T-back swimsuit, while dancing with Travis by the swimming pool.

Elizabeth Gracen . . . . Bridgette
Rachelle Whaley. . . . . Rachelle

Kramer vs. Kramer (1979)

Jane Alexander. . . . . Margaret Phelps
Iris Alhanti . . . . .n.a.
Meryl Streep . . . . Joanna Kramer
JoBeth Williams . . . . Phyllis Bernard
- 0:45—Buns and brief breasts in the hallway meeting Dustin Hoffman's son.

L.A. Bounty (1989)

Sybil Danning . . . . Ruger
Lenore Kasdorf. . . . . Kelly Rhodes
Maxine Wasa . . . . .Model
- 0:07—Right breast while posing for Wings Hauser while he paints. Left breast, getting up. Long shot.
- 0:26—Left breast while posing on couch for Hauser.
- •• 0:38—Breasts lying on couch again.

• *L.A. Confidential* (1997)

Brenda Bakke. . . . . Lana Turner
Kim Basinger . . . . Lynn Bracken
April Breneman . . . . .Look-Alike Dancer
Marisol Padilla Sánchez . . . . .Inez Soto (Rape Victim)
- 0:57—Brief breasts, while gagged and tied to bed. She's bruised and bloodied, so it's not a pretty sight.

Amber Smith . . . . Susan Lefferts
- 0:34—Very brief left breast, twice, dead, when sheet is pulled up so that her mother can identify her.

Sandra Taylor . . . . .Mickey Cohen's Mambo Partner

L.A. Goddess (1992)

Tally Chanel. . . . . Beverly
- •• 0:08—Breasts, while getting dressed in bathroom with Kathy.
- •• 0:17—Breasts and buns, while getting out of the shower.
- ••• 1:07—Buns (nice crotch shot) and breasts in bed while making love with Jeff Conaway and talking on the phone.

Wendy MacDonald . . . . Diane
- •• 0:08—Side of left breast, then breasts while making love with the Sheriff actor in motor home.
- 1:06—Brief buns, while flashing while dancing on table during party.

Kathy Shower . . . . Lisa Moore
- •• 0:00—Full frontal nudity, getting out of the shower.
- •• 0:45—Side view of buns and breasts, getting into and in bathtub.
- ••• 0:53—Nude in spa with Damian.
- 0:56—Left breast, while lying in park with Damian.
- •• 0:58—Breasts while making love in bed with Damian.
- 1:20—Brief breasts in spa with Damian in flashback.

L.A. Story (1991)

Iman . . . . .Cynthia
Cheryl Baker . . . . Changing Room Woman
- 0:18—Brief breasts in dressing room, when Steve Martin sees her.

Frances Fisher . . . . June
Marilu Henner . . . . .Trudi
Victoria Tennant . . . . Sara

• *L.A. Strippers* *(1992; Video Tape)*

Lorraine Dorado . . . . Quisha Cori
- ••• 0:00—Breasts dancing on stage during introduction.
- ••• 0:05—In bra, then nude dancing on stage. Long scene.
- ••• 0:12—Breasts, then nude dancing.

Missy Warner . . . . Missy Warner
- ••• 0:01—Breasts dancing on stage during introduction.
- ••• 0:18—In raincoat, then lingerie, then nude dancing on stage. Long scene.

The Lacemaker *(1977; French)*

Isabelle Huppert . . . . Beatrice
- • 0:50—Briefly nude while getting into bed.
- • 0:57—Breasts under shawl, then nude while getting into bed.
- •• 0:58—Breasts, lying in bed.
- • 1:04—Nude, in her apartment.
- ••• 1:22—Nude, in her apartment with François.

• *Ladies and Gentlemen, The Fabulous Stains* *(1982)*

(Not available on video tape.)

Elizabeth Daily . . . . Motel Maid

Laura Dern . . . . Jessica McNeil

Diane Lane . . . . Corinne Burns
- • 0:31—Brief breasts, under sheer red blouse on stage.
- • 0:53—Brief buns and side of right breast, taking off her towel and getting into shower.

Debbie Rochon . . . . Uncredited Skunkette

Lady Avenger *(1991)*

Michelle Bauer . . . . Annalee
- ••• 0:30—Breasts, making love in bed on top of J.C.
- ••• 0:52—Breasts, making love in bed on top of Ray.

Peggy McIntaggart . . . . Maggie
- ••• 0:18—Breasts in bed with Kevin.

Lady Beware *(1987)*

Diane Lane . . . . Katya Yarno
- ••• 0:46—Breasts in her apartment and in bed making love with Mack.
- •• 0:52—Brief breasts during Jack's flashback when he is in the store.
- •• 0:59—Brief side view breasts in bed with Mack again during another of Jack's flashbacks.
- • 1:02—Very brief breasts in bed with Mack.
- • 1:06—Brief breasts lying in bed behind thin curtain in another of Jack's flashbacks.

Lady Chatterley's Lover *(1981; French/British)*

Sylvia Kristel . . . . Constance Chatterley
- •• 0:25—Nude in front of mirror.
- • 0:59—Brief breasts with the Gardener.
- • 1:04—Brief breasts.
- ••• 1:16—Nude in bedroom with the Gardener.

Lady Cocoa *(1974)*

Lola Falana . . . . Coco
- • 0:45—Left breast lying on bed, pulling up yellow towel. Long shot, hard to see.
- ••• 1:23—Breasts on boat with a guy.

The Lady in Red *(1979)*

Pamela Sue Martin . . . . Polly Franklin
- • 0:07—Right breast, while in bedroom with a guy clutching her clothes.
- ••• 0:20—Breasts in jail with a group of women prisoners waiting to be examined by a nurse.

Francesca "Kitten" Natividad . . . . Uncredited Partygoer
- • 0:39—Brief breasts outside during party.

Mary Woronov . . . . Woman Bankrobber

Lady in Waiting *(1994)*

(Unrated version reviewed.)

Crystal Chappell . . . . Elizabeth
- • 0:39—Buns in T-back, while tied up on bed face-down. Don't see her face.
- • 0:42—Brief side view of buns in T-back and in bra in Michael Nouri's dream.

Meg Foster . . . . n.a.

Janine Lindemulder . . . . Sharon Masters
- •• 0:00—Full frontal nudity, undressing in bedroom with Scott, then on bed.

Fawna MacLaren . . . . Roxie
- •• 0:01—Nude in room while making love with Mr. Bennett and another woman.
- • 0:28—Left breast, then breasts while posing in bedroom.
- • 0:38—Brief left breast, while lying dead on bed.

Sandra Taylor . . . . Lady in Red
- •• 0:09—Breasts, when undressing and rolling her stockings down. Nude while blindfolded and tied by her wrists to the bed.

Shannon Whirry . . . . Lori
- • 0:16—Left breast while making out in car with Michael Nouri.
- ••• 0:30—Breasts, while sitting in bathtub and talking on the phone.
- •• 0:36—Buns and breasts while making love in bed with Nouri.
- •• 0:47—Full frontal nudity in mirror, while putting a shirt on.
- ••• 0:49—Nude, after taking off shirt and taking a shower with her lover and making love while Nouri watches from outside the house.

Lady Jane *(1987; British)*

Helena Bonham Carter . . . . Lady Jane Grey
- • 1:19—Breasts kneeling on the bed with Guilford.
- • 2:09—Side view of right breast and very, very brief breasts sitting by fire with Guilford.

Sara Kestelman . . . . Frances Grey

Lady on the Bus *(1978; Brazilian)*

Sonia Braga . . . . n.a.
- • 0:11—Brief left breast.
- ••• 0:12—Breasts, then buns, then full frontal nudity in bed getting her slip torn off by her newlywed husband. Long struggle scene.
- •• 0:39—Right breast standing with half open dress, then breasts lying in bed, then getting into the pool.
- ••• 0:48—Breasts and buns on the beach after picking up a guy on the bus.
- • 0:54—Brief breasts in bed dreaming.
- • 1:02—Brief breasts in waterfall with bus driver.
- •• 1:05—Breasts in cemetery after picking up another guy on the bus.
- • 1:13—Breasts on the ground with another guy from a bus.
- • 1:16—Left breast sitting on sofa while her husband talks.

Ladykiller *(1996; Made for Cable Movie)*

Renee Ammann . . . . Jennifer
- ••• 0:44—Breasts while wearing panties, when Richard undoes her overalls, then making love with him on the floor.
- •• 0:50—Buns and breasts, while taking a shower behind clear plastic shower curtain.

Landon Hall. . . . . Vicky Gallagher
Jeannie Millar . . . . Nikki
- •• 0:07—Breasts and partial buns in panties, while dancing on stage.
- ••• 0:37—Buns in G-string and breasts, while dancing on stage.
- • 0:55—Brief partial buns in T-back, while lying dead on stage.

Monique Parent . . . . Debbie
- • 0:01—Breasts, while tied by her wrists and killed by killer.

Terri Treas . . . . Capt. Lorraine Hanover

Laguna Heat (1987; Made for Cable Movie)

Rutanya Alda . . . . n.a.
Catherine Hicks . . . . Jane Algernon
- •• 0:50—Breasts and buns, running around the beach with Harry Hamlin.
- •• 1:05—Brief breasts in bed making love with Harry Hamlin, having her head hit the headboard.

The Lair of the White Worm (1988; British)

Sammi Davis-Voss . . . . Mary Trent
Amanda Donohoe . . . . Lady Sylvia Marsh
- • 0:52—Nude, opening a tanning table and turning over.
- • 0:57—Brief left breast licking the blood off a phallic-looking thing.
- • 1:19—Brief breasts jumping out to attack Angus, then walking around her underground lair (her body is painted for the rest of the film).
- • 1:22—Breasts walking up steps with a large phallic thing strapped to her body.

Linzi Drew . . . . Maid/Nun
Tina Shaw . . . . Maid/Nun

Lake Consequence (1992)

(Unrated version reviewed.)

May Karasun . . . . Grace
- • 0:24—Brief breasts, coming up for air from under water in lake.
- •• 0:25—Breasts, getting out of the water to get Joan Severance.
- ••• 0:26—Breasts, lying on float in the middle of the lake with Severance.
- ••• 0:28—Full frontal nudity and brief buns, diving into the lake.
- •• 0:29—Buns and breasts, greeting Billy Zane after getting out of the lake.
- • 0:30—Full frontal nudity, drying herself off and getting dressed. Long shot.
- • 0:47—Left breast, while making out with Xiao in bar.
- ••• 0:50—Breasts close-up getting acupuncture.
- ••• 0:53—Breasts, walking to spa.
- •• 0:55—Breasts in spa with Severance and Zane.
- •• 0:57—Right breast while making love with Zane in spa.

Joan Severance . . . . Irene
- • 0:02—Left breast, while lying in bed.
- • 0:41—Brief breasts several times while making love with Billy Zane.
- ••• 0:50—Full frontal nudity in spa in bathhouse, while making love with Zane.
- ••• 0:54—Breasts in spa making out with Zane and Grace.
- • 1:06—Brief glimpses of right breast in open coat, while struggling in a field with Zane.
- ••• 1:07—Breasts in field with Zane. Oh yeah!
- •• 1:19—Brief side view breasts and buns in bedroom with Zane.

• *Land of the Free* (1998)

Alisa Christensen . . . . Helene
- •• 0:20—Brief breasts, while making love with Fitzpatrick in bed, then more breasts when walking to the bathroom, taking a shower and getting killed.

Land Raiders (1970)

Arlene Dahl . . . . Martha Carden
- • 0:59—Very brief upper half of right breast, sticking out of her top in bed after struggle with George Maharis.

Lap Dancing (1995)

Chanda . . . . Irene
- ••• 0:25—In bra and panties, then nude, while doing strip routine on stage in club. Long scene.
- • 0:45—Brief breasts in flashbacks.
- • 0:52—Breasts, while having sex in dark alley with a customer.

Kim Dawson . . . . Sandy
- ••• 0:38—Nude, when making love with Jimmy in bed, while a blindfolded Lorissa McComas is sitting nearby.
- ••• 0:49—Nude, while doing strip routine on stage. Long scene.

Kimberli Farina. . . . . Lapdancer
Aline Kassel . . . . Jackie
Julianne J. Mantia. . . . . Monica
- • 0:17—Brief breasts and buns in T-back, while lap dancing with a customer.
- ••• 0:41—Nude, while during strip routine on stage in club. Long scene.
- • 0:55—Brief breasts, while lap dancing with a customer.

Tané McClure . . . . Claudia
- • 0:09—Brief buns in T-back, while walking back to get her clothes.
- ••• 0:14—Nude, while doing a strip routine on stage in club. Long scene.
- • 0:21—Buns in T-back in dressing room.
- ••• 0:24—Buns in T-back and breasts, while lap dancing with a customer.
- • 0:45—Brief breasts in flashbacks.
- • 0:57—Brief buns in T-back, going into supply closet with her boyfriend.
- • 1:19—Brief buns in G-string in dressing room.
- ••• 1:23—Nude, while singing and doing a strip routine on stage in club. Long scene.

Lorissa McComas. . . . . Angie
- ••• 0:11—Nude, while making love with Michael on sofa.
- ••• 0:19—Buns in G-string, then breasts, while performing an audition lap dance for Manny.
- •• 0:23—Buns in T-back and breasts, while lap dancing with a customer.
- • 0:33—Brief upper half of left breast, while teasing a grocer in his store with Kim Dawson.
- • 0:45—Brief breasts in flashbacks.
- • 0:55—Buns in G-string while in dressing room.
- ••• 0:59—Buns and breasts, lap dancing with a customer's wife while he watches.
- ••• 1:03—Nude, while doing strip routine on stage. Long scene.
- ••• 1:12—Nude, taking off her dress in front of Sam, then making love with him.
- • 1:23—Buns in panties, during second audition.

Amber Newman . . . . Lapdancer

Las Vegas Weekend (1986)

Vickie Benson . . . . Amanda
• 1:12—Breasts and buns, while making love in bed with Percy.
Tamara Landry . . . . Lea

Laser Moon (1991)

Traci Lords . . . . Barbara Fleck
Crystal Shaw . . . . Jacelyn
• 0:11—Breasts, while making love in bed on top of Cruz.

Lassiter (1984)

Lauren Hutton . . . . Kari Von Fursten
• 0:18—Brief breasts over-the-shoulder shot making love with a guy on the bed just before killing him.
Belinda Mayne . . . . Helen Boardman
••• 0:06—In bra then breasts letting Tom Selleck undress her while her husband is in the other room.
Jane Seymour . . . . Sara
• 0:10—Buns and brief side view of right breast lying on stomach on bed with Tom Selleck.
Jane Wood . . . . Mary Becker

The Last American Virgin (1982)

Diane Franklin . . . . Karen
••• 1:06—Breasts in room above the bleachers with Jason.
•• 1:17—Breasts and almost lower frontal nudity taking off her panties in the clinic.
Louisa Moritz . . . . Carmela
••• 0:42—Breasts and buns in her bedroom with Rick.
Tessa Richarde . . . . Brenda
•• 0:15—Brief breasts walking into the living room when Gary's parents come home.
Kimmy Robertson . . . . Rose

The Last Boy Scout (1991)

Denise Ames . . . . Jacuzzi Party Girl
• 0:11—Brief left breast and buns in swimsuit bottom, while getting out of the spa.
Sara Suzanne Brown . . . . Dancer
• 0:19—Brief breasts and buns in T-back, twice, while dancing in club.
Chelsea Field . . . . Sarah Hollenbeck
Teal Roberts . . . . Dancer

Last Call (1990)

Crisstyn Dante . . . . Hooker
Stella Stevens . . . . Betty
• 0:52—Very brief left nipple popping out of black lingerie top while making love with Jason on a pool table.
Shannon Tweed . . . . Cindy/Audrey
• 0:12—In black body stocking, dancing on stage. Breasts and buns in G-string underneath.
•• 0:29—Right breast, on the floor with William Katt.
•• 0:39—Brief buns, rotating in chair with Katt. Breasts leaning against column.
• 0:40—Breasts on stair railing.
• 1:01—Left breast, while leaning against column and kissing Katt.
• 1:02—Left breast in bed with Katt.
••• 1:05—Breasts making love on roof with Katt.

Last Dance (1992)

Monica Akesson . . . . Body Double
Elaine Hendrix . . . . Kelly
• 0:20—Breasts and buns of body double in bed with Jim. Don't see her face.
• 0:52—Buns in white lingerie outfit while dancing on stage during DTV contest.
Erica Ringstrom . . . . Heather
• 0:48—Buns in G-string outfit, while dancing on stage during DTV contest.
Kimberly Speiss . . . . Meryll
• 1:03—Partial buns, while dancing on stage during DTV contest.

The Last Days of Chez Nous (1991; Australian)

Kerry Fox . . . . Vicki
Lisa Harrow . . . . Beth
• 1:10—Brief breasts, while moving around in bed with Bruno Ganz.

• *The Last Days of Frankie the Fly (1997)*

Vanessa Ann Giorgio . . . . Bathroom Girl
Daryl Hannah . . . . Margaret
• 0:09—Partial buns in sexy outfit while talking with Kiefer Sutherland and Dennis Hopper.
Karen Roe . . . . Sal's Girl

The Last Detail (1973)

Nancy Allen . . . . Nancy
Carol Kane . . . . Young Whore
• 1:02—Brief breasts sitting on bed talking with Randy Quaid. Her hair is in the way, hard to see.

The Last Embrace (1979)

Janet Margolin . . . . Ellie "Eva" Fabian
• 1:10—Brief breasts in bathtub with Bernie, before strangling him.
•• 1:14—Right breast, while reaching for the phone in bed with Roy Scheider.
• 1:20—Left breast in photo that Scheider is looking at with a magnifying glass (it's supposed to be her grandmother).

The Last Emperor (1987)

Joan Chen . . . . Wan Jung
Jade Go . . . . Ar Mo
• 0:10—Right breast in open top after breast feeding the young Pu Yi.
• 0:20—Right breast in open top telling Pu Yi a story.
• 0:29—Right breast in open top breast feeding an older Pu Yi. Long shot.
Vivian Wu . . . . Wen Hsiu

Last Exit to Brooklyn (1990)

Maia Danziger . . . . Mary Black
• 0:10—Out of focus buns and right breast taking off her slip.
• 0:12—Very brief breasts making love with Harry. Breasts after.
Jennifer Jason Leigh . . . . Tralala
•• 1:28—Breasts, opening her blouse in bar after getting drunk.
• 1:33—Breasts getting dragged out of car, placed on mattress, then basically raped by a long line of guys. Long, painful-to-watch scene.
• 1:35—Breasts lying on mattress when Spook comes to save her.

Last Exit to Earth (1996; Made for Cable Movie)

Roma Court . . . . Syb 3
Alex Datcher . . . . Heir Apparent

Kimberly Greist . . . . Eve
Amy Hathaway . . . . Kali
• 0:00—Breasts (nipples are covered with a special-effect appliance), while in time travel contraption.
Katt Shea. . . . . Surgeon Athena
Hilary Shepard. . . . . Lilith
Zoe Trilling . . . . Goldfinger

Last Gasp (1995)

Mimi Craven . . . . Goldie
••• 1:01—Breasts, while making love with Robert Patrick in kitchen.
Joanna Pacula . . . . Nora Weeks
• 0:20—Brief right breast, twice, during dream while making love with her husband.

The Last Good Time (1994)

Olivia D'Abo . . . . Charlotte Zwicki
••• 1:01—Brief breasts, dropping her towel so Armin Mueller-Stahl can see her.
• 1:05—Brief partial right breast, letting Mueller-Stahl feel her breast.
• 1:06—Left breast, while straddling Mueller-Stahl in bed.

The Last Hour (1990)

a.k.a. Concrete War
Raye Hollitt . . . . Adler
Shannon Tweed . . . . Susan
•• 0:05—Breasts in bed, making love with Eric.
• 0:07—Brief buns and side of left breast, in the shower.

The Last Innocent Man (1987; Made for Cable Movie)

Roxanne Hart . . . . Jenny Stafford
••• 1:06—Breasts in bed making love, then sitting up and arguing with Ed Harris in his apartment.
Karen Trumbo. . . . . Officer Marge Hersch

Last Man Standing (1994)

Ava Fabian. . . . . Lucretia
Jillian McWhirter . . . . Anabella
•• 0:12—Breasts, while making love in bed with Jeff Wincott.
• 1:01—Brief breasts, when getting out of bed.

• *Last Man Standing (1996)*

Cassandra Gava. . . . . Barmaid
Karina Lombard. . . . . Felina
• 1:00—Very brief left breast, then brief partial breasts, while burning some paper in her room.

The Last Married Couple in America (1980)

Priscilla Barnes. . . . . Helena Dryden
Sondra Currie . . . . Lainy
•• 1:32—Breasts taking off her clothes in bedroom in front of Natalie Wood, George Segal and her husband.
Catherine Hickland . . . . Rebecca
Jenny Neumann . . . . Nurse

The Last Picture Show (1971)

Eileen Brennan . . . . Genevieve
Ellen Burstyn . . . . Lois Farrow
Kimberly Hyde. . . . . Annie-Annie Martin
•• 0:36—Full frontal nudity, getting out of pool to meet Randy Quaid and Cybill Shepherd.
• 0:37—Breasts several times, sitting at edge of pool with Bobby.
• 0:38—More breasts, sitting on edge of pool in background.
Cloris Leachman . . . . Ruth Popper
Cybill Shepherd. . . . . Jacy Farrow
•• 0:37—Undressing on diving board. Very brief left breast falling onto diving board. Brief breasts tossing bra aside.
• 0:38—Brief left breast jumping into the water.
••• 1:05—Breasts and buns in motel room with Jeff Bridges.
Sharon Taggart . . . . Charlene Duggs
•• 0:11—In bra, then breasts making out in truck with Timothy Bottoms.

Last Resort (1985)

Brenda Bakke. . . . . Veroneeka
•• 0:36—Breasts in the woods with Charles Grodin.
Wally Anne Wharton . . . . Wanda

The Last Ride (1994)

Lori Singer. . . . . Scarlett Stuart
• 0:34—Side of right breast, while taking off towel in front of Mickey Rourke.
•• 0:46—Breasts, while bathing and making love with Rourke in pond outside.
•• 1:04—Brief side view of left breast, then left breast while making love in bed with Rourke. Quick cuts.

• *The Last Riders (1991)*

Kathrin Lautner . . . . Anna
Mimi Lesseos . . . . Feather
• 0:01—Buns, in yellow two piece swimsuit, while walking down the beach.

Last Rites (1988)

Anne Twomey . . . . Zena Pace
Daphne Zuniga . . . . Angela
• 0:04—Very brief breasts running into the bathroom to escape from being shot. Covered with blood, don't see her face. Very brief right breast reaching for a bathrobe. Don't really see anything.
• 0:40—Buns, behind a shower door.
• 0:50—Buns, getting out of bed and standing in front of Tom Berenger.

• *The Last Road (1997)*

Suzi Simpson . . . . Katie
• 0:09—Breasts, while making out in a car with a guy, then getting out.
Julie Strain . . . . Maggie
••• 0:24—In bra and panties, then breasts and buns, while making love with Harry in bed.
••• 0:57—In wet white top, then nude, while fooling around with Harry outdoors under spraying water.
Petra Verkaik . . . . Angel
• 0:07—Breasts in open vest, when signaling start of road race.
••• 0:18—Buns and breasts, while making love in bed with Billy.

The Last Seduction (1994)

Linda Fiorentino. . . . . Bridget Gregory
•• 0:31—Breasts, while walking around the house, gathering her clothes and getting dressed.
• 0:37—Brief side view of buns during pan shot from her feet to her head, while she's lying in bed.
•• 0:50—Very brief breasts, buns, then left breast while making love in bed with Peter Berg.
• 0:53—Very brief partial buns and very, very brief left breast, while getting out of bed.

Last Summer (1969)

Catherine Burns . . . . Rhoda

- 1:31—Very brief breasts struggling with Stacy, Peter and Dan. Long shot.

Barbara Hershey . . . . Sandy

- 0:19—Breasts after taking off her swimsuit top on sailboat with Richard Thomas. Hair is in the way.
- 1:30—Very brief right breast, after taking off her top in the woods.

Last Tango In Paris (1972)

(X-rated, letterbox version.)

Maria Schneider . . . . Jeanne

- 0:15—Lower frontal nudity and very brief buns, rolling on the floor.
- 0:44—Breasts in jeans, walking around the apartment.
- •• 0:53—Left breast, while lying down, then walking to Marlon Brando, then breasts.
- ••• 0:55—Breasts, kneeling while talking to Brando.
- 0:56—Side of left breast.
- 0:57—Breasts, rolling off the bed, onto the floor.
- •• 1:01—Right breast, in bathroom. Breasts in mirror.
- 1:03—Brief breasts in bathroom with Brando while she puts on make-up.
- ••• 1:04—Nude, in bathroom with Brando, then sitting on counter.
- 1:27—Brief lower frontal nudity, pulling up her dress in elevator.
- 1:30—Breasts in bathtub with Brando.
- ••• 1:32—Nude, standing up in bathtub while Brando washes her. More breasts, getting out. Long scene.

The Last Temptation of Christ (1988)

Barbara Hershey . . . . Mary Magdelene

- 0:16—Brief buns behind curtain. Brief right breast making love, then brief breasts.
- 0:17—Buns, while sleeping.
- •• 0:20—Breasts, tempting Jesus.
- 2:12—Brief tip of left breast, lying on ground under Jesus.
- 2:13—Left breast while caressing her pregnant belly.

• *The Last Time I Committed Suicide (1996)*

Claire Forlani . . . . Joan

Marg Helgenberger . . . . Lizzy

Gretchen Mol . . . . Mary Greenway

- 1:13—Very brief silhouette of breasts while in bathtub fooling around with Neal. Long shot.

The Last Tycoon (1976)

Ingrid Boulting . . . . Kathleen Moore

- 0:56—Buns and side of right breast taking off her dress in unfinished beach house in front of Robert De Niro.
- •• 0:58—More buns, lying down afterwards.
- 1:00—Buns, getting up and putting dress on. Very brief side of left breast.
- 1:02—Brief right breast when De Niro takes her dress off.

Anjelica Huston . . . . Edna

Jeanne Moreau . . . . Didi

Theresa Russell . . . . Cecilia Brady

The Last Warrior (1989)

Maria Holvöe . . . . Katherine

- •• 1:24—Right breast, after the Japanese warrior removes her dress.

The Last Winter (1983; Israeli)

Yona Elian . . . . Maya

- •• 0:48—Breasts taking off her robe to get into pool.
- 0:49—Buns, while lying on marble slab with Kathleen Quinlan.

Kathleen Quinlan . . . . Joyce

- •• 0:48—Brief side view of left breast taking off her robe and diving into pool Very brief buns.
- 0:49—Buns, while lying on marble slab, talking with Maya.
- 0:50—Very brief right breast, when sitting up. Long shot, hard to see.

The Last Word (1994)

Michelle Burke . . . . Sara

- •• 0:09—Brief breasts and buns in T-back, when spinning around while dancing on stage.

Holley Chant . . . . Angie

Brittany McCrena . . . . Massage Girl

- 1:06—In bra, then breasts, while giving Timothy Hutton a massage in the bathroom.

Cybill Shepherd . . . . Kiki Taylor

Laura (1979)

a.k.a. Shattered Innocence

Maud Adams . . . . Sarah

Dawn Dunlap . . . . Laura

- 0:20—Brief side view of left breast and buns talking to Maud Adams, then brief side view of right breast putting on robe.
- ••• 0:23—Nude, dancing while being photographed.
- ••• 1:15—Nude, letting Paul feel her so he can sculpt her, then making love with him.
- 1:22—Buns, putting on panties talking to Maud Adams.

Maureen Kerwin . . . . Martine

- 0:03—Brief full frontal nudity getting out of bed and putting white bathrobe on.

Lawman (1971)

Sheree North . . . . Laura Shelby

- ••• 1:19—Right breast, then breasts, while in bed with Burt Lancaster.

The Lawnmower Man (1992)

(Unrated Director's cut reviewed.)

Colleen Coffey . . . . Caroline Angelo

Jenny Wright . . . . Marnie Burke

- •• 1:04—Right breast, while in bed with Jeff Fahey.
- 1:15—Brief right breast, while in bed under Fahey.

Leather Jackets (1991)

Ginger Lynn Allen . . . . Bree

- •• 0:39—Breasts on stage for Mickey's bachelor party. Buns, in G-string. Made up to look like Geisha Girls.

Bridget Fonda . . . . Claudi

- 0:15—Brief breasts on bed with Mickey.

Mary Ella Ross . . . . Student Girl #2

Leaving Las Vegas (1995)

Kim Adams . . . . Sheila

Valeria Golino . . . . Terri

Mariska Hargitay . . . . Hooker at Bar

Carey Lowell . . . . Bank Teller

Emily Procter . . . . Debbie

Elisabeth Shue . . . . Sera

- •• 1:19—Breasts, while making out with Nicolas Cage outside by the pool.

• *Lebensborn* *(1996)*

Melissa Carlton . . . . Kari Berman
- • 0:09—Brief upper half of right breast while taking a shower.
- • 0:20—Breasts, while lying on exam table and getting dressed.
- • 0:40—Brief left breast in open blouse, trying to help her brother get aroused so he can donate sperm.
- • 0:46—Left breast and buns, while starting to make love with Eric in bedroom.
- • 0:49—Brief back side of left breast, when getting out of bed.
- • 1:21—Brief breasts, while dreaming about manually stimulating her brother.
- •• 1:22—Breasts, while dreaming about making love with Eric and then her brother.
- •• 1:33—Breasts, taking off her T-shirt and getting into bed with her brother.

T.J. Myers . . . . Lorelei

Monique Parent . . . . Jocelyn Speer
- • 0:08—Very brief breasts, when Kyle spots her painting in her studio.
- • 0:28—Breasts, while painting nude in her studio when seen by Kyle.
- •• 0:30—Breasts and buns, while seducing Kyle in his bedroom.
- •• 0:33—Nude, when getting out of bed with Kyle
- ••• 0:51—Nude, while making love with Kyle.

La Lectrice *(1989; French)*

a.k.a. The Reader

Miou-Miou . . . . Constance/Marie
- • 1:18—Full frontal nudity lying in bed. Close-up pan shot from lower frontal nudity, then left breast, then right breast.
- • 1:19—Side view of buns, while lying on the floor with the company president.
- • 1:20—Very brief right breast, then lower frontal nudity while getting dressed.

Berangere Bonvoisin . . . . Joel's Mother/Hotel Waitress
- • 1:15—Brief breasts while sitting in bed with Jocelyne and a guy.

Brigitte Catillon . . . . Eric's Mother/Jocelyne
- • 0:27—Brief right breast and buns while lying in bed with a guy. Subtitles get in the way.
- • 1:15—Very brief buns, while lying in bed with the hotel waitress and a guy.

Maria de Medeiros . . . . Silent Nurse

Marianne Denicourt . . . . Bella

Left for Dead *(1978)*

Cindy Girling . . . . Pauline Corte
- •• 0:19—Nude, taking off shirt in bedroom.

Elke Sommer . . . . Magdalene Krushcen
- •• 0:38—Left breast, while posing for photographer.
- • 0:39—Very brief left breast in B&W photo.
- • 0:58—Buns and breasts when police officers lift her up to put plastic under her. Covered with blood, can't see her face.
- • 1:09—Very brief left breast in B&W photo.

Legal Tender *(1991)*

Savannah . . . . Mal's Girl
- •• 0:24—Breasts in bubble bath with brunette girl and Morton Downey Jr.
- •• 0:31—Breasts and buns in G-string bringing phone to Downey.

Wendy MacDonald . . . . Verna Wheeler
- • 0:22—Brief buns in lingerie, while in Morton Downey Jr.'s office. Don't see her face.
- •• 1:20—Long shot of buns and side of left breast taking off robe in front of Downey. Breasts on bed with him.

Jacqueline Palmer . . . . Mal's Girl
- • 0:24—Breasts in bubble bath with blonde girl and Morton Downey Jr.
- •• 0:31—Breasts outside by the swimming pool.

Tanya Roberts . . . . Rikki Rennick
- • 0:41—Buns and breasts making love with Robert Davi. Don't see her face.

The Legend of Hell House *(1973; British)*

Pamela Franklin . . . . Florence Tanner
- • 1:03—Silhouette of breasts while taking off nightgown and getting into bed.

Legends of the Fall *(1994)*

Karina Lombard . . . . Isabel Two
- • 1:35—Brief left breast, while lying in bed with Brad Pitt after getting married.
- • 1:36—Brief partial right breast, while lying in bed with her baby and Pitt.

Julia Ormond . . . . Susannah
- • 0:56—Very brief right breast, while making love with Brad Pitt in bed.

Lenny *(1974)*

Valerie Perrine . . . . Honey Bruce
- ••• 0:14—Breasts in bed when Dustin Hoffman pulls the sheet off her then makes love.
- •• 0:17—Breasts sitting on the floor in a room full of flowers when Hoffman comes in.
- • 0:24—Left breast wearing pastie doing dance in flashback.
- • 0:43—Right breast with Kathryn Witt.

Kathryn Witt . . . . Girl
- • 0:43—Right breast with Valerie Perrine while Dustin Hoffman watches.

Lepke *(1975; U.S./Israeli)*

Mary Wilcox . . . . Marion
- • 1:17—Breasts, while in apartment with Tony Curtis.

Leprechaun 3 *(1995)*

Heidi Lynne . . . . Fantasy Girl
- •• 0:54—Breasts, after removing her top on TV while Mitch watches.
- •• 0:55—Breasts on TV some more, then after coming out of the TV. Buns in lingerie in room with Mitch.
- •• 0:58—Breasts and buns, while on top of Mitch in bed.

Linda Shayne . . . . Nurse

Zoe Trilling . . . . Uncredited Shirley

• *Leprechaun 4 In Space* *(1996)*

Rebekah Carlton-Luff . . . . Princess Zarina
- •• 1:05—Breasts, when opening her top in front of the soldiers.

Lethal Ninja *(1992)*

Kimberleigh Stark . . . . Farida
- •• 1:01—Buns and breasts, while getting out of bath and putting on robe.

Lethal Obsession (1987; German)

a.k.a. The Joker

Tahnee Welch . . . . Daniela Santini

- 0:14—Buns, putting on robe after talking to John on the phone.
- 0:15—Half of left breast, taking off coat to hug John in the kitchen.
- 0:16—Sort of left breast, while in bed with John. Too dark to see anything.
- 1:16—Buns, when getting an injection.

Lethal Pursuit (1989)

Mitzi Kapture . . . . .Debra J.

- •• 0:32—Breasts in motel shower, then getting out. (You can see the top of her swimsuit bottom.)

Lethal Weapon (1987)

Cheryl Baker . . . . Girl in Shower #1

Terri Lynn Doss . . . . Girl in Shower #2

Jackie Swanson . . . . Amanda Hunsacker

- •• 0:01—Brief breasts standing on balcony rail getting ready to jump.

Lethal Weapon 2 (1989)

Patsy Kensit. . . . . Rika Van Den Haas

- •• 1:15—Right breast lying in bed with Mel Gibson.
- •• 1:19—Breasts in bed with Gibson.

Lethal Woman (1988)

Adrienne Pearce . . . . Trudy

Shannon Tweed . . . . Tory

- ••• 1:01—Breasts at the beach with Derek. Brief buns in white bikini bottom.

Merete Van Kamp . . . . Diana/Christine

- 1:23—Very brief side view of left breast, reaching for towel after bath. Hard to see.

Letter to Brezhnev (1986; British)

Alexandra Pigg . . . . Elaine

- •• 0:57—Brief breasts in bed with a guy.

Letters to an Unknown Lover (1985)

Andrea Ferréol. . . . . .Julia

Cherie Lunghi . . . . Helene

Mathilda May . . . . Agnes

- 0:43—Upper half of breasts in bathtub when Gervais opens the door.
- ••• 0:58—Buns and breasts taking off her robe in Gervais' room.

Lianna (1982)

Linda Griffiths . . . . .Lianna

- •• 0:29—Breasts and buns, making love in bed with Ruth. Dark.
- •• 1:26—Right breast, then breasts while lying in bed with Cindy. Long, dark scene.
- •• 1:42—Left breast while lying in bed with Ruth.

Jane Hallaren. . . . . Ruth

- 0:29—Brief left breast lying under Lianna during love making scene in bed. Dark.

Betsy Julia Robinson . . . . Cindy

- •• 1:26—Breasts, while in bed with Lianna.

The Liars' Club (1993)

Shevonne Durkin. . . . . Marla

- 0:13—Very, very brief tip of right breast when standing up when Pat sees her. Left breast when he opens her dress top. Brief lower frontal nudity (dark) when he undoes her panties. Very, very brief left breast when she starts to fall backward.
- •• 0:15—Right breast, then both breasts, when getting raped. (Don't see her face in close-ups.)

• *The Liberation of L. B. Jones* (1970)

Lola Falana . . . . Emma Jones

- 0:19—Very brief breasts walking by the doorway in the bathroom. Very long shot, don't really see anything.

Barbara Hershey . . . . Nella Mundine

Brenda Sykes. . . . . .Jelly

The Lickerish Quartet (1970; Italian)

a.k.a. Erotic Illusion

Erika Remberg . . . . Wife

- •• 1:14—Nude, getting up off sofa and sitting back down, then in B&W film.
- •• 1:15—Breasts, while the girl feels her up. Close-up shot.
- 1:26—Right breast, while in bed in film.

Silvana Venturelli . . . . The Woman

- 0:01—Brief right breast under a guy in B&W porno film.
- •• 0:03—Breasts, after taking off her top in film.
- •• 0:05—Breasts while sitting on bed in film.
- •• 0:06—Breasts, while in bed with another woman.
- 0:30—Breasts, while on couch with a guy in film.
- 0:32—Breasts, while on bed with guy in film.
- 0:47—Lower half of buns under mini-skirt while in library with the father.
- ••• 0:49—Nude, while in library on table and the floor with the father.
- ••• 1:00—Nude, while undressing outside with the son and making love.
- •• 1:10—Breasts, while tied by wrists to bed in film.

Liebestraum (1991)

(Unrated Director's cut reviewed.)

Pamela Gidley . . . . .Jane Kessler

- 1:07—Buns, while taking a shower. Almost breasts, but her arm gets in the way.

Catherine Hicks . . . . Mary Parker

Ele Keats . . . . Actress on Soap Opera

Lies (1984; British)

Miriam Byrd-Nethery. . . . . Night Nurse

Ann Dusenberry . . . . Robyn Wallace

- •• 0:10—Breasts opening the shower curtain in front of her boyfriend.
- 0:11—Right breast while kissing her boyfriend.

The Life and Loves of a She-Devil (1991; Made for Cable Movie; British)

Julie T. Wallace . . . . Ruth

- 0:54—(With commercials.) Brief buns, while walking down hallway.
- 1:05—(Into part 2 with commercials.) brief side view of buns while tied up in bed before getting spanked by the judge.
- 1:06—(With commercials.) Brief buns again.

Life is Sweet *(1991; British)*

Jane Horrocks . . . . Nicola

- 0:50—Breasts in bed with David Thewlis. Hard to see because she has chocolate all over her chest.

Lifeforce *(1985)*

Emma Jacobs. . . . . Crew Member

Mathilda May . . . . Space Girl

- 0:08—Full frontal nudity (upside down) in glass case.
- 0:13—Breasts, lying down in space shuttle. Lit with blue light.
- ••• 0:16—Breasts while sitting up in lab to suck the life out of military guard. Brief full frontal nudity.
- •• 0:17—Breasts again in the lab.
- •• 0:19—Breasts while walking around, then buns.
- ••• 0:20—Breasts, while walking down the stairs. Briefly nude, while fighting with the guards.
- •• 0:44—Breasts with Steve Railsback during his nightmare. Lit with red light.
- 1:10—Brief breasts, whle in space shuttle with Railsback.

Lifeguard *(1975)*

Anne Archer . . . . Cathy

- 1:04—Very brief nipple while kissing Sam Elliott. Need to crank the brightness on your TV to the maximum. It appears in the lower right corner of the screen as the camera pans from right to left.

Sharon Clark . . . . Tina

- 0:07—Brief side view of right breast undressing and getting into the shower.
- 0:08—Buns and brief breasts wrestling with Sam Elliott on the bed.

Kathleen Quinlan . . . . Wendy

Light Sleeper *(1992)*

Dana Delany . . . . Marianne

- ••• 0:46—Right breast, while lying on the floor with Willem Dafoe. Brief left breast when getting up. Lit with green light. (If this was anyone else, it would only get one •.)

Susan Sarandon. . . . . Ann

Like Water for Chocolate *(1993; Mexican)*

a.k.a. Como Agua Para Chocolate

Lumi Cavazos . . . . Tita

- 0:36—Left breast in gaping top when Pedro watches her grind corn.
- 0:47—Brief breasts and lower frontal nudity in small room. Dark.
- •• 1:38—Nude, while making love and getting out of bed and covering Pedro with a blanket.

Claudette Maille . . . . Gertrudis

- •• 0:30—Breasts and buns while taking a shower. Nude, running out of shower house after it catches fire, running and jumping on horse with a guy.
- 1:36—Brief side view of left breast in shower flashback.

The Limbic Region *(1996)*

Corrie Clark. . . . . Lake Girl

Heather Hanson . . . . Reporter #2

Gwynyth Walsh. . . . . Ann Lucca

- 0:33—Very brief right breast, while starting to make love with Edward James Olmos.
- 1:01—Brief lower half of left breast under blouse, when Olmos stops making love with her.

Link *(1986)*

Elisabeth Shue . . . . Jane Chase

- 0:50—Brief right breast and buns, side view of a body double, standing in bathroom getting ready to take a bath while Link watches.

• Linnea Quigley's Horror Workout *(1990; Video Tape)*

Victoria Nesbitt . . . . Missy

Linnea Quigley . . . . Herself

- ••• 0:00—Breasts and buns, taking a shower and drying herself off. Nice.
- ••• 0:09—Breasts in scene from *Assault of the Party Nerds*, making love on top of a guy in bed.
- 0:19—Breasts in still photo from *Return of the Living Dead.*
- •• 0:34—Breasts, while singing and dancing in living room, in scene from *Nightmare Sisters.*
- 0:54—Breasts, while screaming.
- 0:57—Breasts in still photos during end credits.

Lipstick *(1976)*

Margaux Hemingway . . . . Chris McCormick

- •• 0:10—Brief breasts opening the shower door to answer the telephone.
- •• 0:19—Brief breasts during rape attempt, including close-up of side view of left breast.
- 0:24—Buns, lying on bed while rapist runs a knife up her leg and back while she's tied to the bed.
- •• 0:25—Brief breasts getting out of bed.

Mariel Hemingway . . . . Kathy McCormick

Lipstick Camera *(1993)*

Sandahl Bergman . . . . Lilly Miller

- 0:19—Buns, while in T-back panties, while making love with Flynn in bed.
- 1:18—Buns on monitor during video playback.

Ele Keats . . . . Omy Clark

- 0:57—In bra, while making out with Flynn, then left breast while lying back with him.

Charlotte Lewis . . . . Roberta Dailey

Listen to Me *(1989)*

Jami Gertz . . . . Monica Tomanski

Annette Sinclair . . . . Fountain Girl

Yeardley Smith. . . . . Cootz

Nancy Valen . . . . Mia

- 0:06—Very, very brief left breast in bed with Garson when Kirk Cameron first meets him.

Lisztomania *(1975; British)*

Nell Campbell . . . . Olga

- ••• 1:04—Breasts in bed several times with Roger Daltrey when Ringo Starr comes in.
- •• 1:06—Breasts in bed, sitting up and drinking.
- ••• 1:07—More breasts in bed with a gun after Starr leaves.

Anulka Dziubinska . . . . Lola Montez

- •• 0:08—Breasts sitting on Roger Daltrey's lap, kissing him. Nice close up.
- 0:21—Breasts, backstage with Daltrey after the concert.
- 0:39—Breasts, wearing pasties, during Daltrey's nightmare/song and dance number.

Sara Kestelman . . . . Princess Carolyn

Fiona Lewis . . . . Countess Marie

- •• 0:00—Breasts, while in bed, when Roger Daltrey kisses them to the beat of a metronome.
- 0:01—Brief breasts, while swinging a chandelier to Daltrey.

•• 0:03—Brief breasts and buns, while running from chair (long shot). Brief breasts when catching a candle on the bed.

•• 0:04—Brief left breast when her dress top is cut down. Left breast, while sitting inside a piano with Daltrey.

Little Darlings (1980)

Krista Errickson . . . . .Cinder
Kristy McNichol. . . . . Angel
Tatum O'Neal . . . . .Ferris

• 0:35—Very, very brief half of left nipple, sticking out of swimsuit top when she comes up for air after falling into the pool to get Armand Assante's attention.

The Little Death (1995)

Pamela Gidley . . . . .Kelly Hannon

• 0:47—Brief buns, while being placed on edge of spa.

Little Fauss and Big Halsy (1970)

Lauren Hutton. . . . . Rita Nebraska

• 0:44—Nude, while running down a road, then running to hide by a truck.

• 0:45—Buns, while lying in the cab of the truck.

• 1:04—Brief buns, while lying on bed when Robert Redford walks by.

Erin O'Reilly . . . . Sylvene McFall

• 0:11—Brief left breast, while sleeping in bed with the photographer.

Linda Gaye Scott . . . . .Moneth

• 0:37—Brief left breast, while sleeping in bed with another girl.

• 1:23—Buns, while holding a sheet and talking with Michael J. Pollard.

Little Moon & Jud McGraw (1976)

a.k.a. Gone with the West

Stefanie Powers. . . . . Little Moon

• 0:29—Buns, taking a bath outside. At first, hidden behind a bush, then not. Long shot, Don't see her face. Partial right breast, but her hair gets in the way.

Little Nikita (1988)

Loretta Devine . . . . Verna McLaughlin

• 1:03—Very brief left breast in bed after Sidney Poitier jumps out of bed when River Phoenix bursts into their bedroom.

Little Odessa (1994)

Moira Kelly . . . . .Alla Shustervich

•• 0:54—Breasts, while making love in bed with Tim Roth.

Vanessa Redgrave . . . . Irina Shapira

A Little Sex (1982)

Kate Capshaw . . . . Katherine

• 0:10—Brief buns under T-shirt, when running away from table after stuffing a pancake down Tim Matheson's underwear.

• 0:29—Breasts, while sitting on bed next to Matheson. Seen through out-of-focus candles.

Lisa Dunsheath . . . . .Lucy (Down-On Girl)
Carolyn Houlihan . . . . Bathing Suit Model
Wendie Malick . . . . .Philomena

• 0:39—Very, very brief side of left breast in gaping robe when she bends over to put her cigarette down.

The Little Thief (1989; French)

a.k.a. La Petite Voleuse

Nathalie Cardone . . . . Mauricette

•• 1:19—Breasts in convent arguing with a nun, then getting a shot.

Charlotte Gainsbourg . . . . Janine Castang

•• 0:41—Breasts twice, taking off blouse in bedroom with Michel.

Little Vera (1988; U.S.S.R.)

Natalya Negoda . . . . Vera

• 0:15—Very brief breasts and buns getting dressed. Dark, hard to see.

••• 0:50—Breasts making love with Sergei.

•• 1:05—Breasts taking off her dress in the kitchen.

• *Little Witches* (1996)

Clea DuVall . . . . Kelsey

• 0:35—In bra, then brief buns and breasts with the other girls during ceremony.

• 1:25—Brief partial breasts and brief buns, with the other girls, during ceremony. Leaves get in the way.

Landon Hall . . . . .Masked Girl

• 0:02—Partial breasts and brief breasts during ceremony.

Sheeri Rappaport. . . . . Jamie

• 0:09—In bra, then left breast, while caressing herself in confessional when talking with Father Michael.

•• 0:17—Breasts and panties, while stripping out of her school girl uniform in front of window for construction workers.

•• 0:34—In bra, then breasts and side view of buns and side view of lower frontal nudity with the other girls during ceremony.

•• 0:58—Breasts and buns, while in her room with Daniel.

• 1:05—Brief, partial breasts, while kneeling on the floor by herself during ceremony.

•• 1:25—Right breast, brief buns and brief lower frontal nudity, with the other girls during ceremony.

Jennifer Rubin . . . . .Sherilyn
Robin South . . . . Illuminati Girl
Melissa Taub . . . . Erica

• 0:35—In bra, then brief buns and breasts with the other girls during ceremony.

Live Nude Girls (1996)

Kim Cattrall . . . . Jamie

•• 0:26—Buns in lingerie, while talking with Bob.

• 0:30—Buns in lingerie, while talking with the Greenpeace boy and sitting on the table after making love with him.

Olivia D'Abo . . . . .Chris

•• 0:45—Breasts, while starting to make love in bed with Lora Zane.

••• 0:46—Breasts, while in bed with Zane. B&W.

Dana Delany . . . . Jill

•• 0:52—Buns in sheer panties, then bare buns after the mobster Don pulls the panties down and starts spanking her while she's bent over a desk.

Laila Robins . . . . .Rachel

• 0:17—Brief side view of right breast and buns, while sitting at table in neighbor boy's fantasy.

• 1:34—Very brief side view of right breast, while sitting at the table.

Cynthia Stevenson. . . . . Marcy

• 1:34—Brief left breast, when sitting at the table.

Lora Zane . . . . .Georgina

• 0:03—Very brief side view of left breast and buns, while in the shower. Very brief breasts in the shower (closer shot).

- ••• 0:05—Breasts, while lying on table in kitchen, getting covered with flour during fantasy.
- • 0:17—Brief side view of left breast, while sitting at table in neighbor boy's fantasy.
- •• 0:45—Brief breasts, taking off her blouse and getting into bed with Olivia D'Abo.
- •• 0:46—Breasts, while in bed with D'Abo. B&W.

Live Wire *(1992)*

(Unrated version reviewed.)

Lisa Eilbacher. . . . . Terry O'Neill

- ••• 1:01—Brief breasts several times and partial buns, in bath tub and in bed with Pierce Brosnan. Some of the love making scenes in bed were cut for the R-rated version.

Amanda Foreman . . . . Molly

Kira Reed. . . . . n.a.

Tracy Tweed . . . . Rolls Royce Girl

The Living Daylights *(1987)*

Maryam D'Abo . . . . .Kara Milovy

Virginia Hey. . . . . Rubavitch (Colonel Pushkin's girlfriend)

- • 1:10—Brief side view of left breast when James Bond uses her to distract bodyguard.

Catherine Rabett . . . . .Liz

Julie T. Wallace . . . . n.a.

Living in Oblivion *(1995)*

Catherine Keener. . . . . Nicole Springer

- • 0:28—Breasts, while lying in bed in motel room after James Le Gros leaves.
- • 0:57—Breasts, when waking up in bed in the morning. Very, very brief left breast, when closing the shower curtain.

Living to Die *(1990)*

Rebecca Barrington . . . . Married Woman

- • 0:23—In red bra, blindfolded and tied to a lounge chair, then breasts while getting photographed.
- • 0:27—Breasts in chair when Wings Hauser talks to her.

Darcy De Moss . . . . Maggie Sams

- • 0:32—Buns, getting out of spa while Wings Hauser watches without her knowing.
- • 0:33—Buns, in long shot when Hauser fantasizes about dancing with her.
- ••• 0:56—In black bra, then breasts and buns making love with Hauser.
- • 1:20—Breasts in mirror taking off black top for the bad guy.

Wendy MacDonald . . . . Rookie Policewoman

• ***Loaded*** *(1996)*

Bridget Brammall . . . . Shop Assistant

Catherine McCormack. . . . . Rose

- •• 0:36—Breasts, while getting out of her swimsuit.
- • 0:40—Left breast, while in bed with Neil.

Thandie Newton . . . . Zita

Loaded Guns *(1975)*

Ursula Andress. . . . . .Laura

- • 0:32—Buns, lying in bed with a guy.
- ••• 0:33—Breasts and buns getting out of bed. Full frontal nudity in elevator.
- •• 0:40—Nude getting out of bed and putting dress on.
- ••• 0:48—Nude getting into bathtub, breasts in tub, nude getting out and drying herself off.
- • 1:00—Buns while getting undressed and hopping in to bed.
- • 1:02—Brief side view of right breast while getting dressed.

Logan's Run *(1976)*

Jenny Agutter . . . . .Jessica

- • 1:05—Very brief breasts and buns changing into fur coat in ice cave with Michael York.

Farrah Fawcett. . . . . .Holly

Laura Hippe. New You Shop Customer

Candice Rialson . . . . Uncredited Girl with Richard Jordan

London Kills Me *(1991; British)*

Rowena King . . . . Melanie

Emer McCourt. . . . . Sylvie

- • 1:02—Left breast in open blouse, while sleeping.
- ••• 1:05—Breasts, while sitting in bathtub with Clint. Long scene.

Fiona Shaw . . . . Headley

The Lonely Guy *(1983)*

Lamya Derval. . . . . One of "The Seven Deadly Sins"

Robyn Douglass. . . . . Danielle

- • 0:05—Upper half of right breast in sheer nightgown in bed with Raoul while talking to Steve Martin. Great nightgown!
- • 1:03—Very, very brief peek at left nipple when she flashes it for Martin so he'll let her into his party.

Elizabeth Kaitan . . . . .n.a.

Marie Laurin . . . . One of "The Seven Deadly Sins"

Julie Payne. . . . . Rental Agent

Lonely Hearts *(1983; Australian)*

Wendy Hughes . . . . Patricia

- • 1:05—Brief breasts getting out of bed and putting a dress on. Dark, hard to see.

Kris McQuade . . . . Rosemarie

Lonely Hearts *(1991)*

Bibi Besch . . . . Maria Wilson

Joanna Cassidy. . . . . Erin Randall

Beverly D'Angelo . . . . Alma

- • 0:57—Brief side view of right breast, while getting into shower with Roberts.
- • 0:58—Very brief left breast in shower after Roberts gets pushed by Louise.
- • 0:59—Very brief buns, when Roberts punches Louise through the shower door.

Sharon Farrell . . . . Louise

- •• 0:52—Breasts, while lying back on bed in room with Eric Roberts.

Rebecca Street. . . . . Jane Ericson

- • 1:12—Brief side of right breast, while making love on top of Eric Roberts on couch.

The Lonely Lady *(1983)*

Glory Annen . . . . Marion

- • 0:07—Brief left breast in back seat of car with Ray Liotta. Dark, hard to see.

Bibi Besch . . . . Veronica

Carla Romanelli . . . . Carla Maria Peroni

- •• 1:10—Brief breasts taking off her top to make love with Pia Zadora while a guy watches.

Pia Zadora . . . . JeniLee Randall

- • 0:12—Brief breasts getting raped by Ray Liotta, after getting out of the pool.
- •• 0:22—Brief breasts, then left breast, while making love with Walter.
- •• 0:28—Side view breasts lying in bed with Walter.
- •• 0:44—Buns and side view of left breast taking a shower.

- 0:46—Very brief right breast, in bed with George.
- •• 1:05—Left breast, then brief breasts making love with Vinnie.

• *Long Gone (1987; Made for Cable Movie)*

Virginia Madsen . . . . Dixie Lee Boxx
- 0:04—Brief buns several times, while sleeping face down on bed when William Petersen talks with Dermot Mulroney.

• *The Long Kiss Goodnight (1996)*

Geena Davis . . . . .Samantha Caine/Charly
- 0:59—Brief side view of buns, while taking a shower. Hard to see because of all the steam.

Melina Kanakaredes . . . . .Trin

The Long Riders (1980)

Pamela Reed . . . . Belle Starr
- 0:18—Buns, while standing up in bathtub to hug David Carradine. (Don't see her face.)

Savannah Smith Bouchér . . . . Zee

Looker (1981)

Donna Kei Benz. . . . . Ellen
Randi Brooks. . . . . .Girl in Bikini
Pamela Bryant. . . . . Reston Girl
Susan Dey. . . . . Cindy
- 0:36—Buns, then brief breasts in computer imaging device. Breasts in computer monitor.

Melissa Prophet. Commercial Script Girl
Lori Sutton . . . . Reston Girl
Leigh Taylor-Young. . . . . .Jennifer Long
Jeana Tomasina. . . . . Suzy
Terri Welles. . . . . Lisa
- 0:02—Brief breasts getting photographed for operation. In black bra and panties in her apartment a lot.

Vanna White . . . . Reston Girl
Kathryn Witt . . . . Tina Cassidy

Looking for Mr. Goodbar (1977)

Caren Kaye . . . . Rhoda
Diane Keaton . . . . Theresa
- •• 0:11—Right breast in bed making love with her teacher, Martin, then putting blouse on.
- 0:31—Brief left breast over the shoulder when the Doctor playfully kisses her breast.
- •• 1:04—Brief breasts smoking in bed in the morning, then more breasts after Richard Gere leaves.
- ••• 1:17—Breasts making love with Gere after doing a lot of cocaine.
- 1:31—Brief breasts in the bathtub when James brings her a glass of wine.
- •• 2:02—Breasts during rape by Tom Berenger, before he kills her. Hard to see because of strobe lights.

Loose Shoes (1977)

Rikki Marin . . . . Commie Lady
Louisa Moritz . . . . Margie
Misty Rowe. . . . . Louise
Robin Sherwood . . . . .Biker Chic #2
Betty Thomas . . . . .Biker Chick #1
- 0:02—Brief right breast dancing on the table during the *Skateboarders from Hell* sketch.

Susan Tyrrell . . . . .Boobies

• *Los Locos: Posse Rides Again (1997; Made for Cable Movie)*

Melora Walters . . . . .Allison
- 0:20—Brief side of right breast, while skinny dipping in pond.
- 0:21—Breasts and buns, while in pond and walking out.
- 0:56—Lower frontal nudity in bedroom with Mario Van Peebles.
- •• 0:57—Nude, after taking off robe and getting into bathtub with Van Peebles.

• *Loser (1996)*

Peta Wilson . . . . Alyssha Rourke
- •• 0:34—Brief right breast, several times, while making love with Erica in bed.

• *Losin' It (1982)*

Shelley Long . . . . Kathy
Victoria Wells. . . . . Dave's Whore
- 0:39—Breasts, after taking off sheer top in room with Dave. Seen in mirror.

Lost Angels (1989)

Frances Fisher . . . . .Judith Loftis
Jane Hallaren . . . . Grace Willig
Amy Locane . . . . Cheryl Anderson
Nina Siemaszko. . . . . Merilee
- 0:38—Brief breasts and buns, running through courtyard. Long shot, don't really see anything.
- 0:45—Buns, sitting at table outside, undressing and rubbing feces (yuck!) on herself.

The Lost Empire (1983)

Angela Aames . . . . .Heather McClure
- ••• 0:31—Breasts and buns taking a shower while Angel and White Star talk to her.

Deborah Blaisdell. . . . . Girl Recruit
- 0:42—Brief buns and breasts, turning over on exam table.

Raven De La Croix. . . . . .White Star
- ••• 1:05—Breasts with a snake after being drugged by the bad guy.
- •• 1:07—Breasts lying on a table.
- •• 1:08—Breasts, getting up off table and punching a guy.

Annie Gaybis . . . . Prison Referee
- 0:30—Breasts when her top gets ripped off by Angelique Pettyjohn during cat fight.

Tina Merkle . . . . Girl Recruit
Angelique Pettyjohn . . . . .Whiplash
Linda Shayne. . . . . .Cindy Blake

• *Lost Highway (1997)*

Patricia Arquette . . . . Renee Madison/Alice Wakefield
- •• 0:12—Brief side view of right breast and buns, after taking off robe.
- •• 0:15—Breasts (in slow motion), while making love under Bill Pullman.
- ••• 1:32—In bra and panties, then breasts when being forced to strip at gunpoint in front of Robert Loggia.
- 1:54—Breasts and partial buns, while making love outdoors at night, lit by car's headlights. Overexposed shot looks almost like B&W.
- 1:56—Breasts and buns, leaving Getty and walking up the stairs.

Leslie Bega . . . . Raquel

Lisa Boyle . . . . Marian
- 2:04—Brief breasts, while acting in a movie. (She's on the right while another woman is on the left.) B&W.

Natasha Gregson Wagner . . . . Sheila
- 1:10—Breasts, when taking off her blouse in car with Bathazar Getty.

Mink Stole. . . . . .Forewoman

The Lost Honor of Katharina Blum *(1975; German)*

Angela Winkler . . . . Katharina Blum
- •• 0:15—Full frontal nudity, while in bathroom, getting strip searched by policewoman.
- 0:43—Brief right breast, after getting out of the shower.

The Lotus Eaters *(1993; Canadian)*

Michèle Barbara Pelletier . . . . .Anne-Marie Andrews
- 0:58—Side of left breast, when in cabin with Zoe's dad, Hal, while Zoe peeks in with her friend through the window.

Loulou *(1980; French)*

Isabelle Huppert . . . . Nelly
- 0:06—Very, very brief breasts leaning over in bed.
- 0:18—Brief breasts getting out of bed.
- 0:27—Brief breasts turning over in bed.
- •• 0:36—Breasts lying in bed talking on phone. Mostly right breast.
- 0:40—Lower frontal nudity and buns taking off panties and getting into bed.
- •• 0:59—Left breast in bed with André, then breasts taking him to the bathroom.

• ***Love 600*** *(1969; German)*

a.k.a. Stehaufmädchen

Iris Berben. . . . . Eva
- 1:11—Very brief left breast when Erik gets out of bed.

Love and Human Remains *(1995; Canadian)*

Mia Kirshner . . . . Benita
- 1:25—Brief right breast, when her bra is ripped off by Bernie.
- 1:27—Very brief, blurry right breast, when Bernie pushes her on the bed.

Ruth Marshall . . . . Candy
- 0:45—Breasts, while making love with Jerri.
- •• 0:52—Breasts, while in bed with Jerri, then getting out.
- 1:02—Brief, partial breasts, while making love with Robert.

Michèle Barbara Pelletier . . . . n.a.

Polly Shannon . . . . The Second Victim
- 0:36—Very brief breasts, while in bed, struggling with the killer. Dark.

Joanne Vannicola. . . . . Jenni
- 0:45—Brief buns and back side of left breast, while making love with Candy.
- 0:52—Right breast, while lying in bed next to Candy.

Karen Young . . . . The Singer

The Love Butcher *(1982)*

Marilyn Jones . . . . Lena

Robin Sherwood . . . . Sheila
- 0:39—Very brief buns, while putting on swimsuit bottom.
- 0:40—Brief breasts several times, while struggling in pool with killer when he kills her with garden hose.
- 0:41—Buns, while getting carried out of pool by killer. Breasts under water in bathtub, dead.
- 0:43—Brief breasts, while throwing bikini top while in pool.

Love Child *(1982)*

Cheryl King . . . . .Van Inmate

Amy Madigan . . . . Terry Jean Moore
- 0:08—Brief side view of right breast and buns taking a shower in jail while the guards watch.
- •• 0:53—Brief breasts and buns, making love with Beau Bridges in a room at the women's prison.

Margaret Whitton . . . . Jacki Steinberg

Love Circles Around the World *(1984)*

a.k.a. Love Circles

Sophie Berger . . . . Dagmar
- ••• 0:38—Breasts in women's restroom in casino making love with a guy in a tuxedo.
- ••• 0:43—Breasts in steam room wearing a towel around her waist, then making love.

Josephine Jaqueline Jones. . . . . Brigid
- •• 0:18—Breasts, then nude running around her apartment chasing Jack.
- 0:30—Breasts, making love with Count Crispa in his hotel room.

Love Crimes *(1991)*

(Unrated version reviewed.)

Mimi Cochran . . . . Stunt Double for Sean Young

Fern Dorsey . . . . .Colleen Dells
- ••• 0:03—Breasts, getting photographed by Patrick Bergin.

Arnetia Walker . . . . Maria Johnson

Sean Young . . . . Dana Greenway
- •• 0:20—Almost left breast, getting out of bathtub. Buns and partial lower frontal nudity, getting dressed.
- •• 0:55—Breasts in open blouse, yelling at Patrick Bergin.
- 0:57—Brief right breast, on bed in open blouse.
- ••• 0:59—Nude in bathtub.
- ••• 1:01—Breasts, making love with Bergin. Lit with red light.
- ••• 1:03—Full frontal nudity, getting covered with a towel.
- 1:08—Full frontal nudity, in Polaroid that Maria looks at.
- 1:11—More full frontal nudity in Polaroid.
- 1:21—Partial right breast, while taking a shower.
- 1:23—Brief breasts in the shower.
- 1:25—Very brief right breast in gaping robe.
- 1:27—Full frontal nudity in burning Polaroid photograph.

A Love in Germany *(1984; French/German)*

Marie-Christine Barrault. . . . . Maria Wyler
- 0:23—Right breast, in bed with her lover when Pauline peeks from across the way.
- •• 0:28—Right breast in bedroom with Karl. Very brief lower frontal nudity getting back into bed. Long scene.
- ••• 0:43—Breasts in bedroom with Karl. Subtitles get in the way! Long scene.

Hanna Schygulla . . . . Pauline Kropp

Love is a Gun *(1994)*

Carrie Chambers . . . . Ms. Preston's Body Double
- 0:25—Brief back side of right breast in the shower when Eric Roberts sees her.
- 0:43—Left breast, while making love in bed with Roberts.

Kelly Preston . . . . Jean Starr

• ***Love Jones*** *(1996)*

Nia Long . . . . Nina Mosley
- •• 0:31—Brief breasts, several times while making love in bed with Larnez Tate.

Love Letters (1984)
a.k.a. Passion Play
Jamie Lee Curtis . . . . Anna Winter
••• 0:31—Breasts in bathtub reading a letter, then breasts in bed making love with James Keach.
• 0:36—Brief breasts in lifeguard station with Keach.
••• 0:44—Brief breasts admiring a picture taken of her by Keach.
••• 0:46—Breasts and buns in bedroom undressing with Keach.
• 0:49—Breasts in black and white Polaroid photographs that Keach is taking.
• 1:07—Right breast, sticking out of slip, then right breast, while sleeping in bed with Keach.
Sally Kirkland. . . . . Hippie
Amy Madigan . . . . Wendy

Love Lust and Ecstasy (1978)
Ajita Wilson. . . . . Sara
•• 0:02—Nude taking a shower and getting into bed with an old guy.
•• 0:04—Nude making love with a young guy.
•• 0:17—Breasts in bathtub, then making love on bed.
•• 0:22—Breasts making love in a swimming pool, in a river, by a tree.
•• 0:26—Nude getting undressed and taking a shower.
•• 0:35—Full frontal nudity changing clothes.
••• 0:54—Full frontal nudity making love in bed.

The Love Machine (1971)
Madeleine Collinson . . . . Sandy
•• 1:22—Breasts in shower with Robin and her sister when Dyan Cannon discovers them all together. Can't tell who is who.
Mary Collinson . . . . Debbie
•• 1:22—Breasts in shower with Robin and her sister when Dyan Cannon discovers them all together. Can't tell who is who.
Alexandra Hay. . . . . Tina St. Claire
• 0:34—Brief breasts in bed with Robin.
• 0:38—Brief breasts coming around the corner putting blue bathrobe on.
Claudia Jennings . . . . Darlene

Love Matters (1993; Made for Cable Movie)
(Unrated version reviewed.)
Kate Burton. . . . . Deborah
• 0:05—Brief breasts, getting turned over on bed during video playback.
• 0:09—Very brief side view of right breast, while making love in bed with Tony Goldwyn during video playback.
Gina Gershon . . . . Heat
• 0:33—Brief left breast when Tony Goldwyn lays her down.
••• 0:34—Breasts, while on table with Goldwyn. More breasts while making love on kitchen island. Buns when running away.
•• 0:44—Breasts, after turning over and lying under Goldwyn.
• 0:53—Partial left breast, while in shower, talking to Goldwyn.
Annette O'Toole . . . . Julie

Love Scenes (1984)
a.k.a. Ecstacy
Tiffany Bolling. . . . . Val
•• 0:01—Side view of left breast in bed with Peter.
••• 0:06—Breasts getting photographed by Britt Ekland in the house.
• 0:09—Brief breasts opening her bathrobe to show Peter.
• 0:12—Breasts in bathtub with Peter.
••• 0:19—Breasts lying in bed talking with Peter, then making love.
•• 0:43—Breasts acting in a movie when Rick opens her blouse.
•• 0:57—Nude behind shower door, then breasts getting out and talking to Peter.
•• 0:59—Breasts making love tied up on bed with Rick during filming of movie.
•• 1:07—Breasts, then full frontal nudity acting with Elizabeth during filming of movie.
•• 1:17—Full frontal nudity getting out of pool.
•• 1:26—Breasts with Peter on the bed.
Britt Ekland . . . . Annie
Monique Gabrielle. . . . . Uncredited
••• 1:11—Full frontal nudity making love with Rick on bed.
Julie Newmar. . . . . Belinda

• **Love Scenes: Volume 1** (1991; Video Tape)
K.C. Kerrington . . . . Linda Whitney
••• 1:34—Nude, while making love with Tom.
Paula Reve'e . . . . Madilyn Jones
••• 0:20—Nude, while in the room and in the shower with Christopher.

• **Love Scenes: Volume 2** (1992; Video Tape)
Jasaé . . . . Cheryl Lynch
••• 0:16—Breasts, while helping to bathe Marc.
••• 0:18—Breasts and buns, while bathing Marc, then making love on the floor.
••• 0:21—Breasts, while typing in front of a computer, then on chair with Marc.
Tuscany. . . . . Suzanne Coooper
1:21—Sitting in lingerie in hotel room with Lisa.
•• 1:36—Nude, while swimming under water with David, Tom and Lisa.
••• 1:38—Full frontal nudity, while on boat with David and Tom, then during food fight with ice cream and chocolate.
••• 1:45—Nude, during orgy on boat with David, Tom and Lisa.
Annastasia Alexander. . . . . Lisa Carey
•• 1:36—Nude, while swimming under water with David, Tom and Suzanne.
••• 1:38—Breasts, while on boat with David and Tom, then during food fight with ice cream and chocolate.
••• 1:45—Nude, during orgy on boat with David, Tom and Suzanne.
Julie Morrison . . . . Dr. Grace Wells
••• 0:50—Nude, while massaging Travis, then making love in her examination room.
Deborah Stevens . . . . Pamela Carey
••• 1:09—Full frontal nudity, while working out with Chuck, then working with pottery wheel and covering each other with clay.
•• 1:14—Breasts and partial buns in bath with Chuck.
••• 1:17—Nude, while making love in bed with Chuck.

• **Love Scenes: Volume 3** (1993; Video Tape)
Lisa Comshaw . . . . Barbara
1:00—In bra and panties, while watching Andreas dance, seen on monitor.
••• 1:07—Breasts, while making love with Andreas in living room. Dark.

Stevi Conrad . . . . Robin
- •• 0:41—Breasts, while tying Bill up to some trees outside.
- ••• 0:44—Nude, while making love in barn with Bill.

Kelly Jaye . . . . Julianne
- •• 0:09—Nude, while taking a shower in motorhome.
- •• 0:21—Breasts and buns, with Alan outside by camp fire.
- ••• 0:23—Nude, while in the shower in the motorhome and making love in bed with Alan.

Eileen Smith . . . . Laura
- ••• 1:47—Buns in panties and full frontal nudity, while making love with Tom on bed.

Jacqueline St. Claire . . . . Diana
- ••• 1:25—Breasts and buns, while playing with food with four guys.
- ••• 1:29—Nude, while with the four guys.

• Love Skills: A Guide to the Pleasures of Sex *(1984; Video Tape)*

Michelle Bauer . . . . Model
- ••• 0:34—Full frontal nudity, caressing herself in front of a mirror.

Julia Parton . . . . Model
- ••• 0:49—Nude in bed with Barbara Peckinpaugh while a guy watches.

Barbara Peckinpaugh . . . . Model
- •• 0:02—Breasts, falling back into bed.
- ••• 0:09—Nude outside in field, making love with her lover.
- ••• 0:36—Nude, making love in bed with her lover.
- ••• 0:49—Nude in bed with Julie Parton while a guy watches.

Love Strange Love *(1982; Brazilian)*

Xuxa . . . . Tamara
- •• 0:26—Breasts standing on table, getting measured for outfit.
- ••• 0:29—Breasts again when Hugo watches. Long scene.
- •• 0:58—Right breast when she lets Hugo caress it. (Film is reversed since mole above her right breast appears over the left.)
- • 1:00—More right breast.
- •• 1:09—Breasts, stripping out of bear costume during party.
- ••• 1:13—Breasts several times undressing in room. Long scene.
- •• 1:27—Side view of left breast in bed with Hugo.

Vera Fischer . . . . Anna
- •• 0:23—Brief breasts and lower frontal nudity in bathtub. Breasts and buns, getting out.
- •• 0:38—Breasts making love with Dr. Osmar.
- • 0:39—Brief buns, while lying in bed.
- •• 1:19—Breasts in bed with Dr. Osmar when Hugo watches.

Love Trap *(1977)*

a.k.a. Let's Get Laid

Linda Hayden . . . . Gloria

Fiona Richmond . . . . Maxine Lupercal
- •• 0:10—Nude, while in the shower/tub.
- • 0:21—Brief left breast when her lingerie is torn off in Gordon's hand.
- ••• 0:24—Nude, while doing strip routine on stage (wearing a big blonde wig).
- 0:26—Breasts, with a guy in bedroom.
- • 0:27—Breasts and buns in bed with him.
- •• 0:56—Nude, after stripping out of Nazi uniform, then bra and panties, then making love with two girls.
- •• 1:09—Breasts, while in bubble bath, talking to Gordon, then standing up.
- • 1:34—Brief breasts when Gordon pulls her dress top down during filming.

Lisa Taylor . . . . Eleanor
- •• 0:37—Breasts, while answering and talking on the phone.
- • 0:53—Partial lower frontal nudity when talking on the phone to Gordon. Brief breasts, while hanging up the phone.
- • 1:33—Brief left breast while making love on bed with two guys.

• Love Walked In *(1997)*

Aitana Sánchez-Gijón . . . . Vicki Rivas
- • 0:05—Brief left breast, while making love with Denis Leary.
- • 0:26—Partial right breast visible in nightgown, while lying in bed.

Love, Cheat & Steal *(1993; Made for Cable Movie)*

Mädchen Amick . . . . Lauren Harrington
- • 0:26—Buns, when Roberts rips her pants off. Don't see her face.
- • 0:47—Brief back side of right breast, twice, getting out of bed and putting on robe.

Mary Fanaro . . . . Darlene
- •• 0:09—Breasts, making love with Eric Roberts on hood of car.

Susan Lentini . . . . Nun

The Love-Thrill Murders *(1971)*

Joie Addison . . . . Carol
- •• 0:53—Breasts and buns with Chris during party, while everyone else watches.
- •• 1:13—Nude, getting placed on and tied to dining cart.
- ••• 1:17—Breasts, while talking and tied to dining cart, then getting killed.
- • 1:20—Side of right breast and lower frontal nudity, while lying dead on dining cart.

Talie Cochrane . . . . Ruth
- •• 0:24—Breasts and buns, while undressing and talking with Faith.
- ••• 1:03—Nude, while dancing during party.

Francine Middleton . . . . Faith
- •• 0:02—Full frontal nudity, while lying on table during ceremony. Long scene.
- • 0:32—Right breast, while in bed with Maggie.
- • 0:57—Brief buns and partial breasts (seen in mirror), while in bedroom with Maggie.
- •• 1:01—Buns, while standing next to bed as Maggie undresses. Breasts, while making love on bed with Maggie.
- •• 1:09—Breasts, while in bed with Maggie.

Michele Norris . . . . Maggie's Girlfriend
- •• 0:30—Nude, when getting out of bed with Maggie, then dressing.
- •• 0:32—Full frontal nudity, while dressing.

The Lover *(1992)*

(Unrated version reviewed.)

Jane March . . . . The Girl
- •• 0:32—Full frontal nudity in bed with Tony Leung.
- ••• 0:40—Left breast, while making love under Leung.
- ••• 0:42—Full frontal nudity, while lying in bed. Long shot.
- •• 0:43—Buns, while standing in tub, getting washed by Leung.
- ••• 0:44—Breasts, while lying in bed, talking with Leung. Long scene.
- •• 0:47—Left breast, while making love in bed.
- • 0:48—Full frontal nudity, while lying in bed.

•• 0:54—Breasts while making love on the floor with Leung.
••• 0:56—More full frontal nudity on the floor.
••• 0:59—Nude, walking around and watering the plants, getting into bed, then making love.
• 1:02—Brief breasts while making love.
• 1:17—Breasts while washing herself with Leung. Hard to see because bars get in the way.

• ***The Lover's Guide to Sexual Ecstasy: A Sensual Guide to Lovemaking*** *(1992; Video Tape)*

Nikki Dial . . . . Advanced Foreplay
••• 0:25—In white bra, then nude, while making love with her lover.
••• 0:32—Breasts, while making love.
••• 0:36—Nude, while making love in bed in various positions.
••• 0:48—In white bra, then breasts and buns, in female superior positions.
Raven von Bergen . . . . Overture
••• 0:05—Breasts, while in black panties, garter belt and stockings.
•• 0:12—Breasts while modeling jewelry and lingerie.

Lover's Knot *(1995)*

Jennifer Grey . . . . Megan Forrester
• 0:29—Very, very brief upper half of right breast, after sitting up in bed and moving the sheets with Bill Campbell.
• 0:45—Very brief buns, while running through the house in front of Bill Campbell.
Elaine Hendrix. . . . . Robin
Kristin Minter . . . . Cheryl
Tiffany Salerno . . . . Juliet
Marla Sucharetza . . . . Erin

• ***Lover's Leap*** *(1995)*

Sara Suzanne Brown . . . . Rita
••• 0:18—Nude, while making love in bed with Charlie.
••• 0:21—Nude, when walking and standing out on the balcony in the morning.
•• 0:49—Breasts, while sunbathing out in pool with Billie.
Fawna MacLaren. . . . . Billie
•• 0:14—Full frontal nudity, while starting to have sex with Alex in his backyard at night.
•• 0:49—Full frontal nudity, while sunbathing out in pool with Rita.
••• 1:11—Full frontal nudity, while starting to make love with Nick in kitchen.
••• 1:21—Breasts, while playing with herself in bathtub.
Andrea Riave. . . . . Clarine
Carrie Westcott . . . . Johanna
• 0:00—Brief right breast, while on boat with Nick.
••• 0:02—Nude, while making love in the woods with Nick.
• 0:05—Brief breasts, while walking in the woods.
••• 0:36—Breasts and buns, while making love with Alex in living room.
•• 0:38—Nude, while standing on the balcony, then getting dressed inside.
••• 0:55—Nude, while dancing in room, making love with Alex, then in bathroom afterwards.
•• 1:08—Buns and breasts, while making love with Alex on balcony at night.
• 1:17—Brief buns in panties, while lying on the bed, talking on the phone.

Lovers *(1992; Spanish)*

a.k.a. Amantes
Victoria Abril . . . . Luisa
• 0:28—Buns, while lowering herself onto Paco.
Maribel Verdú . . . . Trini
• 0:49—Lower frontal nudity, while lying in bed for Paco.

Lovers Like Us *(1975)*

a.k.a. The Savage
Catherine Deneuve . . . . Nelly
• 1:06—Brief left upper half of left breast in bed with Yves Montand. Dark.
••• 1:09—Breasts sitting up in bed.

Lovers' Lovers *(1993)*

Jennifer Ciesar . . . . Blaire
•• 0:29—Breasts and buns while in the shower.
• 1:07—In white bra and brief breasts while making love with Michael on bed.
1:13—In white bra and panties in bedroom.

• ***Lovers, Liars and Thieves*** *(1996)*

Denise Ames . . . . Flattop
Tamara Kane . . . . Miss Emerson
•• 0:25—Breasts, while making love in bedroom with Cowboy.
Tané McClure . . . . Madam
• 0:00—Breasts, while having sex with a customer in bed.
Monique Parent. . . . . The Teacher
• 0:44—Breasts, while taking a shower, seen through peephole. Very brief lower frontal nudity and partial left breast, when reaching for a towel.
•• 1:09—Breasts and buns, while making love with Cowboy in bed.

The Loves of a French Pussycat *(1976)*

Sybil Danning . . . . Andrea
••• 0:18—Breasts dancing with her boss, then in bed.
•• 0:24—Breasts and buns in swimming pool.
• 0:46—Breasts in bathtub with a guy.
• 1:03—Left breast sticking out of bra, then breasts.

The Loves of a Wall Street Woman *(1989)*

Tara Buckman . . . . Brenda Baxter
• 0:00—Breasts taking a shower, opening the door and getting a towel.
•• 0:06—Breasts changing clothes in locker room in black panties. Nice legs!
••• 0:18—Breasts in bed making love with Alex.
•• 0:31—Breasts in bed with Alex making love.
•• 0:40—Breasts in black panties dressing in locker room.
• 0:46—Brief breasts lying in bed, talking to her lover, side view of buns. Long shot.
••• 1:16—Breasts making love in bed with Alex.

Loving Lulu *(1992)*

Sandahl Bergman . . . . Lulu
••• 0:35—Breasts, making love with Sam.
• 0:42—Brief buns and brief breasts in shower with Sam.
• 0:57—Brief right breast in bathroom, twice, with Sam.
Tanya Boyd . . . . Background

A Low Down Dirty Shame *(1994)*

Devin De Vasquez . . . . Mendoza's Girl
Nikki Fritz . . . . Exotic Dancer
• 1:03—Brief buns in sexy swimsuit, while dancing in a club.

Shawn Lusader . . . . Female Lovemaker
- 0:02—Very brief buns, lower frontal nudity and right breast in hotel bed with a guy when surprised by Jada Pinkett.

Jada Pinkett . . . . .Peaches
Salli Richardson . . . . Angela

Lower Level *(1990)*

Elizabeth Gracen . . . . Hillary
- 0:11—Breasts in back seat of BMW making love with Craig. Long shot.
- 0:12—Very, very brief partial left breast afterwards.
- 0:13—Brief right breast and lower frontal nudity getting dressed. Then in black lingerie.
- •• 0:23—In black lingerie, then brief breasts changing in her office while Sam secretly watches.

Shari Shattuck . . . . .Dawn Simms

Lucky 13 *(1984)*

a.k.a. Running Hot
a.k.a. Highway to Hell

Monica Carrico . . . . .Charlene Andrews
- 0:02—Brief buns and partial left breast under water, while masturbating in bathtub.
- 0:48—Brief buns, after taking off her panties to go skinny dipping.
- •• 0:50—Breasts sitting on a rock after skinny dipping with Eric Stoltz.
- •• 0:51—Breasts and buns after getting out of water and picking up clothes.
- •• 1:03—Breasts in bed making love with Stoltz.
- ••• 1:15—Breasts while lying in bed with Stoltz.

Juliette Cummins. . . . . Jenny

Lunch Box *(1991)*

Ava Cadell. . . . . Maggie Dancer
- 1:01—Brief buns in swimsuit while kneeling next to Waldo by pool.
- 1:03—Brief buns in lingerie while in bed with Waldo.

Felicia Peluso . . . . Annie
- ••• 0:12—In sheer red bra, then nude, while doing strip routine on forklift truck in C.C.'s fantasy. Nice long scene.
- •• 0:40—Partial buns in swimsuit by pool in C.C.'s fantasy.
- •• 1:13—Breasts after taking off sheer red bra in front of C.C. in his room.

Lunch Wagon *(1981)*

a.k.a. Lunch Wagon Girls
a.k.a. Come 'N' Get It

Pamela Bryant . . . . Marcy
- •• 0:04—Breasts while changing tops in room in gas station with Rosanne Katon while a guy watches through key hole.
- 0:55—Left breast, several times, in van with Bif.

Rosanne Katon . . . . Shannon
- 0:01—Brief breasts getting dressed.
- 0:04—Brief side view of left breast changing tops in room in gas station with Pamela Bryant while a guy watches through key hole.
- •• 0:10—Breasts changing again in gas station.

Candy Moore . . . . .Diedra
- •• 0:53—Breasts under sheer robe, then breasts while on couch with Arnie.

Louisa Moritz. . . . . Sunshine
- 0:37—Breasts in spa taking off her swimsuit top.

• ***Lurid Tales: The Castle Queen*** *(1995)*

Kim Dawson . . . . .Older Sister
- •• 0:01—Breasts, while making love with Charles.
- •• 0:23—In black lingerie, then breasts, while making love with Tom.
- 1:12—Very, very brief breasts during flashbacks.

Betsy Lynn George. . . . . .Miranda Dorset
- •• 0:34—Breasts, while her and her sister make love with Tom.
- 1:04—Brief right breast, while making love under Tom.
- 1:12—Very, very brief breasts during flashbacks.

Christi Harris . . . . Amy
- 0:39—Brief right breast, while her and her sister make love with Tom.
- •• 0:51—Breasts, while sitting and posing.
- 1:12—Very, very brief left breast during flashbacks.

Lurkers *(1987)*

Ruth Corrine Collins. . . . . .Jane (Model)
- •• 0:13—Breasts, changing clothes with the other model.

Annie Grindlay. . . . . .Lulu (Model)
- 0:12—Undressing in sheer bra (on the left) with another model.
- •• 0:13—Breasts, while changing clothes with the other model.

Nancy Groff. . . . . .Rita
- 1:07—Partial right breast in bathroom with another woman while Cathy talks.

Christine Moore. . . . . Cathy
- ••• 0:19—Breasts in bed, making love with her boyfriend.
- 0:42—Brief breasts in bubble bath during hallucination scene with her mother.

Debbie Rochon . . . . Uncredited Evil Host

Lust for a Vampire *(1970; British)*

Luan Peters . . . . .Trudi
Pippa Steel. . . . . Susan Pelley
Yutte Stensgaard . . . . Mircalla
- ••• 0:19—Breasts, three times, getting a massage from another school girl.
- •• 0:53—Breasts outside with Lestrange. Left breast when lying down.
- 0:58—Breasts during Lestrange's dream.

Lust for Freedom *(1987)*

Michelle Bauer. . . . . Jackie
- •• 0:37—In bra, then breasts after undressing in prison cell with Lynn.
- 0:40—Lower frontal nudity and left breast when removing her panties.

Crystal Breeze . . . . .Lynn
- •• 0:38—Breasts, after taking off her top in prison cell with Michelle Bauer.
- 0:40—Breasts and brief buns, while kissing Bauer.
- 0:41—Left breast, while kissing Bauer on bed.
- •• 0:42—Close up of breasts, while Bauer makes love with her.
- •• 1:22—Breasts, after taking off her top in prison cell to ask a favor from the guard.

Pamela Gilbert. . . . . Snuff Victim
- •• 0:52—Breasts, while sitting on bed, looking all drugged out before being shot.

Adrian Scott. . . . . Karen
- •• 0:40—Full frontal nudity, after her boyfriend forces her to take off her clothes.
- 0:41—Brief lower frontal nudity with her boyfriend in prison cell.

Luther the Geek (1988)

Stacy Haiduk. . . . . Beth

••• 0:26—Breasts with Rob in the shower, then leaving. Wow!

••• 0:28—Breasts, after taking off her robe in bed, then making love with Rob.

Luzia (Brazilian)

Claudia Ohana . . . . Luzia

• 1:11—Breasts, while swimming in the lake. Brief lower frontal nudity and brief buns, partially visible under water.

• 1:12—Nude, while getting out of the water when Tereza talks with her.

•• 1:26—Breasts, while squatting in corner of room and washing herself off with water from a bowl, then putting on blouse.

• 1:28—Brief left breast in open blouse with a guy.

*M*A*S*H* (1970)

Sally Kellerman . . . . Margaret "Hot Lips" Houlihan

• 0:42—Very, very brief left breast opening her blouse for Frank in her tent.

• 1:11—Very, very brief buns and side view of right breast during shower prank. Long shot, hard to see.

• 1:54—Very brief breasts in a slightly different angle of the shower prank during the credits.

Monica Peterson . . . . Pretty WAC

M. Butterfly (1993)

Annabel Leventon . . . . Frau Baden

•• 0:50—Breasts, while sitting on bed and talking to Jeremy Irons.

Barbara Sukowa . . . . Jeanne Gallimard

Macabre (Italian/Spanish)

Silvana Venturelli. . . . . Annie

• 1:03—Very, very brief right breast, while wrapping a robe around herself.

• 1:05—Brief right breast while lying on bed when Gert checks her out.

Macbeth (1972; British)

Francesca Annis. . . . . Lady Macbeth

• 1:41—Buns, while walking around after the bad guys have attacked and looted the castle. Side view of left breast, hard to see because it's covered by her hair.

Olga Anthony . . . . Dancer

• *Machine Gun Blues* (1995)

Maria Ford . . . . Alba

• 0:53—Buns and breasts, while making love in bed with Nick Cassavetes.

Cynda Williams . . . . Georgia

• 0:18—Very brief left breast, while lying in bed with Nick Cassavetes.

• 0:34—Side of left breast, while sitting in Cassavetes' lap and kissing him.

••• 0:38—In bra, then breasts, while making love in bed with Cassavetes.

Macho Callahan (1970)

Jean Seberg. . . . . Alexandra

• 0:36—Brief buns and partial breast in mirror. (Don't see her face clearly.)

• 1:01—Very brief left breast when David Janssen rips her blouse open. Brief breasts during struggle with him before he rapes her. Brief left breast during rape. (Never see face with body.)

The Mack (1973)

Carol Speed. . . . . Lulu

•• 0:23—Breasts, while lying in bed with Goldie.

Mackenna's Gold (1969)

Julie Newmar. . . . . Hesh-de

• 1:09—Brief breasts and buns under water. Long shots, hard to see anything. Not clear because of all the dirty water. Brief buns, getting out of the pond.

Macon County Line (1974)

Joan Blackman. . . . . Carol Morgan

Cheryl Waters . . . . Jenny

• 0:57—Buns and brief back side of right breast, while undressing in barn.

• 0:58—Buns and lower frontal nudity while in tub with Chris. Very brief right breast, when he dries her off.

Mad Dog and Glory (1993)

Uma Thurman. . . . . Glory

•• 0:56—Left breast, while in bed with Robert De Niro.

• 0:58—Very brief breasts when De Niro gets off her.

The Maddening (1995)

Victoria Bass . . . . Lisa

Angie Dickinson . . . . Georgina Scudder

Mia Sara . . . . Cassie Osborne

• 0:42—Partial left breast, twice, while sitting in bathtub, talking with Angie Dickinson.

• 0:47—Very, very brief side view of left breast, while struggling on the floor with Burt Reynolds when he rips her dress open.

• *Made for Man: Intimate Fantasy* (1992; Video Tape)

Ginger Miller. . . . . Darling Nikki

• 0:03—Buns in G-string, doing strip routine out of black outfit.

• 0:11—Buns, during gelatin wrestling with Baby Driver.

• 0:37—Stripping down to two piece silver swimsuit.

• 0:47—Wrestling with Sugar Ray Rene in lettuce.

• 0:55—Brief left breast, popping out of swimsuit top.

Cindy Rome . . . . Sugar Ray Rene

• 0:23—Stripping out of cave girl outfit down to purple two piece swimsuit.

•• 0:40—Buns, stripping to leopard print two piece swimsuit and wrestling with Ginger Miller.

Made in America (1993)

Nia Long . . . . Zora Mathews

Jennifer Tilly. . . . . Stacy

• 0:13—Very, very brief back side of left breast, when jumping up out of bed. Brief buns and very, very brief back side of left breast while doing cartwheels into the bathroom. Possible body double.

Made in U.S.A. (1988)

Judith Baldwin. . . . . Dorie

Cindi Dietrich . . . . Girl in Trans-Am

Katherine Kelly Lang . . . . Kelly

Lori Singer. . . . . Annie

• 0:26—Brief left breast and very brief lower frontal nudity in the back of a convertible with Dar at night.

Mademoiselle *(1966; French/British)*

Jeanne Moreau . . . . Mademoiselle

•• 1:17—Right breast, while opening her blouse in field in front of her lover. Don't see her face.

Madman *(1982)*

Gaylen Ross. . . . . Betsy

• 0:24—Very brief full frontal nudity, getting into hot tub with T.P.

• *Madonna: The Immaculate Collection* *(1990; Video Tape)*

Madonna . . . . Herself

• 0:18—(1 min., 36 sec. into "Papa Don't Preach.") Very, very brief upper half of right breast after first head throw-back in black strapless outfit. Long shot.

• 0:18—(2 min., 10 sec. into "Papa Don't Preach.") Very, very brief left breast in black strapless outfit when she throws her head back. (After the daughter character she plays walks up the subway stairs.)

• *The Mafu Cage* *(1978)*

a.k.a. My Sister, My Love

Lee Grant . . . . Ellen

Carol Kane . . . . Cissy

• 0:08—Very brief tip of left breast in the bathtub.

Magic *(1978)*

Ann-Margret . . . . .Peggy Ann Snow

••• 0:44—Right breast, lying on her side in bed talking to Anthony Hopkins.

The Magic Bubble *(1992)*

Colleen Camp . . . . Deborah

Betsy Lynn George . . . . Angel

Dayle Haddon . . . . Susan

Shelley Michelle . . . . .Body Double

Diane Salinger. . . . . .Julia

• 0:11—Very, very brief breasts after whipping off towel in front of her husband. Very, very brief buns, walking away. Back side of right breast, while pulling back curtain in front of her husband while he sits on the toilet.

• 1:21—Very brief side of left breast while putting on night-gown.

Magnum Force *(1973)*

Margaret Avery . . . . Prostitute

Suzanne Somers . . . . Uncredited Pool Girl

•• 0:26—In blue swimsuit getting into a swimming pool, brief breasts a couple of times before getting shot, brief breasts floating dead.

Mahler *(1974; British)*

Georgina Hale . . . . Alma Mahler

•• 1:00—Breasts during musical number.

• *Mahogany* *(1975)*

Marisa Mell . . . . .Carlotta Gavin

Diana Ross. . . . . .Tracy

•• 1:25—Very, very brief side view of left breast in gaping white dress, just before taking it off. Very, very brief right breast, while putting on striped robe.

Maiden Quest *(1972)*

a.k.a. The Long Swift Sword of Siegfried

Sybil Danning . . . . Kriemhild

• 0:02—Breasts in bath, surrounded by topless blonde servants.

• 0:04—Breasts in the bath again.

••• 0:10—Nude in tub surrounded by breasts servant girls.

••• 0:12—Breasts on bed, getting rubbed with ointment by the servant girls.

•• 0:35—Breasts while in bed with Siegfried.

• 1:00—Breasts in bed with Siegfried.

••• 1:19—Breasts in bed with Siegfried.

• *The Making of Bar Girls* *(1995; Video Tape)*

Patti Sheehan . . . . Destiny

• 0:19—Breasts, while sitting down in spa and talking on the phone. Shot from different angles than shown in the film.

Nancy Allison Wolfe. . . . . Loretta

•• 0:29—In bra, when in hallway with J.R. Breasts, while in the bedroom with her. These are the same scenes that are seen in the film itself.

• *Making of the "Carousel Girls' Calendar"* *(1993; Video Tape)*

Robin Brown . . . . Miss January

••• 0:09—Nude during photo shoot.

••• 0:13—Nude during interview segment.

Shelly Jones . . . . Miss October

••• 1:07—Breasts and buns during photo shoot.

••• 1:10—Nude during interview segment.

Sam Phillips . . . . Miss September

••• 1:00—Breasts and brief buns during photo shoot.

••• 1:03—Nude during interview segment.

Julie Kristen Smith . . . . Miss February

••• 0:16—Breasts during photo shoot.

••• 0:19—Nude during interview segment.

Sasha Vinni . . . . Miss November

••• 1:13—Full frontal nudity during photo shoot.

••• 1:16—Nude during interview segment.

Dawnya Welsh. . . . . Miss April

••• 0:29—Nude during photo shoot.

••• 0:32—Nude during interview segment.

Malibu Beach *(1978)*

Kim Lankford . . . . Dina

• 0:32—Buns, while running into the ocean.

• 0:34—Brief right breast getting out of the ocean.

• 1:16—Right breast on beach at night with boyfriend.

• 1:19—Brief breasts at top of the stairs.

•• 1:20—Brief breasts when her parents come home.

• 1:21—Breasts in bed with her boyfriend.

Susan Player Jarreau. . . . . Sally

• 0:28—Side view of left breast with boyfriend at night on the beach. Long shot.

• 0:32—Buns, when running into the ocean with her two male friends.

• 0:33—Brief side view of left breast in water. Long shot.

• 0:34—Brief breasts while in the ocean, then breasts while getting dressed by the fire.

Tara Strohmeier. . . . . Glorianna

• 0:08—Breasts kissing her boyfriend at the beach when someone steals her towel.

The Malibu Bikini Shop *(1985)*

Debra Blee. . . . . Jane

Barbra Horan. . . . . Ronnie
- 0:33—In wet tank top during Alan's fantasy.
- 1:13—Most of side of left breast, while kissing Alan in the spa.

Rita Jenrette . . . . Aunt Ida
Jeana Loring . . . . Margie Hill
- •• 0:43—Breasts, dancing on stage during bikini contest (Contestant #4).

Gretchen Palmer . . . . .Woman
Bobbi Pavis . . . . .Stunning Girl
- •• 0:19—Breasts trying on bikini behind two-way glass.

Allene Simmons . . . . Milinda Riley

• Malibu Canyon Nights #1 *(1997; Video Tape)*
Cory Lane . . . . .Herself
- ••• 0:21—In bra and panties, then full frontal nudity, while posing in the woods.

Taylor St. Claire. . . . . .Herself
- ••• 0:31—Nude (wearing a black corset), while posing on bed.

Cher Willis. . . . . .Herself
- ••• 0:11—In lingerie, then nude, while posing in bathtub.

Malibu Express *(1984)*
Sybil Danning . . . . Countess Luciana
- • 0:13—Brief breasts making love in bed with Cody.

Barbara Edwards . . . . May
- •• 0:10—Breasts taking a shower with Kimberly McArthur on the boat.
- •• 1:05—Breasts serving Cody coffee while he talks on the telephone.

Robyn Hilton . . . . Maid Marian
Kimberly McArthur . . . . Faye
- •• 0:10—Breasts taking a shower on the boat with Barbara Edwards.

Shanna McCullough . . . . Uncredited Massage Girl
- •• 0:33—Breasts, several times while giving a guy a rub down.

Lorraine Michaels . . . . Liza Chamberlin
- ••• 0:23—Breasts in the shower making love with Shane, while getting photographed by a camera.

Shelly Taylor Morgan . . . . Anita Chamberlain
- • 0:22—Breasts doing exercises on the floor.
- •• 0:26—Breasts making love with Shane in bed while being video taped. Then right breast while standing by door.

Suzanne M. Regard . . . . Sexy Sally
- • 0:50—Brief breasts, while talking on the telephone.
- •• 1:06—Breasts, while talking on the telephone.

Lori Sutton . . . . Beverly McAfee
- ••• 0:54—Breasts and buns, making love in bed with Cody.

Lynda Wiesmeier. . . . . June Khnockers
- •• 0:04—Breasts in locker room taking jumpsuit off.
- • 1:16—Breasts leaning out of racing car window while a helicopter chases her and Cody.

Malibu Hot Summer *(1981)*
a.k.a. Sizzle Beach

(*Sizzle Beach* is the re-released version with Kevin Costner featured on the cover. It is missing all the nude scenes during the opening credits before 0:06.)

Terry Congie. . . . . .Janice Johnson
- • 0:09—Buns in the shower. Hard to see through the door.
- ••• 0:29—Breasts taking off her top and getting into bed with Steve, then making love.
- • 1:09—Side view of left breast kissing Gary during the party.
- •• 1:11—Breasts making love with Gary the next morning after the party.

Roselyn Royce . . . . Cheryl Rielly
- •• 0:15—On exercise bike, then breasts getting into bed.
- ••• 0:16—Breasts sitting up in bed, buns going to closet to get dressed to go jogging.
- •• 0:52—Breasts on boat with Brent.

Sylvia Wright . . . . Actress at Party
- •• 0:01—Nude, standing up during opening credits.
- ••• 1:07—Breasts fixing her hair in front of mirror, then full frontal nudity talking to Howard.
- • 1:09—Breasts on top of Howard.

Malice *(1993)*
Debrah Farentino . . . . Tanya
- • 0:25—Very brief upper half of right breast, while in bed with Alec Baldwin.
- • 0:26—Brief buns and breasts, while running into the bathroom. Medium long shot.

Nicole Kidman. . . . . Tracy
- •• 0:13—Very brief left breast then buns, when leaning over Bill Pullman in bed.

Sara Melson. . . . . Girl on Bike
Bebe Neuwirth . . . . .Dana
Gwyneth Paltrow. . . . . Paula Bell
Brenda Strong . . . . .Claudia

Malicious *(1974; Italian)*
Laura Antonelli . . . . Angela
- • 1:14—Breasts after undressing while two boys watch from above.
- •• 1:27—Breasts, undressing under flashlight. Hard to see because the light is moving around a lot.
- • 1:29—Breasts and buns running around the house.

Malicious *(1995)*
Sarah Lassez . . . . Laura
- • 0:36—Brief right breast, while making out in the library with Doug.

Molly Ringwald . . . . Melissa Nelson
- 0:23—Very, very brief silhouette of breasts seen through sweater.
- ••• 0:24—Breasts, when making love on top of Doug while his wrists are tied up. Excellent!

Mallrats *(1995)*
Joey Lauren Adams . . . . Gwen
- • 0:29—Brief breasts, while in dressing room before guy's head comes crashing through the wall.

Priscilla Barnes. . . . . .Ivannah
- •• 0:58—Breasts, after opening her blouse and feeling her breasts to "read" the fortunes for the two boys. Ordinarily this would have rated a three, but the second, special-effect nipple on her right breast is rather distracting.

Shannen Doherty . . . . Rene
Claire Forlani . . . . .Brandi
Renée Humphrey. . . . . .Tricia

The Mambo Kings *(1992)*
Stephanie Blake. . . . . .Stripper
Maruschka Detmers. . . . . Dolores Fuentes
- •• 0:47—Breasts several times, making love in bed with Antonio Banderas.

Valerie McIntosh . . . . .Tracy Blair
- •• 1:10—Breasts, getting her bathing suit after Armand Assante discovers her with Antonio Banderas.

Talisa Soto. . . . . Maria Rivera

A Man Called Horse (1970)

Corinna Tsopei . . . . Running Deer
- 1:03—Long shot of buns, before entering sweat house. Side view of left breast kneeling inside the sweat house.
- 1:15—Very brief breasts when startled by Richard Harris' screaming.
- 1:22—Left nipple while in tepee with Harris.
- 1:23—Side of left breast and right breast in tepee with Harris.

A Man for Sale (1982)

Ajita Wilson . . . . .Dancer/Model
- 0:02—Breasts several times posing for photographer with another model.
- 0:26—Breasts and buns, dancing in an erotic ballet show.

A Man in Love (1987)

Jamie Lee Curtis. . . . . Susan Elliot
Greta Scacchi . . . . .Jane Steiner
- ••• 0:31—Breasts with Peter Coyote.
- •• 1:04—Buns and left breast in bed with Coyote.
- • 1:10—Brief side view breasts, when putting black dress on.
- • 1:24—Brief breasts in bed.

Man of Flowers (1984; Australian)

Alyson Best . . . . Lisa
- •• 0:04—Undressing out of clothes, in bra, panties and stockings in front of Charles, then full frontal nudity, then getting dressed.
- •• 0:13—Full frontal nudity after taking off robe and sitting on chair for art class.
- • 0:36—Brief breasts while in bed with a guy.

Victoria Eagger . . . . Angela
- •• 1:08—Breasts, when lying on the floor, then full frontal nudity while putting on her blouse.

• A Man of No Importance (1994; Irish/British)

Tara Fitzgerald. . . . . Adele Rice
- • 1:09—Brief partial breasts, while making love with her boyfriend when Albert Finney sees her.

A Man of Passion (1989)

Maud Adams. . . . . Susana
Elizabeth Ashley. . . . . Gloria
Shari Shattuck . . . . .Teresa
- •• 0:18—Left breast, while posing for Anthony Quinn. Breasts under sheer blouse when leaving the room.
- • 0:20—Brief partial right breast, when caught in bed with Quinn by George.
- • 0:22—Tip of left breast, while sitting on edge of bed.
- • 1:12—Brief breasts, while turning over in bed with Quinn.

Victoria Vera . . . . Nuria
- •• 1:10—Breasts, after taking off her dress at table in front of Anthony Quinn.

The Man Who Fell to Earth (1976; British)

(Uncensored version reviewed.)

Candy Clark . . . . Mary-Lou
- •• 0:42—Breasts in the bathtub, washing her hair and talking to David Bowie.
- •• 0:55—Breasts sitting on bed and blowing out a candle.
- ••• 0:56—Breasts in bed with Bowie.
- ••• 1:26—Full frontal nudity climbing into bed with Bowie after he reveals his true alien self.
- • 1:56—Nude with Bowie, while making love and shooting a gun.

Claudia Jennings . . . . .Uncredited Girl by the Pool
- • 1:42—Breasts, standing by the pool and kissing Bernie Casey.

The Man Who Loved Cat Dancing (1973)

Sarah Miles . . . . .Catherine Crocker
- •• 1:04—Back of left breast, then breasts, after taking off her blouse, then washing herself in water.
- • 1:20—Brief left breast, while in bed with Burt Reynolds.

The Man Who Loved Women (1983)

Julie Andrews. . . . . Marianna
Jennifer Ashley. . . . . .David's Mother
Kim Basinger . . . . Louise "Lulu"
Jill Carroll. . . . . Sue the Baby Sitter
Denise Crosby . . . . Enid
Cindi Dietrich . . . . Darla
Marilu Henner . . . . .Agnes Chapman
- •• 0:18—Brief breasts in bed with Burt Reynolds.

Sharon Hughes . . . . Nurse
Tracy Vaccaro . . . . Legs

The Man Who Wasn't There (1983)

Deborah Dutch . . . . Miss Dawson
Leslie J. Hunt . . . . Nymphet
Lisa Langlois . . . . .Cindy Worth
- •• 0:58—Nude running away from two policemen after turning visible.
- ••• 1:08—Breasts in white panties dancing in her apartment with an invisible Steve Guttenberg.
- • 1:47—Very, very brief upper half of left breast, while throwing bouquet at wedding.

Brinke Stevens . . . . Nymphet
- • 0:45—Buns and brief breasts in the girls' shower, when she gets shampoo from an invisible Steve Guttenberg.

The Man with Two Brains (1983)

Randi Brooks . . . . Fran
- •• 1:11—Brief breasts showing Steve Martin her breasts in front of the hotel. Buns, changing in the hotel room, then wearing black see-through negligee.

Kathleen Turner. . . . . Dolores Benedict
- • 0:08—Right breast when Steve Martin is operating on her in the operating room.
- • 0:36—Buns, in hotel room with a guy about to squeeze her buns when Steve Martin walks in.

Mandingo (1975)

Susan George . . . . Blanche
- • 1:36—Brief breasts in bed with Ken Norton.

Debbi Morgan. . . . . Dite
- • 0:17—Breasts in bed talking to Perry King.

Brenda Sykes . . . . Ellen
- • 0:58—Breasts in bed with Perry King.

Manhunt (1994)

Stephanie Champlin . . . . Woman in Bed
- • 1:12—Breasts, buns and very brief lower frontal nudity in bed with Charlie before getting killed with him.

Jillian McWhirter . . . . Stephanie Williams
Anneliza Scott . . . . .Cop #1

The Manhunters (1980; French/Spanish/German)

Ursula Buchfellner . . . . .Laura Crawford
- • 0:06—Buns and side view breasts, walking around the house. Long shot.
- • 0:08—Breasts taking a bath.

•• 0:10—Breasts in the bathtub.
• 0:15—Full frontal nudity getting pulled out of the tub unconscious.
• 0:19—Brief right breast when a kidnapper opens her blouse while she's tied up.
• 0:43—Very brief breasts, while running through the jungle.
• 0:58—Brief lower frontal nudity, then breasts captured by the natives.
•• 1:04—Breasts, unconscious, while tribe women undress her.
•• 1:05—Full frontal nudity tied to a pole.
•• 1:06—Nude, getting dragged into a hut.
•• 1:10—Full frontal nudity taking a shower under waterfall with three tribe women.
•• 1:12—Full frontal nudity, lying down while three tribe women put flowers on her.
•• 1:23—Breasts and buns, getting carried away by the cannibal creature.
• 1:26—Buns, being carried by the creature.
•• 1:27—Breasts on the ground.
•• 1:29—Buns and right breast, getting carried down the mountain side.
••• 1:30—Breasts on the boat with Peter.

Gisela Hahn. . . . . n.a.

Maniac Cop 2 (1990)

Claudia Christian. . . . . Susan Riley
Laurene Landon . . . . Teresa Mallory
Paula Trickey. . . . . Cheryl
•• 0:41—In orange two piece swimsuit on stage, then breasts and buns in G-string.

Manifesto (1988)

a.k.a. A Night of Love
Gabrielle Anwar . . . . Tina
Camilla Søeberg . . . . Svetlana
••• 0:15—Nude, in bathtub and bedroom with Emile. Long scene.
• 0:19—Brief left breast when Emile cuts off her hair.
•• 1:04—Left breast, several times when Emile is in her room. More left breast cleaning up after Emile accidentally dies.
• 1:15—Brief side of left breast, while making love with Eric Stoltz. Dark. Buns, getting out of bed.
•• 1:16—Breasts and buns unrolling Emile in the rug.
•• 1:23—Breasts sitting in bed with puppies.

• *The Manitou* (1977)

Stella Stevens . . . . Amelia Crusoe
Susan Strasberg. . . . . Karen Tandy
• 1:33—Breasts, while fighting the creature in bed. Really bad special-effects. Too dark to see anything.

Manon of the Spring (1987; French)

Emmanuelle Béart. . . . . Manon
• 0:11—Brief nude dancing around a spring playing a harmonica.

Map of the Human Heart (1992; Australian/Canadian)

Clotilde Courau. . . . . Rainee
Jeanne Moreau . . . . Sister Banville
Anne Parillaud. . . . . Albertine
• 1:14—Partial left breast (close-up), then right breast, while making love with Avik on top of blimp.

Dail Sullivan . . . . Barrage Balloon WAAC

Marathon Man (1976)

Marthe Keller. . . . . Elsa
•• 0:42—Breasts lying on the floor after Dustin Hoffman rolls off her.

Mardi Gras for the Devil (1993)

Margaret Avery . . . . Miss Sadie
Lydie Denier . . . . Valerie
••• 0:50—Breasts, while making love in bed with Robert Davi.

Lesley-Anne Down. . . . . Christine
Trisha Lane . . . . Jackie
•• 0:03—Breasts, while in panties, while simulating sex in front of Michael Ironside.

Maria's Lovers (1985)

Nastassja Kinski . . . . Maria Bosic
• 1:12—Brief right breast, while looking at herself in the mirror.

Anita Morris . . . . Mrs. Wynic
Anna Thomson . . . . Kathy

Marilyn Chambers' Bedtime Stories (1993)

Marilyn Chambers. . . . . Marilyn Chambers
•• 0:02—Breasts, after taking off towel, then opening and adjusting robe.
• 0:04—Brief breasts in bedroom, taking off robe.
• 1:02—Brief right breast on TV.
•• 1:14—Breasts while making love with Bob on bed.
•• 1:15—Breasts while making love with Bob on bed.

Camille Donatacci . . . . Angelique
••• 0:34—Breasts and buns while changing lingerie in bedroom.
••• 0:42—Breasts, while making love with Chris on sofa.
••• 0:55—In pink bra and panties then right breast and buns in Chris' bedroom.

Isabelle Fortea . . . . Tatiana
••• 0:18—Breasts and buns in red G-string, after taking off dress with Bart's help.
••• 0:25—Breasts and buns with Bart, then in shower. Squished breasts against the glass.
• 0:33—Breasts in open solid color robe in bathroom.
• 1:17—Breasts in out take with Bart.

Joan Gerardi . . . . Jane
Theresa Lynn. . . . . Melissa
•• 0:07—Breasts and buns in G-string, while changing lingerie in bedroom in front of mirror.
•• 0:22—Breasts, while on sofa, practicing her acting with Bart.
•• 0:29—Breasts, while making love with Bart on sofa.
•• 0:33—Breasts, while in bathroom with blue towel.
•• 1:17—Breasts, while on couch with Bart in out take.

Donna Salvatore . . . . Letitia
• 0:01—Brief breasts in shower through hole in wall during opening credits.
•• 0:11—Breasts, getting out of shower when Bart peeks through hole in wall.
•• 0:32—Buns in T-back and breasts, while dancing with Bart.
• 0:33—Breasts in open polka dot robe.
• 1:17—Brief breasts in shower out take.

• *Marilyn Chambers: Wet & Wild Fantasies* (1994; Video Tape)

Marilyn Chambers. . . . . Hostess
• 0:18—Partial breasts during segue.
• 0:20—Breasts again during another segue.

- • 0:22—Breasts, while standing in the surf with binoculars. Breasts in a clip from a film.
- • 0:26—Brief breasts, while standing in the surf.
- • 0:28—Brief breasts, while in the surf.
- •• 0:36—Nude while swimming under water.

Beckie Mullen . . . . Pool Cleaner
- •• 0:32—In swimsuit, then breasts by and in the swimming pool.

J. J. North . . . . Exercising Girl 1
- • 0:25—Breasts, while exercising and swimming in pool.

Julia Parton . . . . Girl at the Beach/Shower Girl
- ••• 0:21—Breasts, while making love with her boyfriend at the beach.
- ••• 0:28—Full frontal nudity, while taking a shower.

Jennifer Worthington. . . . . n.a.

The Marilyn Diaries *(1990)*

Tara Buckman . . . . Jane
- •• 0:53—Breasts and buns, taking off robe and getting into bathtub. Left breast, in tub reading diary.
- •• 0:54—Breasts in and getting out of tub. Very brief lower frontal nudity.
- •• 1:27—Breasts in bathtub talking with John.

Marilyn Chambers. . . . . Marilyn
- •• 0:02—Breasts in bathroom with a guy during party.
- •• 0:26—In bra and panties in Istvan's studio, then breasts.
- ••• 0:27—Breasts in panties when Istvan opens her blouse.
- •• 0:45—Breasts in trench coat, opening it up to give the Iranian secret documents.
- • 0:47—Breasts when the Rebel Leader opens her trench coat.
- • 0:48—Breasts with Colonel South.
- •• 0:57—Breasts opening her top for Hollywood producer.
- • 1:10—In swimsuit, then breasts with Roger.
- ••• 1:13—In black lingerie, then breasts making love with Chet.
- • 1:19—Left breast, in flashback with Roger.
- •• 1:25—In slip, then right breast, then breasts with Chet.

The Mark *(1976; Italian)*

Claudine Beccarie . . . . Huana
- •• 0:25—Nude, while leaning out of doorway, walking to bed, lying on it and answering the phone.
- •• 0:36—Breasts, in open blouse, while making love with Francis.
- ••• 0:41—Full frontal nudity, while running in ocean in slow motion. Orange colored tint.
- •• 1:15—Breasts on the beach with Francis. Orange colored tint.

Marked for Death *(1990)*

Tracey Burch . . . . Sexy Girl #1
- • 0:39—Brief breasts on bed with Jimmy when Steven Seagal bursts into the room. (She's the blonde.)

Leslie Danon . . . . Girl #1

Elizabeth Gracen . . . . Melissa

Joanna Pacula . . . . Leslie

Elena Sahagun. . . . . Carmen
- • 0:06—Breasts in room, when shooting Steven Seagal's partner.

Teri Weigel . . . . Sexy Girl #2
- • 0:39—Brief breasts on bed with Jimmy when Steven Seagal bursts into the room. (She's the brunette.)

Marked for Murder *(1990)*

Toni Alessandrini . . . . Toni
- • 0:38—Breasts while serving drinks to Winfield in bar.
- •• 0:40—Breasts while talking with Wings Hauser in bar.
- •• 0:42—Buns in G-string and breasts, when bringing drinks to Hauser.

Tamara Clatterbuck . . . . Barmaid

Victoria Nesbitt . . . . Girlfriend
- •• 0:57—Breasts, while in backyard by pool with Wings Hauser.

Marlowe *(1969)*

Sharon Farrell . . . . Orfamay Quest

Rita Moreno. . . . . Dolores Gonzales
- • 1:29—Buns in G-string, while doing fan dance/strip tease on stage. Brief breasts (with pasties) under jacket.
- •• 1:32—Breasts (with pasties), after taking off jacket while dancing on stage before getting shot. Medium long shot at first, closer shot later.

Mary Wilcox . . . . YWCA Clerk

The Marriage of a Young Stockbroker *(1971)*

Elizabeth Ashley. . . . . Nan
- • 0:49—Very, very brief partial right breast, while adjusting her bikini top.
- • 1:26—Buns through shower door in women's locker room.

Tiffany Bolling . . . . Girl in the Rain

Joanna Shimkus . . . . Lisa Alren
- • 1:27—Very, very brief silhouette of left breast, while going into towel closet with Richard Benjamin.

The Marriage of Maria Braun *(1979; German)*

Hanna Schygulla . . . . Maria Braun
- • 0:22—Brief upper half of right breast, when peeking from behind divider in doctor's office.
- • 0:33—Buns, while lying in bed with her lover.
- • 0:34—Brief buns and left breast, while standing up in doctor's office. Subtitles get in the way.
- •• 1:15—Buns, while dropping sheet in room with her boss.

Married People, Single Sex *(1993)*

Chase Masterson . . . . Beth
- • 0:30—Buns in lingerie, while trying on clothes with her girlfriends.

Shelley Michelle. . . . . Carol
- ••• 0:54—Breasts and buns in G-string, garter belt and stockings while dancing on stage.
- ••• 1:05—Breasts and buns in black G-string, after opening her bathrobe and giving Will a private dance in the kitchen.

Darla Slavens . . . . Fran
- •• 0:03—In white bra and buns in panties while undressing in bedroom. Full frontal nudity, walking to closet.
- •• 0:10—In white bra, then breasts while undressing in bedroom.
- ••• 0:53—Left breast in mirror, while trying out vibrator.

Teri Thompson . . . . Meg
- • 0:33—Right breast after having phone sex with Artie.
- • 0:55—Nude, while talking with Artie on the phone.
- •• 1:18—Breasts and buns when Artie pushes her off him and she puts on robe.

Wendi Westbrook . . . . Shelley
- ••• 0:16—Breasts, in bed with her husband, then getting out and back in bed.
- • 0:31—Buns while in purple lingerie with her girlfriends.

  0:45—In sheer blue lingerie with Richard.

••• 0:48—Right breast under Will, making love while wearing mask. Breasts and very, very brief lower frontal nudity, while getting out of bed and putting on bra.
• 1:03—Right breast, while kneeling on floor in front of Richard.

Married People, Single Sex 2: For Better or Worse *(1994)*

Rainer Grant . . . . Karen
• 0:01—Breasts, while making love in bed with Sam.
• 0:02—Brief buns and breasts, while lying in bed, getting spanked.
••• 0:32—Right breast several times, then breasts while making love in bed with David.
•• 0:53—Brief left breast, then breasts, while in doorway with David.
• 1:11—Very brief partial breasts and buns in bra and panties on bed during fight with Sam.

Tamara Landry . . . . Monica
••• 0:28—Breasts, while in office with John.
• 0:54—Breasts, while crawling on John's desk.
• 0:55—Breasts, while in office with John.
••• 1:17—Breasts, while making love on desk with John in his office.

Tané McClure . . . . House Buyer

Monique Parent . . . . .Valerie
• 0:00—Brief right breast, while making love in bed with David.
• 0:13—Brief breasts, behind sliding glass door, showing off her body for John.
••• 0:14—Breasts, while wearing panties, in the house with John.
•• 0:16—Breasts, when John ties her wrists up with drapery cord and makes love while standing up.
••• 0:18—Breasts, while standing in bedroom and talking with John afterward.
•• 0:35—In slip, then breasts when wearing panties, while talking with John.
•• 0:59—Breasts while wearing panties, taking off her dress in living room in front of David.

Kathy Shower . . . . .Carol
••• 0:47—Breasts, after getting out of shower in bathroom with John.
••• 1:14—Breasts, while lying in bed with John.

Julie Strain. . . . . S&M Woman
•• 1:21—Breasts and buns in panties in motel room bed with David when Karen watches helplessly while tied by her wrists to doorway.

Married to the Mob *(1988)*

Michelle Pfeiffer . . . . .Angela de Marco

Nancy Travis . . . . Karen Lutnick
•• 0:15—Very brief breasts, when getting out of bed. Buns and brief side view of right breast, with Dean Stockwell in hotel room. Breasts in the bathtub.

The Married Woman *(1964; French)*

Macha Meril . . . . .Charlotte
• 0:07—Brief glimpses of breasts while walking around inside house.
• 0:08—Brief side of left breast, when climbing through window from outside.

Martial Law II: Undercover *(1992)*

Bridget Carney . . . . Flash Dancer

Deborah Driggs. . . . . Tiffany
• 0:59—Side of left breast, while taking off lingerie and getting into bed with Billy Drago.
• 1:00—Breasts, rolling off Drago after he passes out.

Denice Duff . . . . Nancy Borelli

Kimber Monroe. . . . . Celeste

Sherrie Rose. . . . . Bree

Mary, Mary, Bloody Mary *(1975)*

Cristina Ferrare . . . . .Mary
•• 0:07—Brief breasts making love with some guy on the couch just before she kills him.
••• 0:41—Breasts when Greta helps pull down Ferrare's top to take a bath.
• 1:12—Bun and brief silhouette of left breast getting out of bed and getting dressed.

Helena Rojo . . . . Greta
• 0:42—Buns and brief breasts getting into bathtub with Cristina Ferrare.

Masala *(1993; Canadian)*

Tova Gallimore . . . . Saraswati
•• 1:00—Full frontal nudity and very brief buns, while making love with Anil in his dream.

Mascara *(1987; French/Belgian)*

Charlotte Rampling . . . . .Gaby Hart
• 1:03—Brief breasts putting on sweater when Michael Sarrazin watches through binoculars.
• 1:18—Right breast, while making love with Chris.

Alexandra Vandernoot. . . . . .Euridice

Masquerade *(1988)*

Kim Cattrall . . . . Mrs. Brooke Morrison
••• 0:04—Breasts in bed with Rob Lowe.

Dana Delany . . . . .Anne Briscoe

Cristen Kauffman. . . . . .Holly

Meg Tilly . . . . Olivia Lawrence

Massacre at Central High *(1976)*

Kimberly Beck . . . . .Theresa
• 0:32—Nude romping in the ocean with David. Long shot, dark, hard to see anything.
•• 0:42—Breasts on the beach making love with Andrew Stevens after a hang glider crash.

Lani O'Grady. . . . . Jane
••• 1:09—Breasts walking out of a tent and getting back into it with Rainbeaux Smith and Robert Carradine.

Cheryl Smith . . . . .Mary
• 0:27—Brief breasts in a classroom getting attacked by some guys.
••• 1:09—Nude walking around on a mountain side with Robert Carradine and Lani O'Grady.

Masseuse *(1995)*

(Unrated version reviewed.)

Griffin Drew . . . . Kristy
• 0:23—Buns, in lingerie in bedroom.
••• 0:24—Breasts, while making love in bed with Jack.
••• 0:50—Breasts, while in bathtub with Connor during her dream.

Sherri Graham . . . . Sheila
•• 0:54—Breasts and buns in lingerie, while in hotel room with Jack.

Gail Harris . . . . Diane
•• 0:08—In bra, then breasts and buns, while making out in office with Jack.

Julianne J. Mantia . . . . Carol
••• 0:56—Breasts, after taking off her bra, then making love with a guy.
Monique Parent . . . . J.J.
••• 0:16—Nude, while standing in pool, tempting the pool guy.
Meaghan Prester . . . . Michelle
••• 1:17—Buns and breasts, while in bedroom with a customer.
Amy Rochelle . . . . Rosa
••• 0:32—Breasts and buns, while making love in bed with Jack when seen by Griffin Drew.
Bianca Rocilili . . . . Gina
•• 1:19—Breasts, while making out with a customer on bed.
Brittany Rollins . . . . Suzy
•• 1:20—Breasts, while in bedroom with a customer.
Brinke Stevens . . . . Hotel Manager

Master of Dragonard Hill (1987)

Kimber Monroe . . . . Jane Abdee
•• 0:08—Breasts making love in bed with Richard.
Claudia Udy . . . . Arabella
••• 0:11—Nude, undressing to seduce Calabar. More breasts and buns while kissing him.
•• 0:14—Silhouette of breasts while making love with Calabar, then breasts.
• 0:58—Brief buns and side of right breast during flash back. Brief right breast when she gets out of bed.

Masterblaster (1986)

Tracey E. Hutchinson . . . . Lisa
••• 0:57—Breasts taking a shower (wearing panties).
Kari Whitman . . . . Jennifer

Mata Hari (1985)

Sylvia Kristel . . . . Mata Hari
••• 0:11—Breasts making love with a guy on a train.
•• 0:31—Breasts standing by window after making love with the soldier.
• 0:35—Breasts making love in empty house by the fireplace.
•• 0:52—Breasts masturbating in bed wearing black stockings.
•• 1:02—Breasts during sword fight with another topless woman.
•• 1:03—Breasts in bed smoking opium and making love with two women.

Matador (1986; Spanish)

Eva Cobo . . . . Eva Soler
•• 0:09—Breasts drying herself off after shower when Angel watches her through binoculars.
• 0:29—Full frontal nudity in bed with Diego.
Carmen Maura . . . . Julie
Assumpta Serna . . . . Maria Cardinal
• 0:03—Breasts taking off wrap and making love with a guy just before she kills him.
••• 1:38—Breasts on floor with Diego. Long shot, hard to see. Breasts in front of the fire.
• 1:41—Brief breasts making love with Diego.
• 1:43—Breasts lying on floor dead.

• *Maui Heat: Swimsuit Edition* (1996)

Kim Dawson . . . . Laura Turner
••• 1:25—Nude, while making love with Jake on the beach at night.
Cory Lane . . . . Shawn Daniels
•• 0:11—Breasts, while changing clothes in bedroom.
••• 0:16—Nude, while making love with Mitch.
Kira Reed . . . . Sara
••• 0:44—Nude, while making love with Mitch.
• 0:54—Buns in swimsuit while walking by the pool.
••• 0:58—Nude, while making love on the beach with Mitch and Karlie.
••• 1:02—Nude, while making love indoors with Mitch and Karlie.
Kimberly Rowe . . . . Dakota
• 0:39—Partial buns in swimsuit, while posing during photo shoot.
•• 0:51—Breasts under sheer red swimsuit. Full frontal nudity, while changing swimsuits.
• 0:54—Breasts, while sunbathing on lounge chair, holding an umbrella.
••• 1:06—Nude, while with Jake at the beach and waterfalls.
Kim Yates . . . . Karlie
••• 0:18—Breasts and buns, while joining Jake in the spa.
• 0:23—Brief left breast, when taking off her swimsuit top.
• 0:24—Buns in swimsuit during photo session.
• 0:33—Buns in swimsuits during photo session.
••• 0:35—Nude, while video taping herself on the bed.
•• 0:52—Breasts, taking off her robe and joining Dakota in pool.
• 0:54—Breasts, while sunbathing on lounge chair.
••• 0:58—Nude, while making love on the beach with Mitch and Sara.
••• 1:02—Nude, while making love indoors with Mitch and Sara.

Mausoleum (1983)

Bobbie Bresee . . . . Susan Farrell
••• 0:25—Breasts and buns wrapping a towel around herself in her bedroom.
•• 0:26—Breasts on the balcony showing herself to the gardener.
• 0:29—Breasts in the garage with the gardener. Brief, dark, hard to see.
• 0:32—Brief left breast, while kissing Marjoe Gortner.
• 1:10—Breasts in the bathtub talking to Gortner. Long shot.
Laura Hippe . . . . Aunt Cora

Maximum Force (1992)

Sherrie Rose . . . . Cody Randal
• 0:59—Breasts, while in bed with Sam Jones.

• *Maximum Revenge* (1997)

Michelle Bauer . . . . Shana
Landon Hall . . . . Tracy Quinn
••• 0:54—Buns and breasts, while making love with Mace.
Monique Parent . . . . Katya
Deanne Power . . . . Wife
••• 0:11—Breasts, while making love with Richard.

• *Maximum Risk* (1996)

Natasha Henstridge . . . . Alex
• 0:45—Brief breasts and partial buns in panties, while changing clothes.
•• 1:10—In black bra, then breasts and brief buns, while making love with Jean-Claude Van Damme in bathroom.

Me & Him (1988; West German)

Ellen Greene . . . . Anette Uttanzi

Carey Lowell . . . . Janet Anderson
- 0:37—Very brief upper half of right breast sticking out of nightgown after turning over in bed with Griffin Dunne.

Mean Dog Blues *(1978)*

Christina Hart . . . . Gloria Kinsman
- •• 1:24—Brief breasts, in house with Gregg Henry.

Kay Lenz . . . . Linda Ramsey
Tina Louise . . . . Donna Lacey
- 1:16—Very brief side view of right breast, while getting up off massage table. Don't see her face very well.

The Mean Season *(1985)*

Mariel Hemingway . . . . Christine Connelly
- •• 0:15—Breasts, while taking a shower.

Mean Streets *(1973)*

Jeannie Bell . . . . Diane
- 0:07—Breasts dancing on stage with pasties on.
- 1:00—Breasts backstage wearing pasties.

Meatballs 4 *(1992)*

Neriah Davis . . . . Neriah
- 0:05—Very brief buns, while getting her red towel pulled up by another girl while walking to the showers.

Kristie Ducati. . . . . Kristi
- 0:05—Very, very brief buns, getting her light blue robe pulled up by Neriah while walking to the showers. Long shot.
- 0:06—Brief side of left breast, while taking a shower with three other girls. (She's on the far right in the first shot.)
- •• 0:37—Breasts, four times, while playing strip charades.
- 0:54—Left breast, while riding behind a guy on a four wheel motorcycle. (She's the one closest to the camera.)

Paige French . . . . Jennifer Lipton
- •• 0:27—Breasts outside with Wes.
- 0:29—Brief breasts, after being splashed with water.

Lauren Hays . . . . Lauren
- 0:05—Brief breasts (she's on the far right), while taking off her black top in cabin with Miche and Hillary.

Monique Noel. . . . . Lovelie #1
Cristy Thom . . . . Hillary
- ••• 0:38—Breasts, taking off her blouse and washing herself off.

Mediterraneo *(1991; Italian)*

Vana Barba . . . . Vassilissa
- •• 1:03—Side of left breast, while in bed with Antonio.

Irene Grazioli. . . . . Pastorella
- ••• 0:36—Breasts with the Munaron brothers.
- 0:52—Brief breasts, swimming in water.

Medium Cool *(1969)*

Mariana Hill . . . . Ruth
- 0:18—Close-up of breast in bed with John.
- •• 0:36—Nude, running around the house frolicking with John.

• Meet Wally Sparks *(1996)*

Cindy Ambuehl . . . . Lola Larue
- 1:10—Very, very brief breasts on fax that David Ogden Stiers slams on his desk. B&W.
- 1:20—Very, very brief left breast in color photo. Difficult to see.

Lesley-Anne Down . . . . Hooker Nurse
Debi Mazar . . . . Sandy Galo

Melanie *(1982)*

Glynnis O'Connor . . . . Melanie
- 0:08—Very brief right breast, while turning over in bed next to Don Johnson.
- •• 0:09—Breasts, while sitting up and putting on a T-shirt, then getting out of bed.

Melody in Love *(1978; German)*

Scarlett Gunden . . . . Angela
- ••• 0:17—Full frontal nudity taking off dress and dancing in front of statue.
- ••• 0:50—Nude with a guy on a boat.
- •• 0:53—Breasts on another boat with Octavio.
- •• 0:59—Buns and breasts in bed talking to Rachel.
- •• 1:12—Full frontal nudity getting a tan on boat with Rachel.
- 1:14—Breasts making love in bed with Rachel and Octavio.

Melvin and Howard *(1980)*

Martine Beswicke . . . . Real Estate Woman
Denise Galik . . . . Lucy
Pamela Reed . . . . Bonnie Dummar
Mary Steenburgen. . . . . Lynda Dummar
- •• 0:31—Breasts and buns, ripping off barmaid outfit and walking out the door.

Men of War *(1994)*

Catherine Bell . . . . Grace
Charlotte Lewis . . . . Loki
- •• 0:44—Breasts, in pond under waterfall, while bathing with the other townspeople.
- •• 0:53—Brief breasts, with Dolph Lundgren, outside at night. A bit dark.

The Men's Club *(1986)*

Penny Baker . . . . Lake
- •• 1:13—Breasts while lying in bed with Treat Williams.

Ann Dusenberry . . . . Page
- •• 1:04—Breasts while lying in bed after making love with Roy Scheider.

Gina Gallego . . . . Felicia
Marilyn Jones. . . . . Allison
- •• 1:21—Breasts, while in bedroom talking to Harvey Keitel, then putting on dress.

Jennifer Jason Leigh . . . . Teensy
Cindy Pickett. . . . . Hannah
Helen Shaver . . . . Sarah (uncredited)
- •• 0:13—Breasts under Roy Scheider in bed, then breasts again, getting back into bed.

Gwen Welles . . . . Redhead

The Mephisto Waltz *(1971)*

Jacqueline Bisset . . . . Paula Clarkson
- 0:48—Very brief right and side view of left breast in bed with Alan Alda.
- •• 1:45—Very brief breasts twice under bloody water in blood covered bathtub, dead. Discovered by Kathleen Widdoes.

Barbara Parkins . . . . Roxanne
- 1:26—Left breast, while kissing Alan Alda during witchcraft sequence.

• Mercenary *(1996)*

Lara Harris . . . . Joanna Ambler
Patricia Skeriotis. . . . . Kurdish Woman
- 0:57—Very brief nude, several times, during fight and after getting killed.

Meridian *(1989)*
a.k.a. Kiss of the Beast
a.k.a. Phantoms
Sherilyn Fenn . . . . Catherine
•• 0:23—White bra and panties, getting clothes taken off by Lawrence, then breasts.
••• 0:28—Breasts in bed with Oliver.
•• 0:51—Breasts getting her blouse ripped open lying in bed.
Charlie Spradling. . . . . Gina
•• 0:22—Breasts getting her blouse torn off by Lawrence while lying on the table.
••• 0:28—Breasts standing next to fireplace, then breasts on the couch. Hot!

• **Mermaids of the Aztec Empire** *(1992; Video Tape)*
Tia. . . . . Mona Brock
•• 0:01—Breasts during opening credits.
••• 0:02—Breasts and buns in G-string at the beach during opening credits.
•• 0:06—Breasts outside with Lori Pallett by pool and under water.
•• 0:10—In bra and panties, then breasts in jewelry store fantasy.
• 0:11—Buns, in swimsuit, by the pool.
• 0:13—Brief buns, while turning over in the spa.
••• 0:14—Breasts and buns in G-string bottom on boat.
••• 0:23—Breasts and buns at the beach. Long scene.
••• 0:31—Breasts and buns in G-string while snorkeling under water.
••• 0:37—Breasts and buns at the beach again.
••• 0:49—Breasts and buns in swimsuit bottoms undressing at the beach during the end credits.
Lori Deann Pallett . . . . Carla Monroe
•• 0:01—Breasts scuba diving under water during the opening credits.
••• 0:04—Breasts, wearing swimsuit bottom, posing for photographer outside by pool.
•• 0:06—Breasts outside by pool and under water.
••• 0:13—Breasts on boat.
••• 0:15—Breasts and buns in swimsuit bottom while scuba diving under water.
•• 0:19—Full frontal nudity during disco fantasy.
••• 0:23—Breasts and buns at the beach. Long scene.
••• 0:33—Breasts, while snorkeling under water.
••• 0:37—Breasts and buns at the beach again.
••• 0:41—Breasts, while scuba diving.
••• 0:45—Breasts in spa by herself, then with a girlfriend.
••• 0:49—Breasts and buns, wearing swimsuit bottom, undressing at the beach during the end credits.

Metamorphosis *(1989)*
Laura Gemser . . . . Prostitute
• 0:37—Very brief breasts several times in Peter's flashback.
• 0:43—Very brief breasts in flashback again.

Miami Blues *(1990)*
Martine Beswicke . . . . Noira
Kerrie Clark . . . . Hooker
Jennifer Jason Leigh. . . . . Susie Waggoner
• 0:07—Very brief upper half of right breast, while changing clothes behind Alec Baldwin.
••• 0:10—Breasts in panties, taking off red dress and getting into bed.
• 0:24—Very, very brief half of right breast while taking a bath. Long shot.
• 0:33—Breasts making love with Baldwin in the kitchen.

• **Miami Hustle** *(1996; Made for Cable Movie)*
Audie England . . . . Jean Ivers
• 0:26—Partial buns in panties while starting to do a strip routine for a customer in bar.
• 0:41—Partial buns in panties in outfit in bar again.
• 0:43—Partial buns in panties in upstairs room with a customer.

Midnight *(1989)*
Rita Gam . . . . Heidi
Kathleen Kinmont . . . . Party
Lynn Redgrave. . . . . Midnight
Karen Witter . . . . Missy Angel
• 0:32—In bed with Mickey. Nice squished breasts against him, but only a very brief side view of left breast.

• **Midnight Blue** *(1996)*
Sung Hi Lee. . . . . Streetwalker
Shelley Michelle. . . . . .Body Double
• 1:12—Brief side of left breast and buns, while lying next to Damian Chapa in his fantasy.
Shauna O'Brien . . . . Sandra
Annabel Schofield . . . . Martine/Georgina
••• 0:11—In bra and panties, then breasts, while making love in hotel room with Chapa.
• 0:15—Breasts, when sitting up in bed and getting out to look at painting.
• 0:46—Brief breasts and buns, in bed during flashbacks.
• 0:55—In bra and panties, then brief right breast, when undressing inside when Chapa watches from outside.
•• 1:11—Breasts, while making love with Chapa in bed.

Midnight Cabaret *(1988)*
Esther Alise . . . . Dancer
Lydie Denier . . . . Woman in White
Laura Harrington . . . . Tanya Richards
• 0:33—Very, very brief upper half of right breast while leaning back.
• 0:34—Very, very brief left breast when a guy sticks his tongue out.
• 0:43—Brief breasts when short guys rip her dress off.
• 0:49—Very brief right breast in gaping nightgown, while bending over to put pants on.
• 1:08—Brief breasts while making love with a guy.
Debra Lamb. . . . . Dancer
Christina Whitaker. . . . . Dancer

Midnight Confessions *(1993)*
(Unrated version reviewed.)
Annastasia Alexander. . . . . Britt
••• 0:37—Nude, while performing oral sex on a customer.
Lisa Comshaw . . . . .Allyn
••• 0:31—Breasts and buns, while making love with Monique Parent.
Diana Cuevas. . . . . Candice
••• 0:51—Breasts and brief buns, while making love with her husband.
Alexa Fiery. . . . . .Nikki
• 0:03—In red bra, then breasts, while undressing in the back seat of a car.
Carol Hoyt. . . . . Vanessa
••• 1:13—Buns in lingerie, then breasts and buns while making love. Don't see her face well.
••• 1:18—Breasts, while taking a shower behind glass door.

Monique Parent . . . . Joni
••• 0:31—Full frontal nudity, while making love with Lisa Comshaw.
Deanne Power . . . . Mrs. Parker
••• 0:14—Breasts and buns, while making love in her house with Ryan.
Amy Rochelle . . . . Renee
••• 0:49—In black leather outfit, then full frontal nudity undressing and then dressing back up.
Julie Strain. . . . . Mariana
•• 0:04—In bra and panties, then breasts and buns, while talking on the phone to the radio talk show host.
•• 0:07—Breasts and buns, while caressing herself and talking on the phone some more.

Midnight Cowboy *(1969)*

Viva. . . . . Gretel McAlbertson
Sylvia Miles . . . . Cass
• 0:20—Brief buns, running into bedroom and jumping onto bed with Jon Voight. More when changing the TV channel with the remote control. Most of her right breast in bed under Voight.
Jennifer Salt. . . . . Annie
• 0:31—Very brief buns, while running away from some bad guys in flashback.
• 0:42—Brief left breast on bed with Voight in flashback.
• 0:49—Very brief breasts in car in B&W flashback. More brief breasts and buns in car and running on porch.
Brenda Vaccaro. . . . . Shirley
• 1:30—Very, very brief out of focus left breast in open fur coat, lying down with Jon Voight.
• 1:31—Very brief left breast when falling back onto bed with Voight.
•• 1:32—Brief right breast, while rolling in bed with Voight.

Midnight Crossing *(1988)*

Kim Cattrall. . . . . Alexa Schubb
Crisstyn Dante. . . . . Body Double for Kim Cattrall
• 0:29—Brief left breast making love on small boat, body double for Kim Cattrall.
Faye Dunaway. . . . . Helen Barton

Midnight Dancer *(1987; Australian)*

a.k.a. Belinda
Robyn Moase . . . . Brenda
• 0:43—Brief breasts while putting on black top.
Mary Regan . . . . Crystal
•• 0:29—Breasts in dressing room, undressing and rubbing make-up on herself.
•• 0:56—In bra, then breasts in panties, changing clothes and getting into bed.
Kathryn Walker . . . . Kathy

Midnight Edition *(1993)*

Sarabeth Tucek . . . . Becky Gallagher
• 0:15—Breasts, after Darryl pushes her back onto the bed and points a gun at her.
Clare Wren . . . . Sarah Travers

Midnight Express *(1978; British)*

Irene Miracle. . . . . Susan
•• 1:40—Breasts in prison visiting booth showing her breasts to Brad Davis so he can masturbate.

Midnight Heat *(1994)*

Mimi Craven . . . . Alison Miller
• 0:08—Brief cleavage in open robe while standing at the window, then very brief breasts, hard to see because of fog on the window.
• 0:10—Breasts (don't see her face), while in bed with Kathrin Nicholson.
••• 0:17—In bra, garter belt and stockings, then breasts, while making love with Tim Matheson.
•• 0:34—Breasts in open robe, while making out with Matheson.
•• 0:36—Left breast, while making love with Matheson.
• 0:37—Breasts, while swimming in the pool, seen through water.
• 0:38—Breasts, while making love with Matheson in pool.
• 0:39—Breasts, while making love with Matheson in bed.
•• 1:02—Left breast, while lying in bed with Matheson.
Kathrin Nicholson . . . . Vivian Grey
• 0:10—Very, very brief blurry right breast, getting up out of bed to answer the door. (She's in bed, caressing Mimi Craven.)

Midnight Tease *(1994)*

Lisa Boyle . . . . Samantha
•• 0:02—Breasts in lingerie outfit, walking up to her stepfather and slicing his throat.
• 0:11—Buns in T-back and in bra, while undressing, then lying on bed.
•• 0:12—Breasts in lingerie outfit, while killing her stepfather in dream.
•• 0:24—Breasts, after opening her leather jacket on table in front of Dr. Saul.
••• 0:37—Breasts, while making love with Dr. Saul in his office.
••• 0:44—Breasts and buns in T-back while dancing on stage with Mantra.
•• 0:47—Breasts while talking with Mantra in dressing room.
•• 0:50—Breasts in lingerie outfit in dream, while slitting Mantra's throat.
••• 0:53—Full frontal nudity while taking a shower behind clear plastic curtain.
•• 0:58—In white bra and panties, then breasts and buns after stripping out of schoolgirl outfit. Intercut with flashbacks of her stepfather's suicide.
Melissa Dutton . . . . Satchi
•• 0:00—Breasts and buns during opening credits.
••• 0:04—Breasts and buns in silver T-back while stripping and dancing on stage.
Nicole Grey . . . . Dusty
••• 0:17—Breasts after stripping out of policewoman's uniform on stage.
Ashlie Rhey . . . . Mantra
•• 0:00—Breasts and buns during opening credits.
••• 0:42—Buns and breasts in black dominatrix outfit while dancing on stage with Samantha.
•• 0:47—Breasts while talking with Samantha in dressing room.
• 0:50—Breasts, when whipping Samantha's stepfather in dream while Samantha kills her.
Stephanie Sumers . . . . Tiffany
•• 0:00—Breasts and buns, while dancing during opening credits.
••• 0:07—Breasts and buns in T-back, while dancing on stage.
••• 0:09—Breasts, while dressing and talking to Samantha in dressing room.

••• 0:12—Nude, while making love on top of Samantha's stepfather, then getting killed in dream.
0:14—Breasts while tied to pole in club with a slit throat and covered with blood.
• 0:50—Breasts with slit throat and blood in dream.

Midnight Tease 2 (1995)

Erin Weidner Ashley. . . . . Shane
• 0:05—Breast breasts and buns in T-back, garter belt and stockings while dancing on stage.
• 0:53—Brief breasts, while dancing on stage.
••• 0:55—Breasts and buns, while dancing on stage.
•• 1:00—Breasts while dancing on stage.

Debra Beatty . . . . Sandra
•• 1:05—Breasts and buns in T-back while dancing on stage with Griffin Drew.

Antonia Dorian . . . . Stephanie

Griffin Drew . . . . Desiree
• 0:04—Brief breasts, while dancing on stage.
• 0:07—Buns in T-back, while in dressing room.
• 0:20—Breasts while in dressing room.
••• 0:37—Doing strip routine on stage, buns in T-back then breasts.
•• 1:05—Buns in T-back and breasts, while dancing on stage with Debra Beatty.

Kimberly Kelley . . . . Jennifer Brennan
•• 0:01—Breasts, while dancing in front of killer before getting killed (she's playing the part of her sister, Amy).
•• 0:12—In bra, then breasts and buns in T-back while doing strip routine on stage.
• 0:15—Breasts under sheer black blouse, while getting dressed.
••• 0:17—Buns and breasts under sheer black bodysuit, then breasts when doing a lap dance for Paul.
•• 0:30—Buns in red bodysuit, then breasts when doing lap dance.
••• 0:52—Breasts while making love in bed.
••• 0:57—Breasts, while dancing on stage and doing strip routine.

Kim Kopf. . . . . Katlin Clark
•• 0:28—Buns in T-back and bra, then breasts.

Tané McClure . . . . Lacy

Tammy Parks. . . . . .Misty
••• 0:06—Breasts and buns in T-back while doing strip routine on stage.
•• 0:09—Breasts and buns in T-back while in dressing room.
• 0:27—Breasts, while dancing in front of the killer before getting killed.

Julie Kristen Smith . . . . .Cherry
••• 0:02—Buns in outfit while dancing on stage in club. In black bra, panties, garter belt and stockings, then breasts.
••• 0:10—Breasts and buns in T-back while dancing on stage.
• 0:20—Breasts, while in dressing room.
• 0:45—Brief breasts, while dancing on stage.
•• 0:47—Breasts and buns in T-back while doing dance for killer before getting killed.

• *Midnight Temptations* (1995)

Ava Fabian. . . . . Raya
• 0:12—Brief buns, while making love with a guy in storage area while Wendy Hamilton watches.
•• 1:14—Breasts, while making love with Jonathon.

Jordana Gowan . . . . .Beach Model
• 1:01—Buns in T-back, after taking off her clothes and walking away on the beach.

Wendy Hamilton . . . . April
•• 0:22—Breasts, while taking a shower.
••• 0:27—Breasts, while making love with Damon. Long scene.
•• 1:08—Breasts and buns in body suit, while making love with Danny.
• 1:20—Brief breasts in flashback.

• *Midnight Temptations 2* (1997)

Jenna Bodnar. . . . . Southern Woman
••• 0:50—Breasts, while making love with the Confederate soldier.

Lucie Malkrabova. . . . . .French Woman
•• 0:37—Breasts, while making love with the French Soldier.

Karolina Mirosova . . . . Revolutionary Woman
•• 1:03—Breasts, while making love with the revolutionary man.
• 1:05—Breasts, while making love with the stable boy.

Midnight Witness (1992)

Lisa Boyle. . . . . .Heidi
•• 1:11—Breasts, while getting out of bed. Buns and breasts some more, seen in mirror.

Kelli Maroney . . . . Devon

Karen Moncrieff. . . . . Katy
• 1:08—Very brief buns, while making love with Paul in bed in motel (don't see her face). Very brief part of right nipple. Very brief right breast, when falling back onto bed (medium long shot).

• *A Midsummer Night's Dream* (1968; British)

Judi Dench. . . . . Titania
• 0:21—Very brief breasts, while running through the woods before meeting Oberon.
• 0:22—Brief breasts, while giving a monologue. She's wearing plant-like pasties.
• 0:32—Brief breasts, several times, while in the woods with the fairies. She has green colored skin and plant-looking pasties.
• 0:51—Brief breasts, while talking to Bottom (he's got a donkey head). Her hair gets in the way.
• 0:53—Breasts, while standing behind Bottom when he's talking with the other fairies. Plant-like pasties get in the way.
• 1:57—Brief breasts, covered with the plant-like pasties again, while walking around in the house.

Helen Mirren . . . . Hermia

Mike's Murder (1984)

Kym Malin. . . . . Beautiful Girl #1

Debra Winger . . . . .Betty
• 0:26—Brief left breast in bathtub.

Mikey (1992)

Josie Bissett . . . . .Jessie

Mimi Craven . . . . Rachel Trenton
•• 0:52—Breasts, sitting in bathtub when Mikey comes into the bathroom to talk.

Ashley Laurence. . . . . Shawn Gilder

Millions (1990)

Carol Alt . . . . Beta

Catherine Hickland . . . . Connie
• 0:36—Buns, getting out of bed to open safe. Don't see her face, probably a body double because the hair is too dark.
• 1:20—Buns, walking away from John Stockwell. Very brief back side of right breast, when she bends over to pick up blouse. Don't see her face.

Lauren Hutton . . . . Christina
Alexandra Paul . . . . Julia
••• 0:44—Breasts while making love in bed with Billy Zane.
• 0:59—Breasts in bed with Zane.

Mind Games *(1996)*
Maria Ford . . . . Ivory/Tess
•• 0:00—Buns and breasts, while making love in bed with Brian Krause.
• 0:04—Brief side view of buns and breasts, while committing suicide in bathtub.
• 0:18—Brief partial right breast, while sitting in bathtub in flashback.
• 0:53—Brief breasts, while making love with Brian Krause.

Mind Twister *(1992)*
(Unrated version reviewed.)
Deborah Dutch . . . . Sheila Harrison
•• 0:01—Brief breasts, after smashing her head through window to scream for help. Left breast, while dead on the floor.
•• 0:04—Breasts, while dead on the floor when photographed by police.
•• 0:05—More brief left breast shots while on the floor. Breasts, while getting put in body bag.
•• 1:22—In bra, then breasts on TV monitor during video playback that Heather watches.
Maria Ford . . . . Melanie Duncan
Erika Nann . . . . Lisa Strahten
••• 0:28—Breasts, while making love in candlelit bathtub with a young stud.
0:33—In black lingerie in bedroom with Daniel.
• 0:37—Breasts, while in bed with Daniel.
0:42—In sheer black body suit in bathroom while talking to Daniel.
0:49—In black bra, panties, garter belt and stockings.
0:54—In black lingerie outfit.
••• 0:56—Breasts and buns, while making love with Heather while getting videotaped by Daniel.
• 1:22—In lingerie on TV monitor during video playback. Buns, while wrestling with Sheila.
Suzanne Slater . . . . Heather Black
••• 0:17—Breasts and partial buns, while making love on sofa with Roy. Long scene.
• 0:39—Inside half of left breast in open robe when pizza delivery guy sees her.
••• 0:56—Breasts and buns, while in bed with Lisa while getting videotaped by Daniel. A little bit of fluorescent paint added to her breasts for color. Great!

Mind, Body & Soul *(1992)*
Toni Alessandrini . . . . Priestess Tura
•• 1:05—Breasts under fishnet body stocking during occult dance in a house.
Ginger Lynn Allen . . . . Brenda
•• 0:13—Breasts in open blouse while getting raped in jail by a guard.
••• 0:17—Breasts while talking with her boyfriend in open blouse and dripping candle wax on him.
••• 1:10—Breasts while lying in bed with her boyfriend, Sean.
Veronica Carothers . . . . Sacrifice Girl
••• 0:02—Breasts when her dress is ripped open during occult ceremony while tied by her wrists.
•• 0:26—Left breast several times and very, very brief right breast in black outfit (her face is covered with a hood) during occult ceremony.

Miracle Beach *(1991)*
Monique Gabrielle . . . . Cindy Beatty
•• 0:03—Breasts in bed with a guy when Scotty comes home. Breasts getting out of bed and getting dressed. (Note in first shot when she's lying in bed, she doesn't have a dress around her waist, then in the next shot when she stands up, she does.)
Michelle Grassnick . . . . Miss Great Britain
• 0:35—Brief buns in swimsuit bottom, then right breast, while lying in bed, talking with Lars.
••• 1:03—Breasts, while trying on swimsuits backstage.
Wendy Kaye . . . . Girl in Bed
• 0:14—Breasts, while lying in bed next to Scotty, then sitting up. (She's on the left.)
Dawn Morgan . . . . Miss Chile
• 0:48—Brief breasts, when winning bingo game.
Brittany York . . . . Girl in Bed
•• 0:14—Breasts, lying in bed next to Scotty, then sitting up. She's on the right.

Mirage *(1995)*
Sean Young . . . . Jennifer Gale
• 0:15—Buns in sexy outfit, while dancing on stage in bar.
• 0:19—Nude, getting out of a steamy shower.
• 1:04—Brief breasts, while lying in bed, opening the covers for Edward James Olmos.
• 1:05—Brief partial buns and side of left breast, while making love in bed with Olmos.

Mirror Images *(1991)*
Lee Anne Beaman . . . . Rebecca
••• 1:11—Buns in G-string, then breasts in conference room, undressing in front of Jeff Conaway and Carter.
Delia Sheppard . . . . Kaitlin/Shauna
•• 0:07—Right breast, while undressing in front of vanity mirror.
•• 0:08—More breasts as Shauna in bed.
• 0:12—Buns, while dancing on stage with a band, wearing a sexy outfit.
••• 0:14—Breasts in bed with Georgio.
••• 0:27—Breasts and buns in G-string, making love with Joey. Long scene.
••• 0:33—Buns in black bra and panties, walking around her sister's apartment. Long scene.
•• 0:39—Right breast, while with a guy with a mask.
••• 0:41—Nude, taking a shower. Great!
••• 0:43—Breasts in bedroom after her shower.
•• 0:48—Left breast, while making love in bed with Julie Strain.
••• 1:29—Breasts in bed in lingerie with the policeman.
Domonique Simone . . . . Slave Girl
••• 0:58—Buns in G-string, then breasts with masked guy.
••• 1:00—Breasts on bed with masked guy and Julie Strain.
Julie Strain . . . . Gina
•• 0:48—Buns and right breast, making love in bed with Kaitlin.
•• 0:49—Buns in black bra and panties.
• 0:57—Buns in black body suit.
••• 0:58—Breasts lying on bed, watching the slave girl and guy with the mask make love.
Janie Wilson . . . . 1st Girl in Commercial
•• 0:17—Breasts (she's on the right) on a guy's shoulders in pool, wrestling with another couple.

Mirror Images II (1993)

Sara Suzanne Brown . . . . Prostitute

••• 0:13—In red bra and panties, then breasts and buns while making love with Clete in motel room. Long scene.

Shannon Whirry . . . . Carrie/Terrie

••• 0:03—Nude, while taking a shower during the opening credits. Then breasts, while making love on top of her twin sister's boyfriend in bed.

• 0:19—Buns in panties and bra while trying on lingerie in front of mirror.

••• 0:25—Full frontal nudity while making love with her female psychologist, Dr. Rubin. Long scene.

••• 0:31—Nude, while making love outside in pool with Dan before getting caught by Phyllis

••• 0:39—In black bra, then full frontal nudity while making love on bed with Clete. She gives him a hot wax treatment. Long scene.

• 0:49—Breasts, while making love in bed with a customer while Jake watches from outside the window. Long shot.

••• 0:56—In black bra and panties, the full frontal nudity while making love in bedroom with a customer.

•• 1:01—In white bra, then breasts and buns in G-string with another woman in hotel room.

••• 1:10—Breasts, while making love in bed with Jake. Long scene.

• 1:27—Breasts while making love with Jake (in B&W).

Mirror Mirror (1990)

Karen Black . . . . Mrs. Gordon

Charlie Spradling. . . . . Charleen Kane

• 1:05—Very, very brief side of left breast, after taking of swimsuit in locker room.

• 1:06—Buns, taking a shower. Brief breasts a couple of times when the hot water pipes break.

• 1:09—Buns, while lying on the floor, dead, covered with blisters.

• *Mirror Mirror III* (1996)

Elizabeth Baldwin . . . . .Carolyn

•• 0:46—Breasts, while making love in bed with Billy Drago.

• 0:49—Very, very brief tip of right breast, when putting bra on.

•• 1:11—Breasts, while making love with a guy in bed.

• 1:13—Brief buns, while walking into bathroom.

Monique Parent . . . . Cassandra

•• 0:03—Nude, while making love with Billy Drago.

•• 0:16—Breasts, while making love with Drago some more.

••• 0:32—Breasts and buns, while making love in bed with Drago and getting out.

•• 0:40—Breasts, while making love with Drago on the floor.

• 0:47—Brief breasts, during flashback.

Mischief (1985)

Jami Gertz . . . . Rosalie

Cristen Kauffman. . . . . Carhop

Kelly Preston . . . . .Marilyn McCauley

••• 0:56—In a bra, then breasts, brief buns and brief partial lower frontal nudity, while seducing and making love with Doug McKeon in her bedroom.

Catherine Mary Stewart. . . . . Bunny

Miss Right (1987; Italian)

Karen Black . . . . Amy

• 0:47—Brief breasts jumping out of bed and running to get a bucket of water to put out a fire.

Dalila Di'Lazzaro . . . . Art Student

Clio Goldsmith . . . . .n.a.

Margot Kidder. . . . . .Juliet

Marie-France Pisier. . . . . .Bebe

•• 0:07—Breasts in open top dress when the reporter discovers her in a dressing room behind a curtain.

Missing in Action (1984)

Lenore Kasdorf. . . . . Ann

• 0:41—Very brief breasts when Chuck Norris sneaks back in room and jumps into bed with her.

Mission Manila (1989)

Tetchie Agbayani. . . . . Maria

Maria Isabel Lopez. . . . . .Jessie

• 0:22—Brief right breast several times in bed while Harry threatens her with knife.

Mississippi Masala (1992)

Sarita Choudhury. . . . . .Mina

• 1:11—Right breast when Denzel Washington sucks on it.

Mississippi Mermaid (1969; French)

Catherine Deneuve . . . . Julie Roussel/Marion Vergano

•• 1:04—Breasts, changing from a blouse to a sweater while standing up in parked car.

•• 1:26—Brief breasts, taking off her blouse in bedroom.

Mistress of the Apes (1979; British)

Barbara Leigh . . . . Laura

••• 0:44—Breasts, washing her blouse in river and putting it on. (Seen through binoculars.)

• 0:46—Breasts, getting her blouse ripped off by jerks.

Suzy Mandel . . . . Secretary

Jenny Neumann. . . . . .Susan Jamison

• 0:23—Brief side of right breast, getting ready for bed in her tent.

• 0:25—Brief half of right breast in open blouse. Very brief right breast, when pushing a guy away.

• 1:08—Back side of left breast and brief breasts while washing her blouse in river and putting it on.

Mo' Better Blues (1990)

Tracy Camilla Johns . . . . Club Patron

Joie Lee . . . . .Indigo Downes

•• 1:06—Right breast while in bed with Denzel Washington.

• 1:08—Very, very brief right breast while pounding the bed and yelling at Denzel Washington.

Cynda Williams . . . . Clarke Betancourt

•• 0:24—Breasts, then left breast after kissing Denzel Washington.

••• 1:07—Breasts on bed when Denzel Washington accidentally calls her "Indigo."

•• 1:28—Left breast while making love in bed with Wesley Snipes.

Mob Boss (1990)

Jasaé . . . . Bar Girl

•• 0:46—Breasts serving drinks to the guys at the table.

Suzanne Ager . . . . Pool Girl

Teagan Clive . . . . .Noelle

Dori Courtney . . . . .Kathryn

••• 0:31—In black bra, talking with Eddie Deezen, then breasts. Nice close-up. Long scene.

Morgan Fairchild . . . . Gina

Sherri Graham . . . . Bar Girl

•• 0:46—Breasts and buns, dancing on stage. Medium long shot.

Debra Lamb . . . . Janise
Tamara Landry . . . . n.a.
Karen Russell . . . . Mary
Brinke Stevens . . . . Sara

Mobsters (1991)

a.k.a. Mobsters—The Evil Empire

Leslie Bega . . . . Anna Lansky
Lara Flynn Boyle . . . . Mara Motes
Ava Fabian . . . . Cute Girl
Jennifer Gatti . . . . Secretary
Anya Longwell . . . . Showgirl
Monique Noel . . . . Showgirl
Bianca Rossini . . . . Rosalie Luciano
Karen Russell . . . . Showgirl
Lynette Walden . . . . Cute Debutante
•• 0:32—Breasts when Richard Grieco undoes her dress.

Model Behavior (1982)

Jade Go . . . . Golden Girl
Jane Hamilton . . . . Uncredited Adult Film Actress
• 0:50—Breasts on TV monitors during playback of adult video.
Kelly Nichols . . . . Anne #2
••• 0:40—Breasts, while taking off her top before the other Anne in front of Dino.
Missy O'Shea . . . . Anne #1
••• 0:40—Breasts, while taking off her top after the other Anne in front of Dino.
Frances Raines . . . . Lily White Girl
Wendy Stuart . . . . Lily White Girl

Model By Day (1994)

(Shown on network TV without the nudity.)
Kim Cayer . . . . Young Woman
Traci Lind . . . . Jae Davis
Shannon Tweed . . . . Shannon
• 0:42—Breasts, while letting the club owner feel her up before she beats him up.
Sean Young . . . . Mercedes

Modern Problems (1981)

Patti D'Arbanville . . . . Darcy
• 0:48—Very brief right breast in bed after Chevy Chase has telekinetic sex with her.

Modern Romance (1981)

Jane Hallaren . . . . Ellen
Kathryn Harrold . . . . Mary Harvard
• 0:46—Very brief breasts and buns taking off robe and getting into bed with Albert Brooks.

The Moderns (1988)

Genevieve Bujold . . . . Libby Valentin
Geraldine Chaplin . . . . Nathalie de Ville
Linda Fiorentino . . . . Rachel Stone
• 0:40—Breasts sitting in bathtub while John Lone shaves her armpits.
• 0:41—Right breast while turning over onto stomach in bathtub.
•• 1:18—Breasts getting out of tub while covered with bubbles to kiss Keith Carradine.

Moll Flanders (1996)

Robin Wright . . . . Moll Flanders
•• 1:00—Right breast, several times, while sitting on couch and posing for paintings.
•• 1:27—Brief right breast in mirror, then left breast while pregnant and reclining on sofa. Left breast, while lying on bed.

Molly & Gina (1993)

Elizabeth Berkley . . . . Kimberly Sweeney
Frances Fisher . . . . Molly
Shana Golden . . . . Sherry
•• 1:05—Breasts, while making love on top of Peter Fonda in bed.
• 1:06—Brief right breast, after rolling over after Fonda leaves the room.
• 1:08—Brief buns in G-string after tossing off her robe.
Natasha Gregson Wagner . . . . Gina
Penny Johnson . . . . Maria
Joanne Lara . . . . Stripper
••• 0:00—Breasts and buns in G-string while dancing on stage during opening credits.
Melanie Smith . . . . Dixie
Stella Stevens . . . . Mrs. Sweeny

• *Moments... The Making of Claire of the Moon (1992)*

Trisha Todd . . . . Claire Jabrowski
•• 0:28—Breasts, while straddling Noel in bed.
•• 0:44—Breasts, several times in outtakes not seen in the film, taking off her sweater after bumping into Noel.
Karen Trumbo . . . . Dr. Noel Benedict
• 0:28—Breasts, with Claire in bed.

Monaco Forever (1984)

Michelle Bauer . . . . Nazi Woman
••• 0:20—In black bra and panties, then breasts, undressing out of Nazi outfit.

Mondo New York (1987)

Phoebe Légerè . . . . Singer
• 0:01—On stage, singing "Marilyn Monroe." Buns and most of lower frontal nudity while writhing on stage in a mini-skirt.
Ann Magnuson . . . . Poetry Reader
Annie Sprinkle . . . . Model/Performer
• 0:17—Nude, painted body with other models during "Rapping & Rocking" segment.

Money for Nothing (1993)

Fionnula Flanagan . . . . Mrs. Coyle
Debi Mazar . . . . Monica Russo
•• 0:39—Breasts, while making love in bed with John Cusack while covered with money.

Money to Burn (1994)

Diana Cuevas . . . . Beach Girl
Melanie Good . . . . Ann
• 0:40—Buns in fishnet body suit, breasts under the suit, while making love with Julie Strain on the floor.
Kymberly Herrin . . . . Linda
Ashlie Rhey . . . . Gina
• 1:02—Nude in bathtub with Don Swayze.
Nicole Sassaman . . . . Rich Girl #1
Julie Strain . . . . Jill
• 0:38—Brief buns in G-string under hiked up dress, several times, while dancing in club.
•• 0:39—Stripping out of her dress down to red bra, panties, garter belt and stockings, then breasts and buns. More when making love with Ann on the floor.

••• 0:42—Nude, waking up and getting dressed.

Money Train *(1995)*

Jennifer Lopez . . . . Grace Santiago

• 0:54—Very brief left breast, twice, then partial right breast, then very brief left breast when Wesley Snipes cups it. Intercut with Woody Harrelson getting beat up.

Monika *(1952; Swedish)*

a.k.a. Sommaren Med Monika

Harriet Andersson . . . . Monika

• 0:42—Brief back side of left breast, while sitting down next to water. Buns while getting up to run to water.

• 1:33—Buns and long shot of right breast in Harry's flashback. This scene lasts longer than the 0:42 one.

Monkey Shines: An Experiment in Fear *(1988)*

Kate McNeil . . . . Melanie Parker

• 1:07—Brief upper half of right breast, while making love with Allan. Dark, hard to see anything.

Patricia Tallman. . . . . Party Guest and Stunts

Janine Turner. . . . . Linda Aikman

• 0:01—Side view of buns, while lying in bed when Jason Beghe wakes up. Don't really see anything.

Joyce Van Patten . . . . Dorothy Mann

Monsignor *(1982)*

Genevieve Bujold. . . . . Clara

••• 1:05—Breasts getting undressed and climbing into bed while talking to Christopher Reeve.

Pamela Prati . . . . 1st Roman Girl

• 1:22—Brief breasts (on the left, wearing necklaces) next to a guy sitting in a chair, with another Roman girl on the right.

Montenegro *(1981; British/Swedish)*

Susan Anspach . . . . Marilyn Jordan

•• 1:08—Full frontal nudity, while taking a shower.

• 1:28—Right breast, while making love with Montenegro.

Monty Python's Life of Brian *(1979; British)*

Sue Jones-Davies . . . . Judith

• 1:04—Brief full frontal nudity, then nude when Brian comes back after opening the window.

Monty Python's the Meaning of Life *(1983; British)*

Patricia Quinn . . . . Professor's Wife

•• 0:25—Breasts, while undressing to give a real sex education demonstration with John Cleese for a classroom full of boys.

Moon in Scorpio *(1987)*

Donna Kei Benz. . . . . Nurse Mitchell

Britt Ekland . . . . Linda

Jillian Kesner . . . . Claire

•• 0:39—Breasts sitting on deck of boat with bathing suit top down.

April Wayne. . . . . Isabel

• 0:32—Brief right breast in bed with a guy.

• 0:35—Brief breasts putting bathing suit on in a bathroom on a boat when a guy opens the door.

The Moon in the Gutter *(1983; French/Italian)*

a.k.a. La Lune dans Le Caniveau

Victoria Abril . . . . Bella

• 0:28—Left breast, while riding on swing and getting felt by Gérard Depardieu.

•• 1:26—Breasts, while lying in bed. Dark.

••• 1:27—Nude, getting out of bed and arguing with Depardieu. Long scene. Subtitles get in the way sometimes.

• 1:50—Upper half of right breast, popping out of the top of her dress when Depardieu leans her back on the counter.

Katia Berger. . . . . Catherine

• 0:04—Right breast a couple of times, while lying dead on sidewalk.

• 1:24—Left breast, dead, while lying on table that Gérard Depardieu looks at during dream-like scene.

• 1:25—Brief right breast in close-up.

Nastassja Kinski . . . . Loretta

• **Moonlight and Valentino** *(1995)*

Gwyneth Paltrow. . . . . Lucy Trager

• 1:15—Right half of buns, after dropping robe in front of her sister because she's insecure about how her body looks. Very, very brief back part of right breast when bending down to pick up her robe. Don't see her face.

Elizabeth Perkins . . . . Rebecca Trager Lott

• 0:27—Brief tip of right breast, while sitting in bathtub. Brief partial right breast when starting to clean the tiles.

• 0:48—Brief buns, while lying in steam room.

Kathleen Turner. . . . . Alberta Russell

Moontrap *(1989)*

Leigh Lombardi . . . . Mera

•• 1:08—Breasts with Walter Koenig in moon tent.

• **More Candid Candid Camera** *(1983; Video Tape)*

Brinke Stevens . . . . Horseriding Student 1

••• 0:00—Buns and lower frontal nudity, learning how to ride a horse "bareback" style.

• **More Tales of the City** *(1998; Made for Cable Movie; Canadian/U.S.)*

Lisa Bronwyn Moore . . . . Bus Ticket Seller

Olympia Dukakis . . . . Anna Madrigal

Barbara Garrick . . . . DeDe Day

Parker Posey . . . . Connie Bradshaw

Nina Siemaszko . . . . Mona Ramsey

•• 1:26—(0:37 into Part 2) Breasts, while changing clothes.

Janine Thériault . . . . Bobby

The Morning After *(1986)*

Kathy Bates . . . . Woman on Mateo Street

Jane Fonda . . . . Alex Sternbergen

• 1:08—Brief breasts making love with Jeff Bridges.

Diane Salinger . . . . Isabel Harding

Mortal Passions *(1989)*

Krista Errickson . . . . Emily

•• 0:08—Brief breasts in bed with Darcy, while tied to the bed. Breasts getting untied and rolling over.

• 0:11—Very brief right breast, rolling back on top of Darcy.

••• 0:40—Breasts after dropping her sheet for Burke, then making love with him.

•• 0:46—Breasts getting into bed with her husband.

Cassandra Gava . . . . Cinda

Sheila Kelley. . . . . Adele

Mortuary Academy *(1988)*

Rebekka Armstrong . . . . Nurse

Vickie Benson . . . . Salesgirl

Megan Blake . . . . Tammy

Laurie Ann Carr . . . . Nurse

Lynn Danielson . . . . Valerie Levitt

Kym Paige . . . . Nurse
Bobbi Pavis . . . . Sexy Dancer
Dona Speir . . . . Nurse
Cheryl Starbuck. . . . . Linda Hollyhead
- 1:08—Breasts, dead, in morgue when Paul Bartel tries to make love with her.

Karen Witter . . . . Christie Doll
Mary Woronov . . . . Mary Purcell

The Mosaic Project (1994)

Colleen Coffey . . . . Ash
Ashlie Rhey . . . . Stewardess
Julie Strain. . . . . Tess
- 0:47—Brief buns in panties, doing a sexy dance during party to distract everybody.

Moscow on the Hudson (1984)

Maria Conchita Alonso . . . . Lucia Lombardo
- •• 1:17—Breasts in bathtub with Robin Williams.

Motel Hell (1980)

Nina Axelrod. . . . . Terry
- •• 1:01—Breasts sitting up in bed to kiss Vincent.
- 1:04—Very brief breasts in tub when Bruce breaks the door down, then getting out of tub.

Rosanne Katon . . . . Suzi

• *Mother Night* (1996)

Sheryl Lee . . . . Hela/Resi Noth
- •• 0:11—Breasts, after taking off her nightgown and getting into bed with Nick Nolte.

Mother's Boys (1994)

Jamie Lee Curtis . . . . Jude
- 0:44—Very brief left nipple in open robe while sitting in chair when Gallagher enters her apartment. Very brief side view of breast in mirror as she turns around. Brief half of left breast in open robe while talking with Gallagher.
- 0:52—Brief side of left breast and buns, when walking past doorway while her son peeks. Don't see her face well.
- 0:55—Buns, standing up in bathtub to show C-section scar to her son. Don't see her face.

Vanessa Redgrave . . . . Lydia

Mountains of the Moon (1989)

Anna Massey. . . . . Mrs. Arundell
Fiona Shaw . . . . Isabel
- •• 0:33—Breasts and very brief lower frontal nudity letting Patrick Bergin wax the hair off her legs.
- •• 1:43—Breasts in bed after Bergin returns from Africa.

Mr. Baseball (1992)

Mary Kohnert . . . . Player's Wife
Carrie Jean Yazel . . . . Coed in Bed
- 0:03—Very, very brief upper half of right breast, while sleeping when Tom Selleck gets out of bed.

• *Mrs. Munck* (1995; Made for Cable Movie)

Kelly Preston . . . . Young Rose
- 0:51—Partial buns, while making love on top of Bruce Dern in bed.

Mrs. Parker and the Vicious Circle (1994)

Jennifer Beals. . . . . Gertrude Benchley
Heather Graham . . . . Mary Kennedy Taylor
Jennifer Jason Leigh . . . . Dorothy Parker
- 0:56—Brief breasts, while turning over in bed with Matthew Broderick.
- 0:57—Brief left breast, while lying under Broderick and kissing him.

Rebecca Miller. . . . . Neyso McMein
Gwyneth Paltrow. . . . . Paula Hunt
- 1:02—Breasts, while sitting in bed when she's discovered by Jennifer Jason Leigh in Matthew Broderick's apartment.

Martha Plimpton . . . . Jane Grant
Lili Taylor. . . . . Edna Ferber

Ms. Don Juan (1973)

Brigitte Bardot. . . . . Joan
- 0:19—Left breast in bathtub.
- •• 1:19—Breasts through fish tank. Buns and left breast, then brief breasts in mirror with Paul.

Jane Birkin . . . . Clara
- 0:58—Lower frontal nudity lying in bed with Brigitte Bardot.
- 1:00—Brief breasts in bed with Bardot. Long shot.
- •• 1:01—Full frontal nudity getting dressed. Brief breasts in open blouse.

Mugsy's Girls (1985)

Darcy Nychols . . . . Madame Antoinette
Kristi Somers . . . . Laurie
- 0:15—Brief breasts several times while mud wrestling.
- •• 0:29—Breasts and buns in bathtub on bus.
- 0:34—Brief breasts holding up sign to get truck driver to stop.

Mulholland Falls (1996)

Alisa Christensen . . . . Spaghetti Girl
Melinda Clarke . . . . Cigarette Girl
Jennifer Connelly. . . . . Alison Pondi
- 0:02—In black bra, panties, garter belt and stockings during opening credits. Breasts when the guy takes her bra off. B&W.
- 0:17—Brief breasts, while kneeling on the bed during playback of B&W film.
- 0:26—Very, very brief side view of left breast, in flashback with Nick Nolte. Color.
- 1:09—Breasts, with Nolte when Melanie Griffith watches B&W film.

Azalea Davila . . . . Perino's Girl
Melanie Griffith . . . . Katherine
Suzanne Solari. . . . . Perino's Girl

• *Murder at 1600* (1997)

Diane Lane . . . . Nina Chance
Mary Moore . . . . Carla Town
- 0:03—Very brief breasts, while making love in a room in the White House at night.
- 0:20—Brief right breast (with blood on it), while lying dead on autopsy table.

Murder Weapon (1989)

Michelle Bauer. . . . . Girl in Shower on TV
- 1:00—Brief left breast on TV that the guys are watching. Scene from *Nightmare Sisters.*

Victoria Nesbitt . . . . Vicki
- ••• 0:05—Breasts in bed with a guy after taking off her swimsuit top, then making love on top of him. Long scene.

Linnea Quigley . . . . Dawn
- 0:08—Buns and very brief side of left breast walking into shower. Long shot.
- •• 0:40—Breasts taking off her top in car.
- •• 0:48—Breasts and buns taking off her top in bedroom.
- ••• 0:50—Breasts in bed on top of a guy. Excellent long scene. Brief buns, getting out of bed.

Karen Russell . . . . Amy
- 0:34—Brief breasts in shower.

Brinke Stevens . . . . Girl in Shower on TV
- 1:00—Brief left breast on TV that the guys are watching. Scene from *Nightmare Sisters.*

• *Murmur of the Heart* (1971; French/Italian/German)

Léa Massari . . . . Clara Chevalier
- •• 1:19—Brief back sides of breasts, while taking a bath, buns when getting out of bath.

Gila von Weitershausen . . . . Freda
- •• 0:44—Breasts, while in bedroom, making love with Laurent, when helping him lose his virginity.
- 0:46—Brief breasts, while hitting Laurent's friend.

Murphy's Law (1986)

Leigh Lombardi . . . . Stewardess
Carrie Snodgress . . . . Joan Freeman
Angel Tompkins . . . . Jan
- 0:19—Breasts doing a strip routine on stage while Charles Bronson watches.
- 0:27—Brief breasts doing another routine.

The Mutations (1973; British)

a.k.a. Freakmaker

Olga Anthony . . . . Bridget
- •• 0:20—Breasts, while lying unconscious on table in Donald Pleasance's laboratory, being undressed by Tom Baker.

Lisa Collings . . . . Prostitute
- 1:04—Breasts, while opening her dress for Tom Baker.

Julie Ege . . . . Hedi
- 1:19—Partial right breast, while in bathtub.
- •• 1:26—Right breast, then breasts, while lying on table in Donald Pleasance's laboratory.

The Mutilator (1983)

Frances Raines . . . . Linda
- •• 0:35—Breasts, while in swimming pool, just before getting killed.

My Beautiful Laundrette (1985; British)

Rita Wolf . . . . Tania
- •• 0:15—Breasts holding blouse up, showing off her breasts outside window to Omar.

My Best Friend's Girl (1984; French)

a.k.a. La Femme du Mon Ami

Isabelle Huppert . . . . Vivian Arthund
- 0:40—Brief left breast peeking out of bathrobe walking around in living room.
- 1:00—Buns, while making love with Thierry Lhermitte while his friend watches.

My Chauffeur (1986)

Cindy Beal . . . . Beebop
Vickie Benson . . . . Party Girl
Jeannine Bisignano . . . . Party Girl
- 1:23—Breasts, several times, after taking off her white blouse in the back of the limousine. (She's the only brunette.)

Leslee Bremmer . . . . Party Girl
- 1:24—Buns and brief breasts in back of the limousine, taking off her yellow outfit.
- 1:25—Breasts, while sleeping when Penn and Teller leave the limousine.

Deborah Foreman . . . . Casey Meadows
Sheila Lussier . . . . Party Girl
- 1:23—Brief breasts after taking off her blue blouse in the back of the limousine.

Darian Mathias . . . . Dolly

My Family (1995)

Bibi Besch . . . . Mrs. Gillespie
Elpidia Carrillo . . . . Isabel Magaña
- 1:26—Brief left breast in bed with Jimmy Smits.
- 1:30—Breasts, after talking and crying with Smits.
- 1:34—Brief right breast, dead, while under plastic cover in morgue.

Jennifer Lopez . . . . Young Maria
Constance Marie . . . . Toni
- 1:05—Very brief right breast, while making love with Scott Bakula in flashback.

Dedee Pfeiffer . . . . Karen Gillespie
Mary Steenburgen . . . . Gloria
Valerie Wildman . . . . Sunny, Gloria's Friend

My Father The Hero (1993)

Katherine Heigl . . . . Nicole
- 0:14—Buns in white, T-back swimsuit, getting up of lounge chair and walking while Gérard Depardieu tries to cover her up.

Lauren Hutton . . . . Megan
Emma Thompson . . . . Uncredited Isabelle

My Father's Wife (1976; Italian)

a.k.a. Confessions of a Frustrated Housewife

Carroll Baker . . . . Lara
- 0:03—Right breast making love in bed with her husband, Antonio.
- •• 0:06—Breasts standing in front of bed talking to Antonio.
- ••• 0:18—Breasts kneeling in bed, then getting out and putting a robe on while wearing beige panties.

Femi Benussi . . . . Patricia
- 0:33—Close up view of left breast.
- •• 0:51—Right breast, while making love in bed with Claudio. Breasts after.

My First Wife (1985; Australian)

Neela Dey . . . . Migrant Teacher
Wendy Hughes . . . . Helen
- 1:00—Brief breasts and lower frontal nudity under water during husband's dream. Don't see her face.
- •• 1:08—In bra, then breasts on the floor with her husband.
- •• 1:10—Breasts in bed lying down, then fighting with her husband. A little dark.

Anna-Maria Monticelli . . . . Hillary

My Life as a Dog (1985; Swedish)

Ing-Marie Carlsson . . . . Berit
- 0:51—Very briefly nude when Ingemar falls through the skylight while trying to peek at her posing as a sculptor's model.

My Man Adam (1986)

Veronica Cartwright . . . . Elaine Swit
- 1:09—Side view of right breast lying on tanning table when Adam steals her car keys. Long shot, hard to see.

Lydia Finzi . . . . Sunbather
- 0:32—Brief breasts sunbathing by the swimming pool when Adam jumps into the pool and angers her.

My New Partner *(1984; French)*

a.k.a. Les Ripoux

Grace de Capitani . . . . Natasha
- 0:38—Brief side of left breast and buns, getting out of bathtub.
- 0:39—Brief buns and side view of left breast, when getting into bathtub. Breasts while talking to Thierry Lhermitte. Medium long shot.

My Own Private Idaho *(1991)*

Chiara Caselli . . . . Carmella
- 1:17—Breasts and buns in very brief, quick cuts with Keanu Reeves.

Melanie Mosely . . . . Lounge Hostess

My Pleasure is My Business *(1974)*

Jayne Eastwood . . . . Isabella
- 1:16—Breasts in bed trying to get His Excellency's attention.
- •• 1:28—Breasts sitting up in bed with blonde guy.

Xaviera Hollander . . . . Gabriele
- •• 0:14—Full frontal nudity in everybody's daydream.
- •• 0:39—Breasts sitting up in bed and putting on a blouse.
- •• 0:40—Breasts getting back into bed.
- ••• 0:59—Breasts and buns taking off clothes to go swimming in the pool, swimming, then getting out.
- •• 1:09—Breasts, buns and very brief lower frontal nudity, underwater in indoor pool with Gus.
- 1:31—Buns and very brief side view of right breast, undressing at party.

• ***My Sex Life... Or How I Got Into an Argument*** *(1996; French)*

Marianne Denicourt . . . . Sylvia
- 0:30—Brief buns, breasts and lower frontal nudity when Paul opens the dressing room door.
- 1:08—Breasts, while lying in bed, getting up and talking with Paul.
- 2:49—(1:27 into tape 2) Brief full frontal nudity, while playing pick-up sticks.

Emmanuelle Devos . . . . Esther
- 0:25—Very, very brief partial right breast, when reaching up to kiss Paul.
- •• 0:46—Brief breasts, when pulling her blouse and bra up in photo booth for Paul.
- 0:47—Brief breasts in developed photograph.
- 2:41—(1:19 into tape 2) Brief full frontal nudity while in the shower.

My Therapist *(1983)*

Marilyn Chambers . . . . Kelly Carson
- •• 0:01—Breasts in sex therapy class.
- •• 0:07—Breasts, then full frontal nudity undressing for Rip. Long scene.
- ••• 0:10—Breasts undressing at home, then full frontal nudity making love on couch. Long scene. Nice. Then brief side view of right breast in shower.
- 0:18—Breasts on sofa with Mike.
- •• 0:21—Breasts taking off and putting red blouse on at home.
- ••• 0:26—Nude in bedroom by herself masturbating on bed.
- ••• 0:32—Breasts exercising on the floor, buns in bed with Mike, breasts in bed getting covered with whipped cream.
- •• 0:41—Left breast and lower frontal nudity fighting with Don while he rips off her clothes.
- •• 1:08—Breasts and brief buns in bed.

Danielle Martin . . . . Francine
- •• 0:29—In bra, garter belt, stockings and panties, then breasts in room with Rip.

My Tutor *(1983)*

Caren Kaye . . . . Terry Green
- •• 0:25—Breasts, while walking into swimming pool.
- •• 0:52—Breasts, while in the pool with Matt Lattanzi.
- ••• 0:55—Right breast, while making love in bed with Lattanzi.

Graem McGavin . . . . Sylvia
- ••• 0:21—In white bra, then breasts in back seat of a car in a parking lot with Matt Lattanzi.

Shelly Taylor Morgan . . . . Louisa

Francesca "Kitten" Natividad . . . . Anna Maria
- ••• 0:10—Breasts in room with Matt Lattanzi, then lying in bed.

Katt Shea . . . . Mud Wrestler
- 0:48—Brief breasts when a guy rips her dress off.

Jewel Shepard . . . . Girl in Phone Booth
- 0:40—Brief left breast in car when Matt Lattanzi fantasizes about making love with her.

Myra Breckinridge *(1970)*

Farrah Fawcett . . . . Mary Ann
- 1:16—Very brief tip of a breast, when Raquel Welch helps put pajama top on her.
- 1:28—Brief tip of left breast, peeking out of nightgown, while lying in bed after Welch turns over.

Marilyn Monroe . . . . Herself
- 1:08—Breasts in B&W version of Playboy centerfold photo.

Genevieve Waite . . . . Dental Patient

• ***Mysteries*** *(1978; Dutch)*

Marina de Graaf . . . . Sara
- 1:22—Buns and sides of breasts, while asleep on top of Rutger Hauer.

Andrea Ferréol . . . . Kamma

Sylvia Kristel . . . . Dany Kielland
- 0:29—Partial right breast, while lying on bed, then right breast and lower frontal nudity while lying in bed with Rutger Hauer.

Mystery Train *(1989)*

Youki Kudoh . . . . Mitzuko
- •• 0:30—In black bra, in bed. Breasts making love with Jun in bed.

Nails *(1992; Made for Cable Movie)*

Anne Archer . . . . Mary Niles

0:16—Breasts and buns belong to body double Shelley Michelle.

Teresa Crespo . . . . Elena Hernandez
- •• 0:44—Breasts, taking off her top in room with Dennis Hopper.

Shelley Michelle . . . . Body Double
- •• 0:16—Breasts and buns, several times body double for Anne Archer during love scene with Dennis Hopper.

Naked *(1993; British)*

Katrin Cartlidge . . . . Sophie
- •• 0:16—Breasts, while making love around the house with David Thewlis.

- •• 1:17—In black bra and panties in bed with Greg Cruttwell. Breasts, while putting on her dress while sitting on bed.
- • 1:23—Brief right breast in gaping dress, when getting up off the floor.

***The Naked Cage** (1985)*

Lucinda Crosby . . . . Rhonda
Flo Gerrish. . . . . Mother
Leslie Huntly . . . . Peaches
Lisa London. . . . . Abbey

- •• 0:22—Breasts in S&M costume with Angel Tompkins.
- •• 0:38—Left breast making out in bed with Angel Tompkins.

Valerie McIntosh . . . . Ruby

- ••• 0:24—Breasts and buns in infirmary, then getting attacked by Smiley. Brief lower frontal nudity.
- • 0:28—Breasts, while hanging by rope, dead.

Stacey Shaffer . . . . Amy

- ••• 1:03—Nude in shower room getting hassled by the other girls.

Shari Shattuck . . . . Michelle

- •• 0:42—Buns and breasts in shower, then getting slashed by Rita during a dream.
- •• 1:00—Left breast getting attacked by Smiley in jail cell, then fighting back.

Angel Tompkins . . . . Diane Wallace

- •• 0:22—In lingerie, then breasts with Abbey.
- • 0:38—Brief right breast, in bed with Abbey.

Christina Whitaker. . . . . Rita

- ••• 0:08—Breasts in bed with Willy.
- • 0:55—Brief breasts in gaping sweatshirt during fight with Sheila.
- • 1:29—Sort of left breast in gaping dress.

***Naked Country** (1985; Australian)*

Neela Dey . . . . Menyan

- • 0:27—Breasts when meeting Mary and Lance.
- •• 0:28—Breasts during wedding ceremony.
- • 1:03—Brief left breast, while on top of cliff.
- • 1:11—Very, very brief breasts during struggle in cave.

***Naked in New York** (1993)*

Colleen Camp . . . . Auditioner
Jill Clayburgh. . . . . Shirley
Mary-Louise Parker . . . . Joanne

- • 0:21—Brief left breast, while making love in bed with Eric Stoltz.

Kathleen Turner. . . . . Dana

***Naked Instinct** (1993)*

Michelle Bauer. . . . . Michelle

- ••• 0:10—Full frontal nudity with Virgin Rich Kid after taking off her maid outfit and making love with him on bed. Long scene.
- ••• 0:13—More full frontal nudity with him on top of her.
- ••• 0:43—Full frontal nudity with Frat Bully and making love with him. Long scene.
- ••• 1:07—Breasts and buns in red panties, making love with the Therapist. Long scene.
- ••• 1:10—Full frontal nudity making love on the floor, with her on top.
- ••• 1:11—More full frontal nudity with him on top.
- ••• 1:13—More full frontal nudity making love on her hands and knees.

Deanne Power. . . . . Joanne

- ••• 0:19—Breasts, in open robe and red panties, watching the pool man masturbate while she plays with herself.
- ••• 0:28—Nude, taking off robe and getting into tub, then making love with the Hot Tub Repairman.
- ••• 0:32—More nude, while making love with him. Long scene.
- ••• 0:36—Full frontal nudity, standing in tub with him.
- ••• 0:54—Nude, making love with the Military Recruit. Long scene.
- ••• 0:59—Nude, making love with the Football Jock.

***Naked Lunch** (1991)*

Judy Davis . . . . Joan Frost/Joan Lee
Monique Mercure . . . . Fadela

- • 1:45—Brief breasts, when first opening her blouse and grabbing her breasts before a cut to her tearing off some special-effect skin to become Roy Scheider.

***Naked Obsession** (1990)*

(Unrated version reviewed.)

Michelle Bauer. . . . . Uncredited Dancer

- • 0:11—Very brief breast, when pulling down her blue blouse after pushing a customer back. Brief breasts, when kneeling on all fours.

Ria Coyne . . . . Cynthia

- •• 0:12—Breasts and buns, while dancing on stage in black lingerie.
- • 0:13—Buns in G-string while dancing.
- •• 0:14—More breasts and buns while dancing.

Maria Ford. . . . . Lynne Hauser

- ••• 0:18—Buns in G-string.
- ••• 0:20—Breasts and buns in G-string, dancing on stage in front of William Katt. Long scene.
- ••• 0:23—Nude, dancing with Katt's necktie.
- •• 0:34—Nude, on stage at end of another dance routine.
- •• 0:44—Breasts in her apartment with Katt.
- ••• 0:45—Breasts and buns on top of Katt in bed while he gently strangles her with his necktie for oxygen deprivation.
- •• 0:47—Breasts in bed after making love with Katt.

Sherri Graham . . . . Waitress
Wendy MacDonald . . . . Saundra Carlyle

- ••• 0:28—In black bra, panties and stockings on the dining table during William Katt's fantasy, then breasts.

Elena Sahagun. . . . . Becky

- ••• 1:10—In white bra, panties, garter belt and stockings while wearing the mask. Breasts and buns in G-string.

Madison Stone . . . . Jezebel

- •• 0:35—In black leather outfit. Buns in G-string and breasts.
- •• 0:37—More breasts and buns.
- • 0:38—More.
- •• 0:39—Brief full frontal nudity.

***Naked Souls** (1995)*

Chantel King . . . . Woman in Bath

- • 0:10—Brief breasts in bathtub before being strangled in B&W flashback.
- • 1:02—Brief breasts, while sitting in bath and being strangled in B&W flashback.

Pamela Lee . . . . Britt

- •• 0:04—Left breast, while kissing Brian Krause in back of art gallery.
- •• 0:42—Left breast, then breasts, while making love with Krause in bed.
- •• 1:18—Breasts, while making love with Krause in bed.

Seana Ryan . . . . Woman in Pool

- • 0:10—Full frontal nudity in and out of pool in B&W flashback.

- 0:12—Brief breasts, while floating dead in pool in B&W flashback.
- 0:36—Nude, while walking next to pool in B&W flashback.
- 0:49—Full frontal nudity, while walking into pool in B&W flashback.
- 1:00—Brief full frontal nudity, while floating dead in pool in B&W flashback.
- 1:02—Nude, while getting out of, then floating dead in pool in B&W flashback.
- 1:16—Full frontal nudity, while floating dead in pool in B&W flashback.

Justina Vail . . . . Amelia

•• 0:27—Breasts, after taking off robe in front of Brian Krause, then climbing into bed with him.

The Naked Truth (1992)

Cindy Ambuehl . . . . Miss Italy
Donna Baltron . . . . Miss Cuba
Maureen Flaherty . . . . Miss Romania
Julie Gray . . . . Miss Hungary
Shelley Michelle . . . . Miss Honduras

•• 0:18—Nude, changing into "something more comfortable" in front of the two Franks.
• 0:22—Buns, in pink sequined G-string two piece swimsuit.

Natasha Pavlova . . . . Miss Bolivia
Shannon Tweed . . . . First Class Stewardess

Naked Vengeance (1985)

Deborah Tranelli . . . . Carla Harris

• 0:25—In black bra, then breasts during gang rape.
••• 0:43—Nude, while walking into the water to seduce a guy before killing him.

Naked Warriors (1973)

a.k.a. The Arena

Pam Grier . . . . Mamawi

•• 0:08—Brief left breast, then lower frontal nudity and side view of right breast getting washed down in court yard.
••• 0:52—Breasts getting oiled up for a battle. Wow!

Lucretia Love . . . . Deidre

• 0:07—Brief breasts, while getting clothes torn off by guards.
•• 0:08—Briefly nude, while getting washed down in court yard.
• 1:08—Brief buns, while bent over riding a horse.

Margaret Markov . . . . Bodicia

• 0:07—Brief breasts getting clothes torn off by guards.
• 0:13—Breasts getting her dress ripped off, then raped during party.
• 0:19—Brief left breast, on floor making love, then right breast and buns.
• 0:52—Brief breasts sitting down, listening to Cornelia.

Rosalba Neri . . . . Cornelia

A Name for Evil (1973)

Samantha Eggar . . . . Joanna Blake

• 0:42—Very brief breasts turning over in bed with Robert Culp. Dark, hard to see.

Sheila Sullivan . . . . Luanna Baxter

• 0:51—Full frontal nudity dancing in the bar with everybody.
• 0:54—Breasts while Robert Culp makes love with her.
• 0:56—Breasts getting dressed.
• 1:17—Nude, skinny dipping with Culp.

The Name of the Rose (1986)

Valentina Vargas . . . . The Girl

••• 0:45—Breasts and buns making love with Christian Slater in the monastery kitchen.

Nashville (1975)

Karen Black . . . . Connie White
Geraldine Chaplin . . . . Opal
Shelley Duvall . . . . L.A. Jane
Cristina Raines . . . . Mary
Gwen Welles . . . . Sueleen Gay

•• 2:09—In bra singing to a room full of men, then breasts doing a strip tease, buns walking up the steps and out of the room.

The Nasty Girl (1989; German)

Lena Stolze . . . . Sonja

• 1:27—Brief breasts and lower frontal nudity, while swimming in water.

National Lampoon Goes to the Movies (1982)

a.k.a. Movie Madness

Candy Clark . . . . Susan Cooper
Olympia Dukakis . . . . Helena
Ann Dusenberry . . . . Dominique
Teresa Ganzel . . . . Diana

••• 0:19—Breasts, while lying in bed with Peter Riegert. Nice, long scene.

Diane Lane . . . . Lisa
Margaret Whitton . . . . First Lady
Mary Woronov . . . . Secretary

National Lampoon's Class Reunion (1982)

Misty Rowe . . . . Cindy Shears

• 0:37—Very brief breasts running around school stage in Hawaiian hula dance outfit.

Marya Small . . . . Iris Augen

National Lampoon's Vacation (1983)

Beverly D'Angelo . . . . Ellen Griswold

•• 0:18—Brief breasts while taking a shower in the motel. (Note she's wearing panties in the shower.)
• 1:19—Brief breasts taking off shirt and jumping into the swimming pool.

Tessa Richarde . . . . Motel Guest

Natural Born Killers (1994)

Juliette Lewis . . . . Mallory

• 0:28—Very, very brief left breast, a few times, in gaping purple slip after climbing on top of Woody Harrelson in bed.

• *Natural Enemy* (1996)

Tia Carrere . . . . Christina
Lenore Zann . . . . Gina

• 0:14—Brief buns, several times, after William McNamara takes her pants off while she's tied to the bed.
• 0:20—Brief breasts, several times, in mirror, while making love with McNamara. Brief buns, when he burns her with a cigarette.

Naughty Nymphs (1972; German)

a.k.a. Passion Pill Swingers
a.k.a. Don't Tell Daddy

Sybil Danning . . . . Elizabeth

••• 0:21—Nude taking a bath while yelling at her two sisters.

• 0:30—Breasts and buns throwing Nicholas out of her bedroom.
•• 0:38—Full frontal nudity running away from Burt.
Christiane Maybach. . . . . Lilly Mae
• 0:29—Breasts in field with Gilbert.
• 0:40—Breasts getting out of car after making love with Gilbert.
•• 0:44—Breasts walking in field with Gilbert.
• 1:03—Breasts talking on phone while sitting in bed.

The Naughty Stewardesses (1978)

a.k.a. Fresh Air
Donna Desmond. . . . . Margie
•• 0:12—Breasts, while leaning out of the shower.
Mikel James. . . . . Diane
•• 0:34—Breasts, while waiting in bed for Ben, then in bed with him.
Marilyn Joi. . . . . Barbara
•• 0:56—Breasts, while dancing by the pool in front of everybody.

Necromancer (1988)

Carla Baron . . . . Gail
• 0:42—Brief breasts getting out of bed with Paul. Dark.
Elizabeth Kaitan. . . . . Julie Johnson
•• 0:41—Breasts in the shower with Carl.
• 0:45—Very brief side view of right breast, taking off dress in front of Paul.
Shannon McLeod . . . . Edna

Necronomicon: Book of the Dead (1993)

Belinda Bauer . . . . Nancy Gallmore
Judith Drake . . . . Mrs. Benedict
Maria Ford . . . . Clara
Denice D. Lewis. . . . . Emma DeLapoer
Bess Meyer . . . . Emily/Amy Osterman
• 0:38—Brief breasts, while taking a shower. Don't see her face, probably a body double.
Millie Perkins . . . . Lena

Necropolis (1987)

LeeAnne Baker. . . . . Eva
• 0:04—Right breast, while dancing in skimpy black outfit during vampire ceremony.
• 0:38—Brief breasts in front of three evil things. (Before she has special make-up to make it look like she has six breasts).
Adriane Lee . . . . Cult Member
Jennifer Stahl. . . . . Cat

Negatives (1968; British)

Glenda Jackson . . . . Vivan
• 0:27—Brief breasts, putting on fur coat in front of mirror.
• 0:30—Very brief left breast, while covering herself with fur coat before sitting up.

Nell (1994)

Jodie Foster . . . . Nell
• 0:40—Nude at night, taking off her dress and going for a swim in the lake.
• 0:42—Breasts and buns, climbing on rock and getting out of the lake.
•• 0:46—Buns and breasts, getting out of water at night while hearing music and starting to cry.
•• 0:53—Breasts, when leaning on rock, then swimming to talk with Natasha Richardson.
• 0:54—Right breast, under the water when Liam Neeson attempts to show her that all men aren't bad.
•• 1:15—Breasts, when she raises her dress in bar when local kid manipulates her.
Natasha Richardson . . . . Paula Olsen

Nemesis (1992)

Jennifer Gatti . . . . Rosaria/German National
Marjean Holden. . . . . San
Deborah Shelton . . . . Julian
• 0:30—Buns, while lying on bed.
•• 0:31—Buns, while standing up and hugging Billy.
• 0:36—Buns, while standing at window. Side view of left breast.
••• 0:37—Full frontal nudity, punching Billy and getting dressed. Looking good! Very buff—she worked out for three and a half hours a day.

• *Nemesis 2: Nebula (1995)*

Tina Coté. . . . . Emily
Sue Price . . . . Alex
• 0:13—Brief buns under grass skirt.
• 0:19—Brief buns under grass skirt during fight with Zumi.
• 0:27—Brief buns under grass skirt, when running around.
• 0:29—Brief buns in G-string after getting rid of her grass skirt.
• 0:37—Buns in G-string and back side of left breast, while changing clothes.

Nemesis 3: Time Lapse (1995)

Sue Price . . . . Alex
• 1:04—Buns in G-string, while getting dressed outside. Great if you like muscular women!

Neon Maniacs (1985)

Marta Kober . . . . Lorraine
Susan Mierisch. . . . . Young Lover
• 0:07—Very brief upper half of right breast while kissing her boyfriend at night.
Leilani Sarelle. . . . . Natalie

Nervous Ticks (1991)

Julie Brown . . . . Nancy Rudman
Lenore Kasdorf. . . . . Katie
Claire Stansfield . . . . Lu
Zoe Trilling . . . . Marci
•• 0:24—Brief breasts in shower when Bill Pullman opens the shower curtains.

Network (1976)

Faye Dunaway . . . . Diana Christensen
• 1:10—Brief left breast twice, taking off clothes in room with William Holden.

Nevada Heat (1982)

a.k.a. Fake-Out
Connie Hair . . . . Roberta
• 0:13—Breasts in the shower scene.
• 0:14—Brief breasts in the shower again. Brief buns in shower (Long shot).
Camelia Kath . . . . Voice #4
Anastassia Stakis . . . . Wooly
• 0:13—Breasts in the shower room scene.
Pia Zadora . . . . Bobbi
• 0:14—Very brief partial right breast and brief buns, in the showers.

• 0:47—Side of left breast, while in bubble bath with Desi Arnaz, Jr.

Never on Tuesday *(1988)*

Claudia Christian . . . . Tuesday

• 0:43—Brief side view of right breast in the shower with Eddie during his fantasy.

• **Never Say Never Again** *(1983)*

Kim Basinger . . . . Domino Vitale

• 1:48—Very brief buns in wet lingerie, when getting pulled onto rescue boat.

Barbara Carrera . . . . Fatima Blush

Pamela Salem . . . . Miss Moneypenny

Never Talk to Strangers *(1995)*

Rebecca De Mornay . . . . Dr. Sarah Taylor

•• 0:34—In black bra, then breasts, while making love with Antonio Banderas.

••• 0:53—Breasts, while making love with Banderas in bed.

Never Too Young to Die *(1986)*

Vanity . . . . Donja Deering

• 1:04—Wearing a bikini swimsuit, putting on suntan lotion. Brief breasts in quick cuts making love with John in a cabin bedroom.

Tara Buckman . . . . Sacrificed Punkette

The New Age *(1994)*

Judy Davis . . . . Katherine Witner

Dana Kaminski . . . . Andrea

Kimberly Kates . . . . Other Katherine

• 1:11—Breasts, in black fishnet lingerie, seen through water in swimming pool.

Paula Marshall . . . . Alison Gale

•• 0:08—Right breast, when lying in bed with Peter Weller, while he makes love to her.

• 1:06—Breasts, while lying face down on massage table in health club. Brief breasts and partial lower frontal nudity, sitting up and putting on robe.

Lisa Pescia . . . . Nova Trainee

Tanya Pohlkotte . . . . Bettina

•• 1:10—Breasts, while wearing black swimsuit bottom, walking into swimming pool. Tattoos on her arm and chest.

• 1:11—Breasts and buns in swimsuit, under the water in the swimming pool while talking with Peter Weller.

Susan Traylor . . . . Ellen Saltonstall

New Crime City: Los Angeles 2020 *(1994)*

Sherrie Rose . . . . Darla

•• 0:52—Nude, taking off robe and starting to make love with Rick Rossovich.

New Eden *(1994)*

Lisa Bonet . . . . Lily

• 1:02—Brief back side of left breast while in bed with Stephen Baldwin.

Heather Hanson . . . . Carmen

New Jack City *(1991)*

Tracy Camilla Johns . . . . Unigua

• 0:40—Buns, while dancing in red bra, panties, garter belt and stockings.

• 0:53—Buns and right breast in bed with Wesley Snipes.

The New Kids *(1985)*

Nikki Fritz . . . . Body Double for Lori Loughlin

• 0:52—Brief buns, partially visible behind plastic shower curtain.

New Year's Evil *(1981)*

Teri Copley . . . . Teenage Girl

• 0:49—Brief right breast in the back of the car with her boyfriend at a drive-in movie. Breast is half sticking out of her white bra. Dark, hard to see anything.

Louisa Moritz . . . . Sally

Taaffe O'Connell . . . . Jane

• **New York Cop** *(1993)*

Theresa Lynn . . . . Babes

• 0:23—Brief buns and brief breasts, while making love in bed with bad guy when interrupted by Toshi.

Mira Sorvino . . . . Maria

New York Nights *(1981)*

Corinne Alphen . . . . The Debutante

•• 0:10—Breasts, making love in the back seat of a limousine with the rock star.

••• 1:38—Breasts dancing in the bedroom while the Financier watches from the bed.

Bobbi Burns . . . . The Authoress

•• 0:16—Breasts on the couch outside with the rock star, then breasts in bed.

Cynthia Lee . . . . The Porn Star

•• 1:15—Breasts in the steam room talking to the prostitute.

••• 1:26—Breasts in office with the financier and making love on his desk.

Missy O'Shea . . . . The Model

•• 0:37—in black bra, panties, garter belt and stockings then breasts taking off bra and getting into bed.

•• 0:40—Breasts while on the floor when the photographer throws her on the floor and rips her bra off.

••• 0:41—Full frontal nudity putting bathrobe on.

• 0:44—Breasts while standing in front of a mirror with short black hair and a mustache getting dressed to look like a guy.

New York Nights *(1994)*

Marilyn Chambers . . . . Barbara Lowery

• 0:21—Breasts, while putting on lingerie for show.

• 0:28—Breasts, with Fred.

• 0:43—Brief breasts, while putting on lingerie.

••• 1:09—Breasts and buns, while making love with Stuart in bed.

• 1:27—Right breast, while making love in bed with a guy.

Susan Napoli . . . . Vicki

•• 0:05—Full frontal nudity while in room with a guy.

•• 0:21—Breasts, while putting on lingerie for show.

••• 0:45—In bra and panties, then full frontal nudity, then making love with Kurt in apartment.

••• 1:03—Breasts and buns, while making love with Chris.

•• 1:25—Nude, while making love with a guy.

Julia Parton . . . . Jessie

• 0:00—Buns in swimsuit on beach.

•• 0:02—Breasts, while making out with a guy on the beach.

•• 0:03—Breasts, while making love with a guy in bed.

• 0:06—Breasts, while making out with a guy. Kind of misty.

••• 0:17—Full frontal nudity in apartment with a guy.

• 0:31—In bra and panties, then buns, while trying on clothes.

•• 0:43—Breasts, in open robe.

- • 0:56—Brief breasts, while in storage room with Gene.
- • 1:02—Buns, when in panties, while trying to put pants on.
- ••• 1:23—Nude, after taking off lingerie with Eric.

Donna Salvatore . . . . Lingerie Girl #1
Jennifer Worthington. . . . . Delivery Woman

- •• 0:23—Full frontal nudity, while in closet with the doorman.
- • 0:25—Brief right breast and buns, while leaving the apartment.

New York's Finest (1988)

Ruth Corrine Collins . . . . Joy Sugarman

- • 0:04—Brief breasts with a bunch of hookers.
- • 0:36—Breasts with her two friends doing push-ups on the floor.
- •• 1:02—Breasts making love on top of a guy talking about diamonds.

Jennifer Delora . . . . Loretta Michaels

- • 0:02—Brief breasts pretending to be a black hooker.
- • 0:04—Brief breasts with a bunch of hookers.
- • 0:36—Breasts with her two friends doing push-ups on the floor.

Jane Hamilton . . . . Bunny
Karen Nielsen . . . . Hooker #1
Heidi Paine . . . . Carley Pointer

- • 0:04—Brief breasts with a bunch of hookers.
- • 0:36—Breasts with her two friends doing push-ups on the floor.

Denise Torek . . . . Hooker #2
Miriam Zucker. . . . . Mrs. Rush

The Newlydeads (1988)

Rebecca Barrington . . . . Blanche

- • 0:08—Right breast, while making out with her fiancee, Bull, in the car.
- • 1:01—Right breast, peeking out of the top of her body suit.
- • 1:02—Brief buns, while on the floor with Bull.

Michele Burger . . . . Bikini Girl
Roxanna Michaels . . . . Lynda

0:23—In lacy black bra and panties, while in bed.

- •• 0:44—Breasts, while in the shower.
- • 0:47—Brief breast, while dead on the shower floor after being stabbed.

Renee Way . . . . Brenda

- • 0:19—Buns and side of right breast, while in spa with her boyfriend.

Next Stop, Greenwich Village (1976)

Denise Galik . . . . Ellen
Ellen Greene . . . . Sarah

- •• 0:15—In white bra, then very brief right breast, then left breast, while on couch on porch with Larry.

Next Year if All Goes Well (1983; French)

Isabelle Adjani . . . . Isabelle

- • 0:27—Brief right breast, lying in bed with Maxime.

Nickel Mountain (1985)

Heather Langencamp . . . . Callie

- ••• 0:24—Breasts in bed lying with Willard.
- • 0:29—Side view of left breast and brief breasts falling on bed with Willard.

Nicole (1972)

a.k.a. The Widow's Revenge

Catherine Bach . . . . Sue

- •• 1:01—Brief breasts, twice, undressing to put on nightgown on boat. Nice shots, but too brief.
- •• 1:10—Very brief side view of breasts, three times, getting felt by Leslie Caron. Don't see either Bach's or Caron's face.

Leslie Caron . . . . Nicole

Night Angel (1989)

Lisa Axelrod . . . . Double
Karen Black . . . . Rita
Debra Feuer. . . . . Kirstie

- • 0:46—Brief side of left breast. Dark.

Night Breed (1990)

Catherine Chevalier . . . . Rachel

- • 1:12—Breasts in police jail, going through a door and killing a cop.

Night Call Nurses (1972)

a.k.a. Young LA Nurses 2

Patti T. Byrne . . . . Barbara

- •• 0:59—Breasts several times in bed with the Doctor.

Lynne Guthrie . . . . Cynthia

- • 0:00—Breasts on hospital roof taking off robe and standing on edge just before jumping off.

Mitte Lawrence . . . . Sandra

- •• 0:49—Breasts, while in bed with a guy.

Dixie Lee Peabody . . . . Robin

- •• 0:35—Breasts taking off clothes in encounter group.
- • 0:39—Brief breasts in Barbara's flashback.

Alana Stewart . . . . Janis

- •• 0:12—Breasts in bed with Zach.
- •• 0:28—Breasts and buns on bed with Kyle.
- • 0:52—Brief right breast twice in shower with Kyle.

Night Club (1989)

Elizabeth Kaitan . . . . Beth/Liza

- •• 0:31—Left breast, while pulling down blouse and caressing herself.
- •• 0:33—Left breast in pulled down blouse on stairwell with Nick.
- ••• 0:36—Breasts on warehouse floor with Nick.
- ••• 0:46—Full frontal nudity, taking off her dress in front of Nick.
- ••• 1:03—Breasts, making love with another guy in front of Nick.

Night Eyes (1990)

(Unrated version reviewed.)

Yvette Buchanan . . . . Baby Doll

- • 0:07—Brief left breast, then breasts making love in bathroom with Ronee.

Barbara Ann Klein . . . . Sleeping Woman

- • 0:02—Brief breasts, while struggling with burglar/rapist.

Tanya Roberts . . . . Nikki

- • 0:20—Side view of left breast, while getting dressed while sitting on bed.
- ••• 1:09—Breasts giving Stevens a massage, then making love. Nice! Buns and left breast, while in the shower making love.
- • 1:27—Buns, making love with Stevens in a chair.

Night Eyes 2 (1991)

Lisa Saxton . . . . Car Rental Girl

- ••• 0:05—Breasts and buns, making love in bed with Jesse.
- • 0:09—Buns, on TV when video tape is played back.

Shannon Tweed. . . . . Marilyn Mejenes

- ••• 0:49—Buns and breasts making love with Andrew Stevens in bed.

••• 1:06—Breasts, making love with Stevens (nice use of raspberries).

Night Eyes 3 (1993)

Monique Parent . . . . Brandy
••• 0:09—Breasts and buns in G-string, stripping out of her clothes in Zoe's house in front of Dan.

Leslie Sachs . . . . Karen

Shannon Tweed . . . . Zoe Clairmont
•• 0:16—Breasts, while getting her clothes ripped off by Dan, then sitting up in bed.
• 0:23—Brief full frontal nudity in shower behind the door.
••• 0:51—Breasts and buns, while making love in bed with Andrew Stevens.
• 0:53—Buns, while lying in bed afterwards.
••• 0:56—Nude, while getting into the shower and in the shower.
••• 1:01—Full frontal nudity, while taking off her robe in front of fireplace.
•• 1:02—Partial buns and breasts, while on top of Stevens.
• 1:15—Brief breasts in B&W photo from security video tape.

Tracy Tweed . . . . Dana Gray
•• 0:25—Left breast, then breasts while in bed with Edgar.
••• 0:40—Breasts and side view of buns, while wearing black G-string panties in dressing room while nonchalantly talking to Andrew Stevens.

• *Night Eyes 4 ...Fatal Passion* (1995)

Paula Barbieri . . . . Dr. Angela Cross
•• 0:01—Buns and breasts, while taking a shower.
•• 0:53—Breasts, while making love with Steve on the floor.
•• 0:59—Breasts and buns, while making love with Steve in a stairwell.
•• 1:06—Breasts, while making love with Steve in bed.
• 1:12—Breasts, while making love with Steve in the kitchen.

Kimberly Kelley . . . . Sara
•• 0:11—Buns and breasts, while sunbathing outside and making out with Roy.
••• 0:29—Breasts and buns, while making love in bed with Roy.
•• 0:33—In bra, then breasts, while seducing Steve.

Jacqueline Lovell . . . . Runaway

Night Fire (1994)

Rochelle Swanson . . . . Gwen
• 0:10—Brief breasts and brief buns in T-back, lifting up her top to flash passing cars while standing up in convertible car.
• 0:21—Brief buns in T-back while fooling around on the bed with Martin Hewitt.
•• 0:29—In black bra, panties and stockings while in bedroom with Hewitt, then breasts and brief partial buns.
• 0:32—Breasts, while in bathtub with Hewitt.
•• 0:36—In red bra and panties, then breasts while in room with Hewitt.
• 0:41—Brief buns in red swimsuit.
•• 0:43—Breasts, when her swimsuit top comes off in spa with Hewitt.
• 0:47—Brief side view of buns, while walking by the spa. Brief buns in swimsuit, when walking back to the house.
• 0:50—Buns in swimsuit, while walking around the house.
•• 0:53—Breasts, when making love outside by fence with Hewitt, while Shannon Tweed watches from inside the house.
• 1:03—Brief breasts, with Hewitt in the spa at night. Medium long shots, then closer shots.
• 1:23—Left breast, while lying in front of Hewitt and talking with Tweed and John Laughlin.

Shannon Tweed . . . . Lydia
•• 0:16—Breasts, while tied and blindfolded on bed.
• 0:36—Breasts, while making love with John Laughlin.
• 1:27—Brief breasts in Polaroid photo. Brief breasts, while in the shower.
• 1:32—Brief breasts in gaping blouse after falling down.

A Night Full of Rain (1978; Italian)

Candice Bergen . . . . Lizzy
•• 1:04—Right breast, while in car with Giancarlo Giannini.

Night Game (1989)

Karen Young . . . . Roxy
• 0:06—Right breast, while in bed with Scheider after he answers the phone.

Night Games (1980)

Joanna Cassidy . . . . Julie Miller
• 0:44—Buns, while skinny dipping in the pool with Cindy Pickett.
•• 0:45—Brief full frontal nudity sitting up.

Cindy Pickett . . . . Valerie St. John
•• 0:05—Brief breasts, while getting scared by her husband in the shower.
• 0:45—Buns and breasts by and in the swimming pool with Joanna Cassidy.
• 0:46—Breasts under sheer blue dress during fantasy sequence with Cassidy.
•• 0:48—Brief full frontal nudity getting out of the pool, then breasts lying down with Cassidy.
••• 1:14—Full frontal nudity standing up in bathtub, then breasts during fantasy with a guy in gold.
•• 1:18—Breasts, while getting out of pool at night.
••• 1:24—Breasts, while sitting up in bed and stretching.

A Night in Heaven (1983)

Sandra Beall . . . . Slick
• 1:09—Brief close up of left breast in shower with Christopher Atkins.

Veronica Gamba . . . . Tammy

Rose McVeigh . . . . Alison

Carrie Snodgress . . . . Mrs. Johnson

Night Moves (1975)

Susan Clark . . . . Ellen
• 1:09—Brief breasts in bed with Gene Hackman.

Melanie Griffith . . . . Delly Grastner
• 0:42—Brief breasts changing tops outside while talking with Gene Hackman.
• 0:46—Nude, saying "hi" from under water beneath a glass bottom boat.
• 0:47—Brief side view of right breast getting out of the water.

Jennifer Warren . . . . Paula
•• 0:56—Breasts in bed with Gene Hackman.
• 0:57—Right breast after making love in bed with Hackman.

Night of the Archer (1994)

Sandahl Bergman . . . . Marla Miles

Barbara Carrera . . . . Victoria de Fleury

Leslie Hardy . . . . Katherine Reggiani
• 1:15—Left breast and buns, while making love with Travis.

Night of the Creeps (1986)

Leslie Ryan . . . . Sorority Girl with Hairbrush 1959

Suzanne Snyder . . . . Lisa
Jill Whitlow . . . . Cynthia Cronenberg
- 0:33—Brief breasts putting nightgown on over her head in her bedroom.

Night of the Cyclone (1990)

Marisa Berenson . . . . .Francoise
Alla Korot . . . . Angelique
- 0:21—Right breast, then brief breasts getting out of the shower.

Kimberleigh Stark . . . . Venna
- 0:01—Brief left breast while posing for the painter.
- 0:40—Breasts on the boat, fighting with the businessman. Breasts on the floor, dead.

Jennifer Steyn . . . . Celeste

Night of the Demons (1987)

(Unrated version reviewed.)

Amelia Kinkade . . . . Angela
- 0:47—Brief buns in panties, garter belt and stockings under dress while doing sexy dance in living room.

Cathy Podewell . . . . Judy
- 0:06—Brief buns, while changing clothes and talking on the phone.

Linnea Quigley . . . . Suzanne
0:10—Buns in panties under short skirt, while bending over to distract the convenience store clerks.
- •• 0:52—Breasts twice, opening her dress top while acting weird. Pushes a tube of lipstick into her left breast. (Don't try this at home kids!)
- 0:56—Lower frontal nudity, lifting her skirt up for Jay.

Jill Terashita . . . . Frannie
- •• 0:57—Breasts while making love with her boyfriend in a coffin.

Night of the Demons 2 (1994)

Christi Harris . . . . Bibi
- •• 0:39—In bra, while in bed with Johnny, then breasts.
- •• 0:41—Right breast, then breasts, while making love in bed with Johnny. Intercut with distracting stuff.

Amelia Kinkade . . . . Angela
Zoe Trilling . . . . .Shirley

The Night of the Following Day (1969)

Pamela Franklin . . . . Girl
- 1:30—Brief breasts, while being helped onto bed by Marlon Brando after she was bound and hung by her wrists.

Rita Moreno . . . . Blonde
- 0:32—Very, very brief tip of left breast, while sitting in bed, wrapping robe around herself.

• Night of the Living Babes (1987; Video Tape)

Blondi . . . . Mondo Zombie Girl Darlene
- ••• 0:12—Breasts wearing dark purple wig and long gloves, with the other Mondo Zombie Girls.
- ••• 0:16—More breasts and buns in bed with Buck.
- 0:50—Breasts on the couch with the other Zombie Girls.
- 0:52—Breasts on the couch again.

Michelle Bauer. . . . . Sue
- •• 0:44—Breasts chained up with Chuck and Buck.
- ••• 0:46—More breasts chained up.
- 0:50—Breasts getting rescued with Lulu.

Teri Lynn Peake . . . . Vesuvia
- ••• 0:25—Breasts and buns in G-string, dancing in front of Chuck and Buck. Long scene.

Connie Woods. . . . . Lulu
- 0:46—Breasts and buns in lingerie, in a cell with Buck.
- ••• 0:48—More breasts in cell with Buck.
- 0:50—Breasts getting rescued with Michelle Bauer.

Night of the Running Man (1994)

Janet Gunn . . . . .Chris Altman
- •• 1:09—Breasts, while making love with Andrew McCarthy.

Kim Lankford . . . . Waitress
Kathrin Lautner . . . . Lady
- •• 0:10—Buns and left breast while making love in bed with Scott Glenn.
- •• 0:11—Nude, walking from bathroom and getting back into bed with Glenn.

Heidi Thomas . . . . Stewardess

• Night of the Scarecrow (1995)

Elizabeth Barondes. . . . . Claire
Martine Beswicke. . . . . .Barbara
Christi Harris . . . . Stephanie
- 0:37—Breasts, while making out in van with Danny.

Night of the Warrior (1991)

Bridget Carney . . . . Sarah
Arlene Dahl . . . . Edie Keane
Sam Jenkins . . . . Hooker
Kathleen Kinmont . . . . Katherine Pierce
- 0:29—Very brief upper half of right breast, while leaning out of the shower to get a towel.
- 1:10—Brief right breast, while making love with Lamas on motorcycle.

Teal Roberts. . . . . Still Model

Night of the Wilding (1990)

Julie Austin. . . . . .Betty
- •• 0:14—Side of left breast, taking off bra in bathroom. Breasts in shower.
- 0:16—More breasts in the shower.
- 0:17—Breasts visible behind shower door.

Kathrin Lautner . . . . Marion
Kimberly Speiss . . . . .Doris

Night Owl (1993)

Caroline Munro . . . . Herself
Suzen Murakoshi . . . . .Woman at Bar
- 0:24—Breasts, while in bathroom after coming home from the bar, before getting killed by Jake.

Ali Thomas. . . . . .Anne
- 0:37—In bra, then left breast while on the floor with Jake.
- 0:38—Left breast, when sleeping, then breasts, while getting up off the floor.
- 0:51—Very brief right breast when Jake lifts his head up and dribbles blood on her after biting her neck.

Karen Wexler . . . . Zohra
- 0:12—Breasts, while making love with Jake in kitchen.

0:14—Breasts, dead, while covered with blood on the floor after Jake bites her neck.
- 0:15—Brief breasts when Jake wipes the blood off her and stuffs her into a garbage bag.

Night Patrol (1985)

Linda Blair . . . . Sue
- 1:19—Brief left breast, in bed with The Unknown Comic.

Francesca "Kitten" Natividad . . . . Hippie Woman
- •• 1:01—Breasts in kitchen with Pat Paulsen, the other police officer and her hippie boyfriend.

Lori Sutton . . . . Edith Hutton
••• 0:47—In white bra, panties, garter belt and stockings, then breasts three times taking off bra in bedroom with the Police officer.

The Night Porter (1974; Italian/U.S.)

Charlotte Rampling . . . . Lucia
•• 0:11—Side nudity being filmed with a movie camera in the concentration camp line.
• 0:13—Nude running around a room while a Nazi taunts her by shooting his gun near her.
••• 1:12—Breasts doing a song and dance number wearing pants, suspenders and a Nazi hat. Long scene.

Night Rhythms (1992)

(Unrated version reviewed.)

Carrie Bittner. . . . . Elaine
••• 0:06—Right breast, then breasts and lower frontal nudity while talking on the phone and playing with herself. Long scene.

Deborah Driggs . . . . Cinnamon
••• 1:15—Left breast, then breasts and lower frontal nudity, making love with Martin Hewitt in bed.
••• 1:19—Breasts, sitting on bed and talking to Hewitt.

Erika Nann . . . . Alex
••• 1:00—Buns in G-string and bra, then breasts, undressing in front of Martin Hewitt and making love with him.

Kristine Rose . . . . Marilyn
••• 0:17—Taking off her blouse at bar with Martin Hewitt, then nude, making love on the bar with him.

Delia Sheppard . . . . Bridget
••• 1:25—Full frontal nudity, making love with Kit in bed. Long scene.

Jamie Stafford . . . . Kit
•• 0:40—Breasts in push-up bra in dressing room.
••• 0:51—Nude, in bed, making love with Lila and Martin Hewitt.
• 0:54—Buns, while watching TV while lying in bed.
••• 0:55—Nude, undressing to take a shower with Lila.
•• 1:23—In sheer black blouse, talking to Delia Sheppard in the radio station.
••• 1:25—Nude, in bed with Sheppard, then getting dressed. Long scene.

Julie Strain. . . . . Linda
••• 0:03—In white bra, then left breast, while talking on the phone and playing with herself.

Tracy Tweed . . . . Honey
••• 0:28—Breasts making love with Martin Hewitt in radio station. Nice, long scene.
••• 0:31—Nude, getting up after changing positions.
•• 0:33—Breasts, lying dead on the floor.

Night School (1980)

Rachel Ward . . . . Eleanor
• 0:25—In sheer white bra and panties, taking off clothes to take a shower. Breasts after taking off bra. Hard to see because she's behind a shower curtain. Brief buns and back side of left breast.
• 0:27—Very brief upper half of right breast, when opening the shower curtain.
•• 0:29—Brief upper half of breasts, and then buns, when her boyfriend rubs red paint all over her in the shower.

Night Shift (1982)

Elizabeth Carder . . . . Dolores
Shannen Doherty . . . . Bluebird
Dawn Dunlap . . . . Maxine
Monique Gabrielle. . . . . Tessie
• 0:55—Brief breasts, while sitting on college guy's shoulders during party in the morgue.

Cassandra Gava . . . . J.J.
Ava Lazar. . . . . Sharon
Shelley Long . . . . Belinda Keaton
Ola Ray . . . . Dawn
K.C. Winkler . . . . Cheryl

The Night They Raided Minsky's (1968)

Britt Ekland . . . . Rachel Schpitendavel
• 1:34—Brief breasts, when her dress accidentally falls down during strip tease routine on stage. Probably a body double because you don't see her face. (A reader has a letter from the director who says it's a body double.)

Night Train to Terror (1985)

Meredith Kennedy. . . . . Dead Redhead
• 0:16—Right breast, while strapped to gurney, before getting killed with a saw by Richard Moll.

Night Train to Venice (1993)

Tahnee Welch . . . . Vera
• 0:48—Silhouette of right breast, while in room on train with Hugh Grant. Don't see her face, but it looks like her.
•• 1:18—Very brief breast, twice, while in bed with Hugh Grant, then breasts.
•• 1:33—Brief left breast, then breasts, while kissing Hugh Grant in bed at end of film. The darn credits get in the way!

Night Visitor (1989)

Shannon Tweed . . . . Lisa Grace
Teresa Vander Woude . . . . Kelly Fremont
Teri Weigel . . . . Victim in Cellar
• 0:50—Brief out of focus breasts changing tops in the cellar.
• 0:55—Right breast, during ceremony. Very brief breasts just before being stabbed.

Night Warning (1982)

Julia Duffy . . . . Julie Linden
• 0:44—Upper half of breasts after Jimmy McNichol gets out of bed.
• 0:46—Brief breasts when McNichol pulls the sheets down.
•• 0:47—Brief breasts when Susan Tyrrell opens the bedroom door.

Susan Tyrrell . . . . Cheryl Roberts
• 0:17—Left breast, sticking out of dress just before she stabs the TV repairman.

The Nightcomers (1971; British)

Stephanie Beacham. . . . . Miss Margaret Jessel
• 0:13—Brief left breast lying in bed having her breasts fondled.
••• 0:30—Breasts in bed with Marlon Brando while a little boy watches through the window.
•• 0:55—Breasts in bed pulling the sheets down.

Nightfall (1988)

Andra Millian. . . . . Anna
• 0:12—Very brief breasts making love with David Birney.
• 0:41—Very brief breasts making love in front of a fire.

Nightforce (1986)

Jeanne Baird . . . . Mrs. Hanson
Linda Blair . . . . Carla
Kathleen Kinmont . . . . Cindy

Claudia Udy . . . . Christy Hanson
•• 0:07—Breasts making love in the stable with Steve during her engagement party.
••• 0:10—Nude, fantasizing in the shower.

The Nightman (1992)

Joanna Kerns . . . . Eve Rhodes
•• 0:47—Buns, while rolling over in bed and sitting up.
Jenny Robertson .Dr. Margaret Rhodes
• 1:25—Very brief right breast in gaping dress when she looks at old things hidden under floor boards.

A Nightmare on Elm Street (1985)

Mimi Craven . . . . Nurse
Heather Langencamp . . . . Nancy Thompson
• 0:32—Very brief right breast, twice, while struggling under water after Freddy pulls her under the water in the bathtub.
Amanda Wyss . . . . Tina Gray

A Nightmare on Elm Street 3: The Dream Warriors (1987)

Stacey Alden . . . . Marcie
••• 0:49—Breasts and buns in white G-string, taking off nurse's uniform and seducing Joey in hospital room. Then giving him the tongue before turning into Freddy Kruger.
Patricia Arquette . . . . Kristen Parker
Heather Langencamp . . . . Nancy Thompson
Jennifer Rubin . . . . Taryn

A Nightmare on Elm Street 4: The Dream Master (1988)

Hope Marie Carlton. . . . . Pin-Up Girl
• 0:21—Brief breasts swimming in a waterbed.
Tuesday Knight . . . . Kristen
Linnea Quigley . . . . Soul from Freddy's Chest
• 1:23—Brief breasts twice, trying to get out of Freddy's body. Don't see her face clearly.

Nightmare Sisters (1987)

Michelle Bauer. . . . . Mickey
••• 0:39—Breasts standing in panties with Melody and Marci after transforming from nerds to sexy women.
••• 0:40—Breasts in the kitchen with Melody and Marci.
••• 0:44—Full frontal nudity in the bathtub with Melody and Marci. Excellent, long scene.
••• 0:47—Breasts in the bathtub. Nice close up.
••• 0:48—Still more breasts in the bathtub.
•• 0:53—Breasts in bed with J.J.
Sandy Brooke . . . . Amanda Detweiler
Linnea Quigley . . . . .Melody
••• 0:39—Breasts, wearing panties, while standing with Mickey and Marci after transforming from nerds to sexy women.
••• 0:40—Breasts in the kitchen with Mickey and Marci.
••• 0:44—Breasts in the bathtub with Mickey and Marci. Excellent, long scene.
••• 0:46—Breasts, while in the bathtub. Nice close up.
••• 0:48—Still more breasts, while in the bathtub.
••• 0:55—Breasts, while dancing and singing in front of Kevin. Long scene.
•• 0:57—Breasts while on the couch with Bud.
Brinke Stevens. . . . . Marci
••• 0:39—Breasts wearing panties, while standing with Melody and Mickey after transforming from nerds to sexy women.
••• 0:40—Breasts while in the kitchen with Melody and Mickey.
••• 0:44—Nude in the bathtub with Melody and Mickey. Excellent, long scene.
••• 0:47—Breasts while in the bathtub. Nice close up.
••• 0:48—Still more buns and breasts in the bathtub.

Nights in White Satin (1987)

Kim Waltrip . . . . .Stevie Hughes
• 0:53—Breasts in bathtub with Walker. Out of focus, hard to see.

Nightscare (1993; British)

Georgina Hale . . . . Sister Romulus
Elizabeth Hurley. . . . . Stephanie Lyell
• 0:19—Right breast, while making love with a guy in bed.
0:21—Brief partial buns, while in bed.

The Nightstalker (1987)

Tally Chanel. . . . . Brenda
• 0:54—Brief frontal nudity lying dead in bed covered with paint. Long shot, hard to see anything.
Joan Chen . . . . Mai Wong
Lydie Denier . . . . First Victim
••• 0:03—Breasts making love with big guy.
Marcia Karr . . . . H.J. Salters
Katherine Kelly Lang . . . . Denise
Sheila Lussier . . . . .n.a.
Ola Ray . . . . Sable Fox
Diane Sommerfield . . . . Lonnie Roberts
• 0:35—Side view of right breast lying dead in morgue.

• *Nighttime Lover (1995)*

a.k.a. Call Girl

Jennifer Leigh Burton . . . . .Cynthia
•• 0:01—Nude, while posing for photographs with another model.
Shari Eckert . . . . Frightened Young Woman
•• 0:31—Breasts, when blindfolded and tied to a post while being caressed by a guy.
Julianne J. Mantia. . . . . Woman in Room 2
••• 0:56—Nude, when a guy rips her top off in room in front of her husband.
Pia Reyes . . . . Tracy
•• 0:01—Breasts and buns, while posing for photographs with another model.
• 0:05—Left breast in B&W still photo. Brief breasts in another B&W photo.
• 1:07—Brief buns in panties in outfit while getting photographed.
• 1:09—Brief breasts in B&W photo.
Domonique Simone. . . . . Prostitute
•• 1:12—Breasts, while getting dressed for photo session, then breasts and buns in G-string during photo session with another prostitute.
• 1:16—Brief left breast in B&W photo and breasts in photo session.
• 1:17—Brief breasts in another photo session and in B&W photos.

Nightwish (1988)

(Unedited version reviewed.)

Alisha Das . . . . .Kim
•• 1:09—Brief breasts, then left breast in open dress caressing herself while lying on the ground.

Elizabeth Kaitan. . . . . .Donna
- 0:04—In wet T-shirt, then brief breasts taking it off during experiment. Long shot.
- 1:10—Briefly in braless, see-through purple dress.

***Nijinsky** (1980; British)*

Henrietta Baynes . . . . Magda
Leslie Browne . . . . Romula
- 1:34—Very brief breasts, twice, on the floor when Nijinksy rips her dress off. Dark.

***Ninja Academy** (1990)*

Michele Burger . . . . .Nudist
Becky LeBeau . . . . .Nudist
- •• 0:26—Nude, carrying plate, then going to swing at nudist colony. Then playing volleyball (she's the first one to hit the ball).

Bonnie Paine. . . . . .Nudist
- 0:26—Brief buns and breasts playing volleyball. (She's the second blonde on the far side of the net who misses the ball.)

***No Place to Hide** (1991)*

Drew Barrymore . . . . .Tinsel Hanley
Lydie Denier . . . . Pamela Hanley
- 0:03—Breasts, after opening her ballet costume in the wings backstage before getting sliced up with a knife.

Dey Young . . . . Karen

***No Small Affair** (1984)*

Judith Baldwin. . . . . Stephanie
- ••• 0:36—In white bra, panties and garter belt, then breasts in Jon Cryer's bedroom trying to seduce him.

Elizabeth Daily . . . . Susan
Demi Moore . . . . .Laura
- 1:34—Very, very brief side view of left breast in bed with Jon Cryer.

Jennifer Tilly . . . . Mona

***No Way Out** (1987)*

Iman . . . . Nina Beka
Sean Young. . . . . Susan Atwell
- ••• 0:13—Side view of left breast, then brief right breast, going into Nina's apartment with Costner.

• ***Nobody Loves Me** (1994; German/French)*

a.k.a. Keiner Liebt Mich

Maria Schrader . . . . .Fanny Fink
- 1:20—Breasts, while bathing with Orfeo in bathtub.

***Nobody's Fool** (1994)*

Melanie Griffith. . . . . .Toby Roebuck
- •• 0:53—Very brief breasts, after pulling up her sweatshirt to flash for Paul Newman in office.

Shannah Laumeister . . . . .Didi
Jessica Tandy. . . . . Miss Beryl

***Nomads** (1986)*

Lesley-Anne Down . . . . .Flax
Anna-Maria Monticelli. . . . . .Niki
- 0:57—Left breast, making love in bed with Pierce Brosnan. Dark, hard to see anything.

Mary Woronov . . . . .Dancing Mary

• ***Norma Jean & Marilyn** (1996; Made for Cable Movie)*

Lindsay Crouse . . . . Natasha Lyress
Ashley Judd . . . . .Norma Jean Dougherty
- ••• 0:02—Breasts, while unclothed in church filled with clothed people during dream.
- •• 0:05—Breasts, after taking off her swimsuit by swimming pool in front of Eddie.
- ••• 0:36—Nude, after taking off robe and posing for photos.
- •• 0:40—Breasts, pulling up her blouse for Johnny.
- 1:54—Brief breasts, cutting her dress open and ripping it off.

Erika Nann. . . . . .Jane Russell
Mira Sorvino . . . . Marilyn Monroe
- 1:00—Brief lower half of buns under sweater, when getting orange juice out of the refrigerator.
- •• 2:01—Brief breasts, pulling open her dress in front of Eddie.

***Normal Life** (1996)*

Ashley Judd . . . . Pam Anderson
- 0:21—Brief right breast several times and very, very brief left breast, while lying in bed and talking with Luke Perry.
- 0:38—Breasts in open blouse, while cutting herself with a knife.
- 0:39—Right breast, while lying in bed when Perry discovers her cuts.
- 0:54—Breasts, while sitting on the bed, holding a gun to her head.
- •• 1:04—Right breast, then brief breasts after having sex in bed with Perry.
- ••• 1:14—Breasts, while making love with Perry in bedroom.
- •• 1:20—Breasts, while depressed when alone in bedroom.

Penelope Milford. . . . . .Adele Anderson

***North Dallas Forty** (1979)*

Dayle Haddon . . . . Charlotte
Savannah Smith Bouchér. . . . . Joanne
- 0:27—Very brief breasts in bed tossing around with Nick Nolte.

• ***Northern Passage** (1994; Canadian)*

Neve Campbell . . . . Nepeese
- 0:16—Brief buns, while walking into the river, long shot.

***Nostradamus** (1993)*

Julia Ormond. . . . . Marie
- ••• 0:34—Left breast, several times, while making love in bed with Tcheky Karyo.

Amanda Plummer . . . . .Catherine De Medici
Diana Quick . . . . Diane De Portier

1:28—Back side of right breast, while getting dressed after sitting for painting.

Assumpta Serna. . . . . .Anne
- 1:13—Right breast, while standing and kissing Tcheky Karyo.

***Not Like Us** (1995; Made for Cable Movie)*

Janet Eilber . . . . Mrs. Bower
Rainer Grant . . . . .Janet
- •• 0:08—Breasts, opening her blouse in old truck in front of hitchhiker.
- 0:09—Brief breasts, while putting on blouse after stabbing the hitchhiker with a needle.
- •• 0:26—Breasts, while outside at night with two guys she picked up from bar.
- ••• 0:54—Breasts, while talking to Peter Onorati in doorway.
- •• 0:55—Breasts, after taking off her jacket to distract a policeman.

Annabelle Gurwitch . . . . Vicki
- 0:49—Breasts, while lying on operating table.
- •• 1:03—Breasts, after putting on her new skin (there's a bit of blood on her).

Joanna Pacula . . . . Anita

Not of This Earth (1988)

Ava Cadell . . . . Second Hooker
- •• 0:41—Breasts in cellar with Paul just before getting killed with two other hookers. Wearing a gold dress.

Kim Dawson . . . . Girl in House
Monique Gabrielle. . . . . Agnes
Roxanne Kernohan . . . . Lead Hooker
- ••• 0:41—Breasts in cellar with Paul just before getting killed with two other hookers. Wearing a blue top.

Becky LeBeau . . . . .Happy Birthday Girl
- ••• 0:47—Breasts doing a Happy Birthday stripper-gram for the old guy.

Traci Lords . . . . Nadine
- •• 0:25—Buns and side view of left breast drying herself off with a towel while talking to Jeremy.
- •• 0:42—Breasts in bed making love with Harry.

Kelli Maroney . . . . Nurse Mary Oxford
Taaffe O'Connell . . . . Damelia
- 0:04—Brief breasts and buns from *Galaxy of Terror* during the opening credits.

Rebecca Perle . . . . .Alien Girl
Cynthia Ann Thompson . . . . Third Hooker (black dress)

Not of This Earth (1995; Made for Cable Movie)

Elizabeth Barondes . . . . Amanda Sayles
- •• 0:35—Breasts, while sunbathing on lounge chair outside.

Not Quite Paradise (1986; British)

a.k.a. Not Quite Jerusalem

Joanna Pacula . . . . Gila
- 1:04—Left breast, lying in bed with Sam Robards.

Not Tonight Darling (1971; British)

Nicola Austine. . . . . At the West Side Health Club
Carol Catkin . . . . Jill
- •• 1:02—Buns and left breast, while in the shower and out. Brief full frontal nudity when getting out of bed.

Luan Peters . . . . Karen
- •• 0:04—Breasts and buns, taking off nightie and getting into bathtub.
- 0:05—Most of right breast, while sitting in tub, wishing her husband would look at her.
- •• 0:20—Breasts, while in bathroom, taking off her nightie while Eddie watches through binoculars.
- •• 0:26—Right breast, while sitting in bathtub. Brief full frontal nudity when getting out.
- ••• 0:38—In white bra, then breasts, while undressing in room with Alex.
- ••• 0:39—Right breast, while making love in bed with Alex. Brief breasts in close-up.
- 0:42—Breasts under sheer top.
- 0:58—Buns, while getting massaged by Joan at the health club.

Nothing Underneath (1985; Italian)

a.k.a. Sotto Il Vestito Niente

Anna Galiena. . . . . n.a.
Renee Simonsen . . . . Barbara
- 0:51—Brief side view of left breast, changing backstage during fashion show.

Novel Desires (1991)

Monica Akesson. . . . . .Model
- ••• 0:17—Buns, then breasts while making love outside during story.
- ••• 0:18—Breasts making love on picnic table with Eric.

Leigh Betchley . . . . Susan
- ••• 0:13—Breasts in warehouse making love with Sandman. Long scene.
- ••• 0:15—More breasts while talking to Sandman.

Lysa Hayland . . . . Linda
Gina Jourard . . . . .Shari
- •• 0:00—Right breast, then breasts in bed with Brian.
- •• 0:03—Breasts while taking a shower.
- •• 0:04—Brief tip of left breast while putting on a stocking. Breasts while getting dressed.

Nowhere to Hide (1987)

Amy Madigan . . . . Barbara Cutter
- 1:04—Brief side view of right breast taking off towel to get dressed in cabin. Long shot, hard to see.

Nowhere to Run (1993)

Rosanna Arquette . . . . .Clydie
- ••• 0:11—In white bra and panties, undressing in bathroom, then nude, getting into the shower while Jean-Claude Van Damme peeks in through the window.
- ••• 1:01—In bra, then breasts while making love in bed with Van Damme.

• *Nude Bowling Party* (1995; Video Tape)

Cory Lane . . . . Tina
- ••• 0:00—Nude throughout.

Jacqueline Lovell . . . . .Barbie
- ••• 0:00—Nude throughout.

Tammy Parks. . . . . .Bambi
- ••• 0:00—Nude throughout.

• *Nude Daydreams* (1993; Video Tape)

Melinda Armstrong . . . . Daydream 1
- ••• 0:01—Nude in and out of lingerie. Long scene.

Stephanie Champlin . . . . Daydream 10
- ••• 0:27—Breasts and partial buns (she's on the right) while playing violin in a musical trio.

Lisa Comshaw . . . . Daydream 7
- ••• 0:22—Nude, while taking a shower.

Diana Cuevas. . . . . Daydream 3
- 0:07—Left breast, while playing piano, when another woman dances around ballet style.

Kelly Jaye . . . . Daydream 8/13
- ••• 0:27—Breasts and partial buns and partial lower frontal nudity (she's on the left) while playing violin in a musical trio.
- ••• 0:40—In black dress, then buns in lingerie, then nude while posing on a stool. Long scene.

Heather Kennedy. . . . . Daydream 12
- ••• 0:36—Buns in red bra and panties, then nude while dancing around (including splits). Long scene.

Monique Parent. . . . . Daydream 4
- ••• 0:12—In black lingerie, then nude while caressing Ashlie Rhey on sofa. Long scene.

Ashlie Rhey . . . . Daydream 5
- ••• 0:12—In black and white lingerie, then nude while caressing Monique Parent on sofa. Long scene.

Jeanine Robért . . . . Daydream 9
- •• 0:27—Right breast (she's in the middle) while playing cello in a musical trio.

• *Nude Models in Hollywood* (1995; Video Tape)

Lucie Malkrabova . . . . Sophia
- •• 0:19—Buns in lingerie, while posing for photographs.
- ••• 0:21—Nude, wearing stockings, while posing for photographs.
- ••• 0:29—Nude, wearing stockings, while dancing next to Natasha.
- ••• 0:38—Nude, while dancing by herself.

Karolina Mirosova . . . . Natasha
- •• 0:10—Buns in lingerie, while posing for photographs.
- ••• 0:13—Nude, while posing for photographs.
- ••• 0:29—Nude, while dancing next to Sophia.
- 0:36—Nude, while dancing by herself.

***Nudity Required* (1989)**

Pamela Bach . . . . Dee Dee

Gail Harris . . . . Midge
- •• 0:36—Breasts, asking Buddy a question. Brief breasts (tenth girl) standing in line.
- ••• 0:37—Breasts doing her song and tap dance audition.
- • 0:44—Breasts while playing in pool.

Becky LeBeau . . . . Melanie
- •• 0:35—Breasts, after taking off pink swimsuit.
- •• 0:36—Brief breasts (third girl) standing in line.
- • 0:37—Breasts, standing behind Scammer.
- • 0:39—Very brief breasts.
- •• 0:41—Breasts while sitting next to Scammer by the pool.

Caroline Lomas . . . . Caroline
- •• 0:36—Brief breasts (fifth girl) standing in line.
- •• 0:37—Breasts doing puppet routine for audition.
- •• 0:38—Breasts while yelling for not having a script.
- • 0:39—Breasts.
- • 0:44—Breasts while sitting on the edge of the pool.

Julie Newmar . . . . Irina
- • 0:57—Side of left breast and side view of buns behind textured shower door with Buddy.

Heidi Paine . . . . Jane

Ty Randolph . . . . Brenda

Misty Regan . . . . Featured Dancer
- • 0:02—Breasts dancing on stage in club.
- • 0:04—Breasts and buns, on stage in G-string.

Edy Williams . . . . Isabella
- ••• 1:05—Breasts, with whip, while acting in movie.
- •• 1:07—More breasts in movie.
- •• 1:09—More right breast.
- •• 1:13—Breasts, during screening of the movie.

***Nudo di Donna* (1984; Italian)**

a.k.a. Portrait of a Woman, Nude

Eleonora Giorgi . . . . Laura
- • 0:11—Very brief left breast, while taking off robe. Subtitles get in the way.
- • 0:12—Right breast, while in the shower, getting consoled.
- • 0:13—Brief upper half breasts, getting into bed.
- •• 0:14—Breasts in bed.
- •• 0:36—Nude, mostly buns, sleeping in bed when Sandro pulls back the covers.
- • 1:12—Brief right breast, while in bed with Sandro.
- • 1:13—Right breast under sheer dress.

***Number One Fan* (1994)**

Renee Ammann. . . . . Blair Madsen
- ••• 0:18—In black bra, in bedroom with Chad McQueen, then breasts and buns while making love with him on the bed.
- • 0:21—Brief right breast, while lying in bed in the morning
- •• 0:26—Breasts, while making love with McQueen in the kitchen.
- • 0:28—Very brief, upper half of right breast, while standing outside with McQueen.
- • 0:39—Brief breasts in open trench coat with Chad McQueen. Brief breasts while straddling over him during struggle.

Gloria Delaney. . . . . Nurse

Suzanne Solari. . . . . Gabrielle
- •• 0:36—Right breast, twice, while making love in bed with Chad McQueen during filming of a movie.
- • 1:11—Buns and breasts, dressing in the background (slightly out of focus) while McQueen does his lines.

Catherine Mary Stewart. Holly Newman

Mary Woronov . . . . Wedding Coordinator

***O Lucky Man!* (1973; British)**

Mary MacLeod . . . . Mary Ball/Salvationist/Vicar's Wife
- • 1:06—Very brief left breast (over the shoulder shot) while letting Malcolm McDowell suck on her breast, after she catches him trying to steal food in church.

Helen Mirren . . . . Patricia Burgess

Christine Noonan . . . . Coffee Trainee/Girl at Stag Party

***Object of Desire* (1991)**

Tara Buckman . . . . Angie
- • 0:12—Breasts, leaning up on massage table.
- ••• 0:14—Breasts, getting dressed so Derrick can see.
- •• 0:23—Breasts, making love with Derrick in her dressing room.
- ••• 0:28—Breasts in bathtub with Derrick.
- • 0:43—Right breast, while making love in bed with Derrick.
- • 0:50—Side view of buns, while lying in bed.
- •• 0:51—Right breast, while sitting up in bed, then full frontal nudity.
- ••• 0:55—Breasts, opening her blouse in Steve's office in front of him.
- ••• 1:09—Full frontal nudity, posing for photographer in studio. Also side view of his buns.
- • 1:12—Brief breasts in magazine photos.
- ••• 1:18—Breasts changing clothes in dressing room.

Laura Gemser . . . . Uncredited Photographer

***Object of Obsession* (1994)**

Erika Anderson . . . . Margaret
- • 0:11—Brief breasts, several times, while making love when imagining herself in a movie that she's watching on TV. Don't see her face.
- •• 0:29—Beasts, while making love in bed with Scott Valentine.
- • 0:46—Brief buns, while making love in bed with Valentine.
- • 1:00—Very, very brief right breast, while shaving her legs in the bathtub.
- • 1:07—Brief partial right breast, while under Harvey in bed.

Alisha Das . . . . Charlotte

Jane Higginson . . . . Vicky

Jennifer MacDonald. . . . . Amy
- •• 1:16—Full frontal nudity, after taking off dress while lying in bed on video playback.

Andrea Riave . . . . Francine
- •• 1:18—Full frontal nudity, while on bed with Scott Valentine in video playback.

Elizabeth Whitcraft . . . . Christy

Obsessed with Lust (1995)

a.k.a. Prelude to Love

Tamara Landry . . . . Jennifer
- •• 0:01—Breasts, while making love with a guy backstage during fashion show.
- •• 0:38—Breasts, when taking off dress and putting on a blouse while talking with David.
- ••• 0:43—Buns in T-back, then breasts and buns, while making love with Carlton on sofa.

Ashlie Rhey . . . . Lanie
- ••• 0:21—Full frontal nudity, while making love with Steve in bed.
- • 0:25—Brief breasts, while sitting up in bed when Steve leaves.
- ••• 1:12—Breasts, while making love with Eric on pool table.

Doria Rone . . . . Carrie
- ••• 0:27—Breasts and buns, while making love on the floor with David. Long scene.
- ••• 0:58—Breasts and partial lower frontal nudity, while making love with Eric in bed. Long scene.

Lynn Wolf . . . . Chloe
- ••• 0:08—Breasts, while making love with Eric in his apartment.

Obsession: A Taste For Fear (1987)

Teagan Clive . . . . Teagan Morrison
- • 0:15—Brief upper half of right breast, when she lies back down in bed.
- • 0:29—Buns, while lying dead, covered with plastic wrap.
- • 0:37—Very brief buns in flashback to 0:29 scene.

Eva Grimaldi . . . . n.a.

Virginia Hey. . . . . Diane
- • 0:02—Breasts, lying in sauna.
- • 0:04—Buns and very brief side view of right breast dropping towel to take a shower.
- •• 0:14—Brief right breast in bed when sheet falls down.
- • 0:37—Most of left breast, while crying.
- • 0:39—Breasts, lying in bed talking to Kim.
- ••• 1:03—Breasts waking up in bed.
- • 1:05—Breasts, getting ready to get dressed. Long shot.
- ••• 1:17—Breasts in hallway with Valerie.
- • 1:19—Brief lower frontal nudity and right breast in bed with Valerie, then buns in bed.
- ••• 1:20—Breasts getting dressed, walking and running around the house when Valerie gets killed.
- • 1:26—Breasts tied up in chair while Paul torments her. Lit with red light.

• *An Occasional Hell* (1996)

Valeria Golino . . . . Elizabeth Laughton
- ••• 0:56—In black bra, then breasts, while making love with Tom Berenger at night.

Ellen Greene . . . . Della

Kari Wührer. . . . . Jeri Gillen
- • 0:00—Very, very brief right breast, while making love in car with Alex. Then brief breasts, covered with blood after he gets shot.
- ••• 0:34—Breasts, while wearing shorts, then panties, when taking photographs outdoors with Alex in Tom Berenger's fantasy.
- • 1:25—Brief breasts in car again when Alex is shot, then when she runs through the woods.

The Octagon (1980)

Carol Bagdasarian . . . . Aura
- • 1:18—Brief side view of right breast, while taking off her blouse, sitting on bed next to Chuck Norris.

Karen Carlson . . . . Justine

Kim Lankford . . . . Nancy

Of Unknown Origin (1983; Canadian)

Jennifer Dale . . . . Lorrie Wells

Shannon Tweed. . . . . Meg Hughes
- • 0:00—Brief side view of right breast taking a shower.

Off Limits (1988)

Thuy Ann Luu . . . . Lanh
- •• 0:48—Breasts dancing on stage in a nightclub.

Amanda Pays. . . . . Nicole

Off the Mark (1986)

Becky LeBeau. . . . . Uncredited Shower Girl
- • 0:52—Brief breasts, after taking off her pink T-shirt in locker room. Brief buns, while walking into showers (2nd to the last girl).

Off the Wall (1982)

Rosanna Arquette . . . . Pam

Jenny Neumann. . . . . Linda

Roselyn Royce . . . . Buxom Blonde
- • 0:35—Left breast, while kissing an inmate in visiting room while the guards watch.
- •• 0:51—Left breast again, while kissing inmate through bars while the guards watch.

Jeana Tomasina . . . . Mrs. Buck Banner

An Officer and a Gentleman (1982)

Lisa Blount. . . . . Lynette Pomeroy

Lisa Eilbacher. . . . . Casey Seeger

Debra Winger . . . . Paula Pokrifki
- ••• 1:05—Brief side view of right breast, then breasts making love with Richard Gere in a motel.

The Offspring (1986)

Martine Beswicke. . . . . Katherine White

Miriam Byrd-Nethery. . . . . Eileen Burnside
- • 0:26—Breasts in bathtub filled with ice while her husband tries to kill her with an ice pick.
- • 0:29—Very brief right breast, dead in bathtub while her husband is downstairs.

Susan Tyrrell . . . . Beth Chandler

Oh, Alfie! (1975; British)

a.k.a. Alfie Darling

Minah Bird. . . . . Gloria

Joan Collins . . . . Fay
- ••• 1:00—Breasts lying in bed after Alfie rolls off her.

Patsy Kensit . . . . Penny

Rula Lenska . . . . Louise
- •• 0:12—Breasts, then left breast in bed after making love with Alfie.

Vicki Michelle . . . . Bird

Annie Ross. . . . . Claire
- •• 1:34—Breasts on top of Alfie in open black dress while he's lying injured in bed.

Sheila White . . . . Norma

Oh, What a Night (1992)

Genevieve Bujold. . . . . Eva

Barbara Williams . . . . Vera
- •• 0:21—Very brief right breast, then very brief breasts, while undressing to go for a swim while Corey Haim watches without her knowledge. Brief breasts in the water and getting out.
- • 0:46—Breasts, while swimming the backstroke in the water while Haim watches again.
- ••• 0:59—Breasts, while swimming the backstroke again and getting out. (This time she knows that Haim is watching.) Nice slow motion shot for a PG-13 film! Very brief wet panties.
- •• 1:15—Left breast, while lying down on her back with Haim in a barn.

Old Gringo (1989)

Jane Fonda . . . . .Harriet Winslow
- • 1:24—Side of left breast, while undressing in front of Jimmy Smits. Sort of brief right breast, while lying in bed and hugging him.

• *The Oldest Profession* (1967)

Nadia Gray . . . . "Paris Today"
Anna Karina . . . . "Anticipation"
Jeanne Moreau . . . . "Mademoiselle Mimi"
Marilu Tolo . . . . "Anticipation"
- • 1:23—Brief side view of left breast, while walking to the bathroom. Shown as a negative image, so it's hard to see.

Olivia (1983)

a.k.a. A Taste of Sin

Suzanna Love . . . . Olivia
- •• 0:34—Buns and breasts making love in bed with Mike.
- •• 0:58—Breasts and buns making love with Mike in the shower.
- • 1:08—Very brief full frontal nudity getting into bed with Richard. Dark, long shot.
- •• 1:09—Buns, lying in bed. Dark. Full frontal nudity getting out of bed and going to the bathroom.

Olivier Olivier (1993; French)

Marina Golovine . . . . Nadine
- • 0:53—Very, very brief buns, when falling on her mom in bed while playing around. Very brief lower half of left breast, while adjusting the sheet.
- • 1:32—Breasts, while in bed with her brother. Don't see her face.

The Omega Man (1971)

Anna Aries. . . . . Woman in Cemetary Crypt
Rosalind Cash . . . . Lisa
- •• 1:09—Side view of left breast and upper half of buns getting out of bed. Buns and breasts sitting in bed.
- • 1:21—Side view breasts in beige underwear while trying on clothes.

On the Edge (1985)

(Unrated version reviewed.)

Pam Grier . . . . Cora
- •• 0:42—Breasts in the mirror, then full frontal nudity making love with Bruce Dern standing up. Then brief left breast. A little dark.

On the Line (1984; Spanish)

Victoria Abril . . . . Engracia
- ••• 0:16—Breasts getting undressed to make love with Mitch.
- • 0:29—Very brief breasts, making love in bed with Mitch.

Once Upon a Time in America (1984)

(Long version reviewed.)

Jennifer Connelly. . . . . Young Deborah
Darlanne Fluegel . . . . Eve
Olga Karlatos. . . . . Woman in the Puppet Theatre
- •• 0:11—Right breast twice when bad guy pokes at her nipple with a gun.

Elizabeth McGovern . . . . Deborah
- • 2:33—(0:32 into tape 2) Brief glimpses of left breast when Robert De Niro tries to rape her in the back seat of a car.

Once Were Warriors (1994; New Zealand)

Rena Owen . . . . Beth Heke
- • 0:29—Brief side view of left breast, while sitting up in bed.

• *The One and Only Phyllis Dixey* (1978)

Lesley-Anne Down. . . . . Phyllis Dixey
- • 0:14—Side view of right breast, long shot, then right breast and buns in closer shot, while kneeling in front of altar in play.
- • 0:29—Left nipple, visible between arm and hands during autobiographical strip tease on stage.
- • 0:30—Very brief side view of buns, during fan dance on stage.
- • 0:31—Brief breasts, after lifting fans at the end of fan dance. Medium long shot.
- • 0:43—Brief breasts, after opening sheer wedding dress during dance on stage.
- • 0:44—Very, very brief right breast when flipping coat from one side to the other.
- • 1:05—Side of right breast and buns, while kneeling at altar. Medium long shot.
- • 1:10—Brief left breast, under fur boa. Seen from side stage. Brief breasts after finishing.

One Deadly Summer (1984; French)

Isabelle Adjani . . . . Eliane
- •• 0:21—Brief breasts changing in the window for Florimond.
- ••• 0:32—Nude, walking in and out of the barn.
- • 0:36—Brief left breast lying in bed when Florimond gets up.
- • 0:40—Buns and breasts taking a bath.
- • 1:41—Part of right breast, getting felt up by an old guy, then right breast then brief breasts.
- •• 1:47—Breasts in bedroom with Florimond.

One Flew Over the Cuckoo's Nest (1975)

Louisa Moritz. . . . . Rose
Marya Small . . . . .Candy
- • 1:00—Very brief side view of left breast, bending over to pick up her clothes on boat.

One from the Heart (1982)

Teri Garr . . . . Frannie
- •• 0:09—Brief breasts getting out of the shower.
- •• 0:40—Side view of right breast changing in. bedroom while Frederic Forrest watches.
- ••• 1:20—Brief breasts in bed when standing up after Forrest drops in though the roof while she's in bed with Raul Julia.

Nastassja Kinski . . . . Leila
- • 1:13—Brief breasts in open blouse when she leans forward after walking on a ball.

• *One Good Turn* (1995)

Suzy Amis . . . . Laura Forrest

Audie England . . . . Kristen
•• 0:49—Breasts, while making love with James Remar on roof of building.
Melanie Good . . . . Newton
• 0:36—Breasts in open blouse, while doing stuff in the kitchen at night.
•• 0:37—Breasts, while making love with James Remar seen by Suzy Amis.

One Man Army (1993)

a.k.a. Kick and Fury
Melissa Anne Moore . . . . Natalie Pierce
••• 0:26—Breasts, while taking a shower and drying herself off.
••• 0:29—Breasts, while making love with Jerry Trimble in bed.
•• 0:33—Left breasts, while taking off her blouse to go for a swim. Breasts while in water after getting shot in the arm.

One Man Force (1989)

Blueberry. . . . . Santiago's Girlfriend
Maria Celedonio . . . . Maria
• 0:30—Brief breasts, twice, while hiding John Matuzak in her apartment. Long shot.
Sharon Farrell . . . . .Shirley
Stacey Q . . . . Lea

One Million Heels B.C. (1993)

Michelle Bauer. . . . . Cavegirl
••• 0:10—Half of right breast, while in skimpy top, under Rose in bed. Nude in the shower with Rose.
•• 0:12—Breasts, while sitting on bed.
••• 0:13—Full frontal nudity while trying on lingerie.
••• 0:21—Nude, while soaping Savannah and Rose in the spa.
• 0:25—Brief full frontal nudity taking off her towel in bedroom.
••• 0:26—Breasts and buns, while getting dressed on bed.
Jerica Fox. . . . . Savannah
••• 0:16—In lingerie, then nude while dancing in living room with Rose.
••• 0:21—Full frontal nudity, while soaping Rose and Bauer in the spa.
• 0:25—Brief full frontal nudity, after taking off her towel in bedroom.
••• 0:26—Full frontal nudity, while getting dressed.

One More Saturday Night (1986)

Moira Harris . . . . Peggy
Bess Meyer . . . . Tobi
• 1:02—Brief breasts in bed with Tom Davis.
Nina Siemaszko. . . . . .Karen Lundahl

One Night Only (1984; Canadian)

a.k.a. For One Night Only
Wendy Lands . . . . Jane
•• 0:36—Breasts taking a bath while Jamie watches through keyhole.
•• 0:38—Brief left breast in open robe.
• 1:15—Brief breasts in bed with policeman.
Helene Udy . . . . Suzanne
• 0:50—Buns and right breast in bed talking with a guy.
• 1:12—Over the shoulder, brief left breast on top of a guy in bed.
Lenore Zann . . . . .Anne
•• 0:20—Breasts while getting dressed in bedroom with Jamie.
• 1:04—Right breast in bedroom with Jamie.
••• 1:19—Breasts and buns while making love with Jamie.

• *One Night Stand* (1994)

a.k.a. Before the Night
Diane Salinger . . . . .Barbara Joslyn
Ally Sheedy . . . . .Mickey Sanderson
• 0:59—Very brief right breast, while making love under A Martinez in flashback.
Jodi Thelen . . . . Janice

• *One Night Stand* (1997)

Lisa Ann Cabasa. . . . . .Armani Model
Amanda Donohoe . . . . .Margaux
Annabelle Gurwitch. . . . . Marie
Nastassja Kinski . . . . Karen
• 0:30—Brief right breast, while making love in bed with Wesley Snipes.
Trula Marcus . . . . .Party Guest
Zoë Nathenson . . . . Mickey
Ione Skye. . . . . .Charlie's Friend
Sabrina Van Tassel. . . . . .Armani Model
Ming-Na Wen . . . . .Mimi
••• 1:04—Breasts, while sleeping in bed next to Wesley Snipes before he covers her up.

One Trick Pony (1980)

Blair Brown . . . . Marion
Joan Hackett . . . . Lonnie Fox
••• 1:21—Nude getting out of bed and getting dressed while talking to Paul Simon.
Mare Winningham. . . . . McDeena Dandridge
•• 0:14—Breasts, while in the bathtub with Paul Simon, smoking a cigarette. Long scene.

One Way Out (1995)

Isabel Gillies. . . . . Betsy
• 1:26—Very brief right breast, while kissing Frank in bedroom.
Annie Golden . . . . Eve
• 1:31—Very brief left breast, in gaping blouse when bending over to help Frank. Slow motion.

One Woman or Two (1986; French)

a.k.a. Une Femme Ou Deux
Zabou . . . . Constance
•• 0:28—Brief breasts pulling up her blouse for Gerard Depardieu.
Sigourney Weaver . . . . .Jessica
•• 1:31—Very brief side view of left breast in bed with Gerard Depardieu.

Open House (1987)

Roxanne Baird . . . . .Allison
•• 1:12—Buns and brief side view of left breast walking to swimming pool, then breasts getting out of the pool before the killer gets her.
Adrienne Barbeau . . . . Lisa Grant
• 0:27—In black lace lingerie, then very brief half of left breast making love with Joseph Bottoms on the floor.
•• 1:15—Brief side view of right breast getting out of bed at night to look at something in her briefcase.
••• 1:16—Brief breasts taking off bathrobe and getting back into bed. Kind of dark.
Tiffany Bolling . . . . Judy Roberts
Cathryn Hartt . . . . .Melody
Mary Stavin . . . . Katie Thatcher

Opposing Force *(1986)*

a.k.a. Hell Camp

Lisa Eichhorn. . . . . .Lieutenant Casey
- • 0:17—Wet T-shirt after going through river.
- ••• 0:33—Breasts getting sprayed with water and dusted with white powder.
- •• 1:03—Breasts after getting raped by Anthony Zerbe in his office, while another officer watches.
- ••• 1:05—Breasts and buns, getting dressed.

Ordeal by Innocence *(1984)*

Faye Dunaway. . . . . Rachel Argyle
Sarah Miles . . . . Mary Durrant
Diana Quick . . . . Gwenda Vaughn
Cassie Stuart . . . . Maureen Clegg
- •• 1:14—Breasts in bed talking to Donald Sutherland.

Orlando *(1993; British)*

Mary MacLeod . . . . First Woman
Tilda Swinton . . . . Orlando
- ••• 0:56—Full frontal nudity while looking at herself in mirror.

Charlotte Valandrey . . . . Sasha

Orpheus Descending *(1990)*

Vanessa Redgrave . . . . Lady Torrance
- •• 1:18—Buns, after taking off her robe and opening curtains to see Kevin Anderson. Shadow of left breast on curtain.

Anne Twomey. . . . . Carol Cutrere

The Osterman Weekend *(1983)*

Meg Foster . . . . Ali Tanner
- • 0:14—Very, very brief tip of right breast after getting nightgown out of closet.

Helen Shaver. . . . . .Virginia Tremayne
- •• 0:24—Breasts in an open blouse yelling at her husband in the bedroom.
- • 0:41—Breasts in the swimming pool when everyone watches on the TV.

Merete Van Kamp . . . . Zuna Brickman
- •• 0:01—Breasts and brief buns in bed on a TV monitor, then breasts getting injected by two intruders.
- • 0:35—Brief breasts on video again while Rutger Hauer watches in the kitchen on TV.
- • 1:30—Breasts again on video during TV show.

Cassie Yates. . . . . Betty Cardone
- •• 0:48—Breasts getting into bed with Chris Sarandon while Rutger Hauer watches on TV.
- • 0:51—Right breast, making love with Sarandon.

Othello *(1995; British)*

Irène Jacob . . . . .Desdemona
- • 0:32—Brief breasts, taking off her dress (long shot) and getting onto bed behind sheer curtain. Right breast, while in bed with Larry Fishburne.

Other Side of Midnight *(1977)*

Marie-France Pisier . . . . .Noëlle Page
- • 0:10—Very brief breasts in bed with Lanchon.
- • 0:28—Buns, in bed with John Beck. Medium long shot.
- • 0:50—Breasts in bathtub, while giving herself an abortion with a coat hanger. Painful to watch!
- •• 1:11—Breasts wearing white slip in room getting dressed in front of Henri.
- ••• 1:17—Full frontal nudity in front of fireplace with Armand, rubbing herself with oil, then making love with ice cubes. Very nice!
- • 1:35—Full frontal nudity taking off dress for Constantin in his room.

Susan Sarandon. . . . . Catherine Douglas
- • 1:10—Breasts in bedroom with John Beck. Long shot, then right breast while lying in bed.

The Other Woman *(1992)*

(Unrated version reviewed.)

Martine Anuszek . . . . Sheila
- •• 0:31—Buns and side of left breast, posing with Traci for Elysse at the beach.
- ••• 0:32—Full frontal nudity, posing with Traci at the beach.
- • 0:33—Breasts and buns, running in the surf. Long shot.
- •• 0:40—Breasts at the beach during Jessica's flashbacks.

Lee Anne Beaman . . . . Jessica Mathews
- ••• 0:17—Nude, undressing and getting into the shower.
- •• 0:40—Breasts in the bathtub.
- •• 0:51—Buns, while lying in bed in the fetal position.
- ••• 1:09—Nude, on the floor making love with Traci. Interesting camera angles.
- ••• 1:13—Nude, getting up and out of bed, taking a shower, then making love with Carl. Long scene.
- •• 1:23—Breasts on floor with Traci during video playback on TV.
- ••• 1:34—Buns, in long shot, taking off robe to greet Zmed. Breasts and buns in bed with him.

Regina Gielser . . . . Neighbor
- •• 0:49—Breasts and buns, while in bed with Jessica's mother during young Jessica's flashback.

Melissa Anne Moore . . . . Elysse
- •• 0:58—Breasts, taking off her blouse while taking pictures during photo shoot.

Jenna Persaud . . . . Traci Collins
- •• 0:21—Breasts under sheer black top in her apartment with her boyfriend.
- ••• 0:22—Breasts taking off her top and getting milk poured on her.
- ••• 0:23—Breasts and buns, making love in kitchen while Jessica secretly watches.
- •• 0:31—Breasts posing with Sheila at the beach for Elysse.
- ••• 0:32—Full frontal nudity at the beach some more.
- • 0:33—Breasts and buns, running in the surf. Long shot.
- •• 0:40—Breasts, during Jessica's flashbacks.
- ••• 0:53—Nude, taking a shower, drying herself off and putting on robe.
- ••• 0:57—Breasts posing with Carl during photo shoot.
- •• 0:59—More breasts during photo shoot.
- ••• 1:09—Breasts and buns, on the floor making love with Jessica. Interesting camera angles.
- • 1:23—Breasts, while on the floor with Jessica during video playback on TV.

Out Cold *(1989)*

Lisa Blount. . . . . Phyllis
Teri Garr . . . . Sunny Cannald
Debra Lamb . . . . Panetti's Dancer
- • 1:04—Brief breasts dancing in G-string on stage. Don't see her face.

Out for Justice *(1991)*

Erin Weidner Ashley. . . . . Hooker
Jo Champa . . . . .Vicky Felino
Gina Gershon . . . . Patti Modono
Athena Massey . . . . .n.a.
Shareen Mitchell . . . . .Laurie Lupo

Julie Strain . . . . Roxanne Ford
- 0:53—Brief side view of right breast in Polaroid photograph that Steven Seagal looks at.
- 1:06—Brief side view of right breast in Polaroid again.
- 1:11—Brief right breast, twice, dead in bed when discovered by Seagal.
- 1:12—Briefly in Polaroid again.

Shannon Whirry . . . . Terry Malloy

Out of Control *(1984)*

Cindi Dietrich . . . . Robin
- 0:29—Breasts taking off her red top. Long shot.

Sherilyn Fenn . . . . Katie

Betsy Russell . . . . Chrissie
- •• 0:29—Breasts taking off her top while playing Strip Spin the Bottle.
- 0:30—Buns, taking off her panties.

Claudia Udy . . . . Tina
- 0:28—In leopard bra and panties playing Strip Spin the Bottle, then very brief breasts taking off her top. Long shot.
- 0:47—Brief left breast getting raped by bad guy on the boat.
- 0:54—Brief left breast, then right breast making love with Cowboy.

Out of Season *(1975; British)*

Susan George . . . . Joanna
- 1:24—Nude, while walking in front of Cliff Robertson. Long shot.

Vanessa Redgrave . . . . .Ann
- 0:35—Breasts, while putting on slip in bedroom.
- 0:53—Full frontal nudity, after throwing open bed covers for Cliff Robertson. Don't see her face.

Out of Sync *(1995)*

Victoria Dillard. . . . . Monica Collins
- •• 1:24—Breasts and buns, taking off her swimsuit and showering.

Renato Powell . . . . Debra B. Collins
- 1:21—Brief right breast, while lying dead in bathtub when discovered by LL Cool J.

Out of the Blue *(1982)*

Sharon Farrell . . . . Kathy
- 1:18—Left breast, when Don Gordon pulls it out of her nightgown and fondles it.

Michele Little. . . . . Girl in Car

Out of the Dark *(1988)*

Starr Andreeff . . . . Camille

Karen Black . . . . Ruth

Bond Bradigan . . . . Hooker/Lee
- •• 1:04—Buns, wearing corset, black stockings and garter belt. Long shot breasts, then breasts in bathroom.

Teresa Crespo . . . . Debbie

Lynn Danielson . . . . Kristi
- 0:09—Brief breasts getting out of bed. More breasts outside getting photographed.
- •• 1:01—Breasts in motel room making love with Kevin.
- 1:06—Left breast, while getting out of bed.

Silvana Gallardo . . . . .McDonald

Karen Mayo-Chandler . . . . Barbara
- 0:16—Brief breasts pulling red dress down wearing black stocking in Kevin's studio.
- ••• 0:17—Breasts and buns posing during photo shoot.

Karen Witter . . . . .Jo Ann

Out on Bail *(1988)*

Adrienne Pearce. . . . . .Maggie

Kathy Shower . . . . .Sally Anne
- 1:01—Brief breasts in shower with Robert Ginty.

The Outing *(1987)*

Michelle Watkins . . . . Faylene
- •• 0:12—Breasts taking off her top, standing by the edge of the swimming pool, then running breasts through the house with panties on.

Outland *(1981)*

Sharon Duce . . . . Prostitute
- 0:30—Right breast, whle lying down in room with drug crazed guy.
- 0:32—Breasts, while entering medical scanning device.

Kika Markham . . . . Carol

The Outlaw Josey Wales *(1976)*

Sondra Locke. . . . . Laura Lee
- •• 1:20—Briefly nude in rape scene.

Outrage *(1993; Spanish)*

a.k.a. Shoot
a.k.a. Dispara

Francesca Neri. . . . . Giuditta/Anna Meltzer
- •• 0:20—Breasts, after taking off robe and putting on blouse in her trailer.
- •• 0:32—Full frontal nudity, while in bed with Antonio Banderas.
- 0:42—Nude, in her trailer at night, getting raped by three punks.
- •• 0:45—Full frontal nudity, while in shower, washing herself off.

Outside the Law *(1994)*

a.k.a. Blood Run
(Unrated version reviewed.)

Kelly Galindo . . . . Greta

Ashley Laurence. . . . . Paige

Stephanie Swinney . . . . Billy
- ••• 0:02—Breasts after taking off swimsuit top, then buns and breasts, in bathtub and getting out. Very, very brief partial lower frontal nudity behind towel.

Anna Thomson . . . . Tanya
- 0:32—Buns under water in pool and getting out. Partial breasts while putting on robe in front of David Bradley.
- ••• 0:33—Breasts, while making love with Bradley on counter of bar. Nice, but some of it is her, and some is a body double.
- 0:49—In white bra, then breasts and buns, while making love with Bradley. Don't see her face, it looks like a body double.

Over the Hill *(1991; Australian)*

Olympia Dukakis . . . . .Alma
- •• 0:56—Breasts, while getting them painted for tribal ceremony.

Sigrid Thornton . . . . .Elizabeth

Over the Wire *(1995)*

Kimberly Blair . . . . Sascha
- ••• 0:00—In bra and panties, when dancing and stripping in front of a guy, then breasts and buns, while making love.

Griffin Drew. . . . . Sally
- ••• 0:51—Nude, while making love in office with Roy.

Landon Hall. . . . . Susan
••• 0:11—In bra and panties, then nude, while making love in bed with Mark.
••• 0:30—Breasts and buns, while making love in bedroom with Bruce.

Shauna O'Brien . . . . Rachel
••• 0:20—Nude, while making love in bed with Mark, when seen by Susan. Long scene.
• 0:47—Breasts, while changing clothes in dressing room.
••• 1:01—Nude, while making love with Bruce in living room, then bathtub.

Brinke Stevens. . . . . .Jenny

Overexposed *(1990)*

Karen Black . . . . Mrs. Trowbridge
Shelley Michelle . . . . Body Double for Catherine Oxenberg
•• 0:54—Left breast several times, buns when taking off panties, lower frontal nudity while in bed with Hank. Wearing a wig with wavy hair.

Overseas *(1991; French)*

Marianne Basler . . . . Gritte
Nicole Garcia . . . . .Zon
• 0:12—Brief breasts behind mosquito net while in bed.
• 0:13—Brief breasts while playing with Paul in the bathroom. Very brief left breast, while reaching for towel.

Pacific Banana *(1980; Australian)*

Alyson Best . . . . Mandy
Luan Peters . . . . Candy Bubbles
•• 1:00—Breasts several times flashing her breasts for Martin.

Pacific Heights *(1990)*

Beverly D'Angelo. . . . . .Ann
• 0:01—Sort of breasts in reflection on TV screen, then right breast, in bed with Michael Keaton.
• 0:03—Very brief buns, turning over on bed when two guys burst in to the house.

Melanie Griffith . . . . .Patty Parker

• ***Painted Hero*** *(1995)*

Michelle Joyner . . . . .Katelin
• 1:24—In bra and panties, while undressing in bedroom. Breasts, after taking off bra (medium long shot, then closer shot.)

Cindy Pickett. . . . . .Sadie
Kiersten Warren. . . . . Teresa
•• 0:22—Breasts, when flashing herself for Dwight Yokam while in the front seat of a car.

Pale Blood *(1990)*

Darcy De Moss . . . . .Cherry
• 0:33—Very, very brief left breast, while opening her robe while posing on couch.

Diana Frank. . . . . .Jenny
•• 0:21—Breasts lying on the bed with Michael when he bites her.
• 0:36—Close up of left breast on TV monitor that Wings Hauser is editing with. Don't see face.
• 0:42—Brief left breast on TV monitor several times while Hauser examines the bite marks.
• 1:03—Very brief breasts when Hauser pulls her dress top down to look at her bite mark.

The Pamela Principle *(1992)*

(Unrated version reviewed.)

Melissa Barrick. . . . . .Uncredited Steve's Girlfriend
••• 0:45—Breasts and buns in red G-string, then lower frontal nudity, while playing strip-card game with Steve.

Kim Burnette . . . . Pamela
•• 0:18—Brief breasts, when Miss Fontana accidentally opens the dressing room door.
••• 0:27—Full frontal nudity, while getting dressed in her bedroom while talking on the phone. In panties, then in bra.
0:34—Breasts under sheer black lingerie.
••• 0:36—Breasts and buns in G-string while stripping out of skirt and stockings in front of Carl, then making love on sofa and the floor.
••• 0:39—Breasts in white panties and stockings while doing splits and stretching out.
• 1:12—Left breast, with Carl in the doorway.
• 1:23—Side of right breast, while taking off dress and putting on bra. Brief buns in G-string while taking off stockings.
••• 1:29—Breasts and brief lower frontal nudity, while making love in bed with Felicia.
•• 1:30—Breasts, while in front of Carl.

Regina Gielser . . . . Felicia
••• 1:27—Buns and breasts, while in bed with Carl and Pamela.

Tamara Landry . . . . Anne Breeding
••• 0:08—Buns, while lying in bed with Carl, then breasts and lower frontal nudity.
•• 0:28—Breasts, while sitting up in bed.
••• 0:48—Breasts, waking up in bed, then buns and lower frontal nudity getting out.
••• 0:57—Breasts, while making love with Carl in the kitchen, then buns in bed.
••• 1:03—Buns and breasts while in the shower.

K.C. Williams . . . . Shannon
• 0:05—Very brief left breast in open blouse with Steve.
••• 0:06—Breasts and partial buns, while in hot tub with Steve.

The Panic in Needle Park *(1971)*

Ruth Alda . . . . Admitting Nurse
Kitty Winn. . . . . Helen
• 0:33—Brief side view of right breast, when reaching over to hug and kiss Al Pacino.
••• 0:42—Breasts, while sitting up in bed next to Pacino, then putting on T-shirt.

Paper Marriage *(1993)*

Sadie Frost. . . . . .Employment Agency Interviewer
Joanna Trzepiechinska . . . . Alicja Straikowska
• 0:41—Very brief breasts, under short top when she raises her arms to hold up tipping armoire. Very brief underside of right breast, while kneeling on the floor to prop up the armoire.

Paper Mask *(1991; British)*

Bridget Brammall. . . . . .Girl in Bed
•• 0:17—Breasts in bed with Matthew, while he is checking out her anatomy.

Amanda Donohoe . . . . .Christine Taylor
• 0:53—Breasts in bed under Matthew, then on top of him.

Barbara Leigh-Hunt . . . . Celia Mumford

Paperback Hero *(1973; Canadian)*

Elizabeth Ashley. . . . . Loretta
••• 0:37—Nude in shower with Keir Dullea. Long scene.
••• 0:39—Breasts, straddling Dullea in the shower.

Dayle Haddon . . . . Joanna
- 0:31—Lower half of buns, under T-shirt while standing behind a bar with Keir Dullea.

• *The Paperboy* *(1994)*

Karyn Dwyer . . . . Brenda
- 0:24—Breasts, while making out with her boyfriend on couch when Johnny peeks in the house.

Krista Errickson . . . . Diana
Alexandra Paul . . . . Melissa

Papillon *(1973)*

Ratna Assan . . . . Zoraima
- 1:54—Breasts, first seeing Steve McQueen.
- •• 1:55—Breasts, helping clean up McQueen on the beach and in the ocean.
- •• 1:56—Breasts, walking on the beach with McQueen.
- •• 1:57—Breasts, getting off boat and watching a guy open oysters.
- •• 2:00—Breasts, on beach, walking with McQueen while holding a torch.

Paradise *(1981)*

Phoebe Cates . . . . Sarah
- •• 0:23—Buns and breasts taking a shower in a cave while Willie Aames watches.
- 0:40—Very brief left breast caressing herself while looking at her reflection in the water.
- 0:43—Buns, getting out of bed to check out Aames' body while he sleeps.
- 0:46—Buns, washing herself in a pond at night.
- •• 0:55—Side view of her silhouette at the beach at night. Nude swimming in the water, viewed from below.
- 1:10—Breasts, while making love with Aames are a body double. Don't see her face.
- ••• 1:12—Nude swimming under water with Aames.
- 1:16—Breasts, while making love with Aames is a body double again.

Paradise *(1991)*

Melanie Griffith . . . . Lily Reed
Sarah Trigger. . . . . Darlene
- 0:14—Brief breasts ironing her clothes in open window while Willard and Billie watch from their tree house. Long shot after. Hard to see her face.

Paradise Motel *(1985)*

Leslee Bremmer. . . . . Uncredited Girl Leaving Room
- 0:38—Breasts buttoning her pink sweater, leaving motel room.

Colleen McDermott. . . . . Debbie
- •• 0:24—Breasts in motel room with Mic, when Sam lets them use a room.

Laurie Smith . . . . Honeymoon Wife
- ••• 0:02—Left breast, then breasts in Honeymoon Suite with her new husband, then making love in bed.

Parallel Lives *(1994; Made for Cable Movie)*

Lindsay Crouse . . . . .Una Pace
- 0:12—Very brief right breast in gaping dress, while bending over to make her bed on the sofa.

Ally Sheedy . . . . Louise
Helen Slater. . . . . .Elsa Freedman
Mira Sorvino . . . . Matty Derosa
JoBeth Williams . . . . .Win Winslow

Paranoia *(1969; Italian/French)*

Carroll Baker . . . . Kathryn West
- 0:13—Buns and partial glimpses of breasts, in shower with Peter.
- 0:16—Very, very brief upper half of right breast when Peter rips her dress.
- •• 0:17—Buns, while lying in bed with Peter.
- 0:25—Brief buns, under mesh black robe.

Colette Descombes . . . . Eva
- ••• 0:45—Breasts in bed with Peter, twice, when discovered by Carroll Baker.
- 0:49—Brief left breast and upper half of right breast.
- ••• 0:50—Left breast, then breasts while sleeping in bed when Baker wakes up. Lit with red light.
- ••• 0:52—Right breast, while in bed with Baker.
- •• 1:02—Brief breasts while sleeping in bed with Peter.
- ••• 1:19—Breasts in bed with Peter, buns while getting out of bed.
- •• 1:22—Breasts in bed while sleeping.

Parasite *(1982)*

Cherie Currie. . . . . Dana
Demi Moore . . . . .Patricia Welles
Joanelle Nadine Romero . . . . .Bo
Cheryl Smith . . . . Captive Girl
- •• 0:08—Breasts tied by wrists in kitchen.
- •• 0:12—Breasts knocking gun out of guy's hands standing behind fence.

Paris, France *(1993; Canadian)*

Leslie Hope . . . . Lucy
- 0:00—Full frontal nudity, while making love with Minter in bed. B&W.
- 0:12—Breasts, while making love in bed with Sloane.
- ••• 0:13—Nude, while getting back into bed.
- 0:14—Breasts, while making love.
- •• 0:18—Right breast, while lying in bed, then nude getting out and getting dressed.
- 0:20—Left breast, while wearing a wig and masturbating when her husband watches in a fantasy. B&W.
- •• 0:30—Left breast in mirror, while shaving her armpit with a straight razor.
- 0:41—Breasts, when making love with Minter in bed while wearing a wig. B&W.
- 0:45—Very brief frontal nudity, when Sloane pushes her away and she sits on sofa.
- ••• 0:46—Breasts, while making love on sofa with Sloane and talking on the phone with her dad.
- 0:48—Frontal nudity in open dress, then brief buns, when she lifts up her dress.
- •• 0:58—Buns, when lying on Minter and writing on his chest. Partial breast when hog-tied and blindfolded while Minter drops hot wax on her. Breasts when he rolls her over. B&W.
- 1:23—Lower frontal nudity, in open robe.
- ••• 1:24—Full frontal nudity in open robe, lying in bed.
- •• 1:26—Buns and left breast, while watching Sloane make love to her husband.
- •• 1:28—Nude, while lying in bed and getting out.

The Park is Mine *(1985; Made for Cable Movie)*

Helen Shaver . . . . .Valery Weaver
- 0:46—Very brief breasts undressing then very, very brief left breast, while catching clothes from Tommy Lee Jones.

Partners (1982)

Iris Alhanti . . . . Jogger
•• 0:21—Breasts in the shower when Ryan O'Neal opens the shower curtain.
Jennifer Ashley . . . . Secretary
Robyn Douglass . . . . Jill
•• 1:00—Brief breasts taking off her top and getting into bed with Ryan O'Neal.
Denise Galik . . . . Clara

Party Camp (1987)

Jewel Shepard . . . . Dyanne Stein
••• 0:57—In white bra and panties, then breasts playing strip poker with the boys.
April Wayne . . . . Nurse Brenda

Party Favors (1987)

Blondi . . . . Bobbi
•• 0:04—Breasts in dressing room, taking off red top and putting on black one.
• 0:23—Brief breasts when blouse pops off while delivering pizza.
••• 0:27—Breasts and buns in G-string doing a strip routine outside.
• 0:31—Brief breasts flapping her blouse to cool off.
••• 1:04—Breasts doing a strip routine in a little girl outfit. Buns, in G-string. More breasts after.
• 1:16—Nude taking off swimsuit next to pool during final credits.
April Dawn Dollarhide . . . . n.a.
Gail Harris . . . . Nicole
• 0:04—Breasts in dressing room with the other three girls changing into blue swimsuit.
• 0:11—Brief left breast in the swimsuit during dance practice.
• 0:12—Breasts during dance practice.
• 0:17—More breasts during dance practice.
•• 0:42—Breasts doing strip routine at anniversary party. Great buns in G-string shots.
••• 1:01—Breasts and buns in G-string after stripping from cheerleader outfit. Lots of bouncing breast shots. Mingling with the men afterwards.
• 1:16—Nude by the swimming pool during the final credits.
Jill Johnson . . . . Trixie
•• 0:04—Breasts in dressing room, taking off blue dress and putting on red swimsuit.
••• 0:35—Breasts in doctor's office taking off her clothes.
••• 1:03—Breasts doing strip routine in cowgirl costume. More breasts after.
• 1:16—Breasts taking off swimsuit next to pool during final credits.

Party Girl (1995)

Parker Posey . . . . Mary
• 0:58—Very brief side of left breast, while getting into the shower with Leo.

Party Incorporated (1989)

a.k.a. Party Girls
Marilyn Chambers . . . . Marilyn Sanders
••• 0:56—In lingerie, then breasts in bedroom with Weston. Nice!
• 1:11—Brief breasts on the beach when Peter takes her swimsuit top off.
Ruth Corrine Collins . . . . Betty
• 0:07—Breasts on desk with Dickie. Long shot.
•• 1:08—Breasts in bed with Weston when Marilyn Chambers comes in.
Jane Hamilton . . . . . Uncredited Whipped Cream Wrestling Girl
Susan Napoli . . . . Uncredited Party Girl
• 0:05—Brief breasts, while wearing a mask and dancing during party with two other girls.
• 0:08—Brief breasts again.
Karen Nielsen . . . . Diane
Debbie Rochon . . . . Trixie
Kimberly Taylor . . . . Felicia
•• 0:26—Breasts shaking her breasts trying an outfit on.
••• 0:39—Breasts and buns in G-string in the bar with the guys.
Christina Veronica . . . . Christina
••• 0:52—Buns and breasts dancing in front of everybody at party.

Party Line (1988)

Greta Blackburn . . . . Angelina
• 0:01—Partial side of left breast in open dress, while standing and kissing Curtis.
•• 0:02—Breasts in bed with Curtis. Brief breasts after rolling off him when Leif Garrett comes in.
Karen Mayo-Chandler . . . . Sugar Lips
•• 0:58—Breasts, opening her blouse while sitting on Garrett's lap.
• 1:01—Brief breasts, while lying dead in field, covered with blood.
Shawn Weatherly . . . . Asst. D.A. Stacy Sloane

Party Plane (1988)

Laura Albert . . . . Uncredited Auditioning Woman
•• 0:30—Breasts, taking off blue dress during audition. She's wearing a white ribbon in her ponytail.
Karen Annarino . . . . Judy
• 0:06—Very brief side view of left breast when Lee peeks through window. Don't see her face.
• 0:10—Very, very brief side of right breast when another guy goes to peek. Don't see her face.
• 0:22—Breasts behind shower door, while putting on towel.
Michele Burger . . . . Carol
• 0:31—Breasts, squirting whipped cream on herself for her audition.
•• 0:38—Breasts doing a strip tease routine on the plane.
••• 1:02—Breasts mud wrestling with Renee on the plane.
• 1:09—Breasts in the cockpit, covered with mud.
•• 1:17—Breasts in serving cart.
Iris Condon . . . . Renee
• 0:29—Buns, in white lingerie during audition.
••• 0:48—Breasts, while on plane doing a strip tease routine.
••• 1:02—Breasts, while mud wrestling with Carol.
• 1:12—Left breast, covered with mud, holding the Mad Bomber.
• 1:17—Left breast, then breasts in trunk with the Doctor.
Jill Johnson . . . . Laurie
••• 0:06—Breasts and buns changing clothes and getting into spa with her two girlfriends. (She's wearing a black swimsuit bottom.)
••• 0:11—Breasts getting out of spa.
•• 0:16—Breasts in pool after being pushed in and her swimsuit top comes off.
•• 0:20—In bra and panties, then breasts on plane doing a strip tease.
Jacqueline Palmer . . . . Suzie
••• 0:06—Breasts and buns changing clothes and getting into spa with her two girlfriends. (She's the dark haired one.)

- ••• 0:11—Breasts again, getting out of spa.
- ••• 0:23—In bra, then breasts doing strip tease routine on plane.
- •• 0:35—Breasts doing another routine on the plane.

Renee Way . . . . .Andy
- ••• 0:01—Breasts, while taking off her blouse to fix the plane.
- ••• 0:06—Breasts, while sitting on edge of spa.
- ••• 0:11—Breasts again, when getting out of spa.
- • 0:12—Brief breasts after dropping her towel while talking to Tim.

Pascali's Island (1988; British)

Helen Mirren . . . . Lydia Neuman
- • 1:00—Left breast, lying in bed with Charles Dance. Long shot.

• *A Passion for Murder* (1996)

a.k.a. Deadlock

Shauna O'Brien . . . . Kirsty
- •• 0:31—Buns in T-back, then breasts, while making love with Nick.
- ••• 0:45—In bra, then breasts and buns , while making love with Nick in barn.

Joli Piccolini . . . . Waitress

Deanne Power . . . . Lisa
- ••• 0:24—Breasts and buns, wearing chaps, while posing outdoors for photos.
- •• 1:16—Brief buns, while lying in bed. Breasts, while in bedroom with Evan.

Ashlie Rhey . . . . Debbie
- • 0:09—Very brief breasts, while sitting in lounge chairs by the pool.
- ••• 0:13—Breasts, while posing for photos with Allison.
- ••• 0:56—Breasts and buns, while making love with Evan in bath.
- • 1:03—Brief beasts, while making love, seen on TV.
- • 1:10—Brief breasts, twice, while making love, seen on TV.

Doria Rone . . . . .Allison
- • 0:09—Very brief breasts, while sitting in lounge chairs by the pool.
- ••• 0:13—Nude, while posing for photos with Debbie.
- ••• 1:05—Buns and breasts, while making love with the detective in kitchen.

The Passion of Beatrice (1988; French)

Julie Delpy . . . . .Béatrice
- • 0:58—Left breast, then breasts getting out of bed.
- ••• 1:11—Side view of right breast, holding dress after getting raped by her father. Nude, running to the door and barricading it with furniture.
- •• 1:12—More nude, arranging furniture.
- ••• 1:13—Full frontal nudity, wiping her crotch and burning her clothes.
- • 1:36—More of right breast, when her father puts soot on her face.
- •• 1:37—Brief left breast, then breasts and brief buns standing with soot on her face. Long shot.
- ••• 1:44—Breasts taking a bath. Subtitles get in the way a bit.

Maïté Maillé . . . . La Noiraude
- • 1:24—Brief left breast, showing Béatrice how she was abused.

Isabelle Nanty . . . . .La Nourrice
- •• 1:53—Right breast, offering her breast milk to Arnaud.

Tina Sportolaro . . . . Mère de François Enfant
- • 0:06—Brief breasts when the young François discovers her in bed with another man and kills him.

A Passion to Kill (1994)

Chelsea Field . . . . Diana
- • 0:16—Buns and side of left breast, while reaching for a towel in bathroom when Scott Bakula sees her.
- • 0:35—In sheer black polka dot blouse in Bakula's office.
- • 0:37—Buns and side of right breast, while in office with Bakula.
- ••• 0:55—Right breast, then breasts, while making love with Bakula in garage, then inside car.

Sheila Kelley. . . . . Beth

Past Midnight (1992; Made for Cable Movie)

Natasha Richardson . . . . Laura Matthews
- ••• 0:48—Breasts while making love in bed with Rutger Hauer.
- • 1:10—Very brief side of left breast, while getting into the shower.

Past Tense (1994; Made for Cable Movie)

Lara Flynn Boyle. . . . . Tory Bass/Sabrina James
- • 0:10—In black bra with Scott Glenn. Brief breasts two times. You don't see her face very well and one is a medium long shot.
- • 0:13—Supposedly her breasts, while making love with another guy during video playback on TV.
- • 0:15—Very brief buns in flashback while on top of Glenn on the floor. Medium long shot.
- • 0:28—Breasts, several times, during video playback on TV. Don't see her face very well.

Sheree Wilson . . . . .Emily Talbert
- •• 1:00—Left breast and most of right breast in open vest in front of Scott Glenn. Definitely not a body double!

Pat Garrett and Billy the Kid (1973)

(Uncut Director's version reviewed.)

Rutanya Alda . . . . .Ruthie Lee
- •• 1:35—Breasts, while sitting on bed with James Coburn. (She's the only girl wearing a necklace.)

Rita Coolidge. . . . . Maria
- •• 1:48—Brief right breast, while sitting on bed and getting undressed with Kris Kristofferson.

Patricia (1984)

Anne Parillaud . . . . Patricia Cook
- •• 0:25—Breasts, opening her jumpsuit top to get attention while trying to hitchhike.
- •• 0:30—Breasts in white panties, running around at a seminary, trying to get away from a group of guys.
- •• 0:31—Breasts in confessional booth.
- • 0:32—Running around some more.
- •• 0:37—Nude making love with Priscilla on bed.
- ••• 0:49—Dancing in two piece swimsuit, then breasts.
- •• 0:50—Breasts while lying on her stomach.
- • 0:52—Brief breasts running into the ocean.
- • 0:53—Brief breasts under water.
- • 0:55—More brief breasts shots under the water.
- ••• 0:56—Nude, getting out of the ocean and lying down on the beach.
- •• 1:09—Breasts taking off her dress and playing bullfight with Harry.
- •• 1:10—Nude, dancing in her room. Hard to see because the curtains get in the way.
- • 1:24—Brief buns while making love with Harry.
- • 1:26—Brief breasts while making love with Harry.
- ••• 1:27—Full frontal nudity making love on top of Harry in bed.

The Patriot (1986)

Simone Griffeth. . . . . Sean
•• 0:49—Brief breasts lying in bed, making love with Ryder.
Lorin Jean Vail . . . . Howard's Girl

Patti Rocks (1988)

Karen Landry. . . . . Patti
• 0:48—Buns, walking from bathroom to bedroom and shutting the door. Long shot.
• 0:48—Very brief right breast in shower with Billy.
•• 1:04—Breasts in bed with Eddie while Billy is out in the living room.

Patty Hearst (1989)

Dana Delany . . . . Celina
Frances Fisher . . . . .Yolanda
Natasha Richardson. . . . . Patricia Hearst
•• 0:13—Breasts, blindfolded in the bathtub while talking to a woman member of the S.L.A.

Pauline at the Beach (1983; French)

Arielle Dombasle . . . . Marion
• 0:24—Brief breasts lying in bed with a guy when her cousin looks in the window.
•• 0:43—Brief breasts in house kissing Henri, while he takes her white dress off.
•• 0:59—Breasts walking down the stairs in a white bikini bottom while putting a white blouse on.

Payback (1988)

Michele Burger . . . . .Laura
• 0:08—Brief breasts sitting up in bed just before getting shot, then brief breasts twice, dead in bed.
Jean Carol . . . . Donna Nathan
••• 0:24—Breasts opening her pink robe for Jason while reclining on couch.

Payback (1994)

(Special director's cut reviewed.)
Katherine Barrese . . . . .Woman in Prison
Lisa Robin Kelly . . . . Teenage Girl
Joan Severance . . . . Rose
•• 0:49—Breasts and partial lower frontal nudity, while making love with C. Thomas Howell in diner kitchen.
••• 0:55—Breasts and brief top of lower frontal nudity while making love with Howell on hood of car.
• 1:05—Brief half of left breast, in open robe.

Payday (1972)

Ahna Capri . . . . Mayleen
• 0:20—Left breast in bed sleeping, then right breast with Rip Torn.
••• 0:21—Breasts sitting up in bed smoking a cigarette and talking to Torn. Long scene.
Elayne Heilveil . . . . .Rosamond
• 1:21—Left breast while lying in bed after Rip Torn gets out of bed.

Peace Maker (1990)

Hilary Shepard . . . . Dori Caisson
• 1:08—Brief upper half of buns, taking off shirt and getting into shower. Brief side view of upper half of left breast, twice while making love with Townsend.

Peephole (1994)

Kristen Trucksess . . . . Sheena
• 0:16—Partial buns in panties, bra and garter belt while undressing in room in front of the Doctor.
• 0:17—Brief upper half of right breast, when raising her hands to wrap a shawl around herself.
• 0:40—Brief partial buns in panties in hiked up T-shirt.
• 0:45—Partial buns, while making out with a guy on the bed. Medium long shot.
••• 0:56—Buns and breasts, after getting out of bed and talking to the Doctor.

The Penitent (1988)

Rona De Ricci . . . . Celia Guerola
• 0:03—Breasts, while changing clothes in bedroom while Raul Julia watches. Mostly in silhouette.
• 0:27—In wet, white blouse, in the water with Armand Assante while he teaches her how to swim.

Pennies from Heaven (1981)

Jessica Harper . . . . Joan
• 0:43—Brief breasts opening her nightgown for Steve Martin.

• The Penthouse All-Pet Workout (1993; Video Tape)

Robin Brown . . . . Pet
• 0:00—Right breast during introduction.
•• 0:03—Brief nude shots while getting undressed and suited up.
••• 0:21—Nude on sofa inside.
••• 0:43—Nude with the other girls, exercising, working with equipment, in the pool and spa.
Jami Dion . . . . Pet
•• 0:00—Nude during introduction.
•• 0:03—Briefly nude, while getting undressed and suited up.
••• 0:28—Nude outside on sculpture and next to fence.
••• 0:43—Nude with the other girls, exercising, working with equipment, in the pool and spa.
Leslie Glass . . . . Pet
•• 0:00—Breasts during introduction.
•• 0:03—Brief nude shots while getting undressed and suited up.
••• 0:38—Nude on chair outside and in pool.
••• 0:43—Nude with the other girls, exercising, working with equipment, in the pool and spa.
Natalie Lennox . . . . Pet
•• 0:00—Full frontal nudity during introduction.
•• 0:03—Brief nude shots while getting undressed and suited up.
••• 0:35—In sheer white body suit, then nude on rocks and in waterfall.
••• 0:43—Nude with the other girls, exercising, working with equipment, in the pool and spa.
Susan Napoli . . . . Pet
•• 0:00—Full frontal nudity during introduction.
•• 0:03—Brief nude shots while getting undressed and suited up.
••• 0:14—Nude on couch inside.
••• 0:43—Nude with the other girls, exercising, working with equipment, in the pool and spa.
Julie Strain . . . . Pet
• 0:00—Breasts during introduction.
•• 0:03—Brief nude shots while getting undressed and suited up.
••• 0:06—Nude while posing outside.

••• 0:43—Nude with the other girls, exercising, working with equipment, in the pool and spa.

• *Penthouse Behind the Scenes* *(1995; Video Tape)*

Celeste . . . . Model
••• 0:10—Nude in interviews and behind the scenes footage.
Leslie Glass . . . . Pet
••• 0:17—Nude in interviews and behind the scenes footage.
Gina LaMarca . . . . Pet
••• 0:25—Nude in interviews and behind the scenes footage.
Natalie Lennox . . . . Pet
••• 0:00—Nude in various segments throughout the video tape.
Shauna O'Brien . . . . Pet
••• 0:00—Nude in various segments throughout the video tape.
Sam Phillips . . . . Pet
••• 0:00—Nude in various segments throughout the video tape.
Bonita Saint . . . . Pet
••• 0:31—Nude in interviews and behind the scenes footage.
Julie Kristen Smith . . . . Pet
••• 0:00—Nude in various segments throughout the video tape.
Natalie Smith . . . . Pet
••• 0:37—Nude in interviews and behind the scenes footage.
Julie Strain . . . . Pet
••• 0:00—Nude in various segments throughout the video tape.

• *Penthouse Centerfold—Julie Strain* *(1991; Video Tape)*

Julie Strain . . . . Pet
••• 0:00—Nude.

• *Penthouse DreamGirls* *(1994; Video Tape)*

Robin Brown . . . . Robin
••• 0:14—Nude, in a house in lingerie, by a window, in a bubble bath.
Lynn Johnson . . . . Lynn
••• 0:45—Full frontal nudity in house.
Brandy Ledford . . . . Brandy
••• 0:10—Nude in a house, on a piano bench, on a sofa.
Janine Lindemulder . . . . Janine
••• 0:23—Nude, with space/alien style silver body paint and costume.
Theresa Presley . . . . Theresa
••• 0:01—Nude by waterfall by pool, in a mansion, on a bed, in a shower/bath.

• *Penthouse Forum Letters: Volume 1* *(1993; Video Tape)*

Jasaé . . . . Three is Definitely Not a Crowd/Carmilla
•• 0:00—Nude in the shower during the opening credits.
••• 0:47—Buns in swimsuit, then breasts, getting lotion rubbed on her by Sandy.
••• 0:51—Nude, undressing in bathroom while Chuck peeks through the door, then taking a bath.
••• 0:54—Full frontal nudity in the shower with Sandy and Chuck.
Amy Lynn Baxter . . . . Maid to Order/The Maid
••• 0:21—Breasts, taking off bra and playing with herself while watching the owners of the house make love. Buns in panties.
Lisa Comshaw . . . . Mystery Caller/Vicky
••• 0:40—In black bra, then breasts in her cubicle, squishing her breasts against the window.
••• 0:41—Nude, dancing in front of a different window.
••• 0:42—Breasts, while making love with Brad by the window.
•• 0:45—Breasts, taking off her clothes in the office with Tanya and Cindy in front of Brad.
Mimi Faillace . . . . The Paint Job/Gina
••• 0:01—Full frontal nudity in bedroom, rubbing lotion on herself and masturbating.
••• 0:05—Nude while making love in kitchen with Mario.
•• 0:09—Left breast, while making love with Mario on the sofa.
••• 0:13—Breasts and buns, while making love in bed with the painter.
Monique Gabrielle . . . . Mystery Caller/Cindy
••• 0:27—Breasts and buns while making love with Brad on the floor in the office.
•• 0:45—Full frontal nudity, taking off her clothes in the office with Tanya and Vicky in front of Brad.
Julie Strain . . . . Reach Out and Touch Someone/Wife
••• 1:09—Breasts on couch having phone sex with her husband. Great if you also like to hear women talk dirty.

• *Penthouse Forum Letters: Volume 2* *(1994; Video Tape)*

Celeste . . . . The Perfect Model/Model
••• 0:18—Nude, while posing, then making love with photographer in studio.
Julia Ann . . . . The Big Switch/Debbie
••• 0:32—Breasts and buns in beige panties while doing strip tease with Cindy in front of their husbands. Nude in hot tub, then nude making love with Dan on bench.
Nicole Broderson . . . . The Loving Nurse/Nurse
••• 0:01—Nude, while making love in hospital bed with a patient.
Bobbi Brown . . . . The Window Washer/Lover
••• 0:46—Nude, making love with another woman on sofa, on kitchen counter and on bed.
Julie Morrison . . . . The Window Washer/Lover
••• 0:46—Nude, making love with another woman on sofa, on kitchen counter and on bed.
Bonita Saint . . . . The Big Switch/Cindy
••• 0:32—Breasts and buns in white panties while doing strip tease with Debbie in front of their husbands. Nude in hot tub, then nude making love with Steve on lounge chair.

• *Penthouse Love Stories* *(1986; Video Tape)*

Colleen Applegate . . . . Service Station Woman
••• 0:10—Nude, making love in a bedroom. Long scene.
Michelle Bauer . . . . Therapist's Patient
••• 0:45—Nude, making love in Therapist's office with his assistant.
Monique Gabrielle . . . . Monique and AC/DC Lover
••• 0:01—Nude in bedroom entertaining herself. A must for Monique fans!
••• 0:18—Nude making love with another woman.
Xaviera Hollander . . . . Herself
Julia Parton . . . . Loveboat Woman
••• 0:51—In white bra and panties in bed. Nude masturbating while the other girls watch. Nice, long, sweaty scene.
Barbara Peckinpaugh . . . . Therapist's Assistant
••• 0:45—Nude, making love in Therapist's office, with the patient.

Shana Ross . . . . AC/DC Lover
••• 0:17—Full frontal nudity in bedroom with Monique Gabrielle.
Vicki Vickers . . . . Snapshot and Loveboat Woman
••• 0:37—Nude, taking pictures of herself.
•• 0:51—Breasts on hammock watching Julie Parton.
•• 0:55—Left breast, twice while lying on hammock.

• *Penthouse Passport to Paradise/Hawaii* (1991; Video Tape)

Amy Lynn Baxter. . . . . Model
••• 0:49—Undressing on boat in white swimsuit top and white panties, then full frontal nudity.
Racquel Darrian. . . . . Model
••• 0:17—Undressing outside by a spa. In lingerie, then nude on a lounge chair and in the spa.
Janine Lindemulder . . . . Model
••• 0:37—Stripping out of a dress and lingerie, then nude dancing during her fantasy.
Sandra Taylor . . . . Model
•• 0:25—Breasts, taking off her top and going down into an underground cave.
••• 0:27—Nude, taking an outdoor shower to wash the dirt off herself.

• *Penthouse Pet of the Year Playoff 1991* (1992; Video Tape)

Amy Lynn Baxter. . . . . Pet
••• 0:02—Full frontal nudity during Hollywood starlet/photographer segment.
••• 0:04—Full frontal nudity on bed during interview.
•• 0:06—Full frontal nudity in still photos.
••• 0:08—Nude, while posing on boat.
••• 0:14—Nude, while posing with large sculptures.
••• 0:19—Nude, while wearing black wig and posing in house and playing with food (including a banana!).
Lynn Johnson . . . . Pet
••• 0:23—Nude in African-theme segment with a man and another woman. Muddy.
• 0:25—Breasts in still photos.
••• 0:26—Nude in B&W and color water-theme segment.
••• 0:28—Nude in mirrored area.
••• 0:30—Nude doing various poses on chair, behind tubular wire screen in studio.
Brandy Ledford . . . . Pet
••• 0:32—Nude in bubble bath.
••• 0:34—Nude doing different things in a house in various lingerie outfits, then in bath again, then covered with rose petals.
••• 0:39—Nude in still photos, then in motion while wearing sunglasses while posing in front of a wall.
••• 0:40—Nude in color and B&W while posing in country setting with different lingerie.
••• 0:43—Nude in science-fiction style segment.
••• 0:45—Buns in G-string and bra, then nude while posing on bed. B&W.
••• 0:50—Nude while posing in a field during end credits.

• *Penthouse Pet of the Year Playoff 1992* (1992; Video Tape)

Nikki Dial . . . . Model
Mahalia Maria. . . . . Pet
••• 0:37—Nude, in the desert, outside around a house, in a wild west theme, in a house and wrestling with another woman, on a bed, in front of a house.
••• 0:57—Nude, outside during the end credits.
Theresa Presley . . . . Pet
••• 0:01—Nude in helicopter, in office, tearing off her clothes in house, fantasy photo shoot, in a car and jumping on a trampoline.
Julie Strain. . . . . Pet
••• 0:16—Nude at the beach, in the house, in the bathtub, outside, at a desk on a bed.

• *Penthouse Pet of the Year Playoff 1993* (1993; Video Tape)

Jami Dion . . . . Pet
••• 0:01—Nude in house, on the beach, on bed, with an old T-bird.
Leslie Glass . . . . Pet
••• 0:11—Nude in back seat of limousine, in TV station (sometimes wearing a blonde wig), in Central Park on horseback, in the desert.
Shauna O'Brien . . . . Pet
••• 0:42—Nude at the beach, in a warehouse, in bathroom while rubbing shaving cream on herself.
Sasha Vinni . . . . Pet
••• 0:20—Nude, outside with a car, in a dance studio, in the back seat of a limousine, in a house, in the shower.
K.C. Williams. . . . . Pet
••• 0:31—Nude on bed, in front of mirror while making herself up and getting dressed, in a house (sometimes wearing a black wig).

• *Penthouse Pet of the Year Winners 1993: Mahalia & Julie* (1994; Video Tape)

Nikki Dial. . . . . Uncredited Cast Member
••• 0:18—Nude, while acting submissive to Mahalia. Wearing sunglasses.
Jami Dion . . . . Sneak Preview of Pet of the Year Playoff
••• 0:30—Nude while posing around a house.
Leslie Glass . . . . Sneak Preview of Pet of the Year Playoff
••• 0:28—Nude in and around Central Park in New York City.
Mahalia Maria . . . . Pet
• 0:01—Full frontal nudity during introduction.
••• 0:18—Full frontal nudity in dominatrix outfit, while dominating Nikki Dial.
••• 0:20—Nude in pool.
••• 0:22—Nude on grass by some flowers, then inside a house.
••• 0:23—More nude while in house wearing a dark wig.
Shauna O'Brien . . . . . . Sneak Preview of Pet of the Year Playoff
••• 0:31—Nude on stairs in empty building.
Julie Strain. . . . . Pet
• 0:00—Brief lower frontal nudity during introduction.
••• 0:01—Nude in bed.
••• 0:04—Nude in chair and making love with a guy.
••• 0:06—Nude, while touching herself while a trio of women work on a film.
••• 0:10—Full frontal nudity, while making love with a guy in a B&W movie.
••• 0:12—Nude in house in a bodysuit, then after ripping it off.
••• 0:16—Nude, while wearing a garter belt and stockings outside and in pool.
•• 0:34—Nude during end credits.
K.C. Williams . . . . Sneak Preview of Pet of the Year Playoff
••• 0:25—In lingerie, then nude on bed and couch.

• *Penthouse Pet of the Year Winners 1994: Gina & Natalie* (1995; Video Tape)

Gina LaMarca . . . . Pet of the Year
- ••• 0:01—Nude on bed in leopard print outfit.
- ••• 0:08—Nude on a motorcycle and with a guy in black leather and chain outfit.
- ••• 0:12—Nude outside by a pool, sometimes in the rain, sometimes not.
- ••• 0:17—Nude as a construction worker (including eating a banana).
- ••• 0:22—Nude after stripping out of clothes outside.

Natalie Smith . . . . .Pet of the Year Runner-Up
- ••• 0:29—Nude, in western theme segment.
- ••• 0:33—Nude in pearl outfit outside in bed.
- ••• 0:37—Nude outside by pool, soaping herself up.
- ••• 0:40—Nude outside in white western outfit.

• *Penthouse Pet of the Year Winners 1994: Sasha & Leslie* (1994; Video Tape)

Leslie Glass . . . . Runner-Up Pet
- ••• 0:30—Breasts then nude in boxing gloves and shorts.
- ••• 0:31—Nude, posing inside and outside a house in color and B&W segments.
- ••• 0:36—Nude in still photos.
- ••• 0:37—Nude while posing in a house.
- ••• 0:38—In lingerie and nude after playing cards with a blonde woman and a guy.
- ••• 0:42—Nude on rooftop in city.
- •• 0:44—Nude in end credits.

Susan Napoli . . . . Pet

Sasha Vinni . . . . Pet of the Year
- ••• 0:00—Breasts, outside of trailer.
- ••• 0:03—Nude on bed.
- ••• 0:08—Breasts, outside with tigers and nude while painted like a tiger.
- ••• 0:14—In lingerie and nude in room.
- ••• 0:19—Sunbathing nude outside.
- ••• 0:23—Nude in front of some seats.

• *Penthouse Satin & Lace: An Erotic History of Lingerie* (1992; Video Tape)

Keisha . . . . .Model

Carrie Bittner. . . . . .Model

Monique Gabrielle. . . . . .Model
- ••• 0:06—Breasts and buns with a blonde woman.
- ••• 0:33—Nude in blonde wig, with lover.
- ••• 0:47—Nude in bed with another blonde.

Brandy Ledford . . . . .Model

Janine Lindemulder . . . . .Model

Carolyn Liu . . . . .Model

Mahalia Maria . . . . .Model

Shauna O'Brien . . . . .Model

Julie Strain. . . . . .Model
- ••• 0:01—Nude with blonde woman.
- ••• 0:09—Nude with blonde woman in elevator.
- ••• 0:29—Nude outside.
- ••• 0:46—Full frontal nudity with three guys.
- ••• 0:49—Full frontal nudity with two blonde women.

• *Penthouse The Great Pet Hunt—Part II* (1993; Video Tape)

Amy Lynn Baxter. . . . . Pet
- ••• 0:34—Breasts and buns in T-back after stripping out of bride outfit on stage. More fun while playing with oil.

Lisa Bradford-Aiton . . . . Pet
- ••• 0:01—Breasts and buns in T-back while dancing on stage. (She's a great dancer.)

Leslie Glass . . . . Pet
- ••• 0:25—Nude after stripping out of maid outfit on stage.

Ashley Lauren . . . . Pet
- ••• 0:18—Nude after stripping out of nurse's outfit.

Theresa Presley . . . . Pet
- ••• 0:41—Nude after stripping out of red dress with white polka dots.

Dominique St. Croix . . . . Pet
- ••• 0:10—Breasts and buns in T-back, then nude while stripping out of dominatrix outfit on stage.

Sandra Taylor . . . . Pet
- ••• 0:50—Breasts and buns in T-back after stripping out of motorcycle mama outfit.

• *Penthouse Women In & Out of Uniform* (1995; Video Tape)

Julia Ann . . . . Pet
- ••• 0:33—Nude as a firewoman, playing around with gushing hoses with Janine Lindemulder.
- ••• 0:38—Nude as a policewoman with Lindemulder and Tiffany Burlingame in squad room.
- ••• 0:41—Nude as a stenographer, in courthouse with Lindemulder and Burlingame.

Tiffany Burlingame. . . . . Pet
- ••• 0:02—Nude as an astronaut in a solo fantasy.
- ••• 0:08—Nude as a dentist assistant, with Tammy Parks in dental office.
- ••• 0:22—Nude as a paramedic, with Parks, while the guy watches from gurney inside ambulance.
- ••• 0:38—Nude as a policewoman with Janine Lindemulder and Julia Ann in squad room.
- ••• 0:41—Nude as a judge, in courthouse with Lindemulder and Julia Ann.

Gina LaMarca . . . . Pet
- ••• 0:16—Nude as a football player with two other women in locker room, then putting on a black dress.
- ••• 0:29—Nude as a business woman, seducing the bellboy while a maid watches from outside the hotel room.

Janine Lindemulder . . . . Pet
- ••• 0:33—Nude as a firewoman, playing around with gushing hoses with Julia Ann.
- ••• 0:38—Nude as a policewoman with Tiffany Burlingame and Julia Ann in squad room.
- ••• 0:41—Nude as a lawyer, in courthouse with Burlingame and Julia Ann.
- ••• 0:45—Nude, as a police detective, when interrogating a guy while he's handcuffed in a chair.

Tammy Parks. . . . . Cast Member
- ••• 0:08—Nude as a dentist assistant, with Tiffany Burlingame in dental office.
- ••• 0:22—Nude as a paramedic, with Parks, while the guy watches from gurney inside ambulance. Wears a leather strap outfit.

Natalie Smith. . . . . Pet
- ••• 0:13—Nude as a painter, while painting on herself outside.
- ••• 0:16—Nude as a football player with two other women in locker room, then putting on a white dress.

• *Penthouse: Fast Cars/Fantasy Women* (1992; Video Tape)

Martine Anuszek . . . . Ferrari California Spyder
- ••• 0:34—In lingerie, then nude, while posing with car.

Tracy Dali . . . . Porsche Speedster 1
••• 0:05—Nude (she's wearing the dark dress), while posing with car in grainy B&W video.

Lynn Johnson . . . . Model

Tamara Landry . . . . Ferrari Testarossa
••• 0:19—In lingerie, then nude, while posing with car.

Brandy Ledford . . . . Mercedes 300 SL
••• 0:15—Nude while washing and posing with car.

Julie Strain. . . . . Mercedes 500 SL/Police Officer
•• 0:27—Breasts, while making love with the driver.

Teri Weigel . . . . Jaguar XK
••• 0:42—Nude, while making love with a guy in several different locations.

• *Penthouse: On the Wild Side* (1988; Video Tape)

Madonna . . . . Madonna
••• 0:14—Full frontal nudity in B&W and color still photographs.

Colleen Applegate. . . . . Colleen
••• 0:39—Breasts in lingerie on bed. Nude on the floor.

Michelle Bauer . . . . Punk or Bust Hairdresser
• 0:32—Breasts in black leather outfit.
••• 0:34—Nude while wearing black leather outfit, making love with Julie Parton.

Alexandra Day. . . . . Honey Pot
••• 0:43—Breasts, getting honey dribbled on her, then getting it licked off by her lover.

Anneka di Lorenzo . . . . Messalina
• 0:54—Nude with Lori Wagner during scenes from *The Making of Caligula.*

Julia Parton . . . . Punk or Bust Customer
••• 0:34—Nude while wearing black leather outfit, making love with Michelle Bauer.

Carina Ragnarsson. . . . . Car Wash
•• 0:16—Breasts and buns in car wash with another woman. Nice and wet.

Teresa Ann Savoy . . . . Druscilla
• 0:51—Breasts in scenes from *Caligula.*

Lori Wagner . . . . Lover
• 0:54—Nude with Anneka de Lorenzo during scenes from *The Making of Caligula.*

• *Penthouse: The Art of Massage* (1996; Video Tape)

Brittany Andrews. . . . . Model

Griffin Drew . . . . Model
••• 0:18—In bra, then full frontal nudity, while making love on desk in office.

Monique Gabrielle . . . . Model
••• 0:21—Breasts, while giving and receiving a massage from a guy.
••• 0:34—Full frontal nudity, while massaging a guy on table with another female model, then receiving a massage by her and two other guys.
••• 0:40—Breasts, while massaging herself.
•• 0:45—Breasts, while massaging a guy on table.
••• 0:51—Nude, while making love with a guy on table.

Jill Kelly . . . . Model
••• 0:02—Nude, while giving a massage, then making love with Vince Voyeur.

Julianne J. Mantia . . . . Model
••• 0:29—Nude, while making love with Rob Lee in bathroom.
••• 0:35—Nude, with another woman and two guys by swimming pool.

Lorissa McComas . . . . Model
••• 0:47—In pink dress, then nude, while dancing and massaging another woman.

Andrea Mountjoy . . . . Model

• *Penthouse: The Ultimate Pet Games* (1996; Video Tape)

Leigh Anderson . . . . Pet
••• 0:13—Nude during badminton segment.
••• 0:17—Nude, while posing in front of a cabin.
••• 0:21—Nude during oil wrestling segment.
••• 0:36—Breasts during pool volleyball game.

Brandi Lee Braxton . . . . Pet
••• 0:02—Nude during obstacle course segment.
••• 0:29—Nude in tug-of-war segment.
••• 0:42—Nude during squirt gun segment.

Tiffany Burlingame . . . . Pet
••• 0:02—Nude during obstacle course segment.
••• 0:13—Nude during badminton segment.
••• 0:21—Nude during oil wrestling segment.
••• 0:29—Nude in tug-of-war segment.
••• 0:33—Nude, while making love with Leslie Glass in cabin (includes the use of honey and chocolate syrup).
••• 0:36—Breasts during pool volleyball game.
••• 0:42—Nude during squirt gun segment.

Leslie Glass . . . . Pet
••• 0:02—Nude during obstacle course segment.
••• 0:13—Nude during badminton segment.
••• 0:21—Nude during oil wrestling segment.
••• 0:29—Nude in tug-of-war segment.
••• 0:33—Nude, while making love with Tiffany Burlingame in cabin (includes the use of honey and chocolate syrup).
••• 0:36—Breasts during pool volleyball game.
0:42—Nude during squirt gun segment.

Andi Sue Irwin. . . . . Pet
••• 0:01—Nude during obstacle course segment.
••• 0:29—Nude in tug-of-war segment.
••• 0:39—Nude, while posing in house.
••• 0:42—Nude during squirt gun segment.

Andrea Mountjoy . . . . Pet
••• 0:13—Nude during badminton segment.
••• 0:21—Nude during oil wrestling segment.
••• 0:25—Nude, while giving a dog a bath, then bathing herself outdoors.
••• 0:36—Breasts during pool volleyball game.

Seana Ryan . . . . Pet
••• 0:02—Nude during obstacle course segment.
••• 0:05—Nude while posing outdoors.
••• 0:29—Nude in tug-of-war segment.
••• 0:42—Nude during squirt gun segment.

Alex Taylor . . . . Pet
••• 0:01—Nude during obstacle course segment.
••• 0:09—Nude, while posing in stagecoach outdoors.
••• 0:29—Nude in tug-of-war segment.
••• 0:42—Nude during squirt gun segment.

The People Next Door (1970)

Cloris Leachman . . . . Tina
• 0:59—Buns and very brief side view of right breast, while getting up out of bed and putting on a robe.

Deborah Winters . . . . Maxie
•• 0:39—Brief left breast and buns, getting out of bed and walking toward her father.
•• 0:57—Nude, walking down the stairs and outside the house while on drugs.

• *The People vs. Larry Flynt* (1996)

Kathleen Kane . . . . 1st Stripper

Courtney Love. . . . . .Althea Leasure
- 0:09—Very brief right breast when pulling up her blouse while dancing on stage.
•• 0:24—Buns and breasts, getting into spa with two other girls.
•• 0:45—Brief breasts, while posing for photos.
- 1:20—Left breast in sheer bra, when waking up in bed.
- 1:44—Brief breasts under sheer net part of outfit.
- 1:49—Full frontal nudity, lying dead under water after drowning in bathtub. Brief left breast when cradled by Woody Harrelson.
•• 2:04—Breasts on television when Harrelson reminisces and watches old video tape.

The Perez Family *(1995)*

Sarita Choudhury . . . . .Josette
Mel Gorham . . . . .Vilma/Raauel
Anjelica Huston . . . . .Carmela Perez
- 0:38—Very brief left breast, while sitting in bubble bath. Very, very brief breasts, when getting up out of bathtub when she's startled by workmen outside the window.

Perfect *(1985)*

Rosalind Allen . . . . .Sterling
Jamie Lee Curtis. . . . . Jessie Wilson
Chelsea Field . . . . Randy
Marilu Henner . . . . Sally
Charlene Jones . . . . .Shotsy
- 0:17—Breasts stripping on stage in a club. Buns in G-string.

Perfect Alibi *(1994)*

Lydie Denier . . . . Janine
- 0:37—Very brief side of left breast and buns, while making love in bed on top of Keith when discovered by Kathleen Quinlan. Dark.
- 0:45—Brief partial left breast, while making love in bed with Keith.

Teri Garr . . . . Laney Tolbert
Kathleen Quinlan . . . . Melanie Bauers

• ***The Perfect Body Contest*** *(1987; Video Tape)*

Blondi . . . . Jennifer
••• 0:46—Buns, in two piece swimsuit, then breasts.
- 0:50—Breasts on stage with the other contestants.

Brandi Downs . . . . Charlene
•• 0:18—Buns, in pink, two piece swimsuit, then breasts.
- 0:50—Breasts on stage with the other contestants.

Beckie Mullen . . . . Beckie
Teal Roberts . . . . Judge
Cindy Rome . . . . Sugar Ray Rene
Susie Santana . . . . Susie Santana
••• 0:38—In black garter belt, stockings, panties and bra. Brief buns and breasts.
- 0:50—Breasts on stage with the other contestants.

• ***The Perfect Husband*** *(1995; Spanish)*

Ana Belén . . . . Theresa Brock
- 0:43—Breasts and buns under sheer white robe while in bathroom.
- 0:45—Brief beasts, while making love with Tim Roth in bed.
- 0:58—Partial breasts, while sitting in mud bath when Roth caresses her.

•• 1:27—Breasts, while in the shower with Roth when discovered by her husband.

Aitana Sánchez-Gijón . . . . .Klara

Perfect Strangers *(1984)*

Anne Carlisle . . . . Sally
- 0:34—Left breast, while making love in bed with Johnny.

Ann Magnuson . . . . .Maida

Perfect Timing *(1984)*

Jo Anne Bates. . . . . Karen
••• 0:21—Nude, while getting ready to have her picture taken.

Nancy Cser . . . . Lacy
••• 0:56—Breasts getting photographed by Harry.
- 0:58—Breasts, making love with Harry.
- 1:01—Breasts.

Papusha Demitro. . . . . Bonnie O. Bendix
•• 0:26—Nude, taking off dress in photo studio and kissing Joe.
- 0:29—Breasts walking with Joe through the living room, then brief nude on the roof.

•• 0:32—Nude, walking into the kitchen and getting chocolate out of the refrigerator.
•• 0:34—Nude in bed with Joe.
••• 0:45—Nude in bedroom with Joe.
•• 1:03—Nude on bed with Joe.

Alexandra Innes. . . . . Salina
•• 1:06—Right breast and buns, posing for Harry.

Mary Elizabeth Rubens. . . . . Judy
- 0:04—In a bra, then breasts in bedroom with Joe.

•• 0:05—Nude, walking to kitchen, then talking with Harry.
- 0:08—Left breast seen through the camera's view finder.
- 0:10—Nude, getting dressed in bedroom.

•• 0:50—Nude, in bed with Joe.
••• 1:00—Nude, discovering Joe's hidden video camera, then going downstairs.

Michele Scarabelli . . . . Charlotte
•• 1:11—Brief buns, then breasts in bed with Harry.
- 1:18—Breasts in bed with Harry during the music video.

Perfect Victims *(1988)*

Nicolette Scorsese . . . . Melissa Cody
Deborah Shelton . . . . Liz Winters
Jackie Swanson . . . . Carrie Marks
•• 0:13—In bra, then left breast, while changing clothes by closet.
- 0:23—Brief left breast, while lying on sofa when Brandon opens her robe while she's drugged out. Brief right breast and lower frontal nudity when he rips off her panties.
- 0:25—Right breast several more times, while lying on sofa when Brandon torments her.

••• 1:15—Left breast and buns, seen through clear shower door. Nice shot for bun lovers!
- 1:16—Brief buns in the shower, seen from above.

Performance *(1970)*

Anita Pallenberg . . . . .Pherber
- 0:44—Side view of left breast, while in bed with Mick Jagger.

••• 0:47—Breasts and buns, while in bathtub with Lucy and Jagger.
- 0:50—Buns, injecting herself with drugs.

•• 1:20—Right breast, while lying on the floor. Then breasts and buns, in bed with Chas.

Ann Sidney . . . . Dana
- 0:01—Very brief breasts and buns.
- 0:24—Brief breasts with Chas in flashbacks.

The Perils of Gwendoline in the Land of the Yik Yak *(1984; French)*

Zabou . . . . Beth

•• 0:36—Breasts, after taking off her blouse in the rain in the forest.

•• 0:57—Breasts while in torture chamber, getting rescued by Tawny Kitaen.

•• 1:04—Breasts after Kitaen escapes.

• 1:11—Buns, in costume during fight.

Tawny Kitaen . . . . Gwendoline

••• 0:36—Breasts in the rain in the forest, taking off her top. More breasts with Willard.

•• 0:52—Buns, while walking around with Willard in costumes.

• 0:55—Buns, falling into jail cell, then in jail cell in costume.

• 0:57—Buns, while rescuing Beth in torture chamber.

•• 1:01—Breasts in S&M costume in front of mirrors.

• 1:04—Brief breasts escaping from chains.

• 1:07—Buns, in costume while riding chariot and next to wall.

• 1:09—Buns, while standing up.

•• 1:11—Buns, in costume during fight. Wearing green ribbon.

•• 1:18—Breasts making love with Willard.

Personal Best *(1982)*

Patrice Donnelly . . . . Tory Skinner

•• 0:17—Nude after making love with Mariel Hemingway.

••• 0:31—Full frontal nudity in steam room with the other women.

• 1:03—Very brief right breast in open blouse and partial lower frontal nudity while getting into bed with Hemingway.

•• 1:10—Nude, while in the steam room with the other women again.

Mariel Hemingway . . . . Chris Cahill

•• 0:18—Brief lower frontal nudity getting examined by Patrice Donnelly, then breasts after making love with her.

•• 0:31—Full frontal nudity in the steam room talking with the other women.

Personal Services *(1987)*

Julie Walters . . . . Cynthia Payne

• 0:21—Very brief side view of left breast, while reaching to turn off radio in the bathtub. Her face is covered with cream.

• **Persons Unknown** *(1995)*

Kelly Lynch . . . . Amanda

• 0:05—Very brief breasts, when rolling over next to Joe Mantegna in bed to show her tattoo.

Pet Sematary II *(1992)*

Darlanne Fluegel . . . . Renee Hallow

• 1:04—Probably a body double wearing a dog mask, breasts on top of Anthony Edwards during nightmare, lit with blue light.

Sarah Trigger . . . . Marjorie Hargrove

Lisa Waltz . . . . Amanda Gilbert

• 0:53—Very brief right breast, while in bed when Clancy Brown rips her nightgown off.

Petit Con *(1986; French)*

Souad Amidou . . . . Salima

•• 0:42—Breasts, after taking off her top and getting into bed, while Michel watches her.

• 0:50—Breasts, while lying in bed, then making love with Michel. Dark.

• 0:53—Breasts, getting out of bed and getting back in.

Caroline Cellier . . . . Annie Choupon

Claudine Delvaux . . . . Maryse

•• 0:28—Right breast, while getting felt up by her husband in front of Michel.

Tanya Lopert . . . . Psychiatrist

Patricia Millardet . . . . Aurore

Pets *(1974)*

Joan Blackman . . . . Geraldine Mills

• 0:46—Brief side view of left breast, while getting out of bed after making love with Bonnie.

Candice Rialson . . . . Bonnie

•• 0:26—Breasts dancing in field while Dan is watching her while he's tied up.

••• 0:33—Breasts making love on top of Dan while he's still tied up.

•• 0:40—Breasts getting into bath at Geraldine's house.

• 0:45—Breasts posing for Geraldine.

••• 1:02—Breasts taking off lingerie in bed with Ron, then making love with him.

Petticoat Planet *(1995)*

Betsy Lynn George . . . . Lily

• 1:11—Breasts, while making love with Steve in saloon.

Elizabeth Kaitan . . . . Delia

• 0:05—Brief buns in white lingerie, while making love with Sarah.

•• 0:10—Breasts and partial buns, while making love with Sarah.

• 0:39—Breasts and partial buns, while making love with Steve in bathtub.

• 0:59—Buns in lingerie, while talking and making love with Steve.

Lesli Kay Sterling . . . . Sheriff Sarah Parker

•• 0:10—Breasts, while making love with Delia.

••• 0:26—Breasts, while dancing in jail cell in front of Steve.

Phantasm II *(1988)*

Sam Phillips . . . . Alchemy

•• 1:00—Breasts making love in bed with Lance.

Stacey Travis . . . . Jeri

• **Phantasm III: Lord of the Dead** *(1994)*

Cindy Ambuehl . . . . Edna

Gloria L. Henry . . . . Rocky

•• 0:52—Brief left breast, then breasts while making love in bed with Reggie.

Sam Phillips . . . . Alchemy

Phantom Empire *(1987)*

Michelle Bauer . . . . Cave Bunny

•• 1:13—Breasts after losing her top during a fight, more breasts until Andrew puts his jacket on her.

Tricia Brown . . . . Cavegirl

Sybil Danning . . . . The Alien Queen

Dawn Wildsmith . . . . Eddy Colchilde

Phantom of the Mall: Eric's Revenge *(1988)*

Crisstyn Dante. . . . . Body Double for Ms. Whitman

•• 0:25—Breasts in bed about five times with Peter.

Morgan Fairchild . . . . Karen Wilton

Kimber Monroe . . . . Suzie

Brinke Stevens . . . . Girl in Dressing Room
- 0:14—Breasts in dressing room and on B&W monitor several times (second room from the left).

Kari Whitman . . . . Melody Austin

• *Phat Beach* (1996)

Corey Anne Chang . . . . Corey
Glori Gold . . . . Glori
Tanya Reid . . . . Ulga
- 0:30—Very brief, partial lower half of buns, while in dancing in hotel room with Durrel.

Phoenix (1995)

Denice Duff . . . . Seline
- •• 0:59—In black bra, then breasts, while making love with McClain in hospital bed.

• *Phoenix* (1998)

Tamara Clatterbuck . . . . Waitress
Annie Fitzgerald . . . . Heist Stripper
Anjelica Huston . . . . Leila
Sandra Taylor . . . . .Video Game Stripper
Kari Wührer . . . . .Katie Shuster
- 1:31—Brief partial buns and very brief left breast, when caught in bed with Xander Berkeley by Ray Liotta.
- 1:33—Brief upper half of breasts, when trying to get Liotta to stop burning the money.
- 1:35—Brief breasts, when getting out of bed.

Phoenix the Warrior (1988)

Veronica Carothers . . . . Suga
Roxanne Kernohan . . . . Meda
- ••• 0:15—Breasts in waterfall (she's the white girl).

Kathleen Kinmont . . . . .Phoenix
Peggy McIntaggart . . . . .Keela

The Piano (1993)

Karen Colston . . . . Bluebeard's Wife
Holly Hunter . . . . .Ada
- ••• 1:02—Nude, while sitting on bed.
- ••• 1:18—Buns then breasts while lying next to Harvey Keitel in bed.
- 1:19—Very brief left nipple when kissing. Close-up shot.

Genevieve Lemon . . . . Nessie

Picasso Trigger (1989)

Cynthia Brimhall . . . . Edy
- •• 0:59—Breasts in weight room with a guy.

Hope Marie Carlton. . . . . Taryn
- ••• 0:56—Breasts and buns in spa with a guy.

Patty Duffek . . . . Patticakes
- •• 1:04—Breasts taking a Jacuzzi bath.

Kym Malin. . . . . Kym
- •• 1:04—Breasts taking a shower.

Dona Speir . . . . Donna
- ••• 0:49—Breasts and buns standing, then making love in bed.

Roberta Vasquez . . . . Pantera

Pick-Up Summer (1979; Canadian)

Joy Boushel . . . . Sally
- ••• 0:56—Breasts playing pinball, then running around.

Karen Stephen. . . . . Donna
- 0:25—Very brief lower half of breast, pulling her T-shirt up to distract someone.
- 0:34—Very, very brief breasts when the boys spray her and she jumps up.

Helene Udy . . . . Suzy
- 0:34—Very, very brief breasts when the boys spray her and she jumps up.

The Pickle (1992)

Linda Carlson. . . . . Bernadette
- •• 0:12—In white bra and panties under stockings, after taking off her clothes in hotel room in front of Danny Aiello, then breasts.

Clotilde Courau . . . . Francoise
- 0:58—Brief half of right breast in gaping bra when she helps Aiello back onto bed.

Rebecca Miller . . . . Carrie
Isabella Rossellini . . . . .Actress in Film
Tiffany Salerno. . . . . Elegant Woman
Ally Sheedy . . . . Molly-Girl

Pie in the Sky (1996)

Anne Heche. . . . . Amy
- 0:24—Brief right breast, while making love with Josh Charles outdoors.

Dey Young . . . . Mrs. Tarnell

• *The Pillow Book* (1995)

Vivian Wu . . . . Nagiko
- •• 0:17—Breasts, with Chinese characters painted on her body, then standing in the rain, as it washes off.
- •• 0:33—Breasts, while Chinese characters are painted on her body.
- •• 0:36—Nude, while a guy paints Chinese characters on her body.
- 0:43—Brief back side of right breast, while sitting in bathtub.
- •• 0:46—Nude, while lying in bed next to a guy.
- •• 0:55—Nude, while standing next to Ewan McGregor, then in bed with him.
- ••• 0:58—Breasts, while sitting in bed as Chinese characters are painted on her.
- •• 1:00—Full frontal nudity, standing up in bathtub.

Pin (1988)

Cyndy Preston . . . . .Ursula
Helene Udy . . . . Marcia Bateman
- ••• 1:03—Breasts in bedroom with Leon.

• *Pink Flamingos* (1972)

Elizabeth Coffey. . . . . .Woman in Park
- •• 1:02—Right "breast," then penis, when flashing Raymond the flasher in the park. (Elizabeth was half way through his sex-change operation at the time.)

Edith Massey . . . . Edy the Egg Lady
Cookie Mueller . . . . Cookie
- •• 0:28—Full frontal nudity, while having sex with Cracker and a chicken.

Mary Vivian Pearce . . . . Cotton
- 1:39—(Note this scene is only available on the Criterion laser disc version. 0:40 into side B of the laser disc.) Breasts, when running from her bed to talk with Divine.

Mink Stole . . . . Connie Marble
- ••• 0:35—Full frontal nudity, while making out and talking with Raymond in bed. Long scene.

Susan Walsh . . . . Suzie, Blonde in Basement
- 0:15—Very brief upper half of right breast in gaping nightgown in pit when Chan hits her.

• 0:35—Brief right nipple sticking out of nightgown when she throws up in pit, after watching Chan inseminate unconscious woman.

Pink Floyd The Wall (1982)

Nell Campbell . . . . .Groupie
Jenny Wright. . . . . .American Groupie
••• 0:41—Breasts, while doing strip tease dance, in back of a truck while it's parked backstage.

Pink Motel (1982)

Terri Berland . . . . .Marlene
••• 1:18—Breasts, dropping her sheet in room in front of Max and Skip.
Cathryn Hartt . . . . Charlene
••• 1:18—Breasts, dropping her sheet in room in front of Max and Skip.
Kathi Sawyer-Young . . . . .Lola
• 0:36—Brief breasts, after opening her bra and falling onto bed with Mark.
••• 0:41—Breasts and buns in panties, trying to coax Mark out of the bathroom. Long scene.
•• 1:13—Breasts, while lying in bed with Mark.

• *Pinocchio's Revenge* (1996)

Rosalind Allen . . . . Jennifer Garrick
• 0:38—Breasts, while making love with David in bed.

Piranha (1978)

Belinda Balaski. . . . . .Betsy
Janie Squire. . . . . Barbara
•• 0:02—Breasts taking off her top to go swimming with her boyfriend.

Piranha (1995; Made for Cable Movie)

Kelly Burns . . . . Gina Green
•• 0:52—Breasts on row boat after taking off her swimsuit top when Wechsler video tapes her. More breasts when in and under the water, getting attacked by the piranha.
Lorissa McComas . . . . Barbara
•• 0:03—In white bra and panties, undressing to go skinny dipping in water tank with Dave. Nude, after undressing and swimming.
Alexandra Paul . . . . Maggie McNamara

The Pit and the Pendulum (1991)

Rona De Ricci . . . . Maria
••• 0:21—Full frontal nudity in front of Lance Henrickson and some other men while being examined.
• 0:28—Brief full frontal nudity during Henrickson's fantasy.
•• 0:59—Full frontal nudity when Henrickson slowly rolls her dress up to admire her before raping her.

A Place Called Today (1972)

Cheri Caffaro. . . . . Cindy Cartwright
•• 0:14—Full frontal nudity covered with oil or something writhing around on the bed.
• 1:21—Brief side view of right breast undressing in the bathroom.
• 1:23—Brief full frontal nudity getting kidnapped by two guys.
•• 1:30—Nude when they take off the blanket.
• 1:35—Brief breasts just before getting killed.
Lana Wood . . . . Carolyn Scheider
••• 0:40—Side view of left breast, then breasts lying down talking to Ron.

The Plague (1992; French/British)

Sandrine Bonnaire . . . . .Martine Rambert
••• 0:53—Breasts, while in bathroom, examining herself for the plague.
Veronica Llinas . . . . .Strip Teaser
• 1:22—Very brief side of right breast and side of buns. Long shot.
•• 1:26—Breasts, while on stage with a rat. Closer shot.
Victoria Tennant . . . . Alice Rieux

Play Misty for Me (1971)

Donna Mills. . . . . Tobie
• 1:10—Brief side view of right breast hugging Clint Eastwood in a pond near a waterfall. Long shot, hard to see.
Jessica Walter. . . . . .Evelyn
• 0:13—Very brief right breast in bed with Clint Eastwood. Lit with blue light. Hard to see anything.

Play Murder For Me (1991)

Tracy Scoggins . . . . .Tricia Merritt
•• 0:37—Right breast, then breasts when her husband sexually attacks her.

Play Nice (1992)

(Unrated version reviewed.)
Robey . . . . Jill/Rapunzel
• 0:28—Side view of right breast, while sitting on top of a victim in bed. Don't see her face.
••• 0:35—Breasts, making love in bed with Jack. Nice, long scene.
•• 0:46—Breasts, making love on the floor with Jack.
••• 1:09—Breasts in bed on top of Jack, then getting out of bed and getting dressed.
Ann Dusenberry . . . . .Pam Crichmore

Play Time (1994)

(Unrated version reviewed.)
Jennifer Leigh Burton. . . . . Lindsey
•• 0:01—Nude, while making love in bed with Joe.
• 0:05—Buns in purple swimsuit by the pool and in the kitchen with Geena.
••• 0:07—Breasts while on lounge chair, rubbing lotion on herself next to Geena.
•• 0:10—Nude in fantasy.
•• 0:11—Breasts and buns, while running into the house with Geena to hide from the pool man.
••• 0:13—Breasts and buns, while dancing and masturbating in front of Geena (who is masturbating on the sofa). Steamy!
••• 0:16—Breasts, while on patio and talking with Geena in the pool.
••• 0:18—Buns in panties and breasts, while undressing for Joe in bedroom.
•• 0:26—Breasts, when undressing in office and caressing Geena while masturbating.
•• 0:32—Right breast, then breasts, while making love with Joe.
••• 0:36—Breasts and partial buns, masturbating and caressing Geena on bed, while Joe watches from closet.
•• 0:41—Full frontal nudity, while sitting in spa and talking with Geena and Joe.
••• 0:44—Breasts and buns in panties in bedroom, caressing Connie while Joe watches.
••• 0:48—Breasts and buns, while making love with Geena and Joe in spa.

••• 0:53—Full frontal nudity while caressing herself in sauna so Brad can see her.
••• 1:03—In sheer blouse and black bra in Brad's office. Breasts and buns in panties after taking off her clothes and making love.
• 1:11—Buns in panties while in bed with Brad.
••• 1:12—Nude, while making love in bed with Brad.
•• 1:14—Breasts, when talking with Brad while lying in bed.
• 1:18—Right breast, then breasts and buns, while in bed with Brad.
••• 1:35—Full frontal nudity, after taking off her swimsuit and rubbing lotion on Geena while the guys watch.

Wendy Hamilton . . . . Brad's Secretary
Candy Loving . . . . Herself
• 1:32—Brief breasts on TV that's playing her video.
Monique Parent . . . . Geena
•• 0:02—Breasts, when lying in bed, enjoying herself, while listening to Lindsey and Joe make love.
•• 0:07—Breasts while on lounge chair, rubbing lotion on herself next to Lindsey.
•• 0:09—Brief left breast in gaping nightie, then partial buns and breasts in fantasy.
•• 0:11—Breasts, while running into the house with Lindsey to hide from the pool man.
••• 0:13—Breasts, when masturbating on sofa while Lindsey dances (and masturbates) in front of her. Steamy!
••• 0:16—Breasts, while on patio and talking with Lindsey in the pool.
••• 0:19—Full frontal nudity, while making love with Brad in bed.
•• 0:26—Breasts, when undressing in office and caressing Lindsey while masturbating.
••• 0:36—Breasts, masturbating and caressing Lindsey on bed, while Joe watches from closet.
•• 0:41—Full frontal nudity, while sitting in spa and talking with Lindsey and Joe.
••• 0:48—Breasts and buns, while making love with Lindsey and Joe in spa.
•• 1:07—Left breast, while in bed, talking on the phone with Joe.
• 1:10—Brief buns, when getting caught making love in the bushes with Joe.
• 1:17—Brief breasts in open robe during argument.
••• 1:35—Full frontal nudity, after taking off her swimsuit and rubbing lotion on Lindsey while the guys watch.
Tammy Parks. . . . . Michelle
•• 1:32—In bra, while undressing in bedroom, then nude with Julie Strain. B&W.
Ashlie Rhey . . . . Connie
•• 0:45—Breasts and buns in panties in bedroom while caressing Lindsey in front of Joe.
Julie Strain. . . . . Sheraton
••• 1:31—Full frontal nudity, while in bed with a young Brad. B&W.
•• 1:32—Nude, in bed with Michelle.

Playback *(1995)*

Traci Adell . . . . Galaxy Club Waitress
Tawny Kitaen . . . . Sara Burgess
• 0:23—Brief left breast, with her husband in bed.
•• 0:40—Breasts, while making love in bed with her husband.
• 0:48—Brief breasts on video playback.
• 0:51—Very brief breasts in video playback in George Hamilton's office.
• 1:27—Brief buns in two piece swimsuit.
Jodi Thelen . . . . Mary
Shannon Whirry. . . . . Karen Stone
• 0:02—Partial buns, while getting dressed in black lingerie.

Playbirds *(1978; British)*

Pat Astley. . . . . Doreen Hamilton
•• 0:00—Breasts posing for photo session.
Suzy Mandel . . . . Lena
•• 0:12—Nude stripping in Playbird office.
Mary Millington. . . . . Lucy Sheridan
••• 0:55—White bra, black garter belt, panties and stockings then nude taking off her clothes during the policewoman audition.
• 1:00—Breasts giving an old man a massage in a massage parlor.
••• 1:05—Breasts making love with another woman from the massage parlor.
••• 1:14—Nude doing a photo session for *Playbird* magazine.

• ***Playboy Celebrity Centerfold: Dian Parkinson*** *(1993; Video Tape)*

Jennifer Lavoie . . . . Playmate
• 0:41—Full frontal nudity in B&W poster, posted on brick wall.
•• 0:42—Nude, while doing various things outside.
••• 0:44—Nude, while dancing and doing gymnastics.
••• 0:47—Nude in still photos.
••• 0:48—Nude with neighbor in hot night fantasy. Some food play.
••• 0:55—Nude in hammock in tropical setting.
Dian Parkinson. . . . . Herself
•• 0:00—Breasts during introduction.
••• 0:05—Nude, after stripping out of a man's business suit in studio.
••• 0:12—In white, bra, garter belt and stockings, then nude while making love with a guy in art gallery fantasy.
••• 0:17—Nude in still photos.
••• 0:20—Nude in desert fantasy.
••• 0:23—Nude in dress while dancing in music video.
••• 0:27—In lingerie, then nude in bedroom fantasy.
• 0:32—Brief breasts while changing clothes by car.
••• 0:35—In white bra in hotel room, then nude making love in robbery fantasy.

• ***Playboy Celebrity Centerfold: Jessica Hahn*** *(1993; Video Tape)*

Kimberli Farina. . . . . Extra
Jessica Hahn. . . . . Herself
•• 0:02—Breasts and buns in an old church by the beach.
••• 0:05—Nude and in lingerie in an old mansion.
••• 0:10—Nude outside with a guy.
•• 0:14—Breasts, in lingerie and swimsuits around town and at a beach.
••• 0:17—Nude in bedroom. Very nice!
••• 0:20—Nude in still photos.
•• 0:21—Nude in wigs in studio. Also wearing lingerie and other outfits.
••• 0:23—Nude, picking an apple off a tree, lying in bed with a snake.
••• 0:26—Nude, checking out different rooms in a hotel, then in a room with a man and a woman.
••• 0:32—In bra and panties on a Merry-Go-Round, then nude.
Echo Johnson. . . . . Playmate
••• 0:39—Nude, doing various modeling things.
••• 0:42—Nude in loft fantasy.
••• 0:45—Nude in still photos.

••• 0:46—Nude in a mansion.

• Playboy Celebrity Centerfold: La Toya Jackson *(1994; Video Tape)*

Neriah Davis . . . . Playmate
••• 0:36—Nude, during music video number out in the country.
••• 0:39—Nude in starry music video number. Sometimes in lingerie.
••• 0:42—Nude in still photos.
••• 0:43—In red bra and panties, then nude in music segment with artwork.
••• 0:47—Nude in farm music video segment.

La Toya Jackson . . . . Herself
•• 0:01—Breasts during introduction.
••• 0:04—Breasts and buns during fantasy bedroom segment.
••• 0:09—Breasts and buns in still photos.
••• 0:12—Breasts, while dancing and doing things around the house.
••• 0:15—Breasts and buns in dance number.
••• 0:19—Breasts in recording studio fantasy.
••• 0:29—In red lingerie, then breasts and buns while making love with a guy in vampire fantasy and playing with a snake.

• Playboy Celebrity Centerfold: Patti Davis *(1994; Video Tape)*

Patti Davis . . . . Herself
•• 0:02—Full frontal nudity while posing in water and on rocks.
••• 0:06—In lingerie, then nude on stage in futuristic fantasy.
••• 0:09—Nude in artistic fantasy with two muscular guys.
••• 0:16—Nude in still photos.
••• 0:19—Nude with a guy in beach fantasy.
••• 0:24—In white bra and panties, then nude while posing on couch.
••• 0:28—Nude in gym and shower in workout segment.
••• 0:37—In lingerie, then in bed with a man and another woman in futuristic dial-a-date fantasy. A few scenes where she's tied to the headboard by her wrists.

Monique Parent . . . . Donna
••• 0:36—Breasts in sexy outfit, then nude in futuristic dial-a-date fantasy with Patti Davis and Greg.

Victoria Zdrok . . . . Playmate
• 0:44—Full frontal nudity in introduction.
••• 0:46—Nude while posing outside.
••• 0:49—Nude in schoolgirl in library fantasy.
••• 0:52—Nude in still photos.
••• 0:53—Nude in various lingerie outfits.
••• 0:56—Nude in mansion fantasy.

• Playboy International Playmates *(1993; Video Tape)*

Cida Costa . . . . Cida
•• 0:04—Buns in still photos.
••• 0:05—Nude on the beach with colored fabric.
••• 0:46—Nude with Christina, trying on clothing at the beach.
••• 0:48—Breasts after taking off clothes and dancing.

Angelique Dijkhuizen . . . . Angelique
••• 0:11—Full frontal nudity in still photos.
••• 0:12—Breasts undressing in bedroom and trying on lingerie and other clothing during cat burglar segment.
••• 0:50—Full frontal nudity in old castle.

Kelly James . . . . Kelly
••• 0:16—Full frontal nudity in still photos. Nude on the beach with sand, a thick rope and a net.
••• 0:30—Nude, walking around the woods with Teresa. Her body is partially painted with stripes.

Teresa Linnane . . . . Teresa
••• 0:28—Full frontal nudity in still photos. Nude, taking off swimsuit and in pool.
••• 0:30—Nude, walking around the woods with Kelly. Her body is partially painted with spots.

Sárka Lukesová . . . . Šharka
••• 0:23—Full frontal nudity in still photos.
•• 0:24—Full frontal nudity, while posing on the floor.
••• 0:25—Full frontal nudity outside in the woods at night.
••• 0:44—Full frontal nudity in old mansion and sitting on couch caressing herself.

Cristina Mortagua . . . . Cristina
••• 0:35—Full frontal nudity in still photos.
••• 0:36—Full frontal nudity on balcony, then taking an outdoor shower. Breasts during recollections of dancing with a guy.
••• 0:46—Nude with Cida, trying on clothing at the beach.
••• 0:48—Breasts taking off clothes and dancing.

Chan Ting . . . . Ting
••• 0:00—Full frontal nudity, on sofa, caressing herself.
••• 0:02—Breasts in still photos.
••• 0:03—Full frontal nudity outside with statue.
•• 0:22—Breasts in restaurant with another woman during food fight.
••• 0:53—Nude, stripping and dancing in basement during interrogation fantasy.

Diana Van Laar . . . . Diana
••• 0:08—Breasts in still photos.
••• 0:09—Nude, in S&M style segment.
••• 0:26—In white lingerie, then nude in schoolgirl fantasy.
••• 0:40—Breasts, while taking a bath.
••• 0:51—Breasts, taking off dress.

• Playboy Night Dreams *(1993; Video Tape)*

Jena Behr. . . . . Arresting Development
••• 0:47—Nude, after stripping out of police officer uniform then making love.

Sharon Cain . . . . Do Not Disturb
••• 0:36—Breasts and buns, when in panties, after getting locked out of her hotel room. Nude, while making love with a guy in his hotel room.

Lisa Comshaw . . . . Night Watch
••• 0:21—In bra, panties, garter belt and stockings in parking structure. Nude, while making love on car.

Monique Parent. . . . . Intimate Strangers
••• 0:12—Lower nudity in sheer black nightgown with guy from restaurant. Nude, while making love in hotel room.

Carrie Westcott . . . . Detour
••• 0:04—Nude after stripping out of bra, panties, garter belt and stockings, after picking up a guy and making love in house.

• Playboy Strip *(1996; Video Tape)*

Vanessa Taylor. . . . . Dancer
••• 0:05—Nude, after stripping out of maid costume on stage, to the surprise of her boyfriend.
••• 0:08—Nude, while getting shaved with a straight razor by another dancer on stage.
••• 0:36—Nude, while dancing by herself and sometime with Raquel.

Necole Velasquez . . . . Dancer
••• 0:41—Nude, while dancing and stripping on stage in warehouse for a guy.
Victoria Vogel . . . . Dancer
••• 0:23—Nude, while dancing and stripping for a customer.
Rachelle Whaley . . . . Dancer
••• 0:06—Nude, after joining another dancer on stage in club.

• *Playboy The Best of Anna Nicole Smith* (1995; Video Tape)

Marilyn Monroe . . . . Herself
•• 0:24—Breasts in B&W and color still photos.
Anna Nicole Smith . . . . Herself
•• 0:00—Breasts, during opening credits.
•• 0:05—Breasts, while dancing in western style bar.
••• 0:07—Nude in still photos.
••• 0:08—Nude, while posing on bed.
• 0:10—Breasts in still photos.
••• 0:12—Nude in B&W country segment.
• 0:15—Buns, while posing for photos.
••• 0:18—Nude, while posing on bed and around the house.
••• 0:25—Nude, while in bubble bath.
••• 0:32—Nude, while making love with a guy in a diner fantasy.
••• 0:37—Nude, while posing on the beach.
••• 0:44—Nude in B&W casino/hotel fantasy with a guy.
•• 0:49—Breasts and buns in still photos.
•• 0:50—Nude, while dancing in front of some muscular guys.
•• 0:52—Nude in still photos.
•• 0:53—Nude in quick cuts of behind-the-camera shots.
•• 0:55—Nude, while posing in bed in B&W.

• *Playboy The Best of Jenny McCarthy* (1996; Video Tape)

Julie Cialini . . . . Herself
••• 0:24—Nude, while dancing with 3 other Playmates with fire and ice from *Wet & Wild: The Locker Room.*
Wendy Hamilton . . . . Herself
••• 0:24—Nude, while dancing with 3 other Playmates with fire and ice from *Wet & Wild: The Locker Room.*
Corinna Harney . . . . Angel
• 0:31—Breasts in backstage scenes while being an angel.
Jenny McCarthy . . . . Herself
•• 0:00—Full frontal nudity (B&W) during introduction.
•• 0:02—Full frontal nudity, while posing around horse race track.
••• 0:08—Nude during schoolgirl, cheerleader, graduation gown segment.
••• 0:13—Full frontal nudity in still photos.
•• 0:14—Nude and in lingerie, while posing outdoors.
••• 0:16—In sheer red dress, then nude outdoors with a water pump.
•• 0:20—Breasts, while sitting in a chair and in lingerie.
••• 0:22—Nude in still photos.
••• 0:24—Nude, while dancing with 3 other Playmates with fire and ice from *Wet & Wild: The Locker Room.*
• 0:29—Brief breasts, while getting dressed.
••• 0:34—Full frontal nudity, in near-death fantasy with two angels.
••• 0:40—Nude on billiard table and dancing in soda fountain fantasy.
••• 0:46—Nude with a guy in old town fantasy.
••• 0:50—Nude, while posing around a house.
••• 0:53—Nude (B&W), while swinging on a swing and lying on some sheets.
Tiffany Sloan . . . . Angel/Nurse
Carrie Westcott . . . . Herself
••• 0:24—Nude, while dancing with 3 other Playmates with fire and ice from *Wet & Wild: The Locker Room.*

• *Playboy The Best of Pamela Anderson* (1995; Video Tape)

Pamela Lee . . . . Herself
•• 0:00—Nude during introduction in lingerie.
• 0:03—In sheer white outfit, then full frontal nudity in winter fantasy.
••• 0:08—Nude in still photos.
••• 0:10—Nude and in lingerie in studio and on bed.
••• 0:14—Nude in studio. Some behind-the-scenes shots.
••• 0:18—Full frontal nudity in motion and in still photos. Some behind-the-scenes shots of her pictorial photos.
••• 0:23—Nude in studio and in a room.
•• 0:25—Buns in panties, then nude, while playing in a bedroom.
••• 0:27—Breasts and partial buns, in music video segment.
•• 0:29—Nude, doing various things around the house.
••• 0:31—Nude, in house, in various pieces of lingerie.
••• 0:33—Nude in water fantasy.
••• 0:36—Full frontal nudity in fantasy with a guy.
••• 0:39—Nude in still photos.
•• 0:42—Nude in lots of different segments.
••• 0:44—Nude in stopped elevator with a guy.
••• 0:46—Nude in and around old mansion.
• 0:49—Buns in still photo with Tommy Lee.
•• 0:51—Full frontal nudity in end segment.

• *Playboy Video Calendar 1989* (1988; Video Tape)

India Allen . . . . January
••• 0:01—Nude.
Lynne Austin . . . . May
••• 0:17—Nude.
Carmen Berg . . . . July
••• 0:25—Nude.
Brandi Brandt . . . . November
••• 0:41—Nude.
Eloise Broady . . . . December
••• 0:45—Nude.
Kimberley Conrad . . . . October
••• 0:38—Nude.
Terri Lynn Doss . . . . March
••• 0:09—Nude.
Rebecca Ferratti . . . . June
••• 0:21—Nude.
Sharry Konopski . . . . April
••• 0:13—Nude.
Diana Lee-Hsu . . . . February
••• 0:05—Nude.
Susie Owens . . . . August
••• 0:29—Nude.
Pamela J. Stein . . . . September
••• 0:33—Nude.

• *Playboy Video Calendar 1990* (1989; Video Tape)

Emily Arth . . . . May
••• 0:23—Nude.
Tawnni Cable . . . . March
••• 0:13—Nude.
Kimberley Conrad . . . . December
••• 1:03—Nude.

Simone Eden . . . . August
••• 0:40—Nude.
Ava Fabian . . . . July
••• 0:34—Nude.
Jennifer Lyn Jackson . . . . September
••• 0:46—Nude.
Shannon Long . . . . November
••• 0:57—Nude.
Fawna MacLaren . . . . January
••• 0:01—Nude.
Pia Reyes . . . . June
••• 0:28—Nude.
Laura Richmond . . . . February
••• 0:07—Nude.
Karin van Breeschooten . . . . October
••• 0:51—Nude.
Miryam van Breeschooten . . . . October
••• 0:51—Nude.
Laurie Wood . . . . April
••• 0:18—Nude.

• ***Playboy Video Calendar 1991*** *(1990; Video Tape)*
Tina Bockrath . . . . January
••• 0:01—Nude.
Deborah Driggs . . . . October
••• 0:40—Nude.
Erika Eleniak . . . . May
••• 0:18—Nude.
Karen Foster . . . . March
Pamela Lee . . . . July
••• 0:26—Nude.
Bonnie Marino . . . . June
••• 0:22—Nude.
Lisa Matthews . . . . September
Peggy McIntaggart . . . . February
••• 0:05—Nude.
Helle Michaelsen . . . . April
••• 0:14—Nude.
Jacqueline Sheen . . . . December
••• 0:49—Nude.
Reneé Tenison . . . . August
••• 0:31—Nude.
Petra Verkaik . . . . November
••• 0:45—Nude.

• ***Playboy Video Calendar 1992*** *(1991; Video Tape)*
Gianna Amore . . . . January
••• 0:01—Nude in Italian restaurant fantasy.
••• 0:02—Nude in classical music fantasy in warehouse.
Stacy Arthur . . . . October
••• 0:39—Buns in lingerie. Full frontal nudity fantasizing in bed.
••• 0:41—Nude in various locations around the house.
Julie Clarke . . . . February
••• 0:05—Breasts on stairs. Nude in warehouse, painting on the floor and on herself.
••• 0:07—Nude, putting oil on herself.
Melissa Evridge . . . . April
••• 0:13—Nude outside in garden.
••• 0:15—Nude in action-movie fantasy in the desert.
Morgan Fox . . . . December
••• 0:48—Nude in aqueduct shoot.
••• 0:49—Breasts and buns in G-string while singing and dancing on stage.
Kerri Kendall . . . . March
••• 0:09—Nude in photo studio.
••• 0:10—In bra, then nude in bedroom.
Christina Leardini . . . . August
••• 0:32—Nude trying on various outfits.
••• 0:33—Nude in old building.
Lisa Matthews . . . . July
•• 0:27—Nude in fashion show fantasy.
••• 0:28—Nude in mansion doing various things.
Lorraine Olivia . . . . May
••• 0:18—Full frontal nudity in the desert.
••• 0:19—Nude in Egyptian bed fantasy.
Cristy Thom . . . . September
••• 0:35—Full frontal nudity walking and posing around the house.
••• 0:37—Nude in room of mirrors.
••• 0:38—Nude in bathtub.
Carrie Jean Yazel . . . . June
••• 0:22—Breasts and buns in kitchen shoot. More when pouring honey on her body.
••• 0:25—Nude, dancing in bar fantasy.
Brittany York . . . . November
••• 0:43—Breasts in lingerie. Nude in studio shoot.
••• 0:45—In black body stocking and nude in oriental style shoot.

• ***Playboy Video Calendar 1993*** *(1992; Video Tape)*
Cheryl Bachman . . . . April
••• 0:14—Nude in studio setting.
••• 0:16—Nude outside on rocks and in bathtub.
Tanya Beyer . . . . March
•• 0:09—Breasts under sheer dress. Full frontal nudity by pool.
••• 0:11—Nude indoors and outdoors.
Cady Cantrell . . . . May
••• 0:19—Nude outside on bridge and in boat.
••• 0:21—Nude in studio setting.
Tonja Christensen . . . . December
••• 0:49—Nude in barn.
••• 0:50—Nude in house.
Samantha Dorman . . . . August
••• 0:33—Full frontal nudity outside in a field and on swing.
••• 0:35—Nude in house in front of fire and on bed.
Wendy Hamilton . . . . October
••• 0:40—Nude, in auto garage setting. Sometimes covered with grease.
••• 0:42—Nude in fire escape setting.
••• 0:43—Nude with old movies projected on her and the walls.
Corinna Harney . . . . June
••• 0:23—Nude, dancing in studio setting.
••• 0:25—Nude outside in the desert.
Tylyn John . . . . November
••• 0:45—Nude on motorcycle in studio and in the rain.
••• 0:47—Nude in house and on balcony.
Wendy Kaye . . . . July
••• 0:28—Nude at the beach.
••• 0:30—Nude in building with graffiti on the walls.
Angela Melini . . . . February
• 0:06—Brief full frontal nudity doing various things outdoors.
••• 0:08—Nude outdoors in Japanese garden.
Suzi Simpson . . . . September
••• 0:37—Nude in cave woman studio setting.
••• 0:39—Nude in haunted house setting.
Anna Nicole Smith . . . . January
•• 0:02—Breasts and buns during Country music number.
••• 0:03—Nude in outdoor Western setting by campfire.

• *Playboy Video Calendar 1994* *(1993; Video Tape)*

Stephanie Adams . . . . April
- ••• 0:15—Nude with brightly colored props in studio.
- ••• 0:17—Nude (down to stockings and garter belt) in hot office fantasy.

Ashley Allen . . . . March
- ••• 0:10—Nude on bed and in various lingerie outfits.
- ••• 0:12—Nude, lit with different lights.

Morena Corwin . . . . November
- ••• 0:42—Breasts and buns, while walking around a house at night. Nude while painting in a field.
- ••• 0:45—Nude in B&W on sofa during dream, then in color when getting up out of bed.

Kimberly Donley . . . . December
- ••• 0:47—Nude, while dancing in a studio with a black and white color theme.
- ••• 0:49—Nude, while on bed.

Amanda Hope . . . . August
- ••• 0:31—Nude, outside in garden, in gazebo and by a pond.
- ••• 0:33—Nude in a house with a clarinet.

Echo Johnson . . . . September
- ••• 0:35—Nude while working out and exercising.
- ••• 0:37—Nude, undressing from a tuxedo.

Jennifer LeRoy . . . . June
- ••• 0:23—Nude in circus setting.
- ••• 0:23—Nude outside in bathtub by a shack.

Barbara Moore . . . . July
- ••• 0:27—Nude in diner while dancing and posing.
- ••• 0:29—Nude on couch and in phone booth during fantasies while waiting at a bar.

Alesha Oreskovich . . . . February
- ••• 0:06—Breasts and buns, posing in a big "O" prop.
- ••• 0:08—Nude, undressing and dancing in an alley.

Tiffany Sloan . . . . May
- ••• 0:19—Nude in bathtub in the desert.
- ••• 0:20—Nude in ballet/dance number in warehouse.

Anna Nicole Smith . . . . January
- ••• 0:04—Full frontal nudity, in country setting, washing herself and rolling around in the hay. B&W.

Nicole Wood . . . . October
- ••• 0:39—Nude while running around a house and posing.
- ••• 0:40—Nude while posing in water-theme backdrops in color and B&W.

• *Playboy Video Calendar 1995* *(1994; Video Tape)*

Arlene Baxter . . . . February
- ••• 0:05—Nude in cabin. Nude in apartment.

Elan Carter . . . . September
- ••• 0:35—Nude posing outside a house. Nude in a large apartment.

Julie Cialini . . . . November
- ••• 0:44—Nude at a beach. Nude in a house.

Neriah Davis . . . . July
- ••• 0:27—Nude outside on and near a train. Nude in starlight fantasy.

Becky Delos Santos . . . . January
- ••• 0:01—Nude in room full on neon lights. Nude in a house.

Anna-Marie Goddard . . . . May
- ••• 0:17—Nude posing in studio. Nude in bayou fantasy.

Elke Jeinsen . . . . April
- ••• 0:13—Nude riding on and posing with a horse. Nude in a house.

Jennifer Lavoie . . . . August
- ••• 0:31—Nude dancing and doing gymnastics. Nude in a hammock and near palm trees.

Shae Marks . . . . October
- ••• 0:39—Nude outside. Nude in a house.

Jenny McCarthy . . . . June
- ••• 0:21—Nude at horse race track. Nude in bar and on pool table.

Carrie Westcott . . . . December
- ••• 0:49—Nude in a greenhouse with water. Nude on different colored beds.

Julianna Young . . . . March
- ••• 0:09—Nude in photo session. Nude outside on rocks.

• *Playboy Video Calendar 1996* *(1995; Video Tape)*

Rhonda Adams . . . . July
- ••• 0:27—Nude in house after surprise birthday party.
- ••• 0:28—Nude in warehouse.

Traci Adell . . . . June
- ••• 0:22—Nude posing in studio in various outfits.
- ••• 0:24—Nude in art studio.

Elisa Bridges . . . . September
- ••• 0:35—Nude outdoors in Western theme segment.
- •• 0:37—Nude in dusty attic type fantasy.

Cindy Brown . . . . February
- •• 0:05—In lingerie and nude in a warehouse. Sometimes playing with basketball.
- ••• 0:07—Nude, on rotating turntable wearing jewelry.

Maria Checa . . . . March
- ••• 0:09—Nude while posing indoors.
- ••• 0:11—In lingerie, while in bedroom.

Julie Cialini . . . . December
- ••• 0:48—Nude in studio posing in chair.
- ••• 0:50—In lingerie then nude in bedroom fantasy.

Danelle Folta . . . . August
- •• 0:31—Nude in house at night.
- ••• 0:33—Nude in studio with a space theme.

Kelly Gallagher . . . . January
- ••• 0:01—In lingerie and nude in an outdoor country setting.
- ••• 0:03—In lingerie and nude in a house at night.

Melissa Holliday . . . . October
- ••• 0:39—Full frontal nudity in magician act.
- •• 0:41—Nude in Casablanca style fantasy.

Stacy Sanches . . . . April
- ••• 0:14—In lingerie and nude while posing outdoors and indoors.
- ••• 0:16—Nude, while posing in studio.

Lisa Marie Scott . . . . May
- ••• 0:18—Nude, while ballet dancing in house.
- ••• 0:20—Nude in bedroom fantasy.

Victoria Zdrok . . . . November
- ••• 0:44—Nude in library fantasy.
- ••• 0:46—Nude in mansion.

• *Playboy Video Calendar 1997* *(1996; Video Tape)*

Gillian Bonner . . . . November
- ••• 0:45—In lingerie and nude, while posing indoors.
- ••• 0:46—In lingerie and nude, while posing in a warehouse.

Kona Carmack . . . . July
- ••• 0:28—Breasts, while posing at the beach.
- ••• 0:29—Nude, while undressing by herself in a deserted train station.

Victoria Fuller . . . . January
- ••• 0:01—Nude, while posing outside.
- ••• 0:03—In lingerie, then nude, while posing indoors.

Heidi Mark . . . . August
- ••• 0:32—Nude, while posing in a studio.
- ••• 0:34—Nude, while undressing in bed and putting on a strap outfit.

Rachel Jeàn Marteen . . . . October
••• 0:41—Nude, while posing outdoors.
••• 0:42—In lingerie and nude, while posing outdoors.

Donna Perry . . . . March
••• 0:10—In lingerie and nude, while posing in a studio, sometimes with a seal.
••• 0:11—In lingerie and nude, while posing indoors and making love with a fantasy guy in bed.

Alicia Rickter . . . . September
••• 0:36—In lingerie and nude while posing in apartment.
••• 0:38—Nude, while posing and dancing in bedroom.

Stacy Sanches . . . . December
••• 0:49—Nude, while dancing and posing in music video segment.
••• 0:52—In lingerie and nude, while posing indoors during a rainy day.

Shauna Sand . . . . February
••• 0:05—In lingerie and nude, while posing indoors.
••• 0:07—In lingerie and nude, while posing outdoors.

Karin Taylor . . . . May
••• 0:19—Nude, while swimming underwater.
••• 0:21—Nude, while posing in bedroom for fantasy guy.

Samantha Torres . . . . April
••• 0:15—Nude, while posing outdoors.
••• 0:16—In lingerie and nude, while posing in bedroom.

Holly Witt . . . . June
••• 0:23—Nude, while posing outdoors after mountain climbing.
••• 0:25—In lingerie, then nude when posing in a house while a guy watches through a telescope.

• ***Playboy Video Calendar 1998*** *(1997; Video Tape)*

Jennifer Allan . . . . April
••• 0:14—Nude, while posing during apartment fantasy.
••• 0:16—Nude, while posing indoors.

Angel Boris . . . . November
••• 0:44—Nude, while posing outdoors.
••• 0:47—Nude, while posing in an auto showroom.

Nadine Chanz . . . . June
••• 0:22—In lingerie and nude, while posing in front of neon signs.
••• 0:24—In lingerie and nude in dark bedroom.

Ulrika Ericsson . . . . October
•• 0:40—Nude, while posing in front of some antiques.
••• 0:41—Nude, while posing in a dark bedroom.

Jami Ferrell . . . . January
••• 0:01—In lingerie and nude while shooting hoops in a warehouse and posing.
••• 0:03—In lingerie and nude while posing on a sofa.

Jennifer Miriam . . . . February
••• 0:05—Nude, while posing outdoors.
0:07—Nude, while posing indoors in bedroom setting.

Kelly Monaco . . . . September
••• 0:35—Nude, while posing in an auto repair shop.
••• 0:38—Nude, while posing on a bed, wearing angel wings.

Victoria Silvstedt . . . . December
•• 0:49—Nude, while posing outdoors.
••• 0:50—Nude, while posing during modeling session.

Carrie Stevens . . . . July
••• 0:27—Nude, while posing outdoors while fishing.
••• 0:29—Nude, while posing in a dressing room.

Priscilla Taylor . . . . March
••• 0:10—Nude, while posing indoors and outdoors with a water theme.
••• 0:12—Nude, while posing indoors.

Lynn Thomas . . . . August
••• 0:31—Nude, while during still photography session.
••• 0:33—In lingerie and nude, while posing in a Japanese style house.

Kimber West . . . . Mary
••• 0:19—Nude, while moving furniture into a house.
••• 0:20—Nude, while posing indoors in the dark.

• ***Playboy Video Centerfold: Anna-Marie Goddard*** *(1994; Video Tape)*

Traci Adell . . . . Runner-Up Playmate
••• 0:43—Nude in lingerie in sequence with a small pool and chair.

Penny Baker . . . . Playmate
• 0:28—Brief breasts, in still photo during retrospective.

Julie Cialini . . . . Runner-Up Playmate
••• 0:39—Nude in beach front (shot in a studio) sequence.

Anna-Marie Goddard . . . . 40th Anniversary Playmate
• 0:00—Full frontal nudity during introduction.
••• 0:02—Nude during studio segment. Sometimes in fishnet body suit and some in B&W.
••• 0:09—Taking off stockings, then full frontal nudity while fantasizing about a man and woman. A little bit of rubbing lotion on herself.
••• 0:14—Nude, in bayou shack.
••• 0:18—Nude in still photos.
••• 0:20—Nude in house in dream wedding sequence.
• 0:27—Nude in end segment.
•• 0:45—Breasts in centerfold still.
•• 0:46—Nude during end credits.

Candy Loving . . . . Playmate
• 0:28—Brief breasts in retrospective.

Fawna MacLaren . . . . Playmate
• 0:29—Brief breasts during retrospective.

• ***Playboy Video Centerfold: Deborah Driggs & Karen Foster*** *(1990; Video Tape)*

Deborah Driggs . . . . Playmate
••• 0:02—Doing a strip tease, other dancing, some in bed. Nude.

Karen Foster . . . . Playmate
••• 0:24—Baton twirling, outside on bed, other miscellaneous things. Nude.

• ***Playboy Video Centerfold: Donna Edmondson*** *(1987; Video Tape)*

Jo Collins . . . . Playmate Update
••• 0:21—Breasts and buns in still photos.

Donna Edmondson . . . . Playmate of the Year 1987
••• 0:00—Nude, behind shower door, in photo session, on sofa in house, in empty house and in the rain.

• ***Playboy Video Centerfold: Dutch Twins*** *(1989; Video Tape)*

Jayne Mansfield . . . . Herself
••• 0:39—Breasts in color and B&W shots from *Promises, Promises.*

Karin van Breeschooten . . . . Playmate
••• 0:00—Nude throughout.

Miryam van Breeschooten . . . . Playmate
••• 0:00—Nude throughout.

- ***Playboy Video Centerfold: Fawna MacLaren***
  (1988; Video Tape)
  Erika Eleniak . . . . .Playmate
  ••• 0:07—In studio, nude.
  Fawna MacLaren . . . . 35th Anniversary Playmate
  ••• 0:11—In front of brick wall. In studio, in bed. Nude.

- ***Playboy Video Centerfold: India Allen***
  (1988; Video Tape)
  India Allen . . . . Playmate of the Year 1988
  ••• 0:05—Nude in still photos.
  •• 0:06—Nude in a field and by the side of a motel.
  ••• 0:09—Nude in and outside of house during the day and at night.
  ••• 0:12—Breasts and buns while exercising. Nice and sweaty.
  •• 0:13—Nude posing on chair in house. Quick cuts.
  ••• 0:15—Nude and in lingerie, while dancing. Color and B&W.
  •• 0:18—Nude while dancing in a sheer dress.
  ••• 0:19—Nude in bed. Lit with a swinging lamp, then continuous light.

- ***Playboy Video Centerfold: Jenny McCarthy***
  (1994; Video Tape)
  Julie Cialini . . . . .Playmate
  • 0:35—Buns while dancing in T-back.
  ••• 0:36—Nude in country setting segment.
  •• 0:40—Breasts and buns in T-back while dancing around in city settings.
  ••• 0:42—Nude in still photos.
  ••• 0:43—Nude in fashion show fantasy.
  ••• 0:45—Nude, when posing in house while thinking about her lover.
  Corinna Harney . . . . Angel
  Jenny McCarthy . . . . Playmate of the Year
  •• 0:00—Full frontal nudity during introduction.
  ••• 0:02—Full frontal nudity, while posing around a race track.
  ••• 0:05—Nude, in pool table/diner fantasy.
  ••• 0:12—Nude in school girl, cheerleader and graduation gown fantasy.
  ••• 0:15—Nude while posing around the house.
  ••• 0:19—Nude in still photos.
  ••• 0:23—Nude in desert town fantasy with a guy.
  ••• 0:28—Full frontal nudity in near-death fantasy.
  Tiffany Sloan . . . . Angel/Nurse
  Rachel Wagner . . . . Cast Member

- ***Playboy Video Centerfold: Julie Lynn Cialini***
  (1995; Video Tape)
  Elisa Bridges . . . . Playmate of the Year Runner-Up
  • 0:42—Briefly nude during introduction.
  ••• 0:43—Nude in colorful house.
  ••• 0:47—Nude, doing things around a farm.
  ••• 0:49—Nude in outdoor bedroom fantasy.
  ••• 0:52—Nude in still photos.
  ••• 0:53—Nude in living doll segment.
  Julie Cialini . . . . Playmate of the Year
  • 0:01—Nude during introduction.
  • 0:02—Breasts and buns in swimsuit while fooling around outside.
  ••• 0:04—Nude, while in a bedroom.
  ••• 0:12—Nude in her apartment during air conditioner repairman fantasy.
  ••• 0:19—Nude in still photos.
  ••• 0:21—Nude, while dancing in studio.
  ••• 0:25—Nude outside, during biker guy fantasy.
  ••• 0:32—Nude during music video/dance segment.
  ••• 0:35—Nude in Victorian house fantasy.

- ***Playboy Video Centerfold: Kerri Kendall***
  (1990; Video Tape)
  Rebekka Armstrong . . . . .Playmate
  ••• 0:33—Nude.
  Connie Brighton . . . . .Playmate
  ••• 0:31—Nude.
  Barbara Edwards . . . . .Playmate
  ••• 0:37—Nude.
  Kim Evenson . . . . .Playmate
  ••• 0:35—Nude.
  Kerri Kendall . . . . .Playmate
  ••• 0:00—Nude throughout.
  Venice Kong . . . . .Playmate
  ••• 0:41—Full frontal nudity.
  Laura Richmond . . . . .Playmate
  ••• 0:39—Nude.

- ***Playboy Video Centerfold: Kimberley Conrad***
  (1989; Video Tape)
  Kimberley Conrad . . . . Playmate of the Year 1989
  ••• 0:00—Nude throughout.
  Candy Loving . . . . Playboy Update
  ••• 0:42—Nude in old still photos.

- ***Playboy Video Centerfold: Lisa Matthews***
  (1991; Video Tape)
  Lisa Matthews . . . . Playmate of the Year 1991
  ••• 0:00—Nude in front of curtains, then in bed, then in medical segment, then at the beach and finally in a fantasy modeling session.
  Lorraine Olivia . . . . .Playmate
  ••• 0:28—Nude in the desert, then washing an old car, then on an airplane, then in Egyptian style bedroom.

- ***Playboy Video Centerfold: Morgan Fox***
  (1991; Video Tape)
  Morgan Fox. . . . . .Playmate
  ••• 0:02—Nude in aqueduct shoot.
  ••• 0:06—Nude in bedroom/factory fantasy.
  • 0:15—Brief silhouette of breasts and buns, several times while dancing.
  ••• 0:18—Nude, taking a bath.
  ••• 0:20—Breasts and buns in still photos.
  ••• 0:22—Breasts and buns in G-string, garter belt and stockings, dancing on stage.
  Wendy Kaye . . . . .Playmate
  ••• 0:27—Nude in different settings.
  ••• 0:30—Nude in American-theme song and dance number.
  ••• 0:31—Breasts and buns in G-string at the beach.
  ••• 0:33—Full frontal nudity in still photos.
  ••• 0:34—Nude while dancing.

- ***Playboy Video Centerfold: Pamela Anderson***
  (1992; Video Tape)
  Wendy Hamilton . . . . .Playmate
  ••• 0:26—Nude throughout.
  Pamela Lee . . . . .Playmate
  ••• 0:00—Nude throughout.

• Playboy Video Centerfold: Peggy McIntagart
(1989; Video Tape)

Julie McCullough. . . . . Playmate
••• 0:35—Nude in still photos and videos.
Peggy McIntaggart . . . . Playmate
••• 0:00—Nude throughout.

• Playboy Video Centerfold: Reneé Tenison
(1990; Video Tape)

Marianne Gravatte . Portrait of a Photographer: Richard Fegley
••• 0:32—Nude, in photo session at the beach.
Reneé Tenison. . . . . Playmate of the Year 1990
••• 0:00—Nude throughout.
Jeana Tomasina. . . . Portrait of a Photographer: Richard Fegley
•• 0:34—Full frontal nudity, posing on piano for centerfold photo.
Shannon Tweed . . . Portrait of a Photographer: Richard Fegley
••• 0:36—Full frontal nudity, posing by bed for centerfold photo.

• Playboy Video Centerfold: Stacy Sanches
(1996; Video Tape)

Donna D'Errico . . . . Playmate
••• 0:36—Nude by old gas station outdoors.
••• 0:39—In lingerie and nude while posing out in the desert.
••• 0:42—Nude, while playing with paint in a studio.
••• 0:45—Nude in still photos.
•• 0:48—In lingerie, then nude in back of limousine with a guy in chauffeur fantasy.
•• 0:50—Breasts and buns by gas station in end segment.
Kim Sanches . . . . Special Appearance
••• 0:16—Nude, while posing in a house, by herself and with her sister, Stacy.
Stacy Sanches . . . . Playmate of the Year
• 0:00—Breasts during introduction.
••• 0:01—Nude, while posing in various outfits outdoors.
••• 0:07—Nude, while dancing in studio with two guys.
••• 0:10—In lingerie, while undressing in house, then nude.
••• 0:15—Nude, while posing in a house, by herself and with her sister, Kim.
••• 0:24—In bra and panties, while bathing a guy, then nude.
••• 0:28—Nude in still photos.
••• 0:31—Nude, while lying on bed and dreaming.
•• 0:34—Full frontal nudity during ending.

• Playboy Video Centerfold: Tawnni Cable
(1990; Video Tape)

Tawnni Cable . . . . Playmate
••• 0:00—Nude throughout.
Jacqueline Sheen. . . . . Playmate
••• 0:14—Nude in Hawaii with Tawnni Cable and Pamela Stein.
Pamela J. Stein . . . . Playmate
••• 0:14—Nude in Hawaii with Tawnni Cable and Jacqueline Sheen.

• Playboy Video Centerfold: Teri Weigel
(1986; Video Tape)

Hope Marie Carlton . . . . Playmate
Dona Speir . . . . Playmate
Teri Weigel . . . . Playmate
••• 0:00—Nude, in shower, taking a bath, in bedroom.
••• 0:15—Nude outside in spa, and modeling lingerie with Dona Speir and Hope Marie Carlton.
••• 0:18—Nude in bed taking off black lingerie outfit.
Cyndi Wood . . . . Playmate Update
••• 0:25—Nude in still photos.

• Playboy Video Centerfold: Tiffany Sloan
(1992; Video Tape)

Tiffany Sloan . . . . Playmate
••• 0:00—Nude in the desert.
•• 0:02—Buns, in aqueduct.
••• 0:03—Nude in factory with fire and ice.
••• 0:09—Nude in warehouse gymnastics and dance routine. Nice.
••• 0:12—Nude in still photos.
••• 0:15—Nude in warehouse song and dance routine.
••• 0:18—Nude in bed in fantasy scene with a guy.
••• 0:23—Nude in the desert.
Anna Nicole Smith. . . . . Playmate Profile
••• 0:26—Nude in country bar.
••• 0:28—Nude at the beach.
••• 0:29—Nude in still photos.
••• 0:30—Nude in bed in Victorian fantasy.
••• 0:32—Nude, dancing in front of male body builders.
••• 0:34—Nude in campfire setting.

• Playboy Video Centerfold: Victoria Silvstedt
(1997; Video Tape)

Shauna Sand . . . . Playmate
••• 0:42—In lingerie and nude, while posing in house.
••• 0:46—Nude and in lingerie in B&W fantasy segment at the beach.
••• 0:50—Nude and in leather outfits while posing with a motorcycle.
••• 0:52—Nude in still photos.
••• 0:54—Nude while posing in bed.
Victoria Silvstedt . . . . Playmate of the Year
•• 0:00—Nude during introduction.
•• 0:02—In lingerie and nude, while dancing and posing outdoors.
••• 0:05—Nude while dancing and posing in a studio.
•• 0:13—Nude when dancing and posing with her (clothed) sister.
••• 0:16—Nude, while making love with her boyfriend in a barn.
••• 0:23—Nude in still photos.
••• 0:25—In lingerie and nude, while posing for photos with a white feather boa.
••• 0:28—Nude, while posing in a house.
••• 0:32—Nude, while posing in rain segment.
••• 0:34—Nude, during Cinderella style fantasy.
•• 0:40—Full frontal nudity, while lying on bed.

• Playboy Video Magazine, Volume 1
(1982; Video Tape)

Ursula Andress. . . . . Herself
•• 0:58—Breasts in still photos from *Playboy* pictorial.
Barbara Carrera . . . . Herself
•• 0:01—Nude in still photos. Nude in scenes from *I, the Jury.*
•• 0:30—Breasts in still photos.
••• 0:32—Nude in scenes from *I, the Jury.*
Lonnie Chin. . . . . Playmate
•• 0:00—Full frontal nudity during introduction.
••• 0:15—Nude outside by pool.
••• 0:19—Nude posing in various clothes in clothes store.
••• 0:21—In bra and panties, then nude in garter belt and stockings in a house.

Bo Derek . . . . Herself
- • 0:02—Breasts in still photos.
- •• 0:56—Breasts in still photos.
- •• 0:57—Breasts in scenes from *Fantasies*.
- •• 0:58—Breasts in still photos.

Linda Evans . . . . Herself
- •• 0:58—Breasts and side view of buns, in still photos from *Playboy* layout.

Brinke Stevens . . . . Marie/Ribald Classic
- • 0:01—Full frontal nudity.
- •• 0:46—Breasts on the bed with Jean-Pierre.
- ••• 0:47—Breasts in bathtub. Full frontal nudity in front of fire.
- •• 0:49—Breasts outside in the garden.

Shannon Tweed . . . . Playmate of the Year
- •• 0:02—Full frontal nudity, posing by bathtub for photo session.
- ••• 1:13—Nude, posing in bed.
- ••• 1:15—Full frontal nudity in photo session.
- ••• 1:21—Full frontal nudity in front of piano, in bathtub and in bed.

• Playboy Video Magazine, Volume 10

(1986; Video Tape)

Rebekka Armstrong . . . . Playmate
- ••• 0:40—Nude in song and dance number in car repair shop.

Kim Basinger . . . . 9 1/2 Weeks
- • 0:32—Brief right breast in ice cube scene.
- • 0:34—Brief right breast during slide show scene.
- • 0:37—Brief breasts in wet stairwell scene.

Cynthia Brimhall . . . . Playmate
- ••• 0:53—Nude in still photos, then in the woods after riding motorcycle and then in the desert.

Judy Norton-Taylor . . . . Herself
- ••• 0:45—Nude in still photos.

Liz Stewart . . . . The Goldner Girls
- •• 0:17—Breasts during modeling session for photographer David Goldner.

• Playboy Video Magazine, Volume 11

(1986; Video Tape)

Pamela Saunders . . . . Playmate
- ••• 0:52—Nude, undressing after party, in still photos and at the beach.

• Playboy Video Magazine, Volume 12

(1987; Video Tape)

Michelle Bauer. . . . . Candid Candid Camera
- •• 0:35—Lower nudity when her skirt falls down whenever she sneezes.

Donna Edmondson . . . . Playmate
- ••• 0:08—Nude in clips from her Playmate video.

Ava Fabian. . . . . Playmate
- ••• 1:08—Nude, in bed, in still photos, in rainy scene, dancing like Kim Basinger in *9 1/2 Weeks*.

Marilyn Monroe . . . . A Loving Tribute to Marilyn Monroe
- •• 1:02—Buns and left breast in still photos by swimming pool from unreleased last film.
- ••• 1:03—Breasts in B&W reference photos for artist Earl Moran. Taken around 1946-50.

Kym Paige . . . . Music Video
- ••• 0:55—Full frontal nudity.

• Playboy Video Magazine, Volume 2

(1983; Video Tape)

Amanda Cleveland . . . . Herself/Playboy Playoffs

Victoria Cooke . . . . Herself/Playboy Playoffs

Kymberly Herrin . . . . Herself/Playboy Playoffs
- • 0:33—Breasts in tug-of-war game.

Sylvia Kristel. . . . . Herself
- ••• 0:16—Breasts in various scenes from her films.

Candy Loving . . . . Playmate
- ••• 0:14—Full frontal nudity posing for her centerfold photograph.

Kym Malin. . . . . Herself/Playboy Playoffs

Kimberly McArthur . . . . Herself/Playboy Playoffs

Jeana Tomasina . . . . Herself/Playboy Playoffs

Lynda Wiesmeier . . . . Playmate
- ••• 1:12—In bra, stockings and garter belt. Undressing then full frontal nudity taking a shower.
- ••• 1:18—Nude, working out in dance studio.

Pamela Zinszer. . . . . Herself/Playboy Playoffs

• Playboy Video Magazine, Volume 3

(1983; Video Tape)

Carol Doda . . . . Carol Doda A San Francisco Monument
- • 0:22—Breasts in B&W before-silicone-injection photo (35 1/2-inch bust).
- •• 0:23—Breasts in B&W after-silicone-injection photo. (44-inch bust). Breasts while dancing on stage.
- • 0:24—Brief breasts and buns, on stage in The Condor Club during her act.
- ••• 0:25—Breasts and buns in G-string. Lit with red light.
- ••• 0:26—Nude, taking off her clothes and running outside in a park. More breasts, on piano in The Condor Club.

Marianne Gravatte. . . . . . . Playboy's Playmate of the Year 1983
- ••• 1:04—Nude in still photos.
- ••• 1:08—Full frontal nudity in bed at beach scene.
- ••• 1:09—Nude at the beach during the day.
- ••• 1:16—Nude while sitting at vanity and in bed.

Charlotte J. Helmcamp . . . . Video Playmate
- ••• 0:12—Nude in bubble bath.
- • 0:14—Full frontal nudity in centerfold still photo.
- ••• 0:17—Nude in house and on bed while wearing a girdle.

• Playboy Video Magazine, Volume 4

(1983; Video Tape)

Penny Baker. . . . . Playmate

Marilyn Chambers . . . . Herself
- •• 0:48—Breasts in scenes from miscellaneous films.

Barbara Edwards . . . . Playmate
- •• 0:20—Breasts on sailboat.
- ••• 0:22—Nude, posing for centerfold photograph.
- ••• 0:24—Full frontal nudity on bed by herself.
- ••• 0:29—Nude, dancing in laser light show.

Linnea Quigley . . . . Flashdancer
- • 0:15—Full frontal nudity.
- •• 0:16—Nude, fighting with Brinke Stevens in the shower.

Brinke Stevens . . . . Flashdancer/Dream Lover
- • 0:15—Very brief lower frontal nudity and buns in orange lingerie.
- ••• 0:16—Nude, fighting over blue towel with Linnea Quigley in the shower.
- ••• 0:43—Nude in a sheet covered chair during fantasy sequence. Best for Brinke fans!

Dorothy Stratten . . . . Playmate
- • 1:09—Brief breasts in black lingerie during photo shoot.
- •• 1:13—Breasts and buns in bubble bath.
- •• 1:19—Breasts posing in dance studio.
- • 1:22—More brief breasts shots from photo shoot.

• **Playboy Video Magazine, Volume 5**
(1983; Video Tape)

Penny Baker . . . . Playmate
••• 1:03—Full frontal nudity, in outdoor bathtub.
•• 1:04—Full frontal nudity on a chair in a field.
•• 1:09—Miscellaneous breasts shots.
••• 1:11—Full frontal nudity in an Asian-theme bedroom set.

Morgan Fairchild. . . . . The Seduction
• 0:43—Brief breasts in scenes from *The Seduction* in pool and bubble bath.

Marianne Gravatte . . . . Playmate
• 0:06—Full frontal nudity outside.
••• 0:09—Nude, posing at beach in a bed set.

Charlotte J. Helmcamp . . . . Playmate
• 0:05—Briefly nude in bubble bath.

Kymberly Herrin . . . . Playmate
• 0:05—Brief full frontal nudity next to car.

Marlene Janssen . . . . Playmate
• 0:05—Brief breasts with rose.

Melinda Mays . . . . Playmate
• 0:05—Brief breasts in hay.

Kimberly McArthur . . . . Playmate
• 0:06—Brief breasts in front of fire.

Susie Scott . . . . Playmate
• 0:05—Brief breasts, while stroking her hair.

Alana Soares . . . . Playmate
• 0:06—Brief breasts on chair.

Heidi Sorenson . . . . Playmate
• 0:06—Brief breasts in library.

Brinke Stevens. . . . . Candid Camera Girl
•• 0:18—Lots of buns shots, during prank learning how to ride a horse "bare back."

Jeana Tomasina. . . . . Playmate
• 0:06—Brief breasts on piano.
• 0:12—Breasts, then full frontal nudity posing on piano.

Shannon Tweed . . . . Playmate
• 0:05—Brief breasts in bathtub.
••• 0:13—Full frontal nudity in bedroom set.

Lynda Wiesmeier. . . . . Playmate
• 0:06—Brief breasts in shower.

• **Playboy Video Magazine, Volume 7**
(1985; Video Tape)

Karen Velez . . . . Playmate
••• 1:01—Breasts and buns on lounge chair, rubbing oil on herself.
••• 1:04—Nude, undressing outside in gazebo and on porch.
••• 1:09—Full frontal nudity undressing in living room.

• **Playboy's 21 Playmates** *(1996; Video Tape)*

Gianna Amore. . . . . Playmate
••• 0:32—Full frontal nudity in still photos.
••• 0:33—Nude in pizza restaurant.

Brandi Brandt . . . . Playmate
••• 0:39—Nude in still photos.
••• 0:40—Nude in biker fantasy.

Lonnie Chin . . . . Playmate
••• 1:10—Nude in still photos.
••• 1:11—Nude in mansion.

Kimberly Donley . . . . Playmate
••• 0:18—Nude in still photos.
••• 0:19—Nude in house.

Kim Evenson . . . . Playmate
••• 0:55—Nude in still photos.
••• 0:56—Full frontal nudity in bedroom.

Rebecca Ferratti. . . . . Playmate
••• 0:10—Nude in still photos.
••• 0:11—Nude in numerous scenes.

Carol Ficatier . . . . Playmate
••• 0:22—Nude in still photos.
••• 0:23—Nude on sailboat.

Morgan Fox. . . . . Playmate
••• 0:25—Nude in still photos.
••• 0:26—Nude in bed and in fantasy.

Charlotte J. Helmcamp . . . . Playmate
••• 0:02—Full frontal nudity in still photos.
••• 0:03—Nude in bedroom.

Kerri Kendall . . . . Playmate
••• 1:03—Full frontal nudity in still photos.
••• 1:04—Nude on sofa.

Sharry Konopski. . . . . Playmate
••• 0:59—Nude in still photos.
••• 1:00—Nude outside in old building and in studio.

Luann Lee . . . . Playmate
••• 0:45—Full frontal nudity in still photos.
••• 0:46—Nude in bedroom.

Shannon Long. . . . . Playmate
••• 0:52—Full frontal nudity in still photos.
••• 0:53—Nude in swimming pool and in the house.

Kimberly McArthur . . . . Playmate
••• 0:42—Nude in still photos.
••• 0:43—Nude while taking a shower and posing on sofa.

Donna Perry . . . . Playmate
••• 0:06—Nude in still photos.
••• 0:07—Nude in outdoor pool scenes.

Pia Reyes . . . . Playmate
••• 0:16—Nude in still photos.
••• 0:17—Nude outdoors in a park.

Leisa Sheridan . . . . Playmate
••• 1:07—Nude in still photos.
••• 1:08—Nude outdoors in swimming pool.

Cathy St. George. . . . . Playmate
••• 0:35—Full frontal nudity in still photos.
••• 0:36—Nude during photo session.

Kelly Tough . . . . Playmate
••• 0:29—Nude in still photos.
••• 0:30—Nude in bedroom.

Shannon Tweed . . . . Playmate
••• 0:14—Nude in still photos.
••• 0:15—Nude in centerfold photo session.

Nicole Wood . . . . Playmate
••• 0:48—Nude in still photos.
••• 0:49—Nude in hotel lobby fantasy.

• **Playboy's 21 Playmates: Volume II**
(1996; Video Tape)

Penny Baker . . . . Playmate
••• 0:32—Nude in still photos.
••• 0:33—Full frontal nudity in oriental theme bedroom.

Carmen Berg. . . . . Playmate
••• 0:25—Full frontal nudity in still photos.
••• 0:26—Nude, while posing and dancing on rooftop and other locations.

Laurie Ann Carr . . . . Playmate
••• 0:06—Nude in still photos.
••• 0:07—In lingerie and nude in house.

Victoria Cooke. . . . . Playmate
••• 0:29—Nude in still photos.
••• 0:30—Full frontal nudity during centerfold photo session.

Devin De Vasquez . . . . Playmate
••• 0:40—Nude in still photos.
••• 0:41—Nude, while posing for photographs.
Simone Eden . . . . Playmate
••• 0:36—Nude in still photos.
••• 0:37—Nude at the beach.
Marianne Gravatte . . . . Playmate
••• 0:02—Nude in still photos.
••• 0:03—Nude on the beach and in bedroom.
Wendy Hamilton . . . . Playmate
••• 1:03—Nude in still photos.
••• 1:04—Nude in auto repair shop fantasy.
Katherine Hushaw . . . . Playmate
••• 0:47—Nude in still photos.
••• 0:48—Nude while picking grapes and playing with them in a vat.
Deborah Nicholle Johnson . . . . Playmate
••• 0:17—Nude in still photos.
••• 0:18—Nude, while stretching and lying in bed after working out.
Venice Kong . . . . Playmate
••• 0:21—Nude in still photos.
••• 0:22—Nude in a river and waterfall.
Barbara Moore . . . . Playmate
••• 1:18—Full frontal nudity in still photos.
••• 1:19—Nude, while doing various things around the house.
Kim Morris . . . . Playmate
••• 0:59—Nude in still photos.
••• 1:00—In lingerie and nude in restaurant fantasy.
Susie Owens . . . . Playmate
••• 0:14—Full frontal nudity in still photos.
••• 0:14—Nude, while dancing in various settings to country music.
Kym Paige . . . . Playmate
••• 1:10—Nude in still photos.
••• 1:11—Nude, while doing various things in studio loft.
Julie Peterson . . . . Playmate
••• 1:07—Full frontal nudity in still photos.
••• 1:07—Nude in fire fantasy sequence.
Donna Smith . . . . Playmate
••• 0:43—Nude in still photos.
••• 0:44—Nude, while swimming in pool and bathing in bathtub.
Liz Stewart . . . . Playmate
••• 0:10—Nude in still photos.
••• 0:11—Nude at the beach.
Roberta Vasquez . . . . Playmate
••• 1:14—Full frontal nudity in still photos.
••• 1:15—Full frontal nudity while undressing in locker room and relaxing in spa.
Petra Verkaik . . . . Playmate
••• 0:55—Nude in still photos.
••• 0:56—Nude outdoors in field, then in studio.
Karen Witter . . . . Playmate
••• 0:51—Nude in still photos.
••• 0:52—Full frontal nudity on sailboat.

• ***Playboy's Cheerleaders*** *(1996; Video Tape)*
Patty Breton . . . . Cheerleader
••• 0:32—Nude (she's the first to take her bra off) outside during car wash with two other cheerleaders.
Julie Cialini . . . . Cheerleader
••• 0:19—Nude, while making love with her football boyfriend in kitchen and playing with food.
Shari Eckert . . . . Cheerleader
Tiffany Granath . . . . Dancer 3
•• 0:39—Brief breasts (she has straight, shoulder length blonde hair), several times during Carmen Elektra music video.
Gina Jackson . . . . Dancer 1/Gina
•• 0:39—Nude during Carmen Elektra music video.
Nichole McAuley . . . . Dancer 2/Nichole
•• 0:39—Nude during Carmen Elektra music video.
Chrissy Ranay . . . . Cheerleader
••• 0:32—Nude (she's the second to take her bra off) outside during car wash with two other cheerleaders.
Cindy Rich . . . . Cheerleader/Cindy
••• 0:32—Nude (she's the third to take her bra off) outside during car wash with two other cheerleaders.

• ***Playboy's College Girls*** *(1994; Video Tape)*
Natasha Alberico . . . . Herself
••• 0:01—Nude, while drying off in bedroom after a shower, then dressing.
••• 0:03—Nude, with a muscular guy in B&W segment.
Angela Cornell . . . . Herself
••• 0:16—Nude, after taking off fencing outfit and popping balloons with fencing sword.
••• 0:18—Nude, while undressing out of sweaters and posing in studio.
Michelle Diamond . . . . Herself
••• 0:11—Nude, while posing on a grand piano.
Catrina Falbo . . . . Herself
••• 0:31—In two piece swimsuit at the beach, then nude.
Jenny McCarthy . . . . Herself
••• 0:43—In bra, then nude, while posing for photos by Ty Erickson.
Tamara Unverzagt . . . . Herself
••• 0:06—Nude while dancing in a deserted building and on a Harley.

• ***Playboy's Erotic Fantasies III*** *(1994; Video Tape)*
Lisa Comshaw . . . . Midnight Madness/Vampiress
••• 0:00—Nude, while making love with a guy and the other vampiress. (She's wearing snake arm bands.)
Tamara Landry . . . . Lube Job/Customer
••• 0:20—Buns in lingerie in car repair shop, then nude while making love with the mechanic.
Monique Parent . . . . Midnight Madness/Vampiress
••• 0:00—Nude, while making love with a guy and the other vampiress. (She's wearing solid arm bands.)
Ashlie Rhey . . . . Final Exam/Teacher
••• 0:39—In white bra, panties and stockings, then full frontal nudity while making love with the student.
Amy Rochelle . . . . Morning Splendor/Horserider
••• 0:14—Breasts in push-up bra, buns in G-string panties, garter belt and lingerie. Then nude while making love in the stable with a guy.

• ***Playboy's Erotic Fantasies: Forbidden Liaisons*** *(1995; Video Tape)*
Jena Behr . . . . Cast Member
Stephanie Champlin . . . . Nice Catch
••• 0:37—In bra, while undressing and making love in the park outside.
Lisa Comshaw . . . . Double Exposure
••• 0:46—Full frontal nudity under and out of sheer white dress, making love in bed with a man and another woman.
Angela Cornell . . . . Satisfaction Guaranteed
••• 0:13—Nude, in fountain with the plumber.

Kim Dawson . . . . Piano Man
••• 0:21—In black lingerie after stripping in restaurant, then nude, while making love on the piano with the piano man.

• *Playboy's Erotic Weekend Getaways* (1992; Video Tape)

Lori Jo Hendrix . . . . Escape: The Desert
•• 0:09—In white bra and panties in moving car. Breasts changing into dress.
••• 0:11—Full frontal nudity while making love in the back seat of the convertible.
••• 0:12—Nude, outside with her lover by the pool.
••• 0:14—Nude, bringing drinks out to the pool.
••• 0:15—Nude, swimming in pool. Some are under water shots.

Michelle Hess . . . . Indulgence: The Spa

Robin Power . . . . Anticipation: The Mountains
••• 0:03—Breasts in cabin with her lover. Buns in G-string.
••• 0:04—Nude in front of fireplace with her lover.
••• 0:06—Breasts in bathtub with her lover, playing with honey and other food.

Sherrie Rose . . . . Adventure: The Beach
••• 0:43—Nude, while making love on sofa with her lover.
••• 0:46—Nude, taking off swimsuit with him, frolicking at the beach, running home, taking an outdoor shower.
••• 0:50—Breasts and very brief buns in pool with her lover.

• *Playboy's Fantasies* (1987; Video Tape)

Barbara Edwards . . . . Fashion
•• 0:00—Full frontal nudity during modeling session.

Monique Gabrielle . . . . Grand Theft
••• 0:25—Nude, in house after stealing jewelry.

Teri Weigel . . . . The Mannequin
••• 0:21—Nude, after coming to life from being a mannequin.

• *Playboy's Fantasies II* (1990; Video Tape)

Lynne Austin . . . . n.a.

Barbara Edwards . . . . The Game/The Secret Garden
••• 0:07—Nude, walking around in garden while a guy watches her.
••• 0:30—Full frontal nudity while trying on different clothes for her lover.

Teri Weigel . . . . Grand Illusions
••• 0:31—Nude outside in the woods during a surveyor's fantasy.

• *Playboy's Girls Next Door: Naughty and Nice* (1998; Video Tape)

Elisa Bridges . . . . Playmate

Daphnee Lynn Duplaix . . . . Naughty Neighbors
••• 0:51—Nude, while stripping with her girlfriend in their neighbor's apartment.

Karen McDougal . . . . Naughty Neighbors
••• 0:51—Nude, while stripping with her girlfriend in their neighbor's apartment.

Kelly Monaco . . . . Afternoon Delight/Katie
••• 0:21—Nude, while frolicking in the woods with Brooke and Josh.

Stacy Sanches . . . . Summer Job/Toni
••• 0:36—Nude, while making love with John in auto repair shop.

Shauna Sand . . . . Virtual Girl/Virtual Girl
••• 0:29—Nude, taking off her clothes, then dancing and giving herself a rubdown.

Carrie Stevens . . . . Picture This/Cindy
••• 0:42—Nude, while undressing and posing by the window, on the bed and giving herself a sponge bath.

• *Playboy's Girls of Radio: Talk, Rock and Shock* (1995; Video Tape)

Seka . . . . Herself
•• 0:43—Left breast, while talking into microphone.

Tempest . . . . Herself
••• 0:06—Nude, while taking a shower, then bathing with Amy Lynn Baxter.

Amy Lynn Baxter . . . . Herself
••• 0:06—Nude, when shaving her legs and pubic region (!) while in bathroom. More nude while taking a bath with Tempest.

Julie Cialini . . . . Herself
••• 0:00—In blue bra and panties, then nude with three other women.

Vanessa Conner . . . . Herself
••• 0:16—In black bra and panties, then nude with four other women.

Lizz Cufari . . . . Herself
••• 0:20—Nude in her office and in swimming pool.

Guadalupe Divina . . . . Herself
••• 0:16—In pink slip, then nude with four other women.

Kimberly Egler . . . . Herself
••• 0:00—In yellow bra and panties, then nude with three other women.

Shelly Jones . . . . Herself
••• 0:40—Nude in and out of various outfits.

Janet Layne . . . . Herself
••• 0:24—Nude, while posing in and on a red Corvette.

Jessica Lee . . . . Herself
••• 0:35—In white lingerie, then nude.

Jenifer Masterman . . . . Herself
••• 0:32—In red bra and panties, then nude while posing on a bar.

Karen Nobis . . . . Herself
••• 0:29—Nude outside in country western theme.

Joy Pons . . . . Herself
••• 0:37—Nude in airplane fantasy.

Diane Ray . . . . Herself
••• 0:16—In white slip, then nude with four other women.

Tracey Ray . . . . Herself
••• 0:11—Nude while working out with various exercise equipment and in sauna.

Tonja Schild . . . . Herself
••• 0:34—In black lingerie, then nude.

• *Playboy's Girls of South Beach* (1996; Video Tape)

Angel Boris . . . . Herself
••• 0:29—Nude while doing various things.

• *Playboy's Girls of Spring Break* (1991; Video Tape)

Tina Bockrath . . . . Herself
••• 0:30—Breasts and buns in panties, while dancing in Western theme segment with Brittney Powell.

Angela Brooks . . . . Herself
•• 0:25—Buns in still photos. Dancing in white lingerie. Breasts and buns in swimming pool.

Wendy Christine . . . . Herself
••• 0:14—Full frontal nudity in still photos.
••• 0:16—Full frontal nudity, in spa at ski resort with her friend, Michelle Mullica.

Kari LaCroix . . . . Herself
••• 0:11—Nude, while posing outdoors next to motorcycle for magazine pictorial.

Brittney Powell . . . . Herself
•• 0:26—Full frontal nudity in still photos.
•• 0:27—Full frontal nudity while posing for photos in studio.
••• 0:30—Breasts and buns in panties, while dancing in Western theme segment with Tina Bockrath.

• ***Playboy's Girls of the Internet*** *(1996; Video Tape)*

Rhonda Adams . . . . Herself
••• 0:10—Nude, while at the beach with two other women.

Tess Hennessy . . . . Girls of the Web
••• 0:19—In black lingerie, then nude while undressing and dancing in office.

Claudine Jennings . . . . Herself
••• 0:01—Nude, while stripping and dancing in the Internet Café, wearing stockings and boots.

Chasey Lain . . . . Herself
••• 0:10—Nude, while stripping and dancing (wearing black gloves and boots) with another woman.

Jacqueline Lovell . . . . Herself
••• 0:40—Nude, while trying on lingerie (she has long hair) and bathing with another woman.

Pam Luu . . . . Girls of the Web
••• 0:21—In lingerie, then nude while stripping and dancing.

Heidi Mark . . . . Herself
••• 0:10—Nude, while at the beach with two other women.

Alesha Oreskovich . . . . Herself
••• 0:10—Nude, while at the beach (she's the brunette one) with two other women.

Ashlie Rhey . . . . Herself
••• 0:31—Nude in virtual reality segment.

Gabriella Skye . . . . Herself
••• 0:36—In lingerie, then nude, while taking off her clothes and dancing for a voyeuristic neighbor.

• ***Playboy's Hard Bodies*** *(1995; Video Tape)*

Kona Carmack . . . . Herself
••• 0:46—Nude, while posing at the beach by herself and two other women.

Casey Gray . . . . Herself
••• 0:11—In lingerie, then nude, while posing outdoors.
••• 0:15—Nude, while posing with Holly Hart in wrestling ring.

Debee Halo . . . . Herself
••• 0:37—Nude, while posing in empty warehouse.

Ahmo Hight . . . . Herself
••• 0:46—Nude, while posing at the beach by herself and two other women.

Jacqueline Lovell . . . . Herself
••• 0:30—Nude while making love with Bobbie Marie on a hilltop.

Christine Lydon . . . . Herself
••• 0:47—Nude, while posing at the beach by herself and two other women.

Bobbie Marie . . . . Herself
••• 0:30—Nude while making love with Sara St. James on a hilltop.

Arlene Rodriguez . . . . Herself
••• 0:20—Breasts, while swimming under water as a mermaid. In lingerie and nude while dancing and posing on land.

• ***Playboy's Hot Latin Ladies*** *(1995; Video Tape)*

Maria Checa . . . . Playmate/Host
••• 0:01—Nude, during introduction and during desert segment.
•• 0:49—Nude during segment.

Stacy Sanches . . . . Stacy/Spanish American
••• 0:20—Nude in office and on the roof.

Samantha Torres . . . . Samantha/Spain
••• 0:15—Nude, while posing in a living room.

• ***Playboy's Hot Wheels & High Heels Biker Babes*** *(1997; Video Tape)*

Avalon Anders . . . . Biker Bash/Avalon
••• 0:33—Nude, while Tylyn video tapes her posing on motorcycle.

Tylyn John . . . . Biker Bash/Tylyn
••• 0:33—Buns in motorcycle leather clothing. Nude while Avalon video tapes her posing on motorcycle.

Cory Lane . . . . Tattoo Mistress/Cory
••• 0:21—Nude, while posing and applyng tattoos.

Bethany Lorraine . . . . Navy Seals/Agent 96
••• 0:03—Nude on boat with a brunette woman and a guy.

Linda O'Neil . . . . The Presentation
••• 0:30—Nude, while posing on motorcycle during sales presentation.

Nikki Schieler . . . . Pool Hall
••• 0:00—Nude, while in pool hall.

Karin Taylor . . . . Space Age Speed
••• 0:12—Nude, while posing on a motorcycle in a studio.

• ***Playboy's How to Reawaken Your Sexual Powers*** *(1992; Video Tape)*

Patricia Ford . . . . Cast Member
• 0:01—Buns in one piece swimsuit while on the beach.
••• 0:04—Nude, while swimming under water, working out on rock and on beach, and massaging her lover.

Lori Jo Hendrix . . . . Cast Member
••• 0:12—Nude with her lover in the woods, a stream, a pond and under a waterfall.
••• 0:45—Nude, outside by beach with her lover. Also on air mattresses and snorkeling under water.

Sam Phillips . . . . Cast Member
••• 0:17—Full frontal nudity while making love with her lover by lava flow.
••• 0:37—Nude while writing love letter, making love by campfire and kissing by waterfall.

Robin Power . . . . Cast Member
••• 0:26—Nude at the beach while standing and touching her lover.
••• 0:43—Nude outside by stream and on blanket with her lover.

Gwen Somers . . . . Cast Member
••• 0:21—Full frontal nudity in the forest with her lover.
••• 0:29—Nude on hammock on sailboat with her lover.

• ***Playboy's Night Calls*** *(1998; Video Tape)*

Doria . . . . Herself
••• 0:00—Nude throughout.

Juli Ashton . . . . Herself
••• 0:00—Nude throughout.

• ***Playboy's Playmate Review*** *(1982; Video Tape)*

Lourdes Estores . . . . Playmate
••• 0:56—Nude at the beach, then under water, then outside near river.

Patty Farinelli . . . . Playmate
••• 0:11—Full frontal nudity during library photo shoot and then by swimming pool.

Vicki Lasseter . . . . Playmate
••• 0:43—Full frontal nudity in office, then in the woods.

Kym Malin . . . . Playmate
••• 0:37—Nude in bar, then on empty stage.
Kimberly McArthur . . . . Playmate
••• 0:19—Nude in sauna, then taking a shower, then in front of fireplace.
Kelly Tough. . . . . Playmate
••• 0:27—Nude, camping, then in bedroom setting.
Shannon Tweed . . . . Playmate
••• 0:47—Nude in bed, then in photo shoot by a table, then by a piano, then in bathtub.
Linda Rhys Vaughn . . . . Playmate
••• 1:06—Nude on horseback, then next to stream.
Lynda Wiesmeier. . . . . Playmate
••• 1:17—Nude undressing and taking a shower. Wow! Then in ballet studio.
Karen Witter . . . . Playmate
••• 0:00—Nude deep sea fishing, then sunbathing on sailboat.

• *Playboy's Playmate Review 1992*

(1992; Video Tape)

Stacy Arthur . . . . Miss January
••• 0:18—Nude, dancing on back of truck, then using a pottery wheel.
Cheryl Bachman . . . . Miss October
••• 0:30—Nude on rooftop and then outside in a field.
Tonja Christensen . . . . Miss November
••• 0:02—Nude in hat and chair scenes in a house.
Julie Clarke . . . . Miss March
••• 0:10—Nude in indoor pool, then in art studio and then on horseback.
Samantha Dorman . . . . Miss September
••• 0:06—Nude on boat, then in laboratory and then in surreal artistic setting.
Wendy Hamilton. . . . . Miss December
••• 0:44—Nude in a house and then dancing next to a car.
Corinna Harney. . . . . Miss August
••• 0:48—Nude posing in a house and then outside.
Wendy Kaye . . . . Miss July
••• 0:36—Nude in patriotic scene and then in a surreal scene.
Christina Leardini . . . . Miss April
••• 0:32—Nude in a car, then in a bed, then inside an old building.
Saskia Linssen . . . . Miss June
••• 0:27—Nude doing futuristic dance and then taking a bath.
Cristy Thom . . . . Miss February
••• 0:22—Nude on motorcycle, then with a snake and then in a house.
Carrie Jean Yazel . . . . Miss May
••• 0:14—Nude outside with piano, then outside in doorway and then in a house.

• *Playboy's Playmate Review 1993*

(1993; Video Tape)

Stephanie Adams . . . . Miss November
••• 0:12—Nude in house and in bed.
Ashley Allen. . . . . Miss August
••• 0:32—Nude in a field and on horseback.
••• 0:33—Nude outside posing by freeway.
Tanya Beyer . . . . Miss February
••• 0:06—Nude, dancing in front of a big screen TV.
••• 0:08—Nude on fountain in front of a house.
Cady Cantrell . . . . Miss April
••• 0:15—Nude while modeling in studio photo session.
••• 0:17—Nude, outside in southern belle style segment.
Morena Corwin . . . . Miss September
••• 0:27—Nude in bed and dancing out in a field with a guy.
••• 0:30—Nude in pool and under water.
Amanda Hope . . . . Miss July
••• 0:19—Nude in pool and in house.
••• 0:21—Nude in military style segment.
Tylyn John . . . . Miss March
••• 0:40—Nude, while doing things around a country home.
••• 0:42—Nude in white studio fantasy.
Angela Melini . . . . Miss June
••• 0:44—Nude in fashion designer fantasy.
••• 0:46—Nude in bedroom while it rains outside.
Barbara Moore . . . . Miss December
••• 0:02—Nude with children's toys in studio.
••• 0:03—Nude, in a stable with a horse.
Suzi Simpson. . . . . Miss January
••• 0:37—Nude while playing billiards.
••• 0:38—Nude in a cabin.
Tiffany Sloan . . . . Miss October
•• 0:48—Lower nudity, while in aqueduct.
••• 0:50—Nude in fire and ice fantasy segment.
Anna Nicole Smith. . . . . Miss May
••• 0:23—Breasts and buns, while at the beach.
••• 0:25—Nude, posing with male bodybuilders.
••• 0:26—Nude in Victorian style fantasy.

• *Playboy's Playmates of the Year: The '80s*

(1989; Video Tape)

India Allen . . . . Playmate of the Year 1988
••• 0:03—Nude, posing in chair.
••• 0:04—Nude, exercising and dancing around the house.
••• 0:06—Nude in bed.
•• 0:52—Breasts in chair. Full frontal nudity in bed.
Kimberley Conrad . . . . Playmate of the Year 1989
••• 0:44—Nude in still photos.
••• 0:49—Full frontal nudity in bathtub and in various scenes around the house.
• 0:53—In lingerie.
Donna Edmondson . . . . Playmate of the Year 1987
••• 0:21—Modeling swimsuits and lingerie. Nude on couch.
••• 0:22—In bra, garter belt and stockings, dancing in strobe light. Lower frontal nudity. Nude seen through open window.
••• 0:23—Nude, taking off her clothes in empty house. Nude in bed.
•• 0:26—Breasts, in the rain.
•• 0:52—Full frontal nudity in bed.
Barbara Edwards . . . . Playmate of the Year 1984
••• 0:13—Nude in still photos.
••• 0:14—Full frontal nudity in centerfold photo session. More in bed.
•• 0:52—Full frontal nudity in bed.
Marianne Gravatte. . . . . Playmate of the Year 1983
••• 0:32—Nude in still photos.
••• 0:33—Nude in bed at the beach during photo session.
•• 0:51—Breasts in bed scene.
Kathy Shower . . . . Playmate of the Year 1986
••• 0:17—Full frontal nudity outside by spa.
••• 0:19—Breasts in still photos. Full frontal nudity, posing in bed.
Dorothy Stratten . . . . Playmate of the Year 1980
••• 0:27—Breasts and buns in various settings during photo session.
•• 0:32—Brief breasts holding flowers in a field.
•• 0:51—Breasts in field.

Shannon Tweed . . . . Playmate of the Year 1982
••• 0:36—Full frontal nudity in photo session in a house.
••• 0:37—Nude in still photos. Nude posing by piano, in bathtub, in bed.
•• 0:51—Full frontal nudity standing by bed.
Karen Velez . . . . Playmate of the Year 1985
••• 0:39—Breasts and buns, in lounge chair, rubbing oil on herself.
••• 0:42—Nude, in a gazebo.
•• 0:52—Right breast in open dress.
Terri Welles . . . . Playmate of the Year 1981
••• 0:08—Nude in still photos.
••• 0:10—Nude at the beach.
••• 0:11—Nude in still photos.
•• 0:51—Breasts coming out of the water.

• *Playboy's Playmates Revisited* (1998; Video Tape)

India Allen . . . . Playmate
••• 0:20—Nude in old footage and still photos.
••• 0:27—Full frontal nudity in new footage.
Cynthia Brimhall . . . . Playmate
••• 0:48—Nude in old footage and still photos.
••• 0:53—Nude in new footage.
Barbara Edwards . . . . Playmate
••• 0:56—Nude in old footage and still photos.
••• 1:00—Nude in new footage.
Ava Fabian. . . . . Playmate
••• 0:39—Nude in old footage and still photos.
••• 0:44—Full frontal nudity in new footage.
Lillian Müller . . . . Playmate
••• 1:03—Nude in old footage and still photos.
••• 1:09—Nude in new footage.
Shauna Sand . . . . Herself
• 0:25—Brief breasts in still photo.
Susie Scott. . . . . Playmate
••• 0:30—Nude in old footage and still photos.
••• 0:36—Nude in new footage.
Kathy Shower . . . . Playmate
••• 0:02—Nude in old footage and still photos.
••• 0:08—Nude in new footage.
Cathy St. George. . . . . Playmate
••• 0:12—Nude in old footage and still photos.
••• 0:17—Full frontal nudity in new footage.
Priscilla Taylor . . . . Herself
• 0:25—Brief breasts in still photo.

• *Playboy's Real Couples: Sex in Dangerous Places* (1995; Video Tape)

Dixie Beck . . . . Up on the Roof/Woman
• 0:45—Brief buns, while mooning the camera at the beach.
••• 0:52—Nude while making love with James and Shayna.
Griffin Drew . . . . Mile High Club/Woman
••• 0:32—Nude, while making love with Bobby in airplane restroom.
Chona Jason . . . . Steamy Encounter/Extra
Shayna Lee . . . . Up on the Roof/Voyeur
••• 0:48—In sheer panties, when caressing herself when watching someone through a telescope. Nude, while making love with Dixie and James.
Shae Marks . . . . .Touching Me, Touching You/Masseuse
••• 0:24—Nude while massaging Carrie Westcott.
Gwen Somers . . . . The Show Room/Woman
•• 0:42—Full frontal nudity, while making love with George in a furniture store.
Carrie Westcott . . . . . . .Touching Me, Touching You/Masseuse
••• 0:24—Nude while massaging Shae Marks.

• *Playboy's Rising Stars and Sexy Starlets* (1996; Video Tape)

Lisa Boyle. . . . . Herself
•• 0:02—Breasts, in strap outfit from *I LIke to Play Games.*
••• 0:05—Nude, while dancing in front of a guy on soundstage.
Kelly Burns. . . . . Herself
•• 0:43—Full frontal nudity, in a clip from *Watch Me.*
••• 0:47—Nude, while making love with a guy in country house segment.
Jennifer Leigh Burton . . . . .Talent
• 0:43—Brief full frontal nudity, while lying down in clip from *Watch Me.*
Anna-Marie Goddard. . . . . Herself
•• 0:51—Breasts, during photo sessions.
••• 0:52—Brief breasts in still photos, then nude while posing some more.
Jacqueline Lovell . . . . .Cowgirl
••• 0:38—Nude, undressing out of cowgirl outfit in barn, then making love with another woman.
Shauna O'Brien . . . . Herself
• 0:55—Brief breasts from *Over the Wire.*
••• 0:56—Nude, while dancing in studio.
Monique Parent. . . . . Herself
•• 0:30—Breasts in clips from some of her films.
••• 0:32—Nude, while making love with a guy in bed.
Ashlie Rhey . . . . Herself
••• 0:26—In lingerie, then nude, while dancing for her boyfriend.
Kate Rodger. . . . . Herself
• 0:37—Right breast in a scene from *Walnut Creek.*
••• 0:38—Breasts, while in barn, then making love with a cowgirl.
Lisa Marie Scott . . . . Herself
•• 0:09—Full frontal nudity in still photos.
•• 0:10—Brief breasts and buns in panties from *The Glass Cage.*
••• 0:12—Nude, while dancing alone, then with a guy in ballet studio.
Julie Strain . . . . Herself
•• 0:17—Full frontal nudity in clips from different films.
••• 0:20—Buns in swimsuit in movie, then nude while posing in a theater.

• *Playboy's Secret Confessions* (1993; Video Tape)

Lisa Comshaw . . . . Here Comes the Judge/Gina
••• 0:50—Full frontal nudity, after taking off the judge's robe and making love with Spike on the judge's bench.
Griffin Drew. . . . . Dream Boy/Elaine
••• 0:04—Full frontal nudity, while making love with Barry in cabin.
Melanie Good . . . . On the Air/Venus
••• 0:12—In bra and panties, then breasts, while making love in radio station with Tony.
Lori Jo Hendrix. . . . . . . Teacher's Pet/Ruth Ann and Twins/Cindy & Sandy
••• 0:26—In green lingerie, then breasts and buns, while making love in bedroom with Jay.
• 0:39—Breasts and buns in hallway and with Stuart.
••• 0:43—Nude in bedroom, then making love with Stuart on the living room floor.
Tamara Landry. . . . . .Jailhouse Rock/Tina
••• 0:34—In red lingerie, then nude, while making love with Rick in jail cell.

Tonya Poole . . . . Wash & Wax/Jogger
••• 0:17—In wet leotard top, while washing the car. Full frontal nudity while making love with Dennis.

Gwen Somers . . . . Teacher's Pet/Marilyn
•• 0:27—Breasts, while making love in bed with Warren. Full frontal nudity and brief buns, while standing on stairs with Jay.

• *Playboy's Secrets of EuroMassage*
(1989; Video Tape)

Amy Rochelle . . . . No. 1 Late Night Passion
••• 0:01—Nude, during massage session on bed.

Teri Weigel . . . . No. 4 Sensual Power of Water
••• 0:23—Nude (including breasts squished against glass), during massage session in the shower, then in spa and on wooden platform. Long scene.

• *Playboy's Sensual Fantasy for Lovers*
(1993; Video Tape)

Jennifer Leigh Burton. . . . . Pretending
0:16—In wet, braless white blouse.
••• 0:17—Nude, in stable after undressing and making love.
• 0:47—Full frontal nudity during review.

Tai Collins . . . . Games
••• 0:05—In white bra and panties, then full frontal nudity while in house, in bathtub, then making love in bed.
• 0:46—Nude during review.
• 0:49—Brief right breast during review.

Shannon McLeod . . . . Risk-Taking
• 0:43—In black bra and panties, then buns, while outside during party with her lover.
••• 0:44—Full frontal nudity while making love outside.

Monique Parent . . . . Secret Desires
0:30—In green bra and panties, while talking on the phone with her lover.
••• 0:32—Full frontal nudity after taking off bra and making love in bed.

Ashlie Rhey . . . . Film Fantasies
••• 0:25—In bra and panties, then nude while making love, in "sheik" fantasy with her lover.
• 0:47—Breasts during review.

• *Playboy's Sex on the Beach: Tropical Heat*
(1997; Video Tape)

Sarah Hutchinson . . . . Bonfire Dance/Sarah
••• 0:07—In Polynesian-style outfit, then nude, while dancing on the sand at night.

Mercy Lopez . . . . Sun Charter/Mercy
••• 0:01—Nude on sailboat with two other women, then in the water by herself.

Shellani Taarud . . . . .Massage/Shellani
••• 0:16—Nude, while getting massaged by another woman.

• *Playboy's Sisters* *(1995; Video Tape)*

Adriana Alexander. . . . . Herself/Friend & Confidant
••• 0:42—Nude while posing with her sister in country farm-house fantasy.

Rachel Furman . . . . Herself/Double Trouble
••• 0:33—Nude when washing the car with her identical twin sister.

Rebecca Furman . . . . Herself/Double Trouble
••• 0:33—Nude when washing the car with her identical twin sister.

Corinna Harney. . . . . .Herself/Natural Woman
••• 0:22—Nude with her sister and four other sisters outdoors.

Christina Leardini . . . . Herself/Cherished Moments
••• 0:27—Nude with her sister in clothing store fantasy.

Mandy Malone . . . . .Herself/Mirror Image
••• 0:15—In lingerie and nude in room and in bathroom with her twin sister.

Mindy Malone. . . . . .Herself/Mirror Image
••• 0:15—In lingerie and nude in room and in bathroom with her twin sister.

Kristina Mateyko . . . . Herself/Natural Woman
••• 0:22—Nude with her sister and four other sisters outdoors.

Kim Sanches . . . . Herself/Loving Competition
••• 0:01—Nude with her sister in boxing workout fantasy.

Stacy Sanches . . . . Herself/Loving Competition
••• 0:01—Nude with her sister in boxing workout fantasy.

• *Playboy's Sorority Girls* *(1997; Video Tape)*

Tracy George. . . . . .Wet & Wild
••• 0:22—Nude outdoors in and by pool with Sterling Dunn.

Shelly Jones . . . . Wash & Dry
••• 0:24—Nude, while dancing by herself in a laundromat.

Tiffany Turner . . . . .Yoga
••• 0:14—Nude, while doing yoga by herself.

• *Playboy's The Girls of Hawaiian Tropic*
(1994; Video Tape)

Ashley Allen. . . . . Hawaiian Earth
••• 0:40—Nude, while posing at a black sand beach.

Deborah Anne. . . . . Paradise
••• 0:01—In white bra and panties, then nude while posing outdoors during the day.

Angel Boris . . . . Moonlit Beach
••• 0:06—Nude, while dancing at the beach at night.

Amy Hayes . . . . .Wild Orchids
••• 0:22—Nude, while posing outdoors in the water.

Shana Hiatt . . . . Volcano
••• 0:52—Nude, while outdoors in the surf at night.

Kristen Holland . . . . Beach Girls
0:39—Nude, while posing with another girl at the beach.

Sarah Hutchinson . . . . Secret Island
••• 0:29—Nude, while doing various things around the beach.

Sung Hi Lee. . . . . Passion Fruit
••• 0:14—Nude, while posing in and by a stream.

Michelle Stanford . . . . .White Sand Beach
••• 0:26—Nude, while posing at the beach during the day.

Shellani Taarud . . . . Lagoon
0:43—Nude, while posing in and beside a lagoon.

• *Playboy's Twins & Sisters Too* *(1997; Video Tape)*

Christine Artecona. Workout Together
••• 0:26—Nude, while working out on exercise equipment with her twin sister.

Jacqueline Artecona. . . . . Workout Together
••• 0:26—Nude, while working out on exercise equipment with her twin sister.

Mandy Malone . . . . Sea Goddesses
••• 0:22—Nude, while frolicking on the beach with her twin sister.

Mindy Malone. . . . . Sea Goddesses
••• 0:22—Nude, while frolicking on the beach with her twin sister.

Leslie Olivan . . . . Special Touch
••• 0:13—Nude with her sister in bathtub segment.

Dawn Willis . . . . Curtain Calls
••• 0:34—In lingerie, then nude, while posing with her twin sister.

Deanna Willis . . . . Curtain Calls
••• 0:34—In lingerie, then nude, while posing with her twin sister.

• Playboy's Women Behaving Badly *(1997; Video Tape)*

Patty Breton . . . . All Wet
••• 0:02—Nude, while undressing in locker room with her two girlfriends in locker room, then taking a shower. (She's wearing earrings.)

Daphnee Lynn Duplaix . . . . Body Paint
••• 0:10—Nude, while in apartment with her girlfriend, then painting each other.

Jami Ferrell . . . . Tie Me Tease Me/Lisa
••• 0:37—Nude, while her husband is tied to the bed

Bethany Lorraine . . . . Ladies Night
••• 0:17—In lingerie, then nude, while dancing on stage in women's club after dancing with male stripper.

Monica Mendez . . . . All Wet
••• 0:01—Nude, while undressing in locker room with her two girlfriends in locker room, then taking a shower.

Layla Roberts . . . . Wanted
••• 0:32—Nude, while bathing, then rubbing oil on herself in old west style segment.

Laura Selway . . . . Body Paint
••• 0:11—Nude, while in apartment with her girlfriend, then painting each other.

• Playboy's Women of Color *(1994; Video Tape)*

Stephanie Adams . . . . Playmate
••• 0:30—Nude, while in motion and in still photos.
••• 0:33—Nude, while posing in studio.
••• 0:35—Nude in warehouse fantasy.

Venice Kong . . . . Playmate
••• 0:20—Nude, when frolicking in the water in Jamaica.

Lorraine Olivia . . . . Playmate
••• 0:04—Nude in motion and in still photos in flight attendant in and out of uniform on airplane set.
••• 0:06—Nude out in the desert and washing an old car.
••• 0:08—Nude in lighted bed.

Robin Power . . . . Weekend Getaway/Sexual Power
••• 0:25—Nude, while making love with a guy in cabin.
•• 0:27—Breasts, while playing with food with a guy in bathtub.
••• 0:38—Nude at the beach with a guy.

Reneé Tenison . . . . Playmate/Hostess
••• 0:01—Breasts and buns, while working out in warehouse.
••• 0:02—Nude in still photos.
••• 0:41—Nude in house, while taking a milk bath.
••• 0:43—Nude in bed and in house.
••• 0:45—Nude in dance/music number.

The Player *(1992)*

Leah Ayres-Hamilton . . . . Sandy
Karen Black . . . . Cameo
Cathy Lee Crosby . . . . Cameo
Kasia Figura . . . . Cameo
Teri Garr . . . . Cameo
Gina Gershon . . . . Whitney Gersh
Anjelica Huston . . . . Cameo
Sally Kellerman . . . . Cameo
Sally Kirkland . . . . Cameo
Marlee Matlin . . . . Cameo
Jennifer Nash . . . . Cameo
Julia Roberts . . . . Cameo
Mimi Rogers . . . . Cameo
Annie Ross . . . . Cameo
Susan Sarandon . . . . Cameo
Greta Scacchi . . . . June Gudmundsdottir
Cynthia Stevenson . . . . Bonnie Sherow
•• 0:19—Breasts, sitting in spa with Tim Robbins.

Playing For Keeps *(1986)*

Monique Mannen . . . . Dancer (Silk's Fantasy)
Mary B. Ward . . . . Chloe
•• 0:49—Breasts, after taking off her sweatshirt outside at night in front of Danny.

Playmaker *(1994)*

Jennifer Rubin . . . . Jamie Harris
••• 0:37—Nude, while lying on piano after Colin Firth cuts her dress off with scissors.
• 0:39—Breasts, after getting out of bed and putting on robe at night.

Belinda Waymouth . . . . Angie

Playroom *(1989)*

a.k.a. Schizo

Lisa Aliff . . . . Jenny
•• 0:23—Breasts making love on top of Christopher.

Kimberly Beck . . . . Secretary
Jamie Rose . . . . Marcy

Pleasure in Paradise *(1992)*

Toni Alessandrini . . . . Lingerie Girl/First
•• 0:51—In black lingerie, then breasts and buns in G-string, while dancing in bar.

Linda Brown . . . . Heather
• 0:02—Full frontal nudity, while getting out of the shower and wrapping a towel around herself.
••• 0:41—Breasts while in bed, making love with Rob. Long scene.

Diane Colton . . . . Tiffany
••• 0:27—In black bra, then breasts while making love with Hansen. Long scene.

Jacqueline Jade . . . . Carol
•• 0:01—Left breast, then breasts while making love in field with a guy at night.

Gina Jourard . . . . Woman
••• 0:06—Breasts, while making in love in bed with Hansen.
• 0:39—Breasts on bed with Hansen.

Honey Lauren . . . . Sandra
••• 0:14—Breasts in lingerie, while making love in bed with Hansen. Long scene.
••• 0:57—Nude in pool, while making love with Hansen, then getting out. Long scene.

Pocahontas, The Legend *(1995)*

Sandrine Holt . . . . Pocahontas
•• 1:01—Breasts, while making love with Miles O'Keeffe.

Point Blank *(1967)*

Angie Dickinson . . . . Chris
• 0:51—Breasts in background putting dress on. Kind of a long shot.

Point Break *(1991)*

Betsy Lynn George . . . . Girl at Party
Debra Lamb . . . . Uncredited Flame Blower at Party
Julie Michaels . . . . Freight Train
• 0:53—Brief breasts in the shower.

• 0:54—Nude, beating up Keanu Reeves in the bathroom during shoot-out. Full frontal nudity while stabbing an FBI agent.

Lori Petty . . . . Tyler

• 1:14—Very brief buns, running out of Keanu Reeves' bedroom.

Point of Impact *(1993)*

Barbara Carrera . . . . Eva

• 0:39—In wet white swimsuit, after getting out of swimming pool.

• 0:40—Very brief breasts, while swimming under water past underwater window.

•• 0:51—Close up of left breast, while making love with Paré.

• 0:53—Brief left breast, after getting out of bed.

••• 0:59—Breasts and buns in T-back, while swimming under water in pool.

•• 1:00—Breasts, while making love outside with Paré.

•• 1:02—Breasts in shower with Paré and on bed in wet sheet.

Point of No Return *(1993)*

Olivia D'Abo . . . . .Angela

Bridget Fonda . . . . Maggie

• 0:49—Brief right breast, while making love with J.P.

Poison Ivy 2: Lily *(1995)*

Belinda Bauer . . . . Angela Falk

Tara Ellison . . . . Catherine

• 0:01—Left breast, while making love with Xander Berkeley on couch.

Victoria Haas . . . . .Bridgette

• 0:11—Brief breasts, while making love in bed with a guy when seen by Alyssa Milano.

Alyssa Milano . . . . Lily

•• 0:43—In black bra, then breasts, while making love with Gredin outside at night. (Some of his artwork gets in the way.)

• 0:51—Brief right breast in open blouse, then breasts while posing for Xander Berkeley.

• 0:53—Very brief left breast, while posing for Berkeley.

• 1:04—Buns and breasts behind patterned glass while making out with Gredin in room during party.

Kate Rodger . . . . Isabel

• 0:05—Brief breasts, while posing as an artist's model for art class.

• 0:17—Brief right breast, while posing in a chair for art class.

• 0:19—Brief right breast again.

• ***Poison Ivy 3: The New Seduction*** *(1996)*

Athena Massey . . . . Rebecca

••• 0:03—In black bra and panties, then breasts, while making love with the pool boy.

Jaime Pressly . . . . Violet

•• 0:12—Buns and breasts, getting into bathtub and taking a bath.

• 0:27—Brief buns in panties, while putting on her slip.

••• 0:30—Breasts and buns in swimsuit bottom, while going for a swim.

• 0:43—Buns, getting out of swimming pool after going for a swim.

••• 0:45—Breasts, while making love with Michael outside at night.

• 0:57—Brief breasts, while starting to make love with Ivan.

••• 0:59—Breasts and buns, while making love with Ivan in bedroom.

• 1:16—Brief breasts, when caught with Ivan by Joy.

Susan Tyrrell . . . . .Mrs. B

Merete Van Kamp . . . . Catherine

Police *(1985; French)*

Sandrine Bonnaire . . . . .Lydie

••• 0:49—Full frontal nudity, undressing in front of Gérard Depardieu, then getting out of the shower.

Sophie Marceau . . . . Noria

• 0:10—Brief left breast in window during police strip search.

• 1:36—Right and left breasts several times, while in bed with Gérard Depardieu

Policewomen *(1974)*

Jeannie Bell . . . . Pam Harris

•• 0:02—Buns and breasts changing clothes during prison break.

••• 1:28—Brief breasts changing into military clothes outside next to truck.

Sondra Currie . . . . .Lacy Bond

••• 0:50—Breasts and buns taking off sheer robe and getting into bed, then making love with Frank.

Susan McIver. . . . . Laura

•• 0:42—Breasts and buns, taking off two piece swimsuit and getting into the shower with Doc.

••• 0:44—Breasts in the shower after Doc leaves.

Laurie Rose . . . . Janette

• 0:02—Brief side of left breast, changing clothes during prison break.

The Pom Pom Girls *(1976)*

Jennifer Ashley. . . . . Laurie

• 1:02—Brief breasts (on the left), taking off her white blouse in locker room. Brief buns, taking off panties and pulling down her cheerleader body suit.

Diane Lee Hart. . . . . Judy

• 1:02—Breasts, in locker room when asking Cheryl Smith to feel for a lump in her breast, then buns, after taking off her panties. Right breast and brief buns, while taking off panties.

Susan Player Jarreau. . . . . Sue Ann

• 0:14—Breasts, when making out with Jesse in the back of his van while parked at burger joint.

• 0:47—Breasts, when making out with Jesse in the back of his van while parked at school.

• 1:02—Brief buns, taking off her panties in locker room with the other girls.

Lisa Reeves . . . . Sally

• 1:02—Brief breasts, pulling black T-shirt over her head.

Cheryl Smith . . . . Roxanne

• 1:02—Very brief breasts, taking off her dress in locker room while talking to Judy.

• 1:03—Brief breasts, while putting her cheerleader top on.

• ***The Pompatus of Love*** *(1996)*

Angela Featherstone . . . . .Times Square Kisser

Jenny McCarthy. . . . . .Alien Babe

Renée Props . . . . Flynn

Mia Sara . . . . .Cynthia

Kristin Scott-Thomas . . . . Caroline

Jennifer Tilly. . . . . .Tarzaan

Dawnya Welsh. . . . . .Leonard's Stripper

• 0:17—Brief side of right breast and buns in T-back while dancing in front of Roscoe Lee Browne in club.

• 0:19—Breasts and buns in T-back, when dancing while Browne talks with Runyon.

• 0:20—Breasts and buns in T-back, when snatching bills from Browne. More breasts in background while getting dressed.

Popcorn and Ice Cream *(1978; West German)*

a.k.a. Sex and Ice Cream

Ursula Buchfellner . . . . Yvonne

••• 0:30—Nude with the hotel manager, Vivi and Bea.

• 0:40—Breasts in open dress at the disco.

Bea Fiedler. . . . . Policewoman

••• 0:47—Full frontal nudity getting dressed.

••• 1:13—Right breast, then breasts in bed with a lover.

••• 1:14—Full frontal nudity in bed some more.

Olivia Pascal Vivi

• 0:26—Full frontal nudity (she's on the right), covered with soap, taking a shower with Bea.

Porky's *(1981; Canadian)*

Kim Cattrall . . . . .Honeywell

• 0:58—Brief buns, then very brief lower frontal nudity after removing skirt to make love in the boy's locker room.

Susan Clark . . . . Cherry Forever

Kaki Hunter . . . . Wendy

• 1:02—Brief full frontal nudity, then brief breasts in the shower scene.

Pat Lee . . . . .Stripper

• 0:33—Brief breasts dancing on stage at Porky's showing her breasts to Pee Wee.

Allene Simmons. . . . . Jackie

• 1:02—Breasts in the shower scene.

Jill Whitlow . . . . .Mindy

Porky's II: The Next Day *(1983; Canadian)*

Cissie Colpitts-Cameron . . . . . . Graveyard Gloria/Sandy Le Toi

• 0:26—Buns in G-string at carnival.

•• 0:39—Breasts and buns in G-string, stripping for Pee Wee at cemetery.

•• 0:40—More breasts, pretending to die.

• 0:42—Breasts, being carried by Meat.

Kaki Hunter . . . . Wendy

Porky's Revenge *(1985; Canadian)*

Kim Evenson . . . . Inga

•• 0:02—Right breast, while opening her graduation gown during Pee Wee's dream.

•• 1:27—Breasts showing Pee Wee that she doesn't have any clothes under her graduation gown.

Kaki Hunter . . . . Wendy

Rose McVeigh . . . . Miss Webster

••• 0:39—In black bra, panties, garter belt and stockings then breasts in her apartment with Mr. Dobish while Pee Wee and his friends secretly watch.

Nancy Valen . . . . Ginger

Portfolio *(1983)*

Carol Alt . . . . Herself

• 0:28—Brief right breast, while adjusting black, see-through blouse.

Kelly Lynch . . . . Elite Model

Shari Shattuck . . . . Elite Model

• ***Portrait in Red*** *(1995)*

Lisa Comshaw . . . . .Rebecca Barlow

• 0:07—Breasts, while having sex in bed with Sam.

•• 0:15—Breasts and partial buns, while taking a shower.

••• 0:20—Nude, while having sex with a doctor on canvas on the floor, then killing him and smearing his blood around.

•• 1:00—Left breast, while having sex on the floor with Adam.

• ***The Portrait of a Lady*** *(1996; British/U.S.)*

Shelley Duvall . . . . Countess Gemini

Barbara Hershey . . . . .Madame Serena

Nicole Kidman. . . . . .Isabel Archer

• 0:59—Brief buns and breasts in B&W fantasy sequence.

Mary-Louise Parker . . . . .Henrietta Stackpole

Posed for Murder *(1988)*

Charlotte J. Helmcamp . . . . Laura Shea

• 0:00—Breasts in photos during opening credits.

••• 0:22—Posing for photos in sheer green teddy, then breasts in sailor's cap, then great breasts shots wearing just a G-string.

• 0:31—Very brief right breast in photo on desk.

••• 0:52—Breasts in bed making love with her boyfriend.

Posse *(1993)*

Pam Grier . . . . Phoebe

Salli Richardson . . . . Lana

• 1:10—Brief buns, while taking off her dress in front of Mario Van Peebles, then brief breasts (don't see her face, but it's her).

•• 1:11—Breasts, while making love with Van Peebles in bed.

Possessed by the Night *(1993)*

Sandahl Bergman . . . . .Peggy Hansen

••• 0:06—Breasts and buns, while making love with Ted Prior in bed.

• 0:08—More right breast and buns, while lying in bed after making love.

0:26—In white bra and panties in bedroom with Prior.

0:58—Briefly in bra in bathroom.

• 0:59—Breasts, while in bathtub.

1:02—In white bra and panties, after undressing while Shannon Tweed hold Prior at gunpoint.

••• 1:03—Breasts, while lying in bed after Prior rips her bra and panties off.

•• 1:14—Breasts, while changing tops in bedroom.

Amy Rochelle. . . . . Bikini Woman/Tina

••• 0:16—Breasts, while giving Scott a back rub, then leaving the room.

Sandra Taylor . . . Uncredited Body Double for Shannon Tweed

••• 1:05—Breasts and buns in panties, while caressing herself. Did this because the film makers didn't need to have Tweed come back to shoot only this one insert scene.

Shannon Tweed. . . . . .Carol McKay

•• 0:42—Breasts, while wiping off her sweat with the tank top.

••• 0:45—In bra on bed with Ted Prior, then breasts and brief lower frontal nudity, while making love with him.

Possession *(1981; French/German)*

Isabelle Adjani . . . . Anna/Helen

• 0:04—Breasts in bed.

• 0:16—Breasts lying in bed when Sam Neill pulls the covers over her.

••• 0:47—Right breast, then breasts lying in bed with Neill.

• 1:08—Right breast, while lying on the floor with Neill, then sitting up.

• ***The Possession of Joel Delaney*** *(1972)*

Shirley MacLaine . . . . .Norah Benson

Barbara Trentham . . . . Sherry Talbot

• 0:32—Brief right breast, several times, while making love under Perry King.

The Postman Always Rings Twice (1981)

Anjelica Huston . . . . Madge
- 1:30—Brief side view left breast sitting in trailer with Jack Nicholson.

Jessica Lange . . . . Cora Papadakis
- 0:18—Pubic hair peeking out of right side of her panties when Nicholson grabs her crotch.
- 1:03—Very, very brief breasts, then very, very brief right breast twice, when Nicholson rips her dress down to simulate a car accident.
- 1:26—Brief lower frontal nudity when Nicholson starts crawling up over her in bed.

• Power 98 (1996)

Leslie Bega . . . . Denise
Tara Ellison . . . . Poker Woman
Leonora Scelfo . . . . Cynthia Berkley
- 0:47—Buns in panties and breasts, while making love with Jason Gedrick.

Power of Attorney (1995; Made for Cable Movie)

Rae Dawn Chong . . . . Joan Armstrong
- ••• 0:50—Breasts, while making love in chair in office with Elias Koteas.

Nina Siemaszko . . . . Maria

• Power Play (1978; Canadian)

Alberta Watson . . . . Donna
- 0:21—Brief breasts, while lying on table getting shocked through her nipples.

Predator 2 (1990)

Maria Conchita Alonso . . . . Leona
Elpidia Carrillo . . . . Anna
Teri Weigel . . . . Columbian Girl
- 0:22—Brief breasts making love on bed. More breasts several times being held on the floor, brief full frontal nudity getting up when the Predator starts his attack.

Preppies (1984)

Nitchie Barrett . . . . Roxanne
- 0:11—Brief breasts changing into waitress costumes with her two friends.

Sharon Cain . . . . Exotic Dancer
Cindy Manion . . . . Jo
- 0:11—Brief breasts changing into waitress costumes with her two friends.
- 0:44—Breasts during party with the three preppie guys.

Katt Shea . . . . Margot
- ••• 0:20—Breasts teasing Richard through the glass door of her house.
- 1:07—Brief breasts after taking off bra in bed.

Lynda Wiesmeier . . . . Trini
- ••• 1:06—Breasts on bed with Mark.

Presumed Guilty (1990)

Holly Floria . . . . Mary Austin
- 1:02—Side view of left breast, very brief lower frontal nudity and buns, while making love with Jessie.

Presumed Innocent (1990)

Bonnie Bedelia . . . . Barbara Sabich
Greta Scacchi . . . . Carolyn Polhemus
- 0:46—Left breast, while making love on desk with Harrison Ford.
- 0:53—Buns, lying in bed on top of Ford.

Pretty Baby (1978)

Mae Mercer . . . . Mama Mosebery
Susan Sarandon . . . . Hattie
- 0:12—Feeding a baby with her left breast, while sitting by the window in the kitchen.
- 0:24—Brief side view, taking a bath.
- ••• 0:39—Breasts on the couch when Keith Carradine photographs her.

Brooke Shields . . . . Violet
- 0:57—Breasts and buns taking a bath.
- 1:26—Breasts posing on couch for Keith Carradine.
- 1:28—Buns, getting thrown out of the room, then trying to get back in.

Pretty Maids All in a Row (1971)

Joy Bang . . . . Rita
- 0:57—Brief breasts in car with Rock Hudson.
- 1:01—Right breast, in car with Hudson. Dark. More right breast, while getting dressed.

Gretchen Burrell . . . . Marjorie
- 0:05—Partial side of right breast, in office with Rock Hudson.
- 0:07—Breasts on the couch in Hudson's office.

Joanna Cameron . . . . Yvonne
Angie Dickinson . . . . Miss Smith
- 1:04—Buns, in long shot, while lying on bed with Ponce.

Aimée Eccles . . . . Hilda
- 1:06—Partial buns while sitting on desk in Rock Hudson's office. Her hair covers most of her right breast.

June Fairchild . . . . Sonya "Sonny" Swingle
- 1:10—Brief breasts and lower frontal nudity, taking Polaroid photos of herself in Rock Hudson's office.

Barbara Leigh . . . . Jean McDrew
- 0:30—Brief partial side view of right breast when she leans over chess board on bed to touch Rock Hudson.

Margaret Markov . . . . Polly
Brenda Sykes . . . . Pamela Wilcox

Pretty Smart (1986)

Patricia Arquette . . . . Zero
Tricia Leigh Fisher . . . . Daphne Ziegler
Julie Kristen Smith . . . . Samantha Falconwright
- •• 0:20—Nude in her room when Daphne sees her.
- •• 0:26—Breasts in bed talking to Jennifer.
- •• 0:40—Breasts in bed.
- •• 0:52—Breasts sitting in lounge by the pool.
- 0:57—Brief left breast, while brushing teeth.
- 1:10—Brief right breast, while making love with boyfriend in bed.
- 1:13—More brief right breast.
- ••• 1:14—Nude, sitting on pillow on top of her boyfriend in bed.

Kim Waltrip . . . . Sara Gentry (the teacher)
- •• 0:53—Breasts, while sunbathing with her students.

Pretty Woman (1990)

Judith Baldwin . . . . Susan
Lucinda Crosby . . . . Olsen Sister
Tracy Dali . . . . n.a.
Shelley Michelle . . . . Body Double for Julia Roberts
Julia Roberts . . . . Vivian Ward
- 1:30—Very, very brief tip of left breast, then right breast, then left breast seen through head board, in bed with Richard Gere. It's her—look especially at the vertical vein that pops out in the middle of her forehead whenever her blood pressure goes up.

Dey Young . . . . Snobby Saleswoman

The Prey (1980)

Gayle Gannes . . . . Gail
- 0:36—Brief breasts putting T-shirt on before the creature attacks her.

Prey of the Chameleon (1992; Made for Cable Movie)

Linda Carol . . . . Nurse
- 0:00—Breasts several times, making love with a guy in restroom. Dark.

Lisa London. . . . . Alice
Michelle McBride . . . . Leslie
Alexandra Paul . . . . Carrie
Daphne Zuniga. . . . . Elizabeth Burrows

• *The Price of Desire (1996)*

Janine Lindemulder. . . . . Lydia
- 0:35—Brief buns and left breast, while having sex with Stephanie Swift in restroom.
- 1:00—Partial breasts in open bra, while trying to seduce Kira Reed in restroom.
- •• 1:32—Breasts, while making love outdoors with Kira Reed and Sinclair.
- 1:34—Full frontal nudity, when opening her robe at night and sitting next to spa.

Kira Reed. . . . . Monica
- •• 0:08—In bra, then breasts, while making love with Mac on car parked on freeway overpass.
- ••• 0:09—Breasts, while making love with Mac in bed.
- 0:25—Brief left breast, while making out with a guy in the parking lot.
- 0:26—Brief left breast, when the guy slams her against the hood of the car.
- 0:41—Buns in panties.
- •• 0:42—Breasts, while talking to her husband.
- •• 0:53—Breasts and buns in panties, while changing clothes.
- ••• 1:10—In bra and panties, then nude, while making love with Sinclair.
- •• 1:16—Breasts and partial buns, while making love with Sinclair out of the rocks by the ocean.
- •• 1:23—Breasts, while sunbathing and reading.
- •• 1:32—In bra, then breasts while making love outdoors with Janine Lindemulder and Sinclair.
- 1:35—Brief buns, when getting out of spa.
- •• 1:37—Briefly nude, while getting dressed in bedroom.

Stephanie Swift. . . . . Girl in Bathroom
- 0:37—Brief full frontal nudity, when stall door opens in restroom with Janine Lindemulder.
- 0:41—Brief right breast, then brief left breast in B&W flashback.

Kim Yates . . . . Hazel
- 0:14—Breasts and buns in T-back, while in yoga position, then getting her outfit.
- •• 0:19—Breasts, while undressing in room when talking with Kira Reed.
- ••• 0:33—Breasts, buns and partial lower frontal nudity, while making love with her boyfriend.
- 1:24—Buns in panties while modeling.

Priceless Beauty (1989; Italian)

Diane Lane . . . . China/Anna
- •• 0:34—Breasts in bed with Christopher Lambert.
- 0:35—Brief left breast, then side of right breast on top of Lambert.

Claudia Ohana. . . . . Lisa

Primal Fear (1996)

Azalea Davila . . . . Linda
- 1:11—Brief breasts, in Archbishop Rushman's office with Edward Norton and another boy seen on sex video playback.

Frances McDormand . . . . Dr. Molly Arrington
Maura Tierney . . . . Naomi Chance

Prime Cut (1972)

Janit Baldwin . . . . Violet
- 0:25—Very brief nude, being swung around when Gene Hackman lifts her up to show to Lee Marvin.
- 0:41—Brief breasts putting on a red dress.

Sissy Spacek. . . . . Poppy
- 0:25—Brief side view of left breast lying in hay, then buns when Gene Hackman lifts her up to show to Lee Marvin.
- ••• 0:30—Breasts sitting in bed, then getting up to try on a dress while Marvin watches.
- 0:32—Close up of breasts though sheer black dress in a restaurant.

Angel Tompkins. . . . . Clarabelle
- 1:03—Very brief left breast sitting up in bed to talk to Lee Marvin.
- 1:04—Very brief back side view of left breast, while jumping out of bed.

Prime Evil (1987)

Amy Brentano . . . . Brett
- ••• 1:13—Breasts removing her gown (she's in the middle) with Cathy and Judy.

Ruth Corrine Collins. . . . . Cathy
- ••• 0:15—Breasts making love with her boyfriend in bed.
- 0:16—More breasts sitting up and getting out of bed.
- ••• 0:27—Breasts, sitting up while the priest talks to her.
- •• 1:13—Left breast, while removing her gown (she's on the left) with Brett and Judy.

Jeanne Marie . . . . Judy
- 1:13—Breasts after removing her gown (she's on the right) with Cathy and Brett.

Christine Moore. . . . . Alexandra Parkman
Miriam Zucker. . . . . Nancy Deans
- •• 0:03—Breasts several times, during sacrificial ceremony.

The Prime of Miss Jean Brodie (1969)

Pamela Franklin . . . . Sandy
- •• 1:21—Breasts posing as a model for Teddy's painting. Brief right breast, while kissing him. Long shot of buns, while getting dressed.

Maggie Smith . . . . Jean Brodie

Prime Target (1991)

Jenilee Harrison . . . . Kathy Bloodstone
- ••• 0:12—Breasts, while lying back in bed with David Heavener. Short, but sweet!
- 0:13—Partial right breast, visible under Heavener's arm.

Sandra Margot . . . . Girl in Shower
- ••• 0:52—Side view of left breast and buns, taking a shower.
- 0:53—Buns, in hotel room after getting out of the shower.

The Prince of Pennsylvania (1988)

Bonnie Bedelia. . . . . Pam Marshetta
Amy Madigan . . . . Carla Headlee
- 0:37—Left breast and buns, while getting out of bed with Keanu Reeves and putting on a robe.

Princess Warrior (1990)

Sharon Lee Jones. . . . . Ovule
- 0:33—Very, very brief buns while jumping through glass. Don't see her face.
- 0:58—Brief breasts a few times, while making love with Bob.
- 1:07—Very brief lower half of buns, while hitting Curette.
- 1:10—Brief buns, while climbing up on back of truck. 1:16—Very brief breasts, while taking off her T-shirt to get into portal. (Note that the image has been blurred so you can't see them clearly.)

Janie Liszewski. . . . . Wet T-Shirt Girl
- 0:10—Buns in swimsuits during contest.

• *Prison Heat* (1992)

Rebecca Chambers . . . . Colleen
- •• 0:15—Breasts, while drying off in the shower room and talking with Audrey.
- ••• 0:43—Breasts, while in the shower with Hellena.

Lori Jo Hendrix . . . . Bonnie
- 0:12—In bra, then brief breasts and buns, while undressing to enter prison.
- •• 0:15—Breasts, while showering next to Michelle.
- •• 0:28—Breasts, while getting raped by Hellena.
- 0:35—Breasts, while getting raped by the warden.
- •• 0:36—Breasts, while showering, getting sick and throwing up.
- ••• 0:48—Full frontal nudity, after undressing in the shower room with the warden.
- ••• 0:51—Nude in the shower room after the warden leaves, slitting her wrist with a piece of the mirror.
- 1:13—In bra in open blouse, then left breast, while getting felt up by the warden.
- 1:15—Left breast, while getting molested on couch by Akim.
- 1:17—More left breast in bra, while getting molested by Akim.

Toni Naples. . . . . Hellena
- •• 0:43—Breasts, while in the shower with Colleen.

Gilya Stern . . . . Michelle
- •• 0:11—In bra, then breasts, while undressing to enter prison.
- •• 0:15—Breasts and very brief buns, while showering next to Bonnie.
- 1:01—In bra, then breasts, while tricking guard.
- 1:03—Brief breasts, while dressing after tricking guard.

Prison Stories, Women on the Inside (1990; Made for Cable Movie)

Rae Dawn Chong . . . . Rhonda
- 0:26—Very brief right breast several times in prison shower with Annabella Sciorra.

Lolita Davidovich. . . . . Lorretta

Silvana Gallardo . . . . Mercedes

Annabella Sciorra . . . . Nicole

Talisa Soto. . . . . Rosina

Rachel Ticotin . . . . Iris
- 0:07—Brief buns, squatting while getting strip searched in jail. Don't see her face.

Private Lessons (1981)

Meridith Baer . . . . Miss Phipps

Pamela Bryant. . . . . Joyce
- 0:03—Very brief right breast, changing in the house while Billy and his friend peep from outside.

Sylvia Kristel . . . . Mallow
- 0:20—Very brief breasts sitting up next to the pool when the sprinklers go on.
- •• 0:24—Breasts and buns, stripping for Billy. Some shots might be a body double.
- •• 0:51—Breasts in bed when she "dies" with Howard Hesseman.
- 1:28—Breasts making love with Billy. Some shots might be a body double.

Private Lessons II (1993; Japanese)

Joanna Pacula . . . . Sophie Morgan
- •• 0:26—Buns, when getting out of swimming pool.
- 0:55—Buns, while lying in bed next to Ken.

Private Lessons—Another Story (1994)

Deirdre Imershein . . . . Jennifer

Mariana Morgan . . . . Lauren
- •• 0:22—Breasts, while in shower reminiscing about Marissa.
- •• 0:43—Breasts and buns, while making love with the chauffeur.
- •• 1:12—Breasts, while making love on the beach during storm with Raul.

Private Obsession (1994)

Shannon Whirry . . . . Emanuelle Griffith
- 0:09—Buns and breasts, while getting dressed in motor home.
- 0:27—Brief breasts, after Richard rips her top off after she tries to squeeze through the pet door.
- •• 0:28—Breasts, when Richard rubs butter on her breasts, to help her slip back through.
- ••• 0:30—Breasts, when in the bathroom, to clean herself off. Nude while in the shower. Sometimes seen on TV monitor.
- ••• 0:56—In black lingerie, after taking off gold dress, for Richard. Nude after taking off bra and panties, and dancing for Richard in only stockings.
- ••• 1:02—Breasts, while making love with Richard in living room.
- 1:07—Breasts, after Richard takes her dress off after her escape attempt.
- 1:08—Buns, while sleeping on the bed, then breasts, sitting up to watch monitor.
- •• 1:12—Breasts and buns, going into bathroom to get glass out of toilet tank.
- 1:14—Nude by the door, listening to Richard yelling.
- 1:25—Breasts, while making love with Richard in bed.
- 1:34—Buns in panties and white bra after undressing in her room.

• *Private Parts* (1972)

Ayn Ruymen . . . . Cheryl Stratton
- ••• 0:57—Breasts and buns, while undressing and getting into bathtub wearing a blindfold, then breasts, seen through peephole.

• *Private Parts* (1997)

Carol Alt . . . . Gloria

Camille Donatacci . . . . Bikini Girl in Westchester

Melanie Good . . . . Brittany Fairchild
- 0:28—Side view of breasts and buns, while getting ready for a bath.
- 0:30—Breasts covered with bubbles, while in bathtub with Howard Stern and Fred Norris.

Jenna Jameson . . . . Mandy
••• 1:29—Nude in the radio station, while giving Howard Stern a massage.
Janine Lindemulder . . . . Camp Director's Wife
Theresa Lynn . . . . Orgasm Woman
•• 0:54—In bra, then breasts when sitting on a speaker while Howard Stern brings her to orgasm over the radio.
Amber Smith . . . . .Julie

Private Passions (1983)

Ulrike Beimpold . . . . .Laura
•• 0:28—Left breast, then breasts in bed with Toni.
Sybil Danning . . . . Katherine

Private Popsicle (1982)

Bea Fiedler . . . . Eva
•• 0:04—In black bra with Bobby. Upper half of left breast, very brief side of right breast, then breasts.
••• 0:06—Full frontal nudity with Bobby in bed.
•• 0:07—More breasts with Bobby.
••• 0:08—Breasts on bed with Hughie.
•• 0:09—More breasts when her husband gets into bed.

Private Resort (1985)

Vickie Benson . . . . Bikini Girl
• 0:21—In blue two piece swimsuit, showing her buns, then brief breasts with Reeves.
• 1:11—Buns and very brief left breast, in locker room, trying to slap Reeves.
Leslie Easterbrook . . . . Bobbie Sue
•• 0:14—Very brief buns taking off swimsuit, then breasts and buns under sheer white nightgown.
Lisa London . . . . Alice
Susan Mechsner . . . . Aerobics Instructor
Hilary Shepard . . . . .Shirley
••• 0:36—Breasts, then buns, taking off her dress in front of Rob Morrow.

Private Road (1987)

Georgette Baker . . . . Maria
••• 0:29—Breasts taking off her dress and getting into bed, then making love with Greg Evigan.
Mitzi Kapture . . . . Helen Milshaw
•• 1:29—Nude, while making love in bed with Greg Evigan.

Private School (1983)

Phoebe Cates . . . . .Christine
• 1:21—Brief buns, while lying in sand with Mathew Modine.
• 1:24—Upper half of buns flashing with the rest of the girls during graduation ceremony.
Sylvia Kristel . . . . .Ms. Copuletta
Kari Lizer . . . . Rita
• 0:30—Very brief left breast popping out of cheerleader's outfit along with the Coach.
Julie Payne . . . . Coach Whelan
• 0:30—Very, very brief left breast popping out of cheerleader's outfit along with Rita.
Betsy Russell . . . . Jordan Leigh-Jensen
• 0:04—Very, very brief right breast and buns when Bubba takes her towel off through window.
••• 0:19—Breasts riding a horse after Kathleen Wilhoite steals her blouse.
• 1:24—Upper half of buns flashing with the rest of the girls during graduation ceremony.
Brinke Stevens . . . . Uncredited School Girl
•• 0:42—Brief breasts and buns in shower room scene. She's the brunette wearing a pony tail who passes in front of the chalkboard.
Lynda Wiesmeier . . . . School Girl
••• 0:42—Nude in shower room scene. First blonde in shower on the left.

Prizzi's Honor (1985)

Anjelica Huston . . . . .Maerose Prizzi
Kathleen Turner . . . . Irene Walker
• 0:30—Very brief left breast making love with Jack Nicholson on bed.

Professional Affair (1994)

Whitney Weston . . . . Belinda
• 0:05—Brief side of right breast, while making love on top of Michael in bed.

• *Profile for Murder (1996)*

Heather Hanson . . . . .Julie Hollis
• 1:14—Breasts and buns, while playing around in the pool with Lance Henriksen.
• 1:15—Brief buns, while floating face down, dead, in the pool.
Fawnia Mondey . . . . Diane Curtis
• 0:02—Breasts, while making love with Lance Henriksen in bed.
•• 0:29—Breasts and partial buns, while making love with Henriksen in flashback.
• 0:34—Very brief breasts, during Joan Severance's fantasy with Henriksen.
Joan Severance . . . . Hanna Carras
•• 0:33—Brief breasts, several times, while playing with herself in bathtub when fantasizing.
• 1:03—Brief partial right breast, while making love with Lance Henriksen in boat.

Programmed to Kill (1987)

a.k.a. The Retaliator
Sandahl Bergman . . . . Samira
• 0:11—Brief side view of right breast taking off T-shirt and leaning over to kiss a guy. Don't see her face.

Project: Alien (1990)

Darlanne Fluegel . . . ."Bird" McNamara
• 0:18—Buns, getting out of bed and putting on a kimono.

Prom Night (1980)

Jamie Lee Curtis . . . . .Kim
Pita Oliver . . . . Vicki
•• 0:35—Brief buns, mooning Mr. Sykes outside of tennis court.
Mary Elizabeth Rubens . . . . Kelly
• 0:59—Very brief right breast making out with Drew in the locker room.
• 1:02—Brief upper half of breasts, standing up to put dress on. Dark.

Prom Night IV: Deliver Us From Evil (1991)

Joy Tanner . . . . Laura
• 0:58—Buns, lying in bed with Jeff. Don't see her face.
• 0:59—Very brief right breast, while making love with Jeff, standing up. Don't see her face.
• 1:00—Buns and back half of right breast, getting out of bed. Don't see her face.

•• 1:01—Breasts in shower. Don't see her face. It looks like a body double because the double's breasts are bigger than Joy's.

Promised Land (1988)

Debi Richter . . . . Pammie
Meg Ryan . . . . Beverly
• 0:22—Very brief side view of left breast in bed with Kiefer Sutherland.

Promises, Promises (1963)

Jayne Mansfield . . . . Sandy Brooks
••• 0:04—Breasts drying herself off with a towel. Same shot also at 0:48.
••• 0:06—Breasts in bed. Same shot also at 0:08, 0:39 and 0:40.
••• 0:59—Buns, kneeling next to bathtub, right breast in bathtub, then breasts drying herself off.

• *Pronto (1997; Made for Cable Movie)*

Therese Kablan . . . . Gloria
• 0:18—Buns in two piece swimsuit.
• 0:22—Brief breasts, three times, while sitting up outside.
• 1:14—Brief breasts, when getting out of the spa.

Proof (1991; Australian)

Genevieve Picot . . . . Celia
•• 0:58—Breasts, in open blouse with Martin.
• 0:59—Brief breasts, while turning around when Martin leaves.

• *The Prophecy II (1997)*

Jennifer Beals . . . . Valerie Rosales
•• 0:16—Very brief upper half of buns, brief breasts, very brief left breast, while making love in bed with Russell Wong.

Prospero's Books (1991; Dutch/French/Italian)

Ute Lemper . . . . Ceres
Isabelle Pasco . . . . Miranda
• 0:13—Tip of left breast, when it peeks out between an opening in her blouse, while lying in bed as John Gielgud sits beside her on the bed.

The Prowler (1981)

Lisa Dunsheath . . . . Sherry
• 0:20—Very brief breasts in the shower (overhead view).
•• 0:21—More breasts and buns in shower, then breasts when Carl opens the door.
• 0:22—More breasts from overhead.
•• 0:23—Breasts, getting killed by the prowler with a pitchfork.
• 1:23—Breasts, dead in the bathtub when Pam discovers her.

Psychic (1992; Made for Cable Movie)

Susan Horton . . . . Woman in Club
•• 0:03—Breasts during opening credits. Very, very brief partial lower frontal nudity, while getting strangled.
• 0:11—Very brief buns and partial left breast, dead, being covered with a sheet.
• 1:17—Very, very brief right breast, being murdered in Zach Galligan's psychic vision.
Andrea Roth . . . . April Morris
• 1:01—Brief buns, partially covered with leaves, lying dead in park.
Catherine Mary Stewart . . . . Laurel
• 0:45—Very brief right breast, twice, at the end of love making scene with Zach Galligan.

Psycho Cop 2 (1992)

Brittany Ashland . . . . Go Go Dancer #1
• 0:21—Breasts on film that the guys are watching at bachelor party. (She's the blonde.)
• 1:17—Breasts and buns in white panties in film during end credits.
Sara Lee Froton . . . . Go Go Dancer #2
• 0:21—Breasts on film that the guys are watching at bachelor party. (She's the brunette.)
• 1:17—Breasts and buns in pink panties in film during end credits.
Melanie Good . . . . Cindy
••• 0:22—Buns in T-back, then breasts under chain bra after stripping out of maid outfit.
•• 0:25—Breasts and buns, while with the two other dancers and the guys.
• 0:33—Breasts, when the guys start worrying about Mike. Buns in outfit for the rest of the film.
Barbara Niven . . . . Sharon
Kimberly Speiss . . . . Chloe
• 0:37—Buns, while falling off of desk with Tony, then standing up and talking to Sharon.
Julie Strain . . . . Stephanie
• 0:19—Brief buns, when elevator door opens.
••• 0:21—Buns in cowboy outfit, then breasts with red star pasties while doing dance routine.
•• 0:25—Breasts and buns, while with the two other dancers and the guys.
• 0:31—Breasts and buns, when Mike comes back.
• 0:33—Breasts, when the guys start worrying about Mike.
• 0:38—Breasts, when putting them in Brian's face.
• 0:41—Breasts, when with Brian. Buns in cowboy outfit for the rest of the film.
Alisa Wilson . . . . Anchorwoman

Psycho From Texas (1981)

Angela Field . . . . Wheeler's Mother
•• 0:09—Breasts and buns, while making love in bed with the salesman.
Linnea Quigley . . . . Barmaid
••• 1:16—Nude, after taking off her dress and dancing in front of Wheeler. (He pours beer on her.) Long scene.

Psycho III (1986)

Juliette Cummins . . . . Red
••• 0:39—Breasts making love with Duke in his motel room, then getting thrown out.
Katt Shea . . . . Patsy
Brinke Stevens . . . . Body Double for Diana Scarwid
•• 0:30—Brief breasts and buns getting ready to take a shower, body doubling for Diana Scarwid.

Psycho IV: The Beginning (1990; Made for Cable Movie)

Sharen Camille . . . . Holly
•• 0:13—In bra, then breasts while in bedroom with Henry Thomas.
Olivia Hussey . . . . Norma Bates
•• 0:49—Breasts in motel room mirror while young Norman, watches through peephole.

Psychopathia Sexualis *(1966)*

a.k.a. On Her Bed of Roses

Pat Barringer . . . . Dancer

••• 0:34—Breasts, while belly dancing during party (she's the second dancer). Long scene.

Psychos in Love *(1987)*

LeeAnne Baker . . . . Heavy Metal Girl

••• 0:25—Breasts, undressing in room in front of Joe.

Patti Chambers . . . . Girl in Bed

•• 0:02—Breasts, sitting in bed and stretching, just before getting killed.

Ruth Corrine Collins . . . . Susan

••• 0:42—Breasts, dancing and undressing in living room in front of Joe when caught by Kate.

Angela Nicholas . . . . Diane

•• 0:04—Breasts while taking a shower, before being killed.

Cecilia Wilde . . . . Nikki

•• 0:08—Breasts, dancing on stage in a bar.

••• 0:14—Buns, in G-string while dancing on stage, then breasts.

•• 0:45—Breasts, dancing on stage with a fluorescent light.

Public Enemy #1 *(1995)*

Alyssa Milano . . . . Amaryllis

• 1:13—Very brief partial buns in short dress when Frank Stallone picks her up after killing her.

Theresa Russell . . . . Kate "Ma" Barker

•• 0:58—Left breast while making love in bed with Eric Roberts.

••• 1:00—Breasts while taking off dress in front of mirror and getting into bed with Roberts.

Pucker Up and Bark Like a Dog *(1989)*

Iris Condon . . . . Stretch Woman

Wendy O. Williams . . . . Butch

Lisa Zane . . . . Taylor Phillips

•• 0:52—Breasts in shower with Max. Left breast, while in bed.

Pump Up the Volume *(1990)*

Ellen Greene . . . . Jan Emerson

Samantha Mathis . . . . Nora Diniro

•• 1:13—Breasts taking off sweater on patio with Christian Slater.

Pumpkinhead II: Blood Wings *(1994)*

Gloria Hendry . . . . Delilah Pettibone

Caren Kaye . . . . Beth Braddock

Linnea Quigley . . . . Nadine

•• 0:41—Breasts, while making love on top of a guy in bed.

Puppet Master *(1989)*

Barbara Crampton . . . . Woman at Carnival

Irene Miracle . . . . Dana Hadley

Kathryn O'Reilly . . . . Carissa Stamford

• 0:41—Left breast in bathtub, covered with bubbles.

• 0:43—Brief left breast getting out of tub. Nipple covered with bubbles.

• 1:11—Right breast under sheer black nightgown, dead sitting at the table. Blood on her face.

Puppet Master II *(1990)*

Charlie Spradling . . . . Wanda

•• 1:04—Breasts getting out of bed and adjusting her panties.

Puppet Master III: Toulon's Revenge *(1990)*

Michelle Bauer Lili

• 0:15—Brief breasts bringing the phone to the General while he takes a bath.

•• 0:43—Breasts, twice, making love on top of the General.

Landon Hall . . . . Uncredited Prostitute

• 0:15—Breasts (she's on right), giving the General a bath.

Jasmine Totschek . . . . Prostitute

• 0:15—Breasts (she's on left), giving the General a bath.

Pure Danger *(1995)*

Elisa Leonetti . . . . Stella

• 0:30—Dancing on stage in bar, then breasts covered with pasties and buns in T-back.

Teri Ann Linn . . . . Becky

• 1:06—Brief partial buns, while in bed with C. Thomas Howell.

Purgatory *(1988)*

Adrienne Pearce . . . . Janine

•• 0:51—Brief breasts in shower scene with Kirsten.

Tanya Roberts . . . . Carly Arnold

• 0:29—Nude, getting into the shower.

• 0:42—Very brief breasts in bed with the Warden.

•• 0:57—Left breast, then brief breasts in bed talking to Tommy.

Purple Hearts *(1984)*

Annie McEnroe . . . . Hallaway

•• 1:23—Brief breasts coming out of the bathroom surprising Ken Wahl and Cheryl Ladd.

Purple Rain *(1984)*

Apollonia . . . . Apollonia

•• 0:20—Brief breasts, after taking off jacket before jumping into lake.

Pyrates *(1991)*

Kyra Sedgwick . . . . Sam

••• 0:19—In sheer lingerie on top of Kevin Bacon in bed, then breasts.

• 0:22—Brief buns, while lying on top of Bacon.

• 0:26—Breasts under water in hot tub with Bacon.

Petra Verkaik . . . . Basia

Q *(1982)*

Bobbi Burns . . . . Sunbather

•• 0:06—Breasts taking off swimsuit top and rubbing lotion on herself.

Candy Clark . . . . Joan

Mary Louise Weller . . . . Mrs. Pauley

Quackser Fortune has a Cousin in the Bronx *(1970; Irish)*

Margot Kidder . . . . Zazel

•• 1:03—Breasts undressing on a chair, then brief right, then breasts when Gene Wilder kisses her.

• 1:05—Side view of left breast, then buns, getting out of bed.

Quake *(1992)*

Erika Anderson . . . . Jenny Sutton

• 0:05—Breasts, getting out of the shower and drying herself off. More breasts, putting on bra.

• 0:40—Breasts in photos from 0:05 in darkroom.

•• 0:50—Breasts on table when Steve Railsback rips her bra off.

•• 0:51—Breasts, in drugged sleep while Railsback takes pictures of her.
• 0:52—More breasts asleep, then awake.

Quartet *(1981; British/French)*
Isabelle Adjani . . . . Marya Zelli
•• 1:06—Breasts in bed with Alan Bates.
Maggie Smith . . . . Lois
Bernice Stegers . . . . Miss Nicholson

Queen Margot *(1994; French)*
a.k.a. La Reine Margot
Isabelle Adjani . . . . Marguerite of Valois (Margot)
•• 1:41—Full frontal nudity, while making love with Le Mole.
Asia Argento . . . . Charlotte
• 1:13—Brief lower frontal nudity while in bed with Henri.
Marina Golovine . . . . Lady in Waiting

Quest For Fire *(1981)*
Joy Boushel . . . . Tribe Member
Rae Dawn Chong . . . . Ika
• 0:37—Breasts and buns, running away from the bad tribe.
• 0:40—Breasts and buns, following the three guys.
• 0:41—Brief breasts behind rocks.
• 0:43—Brief side view of left breast, healing Noah's wound.
• 0:50—Right breast, while sleeping by the fire.
• 0:53—Long shot, side view of left breast after making love.
• 0:54—Breasts shouting to the three guys.
• 1:07—Breasts standing with her tribe.
• 1:10—Breasts and buns, walking through camp at night.
• 1:18—Breasts in a field.
• 1:20—Left breast, turning over to demonstrate the missionary position. Long shot.
• 1:25—Buns and brief left breast running out of bear cave.

Quick *(1993)*
Tia Carrere . . . . Janet Sakamoto
Teri Polo . . . . Quick
• 0:14—Brief buns, while lying face down, handcuffed to bed by Jeff Fahey.
•• 0:42—Breasts, taking off her blouse in front of mirror, then putting on black bra.
•• 1:06—In black bra, then breasts (mostly right breast) while making love in car with Herschel.

The Quick and the Dead *(1994)*
Fay Masterson . . . . Mattie Silk
Sharon Stone . . . . Ellen
• 0:21—Brief right breast in gaping blouse, when bending over after sitting up in bed.

The Quiet Earth *(1985; New Zealand)*
Alison Routledge . . . . Joanne
• 0:49—Brief buns, after making breakfast for Zac.
•• 1:24—Breasts in guard tower making love with Api.

R.P.M. *(1970)*
Ann-Margret . . . . Rhoda
•• 0:07—Brief left breast and buns getting out of bed talking with Anthony Quinn.
Teda Bracci . . . . Student

R.S.V.P. *(1984)*
Jane Hamilton . . . . Mrs. Ellen Edwards
Tamara Landry . . . . Vicky
•• 0:43—Breasts sitting in van taking her top off.
•• 0:48—Breasts making love in the van with two guys.
Suzanne Remey Lawrence . . . . Stripper
•• 0:56—Breasts dancing in a radio station in front of a D.J.
Laurie Senit . . . . Sherry Worth
•• 1:00—Breasts in the shower with Harry Reems.
•• 1:06—Breasts again.
Katt Shea . . . . Rhonda Rivers
• 0:31—Side view of left breast, making love in bed with Jonathan.
Allene Simmons . . . . Patty De Fois Gras
•• 0:13—Breasts taking off red top behind the bar with the bartender.
•• 0:38—Breasts in bed with Mr. Edwards, then buns running to hide in the closet.
•• 0:41—Frontal nudity in room with Mr. Anderson.
••• 0:51—Breasts talking to Toby in the hallway trying to get help for the Governor.
Lynda Wiesmeier . . . . Jennifer Edwards
•• 0:11—Breasts diving into the pool while Toby fantasizes about her being nude.
• 0:19—Breasts in kitchen when Toby fantasizes about her again.
••• 1:21—Nude getting out of the pool and kissing Toby, when she really is nude.

Rabid *(1977; Canadian)*
Marilyn Chambers . . . . Rose
•• 0:14—Breasts in bed.
•• 1:04—Breasts in closet selecting clothes.
•• 1:16—Breasts in white panties getting out of bed.

The Rachel Papers *(1989; British)*
Amanda de Cadenet . . . . Yvonne
Siri Neal . . . . Suki
Ione Skye . . . . Rachel Noyce
•• 0:58—Breasts getting undressed and into bed with Charles. Long shot, then breasts in bed.
••• 1:03—Brief breasts in three scenes. From above in bathtub, in bed and in bathtub again.
•• 1:04—Left breast, making love sitting up with Charles.
• 1:06—Brief breasts sitting up in bathtub.
• 1:08—Brief breasts long shot getting dressed in Charles' room.
• 1:28—Brief breasts kissing Charles in bed during his flashback.

Racing with the Moon *(1984)*
Rutanya Alda . . . . Mrs. Nash
Barbara Howard . . . . Gatsby Girl
Carol Kane . . . . Annie
Elizabeth McGovern . . . . Caddie Winger
• 0:45—Upper half of breast in pond with Sean Penn.

Radio Inside *(1994)*
Elisabeth Shue . . . . Natalie
•• 0:40—Brief left breast in mirror in dressing room.

A Rage in Harlem *(1991)*
Robin Givens . . . . Imabelle
••• 0:32—Buns, while lying in bed with Forest Whitaker.

The Raggedy Rawney *(1988; British)*
Veronica Clifford . . . . The Farmer's Wife
• 0:39—Left breast in open nightgown, while sleeping in bed when a boy peeks in the window.
Zoë Nathenson . . . . Jessie
• 0:44—Buns, after taking off her dress and going skinny dipping while Dexter Fletcher watches.

•• 0:56—Breasts, after sitting up while kissing Fletcher.

Jane Wood . . . . Vie

Ragtime (1981)

Elizabeth McGovern . . . . Evelyn Nesbit

••• 0:52—Breasts in living room sitting on couch and arguing with a lawyer. Very long scene.

Mary Steenburgen. . . . . Mother

The Railway Station Man (1992; Made for Cable Movie)

Julie Christie . . . . .Helen Cuffe

• 0:35—Buns, undressing to go skinny dipping. Brief side of left breast, running into the ocean. Long shot.

• 0:37—Buns, while walking out of the surf. Long shot.

The Rain Killer (1990)

Kirsten Ashley . . . . .Dancer #2

• 0:32—Nude, dancing on stage in club. Backlit too much.

• 0:49—Buns, then brief nude on stage in club. Slightly out of focus.

Tania Coleridge. . . . . Adele

•• 0:28—Breasts on back of couch with Ray Sharkey. Left breast, after rolling onto the floor with Sharkey.

• 0:32—Brief side view of right breast, in bed with Vince.

• 0:53—Very brief tip of left breast, twice, in bubble bath.

Maria Ford . . . . Satin

•• 0:29—Nude, dancing on stage in club. Backlit too much.

••• 0:37—Breasts in bedroom with Jordan, taking off her clothes, getting tied to bed. Long scene.

• 0:41—Breasts lying on her back on bed, dead.

• 0:48—Same scene from 0:41 when Rosewall looks at B&W police photo.

Rain Man (1988)

Valeria Golino . . . . Suzanna

• 0:35—Very brief left breast four times and very, very brief right breast once with open blouse fighting with Tom Cruise after getting out of the bathtub.

Gigi Vorgan. . . . . Voice-Over Actress

The Rain People (1969)

Shirley Knight . . . . Natalie

• 0:15—Breasts walking around in motel room and getting into bed. Long shot.

• 1:36—Very brief buns, with sheet wrapped around her, trying to get out of trailer.

The Rainbow (1989)

Sammi Davis-Voss . . . . .Ursula Brangwen

••• 0:21—Breasts and buns with Amanda Donohoe undressing, running outside in the rain, jumping into the water, then talking by the fireplace.

•• 0:30—Breasts and buns posing for a painter.

• 1:33—Brief right breast and buns getting out of bed.

••• 1:44—Nude running outside with Donohoe.

Amanda Donohoe. . . . . .Winifred Inger

••• 0:21—Nude with Sammi Davis undressing, running outside in the rain, jumping into the water, then talking by the fireplace.

••• 0:43—Full frontal nudity taking off nightgown and getting into bed with Davis, then right breast.

••• 1:44—Nude running outside with Davis.

Glenda Jackson . . . . Anna Brangwen

Rambling Rose (1991)

Laura Dern. . . . . Rose

•• 0:23—Right breast several times, while lying on bench with Robert Duvall while Lucas Haas peeks in.

•• 1:16—Brief right breast, twice, when sheet drops while talking with Duvall in bedroom.

Ramona (1992)

Heidi Von Palleske . . . . Ramona Soco

• 0:04—Brief breasts, while making love with Henry.

•• 0:06—Brief breasts, several times, while rolling over in bed.

• 1:13—Breasts, after taking off blouse in hotel room with Henry.

Rancho Deluxe (1975)

Elizabeth Ashley. . . . . Cora Brown

Patti D'Arbanville. . . . . .Betty Fargo

• 0:14—Very brief back side of right breast, while making love with Jeff Bridges outside.

• 0:15—Side of right breast, while making love some more.

• 0:16—Very, very brief breasts, when jumping up after Bridges puts mask on. Breasts, while running after Bridges in field. Long shot with trees in the way, hard to see anything.

• 1:01—Very brief right breast, while adjusting sheets in bed after Bridges shoots gun.

Rapa Nui (1994)

Sandrine Holt. . . . . Ramana

•• 0:10—Brief breasts, when dancing around fire in the Short Ear village. More breasts, while walking to meet Jason Scott Lee.

••• 0:12—Breasts, while outside with Lee, lying in the grass and talking.

• 0:19—Breasts, while getting hassled by the other Short Ear women in the river.

•• 0:20—Breasts, while walking and talking with Lee.

• 0:22—Breasts, while standing on rock during examination.

• 1:26—Breasts, after seeing iceberg. (Her skin is painted white and she's pregnant.)

Rena Owen . . . . Hitirenga

• 0:19—Breasts, while in the river with the other women.

Tania Simon . . . . Koreto

• 0:19—Breasts, while in the river with the other women.

• 0:24—Left breast, while arguing about small rations.

• 0:24—Brief left breast, while arguing for more food.

Rape of Love (1979; French)

a.k.a. L'Amour Violé

Nathalie Nell . . . . .Nicole

• 0:20—Breasts, while wearing her skirt when running in the woods, trying to get away from the guys.

• 0:21—Breasts, while standing in white panties, after they take her skirt off. Full frontal nudity after they rip her panties off.

•• 0:22—Nude, being held down and brutally raped by the four guys.

• 0:28—Breasts, while being examined by a doctor.

• 0:35—Brief full frontal nudity, while sitting in the bathtub.

Rapid Fire (1992)

Kate Hodge . . . . Karla Withers

• 1:06—Brief breasts, taking off her blouse in bed on top of Brandon Lee. Don't see her face well.

Barbara Ann Klein . . . . .Stunts

Brigitta Stenberg . . . . Rosalyn
- 0:10—Brief side view of right breast, posing in art class. Don't see her face. Long shot breasts, getting up and putting on robe.

Jill Terashita . . . . Stunts

The Rapture *(1991)*

Carole Davis . . . . Angie
- 0:20—Buns, on top of Vic in bed. Most of side of her right breast.
- 0:21—Very brief right breast, then very brief breasts while turning around to talk.

Stephanie Menuez . . . . Diane
- ••• 0:06—Breasts in furniture store with Mimi Rogers, Vic and David Duchovny.

Mimi Rogers . . . . Sharon
- 0:08—Most of her left breast, while lying in bed with David Duchovny.
- •• 0:36—Very brief side view of right breast, dropping nightgown and walking into closet.

• ***Raven*** *(1996)*

Krista Allen . . . . Cali Goodwin
- •• 0:39—Partial right breast, then breasts, while making love with Martin.
- 1:23—Breasts, while making love in bed with Martin.
- 1:25—Brief breasts, when sitting up in bed.

Avalon Anders . . . . .Uncredited Marcia

Kimberly Chase . . . . Sharon

Lauren Hays . . . . Brunette
- •• 0:27—In bra, then breasts, when making out with the Senator in back of limousine.

Raven Hawk *(1995)*

Lisa Comshaw . . . . Uncredited Woman with Senator
- 0:00—Brief breasts (three times), wearing panties and stockings in background while John De Lancie talks on the phone.

Rachel McLish . . . . .Rhyia Shadowfeather
- 0:53—Long shot of buns in loincloth, then brief back side of right breast, while performing ceremony in cave.

• ***The Raven Red Kiss-Off*** *(1990)*

Miriam Byrd-Nethery . . . . Motel Manager

Jennifer Campbell . . . . Ballantyne's Mistress
- 1:10—Brief breasts, while in bed with Bernie, then in background out of focus.

Tracy Scoggins . . . . .Vala Vuvalle

Raw Force *(1981)*

Britt Helfer . . . . Betty
- 0:39—Brief buns and lower frontal nudity when bad guy peeks in through window. Don't see her face.

Jennifer Holmes . . . . Ann Davis

Camille Keaton . . . . Girl in Toilet
- •• 0:28—Breasts, while in bathroom with a guy.
- •• 0:29—Breasts in bathroom again with the guy.
- 0:31—Breasts in bathroom again when he rips her pants off.

Jillian Kesner . . . . Cookie Winchell

Jewel Shepard . . . . Drunk Sexpot
- 0:31—Breasts in black swimsuit, when a guy adjusts her straps and it falls open.

Raw Justice *(1994)*

a.k.a. Good Cop, Bad Cop

April Bogenshutz . . . . Donna
- 0:08—In bra and panties, taking off her clothes. Buns and right breast while getting into the shower.
- ••• 0:09—Full frontal nudity while taking a shower and getting out, then struggling with the killer.

Pamela Lee . . . . Sarah
- ••• 0:40—Breasts, when making out with David Keith in building while standing up.
- •• 0:58—Breasts, while making love with Robert Hayes in hotel room.

The Razor's Edge *(1984)*

Catherine Hicks . . . . Isabel
- 0:43—Brief upper half of left breast, in bed after seeing a cockroach.

Theresa Russell . . . . Sophie

• ***Razorback*** *(1984; Australian)*

Arkie Whitely . . . . .Sarah Cameron
- 0:50—Brief right breast, while showering outdoors when seen by Gregory Harrison.

Re-Animator *(1985)*

(Unrated version reviewed.)

Barbara Crampton . . . . Megan Halsey
- •• 0:10—Brief buns putting panties on, then breasts, putting bra on after making love with Dan.
- •• 1:09—Full frontal nudity, lying unconscious on table getting strapped down.
- 1:10—Breasts getting her breasts fondled by a headless body.
- 1:19—Breasts on the table.

Ready to Wear *(1994)*

a.k.a. Prêt-à-porter

Anouk Aimee . . . . Simone Lowenthal

Kim Basinger . . . . Kitty Porter

Susie Bick . . . . .Model

Anne Canovas . . . . Violetta Romney

Rossy de Palma . . . . Pilar
- 2:05—Brief partial lower frontal nudity while standing with the other models after the "Lo" curtain goes up. (She's standing to the right of the model wearing a wedding veil.)

Kasia Figura . . . . Vivienne
- 1:13—Brief buns, while trying on red dress in background.

Teri Garr . . . . Louise Hamilton

Sally Kellerman . . . . Sissy Wanamaker
- 1:16—Brief breasts, while flashing them for Stephen Rea in hotel room.

Ute Lemper . . . . .Albertine
- 2:02—Lower frontal nudity and buns, wearing a veil and carrying flowers, while on runway with the other models. (She's really pregnant.)
- 2:05—Lower frontal nudity while standing with the other models after the "Lo" curtain goes up.

Sophia Loren . . . . .Isabella de la Fontaine

Tatjana Patitz . . . . Herself

Julia Roberts . . . . Anne Eisenhower

Lili Taylor . . . . .Fiona Ulrich

Tracey Ullman . . . . Nina Scant
- 1:32—Brief buns in G-string panties, while leaving bedroom when Stephen Rea tries to take a photograph of her.

Alexandra Vandernoot . . . . Sky TV Reporter

• *Real Fantasies* (1992)

Tuscany. . . . . The Woman
- •• 0:02—Breasts, while putting on lingerie.
- ••• 0:07—Breasts and buns in black stockings, garter belt and panties, while on piano with Jonathan during fantasy. Long scene.
- ••• 0:11—Breasts and buns in white bodysuit while on chair in another fantasy with Jonathan. Long scene.
- ••• 0:15—Breasts and buns, while making love with Jonathan outside in the spa. Long scene.

Real Men (1987)

Suzanne Slater. . . . . Woman in Bed
- • 0:07—Brief left breast, in bed with James Belushi.

Dyanne Thorne . . . . Dad

A Reason to Believe (1995)

Holly Marie Combs . . . . Sharon
- ••• 1:06—Breasts, after taking off her blouse when making love with Wesley while Jay Underwood watches.

• *Rebecca's Secret* (1997)

Avalon Anders . . . . Ally
- ••• 0:14—Buns in G-string and breasts, while dancing and making love with Jonathan.
- • 0:19—Buns in lingerie, while modeling outdoors.
- ••• 1:04—Breasts, while making love with Jonathan in bed.

Lauren Hays . . . . Gwen
- ••• 0:22—Breasts, while making love with Jonathan in kitchen.
- ••• 0:33—Breasts and buns in lingerie, while making love with a guy.
- ••• 0:55—Buns and breasts, while making love with Jonathan on couch.
- •• 1:09—Breasts and buns, while making love with Max on table.

Amy Rochelle . . . . Rebecca
- •• 0:00—Nude, while swimming in a pool.
- ••• 0:02—Nude, getting up out of bed and taking a bath.
- ••• 0:05—Nude, while making love with Jonathan in the bathroom.
- •• 0:37—Nude, while taking a shower.
- •• 0:39—Breasts and buns, while getting information out of Max.
- ••• 0:46—Nude, while making love with Max in bed.
- ••• 0:58—Nude, while making love with Max in the basement.
- • 1:12—Nude, while getting out of bathtub.
- • 1:16—Breasts during struggle in swimming pool.

Rebel (1985; Australian)

Cassandra Delaney . . . . All-Girl Band Member

Rainee Skinner. . . . . Prostitute in bed
- • 0:37—Brief breasts sitting up in bed.

Rebel Highway: Cool and the Crazy (1994; Made for Cable Movie)

Christine Harnos . . . . Lorraine
- •• 0:43—Breasts, several times, while making love in bed with Michael.

Tuesday Knight . . . . Brenda

Rebel Highway: Girls in Prison (1994; Made for Cable Movie)

Tamara Clatterbuck. . . . . Actress on Newsreel

Anne Heche. . . . . Jennifer
- •• 1:02—Breasts, while walking in showers past the other girls, taking a shower and dropping a bar of soap.

Nicolette Scorsese . . . . Suzy

Ione Skye. . . . . Carol
- • 0:23—Right breast, while in the showers with Melba.
- • 1:02—Very, very brief breasts, while washing Melba's back in the showers.

Bahni Turpin . . . . Melba
- • 0:23—Back side of left breast, while in the showers with Ione Skye.

Rebel Highway: Reform School Girl (1994; Made for Cable Movie)

Aimee Graham . . . . Donna Patterson
- 0:48—In white bra in shack with Carmen.
- • 0:49—Breasts, while making out in shack with Carmen.
- • 0:51—Brief breasts while in shower.

Nicole Grey . . . . Uncredited Girl in Back of Car
- • 0:29—Brief right breast while making out with a guy in back of a convertible car in parking lot.

Elisa Pensler Gabrielli . . . . Velmont Girl

Rebel Love (1985)

Jamie Rose. . . . . Columbine Cromwell
- • 0:43—Very, very brief tip of right breast, while making love in bed under Terence Knox.

Reborn (1978)

Antonella Murgia. . . . . Maria
- • 0:35—Breasts in bed with Michael Moriarty.
- •• 0:37—More breasts in bed with Moriarty.
- ••• 0:38—Nude, getting out of bed.
- ••• 0:39—Nude, walking around in bedroom.

Reckless (1984)

Jennifer Grey . . . . Cathy Bennario

Daryl Hannah . . . . Tracey Prescott
- ••• 0:52—Breasts in furnace room of school making love with Johnny. Lit with red light.

Toni Kalem . . . . Donna

Pamela Springsteen . . . . Karen Sybern

Recruits (1986; Canadian)

Lolita Davidovich. . . . . Susan
- • 0:19—Very brief breasts when Steve bumps into her in the shower room.
- •• 0:54—Right breast, then breasts while making out with Steve in car.
- •• 0:56—Breasts, twice, while driving around in car with Steve, the Governor and his wife.
- •• 0:58—Breasts, while getting out of the car.

Dominique St. Croix . . . . n.a.

Red Blooded American Girl (1988)

Lydie Denier . . . . Rebecca Murrin
- ••• 0:00—Breasts in bed wearing panties, garter belt and stockings. Buns, rolling over. Long scene.

Cindy Fidler. . . . . Nurse

Heather Thomas . . . . Paula Bukowsky

Red Heat (1987; U.S./German)

Linda Blair . . . . Chris Carlson
- ••• 0:56—Breasts in shower room scene.
- ••• 1:01—Brief breasts getting raped by Sylvia Kristel while the male guard watches.

Sue Kiel . . . . Hedda
- • 0:56—Brief breasts in shower room scene (third girl behind Linda Blair). Long shot, hard to see.

Sylvia Kristel . . . . Sofia
•• 0:56—Breasts in shower room scene.
• 1:01—Brief breasts raping Linda Blair.

Red Heat *(1988)*

Gloria Delaney . . . . Intern
Gina Gershon . . . . Cat Manzetti
Gretchen Palmer . . . . Hooker
• 1:20—Breasts and buns in hotel during shoot out.
Gigi Vorgan . . . . Audrey

• ***Red Hot Rock*** *(1984; Video Tape)*

a.k.a. Sexy Shorts (on laser disc)
Monique Gabrielle . . . . Lab Girl
••• 0:06—Breasts and brief buns dancing after throwing off lab coat during "Lovelite" by O'Bryan.
Traci Lords . . . . Miss Georgia
•• 0:41—Breasts several times in open-front swimsuit during beauty pageant during "Gimme Gimme Good Lovin'" by Helix.
•• 0:42—Breasts on stage wearing black outfit with mask, smashing a large avocado during the same song.
Stacey Q . . . . Singer
•• 0:18—Full frontal nudity while in bed with a guy, then a woman during "Screaming in My Pillow" song.
Brinke Stevens . . . . Miss Utah
• 0:41—Brief breasts several times in open-front swimsuit during beauty pageant during "Gimme Gimme Good Lovin'" by Helix.
Lynda Wiesmeier . . . . Girl in Shower
• 0:01—Brief upper half of buns, then breasts taking off bra while a guy peeks into the locker room during "Girls" by Dwight Tilley.
• 0:02—Brief full frontal nudity in the shower. (On the left.)

Red Kiss *(1985; French)*

Marthe Keller . . . . Bronka
Isabelle Nanty . . . . Jeanine
Charlotte Valandrey . . . . Nadia
• 0:52—Very brief right breast, in bed with the photographer. Very dark.
•• 1:21—Very brief right breast, then breasts with the photographer.

• ***Red Line*** *(1995)*

Julie Strain . . . . Crystal
• 0:19—Nude, taking off robe and walking into swimming pool.
• 0:23—Breasts, while making love with Corey Feldman in darkened garage.
Roxana Zal . . . . Gem
••• 0:50—Breasts, while wearing black panties, talking with Chad McQueen in motel room.

Red Scorpion 2 *(1994)*

Suki Kaiser . . . . Donna
Jennifer Rubin . . . . Sam Guiness
• 0:53—In white slip in bedroom, then breasts while in shower. Seen on B&W monitor.

Red Shoe Diaries *(1992; Made for Cable Movie)*

(Unrated video tape version reviewed.)
Brigitte Bako . . . . Alex
• 0:26—Buns and breasts, getting out of bathtub with Jake.
• 0:35—Very brief buns when Tom rips off her panties.
•• 0:36—Several brief breasts shots while making love with Tom in bed.
• 0:40—Brief breasts, leaning back on bed with Tom.
Leana Hall . . . . Ingrid
Anna Karin . . . . Heidi #1
••• 1:29—Breasts, three times, making love with Tom.
Tera Tabrizi . . . . Alex's Friend
Brenda Vaccaro . . . . Martha

Red Sonja *(1985)*

Sandahl Bergman . . . . Queen Gedren
Brigitte Nielsen . . . . Red Sonja
• 0:01—Half of right nipple through torn outfit, while sitting up.

Red-Headed Stranger *(1986)*

Morgan Fairchild . . . . Kaysha
• 0:03—Bathing in stream in wet white dress. Long shot, then closer shot.
Katharine Ross . . . . Laurie

Red-Headed Woman *(1932)*

Jean Harlow . . . . Lil Andrews
• 0:17—Very, very brief right breast when Una Merkel passes over a pajama top and Harlow raises it over her head to put it on.

Reds *(1981)*

Diane Keaton . . . . Louise Bryant
• 0:50—Buns, while standing in the water with Jack Nicholson at night. Very long shot.

Reflections in the Dark *(1995)*

Mimi Rogers . . . . Regina
• 0:26—Buns and breasts, while making love with her husband. Some shots are a body double. Note the body double's moles on her back when you don't see her face.
• 1:00—Buns and breasts, while making love with her husband in bed. Some shots are done by a body double. Note the body double's breasts are smaller than Rogers'.

Reform School Girls *(1986)*

Michelle Bauer . . . . Uncredited Shower Girl
•• 0:25—Breasts, then nude in the shower.
Leslee Bremmer . . . . Uncredited Shower Girl
•• 0:25—Brief breasts in the shower three times. Walking from left to right in the background, full frontal nudity by herself with wet hair, breasts walking from left to right.
Linda Carol . . . . Jennifer Williams
•• 0:05—Nude in the shower.
• 0:56—Breasts in the back of a truck with Norton.
•• 1:13—Breasts getting hosed down by Edna.
Sybil Danning . . . . Warden Sutter
Darcy De Moss . . . . Knox
Sheila Lussier . . . . n.a.
Lorrie Marlow . . . . Shelly
Julia Parton . . . . Uncredited Shower Girl
Sherri Stoner . . . . Lisa
• 1:03—Very brief breasts and buns, lying on stomach in the restroom, getting branded by bad girls.
Wendy O. Williams . . . . Charlie
•• 0:26—Breasts talking to two girls in the shower.

Regenerated Man *(1994)*

Debbie Rochon . . . . Kelley
• 0:37—Breasts in ripped open blouse while being hassled by three biker guys.

Reilly: Ace of Spies (1984)

Jeananne Crowley . . . . .Margaret

•• 0:52—Brief breasts, opening her blouse for her invalid husband.

The Reincarnation of Peter Proud (1975)

Margot Kidder. . . . . Marcia Curtis

• 1:29—Brief breasts sitting in bathtub masturbating while remembering getting raped by husband.

Cornelia Sharpe. . . . . Nora Hayes

•• 0:03—Breasts in bed with Michael Sarrazin, then buns when getting out of bed.

The Rejuvenator (1988)

Vivian Lanko . . . . Elizabeth Warren

• 0:31—Brief breasts in bed with Dr. Ashton while making love. Don't see her face well.

Relentless 3 (1992)

Savannah Smith Bouchér. . . . . Marianne

• 0:10—Very brief breast when Walter starts to kiss it.

0:36—In black bra, then in white bra, while sitting in chair, getting photographed by Walter.

Relentless 4: Ashes to Ashes (1994)

Colleen Coffey. . . . . Jessice Parreti

Rainer Grant . . . . Hairdresser/Victim #1

•• 0:02—Breasts, while making love in bed on top of a guy before getting killed.

• 0:17—Breasts, while lying dead on coroner's table during exam.

Lisa Robin Kelly . . . . Sherry, Cory's Girlfriend

Remember My Name (1978)

Geraldine Chaplin . . . . .Emily

• 1:23—Very brief left breast, lying in bed, then right breast, with Anthony Perkins.

Rendez-Vous (1986; French)

Juliette Binoche . . . . Anne "Nina" Larrieu

• 0:07—Brief breasts in dressing room when Paulot surprises her and Fred.

••• 0:25—Side of left breast, then breasts and buns in empty apartment with Paulot.

•• 0:32—Full frontal nudity in bed with Quentin.

•• 0:35—Buns, then brief breasts in bed with Paulot and Quentin. Full frontal nudity getting out.

•• 1:08—Breasts taking off her top in front of Paulot in the dark, then breasts lying on the floor.

• 1:11—Right breast, making love on the stairs. Dark.

Olimpia Carlisi. . . . . .n.a.

Caroline Faro. . . . . Juliette

• 0:22—Buns, walking up stairs, then full frontal nudity on second floor during play. Buns, while hugging Romeo and falling back into a net.

Renegade: Fighting Cage (1993)

(Nudity added for video release.)

Cie Allman. . . . . Cheetah

•• 0:46—Breasts in bed, while making love with a guy.

Cheryl Bachman . . . . Ring Card Girl

Marjean Holden . . . . Tigress/Sharon Miller

Kathleen Kinmont . . . . Cheyenne

Tamara Landry . . . . Ellen

•• 1:06—Breasts and buns in panties, making love with a guy and another woman.

Ashlie Rhey . . . . Redhead

••• 1:14—Breasts and buns, while in a room with a guy, then making love with him on a small table.

Gwen Somers . . . . Lena

• 1:07—Breasts, while making love with a guy and a blonde woman in bed.

Rented Lips (1988)

Eileen Brennan. . . . . Hotel Desk Clerk

Catlyn Day. . . . . Dancer

Page Leong . . . . Dancer

Monique Mannen . . . . Dancer

Jennifer Tilly. . . . . Mona Lisa

Edy Williams . . . . Heather Darling

• 0:15—Breasts in bed, under Robert Downey, Jr. during playback of porno movie.

Replikator (1994)

Brigitte Bako . . . . .Kathy Mosko

Ilona Staller . . . . Tina

• 0:28—Breasts, in virtual reality visor display.

•• 1:05—Breasts and bun in G-string, while dancing on stage.

••• 1:07—Nude in room and walking to bathtub with Ludo.

•• 1:08—Breasts, while sitting in bathtub.

Repo Jake (1990)

Dana Bentley Konkel . . . . Jenny

Leslie Horan. . . . . Lea

Bonnie Paine . . . . R.V. Girl

•• 0:28—Breasts (mostly left breast) while in R.V. with her boyfriend.

•• 0:29—More breasts, while making love with him.

Jacqueline Palmer . . . . Porn Gal

••• 0:47—Breasts and buns, while on bed, acting in a movie.

Report to the Commissioner (1975)

Susan Blakely. . . . . .Patty Butler

• 1:07—Brief buns, running around in apartment with Slick.

• 1:08—Brief breasts, taking off robe and getting into shower while Michael Moriarty tries to hide.

Noelle North . . . . Samantha

Repossessed (1990)

Belle Avery. . . . . Gym Receptionist

Linda Blair . . . . Nancy Aglet

Charlotte J. Helmcamp . . . . .Incredible Girl

Melissa Anne Moore . . . . Bimbo Student

•• 0:05—Breasts pulling her top down in classroom in front of Leslie Nielsen.

Rescue Force (1989)

Annie Gaybis . . . . Commando

Cynthia Ann Thompson. . . . . Angel

•• 1:17—Breasts, after taking off robe and getting into bubble bath with two other girls.

Rest in Pieces (1987)

Lorin Jean Vail . . . . .Helen Hewitt

•• 0:15—Breasts in the bubble bath.

• 0:17—Breasts hanging onto outside of tub after struggle.

• 0:25—Brief breasts making love in bed with Bob during concert. Dark.

• 0:26—Brief breasts lying under Bob in bed. Dark.

• 0:30—Brief left breast, getting out of bed and putting on robe.

• 0:58—Brief right breast, reaching around to put her right arm into sleeve of robe. Dark.

- •• 1:00—Breasts, getting robe taking off and pushed into swimming pool. More breasts under the water.
- • 1:01—More breasts in the swimming pool.
- • 1:05—Brief side view of left breast getting out of bed and putting on robe.

***Return** (1985)*

Karlene Crockett . . . . Diana
- • 0:46—Breasts sitting up and getting out of bed. Long shot.

Lisa Richards . . . . Ann Stoving

Lenore Zann . . . . Susan

***The Return of Martin Guerre** (1983; French)*

Nathalie Baye . . . . Bertrande de Rols
- • 0:59—Brief side view of left breast, making love in bed on top of Martin. Don't see her face.

***The Return of the Jedi** (1983)*

Caroline Blakiston . . . . Mon Mothma

Femi Taylor . . . . Oola
- • 0:13—Very, very brief blurry right breast, twice, popping out of skimpy outfit, just before falling into pit after dancing for Jabba the Hutt. She's covered with green body paint.

***The Return of the Living Dead** (1985)*

Linnea Quigley . . . . .Trash
- ••• 0:19—Breasts and buns, strip tease and dancing in cemetery. (Lower frontal nudity is covered with some kind of make-up appliance).
- •• 0:25—Breasts and buns, while in cemetery with her boyfriend.
- • 0:37—Breasts and buns, while running around in cemetery when it starts to rain.
- • 0:38—Breasts, while running to the car in the rain (very long shot). Brief breasts while in back seat of car.
- • 0:42—Breasts, while in back seat of car.
- • 0:44—Breasts, while in back seat of car, trying to hold the convertible top closed.
- • 0:46—Brief buns, while running up stairs.
- • 0:49—Buns, while running into the cemetery.
- 1:04—Brief right breast, while in cemetery after seeing a zombie.
- • 1:05—Brief breasts, while walking from the cemetery on the street to catch a streetperson.
- • 1:21—Brief breasts, while running to munch on a policeman in blockade.
- • 1:25—Brief breasts in still photo.
- • 1:27—Breasts, during end credits in cemetery with her boyfriend.

Jewel Shepard . . . . Casey

***Return of the Living Dead 3** (1993)*

Melinda Clarke . . . . .Julie Walker
- •• 0:16—Breasts, while in bed talking with her boyfriend, Curt.
- • 0:17—More breasts, while getting out of bed when Curt's dad comes home.
- • 1:07—Breasts under skimpy outfit after doing some severe body piercing.
- •• 1:25—Brief breasts when getting rescued by Curt.

Pia Reyes . . . . .Alicia

***Return to Frogtown** (1992)*

a.k.a. Frogtown II

Denice Duff. . . . . .Dr. Spangle

Rhonda Shear . . . . .Fuzzy

Linda Singer . . . . Nurse Cloris
- • 0:48—Buns, in sexy outfit in room with Robert D'Zar.
- • 0:50—Brief top of breasts, sticking out of her top while she's on top of D'Zar.

***Return to Horror High** (1987)*

Darcy De Moss . . . . Sheri Haines
- • 0:21—Very brief left breast when her sweater gets lifted up while she's on some guy's back.

Maureen McCormick. . . . . Officer Tyler

Remy O'Neill . . . . Esther Molvania

Kristi Somers . . . . Ginny McCall

***A Return to Salem's Lot** (1988)*

Katja Crosby . . . . Cathy
- •• 0:36—Breasts making love in bed with Joey.
- • 0:48—Side view of right breast kissing Joey outside next to a stream.

***Return to the Blue Lagoon** (1991)*

Milla Jovovich Lilli
- • 0:49—Brief upper half breasts in front of mirror.
- • 1:07—Very brief breasts under water with Richard. Brief breasts under waterfall with Richard.
- • 1:20—Briefly in wet beige blouse, standing up in pond.
- • 1:26—Side view of right breast three times, washing make-up off her face in the pond.
- •• 1:28—Side view of right breast again. Very brief left breast, while picking up her top off rock.
- • 1:30—Side of left breast, while lying on bed and held down.

Lisa Pelikan . . . . Sarah

***Return to Two Moon Junction** (1993)*

Melinda Clarke .Savannah Delongpre
- •• 0:37—Lying in bed in wet white lingerie, then left breast (close-up shot) while fantasizing about Jake.
- • 0:44—Upper half of buns, while in bed with Jake.
- •• 0:45—Buns and back half of right breast, while standing up and putting on dress.
- ••• 0:59—Breasts and very brief lower frontal nudity while making love with Jake.
- •• 1:01—Buns, while getting out of bed and putting a shirt on.
- • 1:09—Breasts, with Jake in bed.

Seana Ryan . . . . .Gena

***Reuben, Reuben** (1983)*

E. Katherine Kerr . . . . Lucille Haxby
- • 0:51—Brief left breast in bedroom, undressing in front of Tom Conti.

Kelly McGillis. . . . . Geneva Spofford

***Reunion** (1989; French/German)*

Maureen Kerwin . . . . Lisa, Henry's Daughter

Amelie Pick . . . . Young Lover
- • 0:47—Brief breasts, twice, while making out in the woods with her boyfriend while two boys watch.

***Revenge** (1990)*

Sally Kirkland. . . . . .Rock Star

Madeleine Stowe. . . . . Miryea
- • 0:44—Side view of buns when Kevin Costner pulls up her dress to make love with her.
- • 1:00—Buns, making love with Costner in jeep. Very brief breasts coming out of the water.
- • 1:07—Very brief breasts when Costner is getting beat up.

Revenge of the Cheerleaders (1976)

Helen Lang . . . . Leslie
- • 0:00—Left breast, changing in back seat of car.
- •• 0:07—Breasts in girl's restroom powdering herself.
- ••• 0:53—Nude with Gail and hiker guy frolicking in the woods.
- •• 0:55—Nude some more making out with the hiker guy with Gail.
- ••• 0:57—Nude walking down road with Gail when stopped by a policeman.
- ••• 1:24—Breasts during Hawaiian party. Nice dancing during the end credits.

Patrice Rohmer . . . . Sesame
- • 0:28—Brief breasts and buns in the boys' shower room.

Cheryl Smith . . . . Heather
- • 0:00—Brief breasts changing tops in back of car. (Blonde on the far right.)
- • 0:28—Buns, in shower room scene.
- • 0:36—Full frontal nudity, but covered with bubbles.

Jerii Woods . . . . Gail
- • 0:00—Breasts, while changing clothes in front left seat of car.
- • 0:05—Lower frontal nudity taking off cheerleader skirt in girls' restroom and putting on panties.
- • 0:26—Brief right breast, while sitting in bleachers with the other cheerleaders.
- ••• 0:28—Nude in boys' shower room scene.
- •• 0:37—Breasts, while sitting up in sleeping bag.
- • 0:44—Brief breasts in front seat of car with David Hasselhoff.
- ••• 0:53—Nude with Leslie and hiker guy while frolicking in the woods.
- •• 0:55—Nude some more making out with the hiker guy with Leslie.
- ••• 0:57—Nude, walking down road with Leslie when stopped by a policeman.
- ••• 1:23—Breasts during Hawaiian party.

Revenge of the Nerds (1984)

Julia Montgomery . . . . Betty
- •• 0:49—Breasts, after taking off robe to take a shower.
- • 1:10—Breasts in photo in pie pan.

Revenge of the Ninja (1983)

Ashley Ferrare . . . . Cathy
- • 0:48—Brief breasts getting attacked by the Sumo Servant in the bedroom.

Rich Girl (1991)

Daphne Cheung . . . . Oriental Temptress
- • 1:14—Breasts, taking off her jacket in back room trying to get Rick to do drugs.

Cherie Currie . . . . Michelle

Maureen Flaherty . . . . Girl in Restroom #1

Jill Schoelen . . . . Courtney

Melanie Tomlin . . . . Diana
- • 0:03—Half of left breast, while in bed with Jeffrey.
- • 0:04—Almost side of left breast again, while looking for her keys.

Richard's Things (1980; British)

Amanda Redman . . . . Josie
- •• 0:51—Breasts, while lying in bed talking to Liv Ullman.

Liv Ullmann . . . . Kate
- • 0:12—Very, very brief left breast, while wrapping a towel around herself.

Ricochet (1991)

Viveka Davis . . . . Babysitter

Victoria Dillard . . . . Alice

Linda Doná . . . . Wanda
- •• 1:03—Breasts, undoing her dress, then buns, getting on bed to make love with Denzel Washington while he's drugged.
- • 1:16—Buns, on top of Washington during video playback.

Susan Lentini . . . . Reporter

Heidi Thomas . . . . Reporter

• Ridicule (1996; French)

Fanny Ardant . . . . Countess of Blayac
- • 0:06—Brief buns and side of left breast while getting powdered. Long shot.

Rikky & Pete (1988; Australian)

Tetchie Agbayani . . . . Flossie
- • 0:58—Brief upper half of left breast in bed with Pete when Rikky accidentally sees them in bed.
- ••• 1:30—Breasts in black panties dancing outside the jail while Pete watches from inside.

Ring of Fire (1991)

Maria Ford . . . . Julie
- •• 1:12—In black lingerie, then breasts, making love with Don Wilson.
- • 1:14—Brief left breast, lying in bed, while he undresses her.
- ••• 1:15—Breasts, several, lying on her back in bed while making love.
- • 1:17—Brief breasts, sitting up in bed afterward.

Lisa Saxton . . . . Linda
- •• 0:10—Breasts and buns in several times, making love with Brad. Intercut with martial arts fight.
- •• 0:18—Brief buns, in G-string swimsuit, getting into spa with Brad. Breasts in spa.
- ••• 0:22—Breasts and buns in bathroom, while talking to Maria Ford.

Ring of Steel (1994)

Carol Alt . . . . Tanya

Darlene Vogel . . . . Elena Carter
- •• 0:15—Left breast, then breasts, while making love with Alex.

• Ringer (1996)

Maud Adams . . . . Leslie Polokoff

Lisa Marie Scott . . . . Shimeka
- •• 0:30—Buns and breasts in panties, garter belt and stockings while dressing being assisted by Shannon Whirry.
- •• 0:38—Nude, undressing and joining Shannon Whirry and Malcolm McDowell in hot tub.

Shannon Whirry . . . . Kristin/Tracy
- • 0:02—Brief buns in panties. Don't see her face.
- • 0:05—Breasts, while making love with her husband on the floor.
- •• 0:37—Nude, getting in and out of hot tub with Malcolm McDowell.
- •• 1:28—Breasts and brief partial buns, while making love with Timothy Bottoms in bed.

Rising Sun (1993)

Tia Carrere . . . . Jingo Asakuma

Tylyn John . . . . Redhead
- ••• 0:56—Breasts, while sitting next to Eddie and when he licks sake off her left breast.

•• 0:58—Breasts and buns, while jumping onto and riding on Wesley Snipes' back.

Shelley Michelle . . . . Blonde

• 0:44—Very, very brief buns in black G-string, when her dress flies up while spinning around during party.

•• 0:56—Breasts, while lying down on her back with sushi on her front. More breasts when police bust in.

Tatjana Patitz . . . . Cheryl Lynn Austin

• 0:06—Upper half of buns and side of right breast, while sitting in front of vanity in her apartment.

•• 0:10—Very brief lower frontal nudity and breasts, getting her dress ripped open while on board room table.

• 0:52—Very brief right breast, on video monitor during playback of murder surveillance video.

• 1:44—Brief half of right breast in open dress during Wesley Snipes' daydream after being shot. Out of focus.

Tamara Tunie . . . . Lauren

Risk (1993)

Karen Sillas . . . . Maya

•• 0:04—Breasts and buns, while sitting as an artist's model then getting up. Medium long shot.

• 0:05—Left breast, while changing tops in her apartment.

• 0:11—Very brief partial right breast, while getting into bathtub with Joe.

••• 0:19—Breasts, after taking off robe in art classroom and posing in a chair.

• 0:21—Brief breasts, getting up from chair, when Joe gets caught starting to take off his clothes.

Risky Business (1983)

Cynthia Baker . . . . Test Teacher

Rebecca De Mornay . . . . Lana

• 0:28—Briefly nude, while standing by the window with Tom Cruise.

Lora Staley . . . . Call Girl

River of Death (1990)

Sarah Maur-Thorp. . . . . Anna Blakesley

• 0:14—Very brief left breast while in tent with Michael Dudikoff.

A River Runs Through It (1992)

Emily Lloyd . . . . Jessie Burns

Susan Traylor . . . . Rawhide

• 1:17—Buns, sleeping in the woods with Neal. Don't see her face.

River's Edge (1987)

Danyi Deats . . . . Jamie

• 0:03—Breasts, dead lying next to river with her killer. (All the shots of her breasts in this film aren't exciting unless you like looking at dead bodies).

• 0:15—Close up breasts, then full frontal nudity when Crispin Glover pokes her with a stick.

• 0:16—Full frontal nudity when the three boys leave.

• 0:22—Full frontal nudity when all the kids come to see her body. (She's starting to look very discolored).

• 0:24—Right breast when everybody leaves.

• 0:30—Right breast when her body is dumped in the river.

Ione Skye . . . . Clarissa

Road to Ruin (1992)

Eleonore Klarwein . . . . Girl Friend

•• 0:03—Breasts and buns, getting out of bed and walking into bathroom.

Carey Lowell . . . . Jessie Taylor

• 0:25—Lower half of buns, while sitting in bed with Peter Weller.

• 0:26—Very, very brief buns, when Weller pulls her onto the bed.

Road to Salina (1969; French/Italian)

Mimsy Farmer . . . . Billie

••• 0:23—Breasts and buns, undressing and running to beach with Jonas. Nude, while swimming under water.

•• 0:24—Buns and breasts, while lying on the beach with Jonas.

• 0:40—Buns and brief right breast while taking a shower. Seen through lattice work.

•• 0:41—Nude in bed with Jonas.

• 0:42—Breasts, while making love with Jonas in tent.

• 0:44—Breasts and buns, while running out of the tent into the water. Nude in the water.

• 0:56—Brief right breast in bed with Jonas.

• 1:28—Buns and brief breasts after taking a shower outside and wrapping a towel around herself.

• 1:29—Briefly nude, while rolling over in bed.

The Road to Wellville (1994)

Lara Flynn Boyle . . . . Ida Muntz

•• 0:16—Breasts, while sitting on bed in Matthew Broderick's fantasy.

••• 0:55—Breasts, while sitting in bed, talking with Broderick. Nice long scene, although she's made up to look sick.

Bridget Fonda . . . . Eleanor Lightbody

• 0:23—Breasts, while bathing in milk bath.

• 1:46—Right breast, while getting sexually manipulated by Dr. Spitzvogel in the woods.

Traci Lind . . . . Nurse Irene Graves

•• 0:15—Buns and side of left breast in elevator in Matthew Broderick's fantasy.

Camryn Manheim . . . . Virginia Cranchill

• 1:02—Buns, while lying down and talking with Bridget Fonda.

Roadhouse (1989)

Jasaé . . . . Strip Joint Girl

Laura Albert. . . . . Strip Joint Girl

•• 0:45—Breasts and buns dancing on stage, wearing a hat.

Lisa Axelrod. . . . . Party Girl

Cheryl Baker . . . . Well-Endowed Wife

Sylvia Baker . . . . Table Dancer

Michele Burger . . . . Strip Joint Girl

Terri Lynn Doss . . . . Cody's Girlfriend

Kymberly Herrin . . . . Party Girl

Pamela Jackson . . . . Strip Joint Girl

Susan Lentini . . . . Bandstand Babe

Kelly Lynch . . . . Doc

•• 1:04—Breasts and buns getting out of bed with a sheet wrapped around her.

Kym Malin. . . . . Party Girl

Julie Michaels . . . . Denise

••• 1:18—Breasts dancing on stage in club in front of Patrick Swayze.

Monique Noel. . . . . Uncredited Barfly

Heidi Paine . . . . Party Girl

Jacqueline Palmer . . . . Party Girl

Patricia Tallman. . . . . Bandstand Babe

Christina Veronica . . . . Strip Joint Girl

Roadhouse 66 (1984)

Kaaren Lee . . . . Jesse Duran
- •• 1:00—Breasts, taking off her top to go skinny dipping with Willem Dafoe. Dark.

Kate Vernon . . . . Melissa Duran
- • 1:03—Brief breasts in back of car with Judge Reinhold. Dark.

Robot Jox (1990)

Anne-Marie Johnson . . . . Athena
- •• 0:35—Buns, while walking to the showers after talking with Achilles and Tex.

• *Rock Video Girls* (1991; Video Tape)

Kim Anderson . . . . Herself
- • 0:02—Dancing in wet T-shirt. Buns and brief breasts on the beach (some in B&W).

Susan Ashley . . . . Herself

Beckie Mullen . . . . Herself

Sam Phillips . . . . Herself
- •• 0:47—Brief breasts and buns quite a few times, while wearing a G-string.

Aleisa Shirley . . . . Herself

Judette Warren . . . . Herself

Kari Whitman . . . . Small Town Girl
- • 0:31—Breasts under sheer white nightie.

• *Rock Video Girls 2* (1992; Video Tape)

Blueberry . . . . Herself
- • 0:28—Buns in G-string under sheer body stocking.

Monique Biffignani . . . . Herself
- • 0:49—Right breast under gauze and buns in G-string after being unwrapped as a mummy.

Peggy McIntaggart . . . . Herself

Shauna O'Brien . . . . Herself
- ••• 0:33—Breasts in shower during music video.

Shannon Stiles . . . . Herself

Sándra Wild . . . . Herself
- ••• 0:21—Breasts taking off her tank top by water pump in music video.

The Rocky Horror Picture Show (1975; British)

Nell Campbell . . . . Columbia
- • 1:17—Top of breasts popping out of her blouse during song and dance on stage.

Patricia Quinn . . . . Magenta

Susan Sarandon . . . . Janet Weiss

Koo Stark . . . . Bridesmaid

Roller Blade (1986)

Michelle Bauer . . . . Bod Sister
- • 0:11—Breasts, being held by Satacoy's Devils.
- ••• 0:13—More breasts and buns in G-string during fight. Long scene.
- • 0:16—Brief breasts twice, getting rescued by the Sisters.
- •• 0:33—Breasts during ceremony with the other two Bod Sisters. Buns also.
- ••• 0:35—Full frontal nudity after dip in hot tub. (Second to leave the tub.)
- •• 0:40—Nude, on skates with the other two Bod Sisters. (She's on the left.)

Barbara Peckinpaugh . . . . Bod Sister
- •• 0:33—Breasts during ceremony. Cut on her throat is unappealing.
- ••• 0:35—Full frontal nudity after dip in hot tub with the other two Bod Sisters. (She's the first to leave.)
- •• 0:40—Nude, on skates with the other two Bod Sisters. (She's in the middle.)

Suzanne Solari . . . . Sister Sharon Cross
- • 0:04—Buns, in G-string, while lying in bed.
- • 1:21—Brief upper half of right breast, taking off suit. Buns in G-string.

RollerBlade Warriors: Taken By Force (1988)

Susan Jones . . . . Slave Girl #2
- •• 0:20—Breasts, while getting hassled by two guys.
- ••• 0:23—Breasts, while walking through the desert.

Elizabeth Kaitan . . . . Gretchen Hope
- • 0:51—Breasts, while tied to large spool and getting raped by Marachek.
- • 1:03—Very brief breasts, several times, while getting raped in B&W vision.

Kathleen Kinmont . . . . Karin Crosse

Suzanne Solari . . . . Sharon Crosse

Lisa Toothman . . . . Slave Girl #1
- •• 0:21—Breasts after getting her top ripped off by two guys.
- ••• 0:23—Breasts, while walking through the desert.

Rolling Thunder (1977)

Linda Haynes . . . . Linda Forchet

Lisa Richards . . . . Janet

Cassie Yates . . . . Candy
- ••• 1:31—Breasts while undressing in bedroom with Tommy Lee Jones.
- • 1:32—Right breast, while sitting on bed with Jones.
- • 1:33—Right breast, when Jones sits up in bed.

Romance with a Double Bass (1974; British)

Connie Booth . . . . Princess Costanza
- •• 0:10—Very brief buns, going into the water to retrieve her fishing float, then full frontal nudity while yelling at a guy who steals her clothes.
- •• 0:11—Full frontal nudity, while walking around, looking for her clothes.
- ••• 0:18—Breasts, while holding her hand over her eyes.
- •• 0:20—Brief left breast, while reaching up to close the bass case.

The Romantic Englishwoman (1975; British/French)

Nathalie Delon . . . . Miranda

Glenda Jackson . . . . Elizabeth
- • 0:30—Brief full frontal nudity outside, taking robe off in front of Michael Caine.
- • 0:31—Buns, walking back into the house.
- • 1:08—Side view of right breast sitting at edge of pool talking to Thomas.
- • 1:45—Very, very brief breasts while in bed talking with Thomas.

Kate Nelligan . . . . Isabel

Romeo and Juliet (1968; British/Italian)

Olivia Hussey . . . . Juliet
- • 1:37—Very brief breasts rolling over and getting out of bed with Romeo.

Romeo Is Bleeding (1994)

Victoria Bastell . . . . Girl #1
- • 0:03—Breasts, (she's the blonde) while frolicking in bed with a brunette woman and a guy. Very brief buns in panties in mirror.
- • 0:31—Breasts, in room with a brunette woman and a guy.

Juliette Lewis . . . . Sheri

Lena Olin . . . . .Mona Demakov
•• 1:20—Breasts under leather outfit with fake arm.
•• 1:22—More breasts in the leather outfit.
• 1:29—Buns in sexy black bodysuit.
Annabella Sciorra . . . . Natalie

Romper Stomper *(1993; Australian)*

Jacqueline McKenzie . . . . .Gabe
•• 0:18—Breasts, while making love with Hando at the gang's hangout.
••• 1:11—Breasts, while making love with Davey in bed.

Roosters *(1993)*

Maria Conchita Alonso . . . . Chata
Sonia Braga. . . . . .Juana
•• 0:26—Right breast and lower frontal nudity, while lying in bed with Edward James Olmos.
Sarah Lassez . . . . .Angela
Maude Winchester . . . . Waitress

Roots of Evil *(1991)*

(Unrated version reviewed.)
Jasaé . . . . .Subway Hooker
••• 1:05—Breasts taking off her top in subway stairwell, then getting killed by the bad guy.
Yvette Buchanan . . . . Hooker
Daphne Cheung . . . . .Tina
••• 0:09—Breasts in alley with a customer.
Jillian Kesner . . . . Brenda
••• 0:27—Breasts, giving Alex Cord a back massage in bed.
• 0:30—Brief breasts, getting up out of bed.
Deanna Lund . . . . Marissa
• 0:19—Most of left breast, then brief right breast, while making love in bed with Johnny.
•• 0:20—More right breast, while making love.
•• 0:21—Still more right breast.
••• 1:33—Right breast, then breasts while lying in bed with Brinke Stevens.
Jewel Shepard . . . . Wanda
• 1:31—Brief right breast, a couple of times, when it pops out of her blouse while she's in police station.
Delia Sheppard . . . . Monica
••• 0:04—Breasts and buns in G-string, dancing on stage.
• 0:07—Breasts and buns, while on stage when wounded guy disturbs her act.
••• 0:38—Buns in outfit, then breasts dancing on stage.
••• 0:41—More buns and breasts in bed, making love with Johnny. Long scene.
Donna Spangler . . . . Scarlett
•• 0:04—Breasts, getting attacked by the crazy guy, then killed.
• 0:07—Brief breasts, dead, covered with blood when Alex Cord discovers her.
Brinke Stevens. . . . . .Candy
•• 1:33—Right breast, then breasts while sitting on bed talking to Deanna Lund.

Rosebud *(1975)*

Brigitte Ariel . . . . .Sabine
• 0:11—Very, Very brief part of right breast, while lying in bed when her boyfriend, Patrice, sits up. Brief left breast, when scooting up behind him.
• 0:19—Buns while sleeping on bed, then lower frontal nudity after terrorist wakes her up. Buns, while standing on deck of boat (she's first in line).
Debra Berger. . . . . Gertrude Fryer
• 0:19—Brief upper half of buns, while on deck of boat with the other girls and the terrorists (she's last in line).
Kim Cattrall . . . . Joyce Donovan
• 0:19—Buns, while on deck of boat with the other girls and the terrorists (she's fourth in line).
Adrienne Corri. . . . . .Lady Carter
Isabelle Huppert . . . . Helene Nikolaos
• 0:19—Buns, while on deck of boat with the other girls and the terrorists (she's second in line).
• 1:40—Partial side view of right breast in gaping robe, while lying back in bed with Peter O'Toole.
Lalla Ward . . . . Margaret Carter
• 0:19—Buns, while on deck of boat with the other girls and the terrorists (she's third in line).

The Rosebud Beach Hotel *(1985)*

Julie Always . . . . .Bellhop
•• 0:22—Breasts, in open blouse, undressing with two other bellhops. She's the blonde on the left.
•• 0:44—Breasts, playing spin the grenade, with two guys and the two other bellhops. She's on the left.
Colleen Camp . . . . Tracy
Cherie Currie. . . . . .Cherie
Fran Drescher . . . . Linda
Monique Gabrielle. . . . . Lisa
•• 0:22—Breasts and buns undressing in hotel room with two other girls. She's on the right.
•• 0:44—Breasts taking off her red top in basement with two other girls and two guys.
• 0:56—In black see-through nightie in hotel room with Peter Scolari.
Dirga McBroom. . . . . .Bellhop
• 0:49—Buns, then breasts, standing with the other bell hops, outfitted with military attire. (She's the one at the far end, furthest from the camera.)
Tina Merkle . . . . .Bellhop
• 0:49—Breasts, standing in line. Closest to the camera.
Julia Parton . . . . .Bellhop
•• 0:49—Buns, then breasts, standing in line. Second from the camera.

Rosemary's Baby *(1968)*

Mia Farrow . . . . Rosemary Woodhouse
• 0:10—Brief left breast in room in new apartment on floor with John Cassavetes. Hard to see anything.
• 0:43—Brief close up of her breasts while she's sitting on a boat during a nightmare.
•• 0:44—Buns walking on boat, then breasts during impregnation scene with the devil.
Victoria Vetri . . . . Terry Fionoffrio

Round Numbers *(1990)*

India Allen . . . . Swimsuit Model
Hope Marie Carlton. . . . . .Mitzi
• 0:39—Left breast, twice, while turning around in steam room in Kate Mulgrew's imagination.
Samantha Eggar . . . . .Anne

Round Trip to Heaven *(1992)*

Tara Buckman . . . . Phyllis
Lauren Hays. . . . . Contestant
Julie McCullough. . . . . .Lucille
Cyndi Pass. . . . . Cindy

Brittney Powell . . . . Contestant
- 0:36—Brief breasts, while putting on dark gray, one piece swimsuit in dressing room.

Amy Rochelle . . . . Yvette
- ••• 0:19—In black bra and G-string in bedroom with Corey Feldman, then breasts and buns on top of him in bed.

Kristine Rose . . . . Tina

Denise Zakovich . . . . Miss Moscow
- •• 1:06—Buns and upper half breasts, undressing in bedroom.
- ••• 1:07—Breasts, opening her towel for Zach Galligan.
- • 1:12—Very brief right breast, while in bed with Galligan.

• *Rumpelstiltskin (1995)*

Judith Drake . . . . Woman Deputy

Kim Johnston-Ulrich . . . . Shelly Stewart
- • 0:23—Very brief back side of right breast, then buns, while getting out of bed. Don't see her face well.

Valerie Wildman . . . . Nedda

Runaway (1984)

Kirstie Alley . . . . Jackie

Cec Verrell. . . . . Hooker
- •• 0:44—Breasts in hotel bathroom while Tom Selleck sneaks into her room.

Running Out of Luck (1986)

Rae Dawn Chong . . . . .Slave Girl
- •• 0:42—Left breast, while hugging Mick Jagger, then again while lying in bed with him.
- •• 1:12—Left breast painting some kind of drug laced solution on herself.
- •• 1:14—Right breast, while in prison office offering her breast to the warden.
- • 1:21—Buns and left breast, in bed with Jagger during a flashback.

Jerry Hall . . . . Herself

Running Scared (1986)

Darlanne Fluegel . . . . Anna Costanzo

Tracy Reed . . . . Maryann
- • 0:18—Brief buns.
- • 1:30—Very brief breasts in bed with Gregory Hines.

Rush (1991)

Jennifer Jason Leigh . . . . .Kristen Cates
- • 1:09—Brief buns, when Jason Patric takes off her pajama bottoms and forces himself on her.

Rush Week (1989)

Laura Burkett. . . . . Rebecca Winters
- •• 0:43—Breasts in the shower, talking to Jonelle.
- • 0:55—Brief breasts getting dressed after modeling session.

Kathleen Kinmont . . . . Julie Ann McGuffin
- • 0:07—Brief breasts several times during modeling session. Buns in G-string getting dressed. Long shot.

Ruthless People (1986)

Jeannine Bisignano . . . . Hooker in Car
- • 0:40—Breasts in the same scene three times on TV while Danny De Vito watches.
- • 0:49—Left breast hanging out of the car when the Chief of Police watches on TV. Closest shot.

Laura Cruikshank. . . . . n.a.

Anita Morris . . . . .Carol

Helen Slater. . . . . Sandy Kessler

Ryan's Daughter (1970)

Sarah Miles . . . . Rosy Ryan
- • 1:32—Brief right breast, in open red blouse, while outside with Major Doryan.
- • 1:36—Very brief right breast, when reaching up to hug Doryan while lying on the ground together.

S.A.S. San Salvador (1982)

Sybil Danning . . . . Countess Alexandra
- • 0:07—Brief left breast, while lying on the couch and kissing Malko.

Catherine Jarrett . . . . Rosa
- ••• 0:28—Buns and breasts, taking off swimsuit in bathroom, then taking a shower.

S.F.W. (1994)

Joey Lauren Adams . . . . Monica Dice
- • 0:31—Brief upper half of right breast, then left breast, while making love in bed with Stephen Dorff.

Kathryn Atwood . . . . Pebbles Goren

Pamela Gidley . . . . Janet Streeter

Natasha Gregson Wagner . . . . Kristen

Melissa Lechner . . . . .Sandy Hooten
- • 0:46—Brief side of right breast, while in bathtub.
- • 0:50—Brief breasts after dropping her towel after professing her love for Stephen Dorff.

Annie McEnroe . . . . .Dolly

S.O.B. (1981)

Julie Andrews. . . . . .Sally Miles
- •• 1:19—Breasts pulling the top off her red dress during the filming of a movie.

Rosanna Arquette . . . . Babs
- • 0:21—Brief breasts taking off white T-shirt on the deck of the house. Long shot, hard to see.

Marisa Berenson . . . . Mavis
- •• 1:20—Breasts in bed with Robert Vaughn.

Gisele Lindley . . . . .n.a.

Gay Rowan . . . . .n.a.

Sacred Cargo (1995)

Anna Karin. . . . . Sasha Rosanov
- • 1:06—Very brief side view of left breast while making love with Chris Penn.

Sacrilege (1986)

Myriem Roussel . . . . Sister Virginia Maria di Leva
- ••• 0:50—Full frontal nudity, when making love with a guy, while two other sisters watch.

The Sailor Who Fell From Grace with the Sea (1976)

Sarah Miles . . . . Anne Osborne
- • 0:18—Breasts sitting at the vanity getting dressed while her son watches through peephole.
- •• 0:23—Breasts, fantasizing about her husband.
- •• 0:42—Breasts, then nude, while making love with Kris Kristofferson.
- • 1:15—Brief right breast, while in bed with Kristofferson.

Saints and Sinners (1994)

Jennifer Rubin . . . . Eva
- • 0:03—Buns in short nightie, after kicking the covers off herself while lying in bed.
- ••• 0:31—In black bra and panties, then breasts, while making love with Damian Chapa.

• 0:42—Breasts, while making love with Chapa and Scott Plank at the same time.
•• 0:43—Breasts, while lying in bed and talking with Chapa and Plank, then getting out of bed and putting on blouse.
• 0:45—Brief breasts, taking off her blouse and going into the bathroom.
• 0:57—Breasts, while making love in bed with Chapa and Plank again.

Salmonberries *(1991; German)*
k.d. lang . . . . Kotzebue
••• 0:13—Brief full frontal nudity while standing in the library.

Salomé *(1986; Italian)*
Jo Champa . . . . Salomé
•• 1:12—Nude under blue dress while dancing around.
• 1:20—Full frontal nudity under sheer blue dress while in jail cell.
• 1:27—Full frontal nudity in sheer dress while walking around.
Pamela Salem . . . . Herodias
• 0:05—Brief left breast, when her top gets ripped off.
• 0:26—Left breast when servant girl helps take her dress off.
• 0:27—Left breast and lower frontal nudity while standing in front of pool. Medium long shot.

Salome's Last Dance *(1987)*
Linzi Drew. . . . . 1st Slave
•• 0:08—Breasts in black costume around a cage.
•• 0:52—Breasts during dance number.
Glenda Jackson . . . . Herodias/Lady Alice
Tina Shaw. . . . . 2nd Slave
•• 0:08—Breasts in black costume around a cage.
•• 0:52—Breasts during dance number.

Salvador *(1986)*
Elpidia Carrillo. . . . . Maria
• 0:21—Very brief right breast, lying in a hammock with James Woods. Very brief buns and side of left breast when getting out of the hammock.
Cynthia Gibb . . . . Cathy Moore
Valerie Wildman . . . . Pauline Axelrod

Sammy and Rosie Get Laid *(1987; British)*
Frances Barber . . . . Rosie Hobbs
• 1:09—Very brief breasts, while bending over to kiss Danny. More brief breasts while making love (short cuts).
1:21—Partial right breast while sitting in bubble bath with Sammy.
Claire Bloom . . . . Alice
Wendy Gazelle . . . . Anna
•• 0:03—Buns, while lying in bed with Sammy.
• 1:10—Breasts, while lying under Sammy. Seen on the top of a three segment split screen. Don't see her face.

Santa Sangre *(1989; Italian/Spanish)*
Blanca Guerra . . . . Concha
• 0:34—Half of buns, while wearing a sexy circus outfit.

Satan's Princess *(1989)*
Lydie Denier . . . . Nicole St. James
• 0:27—Full frontal nudity, getting out of pool.
••• 0:28—Full frontal nudity, next to bed and in bed with Karen.
••• 0:45—Breasts and buns, making love in bed with Robert Forster.
Leslie Huntly . . . . Karen Rhodes
••• 0:27—Breasts sitting on bed and in bed with Nicole.
Marilyn Joi. . . . . Hooker
Caren Kaye . . . . Leah
Debra Lamb . . . . Fire Eater/Dancer
•• 0:23—Breasts in G-string doing a fire dance in club.
• 0:25—Breasts, doing more dancing. Long shot.
Rena Riffel . . . . Erica Dunn
•• 0:16—Breasts getting white dress torn open, then killed with a knife.

Satanic Attraction *(1991; Italian)*
Gabriela Toscano. . . . . Fernanda
• 0:43—Partial left breast, making love with Lionel. Brief side view of left breast, eating fruit afterwards.

Saturday Night Special *(1994)*
(Unrated version reviewed.)
Deborah Dutch . . . . Uncredited Singer
Maria Ford. . . . . Darlene
••• 0:37—Breasts, while making love with Travis in the woods.
••• 0:50—Breasts, while making love with Travis on bed. Buns, when lying down afterwards. Great!
Nikki Fritz . . . . Uncredited Line Dancer

Saturn 3 *(1980)*
Farrah Fawcett. . . . . Alex
•• 0:17—Brief right breast taking off towel and running to Kirk Douglas after taking a shower.

• ***Savage*** *(1995)*
Kristin Minter . . . . Marie Beloc
••• 0:18—Breasts and buns, when having sex in bed with a guy, then getting out and looking at a computer monitor, then talking on the telephone. A bit on the dark side.
Victoria Morsell . . . . Julie Verne

Savage Attraction *(1983; Australian)*
Kerry Mack . . . . Christine Maresch
••• 0:10—Breasts, getting out of shower and putting on robe.
• 0:11—Breasts behind shower door, making love with Walter.
•• 0:17—Breasts sitting at the end of the bed.
•• 0:59—Breasts undressing in bedroom, then in bathtub with Walter.
••• 1:04—Breasts getting her blouse unbuttoned, then breasts in bed with Walter.

Savage Beach *(1989)*
Hope Marie Carlton. . . . . Taryn
• 0:32—Breasts changing clothes in airplane with Dona Speir.
•• 0:48—Nude, going for a swim on the beach with Speir.
Patty Duffek . . . . Patticakes
• 0:06—Breasts in spa with Lisa London, Dona Speir and Hope Marie Carlton.
•• 0:50—Breasts changing clothes.
Lisa London. . . . . Rocky
• 0:06—Breasts in spa with Patty Duffek, Dona Speir and Hope Marie Carlton.
•• 0:50—Breasts changing clothes.
Dona Speir . . . . Dona
• 0:32—Breasts changing clothes in airplane with Hope Marie Carlton.
•• 0:48—Nude, going for a swim on the beach with Carlton.

Maxine Wasa . . . . Sexy Beauty
••• 0:08—Side view of left breast, in pool with Shane, then breasts getting out of pool.
••• 0:10—Breasts while Shane talks on the phone.
Teri Weigel . . . . Anjelica
••• 0:33—Breasts taking off black teddy and getting into bed to make love.
•• 0:47—Breasts making love in the back seat of car.

Savage Dawn *(1984)*

Wendy Barry . . . . Lipservice
• 1:01—Breasts, after taking off top in room in front of Richard Lynch.
•• 1:03—Breasts and buns after getting up with Lynch, then getting dressed.
Karen Black . . . . Rachel
Elizabeth Kaitan . . . . Becky Sue
• 0:17—Right breast, while getting mauled by the bad guys.
Janice Renney . . . . Susan
Claudia Udy . . . . Katie Rand

Savage Messiah *(1972; British)*

Maggy Maxwell . . . . Tart
•• 0:39—Nude, undressing in bedroom and posing for a guy doing sketches.
Helen Mirren . . . . Gosh Smith-Boyle
••• 0:39—Full frontal nudity, posing for sketches while walking up and down stairs and around. Nice long scene.
•• 1:15—Brief buns, while covering herself up.

Savage Nights *(1992; French)*

a.k.a. Les Nuits Fauves
Romane Bohringer . . . . Laura
• 0:29—Half of left breast, while making love in bed with Jean.
• 0:30—Left breast.
• 0:34—Full frontal nudity while going to closet to get a T-shirt. Dark, medium long shot.
••• 0:41—Left breasts, then breasts, while in bed with Jean.
Maria Schneider . . . . Noria

Savage Streets *(1984)*

Linda Blair . . . . Brenda
••• 1:05—Breasts, while sitting in the bathtub thinking.
Debra Blee . . . . Rachel
Marcia Karr . . . . Stevie
Rebecca Perle . . . . Cindy Clark
•• 0:53—Brief breasts in biology class getting her top torn off by Linda Blair.
Linnea Quigley . . . . Heather
• 0:28—Breasts getting raped by the jerks.
Suzanne Slater . . . . Uncredited
•• 0:09—Breasts being held by jerks when they yank her tube top down.
Kristi Somers . . . . Valerie

Save Me *(1993)*

(Unrated version reviewed.)
Lysette Anthony . . . . Ellie
0:31—Upper half of right breast in bra, while making love in convertible Mustang with Hamlin.
••• 0:39—Nude, while sleeping then making love in bed with Hamlin.
•• 0:49—Breasts in spa with Hamlin. Long shot of buns, when getting out. Breasts again while putting on swimsuit.
••• 0:52—In bra, then breasts while making love with Hamlin in front of fireplace.
• 1:05—Breasts, when Hamlin forces himself on her in stairway of parking garage.
Olivia Hussey . . . . Gail
Ashlie Rhey . . . . Customer
••• 0:21—Nude, while trying on lingerie after Lysette Anthony shows Harry Hamlin secret one-way mirror in dressing room in lingerie store.
Kristine Rose . . . . Cheryl

Sawbones *(1995; Made for Cable Movie)*

Cheryl Bartel . . . . Beautiful Woman
•• 0:40—Breasts, while lying on operating table, unable to move.
• 0:55—Breasts, several times, while lying dead on coroner's examination table.
Barbara Carrera . . . . Rita Baldwin
• 1:06—Buns, several times, while lying on operating table. Don't see her face very well.
Nina Siemaszko . . . . Jenny Sloan

Say Yes *(1986)*

Lissa Layng . . . . Annie
•• 1:06—Breasts, getting her dress ripped off.
• 1:07—More breasts, putting on jacket in restroom.

Scandal *(1989)*

(Unrated version reviewed.)
Britt Ekland . . . . Mariella Novotny
•• 0:31—Breasts, while lying on table with John Hurt.
• 0:51—Right breast, while talking with Hurt and Joanne Whalley.
Bridget Fonda . . . . Mandy Rice-Davis
• 0:20—Brief breasts dressed as an Indian dancing while Joanne Whalley tries to upstage her.
• 0:53—In white lingerie, then brief lower frontal nudity under sheer nightgown in room with a guy.
• 1:05—Brief buns, while walking back into bedroom. Long shot.
Arkie Whitely . . . . Vicky

Scanners III: The Takeover *(1992)*

Liliana Komorowska . . . . Helena Monet
•• 0:32—Breasts in and out of spa, talking with her dad.
• 0:35—Brief right breast, while sitting up.

Scarecrow *(1973)*

Rutanya Alda . . . . Woman in Camper
Eileen Brennan . . . . Darlene
• 0:27—Brief breasts in bed when Gene Hackman takes off her bra and grabs her breasts.
Dorothy Tristan . . . . Coley

Scarface *(1983)*

Angela Aames . . . . Woman at the Babylon Club
Lana Clarkson . . . . Woman at the Babylon Club
Emilia Crow . . . . Echevera
Jeanette Linné . . . . Woman at the Babylon Club
Mary Elizabeth Mastrantonio . . . . Gina
• 2:36—(0:39 into tape 2) Very, very brief left breast when she gets shot and her nightgown opens up.
Shelly Taylor Morgan . . . . Woman at the Babylon Club
Michelle Pfeiffer . . . . Elvira
Katt Shea . . . . Woman at the Babylon Club

Scarlet Letter (1995)

Lisa Jolliff-Andoh . . . . Mituba
- 0:50—Very brief left breast, when bending over before getting into tub. Partial left breast while sitting in the tub, holding a candle.

Demi Moore . . . . Hester Prynne
- 0:36—Brief breasts under dress while she bathes herself.
- •• 0:37—Partial buns and side of left breast while standing in tub when spied on by Mituba.

Diane Salinger. . . . . .Margaret Bellingham
Amy Wright . . . . Goody Gotwick

Scarred (1983)

Annie Gaybis. . . . . .Movie Girl
- •• 0:32—Breasts, while straddling a guy in bed during filming of a movie.

Jennifer Mayo . . . . Ruby
- ••• 0:18—Breasts, undressing in bedroom in front of a customer, lying in bed, then making love. Long scene.
- 0:21—Breasts, while lying in bed afterward.
- 0:27—Breasts in bathtub, getting red paint washed off by a friend.
- 0:29—Left breast, while sitting in bathtub.

Alexis Schreiner. . . . . .Movie Girl
- 0:32—Breasts, while dancing during filming of a movie. (She's the auburn hair girl wearing a gold necklace.)

Scenes from the Class Struggle in Beverly Hills (1989)

Jacqueline Bisset . . . . .Clare
Arnetia Walker. . . . . .To-Bel
- 0:37—Breasts making love with Ray Sharkey on the sofa.
- •• 1:10—Breasts in bed waking up with Wallace Shawn.
- ••• 1:23—Breasts making love on top of Ed Begley, Jr. on the floor.

Mary Woronov . . . . Lizabeth
- ••• 1:06—In black lingerie, then breasts in bedroom, then in bed with Robert Beltran.

Schizo (1977; British)

a.k.a. Amok
a.k.a. Blood of the Undead

Stephanie Beacham. . . . . Beth
Lynne Frederick. . . . . Samantha
0:26—In white bra and panties, while changing clothes in bedroom.
- •• 0:29—Breasts and buns, while walking to and taking a shower.
- 0:56—Brief frontal nudity, while getting into bed.

Schizoid (1980)

Flo Gerrish . . . . Pat
Mariana Hill . . . . .Julie
- 0:58—Left breast, while making love in bed with Klaus Kinski. Dark, hard to see.

Donna Wilkes . . . . Allison Foles
- 0:12—Breasts taking off her bra in bathroom while Klaus Kinski watches. Buns, getting into the shower. Out of focus shots.
- •• 0:13—Side view breasts getting into the shower.

School Spirit (1985)

Leslee Bremmer. . . . . Sandy
- 1:18—Breasts on a guy's shoulder in pool. (She's on the right, wearing red swimsuit bottoms.)

Linda Carol . . . . .Hogette
Roberta Collins . . . . Helen Grimshaw
Jackie Easton . . . . Hogette
Julie Gray. . . . . Kendall
Marlene Janssen . . . . Sleeping Princess
- •• 0:16—Breasts in shower room, shaving her legs.
- •• 0:42—Breasts and buns, sleeping when old guy goes invisible to peek at her.

Marta Kober . . . . Ursula
Becky LeBeau. . . . . Hogette
- 1:07—Breasts sliding down water slide at dance, wearing black and white swimsuit bottom.

Pamela Ward . . . . Girl in Sorority Room
- ••• 0:15—Buns, then breasts in her room while Billy is invisible.
- ••• 0:16—More breasts and buns with other women in shower room.

• *Sci-Fighters (1996; Canadian)*

Karen Elkin . . . . Zombie Woman
- 0:57—Breasts, while lying on bed in Billy Drago's room. Eye pattern artwork is drawn on her breasts.
- 0:59—Brief breasts, while lying on the bed. Brief buns, when the bed is tipped over and she rolls over on the floor.

Jayne Heitmeyer . . . . Kirbie
- 1:23—Very brief upper half of left breast, when Billy Drago struggles with her on the floor and he yanks her bra up.

Doris Milmore . . . . Hooker
Donna Sarrasin . . . . .Tricia
- 0:45—Brief breasts, while convulsing on laboratory table. Covered with unappealing makeup on her body.
- 0:46—Brief left breast, after dying on the table.

Scissors (1990)

Vicki Frederick . . . . .Nancy Leahy
Michelle Phillips. . . . . Ann Carter
Sharon Stone. . . . . .Angela Anderson
- 0:04—Upper half of left breast, while sitting up after attack in elevator.
- •• 0:12—Breasts changing clothes.

Scorchy (1971)

Connie Stevens . . . . Jackie Parker
- •• 0:23—Open blouse, revealing left bra cup while talking on the telephone. Brief breasts swimming in the water after taking off bathing suit top.
- •• 0:52—Side view left breast, taking a shower.
- ••• 0:56—Brief right breast making love in bed with Greg Evigan. Breasts getting tied to the bed by the thieves. Kind of a long shot and a little dark and hard to see.
- 1:00—Brief breasts getting covered with a sheet by the good guy.

Score! (1973)

Lynn Lowry . . . . .Betsy
- 0:35—Left breast, sticking out of lingerie outfit.
- 0:38—Brief full frontal nudity, in lingerie outfit while dancing.
- 0:40—Breasts, in lingerie, while sitting on the floor with Eddie.
- 1:01—Brief lower frontal nudity while in bed with Elvira.
- 1:06—Brief left breast in reflection in mirror.
- 1:07—Breasts in lingerie in bed with Elvira.
- •• 1:15—Brief right breast and lower frontal nudity in bed with Elvira.
- •• 1:22—Full frontal nudity, while in bed, then talking to Eddie.

Claire Wilbur . . . . Elvira
- 0:01—Brief breasts, while making love with Jack.
- 0:04—Brief buns, after taking off overcoat.
- 0:13—Left breast, while on bed in open blouse, lying on bed for Lynn Lowry to take a picture.

••• 0:20—Full frontal nudity after taking off her robe in front of Mike. Buns, while making love.
- 0:33—Brief breasts, while taking off bra.
- 0:53—Brief right breast while sitting back in bed.

•• 0:59—Breasts, after taking off her dress to go to sleep with Betsy.
- 1:02—Brief left breast, while in bed with Betsy.

••• 1:09—Full frontal nudity while standing up in bed, making love with Betsy.

••• 1:12—Breasts, while making love with Lynn.
- 1:15—Breasts, while waking up in bed.
- 1:22—Right breast, while in bed with everybody.
- 1:24—Breasts, while in bed.

Scorned *(1993)*

Anya Longwell. . . . . The Woman
Kim Morgan Greene . . . . Marina Weston

•• 0:42—Brief breasts, while sitting in bubble bath and getting out. Buns, when Shannon Tweed helps dry her off.

••• 1:09—Left breast, then breasts while in bed when Tweed makes love with her.
- 1:28—Breasts, while crying in shower after discovering her birds are dead.

Leslie Sachs . . . . Alex's Secretary
Shannon Tweed . . . . Patricia Langley/Amanda Chessfield

•• 0:50—Breasts, after taking off bra with Robey, then in bed.

•• 0:59—Left breast and buns, while making love on top of Robey in bed.

•• 1:19—In bra, then breasts, while making love on bed with Robey.

Scream Dream *(1989)*

Melissa Anne Moore . . . . Jamie Summers

••• 0:39—Breasts in black panties in room with Derrick. Then straddling him.

•• 0:58—Breasts in dressing room pulling her top down during transformation into monster.

• ***Scream Queen Hot Tub Party*** *(1991; Video Tape)*

Michelle Bauer. . . . . Herself

•• 0:00—Full frontal nudity during opening credits.

•• 0:07—Breasts taking off pink outfit and putting on red teddy.
- 0:12—Buns, while walking up the stairs.

••• 0:33—Nude, stripping out of blue dress in scene from *Hollywood Chainsaw Hookers.* Long scene.

••• 0:38—In black lingerie, then stripping to breasts to demonstrate the proper Scream Queen use of a chainsaw.

••• 0:44—Breasts taking off her swimsuit top and soaping up with the other girls.

•• 0:46—Breasts in still shot during the end credits.

Bridget Carney . . . . Shayne

••• 0:17—Breasts and buns in shower from *Hard to Die.*

Deborah Dutch . . . . Jackie Webster

•• 0:19—Breasts, taking off towel and getting into shower from *Hard to Die.*

Monique Gabrielle. . . . . Herself

•• 0:07—Breasts, taking off blue outfit and putting on white teddy.
- 0:12—Buns, while walking up the stairs.

••• 0:21—Breasts and buns making love with a guy from *Emmanuelle 5.*

••• 0:23—Breasts taking off bra in front of mirror from *Evil Toons.*

••• 0:25—Breasts in black panties demonstrating the Dance of the Vampires.

••• 0:44—Breasts taking off her swimsuit top and soaping up with the other girls.

•• 0:46—Breasts in still shot during the end credits.

Roxanne Kernohan . . . . Herself

•• 0:07—Breasts, taking off black dress and putting on sheer black robe.
- 0:12—Buns, while walking up the stairs.

•• 0:43—Breasts, struggling with a monster in basement.

••• 0:44—Breasts taking off her swimsuit top and soaping up with the other girls.

•• 0:46—Breasts in still shot during the end credits.

Kelli Maroney . . . . Herself

•• 0:07—Breasts after taking off flower print blouse and putting on pink teddy.
- 0:12—Buns, while walking up the stairs.

••• 0:30—Breasts and buns after stripping out of cheerleader outfit, rubbing lotion on herself and demonstrating the proper Scream Queen way to pump iron.

••• 0:44—Breasts taking off her swimsuit top and soaping up with the other girls.

•• 0:46—Breasts in still shot during the end credits.

Michele Michaels. . . . . Trish

•• 0:14—Breasts and buns in shower scene from *Slumber Party Massacre.*

Melissa Anne Moore . . . . Jessica
- 0:00—Breasts during opening credits.

••• 0:17—Breasts opening her towel, then in the shower from *Sorority House Massacre 2.*

Linnea Quigley . . . . Samantha
- 0:01—Breasts during opening credits.

•• 0:36—Breasts with painted body, doing double chainsaw dance from *Hollywood Chainsaw Hookers.*

Brinke Stevens . . . . Herself

•• 0:07—Breasts, taking off white outfit and putting on black teddy.
- 0:12—Buns, while walking up the stairs.

•• 0:14—Buns and breasts in shower scene from *Slumber Party Massacre.*

••• 0:19—Breasts and buns, demonstrating the proper Scream Queen way to take a shower.

••• 0:44—Breasts taking off her swimsuit top and soaping up with the other girls.

•• 0:46—Breasts in still shot during the end credits.

Stacia Zhivago. . . . . Kimberly

••• 0:16—Nude, in shower scene from *Sorority House Massacre 2.*

Screen Test *(1986)*

Michelle Bauer. . . . . Dancer/Ninja Girl

•• 0:04—Breasts dancing on stage.

••• 0:42—Nude, with Monique Gabrielle, making love in a boy's dream.

Deborah Blaisdell. . . . . Dancer
- 1:20—Brief breasts, twice, dancing on stage. Long shot.

Monique Gabrielle. . . . . Roxanne

•• 0:06—Breasts taking off clothes in back room in front of a young boy.

••• 0:42—Nude, with Michelle Bauer, seducing a boy in his day dream.

•• 1:20—Breasts taking off her top for a guy.

Screwball Hotel *(1988)*

Corinne Alphen . . . . Cherry Amour
• 0:46—Buns, in black outfit on bed with Norman.
Gianna Amore . . . . Mary Beth
Lisa Bradford-Aiton . . . . Punk Singer
Andi Bruce . . . . Bobbi Jo
Lori Deann Pallett . . . . Candy
••• 0:26—Breasts in the shower while Herbie is accidentally in there with her.
Reneé Shugart . . . . Blue Bell

Screwballs *(1983)*

Kim Cayer . . . . Brunette Cheerleader
Raven De La Croix . . . . Miss Anna Tomical
••• 1:08—Breasts during strip routine in nightclub.
Linda Shayne . . . . Bootsie Goodhead
••• 0:43—Right breast, while in back of van at drive-in theater, then breasts.

Sea of Love *(1989)*

Ellen Barkin . . . . Helen Cruger
• 1:13—Brief upper half of buns, while lying in bed with Pacino.

The Sea Wolves *(1980; British)*

Barbara Kellermann . . . . Mrs. Cromwell
• 0:32—Brief right breast, while holding champagne bottle, then brief right breast throwing it at gunman in room with Roger Moore.

Season of Fear *(1989)*

Clare Wren . . . . Sarah Drummond
• 0:22—Brief, partial left breast, while in bed with Mick. Long shot, hard to see.
• 0:25—Brief full frontal nudity, seen behind shower door.
• 0:42—Side view of left breast, while making love on top of Mick. Very, very brief left breast, when turning over after hearing a noise outside.

Second Time Lucky *(1986)*

Diane Franklin . . . . Eve
•• 0:13—Breasts a lot during first sequence in the Garden of Eden with Adam.
••• 0:28—Brief full frontal nudity running to Adam after trying an apple.
• 0:41—Left breast, while taking top of dress down.
••• 1:01—Breasts, opening her blouse in defiance, while standing in front of a firing squad.

Secret Admirer *(1985)*

Kelly Preston . . . . Deborah Anne Fimple
•• 0:53—Brief breasts in car with C. Thomas Howell.
• 1:17—Very brief breasts in and out of bed.
Leigh Taylor-Young . . . . Elizabeth Fimple
Dee Wallace Stone . . . . Connie Ryan

Secret Fantasy *(1981)*

Laura Antonelli . . . . Costanza Vivaldi
••• 0:16—In black bra in Doctor's office, then left breast, then breasts getting examined.
•• 0:18—In black bra and panties in another Doctor's office. Breasts and buns.
•• 0:19—Breasts getting X-rayed. Brief breasts lying down.
•• 0:32—Breasts and buns when Nicolo drugs her and takes Polaroid photos of her.
•• 0:49—Breasts and buns posing around the house for Nicolo while he takes Polaroid photos.
•• 0:53—Breasts and buns during Nicolo's dream.
••• 1:12—Breasts in Doctor's office.
•• 1:14—Breasts and buns in room with another guy.
•• 1:16—Breasts on train while workers "accidentally" see her.
•• 1:20—Breasts on bed after being carried from bathtub.
•• 1:25—Breasts dropping dress during opera.
•• 1:27—More breasts scenes from 0:49.

Secret Games *(1991)*

(Unrated version reviewed.)
Michele Brin . . . . Julianne
•• 0:03—Left breast, while lying in bed with Billy Drago.
••• 0:08—Breasts and buns, while taking a shower.
•• 0:09—Breasts under sheer white robe, trying to entice Drago.
• 0:12—Brief left breast, while getting out of bed. Breasts, while picking clothes out of closet.
••• 0:34—Breasts, sunbathing with the other girls. (She's wearing brown framed sunglasses.)
••• 0:38—Breasts in bed, making love with Martin Hewitt.
••• 0:43—Buns and breasts making love in bed with Drago.
••• 0:48—Breasts, while tied to the bed.
••• 0:54—In white bra and panties, then nude taking them off and putting new ones on.
••• 1:10—Breasts, while lying in bed with Hewitt.
••• 1:13—Breasts and buns, making love with Hewitt in bathtub.
•• 1:15—Breasts under sheer robe.
•• 1:32—Buns in G-string, then breasts, getting into bed and making love with Drago.
Monique Parent . . . . Robin
• 0:33—Right breast, buns and crotch, while in bed with Julianne.
Catya Sassoon . . . . Sandra
••• 0:21—Breasts during modeling session with the other girls. (She's the only brunette.)
••• 0:26—Breasts, making love in bed with Emil.
•• 0:34—Breasts in yellow bikini bottoms, sunbathing with the other girls.
••• 0:40—Breasts, getting out of the swimming pool and lying on lounge chair.
Delia Sheppard . . . . Celeste
• 0:38—Breasts under sheer black body suit.
• 0:45—Buns, under sheer robe.
•• 0:48—Breasts with her lover, while watching Julianne and Eric on TV.
Brittany York . . . . Nun

Secret Games 2—The Escort *(1993)*

(Unrated version reviewed.)
Sara Suzanne Brown . . . . Irene
••• 0:32—Undressing in bedroom, then nude while making love with Martin Hewitt in bed.
• 0:53—Breasts, while making love next to dining room table with Hewitt.
•• 1:00—Breasts, while lying in bed with Hewitt.
••• 1:20—Nude, while making love with Hewitt in bed.
Jennifer Peace . . . . Darci
••• 0:47—Full frontal nudity, while making love with Martin Hewitt in bed.
• 1:05—Breasts, in flashbacks.
Amy Rochelle . . . . Stacey
••• 0:09—Full frontal nudity, while making love with Martin Hewitt in front of fireplace.
••• 0:16—Nude, while in bedroom then making love with Hewitt on dining room table.

•• 0:19—Breasts, while sitting in bed with Hewitt and talking.
••• 0:21—Breasts in video playback and in bed while talking with Hewitt on the phone.
••• 0:24—Nude, after taking off coat, covering Hewitt with birthday cake and in the shower with him and Lisa.
•• 0:26—Breasts and buns while making love in bed with Lisa and Hewitt.
• 0:37—Breasts, several times in flashback.
• 0:38—Breasts on video playback.
••• 0:41—Breasts, while making love with Hector in bed while Hewitt watches.
••• 0:54—Breasts, while modeling clothes for Hewitt in bedroom.
••• 0:57—Breasts, while making love with Hewitt in newlywed fantasy.
•• 1:04—Breasts and buns, while making love on top of Hewitt in flashbacks.
•• 1:11—Breasts, while in bed with Hector while talking on the phone.
•• 1:13—Breasts on video playback.
• 1:16—Brief breasts on video playback.

Holly Spencer . . . . Lisa
••• 0:24—Nude, after taking off coat, covering Hewitt with birthday cake and in the shower with him and Stacey.
•• 0:26—Breasts and buns while making love in bed with Stacey and Hewitt.
•• 1:05—Breasts in flashbacks.

Secret Games 3 *(1994)*

(Unrated version reviewed.)

Jasaé . . . . Uncredited Lover
•• 0:21—Full frontal nudity, while making love in bed with a redhead woman.

May Karasun . . . . Gwen
••• 0:17—Left breast, then breasts and buns in G-string, while making love in room with Peter. Sometimes seen on monitor.

Tammy Parks. . . . . Uncredited Lover
• 0:21—Buns and partial breasts, while making love with a brunette woman on bed.

Brenda Swanson . . . . Ruthie

Rochelle Swanson . . . . Diana Larson
• 0:00—Breasts, while in bathtub.
•• 0:02—Breasts, while in bathtub, then making love with a fantasy guy.
•• 0:07—Breasts and buns, while making love with Terrell in daydream.
• 0:09—Brief buns in daydream.
••• 0:28—In white bra and panties, then breasts in room and on monitor while making love on bed with Jack.
•• 0:32—In white bra and panties, then breasts and buns, undressing and getting into bathtub.
••• 0:40—Breasts and buns in black panties in bedroom with Terrell.
•• 0:43—Buns, getting into bathtub. Breasts, while sitting in tub and getting out.
•• 0:50—Breasts, while making love on bed with Terrell.
• 0:56—Brief breasts on TV monitor while making love with Terrell.
••• 0:58—In white bra, then breasts and buns, while making love with Terrell in bed.
• 1:01—Brief breasts in bathtub while talking to her husband.
•• 1:03—Right breast, then breasts while making love in front of the fire with her husband.
• 1:27—Brief right breast, while in bathtub.

The Secret of My Success *(1987)*

Ashley Laurence. . . . . Fletcher

Helen Slater . . . . Christy

Margaret Whitton . . . . Vera Prescott
• 0:31—Very brief breasts taking off swimsuit top in swimming pool with Michael J. Fox.

Secret Places *(1984; British)*

Jenny Agutter . . . . .Miss Lowrie

Claudine Auger . . . . .Sophy Meister

Veronica Clifford . . . . Miss Mallard

Cassie Stuart . . . . Nina
• 0:07—Brief breasts, after pulling up her blouse to show off her breasts to her girlfriends.
• 1:15—Brief left breast, getting into bathtub with the help of her girlfriends. (She's drunk.)

The Secret Rapture *(1994; British)*

Juliet Stevenson . . . . Isobel Coleridge
••• 0:23—Full frontal nudity, taking off blouse and getting into bed with a guy.
•• 0:24—Breasts, while making love with him in bed.
•• 0:29—Brief side of right breast, when standing up with him, then breasts, while making love on desk.
•• 0:48—Left breast, then breasts, while in bed with him.
• 1:04—Brief right breast, while taking shower. Overhead view.
•• 1:07—Brief full frontal nudity, while walking to bed in flashback.
• 1:09—Brief breasts, while getting into bed in flashback.
1:24—Brief side of right breast, while washing herself off.

Secret Sins *(1992)*

Michelle McIntosh. . . . . Sara Jenson
• 0:29—Tip of right breast, sticking out of bubbles in bubble bath, then putting on bra in bedroom while wearing panties.
•• 0:43—Breasts, while making love with Johnny on sofa and in living room.

Taylor Wayne. . . . . Blonde Temptress
• 0:13—Right breast while in porno film.

Secrets *(1971)*

Jacqueline Bisset . . . . Jenny
• 0:49—Very brief lower frontal nudity, putting panties on while wearing a black dress.
••• 1:02—Brief buns and a lot of breasts on bed making love with Raoul.

Shirley Knight . . . . Beatrice

The Secrets of Love—Three Rakish Tales *(1986)*

Lucienne Bruinooge. . . . . Marietta
• 0:02—Buns, while getting spanking.
•• 0:27—Breasts, while lying in bed.

Olivia Brunaux. . . . . Célestine
• 1:03—Brief breasts and buns fantasizing.
••• 1:14—Breasts and buns in the greenhouse making love.
••• 1:18—Breasts while kneeling in the greenhouse and making love.

Tina Shaw . . . . The Weaver's Wife
••• 0:10—Breasts in bed with Luke.
••• 0:17—Breasts in the barn.

• *Secrets of Making Love... To the Same Person Forever* (1991; Video Tape)

Rachel Ryan. . . . . Blonde Girl/Boat
- ••• 0:04—Breasts in boat and on river bank with her lover.
- •• 0:47—Breasts in boat again.

Teri Weigel . . . . Mirror, Spa & Bed
- ••• 0:33—Breasts and buns in front of mirror, in spa and tied up in bed.
- • 0:48—Breasts and lower frontal nudity in spa and in bed.

Seduce Me: Pamela Principle 2 (1994)

India Allen. . . . . Elaine
- •• 0:19—Breasts when Charles opens her pajamas in bed to try to make love with her.
- ••• 0:27—Breasts and buns, while taking a shower.
- •• 1:13—Nude, walking outside and getting into spa, then in spa. Medium long shots.
- ••• 1:25—Nude, when making love with her lover in shower while Charles watches from outside.

Sara Bellomo. . . . . .Inger
- •• 0:33—Breasts, twice, while walking past Charles in house.
- • 0:50—Breasts, while sitting in spa. (She's on the left.)
- •• 1:01—Breasts, while making love (loudly) on bed when Charles passes by open door. Dark.

Shannon McLeod . . . . .Melinda
- • 0:50—Very brief breasts, while in spa.

Shauna O'Brien. . . . . Michelle
- ••• 0:15—Breasts and buns in G-string, after taking off lingerie for photo session.

Tonya Poole . . . . Eve
- ••• 0:58—Breasts, while posing during photo shoot in studio.

Cathleen Raymond . . . . Cindy
- • 0:03—Breast, while in background, changing clothes. Out of focus.
- ••• 0:04—Breasts and buns in G-string, after taking off lingerie during photo session. Long scene.

Elizabeth Sandifer . . . . Jill
- • 1:13—Buns and breasts, while walking to spa, then in spa. Medium long shot.

Alina Thompson . . . . Pamela
- ••• 0:23—Buns in sexy swimsuit, then breasts during photo session.
- • 0:33—Brief lower half of buns, while walking up stairs in short dress.
- ••• 0:35—Breasts and buns, opening towel, then getting dressed.
- ••• 0:37—Nude, changing clothes then posing for photos outside. Some in B&W. Long scene.
- •• 0:44—Buns in G-string and left breast while making love with Charles in kitchen.
- • 0:49—Brief right breast and buns in swimsuit bottom while getting out of spa.
- ••• 1:16—Breasts and buns, while making love in bed with Charles.

The Seducers (1970)

a.k.a. Sensation
a.k.a. Top Sensation

Edwige Fenech . . . . .Ulla
- • 0:10—Very brief side of right breast, after Tony pulls her top down.
- • 0:11—Brief buns, under towel while walking in hallway.
- ••• 0:13—Breasts, after taking off her top and rubbing suntan lotion on Paula.
- • 0:22—Brief left breast, after opening her robe to let a goat lick her while Aldo takes pictures.
- •• 1:10—Breasts, while on boat deck with Andrew.
- •• 1:12—Breasts, a couple of more times with Andrew.

Rosalba Neri . . . . .Paula
- •• 0:06—Breasts, under lots of necklaces, in cabin with Mudy. Partial buns in panties.
- ••• 0:12—Buns, while sunbathing on boat, then brief left breast.
- •• 0:13—Right breast with Ulla on boat deck.
- • 0:35—Brief buns, pulling down her swimsuit bottom to show off her tan.
- • 0:54—Brief breasts, while on boat deck with Andrew.
- • 1:05—Upper half of buns, when Andrew pulls her swimsuit down.

The Seduction (1982)

Colleen Camp . . . . Robin

Morgan Fairchild . . . . Jamie
- • 0:02—Brief breasts under water, swimming in pool.
- • 0:05—Very brief left breast, getting out of the pool to answer the telephone.
- •• 0:51—Breasts pinning her hair up for her bath, then brief left breast in bathtub covered with bubbles.
- • 1:21—Breasts getting into bed. Kind of dark, hard to see anything.

Cathryn Hartt . . . . Teleprompter Girl

Seduction of Innocence (1994)

T.J. Myers . . . . .Tammy
- • 1:06—Buns in panties and bra in front of mirror.

Danielle Petty . . . . .Star
- •• 0:15—Breasts, while dancing with a customer.
- • 0:16—Breasts, while in office.

Angela Wright. . . . . .Gretchen

See No Evil, Hear No Evil (1989)

Joan Severance . . . . Eve
- •• 1:08—Breasts in and leaning out of the shower while Gene Wilder tries to get her bag.

Senior Week (1987)

Vicki Darnell . . . . Everett's Dream Teacher
- •• 0:03—Breasts during classroom fantasy.

Miriam Zucker. . . . . Princeton Dream Girl
- •• 0:42—Breasts during dream.

Seniors (1978)

Priscilla Barnes. . . . . Sylvia
- •• 0:18—Breasts at the top of the stairs while Arnold climbs up the stairs while the rest of the guys watch.

Sensation (1994)

Claire Stansfield. . . . . .Paula
- ••• 1:03—In black bra, panties, garter belt and stockings, then buns and breasts, while making love on sofa with Eric Roberts.

Kari Wührer. . . . . Lila Reed
- • 0:01—Brief buns in G-string while getting out of bed. Long shot.
- • 0:23—Breasts under overalls while painting in her studio.
- •• 0:33—Brief breasts, quite a few times on cafeteria table with Eric Roberts in her vision. Lit with blue light.
- •• 0:39—Breasts and buns, after taking off robe and putting on slip. Kind of dark.
- ••• 0:41—Breasts and buns in T-back, while dancing in her living room at night.

- • 0:53—Brief breasts and buns in the shower and getting out. Seen from above.
- •• 0:55—Right breast, while in bed with Roberts when she imagines Carrie is her.
- ••• 1:08—Full frontal nudity, while making love in bed with Roberts.
- •• 1:14—Breasts, while on bed, making love with Roberts, when she imagines him strangling her.
- • 1:32—Very brief partial right breast while in bed with Roberts.

Sensations *(1988)*

Jennifer Delora . . . . Della Randall
- • 0:11—Brief breasts talking to Jenny to wake her up.
- • 0:13—Brief breasts a couple of times in open robe.
- •• 0:38—Breasts making love with a guy on bed.

Jane Hamilton . . . . Tippy
Rebecca Lynn . . . . Jenny Hunter
- • 0:11—Breasts, sleeping on couch.
- •• 0:23—Breasts talking on the telephone.
- •• 1:09—Breasts making love in bed with Brian.

Karen Nielsen . . . . Scared Woman
Jacqueline Palmer . . . . Tess
Denise Torek . . . . Phone Girl #2
- • 0:23—Breasts talking on the phone sex line.

Miriam Zucker. . . . . Cookie Woman
- • 0:06—Breasts on couch making love with a guy while Jenny and Brian watch.

The Sensuous Nurse *(1975; Italian)*

Ursula Andress. . . . . Anna
- •• 0:16—Breasts and buns in bed after making love with Benito.
- •• 0:22—Nude swimming in pool while Adonais watches.
- ••• 0:50—Nude slowly stripping and getting in bed with Adonais.
- ••• 1:10—Nude getting into bed.

Luciana Paluzzi . . . . Jole Carpa
- •• 0:20—Breasts in room, ripping off her clothes and reluctantly making love with Benito.

Carla Romanelli . . . . Tosca
- •• 0:06—Breasts, then nude standing in the winery, then running around.
- •• 0:41—Nude, in basement, playing army, then making love with bearded guy.

A Sensuous Summer *(1991)*

Lori Jo Hendrix . . . . Dream Girl/Beach
- ••• 0:16—Nude on beach with dark haired girl in Jinx's dream.
- •• 0:24—Breasts while kneeling on one knee in Jinx's dream.
- •• 0:39—Breasts again while kneeling on one knee in Jinx's dream.

Gina Jourard . . . . .Tracy
- ••• 0:09—Breasts while making love in bed with Alex.

Brittany McCrena . . . . Jill
- •• 0:00—Breasts while making love in bed with Bobby in flashback.
- •• 0:11—Breasts while making love with Bobby in flashback. Buns in swimsuit.
- ••• 0:59—In black bra then breasts while making love with Bobby.

The Sentinel *(1977)*

Beverly D'Angelo. . . . . Sandra
- • 0:33—Brief breasts playing cymbals during Raines' nightmare (in B&W).
- • 1:24—Brief breasts long shot with zombie make-up, munching on a dead Chris Sarandon.

Sylvia Miles . . . . Gerde
- • 0:33—Brief left breast, three times, standing behind Beverly D'Angelo. Right breast, while ripping dress off Christina Raines. B&W dream.
- • 1:23—Brief breasts, three times, with D'Angelo made up to look like zombies, munching on a dead Chris Sarandon.
- • 1:27—Very brief right breast during big zombie scene.
- • 1:28—Brief breasts when the zombies start dying.

Cristina Raines. . . . . Alison Parker
- • 0:18—Briefly in sheer beige bra, putting her blouse on.
- • 0:33—Very, very brief left breast immediately after Sylvia Miles rips her dress off. B&W dream sequence.

Separate Lives *(1995)*

Linda Hamilton . . . . Lauren Porter/Lena
- •• 1:14—Brief right breast, when Jim Belushi kisses her breast on kitchen table.

Separate Vacations *(1985; Canadian)*

Susan Almgren . . . . Helene Gilbert
- •• 1:05—Breasts and buns in G-string before getting into bed and then in bed with David Naughton.
- • 1:07—Breasts and buns in bed, then in bathroom with Naughton.

Nancy Cser . . . . Stewardess
Jennifer Dale . . . . Sarah Moore
- • 0:17—Brief right breast in bed with her husband after son accidentally comes into their bedroom.
- •• 1:14—Breasts on bed with Jeff after having a fight with her husband.
- • 1:19—Brief right breast, in bed with her husband.

Blanca Guerra . . . . Alicia
- • 0:56—Breasts on the bed with David Naughton when she turns out to be a hooker.

Laura Henry. . . . . Nancy
Sherry Miller . . . . Sandy

Separate Ways *(1979)*

Karen Black . . . . Valentine Colby
- • 0:04—Breasts and in panties changing while her husband talks on the phone, then in bra. Long shot.
- •• 0:18—Breasts in bed, while making love with Tony Lo Bianco.
- •• 0:36—Breasts taking a shower, then getting out.

Pamela Bryant . . . . .Cocktail Waitress
Sybil Danning . . . . Mary

Serial *(1980)*

Sally Kellerman . . . . Martha
- ••• 0:03—Breasts sitting on the floor with a guy.

Patch Mackenzie . . . . Stella
- • 0:59—Brief breasts in mirror in swinger's club with Martin Mull.

Stacey Nelkin. . . . . Marlene
Robin Sherwood . . . . Woman

The Serpent and the Rainbow *(1988)*

Cathy Tyson . . . . Dr. Marielle Duchamp
- • 0:41—Brief breasts making love with Dennis. Probably a body double, don't see her face.

Dey Young . . . . Mrs. Cassedy

The Serpent of Death *(1989)*

Camilla More. . . . . Rene
- •• 0:15—Brief breasts in bed with Jeff Fahey.

•• 1:22—Brief left breast while in bed, then breasts and buns, getting out of bed (in mirror).

Serpico *(1973)*

Cornelia Sharpe. . . . . .Leslie
•• 0:41—Breasts in bathtub with Al Pacino.

• *Set It Off* *(1996)*

Tamara Clatterbuck. Luther's Girlfriend
• 1:20—Brief breasts, while making love with Luther in bed.
Vivica A. Fox . . . . Frankie
Samantha MacLachlan . . . . Ursula
• 0:53—Buns and brief side view of left breast in swimsuit while dancing in front of Queen Latifah.
Jada Pinkett. . . . . Stony

The Set-Up *(1995; Made for Cable Movie)*

Margaret Avery . . . . .Olivia Dubois
Mia Sara . . . . Gina Sands
• 0:23—Brief breasts, several times, while making love in bed with Billy Zane.
• 1:10—Breasts, while making love in office with James Russo. Quick cuts.

Seven *(1979)*

Susan Lynn Kiger. . . . . Jennie
••• 0:58—Breasts, while sitting on bed, then getting up and walking around in the kitchen, making coffee, then putting her swimsuit top on.
• 1:15—Brief breasts, while taking off swimsuit top to change outside by car.
Barbara Leigh . . . . .Alexa
0:17—Briefly in braless, semi-sheer yellow blouse.

The Seventh Sign *(1988)*

Demi Moore . . . . Abby Quinn
• 1:03—Brief breasts, taking off bathrobe to take a bath. Her pregnant belly is not real—it's a full body prosthetic. Brief breasts when sitting in bathtub.
• 1:04—Brief tip of left breast, while sitting in bathtub and rubbing her belly.

A Severed Head *(1971; British)*

Claire Bloom . . . . .Honor Klein
• 1:10—Breasts, while leaning up, then right breast while sitting up in bed with Richard Attenborough.
Jennie Linden . . . . Georgie Hands
• 0:02—Buns, while rolling over on the floor with Ian Holm.

• *Sex and the Other Man* *(1996)*

Kari Wührer. . . . . .Jessica
• 0:27—Breasts, while making love with Ron Eldard in bed when Stanley Tucci is forced to watch.
••• 0:50—Full frontal nudity and side view of buns, while making love with Eldard again when Tucci has to watch.

Sex and the Single Alien *(1993)*

Annastasia Alexander . . . . Roxana
••• 0:09—Breasts and buns in string lingerie, while dancing on stage.
•• 0:25—Breasts, while dancing on stage.
Skye Blue . . . . Ruth
•• 0:45—Breasts and buns, while dancing on stage with Merry.
•• 1:08—Breasts in white lingerie while dancing on stage again with Merry.
Diana Cuevas . . . . Merry
•• 0:45—Breasts and buns, while dancing on stage with Ruth.
•• 1:08—Breasts in black lingerie while dancing on stage again with Ruth.
Michelle Hess . . . . Meg
•• 0:04—Buns in sexy outfit, while walking to Olivia's house and talking with her.
Monique Parent. . . . . .Jennifer
Deanne Power . . . . .Rachel
••• 0:00—Breasts and buns in G-string, while dancing on stage during opening credits.
•• 0:12—Breasts, while dancing on stage in black panties.
• 1:13—Breasts, while dancing on stage.
Mihaella Stoicov . . . . .Thousand Ways
••• 0:19—Breasts and buns in T-back, dancing while wearing a mask.
• 0:23—Brief buns in T-back, while talking backstage with Sam.
••• 1:10—Breasts and buns, while dancing on stage, wearing a mask.
• 1:25—Brief breasts and buns, while dancing on stage, wearing a mask.

The Sex and Violence Family Hour *(1983; Canadian)*

Toni Alessandrini . . . . Body Flash Dancer
•• 1:05—Buns in one piece leotard, while dancing in a studio. Nude after taking it off to put on a robe.
Cheryl Baker . . . . Body Flash Dancer
•• 1:16—Nude after taking off one piece swimsuit during interview.
Kim Morris . . . . Body Flash Dancer
••• 0:57—Breasts, buns in T-back and lower frontal nudity, while dancing in a studio and on couch in interview.
Jewel Shepard . . . . Body Flash Dancer
••• 1:09—Buns and partial lower frontal nudity in T-back, breasts under short black top, while dancing in studio. Nude during interview.

Sex Appeal *(1986)*

Tally Chanel . . . . .Corinne
• 1:22—Brief breasts at the door of Tony's apartment when he opens the door while fantasizing about her.
Samantha Fox . . . . Sheila
••• 1:14—In black lingerie, then breasts and buns in black G-string with Rhonda. Long scene.
Jane Hamilton . . . . Monica
••• 0:58—Breasts dancing on the bed with Tony in his apartment. Long scene.
Kim Kafkaloff . . . . Stephanie
•• 0:29—Buns, in G-string in Tony's bachelor pad. Breasts dancing and on bed.
Marcia Karr . . . . .Christina
• 1:12—Brief left breast, then in bra and panties on bed with her boyfriend.
Taija Rae . . . . .Rhonda
•• 1:14—In black lingerie, then breasts in black push-up teddy with Sheila.
Suzanne Vale. . . . . Audrey
•• 0:00—Breasts, while on the couch making out with Tony.

Sex Crimes *(1991)*

Kirsten Ashley . . . . Dancer
Grace Morley. . . . . .Cynthia
• 0:13—Buns in swimsuit in club. Very, very brief left breast, while taking off her swimsuit top in dressing room.

- 0:36—Buns in G-string and red pasties while dancing in club. More in dressing room.

Maria Richwine . . . . Rosanna
- 0:09—Very brief tip of right breast, while sitting in bathtub, covered with bruises and cuts after getting raped.
- 1:19—Brief breast in mirror, while taking a shower.

Sex Crimes *(1992)*

Millicent Sheridan . . . . Demon Lover
- •• 0:23—Buns, then breasts, while making love with J.J. in his nightmare. (She's wearing deformed face make-up.)
- • 0:32—Breasts, while in bed with J.J.—ugly make-up still on.

Deborah Stevens . . . . Hooker

Sex on the Run *(1979; German/French/Italian)*

a.k.a. Some Like It Cool
a.k.a. Casanova and Co.

Jeannie Bell . . . . Slave Girl
- ••• 0:01—Breasts, reading book in large bath with Marisa Berenson.
- ••• 0:24—Breasts, giving Berenson a back massage.

Marisa Berenson . . . . The Caliph's Wife

Britt Ekland . . . . Countess Trivulsi
- • 0:44—Left breast while making love in bed with Tony Curtis (don't see her face).

Andrea Ferréol . . . . Beatrice

Sylva Koscina . . . . Jelsamina
- ••• 0:28—Breasts and brief buns dropping her top for Tony Curtis, then walking around with the "other" Tony Curtis.
- •• 1:20—Breasts talking to her husband.

Marisa Mell . . . . Francesca
- • 0:52—Very, very brief left breast, while getting out of bed with Tony Curtis.

Lillian Müller . . . . Angela
- ••• 0:15—Second woman (blonde) to take off her clothes with the other two women, nude. Long scene.

Olivia Pascal . . . . Convent Girl
- ••• 0:15—First woman (brunette) to take off her clothes with the other two women, full frontal nudity. Long scene.

Carla Romanelli . . . . Dice Girl
- •• 0:58—Breasts and buns with two other women, losing their clothes during dice game.

Sex Through a Window *(1977)*

Jackie Giroux . . . . Barbie

Cheryl King . . . . Nurse
- • 0:19—In bra and panties, under sheer white pantyhose, then breasts after taking off bra, while John watches her through a telephoto lens.

Kate Woodville . . . . Sally Norman
- •• 0:29—Left breast, after sitting up in bed after John sits up, then brief breasts while turning over in bed.
- ••• 1:15—Breasts, while making love in bed and after with John.

Sex with a Smile *(1976; Italian)*

Barbara Bouchet . . . . "One for the Money" segment
- ••• 0:50—Breasts sitting up in bed with a guy in bed, then lying down, wearing glasses.

Edwige Fenech . . . . Dream Girl
- •• 0:03—Breasts tied to bed with two holes cut in her red dress top.
- • 0:09—Buns, in jail cell in court when the guy pulls her panties down with his sword.
- •• 0:13—Brief breasts in bed with Dracula taking off her top and hugging him.
- • 0:16—Breasts in bathtub. Long shot.

Dayle Haddon . . . . The Girl
- •• 0:23—Breasts, covered with bubbles in the bathtub.
- • 0:43—Buns, taking off robe to take a shower, then brief breasts with Marty Feldman.

Sydne Rome . . . . "A Dog's Day" segment

Sexpot *(1986)*

Ruth Corrine Collins. . . . . Ivy Barrington
- •• 0:09—Breasts on table, taking her dress off for Phillip.
- • 0:41—Buns, in Damon's arms.
- •• 0:51—Left breast, while in shower talking to Boopsie.

Jennifer Delora. . . . . Barbara
- ••• 0:28—In bra, then breasts with her two sisters when their bras pop off. (She's in the middle.)
- •• 0:36—Breasts on bed with Gorilla.
- • 1:32—Breasts during outtakes of 0:28 scene.

Jane Hamilton . . . . Beth
- ••• 0:28—In bra, then breasts with her two sisters when their bras pop off. (She's on the right.)
- • 1:32—Breasts during outtakes of 0:28 scene.

Christina Veronica . . . . Betty
- ••• 0:28—In bra, then breasts with her two sisters when their bras pop off. (She's on the left.)
- •• 0:46—Breasts taking off her top in boat with Gorilla.
- • 0:54—Breasts lying on the grass with Gorilla.
- • 1:28—Breasts during outtakes of 0:28 scene.

Sexual Intent *(1994)*

Michele Brin . . . . Barbara Hayden
- • 0:28—Breasts, on balcony after John talks to her on cellular phone. Long shot.
- • 0:47—Breasts during fantasy with John while she's watching video tape of an interview.
- ••• 0:49—In bra and panties, then breasts and buns while making love with John in her office.
- •• 0:54—Breasts, while sitting in bathtub.

Vanessa Ann Giorgio . . . . Chris
- •• 0:32—In black bra, then breasts, while in bedroom with John.

Sexual Malice *(1993)*

(Unrated version reviewed.)

Diana Barton . . . . Christine
- • 0:13—Brief buns in panties, taking off robe and getting into bed.
- ••• 0:32—Breasts in shower, then nude getting out and putting on a robe.
- •• 0:33—Left breast in open robe, looking at herself in the mirror.
- ••• 0:36—Breasts and buns in hotel room when takes her robe off and makes love with her in bed.
- •• 0:42—Breasts while making love in surf under pier at the beach.
- ••• 0:48—In white bra, panties and stockings, then buns and breasts while making love.
- •• 0:55—Breasts and buns while making love in dressing room of clothing store.
- ••• 1:04—Breasts, while in bed with a black girl while Quinn takes photos.
- • 1:13—Breasts, while in spa with Edward Albert.

Sam Phillips . . . . Nicole
- ••• 1:30—Brief buns in raised skirt, then breasts, while making love with Edward Albert on sofa.

Kathy Shower . . . . .Laura Altman
••• 0:10—Breasts, while making love on pool table with a guy when Christine peeks in room.

Sexual Outlaws *(1993)*

Kim Dawson . . . . Jeannie
••• 0:05—Breasts and buns in panties, then nude while changing lingerie, then posing on bed.
••• 0:07—Breasts and buns, while posing on bed.
••• 0:09—Breasts, while in bed with Rita.
Nicole Grey . . . . Rita
••• 0:09—Breasts, after taking off her top with Jeannie, then making love in hotel room.
Monique Parent . . . . Uncredited Annie
••• 0:31—In green bra, while sitting on bed and posing for John, then breasts while making love with him.
Jennifer Peace . . . . Betty
••• 0:10—Breasts, in lingerie and after taking it off with Frank while acting for a video.
••• 0:13—Breasts with Frank and Harriet for video.
Elizabeth Sandifer . . . . Lisa Bauer
• 0:39—Partial buns in G-string in bedroom.
••• 0:41—Breasts, after taking off bra and posing for John for ad. Also putting on stockings.
• 0:46—Upper half of breasts while in bathtub.
••• 0:47—In black lingerie, then breasts, while posing for photos.
•• 1:25—Breasts while making love with Mitch Gaylord.

Sexual Response *(1992)*

(Unrated version reviewed.)
Shannon Tweed . . . . Eve
••• 0:25—Breasts in studio with Edge, while he checks her out.
••• 0:29—Breasts, making love with him. Long scene.
••• 0:31—Full frontal nudity, lying in bed, then sitting up.
••• 0:43—Breasts, while making love in her house with Edge.
•• 0:51—Breasts in pool at night with Edge.
•• 0:52—Full frontal nudity, getting up out of bed and putting robe on.
•• 0:55—Breasts in study with Edge.
••• 1:07—Breasts and buns, while taking a shower. Nude, getting out and drying herself off.

• ***Sexual Roulette*** *(1996)*

(Unrated version reviewed.)
Ashley Bates . . . . Nikki
•• 0:09—Breasts and buns in T-back, while dancing on stage, then coming to talk at the bar.
Gabriella Hall. . . . . Sally Wills
•• 0:03—Full frontal nudity, while making love with her husband in the shower.
••• 0:15—In bra, then nude, while making love with her husband at home.
••• 0:29—Nude, while making love with her husband in hotel bathroom and bedroom.
•• 1:17—Breasts and buns, while making love with the other guy in bed.
Tané McClure . . . . .Sherry Landis
••• 0:26—Nude, while making love with Jed in several locations.
••• 0:45—Breasts, while making love with Jed in her suite.
• 0:50—Brief breasts, while sitting up in bed with Jed.
• 1:07—Breasts, while sitting in bed with Jed.
•• 1:08—Breasts and buns, while making love with Jed in bed.
Stacy Warfel . . . . Laura
••• 1:01—Partial buns under short skirt, then breasts, while making love with Jed in suite, while Tané McClure watches.
• 1:07—Full frontal nudity, while sitting in bed and after getting out.

Shadow of the Wolf *(1992)*

Jennifer Tilly. . . . . Iglyook
• 0:21—Very brief right breast under Lou Diamond Phillips.
• 0:22—Very, very brief left breast when Phillips is on top of her and holds her arms down.
•• 1:27—Very brief breasts, after taking off her clothes, then making love with Phillips.

Shadow Play *(1986)*

Cloris Leachman . . . . Millie Crown
Dee Wallace Stone. . . . . Morgan Hanna
• 1:06—Brief breasts making love with Ron Kuhlman. Kind of dark and hard to see.

ShadowHunter *(1992)*

Beth Broderick. . . . . .Bobby Cain
Gloria Reuben . . . . Cayla
• 0:07—Buns, lifting up her skirt to tempt Scott Glenn. Don't see her face and slightly out of focus.

Shadows Run Black *(1981)*

Terry Congie . . . . Lee Faulkner
•• 0:22—Breasts, going for a swim in pool at night.
• 0:23—Breasts under water.
Barbara Peckinpaugh. . . . . Sandy
••• 0:57—Full frontal nudity, undressing in bedroom.
•• 0:58—Buns and very, very brief breasts getting into the shower.
••• 0:59—Full frontal nudity, drying herself off. Nude, walking around the house. Long scene.
•• 1:01—Nude, in the bathroom, trying to avoid the killer.

Shadowzone *(1989)*

Maureen Flaherty . . . . Jenna
•• 0:13—Breasts, while lying under plastic cover.
• 0:18—Breasts, while lying on table during operation.
•• 1:11—Breasts again under plastic cover several times.
•• 1:17—Brief breasts again, then full frontal nudity.
• 1:24—Breasts, after reviving under the plastic cover.
Shawn Weatherly . . . . Dr. Kidwell

Shaft *(1971)*

Margaret Warncke. . . . . Linda
• 1:04—Very brief breasts while getting into the shower with Richard Roundtree.

Shaft in Africa *(1973)*

Neda Arneric . . . . Jazar
•• 1:19—Buns and breasts, after taking off dress in cabin on boat with Richard Roundtree.
•• 1:20—Very brief lower frontal nudity, then buns and breasts when Roundtree brings her into the bathroom.
•• 1:21—Breasts and buns, in bed with Roundtree.
• 1:23—Brief partial right breast, lying in bed. Buns and partial breasts, sitting up.

• ***Shalako*** *(1968; British)*

Brigitte Bardot. . . . . Countess Irini Lazaar
• 1:38—Brief partial back side of right breast, when Sean Connery catches her washing herself.

Shallow Grave *(1994; British)*
Kerry Fox. . . . . Juliet Miller
•• 0:10—Brief breasts, getting her mail from Ewan McGregor.

• **Shameless** *(1994; British)*
Claire Bloom . . . . .Liz
Louise Delamere . . . . Sandy
•• 0:25—Breasts, after Tony pulls her dress down while standing in front of open window.
• 1:32—Very brief right breast, in B&W movie.
Elizabeth Hurley . . . . .Antonia Dyer
••• 0:35—Breasts, while making love with C. Thomas Howell in bed.

The Shaming *(1979)*
a.k.a. Good Luck, Miss Wyckoff
a.k.a. The Sin
Anne Heywood . . . . Evelyn Wyckoff
••• 0:49—Right breast, then breasts in open blouse after being raped by Rafe in her classroom.
• 0:52—Breasts, while making love with Rafe on classroom floor.

Shampoo *(1975)*
Julie Christie . . . . Jackie
Lee Grant . . . . Felicia
• 0:03—Brief breasts in bed sitting up and putting bra on talking to Warren Beatty. Long shot, hard to see.
Goldie Hawn . . . . Jill
Sharon Kelly . . . . Painted Lady
• 1:17—Brief breasts covered with tattoos all over her body during party. Lit with strobe light.
Susan McIver. . . . . Customer

Sharky's Machine *(1981)*
Sue Francis Pai. . . . . Siakwan
Rachel Ward . . . . .Dominoe
Aarika Wells. . . . . .Tiffany
• 0:52—Brief side view breasts (mostly silhouette) in Rachel Ward's apartment.

Shattered *(1991)*
Greta Scacchi . . . . Judith Merrick
•• 0:14—Breasts, turning over in bed.
• 0:16—Breasts in a strip of B&W photos that Tom Berenger looks at.
• 0:36—Breasts in B&W photos in Bob Hoskins' office. Brief breasts in flashback.
•• 1:24—Breasts during love-making flashback.

Shattered Image *(1993)*
Bo Derek . . . . Helen
• 1:12—Breasts, under water in spa, while talking with Jack Scalia.

She *(1983)*
Sandahl Bergman . . . . She
•• 0:22—Breasts getting into a pool of water to clean her wounds after sword fight.

She'll be Wearing Pink Pyjamas *(1985; British)*
Maureen O'Brien. . . . . Joan
• 0:46—Brief breasts making love in bed with Tom. Dark.
Alyson Spiro . . . . .Anita
•• 0:07—Nude talking to Julie Walters in the shower.
•• 0:58—Nude, undressing and going skinny dipping in mountain lake with Julie Walters, then getting out. Nice buns shot while walking into the lake.
Julie Walters. . . . . Fran
••• 0:07—Full frontal nudity taking a shower with the other women. Long scene.
•• 0:58—Nude, undressing and going skinny dipping in mountain lake, then getting out. Nice bun shot walking into the lake.
Jane Wood. . . . . Jude
• 0:07—Nude, shaving her legs in the women's shower room.

She's Gotta Have It *(1987)*
Tracy Camilla Johns . . . . .Nola Darling
••• 0:05—Breasts, making love in bed with Jamie.
•• 0:25—Brief left breast taking off leotard with Greer. More breasts waiting for him to undress.
•• 0:27—Breasts and buns in bed with Greer.
• 0:38—Breasts, close up of breast, while making love with Spike Lee.
•• 0:41—Left breast, while lying in bed with Lee.
•• 1:05—Breasts, twice, in bed masturbating.
Joie Lee . . . . Clorinda Bradford

Sheba, Baby *(1975)*
Pam Grier . . . . Sheba Shayne
• 0:26—Side view of left breast, while lying in bed with Brick.

Sheena *(1984)*
Nancy Paul . . . . Betsy Ames
Tanya Roberts . . . . Sheena
•• 0:18—Breasts and buns taking a shower under a waterfall. Full frontal nudity (long shot), diving into the water.
••• 0:54—Nude taking a bath in a pond while Ted Wass watches.

• **Shelter** *(1997)*
Brenda Bakke. . . . . Helena
• 0:25—Brief upper half of right breast in bloody, open blouse in car.
• 1:02—Brief breasts, several times, while making love with Martin.
Anna Karin. . . . . Rana

The Sheltering Sky *(1990)*
Amina Annabi . . . . Mahrnia
•• 0:20—Left breast, then breasts in tent with John Malkovich.
•• 0:22—Right breast while lying down with Malkovich, breasts when he gets up.
Debra Winger . . . . Kit Moresby
• 0:13—Upper half of lower frontal nudity in open robe when John Malkovich caresses her stomach.
• 0:24—Buns, when getting out of bed.
• 0:41—Very brief breasts grabbing sheets and getting out of bed with Tunner.
• 1:58—Lower frontal nudity and sort of buns, while getting undressed with Belqassim.

• **Shine** *(1996; Australian)*
Lynn Redgrave. . . . . .Gillian
• 1:36—Brief left breasts (dark) while lying under Geoffrey Rush in bed.

The Shining (1980)

Lia Beldam . . . . Young Woman in Bath
••• 1:12—Full frontal nudity getting out of bathtub while Jack Nicholson watches.
Shelley Duvall . . . . Wendy Torrance

Shining Through (1992)

Melanie Griffith . . . . .Linda Voss
•• 0:22—Breasts, making love in bed on top of Michael Douglas.
Lisa Orgolini . . . . Girl in Canteen
Joely Richardson . . . . .Margrete von Eberstien

Shirley Valentine (1989; British)

Pauline Collins. . . . . Shirley Valentine
• 0:13—Brief left breast, while giving Joe a shampoo in the bathtub.
•• 1:17—Brief breasts, while jumping from the boat into the water. Very brief breasts in the water.
•• 1:19—Buns, while hugging Tom Conti (possible body double—don't see her face). Left breast several times, while lying on deck, kissing Conti.
Joanna Lumley . . . . Marjorie

Shock 'Em Dead (1990)

Suzanne Ager . . . . Groupie 3
Kathleen Kane. . . . . Pizza Girl 2
Traci Lords . . . . .Lindsay Roberts
Jackie Moen . . . . Groupie 4
•• 1:05—Breasts, taking off her top to tempt Martin.
Karen Russell. . . . . Michelle
•• 0:16—In lingerie, then breasts twice with Martin.
Laurel Wiley . . . . .Monique
• 0:26—Brief breasts, pulling her top down to show Martin her scar. Don't see her face.

• *Shoot Out* (1971)

Rita Gam. . . . . Emma
• 0:13—Brief right breast, when sitting up in bed with Gregory Peck. Seen through bed post.
Susan Tyrrell . . . . Alma
• 0:13—Right breast, while in bed with Bobby Jay.

Short Cuts (1993)

Anne Archer . . . . Claire Kane
• 1:49—(0:6 into Part 2) Very brief side view of buns, while hiking up nightgown and sitting on edge of tub.
Jennifer Jason Leigh. . . . . .Lois Kaiser
Frances McDormand. . . . . Betty Weathers
• 0:46—Very brief left breast and partial lower frontal nudity, while walking past doorway. Brief left breast and lower frontal nudity, while peeking around doorway and wrapping a towel around herself.
Julianne Moore . . . . Marian Wyman
••• 2:22—(0:39 into Part 2) Buns and lower frontal nudity in top part of outfit, after having to take off the skirt to clean it. Long scene.
Annie Ross. . . . . .Tess Trainer
Lori Singer. . . . . Zoe Trainer
•• 0:48—Nude, stripping out of her clothes, then jumping in pool and floating. Seen through a fence.
Madeleine Stowe . . . . .Sherri Shepard
•• 1:20—Left breast, while posing for painting by Julianne Moore.
• 2:07—(0:24 into Part 2) Brief left breast, while turning over in bed.

Lili Taylor. . . . . Honey Bush

The Shout (1979; British)

Carol Drinkwater . . . . Wife
Susannah York. . . . . Rachel Fielding
•• 0:53—Brief breasts changing from a bathrobe to a blouse in bedroom.
• 1:02—Briefly nude, in upstairs room getting ready to make love with Alan Bates.
• 1:05—Brief buns, standing at end of hallway.
• 1:11—Breasts in bathtub with John Hurt.
• 1:18—Brief breasts getting up from bed with Bates. Long shot, hard to see anything.

Showdown in Little Tokyo (1991)

Renee Ammann. . . . . Angel
•• 0:15—In black bra. Breasts in lingerie and stockings (mostly right breast) just before getting killed.
• 0:34—Right breast, on TV during playback of her execution.
Tia Carrere . . . . .Minako
Tera Tabrizi . . . . Pool Girl
• 0:13—Brief breasts, walking into pool during party.

Showgirl Murders (1995)

Maria Ford. . . . . Jessica Cross
•• 0:01—Breasts and buns in T-back while dancing on stage.
••• 0:13—Buns and breasts in T-back while dancing on stage.
•• 0:21—Buns in T-back, while wearing a black wig, doing strip routine on stage.
•• 0:31—Buns in T-back and breasts under sheer top, then breasts while dancing on stage.
•• 0:37—Breasts and buns while wearing a S&M outfit and dancing on stage.
••• 0:47—In silver outfit, then breasts and buns in T-back, dancing on stage with Nikki Fritz. Dribbling hot wax on Fritz.
•• 0:50—Breasts while making love with Mitch in the kitchen.
•• 0:55—Breasts and buns in T-back on stage, pouring liquid on herself while writhing around in one of those large cup props.
• 1:03—Very brief partial left breast, while making love with Mitch.
•• 1:05—Breasts and buns in T-back, while dancing on stage in bridal outfit.
•• 1:07—Breasts and buns in T-back, covered with fluorescent paint, while dancing on stage with another woman and a man.
• 1:16—Brief breasts in flashbacks.
•• 1:19—Breasts, while dancing on stage.
Nikki Fritz . . . . Dancer
••• 0:47—In green outfit, then breasts and buns, while dancing on stage with Maria Ford. Then getting hot wax dribbled on her by Ford.

Showgirls (1995)

(NC-17 version reviewed.)
Elizabeth Berkley . . . . Nomi Malone
••• 0:23—Breasts and buns in T-back, while doing strip routine on stage at Cheetah's.
••• 0:25—Breasts and buns in T-back backstage.
••• 0:28—Breasts and buns in T-back, then nude when doing lap dance for Kyle MacLachlan while Gina Gershon watches.
•• 0:35—Nude, while dancing on stage with Penny.
• 0:36—Breasts, while walking and talking to Phil.

- ••• 0:40—Breasts after taking off her bra during audition and afterward while talking with Gershon.
- ••• 0:47—Breasts, while dancing with James in his house.
- ••• 1:00—Breasts and buns in T-back, during dance number on stage.
- •• 1:01—Breasts and buns in G-string, while walking down the stairs backstage.
- •• 1:10—Breasts when Gershon pulls her top off and kisses her.
- ••• 1:11—Breasts and buns in G-string, while backstage behind Nicky, sitting at make-up table.
- ••• 1:24—Nude, after taking off dress and going for a swim in MacLachlan's pool, then making love with him. Nice!!
- • 1:26—Brief buns, while getting dressed.
- • 1:29—Buns in G-string during audition.
- ••• 1:38—Breasts in leather outfit and buns in G-string while dancing on stage.
- •• 1:40—Breasts, while running down the stairs.
- ••• 1:43—Breasts and buns in G-string, while dancing on stage.
- •• 1:56—Breasts after taking off her top with Carver, then beating him up.

Lisa Boyle . . . . Sonny
Ungela Brockman . . . . Annie
- • 0:09—Brief breasts in dressing room, when Gay passes by.
- • 1:17—Buns, while getting dressed backstage.

Bethany Chesser . . . . Finalist Dancer
- ••• 0:40—Breasts while dancing during final audition with Elizabeth Berkley and another dancer.

Maria Diaz. . . . . Yoga Dancer
- ••• 0:40—Breasts while dancing during final audition with Elizabeth Berkley and another dancer.

Annie Gaybis. . . . . .Uncredited Cheetahs Dancer
Gina Gershon . . . . Cristal
- • 0:09—Brief buns in G-string in her dressing room.
- ••• 0:10—Breasts and buns in G-string, while dancing on stage.
- ••• 0:13—Breasts, while undressing and taking off her make-up in dressing room.
- • 0:59—Brief breasts backstage with Kyle MacLachlan.
- ••• 1:00—Breasts and buns in T-back, during dance number on stage.
- • 1:01—Breasts and buns in G-string, while walking down the stairs backstage.
- • 1:18—Breasts, while dancing on stage in sheer bodysuit.
- ••• 1:39—Breasts and buns in G-string while dancing on stage.
- • 1:40—Brief breasts, while running down the stairs.

Caroline Key Johnson . . . . Nadia
Michelle Johnston . . . . Gay
Kristen Knittle . . . . Al Torres' Girl
Mason Marconi. . . . . .Uncredited Cheetahs Dancer
- • 0:25—Breasts and buns on stage when camera pans across the room. (She's the dancer closest to the camera.)

Danté McCarthy . . . . Carmi
- •• 0:19—Breasts and buns in T-back, when asking Elizabeth Berkley if her breasts look bigger.

Bobbie Phillips. . . . . Dee
- •• 0:19—Breasts, while standing behind Carmi and holding a snake.
- • 0:31—Breasts under sheer purple bodysuit backstage after Elizabeth Berkley's lap dance.
- • 0:49—Breasts and buns in G-string, while sitting down (wearing sunglasses), then standing up.

Gina Ravera . . . . Molly Abrams
- • 1:50—Brief buns, while getting raped by Carver and his goons.

Rena Riffel . . . . Penny
- • 0:24—Nude on stage.
- • 0:26—Breasts and buns in G-string, after taking off robe and stepping onto stage.
- • 0:27—Breasts and buns in G-string as Elizabeth Berkley walks into the lap dance room.
- •• 0:35—Nude, while on stage dancing with Berkley.
- • 0:51—Brief buns (long shot) at James' place when seen by Berkley. Very brief partial left breast under robe, then breasts when James caresses her.

Melinda Songer. . . . . Nicky
- • 1:11—Breasts, while standing in front of Elizabeth Berkley backstage.
- • 1:13—Breasts, while sitting at make-up table, talking with Berkley.
- • 1:29—Buns in G-string during audition.
- • 1:40—Brief breasts, while running down the stairs.

Judette Warren . . . . Spelling Dancer
Melissa Williams. . . . . Julie
- • 1:11—Brief breasts, while sitting at her make-up table backstage. Brief buns in T-back when she carries her daughter away.
- • 1:40—Brief breasts, while running down the stairs.

The Sicilian *(1987)*

(Director's uncut version reviewed.)

Barbara Sukowa. . . . . Camilia Duchess of Crotone
- •• 0:05—Buns and brief breasts taking a bath, three times.
- • 0:07—Brief right breast reading Time magazine. Full frontal nudity in the mirror standing up in the tub.
- • 0:08—Brief right breast standing at the window watching Christopher Lambert steal a horse.
- ••• 1:01—In bra, then breasts in bedroom with Lambert. More breasts, then nude. Long scene.

Sid and Nancy *(1986; British)*

Courtney Love. . . . . Gretchen
Patti Tippo. . . . . .Tanned and Sultry Blonde
Chloe Webb . . . . .Nancy
- • 0:21—Left breast, under Sid's arm in bed with him. Covered up, hard to see.
- •• 0:44—Breasts in bed after making love, then arguing with Sid.

Side Out *(1990)*

Hope Marie Carlton. . . . . .Vanna
Harley Jane Kozak . . . . Kate Jacobs
- • 0:53—Brief left breast, then out of focus left breast, while in bed with Peter Horton.

Side Roads *(1988)*

Ingrid Vold . . . . Bonnie Velasco
- • 0:29—Brief breasts in motel room, getting undressed and carried into bed by Joe.
- • 1:45—Brief breasts in mirror, getting out of bed.

Siesta *(1987)*

Ellen Barkin . . . . Diane
- ••• 0:03—Brief full frontal nudity long shot taking off red dress, breasts, brief buns standing up, then full frontal nudity lying down.

- 1:22—Right nipple sticking out of dress while imagining she's with Gabriel Byrne instead of the reality of getting raped by taxi driver.
- 1:23—Brief lower frontal nudity, very brief silhouette of a breast, then brief buns some more while with Byrne. Dark, hard to see.
- 1:24—Lower frontal nudity, with torn dress while lying in bed after the taxi driver gets up.
- 1:26—Very brief lower frontal nudity, while running down road and her dress flies up as police cars pass by.
- 1:28—Very brief side view of right breast putting on dress in bed just before Isabella Rossellini comes into the bedroom to attack her. Long distance shot.

Jodie Foster . . . . Nancy
Grace Jones . . . . Conchita
Isabella Rossellini . . . . Marie
Anastassia Stakis . . . . Desdra

Sign of the Cross (1932)

Claudette Colbert . . . . Poppaea
- 0:19—Very, very brief upper half of breasts, several times, while in milk bath.
- 0:21—Very, very brief upper half of areola on left breast when telling Dacia to get in milk bath.

Silence Like Glass (1989)

Kathleen Doyle . . . . Mrs. Jacoby
Jami Gertz . . . . Eva March
- 1:31—Very brief left breast, during defibrillation on operating table. Possible body double. The Doctor's arm covers her face.

Dayle Haddon . . . . Darlene Meyers
Martha Plimpton . . . . Claudia Jacoby

The Silencer (1992)

Lynette Walden . . . . Angel
- ••• 0:09—Breasts and buns, taking off clothes and getting into bathtub with her boyfriend.
- •• 0:10—More breasts, while making love with him in the bathtub.

• *Silent Hunter* (1995)

Lynne Adams . . . . Anna
- 1:03—Very brief left breast, while pulling up her blouse to taunt Miles O'Keeffe.

Silent Madness (1984)

Elizabeth Kaitan . . . . Barbara
Belinda Montgomery . . . . Joan Gillmore
April Daisy White . . . . Susan
- 0:06—Breasts, while changing tops at back of van.

Silent Night, Deadly Night (1984)

Tara Buckman . . . . Mother (Ellie)
- 0:12—Brief right breast twice when the killer dressed as Santa Claus, rips her blouse open. Breasts lying dead with slit throat.
- 0:18—Very, very brief breasts during Billy's flashback.
- 0:43—Brief breasts a couple of times again in another of Billy's flashbacks.

Toni Nero . . . . Pamela
- 0:30—Brief right breast twice just before Billy gets stabbed during fantasy scene.
- 0:42—Breasts in stock room when Andy attacks her.
- 0:44—Breasts while in stock room struggling with Billy, then getting killed by him.

Linnea Quigley . . . . Denise
- ••• 0:52—Breasts while on pool table with Tommy, then putting on shorts and walking around the house. More breasts, while impaled on antlers.

Silent Night, Deadly Night 4: Initiation (1990)

Maud Adams . . . . Fima
Marjean Holden . . . . Jane
Neith Hunter . . . . Kim
- 0:03—Brief breasts several times in bed with Hank.
- 0:47—Brief breasts during occult ceremony when a worm comes out of her mouth.
- 1:05—Right breast, while lying on floor. Long shot.
- 1:06—Breasts, covered with gunk, when transforming into a worm.
- 1:07—Very brief side of right breast, while sitting up.

Silent Night, Deadly Night III: Better Watch Out! (1989)

Laura Harring . . . . Jerri
- ••• 0:48—Breasts, while in bathtub with her boyfriend, Chris.

Silent Night, Deadly Night, Part 2 (1986)

Tara Buckman . . . . Mother
- 0:09—Very brief right breast, with Santa Claus during flashback.
- 0:14—Very brief breasts on ground during flashback.
- 0:22—Very, very brief blurry breasts during flashback.
- 0:47—Very, very brief breasts during flashback.

Elizabeth Kaitan . . . . Jennifer
- 0:58—Most of right breast, then buns, while kissing Ricky.

Toni Nero . . . . Pamela
- •• 0:22—Breasts in back of toy store in flashback from *Silent Night, Deadly Night*.

Linnea Quigley . . . . Denise
- ••• 0:26—Breasts on pool table and getting dressed flashback from *Silent Night, Deadly Night*.

The Silent Partner (1978)

Gail Dahms . . . . Louise
- 0:31—Right breast in bathroom with another guy when Elliott Gould surprises them.

Céline Lomez . . . . Elaine
- 1:05—Side view of left breast, then breasts, then buns with Elliott Gould.

Susannah York . . . . Julie
- 0:38—Very brief right breast pulling her dress back up with Elliott Gould.

Silent Rage (1982)

Toni Kalem . . . . Alison Halman
- •• 0:22—Side view of left breast, then breasts, while in bed with Chuck Norris.
- •• 0:46—Right breast, while lying in bed with Norris.

Silent Scream (1980)

Rebecca Balding . . . . Scotty Parker
- 0:50—Brief right breast while making love in bed with Jack.

Silk 2 (1989)

Monique Gabrielle . . . . Jenny "Silk" Sleighton
- ••• 0:27—Breasts, then full frontal nudity taking a shower while killer stalks around outside.
- 0:28—Very, very brief blurry right breast in open robe when she's on the sofa during fight.
- 0:29—Brief breasts doing a round house kick on the bad guy. Right breast several times during the fight.

••• 0:55—Breasts taking off her blouse and making love on bed. Too much diffusion!

Silk Degrees *(1994)*

India Allen . . . . Sheila
•• 0:02—Breasts, while making love in bed with Degrillo.

Katherine Armstrong . . . . Nicole
• 1:05—Very, very brief breast, when in water, while killing Mark Hamill.

Adrienne Barbeau . . . . Violet

Angela Melini . . . . Bonnie

Deborah Shelton . . . . Alex Ramsey
• 0:49—Full frontal nudity behind plastic shower curtain.
•• 0:56—Breasts, while making love with Marc Singer in cabin.

Silk n' Sabotage *(1994)*

Stephanie Champlin . . . . Lynn
•• 0:00—Breasts, while taking a shower.
• 0:01—Brief breasts after taking off towel in bedroom.
••• 0:03—Nude, while making love on sofa with Toby.
••• 0:05—In bra, then breasts, while trying on lingerie in bedroom.
• 0:06—Buns in black lingerie outfit.
•• 0:12—Breasts, while making love with Toby.
•• 0:16—Breasts, while looking at herself in bathroom mirror.
• 0:23—Buns in blue T-back swimsuit while at the beach with the other two girls.
••• 0:29—Brief buns in white T-back, when undressing in bedroom and rubbing lotion on her legs. Breasts and buns, while getting dressed and posing in front of mirror.

Nicole Grey . . . . Jerri
• 0:07—Buns, while in lingerie during lingerie sales party.

Aline Kassman . . . . Tracy
• 0:53—In a black teddy, then breasts with Michael on boat.

Julie Kruis . . . . Jamie
• 0:33—Brief breasts and buns in B&W dream with Michael.
• 0:38—Breasts, while changing clothes in bathroom.
• 0:45—Brief breasts, while in the pool with Michael.
••• 0:46—Buns in swimsuit bottom, then breasts and lower frontal nudity while making love in bedroom with Michael.
•• 0:54—Breasts, while in the shower.
•• 1:07—Breasts, while making love in bedroom with Robert.

Gloria Pryor . . . . TV Interviewer

Cherilyn Shea . . . . Dagny
•• 0:02—Breasts, while making love in bed with Tyler.
•• 0:03—Breasts, while making love some more.
••• 0:12—Breasts, while making love in bed with Tyler.

Silkwood *(1984)*

E. Katherine Kerr . . . . Gilda Schultz

Meryl Streep . . . . Karen Silkwood
• 0:24—Very brief glimpse of upper half of left breast when she flashes it in nuclear reactor office.

The Silver Strand *(1995; Made for Cable Movie)*

Helen Jones . . . . Rose Guttierez

Nicollette Sheridan . . . . Michelle Hughes
• 0:44—Very, very brief side of right breast, while in bunker with Del Piso. Partial buns when he takes off her panties.
• 0:49—Brief buns and breasts, while swimming under water in pool with Del Piso. (Mostly seen in silhouette.)

Simply Irresistible *(1983)*

(R-rated version. *Irresistible* is the X-rated version.)

Nicole Black . . . . Mata Hari
•• 1:14—Full frontal nudity, while tied to a chair.

Samantha Fox . . . . Arlene Brooks
• 1:20—In see-through white nightgown, then brief peeks at right breast when nightgown gapes open.

Gina Gianetti . . . . Sunshine
•• 0:49—Breasts in motel room with Walter and Juliet.

Dorothy LeMay . . . . Hitchhiker
••• 0:09—Nude in office with Walter.

Gayle Sterling . . . . Juliet
•• 0:40—Breasts and buns in bed with Walter.

Sincerely Charlotte *(1986; French)*

Caroline Faro . . . . Irene the Baby Sitter

Isabelle Huppert . . . . Charlotte
• 0:20—Brief breasts while in bathtub. Long shot, out of focus.
• 1:07—Very brief left breast, while changing into red dress in the back seat of the car.
•• 1:15—Breasts in bed with Mathieu. Kind of dark.

Tina Sportolaro . . . . n.a.

Sinful Intrigue *(1995)*

Griffin Drew . . . . Cindy
••• 0:20—Breasts and buns in office, while making love with Adam.
•• 0:39—Breasts, while making love with Chona Jason and Adam.

Casey Gray . . . . Dancer #2
• 0:47—Brief breasts, while walking by swimming pool (medium long shot), then breasts, when massaging another woman (closer shot).

Chona Jason . . . . Mei-Ling
• 0:21—Buns and breasts (she's on the right), while in bathtub with Bianca Rocilili.
•• 0:39—Breasts, while making love with Adam and Griffin Drew.
• 0:47—Brief breasts (she's on the far left), while sipping a margarita in the backyard. Medium long shot, then closer shot.

Kristen Knittle . . . . Jake's Wife
•• 0:06—Breasts, while making love with Jake in his flashback.

Cory Lane . . . . Denise
•• 0:57—Breasts and buns, while in shower.

Kristina Mateyko . . . . Girl #1

Kathleen Mazzotta . . . . Girl #3
• 0:47—Brief breasts (she's the redhead), while sipping a margarita in the backyard. Medium long shot, then closer shot.

Lorissa McComas . . . . Jean

Beckie Mullen . . . . Steph
• 0:02—Breasts, after getting her T-shirt ripped off in kitchen by Adam. Dark.
••• 0:03—Brief buns seen through open back of shirt, then breasts, while taking a bath.
••• 0:27—In white bra, then breasts and buns in T-back, in bedroom and bathroom with Adam. Long scene
•• 0:29—Breasts in black leather and chain outfit, while standing in bathroom, looking at herself in the mirror.
••• 0:30—Breasts, when making love in bed on top of Adam while wearing the outfit.
• 0:45—Side view of left breast and buns in T-back, taking off robe and putting on a bra.
•• 0:52—Breasts, after taking off her robe in front of Jake

••• 1:03—In white bra, then breasts, while tied by her wrists to the bed.

Pia Reyes . . . . Yvette

• 0:18—Breasts, quite a few times, under sheer body suit while talking with Beckie Mullen.

Bianca Rocilili . . . . Hispanic Girl

• 0:21—Brief buns and breasts (she's on the left) while in bathtub.

• 0:38—Breasts, while sitting in bathtub.

Vanessa Taylor . . . . Laurie

•• 0:11—Breasts, while making out with Mr. Dorsey on his lap in his office.

Sharon Turner. . . . . Gorgeous Girl

• 0:37—Brief breasts in mirror, while applying lip gloss on another girl's lips. Buns in black T-back and breasts, while walking to, then sitting on the edge of bathtub.

Heather Ward . . . . Rebecca

• *Single Alien Seeks Horny Earth Girl* *(1995; Video Tape)*

Lisa Comshaw. . . . . Traci

•• 0:00—Nude in small window.

••• 0:03—Nude, while undressing and taking a shower.

• 0:10—Brief full frontal nudity in open robe.

••• 0:26—Breasts, while starting to make love with Zing, then putting her bra back on.

••• 0:34—Nude, after taking off lingerie and making love with Zing in bedroom.

••• 0:38—Breasts, while lying in bed with her wrists tied to the bed, making love with Zing.

Single White Female *(1992)*

Christina Capetillo. . . . . Exotic Applicant

Bridget Fonda . . . . .Allie

• 0:04—Very, very brief right breast, while getting out of bed with Sam. Very brief side view of right breast, then buns, while walking to turn off answering machine.

• 0:05—Brief breasts, grabbing her clothes.

• 0:34—Buns and brief breasts, getting out of bed. Dark.

• 1:18—Brief right breast, in gaping nightgown while kneeling on bathroom floor after throwing up in the toilet.

• 1:20—Brief silhouette of left breast, while changing clothes.

Jennifer Jason Leigh. . . . . .Hedy Carlson

••• 0:18—Breasts, changing clothes in her room in front of Bridget Fonda.

• 0:29—Upper half of breasts, while in bathtub.

•• 0:37—Breasts, masturbating in bed while Fonda peeks in bedroom.

••• 1:04—Breasts in the shower, then full frontal nudity, getting out.

•• 1:09—Breasts, getting into bed with Sam.

• 1:10—Breasts, while in bed with Sam.

Sins of Desire *(1992)*

(Unrated version reviewed.)

Gail Harris . . . . Monica Waldman

• 0:00—Breasts in quick clips, while making love with Scott during nightmare.

Becky LeBeau . . . . Sandy

••• 0:23—Nude, stripping and dancing (she's the blonde on the left) with Clarise in front of Mr. O'Connor. Long scene.

Monique Parent . . . . .Clarise

••• 0:23—Nude, stripping and dancing (she's the redhead on the right) with Sandy in front of Mr. O'Connor. Long scene.

Tanya Roberts . . . . .Kay Egan

• 0:50—Buns, while in panties in bed with Barry.

••• 0:51—Nude, while making love in bed with Barry. Long scene.

• 1:06—Breasts under patterned black body suit with Jessica.

• 1:10—Brief left breast, under body suit.

Pamela Runo . . . . .Rachel

••• 0:12—Right breast while in bubble bath, covered with bubbles, then rinsed off. Breasts and buns, getting out and walking down hall.

Delia Sheppard . . . . Jessica Callister

••• 0:10—Full frontal nudity, while tied by her wrists in bed with Scott.

••• 0:45—Breasts and buns, while making love on the floor with Scott. Nice close-ups.

Carrie Stevens . . . . Pam

Roberta Vasquez . . . . Motel Girl

Sins of the Night *(1993)*

(Unrated version reviewed.)

Lee Anne Beaman . . . . Sue Ellen

•• 0:46—In black bra and G-string panties under sheer robe while drunk in her house, then breasts.

Michele Brin . . . . Laura Winters

• 0:05—In black bra and panties in her house with her lover. Brief buns in G-string while Jack takes photos.

••• 0:06—Breasts, while making love with her lover. Long scene.

•• 0:14—Breasts and buns, getting out of bed.

Michelle Moffett . . . . Kay

••• 0:20—In black bra, then breasts and lower frontal nudity while making love in bed with Jack. Long scene.

•• 0:22—Breasts and very brief buns, getting out of bed.

Deborah Shelton . . . . .Roxanne Flowers

••• 0:48—Breasts, while making love with Jack. Some nice close-ups! Great, long scene.

•• 0:58—Breasts during Jack's recollections.

••• 1:03—Breasts and buns, while making love with Jack. Long scene.

Courtney Taylor. . . . . Danielle

• 1:20—In black bra and panties, then breasts in room with Deborah Shelton and Miles O'Keeffe. Medium long shot. Side of right breast in closer shot.

Sirens *(1994; Australian)*

Portia de Rossi . . . . Giddy

•• 1:15—Full frontal nudity while posing for painting.

•• 1:24—Breasts while in pond with Elle Macpherson and Pru in Estelle's fantasy.

• 1:30—Brief full frontal nudity on rock formation. Medium long shot. She's the first from the left.

Tara Fitzgerald. . . . . Estella Campion

• 0:19—Brief breasts, while changing behind divider.

•• 1:00—Brief breasts, while running outside. Brief full frontal nudity in church during daydream.

• 1:11—Right breast and brief lower frontal nudity in studio with Devlin.

• 1:30—Brief full frontal nudity on rock formation. Medium long shot. She's the fifth from the left.

Elle Macpherson . . . . .Sheela

•• 0:25—Breasts and buns, while in pond with Pru.

••• 0:26—Breasts, while in pond with Pru talking to Devlin.

•• 0:30—Full frontal nudity, while posing.

•• 0:45—Buns and right breast, then breasts while posing.

•• 1:15—Breasts and partial lower frontal nudity while posing for painting.

••• 1:24—Breasts, in pond with Pru and Giddy during Estella's fantasy.
• 1:30—Brief full frontal nudity on rock formation. Medium long shot. She's the fourth from the left.

Pamela Rabe . . . . Rose Lindsay
•• 0:52—Nude, undressing to pose for Sam Neill.
• 1:15—Breasts, while posing for painting.
• 1:30—Brief full frontal nudity on rock formation. Medium long shot. She's the third from the left.

Sister Sister *(1987)*

Jennifer Jason Leigh . . . . Lucy Bonnard
•• 0:01—Breasts making love during a dream.
•• 0:53—Left breast, while making love with Stoltz in her bedroom.
• 0:58—Breasts in bathtub surrounded by candles.

The Sister-In-Law *(1974)*

Meridith Baer . . . . Deborah Holt
• 0:58—Breasts, while lying down on the ground in the woods to make love with John Savage.
• 1:00—Left breast, while kissing John Savage.

Sisters *(1973)*

Margot Kidder . . . . Danielle Breton
• 0:11—Very brief left breast, undressing while walking down hallway. Long shot.
• 0:14—Breasts opening her robe on couch for her new boyfriend. Shadows make it hard to see.

Jennifer Salt . . . . Grace Collier

Sitting Ducks *(1978)*

Patrice Townsend . . . . Jenny
••• 0:55—Breasts, taking off her blouse in room with Sid.
•• 0:58—Buns and brief left breast, sitting up in bed with Simon after getting seen by Leona.

Skeeter *(1994)*

Tracy Griffith . . . . Sarah
• 0:59—Brief breasts, while sitting on bed with Boone after making love. Medium long shot.

Saxon Trainor . . . . Dr. Jill Wylde

Sketch Artist *(1992; Made for Cable Movie)*

Belle Avery . . . . Krista
• 1:11—Right breast, while making love with Paul by swimming pool. Long shot, don't see her face very well.

Drew Barrymore . . . . Daisy
Stacy Haiduk . . . . Claire
Charlotte Lewis . . . . Leese
••• 0:02—Breasts, while making love on sofa. Buns in G-string, side of right breast, while changing CD. (Does this woman have the most awesome waist-to-chest ratio or what?)

Sean Young . . . . Rayanne
•• 0:52—Right breast, several times while making love in bed with Fahey.

Ski School *(1990)*

Ava Fabian . . . . Victoria
••• 0:53—In white bra and panties, then breasts making love with Johnny.

Charlie Spradling . . . . Paulette
Darlene Vogel . . . . Lori
• 1:03—Breasts in bed with Johnny.

Ski School 2 *(1994)*

Wendy Hamilton . . . . Lois Schnitzelbank
••• 0:23—Buns and breasts, when wearing ski boots, while doing a painting of a geeky guy out in the snow.
•• 0:55—Breasts while outside, doing a painting.
••• 0:56—In purple bra and panties, then breasts and buns, while making love with Alex.

Skin Art *(1993)*

Ariane . . . . Lin
• 1:00—Left breast when Will pulls her lingerie top down and kisses her.

Skin Deep *(1989)*

Diana Barton . . . . Helena
Denise Crosby . . . . Angie Smith
Chelsea Field . . . . Amy
Raye Hollitt . . . . Lonnie
• 0:26—Brief side view breasts and buns getting undressed and into bed with John Ritter.

Heidi Paine . . . . Tina
• 0:01—Brief side view breasts sitting on John Ritter's lap while Denise Crosby watches.

Brenda Swanson . . . . Emily

Skyscraper *(1996)*

Deirdre Imershein . . . . Natasha
Anna Nicole Smith . . . . Carrie Wink
•• 0:10—Breasts and buns, while taking a shower.
••• 0:11—Breasts, while making love in bed with her husband.
••• 0:52—Breasts in open dress top, while making love with her husband outdoors.
•• 1:15—Breasts, while getting raped in office by bad guy.

Slam Dance *(1987; U.S./British)*

Virginia Madsen . . . . Yolanda Caldwell
Mary Elizabeth Mastrantonio . . . . Helen Drood
Lisa Niemi . . . . Ms. Schell
••• 0:54—Nude in Tom Hulce's apartment.
• 1:00—Breasts, dead, lying on the floor in Hulce's apartment.

Millie Perkins . . . . Bobbie Nye

Slammer Girls *(1987)*

Beth Broderick . . . . Abigail
Sharon Cain . . . . Rita
• 0:23—Brief breasts changing clothes under table in the prison cafeteria.
•• 1:01—Breasts walking around an electric chair trying to distract a prison guard.

Tally Chanel . . . . Candy Treat
• 0:56—Buns, in G-string, doing a dance routine wearing feathery pasties for the Governor in the hospital.

Samantha Fox . . . . Mosquito
•• 0:17—Breasts in the shower hassling Melody with Tank.

Jane Hamilton . . . . Miss Crabapples
Devon Jenkin . . . . Melody Campbell
• 0:12—Brief breasts getting lingerie ripped off by the prison matron.
• 0:16—Brief breasts getting blouse ripped off by Tank in the shower.

Kim Kafkaloff . . . . Ginny
• 0:23—Brief breasts changing clothes under table in the prison cafeteria.

Sharon Kelly . . . . Professor
- • 0:23—Brief breasts, while changing clothes under table in the prison cafeteria.
- •• 0:34—Breasts, while squishing them against the window during prison visiting hours.
- •• 0:36—Breasts with an inflatable male doll.

Adriane Lee . . . . Dead Convict
Maria Machart . . . . Hooker
- •• 0:06—Breasts, getting fondled by a cop.

Darcy Nychols . . . . Tank
- • 0:17—Breasts ripping blouse open while hassling Melody.

Slap Shot (1977)

Lindsay Crouse . . . . Lily Braden
Melinda Dillon . . . . Suzanne
- ••• 0:30—Right breast, lying in bed with Paul Newman, then breasts sitting up and talking. Nice, long scene.

Jennifer Warren . . . . Francine Dunlop

The Slasher (1975)

Sylva Koscina . . . . Barbara
- •• 0:17—Left breast lying down getting a massage.
- •• 1:18—Breasts undressing and putting a robe on at her lover's house. Left breast after getting stabbed.

Slaughter (1972)

Marlene Clark . . . . Kim Walker
- • 0:11—Very brief buns and right breast, getting thrown out of room by Jim Brown.

Stella Stevens . . . . Ann
- •• 0:47—Left breast, several times in bed with Jim Brown.
- • 0:55—Left breast, making love in bed with Brown again. Dark.
- • 0:57—Brief right breast, in bed afterwards. Close up shot.
- ••• 1:14—Buns and breasts taking a shower and getting out. This is her best nude scene.

Slaughterhouse Five (1972)

Valerie Perrine . . . . Montana Wildhack
- • 0:39—Breasts in *Playboy* magazine as a Playmate.
- • 0:43—Breasts getting into the bathtub.
- ••• 1:27—Breasts in a dome with Michael Sacks.

Slaughterhouse Rock (1988)

Toni Basil . . . . Sammy Mitchell
Hope Marie Carlton . . . . Krista Halpern
- • 0:09—Brief right breast, taking off her top in bedroom with her boyfriend.
- •• 0:49—Breasts, getting raped by Richard as he turns into a monster.

Slave of Dreams (1995; Made for Cable Movie)

Sherilyn Fenn . . . . Zulaikha
- • 0:26—Almost buns, then brief left breast, while making love on the ground with Joseph in a dream.
- • 0:40—Brief buns, while standing before getting a bath.
- 1:31—Partial left breast, while breast feeding her baby.

Slave of the Cannibal God (1979; Italian)

Ursula Andress . . . . n.a.
- •• 0:33—Breasts taking off shirt and putting on a T-shirt.
- ••• 1:07—Nude getting tied to a pole by the Cannibal People and covered with red paint.
- • 1:20—Brief peek at buns under her skirt when running away from the Cannibal People.

Slavegirls from Beyond Infinity (1987)

Cindy Beal . . . . Tisa
- ••• 0:36—Breasts on beach wearing white panties.
- • 1:05—Left breast leaning back on table while getting attacked by Zed.

Elizabeth Kaitan . . . . Daria
- ••• 0:38—Breasts undressing and jumping into bed with Rik.

Brinke Stevens . . . . Shala
- • 0:29—Chained up wearing black lingerie. Brief right breast.
- • 0:31—Brief side view of left breast on table. Nice pan from her feet to her head while she's lying on her back.

Slavers (1977)

Britt Ekland . . . . Anna
- • 0:40—Breasts undressing in front of Ron Ely.

Slaves of New York (1989)

Madeleine Potter . . . . Daria
- • 1:14—Breasts making love with Stash on chair. Mostly see left breast. Dark.

Sleep With Me (1994)

Joey Lauren Adams . . . . Lauren
Vanessa Angel . . . . Marianne
Parker Posey . . . . Athena
- • 0:56—Breasts, after taking off her blouse while straddling Eric Stoltz on sofa.
- • 0:58—Brief breasts, while getting up off the floor after Stoltz changes his mind. Slightly out of focus.

Meg Tilly . . . . Sarah
Susan Traylor . . . . Deborah

Sleepaway Camp II: Unhappy Campers (1988)

Carol Chambers . . . . Brooke
Valerie Hartman . . . . Ally
- ••• 0:06—Breasts waking up and stretching in bed, then standing next to bathroom.
- • 0:33—Breasts in Polaroid photographs that Angela confiscates from the boys.
- ••• 0:39—In beige bra, then breasts in restroom stall with Rob.
- ••• 0:43—Breasts making love in the woods with Rob, then getting dressed. Nice!

Susan Marie Snyder . . . . Mare
- • 0:08—Brief breasts lifting up her T-shirt.
- • 0:24—Brief breasts flashing in boys' cabin.
- • 0:33—Breasts in Polaroid photograph that Angela confiscates from the boys.

Pamela Springsteen . . . . Angela

Sleepaway Camp III: Teenage Wasteland (1989)

Tracy Griffith . . . . Marcia Holland
Pamela Springsteen . . . . Angela Baker
Jill Terashita . . . . Arab
- •• 0:16—Breasts putting sweatshirt on.

The Sleeping Car (1990)

Judie Aronson . . . . Kim
- •• 0:42—Brief breasts on top of David Naughton making love. Brief breasts three times after he hallucinates.

Sandra Margot . . . . 19-Year Old Girl
- •• 0:00—Brief breasts shots taking off clothes then making love with a guy. Left breast while making love.

Dani Minnick . . . . Joanne

• ***Slipping into Darkness*** *(1988)*

Anastasia Fielding . . . . Genevieve
- 0:38—Brief breasts, after taking off her lingerie in graveyard with Otis.
- 0:43—Breasts, while lying dead on grave and being carried to another grave. Fairly long scene.

Michelle Johnson. . . . . Carlyle
Cristen Kauffman. . . . . Alex
- 0:39—Brief breasts, after T-bone rips her blouse open.

Sliver *(1993)*

Colleen Camp . . . . Judy Marks
Amanda Foreman . . . . Samantha Moore
Allison Mackie . . . . Naomi Singer
- 1:36—Brief buns, while making love on top of William Baldwin on video playback. B&W.

Sharon Stone. . . . . Carly Norris
- 0:14—Brief left breast, while in bathtub.
- 0:43—Buns, in black bra, while making love on William Baldwin's lap.
- 0:44—Half of right breast, while under Baldwin.
- •• 0:45—Brief left breast, while getting up out of bed. Side view breasts and buns, while getting dressed.
- •• 0:46—Buns and breasts, while taking off her top again.

Sloane *(1984)*

Debra Blee . . . . Cynthia Thursby
- 0:15—Very brief breasts during attempted rape.

Ann Milhench . . . . Janice Thursby
- •• 0:02—Breasts and buns getting out of shower and being held by kidnappers.

Slow Burn *(1986)*

Beverly D'Angelo. . . . . Laine Fleischer
- 1:01—Breasts making love with Eric Roberts. Don't see her face. Part of lower frontal nudity showing tattoo.

Slumber Party '57 *(1976)*

Mary Ann Appleseth . . . . Jo Ann
- •• 1:18—Left breast with movie star getting interviewed. Don't see her face. Breasts a couple of more times, but still don't see her face.

Bridget Holloman . . . . Bonnie May
- 0:10—Breasts with her five girl friends during swimming pool scene. Hard to tell who is who.
- 0:26—Left breast in truck with her cousin Cal.

Joyce Jillson . . . . Gladys
Janice Karman . . . . Hank
- •• 1:06—Breasts, sitting watching Smitty and David make love in the stable.

Noelle North . . . . Angie
- •• 0:37—Buns, then breasts in bed with a party guest of her parents.

Cheryl Smith . . . . Sherry
Debra Winger . . . . Debbie
- 0:10—Breasts with her five girl friends during swimming pool scene. Hard to tell who is who.
- ••• 0:53—Breasts three times, lying down, making out with Bud.

Janet Wood . . . . Smitty
- 0:10—Breasts with her five girl friends during swimming pool scene. Hard to tell who is who.
- •• 1:06—Left breast, then breasts in stable with David while his sister watches.

The Slumber Party Massacre *(1982)*

Debra De Liso . . . . Kim
- 0:08—Very brief breasts getting soap from Trish in the shower.
- •• 0:29—In beige bra and panties, then breasts putting on a U.S.A. shirt while changing with the other girls.

Gina Mari . . . . Diane
- 0:43—Close up of right breast while making out in car with Daryl. Don't see her face.

Michele Michaels. . . . . Trish
- •• 0:01—Breasts, in white panties, while getting dressed.
- •• 0:08—Buns, then brief breasts while passing the soap to Kim.
- •• 0:29—Breasts, in white panties, while putting shirt on while two boys watch from outside.

Brinke Stevens . . . . Linda
- •• 0:07—Buns, then breasts taking a shower during girls' locker room scene.

Slumber Party Massacre II *(1987)*

Juliette Cummins . . . . Sheila
- •• 0:24—In black bra, then breasts in living room during a party with her girlfriends.

Heidi Kozak . . . . Sally
Kimberly McArthur . . . . Amy

A Small Circle of Friends *(1980)*

Karen Allen . . . . Jessica
- 0:47—Brief breasts in bathroom with Brad Davis. Don't see her face.
- 0:48—Very brief breasts, pushing Davis off her. Then very, very brief half of left breast turning around to walk to the mirror.

Shelley Long . . . . Alice

Smash Palace *(1981; New Zealand)*

Anna-Maria Monticelli . . . . Jacqui Shaw
- 0:21—Silhouette of right breast changing while sitting on the edge of the bed.
- ••• 0:39—Breasts in bed after arguing, then making up with Bruno Lawrence.

Smile *(1974)*

Colleen Camp . . . . Connie Thompson
- 0:47—Side profile of right breast and buns in dressing room while Little Bob is outside taking pictures.

Melanie Griffith . . . . Karen Love
- 0:34—Very, very brief side view of right breast in dressing room, just before passing behind a rack of clothes.
- 0:47—Very brief side view of right breast, then side view of left breast when Little Bob is outside taking pictures.
- 0:48—Very brief breasts as Polaroid photograph that Little Bob took develops.
- 1:51—Breasts in the same Polaroid in the policeman's sun visor.

Annette O'Toole . . . . Doria Houston
Joan Prather. . . . . Robin
- 0:47—Brief buns in dressing room, while taking off pants while Little Bob is outside taking pictures. (She's wearing a pink ribbon in her hair.)

• ***Smilla's Sense of Snow*** *(1997)*

Julia Ormond. . . . . Smilla Jaspersen
- 1:06—Brief, partial buns, while lying on top of Gabriel Byrne.

Vanessa Redgrave . . . . Elsa Lübing

Smoke Screen (1988)

Kim Cattrall . . . . .Odessa Muldoon
- • 0:31—Brief half of right breast, while sitting in bed with sheet pulled up on her.
- •• 1:16—Breasts in bed on top of Gerald.
- ••• 1:17—Breasts lying in bed under Gerald while he kisses her breasts.

Smooth Talker (1990)

Suzanne Ager . . . . .Candy (The 976-GIRL)
- • 0:23—Left breast and partial buns, while lying on the floor dead.
- • 0:24—More left breast, while lying dead on the floor. Lit with red light.
- • 0:35—Left breast, while lying dead on the floor. Very brief buns in G-string.

Julie Austin . . . . .Ms. Weston

Blair Weickgenant . . . . .Lisa Charles
- • 0:33—Breasts, lying in bed and sitting up during Carl's B&W fantasy.

SnakeEater (1988)

Josie Bell . . . . The Kid
- • 0:39—Very brief side view of right breast and buns, when walking past open doorway while Lorenzo Lamas watches. Medium long shot.

Mowava Pryor . . . . Chloe
- ••• 0:07—In bra and panties, then breasts and buns, while undressing in room with Lorenzo Lamas to prove each other is not a cop.
- • 0:10—Breasts, while lying down, then getting up.

SnakeEater III ...His Law (1992)

Holly Chester . . . . Fran
- ••• 0:30—Breasts and buns in G-string while dancing on stage in club.

Tracy Cook . . . . Hildy Gardener
- ••• 0:27—Breasts, while making love with Lorenzo Lamas in bedroom.

Snapdragon (1993)

Chelsea Field . . . . .Peckham

Pamela Lee . . . . .Felicity
- • 0:06—Brief side view of right breast, while making love on top of a guy in bed before killing him.
- • 0:26—Right breast, while making love on top of another guy in bed before killing him.
- ••• 0:55—Breasts and buns, while making love in bed on top of Steven Bauer in his dream.
- • 1:06—In white bra and panties, then left breast and buns while making love on top of Bauer on the floor.
- ••• 1:22—Breasts and buns, while making love with Bauer.

Diana Lee-Hsu . . . . Professor Huan

Society (1989)

Devin De Vasquez . . . . .Clarisa
- ••• 0:37—Breasts, making love in bed with Billy.
- • 0:40—Left breast, while on sofa with Billy when her mother comes home.

Heidi Kozak . . . . Shauna

Caroline Lomas . . . . Extra

• Soft Bodies (1988; Video Tape)

Becky LeBeau . . . . .Herself
- ••• 0:01—In two piece swimsuit, then breasts in swimming pool.
- •• 0:08—On bed during photo session in various lingerie, then breasts and buns in G-string.
- ••• 0:16—In bra and panties, then breasts on bed.

• Soft Bodies Invitational (1990; Video Tape)

Becky LeBeau . . . . Herself
- • 0:00—Buns, under short skirt playing tennis with Julia Parton.
- ••• 0:15—Breasts while posing with Parton in photo session.
- •• 0:24—In two piece swimsuit, then breasts while arguing with Parton about who has better breasts.
- ••• 0:38—In red bra and panties outside on bridge, then breasts.
- ••• 0:44—Breasts and buns in G-string in spa.

Julia Parton . . . . Nina Alexander
- • 0:00—Buns, under short skirt, playing tennis with Becky LeBeau.
- ••• 0:03—In lingerie during photo session, then breasts and buns in G-string. Long scene.
- ••• 0:15—Breasts posing with LeBeau.
- ••• 0:18—Outside in dress, then undressing to two piece swimsuit, then breasts. Long scene.
- •• 0:24—In two piece swimsuit, then breasts arguing with LeBeau about who has better breasts.
- ••• 0:28—In two piece swimsuit, then breasts by the pool.

• Soft Bodies: All American Girls (1997; Video Tape)

Becky LeBeau . . . . Herself
- •• 0:01—Breasts, while frolicking outside with Candace.
- ••• 0:39—In bra and panties, when nude, while posing on bed.
- ••• 0:43—In schoolgirl outfit, then nude, while posing outdoors.
- ••• 0:48—In bra and panties, then nude, while posing indoors.
- ••• 0:52—In swimsuit, then nude, while posing outdoors in the pool.

Kira Reed . . . . Herself
- ••• 0:02—In lingerie, then nude, while posing indoors on sofa.
- ••• 0:06—In dress, then nude, while posing outdoors.
- ••• 0:10—In lingerie, then nude, while posing indoors.

• Soft Bodies: Beyond Blonde (1995; Video Tape)

Heather Kennedy . . . . Herself
- ••• 0:15—Buns in sheer lingerie outfit, then nude on stairs.
- ••• 0:23—In dress, then nude, while outside in garden.
- •• 0:29—In skimpy outfit, then breasts, during pillow fight in bed with Becky LeBeau.
- ••• 0:30—Buns in two piece swimsuit, then nude while posing on and around chair next to pool.

Becky LeBeau . . . . Herself
- •• 0:01—Breasts and buns in swimsuit, while playing tetherball in pool with Rachel Love.
- •• 0:11—Breasts, while posing in pool with Love.
- •• 0:29—In skimpy outfit, then breasts, during pillow fight in bed with Heather Kennedy.
- ••• 0:37—In lingerie, then nude, while posing on bed.
- ••• 0:44—In two piece swimsuit, then nude in pool.
- ••• 0:49—In white lingerie, then nude on chair inside.

Rachel Love . . . . Herself
- •• 0:01—Breasts and buns in swimsuit, while playing tetherball in pool with Becky LeBeau.
- ••• 0:02—In bra and panties, then nude while posing in chair.
- ••• 0:09—In two piece swimsuit, then nude by and in pool with LeBeau.
- ••• 0:13—In robe, then full frontal nudity in the shower.

• *Soft Bodies: Curves Ahead* (1991; Video Tape)

Becky LeBeau . . . . Herself

- • 0:00—Buns in G-string, while playing Frisbee with Kylie Rose.
- ••• 0:32—Breasts in pool with Tamara. Buns and partial lower frontal nudity. Long scene.
- ••• 0:36—Breasts while posing for photographs in various outfits.
- ••• 0:41—On balcony in two piece swimsuit, then breasts and buns taking an outdoor shower. Long scene.
- ••• 0:45—Breasts and buns in G-string, posing on bed for photo session in various lingerie. Long scene.
- ••• 0:51—In two piece swimsuit outside at night in spa. Breasts and buns in G-string. Long scene.

Tamara Lee . . . . Herself

- ••• 0:23—In lingerie on chair, then breasts during photo session. Brief lower frontal nudity under sheer lingerie. Long scene.
- ••• 0:31—In chair by pool. Breasts and partial lower frontal nudity.

• *Soft Bodies: Double Exposure* (1994; Video Tape)

Danni Ashe . . . . Herself

- ••• 0:02—In blue bra and panties, then nude, on sofa.
- ••• 0:10—In sheer white lingerie, then nude outside.
- ••• 0:14—In blue two piece swimsuit, then nude in spa.

Becky LeBeau . . . . Herself

- •• 0:27—Breasts and buns in panties, while rehearsing with Julia Parton outside.
- ••• 0:38—In lingerie, then nude, while posing on bed.
- ••• 0:46—In two piece swimsuit, then nude, while posing in spa.
- ••• 0:52—In two piece outfit, then full frontal nudity, while posing on swinging chair outside.

Julia Parton . . . . Herself

- ••• 0:18—In purple lingerie, then nude on sofa.
- •• 0:27—Breasts and buns in panties, while rehearsing with Becky LeBeau outside.
- ••• 0:28—In dress, then nude, while posing on chair outside.
- ••• 0:33—In lingerie, then nude, while posing on chair inside.

• *Soft Bodies: Party Favors* (1992; Video Tape)

Antonia Dorian . . . . Herself

- ••• 0:03—In black bra and panties in bed, then breasts and buns during photo session.
- ••• 0:08—Breasts, while on hammock outside.
- ••• 0:11—In white lace dress in living room by piano. Breasts and buns in G-string.
- ••• 0:18—Breasts and buns outside by pool with Becky LeBeau.

Julia Hayes . . . . Herself

- ••• 0:22—Buns in sheer nightie, while posing on bed, then breasts during photo session.
- ••• 0:29—In bra and panties on couch, then breasts and buns.
- ••• 0:35—Breasts and buns, on floating bed in pool with Becky LeBeau.

Becky LeBeau . . . . Herself

- ••• 0:35—Breasts and buns, on floating bed in pool with Julia Hayes.
- ••• 0:39—Breasts and buns posing in bed in various lingerie outfits.
- ••• 0:46—Breasts and buns on couch.
- ••• 0:52—On balcony taking off dress, then in white lingerie, then breasts and buns.

• *Soft Bodies: Pillow Talk* (1996; Video Tape)

Danni Ashe . . . . Herself

- ••• 0:02—In lingerie, then nude, while posing on chair indoors.
- ••• 0:08—In dress, then nude, while posing on chair outdoors.
- ••• 0:12—In bra and panties, then nude in bathroom, then in bubble bath.
- •• 0:37—Breasts, after taking off her top and doing cheerleader moves outdoors with Becky LeBeau.

Becky LeBeau . . . . Herself

- •• 0:37—Breasts, after taking off her top and doing cheerleader moves outdoors with Danni Ashe.
- ••• 0:38—In bra and panties, then nude, while posing in dining area.
- ••• 0:43—In bra and panties, then nude, while posing on bed.
- ••• 0:48—In dress, then nude, while posing on sofa.

Lori Morrissey . . . . Herself

- ••• 0:22—In lingerie, while posing in front of doors, then nude.
- ••• 0:26—In shirt and short pants, then lingerie, then nude outdoors.
- ••• 0:31—In a slip, then nude, while posing next to swimming pool.

• *Soft Bodies: Show 'n Tell* (1995; Video Tape)

Becky LeBeau . . . . Herself

- •• 0:13—Breasts, while in swimming pool with St. Clair.
- •• 0:16—Breasts and buns in swimsuit while washing and posing next to car with St. Clair.
- ••• 0:33—In lingerie, then nude, while posing indoors near entry way.
- ••• 0:44—In dress, then nude, while posing outside.
- ••• 0:47—In lingerie, then nude, while posing in bedroom.

Mason Marconi . . . . Herself

- ••• 0:19—In lingerie and nude, while posing in bedroom.
- ••• 0:26—In schoolgirl outfit, then nude while posing outside.
- ••• 0:33—Nude, while posing by swimming pool.

Taylor St. Claire . . . . Herself

- ••• 0:02—In lingerie, then nude while posing on sofa.
- ••• 0:08—Nude in swimming pool, by herself and with LeBeau.
- ••• 0:16—Nude, while washing and posing next to car with LeBeau.

• *Soft Bodies: Squeeze Play* (1993; Video Tape)

Tuscany . . . . Victoria King

- ••• 0:03—In bra and panties, then nude on bed.
- ••• 0:09—Breasts and buns in bathtub.
- ••• 0:15—Breasts and partial buns in cut-offs, while washing windows with Becky LeBeau.
- ••• 0:19—In T-shirt and cut-offs, then breasts and partial buns, while posing outside on stepladder.

Elayne Dahl . . . . Herself

- ••• 0:21—In lingerie, then nude on bed.
- ••• 0:27—In lingerie, then breasts and buns on bed with Becky LeBeau.
- ••• 0:29—In dress, then in bra and panties, then nude on sofa.
- •• 0:35—In outfit, then breasts, while outside on chair.

Becky LeBeau . . . . Herself

- ••• 0:15—Breasts and partial buns in cut-offs, while washing windows with Tuscany.
- ••• 0:27—In lingerie, then breasts and buns on bed with Elayne Dahl.
- ••• 0:37—In bra and panties, then nude in front of and on bar.
- ••• 0:47—In a dress, then in bra and panties, then nude on sofa.
- ••• 0:51—In bra and panties, then nude on bed.

Soft Deceit *(1994)*

Krista Bridges . . . . Ed's Girlfriend
- 0:07—Left breast, while sleeping in bed, brief breasts, when Ed gets up out of bed.
- 0:08—Brief side view of left breast, when Ed gets back in bed to kiss her.

Kate Vernon . . . . Anne Fowler
- 0:43—Right breast in pulled down blouse when making love with Patrick Bergin in the woods.
- •• 0:58—Side view of right breast, while making love with Bergin on staircase railing in her house.

Gwynyth Walsh. . . . . Captain Brock

Soft Kill *(1994)*

Kim Morgan Greene . . . . Kimberly Lewis
- ••• 0:02—Right breast when lying in bed. Breasts, after sitting up with Jack and rearranging the covers. Long scene. Lower frontal nudity while opening the door.

Carrie-Anne Moss . . . . Jane Tanner
- 1:10—In white bra, then breasts while making love with Jack.

Soft Touch *(1987; Made for Cable Movie)*

(Shown on *The Playboy Channel* as *Birds in Paradise*.)

Jennifer Inch . . . . Tracy Anderson
- 0:01—Full frontal nudity during the opening credits.
- 0:02—Breasts with her two girlfriends during the opening credits.
- ••• 0:17—Breasts exercising on the floor, walking around the room, then lying on bed. Long scene.
- 0:20—Full frontal nudity getting out of bed.
- •• 0:23—Breasts in bed.
- ••• 0:50—Breasts sunbathing on boat with Carrie.
- •• 1:01—Full frontal nudity, sitting on towel, watching Carrie.
- 1:02—Full frontal nudity, waving to a dolphin.
- •• 1:04—Breasts at night by campfire with Carrie.
- ••• 1:05—Brief left breast, then breasts putting on skirt and walking around the island.
- •• 1:13—Breasts in hut with island guy.
- 1:19—Breasts in stills during the end credits.

Jeanine Louise . . . . Carrie Crawford
- 0:00—Breasts during opening credits.
- 0:02—Breasts with her two girlfriends during the opening credits.
- 0:03—Brief breasts getting out of the shower.
- 0:17—Breasts seen in mirror, while taking a shower.
- •• 0:19—Full frontal nudity during pillow fight on bed.
- •• 0:23—Breasts in bed with the other two girls.
- 0:27—Breasts in T-shirt, leaning over to wash car.
- 0:32—Breasts with Neill in open dress.
- ••• 0:35—Dancing on stage in red lingerie, then breasts and buns in G-string.
- •• 0:41—Full frontal nudity walking in water with a guy.
- ••• 0:50—Breasts sunbathing on the boat with Tracy.
- 1:01—Nude, swinging into water. Long shot.
- 1:02—Buns, waving to a dolphin.
- 1:04—Breasts at night by campfire with Tracy.
- 1:05—Brief left breast, while sleeping.
- 1:06—Breasts when Tracy wakes her up.
- 1:19—Breasts in stills during the end credits.

Sue Morrow . . . . Ashley Keyes
- 0:01—Breasts during opening credits.
- 0:02—Breasts with her two girlfriends during the opening credits.
- •• 0:19—Breasts taking off her T-shirt in bed. More breasts sleeping, then waking up.
- 0:20—Breasts getting out of bed.
- •• 0:22—Breasts making love with a guy.
- 0:23—Breasts in bed.
- •• 0:53—Breasts on bed with Ensign Landers.
- ••• 0:59—Breasts and buns in play pool with Landers.
- 1:19—Breasts in stills during end credits.

Jennifer Wyhl. . . . . Nancy
- 0:00—Breasts during opening credits.

Soft Touch II *(1987; Made for Cable Movie)*

(Shown on *The Playboy Channel* as *Birds in Paradise*.)

Jennifer Inch . . . . Tracy Anderson
- 0:01—Breasts during opening credits.
- 0:02—Breasts with her two girlfriends during opening credits.
- •• 0:14—Breasts dancing in Harry's bar by herself.
- 0:27—Full frontal nudity on stage at Harry's after robbers tell her to strip.
- 0:29—Side of left breast tied to Neill on bed.
- 0:31—Breasts tied up when Ashley and Carrie discover her.
- •• 0:52—Full frontal nudity during strip poker game, then covered with whipped cream.
- 0:57—Full frontal nudity getting out of bed.

Jeanine Louise . . . . Carrie Crawford
- 0:00—Breasts during opening credits.
- 0:02—Breasts with her two girlfriends during opening credits.
- •• 0:24—Breasts in bed feeling herself.
- •• 0:41—Full frontal nudity undressing and putting swimsuit on.
- 0:51—Breasts with her diving instructor.

Sue Morrow . . . . Ashley Keyes
- 0:01—Breasts during opening credits.
- 0:02—Breasts with her two girlfriends during the opening credits.
- •• 0:26—Breasts while sunbathing on boat.
- 0:50—Brief breasts in the water.
- 0:52—Breasts during strip poker game, then covered with whipped cream.
- •• 0:56—Full frontal nudity getting out of bed.

Jennifer Wyhl. . . . . Nancy
- 0:01—Breasts during opening credits.
- 0:05—Breasts in bed with Neill.
- 0:18—Breasts undressing for robbers. Brief full frontal nudity.
- •• 0:57—Breasts in bed with Neill.
- •• 1:01—Full frontal nudity in bed with Neill.

Solar Crisis *(1992)*

Brenda Bakke. . . . . Claire Beeson

Silvana Gallardo. . . . . T.C.

Annabel Schofield . . . . Alex Noffe
- •• 0:34—Breasts in the shower.
- •• 0:35—Breasts, sitting in chair, getting her mind probed.
- •• 0:54—Brief breasts during recollection of shower scene. Slightly distorted and out of focus.

Soldier Blue *(1970)*

Candice Bergen. . . . . Cresta Marybelle Lee
- 0:57—Close-up of buns, in open skirt while in back of wagon when Peter Strauss tries to cover her up. Don't see her face.

Soldier of Orange *(1977; Dutch)*

Susan Penhaligon . . . . Susan
- • 1:34—Brief breasts kissing her boyfriend when Rutger Hauer sees them through the window. Medium long shot.
- ••• 1:36—Breasts in bed with her boyfriend and Hauer.

A Soldier's Tale *(1988; New Zealand)*

Marianne Basler. . . . . Belle
- • 0:19—Brief breasts, while undressing in bedroom for Gabriel Byrne.
- •• 0:21—Breasts in bed with Byrne.
- •• 1:02—Buns and brief breasts while washing herself when Byrne sees her.

Sole Survivor *(1982)*

Anita Skinner. . . . . Denise Watson
- • 0:29—Very, very brief right breast in bed with Dr. Richardson. Brief side view of right breast when he jumps out of bed.

Brinke Stevens. . . . . Jennifer
- •• 0:45—Breasts after taking off bra while playing strip poker.

Solitaire for 2 *(1995; British)*

Maryam D'Abo . . . . Caroline
Amanda Pays. . . . . Katie
- • 0:57—Right breast, while making love in bed with Daniel.

Liza Walker . . . . Lucy

Some Call It Loving *(1972)*

Tisa Farrow . . . . Jennifer
- ••• 1:17—Breasts, while in bed with Troy.

Brandy Herred. . . . . Cheerleader
- ••• 1:12—Nude dancing in a club doing a strip tease dance in a cheerleader outfit.

Carol White. . . . . Scarlett

Some Girls *(1988)*

a.k.a. Sisters

Jennifer Connelly. . . . . Gabriella
Sheila Kelley . . . . Irenka
- • 0:13—Breasts and buns, while getting something at the end of the hall while Patrick Dempsey watches. Long shot, hard to see.
- • 1:01—Breasts in window while Dempsey watches from outside. Long shot, hard to see.

Something Wild *(1986)*

Melanie Griffith . . . . "Lulu"/Audrey Hankel
- ••• 0:16—Strips to breasts in bed with Jeff Daniels.
- • 0:24—Buns and brief breasts, while looking out the window.

Anna Thomson . . . . The Girl in 3F

Sometimes They Come Back ...Again *(1995)*

Jennifer Aspen . . . . Maria Moore
- •• 1:13—Left breast, after taking off her blouse, while with Vinnie.

Leslie Danon . . . . Lisa Porter
- • 0:12—Brief breasts, when her dress is pulled off by her girl friend.

Songwriter *(1984)*

Melinda Dillon. . . . . Honey Carder
Sage Parker . . . . Pattie McLeish
- • 1:01—Brief breasts, in bed when Rip Torn catches her in bed with Sam.

Sorceress *(1982)*

a.k.a. The Devil's Advocate

Ana de Sade . . . . Delisia
Lee Anne Harris . . . . Mira
- ••• 0:11—Breasts (on the left) greeting the creature with her sister. Upper half of buns, getting dressed.
- •• 0:29—Breasts (she's the second one) undressing with her sister in front of Erlick and Baldar.

Lynette Harris . . . . Mara
- ••• 0:11—Breasts (on the right) greeting the creature with her sister.
- ••• 0:29—Breasts (she's the first one) undressing with her sister in front of Erlick and Baldar.

Sorceress *(1994)*

Linda Blair . . . . Amelia
Antonia Dorian . . . . Trisha
Kristie Ducati . . . . Kathy
- ••• 1:12—Nude, while taking a shower. Long scene.
- • 1:19—Breasts behind shower door. Buns and right breast, while lying unconscious on the shower floor.
- • 1:20—Right breast, while lying unconscious on floor again.

Toni Naples . . . . Maria
- •• 0:17—Breasts under sheer black bodysuit. Breasts after taking off top and joining Larry and Julie Strain in bed.
- • 0:36—Left breast in open blouse, after fighting in bed with Larry.
- ••• 0:53—Buns and breasts, while on bed with Julie Strain and Rochelle Swanson.

Julie Strain . . . . Erica
- ••• 0:00—Breasts under sheer black robe, then breasts while rubbing oil on herself.
- ••• 0:16—Breasts in red push-up bra, while making love on top of Larry in bed.
- • 0:19—Buns, while lying on top of Larry in front of fire in flashback.
- ••• 0:53—Breasts, while on bed with Toni Naples and Rochelle Swanson.

Rochelle Swanson . . . . Carol
- ••• 0:23—Breasts and buns (wearing a blonde wig), while making love in bed with Larry.
- ••• 0:51—Buns and breasts (wearing blonde wig) while making love in bed in her dream with Julie Strain and Toni Naples.
- 1:01—In sexy black lingerie in bedroom with Larry (no more wig).
- •• 1:16—Breasts, while undressing in sauna.
- •• 1:19—Breasts in panties after taking off towel and putting on bra.

Sorority Babes in the Slimeball Bowl-O-Rama *(1988)*

Carla Baron . . . . Frankie
Michelle Bauer. . . . . Lisa
- ••• 0:12—Breasts, while brushing herself in the front of mirror when Brinke Stevens takes a shower.
- • 0:14—Brief full frontal nudity when the three nerds fall into the bathroom.
- ••• 0:40—Breasts, while taking off her bra.
- ••• 0:43—More breasts, while undoing garter belt.
- •• 0:46—More breasts, while in locker room.
- •• 0:47—More breasts, while taking off stockings.
- • 1:04—Full frontal nudity, while sitting on the floor by herself.

•• 1:05—Full frontal nudity, while getting up after the lights go out. Kind of dark.

Linnea Quigley . . . . Spider

Brinke Stevens. . . . . Taffy

••• 0:12—Nude, while showering off whipped cream in bathtub when talking to Michelle Bauer. Excellent long scene!

Sorority Girls and the Creature from Hell (1990)

Dori Courtney . . . . Belinda

•• 0:06—Breasts, while drying herself off after shower. (Wearing panties.)

••• 0:08—More breasts, still drying herself off.

• 0:12—Brief right breast, while in car with J.J.

••• 0:35—Breasts while in spa with J.J.

• 0:37—Buns, then left breast, while in spa during Gerald's fantasy.

••• 0:41—Breasts after taking off her top by stream while J.J. gets killed.

•• 0:43—Breasts, while running around at night getting chased by the creature.

Vicki Darnell . . . . Dancer

• 0:17—Breasts in bar in open blouse, while dancing on stage. Lit with red light.

• 0:24—More breasts dancing on stage.

Deborah Dutch . . . . Mary Anne

• 0:08—Very brief, side of left breast while changing clothes in background.

• 0:32—Lower half of left breast, while dancing in cabin.

Gloria Hylton. . . . . Kristina

Kelli Lee . . . . Body Double for Dori Courtney

• 0:23—Breasts, while in bedroom with J.J.

• 0:36—Breasts, while pretending to be strangled by Skip in the spa. Buns, when getting out.

Ashley St. Jon . . . . Bar Patron

Sorority House Massacre (1987)

Nicole Rio . . . . Tracy

•• 0:20—In a sheer bra changing clothes with two other girls in a bedroom.

•• 0:49—Breasts in a tepee with her boyfriend, Craig, just before getting killed.

Sorority House Massacre 2 (1990)

Savannah . . . . Satana

•• 0:43—Breasts and buns in G-string, dancing in club.

Dana Bentley Konkel . . . . Janey

••• 0:23—Breasts in bedroom talking to Suzanne and looking in the mirror. Buns, while getting dressed in black bodysuit.

• 0:48—Left breast, sticking out of bodysuit, covered with blood, when the girls discover her dead.

Bridget Carney . . . . Candy

••• 0:40—Breasts and buns in G-string, dancing in club.

Gail Harris . . . . Linda

•• 0:25—In bra and panties, then breasts while changing clothes.

• 1:00—Brief breasts, sitting up in bathtub filled with bloody water to strangle Linda.

Melissa Anne Moore . . . . Jessica

••• 0:22—Breasts, talking to Kimberly, then taking a shower.

• 0:53—Buns, while going up the stairs.

Toni Naples. . . . . Sgt. Shawlee

Michelle Verran . . . . Suzanne

••• 0:23—Buns in panties, then breasts changing clothes.

Stacia Zhivago . . . . Kimberly

••• 0:21—Nude, taking a shower.

• 0:53—Buns, while going up the stairs.

• 0:55—Brief buns, while going up the stairs.

Sorority House Party (1992)

Avalon Anders . . . . Miranda

• 1:05—Breasts and buns under sheer purple body suit.

Debra Beatty . . . . Mennonite Fury Woman

April Lerman . . . . Alex

••• 0:50—Breasts, while making love on bed with Jamie Z.

• 1:00—Right breast, while in bubble bath with Jamie.

Geraldina Marsilo . . . . Party Guest (Streaker)

• 0:04—Breasts, while walking by pool during party. Medium long shot.

Nicole Sassaman . . . . Topless Sorority Girl

•• 0:39—Breasts, opening Alex's bedroom door to ask for a bra.

Elizabeth Zimmie. . . . . Screaming Sorority Girl

• *Soul Hustler* (1975)

Nai Bonet . . . . Helena

• 0:54—Very, very brief buns, when putting on night shirt in bedroom with Fabian Forte.

South Beach (1992)

a.k.a. Night Caller

Vanity . . . . Jennifer Derringer

Stella Stevens . . . . Nancy

Robin Trapp . . . . Casey

••• 0:59—Buns, while making love with Fred Williamson. Nice close-up of breasts.

• *South Beach Academy* (1997)

Angel Boris . . . . Extra

Julie Cialini . . . . Phyllis Glass

Elizabeth Kaitan . . . . Shannon McSorley

• 1:21—Breasts, while making love with Harry at night.

Lorelei Leslie . . . . Harley

• 1:21—Breasts and partial buns, while making love with Corey Feldman at the beach at night.

South of Reno (1987)

Lisa Blount. . . . . Anette Clark

Danitza Kingsley . . . . Louise

Julia Montgomery . . . . Susan

• 1:22—Brief breasts, while kissing Martin. Dark, hard to see.

The Southern Star (1969; French/British)

Ursula Andress. . . . . Erica Kramer

• 1:07—Buns, walking into lake to wash herself. Long shot.

• 1:08—Breasts seen through water while she talks to George Segal.

Spaced Out (1980; British)

a.k.a. Outer Touch

Glory Annen . . . . Cosia

••• 0:23—Breasts talking to the other two space women. Long scene.

• 0:31—Very brief breasts changing clothes while dancing.

•• 0:43—Breasts in bed with Willy.

••• 1:08—Breasts lying down.

Ava Cadell . . . . Partha

•• 0:41—Left breast making love on bed with Cliff.

•• 0:42—Nude wrestling on bed with Cliff.

• 0:43—Brief left breast lying in bed alone.

•• 1:08—Breasts sitting on bed.

Kate Ferguson . . . . Skipper
• 1:07—Brief breasts making love with Willy in bed. Lit with red light.

Spanking the Monkey (1994)

Alberta Watson . . . . Susan Aibelli
• 0:12—Full frontal nudity, when getting into the shower. Brief right breast, while in the shower, assisted by her son.

Speaking Parts (1989; Canadian)

Cindy Fidler. . . . . Woman at Party
Arsinée Khanjian . . . . Lisa
Gabrielle Rose . . . . Clara
•• 0:41—Right breast, on TV monitor, masturbating with Lance, then breasts, while getting dressed.

Special Effects (1984)

Zoe Tamerlis . . . . Amelia/Elaine
• 0:01—Side view of right breast, wearing pasties during photo session.
• 0:16—Brief breasts sitting by pool with Eric Bogosian.
•• 0:19—Breasts getting into bed and in bed with Bogosian.
• 0:22—Breasts, dead in spa while Bogosian washes her off.
• 0:44—Brief breasts in moviola that Bogosian watches.
•• 1:12—Breasts making love on bed with Keefe.
• 1:17—Breasts getting into bed during filming of movie. Brief breasts during Bogosian's flashbacks.
• 1:20—More left breast shots on moviola getting strangled.
••• 1:33—Breasts with Bogosian when he takes her dress off.
• 1:35—Breasts sitting on bed kissing Bogosian. More breasts and more flashbacks.
• 1:40—Brief breasts during struggle. Dark.

The Specialist (1975)

Ahna Capri . . . . Londa Wyeth
••• 0:10—Breasts, while in bed, talking on the phone.
••• 0:28—Breasts on couch, posing for Bert.
•• 1:09—Breasts, sitting up in bed and putting robe on.
Christiane Schmidtmer . . . . Nude Model
••• 0:12—Breasts, while posing for artist, then buns when she gets up to leave.

The Specialist (1994)

Victoria Bass . . . . Socialite
Sharon Stone. . . . . .May Munro
• 0:29—Left breast and buns in panties in her house.
•• 1:14—Breasts and buns, in the shower with Sylvester Stallone.

Species (1995)

Marg Helgenberger. . . . . .Laura
• 1:21—Very, very brief tip of right breast, when yanking off Michael Madsen's socks. Very brief left breast, getting up to pull his underwear down.
Natasha Henstridge. . . . . Sil
• 0:18—Brief breasts and very brief lower frontal nudity, after hatching from alien cocoon. Covered with gunk.
•• 0:36—Breasts, while wearing white panties, getting dressed in motel room.
• 0:42—Brief breasts, after taking off bra in bathroom in front of Robby.
• 0:44—Brief breasts, while taking a shower to wash blood off herself. Hard to see through the door.
•• 0:53—Breasts, while in the hot tub with John.
• 0:59—Brief breasts, when running outside, then brief breasts, while getting into car.
•• 1:22—Breasts, after taking off dress in hotel room with Alfred Molina.
•• 1:25—Left breast, while making love on top of Alfred Molina.

• *Specimen* (1995; Canadian)

Michelle Johnson . . . . Sarah
Carmelina Lamanna. . . . . Carol Hillary
• 0:19—Buns, after taking off nightgown and walking in the woods at night.
•• 0:50—Very, very brief buns in flashback, then nude, walking into lake.
• 0:52—Brief breasts, after turning around in the lake.

Spellbinder (1988)

Alexandra Morgan. . . . . Pamela
Kelly Preston . . . . .Miranda Reed
••• 0:19—Breasts in bed making love with Timothy Daly.

Spetters (1980; Dutch)

Reneé Soutendijk. . . . . Fientje
•• 1:12—Breasts making love in trailer with Jeff.

• *Spice Exposed* (1997; Video Tape)

Geri Haliwell . . . . .Ginger Spice
•• 0:00—Nude in still photos throughout.

• *Spirit Lost* (1996)

Tamara Tunie . . . . .Anne
Cynda Williams . . . . Arabella
•• 0:32—Side of left breast, then left and right breasts, while making love with Leon on the floor.
•• 0:41—Breasts, while making love with Leon in bed.
• 1:00—Brief left breast, when covering herself with the comforter.
• 1:22—Brief breasts, while making love on top of Leon in bed when confronted by his wife.

• *Spirit of the Night* (1994)

Jenna Bodnar. . . . . Tara Wexford
• 0:01—Brief buns in panties and brief partial right breast, while making out with a guy in a daydream.
• 0:18—In bra, then brief breasts, while making out with Michelle and Alek on sofa.
• 0:27—Brief breasts, when the spirit takes off her clothes and enters her body.
• 0:28—Buns while in the shower. Brief breast, while examining herself in the bathroom, very brief full frontal nudity after knocking a glass off the shelf.
••• 0:42—Full frontal nudity, while caressing herself outdoors at night. Long scene.
• 0:47—Very brief full frontal nudity in bedroom during flashback.
••• 0:49—In wet body suit, then nude, while posing for photographs, then making love with Jacob. Great, long scene.
• 1:11—Breasts in B&W photos.
Carmen Lacatus. . . . . Cocktail Waitress/Lover in Study
• 1:09—Breasts, while making love with a man in study when seen by Tara.
Blair Valk . . . . Michelle
• 0:20—In bra, then breasts, while making love with Alek on sofa while Tara watches.
• 0:37—Full frontal nudity, after taking off her towel and climbing onto piano.

Spirits *(1991)*
Michelle Bauer . . . . Sister Mary
••• 0:21—Breasts, taking off nun's habit, trying to seduce Erik Estrada. Brief lower frontal nudity and buns also. Long scene.
Kaitlin Hopkins . . . . Succubus/Mrs. Heron
•• 0:36—Breasts, several times, in bed on top of Harry. Then in gross make-up.
Kathrin Lautner . . . . Beth
Carol Lynley . . . . Sister Jillian
Sandra Margot . . . . Nun Demon
Brinke Stevens . . . . Amy Goldwyn

Spitfire *(1994)*
Debra Jo Fondren . . . . Amanda Case
•• 0:00—Breasts, after taking off her top in front of Lance Henriksen.
••• 0:01—Breasts, while lying in bed with Henriksen after Sarah Douglas and her men burst into the room.
•• 0:03—Breasts, after getting shot and talking to Henriksen.

Splash *(1984)*
Daryl Hannah . . . . Madison
• 0:24—Partial buns, while running into the water at the beach. Looks like the bottom of her hair is taped to her buns.
• 0:27—Brief right breast, swimming under water, entering the sunken ship.
• 0:28—Buns, while walking around the Statue of Liberty.
• 1:26—Brief right, then left breast while in tank when Eugene Levy looks at her.
• 1:44—Brief right breast, under water when frogman grabs her from behind.
Amy Ingersoll . . . . Reporter
Valerie Wildman . . . . Wedding Guest

Split Second *(1992)*
Kim Cattrall . . . . Michelle
•• 0:43—Breasts in the shower.
•• 0:45—Breasts in the shower, when Rutger Hauer opens the curtains.
Tina Shaw . . . . Nightclub Stripper
•• 0:07—Breasts, dancing in club in black S&M outfit, wearing a mask over her head.

Splitting Heirs *(1993)*
Sadie Frost . . . . Angela
Barbara Hershey . . . . Duchess Lucinda
Catherine Zeta Jones . . . . Kitty
• 0:39—Swimming in lap pool (hard to see anything because of the water distortion.) Brief buns and back half of left breast, while getting out of the pool. Long shot.

The Sporting Club *(1971)*
Margaret Blye . . . . Janey
• 0:31—Breasts, sunbathing on rock when seen by James. Medium long shot.
Jo Ann Harris . . . . Lu
••• 0:55—Breasts (mostly right breast) while in the woods, talking to James.

• **Sports Illustrated's 25th Anniversary Swimsuit Video** *(1989; Video Tape)*
(The version shown on HBO left out two music video segments at the end. If you like buns, definitely watch the video tape!)
Carol Alt . . . . Model
Rachel Hunter . . . . Model
• 0:03—Right breast in see-through black swimsuit with white stars on it.
Elle Macpherson . . . . Model
• 0:23—Very, very brief lower breasts, when readjusting her yellow tank top.

• **Sports Illustrated: 1994 Swimsuit Issue Video** *(1994; Video Tape)*
(Unedited Version reviewed.)
Angie Everhart . . . . Model
Rachel Hunter . . . . Model
Elle Macpherson . . . . Model
Ingrid Seynhaeve . . . . Model
• 0:00—Very, very brief right breast when adjusting fishnet top.
Patricia Velasquez . . . . Model
• 0:34—Brief breasts under sheer white swimsuit. Buns in other swimsuit.
• 0:36—Very, very brief right breast, when covering her breast while holding a fan while posing for photos in Bali.

The Spring *(1989)*
Shari Shattuck . . . . Dyanne
• 0:00—Nude, several times, swimming under the water. Shot from under water.
• 0:50—Breasts and buns, swimming under water.
•• 0:51—Breasts, getting out of the water.
•• 0:59—Brief breasts, turning over in bed with Dack Rambo.
• 1:05—Standing up in wet lingerie, then swimming under water.
Virginia Watson . . . . Pafinya
•• 0:45—Breasts taking off her top in front of Dack Rambo in his hotel room.

Spring Break *(1983; Canadian)*
Corinne Alphen . . . . Joan
Nikki Fritz . . . . Girl In Corvette
••• 0:24—Breasts taking off clothes in room with Stu and O.T.
Sheila Kennedy . . . . Carla
•• 0:49—Breasts during wet T-shirt contest.

Spring Fever USA *(1988)*
a.k.a. Lauderdale
Amy Lynn Baxter . . . . Amy (Car Wash Girl)
Janine Lindemulder . . . . Heather Lipton
•• 0:14—Taking off her stockings, then brief breasts undressing for bath, then taking a bath.
Cari Mayor . . . . Girl on Campus
Anne Marie Oliver . . . . Rita Durango
•• 1:02—Breasts, during wet T-shirt contest.
Sherrie Rose . . . . Vinyl Vixen #1
Reneé Shugart . . . . Beach Beauty

Spring Symphony *(1983)*
Nastassja Kinski . . . . Clara
• 0:29—Brief left breast, when it pops out of her corset when she tries on a dress.

The Spy Within *(1994)*
a.k.a. Flight of the Dove
Theresa Russell . . . . Alex Canis
••• 0:19—In black bra, then breasts, while making love with Scott Glenn inside.
• 0:47—Partial left breast and brief partial right breast when taking a shower and talking to Glenn.

- 1:07—Brief partial buns and brief partial side of right breast, while making love in bed with Glenn.

Spymaker—The Secret Life of Ian Flemming (1990; Made for Cable Movie)

Ingrid Held . . . . Countess de Tubinville
- 0:59—Very brief side view of right breast, while getting knocked unconscious by Jason Connery.

The Squeeze (1977; British)

Carol White. . . . . Jill
- ••• 0:58—Nude, after taking off her clothes in front of the three bad guys. Long scene.

Squeeze Play (1979)

Jennifer Hetrick . . . . Samantha
- •• 0:00—Breasts in bed after making love.
- • 0:26—Right breast, brief breasts with Wes on the floor.

Stacey! (1973)

a.k.a. Stacey and Her Gangbusters

Anitra Ford . . . . Tish Chambers
- •• 0:13—Breasts in bed making love with Frank.

Cristina Raines. . . . . Pamela Chambers

Anne Randall. . . . . .Stacey Hansen
- ••• 0:01—Breasts taking off her driving jump suit.
- ••• 0:12—Breasts changing clothes.
- ••• 0:39—Breasts in bed with Bob.

Stag (1997; Made for Cable Movie)

Taylor Dayne. . . . . .Serena
- • 0:16—Brief buns, when in bathroom with John Stockwell.
- • 0:24—Brief partial buns, when being carried up the stairs.

• *Stakeout* (1987)

Madeleine Stowe. . . . . Maira McGuire
- • 0:43—Buns and brief side view of right breast getting a towel after taking a shower while Richard Dreyfuss watches her.

Star 80 (1983)

Carroll Baker . . . . Dorothy's Mother

Lonnie Chin. . . . . Playboy Mansion Guest

Deborah Geffner . . . . Billie

Tabitha Harrington . . . . Blonde

Mariel Hemingway . . . . Dorothy Stratten
- •• 0:00—Breasts in still photos during opening credits.
- • 0:02—Breasts lying on bed in Paul's flashbacks.
- ••• 0:22—Breasts during Polaroid photo session with Paul
- • 0:25—Breasts during professional photography session. Long shot.
- • 0:36—Brief breasts during photo session.
- • 0:57—Right breast, in centerfold photo on wall.
- • 1:04—Upper half of breasts, in bathtub.
- • 1:05—Brief breasts in photo shoot flashback.
- • 1:17—Brief breasts during layout flashbacks.
- • 1:20—Very brief breasts in photos on the wall.
- •• 1:33—Breasts undressing before getting killed by Paul. More brief breasts layout flashbacks.

Lorraine Michaels . . . . Paul's Party Guest

Cathy St. George. . . . . Playboy Mansion Guest

Kathryn Witt . . . . Robin

• *Star Portal* (1997)

Athena Massey . . . . Quad Rena/Sarah
- • 0:17—Brief breasts, when taking off her hospital gown in front of Steven Bauer.
- •• 0:24—Breasts, while in bedroom with her boyfriend, in flashbacks and when picking out a dress.
- ••• 0:46—Breasts and buns, while taking a shower.
- • 0:49—Brief breasts, while sitting up in bed and talking with Bauer.
- • 0:52—Brief full frontal nudity, when standing up in bed and walking out from behind bead curtain.

Star Slammer—The Escape (1986)

Bobbie Bresee . . . . Marai

Sandy Brooke . . . . Taura
- ••• 0:21—Breasts in jail putting a new top on. In braless white T-shirt for most of the rest of the film.
- •• 1:09—Breasts changing into a clean top.

Dawn Wildsmith . . . . Muffin

• *Starlet Screen Test* (1986; Video Tape)

Leslee Bremmer. . . . . Leslee
- ••• 0:11—Nude, taking off towel in hot tub.

Gail Harris . . . . Susan
- ••• 0:31—In robe, on red sofa, then in bra and panties, then nude.

• *Starlet Screen Test II* (1991; Video Tape)

Jasaé . . . . .Jasae
- ••• 0:05—Nude on couch (same segment from *Centerfold Screen Test, Take 3.*)

Sylvia Baker . . . . Herself
- ••• 0:01—Nude on couch (same segment from *Centerfold Screen Test, Take 3.*)

Leslee Bremmer. . . . . Lauren
- ••• 0:41—Breasts and buns, in swimsuit bottom, dancing on stage.

Sheila Lussier. . . . . Dusty Rose
- ••• 0:31—Breasts, posing on car (same segment from *Centerfold Screen Test.*)

• *Starlet Screen Test III* (1992; Video Tape)

Brittany Ashland . . . . Brigitte Williams
- ••• 0:34—Breasts in silhouette during audition, then nude with the lights on and playing with ice.

Lori Jo Hendrix. . . . . Sherry Miller
- ••• 0:09—In bra, then breasts while kneeling on table.

Carrie Janisse . . . . Alexa Jones
- ••• 0:14—Breasts, while sitting on table, then full frontal nudity while getting dressed.

• *Starlets Exposed!* (1990; Video Tape)

Iris Condon . . . . Iris
- • 0:04—Brief breasts doing strippergram in office.
- ••• 0:05—Nude, taking a bubble bath and drying herself off.

• *Starlets Exposed! Volume II* (1991; Video Tape)

Leslee Bremmer. . . . . Leslee
- ••• 0:40—Breasts, then nude, taking off two piece swimsuit in garden.

Venus De Light . . . . Venus
- ••• 0:43—Buns in G-string, then breasts dancing on stage with a life-size dummy and in a giant champagne glass.

Brandi Downs . . . . .Charlene
- ••• 0:21—Buns in pink two piece swimsuit, then breasts on stage doing strip routine.

Gail Harris . . . . .Gail
- ••• 0:07—Nude, taking off robe, taking a shower, then drying herself off.

Teri Lynn Peake . . . . Lenee
- ••• 0:52—Nude outside and in a hot tub.

Starquest *(1995)*

Brenda Bakke . . . . Zinovitz
Lisa Boyle . . . . Veiled Woman
••• 0:45—Breasts while posing in desert during virtual reality session.
Ming-Na Wen . . . . Han

• **Starship Troopers** *(1996)*

Laura Albert . . . . Stunts
Ungela Brockman . . . . Corporal Birdie
Tami-Adrian George . . . . Djana'D
• 0:29—Very brief left breast, while in the co-ed showers.
• 0:30—Very brief left breast, when giving Casper Van Dien a quick spank when he leaves the co-ed showers.
Lenore Kasdorf . . . . Mrs. RIco
Blake Lindsley . . . . Katrina
• 0:28—Brief side of left breast, five times, while in the co-ed showers.
• 0:30—Very brief buns, when mooning the camera next to Shujimi.
Dina Meyer . . . . Dizzy Flores
•• 0:29—Breasts, after taking off her blouse in co-ed showers.
••• 1:21—Breasts, while taking off her T-shirt with Casper Van Dien. Later, brief breasts when hiding under the covers.
Brenda Strong . . . . Captain Deladier

Starting Over *(1979)*

Candice Bergen . . . . Jessica Potter
• 1:29—Very, very brief left breast in bed with Reynolds when he undoes her top. You see her breast just before the scene dissolves into the next one. Long shot, hard to see.
Jill Clayburgh . . . . Marilyn Holmberg
• 0:45—Very brief upper half of breasts taking a shower while Burt Reynolds waits outside.
Mary Kay Place . . . . Marie

State of Grace *(1990)*

Sandra Beall . . . . Steve's Date
Robin Wright . . . . Kathleen
•• 0:38—Breasts making love standing up with Sean Penn in the hall. Dark.
• 1:58—Brief side of right breast taking off towel and putting on blouse.

State Park *(1988; Canadian)*

Crisstyn Dante . . . . Blond in Net
• 0:45—Very, very brief left breast putting swimsuit top back on after being rescued from net by the guy in the bear costume.
Shana Golden . . . . Blond in Shower
• 0:46—Breasts taking a shower outside while park ranger watches. Long shot.
Jennifer Inch . . . . Linnie
• 0:34—Brief right breast, undoing swimsuit top while sunbathing.
• 0:39—Brief breasts, taking off swimsuit top while cutting Raymond's hair.
Isabelle Mejias . . . . Marsha

Stateline Motel *(1975; Italian)*

a.k.a. Last Chance for a Born Loser
Ursula Andress . . . . Michelle Nolton
••• 0:34—Left breast, then breasts on bed with Oleg.
Barbara Bach . . . . Emily

Stay As You Are *(1978; Italian)*

English language version.
Barbara De Rossi . . . . n.a.
Nastassja Kinski . . . . Francesca
• 0:07—Left breast, while sleeping in bed.
• 1:00—Breasts, undressing and sitting in bed. Brief side of left breast, while lying in bed.
••• 1:02—Buns, while lying in bed, then full frontal nudity sitting up and covering herself with a sheet.
••• 1:27—Left breast, then breasts and brief buns in bed with Marcello Mastroianni. Long scene.
••• 1:28—Breasts, sitting up in bed, talking with Mastroianni.
••• 1:30—Nude, fooling around at the table with Mastroianni. Long scene. Nice bun shots.
•• 1:33—Breasts in bedroom at night. Mostly silhouette.

Stay Hungry *(1976)*

Joanna Cassidy . . . . Joe Mason
Sally Field . . . . Mary Kay Farnsworth
• 0:27—Buns, then very, very brief side view of left breast jumping back into bed. Very fast, everything is a blur, hard to see anything.
Laura Hippe . . . . May Ruth
• 1:19—Brief buns, hanging upside down in gym.
Helena Kallianiotes . . . . Anita

Staying Together *(1989)*

Melinda Dillon . . . . Eileen McDermott
Sheila Kelley . . . . Beth Harper
Daphne Zuniga . . . . Beverly Young
•• 0:56—Buns, lying in bed with Kit. Nice, long buns scene.

The Steagle *(1971)*

Cloris Leachman . . . . Rita Weiss
Susan Tyrrell . . . . Louise
• 0:48—Brief left breast twice, lying on bed with Richard Benjamin.

Stealing Beauty *(1996)*

Stefania Sandrelli . . . . Noemi
Liv Tyler . . . . Lucy
•• 0:48—Brief right breast while reaching up in bathtub.
•• 1:02—Left breast, after pulling her dress aside, sitting next to tree.
• 1:48—Partial breasts, while making love with a guy.
• 1:51—Very brief partial crotch, while making love on the ground with the guy.
Rachel Weisz . . . . Miranda
•• 0:11—Left breast and brief upper half of lower frontal nudity, while lying on a cot next to pool.

Stealing Heaven *(1988; British/Yugoslavian)*

Victoria Burgoyne . . . . Prostitute
• 0:28—Left breast, taking off her top. Side view of right breast and buns.
•• 0:29—Breasts lying in bed.
Cassie Stuart . . . . Petronilla
Kim Thomson . . . . Heloise
• 0:42—Side of left breast kneeling on floor with steam. Long shot.
•• 0:43—Closer view of left breast.
••• 0:47—Breasts and very brief lower frontal nudity lying in bed with Abelard. More left breast afterwards.
• 1:07—Nude, left side view on top of Abelard in bed. Long shot.

***Steaming** (1985; British)*
Felicity Dean . . . . Dawn
•• 1:12—Breasts, while painting on herself.
Patti Love . . . . Josie
• 0:08—Frontal nudity, while getting undressed.
• 0:45—Brief breasts.
• 1:30—Breasts, while jumping around in the pool.
Sarah Miles . . . . Sarah
•• 0:23—Breasts while getting into pool with Vanessa Redgrave.
•• 0:49—Breasts while getting undressed.
•• 1:31—Nude while lying down next to pool.
Vanessa Redgrave . . . . Nancy
• 1:32—Buns and brief side view of right breast getting into pool.

***Steel and Lace** (1990)*
Stacy Haiduk . . . . Alison
Brenda Swanson . . . . Miss Fairweather
•• 0:58—Breasts in lunchroom, opening her blouse in front of one of the bad guys on the table.
Clare Wren . . . . Gally

***The Stepfather** (1987)*
Gabrielle Rose . . . . Dorothy
Jill Schoelen . . . . Stephanie Maine
•• 1:16—Buns and brief side of right breast, while getting into the shower. Breasts in the shower.

***Stepfather III: Father's Day** (1992)*
Priscilla Barnes . . . . Christine Davis
• 1:27—Very brief buns, sitting down in bubble bath.
Season Hubley . . . . Jennifer Ashley
Brenda Strong . . . . Crime Search Reporter

• ***The Stepford Wives** (1975)*
Judith Baldwin . . . . Mrs. Cornell
Tina Louise . . . . Charmaine
Paula Prentiss . . . . Bobby
Katharine Ross . . . . Joanna
1:49—Prosthetic breasts under sheer nightgown of robotic Katharine Ross.
Dee Wallace Stone . . . . Nettie the Maid

***Steppenwolf** (1974)*
Carla Romanelli . . . . Maria
••• 0:59—Breasts sitting on bed with Max von Sydow. Long scene.
Dominique Sanda . . . . Hermine
• 1:40—Brief lower frontal nudity, while sleeping with a guy.
• 1:41—Very brief left breast, waking up and rolling over to hug Max Von Sydow.

***Stewardess School** (1987)*
Sandahl Bergman . . . . Wanda Polanski
Corinne Bohrer . . . . Cindy Adams
Vicki Frederick . . . . Miss Grummet
Leslie Huntly . . . . Alison Hanover
•• 0:46—Breasts, doing a strip tease on a table at a party at her house.
Julia Montgomery . . . . Pimmie Polk

***Still of the Night** (1982)*
Sara Botsford . . . . Gail Phillips
Meryl Streep . . . . Brooke Reynolds
• 0:22—Side view of right breast and buns taking off robe for the massage guy. Long shot, don't see her face.
Jessica Tandy . . . . Grace Rice

***Stitches** (1985)*
Lucinda Crosby . . . . Nurse #5
Deborah Fallender . . . . Nurse #1
Jenny Neumann . . . . Joan
Rebecca Perle . . . . Bambi Belinka
••• 0:33—Breasts during female medical student's class where they examine each other.
• 1:00—Brief breasts on bed with Parker Stevenson when discovered by Nancy.

• ***Stolen Hearts** (1995)*
Landon Hall . . . . Tess
• 0:51—Brief right breast during a dream.
••• 1:19—Breasts while making love with Justin.
Lori Jo Hendrix . . . . Sherrie
•• 0:23—In bra, then breasts and partial buns, while making love with David in storage room.
• 0:50—Brief buns in T-back, while starting her routine on stage.
• 0:57—Breasts, while making love with Brandon in spa.
Tammy Parks . . . . Diana
•• 0:37—In lingerie, then buns in T-back, then breasts while dancing on stage.
• 0:38—Breasts and buns in T-back, while backstage.
• 0:49—Breasts and buns in T-back, while dancing on stage.

***Stone Cold** (1991)*
Laura Albert . . . . Joe's Girlfriend
• 0:11—Buns, in bed when waking up. Very brief right breast.
Arabella Holzbog . . . . Nancy
Tracey E. Hutchinson . . . . Pool Playing Chick
• 0:25—Brief breasts, playing pool with the guys.
Brenda Lynn Klemme . . . . Marie

***Stone Cold Dead** (1979; Canadian)*
Jennifer Dale . . . . Claudia Grissom
••• 0:05—Breasts, dancing on stage.
Monique Mercure . . . . Dr. Bouvier
Belinda Montgomery . . . . Sandy MacAuley
Linnea Quigley . . . . First Victim
• 0:03—Very brief right breast after getting shot through shower door. Buns after falling to the floor.
Alberta Watson . . . . Olivia Page

***The Stoned Age** (1994)*
Renee Ammann . . . . Lanie
•• 0:46—Brief breasts in bedroom with Hubbs, then brief right breast in bed with him.
• 0:47—Brief breasts, while sitting up in bed when Joe interrupts her session with Hubbs.
• 0:58—Brief breasts, while making love with Hubbs in bed.
• 1:06—Left breast, twice, while sleeping in bed when Joe comes in the room.
• 1:08—Left breast, twice again, after Joe's hallucination.
Judith Drake . . . . Mrs. Hankey

***Stormquest** (1988)*
Kai Baker . . . . Arr
• 0:37—Very, very brief left breast, while struggling with Zar in the water.
Christina Whitaker . . . . Asha

Stormswept (1994)

Julie Hughes . . . . Brianna
•• 0:54—Breasts, while making love in bed with Kelly.
••• 1:26—Breasts in open robe and panties, while on couch during hypnosis session.
•• 1:29—Breasts, while making love in pantry with Eugene.
Kathleen Kinmont . . . . .Missy
Kim Kopf. . . . . Maria
Lorissa McComas . . . . Kelly
••• 0:53—Breasts, while making love in bed with Brianna.
••• 1:33—Nude, after taking off her robe in room in front of Eugene.
Melissa Anne Moore . . . . Dottie
•• 0:33—Breasts, when her towel falls off while talking to Brianna.
• 0:40—Breasts in open robe, while sitting on bed.
••• 1:10—Breasts, while making love on table with Damon.

Stormy Monday (1988)

Catherine Chevalier. . . . . .Cosmo's Secretary
Melanie Griffith. . . . . Kate
• 1:11—Very brief left breast, while making love in bed with Brendan.

The Story of "O" (1975; French)

Corrine Clery. . . . . O
•• 0:04—Breasts in the back of car when her boyfriend pulls her blouse down and rips her bra off.
••• 0:08—Breasts, getting made up by two women.
•• 0:10—Left breast, while getting checked out.
•• 0:13—Frontal nudity, chained to chandelier and whipped.
•• 0:14—Breasts on couch.
•• 0:16—Breasts getting out of tub and sitting on bed.
••• 0:18—Breasts and brief buns, getting out of bed and whipped. Frontal nudity, getting up.
••• 0:20—Frontal nudity with two guys.
••• 0:22—Breasts, sitting in front of a mirror.
•• 0:24—Breasts, watching another woman have sex in library.
••• 0:27—Breasts sitting at table and eating.
••• 0:29—Breasts getting a bath.
•• 0:30—Breasts being led around blindfolded.
•• 0:33—Brief breasts, getting whipped and eating.
•• 0:42—Buns, while bent over sofa.
••• 0:43—Breasts with older man on sofa.
••• 0:44—Nude, taking off her skirt.
••• 0:59—Frontal nudity, reclining on bed, then sitting up.
•• 1:02—Breasts in room with older man when he opens her blouse.
••• 1:05—Breasts and buns in bedroom.
••• 1:06—Nude with other women, getting dressed in a corset.
••• 1:08—Breasts, getting chained to posts and whipped.
•• 1:13—Breasts in bed with another woman.
•• 1:14—Breasts before getting branded.
••• 1:17—Frontal nudity, getting out of tub and putting on robe.
•• 1:19—Breasts getting her blouse opened and breast sucked.
••• 1:21—Nude, making love in bed. Slightly overexposed.
••• 1:26—Tied up to posts by wrists.
•• 1:32—Breasts in open cape, while wearing a mask. Frontal nudity getting cape removed.
Vibeke Knudsen . . . . n.a.

The Story of "O" Continues (1981; French)

a.k.a. Les Fruits de la Passion
Arielle Dombasle . . . . Nathalie
• 0:17—Brief left breast, lying on her stomach in bed with Klaus Kinski.
••• 0:40—Full frontal nudity on bed, making love in front of O.
• 1:00—Very, very brief left breast, while grabbing her blouse out of Kinski's hands.
Isabelle Illiers . . . . O
••• 0:06—Breasts in chair, getting made up.
•• 0:08—Breasts and buns, walking up stairs.
• 0:10—Breasts sitting in bed.
•• 0:11—Breasts sitting in bed putting up Klaus Kinski's picture on the wall.
•• 0:12—Breasts and buns getting out of bed and walking around the room.
• 0:13—Tip of right breast, while looking out the window.
•• 0:18—Breasts looking out the window.
• 0:24—Brief left breast, under her dress.
• 0:26—Tips of breasts, sticking out of dress top.
•• 0:27—Breasts and buns in chair, more in room with a customer.
• 0:35—Breasts, sitting while looking at Kinski.
•• 0:36—Brief left breast, then full frontal nudity lying on bed during fantasy.
•• 0:40—Full frontal nudity, while getting chained up by Kinski.
•• 0:58—Full frontal nudity running in slow-motion during boy's fantasy.
•• 1:02—Breasts in room with the boy.
•• 1:04—Breasts making love with the boy.

Story of a Love Story (1973; French/Italian)

a.k.a. Impossible Object
Léa Massari . . . . .Hipolita
Dominique Sanda . . . . Nathalie
0:13—Briefly in wet dress in the surf.
• 0:21—Breasts, after taking off nightgown in bathroom while talking to Georges.
• 0:26—Breasts in open blouse, with Georges in his office.
• 1:11—Breasts, while undressing in front of Alan Bates.
• 1:13—Brief left breast, while turning over in bed.
•• 1:23—Breasts while pregnant and brushing her hair.
• 1:24—Brief breasts, while lying on sofa in Bates' lap.
• 1:27—Partial left breast while breast feeding a baby.
• 1:28—Breasts while making love in bed with Bates.
• 1:31—Brief left breast, when moving her hair away to breast feed her baby.

The Story of Fausta (1988; Brazilian)

Betty Faria . . . . .Fausta
• 1:10—Left breast, while leaning out of the shower to talk to Lourdes.

Storyville (1992)

Charlotte Lewis . . . . Lee
•• 0:17—Buns, taking off martial arts outfit and getting into hot tub. Brief breasts, sitting down (medium long shot).
• 0:18—Brief upper half of breasts, in hot tub with James Spader.

Straight Time (1978)

Kathy Bates . . . . Selma Darin
Theresa Russell . . . . Jenny Mercer
••• 1:00—Left breast, while in bed with Dustin Hoffman. Don't see her face.

Strange Days (1995)

Brigitte Bako .... Iris

- 0:54—Breasts and very brief lower frontal nudity when the killer rips her blouse open, rapes and kills her in replay of a clip.

Angela Bassett.................. Lornette "Mace" Mason

Kylie Ireland .... Stoned Looking Girl

- 0:07—Breasts, seen from her point of view during playback of clip.

Honey Labrador .... Beach Beauty

Juliette Lewis .... Faith Justin

- ••• 0:15—Breasts, after taking off her top in her apartment with Ralph Fiennes, when he replays an old clip.
- 0:43—Singing on stage in chain top.
- 0:45—Very brief back side of left breast under gaping top when bending over sink, washing herself.
- ••• 0:46—Breasts, after taking off chain top backstage while talking to Fiennes.

Strange Shadows in an Empty Room (1976)

Tisa Farrow .... n.a.

Carole Laure .... Louise

- ••• 1:29—Brief breasts, while running around the house and frolicking with Mrs. Wilkinson and Fred. Breasts while in slow motion, when beating Mrs. Wilkinson to death.

The Stranger (1986)

Bonnie Bedelia............................ Alice Kildee

- 0:15—Brief right breast sticking up from behind her lover's arm making love in bed during flashback sequence (B&W).
- 0:19—Brief left breast turning over in hospital bed when a guy walks in. Long shot, hard to see.
- •• 0:38—Right breast again making love (B&W).

The Stranger (1994)

Ginger Lynn Allen .... Sally Womack

Kathy Long .... The Stranger

- •• 1:14—Buns and breasts, while making love on bed with Eric Pierpoint.

Stranger By Night (1994)

Jennifer Rubin .... Anne Richmond

- ••• 0:57—Breasts, while making love in bed with Steven Bauer.

Stranglehold (1994)

Jillian McWhirter .... Helen Filmore

- 1:00—In bra, then breasts, while starting to make out with Richter. Don't see her face.

Straw Dogs (1972)

Susan George .... Amy

- •• 0:32—Breasts taking off sweater, tossing it down to Dustin Hoffman, then looking out the door at the workers.
- ••• 1:00—Breasts on couch getting raped by one of the construction workers.

Street Hunter (1990)

Susan Napoli............................. Eddie's Girl

- •• 0:40—Breasts in bed with Eddie (she's on the left, wearing white panties).

Street Law (1994)

a.k.a. Jungle Law

Christina Cox .... Kelly

- 0:43—Brief close-up of buns, when Luis is feeling her up in raised skirt. Don't see her face.
- 0:44—Brief close-up of buns again.
- 1:08—Breasts, while making love in bed with Jeff Wincott. Don't see her face. In one shot you can see tape over her breasts.

Street Music (1982)

Elizabeth Daily .... Sadie

- 0:00—Nude behind shower door (can't see anything), then brief right breast while reaching for towel.
- •• 0:24—Partial lower frontal nudity and left breast with Eddie.
- 1:07—Brief breasts while on top of Eddie on the floor.
- •• 1:08—Brief breasts while getting dressed.

• *Street Smart* (1987)

Lynne Adams................................ Reporter

Marie Barrientos .... Hispanic Prostitute

- 0:06—Brief breasts and buns, when getting beat up by a customer when Morgan Freeman opens the door.

Mimi Rogers .... Alison Parker

Streets (1989)

Starr Andreeff .... Policewoman on Horse

Christina Applegate............................... Dawn

1:09—Very, very brief almost side view of left breast, while kissing her boyfriend, Sy. His hand is over her breast. Not really a nude scene, but I'm including it because people might send this in as an addition.

Julie Jay .... Dawn's Tattooed Roommate

- 0:20—Brief breasts, twice, pulling her blouse closed when Christina Applegate talks to her.

Kay Lenz .... Sergeant

Streets of Fire (1984)

Elizabeth Daily.............................. Baby Doll

Marine Jahan .... "Torchie's" Dancer

- 0:28—Buns in G-string, while dancing in club.
- 0:35—Very brief right breast under body stocking, then almost breasts under stocking when taking off T-shirt.

Diane Lane .... Ellen Aim

Amy Madigan .... McCoy

Streets of Rage (1993)

Mimi Lesseos........................... Melody Sails

- 0:33—Buns and brief side view of breasts after taking off robe and getting into shower. Breasts, sort of visible behind shower door.

Streetwalkin' (1985)

Khandi Alexander .... Star

Samantha Fox .... Topless Dancer

- 0:22—Breasts, dancing on stage in nightclub (She's the one wearing a head band).
- 0:27—More breasts, dancing on stage.
- 0:29—More breasts, dancing on stage.
- 0:56—Breasts, giving Antonio Fargas a massage at the bar.

Annie Golden .... Phoebe

Melissa Leo .... Cookie

- 0:05—Brief breasts taking off red blouse in front of mirror.
- •• 0:15—Breasts, stripping and taking off her top for a customer.
- 0:18—Brief right breast, having sex with her pimp on the floor.
- 0:44—Breasts, taking off her top and sitting on bed with a customer (long shot seen in mirror).
- 0:53—Buns in body suit, while in hotel room with customer.

Julie Newmar........................... Queen Bee

Deborah Offner . . . . Heather

Strike a Pose (1993)

Debra Beatty . . . . Model

Michele Brin . . . . Miranda Cross

••• 0:06—Breasts, while making love with Nick at night outside by a fire. Long scene.

••• 0:32—In black bra and panties, then breasts while making love with Nick. Long scene.

• 0:40—Buns in panties that are squished against a glass door.

••• 1:06—Brief left breast in bed, then breasts and buns while making love with Nick.

Diana Cuevas . . . . Model

Tamara Landry . . . . Candy

••• 0:23—In black bra, panties and stockings, then nude with Carl. Long scene.

••• 1:01—Breasts, while making love on bed.

Striking Point (1994)

Tracy Spaulding . . . . Tina Wells

••• 0:22—Buns and breasts, when dancing on stage in a black T-back, then in black bra while talking to the two policemen.

Stripes (1981)

Sue Bowser . . . . Mud Wrestler

Dawn Clark . . . . Mud Wrestler

Roberta Leighton . . . . Anita

• 0:07—Breasts, while wearing blue panties, then putting her shirt on and talking to Bill Murray.

Susan Mechsner . . . . Mud Wrestler

• 0:56—Brief breasts, while kneeling on the ground to the left of John Candy. Brief breasts, when punching Candy in the stomach after the police arrive (she's in the front to the left). Covered with mud.

P.J. Soles . . . . Stella

Sean Young . . . . Louise Cooper

Stripped to Kill (1987)

Michelle Foreman . . . . Angel

••• 0:02—Breasts dancing on stage for Norman Fell.

Debra Lamb . . . . Amateur Dancer

Kay Lenz . . . . Cody Sheehan

•• 0:23—Breasts dancing on stage.

••• 0:47—Breasts dancing in white lingerie.

Lucia Lexington . . . . Brandy

•• 0:35—Breasts dancing on stage.

Deborah Ann Nassar . . . . Dazzle

••• 0:07—Breasts wearing a G-string dancing on stage with a motorcycle prop.

Stripped to Kill II (1988)

Jeannine Bisignano . . . . Sonny

• 0:06—Buns, while wearing a black bra in dressing room.

••• 0:38—Breasts and buns during strip dance routine in white lingerie.

Maria Ford . . . . Shady

•• 0:21—Breasts, dancing on table in front of the detective. Buns, walking away.

• 0:40—Brief upper half of left breast in the alley with the detective.

•• 0:52—Breasts and buns during dance routine.

Lisa Glaser . . . . Victoria

•• 0:01—Breasts and buns in G-string doing a strip dance routine during Shadey's nightmare.

Marjean Holden . . . . Something Else

•• 0:17—Breasts during strip dance routine.

Debra Lamb . . . . Mantra

•• 0:04—Breasts during strip dance routine.

••• 0:42—Breasts in black lingerie during strip dance routine.

Karen Mayo-Chandler . . . . Cassandra

•• 0:18—Breasts taking off her top for a customer.

Stripper (1985)

Sara Costa . . . . Herself

••• 0:16—Breasts doing strip dance routine.

••• 0:46—Breasts and buns dancing on stage in a G-string.

••• 1:12—Breasts doing another strip routine.

Venus De Light . . . . Herself

• 0:59—Brief breasts, on stage, blowing fire.

••• 1:07—Breasts and buns in black G-string, doing routine on stage, using fire.

Suzanne Primeaux . . . . Herself

•• 0:03—Breasts dancing on stage, kneeling on her left knee. Very brief buns in G-string.

• *The Stripper of the Year* (1986; Video Tape)

Venus De Light . . . . Venus De Light

••• 0:37—Nude, doing strip routine that includes fire tricks.

•• 0:53—Breasts on stage with the other contestants.

••• 0:55—Breasts as a finalist, then in dance-off.

•• 0:56—Breasts as the winner.

Gail Harris . . . . Billy Jean

••• 0:32—Nude, stripping from red overalls and a hat.

•• 0:53—Breasts on stage with the other contestants.

Francesca "Kitten" Natividad . . . . Kitten

••• 0:51—Nude, stripping out of black outfit.

•• 0:53—Breasts on stage with the other contestants.

Teri Lynn Peake . . . . Lenee

••• 0:47—Nude, stripping out of red sequined dress.

•• 0:53—Breasts, on stage with the other contestants.

•• 0:54—Breasts, as a finalist.

••• 0:55—Breasts, as a finalist, then in dance-off.

Ashley St. Jon . . . . Judge

Stripshow (1995)

Kaitlyn Ashley . . . . Dancer

• 0:10—Buns in T-back, then breasts while dancing on stage.

• 0:40—Breasts and buns in T-back, while on stage.

•• 1:12—Breasts while on stage.

•• 1:15—Breasts and buns in T-back, while dancing on stage, intercut with Tané McClure.

Tané McClure . . . . Raquel

• 0:00—Breasts and buns in quick cuts.

•• 0:05—Breasts, while making love with Cowboy. Buns in T-back afterward.

• 0:33—Breasts in flashbacks.

••• 0:37—Breasts and buns while making love with Monique Parent in shack.

••• 0:43—Breasts while making love with Cowboy in the back of his truck.

• 1:11—Breasts and buns while dancing. Quick cuts.

•• 1:15—Breasts, while dancing. Quick cuts. Intercut with another dancer.

Monique Parent . . . . Kara

• 0:12—Buns in swimsuit bottom outside, getting ready to sunbathe.

••• 0:37—Buns and lower frontal nudity, while making love with Tané McClure in shack.

• 0:46—Buns, while lying in bed.

••• 0:52—Nude, stripping in motel room in front of McClure and Cowboy, then playing with herself.
• 1:02—Buns and breasts, bending over in bed, while having sex with Cowboy.
•• 1:13—Breasts, while on stage, reluctantly taking off her dress.

Striptease (1996)

(R-rated version reviewed.)

Daphnee Lynn Duplaix . . . . Uncredited Dancer
• 0:03—Breasts, while dancing in the background.
• 0:34—Brief breasts, while putting her dress on as she walks by Demi Moore, who is talking on the phone.

Frances Fisher . . . . Donna Garcia

Demi Moore . . . . Erin Grant
• 0:10—Brief buns in G-string, while running off the stage.
•• 0:16—Buns in T-back and sheer black bra, while dancing on stage.
•• 0:43—Breasts, while dancing around and singing when drying her hair in her bedroom (towel around her neck gets in the way).
••• 0:56—Buns in T-back and breasts, while dancing on stage.
••• 1:15—Buns in T-back and in bra, then breasts while dancing on boat in front of Burt Reynolds.

Pandora Peaks . . . . Urbana Sprawl
• 0:03—Breasts, while dancing on stage. Medium long shot.

Rena Riffel . . . . Tiffany Glass
• 0:02—Breasts and buns in T-back while dancing on stage during opening credits.

Dina Spybey . . . . Monique Jr.
•• 0:05—Buns in T-back and breasts, while dancing on stage.
• 0:36—Breasts, while dancing on stage in background, when Demi Moore talks with Armand Assante.

Tiffany Turner . . . . Uncredited Dancer

Barbara Alyn Woods . . . . Lorelei
•• 0:38—Breasts and buns in T-back, while dancing on stage with a snake.

• *Stripteaser 2* (1997)

Kimberly Blair . . . . Lisa

Lisa Ann Brown . . . . Sindy
••• 0:05—Breasts and buns in red T-back, while dancing on stage. Long scene.
••• 0:25—Breasts and buns in T-back, while dancing on stage with Sylvia.
•• 0:41—Breasts and buns, while dancing on stage with Sylvia.
• 0:46—Breasts, while showing Angie around the upstairs room.
• 0:48—Breasts, while showing Angie around the upstairs room.
•• 0:57—Breasts, while chained by her wrists in upstairs room.
••• 1:01—Breasts and buns in panties on stage with Junior in dream.
•• 1:08—Breasts and buns, while dancing for customers in upstairs room (wearing mask).

Kim Dawson . . . . Daphne Gulliani
••• 0:37—In bra, then breasts and partial buns, while making love with Nick in office.

Stacey Leigh Mobley . . . . Angie
••• 0:28—Breasts and buns in T-back.
••• 0:34—Breasts and buns in T-back, while dancing on stage.
•• 0:38—Left breast, then breasts, while listening to the goings on in the office.
• 0:48—Breasts, while getting shown around upstairs.
•• 0:51—Breasts and buns in T-back, while in S&M room with the police chief.
•• 1:00—Breasts and buns, while making love with Marty in bedroom at night.
• 1:03—Buns, while asleep on top of Marty in the morning.
• 1:12—Breasts, covered with blood.

Taylor St. Claire . . . . Junior Samples
•• 0:03—Breasts and buns in panties, while dancing on stage with Sylvia.
• 0:09—Breasts and buns in black T-back, while in dressing room.
••• 0:10—Breasts and buns in T-back, while dancing on stage.
•• 0:47—Breasts and brief buns in T-back, while talking with Bronson.
••• 1:01—Breasts and buns in panties on stage with Sindy in dream.
•• 1:08—Breasts and buns, while dancing for customers in upstairs room (wearing mask).

Stripteasers (1995)

Maria Ford . . . . Christina Loren
••• 0:00—In bra and panties, then breasts and buns in panties while doing strip routine on stage.
•• 0:04—In bridal gown, then breasts and buns in panties while doing strip routine on stage.
• 0:33—Brief breasts, after being forced to perform oral sex on Carey.
• 0:41—Brief breasts with Carey.
•• 0:53—Buns and breasts, while dancing on stage in patriotic outfit.

Nikki Fritz . . . . Sandra
••• 0:08—Buns then breasts, while doing strip tease dance on stage.
• 1:08—Brief buns in T-back, while leaping over the bar to get a shot gun.

Ann-Marie Holman . . . . Kitten
••• 0:41—In black bra and panties, then nude doing strip tease in front of the gunman.

Linnea Quigley . . . . Uncredited Waitress

Bianca Rocilili. . . . . Housewife
• 0:22—Buns in lingerie, seen in phony porno film seen on TV at Arnie's apartment.
• 0:23—Breasts, squished against shower door on TV.
• 0:25—More breasts on TV in the background.
• 0:27—More brief breasts on TV.

The Stud (1978; British)

Minah Bird. . . . . Molly
•• 0:26—Breasts in bed when Tony is talking on the telephone.

Joan Collins . . . . Fontaine
• 0:10—Brief left breast making love with Tony in the elevator.
• 1:03—Brief breasts taking off dress to get in pool.
• 1:04—Nude in the pool with Tony.

Emma Jacobs . . . . Alexandra
•• 0:44—In bra, then breasts taking bra off in bedroom.
• 0:48—Close up of breasts making love with Tony in his dark apartment.
• 1:14—Breasts in bed with Tony, yelling at him.

Sue Lloyd. . . . . Vanessa
• 1:04—Breasts in the swimming pool with Joan Collins and Tony.

Natalie Ogle . . . . Maddy

Student Affairs (1987)

Deborah Blaisdell . . . . Kelly
••• 0:26—Breasts sitting up in bed talking to a guy.
Beth Broderick. . . . . Alexis
Jane Hamilton . . . . Veronica
•• 0:48—Breasts changing in dressing room, showing herself off to a guy.
• 0:51—Brief breasts in a school room during a movie.
•• 0:56—In black lingerie outfit, then breasts in bedroom while she tape records everything.
Jeanne Marie. . . . . Robin Ready
• 0:35—Brief breasts wearing black panties in bed trying to seduce a guy.
••• 0:41—Breasts making love with another guy, while banging her back against the wall.
• 0:44—Very brief breasts in VW with a nerd.
• 1:09—Very brief breasts falling out of a trailer home filled with water.

The Student Body (1975)

June Fairchild . . . . .Mitzi Mashall
• 0:15—Brief breasts and buns, running and jumping into the pool during party. Brief long shot breasts, while in the pool.
•• 0:21—Breasts getting into bed.
Jillian Kesner . . . . Carrie Rafferty
•• 0:29—Left breast, making out with Carter in the car.

Student Confidential (1987)

Katherine Kriss . . . . Elaine's Friend
Susie Scott . . . . .Susan Bishop
• 0:02—Lying in bed covered with a gold sheet. Sort of right breast through her hair.
•• 1:26—Full frontal nudity standing in front of Greg.

The Student Nurses (1970)

a.k.a. Young LA Nurses
Karen Carlson . . . . Phred
• 0:08—Breasts in bed with the wrong guy.
••• 0:50—In bed with Jim, breasts and buns getting out, then breasts sitting in chair. Long scene.
• 1:02—Brief breasts in bed.
Elaine Giftos . . . . Sharon
• 1:14—Brief breasts undressing and getting into bed with terminally ill boy. Dark, hard to see.
Barbara Leigh . . . . Priscilla
••• 0:43—Breasts on the beach with Les. Long scene.

The Stunt Man (1980)

Barbara Hershey . . . . Nina
• 1:29—Buns and side view of left breast in bed in a movie within a movie while everybody is watching in a screening room.

• *Subliminal Seduction* (1996; Made for Cable Movie)

Griffin Drew . . . . .Kim
•• 0:09—Breasts and buns in T-back, while a guy undoes her dress when she's hypnotized.
• 1:04—Very, very brief right breast in flashback.
Rainer Grant . . . . Angie
•• 0:32—Right breast and buns, while making love with Ian Ziering.
Jillian Kesner . . . . .Cheri
Katherine Kelly Lang . . . . Debbie Danver
••• 0:10—Nude, while making love with Ian Ziering in bathtub.
••• 0:22—Breasts and side view of buns, while making love with Ziering in shower.
Kim Morgan Greene . . . . Meg
Stella Stevens . . . . .Mrs. Beecham
Dee Wallace Stone. . . . . Sissy Bonner

Submission (1976; Italian)

Andrea Ferréol. . . . . .Juliet
•• 0:43—Breasts in room with Franco Nero and Elaine.
Lisa Gastoni. . . . . Elaine
• 0:28—Lower frontal nudity, while on the floor behind the counter with Franco Nero.
• 0:30—Left breast, while talking on the phone with her husband while Nero fondles her.
•• 0:32—Breasts and buns, making love on bed with Nero. Slightly out of focus.
•• 0:33—Breasts getting out of bed to talk to her daughter.
••• 0:43—Breasts in room with Juliet and Nero. Long scene.
••• 0:45—More breasts on the floor yelling at Nero.
• 0:54—Brief lower frontal nudity in slip, while sitting on floor with Nero.
••• 0:57—Left breast, while wearing slip, walking in front of pharmacy. Then full frontal nudity while wearing only stockings. Long scene.
•• 1:00—Breasts in pharmacy with Nero, singing and dancing.
•• 1:28—Breasts when Nero cuts her slip open. Nice close up.
•• 1:29—Breasts getting up out of bed.
Claudia Marsani. . . . . .Justine

Subspecies (1990)

Michelle McBride. . . . . Lillian
• 0:34—Left breast, while sleeping in bed when the vampire comes to get her.
Laura Tate . . . . Michelle

Sudden Impact (1983)

Sondra Locke. . . . . Jennifer Spencer
Lisa London. . . . . .Young Hooker
•• 1:04—Breasts in bathroom, walking to Nick in the bed.

Sudden Thunder (1990)

Andrea Lamatsch. . . . . .Patricia Merrill
• 0:18—Right breast, while getting raped by jerks in the woods and brief breasts after escaping from them.
••• 0:27—Nude, while skinny dipping in pond (some body parts are visible under the water).

Sugar Cookies (1973)

Maureen Byrnes . . . . Dola
•• 0:37—Right breast while Gus is on top of her, then breasts and buns.
Lynn Lowry . . . . Alta/Julie
••• 0:03—Brief breasts falling out of hammock, then breasts on couch with Max, then nude. Long scene. (Brunette wig as Alta.)
• 0:13—Brief right breast in B & W photo.
• 0:14—Left breast while lying on autopsy table.
•• 0:20—Breasts in movie.
•• 0:52—Breasts taking off clothes for Mary Woronov. Breasts on bed. (Blonde as Julie.)
••• 1:00—Breasts and buns with Woronov in bedroom, nude while wrestling with her.
• 1:04—Breasts with Woronov in bathtub.
••• 1:06—Nude in bed with Woronov. Long scene.
•• 1:11—Right breast outside displaying herself to Max.

- 1:16—Right breast, then breasts making love with Woronov.
- ••• 1:20—Nude with Woronov and Max. Long scene.

Monique Van Vooren . . . . Helene
Jennifer Welles. . . . . .Max's Secretary

- • 0:28—Breasts in red panties in Max's office while he talks on the phone, then lower frontal nudity.
- •• 0:56—Full frontal nudity getting dressed.

Mary Woronov . . . . Camila

- ••• 0:10—Breasts in bathtub, then wearing white panties exercising breasts on the floor. Long scene.
- • 1:04—Breasts with Julie in the bathtub.
- • 1:07—Brief breasts, then left breast, making love with Julie.
- • 1:17—Brief right breast when Lynn Lowry yanks her dress up.

Sugarbaby (1985; German)

a.k.a. Zuckerbaby

Marianne Sägebrecht . . . . Marianne

- •• 0:44—Breasts, while undressing with Huber.
- 0:48—Partial right breast, under bubbles in bubble bath with Huber.
- • 0:59—Breasts, while sitting in bubble bath with Huber.

• *Suite 16* (1996)

Géraldine Pailhas. . . . . Helen

- • 1:20—Brief right breast when Chris caresses her while Pete Postlethwaite watches.

Summer Affair (1979)

Ornella Muti . . . . Lisa

- • 0:44—Silhouette of breasts in cave by the water.
- • 1:00—Brief breasts getting chased around in the grass and by the beach.

Summer Dreams: The Story of the Beach Boys (1990)

(Originally a made for TV movie.)

Linda Doná . . . . Karen Lamm

- • 1:06—Silhouette of breasts while making love with Dennis Wilson.

Summer Heat (1987)

Kathy Bates . . . . .Ruth Stanton
Miriam Byrd-Nethery. . . . . .Aunt Patty
Lori Singer. . . . . Roxy

- •• 0:36—Breasts in bed with Jack. Kind of dark and hard to see.

Summer Job (1989)

Amy Lynn Baxter. . . . . Susan

- •• 0:10—Breasts changing in room with the other three girls. More breasts sitting on bed.
- • 0:34—Brief breasts when her swimsuit top pops off after saving a guy in swimming pool.
- • 0:45—In white lingerie, brief breasts on stairs, flashing her breasts (wearing curlers).
- • 1:23—Breasts pulling her top down talking to Mr. Burns.

Chona Jason . . . . Beautiful Lady
Cari Mayor . . . . Donna

- • 0:10—Brief breasts twice, taking off her top before and after Herman comes into the room.

Anne Marie Oliver . . . . Kathy's Friend #2
Sherrie Rose . . . . Kathy Shields

- • 0:52—Buns, while walking around in swimsuit and jacket.
- •• 0:53—Breasts taking off swimsuit top kneeling by the phone, then brief buns standing up.
- •• 1:24—Brief breasts taking off her yellow top on the beach talking to Bruce.

Reneé Shugart . . . . Karen

- •• 0:42—Breasts taking off her top. Long shot, dark.
- • 0:45—In white lingerie, standing on stairs, then very brief left breast flashing.

Summer Lovers (1982)

Daryl Hannah . . . . .Cathy Featherstone

- • 0:07—Very brief breasts getting out of bed.
- • 0:54—Buns, while lying on rock with Valerie Quennessen watching Michael dive off a rock.
- • 1:03—Brief right breast sweeping the balcony.

Valerie Quennessen . . . . Lina

- • 0:12—Breasts, while on balcony.
- ••• 0:19—Nude on the beach with Michael.
- • 0:23—Brief breasts in a cave with Michael.
- •• 0:30—Breasts, while lying on the floor with Michael.
- • 0:54—Buns, while lying on a rock with Daryl Hannah watching Michael dive off a rock.
- • 1:03—Left breast, while in bed.
- •• 1:05—Breasts while dancing on the balcony.
- •• 1:09—Breasts while on the beach.

Summer Night (1987; Italian)

Mariangela Melato. . . . . Signora Bolk

- •• 0:26—Breasts behind gauze net over bed making love with a German guy.
- •• 1:02—Breasts while on the bed making love with the prisoner.
- •• 1:09—Breasts again.
- ••• 1:13—Buns, while walking out of the ocean, then breasts.

Summer School Teachers (1975)

Pat Anderson . . . . Sally

- •• 0:52—Breasts and buns, posing for photos, then in bed with Bob.
- • 1:05—Side view of right breast in photo in magazine.

Rhonda Leigh Hopkins. . . . . Denise

- • 0:45—Breasts making love with a guy. Close up of a breast.

Candice Rialson . . . . .Conklin T.

- • 0:14—Breasts and buns when Mr. Lacey fantasizes about what she looks like. Don't see her face, but it looks like her.
- ••• 0:38—Breasts outside with other teacher, kissing on the ground.

A Summer Story (1988)

Imogen Stubbs . . . . Megan David

- •• 0:36—Left breast several times, then right breast while making love with Frank in barn.
- • 0:41—Very, very brief buns, while frolicking in pond at night with Frank.
- • 1:03—Very brief silhouette of left breast during Frank's flashback sequence.

Susannah York. . . . . Mrs. Narracrombe

Summer's Games (1987)

Amy Lynn Baxter . . . . Boxer/Girl from Penthouse

- •• 0:04—Breasts opening her swimsuit top after contest. (1st place winner.)
- •• 0:18—Breasts during boxing match.

Andi Bruce. . . . . News Anchor

- • 0:12—Brief right breast, while turning around to look at monitor.

• 0:42—Breasts turning around to look at the monitor.

Lori Deann Pallett . . . . .Torch Carrier

• 0:00—Half breasts running in short T-shirt carrying torch.

•• 0:04—Breasts opening her swimsuit top after contest. (2nd place winner.)

Teri Lynn Peake. . . . . .Penthouse Girl

Cindy Rome . . . . Boxer

Sunday, Bloody Sunday *(1971)*

Caroline Blakiston . . . . Rowing Wife

• 1:09—Brief right breast in open dress during fight at party.

Glenda Jackson . . . . Alex Greville

• 0:10—Brief breasts, taking off her nightshirt and getting into bed with a guy.

• 1:11—Brief right breast, when wrapping a shawl around herself before getting out of bed.

• 1:15—Very brief breasts, when getting off the floor and wrapping a shawl around herself.

Sunset Grill *(1992)*

Alexandra Paul . . . . Anita

••• 1:14—Breasts and upper half of buns, while on top of Peter Weller in bed. Nice.

•• 1:15—Very brief buns, while rolling over on her back, then right breast.

Lori Singer. . . . . Loren

•• 0:57—Breasts, taking off bra and putting on robe.

• 0:58—Brief full frontal nudity sitting down in open robe. Left breast, while sitting down in tub.

••• 0:59—Breasts and buns, with Peter Weller in bathtub.

••• 1:15—Breasts, sitting up in bed after making love with Weller. Covered with sweat.

Sándra Wild . . . . Mrs. Pietrowski

• 0:03—Out-of-focus breasts, while making love. Seen through telephoto camera lens.

••• 0:04—Breasts in bed with her lover, then nude while struggling in bedroom with her husband.

Sunset Heat *(1991)*

a.k.a. Midnight Heat

(Unrated version reviewed.)

Daphne Ashbrook . . . . .Julie

• 1:06—Brief breasts in silhouette, while making love with Michael Paré. Dark.

•• 1:07—More breasts, while on top of Paré, then lying down.

Bridget Butler . . . . Lady in New York

• 0:00—Buns, lying in bed.

• 0:01—Buns, when Michael Paré takes off her shirt. Buns and partial left breast lying on him in bed.

Kerrie Clark . . . . .Brandon's Model

Tracy Dali . . . . Carl's Pool Girl

•• 1:08—Breasts in pool with Dennis Hopper. Breasts and buns, getting out of pool while wearing a G-string.

Elena Sahagun . . . . .Brandon's Model

Julie Strain. . . . . Carl's Breakfast Girl/Party Statuette

•• 0:51—Breasts, covered with silver paint, made up to look like a statue at the party.

Tracy Tweed . . . . Lena

••• 0:19—Breasts making love with Michael Paré. Nice, long scene.

••• 0:22—Breasts and buns, making love with Paré on stairs, sofa and the floor.

••• 0:24—Breasts, lying on the floor when the bad guys come in. Brief partial right breast, standing up and covering herself with a jacket.

Sunset Strip *(1992)*

Cameron . . . . Crystal

•• 0:17—Breasts and buns in G-string, while dancing on stage.

•• 0:38—In red dress, then breasts while doing strip routine.

•• 1:03—In dress, then breasts while stripping. Buns in body stocking.

• 1:16—Breasts in music video.

Bridget Butler . . . . Candice

Michelle Clunie . . . . .Jonesy

••• 0:23—In black skirt and bra, then breasts and buns in G-string, while doing routine on stage.

• 1:16—Breasts in music video.

Michelle Foreman . . . . .Heather

•• 0:29—In black bra and G-string, while practicing her dance routine in her living room.

•• 1:24—Buns in G-string, while dancing during contest.

•• 1:28—Breasts while in the shower with Jeff Conaway. Don't see her face well, but it looks like her.

••• 1:30—Buns in G-string, while dancing on stage and breasts (finally!) at the end.

Lori Jo Hendrix . . . . .Tammy

•• 0:54—Breasts, after taking off her swimsuit top for Crystal's video camera.

••• 1:12—Breasts and buns in G-string, while doing strip routine on stage.

• 1:16—Breasts in music video.

Shelley Michelle. . . . . Veronica

Tonya Moon . . . . Amateur Dancer

•• 0:33—Breasts, while dancing on stage in black shorts.

Superchick *(1978)*

Uschi Digard . . . . .Mayday

••• 0:42—Buns and breasts getting whipped acting during the making of a film, then talking to three people.

Flo Gerrish. . . . . Funky Jane

Joyce Jillson . . . . Tara B. True/Superchick

• 0:03—Brief upper half of right breast leaning back in bathtub.

•• 0:06—Breasts in bed throwing cards up.

• 0:16—Brief breasts under net on boat with Johnny.

• 0:29—Brief right breast several times in airplane restroom with a Marine.

• 1:12—Buns, frolicking in the ocean with Johnny. Don't see her face.

• 1:27—Close up of breasts (probably body double) when sweater pops open.

Candy Samples . . . . .Lady on Boat

••• 0:08—Breasts in bed with Johnny on boat.

Superfly *(1972)*

Sheila Frazier . . . . .Georgia

•• 0:40—Breasts and buns, making love in the bathtub with Superfly.

• ***The Supergrass*** *(1985; British)*

Jennifer Saunders. . . . . Lesley

•• 0:44—In white bra and black panties, then side of right breast when changing into her pajamas in hotel room.

• ***Supermodel Invasion*** *(1996)*

Lucie Malkrabova . . . . Model 5

••• 0:31—In swimsuit, then nude, while posing by the pool.

• 0:48—Full frontal nudity, while standing and posing.

Karolina Mirosova . . . . Model 3
••• 0:10—Breasts and buns, while posing in lingerie on balcony.
••• 0:42—Nude, while rolling on the floor, then standing and posing.
Darina Vanickova. . . . . Model 2
•• 0:09—Brief breasts, while posing.
•• 0:34—Breasts, while lying by the pool.

• *Supermodels Go Wild (1993; Video Tape)*
Jena Behr. . . . . Model
••• 0:00—Nude throughout.

Superstar: The Life and Times of Andy Warhol (1990)
Viva. . . . . Herself
• 0:26—Very brief right breast, while raising blouse to breast feed a baby.
• 0:49—Brief breasts, while lying in bed on right side of split screen in a clip from another film.

Surf II (1984)
Corinne Bohrer . . . . Cindy Lou
Britt Helfer. . . . . Hot Potato #2
•• 0:25—Breasts taking off bikini top with her friend in lifeguard station at beach with Eric Stoltz and his friend.
•• 0:27—Brief breasts with her friend, after dropping towel when she raises her hands for the police.
Linda Kerridge. . . . . Sparkle
Joy Michael . . . . Hot Potato #1
•• 0:25—Breasts taking off bikini top with her friend in lifeguard station at beach with Eric Stoltz and his friend.
•• 0:27—Brief breasts with her friend, after dropping towel when she raises her hands for the police.
Carol Wayne . . . . Mrs. O'Finlay

Surf Nazis Must Die (1986)
Bobbie Bresee . . . . Smeg's Mom
Cristina Garcia. . . . . Waitress
• 0:21—Breasts pulling her top up for Wheels while sitting on his lap.
Dawn Wildsmith . . . . Eva
• 0:25—Breasts being fondled at the beach wearing a wet suit by Adolf. Mostly right breast.

Surf, Sand and Sex (1994)
Debra Beatty . . . . Second Woman
••• 0:12—Breasts and buns, while fantasizing about doing a strip dance routine in front of one customer in gentleman's club, then making love with him on stage. Long scene.
• 1:08—Breasts again during end credits.
Kim Dawson . . . . First Woman
••• 0:03—Full frontal nudity, in bathtub, then making love on bed with her first husband. Nice, long scene.
Lauren Hays . . . . Hostess
1:04—Brief buns in two piece swimsuit during end credits.
Tamara Landry . . . . Fifth Woman
••• 0:44—In bra, then breasts and very brief partial buns, while making love with a policeman in her house. Long scene.
Tané McClure . . . . Uncredited Fourth Woman
••• 0:34—Breasts, while making love with Nick in a restaurant. Very brief partial lower frontal nudity. Lit with red light. Long scene.
•• 1:09—Breasts, during end credits.

Danielle Petty . . . . Sixth Woman
••• 0:54—In bra, then breasts, buns and very, very brief partial lower frontal nudity, when making love with a guy she met while hiking in the mountains.
• 1:10—Breasts, during end credits.
Gwen Somers . . . . Suzanne
••• 0:27—Breasts while making love with Kato Kaelin on hood of car. Wearing sunglasses the entire time.

Surfacing (1980)
Kathleen Beller. . . . . Kate
• 0:22—Very brief buns, pulling down pants to change. Dark, hard to see.
• 0:23—Very brief right breast undressing. Dark, hard to see.
• 0:24—Very, very brief breasts turning over in bed.
• 0:25—Buns, while standing next to bed.
••• 1:23—Breasts washing herself in the water. One long shot, one side view of right breast.

The Surgeon (1995; German/U.S.)
a.k.a. Exquisite Tenderness
Isabel Glasser. . . . . Dr. Theresa McCann
•• 0:55—Nude, while frolicking in the pool with James Remar, then getting out.
Juliette Jeffers. . . . . Lisa Wilson
• 0:51—Left breast, while making love with her boyfriend, Tommy, when she's in hospital bed.
Kendra Tucker . . . . TV Nurse (Soap Opera)

The Surrogate (1984; Canadian)
Carole Laure . . . . Anouk Vanderlin
• 0:48—Very brief breasts when Frank rips her blouse open in his apartment.
Barbara Law. . . . . Maggie Simpson
Marilyn Lightstone. Dr. Harriet Forman
Shannon Tweed. . . . . Lee Wake
••• 0:03—Breasts taking a Jacuzzi bath.
• 0:42—Brief breasts changing in bedroom, then in bra getting dressed. Long shot.
••• 1:02—Breasts in sauna talking with Frank. Long scene.

Survival Quest (1989)
Catherine Keener. . . . . Cheryl
Traci Lind . . . . Olivia
• 0:50—Breasts, while bathing in a stream while seen by Gray. Long shot.

• *Surviving Picasso (1996)*
Natascha McElhone. . . . . Francoise
•• 0:20—Full frontal nudity, while posing for Anthony Hopkins in his studio.
Julianne Moore . . . . Dora
Diane Venora. . . . . Jacqueline

Survivor (1987)
Sue Kiel . . . . The Woman
••• 0:33—Right breast, then breasts and buns making love with Survivor in hammock. Long scene.

Suspect Device (1995; Made for Cable Movie)
Jill Pierce . . . . Operator
Heidi Sorenson . . . . Kristen
•• 0:05—Breasts and buns, after taking off nightgown then making love in bed with C. Thomas Howell.
Stacey Travis . . . . Jessica

Suspicious Agenda (1994)
Rachel Hayward . . . . Roxanne
- •• 0:17—Left breast and side view of buns, while lying in bed.
- • 0:18—Left breast (close-up) while kissing Richard Grieco in bed.
- • 0:19—Breasts, when sitting up in bed.
- •• 0:20—Breasts after Grieco leaves.

Suzanne (1973)
a.k.a. The Second Coming of Suzanne
(*Suzanne* has nudity in it, *The Second Coming of Suzanne* has the nudity cut out.)
Sondra Locke . . . . Suzanne
- •• 0:27—Breasts sitting, looking at a guy. Brief left breast several times lying down.
- ••• 0:29—Breasts lying down.

Suzanne (1980; Canadian)
Jennifer Dale . . . . Suzanne
- •• 0:29—Breasts when boyfriend lifts her sweatshirt up when she's sitting on couch doing homework.
- •• 0:53—Breasts with Nicky on the floor.

Gina Dick . . . . Marilyn

Swamp Thing (1981)
Adrienne Barbeau . . . . Alice Cable
- • 1:03—Side view of left breast washing herself off in the swamp. Long shot.

Mimi Craven . . . . Secretary

Swann in Love (1984; French/German)
a.k.a. Un Amour de Swann
Marie-Christine Barrault . . . . Madame Verdunn
Ornella Muti . . . . Odette de Crêcy
- •• 1:15—Brief left breast, making love with Jeremy Irons.
- ••• 1:28—Breasts sitting on bed talking to Irons.

Swashbuckler (1976)
Rutanya Alda . . . . Bath Attendant
Genevieve Bujold . . . . Jane Barnet
- • 1:00—Very brief side view nude, diving from the ship into the water. Long shot, don't really see anything.
- • 1:01—Buns and brief side of left breast seen from under water.

Anjelica Huston . . . . Woman of Dark Visage
Lisa Moore . . . . Pirates' Lady
Dorothy Tristan . . . . Alice
Brenda Venus . . . . Bath Attendant

The Sweeper (1995)
Keisha . . . . Mall Mother
Kristen Dalton . . . . Rachel
- •• 1:04—Buns and breasts behind shower curtain, then behind glass, while making love with C. Thomas Howell.

Janet Gunn . . . . Melissa
Kathrin Lautner . . . . Amy
Cynda Williams . . . . Diane

Sweet Country (1985)
Jane Alexander . . . . Anna
- • 1:39—Brief side view of left breast after getting out of bed.

Carole Laure . . . . Eva
- •• 0:31—Breasts changing in apartment while Randy Quaid watches.
- • 0:43—Nude in auditorium with other women prisoners.
- ••• 1:13—Nude in bed with Quaid.

Irene Papas . . . . Mrs. Araya
Joanna Pettet . . . . Monica

Sweet Hearts Dance (1988)
Holly Marie Combs . . . . Debs Boon
Elizabeth Perkins . . . . Adie Nims
Susan Sarandon . . . . Sandra Boon
- • 1:25—Very, very brief left breast, then very brief right breast, under white bathrobe arguing with Don Johnson in the bathroom.

• *The Sweet Hereafter* (1997; Canadian)
Arsinée Khanjian . . . . Wanda Otto
Fides Krucker . . . . Klara
- • 0:01—Brief upper half of right breast, while sleeping in bed next to her baby and her husband.

Stephanie Morgenstern . . . . Allison
Gabrielle Rose . . . . Dolores Driscoll
Alberta Watson . . . . Risa Walker
- • 0:45—Brief breasts, after turning away from the window then lying on the bed, while talking with Bruce Greenwood.
- •• 0:46—Brief full frontal nudity, while putting her panties on.

Sweet Justice (1991)
Finn Carter . . . . Sunny Justice
Catherine Hickland . . . . Chris Barnes
- • 0:52—Brief buns and left breast, getting into spa. (You don't see her face clearly, it looks like a body double because her hair is different.)
- •• 0:53—Brief upper half of left breast, while sitting in spa. This is definitely her!

Marjean Holden . . . . MJ
Kathleen Kinmont . . . . Heather
Michelle McCormick . . . . Kim
- • 0:44—Buns in sexy outfit while dancing on stage in club.

Cheryl Paris . . . . Suzanne
- •• 0:12—Brief breasts while making love with Singer standing up by tree.

Patricia Tallman . . . . Josie

Sweet Killing (1992; Canadian/French)
Andrea Ferréol . . . . Louise Cross
Leslie Hope . . . . Eva Bishop
- •• 0:36—Right breast and partial left breast, while making love with Alan.

Sweet Murder (1990)
Embeth Davidtz . . . . Laurie Shannon
- • 0:40—Brief breasts behind wet shower door. Can't really see anything.

Helene Udy . . . . Lisa Smith
- •• 0:44—Brief buns, twice, while standing in doorway in Dell's apartment.
- •• 0:47—Breasts in bed while talking to Dell, then nude, getting out of bed while he's asleep.
- • 0:48—Brief nude while stabbing Dell with a knife.
- • 0:49—Buns and right breast while dragging Dell out of the bedroom.

Sweet Perfection (1988)
a.k.a. The Perfect Model
Liza Cruzat . . . . Linda Johnson
- • 0:31—Left breast, in bed with Mario. Don't see her face. Probably a body double.

Sweet Poison (1991)

Patricia Healy. . . . . Charlene
- • 0:01—Breasts and buns, while straddling her husband in bed.
- ••• 1:05—Breasts, dropping her towel in front of Bauer in the bathroom.
- •• 1:08—Side view breasts, straddling Bauer in bed.

Sweet Revenge (1987)

Nancy Allen. . . . . Jillian Grey
Gina Gershon . . . . K.C.
- • 0:41—Brief breasts in water under a waterfall with Lee.

Michele Little. . . . . Lee
- • 0:41—Brief breasts in water under a waterfall with K.C.

Sweet Sixteen (1982)

Sharon Farrell . . . . Kathy
Aleisa Shirley . . . . Melissa Morgan
- • 0:16—Side view of body, nude, taking a shower.
- • 1:11—Breasts undressing to go skinny dipping with Hank. Dark, hard to see.
- • 1:13—Breasts, getting out of the water.

Susan Strasberg. . . . . Joanne Morgan

Sweet Sugar (1972)

a.k.a. Hellfire on Ice

Pamela Collins. . . . . Dolores
- • 0:26—Brief breasts when doctor tears her bra off.
- ••• 0:50—Breasts in the shower with Phyllis Davis.

Phyllis Davis. . . . . Sugar
- ••• 0:34—Breasts in bed with a guard.
- ••• 0:50—Breasts in the shower with Dolores.
- •• 0:57—Brief breasts in the bathroom.

Ella Edwards . . . . Simone
- • 0:58—Breasts in bed with Mojo.

Jackie Giroux. . . . . Fara
- •• 0:33—Breasts, skinny dipping in stream with Dolores.

Sweet William (1980; British)

Jenny Agutter . . . . Ann
- • 0:27—Buns, while standing on balcony with Sam Waterston.
- •• 0:28—Breasts sitting on edge of the bed while talking with Waterston.
- • 0:44—Brief left breast when Waterston takes her blouse off in the living room.

Anna Massey. . . . . Edna

Sweetie (1989; Australian)

Karen Colston . . . . Kay
- •• 0:24—Very brief side of right breast while sitting up in bed, then breasts in bed with Lou.
- • 0:25—Right breast while sitting up in bed and putting bra on.

Genevieve Lemon . . . . Sweetie
- •• 1:23—Breasts in tree house (she's covered with paint).
- • 1:25—Brief buns, mooning her dad.

Swept Away (1975; Italian)

a.k.a. Swept Away...by an unusual destiny in the blue sea of august

Mariangela Melato . . . . Raffaela Lenzetti
- •• 1:10—Breasts on the sand when Giancarlo Giannini catches her and makes love with her.

The Swindle (1991)

Jasaé . . . . Nina
- ••• 0:28—Nude, posing for Tom while he video tapes her. Long scene.
- ••• 0:31—Nude, making love with Tom.
- ••• 0:36—Breasts in back of limousine with Dude.

Monica Akesson. . . . . Tom's Last Hurrah
- ••• 1:17—Breasts, then full frontal nudity, posing on couch for Tom.

Gloria Pryor . . . . Claudia
- •• 1:15—Breasts with Tom.

Swing Shift (1984)

Goldie Hawn . . . . Kay Walsh
Holly Hunter . . . . Jeannie Sherman
Penny Johnson. . . . . Genevieve
Lisa Pelikan . . . . Violet Mulligan
Alana Stewart . . . . Frankie Parker
- • 0:11—Buns in B&W photo that Christine Lahti shows to Fred Ward. Possible photo composite.

The Swinging Cheerleaders (1974)

Colleen Camp . . . . Mary Ann
Sandra Dempsey . . . . 1st Girl at Tryout
Rosanne Katon. . . . . Lisa
- •• 0:25—Breasts taking off her blouse in her teacher's office. Half of right breast while he talks on the phone.

Cheryl Smith . . . . Andrea
- •• 0:12—Breasts taking off her bra and putting sheer blouse on.
- • 0:17—Left breast, several times, sitting in bed with Ross.

Switch (1991)

Lysette Anthony. . . . . Liz
- • 0:05—Brief breasts in spa with JoBeth Williams and Felicia, trying to kill Steve.

Ellen Barkin . . . . Amanda Brooks/Steve
Lorraine Bracco . . . . Sheila Faxton
Linda Doná . . . . Gay Club Patron
Catherine Keener. . . . . Steve's Secretary
Victoria Mahoney . . . . Felicia
Karen Medak . . . . Saleswoman
Jackie Moen . . . . Girl at City Grille
JoBeth Williams . . . . Margo Brofman
Rebecca Wood. . . . . Gay Club Patron

Switchblade Sisters (1975)

Marlene Clark . . . . Muff
Janice Karman . . . . Bunnie
Robin Lee . . . . Lace
- • 0:48—Breasts sitting up in bed to talk to Dominic. Dark.

Joanne Nail . . . . Maggie
- • 0:21—Very, very brief right breast in ripped blouse when she tries to rip Dominic's shirt off.

Jerii Woods . . . . Toby

The Sword and the Sorcerer (1982)

Kathleen Beller. . . . . Alana
- • 0:54—Side view of buns, lying face down getting oil rubbed all over her.

Shelly Taylor Morgan. . . . . Bar-Bra
- • 0:54—Brief breasts when Lee Horsley crashes through the window and almost lands on her.

Sword of Honor *(1994)*

Sophia Crawford . . . . Vicky

- • 0:43—In bra and panties with Johnny, then (muscular) buns and brief right breast, twice.

Sylvester *(1985)*

Melissa Gilbert . . . . Charlie

- • 0:23—Very, very brief breasts struggling with a guy in truck cab. Seen through a dirty windshield.
- •• 0:24—Very brief left breast after Richard Farnsworth runs down the stairs to help her. Seen from the open door of the truck.

T-Force *(1994)*

Jane Higginson . . . . Hostage

Jennifer MacDonald . . . . Mandragora

- • 0:56—Breasts, while outside with Adam, finding out if she can procreate. Don't see her face.

Rochelle Swanson . . . . Cocktail Waitress

Taffin *(1988; U.S./British)*

Alison Doody . . . . Charlotte

- • 0:14—Very, very brief side view of right breast when Pierce Brosnan rips her blouse open. Long shot, hard to see.

Tina Shaw . . . . Lola the Stripper

- •• 1:04—Breasts doing routine in a club.

Tai-Pan *(1986)*

Joan Chen . . . . May May

- • 0:56—Brief left breast washing herself, hard to see anything.

Kyra Sedgwick . . . . Tess

Janine Turner . . . . Shevaun

Tainted

Shari Shattuck . . . . Cathy

- •• 0:09—Buns, while lying on top of Frank.
- ••• 0:27—Breasts in bubble bath, getting up, drying herself off, then putting on white bra while wearing panties.
- ••• 0:49—Breasts taking a shower.
- • 0:51—Brief side view of left breast in the shower again.

Tainted Love *(1995)*

Lee Anne Beaman . . . . Sara Baldwin

- • 0:24—Brief breasts, while in bathtub.
- •• 0:29—Breasts and partial buns, while talking with Chantal in steam room.
- • 0:41—Brief buns, while walking into spa and talking with Chantal.
- •• 0:53—Breasts, while making love with Michael on boat.
- • 0:54—Buns in T-back, while kissing Michael on boat.
- •• 1:03—Breasts, while making love with Michael in back seat of limousine.
- • 1:19—In black bra, then buns in panties, while in her apartment with Michael.

Dixie Beck . . . . Marie

Kelly Burns . . . . Chantal Benteen

- • 0:27—Brief breasts, while changing clothes in locker room.
- •• 0:29—Full frontal nudity, while talking with Sara in steam room.
- •• 0:58—In black bra, then breasts and buns, while making love with Franz on factory floor.
- • 1:00—Breasts, while lying dead on bed with her wrists tied to the bed.

Nicole Gian . . . . Pauline

- •• 0:06—In lingerie, then breasts while undressing in bedroom in front of a police officer.

Caroline Key Johnson. . . . . Chloe

Nici Sterling . . . . Carol Spencer

- • 0:17—Full frontal nudity, while lying dead in bed with her wrists tied to bed. More in photos.

Take Two *(1988)*

Robin Mattson. . . . . Susan Bentley

- •• 0:25—Brief breasts taking a shower.
- ••• 0:29—Breasts in bed with Goodeve.
- ••• 0:45—Right breast in shower, then breasts getting into bed.
- • 0:47—Brief breasts getting out of bed and putting an overcoat on.
- ••• 1:28—Breasts taking a shower after shooting Goodeve in bed.

Karen Mayo-Chandler . . . . Dorothy

- •• 1:17—Brief breasts on bed when her gold dress is pulled down a bit.

Suzanne Slater. . . . . Sherrie

- •• 0:11—Breasts in office talking with Grant Goodeve, wearing panties, garter belt and stockings.
- • 1:00—Breasts undressing to get into hot tub wearing black underwear bottom.

• The Takeover *(1994)*

Arlene Rodriguez . . . . Brandi

- •• 0:00—Buns in two piece outfit, then breasts, while dancing on stage in club.

Cali Timmins . . . . Kathy

- • 1:12—Brief left breast, several times, while making love in bed with Jonathan.

Takin' It All Off *(1987)*

Gail Harris . . . . Hannah McCall

- ••• 0:03—Breasts in red leotard and head band, in dance studio.
- ••• 0:11—Full frontal nudity in the showers (she's in the back on the right.)
- ••• 0:28—Nude, doing strip routine outside.
- •• 1:24—Nude, dancing with the other girls on stage.
- • 1:29—Breasts in crate backstage with Hadem.

Becky LeBeau. . . . . Becky

- •• 0:03—Breasts in pink leotard in dance studio.
- ••• 0:11—Nude in the showers (she's in the back on the left).
- •• 0:16—Breasts and brief full frontal nudity getting introduced to Allison.
- ••• 0:23—In black bra and panties, then nude doing a strip routine outside.
- • 0:35—Brief full frontal nudity pushing Elliot into the pool.
- • 0:36—Brief breasts in studio with Allison again.
- • 0:36—Brief left breast in dance studio with Allison.
- •• 1:23—Nude, dancing with the other girls on stage.

Francesca "Kitten" Natividad . . . . Betty Bigones

- ••• 0:12—Nude, washing herself in the shower.
- •• 0:39—Nude, on stage in a giant glass, then breasts backstage in her dressing room.
- •• 0:42—Breasts in flashbacks from *Takin' It Off.*
- •• 0:46—Breasts in group in the studio.
- ••• 0:53—Nude, dancing on the deck outside. Some nice slow motion shots.
- •• 1:16—Breasts on stage in club.
- ••• 1:23—Nude, dancing with the other girls on stage.

Jean Poremba . . . . Allison
- • 0:36—Buns in G-string and in pink bra.
- ••• 0:49—In white lingerie, then breasts, then nude dancing.
- ••• 0:58—Breasts and buns in G-string, dancing outside when she hears the music.
- ••• 0:59—Nude dancing in a park.
- •• 1:01—Nude dancing in a laundromat.
- ••• 1:03—Nude dancing in a restaurant.
- ••• 1:07—Nude in shower with Adam.
- •• 1:13—Breasts dancing for the music in a studio.
- ••• 1:23—Nude, dancing with the other girls on stage.

Takin' It Off *(1984)*

Francesca "Kitten" Natividad. . . . . Betty Bigones
- •• 0:01—Breasts dancing on stage.
- ••• 0:04—Breasts and buns dancing on stage.
- •• 0:29—Breasts in the Doctor's office.
- ••• 0:32—Nude dancing in the Psychiatrist's office.
- ••• 0:39—Nude in bed with a guy during fantasy sequence playing with vegetables and fruits.
- •• 0:49—Breasts in bed covered with popcorn.
- • 0:51—Nude doing a dance routine in the library.
- ••• 1:09—Nude splashing around in a clear plastic bathtub on stage.
- •• 1:20—Nude at a fat farm dancing.
- •• 1:24—Nude running in the woods in slow motion.

Angelique Pettyjohn . . . . Anita Little

Ashley St. Jon . . . . Sin
- ••• 0:20—Breasts and buns doing two dance routines on stage.
- •• 0:53—Nude, stripping and dancing in the library.

Taking Care of Business *(1990)*

Jill Johnson . . . . Tennis Court Girl

Loryn Locklin. . . . . Jewel
- • 0:42—Buns and very brief side view, twice, seen through door, changing by the pool. Then in black two piece swimsuit.

Taking the Heat *(1993)*

Lynn Whitfield. . . . . Carolyn

Rachel York . . . . Susan
- •• 0:19—Left breast, while enthusiastically making love in bed on top of George Segal. Very, very brief breasts when changing positions to under the sheets.

Tales From the Darkside, The Movie *(1990)*

Rae Dawn Chong . . . . Carola
- • 1:09—Left breast in blue light, twice, with James Remar. Don't see her face.

Deborah Harry . . . . Betty

Julianne Moore . . . . Susan

Tales of Erotica *(1995)*

Henrietta Baynes . . . . Mrs. Kirsch
- • 0:30—Brief upper half of breasts, while wearing lingerie and playing with a vibrator by herself.

Mira Sorvino . . . . Teresa

Cynda Williams . . . . Davida Urked
- •• 1:30—Breasts and buns, getting out of bubble bath and walking to the front door. Covered with bubbles.
- • 1:31—Brief breasts, getting back into the bathtub.
- • 1:32—Brief breasts, moving back in bathtub. Upper half of breasts, while sitting in bathtub.
- • 1:34—Brief breasts, while turning around in bathtub.
- • 1:36—Buns, while standing up in bathtub. Brief close up shot of buns.
- • 1:38—Brief buns in video playback.

Tales of Ordinary Madness *(1983; Italian)*

Katia Berger. . . . . Girl on Beach
- ••• 1:30—Full frontal nudity, taking off her clothes in front of Ben Gazzara at the beach.

Judith Drake . . . . Fat Woman
- • 0:49—Buns, in bra and panties in her bedroom with Ben Gazzara, then left breast when he fondles her.

Tanya Lopert . . . . Vicky
- • 0:58—Buns, then breasts in bedroom with Pepito and Ben Gazzara.

Ornella Muti . . . . Cass
- •• 0:37—Buns, four times, while standing at window in room with Ben Gazzara. Medium long shot.
- • 1:06—Buns, while standing at the beach and feeding the seagulls. One medium long shot and one long shot.

Susan Tyrrell . . . . Vera
- • 0:19—Right nipple, seen in between strings in bra when she's lying on the floor.
- • 0:20—Upper half of breasts, in between strings in bra. Lower frontal nudity.
- •• 0:22—Lower frontal nudity and upper half of breasts in bra, while standing by the door. Brief buns, while getting carried to bed by Ben Gazzara.
- •• 0:23—Upper half of breasts, buns and lower frontal nudity while lying in bed.

Talking Walls *(1982)*

Judith Baldwin . . . . n.a.

Elizabeth Carder . . . . Bored Girl
- •• 0:20—Breasts, making love in the Sheep Room.
- • 1:09—Very brief left breast, in bed.

Sybil Danning . . . . Bathing Beauty

Sally Kirkland . . . . Hooker

Marie Laurin . . . . Jeanne

Kathi Sawyer-Young. . . . . n.a.

June Wilkinson. . . . . Blonde
- • 0:13—Brief left breast, in car room, getting green towel yanked off.
- • 0:14—Very, very brief left breast in car room again. Dark.
- •• 1:08—Brief breasts, getting green towel taken off.

The Tall Guy *(1990; British)*

Anna Massey . . . . Mary

Emma Thompson . . . . Kate
- ••• 0:33—Very brief right breast, brief buns, then breasts during funny love making scene with Jeff Goldblum.

Tango & Cash *(1989)*

Dori Courtney . . . . Dressing Room Girl
- • 1:06—Breasts, sitting in chair looking in the mirror in the background. Long shot.

Teri Hatcher. . . . . Kiki

Roxanne Kernohan . . . . Dressing Room Girl
- • 1:06—Brief breasts in dressing room with three other girls. She's the second one in the middle.

Tamara Landry. . . . . Girl in Bar

Christie Mucciante. . . . . Dressing Room Girl
- • 1:06—Brief breasts in dressing room. (She's the first topless blonde.)

Tanya's Island (1980; Canadian)

Vanity . . . . Tanya
- • 0:04—Very brief breasts and buns covered with paint during B&W segment.
- ••• 0:07—Nude caressing herself and dancing during the opening credits.
- •• 0:09—Nude making love on the beach.
- • 0:11—Brief right breast, while talking to Lobo.
- •• 0:19—Brief breasts on the beach with Lobo, then more breasts while yelling at him.
- • 0:28—Mostly breasts in flimsy halter top exploring a cave.
- • 0:33—Full frontal nudity undressing in tent.
- • 0:35—Left breast sleeping. Dark, hard to see.
- • 0:37—Buns while sleeping.
- • 0:40—Breasts superimposed over another scene.
- • 0:48—Brief buns swimming in the ocean.
- •• 0:51—Full frontal nudity walking out of the ocean and getting dressed.
- • 0:53—Brief breasts in open blouse.
- •• 1:08—Breasts in middle of compound when Lobo rapes her in front of Blue.
- • 1:16—Full frontal nudity running through the jungle in slow motion. Brief buns.

Target (1985)

Ilona Grubel . . . . Carla
- • 1:12—Brief breasts in bed with Matt Dillon.

• *Target of Seduction* (1995)

Tané McClure . . . . Lauren
- • 0:04—Breasts, while dressing in front of mirror.
- ••• 0:18—Breasts and buns in T-back, while checking herself out in the mirror.
- ••• 0:25—Breasts and buns, while making love in bed with her boyfriend.
- • 0:50—Breasts, while putting make up on in dressing room.
- • 1:05—Left breast, while sleeping in bed.

Wendy Sage . . . . Alex
- • 0:59—Breasts and buns, while taking a shower. Don't see her face.

Tarzan, The Ape Man (1981)

Bo Derek . . . . Jane
- ••• 0:43—Nude taking a bath in the ocean, then in a wet white dress.
- • 1:35—Brief breasts painted all white.
- • 1:45—Breasts washing all the white paint off in the river with Tarzan.
- •• 1:47—Breasts during the ending credits playing with Tarzan and the orangutan. (When I saw this film in a movie theater, the entire audience actually stayed to watch the credits!)

Tattoo (1981)

Maud Adams . . . . Maddy
- • 0:22—Very brief breasts taking off clothes and putting a bathrobe on.
- •• 0:23—Breasts opening bathrobe so Bruce Dern can start painting.
- •• 0:25—Brief breasts getting into the shower to take off body paint.
- •• 0:58—Brief breasts and buns getting out of bed.
- •• 1:04—Breasts, knocked out on table before Dern starts tattooing her.
- ••• 1:07—Breasts looking at herself in the mirror with a few tattoos on.
- •• 1:24—Breasts lying on table masturbating while Dern watches through peep hole in the door.
- ••• 1:36—Full frontal nudity taking off robe then making love with Dern (her body is covered with tattoos).

E. Katherine Kerr . . . . Wife

Taxi Dancers (1993)

Michelle Hess . . . . Candy

Brittany McCrena . . . . Billie
- •• 0:16—Breasts, while changing clothes in room with Star.
- ••• 0:27—Breasts, while making love on billiard table with Bobby.
- ••• 0:44—Breasts (mostly left breast) while making love with Bobby in van.
- 0:45—Partial right breast, when waking up in the morning with Bobby.

The Teacher (1974)

Angel Tompkins . . . . Diane Marshall
- ••• 0:09—Breasts on a boat taking off her swimsuit.
- ••• 0:12—More breasts on the boat getting a suntan.
- ••• 0:36—Breasts taking off her top in bedroom, then buns and breasts taking a shower.
- • 0:41—Brief right breast lying back on bed.
- •• 0:43—Brief breasts opening her bathrobe for Jay North.
- •• 0:47—Side view of right breast lying on bed, then right breast from above.
- •• 0:52—Breasts in boat after making love.

Teachers (1984)

Laura Dern . . . . Diane

Lee Grant . . . . Dr. Burke

Julia Jennings . . . . The Blonde
- •• 0:05—Brief left breast, while sitting up in bed with Nick Nolte.

JoBeth Williams . . . . Lisa
- • 1:39—Brief breasts taking off clothes and running down school hallway yelling at Nick Nolte.

Ted & Venus (1991)

Elvira . . . . Lisa

Kim Adams . . . . Linda
- • 0:16—In sheer leotard in dance studio.
- ••• 0:30—Breasts, reciting poetry while in bed at night.

Pamella D'Pella . . . . Gloria
- ••• 0:17—Breasts while undressing in locker room while talking to Linda.

Carol Kane . . . . Colette/Colette's Twin Sister

Teen Lust (1978)

a.k.a. Girls Next Door

Kirsten Baker . . . . Carol Hill
- • 0:45—Brief side view of left breast, while changing clothes in her bedroom.

Teenage Bonnie and Klepto Clyde (1993)

Maureen Flannigan . . . . Bonnie
- • 0:26—Very brief breasts, while climbing into back seat of car.
- ••• 0:34—In black bra and panties, lying on bed when Clyde pours money all over her. Right breast after taking off bra. Breasts while making love.

Connie Hair . . . . Waitress

Teenage Exorcist (1992)

Jasaé . . . . Dead Woman
- 0:01—Brief breasts, dead with a slashed throat, on stairway when discovered by the maid.
- 0:16—Brief breasts, several times, during nightmare while Brinke Stevens is sleeping.

Elena Sahagun. . . . . Sally
- 0:09—Brief side view of right breast and buns in panties, while putting robe on.
- 0:31—Buns and brief side of right breast, while getting into the shower.
- •• 0:32—Buns and right breast, while getting soaped up by creature's hand. Sort of frontal nudity behind fabric shower curtain.

Brinke Stevens. . . . . Dianne
- 1:03—Brief partial buns in sexy, skimpy outfit, while walking down stairs with Eddie Deezen.
- 1:06—More brief partial buns.
- 1:13—Partial buns, during struggle with Elena Sahagan.
- 1:13—More partial buns, while bending over Jay Richardson.
- 1:16—Partial buns under fishnet stockings with Deezen.

Teenage Seductress

Sondra Currie . . . . Terry
- ••• 0:14—Buns, while taking off robe in bedroom. Breasts, while looking at herself in bathroom mirror.
- ••• 0:16—Breasts, while in front of mirror again. More breasts while taking a shower.
- 0:24—Breasts, while in bed, trying to get Preston to join her.
- 1:14—Brief partial right breast, while lying on bed with Preston.

The Tempest (1982)

Molly Ringwald . . . . Miranda

Susan Sarandon. . . . . Aretha
- 1:57—Brief right, then left breasts in open T-shirt saving someone in the water.

• *Temptation of a Monk* (1993; Hong Kong)

Joan Chen . . . . Princess Scarlet/Violet
- •• 1:39—Breast and upper half of buns, after opening her robe. (She has a shaved, bald head.)

Temptress (1994)

Kim Delaney . . . . Karin Swann
- •• 0:14—Breasts, while making love with Chris Sarandon.
- 0:44—Buns, making love on bed with Sarandon.

Barbara Moore . . . . Champagne Glass Model
- ••• 0:18—Breasts, while posing in a large champagne glass during photo session.

Dee Wallace Stone . . . . Allison Mackie

Jessica Walter. . . . . Dr. Phyllis Evergreen

Tender Loving Care (1974)

Donna Desmond. . . . . Karen Jordan
- ••• 0:26—Breasts on waterbed with Reno, brief lower frontal nudity, making love. Long scene.
- 0:39—Breasts and very brief buns getting out of bed.
- •• 0:55—Brief buns and breasts on bed with Dr. Traynor.

• *Tender Loving Care* (1993)

Antonia Dorian . . . . Nursing Grad

Nicole Durant . . . . Tough Beach Girl

Deborah Dutch . . . . Tough Beach Girl/Party Girl
- •• 1:07—Breasts, while in spa with a blonde party girl.

Lori Morrissey . . . . Candy
- ••• 0:15—Breasts, while running and sunbathing at the beach.

Deanne Power. . . . . Veronica
- ••• 0:53—Breasts, while sitting on Julio's lap.
- ••• 0:55—Buns and breasts, while dancing and stripping in front of the doctor in his office.

Rhonda Shear . . . . Gretchen

Lisa M. Throw . . . . Stacy
- ••• 0:06—Breasts, sleeping, waking up, then taking a shower.

Terminal Choice (1985; Canadian)

Teri Austin. . . . . Lylah Crane
- 0:14—Full frontal nudity, covered with blood on operating table. Long shot.
- 0:21—Right breast, on table being examined by Ellen Barkin. Dead, covered with dried blood.
- 0:26—Very brief left breast under plastic on table, hard to see.

Ellen Barkin . . . . Mary O'Connor

Chapelle Jaffe. . . . . Mrs. Dodson

Diane Venora. . . . . Anna
- 0:48—Brief left breast, making love in bed with Frank. Don't see her face.

Sandra Warren. . . . . Nurse Tipton

Cheryl-Ann Wilson. . . . . Nurse Fields

Terminal Entry (1986)

Barbara Edwards . . . . Lady Electric
- ••• 0:05—Breasts taking a shower and getting a towel during video game scene.

Jill Terashita . . . . Gwen

Terminal Exposure (1988)

Tara Buckman . . . . Mrs. Karrothers

Hope Marie Carlton. . . . . Christie
- ••• 1:11—Breasts in bathtub licking ice cream off a guy.

Ava Fabian. . . . . Bruce's Girl

Luann Lee . . . . Bruce's Girl

Nicole Rio . . . . Hostage Girl

Terminal Island (1973)

Phyllis Davis. . . . . Joy Lange
- ••• 0:39—Breasts and buns in a pond, full frontal nudity getting out, then more breasts putting blouse on while a guy watches.

Marta Kristen. . . . . Lee Phillips

Barbara Leigh . . . . Bunny Campbell
- ••• 0:22—Breasts and buns undressing in room while Bobbie watches from the bed.

Terminal Justice (1995)

Kari Wührer . . . . Pamela
- •• 0:47—Brief breasts, while in the bathroom when Lorenzo Lamas talks with her.
- ••• 1:04—Breasts, while making love with Lamas in bed.

Terminal Virus (1995; Made for Cable Movie)

Kelly Burns. . . . . Shara
- •• 0:55—Breasts, while making love in the lab with Joe.

Nikki Fritz . . . . Casandra
- •• 0:04—Breasts, while running away from the bad guy.
- 0:05—Very brief breasts, while getting up off the ground.
- 0:06—Breasts, while running away from some more bad guys, then climbing into car.

Bianca Rocilili . . . . Uncredited Woman on TV
•• 0:40—Breasts, while making love on phony porno video tape seen on TV.
Elena Sahagun . . . . Blanca
• 0:32—Very brief side of right breast, then buns, while undressing and joining two other nude women in the bath outside.
•• 1:09—Breasts, after taking off top during strip poker game.
Cristina Villiegas . . . . Cristina
• 0:32—Nude, while bathing outside when joined by Elena Sahagun. (She's the one furthest from Sahagun.)

The Terminator (1984)

Linda Hamilton . . . . Sarah Connor
•• 1:18—Brief breasts about four times making love on top of Michael Biehn in motel room.

Terms of Endearment (1983)

Shirley MacLaine . . . . Aurora Greenway
• 1:00—Very, very brief right breast wrestling with Jack Nicholson in the ocean when she finally frees his hand from her breast. One frame. Hard to see, but for the sake of thoroughness....
Michelle Watkins . . . . Woman
Debra Winger . . . . Emma Greenway Horton

Terror at the Opera (1989; Italian)

Barbara Cupisti . . . . Albertini
Cristina Marsillach . . . . Betty
• 0:23—Brief left breast during nightmare. Brief breasts, sitting up in bed and screaming.
Daria Nicolodi . . . . Mira

Terror in the Aisles (1984)

Nancy Allen . . . . Hostess
Susan Backlinie . . . . Swimmer
• 0:51—Breasts, under water from *Jaws.*
Kirsten Baker . . . . Terry
•• 1:03—Breasts and buns, undressing to go skinny dipping from *Friday the 13th, Part II.*
Morgan Fairchild . . . . Jamie
•• 1:06—Breasts in mirror in scene from *The Seduction.*
• 1:08—Brief left breast, getting out of pool from *The Seduction.*
Sandy Johnson . . . . Judith Meyers
• 0:15—Brief breasts in scene from *Halloween.*
Victoria Lynn Johnson . . . . . . Body Double for Angie Dickinson
• 1:07—Breasts in shower from Angie Dickinson's shower scene in *Dressed to Kill.*
P.J. Soles . . . . Lynda
• 0:24—Brief breasts in scene from *Halloween.*

The Terror on Alcatraz (1986)

Sandy Brooke . . . . Mona
• 0:05—Right breast on bed getting burned with a cigarette by Frank.
Alisa Wilson . . . . Clarissa
• 1:14—Brief breasts opening her blouse to distract Frank, so she can get away from him.

• *Terror on Tape* (1985; Video Tape)

Michelle Bauer . . . . Unsatisfied Video Store Customer
Lenka Novak . . . . Suzy
• 0:00—Breasts in scene from *Vampire Hookers.*

Terror Train (1980; Canadian)

Vanity . . . . Merry
Joy Boushel . . . . Pet
•• 0:49—Breasts, while wearing panties in sleeper room on train with Mo.
Jamie Lee Curtis . . . . Alena
Sandra Warren . . . . Mitchy

The Terror Within II (1992)

Clare Hoak . . . . Ariel
• 0:25—Brief side view of right breast, while in front of fire with Andrew Stevens.
Stella Stevens . . . . Kara
Barbara Alyn Woods . . . . Sharon
•• 0:28—Buns and breasts while in bed with Jamie.

Tess (1979; French/British)

Arielle Dombasle . . . . Mercy Chant
Suzanna Hamilton . . . . Izz
Nastassja Kinski . . . . Tess Durbeyfield
• 0:47—Brief left breast, opening blouse in field to feed her baby.

Test Tube Teens From the Year 2000 (1993)

a.k.a. Virgin Hunters
Robin Joi Brown . . . . Victoria
••• 0:31—Breasts, in the showers (she's on the left) with Annie while Vin and Naldo watch.
Sara Suzanne Brown . . . . Reena
•• 0:03—In black bra and panties, then buns in panties and breasts stripping out of her jumpsuit during Vin's day dream.
Morgan Fairchild . . . . Camella Swales
Charlie Spradling . . . . Girl on TV
• 0:23—Breasts in scenes from *Meridian: Kiss of the Beast* being shown on TV.
Laurel Wiley . . . . Annie
••• 0:30—Breasts, taking off towel and in the showers (she's on the right) with Victoria while Vin and Naldo watch.

Texas Detour (1977)

Priscilla Barnes . . . . Claudia Hunter
••• 1:03—Breasts, changing clothes and walking around in bedroom. Wearing white panties. This is her best breasts scene.
• 1:11—Breasts sitting up in bed with Patrick Wayne.
Lindsay Bloom . . . . Sugar McCarthy

Texas Lightning (1980)

Maureen McCormick . . . . Fay
• 1:04—Very brief upper half of right breast popping out of slip while struggling on bed with two jerks. Long shot, hard to see.
Danone Simpson . . . . n.a.

• *Thanks of a Grateful Nation* (1998; Made for Cable Movie)

Cynthia Dale . . . . Lisa Tuite
Karyn Dwyer . . . . Deeni
Marg Helgenberger . . . . Jerrilinn Folz
Jennifer Jason Leigh . . . . Teri Small
• 0:10—Brief breasts, while making love with Chris in bed.
• 0:38—Brief breasts, while lying in bed with Chris.

That Cold Day in the Park (1969)

Suzanne Benton . . . . Nina
• 0:38—Side view of left breast putting top on. Long shot.
• 1:05—Breasts taking off her clothes and getting into the bathtub. Another long shot.

That Obscure Object of Desire (1977; French/Spanish)

Carole Bouquet . . . . Conchita
- ••• 0:53—Breasts in bedroom.
- ••• 1:01—Breasts in bed with Fernando Rey.

Angela Molina . . . . Conchita
- • 0:53—Brief breasts in bathroom.
- •• 1:20—Nude dancing in front of a group of tourists.
- • 1:29—Brief breasts behind a gate taunting Fernando Rey.

There Was a Crooked Man (1970)

Jeanne Cooper . . . . Prostitute
- • 0:18—Brief left breast trying to seduce the sheriff, Henry Fonda, in a room.

Lee Grant . . . . Mrs. Bullard

Pamela Hensley . . . . Edwina
- • 0:12—Very brief left breast lying on pool table with a guy.

There's a Girl in My Soup (1970)

Gabrielle Drake . . . . Julia Halford-Smythe
- • 0:09—In beige bra with Peter Sellers, brief left breast in bed with him. Don't see her face well, but it is her.

Goldie Hawn . . . . Marion
- • 0:37—Buns and very brief right side view of her body getting out of bed and walking to a closet to get a robe. Long shot.

Geraldine Sherman . . . . Caroline
- •• 0:43—Breasts in bed, then getting out after Goldie Hawn splashes water on her.

They Bite (1991)

Susie Owens . . . . Kate
- • 1:01—Right breast, while lying on the beach after getting attacked.
- ••• 1:02—Breasts and buns, while in bed on top of a guy before killing him.

Blake Pickett . . . . Model
- ••• 0:03—Left breast, then breasts and buns, taking off swimsuit for the photographer. More breasts in the water, struggling with the monster.

Christina Veronica . . . . Tammy
- ••• 0:20—Breasts in bed during porno movie shoot.
- ••• 0:55—Breasts, sunbathing on the beach while a guy rubs suntan lotion on her.
- • 1:03—Breasts on the beach during playback of film.
- •• 1:08—Breasts on boat, getting attacked by monster.
- • 1:09—Breasts in water, struggling with the monster.
- • 1:10—Brief breasts on beach during playback of film.

They Only Kill Their Masters (1972)

Katharine Ross . . . . Kate
- • 1:00—Very brief upper half of buns and very, very brief back side of right breast, when getting out of bed.

They're Playing with Fire (1984)

Sybil Danning . . . . Diane Stevens
- ••• 0:08—Breasts and buns making love on top of Jay in bed on boat. Nice!
- •• 0:10—Breasts and buns getting out of shower, then brief side view of right breast.
- •• 0:47—In black bra and slip, at home with Michael, then panties, then breasts and buns getting into shower.
- ••• 1:12—In white bra and panties in room with Jay then breasts.

Thief of Hearts (1984)

(Special Home Video Version reviewed.)

Annette Sinclair . . . . College Girl #1

Romy Walthall . . . . Nicole
- ••• 0:12—Full frontal nudity with Steven Bauer getting dressed.

Barbara Williams . . . . Mickey Davis
- • 0:46—Right breast in bathtub when her husband comes in and tries to read her diary.
- ••• 0:53—Breasts, while making love with Steven Bauer in his condo. Very brief lower frontal nudity when Bauer picks her up.

Thieves Like Us (1974)

Shelley Duvall . . . . Keechie
- • 1:16—Brief upper half of left breast, several times, while in bathtub.
- •• 1:17—Brief breasts and partial lower frontal nudity, then buns, standing up, getting out of tub and drying herself off.
- •• 1:18—Brief back side of right breast, while putting on nightgown.

Thieves of Fortune (1989)

Claudia Udy . . . . Marissa

Shawn Weatherly . . . . Peter
- • 1:09—Brief breasts several times, taking a shower (while wearing beard and mustache disguise).
- ••• 1:21—Breasts in white panties distracting tribe so she can get away.

A Thin Line Between Love and Hate (1995)

Stacii Jae Johnson . . . . Peaches

Lynn Whitfield . . . . Brandi
- •• 0:53—Brief right breast, then brief left breast, while making love in bed with Martin Lawrence.

Think Dirty (1970; British)

a.k.a. Every Home Should Have One

Veronica Clifford . . . . Hot Dog Girl

Julie Ege . . . . Inga
- • 0:43—Brief full frontal nudity, twice, in photo that Marty Feldman looks at.
- •• 0:44—Brief breasts in another photo. Breasts and buns, while running around in a "documentary" about Sweden with Marty Feldman, then in a "Swedish" film.

Annabel Leventon . . . . Chandler's Secretary

This Gun for Hire (1990; Made for Cable Movie)

Nancy Everhard . . . . Anne
- •• 1:03—Buns and breasts, after taking off panties and sitting down in bathtub.
- • 1:07—Buns, when walking toward Robert Wagner.

• *This World, then the Fireworks* (1997)

Gina Gershon . . . . Carol
- • 0:12—Right breast, sticking out of slip, while lying in bed and talking with Billy Zane.
- • 1:27—Brief right breast in flashback of 0:12 scene.

Elizabeth Imboden . . . . Neighbor's Wife
- • 0:00—Brief buns, very brief lower frontal nudity and very brief right breast, while making love with another man in bed and getting caught.

Sheryl Lee . . . . Lois
- •• 0:30—Breasts, while making love in bed with Billy Zane. Lit with blue light.

• 0:52—In lingerie, then brief breasts, while fooling around on bed. Very brief tip of right breast, while sitting in bathtub.

Those Lips, Those Eyes *(1980)*

Glynnis O'Connor . . . . Ramona
- • 0:37—Left breast in car with Tom Hulce. Dark, hard to see.
- •• 1:12—Breasts and buns on bed with Tom Hulce. Dark.

• ***A Thousand Acres*** *(1997)*

Jessica Lange . . . . Ginny Cook Smith
Jennifer Jason Leigh . . . . Caroline Cook
Michelle Pfeiffer . . . . Rose Cook Lewis
- • 0:16—Brief right breast (with left breast covered with a prosthetic appliance to make it appear she has lost a breast to surgery) while lying down during medical exam. (The entire chest area below her neck is probably a prosthetic appliance, I haven't been able to get positive verification yet.)

Three Days to a Kill *(1991)*

Kim Dakour . . . . Yolanda
- •• 0:31—Buns in white T-back, then breasts wearing tasseled pasties while dancing on stage.
- • 1:11—Brief breasts, while fighting with Pepe on couch when he rapes her.
- • 1:12—Brief buns, while lying on her stomach on the couch.

Threesome *(1994)*

Lara Flynn Boyle . . . . Alex
- • 0:52—Buns, while walking and diving into lake to go skinny dipping.
- • 0:54—Partial buns, while lying on lake shore with Baldwin and Charles.
- • 1:21—Partial buns, while lying in bed between Baldwin and Charles.

Threshold *(1983; Canadian)*

Mare Winningham . . . . Carol Severance
- • 0:56—Brief full frontal nudity, lying on operating table, then side view of left breast getting prepped for surgery.

Thrilled to Death *(1988)*

Rebecca Lynn . . . . Elaine Jackson
- • 0:01—Breasts twice when Baxter opens her blouse.
- •• 0:31—Breasts in locker room talking to Nan.

Christine Moore . . . . Nan Christie
- ••• 0:38—Breasts in office with Mr. Dance just before killing him.

Karen Nielsen . . . . n.a.
Christina Veronica . . . . Satin
- •• 0:33—Breasts talking to Cliff during porno film shoot.

Thumb Tripping *(1972)*

Meg Foster . . . . Shay
- • 1:19—Very, very brief breasts leaning back in field with Jack. Long shot.
- • 1:20—Breasts at night. Face is turned away from the camera.

Mariana Hill . . . . Lynn
- • 1:14—In black bra, then very, very brief left breast when Jack comes to cover her up.
- • 1:19—Breasts frolicking in the water with Gary.

Joyce Van Patten . . . . Mother

Thunder Alley *(1985)*

Melanie Kinnaman . . . . Star
- • 0:52—Brief breasts under water in pool talking to a Richie. Side view of right breast, talking to Donnie.
- •• 1:14—Breasts and buns, making love on bed with Richie, then getting out.

Susan McIver . . . . Redhead
Jill Schoelen . . . . Beth
- • 0:55—Very, very brief left breast and side view of buns, when Richie sits up while she's lying on her stomach on rocks.

• ***Thunder and Mud*** *(1989; Video Tape)*

Lorraine Dorado . . . . Quisha/Sex Toy
- • 1:02—Buns, while mud wrestling in white top and pink bikini bottom.
- ••• 1:06—Breasts, covered with mud after Leslie rips her top off.

Jessica Hahn . . . . Hostess
Sandra Margot . . . . Tiffany
Wally Anne Wharton . . . . Wanda Wallinsky

Thunderbolt and Lightfoot *(1974)*

Catherine Bach . . . . Melody
June Fairchild . . . . Gloria
- • 0:20—Very brief right breast and buns, while getting dressed in the bathroom after making love with Clint Eastwood.

Leslie Oliver . . . . Teenage Girl
- •• 1:16—Brief breasts in bed when robbers break in and George Kennedy watches her.
- • 1:31—Brief buns, tied up with her boyfriend in bed.

Luanne Roberts . . . . Suburban Housewife
- • 0:57—Brief full frontal nudity standing behind a sliding glass door tempting Jeff Bridges.

Tie Me Up! Tie Me Down! *(1990; Spanish)*

Victoria Abril . . . . Marina Osorio
- ••• 0:24—Full frontal nudity playing with a frogman toy in the bathtub.
- • 0:34—Buns and brief side of right breast, getting dressed.
- •• 0:44—Breasts while changing clothes, then on TV while Maximo watches.
- •• 1:09—Breasts while changing clothes.
- ••• 1:16—Right breast, then breasts while making love in bed with Ricky.

Maria Barranco . . . . Médica
Rossy de Palma . . . . Drug Dealer on Scooter

• ***The Tie That Binds*** *(1995)*

Daryl Hannah . . . . Leann Netherwood
Moira Kelly . . . . Dana Clifton
- • 0:23—Partial side of left breast while in bed with Vincent Spano. Very, very brief partial right breast when he rolls off the top of her.
- • 0:24—Brief left breast as Spano works his way down her torso with kisses.

Cynda Williams . . . . Lisa-Marie Chandler

Tiffany Jones *(1973; British)*

Anouska Hempel . . . . Tiffany Jones
- • 0:02—Brief breasts walking in from the surf in wet white dress.
- •• 0:13—Breasts in bath. Buns also, getting out.
- • 0:18—Brief left breast, taking off her top in front of bright light.

- • 0:23—Breasts, several times, changing clothes in her bedroom.
- •• 0:24—Breasts walking around her apartment in white panties.
- • 0:31—Breasts in bubble bath.
- • 0:32—Brief left breast, wrapping an orange towel around herself.
- ••• 0:39—Lying on table in black and red bra, then breasts. More right breast.
- • 0:41—Side view breasts, covered with sweat.
- •• 0:55—Breasts, partial lower frontal nudity, taking a shower.
- • 1:26—Breasts, running outside in a field when guys rip off her dress.

A Tiger's Tale *(1988)*

Ann-Margret . . . . Rose
- • 0:45—Side view of left breast in bra, then breasts jumping up after fire ants start biting her. Brief buns running along a hill. Long shot, probably a body double.

Traci Lind . . . . Penny
Leigh Lombardi . . . . Marcia
Kelly Preston . . . . Shirley
- •• 0:03—Breasts in the car, letting C. Thomas Howell open her blouse and look at her breasts.

Angel Tompkins . . . . La Vonne

Tigers in Lipstick *(1979)*

Ursula Andress . . . . The Stroller and The Widow
- • 0:50—Very brief breasts when top of slip accidentally falls down.
- • 0:51—More breasts with the photographer.

Laura Antonelli . . . . The Pick Up
Sylvia Kristel . . . . The Girl
- • 0:04—Breasts in photograph on the sand.
- •• 0:09—Breasts lying in bed with The Arab.
- •• 0:16—Lying in bed in red lingerie, then left breast for awhile.

Tightrope *(1984)*

Randi Brooks . . . . Jamie Cory
- ••• 0:20—Nude, taking off her robe and getting into the spa.
- • 0:24—Buns and side of left breast, dead in the spa while Clint Eastwood looks at her.

Genevieve Bujold . . . . Beryl Thibodeaux
Margaret Howell . . . . Judy Harper
- • 0:44—Brief left breast viewed from above in a room with Clint Eastwood.

Rebecca Perle . . . . Becky Jacklin
Jamie Rose . . . . Melanie Silber
- • 0:07—Buns, lying face down on bed, dead.

The Tigress *(1992)*

Belinda Mayne . . . . Elsy
Valentina Vargas . . . . Tigress/Pauline
- •• 0:06—Nude, undressing in room and lying in bed with James Remar.
- •• 0:10—Nude, sitting up in bed, then getting out and leaving the room.
- •• 0:18—Nude, getting out of bed and getting dressed.
- •• 0:45—Right breast, while in room when Remar pulls her dress down.
- •• 0:48—Buns, while in bed with Remar.
- • 0:52—Brief breasts, while changing clothes in room.
- ••• 0:53—Breasts when Remar opens her blouse and massages her breasts.
- • 1:03—Half of left breast while primping herself in front of mirror.

Till Death Do Us Part *(1991)*

Embeth Davidtz . . . . Cat
Rebecca Jenkins . . . . Sandra Stockton
Ashley Judd . . . . Gwen Fox
Jennifer Runyon . . . . Judy
- • 1:02—Breasts and buns in T-back, undressing in bathroom. Don't see her face.

Leilani Sarelle . . . . Gloria

Till Marriage Do Us Part *(1974; Italian)*

Laura Antonelli . . . . Eugenia
- •• 0:58—Nude in the barn, while lying on hay after guy takes off her clothes.
- •• 1:02—Full frontal nudity standing up in bathtub while maid washes her.
- •• 1:07—Right breast with chauffeur in barn.
- •• 1:36—Breasts surrounded by feathers on the bed while priest is talking.

Karin Schubert . . . . Evelyn

Till the End of the Night *(1994)*

Mary Fanaro . . . . Faith
- • 0:16—Brief breasts, while making love in bed with Drew.

Katherine Kelly Lang . . . . Diana Davenport
- • 0:04—Very, very brief breast in mirror, while making love with her husband in bed.

Time Barbarians *(1990)*

Ingrid Vold . . . . Wizard
- • 0:45—Breasts visible under sheer white gown.

Sheila Young . . . . Minomo
- •• 0:19—Breasts, (she's the blonde one) while bathing with a brunette woman in the water.

A Time to Die *(1991)*

Nitchie Barrett . . . . Sheila
- • 0:12—Buns, getting out of bed.
- •• 0:16—Breasts making love in bed with Sam.

Daphne Cheung . . . . Sunshine
Traci Lords . . . . Jackie
Nicole Picard . . . . Patti

Timebomb *(1990)*

Julie Brown . . . . Uncredited Waitress at Al's Diner
Patsy Kensit . . . . Dr. Anna Nolmar
- •• 1:15—Breasts, mostly left breast, making love with Michael Biehn in bed. Partial buns also.

Tracy Scoggins . . . . Ms. Blue
Sheila Young . . . . Nude Film Star
- • 0:50—Brief breasts, several times (mostly out of focus) in adult theater during shoot out.

Timecop *(1994)*

Laura Murdoch . . . . Virtual Reality Woman
- •• 0:38—Full frontal nudity, while in bed in virtual reality image that Ricky is experiencing.

Gloria Reuben . . . . Sarah Fielding
Gabrielle Rose . . . . Judge Marshall
Mia Sara . . . . Melissa
- •• 0:10—Brief breasts, while making love in bed with Jean-Claude Van Damme.

The Tin Drum *(1979; German)*

Andrea Ferréol . . . . Lina Greff

Angela Winkler . . . . Agnes Matzerath
•• 0:38—Very brief right breast after taking off clothes in room with Jan. Buns and side view of left breast in bed with him.

Tintorera (1977)

Jennifer Ashley . . . . Kelly
• 0:27—Buns and brief side of left breast, taking off her dress and swimming to the boat. She's the first one to undress.
•• 0:28—Breasts and buns, while on boat deck and getting into hammock with Steven.
•• 0:29—Breasts, when sleeping in hammock and getting out. Brief nude in water, while swimming from the boat.
• 1:11—Breasts, while taking off her yellow top. Dark.
• 1:12—Brief breasts, while doing backstroke in water near Cynthia.
• 1:14—Brief breasts, while getting pulled out of the water by Steven, then lying on her back on beach.

Priscilla Barnes. . . . . Girl from Bar
• 1:12—Brief breasts, while pouring beer over her head. Breasts seen from under water, while she turns around while wearing white panties. Breasts, while dropping her beer in the water.
• 1:14—Breasts, while on the beach after the shark attack (on the left).

Susan George . . . . Gabriella
• 0:42—Brief breasts waking up Steven in hammock.

Fiona Lewis . . . . Patricia
• 0:20—Brief side view (silhouette) of left breast while in hallway. Breasts and buns, while walking to the ocean (long shot).
•• 0:22—Nude, while swimming under water just before getting eaten by a shark. Don't see her face.

Laura Lyons. . . . . Cynthia
• 0:27—Buns and brief side of left breast, taking off her dress to swim to boat. She's the second one to take off her dress.
• 0:28—Full frontal nudity, while dancing on boat deck.
• 0:29—Left breast and brief buns, while getting into hammock with Steven.
• 0:30—Brief buns, while swimming in water.

TNT Jackson (1975)

Pat Anderson. . . . . Elaine
•• 0:58—Buns and breasts, getting out of the shower and putting robe on.

Jeannie Bell . . . . Diana "TNT" Jackson
••• 0:43—Breasts, getting her blouse ripped off by the bad guys. More breasts during fight (notice her panties change from black to white to black).
• 0:45—Brief breasts, almost hitting Joe.
••• 0:50—Breasts, while making love with Charlie.

To Die For (1995)

Nicole Kidman . . . . Suzanne Stone
• 0:54—Partial buns in purple bra and panties seen in reflection in the mirror.

Susan Traylor . . . . Faye Stone

To Die For 2 (1991)

a.k.a. Son of Darkness: To Die For II

Rosalind Allen . . . . Nina
• 0:37—Breasts a few times in bed, while making love with Max.

Kathryn Atwood . . . . Nurse

Remy O'Neill. . . . . Jane

Amanda Wyss . . . . Celia

• To Gillian on her 37th Birthday (1996)

Claire Danes . . . . Rachel Lewis
• 0:40—Brief buns in swimsuit, while walking on the beach next to Cindy.
• 0:41—Buns, while standing in swimsuit at the beach.

Laurie Fortier. . . . . Cindy Bayles
• 0:16—Brief buns, then buns in blue T-back swimsuit, while talking with Claire Danes in bedroom.
• 0:40—Brief buns in swimsuit, while walking on the beach next to Danes.
• 0:41—Buns, while standing in swimsuit at the beach.

Michelle Pfeiffer. . . . . Gillian Lewis

To Kill a Clown (1971)

Blythe Danner . . . . Lily Frischer
• 1:10—Side view of left breast sitting on bed talking to Alan Alda. Hair covers breast, hard to see. Buns, getting up and running out of the house.

To Live and Die in L.A. (1985)

Debra Feuer. . . . . Bianca Torres
• 0:58—Side view of buns, while lying on bed, watching Willem Dafoe burn the counterfeit money. Long shot.
• 1:47—Brief breasts on video tape being played back on TV in empty house, hard to see anything.

Darlanne Fluegel . . . . Ruth Lanier
•• 0:44—Brief breasts and buns, in bed when William Petersen comes home.
• 1:50—Very brief breasts on bed with Petersen in a flashback.

Jackie Giroux . . . . Claudia Leith

To Protect and Serve (1992)

Lezlie Deane . . . . Harriet
• 0:47—Brief breasts in front of fireplace with C. Thomas Howell. Hard to see because candles get in the way.
• 0:51—Brief breasts, getting up off the floor.
• 1:18—Brief side view of left breast in mirror in bathroom. Long shot.

Janine Stillo . . . . Counter Girl

Zoe Trilling . . . . Beverly
• 0:24—Breasts in bed with a guy. Lit with strobe light.

To Sleep with a Vampire (1992)

Kristine Rose . . . . Prom Queen

Charlie Spradling. . . . . Nina
• 0:04—On stage in black lingerie, then buns in T-back.
••• 0:05—Breasts and buns in push up bra and T-back while dancing on stage.
••• 0:59—In red top and red T-back on stage, breasts and buns. Excellent close up of breasts.
••• 1:03—Breasts while making love on stage with Scott Valentine.

Ingrid Vold . . . . Stripper #1
••• 0:06—Breasts, while dancing on stage. (Wearing a wig.)
• 0:07—Brief breasts on stage (seen in B&W through the vampire's eyes.)

To the Devil, a Daughter (1976; British/German)

Nastassja Kinski . . . . Catherine Beddows
••• 1:24—Full frontal nudity, taking off her robe outside and walking towards Richard Widmark in slow motion.

To the Limit (1995)

Lydie Denier . . . . Frannie

Rebecca Ferratti. . . . . Lupe

Kathrin Lautner . . . . Nurse Ellen
Kathy Shower . . . . Vinnie
- 0:30—Breasts and partial buns, while making love with a guy in bed.

Anna Nicole Smith . . . . Colette
- ••• 0:06—Breasts, while taking a bath and enjoying herself. Very brief lower frontal nudity when standing up to get out.
- ••• 0:11—Breasts, while making love in bed with Michael Nouri.
- ••• 1:13—Full frontal nudity, while taking a shower and enjoying herself.
- •• 1:17—Breasts, while making love with Frank in bed.
- • 1:22—Breasts and brief buns in T-back, while getting out of bed.

Catherine Weber . . . . Mona
- • 0:21—Brief breasts, while getting strangled for failing to kill Frank.

Tobe Hooper's Night Terrors *(1993)*

Zoe Trilling . . . . Genie
- ••• 0:35—Buns and breasts, while making love with Mahmoud.
- •• 0:37—In bra, then breasts, when Mahmoud makes love with her on bed.
- • 1:04—Buns, several times, while lying in bed with Sabina.

• ***Tokyo Decadence*** *(1992; Japanese)*

Miho Nikaido . . . . Ai
- ••• 0:00—Breasts, while strapped, bound and gagged in a chair for a customer.
- • 0:11—Buns in lingerie, while talking on the phone.
- •• 0:13—Buns in and out of panties, while standing on window sill for Mr. Ishioka.
- •• 0:24—Buns in panties, then buns and breasts in bathroom.
- ••• 0:26—Buns and breasts, while crawling on the floor, then watching Yuko have sex with Mr. Ishioka.
- •• 0:33—Breasts, while cleaning herself in the bathroom.
- • 0:45—Partial buns, while in lingerie in hotel room with a customer.
- ••• 1:07—Breasts, while standing in front of mirror when Saki takes her dress off, then when having sex with Saki while Turtle Face guy watches.

• ***Tollbooth*** *(1994)*

Fairuza Balk . . . . Doris
- • 0:20—Very, very brief blurry breasts, while making love in bed on top of Will Patton (right after the doll is stuck in the garbage disposal).
- • 0:21—Very, very brief blurry breasts, while making love on top of Patton some more (right after the garbage disposal starts). Very, very brief breasts seen through the blinds.

• ***Tom Jones: Part 2*** *(1998; Made for Cable Movie)*

Lindsay Duncan . . . . Lady Bellaston
- •• 1:41—Brief breasts, after opening the door to show herself to Tom Jones. You can't see her face clearly, because she's wearing a mask, so it's probably a body double. (The body double's shoulders look wider than Duncan's.)

The Tomb *(1987)*

Michelle Bauer . . . . Nefartis
Sybil Danning . . . . Jade
Francesca "Kitten" Natividad . . . . Stripper
- ••• 0:19—Breasts and buns in G-string dancing on stage.
- • 0:21—Brief breasts again.

Dawn Wildsmith . . . . Anna Conda
- ••• 0:54—Breasts taking off robe in room with Michelle Bauer, then getting pushed onto a bed full of snakes.

Tomboy *(1985)*

Michelle Bauer . . . . Uncredited Girl in Corvette
- • 1:16—Brief breasts, while opening her dress in Corvette.

Betsy Russell . . . . Tomasina "Tommy" Boyd
- •• 0:44—In wet T-shirt, then brief breasts after landing in the water with her motorcycle.
- •• 0:59—Breasts making love with the race car driver in an exercise room.

Kristi Somers . . . . Seville Ritz
- •• 0:14—Breasts taking a shower while talking to Betsy Russell.
- • 0:53—Brief breasts stripping at a party.

Cynthia Ann Thompson . . . . Amanda
- • 0:23—Brief right breast getting out of car in auto repair shop.
- •• 1:02—Breasts delivering drinks to two guys in the swimming pool.

Tomcat: Dangerous Desires *(1993)*

Maryam D'Abo . . . . Jacki
- ••• 0:07—Breasts in bathroom mirror with Richard Grieco.

Christine Lippa . . . . Randi
- • 0:56—Buns, while lying on bed and talking to Richard Grieco.

Natalie Radford . . . . Imogen
- ••• 1:04—Brief left breast, then breasts and lower frontal nudity in bed with Richard Grieco.
- •• 1:08—Brief buns and breasts in bed some more.
- •• 1:09—More breasts while sitting in bed and watching video tape on TV.

• ***Tonya & Jeff's Wedding Night*** *(1994; Video Tape)*

Tonya Harding . . . . Herself
- ••• 0:00—Nude, while making love with Jeff Gilloly on their wedding night. Long scene.

Too Fast, Too Young *(1995)*

Kasia Figura . . . . Kaddy Havel
- • 0:10—Buns in panties and bra after taking off robe and walking around indoors.
- • 0:42—Brief buns, while lying in bed with Dalton.
- • 0:44—Very brief buns and breasts, while lying in bed with Dalton and after he gets out.

Too Hot To Handle *(1975)*

Cheri Caffaro . . . . Samantha Fox
- •• 0:06—Breasts wearing a black push-up bra and buns in black G-string.
- • 0:13—Full frontal nudity lying on boat.
- ••• 0:39—Breasts making love in bed with Dominco.
- ••• 0:55—Full frontal nudity taking off clothes and lying in bed.
- • 1:06—Brief left breast in bed with Dominco.

Too Scared to Scream *(1985)*

Anne Archer . . . . Kate
Victoria Bass . . . . Cynthia Oberman
- ••• 0:08—Breasts and buns, undressing and hanging up her dress in closet, then walking to shower.
- •• 0:10—Brief breasts, getting out of the shower.

Karen Rushmore . . . . Nadine
- ••• 0:51—Breasts in sauna, rubbing oil on herself.
- ••• 0:52—Breasts, lying in sauna.

••• 0:53—Buns and breasts in spa.

The Toolbox Murders (1978)

Marciee Drake. . . . . Debbie

•• 0:09—In wet blouse, then breasts taking it off and putting a dry one on.

Evelyn Guerrero . . . . Maria

Kelly Nichols . . . . Dee Ann

••• 0:22—Right breast, then breasts taking a bath and enjoying herself. Long scene. Nude, running around trying to get away from Cameron Mitchell.

• 0:32—Breasts, while dead in her apartment and later on the coroner's table.

Top Model (1989; Italian)

Laura Gemser . . . . Dorothy/Eve

• 0:44—Brief right breast and buns, frolicking with the cowboy.

Jessica Moore . . . . Sarah Asproon/Gloria

••• 0:03—Nude, posing for photographer customer in his loft with mannequins, then talking on the phone.

• 0:08—Breasts in dressing room, when seen by Cliff.

•• 0:23—Buns and brief side of right breast, undressing in front of a customer.

•• 0:24—Breasts, rubbing oil on him.

•• 0:30—Full frontal nudity, in her bedroom when Peter blackmails her.

••• 0:35—Nude in photographer customer's loft again.

• 0:40—Brief buns, turning over in bed.

•• 0:43—Breasts on couch, making love (disinterestedly) with cowboy.

• 0:56—Buns and partial right breast, while getting dressed.

••• 1:00—Breasts making love with Cliff on sofa, then sleeping afterward.

•• 1:04—Nude, undressing and walking down hallway.

••• 1:08—Nude, in hotel room, making love with Cliff.

••• 1:19—Buns, with Cliff in stairwell. Breasts and buns in bathroom with him.

Total Eclipse (1995; French/British)

Romane Bohringer . . . . Mathilde

• 0:37—Very brief partial left breast, when covering herself up after breast feeding.

••• 0:51—Buns, while lying face down on bed, then breasts, with David Thewlis in bed and out.

Total Exposure (1991)

Martina Castel. . . . . Cissy

• 1:06—Breasts in spa being questioned by a guy with a gun.

Deborah Driggs . . . . Kathy

••• 0:08—Breasts dancing in front of Jeff Conaway, then making love in bed with him. Long scene.

• 0:22—Brief side view breasts in B&W photos that Conaway looks at.

• 0:24—Brief buns in black G-string and side of right breast changing clothes in locker room.

•• 0:25—Breasts and buns, trying to beat up Season Hubley.

Linda Hoffman . . . . Patty

Season Hubley . . . . Andi Robinson

• 0:07—Buns, while getting into hot tub. Probably a body double.

Kristine Rose . . . . Rita

Total Recall (1990)

Sharon Stone. . . . . Lori

• 0:04—Brief right breast in gaping lingerie when leaning over Arnold Schwarzenegger in bed.

Rachel Ticotin . . . . Melina

Totally Exposed (1991)

Tina Bockrath . . . . Lillian Tucker

•• 0:00—Buns and breasts, turning over on tanning table during opening credits.

• 0:01—Brief full frontal nudity, lying on tanning table.

•• 0:03—Briefly nude, while getting out of bed and putting on towel, talking to Bill.

••• 1:01—Full frontal nudity, turning over on tanning table. Full frontal nudity, dropping her towel in reception area.

••• 1:02—Buns, walking back to the room. Nude, taking off towel and lying on massage table.

••• 1:04—Nude, sitting up on table and standing up with Bill.

Jacqueline Jade . . . . Eleanor

••• 0:05—Full frontal nudity, taking off towel and lying on tanning table.

•• 0:08—Nude, on massage table, talking with Bill.

•• 0:09—Brief breasts, turning over on table, trying to make the moves on Bill.

•• 0:10—Brief breasts, sitting up.

•• 0:57—Nude, taking off towel and getting on massage table.

••• 0:58—Full frontal nudity, turning over to talk to Bill.

Kelli Konop . . . . Sue

• 0:18—Undressing to take a shower. Brief right breast, bending over to take off panties. Brief side view of left breast, while getting into the shower.

• 0:19—Sort of breasts, while washing herself in the shower. Her arms get in the way.

Honey Lauren . . . . Linda

•• 0:41—Full frontal nudity, taking off towel in massage room.

Toto the Hero (1991; French)

Mireille Perrier. . . . . Adult Evelyne

••• 1:04—Breasts, while sitting up in bed and turning around after making love with Thomas.

The Touch (1971; U.S./Swedish)

Bibi Andersson. . . . . Karen Vergerus

• 0:31—Breasts, while in bed with Elliott Gould.

••• 0:56—Breasts, while kissing Gould.

• 1:13—Very, very brief right breast, when washing Gould's hair in the sink.

• *Touch (1996)*

Maria Celedonio . . . . Alisha

Lolita Davidovich. . . . . Antoinette Baker

Bridget Fonda . . . . Lynn Faulkner

• 0:54—Very brief, partial buns, while lying in bed with Skeet Ulrich.

Gina Gershon . . . . Debra Lusanne

Casey Gray . . . . Stripper

Tamlyn Tomita . . . . Prosecutor

Tough Guys (1986)

Darlanne Fluegel . . . . Skye Foster

• 0:47—Very brief side view of right breast, leaning over to kiss Kirk Douglas.

Lisa Pescia . . . . Customer #1

Hilary Shepard. . . . . Sandy

Tough Guys Don't Dance (1987)

Frances Fisher . . . . Jessica Pond
Isabella Rossellini . . . . .Madeleine
Debra Sandlund . . . . Patty Lareine
•• 1:24—Breasts ripping her blouse off to kiss the policeman after they have killed and buried another woman.
• 1:24—Very brief left breast, twice, in bed with Ryan O'Neal. Long shot.

Tower of Evil (1972; British)

a.k.a. Beyond the Fog
Candace Glendenning. . . . . Penny
• 0:07—Breasts, screaming and killing a fisherman with a knife.
• 0:12—Brief buns, while running up steps.
• 0:13—Brief breasts, lying down with Gary during flashback.
• 0:14—Brief buns, after swim with Gary, then breasts drying off.
•• 0:15—Breasts, lying down with Gary.
• 0:39—Breasts and buns, getting up and walking with Gary. Breasts, stopping to kiss him.
• 0:40—Buns and breasts when Gary gets killed. Very brief breasts several times, getting blood spattered on her.
• 0:41—Breasts, running.
Seretta Wilson . . . . Mae
• 0:34—Very, very brief breasts, lying in bed in flashbacks. Then breasts, sleeping in bed.
•• 0:35—Breasts, while sleeping in bed.
• 0:38—More breasts, while sleeping in bed.
• 0:39—Very, very brief breasts, getting the covers taken off before getting killed.
• 0:41—Very brief breasts, dead, covered with blood.

The Toxic Avenger (1985)

Cindy Manion . . . . .Julie
••• 0:15—Breasts, after untying her swimsuit top in front of Melvin.

The Toxic Avenger: Part II (1988)

Phoebe Légerè . . . . Claire
• 0:31—Brief right breast, while caressing herself while making out with the Toxic Avenger.

Toy Soldiers (1983)

Terri Garber. . . . . Amy
• 0:18—Brief right breast taking off her tank top when the army guys force her. Her head is down.
Tracy Scoggins . . . . .Monique

Traces of Red (1992)

Victoria Bass . . . . .Susan Dobson
Lorraine Bracco . . . . .Ellen Schofield
Katheryn Culliver Pierce. Kimberly Davis
•• 0:11—Breasts in bed, dead with blood on her during James Belushi's recollection.
Faye Grant. . . . . Beth Frayn
• 0:52—Buns in T-back under sheer dress.
Michelle Joyner . . . . Morgan Cassidy
• 0:08—In black bra, in bedroom with James Belushi. Brief breasts making love.
•• 0:24—Left breast, while lying dead in bed when Belushi sees her.
Melanie Tomlin . . . . Amanda

Tracks (1977)

Sally Kirkland . . . . Uncredited
Taryn Power . . . . Stephanie
• 0:32—Brief side view of right breast changing in her room on the train. Don't see her face.
• 1:15—Brief left breast making love with Dennis Hopper in a field.

Tracks of a Killer (1995)

Kelly Le Brock . . . . Claire Hawkner
Courtney Taylor. . . . . Bella
• 0:07—Left breast, while taking off her clothes in office with Patrick.
•• 0:17—Breasts, while in bed when Patrick rips off her lingerie and makes love in bed.

Trade-Off (1994; Made for Cable Movie)

Theresa Russell. . . . . Jackie Daniels
• 0:18—Breasts, while making love in bed with Adam Baldwin.
• 0:40—Brief breasts in the bathtub with Baldwin. Covered with bubbles.

Trading Places (1983)

Jamie Lee Curtis. . . . . Ophelia
••• 1:00—Breasts in black panties after taking red dress off in bathroom while Dan Aykroyd watches.
••• 1:09—Breasts and black panties taking off halter top and pants getting into bed with a sick Aykroyd.

The Tragedy of a Ridiculous Man (1981; Italian)

Anouk Aimee. . . . . Barbara Spaggiari
Olimpia Carlisi . . . . Chiromat
Laura Morante . . . . Laura
••• 1:30—Breasts taking off her sweater in front of Primo because she's "uneasy."

• *Trainspotting* (1996; British)

Kelly MacDonald . . . . Diane
• 0:25—Breasts, while undressing in her bedroom.
•• 0:26—Brief breasts, several times while making love with Ewan McGregor. Very brief lower frontal nudity when getting dressed.

Transformations (1988)

Ann Margaret Hughes . . . . .Myra
• 0:42—Right breast, then breasts under Rex Smith in bed.
• 0:43—More breasts, dead in bed.
Lisa Langlois . . . . Miranda
Pamela Prati. . . . . .Woman Succubus
••• 0:05—Breasts and buns making love on top of Rex Smith in bed. She starts transforming into a creature.
• 0:21—Brief breasts again during Smith's flashback.
• 0:24—Brief breasts again, while transforming.
• 0:26—Brief breasts again, while transforming.
Cec Verrell. . . . . .Antonia

Trapped (1993)

a.k.a. The Killing Jar
Cie Allman. . . . . Buxom Blonde
Pamela Bryant . . . . .Laura Armstrong
• 0:04—Brief breasts on TV monitor.
• 0:05—Brief buns and right breast in mirror while changing clothes in the bathroom.
•• 0:11—Breasts, while starting to make love in backyard with Curtis.

- 0:15—Brief breasts in bathroom with her husband while he fantasizes about Monica.
- 0:24—Breasts, while on TV.
- •• 0:27—Breasts, while in shower, getting out and getting dressed.
- 0:29—Brief right breast when it slips out of nightgown while she lies in bed.
- 0:32—Brief left breast when masked guy cuts her nightgown strap open.
- 0:48—Brief side of left breast on TV.
- ••• 0:50—Nude, getting into bathtub, in bathtub, then getting dragged around house by guy.

Alina Thompson . . . . Monica

- 0:16—In sheer white lingerie outfit in bedroom with Alan.
- 0:26—Right breast while in bed with Alan in Laura's imagination.
- ••• 0:33—In two piece swimsuit, then nude, while making love with Alan outside by pool.
- •• 0:37—Nude, undressing and going for a swim in the pool, then getting killed.

Trapped Alive *(1988)*

Elizabeth Kent . . . . Rachel

- 0:28—Brief left breast, then breasts, while making love on the floor with Billy.

• ***Trashy Ladies Wrestling*** *(1987; Video Tape)*

Gail Harris . . . . Fifi

- •• 0:02—Buns in G-string, black bra, garter belt and stockings. Breasts getting oil dribbled on her.

Debra Lamb . . . . n.a.

- •• 0:48—In black and silver S&M costume. Buns in G-string.

Becky LeBeau . . . . Round Girl

Trauma *(1992)*

Asia Argento . . . . Aura Petrescu

- •• 0:27—Breasts, after taking off bra in bathroom.

Laura Johnson . . . . Grace Harrington

- 0:38—Breast, while making love in bed with David and after he leaves.

Traveling Man *(1989; Made for Cable Movie)*

Ingrid Buxbaum . . . . Uncredited Salesgirl

- ••• 0:05—Breasts and buns while wearing G-string, dancing during sales meeting.

Traxx *(1988)*

Priscilla Barnes . . . . Mayor Alexandria Cray

Suzanne Primeaux . . . . Hooker #1

- •• 0:37—Breasts, dancing on stage while wearing a mask.

Treacherous *(1993)*

Anastacia Belmonte . . . . Maria

Tia Carrere . . . . Dr. Jessica Jamison

Randi Ingerman . . . . Lisa Rivers

- 0:01—Brief buns, when getting a massage from another woman. Brief breasts while C. Thomas Howell watches.
- 0:03—Very brief right breast, when Howell joins her in bed.
- 0:34—Very, very brief breasts, in spa with Howell after she takes her swimsuit top off.
- 0:49—Breasts and buns in T-back under sheer black patterned body suit in bathroom while getting dressed.
- ••• 0:53—Breasts and buns in T-back, while making love in bed with Damon.
- 0:57—Very brief buns and left breast, while getting out of bed.

Trial By Jury *(1994)*

Karina Arroyave . . . . Mercedes

Kathleen Quinlan . . . . Wanda

- 0:04—Brief buns, while dancing in room wearing black bra, panties, garter belt and stockings (in a blonde wig) in front of Limpy.

Margaret Whitton . . . . Jane Lyle

Tribute *(1980; Canadian)*

Kim Cattrall . . . . Sally Haines

Gale Garnett . . . . Hilary

- ••• 1:39—Breasts, while taking off her nurse outfit in front of Jack Lemmon. (Pretty amazing for a PG movie!)
- 1:42—Brief half of right breast, while standing up.

Trick or Treat *(1986)*

Lisa Orgolini . . . . Leslie Graham

Elise Richards . . . . Genie Wooster

- •• 0:39—In black bra, then breasts in back seat of car when taken over by evil spirits.
- •• 0:41—Very brief breasts, getting attacked by monster, then breasts when unconscious and found by Tim.

• ***Tricks*** *(1997; Made for Cable Movie)*

Tyne Daly . . . . Sarah

Mimi Rogers . . . . Jackie

- 1:09—Brief breasts, while making love with Adam in bed. (Don't see her face.)

Elizabeth Carol Savenkoff . . . . Daria

- •• 0:49—Breasts, during strip tease dance in front of Adam during party.

• ***The Trigger Effect*** *(1996)*

Elisabeth Shue . . . . Annie

- 0:11—Very brief, left nipple when she fondles herself while talking with Kyle MacLachlan.

The Trip *(1967)*

Susan Strasberg . . . . Sally Groves

- 0:17—Very brief left breast, while making love with Peter Fonda in bed. Very difficult to see because it's lit with psychedelic lights.

Triplecross *(1994; Made for Cable Movie)*

Lara Daans . . . . Tiny's Pal

Susan Horton . . . . Girl in Club

Ashley Laurence . . . . Julia

- •• 0:41—Breasts, while making out with Paré.
- ••• 0:42—Breasts, while making out with Paré on bed.
- •• 0:43—Breasts and partial buns, while making love with Paré.
- 0:48—Partial left breast, while in bubble bath with Paré.

The Trojan Women *(1972; British)*

Genevieve Bujold . . . . Cassandra

Irene Papas . . . . Helen

- 1:11—Very brief breasts, kneeling down to bathe in a pan of water. Seen between slats in wall. Long shot.
- 1:12—Brief breasts and very brief side view of buns, standing up and moving away from the slat wall when the women start throwing stones.

Vanessa Redgrave . . . . Andromache

• ***Tromeo & Juliet*** *(1995)*

(Unrated director's cut reviewed.)

Debbie Rochon . . . . Ness

- •• 0:17—Right breast, while making out with Juliet on bed.

Carolyn R. Smith . . . . Pauline
Jacqueline Tavarez. . . . . Rosy
••• 0:10—Breasts, while making love with a guy and talking on the phone.

Tropic of Cancer (1970)

Ellen Burstyn . . . . Mona
••• 0:02—Full frontal nudity, while lying on bed.
•• 0:03—Right breast while lying on her back in bed.
•• 0:04—Nude, getting out of bed to get bugs off her.
Magali Noel . . . . The Princess
••• 0:17—In sheer bra, then breasts after taking off her bra while sitting in bed in front of a guy.
Sheila Steafel. . . . . .Tania
•• 0:25—Breasts, while ballet dancing in studio while wearing only a tutu.
Nadia Vasil . . . . Madame Hamilton's Girl
•• 0:32—Full frontal nudity in open dresses with other girls in room.

Tropical Heat (1993)

Lee Anne Beaman . . . . .Carolyn
••• 0:10—Nude, taking her clothes off outside by swimming pool, then getting in and making love with Rick Rossovich. Long scene.
•• 0:14—Breasts, while sitting at bar in swimming pool with Rossovich.
Maryam D'Abo . . . . Beverly
•• 0:36—Breasts, several times, while in waterfall with Rick Rossovich.
••• 0:47—Breasts in bathtub, giving Rossovich a shave.
• 0:49—Partial left breast, while lying in bed and making love with Rossovich.
• 0:50—Brief breasts in bed, while under Rossovich.
••• 0:51—Breasts while in bed with Rossovich.
Asha Siewkumar . . . . Kamala
•• 0:45—Brief breasts, while opening her blouse in front of Rick Rossovich.
••• 1:09—Breasts and buns, undressing in front of mirror and walking into bathroom.
••• 1:10—Breasts and buns, while getting out of the shower, drying herself off and walking out of the bathroom.
••• 1:16—Buns and breasts while making love in bed with Rossovich.

Tropical Snow (1989)

Madeleine Stowe. . . . . Marina
• 0:05—Very brief side view of left breast putting red dress on.
• 0:11—Buns, lying in bed. Very brief right breast sitting up. (I wish they could have panned the camera to the right!)
•• 0:24—Breasts in mirror putting red dress on.
• 0:32—Buns, while lying on top of Tavo in bed.
• 0:54—Brief breasts making love in the water with Tavo. Then buns, lying on the beach (long shot.)
• 1:22—Long shot side view of right breast in water with Tavo.

Trouble Bound (1992)

Ginger Lynn Allen . . . . Uncredited Adult Film Actress
•• 0:22—Breasts on TV in motel room that Kit and Harry are watching.
Patricia Arquette . . . . .Kit

Trouble in Mind (1986)

Genevieve Bujold. . . . . Wanda
Lori Singer. . . . . Georgia
• 1:01—Very brief left breast, in bed with Kris Kristofferson.

The Trouble with Dick (1986)

Susan Dey . . . . Diane
Elaine Giftos. . . . . Sheila
Elizabeth Gorcey . . . . Haley
• 0:13—Very brief left breast in gaping T-shirt while she lies on bed, plays with a toy and laughs.
• 0:26—Lower half of buns under robe on sofa with Dick.
• 0:27—Half of right breast on top of Dick in bed.

Truck Stop Women (1974)

Uschi Digard . . . . .Truck Stop Woman
•• 0:18—Breasts getting arrested in the parking lot by the police officer, then buns and breasts getting frisked in a room.
Claudia Jennings . . . . Rose
• 0:27—Brief breasts taking off blouse and getting into bed.
• 0:48—Brief side view of right breast in mirror, while getting dressed.
• 1:10—Brief breasts wrapping and unwrapping a towel around herself.

Truck Turner (1974)

Annik Borel . . . . .Stalingrad
• 0:38—Brief breasts, twice, in slow motion while running to stab Isaac Hayes' partner.
Tara Strohmeier. . . . . .Turnpike

True Blood (1989)

Sherilyn Fenn. . . . . Jennifer Scott
• 1:22—Very brief right breast, while in closet trying to stab Spider with a piece of mirror.

True Lies (1994)

Tia Carrere. . . . . .Juno Skinner
Jamie Lee Curtis. . . . . .Helen Tasker
• 1:20—In black bra, buns in sexy panties, while doing strip routine in front of Arnold Schwarzenegger.

True Romance (1993)

(Unrated version reviewed.)
Patricia Arquette . . . . Alabama Whitman
• 0:11—Brief breasts, while lying in bed with Christian Slater. [On the wide screen laser disc version only: Right breast two more times and partial left breast (••).]
Anna Thomson . . . . Lucy

• *Truth or Consequences, N.M.* (1997)

Kim Dickens. . . . . Addy Monroe
• 1:24—Breasts, while making love in bed under Ray.

Truth or Dare (1991)

Madonna. . . . . Herself
••• 0:44—Brief breasts changing clothes backstage. B&W.
• 1:35—Very brief half of left breast, while wearing robe and jumping up. B&W.
Sandra Bernhard . . . . Herself

Tryst (1994)

Barbara Carrera . . . . Julia
• 1:03—Partial right breast, then left breast while making love in bed with Todd.

Jamie Luner . . . . Mindy
- 0:41—In black bra and panties, then back side of left breast, while changing clothes when Danny peeks through hole in wall and photographs her.
- 1:12—Back side of right breast, while changing clothes in motel room.
- •• 1:13—Breasts, while struggling with Danny and getting raped in hotel room.

Tuff Turf *(1984)*

Kim Richards . . . . Frankie Croyden
- 1:29—Brief breasts supposedly of a body double (Fiona Morris) in bedroom with James Spader but I have heard from a very reliable source that it really was her.

Catya Sassoon . . . . Feather

The Tunnel *(1987; Spanish)*

Jane Seymour . . . . Maria
- 0:29—Very brief left breast, while in bed with Peter Weller when the sheet is pulled down.
- •• 0:44—Brief right breast, while getting dressed, throwing off her robe.
- 0:48—Very brief, buns in pulled up skirt while struggling with Weller on the floor.
- 1:43—Brief buns behind textured glass divider, while changing clothes.

Tunnel Vision *(1995; Australian)*

Catherine Zeta Jones . . . . Bunny

Patsy Kensit . . . . Kelly Wheatstone

Vanessa Steele . . . . Rachel Kossinger
- 0:41—Very, very brief left breast when girl dressed in bunny suit discovers her. Lit with flashlight.

Tunnelvision *(1976)*

Betty Thomas . . . . Brigit Bert Richards
- 0:19—Breasts in pasties, during game show. Long scene. (She jumps up and down a lot.)

Turkish Delight *(1974; Dutch)*

Monique Van De Ven . . . . Olga
- •• 0:24—Breasts when Rutger Hauer opens her blouse, then nude on the bed.
- •• 0:27—Breasts, waking up in bed.
- ••• 0:33—Breasts on bed with Hauer, then nude getting up to fix flowers.
- 0:42—Buns, with Hauer at the beach.
- •• 0:46—Breasts modeling for Hauer, then brief nude running around outside.
- •• 0:54—Breasts in bed with open blouse with flowers.
- 1:04—In wet T-shirt in the rain with Hauer, then brief breasts coming down the stairs.

The Turn-On *(1989)*

a.k.a. Le Clic

Maria Ford . . . . Maria
- ••• 0:21—Breasts, then nude while dancing on stage after getting turned on by the black box.

Florence Guerin . . . . Claudia Christiani
- •• 0:02—Buns and breasts in mirror.
- ••• 0:34—Breasts, while looking at herself in dressing room mirror and caressing herself.
- •• 0:54—Breasts, while walking through the woods and taking off her clothes.
- ••• 0:56—Nude, while playing with herself in the woods, then getting tied up and carried away on a guy's shoulders. Long scene.
- ••• 1:07—Breasts and buns, while on the beach with Dr. Fez. Nude, fighting with her husband and running away into the house.

Marjean Holden . . . . Voodoo Priestess

Debra Lamb . . . . Assistant in White Dress

Toni Naples . . . . Harold's Wife
- ••• 0:31—Nude, during ceremony and after getting turned on by the black box.

• ***The Turning*** *(1992)*

Nancy Allen . . . . Glory Lawson

Gillian Anderson . . . . April Cavanaugh
- 0:47—In bra, then very brief side of left breast when the bra is pulled down.
- •• 0:48—Very brief right breast, seen from over her left shoulder as Clifford eases her backward.

The Turning Point *(1977)*

Leslie Browne . . . . Emilia Rogers
- 0:51—Brief side view of right breast, while lying in bed with Mikhail Baryshnikov at the end of the love scene. Don't see her face.

Shirley MacLaine . . . . DeeDee

Turtle Beach *(1992; Australian)*

a.k.a. The Killing Beach

Joan Chen . . . . Minou
- ••• 0:07—Brief buns, dropping robe and leaving room while talking to Greta Scacchi.

Greta Scacchi . . . . Judith
- 0:44—Upper half of buns and almost breasts, making love.

Tusks *(1990)*

Lucy Gutteridge . . . . Micah Hill
- •• 0:23—Breasts in tub taking a bath.

Tuxedo Warrior *(1970)*

Holly Palance . . . . Sally
- •• 0:32—Breasts, while making love in bed with Cliff.
- 0:40—Brief breasts, while putting on a robe.
- •• 0:55—Breasts, while in bed with Cliff.

Carol Royle . . . . Lisa
- •• 0:35—Breasts, while lying in bed and talking with Cliff.

Twelfth Night *(1988; Italian)*

Viju Krim . . . . Maria
- •• 1:09—Breasts, dancing in tavern in open top.

Ajita Wilson . . . . Antonia
- •• 0:50—Buns, taking off her dress and walking into stream with a guy.
- 0:51—Very brief breasts, making love with him in the stream.
- •• 1:11—Right breast, hanging out of black dress, dancing in tavern.

Twenty Bucks *(1993)*

Sam Jenkins . . . . Anna Holiday

Elisabeth Shue . . . . Emily Adams

Nina Siemaszko . . . . Bank Teller

Melora Walters . . . . Stripper
- •• 0:14—Buns and breasts, while getting ready for bachelor party in bathroom.
- •• 0:15—Buns in G-string, then breasts, while dancing during bachelor party.
- 0:18—Brief breasts, getting dressed in bathroom.
- 0:20—Brief breasts, while on fire escape.

Chloe Webb . . . . Uncredited Convenience Store Clerk

Twenty-One (1991; British)
Veronica Clifford . . . . Bobby's Aunt
Patsy Kensit. . . . . Katie
••• 1:17—Breasts in reflection in bathroom mirror undressing, then dressing.

Twice a Woman (1979)
Bibi Andersson . . . . .Laura
• 0:05—Breasts taking off her bra and putting a blouse on.
• 0:06—Brief side view of left breast, getting into bed, brief left breast lying back in bed.
Sandrine Dumas . . . . Sylvia
• 0:06—Breasts, kneeling on the bed, then more brief breasts in bed with Bibi Andersson.
••• 0:47—Brief right breast, then breasts in bed with Andersson. Long scene.
• 1:15—Left breast, lying in bed with Anthony Perkins. Long shot.
••• 1:23—Breasts with Andersson.

Twice Dead (1989)
Charlie Spradling. . . . . Tina
•• 1:11—Breasts taking off jacket next to bed.
••• 1:14—Breasts making love with her boyfriend in bed.
• 1:18—Brief breasts dead in bed.
Jill Whitlow . . . . .Robin/Myrna

Twin Peaks: Fire Walk With Me (1992)
Mädchen Amick . . . . Shelly Johnson
Annie Gaybis . . . . Uncredited Dancer on Stage
• 1:15—Breasts, dancing on stage. Lit with red light.
• 1:16—More breasts and very brief buns, while on stage.
• 1:18—More breasts while on stage.
Pamela Gidley . . . . Teresa Banks
Heather Graham . . . . Annie Blackburn
Moira Kelly . . . . Donna Hayward
•• 1:22—Breasts, while lying on table in cabin.
Sheryl Lee . . . . Laura Palmer
• 0:37—Very brief breasts, letting her boyfriend feel her breast.
•• 1:18—Breasts when a guy takes off her dress in cabin.
••• 1:19—Breasts, while talking with Ronette at table.
••• 1:21—More breasts in cabin and while sitting at the table with Ronette. More breasts when getting up.
• 1:49—Side view of buns and upper half of right breast (wearing lingerie) while lying in bed and rolling over.
• 1:58—Brief upper half of left breast while dancing in lingerie in cabin.
•• 1:59—Breasts, while struggling on bed with big guy.
• 2:01—Brief breasts talking with her dad in the cabin.

Twin Sisters (1992; Made for Cable Movie)
Susan Almgren . . . . Sophie
•• 0:06—Breasts and buns, while making love in bed with a guy.

Twins of Evil (1971; British)
Madeleine Collinson . . . . Freida Gelhorn
•• 1:07—Right breast, then brief breasts undoing dress, then full frontal nudity after turning into a vampire in bedroom.
Mary Collinson . . . . .Maria Gelhorn
Luan Peters . . . . Gerta
Maggie Wright . . . . Aleta

The Twist (1976)
Ann-Margret . . . . .Charlie Minerva
Sybil Danning . . . . Jacques' Secretary
•• 1:24—Brief breasts sitting next to Bruce Dern during his daydream.
Sydne Rome . . . . Nathalie

Twisted Justice (1990)
Julie Austin. . . . . Andrea Leyton
Karen Black . . . . Mrs. Granger
Bonnie Paine . . . . Hooker
•• 0:11—Breasts, wearing black panties and stockings, while getting photographed.
Tanya Roberts . . . . Secretary
Shannon Tweed. . . . . .Hinkle

Twisted Love (1994)
Donna Eskra . . . . .Penny
•• 0:04—Breasts, several times, while making out with Mark Paul Gosselar in a room during a party. Breasts, during introduction to Beau.
Lisa Dean Ryan . . . . Janna
• 0:48—Buns in T-back, taking off slip and getting into bed with Beau. Dark.
Janet Wood . . . . Nurse

Twisted Obsession (1990)
Arielle Dombasle . . . . Marion Derain
Miranda Richardson. . . . . .Marilyn
Liza Walker . . . . Jenny Greene
• 1:12—Lower frontal nudity while lying down. (Don't see her face.)
• 1:35—Brief breasts in blue light when Jeff Goldblum sees her.

Twisted Passion (1995)
a.k.a. Shades of Gray
Lee Anne Beaman . . . . Truck Stop Waitress
Kelly Burns. . . . . .Gray Goodman
•• 0:09—Breasts, when Jack opens her dress, then makes love with her.
••• 0:41—Breasts and buns, when making love with Frank at night. Playing with fluorescent paint on each other, then in the shower.
Wendy MacDonald . . . . Head Nurse
Kathy Shower . . . . .Joyce Walker

• Two Deaths (1994; British)
Sonia Braga . . . . Ana Puscasu
•• 0:44—Breasts, when Michael Gambon takes her top off during dinner party in front of several men.
•• 1:23—Breasts, while Gambon gropes her.
Lisa Orgolini . . . . Young Ana
• 0:29—Brief breasts, when sitting up in bed when the young Daniel visits her at night.
•• 1:09—Nude after undressing in young Daniel's medical office.

Two Moon Junction (1988)
Sherilyn Fenn. . . . . April
••• 0:07—Breasts and brief buns, while taking a shower in the country club shower room.
•• 0:27—Brief breasts on the floor kissing Perry.
•• 0:42—Breasts in gas station restroom changing camisole tops with Kristy McNichol.
• 0:54—Brief breasts making love with Perry in a motel room.
••• 1:24—Nude at Two Moon Junction making love with Perry. Very hot!

- 1:40—Brief left breast, brief lower frontal nudity and buns in the shower with Perry.

Milla Jovovich . . . . Samantha
Kristy McNichol. . . . . .Patti Jean

- •• 0:42—Breasts in gas station restroom changing camisole tops with Sherilyn Fenn.

Millie Perkins. . . . . .Mrs. Delongpre

Two Small Bodies *(1993)*

Suzy Amis . . . . Eileen Maloney

- 0:57—Very, very brief back side view of right breast after taking off bra.

Two to Tango *(1988)*

Adrianne Sachs . . . . Cecilia Lorca

- •• 0:29—Side of left breast and buns in bedroom with Lucky Lara. More left breast while Dan Stroud watches through camera.
- •• 0:59—Breasts and buns in bed with Dan Stroud.

Twogether *(1992)*

(Unrated version reviewed.)

Brenda Bakke . . . . .Allison McKenzie

- •• 0:08—Breasts and buns, while making love in bed with Nick Cassavetes.
- •• 0:10—Brief breasts, several times, while making love with Cassavetes.
- •• 0:24—Lower frontal nudity, while posing in a bra for drawing by Cassavetes.
- 1:50—Brief buns and partial breasts with Cassavetes in bed in flashback.

Deborah Driggs . . . . .Beach Babe/Melissa

- 1:29—Brief right breast, while lying in bed with Nick Cassavetes.

Lisa Saxton . . . . Naked Lady in Bed

- 0:01—Brief buns, while turning over in bed next to Nick Cassavetes.

• ***U Turn*** *(1997)*

Claire Danes . . . . .Jenny
Jennifer Lopez. . . . . .Grace McKenna

- 1:46—Very brief left breast, twice, while making love with Nick Nolte during flashback montage.

Liv Tyler . . . . Girl in Bus Station

Ultimate Desires *(1991)*

a.k.a. Silhouette

Sheri Able . . . . .Carlos' Girlfriend
Holly Chester . . . . Streetgirl
Robyn Kelly. . . . . Streetgirl
Tracy Scoggins . . . . Samantha Stewart

- 0:59—Very brief buns and side of left breast taking off her dress and walking out of the room.
- ••• 1:10—Breasts, several times, in bed with Singer.

• ***Ultimate Sensual Massage*** *(1991; Video Tape)*

Rebekka Armstrong. . . . . Seduction

- ••• 0:39—Nude, during massage session in surreal outdoor setting.

Linda Singer . . . . Awakening

- ••• 0:02—Breasts and buns, during massage session in bed.

Ultraviolet *(1992)*

Patricia Healy . . . . Kristen Halsey

- 0:21—Brief breasts, after taking off blouse and posing for Esai Morales in motor home.
- ••• 0:50—In wet bra and panties, coming out of the pond. Side view of buns, then breasts while posing for Morales.
- ••• 0:52—More buns in panties and breasts in pond with Morales and struggling with him.

The Unbearable Lightness of Being *(1988)*

Juliette Binoche . . . . .Tereza

- 1:33—Brief breasts while jumping onto couch.
- 1:35—Buns, while lying on couch when Lena Olin pulls her panties down.
- 1:36—Buns, while sitting in front of fire being photographed, then running around, when trying to hide.
- 1:53—Very brief left breast, then very, very brief right breast, while in bed with Lewis.
- 2:18—Left breast and lower frontal nudity in The Engineer's apartment.

Consuela de Haviland . . . . Tall Brunette

- •• 2:10—In black bra, then lower nudity and side view of right breast while trying to seduce Daniel Day Lewis.

Lena Olin. . . . . .Sabina

- •• 0:03—Breasts in bed with Daniel Day Lewis, then while looking in a mirror.
- 0:27—Brief back side of right breast and upper half of buns, while making love in bed with Lewis.
- •• 1:29—Breasts and buns while Juliette Binoche photographs her.
- 1:43—Very brief left breast, in bed with Lewis.
- 2:32—Brief breasts in B&W photo found in a drawer by Lewis.

The Unborn *(1991)*

Brooke Adams . . . . Virginia Marshall

- 1:12—Right breast, while breast feeding her baby creature.

Uncaged *(1991)*

a.k.a. Angel in Red

Sean'a Arthur . . . . Dancer

- •• 0:44—Buns in lingerie. Breasts dancing on stage.

Leslie Bega . . . . .Micki

- •• 0:02—Breasts on top of a customer, in bed.
- •• 0:16—Breasts in bed with Evan.
- 0:42—Brief breasts with Evan on the floor.

Pamella D'Pella . . . . Ros
Monique Gabrielle. . . . . Beautiful Hooker
Elena Sahagun. . . . . Joey

• ***Unconditional Love*** *(1994)*

Aleksandra Kaniak . . . . Mary Chambers

- 0:11—Breasts, while taking a shower outdoors, when spotted by Steve.
- •• 0:38—Breasts, while making love with Steve in his studio.
- •• 0:51—Full frontal nudity, while posing for Steve in his studio.

Under Lock and Key *(1994)*

Trisha Berdot. . . . . Zelda

- •• 0:03—Breasts and buns while in the shower.

Tamara Carrera . . . . Inmate
Barbara Niven . . . . Tina
Stephanie Ann Smith. . . . . Sarah

- 0:02—Breasts, while getting up out of bed in cell.
- 0:05—Breasts, while getting menaced by Zelda and her two friends.
- ••• 0:13—Nude in the showers with Danielle.
- •• 0:14—Nude, while getting hassled by Wincott.
- ••• 0:25—Nude, while getting examined by the doctor.

Wendi Westbrook . . . . Danielle Peters
- 0:11—Breasts, when changing clothes while sitting on bed in cell.

••• 0:13—Nude, with Sarah in the showers.
- 0:18—Nude while getting undressed for "conjugal visit."
- 0:19—Partial left breast, while in bed during "conjugal visit."

•• 0:50—Nude, getting undressed, taking a shower, and getting out.

Under Siege *(1992)*

Erika Eleniak . . . . Jordan Tate

•• 0:43—Buns in T-back, then brief breasts in open coat, while popping out of cake.

Under Suspicion *(1992)*

Maggie O'Neill . . . . Hazel
- 0:02—Breasts and lower frontal nudity in shower with Liam Neeson.
- 0:03—Very brief right breast, while ducking to avoid shotgun blast.

The Underachievers *(1987)*

Barbara Carrera . . . . Katherine

Becky LeBeau . . . . Ginger Bronsky

••• 0:40—Breasts in swimming pool playing with an inflatable alligator after her exercise class has left.

Jewel Shepard . . . . Sci-Fi Teacher
- 0:27—Breasts ripping off her Star Trek uniform when someone enters her classroom. Dark, hard to see.

Susan Tyrrell . . . . Mrs. Grant

Undercover *(1995)*

(Unrated version reviewed.)

Meg Foster . . . . Mrs. V

Athena Massey . . . . Cindy Hanen
- 0:00—Brief breast and buns, while getting dressed during opening credits. Don't see her face.

•• 0:13—Buns and left breast, while making love in bed with Hunt.

•• 0:21—Breasts, while undressing in front of Meg Foster for her audition.

•• 0:31—In black bra, then breasts in front of Mr. Ralston.
- 0:45—Breasts under sheer black blouse.

••• 0:55—Breasts and buns doing a strip routine in front of a customer, then making love with him. Very, very brief partial lower frontal nudity when she pulls her dress up.

0:59—Brief buns under sheer nightgown.

••• 1:04—Breasts and buns in black rubber outfit in room with a customer, then making love with him on a chair.
- 1:11—Buns in T-back in sheer black robe.

•• 1:15—Breasts with a customer and his wife.

••• 1:16—Breasts and buns while making love in bed with the customer and his wife.

••• 1:21—Breasts while in bathtub. Breasts and buns in flashbacks.

••• 1:32—Nude, while making love with Hunt in bed.

Mari Morrow . . . . Victoria

Rena Riffel . . . . Rain
- 0:37—Brief full frontal nudity while in bathtub with another blonde woman on TV monitor.

•• 0:39—Breasts and brief buns, while in bathtub with the other blonde.

••• 0:43—In black lingerie, then breasts and buns while doing strip routine in front of Cindy.

•• 0:46—Breasts and buns after undressing out of purple outfit.
- 0:48—Left breast, then breasts while making love with mystery guy.

The Underneath *(1994)*

Shelley Duvall . . . . Nurse

Alison Elliott. . . . . .Rachel
- 0:39—Very brief buns, while rolling over with Peter Gallagher. Dark.

Elisabeth Shue . . . . Susan

• ***The Understudy: Graveyard Shift II*** *(1988)*

Wendy Gazelle. . . . . Camilla Turner/Patti Venus

Ilse Von Glatz. . . . . Ash
- 0:49—Very brief side view of right breast and several very, very brief and brief breasts shots in bed with Baisez.

Undertow *(1995)*

Mia Sara . . . . Willie Yates

••• 0:51—Breasts, while taking a shower, then making out with Lou Diamond Phillips.

• ***Underworld*** *(1996)*

Cristi Conaway . . . . Julianne

Traci Lords. . . . . .Anna

Heidi Schanz . . . . Simone/Joyce Alt

•• 0:01—In red lingerie, then breasts, while modeling lingerie during show.

Annabella Sciorra. . . . . Dr. Leah

Unexpected Encounters, Vol. 3 *(1988)*

Jasaé . . . . Neighbor

••• 0:32—Doing strip tease in front of guitar playing neighbor. Buns in G-string and breasts.

Charlie Spradling. . . . . Woman in House

••• 0:50—In lingerie, then breasts on sofa with the gardener.

Unfaithfully Yours *(1984)*

Jane Hallaren . . . . .Janet

Nastassja Kinski . . . . Daniella Eastman
- 0:37—Breasts and buns in the shower.

Cassie Yates. . . . . Carla Robbins

The Unholy *(1988)*

Jill Carroll. . . . . Millie
- 1:10—Very brief upper half of left breast, while talking in the courtyard with Ben Cross.

Unholy Rollers *(1972)*

a.k.a. Leader of the Pack

Roberta Collins . . . . .Jennifer

Claudia Jennings . . . . Karen Walker

••• 0:32—Breasts on pool table, getting gang stripped by the other girls, then walking around and yelling at them.
- 0:38—Buns on top of Nick, on table in the middle of the roller derby rink.

•• 1:15—Breasts, twice, while changing clothes in locker room, then in bra and panties.

Charlene Jones. . . . . Beverly

Candice Roman . . . . Donna

••• 0:06—Breasts in bed with Greg when Karen comes home.

•• 0:12—Breasts, dancing on stage in club next to a brunette dancer.
- 0:13—More breasts in background.
- 0:14—More breasts in background.

Uninhibited (1993)

Leigh Betchley. . . . . .Rocket's Wife
••• 0:54—Breasts, while making love on top of Escobar.
Mimi Faillace. . . . . Rocco Gambino's Wife
• 0:18—Right breast, while making out with Gambino.
Kelly Jaye. . . . . .Girl in Bed
• 0:00—Breasts, while getting out of bed and getting dressed.
Asha Siewkumar . . . . Cassandra
•• 1:12—Breasts, while making love with Jugginson.
Domonique Simone . . . . Detective Jordan's Wife
•• 0:02—Breasts, while in bed by herself, then making love with Detective Jordan.
K.C. Williams. . . . . Detective Jugginson
•• 0:58—Right breast, while lying in bed, talking on the phone with Detective Gunn.
•• 1:08—Breasts and buns, while in bathtub. Buns in sheer white outfit.
• 1:10—In sheer white outfit again. Buns, while talking with Cassandra.
•• 1:11—Breasts, while making love with Cassandra.
•• 1:24—Buns in G-string, while putting on make-up and in bed with Gunn.
••• 1:27—Breasts, while making love in bed with Gunn.

Unlawful Entry (1992)

Deborah Offner. . . . . Penny
Sherrie Rose . . . . Girl in Jeep
•• 0:42—Breasts, making love with Ray Liotta in police car, then getting thrown out.
Madeleine Stowe . . . . .Karen Carr
••• 0:56—Breasts and partial buns, while making love on top of Kurt Russell in bed.

An Unmarried Woman (1978)

Jill Clayburgh . . . . Erica
•• 0:12—Brief breasts getting dressed for bed, kind of dark and hard to see.
•• 1:10—In bra and panties in guy's apartment, then brief breasts lying on bed.

The Unnameable (1988)

Laura Albert . . . . .Wendy Barnes
•• 0:46—Left breast while lying on floor kissing John, then brief buns when he pulls her panties down.

The Unnameable II (1992)

Laura Albert . . . . Guest Corpse
Maria Ford . . . . .Alyda Winthrop
•• 0:52—Buns, when her long hair moves out of the way. Partial tip of right breast when looking at the telephone.
• 0:53—Brief buns and side of right breast in bedroom.
•• 0:54—Buns and breasts while checking out the bed.
• 0:57—Brief buns, while getting out of bed.
•• 0:58—Buns and brief breasts in bedroom with Mary.
• 1:01—Right breast in gaping nightgown while kneeling on elevator floor.
• 1:22—Brief glimpses of right breast in gaping nightgown.
• 1:32—Very brief right breast in gaping nightgown while crawling on the floor.
Julie Strain. . . . . Creature

The Unspeakable (1996; Made for Cable Movie)

a.k.a. Shadow of a Scream
Elizabeth Costello . . . . .Mary Dumaski
Athena Massey . . . . Alice Redmond
• 0:00—Breasts in quick cuts during opening credits.
• 0:18—Breasts, while having rough sex with Cyril O'Reilly in bedroom.
•• 0:47—Breasts, while taking a shower. Overhead shots, then normal shots, when Cyril O'Reilly scares her.
• 1:16—In bra, with David Chokachi. Brief partial buns in panties.
•• 1:19—Breasts, while being threatened by Chokachi. Very brief buns and lower frontal nudity, lying back on bed.

Until September (1984)

Karen Allen . . . . .Mo Alexander
•• 0:41—Breasts in bed making love with Thierry Lhermitte.
•• 1:13—Breasts and buns walking from bed to Lhermitte.
• 1:25—Brief breasts jumping out of bathtub.
Maryam D'Abo . . . . Nathalie
Marika Green . . . . Banker

Until the End of the World (1991)

Lois Chiles . . . . Elsa Farber
Solveig Dommartin . . . . .Claire Tourneur
••• 0:34—Left breast, then breasts, then full frontal nudity in bedroom with William Hurt and Winter.
Jeanne Moreau . . . . Edith Farber

Unveiled (1993)

Lisa Zane. . . . . Stephania Montgomery
• 1:06—Very, very brief left breast in gaping gown, while bending over to pick stuff up off the floor.

Up 'n' Coming (1987)

(R-rated version reviewed, X-rated version available.)
Marilyn Chambers. . . . . Cassie
••• 0:01—Nude, getting out of bed and taking a shower.
•• 0:08—Breasts making love in bed with the record producer.
• 0:30—Brief breasts in bed with two guys.
•• 0:47—Full frontal nudity getting suntan lotion rubbed on her by another woman.
•• 0:55—Breasts taking off her top at radio station.
Lisa De Leeuw . . . . Altheah Anderson
• 0:33—Very brief breasts by the pool when her robe opens.
• 0:48—Brief breasts, while walking around the house when her robe opens.
•• 0:49—Left breast talking with a guy, then breasts while walking into the bedroom.
Monique Gabrielle. . . . . Boat Girl #1
• 0:39—Breasts wearing white shorts on boat. Long shot.
• 0:40—More brief nude shots on the boat.
Loni Saunders . . . . Dixanne
• 0:19—Breasts, while kissing a guy on the bus.

Up in Smoke (1978)

Madeleine Collinson . . . . Pinup
• 0:44—Brief breasts in centerfold photo on inside of restroom stall door.
Mary Collinson . . . . Pinup
• 0:44—Brief breasts in centerfold photo on inside of restroom stall door.
June Fairchild. . . . . Ajax Lady
Louisa Moritz. . . . . Officer Gloria
Cheryl Smith . . . . Laughing Lady
Wally Anne Wharton . . . . Debbie

Up Pompeii (1971; British)

Veronica Clifford . . . . Boobia

Julie Ege . . . . Voluptua
- 0:45—Partial right breast, while she thinks she seducing Ludicrus. There is some kind of jewelry covering her right nipple.

Madeline Smith . . . . Erotica
- 0:35—Breasts while in bubble bath.

Up the Creek (1984)

Julia Montgomery . . . . Lisa
Jennifer Runyon . . . . Heather Merriweather
Lori Sutton . . . . Cute Girl
- 0:40—Brief breasts, twice, after ripping open her blouse to get a crowd excited while cheerleading.

Jeana Tomasina . . . . Molly
Peggy Trentini . . . . Co-Ed
- 1:25—Left breast, in cabin with James B. Sikking.
- 1:27—Breasts, while in room with Sikking before mud slide hits the cabin.

Romy Walthall . . . . Corky

Used Cars (1980)

Cheryl Rixon . . . . Margaret
- •• 0:29—Breasts after getting her dress torn off during a used car commercial.

Betty Thomas . . . . Bunny
- 0:37—Dancing on top of a car next to Kurt Russell wearing pasties to attract customers (wearing a brunette wig).

Vagabond (1985; French)

Sandrine Bonnaire . . . . Mona
Macha Meril . . . . Madame Landier
- •• 0:45—Breasts, while sitting in the bathtub and talking on the phone.

Valentino (1977; British)

Leslie Caron . . . . Nazimova
Carol Kane . . . . Fatty's Girl
Jennie Linden . . . . Agnes Ayres
Penelope Milford . . . . Lorna Sinclair
- ••• 1:28—Nude, while making love with Rudolf Nureyev in bedroom. Long scene.

Michelle Phillips . . . . Natasha Rambova
- 0:53—Brief buns, enticing Rudolf Nureyev into tent.
- 0:54—Brief lower frontal nudity, when sitting up in bed.
- ••• 0:55—Brief left breast when Nureyev moves her hair out of the way. Breasts, while getting up and out of bed.
- •• 1:39—Brief right breast, after Nureyev rolls off her.

Linda Thorson . . . . Billie Streeter
- 0:14—Brief left breast, under a guy in bed.

Valentino Returns (1988)

Veronica Cartwright . . . . Pat Gibbs
- ••• 0:33—Breasts, while sitting in bed with Frederic Forrest. Fairly long scene.

Jenny Wright . . . . Sylvia Fuller

Valet Girls (1987)

Barbara Dare . . . . Uncredited Party Girl
- 1:10—Brief breasts, getting photographed while sitting on railing.
- 1:14—Brief breasts, popping out of birthday cake and putting a pie in Dirk's face.

Kim Gillingham . . . . Madonna Wannabe
Mary Kohnert . . . . Carnation
Elise Richards . . . . Cindy

Valley Girl (1983)

Colleen Camp . . . . Sarah Richman
Elizabeth Daily . . . . Loryn
- •• 0:16—In bra through open jumpsuit, then brief breasts on bed with Tommy.

Deborah Foreman . . . . Julie
Joyce Hyser . . . . Joyce

Valley of the Dolls (1967)

Patty Duke . . . . Neely O'Hara
Lee Grant . . . . Miriam
Susan Hayward . . . . Helen Lawson
Barbara Parkins . . . . Anne Welles
- 0:28—Very brief silhouette of a breast, when taking off nightgown and getting into bed.

Sharon Tate . . . . Jennifer North
- 1:21—In bra, acting in a movie. Very, very brief left breast in bed with a guy (curtain gets in the way).
- 1:23—Very brief side view of right breast, while sitting up in bed.

Corinna Tsopei . . . . Telephone Girl

• *Valmont* (1989)

Fairuza Balk . . . . Cécile
- 1:16—Buns, when Valmont kisses her and plays with her before deflowering her. Don't see her face with the rest of her body.

Annette Bening . . . . Marquise de Merteuil
- 0:10—Very brief, hard to see right breast, while reaching up to kiss Jeffrey Jones.

Sandrine Dumas . . . . Martine
Meg Tilly . . . . Tourvel

The Vals (1982)

Tiffany Bolling . . . . Valley Attorney and Parent
Gina Calabrese . . . . Annie
- 0:04—Breasts changing clothes in bedroom with three of her friends. Long shot, hard to see.
- 0:15—Right breast, while making love with a guy at a party.

Jill Carroll . . . . Sam

Vamp (1986)

Tricia Brown . . . . Candi
- 0:32—Brief breasts doing strip tease.

Grace Jones . . . . Katrina
- 0:23—Breasts under wire bra, dancing on stage. Body is painted, so it's difficult to see.

Lisa Lyon . . . . Cimmaron
Tanya Papanicolas . . . . Waitress
Dedee Pfeiffer . . . . Amaretto

Vampire at Midnight (1988)

Esther Alise . . . . Lucia Giannini
- ••• 1:01—In black lingerie, then breasts and buns while taking off clothes to wish Roger a happy birthday.

Barbara Hammond . . . . Kelly
- •• 0:07—Breasts and buns, getting out of the shower and drying herself off.
- 0:16—Left breast, dead, in Victor's car trunk. Blood on her.

Jeanie Moore . . . . Amalia
- •• 0:32—Breasts getting up to run an errand.

Christina Whitaker . . . . Ingrid

***Vampire Cop** (1990)*
Melissa Anne Moore . . . . Melanie Roberts
- ••• 0:46—Breasts in bed with the Vampire Cop.
- •• 0:51—Right breast, sitting in bed talking with Hans.
- • 1:21—Right breast, in bed on the phone during end credits.

***Vampire Hookers** (1979)*
Lenka Novak . . . . Suzy
- •• 0:51—Breasts in bed during the orgy with the guy and the other two Vampire Hookers.

• ***Vampire Journals** (1996)*
Starr Andreeff . . . . .Iris
Elvira Deatcu . . . . .Dreamy Girl
Floriela Grappini . . . . .Serena
- • 0:59—Breasts, while in bed with Zachary before biting him and turning him into a vampire.

***Vampire Lovers** (1970; British)*
Kate O'Mara . . . . Madame Perrodot
Ingrid Pitt . . . . Marcilla/Carmilla
- •• 0:32—Breasts and buns in the bathtub and reflection in the mirror talking to Emma.

Madeline Smith. . . . . Emma
- •• 0:32—Breasts trying on a dress in the bedroom after Carmilla has taken a bath.
- • 0:49—Breasts in bed, getting her top pulled down by Carmilla.

Pippa Steel . . . . .Laura
- • 0:24—Left breast in bed when the doctor pulls her top down to listen to her heart beat.

***Vampire Vixens From Venus** (1995)*
Michelle Bauer . . . . Shampay
- •• 0:58—Breasts, while on the floor with her boyfriend.

Leslie Glass . . . . Omay
- •• 0:20—Breasts in open dress top, behind a guy on the couch.
- •• 0:31—Breasts, while putting on make-up in bathroom.
- • 0:41—Breasts, while dancing on stage.
- • 1:07—Breasts, while greeting policemen at the door.

Theresa Lynn. . . . . Shirley
- • 0:05—Breasts after pulling down her blouse, to get some attention while hitchhiking.
- • 0:20—Breasts in pulled down blouse, while on the sofa with a guy.
- • 0:40—Brief breasts, while dancing on stage.
- • 1:07—Breasts, while greeting policemen at the door.

J. J. North . . . . Arylai
- • 0:18—Left breast, while on couch with a guy.
- • 1:07—Left breast, while greeting policemen at the door.

***Vampire's Kiss** (1989)*
Maria Conchita Alonso . . . . .Alva
Elizabeth Ashley . . . . Dr. Glaser
Jennifer Beals. . . . . Rachel
Kasi Lemmons. . . . . Jackie
- •• 0:05—In black bra and panties, then breasts in living room with Nicolas Cage.

***Vampirella** (1996; Made for Cable Movie)*
Antonia Dorian . . . . Vampire Girl #2
Corinna Harney. . . . . Sallah
- •• 0:42—Breasts, while changing clothes in room.

Talisa Soto. . . . . Vampirella
Peggy Trentini . . . . Vampire Girl #1
- • 0:51—Breasts, while lying on sofa and pulling her top down to distract Adam.

***Vampyres** (1974; British)*
Anulka Dziubinska . . . . Miriam
- • 0:00—Brief full frontal nudity in bed with Fran, kissing each other before getting shot.
- • 0:43—Breasts taking a shower with Fran.
- ••• 0:58—Breasts and buns in bed with Fran, drinking Ted's blood. Brief lower frontal nudity.

Sally Faulkner . . . . Harriet
- • 1:14—Side of left breast, partial buns, then right breast while making love with John in the trailer.
- •• 1:22—Full frontal nudity getting her clothes ripped off by Fran and Miriam in the wine cellar before being killed.

Marianne Morris . . . . Fran
- •• 0:00—Breasts, then full frontal nudity in bed with Miriam, kissing each other before getting shot.
- ••• 0:20—Side of right breast, then breasts in bed with Ted, drinking wine, then making love.
- • 0:23—Buns, lying in bed when Ted gets out.
- ••• 0:39—In black bra, panties, garter belt and stockings, then taking them off in front of Ted. Breasts and buns, then in bed.
- ••• 0:43—Breasts getting kissed by Miriam in the shower.
- •• 0:56—Breasts taking off dress in front of Ted and getting into bed. Partial lower frontal nudity getting into bed.
- •• 0:58—Breasts and brief lower frontal nudity in bed with Miriam, drinking Ted's blood.
- • 1:00—Full frontal nudity getting dragged out of bed by Miriam.
- • 1:18—Brief left breast, getting fondled by the Playboy guy in the wine cellar.

***The Van** (1977)*
Marcie Barkin . . . . Sue
- • 0:52—Brief breasts and very brief partial buns, while making love with Jack in back of van.
- • 0:54—Very brief right breast, twice, while lying in back of van with Jack.

Connie Lisa Marie . . . . Sally
- • 0:40—In wet T-shirt, while talking to Bobby.
- • 1:00—Brief right breast when changing clothes in house while bobby watches her through binoculars.
- •• 1:03—Breasts and partial buns after taking off robe, then making love with Bobby in back of van.
- • 1:05—Brief breasts, while getting dressed.

***Van Nuys Blvd.** (1979)*
Nancy McCauley. . . . . Mooner/Flasher
- • 0:11—Brief buns, while mooning Chooch out the window of her car.
- • 0:13—Brief breasts, while opening her jacket to flash Chooch and the police man.

Melissa Prophet. . . . . Camille
Suzanne Severeid . . . . Jo
- ••• 0:02—Breasts and buns, bringing a beer to Bobby, then sitting and watching TV.

Tara Strohmeier. . . . . Wanda
- •• 0:21—Breasts, while playing around with food with Bobby in the back of his van.
- • 0:51—Brief breasts, flashing while hitchhiking to get a ride.

Cyndi Wood . . . . Moon
- •• 0:57—Left breast outside on boat with Bobby, then breasts, while making love in bed with him.

Vanessa (1977; West German)

Olivia Pascal . . . . Vanessa

••• 0:08—Nude undressing, taking a bath and getting washed by Jackie. Long scene.
••• 0:16—Buns, then full frontal nudity getting a massage.
• 0:26—Breasts, while getting fitted for new clothes.
• 0:47—Full frontal nudity when Adrian rips her clothes off.
••• 0:56—Full frontal nudity on beach with Jackie.
••• 1:05—Nude making love with Jackie in bed. Nice close up of left breast.
•• 1:19—Full frontal nudity lying on the table.
•• 1:27—Breasts, wearing white panties, garter belt and stockings shackled up by Kenneth.

Vanishing Point (1971)

Gilda Texter . . . . Nude Rider

• 1:17—Breasts while riding motorcycle outside.
••• 1:19—Breasts riding motorcycle and walking around without wearing any clothes. Long scene.

Velvet Dreams (1991; Italian)

Alicia Moro . . . . n.a.

Kathy Shower . . . . Laura

•• 0:15—Left breast, while making love with Paul in the dressing room.
• 0:35—Brief buns, while getting a massage.
•• 0:42—Breasts, tied to a tree during her writing fantasy.

The Velvet Vampire (1971)

Sherry Miles . . . . Susan Ritter

• 0:08—Brief breasts in bed with Lee.
••• 0:18—Breasts sitting up in bed, then making love with Lee.
• 0:21—Breasts in bed in desert during dream scene.
••• 0:22—Breasts sitting up in bed and turning on the light.
• 0:42—Breasts in bed during desert dream scene, long shot.
• 0:55—Breasts in bed during desert dream scene.
••• 0:56—Breasts in bed in desert scene, closer shot with Diane.
• 1:19—Brief breasts in desert scene during flashback.

Celeste Yarnell . . . . Diane Le Fanu

• 0:32—Brief breasts, while zipping up her blouse after trying to seduce Lee.
•• 0:42—Breasts in desert scene when Lee pulls her blouse down.
••• 0:45—Breasts, while on the floor, making love with Lee.
•• 0:55—Breasts in desert scene with Lee.
• 0:57—Side view of buns, lying on top of someone in a coffin.
•• 1:02—Breasts, while in bed with Lee.

Vendetta (1986)

Roberta Collins . . . . Miss Dice

Marta Kober . . . . Sylvia

• 1:10—Very brief, dark, right breast in open blouse, in her prison cell with the guard.

Sandy Martin . . . . Kay Butler

• 0:34—Brief left breast, while making love with her boyfriend. Don't see her face.

Dirga McBroom . . . . Willow

Joanelle Nadine Romero . . . . Elena

Marianne Taylor . . . . Star

Vengeance... One by One

Romy Schneider . . . . n.a.

• 0:28—Very brief left breast when a soldier rips her bra open during struggle.

Venus in Furs (1970)

(Original version reviewed.)

Margareth Lee . . . . Olga

• 0:53—Buns, lying on floor with Maria.
• 0:54—Buns, while walking and holding candelabra.

Maria Rohm . . . . Wanda Reed

• 0:05—Breasts, while dead on the beach.
• 0:08—Breasts in stockings and panties, getting whipped by Olga.
•• 0:10—Breasts before getting stabbed by Klaus Kinski.
• 0:11—More breasts on beach, dead.
• 0:17—Brief breasts.
• 0:21—Right breast several times, making love in bed with a guy.
••• 0:22—Breasts, lying in bed with the guy afterwards.
• 0:23—Brief breasts on beach again.
• 0:32—Breasts, dead on the beach with two cuts.
• 0:43—Breasts on couch when Olga opens her blouse.
•• 0:45—Breasts in bed.
•• 0:52—Breasts posing for Olga.
• 0:54—Breasts, dead.
•• 0:56—Breasts walking down stairs, wearing panties.
• 0:59—Breasts in bed again.
• 1:02—Brief side view of right breast, hugging Jimmy.
• 1:05—Left breast while acting as a slave girl.
• 1:06—Brief breasts seen through sheer curtain.
• 1:09—Very brief right breast, dead.
•• 1:10—Left breast, with Klaus Kinski.
• 1:12—Buns, whlie lying on couch.

• *Venus Rising* (1995)

Audie England . . . . Eve

• 0:20—Very brief partial right breast while taking a bath.
• 1:00—Breasts, while making love on bed with Billy Wirth.

Morgan Fairchild . . . . Peyton

• *Very Close Quarters* (1984)

Kathleen Doyle . . . . Irina

• 0:36—Brief buns in panties, when mooning Alex.

Lee Taylor Allen . . . . Vera

•• 0:12—Right breast, while in bathtub with Luda in Vadik's imagination. Breasts in bathtub when old guy peeks through keyhole.

Vice Academy (1988)

Ginger Lynn Allen . . . . Holly

• 1:20—Buns, in white lingerie outfit when graduation robe gets torn off.

Linnea Quigley . . . . Didi

••• 0:45—Breasts making love with Chuck while he's handcuffed.

Karen Russell . . . . Shawnee

•• 0:09—Breasts exposing herself to Dwayne to disarm him.
•• 1:13—Breasts pulling her top down to distract a bad guy.

Vice Academy, Part 2 (1990)

Toni Alessandrini . . . . Aphrodisia

• 0:33—Breasts in dressing room.
••• 0:34—Breasts and buns in G-string, dancing in club.

Ginger Lynn Allen . . . . Holly

• 0:44—Buns in black bra, panties, garter belt and stockings.
•• 1:04—Buns in G-string, then breasts dancing with Linnea Quigley on stage at club.

Teagan Clive . . . . Bimbo Cop

Dee Hengstler . . . . Felatia

Melissa Anne Moore . . . . Glaze

Linnea Quigley . . . . Didi
•• 1:04—Buns in G-string, then breasts dancing with Ginger Lynn Allen on stage at club.

Vice Academy, Part 3 (1991)

Toni Alessandrini . . . . Stripper
•• 0:26—Breasts taking off dress on stage.
•• 0:27—More breasts on stage (about five times).
• 0:28—More breasts giving her money to the robbers.
• 0:34—Buns in G-string, while dancing on stage.
Ginger Lynn Allen . . . . Holly
Veronica Carothers . . . . Loretta
Darcy De Moss . . . . Uncredited Samantha
Dee Hengstler . . . . Lulu
Elizabeth Kaitan . . . . Candy
••• 0:12—Breasts in back of van with her boyfriend.
Julia Parton . . . . Melanie/Malathion
•• 0:44—Breasts, opening her blouse after seeing all the money.

Vice Academy, Part 4 (1994)

Veronica Carothers . . . . Amber
• 0:11—Brief partial buns, while getting a tattoo from Scabia.
Deborah Dutch . . . . Bar Hooker
Elizabeth Kaitan . . . . Candy
•• 0:46—Breasts, after taking off her dress top, while trying to seduce Anvil in his garage.
Honey Lauren . . . . Tiffany Berkowitz
Julia Parton . . . . Malathion
• 0:06—Buns in two piece swimsuit, getting clothes from Debbie Dutch in club.
•• 0:08—Breasts, while stripping out of dress in garage in front of Anvil.
Robin Sheridan . . . . Scabia
• 0:14—Brief partial right breast poking out of bra during struggle on sofa with Amber.

• *Vice Girls* (1995)

Lana Clarkson . . . . Jan Cooper
•• 0:11—Breasts, while making out in restroom with John.
Madeline Knight . . . . Michelle
• 0:04—Buns in T-back under fishnet dress.
• 0:08—Breasts, after taking off dress while being video taped.
•• 0:11—Breasts, while being video taped in bedroom.
Peggy Trentini . . . . Top Popper
• 0:41—Brief breasts, when taking off her black dress top while talking with a guy at party.
Heather Ward . . . . Dominique Star
• 0:32—Brief breasts, three times, while pulling down her dress top during autograph session at video store.

Vice Squad (1982)

Season Hubley . . . . Princess
•• 0:57—Brief left breast and buns, wearing garter belt and stockings, getting out of bed after making love with a John.
• 0:58—More buns, under sheer panties while fighting with the John.
Cheryl Smith . . . . White Prostitute

• *Vicious Circles* (1997)

(Unrated version reviewed.)
Carolyn Lowery . . . . Andrea
• 0:05—Brief breasts, while flashing herself to Paul Hipp.
•• 0:10—Breasts, while sitting in steam room with Helga.
• 0:17—Brief partial breasts during examination.
•• 0:31—Breasts and buns, while posing when wearing harness.
••• 0:42—In bra and panties, then breasts, while dancing in front of mirror. Sometimes difficult to see because of the hallucination effect.
• 0:47—Brief right breast, when sitting up during massage.
0:55—Partial breasts, while wearing harness
•• 1:09—Breasts in harness after taking off her blouse, while talking with Stan.
• 1:14—Brief breasts and partial lower frontal nudity, standing up out of bath.
• 1:15—Brief lower frontal nudity, with green pubic hair.
• 1:16—Very brief breast and lower frontal nudity, looking at herself in the mirror.
•• 1:17—Breasts and buns in harness, while posing for Ben Gazzara.
Camilla Overbye Roos . . . . Helga
•• 0:10—Breasts, while sitting in steam room with Carolyn Lowry.

Victim of Desire (1994)

Julie Strain . . . . Linda Hammond
•• 0:10—Nude, taking a shower.
••• 0:12—Breasts and buns in red panties, while making love with Wings Hauser on the floor at night. Nice finger sucking!
Shannon Tweed . . . . Carla Duvall
•• 0:21—In black lingerie outfit, then breasts, when changing clothes in bedroom while talking to Marc Singer.
••• 0:41—In white bra, then breasts and buns, while making love with Singer.
••• 0:52—Breasts and buns, while lying in bed after Singer sneaks back in the house, then making love.

Video Vixens (1973)

Angela Carnon . . . . Mrs. Gordon
•• 1:13—Full frontal nudity making love with Mr. Gordon in bed in various positions. Shot at fast speed.
Sandra Dempsey . . . . Actress
•• 0:05—Full frontal nudity, lying down getting make-up put on.
Marva Farmer . . . . Girl
•• 0:59—Full frontal nudity in the swimming pool with three other women during commercial.
Robyn Hilton . . . . Inga
•• 1:18—Breasts, opening her top in a room full of reporters.
Kimberly Hyde . . . . Claudine
Terri Johnson . . . . Anita
•• 0:43—Full frontal nudity, talking with her mother in bedroom during commercial.
Cheryl Smith . . . . Twinkle Twat Girl
••• 0:24—Full frontal nudity doing a commercial, sitting next to pool.
Robyn Whitting . . . . Patient and Virginia
•• 0:40—Breasts, then nude on couch in psychiatrist's office. In B&W.
•• 0:52—Full frontal nudity acting in bed with Rex for a film. In B&W.
Linda York . . . . Dial-A-Snatch Girl
•• 0:34—Nude on a turntable during a commercial, getting felt by four blindfolded guys.

Videodrome *(1983; Canadian)*

Deborah Harry . . . . Nicki Brand

•• 0:16—Breasts rolling over on the floor when James Woods is piercing her ear with a pin.

• **Vincent and Theo** *(1990; British/French/U.S.)*

Anne Canovas . . . . Marie

• 0:32—Three very, very brief breast shots in gaping nightgown, when getting up off the floor and yelling at Paul Rhys.

Johanna Ter Steege . . . . Jo Bonger

Vindicator *(1986; Canadian)*

a.k.a. Frankenstein '88

Caroline Arnold . . . . Lisa

•• 0:40—Breasts in bed with a jerk, then putting her blouse on.

Teri Austin . . . . Lauren Lehman

• 0:30—Very brief left breast and buns in mirror getting out of the bubble bath covered with bubbles. Long shot, hard to see anything.

Pam Grier . . . . Hunter

Violated *(1987)*

Sharon Cain . . . . Party Guest

Samantha Fox . . . . Joan

• 0:52—Breasts, while in bed with Marilyn on video playback.

Carol Francis . . . . Katy Carson

•• 0:22—Breasts, while taking off her outfit during party, then diving into pool.

Elizabeth Kaitan . . . . Liz Grant

•• 0:03—Breasts and lower frontal nudity while Frank rapes her in bedroom.

• 0:53—Very brief right breast several times while getting raped by Frank. Seen on video playback.

••• 0:59—Breasts and buns, while in bed with a customer.

April Daisy White . . . . Lisa Robb

••• 0:16—Breasts, while wearing panties while getting dressed in bedroom while talking to her little brother.

•• 0:22—Breasts, after taking off her dress and diving into pool.

•• 0:25—Full frontal nudity while getting raped in bedroom by Jack while Marilyn and Frank help.

• 0:28—Breasts and lower frontal nudity while washing herself off in bathtub.

•• 0:40—Breasts in flashback of rape scene.

• 0:53—Full frontal nudity in flashback of rape scene.

• 1:08—Breasts on video playback of taking her dress off by pool.

Virgin High *(1990)*

Michelle Bauer . . . . Miss Bush

Tracy Dali . . . . Christy

•• 0:04—Brief breasts several times when her blouse and bra pop open while talking to her parents.

Maureen La Vette . . . . Mrs. Murphy

Linnea Quigley . . . . Kathleen

•• 0:24—Breasts, nonchalantly making love on top of Derrick.

•• 0:55—Brief breasts several times on top of Derrick, then breasts.

• 1:21—Breasts in photo during party.

Donna Spangler . . . . Uncredited Car Wash Girl

Virgin Witch *(1971; British)*

Patricia Haines . . . . Sybil Waite

•• 0:50—Breasts, during ceremony when Gerald makes love with Christine.

• 0:52—Brief left breast, while lying in bed after Christine gets out.

Ann Michelle . . . . Christine

• 0:00—Brief right breast, during opening credits.

••• 0:06—Breasts and lower frontal nudity, after undressing and getting her body measured by Sybil.

•• 0:17—Breasts, undressing and standing by doorway, then prancing around outside for Peter the photographer.

••• 0:23—Brief breasts, while lying on car, then more breasts while standing next to it and posing.

••• 0:27—Full frontal nudity, while posing for photographer outside. Buns while making love with him.

•• 0:33—Nude, undressing and taking a shower.

••• 0:47—Nude, while standing, then lying on table during ceremony.

•• 0:52—Breasts, while getting out of bed with Sybil.

•• 1:20—Breasts, during ceremony.

• 1:23—Breasts, while getting dressed.

Vicki Michelle . . . . Betty

• 0:00—Brief breasts, while sitting up during opening credits.

•• 0:31—Breasts, while sitting in bathtub. Nude, getting out. Seen through fish-eye lens.

•• 1:17—Buns, during witches' ceremony. Left breast, then breasts while lying on table.

• 1:23—Brief left breast, while on the ground with Johnny.

• 1:25—Left breast, when Johnny gets up off her.

Virtual Combat *(1995)*

Dawn Ann Billings . . . . Greta

Athena Massey . . . . Liana

• 0:15—Brief breasts in virtual reality program. Then in bra and panties in real life.

•• 0:51—Breasts, while making love with Don "The Dragon" Wilson.

Stella Stevens . . . . Mary

Peggy Trentini . . . . Debbie

•• 0:09—Full frontal nudity getting out of bubble bath during a guy's virtual reality session.

Virtual Desire *(1995)*

Annette Burger . . . . Cora

••• 0:50—In tight, white braless dress, then nude while making love with Brad. Long scene.

Marcia Gray . . . . Stranger

••• 1:13—In bra and panties outside in the woods with Brad, then breasts while making love. Long scene.

Gail Harris . . . . Wendy

••• 0:54—Nude, after stripping out of her clothes in back yard in front of Brad and in swimming pool.

•• 1:01—Full frontal nudity after getting out of the pool.

••• 1:05—Full frontal nudity, when making love with Brad on the floor while he is blindfolded.

Lorissa McComas . . . . Julie

• 0:43—Brief buns in panties and breasts.

••• 0:57—Buns in panties and breasts after stripping by the dinner table in front of Brad, then making love with him. Also see brief partial lower frontal nudity. Long scene.

Tammy Parks . . . . Susan

••• 0:11—Left breast, then breasts, while making love on the sofa with Brad.

••• 0:17—Stripping outside by hot tub in front of Brad. In white lingerie outfit, then nude while making love with him in the hot tub. Long scene.
•• 0:36—Breasts and buns, while making love on the sofa with Brad.

Taylor St. Claire . . . . Taylor
••• 0:46—Stripping down to black bra, panties, garter belt and stockings, then breasts and buns in panties.

Julie Strain . . . . Sascha
••• 0:25—Nude, while taking a shower when Brad peeks in the window.
••• 0:30—Full frontal nudity, while making love with Brad in the living room. Long scene.

Peggy Trentini . . . . Beth
••• 0:41—Stripping on office table, in black lingerie outfit, then breasts and buns in panties.

Catherine Weber . . . . Molly
• 0:43—Brief breasts, while making out with Brad on tennis court.

Virtual Encounters (1995)

(Unrated version reviewed.)

Michelle Barry . . . . Policewoman/S&M Girl 2
••• 0:29—Stripping on stage while dressed as a policewoman. In black bra and T-back, then nude after dancing and taking off all her clothes, then making love with a guy on stage. Long scene.
••• 1:07—Full frontal nudity in black outfit, while making love and dribbling hot candle wax on the other girl.

Ashley Bates . . . . Erica

Sara Bellomo . . . . First Encounter Woman
••• 0:12—Nude, while making love with a guy in outdoor setting during first VR experience. (This is part of a clip from *Cave Girl Island*.)

Sindee Coxx . . . . S&M Girl 1
••• 1:07—Full frontal nudity, in red outfit, while tied to the table, making love with another woman, getting hot candle wax dribbled on her.

Elizabeth Kaitan . . . . Amy
•• 0:42—Nude, while in the shower, fantasizing about making love with Michael.
••• 1:15—In sheer white nightgown, then breasts, while making love with Michael.
•• 1:22—Full frontal nudity, while making love with Michael in office.

Jill Kelly . . . . Cave Girl
••• 1:00—Nude, while making love with a cave guy in cave.

Jacqueline Lovell . . . . Kika
••• 0:19—In bra and panties, then full frontal nudity, while making love with Tricia Yen.

Lori Morrissey . . . . Candle Girl
••• 0:15—Nude, when making love with the Candle Boy in bed surrounded by lit candles while Elizabeth Kaitan watches.

Cathleen Raymond . . . . Rain Dancer 1
••• 0:50—In pink dress, then nude after stripping and making love with another woman in the rain (wearing sunglasses the entire time). Long scene.

Taylor St. Claire . . . . Maggie/Rain Dancer 2
•• 0:00—Breasts, when caressing herself while wearing VR helmet.
••• 0:50—In blue dress, then nude after stripping and making love with another woman in the rain (wearing sunglasses the entire time). Long scene.

Tricia Yen . . . . Miko
••• 0:19—In bra and panties, then breasts, while making love with Sara St. James.

Virtual Seduction (1995; Made for Cable Movie)

Donna Baltron . . . . 2nd Woman at Restaurant

Carrie Genzel . . . . Paris
•• 0:46—Breasts and buns, while making love with Jeff Fahey in paint studio, rubbing rubs paint over each other.

Lynn Oddo . . . . Woman at Restaurant

Marla Sucharetza . . . . Coat Girl

Meadow Williams . . . . Hostess

Vital Signs (1989)

Diane Lane . . . . Gina Wyler
••• 1:11—In white bra, then breasts making love with Michael in the basement.

Gigi Vorgan . . . . Nell

Volere Volare (1991; Italian)

Angela Finocchiaro . . . . Martina
0:05—Very, very brief nipple, while rolling over in bed.
••• 0:06—Nude, after getting out of bed and carrying two cups of coffee around, then in bathroom while two identical twin guys watch her.
•• 0:10—Buns, while lying on table in kitchen getting chocolate poured over her by a chef.
• 0:52—Side of left breast and buns, while kneeling on the bed.
• 1:09—Buns, while taking a shower. Subtitles get in the way.
•• 1:11—Brief left breast, while bending over to peek under covers of the bed. Subtitles get in the way. Right breast while sitting in bed with Maurizio.
• 1:15—Very, very brief breasts in open blouse, while running out of the bedroom.
• 1:25—Brief breasts, while getting into bed with the animated Maurizio. Subtitles get in the way.
• 1:26—Right breast, in bed with animated Maurizio.
•• 1:27—Nude, while frolicking in bed with animated Maurizio. Medium long shot.

The Voyeur (1994)

Kim Dawson . . . . Brenda
•• 0:09—In pink bra, then breasts, while making out in bathroom with James during party.
• 0:21—Upper half of breasts and buns, while posing in lingerie in front of mirror.
• 0:25—Buns and upper half of breasts in lingerie, while making love with James in daydream.
• 0:31—Partial right breast in open blouse in James' daydream.
•• 0:33—Breasts in open blouse, while making love with James in his daydream.
••• 0:38—Upper half of breasts and buns in lingerie, while making love in room with James. Long scene.
••• 0:44—Nude, after taking off bra and panties, when making love in bed with James while his wrists are tied to the bed.
••• 0:55—Breasts on lounge chair, while James rubs lotion on her in front of some onlookers in his fantasy.
•• 0:56—Breasts, while wearing red panties, then putting on red dress, in bedroom with James.
••• 1:12—Nude, while making love with James in bed. Nice long scene.

Belinda Farrell . . . . Aunt Helen

Gwen Somers . . . . Woman at Poolside
••• 0:52—Full frontal nudity, while the pool guy rubs lotion on her in Brenda's fantasy.

W. B., Blue and the Bean *(1988)*
a.k.a. Bail Out
Linda Blair . . . . Nettie
Debra Lamb . . . . Motel Clerk
• 0:42—Full frontal nudity opening door in motel to talk to David Hasselhoff.

• **Walkabout** *(1971; Australian/U.S.)*
Jenny Agutter . . . . Girl
•• 0:57—Nude, while swimming in the water.
•• 1:00—Breasts, while getting dressed.
•• 1:19—Breasts, when surprised in the house by David Gulpilil.
•• 1:37—Nude, when swimming outdoors with her little brother and Gulpilil.

Wall Street *(1987)*
Daryl Hannah . . . . Darian Taylor
Annie McEnroe . . . . Muffie Livingston
Sylvia Miles . . . . Realtor
Suzen Murakoshi . . . . Girl in Bed
• 0:13—Brief full frontal nudity getting out of bed and walking past the camera in Charlie Sheen's bedroom (slightly out of focus).
Millie Perkins . . . . Mrs. Fox
Andrea Thompson . . . . Hooker
Tamara Tunie . . . . Carolyn
Monique Van Vooren . . . . Woman at "21"
Sean Young . . . . Kate Gekko

The War of the Roses *(1989)*
Susan Isaacs . . . . Auctioneer's Assistant
Marianne Sägebrecht . . . . Susan
Kathleen Turner . . . . Barbara Rose
• 0:08—Very brief left breast, while lying in bed with Douglas and she moves the sheets.
• 0:33—Very, very brief lower frontal nudity, after squeezing Douglas' waist with her legs in bed.

Warlock: The Armageddon *(1993)*
Dawn Ann Billings . . . . Amanda Sloan
• 0:10—Very brief side of left breast, walking through hallway while taking off robe. Brief breasts, while walking past doorway.
Wendy Hamilton . . . . Model
Paula Marshall . . . . Samantha Ellison
Michelle Moffett . . . . Celine
Elizabeth Nottoli . . . . Model 3
• 0:29—Very brief breasts under sheer black blouse, while backstage during fashion show. (She's blowing a bubble with bubble gum.)
Joanna Pacula . . . . Paula Darc
Rebecca Street . . . . Kate

Warlords *(1988)*
Michelle Bauer . . . . Harem Girl
••• 0:14—Breasts, getting her top ripped off, then shot by a bad guy.
Greta Gibson . . . . Harem Girl
•• 1:05—Breasts in tent with the other harem girls. Holding a snake.
•• 1:09—Breasts again.
Debra Lamb . . . . Harem Girl
••• 0:14—Breasts, getting her blouse ripped off by a bad guy, then kidnapped.
••• 0:17—Breasts in harem pants while shackled to another girl.
Victoria Sellers . . . . Desert Girl
• 0:06—Getting out of car and running into the desert while wearing the sheer white top.
Brinke Stevens . . . . Dow's Wife
Dawn Wildsmith . . . . Danny

Warlords 3000 *(1992)*
April Dawn Dollarhide . . . . Terrified Girl
• 0:11—Breasts, while struggling in room with bad guys who are trying to rape her.
Denice Duff . . . . Anani
••• 0:50—Breasts, after taking off blouse in front of Nova, then making love and sleeping after.
Ty Randolph . . . . Bull Woman
Nicole Vasilopoulos . . . . Ox's Wife
•• 0:23—Breasts, in open blouse in bedroom with Ox.

Warm Summer Rain *(1989)*
Kelly Lynch . . . . Kate
• 0:03—Brief breasts and side view of buns in B&W lying on floor during suicide attempt. Quick cuts breasts getting shocked to start her heart.
•• 0:23—Full frontal nudity when Guy gets off her in bed.
•• 0:24—Side view of right breast in bed, then breasts.
••• 0:58—Buns then breasts, getting washed by Guy on the table.
••• 1:07—Brief buns making love. Quick cuts full frontal nudity spinning around. Side view of left breast with Guy.
••• 1:09—Nude picking up belongings and running out of burning house with Guy.

The Warrior and the Sorceress *(1984)*
Maria Socas . . . . Naja
••• 0:15—Breasts wearing robe and bikini bottoms in room with Zeg. Sort of brief buns, leaving the room.
•• 0:22—Breasts standing by a wagon at night.
•• 0:27—Breasts in room with David Carradine. Dark. Most of buns when leaving the room.
•• 0:31—Breasts and buns climbing down wall.
• 0:34—Brief breasts, then left breast with rope around her neck at the well.
• 0:44—Breasts when Carradine rescues her.
• 0:47—Breasts walking around outside.
• 0:57—More breasts outside.
• 1:00—Breasts watching a guy pound a sword.
• 1:05—Breasts under a tent after Carradine uses the sword. Long shot.
• 1:09—Breasts during big fight scene.
• 1:14—Breasts next to well. Long shot.

Warrior Queen *(1987)*
Tally Chanel . . . . Vespa
••• 0:09—Breasts hanging on a rope, being auctioned.
••• 0:20—Breasts and buns with Chloe.
•• 0:37—Nude, before attempted rape by Goliath.
•• 0:58—Breasts during rape by Goliath.
Sybil Danning . . . . Berenice
Samantha Fox . . . . Philomena/Augusta
••• 0:31—Nude, doing a dance with a snake during orgy scene.

• 1:03—Brief right breast after unsuccessfully trying to seduce Marcus.

Josephine Jaqueline Jones . . . . Chloe

••• 0:20—Breasts, while making love with Vespa.

Wasp Woman (1995; Made for Cable Movie)

Antonia Dorian . . . . Roommate

Maria Ford . . . . Caitlin

• 0:22—Buns in two piece swimsuit, while posing for photos on the beach.

•• 0:25—Full frontal nudity, while making love on the beach with Alec.

Jennifer Rubin . . . . Janice

Julie Kristen Smith . . . . Carla

Watch It (1993)

Suzy Amis . . . . Anne

Jordana Capra . . . . Call Girl

• 1:26—Brief partial buns, while making love with Michael in coat room during concert.

Cynthia Stevenson . . . . Ellen

Lili Taylor . . . . Brenda

Watch Me (1995)

Kelly Burns . . . . Elise

• 0:00—Buns in panties and left breast during opening credits.

••• 0:18—Full frontal nudity, after pouring breakfast drink on herself and rubbing it all over while watching Alex and Samantha make love in other apartment.

• 0:30—Brief breasts, when caressing herself while watching Alex and Samantha make love in other apartment.

••• 0:32—Full frontal nudity, while caressing herself more after seeing Paul photographing her from another apartment.

• 0:36—Brief partial breasts in B&W photos.

• 0:40—Brief breasts in video playback.

•• 0:42—Breasts, while changing blouses in laundry room with Samantha.

• 0:44—Brief breast in video playback.

• 0:52—Breasts, caressing herself while watching Paul and Samantha make love in other apartment.

• 0:55—Brief buns in panties under short skirt, while dancing by herself in front of mirror.

•• 0:59—Breasts, while in studio, being photographed by Paul.

••• 1:18—Nude, while making love with Paul.

Jennifer Leigh Burton. . . . . Samantha

• 0:04—Brief breasts while on sofa.

••• 0:08—Nude, while making love with Alex. He has her tied by her wrists and blindfolded.

••• 0:16—Full frontal nudity, while lying on table when Alex blindfolds her, rubs raw egg on her body, then makes love with her.

••• 0:30—Full frontal nudity, when blindfolded, making love with Alex while Elise watches from other apartment.

• 0:44—In black lingerie, then buns and breasts, while undressing when Paul video tapes her.

••• 0:49—Nude while being video taped some more, then making love with Paul.

••• 1:00—Nude, while making love with Alex during Elise's flashback.

•• 1:14—Buns, while in kitchen with Alex. Full frontal nudity, while blindfolded in chair with Alex.

Sheila Redgate . . . . Sherry

• 0:04—Full frontal nudity, while posing for Paul, the photographer. (She has blonde hair.)

Lynn Wolf . . . . Nadia

•• 0:06—Breasts, while posing on sofa and talking with Paul.

•• 0:13—Breasts, while posing on table in studio for Paul.

••• 0:21—Nude, after taking off her sweater and looking out window while Paul photographs her.

Watchers II (1990)

Keisha . . . . Woman at Hotel

Irene Miracle . . . . Sarah Ferguson

••• 0:40—Side view in black bra, then breasts a few times in the bathtub.

Tracy Scoggins . . . . Barbara White

Mary Woronov . . . . Dr. Glatman

The Waterdance (1991)

Susan Gibney . . . . Cheryl Lynn

Helen Hunt . . . . Anna

••• 0:51—Breasts in bed, making love with Eric Stoltz.

•• 0:52—Brief buns and brief right breast, coming back to the bed to clean up.

Elizabeth Peña . . . . Rosa

Barbara Alyn Woods . . . . Annabelle Lee

• 1:24—Buns, in G-string, while on stage in a strip club.

Waterland (1992; British/U.S.)

Cara Buono . . . . Jody Dobson

• 0:38—Brief breasts, while sitting in chair in classroom during Jeremy Irons' daydream.

Lena Headey . . . . Young Mary

• 0:16—In braless white undershirt, then brief breasts while making love with Tom in train.

••• 0:20—Breasts, while talking with Tom.

Siri Neal. . . . . Helen Atkinson

• 0:40—Brief side view of breast in mirror while rubbing her legs. Long shot at far left of TV screen.

• *Wavelength* (1982)

Cherie Currie. . . . . Iris Longacre

• 0:09—Brief side view of right breast and buns getting out of bed. Dark, don't really see anything.

We're No Angels (1989)

Demi Moore . . . . Molly

• 0:18—One long shot, then two brief side views of left breast when Robert De Niro watches from outside. Reflections in the window make it hard to see.

• *Weapons of Mass Distraction* (1997; Made for Cable Movie)

Alex Kingston . . . . Verity Graham

Sung Hi Lee. . . . . Kelly

Heidi Mark . . . . Cricket Paige

• 0:12—In bra and panties, then brief breasts, while jumping on bed in hotel room with Marvel. Seen through B&W video camera hidden in stuffed dog.

Cherie Michan. . . . . Nanci Gross

Mimi Rogers . . . . Ariel Powers

A Wedding (1978)

Geraldine Chaplin . . . . Rita Billingsley

Mia Farrow . . . . Buffy Brenner

••• 1:10—Breasts posing in front of a painting, while wearing a wedding veil.

Lauren Hutton. . . . . Florence Farmer

Weekend Pass *(1984)*

Sara Costa . . . . Tuesday Del Mundo
••• 0:07—Buns in G-string, then breasts during strip dance routine on stage.
Graem McGavin . . . . Tawny Ryatt
Valerie McIntosh . . . . .Etta
Hilary Shepard. . . . . Cindy Hazard
•• 1:05—In red bra, then breasts taking off bra.
• 1:07—Buns and breasts getting into bathtub.
Annette Sinclair. . . . . Maxine
Cheryl Song . . . . .Chop Suzi
• 0:26—Breasts while giving a guy a massage.
Ashley St. Jon . . . . Xylene B-12
•• 0:13—Breasts dancing on stage.

Weekend Warriors *(1986)*

Monique Gabrielle. . . . . .Showgirl on plane
•• 0:51—Brief breasts taking off top with other showgirls.
Brenda Strong. . . . . Danny El Dubois
• 0:44—Breasts, lit from the side, standing in the dark.

Weird Science *(1985)*

Judie Aronson . . . . Hilly
Kelly Le Brock . . . . Lisa
Kym Malin. . . . . Girl Playing Piano
• 0:55—Brief breasts several times as her clothes get torn off by the strong wind and she gets sucked up and out of the chimney.
Renée Props . . . . One of The Weenies
Suzanne Snyder. . . . . Deb
Jill Whitlow . . . . .Perfume Salesgirl

Welcome Home Roxy Carmichael *(1990)*

Ava Fabian. . . . . .Roxy Carmichael
• 0:10—Buns under the water in swimming pool, then more buns when getting out.
Frances Fisher . . . . Rochelle Bossetti
Laila Robins. . . . . Elizabeth Zaks

Welcome to 18 *(1986)*

Mariska Hargitay . . . . Joey
• 0:26—Buns, while taking a shower when video camera is taping her.
• 0:43—Buns, while watching herself on the videotape playback.
Cristen Kauffman. . . . . Talia

Welcome to Arrow Beach *(1973)*

a.k.a. Tender Flesh
Meg Foster . . . . Robbin Stanley
• 0:12—Buns and brief side view of right breast getting undressed to skinny dip in the ocean. Don't see her face.
•• 0:40—Breasts getting out of bed.
Joanna Pettet. . . . . Grace Henry

Welcome to L.A. *(1977)*

Geraldine Chaplin . . . . .Karen Hood
•• 1:28—Full frontal nudity standing in Keith Carradine's living room.
Lauren Hutton. . . . . Nora Bruce
• 0:56—Very brief, obscured glimpse of left breast under red light in photo darkroom.
Sally Kellerman . . . . Ann Goode
Sissy Spacek . . . . Linda Murray
•• 0:51—Brief breasts after bringing presents into Keith Carradine's bedroom.

Wes Craven's Mind Ripper *(1995)*

Natasha Gregson Wagner . . . . Wendy
Claire Stansfield . . . . Joanne
• 0:04—Brief buns, when getting into, then in the shower.

Wet and Wild Summer! *(1992; Australian)*

a.k.a. Exchange Lifeguards
Vanessa Steele . . . . .Charlene
•• 1:25—Breasts, opening her leather jacket to distract the other lifeguard boat.

• **Wet Water T's** *(1987; Video Tape)*

Lois Ayer . . . . Herself
••• 0:55—Breasts during boxing match. Long scene.
Amy Lynn Baxter . . . . Herself
••• 0:33—Breasts in black lingerie bottoms, then buns in G-string, dancing on stage in a contest.
•• 0:38—Breasts during judging.
•• 0:39—Breasts during semi-finals.
••• 0:40—Breasts dancing with the other women during semi-final judging.
••• 0:43—Breasts during finals.
•• 0:47—Breasts during final judging.
••• 0:48—Breasts dancing after winning first place.
Teri Lynn Peake . . . . Herself
••• 0:13—Breasts and buns, dancing on stage in white G-string, in a contest.
•• 0:36—Breasts again during judging.
•• 0:39—Breasts during semi-finals.
••• 0:40—Breasts dancing with the other women.
••• 0:43—Breasts dancing during finals.
•• 0:46—Breasts during final judging.

Wetherby *(1985; British)*

Suzanna Hamilton . . . . .Karen Creasy
Vanessa Redgrave . . . . Jean Travers
Joely Richardson . . . . .Young Jean Travers
•• 1:10—Breasts in room with Jim when he takes off her coat.

What the Peeper Saw *(1971; British)*

a.k.a. Night Hair Child
Britt Ekland . . . . Elise
• 0:38—Sort of side view of left breast in bed. Don't really see anything.

Wheels of Fire *(1984)*

a.k.a. Desert Warrior
Laura Banks . . . . Stinger
• 0:49—Brief breasts when Trace rips her top open outside.
Lynda Wiesmeier . . . . Arlie
••• 0:18—Breasts on the ground, being held down by two bad guys, then getting tied to hood of car.
•• 0:20—More breasts, long shot, tied to hood of car.
• 0:22—More breasts while tied to the hood of the car.
•• 0:23—Breasts, being brought into tent.
••• 0:34—Breasts, chained up in tent and trying to escape. Long scene.
•• 0:45—Left breast, while lying on cot.
•• 0:47—Breasts outside, fighting off crowd of guys.

• **When Night is Falling** *(1995; Canadian)*

Pascale Bussières . . . . .Camille
• 0:00—Full frontal nudity, while swimming under water, sometimes with another woman. Sometimes it's hard to see because of the distorted view.

- 0:50—Brief side view of left breast, while making love in bed with Martin.
- •• 0:56—Breasts, while making love in bed with Petra.
- 1:08—Right breast, while making love in bed with Petra.
- 1:11—Brief breasts, when sitting up in bed with Petra.
- 1:13—Very brief partial left breast, after throwing pillow aside to get out of bed.

1:22—Partial breasts, while swimming under water.
- 1:25—Brief buns, while lying on top of Petra.

Rachael Crawford . . . . Petra
- 0:57—Brief breasts, while making love in bed on top of Camille.

Fides Krucker. . . . . Roaring Woman

• When the Bullet Hits the Bone
(1996; Made for Cable Movie)

Lisa Boyle . . . . Uncredited Desert Girl
- •• 0:25—Brief breasts, while in desert in Michelle Johnson's vision.

Michelle Johnson. . . . . Lisa

When the Party's Over *(1991)*

Elizabeth Berridge . . . . Frankie
Rae Dawn Chong . . . . MJ
- 0:03—Brief buns, while getting out of bed.

When Women Had Tails *(1970; Italian)*

Senta Berger . . . . Felli
- 0:22—Buns, while lying in pit.
- 1:08—Buns, while getting carried around.
- 1:30—Buns, after her boyfriend gets caught in tree.

When Women Lost Their Tails *(1971; Italian)*

Senta Berger . . . . Felli
- 0:13—Very long shot of buns, while walking into pond.

Where Evil Lies *(1994)*

Roma Court . . . . Sadako
- •• 0:42—Breasts and buns in panties, after undressing and making love with Kurt in front of the imprisoned girls.

Nikki Fritz . . . . Alex
- 0:00—Buns in outfit, while posing for still photos.
- 0:02—Very brief peeks at breasts and buns in G-string, while posing for photos.
- 0:04—Buns, in outfit when fooling around with her friends.
- ••• 0:19—Nude, doing strip tease dance on stage.
- ••• 0:58—Breasts and buns in outfit, while dancing on stage.
- ••• 1:00—Breasts, while making love with Kurt.

Ann-Marie Holman . . . . Uncredited Dancer
- 1:07—Brief breasts, while dancing on stage. (Clip is from *Stripteasers.*)

Bianca Rocilili . . . . Dancer
- ••• 0:09—In bra and buns in G-string, then breasts while doing strip routine on stage in club. Very good, well photographed, long scene.
- 0:46—Buns in G-string, while dancing on stage.
- 0:48—Breasts, while dancing on stage.

Where the Heart Is *(1990)*

Suzy Amis . . . . Chloe McBain
- 0:08—Breasts during her art film. Artfully covered with paint, with a bird. Breasts again in the third segment.
- 0:09—Breasts during the film again. Hard to see because of the paint. Last segment while she narrates.

Joanna Cassidy . . . . Jean McBain
Sheila Kelley . . . . Sheryl

Uma Thurman . . . . Daphne McBain
- 0:08—Breasts during art film, but her entire body is artfully painted to match the background paintings. The second segment.
- 0:40—More breasts with body painted posing for her sister. Long shot.
- 1:16—In slide of painting taken at 0:40.
- 1:43—Same painting from 0:40 during the end credits.

• Where Truth Lies *(1995)*

Kim Cattrall . . . . Racquel Chambers
Janine Stillo . . . . Body Double for Candice Daly
- 0:45—Very brief breasts, three times, while making love with Eric Pierpoint, seen in John Savage's vision.
- 1:00—Breasts, while making love with Pierpoint when seen by Savage.

The Whispering *(1994)*

Leslie Danon . . . . Lisa Smyths
Tiffany Salerno. . . . . Jenna
- 0:09—Breasts, while making love in bed with Leif Garrett. Don't see her face.

Whispers *(1989)*

Linda Singer . . . . Prostitute
Victoria Tennant . . . . Hilary Thomas
- 0:42—Brief partial left breast, while in bed with Chris Sarandon. The later scenes in bathtub and on stairs look like a body double.

Whispers in the Dark *(1992)*

Jill Clayburgh. . . . . Sarah Green
Annabella Sciorra. . . . . Ann Hecker
- 1:25—Buns in mirror in front of closet (don't see her face). Partial left breast.

Deborah Unger . . . . Eve Abergray
- 0:14—Breasts during dream visualizations. Don't see her face.
- 0:24—Brief breasts during visualization by Sciorra. Don't see her face.
- 0:37—Brief breasts during Sciorra's dream.
- 0:38—Buns and side view of left breast, dead, while hanging by her neck.

White Dog *(1982)*

Kristy McNichol. . . . . Julie Sawyer
- 1:25—Most of the inside of breasts in gaping tank top when bending over to help lift dog off Burl Ives.

Lynne Moody . . . . Molly

White Fire *(1985)*

Belinda Mayne . . . . Ingrid
- •• 0:33—Nude, while swimming in pool.
- ••• 0:34—Nude, swimming in pool, then getting out and taking a shower.
- •• 0:35—Nude, after Robert Ginty steals her towel.
- •• 0:37—Nude, standing up in pool and getting out and going up stairs.
- •• 1:16—Breasts, when taking off her dress while on boat with Ginty.

White Hot *(1988)*

a.k.a. Crack In the Mirror

Sally Kirkland . . . . Harriet
Tawny Kitaen . . . . Vanessa
- 1:04—Brief half of lower frontal nudity, when sitting up in bed.

Anna Thomson . . . . Heather
••• 0:04—In bra, then breasts when undressing for drug dealer in exchange for cocaine.

White Light *(1990)*

Allison Hossack . . . . Rachel Rutledge
• 1:22—Very, very brief lower half of left breast, while in front of the fireplace with Martin Cove.
• 1:23—Brief buns and breasts several times, while making love on the floor with Cove.

Heidi Von Palleske . . . . Debra Halifax

White Men Can't Jump *(1992)*

Rosie Perez . . . . Gloria Clemente
•• 0:36—Breasts in shower and making love in bed with Woody Harrelson.
• 0:39—Brief right breast, while sitting up in bed.
• 0:40—Very brief side of right breast, three times, while getting out of bed quickly.

White Mischief *(1988)*

Geraldine Chaplin . . . . Nina

Sarah Miles . . . . Alice

Jacqueline Pearce . . . . Idina
•• 0:07—Buns, then breasts several times while standing up in the bathtub and talking with her male and female friends.

Greta Scacchi . . . . Diana Broughton
•• 0:16—Breasts taking a bath while an old man watches through a peephole in the wall.
•• 0:24—Brief breasts in bedroom with her husband.
•• 0:29—Brief breasts taking off bathing suit top in the ocean in front of Charles Dance.
•• 0:30—Breasts while lying in bed, then talking to Dance.
•• 0:49—Breasts while sitting in bed and talking to Dance.

White Palace *(1990)*

Kathy Bates . . . . Rosemary Powers

Eileen Brennan . . . . Judy

Barbara Howard . . . . Sherri Klugman

Rachel Levin . . . . Rachel

Susan Sarandon. . . . . Nora Baker
••• 0:28—Breasts on top of James Spader. Great shots of right breast.
• 0:38—Breasts on bed with Spader.

White Sands *(1992)*

Mary Elizabeth Mastrantonio. . . . . Lane Bodine
• 1:11—Brief left breast in shower with Willem Dafoe. You see her face, so this shot is really her.

Mimi Rogers . . . . Uncredited Molly Dolezal

Tera Tabrizi . . . . Body Double for Mary Elizabeth Mastrontonio
•• 1:10—Left breast and upper half of buns in the shower undressing in the shower with Willem Dafoe. Don't see face, so it's probably Tera.

Maura Tierney. . . . . Noreen

White Tiger *(1995)*

Kelly Benson . . . . The Brunette
• 0:27—Breasts, while sitting up in bed with Cary Hiroyuki Tagawa.

Lisa Langlois . . . . Joanne Grogan

Julia Nickson . . . . Jade
••• 1:04—Breasts, while making love with Gary Daniels.

• Whitesnake—Trilogy *(1987; Video Tape)*

Tawny Kitaen. . . . . The Girl
• 0:10—(2 min., 17 sec. into "Here I Go Again.") Very brief right breast, leaning out of car.
• 0:18—Most of her buns, while kissing David Coverdale in out-take from "Is This Love."

Whore *(1991)*

a.k.a. If you're afraid to say it... Just see it

Ginger Lynn Allen . . . . Wounded Girl

Stephanie Blake . . . . Stripper in Big T's
• 0:35—Buns, in G-string on stage.
••• 0:36—Breasts, dancing on stage in a club.

Alisa Christensen . . . . Lady in Toilet

Dori Courtney . . . . Topless woman on TV
• 0:14—Brief breasts on TV in old folks home in a scene from *Mob Boss*.

Theresa Russell. . . . . Liz
•• 0:13—Breasts and buns in G-string outfit, taking off her coat.
••• 0:25—In black bra, doing sit-ups. Breasts making love in spa with Blake.
• 1:18—Brief buns, in open skirt in back of car with a customer.

Whore 2 *(1994)*

Erin McMurtry . . . . Lisa

Marla Sucharetza . . . . Lori
•• 0:33—Breasts and buns in panties in bathroom.
• 0:59—Breasts while dancing on stage in club.
•• 1:07—Breasts and buns in panties, after taking off her dress for Nico.

Whose Child Am I? *(1974; British)*

Sally Faulkner. . . . . n.a.

Kate O'Mara . . . . Barbara Martin
••• 0:00—Breasts and buns, while making love with her husband in bed.
•• 0:06—Breasts, while reading the newspaper in bed next to her husband.
••• 0:25—In bra, then nude, while in hospital room with Michael, then starting to make love with him to get pregnant.
••• 0:32—Nude, while in bathroom, then in bed with Michael.

Whose Life Is It, Anyway? *(1981)*

Janet Eilber . . . . Patty
•• 0:30—Nude, ballet dancing during B&W dream sequence.
• 1:13—Very brief side of left breast when her back is turned while changing clothes.

Kaki Hunter . . . . Mary Jo

Lissa Layng . . . . 1st Nurse

The Wicked Lady *(1983; British)*

Glynnis Barber . . . . Caroline
••• 0:58—Breasts and buns making love with Kit in the living room. Possible body double.

Faye Dunaway. . . . . Barbara Skelton

Marina Sirtis . . . . Jackson's Girl
••• 1:06—Full frontal nudity in and getting out of bed when Faye Dunaway discovers her in bed with Alan Bates.
••• 1:20—Breasts getting whipped by Dunaway during their fight during Bates' hanging.

Wicked Stepmother *(1989)*

Colleen Camp . . . . Jenny

Barbara Carrera . . . . Priscilla
- 1:14—Very, very brief upper half of right breast peeking out of the top of her dress when she flips her head back while seducing Steve.

Laurene Landon . . . . Vanilla

The Wicker Man (1973; British)

Britt Ekland . . . . Willow
- ••• 0:58—Breasts in bed knocking on the wall, then more breasts and buns getting up and walking around the bedroom. Long scene. Body double used when you don't see her face when pounding on the wall. (Britt's hair is shorter than the body double's.)

Lorraine Peters . . . . Girl on Grave
- • 0:22—Side view of right breast sitting on grave, crying. Dark, long shot, hard to see.

Ingrid Pitt . . . . Librarian
- •• 1:11—Brief breasts in bathtub seen by Edward Woodward.

Wide Sargasso Sea (1993)

(Unrated version reviewed.)

Martine Beswicke . . . . Aunt Cora

Rowena King. . . . . Amelie
- • 0:54—Briefly nude in open window, while showing off for Rochester.
- ••• 1:16—Breasts, while making love standing up outside with Rochester.
- ••• 1:17—Full frontal nudity in bed, then getting out and getting dressed.

Karina Lombard . . . . Antoinette
- ••• 0:31—Buns and breasts, with her new husband, Rochester.
- •• 0:37—Breasts and partial frontal nudity while making love in bedroom with Rochester.
- •• 0:42—Buns and partial breasts, in wet white clothes. Left breast and buns while in bed with Rochester.
- ••• 0:52—Breasts while in bed before making love and after.
- • 0:55—Right breast, while sitting in bed.
- • 1:13—Breasts, while sitting in bed.

Rachel Ward . . . . Annette Cosway

Widow's Kiss (1995)

Beverly D'Angelo. . . . . Vivian Fairchild
- • 0:15—Partial right breast, while lying in bed under Bruce Davison.
- • 1:14—Right breast, while making love in bed with Paul.

Leslie Horan . . . . Kelly Givens
- •• 0:40—In white bra, then breasts and side view of buns with Mackenzie Astin.

Wifemistress (1977; Italian)

Laura Antonelli . . . . Antonia De Angelis
- • 1:22—Brief upper half of left breast in bed with Clara and her husband.

Olga Karlatos . . . . Miss Paula Pagano, M.D.
- •• 0:42—Breasts undressing in room with Laura Antonelli. Right breast and part of left breast lying in bed with Marcello Mastroianni.
- • 0:46—Brief breasts in bed with Mastroianni and Clara.

Wild at Heart (1990)

Lisa Ann Cabasa . . . . Reindeer Dancer
- •• 0:30—Breasts standing while Mr. Reindeer talks on the phone. More breasts dancing in front of him.

Laura Dern . . . . Lula
- ••• 0:07—Breasts putting on black halter top.
- •• 0:26—Left breast, then breasts sitting on Nicolas Cage's lap in bed.
- •• 0:35—Breasts wriggling around in bed with Cage.
- • 0:41—Brief breasts several times making love with Cage. Hard to see because it keeps going overexposed. Great moaning, though.

Sherilyn Fenn. . . . . Girl in Accident

Sheryl Lee . . . . Good Witch

Isabella Rossellini . . . . Perdita

Mia M. Ruiz. . . . . Mr. Reindeer's Resident Valet #1
- •• 0:32—Breasts standing next to Mr. Reindeer on the right, holding a tray. Long scene.

Charlie Spradling. . . . . Irma
- •• 0:40—Brief breasts in bed during flashback.

• Wild Bikinis (1987; Video Tape)

Jasaé . . . . Herself
- ••• 0:32—Breasts on swing, then pushing Brandi on swing from *Becky Bubbles*.
- ••• 0:35—Breasts playing with ball on the grass.
- ••• 0:37—Breasts on swing, drinking wine.
- • 0:55—Breasts on swing, making a funny face.

Lorraine Dorado . . . . Herself
- ••• 0:10—Breasts in pool and buns in swimsuit from *Becky Bubbles*.
- •• 0:35—Breasts playing with a ball on the grass with Jasaé.

Brandi Downs . . . . Herself
- • 0:09—Brief side of right breast, lying next to pool from *Becky Bubbles*.

Ginger Miller. . . . . Herself
- • 0:23—Buns in white two piece swimsuit, while rubbing oil on herself.
- • 0:26—Buns, while on pool float with Beckie Mullen.

Beckie Mullen . . . . Herself

Wild Cactus (1992)

(Unrated version reviewed.)

India Allen. . . . . Alex
- ••• 0:21—Buns and breasts, making love in bed on top of Naughton.
- ••• 0:34—Breasts, while pouring maple syrup on herself and making love with Naughton in the kitchen. Yummy!
- ••• 1:10—Nude, getting into and out of the shower.
- ••• 1:13—Nude, getting lotion rubbed on her by Maggie.
- •• 1:18—Breasts, while making love in bed with Randall.
- •• 1:20—Lower frontal nudity when Randall gets out of bed.

Carrie Chambers . . . . Waitress

Anna Karin . . . . Inga
- ••• 0:09—In black lingerie, then breasts and buns after undressing and making love on bed with Randall.
- ••• 0:14—Breasts while tied by her wrists to the bed by Randall.

Wendy MacDonald . . . . Abby

Michelle Moffett . . . . Maggie
- •• 0:20—Breasts while making love with Randall on trunk of car outside at night.
- ••• 0:58—Nude, taking a shower and getting out to talk to Alex.
- • 1:00—Brief buns, while walking into bedroom.
- ••• 1:14—Breasts, while sitting in bed with Alex, then buns in sheer black panties.

Kathy Shower . . . . Celeste
- •• 0:52—Breasts, while lying in bed.
- •• 1:16—Breasts in bed with bullet through her head, when discovered by Philip.

Wild Child (1991)

Crystal Breeze . . . . Jan
- • 0:30—Breasts, while sitting on the edge of the pool, then running around in black swimsuit bottoms.
- ••• 0:59—Breasts, while making love with Jack in the kitchen. Long scene.

K.C. Kerrington . . . . Linda
- ••• 0:16—Buns in lingerie, while bending over bathtub. Breasts and buns, while making love with Pete in bathtub. Long scene.
- • 0:29—Breasts, while in the swimming pool.

Jasmine Totschek. . . . . Katrina
- ••• 0:51—Breasts, while making love with Johnny in bed. Nice, long scene.

Missy Warner . . . . Laurie
- •• 0:01—Breasts, while sitting on chair on balcony.
- ••• 0:04—Breasts and buns, while making love with Jon in the pool, then talking afterward. Long scene.
- •• 0:29—Breasts while in swimming pool after her top comes off, then getting out.
- ••• 1:10—In white bra and panties, then breasts, while making love on bed with Todd.

The Wild Life (1984)

Sherilyn Fenn . . . . Penny Hallin
Tracey E. Hutchinson. . . . . Poker Girl #2
- • 1:23—Brief breasts in a room full of guys and girls playing strip poker when Lea Thompson looks in.

Leigh Lombardi. . . . . Stewardess
Francesca "Kitten" Natividad. . . . . Stripper #2
- ••• 0:50—Breasts doing strip routine in a bar just before a fight breaks out.

Ashley St. Jon . . . . Stripper #1
- ••• 0:47—Breasts and brief buns doing strip tease routine in front of Christopher Penn and his friends.

Lea Thompson . . . . Anita
Jenny Wright. . . . . Eileen
- •• 0:22—In bra and panties, then breasts changing in her bedroom while Christopher Penn watches from the window.

Wild Man (1988)

Ginger Lynn Allen . . . . Dawn Hall
- •• 0:24—Breasts taking off her dress in front of Eric, then making love with him.

Michelle Bauer. . . . . Trisha Collins
- • 1:02—In sheer white lingerie with Eric. Buns also.
- ••• 1:06—Breasts on couch making love with Eric. Brief lower frontal nudity.

Jeanie Moore. . . . . Lady at Pool

Wild Obsession (1992; Italian)

Victoria Mahoney . . . . Veronica
- •• 0:06—Breasts and buns, while dancing on stage.
- • 0:44—Brief side of right breast, after taking off bra in dressing room while talking with Victor.
- ••• 1:16—Breasts, after taking off her top. Buns in G-string panties getting into bed with Victor and talking with him.

Grazyna Szapolowska . . . . Caroline
- • 1:29—Very, very brief partial left breast in gaping blouse when she wipes her hands on towel in bathroom.

Wild Orchid (1990)

Jacqueline Bisset . . . . Claudia
Carré Otis . . . . Emily Reed
- •• 0:51—Left breast in mirror looking at herself while getting dressed.
- ••• 1:01—Breasts when a guy takes off her dress while Mickey Rourke watches.
- ••• 1:02—Right breast, then breasts while on the floor with Bruce Greenwood.
- • 1:31—Brief breasts in flashback with Greenwood.
- • 1:42—Breasts while opening her blouse for Rourke.
- ••• 1:44—Nude while making love with Rourke. Nice and sweaty.

Assumpta Serna. . . . . Hanna
- ••• 0:39—Breasts at the beach and in the limousine. Very erotic.

Wild Orchid II: Two Shades of Blue (1992)

Lydie Denier . . . . Dominique
- ••• 0:28—Breasts, undressing from lingerie while Blue and Elle watch.

Wendy Hughes . . . . Elle
Victoria Mahoney . . . . Mary
Gloria Reuben . . . . Celeste
- •• 0:32—Breasts on floor in front of fire when Mona and Blue peek in the rooms. (She's wearing a blonde wig.)

Nina Siemaszko . . . . Blue
- ••• 0:27—Breasts and buns, getting undressed in front of Wendy Hughes.
- •• 0:43—Breasts and buns in steam room with a customer.
- •• 0:58—Breasts in panties, garter belt and stockings while undressing for Josh.
- ••• 1:06—Breasts while humiliating J. J. in front of everyone at a party.

• Wild Reeds (1994; French)

Elodie Bouchez . . . . Maite
- • 1:39—Brief right breast, while out in the woods with Henri, then brief partial right breast, while sitting on the ground. Very brief left breast after lying on her back just before Henri starts to feel her. Brief lower frontal nudity, while lying on her back.

Wild Side (1995)

(Unrated version reviewed.)

Joan Chen . . . . Virginia Chow
- • 0:39—Brief inside half of right breast, in open jacket with Anne Heche.
- ••• 0:40—Breasts, while making love in bed with Heche. You don't see as much of Chen as you do of Heche, but the scene is very erotic!

Anne Heche. . . . . Alex Lee
- ••• 0:13—Breasts, while making love on top of Christopher Walken in bed.
- ••• 0:40—Breasts and buns, while making love in bed with Joan Chen.
- •• 0:54—Breasts, while in dressing room with Chen.
- •• 0:55—Breasts and partial buns, while putting on a bustier in dressing room.

Wild Zone (1989)

Cristobel D'Ortez. . . . . Mary
- •• 1:19—Breasts in the brush, getting molested by a bad guy.

Carla Herd . . . . Nicole Laroche

Wildcats (1986)

Goldie Hawn . . . . Molly
- • 0:30—Brief breasts while in bathtub.

Wilder Napalm (1993)

Debra Winger . . . . Vida
- 0:09—Left breast, after falling into bed with Arliss Howard.

Wildest Dreams (1987)

Deborah Blaisdell . . . . Joan Peabody
- 1:10—Brief breasts during fight on floor with two other women.

Ruth Corrine Collins . . . . Stella
- ••• 0:22—Breasts wearing panties in bedroom on bed with Bobby.
- • 1:10—Brief breasts fighting on floor with two other women.

Nicole Grey. . . . . Girl on Street
Jane Hamilton . . . . Ruth Delaney
Jill Johnson . . . . Rachel Richards
- •• 0:51—Breasts on bed underneath Bobby in a net.
- • 1:10—Brief breasts during fight with two other women.

Jeanne Marie. . . . . Isabelle
- •• 0:35—Breasts in panties in bedroom with Bobby.

Susan Napoli. . . . . Punk #4
- • 0:21—Brief left breast, leaning backwards on couch with her boyfriend.

Angela Nicholas . . . . Claudia
- •• 1:01—Breasts typing on computer doing Bobby's book keeping.

Karen Nielsen . . . . Punk #2
- • 0:21—Left breast, while sitting on couch.

Heidi Paine . . . . Dancee
- • 0:23—Breasts, while being held in the arms of a gladiator in Bobby's bedroom.

Miriam Zucker. . . . . Customer

Wilding, The Children of Violence (1990)

Catlyn Day . . . . Officer Breedlove
Susan Jones. . . . . Alley Rape Victim
- • 1:16—Breasts outside struggling with Jason and Bobby on the ground.

Jackie Moen . . . . Car Rape Victim
- • 0:23—Very brief right breast in back of car with her boyfriend when the gang of kids terrorizes them.

Karen Russell . . . . Cathy
- •• 0:20—Breasts in bedroom when Wings Hauser pulls her lingerie down.

Willie and Phil (1980)

Kristine DeBell. . . . . Rena
- • 1:36—Breasts on the beach (mostly silhouette). Brief side of left breast.

Jerry Hall . . . . Karen
- • 0:05—Brief breasts getting dressed in bedroom with Phil.

Kaki Hunter. . . . . Patti Sutherland
Margot Kidder . . . . Jeanette Sutherland
- • 0:36—Brief breasts in bed when Phil opens up her blouse. Long shot.
- • 0:47—Brief breasts playing in a lake with Willie and Phil.

Wimps (1987)

Deborah Blaisdell . . . . Roxanne Chandless
- • 1:22—Brief breasts and buns taking off clothes and getting into bed with Francis in bedroom.

Jane Hamilton . . . . Tracy
- • 0:40—Lifting up her sweater and shaking her breasts in the back of the car with Francis. Too dark to see anything.
- •• 0:44—Breasts and buns taking off sweater in a restaurant.

Gretchen Kingsley . . . . Debbie
Jeanne Marie . . . . Janice
- •• 0:20—Breasts in bed taking off top with Charles.

Annie Sprinkle . . . . Head Stripper
- •• 1:12—Breasts on stage with two other strippers, teasing Francis.

Windrider (1986; Australian)

Nicole Kidman. . . . . Jade
- • 0:40—Brief breasts in the shower with Tom Burlinson.
- •• 0:42—Brief buns and breasts in bed with Burlinson.
- • 0:43—Brief left breast on top of Burlinson in bed. Dark.
- ••• 0:47—Buns and very brief back side of left and right breasts, getting out of bed and putting on robe.

Wings (1927)

Clara Bow . . . . Mary Preston
- • 1:22—It looks like very, very brief left breast (blurry) when military guys walk in on her and she stands up straight while in front of a mirror.

Wings of Desire (1987)

a.k.a. Der Himmel Uber Berlin

Solveig Dommartin . . . . Marion
- • 0:34—Brief side of left breast, while putting robe on. (The film changes from B&W to color.)

• Wings of Fame (1990; Dutch)

Andrea Ferréol. . . . . Theresa
Marie Trintignant . . . . Bianca
- • 1:10—Very brief partial buns, while making love in Colin Firth's lap.
- •• 1:11—Buns and lower frontal nudity, while walking around the room and talking with Firth.

• The Wings of the Dove (1997; British)

Helena Bonham Carter . . . . Kate Croy
- ••• 1:30—Nude, while sitting on bed in bedroom, then making love with Merton.

Alison Elliott . . . . Milly Theale
Charlotte Rampling . . . . Aunt Maud

Winter Kills (1979)

Belinda Bauer . . . . Yvette Malone
- •• 0:46—Breasts making love in bed with Jeff Bridges, then getting out of bed.
- • 1:25—Breasts, dead as a corpse when sheet uncovers her body.

Tisa Farrow . . . . Nurse Two
Amanda Jones . . . . Beautiful Woman Seven
Candice Rialson . . . . Second Blonde Girl

Winter of Our Dreams (1981)

Judy Davis . . . . Lou
- • 0:19—Brief left breast sticking out of yellow robe in bed with Pete.
- • 0:26—Very brief side view of left breast taking off top to change. Long shot.
- •• 0:48—Breasts taking off top and getting into bed with Bryan Brown, then brief right breast lying down with him.

Cathy Downes. . . . . Gretel
- • 0:41—Brief right breast putting top on while talking to Judy Davis.
- •• 1:04—Breasts sitting up in bed at night.
- • 1:11—Breasts sitting up in bed while Bryan Brown and Davis talk.

Wish Me Luck (1995)

(Unrated version reviewed.)

Avalon Anders . . . . Geanie
- ••• 0:00—Breasts during opening credits.
- ••• 0:16—Breasts, while in shower in the locker room.
- • 0:19—Breasts in front of lockers, then in bra.
- •• 1:01—Breasts, while making love in bed with a guy.
- ••• 1:25—Breasts, while dancing during the end credits.

April Breneman . . . . Joyce

Stephanie Champlin . . . . Stephanie
- •• 0:16—Breasts, while in the shower in the locker room.
- • 0:42—Brief buns in T-back under sheer black robe when she bends over.
- •• 0:47—Buns in panties and bra, then breasts in front of Eddie.
- • 0:48—Breasts and buns in panties in bed, while talking with Eddie.

Christine Harte . . . . Rachel
- •• 0:33—Breasts in fantasy with the Dream Man.

Lorissa McComas. . . . . Heather
- • 0:39—In white bra and buns in panties getting out of her clothes.
- •• 0:43—In bra and panties, then buns and breasts with Eddie on sofa.

Joli Piccolini. . . . . Dream Girl
- ••• 0:08—Full frontal nudity (she's the redhead), while frolicking in bed and making love with a blonde Dream Girl.

Gloria Pryor. . . . . Tierra

Catherine Sugg . . . . Dream Girl
- ••• 0:08—Breasts (she's the blonde), while frolicking in bed and making love with a redhead Dream Girl.

Wish You Were Here (1987)

Emily Lloyd . . . . Lynda
- • 0:43—Buns, while singing in the alley and lifting up her skirt to moon an older neighbor woman.

Witch Hunt (1995; Made for Cable Movie)

Debi Mazar . . . . Manicurist

Penelope Ann Miller . . . . Kim Hudson

Jill Pierce . . . . Marie
- • 1:29—Breasts, while in bathtub when Eric Bogosian keeps putting her head under the water.

The Witch Who Came From the Sea (1976)

Roberta Collins . . . . Clarissa

Lynne Guthrie. . . . . Carol

Millie Perkins. . . . . Molly
- • 0:14—Brief left breast, while talking with two guy who smoke drugs.
- •• 0:16—Breasts, when putting on blouse in bedroom while talking to the two guys and tying them up.
- • 0:17—Right breast in open blouse while guy in bed plays with her left breast using his foot.
- • 0:30—Breasts, while lying back in bed and talking with a guy.
- •• 0:41—Breasts, while lying on her back, getting a tattoo.
- •• 1:00—Breasts, while lying on her back with a guy.
- • 1:01—Very, very brief left breast, when getting out of bed, upper half of breasts, when walking to the bathroom.
- •• 1:02—Breasts, after killing guy with razor in bathroom.

Witchboard (1987)

Tawny Kitaen . . . . Linda
- • 1:26—Nude, stuck in the shower and breaking the glass doors to get out.

Judy Tatum . . . . Dr. Gelineau

Witchboard 2: The Devil's Doorway (1993)

Julie Michaels. . . . . Susan
- • 1:17—Brief breasts, in B&W photos that Russel looks at.

• *Witchboard: The Possession* (1995)

Locky Lambert. . . . . Julie
- • 0:04—Left breast, while making love in bed with Brian.
- •• 0:44—In black bra, panties and stockings with Brian in living room, then breasts while making love.
- •• 0:46—Breasts, while sitting up in bed.
- • 0:57—Breasts, while making love in bed with Brian.

Donna Sarrasin . . . . Lisa
- • 1:03—Brief breasts in white panties, when Brian comes to get her. Brief breasts, while crawling across the bed.
- •• 1:04—Right breast, then breasts in bathroom, just before Brian kills her with broken glass.

Witchcraft 6: The Devil's Mistress (1993)

(Unrated version reviewed.)

Debra Beatty . . . . Keli
- ••• 0:50—Breasts, while sitting in bubble bath, then nude, while making love with Will in the tub.
- ••• 1:06—Full frontal nudity getting into the bathtub, then washing herself.
- • 1:11—Brief right breast, while washing herself.

Stephanie Champlin . . . . 1st Victim
- • 0:02—Breasts, while lying dead in trunk of car.

Shannon McLeod . . . . Cat
- •• 0:17—In bra, then right breast, while making love with Jonathan in front seat of car.
- • 0:42—Brief lower frontal nudity, while cutting a string off her mini skirt.
- • 1:01—Left breast, while making love with Will in his office.
- ••• 1:13—Breasts, while making love with Jonathan on trunk of car.

Stephanie Swinney . . . . Mary
- ••• 0:13—Breasts, while making love in the kitchen with Jonathan.
- • 0:25—Full frontal nudity, dead, while lying on table in morgue and also in flashbacks.

Witchcraft 7: Judgement Hour (1995)

(Unrated version reviewed.)

Kimberly Blair . . . . Gina
- ••• 0:09—Full frontal nudity, getting out of shower and drying herself off, then putting on panties and bra. Long scene.
- ••• 0:11—Breasts and very brief lower frontal nudity, after taking off bra and making love with her boyfriend in bed. Long scene.
- • 0:15—Buns in panties, after police raid the apartment.

April Breneman . . . . Keli
- •• 0:40—Nude, while making love with Will in bed.
- •• 0:57—Nude, while making love with Will in the living room.
- •• 1:08—Breast, while in bed with Martin.

Alisa Christensen . . . . Lutz

Mai-Lis Holmes . . . . Sally
- •• 1:02—Breasts and buns in leather outfit, while being a dominatrix to a guy, then during fight with police.

Aline Kassel . . . . Emily
- •• 1:05—Brief breasts, twice, while making love in bed with Jack.

Ashlie Rhey . . . . Rachel
- •• 0:03—Breasts and brief partial lower frontal nudity, while making love with Martin. Extreme close-ups of nipples.
- ••• 0:08—Breasts, while on operating table in hospital, when they defibrillate her several times to get her heart started.
- •• 0:21—Buns in open back of hospital gown, while running away from hospital.
- ••• 0:23—Buns, then breasts, while making love with jogger outside, then during fight with police.
- •• 0:52—Full frontal nudity on video monitor that the policemen watch, while she makes love with the invisible vampire.

Witchcraft 8: Salems Ghost *(1994)*

Mai-Lis Holmes . . . . Cathy
- •• 1:09—Brief breasts, while making love with Sonny in the house.

Kim Kopf. . . . . Mary Ann Dunaway
- •• 0:10—Breasts, while playing with food and making love with her husband in the kitchen.
- ••• 0:38—Nude, while making love with her husband on the bed.
- • 0:41—Left breast, while sitting on bed with McArthur during dream.
- ••• 0:48—Breasts, while caressing herself in the bathroom and then the bathtub. Very brief lower frontal nudity when going under the water in the bathtub.
- • 1:03—Buns in T-back, while in bed with McArthur in dream.

Witchcraft II: The Temptress *(1989)*

Mia M. Ruiz. . . . . Michelle
- • 0:27—Brief breasts several times making love with a guy on the floor during William's hallucination.

Delia Sheppard . . . . Dolores
- •• 1:20—Brief breasts several times with William.

Witchcraft III: The Kiss of Death *(1991)*

Leana Hall . . . . Roxy
- •• 1:08—Breasts on bed with William making love when Charlotte gets trapped in the room.

Alexa Jago . . . . .Marlena
- • 0:04—Brief breasts in open dress in alley with Louis before he kills her.

Lisa Toothman . . . . .Charlotte
- •• 1:02—Buns and breasts in shower with Louis while William has a bad dream.
- •• 1:12—Left breast, while on bed with Louis, against her will.

Witchcraft IV: Virgin Heart *(1992)*

Julie Strain. . . . . Belladonna
- • 0:25—Buns, while dancing on stage in a red bra and red G-string.
- ••• 0:27—Breasts, dancing on stage.
- •• 0:46—Breasts on the floor with Santara.
- • 0:49—Brief breasts in open dress on couch with Will.
- • 1:15—Breasts, lying on couch in her dressing room while Will tries to talk to her.

Sunset Thomas . . . . Nora Breckenridge
- • 0:02—Brief tip of right breast, outside with Pete at night when he tries to make some moves on her.
- • 0:11—Very brief breasts, twice, lying with blood covering her chest.

Witchcraft V: Dance with the Devil *(1993)*

Annastasia Alexander. . . . . Sacrifice
- ••• 1:15—Nude, undressing and getting sacrificed on table. Long scene.

Kim Bolin. . . . . .Secretary
- ••• 1:09—Breasts, while making love with the Reverend on the sofa.

Nicole Sassaman . . . . Marta
- • 0:03—Brief breasts in open bra, just before the customer gets killed.
- ••• 0:30—Breasts in bed, while making love with Bill while Keli is asleep.
- • 0:51—Breasts under sheer black blouse.
- ••• 0:55—Breasts with Bill at the top of the stairs.

Carolyn Taye-Loren . . . . Keli
- ••• 1:01—Breasts while making love with Bill under leaky water pipes in the basement.

Witchfire *(1986)*

Vanessa Blanchard. . . . . .Liz
- •• 0:52—Brief breasts in bed and then the shower.

The Witching *(1983)*

a.k.a. Necromancy

(Originally filmed in 1971 as *Necromancy*, additional scenes were added and re-released in 1983.)

Sue Bernard. . . . . .Nancy
- • 1:03—Brief breasts in bed with Michael Ontkean.

Pamela Franklin . . . . Lori
- •• 0:38—Breasts lying in bed during nightmare.
- • 1:07—Brief breasts putting on black robe.
- • 1:17—Brief breasts in several quick cuts.

Annie Gaybis . . . . .Spirit

Barbara Peckinpaugh. . . . . Jennie
- ••• 0:02—Breasts and buns in open gown during occult ceremony. Brief full frontal nudity holding a doll up.

Laurie Senit . . . . Witches Coven

Brinke Stevens. . . . . Black Sabbath Member

Witchtrap *(1989)*

Linnea Quigley . . . . .Ginger Kowoski
- ••• 0:34—Nude taking off robe and getting into the shower.
- •• 0:36—Breasts just before getting killed when the shower head goes into her neck.

Judy Tatum . . . . Agnes Goldberg
- •• 0:05—Breasts in the bathtub.

With a Song in My Heart *(1952)*

Susan Hayward . . . . Jane Froman
- • 0:48—Very brief upper half of left breast, when it pops out of the top of her strapless dress during song and dance number when she lifts her right arm over her dancing partner's head.

Without Mercy *(1996)*

Ayu Azhari. . . . . Tanya
- • 0:30—Very brief breasts with John by sofa.
- • 0:31—Brief breasts, several times, while making love in bathtub with John.
- • 0:54—Buns, while in bed with John.

Without You I'm Nothing *(1990)*

Sandra Bernhard . . . . Various Characters
- ••• 1:20—Dancing in very small pasties on stage. Buns in very small G-string. Long scene.

Witness *(1985)*

Kelly McGillis . . . . Rachel
••• 1:18—Breasts taking off her top to take a bath while Harrison Ford watches.

Wizards of the Demon Sword *(1990)*

a.k.a. Demon Sword

Heidi Paine . . . . Melina
• 0:39—Left breast, while lying with Thane, then trying to stab him with a knife.

Dawn Wildsmith . . . . Selena

Wolf Lake *(1978)*

a.k.a. Survive the Night at Wolf Lake

Robin Mattson . . . . Linda
• 0:54—Brief full frontal nudity during rape in cabin. Dark.
• 0:55—Brief breasts afterwards.

The Woman in Red *(1984)*

Kelly Le Brock . . . . Charlotte
• 1:13—Brief right breast, getting into bed. Too far to see anything.
• 1:15—Brief lower frontal nudity getting out of bed when her husband comes home. Very brief left breast, but it's blurry and hard to see.

Woman of Desire *(1993)*

(Unrated version reviewed.)

Bo Derek . . . . Christina Ford
• 0:07—Very brief right breast, while turning over in bed with Steven Bauer.
• 0:14—Breasts, in photo that a detective finds on boat.
••• 0:19—Breasts, while sunbathing on boat, then nude after taking off bikini bottoms and diving into the water.
0:33—Breasts, while getting out of bed. Seen in "flashback-vision."
•• 0:40—Breasts, while taking off blouse and putting on leather jacket in front of Jeff Fahey.
••• 0:41—Breasts and buns while making love with Fahey on a motorcycle inside. Great!
•• 0:51—Breasts, in shower with Fahey.
• 0:57—Breasts on floor, while making love with Fahey.
1:07—Sort of breasts on boat while sunbathing. Seen in "flashback-vision."

Kimberleigh Stark . . . . Nurse Vivian Donner

A Woman's Tale *(1991; Australian)*

Gosia Dobrowolska . . . . Anna
• 0:29—Brief breasts, while putting on blouse when standing at the door.

Victoria Eagger . . . . Nurse 1

Sheila Florance . . . . Martha
• 0:07—Breasts, after leaning back in the bathtub. Dark. Check this out if you like really old women.

A Woman, Her Men and Her Futon *(1992)*

Kathryn Atwood . . . . Waitress #2

Delaune Michel . . . . Gail

Jennifer Rubin . . . . Helen
•• 0:22—Breasts, making love in bed with Randy.
••• 0:31—Breasts, lying in bed with Donald.
• 0:35—Brief breasts, while making love in bed with Randy.
•• 1:04—Breasts, lying in bed and starting to make love with Donald.

Women & Men: Stories of Seduction *(1990; Made for Cable Movie)*

Melanie Griffith . . . . Hadley

Elizabeth McGovern . . . . Vicki
••• 0:22—Breasts when Bridges takes her top off when she lies back in bed.

Molly Ringwald . . . . Kit

• ***Women From Down Under*** *(1995; Australian/New Zealand)*

Lynette Curran . . . . Just Desserts/Mrs. Fullilove

Genevieve Lemon . Excursion to the Bridge of Friendship/Grace

Mary Regan . . . . . . Excursion to the Bridge of Friendship/Shelly

Tania Simon . . . . Peach/Sal

Jenny Vuletic . . . . Jumping the Gun/Host
• 0:42—Breasts, while waking up next to another woman in the morning.

Women in Love *(1971)*

Glenda Jackson . . . . Gudrun Brangwen
••• 1:20—Breasts taking off her blouse on the bed with Oliver Reed watching her, then making love.
•• 1:49—Brief left breast making love with Reed in bed again.

Jennie Linden . . . . Ursula Bragwen
• 0:38—Brief breasts skinny dipping in the river with Glenda Jackson.
• 1:11—Brief breasts in a field with Alan Bates. Scene is shown sideways.

Women on the Verge of a Nervous Breakdown *(1988; Spanish)*

Maria Barranco . . . . Candela

Rossy de Palma . . . . Marisa

Carmen Maura . . . . Pepa Marcos
• 0:57—Inner half of breasts visible under sheer portion of black lingerie while changing clothes.

The Women's Club *(1987)*

Maud Adams . . . . Angie Blake

Dotty Coloroso . . . . Cali
• 0:11—Brief breasts getting angrily out of bed with Michael Paré.

Pamela Ward . . . . Fashion Show Woman

Wonderland *(1989; British)*

Julie Graham . . . . Hazel
•• 1:11—Nude, taking off her clothes at the beach while talking to Eddie.

Clare Higgins . . . . Eve

Working Girl *(1989)*

Olympia Dukakis . . . . Personnel Director

Barbara Garrick . . . . Phyllis Trask

Melanie Griffith . . . . Tess McGill
• 1:18—Very, very brief right breast turning over in bed with Ford.
• 1:20—Breasts, vacuuming. Long shot seen from the other end of the hall.

Sigourney Weaver . . . . Katherine Parker

Elizabeth Whitcraft . . . . Doreen DiMucci
•• 0:29—Breasts, while on bed on Alec Baldwin when Melanie Griffith opens the door.

The Working Girls *(1973)*

Elvira . . . . Katya
••• 0:20—Breasts, dancing on stage.

Lynne Guthrie . . . . Jill
••• 0:43—Breasts, dancing on stage at club.
•• 0:48—Breasts in swimming pool with Nick.
Laurie Rose . . . . Denise

World According to Garp (1982)

Glenn Close . . . . Jenny Fields
Amanda Plummer . . . . Ellen James
Jessica Tandy . . . . Mrs. Fields
Jenny Wright . . . . Curbie
•• 0:33—Brief breasts behind the bushes with Robin Williams giving him "something to write about."

The World is Full of Married Men (1979; British)

Carroll Baker . . . . Linda Cooper
• 0:19—Brief left breast, while sitting up in bathtub covered with bubbles.
Georgina Hale . . . . Lori Grossman

The Wraith (1986)

Vickie Benson . . . . Waitress
• 0:59—Breasts in bed with Packard when Loomis interrupts them.
Sherilyn Fenn . . . . Keri
• 0:13—Very brief breasts when Packard's gang catches her in bed with Jamie.
• 1:02—Brief breasts during flashback when caught in bed by Packard's gang.
• 1:03—Very brief right breast, pulling her swimsuit top off in pond with Charlie Sheen.

Write to Kill (1990)

Joan Severance . . . . Belle Washburn
••• 1:01—Breasts, making love in bed with Valentine.
• 1:04—Very brief, blurry breasts when Valentine tosses her a blouse.

The Wrong Man (1993; Made for Cable Movie)

Rosanna Arquette . . . . Missy
•• 0:34—Buns in black panties, then breasts, taking off her dress at the beach and going into the water. Medium long shot.
••• 1:15—Breasts after taking off bra and dancing on table in room, then putting on dress afterwards. Very nice, long scene.
• 1:23—Very, very brief part of right breast in open robe and very brief side view of buns while in bed on top of Anderson.

Wyatt Earp (1994)

Alison Elliott . . . . Lou Earp
Joanna Going . . . . Josie Marcus
• 1:53—(0:14 into tape 2) Brief breasts, in B&W photo that Mark Harmon is showing to everybody in the saloon.
• 2:03—(0:24 into tape 2) Very brief right breast, while in bed, kissing Kevin Costner.
Isabella Rossellini . . . . Big Nose Kate
JoBeth Williams . . . . Bessie Earp
Mare Winningham . . . . Mattie Blaylock

Xtro (1982)

Maryam D'Abo . . . . Analise
••• 0:25—Breasts making love with her boyfriend on the floor in her bedroom.
•• 0:56—Brief breasts with her boyfriend again.
Bernice Stegers . . . . Rachel Phillips

Yanks (1979)

Lisa Eichhorn . . . . Jean Moreton
• 1:48—Brief breasts in bed when Richard Gere rolls off her.
Vanessa Redgrave . . . . Helen
• 1:25—Brief side of left breast and buns, taking off robe and getting into bed.
Annie Ross . . . . Red Cross Lady

The Year of the Dragon (1985)

Ariane . . . . Tracy Tzu
• 0:59—Very brief breasts when Mickey Rourke rips her blouse off in her apartment.
•• 1:14—Nude, taking a shower in her apartment.
•• 1:18—Breasts straddling Rourke, while making love on the bed.

Year of the Gun (1991)

Valeria Golino . . . . Lia Spinelli
••• 0:17—Breasts, making love in bed with Andrew McCarthy.
• 0:25—Half of buns and side of right breast, lying in bed with McCarthy.
Sharon Stone . . . . Alison King
• 1:00—Brief left breast, while standing against the door, with Andrew McCarthy. Long shot.
• 1:01—Side of left breast, while making love on bed.

You Can't Hurry Love (1984)

Bridget Fonda . . . . Peggy
Sally Kellerman . . . . Kelly Bones
Danitza Kingsley . . . . Tracey
Kristy McNichol . . . . Rhonda
Kimber Monroe . . . . Brenda
Jean Poremba . . . . Model in Back
• 0:05—Breasts posing in the backyard getting photographed.
•• 0:48—Nude in backyard again getting photographed.
Merete Van Kamp . . . . Monique

You've Got to Have Heart (Italian)

a.k.a. At Last, At Last
Carroll Baker . . . . Lucia
•• 1:23—Left breast, while in cabin, consoling Giovanni.
•• 1:24—More left breast, while with Giovanni.
•• 1:25—Right breast while making love.
Edwige Fenech . . . . Valentina
••• 0:10—Breasts and buns, while taking off nightgown for Giovanni.
• 0:11—Brief side view of left breast, while sitting up on the floor with Giovanni.
••• 0:20—Nude in bedroom with Giovanni.
••• 0:26—Right breast, when Giovanni gets out of bed.
•• 0:43—Left breast, while entertaining herself and fantasizing.
••• 0:47—Breasts, while on boat getting lotion rubbed on her by Brigitte.
••• 0:53—Breasts and buns in G-string when Giovanni takes off her body suit.
• 0:58—Right breast, while getting molested by Uncle Frederico.
•• 1:20—Breasts while getting out of her wet dress in tent.
•• 1:24—Breasts in tent while making love with another man.
•• 1:25—Right breast while making love.
• 1:32—Brief full frontal nudity in bedroom during argument.

Young Doctors in Love (1982)

Jaime Lyn Bauer. . . . . Cameo
Kimberly McArthur . . . . .Jyll Omato
•• 0:58—Breasts in front of Dabney Coleman after taking off her Santa Claus outfit in his study.
Pamela Reed . . . . Norine Sprockett
Tessa Richarde. . . . . Rocco's Wife
Peggy Trentini. . . . . Christmas Elf
•• 0:55—Brief breasts greeting visitors to the party.
• 0:57—Breasts again sitting on couch.
Janine Turner. . . . . Cameo
Sean Young. . . . . Dr. Stephanie Brody

Young Guns II (1990)

Ginger Lynn Allen . . . . Dove
Jenny Wright. . . . . Jane Greathouse
• 1:07—Buns, taking off her clothes, getting on a horse and riding away. Hair covers breasts.
• 1:38—Buns, while walking down stairs during epilogue.

Young Lady Chatterley (1977)

Lindsay Freeman . . . . Sybil, Light-Duty Maid
• 1:35—Brief left breast, while on the floor, covered with cake.
Harlee McBride . . . . Cynthia Chatterley
•• 0:19—Nude masturbating in front of mirror.
• 0:28—Brief breasts with young boy.
••• 0:41—Nude in bathtub while maid washes her.
••• 0:52—Nude in back of car with the hitchhiker while the chauffeur is driving.
••• 1:03—Nude in the garden with the sprinklers on making love with the Gardener.
••• 1:31—Breasts and buns in bed with the gardener.
Ann Michelle. . . . . .Gwen, Roommate

Young Lady Chatterley II (1986)

Wendy Barry .Sybil, Maid in Hot House
• 0:12—Breasts in hot house with the Gardener.
Sybil Danning . . . . .Judith Grimmer
••• 1:02—Breasts in the hut on the table with the Gardener.
Alexandra Day. . . . . Jenny, Maid in Hut
••• 0:06—Breasts and buns in hut on the bed with the Gardener.
••• 0:28—Breasts taking bath with Harlee McBride.
Monique Gabrielle. . . . . Eunice, Maid in Woods
•• 0:15—Breasts in the woods with the Gardener.
••• 0:43—Breasts in bed with Virgil.
Harlee McBride . . . . Cynthia Chatterley
•• 0:20—Breasts getting a massage with Eleanor.
•• 0:22—Full frontal nudity during flashback to the first time she made love with Robert.
••• 0:28—Breasts taking a bath with Jenny.
••• 0:35—Breasts in library seducing Virgil.
••• 0:50—Breasts in back of the car with the Count.
••• 0:58—Breasts in the garden with Robert.
Allene Simmons. . . . . Marta, Maid in Bed

Young Nurses in Love (1987)

Beth Broderick. . . . . .Putnam
Jennifer Delora . . . . Bunny
Jane Hamilton . . . . Franchesca
•• 1:05—Breasts on top of a guy on a gurney.
Jeanne Marie. . . . . Nurse Ellis Smith
• 0:31—Brief side view of left breast in mirror with Dr. Riley.
•• 1:09—Breasts in panties, getting into bed with Dr. Riley.
Sharon Moran . . . . Bambi/Bibi
Annie Sprinkle . . . . Twin Falls
•• 0:23—Breasts getting measured by Dr. Spencer.

The Young Warriors (1983; U.S./Canadian)

Anne Lockhart . . . . Lucy
•• 0:42—Breasts and buns making love with Kevin on the bed. Looks like a body double.
Linnea Quigley . . . . Ginger
• 0:05—Nude in and getting out of bed in bedroom.

Youngblood (1986)

Fionnula Flanagan . . . . .Miss McGill
Cynthia Gibb. . . . . Jessie Chadwick
• 0:50—Brief breasts and buns making love with Rob Lowe in his room.

Your Ticket is No Longer Valid (1982)

Jennifer Dale . . . . Laura
•• 0:27—In black panties, then breasts when her husband fantasizes, then makes love with her.
• 1:23—Left breast in bed with Montoya, then sitting, waiting for Richard Harris.

• *Zafarinas (1994; Spanish)*

a.k.a. Morirás en Chafarinas
Maria Barranco . . . . Elisa
• 0:51—Very, very brief side view of right breast in open military shirt when she shifts position in bed with Jorge Sanz.
• 0:52—Very, very brief upper half of right breast, just before opening the shower curtain to leave the shower. The US version cuts off the bottom of the screen with a black bar for the subtitles, so more may be seen in the original, non-subtitled version.

Zandalee (1991)

(Unrated version reviewed.)
Erika Anderson. . . . . Zandalee Martin
••• 0:02—Nude, taking off robe and dancing around the room.
••• 0:21—Nude, undressing, then in bed with Judge Reinhold. Long scene.
•• 0:30—Right breast, then breasts making love in bed with Nicolas Cage.
•• 0:32—Breasts as Cage paints on her with his finger.
••• 0:45—Left breast, then breasts and lower frontal nudity on floor with Cage.
•• 0:47—Nude, getting massaged by Cage with an oil and cocaine mixture.
• 0:48—Brief breasts getting into bed with Reinhold. Slightly out of focus.
•• 1:09—Breasts opening her dress for Reinhold while lying on a river bank, then making love with him at night in bed.

Zapped! (1982)

Corinne Bohrer . . . . Cindy
Rosanne Katon. . . . . Donna
Jewel Shepard . . . . .Uncredited Girl in Car
• 0:39—Brief breasts after red and white top pops off when Scott Baio uses his Telekinesis on her.
Marya Small. . . . . Mrs. Springboro
Heather Thomas . . . . .Jane Mitchell
1:29—Body double brief breasts when Scott Baio drops her dress during the dance.

Zardoz (1974; British)

Sara Kestelman .... May
- 1:04—Left breast, in open blouse, under sheet with Sean Connery.
- 1:05—Very brief breasts grabbing Connery from behind during struggle.

Charlotte Rampling.......................... Consuella
- 0:29—Breasts under yellow net blouse.
- 1:05—Very brief left breast, when Sean Connery grabs her during struggle.
- 1:26—Wearing yellow blouse, trying to kill Connery.
- 1:44—Very brief right breast feeding her baby in time lapse scene at the end of the film.

A Zed and Two Noughts (1985; British)

Frances Barber ....Venus de Milo
- ••• 0:22—Breasts, sitting in bed, talking to Oliver, then nude while getting thrown out of his place.

Andrea Ferréol..............................Alba Bewick

Guusje Van Tilborgh ....Caterina Bolnes
- 0:42—Brief lower frontal nudity when Oliver lifts her skirt up in restroom to check to see what kind of panties she's wearing.
- 0:51—Lower frontal nudity, then very brief breasts while posing for photo by Van Meegeren.

Zipperface (1991)

Rikki Brando .... Sherry

Laureen E. Clair............................... Elizabeth
- 0:23—Brief breasts, while putting on lingerie in front of mirror.

Zombie (1980)

Tisa Farrow .... Anne Bolles

Olga Karlatos .... Mrs. Menard
- 0:40—Breasts and buns taking a shower.

Zombie Island Massacre (1984)

Rita Jenrette .... Sandy
- ••• 0:01—Breasts taking a shower while Joe sneaks up on her. Breasts in bed with Joe.
- •• 0:10—Brief right breast with open blouse, in boat with Joe. Left breast with him on the couch.

OTHER SOURCES

Back issues of *Playboy* magazine can be purchased through *The Playboy Catalog*. Their catalog is free by calling (800) 423-9494. They have a large assortment of *Playboy* magazine back issues from the 1960's to the present. They also sell *Playboy* Video Magazines, *Playboy* Video Centerfolds and other video tapes listed in this book such as *Nudity Required* and the *Mermaid* series. Their web site is at www.playboy.com/catalog

If you can't find the video tapes listed in *The Bare Facts Video Guide* for rent at your local video tape rental stores, an excellent source for purchasing video tapes is *Movies Unlimited*. Their catalog costs $7.95 plus $3.00 shipping, but you get a $5.00 credit voucher to use on your order. The address is:

Movies Unlimited
3015 Darnell Road
Philadelphia, PA 19154-3295
(800) 4-MOVIES
(215) 637-4444 - Outside of the United States
www.moviesunlimited.com

Another source for locating hard to find video tapes is *Critics' Choice*. They have thousands of titles in their warehouse. Their order line is open 24 hours a day, 7 days a week. Their telephone number is (800) 367-7765. The *Critics' Choice Video Search Line* has access to over 70,000 movies. Their phone number is (800) 729-0833. It is open Monday through Friday, from 8am to 6pm, Central Time. Their web site is at www.ccvideo.com

An excellent magazine that you should definitely check out is *Celebrity Sleuth*. In it, you'll find photographs of many celebrities that don't or won't do nudity for video tapes. People like Jackie Onassis, Deidre Hall and Caroline Munro are featured in various issues of *Celebrity Sleuth*.

Celebrity Sleuth
P.O. Box 273
West Redding, CT 06896

If you are interested in writing to your favorite actor or actress to get an autograph or ask a question, you'll want to purchase *Celebrity Access—The Directory 6th Edition*. The book lists thousands of celebrity addresses. The cost is (Taxes, postage and handling are already included): For orders in the U.S. the cost is $26. California orders are $27, Orders outside of the U.S. are $30.00. Write or call:

Celebrity Access Publications
20 Sunnyside Avenue, Suite A241
Mill Valley, CA 94941
(415) 389-8133

Brinke Steven's *Private Collection* video tape can be purchased directly from her (she also has a fan club). Write to her at:

Brinke Stevens Fan Club
8033 Sunset Boulevard, Suite 557
Hollywood, CA 90046

Melissa Anne Moore has a fan club. Write to her at:

Melissa Anne Moore Fan Club
P.O. Box 55
Versailles, KY 40383

Taylor St. Claire has a fan club. Write to her at:

Taylor St. Claire Fan Club
P.O. Box 5336
Chatsworth, CA 91313

Tracy Dali has a fan club. Write to her at:

Traci Dali Fan Club
c/o Promotions Plus
7272 E. Broadway, Suite 230
Tucson, AZ 85710

Purrfect Productions has video tapes that you won't find anywhere else for sale. They feature Monique Gabrielle, Julie Strain, Rhonda Shear, Linnea Quigley and Dian Parkinson. They also have some special *very* hot tapes featuring Julie Kristen Smith and others. Ask for "The Bare Facts Discount" when ordering. Contact them at:

Purrfect Productions (BF)
P.O. Box 430
Newbury Park, CA 91320
(800) 642-8183 for credit card orders only from 8am to 11pm PST

Becky LeBeau's video tapes and still photos can be purchased directly from her (she also has a fan club). Call or write:

Soft Bodies
505 S. Beverly Drive, Suite 973
Beverly Hills, CA 90212
(800) 622-9920
(310) 558-3191 - Outside the United States

The Vice Academy series of movies has a fan club. You can write to Linnea, Ginger, Liz and Julia. Write to (enclose a self-addressed, stamped envelope):

The Vice Academy Fan Club
P.O. Box 480593
Los Angeles, CA 90048

Video Oyster has a catalog of hard-to-find video tapes for sale called *Pearls Magazine*. Issue #7 is $3.77, back issues are $3 each or subscriptions are $22.22 for *Pearls* 1-12. The issues come out about two per year. Video Oyster will also search for a video tape for free. Tell them The Bare Facts sent you. Video Oyster will be doing auctions soon.

Video Oyster
145 West 12th Street
New York, NY 10011
(212) 989-3300
(212) 989-3533 - Fax

Hot Body International and *Hot Body Video Magazine* video tapes may be purchased from Hot Body International. Tell them The Bare Facts sent you. Call them at:

Hot Body International
401 Levering Avenue
Los Angeles, CA 90024
(800) 336-4321

VideoMania is a good newspaper to place a classified ad to reach other video enthusiasts who might be able to locate hard to find video tapes for trade or purchase. Published monthly, it costs $11.97 per year. Contact:

VideoMania
P.O. Box 47
Princeton, WI 54968

Perfect 10 Video sells hundreds of video tapes, photos and calendars. Their selection includes video tapes with nudity such as *Dream Babies*, *Becky Bubbles* and *In Search of the Perfect 10* plus a large selection of bikini contests. Call or write for their catalog ($2.00). Tell them The Bare Facts sent you.

Perfect 10 Video
11684 Ventura Blvd., Suite 589
Studio City, CA 91604
(800) GIRL-USA

Femme Fatales is a great magazine with in-depth interviews, stories and photos about B-movie beauties such as Brinke Stevens, Julie Strain, Robey, Debra Lamb and Patricia Tallman. *Femme Fatales* is a monthly magazine put out by the same people who do *Cinefantastique*. For information write to:

Femme Fatales
P.O. Box 270
Oak Park, IL 60303

For Beta format fans, contact Joe Korpsak, the owner of Absolute Beta Videos. They sell new and used Beta video tapes in addition to reconditioned Beta VCR's and accessories. They can be reached at:

Absolute Beta Videos
225 East Main Street
P.O. Box 130
Remington, VA 22734
(540) 439-3259
www.AbsoluteBeta.com

If you are interested in viewing the Rob Lowe video tape that he accidentally made in 1989, you can purchase it from Al Goldstein, publisher of *Screw* magazine. His New York cable TV show, *Midnight Blue*, showed some of the footage on show #672. The cost is $29.95, you need to specify VHS or Beta. Contact:

Media Ranch, Inc.
P.O. Box 432
Old Chelsea Station
New York, NY 10013

REFERENCES

The Complete Directory to Prime Time Network TV Shows, 1946–Present [Sixth Edition]
Tim Brooks and Earle Marsh
Ballantine, 1995

The Motion Picture Guide
Baseline II, 1997
1984 through 1997 Editions

The TV Encyclopedia
David Inman
The Putnam Publishing Group, 1991

Video Movie Guide 1997
Mick Martin and Marsha Porter
Ballantine, 1996

Adult Video News magazine
8600 West Chester Pike, Suite 300
Upper Darby, PA 19082
Various issues from 1990–1998

Entertainment Weekly magazine
Entertainment Weekly Inc.
1675 Broadway, New York, NY 10019
Various issues from 1990–1998

Playboy magazine
919 North Michigan Avenue, Chicago, IL 60611
Various issues from 1972–1998

Penthouse magazine
1965 Broadway, New York, NY 10023-5965
Various issues from 1972–1998

The San Jose Mercury News newspaper
750 Ridder Park Drive, San Jose, CA 95190
Various issues from 1987–1998

Sight and Sound magazine
21 Stephen Street
London W1P 1PL, England
Various issues from 1990–1996

TV Guide magazine
Triangle Publications Inc.
100 Matsonford Road, Radnor, PA 19088
Various issues from 1987–1998

Online References:

The Internet Movie Database
http://us.imdb.com/

The Internet Adult Film Database
http://homepage.eznet.net/~rwilhelm/asm/dbsearch.html

A moderated newsgroup for discussing erotic films
rec.arts.movies.erotica

ABOUT THE AUTHOR

Craig Hosoda is a Software Engineer. He grew up in Silicon Valley, California, then went to the University of California at Berkeley where he graduated with a B.S. degree in Electrical Engineering and Computer Science. After graduation, he worked at Hewlett-Packard for two years before getting a programming job at Industrial Light and Magic, George Lucas' special effects division of Lucasfilm Ltd. (Craig's film credits can be found in *The Golden Child*, *The Goonies* and **batteries not included*.)

While working at ILM, the seeds for *The Bare Facts Video Guide* were planted during a casual conversation one day with his friend, Marty Brenneis. While working on the film, *Howard the Duck*, Marty asked Craig about Lea Thompson's film credits. When Marty didn't know about her nude scene in *All the Right Moves*, Craig thought, "There should be a book that lists this type of important information in one place..."

After returning to Silicon Valley in 1987 to raise a family with his wife, he began research for the book during the evenings while working as a software engineer during the day. Unfortunately, it was difficult to balance a full-time job, work on *The Bare Facts* and have time for his family, so in July 1990, he quit his regular job to devote his life to uncovering the bare facts.

HOW THIS BOOK WAS CREATED

This book was published using the latest in database publishing techniques on an Apple Macintosh computer. A custom ACI *4th Dimension* database was created to keep track of the data. An export module was written in *4th Dimension* that outputs the information with *FrameMaker* format tags into a text file. The text file was read into Frame Technology's *FrameMaker* and cleaned up a bit. The files were copied onto an Iomega Zip disk and sent to the Printer where the camera-ready copy was output on a Linotronic phototypesetter.